The Decorative Workshop

PICTURE FRAMING

The Decorative Workshop

PICTURE FRAMING

MOYRA BYFORD

FRIEDMAN/FAIRFAX
PUBLISHERS

To William

A FRIEDMAN/FAIRFAX BOOK

Published by Michael Friedman Publishing Group, Inc.
by arrangement with Merehurst Ltd, Ferry House, 51-57 Lacy
Road, Putney, London SW15 1PR

© 1996 Merehurst Ltd

Library of Congress Cataloging-in-Publication Data
available upon request.

ISBN 1-56799-262-5 (paperback)
ISBN 1-56799-255-2 (hardcover)

Edited by David Holloway
Designed by Lisa Tai
Photography by Tony Robbins (pages 2, 7, 39, 41, 45, 47, 51, 55,
57, 61, 65, 67, 71, 73, 77, 79, 83, 85, and 89) and Mark Gatehouse
(pages 9–37, 40, 42–44, 48–50, 52–54, 58–60, 62–64, 68–70, 72,
74–76, 78, 80–82, 84, 86–88, and 91–93)
Illustrations by King & King

Originally published as *Decorative Picture Framing*.

Typeset by Servis Filmsetting Ltd.
Color separations and printing by Toppan, Singapore

For bulk purchases and special sales, please contact:
Friedman/Fairfax Publishers
Attention: Sales Department
15 West 26th Street
New York, New York 10010
212/685-6610 FAX 212/685-1307

Contents

Introduction

Everyone has things that they want to have framed, maybe a family heirloom, old photographs, the first paintings that children brought back from school or just some holiday mementoes. I think it is more personal and a lot more fun to frame these things yourself and, what is more, it is not necessary to be a technical expert to make and decorate the frames that are in this book.

I started framing about twenty-five years ago and in those days styles were still very conventional – the main idea being that frames should last. Nowadays, fashions have changed considerably with pictures being thought of as part of the decor of the room, almost becoming disposable. While I do not altogether agree with our new throwaway world, I have tried to put together a selection of projects in this book that not only show some of the traditional forms of presentation, but also give you some more exciting ways of showing things off that may not be quite so long-lasting, but are great fun!

In this book, I have tried to describe both the "traditional" methods of framing and some modern contemporary treatments. Oil paintings, for example, traditionally were, and still are, framed with wide moldings without glass. This is not always easy, and for this book I have bent the rules a little and suggested another way of creating the same effect. Watercolors, on the other hand, are traditionally framed with a rather narrower molding and a washlined mat so I have included a very classically framed watercolor for you.

There are many other reasons why pictures are framed. Framing will not only make the picture look better and more important, but will also protect it from dirt and damage, make it more portable, and make it easier to hang on the wall to create a focal point in a room.

There are also many things other than pictures that we want to preserve and display and framing them is the answer, even if they are of no intrinsic value. Once framing materials were mass produced in the nineteenth century, the Victorians could afford to feel much the same as we do, and a humble greeting card with a mat and frame was just as popular then as it is now.

The idea of decorating mats also became popular in the nineteenth century, later to be dropped for a more austere and plain look. Another revived nineteenth-century craft was decorating the frame molding with collage and relief work. We are fortunate today because there are so many paints, dyes, and stains available.

The big revolution in picture framing, however, has occurred in the last thirty years and is the availability of reasonably priced hand-operated equipment for the home picture framer to use. There is now an enormous and almost overwhelming choice in this area for anyone who wants to make their own frames. I shall be showing you how to make a frame and cut a mat before we start on the projects, but if you do not want to have a go at this, you can get your local picture framer to cut your molding pieces and your mats, which leaves you just the fun of decorating. And, of course, you can decorate ready-made frames and mats – or restored secondhand ones.

I hope that the sixteen projects I have chosen for this book not only guide you, but also inspire you to continue to frame more and more interesting objects.

Equipment and Materials

A lot of decorative picture framing can be done with normal tools or equipment. But for good results, one or two specialist items will need to be bought and you will want a warm, well-lit place where you can work. Much of the equipment and materials you need can be bought from art shops and do-it-yourself stores, but for some of the more specialized things you may need to go to a picture framing supplier.

Equipment and materials

TO MAKE IT EASIER FOR YOU TO DECIDE HOW MUCH you want to do, I have divided this section into four parts – making and assembling frames, decorating frames, cutting mats, and decorating mats. I appreciate that not everyone will want to learn how to cut and join moldings to make frames, but will prefer to go straight to the decoration stage. This is fine, just ask your local picture framers to cut the pieces for you and go ahead with the decorating. If you talk to them nicely, they may assemble the frame for you afterward, or you may decide to invest in a clamp to do this yourself – which has the added bonus that you can also strengthen old frames. The choice is yours. Similarly with mats, you can have them cut, or learn the art of mat cutting yourself before you start to express your individuality in the decoration. With this in mind, I have suggested basic kits for each section, which you would need for almost every framing project you tackle.

Making and assembling frames

The basic requirement for making a picture frame is cutting four pieces of picture frame molding to the correct size with their ends cut at an angle of exactly 45° (known as a miter) and then to join them together to form a perfect rectangle with square corners. Picture frame molding is different from ordinary wood molding in that it has a square cutout – the rabbet – to hold the picture, glass, mat, and backing board.

MITER SAW

If you want to make your own frames – which, financially, is a very beneficial thing to do – you will need to purchase a good saw. A tenon saw and simple miter box can be used to cut miters, but will not give you a good enough cut to make the accurate corners necessary for picture framing. A far better tool is a **miter saw** and

there is an excellent range of inexpensive ones available. The saw has a machined metal bed for supporting the molding and a fine-toothed saw blade that can be swung from side to side and locked in position to give 45° angles in both directions, making beautiful, smooth cuts which join together perfectly for the frame corners. It can also be used to cut other angles for multisided frames – see the project on page 84 – and fixed settings are provided for these angles as well as 45°. Be sure that you buy a saw that has a detachable blade that can be replaced when it becomes blunt; some miter saws have a clamp for securing the molding and some have a depth stop which is a help for repetitive cutting.

CLAMPS

The band clamp is the simplest and cheapest type of clamp for holding a picture frame while it is being joined with adhesive. It has a roll of plastic webbing coiled within the main body which can be pulled out to the distance around your frame. One corner of the frame is held by the body of the clamp; the other corners are held in place with molded plastic shapes through which the band threads. The band can be locked and then tightened by means of a knob on the clamp body which pulls the whole frame together.

ADHESIVES

I find that most brands of wood glue are perfectly satisfactory for frame making, though I always use the belt and braces method of pinning frame corners as well as gluing them. Always remove excess glue with a cotton swab before it dries.

HAMMER

A small hammer is the best for putting in panel pins and other delicate jobs. Choose the type that has a round head on one side and a flat head on the other. You will also need a narrow nail set for driving panel pins home without damaging the wood.

DIMENSIONS
Throughout the book I have given both imperial measurements (ft and in) and metric (m, cm, and mm). Work with whichever you feel more comfortable, but don't mix them. Normally, I have given exact equivalents – such as 1in (2.5cm) – but where the metric measurement is an alternative I have given it as ½in (or 1.5cm).

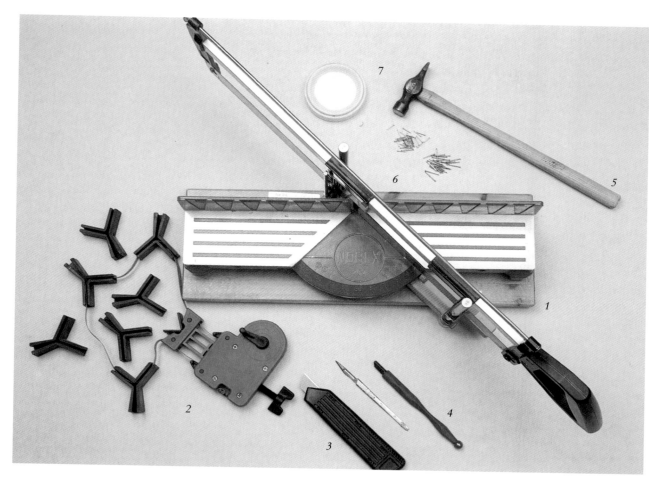

Basic Framing Kit

1 *Miter saw*

2 *Band clamp*

3 *Mat knife and X-Acto knife*

4 *Glass cutter*

5 *Hammer*

6 *Panel pins ½ inch (12mm)
and 1 inch (2.5cm)*

7 *Wood glue*

SMALL CRAFT KNIVES

A mat (Stanley-type craft) knife (preferably the retractable type) is indispensable in the picture framing workshop, but be sure to have plenty of spare blades. An X-Acto knife is also very useful for precise work.

GLASS CUTTER

If you need to cut glass, the best glass cutters have an oil reservoir which dispenses a small amount of oil onto the glass every time pressure is applied. This makes cutting a lot easier.

MOLDINGS

You can buy an absolutely massive range of *finished* moldings, but if you choose one of these you cannot usually decorate it further.

My own favorite moldings are the plain, *unfinished*, wood moldings now available. These are perfect for decoration and are available in oak and pine as well as other woods. Different effects can be obtained with the same dyes on different woods and so an infinite range of colors can be made. The other advantage of these moldings is that you can avoid waste by cutting the four pieces for a frame before coloring, leaving the remnant of the length of molding to be stained a different color for another frame. Most moldings are sold in lengths from 6 feet 6 inches to 10 feet (2 to 3 meters), and once you have cut a frame from a finished molding you can often be left with a virtually unusable piece which is not big enough for another whole frame.

When buying moldings, you will need to know some of the words used to describe the main shapes. A

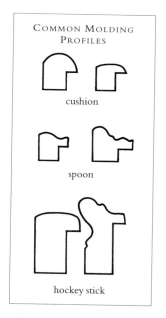

COMMON MOLDING
PROFILES

cushion

spoon

hockey stick

flat molding is what it says, while a **cushion** molding has a gently curved front face. I like to use **hockey stick** molding, which has a curved face, but a very deep rabbet, and you will find a variety of ornately shaped moldings known as **scoop** or **spoon**. One technical term you will come across is the "sight edge" – this is the part of the molding (or the mat) closest to the picture. Sometimes, you will want to decorate this.

BACKING BOARDS
A picture is backed for protection and thick cardboard or hardboard can be used. Hardboard used for picture framing is smooth on both sides and yet only 2mm thick, so it does not fill up too much space in the rabbet. It can be bought in large sheets which will do for several pictures, or you may be able to buy smaller pieces from your local picture framer.

GLASS
Glass is used to protect watercolors, prints, and other pictures with a mat, but oil paintings and acrylics are traditionally not glazed. Sometimes a coat of varnish will suffice for protection on items that will be short-lived. If you need to use glass and feel unhappy about the idea of cutting it, your local glass retailer is quite used to cutting individual pieces. This may cost a little more, but you will save on bandages! Make sure you ask for 2mm picture glass and never try to use old pieces of 3mm or 4mm window glass, which will make the frame too heavy.

Basic Assembly Kit

1 Glass cleaner

2 Bradawl

3 Gummed brown paper tape

4 Pushmate and tabs

5 Screw eyes

6 Masking tape

7 Nylon picture cord (medium thickness)

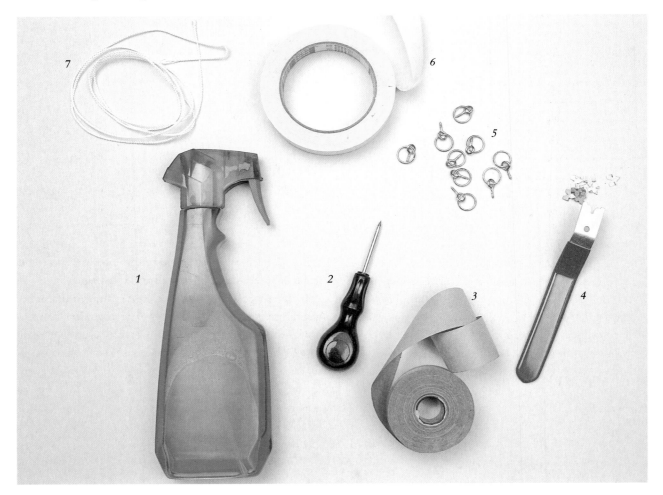

GLASS CLEANER

Just before the frame is assembled, you must clean the glass thoroughly. I find most types of spray-on clear glass cleaner perfectly adequate for this.

FASTENING DEVICES

The glass, mat, picture, and backing board all need to be secured into the frame. The cheapest way to do this is with panel pins and a hammer (which, for most frames, you will need anyway for strengthening the corners), but it is a very difficult method and almost impossible to get a tight fit.

A "Pushmate" is a more sophisticated way of achieving the same result. This device pushes small, shaped tabs into the inner sides of the frame to hold everything in place. Similar results can be achieved using a brad gun, which fires metal pieces into the frame.

TAPE

The backs of pictures are traditionally finished with gummed brown paper tape about 1⅝ inches (4cm) wide. This keeps out the dirt and makes a nice, neat finish. Masking tape is useful for a variety of jobs and the most common width that I use is 1 inch (2.5cm).

NAILS, SCREW EYES, AND HOOKS

The very thinnest panel pins are used to pin corners together. Use ½ inch (12mm) pins for narrow moldings and 1 inch (2.5cm) ones for wider moldings.

Use a mediumweight screw eye for the hanging cord – some screw eyes have an additional ring which allows the cord to lie flatter. A bradawl is the best tool for starting the hole for a screw eye. Alternatively, for a small decorative frame, you can use an ornamental hanger screwed to the top of the frame at the back.

CORD VERSUS WIRE

I have always preferred to use nylon cord rather than picture wire to hang pictures as it is available in a range of thicknesses and is very durable. Do not attempt to hang a picture on cord that is too fine, or use string or any other unsuitable material.

Cutting mat

You can cut a mat to size with a mat knife (used along the side of a suitable metal straightedge), but one of the most important jobs in picture framing is cutting the beveled-edge opening in the mat which reveals the picture underneath.

HAND-HELD MAT CUTTER

For cutting a beveled-edge opening, the most basic piece of equipment that you can buy is a hand-held mat cutter, and you can do a lot of work with it before you feel the need to move on to something more extravagant. Some people always cut their mats with a hand-held cutter, and I certainly have one or two by me for small jobs in the studio.

There are many cutters on the market, but your choice should be determined by some basic factors. Hand-held cutters all depend on running the cutter along a line that you have previously drawn on your matboard. It is therefore imperative that you choose a cutter that allows you to see the start and finish of the line that you have marked. Curiously, not all cutters allow you to do this, so it is a point to watch.

Some cutters have their own straightedge which they hook on to and run along, and these are a little more expensive. Otherwise, the cutter has to run along a separate straightedge which can be a little difficult to hold steady and this may influence your choice. Lastly, there is the choice of a fixed blade or a retractable blade. I find that I have no difficulty with either, but you may feel that a retractable blade is easier to manage.

If you are going to do a lot of mat cutting, it might be worth investing in a more sophisticated (and, of course, more expensive!) tool, which has the straightedge attached to a board, which holds the mat firm. Some of these cutters have adjustable stops at the ends so that you do not have to mark out your mat, but some still require you to draw your rectangle with the crosses at the corners.

Some subjects require a circular or oval opening to be cut in the mat. If you want to do this yourself, you really need to buy a circle or oval/circle mat cutter.

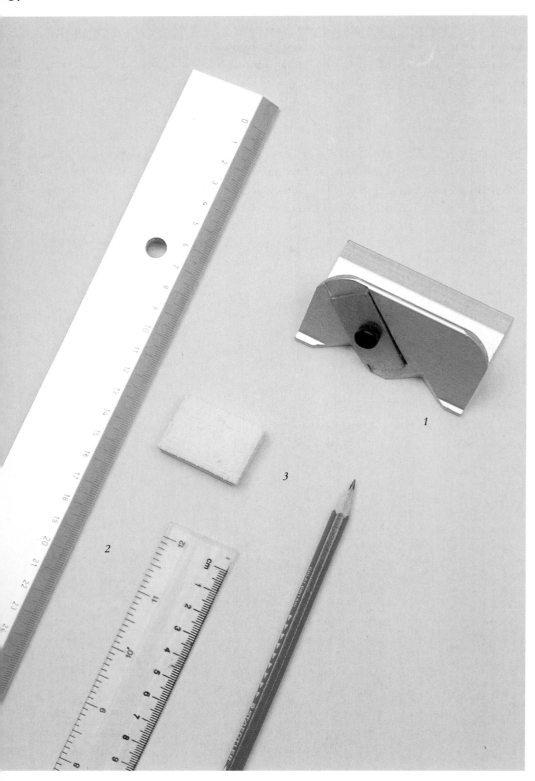

However, these are expensive and to start with you can buy mats with ovals and circles already cut or ask your local picture framers to do the cutting for you.

STRAIGHTEDGES AND RULERS

A good quality metal straightedge of at least 18 inches (or 50cm) is essential if you intend to use a simple hand-held cutter. If you want to cut mats from full-size sheets of matboard you will need a straightedge of 3 feet (or 1m). In addition to this a 3 foot (or 1m) clear plastic ruler with beveled edges and marked in both inches and centimeters is invaluable.

MATBOARD

There is an overwhelming selection of matboard available in different colors (including gold and silver) and with different finishes (including cloud, flannel, and textured as well as plain).

Matboard comes in large sizes – 44 × 32 inches (112 × 81.5cm) – so each sheet can be cut into several mats. It is therefore best to select neutral shades to start with to give you maximum versatility and avoid waste. Some art shops and picture framers will sell half sheets, but these usually work out to be more expensive.

TAPE

Double-sided adhesive tape is used for fastening double mats together and masking tape is used for holding the picture to the mat.

PENCILS AND ERASERS

Matboard marks very easily so clean hands are a must. A very sharp HB pencil used lightly is the only acceptable marker. Never use a ballpoint pen on matboard. Some dirty marks can be removed with a putty eraser that is obtainable in art shops.

Basic Mat Cutting Kit

1 *Hand-held mat cutter*
2 *Straightedge and ruler*
3 *HB pencil and putty eraser*

Decorating frames

There are many ways in which you can decorate picture frames and most decoration – painting, staining, liming, and waxing of the wood, for example – is carried out on the molding after it has been cut, but before it is joined. This makes it easier to get an even coating.

Brushes and sponges

I use the best quality narrow household paint brushes for painting frames as I find that the natural bristles withstand both oil and acrylic paint and last well. Beware of cheap brushes as they will tend to lose their bristles. You will also need some artist's brushes for finer decoration and touching up. You can try both natural and synthetic sponges for decoration as they will give different effects. I always feel that natural sponges should give the best results – but then end up using a small piece cut off a synthetic sponge!

Wood dyes

There is an excellent range of water-based wood dyes that have been developed to use with plain, unfinished moldings. They come in two ranges – pastel colors and natural wood colors. Spirit-based wood dyes produce a very strong, hard color and are available in a small basic range of shades.

Basic Frame Decorating Kit

(These items can be bought gradually)

1 *Small pots of wood dye*
2 *Paints*
3 *Collection of sponges*
4 *Self-hardening modeling clay*
5 *Liming wax and a selection of other waxes*
6 *Artist's brushes*
New, narrow household paintbrushes (not shown)

PAINTS

The new artist's paints are excellent for decorating moldings. They can be mixed to produce a solid opaque effect or diluted with water to produce a more translucent finish. I also use small sample ("tester") pots of household acrylic paint and I like to have a selection of small cans of gloss paint – the basic colors of red, green, blue, yellow, white, and black are the most useful.

Have a look in art shops for gold paints. Most makes come in different shades of gold and it is a good idea to have several on hand to blend with golds on finished moldings and also with gold matboard.

WAXES

My favorite wax has to be liming wax, which is very effective when used on a strong-grained wood such as oak. It seems a wasteful sort of process because it is worked into the wood and then almost immediately rubbed off again, but a small amount is left in the grain and the effect is quite miraculous. Wood-colored waxes are also very useful for adding depth of color. Similarly gold waxes can be used to add a little shimmer to a color.

METAL LEAF

An effective way of decorating a frame is with metal leaf, which can be used either on bare wood or on stained or painted wood. It is attached by means of gold size which is painted on. Metal leaf is very cheap and comes in a roll approximately 1¼ to 1½ inches (3 to 4cm) wide with a paper backing. It is not easy to handle, however, and to start with I would advise using it in small patches.

MODELING CLAY

I use self-hardening modeling clay when I want to build up a frame to produce a relief effect. This is very easy to work, yet sets hard and can be sanded if necessary. I also use it if I want to attach things such as shells to a frame, and it makes a very good filler. Alternatively, ceramic tile adhesive is useful for attaching things to frames and has the advantage of being pure white.

Decorating mats

I feel that mat decoration is one of the most exciting parts of picture framing as it allows you to add a very personal touch to the whole picture.

CORNER GAUGE

The most essential piece of equipment for decorating mats is a graduated corner gauge. This is a piece of clear plastic with a short ruler or a right angle which tucks neatly into the corner of the beveled-edge opening in the mat to allow you to measure and mark across the mat at the corners.

PENS

The most sophisticated pen is an artist's ruling pen. This is stainless steel and the distance between the two parts of the tip can be adjusted with a thumbscrew to alter the width of the line. The pen is loaded with paint and care must be taken to put sufficient paint into it to complete a line without putting so much paint in that it blots. With practice, this pen will become your best friend.

Some felt-tip pens can be used for drawing lines on a mat, but they should be capable of a very fine and crisp line. Nothing is worse than lines drawn around a mat with a child's garish felt-tip pen. Gold and silver felt-tip pens are, however, very effective and are a good standby in the workshop.

BRUSHES AND SPONGES

Only the very best artist's sable brushes should be used for decorating mats. For free-hand decoration you will need the usual pointed round brushes in a selection of sizes. For washlining, you will need a good quality flat brush; the size I use most is ½ inch (12mm). A selection of sponges is useful, particularly a new synthetic bath sponge which can be cut into shaped pieces.

OTHER BITS AND PIECES

White paper towels, cotton wool, cotton swabs, and scraps of cardboard can all be used to decorate mats. A child's airbrush (used with its colored felt-tip pens) and spray bottles are also useful.

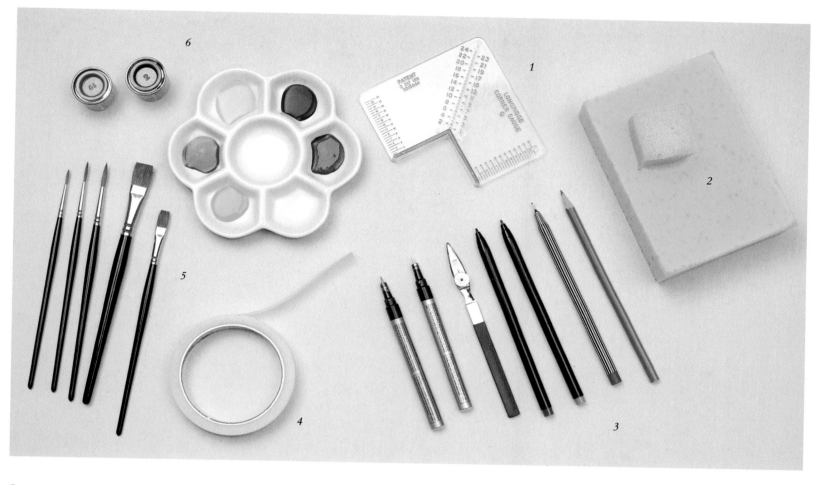

SELF-ADHESIVE DECORATIONS

Rolls of printed borders are available to apply to a mat for a very quick, instant effect. This is cheating, but in some instances they can look very effective and it is good to know how to apply them – see the *Print of Old Master* project on page 50.

You can also get sheets of self-adhesive corners and flourishes which, when used sparingly, can look very good. Lastly, there is self-adhesive lettering, which is applied rather laboriously letter by letter, but is very useful if you need to make a title and are not enough of a calligrapher to print the letters yourself.

TAPE

The only tape that you dare to apply to the **face** of a mat is no-stick tape; any other type of tape will drag the surface off the board. No-stick tape is marvelous for creating a mask so that you can make a decorative border, and a roll of it is essential equipment for any mat decorator. You can also obtain sheets of low-tack masking film for making stencils.

PAINTS

I use the new type of artist's paints extensively in mat decoration as they are so versatile. They can be applied thickly straight from the pot, or diluted to form a watercolor. In a slightly diluted state they are excellent in a ruling pen for ruling lines.

Artist's watercolors can also be used in mat decoration. Free-hand decorations are fine with pan or tube watercolors, but I prefer the liquid watercolors for spraying as there is no danger of lumps.

Basic Mat Decorating Kit

1. *Corner gauge*
2. *Selection of sponges*
3. *Pencil, felt-tip pens, ruling pen, gold and silver pens*
4. *No-stick tape*
5. *Sable artist's brushes (Nos 1, 3, and 5) and flat brushes (12mm/6mm – ½ inch and ¼ inch)*
6. *Paints, either a set of the new artist's paints or watercolors*

Basic Framing Techniques

When you start framing and mat cutting, you will need some scraps of molding and pieces of matboard to practice on. My local picture framing shop often has these for sale very cheaply, and they are absolutely ideal to learn with. They can be made into small frames that can then be used for things like photographs and will give you practice without too much expense.

Basic framing techniques

A GOOD "PRACTICE" FRAME TO MAKE IS 8 BY 6 INCHES (or 20 by 15cm), which can later be used with or without a mat for framing standard-size photographs.

USING THE MITER SAW

To cut the frame molding, start by swinging the saw blade to the left and lock it in the 45° position. Lift the saw blade gently in your right hand, place the end of the molding underneath it with the rabbet facing you and gently lower the blade onto the molding. Hold the molding firmly with your left hand, pressing it down and against the back of the saw bed. Draw the handle toward you for the first cut, then saw gently and evenly all the way through the molding.

The measurement for the frame is taken on the inside of the rabbet and a small allowance of 2mm is added to the measurement for "ease" so that the glass, mat, and backing will slip into the finished frame easily. For your practice frame mark $7^{15}/_{16}$ inch (20.2cm), the measurement for the long side of the frame, on the inside edge of the rabbet and then continue the line round onto the top of the molding above the back of the rabbet. Swing the saw blade to the right and lock it in position. Lift the blade and insert the molding, positioning it so that the cut will cross your mark. Cut as before. This is now your master piece that you can use to measure the other long side – or, if you are making a set of frames the same size, all the long sides.

▶ *To make the first cut with the miter saw, swing the blade to the left and cut off the end of the molding with the rabbet facing you.*

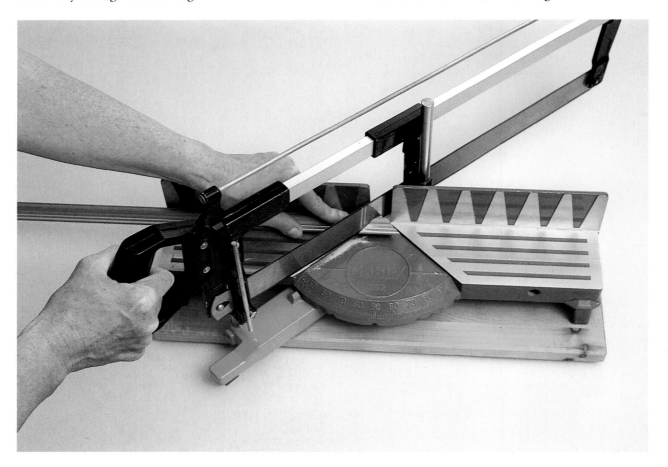

To cut the second piece of this length make the preliminary cut with the saw blade on the left-hand side, then put the length of molding back to back with the master to mark the required length on the back. Move the blade to the right and make the second cut.

Repeat this whole process for the two short sides of the frame – in this instance, making these 6 inches (15.2cm) long. Always cut the long sides of any frame first – if you make a mistake on one, it can be cut down to make a short side!

READY-MADE FRAMES

Widely available, these are a good, quick alternative for use around a decorated mat. They are normally sold complete with glass, but in my experience the backing boards provided are not of the quality of 2mm hard-board and so may need substituting.

GLUING AND CLAMPING

The four pieces of molding are now put into a band clamp. Release the lock on the clamp and draw the band out to roughly the shape of the frame, slotting it through the three corner pieces. Adjust the clamp and the four lengths of molding until everything is square. Remove the two short lengths and spread wood glue sparingly on both ends so that all four corners will be glued. Replace and then tighten the band slightly and lock in position checking that the four corners are square and the whole frame is straight, and start to apply pressure by tightening. The glue will be squeezed out of the joints and should be wiped away with a cotton swab so that you can see whether the corners are still positioned correctly. Continue tightening until the band is twanging, remove any excess glue, and then leave two to three hours for the glue to set.

PINNING

For anything other than small, lightweight frames, the corners should be reinforced with panel pins. With the frame held upright, hammer the pins in gently – a narrow nail punch can be used to drive the pinhead

▲ *After transferring the frame measurement onto the molding, swing the saw blade to the right, positioning the* molding at the mark and make the second cut, again holding the molding firmly in place. ▼ *Use the first cut length of molding as a "master" to mark the length of the opposite piece.*

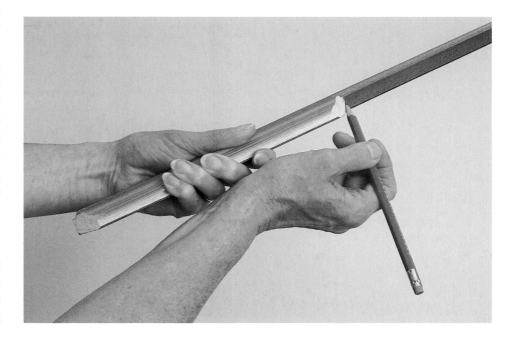

▶ *To join the frame, position the molding in the clamp with plastic support pieces at each corner and apply glue to both ends of each short piece of molding.*

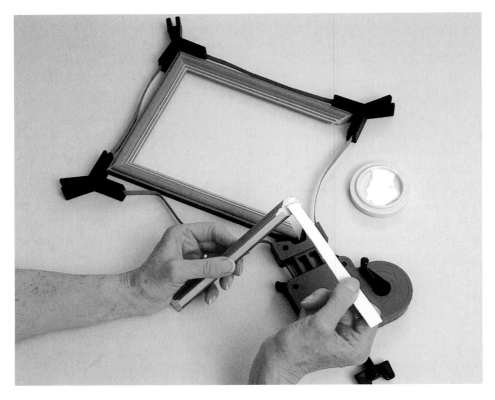

▼ *Lock the clamp, checking that each corner is square and removing excess glue, then continue tightening the clamp and leave 2 to 3 hours until the glue has set.*

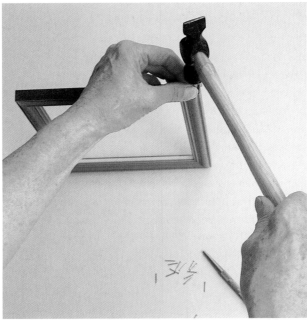

▲ *Stand the frame upright on a flat surface when hammering in reinforcing panel pins at the corners.*

below the surface and the tiny holes filled (and, if necessary, touched up with paint or stain) afterward.

ASSEMBLY

The backing board and glass (and mat, if required) are all cut to the same measurement – for our practice frame, this is 8 × 6 inches (or 20 × 15cm) – and they should slip into the frame easily as it has been cut fractionally bigger.

To cut the backing board – usually 2mm hardboard – first mark it out to size with a pencil and ruler and then score twice along the marked lines with a mat knife against a straightedge. If you move the scored line to the edge of a table and "crack" the board down and then up, you will find that it will break easily along the line. Any slightly rough edges can be sanded away. See page 26 for mat-cutting techniques.

If you are having your glass cut for you, take the frame along to the glass retailer so that it can be made exactly the right size. If you want to have a go yourself, mark out the size with a felt-tip pen and use your glass cutter against a straightedge to make one firm score. You will hear the scratch when the glass is being scored correctly. Place the scored line along the edge of a piece of board or over a matchstick and press down gently. The glass should break cleanly along the line. It is best to have some spare pieces of glass to practice on until you become confident.

To clean the glass, use glass cleaner and a soft cloth. Immediately after the glass has been cleaned, put it in the frame followed by the mat, picture, and finally the backing board. Do not delay in doing this or specks of dust will fall on the glass and you will have to start cleaning all over again. The backing board needs to be fastened firmly in place with either hammer and pins or a Pushmate. The pins or securing tabs need to be about 3 inches (or 8cm) apart and spaced out evenly around the frame.

The back of the frame is then sealed against dirt and insects with gummed brown paper tape. Tear off four pieces of tape that are longer than the sides of the frame, dampen one at a time with a wet sponge and place it neatly and evenly on the back of the frame covering the join and slightly away from the edge. Tape two opposite sides first, then tape the other two sides allowing the tapes to cross at the corners. Put the frame somewhere flat to dry, which will take about an hour, then carefully trim the excess tape away. The back should now look neat as well as being properly sealed.

Screw eyes are placed roughly one-third of the way down the side of the frame and in the center of the underside of the molding. Make a starter hole with a bradawl, then screw in the eye to the hilt by hand.

The hanging cord is threaded through the screw eyes and I always think it is best used double. The ends are

▼ *To cut hardboard, make a double score along the marked line and "crack" it across a table edge. Use sandpaper to smooth the edges.*

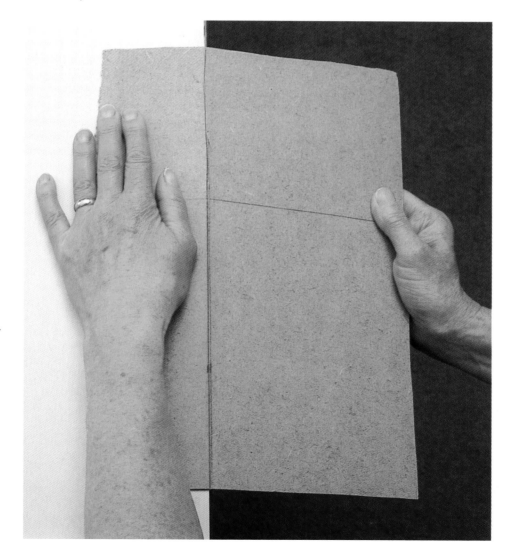

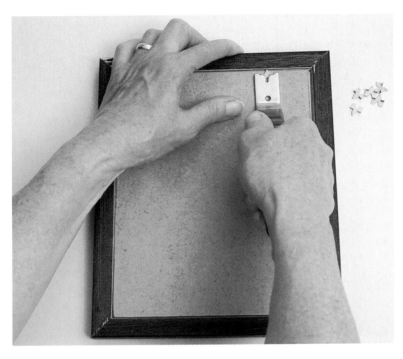

▲ *The glass, mat, picture, and backing board can easily be secured into the frame using a Pushmate and tabs.*

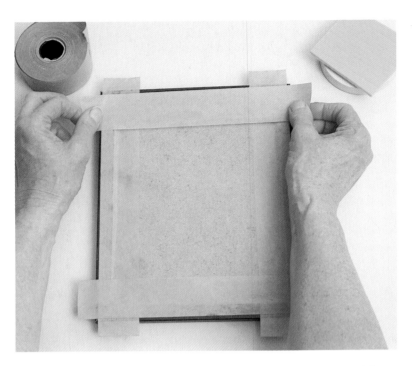

▲ *Finish off the assembly by applying gummed brown paper tape all around the back to give a neat result.*

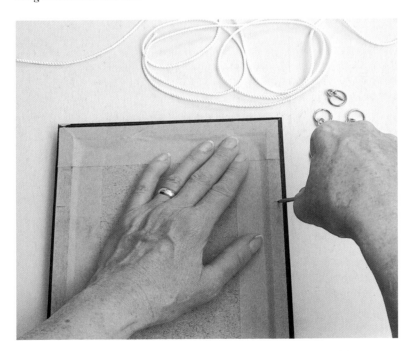

▲ *Use a bradawl to start the holes for the screw eyes about one-third of the way down from the top of the frame.*

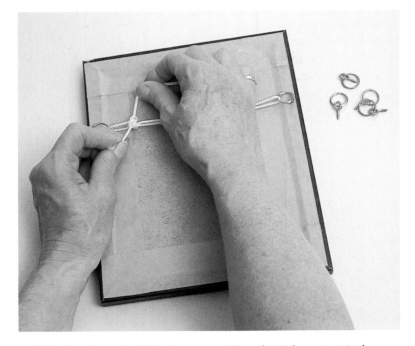

▲ *Fix the hanging cord with the knot to one side so that it does not get in the way of the picture hook.*

tied around both pieces of the cord and the knot is made to one side so that it does not interfere with the hook when the picture is hung.

MAKING FRAMES FROM OTHER MATERIALS

There is no need to use conventional moldings to make a picture frame. Frames can equally well be made from a flat piece of wood (plywood is a good choice) with the appropriate size hole cut in the middle to form an opening. The wood can then be painted, stained, or decorated as required. However, some arrangement has then to be made on the back to contain the glass, picture, and backing board. I have shown such a frame in my *Miniature beaded frames* project on page 56 and *Kitchen poster* project on page 78.

Cheap frames can also be made from cardboard or corrugated paper, where maximum advantage can be taken of the lined effect. These frames do not last very well, however, and so are really suitable only for use with photographs or other "temporary" pictures.

REJUVENATING OLD FRAMES

When I want an old frame, my first port of call is the local garage sale. Quite good frames can be picked up cheaply and if you are lucky they have their glass and backing board intact, so everything can be recycled. Another good source of supply is the local saleroom or auction house. Try to go to a household sale rather than an antiques sale and you should find boxes of discarded frames among the various lots.

Sometimes the corners on old frames will be a little loose and need to be strengthened. Insert a little wood glue into the corners, put the frame into your band clamp, tighten the whole thing up, and leave the glue to dry. To make sure that the corners of large frames are strong, hammer in a 2 inch (5cm) oval nail (with the long side along the grain) in each corner, then cover the head with a little filler.

Most old wood frames benefit from a rub over with fine steel wool. This will get rid of any dirt and grime and prepare the surface for painting. Do not, however, use steel wool on gilt frames.

CHOOSING MAT PROPORTIONS

The size border you need on your mat depends partly on the size picture you are framing and the effect you want to achieve – some small pictures, for example, can look good in a mat with narrow borders, while others might need a wider border. There are no rules about this, so take your time experimenting with mat-board scraps until you get the effect you are happy with.

You will usually need wider borders when you want to add decoration to the mat – the amount you need for this depends on the type and size of the decorative effect. Once you have decided on the proportions of the mat, the matboard has to be cut to size and then the beveled-edge opening made.

CUTTING MATS TO SIZE

To cut a mat to size, first mark out the measurements on a large sheet or matboard, trying to minimize any wastage. Place the sheet on a piece of spare backing board and cut through the matboard firmly with a mat knife. For our practice frame, the mat is 8 by 6 inches (or 20 by 15cm).

▼ *Use fine steel wool to clean up an old frame.*

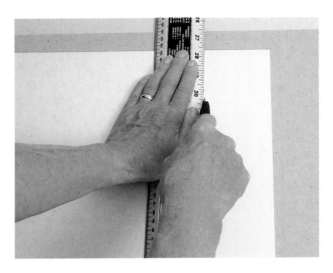

▲ *Cut matboard to size on some spare backing board with a mat knife along a firmly held straightedge.*

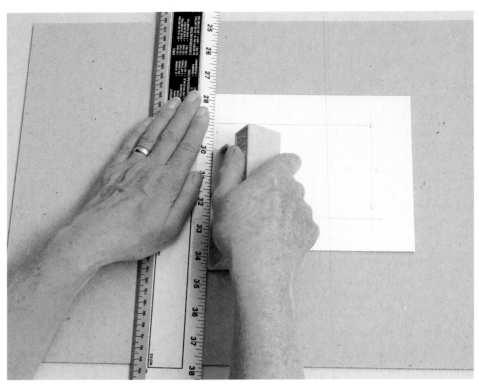

▶ *Once the size of the opening has been marked out on the back of the mat, position your straightedge correctly, and use a hand-held mat cutter to cut the first bevel.*

▶ *After cutting around all four edges of the opening (rotating the mat clockwise for each cut), the center "fallout" should come away easily. If not, use an X-Acto knife to remove it.*

CUTTING THE OPENING

A good size border for the mat to fit our practice frame would be 1¼ inches (3cm). You can use the width of your ruler to mark this out – this time on the back of the matboard – making lines parallel to the edge, adding ³⁄₁₆ inch (5mm) to the bottom border and crossing the lines at the corners.

Position your straightedge and hand-held mat cutter parallel to the line so that, when inserted, the blade of the cutter will start at the cross and run along the line. When you are satisfied that you are in position, insert the blade and push along the line, stopping at the cross at the other end. Take your blade out, turn the mat clockwise and reposition the cutter on the next side and repeat the process until all four sides are cut and the center comes away: this is called the "fallout." You will probably need to practice with your cutter for a little while to attain perfectly straight sides and crisp corners without overcuts. If you undercut a corner slightly, use an X-Acto knife to remove the fallout.

CUTTING A DOUBLE MAT

If two pieces of matboard are cut to the same overall size, but given different widths of border, it is possible to get an interesting effect when they are placed together. Two different colors can be used, but two mats of the same color are also surprisingly effective. The two mats are held together with double-sided adhesive tape. A small piece of tape is placed on each side of the lower mat called the "inner," well back from the cut edge, the protective paper is peeled off, and the "outer" or top mat is carefully placed in position. Double-sided adhesive tape is very sticky so you have only one chance to get the position correct.

FASTENING A PRINT TO A MAT

The simplest way of doing this is with masking tape. Lay the print faceup on the table, then slip two pieces of masking tape about 3 inches (or 8cm) long under the print and diagonally across the top corners. Hold the mat over the print in the correct position and gently lower it onto the print checking all the time that it is in

◄ *A double mat allows you to have two borders of different widths in the same or contrasting colors.*

▼ *To fasten a picture to its mat, place the picture faceup on a surface with masking tape diagonally across the top corners and position and press down the mat exactly where you want it. Add more tape on the back of the picture if necessary.*

the right place. When it is on the print, press firmly on the top corners and it should be held sufficiently for you to be able to turn the whole thing over. More tape can then be applied on the other side if necessary.

Basic Decorative Techniques

Decoration can be applied to the frame, to the mat, or to both, depending on the picture that is being framed. There is obviously more scope for decoration when the frame is around something plain like a mirror, a memo board, or even an old sepia photograph, but when decoration is going to be used with a painting or colored print the whole effect must harmonize.

Decorating frames

ALL FRAMES ARE DYED AFTER THEY ARE CUT AND before they are assembled. This avoids the uneven effect that may occur if glue has been squeezed onto the surface of the molding at the corners, which would have the effect of sealing the wood and preventing the dye from taking properly.

DYEING

I apply water-based dye with wads of cotton wool and wear rubber gloves. Pour a small amount of dye onto the cotton wool and apply it directly and evenly to the first molding. Make sure that the edges and the back of the molding are also covered. Repeat this on the other three pieces of molding and leave to dry.

Exciting color variations can be obtained by putting one dye over another, and a different effect is achieved when the second color is applied before the first one has dried. You should therefore save all your scraps so that you can experiment with them and find color combinations that you like. For example, if you are using rose and lavender dyes, apply the rose first, then, while it is still wet, apply the lavender. Repeat, this time waiting until the rose dye is dry. This will produce two completely different colors – and if you put the lavender on first and then the rose, you can get two more colors.

Further experiments can be made with combinations of the pastel colors and the wood colors which produce a range of more subtle shades. The important thing to remember is that the color you finally select must blend with and complement the picture and mat that will be in the frame.

Spirit-based dyes are very intense and should only be used when you need a hard, bright color. They can also be applied with cotton wool wads, but should be used sparingly, one coat usually being sufficient.

USING WAX

Liming wax is most effective when used on a strongly grained wood such as oak and is particularly pleasing if it is applied after water-based dyes, although it can be applied on bare wood. Allow the wood to dry completely if it has been dyed, then apply the liming wax liberally with a pad of steel wool, rubbing it into the grain of the wood. If you are liming a small or medium-size frame, you can work the liming wax into all four pieces before you start to rub it off, but if you are working on a large frame, it is best to work on just two pieces at a time because the liming wax has to be rubbed off within a few minutes and should **never** be allowed to dry because it sets hard.

Clear wax on a soft cloth are used to rub the liming wax off and will simultaneously produce a very pleasant sheen on the wood. If your molding has a sculptured profile it is very good to leave some liming wax in the grooves to accentuate the effect.

The color of the wood (or the dyed wood) molding can be changed by the application of colored waxes.

▼ *The best way to apply dye to wood molding is with wads of cotton wool.*

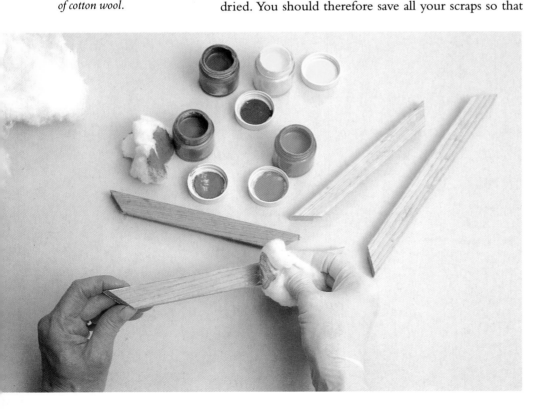

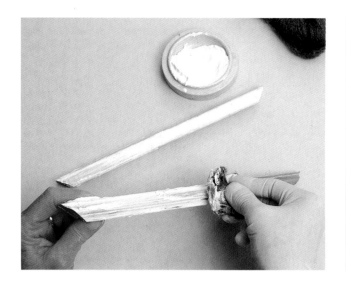

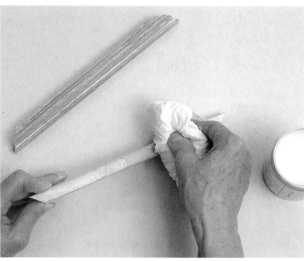

◄◄ *Liming wax is applied liberally to a plain or dyed molding using steel wool.*

◄ *Before it dries, rub off the liming wax using clear wax and a soft cloth.*

These are available in a range of wood colors and the darker colors are particularly useful for darkening down a rather brash dye. The method of application is simply to rub on sparingly with a cloth and then to buff it off. If you have not achieved sufficient density, the process can be repeated.

A gold wax can also be used to change the color of dyed wood slightly or to heighten a certain part of the molding. Apply with an old toothbrush, or even your finger if you wish to cover large areas, and use a circular motion when applying to eliminate uneven application.

Buffing with a soft cloth will help to spread the wax and take away any excess. If you want to gild one specific edge of a molding, it is better to use gold paint, which will give you a crisper finish.

COLORED VARNISHES

You can buy colored varnishes in a small range of colors which can be applied to bare wood with a paintbrush. I find that the best method of application is to apply several thin coats to get the color you want, as one heavy application tends to run and form pools.

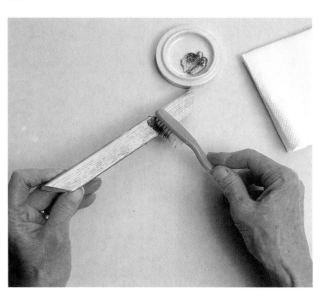

◄◄ *Colored waxes, applied with a cloth (or strong tissue), can change the color of wood.*

◄ *Apply gold wax with an old toothbrush (or your finger) and buff with a soft cloth.*

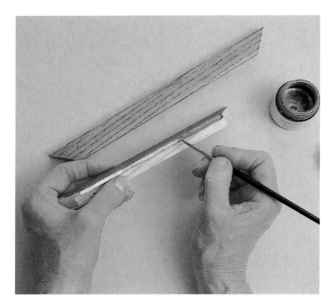

▲ *A gold "sight edge" can be created by using gold paint applied with a fine artist's brush.*

▶ *Metal leaf can be applied to a frame in any pattern you like, once gold size has been "painted" onto the molding. After the backing paper has been peeled off, excess leaf can be removed with a brush.*

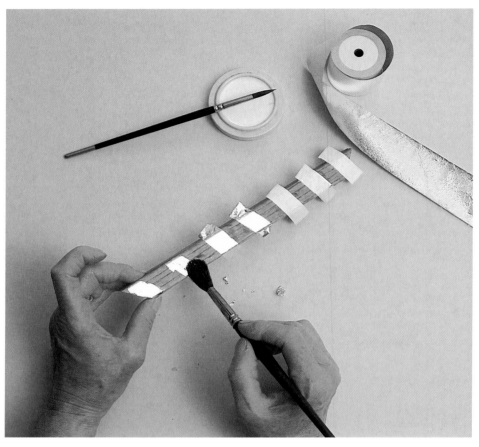

USING PAINT

The small jars of paint sold for model making are ideal for decorating frames – they are sold with either matte or gloss finishes. Apply with a paintbrush and leave plenty of time for each coat to dry. When you apply the paint to bare wood you will probably find that you need three coats to give a really good finish.

The new water-based artist's paints are also ideal. The colors can be mixed, but are quick to dry and the brushes can be washed out in water. Because this paint does not soak into the wood like water-based wood dyes, it produces a different, rather more opaque effect. A good combination can be achieved on molding with a sculptured profile by carefully applying water-based dye to one part of the molding, allowing it to dry, then mixing artist's paint to exactly the same color and painting it on the rest of the molding. This produces an inter-

esting gradation of color. I find this paint is also the best for sponging onto molding and for stenciling no-frame frames on borders. I use the paint without dilution to produce a rather crusty effect, but I mix the colors to blend with areas in the picture.

Gold paint can be used to give a sight edge or a thin gold line. All gold paint requires stirring very carefully and should be applied with a fine artist's brush which should be thoroughly cleaned afterward.

APPLYING METAL LEAF

First paint the gold size onto the frame in the desired pattern, allow the size to become tacky, then carefully cut off small pieces of the metal leaf together with its backing paper and apply to the sized areas. It will stick instantly, the backing paper can be peeled off, and any excess leaf can be brushed away with a soft brush.

Decorating mats

There is a wonderful choice of ways in which you can decorate a mat, all of which are carried out after the opening has been cut to the finished size.

LINING RECTANGULAR MATS

The simplest form of mat decoration is lining and, with normal rectangular and square mats, starts with the use of a corner gauge.

Take the practice mat that you cut earlier, tuck the gauge into the cut corner of the opening, and mark off the same two or three measurements on each corner. These, when joined up, will give lines to lead the eye into the picture. This is ample for a mat with borders of 1¼ inches (3cm). If you want to draw more lines (or to have a washline – see page 36), the borders would have to be cut wider to accommodate them.

With a beveled-edge ruler turned on its face to avoid blotting, carefully join the marks to form lines. Try using felt-tip pens in subtle colors, gold pens, and also a ruling pen filled with paint for different effects.

Now, with the ruling pen, try mixing colors, aiming for a range that complements a picture. There is nothing quite as nice as a line drawn with a ruling pen, for not only can you choose your own colors, but you can alter the width of the line as well. I use either watercolor or diluted artist's colors in ruling pens: both are equally good. If you want a gold line, mix gold acrylic paint with a little water and keep it in a small screw-top jar; it should last for several weeks.

APPLIED DECORATIONS

The next thing to try is using your corner gauge to mark out for applied self-adhesive strip decoration. Tuck the gauge into the corners of the opening and mark points that are well away from the cut edge. Hold the strip roughly along the sides of the mat and tear off four pieces that will be long enough to cross at the corners. Remove the backing paper and gently line the strip up to the marks taking care that it is not pressed down until it is correctly positioned. Then press the center of each strip lightly to hold it in place.

▼ *Lines can be drawn with felt-tip pens, gold pens, or a ruling pen, used against a ruler held with its bevel edge facing downward.*

▲ *The starting point for most mat decoration is to use a corner gauge, tucked into the corner of the opening, to mark the position of the decoration across the corners.*

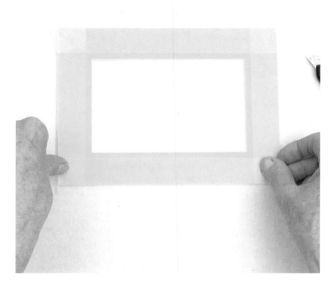

◄ *To apply self-adhesive strip decoration, first use a corner gauge to mark its position and then carefully lay the strips between the marks.*

► *When just one area of the mat is to be decorated, apply lengths of wide no-stick tape around the mat, after first marking it out with a corner gauge.*

▼ *Sponging a masked mat is an easy method of decoration and can be done with any number of colors to match the picture.*

Using a very sharp X-Acto or mat knife and a small straightedge, the corners can now be mitered. Cut carefully on the same line through the top layer and the lower layer, removing the excess. The two cut edges should fit neatly together forming a perfect miter.

The corner gauge is also used to mark mats before applying instant corner motifs and flourishes. These need to be used with discretion but can be very effective. They can be used on their own or combined with lines.

MASKING MATS

For techniques such as sponging or spraying, you will need to make a mask. This is done by covering parts of the mat with no-stick tape leaving an area exposed for decoration.

With your practice mat, tuck the corner gauge into the corners of the opening and mark off two measurements about ⅝ inch (1.5cm) apart. Between these marks is the area that will be decorated. Tape the outer line first using your marks as the guide and crossing the tape at the corners. More care is needed at the corners when taping the inner line – these can either be mitered or crossed providing that no tape protrudes onto the area between the two tape lines.

SPONGING

This is one of the easiest forms of mat decoration. First mask the mat, then cut pieces from a synthetic sponge keeping a separate piece for every color that you want to use. Using slightly diluted artist's paint, mix three colors – preferably one dark, one medium, and one pale – that blend with the picture and choose the darkest of the three to start with. Dip the sponge into the paint and get rid of any excess on a piece of paper towel. Pat the sponge onto the exposed area of the mat at intervals all around, keeping the application even.

Allow a short while for this to dry and then repeat the process with the medium color, filling in any gaps that may have been left. Finally, and very delicately, apply the pale color taking care that it does not obscure the other two colors. When all the paint is thoroughly dry remove the tape and you should have a mottled border with clean, straight edges. This can be further enhanced with gold lines.

SPRAYING

Mask the mat as before and mix watercolors that will blend with the picture or use a child's airbrush, selecting the colored felt-tip pens that will suit. Spray one color sparingly onto the exposed area and immediately spray on another. You will find that this has the effect of color mixing so that blue and yellow will look green, and blue and red will look purple. A third color can be used to enhance the effect, either all around or in selected areas.

Try masking with a scrap piece of matboard and changing the colors as you go to produce a candy-stripe effect, or mask with a combination of other shapes and tape to produce interesting patterns.

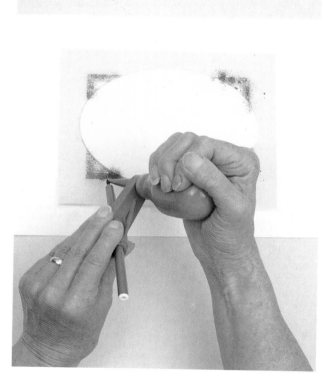

▲ *A child's airbrush, used with different colors of felt-tip pen, provides a delicate but effective method of mat decoration.*

▲ *Using an oval mask with a child's airbrush (as in the photograph left) produces this interesting decorative effect.*

DECORATING WITH CUT SHAPES OR SWABS

The exposed area of a masked mat can be decorated with cut shapes of board dipped into paint, cotton swabs dipped into paint, or any other ingenious idea that you may have for transferring paint onto the surface. An effective method that I use frequently is to dip the edge of a thick piece of cardboard into the paint, putting the edge down onto the exposed area and dragging it slightly so that it makes an attractive graded mark. A second color can be added between the first marks if required. I have used both cardboard and swabs in my *Child's painting* project on page 60.

WASHLINING

This traditional form of mat decoration for watercolors is a much sought-after skill and the mat must be cut with much wider borders than usual, 3½ to 4 inches (9 to 10cm), to accommodate it. The marks for the lines are made using the corner gauge, as for normal lining, but the design can vary.

A good combination for washlining is to make marks at ³⁄₁₆ inch, ⅜ inch, 1¼ inches, and 2 inches (5mm, 1cm, 3cm, and 5cm). The inside mark at ³⁄₁₆ inch is called the *sight line*, the two middle marks at ⅜ inch and 1¼ inches will be either side of the *wash*, and the outer mark at 2 inches is called the *lead line*. The whole point of a washline is that it leads the eye comfortably into the watercolor and blends and harmonizes with it, so the colors must be picked out of the picture and each watercolor should be given its own washline. This makes the whole thing very special.

Mix two washes of paint in separate containers, choosing one dark color and one light color to blend with the painting. Adjust the ruling pen to a medium line and fill it with the darker of the two washes. Turn a ruler facedown to avoid blotting and position it on the

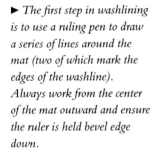

► *The first step in washlining is to use a ruling pen to draw a series of lines around the mat (two of which mark the edges of the washline). Always work from the center of the mat outward and ensure the ruler is held bevel edge down.*

outside of the mat lined up on the inner (sight line) marks. Carefully rule the first line, turn the mat, reposition the ruler, refill the pen, and rule the next line. Provided the ruler is kept on the outside of the mat, all four inner sight lines can be ruled like this without waiting for the paint to dry on the previous one as there will be no chance of smudging.

Clean out the pen, adjust to widen the line, and refill using the paler of the two washes. Position the ruler on the next set of marks (the inside of the washline) and rule the next line around the mat, turning it and refilling the pen each time. Move the ruler to the next set of marks and repeat the process with the same color paint. Lastly, clean out the pen again, adjust it back to a medium line, fill it with the darker color, and draw the outer set of lines for the lead line.

Although this seems like a lengthy process there can be no shortcuts without either waiting for each line to dry, or smudging the previous line, but I find that a rhythm develops which makes it quite pleasant to do.

An option is to put an additional fine gold line on the outside of the outer (lead) line and close to it, which is done with a mix of gold acrylic paint and water. This gives the washline a little sparkle without making it look vulgar. Allow all the lines to become completely dry before progressing to the wash.

Take a little of the paler color and dilute it in a third dish to make the wash, using a lot of water until it is very faint. With a ½ inch (12mm) flat sable artist's brush carefully paint plain clean water between the two washline markers around the mat without stopping. Immediately paint the pale wash around the mat, taking care to keep within your ruled lines. The fact that water has been painted on first will help the wash disperse and spread, but there is no worry about the lines smudging providing they were completely dry before you started.

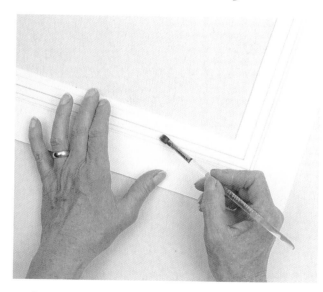

▲ *After mixing the wash color you need (so that it is ready), "paint" the area for the washline between the lines with plain clean water, working around the mat without stopping.*

▶ *Immediately after the clean water has been applied, use the same brush to apply the pale wash, taking care to stay within the ruled lines.*

Projects

Τ he basic framing techniques and the basic decoration techniques now have to be combined to suit the item to be framed. This is enormous fun and the ideas are endless. The inspiration can start with the design and finish of an old frame, with the picture itself, or even with the color of a piece of matboard.

Sepia photograph

A friend recently brought me an old photograph of her great-grandmother to frame. It is a lovely sepia color and I was able to find an old oak frame to cut down for it. I also had fun experimenting with some new instant mat decorations.

You will need

Preparation
- Old oak frame to be cut down
- Precut mat in pale peach with an oval opening
- Basic framing kit

Decoration
- Spirit-based wood dye in medium oak
- Sheet of adhesive mat decorations in sepia

Assembly
- Basic assembly kit

PREPARATION

When you are cutting down a old frame, try to choose one that is much larger than you need because then it does not matter if you damage the corners when you take it apart. This can happen as you try to remove the excessively long nails that were always used on old frames: if these nails are not removed and the saw hits one, it blunts the blade very quickly. If the frame has still got its glass and backing board, you can reuse these, cutting them down to size.

When a frame is being cut down, it is far better to make new cuts on all the corners, even if some of them do not look too bad. New cuts will ensure that the frame will fit together perfectly, so the first task is to cut the long sides to 10 inches (or 25cm) plus ease and the short sides to 8 inches (or 20cm) plus ease and join them as normal.

While I was pinning my frame I noticed that there were one or two rough pieces at the corners, so I disguised these with a little medium oak spirit-based dye spread over the frame with a wad of cotton wool.

An oval opening in the mat not only looks attractive but is very appropriate for this period photograph. You may be able to buy a ready-made mat with an oval already cut in it; if not, ask your local picture framer to cut an oval in pale peach matboard with the border at the bottom wider than at the top and sides to accommodate the design.

DECORATION

You will not want to overdo the decoration on this mat, so choose two designs from the sheet that make a pair. As mat decorations like these are very conveniently printed on clear squared plastic it is easy to experiment with where to place each design. When you have finally decided on the positions, measure and make guide marks and then transfer the designs onto the board by scribbling on the surface of the plastic with a pencil or ballpoint pen.

ASSEMBLY

Lay the photograph faceup on the table and use two pieces of masking tape across the corners to fasten the mat in place as described on page 27. You can then turn the photograph and mat over and apply additional pieces of masking tape to make it really secure.

1 If there are any rough or damaged corners of the frame once you have cut it down and reassembled it, disguise these with spirit-based wood dye applied with cotton wool.

The glass and backing board need to be cut down to the same measurement as the mat. If you are cutting down old glass, take care that you cut the piece of glass from the center, away from the dirty edges. This may seem a little wasteful but the scraps can rarely be used, and the edges are usually almost impossible to clean.

The frame is assembled in the normal way and a normal strength cord used. Alternatively, if the photograph and frame are fairly small and light, a small decorative hanger could be pinned on the top at the back or, for standing on a shelf or cupboard, a stand-up or "strut" back can be attached.

2 Decide where you want to put your applied decorations and then make a light pencil mark on the mat.

3 Position the sheet of decorations over your marks and transfer the design onto the mat by rubbing the back of the sheet with a pencil or a ballpoint pen.

4 Once all the decoration has been applied to the mat, it can be secured to the photograph and assembled into the frame in the normal way.

Shell mirror

I found this collection of shells at a garage sale and decided that they would make a good decoration for a bathroom mirror. The shells are large so I needed to use a molding with a wide, flat profile so that I could stick the arrangements safely to it.

PREPARATION

First cut the molding into four pieces with an inside measurement of 9 inches (23cm), rub down with steel wool, and wax each piece with clear wax, applied with a soft cloth, before joining them to make the frame.

DECORATION

With the frame flat on a table, you can start to arrange the shells on it. It's best to place the largest shells in the center and arrange the others in clusters around them to produce a symmetrical pattern. Where the shells have interesting mother-of-pearl on the inside, reverse them so that this will show.

Once you are happy with the arrangement, gently remove the shells from each side at a time, so that you can replace them in exactly the same order with generous helpings of wood glue and then allow everything to dry overnight.

The next day you hope to find that everything is firm and dry. But, because of the lovely curving shapes of the shells, you may find some big gaps between them and the frame that need to be filled with the clay. Each gaping hole should be filled, smoothed off with a cotton swab dipped into water, and allowed to dry for two days. It is easy to tell when the clay is dry because it turns from a rather gray color to white. Check the effect carefully and sand off any remaining rough edges with fine sandpaper.

ASSEMBLY

When the clay is completely dry, put the frame facedown on a soft cushion to protect the shells and place the piece of mirror into it. This should always be a snug

1 After cutting the molding to size, rub it down to a smooth finish with fine-grade steel wool.

2 Apply clear wax to the molding with a cloth or paper towel once the surface is smooth.

fit, as should the hardboard that is placed on top. Now fasten the "sandwich" securely as normal, taking care not to press down too hard, which could damage the fragile shells.

Finally, with the mirror still facedown on the cushion, tape the back and fit screw eyes plus a medium thickness picture cord, used double thickness because of the weight of the mirror.

3 Take some time arranging the shells to produce a symmetrical pattern with the biggest shells in the center of each arrangement. Reverse any mother-of-pearl shells.

4 The individual shells are held in place with wood glue once you are happy with the arrangement and, when the glue has dried, any gaps are filled with clay.

Kitchen memo board

My love affair with blue-and-white pottery started years ago and I use it all the time, hanging my chipped plates on the kitchen walls. But inevitably there are breakages, which I hate to throw away. I needed a kitchen memo board, so decided to smash my breakages into even smaller pieces and use them as a mosaic. I have even been able to add blue and white shards that I dug up in the garden. It is interesting to think that I am not the first person in this old house that liked blue-and-white pottery.

You will need

Preparation
- Old frame
- Corkboard to fit it
- White acrylic paint
- White gloss paint
- Fine sandpaper
- 000 steel wool

Decoration
- Selection of broken pottery
- Heavy hammer
- Heavy-duty clear plastic bag
- Ceramic tile adhesive/grout
- Clear varnish
- Blue gloss paint

Assembly
- Basic assembly kit

PREPARATION

An old frame is often very dirty (this one was found in a box of junk at an auction), so the first job is usually to clean it thoroughly, then lightly sand it, and finally give it a good rub with steel wool to remove any grease. When the frame is ready, undercoat it with acrylic paint and then paint two coats of gloss on the back, the top of the rabbett, and the sight edge. Also apply two coats of white acrylic paint to the smooth side of the corkboard allowing the first coat to dry before applying the second.

1 The best way to break up china or pottery is to put it into a plastic bag and then hit it with a hammer, holding the neck of the bag tightly.

DECORATION

You will need to wash the pieces of broken pottery and sort them into types and colors – I found that there were many different blues. Then put all the pieces of each type into a plastic bag and, holding the neck tightly to prevent pieces flying about, smash them into tiny pieces with the hammer. The resulting collection of shards can then be tipped on to a sheet of paper and sorted. Discard boring plain white pieces and also pieces that are too curved or shaped on the back to lie down properly, but you might like to keep pieces that have the maker's name in blue because they are fun to include. Soon you will be surrounded by piles of broken pottery in different blues on separate sheets of paper.

There is usually an applicator included in a container of ceramic tile adhesive but it is rather clumsy and large for this purpose, so cut a strip off it to make a more delicate tool. You also need a narrow-bladed tool (I used a palette knife) to help in positioning the shards.

Apply a generous amount of adhesive to the top of the frame, covering about 4 inches (10cm), and smooth it out with the applicator trying to line it up at the sides. Select from the piles of shards and start to nestle each piece into the adhesive taking care that they are level and also that no two pieces from the same plate are side by side. When the first section is complete, tidy up the edges with a cotton swab dipped in water, removing any overhanging adhesive and smooth it off.

As tile adhesive/grout starts to dry out quite quickly forming a hard crust, you must not leave a section half completed, so this decoration means progressing around the frame in small steps. When one section is finished, a new one can be started immediately, the next day, or even the next week, so there is no need to labor over this rather long job.

The next stage is to grout between the pieces of pottery where necessary. Delicately add more tile adhesive/grout between the pieces with a cotton swab, clean

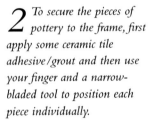

2 To secure the pieces of pottery to the frame, first apply some ceramic tile adhesive/grout and then use your finger and a narrow-bladed tool to position each piece individually.

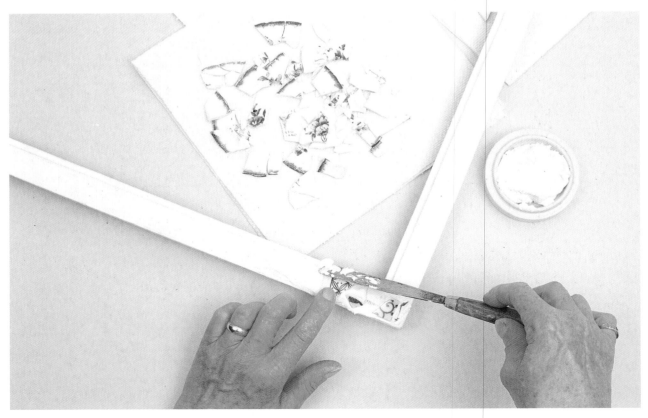

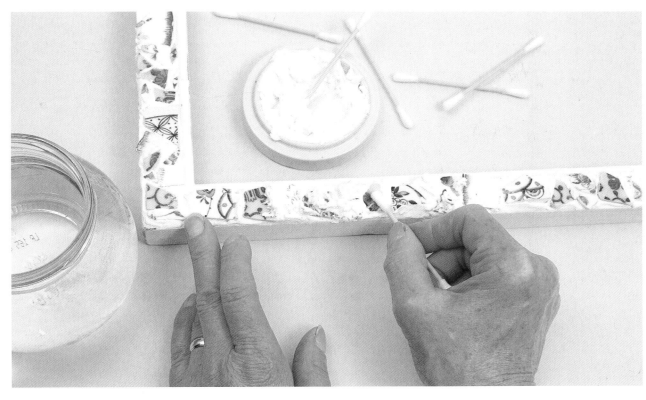

3 *Once all the pieces of pottery have been attached, add more adhesive/grout to fill the gaps between the pieces and polish the surface of each piece with a cotton swab.*

4 *To give the corkboard a border, draw faint pencil lines in from the edge and paint between them with a fine brush and the color of your choice.*

up immediately with another swab dipped in water, and finish off by polishing each shard with a dry swab. Also fill any gaps in the adhesive on the edges at this stage.

The decoration must be left to dry completely before the final inspection when any overhangs can be easily sanded off.

If you want a border on the corkboard, no-stick tape is no good as a mask because the board is so absorbent that the paint seeps underneath, so it is best to paint it by hand. Measure 1½ inches (4cm) in from all four edges of the corkboard, then a further ³⁄₁₆ inch (5mm) all around for the inner edge and rule faint pencil lines. With blue gloss paint and a fine artist's brush carefully paint between these lines.

ASSEMBLY

Lay the frame facedown on a soft cloth to protect the surface, place the corkboard in it, and assemble in the normal way, using large screw eyes and double-thickness nylon cord as the frame will be heavy.

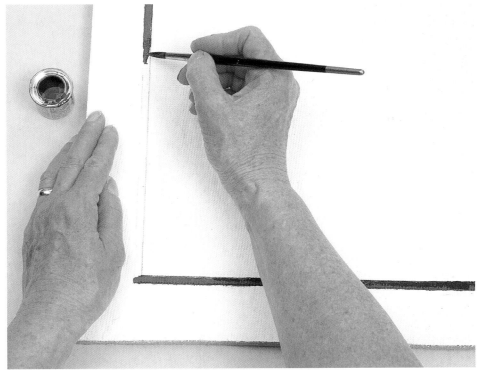

Print of Old Master

This beautiful reproduction of Giotto's Saint Francis was on a calendar and I admired the composition and rich colors. I deliberately picked an ivory color for the double mat to accentuate the richness and then used an applied marbled decoration. To complete the look, I searched for a molding that had a classic but "distressed" finish in old gold.

You will need

Preparation
- Print
- Length of old gold molding 1½ inches (4cm) wide
- Two pieces of mat board in ivory
- Basic framing kit
- Basic mat cutting kit

Decoration
- Two rolls of marbled mat decoration in brown ⅝ inch and ¼ inch (or 1.5cm and 6mm) wide
- Double-sided tape
- Basic mat decoration kit

Assembly
- Glass
- Hardboard
- Basic assembly kit

PREPARATION

Cut two pieces of molding 22 inches (56cm) plus ease and two pieces 18¼ inches (46.5cm) plus ease and make the frame as normal. While the adhesive is setting, you can cut the two ivory mats to the same overall size, but one with equal borders of 2¾ inches (7cm) and the other with equal borders of 3½ inches (9cm).

DECORATION

Using a corner gauge set into the corners of the opening, mark both boards at ¼ inch (or 6mm). Then tear off four pieces of the narrower marbled decoration and apply them to the mat with the wider borders and, similarly apply four lengths of the wider marbled mat decoration to the mat with the narrower borders, mitering both decorative strips neatly at the corners and removing the excess as described on page 34.

Fasten the double mat together as described on page 27. Be very careful to align the two mats when you do this as double-sided tape is extremely sticky and it is very difficult to separate two mats that have been incorrectly stuck together.

1 Once the position of the marbled decoration has been marked out on the mats, it can be applied, using tiny slips of paper at the corners to prevent the ends from sticking down.

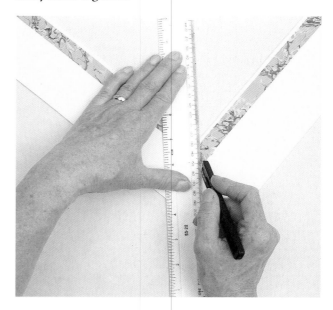

2 Each corner should be mitered with an X-Acto knife, cutting through both strips at the same time, and the excess (and the paper slips) removed.

ASSEMBLY

Place the print faceup on a table and slip two pieces of masking tape under it projecting out top and bottom, then lower the double mat onto the print, pressing down when it is in the correct position. Place the frame facedown on a table, clean the glass, and put it into the frame immediately followed by the double mat and finally the backing board. Fasten securely and tape the back. As this picture is not very heavy, standard screw eyes and mediumweight cord can be used.

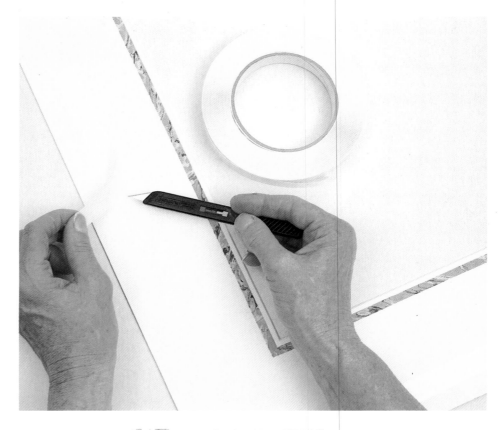

3 *The double mat is held together with double-sided adhesive tape. Stick this down firmly to the lower mat before removing the backing tape.*

4 *Take great care when positioning the upper mat on top of the lower one — the adhesive tape is very strong and mistakes are almost impossible to correct.*

Print-room effect

I visited a splendid print room in a large country house recently and have been very influenced by it. But instead of having a whole room covered with prints, which was the eighteenth-century fashion, I decided to decorate just a small wall area in the same way.

First, I selected one or two fashion prints from my own collection that I particularly liked. Then I hunted through my books for a good selection of engravings of frames and borders. I took the prints, frames, and borders to be photocopied, making sure that the frames were enlarged so that they fitted the fashion prints exactly.

You will need

Preparation
- One or two fashion prints (or photocopies)
- Prints of borders and frames (or photocopies)
- Plain white paper
- Glass sheets
- Cat litter tray
- Cold tea
- Weights

Decoration and assembly
- Wallpaper paste
- Reusable adhesive
- Artist's matte varnish

PREPARATION

The only trouble with normal photocopying paper is that it is so very white and somehow the alternative cream paper was also not the color that I wanted, so I decided to stain everything myself. To do this, make up a weak tea mixture, pour it into a large shallow dish (a cat litter tray is an ideal shape), put a piece of glass into the tray and lay a print in the liquid for a few minutes until it is ivory colored. Then lift out the glass with the print on it and drain off the excess liquid.

The prints will dry quite happily on the pieces of glass, but if they become a little crinkled, put them between plain white paper under a board with some weights on top for a day or two.

1 A mixture of cold weak tea in a large shallow dish is an ideal way of staining prints to a uniform ivory color. The print is placed on a sheet of glass and lifted out after a few minutes. Leave on the glass to dry.

DECORATION

Cut out the frames and the prints, lay them on a flat surface, and move them around until you are happy with the overall arrangement.

Mark the wall lightly with a pencil to give an indication of the position of each piece, fasten them temporarily to the wall with reusable adhesive, and stand back to check the proportions and overall effect.

ASSEMBLY

When you are satisfied you have got the positions right, mix some wallpaper paste following the instructions for standard wallpaper, coat the back of each print and place it in its position on the wall, using a soft, clean cloth to smooth it flat without rubbing too hard. Then start to build up the pattern of "frames" and borders, pasting and placing one piece at a time.

When the whole area is completely dry, protect the entire design with two coats of artist's matte varnish.

2 Once dry after staining, cut out the prints and the photocopied "frames" and arrange them roughly on a flat surface.

3 On your flat surface, try different combinations of print, "frame," and decorative border, moving them around until you have achieved the effect you want.

4 Having tried various positions and arrangements for the pictures, stick the prints, frames, and decorative borders to the wall using wallpaper paste and protect with varnish.

Miniature beaded frames

I wanted to make some photograph frames that I could stand in a group together and maybe add to in the future. I like the decoration on jewelry and enamelware that was popular in the 1930s, so thought that I would try to simulate it using beads instead of precious stones.

You will need

Preparation
- Scrap plywood
- Sandpaper
- Fine-grade (000) steel wool
- Saws for wood

Decoration
- Small threaded dress beads in various colors
- Artist's paint in colors to blend
- White glue
- Artists' clear varnish

Assembly
- Small pieces of acetate film
- Small stand-up back for each frame
- Hardboard
- Mat knife and straight-edge
- Basic assembly kit

PREPARATION

The size of the frames will obviously depend on the photographs you are using and the cutout can be any shape you want – square, rectangular, round, or oval. For these photographs, I decided to make one rectangular frame 3¼ × 4 inches (or 8.5 × 10.5cm) with a 1⅜- by 2-inch (3.5 × 5cm) cutout and a second oval frame with the same overall dimensions, but with an oval opening – see the shapes below.

If you have the correct saws, you may be able to make your own cutouts, but this is something you might want to leave (as I did) to a carpenter friend.

Cutting plywood is not difficult once you have marked out the shape – you can cut it to size with a tenon saw and cut the opening with a pad saw (drilling one or more holes to start the saw off). If you own (or can borrow) an electric jigsaw, it will make the cutting that much faster.

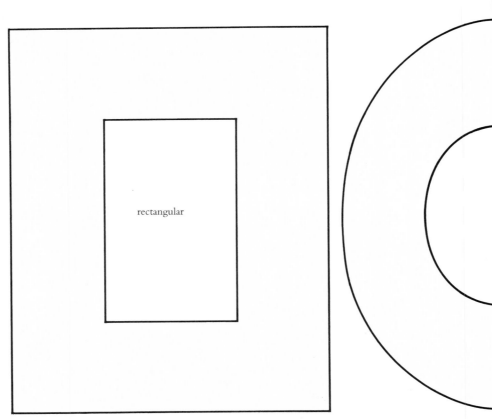

rectangular

oval

The shapes for the frames

1 With the frames cut to size from plywood, and sanded and rubbed with steel wool until smooth, start by marking out each frame into different areas with lines running in different directions.

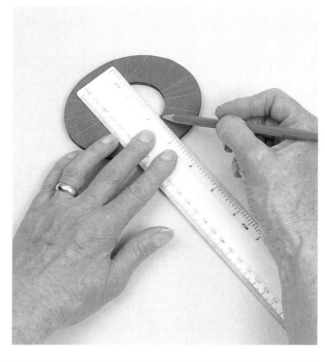

DECORATION

Once the frames have been cut to size, sand each one carefully and then rub with steel wool until they are silky smooth. Work out what color scheme you are going to use – I used two coats of paynes gray on the rectangular frame and two coats of terra-cotta on the oval frame.

When the paint is dry, mark out the shapes you want with pencil on the frames to act as a guide while sticking on the beads. To reflect the most light and to make the beads sparkle, they should be laid in different directions – so divide the area up as much as possible.

Coat one small area with glue and then, very carefully, break the loop of thread on one line of beads. Holding both ends of the thread, lay the line of beads into the glue and hold it there for a few seconds. Once the beads have settled into the glue, you can gently withdraw the thread.

Repeat this process with the next line and continue until the whole glued area has been filled with beads. Then move on to the next area of the same color and repeat the process. When you want to divide two colors with a different line, use the same method, but with greater care on the longer strings of beads.

When the whole frame is filled with beads, allow it to dry and set overnight and then coat the surface liberally with artist's clear varnish in order to secure all the beads from the top. This will take a further two hours to dry.

ASSEMBLY

Using a mat knife and a small straightedge, cut three short hardboard strips ¼ inch (6mm) wide and six strips ⅛ inch (3mm) wide for each frame. Cut the strips into lengths and stick the narrower strips together in pairs. When the glue has set, stick each pair to the wider strip, so that one of the long edges lines up to make a L-shaped channel.

2 Coat one area with glue, then break one end of the thread and lay a line of beads into the glue before withdrawing the thread.

Now cut down a stand-up back so that it will cover the opening in the frame and also trim the support leg making sure that the frame will stand up, leaning slightly backward as it should. Tape the stand-up back temporarily into position and place the hardboard channels on either side and below it. When it is all correct, glue the channels in place and leave to set.

Glass would make these frames too heavy, so it would be better to use acetate film to protect the photographs: simply cut a small rectangle of film which can be slid into place with the photograph into the channels together with the stand-up back.

3 Each glued area is filled with beads running in the same direction – but the direction is altered for the adjacent area to reflect light and to make the beads sparkle.

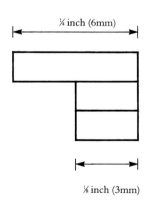

¼ inch (6mm)

⅛ inch (3mm)

The three hardboard strips are glued together as shown to form the L-shaped channels.

4 To provide support for the photograph and also for the stand-up back, the L-shaped hardboard channels are glued to the back of the frame.

Child's painting

Children's or grandchildren's paintings are such fun to display, but I feel that framing them with the conventional mat and frame is a little too formal. On the other hand, if they are just taped on the wall they can get torn. This project, using a corkboard backing and a painted mat, is an answer to both problems, creating a bright, lively yet inexpensive presentation that will make everyone proud.

You will need

Preparation
- Child's painting
- Corkboard 4 inches (10cm) larger all around than the painting
- Deep blue matboard the same size as the corkboard
- Wood sealer
- Basic mat cutting kit

Decoration
- Artist's paints in colors to suit the painting
- Basic mat decoration kit

Assembly
- Masking tape
- White glue
- Wooden board and weights

PREPARATION

The edges of corkboard are often a little rough and crumbly, so start by sanding them gently and apply two coats of wood sealer, extending it slightly over the edges onto the front and back of the corkboard. The first coat will be sucked in immediately, but a second coat should be sufficient to give a base for paint.

When the sealer is dry, turn the corkboard facedown, and on the rough reverse side of the board mark a point 3 inches (7.5cm) down from the top and in the center. To make the hanger hole, draw a short line of about ¾ inch (2cm) at this point as a guide and then two more lines of the same length to form an upside-down triangle.

Use an X-Acto knife and a small straightedge as a guide to cut around the triangle and remove enough of the corkboard to enable a wall-mounted nail or picture hook to lodge inside it.

On the matboard, measure and mark a border 4 inches (10cm) wide all around and use a hand-held mat cutter to cut the opening.

DECORATION

Using no-stick tape, mask ¾ inch (2cm) away from the opening all around and cut a small piece of sponge into a semicircular shape to reflect the shapes on the painting. Using a suitable color paint (I chose orange), sponge the matboard all around the opening.

Then mask again, leaving a 1 inch (2.5cm) gap and sponge all around with the paint color again, leaving a gap of matboard between the two sponged areas, and on the other side of the tape, paint a solid line of a different color (in this case, olive green).

When all this paint has dried, complete the decoration by painting some spots within the sponging in a third color (I used scarlet) and add a broken line against it in the first color (orange), using the edge of a piece of cardboard to apply the paint.

Finally remove the tape and finish off by painting some random olive-green patterns in the gap left by the masking tape.

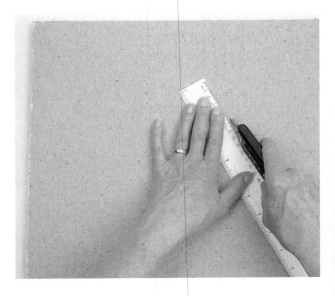

1 To enable the painting to be hung on a wall, a triangular recess is made in the back with the point of the triangle at the top. Cut out the triangular shape with an X-Acto knife, cutting halfway through the board before gouging out the waste.

ASSEMBLY

Fasten the painting firmly to the mat with masking tape, making sure that it is flat and secure. Because of the absorbency of the corkboard, coat the front of it with white glue fairly generously and also spread a thin skim to the back of the matboard but not the picture. Stick the two boards together, taking care to position the matboard exactly onto the corkboard, wipe away any excess glue from the edges, place a wooden board and weights on top, and leave it to dry.

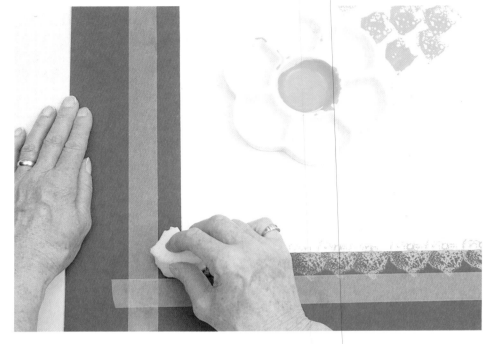

2 Mask off an area of the matboard around the opening with no-stick tape and sponge all around.

3 A second strip of no-stick tape marks the edge of the outer sponged area and provides an edge along which the solid line is painted in a different color.

4 An attractive effect can be created by adding colored spots within the sponging and then using the edge of a piece of cardboard to apply more paint of the first color outside the line.

Oil painting on board

An oil painting is usually surrounded with a conventional wide gold frame. But I wanted to give this contemporary oil-on-board a different treatment, while still leading the eye into the painting. By framing the oil-on-board in a narrow molding and then raising it from the dark background, the painting is made to look more three-dimensional and seems to acquire depth.

You will need

Preparation
- Oil painting on board
- Plain molding in a deep "hockey stick" profile
- Thick plywood 2⅛ inches (or 5.5cm) larger all around than the painting
- Basic framing kit

Decoration
- Basic frame decoration kit

Assembly
- Wood glue
- Basic assembly kit

PREPARATION

Cut the frame moldings to the size of the oil-on-board – in this case a standard 22 × 16 inches (56 × 40cm) size – plus ease. The plywood should be cut 4⅜ inches (11cm) larger – a lumber supplier will do this for you if you do not have the saws or the confidence to do it accurately yourself.

DECORATION

Color the four pieces of molding with two wood dyes, applying the second before the first one has dried. Pick one of the colors in the painting to dye the frame; for this picture, I found using lavender and antique pine dyes blended with the background and matched the shadows on the man's face.

Then make a thick mix of color for the backing board which blends with another part of the painting – in this case, the deep greeny purple in the pullover. This mix is applied in two coats over the edges of the board and 3 inches (7.5cm) onto the surface all around.

ASSEMBLY

Make up the frame as normal, giving it two coats of clear wax polish to create a sheen and to seal the surface, and fasten the oil painting into the frame.

Mark the backing board carefully 2 inches (5cm) in from the edges and make small unobtrusive marks on each edge as guides. Apply wood glue fairly generously to the back face of the molding and then lower it gently and carefully into position using the guide marks. Leave the whole thing for twenty-four hours to make sure

that it is perfectly dry before trying to pick it up.

Position screw eyes 3 inches (7.5cm) down from the top and use a double thickness of medium cord to take the weight of the assembled frame.

1 Once the four lengths of molding have been cut to size, color them using cotton wool to apply a dye (or a combination of dyes) to match a color in the oil painting.

2 *Mix a second, stronger color, again matching it to the painting, and apply it with a sponge to the edges and outer surface of the board.*

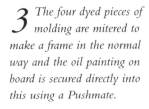

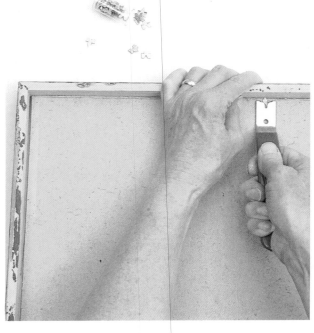

3 *The four dyed pieces of molding are mitered to make a frame in the normal way and the oil painting on board is secured directly into this using a Pushmate.*

4 *With light guide marks on the backing board, apply wood glue to the back of the frame and lower it gently into place. Leave for twenty-four hours before trying to pick it up.*

Set of flower prints

Sets of prints are always nice to have, and these four flower prints by Charles Rennie Mackintosh are ideal for creating coordinated mats and frames. I liked the delicate colors on the flowers, so have used pastel colors and a textured matboard in a cloud design. In order to make the frames look light, I stained and limed the molding to blend.

You will need

Preparation
- Set of prints
- Two lengths of plain oak molding about 1¼ inches (3cm) wide
- Matboard in pink cloud
- Glass
- Hardboard
- Basic framing kit
- Basic mat cutting kit

Decoration
- Water-based dye in lavender and rose
- 000 steel wool
- Clear wax
- Artist's paints
- Basic frame decoration kit
- Basic mat decoration kit

Assembly
- Basic assembly kit

PREPARATION

Cut eight pieces of molding 10¼ inches (26cm) plus ease, and eight pieces 8½ inches (21.5cm) plus ease and cut four pieces of matboard and four pieces of hardboard exactly 10¼ × 8½ inches (26 × 21.5cm). Then cut the four mats to the same size with equal borders of 1½ inches (4cm) all around.

DECORATION

Dye the molding pieces first with a light coat of rose, and then immediately with lavender and leave to dry. Because of the number of pieces, work on just two at a time, then another two and so on, to make sure that the rose dye does not dry and produce a different color.

Take a pad of steel wool and rub in a generous amount of liming wax on two of the lengths, and then rub it off with a soft cloth dipped into clear wax until the liming wax is left only in the grain and in the grooves of the molding profile. Repeat with two more lengths and continue until all sixteen lengths have been treated and are the same color. Then assemble the four frames as normal.

Mask the mats with two borders of no-stick tape so that there is an exposed area ⅛ inch (3mm) from the opening and ⅜ inch (1cm) wide.

Now look at the four prints and mix the artist's paint into two colors to blend with the colors on the flowers and leaves – I chose a deep red and a dusty green. Find a sponge with very tiny holes and cut off a small piece. Sponge the stronger color on first, allowing the mat color to show through and, when it is dry, sponge on the

second color. If you want to create highlights, finish by sponging on a light coating of gold acrylic paint mixed with water.

When all the paint is dry, remove the tape and rule two gold lines with a gold pen, one on the sight edge, and one ⅝ inch (1.5cm) from the sight edge.

ASSEMBLY

Fasten the prints to the mats, clean the glass, and assemble the pictures. It is important when you are tackling a set of pictures like this that each one is completed before the next is started so that dust does not fall onto the glass you have already cleaned.

1 It's worth experimenting with different colors of dye, applying them in different orders, both before and after the first one has dried. Here, I am putting on lavender dye before the previously applied rose dye has dried.

2 *Liming wax is applied to the dyed molding with steel wool and rubbed off with a cloth dipped in clear wax. On a frame of this size, work on just two lengths at a time.*

3 *With the mat masked by two strips of no-stick tape, sponge on the colors you have chosen. Here, I am applying a dusty green on top of deep red, to be followed by a light coating of gold to create highlights.*

4 *Gold lines always enhance pictures like this. I have chosen to use two – one around the sponged decoration and one along the sight edge (the bevel of the mat opening).*

Underwater fish

It is always fun to use the mat and frame as an extension of a picture, either by continuing the painting onto the mat or, as I have done here, by using decorations suggested by the picture. I wanted to do something a little different with this nineteenth-century engraving of a fish, so I made a mat and frame that suggested an underwater theme.

You will need

Preparation
• Engraving of a fish
• Plain molding with a flat profile 1½ inches (4cm) wide
• Matboard in ivory and green pear
• Basic framing kit
• Basic mat cutting kit

Decoration
• Watercolors in shades of green
• Sheet of paper
• Hand-spray bottles
• Small jar of pale green acrylic paint

Assembly
• Glass
• Hardboard
• Double-sided tape
• Basic assembly kit

PREPARATION

Cut the molding to 14 and 11 inches (or 35 and 28cm) plus ease and the mats to the exact measurements. Give the inner mat in green pear 3-inch (7.5cm) borders and the outer, ivory, mat 2¾-inch (7cm) borders.

DECORATION

Give the four pieces of molding two coats of pale green acrylic paint and put aside to dry. Then cut a continuous curving shape along a piece of paper to create a mask which you can move easily, then mix three shades of green watercolor to enable you to spray the mat. Put the three colors into small hand-spray bottles. It is important to make sure that enough paint of each color is mixed so that there is no danger of running out partway through the spraying.

Place the mask diagonally across the ivory mat in the top left-hand corner and spray on the first green color. Then move the mask about 2¾ inches (7cm) down, keeping it roughly parallel, and spray again, repeating the process until you reach the bottom right-hand corner.

Change to a different color of green, place the mask in the top left-hand corner again, but a little way away from the first spray, and repeat the spraying across the

1 Using a curved mask (cut from paper), spray on the first green color with a simple hand spray bottle.

mat. To get the curves overlapping and the colors tending to merge (which was exactly the effect that I wanted), take care not to place the mask exactly in line with the previous spray. The third color can now be sprayed in between the others so that the complete surface of the mat is covered to give an underwater effect. To complete the mat, paint the sight edge in gold using a very fine sable brush.

Dip your finger into the gold paste and smear it across the surface of the frame in an irregular pattern and then buff it with a soft cloth, making long, gentle strokes to allow the pale green to show through.

Finally, using a cotton swab dipped in gold paint, make marks the shape of fish scales in arbitrary groups around the frame. The sight edge and the outer edge of the frame are left plain.

Assembly

Fasten the two mats together using double-sided tape so that ¼ inch (6mm) of green pear shows, and then fasten the engraving behind the opening using masking tape. Assemble the frame in the normal way.

2 After spraying on the second and third green colors (taking care to place the mask in a different position each time), the mat is completed by painting the sight edge of the mat with gold paint using a fine sable brush.

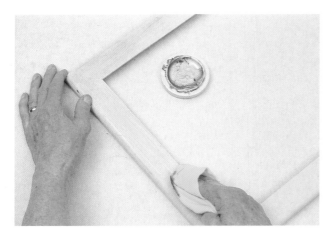

3 The frame has already been painted with pale green acrylic paint, which is enhanced by gold paste smeared across the surface and buffed with a soft cloth.

4 To complete the effect, fish "scales" are painted on the frame using a cotton swab dipped in gold paint, positioning them in groups around the frame.

Five variations with metal leaf

I wanted to create a group of small frames with a sparkle to hang in a dull corner, so I made these five different little frames, painted or stained them and decorated them with metal leaf or gold wax, so that they could hang together.

You will need

Preparation
- Five small pictures or decorations
- Scraps of two or three profiles of narrow molding
- Basic framing kit

Decoration
- Metal leaf
- Gold size
- Basic frame decoration kit

ASSEMBLY
- Five pieces of glass to fit frames if decorative items are not too thick
- Five pieces of hardboard to fit frames
- Basic assembly kit

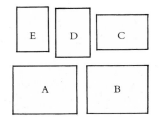

KEY TO PICTURE

PREPARATION

Cut two frames 8 × 6 inches (or 20 × 15cm) from one molding and three frames 6 × 4 inches (or 15 × 10cm) from the other.

The finished frames are shown in the photograph opposite – Frame A (the leaf impressions) is at the bottom left and the letters then go around counter-clockwise to the top left. As I wanted each frame to be decorated differently, I colored them as follows:

Frame A Dyed with rose and before it was dry again with mahogany.
Frame B Dyed with lavender and then immediately with old pine.
Frame C Painted with red oxide.
Frame D Dyed with lavender, then rose.
Frame E Dyed with apple, then lavender.

When the moldings are dry, all five frames can be joined in the normal way.

DECORATION

The technique for applying gold leaf to a frame is described and illustrated on page 32.
Frame A Using a cotton swab dipped into gold size, make random spots around the frame. When the size is tacky (about 20 minutes), apply small pieces of metal leaf to each spot, pressing them down firmly, remove the paper backing, and brush away any excess.
Frame B Using a brush dipped into gold size, paint diagonal lines around the frame and then apply the metal leaf in the same way.
Frame C Coat the whole frame with gold size, apply metal leaf all around, then use rose dye over the leaf to create an antiqued look.

Frame D Lightly rub the frame with gold wax and burnish with a soft cloth.
Frame E Dip a cotton swab into lavender stain and make random dots around the frame. Repeat with black dots and mask the sides of the frame before painting a black border around the outside back edge of the frame. When the paint is dry, dip a swab into gold size and make more dots. Apply metal leaf as before.

ASSEMBLY

Assemble the frames as normal and pin decorative wreath-top hangers to the center top of each frame.

1 All the frames are painted or dyed in different ways. Here, I am applying red oxide paint to Frame C which will hang on the right of the top row.

2 On top of the apple and lavender dyes of this frame (Frame E), to hang at the top left, a combination of lavender dye and black paint spots were used, with gold leaf spots as a contrast. Here I am applying the gold size.

3 For this frame (Frame D), which had been dyed with lavender and then rose and will hang at the top center, I used gold wax which I burnished with a soft cloth.

4 For this frame (Frame C), which I painted with red oxide in Step 1, gold size was used to coat the whole frame, with metal leaf applied all around and a final light coating of rose dye to give an "antique" effect.

Greeting card

There are so many greeting cards on sale now that I would like to frame. I was attracted to this one because of the compact composition and the bright colors which I felt would look good if they were to be echoed in the mat decoration.

You will need

Preparation
- Greeting card in bold colors
- Short length of narrow, plain molding
- Matboard in pampas
- Basic framing kit
- Basic mat cutting kit

Decoration
- Spirit-based wood dye in blue
- Child's felt-tip pen airbrush
- Basic mat decoration kit

Assembly
- Hardboard
- Glass
- Basic assembly kit

PREPARATION

Cut the matboard, backing board, and glass to 9½ × 8 inches (24 × 20cm) and cut the molding to the same size plus ease. Cut the opening in the mat to give 1½ inches (4cm) equal borders.

DECORATION

Stain all four pieces of molding with one coat of blue spirit-based dye and leave to dry.

Mask the mat with no-stick tape, leaving an exposed area ¼ inch (6mm) away from the sight edge and ⅝ inch (1.5cm) wide. The felt-tip pen kit that came with a child's airbrush had the colors I needed to blend with the picture, but you should experiment for the best effect. I decided on a candy-striped effect using a scrap of matboard as a very simple mask. To do this, first insert a blue pen into the airbrush and, with the mask lying diagonally across the tape, spray a small area. Then change the pen to red, move the mask along a little and spray again, and, finally, changing the pen to yellow, move the mask by an equal amount and spray a third time. After the yellow stripe, leave a larger gap so that the green of the mat shows through and then start the sequence again.

When you reach a corner, turn the mat and start down the next side. On the last side, judge the amount of space left by eye to make sure that the sequence will fit in.

The ink dries immediately, so you will be able to remove the tape and rule gold lines either side of the band of candy stripe and two more outside to finish off.

ASSEMBLY

Assemble the frame in the normal way.

1 Cut the molding to the required size and stain it with a color to suit one of the main colors in the greeting card chosen.

2 To achieve this "candy-striped" effect, use at least three colors plus the base color of the matboard. Mask the matboard and spray with the child's airbrush, with the appropriate color felt-tip pen inserted, moving the cardboard mask an equal amount each time.

3 At each corner, try to finish with a whole stripe and then turn the mat to work along the next side. At the last corner, make sure the sequence is completed.

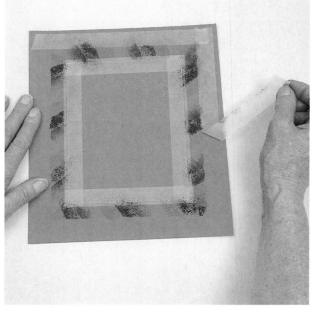

4 As soon as you have finished spraying, remove the no-stick tape and rule the gold lines.

Kitchen poster

I wanted to frame this reproduction of an old poster for my kitchen with an "antiqued" finish and so decided to use a sprayed technique which gives the appearance of an old piece of fabric.

You will need

Preparation
- Old poster on board
- ⅜ inch (9mm) plywood
- Wood sealer

Decoration
- Artist's paints in parchment, brilliant orange, cadmium red, and magenta
- Hand-spray bottle
- Basic frame decoration kit

Assembly
- Mat knife and straightedge
- Hardboard
- Wood glue

PREPARATION

You will need the plywood cut to size with an opening leaving 2¾ inch (7cm) borders all around the poster. If you do not feel up to this, a carpenter will be able to do it for you. Sand the cut board thoroughly, particularly on the edges, rub it with fine steel wool, and finally coat it all over with wood sealer.

DECORATION

Use a brush to apply two coats of a pale ivory color – which you can get by mixing parchment and a little brilliant orange – to the plywood frame, rubbing the whole surface down with steel wool between coats. When the second coat is dry, make small pencil marks at 3 inch (7.5cm) intervals to mark the centers of the stripes.

Make a watery mixture in a soft pink color, using magenta and cadmium red, and put it into a hand-spray bottle. Using two pieces of scrap cardboard as masks, spray stripes around the frame at each pencil mark – before these are dry, run a brush through each stripe to even it out and continue the stripe onto the sight edge and the outside edge of the board.

When the stripes are totally dry, rub them down with fine steel wool, revealing the background color in patches to produce the antiqued effect. Finally, mix the pale ivory shade again, put it into the spray bottle, and spray the whole frame lightly.

ASSEMBLY

To make channels to hold the poster, cut six strips of hardboard with a mat knife about 16 to 18 inches (or 40 to 45 cm) long and ⅜ inch (1cm) wide and glue them together in pairs. Then cut three 1¼ inches (3cm) wide

hardboard strips the same length and glue one of these to each pair of the narrow strips to make L-shaped channels (see the drawing on page 59). When the glue is dry, tape the poster behind the opening on the board, then place the L-shaped channels in position. One is placed at the bottom to support the poster (and, if necessary, to hold the weight of protective glass) and the other two on either side to hold the poster in position. When you are totally satisfied that all three are correct, release the poster and tack the channels in place using ½ inch (12mm) panel pins and a hammer. The poster can now be slid back into position in the channels.

1 With the plywood "frame" cut to size and with the correct opening, start the decoration by applying two coats of the background paint color.

2 An ordinary hand-spray bottle is ideal for spraying stripes in a second color. Simply mask off the area to be sprayed with two strips of scrap matboard.

3 Use fine steel wool to rub through the colored stripes once the paint has dried to produce an "antique" effect.

4 Make three L-shaped channels from one wide and two narrow strips of hardboard and position them on the back of the frame to hold the poster in place.

Watercolor

If you paint or collect watercolors and want to frame them, there is only one way to decorate the mat and that is with a washline. Colored prints can benefit from this treatment as well, and although it takes a little practice, it is effective when it is done and adds a lot to the painting.

You will need

Preparation
- Watercolor
- Plain molding ¾ inch (2cm) wide
- Matboard in ivory
- Basic framing kit
- Basic mat cutting kit

Decoration
- Basic mat decoration kit
- Basic frame decoration kit

Assembly
- Basic assembly kit

PREPARATION

Start by calculating the measurement for the mat because, when a washline is going to be done, the mat must be cut with wider borders than normal. Measure the watercolor itself, allowing a small amount for the part tucked under the mat, then add the width of border to arrive at the final measurement. In this case, the watercolor measured 13¾ × 12¼ inch (35 × 31cm) and, since it was rather large, I felt that I needed a generous border so I added 3¾ inches (9.5cm) to the top and sides, and 4½ inches (11.5cm) to the bottom. This gave a total measurement of 21¼ × 20½ inches (54 × 52 cm) which is, of course, also the size for the glass and hardboard.

Cut the opening in the mat and then the four pieces of molding for the frame, allowing ease.

DECORATION

The technique of washlining is described in detail in the *Basic decorative techniques* chapter, but before you embark on this part of the project it would be a good idea to become totally confident with your ruling pen by using it for basic lines on a few mats, changing the line width and learning how to handle it with the ruler.

For this particular watercolor, I mixed two diluted colors to blend, picking one from the bridge (orangy-red) and one from the water (blue).

1 The colors that you are going to use for the decoration should be matched to the colors of the picture.

2 The starting point with washlining is to rule the lines in your chosen colors, starting from the inside of the mat and working outward line by line.

3 Making sure your wash color is mixed and ready, start the washline by applying clean water between the two lines and then follow this immediately with the wash itself.

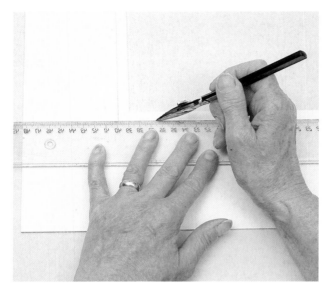

Work out the spacing of your lines using the corner gauge: I decided on ⅜ inch (1.5cm) for the sight line, 1¼ inches (3cm) and 2⅛ inches (5.5cm) for the wash and 2⅝ inches (6.7cm) and 2¾ inches (7cm) for the lead lines. It's always a good idea to experiment with your proposed pattern on a small piece of matboard and work out where you are going to have the colors when you are introducing more lines.

I decided to make the sides of the wash and the wash itself in the first color, and the other lines in the second color, plus a gold line by the side of the wash if I felt it was needed once the washline had been done.

Using the technique described on pages 36 and 37, rule the lines and allow them to dry. Dilute the first color (here, orangy-red) for the wash and "paint" the washline with plain clean water. Then, before this has had a chance to dry, apply the wash over the water-covered area between the lines.

To decorate the frame I mixed a thicker mixture of the second color (blue) with a little pale gray, coating all four pieces of molding generously and then rubbing off with cotton wool before the paint was quite dry to give a "washed-out" appearance.

ASSEMBLY
Assemble the frame in the normal way.

4 The final part of the decoration is to paint the frame in one of the matching colors. Using cotton wool (or a soft cloth) to rub the paint before it dries gives a "washed-out" appearance.

Octagonal frame

Multisided frame cutting is always impressive, but all it really needs is stamina! Miter saws are marked on the base, not only for the conventional 45° angles for a four-sided frame, but also for frames with five, six, and eight sides. These multisided frames look good with flower paintings, embroideries, or portrait photographs and they are always noticed and admired. I recently rediscovered a little machine embroidery that I did years ago and have given it a wide frame and a mat to make it stand out when hung on a wall.

You will need

Preparation
• Embroidery or flower painting
• Wide gold molding
• Scrap piece of matboard in ivory
• Circle mat cutter (optional)
• Paper
• Basic framing kit

Assembly
• Glass
• Hardboard
• Basic assembly kit

PREPARATION

Measure the size of your embroidery to work out the size of opening you need in the mat. I cut my own circular opening – but unless you have a circle mat cutter, you will probably want to ask a professional picture framer to do this for you. Then consider how much of the mat you want to show – in this case, I decided I did not need more than ¾ inch (2cm). To this measurement, add the width of the frame rabbet (the one I used

was rather wide at ⅜ inch [1cm]) to give the border size – in my case, the opening was 6 inches (15.5cm), giving an overall size of 8½ inches (21.5cm) – and draw a square of this overall size on a piece of paper, which you can then use to work out the dimensions of the octagon – see page 86 for details of how to do this.

Study the base of your miter saw, and you should see the symbol for an eight-sided frame. You will find that the saw blade will lock into this position (at 67.5°).

1 Once you have worked out the length of the sides of the octagon, it is cut in the normal way, except that the saw blade is set to the eight-sided frame symbol on the saw body.

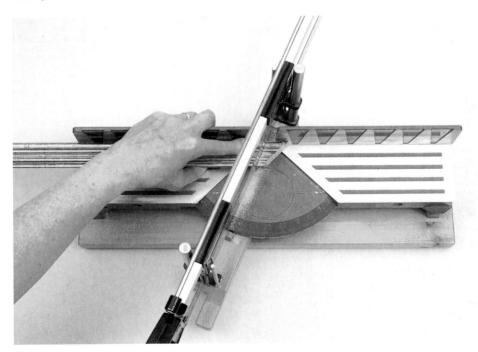

Choosing an eight-sided frame means that you have twice as much cutting as usual and it is important when you cut your first multisided frame to understand that there is a lot of waste when you cut, so do allow enough molding before you start.

Set your saw to the eight-sided symbol and cut the molding as usual. Then cut angles off the corners of the matboard to suit the octagonal frame.

DRAWING OUT THE OCTAGON

Take the piece of paper on which you have drawn your square and draw diagonal lines from corner to corner to make a cross. You now need to ascertain how much of each corner needs to be cut off to make an octagon with each of its eight sides the same length. This is done by measuring half the size of the square – in my case, 4¼ inches (10.75cm) – out from the center, parallel with each of the diagonal lines, using the width of the ruler to make your marks either side of the line. Then do the same for each of the other three corners.

In each corner, you will now have two marks, which when you join them up, continuing the lines to the edges of the square, will give you an octagon.

The eight sides will all be the same length and it is this measurement that you use for cutting your molding (for my frame 3½ inches [9cm]). The octagon shape can also be used as a pattern for cutting the mat, the backing, and the glass – or, for the glass, you can take the completed frame along to your local glass retailer who will cut the glass to size for you.

HOW TO WORK OUT THE OCTAGON

To work out the size of the octagon, first determine the size of opening and mat border, then draw a square of this size (L). Draw diagonals and mark half the width of the square at each corner from the center. Make two marks at each corner and join them up to form the octagon shape.

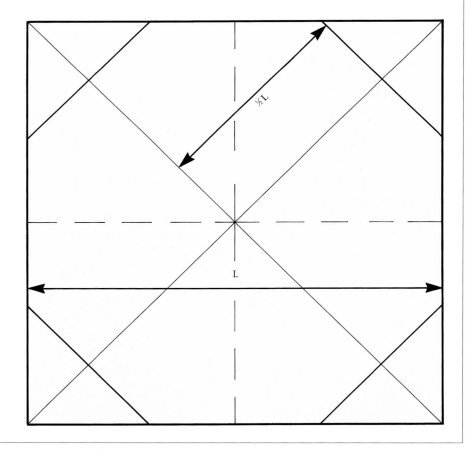

ASSEMBLY

Prepare the band clamp by using all the corner supports provided and fitting the eight pieces of molding into it. To ensure every joint is glued, I usually take out alternate pieces and apply glue to both ends – but, of course, one end of each piece could be coated. The clamp is tightened in the usual way and the resulting frame carefully pinned in the corners when it is dry.

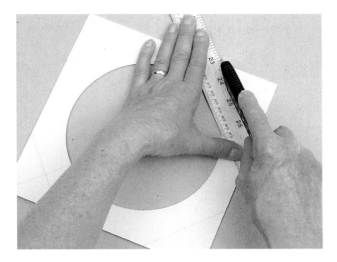

2 The square mat, with its circular opening, needs to have its corners cut off to suit the size of the octagon.

3 To join an octagonal frame, you will need to use all the corner supports supplied with the band clamp. Before tightening, take out alternate pieces and apply glue to both ends before replacing them.

Clown mirror

Adding extensions to a frame is another exciting form of decoration and is particularly suited to mirrors. If they are built on the outside of the frame, they tend to be vulnerable to knocks, but an extension inward on a frame holds endless possibilities and is protected from damage.

For this "clown" mirror, I wanted the clown to dominate the design and occupy the bottom of the frame. I decided that a rectangular shape would be best and as I did not want to tie the design to a particular color scheme, I decided to use four colors and white for the decoration.

You will need

Preparation
- Mirror glass
- Molding with a flat top profile
- Scraps of plywood the same thickness as the sight edge of the molding
- Coping saw
- Basic framing kit

Decoration
- White paper
- Tracing paper
- Self-hardening clay
- Small cans of gloss paint (I chose red, yellow, blue, green, and white)
- Small can of white matte model-makers' paint
- 3 Styrofoam or wooden balls
- No-stick tape
- Basic frame decoration kit

Assembly
- Basic assembly kit

PREPARATION

Draw the clown design on a piece of paper and mark out a suitable size frame with the width of molding you are using, taking care that most of the clown's body will be on the frame without too many projections going over the mirror – I finally settled for just two projections, one for the clown's arm and one for his knee. Keep this design as your master, tracing it onto tracing paper, then transfer it to the frame by the old method of scribbling on the back of the lines and drawing over the design onto the frame.

Then trace the extensions onto a small piece of plywood, cut them out with a coping saw, and sand any rough edges. You will have to support the extensions

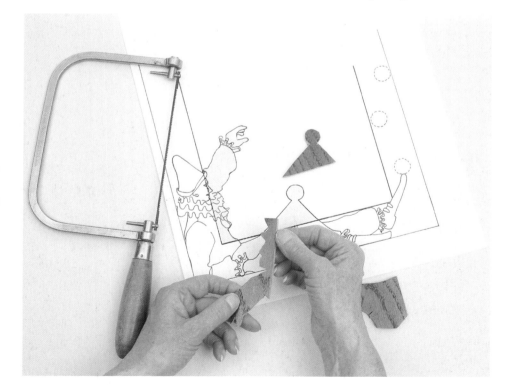

1 *Once you have traced the basic clown design onto paper and transferred it to the frame, cut plywood pieces to match the parts of the design extending from the frame.*

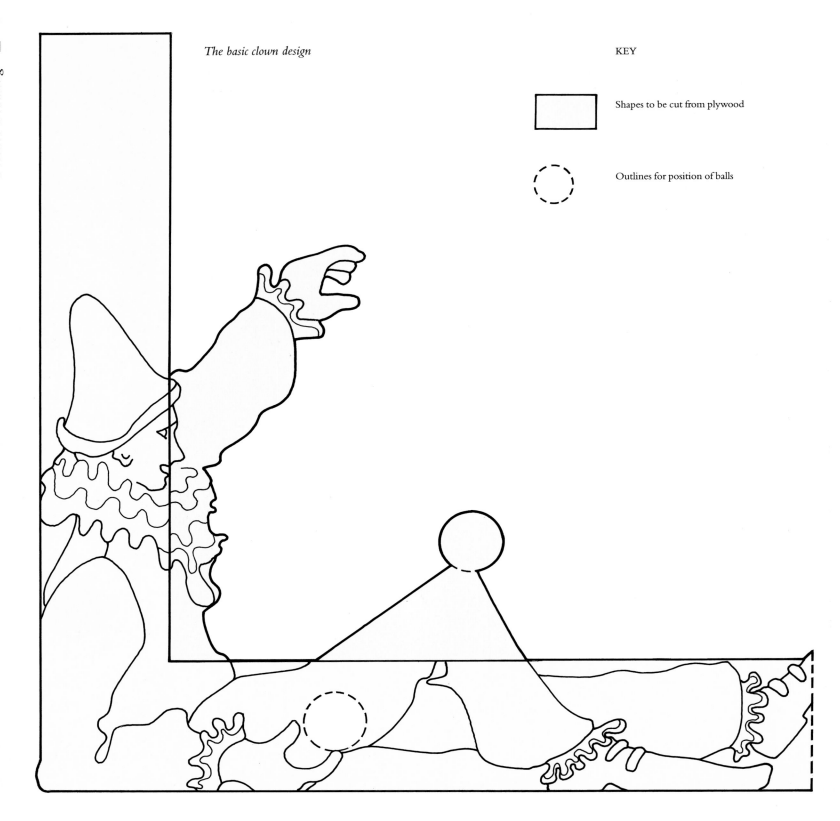

The basic clown design

KEY

Shapes to be cut from plywood

Outlines for position of balls

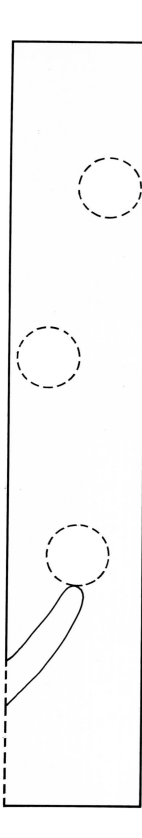

while they are being glued in place – a good way of doing this is with a pile of matboard scraps, adjusting the level until the extensions are exactly in position. When you are satisfied, apply adhesive to the edge of the extensions, place them in position, and allow them to dry without moving.

I had debated for a while about whether to paint the individual pieces of molding before making the frame, but finally decided against it on the grounds that the clay is messy to use and also needs sanding when it is dry and this could damage the paintwork.

DECORATION

Once the adhesive is dry, tape the pile of matboard to the back of the extensions to act as a support while you are modeling the clay. Taking a small piece of clay at a time, start to model the clown in relief, suggesting just

enough form to make him stand out from the frame. Apply a basic coverage and then allow the clay to dry overnight before building up a little more in places such as the brim of the hat, the ruffles round his neck, and his right arm. As you are working, use a cotton swab dipped in water to smooth off areas as this eliminates a lot of subsequent sanding. This type of clay is very good tempered as you can add new damp pieces to it when it is dry, as well as sanding or even carving it.

In places like the trousers, you need put on very little clay, relying on the curving lines of the paint to give the illusion of form. I also left flat areas on the knee and trousers for the half balls to lie. You can put a little form into the face but again it is best to rely on the painting to give subsequent detail.

When you are happy with the result, the painting can begin. Use no-stick tape as a mask on the corners of the

2 With the frame extensions glued in place and supported by piles of scrap matboard, start modeling the clay in the corner. Apply just a small amount of clay at a time and use a cotton swab dipped in water to smooth out each area.

3 After leaving the first application of clay to dry overnight, you can carry on building up the clown shape, adding clay where necessary to create the details.

molding and paint each side of the frame individually with three coats of paint, using one of the four colors so that each side is different. Paint carefully around the modeling of the clown and complete the frame before starting to paint the clown itself.

The hat and shirt of the clown are painted in gloss white, and the mask, ruffles, and trouser background in matte white. Mix up a pink color for his neck and hands with matte white and a brush-tip full of red gloss. Paint his shoes two different colors taking care that they contrast with their backgrounds, and paint the laces different colors again. The checks on the trousers can be painted with curving lines to suggest the roundness of the legs using alternate wide and narrow lines in green one way and narrow lines in yellow the other way.

Lastly, enhance his ruffles with edges of blue and red using a very fine brush and, mixing a little blue-gray with matte white and a brush-tip full of blue, paint the shadows on his face and in the ruffles.

Cut the Styrofoam balls carefully in half using a mat knife (use a fine-toothed saw for wooden balls), paint them in matte white, and stick them in place using wood glue to give the idea that they are actually being juggled by the clown.

ASSEMBLY

Lay the frame facedown on a blanket to protect the surface and secure the mirror and backing board. The final half ball is then stuck onto the mirror with wood glue and left to dry overnight.

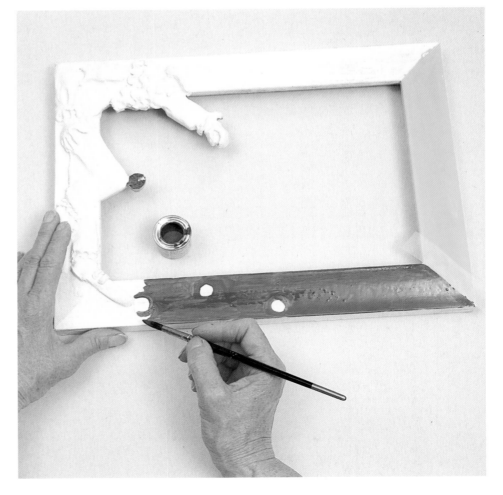

4 Each side of the frame is painted in a different color. Once three coats have been applied to one side (above), use no-stick tape to mask it at the corner before painting the next side in another color (right).

5 Painting the clown is detailed work, but you can have a lot of fun using the different bright colors. Make sure you use the shaped painted lines to suggest the form of, for example, his trousers.

6 The Styrofoam or wooden balls are cut in half, painted white, and stuck in place with wood glue. Position the last ball on the mirror close to the clown's hand.

Suppliers

Most woodworking tools (including miter saws) and general supplies can be bought from your local hardware store or home center; picture framing suppliers will have a better selection, but may have a minimum order. Self-hardening modeling clay is available from most art supply stores, and finished frames and ready-cut mats can be bought from art shops or local picture framers. Listed below are companies who can provide supplies by mail order.

American Frame Corp.
1340 Tomahawk Drive
Maumee, OH 43567
800-537-0944
Metal and wood section frames

ASW (Art Supply Warehouse)
360 Main Avenue
Norwalk, CT 06851
800-243-5038
General art supplies

Chroma Acrylics
P.O. Box 510
Hainesport, NY 08036
6090-261-3452
Artists' paints and mediums

Deco Art
P.O. Box 360
Stanford, KY
606-365-9739
Paints

Graphik Dimensions, Ltd., Dept. AA
41–23 Haight Street
Flushing, NY 11355
800-221-0262
Frames, framing tools, general art supplies

Jerry's Artarama
P.O. Box 1105
New Hyde Park, NY 11040
800-221-2323
Framing tools and materials

Index

ACKNOWLEDGMENTS
I would like to thank William for all his help, Sibile for her photocopying skills, and Sarah for her paintings.

PSYCHOLOGY

PSYCHOLOGY

from
inquiry
to
understanding

SECOND EDITION

PSYCHOLOGY

from
inquiry
to
understanding

SECOND EDITION

SCOTT O. LILIENFELD
Emory University

STEVEN JAY LYNN
Binghamton University

LAURA L. NAMY
Emory University

NANCY J. WOOLF
University of California
at Los Angeles

PEARSON

BOSTON   NEW YORK   SAN FRANCISCO
MEXICO CITY   MONTREAL   TORONTO   LONDON   MADRID   MUNICH   PARIS
HONG KONG   SINGAPORE   TOKYO   CAPE TOWN   SYDNEY

Editor in Chief: Jessica Mosher
Executive Editor: Stephen Frail
Editorial Assistant: Kerri Hart-Morris
Director of Development: Sharon Geary
Senior Development Editor: Julie Swasey
Director of Marketing: Brandy Dawson
Executive Marketing Manager: Jeanette Koskinas
Marketing Assistant: Shauna Fishweicher
Managing Editor: Maureen Richardson
Project Manager: Marianne Peters-Riordan
Senior Operations Manager: Nick Sklitsis
Senior Operations Specialist: Sherry Lewis
Senior Art Director: Nancy Wells

Text and Cover Designer: Anne DeMarinis
Manager, Visual Research: Beth Brenzel
Photo Researcher: Nancy Tobin
Manager, Rights and Permissions: Zina Arabia
Manager, Cover Visual Research & Permissions: Karen Sanatar
Cover Art: Smiling Lady: Masterfile RF; Frame: Istochphoto
Director, Digital Media: Brian Hyland
Senior Digital Media Editor: Paul DeLuca
Full-Service Project Management: Francesca Monaco/Prepare
Composition: Prepare, Inc.
Printer/Binder: Courier Companies, Inc.
Cover Printer: Lehigh/Phoenix
Text Font: Minion 9/11

Credits and acknowledgments borrowed from other sources and reproduced, with permission, in this textbook appear on appropriate page within text (or on starting on page CR-1).

Many of the designations by manufacturers and seller to distinguish their products are claimed as trademarks. Where those designations appear in this book, and the publisher was aware of a trademark claim, the designations have been printed in initial caps or all caps.

Library of Congress Cataloging-in-Publication Data
Psychology : from inquiry to understanding / Scott O. Lilienfeld . . . [et al.]. —
2nd ed.
    p. cm.
ISBN-10: 0-205-83206-7
ISBN-13: 978-0-205-83206-4
1. Psychology. I. Lilienfeld, Scott O.
BF121.P7625 2011
150—dc22

2010024862

10 9 8 7 6 5 4 3 2 1

Student Edition:
Case: ISBN 10: 0-205-83206-7
       ISBN 13: 978-0-205-83206-4
Paper: ISBN 10: 0-205-00160-2
        ISBN 13: 978-0-205-00160-6

Exam Edition:
ISBN 10: 0-205-00167-X
ISBN 13: 978-0-205-00167-5

A La Carte Edition:
ISBN 10: 0-205-00175-0
ISBN 13: 978-0-205-00175-0

Allyn & Bacon
is an imprint of

www.pearsonhighered.com

*We dedicate this book
to Barry Lane Beyerstein
(1947–2007),
great scholar
and valued friend.*

*My deepest gratitude
to David Lykken,
Paul Meehl,
Tom Bouchard,
Auke Tellegen, and my
other graduate mentors
for an invaluable gift
that I will always cherish:
scientific thinking.*
—Scott Lilienfeld

*To Fern Pritikin Lynn,
my heart and my soul.*
—Steven Jay Lynn

*To my guys:
Stanny and the Rodent.*
—Laura Namy

*To Larry, Lawson,
and Ashley.*
—Nancy Woolf

BRIEF CONTENTS

CONTENTS

4 SENSATION AND PERCEPTION
how we sense and conceptualize the world 122

5 CONSCIOUSNESS
expanding the boundaries of psychological inquiry 164

6 LEARNING
how nurture changes us 200

10 HUMAN DEVELOPMENT
how and why we change   358

11 EMOTION AND MOTIVATION
what moves us   404

12 STRESS, COPING, AND HEALTH
the mind–body interconnection   454

15 PSYCHOLOGICAL DISORDERS
when adaptation breaks down 582

16 PSYCHOLOGICAL AND BIOLOGICAL TREATMENTS
helping people change 630

"What are infants' earliest memories?" "Does watching violence on TV really teach children to become violent?" "Is human intelligence related to brain size?" "Is it usually dangerous to wake up sleepwalkers?" "Do genes contribute to obesity?" "Is the polygraph test really a 'lie detector'?" "Should we trust most self-help books?"

Every day, our students encounter a host of questions that challenge their understanding of themselves and others. Whether it's from the Internet, television programs, radio call-in shows, movies, self-help books, or advice from friends, our students' daily lives are a steady stream of information—and often misinformation—about intelligence testing, parenting, romantic relationships, mental illness, drug abuse, psychotherapy, and a host of other topics. Much of the time, the questions about these issues that most fascinate students are precisely those that psychologists routinely confront in their research, teaching, and practice.

As we begin our study of psychology, it's crucial to understand that we're *all* psychologists. We need to be able to evaluate the bewildering variety of claims from the vast world of popular psychology. Without a framework for evaluating evidence, making sense of these often contradictory findings can be a bewildering task for anyone. It's no surprise that the untrained student can find claims regarding memory- and mood-enhancing drugs, the overprescription of stimulants, the effectiveness of Prozac, and the genetic bases of psychiatric disorders, to name only a few examples, difficult to evaluate. Moreover, it is hard for those who haven't been taught to think scientifically to make sense of extraordinary psychological claims that lie on the fringes of scientific knowledge, such as extrasensory perception, subliminal persuasion, astrology, alien abductions, lie-detector testing, handwriting analysis, and inkblot tests, among many others. Without a guide for distinguishing good from bad evidence, our students are left to their own devices when it comes to weighing the merits of these claims.

Our goal in this text, therefore, is to empower readers to apply scientific thinking to the psychology of their everyday lives. By applying scientific thinking—thinking that helps protect us against our tendencies to make mistakes—we can better evaluate claims about both laboratory research and daily life. In the end, we hope that students will emerge with the "psychological smarts," or open-minded skepticism, needed to distinguish psychological misinformation from psychological information. We'll consistently urge students to keep an open mind to new claims, but to insist on evidence. Indeed, our overarching motto is that of space scientist James Oberg (sometimes referred to as "Oberg's dictum"): *Keeping an open mind is a virtue, just so long as it is not so open that our brains fall out.*

WHAT'S NEW IN THIS EDITION?

Psychology: From Inquiry to Understanding continues its commitment to emphasize the importance of scientific thinking skills. In the Second Edition, we've focused on providing even more opportunities for students to *apply* these skills to a variety of real-life scenarios. In addition, thanks to the ongoing support and feedback from instructors and students of our text, the Second Edition reflects many insightful and innovative updates that we believe enhance the text. Among the key changes made to the Second Edition are the following:

New Features and Pedagogy

- New "Evaluating Claims" feature in every chapter allows students to apply their scientific thinking skills to evaluate claims based on those found in actual advertisements and websites

- Redesigned callouts for the Six Scientific Thinking Principles now include brief questions that remind students of the key issues to consider when evaluating a claim
- "Your Complete Review System" now ties summary and assessment material to learning objectives and includes new "Apply Your Scientific Thinking Skills" questions (sample responses are provided in the Instructor's Manual so that these can be used for homework assignments)
- New MyPsychLab icons integrated in the text guide students to available Web-based practice quizzes, tutorials, videos and simulations that consolidate the knowledge they acquired from the textbook. The icons are not exhaustive—many more resources are available than those highlighted in the text—but they draw attention to some of the most high-interest materials available at www.mypsychlab.com
- Numbered learning objectives highlight major concepts in every section and can be used by instructors to assess student knowledge of the course material
- New interactive photo captions—with answers—test students' knowledge of the chapter content and their ability to think scientifically. This feature was inspired in part by recent work by Henry Roediger (Washington University) and others showing that periodic testing of knowledge is a powerful way of enhancing student learning

New Content and Updated Research

- **A new introductory Chapter 1 (Psychology and Scientific Thinking)** was formed by streamlining and reorganizing material from the first edition's Prologue and Chapter 1
- **Chapter 2 (Research Methods)** includes a new discussion of operational definitions and a new table reviewing the advantages and disadvantages of various research designs
- **Chapter 3 (Biological Psychology)** has been reorganized to follow a micro to macro (neurons to brain) organization. The chapter also includes expanded coverage of glial cells and neurotransmitters as well as a new section on interpreting and misinterpreting brain scans
- **Chapter 4 (Sensation and Perception)** includes new research on noise-induced hearing loss, cultural influences on food preferences, and fMRI studies of brain activity in response to ESP-related stimuli
- **Chapter 5 (Consciousness)** includes an expanded discussion of consciousness and updated coverage of hypnosis and the long-term physical and psychological effects of marijuana
- **Chapter 6 (Learning)** includes an expanded discussion of reinforcement and punishment, covering both positive and negative punishment
- **Chapter 7 (Memory)** includes new research on cultural differences in field vs. observer memories, eyewitness testimony, and the use of prescription drugs as cognitive enhancers
- **Chapter 8 (Language, Thinking, and Reasoning)** now includes sections on decision making and on problem solving approaches as well as on cutting-edge topics in cognitive psychology including embodied cognition and neuroeconomics
- **Chapter 9 (Intelligence and IQ Testing)** includes new research by Keith Stanovich on irrational thinking and intelligence, updated coverage of the WAIS-IV intelligence test, and expanded coverage of the validity of IQ scores
- **Chapter 10 (Human Development)** now follows a topical organization, with sections on physical and motor development, cognitive development, and social and moral development across the lifespan. The chapter also includes increased coverage of adolescence and adulthood, including new discussions of emerging adulthood, nontraditional families, and job satisfaction

- **Chapter 11 (Emotion and Motivation)** includes a new discussion of body language experts, new research on brain scanning techniques of lie detection, and expanded sections on sexual orientation and evolutionary models of attraction

- **Chapter 12 (Stress, Coping, and Health)** includes updated material on the tend and befriend reaction to stress, new research on how stress contributes to coronary heart disease, and expanded coverage of emotional control

- **Chapter 13 (Social Psychology)** includes new research on the psychological effects of solitary confinement, updated examples of crowd behavior, groupthink, and bystander nonintervention, and an expanded discussion of central and peripheral routes to persuasion

- **Chapter 14 (Personality)** includes updated and expanded research on the Big Five model of personality and the NEO personality inventory as well as updated research on behavior-genetic studies

- **Chapter 15 (Psychological Disorders)** includes new research on obsessive-compulsive disorder, cultural influences on depression, the emotional cascade model of borderline personality disorder, and a new section on controversies concerning childhood disorders, such as autism, ADHD, and early-onset bipolar disorder

- **Chapter 16 (Psychological and Biological Treatments)** includes an overview of meta-analysis, updated coverage of cognitive-behavioral therapies (including a new section on third wave therapies), and an expanded discussion of common factors in psychotherapy

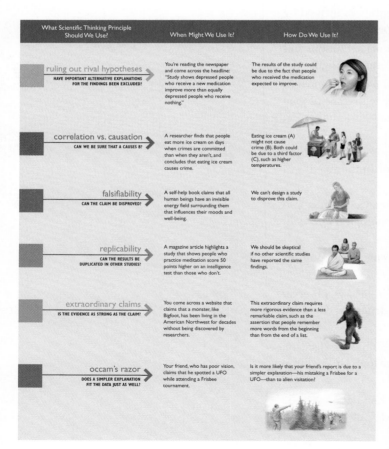

FROM INQUIRY TO UNDERSTANDING: THE FRAMEWORK IN ACTION

As instructors, we find that students new to psychology tend to learn best when information is presented within a clear, effective, and meaningful framework—one that encourages inquiry along the path to understanding. As part of the inquiry to understanding framework, our pedagogical features and assessment tools work to empower students to develop a more critical eye in understanding the psychological world and their place in it.

Thinking Scientifically

In Chapter 1, we introduce readers to the **Six Principles of Scientific Thinking** that are the framework for lifelong learning of psychology. Colored arrows appear in the margins whenever the principles are referenced to reinforce these scientific thinking principles in readers' minds. In this way, readers come to understand these principles as key skills for evaluating claims in scientific research and in everyday life.

Applications of Scientific Thinking

In keeping with the text's theme, a new **Evaluating Claims** feature prompts students to use scientific thinking skills to evaluate claims they are likely to encounter in various forms of media. Answers are provided at the end of the text.

Apply Your Scientific Thinking Skills questions (located at the end of each chapter) invite students to investigate current topics of debate or controversy and use their scientific thinking skills to make informed judgments about them. Sample answers to these questions appear in the Instructor's Resource Manual, making them ideal for outside research and writing assignments.

Throughout this text, we introduce a variety of misconceptions often held by introductory psychology students and use them as starting points for discussions of genuine scientific knowledge. We also present pieces of psychological knowledge that violate common sense, but that are true. Located in the margins of every chapter, **Factoids** present interesting and surprising facts, and **Fictoids** present widely held beliefs that are false or unsupported.

Each chapter also contains a **PsychoMythology** box focusing in depth on a widespread psychological misconception. In this way, students will come to recognize that their commonsense intuitions about the psychological world are not always correct and that scientific methods are needed to separate accurate from inaccurate claims.

Integrated Cultural Content

Wherever relevant, we highlight noteworthy and well-replicated research findings bearing on cultural and ethnic differences. By doing so, students should come to understand that many psychological principles have boundary conditions and that much of scientific psychology focuses as much on differences as commonalities.

A FOCUS ON MEANINGFUL PEDAGOGY: HELPING STUDENTS SUCCEED IN PSYCHOLOGY

Our goal of applying scientific thinking to the psychology of everyday life is reflected in the text's pedagogical plan. The features in the text, the end-of-chapter review, our online MyPsychLab resource, and the print and media supplements were designed to help students achieve a mastery of the subject and succeed in the course.

HOW DOES THE PEDAGOGY HELP STUDENTS IDENTIFY THE KEY CONCEPTS IN PSYCHOLOGY?

Think About It questions, located at the start of every chapter, highlight some of the common questions that students have about psychology. Together with the **Chapter Outline**, they also serve to preview the key topics that will be discussed in each chapter. Each chapter is organized around **Numbered Learning Objectives**, which are listed at the start of each major section. These objectives allow instructors to assess their students' knowledge of the course material. The end-of-chapter summary and assessment material is also organized around these objectives. Students' understanding of important terminology is enhanced with our on-page **Glossary.**

APPLY YOUR SCIENTIFIC THINKING SKILLS

Use your scientific thinking skills to answer the following questions, referencing specific scientific thinking principles and common errors in reasoning whenever possible.

1. Parents now have an amazing amount of parenting advice at their disposal in books, on websites, and through parent listservs and chat rooms. Research three sources of parenting information and create a list of the key topics they address (such as getting one's infant to sleep or eat better, or disciplining one's child). What assumptions do they make about the role of nature versus nurture in parenting and how do these assumptions correspond to scientific research? Are there rival hypotheses about children's behaviors that these sources neglected to consider?

2. As we've learned, the frontal lobes don't fully mature until late adolescence or early adulthood, a biological reality that may affect teenage decision making. There is active debate regarding how many teenage behavioral problems stem from the "teen brain." Find three examples of media articles related to this issue, such as debates over changing the age at which teens can enlist in the military, drink alcohol legally, obtain a driving license, or even stay out during an age-related "curfew." What arguments does each side use to support its case? What scientific or logical errors, if any, does each side make?

3. Based on the research that we've discussed regarding the changes that come with age, what features would you include if someone asked you to design a senior center to help healthy aging adults maintain their physical, cognitive, and social well-being? What evidence would you cite to support each of your decisions?

FICTOID

MYTH: *Dyslexia* is defined as a tendency to transpose letters in words (like spelling the word *read* as "raed") or to perceive letters or numbers backward (like seeing a *b* as a *d*).

REALITY: Only some people with dyslexia (which means "reading difficult problems; more children display these problem age but don't develop dyslexia. people with dyslexia literally p words backward.

FACTOID

People with severe mental illnesses, like schizophrenia, are much more likely to be victims than perpetrators of violence (Teplin et al., 2005), probably because they often experience difficulty defending themselves against attack or avoiding dangerous situations.

psychomythology

HOW ACCURATE IS CRIMINAL PROFILING?

Another practice whose popularity may derive in part from the P.T. Barnum effect is *criminal profiling*, a technique depicted in the 1991 movie *The Silence of the Lambs* and such television shows as *Criminal Minds* and *Law and Order*. Criminal profilers at the FBI and other law enforcement agencies claim to draw detailed inferences about perpetrators' personality traits and motives from the pattern of crimes committed.

It's true that we can often guess certain characteristics of criminals at better-than-chance levels. If we're investigating a homicide, we'll do better than flipping a coin by guessing that the murderer was a male (most murders are committed by men) between the ages of 15 and 25 (most murders are committed by adolescents and young adults) who suffers from psychological problems (most murderers suffer from psychological problems). But criminal profilers purport to go considerably beyond such widely available statistics. They typically claim to possess unique expertise and to be able to harness their years of accumulated experience to outperform statistical formulas.

THE THREE PROCESSES OF MEMORY
7.4 Identify methods for connecting new information to existing knowledge.
7.5 Identify the role that schemas play in the storage of memories.
7.6 Distinguish ways of measuring memory.
7.7 Describe how the relation between encoding and retrieval conditions influences remembering.

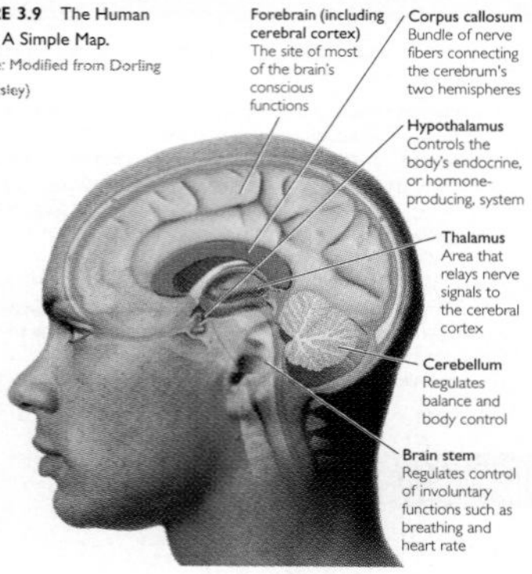
Forebrain (including cerebral cortex)
The site of most of the brain's conscious functions
Corpus callosum
Bundle of nerve fibers connecting the cerebrum's two hemispheres
Hypothalamus
Controls the body's endocrine, or hormone-producing, system
Thalamus
Area that relays nerve signals to the cerebral cortex
Cerebellum
Regulates balance and body control
Brain stem
Regulates control of involuntary functions such as breathing and heart rate

FIGURE 3.9 The Human Brain: A Simple Map.
(*Source:* Modified from Dorling Kindersley)

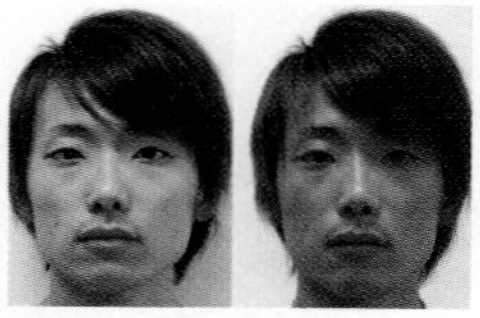

? Like some people of Asian heritage, this person shows a pronounced flushing response after having a drink, as seen in this before and after panel. **Based on the research literature, is he likely to be at increased or decreased risk for alcohol problems in later life compared with most people?** (See answer upside-down at bottom of page).

Study and **Review** on **mypsychlab.com**
Explore on **mypsychlab.com**
Listen on **mypsychlab.com**
Simulate on **mypsychlab.com**
Watch on **mypsychlab.com**

HOW DOES THE PEDAGOGY HELP GUIDE STUDENTS' UNDERSTANDING OF CONCEPTS?

Color-coded biological art orients students at both the micro and macro levels as they move throughout the text and forge connections among concepts. **Interactive photo captions** test students on their scientific thinking skills and invite them to evaluate whether or not the photo is an accurate depiction of psychological phenomena. Answers appear at the bottom of the page.

HOW DOES THE PEDAGOGY HELP STUDENTS TO REINFORCE WHAT THEY'VE LEARNED?

At the end of each major topic heading, we provide an **Assess Your Knowledge: Fact or Fiction?** review of selected material to further reinforce concept comprehension and foster students' ability to distinguish psychological fact from fiction. Throughout the text, **MyPsychLab** icons direct students to additional online study and review material such as videos, simulations, and practice quizzes and customized study plans.

assess your knowledge — **FACT OR FICTION?**

1. Piaget argued that development was domain-general and continuous. **True / False**
2. Vygotsky's theory proposes that individual children vary in the age at which they achieve developmental readiness for particular cognitive abilities. **True / False**
3. The ability to count precise quantities is absent in some cultures. **True / False**
4. Adolescents may not always make mature decisions about engaging in risky behaviors because their frontal lobes aren't fully mature. **True / False**
5. Older adults perform worse than younger adults on tests that require memory for random lists of words, but perform better on tests of knowledge and vocabulary. **True / False**

Answers: 1. F (p. 372); 2. T (p. 376); 3. T (p. 380); 4. T (p. 381); 5. T (p. 382)

HOW DOES THE PEDAGOGY HELP STUDENTS SYNTHESIZE INFORMATION AND ASSESS THEIR KNOWLEDGE?

Your Complete Review System, located at the end of every chapter, includes a summary, quiz questions, and visual activities, all organized by the major chapter sections and tied to chapter learning objectives. **Apply Your Scientific Thinking Principles** questions challenge students to research and evaluate current event topics. A complete list of key terms is also provided.

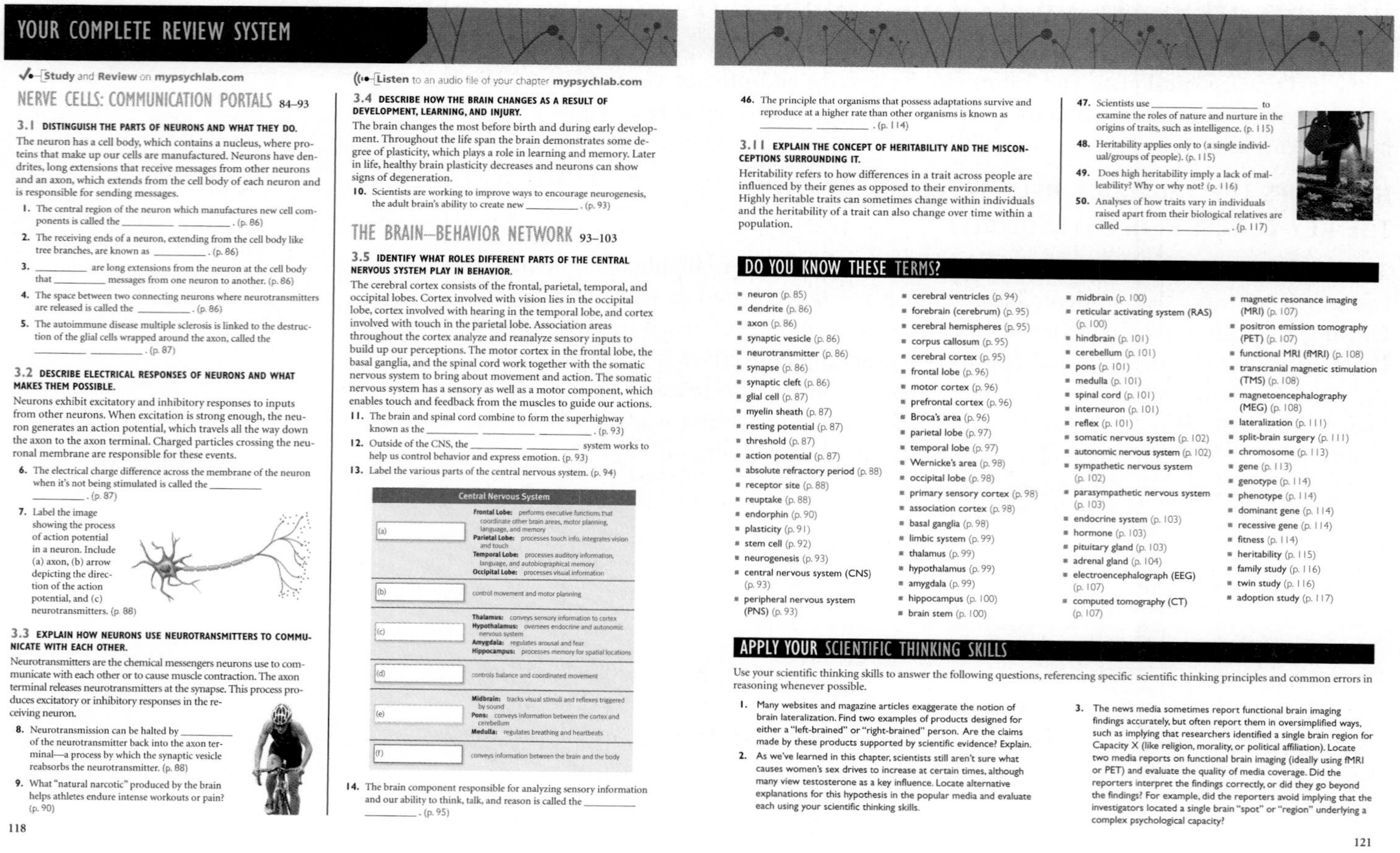

YOUR COMPLETE REVIEW SYSTEM

Study and **Review** on **mypsychlab.com**

NERVE CELLS: COMMUNICATION PORTALS 84–93

3.1 DISTINGUISH THE PARTS OF NEURONS AND WHAT THEY DO.

The neuron has a cell body, which contains a nucleus, where proteins that make up our cells are manufactured. Neurons have dendrites, long extensions that receive messages from other neurons and an axon, which extends from the cell body of each neuron and is responsible for sending messages.

1. The central region of the neuron which manufactures new cell components is called the ________ ________. (p. 86)
2. The receiving ends of a neuron, extending from the cell body like tree branches, are known as ________. (p. 86)
3. ________ are long extensions from the neuron at the cell body that ________ messages from one neuron to another. (p. 86)
4. The space between two connecting neurons where neurotransmitters are released is called the ________. (p. 86)
5. The autoimmune disease multiple sclerosis is linked to the destruction of the glial cells wrapped around the axon, called the ________ ________. (p. 87)

3.2 DESCRIBE ELECTRICAL RESPONSES OF NEURONS AND WHAT MAKES THEM POSSIBLE.

Neurons exhibit excitatory and inhibitory responses to inputs from other neurons. When excitation is strong enough, the neuron generates an action potential, which travels all the way down the axon to the axon terminal. Charged particles crossing the neuronal membrane are responsible for these events.

6. The electrical charge difference across the membrane of the neuron when it's not being stimulated is called the ________ ________. (p. 87)
7. Label the image showing the process of action potential in a neuron. Include (a) axon, (b) arrow depicting the direction of the action potential, and (c) neurotransmitters. (p. 88)

3.3 EXPLAIN HOW NEURONS USE NEUROTRANSMITTERS TO COMMUNICATE WITH EACH OTHER.

Neurotransmitters are the chemical messengers neurons use to communicate with each other or to cause muscle contraction. The axon terminal releases neurotransmitters at the synapse. This process produces excitatory or inhibitory responses in the receiving neuron.

8. Neurotransmission can be halted by ________ of the neurotransmitter back into the axon terminal—a process by which the synaptic vesicle reabsorbs the neurotransmitter. (p. 88)
9. What "natural narcotic" produced by the brain helps athletes endure intense workouts or pain? (p. 90)

118

Listen to an audio file of your chapter **mypsychlab.com**

3.4 DESCRIBE HOW THE BRAIN CHANGES AS A RESULT OF DEVELOPMENT, LEARNING, AND INJURY.

The brain changes the most before birth and during early development. Throughout the life span the brain demonstrates some degree of plasticity, which plays a role in learning and memory. Later in life, healthy brain plasticity decreases and neurons can show signs of degeneration.

10. Scientists are working to improve ways to encourage neurogenesis, the adult brain's ability to create new ________. (p. 93)

THE BRAIN–BEHAVIOR NETWORK 93–103

3.5 IDENTIFY WHAT ROLES DIFFERENT PARTS OF THE CENTRAL NERVOUS SYSTEM PLAY IN BEHAVIOR.

The cerebral cortex consists of the frontal, parietal, temporal, and occipital lobes. Cortex involved with vision lies in the occipital lobe, cortex involved with hearing in the temporal lobe, and cortex involved with touch in the parietal lobe. Association areas throughout the cortex analyze and reanalyze sensory inputs to build up our perceptions. The motor cortex in the frontal lobe, the basal ganglia, and the spinal cord work together with the somatic nervous system to bring about movement and action. The somatic nervous system has a sensory as well as a motor component, which enables touch and feedback from the muscles to guide our actions.

11. The brain and spinal cord combine to form the superhighway known as the ________ ________ ________. (p. 93)
12. Outside of the CNS, the ________ ________ system works to help us control behavior and express emotion. (p. 93)
13. Label the various parts of the central nervous system. (p. 94)

Central Nervous System	
(a)	**Frontal Lobe:** performs executive functions that coordinate other brain areas, motor planning, language, and memory **Parietal Lobe:** processes touch info. integrates vision and touch **Temporal Lobe:** processes auditory information, language, and autobiographical memory **Occipital Lobe:** processes visual information
(b)	control movement and motor planning
(c)	**Thalamus:** conveys sensory information to cortex **Hypothalamus:** oversees endocrine and autonomic nervous system **Amygdala:** regulates arousal and fear **Hippocampus:** processes memory for spatial locations
(d)	controls balance and coordinated movement
(e)	**Midbrain:** tracks visual stimuli and reflexes triggered by sound **Pons:** conveys information between the cortex and cerebellum **Medulla:** regulates breathing and heartbeats
(f)	conveys information between the brain and the body

14. The brain component responsible for analyzing sensory information and our ability to think, talk, and reason is called the ________ ________. (p. 95)

46. The principle that organisms that possess adaptations survive and reproduce at a higher rate than other organisms is known as ________ ________. (p. 114)

3.11 EXPLAIN THE CONCEPT OF HERITABILITY AND THE MISCONCEPTIONS SURROUNDING IT.

Heritability refers to how differences in a trait across people are influenced by their genes as opposed to their environments. Highly heritable traits can sometimes change within individuals and the heritability of a trait can also change over time within a population.

47. Scientists use ________ ________ to examine the roles of nature and nurture in the origins of traits, such as intelligence. (p. 115)
48. Heritability applies only to (a single individual/groups of people). (p. 115)
49. Does high heritability imply a lack of malleability? Why or why not? (p. 116)
50. Analyses of how traits vary in individuals raised apart from their biological relatives are called ________ ________. (p. 117)

DO YOU KNOW THESE TERMS?

- neuron (p. 85)
- dendrite (p. 86)
- axon (p. 86)
- synaptic vesicle (p. 86)
- neurotransmitter (p. 86)
- synapse (p. 86)
- synaptic cleft (p. 86)
- glial cell (p. 87)
- myelin sheath (p. 87)
- resting potential (p. 87)
- threshold (p. 87)
- action potential (p. 87)
- absolute refractory period (p. 88)
- receptor site (p. 88)
- reuptake (p. 88)
- endorphin (p. 90)
- plasticity (p. 91)
- stem cell (p. 92)
- neurogenesis (p. 93)
- central nervous system (CNS) (p. 93)
- peripheral nervous system (PNS) (p. 93)
- cerebral ventricles (p. 94)
- forebrain (cerebrum) (p. 95)
- cerebral hemispheres (p. 95)
- corpus callosum (p. 95)
- cerebral cortex (p. 95)
- frontal lobe (p. 96)
- motor cortex (p. 96)
- prefrontal cortex (p. 96)
- Broca's area (p. 96)
- parietal lobe (p. 97)
- temporal lobe (p. 97)
- Wernicke's area (p. 98)
- occipital lobe (p. 98)
- primary sensory cortex (p. 98)
- association cortex (p. 98)
- basal ganglia (p. 98)
- limbic system (p. 99)
- thalamus (p. 99)
- hypothalamus (p. 99)
- amygdala (p. 99)
- hippocampus (p. 100)
- brain stem (p. 100)
- midbrain (p. 100)
- reticular activating system (RAS) (p. 100)
- hindbrain (p. 101)
- cerebellum (p. 101)
- pons (p. 101)
- medulla (p. 101)
- spinal cord (p. 101)
- interneuron (p. 101)
- reflex (p. 101)
- somatic nervous system (p. 102)
- autonomic nervous system (p. 102)
- sympathetic nervous system (p. 102)
- parasympathetic nervous system (p. 103)
- endocrine system (p. 103)
- hormone (p. 103)
- pituitary gland (p. 103)
- adrenal gland (p. 104)
- electroencephalograph (EEG) (p. 107)
- computed tomography (CT) (p. 107)
- magnetic resonance imaging (MRI) (p. 107)
- positron emission tomography (PET) (p. 107)
- functional MRI (fMRI) (p. 108)
- transcranial magnetic stimulation (TMS) (p. 108)
- magnetoencephalography (MEG) (p. 108)
- lateralization (p. 111)
- split-brain surgery (p. 111)
- chromosome (p. 113)
- gene (p. 113)
- genotype (p. 114)
- phenotype (p. 114)
- dominant gene (p. 114)
- recessive gene (p. 114)
- fitness (p. 114)
- heritability (p. 115)
- family study (p. 116)
- twin study (p. 116)
- adoption study (p. 117)

APPLY YOUR SCIENTIFIC THINKING SKILLS

Use your scientific thinking skills to answer the following questions, referencing specific scientific thinking principles and common errors in reasoning whenever possible.

1. Many websites and magazine articles exaggerate the notion of brain lateralization. Find two examples of products designed for either a "left-brained" or "right-brained" person. Are the claims made by these products supported by scientific evidence? Explain.
2. As we've learned in this chapter, scientists still aren't sure what causes women's sex drives to increase at certain times, although many view testosterone as a key influence. Locate alternative explanations for this hypothesis in the popular media and evaluate each using your scientific thinking skills.
3. The news media sometimes report functional brain imaging findings accurately, but often report them in oversimplified ways, such as implying that researchers identified a single brain region for Capacity X (like religion, morality, or political affiliation). Locate two media reports on functional brain imaging (ideally using fMRI or PET) and evaluate the quality of media coverage. Did the reporters interpret the findings correctly, or did they go beyond the findings? For example, did the reporters avoid implying that the investigators located a single brain "spot" or "region" underlying a complex psychological capacity?

121

PUTTING SCIENTIFIC THINKING TO THE TEST: INNOVATIVE AND INTEGRATED SUPPLEMENTS

Psychology: From Inquiry to Understanding is accompanied by a collection of teaching and learning supplements designed to reinforce the scientific thinking skills from the text. These supplements "put scientific thinking to the test" by reinforcing our framework for evaluating claims and assessing students' ability to think scientifically in a variety of psychological and real-world situations.

PRINTABLE TEST ITEM FILE (ISBN 0-205-00162-9)

The thoroughly updated and revised test bank, authored by Jason Spiegelman (Community College of Baltimore County) and Nicholas Greco IV, contains over 2,000 multiple choice, fill-in-the-blank, short-answer, and essay questions—each referenced to the relevant page in the textbook. Many of these questions are designed to test students' scientific thinking skills. An additional feature of the test bank is the inclusion of rationales for the correct answer in the conceptual and applied multiple-choice questions. The rationales help instructors to evaluate the questions they are choosing for their tests and give instructors the option to use the rationales as an answer key for their students. Feedback from customers indicates that this unique feature is useful for ensuring quality and quick responses to student queries.

A two-page Total Assessment Guide chapter overview makes creating tests easier by listing all of the test items in an easy-to-reference grid. The Total Assessment Guide organizes all test items by text section and question type/level of difficulty. All multiple-choice questions are categorized as factual, conceptual, or applied. The Test Item File is available in Microsoft Word and PDF formats on the Instructor's DVD (ISBN: 0-205-00317-6) and also online at http://www.pearsonhighered.com/irc.

NEW MYTEST mypearsontest ☑ (WWW.PEARSONMYTEST.COM)

The Second Edition test bank comes with Pearson MyTest, a powerful assessment-generation program that helps instructors easily create and print quizzes and exams. Instructors can do this online, allowing flexibility and the ability to efficiently manage assessments at any time. Instructors can easily access existing questions and edit, create, and store using simple drag-and-drop and Word-like controls. Each question comes with information on its level of difficulty and related page number in the text, mapped to the appropriate learning objective. For more information go to www.PearsonMyTest.com.

BLACKBOARD TEST ITEM FILE/WEBCT TEST ITEM FILE

For instructors who only need the test item file, we offer the complete test item file in BlackBoard and WebCT format. To access this feature, go to the Instructor's Resource Center at http://pearsonhighered.com/irc.

NEW INTERACTIVE POWERPOINT SLIDES

These slides, available on the Instructor's DVD (ISBN: 0-205-00317-6), bring the Lilienfeld et al. design right into the classroom, drawing students into the lecture and providing wonderful interactive activities, visuals, and videos. A video walk-through is available and provides clear guidelines on using and customizing the slides. The slides are built around the text's learning objectives and offer many links across content areas. Icons integrated throughout the slides indicate interactive exercises, simulations, and activities that can be accessed directly from the slides if instructors want to use these resources in the classroom.

STANDARD LECTURE POWERPOINT SLIDES

Created by Caleb Lack (University of Central Oklahoma), in a more traditional format with excerpts of the text material, photos, and art work, these slides are available on the Instructor's DVD (ISBN: 0-205-00317-6) and also online at http://www.pearsonhighered.com/irc.

CLASSROOM RESPONSE SYSTEM (CRS) POWERPOINT SLIDES

Authored by Cathleen Campbell-Raufer (Illinois State University), Classroom Response System questions ("clicker" questions) are intended to form the basis for class discussions as well as lectures. The incorporation of the CRS questions into each chapter's slideshow facilitates the use of "clickers"—small hardware devices similar to remote controls, which process student responses to questions and interpret and display results in real time. CRS questions are a great way to get students involved in what they are learning, especially because many of these questions address specific scientific thinking skills highlighted in the textbook. These questions are available on the Instructor's DVD (**ISBN: 0-205-00317-6**) and also online at http://pearsonhighered.com/irc.

INSTRUCTOR'S RESOURCE MANUAL

Authored by Jason Warnick (Arkansas Tech University), the Instructor's Resource Manual gives you unparalleled access to a huge selection of classroom-proven assets. First-time instructors will appreciate the detailed introduction to teaching the introductory psychology course, with suggestions for preparing for the course, sample syllabi, and current trends and strategies for successful teaching. Each chapter offers activities, exercises, assignments, handouts, and demos for in-class, as well as guidelines for integrating media resources into the classroom and syllabus. The material is organized in an easy-to-use Chapter Lecture Outline. This resource saves prep work and helps you make maximum use of classroom time. A unique hyperlinking system allows for easy reviewing of relevant sections and resources. The IRM is available for download from the Instructor's Resource Center at http://www.pearsonhighered.com/irc or from the Instructor's DVD (**ISBN: 0-205-00317-6**).

APA CORRELATION GUIDE

This detailed correlation guide, which appears in the Instructor's Manual, shows how the learning outcomes in the text and the test bank questions correspond to the APA Learning Goals and Outcomes.

INSTRUCTOR'S RESOURCE DVD (ISBN 0-205-00317-6)

Bringing all of the Second Edition's instructor resources together in one place, the Instructor's DVD offers both versions of the PowerPoint presentations, the Classroom Response System (CRS), the electronic files for the Instructor's Resource Manual materials, and the Test Item File to help instructors customize their lecture notes.

MYCLASSPREP

New from Pearson, MyClassPrep makes lecture preparation simpler and less time-consuming. It collects the very best class presentation resources—art and figures from our leading texts, videos, lecture activities, classroom activities, demonstrations, and much more—in one convenient online destination. You may search through MyClassPrep's extensive database of tools by content topic (arranged by standard topics within the psychology curriculum) or by content type (video, audio, simulation, Word documents, etc.). You can select resources appropriate for your lecture, many of which can be downloaded directly. Or you may build your own folder of resources and present from within MyClassPrep. MyClassPrep can be accessed via the Instructor's Resources tab within MyPsychLab. Please contact your Pearson representative for access to MyPsychLab.

INTRODUCTORY PSYCHOLOGY TEACHING FILMS BOXED SET (ISBN 0-13-175432-7)

This multi-DVD set of videos includes 100 short video clips of 5 to 10 minutes in length from many of the most popular video sources for psychology content, such as ABC News, Films for the Humanities series, PBS, and Pennsylvania State Media Sales Video Classics. Annual update volumes are also available (2009 volume ISBN 0-205-65280-8, 2010 volume ISBN 0-13-605401-3).

STUDENT STUDY GUIDE (ISBN 0-205-83883-9)

Authored by Annette Kujawski Taylor (University of San Diego), the study guide is filled with review material, in-depth activities, and self-assessments. Special sections devoted to study skills, concept mapping, and the evaluation of websites appear at the start of the guide.

MYPSYCHLAB . . . SAVE TIME. IMPROVE RESULTS. PUT SCIENTIFIC THINKING TO THE TEST.

Across the country, from small community colleges to large public universities, a trend is emerging: Introductory psychology enrollments are increasing and available resources can't keep pace. Many instructors are finding that their time is being stretched to the limit. Yet continual feedback is an important contributor to successful student progress. For this reason, the APA strongly recommends the use of student self-assessment tools and embedded questions and assignments (see http://www.apa.org/ed/eval_strategies.html for more information). In response to these demands, Pearson's MyPsychLab (MPL) provides students with useful and engaging self-assessment tools and offers instructors flexibility in assessing and tracking student progress.

What Is MyPsychLab?

MyPsychLab is a learning and assessment tool that enables instructors to assess student performance and adapt course content without investing additional time or resources. Instructors decide the extent of integration, from independent self-assessment for students to total course management. Students benefit from an easy-to-use site at which they can test themselves on key content, track their progress, and create individually tailored study plans. By transferring faculty members' most time-consuming tasks—content delivery, student assessment, and grading—to

automated tools, MyPsychLab allows teachers to spend more quality time with students. For sample syllabi with ideas on incorporating content, go to http://www.mypsychlab.com.

MyPsychLab Includes:

- **An interactive eBook** with highlighting and note-taking features and powerful embedded media including simulations, podcasts, more than 200 video clips (available in closed caption), and an **interactive timeline** that presents the history of psychology.

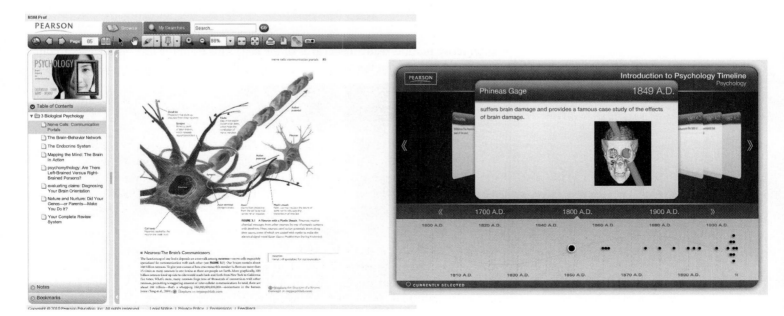

- **New Pearson Psychology Experiments Tool** presents a suite of data-generating study demonstrations, self-inventories, and surveys that allow students to experience firsthand some of the main concepts covered in the textbook. Each item in the Experiments Tool generates anonymous class data that instructors can download and use for in class lectures or homework assignments. With over 50 assignable demonstrations such as the Implicit Association Test, Roediger Effect, Inter-hemispheric Transfer Time, the IPIP-Neo Personality Inventory, Buss Mate Preference Survey, and general surveys, the Experiments Tool holds students accountable for *doing* psychology.

- Within each chapter, a **Psychology in the News activity** presents students with a real news story and then asks students to apply the six scientific thinking principles to think scientifically about the claims introduced in the story.

- **A Gradebook for instructors**, and the availability of full course management capabilities for instructors teaching online or hybrid courses.

- **Audio files of each chapter**, which benefit blind students and others who prefer sound-based materials, and conform to ADA guidelines.

- **A new podcasting tool** with pre-loaded podcasts, permitting instructors to easily record and upload podcasts of their own lectures for students to access.

- **Audio podcasts** present a hot topic in the field of psychology and utilize the scientific thinking framework to evaluate the issues thoughtfully.

- **Many opportunities for self-testing**, including pre- and post-tests, customized study plans, and eBook self-assessments.

- **Interactive mobile-ready flash cards** of the key terms from the text—students can build their own stacks, print the cards, or export their flash cards to their cellphone.

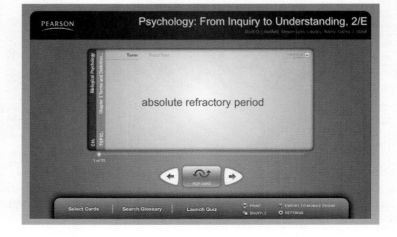

MyPsychLab for BlackBoard/MyPsychLab for WebCT

The customized BlackBoard cartridge and WebCT epack include the complete Test Item File, each chapter's Learning Objectives, Glossary Flash Cards, Chapter Summaries, a link to MyPsychLab, and Chapter Exams. Ask your Pearson representative about custom offerings for other learning management systems.

Assessment and Ability to Adapt

MyPsychLab is designed with instructor flexibility in mind—you decide the extent of integration into your course—from independent self-assessment for students, to total course management. By transferring faculty members' most time-consuming tasks—content delivery, student assessment, and grading—to automated tools, MyPsychLab enables faculty to spend more quality time with students. For sample syllabi with ideas on incorporating MPL, see the Instructor's Manual as well as online at www.mypsychlab.com. Instructors are provided with the results of the diagnostic tests—by students as well as an aggregate report of their class.

For more information on MyPsychLab go to www.mypsychlab.com

SUPPLEMENTARY TEXTS FOR YOUR INTRODUCTORY PSYCHOLOGY COURSE

Contact your Pearson Education representative to package any of the following supplementary texts with *Psychology,* Second Edition. A package ISBN is required for your bookstore order.

CURRENT DIRECTIONS IN INTRODUCTORY PSYCHOLOGY, SECOND EDITION (ISBN 0-13-714350-8)

The second edition of this reader includes more than 20 articles selected for undergraduates from *Current Directions in Psychological Science.* These timely, cutting-edge, and accessible articles allow instructors to show students how psychologists go about their research and how they apply it to real-world problems.

FORTY STUDIES THAT CHANGED PSYCHOLOGY, SIXTH EDITION (ISBN 0-13-603599-X)

Presenting the seminal research studies that have shaped modern psychological study, this brief supplement by Roger Hock (Mendocino College) provides an overview of the thinking that gave rise to each study, its research design, its findings, and its impact on current thinking in the discipline.

THE PSYCHOLOGY MAJOR: CAREERS AND STRATEGIES FOR SUCCESS, FOURTH EDITION (ISBN: 0-205-68468-8)

This paperback by Eric Landrum (Idaho State University) and Stephen Davis (Emporia State University) provides valuable information about career options available to psychology majors, tips for improving academic performance, and a guide to the APA style of reporting research.

COLLEGE TEACHING TIPS (ISBN 0-13-614317-2)

This guide by Fred W. Whitford (Montana State University) helps new instructors or graduate teaching assistants manage complex tasks required to teach an introductory course effectively. The author has used his own teaching experience over the past 25 years to illustrate some of the problems a new instructor may expect to face.

PSYCHOBABBLE AND BIOBUNK: USING PSYCHOLOGY TO THINK CRITICALLY ABOUT ISSUES IN THE NEWS, THIRD EDITION (ISBN 0-205-01591-3)

This handbook features a selection of opinion essays and book reviews by Carol Tavris, written for the *Los Angeles Times,* the *New York Times, Scientific American,* and other publications. These essays, which apply psychological research and principles of scientific and critical thinking to issues in the news, may be used to encourage debate in the classroom or as a basis for student papers.

READINGS IN PSEUDOSCIENCE AND THE PARANORMAL (ISBN 0-13-194101-1)
This topically organized text integrates naturally with the flow of all introductory psychology courses presenting the differences between science and pseudoscience in a fun and interesting way. Timothy Lawson uses original sources to address the numerous pseudoscientific claims that students are exposed to through the media, the Internet and pop psychology books.

HOW TO THINK STRAIGHT ABOUT PSYCHOLOGY, NINTH EDITION (ISBN 0-205-68590-0)
Keith Stanovich's widely used and highly acclaimed book helps students become more discriminating consumers of psychological information, helping them recognize pseudoscience and be able to distinguish it from true psychological research. Stanovich helps instructors teach critical thinking skills within the rich context of psychology. It is the leading text of its kind.

ACCESSING ALL RESOURCES

For a list of all student resources available with *Psychology: From Inquiry to Understanding*, Second Edition, go to www.mypearsonstore.com, enter the text ISBN (0-205-83206-7) and check out the "Everything That Goes with It" section under the book cover.

For access to all instructor supplements for *Psychology: From Inquiry to Understanding*, **Second Edition go to** http://pearsonhighered.com/irc and follow the directions to register (or log in if you already have a Pearson user name and password). Once you have registered and your status as an instructor is verified, you will be e-mailed a log-in name and password. Use your log-in name and password to access the catalog. Click on the "online catalog" link, click on "psychology" followed by "introductory psychology" and then the Lilienfeld/Lynn/Namy/Woolf, *Psychology: From Inquiry to Understanding*, Second Edition text. Under the description of each supplement is a link that allows you to download and save the supplement to your desktop.

You can request hard copies of the supplements through your Pearson sales representative. If you do not know your sales representative, go to http://www.pearsonhighered.com/replocator/ and follow the directions. For technical support for any of your Pearson products, you and your students can contact http://247.pearsoned.com.

A FINAL WORD & THANKS

For the four authors, writing this book has been a great deal of work, but it's also been a labor of love. When we began this undertaking, we as authors could never have imagined the number of committed, selfless, and enthusiastic colleagues in the psychology community who would join us on this path to making our textbook a reality. During the long months of writing and revising, the feedback and support from fellow instructors, researchers, and students helped keep our energy high and our minds sharp. We stand in awe of their love of the discipline and the enthusiasm and imagination each of these individuals brings to the psychology classroom every day. This text is the culmination of their ongoing support from first to final draft and then subsequent revision, and we are forever grateful to them.

In addition, the authors would like to extend our heartfelt gratitude and sincere thanks to a host of people on the Pearson team. We consider ourselves remarkably fortunate to have worked with such an uncommonly dedicated, talented, and genuinely kind group of people. Needless to say, this project was a monumental team effort, and every member of the team played an invaluable role in its inception. We owe special thanks to Jessica Mosher, Editor-in-Chief, and Stephen Frail, Executive Editor, for the enthusiasm, creativity, and support they brought to the project; to Susan Hartman (our original Editor-in-Chief) for her exceptional professionalism, generosity, support, and grace under pressure, not to mention her undying commitment to the project; Marianne Peters-Riordan, our production manager, for her high-quality work and wonderful attitude; Sharon Geary, Director of Development, and Julie Swasey, our developmental editor, for their unending encouragement, good cheer, and invaluable assistance in polishing our prose and sharpening our ideas; and to Jeanette Koskinas, Executive Marketing Manager, for her energy, creativity, and contagious enthusiasm.

Warm thanks also go to many, many others, especially Maria Piper, art coordination; Beth Brenzel and Nancy Tobin, photo research; Charles Morris and Kathleen Karcher, permissions research; Anne DeMarinis and Nancy Wells, interior and cover design; Angela Pica, copyediting; Francesca Monaco, full-service vendor coordination; Kerri Hart-Morris, supplements managing and hiring; and Paul DeLuca, coordination of MyPsychLab. Special thanks go to Lisa Hamlett for her profound dedication and invaluable help with references.

Steven Lynn extends his deepest appreciation to Fern Pritikin Lynn for her discerning editorial assistance, and to Jessica Lynn for her helpful comments and insights concerning preliminary versions of the manuscript.

Last but by no means least, we thank the countless others who helped in small but significant ways in bringing this text to fruition. The feedback from users of the text has been especially helpful and we welcome others to share their experiences using the Second Edition by writing to Scott Lilienfeld at slilien@emory.edu.

Our Review Panel

We are indebted to the members of our Review Panel from the First and Second Editions who evaluated chapters and provided expert analysis on critical topic areas. Others served on an advisory council, participated in focus groups, conducted usability studies, ran class testing of chapters, and attended our faculty forums for the text. Their input proved invaluable to us, and we thank them for it.

ALABAMA
Clarissa Arms-Chavez, Auburn University–Montgomery
Charles Brown, University of South Alabama
Samuel Jones, Jefferson State Community College
David Payne, Wallace Community College
Christopher Robinson, University of Alabama–Birmingham
Eric Seemann, University of Alabama–Huntsville
Royce Simpson, Spring Hill College

ARIZONA
Lindette Lent Baas, Arizona Western College
Linda Ruehlman, Arizona State University

ARKANSAS
James Becker, Pulaski Technical College
Yousef Fahoum, University of Arkansas–Little Rock
Robert Hines, University of Arkansas–Little Rock
Travis Langley, Henderson State University
David Osburn, Arkansas Tech University
David A. Schroeder, University of Arkansas
Jason Warnick, Arkansas Tech University
Karen Yanowitz, Arkansas State University

CALIFORNIA
Mark Akiyama, Diablo Valley College
Matt Bell, Santa Clara University
John Billimek, California State University–Long Beach
David E. Campbell, Humboldt State University
G. William Domhoff, University of California–Santa Cruz
Glenn Callaghan, San Jose State University
Kimberley Duff, Cerritos College
Debra L. Golden, Grossmont College
Margaret Lynch, San Francisco State University
Janie Nath, Cerritos College
Ann Renken, University of Southern California

Amira Rezec, Saddleback College
Scott Roesch, San Diego State University
Catherine Sandhofer, University of California–Los Angeles
Dr. Martin van den Berg, California State University, Chico
Dean Yoshizumi, Sierra College

COLORADO
Pamela Ansburg, Metropolitan State College of Denver
Mark Basham, Regis University
Stefanie M. Bell, Pikes Peak Community College
Layton Seth Curl, Metropolitan State College of Denver
Linda Lockwood, Metropolitan State College of Denver
Peggy Norwood, Red Rocks Community College
Laura Sherrick, Front Range Community College–Westminster
Michael Zinser, University of Colorado–Denver

CONNECTICUT
Marlene Adelman, Norwalk Community College
Nathan Brody, Wesleyan University
Luis A. Cordon, Eastern Connecticut State University
Carlotta Ocampo, Trinity College
Amy Van Buren, Sacred Heart University

DELAWARE
Jack Barnhardt, Wesley College
Carrie Veronica Smith, University of Delaware

FLORIDA
Ted Barker, Northwest Florida State College
Job Clement, Daytona Beach Community College
Bethany Fleck, University of Tampa
Vicki Gier, University of South Florida
Gladys Green, State College of Florida
R. J. Grisham, Indian River Community College
James Jakubow, Florida Atlantic University
Glenn Musgrove, Broward Community College–Central

Jermaine Robertson, Florida A&M University
Lawrence Siegel, Palm Beach State College
Richard W. Townsend, Miami-Dade College–Kendall
Barbara VanHorn, Indian River Community College

GEORGIA

Richard Catrambone, Georgia Institute of Technology
Gregory M. Corso, Georgia Institute of Technology
Janet Frick, University of Georgia
Deborah Garfin, Georgia State University
Adam Goodie, University of Georgia
Mark Griffin, Georgia Perimeter College–Dunwoody
Amy Hackney-Hansen, Georgia Southern University
Katherine Kipp, Gainesville State College
William McIntosh, Georgia Southern University
Dominic Parrott, Georgia State University
Alan Pope, University of West Georgia
Amy Skinner, Gordon College
Robert Barry Stennett, Gainesville State College
James Stringham, University of Georgia
Richard Topolski, Augusta State University
Chantal Tusher, Georgia State University
Cynthia Vance, Piedmont College
Thresa Yancey, Georgia Southern University

HAWAII

Howard Markowitz, Hawaii Pacific University
Tanya Renner, Kapi'olani Community College

IDAHO

Tera Letzring, Idaho State University
Christopher Lowry, BYU Idaho
Steven E. Meier, University of Idaho
Randy Simonson, College of Southern Idaho

ILLINOIS

Jason Barker, University of Illinois at Springfield
Jessica Carpenter, Elgin Community College
Lorelei A. Carvajal, Triton Community College
Michael G. Dudley, Southern Illinois University–Edwardsville
Joseph R. Ferrari, DePaul University
Marjorie A. Getz, Bradley University
Allen Huffcutt, Bradley University
James Johnson, Illinois State University
Dawn McBride, Illinois State University
Margaret Nauta, Illinois State University
Cindy Nordstrom, Southern Illinois University–Edwardsville
John Skowronski, Northern Illinois University
Dale Smith, Olivet Nazarene University
Jeffrey Wagman, Illinois State University

INDIANA

Cathy Alsman, IvyTech Community College of Indiana
Brad Brubaker, Indiana State University
Johnathan Forbey, Ball State University
Robin Morgan, Indiana University Southeast
Cynthia O'Dell, Indiana University Northwest
Larry Pace, Anderson University
Anré Venter, University of Notre Dame

IOWA

Jennifer Bellingtier, University of Northern Iowa
Susan R. Burns, Morningside College

Doug Gentile, Iowa State University
Jennifer Grossheim, University of Northern Iowa
James Rodgers, Hawkeye Community College
Nicholas Schwab, University of Northern Iowa

KANSAS

Mary Coplen, Hutchinson Community College
Tammy Hutcheson, Garden City Community College

KENTUCKY

Joseph Bilotta, Western Kentucky University
Eric L. Bruns, Campbellsville University
Kelly Hagan, Bluegrass Community and Technical College
Paul M. Kasenow, Henderson Community College
Richard Miller, Western Kentucky University
Thomas W. Williams, Western Kentucky University

LOUISIANA

Michael Dreznick, Our Lake of the Lake College
Matthew I. Isaak, University of Louisiana–Lafayette
Gary J. Greguras, Louisiana State University
Mike Majors, Delgado Community College
Jack Palmer, University of Louisiana at Monroe

MAINE

Michelle Rivera, University of Maine

MARYLAND

Thomas Capo, University of Maryland
Cynthia Koenig, St. Mary's College of Maryland
Ann McKim, Goucher College
Mark Walter, Salisbury University

MASSACHUSETTS

Louis E. Banderet, Northeastern University
John Bickford, University of Massachusetts–Amherst
Anne Marie Perry, Massasoit Community College
Amy Shapiro, University of Massachusetts, Dartmouth

MICHIGAN

Renee Babcock, Central Michigan University
David Baskind, Delta College
Katherine Corker, Michigan State University
Joseph M. Fitzgerald, Wayne State University
Bryan Gibson, Central Michigan University
Linda Jackson, Michigan State University
Mary B. Lewis, Oakland University

MINNESOTA

Thomas Brothen, University of Minnesota
Ben Denkinger, Hamline University/Augsburg University
Randy Gordon, University of Minnesota–Duluth
Brenda E. Koneczny, Lake Superior College
Na'im Madyun, University of Minnesota–Twin Cities
Joe Melcher, St. Cloud State University

MISSISSIPPI

Tammy D. Barry, University of Southern Mississippi
David Echevarria, University of Southern Mississippi
Linda Fayard, Mississippi Gulf Coast Community College
Melissa Kelly, Millsaps College
David Marcus, University of Southern Mississippi
Todd Smitherman, University of Mississippi

MISSOURI

Michele Y. Breault, Truman State University
Jay Brown, Southwest Missouri State University

Carla Edwards, Northwest Missouri State University
Matthew Fanetti, Missouri State University
Donald Fischer, Missouri State University
Rebecca Hendrix, Northwest Missouri State University
Melinda Russell-Stamp, Northwest Missouri State University

NEBRASKA
Jean Mandernach, University of Nebraska at Kearney

NEW HAMPSHIRE
Francis Catano, Southern New Hampshire University
Jane Dwyer, Rivier College
Mike Mangan, University of New Hampshire

NEW JERSEY
Fred Bonato, St. Peter's College
Bruce J. Diamond, William Paterson University
Christine Floether, Centenary College
Elissa Koplik, Bloomfield College
Elaine Olaoye, Brookdale Community College
John Ruscio, The College of New Jersey
Jakob Steinberg, Fairleigh Dickinson University
Keith Williams, Richard Stockton College of New Jersey
Tara Woolfolk, Rutgers University–Camden

NEW MEXICO
Kathryn Demitrakis, Central New Mexico Community College
Richard M. Gorman, Central New Mexico Community College
Michael Hillard, Albuquerque Tech Vocational Institute
James R. Johnson, Central New Mexico Community College
Ron Salazar, San Juan College
Paul Vonnahme, New Mexico State University

NEW YORK
Michael Benhar, Suffolk County Community College
Robin Cautin, Manhattanville College
Christopher Chabris, Union College
Jennifer Cina, Barnard College
Dale Doty, Monroe Community College
Robert Dushay, Morrisville State College
Melvyn King, SUNY Cortland
Michie Odle, SUNY Cortland
Tibor Palfai, Syracuse University
Celia Reaves, Monroe Community College
Dennis T. Regan, Cornell University
Wayne Robinson, Monroe Community College
Jennifer Yanowitz, Utica College

NORTH CAROLINA
Rebecca Hester, Western Carolina University
Michael J. Kane, University of North Carolina–Greensboro
Amy Lyndon, East Carolina University
Mark O'DeKirk, Meredith College

NORTH DAKOTA
Caitlin Schultz, University of North Dakota
Jeff Weatherly, University of North Dakota

OHIO
Eynav Accortt, Miami University
Monali Chowdhury, Ohio State University
Lorry Cology, Owens Community College
Anastasia Dimitropoulos White, Case Western Reserve University
David R. Entwistle, Malone College
Stephen Flora, Youngstown State University
Ellen Furlong, Ohio State University

Joseph P. Green, Ohio State University–Lima
Traci Haynes, Columbus State Community College
Lance Jones, Bowling Green State University
Robin Lightner, University of Cincinnati
Wanda McCarthy, University of Cincinnati–Clermont College
Barbara McMasters, University of Cincinnati–Raymond Walters College
Barbara Oswald, University of Cincinnati–Raymond Walters College
Meera Rastogi, University of Cincinnati–Clermont College
Wayne Shebilske, Wright State University
Vivian Smith, Lakeland Community College
Colin William, Columbus State Community College

OKLAHOMA
Laura Gruntmeir, Redlands Community College
Caleb W. Lack, University of Central Oklahoma
Kevin M.P. Woller, Rogers State University

OREGON
Alyson Burns-Glover, Pacific University
Deana Julka, University of Portland
Tony Obradovich, Portland Community College

PENNSYLVANIA
Robert Brill, Moravian College
Gayle L. Brosnan Watters, Slippery Rock University
Mark Cloud, Lock Haven University
Perri B. Druen, York College of Pennsylvania
Audrey M. Ervin, Delaware County Community College
Roy Fontaine, Pennsylvania College of Technology
William F. Ford, Bucks County Community College
Robert Hensley, Mansfield University
Barbara Radigan, Community College of Allegheny County
Reece Rahman, University of Pittsburgh at Johnstown
David R. Widman, Juniata College

RHODE ISLAND
David Alfano, Community College of Rhode Island

SOUTH CAROLINA
Chelsea Fry, Midlands Technical College
Dr. Tharon Howard, Clemson University
Lloyd R. Pilkington, Midlands Technical College
Frank Provenzano, Greenville Technical College
Kathy Weatherford, Trident Technical College

SOUTH DAKOTA
Brady J. Phelps, South Dakota State University

TENNESSEE
Gina Andrews, Volunteer State Community College
Andrea Clements, Eastern Tennessee State University
Vicki Dretchen, Volunteer State Community College
Brian Johnson, University of Tennessee at Martin
Colin Key, University of Tennessee at Martin
Angelina MacKewn, University of Tennessee at Martin

TEXAS
Michael C. Boyle, Sam Houston State University
Veda Brown, Prairie View A&M University
Catherine Camilletti, University of Texas at El Paso
Celeste Favela, El Paso Community College
Daniel J. Fox, Sam Houston State University
C. Allen Gorman, Angelo State University
Erin Hardin, Texas Tech University
Bert Hayslip, Jr., University of North Texas
Joanne Hsu, Houston Community College–Town and Country

Kevin W. Jolly, University of Texas at El Paso
Shirin Khosropour, Austin Community College
Don Lucas, Northwest Vista College
Jason Moses, El Paso Community College
Wendy Ann Olson, Texas A&M University
Wade C. Rowatt, Baylor University
Valerie T. Smith, Collin County Community College
Jeanne Spaulding, Houston Community College–Town and Country
Susan Spooner, McLennan Community College
Jennifer Vencill, Texas Tech University
Anton Villado, Rice University
Sharon Wiederstein, Blinn College, Bryan

UTAH
Scott C. Bates, Utah State University
Joseph Horvat, Weber State University
Cameron John, Utah Valley University
Kerry Jordan, Utah State University

VERMONT
Michael Zvolensky, University of Vermont

VIRGINIA
Keith P. Corodimas, Lynchburg College
Jeff D. Green, Virginia Commonwealth University
Natalie Lawrence, James Madison University
Kymberly Richard, Northern Virginia Community College
Mary Ann Schmitt, North Virginia Community College–Manassas

WASHINGTON
Ronald Boothe, University of Washington–Tacoma
Kevin King, University of Washington
Susan D. Lonborg, Central Washington University
Thomas J. Mount, Yakima Valley Community College

Jacqueline Pickrell, University of Washington
Heidi Shaw, Yakima Valley Community College
Alexandra Terrill, Washington State University–Vancouver
John W. Wright, Washington State University

WASHINGTON DC
Laura M. Juliano, American University

WEST VIRGINIA
Tammy McClain, West Liberty State College

WISCONSIN
Sylvia Beyer, University of Wisconsin–Parkside
Tracie Blumentritt, University of Wisconsin–LaCrosse
Dawn Delaney, Madison Area Technical College
Jeffrey B. Henriques, University of Wisconsin–Madison

We would also like to thank the following instructors from outside the United States who offered feedback on the text:
Nicole D. Anderson, Grant MacEwan College
Etzel Cardena, University of Lund
Helene Deacon, Dalhousie University
Matthew Holahan, Carleton University
Mark Holder, UBC, Okanagan
Lynne Honey, Grant MacEwan College
Kenneth W. Johns, University of Winnipeg
Sonya Major, Acadia University
Michael McIntyre, University of Winnipeg
Kim O'Neil, Carleton University
Lisa Sinclair, University of Winnipeg
Patrice Smith, Carleton University
Jennifer Steeves, York University
Gillian Watson, University of British Columbia

Scott O. Lilienfeld received his B.A. in Psychology from Cornell University in 1982 and his Ph.D. in Clinical Psychology from the University of Minnesota in 1990. He completed his clinical internship at Western Psychiatric Institute and Clinic in Pittsburgh, Pennsylvania, from 1986 to 1987. He was Assistant Professor in the Department of Psychology at SUNY Albany from 1990 to 1994 and now is Professor of Psychology at Emory University. He is a Fellow of the Association of Psychological Science and was the recipient of the 1998 David Shakow Award from Division 12 (Clinical Psychology) of the American Psychological Association for Early Career Contributions to Clinical Psychology. Dr. Lilienfeld is a past president of the Society for a Science of Clinical Psychology within Division 12. He is the founder and editor of the *Scientific Review of Mental Health Practice,* Associate Editor of *Applied and Preventive Psychology,* and a regular columnist for *Scientific American Mind* magazine. He has authored or coauthored seven books and over 200 journal articles and chapters. Dr. Lilienfeld has also been a participant in Emory University's "Great Teachers" lecturer series, as well as the Distinguished Speaker for the Psi Chi Honor Society at the American Psychological Association and numerous other national conventions.

Steven Jay Lynn received his B.A. in Psychology from the University of Michigan and his Ph.D. in Clinical Psychology from Indiana University. He completed an NIMH Postdoctoral Fellowship at Lafayette Clinic, Detroit, Michigan, in 1976 and is now Distinguished Professor of Psychology at Binghamton University (SUNY), where he is the director of the Psychological Clinic. Dr. Lynn is a fellow of numerous professional organizations, including the American Psychological Association and the American Psychological Society, and he was the recipient of the Chancellor's Award of the State University of New York for Scholarship and Creative Activities. Dr. Lynn has authored or edited 19 books and more than 270 other publications, and was recently named on a list of "Top Producers of Scholarly Publications in Clinical Psychology Ph.D. Programs" (2000–2004/Stewart, Wu, & Roberts, 2007, *Journal of Clinical Psychology*). Dr. Lynn has served as the editor of a book series for the American Psychological Association, and he has served on 11 editorial boards, including the *Journal of Abnormal Psychology*. Dr. Lynn's research has been supported by the National Institute of Mental Health and the Ohio Department of Mental Health.

Laura L. Namy received her B.A. in Philosophy and Psychology from Indiana University in 1993 and her doctorate in Cognitive Psychology at Northwestern University in 1998. She is now Associate Professor of Psychology and Core Faculty in Linguistics at Emory University. Dr. Namy is the editor of the *Journal of Cognition and Development*. At Emory, she is Director of the Emory Child Study Center and Associate Director of the Center for Mind, Brain, and Culture. Her research focuses on the origins and development of verbal and nonverbal symbol use in young children, sound symbolism in natural language, and the role of comparison in conceptual development.

Nancy J. Woolf received her B.S. in Psychobiology at UCLA in 1978 and her Ph.D. in Neuroscience at UCLA School of Medicine in 1983. She is Adjunct Professor in the Department of Psychology at UCLA. Her specialization is behavioral neuroscience, and her research spans the organization of acetylcholine systems, neural plasticity, memory, neural degeneration, Alzheimer's disease, and consciousness. In 1990 she won the Colby Prize from the Sigma Kappa Foundation, awarded for her achievements in scientific research in Alzheimer disease. In 2002 she received the Academic Advancement Program Faculty Recognition Award. She also received a Distinguished Teaching Award from the Psychology Department at UCLA in 2008. Dr. Woolf is currently on the editorial boards of *Science and Consciousness Review* and *Journal of Nanoneuroscience.*

PSYCHOLOGY AND SCIENTIFIC THINKING

a framework for everyday life

THINK ABOUT IT

IS PSYCHOLOGY MOSTLY JUST COMMON SENSE?

SHOULD WE TRUST MOST SELF-HELP BOOKS?

IS PSYCHOLOGY REALLY A SCIENCE?

ARE CLAIMS THAT CAN'T BE PROVEN WRONG SCIENTIFIC?

ARE ALL CLINICAL PSYCHOLOGISTS PSYCHOTHERAPISTS?

[Handwritten note:] Psychology: scientific study of the mind, brain, and behavior.

[Handwritten note:] ✱ Levels of analysis:
- Lower rungs = brain
  - thoughts, feelings, and emotions
  - biological influences
- Higher rungs = mind
  - social and cultural influences
  - social influences.

[Handwritten note:] Common sense is not the key

[Handwritten note:] ✱✱ Can't understand psychology by only focusing on one of the levels of analysis.

[Handwritten note:] Psychology does not have simple answers

test of popular psychology knowledge

1. Most people use only about 10 percent of their brain capacity. **True / False**

2. Newborn babies are virtually blind and deaf. **True / False**

3. Hypnosis enhances the accuracy of our memories. **True / False**

4. All people with dyslexia see words backward (like *tac* instead of *cat*). **True / False**

5. In general, it's better to express anger than to hold it in. **True / False**

6. The lie-detector (polygraph) test is 90 to 95 percent accurate at detecting falsehoods. **True / False**

7. People tend to be romantically attracted to individuals who are opposite to them in personality and attitudes. **True / False**

8. The more people present at an emergency, the more likely it is that at least one of them will help. **True / False**

9. People with schizophrenia have more than one personality. **True / False**

10. All effective psychotherapies require clients to get to the root of their problems in childhood. **True / False**

For most of you reading this text, this is your first psychology course. But you may believe you've learned a lot about psychology already from watching television programs and movies, listening to radio call-in shows, reading self-help books and popular magazines, surfing the Internet, and talking to friends. In short, most of your psychology knowledge probably derives from the popular psychology industry: a sprawling network of everyday sources of information about human behavior.

Take a moment to review the 10 test questions above. Beginning psychology students typically assume they know the answers to most of them. That's hardly surprising, as these assertions have become part of popular psychology lore. Yet most students are surprised to learn that *all* 10 of these statements are false! This little exercise illustrates a take-home message we'll emphasize throughout the text: *Although common sense can be enormously useful for some purposes, it's sometimes completely wrong* (Chabris & Simons, 2010). This can be especially true in psychology, a field that strikes many of us as self-evident, even obvious. In a sense, we're *all* psychologists, because we deal with psychological phenomena, like love, friendship, anger, stress, happiness, sleep, memory, and language, in our daily lives (Lilienfeld et al., 2009). But as we'll soon discover, everyday experience doesn't necessarily make us an expert (Kahneman & Klein, 2009).

WHAT IS PSYCHOLOGY? SCIENCE VERSUS INTUITION

1.1 Explain why psychology is more than just common sense.

1.2 Explain the importance of science as a set of safeguards against biases.

William James (1842–1910), often regarded as the founder of American psychology, once described psychology as a "nasty little subject." As James noted, psychology is difficult to study, and simple explanations are few and far between. If you enrolled in this course expecting simple answers to psychological questions, like why you become angry or fall in love, you may be disappointed. But if you enrolled in the hopes of acquiring more insight into the hows and whys of human behavior, stay tuned, because a host of delightful surprises are in store. When reading this textbook, prepare to find many of your preconceptions about psychology challenged; to learn new ways of thinking about the causes of your everyday thoughts, feelings, and actions; and to apply these ways of thinking to evaluating psychological claims in your everyday life.

psychology
the scientific study of the mind, brain, and behavior

levels of analysis
rungs on a ladder of analysis, with lower levels tied most closely to biological influences and higher levels tied most closely to social influences

multiply determined
caused by many factors

[handwritten: Mind = brain in action]

[handwritten: Scientific psychologists study what causes behavior in humans and animals]

[handwritten: "And I said, "oh my! what a marvelous tune"]

Psychology and Levels of Analysis

The first question often posed in introductory psychology textbooks could hardly seem simpler: "What is psychology?" Although psychologists disagree about many things, they agree on one thing: Psychology isn't easy to define (Henriques, 2004; Lilienfeld, 2004). For the purposes of this text, we'll simply refer to **psychology** as the scientific study of the mind, brain, and behavior.

Another way of making this point is to describe psychology as a discipline that spans multiple **levels of analysis**. We can think of levels of analysis as rungs on a ladder, with the lower rungs tied most closely to biological influences and the higher rungs tied most closely to social influences (Ilardi & Feldman, 2001). The levels of analysis in psychology stretch all the way from molecules to brain structures on the low rungs to thoughts, feelings, and emotions, and to social and cultural influences at the high rungs, with many levels in between (Cacioppo et al., 2000) (see **FIGURE 1.1**). The lower rungs are more closely tied to what we traditionally call "the brain," the higher rungs to what we traditionally call "the mind." But it's crucial to understand that "brain" and "mind" are just different ways of describing the same "stuff," but at different levels of analysis: As we'll learn in Chapter 3, the "mind" is just the brain in action. Although scientific psychologists may differ in which rungs they choose to investigate, they're united by a shared commitment to understanding the causes of human and animal behavior.

We'll cover all of these levels of analysis in coming chapters. When doing so, we'll keep one crucial guideline in mind: *We can't understand psychology by focusing on only one level of analysis.* That's because each level tells us something different, and we gain new knowledge from each vantage point. Some psychologists believe that biological factors— like the actions of the brain and its billions of nerve cells—are most critical for understanding the causes of behavior. Others believe that social factors—like parenting practices, peer influences, and culture—are most critical for understanding the causes of behavior (Meehl, 1972). In this text, we'll steer away from these two extremes, because both biological and social factors are essential for a complete understanding of psychology (Kendler, 2005).

[handwritten: Taking biological and social factors together to understand psychology more fully.]

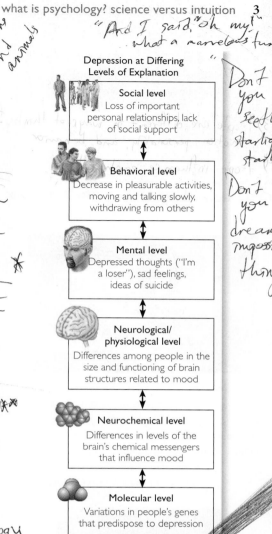

Depression at Differing Levels of Explanation

Social level
Loss of important personal relationships, lack of social support

Behavioral level
Decrease in pleasurable activities, moving and talking slowly, withdrawing from others

Mental level
Depressed thoughts ("I'm a loser"), sad feelings, ideas of suicide

Neurological/ physiological level
Differences among people in the size and functioning of brain structures related to mood

Neurochemical level
Differences in levels of the brain's chemical messengers that influence mood

Molecular level
Variations in people's genes that predispose to depression

[handwritten: Don't you see the starlight starlight? Don't you dream impossible things?]

FIGURE 1.1 Levels of Analysis in Depression. We can view psychological phenomena, in this case the disorder of depression, at multiple levels of analysis, with lower levels being more biological and higher levels being more social. Each level provides us with unique information and offers us a distinctive view of the phenomenon at hand. (*Source:* Adapted from Ilardi, Rand, & Karwoski, 2007)

What Makes Psychology Challenging—and Fascinating

A host of challenges make psychology complicated; it's precisely these challenges that also make psychology fascinating, because each challenge contributes to scientific mysteries that psychologists have yet to solve. Here, we'll touch briefly on five challenges that we'll be revisiting throughout the text.

First, human behavior is difficult to predict, in part because almost all actions are **multiply determined**, that is, produced by many factors. That's why we need to be profoundly skeptical of *single-variable explanations* of behavior, which are widespread in popular psychology. We may be tempted to explain complex human behaviors, like violence, in terms of a single causal factor, like either poverty or genes, but we'd almost surely be wrong because such behaviors are due to the interplay of an enormous array of factors.

[handwritten: 1) because you trip and don't catch yourself in time 2) for non-apparent reasons 3) angry stuff, anger-making things]

Each of these panels from everyday life poses a different psychological question: (1) Why do we fall in love? (2) Why do some of us become depressed for no apparent reason? (3) What makes us angry? Although the science of psychology doesn't provide easy answers to any of these questions, it does offer valuable insights into them.

1) Human behavior is unpredictable because it has many factors
2) Psychological influences tend to ~~not~~ be ~~independent~~ interconnected.

Psychology may not be one of the traditional "hard sciences," like chemistry, but many of its fundamental questions are even harder to answer.

3) People are different in ways of thinking, emotion, personality, and behavior
4) People influence each other
5) Culture shapes a person's behavior.

Second, psychological influences are rarely independent of each other, making it difficult to pin down which cause or causes are operating. Imagine yourself a scientist attempting to explain why some women develop *anorexia nervosa*, a severe eating disorder we'll discuss in Chapter 11. You could start by identifying several factors that might contribute to anorexia nervosa, like anxiety-proneness, compulsive exercise, perfectionism, excessive concern with body image, and exposure to television programs that feature thin models. Let's say that you now want to focus on just one of these potential influences, like perfectionism. Here's the problem: Women who are perfectionists also tend to be anxious, to exercise a lot, to be overly concerned with their body image, to watch television programs that feature thin models, and so on. The fact that all of these factors tend to be interrelated makes it tricky to pinpoint which actually contributes to anorexia nervosa. They could all be playing a role, but it's hard to know for sure.

In the museum of everyday life, causation isn't a one-way street. In conversations, one person influences a second person, who in turn influences the first person, who in turn influences the second person, and so on. This principle, called *reciprocal determinism,* makes it challenging to pinpoint the causes of behavior.

Third, people differ from each other in thinking, emotion, personality, and behavior. These **individual differences** help to explain why we each respond in different ways to the same objective situation, such as an insulting comment from a boss (Harkness & Lilienfeld, 1997). Entire fields of psychology, such as the study of intelligence, interests, personality, and mental illness, focus on individual differences (Lubinski, 2000). Individual differences make psychology challenging because they make it difficult to come up with explanations of behavior that apply to everyone.

Fourth, people often influence each other, making psychology unimaginably more complicated than disciplines like chemistry, in which we can isolate substances in test tubes (Wachtel, 1973). For example, if you're an extraverted person, you're likely to make the people around you more outgoing. In turn, their outgoing behavior may "feed back" to make you even more extraverted, and so on. This is an example of what Albert Bandura (1973) called *reciprocal determinism*—the fact that we mutually influence each others' behavior (see Chapter 14). Reciprocal determinism makes it difficult to know what's causing what.

In a study by Chua, Boland, and Nisbett (2005), European Americans tend to focus more on the central details of photographs, like the tiger itself (top), whereas Asian Americans tend to focus more on the peripheral details, like the rocks and leaves surrounding the tiger (bottom).

Fifth, people's behavior is often shaped by culture. Cultural differences, like individual differences, place limits on the generalizations that psychologists can draw about human nature (Henrich, Heine, & Norenzayan, 2009). To take one example, Richard Nisbett and his colleagues found that European American and Chinese participants often attend to strikingly different things in pictures (Chua, Boland, & Nisbett, 2005). In one case, they showed people a photograph of a tiger walking on rocks next to a river. Using eye-tracking technology, which allows researchers to determine where people are moving their eyes, they found that European Americans tend to look mostly at the tiger, whereas Chinese tend to look mostly at the plants and rocks surrounding it. This finding dovetails with evidence that European Americans tend to focus on central details, whereas Asian Americans tend to focus on peripheral or incidental details (Nisbett, 2003; Nisbett et al., 2001).

Social scientists sometimes distinguish between emic and etic approaches to cross-cultural psychology. In an *emic* approach, investigators study the behavior of a culture from the perspective of a "native" or insider, whereas in an *etic* approach, they study the behavior of a culture from the perspective of an outsider (Harris, 1976). A researcher using an emic approach studying the personality of inhabitants of an isolated Pacific Island would probably rely on personality terms used by members of that culture. In contrast, a researcher using an etic approach would probably adapt and translate personality terms used by Western culture, like shyness and extraversion, to that culture. Each approach has its pluses and minuses. Investigators who adopt an emic approach may better understand the unique characteristics of a culture, but they may overlook characteristics that this culture shares with others. In contrast, investigators who adopt an etic approach may be better able to view this culture within the broader perspective of other cultures, but they may unintentionally impose perspectives from their own culture onto others.

emic = perspective of native etic = perspective of outsider

individual differences
variations among people in their thinking, emotion, personality, and behavior

■ Why We Can't Always Trust Our Common Sense

To understand why others act as they do, most of us trust our common sense—our gut intuitions about how the social world works. This reliance is tempting, because children and adults alike tend to regard psychology as "easier" and more self-evident than physics, chemistry, biology, and most other sciences (Keil, Lockhart, & Schlegel, 2010). Yet, as we've already discovered, our intuitive understanding of ourselves and the world is frequently mistaken (Cacioppo, 2004; van Hecke, 2007). In fact, as the quiz at the start of this chapter showed us, sometimes our commonsensical understanding of psychology isn't merely incorrect but entirely backward. For example, although many people believe the old adage "There's safety in numbers," psychological research actually shows that the more people present at an emergency, the *less* likely it is that at least one of them will help (Darley & Latané, 1968a; Latané & Nida, 1981; see Chapter 13).

Here's another illustration of why we can't always trust our common sense. Read the following well-known proverbs, most of which deal with human behavior, and ask yourself whether you agree with them:

1. Birds of a feather flock together.
2. Absence makes the heart grow fonder.
3. Better safe than sorry.
4. Two heads are better than one.
5. Actions speak louder than words.
6. Opposites attract.
7. Out of sight, out of mind.
8. Nothing ventured, nothing gained.
9. Too many cooks spoil the broth.
10. The pen is mightier than the sword.

Why are marriages like that of Mary Matalin, a prominent conservative political strategist, and James Carville, a prominent liberal political strategist, rare?

These proverbs all ring true, don't they? Yet each proverb contradicts the proverb across from it! So our common sense can lead us to believe two things that can't both be true simultaneously—or at least that are largely at odds with each other. Strangely enough, in most cases we never notice the contradictions until other people, like the authors of an introductory psychology textbook, point them out to us. This example reminds us of why scientific psychology doesn't rely exclusively on intuition, speculation, or common sense.

Naive Realism = the world as we see it.

NAIVE REALISM: IS SEEING BELIEVING? We trust our common sense largely because we're prone to **naive realism**: the belief that we see the world precisely as it is (Lilienfeld, Lohr, & Olatanji, 2008; Ross & Ward, 1996). We assume that "seeing is believing" and trust our intuitive perceptions of the world and ourselves. In daily life, naive realism often serves us well. If we're driving down a one-lane road and see a tractor trailer barreling toward us at 85 miles per hour, it's a wise idea to get out of the way. Much of the time, we *should* trust our perceptions.

Yet appearances can sometimes be deceiving. The earth *seems* flat. The sun *seems* to revolve around the earth (see **FIGURE 1.2** for another example of deceptive appearances). Yet in both cases, our intuitions are wrong. Similarly, naive realism can trip us up when it comes to evaluating ourselves and others. Our common sense assures us that people who don't share our political views are biased but that we're objective. Yet psychological research demonstrates that just about all of us tend to evaluate political issues in a biased fashion (Pronin, Gilovich, & Ross, 2004). So our tendencies toward naive realism can lead us to draw incorrect conclusions about human nature. In many cases, "believing is seeing" rather than the reverse: Our beliefs shape our perceptions of the world (Gilovich, 1991).

WHEN OUR COMMON SENSE IS RIGHT. That's not to say that our common sense is always wrong. Our intuition comes in handy in many situations and sometimes guides us to the truth (Gigerenzer, 2007; Gladwell, 2005; Myers, 2002). For example, our snap (five-second) judgments about whether someone we've just watched on a videotape is trustworthy or untrustworthy tend to be right more often than we'd expect by chance (Fowler, Lilienfeld, & Patrick, 2009). Common sense can also be a helpful guide for generating hypotheses that scientists can later test in rigorous investigations (Redding, 1998). Moreover, some everyday psychological notions are indeed correct. For example, most people believe that happy employees tend to be more productive on the job than unhappy employees, and research shows that they're right (Kluger & Tikochinsky, 2001).

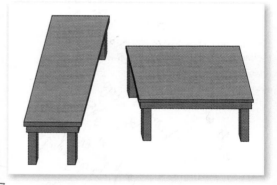

FIGURE 1.2 Naive Realism Can Fool Us. Even though our perceptions are often accurate, we can't always trust them to provide us with an error-free picture of the world. In this case, take a look at *Shepard's tables*, courtesy of psychologist Roger Shepard. Believe it or not, the tops of these tables are identical in size: One can be directly superimposed on top of the other (get out a ruler if you don't believe us!). (*Source:* Shepard, 1990)

> **naive realism**
> belief that we see the world precisely as it is

Answer: Despite the commonsense belief that opposites attract, psychological research shows that people are generally drawn to others who are similar to them in beliefs and values.

Here's another case in which our naive realism can trick us. Take a look at these two upside-down photos of Barack Obama. They look quite similar, if not identical. Now turn your book upside down.

But to think scientifically, we must learn when—and when not—to trust our common sense. Doing so will help us become more informed consumers of popular psychology and make better real-world decisions. One of our major goals in this text is to provide you with a framework of scientific thinking tools for making this crucial distinction. This thinking framework can help you to better evaluate psychological claims in everyday life.

■ Psychology as a Science

A few years ago, one of our academic colleagues was advising a psychology major about his career plans. Out of curiosity, he asked the student, "So why did you decide to go into psychology?" He responded, "Well, I took a lot of science courses and realized I didn't like science, so I picked psychology instead."

We're going to try to persuade you that the student was wrong—not about selecting a psychology major, that is, but about psychology not being a science. A central theme of this text is that modern psychology, or at least hefty chunks of it, are scientific. But what does the word *science* really mean, anyway?

Most students think that *science* is just a word for all of that really complicated stuff they learn in their biology, chemistry, and physics classes. But science isn't a body of knowledge. Instead, it's an *approach* to evidence (Bunge, 1998). Specifically, science consists of a set of attitudes and skills designed to prevent us from fooling ourselves. Science begins with *empiricism*, the premise that knowledge should initially be acquired through observation. Yet such observation is only a rough starting point for obtaining psychological knowledge. As the phenomenon of naive realism reminds us, it isn't sufficient by itself, because our observations can fool us. So science refines our initial observations, subjecting them to stringent tests to determine whether they are accurate. The observations that stand up to rigorous examination are retained; those that don't are revised or discarded.

You may have heard the humorous saying: "Everyone is entitled to my opinion." In everyday life, this saying can be helpful in a pinch, especially when we're in the midst of an argument. Yet in science, this saying doesn't pass muster. Many people believe they don't need science to get them closer to the truth, because they assume that psychology is just a matter of opinion. "If it seems true to me," they assume, "it probably is." Yet adopting a scientific mindset requires us to abandon this comforting way of thinking. Psychology is more than a matter of opinion: It's a matter of finding out which explanations best fit the data about how our minds work. Hard-nosed as it may sound, some psychological explanations are just plain better than others.

WHAT IS A SCIENTIFIC THEORY? Few terms in science have generated more confusion than the deceptively simple term *theory*. Some of this confusion has contributed to serious misunderstandings about how science works. We'll first examine what a scientific theory is, and then address two misconceptions about what a scientific theory *isn't*.

A **scientific theory** is an explanation for a large number of findings in the natural world, including the psychological world. A scientific theory offers an account that ties multiple findings together into one pretty package.

But good scientific theories do more than account for existing data. They generate predictions regarding new data we haven't yet observed. For a theory to be scientific, it must generate novel predictions that researchers can test. Scientists call a testable prediction a **hypothesis**. In other words, theories are general explanations, whereas hypotheses are specific predictions derived from these explanations (Bolles, 1962; Meehl, 1967). Based on their tests of hypotheses, scientists can provisionally accept the theory that generated these hypotheses, reject this theory outright, or revise it (Proctor & Capaldi, 2006).

Misconception 1: *A theory explains one specific event.* The first misunderstanding is that a theory is a specific explanation for an event. The popular media get this distinction wrong much of the time. We'll often hear television reporters say something like, "The most likely theory for the robbery at the downtown bank is that it was committed by two former bank employees who dressed up as armed guards." But this isn't a "theory" of the robbery. For one thing, it attempts to explain only one event rather than a variety of diverse observations. It also doesn't generate testable predictions. In contrast, *forensic psychologists*—those who study the causes and treatment of criminal behavior—have constructed general theories that attempt to explain why certain people steal and to forecast when people are most likely to steal (Katz, 1988).

Misconception 2: *A theory is just an educated guess.* A second myth is that a scientific theory is merely a guess about how the world works. People will often dismiss a theoretical explanation on these grounds, arguing that it's "just a theory."

This last phrase implies mistakenly that some explanations about the natural world are "more than theories." In fact, *all* general scientific explanations about how the world works are theories. A few theories are extremely well supported by multiple lines of evidence; for example, the Big Bang theory, which proposes that the universe began in a gigantic explosion about 14 billion years ago, helps scientists to explain a diverse array of observations. They include the findings that (a) galaxies are rushing away from each other at remarkable speeds, (b) the universe exhibits a background radiation suggestive of the remnants of a tremendous explosion, and (c) powerful telescopes reveal that the oldest galaxies originated about 14 billion years ago, right around the time predicted by the Big Bang theory. Like all scientific theories, the Big Bang theory can never be "proved" because it's always conceivable that a better explanation might come along one day. Nevertheless, because this theory is consistent with many differing lines of evidence, the overwhelming majority of scientists accept it as a good explanation. Darwinian evolution, the Big Bang, and other well-established theories aren't guesses about how the world works, because they've been substantiated over and over again by independent investigators. In contrast, many other scientific theories are only moderately well supported, and still others are questionable or entirely discredited. Not all theories are created equal.

So, when we hear that a scientific explanation is "just a theory," we should remember that theories aren't just guesses. Some theories have survived repeated efforts to refute them and are well-confirmed models of how the world works (Kitcher, 2009).

SCIENCE AS A SAFEGUARD AGAINST BIAS: PROTECTING US FROM OURSELVES. Some people assume incorrectly that scientists are objective and free of biases. Yet scientists are human and have their biases, too (Mahoney & DeMonbreun, 1977). But the best scientists

---

This textbook contains material on evolution. Evolution is a theory, not a fact, regarding the origin of living things. This material should be approached with an open mind, studied carefully, and critically considered.

Approved by
Cobb County Board of Education
Thursday, March 28, 2002

Some creationists have argued that evolution is "just a theory." Cobb County, Georgia, briefly required high school biology textbooks to carry this sticker (Pinker, 2002).

scientific theory
explanation for a large number of findings in the natural world

hypothesis
testable prediction derived from a scientific theory

Even the best scientists can be taken by bias.
- confirmation bias = tendency to search for or interpret new info to confirm one's perceptions or beliefs
- belief perseverance = tendency to continue believing in your own beliefs even when evidence proves otherwise

Arthur Darbishire (1879–1915), a British geneticist and mathematician. Darbishire's favorite saying was that the attitude of the scientist should be "one of continual, unceasing, and active distrust of oneself."

are aware of their biases and try to find ways of compensating for them. This principle applies to all scientists, including psychological scientists—those who study mind, brain, and behavior. In particular, the best scientists realize that they *want* their pet theories to turn out to be correct. After all, they've invested months or even years in designing and running a study to test a theory, sometimes a theory they've developed. If the results of the study are negative, they'll often be bitterly disappointed. They also know that because of this deep personal investment, they may bias the results unintentionally to make them turn out the way they want (Greenwald et al., 1986). Scientists are prone to self-deception, just like the rest of us. There are several traps into which scientists can fall unless they're careful. We'll discuss two of the most crucial next.

Confirmation Bias. To protect themselves against bias, good scientists adopt procedural safeguards against errors, especially errors that could work in their favor (see Chapter 2). In other words, scientific methods are tools for overcoming **confirmation bias**: the tendency to seek out evidence that supports our beliefs and deny, dismiss, or distort evidence that contradicts them (Nickerson, 1998; Risen & Gilovich, 2007). We can sum up confirmation bias in five words: *Seek and ye shall find.*

Because of confirmation bias, our preconceptions often lead us to focus on evidence that supports our beliefs, resulting in psychological tunnel vision. One of the simplest demonstrations of confirmation bias comes from research on the *Wason selection task* (Wason, 1966), an example of which we can find in **FIGURE 1.3**. You'll see four cards, each of which has a number on one side and a letter on the other. Your task is to determine whether the following hypothesis is correct: *All cards that have a vowel on one side have an odd number on the other*. To test this hypothesis, you need to select *two* cards to turn over. Which two will you pick? Decide on your two cards before reading on. **Explore**

Most people pick the cards showing E and 5. If you selected E, you were right, so give yourself one point there. But if you selected 5, you've fallen prey to confirmation bias, although you'd be in good company because most people make this mistake. Although 5 *seems* to be a correct choice, it can only confirm the hypothesis, not disconfirm it. Think of it this way: If there's a vowel on the other side of the 5 card, that doesn't rule out the possibility that the 4 card also has a vowel on the other side, which would disconfirm the hypothesis. So the 4 card is actually the other card to turn over, as that's the only other card that could demonstrate that the hypothesis is wrong.

Confirmation bias wouldn't be especially interesting if it were limited to cards. What makes confirmation bias so important is that it extends to many areas of our daily lives (Nickerson, 1998). For example, research shows that confirmation bias affects how we evaluate candidates for political office—including those on both the left and right sides of the political spectrum. Research shows that if we agree with a candidate's political views, we quickly forgive her for contradicting herself, but if we disagree with a candidate's views, we criticize her as a "flip-flopper" (Tavris & Aronson, 2007; Westen et al., 2006). Similarly, in a classic study of a hotly contested football game, Dartmouth fans saw Princeton players as "dirty" and as committing many penalties, while Princeton fans saw Dartmouth players in exactly the same light (Hastorf & Cantril, 1954). When it comes to judging right and wrong, our side almost always seems to be in the right, the other side in the wrong.

FICTOID

MYTH: Physicists and other "hard" scientists are more skeptical about most extraordinary claims, like extrasensory perception, than psychologists are.

REALITY: Academic psychologists are more skeptical of many controversial claims than their colleagues in more traditional sciences are, perhaps because psychologists are aware of how biases can influence the interpretation of data. For example, psychologists are considerably less likely to believe that extrasensory perception is an established scientific fact than physicists, chemists, and biologists are (Wagner & Monnet, 1979).

Explore the Confirmation Bias on **mypsychlab.com**

Here are four cards. Each of them has a letter on one side and a number on the other side. Two of these cards are shown with the letter side up, and two with the number side up.

E C 5 4

Indicate which of these cards you have to turn over in order to determine whether the following claim is true:

If a card has a vowel on one side, then it has an odd number on the other side.

FIGURE 1.3 Diagram of Wason Selection Task. In the Wason selection task, you must pick two cards to test the hypothesis that all cards that have a vowel on one side have an odd number on the other. Which two will you select?

confirmation bias
tendency to seek out evidence that supports our hypotheses and deny, dismiss, or distort evidence that contradicts them

Although we'll be encountering a variety of biases in this text, we can think of confirmation bias as the "mother of all biases." That's because it's the bias that can most easily fool us into seeing what we want to see. For that reason, it's the most crucial bias that psychologists need to counteract. What distinguishes psychological scientists from nonscientists is that the former adopt systematic safeguards to protect against confirmation bias, whereas the latter don't (Lilienfeld, Ammirati, & Landfield, 2009). We'll learn about these safeguards in Chapter 2.

Belief Perseverance. Confirmation bias predisposes us to another shortcoming to which we're all prone: **belief perseverance**. Belief perseverance refers to the tendency to stick to our initial beliefs even when evidence contradicts them. In everyday language, belief perseverance is the "don't confuse me with the facts" effect. Because none of us wants to think we're wrong, we're usually reluctant to give up our cherished notions. In a striking demonstration of belief perseverance, Lee Ross and his colleagues asked students to inspect 50 suicide notes and determine which were real and which were fake (in reality, half were real, half fake). They then gave students feedback on how we'll they'd done—they told some students they were usually right, others they were usually wrong. Unbeknownst to the students, this feedback was unrelated to their actual performance. Yet even after the researchers informed the students that the feedback was bogus, students based their estimates of ability on the feedback they'd received. Students told they were good at detecting real suicide notes were convinced they were better at it than students told they were bad at it (Ross, Lepper, & Hubbard, 1975).

Beliefs endure. Even when informed that we're wrong, we don't completely wipe our mental slates clean and start from scratch.

■ Metaphysical Claims: The Boundaries of Science

It's essential to distinguish scientific claims from **metaphysical claims**: assertions about the world that we can't test (Popper, 1965). Metaphysical claims include assertions about the existence of God, the soul, and the afterlife. These claims differ from scientific claims in that we could never test them using scientific methods. (How could we design a scientific test to conclusively disprove the existence of God?).

This point doesn't mean that metaphysical claims are wrong, let alone unimportant. To the contrary, many thoughtful scholars would contend that questions concerning the existence of God are even more significant and profound than

Frequently, newspapers present headlines of medical and psychological findings, only to retract them weeks or months later. How can we know how much trust to place in them?

belief perseverance
tendency to stick to our initial beliefs even when evidence contradicts them

metaphysical claim
assertion about the world that is not testable

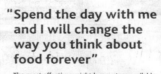

? Which of these claims is metaphysical and which is probably pseudoscientific? (See answer upside down on bottom of page.)

Answer: Image on left is probably pseudoscientific, because it makes extreme claims that aren't supported by evidence; Image on right is metaphysical because it makes a claim that science cannot test.

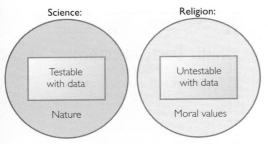

FIGURE 1.4 Nonoverlapping Realms. Scientist Stephen Jay Gould (1997) argued that science and religion are entirely different and nonoverlapping realms of understanding the world. Science deals with testable claims about the natural world that can be answered with data, whereas religion deals with untestable claims about moral values that can't be answered with data. Although not all scientists and theologians accept Gould's model, we adopt it for the purposes of this textbook. (*Source:* Gould, 1997)

[handwritten margin note: Science can be tested, but only to an extent. Science is constantly being revised. Scientists know they may be wrong]

scientific questions. Moreover, regardless of our beliefs about religion, we need to treat these questions with the profound respect they deserve. But it's crucial to understand that there are certain questions about the world that science can—and can't—answer (Gould, 1997). Science has its limits. So it needs to respect the boundaries of religion and other metaphysical domains. Testable claims fall within the province of science; untestable claims don't (see **FIGURE 1.4**). Moreover, according to many (although admittedly not all) scholars, there's no inherent conflict between science and the vast majority of religious claims (Dean, 2005). One can quite comfortably adhere to one's religious views while embracing psychology's scientific tools (see Chapter 2) and findings.

■ Recognizing That We Might Be Wrong

Good scientists are keenly aware they might be mistaken (Sagan, 1995). In fact, initial scientific conclusions are often wrong or at least partly off base. Medical findings are prime examples. Eating lots of chocolate reduces your risk for heart disease; oops, no, it doesn't (I'd bet you were disappointed to learn that). Drinking a little red wine now and then is good for you; no, actually, it's bad for you. And on and on it goes. It's no wonder that many people just throw up their hands and give up reading medical reports altogether. One researcher (Ioannidis, 2005) found that about a third of findings from published medical studies don't hold up in later studies (of course, we have to wonder: Do we know that the results of *this* analysis will hold up?). But the beauty of this messy process is that scientific knowledge is almost always tentative and potentially open to revision. The fact that science is a process of continually revising and updating findings lends it strength as a method of inquiry. It does mean, though, that we usually acquire knowledge slowly and in small bits and pieces.

One way of characterizing this process is to describe science, including psychological science, as a *prescription for humility* (McFall, 1996). Good scientists never claim to "prove" their theories and try to avoid committing to definitive conclusions unless the evidence supports them overwhelmingly. Such phrases as "suggests," "appears," and "raises the possibility that" are widespread in scientific writing and allow scientists to remain tentative in their interpretations of findings. Many beginning students understandably find this hemming and hawing frustrating. *Duh.*

Yet as Carl Sagan (1995) observed, the best scientists hear a little voice in their heads that keeps repeating the same words: "But I might be wrong." Science forces us to question our findings and conclusions, and encourages us to ferret out mistakes in our belief systems (O'Donohue, Lilienfeld, & Fowler, 2007). Science also forces us to attend to data that aren't to our liking, whether or not we want to—and often we don't. In this respect, good scientists differ from politicians, who rarely admit when they've made a mistake and are often punished when they do. *Scientists (the good ones) ≠ Politicians.*

✓—Study and Review on **mypsychlab.com**

---

assess your knowledge   **FACT OR FICTION?**

1. Psychology involves studying the mind at one specific level of explanation. **True / False**

2. Science is a body of knowledge consisting of all of the findings that scientists have discovered. **True / False**

3. Scientific theories are general explanations and hypotheses are specific predictions derived from these explanations. **True / False**

4. Good scientists are confident they're right, so they don't need to protect themselves against confirmation bias. **True / False**

5. Metaphysical claims are not testable. **True / False**

Answers: 1. F (p.3); 2. F (p.6); 3. T (p.7); 4. F (p.8); 5. T (p.9)

PSYCHOLOGICAL PSEUDOSCIENCE: IMPOSTERS OF SCIENCE

1.3 Describe psychological pseudoscience and distinguish it from psychological science.

1.4 Identify reasons we are drawn to pseudoscience.

Of course, you might have enrolled in this course to understand yourself, your friends, or a boyfriend or girlfriend. If so, you might well be thinking, "But I don't want to become a scientist. In fact, I'm not even interested in research. I just want to understand people."

Actually, we're not trying to persuade you to become a scientist. Instead, our goal is to persuade you to *think scientifically:* to become aware of your biases and to take advantage of the tools of the scientific method to try to overcome them. By acquiring these skills, you'll make better educated choices in your everyday life, such as what weight loss plan to choose, what psychotherapy to recommend to a friend, or maybe even what potential romantic partner is a better long-term bet. You'll also learn how to avoid being tricked by bogus claims. Not everyone needs to become a scientist, but just about everyone can learn to think like one.

■ The Amazing Growth of Popular Psychology

Distinguishing real from bogus claims is crucial, because the popular psychology industry is huge and growing rapidly. On the positive side, this fact means that the American public has unprecedented access to psychological knowledge. On the negative side, the remarkable growth of popular psychology has led not only to an information explosion but to a *misinformation explosion* because there's scant quality control over what this industry produces.

For example, about 3,500 self-help books are published every year (Arkowitz & Lilienfeld, 2006, see Chapter 16). Some of these books are effective for treating depression, anxiety, and other psychological problems, but about 95 percent of all self-help books are untested (Gould & Clum, 1993; Gregory et al., 2004; Rosen, 1993) and recent evidence suggests that a few may even make people worse (Haeffel, 2010; Rosen, 1993; Salerno, 2005).

Coinciding with the rapid expansion of the popular psychology industry is the enormous growth of treatments and products that claim to cure almost every imaginable psychological ailment. There are well over 500 "brands" of psychotherapy (Eisner, 2000), with new ones being added every year. Fortunately, as we'll learn in Chapter 16, research shows that some of these treatments are clearly helpful for numerous psychological problems. Yet the substantial majority of psychotherapies remain untested, so we don't know whether they help (Baker, McFall, & Shoham, 2009). Some may even be harmful (Lilienfeld, 2007).

Some self-help books base their recommendations on solid research about psychological problems and their treatment. We can often find excellent articles in the *New York Times, Scientific American Mind,* and *Discover* magazines and other media outlets that present high-quality information regarding scientific psychology. In addition, hundreds of websites provide helpful information and advice concerning numerous psychological topics, like memory, personality testing, and psychological disorders and their treatment (see **TABLE 1.1** on page 12). Yet other websites contain misleanding or erroneous information, so we need to be armed with accurate knowledge to evaluate them.

■ What is Pseudoscience?

These facts highlight a crucial point: We need to distinguish claims that are genuinely scientific from those that are merely imposters of science. An imposter of science is **pseudoscience**: a set of claims that *seem* scientific but aren't. In particular, *pseudoscience lacks the safeguards against confirmation bias and belief perseverance that characterize science.* We must be careful to distinguish pseudoscientific claims from metaphysical claims, which as we've seen, are untestable and therefore lie outside the realm of science. In principle, at least, we can test pseudoscientific claims, although the proponents of these claims often avoid subjecting them to rigorous examination. ●—|Explore

Subliminal self-help tapes supposedly influence behavior by means of messages delivered to the unconscious. But do they really work?

● |Explore the Pseudoscience of Astrology on **mypsychlab.com**

pseudoscience
set of claims that seems scientific but aren't

TABLE I.I Some Trustworthy Websites for Scientific Psychology.

ORGANIZATION / URL	
American Psychological Association www.apa.org	Society for Research in Child Development www.srcd.org
Association for Psychological Science www.psychologicalscience.org	Society for Personality and Social Psychology www.spsp.org
Canadian Psychological Association www.cpa.ca	Society for Research in Psychopathology www.psychopathology.org
American Psychiatric Association www.psych.org	Society for a Science of Clinical Psychology www.sscpweb.org
Society for General Psychology www.apa.org/divisions/div1/div1homepage.html	Scientific Review of Mental Health Practice www.srmhp.org
Association for Behavioral and Cognitive Therapies www.aabt.org	Center for Evidence-Based Mental Health http://cebmh.warne.ox.ac.uk/cebmh/
Psychonomic Society www.psychonomic.org	Empirically Supported Treatments for Psychological Disorders www.apa.org/divisions/div12/rev_est
Association for Behavior Analysis, Intl. www.abainternational.org	National Institute of Mental Health www.nimh.nih.gov

[handwritten margin note: Pseudoscience and questionable beliefs. • Extrasensory perception • haunted houses, ghosts • telepathy • astrology]

Pseudoscientific and otherwise questionable claims have increasingly altered the landscape of modern life.

Pseudoscientific and other questionable beliefs are widespread. A recent survey of the U.S. public shows that 41 percent of us believe in extrasensory perception (ESP); over 30 percent of us in haunted houses, ghosts, and telepathy; and 25 percent of us in astrology (Musella, 2005). The fact that many Americans *entertain* the possibility of such beliefs isn't by itself worrisome, because a certain amount of open-mindedness is essential for scientific thinking. Instead, what's troubling is that many Americans appear convinced that such claims are correct even though the scientific evidence for them is either weak, as in the case of ESP, or essentially nonexistent, as in the case of astrology. Moreover, it's troubling that many poorly supported beliefs are more popular, or at least more widespread, than well-supported beliefs. To take merely one example, there are about 20 times as many astrologers as astronomers in the United States (Gilovich, 1991).   *[handwritten: Wow—]*

WARNING SIGNS OF PSEUDOSCIENCE. Numerous warning signs can help us distinguish science from pseudoscience; we've listed some of the most useful ones in **TABLE I.2**. They're extremely helpful rules of thumb, so useful in fact that we'll draw on many of them in later chapters to help us become more informed consumers of psychological claims. We can—and should—also use them in everyday life. None of these signs is by itself proof positive that a set of claims is pseudoscientific. Nevertheless, the more of these signs we see, the more skeptical of these claims we should become.

[handwritten: Look at the signs --]

Here, we'll discuss three of the most crucial of these warning signs.

Overuse of ad hoc immunizing hypotheses: Yes, we know this one is a mouthful. But it's actually not as complicated as it appears, because an **ad hoc immunizing hypothesis** is just an escape hatch or loophole that defenders of a theory use to protect this theory from being disproven. For example, some psychics have claimed to perform remarkable feats of ESP, like reading others' minds or forecasting the future, in the real world. But when brought into the laboratory and tested under tightly controlled conditions, most have bombed, performing no better than chance. Some of these psychics and their proponents have invoked an ad hoc immunizing hypothesis to explain away these failures: The skepti-

ad hoc immunizing hypothesis
escape hatch or loophole that defenders of a theory use to protect their theory from falsification

TABLE 1.2 Some Warning Signs That Can Help Us Recognize Pseudoscience.

SIGN OF PSEUDOSCIENCE	EXAMPLE
Exaggerated claims	Three simple steps will change your love life forever!
Overreliance on anecdotes	This woman practiced yoga daily for three weeks and hasn't had a day of depression since.
Absence of connectivity to other research	Amazing new innovations in research have shown that eye massage results in reading speeds 10 times faster than average!
Lack of review by other scholars (called *peer review*) or replication by independent labs	Fifty studies conducted by the company all show overwhelming success!
Lack of self-correction when contrary evidence is published	Although some scientists say that we use almost all our brains, we've found a way to harness additional brain power previously undiscovered.
Meaningless "psychobabble" that uses fancy scientific-sounding terms that don't make sense	Sine-wave filtered auditory stimulation is carefully designed to encourage maximal orbitofrontal dendritic development.
Talk of "proof" instead of "evidence"	Our new program is proven to reduce social anxiety by at least 50 percent!

cal "vibes" of the experimenters are somehow interfering with psychic powers (Carroll, 2003; Lilienfeld, 1999c). Although this hypothesis isn't necessarily wrong, it makes the psychics' claims essentially impossible to test.

Lack of self-correction: As we've learned, many scientific claims turn out to be wrong. That may seem like a weakness of science, but it's actually a strength. That's because in science, wrong claims tend to be weeded out eventually, even though it often takes a while. In contrast, in most pseudosciences, wrong claims never seem to go away, because their proponents fall prey to belief perseverance, clinging to them stubbornly despite contrary evidence. Moreover, pseudoscientific claims are rarely updated in light of new data. Most forms of astrology have remained almost identical for about 4,000 years (Hines, 2003) despite the discovery of outer planets in the solar system (Uranus and Neptune) that were unknown in ancient times.

Overreliance on anecdotes: There's an old saying that "the plural of anecdote isn't fact" (Park, 2003). A mountain of numerous anecdotes may seem impressive, but it shouldn't persuade us to put much stock in others' claims. Most anecdotes are *I know a person who* assertions (Nisbett & Ross, 1980; Stanovich, 2009). This kind of secondhand evidence—"I know a person who says his self-esteem skyrocketed after receiving hypnosis," "I know someone who tried to commit suicide after taking an antidepressant"—is commonplace in everyday life. So is firsthand evidence—"I felt less depressed after taking this herbal remedy"—that's based on subjective impressions.

Pseudosciences tend to rely heavily on anecdotal evidence. In many cases, they base claims on the dramatic reports of one or two individuals: "I lost 85 pounds in three weeks on the Matzo Ball Soup Weight Loss Program." Compelling as this anecdote may appear, it doesn't constitute good scientific evidence (Davison & Lazarus, 2007; Loftus & Guyer, 2002). For one thing, anecdotes don't tell us anything about cause and effect. Maybe the Matzo Ball Soup Weight Loss Program caused the person to lose 85 pounds, but maybe other factors were responsible. Perhaps he went on an additional diet or started to exercise frantically during that time. Or perhaps he underwent drastic weight loss surgery during

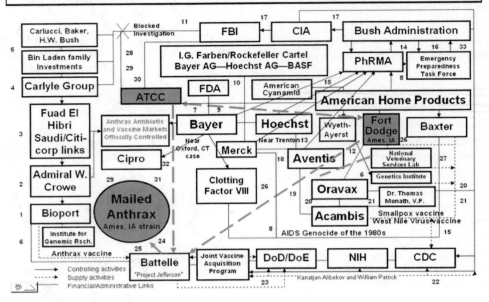

Military-Industrial Suspects and Contractors Linked to the Anthrax Mailings Mystery

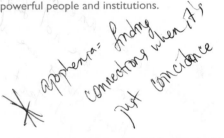

Conspiracy theories are manifestations of apophenia. Believers in conspiracies often claim to detect hidden interconnections among powerful people and institutions.

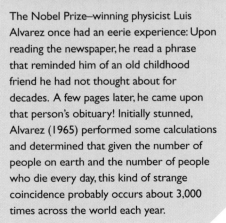

[handwritten note: apophenia= finding connections when it's just coincidence]

FACTOID +

The Nobel Prize–winning physicist Luis Alvarez once had an eerie experience: Upon reading the newspaper, he read a phrase that reminded him of an old childhood friend he had not thought about for decades. A few pages later, he came upon that person's obituary! Initially stunned, Alvarez (1965) performed some calculations and determined that given the number of people on earth and the number of people who die every day, this kind of strange coincidence probably occurs about 3,000 times across the world each year.

apophenia
tendency to perceive meaningful connections among unrelated phenomena

this time, but didn't bother to mention it. Anecdotes also don't tell us anything about how representative the cases are. Perhaps most people who went on the Matzo Ball Soup Weight Loss Program gained weight, but we never heard from them. Finally, anecdotes are often difficult to verify. Do we really know for sure that he lost 85 pounds? We're taking his word for it, which is a risky idea.

Simply put, most anecdotes are extremely difficult to interpret as evidence. As Paul Meehl (1995) put it, "The clear message of history is that the anecdotal method delivers both wheat and chaff, but it does not enable us to tell which is which" (p. 1019).

WHY ARE WE DRAWN TO PSEUDOSCIENCE?

There are a host of reasons why so many of us are drawn to pseudoscientific beliefs.

Perhaps the central reason stems from the way our brains work. *Our brains are predisposed to make order out of disorder and find sense in nonsense.* This tendency is generally adaptive, as it helps us to simplify the often bewildering world in which we live (Alcock, 1995; Pinker, 1997). Without it, we'd be constantly overwhelmed by endless streams of information we don't have the time or ability to process. Yet this adaptive tendency can sometimes lead us astray because it can cause us to perceive meaningful patterns even when they're not there (Davis, 2009; Shermer, 2008).

The Search for Meaningful Connections. Our tendency to seek out patterns sometimes goes too far, leading us to experience **apophenia**: perceiving meaningful connections among unrelated and even random phenomena (Carroll, 2003). We all fall victim to apophenia from time to time. If we think of a friend with whom we haven't spoken in a few months and immediately afterward receive a phone call from her, we may jump to the conclusion that this striking co-occurrence stems from ESP. Well, it *might.*

But it's also entirely possible, if not likely, that these two events happened at about the same time by chance alone. For a moment, think of the number of times one of your old friends comes to mind, and then think of the number of phone calls you receive each month. You'll realize that the laws of probability make it likely that at least once over the next few years, you'll be thinking of an old friend at about the same time she calls.

Another manifestation of apophenia is our tendency to detect eerie coincidences among persons or events. To take one example, read through each of the uncanny similarities between Abraham Lincoln and John F. Kennedy, two American presidents who were the victims of assassination, listed in **TABLE 1.3**.

Pretty amazing stuff, isn't it? So extraordinary, in fact, that some writers have argued that Lincoln and Kennedy are somehow linked by supernatural forces (Leavy, 1992). In actuality, though, coincidences are everywhere. They're surprisingly easy to detect if we make the effort to look for them. Because of apophenia, we may attribute paranormal significance to coincidences that are due to chance. The term *paranormal* describes phenomena, like ESP, that fall outside the boundaries of traditional science. Moreover, we often fall victim to confirmation bias and neglect to consider evidence that *doesn't* support our hypothesis. Because we typically find coincidences to be far more interesting than noncoincidences, we tend to forget that Lincoln was a Republican whereas Kennedy was a Democrat; that Lincoln was shot in Washington, DC, whereas Kennedy was shot in Dallas; that Lincoln had a beard, but Kennedy didn't, and on and on. Recall that scientific thinking is designed to counteract confirmation bias. To do so, we must seek out evidence that contradicts our ideas.

[handwritten note: In order to confirm, must be sure nothing contradicts the idea.]

TABLE 1.3 Some Eerie Commonalities between Abraham Lincoln and John F. Kennedy.

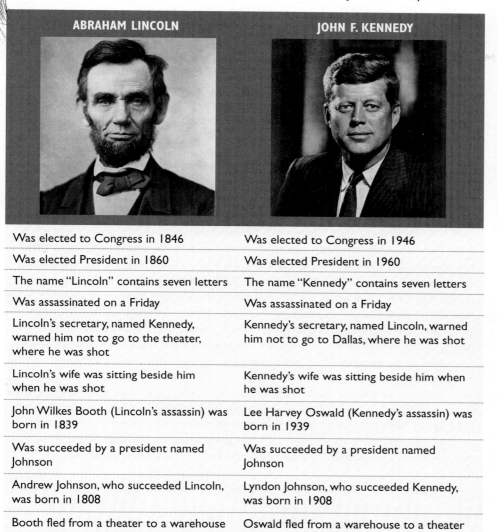

ABRAHAM LINCOLN	JOHN F. KENNEDY
Was elected to Congress in 1846	Was elected to Congress in 1946
Was elected President in 1860	Was elected President in 1960
The name "Lincoln" contains seven letters	The name "Kennedy" contains seven letters
Was assassinated on a Friday	Was assassinated on a Friday
Lincoln's secretary, named Kennedy, warned him not to go to the theater, where he was shot	Kennedy's secretary, named Lincoln, warned him not to go to Dallas, where he was shot
Lincoln's wife was sitting beside him when he was shot	Kennedy's wife was sitting beside him when he was shot
John Wilkes Booth (Lincoln's assassin) was born in 1839	Lee Harvey Oswald (Kennedy's assassin) was born in 1939
Was succeeded by a president named Johnson	Was succeeded by a president named Johnson
Andrew Johnson, who succeeded Lincoln, was born in 1808	Lyndon Johnson, who succeeded Kennedy, was born in 1908
Booth fled from a theater to a warehouse	Oswald fled from a warehouse to a theater
Booth was killed before his trial	Oswald was killed before his trial

Fascinating but nothing more than coincidences, definitely not supernatural stuff.

Another example of our tendency to find patterns is the phenomenon of **pareidolia**: seeing meaningful images in meaningless visual stimuli. Any of us who's looked at a cloud and perceived the vague shape of an animal has experienced pareidolia, as has any of us who's seen the oddly misshapen face of a "man" in the moon. A more stunning example comes from the photograph in **FIGURE 1.5a**. In 1976, the *Mars Viking Orbiter* snapped an image of a set of features on the Martian surface. As we can see, these features bear an eerie resemblance to a human face. So eerie, in fact, that some individuals maintained that the "Face on Mars" offered conclusive proof of intelligent life on the Red Planet (Hoagland, 1987). In 2001, during a mission of a different spacecraft, the *Mars Global Surveyor*, the National Aeronautics and Space Administration (NASA) decided to adopt a scientific approach to the Face on Mars. They were open-minded but demanded evidence. They swooped down much closer to the face, and pointed the *Surveyor*'s cameras directly at it. If we look at **FIGURE 1.5b**, we'll see what they found: absolutely nothing. The pareidolia in this instance was a consequence of a peculiar configuration of rocks and shadows present at the angle at which the photographs were taken in 1976, a camera artifact in the original photograph that just happened to place a black dot where a nostril should be, and perhaps most important, our innate tendency to perceive meaningful faces in what are basically random visual stimuli (see Chapter 11).

✗ pareidolia = apophenia for the eyes.

Pareidolia can lead us to perceive meaningful people or objects in largely random stimuli. The "nun bun," a cinnamon roll resembling the face of nun Mother Teresa, was discovered in 1996 in a Nashville, Tennessee, coffee shop.

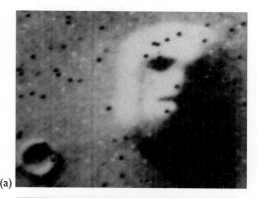

(a)

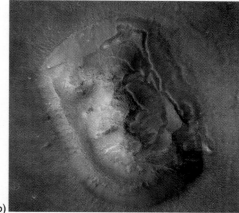

(b)

FIGURE 1.5 Face on Mars. At the top (a) is the remarkable "Face on Mars" photo taken by the *Mars Viking Orbiter* in 1976. Some argued that this face provided conclusive proof of intelligent life on other planets. Below (b) is a more detailed photograph of the Face on Mars taken in 2001, which revealed that this "face" was just an illusion.

pareidolia
tendency to perceive meaningful images in meaningless visual stimuli

TABLE 1.4 Is the Hot Hand a Reality or an Illusion? Let's look at the data from these two players on the Philadelphia 76ers to help us find out.

	ERVING	TONEY
P(h/mmm)	0.52	0.52
P(h/mm)	0.51	0.53
P(h/m)	0.51	0.51
P(h/h)	0.53	0.43
P(h/hh)	0.52	0.40
P(h/hhh)	0.48	0.32

(*Source:* Gilovich, 1991)

FICTOID ✖

MYTH: "Streaks" of several consecutive heads (H) or tails (T) in a row when flipping a coin, like HTTHTTTTTHHHTHHTTHH, are evidence of a nonrandom sequence.

REALITY: Streaks like this are both widespread and inevitable in long random sequences. Indeed, the sequence above is almost perfectly random (Gilovich, 1991). Because we tend to underestimate the probability of consecutive sequences, we're prone to attributing more significance to these sequences than they deserve ("Wow . . . I'm on a winning streak!").

THE HOT HAND: REALITY OR ILLUSION?

Because we're meaning-seeking organisms, we find it almost impossible *not* to detect patterns in random data. If we flip a coin four times and it comes up heads all four times, we may begin to think we're on a streak. Instead, we're probably just being fooled by randomness (Mlodinow, 2008; Taleb, 2004). The same phenomenon extends to sports.

Basketball players, coaches, and fans are fond of talking about the "hot hand." Once a player has made three or four shots in a row, he's "hot," "in the zone," and "on a roll." One television basketball announcer, former star center Bill Walton, once criticized a team's players for not getting the ball to a fellow player who'd just made several consecutive baskets ("He's got the hot hand—get him the ball!"). It certainly *seems* as though basketball players go on streaks. Do they?

To find out, Thomas Gilovich and his colleagues got hold of the shooting records of the 1980–1981 Philadelphia 76ers, then the only basketball team to keep precise records of which player made which shot in which order (Gilovich, Vallone, & Tversky, 1985). Let's look at **TABLE 1.4**, which displays the results of two representative players on the 76ers (you basketball fans out there may recognize "Erving" as the famous "Dr. J," widely regarded as one of the greatest players of all time). There we can see six rows, with *h* standing for a hit, that is, a successful shot, and *m* standing for a miss, that is, an unsuccessful shot. As we move from top to bottom, we see six different probabilities (abbreviated with *P*), starting with the probability of a successful shot (a hit) following three misses, then the probability of a successful shot following two misses, all the way (in the sixth and final row) to the probability of a successful shot following three successful shots.

If the hot hand is real, we should see the probabilities of a successful shot increasing from top to bottom. Once a player has made a few shots in a row, he should be more likely to make another. But as we can see from the data on these two players, *there's no evidence for the hot hand.* The proportions don't go up and, in fact, go down slightly (perhaps we should call this the "cool hand"?). Gilovich and his colleagues found the same pattern for all the other 76ers' players.

Perhaps the absence of a hot hand is due to the fact that once a player has made several shots in a row, the defensive team makes adjustments, making it tougher for him to make another shot. To rule out this possibility, Gilovich and his colleagues examined foul shots, which are immune from this problem because players attempt these shots without any interference from the defensive team. Once again, they found no hint of "streaky" shooting.

Later researchers have similarly found little or no evidence for "streaky performance" in other sports, including golf and baseball (Bar-Eli, Avugos, & Raab, 2006; Clark, 2005; Mlodinow, 2008). Still, belief perseverance makes it unlikely that these findings will shake the convictions of dyed-in-the-wool hot-hand believers. When told about the results of the Gilovich hot-hand study, late Hall of Fame basketball coach Red Auerbach replied, "Who is this guy? So he makes a study. I couldn't care less." The hot hand may be an illusion, but it's a remarkably stubborn one.

[handwritten: Rosencrantz and Guildenstern Are Dead! Corn scene.]

Finding Comfort in Our Beliefs. Another reason for the popularity of pseudoscience is motivational: We believe because we want to believe. As the old saying goes, "hope springs eternal": Many pseudoscientific claims, such as astrology, may give us comfort because they seem to offer us a sense of control over an often unpredictable world (Shermer, 2002). Research suggests that we're especially likely to seek out and find patterns when we feel a loss of control over our surroundings. Jennifer Whitson and Adam Galinsky (2008) deprived some participants of a sense of control—for example, by having them try to solve an unsolvable puzzle or recall a life experience in which they lacked control—and found that they were more likely than other participants to perceive conspiracies, embrace superstitious beliefs, and detect patterns in meaningless visual stimuli (see **FIGURE 1.6**). Whitson and Galinsky's results may help

[handwritten left margin: People believe pseudosciences because it comforts them]

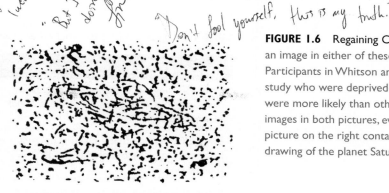

(handwritten annotations at top: "...watch both my eyes were faded out of luck" "But I'm doing fine" "Don't fool yourself, this is my truth.")

FIGURE 1.6 Regaining Control. Do you see an image in either of these pictures? Participants in Whitson and Galinsky's (2008) study who were deprived of a sense of control were more likely than other participants to see images in both pictures, even though only the picture on the right contains an image (a faint drawing of the planet Saturn).

to explain why so many of us believe in astrology, ESP, and other belief systems that claim to foretell the future: They lend a sense of control over the uncontrollable.

According to **terror management theory**, our awareness of our own inevitable death leaves many of us with an underlying sense of terror (Solomon, Greenberg, & Pyszczynski, 2000). We cope with these feelings of terror, advocates of this theory propose, by adopting cultural worldviews that reassure us that our lives possess a broader meaning and purpose—one that extends well beyond our vanishingly brief existence on this planet.

Terror management researchers typically test this model by manipulating *mortality salience:* the extent to which thoughts of death are foremost in our minds. They may ask participants to think about the emotions they experience when contemplating their deaths or to imagine themselves dying (Friedman & Arndt, 2005). Numerous studies demonstrate that manipulating mortality salience makes many people more likely to adopt certain reassuring cultural perspectives (Pyszczynski, Solomon, & Greenberg, 2003).

Can terror management theory help to explain the popularity of certain paranormal beliefs, such as astrology, ESP, and communication with the dead? Perhaps. Our society's widespread beliefs in life after death and reincarnation may stem in part from the terror that stems from knowing we'll eventually die (Lindeman, 1998; Norenzayan & Hansen, 2006). Two researchers (Morier & Podlipentseva, 1997) found that compared with other participants, participants who underwent a mortality salience manipulation reported higher levels of beliefs in the paranormal, such as ESP, ghosts, reincarnation, and astrology. It's likely that such beliefs are comforting to many of us, especially when confronted with reminders of our demise, because they imply the existence of a dimension beyond our own.

Of course, terror management theory doesn't demonstrate that paranormal claims are false; we still need to evaluate these claims on their own merits. Instead, this theory suggests that we're likely to hold many paranormal beliefs regardless of whether they're correct.

(handwritten: "That's sick!")

According to terror management theory, reminders of our death can lead us to adopt comforting worldviews—perhaps, in some cases, beliefs in the paranormal.

(handwritten note: Terror Management = terror caused by being aware of own deaths. Relieved (kind of) with cultural beliefs.)

(handwritten note: logical fallacies - traps that lead to mistaken conclusions because of intuitive sense)

THINKING CLEARLY: AN ANTIDOTE AGAINST PSEUDOSCIENCE. To avoid being seduced by the charms of pseudoscience, we must learn to avoid commonplace pitfalls in reasoning. Students new to psychology commonly fall prey to *logical fallacies:* traps in thinking that can lead to mistaken conclusions. It's easy for all of us to make these errors, because they seem to make intuitive sense. We should remember that scientific thinking often requires us to cast aside our beloved intuitions, although doing so can be extremely difficult.

Here we'll examine three especially important logical fallacies that are essential to bear in mind when evaluating psychological claims; we can find other useful fallacies in **TABLE 1.5** on page 18. All of them can help us separate science from pseudoscience.

Emotional Reasoning Fallacy. "The idea that day care might have negative emotional effects on children gets me really upset, so I refuse to believe it."

The *emotional reasoning fallacy* is the error of using our emotions as guides for evaluating the validity of a claim (some psychologists also refer to this error as the *affect heuristic*;

terror management theory
theory proposing that our awareness of our death leaves us with an underlying sense of terror with which we cope by adopting reassuring cultural worldviews

TABLE 1.5 Logical Fallacies to Avoid When Evaluating Psychological Claims.

LOGICAL FALLACY	EXAMPLE OF THE FALLACY
Error of using our emotions as guides for evaluating the validity of a claim (*emotional reasoning fallacy*)	"The idea that day care might have negative emotional effects on children gets me really upset, so I refuse to believe it."
Error of assuming that a claim is correct just because many people believe it (*bandwagon fallacy*)	"Lots of people I know believe in astrology, so there's got to be something to it."
Error of framing a question as though we can only answer it in one of two extreme ways (*either-or fallacy*)	"I just read in my psychology textbook that some people with schizophrenia were treated extremely well by their parents when they were growing up. This means that schizophrenia can't be due to environmental factors and therefore must be completely genetic."
Error of believing we're immune from errors in thinking that afflict other people (*not me fallacy*)	"My psychology professor keeps talking about how the scientific method is important for overcoming biases. But these biases don't apply to me, because *I'm* objective."
Error of accepting a claim merely because an authority figure endorses it (*appeal to authority fallacy*)	"My professor says that psychotherapy is worthless; because I trust my professor, she must be right."
Error of confusing the correctness of a belief with its origins or genesis (*genetic fallacy*)	"Freud's views about personality development can't be right, because Freud's thinking was shaped by sexist views popular at the time."
Error of assuming that a belief must be valid just because it's been around for a long time (*argument from antiquity fallacy*)	"There must be something to the Rorschach Inkblot Test, because psychologists have been using it for decades."
Error of confusing the validity of an idea with its potential real-world consequences (*argument from adverse consequences fallacy*)	"IQ can't be influenced by genetic factors, because if that were true it would give the government an excuse to prevent low-IQ individuals from reproducing."
Error of assuming that a claim must be true because no one has shown it to be false (*appeal to ignorance fallacy*)	"No scientist has been able to explain away every reported case of ESP, so ESP probably exists."
Error of inferring a moral judgment from a scientific fact (*naturalistic fallacy*)	"Evolutionary psychologists say that sexual infidelity is a product of natural selection. Therefore, sexual infidelity is ethically justifiable."
Error of drawing a conclusion on the basis of insufficient evidence (*hasty generalization fallacy*)	"All three people I know who are severely depressed had strict fathers, so severe depression is clearly associated with having a strict father."
Error of basing a claim on the same claim reworded in slightly different terms (*circular reasoning fallacy*)	"Dr. Smith's theory of personality is the best, because it seems to have the most evidence supporting it."

Slovic & Peters, 2006). If we're honest with ourselves, we'll realize that findings that challenge our preexisting beliefs often make us angry, whereas findings that confirm these beliefs often make us happy or at least relieved. We shouldn't make the mistake of assuming that because a scientific claim makes us feel uncomfortable or indignant, it must be wrong.

SIX PRINCIPLES OF SCIENTIFIC THINKING

These six principles of scientific thinking, introduced on page 21 and used throughout the text, will help you evaluate claims in research and everyday life.

What Scientific Thinking Principle Should We Use?	When Might We Use It?	How Do We Use It?
ruling out rival hypotheses HAVE IMPORTANT ALTERNATIVE EXPLANATIONS FOR THE FINDINGS BEEN EXCLUDED?	You're reading the newspaper and come across the headline: "Study shows depressed people who receive a new medication improve more than equally depressed people who receive nothing."	The results of the study could be due to the fact that people who received the medication expected to improve.
correlation vs. causation CAN WE BE SURE THAT A CAUSES B?	A researcher finds that people eat more ice cream on days when crimes are committed than when they aren't, and concludes that eating ice cream causes crime.	Eating ice cream (A) might not cause crime (B). Both could be due to a third factor (C), such as higher temperatures.
falsifiability CAN THE CLAIM BE DISPROVED?	A self-help book claims that all human beings have an invisible energy field surrounding them that influences their moods and well-being.	We can't design a study to disprove this claim.
replicability CAN THE RESULTS BE DUPLICATED IN OTHER STUDIES?	A magazine article highlights a study that shows people who practice meditation score 50 points higher on an intelligence test than those who don't.	We should be skeptical if no other scientific studies have reported the same findings.
extraordinary claims IS THE EVIDENCE AS STRONG AS THE CLAIM?	You come across a website that claims that a monster, like Bigfoot, has been living in the American Northwest for decades without being discovered by researchers.	This extraordinary claim requires more rigorous evidence than a less remarkable claim, such as the assertion that people remember more words from the beginning than from the end of a list.
occam's razor DOES A SIMPLER EXPLANATION FIT THE DATA JUST AS WELL?	Your friend, who has poor vision, claims that he spotted a UFO while attending a Frisbee tournament.	Is it more likely that your friend's report is due to a simpler explanation—his mistaking a Frisbee for a UFO—than to alien visitation?

SOME WARNING SIGNS OF PSEUDOSCIENTIFIC CLAIMS

These warning signs, which are discussed on page 12, will help you distinguish scientific from pseudoscientific claims so that you can become a more informed consumer.

Sign of Pseudoscience	Explanation	Example
Exaggerated claims	Pseudoscience tends to promise remarkable or dramatic cures, but rarely delivers the goods. Remember — extraordinary claims require extraordinary evidence.	
Overreliance on anecdotes	Pseudoscience tends to rely heavily on anecdotal evidence ("I know a person who" assertions). Anecdotes have three major limitations: they don't tell us anything about cause and effect, they don't tell us how representative the cases are, and they are difficult to verify.	
Absence of connectivity to other research	Most sciences are cumulative: new findings build on or "connect up with" previous findings. In contrast, pseudoscience neglects previous research and purport to create grand new ideas.	
Lack of review by other scholars (called peer review) or replication by independent labs	Most pseudoscience bypasses peer review and relies on anecdotes or conducts informal research that's never submitted to scientific journals. Many of these research studies are conducted "in-house" so there is no way to evaluate if they were conducted properly.	
Lack of self-correction when contrary evidence is published	Unlike science, in which incorrect claims tend to be weeded out eventually, in pseudoscience, incorrect claims never seem to go away because their proponents cling to them stubbornly despite contrary evidence.	
Meaningless "psychobable" that uses fancy scientific-sounding terms that don't make sense	Pseudoscience attempts to lure consumers into accepting claims by peppering their advertising with technical terms that are devoid of meaning.	
Talk of "proof" instead of "evidence"	Scientific knowledge is rarely, if ever, conclusive. In contrast pseudoscience tends to promise products or treatments that have been "proven" effective.	

In the case of scientific questions concerning the psychological effects of day care, which are scientifically controversial (Belsky, 1988; Hunt, 1999), we need to keep an open mind to the data, regardless of whether they confirm or disconfirm our preconceptions.

Bandwagon Fallacy. "Lots of people I know believe in astrology, so there's got to be something to it."

The *bandwagon fallacy* is the error of assuming that a claim is correct just because many people believe it. It's an error because popular opinion isn't a dependable guide to the accuracy of an assertion. Prior to 1500, almost everyone believed the sun revolved around the earth, rather than vice versa, but they were woefully mistaken.

Not Me Fallacy. "My psychology professor keeps talking about how the scientific method is important for overcoming biases. But these biases don't apply to me, because *I'm* objective."

The *not me fallacy* is the error of believing that we're immune from errors in thinking that afflict other people. This fallacy can get us into deep trouble, because it can lead us to conclude mistakenly that we don't require the safeguards of the scientific method. Many pseudoscientists fall into this trap: They're so certain their claims are right—and uncontaminated by mistakes in their thinking—that they don't bother to conduct scientific studies to test these claims. Social psychologists have recently uncovered a fascinating phenomenon called *bias blind spot,* which means that most people are unaware of their biases but keenly aware of them in others (Pronin, Gilovich, & Ross, 2004). None of us believes we have an accent because we live with our accents all of the time. Similarly, few of us believe that we have biases, because we've grown accustomed to seeing the world through our own psychological lenses. To see the not me fallacy at work, watch a debate between two intelligent people who hold extremely polarized views on a political issue. More likely than not, you'll see that the debate participants are quite adept at pointing out biases in their opponents, but entirely oblivious of their own equally glaring biases.

■ The Dangers of Pseudoscience: Why Should We Care?

Up to this point, we've been making a big deal about pseudoscience. But why should we care about it? After all, isn't a great deal of pseudoscience, like astrology, pretty harmless? In fact, pseudoscience can be dangerous, even deadly. This point applies to a variety of questionable claims that we encounter in everyday life. There are three major reasons why we should all be concerned about pseudoscience.

- **Opportunity Cost: What We Give Up.** Pseudoscientific treatments for mental disorders can lead people to forgo opportunities to seek effective treatments. As a consequence, even treatments that are themselves harmless can cause harm indirectly by causing people to forfeit the chance to obtain a treatment that works. For example, a major community survey (Kessler et al., 2001) revealed that Americans with severe depression or anxiety attacks more often received scientifically unsupported treatments than scientifically supported treatments, like cognitive-behavioral therapy (see Chapter 16). The unsupported treatments included acupuncture, which hasn't been shown to work for depression despite a few scattered positive findings; laughter therapy, which is based on the untested notion that laughing can cure depression; and energy therapy, which is based on the untestable notion that all people possess invisible energy fields that influence their moods. Although some future research might reveal some of these treatments to be helpful in certain cases, consumers who seek them out are rolling the dice with their mental health.

- **Direct Harm.** Pseudoscientific treatments sometimes do dreadful harm to those who receive them, causing psychological or physical damage—occasionally even death. The tragic case of Candace Newmaker, a 10-year-old child who received treatment for her behavioral problems in Evergreen, Colorado, in 2000, illustrates

The bandwagon fallacy reminds us that the number of people who hold a belief isn't a dependable barometer of its accuracy.

Fallacies:

1- Emotional Reasoning: using emotions to ~~prove~~ understand validity of a claim

2- Bandwagon: believing a claim is correct because so many others do too.

3- Not Me: believe the self does not make errors that others do, and such.

Dangers of Pseudoscience:

- forgo effective treatments. take part in scientifically unsupported treatments.

- direct harm, like death from "rebirthing treatment"

- the lack of ~~them~~ scientific thought.

Candace Newmaker was a tragic victim of a pseudoscientific treatment called rebirthing therapy. She died of suffocation at age 10 after her therapists wrapped her in a flannel blanket and squeezed her to simulate birth contractions.

✓●─ **Study** and **Review** on **mypsychlab.com**

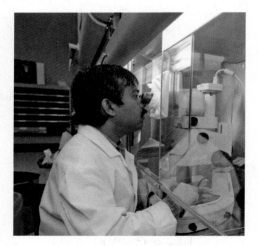

Stem cell research is controversial on both scientific and ethical grounds. To evaluate this and other controversies properly, we need to be able to think critically about the potential costs and benefits of such research.

((●─ **Listen** to the Psychology in the News podcast on **mypsychlab.com**

---

scientific skepticism
approach of evaluating all claims with an open mind but insisting on persuasive evidence before accepting them

---

this point (Mercer, Sarner, & Rosa, 2003). Candace received a treatment called *rebirthing therapy*, which is premised on the scientifically doubtful notion that children's behavioral problems are attributable to difficulties in forming attachments to their parents that stem from birth—in some cases, even before birth. During rebirthing, children or adolescents reenact the trauma of birth with the "assistance" of one or more therapists (Mercer, 2002). During Candace's rebirthing session, two therapists wrapped her in a flannel blanket, sat on her, and squeezed her repeatedly in an effort to simulate birth contractions. During the 40-minute session, Candace vomited several times and begged the therapists for air, complaining desperately that she couldn't breathe and felt as though she was going to die. When Candace was unwrapped from her symbolic "birth canal," she was dead (Mercer, Sarner, & Rosa, 2003). Sick.

- **An Inability to Think Scientifically as Citizens.** Scientific thinking skills aren't just important for evaluating psychological claims—we can apply them to all aspects of our lives. In our increasingly complex scientific and technological society, we need scientific thinking skills to reach educated decisions about global warming, genetic engineering, stem cell research, novel medical treatments, parenting and teaching practices, among dozens of other claims.

The take-home message is clear: Pseudoscience matters. That's what makes scientific thinking so critical: Although far from foolproof, it's our best safeguard against human error.

---

assess your knowledge   FACT OR FICTION?

1. Most self-help books and psychotherapies have been tested. **True / False**

2. Humans' tendency to see patterns in random data is entirely maladaptive. **True / False**

3. According to terror management theory, our fears of death are an important reason for pseudoscientific beliefs. **True / False**

4. The fact that many people believe in a claim is a good indicator of its validity. **True / False**

5. Pseudoscientific treatments can cause both direct and indirect harm. **True / False**

Answers: 1. F (p.11); 2. F (p.14); 3. T (p.17); 4. F (p.19); 5. T (p.19)

SCIENTIFIC THINKING: DISTINGUISHING FACT FROM FICTION

1.5   Identify the key features of scientific skepticism.

1.6   Identify and explain the text's six principles of scientific thinking.

Given that the world of popular psychology is chock-full of remarkable claims, how can we distinguish psychological fact—that is, the body of psychological findings that are so dependable we can safely regard them as true—from psychological fiction?

■ Scientific Skepticism

The approach we'll emphasize throughout this text is **scientific skepticism**. To many people, *skepticism* implies closed-mindedness, but nothing could be further from the truth. The term *skepticism* derives from the Greek word *skeptikos*, meaning "to consider carefully" (Shermer, 2002). The scientific skeptic evaluates all claims with an open mind but insists on persuasive evidence before accepting them. ((●─ **Listen**

As astronomer Carl Sagan (1995) noted, to be a scientific skeptic, we must adopt two attitudes that may seem contradictory but aren't: first, a willingness to keep an open mind to all claims and, second, a willingness to accept claims only after researchers have subjected them to careful scientific tests. Scientific skeptics are willing to change their minds when confronted

Scientific skeptic:
- will to keep open mind
- will to accept only after careful scientific tests

Evidence must be persuasive enough to change mind.

Open-minded but wait for evidence.

with evidence that challenges their preconceptions. At the same time, they change their minds only when this evidence is persuasive. The motto of the scientific skeptic is the Missouri principle, which we'll find on many Missouri license plates: "Show me" (Dawes, 1994).

Another feature of scientific skepticism is an unwillingness to accept claims on the basis of authority alone. Scientific skeptics evaluate claims on their own merits and refuse to accept them until they meet a high standard of evidence. Of course, in everyday life we're often forced to accept the word of authorities simply because we don't possess the expertise, time, or resources to evaluate every claim on our own. Most of us are willing to accept the claim that our local governments keep our drinking water safe without conducting our own chemical tests. While reading this chapter, you're also placing trust in us—the authors, that is—to provide you with accurate information about psychology. Still, this doesn't mean you should blindly accept everything we've written hook, line, and sinker. Consider what we've written with an open mind but evaluate it skeptically. If you disagree with something we've written, be sure to get a second opinion by asking your instructor.

The license plate of the state of Missouri captures the central motto of scientific skepticism.

" …and, as you go out into the world, I predict that you will, gradually and imperceptibly, forget all you ever learned at this university."

You'll probably forget many of the things you'll learn in college. But you'll be able to use the approach of scientific skepticism throughout your life to evaluate claims. (© Science CartoonsPlus.com)

■ A Basic Framework for Scientific Thinking

The hallmark of scientific skepticism is **critical thinking**. Many students misunderstand the word *critical* in *critical thinking*, assuming incorrectly that it entails a tendency to attack all claims. In fact, critical thinking is a set of skills for evaluating all claims in an open-minded and careful fashion. We can also think of critical thinking in psychology as *scientific thinking*, as it's the form of thinking that allows us to evaluate scientific claims, not only in the laboratory but in everyday life (Willingham, 2007).

Critical thinking = evaluate things with an open mind and careful fashion. Also, overcoming biases.

Just as important, scientific thinking is a set of skills for overcoming our own biases, especially confirmation bias, which as we've learned can blind us to evidence we'd prefer to ignore (Alcock, 1995). In particular, in this text we'll be emphasizing *six* principles of scientific thinking (Bartz, 2002; Lett, 1990). We should bear this framework of principles in mind when evaluating all psychological claims, including claims in the media, self-help books, the Internet, your introductory psychology course, and, yes, even this textbook.

These six scientific thinking principles are so crucial that beginning in Chapter 2, we'll indicate each of them with a different-colored icon you'll see throughout the text. Whenever one of these principles arises in our discussion, we'll display that icon in the margin to remind you of the principle that goes along with it (see **FIGURE 1.7** on page 22).

? Scientific thinking involves ruling out rival hypotheses. In this case, do we know that this woman's weight loss was due to a specific diet plan? **What might be some alternative explanations for her weight loss?** (See answer upside down at bottom of page.)

SCIENTIFIC THINKING PRINCIPLE #1: *RULING OUT RIVAL HYPOTHESES.* Most psychological findings we'll hear about on television or read about online lend themselves to multiple explanations. Yet, more often than not, the media report only one explanation. We shouldn't automatically assume it's correct. Instead, we should ask ourselves: Is this the only good explanation for this finding? Have we ruled out other important competing explanations (Huck & Sandler, 1979; Platt, 1964)?

Let's take a popular treatment for anxiety disorders: eye movement desensitization and reprocessing (EMDR; see Chapter 16). Introduced by Francine Shapiro (1989), EMDR asks clients to track the therapist's back-and-forth finger movements with their eyes while imagining distressing memories that are the source of their anxiety, such as the recollection of seeing someone being killed. Proponents of EMDR have consistently maintained that it's

critical thinking
set of skills for evaluating all claims in an open-minded and careful fashion

Answer: During this time, she might have exercised or used another diet plan. Or perhaps, the larger pants she's holding up were never hers to begin with.

What Scientific Thinking Principle Should We Use?	When Might We Use It?	How Do We Use It?
ruling out rival hypotheses HAVE IMPORTANT ALTERNATIVE EXPLANATIONS FOR THE FINDINGS BEEN EXCLUDED?	You're reading the newspaper and come across the headline: "Study shows depressed people who receive a new medication improve more than equally depressed people who receive nothing."	The results of the study could be due to the fact that people who received the medication expected to improve. 
correlation vs. causation CAN WE BE SURE THAT A CAUSES B?	A researcher finds that people eat more ice cream on days when crimes are committed than when they aren't, and concludes that eating ice cream causes crime.	Eating ice cream (A) might not cause crime (B). Both could be due to a third factor (C), such as higher temperatures. 
falsifiability CAN THE CLAIM BE DISPROVED?	A self-help book claims that all human beings have an invisible energy field surrounding them that influences their moods and well-being.	We can't design a study to disprove this claim. 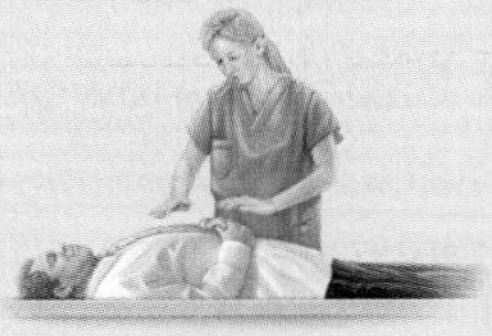
replicability CAN THE RESULTS BE DUPLICATED IN OTHER STUDIES?	A magazine article highlights a study that shows people who practice meditation score 50 points higher on an intelligence test than those who don't.	We should be skeptical if no other scientific studies have reported the same findings. 
extraordinary claims IS THE EVIDENCE AS STRONG AS THE CLAIM?	You come across a website that claims that a monster, like Bigfoot, has been living in the American Northwest for decades without being discovered by researchers.	This extraordinary claim requires more rigorous evidence than a less remarkable claim, such as the assertion that people remember more words from the beginning than from the end of a list. 
occam's razor DOES A SIMPLER EXPLANATION FIT THE DATA JUST AS WELL?	Your friend, who has poor vision, claims that he spotted a UFO while attending a Frisbee tournament.	Is it more likely that your friend's report is due to a simpler explanation—his mistaking a Frisbee for a UFO—than to alien visitation? 

FIGURE 1.7   The Six Principles of Scientific Thinking That Are Used Throughout This Textbook.

far more effective and efficient than other treatments for anxiety disorders. Some have claimed that these eye movements somehow synchronize the brain's two hemispheres or stimulate brain mechanisms that speed up the processing of emotional memories.

Here's the problem: A slew of well-controlled studies show that the eye movements of EMDR don't contribute to its effectiveness. EMDR works just as well when people stare straight ahead at an immobile dot while thinking about the source of their anxiety (Davidson & Parker, 2001; Lohr, Tolin, & Lilienfeld, 1998). Most EMDR advocates neglected to consider a rival explanation for EMDR's success: EMDR asks patients to expose themselves to anxiety-provoking imagery. Researchers and therapists alike have long known that prolonged exposure itself can be therapeutic (Bisson, 2007; Lohr et al., 2003; see Chapter 16). By not excluding the rival hypothesis that EMDR's effectiveness stemmed from exposure rather than eye movements, EMDR advocates made claims that ran well ahead of the data.

The bottom line: Whenever we evaluate a psychological claim, we should ask ourselves whether we've excluded other plausible explanations for it.

SCIENTIFIC THINKING PRINCIPLE #2: *CORRELATION ISN'T CAUSATION.* Perhaps the most common mistake psychology students make when interpreting studies is to conclude that when two things are associated with each other—or what psychologists call "correlated" with each other—one thing must cause the other. This point leads us to one of the most crucial principles in this book (get your highlighters out for this one): *Correlational designs don't permit causal inferences,* or, putting it less formally, *correlation isn't causation.* When we conclude that a correlation means causation, we've committed the **correlation–causation fallacy.** This conclusion is a fallacy because the fact that two variables are correlated doesn't necessarily mean that one causes the other (see Chapter 2). Incidentally, a **variable** is anything that can *vary,* like height, IQ, or extraversion. Let's see why correlation isn't causation.

If we start with two variables, A and B, that are correlated, there are three major explanations for this correlation.

1. A → B. It's possible that variable A causes variable B.   *like Pavlov's dogs.*
2. B → A. It's possible that variable B causes variable A.
   So far, so good. But many people forget that there's also a third possibility, namely, that:
3. C ⟋↗ A ⟍↘ B   *3rd variable problem.*

In this third scenario, there's a third variable, C, that causes *both* A and B. This scenario is known as the *third variable problem.* It's a problem because it can lead us to conclude mistakenly that A and B are causally related to each other when they're not. For example, researchers found that teenagers who listen to music with lots of sexual lyrics have sexual intercourse more often than teenagers who listen to music with tamer lyrics (Martino et al., 2006). So listening to sexual lyrics is *correlated* with sexual behavior. One newspaper summarized the findings of this study with an attention-grabbing headline: "Sexual lyrics prompt teens to have sex" (Tanner, 2006). Like many headlines, this one went well beyond the data. It's indeed possible that music with sexual lyrics (A) causes sexual behavior (B). But it's also possible that sexual behavior (B) causes teens to listen to music with sexual lyrics (A), or that a third variable, like impulsivity (C), both causes teens to listen to music with sexual lyrics *and* engage in sexual behavior. Given the data reported by the authors, there's no way to know. *Correlation isn't causation.* This point is so crucial that we'll revisit it in Chapter 2.

The bottom line: We should remember that a correlation between two things doesn't demonstrate a causal connection between them.

SCIENTIFIC THINKING PRINCIPLE #3: *FALSIFIABILITY.* Philosopher of science Sir Karl Popper (1965) observed that for a claim to be meaningful, it must be **falsifiable,** that is, capable of being disproved. If a theory isn't falsifiable, we can't test it. Some students misunderstand this point, confusing the question of whether a theory is *falsifiable* with whether it's *false.* The

THE FAMILY CIRCUS.   **By Bil Keane**

8-5
© 1998 Bil Keane, Inc.
Dist. by Cowles Syrd., Inc.

"I wish they didn't turn on that seatbelt sign so much! Every time they do, it gets bumpy."

Correlation isn't always causation.
(Family Circus © Bil Keane, Inc. King Features Syndicate)

Scientific Thinking Principles

1 - Rule out rival hypotheses

2 - Correlation ≠ Causation

3 - Claims that are meaningful must be falsifiable (can be disproved).

4 - Replicability ... study should be able to be duplicated.

5 - If a claim is extraordinary and has extraordinary evidence, tread with caution.

6 - Occam's Razor:
KISS = keep it simple, stupid
- sometimes the best explanation is the simplest one.

correlation–causation fallacy
error of assuming that because one thing is associated with another, it must cause the other

variable
anything that can vary

falsifiable
capable of being disproved

Some television shows, like *Medium*, feature "psychic detectives," people with supposed extrasensory powers who can help police to locate missing people. Yet psychic detectives' predictions are typically so vague—"I see a body near water," "The body is near a wooded area"—that they're virtually impossible to falsify.

Replrability = duplication shows relrability

ESP researchers often ask subjects to predict the outcomes of random events. Yet ESP findings have proven difficult to replicate.

principle of falsifiability doesn't mean that a theory must be false to be meaningful. Instead, it means that for a theory to be meaningful, it *could* be proven wrong if there were certain types of evidence against it. For a claim to be falsifiable, its proponent must state clearly *in advance,* not after the fact, which findings would count as evidence for and against the claim (Dienes, 2008; Proctor & Capaldi, 2006).

A key implication of the falsifiability principle is that a theory that explains everything—a theory that can account for every conceivable outcome—in effect explains nothing. That's because a good scientific theory must predict only certain outcomes, but not others. If a friend told you he was a master "psychic sports forecaster" and predicted with great confidence that, "Tomorrow, all of the major league baseball teams that are playing a game will either win or lose," you'd probably start giggling. By predicting every potential outcome, your friend hasn't really predicted anything.

If your friend instead forecasted "The New York Yankees and New York Mets will both win tomorrow by three runs, but the Boston Red Sox and Los Angeles Dodgers will lose by one run," this prediction could be either correct or incorrect. There's a possibility he'll be wrong—the prediction is falsifiable. If he's right, it wouldn't prove he's psychic, of course, but it might make you at least wonder whether he has some special predictive abilities.

The bottom line: Whenever we evaluate a psychological claim, we should ask ourselves whether one could in principle disprove it or whether it's consistent with any conceivable body of evidence. *Like the Big Bang Theory and Darwin and all.*

SCIENTIFIC THINKING PRINCIPLE #4: *REPLICABILITY.* Barely a week goes by that we don't hear about another stunning psychological finding on the evening news: "Researchers at Cupcake State University detect a new gene linked to excessive shopping"; "Investigators at the University of Antarctica at Igloo report that alcoholism is associated with a heightened risk of murdering one's spouse"; "Nobel Prize–winning professor at Cucumber State College isolates brain area responsible for the enjoyment of popcorn." One problem with these conclusions, in addition to the fact that the news media often tell us nothing about the design of the studies on which they're based, is that the findings often haven't been replicated. **Replicability** means that a study's findings can be duplicated consistently. If they can't be duplicated, it increases the odds that the original findings were due to chance. *We shouldn't place too much stock in a psychological finding until it's been replicated.*

Most replications aren't exact duplications of the original researchers' methods. Most involve minor variations in the original design, or extending this design to different participants, including those in different cultures, races, or geographical locations. The more we can replicate our findings using different subjects in different settings, the more confidence we can place in them (Schmidt, 2009; Shadish, Cook, & Campbell, 2002).

We should bear in mind that the media are far more likely to report initial positive findings than failures to replicate. The initial findings may be especially fascinating or sensational, whereas replication failures are often disappointing: They don't make for juicy news stories. It's especially crucial that investigators other than the original researchers replicate the results because this increases our confidence in them. If I tell you that I've created a recipe for the world's most delicious veal parmigiana, but it turns out that every other chef who follows my recipe ends up with a meal that tastes like an old piece of cardboard smothered in rotten cheese and six-month-old tomato sauce, you'd be justifiably skeptical. Maybe I flat-out lied about my recipe. Or perhaps I wasn't actually following the recipe very closely and was instead tossing in ingredients that weren't even in the recipe. Or perhaps I'm such an extraordinary chef that nobody else can come close to replicating my miraculous culinary feats. In any case, you'd have every right to doubt my recipe until someone else replicated it. The same goes for psychological research.

replicability
when a study's findings are able to be duplicated, ideally by independent investigators

The literature on ESP offers an excellent example of why replicability is so essential (see Chapter 4). Every once in a blue moon, a researcher reports a striking new finding that seemingly confirms the existence of ESP. Yet time and again, independent researchers haven't been able to replicate these tantalizing results (Gilovich, 1991; Hyman, 1989; Lilienfeld, 1999c), which might lead a skeptical observer to wonder if many of the initial positive findings were due to chance.

like a chemistry lab.

The bottom line: Whenever we evaluate a psychological claim, we should ask ourselves whether independent investigators have replicated the findings that support this claim; otherwise, the findings might be a one-time-only fluke.

SCIENTIFIC THINKING PRINCIPLE #5: *EXTRAORDINARY CLAIMS REQUIRE EXTRAORDINARY EVIDENCE.* (Throughout the book, we'll be abbreviating this principle as "Extraordinary Claims.") This principle was proposed in slightly different terms by 18th century Scottish philosopher David Hume (Sagan, 1995; Truzzi, 1978). According to Hume, the more a claim contradicts what we already know, the more persuasive the evidence for this claim must be before we accept it.

A handful of researchers believe that every night hundreds or even thousands of Americans are being lifted magically out of their beds, brought aboard flying saucers, and experimented on by aliens, only to be returned safely to their beds hours later (Clancy, 2005). According to some alien abduction advocates, aliens are extracting semen from human males to impregnate female aliens in an effort to create a race of alien–human hybrids. *Weird.*

According to a few researchers, tens of thousands of Americans have been abducted by aliens and brought aboard spaceships to be experimented on. Could it really be happening, and how would we know?

Of course, alien abduction proponents *might* be right, and we shouldn't dismiss their claims out of hand. But their claims are pretty darned extraordinary, especially because they imply that tens of thousands of invading flying saucers from other solar systems have inexplicably managed to escape detection by hundreds of astronomers, not to mention air traffic controllers and radar operators. Alien abduction proponents have been unable to provide even a shred of concrete evidence that supposed abductees have actually encountered extraterrestrials—say, a convincing photograph of an alien, a tiny piece of a metal probe inserted by an alien, or even a strand of hair or shred of skin from an alien. Thus far, all that alien abduction proponents have to show for their claims are the self-reports of supposed abductees. Extraordinary claims, but decidedly ordinary evidence.

The bottom line: Whenever we evaluate a psychological claim, we should ask ourselves whether this claim runs counter to many things we know already and, if it does, whether the evidence is as extraordinary as the claim.

SCIENTIFIC THINKING PRINCIPLE #6: *OCCAM'S RAZOR.* Occam's Razor, named after 14th century British philosopher and monk Sir William of Occam, is also called the "principle of parsimony" (*parsimony* means logical simplicity). According to Occam's Razor, if two explanations account equally well for a phenomenon, we should generally select the more parsimonious one. Good researchers use Occam's Razor to "shave off" needlessly complicated explanations to arrive at the simplest explanation that does a good job of accounting for the evidence. Scientists of a romantic persuasion refer to Occam's Razor as the principle of KISS: Keep it simple, stupid. Occam's Razor is only a guideline, not a hard-and-fast rule (Uttal, 2003). Every once in a while the best explanation for a phenomenon is the most complex, not the simplest. But Occam's Razor is a helpful rule of thumb, as it's right far more often than wrong.

During the late 1970s and 1980s, hundreds of mysterious designs, called crop circles, began appearing in wheat fields in England. Most of these designs were remarkably intricate. How on Earth (pun intended) can we explain these designs? Many believers in the paranormal concluded that these designs originated not on Earth but on distant planets. The crop circles, they concluded, are proof positive of alien visitations to our world.

Occam chooses a razor

KISS = Keep it simple stupid.

There are two explanations for crop circles, one supernatural and the other natural. Which should we believe?

The crop circle excitement came crashing down in 1991, when two British men, David Bower and Doug Chorley, confessed to creating the crop circles as a barroom prank intended to poke fun at uncritical believers in extraterrestrials. They even demonstrated on camera how they used wooden planks and rope to stomp through tall fields of wheat and craft the complex designs. Occam's Razor reminds us that when confronted with two explanations that fit the evidence equally well, we should generally select the simpler one—in this case, human pranksters. *Nice.*

The bottom line: Whenever we evaluate a psychological claim, we should ask ourselves whether the explanation offered is the simplest explanation that accounts for the data or whether simpler explanations can account for the data equally well.

Answers are located at the end of the text.

HEALTH BENEFITS OF FRUITS AND VEGETABLES

evaluating CLAIMS

We all know the importance of eating a balanced diet with plenty of fruits and vegetables. Yet many popular media sources exaggerate the health benefits of fruits and vegetables and even make dangerous claims about their ability to cure serious illnesses like diabetes or cancer. Let's evaluate some of these claims, which are modeled after actual advertisements.

"*Studies show* that eating walnuts *may* reduce your risk and delay the onset of Alzheimer's."
The use of the qualifying word "may" renders the claim difficult or impossible to falsify. What would we need to know about how these studies were conducted to validate the claim?

"Eating peaches gives you energy and makes you feel *light and fresh* throughout the year."
This claim is vague and difficult to falsify. How would you define or measure "light and fresh"?

"Avoid drugs or surgery and find a *completely natural* cure for your disease."
The phrase "completely natural" implies that the cure is safer than drugs or surgery. Can you think of any natural substances (including fruits and vegetables) that are dangerous or even fatal?

"These natural cures come from *ancient cultures* and have been handed down for thousands of years."
Does the fact that something has been around for a long time mean it is trustworthy? What logical fallacy does this ad commit?

✓—Study and Review on **mypsychlab.com**

assess your knowledge

FACT OR FICTION?

1. Scientific skepticism requires a willingness to keep an open mind to all claims. **True** / **False**
2. When evaluating a psychological claim, we should consider other plausible explanations for it. **True** / **False**
3. The fact that two things are related doesn't mean that one directly influences the other. **True** / **False**
   can be disprovable
4. Falsifiability means that a theory must be false to be meaningful. **True** / **False**
5. When psychological findings are replicated, it's especially important that the replications be conducted by the same team of investigators. **True** / **False**

Answers: 1. T (p.20); 2. T (p.23); 3. T (p.23); 4. F (p.24); 5. F (p.24)

PSYCHOLOGY'S PAST AND PRESENT: WHAT A LONG, STRANGE TRIP IT'S BEEN

1.7 Identify the major theoretical frameworks of psychology.

1.8 Describe different types of psychologists and identify what each of them does.

1.9 Describe the two great debates that have shaped the field of psychology.

1.10 Describe how psychological research affects our daily lives.

How did psychology emerge as a discipline, and has it always been plagued by pseudoscience? The scientific approach to the study of the mind, brain, and behavior emerged slowly, and the field's initial attempts displayed many of the weaknesses that pseudoscientific approaches possess today. Informal attempts to study and explain how our minds work have been with us for thousands of years. But psychology as a science has existed for only about 130 years, and many of those years were spent refining techniques to develop research methods that were free from bias (Coon, 1992). Throughout its history, psychology has struggled with many of the same challenges that we confront today when reasoning about psychological research. So, it's important to understand how psychology evolved as a scientific discipline—that is, a discipline that relies on systematic research methods to avoid being fooled.

Explore the Psychology Timeline on **mypsychlab.com**

■ Psychology's Early History

We'll start our journey with a capsule summary of psychology's bumpy road from non-science to science (a timeline of significant events in the evolution of scientific psychology can be seen in **FIGURE 1.8** on page 28). **Explore**

For many centuries, the field of psychology was difficult to distinguish from philosophy. Most academic psychologists held positions in departments of philosophy (psychology departments didn't even exist back then) and didn't conduct experimental research. Instead, they mostly sat and contemplated the human mind from the armchair. In essence, they relied on common sense.

Yet beginning in the late 1800s, the landscape of psychology changed dramatically. In 1879, Wilhelm Wundt (1832–1920) developed the first full-fledged psychological laboratory in Leipzig, Germany. Most of Wundt's investigations and those of his students focused on basic questions concerning our mental experiences: How different must two colors be for us to tell them apart? How long does it take us to react to a sound? What thoughts come to mind when we solve a math problem? Wundt used a combination of experimental methods, including reaction time procedures, and a technique called **introspection**, which required trained observers to carefully reflect and report on their mental experiences. Introspectionists might ask participants to look at an object, say an apple, and carefully report everything they saw. In many respects, the pioneering work of Wundt marked the beginnings of psychology as a science. Soon, psychologists elsewhere around the world followed Wundt's bold lead and opened laboratories in departments of psychology.

Before becoming a science, psychology also needed to break free from another influence: spiritualism. The term "psychology" literally means the study of the "psyche," that is, spirit or soul. In the mid and late 1800s, Americans became fascinated with spirit mediums, people who claimed to contact the dead, often during séances (Blum, 2006). These were group sessions that took place in darkened rooms, in which mediums attempted to "channel" the spirits of deceased individuals. Americans were equally enchanted with psychics, individuals who claimed to possess powers of mind reading and other extrasensory abilities (see Chapter 5). Many famous psychologists of the day invested a great deal of time and effort in the search for these paranormal capacities (Benjamin & Baker, 2004; Blum, 2006). They ultimately failed, and psychology eventually developed a respectful distance from spiritualism. It did so largely by creating a new field: the psychology of human error and self-deception. Rather than asking whether extrasensory powers exist, a growing number of psychologists in the late 1800s began to ask the equally fascinating question of how people can fool themselves into believing things that aren't supported by evidence (Coon, 1992)—a central theme of this book.

Wilhelm Wundt (*right*) in the world's first psychology laboratory. Wundt is generally credited with launching psychology as a laboratory science in 1879.

FICTOID

MYTH: Some psychics can "channel" messages from dead people to their loved ones and friends.

REALITY: Maybe, but unlikely. No psychic channeler has ever passed a carefully controlled scientific test (Hyman, 2003).

---

introspection
method by which trained observers carefully reflect and report on their mental experiences

1649: René Descartes writes about the mind–body problem

Late 1700s: Frans Anton Mesmer discovers principles of hypnosis

Early 1800s: Due to efforts of Franz Joseph Gall and Joseph Spurzheim, phrenology becomes immensely popular in Europe and the United States

1850: Gustav Fechner experiences crucial insight linking physical changes in the external world to subjective changes in perception; leads to establishment of psychophysics

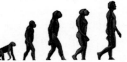

1859: Charles Darwin writes *Origin of Species*

1875: William James creates small psychological laboratory at Harvard University

1879: Wilhelm Wundt creates world's first formal psychological laboratory, launching psychology as an experimental science

1881: Wundt establishes first psychology journal

1883: J. Stanley Hall, one of Wundt's students, opens first major psychology laboratory in the United States, at Johns Hopkins University

1888: James McKeen Cattell becomes first professor of psychology in the United States

1889: Sir Francis Galton introduces concept of correlation, allowing psychologists to quantify associations among variables

1890: William James writes *Principles of Psychology*

1892: American Psychological Association (APA) founded

1896: Lightmer Witmer creates first psychological clinic at the University of Pennsylvania, launching field of clinical psychology

1900: Sigmund Freud writes *The Interpretation of Dreams*, landmark book in the history of psychoanalysis

1904: Mary Calkins is first woman elected president of the American Psychological Association

1967: Ulric Neisser writes *Cognitive Psychology*; helps to launch field of cognitive psychology

1963: Stanley Milgram publishes classic laboratory studies of obedience

1958: Joseph Wolpe writes *Psychotherapy by Reciprocal Inhibition*, helping to launch field of behavioral therapy

1954: Paul Meehl writes *Clinical versus Statistical Prediction*, first major book to describe both the strengths and weaknesses of clinical judgment

1953: Rapid eye movement (REM) sleep discovered

1953: Francis Crick and James Watson discover structure of DNA, launching genetic revolution

1952: Antipsychotic drug Thorazine tested in France, launching modern era of psychopharmacology

1949: Conference held at University of Colorado at Boulder to outline principles of scientific clinical psychology; founding of the "Boulder" (scientist-practitioner) model of clinical training

1938: B. F. Skinner writes *The Behavior of Organisms*

1935: Kurt Koffka writes *Principles of Gestalt Psychology*

1920s: Gordon Allport helps to initiate field of personality trait psychology

1920: Jean Piaget writes *The Child's Conception of the World*

1913: John B. Watson writes *Psychology as Behavior*, launching field of behaviorism

1911: E. L. Thorndike discovers instrumental (later called operant) conditioning

1910: Ivan Pavlov discovers classical conditioning

1907: Oscar Pfungst demonstrates that the amazing counting horse, Clever Hans, responds to cues from observers; demonstrates power of expectancies

1905: Alfred Binet and Henri Simon develop first intelligence test

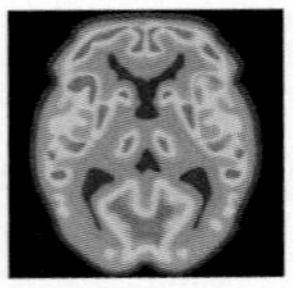

1974: Positron emission tomography (PET) scanning introduced, launching field of functional brain imaging

1974: Elizabeth Loftus and Robert Palmer publish paper showing that memory is more reconstructive than previously believed

1976: Founding of Committee for the Scientific Investigation of Claims of the Paranormal, first major organization to apply scientific skepticism to paranormal claims

1977: First use of statistical technique of meta-analysis, which allows researchers to systematically combine results of multiple studies; demonstrated that psychotherapy is effective

1980: *Diagnostic and Statistical Manual of Mental Disorders,* Third Edition (*DSM-III*) published; helps standardize the diagnosis of mental disorders

1980s: Recovered memory craze sweeps across America; pits academic researchers against many clinicians

1988: Many scientifically oriented psychologists break off from APA to found American Psychological Society (APS)

1990: Thomas Bouchard and colleagues publish major results of Minnesota Study of Twins Reared Apart, demonstrating substantial genetic bases for intelligence, personality, and other individual differences

1995: Task force of Division 12 (Society of Clinical Psychology) of American Psychological Association publishes list of, and criteria for, empirically supported psychotherapies

2000: Human genome sequenced

2002: Daniel Kahneman becomes first Ph.D. psychologist to win Nobel Prize; honored for his pioneering work (with the late Amos Tversky) on biases and heuristics

2004: APS members vote to change name to Association for Psychological Science

2009: New graduate accreditation system proposed to place psychotherapy training on a firmer scientific footing.

FIGURE 1.8 Timeline of Major Events in Scientific Psychology.

■ The Great Theoretical Frameworks of Psychology

Almost since its inception, psychological science has confronted a thorny question: What unifying theoretical perspective best explains behavior?

Five major theoretical perspectives—structuralism, functionalism, behaviorism, psychoanalysis, and cognitivism—have played pivotal roles in shaping contemporary psychological thought. Many beginning psychology students understandably ask, "Which of these perspectives is the right one?" As it turns out, the answer isn't entirely clear. Each theoretical viewpoint has something valuable to contribute to scientific psychology, but each has its limitations (see **TABLE 1.6**). In some cases, these differing viewpoints may not be contradictory, as they may be explaining behavior at different levels of analysis. As we wind our way through these five frameworks, we'll discover that psychology's view of what constitutes a scientific approach to behavior has changed over time. Indeed, it continues to evolve even today.

STRUCTURALISM: THE ELEMENTS OF THE MIND. Edward Bradford Titchener (1867–1927), a British student of Wundt who emigrated to the United States, founded the field of structuralism. **Structuralism** aimed to identify the basic elements, or "structures,"

> **structuralism**
> school of psychology that aimed to identify the basic elements of psychological experience

TABLE 1.6 The Theoretical Perspectives That Shaped Psychology.

PERSPECTIVE	LEADING FIGURES	SCIENTIFIC GOAL	LASTING SCIENTIFIC INFLUENCE
Structuralism ◀ E.B. Titchener	E. B. Titchener	Uses introspection to identify basic elements or "structures" of experience	Emphasis on the importance of systematic observation to the study of conscious experience
Functionalism ◀ William James	William James; influenced by Charles Darwin	To understand the functions or adaptive purposes of our thoughts, feelings, and behaviors	Has been absorbed into psychology and continues to influence it indirectly in many ways
Behaviorism ◀ B. F. Skinner	John B. Watson; B. F. Skinner	To uncover the general principles of learning that explain all behaviors; focus is largely on observable behavior	Influential in models of human and animal learning and among the first to focus on need for objective research
Cognitivism ◀ Jean Piaget	Jean Piaget; Ulric Neisser	To examine the role of mental processes on behavior	Influential in many areas, such as language, problem solving, concept formation, intelligence, memory, and psychotherapy
Psychoanalysis ◀ Sigmund Freud	Sigmund Freud	To uncover the role of unconscious psychological processes and early life experiences in behavior	Understanding that much of our mental processing goes on outside of conscious awareness

[handwritten: Structuralism = understand basic elements/structures of psychological experience (what?)]

[handwritten: Functionalism = understand functions of psychological characters, (why?) like thoughts, feelings, and behaviors]

of psychological experience. Adopting Wundt's method of introspection, structuralists dreamed of creating a comprehensive "map" of the elements of consciousness—which they believed consisted of sensations, images, and feelings—much like the periodic table of the elements we can find in every chemistry classroom (Evans, 1972).

Structuralism eventually ran out of steam. At least two major problems eventually did it in. First, even highly trained introspectionists often disagreed on their subjective reports. Second, German psychologist Oswald Kulpe (1862–1915) showed that subjects asked to solve certain mental problems engage in *imageless thought*: thinking unaccompanied by conscious experience. If we ask an introspecting subject to add 10 and 5, she'll quickly respond "15," but she'll usually be unable to report what came to her mind when performing this calculation (Hergenhahn, 2000). The phenomenon of imageless thought dealt a serious body blow to structuralism because it demonstrated that some important aspects of human psychology lie outside of conscious awareness.

Structuralism correctly emphasized the importance of *systematic observation* to the study of conscious experience. Nevertheless, structuralists went astray by assuming that a single, imperfect method—introspection—could provide all of the information needed for a complete science of psychology. In the time since introspectionism came and went, psychologists have learned that multiple methods are almost always needed to understand complex psychological phenomena (Cook, 1985; Figueredo, 1993).

FUNCTIONALISM: PSYCHOLOGY MEETS DARWIN. Proponents of **functionalism** strove to understand the adaptive purposes, or functions, of psychological characteristics, such as thoughts, feelings, and behaviors (Hunt, 1993). Whereas structuralists asked "what" questions, like "What is conscious thought like?" functionalists asked "why" questions, like "Why do we sometimes forget things?" The founder of functionalism, William James, rejected structuralists' approach and methods, arguing that careful introspection doesn't yield a fixed number of static elements of consciousness but rather an ever-changing "stream of consciousness," a famous phrase he coined. James is also famous for writing the influential text *Principles of Psychology* (1890), which introduced the science of psychology to the general public.

The functionalists of the late 1800s were influenced substantially by biologist Charles Darwin's (1809–1882) still-young theory of **natural selection**, which emphasized that physical and behavioral characteristics evolved because they increased the chances of their survival and reproduction. The functionalists believed that Darwin's theory applied to psychological characteristics, too. Just as the trunk of an elephant serves useful survival functions, such as snaring distant water and food, the human memory system, for example, must similarly serve a purpose. It's the job of psychologists, functionalists maintained, to act as "detectives," figuring out the evolved functions that psychological characteristics serve for organisms.

Like structuralism, functionalism doesn't exist in its original form today. Instead, functionalism was gradually absorbed into mainstream scientific psychology and continues to influence it indirectly in many ways.

BEHAVIORISM: THE LAWS OF LEARNING. By the early twentieth century, many American psychologists were growing impatient with the touchy-feely nature of their discipline. In particular, they believed that Titchener and other introspectionists were leading psychology down a misguided path. For these critics, the study of consciousness was a waste of time because researchers could never verify conclusively the existence of the basic elements of mental experience. Psychological science, they contended, must be objective, not subjective.

Foremost among these critics was a flamboyant American psychologist, John B. Watson (1878–1958). Watson was a founder of the still-influential school of **behaviorism**, which focuses on uncovering the general principles of learning underlying human and animal behavior. For Watson (1913), the proper subject matter of psychology was observable behavior, plain and simple. Subjective reports of conscious experience should play no part in psychology. If it followed his brave lead, Watson proclaimed, psychology could become just as scientific as physics, chemistry, and other "hard" sciences.

Watson, like his follower Burrhus Frederic (B.F.) Skinner (1904–1990), insisted that psychology should aspire to uncover the general laws of learning that explain all behaviors,

Charles Darwin's theory of evolution by natural selection was a significant influence on functionalism, which strove to understand the adaptive purposes of psychological characteristics.

[handwritten: Behaviorism = understanding by looking from the outside, at observable behavior.]

functionalism
school of psychology that aimed to understand the adaptive purposes of psychological characteristics

natural selection
principle that organisms that possess adaptations survive and reproduce at a higher rate than other organisms

behaviorism
school of psychology that focuses on uncovering the general laws of learning by looking at observable behavior

Cognitivism = thinking is key to psychology. Thinking and the way the brain functions correlate.

Psychoanalysis = internal psychological processes, (impulses, thoughts, memories of which we're unaware), unconscious drives.

whether they be riding a bicycle, eating a sandwich, or becoming depressed. All of these behaviors, they proposed, are products of a handful of basic learning principles (see Chapter 6). Moreover, according to Watson and Skinner, we don't need to peer "inside" the organism to grasp these principles. We can comprehend human behavior exclusively by looking *outside* the organism, to rewards and punishments delivered by the environment. For traditional behaviorists, the human mind is a black box: We know what goes into it and what comes out of it, but we needn't worry about what happens between the inputs and the outputs. For this reason, psychologists sometimes call behaviorism *black box psychology.*

Behaviorism has left a stamp on scientific psychology that continues to be felt today. By identifying the fundamental laws of learning that help to explain human and animal behavior, behaviorists placed psychology on firmer scientific footing. Although early behaviorists' deep mistrust of subjective observations of conscious experience probably went too far, these psychologists properly warned us of the hazards of relying too heavily on reports that we can't verify objectively.

COGNITIVISM: OPENING THE BLACK BOX. Beginning in the 1950s and 1960s, growing numbers of psychologists grew disillusioned with behaviorists' neglect of *cognition,* the term psychologists use to describe the mental processes involved in different aspects of thinking. Although some behaviorists acknowledged that humans and even many intelligent animals do think, they viewed thinking as merely another form of behavior. Proponents of **cognitive psychology**, in contrast, argued that our thinking affects our behavior in powerful ways. For example, Swiss psychologist Jean Piaget (1896–1980) argued compellingly that children conceptualize the world in markedly different ways than do adults (see Chapter 10). Later, led by Ulric Neisser (1928–), cognitivists argued that thinking is so central to psychology that it merits a separate discipline in its own right (Neisser, 1967; see Chapter 8).

According to cognitivists, a psychology based solely on rewards and punishments will never be adequate because our *interpretation* of rewards and punishments is a crucial determinant of our behavior. Take a student who receives a B+ on his first psychology exam. A student accustomed to getting Fs on his tests might regard this grade as a reward, whereas a student accustomed to As might view it as a punishment. Without understanding how people evaluate information, cognitivists maintain, we'll never fully grasp the causes of their behavior. Moreover, according to cognitivists, we often learn not merely by rewards and punishments but by *insight,* that is, by grasping the underlying nature of problems (see Chapter 8).

Cognitive psychology is a thriving approach today, and its tentacles have spread to such diverse domains as language, problem solving, concept formation, intelligence, memory, and even psychotherapy. By focusing not merely on rewards and punishments but on organisms' interpretation of them, cognitivism has encouraged psychologists to peek inside the black box to examine the connections between inputs and outputs. Moreover, cognitivism has increasingly established strong linkages to the study of brain functioning, allowing psychologists to better understand the physiological bases of thinking, memory, and other mental functions (Ilardi & Feldman, 2001). A burgeoning field, **cognitive neuroscience**, which examines the relation between brain functioning and thinking, has come to the fore over the past decade or so (Gazzaniga, Ivry, & Mangun, 2002). Cognitive neuroscience and the allied field of affective neuroscience (Panksepp, 2004), which examines the relation between brain functioning and emotion, hold out the promise of allowing us to better understand the biological processes associated with thinking and feeling.

PSYCHOANALYSIS: THE DEPTHS OF THE UNCONSCIOUS. Around the time that behaviorism was becoming dominant in the United States, a parallel movement was gathering momentum in Europe. This field, psychoanalysis, was founded by Viennese neurologist Sigmund Freud (1856–1939). In sharp contrast to behaviorism, **psychoanalysis** focused on internal psychological processes, especially impulses, thoughts, and memories of which we're unaware. According to Freud (1900) and other psychoanalysts, the primary influences on behavior aren't forces outside the organism, like rewards and punishments, but rather unconscious drives, especially sexuality and aggression.

John B. Watson, one of the founders of behaviorism. Watson's stubborn insistence on scientific rigor made him a hero to some and an enemy to others.

Two students may react to the same grade on a test—say a B+—in markedly different ways. One may be pleased, the other disappointed. Cognitive psychologists would say that these differing reactions stem from the students' differing interpretations of what these grades mean to them.

cognitive psychology
school of psychology that proposes that thinking is central to understanding behavior

cognitive neuroscience
relatively new field of psychology that examines the relation between brain functioning and thinking

psychoanalysis
school of psychology, founded by Sigmund Freud, that focuses on internal psychological processes of which we're unaware

The couch that Sigmund Freud used to psychoanalyze his patients, now located in the Freud museum in London, England. Contrary to popular conception, most psychologists aren't psychotherapists, and most psychotherapists aren't even psychoanalysts. Nor do most modern therapists ask patients to recline on couches.

Psychoanalysts maintain that much of our everyday psychological life is filled with symbols—things that represent other things (Loevinger, 1987; Moore & Fine, 1995). For example, if you refer accidentally to one of your female professors as "Mom," Freudians would be unlikely to treat this embarrassing blooper as an isolated mistake. Instead, they'd quickly suggest that your professor probably reminds you of your mother, which may be a good reason to transfer to a different course. The goal of the psychoanalyst is to decode the symbolic meaning of our slips of the tongue (or *Freudian slips,* as they're often called), dreams, and psychological symptoms. By doing so, psychoanalysts contend, they can get to the roots of our deep-seated psychological conflicts. Psychoanalysts also place considerably more emphasis than do other schools of thought on the role of infant and childhood experience. For Freud and others, the core of our personalities is molded in the first few years of life.

The influence of Freud and psychoanalysis on scientific psychology is controversial. On the one hand, some critics insist that psychoanalysis retarded the progress of scientific psychology because it focused heavily on unconscious processes that are difficult or impossible to falsify. As we'll learn in Chapter 14, these critics probably have a point (Crews, 2005; Esterson, 1993). On the other hand, at least some psychoanalytic claims, such as the assertion that a great deal of important mental processing goes on outside of conscious awareness, have held up well in scientific research (Westen, 1998; Wilson, 2002). It's not clear, however, whether the Freudian view of the unconscious bears anything more than a superficial resemblance to more contemporary views of unconscious processing (Kihlstrom, 1987; see Chapter 14).

■ The Multifaceted World of Modern Psychology

Psychology isn't just one discipline, but rather an assortment of many subdisciplines. These subdisciplines differ widely in their preferred level of analysis, ranging all the way from biological to cultural. In most major psychology departments, we can find researchers examining areas as varied as the neurological bases of visual perception, the mechanisms of memory, the causes of prejudice, and the treatment of depression.

THE GROWTH OF A FIELD. Today, there are about 500,000 psychologists worldwide (Kassin, 2004), with more than 100,000 in the United States alone (McFall, 2006). The American Psychological Association (APA), founded in 1892 and now the world's largest association of psychologists, consists of more than 150,000 members. (To give us a sense of how much the field has grown, there were only 150 APA members in 1900.) The percentage of women and minorities within the APA has grown steadily, too. These members' interests span such topics as addiction, art psychology, clinical psychology, hypnosis, law and psychology, media psychology, mental retardation, neuroscience, psychology and religion, sports psychology, the psychology of women, and gay, lesbian, bisexual, and transgendered issues.

TYPES OF PSYCHOLOGISTS: FACT AND FICTION. FIGURE 1.9 shows a breakdown of the settings in which psychologists work. As we can see, some work primarily in research settings, others primarily in practice settings. **TABLE 1.7** describes a few of the most important types of psychologists whose work we'll encounter in this book. It also dispels common misconceptions about what each type of psychologist does. **Explore**

As we can see, the field of psychology is remarkably diverse, as are the types of careers psychology majors pursue. Moreover, the face of psychology is changing, with more

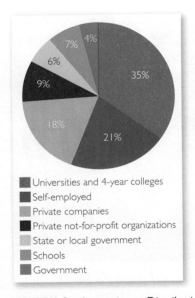

Universities and 4-year colleges
Self-employed
Private companies
Private not-for-profit organizations
State or local government
Schools
Government

FIGURE 1.9 Approximate Distribution of Psychologists in Different Settings.
Psychologists are employed in a diverse array of settings. (*Source:* Data from National Science Foundation, 2003)

Explore Psychologists at Work on
mypsychlab.com

Psychologists Elizabeth Loftus (1) and Paul Meehl (2) are far less well known to the general public than psychologists Dr. Phil (3) and John Gray (4), but they've had a much greater impact on how we think about ourselves and the world.

(1)   (2)   (3)   (4)

TABLE 1.7 Types of Psychologists, What They Do, and What They Don't Do.

TYPE OF PSYCHOLOGIST	WHAT DO THEY DO?	FREQUENT MISCONCEPTION AND TRUTH
Clinical Psychologist 	• Perform assessment, diagnosis, and treatment of mental disorders • Conduct research on people with mental disorders • Work in colleges and universities, mental health centers, or private practice	*Misconception: You need a Ph.D. to become a therapist.* • **Truth:** Most clinical psychology Ph.D. programs are highly research oriented. Other options for therapists are a Psy.D. (doctor of psychology), which focuses on training therapists rather than researchers, or an M.S.W., a master's degree in social work, which also focuses on training therapists.
Counseling Psychologist	• Work with people experiencing temporary or relatively self-contained life problems, like marital conflict, sexual difficulties, occupational stressors, or career uncertainty • Work in counseling centers, hospitals, or private practice (although some work in academic and research settings)	*Misconception: Counseling psychology is pretty much the same as clinical psychology.* • **Truth:** Whereas clinical psychologists work with people with serious mental disorders like severe depression, most counseling psychologists don't.
School Psychologist	• Work with teachers, parents, and children to remedy students' behavioral, emotional, and learning difficulties	*Misconception: School psychology is another term for educational psychology.* • **Truth:** Educational psychology is a substantially different discipline that focuses on helping instructors identify better methods for teaching and evaluating learning.
Developmental Psychologist	• Study how and why people change over time • Conduct research on infants', children's, and sometimes adults' and elderly people's emotional, physiological, and cognitive processes and how these change with age	*Misconception: Developmental psychologists spend most of their time on their hands and knees playing with children.* • **Truth:** Most spend their time in the laboratory, collecting and analyzing data.
Experimental Psychologist	• Use research methods to study memory, language, thinking and social behaviors of humans • Work primarily in research settings	*Misconception: Experimental psychologists do all of their work in psychological laboratories.* • **Truth:** Many conduct research in real-world settings, examining how people acquire language, remember events, apply mental concepts, and the like, in everyday life.
Biological Psychologist	• Examine the physiological bases of behavior in animals and humans • Most work in research settings	*Misconception: All biological psychologists use invasive methods in their research.* • **Truth:** Although many biological psychologists create brain lesions in animals to examine their effects on behavior, others use brain imaging methods that don't require investigators to damage organisms' nervous systems.
Forensic Psychologist 	• Work in prisons, jails, and other settings to assess and diagnose inmates and assist with their rehabilitation and treatment • Others conduct research on eyewitness testimony or jury decision making • Typically hold degrees in clinical or counseling psychology	*Misconception: Most forensic psychologists are criminal profilers, like those employed by the FBI.* • **Truth:** Criminal profiling is a small and controversial (as we'll learn in Chapter 14) subspecialty within forensic psychology.
Industrial-Organizational Psychologists 	• Work in companies and businesses to help select productive employees, evaluate performance, examine the effects of different working or living conditions on people's behavior (called *environmental psychologists*) • Design equipment to maximize employee performance and minimize accidents (called *human factors or engineering psychologists*)	*Misconception: Most industrial/organizational psychologists work on a one-to-one basis with employees to increase their motivation and productivity.* • **Truth:** Most spend their time constructing tests and selection procedures or implementing organizational changes to improve worker productivity or satisfaction.

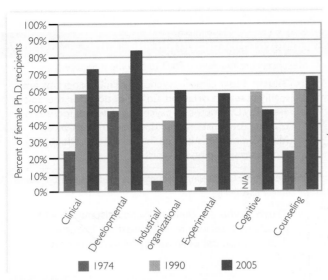

FIGURE 1.10   The Face of Psychology Has Changed Dramatically over the Past Three Decades.   Across most areas, the percentage of women earning doctoral degrees has increased. In clinical and developmental psychology, women comprise three-fourths to four-fifths of those attaining Ph.D.s. (Source: www.apa.org/monitor/jun07/changing.html)

FICTOID ✖

MYTH: If you want to become a psychotherapist, you don't need to learn about research.

REALITY: The "scientist–practitioner model" of training—often called the "Boulder model" because it was formulated over 60 years ago at a conference in Boulder, Colorado—is the predominant model for educating clinical psychology Ph.D. students. This model requires all graduate students, even those who intend to become therapists, to receive extensive training in how to interpret psychological research.

---

evolutionary psychology
discipline that applies Darwin's theory of natural selection to human and animal behavior

"The title of my science project is 'My Little Brother: Nature or Nurture.'"

---

women and minorities entering many of its subfields (see **FIGURE 1.10**). Despite their differences in content, all of these areas of psychology have one thing in common: Most of the psychologists who specialize in them rely on scientific methods (see Chapter 2). Specifically, they use scientific methods to generate new findings about human or animal behavior, or use existing findings to enhance human welfare. But as we've discussed, many pseudoscientists try to lead us to believe that they're using a genuinely scientific approach. Throughout this text, we'll highlight ways that pseudoscience has infiltrated popular beliefs about psychology and ways that good science has helped to guard us against pseudoscience.

■ The Great Debates of Psychology

Now that we've learned a bit about the past and present of psychology, we need to set the stage for things to come. Two great debates have shaped the field of psychology since its inception and seem likely to continue to shape it in the future. Because these debates are alive and well, we'll find traces of them in virtually all of the chapters of this text.

THE NATURE–NURTURE DEBATE.   The nature–nurture debate poses the following question: *Are our behaviors attributable mostly to our genes (nature) or to our rearing environments (nurture)?*

As we'll discover later in this text, the nature–nurture debate has proven especially controversial in the domains of intelligence, personality, and psychopathology (mental illness). Like most major debates in psychology, this one has a lengthy history. Many early thinkers, such as British philosopher John Locke (1632–1704), likened the human mind at birth to white paper that hadn't been written on. Others after him referred to the mind as a *tabula rasa* ("blank slate"). For Locke and his followers, we enter the world with no genetic preconceptions or preconceived ideas: We're shaped exclusively by our environments (Pinker, 2002).

For much of the 20th century, most psychologists assumed that virtually all human behavior was exclusively a product of learning. But research conducted by *behavior geneticists,* who use sophisticated designs such as twin and adoption studies (see Chapter 3), shows that the most important psychological traits, including intelligence, interests, personality, and many mental illnesses, are influenced substantially by genes. Increasingly, modern psychologists have come to recognize that human behavior is attributable not only to our environments but to our genes (Bouchard, 2004; Harris, 2002; Pinker, 2002).

Current Status of the Nature–Nurture Debate.   Some people have declared the nature–nurture debate dead (Ferris, 1996), because just about everyone now agrees that both genes and environment play crucial roles in most human behaviors. Yet this debate is far from dead because we still have a great deal to learn about how much nature or nurture contributes to different behaviors and how nature and nurture work together. Indeed, we'll discover in later chapters that the old dichotomy between nature and nurture is far less clear-cut—and far more interesting—than once believed. Nature and nurture sometimes intersect in complex and surprising ways (see Chapters 6, 10, and 14).

Evolutionary Psychology.   One domain of psychology that's shed light on the nature–nurture debate is **evolutionary psychology**, sometimes also called *sociobiology*: a discipline that applies Darwin's theory of natural selection to human and animal behavior

(Barkow, Cosmides, & Tooby, 1992; Dennett, 1995; Tooby & Cosmides, 1989). It begins with the assumption, shared by William James and other functionalists, that many human psychological systems, like memory, emotion, and personality, serve key adaptive functions: They help organisms survive and reproduce. Darwin and his followers suggested that natural selection favored certain kinds of mental traits, just as it did physical ones, like our hands, livers, and hearts.

Biologists refer to *fitness* as the extent to which a trait increases the chances that organisms that possess this trait will survive and reproduce at a higher rate than competitors who lack it (see Chapter 3). Fitness has nothing to do, by the way, with how strong or powerful an organism is. By surviving and reproducing at higher rates than other organisms, more fit organisms pass on their genes more successfully to later generations. For example, humans who have at least some degree of anxiety probably survived at higher rates than humans who lacked it, because anxiety serves an essential function: It warns us of impending danger (Barlow, 2000).

Still, evolutionary psychology has received more than its share of criticism (Kitcher, 1985; Panksepp & Panksepp, 2000). Many of its predictions are extremely difficult to falsify. In part, that's because behavior, unlike the bones of dinosaurs, early humans, and other animals, doesn't leave fossils. As a consequence, it's far more challenging to determine the evolutionary functions of anxiety or depression than the functions of birds' wings. For example, two researchers speculated that male baldness serves an evolutionary function, because women supposedly perceive a receding hairline as a sign of maturity (Muscarella & Cunningham, 1996). But if it turned out that women preferred men with lots of hair to bald men, it would be easy to cook up an explanation for that finding ("Women perceive men with a full head of hair as stronger and more athletic."). Evolutionary explanations could account for either outcome. Evolutionary psychology has the potential to be an important unifying framework for psychology (Buss, 1995), but we should beware of evolutionary explanations that can fit almost any piece of evidence after the fact (de Waal, 2002).

The fact that American men spend billions of dollars per year on hair replacement treatments is difficult to square with evolutionary hypotheses suggesting that women prefer bald men. The bottom line: Beware of unfalsifiable evolutionary stories.

THE FREE WILL–DETERMINISM DEBATE. The free will–determinism debate poses the following question: *To what extent are our behaviors freely selected rather than caused by factors outside of our control?*

Most of us like to believe that we're free to select any course of events we wish. Fewer truths seem more self-evident than the fact that we're free to do what we want whenever we want. You may believe that at this very moment you can decide to either continue reading to the end of the chapter or take a well-deserved break to watch TV. Indeed, our legal system is premised on the concept of free will. We punish criminals because they're supposedly free to abide by the law but choose otherwise. One major exception, of course, is the insanity defense, in which the legal system assumes that severe mental illness can interfere with people's free will (Hoffman & Morse, 2006; Stone, 1982). Some prominent psychologists agree that we all possess free will (Baumeister, 2008).

Yet many other psychologists maintain that free will is actually an illusion (Sappington, 1990; Wegner, 2002). It's such a powerful illusion, they insist, that we have a hard time imagining it could be an illusion. Some psychologists, like behaviorist B. F. Skinner (1971), argue that our sense of free will stems from the fact that we aren't consciously aware of the thousands of subtle environmental influences impinging on our behavior at any given moment. Much like puppets in a play who don't realize that actors are pulling their strings, we conclude mistakenly that we're free simply because we don't realize all of the influences acting on our behavior. For Skinner and others, our behaviors are completely determined: caused by preceding influences.

Some psychologists argue that most or even all of our behaviors are generated *automatically*—that is, without conscious awareness (Kirsch & Lynn, 1999; Libet, 1985). We may even come to believe that something or someone else is producing behaviors we ourselves are generating. For example, people who engage in *automatic writing*—writing sentences while seemingly in a trance—typically insist they're being compelled to do so by some outside force. But there's overwhelming evidence that they're generating this behavior themselves, although unconsciously (Wegner, 2002). According to many determinists, our everyday behaviors are produced in the same way—triggered automatically by influences of which we're unaware (Bargh & Chartrand, 1999).

FACTOID

Inducing students to believe in determinism—by having them read a scientific passage suggesting that free will is an illusion—makes them more likely to cheat on a test in the laboratory (Vohs & Schooler, 2008). So regardless of whether free will exists, belief in it may serve a useful function—inhibiting unethical behavior.

How Psychology Affects Our Lives

Basic = how mind works.

Applied: real-world

As we'll discover throughout this text, psychological science and scientific thinking offer important applications for a variety of aspects of everyday life. Psychological scientists often distinguish basic from applied research. **Basic research** examines how the mind works, whereas **applied research** examines how we can use basic research to solve real-world problems. Within most large psychology departments, we'll find a healthy mix of people conducting basic research, such as investigators who study the laws of learning, and applied research, such as investigators who study how to help people cope with the psychological burden of cancer.

APPLICATIONS OF PSYCHOLOGICAL RESEARCH. Surveys show that although most Americans hold positive views toward psychology, few are aware of the substantial impact on psychology on their everyday lives (Wood, Jones, & Benjamin, 1986). Indeed, psychological science has found its way into far more aspects of contemporary society than most of us realize (Salzinger, 2002; Zimbardo, 2004a). Let's look at a sampling of these applications; we can discover more about these and other examples on a free pamphlet produced by the American Psychological Association: http://www.decadeofbehavior.org/BehaviorMattersBooklet.pdf.

Increasingly, today's fire trucks are lime-yellow rather than red. That's because psychological research has demonstrated that lime-yellow objects are easier to spot in the dark than red objects.

- If you live in or near a big city, you may have noticed a gradual change in the color of fire engines. Although old fire engines were bright red, most new ones are lime-yellow. That's because psychological researchers who study perception found that lime-yellow objects are easier to detect in the dark. Indeed, lime-yellow fire trucks are only about half as likely to be involved in traffic accidents as red fire trucks (American Psychological Association, 2003; Solomon & King, 1995).
- As a car driver, have you ever had to slam on your brakes to avoid hitting a driver directly in front of you who stopped short suddenly? If so, and if you managed to avoid a bad accident, you may have John Voevodsky to thank. For decades, cars had only two brake lights. In the early 1970s, Voevodsky hit on the bright (pun intended) idea of placing a third brake light at the base of cars' back windshields. He reasoned that this additional visual information would decrease the risk of rear-end collisions. He conducted a 10-month study of taxis with and without the new brake lights and found a 61 percent lower rate of rear-end accidents in the first group (Voevodsky, 1974). As a result of his research, all new American cars have three brake lights.

Smart move.

Thanks to psychological research, advertisers know that placing a model's face on the left and written text on the right of an advertisement best captures readers' attention.

- If you're anything like the average American, you see more than 100 commercial messages every day. The chances are that psychologists had a hand in crafting many of them. The founder of behaviorism, John B. Watson, pioneered the application of psychology to advertising in the 1920s and 1930s. Today, psychological researchers still contribute to the marketing success of companies. For instance, psychologists who study magazine advertisements have discovered that human faces better capture readers' attention on the left rather than on the right side of pages. Written text, in contrast, better captures readers' attention on the right rather than on the left side of pages (Clay, 2002).
- To get into college, you probably had to take one or more tests, like the SAT or ACT. If so, you can thank—or blame—psychologists with expertise in measuring academic achievement and knowledge, who were primarily responsible for developing these measures (Zimbardo, 2004a). Although these tests are far from perfect predictors of academic performance, they do significantly better than chance in forecasting how students perform in college (Geiser & Studley, 2002; Sackett, Borneman, & Connelly, 2008; see Chapter 9).
- Police officers often ask victims of violent crimes to select a suspect from a lineup. When doing so, they've traditionally used *simultaneous lineups,* in which one or more suspects and several decoys (people who aren't really suspects) are lined up

basic research
research examining how the mind works

applied research
research examining how we can use basic research to solve real-world problems

sequential > simultaneous

in a row, often of five to eight individuals (see Chapter 7). These are the kinds of lineups we've most often seen on television crime shows. Yet psychological research shows that *sequential lineups*—those in which victims view each person individually and then decide whether he or she was the perpetrator of the crime—are generally more accurate than simultaneous lineups (Cutler & Wells, 2009; Steblay et al., 2003; Wells, Memon, & Penrod, 2006). As a result of this research, police departments around the United States are increasingly using sequential rather than simultaneous lineups.

- For many years, many American public schools were legally required to be racially segregated. Before 1954, the law of the land in the United States was that "separate but equal" facilities were sufficient to guarantee racial equality. But based in part on the pioneering research of psychologists Kenneth and Mamie Clark (1950), who demonstrated that African American children preferred White to African American dolls, the U.S. Supreme Court decided—in the landmark 1954 case of *Brown v. Board of Education of Topeka, Kansas*—that school segregation exerted a negative impact on the self-esteem of African American children.

So, far more than most of us realize, the fruits of psychological research are all around us. Psychology has dramatically altered the landscape of everyday life.

A classic simultaneous eyewitness lineup. Although police commonly use such lineups, most research suggests that they're more prone to error than sequential lineups.

THINKING SCIENTIFICALLY: IT'S A WAY OF LIFE. As you embark on your journey to the rest of the field of psychology, we leave you with one crucial take-home point: Learning to think scientifically will help you make better decisions not only in this course and other psychology courses, but in everyday life. Each day, the news and entertainment media bombard us with confusing and contradictory claims about a host of topics: herbal remedies, weight loss plans, parenting methods, insomnia treatments, speed-reading courses, urban legends, political conspiracy theories, unidentified flying objects, and "overnight cures" for mental disorders, to name only a few. Some of these claims are at least partly true, whereas others are entirely bogus. Yet the media typically offer little guidance for sorting out which claims are scientific, pseudoscientific, or a bit of both. It's scarcely any wonder that we're often tempted to throw up our hands in despair and ask "What I am supposed to believe?"

The classic doll studies of Kenneth and Mamie Clark paved the way for the 1954 Supreme Court decision of *Brown v. Board of Education,* which mandated racial integration of public schools.

Fortunately, the scientific thinking skills you've encountered in this chapter—and that you'll come to know and (we hope!) love in later chapters—can assist you in successfully navigating the bewildering world of popular psychology and popular culture. The trick is to bear three words in mind throughout this text and in daily life: "Insist on evidence." By recognizing that common sense can take us only so far in evaluating claims, we can come to appreciate the need for scientific evidence to avoid being fooled—and to avoid fooling ourselves. But how do we collect this scientific evidence, and how do we evaluate it? We're about to find out in the next chapter.

INSIST ON EVIDENCE!

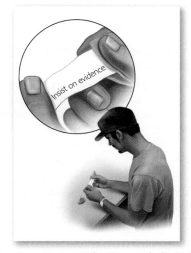

assess your knowledge   FACT OR FICTION?

1. Behaviorism focuses on uncovering the general laws of learning in animals, but not humans. **True / False**

2. Cognitive psychologists argue that we need to understand how organisms interpret rewards and punishments. **True / False** *thinking*

3. Advocates of determinism believe that free will is an illusion. **True / False**

4. Studying color discrimination in the lab is basic research, whereas testing which color fire truck results in the fewest traffic accidents is applied research. **True / False**

5. Achievement tests, such as the SAT, do no better than chance at predicting how students will perform in college. **True / False** *do better than chance*

Answers: 1. F (p.30); 2. T (p.31); 3. T (p.35); 4. T (p.36); 5. F (p.36)

When it comes to evaluating psychological claims in the news or entertainment media, there's a simple bottom-line message: We should always insist on rigorous research evidence.

✓ **Study** and **Review** on **mypsychlab.com**

WHAT IS PSYCHOLOGY? SCIENCE VERSUS INTUITION 2–10

1.1 EXPLAIN WHY PSYCHOLOGY IS MORE THAN JUST COMMON SENSE.

Psychology is the scientific study of the mind, brain, and behavior. Although we often rely on our common sense to understand the psychological world, our intuitive understanding of ourselves and others is often mistaken. Naive realism is the error of believing that we see the world precisely as it is. It can lead us to false beliefs about ourselves and our world, such as believing that our perceptions and memories are always accurate.

1. Which would be a better description of naive realism, "seeing is believing" or "believing is seeing"? (p. 5)

2. What does Shepard's table illusion tell us about our ability to trust our own intuitions and experiences? (p. 5)

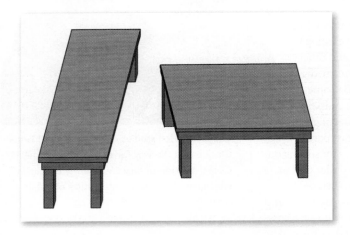

3. Our common sense (is/isn't) always wrong. (p. 5)

1.2 EXPLAIN THE IMPORTANCE OF SCIENCE AS A SET OF SAFEGUARDS AGAINST BIASES.

Confirmation bias is the tendency to seek out evidence that supports our hypotheses and deny, dismiss, or distort evidence that doesn't. Belief perseverance is the tendency to cling to our beliefs despite contrary evidence. The scientific method is a set of safeguards against these two errors.

4. Science is a(n) _____ to evidence. (p. 6)

5. A scientific model like the Big Bang theory, which provides an explanation for a large number of findings in the natural world, is known as a _____ _____. (p. 7)

6. In scientific research, _____ are general explanations, whereas _____ are specific predictions derived from these explanations. (p. 7)

7. Review each of the statements in the table below and identify whether each is a theory (T) or hypothesis (H). (p. 7)

T OR H	EXPLANATION
1. _____	Sarah's motivation for cheating on the test was fear of failure.
2. _____	Darwin's evolutionary model explains the changes in species over time.
3. _____	The universe began in a gigantic explosion about 14 billion years ago.
4. _____	Our motivation to help a stranger in need is influenced by the number of people present.
5. _____	Crime rates in Nashville increase as the temperature rises.

8. When presented with both contradictory and supportive evidence regarding a hypothesis we are researching, our tendency to disregard the contradictory evidence is our _____ _____. (p. 8)

9. Our _____ _____ kicks in when we refuse to admit our beliefs are incorrect in the face of evidence that contradicts them. (p. 9)

10. Metaphysical claims, such as the existence of God, the soul, or the afterlife, differ from pseudoscientific claims in that they aren't _____. (p. 9)

PSYCHOLOGICAL PSEUDOSCIENCE: IMPOSTERS OF SCIENCE 11–20

1.3 DESCRIBE PSYCHOLOGICAL PSEUDOSCIENCE AND DISTINGUISH IT FROM PSYCHOLOGICAL SCIENCE.

Pseudoscientific claims appear scientific but don't play by the rules of science. In particular, pseudoscience lacks the safeguards against confirmation bias and belief perseverance that characterize science.

11. The growth of popular psychology has led to a _____ explosion. (p. 11)

12. About _____ percent of self-help books are untested. (p. 11)

13. There are over 500 "brands" of _____, with new ones being added every year. (p. 11)

14. A recent survey of the American public shows that pseudoscientific and other questionable beliefs are (rare/widespread). (p. 12)

15. Match the warning signs of pseudoscience with the examples shown. (p. 13)

EXAMPLE	SIGN OF PSEUDOSCIENCE
1. _____ Three simple steps will change your love life forever!	a. Meaningless "psychobabble" that uses fancy scientific-sounding terms that don't make sense
2. _____ This woman practiced yoga daily for three weeks and hasn't had a day of depression since.	b. Exaggerated claims
3. _____ Amazing new innovations in research have shown that eye massage results in reading speeds 10 times faster than average!	c. Overreliance on anecdotes
4. _____ Fifty studies conducted by the company all show overwhelming success!	d. Lack of self-correction when contrary evidence is published
5. _____ Although some scientists say that we use almost all of our brain, we've found a way to harness additional brain power previously undiscovered.	e. Absence of connectivity to other research
6. _____ Sine-wave filtered auditory stimulation is carefully designed to encourage maximal orbitofrontal dendritic development.	f. Talk of "proof" instead of "evidence"
7. _____ Our new program is proven to reduce social anxiety by at least 50 percent!	g. Lack of review by other scholars (called *peer review*) or replication by independent labs

1.4 IDENTIFY REASONS WE ARE DRAWN TO PSEUDOSCIENCE.

We are drawn to pseudoscientific beliefs because the human mind tends to perceive sense in nonsense and order in disorder. Although generally adaptive, this tendency can lead us to see patterns when they don't exist. Pseudoscientific claims can result in opportunity costs and direct harm due to dangerous treatments. They can also lead us to think less scientifically about other important domains of modern life.

16. Although the tendency to make order out of disorder is generally _____, it can lead us astray into pseudoscientific thinking. (p. 14)

17. Apophenia is the tendency for us to make meaningful connections among (related/unrelated) phenomena. (p. 14)

18. We may attribute paranormal significance to coincidences that are probably due to _____. (p. 14)

19. The tendency to see meaningful images in meaningless visual stimuli is called _____. (p. 15)

20. According to _____ _____ theory, our awareness of our own inevitable death leaves many of us with an underlying sense of terror. (p. 17)

SCIENTIFIC THINKING: DISTINGUISHING FACT FROM FICTION 20–26

1.5 IDENTIFY THE KEY FEATURES OF SCIENTIFIC SKEPTICISM.

Scientific skepticism requires us to evaluate all claims with an open mind but to insist on compelling evidence before accepting them. Scientific skeptics evaluate claims on their own merits and are unwilling to accept them on the basis of authority alone.

21. Being open-minded but conservative about accepting claims without evidence is _____ _____. (p. 20)

1.6 IDENTIFY AND EXPLAIN THE TEXT'S SIX PRINCIPLES OF SCIENTIFIC THINKING.

Six key scientific thinking principles are ruling out rival hypotheses, correlation versus causation, falsifiability, replicability, extraordinary claims, and Occam's Razor.

22. The skill set for evaluating all claims in an open-minded and careful manner, both inside and outside the classroom or laboratory, is called _____ _____. (p. 21)

23. Scientific thinking (can/can't) be applied to claims in the media, Internet, self-help books, and any other information outlet outside the psychology laboratory. (p. 21)

Answers are located at the end of the text.

24. When evaluating a claim, we should ask ourselves whether we're excluded other plausible _____ for it. (p. 21)

25. The assumption that because one thing is associated with another, it must cause the other is the definition of the _____ _____ . (p. 23)

26. A claim is considered _____ if it could in principle be disproved. (p. 23)

27. The ability of others to consistently duplicate a study's findings is called _____. (p. 24)

28. Occam's Razor is also called the principle of _____. (p. 25)

29. How would you use Occam's Razor to select among different explanations for crop circles like this one? (p. 26)

30. Match the scientific thinking principle (left) with the accurate description (right). (pp. 21–26).

NAME OF SCIENTIFIC THINKING PRINCIPLE	EXPLANATION OF SCIENTIFIC THINKING PRINCIPLE
1. _____ Ruling Out Rival Hypotheses	a. Claims must be capable of being disproved.
2. _____ Correlation versus Causation	b. If two hypotheses explain a phenomenon equally well, we should generally select the simpler one.
3. _____ Falsifiability	c. The fact that two things are associated with each other doesn't mean that one causes the other.
4. _____ Replicability	d. The more a claim contradicts what we already know, the more persuasive the evidence for this claim must be before we should accept it.
5. _____ Extraordinary Claims	e. A finding must be capable of being duplicated by independent researchers following the same "recipe."
6. _____ Occam's Razor	f. Findings consistent with several hypotheses require additional research to eliminate these hypotheses.

PSYCHOLOGY'S PAST AND PRESENT: WHAT A LONG, STRANGE TRIP IT'S BEEN 27–37

1.7 IDENTIFY THE MAJOR THEORETICAL FRAMEWORKS OF PSYCHOLOGY.

Five major theoretical orientations have played key roles in shaping the field. Structuralism aimed to identify the basic elements of experience through the method of introspection. Functionalism hoped to understand the adaptive purposes of behavior. Behaviorism grew out of the belief that psychological science must be completely objective and derived from laws of learning. The cognitive view emphasized the importance of mental processes in understanding behavior. Psychoanalysis focused on unconscious processes and urges as causes of behavior.

31. Structuralism aimed to identify the basic elements of thought through _____. (p. 27)

32. For traditional behaviorists, the human mind is a _____ _____: We know what goes into it and what comes out of it, but we needn't worry about what happens between inputs and outputs. (p. 31)

33. Cognitivists believe our _____ of rewards and punishments is a crucial determinant of our behavior. (p. 31)

1.8 DESCRIBE DIFFERENT TYPES OF PSYCHOLOGISTS AND IDENTIFY WHAT EACH OF THEM DOES.

There are many types of psychologists. Clinical and counseling psychologists often conduct therapy. School psychologists develop intervention programs for children in school settings. Industrial/organizational psychologists often work in companies and business and are involved in maximizing employee performance. Many forensic psychologists work in prisons or court settings. Many other psychologists conduct research. For example, developmental psychologists study systematic change in individuals over time. Experimental psychologists study learning and thinking, and biological psychologists study the biological basis of behavior.

34. You (need/don't need) a Ph.D. to become a therapist. (p. 33)

35. How do developmental psychologists spend the bulk of their time? (p. 33)

Developmental Psychologist

1.9 DESCRIBE THE TWO GREAT DEBATES THAT HAVE SHAPED THE FIELD OF PSYCHOLOGY.

The two great debates are the nature–nurture debate, which asks whether our behaviors are attributable mostly to our genes (nature) or our rearing environments (nurture), and the free will–determinism debate, which asks to what extent our behaviors are freely selected rather than caused by factors outside our control. Both debates continue to shape the field of psychology.

36. _____ _____, a discipline that applies Darwin's theory of natural selection to human and animal behavior, has shed light on the nature–nurture debate. (p. 34)

37. Many psychologists, such as B. F. Skinner, believe that free will is a(n) _____. (p. 35)

1.10 DESCRIBE HOW PSYCHOLOGICAL RESEARCH AFFECTS OUR DAILY LIVES.

Psychological research has shown how psychology can be applied to such diverse fields as advertising, public safety, the criminal justice system, and education.

38. _____ research examines how the mind works, whereas _____ research examines how we use research to solve real-world problems. (p. 36)

39. What have psychologists who study magazine advertisements learned about how best to capture readers' attention? (p. 36)

40. Psychologists with expertise in measuring academic achievement and knowledge were primarily responsible for developing the _____ and _____ tests. (p. 36)

DO YOU KNOW THESE TERMS?

- psychology (p. 3)
- levels of analysis (p. 3)
- multiply determined (p. 3)
- individual differences (p. 4)
- naive realism (p. 5)
- scientific theory (p. 7)
- hypothesis (p. 7)
- confirmation bias (p. 8)
- belief perseverance (p. 9)

- metaphysical claim (p. 9)
- pseudoscience (p. 11)
- ad hoc immunizing hypothesis (p. 12)
- apophenia (p. 14)
- pareidolia (p. 15)
- terror management theory (p. 17)
- scientific skepticism (p. 20)
- critical thinking (p. 21)

- correlation–causation fallacy (p. 23)
- variable (p. 23)
- falsifiable (p. 23)
- replicability (p. 24)
- introspection (p. 27)
- structuralism (p. 29)
- functionalism (p. 30)
- natural selection (p. 30)

- behaviorism (p. 30)
- cognitive psychology (p. 31)
- cognitive neuroscience (p. 31)
- psychoanalysis (p. 31)
- evolutionary psychology (p. 34)
- basic research (p. 36)
- applied research (p. 36)

APPLY YOUR SCIENTIFIC THINKING SKILLS

Use your scientific thinking skills to answer the following questions, referencing specific scientific thinking principles and common errors in reasoning whenever possible.

1. Psychology is a discipline that spans many levels of analysis, yet the popular media often assigns only a single cause to a complex issue. Locate three media articles on an issue, such as homelessness or terrorism, and compare their views on the root causes and possible solutions to this issue. How many levels of analysis does each article consider?

2. How can our scientific thinking skills help us to evaluate the seemingly conflicting news we hear about nutrition and exercise? Choose a health topic to investigate further (for example: How much exercise do we need each day? Is drinking red wine every day healthy? Should we limit our intake of carbohydrates?) and locate three articles with conflicting views on the topic. What errors or logical fallacies do the articles

commit? How can you evaluate the accuracy of the articles and advice they provide?

3. Confirmation bias is widespread in everyday life, especially in the world of politics. Take a political issue that's been controversial in recent months (such as health care, our nation's approach to terrorism, or abortion), and locate two opinion pieces that adopt opposing stances on this issue. Did each author attempt to avoid confirmation bias—for example, by acknowledging and thoughtfully discussing arguments that might challenge his or her position—or instead fall victim to confirmation bias? Did each author try to interpret contrary evidence in a fair or in a biased fashion? Explain your answer with reference to one or more specific examples in each case.

2 RESEARCH METHODS

safeguards against error

THINK ABOUT IT

DO WE REALLY NEED RESEARCH DESIGNS TO FIGURE OUT THE ANSWERS TO PSYCHOLOGICAL QUESTIONS?

HOW DO OUR INTUITIONS SOMETIMES DECEIVE US?

CAN WE PERCEIVE STATISTICAL ASSOCIATIONS EVEN WHEN THEY DON'T EXIST?

WHAT'S AN "EXPERIMENT," AND IS IT JUST LIKE ANY OTHER PSYCHOLOGICAL STUDY?

HOW CAN WE BE FOOLED BY STATISTICS?

Autism is a motor disorder, not a mental disorder.

Facilitated communication in action. The rationale is that, because of a severe motor impairment, some children with autism are unable to speak or type on their own. Therefore, with the help of a facilitator, they can supposedly type out complete sentences on a keyboard or letter pad. Is it too good to be true?

extraordinary claims

IS THE EVIDENCE AS STRONG AS THE CLAIM?

Jenny Storch was 14 years old, but she was no ordinary teenager. She was mute. Like all people with infantile autism, a severe psychological disorder that begins in early childhood (see Chapter 15), Jenny's language and ability to bond with others were severely impaired. Like three-fourths of individuals with infantile autism (American Psychiatric Association, 2000), Jenny had mental retardation. And, like all parents of children with infantile autism, Mark and Laura Storch were desperate to find some means of connecting emotionally with their child.

In the fall of 1991, Mark and Laura Storch had enrolled Jenny in the Devereux School in Red Hook, New York. Only a year before, Douglas Biklen, a professor of education at Syracuse University, had published an article announcing the development of a technique called *facilitated communication*. Developed in Australia, facilitated communication was a stunning breakthrough in the treatment of infantile autism—or so it seemed.

Facilitated communication possessed a charming simplicity that somehow rang true. A "facilitator" sits next to the child with autism, who in turn sits in front of a computer keyboard or letter pad. According to Biklen, the facilitator must be present because infantile autism is actually a motor (movement) disorder, not a mental disorder as scientists had long assumed. Boldly challenging conventional wisdom, Biklen (1990) proclaimed that children with autism are just as intelligent as other children. But they suffer from a severe motor disorder that prevents them from talking or typing on their own. By holding the child's hands ever so gently, the facilitator permits the child to communicate by typing out words. Not just isolated words, like *Mommy,* but complete sentences like, *Mommy, I want you to know that I love you even though I can't speak.* Using facilitated communication, one child with autism even asked his mother to change his medication after reading an article in a medical journal (Mann, 2005). Facilitated communication was the long-sought-after bridge between the hopelessly isolated world of children with autism and the adult world of social interaction.

The psychiatric aides at Devereux had heard about facilitated communication, which was beginning to spread like wildfire throughout the autism treatment community. Thousands of mental health and education professionals across America were using it with apparently astonishing effects. Almost immediately after trying facilitated communication with Jenny, the Devereux aides similarly reported amazing results. For the first time, Jenny produced eloquent statements describing her innermost thoughts and feelings, including her deep love for her parents. The emotional bond with Jenny that Mark and Laura Storch had dreamt of for 14 years was at last a reality.

Yet the Storchs' joy proved to be short-lived. In November 1991, Mark Storch received a startling piece of news that was to forever change his life. With the aid of a facilitator, Jenny had begun to type out allegations of brutal sexual abuse against him. When all was said and done, Jenny had typed out 200 gruesome accusations of rape, all supposedly perpetrated by her father. A second facilitator, who'd heard about these accusations, reported similar findings while assisting Jenny at the keyboard.

Although there was no physical evidence against Mark Storch, the Department of Social Services in Ulster County, New York, restricted contact between Jenny and her parents and removed Jenny from the Storch home. Jenny was eventually returned to her parents following a legal challenge, but not before Mark Storch's reputation had been stained.

The claims of facilitated communication proponents seemed extraordinary. Was the evidence for these claims equally extraordinary?

Since Douglas Biklen introduced facilitated communication to the United States, dozens of investigators have examined this procedure under tightly controlled laboratory conditions. In a typical study, the facilitator and child are seated in adjoining cubicles. A wall separates them, but an opening between them permits hand-to-hand contact on a keyboard (see **FIGURE 2.1**). Then, researchers flash two different pictures on adjacent screens, one of which is seen only by the facilitator and the other of which is seen only by the child. The facilitator might view a photograph of a dog, the child a photograph of a cat. The crucial question is this: Will the word typed out by the child be the picture shown to the facilitator—*dog*—or the picture shown to the child—*cat*?

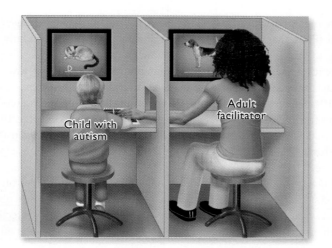

FIGURE 2.1 Putting Facilitated Communication to the Test. By placing a child with autism and the facilitator in adjoining cubicles and flashing different pictures to each of them on some trials, researchers demonstrated that the "facilitated communications" emanated from the mind of the facilitator, not the child.

The results of these studies were as stunning as they were unanimous. In virtually 100 percent of trials, the typed word corresponded to the picture flashed to the facilitator, not the child (Jacobson, Mulick, & Schwartz, 1995; Romancyzk et al., 2003). Unbelievable as it seems, facilitated communication originates entirely from the minds of facilitators. *Unbeknownst to facilitators, their hands are effortlessly guiding the fingers of children toward the keyboard, and the resulting words are coming from their minds, not the children's.* Scientists, who'd known about a similar phenomenon for decades before facilitated communication appeared on the scene, term it the *ideomotor effect,* because facilitators' ideas are unknowingly influencing their movements (Wegner, 2002). The facilitated communication keyboard turns out to be nothing more than a modern version of the Ouija board, a popular device used by spiritualists to communicate with the dead. Regrettably, proponents of facilitated communication neglected to consider rival hypotheses for its apparent effects.

> *[handwritten margin note: Facilitated communication is actually the communication of the facilitator, not the child.]*

◄ ruling out rival hypotheses

HAVE IMPORTANT ALTERNATIVE EXPLANATIONS FOR THE FINDINGS BEEN EXCLUDED?

THE BEAUTY AND NECESSITY OF GOOD RESEARCH DESIGN

2.1 Identify heuristics and biases that prevent us from thinking scientifically about psychology.

The facilitated communication story imparts an invaluable lesson that we'll highlight throughout this book: *Research design matters.* This story is also a powerful illustration of the triumph of good science over pseudoscience.

■ Why We Need Research Designs

Many beginning psychology students understandably wonder why they need to learn about research design. Some of you may be puzzling over the same thing: "I took this course to learn about people, not about numbers." The facilitated communication story tells us the answer. Without research designs, even intelligent people can be fooled. After all, the Devereux aides who worked with Jenny Storch "knew" that facilitated communication worked: Their naïve realism (see Chapter 1) led them to see Jenny's abuse allegations "with their own eyes." But like many advocates of pseudoscientific techniques, they were the victims of an illusion. Their confirmation bias (see Chapter 1) led them to see what they hoped to see. Had the proponents of other facilitated communication made use of some of the research designs we'll discuss in this chapter, they wouldn't have been fooled. As we learned in Chapter 1, the scientific method is a toolbox set of thinking skills that helps us to avoid being tricked by our own biases, including confirmation bias. In this chapter, we'll learn what these skills are and how we can use them to evaluate claims, both in psychology courses and in everyday life.

Let's take another tragic example. For several decades of the early twentieth century, mental health professionals were convinced that the technique of **prefrontal lobotomy** (referred to in popular lingo as a "lobotomy") was an effective treatment for schizophrenia

The facilitated communication keyboard appears to be little more than a modern version of the Ouija board, which is used widely in spiritual circles to supposedly "contact" the dead. Both rely on the ideomotor effect.

prefrontal lobotomy
surgical procedure that severs fibers connecting the frontal lobes of the brain from the underlying thalamus

and other severe mental disorders (see Chapter 16). Surgeons who used this technique severed the neural fibers that connect the brain's frontal lobes to the underlying thalamus (**FIGURE 2.2**).

The scientific world was so certain that prefrontal lobotomy was a remarkable breakthrough that they awarded its developer, Portuguese neurosurgeon Egas Moniz, the Nobel Prize in 1949. As in the case of facilitated communication, stunning reports of the effectiveness of prefrontal lobotomy were based almost exclusively on subjective clinical reports. One physician who performed lobotomies proclaimed, "I am a sensitive observer, and my conclusion is that a vast majority of my patients get better as opposed to worse after my treatment" (see Dawes, 1994, p. 48).

Like proponents of facilitated communication, believers in prefrontal lobotomy didn't conduct systematic research. They simply assumed that their clinical observations—"I can see that it works"—were sufficient evidence for this treatment's effectiveness. They were wrong; when scientists finally performed controlled studies on the effectiveness of prefrontal lobotomy, they found it to be virtually useless. The operation certainly produced radical changes in behavior, but it didn't target the specific behaviors associated with severe mental illness. Moreover, it created a host of other problems, including extreme apathy (Valenstein, 1986). Again, observers' naïve realism and confirmation bias had deceived them. Nowadays, prefrontal lobotomy is little more than a relic of an earlier pseudoscientific era of mental health treatment. Research design matters.

Think: One Flew Over the Cuckoo's Nest (handwritten)

■ Heuristics and Biases: How We Can be Fooled

At this point, you may be feeling a bit defensive. At first glance, the authors of your text may seem to be implying that many people, perhaps you included, are foolish. But we shouldn't take any of this personally, because one of our central themes is that we can *all* be fooled, and that includes your text's authors.

How can we all be fooled so easily? A key finding emerging from the past few decades of research is that *the same psychological processes that serve us well in most situations also predispose us to errors in thinking.* That is, most mistaken thinking is cut from the same cloth as useful thinking (Ariely, 2008; Lehrer, 2009; Pinker, 1997). ⊙—[**Simulate**

HEURISTICS: DOUBLE-EDGED SWORDS. Psychologists have identified several **heuristics**—mental shortcuts or rules of thumb—that help us to streamline our thinking and make sense of our world. These heuristics probably have evolutionary survival value, because without them we'd quickly become overwhelmed by the tens of thousands of pieces of information with which we're bombarded every day. According to cognitive psychologists (psychologists who study thought; see Chapters 1 and 8), we're all *cognitive misers* (Fiske & Taylor, 1991). That is, we're mentally lazy and try to conserve our mental energies by simplifying the world. Just as a miser doesn't spend much money, a cognitive miser doesn't expend any more effort in thinking than is necessary.

Although our heuristics work well most of the time (Gigerenzer, 2007; Krueger & Funder, 2005; Shepperd & Koch, 2005), they occasionally get us into trouble. In some cases, they can lead us to not merely simplify reality, but to *oversimplify* it. Although most heuristics are generally helpful, the modern world sometimes presents us with complicated information for which these shortcuts weren't intended. The good news is that research designs can help us avoid the pitfalls that can result from misapplying heuristics.

To understand the concept of a heuristic, try to answer the following question. *Imagine that you are in Reno, Nevada. If you wanted to get to San Diego, California, what compass direction would you take? Close your eyes for a moment and picture how you'd get there* (Piatelli-Palmarini, 1994).

Well, we'd of course need to go southwest to get to San Diego from Reno, because California is west of Nevada, right? Wrong! Actually, to get from Reno to San Diego, we would go *southeast*, not southwest. If you don't believe us, look at **FIGURE 2.3** on the next page.

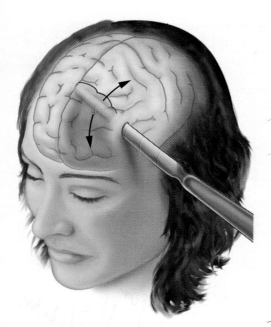

FIGURE 2.2 The Prefrontal Lobotomy. In a prefrontal lobotomy, the surgeon severs the fibers connecting the brain's frontal lobes from the underlying thalamus.

Mistaken thinking IS similar to useful thinking (handwritten)

 Simulate Heuristics on **mypsychlab.com**

FACTOID +

About 50,000 Americans received prefrontal lobotomies; most of them were performed in the late 1940s and early 1950s. Some of these people are still alive today.

heuristics = mental shortcuts. (handwritten)

heuristic
mental shortcut that helps us to streamline our thinking and make sense of our world

representativeness heuristic
heuristic that involves judging the probability of an event by its superficial similarity to a prototype

base rate
how common a characteristic or behavior is in the general population

If you got this one wrong (and, if you did, don't feel bad, because your book's authors did, too!), you almost certainly relied on a heuristic: *California is west of Nevada, and San Diego is at the bottom of California, whereas Reno has a lot more land south of it before you hit Mexico.* What you either forgot or didn't know is that a large chunk of California (the bottom third or so) is actually *east* of Nevada. Of course, for most geographical questions (such as, "Is St. Louis east or west of Los Angeles?") these kinds of mental shortcuts work just fine. But in this case the heuristic tripped us up.

THE REPRESENTATIVENESS HEURISTIC: LIKE GOES WITH LIKE. Two Israeli psychologists who emigrated to the United States, Daniel Kahneman and Amos Tversky, pioneered the study of heuristics. Their research fundamentally changed how psychologists think about thinking. Indeed, in 2002, Kahneman became the first Ph.D. psychologist to be awarded a Nobel Prize (unfortunately, Tversky had died in 1996 and therefore was not eligible for the award). Kahneman and Tversky focused on several heuristics, two of which we'll discuss here. They termed the first *representativeness* (Kahneman, Slovic, & Tversky, 1982; Tversky & Kahneman, 1974). When we use the **representativeness heuristic**, we judge the probability of an event by its superficial similarity to a prototype; that is, we judge a book by its cover. According to this heuristic, "Like goes with like." Imagine that on the first day of your introductory psychology class you sit next to Roger, whom you've never met. You have a few minutes before the class begins, so you try to strike up a conversation with him. Despite your best efforts, Roger says almost nothing. He appears painfully shy, looks away from you when you ask him a question, stammers, and finally manages to blurt out a few awkward words about being a member of the college chess team and treasurer of the local Star Trek fan club.

Based on your brief interaction, would you say that Roger is more likely to be a major in communications or in computer science? You're more likely to pick the latter, and you'd probably be right. You relied on a representativeness heuristic to answer this question, because Roger matched your stereotype (see Chapter 13) of a computer science major far better than your stereotype of a communications major. According to the representativeness heuristic, we judge the similarity between two things by gauging the extent to which they resemble each other superficially. In many cases, this strategy works—or works well enough—in everyday life.

Let's consider a different example. Imagine that on the second day of class you sit next to a woman who introduces herself as Amy Chang. Amy is soft-spoken but polite, and describes herself as having grown up in the Chinatown section of San Francisco. In response to a question about her interests, she mentions that she's vice president of the college Chinese Students' Association.

Based on your brief interaction, would you say that Amy is more likely to be a psychology major or an Asian American studies major? You'd probably pick the latter. Yet in this case, you'd probably be wrong. Why?

Although Amy fits your stereotype of an Asian American studies major better than your stereotype of a psychology major, you probably forgot one crucial fact: There are many more psychology majors in your college than Asian American studies majors. By focusing too heavily on the superficial similarity of Amy to your stereotype of an Asian American studies major—by relying too heavily on the representativeness heuristic—you neglected to consider what psychologists call the extremely low *base rate* of this major.

Base rate is a fancy term for how common a behavior or characteristic is (Finn & Kamphuis, 1995; Meehl & Rosen, 1955). When we say that alcoholism has a base rate of about 5 percent in the U.S. population (American Psychiatric Association, 2000), we mean that about one in 20 Americans experiences alcoholism at any given time. When evaluating the probability that a person (for example, Amy) belongs to a category (for example, Asian American studies major), we need to consider not only how similar that person is to other members of the category, but also the base rate of this category. We commit the *base rate fallacy* when we neglect to consider base rates, as we'd have done if we'd concluded that Amy was more likely to be an Asian American studies major than a psychology major.

Daniel Kahneman of Princeton University (*left*) was the first Ph.D. psychologist to be awarded a Nobel Prize. The Nobel Committee recognized him for his groundbreaking work on the cognitive sources of human irrationality.

FIGURE 2.3 In Which Compass Direction Would You Travel to Get from Reno, Nevada, to San Diego, California? If you didn't guess southeast (which is the correct answer), you're not alone. By relying on a heuristic—that is, a mental shortcut—we can sometimes be fooled.

Our mental images of Michigan (*top*) and Detroit, Michigan (*bottom*), conjure up markedly different estimates of violent crime. In this case, the availability heuristic can lead us to faulty conclusions.

availability heuristic
heuristic that involves estimating the likelihood of an occurrence based on the ease with which it comes to our minds

cognitive biases
systematic errors in thinking

hindsight bias
tendency to overestimate how well we could have successfully forecasted known outcomes

overconfidence
tendency to overestimate our ability to make correct predictions

THE AVAILABILITY HEURISTIC: "OFF THE TOP OF MY HEAD . . ." Kahneman and Tversky termed the second heuristic *availability*. Using the **availability heuristic**, we estimate the likelihood of an occurrence based on the ease with which it comes to our minds—on how "available" it is in our memories (Kahneman et al., 1982). Like representativeness, availability often works well. If I ask you whether there's a higher density of trees (a) on your college campus or (b) in the downtown area of the nearest major city, you're likely to answer (a). Odds are you'd be right (unless, of course, your college campus is *in* a downtown area!). When answering this question, it's unlikely you actually calculated the precise proportion of trees you've observed in each place. Instead, you probably called to mind mental images of your campus and of the downtown area of the nearest big city, and you recalled correctly that the former contains a higher density of trees than the latter.

But now consider this example, which you may want to try on your friends (Jaffe, 2004). Ask half of your friends to guess the number of murders per year in Michigan, and average the answers. Then ask the other half to guess the number of murders per year in the city of Detroit, Michigan, and again average the answers. (If one or more of your friends are from Michigan, this example might not work, so you may want to try substituting Illinois for Michigan and Chicago for Detroit.) If the results of your informal "poll" are anything like those of Kahneman, you're likely to find that your friends give higher estimates for the number of murders in Detroit, Michigan, than for the entire state of Michigan! Kahneman found that when he asked people about the state of Michigan they estimated about 100 murders per year, whereas when he asked people about the city of Detroit they estimated about 200 murders per year.

This paradoxical result is almost certainly due to our reliance on the availability heuristic. When we imagine the state of Michigan, we conjure up images of sprawling farms and peaceful suburbs. Yet when we imagine the city of Detroit, we conjure up images of bustling inner-city areas and rundown buildings. So thinking of Detroit makes us think of more dangerous areas and therefore more murders.

We should keep heuristics in mind, because we'll soon learn that many research methods help us to avoid the mistakes that arise from applying them uncritically. As Kahneman and Tversky noted, however, it's not only heuristics that can lead us astray. We can also fall prey to a variety of **cognitive biases**—systematic errors in thinking.

■ Cognitive Biases

As we'll recall from Chapter 1, *confirmation bias* is our natural tendency to seek out evidence that supports our hypotheses and to deny, dismiss, or distort evidence that doesn't. One crucial function of the scientific method, as we've seen, is to help us compensate for this bias. By forcing us to adopt safeguards against confirming our pet hypotheses, this method makes us less likely to trick ourselves.

Yet confirmation bias is only one bias that can lead us to draw misleading conclusions. Two others are hindsight bias and overconfidence.

HINDSIGHT BIAS. **Hindsight bias**, also known as the "I knew it all along effect," refers to our tendency to overestimate how well we could have successfully forecasted known outcomes (Fischoff, 1975; Kunda, 1999). As the old saying goes, "Hindsight is always 20/20." Following the terrorist attacks of September 11, 2001, many pundits and politicians engaged in "Monday-morning quarterbacking" regarding what could or should have been done to prevent these attacks: better airport security, better covert intelligence, better warnings to the public, better prosecution of known terrorists, and so on. There may well have been some truth to each of these after-the-fact recommendations, but they miss a crucial point: Once an event has occurred, it's awfully easy in retrospect to "predict" it and then suggest ways in which we could have prevented it. As Nobel Prize–winning physicist Niels Bohr joked, "Prediction is difficult, especially for the future."

OVERCONFIDENCE. Related to hindsight bias is **overconfidence**: our tendency to overestimate our ability to make correct predictions. Across a wide variety of tasks, most of us are more confident in our predictive abilities than we should be (Hoffrage, 2004; Smith & Dumont, 2002). Try answering the following four questions:

1. Which city is farther north—Rome, Italy, or New York City?
2. Is absinthe a precious stone or a liqueur?
3. How old was Dr. Martin Luther King when he was assassinated, 39 or 49?
4. How many bones are in the human body, 107 or 206?

Then, using a 0–100 scale, estimate how confident you are regarding whether each answer is correct (with 0 being "I am not confident at all" and 100 being "I am completely confident"). Now, look at the bottom of page 50 to find the correct answers to these questions. Researchers typically find that for the questions we get wrong, we're much more confident than we should have been that we got them right.

We're overconfident in many domains of our lives. A national survey of nearly a million high school seniors revealed that 100 percent (yes, all of them!) believed they were *above* average in their ability to get along with others. Twenty-five percent believed that they were in the top 1 percent (College Board, 1976–1977). A survey of college professors revealed that 94 percent believed they were better scholars than their colleagues (Cross, 1977). Obviously, we can't all be above average, but most of us think we are. Some psychologists have referred to this belief as the "Lake Wobegon effect" after the fictional town (in Garrison Keillor's popular radio show, *A Prairie Home Companion*) in which "all the women are strong, all the men are good-looking, and all the children are above average."

Psychologist Philip Tetlock (2005) demonstrated that television and radio political pundits—so-called talking heads—are also prone to overconfidence, especially when it comes to predicting domestic and foreign policy events ("Will Congress pass the new healthcare bill?" "Who will be the next Republican nominee for president?"), even though they're often wildly wrong. Moreover, Tetlock found that the more extreme pundits were in their political views, whether liberal or conservative, the *less* likely their predictions were to be accurate. Moderates are typically more accurate in their predictions, perhaps because they tend to possess a better appreciation of alternative points of view.

Heuristics and biases can make us sure we're right when we're not. As a consequence, we can not only draw false conclusions, but become convinced of them. Not to worry: The scientific method is here to come to the rescue.

✓•—[**Study** and **Review** on **mypsychlab.com**

assess your knowledge   FACT OR FICTION?

1. Psychological research suggests that we're all capable of being fooled by our heuristics. **True / False**

2. The psychological processes that give rise to heuristics are generally maladaptive. **True / False**

3. The representativeness heuristic often leads us to attend too closely to base rates. **True / False** *does not*

4. Most of us tend to be less confident than we should be when making predictions about future events. **True / False**

Answers: 1. T (p. 46); 2. F (p. 46); 3. F (p. 47); 4. F (p. 49)

THE SCIENTIFIC METHOD: TOOLBOX OF SKILLS

2.2 Describe the advantages and disadvantages of using naturalistic observation, case studies, self-report measures, and surveys.

2.3 Describe the role of correlational designs and distinguish correlation from causation.

2.4 Identify the components of an experiment and the potential pitfalls that can lead to faulty conclusions.

FACTOID

Are there more words in the English language with the letter *k* as the first letter in the word or the third letter in the word? If you're like most people, you guessed that there are more words beginning with the letter *k* than with *k* in the third position. In fact, there are more than twice as many words with *k* in the third position as there are words beginning with the letter *k*. Most of us get this question wrong because we rely on the availability heuristic: Because of how our brains categorize words, we find it easier to think of words with *k* in the first position (like *kite* and *kill*) than words with *k* in the third position (like *bike* and *cake*).

? Nostradamus was a 16th-century prophet whose four-line poems supposedly foretold the future. Here's a famous one:

Beasts ferocious with hunger will cross the rivers,
The greater part of the battlefield will be against the Hister.
Into a cage of iron will the great one be drawn,
When the child of Germany observes nothing.

After reading it, can you guess what historical event it supposedly predicted? (the answer is upside down at the bottom of this page). Odds are high you won't. Yet after discovering the answer, you're likely to find that the poem fits the event quite well. People's beliefs that Nostradamus forecasted the future probably reflect hindsight bias, because his poems make sense once we know what they're supposed to predict (Yafeh & Heath, 2003).

Answer: Adolph Hitler's rise to power.

TABLE 2.1 Advantages and Disadvantages of Research Designs.

	ADVANTAGES	DISADVANTAGES
Naturalistic Observation	High in external validity	Low in internal validity Doesn't allow us to infer causation
Case Studies	Can provide existence proofs Allow us to study rare or unusual phenomena Can offer insights for later systematic testing	Are typically anecdotal Don't allow us to infer causation
Correlational Designs	Can help us to predict behavior	Don't allow us to infer causation
Experimental Designs	Allow us to infer causation High in internal validity	Can sometimes be low in external validity

In actuality, the heading of this section is a bit of a fib, because there's no *single* scientific method. "The" scientific method is a myth, because the techniques that psychologists use are very different from those that their colleagues in chemistry, physics, and biology use (Bauer, 1992).

As we discovered in Chapter 1, the scientific method is a toolbox of skills designed to counteract our tendency to fool ourselves—specifically, to be tricked by our heuristics and cognitive biases. All of the tools we'll describe have one major thing in common: They permit us to test *hypotheses,* which as we learned in Chapter 1 are predictions often derived from broader theories. If these hypotheses are confirmed, our confidence in the theory is strengthened, although we should recall that this theory is never "proven." If these hypotheses are disconfirmed, scientists often revise this theory or abandon it entirely. This toolbox of the scientific method isn't perfect by any means, but it's the best set of safeguards against bias we have. Let's now open up this toolbox and peek at what's inside (see **TABLE 2.1**).

■ Naturalistic Observation: Studying Humans "In the Wild"

Let's say we wanted to conduct a study to find out about laughter. How often do people laugh in the real world? What makes them laugh? Do men laugh more often than women? In what settings are people most likely to laugh? We could try to answer these questions by bringing people into our laboratory and observing their laughter across various situations. But it's unlikely we'd be able to re-create the full range of situations that trigger laughter. Moreover, even if we observed participants without their knowing it, their laughter could still have been influenced by the fact that they were in a laboratory. Among other things, they may have been more nervous or less spontaneous than in the real world.

One way of getting around these problems is **naturalistic observation**: watching behavior in real-world settings without trying to manipulate people's behavior. That is, we watch behavior unfold "naturally" without intervening in it. We can perform naturalistic observation using a video camera or tape recorder or, if we're willing to go low-tech, only a paper and pencil. Many psychologists who study animals, such as chimpanzees, in their natural habitats use naturalistic observation, although psychologists who study humans sometimes use it, too. By doing so, we can better understand the range of behaviors displayed by individuals in the "real world," as well as the situations in which they occur.

Robert Provine (1996, 2000) relied on naturalistic observation in an investigation of human laughter. He eavesdropped on 1,200 instances of laughter in social situations—shopping malls, restaurants, and street corners—and recorded the gender of the laugher and "laughee," the remarks that preceded laughter, and others' reactions to laughter. He found that women laugh much more than men in social situations. Surprisingly, he discovered that less than 20 percent of laughing incidents are preceded by statements that could

Researcher Jane Goodall has spent much of her career using techniques of naturalistic observation with chimpanzees in Gombe, Kenya. As we'll learn in Chapter 13, her work strongly suggests that warfare is not unique to humans.

naturalistic observation
watching behavior in real-world settings without trying to manipulate the situation

remotely be described as funny. Instead, most cases of laughter are preceded by quite ordinary comments (like "It was nice meeting you, too."). Provine also found that speakers laugh considerably more than listeners, a finding painfully familiar to any of us who've had the experience of laughing out loud at one of our jokes while our friends looked back at us with a blank stare. Provine's work, which would have been difficult to pull off in a laboratory, sheds new light on the interpersonal triggers and consequences of laughter.

The major advantage of naturalistic designs is that they're often high in **external validity**: the extent to which we can generalize our findings to real-world settings (Neisser & Hyman, 1999). Because psychologists apply these designs to organisms as they go about their everyday business, their findings are frequently relevant to the real world. Some psychologists contend that naturalistic designs almost always have higher external validity than laboratory experiments, although actually there's not much research support for this claim (Mook, 1983).

Still, naturalistic designs have a disadvantage. They tend to be low in **internal validity**: the extent to which we can draw cause-and-effect inferences. As we'll soon learn, well-conducted laboratory experiments are high in internal validity, because we can manipulate the key variables ourselves. In contrast, in naturalistic designs we have no control over these variables and need to wait for behavior to unfold before our eyes. In addition, naturalistic designs can be problematic if people know they're being observed, as this knowledge can affect their behavior.

■ Case Study Designs: Getting to Know You

One of the simplest designs in the psychologist's investigative toolbox is the case study. In a **case study**, researchers examine one person or a small number of people, often over an extended period of time (Davison & Lazarus, 2007). An investigator could spend 10 or even 20 years studying one person with schizophrenia, carefully documenting his childhood experiences, academic and job performance, family life, friendships, psychological treatment, and the ups and downs of his mental problems. There's no single "recipe" for a case study. Some researchers might observe a person over time, others might administer questionnaires, and still others might conduct repeated interviews.

Case studies can be helpful in providing **existence proofs**: demonstrations that a given psychological phenomenon can occur. As we'll learn in Chapter 7, one of the most heated controversies in psychology surrounds the question of "recovered memories" of child abuse. Can individuals completely forget episodes of childhood sexual abuse for years or even decades, only to remember them, often with the aid of a psychotherapist, in perfectly accurate form in adulthood? To demonstrate the possibility of recovered memories, all we'd need is *one* clear-cut case of a person who'd forgotten an abuse memory for decades and then recalled it suddenly. Although there have been several suggestive existence proofs of recovered memories (Duggal & Sroufe, 1998; Schooler, 1997), none has been entirely convincing (McNally, 2003).

Case studies also provide a valuable opportunity to study rare or unusual phenomena that are difficult or impossible to re-create in the laboratory, such as people with atypical symptoms or rare types of brain damage. Richard McNally and Brian Lukach (1991) reported a case history of a man who exposed himself sexually to large dogs, and obtained sexual gratification from doing so, a condition known as "zoophilic exhibitionism." To treat this man's condition, they developed a six-month program that incorporated techniques designed to enhance his sexual arousal in response to women and snuff out his sexual response to dogs. Needless to say, researchers could wait around for decades in the laboratory before accumulating a sample of fifty or even five individuals with this bizarre condition. McNally and Lukach's single case provided helpful insights into the treatment of this condition that laboratory research couldn't.

Case studies can also offer useful insights that researchers can test in systematic investigations (Davison & Lazarus, 2007). For example, in the 1960s, psychiatrist Aaron Beck was conducting psychotherapy with a female client who appeared anxious during the

Case studies can sometimes provide access to the rare or unusual. For example, people with the condition of Capgras' syndrome believe that their relatives or loved ones have been replaced by identical-looking doubles. The study of this condition has shed light on neurological and psychological processes involved in identifying other people.

external validity
extent to which we can generalize findings to real-world settings

internal validity
extent to which we can draw cause-and-effect inferences from a study

case study
research design that examines one person or a small number of people in depth, often over an extended time period

existence proof
demonstration that a given psychological phenomenon can occur

session (Smith, 2009). When Beck asked her why she was nervous, she reluctantly admitted she was afraid she was boring him. Beck probed in more depth, discovering that she harbored the irrational idea that just about everyone found her boring. From these and other informal observations, Beck pieced together a now influential form of therapy (about which we'll learn in Chapter 16) based on the premise that people's emotional distress stems from their deep-seated irrational beliefs.

Nevertheless, if we're not careful, case studies can lead to misleading, even disastrously wrong, conclusions. As we discovered in Chapter 1, the *plural of anecdote isn't fact*. Hundreds of observations purporting to show that facilitated communication is effective for autism aren't sufficient to conclude that it's effective, because carefully controlled studies have pinpointed alternative explanations for its effects. As a consequence, case studies almost never lend themselves to systematic tests of hypotheses about *why* a given phenomenon occurred. Nevertheless, they're often an invaluable way to generate hypotheses that psychologists can test in well-conducted studies.

■ Self-Report Measures and Surveys: Asking People about Themselves and Others

Psychologists frequently use *self-report measures,* often called questionnaires, to assess a variety of characteristics, such as personality traits, mental illnesses, and interests. Closely related to self-report measures are *surveys,* which psychologists typically use to measure people's opinions and attitudes.

RANDOM SELECTION: THE KEY TO GENERALIZABILITY. Imagine being hired by a research firm to gauge people's attitudes toward a new brand of toothpaste, Brightooth, which supposedly prevents 99.99 percent of cavities. How should we do it? We could flag people off the street, pay them money to brush their teeth with Brightooth, and measure their reactions to Brightooth on a survey. Is this a good approach?

No, because the people on your neighborhood street probably aren't typical of people in general. Moreover, some people will almost surely refuse to participate, and they may differ from those who agreed to participate. For example, people with especially bad teeth might refuse to try Brightooth, and they may be the very people to whom Brightooth executives would most want to market their product.

A better approach would be to identify a representative sample of the population, and administer our survey to people drawn from that sample. For example, we could look at U.S. population census data, scramble all of the names, and try to contact every 10,000th person listed. This approach, often used in survey research, is called **random selection**. In random selection, every person in the population has an equal chance of being chosen to participate. Random selection is crucial if we want to generalize our results to the broader population. Political pollsters keep themselves awake at night worrying about random selection. If their selection of survey respondents from the population is nonrandom, their election forecasts may well be skewed.

An example of how nonrandom selection can lead to wildly misleading conclusions comes from the infamous *Hite Report on Love, Passion and Emotional Violence* (1987). In the mid-1980s, sex researcher Shere Hite sent out 100,000 surveys to American women inquiring about their relationships with men. She'd identified potential survey respondents from lists of subscribers to women's magazines. Hite's findings were so startling that *Time* magazine and other prominent publications featured them as their cover story. Here's a sampling of Hite's findings:

- 70 percent of women married five or more years say they've had extramarital affairs.
- 87 percent of married women say their closest emotional relationship is with someone other than their husband.
- 95 percent of women say they're "emotionally and psychologically harassed" by their love partner.
- 98 percent of women say they're generally unsatisfied with their present love relationship.

---

ruling out rival hypotheses

HAVE IMPORTANT ALTERNATIVE EXPLANATIONS FOR THE FINDINGS BEEN EXCLUDED?

FICTOID ✕

MYTH: When conducting surveys, larger samples are always better.

REALITY: A poll of over 100,000 people is virtually useless if it's nonrandom. In fact, it's far better to conduct a poll of 100 people we've selected randomly than a poll of 100 million people we've selected nonrandomly. In large samples, biases can become magnified.

---

random selection
procedure that ensures every person in a population has an equal chance of being chosen to participate

Sad people.

That's pretty depressing news, to put it mildly. Yet lost in the furor over Hite's findings was one crucial point: Only 4.5 percent of her sample had responded to her survey. What's more, Hite had no way of knowing whether this 4.5 percent was representative of her full sample. Interestingly, a poll conducted by the Harris organization at around the same time used random selection and reported results virtually opposite to Hite's. In their better-conducted survey, 89 percent of women said they were generally satisfied with their current relationship, and only a small minority reported extramarital affairs. More likely than not, Hite's high percentages resulted from nonrandom selection: The 4.5 percent of participants who responded to her survey were probably the very women experiencing the most relationship problems to begin with and therefore the most motivated to participate.

EVALUATING MEASURES. When evaluating the results from any dependent variable or measure, we need to ask two critical questions: Is our measure reliable? Is it valid?

Reliability refers to consistency of measurement. For example, a reliable questionnaire yields similar scores over time; this type of reliability is called *test-retest reliability*. To assess test-retest reliability, we could administer a personality questionnaire to a large group of people today and readminister it in two months. If the measure is reasonably reliable, participants' scores should be similar at both times. Reliability also applies to interviews and observational data. *Interrater reliability* is the extent to which different people who conduct an interview, or make behavioral observations, agree on the characteristics they're measuring. If two psychologists who interview all patients in a psychiatric hospital unit disagree on most of their diagnoses—for example, if one psychologist diagnoses most of the patients as having schizophrenia and the other psychologist diagnoses most of the patients as having depression, then their interrater reliability will be low.

Democrat Harry Truman at his presidential victory rally (*left*), famously holding up an early edition of the *Chicago Daily Tribune* incorrectly proclaiming Republican Thomas Dewey the winner of the 1948 presidential election. In fact, Truman won by nearly five percentage points. The pollsters got it wrong largely because they based their survey results on people with telephones. Back in 1948, considerably more Republicans (who tended to be richer) owned telephones than Democrats, resulting in a skewed preelection prediction.

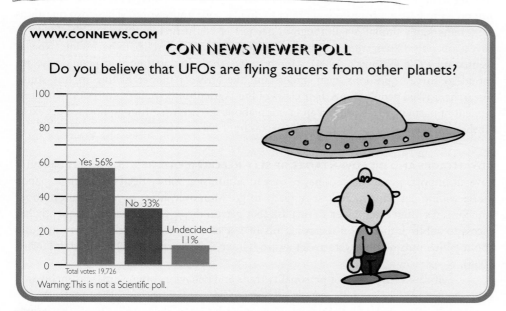

WWW.CONNEWS.COM

CON NEWS VIEWER POLL

Do you believe that UFOs are flying saucers from other planets?

Yes 56%
No 33%
Undecided 11%

Total votes: 19,726

Warning: This is not a Scientific poll.

? Frequently, one will see polls in the news or Internet that carry the disclaimer "This is not a scientific poll" (Of course, one then has to wonder: Why report the results?) **Why is this poll not scientific?** (See answer upside down on bottom of page.)

These two thermometers are providing different readings for the temperature in an almost identical location. Psychologists might say that these thermometers display less-than-perfect interrater reliability.

Answer: The poll isn't scientific because it's based on people who logged onto the website, who are probably not a representative sample of all people who watch Con News—and almost certainly not of all Americans.

reliability
consistency of measurement

Reliability = Consistency of measurements

Validity = truth in measurement.

Validity is the extent to which a measure assesses what it purports (claims) to measure. We can think of validity as "truth in advertising." If we went to a computer store, purchased a fancy package labeled "iPhone" and on opening it discovered an old wristwatch, we'd demand our money back (unless we really needed a wristwatch). Similarly, if a questionnaire we're administering purports to be a valid measure of introversion, but studies show it's really measuring anxiety, then this measure isn't valid. As users of the test, we should similarly demand our money back.

Reliability and validity are different concepts, although people routinely confuse them. In courts of law, we'll frequently hear debates about whether the polygraph (or so-called lie-detector) test is scientifically "reliable." But as we'll learn in Chapter 11, the central question concerning the polygraph isn't its reliability, because it typically yields fairly consistent scores over time. Instead, the central question is its validity, because many critics maintain that the polygraph actually detects emotional arousal, not lies (Lykken, 1998; Ruscio; 2005).

Reliability is necessary for validity, because we need to measure something consistently before we can measure it well. Imagine trying to measure the floors and walls of an apartment using a ruler made of Silly Putty, that is, a ruler whose length changes each time we pick it up. Our efforts at accurate measurement would be doomed. Nevertheless, reliability isn't sufficient for validity. Although a test must be reliable to be valid, a reliable test can be completely invalid. Imagine we've developed a new measure of intelligence, the "Distance Index-Middle Width Intelligence Test" (DIMWIT), which subtracts the width of our index finger from that of our middle finger. The DIMWIT would be a highly reliable measure of intelligence, because the widths of our fingers are unlikely to change much over time (high test-retest reliability) and are likely to be measured similarly by different raters (high interrater reliability). But the DIMWIT would be a completely invalid measure of intelligence, because finger width has nothing to do with intelligence. hence, the name.

When interpreting the results of self-report measures and surveys, we should bear in mind that we can obtain quite different answers depending on how we phrase the questions (Schwarz, 1999; Smith, Schwarz, & Roberts, 2006). One researcher administered surveys to 300 women homemakers. In some surveys, women answered the question "Would you like to have a job, if this were possible?," whereas others answered the question "Would you prefer to have a job, or do you prefer to do just your housework?" These two questions seem remarkably similar. Yet although 81 percent asked the first question said they'd like to have a job, only 32 percent asked the second question said they'd like to have a job (Noelle-Neumann, 1970; Walonick, 1994). Moreover, we shouldn't assume that people who respond to survey questions even understand the answers they're giving. In one study, researchers asked people about their views of the "Agricultural Trade Act of 1978." About 30 percent of participants expressed an opinion about this act, even though no such act exists (Bishop, Oldendick, & Tuchfarber, 1986; Schwarz, 1999).

ADVANTAGES AND DISADVANTAGES OF SELF-REPORT MEASURES. Self-report measures have an important advantage: They're easy to administer. All we need are a pencil, paper, and a willing participant, and we're ready to go. Moreover, if we have a question about someone, it's often a good idea to first ask that person directly. That person frequently has access to subtle information regarding his or her emotional states, like anxiety or guilt, about which outside observers aren't aware (Grove & Tellegen, 1991; Lilienfeld & Fowler, 2006).

Self-report measures of personality traits and behaviors often work reasonably well (see Chapter 14). For example, people's reports of how outgoing or shy they are tend to be moderately associated with the reports of people who know them well. These associations are somewhat higher for more observable traits, like extraversion, than for less observable traits, like anxiety (Gosling, Rentfrow, & Swann, 2003; Kenrick & Funder, 1988).

Yet self-report measures have their disadvantages, too. First, they typically assume that respondents possess enough insight into their personality characteristics to report on

A widely publicized 1992 poll by the Roper organization asked Americans the following confusing question, which contained two negatives: "Does it seem possible or does it seem impossible to you that the Nazi extermination of the Jews never happened?" A shocking 22 percent of respondents replied that the Holocaust may not have happened. Yet when a later poll asked the question more clearly, this number dropped to only 1 percent. Survey wording counts.

validity
extent to which a measure assesses what it purports to measure

them accurately (Oltmanns & Turkheimer, 2009). This assumption is questionable for certain groups of people. For example, people with high levels of narcissistic personality traits, like self-centeredness and excessive self-confidence (the word *narcissistic* derives from the Greek mythological character Narcissus, who fell in love with his reflection in the water), view themselves more positively than others do (John & Robins, 1994). Narcissistic people tend to perceive themselves through rose-colored glasses.

Second, self-report questionnaires typically assume that participants are honest in their responses. Imagine that a company required you to take a personality test for a job you really wanted. Would you be completely frank in your evaluation of yourself, or would you minimize your personality quirks? Not surprisingly, some respondents engage in **response sets**—tendencies to distort their answers to items, often in a socially desirable direction. (Edens, Buffington, & Tomicic, 2001; Paulhus, 1991).

Two especially problematic response sets are positive impression management and malingering. *Positive impression management* is the tendency to make ourselves look better than we are (Paulhus, 1991). We're especially likely to engage in this response set when applying for an important job. Positive impression management can make it difficult to trust people's reports of their abilities and achievements. For example, college students overstate their SAT scores by an average of 17 points (Hagen, 2001).

A nearly opposite response set is *malingering,* the tendency to make ourselves appear psychologically disturbed with the aim of achieving a clear-cut personal goal (Rogers, 1997). We're especially likely to observe this response set among people who are trying to obtain financial compensation for an injury or mistreatment on the job, or among people trying to escape military duty—in the last case, perhaps by faking insanity (see Chapter 15).

RATING DATA: HOW DO THEY RATE? An alternative to asking people about themselves is asking others who know them well to provide ratings on them. In many job settings, employers rate their employees' work productivity and cooperativeness in routine evaluations. Rating data can circumvent some of the problems with self-report data, because observers may not have the same "blind spots" as the people they're rating (who are often called the "targets" of the rating). Imagine asking your introductory psychology instructor, "How good a job do you think you did in teaching this course?" It's unlikely she'd say "Just awful."

Nevertheless, like self-report measures, rating data have their drawbacks, in particular the *halo effect.* This is the tendency of ratings of one positive characteristic to "spill over" to influence the ratings of other positive characteristics (Guilford, 1954). Raters who fall prey to the halo effect seem almost to regard the targets as "angels"—hence the halo—who can do no wrong. If we find an employee physically attractive, we may unknowingly allow this perception to influence our ratings of his or her other features, such as conscientiousness and productivity. Indeed, people perceive physically attractive people as more successful, confident, assertive, and intelligent than other people even though these differences often don't reflect objective reality (Dion, Berscheid, & Walster, 1972; Eagly et al., 1991).

Student course evaluations of teaching are especially vulnerable to halo effects, because if you like a teacher personally you're likely to give him "a break" on the quality of his teaching. In one study, Richard Nisbett and Timothy Wilson (1977) placed participants into one of two conditions. Some participants watched a videotape of a college professor with a foreign accent who was friendly to his students; others watched a videotape of the same professor who was unfriendly to his students. Participants watching the videotapes not only liked the friendly professor better, but rated his physical appearance, mannerisms, and accent more positively. Students who like their professors also tend to give them high ratings on characteristics that are largely irrelevant to teaching effectiveness, like the quality of the classroom audiovisual equipment and the readability of their handwriting (Greenwald & Gillmore, 1997; Williams & Ceci, 1997).

People often perceive highly attractive individuals as possessing many other desirable attributes. This phenomenon is one illustration of the halo effect.

FACTOID

The converse of the halo effect is called the *horns effect*—picture a devil's horns—or pitchfork effect. In this effect, the ratings of one negative trait, such as arrogance, spill over to influence the ratings of other negative traits (Corsini, 1999).

response set
tendency of research participants to distort their responses to questionnaire items

■ Correlational Designs

Another essential research method in the psychologist's toolbox is the correlational design. When using a **correlational design**, psychologists examine the extent to which two variables are associated. Recall from Chapter 1 that a *variable* is anything that can take on different values across individuals, like impulsivity, creativity, or religiosity. When we think of the word *correlate*, we should decompose it into its two parts: *co-* and *relate*. If two things are correlated, they relate to each other—not interpersonally, that is, but statistically.

IDENTIFYING CORRELATIONAL DESIGNS. Identifying a correlational design can be tricky at first, because investigators who use this design—and news reporters who describe it—don't always use the word *correlated* in their description of findings. Instead, they'll often use terms like *associated, related, linked,* or *went together.* Whenever researchers conduct a study of the extent to which two variables "travel together," their design is correlational even if they don't describe it that way. ◉─ Watch

CORRELATIONS: A BEGINNER'S GUIDE. Before we go any further, let's lay some groundwork by examining two basic facts about correlations:

1. Correlations can be *positive, zero,* or *negative.* A positive correlation means that as the value of one variable changes, the other goes in the same direction: If one goes up, the other goes up, and if one goes down, the other goes down. If the number of friends children have is positively correlated with how outgoing these children are, then more outgoing children have more friends and less outgoing children have fewer friends. A zero correlation means that the variables don't go together. If math ability has a zero correlation with singing ability, then knowing that someone is good at math tells us nothing about his singing ability. A negative correlation means that as the value of one variable changes, the other goes in the opposite direction: If one goes up, the other goes down, and vice versa. If social anxiety is negatively correlated with perceived physical attractiveness, then more socially anxious people would be rated as less attractive, and less socially anxious people as more attractive.

2. Correlation coefficients (the statistics that psychologists use to measure correlations), at least the ones we'll be discussing in this textbook, range in value from −1.0 to 1.0. A correlation coefficient of −1.0 is a perfect negative correlation, whereas a correlation coefficient of +1.0 is a perfect positive correlation. We won't talk about how to calculate correlation coefficients, because the mathematics of doing so gets pretty technical (those of you who are really ambitious can check out http://www.easycalculation.com/statistics/correlation.php to learn how to calculate a correlation coefficient). Values lower than 1.0 (either positive or negative values), such as .23 or .69, indicate a less-than-perfect correlation coefficient. To find how strong a correlation coefficient is, we need to look at its *absolute value,* that is, the size of the coefficient without the plus or minus sign in front of it. The absolute value of a correlation coefficient of +.27 is .27, and the absolute value of a correlation coefficient of −.27 is also .27. Both correlation coefficients are equally large in size—and equally informative—but they're going in opposite directions.

THE SCATTERPLOT. FIGURE 2.4 shows three panels depicting three types of correlations. Each panel shows a **scatterplot**: a grouping of points on a two-dimensional graph. Each dot on the scatterplot depicts a person. As we can see, each person differs from other persons in his or her scores on one or both variables.

The panel on the left displays a fictional scatterplot of a moderate ($r = -.5$) negative correlation, in this case, the association between the average number of beers that students drink the night before their first psychology exam and their scores on that exam. We can tell that this correlation coefficient is negative because the clump of dots goes from higher

Watch Research Methods on
mypsychlab.com

correlational design
research design that examines the extent to which two variables are associated

scatterplot
grouping of points on a two-dimensional graph in which each dot represents a single person's data

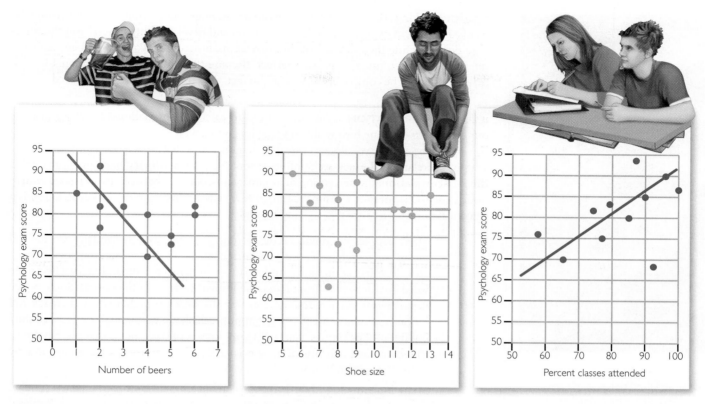

FIGURE 2.4   Diagram of Three Scatterplots. Scatterplot (*left*) depicts a moderate negative correlation (r = −.5); scatterplot (*middle*) depicts a zero correlation; and scatterplot (*right*) depicts a moderate positive correlation (r = .5).

on the left of the graph to lower on the right of the graph. Because this correlation is negative, it means that the more beers students drink, the worse they tend to do on their first psychology exam. Note that this negative correlation isn't perfect (it's not r = −1.0). That means that some students drink a lot of beer and still do well on their first psychology exam and that some students drink almost no beer and still do poorly on their first psychology exam.

In the middle panel is a fictional scatterplot of a zero (r = 0) correlation coefficient, in this case the association between the students' shoe sizes and scores on their first psychology exam. The easiest way to identify a zero correlation is that the scatterplot looks like a blob of dots that's pointing neither upward nor downward. This zero correlation means there's no association whatsoever between students' shoe sizes and how well they do on their first psychology exam. Knowing one variable tells us absolutely nothing about the other (that's good news for those of us with tiny feet).

The panel on the right shows a fictional scatterplot of a moderate (r = .5) positive correlation, in this case, the association between students' attendance in their psychology course and their scores on their first psychology exam. Here, the clump of dots goes from lower on the left of the graph to higher on the right of the graph. This positive correlation means that the more psychology classes students attend, the better they tend to do on their first psychology exam. Because the correlation isn't perfect (it's not r = 1.0), there will always be the inevitable annoying students who don't attend any classes yet do well on their exams, and the incredibly frustrated souls who attend all of their classes and still do poorly.

Remember that unless a correlation coefficient is perfect, that is, 1.0 or −1.0, there will always be exceptions to the general trend. Because virtually all correlations in psychology have an absolute value of less than one, *psychology is a science of exceptions*. To argue against the existence of a correlation, it's tempting to resort to "I know a person who . . ." reasoning (see Chapter 1). So if we're trying to refute the overwhelming evidence that

Just because we know one person who was a lifelong smoker and lived to a ripe old age doesn't mean there's no correlation between smoking and serious illnesses, like lung cancer and heart disease. Exceptions don't invalidate the existence of correlations.

Although legend has it that animals and humans behave strangely during full moons, research evidence demonstrates that this supposed correlation is an illusion.

illusory correlation
perception of a statistical association between two variables where none exists

cigarette smoking is correlated with lung cancer, we might insist, "But I know a person who smoked five packs of cigarettes a day for 40 years and never got lung cancer." But this anecdote doesn't refute the existence of the correlation, because the correlation between cigarette smoking and lung cancer isn't perfect. Because the correlation is less than 1.0, such exceptions are to be completely expected—in fact, they're mathematically required.

ILLUSORY CORRELATION. Why do we need to calculate correlations? Can't we just use our eyeballs to estimate how well two variables go together?

No, because psychological research demonstrates that we're poor at estimating the sizes of correlations. In fact, we're often prone to an extraordinary phenomenon termed **illusory correlation**: the perception of a statistical association between two variables where none exists (Chapman & Chapman, 1967, 1969; Dawes, 2006). An illusory correlation is a statistical mirage. Here are two striking examples:

1. Many people are convinced of a strong statistical association between the full moon and a variety of strange occurrences, like violent crimes, suicides, psychiatric hospital admissions, and births—the so-called lunar lunacy effect (the word *lunatic* derives from *Luna*, the Roman goddess of the moon). Some police departments even put more cops on the beat on nights when there's a full moon, and many emergency room nurses insist that more babies are born during full moons (Hines, 2003). Yet a mountain of data shows that the full moon isn't correlated with any of these events: that is, the correlation is almost exactly $r = 0$ (Plait, 2002; Rotton & Kelly, 1985).

2. Many individuals with arthritis are convinced their joint pain increases during rainy weather, yet carefully conducted studies show no association between joint pain and rainy weather (Quick, 1999).

Illusory Correlation and Superstition. Illusory correlations form the basis of many superstitions (Vyse, 2000). Take the case of Wade Boggs, Hall of Fame baseball player and one of the game's greatest hitters. For 20 years, Boggs ate chicken before every game, believing this peculiar habit was correlated with successful performance in the batter's box. Boggs eventually became so skilled at cooking chicken that he even wrote a cookbook called *Fowl Tips*. It's unlikely that eating chicken and belting 95-mile-an-hour fastballs into the outfield have much to do with each other, but Boggs perceived such an association. Countless other superstitions, like keeping a rabbit's foot for good luck and not walking under ladders to avoid bad luck, probably also stem in part from illusory correlation (see Chapter 6).   Luck does not exist.

Why We Fall Prey to Illusory Correlation. So you may be wondering: How on earth could so many people be so wrong? We're all susceptible to illusory correlation; this phenomenon is an inescapable fact of everyday life. We can think of much of everyday life in terms of a table of four probabilities, like that shown in **TABLE 2.2**.

Returning to the lunar lunacy effect, there are four possible relations between the phase of the moon and whether a crime is committed. The upper left-hand (A) cell of the table consists of cases in which there was a full moon and a crime occurred. The upper right-hand (B) cell consists of cases in which there was a full moon and no crime occurred. The bottom left-hand (C) cell consists of cases in which there was no full moon and a crime occurred. Finally, the bottom right-hand (D) cell consists of cases in which there was no full moon and no crime.

Decades of psychological research lead to one inescapable conclusion: We tend to pay too much attention to the *upper left-hand (A) cell* of the table (Gilovich, 1991). This cell is especially interesting to us, because it typically fits what we expect to see, causing our confirmation bias to kick in. In the case of the lunar lunacy effect, instances in which there was both a full moon and a crime are especially memorable ("See, just like I've always said, weird things happen during full moons."). Moreover, when we think about what occurs during full moons, we rely on the availability heuristic, so we tend to remember instances

TABLE 2.2 The Great Fourfold Table of Life.

		DID A CRIME OCCUR?	
		YES	**NO**
Did a Full Moon Occur?	**Yes**	(A) Full moon + crime	(B) Full moon + no crime
	No	(C) No full moon + crime	(D) No full moon + no crime

MYTH: People who adopt a child after years of unsuccessfully trying to have one of their own are more likely to conceive successfully shortly following the adoption.

REALITY: Studies show that this correlation is entirely illusory (Gilovich, 1991). To find out why many people hold this belief, read on about the causes of illusory correlation.

that come most easily to mind. In this case, these instances are usually those that grab our attention, namely, those that fall into the (A) cell.

Unfortunately, our minds aren't good at detecting and remembering *nonevents*, that is, things that don't happen. It's unlikely we're going to rush home excitedly to tell our friend, "Wow, you're not going to believe this. There was a full moon tonight, and nothing happened!" Our uneven attention to the different cells in the table leads us to perceive illusory correlations.

How can we avoid or at least minimize our tendencies toward illusory correlation? Probably the best way is to force ourselves to keep track of disconfirming instances—to give the other three cells of the table a little more of our time and attention. When James Alcock and his students asked a group of participants who claimed they could predict the future from their dreams—so-called prophetic dreamers—to keep careful track of their dreams by using a diary, their beliefs that they were prophetic dreamers vanished (Hines, 2003). By encouraging participants to record all of their dreams, Alcock forced them to attend to the (B) cell, the cell consisting of cases that disconfirm prophetic dreams.

The phenomenon of illusory correlation explains why we can't rely on our subjective impressions to tell us whether two variables are associated—and why we need correlational designs. Our intuitions often mislead us, especially when we've learned to expect two things to go together (Myers, 2002). Indeed, adults may be more prone to illusory correlation than children, because they've built up expectations about whether certain events—like full moons and odd behavior—go together (Kuhn, 2007).

CORRELATION VERSUS CAUSATION: JUMPING THE GUN. Correlational designs can be extremely useful for determining whether two (or more) variables are related. As a result, they can help us to predict behavior. For example, they can help us discover which variables—like personality traits or history of crimes—predict which inmates will reoffend after being released from prison, or what life habits—like heavy drinking or cigarette smoking—predict heart disease. Nevertheless, there are important limitations to the conclusions we can draw from correlational designs. As we learned in Chapter 1, the most common mistake we can make when interpreting these designs is to jump the gun and draw *causal* conclusions from them: Correlation doesn't necessarily mean causation. Although a correlation *sometimes* results from a causal relationship, we can't tell from a correlational study alone whether the relationship is causal.

Incidentally, we shouldn't confuse the correlation versus causation fallacy—the error of equating correlation with causation (see Chapter 1)—with illusory correlation. Illusory correlation refers to perceiving a correlation where none exists. In the case of the correlation versus causation fallacy, a correlation exists, but we mistakenly interpret it as implying a causal association. Let's look at two examples of how a correlation between variables *A* and *B* can actually be due to a third variable, *C*, rather than to a direct causal association between variables *A* and *B*. ✦ Explore

1. A statistician with too much time on his hands once uncovered a substantial negative correlation between the number of Ph.D. degrees awarded in a state within the United States and the number of mules in that state (Lilienfeld, 1995). Yes, *mules*. Does this negative correlation imply that the number of Ph.D.

Many superstitions, such as avoiding walking under ladders, probably stem from illusory correlation.

correlation vs. causation

CAN WE BE SURE THAT A CAUSES B?

✦ Explore Correlations Do Not Show Causation on **mypsychlab.com**

? There's a positive correlation between the amount of ice cream consumed and the number of violent crimes committed on that same day, but that doesn't mean that eating ice cream causes crime. **Can you think of a third variable that might explain this correlation?** (See answer upside down on bottom of page.)

FIGURE 2.5 Examples of Newspaper Headlines That Confuse Correlation with Causation. Here are some actual newspaper headlines that suggest a causal association between two variables. Can you think of alternative explanations for the findings reported in each headline? (See http://jonathan.mueller.faculty.noctrl.edu/100/correlation_or_causation.htm for a good source of other newspaper headlines incorrectly suggesting causation from correlational findings.)

degrees (A) influences the number of mules (B)? It's possible—perhaps people with Ph.D.s have something against mules and campaign vigorously to have them relocated to neighboring states. But this scenario seems rather unlikely. Or does this negative correlation instead imply that mules (B) cause people with Ph.D. degrees (A) to flee the state? Maybe, but don't bet on it. Before reading the next paragraph, ask yourself whether there's a third explanation.

Indeed there is. Although we don't know for sure, the most likely explanation is that a third variable, C, is correlated with both A and B. In this case, the most probable culprit for this third variable is *rural versus urban status*. States with large rural areas, like Wyoming, contain many mules and few universities. In contrast, states with many urban (big city) areas, like New York, contain few mules and many universities. So in this case, the correlation between variables A and B is almost certainly due to a third variable, C.

2. One team of researchers found a positive correlation over time between the number of babies born in Berlin, Germany (A), and the number of storks in nearby areas (B) (Hofer, Przyrembel, & Verleger, 2004). Specifically, over a 30 year period, more births were consistently accompanied by more storks. As the authors themselves noted, this correlation doesn't demonstrate that storks deliver babies. Instead, a more likely explanation is a third variable, population size (C): Highly populated city areas are characterized by large numbers of both births and birds.

Observational and case studies allow us to describe the state of the psychological world, but rarely allow us to generate predictions about the future. In contrast, correlational designs often do. If SAT scores are correlated with college grades, then knowing people's SAT scores allows us to forecast—although by no means perfectly—what their grades will be. Nevertheless, our conclusions from correlational research are almost always limited because we can't be sure *why* these predicted relationships exist.

Low Self-Esteem "Shrinks Brain"

A Surprising Secret to a Long Life: Stay in School

Housework Cuts Breast Cancer Risk

Fear of hell makes us richer, Fed says

Wearing a helmet puts cyclists at risk, suggests research

Winning World Cup lowers heart attack deaths

Eating fish prevents crime

We shouldn't rely on the news media to help us distinguish correlation from causation, because they frequently fall prey to the correlation versus causation fallacy (see some examples of misleading headlines in **FIGURE 2.5**). Take, for example, the headline "Low Self-Esteem Shrinks Brain." The article reports a correlation: Self-esteem is negatively correlated with brain size. Yet the article's title implies a causal association between low self-esteem and brain size. Although it's possible that low self-esteem "shrinks" people's brains, it's also possible that shrinking brains lower people's self-esteem. Alternatively, it's possible that an undetected third variable, such as alcohol use, contributes to both low self-esteem and smaller brains (people who drink heavily may both think more poorly of themselves and suffer long-term brain damage). *The bottom line:* Be on the lookout for headlines or news stories that proclaim a causal association between two variables. If the study is based on correlational data alone, we know they're taking their conclusions too far.

■ Experimental Designs

If observational designs, case studies, and correlational designs don't allow us to draw cause-and-effect conclusions, what kinds of designs do? The answer: Experimental designs, often known simply as "experiments." These designs differ from other designs in one crucial way: *They permit cause-and-effect inferences.* To see why, we need to understand that in correlational designs researchers are measuring preexisting differences in participants, like age, gender, IQ, and extraversion. In contrast, in experimental designs researchers are *manipulating* variables to see whether these manipulations produce differences in participants' behavior. Putting it another way, in correlational designs the differences among participants are *measured*, whereas in experimental designs they're *created*.

WHAT MAKES A STUDY AN EXPERIMENT: TWO COMPONENTS. Although news reporters frequently use the term *experiment* rather loosely to refer to any kind of research study, this term actually carries a specific meaning in psychology. To be precise, an **experiment** consists of *two* ingredients:

1. Random assignment of participants to conditions
2. Manipulation of an independent variable

Both of these ingredients are necessary for the recipe; if a study doesn't contain both of them, it's *not* an experiment. Let's look at each in turn.

Random Assignment. By **random assignment**, we mean that the experimenter randomly sorts participants into one of two groups. By doing so, we tend to cancel out preexisting differences between the two groups, such as differences in their gender, race, or personality traits. One of these two groups is the **experimental group**: This group receives the manipulation. The other is the **control group**: This group doesn't receive the manipulation. As we learned in Chapter 1, scientific thinking doesn't come naturally to the human species. When viewed through this lens, it's perhaps not surprising that the concept of the control group didn't clearly emerge in psychology until the turn of the twentieth century (Coover & Angell, 1907; Dehue, 2005).

To take an example of random assignment, let's imagine we wanted to determine whether a new drug, Miraculin, is effective for treating depression. We'd start with a large sample of individuals with depression. We'd then randomly assign (say, by flipping a coin) half of the participants to an experimental group, which receives Miraculin, and the other half to a control group, which doesn't receive Miraculin.

Incidentally, we shouldn't confuse random assignment with *random selection*, which, as we discussed earlier, is a procedure that allows every person an equal chance to participate. Here's how to remember the difference: Random selection deals with how we initially choose our participants, whereas random assignment deals with how we assign our participants *after we've already chosen them.*

Manipulation of an Independent Variable. The second ingredient of an experiment is manipulation of an independent variable. An **independent variable** is the variable the experimenter manipulates. The **dependent variable** is the variable that the experimenter measures to see whether this manipulation has had an effect. To remember this distinction, think about the fact that the dependent variable is "dependent on" the level of the independent variable. In the experiment using Miraculin as a treatment for depression, the independent variable is the presence versus absence of Miraculin. The dependent variable is the level of participants' depression following the experimental manipulation.

When we define our independent and dependent variables for the purposes of a study, we're providing what some psychologists call an **operational definition**—a working definition of what they're measuring. Specifying how we're measuring our variables of interest is important because different researchers may define the same variables in different ways and end up with different conclusions as a result. Imagine that two researchers used two different doses of Miraculin and measured depression using two different scales. They might end up drawing different conclusions about Miraculin's effectiveness because their measures told different stories. Still, operational definitions aren't like "dictionary" definitions of a word, in which just about all dictionaries agree on the "right" definition (Green, 1992). Different researchers can adopt different operational definitions for their own purposes.

MCHUMOR.com by T. McCracken

McWIT LABS · CONTROL GROUP · OUT OF CONTROL GROUP

The control group is an essential part of the "recipe" for a psychological experiment.

[handwritten notes: Correlational Design: observation, correlation. Experimental Design: manipulation, cause and effect. — randomized participants — manipulation of ind. variable]

experiment
research design characterized by random assignment of participants to conditions and manipulation of an independent variable

random assignment
randomly sorting participants into two groups

experimental group
in an experiment, the group of participants that receives the manipulation

control group
in an experiment, the group of participants that doesn't receive the manipulation

independent variable
variable that an experimenter manipulates

dependent variable
variable that an experimenter measures to see whether the manipulation has an effect

operational definition
a working definition of what a researcher is measuring

CONFOUNDS: A SOURCE OF FALSE CONCLUSIONS. For an experiment to possess adequate internal validity—which is needed to draw cause-and-effect conclusions—the level of the independent variable must be the *only* difference between the experimental and control groups. If there's some other difference between these groups, there's no way of knowing whether the independent variable really exerted an effect on the dependent variable. Psychologists use the term *confounding variable,* or confound, to refer to any difference between the experimental and control groups other than the independent variable. In our depression treatment example, let's imagine that the patients who received Miraculin also received a few sessions of psychotherapy. This additional treatment would be a confounding variable, because it's a variable other than the independent variable that differed between the experimental and control groups. This confounding variable makes it impossible for us to determine whether the differences between groups on the dependent variable (level of depression) were due to Miraculin, psychotherapy, or both.

CAUSE AND EFFECT: PERMISSION TO INFER. The two major features of an experiment—random assignment to conditions and manipulation of an independent variable—permit us to infer cause-and-effect relations if we've done the study right. To decide whether to infer cause-and-effect relations from a study, here's a tip that will work 100 percent of the time. *First,* using the criteria we've outlined, ask yourself whether a study is an experiment. *Second,* if it isn't an experiment, don't draw causal conclusions from it, no matter how tempting it might be to do so.

Before going further, let's make sure the major points concerning experimental designs are clear. Read this description of a study, and then answer the four questions below it. (You can find the answers upside down on the bottom of page 63.)

Acupuncture Study: Assess Your Knowledge. A researcher hypothesizes that acupuncture, an ancient Chinese medical practice that involves inserting thin needles in specific places on the body (see Chapter 12), can allow stressed-out psychology students to decrease their anxiety. She randomly assigns half of her participants to undergo acupuncture and half to receive no treatment. Two months later, she measures their anxiety levels and finds that people who received acupuncture are less stressed out than other participants, who received no treatment.

1. Is this a correlational or an experimental design?
2. What are the independent and dependent variables?
3. Is there a confound in this design? If so, what is it?
4. Can we infer cause and effect from this study? Why or why not?

PITFALLS IN EXPERIMENTAL DESIGN. Like correlational designs, experimental designs can be tricky to interpret, because there are numerous pitfalls to beware of when evaluating them. We'll focus on the most important traps here.

The Placebo Effect. To understand the first major pitfall in experiments, imagine we've developed what we believe to be a new wonder drug that treats hyperactivity (now called attention-deficit/hyperactivity disorder; see Chapter 15) in children. We randomly assign half of our participants with this condition to receive the drug and the other half to receive no treatment. At the conclusion of our study, we find that children who received the drug are much less hyperactive than children who received nothing. That's good news, to be sure, but does it mean we can now break out the champagne and celebrate the news that the drug is effective? Before reading the next paragraph, try to answer this question yourself.

If you answered no, you were right. The reason we can't pop the corks on our champagne bottles is that we haven't controlled for the placebo effect. The term *placebo* derives from the Latin for "I will please." The **placebo effect** is improvement resulting from the mere expectation of improvement (Kaptchuk, 2002; Kirsch, 2010). Participants who received the drug may have gotten better merely because they knew they were receiving treat-

Does yoga help people to lower their blood pressure and relieve stress? Only an experiment, with random assignment to conditions and manipulation of an independent variable, gives us permission to infer a cause-and-effect relationship.

This joke advertisement reminds us that the effects of placebos can sometimes be just as powerful as those of real medications.

placebo effect
improvement resulting from the mere expectation of improvement

ment. This knowledge could have instilled confidence or exerted a calming influence. The placebo effect is a powerful reminder that expectations can create reality.

In medication research, researchers typically control for the placebo effect by administering a sugar pill (sometimes referred to as a "dummy pill," although this term isn't meant as an insult to either the researchers or patients), which is itself often called a *placebo*, to members of the control group. In this way, patients in both the experimental and control groups don't know whether they're taking the actual medication or a placebo, so they're roughly equated in their expectations of improvement. In the Miraculin study, a placebo effect might have been operating, because the participants in the control group didn't receive a placebo—they received nothing. As a result, participants in the experimental group might have improved more than those in the control group because they knew they were getting treatment.

To avoid placebo effects, it's critical that patients not know whether they're receiving the real medication or a placebo. That is, patients must remain **blind** to the condition to which they've been assigned, namely, experimental or control. If patients aren't blind to their condition, then the experiment is essentially ruined, because the patients differ in their expectations of improvement.

Two different things can happen if the "blind is broken," which is psychological lingo for what happens when patients find out which group (experimental or control) they're in. First, patients in the experimental group (the ones receiving the drug) might improve more than patients in the control group (the ones receiving the placebo) because they know their treatment is real rather than fake. Second, patients in the control group might become resentful that they're receiving a placebo and try to "beat out" the patients in the experimental group ("Hey, we're going to show those experimenters what we're really made of.").

Placebo effects are just as real as those of actual drugs (Mayberg et al., 2002) and worthy of psychological investigation in their own right (see Chapters 12 and 16). Placebos show many of the same characteristics as do real drugs, such as having a more powerful effect at higher doses (Buckalew & Ross, 1981; Rickels et al., 1970). Placebos injected through a needle (researchers usually use a salt and water solution for this purpose) tend to show more rapid and powerful effects than placebos that are swallowed (Buckalew & Ross, 1981), probably because people assume that injectable placebos enter the bloodstream more quickly than pill placebos. Some patients even become addicted to placebo pills (Mintz, 1977). And placebos we believe to be more expensive tend to work better than placebos we believe to be cheaper (Ariely, 2008), probably because we rely on a heuristic that if something costs more, it's probably more effective.

Moreover, some researchers maintain that up to 80 percent of the effectiveness of antidepressants is attributable to placebo effects (Kirsch, 2010; Kirsch & Saperstein, 1998), although others suspect the true percentage is somewhat lower (Dawes, 1998; Klein, 1998). There are indications that placebos are equivalent to antidepressant medication in all but severe cases of depression, in which antidepressants have a clear edge over placebos (Fournier et al., 2010; Kirsch, Deacon, & Huedo-Medina, 2008). Placebo effects also aren't equally powerful for all conditions. They generally exert their strongest effects on subjective reports of depression and pain, but their effects on objective measures of physical illnesses, such as cancer and heart disease, are weaker (Hröbjartsson & Götzsche, 2001). Also, the effects of placebos may be more short-lived than those of actual medications (Rothschild & Quitkin, 1992).

The Nocebo Effect. The placebo effect has an "evil twin" of sorts: the nocebo effect (Benedetti, Lanotte, & Lopiano, 2007; Kirsch, 1999). The *nocebo effect* is harm resulting from the mere expectation of harm (*nocebo* comes from the Latin phrase meaning "to harm"). The ancient African, and later Caribbean, practice of voodoo presumably capitalizes on the nocebo effect: People who believe that others are sticking them with pins sometimes experience pain themselves. In one study, individuals who were allergic to roses sneezed when presented with fake roses (Reid, 2002). In another, researchers deceived a

"FIND OUT WHO SET UP THIS EXPERIMENT. IT SEEMS THAT HALF OF THE PATIENTS WERE GIVEN A PLACEBO, AND THE OTHER HALF WERE GIVEN A DIFFERENT PLACEBO."

(© ScienceCartoonsPlus.com)

blind
unaware of whether one is in the experimental or control group

Answers to questions on page 62:

(1) This study is experimental because there's random assignment to groups and the experimenter manipulated whether or not participants received treatment.

(2) The independent variable is the presence versus absence of acupuncture treatment. The dependent variable is the anxiety level of participants.

(3) There is a potential confound in that those who received acupuncture knew they were receiving treatment. Their lower anxiety may have been the result of expectations that they'd be feeling better following treatment.

(4) Yes. Because of the confound, we don't know why the experimental group was less anxious. But we can conclude that something about the treatment reduced anxiety.

"IT WAS MORE OF A 'TRIPLE-BLIND' TEST. THE PATIENTS DIDN'T KNOW WHICH ONES WERE GETTING THE REAL DRUG, THE DOCTORS DIDN'T KNOW, AND, I'M AFRAID, NOBODY KNEW."

(© ScienceCartoonsPlus.com)

experimenter expectancy effect
phenomenon in which researchers' hypotheses lead them to unintentionally bias the outcome of a study

extraordinary claims

IS THE EVIDENCE AS STRONG AS THE CLAIM?

double-blind
when neither researchers nor participants are aware of who's in the experimental or control group

Answer: Nocebo effect—the expectation of pain can itself create pain.

group of college students into believing that an electric current being passed into their heads could produce a headache. More than two-thirds of the students reported headaches, even though the current was imaginary (Morse, 1999).

The Experimenter Expectancy Effect. Including a control condition that provides a placebo treatment is extremely important, as is keeping participants blind to their condition assignment. Still, there's one more potential concern with experimental designs. In some cases, the participant doesn't know the condition assignment, but the experimenter does.

When this happens, a nasty problem can arise: The **experimenter expectancy effect** or *Rosenthal effect.* It occurs when researchers' hypotheses lead them to unintentionally bias the outcome of a study. You may want to underline the word *unintentionally* in the previous sentence, because this effect doesn't refer to deliberate "fudging" or making up of data, which fortunately happens only rarely in science. Instead, in the experimenter expectancy effect, researchers' biases subtly affect the results. In some cases, researchers may end up confirming their hypotheses even when these hypotheses are wrong.

Because of this effect, it's essential that experiments be conducted whenever possible in a **double-blind** fashion. By double-blind, we mean that neither researchers nor participants know who's in the experimental or control group. By voluntarily shielding themselves from the knowledge of which subjects are in which group, researchers are guarding themselves against confirmation bias.

One of the oldest and best-known examples of the experimenter expectancy effect is the infamous tale of German teacher Wilhelm von Osten and his horse. In 1900, von Osten had purchased a handsome Arabian stallion, known in the psychological literature as Clever Hans, who seemingly displayed astonishing mathematical abilities. By tapping with his hooves, Clever Hans responded correctly to mathematical questions from von Osten (such as, "How much is 8 plus 3?"). He even calculated square roots and could tell the time of day. Understandably, von Osten was so proud of Clever Hans that he began showing him off in public for large throngs of amazed spectators.

You might be wondering whether Clever Hans's feats were the result of trickery. A panel of 13 psychologists who investigated Clever Hans witnessed no evidence of fraud on von Osten's part, and concluded that Clever Hans possessed the arithmetic abilities of a 14-year-old human. Moreover, Clever Hans seemed to be a true-blue math whiz, because he could add and subtract even when von Osten wasn't posing the questions.

Nevertheless, psychologist Oscar Pfungst was skeptical of just how clever Clever Hans really was, and in 1904 he launched a series of careful observations. In this case, Pfungst did something that previous psychologists didn't think to do: He focused not on the horse, but on the people asking him questions. When he did, he found that von Osten and others were *unintentionally cuing* the horse to produce correct answers. Pfungst found that Clever Hans's questioners almost invariably tightened their muscles immediately before the correct answer. When Pfungst prevented Clever Hans from seeing the questioner or anyone else who knew the correct answer, the horse did no better than chance. The puzzle was solved: Clever Hans was cleverly detecting subtle physical cues emitted by questioners.

The Clever Hans story was one of the first demonstrations of the experimenter expectancy effect. It showed that people can—even without their knowledge—give off cues that affect a subject's behavior, even when that subject is a horse. This story also reminds us that an extraordinary claim, in this case that a horse can perform arithmetic, requires extraordinary evidence. Von Osten's claims were extraordinary, but his evidence wasn't. Interestingly, in a play on words, some authors have referred to facilitated communication, which we encountered at the beginning of this chapter, as the "phenomenon of Clever Hands" (Wegner, Fuller, & Sparrow, 2003), because it too appeared to be the result of an experimenter expectancy effect.

We mentioned that the experimenter expectancy effect is also called the Rosenthal effect. That's because in the 1960s psychologist Robert Rosenthal conducted an elegant series of experiments that persuaded the psychological community that experimenter expectancy effects were genuine. In one of these experiments, Rosenthal and Fode (1963) randomly assigned some psychology students a group of five so-called maze bright rats—rats bred over many generations to run mazes quickly—and other students a group of five so-called maze dull rats—rats bred over many generations to run mazes slowly. Note that this is an experiment, because Rosenthal and Fode randomly assigned students to groups and manipulated which type of rat the students supposedly received. They then asked students to run the rats in mazes and to record each rat's completion time. But there was a catch: Rosenthal and Fode had fibbed. They had randomly assigned rats to the students rather than the other way around. The story about the "maze bright" and "maze dull" rats was all cooked up. Yet when Rosenthal and Fode tabulated their results, they found that students assigned the "maze bright" rats reported 29 percent faster maze running times than did students assigned the "maze dull" rats. In some unknown fashion, the students had influenced their rats' running times.

Demand Characteristics. A final potential pitfall of psychological research can be difficult to eliminate. Research participants can pick up cues, known as **demand characteristics**, from an experiment that allow them to generate guesses regarding the experimenter's hypotheses (Orne, 1962; Rosnow, 2002). In some cases, participants' guesses about what the experimenter is up to may be correct; in other cases, they may not. The problem is that when participants think they know how the experimenter wants them to act, they may alter their behavior accordingly. So whether they've guessed right or wrong, their beliefs are preventing researchers from getting an unbiased view of participants' thoughts and behaviors. To combat demand characteristics, researchers may try to disguise the purpose of the study. Alternatively, they may include "distractor" tasks or "filler" items—measures unrelated to the question of interest. These items help to prevent participants from altering their responses in ways they think the experimenters are looking for.

Clever Hans performing in public. If one can observe powerful experimenter (in this case, owner) expectancy effects even in animals, how powerful might such effects be in humans?

psychomythology

LABORATORY RESEARCH DOESN'T APPLY TO THE REAL WORLD, RIGHT?

Beginning psychology students often assume that most laboratory research doesn't generalize to the real world. This assumption seems reasonable at first blush, because behavior that emerges in the artificial confines of the laboratory doesn't always mirror behavior in natural settings. Moreover, psychologists conduct a great deal of their research on college students, who tend to be more intelligent, more self-absorbed, less certain of their identities, and more reliant on social approval than noncollege participants. Indeed, about 75 percent of published studies of interpersonal interactions are conducted on undergraduates (Sears, 1986). It's not always clear how generalizable these findings are to the rest of humanity (Henrich, Heine, & Norenzayan, 2010; Peterson, 2000).

But is the "truism" that laboratory research is low in external validity—generalizability to the real world—true? As Douglas Mook (1983) pointed out, high internal validity can often lead to high external validity. That's because carefully controlled experiments generate conclusions that are more trustworthy and more likely to apply to the real world than are loosely controlled studies. In addition, the results of carefully controlled experiments are typically more likely to replicate than the results of loosely controlled studies.

Craig Anderson, James Lindsay, and Brad Bushman (1999) took a systematic look at this issue. They examined the correspondence between laboratory studies of various psychological phenomena—including aggression, helping, leadership, interpersonal perception, performance on exams, and the causes of depressed mood—as measured in both the laboratory and real world. Anderson and his colleagues computed how large the effects were in both laboratory and real-world studies and correlated these effects. For example, in studies of the relation between watching violent television and aggressive behavior, they examined the correspondence between findings from controlled laboratory studies—in which investigators

FACTOID +

Clever Hans wasn't the only horse to fool dozens of people. In the 1920s, Lady Wonder, a horse in Richmond, Virginia, amazed observers by what appeared to be psychic abilities. She answered her trainer's questions by arranging alphabet blocks with her mouth, including questions that only her trainer knew. A magician, Milbourne Christopher, later determined that when the trainer didn't know the right answer to the question, Lady Wonder performed no better than chance.

 replicability

CAN THE RESULTS BE DUPLICATED IN OTHER STUDIES?

demand characteristics
cues that participants pick up from a study that allow them to generate guesses regarding the researcher's hypotheses

Size of finding in the laboratory

FIGURE 2.6   Does Laboratory Research Relate to the Real World? This scatterplot displays the data from the findings of studies in the laboratory versus the real world from Anderson, Lindsay, and Bushman (1999).

✓—Study and Review on **mypsychlab.com**

randomly assign participants to watch either violent television or nonviolent television, and then measure their aggression—and real-world studies—in which investigators observe people's television viewing habits and aggression in daily life.

Contrary to what many psychologists have assumed, Anderson and his collaborators found the correlation between the sizes of the effects in laboratory and real-world studies to be *r* = .73, which is a high association (see **FIGURE 2.6**). Laboratory research often generalizes surprisingly well to the real world.

Even so, we shouldn't simply assume that a laboratory study has high external validity. The best approach is to examine both well-controlled laboratory experiments and studies using naturalistic observation to make sure that the results from both research designs converge. If they do, that should make us more confident in our conclusions (Shadish, Cook, & Campbell, 2002). If they don't, that should make us scratch our heads and try to figure out what's accounting for the difference.

---

assess your knowledge   FACT OR FICTION?

1. Case studies can sometimes provide existence proofs of psychological phenomena. **True** / **False**

2. Rating data can be biased because some respondents allow their ratings of one positive characteristic to spill over to other positive characteristics. **True** / **False**

3. A correlation of −.8 is just as large in magnitude as a correlation of +.8. **True** / **False**

4. Experiments are characterized by two, and only two, features. **True** / **False**

5. To control for experimenter expectancy effects, only participants need to be blind to who's in the experimental and control groups. **True** / **False**

Answers: 1. T (p.51); 2. T (p.55); 3. T (p.56); 4. T (p.61); 5. F (p.64)

ETHICAL ISSUES IN RESEARCH DESIGN

2.5   Explain the ethical obligations of researchers toward their research participants.

2.6   Describe both sides of the debate on the use of animals as research subjects.

When designing and conducting research studies, psychologists need to worry about more than their scientific value. The ethics of these studies also matter. Although psychology adheres to the same basic scientific principles as other sciences, let's face it: A chemist needn't worry about hurting his mineral's feelings, and a physicist needn't be concerned about the long-term emotional well-being of a neutron. The scientific study of people and their behavior raises unique concerns.

Many philosophers believe—and the authors of this text agree—that science itself is value-neutral. Because science is a search for the truth, it's neither inherently good nor bad. This fact doesn't imply, though, that scientific *research* is value-neutral, as there are both ethical and unethical ways of searching for the truth. Moreover, we may not all agree on which ways of searching for the truth are ethical. We'd probably all agree that it's acceptable to learn about brain damage by studying the behavior of people with brain damage on laboratory tasks of learning, just so long as these tasks aren't overly stressful. We'd also all agree (we hope!) that it's unacceptable for us to learn about brain damage by hitting people over the head with baseball bats and then testing their motor coordination by measuring how often they fall down a flight of stairs. Nevertheless, we might not all agree on whether it's acceptable to learn about brain damage by creating severe lesions (wounds) in the brains of cats and examining their effects on cats' responses to fear-provoking stimuli (like scary dogs). In many cases, the question of whether research is ethical isn't clear-cut.

■ Tuskegee: A Shameful Moral Tale

Scientists have learned the hard way that their thirst for knowledge can blind them to crucial ethical considerations. One deeply troubling example comes from the Tuskegee study performed by the United States Public Health Service, an agency of the United States Government, from 1932 to 1972 (Jones, 1993). During this time, a number of researchers wanted to learn more about the natural course of syphilis, a sexually transmitted disease. What happens, they wondered, to syphilis over time if left untreated?

The "subjects" in this study were 399 African American men living in the poorest rural areas of Alabama who'd been diagnosed with syphilis. Remarkably, the researchers never informed these men that they had syphilis, nor that an effective treatment for syphilis, namely, antibiotics, had become available. Indeed, the subjects didn't even know they were subjects, as researchers hadn't informed them of that crucial piece of information. Instead, the researchers merely tracked subjects' progress over time, withholding all medical information and all available treatments. By the end of the study, 28 men had died of syphilis, 100 had died of syphilis-related complications, 40 of the men's wives had been infected with syphilis, and 19 children had been born with syphilis. In 1997—25 years after the termination of this study—then President Bill Clinton, on behalf of the United States government, offered a formal apology for the Tuskegee study to the study's eight remaining survivors.

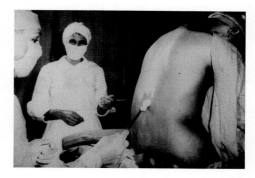

In this 1933 photograph, an African American subject undergoes a painful medical procedure (spinal tap) as part of the Tuskegee study. This study demonstrates the tragic consequences of ignoring crucial ethical considerations in research.

■ Ethical Guidelines for Human Research

If any good at all came out of the horrific Tuskegee study and other ethical catastrophes in scientific research, it was a heightened appreciation for protecting human subjects' rights. Fortunately, researchers could never perform the Tuskegee study today, at least not in the United States. That's because every major American research college and university has at least one *institutional review board* (IRB), which reviews all research carefully with an eye toward protecting participants against abuses. IRBs typically consist of faculty members drawn from various departments within a college or university, as well as one or more outside members, such as a person drawn from the community surrounding the college or university.

INFORMED CONSENT. IRBs insist on a procedure called **informed consent**: Researchers must tell subjects what they're getting into before asking them to participate. During the informed consent process, participants can ask questions about the study and learn more about what will be involved. The Tuskegee subjects never received informed consent, and we can be certain they wouldn't have agreed to participate had they known they wouldn't be receiving treatment for a potentially fatal illness.

Nevertheless, IRBs may sometimes allow researchers to forgo certain elements of informed consent. In particular, some psychological research entails *deception*. When researchers use deception, they deliberately mislead participants about the study's design or purpose. In one of the most controversial studies in the history of psychology (see Chapter 13), Stanley Milgram (1963), then at Yale University, invited volunteers to participate in a study of the "effects of punishment on learning." The experimenter deceived participants into believing they were administering painful electric shocks of increasing intensity to another participant, who made repeated errors on a learning task. In reality, the other "participant" was actually a *confederate* (a research assistant who plays the part of a participant) of the experimenter, and never received any shocks. Moreover, Milgram had no interest in the effects of punishment on learning; he was actually interested in the influence of authority figures on obedience. Many of the actual participants experienced considerable distress during the procedure, and some were understandably troubled by the fact that they delivered what they believed to be extremely painful—even potentially fatal—electric shocks to an innocent person.

FACTOID

The award for the most ethically questionable research on humans published in a psychology journal may well go to an early 1960s study in which investigators wanted to determine the effects of fear on attention. A pilot informed ten U.S. soldiers on board what they believed to be a routine training flight that the plane's engine and landing gear were malfunctioning and that he was going to attempt to crash-land in the ocean. In fact, the pilot had deceived the soldiers: The plane was just fine. The researchers found that these soldiers made more errors filling out paperwork forms than did a control group of soldiers on the ground (Boese, 2007). Needless to say, the bizarre investigation could never make it past any modern-day IRB.

informed consent
informing research participants of what is involved in a study before asking them to participate

Was Milgram's elaborate deception justified? Milgram (1964) argued that the hoax was required to pull off the study, because informing subjects of its true purpose would have generated obvious demand characteristics. He further noted that he went out of his way to later explain the study's true purpose to participants and assure them that their obedience wasn't a sign of cruelty or psychological disturbance. In addition, he sent a questionnaire to all subjects after the studies were completed and found that only 1.3 percent reported any negative emotional aftereffects. In contrast, Diana Baumrind (1964) argued that Milgram's study wasn't worth the knowledge or psychological distress it generated. Milgram's failure to provide subjects with full informed consent, she maintained, was ethically indefensible. Simply put, Milgram's subjects didn't know what they were getting into when they volunteered.

The debate concerning the ethics of Milgram's study continues to this day (Blass, 2004). Although we won't try to resolve this controversy here, we'll say only that the ethical standards of the American Psychological Association (2002) affirm that deception is justified only when (a) researchers couldn't have performed the study without the deception and (b) the scientific knowledge to be gained from the study outweighs its costs (see **TABLE 2.3**). Needless to say, evaluating (b) isn't easy, and it's up to researchers—and ultimately, the IRB—to decide whether the potential scientific benefits of a study are sufficient to justify deception. Over the years, IRBs—which didn't exist in Milgram's day—have become more stringent about the need for informed consent. 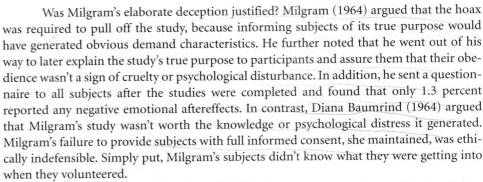 Simulate

 Simulate Ethics in Psychological Research on **mypsychlab.com**

DEBRIEFING: EDUCATING PARTICIPANTS. IRBs may also request that a full debriefing be performed at the conclusion of the research session. *Debriefing* is a process whereby researchers inform participants what the study was about. In some cases, researchers use debriefings to explain their hypotheses in nontechnical language. By administering a debriefing, the study becomes a learning experience for not only the investigator, but also the subject.

TABLE 2.3 APA Ethical Principles for Human Research. Psychological researchers must carefully weigh the potential scientific benefits of their research against the potential danger to participants. In 2002, the American Psychological Association (APA) published a code of ethics to govern all research with human participants. The following is a summary of the key ethical principles.

Scientific knowledge — Potential harm to subjects

Informed Consent

- Research participants should be fully informed of the purpose of the research, its expected duration, and any potential risks, discomfort, or adverse effects associated with it.
- Participants should enter the study voluntarily and be informed of their right to withdraw from it at any time.
- A contact who can answer questions about the research and the participant's rights should be provided.

Protection from Harm and Discomfort

- Psychologists must take reasonable steps to avoid harm to research participants.

Deception and Debriefing

- When deceptive techniques are used in research, the participants should be informed of the deception as soon as possible after the deception takes place.
- Participants should not be deceived about research procedures that may cause the participants physical pain or emotional distress.
- Once the research study has concluded, participants should not only be informed of the deception but fully debriefed about the true nature of the research and its results.

■ Ethical Issues in Animal Research

Few topics generate as much anger and discomfort as animal research. This is especially true of *invasive* research, in which investigators cause physical harm to animals. In psychology departments, invasive research most often takes the form of producing lesions in animals' brains, usually by means of surgery, and observing their effects on animals' behavior (see Chapter 3). About 7 to 8 percent of published research in psychology relies on animals (American Psychological Association, 2008) with the overwhelming majority of studies conducted on rodents (especially rats and mice) and birds. The goal of such research is to generate ideas about how the brain relates to behavior in animals—and how these findings generalize to humans—without inflicting harm on people.

A great deal of animal research remains intensely controversial. It will probably always remain this way, given the complex ethical questions involved.

Many animal rights activists have raised useful concerns regarding the ethical treatment of animals and have underscored the need for adequate housing and feeding conditions (Marino, 2009; Ott, 1995). In contrast, others have gone to extremes that many critics would describe as unethical in themselves. Some have ransacked laboratories and liberated animals. In 1999, the Animal Liberation Front attacked several psychology laboratories at the University of Minnesota, releasing rats and pigeons and inflicting about $2 million worth of damage (Azar, 1999; Hunt, 1999). Incidentally, most individuals on both sides of the animal rights debate agree that liberating animals is a dreadful idea, because many or most animals die shortly after being released. ◉─┤Watch

These excessive tactics aside, the ethical issues here aren't easily resolved. Some commentators maintain that the deaths of approximately 20 million laboratory animals every year (Cunningham, 1993) aren't worth the cost. For many critics, the knowledge gleaned from animal research on aggression, fear, learning, memory, and related topics is of such doubtful external validity to humans as to be virtually useless (Ulrich, 1991).

◉─┤**Watch** Animal Rights Terrorists on **mypsychlab.com**

This position has some merit but may be too extreme. Some animal research has led to direct benefits to humans, as well as immensely useful knowledge in its own right. Many psychological treatments, especially those based on principles of learning (see Chapter 6), derived from animal research. Without animal research, we'd know relatively little about the physiology of the brain (Domjan & Purdy, 1995). Moreover, to answer many critical psychological questions, there are simply no good alternatives to using animals (Gallup & Suarez, 1985). For example, without animals we'd be unable to test the safety and effectiveness of many medications.

None of this tells us when we should and shouldn't use animals in research. Nevertheless, it's clear that animal research has yielded enormously important insights about the brain and behavior and that psychologists are likely to rely on such research for some time to come. It's also clear that animal researchers must weigh carefully the potential scientific gains of their inquiries against the costs in death and suffering they produce. Because reasonable people will inevitably disagree about how to weigh these pros and cons, the intense controversy surrounding animal research is unlikely to subside anytime soon.

---

assess your knowledge   FACT OR FICTION?

✓●─┤**Study** and **Review** on **mypsychlab.com**

1. The Tuskegee study violated the principles of informed consent. **True / False**

2. Milgram's study would be considered unethical today because the shock could have caused injury or death. **True / False**

3. In debriefing, the researcher informs participants of what will happen in the procedure before asking them to participate. **True / False**

4. Before conducting invasive research on animals, investigators must weigh carefully the potential scientific benefits of this research against the costs of animal death and suffering. **True / False**

Answers: 1. T (p. 67); 2. F (p. 68); 3. F (p. 68); 4. T (p. 69)

FORMULA APPRECIATION CLASS
AT THE MATH MUSEUM

(© ScienceCartoonsPlus.com)

Central tendency:
mean = average
median = middle
mode = most

Simulate Doing Simple Statistics on
mypsychlab.com

STATISTICS: THE LANGUAGE OF PSYCHOLOGICAL RESEARCH

2.7   Identify uses of various measures of central tendency and variability.

2.8   Explain how inferential statistics can help us to determine whether we can generalize from our sample to the full population.

2.9   Show how statistics can be misused for purposes of persuasion.

Up to this point, we've mostly spared you the gory mathematical details of psychological research. Aside from correlation coefficients, we haven't said much about how psychologists analyze their findings. Still, to understand psychological research and how to interpret it, we need to know a bit about **statistics**: the application of mathematics to describing and analyzing data. For you math phobics (or "arithmophobics," if you want to impress your friends with a technical term) out there, there's no cause for alarm. We promise to keep things simple.

■ Descriptive Statistics: What's What? *Math!* ☺

Psychologists use two kinds of statistics. The first are **descriptive statistics**. They do exactly what the name implies: describe data. Using descriptive statistics on a sample of 100 men and 100 hundred women whose levels of extraversion we assess using a self-report measure, we could ask the following questions:

- What's the average level of extraversion in this sample?
- What's the average level of extraversion among men, and what's the average level of extraversion among women?
- How much do all of our participants, as well as men and women separately, vary in how extraverted they are?

To maintain our promise we'd keep things simple, we'll discuss only two major types of descriptive statistics. The first is the **central tendency**, which gives us a sense of the "central" score in our data set or where the group tends to cluster. In turn, there are three measures of central tendency: mean, median, and mode (known as the "three Ms"). Follow along in **TABLE 2.4a** (the left half of the table below) as we calculate each. Simulate

The **mean**, also known as the average, is just the total score divided by the number of people. If our sample consists of five people as shown in the table, the mean IQ is simply the total of the five scores divided by five, which happens to be 102.

The **median**, which we shouldn't confuse with that patch of grass in the middle of a highway, is the middle score in our data set. We obtain the median by lining up our scores in order and finding the middle one. So in this case, we'd line up the five IQ scores in order from lowest to highest, and find that 100 is the median because it's the score smack in the middle of the distribution.

The **mode** is the most frequent score in our data set. In this case, the mode is 120, because two people in our sample received scores of 120 on the IQ test and one person each received other scores.

TABLE 2.4 The Three Ms: Mean, Median, and Mode.

(a)	(b)
Sample IQ scores: 100, 90, 80, 120, 120	**Sample IQ scores:** 80, 85, 95, 95, 220
Mean: (100 + 90 + 80 + 120 + 120)/5 = 102	**Mean:** (80 + 85 + 95 + 95 + 220)/5 = 116
Median: order scores from lowest to highest: 80, 90, 100, 120, 120; middle score is 100	**Median:** 95
Mode: only 120 appears twice in the data set, so it's the most common score.	**Mode:** 95
	Note: Mean is affected by one extreme score, but median and mode aren't.

statistics
application of mathematics to describing and analyzing data

descriptive statistics
numerical characterizations that describe data

central tendency
measure of the "central" scores in a data set, or where the group tends to cluster

mean
average; a measure of central tendency

median
middle score in a data set; a measure of central tendency

mode
most frequent score in a data set; a measure of central tendency

As we can see, the three Ms sometimes give us rather different measures of central tendency. In this case, the mean and median were close to each other, but the mode was much higher than both. The mean is generally the best statistic to report when our data form a bell-shaped or "normal" distribution, as we can see in the top panel of **FIGURE 2.7**. But what happens when our distribution is "skewed," that is, tilted sharply to one side or the other, as in the bottom panels? Here the mean provides a misleading picture of the central tendency, so it's better to use the median or mode instead, as these statistics are less affected by extreme scores at either the low or high end.

To hammer this point home, let's look at **TABLE 2.4b** to see what happens to our measures of central tendency. The mean of this distribution is 116, but four of the scores are much below 116, and the only reason the mean is this high is the presence of one person who scored 220 (who in technical terms is an *outlier,* because his or her score lies way outside the other scores). In contrast, both the median and mode are 95, which capture the central tendency of the distribution much better.

The second type of descriptive statistic is **variability** (sometimes called dispersion), which gives us a sense of how loosely or tightly bunched the scores are. Consider the following two sets of IQ scores from five people:

- 80, 85, 85, 90, 95
- 25, 65, 70, 125, 150

In both groups of scores, the mean is 87. But the second set of scores is much more spread out than the first. So we need some means of describing the differences in variability in these two data sets.

The simplest measure of variability is the **range**. The range is the difference between the highest and lowest scores. In the first set of IQ scores, the range is only 15, whereas in the second set the range is 125. So the range tells us that although the two sets of scores have a similar central tendency, their variability is wildly different (as in **FIGURE 2.8a**). Although the range is the easiest measure of variability to calculate, it can be deceptive because, as shown in **FIGURE 2.8b**, two data sets with the same range can display a very different distribution of scores across that range. To compensate for this problem, psychologists often use another measure called the **standard deviation** to depict variability. This measure is less likely to be deceptive than the range because it takes into account how far *each* data point is from the mean, rather than simply how widely scattered the most extreme scores are.

■ Inferential Statistics: Testing Hypotheses

In addition to descriptive statistics, psychologists use **inferential statistics**, which allow us to determine how much we can generalize findings from our sample to the full population. When using inferential statistics, we're asking whether we can draw "inferences" (conclusions) regarding whether the differences we've observed in our sample apply to similar samples. Earlier, we mentioned a study of 100 men and 100 women who took a self-report measure of extraversion. In this study, inferential statistics allow us to find out whether the differences we've observed in extraversion between men and women are believable, or if they're just a fluke occurrence in our sample. Let's imagine we calculated the means for men and women (we first verified that the distribution of scores in both men and women approximated a bell curve). After doing so, we found that men scored 10.4 on our extraversion scale

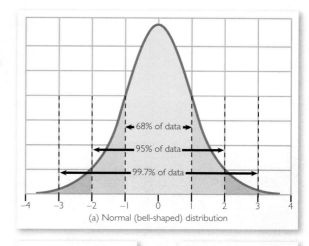

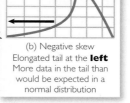

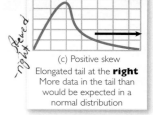

(a) Normal (bell-shaped) distribution

(b) Negative skew
Elongated tail at the **left**
More data in the tail than would be expected in a normal distribution

(c) Positive skew
Elongated tail at the **right**
More data in the tail than would be expected in a normal distribution

FIGURE 2.7 Distribution Curves. (a) a normal (bell-shaped) distribution, (b) a markedly negative skewed distribution, and (c) a markedly positive skewed distribution.

The Psychologist

09-04-2010

NEWSWIRE

50% of Americans Below Average in IQ

Rutters News Agency: A shocking 50% of Americans are below average in IQ, reported a team of psychologists today at the Annual Meeting of the American Society of Psychology and Pseudoscience. The researchers, from Nonexistent State University, administered IQ tests to a sample of 6,000 Americans and found that fully half scored below the mean of their sample.

What's wrong with this (fake) newspaper headline?

FIGURE 2.8 The Range versus the Standard Deviation. These two number lines display data sets with the same *range* but different *standard deviations*. The variability is more tightly clustered in (a) than in (b), so the standard deviation in (a) will be smaller.

variability
measure of how loosely or tightly bunched scores are

range
difference between the highest and lowest scores; a measure of dispersion

standard deviation
measure of dispersion that takes into account how far each data point is from the mean

inferential statistics
mathematical methods that allow us to determine whether we can generalize findings from our sample to the full population

(the scores range from 0 to 15) and that women scored 9.9. So, *in our sample,* men are more extraverted, or at least say they are, than women. Can we now conclude that men are more extraverted than women in general? How can we rule out the possibility that this small sex difference in our sample is due to chance? That's where inferential statistics enter the picture.

STATISTICAL SIGNIFICANCE. To figure out whether the difference we've observed in our sample is a believable (real) one, we need to conduct statistical tests to determine whether we can generalize our findings to the broader population. To do so, we can use a variety of statistics depending on the research design. But regardless of which test we use, we generally use a .05 level of confidence when deciding whether a finding is trustworthy. This minimum level—five in 100—is taken as the probability that the finding occurred by chance. When the finding would have occurred by chance less than five in 100 times, we say that it's *statistically significant.* A statistically significant result is believable; it's probably a real difference in our sample. In psychology journals, we'll often see the expression "$p < .05$," meaning that the probability (the lowercase p stands for probability) that our finding would have occurred by chance alone is less than five in 100, or one in 20.

PRACTICAL SIGNIFICANCE. Writer Gertrude Stein said that "a difference is a difference that makes a difference." Stein's quotation reminds us not to confuse statistical significance with *practical significance,* that is, real-world importance. A finding can be statistically significant yet be of virtually no real-world importance. To understand this point, we need to understand that a major determinant of statistical significance is sample size. The larger the sample size, the greater the odds (all else being equal) that a result will be statistically significant (Meehl, 1978; Schmidt, 1992). With huge sample sizes, virtually all findings—even tiny ones—will be statistically significant.

If we were to find a correlation of $r = .06$ between IQ and nose length in a sample of 500,000 people, this correlation would be statistically significant at the $p < .05$ level. Yet it's so miniscule in magnitude that it would be essentially useless for predicting anything.

■ How People Lie with Statistics

Humorist Mark Twain once said there are three kinds of untruths: "lies, damned lies, and statistics." Because many people's eyes glaze over when they see lots of numbers, it's easy to fool them with statistical sleight of hand. Here, we'll provide three examples of how people can misuse statistics. Our goal, of course, isn't to encourage you to lie with statistics, but to equip you with scientific thinking skills for spotting statistical abuses (Huck, 2008; Huff, 1954).

EXAMPLE I

Your Congressional Representative, Ms. Dee Section, is running for reelection. As part of her platform, she's proposed a new tax plan for everyone in your state. According to the "fine print" in Ms. Section's plan, 99 percent of people in your state will receive a $100 tax cut this year. The remaining 1 percent, who make over $3 million per year, will receive a tax cut of $500,000 (according to Ms. Section, this large tax cut for the richest people is necessary because she gets her biggest campaign contributions from them).

Based on this plan, Ms. Dee Section announces at a press conference, "If I'm elected and my tax plan goes through, the average person in our state will receive a tax cut of $5,099." Watching this press conference on television, you think, "Wow . . . what a deal! I'm definitely going to vote for Dee Section. If she wins, I'll have over 5,000 extra bucks in my bank account."

Question: *Why should you be skeptical of Dee Section's claim?*

Answer: Ms. Dee Section has engaged in a not-especially-subtle deception, suggesting that she's aptly named. She assures us that under her plan the "average person" in her state will receive a tax cut of $5,099. In one respect she's right, because the *mean* tax cut is indeed $5,099. But in this case, the mean is highly misleading, because under Section's plan virtually everyone in her state will receive only a $100 tax cut. Only the richest of the rich will receive a tax cut of $500,000, making the mean highly unrepresentative of the cen-

A large sample size can yield a statistically significant result, but this result may have little or no practical significance.

"There are lies, damn lies, and statistics. We're looking for someone who can make all three of these work for us."

(© www.CartoonStock.com)

tral tendency. Dee Section should have instead reported the median or mode, which are both only $100, as measures of central tendency. As we learned earlier, the median and mode are less affected by extreme scores than the mean.

EXAMPLE 2

A researcher, Dr. Faulty Conclusion, conducts a study to demonstrate that transcendental meditation (TM), a form of relaxation that originated in East Asian cultures, reduces crime rates. According to Dr. Conclusion, towns whose citizens are taught to practice TM will experience a dramatic drop in arrests. He finds a small town, Pancake, Iowa (population 300), and teaches all citizens of Pancake to practice TM. For his control group, he identifies a small neighboring town in Iowa, called Waffle (population also 300), and doesn't introduce them to TM. According to Dr. Conclusion, Waffle is a good control group for Pancake, because it has the same population, ethnic makeup, income, and initial arrest rates.

Two months after the introduction of TM to Pancake, Dr. Conclusion measures the arrest rates in Pancake and Waffle. At a major conference, he proudly announces that although the arrest rates in Waffle stayed exactly the same, the arrest rates in Pancake experienced a spectacular plunge. To demonstrate this astonishing effect, he directs the audience to a graph (see **FIGURE 2.9**). As he does, the audience gasps in astonishment. "As you can see from this graph," Conclusion proclaims, "the arrest rates in Pancake were initially very high. But after I taught Pancake's citizens TM, their arrest rates two months later were much, much lower." Dr. Conclusion concludes triumphantly, "Our findings show beyond a shadow of a doubt that TM reduces crime rates."

Question: *What's wrong with Dr. Conclusion's conclusion?*

Answer: Dr. Conclusion's graph in Figure 2.9 sure looks impressive, doesn't it? The arrest rates have indeed gone down from the beginning to the end of the study. But let's take a good close look at the *y* axis (that's the vertical axis) of the graph. Can we see anything suspicious about it?

Dr. Conclusion has tricked us, or perhaps he's tricked himself. The *y* axis starts at 15.5 arrests per month and goes up to 16 arrests per month. In fact, Dr. Conclusion has demonstrated only that the arrest rate in Pancake declined from 15.9 arrests per month to 15.6 arrests per month—a grand total of less than one-third of an arrest per month! That's hardly worth writing home about, let alone mastering TM for.

Dr. Conclusion used what's termed a "truncated line graph." That kind of graph is a real "no-no" in statistics, although many researchers still use it (Huff, 1954; Smith, 2001). In this kind of graph, the *y* axis starts not at the lowest possible score, where it should start (in this case, it should start at zero, because that's the lowest possible number of arrests per month), but somewhere close to the highest possible score. By using a truncated line graph, Dr. Conclusion made the apparent effects of TM appear huge when in fact they were pitifully small.

EXAMPLE 3

Ms. Representation conducts a study to determine the association between nationality and drinking patterns. According to Professor Representation's new "Grand Unified Theory of Drinking Behavior," people of German descent are at higher risk for alcoholism than people of Norwegian descent. To test this hypothesis, she begins with a randomly selected sample of 10,000 people from the city of Inebriated, Indiana. She administers a survey to all participants inquiring about their drinking habits and national background. When she analyzes her data, she finds that 1,200 citizens of Inebriated meet official diagnostic criteria for alcoholism. Of these 1,200 individuals, 450 are of German descent, whereas only 30 are of Norwegian descent—a 15-fold difference! She conducts a statistical test (we won't trouble you with the precise mathematics) and determines that this amazingly large difference is statistically significant at $p < .05$. At the annual convention of the International Society of Really, Really Smart Alcoholism Researchers, Ms. Representation asserts, "My bold hypothesis has been confirmed. I can conclude confidently that Germans are at higher risk for alcoholism than Norwegians."

Question: *Why are Ms. Representation's conclusions about drinking all washed up?*

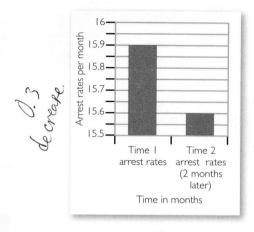

0.3 decrease

FIGURE 2.9 Arrest Rates Before and After Transcendental Meditation. Arrest rates per month in Pancake before (*left*) and after (*right*) introduction of transcendental meditation.

To evaluate claims about statistics on the Internet, we must equip ourselves with tools that protect us against errors in reasoning.

Answer: Remember the _base rate fallacy_ we introduced in this chapter? When interpreting findings, it's easy to forget about base rates. That's because base rates often "lurk in the distance" of our minds and aren't especially vivid. In this case, Ms. Representation forgot to take a crucial fact into account: In Inebriated, Indiana, the base rate of people of German descent is 25 times higher than the base rate of people of Norwegian descent. As a result, the fact that there are 15 times more German than Norwegian alcoholics in Inebriated doesn't support her hypothesis. In fact, given there are 25 times more Germans than Norwegians in Inebriated, the data actually run _opposite_ to Ms. Representation's hypothesis: The percentage of alcoholic Norwegians is higher than the percentage of alcoholic Germans!

The bottom line: _Don't trust all of the statistics you read in a newspaper_.

Bear in mind that we've focused here on misuses and abuses of statistics. That's because we want to immunize you against statistical errors you're likely to encounter in the newspaper as well as on TV and the Internet. But you shouldn't conclude from our examples that we can _never_ trust statistics. As we'll learn throughout this text, statistics are a wonderful set of tools that can help us to understand behavior. When evaluating statistics, it's best to steer a middle course between dismissing them out of hand and accepting them uncritically. As is so often the case in psychology, remember that we should keep our minds open, but not so open that our brains fall out.

✓• Study and Review on mypsychlab.com

assess your knowledge   FACT OR FICTION?

1. The mean is not always the best measure of central tendency. **True / False**

2. The mode and standard deviation are both measures of variability. **True / False**

3. All statistically significant findings are important and large in size. **True / False**

4. Researchers can easily manipulate statistics to make it appear that their hypotheses are confirmed even when they're not. **True / False**

Answers: 1. T (p.71); 2. F (p.71); 3. F (p.72); 4. T (p.72)

EVALUATING PSYCHOLOGICAL RESEARCH

2.10   Identify flaws in research designs.

2.11   Identify skills for evaluating psychological claims in the popular media.

Every day, the Internet, newspapers, and television stations bombard us with the results of psychological and medical studies. Some of these studies are trustworthy, yet many others aren't. How can we sort out which are which?

■ Becoming a Peer Reviewer

Nearly all psychological journals send submitted articles to outside reviewers, who screen the articles carefully for quality control. As we'll recall, this often ego-bruising process is called _peer review_ (see Chapter 1, Table 1.2). One crucial task of peer reviewers is to identify flaws that could undermine a study's findings and conclusions. Now that we've learned the key ingredients of a psychological experiment and the pitfalls that can cause experiments to go wrong, let's try our hands at becoming peer reviewers. Doing so will allow us to become better consumers of real-world research.

We'll present descriptions of three studies, each of which contains at least one hidden flaw. Read each study and try to figure out what's wrong with it. Once you've done so, read the paragraph below it to see how close you came.

Ready? Here goes.

"THAT'S IT? THAT'S PEER REVIEW?"

(© ScienceCartoonsPlus.com)

STUDY 1

An investigator, Dr. Sudo Sigh-Ents, sets out to test the hypothesis that subliminal self-help tapes (see Chapter 4) increase self-esteem. She randomly selects 50 college freshmen from the subject pool to receive a commercially available subliminal self-help tape. She asks them to play the tape for two months each night for one hour before going to sleep (which is consistent with the standard instructions on the tape). Dr. Sigh-Ents measures participants' self-esteem at the start of the study and again after two months. She finds that their self-esteem has increased significantly over these two months, and concludes that "subliminal self-help tapes increase self-esteem."

Question: *What's wrong with this experiment?*

Answer: What's wrong with this "experiment" is that it's not even an experiment. There's no random assignment of participants to experimental and control groups; in fact, there's no control group at all. There's also no manipulation of an independent variable. Remember that a variable is something that varies. In this case, there's no independent variable because all participants received the same manipulation, namely, playing the subliminal self-help tape every night. As a result, we can't know whether the increase in self-esteem was really due to the tape. It could have been due to any number of other factors, such as placebo effects or increases in self-esteem that might often occur over the course of one's freshman year.

STUDY 2

A researcher, Dr. Art E. Fact, is interested in determining whether a new treatment, Anger Expression Therapy, is effective in treating anxiety. He randomly assigns 100 individuals with anxiety disorders to two groups. The experimental group receives Anger Expression Therapy (which is administered by Dr. Fact himself), whereas the control group is placed on a waiting list and receives no treatment. At the conclusion of six months, Dr. Fact finds that the rate of anxiety disorders is significantly lower in the experimental group than in the control group. He concludes, "Anger Expression Therapy is helpful in the treatment of anxiety disorders."

Question: *What's wrong with this experiment?*

Answer: On its surface, this experiment looks okay. There's random assignment of participants to experimental and control groups, and manipulation of an independent variable, namely, the presence versus absence of Anger Expression Therapy. But Dr. Fact hasn't controlled for two crucial pitfalls. First, he hasn't controlled for the placebo effect, because people receiving Anger Expression Therapy know they're receiving a treatment, and people in the control group know they're not. To control for this problem, Dr. Fact should probably have built in an *attention-placebo control condition:* A condition in which a counselor provides attention, but no formal psychotherapy, to patients (for example, the counselor could simply chat with her patients once a week). Second, Dr. Fact hasn't controlled for the experimenter expectancy effect. He knows which patients are in which group and could subtly influence patients who are receiving Anger Expression Therapy to improve or report better results.

STUDY 3

Dr. E. Roney Us wants to find out whether listening to loud rock music impairs students' performance on psychology tests. She randomly assigns 50 college students in Psychology 101 to listen to loud rock music for two hours (from 7 P.M. to 9 P.M.) every day for one week. Dr. Us asks her research assistant to randomly assign 50 other college students in Psychology 101 to use these same two hours to do whatever they like, except that they can't listen to loud rock music during this time period. She has no contact with the subjects in either group throughout the week and doesn't know who's in which group, although she monitors their music listening by means of a secret recording device hidden in their dorm rooms (because this study involves deception, Dr. Us needed to persuade the IRB that it was scientifically important). At the end of the week, she examines their scores on their first Psychology 101 test (she doesn't know the Psychology 101 instructor and has no contact with him) and finds that students who listen to loud rock music do significantly worse than other students. Dr. Us concludes that "listening to loud rock music impairs students' performance on psychology tests."

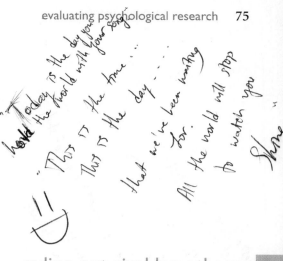

◄ **ruling out rival hypotheses**

HAVE IMPORTANT ALTERNATIVE EXPLANATIONS FOR THE FINDINGS BEEN EXCLUDED?

? In an experiment on marital therapy for anger problems, a researcher could examine whether individuals who receive a specific treatment show less anger than people who don't receive this treatment. **In such a study, what's the independent variable? What's the dependent variable?** (See the answers upside down at the bottom of this page.)

Answers: Independent variable—whether client receives a marital therapy for anger; dependent variable—the level of client's anger at the end of the study.

Question: *What's wrong with this experiment?*

Answer: Again, this study looks pretty decent at first glance. There's random assignment of participants to conditions, and manipulation of an independent variable—either listening to, or not listening to, loud rock music. In addition, Dr. Us has ensured that she's blind to who's in the experimental and control groups and that she has no contact with either the participants or instructor during this time. But Dr. Us has forgotten to control for one crucial confound: Subjects in the control group could have used the extra time to study for their exams. As a result, it's impossible to know whether rock music leads to poorer test performance or whether extra study time leads to better test performance. Both could be true, but we don't know for sure.

■ Most Reporters Aren't Scientists: Evaluating Psychology in the Media

Few major American newspapers hire reporters with any formal psychological training—the *New York Times* is a notable exception—so we shouldn't assume that people who write news stories about psychology are trained to distinguish psychological fact from fiction (Stanovich, 2009). Most aren't. This means that news stories are prone to faulty conclusions because reporters rely on the same heuristics and biases that we all do.

When evaluating the accuracy of psychological reports in the media, it's worth keeping some tips in mind. First, we should *consider the source* (Gilovich, 1991). We should generally place more confidence in a finding reported in a reputable science magazine (like *Scientific American Mind* or *Discover*) than in a supermarket tabloid (like the *National Enquirer*) or a popular magazine (like *People* or *Vogue*). This "consider the source" principle also applies to websites (refer back to Chapter 1, p. 11). Moreover, we should place more trust in findings from primary sources, such as the original journal articles themselves (if we can look them up in the library or on the Internet) than from secondary sources, such as newspapers, magazines, or websites that merely report findings from primary sources.

Second, we need to be on the lookout for excessive *sharpening* and *leveling* (Gilovich, 1991). *Sharpening* refers to the tendency to exaggerate the gist, or central message, of a study, whereas *leveling* refers to the tendency to minimize the less central details of a study. Sharpening and leveling often result in a "good story," because they end up bringing the most important facts of a study into sharper focus. Of course, secondary sources in the news media need to engage in a certain amount of sharpening and leveling when reporting studies, because they can't possibly describe every minor detail of an investigation. Still, too much sharpening and leveling can result in a misleading picture. If an investigator discovers that a new medication is effective for 35 percent of people with anxiety disorders, but that a placebo is effective for 33 percent of people with anxiety disorders, the newspaper editor may lead off the story with this eye-popping headline: "Breakthrough: New Medication Outperforms Other Pills in Treating Anxiety." This headline isn't literally wrong, but it oversimplifies greatly what the researcher found.

Third, we can easily be misled by seemingly "balanced" coverage of a story. There's a crucial difference between genuine scientific controversy and the kind of balanced coverage that news reporters create by ensuring that representatives from both sides of the story receive equal air time. When covering a psychological story, the news media usually try to include comments from "experts" (we place this term in quotation marks, because they're not always genuine experts) on opposing sides of an issue to make the story appear more balanced.

The problem is that "balanced coverage" sometimes creates *pseudosymmetry* (Park, 2002): the appearance of a scientific controversy where none exists. A newspaper might feature a story about a study that provides scientific evidence against extrasensory perception (ESP). They might devote the first four paragraphs to a description of the study but the last four paragraphs to impassioned critiques of the study from ESP advocates. This coverage may create the impression that the scientific evidence for ESP is split right down the middle, with about half of the research supporting it and about half disputing it. It's easy to overlook the fact that there was no scientific evidence in the last four paragraphs, only crit-

When evaluating media claims, we often need to consider the source.

[Handwritten margin notes:] Evaluating Psychology in Media: 1. Consider the source. 2. Look out for: "sharpening" = exaggerate the gist of study; "leveling" = minimize less central details to study. 3. Pseudosymmetry = appearance of a non-existing scientific controversy.

icisms of the evidence against ESP. Moreover, the article might fail to note that the scientific evidence regarding ESP is overwhelmingly negative (Hines, 2003; see Chapter 4).

One reason why most of us find it difficult to think scientifically about research evidence is that we're constantly bombarded with media reports that (unintentionally) provide us with poor role models for interpreting research (Lilienfeld, Ruscio, & Lynn, 2008; Stanovich, 2009). Bearing these tips in mind should help us become better consumers of psychological science in everyday life.

Answers are located at the end of the text.

HAIR-LOSS REMEDIES

evaluating CLAIMS

"Grow back a full head of hair in only three weeks!" Sounds great (for those of us who've experienced hair loss), but is it too good to be true? Let's evaluate some of these claims, which are modeled after actual ads for hair-loss remedies.

"Call us now to learn more about the *advantages and highlights* of our product."
Beware of ads that only focus on the advantages of their products. What questions would you have about potential disadvantages or side effects?

"Thousands of others have seen results—read their *testimonials.*"
Can we rely on testimonial or anecdotal evidence alone? Why or why not?

"Use our supplements and grow back your hair *without the use of chemicals* or surgery."
Why is the claim that this supplement doesn't contain chemicals implausible?

"Our hair-loss cure is *doctor approved* and recommended."
Does the fact that doctors approve this cure make it more legitimate in your eyes? What questions would you ask about the number and type of doctors who approve of this product?

---

assess your knowledge   FACT OR FICTION?

✓●⎯[**Study** and **Review** on **mypsychlab.com**

1. Few psychological journals use a peer-review process. **True / False**

2. When evaluating the quality of a study, we must be on the lookout for potential confounds, expectancy effects, and nonrandom assignment to experimental and control groups. **True / False**

3. Most newspaper reporters who write stories about psychology have advanced degrees in psychology. **True / False**

4. "Balanced" coverage of a psychology story is sometimes inaccurate. **True / False**

Answers: 1. F (p.74); 2. T (p.74–76); 3. F (p.76); 4. T (p.76)

YOUR COMPLETE REVIEW SYSTEM

✓•─Study and Review on **mypsychlab.com**

THE BEAUTY AND NECESSITY OF GOOD RESEARCH DESIGN 45–49

2.1 IDENTIFY HEURISTICS AND BIASES THAT MAKE RESEARCH DESIGNS NECESSARY.

Our heuristics are useful in most everyday circumstances but can sometimes steer us wrong. Representativeness and availability heuristics can lead us to rely too heavily on inaccurate measures of the probability of events. Such errors as hindsight bias and overconfidence can lead us to overestimate our ability to predict outcomes accurately. Research designs help to safeguard us against all of these thinking errors.

1. How can we explain that most people say they'd have to travel southwest to get from Reno to San Diego? (p. 47)

2. Kahneman and Tversky pioneered the study of _____: mental shortcuts that help us make sense of the world. (p. 47)

3. When we use the _____ heuristic, we're essentially judging a book by its cover. (p. 47)

4. A _____ _____ is another term for how common a characteristic or behavior is. (p. 47)

5. The _____ heuristic involves estimating the likelihood of an occurrence based on the ease with which it comes to our minds. (p. 48)

6. _____ _____ are systematic errors in thinking. (p. 48)

7. In addition to confirmation bias, two other tendencies that can lead us to draw misleading conclusions are _____ _____ and _____. (p. 48)

8. Once an event occurs, if you say, "I knew that was going to happen," you might be engaging in _____ _____. (p. 48)

9. Most of us tend to engage in _____ when we overestimate our ability to make correct predictions. (p. 48)

10. Name one major historical event that Nostradamus was supposed to have predicted. (p. 49)

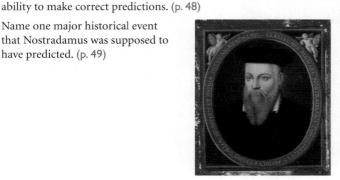

((•─Listen to an audio file of your chapter on **mypsychlab.com**

THE SCIENTIFIC METHOD: TOOLBOX OF SKILLS 49–66

2.2 DESCRIBE THE ADVANTAGES AND DISADVANTAGES OF USING NATURALISTIC OBSERVATION, CASE STUDIES, SELF-REPORT MEASURES, AND SURVEYS.

Naturalistic observation, case studies, self-report measures, and surveys are all important research designs. Naturalistic observation involves recording behaviors in real-world settings, but is often not carefully controlled. Case studies involve examining one or a few individuals over long periods of time; these designs are often useful in generating hypotheses but are typically limited in testing them rigorously. Self-report measures and surveys ask people about themselves; they can provide a wealth of useful information, but have certain disadvantages, especially response sets.

11. Although the major advantage of naturalistic designs is that they are often high in _____ _____, or the extent to which we can generalize our findings to real-world settings, they also tend to be low in _____ _____, or the extent to which we can draw cause-and-effect inferences. (p. 51)

12. Using your knowledge of random selection, explain what pollsters did wrong in reporting the 1948 presidential election results. (p. 53)

13. When evaluating results, we need to be able to evaluate the consistency of the measurement, or _____, and the extent to which a measure assesses what it claims to measure, or _____. (pp. 53–54)

14. In using _____ _____, psychologists need to evaluate whether questionnaire respondents engaged in _____ _____. (p. 55)

2.3 DESCRIBE THE ROLE OF CORRELATIONAL DESIGNS AND DISTINGUISH CORRELATION FROM CAUSATION.

Correlational studies allow us to establish the relations among two or more measures, but do not allow causal conclusions.

15. A positive correlation means that as the value of one variable changes, the other goes in (the same/a different) direction. (p. 56)

2.4 IDENTIFY THE COMPONENTS OF AN EXPERIMENT AND THE POTENTIAL PITFALLS THAT CAN LEAD TO FAULTY CONCLUSIONS.

Experimental designs involve random assignment of participants to conditions and manipulation of an independent variable, and when conducted properly, permit us to draw conclusions about the causes of a psychological intervention. Placebo effects and experimenter expectancy effects are examples of pitfalls in experimental designs that can lead us to draw false conclusions.

16. If a study is an experiment we (can/can't) infer cause and effect, but if the study is correlational we (can/can't). (p. 61)

17. A(n) _____ is a research design that consists of two components: 1) a random assignment of participants to conditions, and 2) manipulation of an independent variable. (p. 61)

18. The group of participants in a study that doesn't receive the manipulation is the _____ group. (p. 61)

19. To avoid the _____ effect during medication research, it's crucial that the subject remain _____ to whether he/she has been assigned to the experimental group. (p. 63)

20. How does this photo illustrate the nocebo effect? (p. 64)

ETHICAL ISSUES IN RESEARCH DESIGN 66–69

2.5 EXPLAIN THE ETHICAL OBLIGATIONS OF RESEARCHERS TOWARD THEIR RESEARCH PARTICIPANTS.

Concerns about ethical treatment of research participants have led research facilities, such as colleges and universities, to establish institutional review boards that review all research involving human participants and require informed consent by participants. In some cases, they may also require a full debriefing at the conclusion of the research session.

21. In the Tuskegee study performed by the U.S. government starting in 1932, the researchers never informed the subjects that they had _____, nor did they inform them that _____ were available to treat the disease. (p. 67)

22. What important changes have been made to research procedures in the United States to ensure that an ethical catastrophe like the Tuskegee study doesn't happen again? (p. 67)

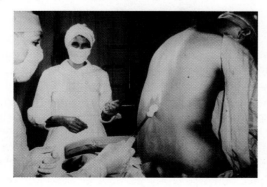

23. The process in which researchers tell participants what's involved in a study is called _____ _____. (p. 67)

24. Milgram's controversial study relied on _____ because he deliberately misled the participants about the study's purpose. (p. 67)

25. _____ is a process whereby researchers inform participants what the study was about. (p. 68)

26. The _____ _____ _____ published a code of ethics to govern all research with human participants. (p. 68)

2.6 DESCRIBE BOTH SIDES OF THE DEBATE ON THE USE OF ANIMALS AS RESEARCH SUBJECTS.

Animal research has led to clear benefits in our understanding of human learning, brain physiology, and psychological treatment, to mention only a few advances. To answer many critical psychological questions, there are simply no good alternatives to using animals. Nevertheless, many critics have raised useful questions about the treatment of laboratory animals and emphasized the need for adequate housing and feeding conditions. Many protest the large number of laboratory animals killed each year and question whether animal research offers sufficient external validity to justify its use.

27. The goal of a(n) _____ research study on animals is to learn how the brain relates to behavior in humans without having to inflict harm on people. (pp. 69)

28. About _____ percent of published psychology research relies on animals. (p. 69)

29. Animal researchers must carefully weigh the potential _____ _____ against the costs in death and suffering they produce. (p. 69)

30. What are some of the arguments for and against the ethics of animal testing? (p. 69)

STATISTICS: THE LANGUAGE OF PSYCHOLOGICAL RESEARCH 70–74

2.7 IDENTIFY USES OF VARIOUS MEASURES OF CENTRAL TENDENCY AND VARIABILITY.

Three measures of central tendency are the mean, median, and mode. The mean is the average of all scores. The median is the middle score. The mode is the most frequent score. The mean is the most widely used measure but is the most sensitive to extreme scores. Two measures of variability are the range and standard deviation. The range is a more intuitive measure of variability, but can yield a deceptive picture of how spread out individual scores are. The standard deviation is a better measure of variability, although it's more difficult to calculate.

31. In _____ statistics, the _____ _____ provides a sense of the "central" score in a data set, or where the group tends to cluster. (p. 70)

32. Match up the measure to the definition (p. 70)

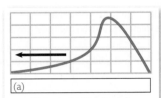 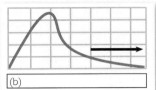

_____ Mode	1. Middle score in a data set
_____ Mean	2. Most frequent score in a data set
_____ Median	3. Average score in a data set

33. The best measure of central tendency to report when the data form a "bell-shaped" or normal distribution is the _____. (p. 71)

34. Another type of descriptive statistic is _____, which gives a sense of how loosely or tightly bunched the data are. (p. 71)

35. The difference between the highest and lowest scores is the _____. (p. 71)

36. The _____ _____ takes into account how far each data point is from the mean. (p. 71)

37. Using your knowledge of distribution curves, label these two different types of skews. (p. 71)

(a) Elongated tail at the **left**
More data in the tail than would be expected in a normal distribution

(b) Elongated tail at the **right**
More data in the tail than would be expected in a normal distribution

2.8 EXPLAIN HOW INFERENTIAL STATISTICS CAN HELP US TO DETERMINE WHETHER WE CAN GENERALIZE FROM OUR SAMPLE TO THE FULL POPULATION.

Inferential statistics allow us to determine how much we can generalize findings from our sample to the full population. Not all statistically significant findings are large enough in magnitude to make a real-world difference, so we must also consider practical significance when evaluating the implications of our results.

38. When using inferential statistics, we're asking whether we can draw "inferences" (or _____) regarding whether the differences we've observed in our sample apply to other samples drawn from the same population. (p. 71)

39. The larger the sample size, the (greater/lesser) the odds that a result will be statistically significant. (p. 72)

2.9 SHOW HOW STATISTICS CAN BE MISUSED FOR PURPOSES OF PERSUASION.

Reporting measures of central tendency that are nonrepresentative of most participants, creating visual representations that exagger-

ate effects, and failing to take base rates into account are all frequent methods of manipulating statistics for the purposes of persuasion.

40. In a _____ _____ _____, the *y* axis starts somewhere close to the highest possible score, instead of at the lowest score, where it should start. (p. 73)

EVALUATING PSYCHOLOGICAL RESEARCH

74–77

2.10 IDENTIFY FLAWS IN RESEARCH DESIGNS.

Good experimental design requires not only random assignment and manipulation of an independent variable, but also inclusion of an appropriate control condition to rule out placebo effects. Most important, it requires careful attention to the possibility of alternative explanations of observed effects.

41. The crucial task of a _____ _____ is to identify flaws that could undermine a study's findings. (p. 74)

42. By definition, an experiment is flawed if it doesn't include a manipulation of a(n) _____ _____. (p. 75)

43. In Study 1, the researcher puts all the subjects in a single group and is therefore lacking a necessary _____ group. (p. 75)

44. In Study 2, the researcher hasn't controlled for the _____ effect because participants are aware of whether or not they are receiving treatment. (p. 75)

45. In Study 2, the researcher knows which participants are in which groups, so he has created an opportunity for the _____ _____ effect. (p. 75)

46. In Study 3, the researcher protected her study from the experimenter expectancy effect by ensuring that she was _____ as to who was in the experimental control and who was in the control group. (p. 76)

2.11 IDENTIFY SKILLS FOR EVALUATING PSYCHOLOGICAL CLAIMS IN THE POPULAR MEDIA.

To evaluate psychological claims in the news and elsewhere in the popular media, we should bear in mind that few reporters have formal psychological training. When considering media claims, we should consider the source, beware of excessive sharpening and leveling, and be on the lookout for pseudosymmetry.

47. News stories about psychology (are/are not) typically written by people who have formal training in psychology. (p. 76)

48. When evaluating the legitimacy of psychological reports in the media, one should consider the _____. (p. 76)

49. _____ refers to the tendency to exaggerate the central message of a study, whereas _____ refers to the tendency to minimize the less central details of a study. (p. 76)

50. When a news story mistakenly suggests that experts are equally divided over a topic, it creates _____. (p. 76)

DO YOU KNOW THESE TERMS?

- prefrontal lobotomy (p. 45)
- heuristic (p. 46)
- representativeness heuristic (p. 47)
- base rate (p. 47)
- availability heuristic (p. 48)
- cognitive biases (p. 48)
- hindsight bias (p. 48)
- overconfidence (p. 48)
- naturalistic observation (p. 50)
- external validity (p. 51)
- internal validity (p. 51)

- case study (p. 51)
- existence proof (p. 51)
- random selection (p. 52)
- reliability (p. 53)
- validity (p. 54)
- response set (p. 55)
- correlational design (p. 56)
- scatterplot (p. 56)
- illusory correlation (p. 58)
- experiment (p. 61)
- random assignment (p. 61)
- experimental group (p. 61)

- control group (p. 61)
- independent variable (p. 61)
- dependent variable (p. 61)
- operational definition (p. 61)
- placebo effect (p. 62)
- blind (p. 63)
- experimenter expectancy effect (p. 64)
- double-blind (p. 64)
- demand characteristics (p. 65)
- informed consent (p. 67)
- statistics (p. 70)

- descriptive statistics (p. 70)
- central tendency (p. 70)
- mean (p. 70)
- median (p. 70)
- mode (p. 70)
- variability (p. 71)
- range (p. 71)
- standard deviation (p. 71)
- inferential statistics (p. 71)

APPLY YOUR SCIENTIFIC THINKING SKILLS

Use your scientific thinking skills to answer the following questions, referencing specific scientific thinking principles and common errors reasoning whenever possible.

1. Many media sources report findings showing an association between violent video games or violent song lyrics, on one hand, and violent behavior, on the other. Locate two examples of such media reports (check websites, newspapers, and magazines) and use your scientific thinking skills to determine whether the sources properly interpreted the original study's findings. If the study was correlational, did the reporters infer a causal relationship between the variables?

2. As we've learned, the results of a poll can vary based on the sample, as well as on the wording of the questions. Pick a current

social or political issue (such as abortion or global warming) and identify three polls on that issue (such as Gallup or cable news polls). How does the wording vary? How were individuals sampled? To what extent might these differences have contributed to differences in results across the polls?

3. Most of us have heard the statistic that half of all marriages end in divorce. Is this claim really true? Research different statistics concerning marriage and divorce rates in the United States and explain how they support or refute this claim.

3 BIOLOGICAL PSYCHOLOGY

bridging the levels of analysis

correlation vs. causation

CAN WE BE SURE THAT A CAUSES B?

FICTOID ✖

MYTH: The brain is gray in color.

REALITY: The living brain is a mixture of white, red, pink, and black colors.

In the early 21st century, we take for granted the fact that the brain is the seat of psychological activity. When we struggle with a difficult homework problem, we say that "our brains hurt," when we consult friends for advice about a complicated question, we "pick their brains," and when we insult others' intelligence, we call them "bird brains." Yet throughout much of human history, it seemed obvious that the brain *wasn't* the prime location for our thoughts, memories, and emotions.

For example, the ancient Egyptians believed that the heart was the seat of the human soul and the brain was irrelevant to mental life (Finger, 2000; Raulin, 2003). Egyptians often prepared corpses for mummification by scooping their brains out through the nostrils using an iron hook (you'll be pleased to know that no drawings of this practice survive today) (Leek, 1969). Although some ancient Greeks correctly pinpointed the brain as the source of the psyche, others, like the great philosopher Aristotle, were convinced that the brain functions merely as a radiator, cooling the heart when it becomes overheated. Even today, we can find holdovers of this way of thinking in our everyday language. When we memorize something, we come to know it "by heart" (Finger, 2000). When we're devastated by the loss of a romantic relationship, we feel "heartbroken."

Why were so many of the ancients certain that the heart, not the brain, was the source of mental activity? It's almost surely because they trusted their "common sense," which as we've learned is often a poor signpost of scientific truth (Chapter 1). They noticed that when people become excited, angry, or scared, their hearts pound quickly, whereas their brains seem to do little or nothing. Therefore, they reasoned, the heart must be causing these emotional reactions. By confusing correlation with causation, the ancients' intuitions misled them.

Today, we recognize that the mushy organ lying between our two ears is by far the most complicated structure in the known universe. Our brain has the consistency of gelatin, and it weighs a mere three pounds. Despite its rather unimpressive appearance, it's capable of astonishing feats. As poet Robert Frost wrote, "The brain is a wonderful organ. It starts working the moment you get up in the morning and does not stop until you get into the office."

In recent decades, scientists have made numerous technological strides that have taught us a great deal about how our brains work. Researchers who study the relationship between the nervous system—a communication network consisting of nerve cells, both inside and outside of the brain and spinal cord—and behavior go by the names of *biological psychologists* or *neuroscientists*. By linking brain to behavior, these scientists bridge multiple levels of analysis within psychology (see Chapter 1). As we explore what biological psychologists have discovered about the brain, we'll compare our current state-of-the-art knowledge with misconceptions that have arisen along the way (Aamodt & Wang, 2008). The history of our evolving understanding of the brain provides a wonderful example of the self-correcting nature of science (see Chapter 1). Over time, mistaken beliefs about the brain have gradually been replaced by more accurate knowledge (Finger, 2000).

NERVE CELLS: COMMUNICATION PORTALS

3.1 Distinguish the parts of neurons and what they do.

3.2 Describe electrical responses of neurons and what makes them possible.

3.3 Explain how neurons use neurotransmitters to communicate with each other.

3.4 Describe how the brain changes as a result of development, learning, and injury.

If we wanted to figure out how a car works, we'd open it up and identify its parts, like its engine, carburetor, and transmission, and then try to figure out how they operate in tandem. Similarly, to understand how our brain works, we first need to get a handle on its key components and determine how they cooperate. To do so, we'll start with the brain's most basic unit of communication: its cells. Then, we'll examine how these cells work in concert to generate our thoughts, feelings, and behaviors.

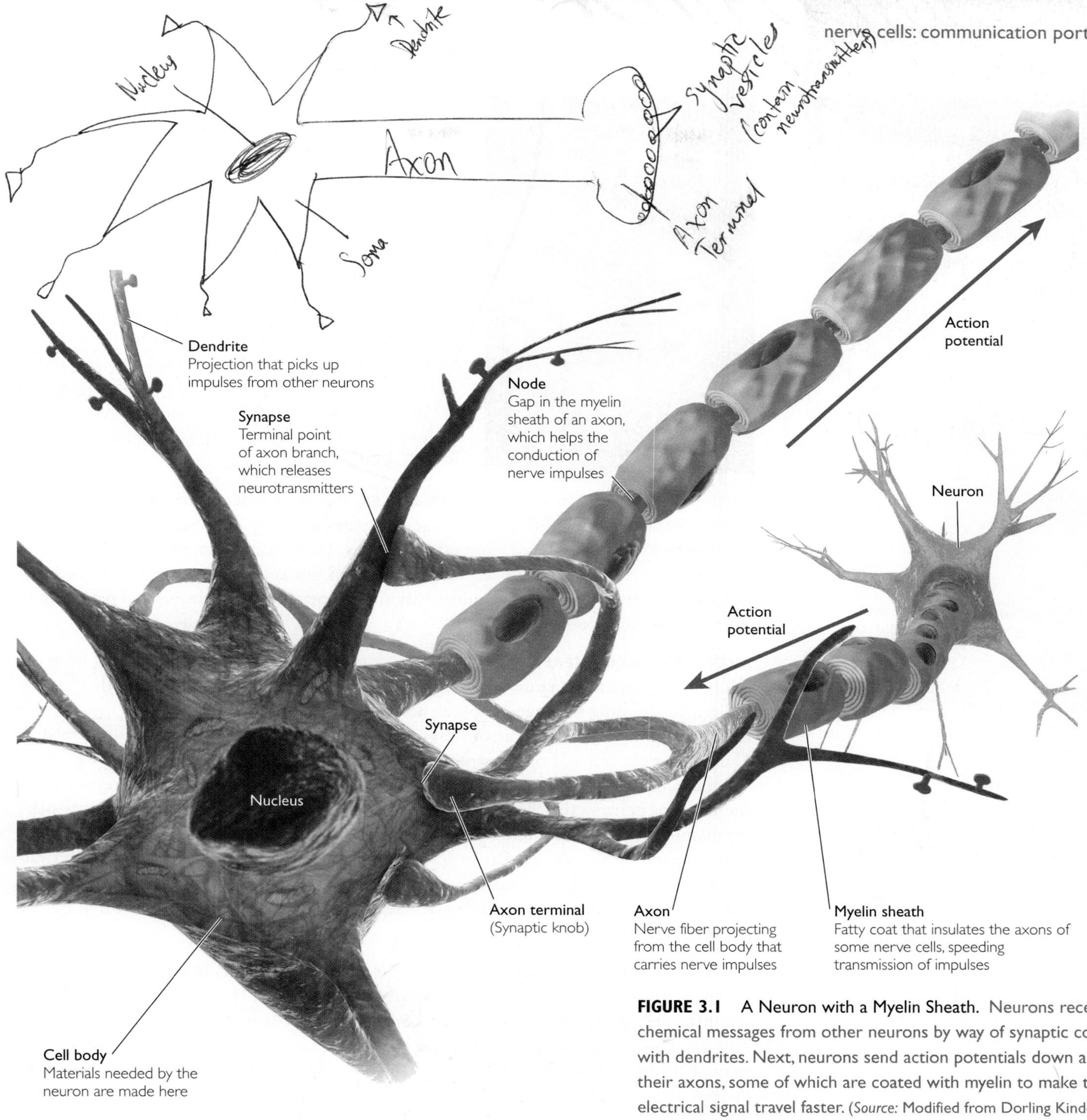

Hand-drawn labels: Nucleus, Dendrite, Axon, Soma, Synaptic Vesicles (contain neurotransmitters), Axon Terminal

Dendrite
Projection that picks up impulses from other neurons

Synapse
Terminal point of axon branch, which releases neurotransmitters

Node
Gap in the myelin sheath of an axon, which helps the conduction of nerve impulses

Action potential

Neuron

Action potential

Synapse

Nucleus

Cell body
Materials needed by the neuron are made here

Axon terminal
(Synaptic knob)

Axon
Nerve fiber projecting from the cell body that carries nerve impulses

Myelin sheath
Fatty coat that insulates the axons of some nerve cells, speeding transmission of impulses

FIGURE 3.1 **A Neuron with a Myelin Sheath.** Neurons receive chemical messages from other neurons by way of synaptic contacts with dendrites. Next, neurons send action potentials down along their axons, some of which are coated with myelin to make the electrical signal travel faster. (*Source:* Modified from Dorling Kindersley)

■ Neurons: The Brain's Communicators

The functioning of our brain depends on cross-talk among **neurons**—nerve cells exquisitely specialized for communication with each other (see **FIGURE 3.1**). Our brains contain about 100 billion neurons. To give you a sense of how enormous this number is, there are more than 15 times as many neurons in our brains as there are people on Earth. More graphically, 100 billion neurons lined up side to side would reach back and forth from New York to California five times. What's more, many neurons forge tens of thousands of connections with other neurons, permitting a staggering amount of inter-cellular communication. In total, there are about 160 trillion—that's a whopping 160,000,000,000,000—connections in the human brain (Tang et al., 2001). ●—Explore

neuron
nerve cell specialized for communication

●—Explore the Structure of a Neuron on mypsychlab.com

FICTOID ✖

MYTH: As adults, we lose about 100,000 neurons each day.

REALITY: Although we do lose neurons each day, the actual number is considerably lower, perhaps one-tenth of that (Juan, 2006).

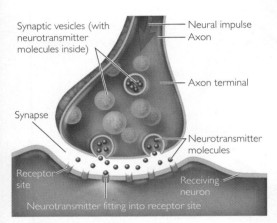

FIGURE 3.2   **The Axon Terminal.** The axon terminal contains synaptic vesicles filled with neurotransmitter molecules.

dendrite
portion of neuron that receives signals

axon
portion of neuron that sends signals

synaptic vesicle
spherical sac containing neurotransmitters

neurotransmitter
chemical messenger specialized for communication from neuron to neuron

synapse
space between two connecting neurons through which messages are transmitted chemically

synaptic cleft
a gap into which neurotransmitters are released from the axon terminal

falsifiability
CAN THE CLAIM BE DISPROVED?

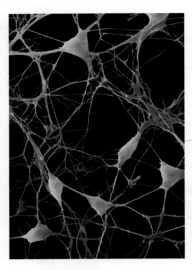

Neurons and their dendrites (shown stained pink) with their nuclei (shown stained purple).

Although many cells have simple and regular shapes, neurons are different. In fact, from a biological perspective, they're downright strange. They have long—sometimes extremely long—extensions, which help them respond to stimulation from other neurons and communicate. Neurons contain several other components that collaborate to help our nervous systems function.

THE CELL BODY.   The *cell body*, also called the soma, is the central region of the neuron. It manufactures new cell components, which consist of small and large molecules (refer to Figure 3.1). Because the cell body contains the nucleus, where proteins are manufactured, damage to this part of the neuron is fatal. The cell body also provides continual renewal of cell components.

DENDRITES.   Neurons differ from other cells in their branchlike extensions for receiving information from other neurons. These extensions, which we can liken to the receivers on our cell phones, are **dendrites**. Dendrites spread out to "listen in" on information from neighboring neurons and pass it on to the cell body (refer to Figure 3.1).

AXONS AND AXON TERMINALS.   **Axons** are long tail-like extensions protruding from the cell body. We can liken axons to the transmitters on our cell phones, because they're specialized for sending messages to other neurons. Unlike dendrites, axons are usually very thin near the cell body. This narrowness creates a *trigger zone,* an area that's easily activated. The *axon terminal* is a knoblike structure at the far end of the axon (see **FIGURE 3.2**). Axon terminals, in turn, contain **synaptic vesicles**, tiny spheres that contain **neurotransmitters**, chemical messengers that neurons use to communicate with each other. Synaptic vesicles are manufactured in the cell body and travel down the length of the axon. We might think of the synaptic vesicles as similar to gel capsules filled with cold medicine. When we swallow a capsule, its exterior dissolves and the medicine inside it moves down our digestive tracts. Similarly, when the synaptic vesicle reaches the end of the axon terminal, it bursts, releasing neurotransmitters.

SYNAPSES.   Neurotransmitters then enter the **synapse**, a miniscule fluid-filled space between neurons through which neurotransmitters travel. The synapse consists of a **synaptic cleft**, a gap into which neurotransmitters are released from the axon terminal. This gap is surrounded by small patches of membrane on each side, one on the sending axon of the first neuron and the other on the receiving dendrite of the second neuron. As neurotransmitters are released from the axon of a cell into the synapse, they're quickly picked up by the dendrites of nearby neurons, just as phone receivers quickly pick up signals from other phones.

British neuroscientist Sir Charles Sherrington was one of the first to hypothesize the existence of synapses. He measured how long it took muscles to become active following nerve stimulation. From these data, he inferred the existence of microscopic spaces between neurons themselves and between neurons and muscle cells (Pearce, 2004). At the time, no microscopes were powerful enough to observe these spaces. Consequently, some scientists believed that all neurons melded together into one giant net. But Sherrington (1906) argued that neurons are separate cells that communicated with each other and with muscle cells. What he hypothesized could have been falsified had he been wrong. Spanish scientist Santiago Ramón y Cajal showed that Sherrington was right using a staining technique that demonstrated the existence of individual neurons. Later studies using powerful *electron microscopes* confirmed that tiny gaps allowing communication between neurons, which we now recognize as synapses, indeed exist (Davis, 2006).

GLIAL CELLS: SUPPORTING ACTORS OR KEY PLAYERS? But neurons aren't the only players in our nervous systems: **Glial cells** (glial means glue) are also remarkably plentiful. Scientists once regarded them as nothing more than bit-part actors in the nervous system that surround the synapse and provide protective scaffolding for the neurons they hold in place. Nevertheless, over the past 20 years or so, researchers have realized that glial cells are star performers in their own right (Fields, 2009).

What accounts for their elevated status? It's more than the star shape of *astrocytes* (astro means star in Greek), the most abundant of glial cells. A single astrocyte interacts with as many as 300,000–1,000,000 neurons. The well-connected astrocytes communicate closely with neurons, increase the reliability of their transmission, control blood flow in the brain, and play a vital role in the development of the embryo (Metea & Newman, 2006). Astrocytes, in concert with other glial cells, are intimately involved in thought, memory, and the immune system (Gibbs & Bowser, 2009; Koob, 2009). Although researchers once thought that glial cells greatly outnumbered neurons, by as much as 10:1, recent research suggests that the ratio is much lower, and closer to 1:1 (Azevedo et al., 2009).

We can find astrocytes in great supply in the *blood–brain barrier*, a fatty coating that wraps around tiny blood vessels. As a result, large molecules, highly charged particles, and molecules that dissolve in water but not in fat are blocked from entering the brain. The blood-brain barrier is the brain's way of protecting itself from infection by bacteria and other intruders. Treatments that target glial cells may assist in treating a variety of conditions related to the number and activity of glial cells, including depression and schizophrenia (Cotter, Pariant, & Everall, 2001; Schroeter et al., 2009), as well as inflammation, chronic pain, and Alzheimer's disease and other degenerative conditions (Suter et al., 2007).

Another type of glial cell, called an *oligodendrocyte*, promotes new connections among nerve cells and releases chemicals to aid in healing. In addition, this cell produces an insulating wrapper around axons called the **myelin sheath**. This sheath contains numerous gaps all the way along the axon called *nodes*, which help the neuron conduct electricity more efficiently (refer again to Figure 3.1). Much like a person playing hopscotch, the neural signal jumps from node to node, speeding up its transmission. In the autoimmune disease of multiple sclerosis, the myelin sheaths surrounding neurons are "eaten away," resulting in a progressive loss of insulation of neural messages. As a consequence, these messages become hopelessly scrambled, resulting in a wide variety of physical and emotional symptoms. Glial cells also clear away debris, acting as the brain's cellular garbage disposals. We hope you'll agree that if glial cells don't deserve an academy award for their versatile performance in the nervous system, they at least merit a nomination.

■ Electrifying Thought

Neurons respond to neurotransmitters by generating electrical activity (see **FIGURE 3.3** on page 88). We know this because scientists have recorded electrical activity from neurons using *electrodes*, small devices made from wire or fine glass tubes. These electrodes allow them to measure the *potential difference* in electrical charge inside versus outside the neuron. The basis of all electrical responses in neurons depends on an uneven distribution of charged particles across the membrane surrounding the neuron (see Figure 3.3). Some particles are positively charged, others negatively charged. When there are no neurotransmitters acting on the neuron, the membrane is at the **resting potential**. In this baseline state, when the neuron isn't doing much of anything, there are more negative particles inside than outside the neuron. In some large neurons, the voltage of the resting potential can be about one-twentieth that of a flashlight battery, or about –60 millivolts (the negative sign means the inside charge is more negative than outside). While at rest, particles of both types are flowing in and out of the membrane. When the electrical charge inside the neuron reaches a high enough level relative to the outside, called the **threshold**, an action potential occurs.

ACTION POTENTIALS. **Action potentials** are abrupt waves of electric discharge triggered by a change in charge inside the axon. When this change occurs, we can describe the neuron as "firing," similar to the firing of a gun. Much like a gun, neurons obey the "all or none" law:

glial cell
cell in nervous system that plays a role in the formation of myelin and the blood–brain barrier, responds to injury, removes debris, and enhances learning and memory

myelin sheath
glial cells wrapped around axons that act as insulators of the neuron's signal

resting potential
electrical charge difference (–60 millivolts) across the neuronal membrane, when the neuron is not being stimulated or inhibited

threshold
membrane potential necessary to trigger an action potential

action potential
electrical impulse that travels down the axon triggering the release of neurotransmitters

---

Handwritten margin notes:

Myelin sheath contains gaps along the axon called nodes which help neurons conduct electricity efficiently

Glial cells:
- astrocyte
- oligodendrocyte
- also clear away debris (cellular garbage disposal)

Astrocyte (star shaped, most abundant of glial cells) interacts with 300,000 – 1 million neurons.
- increase reliability of transmission
- control blood flow in brain
- vital role in development of embryo
- involved in thought, memory, and immune system.

Many astrocytes in blood-brain barrier (fatty coating wrapped around tiny blood vessels)

Myelin sheath has nodes which help efficiently conducting electricity

oligodendrocyte = promotes connections in nerve cells and releases chemicals to help with healing. Produces myelin sheath.

For Protection against infections and such.

resting potential node outside

inside charge is more negative than the outside charge. no neurotransmitters!

Action potential = waves of electric discharge triggered by a change in charge inside axon.

FIGURE 3.3   The Action Potential. When a neuron is at rest there are positive and negative ions on both sides of the membrane. During an action potential, positive ions rush in and then out of the axon. This process recurs along the axon until the axon terminal releases neurotransmitters. (*Source:* Adapted from Sternberg, 2004a)

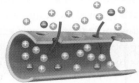

At rest.

During an action potential, positive particles rapidly flow into the axon.

When the inside of the axon accumulates maximal levels of positive charge, positive particles begin to flow back out of the axon.

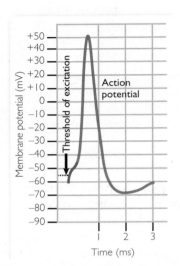

FIGURE 3.4   Voltage across the Membrane during the Action Potential. The membrane potential needed to trigger an action potential is called the *threshold*. Many neurons have a threshold of −55 mV. That means only 5 mV of current above resting (at −60 mV) is needed to trigger an action potential. (*Source:* Adapted from Sternberg, 2004a)

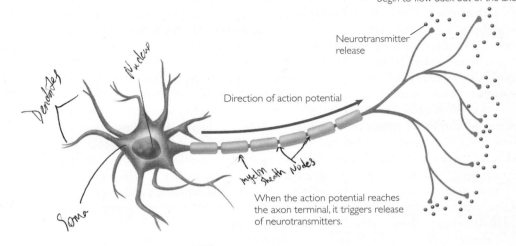

Neurotransmitter release

Direction of action potential

When the action potential reaches the axon terminal, it triggers release of neurotransmitters.

FACTOID +

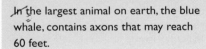

In the largest animal on earth, the blue whale, contains axons that may reach 60 feet.

absolute refractory period
time during which another action potential is impossible; limits maximal firing rate

receptor site
location that uniquely recognizes a neurotransmitter

reuptake
means of recycling neurotransmitters

They either fire or they don't (you wouldn't accuse a criminal of "sort of shooting at me"). Action potentials originate in the trigger zone near the cell body and continue all the way down the axon to the axon terminal. During an action potential, positively charged particles flow rapidly into the axon and then just as rapidly flow out, causing a spike in positive charge followed by a sudden decrease in charge, with the inside charge ending up at a slightly more negative level than its original resting value (see **FIGURES** 3.3 and **3.4**). These sudden shifts in charge produce a release of electricity. When the electrical charge reaches the axon terminal, it triggers the release of neurotransmitters—chemical messengers—into the synapse.

THE ABSOLUTE REFRACTORY PERIOD. Neurons can fire extremely rapidly, at rates of 100 to 1,000 times per second. At this very moment, energy is traveling down tens of millions of your axons at breakneck speeds of about 220 miles per hour. Each action potential is followed by an **absolute refractory period**, a brief interval during which another action potential can't occur. This period limits the *maximal firing rate,* the fastest rate at which a neuron can fire, much as it takes us awhile to reload some guns after firing them. The rate at which action potentials travel becomes an issue in very long axons, such as the sciatic nerve, which runs from the spinal cord down the leg. Remarkably, in humans this axon extends an average of three feet.

■ Chemical Communication: Neurotransmission

Whereas electrical events transmit information *within* neurons, chemical events initiated by neurotransmitters orchestrate communication *among* neurons. After neurotransmsitter molecules are released into the synapse, they bind with **receptor sites** along the dendrites of neighboring neurons. Different receptor sites recognize different types of neurotransmitters. Researchers typically invoke a lock-and-key analogy to describe this specificity (see **FIGURE 3.5**). We can think of each neurotransmitter as a key that fits only its own type of receptor, or lock.

Neurotransmission can be halted by **reuptake** of the neurotransmitter back into the axon terminal—a process by which the synaptic vesicle reabsorbs the neurotransmitter. We can think of release and reuptake of the neurotransmitter as analogous to letting some liquid drip out of the bottom of a straw (release) and then sucking it back up again (reuptake). Reuptake is one of nature's recycling mechanisms.

NEUROTRANSMITTERS. Different neurotransmitters are different messengers, each with a slightly different thing to say. Some *excite* the nervous system, increasing its activity, whereas others *inhibit* the nervous system, decreasing its activity. Some play a role in movement, others in pain perception, and still others in thinking and emotion. Let's now meet a few of the more prominent neurotransmitters (see **TABLE 3.1**).

Glutamate and GABA. *Glutamate* and gamma-aminobutyric acid (*GABA*) are the most common neurotransmitters in the central nervous system (CNS). Neurons in virtually every brain area use these neurotransmitters to communicate with each other (Fagg & Foster, 1983). Glutamate rapidly excites neurons, increasing the likelihood that they'll communicate with other neurons. The release of glutamate is associated with enhanced learning and memory (see Chapter 7). When elevated, glutamate may also contribute to schizophrenia and other mental disorders, because in high doses it can be toxic, damaging neural receptors by overstimulating them (Goff & Coyle, 2001; Karlsson et al., 2008).

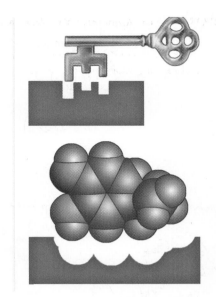

FIGURE 3.5 The Lock-and-Key Model of Neurotransmitter Binding to Receptor Sites. Receptor sites are specialized to receive only certain types of neurotransmitters.

TABLE 3.1 Neurotransmitters and Their Major Functional Roles.

NEUROTRANSMITTER	SELECTED ROLES	DRUGS THAT INTERACT WITH THE NEUROTRANSMITTER SYSTEM
Glutamate	Main excitatory neurotransmitter in the nervous system; participates in relay of sensory information and learning	*Alcohol* and *memory enhancers* interact with N-methyl-D-aspartate (NMDA) receptors, a specific type of glutamate receptor.
Gamma-aminobutyric acid (GABA)	Main inhibitory neurotransmitter in the nervous system	*Alcohol* and *antianxiety drugs* increase GABA activity.
Acetylcholine (ACh)	Muscle contraction (PNS) Cortical arousal (CNS)	*Nicotine* stimulates ACh receptors. *Memory enhancers* increase ACh. *Insecticides* block the breakdown of ACh. *Botox* causes paralysis by blocking ACh.
Norepinephrine (NE)	Brain arousal and other functions like mood, hunger, and sleep	*Amphetamine* and *methamphetamine* increase NE.
Dopamine	Motor function and reward	*L-Dopa,* which increases dopamine, is used to treat *Parkinson*'s disease. *Antipsychotic drugs,* which block dopamine action, are used to treat schizophrenia.
Serotonin	Mood and temperature regulation, aggression, and sleep cycles	*Serotonin-selective reuptake inhibitor (SSRI) antidepressants* are used to treat depression.
Endorphins	Pain reduction	*Narcotic drugs*—codeine, morphine, and heroin—reduce pain and produce euphoria.
Anandamide	Pain reduction, increase in appetite	*Tetrahydrocannabinol (THC)*—found in marijuana—produces euphoria.

(*Source:* Adapted from Carlson et al., 2007)

GABA, in contrast, inhibits neurons, thereby dampening neural activity. That's why most antianxiety drugs bind to GABA receptors. GABA is a workhorse in our nervous systems, playing critical roles in learning, memory, and sleep (Gottesman, 2002; Jacobson et al., 2007; Wang & Kriegstein, 2009). Scientists are intrigued by the promise of drugs that target GABA to one day treat a variety of conditions, including insomnia, depression, and epilepsy (Gerard & Aybala, 2007; Mann & Mody, 2008; Winkelman et al., 2008).

Acetylcholine. The neurotransmitter acetylcholine plays roles in arousal, selective attention, sleep (see Chapter 5), and memory (McKinney & Jacksonville, 2005; Woolf, 1991). In the neurological disorder of Alzheimer's disease, neurons containing acetylcholine (and several other neurotransmitters) are progressively destroyed, leading to severe memory loss (see Chapter 7). Medications that alleviate some of the symptoms of Alzheimer's, like the drug Aricept (its generic name is Donezepil), boost acetylcholine levels in the brain. Neurons that connect directly to muscle cells also release acetylcholine, allowing them to trigger movement. That's how most insecticides work; they limit the breakdown of acetycholine (allowing more acetylcholine to stick around the synapse), causing insects to engage in uncontrolled motor activity that eventually kills them.

Monoamines. *Norepinephrine, dopamine,* and *serotonin* are the monoamine neurotransmitters (they're called "monoamines" because they contain only one amino acid, the building block of proteins). Dopamine plays an especially critical role in the rewarding experiences that occur when we seek out or accomplish goals, whether they be sex, a fine meal, or a gambling jackpot. Research even shows that brain areas rich in dopamine become active when we hear a funny joke (Mobbs et al., 2003). Norepinephrine and serotonin activate or deactivate various parts of the brain, influencing arousal and our readiness to respond to stimuli (Jones, 2003).

Neuropeptides. Neuropeptides are short strings of amino acids in the nervous system. They act somewhat like neurotransmitters, but their roles are typically more specialized. **Endorphins** are a type of neuropeptide that play a specialized role in pain reduction (Holden, Jeong, & Forrest, 2005). Endorphins were discovered in the early 1970s by neuroscientists Candace Pert and Solomon Snyder, who hoped to pinpoint the physiological mechanisms of opioids, drugs like morphine and codeine that produce pain relief and euphoria. Remarkably, they discovered that our brains contain their very own receptors for naturally occurring opioids—endorphins (Pert, Pasternak, & Snyder, 1973). So human-made opioids, like morphine, exert their effects by "hijacking" the endorphin system, binding to endorphin receptors and mimicking their effects. Our brains contain a host of other neuropeptides; some regulate hunger and satiety (fullness), and others learning and memory.

Anandamide. Just as we knew about opiates long before we knew about endogenous opioids, we knew about marijuana and its active ingredient, *tetrahydrocannabinol* (THC), long before we knew about anandamide. Cells in our bodies, like neurons, make anandamide, which binds to the same receptors as THC. *Anandamide* plays roles in eating, motivation, memory, and sleep.

NEUROTRANSMITTERS AND PSYCHOACTIVE DRUGS. Scientists have developed specific medications to target the production or inhibition of certain neurotransmitters (refer again to Table 3.1). Drugs that interact with neurotransmitter systems are called *psychoactive,* meaning they affect mood, arousal, or behavior (see Chapter 5).

Knowing how psychoactive drugs interact with neurotransmitter systems allows us to predict how they'll affect us psychologically. Opiates, such as codeine and morphine, function as *agonists,* meaning they increase receptor site activity. Specifically, they reduce our emotional response to painful stimuli by binding with opioid receptors (the receptors discovered by Pert and Snyder) and mimicking endorphins (Evans, 2004). Tranquilizers, like Xanax (whose generic name is Alprazolam), diminish anxiety by stimulating GABA receptor sites, thereby tamping down neuronal activity (Roy-Byrne, 2005). As we've already seen with insecticides, still other drugs block the reuptake of neurotransmitters. Many anti-

Athletes, like this bicyclist, often rely on their endorphins to push them through intense pain.

endorphin
chemical in the brain that plays a specialized role in pain reduction

Acetylcholine = arousal, selective attention, sleep, memory

- destruction of acetylcholine
   = memory loss
   (Alzheimer's)

- triggers movement

Monoamines (norepinephrine, dopamine, serotonin)
activate or deactivate different parts of brain to influence arousal and readiness in response to stimuli.
rewarding experiences

Neuropeptides
- endorphins = pain reduction

Anandamide = eating motivation memory and sleep

Psychoactive = affect mood, arousal, behavior

agonists = increase receptor site activity
- reduce emotional response to painful stimuli, mimic endorphins

[handwritten: antagonist – decrease receptor site activity]

depressants, like Prozac (whose generic name is Fluoxetine), inhibit the reuptake of certain neurotransmitters, especially serotonin, from the synapse (Schatzberg, 1998). By allowing these neurotransmitters to remain in the synapse longer than usual, these medications enhance these neurotransmitters' effects on receptor sites—much as we can heighten the pleasurable sensations of a delicious food by keeping it in our mouths a bit longer than usual.

Some drugs work in the opposite way, functioning as receptor *antagonists,* meaning they decrease receptor site activity. Most medications used to treat schizophrenia—a severe mental disorder we'll describe more fully in Chapter 15—block dopamine receptors by binding to them and then blocking dopamine from binding to the receptors themselves (Bennett, 1998; Compton & Broussard, 2009).

■ Neural Plasticity: How and When the Brain Changes

We'll conclude our guided tour of neurons by looking at the ability of the nervous system to change. Nature—our genetic makeup—influences what kind of changes are possible and when they'll occur during the long and winding road from birth to old age. Nurture, consisting of learning, life events, injuries, and illnesses, affects our genetically influenced course. Scientists use the term **plasticity** to describe the nervous system's ability to change. We can talk about brain circuits being "hardwired" when they don't change much, if at all.

But in fact, few human behaviors are "hardwired," even though the popular media frequently use this term to refer to genetically influenced characteristics. That's because the nervous system is continually changing, by leaps and bounds, as in early development, or more subtly, as with learning. Unfortunately, the nervous system often doesn't change enough following injury, which can lead to permanent paralysis and disability.

NEURAL PLASTICITY OVER DEVELOPMENT. Typically, our brain is most capable of changing during early development, when much of our nervous system has yet to be set in place. Our brains don't mature fully until late adolescence or early adulthood. This means the period of heightened plasticity in the human brain is lengthy, with some parts maturing faster than others. 👁 Watch

The network of neurons in the brain changes over the course of development in four primary ways:

1. *growth* of dendrites and axons;
2. *synaptogenesis,* the formation of new synapses;
3. *pruning,* consisting of the death of certain neurons and the retraction of axons to remove connections that aren't useful; and
4. *myelination,* the insulation of axons with a myelin sheath.

Of these four steps, pruning is probably the most surprising. During pruning, as many as 70 percent of neurons die off. This process is helpful, though, because it streamlines neural organization, enhancing communication among brain structures (Oppenheim, 1991). In a real sense, less is more, because with pruning our brains can process information more efficiently with fewer neurons. One theory of infantile autism (see Chapter 15) suggests that this disorder is caused by inadequate pruning (Hill & Frith, 2003), which may explain why individuals with autism tend to have unusually large brains (Herbert, 2005).

Late maturation of certain cortical areas has fueled interest in the brains of teenagers and how their brain maturation—or lack thereof—affects their decision making (Steinberg, 2008). By age 12, the human brain is adult in size and weight. Nonetheless, adolescent brain activity patterns—such as those shown by brain imaging techniques we'll soon discuss—are still far different from those of adults (see Chapter 10).

NEURAL PLASTICITY AND LEARNING. Our brains change as we learn. The simplest change occurs when synapses simply perform better, that is, show stronger and more prolonged excitatory responses. Researchers call this phenomenon potentiation, and when it's

[handwritten: potentiation – when synapses show stronger and more prolonged excitatory responses]

[handwritten notes in right margin:]
Nature = genetic makeup
Nurture = growing up, affects genetically influenced course of action.
Plasticity = ability to change.

👁 **Watch** Brain Building on **mypsychlab.com**

[handwritten: Growth of dendrites and axons; dendrites, nucleus, Schwann cell, Myelin, axon terminal, Axon, Soma]
Synaptogenesis = formation of new synapses
Pruning = 70% of neurons die → neural organization, so better communication in brain
Myelination = insulation of axons with MYELIN sheath

plasticity
ability of the nervous system to change

enduring, *long-term potentiation* (LTP) (see Chapter 7). Many scientists believe that *structural* plasticity, in the form of altered neuronal shape, is also critical for learning. A number of investigators have demonstrated learning-related structural changes in both axons and dendrites (Woolf, 2006). In one study, researchers trained rats to swim to a platform hidden in a tub of milky water. By the time the rats became adept at doing so, axons entering a part of their brains relevant to spatial ability had expanded (Holahan et al., 2006). Exposure to enriched environments also results in structural enhancements to dendrites (see **FIGURE 3.6**). Two studies compared rats exposed to an enriched environment—such as large cages with multiple animals, toys, and running wheels—with rats exposed to a standard environment of a cage with only two animals and no objects (Freire & Cheng, 2004; Leggio et al., 2005). Enriched environments led to more elaborate dendrites with more branches.

NEURAL PLASTICITY FOLLOWING INJURY AND DEGENERATION. In adults, brain plasticity decreases sharply, occurring only on a small scale, such as with learning. The human brain and spinal cord exhibit only limited regeneration following injury or serious illness. Yet certain brain regions can sometimes take over the functions previously performed by others. For example, in blind people, the capacity to read Braille (a system of raised dots that correspond to letters in the alphabet) with the fingers is taken over by brain regions associated with vision in sighted people (Hamilton & Pascual-Leone, 1998).

Not surprisingly, scientists are focused on finding ways to get around the barriers that prevent brain and spinal cord axons from growing back following injury (Maier & Schwab, 2006). Some humans and animals recover sensory and motor function following certain treatments, but the degree of recovery varies greatly (Bradbury & McMahon, 2006; Jones et al., 2001). Because degenerative disorders, such as Alzheimer's disease and Parkinson's disease, pose enormous challenges to society, scientists are actively investigating ways of preventing damage or enabling the brain to heal itself.

Stem Cells. You've probably heard or read about research on **stem cells**, especially embryonic stem cells, in the news. The reason they've garnered so much attention is that they have the potential to become a wide variety of specialized cells (see **FIGURE 3.7**). This is akin to being a first-year undergraduate who has yet to declare a major: He or she might become nearly anything. Once the cell begins to specialize, however, the cell type becomes more permanently cast, much like an undergraduate who's spent three years taking pre-med courses. Stem cells offer several ways of treating diseases marked by neural degeneration (Fukuda & Takahashi, 2005; Miller, 2006; Muller, Snyder, & Loring, 2006). For example, researchers can implant stem cells directly into the host's nervous system and induce them to grow and replace damaged cells. In addition, researchers can genetically engineer stem cells so that the cells can administer *gene therapy*—that is, provide the patient with replacement genes.

Yet stem cell research is exceedingly controversial for ethical reasons. Its advocates point to its potential for treating serious diseases, including Alzheimer's, diabetes, and certain cancers, but its opponents point out that such research requires investigators to destroy lab-created balls of cells that are four or five days old (which at that stage are smaller than the period at the end of this sentence). For stem cell research opponents, these cells are an early form of human life. As we learned in Chapter 1, certain profoundly important questions are metaphysical and therefore lie outside the boundaries of science: Science deals only with testable claims within the realm of the natural world (Gould, 1997). The question of whether

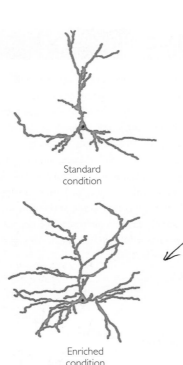

FIGURE 3.6 Neurons in Standard and Enriched Conditions. Neurons from rats reared in standard (*top*) or enriched (*bottom*) conditions. Note the increase in branching and extension of dendrites in the enriched condition. (*Source:* Giuseppa Leggio et al., 2005)

Stem cells = cells that may specialize into almost any type of cell. (also can provide gene therapy (provide patient with replacement genes))

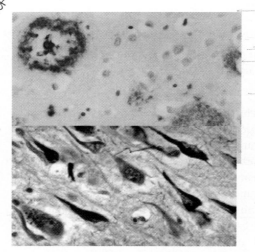

Senile plaques (*top*) and neurofibrillary tangles (*bottom*) in a brain of a patient with Alzheimer's disease. This degeneration in several brain regions may contribute to the memory loss and intellectual decline associated with the disorder (see Chapter 7).

stem cell
a cell, often originating in embryos, having the capacity to differentiate into a more specialized cell

stem cell research may one day cure diseases falls within the scope of science, but the question of whether such research is ethical doesn't. Nor, in all likelihood, can science ever resolve definitively the question of when human life begins (Buckle, Dawson, & Singer, 1989). As a consequence, reasonable people will continue to disagree on whether stem cell research should be performed.

Neurogenesis. There's another way that researchers may be able to get around the lack of regeneration following injury and neural degeneration. **Neurogenesis** is the creation of new neurons in the adult brain. Less than 20 years ago, most scientists were quite sure that we're born with all the neurons we'll ever have. Then Fred Gage (interestingly, a descendant of Phineas Gage, whom we'll meet later in the chapter), Elizabeth Gould, and their colleagues discovered that in adult monkeys, neurogenesis occurs in certain brain areas (Gage, 2002; Gould & Gross, 2002). The odds are high that neurogenesis occurs in adult human brains, too.

Why does neurogenesis occur in adults? One possibility is that it plays a role in learning (Aimone, Wiles, & Gage, 2006). Another role may be aiding recovery following brain injury. By triggering neurogenesis, scientists may one day be able to induce the adult nervous system to heal itself (Kozorovitskiy & Gould, 2003; Lie et al., 2004).

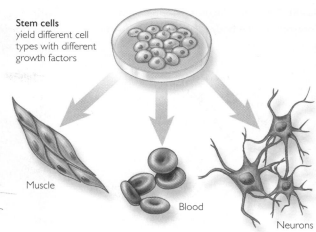

Stem cells yield different cell types with different growth factors

Muscle

Blood

Neurons

FIGURE 3.7 Stem Cells and Growth Factors. Stem cells have the capacity to become many different cell types depending on the growth factors to which they're exposed.

✔ **Study** and **Review** on **mypsychlab.com**

---

assess your knowledge   **FACT OR FICTION?**

1. Dendrites are the sending portions of neurons. **True / False**

2. Positive particles flowing into the neuron inhibit its action. **True / False**

3. Neurotransmitters send messages between neurons. **True / False**

4. Some antidepressants block the reuptake of serotonin from the synapse. **True / False**

5. Neurogenesis is the same thing as pruning. **True / False**

Answers: 1. F (p. 86); 2. F (p. 88); 3. T (p. 88); 4. T (pp. 90–91); 5. F (p. 93)

THE BRAIN–BEHAVIOR NETWORK

3.5 Identify what roles different parts of the central nervous system play in behavior.

3.6 Clarify how the somatic and autonomic nervous systems work in emergency and everyday situations.

The connections among neurons provide the physiological bases of our thoughts, emotions, and behaviors. But how do we get from electrical charges and release of neurotransmitters to complex behaviors, like writing a term paper or asking someone out for a date? Let's say we decide to walk to a vending machine to buy a can of soda. How does our brain, this motley collection of billions of neurons, accomplish this feat? First, our brain makes a conscious decision to do so—or so it would seem. Second, our nervous system propels our body into action. Third, we need to locate and operate the vending machine. We must accurately identify the machine based on how it looks and feels, insert the right amount of money, and finally retrieve our soda to take a well-deserved sip. Communication among neurons in the vast network of connections we call our nervous system allows us to take these complex actions for granted.

We can think of our nervous system as a superhighway with a two-way flow of traffic. Sensory information comes into—and decisions to act come out of—the **central nervous system (CNS)**, composed of the brain and spinal cord. Scientists call all the nerves that extend outside of the CNS the **peripheral nervous system (PNS)** (see **FIGURE 3.8** on page 94). The PNS is further divided into the somatic nervous system, which controls voluntary behavior, and the autonomic nervous system, which controls nonvoluntary, that is, automatic, functions of the body (see Chapter 11).

neurogenesis
creation of new neurons in the adult brain

central nervous system (CNS)
part of nervous system containing brain and spinal cord that controls the mind and behavior

peripheral nervous system (PNS)
nerves in the body that extend outside the central nervous system (CNS)

FIGURE 3.8 The Nervous System Exerts Control over the Body. (*Source:* Modified from Dorling Kindersley)

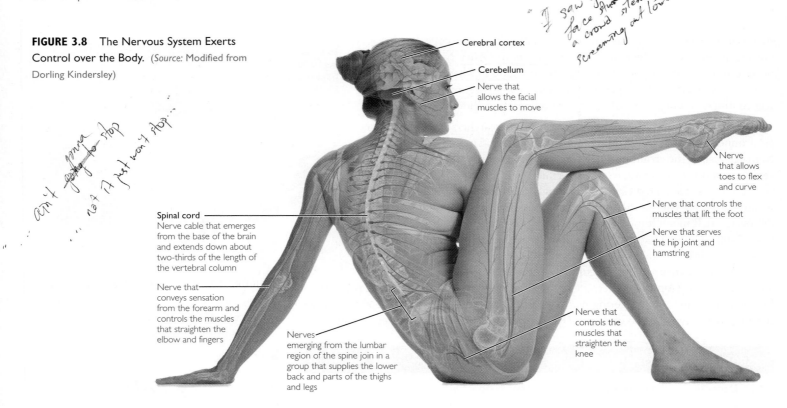

Cerebral cortex

Cerebellum

Nerve that allows the facial muscles to move

Nerve that allows toes to flex and curve

Nerve that controls the muscles that lift the foot

Nerve that serves the hip joint and hamstring

Nerve that controls the muscles that straighten the knee

Nerves emerging from the lumbar region of the spine join in a group that supplies the lower back and parts of the thighs and legs

Nerve that conveys sensation from the forearm and controls the muscles that straighten the elbow and fingers

Spinal cord
Nerve cable that emerges from the base of the brain and extends down about two-thirds of the length of the vertebral column

■ The Central Nervous System: The Command Center

Scientists divide the CNS into distinct sections or systems (see **TABLE 3.2**). The brain and spinal cord are protected by *meninges*, three thin layers of membranes. Further protection is afforded by the **cerebral ventricles**, fluid-filled pockets that extend throughout the entire

TABLE 3.2 The Organization of the Central Nervous System.

Central Nervous System		
Cortex	**Frontal Lobe:** performs executive functions that coordinate other brain areas, motor planning, language, and memory	
	Parietal Lobe: processes touch information, integrates vision and touch	
	Temporal Lobe: processes auditory information, language, and autobiographical memory	
	Occipital Lobe: processes visual information	
Basal Ganglia	control movement and motor planning	
Limbic system	**Thalamus:** conveys sensory information to cortex	
	Hypothalamus: oversees endocrine and autonomic nervous system	
	Amygdala: regulates arousal and fear	
	Hippocampus: processes memory for spatial locations	
Cerebellum	controls balance and coordinated movement	
Brain Stem	**Midbrain:** tracks visual stimuli and reflexes triggered by sound	
	Pons: conveys information between the cortex and cerebellum	
	Medulla: regulates breathing and heartbeats	
Spinal Cord	conveys information between the brain and the rest of the body	

cerebral ventricles
pockets in the brain that contain cerebrospinal fluid (CSF), which provide the brain with nutrients and cushion against injury

FIGURE 3.9 The Human Brain: A Simple Map.

(*Source:* Modified from Dorling Kindersley)

[handwritten: Cerebrum, most developed area of brain.]

[handwritten: Corpus callosum → connects both hemispheres and allows them to communicate]

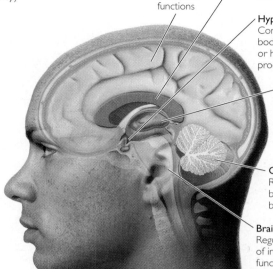

Forebrain (including cerebral cortex) The site of most of the brain's conscious functions

Corpus callosum Bundle of nerve fibers connecting the cerebrum's two hemispheres

Hypothalamus Controls the body's endocrine, or hormone-producing, system

Thalamus Area that relays nerve signals to the cerebral cortex

Cerebellum Regulates balance and body control

Brain stem Regulates control of involuntary functions such as breathing and heart rate

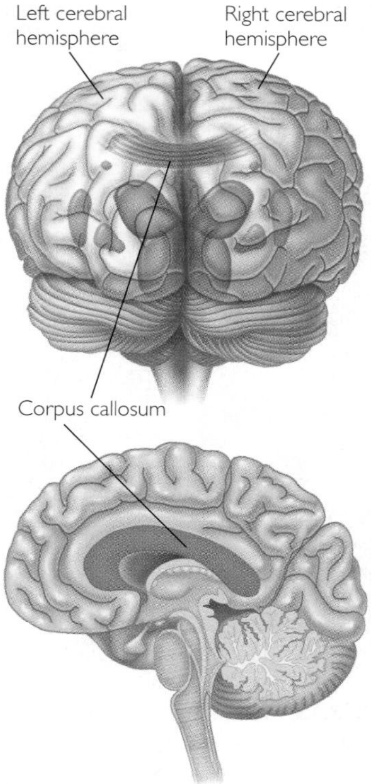

Left cerebral hemisphere

Right cerebral hemisphere

Corpus callosum

FIGURE 3.10 The Cerebral Hemispheres and the Corpus Callosum. The corpus callosum connects the two cerebral hemispheres.

[handwritten: "...from a thousand miles apart."]

[handwritten: Forebrain = most developed brain - 2 hemispheres connected by corpus callosum]

brain and spinal cord. A clear liquid, called *cerebrospinal fluid* (CSF), runs through these ventricles and bathes our brain and spinal cord, providing nutrients and cushioning us against injury. This fluid is the CNS's shock absorber, allowing us to move our heads rapidly in everyday life without sustaining brain damage.

As we review different brain regions, bear in mind that although these regions serve different functions, they cooperate seamlessly with each other to generate our thoughts, feelings, and behaviors (see **FIGURE 3.9**). We'll begin our guided tour of the brain with the part of the brain studied most extensively by psychologists.

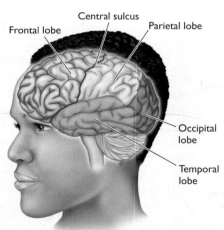

Central sulcus

Frontal lobe

Parietal lobe

Occipital lobe

Temporal lobe

FIGURE 3.11 The Four Lobes of the Cerebral Cortex. The cerebral cortex consists of four interacting lobes: frontal, parietal, temporal, and occipital.

THE CEREBRAL CORTEX. The *cerebrum* or **forebrain**, is the most highly developed area of the human brain. It gives us our advanced intellectual abilities—which explains why it's of such keen interest to psychologists.

The cerebrum consists of two **cerebral hemispheres** (see **FIGURE 3.10**). These hemispheres look alike but serve somewhat different functions. Nevertheless, like two figure skaters in a pairs competition, they communicate and cooperate continually. The huge band of fibers connecting the **corpus callosum**, meaning "colossal body" in Latin, connects the two hemispheres and permits them to communicate (see Figure 3.10).

The largest component of the cerebrum is the **cerebral cortex**, which contains some 12 to 20 billion neurons. The cortex is the outermost part of the cerebrum. It's aptly named, because *cortex* means "bark," as the cortex surrounds the hemispheres much like bark on a tree. The cerebral cortex analyzes sensory information, helping us to perform complex brain functions, including reasoning and language.

The cortex contains four regions called *lobes*, each associated with somewhat different functions (see **FIGURE 3.11**). Each of our hemispheres contains the same four lobes.

forebrain (cerebrum) forward part of the brain that allows advanced intellectual abilities

cerebral hemispheres two halves of the cerebral cortex, each of which serve distinct yet highly integrated functions

corpus callosum large band of fibers connecting the two cerebral hemispheres

cerebral cortex outermost part of forebrain, responsible for analyzing sensory processing and higher brain functions

[handwritten: largest component of cerebrum, Cerebral cortex = 12 to 20 billion neurons surrounds hemispheres, outermost part of cerebrum. - reasoning, language.]

All that you want is in front of you.
All that you need is love-

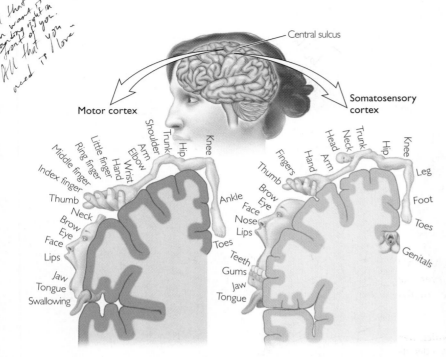

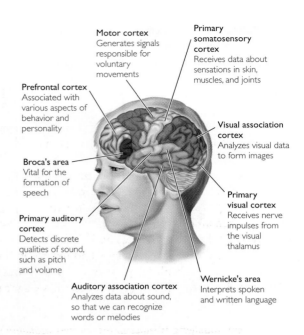

FIGURE 3.12 Representation of the Body Mapped onto the Motor and Sensory Areas of the Cerebral Cortex. The brain networks with the body in a systematic way, with specific regions of both the motor and somatosensory cortex mapping onto specific regions of the body. (*Source:* Adapted from Marieb & Hoehn, 2007)

FIGURE 3.13 Selected Areas of the Cerebral Cortex. The prefrontal cortex controls various aspects of behavior and personality. Broca's area is vital for the formation of speech, and Wernicke's area interprets spoken and written language. Other cortical areas include the motor cortex, primary sensory areas, and association areas.

Cortex contains 4 Lobes:

→ Frontal = motor function (movement), language, and memory
- executive functioning (oversee other cognitive functions)

Central sulcus = deep groove that ~~that~~ separates frontal lobe from rest of the cortex
Motor cortex: next to central sulcus, controls body movement
prefrontal cortex= in front of motor cortex for thinking, planning, and language, mood, personality, self-awareness

frontal lobe
forward part of cerebral cortex responsible for motor function, language, memory, and planning

motor cortex
part of frontal lobe responsible for body movement

prefrontal cortex
part of frontal lobe responsible for thinking, planning, and language

Broca's area
language area in the prefrontal cortex that helps to control speech production

Frontal Lobes. The **frontal lobes** lie in the forward part of the cerebral cortex. If you touch your forehead right now, your fingers are less than an inch away from your frontal lobes. The frontal lobes assist us in motor function (movement), language, and memory. They also oversee and organize most other brain functions, a process called *executive functioning.* Just as the U.S. president exerts control over the members of his (and surely one day, her) Cabinet, the brain's executive function provides a kind of top-level governance over other cognitive functions.

In most people's brains, a deep groove, called the *central sulcus,* separates the frontal lobe from the rest of the cortex. The **motor cortex** is the part of the frontal lobe that lies next to the central sulcus. We owe much of our knowledge of how the motor cortex works to Canadian neurosurgeon Wilder Penfield (1958), who applied mild electrical shocks to the motor cortex of patients who were awake during surgery for epilepsy (because the brain doesn't contain pain receptors, one can accomplish this procedure without hurting patients). He elicited movements ranging from small muscle twitches to large and complex bodily movements. Penfield found that each part of the motor cortex controlled a specific part of the body, with regions requiring more precise motor control, like our fingers, consuming more cortical space (see **FIGURE 3.12**).

In front of the motor cortex lies a large expanse of the frontal lobe called the **prefrontal cortex**, which is responsible for thinking, planning, and language (see **FIGURE 3.13**). One region of the prefrontal cortex, **Broca's area**, was named after French surgeon Paul Broca, who discovered that this site plays a key role in language production (Broca, 1861). Broca found that this site was damaged in many patients who were having trouble producing speech. His first patient with this strange condition, named "Tan" in the research literature, responded only with the word "Tan" when asked questions. It didn't take long for Broca to recognize that brain damage in Tan and other patients with this speech disorder was almost always located in the left cerebral hemisphere. Many researchers have replicated this finding.

replicability

CAN THE RESULTS BE DUPLICATED IN OTHER STUDIES?

Broca's area (in prefrontal cortex) = responsible for speech production

[Handwritten annotations at top: "Do you know what your lobe is?" "Praying that you make it..." "all I need is the air I breathe and a place to rest my head"]

The prefrontal cortex, which receives information from many other regions of the cerebral cortex, also contributes to mood, personality, and self-awareness (Chayer & Freedman, 2001; Fuster, 2000). The tragic story of Phineas Gage demonstrates how crucial the prefrontal cortex can be to personality.

Gage was a railroad foreman who experienced a horrific accident in 1848. His job was to build railroad tracks running through rural Vermont. Gage was performing his usual task of filling holes with gunpowder to break up stubborn rock formations. He was pressing gunpowder into one hole with a tamping iron when an explosion suddenly propelled the iron with great thrust through his head. The iron pierced Gage's face under his cheekbone and destroyed much of his prefrontal cortex. Remarkably, Gage survived but he was never the same. His physician, J. M. Harlow (1848), describes Gage's personality after the accident as

> fitful, irreverent, indulging at times in the grossest profanity (which was not previously his custom) . . . his mind was radically changed, so decidedly that his friends and acquaintances said he was "no longer Gage."

Admittedly, we don't know exactly what Gage was like before the accident, and some scholars have contended that his personality didn't change as much as is often claimed (Macmillan, 2000). We do know more about the exact location of Gage's brain damage, however. Hanna Damasio and her colleagues (1994) examined the skull of Phineas Gage with brain imaging techniques and confirmed that both the right and left sides of his prefrontal cortex were seriously damaged.

Parietal Lobe. The **parietal lobe** is the upper middle part of the cerebral cortex lying behind the frontal lobe (refer to Figure 3.11). The region of the parietal lobe lying just behind the central sulcus next to the motor cortex is the somatosensory cortex, which is sensitive to touch, including pressure and pain, and temperature (Figure 3.12). The parietal lobe helps us track objects' locations (Nachev & Husain, 2006; Shomstein & Yantis, 2006), shapes, and orientations. It also helps us process others' actions and represent numbers (Gobel & Rushworth, 2004). The parietal lobe communicates visual and touch information to the motor cortex every time we reach, grasp, and move our eyes (Culham & Valyear, 2006). Imagine that you ask your roommate to put a blank CD in your bookbag because you need to copy an assignment for him. You grab your bookbag, head off to school, and forget about it until you're in the library sitting at the computer terminal and then you reach into your bag. What do you expect to feel? A CD or disk case, or maybe a soft sleeve? You're probably not sure how, or even if, your roommate packaged the blank CD, but you can construct a mental image of the possibilities. So you can translate what your fingers feel into how the CD will look when you pull it out of your pocket. That's a parietal lobe function.

Temporal Lobe. The **temporal lobe** is the prime site of hearing, understanding language, and storing memories of our past (look again at Figure 3.11). This lobe is separated from the rest of the cortex by a horizontal groove called the *lateral fissure*.

The top of the temporal lobe contains the *auditory cortex*, the part of the cortex devoted to hearing (see Chapter 4). The language area in the temporal lobe is called

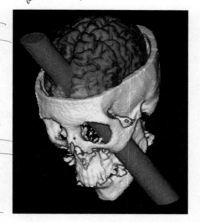

A computer-generated image showing the tamping iron that pierced through the skull and frontal lobes of Phineas Gage.

[Handwritten notes: Parietal Lobe = behind frontal lobe, upper middle part of cortex; somatosensory cortex = touch; temperature (pressure and pain); tracks objects' locations, shapes, orientations, process others' actions, represent numbers; communicates visual and touch info to motor cortex]

In 2009, this photograph of a man believed by historians to be Phineas Gage (whose appearance was previously unknown) surfaced (Wilgus & Wilgus, 2009). One can clearly see (a) Gage holding the huge tamping rod that passed through his frontal lobes, (b) his missing left eye, which was destroyed by the rod, and (c) a tuft of hair on the left side of his head, presumably covering the region of his scalp from which the rod exited.

[Handwritten: Temporal Lobe = hearing, understanding language, storing memories of past; lateral fissure (horizontal groove) = lobe is separated from rest of cortex by this]

parietal lobe
upper middle part of the cerebral cortex lying behind the frontal lobe that is specialized for touch and perception

temporal lobe
lower part of cerebral cortex that plays roles in hearing, understanding language, and memory

[Handwritten: auditory cortex (top of temporal lobe) = hearing]

Boxer Muhammad Ali (*left*) and actor Michael J. Fox (*right*) both live with Parkinson's disease. Ali and his wife, Lonnie, founded the Muhammad Ali Parkinson Center and created *Ali Care*, a special fund for people with Parkinson's disease. The computerized tomography scan (see p. 107) on the right shows the dramatic loss of dopamine neurons, which naturally contain a dark pigment, in a brain affected by Parkinson's disease. The ventricles, shown in blue in the middle of the brain, are abnormally large due to the death of surrounding brain tissue.

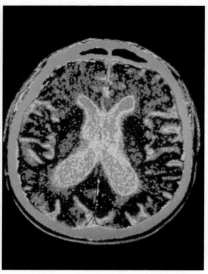

Wernicke's area, although this area also includes the lower parietal lobe (look again at Figure 3.13). It's located slightly above and behind your left ear (unless you're a lefty, in which case it might be above your right ear). Damage to Wernicke's area results in severe difficulties with understanding speech. Moreover, patients with damage to this area tend to speak mostly in gibberish, probably because they don't realize that the words coming out of their mouths don't make sense. When asked whether his last name was "Brown," one patient with damage to this area responded, "What it is here, then let me see. I just don't know. No, I not going to eat any sigh, no."

The lower part of the temporal lobe is critical to storing memories of autobiographical events (see Chapter 7). Penfield (1958) discovered that stimulating this region with electrical probes elicited memories, like vivid recollections of "a certain song" or "the view from a childhood window." Yet psychologists today aren't certain if stimulating the brain elicits genuine memories of past events or instead altered perceptions, making them closer to hallucinations (Schacter, 1996). Indeed, this alternative hypothesis is difficult to rule out.

Occipital Lobe. At the very back of our brain lies the **occipital lobe,** containing the *visual cortex,* dedicated to seeing. Compared with most animals, we human beings are highly dependent on our visual systems—we've even been called the "visual primate" (Angier, 2009)—so it stands to reason that we have an awful lot of cortical real estate devoted to seeing. Still, we're by no means the only highly visual creatures. For each species, the amount of sensory cortex of each type is proportional to the degree to which it relies on that sense. Ghost bats depend highly on sound cues and have proportionally more auditory cortex; the platypus relies heavily on touch cues and has proportionally more touch cortex; and squirrels, like humans, rely strongly on visual inputs and have proportionally more visual cortex (Krubitzer & Kaas, 2005).

Cortical Hierarchies. When information from the outside world is transmitted by a particular sense (like sight, hearing, or touch), it reaches the **primary sensory cortex** specific to that sense (look at Figure 3.13 again). After the eye, ear, or skin transmits sense information to the primary sensory cortex, it's passed on to another area for that sense called the **association cortex,** which is spread throughout all four of the brain's lobes. The association cortex integrates information to perform more complex functions, such as pulling together size, shape, color, and location information to identify an object (see Chapter 4). The overall organization of the cortex is "hierarchical" because processing becomes increasingly complex as information is passed up the network.

THE BASAL GANGLIA. The **basal ganglia** are structures buried deep inside the cortex that help to control movement. Damage to the basal ganglia contributes to Parkinson's disease,

---

ruling out rival hypotheses

HAVE IMPORTANT ALTERNATIVE EXPLANATIONS FOR THE FINDINGS BEEN EXCLUDED?

Wernicke's area
part of the temporal lobe involved in understanding speech

occipital lobe
back part of cerebral cortex specialized for vision

primary sensory cortex
regions of the cerebral cortex that initially process information from the senses

association cortex
regions of the cerebral cortex that integrate simpler functions to perform more complex functions

basal ganglia
structures in the forebrain that help to control movement

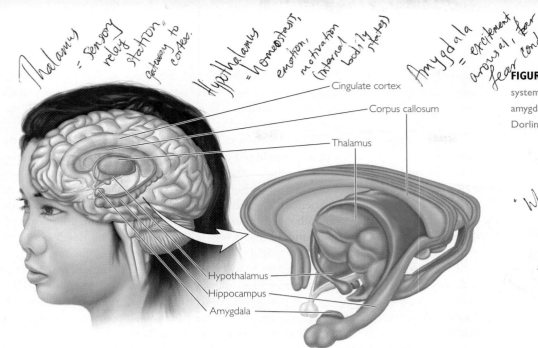

Cingulate cortex
Corpus callosum
Thalamus
Hypothalamus
Hippocampus
Amygdala

FIGURE 3.14 **The Limbic System.** The limbic system consists mainly of the thalamus, hypothalamus, amygdala, and hippocampus. (Left art modified from Dorling Kindersley and right art from Kalat, 2007)

[Handwritten margin notes: Thalamus = sensory relay station, gateway to cortex. Hypothalamus = "homeostasis," emotion, motivation (internal bodily states). Amygdala = excitement, arousal, fear, fear conditioning.]

[Handwritten: "What's your vice? You know mine's the illusion."]

[Handwritten: "So jump in my step, as I rush to see you"]

[Handwritten: Basal ganglia = structures deep inside cortex that help control movement]

[Handwritten: Primary sensory cortex → Association cortex → Basal ganglia → Motor cortex]

[Handwritten: Limbic System = blood pressure, heart rate, respiration, perspiration, emotions, smell, motivation, memory]

[Handwritten: "from the outside looking in"]

resulting in a lack of control over movement and uncontrollable tremors. After sensory information reaches primary and association areas, it's transmitted to the basal ganglia, which calculate a course of action and transmit it to the motor cortex.

The basal ganglia also allow us to perform movements to obtain rewards (Graybiel et al., 1994). When we anticipate a pleasurable outcome, such as a tasty sandwich or hot date, we depend on activity in our basal ganglia.

THE LIMBIC SYSTEM. The diverse parts of the brain dedicated to emotion are housed within the **limbic system** (Lambert, 2003; McClean, 1990), a set of highly interconnected brain regions. In contrast to the cortex, which processes information about external stimuli, the limbic system processes information about our internal states, such as blood pressure, heart rate, respiration, and perspiration, as well as our emotions. It's the latter that we'll focus on here. *[Handwritten: Cortex = external stimuli; Limbic = internal states]*

We can think of the limbic system as the brain's *emotional center* (see **FIGURE 3.14**). Limbic system structures also play roles in smell, motivation, and memory. The limbic system evolved out of the primitive olfactory system (dedicated to smell), that controlled various survival behaviors in early mammals. As anyone who's walked a dog knows, smell remains vitally important to many animals. ✦ Explore

We'll explore four areas of the limbic system: the thalamus, the hypothalamus, the amygdala, and the hippocampus. Each area plays specific roles, although it cooperates with other regions. The term **thalamus** derives from the Greek word for bedroom or chamber. But the thalamus is more than one room, because it contains many areas, each of which connects to a specific region of the cerebral cortex. We can think of the thalamus as a sensory relay station. The vast majority of sensory information first passes through its doors, undergoing some initial processing, before traveling on to the cortex (refer again to Figure 3.14).

The **hypothalamus**, located on the floor of the brain, regulates and maintains constant internal bodily states. Different areas of the hypothalamus play various roles in emotion and motivation. Some play roles in regulating hunger, thirst, sexual motivation, or other emotional behaviors (see Chapter 11). The hypothalamus also helps control our body temperature, acting much like a thermostat that adjusts our home's temperature in response to indoor changes in temperature. *[Handwritten: (homeostasis)]*

The **amygdala** is named for its almond shape (*amygdala* is Greek for "almond"). Excitement, arousal, and fear are all part of its job description. The amygdala kicks into high gear when teenagers play violent video games (Mathews et al., 2006), or when we view fearful faces (Killgore & Yergelun-Todd, 2005). It also plays a key role in fear conditioning, a process by which animals, including humans, learn to predict when something scary is about to happen

✦ **Explore** the Limbic System on **mypsychlab.com**

limbic system
emotional center of brain that also plays roles in smell, motivation, and memory

thalamus
gateway from the sense organs to the primary sensory cortex

hypothalamus
part of the brain responsible for maintaining a constant internal state

amygdala
part of limbic system that plays key roles in fear, excitement, and arousal

"When we were children we'd play out in the street just doped in fairytale. When we were children we'd say that we don't know the meaning of fear."

(Davis & Shi, 2000; LeDoux, 2000). Ralph Adolphs and colleagues verified the role of the amygdala in fear in a 30-year-old woman whose left and right amygdalas were almost entirely destroyed by disease. Although she had no difficulty identifying faces, she was markedly impaired in detecting fear in these faces (Adolphs et al., 1994).

The **hippocampus** plays crucial roles in memory, especially spatial memory—the memory of the physical layout of things in our environment. When we make a mental map of how to get from one place to another, we're using our hippocampus. This may explain why a portion of the hippocampus is larger in London taxi drivers than in non–taxi drivers and is especially large in experienced taxi drivers (Maguire et al., 2000). This correlation could mean either that people with greater amounts of experience navigating complex environments develop larger hippocampi or that people with larger hippocampi seek out occupations, like taxi driving, that rely on spatial navigation. One study that could help us figure out what's causing what would be to examine whether cab drivers' hippocampi become larger as they acquire more driving experience. Although researchers haven't yet conducted this study, they've looked at this issue in people who've recently learned to juggle. Sure enough, they've found evidence for short-term increases in the size of the hippocampus, suggesting that this brain area can change in size in response to learning (Boyke et al., 2008).

Damage to the hippocampus causes problems with forming new memories, but leaves old memories intact (see Chapter 7). One hypothesis is that the hippocampus stores memories temporarily before transferring them to other sites, such as the cortex, for permanent storage (Sanchez-Andres, Olds, & Alkon, 1993). The *multiple trace theory* is a rival hypothesis of memory storage in the hippocampus (Moscovitch et al., 2005). According to this theory, memories are initially stored at multiple sites. Over time, storage becomes stronger at some sites but weaker at others. The multiple trace theory avoids the need to "transfer" memory from the hippocampus to the cortex. According to this model, memories are already stored in the cortex and merely strengthen over time.

THE BRAIN STEM. The **brain stem**, housed inside the cortex and located at the very back of our brains, contains the *midbrain, pons,* and the *medulla* (see **FIGURE 3.15**). The brain

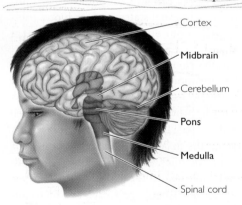

stem performs some of the basic bodily functions that keep us alive. It also serves as a relay station between the cortex and the rest of the nervous system. The **midbrain**, in turn, plays an important role in movement. It also controls the tracking of visual stimuli and reflexes triggered by sound, like jumping after we're startled by a car backfiring.

Reticular Activating System. The **reticular activating system (RAS)** connects to the forebrain and cerebral cortex; this system plays a key role in arousal. Turn off a dog's RAS, for example, and it instantly falls asleep. Damage to the RAS can result in a coma. Some scientists even believe that many knockdowns in boxing result from a temporary compression of the RAS following a powerful punch (Weisberg, Garcia, & Strub, 1996).

The pathways emanating from the RAS activate the cortex by jacking up the *signal-to-noise ratio* among neurons in the brain (Gu, 2002). When it's working well, a cell phone produces sound with a high signal-to-noise ratio so that each caller can understand the other's messages. When there's a great deal of background static—resulting in a low signal-to-noise ratio—callers find it difficult to understand each other (see Chapter 4).

A possible example of this problem occurs in attention-deficit/hyperactivity disorder (ADHD), a disorder originating in childhood (see Chapter 15). ADHD is marked by inattention, overactivity, and impulsivity. Stimulant drugs used to treat ADHD, such as methylphenidate (often marketed under the brand name Ritalin), appear to increase the

correlation vs. causation

CAN WE BE SURE THAT A CAUSES B?

Hippocampus = memory
(spatial memory = memory of physical layout in environment)

ruling out rival hypotheses

HAVE IMPORTANT ALTERNATIVE EXPLANATIONS FOR THE FINDINGS BEEN EXCLUDED?

The hippocampi of taxi drivers seem to be especially large, although the causal direction of this finding is unclear.

FIGURE 3.15   The Brain Stem. The brain stem is located at the top of the spinal cord, below the cortex.

Labels in figure: Cortex, Midbrain, Cerebellum, Pons, Medulla, Spinal cord

hippocampus
part of the brain that plays a role in spatial memory

brain stem
part of the brain between the spinal cord and cerebral cortex that contains the midbrain, pons, and medulla

midbrain
part of the brain stem that contributes to movement, tracking of visual stimuli, and reflexes triggered by sound

reticular activating system (RAS)
brain area that plays a key role in arousal

[Handwritten margin notes: Brain stem (rest de cortex) (at back of brain) - midbrain = movement, tracks visual and stimuli, reflexes by sound - Pons "dreams" connects cortex to cerebellum - medulla "breathing, heartbeat, other vital functions" (damage can cause irreversible coma) | Cerebellum: predominant role in balance, coordination in movement, motor skills, also executive, spatial, and linguistic abilities]

signal-to-noise ratio in the prefrontal cortex (Devilbiss & Berridge, 2006). One hypothesis is that these drugs mimic activity in the RAS and neighboring brain regions, but other explanations are possible. For example, methylphenidate boosts levels of the neurotransmitter dopamine, which may be responsible for increases in attention and decreases in impulsivity (Volkow et al., 2005). *[Handwritten: Reticular Activating system (RAS) connects forebrain and cortex; arousal (damage causes coma)]*

The Cerebellum, Pons, and Medulla. Below the midbrain lies the **hindbrain**, which consists of the *cerebellum*, *pons*, and *medulla*, the last two being part of the brain stem. *Cerebellum* is Latin for "little brain," and in many respects the cerebellum is a miniature version of the cortex. The **cerebellum** plays a predominant role in our sense of balance and enables us to coordinate movement and learn motor skills. Among other things, it helps prevent us from falling down. But in recent years, scientists have come to realize that the cerebellum does more: It also contributes to executive, spatial, and linguistic abilities (Schmahmann, 2004). The **pons**, which as we'll learn in Chapter 5 plays a crucial role in triggering dreams, connects the cortex to the cerebellum.

The **medulla** regulates breathing, heartbeat, and other vital functions. Damage to the medulla can cause *brain death,* which scientists define as irreversible coma. People who are brain dead are totally unaware of their surroundings and unresponsive, even to ordinarily very painful stimuli. They show no signs of spontaneous movement, respiration, or reflex activity.

People often confuse a *persistent vegetative state,* or cortical death, with brain death, but the two aren't identical. Terri Schiavo made headlines in 2005 as the woman who had lain in a persistent vegetative state for 15 years. Schiavo collapsed in her Florida home in 1990 following temporary cardiac arrest, depriving her brain of oxygen and resulting in severe brain damage. The deep structures in her brain stem that control breathing, heart rate, digestion, and certain reflexive responses were still operating, so Schiavo wasn't brain dead, as much of the news media reported incorrectly. Nevertheless, her higher cerebral structures, necessary for awareness of herself and her environment, were damaged permanently. Her doctors knew that much of her cortex had withered away, and an autopsy later showed that she'd lost about half of her brain.

Those who believe that death of the higher brain centers essential for consciousness is equivalent to actual death felt that Schiavo had, in fact, died 15 years earlier. Nevertheless, her death raises difficult and troubling questions that science can't fully resolve: Should brain death be the true criterion for death, or should this criterion instead be the permanent loss of consciousness? *[Handwritten: Sensory nerves, motor nerves, interneurons]*

THE SPINAL CORD. The **spinal cord** extends from our brain stem and runs down the middle of our backs, conveying information between the brain and the rest of the body. *Nerves* extend from neurons to the body, traveling in two directions much like the traffic on a two-lane highway. Sensory information is carried from the body to the brain by way of *sensory nerves;* motor commands are carried from the brain to the body by way of *motor nerves.* The spinal cord also contains sensory neurons that contact **interneurons**, neurons that send messages to other neurons located nearby. Interneurons connect sensory nerves with motor nerves within the spinal cord without having to report back to the brain. Interneurons explain how **reflexes**, automatic motor responses to sensory stimuli, can occur.

Consider an automatic behavior called the stretch reflex, which relies only on the spinal cord. We're carrying our books in our arms, but over time our grasp releases ever so slightly without our even noticing. Our sensory nerves detect the muscle stretch and relay this information to the spinal cord. Interneurons intervene and motor neurons automatically send messages that cause our arm muscles to contract. Without our ever knowing it, a simple reflex causes our arm muscles to tighten, preventing us from dropping our books (see **FIGURE 3.16**).

■ The Peripheral Nervous System

Thus far, we've examined the inner workings of the CNS—the central nervous system. Now let's briefly examine the peripheral nervous system (PNS), the part of the nervous system consisting of the nerves that extend outside of the CNS. The PNS itself contains two branches, somatic and autonomic.

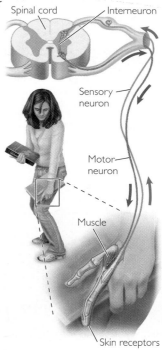

Spinal cord · Interneuron · Sensory neuron · Motor neuron · Muscle · Skin receptors

FIGURE 3.16 **The Spinal Reflex.** We detect even small amounts of muscle stretch and compensate by contraction. In this way we can maintain balance or keep from losing our grip.

[Handwritten: "I stared at the sun...just to see with all of the faces, you were the one next to me."]

hindbrain
region below the midbrain that contains the cerebellum, pons, and medulla

cerebellum
brain structure responsible for our sense of balance

pons
part of the brain stem that connects the cortex with the cerebellum

medulla
part of brain stem involved in basic functions, such as heartbeat and breathing

spinal cord
thick bundle of nerves that conveys signals between the brain and the body

interneuron
neuron that sends messages to other neurons nearby *[Handwritten: without having to go back to the brain.]*

reflex
an automatic motor response to a sensory stimulus

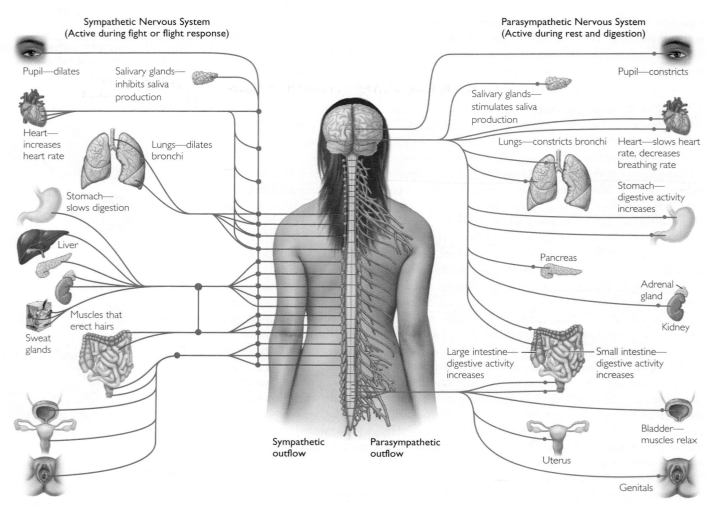

Sympathetic Nervous System
(Active during fight or flight response)

Pupil—dilates

Salivary glands—inhibits saliva production

Heart—increases heart rate

Lungs—dilates bronchi

Stomach—slows digestion

Liver

Muscles that erect hairs

Sweat glands

Sympathetic outflow

Parasympathetic Nervous System
(Active during rest and digestion)

Pupil—constricts

Salivary glands—stimulates saliva production

Lungs—constricts bronchi

Heart—slows heart rate, decreases breathing rate

Stomach—digestive activity increases

Pancreas

Adrenal gland

Kidney

Large intestine—digestive activity increases

Small intestine—digestive activity increases

Parasympathetic outflow

Uterus

Bladder—muscles relax

Genitals

FIGURE 3.17   The Autonomic Nervous System (Female Shown). The sympathetic and parasympathetic divisions of the autonomic nervous system control the internal organs and glands.

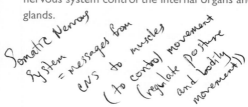

somatic nervous system
part of the nervous system that conveys information between the CNS and the body, controlling and coordinating voluntary movement

autonomic nervous system
part of the nervous system controlling the involuntary actions of our internal organs and glands, which (along with the limbic system) participates in emotion regulation

sympathetic nervous system
division of the autonomic nervous system engaged during a crisis or after actions requiring fight or flight

THE SOMATIC NERVOUS SYSTEM. The **somatic nervous system** carries messages from the CNS to muscles throughout the body, controlling movement (look back to Figure 3.8). Whenever we stabilize or move our many joints, the CNS cooperates with the somatic nervous system to regulate our posture and bodily movement.

Let's review what happens when we decide to stroll over to the vending machine to purchase a can of soda. Sensory inputs of all types reach the cortex. Then all parts of the cortex send information to the basal ganglia. The basal ganglia contribute to our decision about what to do and relay that information to the motor cortex. Next up, the motor cortex sends commands to the spinal cord, activating motor neurons. These motor neurons send messages through nerves that reach muscles throughout the body and trigger muscle contractions. We walk, reach, touch, and grasp. Our brain triggers all of these movements, but our somatic nervous system carries them out. After we finish our drink, our somatic nervous system keeps working, enabling us to walk away—ideally, to the nearest recycling container.

THE AUTONOMIC NERVOUS SYSTEM. The brain and spinal cord interact with our somatic nervous system to bring about sensation and behavior. In much the same way, the brain, especially the limbic system, interacts with the **autonomic nervous system** to regulate emotion and internal physical states. The autonomic nervous system is the part of the nervous system that controls the involuntary actions of our organs and glands; along with the limbic system, it helps to regulate our emotions. The autonomic nervous system, in turn, consists of two divisions: sympathetic and parasympathetic (see **FIGURE 3.17**). These two divisions work in opposing directions, so that when one is active, the other is passive. The **sympathetic nervous system** is active during emotional arousal, especially during crises. This system mobilizes the *fight-or-flight response*, described by Walter Cannon in 1929 (see

[handwritten notes at top: Autonomic Nervous System = regulate emotion and internal physical states → Sympathetic: active during emotional arousal (during crises), increased heart rate, respiration, and perspiration → parasympathetic: active during rest and digestion.]

Chapter 12). Cannon noticed that when we encounter threats, like the sight of a huge predator charging toward us, our sympathetic nervous system becomes aroused and prepares us for fighting or fleeing. Sympathetic activation triggers a variety of physical responses helpful for reacting in a crisis, including increased heart rate (allowing more blood to flow into our extremities), respiration, and perspiration. Autonomic nerves that reach the heart, diaphragm, and sweat glands control these reactions. The **parasympathetic nervous system**, in contrast, is active during rest and digestion. This system kicks into gear when there's no threat on our mental radar screens.

---

assess your knowledge — FACT OR FICTION?

1. The cortex is divided into the frontal, parietal, temporal, and hippocampal lobes. **True / False**

2. The basal ganglia control sensation. **True / False**

3. The amygdala plays a key role in fear. **True / False**

4. The cerebellum regulates only our sense of balance. **True / False**

5. There are two divisions of the autonomic nervous system. **True / False**

Answers: 1. F (p. 95); 2. F (p. 98); 3. T (p. 99); 4. F (p. 101); 5. T (p. 102)

---

parasympathetic nervous system
division of autonomic nervous system that controls rest and digestion

endocrine system
system of glands and hormones that controls secretion of blood-borne chemical messengers

hormone
chemical released into the bloodstream that influences particular organs and glands

pituitary gland
master gland that, under the control of the hypothalamus, directs the other glands of the body

✓ Study and Review on **mypsychlab.com**

[handwritten note: "You can feel the washing light start to tremble to see in. what you know out to see in. You can see a life out the window tonight."]

THE ENDOCRINE SYSTEM

3.7 Describe what hormones are and how they affect behavior.

The limbic system also cooperates with the **endocrine system** to regulate emotion. The endocrine system is separate from, but interfaces with, the nervous system, and consists of glands that release **hormones**, molecules that influence particular organs, into the bloodstream (see **FIGURE 3.18**). Hormones differ from neurotransmitters in that they're carried through our blood vessels rather than our nerves, so they're much slower in their actions. We can think of hormonal messages as a bit like regular mail and neurotransmitter messages as a bit like e-mail. But hormones tend to outlast neurotransmitters in their effects, so their eventual impact tends to be more enduring.

■ The Pituitary Gland and Pituitary Hormones

The **pituitary gland** controls the other glands in the body; for this reason, it was once called the "master gland," although scientists have now realized that it depends heavily on the actions of other glands, too. The pituitary gland, in turn, is under the control of the hypothalamus. The pituitary releases a variety of hormones that serve numerous functions, ranging all the way from regulating physical growth, controlling blood pressure, and determining how much water we retain in our kidneys. One pituitary hormone called *oxytocin* is responsible for a several reproductive functions, including stretching the cervix and vagina during birth and aiding milk flow in nursing mothers. Oxytocin also plays essential roles in maternal and romantic love (Esch & Stefano, 2005). Scientists have identified two closely related species of voles (a type of rodent) that differ in their pair bonding: The males of one species are promiscuous, flitting from attractive partner to another, whereas the males of the other remain faithfully devoted to one partner for life. Only in the brains of the loyal voles are oxytocin receptors linked to the dopamine system, which as we've learned influences the experience of reward (Young & Wang, 2004). For male voles, at least, remaining faithful isn't a chore: It's literally a labor of love. Oxytocin may also influence

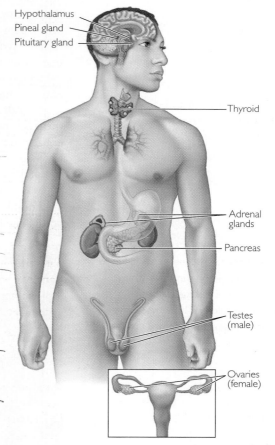

Hypothalamus
Pineal gland
Pituitary gland

Thyroid

Adrenal glands

Pancreas

Testes (male)

Ovaries (female)

FIGURE 3.18 **The Major Endocrine Glands of the Body.** Endocrine glands throughout the body play specialized roles.

Although these two vole species (the prairie vole on the left and the montane vole on the right) look quite similar, they differ in their "personalities," at least when it comes to romance. The male prairie vole stays loyal to one partner, but the male montane vole doesn't. The difference lies in their oxytocin systems.

how much we trust others. In one study, men exposed to a nasal spray containing oxytocin were more likely than others to hand over money to their team partners in a risky investment game (Kosfeld et al., 2005; Rilling, King-Cassas, & Sanfey, 2008).

■ The Adrenal Glands and Adrenaline

Psychologists sometimes call the **adrenal glands** the emergency centers of the body. Located atop of the kidneys, they manufacture the hormones *adrenaline* and *cortisol.* Adrenaline boosts energy production in muscle cells, thrusting them into action, while conserving as much energy as possible. Nerves of the sympathetic nervous system signal the adrenal glands to release adrenaline. Adrenaline triggers many actions, including (1) contraction of our heart muscle and constriction of our blood vessels to provide more blood to the body, (2) opening the bronchioles (tiny airways) of the lungs to allow inhalation of more air, (3) breakdown of fat into fatty acids, providing us with more fuel, (4) breakdown of glycogen (a carbohydrate) into glucose (a sugar) to energize our muscles, and (5) opening the pupils of our eyes to enable better sight during emergencies. Adrenaline also inhibits gastrointestinal secretions, explaining why we often lose our appetites when we feel nervous, as when anticipating a big job interview or final exam. ◆⊢Explore

⊕⊢Explore the Endocrine System on **mypsychlab.com**

Adrenaline allows people to perform amazing feats in crisis situations, although these acts are constrained by people's physical limitations. One desperate mother was energized to lift a heavy automobile to save her trapped infant (Solomon, 2002). She probably had evolution to thank, as natural selection has almost surely predisposed the sympathetic nervous system to react to dangerous stimuli to prepare us for counterattack (fight) or escape (flight). But adrenaline isn't activated only during threatening situations. Pleasurable and exciting activities, like race car driving and skydiving, can also produce adrenaline rushes.

? If this rhinoceros suddenly charged at the three people on this African safari, which branch of their autonomic nervous systems would (we hope!) become activated? (See answer upside down at bottom of page.)

adrenal gland
tissue located on top of the kidneys that releases adrenaline and cortisol during states of emotional arousal

Answer: Sympathetic.

Like adrenaline, cortisol increases in response to physical and psychological stressors. Not surprisingly, some anxiety disorders are associated with elevated levels of cortisol (Mantello et al., 2008). Cortisol regulates blood pressure and cardiovascular function, as well as the body's use of proteins, carbohydrates, and fats. The way in which cortisol regulates nutrients has led some researchers to suggest that it regulates body weight, leading to the development of the popular *cortisol diet*. Proponents of this diet claim that elevated cortisol produced by stress causes weight gain (Talbott, 2002). The solution: Reduce stress, increase exercise, and monitor nutrition—reasonable advice for those of us who want to lose weight. Some people want a quick fix, however, so health food supplement outlets are happy to oblige by selling cortisol blockers. Unfortunately, there's little scientific evidence that these supplements work better than dieting measures that naturally inactivate the body's cortisol.

■ Sexual Reproductive Glands and Sex Hormones

The sexual reproductive glands are the testes in males and ovaries in females (refer back to Figure 3.18). Most of us think of *sex hormones* as either male or female. After all, the testes make the male sex hormone, called *testosterone*, and the ovaries make the female sex hormone, called *estrogen*. Although testosterone is correlated with aggression, the interpretation of this association is controversial. Some authors have argued that a certain minimal level of testosterone is needed for humans and other animals to engage in aggression (Dabbs & Dabbs, 2000), but that above that level testosterone isn't correlated with aggression. Moreover, above that level, these authors contend, aggressive behavior actually causes heightened testosterone rather than the other way around (Sapolsky, 1997).

Although males and females do have more of their own type of sex hormone, both sexes manufacture some amount of the sex hormone associated with the opposite sex. Women's bodies produce about one-twentieth the amount of testosterone as those of males. That's because the ovaries also make testosterone, and the adrenal gland makes low amounts of testosterone in both sexes. Conversely, the testes manufacture estrogen, but in low levels (Hess, 2003).

Scientists have long debated the relationship between sex hormones and sex drive (Bancroft, 2005). Most scientists believe that testosterone, which increases sex drive in men, also increases sex drive in women, but to a lesser degree. Australian researchers conducted a survey of 18- to 75-year-old women regarding their sexual arousal and frequency of orgasm (Davis et al., 2005). They found no correlation between the levels of male sex hormone in a woman's blood and her sex drive. However, the study relied exclusively on self-reports and contained no controls for demand characteristics (see Chapter 2). Most researchers still accept the hypothesis that testosterone influences female sex drive, but additional research from multiple laboratories must be conducted before we can draw firm conclusions.

FACTOID

The thrill of watching others win can increase testosterone in sports fans. Males watching World Cup soccer matches showed increased testosterone levels in their saliva if their favorite team won, but decreased testosterone levels if their favorite team lost (Bernhardt et al., 1998).

◀ **correlation vs. causation**

CAN WE BE SURE THAT A CAUSES B?

Testosterone does not cause aggression.
Aggression causes heightened testosterone.

◀ **replicability**

CAN THE RESULTS BE DUPLICATED IN OTHER STUDIES?

---

assess your knowledge　　　　　　**FACT OR FICTION?**　　✓—[Study and Review on mypsychlab.com

1. Hormones are more rapid in their actions than neurotransmitters. **True / False**

2. Adrenaline sometimes allows people to perform amazing physical feats. **True / False**

3. Cortisol tends to increase in response to stressors. **True / False**

4. Women have no testosterone. **True / False**

Answers: 1. F (p. 103); 2. T (p. 104); 3. T (p. 105); 4. F (p. 105)

MAPPING THE MIND: THE BRAIN IN ACTION

3.8   Identify different brain-stimulating, -recording, and -imaging techniques.

3.9   Evaluate results demonstrating the brain's localization of function.

Although many questions about the brain remain unanswered, we know far, far more about it today than we did 200, or even 20, years ago. For this, we owe psychologists and related scientists who've developed a host of methods to explore the brain and its functioning a major debt of gratitude. ((•—**Listen**

■ A Tour of Brain-Mapping Methods

Many advances over the past two centuries have enabled scientists to measure brain activity, resulting in a better understanding of how the most complicated organ in the known universe works. But brain research tools weren't always grounded in solid science. Some of the earliest methods were fundamentally flawed, but they paved the way for the newer and improved methods used today.

PHRENOLOGY: AN INCORRECT MAP OF THE MIND. Phrenology—sometimes jokingly called "bumpology"—was one of the first attempts to map mind onto brain. This theory was wildly popular in the 1800s, when phrenologists assessed enlargements of the skull—literally bumps on the head—and attributed various personality and intellectual characteristics to those who sought their "expertise." Phrenologists assumed that bumps on the skull corresponded to brain enlargements, and that these brain enlargements were linked directly to psychological capacities. From the 1820s through the 1840s, thousands of phrenology shops popped up in Europe and North America. Anyone could go to a phrenology parlor to discover his or her psychological makeup. This popular practice was the origin of the familiar expression "having one's head examined."

The founder of phrenology, Viennese physician Franz Joseph Gall (1758–1828), began with some valid assumptions about the brain. He correctly predicted a positive relationship between enlargements in a handful of brain areas and certain traits and abilities, like language. Nevertheless, the up to 37 different traits that phrenologists described—aggressiveness, vanity, friendliness, and happiness among them—are vastly different from the functions scientists studying the brain today assign to different brain areas. What's more, Gall and others based their hypotheses about the supposed associations between brain areas and personality traits almost entirely on anecdotal observations, which we've learned (see Chapter 1) are often subject to a host of errors.

Still, phrenology had one virtue: It was falsifiable. Ironically, this lone asset proved to be its undoing. Eventually, researchers discovered that patients with damage to specific brain areas didn't experience the kinds of psychological deficits the phrenologists predicted. Even more critically, because the shape of the outer surface of the skull doesn't closely match that of the underlying brain, phrenologists weren't even measuring bumps on the brain, as they'd believed. These discoveries ultimately led to the demise of phrenology as an approach.

BRAIN DAMAGE: UNDERSTANDING HOW THE BRAIN WORKS BY SEEING HOW IT DOESN'T. New methods quickly arose to fill the void left by phrenology. Foremost among them were methods of studying psychological functioning following damage to specific brain regions. We've already mentioned the pioneering work of Broca and others that linked specific areas of the cerebral cortex to specific functions. More recently, scientists have created lesions, that is, areas of damage, in experimental animals using stereotaxic methods, techniques that permit them to pinpoint the location of specific brain areas using coordinates, much like those navigators use on a map. Today, *neuropsychologists* rely on sophisticated psychological tests, like measures of reasoning, attention, and verbal and spatial ability, to infer the location of brain dysfunction in human patients. Neuropsychological tests, which require specialized training to administer, score, and interpret, include laboratory, computer-

((•—**Listen** to the Brain Mapping Podcast on **mypsychlab.com**

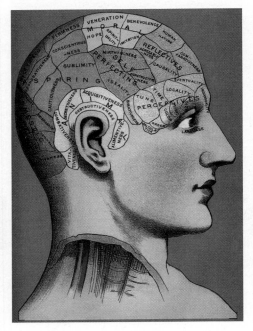

A phrenologist's chart showing where certain psychological traits are supposedly associated with bumps on the skull.

falsifiability

CAN THE CLAIM BE DISPROVED?

FACTOID ✚

Mark Twain (1835-1910), often considered America's greatest humorist, once underwent a phrenology reading from Lorenzo Fowler, probably the foremost U.S. proponent of phrenology. Fowler, who was then proponent of Twain's identity, informed Twain that the pattern of bumps on his skull indicated that he had an entirely unremarkable personality with one exception: He lacked a sense of humor. When Twain returned three months later and identified himself, Fowler "discovered" a large skull bump corresponding to humor (Lopez, 2002).

ized, and paper-and-pencil measures designed to assess patients' cognitive strengths and weaknesses (Lezak, Howieson, & Loring, 2004).

ELECTRICAL STIMULATION AND RECORDING OF NERVOUS SYSTEM ACTIVITY. Although early studies of function following brain damage provided valuable insights into which brain areas are responsible for which behaviors, many questions remained. Researchers soon discovered that stimulating parts of the human motor cortex in patients undergoing brain surgery produced extremely specific movements (Penfield, 1958). This finding, among others, led to the hypothesis that neurons use electrical activity to send information. But to test that hypothesis, scientists needed to record electrical activity from the nervous system.

To that end, Hans Berger (1929) developed the **electroencephalograph (EEG)**, a device—still widely used today—that measures electrical activity generated by the brain (see **FIGURE 3.19**). Patterns and sequences in the EEG allow scientists to infer whether a person is awake or asleep, dreaming or not, and to tell which regions of the brain are active during specific tasks. To obtain an EEG record, researchers record electrical activity from multiple electrodes placed on the scalp's surface.

Because the EEG is noninvasive (that is, it doesn't require us to penetrate bodily tissue), scientists frequently use it in both animal and human studies. EEGs can detect very rapid changes in the electrical activity of the brain occurring in the range of milliseconds (one-thousandths of seconds). Even today, researchers use EEGs to study brain activity in the brains of individuals with schizophrenia, epilepsy, and other psychiatric and neurological disorders as well as those without disorders. But EEGs have a few disadvantages. Because they show averaged neural activity that reaches the surface of the scalp, they tell us little, if anything, about what's happening inside neurons. In this respect, interpreting EEGs is a bit like trying to understand the mental states of individual people in a stadium with 100,000 football fans by measuring how often they cheer, clap, or boo in response to plays on the field; we'll certainly do better than chance, but we'll make lots of mistakes too. EEGs also aren't especially good for determining exactly where in the brain the activity is occurring.

BRAIN SCANS. Although electrical recording and stimulation provided the initial routes for mapping mind functions onto brain areas, a virtual revolution in brain research occurred with the advent of brain scans, or *neuroimaging*. As a group, these imaging methods enable us to peer inside the brain's structure (that is, its appearance), its function (that is, its activity), and sometimes both.

CT Scans and MRI Images. In the mid-1970s, independent teams of researchers developed **computed tomography (CT)** and **magnetic resonance imaging (MRI)**, both of which allow us to visualize the brain's structure (Hounsfield, 1973; Lauterbur, 1973). The CT scan is a three-dimensional reconstruction of multiple X-rays taken through a part of the body, such as the brain. As a result, it shows far more detail than an individual X-ray. The MRI shows structural detail using a different principle. The MRI scanner measures the release of energy from water in biological tissues following exposure to a magnetic field. MRI images are superior to CT scans for detecting soft tissues, such as brain tumors.

PET. CT and MRI scans show only the brain's structure, not its activity. Therefore, neuroscientists interested in thought and emotion typically turn to *functional imaging* techniques like **positron emission tomography (PET)**, which measures changes in the brain's

Alert EEG reading

FIGURE 3.19
Electroencephalograph (EEG). An EEG reading during wakefulness.

FICTOID

MYTH: Research using brain imaging is more "scientific" than other psychological research.

REALITY: Brain imaging research can be extremely useful but, like all research, can be misused and abused. Yet because it seems scientific, we can be more persuaded by brain imaging research than we should be. In fact, studies show that undergraduates are more impressed by claims accompanied by brain imaging findings than research that isn't, even when the claims are bogus (McCabe & Castel, 2008; Weisberg et al., 2008).

electroencephalograph (EEG)
recording of brain's electrical activity at the surface of the skull

computed tomography (CT)
a scanning technique using multiple X-rays to construct three-dimensional images

magnetic resonance imaging (MRI)
technique that uses magnetic fields to indirectly visualize brain structure

positron emission tomography (PET)
imaging technique that measures consumption of glucose-like molecules, yielding a picture of neural activity in different regions of the brain

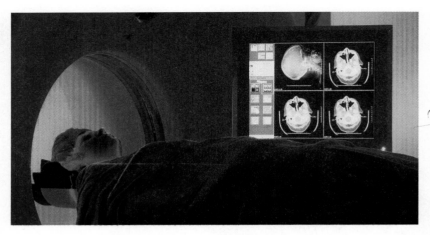

Magnetic resonance imaging (MRI) is a noninvasive procedure that reveals high-resolution images of soft tissue, such as the brain.

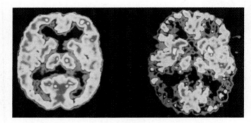

PET scans show more regions displaying low activity (blue and black areas) in an Alzheimer's disease brain (*right*) than a control brain (*left*), whereas the control brain displays more areas showing high activity (red and yellow).

correlation vs. causation

CAN WE BE SURE THAT A CAUSES B?

functional MRI (fMRI)
technique that uses magnetic fields to visualize brain activity using the BOLD response

transcranial magnetic stimulation (TMS)
technique that applies strong and quickly changing magnetic fields to the surface of the skull that can either enhance or interrupt brain function

magnetoencephalography (MEG)
technique that measures brain activity by detecting tiny magnetic fields generated by the brain

activity in response to stimuli. PET relies on the fact that neurons, like other cells, increase their consumption of glucose (a sugar) when they're active. We can think of glucose as the brain's gasoline. PET requires the injection of radioactive glucose-like molecules into patients. Although they're radioactive, they're short-lived, so they do little or no harm. The scanner measures where in the brain most of these glucose-like molecules are consumed, allowing neuroscientists to figure out which brain regions are most active during a task. Clinicians can also use PET scans to see how brain activity changes when patients take a medication. Because PET is invasive, researchers continued to work to develop functional imaging methods that wouldn't require injections of radioactive molecules.

fMRI. In 1990, researchers discovered that as neural activity quickens, there's an increase in oxygenated blood in response to heightened demand (Ogawa et al., 1990). The discovery of this response, known as the *blood oxygenation level dependent* (BOLD) response, enabled the development of the **functional MRI (fMRI)**. Because fMRI measures the change in blood oxygen level, it's an indirect correlate of neural activity. Neuroscientists frequently use fMRI to image brain activity in response to specific tasks, like looking at emotional faces or solving math problems (Marsh et al., 2008). The fMRI relies on magnetic fields, as does MRI. fMRI's strength, especially compared with PET, is its ability to provide detailed images of activity in small brain regions and over brief time intervals. Nevertheless, in contrast to PET and some other imaging techniques, fMRI is extremely sensitive to motion, so researchers often have to toss out fMRI data if participants move too much.

MAGNETIC STIMULATION AND RECORDING. **Transcranial magnetic stimulation** (**TMS**) applies strong and quickly changing magnetic fields to the skull to create electric fields in the brain. Depending on the level of stimulation, TMS can either enhance or interrupt brain function in a specific region. TMS offers useful insights regarding which brain areas are involved in different psychological processes. For example, if TMS interrupts functioning in the temporal lobe and the subject displays (temporary!) language impairment as a result, we can conclude that the temporal lobe is important for language processing. Because it allows us to manipulate brain areas directly, TMS is the only noninvasive brain imaging technique that allows us to infer causation—all other techniques can only *correlate* brain activation with psychological processing. Some reports suggest that TMS provides relief for depression and may decrease auditory hallucinations, that is, the hearing of sounds, typically voices (Saba, Schurhoff, & Leboyer, 2006). *Repetitive TMS* (rTMS) also shows promise as a treatment for depression (Rachid & Bertschy, 2006).

A final imaging technique is **magnetoencephalography** (**MEG**), which detects electrical activity in the brain by measuring tiny magnetic fields (Vrba & Robinson, 2001). In this way, MEG reveals patterns of magnetic fields on the skull's surface, thereby revealing which brain areas are becoming active in response to stimuli. MEG's strength is its ability to track brain changes over extremely small time intervals. In contrast to PET and fMRI scans, which measure activity changes second by second, MEG measures activity changes millisecond by millisecond.

How to Interpret—and Misinterpret—Brain Scans. PET, fMRI, and other functional brain imaging techniques have taught us a great deal about how the brain's activity changes in response to different stimuli. They've also helped scientists to uncover deficits in the brain functioning of people with certain psychiatric disorders. For example, they've revealed that schizophrenia, a severe disorder of thought and emotion marked by a loss of contact with reality, is often associated with underactivity of the frontal lobes (Andreasen et al., 1997; see Chapter 15).

Yet it's extremely easy to misinterpret brain scans, largely because many laypersons and even newspaper reporters hold misunderstandings of how they work (Racine, BarIlan, & Illes, 2006). For one thing, many people assume that functional brain images, like the multicolor images generated by PET and fMRI scans, are like photographs of the brain in action (Roskies, 2007). They aren't. In most cases, these images are produced by subtracting brain activity on a "control" task from brain activity on an "experimental" task, which is of primary interest to the researchers. For example, if researchers wanted to find out how people with clinical depression process sad faces, they could subtract the brain's activity following neutral faces from its activity following sad faces. So although we're seeing one image, it's actually one image subtracted from another. Moreover, the pretty colors in these images are arbitrary and superimposed by researchers. They don't correspond directly to the brain's activity (Shermer, 2008). Making matters more complicated, when a brain area

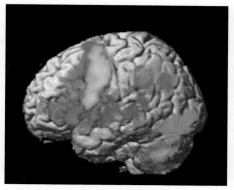

An fMRI of the brain showing areas that were active when subjects remembered something they saw (*green*), something they heard (*red*), or both (*yellow*). (*Source:* M. Kirschen/Stanford University)

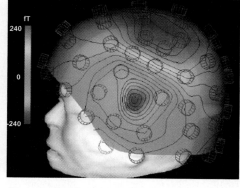

An example of magnetoencephalography (MEG) illustrating the presence of magnetic fields on the surface of the cerebral cortex. (*Source:* Arye Nehorai/Washington University, St. Louis)

"lights up" on a brain scan, we know only that neurons in that region are becoming more active. They might actually be *inhibiting* other neurons rather than exciting them.

Another complexity is introduced by the fact that when researchers conduct the calculations that go into brain scans, they're typically comparing the activity of hundreds of brain areas across neutral versus experimental tasks (Vul et al., 2009). As a result, there's a risk of chance findings—those that won't replicate in later studies. To make this point, one mischievous team of researchers (Bennett et al., 2009) placed a dead salmon in a brain scanner, flashed it photographs of people in social situations, and asked the salmon to guess which emotions the people were experiencing (no, we're not making this up). Remarkably, the investigators "found" an area in the salmon's brain that became active in response to the task. In reality, of course, this activation was just a statistical artifact, a result of the fact that they'd computed so many analyses that a few were likely to be statistically significant (see Chapter 2) by chance. This finding is a needed reminder that we should view many brain imaging findings with a bit of caution until other investigators have replicated them.

■ How Much of Our Brain Do We Use?

Despite having so much information available today regarding the relationship between brain and behavior, scores of misconceptions about the brain abound. One widely held myth is that most of us use only 10 percent of our brain (Beyerstein, 1999). What could we do if we could access the other 90 percent? Would we find the cure for cancer, acquire great wealth, or write our own psychology textbook?

The 10-percent myth gained its toehold at around the same time as phrenology, in the late 1800s. William James (1842–1910), one of the fathers of psychology (see Chapter 1), wrote that most people fulfill only a small percent of their intellectual potential. Some people misconstrued James to mean that we only use about 10 percent of our brain. As the 10-percent myth was repeated, it acquired the status of an urban legend (see Chapter 13).

Early difficulties in identifying which brain regions controlled which functions probably reinforced this misconception. In 1929, Karl Lashley showed that there was no single memory area in the brain (see Chapter 7). He made multiple knife cuts in the brains of rats and tested them on mazes. He found that no specific cortical area was more critical to maze learning than any other. Lashley's results were ripe for misinterpretation

> **replicability**
>
> **CAN THE RESULTS BE DUPLICATED IN OTHER STUDIES?**

A "Fishy" Result? Researchers (Bennett et al., 2009) showed that even a dead salmon can seem to be responding to stimuli—see the red regions of "brain activation"—using standard imaging techniques (to see how, read the text). This finding doesn't show that brain imaging techniques aren't useful, of course, but they show that positive findings can sometimes arise by chance.

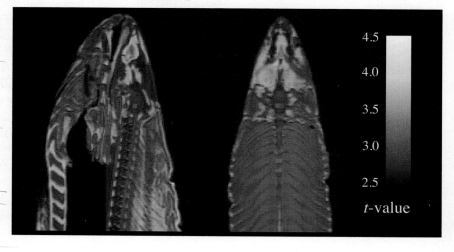

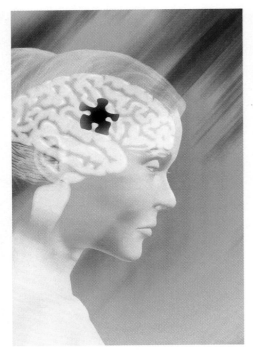

Contrary to popular psychology claims that we use only 10% of our brain, we use most or even all of our brain capacity virtually all of the time.

as evidence for "silent" areas in the cerebral cortex—those that presumably did nothing. In fact, we know today that these supposedly silent areas comprise much of the association cortex, which as we've already learned serves invaluable functions. Given how appealing the idea of tapping into our full potential is, it's no wonder that scores of pop psychology writers and so-called self-improvement experts have assured us they know how to harness our brain's full potential. Some authors of self-help books who were particularly fond of the 10-percent myth liberally misquoted scientists as saying that 90 percent of the brain isn't doing anything. Believers in psychic phenomena have even spun the fanciful story that because scientists don't know what 90 percent of the brain is doing, it must be serving a psychic purpose, like extrasensory perception (ESP) (Clark, 1997).

Today, we now know enough about the brain that we can safely conclude that every brain region has a function. Specialists in clinical neurology and neuropsychology, who deal with the effects of brain damage, have shown that losses of even small areas of certain parts of the brain can cause devastating, often permanent, losses of function (Sacks, 1985). Even when brain damage doesn't cause severe deficits, it produces some change in behavior, however subtle.

The fatal blow against the 10-percent myth, however, finally came from neuroimaging and brain stimulation studies. No one's ever discovered any perpetually silent areas, nor is it the case that 90 percent of the brain produces nothing of psychological interest when stimulated. All brain areas become active on brain scans at one time or another as we think, feel, and perceive (Beyerstein, 1999).

■ Which Parts of Our Brain Do We Use for What?

Scientists refer to *localization of function* when they identify brain areas that are active during a specific psychological task over and above a baseline rate of activity. We should be careful not to overemphasize localization of function, though, and we need to be especially cautious in our interpretations of neuroimaging results. William Uttal (2001) warned that researchers are too quick to assign narrowly defined functions to specific brain regions. He pointed out that we can't always dissect higher brain functions into narrower components. Take visual perception, for example: Can we divide it into neat and tidy subcomponents dealing with color, form, and motion, as the cortical localization of functions might imply, or is visual perception a unified experience supported by multiple regions? It's almost certainly the latter.

Regrettably, much of the popular media hasn't taken Uttal's useful cautions to heart. On a virtually weekly basis, we'll encounter news headlines like "Alcoholism Center in Brain Located" or "Brain Basis of Jealousy Found" (Cacioppo et al., 2003). To take another example, in the late 1990s and as recently as 2009, some newspapers announced the discovery of a "God spot" in the brain when scientists found that certain areas of the frontal lobes become active when individuals think of God. Yet most brain imaging research shows that religious experiences activate a wide variety of brain areas, not just one (Beauregard & Paquette, 2006). As Uttal reminds us, few if any complex psychological functions are likely to be confined to a single brain area. ⊙→ **Simulate**

⊙→ **Simulate** the Hemispheric Experiment on **mypsychlab.com**

Just as multiple brain regions contribute to each psychological function, individual brain areas contribute to multiple psychological functions. Broca's area, well known to play a role in speech, also becomes active when we notice that a musical note is off key (Limb, 2006). There's enhanced activity in the amygdala and other limbic regions when we listen to inspiring music, even though these regions aren't traditionally known as "musical areas" (Blood & Zatorre, 2001). The rule of thumb is that each brain region participates in many functions—some expected, some unexpected—so coordination across multiple brain regions contributes to each function.

Some news sources refer to the possibility of a God spot in the brain as identified by imaging research. Yet most scientists, like Dr. Andrew Newberg (shown here), argue that the localization of religion and other complex cognitive capacities to one or two brain regions is extremely unlikely.

■ Which Side of Our Brain Do We Use for What?

As we've learned, the cerebral cortex consists of two hemispheres, which are connected largely by the corpus callosum. Although they work together closely to coordinate functions, each hemisphere serves different functions. Many functions rely on one cerebral

Lateralization = hemisphere favoritism.

hemisphere more than the other; scientists call this phenomenon **lateralization** (see **TABLE 3.3**). Many lateralized functions concern specific language and verbal skills.

Roger Sperry (1974) won the Nobel Prize for showing that the two hemispheres serve different functions, such as different levels of language ability. His remarkable studies examined patients who underwent **split-brain surgery** because their doctors couldn't control their epilepsy with medication. In this exceedingly rare operation, neurosurgeons separate a patient's hemispheres by severing the corpus callosum. Split-brain surgery typically offers relief from seizures, and patients behave normally under most conditions.

Nevertheless, carefully designed studies reveal surprising deficits in split brain patients. Specifically, they experience a bizarre fragmenting of mental functions that we normally experience as integrated. Putting it a bit differently, the two hemispheres of split-brain subjects display somewhat different abilities, even though these individuals experience themselves as unified persons (Gazzaniga, 2000; Zaidel, 1994).

Here's what Sperry and his colleagues did. They presented stimuli, such as written words, to either patients' right or left *visual field*. The right visual field is the right half of information entering each eye, and the left visual field is the left half of information entering each eye. To understand why researchers present stimuli to only one visual field, we need to know that in normal brains most visual information from either the left or right visual field ends up on the opposite side of the visual cortex. The brain's design also results in crossing over for motor control: The left hemisphere controls the right hand, the right hemisphere controls the left hand.

Because corpus callosum transfers information between the two hemispheres, cutting it prevents most visual information in each visual field from reaching the visual cortex on the same side. As a consequence, we often see a stunning separation of functions. In one extreme case, a split-brain subject complained that his left hand wouldn't cooperate with his right hand. His left hand misbehaved frequently; it turned off TV shows while he was in the middle of watching them and frequently hit family members against his will (Joseph, 1988).

Split-brain subjects often experience difficulties integrating information presented to separate hemispheres, but find a way to explain away or make sense of their bewildering behaviors. In one study, researchers flashed a chicken claw to a split-brain patient's left hemisphere and a snow scene to his right hemisphere (see **FIGURE 3.20**). When asked to match what he saw with a set of choices, he pointed to a shovel with his left hand (controlled by his right hemisphere) but said "chicken" (because speech is controlled by his left hemisphere). When asked to explain these actions, he said, "I saw a claw and I picked the chicken, and you have to clean out the chicken shed with a shovel."

TABLE 3.3 Lateralized Functions

LEFT HEMISPHERE
Fine-tuned language skills
• Speech comprehension
• Speech production
• Phonology
• Syntax
• Reading
• Writing
Actions
• Making facial expressions
• Motion detection

RIGHT HEMISPHERE
Coarse language skills
• Simple speech
• Simple writing
• Tone of voice
Visuospatial skills
• Perceptual grouping
• Face perception

(*Source:* Adapted from Gazzaniga, 2000)

? This man has suffered a stroke that affected the left side of his face. **On what side of his brain did his stroke probably occur, and why?** (See answer upside down on bottom of page.)

lateralization
cognitive function that relies more on one side of the brain than the other

split-brain surgery
procedure that involves severing the corpus callosum to reduce the spread of epileptic seizures

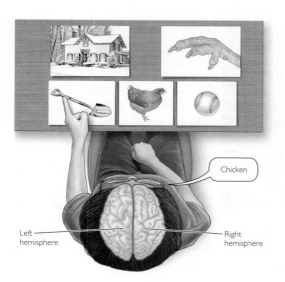

Chicken

Left hemisphere

Right hemisphere

FIGURE 3.20 Split-Brain Subject. This woman's right hemisphere recognizes the snow scene and leads her to point to the shovel, but her left hemisphere recognizes the claw and indicates verbally that the chicken is the matching object.

ARE THERE LEFT-BRAINED VERSUS RIGHT-BRAINED PERSONS?

Despite the great scientific contribution of split-brain studies, the popular notion that normal people are either "left-brained" or "right-brained" is a misconception. According to this myth, left-brained people are scholarly, logical, and analytical, and right-brained people are artistic, creative, and emotional. One Internet blogger tried to explain the differences between people's political beliefs in terms of the left–right brain distinction; conservatives, he claimed, tend to be left-brained and liberals right-brained (Block, 2006). Yet these claims are vast oversimplifications of a small nugget of truth, because research demonstrates that we use both sides of our brain in a complementary way (Corballis, 1999; Hines, 1987). Furthermore, the corpus callosum and other interconnections ensure that both hemispheres are in continual communication.

We can trace the myth of exaggerated left brain versus right brain differences to misinterpretations of accurate science. Self-help books incorporating the topic have flourished. Robert E. Ornstein was among those to promote the idea of using different ways to tap into

"Roger doesn't use the left side of his brain or the right side. He just uses the middle."

Still, we must guard against taking lateralization of function to an extreme. Remarkably, it's possible to live with only half a brain, that is, only one hemisphere. Indeed, a number of people have survived operations to remove one hemisphere to spare the brain from serious disease. Their outlook is best when surgeons perform the operation in childhood, which gives the remaining hemisphere a better chance to assume the functions of the missing hemisphere (Kenneally, 2006). The fact that many children who undergo this procedure develop almost normally suggests that functional localization isn't a foregone conclusion.

DIAGNOSING YOUR BRAIN ORIENTATION   evaluating CLAIMS

Many online quizzes claim to identify you as either "left-brained" or "right-brained" based on which direction you see an image move, whether you can find an image hidden in an ambiguous photo, or your answers to a series of multiple-choice questions. Other websites and books claim to help you improve your brain's nondominant side. Let's evaluate some of these claims, which are modeled after actual tests and products related to brain lateralization.

"*Left-brained people* are more likely to focus on details and logic and to follow rules and schedules. They do well in math and science. *Right-brained people* are more likely to be deep thinkers or dreamers, and to act more spontaneously. They excel in the social sciences and the arts."

The ad implies incorrectly that some people are left-brained and others right-brained, when in fact the left and right hemispheres differ only in emphasis.

"This *quick test* can help you determine your dominant side in just a few seconds."

This extraordinary claim isn't supported by extraordinary evidence. Furthermore, what would we need to know about this test to determine if it's valid?

"Use these exercises to improve the information flow between your left and right brain and *improve your performance* on spelling tests and listening comprehension."

There's no research to support the claim that these exercises will improve your academic performance.

Answers are located at the end of the text.

our creative right brains versus our intellectual left brains in his 1997 book *The Right Mind: Making Sense of the Hemispheres*. Right brain–oriented educational programs for children sprang up that deemphasized getting the correct answers on tests in favor of developing creative ability. Such programs as the "Applied Creative Thinking Workshop" trained business managers to use their right brain (Herrmann, 1996). For a mere $195, "whole brain learning" supposedly expanded the mind in new ways using "megasubliminal messages," heard only by the left or the right brain (Corballis, 1999). Although there's nothing wrong with trying to be more creative by using our minds in different ways, using both hemispheres in tandem works far better.

Supposedly, we can also use left-brain, right-brain differences to treat mood disorders or anger. There are even sunglasses with flip-up side panels designed to selectively increase light to either the left or right hemisphere. Nevertheless, there's little or no scientific support for "goggle therapy" (Lilienfeld, 1999a). The magazine *Consumer Reports* (2006) couldn't confirm the claim that the sunglasses reduced anger or other negative feelings, with seven out of 12 subjects reporting no change. Surely, more evidence is required before we can interpret an extraordinary claim of this kind as scientifically supported.

Left-side, right-side flip-up sunglasses designed to improve mental state.

extraordinary claims
IS THE EVIDENCE AS STRONG AS THE CLAIM?

---

assess your knowledge · FACT OR FICTION?

✓ **Study** and **Review** on **mypsychlab.com**

1. PET scans detect changes in cerebral blood flow that tend to accompany neural activity. **True / False**

2. Most people use only about 10 percent of their brain. **True / False**

3. Psychological functions are strictly localized to specific areas of the cerebral cortex. **True / False**

4. Split-brain subjects are impaired at integrating information from both visual fields. **True / False**

Answers: 1. F (pp. 107–108); 2. F (p. 110); 3. F (p. 110); 4. T (p. 111)

NATURE AND NURTURE: DID YOUR GENES—OR PARENTS—MAKE YOU DO IT?

3.10 Describe genes and how they influence psychological traits.

3.11 Explain the concept of heritability and the misconceptions surrounding it.

Up to this point in the chapter, we've said relatively little about how what influences shape the development of our brains. Our nervous system, of course, is shaped by both our genes (nature) and our environments (nurture)—everything that affects us after fertilization. But how do nature and nurture operate to shape our physiological, and ultimately our psychological, makeup?

■ How We Come to be Who We Are

As little as 150 years ago, even the smartest of scientists knew almost nothing about how we humans come to be. Today, the average educated person knows more about the origins of human life and the human brain than did Charles Darwin. We're remarkably fortunate to be armed with scientific principles concerning heredity, adaptation, and evolution that enable us to understand the origins of many of our psychological characteristics.

THE BIOLOGICAL MATERIAL OF HEREDITY. In 1866, a monk named Gregor Mendel published his classic treatise on inheritance based on his research on pea plants, but Mendel didn't understand how the characteristics of these plants, like their height, shape, and color, were transmitted across generations. We now know that both plants and animals possess **chromosomes** (see **FIGURE 3.21**), slender threads inside the cell's nucleus that carry **genes**, the

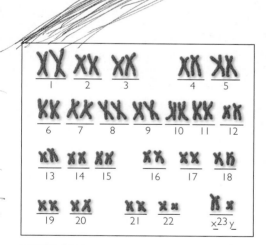

FIGURE 3.21 Human Chromosomes. Humans have 46 chromosomes. Males have an XY pair and females have an XX pair. The other 22 pairs of chromosomes aren't sex linked.

chromosome
slender thread inside a cell's nucleus that carries genes

gene
genetic material, composed of deoxyribonucleic acid (DNA)

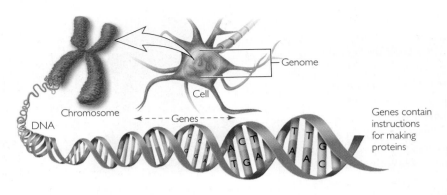

FIGURE 3.22   **Genetic Expression.** The nucleus of the neuron houses chromosomes, which contain strands of DNA. They store codes for constructing proteins needed by the cell.

Explore Dominant and Recessive Traits on **mypsychlab.com**

genotype
our genetic makeup

phenotype
our observable traits

dominant gene
gene that masks other genes' effects

recessive gene
gene that is expressed only in the absence of a dominant gene

fitness
organisms' capacity to pass on their genes

genetic material (we humans have 46 chromosomes). Genes, in turn, are composed of deoxyribonucleic acid (DNA), a remarkable substance shaped like a double helix that stores everything cells need to replicate (reproduce) themselves (see **FIGURE 3.22**). The *genome* consists of a full set of chromosomes and the heritable traits associated with them. The monumental *Human Genome Project,* which characterized all human genes, was completed in 2001. This project has garnered enormous attention and stirred great hopes, as it holds out the promise of treating—and perhaps one day curing—many human disorders, including mental disorders influenced by genes (Plomin & Crabbe, 2000).

GENOTYPE VERSUS PHENOTYPE.   Our genetic makeup, the set of genes transmitted from our parents to us, is our **genotype**. In contrast, our **phenotype** is our set of observable traits. We can't easily infer people's genotypes by observing their phenotypes in part because some genes are **dominant**, meaning they mask other genes' effects. In contrast, other genes are **recessive**, meaning they're expressed only in the absence of a dominant gene.

Eye, hair, and even skin color are influenced by combinations of recessive and dominant genes. For example, two brown-eyed parents could have a blue-eyed child because the child inherited recessive genes for blue eyes from both parents. **Explore**

BEHAVIORAL ADAPTATION.   Charles Darwin's classic book *On the Origin of Species* (1859) introduced the broad brush strokes of his theory of evolution by natural selection (see Chapter 1). Darwin hypothesized that populations of organisms change over time by selective breeding among individuals within the population who possess an adaptive advantage. According to these principles, some organisms possess *adaptations* that make them better suited to their environments. They survive and reproduce at higher rates than other organisms. Many adaptations are physical changes that enable organisms to better adjust to or manipulate their environments. An opposable thumb—one that can be moved away from the other fingers—for example, greatly enhanced our hand function. Compared with other organisms, those with successful adaptations have heightened levels of **fitness**, meaning they have a better chance of passing on their genes to later generations.

Other adaptations are behavioral. Indeed, the field of evolutionary psychology (Chapter 1) examines the potential adaptive functions of psychological traits (Buss, 1995). According to most evolutionary psychologists, aggressive behavior is an adaptation, because it enables organisms to obtain more resources. Too much aggression, however, is usually maladaptive, meaning it often decreases organisms' chances of survival or reproduction, perhaps because they're likely to be killed in fights or because their aggression scares off potential mates. But evolutionary psychology is controversial, largely because it's difficult to know whether a psychological trait is a direct product of natural selection (Panksepp & Panksepp, 2000). In contrast to bones and some other physical characteristics, psychological traits don't leave fossils, so we need to make educated guesses about these traits' past adaptive functions. For example, is religion an evolutionary adaptation, perhaps because it helps us to cement social ties? It's difficult to know (Boyer, 2003). Or what about morality, jealousy, artistic ability, and scores of other psychological traits? In all of these cases, we may never know whether they're direct products of natural selection as opposed to indirect byproducts of other traits that have been selected. Nevertheless, it's likely that some psychological characteristics, like anxiety, disgust, happiness, and other emotions are adaptations that prepare organisms to react to certain stimuli (Nesse & Elsworth, 2009). Anxiety, for example, predisposes us to attend to potential threats, like predators (see Chapters 11 and 15).

HUMAN BRAIN EVOLUTION.   The relationship between the human nervous system and behavior has been finely tuned over millions of years of evolution (Cartwright, 2000). Brain regions with complicated functions, such as the cortex, have evolved the most (Karlen & Krubitzer, 2006). As a result, our behaviors are more complex and flexible than those of other animals, allowing us to respond in many more ways to a given situation.

What makes us so distinctive in the animal kingdom? Fossil and genetic evidence suggests that somewhere between six and seven million years ago, humans and apes split off from a shared ancestor. After that critical fork in the evolutionary road, we went our separate ways. The human line eventually resulted in our species, *Homo sapiens*, whereas the ape line resulted in chimpanzees, gorillas, and orangutans (the "great apes"). We often fail to appreciate that *Homo sapiens* have been around for only about one percent of the total time period of the human race (Calvin, 2004).

Around the time of our divergence from apes, our brains weren't that much larger than theirs. Then, around three to four million years ago, something dramatic happened, although we don't know why. We do know that within a span of only a few million years—a mere blink of an eye in the earth's 4.5-billion-year history—one tiny area of the human genome changed about 70 times more rapidly than other areas, resulting in significant changes in the cortex (Pollard et al., 2006). The human brain mushroomed in size, more than tripling from less than 400 grams—a bit less than a pound—to its present hefty weight of 1,300 grams—about three pounds (Holloway, 1983). The brains of modern great apes weigh between 300 and 500 grams, even though their overall body size doesn't differ that much from humans' (Bradbury, 2005).

Relative to our body size, we're proportionally the biggest-brained animals (we need to correct for body size, because large animals, like whales and elephants, have huge brains in part because their bodies are also huge). Second in line are dolphins (Marino, McShea, & Uhen, 2004), followed by chimpanzees and other great apes. Research suggests that across species, relative brain size—brain size corrected for body size—is associated with behaviors we typically regard as intelligent (Jerison, 1983). For example, big-brained animals tend to have especially large and complex social networks (Dunbar, 2003).

■ Behavioral Genetics: How We Study Heritability

Scientists use *behavioral genetics* to examine the influence of nature and nurture on psychological traits, such as intelligence (see Chapter 9). In reality, behavioral genetic designs are misnamed, because they permit us to look at the roles of both genes *and* environment in behavior (Waldman, 2005).

Behavioral genetic designs also allow us to estimate the **heritability** of traits and diseases. By heritability, we mean the extent to which genes contribute to differences in a trait *among individuals*. Typically, we express heritability as a percentage. So, if the heritability of a trait is 60 percent, that means that more than half of the differences *among individuals* in their levels of that trait are due to differences in their genes. By definition, the other 40 percent is due to differences in their environments. Some traits, like height, are highly heritable; The heritability of height in adults is between 70 and 80 percent (Silventoinen et al., 2003). In contrast, other traits, like religious affiliation (which religion we choose), are due almost entirely to environment and therefore have a heritability of about zero. Our religious affiliation, not surprisingly, is influenced substantially by the beliefs with which we were raised. Interestingly, though, *religiosity*, the depth of our religious belief, is moderately heritable (Turkheimer, 1998), perhaps because it stems partly from personality traits are themselves heritable (see Chapter 14).

THREE MAJOR MISCONCEPTIONS ABOUT HERITABILITY. Heritability isn't as simple a concept as it appears, and it confuses even some psychologists. So before discussing how psychologists use heritability in different studies, we'll first address three misunderstandings about what heritability is—and isn't:

> **Misconception 1:** *Heritability applies to a single individual rather than to differences among individuals.* Heritability applies only to groups of people. If someone asks you, "What's the heritability of your IQ?" you should promptly hand that person a copy of this chapter. Heritability tells us about the causes of differences among people, not within a person.

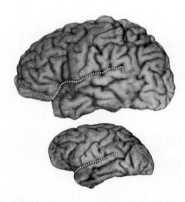

The brain of a human (*top*) and that of a chimpanzee (*bottom*). The human brain is about three times larger, even though humans are only about two times as large overall.

? The distinction of the largest brain in the animal kingdom—between 15 and 20 pounds—goes to the sperm whale. **Does this mean that sperm whales are the most intelligent creatures? Why or why not?** (See answer upside down on bottom of page.)

[handwritten margin notes:]
Heritability = variation ⇄ percentage in a trait across individuals because of genes.
- heritability tells causes of differences among groups, not individuals
- heritability does not speak of a trait's alterability, just of its variation
- heritability is not a fixed number.

heritability
percentage of the variability in a trait across individuals that is due to genes

Even though differences in height among plants may be largely heritable, watering these plants—an environmental manipulation—can result in substantial increases in their height. The bottom line: High heritability doesn't imply unchangeability.

Misconception 2: *Heritability tells us whether a trait can be changed.* Many people believe that if a trait is highly heritable, then by definition we can't change it. Yet heritability technically says little or nothing about how malleable (alterable) a trait is. A trait can in principle have a heritability of 100 percent and still be extremely malleable. Imagine 10 plants that differ markedly in height, with some of them only two or three inches tall and others five or six inches tall. Further imagine that they're only a few days old and that since their germination we've exposed them to *exactly equal* environmental conditions: the same amount of water and identical soil and lighting conditions. What's the heritability of height in this group of plants? It's 100 percent: The causes of differences in their heights *must be* completely genetic, because we've kept all environmental influences constant. Now imagine we suddenly decide to stop watering these plants and providing them with light. All of the plants will soon die, and their heights will become zero inches. So, even though the heritability of height in these plants was 100 percent, we can easily change their heights by changing their environments.

Behavioral geneticists refer to *reaction range* as the extent to which genes set limits on how much a trait can change in response to new environments (Gottlieb, 2003; Platt & Sanislow, 1988). Eye color has a limited reaction range, because it won't change much over our lifetimes, even in the presence of radical environmental changes. In contrast, at least some genetically influenced psychological traits, like intelligence, probably have a larger reaction range, because they can change—in either a positive or negative direction—in response to environmental changes, like early enrichment or early deprivation. As we'll learn in Chapter 9, however, the true reaction range of intelligence is unknown.

Misconception 3: *Heritability is a fixed number.* Heritability can differ dramatically across different time periods and populations. Remember that heritability is the extent to which differences among people in a trait are due to genetic influences. So if we reduce the range of environmental influences on a trait within a population, the heritability of that trait will increase because more of the differences in that trait will be due to genetic factors. Conversely, if we increase the range of environmental influences on a trait within a population, heritability will go down because fewer of the differences in that trait will be due to genetic factors.

BEHAVIORAL GENETIC DESIGNS. Scientists estimate heritability using one of three behavioral genetic designs: *family studies, twin studies,* and *adoption studies.* In such studies, scientists track the presence or absence of a trait among different relatives. These studies help them determine how much both genes and environment contribute to that trait.

Family Studies. In **family studies**, researchers examine the extent to which a characteristic "runs" or goes together in intact families, namely, those in which all family members are raised in the same home. This information can be useful for estimating the risk of a disorder among the relatives of people afflicted with that disorder. Nevertheless, family studies have crucial drawback: Relatives share a similar environment as well as similar genetic material. As a consequence, family studies don't allow us to disentangle the effects of nature from nurture. Investigators have therefore turned to more informative research designs to separate these influences and rule out alternative hypotheses about the effects of genes versus environments.

Twin Studies. To understand **twin studies**, most of which examine differences between identical and fraternal twins in traits, we first need to say a bit about the birds and the bees. Two different things can happen when a sperm fertilizes an egg. First, a single sperm may fertilize a single egg, producing a *zygote*, or fertilized egg (see Chapter 10). For reasons that scientists still don't fully understand, that zygote occasionally (in about one in 250 births) splits into two, yielding two identical genetic copies. Researchers refer to these identical twins as *monozygotic* (MZ), because they originate from one zygote. Identical twins are essentially genetic clones of each other because they share 100 percent of their

ruling out rival hypotheses

HAVE IMPORTANT ALTERNATIVE EXPLANATIONS FOR THE FINDINGS BEEN EXCLUDED?

family study
analysis of how characteristics run in intact families

twin study
analysis of how traits differ in identical versus fraternal twins

genes. In other cases, two different sperm may fertilize two different eggs, resulting in two zygotes. These twins are *dizygotic* (DZ), or, more loosely, fraternal. In contrast to identical twins, fraternal twins share only 50 percent of their genes on average and are no more alike genetically than ordinary brothers or sisters. Fraternal twins (and triplets, quadruplets, and so on) are more likely to occur in women undergoing fertility treatments to encourage eggs to be produced and released. But fertility treatments have no effect on the frequency of identical twins, because they don't affect whether a single egg will split.

The logic of twin studies rests on the fact that identical twins are more similar genetically than are fraternal twins. Consequently, if identical twins are more alike on a psychological characteristic, such as intelligence or extraversion, than are fraternal twins, we can infer that this characteristic is genetically influenced, assuming the environmental influences on the characteristic we're studying are the same in identical and fraternal twins (Kendler et al., 1993).

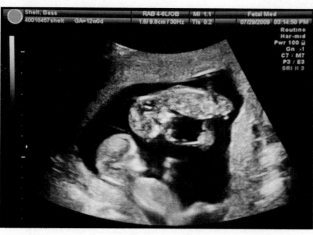

Identical twin fetuses developing in utero. Behavior geneticists compare identical with fraternal twins to estimate genetic and environmental influences on psychological traits.

Adoption Studies. As we've noted, studies of intact family members are limited because they can't disentangle genetic from environmental influences. To address this shortcoming, psychologists have turned to **adoption studies**, which examine the extent to which children adopted into new homes resemble their adoptive as opposed to their biological parents. Children adopted into other homes share genes, but not environment, with their biological relatives. As a consequence, if adopted children resemble their biological parents on a psychological characteristic, we can typically assume it's genetically influenced.

One potential confound in adoption studies is *selective placement:* Adoption agencies frequently place children in homes similar to those of their biological parents (DeFries & Plomin, 1978). This confound can lead investigators to mistakenly interpret the similarity between adoptive children and their biological parents as a genetic effect. In adoption studies, researchers try to control for selective placement by correcting statistically for the correlation between biological and adoptive parents in their psychological characteristics.

As we'll discover in later chapters, psychologists have come to appreciate that genetic and environmental influences intersect in complex ways to shape our nervous systems, thoughts, feelings, and behaviors. For example, they've learned that people with certain genetic makeups tend to seek out certain environments (Plomin, DeFries, & McClearn, 1977) and react differently than people with other genetic makeups to certain environments (Kim-Cohen et al., 2006; see Chapter 10). They've also learned that many environmental influences, like life stressors and maternal affection, actually work in part by turning certain genes on or off (Weaver et al., 2004). Nature and nurture, although different sources of psychological influence, are turning out to be far more intertwined than we'd realized.

---

assess your knowledge　　　　**FACT OR FICTION?**　　✓•⌐Study and Review on mypsychlab.com

1. Brain evolution is responsible for humans' advanced abilities. **True / False**

2. The fact that the human brain is smaller than an elephant's shows that brain size is unrelated to intelligence. **True / False**

3. Heritability values can't change over time within a population. **True / False**

4. Identical twins have similar phenotypes (observable traits) but may have different genotypes (sets of genes). **True / False**

5. Adoption studies are useful for distinguishing nature influences from nurture influences. **True / False**

Answers: 1. T (pp. 114–115); 2. F (p. 115); 3. F (p. 116); 4. F (pp. 116–117); 5. T (pp. 117)

adoption study
analysis of how traits vary in individuals raised apart from their biological relatives

NERVE CELLS: COMMUNICATION PORTALS 84–93

3.1 DISTINGUISH THE PARTS OF NEURONS AND WHAT THEY DO.

The neuron has a cell body, which contains a nucleus, where proteins that make up our cells are manufactured. Neurons have dendrites, long extensions that receive messages from other neurons and an axon, which extends from the cell body of each neuron and is responsible for sending messages.

1. The central region of the neuron which manufactures new cell components is called the _____ _____ . (p. 86)

2. The receiving ends of a neuron, extending from the cell body like tree branches, are known as _____ . (p. 86)

3. _____ are long extensions from the neuron at the cell body that _____ messages from one neuron to another. (p. 86)

4. The space between two connecting neurons where neurotransmitters are released is called the _____ . (p. 86)

5. The autoimmune disease multiple sclerosis is linked to the destruction of the glial cells wrapped around the axon, called the _____ _____ . (p. 87)

3.2 DESCRIBE ELECTRICAL RESPONSES OF NEURONS AND WHAT MAKES THEM POSSIBLE.

Neurons exhibit excitatory and inhibitory responses to inputs from other neurons. When excitation is strong enough, the neuron generates an action potential, which travels all the way down the axon to the axon terminal. Charged particles crossing the neuronal membrane are responsible for these events.

6. The electrical charge difference across the membrane of the neuron when it's not being stimulated is called the _____ _____ . (p. 87)

7. Label the image showing the process of action potential in a neuron. Include (a) axon, (b) arrow depicting the direction of the action potential, and (c) neurotransmitters. (p. 88)

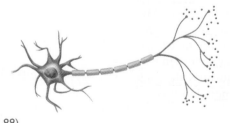

3.3 EXPLAIN HOW NEURONS USE NEUROTRANSMITTERS TO COMMUNICATE WITH EACH OTHER.

Neurotransmitters are the chemical messengers neurons use to communicate with each other or to cause muscle contraction. The axon terminal releases neurotransmitters at the synapse. This process produces excitatory or inhibitory responses in the receiving neuron.

8. Neurotransmission can be halted by _____ of the neurotransmitter back into the axon terminal—a process by which the synaptic vesicle reabsorbs the neurotransmitter. (p. 88)

9. What "natural narcotic" produced by the brain helps athletes endure intense workouts or pain? (p. 90)

3.4 DESCRIBE HOW THE BRAIN CHANGES AS A RESULT OF DEVELOPMENT, LEARNING, AND INJURY.

The brain changes the most before birth and during early development. Throughout the life span the brain demonstrates some degree of plasticity, which plays a role in learning and memory. Later in life, healthy brain plasticity decreases and neurons can show signs of degeneration.

10. Scientists are working to improve ways to encourage neurogenesis, the adult brain's ability to create new _____ . (p. 93)

THE BRAIN—BEHAVIOR NETWORK 93–103

3.5 IDENTIFY WHAT ROLES DIFFERENT PARTS OF THE CENTRAL NERVOUS SYSTEM PLAY IN BEHAVIOR.

The cerebral cortex consists of the frontal, parietal, temporal, and occipital lobes. Cortex involved with vision lies in the occipital lobe, cortex involved with hearing in the temporal lobe, and cortex involved with touch in the parietal lobe. Association areas throughout the cortex analyze and reanalyze sensory inputs to build up our perceptions. The motor cortex in the frontal lobe, the basal ganglia, and the spinal cord work together with the somatic nervous system to bring about movement and action. The somatic nervous system has a sensory as well as a motor component, which enables touch and feedback from the muscles to guide our actions.

11. The brain and spinal cord combine to form the superhighway known as the _____ _____ _____ . (p. 93)

12. Outside of the CNS, the _____ _____ system works to help us control behavior and express emotion. (p. 93)

13. Label the various parts of the central nervous system. (p. 94)

Central Nervous System	
(a)	**Frontal Lobe:** performs executive functions that coordinate other brain areas, motor planning, language, and memory **Parietal Lobe:** processes touch info, integrates vision and touch **Temporal Lobe:** processes auditory information, language, and autobiographical memory **Occipital Lobe:** processes visual information
(b)	control movement and motor planning
(c)	**Thalamus:** conveys sensory information to cortex **Hypothalamus:** oversees endocrine and autonomic nervous system **Amygdala:** regulates arousal and fear **Hippocampus:** processes memory for spatial locations
(d)	controls balance and coordinated movement
(e)	**Midbrain:** tracks visual stimuli and reflexes triggered by sound **Pons:** conveys information between the cortex and cerebellum **Medulla:** regulates breathing and heartbeats
(f)	conveys information between the brain and the body

14. The brain component responsible for analyzing sensory information and our ability to think, talk, and reason is called the _____ _____ . (p. 95)

15. Fill in the function of each brain component identified in this figure. (p. 96)

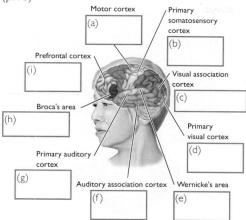

Motor cortex
(a)

Primary somatosensory cortex
(b)

Prefrontal cortex
(i)

Visual association cortex
(c)

Broca's area
(h)

Primary visual cortex
(d)

Primary auditory cortex
(g)

Auditory association cortex
(f)

Wernicke's area
(e)

16. Parkinson's disease is the result of damage to the _____ _____ , which play a critical role in voluntary movement. (p. 98)

17. The _____ _____ system connects to the forebrain and cerebral cortex and plays a key role in arousal. (p. 100)

3.6 CLARIFY HOW THE SOMATIC AND AUTONOMIC NERVOUS SYSTEMS WORK IN EMERGENCY AND EVERYDAY SITUATIONS.

The somatic nervous system carries messages from the CNS to the body's muscles. The autonomic nervous system consists of the parasympathetic and sympathetic divisions. Whereas the parasympathetic nervous system is active during rest and digestion, the sympathetic division propels the body into action during an emergency or crisis. Sympathetic arousal also occurs in response to everyday stressors.

18. Our ability to execute messages or commands of our central nervous system, through physical action, is dependent on the _____ _____ system. (p. 102)

19. Our ability to react physically to a perceived threat is dependent on the _____ division of the autonomic system. (p. 103)

20. Sympathetic activation triggers a variety of physical responses, including increased heart rate, _____ , and _____ . (p. 103)

THE ENDOCRINE SYSTEM 103–105

3.7 DESCRIBE WHAT HORMONES ARE AND HOW THEY AFFECT BEHAVIOR.

Hormones are chemicals released into the bloodstream that trigger specific effects in the body. Activation of the sympathetic nervous system triggers the release of adrenaline and cortisol by the adrenal glands, which energize our bodies. Sex hormones control sexual responses.

21. The limbic system in the brain also cooperates with the _____ _____ in the body to regulate emotion. (p. 103)

22. The gland once called the the "master gland" which, under the control of the hypothalamus, directs all other body glands is known as the _____ _____ . (p. 103)

23. Label the major endocrine glands of the body. (p. 103)

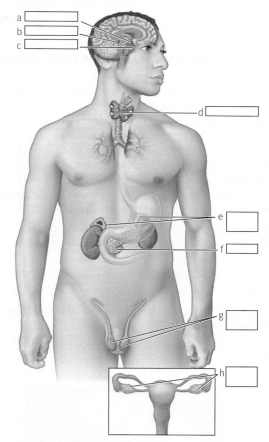

a
b
c
d
e
f
g
h

24. The pituitary hormone called _____ is responsible for a variety of reproductive functions including stretching the cervix and vagina during birth and aiding milk flow in nursing mothers. (p. 103)

25. Psychologists sometimes call the _____ _____ the emergency centers of the body. (p. 104)

26. When under threat or attack, how does the body prepare for fight or flight? (p. 104)

27. Many anxiety disorders are associated with elevated levels of _____ . (p. 105)

28. The testes make the male sex hormone, called _____, and the ovaries make the female sex hormone, called _____ . (p. 105)

29. Males and females (do/don't) both manufacture some amount of sex hormone associated with the opposite sex. (p. 105)

30. Most researchers (accept/reject) the hypothesis that testosterone influences female sex drive. (p. 105)

MAPPING THE MIND: THE BRAIN IN ACTION

106–113

3.8 IDENTIFY THE DIFFERENT BRAIN-STIMULATING, -RECORDING, AND -IMAGING TECHNIQUES.

Electrical stimulation of the brain can elicit vivid imagery or movement. Methods such as electroencephalography (EEG) and magnetoencephalography (MEG) enable researchers to record brain activity. Imaging techniques provide a way to see the brain's structure or function. The first imaging techniques included computed tomography (CT) and magnetic resonance imaging (MRI). Imaging techniques that allow us to see how the brain's activity changes in response to psychological stimuli include positron emission tomography (PET) and functional MRI (fMRI).

31. Franz Joseph Gall made one of the earliest attempts to connect mind and brain by measuring head bumps, a technique known as _____ . (p. 106)

32. Early efforts by Hans Berger to measure electrical activity in the brain resulted in the development of the _____ . (p. 107)

33. Neuroscientists interested in measuring thought and emotion (would/wouldn't) employ a CT scan. (p. 107)

34. What do functional MRIs (fMRI), such as the one pictured here, measure? (p. 109)

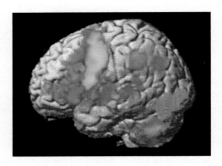

3.9 EVALUATE RESULTS DEMONSTRATING THE BRAIN'S LOCALIZATION OF FUNCTION.

Stimulating, recording, and imaging techniques have shown that specific brain areas correspond to specific functions. Although these results provide valuable insight into how our brains delegate the many tasks we perform, many parts of the brain contribute to each specific task. Because individual brain areas participate in multiple functions, many cognitive functions cannot be neatly localized.

35. Neuroscientists have confirmed that there (are/aren't) parts of the brain that remain completely inactive and unutilized. (p. 110)

36. The phenomenon known as _____ explains how many cognitive functions rely on one cerebral hemisphere more than another. (pp. 110–111)

37. Severing the corpus callosum to reduce the incidence of epileptic seizures is known as _____ surgery. (p. 111)

38. In this experiment, researchers flashed a chicken claw to a split-brain patient's left hemisphere and a snow scene to his right hemisphere. How can we explain his response? (p. 111)

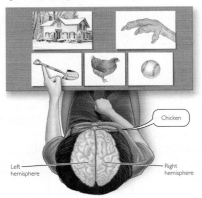

39. The _____ hemisphere of the brain is related to coarse language skills and visuospatial skills whereas the _____ hemisphere is related to fine-tuned language skills and actions. (p. 111)

40. Artists and other creative thinkers (are/aren't) able to make use only of their right hemisphere. (p. 112)

NATURE AND NURTURE: DID YOUR GENES—OR PARENTS—MAKE YOU DO IT? 113–117

3.10 DESCRIBE GENES AND HOW THEY INFLUENCE PSYCHOLOGICAL TRAITS.

Genes are composed of deoxyribonucleic acid (DNA), which are arranged on chromosomes. We inherit this genetic material from our parents. Each gene carries a code to manufacture a specific protein. These proteins influence our observable physical and psychological traits.

41. How many chromosomes do humans have? How many are sex-linked? (p. 113)

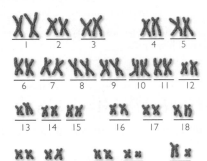

42. _____ are the thin threads within a nucleus that carry genes. (p. 113)

43. _____ are made up of deoxyribonucleic acid (DNA), the material that stores everything cells need to reproduce themselves. (p. 114)

44. Our _____ is the set of our observable traits, and our genetic makeup is our _____. (p. 114)

45. (Recessive/Dominant) genes work to mask other genes' effects. (p. 114)

46. The principle that organisms that possess adaptations survive and reproduce at a higher rate than other organisms is known as _____ _____ . (p. 114)

3.11 EXPLAIN THE CONCEPT OF HERITABILITY AND THE MISCONCEPTIONS SURROUNDING IT.

Heritability refers to how differences in a trait across people are influenced by their genes as opposed to their environments. Highly heritable traits can sometimes change within individuals and the heritability of a trait can also change over time within a population.

47. Scientists use _____ _____ to examine the roles of nature and nurture in the origins of traits, such as intelligence. (p. 115)

48. Heritability applies only to (a single individual/groups of people). (p. 115)

49. Does high heritability imply a lack of malleability? Why or why not? (p. 116)

50. Analyses of how traits vary in individuals raised apart from their biological relatives are called _____ _____ . (p. 117)

DO YOU KNOW THESE TERMS?

- neuron (p. 85)
- dendrite (p. 86)
- axon (p. 86)
- synaptic vesicle (p. 86)
- neurotransmitter (p. 86)
- synapse (p. 86)
- synaptic cleft (p. 86)
- glial cell (p. 87)
- myelin sheath (p. 87)
- resting potential (p. 87)
- threshold (p. 87)
- action potential (p. 87)
- absolute refractory period (p. 88)
- receptor site (p. 88)
- reuptake (p. 88)
- endorphin (p. 90)
- plasticity (p. 91)
- stem cell (p. 92)
- neurogenesis (p. 93)
- central nervous system (CNS) (p. 93)
- peripheral nervous system (PNS) (p. 93)

- cerebral ventricles (p. 94)
- forebrain (cerebrum) (p. 95)
- cerebral hemispheres (p. 95)
- corpus callosum (p. 95)
- cerebral cortex (p. 95)
- frontal lobe (p. 96)
- motor cortex (p. 96)
- prefrontal cortex (p. 96)
- Broca's area (p. 96)
- parietal lobe (p. 97)
- temporal lobe (p. 97)
- Wernicke's area (p. 98)
- occipital lobe (p. 98)
- primary sensory cortex (p. 98)
- association cortex (p. 98)
- basal ganglia (p. 98)
- limbic system (p. 99)
- thalamus (p. 99)
- hypothalamus (p. 99)
- amygdala (p. 99)
- hippocampus (p. 100)
- brain stem (p. 100)

- midbrain (p. 100)
- reticular activating system (RAS) (p. 100)
- hindbrain (p. 101)
- cerebellum (p. 101)
- pons (p. 101)
- medulla (p. 101)
- spinal cord (p. 101)
- interneuron (p. 101)
- reflex (p. 101)
- somatic nervous system (p. 102)
- autonomic nervous system (p. 102)
- sympathetic nervous system (p. 102)
- parasympathetic nervous system (p. 103)
- endocrine system (p. 103)
- hormone (p. 103)
- pituitary gland (p. 103)
- adrenal gland (p. 104)
- electroencephalograph (EEG) (p. 107)
- computed tomography (CT) (p. 107)

- magnetic resonance imaging (MRI) (p. 107)
- positron emission tomography (PET) (p. 107)
- functional MRI (fMRI) (p. 108)
- transcranial magnetic stimulation (TMS) (p. 108)
- magnetoencephalography (MEG) (p. 108)
- lateralization (p. 111)
- split-brain surgery (p. 111)
- chromosome (p. 113)
- gene (p. 113)
- genotype (p. 114)
- phenotype (p. 114)
- dominant gene (p. 114)
- recessive gene (p. 114)
- fitness (p. 114)
- heritability (p. 115)
- family study (p. 116)
- twin study (p. 116)
- adoption study (p. 117)

APPLY YOUR SCIENTIFIC THINKING SKILLS

Use your scientific thinking skills to answer the following questions, referencing specific scientific thinking principles and common errors in reasoning whenever possible.

1. Many websites and magazine articles exaggerate the notion of brain lateralization. Find two examples of products designed for either a "left-brained" or "right-brained" person. Are the claims made by these products supported by scientific evidence? Explain.

2. As we've learned in this chapter, scientists still aren't sure what causes women's sex drives to increase at certain times, although many view testosterone as a key influence. Locate alternative explanations for this hypothesis in the popular media and evaluate each using your scientific thinking skills.

3. The news media sometimes report functional brain imaging findings accurately, but often report them in oversimplified ways, such as implying that researchers identified a single brain region for Capacity X (like religion, morality, or political affiliation). Locate two media reports on functional brain imaging (ideally using fMRI or PET) and evaluate the quality of media coverage. Did the reporters interpret the findings correctly, or did they go beyond the findings? For example, did the reporters avoid implying that the investigators located a single brain "spot" or "region" underlying a complex psychological capacity?

4 SENSATION AND PERCEPTION

how we sense and conceptualize the world

THINK ABOUT IT

CAN WE PERCEIVE INVISIBLE STIMULI?

CAN WE "READ" SOMEONE ELSE'S THOUGHTS?

CAN OUR EYES DETECT ONLY A SINGLE PARTICLE OF LIGHT?

CAN CERTAIN BLIND PEOPLE STILL "SEE" SOME OF THEIR SURROUNDINGS?

DO SOME PEOPLE "TASTE" SHAPES OR "HEAR" COLORS?

Before you read any further, try the exercise in **FIGURE 4.1** below. Were you surprised that the white "X" disappeared from view? Were you even more surprised that you filled the missing space occupied by the "X" with a mental image exactly matching the fancy background pattern?

Sensation and perception are the underlying processes operating in this visual illusion; it's an **illusion** because the way you perceived the stimulus doesn't match its physical reality. Your brain—not your eyes—perceived a complete pattern even though some of it was missing. **Sensation** refers to the detection of physical energy by our sense organs, including our eyes, ears, skin, nose, and tongue, which then relay information to the brain (see Chapter 3). **Perception** is the brain's *interpretation* of these raw sensory inputs. Simplifying things just a bit, sensation first allows us to pick up the signals in our environments, and perception then allows us to assemble these signals into something meaningful.

We often assume that our sensory systems are infallible and that our perceptions are perfect representations of the world around us. As we learned in Chapter 1, we term these beliefs *naive realism*. We'll discover in this chapter that naive realism is wrong, because the world isn't precisely as we see it. Somewhere in our brains we reconstructed that fancy pattern in the figure and put it smack in the middle of the empty space, a perceptual process called *filling-in*. Most of the time, filling-in is adaptive, as it helps us make sense of our often confusing and chaotic perceptual worlds. But sometimes it can fool us, as in the case of visual illusions.

Perception researchers have studied filling-in by showing participants incomplete objects on computer screens and determining which *pixels*, or picture elements, subjects rely on to make perceptual judgments (Gold et al., 2000). The pixels that participants use to perceive images are often located next to regions where there's no sensory information, demonstrating that we interpolate—or mix—illusory with sensory-based information to arrive at perceptual decisions. We often blend the real with the imagined, going beyond the information given to us. By doing so, we simplify the world, but often make better sense of it in the process.

FIGURE 4.1 Separating Sensation from Perception. Hold this page about 10 inches from your face. Close your right eye and keep focusing on the white circle. Can you see the white *X*? Now slowly move the page toward your face and then away from it; at some point the white *X* will disappear and then reappear. Surprisingly, your brain supplies an illusory background pattern that fills in the white space occupied by the X. (*Source: Glynn, 1999*)

TWO SIDES OF THE COIN: SENSATION AND PERCEPTION

4.1 Identify the basic principles that apply to all senses.

4.2 Track how our minds build up perceptions.

4.3 Analyze the scientific support for and against ESP.

How do signals that make contact with our sense organs—like our eyes, ears, and tongue—become translated into information that our brains can interpret and act on? And how does the raw sensory information delivered to our brains become integrated with what we already know about the world, allowing us to recognize objects, avoid accidents, and (we hope) find our way out the door each morning?

Here's how. Our brain picks and chooses among the types of sensory information it uses, often relying on expectations and prior experiences to fill in the gaps and simplify processing. The end result often differs from the sum of its parts—and sometimes it's a completely wrong number! Errors in perception, like the illusion in Figure 4.1 and others we'll examine in this chapter, are often informative, not to mention fun. They show us which parts of our sensory experiences are accurate and which parts our brains fill in for us.

We'll first discover what our sensory systems can accomplish and how they manage to transform physical signals in the outside world into neural activity in the "inside world"—our brains. Then we'll explore how and when our brains flesh out the details, moving beyond the raw sensory information available to us.

■ Sensation: Our Senses as Detectives

Our senses enable us to see majestic scenery, hear glorious music, feel a loving touch, maintain balance, and taste wonderful food. Despite their differences, all of our senses rely on a mere handful of basic principles.

illusion
perception in which the way we perceive a stimulus doesn't match its physical reality

sensation
detection of physical energy by sense organs, which then send information to the brain

perception
the brain's interpretation of raw sensory inputs

[handwritten: Transduction: Nervous System converts external stimuli into electrical signals within neurons]

TRANSDUCTION: GOING FROM THE OUTSIDE WORLD TO WITHIN.

The first step in sensation is converting external energies or substances into a "language" the nervous system understands, such as the action potential (see Chapter 3). **Transduction** is the process by which the nervous system converts an external stimulus, like light or sound, into electrical signals within neurons. A specific type of **sense receptor**, or specialized cell, transduces a specific stimulus. As we'll learn, specialized cells at the back of the eye transduce light, cells in a spiral-shaped organ in the ear transduce sound, odd-looking endings attached to axons embedded in deep layers of the skin transduce pressure, receptor cells lining the inside of the nose transduce airborne odorants, and taste buds transduce chemicals containing flavor.

(© ScienceCartoonsPlus.com)

For all of our senses, activation is greatest when we first detect a stimulus. After that, our response declines in strength, a process called **sensory adaptation**. What happens when we sit on a chair? After a few seconds, we no longer notice it, unless it's an extremely hard seat, or worse, has a thumbtack on it. The adaptation takes place at the level of the sense receptor. This receptor reacts strongly at first and then tamps down its level of responding to conserve energy and attentional resources. If we didn't engage in sensory adaptation, we'd be attending to just about everything around us, all of the time.

PSYCHOPHYSICS: MEASURING THE BARELY DETECTABLE.

Back in the 19th century, when psychology was gradually distinguishing itself as a science apart from philosophy (see Chapter 1), many researchers focused on sensation and perception. In 1860, German scientist Gustav Fechner published a landmark work on perception. Out of his efforts grew **psychophysics**, the study of how we perceive sensory stimuli based on their physical characteristics.

Absolute Threshold. Imagine that a researcher fits us with a pair of headphones and places us in a quiet room. She asks repeatedly if we've heard one of many very faint tones. Detection isn't an all-or-none state of affairs because human error increases as stimuli become weaker in magnitude. Psychophysicists study phenomena like the **absolute threshold** of a stimulus—the lowest level of a stimulus we can detect on 50 percent of the trials when no other stimuli of that type are present. Absolute thresholds demonstrate how remarkably sensitive our sensory systems are. On a clear night, our visual systems can detect a single candle from 30 miles away. We can detect a smell from as few as 50 airborne odorant molecules; the salamander's exquisitely sensitive sniffer can pull off this feat with only one (Menini, Picco, & Firestein, 1995).

Just Noticeable Difference. Just how much of a difference in a stimulus makes a difference? The **just noticeable difference (JND)** is the smallest change in the intensity of a stimulus that we can detect. The JND is relevant to our ability to distinguish a stronger from a weaker stimulus, like a soft noise from a slightly louder noise. Imagine we're playing a song on an iPod but the volume is turned so low that we can't hear it. If we nudge the volume dial up to the point at which we can *just* begin to make out the song, that's a JND. **Weber's law** states that there's a constant proportional relationship between the JND and the original stimulus intensity (see **FIGURE 4.2**). In plain language, the stronger the stimulus, the bigger the change needed for a change in stimulus intensity to be noticeable. Imagine how much light we'd need to add to a brightly lit kitchen to notice an increase in illumination compared with the amount of light we'd need to add to a dark bedroom to notice a change in illumination. We'd need a lot of light in the first case and only a smidgeon in the second.

transduction
the process of converting an external energy or substance into electrical activity within neurons

sense receptor
specialized cell responsible for converting external stimuli into neural activity for a specific sensory system

sensory adaptation
activation is greatest when a stimulus is first detected

psychophysics
the study of how we perceive sensory stimuli based on their physical characteristics

absolute threshold
lowest level of a stimulus needed for the nervous system to detect a change 50 percent of the time

just noticeable difference (JND)
the smallest change in the intensity of a stimulus that we can detect

Weber's Law
there is a constant proportional relationship between the JND and original stimulus intensity

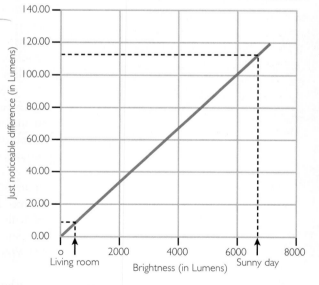

FIGURE 4.2 Just Noticeable Differences (JNDs) Adhere to Weber's Law. In this example, changes in light are shown measured in lumens, which are units equaling the amount of light generated by one candle standing one foot away. Weber's law states that the brighter the light, the more change in brightness is required for us to be able to notice a difference.

TABLE 4.1 Distinguishing Signal from Noise. In signal detection theory there are true positives, false negatives, false positives, and true negatives. Subject biases affect the probability of "yes" and "no" responses to the question "Was there a stimulus?"

	RESPOND "YES"	RESPOND "NO"
Stimulus present	True Positive	False Negative
Stimulus absent	False Positive	True Negative

Signal Detection Theory. David Green and John Swets (1966) developed **signal detection theory** to describe how we detect stimuli under uncertain conditions, as when we're trying to figure out what a friend is saying on a cell phone when there's a lot of static in the connection—that is, when there's high background noise. We'll need to increase the signal by shouting over the static or else our friend won't understand us. If we have a good connection, however, our friend can easily understand us without our shouting. This example illustrates the *signal-to-noise ratio*: It becomes harder to detect a signal as background noise increases.

Green and Swets were also interested in *response biases*, or tendencies to make one type of guess over another when we're in doubt about whether a weak signal is present or absent under noisy conditions. They developed a clever way to take into account some people's tendency to say "yes" when they're uncertain and other people's tendency to say "no" when they're uncertain. Instead of always delivering a sound, they sometimes presented a sound, sometimes not. This procedure allowed them to detect and account for subjects' response biases. As we can see in **TABLE 4.1**, subjects can report that they heard a sound when it was present (a *true positive*, or hit), deny hearing a sound when it was present (a *false negative*, or miss), report hearing a sound that wasn't there (a *false positive*, or false alarm), or deny hearing a sound that wasn't there (a *true negative*, or correct rejection). The frequency of false negatives and false positives helps us measure how biased subjects are to respond "yes" or "no" in general.

Sensory Systems Stick to One Sense—Or Do They? Back in 1826, Johannes Müller proposed the doctrine of *specific nerve energies*, which states that even though there are many distinct stimulus energies—like light, sound, or touch—the sensation we experience is determined by the nature of the sense receptor, not the stimulus. To get a sense (pun intended) of this principle in action, the next time you rub your eyes shortly after waking up, try to notice *phosphenes*—vivid sensations of light caused by pressure on your eye's receptor cells. Many phosphenes look like sparks, and some even look like multicolored shapes in a kaleidoscope. Perhaps not surprisingly, some people have speculated that phosphenes may explain certain reports of ghosts and UFOs (Neher, 1990).

Why do phosphenes occur? In the cerebral cortex, different areas are devoted to different senses (see Chapter 3). It doesn't matter to our brain whether light or touch activated the sense receptor: Our brains react the same way in either case. That is, once our visual sense receptors send their signals to the cortex, the brain interprets their input as visual, regardless of how our receptors were stimulated in the first place.

Most areas of the cortex are connected to cortical areas devoted to the same sense: Vision areas tend to be connected to other vision areas, hearing areas to other hearing areas, and so on. Yet scientists have found many examples of cross-modal processing that produce different perceptual experiences than either modality provides by itself. One striking example is the *McGurk effect* (Jones & Callan, 2003; McGurk & MacDonald, 1976). This effect demonstrates that we integrate visual and auditory information when processing spoken language, and our brains automatically calculate the most probable sound given the information from the two sources. In the McGurk effect, hearing the audio track of one syllable (such as "ba") spoken repeatedly while seeing a video track of a different syllable being spoken (such as "ga") produces the perceptual experience of a different third sound (such as "da"). This third sound is the brain's best "guess" at integrating the two conflicting sources of information (see Chapter 8).

Another fascinating example is the *rubber hand illusion*, which shows how our senses of touch and sight interact to create a false perceptual experience (Erhsson, Spence, & Passingham, 2004; Knox et al., 2006). This illusion involves placing a rubber hand on top of a table with the precise positioning that a subject's hand would have if she were resting it on the table. The subject's hand is placed under the table, out of her view. A researcher simultaneously strokes the subject's hidden hand and rubber hand gently with a paintbrush. When the strokes match each other, the subject experiences an eerie illusion: The rubber hand seems to be her own hand.

As we've seen, these cross-modal effects may reflect "cross-talk" among different brain regions. But there's an alternative explanation: In some cases, a single brain region may serve double duty, helping to process multiple senses. For example, neurons in the auditory cortex

signal detection theory
theory regarding how stimuli are detected under different conditions

ruling out rival hypotheses >

HAVE IMPORTANT ALTERNATIVE EXPLANATIONS FOR THE FINDINGS BEEN EXCLUDED?

tuned to sound also respond weakly to touch (Fu et al., 2003). Visual stimuli enhance touch perception in the somatosensory cortex (Taylor-Clarke, Kennett, & Haggard, 2002). The reading of Braille by people blind from birth activates their visual cortex (Gizewski et al., 2003; see Chapter 3). And monkeys viewing videos with sound display increased activity in their primary auditory cortex compared with exposure to sound alone (Kayser et al., 2007).

Sir Francis Galton (1880) was the first to describe **synesthesia**, a rare condition in which people experience cross-modal sensations, like hearing sounds when they see colors—sometimes called "colored hearing"—or even tasting colors (Cytowic, 1993; Cytowic & Eagleman, 2009). Synesthesia may be an extreme version of the cross-modal responses that most of us experience from time to time (Rader & Tellegen, 1987). The great Finnish composer Jean Sibelius saw notes as colors and even claimed to smell them. In one case, he asked a worker to repaint his kitchen stove in the key of F major. The most common form of synesthesia is *grapheme-color synesthesia*, in which a "6" may always seem red and a "5" green. In *lexical-taste synesthesia*, words have associated tastes, and in still other synesthesias, letters take on "personality traits," such as an *A* being perceived as bold. No one knows for sure how widespread synesthesia is, but some estimates put it at no higher than about 1 in 2,500 people (Baron-Cohen et al., 1993).

In the past, some scientists questioned the authenticity of synesthesia and accused synesthetes of having overly vivid imaginations, seeking attention, or even taking hallucinogenic drugs. Yet research demonstrates that the condition is genuine (Ramachandran & Hubbard, 2001). **FIGURE 4.3** illustrates a clever test that detects grapheme-color synesthesia. Specific parts of the visual cortex become active during most synesthesia experiences, verifying that these experiences are associated with brain activity (Paulesu et al., 1995; Ramachandran & Hubbard, 2001).

■ Perception: When Our Senses Meet Our Brains

Now that we've learned how we process sensory information, we'll embark on an exciting voyage into how our minds organize the bits of sensory data into more meaningful concepts. What's so remarkable about our brain's ability to bring together so much data is that it doesn't rely only on what's in our sensory field. Our brain pieces together (a) what's in the sensory field, along with (b) what was just there a moment ago, and (c) what we remember from our past. Just as we perceive the broad strokes of a stimulus, we remember the typical characteristics of objects. When we perceive the world, we sacrifice small details in favor of crisp and often more meaningful representations. In most cases, the trade-off is well worth it, because it helps us make sense of our surroundings.

PARALLEL PROCESSING: THE WAY OUR BRAIN MULTITASKS. We can attend to many sense modalities simultaneously, a phenomenon called **parallel processing** (Rumelhart & McClelland, 1987). Two important concepts that go along with parallel processing are **bottom-up** and **top-down processing** (see Chapter 8). In bottom-up processing, we construct a whole stimulus from its parts. An example is perceiving an object on the basis of its edges. Bottom-up processing starts with the raw stimuli we perceive and ends with our synthesizing them into a meaningful concept. This kind of processing begins with activity in the primary visual cortex (see Chapter 3), followed by processing in the association cortex. In contrast, top-down processing starts with our beliefs and expectations, which we then impose on the raw stimuli we perceive. Top-down processing starts with processing in the association cortex, followed by processing in the primary visual cortex.

Some perceptions rely more heavily on bottom-up processing (Koch, 1993), others on top-down processing (McClelland & Plaut, 1993). In most cases, though, these two kinds of processing work hand in hand (Patel & Sathian, 2000). We can illustrate this point by how we process ambiguous figures (see **FIGURE 4.4**). Depending on our expectations, we typically perceive these figures differently. The top-down influence that we're thinking of a jazz musician biases our bottom-up processing of

FIGURE 4.3 Are You Synesthetic? Although most of us see the top image as a bunch of jumbled numbers, some grapheme-color synesthetes perceive it as looking like the image on the bottom. Synesthesia makes it much easier to find the 2s embedded in a field of 5s. (*Source:* Adapted from Ramachandran & Hubbard, 2001)

---

synesthesia
a condition in which people experience cross-modal sensations

parallel processing
the ability to attend to many sense modalities simultaneously

bottom-up processing
processing in which a whole is constructed from parts

top-down processing
conceptually driven processing influenced by beliefs and expectancies

---

FIGURE 4.4 What Do You See? Due to the influence of top-down processing, reading the caption "saxophone player" beneath this ambiguous figure tends to produce a different perception than reading the caption "woman."

THE BAT

FIGURE 4.5   Context Influences Perception. Depending on the perceptual set provided by the context of the surrounding letters, the middle letter can appear as an "H" or as an "A." Most of us read this phrase as "THE BAT" because of the context.

FIGURE 4.6   An Example of Perceptual Set. Depending on our perspective, the drawing on top can appear to be a young woman or an old one. Which did you perceive first? Look at the biased pictures (turn the page upside down) to alter your perceptual set. (*Source:* Hill, 1915)

FIGURE 4.7   Shape Constancy. We perceive a door as a door whether it appears as a rectangle or a trapezoid.

perceptual set
set formed when expectations influence perceptions

perceptual constancy
the process by which we perceive stimuli consistently across varied conditions

selective attention
process of selecting one sensory channel and ignoring or minimizing others

the shapes in Figure 4.4 and increases the chances we'll perceive a saxophone player. In contrast, if our top-down expectation were of a woman's face, our sensory-based bottom-up processing would change accordingly. (Can you see both figures?)

PERCEPTUAL HYPOTHESES: GUESSING WHAT'S OUT THERE.   Because our brains rely so much on our knowledge and experiences, we can usually get away with economizing in our sensory processing and making educated guesses about what sensory information is telling us. Moreover, a pretty decent guess with fewer neurons is more efficient than a more certain answer with a huge number of neurons. As cognitive misers (see Chapter 2), we generally try to get by with as little neural firepower as we can.

Perceptual Sets.   We form a **perceptual set** when our expectations influence our perceptions—an example of top-down processing. We may perceive a misshapen letter as an "H" or as an "A" depending on the surrounding letters and the words that would result from our interpretation (see **FIGURE 4.5**). We also tend to perceive the world in accord with our preconceptions. An ambiguous cartoon drawn by W. E. Hill raises the question: Is it a young woman or an old witch? Participants placed in the perceptual set of a young woman by viewing a version of the cartoon exaggerating those features (see **FIGURE 4.6**) reported seeing a young woman. In contrast, participants placed in the perceptual set of an old woman by viewing a version of the cartoon exaggerating those features reported seeing an old woman (Boring, 1930).

Perceptual Constancy.   The process by which we perceive stimuli consistently across varied conditions is **perceptual constancy**. Without perceptual constancy, we'd be hopelessly confused, because we'd be seeing our worlds as continually changing. We'd even have trouble reading the words on this page if our heads were moving very slightly, because the page looks a tiny bit different from each angle. Yet our brain allows us to correct from these minor changes. There are several kinds of perceptual constancy: shape, size, and color constancy. Consider a door we view from differing perspectives (see **FIGURE 4.7**). Because of *shape constancy,* we still see a door as a door whether it's completely shut, barely open, or more fully open, even though these shapes look almost nothing like each other.

Or take *size constancy,* our ability to perceive objects as the same size no matter how far away they are from us. When a friend walks away from us, her image becomes smaller. But we almost never realize this is happening, nor do we conclude that our friend is mysteriously shrinking. Outside of our conscious awareness, our brains mentally enlarge figures far away from us so that they appear more like similar objects in the same scene.

Color constancy is our ability to perceive color consistently across different levels of lighting. Consider a group of firemen dressed in bright yellow jackets. Their jackets look bright yellow even in very low levels of ambient light. That's because we evaluate the color of an object in the context of background light and surrounding colors. Take a moment to examine **FIGURE 4.8**. The checkerboard appears to contain all black and white squares, but

The man standing toward the back of the bridge looks to be of normal size, but the exact duplicate image appears in the foreground and looks like a toy because of size constancy.

FIGURE 4.8   The Checker-Shadow Illusion. We perceive a checkerboard pattern of black and white alternating squares, and because of color constancy, we ignore the dramatic change due to the shadow cast by the green cylinder. Believe it or not, the A and B squares are identical. (*Source:* © 1995 Edward H. Adelson)

they're actually varying shades of gray. Remarkably, the A and B squares (one from the black set and one from the white set) are exactly the same shade of gray. Dale Purves and colleagues (2002) applied the same principle to cubes composed of smaller squares that appear to be of different colors, even though some of the smaller squares are actually gray (see **FIGURE 4.9**). We base our perception of color in these smaller squares on the surrounding context.

THE ROLE OF ATTENTION. In a world in which our brains are immersed in a sea of sensory input, flexible attention is critical to our survival and well-being. To zero in on a video game we play in the park, for example, we must ignore that speck of dust on our shirt, the shifting breeze, and the riot of colors and sounds in the neighborhood. Yet at any moment we must be prepared to use sensory information that heralds a potential threat, such as an approaching thunderstorm. Fortunately, we're superbly well equipped to meet the challenges of our rich and ever-changing sensory environments.

Selective Attention: How We Focus on Specific Inputs. If we're constantly receiving inputs from all our sensory channels, like a TV set with all channels switched on at once, how do we keep from becoming hopelessly bewildered? **Selective attention** allows us to select one channel and turn off the others, or at least turn down their volume. The major brain regions that control selective attention are the reticular activating system (RAS) and forebrain (see Chapter 3). These areas activate regions of the cerebral cortex, such as the frontal cortex, during selective attention. ⊙▸⎾**Simulate**

Donald Broadbent's (1957) *filter theory of attention* views attention as a bottleneck through which information passes. This mental filter enables us to pay attention to important stimuli and ignore others. Broadbent tested his theory using a task called *dichotic listening*—in which subjects hear two different messages, one delivered to the left ear and one to the right ear. When Broadbent asked subjects to ignore messages delivered to one of the ears, they seemed to know little or nothing about these messages. Anne Treisman (1960) replicated these findings, elaborating on them by asking subjects to repeat the messages they heard, a technique called *shadowing*. Although subjects could only repeat the messages to which they'd attended, they'd sometimes mix in some of the information they were supposed to ignore, especially if it made sense to add it. If the attended ear heard, "I saw the girl . . . song was wishing," and the unattended ear heard, "me that bird . . . jumping in the street," a participant might hear "I saw the girl jumping in the street," because the combination forms a meaningful sentence. The information we've supposedly filtered out of our attention is still being processed at some level—even when we're not aware of it (Beaman, Bridges, & Scott, 2007).

An attention-related phenomenon called the *cocktail party effect* refers to our ability to pick out an important message, like our name, in a conversation that doesn't involve us. We don't typically notice what other people are saying in a noisy restaurant or at a party unless it's relevant to us—and then suddenly, we perk up. This finding tells us that the filter inside our brain, which selects what will and won't receive our attention, is more complex than just an "on" or "off" switch. Even when seemingly "off," it's ready to spring into action if it perceives something significant (see **FIGURE 4.10**).

Inattentional Blindness. Before reading on, try the ESP trick in **FIGURE 4.11** below. We're going to try to read your mind. Then come back and read the next paragraph.

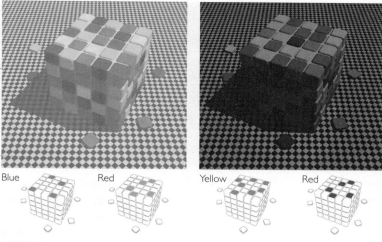

Blue   Red   Yellow   Red

FIGURE 4.9 Color Perception Depends on Context. Gray can appear like a color depending on surrounding colors. The blue-colored squares on the top of the cube at the left are actually gray (*see map below the cube*). Similarly, the yellow-colored squares on the top of the cube at the right are actually gray (*see map below the cube*). (*Source:* © Dale Purves and R. Beau Lotto, 2002)

⊙▸**Simulate** Selective Attention on **mypsychlab.com**

replicability

CAN THE RESULTS BE DUPLICATED IN OTHER STUDIES?

FIGURE 4.10 The Cocktail Party Effect. The cocktail party effect helps explain how we can become aware of stimuli outside of our immediate attention when it's relevant to us—like our names.

FIGURE 4.11 An ESP Trick? Try It and Find Out. Try this "ESP trick," adapted from a demonstration by Clifford Pickover. This remarkable trick will demonstrate that we—the authors of this book—can read your mind! Select **one** of the six cards and be sure to recall it. To help you remember it, repeat its name out loud several times. Once you're sure you have the card in mind, turn to page 133.

In these frames from the video clip, a woman in a gorilla suit fails to catch the attention of most subjects, who are too busy counting basketball passes.

© 2005, Daniel J. Simons

We're surprisingly poor at detecting stimuli in plain sight when our attention is focused elsewhere (Henderson & Hollingworth, 1999; Levin & Simons, 1997; McConkie & Currie, 1996). In an astonishing demonstration of this phenomenon, called **inattentional blindness**, Daniel Simons and Christopher Chabris (1999, 2010) asked subjects to watch a videotape of people tossing a basketball back and forth quickly, and required them to keep track of the number of passes. Then, smack in the middle of the videotape, a woman dressed in a gorilla suit strolled across the scene for a full nine seconds. Remarkably, about half the subjects failed to notice the hairy misfit even though she paused to face the camera and thump her chest. This and other findings demonstrate that we often need to pay close attention to pick out even dramatic changes in our environments (Koivisto & Revonsuo, 2007; Rensink, O'Regan, & Clark, 1997).

A closely related phenomenon, called *change blindness,* is a failure to detect obvious changes in one's environment (if you've tried the ESP trick we mentioned, you'll know what we mean). Change blindness is a particular concern for airplane pilots, who may fail to notice another plane taxiing across the runway as they're preparing to land (Podczerwinski, Wickens, & Alexander, 2002). You may be relieved to hear that industrial/organizational psychologists (see Chapter 1) are working actively with aviation agencies to reduce the incidence of this problem.

THE BINDING PROBLEM: PUTTING THE PIECES TOGETHER. The *binding problem* is one of the great mysteries of psychology. When we perceive an apple, different regions of our brains process different aspects of it. Yet somehow—we don't really know how—our brains manage to combine or "bind" these diverse pieces of information into a unified whole. An apple looks red and round, feels smooth, tastes sweet and tart, and smells, well, like an apple. Any one of its characteristics in isolation isn't an apple or even a part of an apple (that would be an apple slice). One hypothesis is that rapid, coordinated activity across multiple cortical areas assists in binding (Engel & Singer, 2001). Binding may explain many aspects of perception and attention. When we see the world, we rely on shape, motion, color, and depth cues, each of which requires different amounts of time to detect individually (Bartels & Zeki, 2006). Yet our minds seamlessly combine these visual cues into a unified perception of a scene.

Subliminal Information Processing. Over the past few decades, scientists have discovered that we process many of the sensory inputs to which we're exposed unconsciously, and that many of our actions occur with little or no forethought or deliberation (see Chapter 1; Hassin, Uleman, & Bargh, 2005). Consider that our lives would grind to a standstill if we had to think carefully before uttering every word, typing every sentence, or making the minor corrections in steering needed to drive a car safely. Under ordinary circumstances, we don't direct our attention consciously to these activities, yet we constantly adjust to the flow of sensory experience. Might some sensory inputs be so subtle that they aren't registered consciously, yet still affect our everyday lives? Put another way, if we can detect stimuli without our knowing it, does that affect our behavior? ((•— **Listen**

Subliminal Perception. You're home on a Sunday afternoon, curled up on your couch watching a movie on TV. Suddenly, within a span of a few minutes you see three or four extremely quick flashes of light on the screen. Only a few minutes later, you're seized with an uncontrollable desire to eat a cheeseburger. Did the advertiser fiendishly insert several photographs of a cheeseburger in the midst of the film, so rapidly you couldn't detect them? The American public has long been fascinated with the possibility of **subliminal perception**—the processing of sensory information that occurs below the limen, that is, the level of conscious awareness (Cheesman & Merikle, 1986; Rogers & Smith, 1993). To study subliminal perception, researchers typically present a word or photograph very quickly, say at 50 milliseconds (one twentieth of a second). They frequently follow this stimulus immediately with a *mask,* another stimulus (like a pattern of dots or lines) that blocks out mental

((•— **Listen** to the Subliminal Messages podcast on **mypsychlab.com**

inattentional blindness
failure to detect stimuli that are in plain sight when our attention is focused elsewhere

subliminal perception
perception below the limen or threshold of conscious awareness

[handwritten margin note: " I don't walk right, not like I used to. So I pump my step, as I rush to see you. I could be happy here..."]

processing of the subliminal stimulus. When subjects can't correctly identify the content of the stimulus at better than chance levels, researchers deem it subliminal.

The claim for subliminal perception may seem extraordinary, but the evidence for it is compelling (Seitz & Watanabe, 2003). When investigators subliminally trigger emotions by exposing subjects to words related to anger, these subjects are more likely to rate other people as hostile (Bargh & Pietromonaco, 1982). In one study, researchers asked graduate students in psychology to list ideas for research projects. Researchers then exposed them subliminally to photographs of either (a) the smiling face of a postdoctoral research assistant in their laboratory or (b) the scowling face of their primary professor. Despite being unable to identify what they saw, graduate students who saw their faculty mentor's contemptuous face rated their research ideas less positively than did those who saw their colleague's smiling face (Baldwin, Carrell, & Lopez, 1990). In another study, researchers subliminally presented subjects with words such as church, saint, and preacher, and then provided them with an opportunity to cheat on a different task. None of the subjects who subliminally received religious words cheated, compared with 20 percent of those who subliminally received neutral, nonreligious words (Randolph-Seng & Nielson, 2007). For unclear reasons, the effects of subliminal information often vanish when subjects become aware of or even suspect attempts to influence them subliminally (Glaser & Kihlstrom, 2005).

Subliminal Persuasion. Even though we're subject to subliminal perception, that doesn't mean we numbly succumb to *subliminal persuasion,* that is, subthreshold influences over our votes in elections, product choices, and life decisions. Subliminally presented words related to thirst, such as "drink," may slightly influence how much people drink, but specific words related to brand names, such as "cola," don't influence beverage choice (Dijksterhuis, Aarts, & Smith, 2005). Some researchers contend that subliminal persuasion is possible (Randolph-Seng & Mather, 2009). Yet it's probably unlikely in most cases because we can't engage in much, if any, in-depth processing of the *meaning* of subliminal stimuli (Rosen, Glasgow, & Moore, 2003). As a result, these stimuli probably can't produce large-scale or enduring changes in our attitudes, let alone our decisions.

Still, subliminal self-help audiotapes and videotapes are a multimillion-dollar-a-year industry in the United States alone. They purportedly contain repeated subliminal messages (such as "Feel better about yourself") designed to influence our behavior or emotions. In stores and on the Internet, we can find subliminal tapes for self-esteem, memory, sexual performance, and weight loss (Rosen et al., 2003).

Yet scores of studies show that subliminal self-help tapes are ineffective (Eich & Hyman, 1991; Moore, 1992). In one clever investigation, Anthony Greenwald and his colleagues examined the effectiveness of subliminal audiotapes designed to enhance memory or self-esteem. They switched the labels on half of the tapes, so that half of the participants received the tapes they believed they'd received, and half received the other set of tapes. On objective tests of memory and self-esteem, all of the tapes were useless. Yet participants *thought* they'd improved, and their reports corresponded to the tape they *thought* they'd received. So those who thought they'd received self-esteem tapes said their self-esteem improved even when they received memory tapes, and vice versa for those who believed they'd received memory tapes. The authors termed this phenomenon the *illusory placebo effect:* Subjects didn't improve at all, but they thought they had (Greenwald et al., 1991). Phil Merikle (1988) uncovered another reason why subliminal self-help tapes don't work: His auditory analyses revealed that many of these tapes contain no message at all!

Some people even claim that *reversed* subliminal messages influence behavior. In 1990, the rock band Judas Priest was put on trial for the suicide of a teenager and the attempted suicide of another. While listening to a Judas Priest song, the boys supposedly heard the words "Do it" played backward. The prosecution claimed that this reversed message led the boys to shoot themselves. In the end, the members of Judas Priest were acquitted (Moore, 1996). As the expert witnesses noted, forward subliminal messages can't produce major changes in behavior, so it's even less likely that backward messages can do so. In some cases, extraordinary claims remain just that—extraordinary claims with no scientific support.

Break out the frosty bottle

and keep your tonics dry!

 In this famous magazine advertisement for Gilbey's Gin, some viewers claimed to spot the word "sex" in the three ice cubes in the glass on the right. Is this a subliminal advertisement? (See answer upside down on bottom of page.)

FICTOID ✕

MYTH: In the late 1950s, advertisers subliminally flashed the words "Eat popcorn" and "Drink Coke" during films in a New Jersey movie theater over the span of several weeks. The rates of popcorn and Coca-Cola consumption in the theater skyrocketed.

REALITY: The originator of this claim, advertising expert James Vicary, later admitted that it was a hoax cooked up to generate publicity for his failing business (Pratkanis, 1992).

Answer: No, because even if the viewers were right, they could see the word "sex," By definition, a subliminal image is one we can't consciously detect.

SUBLIMINAL PERSUASION CDS

evaluating **CLAIMS**

The Internet is chock-full of advertisements for subliminal self-help CDs that promise to change your life, despite the fact that scientific research shows these products to be ineffective. The manufacturers of these CDs claim to be able to send messages to your unconscious mind that influence your actions. Let's evaluate some of these claims, which are modeled after actual advertisements for subliminal persuasion CDs.

"Over one million people have discovered the power of our CDs."
Does the sheer number of people who purchase a product provide evidence of its effectiveness? Is there necessarily a correlation between how many people use a product and its effectiveness?

"Your CDs are the best I've ever tried—they changed my life!"—Andrew from Atlanta, GA"
Why are claims based only on testimonials and anecdotal evidence not trustworthy?

"Our CDs will improve all aspects of your life. You will conquer your fears, increase your IQ, lose weight, and attract a mate."
Extraordinary claims about subliminal persuasion require extraordinary evidence, and the ad provides no such evidence. To date, scientists have failed to document the ability of subliminal persuasion to produce profound personal changes.

■ Extrasensory Perception (ESP): Fact or Fiction?

If we can respond to words that appear as flashes of light well below the threshold of consciousness, might we somehow perceive certain stimuli without using one of the established senses, like seeing or hearing? This question takes us into the mysterious realm of **extrasensory perception (ESP)**. Proponents of ESP argue that we can perceive events outside of the known channels of sensation, like seeing, hearing, and touch.

("It's like I have ESP or something.")

WHAT'S ESP, ANYWAY? *Parapsychologists*—investigators who study ESP and related psychic phenomena—have subdivided ESP into three major types (Hines, 2003; Hyman, 1989):

1. **Precognition:** predicting events before they occur through paranormal means, that is, mechanisms that lie outside of traditional science. (You knew we were going to say that, didn't you?);
2. **Telepathy:** reading other people's minds; and
3. **Clairvoyance:** detecting the presence of objects or people that are hidden from view.

Closely related to ESP, although usually distinguished from it, is *psychokinesis*: Moving objects by mental power alone.

SCIENTIFIC EVIDENCE FOR ESP. In the 1930s, Joseph B. Rhine, who coined the term *extrasensory perception*, launched the full-scale study of ESP. Rhine used a set of stimuli called *Zener cards,* which consist of five standard symbols: squiggly lines, star, circle, plus sign, and square. He presented these cards to subjects in random order and asked them to guess which card would appear (precognition), which card another subject had in mind (telepathy), and which card was hidden from view (clairvoyance). Rhine (1934) initially reported positive results, as his subjects averaged about seven correct Zener card identifications per deck of 25, where five would be chance performance.

---

extrasensory perception (ESP)
perception of events outside the known channels of sensation

The Zener cards, named after a collaborator of Joseph B. Rhine, have been used widely in ESP research.

But there was a problem, one that has dogged ESP research for well over a century: Try as they might, other investigators couldn't replicate Rhine's findings. Moreover, scientists later pointed out serious flaws in Rhine's methods. Some of the Zener cards were so worn down or poorly manufactured that subjects could see the imprint of the symbols through the backs of the cards (Alcock, 1990; Gilovich, 1991). In other cases, scientists found that Rhine and his colleagues hadn't properly randomized the order of the cards, rendering his analyses essentially meaningless. Eventually, enthusiasm for Zener card research dried up.

More recently, considerable excitement has been generated by findings using the *Ganzfeld technique.* According to ESP proponents, the mental information detected by ESP "receivers" is an extremely weak signal that's typically obscured by irrelevant stimuli in the environment. By placing subjects in a uniform sensory field, the Ganzfeld technique decreases the amount of extraneous noise relative to ESP signal, supposedly permitting researchers to uncover weak ESP effects (Lilienfeld, 1999c).

Here's how it works. As a "receiver," you sit in a chamber while the experimenter covers your eyes with goggles that look like the halves of ping-pong balls, directs a red floodlight toward your eyes, and pipes white noise into your ears through headphones. Down the hall, another person (the "sender") sits in a soundproof room attempting to mentally transmit a picture to you, perhaps a photograph of a specific building on your campus. Meanwhile, the experimenter asks you to report all mental images that come to mind. Finally, she presents you with four pictures, only one of which the sender down the hall had viewed. Your job is to rate the extent to which each picture matches the mental imagery you experienced.

In 1994, Daryl Bem and Charles Honorton analyzed multiple studies of the Ganzfeld technique and appeared to find convincing evidence for ESP. Their subjects obtained accurate response rates of approximately 35 percent, exceeding chance performance of 25 percent. Yet parapsychologists' optimism was again short-lived. In 1999, Julie Milton and Richard Wiseman published an updated statistical overview of Ganzfeld studies that Bem and Honorton (1994) hadn't reviewed. In contrast to Bem and Honorton, Milton and Wiseman (1999) found that the size of Ganzfeld effects was small and corresponded to chance differences in performance.

Other ESP paradigms have proven equally disappointing. For example, research conducted over three decades ago suggested that people could mentally transmit images to dreaming subjects (Ullman, Krippner, & Vaughn, 1973). Yet later investigators couldn't replicate these results, either. All of these findings underscore the absence of a feature that's a hallmark of mature sciences: an "experimental recipe" that yields replicable results across independent laboratories (Hyman, 1989).

Recently, Samuel Moulton and Stephen Kosslyn (2008) tried a different tack by examining brain activity in response to ESP-related and non-ESP-related stimuli. Their study takes advantage of the finding that the brain reacts in a distinct way to novel versus previously seen stimuli. Moulton and Kosslyn placed subjects in an fMRI scanner (see Chapter 3) and showed them two photographs. In another room, a person tried to mentally "send" one of the two photos, and the subject tried to guess which of the two photos it was. If ESP were genuine, the brain should react as if the "sent" image were seen previously. The results revealed no differences in patterns of brain activity in response to ESP versus non-ESP stimuli, disconfirming the ESP hypothesis.

Unlike other areas of psychology, which contain terms for positive findings, parapsychology contains terms for negative findings, that is, effects that explain why researchers *don't* find the results they're seeking. The *experimenter effect* refers to the tendency of skeptical experimenters to inhibit ESP; the *decline effect* refers to the tendency for initial positive ESP results to disappear over time; and *psi missing* refers to significantly *worse* than chance performance on ESP tasks (Gilovich, 1991). Yet these terms appear to be little more than ad hoc hypotheses (see Chapter 1) for explaining away negative findings. Some ESP proponents have even argued that psi missing

replicability
CAN THE RESULTS BE DUPLICATED IN OTHER STUDIES?

 See, we read your mind! Now look at the cards again; you'll notice that one is missing. We've removed the card you picked! **How did we do it?** (See answer upside down.)

A subject in a Ganzfeld experiment attempting to receive images from a sender. The uniform sensory field he's experiencing is designed to minimize visual and auditory "noise" from the environment, supposedly permitting him to detect otherwise weak ESP signals.

replicability
CAN THE RESULTS BE DUPLICATED IN OTHER STUDIES?

Answer: It's not an ESP trick after all. All five cards are different from those in the initial batch, but you probably didn't notice the change. The trick illustrates change blindness, a failure to notice obvious alterations in our environments.

falsifiability

CAN THE CLAIM BE DISPROVED?

extraordinary claims

IS THE EVIDENCE AS STRONG AS THE CLAIM?

replicability

CAN THE RESULTS BE
DUPLICATED IN OTHER STUDIES?

FACTOID

Beginning in 1972, the U.S. government invested $20 million in the Stargate program to study the ability of "remote viewers" to acquire militarily useful information in distant places, like the locations of nuclear facilities in enemy countries through clairvoyance. The government discontinued the program in 1995, apparently because the remote viewers provided no useful information. They often claimed to pinpoint secret military sites with great accuracy, but follow-up investigations showed them to be wildly wrong (Hyman, 1996).

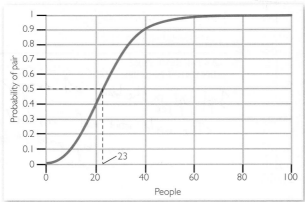

FIGURE 4.12 The "Birthday Paradox." As we reach a group size of 23 people, the probability that at least two people share the same birthday exceeds 0.5, or 50 percent. Research demonstrates that most people markedly underestimate the likelihood of this and other coincidences, sometimes leading them to attribute these coincidences to paranormal events.

demonstrates the existence of ESP, because below chance performance indicates that subjects with ESP are deliberately selecting incorrect answers! These ad hoc hypotheses render claims about ESP extremely difficult to falsify.

WHY PEOPLE BELIEVE IN ESP. The findings we've reviewed suggest that the extraordinary claim of ESP isn't matched by equally extraordinary evidence. Yet surveys indicate that 41 percent of American adults believe in ESP (Haraldsson & Houtkooper, 1991; Moore, 2005). Moreover, two-thirds of Americans say they've had a psychic experience, like a dream foretelling the death of a loved one or a premonition about a car accident that came true (Greeley, 1987). In light of more than 150 years of failed replications, it's reasonable to ask why our beliefs in ESP are so strong given that the research evidence for it is so weak.

Illusory correlation (see Chapter 2) offers one likely answer. We attend to and recall events that are striking coincidences, and ignore or forget events that aren't. Imagine we're in a new city and thinking of an old friend we haven't seen in years. A few hours later, we run into that friend on the street. "What a coincidence!" we tell ourselves. This remarkable event is evidence of ESP, right? Perhaps. But we're forgetting about the thousands of times we've been in new cities and thought about old friends whom we never encountered (Presley, 1997).

Further contributing to belief in ESP is our tendency to underestimate the frequency of coincidences (see Chapter 1). Most of us don't realize just how probable certain seemingly "improbable" events are. Take a crack at this question: *How large must a group of people be before the probability of two people sharing the same birthday exceeds 50 percent?*

Many subjects respond with answers like 365, 100, or even 1,000. To most people's surprise, the correct answer is 23. That is, in a group of 23 people it's more likely than not that at least two people have the same birthday (see **FIGURE 4.12**). Once we get up to a group of 60 people, the odds exceed 99 percent. Because we tend to underestimate the likelihood of coincidences, we may be inclined to attribute them incorrectly to psychic phenomena.

FAILED PSYCHIC PREDICTIONS. For many years, science journalist Gene Emery tracked failed psychic predictions. In 2005, he found that psychics predicted that an airplane would crash into the Egyptian pyramids, astronauts would discover a Nazi flag planted on the moon, the earth's magnetic field would reverse, and a participant on a television reality show would cannibalize one of the contestants. Conversely, no psychic predicted any of the significant events that *did* occur in 2005, like Hurricane Katrina, which inflicted terrible loss of life and property damage on New Orleans and neighboring areas (Emery, 2005).

Multiple End Points. Many psychic forecasters make use of *multiple end points,* meaning they keep their predictions so open-ended that they're consistent with almost any conceivable set of outcomes (Gilovich, 1991). A psychic may predict, "A celebrity will get caught in a scandal this year." But aside from being vague, this prediction is extremely open-ended. What counts as a "celebrity"? Sure, we'd all agree that Paris Hilton and Brad Pitt are celebrities, but does our congressional representative count? What about a local television newscaster? Similarly, what counts as a "scandal"?

Cold Reading. What about psychics, like John Edward or James von Pragh, who claim to tell us things about ourselves or our dead relatives that they couldn't possibly have known? Most of these psychics probably rely on a set of skills known as *cold reading,* the art of persuading people we've just met that we know all about them (Hines, 2003; Hyman, 1977). If you want to impress your friends with a cold reading, **TABLE 4.2** contains some tips to keep in mind.

Cold reading works for one major reason: As we've learned in earlier chapters, we humans seek meaning in our worlds and often find it even when it's not there. So in many respects we're reading into the cold reading at least as much as the cold reader is reading into us.

TABLE 4.2 Cold-Reading Techniques.

TECHNIQUE	EXAMPLE
Let the person know at the outset that you won't be perfect.	"I pick up a lot of different signals. Some will be accurate, but others may not be."
Start off with a *stock spiel,* a list of general statements that apply to just about everyone.	"You've recently been struggling with some tough decisions in life."
Fish for details by peppering your reading with vague probes.	"I'm sensing that someone with the letter *M* or maybe *N* has been important in your life lately."
Use the technique of *sleight of tongue,* meaning that you toss out so many guesses in rapid-fire fashion that at least a few of them are bound to be right.	"Has your father been ill?"; "How about your mother?"; "Hmmm . . . I sense that someone in your family is ill or worried about getting ill."
Use a prop.	A crystal ball, set of tarot cards, or horoscope convey the impression that you're basing your reading on mystical information to which you have special access.
Make use of *population stereotypes,* responses or characteristics reported by many or even most people.	"I believe you have a piece of clothing, like an old dress or blouse, that you haven't worn in years but have kept for sentimental value."
Look for physical cues to the individual's personality or life history.	A traditional manner of dress often suggests a conventional and proper person, a great deal of shiny jewelry often suggests a flamboyant person, and so on.
Remember that "flattery will get you everywhere."	Tell people what they want to hear, like "I see a great romance on the horizon."

(*Source:* Hines, 2003; Hyman, 1977; Rowland, 2001)

*Complete BS.
First ESP, now Cold Reading.*

Crystal ball readers claim to be able to tell us a great deal about ourselves and our futures. Yet many of them probably rely on cold-reading techniques that most of us could duplicate with relatively little training.

FACTOID +

To persuade people you have ESP, try the following demonstration in a large group of friends. Tell them, "I want you to think of an odd two-digit number that's less than 50, the only catch being that the two digits must be different—because that would make it too easy for me." Give them a few moments, and say, "I get the sense that some of you were thinking of 37." Then pause and say, "I was initially thinking of 35, but changed my mind. Was I close?" Research shows that slightly more than half of people will pick either 37 or 35, which are population stereotypes (see Table 4.2) that can convince many people you possess telepathic powers (French, 1992; Hines, 2003).

---

assess your knowledge — FACT OR FICTION?

1. Perception is an exact translation of our sensory experiences into neural activity. **True / False**

2. In signal detection theory, false positives and false negatives help us measure how much someone is paying attention. **True / False**

3. Cross-modal activation produces different perceptual experiences than either modality provides by itself. **True / False**

4. Subliminal perception typically influences our behavioral choices. **True / False**

5. Belief in ESP can be partly explained by our tendency to underestimate the probability of coincidences. **True / False**

Answers: 1. F (p. 124); 2. F (p. 126); 3. T (p. 126); 4. F (p. 131); 5. T (p. 134)

 Study and **Review** on **mypsychlab.com**

SEEING: THE VISUAL SYSTEM

4.4 Explain how the eye starts the visual process.

4.5 Identify the different kinds of visual perception.

4.6 Describe different visual problems.

The first thing we see after awakening is typically unbiased by any previous image. If we're on vacation and sleeping somewhere new, we may not recognize our surroundings for a moment or two. Building up an image involves many external elements, such as light, biological systems in the eye and brain that process images for us, and our past experiences.

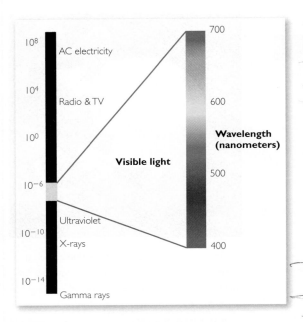

FIGURE 4.13 The Visible Spectrum Is a Subset of the Electromagnetic Spectrum. Visible light is electromagnetic energy between ultraviolet and infrared. Humans are sensitive to wavelengths ranging from slightly less than 400 nanometers (violet) to slightly more than 700 nanometers (red).

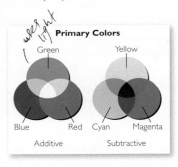

FIGURE 4.14 Additive and Subtractive Color Mixing. Additive color mixing of light differs from subtractive color mixing of paint.

hue
color of light

pupil
circular hole through which light enters the eye

cornea
part of the eye containing transparent cells that focus light on the retina

lens
part of the eye that changes curvature to keep images in focus

■ Light: The Energy of Life

One of the central players in our perception of the world is light, a form of electromagnetic energy—energy composed of fluctuating electric and magnetic waves. Visible light has a *wavelength* in the hundreds of nanometers (a nanometer is one billionth of a meter). As we can see in **FIGURE 4.13**, we respond only to a narrow range of wavelengths of light; this range is the human visible spectrum. Each animal species detects a specific visible range, which can extend slightly above or below the human visible spectrum. Butterflies are sensitive to all of the wavelengths we detect in addition to ultraviolet light, which has a shorter wavelength than violet light. We might assume that the human visible spectrum is fixed, but increasing the amount of vitamin A in our diets can increase our ability to see infrared light, which has a longer wavelength than red light (Rubin & Walls, 1969).

When light reaches an object, part of that light gets reflected by the object and part gets absorbed. Our perception of an object's *brightness* is influenced directly by the intensity of the reflected light that reaches our eyes. Completely white objects reflect all of the light shone on them and absorb none of it, whereas black objects do the opposite. So white and black aren't really "colors": white is the presence of all colors, black the absence of them. The brightness of an object depends not only on the amount of reflected light, but on the overall lighting surrounding the object.

Psychologists call the color of light **hue**. We're maximally attuned to three primary colors of light: red, green, and blue. The mixing of varying amounts of these three colors—called *additive color mixing*—can produce any color (see **FIGURE 4.14**). Mixing equal amounts of red, green, and blue light produces white light. This process differs from the mixing of colored pigments in paint or ink, called *subtractive color mixing*. As we can see in most printer color ink cartridges, the primary colors of pigment are yellow, cyan, and magenta. Mixing them produces a dark color because each pigment absorbs certain wavelengths. Combining them absorbs most or all wavelengths, leaving little or no color (see Figure 4.14).

■ The Eye: How We Represent the Visual Realm

Without our eyes we couldn't sense or perceive much of anything about light, aside from the heat it generates. Keep an "eye" on **FIGURE 4.15** as we tour the structures of the eye.

HOW LIGHT ENTERS THE EYE. Different parts of our eye allow in varying amounts of light, permitting us to see either in bright sunshine or in a dark theater. Structures toward the front of the eyeball influence how much light enters our eye, and they focus the incoming light rays to form an image at the back of the eye.

The Sclera, Iris, and Pupil. Although poets have told us that the eyes are the windows to the soul, when we look people squarely in the eye all we can see is their sclera, iris, and pupil. The sclera is simply the white of the eye. The iris is the colored part of the eye, and is usually blue, brown, green, or hazel. The chemicals responsible for eye color are called *pigments*. Only two pigments—melanin, which is brown, and lipochrome, which is yellowish-brown—account for all of the remarkable variations in eye colors. Blue eyes contain a small amount of yellow pigment and little or no brown pigment; green and hazel eyes, an intermediate amount of brown pigment; and brown eyes, a lot of brown pigment. The reason blue eyes appear blue, and not yellow, is that blue light is scattered more by irises containing less pigment. Popular belief notwithstanding, our irises don't change color over brief periods of time, although they may seem to do so depending on lighting conditions. Like the shutter of a camera, the iris controls how much light enters our eyes.

The **pupil** is a circular hole through which light enters the eye. The closing of the pupil is a reflex response to light or objects coming toward us. If we walk out of a building into bright sunshine, our eyes respond with the *pupillary reflex* to decrease the amount of light allowed into them. This reflex occurs simultaneously in both eyes (unless there's neurological damage), so shining a flashlight into one eye triggers it in both.

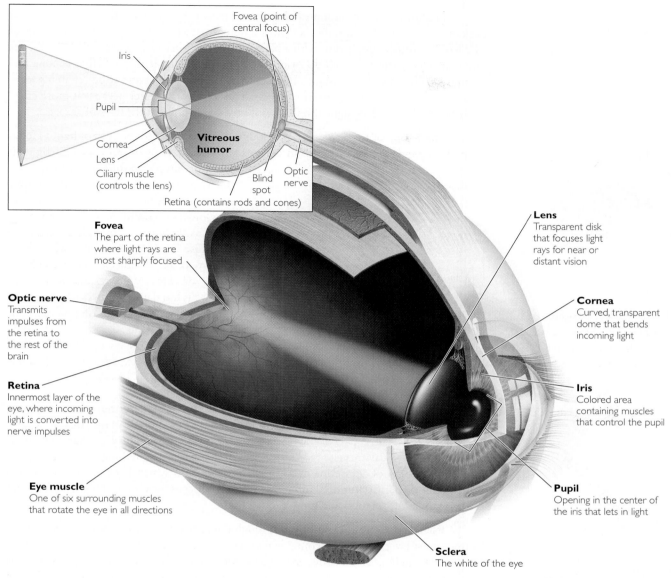

Fovea (point of central focus)

Iris

Pupil

Cornea

Lens

Ciliary muscle (controls the lens)

Vitreous humor

Blind spot

Optic nerve

Retina (contains rods and cones)

Fovea
The part of the retina where light rays are most sharply focused

Optic nerve
Transmits impulses from the retina to the rest of the brain

Retina
Innermost layer of the eye, where incoming light is converted into nerve impulses

Eye muscle
One of six surrounding muscles that rotate the eye in all directions

Lens
Transparent disk that focuses light rays for near or distant vision

Cornea
Curved, transparent dome that bends incoming light

Iris
Colored area containing muscles that control the pupil

Pupil
Opening in the center of the iris that lets in light

Sclera
The white of the eye

FIGURE 4.15 The Key Parts of the Eye.
(*Source:* Adapted from Dorling Kindersley)

The dilation (expansion) of the pupil also has psychological significance. Our pupils dilate when we're trying to process complex information, like difficult math problems (Beatty, 1982; Karatekin, 2004). They also dilate when we view someone we find physically attractive (Tombs & Silverman, 2004). This finding may help to explain why people find faces with large pupils more attractive than faces with small pupils, even when they're oblivious to this physical difference (Hess, 1965; Tomlinson, Hicks, & Pelligrini, 1978). Researchers found that when they're in the fertile phase of their menstrual cycles, women are especially prone to prefer men with large pupils (Caryl et al., 2009). For centuries European women applied a juice from a poisonous plant called *belladonna* (Italian for "beautiful woman"), sometimes also called deadly nightshade, to their eyes to dilate their pupils, and thereby make themselves more attractive to men. Today, magazine photographers often enlarge the pupils of models, reasoning it will increase their appeal.

The Cornea, Lens, and Eye Muscles. The **cornea** is a curved, transparent layer covering the iris and pupil. Its shape bends incoming light to focus the incoming visual image at the back of the eye. The **lens** also bends light, but unlike the cornea, the lens changes its curvature, allowing us to fine-tune the visual image. The lens consists of some of the most unusual cells in the body: They're completely transparent, allowing light to pass through them.

Research demonstrates that men tend to find the faces of women with larger pupils (in this case, the face on the left) more attractive than those with smaller pupils, even when they're unaware of the reason for their preference. (*Source:* Hess, 1965; Tombs & Silverman, 2004)

In a process called **accommodation**, the lenses change shape to focus light on the back of the eyes; in this way, they adapt to different perceived distances of objects. So, nature has generously supplied us with a pair of "internal" corrective lenses, although they're often far from perfect. Accommodation can either make the lens "flat" (that is, long and skinny) enabling us to see distant objects, or "fat" (that is, short and wide) enabling us to focus on nearby objects. For nearby objects, a fat lens works better because it more effectively bends the scattered light and focuses it on a single point at the back of the eye.

The Shape of the Eye. How much our eyes need to bend the path of light to focus properly depends on the curve of our corneas and overall shape of our eyes. Nearsightedness, or *myopia*, results when images are focused in front of the rear of the eye due to our cornea being too steep or our eyes too long (see **FIGURE** 4.16a). Nearsightedness, as the name implies, is an ability to see close objects well coupled with an inability to see far objects well. Farsightedness, or *hyperopia*, results when our cornea is too flat or our eyes too short (see

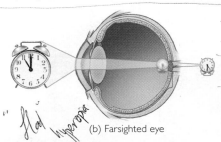

(b) Farsighted eye

FIGURE 4.16b). Farsightedness, as the name implies, is an ability to see far objects well coupled with an inability to see near objects well. Our vision tends to worsen as we become older. That's because our lens can accommodate and overcome the effects of most mildly misshapen eyeballs until it loses its flexibility due to aging. This explains why only a few first-graders need eyeglasses, whereas most senior citizens do.

THE RETINA: CHANGING LIGHT INTO NEURAL ACTIVITY. The **retina**, which according to many scholars is technically part of the brain, is a thin membrane at the back of the eye. The **fovea** is the central part of the retina and is responsible for **acuity**, or sharpness of vision. We need a sharp image to read, drive, sew, or do just about anything requiring fine detail. We can think of the retina as a "movie screen" onto which light from the world is projected. It contains a hundred million sense receptor cells for vision, along with cells that process visual information and send it to the brain.

Rods and Cones. Light passes through the retina to sense receptor cells located in its outermost layer. The retina contains two types of receptor cells. The far more plentiful **rods**, which are long and narrow, enable us to see basic shapes and forms. We rely on rods to see in low levels of light. When we enter a dimly lit room, like a movie theater, from a bright environment, **dark adaptation** occurs. Dark adaptation takes about 30 minutes, or about the time it takes rods to regain their maximum sensitivity to light (Lamb & Pugh, 2004). Some have even speculated that pirates of old, who spent many long, dark nights at sea, might have worn eye patches to facilitate dark adaptation. There are no rods in the fovea, which explains why we should tilt our heads slightly to the side to see a dim star at night. Paradoxically, we can see the star better by *not* looking at it directly. By relying on our peripheral vision, we allow more light to fall on our rods.

The less numerous **cones**, which are shaped like—you guessed it—small cones, give us our color vision. We put our cones to work when reading because they're sensitive to detail; however, cones also require more light than do rods. That's why most of us have trouble reading in a dark room.

Different types of receptor cells contain *photopigments*, chemicals that change following exposure to light. The photopigment in rods is *rhodopsin*. Vitamin A, found in abundance in carrots, is needed to make rhodopsin. This fact led to the urban legend that eating carrots is good for our vision. Unfortunately, the only time vitamin A improves vision in the visual spectrum is when vision is impaired due to vitamin A deficiency.

The Optic Nerve. The *ganglion cells,* cells in the retinal circuit that contain axons, bundle all their axons together and depart the eye to reach the brain. The **optic nerve**, which contains the axons of ganglion cells, travels from the retina to the rest of the brain.

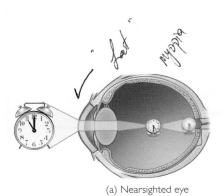

(a) Nearsighted eye

FIGURE 4.16 **Nearsighted and Farsighted Eyes.** Nearsightedness or farsightedness results when light is focused in front of or behind the retina, respectively. (*Source:* Adapted from St. Luke's Cataract & Laser Institute)

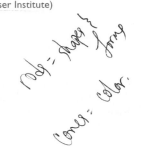

accommodation
changing the shape of the lens to focus on objects near or far

retina
membrane at the back of the eye responsible for converting light into neural activity

fovea
central portion of the retina

acuity
sharpness of vision

rods
receptor cells in the retina allowing us to see in low levels of light

dark adaptation
time in dark before rods regain maximum light sensitivity

cones
receptor cells in the retina allowing us to see in color

optic nerve
nerve that travels from the retina to the brain

Handwritten annotations (top): Optic nerves of comprise of ganglion cells which contain axons → Optic nerves come to optic chiasm. half go, other half stay. → become optic tracts → optic tract send most axons to visual part of thalamus then primary visual cortex (V1) → remaining axons go to midbrain, superior colliculus (reflexes)

After the optic nerves leave both eyes, they come to a fork in the road called the *optic chiasm*. Half of the axons cross in the optic chiasm and the other half stay on the same side. Within a short distance, the optic nerves enter the brain, turning into the optic tracts. The optic tracts send most of their axons to the visual part of the thalamus and then to the primary visual cortex—called V1—the primary route for visual perception (see **FIGURE 4.17**). The remaining axons go to structures in the midbrain (see Chapter 3), particularly the *superior colliculus*. These axons play a key role in reflexes, like turning our heads to follow something interesting.

The place where optic nerve connects to the retina is a **blind spot**, a part of the visual field that we can't see. It's a region of the retina containing no rods and totally devoid of sense receptors (refer back to Figure 4.15). We have a blind spot because the axons of ganglion cells push everything else aside. The exercise we performed at the outset of this chapter made use of the blind spot to generate an illusion (refer back to Figure 4.1). Our blind spot is there all of the time, creating perhaps the most remarkable of all visual illusions—one we experience every moment of our seeing lives. Our brain fills in the gaps created by the blind spot, and because each of our eyes supplies us with a slightly different picture of the world, we don't ordinarily notice it. ◉ **Watch**

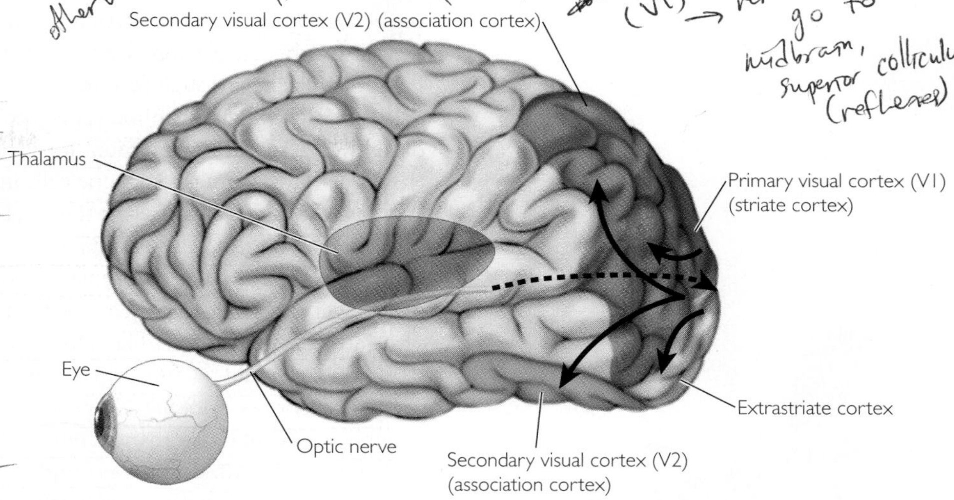

Handwritten (margin): "All I need is the art, breathe and a place to rest my head." "Do you think you can find it? Better than you had it?"

■ Visual Perception

Now that we we've learned how our nervous system gathers and transmits visual information, we can find out how we perceive shape, motion, color, and depth, all of which are handled by different parts of the visual cortex (refer back to Figure 4.17). Even though different parts of the brain process different aspects of visual perception, we perceive whole objects and unified scenes, not isolated components. By compensating for missing information, our perceptual systems help us make sense of the world, but they occasionally out-and-out deceive us along the way.

HOW WE PERCEIVE SHAPE AND CONTOUR. In the 1960s, David Hubel and Torsten Wiesel sought to unlock the secrets of how we perceive shape and form; their work eventually garnered them a Nobel Prize. They used cats as subjects because their visual systems are much like ours. Hubel and Wiesel recorded electrical activity in the visual cortexes of cats while presenting them with visual stimuli on a screen (see **FIGURE 4.18**). At first, they were unaware of which stimuli would work best, so they tried many types, including bright and dark spots. At one point, they put up a different kind of stimulus on the screen, a long slit of light. As the story goes, one of their slides jammed in the slide projector slightly off-center, producing a slit of light (Horgan, 1999). Cells in V1 suddenly went haywire, fir-

Figure 4.17

Labels: Secondary visual cortex (V2) (association cortex); Thalamus; Eye; Optic nerve; Primary visual cortex (V1) (striate cortex); Extrastriate cortex; Secondary visual cortex (V2) (association cortex)

FIGURE 4.17 Perception and the Visual Cortex. Visual information from the retina travels to the visual thalamus. Next, the visual thalamus sends inputs to the primary visual cortex (V1), then along two visual pathways to the secondary visual cortex (V2; see p. 140). One pathway leads to the parietal lobe, which processes visual form, position, and motion; and one to the temporal lobe, which processes visual form and color.

◉ **Watch** the Blindspot video on **mypsychlab.com**

FICTOID ✖

MYTH: Our eyes emit tiny particles of light, which allow us to perceive our surroundings.

REALITY: Many children and about 50 percent of college students (including those who've taken introductory psychology classes) harbor this belief, often called "emission theory" (Winer et al., 2002). Nevertheless, there's no scientific evidence for this theory, and considerable evidence against it.

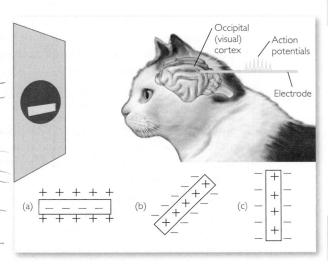

Labels: Occipital (visual) cortex; Action potentials; Electrode; (a) (b) (c)

FIGURE 4.18 Cells Respond to Slits of Light of a Particular Orientation. *Top:* Hubel and Wiesel studied activity in the visual cortex of cats viewing slits of light on a screen. *Bottom:* Visual responses were specific to slits of dark on light (minuses on pluses—a) or light on dark (pluses on minuses—b) that were of particular orientations, such as horizontal, oblique, or vertical—c). Cells in the visual cortex also detected edges.

blind spot
part of the visual field we can't see because of an absence of rods and cones

ing action potentials at an amazingly high rate when the slit moved across the screen. Motivated by this surprising result, Hubel and Wiesel devoted years to figuring out which types of slits elicited such responses.

Here's what they found (Hubel & Wiesel, 1962; 1963). Many cells in V1 respond to slits of light of a specific orientation, for example, vertical, horizontal, or oblique lines or edges (refer again to Figure 4.18). Some cells in the visual cortex, *simple cells,* display distinctive responses to slits of a specific orientation, but these slits need to be in a specific location. Other cells, *complex cells,* are also orientation-specific, but their responses are less restricted to one location. This feature makes complex cells much more advanced than simple cells. Here's why.

Let's say we've learned a concept in our psychology class that allows us to give simple yes or no answers to questions, like "Do some cells in V1 respond to slits of light of a specific orientation?" That would be similar to a simple cell responding: Yes, this part of the visual field sees a vertical line, or no, it doesn't. Now suppose our professor has a nasty reputation for requiring us to apply a concept rather than merely regurgitate it (don't you hate that?). Applying a concept is analogous to the workings of a complex cell. A complex cell responds to the abstract idea of a line of a specific orientation, and for this reason, it may well represent the first cell in which sensation transitions to perception. So the simplest idea in our minds may be a straight line.

Feature Detection. Our ability to use certain minimal patterns to identify objects is called *feature detection.* Although simple and complex cells are **feature detector cells** in that they detect lines and edges, there are more complex feature detector cells at higher, that is, later levels of visual processing. They detect lines of specific lengths, complex shapes, and even moving objects. We use our ability to detect edges and corners to perceive many human-made objects, like furniture, laptops, and even the corners of the page you're reading at this moment.

As we saw in Figure 4.17, visual information travels from V1 to higher visual areas, called V2, along two major routes, one of which travels to the upper parts of the parietal lobe, and the other of which travels to the lower part of the temporal lobe (see Chapter 3). Numerous researchers have proposed a model of visual processing in which successively higher cortical regions process more and more complex shapes (Riesenhuber & Poggio, 1999). The many visual processing areas of the cortex enable us to progress from perceiving basic shapes to the enormously complex objects we see in our everyday worlds.

Gestalt Principles. As we learned in our discussion of top-down processing, much of our visual perception involves analyzing an image in the context of its surroundings and our expectations. Our brains often provide missing information about outlines, a phenomenon called *subjective contours.* Gaetano Kanizsa sparked interest in this phenomenon in 1955. His figures illustrate how a mere hint of three or four corners can give rise to the perception of an imaginary shape (see **FIGURE 4.19**).

Gestalt principles are rules governing how we perceive objects as wholes within their overall context (*Gestalt* is a German word roughly meaning "whole"). Gestalt principles of perception help to explain why we see much of our world as consisting of unified figures or forms rather than confusing jumbles of lines and curves. These principles provide a road map for how we make sense of our perceptual worlds. ◉──|Watch

Here are the main Gestalt principles, formulated by psychologists Max Wertheimer, Wolfgang Kohler, and Kurt Koffka in the early 20th century (see **FIGURE 4.20**):

1. **Proximity:** Objects physically close to each other tend to be perceived as unified wholes (Figure 4.20a).

2. **Similarity:** All things being equal, we see similar objects as comprising a whole, much more so than dissimilar objects. If patterns of red circles and yellow circles are randomly mixed, we perceive nothing special. But if the red and yellow circles are lined up horizontally, we perceive separate rows of circles (Figure 4.20b).

3. **Continuity:** We still perceive objects as wholes, even if other objects block part of them. The Gestalt principle of continuity leads us to perceive the cross shown in Figure 4.20c as one long vertical line crossing over one long horizontal line rather than four smaller line segments joining together.

We're not alone when it comes to detecting edges and corners. In this example, a computer program detects edges (*blue*) and corners (*red*).

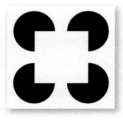

FIGURE 4.19 Kanizsa Square. This Kanizsa square illustrates subjective contours. The square you perceive in the middle of this figure is imaginary. (*Source:* Herrmann & Friederici, 2001)

◉──|Watch Gestalt Laws of Perception on **mypsychlab.com**

feature detector cell
cell that detects lines send edges

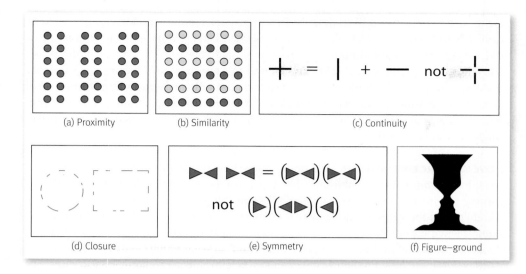

FIGURE 4.20 Gestalt Principles of Perception. As Gestalt psychologists discovered, we use a variety of principles to help us organize the world.

(a) Proximity (b) Similarity (c) Continuity

(d) Closure (e) Symmetry (f) Figure–ground

4. **Closure:** When partial visual information is present, our brains fill in what's missing. When the missing information is a contour, this principle is essentially the same as subjective contours. This Gestalt principle is the main illusion in the Kanizsa figures (Figure 4.20d).

5. **Symmetry:** We perceive objects that are symmetrically arranged as wholes more often than those that aren't. Figure 4.20e demonstrates that two symmetrical figures tend to be grouped together as a single unit.

6. **Figure–ground:** Perceptually, we make an instantaneous decision to focus attention on what we believe to be the central figure, and largely ignore what we believe to be the background. We can view some figures, such as Rubin's vase illusion, in two ways (Figure 4.20f). The vase can be the figure, in which case we ignore the background. If we look again, we can see an image in the background: two faces looking at each other.

Rubin's vase illusion is an example of a *bistable* image, one we can perceive in two ways. Another example is the Necker Cube in **FIGURE 4.21**. When we look at bistable images, we can typically perceive them only one way at a time, and there are limits to how quickly we can shift from one view to the other. A concept related to the bistable image is *emergence*—a perceptual gestalt that almost jumps out from the page and hits us all at once. Try to find the Dalmatian dog in the photo on this page. If you have trouble, keep staring at the black-and-white photo until the dog emerges. It's worth the wait.

Face Recognition. Our ability to recognize familiar faces, including our own, lies at the core of our social selves. After all, don't we refer to a friend as "a familiar face"? Even nonhuman primates can recognize faces (Pinsk et al., 2005).

We don't need an exact picture of a face to recognize it. Caricature artists have long capitalized on this fact and amused us with their drawings of famous faces, usually with some feature exaggerated way out of proportion. Yet we can recognize wacky faces because our brains get by with only partial information, filling in the rest for us. Do individual neurons respond specifically to certain faces? Scientists have known for some time that the lower part of the temporal lobe responds to faces (refer back to Figure 4.17). As we'll learn in Chapter 7, researchers have identified neurons in the human hippocampus that fire selectively in response to celebrity faces, such as those of Jennifer Aniston and Halle Berry (Quiroga et al., 2005). In the 1960s, Jerry Lettvin half-jokingly proposed that each neuron might store a single memory, like the recollection of our grandmother sitting in our living room when we were children. He coined

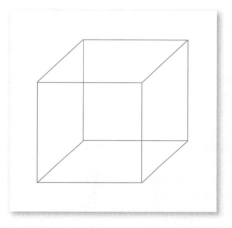

FIGURE 4.21 The Necker Cube. The Necker cube is an example of a bistable image.

Embedded in this photograph is an image of a Dalmatian dog. Can you find it?

falsifiability

CAN THE CLAIM BE DISPROVED?

the term "grandmother cell" to describe this straw person argument, assuming it could be easily falsified (Horgan, 2005). Certain neurons, such as those responding to Jennifer Aniston, are suggestive of grandmother cells, but we shouldn't be too quick to accept this possibility. Even though individual cells may respond to Aniston, many other neurons in other brain regions probably chime in, too. Researchers can only make recordings from a small number of neurons at once, so we don't know what the rest of the brain is doing. At present, the most parsimonious hypothesis is that sprawling networks of neurons, rather than single cells, are responsible for face recognition.

occam's razor

DOES A SIMPLER EXPLANATION FIT THE DATA JUST AS WELL?

HOW WE PERCEIVE MOTION. The brain judges how things in our world are constantly changing by comparing visual frames, like those in a movie. Perceiving the motion of a car coming toward us as we cross the street relies on this kind of motion detection, and we couldn't cross the street, let alone drive a car, without it. We can also be fooled into seeing motion when it's not there. Moving closer to and farther from certain clever designs produces the illusion of motion, as we can see in **FIGURE 4.22**. The *phi phenomenon,* discovered by Max Wertheimer, is the illusory perception of movement produced by the successive flashing of images, like the flashing lights that seem to circle around a movie marquee. These lights are actually jumping from one spot on the marquee to another, but they appear continuous. The phi phenomenon shows that our perceptions of what's moving and what's not are based on only partial information, with our brains taking their best guesses about what's missing. Luckily, many of these guesses are accurate, or at least accurate enough for us to get along in everyday life.

FIGURE 4.22 Moving Spiral Illusion. Focus on the plus sign in the middle of the figure and move the page closer to your face and then farther away. The two rings should appear to move in opposite directions, and those directions should reverse when you reverse the direction in which you move the page. (*Source:* cooopticalillusions.com)

HOW WE PERCEIVE COLOR. Color delights our senses and stirs our imagination, but how does the brain perceive it? Scientists have discovered that we use the lower visual pathway leading to the temporal lobe to process color (refer back to Figure 4.17), but it hardly starts there. Different theories of color perception explain different aspects of our ability to detect color, enabling us to see the world, watch TV, and enjoy movies, all in vibrant color.

Trichromatic Theory. Trichromatic theory proposes that we base our color vision on three primary colors—blue, green, and red. Trichromatic theory dovetails with our having three kinds of cones, each maximally sensitive to different wavelengths of light. Given that the three types of cones were discovered in the 1960s (Brown & Wald, 1964), it's perhaps surprising that Thomas Young and Hermann von Helmholtz described trichromatic theory over a century earlier. Young (1802) suggested that our vision is sensitive to three primary colors of light, and von Helmholtz (1850) replicated and extended his proposal by examining the colors that color-blind subjects could see. The Young-Helmholtz trichromatic theory of color vision was born.

replicability

CAN THE RESULTS BE DUPLICATED IN OTHER STUDIES?

Persons with **color blindness** can't see all colors. Color blindness is most often due to the absence or reduced number of one or more types of cones stemming from genetic abnormalities.

trichromatic theory
idea that color vision is based on our sensitivity to three primary colors

color blindness
inability to see some or all colors

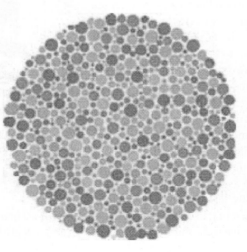

FIGURE 4.23 The Ishihara Test for Red-Green Color Blindness. If you can't see the two-digit number, you probably have red-green color blindness. This condition is common, especially among males.

Still another cause is damage to a brain area related to color vision. Contrary to a popular misconception, *monochromats*—who have only one type of cone and thereby lose all color vision—are extremely rare, making up only about 0.0007 percent of the population. Most color-blind individuals can perceive a good deal of their world in color because they're *dichromats,* meaning they have two cones and are missing only one. Red-green dichromats see considerable color but can't distinguish reds as well as can people with normal color vision. We can find a test for red-green color blindness in **FIGURE 4.23**; many males have this condition but don't know it because it doesn't interfere much with their everyday functioning.

Humans, apes, and some monkeys are *trichromats*, meaning we and our close primate relatives possess three kinds of cones. Most other mammals, including dogs and cats, see the world with only two cones, much like people with red-green color blindness (the most frequent form of color blindness). Trichromatic vision evolved about 35 million years ago, perhaps because it allowed animals to easily pick ripe fruit out of a green background. Recent fossil evidence suggests an alternative hypothesis, namely, that trichromatic vision may have enabled primates to find young, reddish, tender leaves that were nutritionally superior (Simon-Moffat, 2002). All scientists agree that seeing more colors gave our ancestors a leg up in foraging for food.

Opponent Process Theory. Trichromatic theory accounts nicely for how our three cone types work together to detect the full range of colors. But further research revealed a phenomenon that trichromatic theory can't explain—afterimages. Afterimages occur when we've stared at one color for a long time and then look away. We'll often see a different colored replica of the same image, as in **FIGURE 4.24**. Trichromatic theory doesn't easily explain why looking at one color consistently results in seeing another color in the afterimage, such as afterimages for red always appearing green. It turns out that afterimages arise from the visual cortex's processing of information from our rods and cones.

Stage magicians—people who rely on illusions to create the appearance of "magic" —use afterimages to their advantage in the Great Tomsoni's Colored Dress Trick. In this trick, the magician appears to transform the tiny white dress his assistant is wearing into a red dress. For the first part of the trick, a bright red spotlight is beamed on the woman, making her dress appear red. Not much of a trick, the magician jokes. After all, a white dress would appear red in this lighting. But then an amazing thing happens. At the magician's command, a brilliant white light is shined on the woman. Presto change-o! In this light, the amazed audience can plainly see that the dress is red. What happened? After the red light is turned off, the audience continues to see a red afterimage of the assistant. The red image persists in the dark just long enough for the woman to remove the white dress that covered the red dress she was wearing underneath all along. So when the white light illuminates the woman, she's clad in red for all to see. Scientists are now collaborating with famous magicians, including James "The Amazing" Randi and Teller (of Penn and Teller), to gain insight into perception and attention by studying the illusions they create in their craft (Macknik et al., 2008).

Some people occasionally report faint negative afterimages surrounding objects or other individuals. This phenomenon may have given rise to the paranormal idea that we're all encircled by mystical "auras" consisting of psychical energy (Neher, 1990). Nevertheless, because no one's been able to photograph auras under carefully controlled conditions, there's no support for this extraordinary claim (Nickel, 2000).

A competing model, **opponent process theory**, holds that we perceive colors in terms of three pairs of opponent cells: red or green, blue or yellow, or black or white. Afterimages, which appear in complementary colors, illustrate opponent processing. Ganglion cells of the retina and cells in the visual area of the thalamus that respond to red spots are inhibited by green spots. Other cells show the opposite responses, and still others distinguish yellow from blue spots. Our nervous system uses both trichromatic and opponent processing principles during color vision, but different neurons rely on one principle more than the other. There's a useful lesson here that applies to many controversies in science: Two ideas that seem contradictory are sometimes both partly correct—they're merely describing differing aspects of the same phenomenon.

ruling out rival hypotheses
HAVE IMPORTANT ALTERNATIVE EXPLANATIONS FOR THE FINDINGS BEEN EXCLUDED?

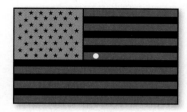

FIGURE 4.24 Opponent Processes in Action. Find a patch of blank white wall or place a blank sheet of white paper nearby before you begin. Then relax your eyes and fix your gaze on the white dot in the image above for at least 30 seconds without looking around or away. Afterward, stare at the white wall or paper for a few seconds. What do you see?

opponent process theory
theory that we perceive colors in terms of three pairs of opponent colors: either red or green, blue or yellow, or black or white

? Uri Geller claims to bend spoons with paranormal abilities. Yet many people who make no such claims can perform the spoon trick using illusions and gimmicks. Can you think of ways in which magicians might fool us into thinking they're actually bending spoons?

extraordinary claims
IS THE EVIDENCE AS STRONG AS THE CLAIM?
ruling out rival hypotheses
HAVE IMPORTANT ALTERNATIVE EXPLANATIONS FOR THE FINDINGS BEEN EXCLUDED?

Answer: A magician can (a) replace the spoon with another that's already bent, (b) physically bend the spoon by distracting onlookers, and (c) convince spectators the spoon is still bending by moving it back and forth rapidly.

This painting depicts a scene that provides monocular cues to depth.

a. Relative size: The house is drawn approximately as high as the fence post, but we know the house is much bigger, so it must be considerably farther away.

b. Texture gradient: The grasses in front of the fence are drawn as individual blades but those in the field behind are shown with almost no detail.

c. Interposition: The tree at the corner of the house is blocking part of the house, so we know that the tree is closer to us than the house is.

depth perception
ability to judge distance and three-dimensional relations

monocular depth cues
stimuli that enable us to judge depth using only one eye

binocular depth cues
stimuli that enable us to judge depth using both eyes

This lithograph by M. C. Escher titled *Belvedere* (1958) features two vanishing points, resulting in an impossible structure. Can you locate the vanishing points off the page?

HOW WE PERCEIVE DEPTH. Depth perception is the ability to see spatial relations in three dimensions; it enables us to reach for a glass and grasp it rather than knock it over and spill its contents. We need to have some idea of how close or far we are from objects to navigate around our environments. We use two kinds of cues to gauge depth: **monocular depth cues**, which rely on one eye alone, and **binocular depth cues**, which require both eyes.

Monocular Cues. We can perceive three dimensions using only one eye. We do so by relying on *pictorial cues* to give us a sense of what's located where in stationary scenes. The following pictorial cues help us to perceive depth.

- **Relative size:** All things being equal, more distant objects look smaller than closer objects.
- **Texture gradient:** The texture of objects becomes less apparent as objects move farther away.
- **Interposition:** One object that's closer blocks our view of an object behind it. From this fact, we know which object is closer and which is farther away.
- **Linear perspective:** The outlines of rooms or buildings converge as distance increases, a fact exploited by artists. We can trace most lines in a scene to a point where they meet—the *vanishing point*. In reality, lines in parallel never meet, but they appear to do so at great distances. Some *impossible figures*—figures that break physical laws—possess more than one vanishing point. Artist M. C. Escher was fond of violating this rule in his prints.
- **Height in plane:** In a scene, distant objects tend to appear higher, and nearer objects lower.
- **Light and shadow:** Objects cast shadows that give us a sense of their three-dimensional form.

One additional monocular cue that's not pictorial is *motion parallax:* the ability to judge the distance of moving objects from their speed. Nearby objects seem to move faster than those far away traveling at the same speed. Motion parallax also works when we're moving. Stationary objects nearer to us pass us more quickly than objects farther away, a fact we'll discover when looking out of the windows of a moving car. Our brains quickly compute these differences in speed and calculate approximate distances from us.

Binocular Cues. Our visual system is set up so that we view each of our two visual fields with both eyes. We'll recall that half of the axons in the optic nerve cross to the other side and half stay on the same side before entering the brain. Visual information from both sides is sent to neighboring cells in the visual cortex, where our brains can make comparisons. These comparisons form the basis of binocular depth perception; we use several binocular cues to perceive depth in our worlds.

- **Binocular disparity:** Like the two lenses from a pair of binoculars, our left and right eyes transmit quite different information for near objects but see distant objects similarly. To demonstrate this cue, close one of your eyes and hold a pen up about a foot away from your face, lining the top of it up with a distant point on the wall (like a doorknob or corner of a picture frame). Then, hold the pen steady while alternating which of your eyes is open. You'll find that although the pen is lined up with one eye, it's no longer lined up when you switch to the other eye. Each eye sees the world a bit differently, and our brains ingeniously make use of this information to judge depth.

- **Binocular convergence:** When we look at nearby objects, we focus on them reflexively by using our eye muscles to turn our eyes inward, a phenomenon called *convergence.* Our brains are aware of how much our eyes are converging, and use this information to estimate distance.

Depth Perception Appears in Infancy.   We can judge depth as soon as we learn to crawl. Eleanor Gibson established this phenomenon in a classic setup called the *visual cliff* (Gibson, 1991; Gibson & Walk, 1960). The typical visual cliff consists of a table and a floor several feet below, both covered by a checkered cloth. A clear glass surface extends from the table out over the floor, creating the appearance of a sudden drop. Infants between 6 and 14 months of age hesitate to crawl over the glass elevated several feet above the floor, even when their mothers beckon. The visual cliff demonstrates that depth cues present soon after birth are probably partly innate, although they surely develop with experience. 👁—|Watch

WHEN PERCEPTION DECEIVES US.   Sometimes the best way to understand how something works is to see how it doesn't work—or works in unusual circumstances. We've already examined some illusions that illustrate principles of sensation and perception. Now we'll examine further how illusions and other unusual phenomena shed light on everyday perception.

- The *moon illusion,* which has fascinated people for centuries, is the illusion that the moon appears larger when it's near the horizon than high in the sky. Scientists have put forth several explanations for this illusion, but none is universally accepted. A common misconception is that the moon appears larger near the horizon due to a magnification effect caused by the earth's atmosphere. But we can easily refute this hypothesis. Although the earth's atmosphere does alter the moon's color at the horizon, it doesn't enlarge it. Let's contrast this common misconception with a few better-supported explanations. The first is that the moon illusion is due to errors in perceived distance. The moon is some 240,000 miles away, a huge distance we've had little experience judging. When the moon is high in the sky, there's nothing else around for comparison. In contrast, when the moon is near the horizon, we may perceive it as farther away because we can see it next to things we know to be far away, like buildings, mountains, and trees. Because we know these things are large, we perceive the moon as larger still. Another explanation is that we're mistaken about the three-dimensional space in which we live, along with the moon. For example, many people have the misperception that the sky is shaped like a flattened dome, leading us to see the moon as farther away on the horizon than at the top of the sky (Rock & Kaufman, 1962; Ross & Plug, 2002).

- The startling *Ames room illusion,* developed by Adelbert Ames, Jr. (1946), is shown in **FIGURE 4.25** on page 146. This distorted room is actually trapezoidal; the walls are slanted and the ceiling and floor are at an incline. Insert two people of the same size and the Ames room creates the bizarre impression of a giant person on the side of the room where the ceiling is lower (but doesn't appear to be) and of a tiny person on the side of the room where the ceiling is higher. This illusion is due to the relative size principle. The height of the ceiling is the key to the illusion, and the other distortions in the room are only necessary to make the room appear normal to the observer. Hollywood special effects wizards have capitalized on this principle in movies such as the *Lord of the Rings* and *Charlie and the Chocolate Factory* to make some characters appear gargantuan and others dwarf-like.

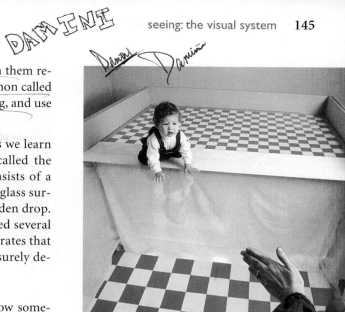

The visual cliff tests infants' ability to judge depth.

👁—|**Watch**   Eleanor Gibson, Richard Walk, and the Visual Cliff on **mypsychlab.com**

◄ falsifiability
CAN THE CLAIM BE DISPROVED?

The moon illusion causes us to perceive the moon as larger near the horizon than high in the sky. Here, the moon looks huge at the San Francisco skyline.

FIGURE 4.25   The Ames Room.   Viewed through a small peephole, the Ames room makes small people look impossibly large and large people look impossibly small. Who is the younger and smaller child in this picture?

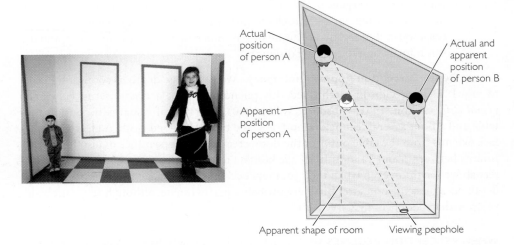

Actual position of person A

Actual and apparent position of person B

Apparent position of person A

Apparent shape of room   Viewing peephole

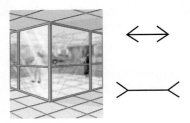

(a) Which horizontal line is longer?

(b) Which line above is longer, and which circle is bigger?

(c) Which line is longer?

(d) Which center circle is bigger?

FIGURE 4.26   How Well Can You Judge Relative Size?   The Müller-Lyer (a), Ponzo (b), horizontal–vertical (c), and Ebbinghaus–Titchener (d) illusions.

replicability

CAN THE RESULTS BE DUPLICATED IN OTHER STUDIES?

- In the *Müller-Lyer illusion*, a line of identical length appears longer when it ends in a set of arrowheads pointing inward than in a set of arrowheads pointing outward (see **FIGURE 4.26a**). That's because we perceive lines as part of a larger context. Three researchers (Segall, Campbell, & Herskovitz, 1966) found that people from different cultures displayed differing reactions to the Müller-Lyer illusion. The Zulu, who live in round huts and plow their fields in circles rather than rows, are less susceptible to the Müller-Lyer illusion, probably because they have less experience with linear environments (McCauley & Henrich, 2006).

- In the *Ponzo illusion*, also called the railroad tracks illusion, converging lines enclose two objects of identical size, leading us to perceive the object closer to the converging lines as larger (see **FIGURE 4.26b**). Our brain "assumes" that the object closer to the converging lines is farther away—usually it would be correct in this guess—and compensates for this knowledge by making the object look bigger.

- The *horizontal–vertical illusion* causes us to perceive the vertical part of an upside-down "T" as longer than the horizontal part, because the horizontal part is divided in half by the vertical part (see **FIGURE 4.26c**).

- The *Ebbinghaus–Titchener* illusion leads us to perceive a circle as larger when surrounded by smaller circles and smaller when surrounded by larger circles (see **FIGURE 4.26d**). Although this illusion fools our eyes, it doesn't fool our hands! Studies in which subjects have to reach for the center circle indicate that their grasp remains on target (Milner & Goodale, 1995), although some scientists have recently challenged this finding (Franz et al., 2003).

■ When We Can't See or Perceive Visually

We've learned how we see, and how we don't always see exactly what's there. Yet some 40 million people worldwide can't see at all.

BLINDNESS.   Blindness is the inability to see, or more specifically, the presence of vision less than or equal to 20/200 on the familiar Snellen eye chart, on which 20/20 is perfect vision. For people with 20/200 vision, objects at 20 feet appear as they would at 200 feet in a normally sighted person. We can find the major causes of blindness worldwide in **TABLE 4.3**; it's worth noting that blindness is more frequent in underdeveloped countries.

The blind cope with their loss of vision in various ways—often relying more on other senses, including touch. This issue has been controversial over the years, with studies both replicating and contradicting a heightened sense of touch in the blind. Recent studies suggest that tactile (touch) sensitivity is indeed heightened in blind adults,

TABLE 4.3 Major Causes of Blindness.

CAUSE OF BLINDNESS	PERCENT OF ALL BLIND PERSONS WORLDWIDE	TREATABLE
Cataract	47.8%	Yes
Glaucoma	12.3%	Yes
Macular degeneration	8.7%	No
Diabetic retinopathy	4.8%	No
Childhood blindness	3.9%	Some types are treatable

(*Source:* Data reported by the World Health Organization based on the 2002 population)

giving them the same sensitivity as someone 23 years younger (Goldreich & Kanics, 2003). It's further known that the visual cortex of blind persons undergoes profound changes in function, rendering it sensitive to touch inputs (Sadato, 2005). This means they can devote more cortex—somatosensory cortex and visual cortex—to a touch task, such as reading Braille. As we learned in Chapter 3, this phenomenon illustrates brain plasticity, in which some brain regions gradually take over the jobs previously assigned to others.

MOTION BLINDNESS. Motion blindness is a serious disorder in which patients can't seamlessly string still images processed by their brains into the perception of ongoing motion. As we noted earlier, motion perception is much like creating a movie in our heads. Actual movies contain 24 frames of still photos per second, creating the illusory perception of motion. In patients with motion blindness, many of these "frames" are missing. This disability interferes with many simple tasks, like crossing the street. Imagine a car appearing to be 100 feet away and then suddenly jumping to only one foot away a second or two later. Needless to say, the experience would be terrifying. Life indoors isn't much better. Simply pouring a cup of coffee can be enormously challenging, because the person doesn't see the cup fill up. First, it's empty and then is overflowing with coffee onto the floor only a moment later.

VISUAL AGNOSIA. *Visual agnosia* is a deficit in perceiving objects. A person with this condition can tell us the shape and color of an object, but can't recognize or name it. At a dinner party, such a person might say, "please pass that eight-inch silver thing with a round end" rather than, "please pass the serving spoon." Oliver Sacks's 1985 book, *The Man Who Mistook His Wife for a Hat,* includes a case study of a man with visual agnosia who did exactly as the title suggests; he misperceived his wife as a fashion accessory.

BLINDSIGHT. *Blindsight* is the remarkable phenomenon in which blind people who've experienced damage to a specific area of their cortex can still make correct guesses about the visual appearance of things around them (Hamm et al., 2003). Larry Weiskrantz (1986) asked so-called cortically blind subjects whether they saw stimuli consisting of stripes arranged either vertically or horizontally within circles. When these subjects answered at better-than-chance levels—while reporting they *saw nothing*—many scientists were baffled. Because blindsight operates outside the bounds of conscious activity, some nonscientists have suggested that it may be a paranormal phenomenon. Yet there's a parsimonious natural explanation: People with blindsight have suffered damage to V1, the primary visual cortex, so that route of information flow to visual association areas is blocked. Coarser visual information still reaches the visual association cortex through an alternative pathway and bypasses V1. This visual information probably accounts for blindsight (Moore et al., 1995; Stoerig & Cowey, 1997; Weiskrantz, 1986).

Gisela Leibold is unable to detect motion. She's understandably concerned about important information she might miss riding down an escalator in Munich.

◄ **occam's razor**

DOES A SIMPLER EXPLANATION FIT THE DATA JUST AS WELL?

Study and Review on mypsychlab.com

HEARING: THE AUDITORY SYSTEM

4.7   Explain how the ear starts the auditory process.

4.8   Identify the different kinds of auditory perception.

If a tree falls in the forest and no one is around to hear it, does it make a sound? Ponder that age-old question while we explore our sense of hearing: **audition**. Next to vision, hearing is probably the sensory modality we rely on most to acquire information about our world.

■ Sound: Mechanical Vibration

Sound is vibration, a kind of mechanical energy traveling through a medium, usually air. The disturbance created by vibration of molecules of air produces sound waves. Sound waves can travel through any gas, liquid, or solid, but we hear them best when they travel through air. In a perfectly empty space (a vacuum), there can't be sound because there aren't any airborne molecules to vibrate. That should help us answer our opening question: Because there are air molecules in the forest, a falling tree most definitely makes a loud thud even if nobody can hear it.

PITCH. Sounds have *pitch,* which corresponds to the frequency of the wave. Higher frequency corresponds to higher pitch, lower frequency to lower pitch. Scientists measure pitch in cycles per second, or hertz (Hz) (see **FIGURE 4.27**). The human ear can pick up frequencies ranging from about 20 to 20,000 Hz (see **FIGURE 4.28**). When it comes to sensitivity to pitch, age matters. Younger people are more sensitive to higher pitch tones than older adults. A new ring tone for cell phones has ingeniously exploited this simple fact of nature, allowing teenagers to hear their cell phones ring while many of their parents or teachers can't (Vitello, 2006). ⊙ Watch

Watch Ear Ringing on mypsychlab.com

audition
our sense of hearing

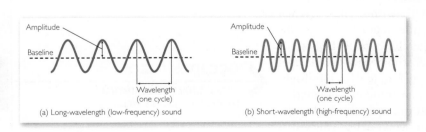

FIGURE 4.27 Sound Wave Frequency and Amplitude. Sound wave frequency (cycles per second) is the inverse of wavelength (cycle width). Sound wave amplitude is the height of the cycle. The frequency for middle C (a) is lower than that for middle A (b).

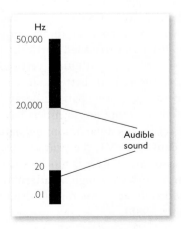

FIGURE 4.28 The Audible Spectrum (in Hz). The human ear is sensitive to mechanical vibration from about 20 Hz to 20,000 Hz.

LOUDNESS. The amplitude—or height—of the sound wave corresponds to *loudness,* measured in decibels (dB) (refer again to Figure 4.27). Loud noise results in increased wave amplitude because there's more mechanical disturbance, that is, more vibrating airborne molecules. **TABLE 4.4** lists various common sounds and their typical loudness.

TIMBRE. **Timbre** refers to the quality or complexity of the sound. Different musical instruments sound different because they differ in timbre, and the same holds for human voices.

■ The Structure and Function of the Ear

Just as sense receptors for vision transduce light into neural activity, sense receptors for hearing transduce sound into neural activity. The ear has three parts: outer, middle, and inner, each of which performs a different job (see **FIGURE 4.29** on page 150). The *outer ear*, consisting of the *pinna* (the part of the ear we see, namely, its skin and cartilage flap) and ear canal, has the simplest function; it funnels sound waves onto the *eardrum*. Explore

On the other side of the eardrum lies the *middle ear*, containing the *ossicles*—the three tiniest bones in the body—named the hammer, anvil, and stirrup, after their shapes. These ossicles vibrate at the frequency of the sound wave, transmitting it from the eardrum to the inner ear.

Once sound waves enter the *inner ear*, the **cochlea** converts vibration into neural activity. The term *cochlea* derives from the Greek word *kokhlias,* meaning "snail" or "screw," and as its name implies, it's spiral in shape. The outer part of the cochlea is bony, but its inner cavity is filled with a thick fluid. Vibrations from sound waves disturb this fluid and travel to the base of the cochlea, where pressure is released and transduction occurs.

Also located in the inner ear, the **organ of Corti** and **basilar membrane** are critical to hearing because *hair cells* are embedded within them (see Figure 4.29). Hair cells are where transduction of auditory information takes place: They convert acoustic information into action potentials. Here's how. Hair cells contain cilia (hairlike structures) that protrude into the fluid of the cochlea. When sound waves travel through the cochlea, the resulting pressure deflects these cilia, exciting the hair cells (Roberts, Howard, & Hudspeth, 1988). That information feeds into the *auditory nerve,* which travels to the brain, through the thalamus, which we'll recall from Chapter 3 is a sensory relay station.

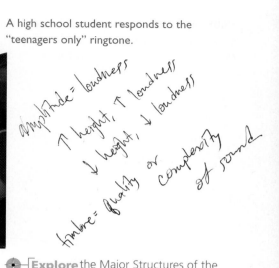

A high school student responds to the "teenagers only" ringtone.

 Explore the Major Structures of the Ear on **mypsychlab.com**

FICTOID ✕

MYTH: Some psychics claim to possess clairaudience, or "clear hearing." Clairaudience is hearing voices, music, or other sounds having a supernatural rather than physical source.

REALITY: There's no scientific evidence for clairaudience.

TABLE 4.4 Common Sounds. This decibel (dB) table compares some common sounds and shows how they rank in potential harm to hearing.

SOUND	NOISE LEVEL (DB)	EFFECT
Jet Engines (near)	140	We begin to feel pain at about 125 dB
Rock Concerts (varies)	110–140	
Thunderclap (near)	120	Regular exposure to sound over 100 dB for more than one minute risks permanent hearing loss
Power Saw (chainsaw)	110	
Garbage Truck/ Cement Mixer	100	No more than 15 minutes of unprotected exposure is recommended for sounds between 90 and 100 dB
Motorcycle (25 ft)	88	Very annoying
Lawn Mower	85–90	85 dB is the level at which hearing damage (after eight hours) begins
Average City Traffic	80	Annoying; interferes with conversation; constant exposure may cause damage
Vacuum Cleaner	70	Intrusive; interferes with telephone conversation
Normal Conversation	50–65	Comfortable hearing levels are under 60 dB
Whisper	30	Very quiet
Rustling Leaves	20	Just audible

(*Source:* NIDCD)

timbre
complexity or quality of sound that makes musical instruments, human voices, or other sources sound unique

cochlea
bony, spiral-shaped sense organ used for hearing

organ of Corti
tissue containing the hair cells necessary for hearing

basilar membrane
membrane supporting the organ of Corti and hair cells in the cochlea

FIGURE 4.29 The Human Ear and Its Parts. A cutaway section through the human ear, and a close-up diagram of the hair cells. (*Source:* Adapted from Dorling Kindersley)

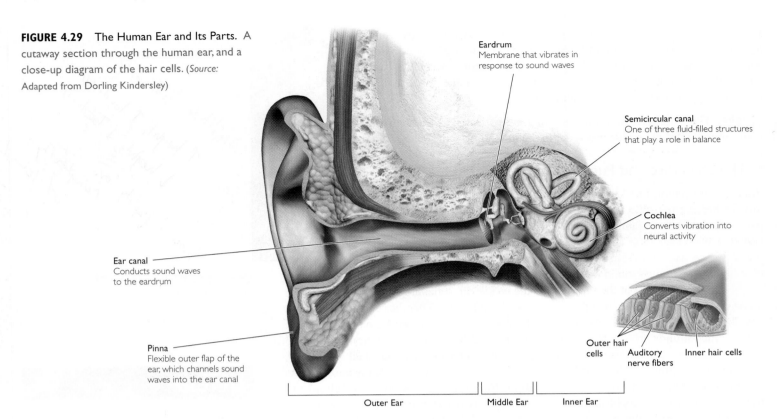

Eardrum
Membrane that vibrates in response to sound waves

Semicircular canal
One of three fluid-filled structures that play a role in balance

Cochlea
Converts vibration into neural activity

Ear canal
Conducts sound waves to the eardrum

Pinna
Flexible outer flap of the ear, which channels sound waves into the ear canal

Outer hair cells   Auditory nerve fibers   Inner hair cells

Outer Ear   Middle Ear   Inner Ear

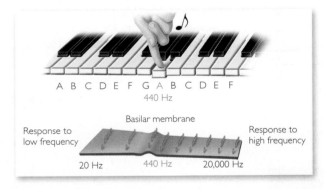

A B C D E F G A B C D E F
440 Hz

Basilar membrane

Response to low frequency

Response to high frequency

20 Hz   440 Hz   20,000 Hz

FIGURE 4.30 The Tone-Based Organization of the Basilar Membrane. Hair cells at the base of the basilar membrane respond to high-pitched tones, whereas hair cells at the top of the basilar membrane respond to low-pitched tones.

Explore the Frequency and Amplitude of Sound Waves on **mypsychlab.com**

place theory
specific place along the basilar membrane matches a tone with a specific pitch

frequency theory
rate at which neurons fire the action potential reproduces the pitch

■ Auditory Perception

Once the auditory nerve enters the brain, it makes contacts with the brain stem, which sends auditory information higher—all the way up the auditory cortex. At each stage, perception becomes increasingly complex. In this respect, auditory perception is like visual perception.

PITCH PERCEPTION. The primary auditory cortex processes different tones in different places (see **FIGURE 4.30**). That's because each place receives information from a specific place in the basilar membrane. Hair cells located at the base of the basilar membrane are most excited by high-pitched tones, whereas hair cells at the top of the basilar membrane are most excited by low-pitched tones. Scientists call this mode of pitch perception **place theory**, because a specific place along the basilar membrane—and in the auditory cortex, too—matches a tone with a specific pitch (Békésy, 1949). Place theory accounts only for our perception of high-pitched tones, namely those from 5,000 to 20,000 Hz. Explore

There are two routes to perceiving low-pitched tones. We'll discuss the simpler way first. In **frequency theory,** the rate at which neurons fire action potentials faithfully reproduces the pitch. This method works well up to 100 Hz, because many neurons have maximal firing rates near that limit. *Volley theory* is a variation of frequency theory that works for tones between 100 and 5,000 Hz. According to volley theory, sets of neurons fire at their highest rate, say 100 Hz, slightly out of sync with each other to reach overall rates up to 5,000 Hz.

When it comes to listening to music, we're sensitive not only to different tones, but to the arrangement of tones into melodies (Weinberger, 2006). We react differently to pleasant and unpleasant melodies. In one study, music that literally provoked feelings of "chills" or "shivers" boosted activity in the same brain regions corresponding to euphoric responses to sex, food, and drugs (Blood & Zatorre, 2001). So there may be a good reason why "sex," "drugs," and "rock and roll" often go together.

LOCALIZATION OF SOUND. We use various brain centers to localize (locate) sounds with respect to our bodies. When the auditory nerve enters the brain stem, some of its axons connect with cells on the same side of the brain, but the rest cross over to the other side of the brain. This clever arrangement enables information from both ears to reach the same structures in the brain stem. Because the two sources of information take different routes, they arrive at the brain stem slightly out of sync with each other. Our brains compare this difference between our ears—a so-called *binaural cue*—to localize sound sources (**FIGURE 4.31**). There's also a loudness difference between our ears, because the ear closest to the sound source is in the direct path of the sound wave, whereas the ear farthest away is in a *sound shadow,* created by our head. We rely mostly on binaural cues to detect the source of sounds. But we also use *monaural cues,* heard by one ear only. The cues help us distinguish sounds that are clear from those that are muffled due to obstruction by the ear, head, and shoulders, allowing us to figure out where sounds are coming from.

ECHOLOCATION. Certain animals, such as bats, dolphins, and many whales, emit sounds and listen to their echoes to determine their distance from a wall or barrier, a phenomenon called *echolocation.* Small bats emit high-pitched sounds ranging from 14,000 to 100,000 Hz, most of which we can't hear.

Remarkably, there's evidence that humans are capable of a crude form of echolocation. Near-sighted people display better echolocation skills than normal-sighted individuals (Despres, Candas, & Dufour, 2005). This correlation suggests that people hone echolocation skills if they need them, but scientists haven't experimentally verified direct causation. Human echolocation may account for the fact that blind persons can sometimes detect objects a few feet away from them. This seems likely in the case of Ben Underwood, who was blinded at age three by retinal cancer. Ben learned to make clicking noises that bounced off surfaces and clued him in to his surroundings. He rides his skateboard and plays basketball and video games. Ben is a rare example of what's possible, although his doctors point out that Ben was sighted for his first few years, long enough for him to acquire a perspective of the world.

■ When We Can't Hear

About one in 1,000 people are deaf: They suffer from a profound loss of hearing. Many others have hearing deficits, called being "hard of hearing." There are several causes of deafness, some largely genetic, others deriving from disease, injury, or exposure to loud noise (Willems, 2000). *Conductive deafness* is due to a malfunctioning of the ear, especially a failure of the eardrum or the ossicles of the inner ear. In contrast, *nerve deafness* is due to damage to the auditory nerve.

If your grandmother warns you to "Turn down the sound on your iPod, or you'll go deaf by the time you're my age," there's more than a ring of truth in her warning. Loud sounds, especially those that last a long time or are repeated, can damage our hair cells and lead to *noise-induced hearing loss.* This type of hearing loss is often accompanied by tinnitus, a ringing, roaring, hissing, or buzzing sound in the ears that can be deeply disturbing (Nondahl et al., 2007). Hearing loss can also occur after exposure to one extremely loud sound, such as an explosion. But most of us lose some hearing ability as we age—especially for high frequency sounds—as a by-product of the loss of sensory cells and degeneration of the auditory nerve, even if we've never attended a rock concert without earplugs (Ohlemiller & Frisina, 2008).

Ben Underwood has developed an amazing ability to use human echolocation to overcome many of the limitations of his blindness. Humans don't usually rely much on echolocation, although many whales do.

correlation vs. causation
CAN WE BE SURE THAT A CAUSES B?

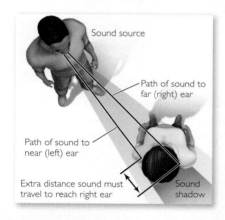

FIGURE 4.31   How We Locate Sounds. When someone standing to our left speaks to us, the sound reaches our left ear slightly earlier than it reaches our right. Also, the intensity detected by the left ear is greater than the intensity detected by the right ear, because the right ear lies in a sound shadow produced by the head and shoulders.

Study and **Review** on **mypsychlab.com**

assess your knowledge   FACT OR FICTION?

1. Sound waves are converted to neural impulses by creating vibrations of fluid inside the cochlea. **True / False**
2. Place theory states that each hair cell in the inner ear has a particular pitch or frequency to which it's most responsive. **True / False**
3. We can determine the location of a sound because the pitch seems higher in the closer ear. **True / False**
4. Only nonhuman animals, like bats, engage in echolocation. **True / False**
5. As we age, we tend to lose hearing for low-pitched sounds more than high-pitched sounds. **True / False**

*Sweet, salty, sour,
bitter, umami*

SMELL AND TASTE: THE SENSUAL SENSES

4.9　Identify how we sense and perceive odors and tastes.

Without smell and taste many of our everyday experiences would be bland. Cuisines of the world feature characteristic spices that enliven their dishes. Similarly, smell and taste stimulate our senses and elevate our spirits. The term "comfort food" refers to familiar dishes that we crave because of the warm memories they evoke.

Smell is also called **olfaction**, and taste **gustation**. These senses work hand in hand, enhancing our liking of some foods and our disliking of others. Smell and taste are the chemical senses because we derive these sensory experiences from chemicals in substances.

Animals use their sense of smell for many purposes—tracking prey, establishing territories, and recognizing the opposite sex, to name but a few. We humans aren't the most smell-oriented of creatures. The average dog is at least 100,000 times more sensitive to smell than we are, which explains why police use trained dogs rather than nosy people to sniff for bombs and banned substances.

The most critical function of our chemical senses is to sample our food before swallowing it. The smell and taste of sour milk are powerful stimuli that few of us can ignore even if we want to. An unfamiliar bitter taste may signal dangerous bacteria or poison in our food. We develop food preferences for "safe" foods and base them on a combination of smell and taste. One study of young French women found that only those who already liked red meat—its smell and its taste—responded favorably to pictures of it (Audebert, Deiss, & Rousset, 2006). We like what smells and tastes good to us.

Culture also shapes what we perceive as delicious or disgusting. The prospect of eating sacred cow meat (as in a hamburger) would be as off-putting to Hindus as eating fried tarantulas, a delicacy in Cambodia, or Casu Marzu, a Sardinian cheese filled with insect larvae, would be to most Americans. Even within a society there are pronounced differences in food choices, as American meat lovers and vegans enjoy vastly different diets. We can acquire food preferences by means of learning, including modeling of eating behaviors (see Chapter 6); parental approval of food choices; and availability of foods (Rozin, 2006).

■ What are Odors and Flavors?

Odors are airborne chemicals that interact with receptors in the lining of our nasal passages. Our noses are veritable smell connoisseurs, capable of detecting between 2,000 and 4,000 different odors. Not everything, though, has an odor. (We bet you're pleased to hear that!) Clean water, for example, has no odor or taste. Not all animals smell airborne molecules. The star-nosed mole, named for its peculiarly shaped snout, can detect odors underwater (Catania, 2006). The animal blows out air bubbles and "sniffs" them back in to find food underwater and underground.

In contrast, we can detect only a few tastes. We're sensitive to five basic tastes—sweet, salty, sour, bitter, and umami, the last of which is a recently uncovered "meaty" or "savory" taste. There's preliminary evidence for a sixth taste, one for fatty foods (Gilbertson et al., 1997).

■ Sense Receptors for Smell and Taste

We humans have over 1,000 olfactory (smell) genes, 347 of which code for olfactory receptors (Buck & Axel, 1991). Each olfactory neuron contains a single type of olfactory receptor, which "recognizes" an odorant on the basis of its shape. This lock-and-key concept is similar to how neurotransmitters bind to receptor sites (see Chapter 3). When olfactory receptors come into contact with odor molecules, action potentials in olfactory neurons are triggered.

We detect taste with **taste buds** on our tongues. Bumps on the tongue called *papillae* contain numerous taste buds (**FIGURE 4.32**). There are separate taste buds for sweet, salty, sour, bitter, and umami (Chandrashekar et al., 2006).

It's a myth, however, that a "tongue taste map" describes the tongue's sensitivity to different flavors, even though some books still contain this map (see **FIGURE 4.33**). In reality, there's only a weak tendency for individual taste receptors to concentrate at certain locations on the tongue, and any location on the tongue is at least slightly sensitive to all tastes. Try this

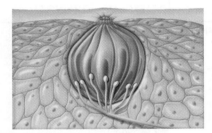

FIGURE 4.32　How We Detect Taste. The tongue contains many taste buds, which transmit information to the brain as shown in this close-up.

like phrenology!

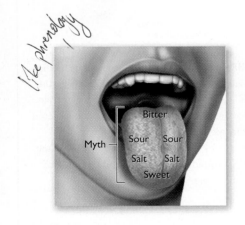

FIGURE 4.33　The "Tongue Taste Map" Myth. Although diagrams of the tongue, like this one, appear in many popular sources, they're more fiction than fact.

olfaction
our sense of smell

gustation
our sense of taste

taste bud
sense receptor in the tongue that responds to sweet, salty, sour, bitter, umami, and perhaps fat

exercise: Place a bit of salt on the tip of your tongue. Can you taste it? Now try placing a small amount of sugar on the back of your tongue. Chances are good you'll taste both the salt and the sugar, even though you placed them outside the mythical "tongue" taste map. That's because receptors that detect sweet tastes are often located on the tip of the tongue and receptors that detect salt are often on the sides, but there's a good mix of receptors everywhere on the tongue.

Umami taste receptors were controversial until physiological studies replicated earlier results and showed that these receptors were present on taste buds (Chandrashekar et al., 2006). That was nearly a century after 1908, when Kikunae Ikeda isolated the molecules responsible for the savory flavor found in many Japanese foods, such as broth or dried seaweed (Yamaguchi & Ninomiya, 2000). These molecules producing a savory or meaty flavor all had one thing in common: They contained a lot of the neurotransmitter glutamate (see Chapter 3). Monosodium glutamate (MSG), a derivative of glutamate, is a well-known flavor enhancer (the commercial flavor enhancer *Accent* consists almost entirely of MSG). Today, most scientists consider umami the fifth taste.

replicability

CAN THE RESULTS BE DUPLICATED IN OTHER STUDIES?

A similar controversy swirls around taste receptors for fat. It's clear that fat does something to our tongues. Richard Mattes (2005) and his associates found that merely putting fat on people's tongues alters their blood levels of fat. This means that as soon as fat enters our mouths it starts to affect our bodies' metabolism of fat. At first, researchers thought the responses were triggered by an olfactory receptor for fat. This hypothesis was ruled out when they showed that smelling fat didn't alter blood levels of fat; the fat had to make contact with the tongue.

ruling out rival hypotheses

HAVE IMPORTANT ALTERNATIVE EXPLANATIONS FOR THE FINDINGS BEEN EXCLUDED?

With only five or six taste receptors, why do we taste so many flavors? The secret lies in the fact that our taste perception is biased strongly by our sense of smell, which explains why we find food much less tasty when our noses are stuffed from a cold. Far more than we realize, we find certain foods "delicious" because of their smell. If you're not persuaded, try this exercise. Buy some multiflavored jelly beans, open the bag, and close your eyes so you can't see which color you're picking. Then pinch your nose with one hand and pop a jelly bean into your mouth. At first you won't be able to identify the flavor. Then gradually release your fingers from your nose and you'll be able to perceive the jelly bean's taste.

Our tongues differ in their number of taste receptors. Linda Bartoshuk (2004) calls those of us with a marked overabundance of taste buds—about 25 percent of people—"supertasters." If you find broccoli and coffee to be unbearably bitter, and sugary foods to be unbearably sweet, the odds are high you're a supertaster. At age 10, supertasters are most likely to be in the lowest 10 percent of height, probably a result of their sensitivity to bitter tastes and their fussy eating habits (Golding et al., 2009). Supertasters, who are overrepresented among women and people of African or Asian descent, are also especially sensitive to oral pain, and tend to avoid bitter tastes as a result. They also tend to avoid bitter tastes in alcohol and smoking tobacco, which may make them healthier than the rest of us (Bartoshuk, 2004).

■ Olfactory and Gustatory Perception

Our perceptions of smell and taste are often remarkably sensitive, and more informative than we consciously realize, although we're often not especially good at identifying odors by name. Babies can identify their mothers' odor and siblings can recognize each other on the basis of odor. Research suggests that women can even tell whether people just watched a happy or a sad movie from samples of their armpit odor (Wysocki & Preti, 2004). Should we perhaps call sad movies sweat-jerkers rather than tear-jerkers?

How do odors and tastes excite our receptors for smell and taste? After odors interact with sense receptors in the nasal passages, the resulting information enters the brain, reaching the olfactory cortex and parts of the limbic system (see **FIGURE 4.34** on page 154). Similarly, after taste information interacts with taste buds, it enters the brain, reaching a taste-related area called gustatory cortex, somatosensory cortex (because food also has texture), and parts of the limbic system. A region of the frontal cortex (see Chapter 3) is a site of convergence for smell and taste (Rolls, 2004).

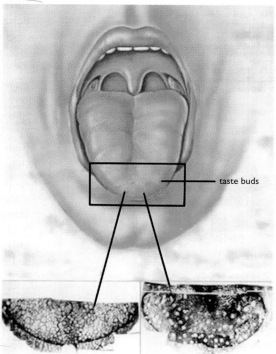

taste buds

? The two photographs above show the tongues of two people, one a supertaster and one a non-supertaster. The small circles on each tongue are taste buds. Which tongue belongs to a supertaster and why? (See answer upside down on bottom of page.)

Answer: The tongue on the left, because supertasters have more taste buds on their tongues than do other people.

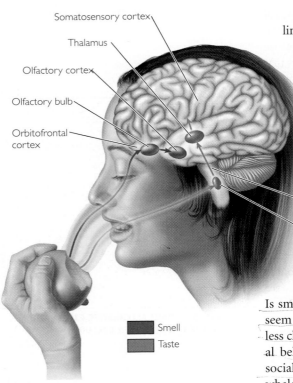

Smell

Taste

FIGURE 4.34   **Smell and Taste.** Our senses of smell and taste enter the brain by different routes but converge in the orbitofrontal cortex.

ruling out rival hypotheses

HAVE IMPORTANT ALTERNATIVE EXPLANATIONS FOR THE FINDINGS BEEN EXCLUDED?

Advocates of aromatherapy claim that essential oils derived from plants have special healing powers. Many claim that such oils can cure depression, anxiety disorders, insomnia, and other ailments. Although the pleasant smells of such plants can no doubt lift our moods a bit, there's little evidence that they possess magical curative power (McCutcheon, 1996).

pheromone
odorless chemical that serves as a social signal to members of one's species

somatosensory
our sense of touch, temperature, and pain

We analyze the intensity of smell and determine whether it's pleasing. Parts of the limbic system, such as the amygdala, help us to distinguish pleasant from disgusting smells (Anderson et al., 2003). Taste can also be pleasant or disgusting; "disgust," not surprisingly, means "bad taste" (see Chapter 11). Both tasting disgusting food and viewing facial expressions of disgust (see Chapter 11) activate the gustatory cortex (Wicker et al., 2003). Moreover, persons who suffer damage to the gustatory cortex don't experience disgust (Calder et al., 2000). These results underscore the powerful links among smell, taste, and emotion.

Emotional disorders, like anxiety and depression, can distort taste perception (Heath et al., 2006). Certain neurotransmitters, such as serotonin and norepinephrine—the same chemical messengers whose activity is enhanced by antidepressants (see Chapters 3 and 16)—make us more sensitive to tastes. Tom Heath and his colleagues (2006) found that antidepressant drugs rendered subjects more sensitive to various combinations of sweet, sour, and bitter tastes. Their research may shed light on appetite loss, which is a frequent symptom of depression.

Smell plays a particularly strong role in sexual behavior. Mice with a genetic defect in smell don't even bother to mate (Mandiyan, Coats, & Shah, 2005). Is smell central to human sexuality, too? Many perfume and cologne manufacturers sure seem to think so. Curiously, though, it may not be fragrant odors, but **pheromones**—odorless chemicals that serve as social signals to members of one's species—that alter our sexual behavior. There's evidence that rodents respond to pheromones during mating and social behavior (Biasi, Silvotti, & Tirindelli, 2001). So do most other mammals, including whales and horses (Fields, 2007). Most mammals use the *vomeronasal organ,* located in the bone between the nose and the mouth, to detect pheromones. The vomeronasal organ doesn't develop in humans (Witt & Wozniak, 2006), causing some to suggest that humans are insensitive to pheromones. An alternative hypothesis is that humans detect pheromones via a different route. This idea is supported by the discovery of human pheromones (Pearson, 2006). A nerve that's only recently received attention, called "nerve zero," may step in to enable pheromones to trigger responses in the "hot-button sex regions of the brain" (Fields, 2007).

Still, we should be cautious about shelling out sizable chunks of our salaries on pheromone-based products that promise to stir up romance. Scientific evidence suggests they probably won't work. Pheromones are large molecules, so although it's easy to transfer a pheromone from one person to another during a passionate kiss, sending them across a restaurant table is definitely a stretch. Moreover, there's far more to human romance than physical chemistry; psychological chemistry matters, too (see Chapter 11).

Smells other than pheromones may contribute to human sexual behavior. Remarkably, human sperm cells may contain smell receptors that help them to find their way to female eggs (Spehr et al., 2003). Sometimes truth *is* stranger than fiction.

Haha

■ When We Can't Smell or Taste

About two million Americans suffer from disorders of taste, smell, or both. Gradual loss of taste and smell can be a part of normal aging, as the number of taste buds, routinely replaced when we're younger, declines. But these losses can also result from diseases, such as diabetes and high blood pressure.

There are many disorders of olfaction (Hirsch, 2003). Although not as serious as blindness or deafness, they can pose several dangers, such as an inability to detect gas leaks and smell spoiled food before we eat it. Damage to the olfactory nerve, along with brain damage caused by such disorders as Parkinson's and Alzheimer's disease (see Chapter 3), can damage our sense of smell and ability to identify odors (Doty, Deems, & Stellar, 1988; Murphy, 1999; Wilson et al., 2007).

Losing our sense of taste can also produce negative health consequences. Cancer patients who lose their sense of taste have a worse prognosis than other patients, because they eat less and die sooner (Schiffman & Graham, 2000). This effect isn't due merely to a lack of nutrition. Adding flavor enhancers to the diet appreciably improves patients' health status. So taste may add an essential "zest" to life; a psychological flavoring that can help to ward off disease by boosting appetite.

✔• Study and Review on mypsychlab.com

assess your knowledge   FACT OR FICTION?

1. The most critical function of our chemical senses is to sample our food before we swallow it. **True / False**

2. Humans can detect only a small number of odors but thousands of tastes. **True / False**

3. There's good evidence for a "tongue taste map," with specific taste receptors located on specific parts of the tongue. **True / False**

4. The limbic system plays a key role in smell and taste perception. **True / False**

5. The vomeronasal organ helps to detect pheromones in many mammals but doesn't develop in humans. **True / False**

Answers: 1. T (p. 152); 2. F (p. 152); 3. F (p. 153); 4. T (p. 152); 5. T (p. 154)

Perfume manufacturers have long advertised fragrances as increasing attraction and romance. But at least in nonhuman animals, the chemicals that produce the most potent effects on sexual behaviors are actually odorless pheromones.

OUR BODY SENSES: TOUCH, BODY POSITION, AND BALANCE

4.10 Describe the three different body senses.

4.11 Explain how pain perception differs from touch perception.

4.12 Describe the field of psychology called human factors.

It was the summer of 1974 and all eyes were focused on daredevil Philippe Petit, who navigated ever so skillfully across a tightrope of steel cable that stretched from one of the Twin Towers of New York City's World Trade Center to the other. Each time he lowered his foot onto the cable he relied on his sense of touch. Each time he moved forward he relied on his senses of body position and balance. One miscalculation and he would have plummeted nearly a quarter of a mile to the ground.

Fortunately for Petit, he, like the rest of us, has three body senses that work in tandem. The system we use for touch and pain is the **somatosensory** (*somato-*, for "body") system. We also have a body position sense, called *proprioception*, or *kinesthetic* sense, and a sense of equilibrium or balance, called the *vestibular sense*.

Bystanders looked on as tightrope artist Philippe Petit made his way across the chasm between the Twin Towers of the World Trade Center on August 7, 1974.

■ The Somatosensory System: Touch and Pain

The stimuli that activate the somatosensory system come in a variety of types. In this respect, this sense differs from vision and audition, each of which is devoted mainly to a single stimulus type.

PRESSURE, TEMPERATURE, AND INJURY. Our somatosensory system responds to stimuli applied to the skin, such as light touch or deep pressure, hot or cold temperature, or chemical or mechanical (touch-related) injury that produces pain. Somatosensory stimuli can be very specific, such as the embossed patterns of a letter written in Braille, or generalized to a large area of the body. Damage to internal organs sometimes causes "referred pain"—pain in a different location—such as an ache felt throughout the left arm and shoulder during a heart attack.

SPECIALIZED AND FREE NERVE ENDINGS IN THE SKIN. We sense light touch and deep pressure with *mechanoreceptors*, specialized nerve endings located on the ends of sensory nerves in the skin (see **FIGURE 4.35** on page 156). One example is the Pacinian corpuscle named after anatomist Filippo Pacini, who discovered them in 1831. Other specialized nerve endings are sensitive to temperature (refer again to Figure 4.35).

We sense touch, temperature, and especially pain with *free nerve endings*, which are far more plentiful than specialized nerve endings (refer once more to Figure 4.35). Nerve endings of all types are distributed unevenly across our body surface. Most of them are in

FICTOID   ✖

MYTH: Consuming ice cream or other cold substances too quickly causes pain in our brains.

REALITY: "Brain freeze," as it's sometimes called, doesn't affect the brain at all. It's produced by a constriction of blood vessels in the roof of our mouths in response to intense cold temperatures, followed by an expansion of these blood vessels, producing pain.

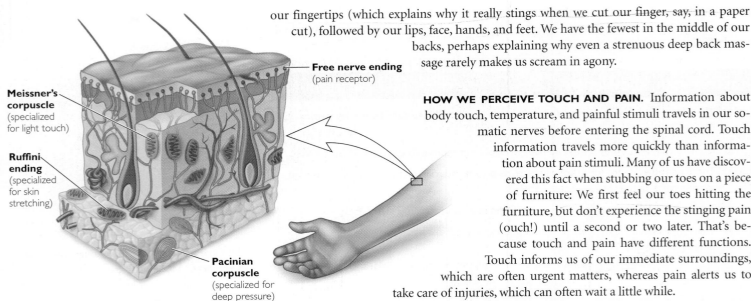

Meissner's
corpuscle
(specialized
for light touch)

Ruffini
ending
(specialized
for skin
stretching)

Free nerve ending
(pain receptor)

Pacinian
corpuscle
(specialized for
deep pressure)

FIGURE 4.35   The Sense of Touch. The skin contains many specialized and free nerve endings that detect mechanical pressure, temperature, and pain.

our fingertips (which explains why it really stings when we cut our finger, say, in a paper cut), followed by our lips, face, hands, and feet. We have the fewest in the middle of our backs, perhaps explaining why even a strenuous deep back massage rarely makes us scream in agony.

HOW WE PERCEIVE TOUCH AND PAIN. Information about body touch, temperature, and painful stimuli travels in our somatic nerves before entering the spinal cord. Touch information travels more quickly than information about pain stimuli. Many of us have discovered this fact when stubbing our toes on a piece of furniture: We first feel our toes hitting the furniture, but don't experience the stinging pain (ouch!) until a second or two later. That's because touch and pain have different functions. Touch informs us of our immediate surroundings, which are often urgent matters, whereas pain alerts us to take care of injuries, which can often wait a little while.

Often touch and pain information activate local spinal reflexes (see Chapter 3) before traveling to brain sites dedicated to perception. In some cases, painful stimuli trigger the *withdrawal reflex*. When we touch a fire or hot stove, we pull away immediately to avoid getting burned.

After activating spinal reflexes, touch and pain information travels upward through parts of the brain stem and thalamus to reach the somatosensory cortex (Bushnell et al., 1999). Additional cortical areas are active during the localization of touch information, such as association areas of the parietal lobe.

As we've all discovered, pain comes in many varieties: sharp, stabbing, throbbing, burning, and aching. Many of the types of pain perception relate to the pain-causing stimulus—thermal (heat-related), chemical, or mechanical. Pain can also be acute, that is, short-lived, or chronic, that is, enduring, perhaps even lasting years. Each kind of pain-producing stimulus has a *threshold*, or point at which we perceive it as painful. People differ in their pain thresholds. Surprisingly, one study showed that people with naturally red hair require more anesthetic than do people with other hair colors (Liem et al., 2004). Of course, this correlational finding doesn't mean that red hair causes lower pain thresholds. Instead, some of the differences in people's thresholds are probably due to genetic factors that happen to be associated with hair color.

We can't localize pain as precisely as touch. Moreover, pain has a large emotional component. That's because pain information goes partly to the somatosensory cortex and partly to limbic centers in the brain stem and forebrain. The experience of pain is frequently associated with anxiety, uncertainty, and helplessness. Scientists believe we can control pain in part by controlling our thoughts and emotions in reaction to painful stimuli (Moore, 2008). This belief has been bolstered by stories of people withstanding excruciating pain during combat, natural childbirth, or right-of-passage ceremonies.

According to the **gate control model** of Ronald Melzack and Patrick Wall (1965, 1970), pain under these circumstances is blocked from consciousness because neural mechanisms in the spinal cord function as a "gate," controlling the flow of sensory input to the central nervous system. The gate-control model can account for how pain varies from situation to situation depending on our psychological state. Most of us have experienced becoming so absorbed in an event, such as an interesting conversation or television program, that we "forgot" the pain we were feeling from a headache or a trip to the dentist's office. The gate control model proposes that the stimulation we experience competes with and blocks the pain from consciousness. Because pain demands attention, distraction is an effective way of short-circuiting painful sensations (Eccleston & Crombez, 1999; McCaul & Malott, 1984). Scientists discovered that they could relieve the pain of burn patients undergoing physical therapy, wound care, and painful skin grafts by immersing them in a virtual environment populated by snowmen and igloos (Hoffman & Patterson, 2005). Researchers used the fact

correlation vs. causation

CAN WE BE SURE THAT A CAUSES B?

gate control model
idea that pain is blocked or gated from consciousness by neural mechanisms in spinal cord

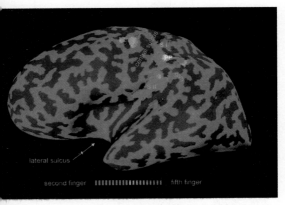

lateral sulcus

second finger ||||||||||||||| fifth finger

Touch to our fingers, in this case the second and fifth digits, activates many cortical areas, as shown in this fMRI scan. (*Source:* Ruben et al., 2001)

that vision and somatic (body) sense interact to demonstrate that subjects can reduce pain sensations by simply looking at their left hand, or at a reflected image of their hand in a mirror (Longo et al., 2009). These effects were absent when subjects looked at another person's hand or an object. On the flip side, dwelling on catastrophic thoughts and expectations about pain (such as "I won't be able to bear it") can open the floodgates of distress.

What's the evidence for the involvement of the spinal cord in the gate control model? Patrick Wall (2000) showed that the brain controls activity in the spinal cord, enabling us to turn up, damp down, or in some cases ignore pain. As we learned in Chapter 3, the placebo effect exerts a strong response on subjective reports of pain. Falk Eippert and his colleagues (Eippert et al., 2009) used brain imaging to demonstrate that pain-related activity in the spinal cord is sharply reduced when subjects receive an application of a placebo cream they're told would alleviate pain. Placebos may also stimulate the body's production of its natural painkillers: endorphins (see Chapter 3; Glasser & Frishman, 2008). Scientists are investigating ways of boosting endorphins while deactivating glial cells (see Chapter 3) in the spinal cord that amplify pain (Bartley, 2009; Watkins & Maier, 2002).

For many years the scientific consensus has been that we can ignore pain, or at least withstand it, with a stoic mind-set (Szasz, 1989). There's evidence that people of certain cultural backgrounds, such as American Indians, Cambodians, Chinese, and Germans, are more reserved and less likely to communicate openly about pain, whereas South and Central Americans consider it more acceptable to moan and cry out when in pain (Ondeck, 2003). Although these descriptions of average behavior may help physicians deal with diverse populations, the premise that pain perception varies with ethnicity isn't universally accepted. An alternative hypothesis is that health care professionals treat certain ethnic groups differently. Blacks and Hispanics are less likely than Caucasians to receive analgesic (anti-pain) medication during emergency room visits (Bonham, 2001), which could account for some of the differences in reports of pain.

Are there any unusual activities for which a stoic mind-set may come in handy? Some popular psychology gurus certainly think so. Firewalkers, popular in India, Japan, North Africa, and the Polynesian islands, have walked 20- to 40-foot-long beds of burning embers. Although the practice has been around since as early as 1200 B.C., there's recently been a glut of "Firewalking Seminars" in California, New York, and other states. These motivational classes promise ordinary people everything from heightened self-confidence to spiritual enlightenment—all by walking down an 8- to 12-foot-long path of burning embers. Contrary to what we might learn at these seminars, success in firewalking has nothing to do with pain sensitivity and everything to do with physics. The type of coal or wood used in firewalking has a low rate of heat exchange, such that it burns red hot in the center while remaining less hot on the outside (Kurtus, 2000). So any of us can firewalk successfully just so long as we walk (or even better, run) over the burning embers quickly enough. Still, accidents can occur if the fire isn't prepared properly or if the firewalker walks too slowly.

PHANTOM LIMB ILLUSION. Persons with amputated limbs often experience the eerie phenomenon of **phantom pain**, pain or discomfort in the missing limb. About 50 to 80 percent of amputees experience phantom limb sensations (Sherman, Sherman, & Parker 1984). The missing limb often feels as if it's in an uncomfortably distorted position.

Vilayanur Ramachandran and colleagues developed a creative treatment for phantom limb pain called the mirror box (Ramachandran & Rogers-Ramachandran, 1996). Phantom limb patients position their other limb so that it's reflected in exactly the position that the amputated limb would assume. Then the patient performs the "mirror equivalent" of the exercise the amputated limb needs to relieve a cramp or otherwise get comfortable. For the mirror box to relieve pain or discomfort in the amputated limb, the illusion must be realistic. Some subjects report pain relief the first time the illusion works, but not thereafter. In many cases, the mirror box causes the phantom limb pain to disappear permanently (Ramachandran & Altschuler, 2009).

PAIN INSENSITIVITY. Just as some people are blind or deaf, others experience disorders that impair their ability to sense pain. Although pain isn't fun, research on pain insensitivity shows that pain serves an essential function. Pain insensitivity present from birth is an extremely rare condition that is sometimes inherited (Victor & Ropper, 2001). Children with

Why do you think the designers of this virtual world chose imagery of snowmen and igloos for burn patients? What imagery would you choose, and why? (*Source:* University of Washington Harborview/HIT Lab's Snow World, Image by Stephen Dagadakis)

> ruling out rival hypotheses

HAVE IMPORTANT ALTERNATIVE EXPLANATIONS FOR THE FINDINGS BEEN EXCLUDED?

The mirror box consists of a two-chamber box with a mirror in the center. When the subject looks at her right hand in the box, it creates the illusion that the mirror image of her right hand is her left hand. This box can sometimes alleviate the discomfort of phantom limb pain by positioning the intact limb as the phantom limb appears to be positioned, and then moving it to a more comfortable position. (*Source:* Ramachandran & Rogers-Ramachandran, 1996)

phantom pain
pain or discomfort felt in an amputated limb

Ashlyn Blocker has congenital insensitivity to pain with anhidrosis. *Congenital* means "present at birth," and *anhidrosis* means "inability to sweat." CIPA is a rare disorder that renders people unable to detect pain or temperature; those affected also can't regulate body temperature well because of an inability to sweat. Her parents and teachers need to monitor her constantly because she's prone to eating scalding hot food without the slightest hesitation. She may badly injure herself on the playground and continue to play.

inherited pain insensitivity usually have a normal ability to discriminate touch, although not necessarily temperature. For the most part, they're completely unable to detect painful stimuli. In some cases, they chew off parts of their bodies, like their fingertips or the ends of their tongues, or suffer bone fractures without realizing it. Needless to say, this condition can be exceedingly dangerous. Other individuals show an indifference to painful stimuli: They can identify the type of pain, but experience no significant discomfort from it.

■ Proprioception and Vestibular Sense: Body Position and Balance

Right at this moment you're probably sitting somewhere. You may not be thinking about body control or keeping your head and shoulders up, because your brain is kindly taking care of all that for you. If you decided to stand up and grab a snack, you'd need to maintain posture and balance, as well as navigate bodily motion. **Proprioception**, also called our kinesthetic sense, helps us keep track of where we are and move efficiently. The **vestibular sense**, also called our sense of equilibrium, enables us to sense and maintain our balance as we move about. Our senses of body position and balance work together.

PROPRIOCEPTORS: TELLING THE INSIDE STORY. We use *proprioceptors* to sense muscle stretch and force. From these two sources of information we can tell what our bodies are doing, even with our eyes closed. There are two kinds of proprioceptors: stretch receptors embedded in our muscles, and force detectors embedded in our muscle tendons. Proprio-

---

proprioception
our sense of body position

vestibular sense
our sense of equilibrium or balance

semicircular canals
three fluid-filled canals in the inner ear responsible for our sense of balance

---

ruling out rival hypotheses

HAVE IMPORTANT ALTERNATIVE EXPLANATIONS FOR THE FINDINGS BEEN EXCLUDED?

psychomythology

PSYCHIC HEALING OF CHRONIC PAIN

Many people believe in the power of mind over pain, but some individuals claim to possess supernatural abilities or "gifts" that enable them to reduce others' pain. Is this fact or fiction? In the summer of 2003, the Australian television show *A Current Affair* approached psychologists at the University of Bond to conduct a double-blind, randomized, controlled test of psychic healing powers.

Using a newspaper advertisement, the researchers located volunteers suffering from pain caused by cancer, chronic back conditions, and fibromyalgia (a chronic condition of muscle, joint, and bone pain and fatigue) (Lyvers, Barling, & Harding-Clark, 2006). The researchers assigned half of the chronic pain subjects to a group that received psychic healing and the other half to a control condition that didn't. Neither the subjects nor those interacting with them knew who was assigned to which group. In the healing condition, the psychic healer viewed and touched photographs of the chronic pain subjects in another room. The healer was given all the time deemed necessary.

The researchers used the McGill Pain Questionnaire (Melzack, 1975) to test chronic pain subjects' level of discomfort before and after the trial. Then, researchers compared their before and after scores. On average the scores showed no change before and after treatment, with half the subjects reporting more pain and half reporting less pain regardless of whether psychic healing occurred.

These results agreed with earlier results obtained by British researchers on spiritual healing (Abbot et al., 2001). In a study of 120 chronic pain sufferers, they similarly used the McGill Pain Questionnaire. These researchers compared pain reports before and after face-to-face versus distant spiritual healing compared with no spiritual healing. The results suggested that despite the popularity of spiritual healing in England, this method lacks scientific support. A different research team, however, reported an improvement in neck pain following spiritual healing (Gerard, Amith, & Simpson, 2003). But because their study lacked a placebo treatment or blinding of the therapist, these authors couldn't rule out a placebo effect (see Chapter 2).

Lyvers and colleagues (2006) addressed the placebo effect with a double-blind design, and rated their chronic pain subjects on a five-point scale that assessed the degree to which subjects believed in psychic phenomena. They found no correlation between psychic healing and decreased pain; however, they found that decreases in reported pain correlated with increased belief in psychic phenomena. So beliefs in the paranormal may create reality, at least psychological reality.

ceptive information enters the spinal cord and travels upward through the brain stem and thalamus to reach the somatosensory and motor cortexes (Naito, 2004). There, our brains combine information from our muscles and tendons, along with a sense of our intentions, to obtain a perception of our body's location (Proske, 2006).

THE VESTIBULAR SENSE: A BALANCING ACT. In addition to the cochlea, the inner ear contains three **semicircular canals** (see **FIGURE 4.36**). These canals, which are filled with fluid, sense equilibrium and help us maintain our balance. Vestibular information reaches parts of the brain stem that control eye muscles and triggers reflexes that coordinate eye and head movements (Highstein, Fay, & Popper, 2004). Vestibular information also travels to the cerebellum, which controls bodily responses that enable us to catch our balance when we're falling.

The vestibular sense isn't heavily represented in our cerebral cortex, so our awareness of this sense is limited. We typically become aware of this sense only when we lose our sense of balance or experience dramatic mismatches between our vestibular and visual inputs, which occur when our vestibular system and our eyes tell us different things. We commonly experience dizziness and nausea following these mismatches, such as when we're moving quickly in a car while not looking outside at the road whizzing past us.

■ Ergonomics: Human Engineering

How do our bodies interact with new technologies? A field of psychology called *human factors* optimizes technology to better suit our sensory and perceptual capabilities. We can use what we know about human psychology and sensory systems—ranging from our body position sense to vision—to build more *ergonomic,* or worker-friendly, gadgets and tools of the trade.

As Donald Norman (1998) pointed out, many everyday objects are designed without the perceptual experiences of users in mind. As a result, they can be extremely difficult to figure out how to operate. Have you ever tried to repeatedly push open a door that needed to be pulled open, or spent several minutes trying to figure out how to turn on a shower in an apartment or hotel room? Poor design kept the United States in limbo for five weeks following the 2000 presidential election between George W. Bush and Al Gore, when a bewildering election ballot in some Florida counties left state officials unable to figure out which candidate voters picked.

Fortunately, human factors psychologists have applied their extensive knowledge of sensation and perception to improve the design of many everyday devices. To take just one example, many people hold jobs that require them to sit at a computer terminal most of the day. This means that a new design for a computer screen, keyboard, or mouse that enables them to better reach for their computers or see their screens can increase their efficiency. Human factors psychologists design not only computer components, but devices that assist surgeons in performing delicate operations, workstations to improve comfort and decrease injuries on the job, and control panels on aircraft carriers, to make them safer and easier to use. The psychology of human factors reminds us that much of what we know about sensation and perception has useful applications to many domains of everyday life.

✓●─ **Study** and **Review** on **mypsychlab.com**

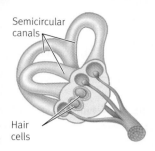

FIGURE 4.36 **How We Sense Motion.** The semicircular canals of the inner ear detect movement and gravity.

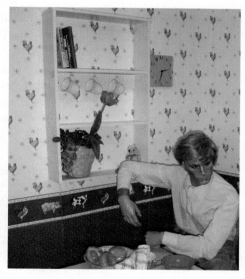

This room is designed to rotate around subjects seated at the table. Illusory movement and scene distortions often result. *(Source: Palmisano et al., 2006)*

? Psychologist Donald Norman, posing in his office behind a teapot. Can you figure out what makes this teapot design a poor one? (See answer upside down on bottom of page.)

assess your knowledge	FACT OR FICTION?

1. Pain information travels more quickly to the spinal cord than does touch information. **True / False**

2. Pain thresholds vary depending on the person and type of pain (stabbing, burning, or aching, for example). **True / False**

3. Firewalking requires both an insensitivity to pain and extremely high levels of motivation. **True / False**

4. Proprioception enables us to coordinate our movements without having to look at our bodies. **True / False**

5. The inner ear plays a key role in our ability to keep our balance. **True / False**

Answers: 1. F (p. 156); 2. T (p. 156); 3. F (p. 157); 4. T (p. 158); 5. T (p. 159)

TWO SIDES OF THE COIN: SENSATION AND PERCEPTION 124–135

4.1 IDENTIFY THE BASIC PRINCIPLES THAT APPLY TO ALL SENSES.

Transduction is the process of converting an external energy, such as light or sound vibration, into electrical activity within neurons. The doctrine of specific nerve energies refers to how each of the sensory modalities (vision, hearing, touch, and so on) is handled by specific regions of the brain, especially specific regions of the cerebral cortex (visual cortex, auditory cortex, and so on). Even though most connections in the brain are faithful to one sense modality, brain regions often respond to information from a different sense. For example, what we see affects what we hear when watching video with sound.

1. The process of converting external stimulus energy into neural activity is called _____. (p. 125)

2. A _____ _____ is a specialized cell that transduces a specific stimulus. (p. 125)

3. The _____ _____ is the lowest level of a stimulus needed for the nervous system to detect a change 50 percent of the time. (p. 125)

4. The _____ _____ _____ tells us how easily we can detect changes in stimulus intensity. (p. 125)

5. Sir Francis Galton (1880) was the first to describe _____, a condition in which people experience cross-modal sensations, like hearing sounds when they see colors—sometimes called "colored hearing"—or even tasting colors. (p. 127)

4.2 TRACK HOW OUR MINDS BUILD UP PERCEPTIONS.

Information travels from primary sensory to secondary sensory cortex and then on to association cortex. Along the way, perception becomes increasingly complex. We also process many different inputs simultaneously, a phenomenon called parallel processing. All of the processing comes together to generate an integrated perceptual experience, a process referred to as binding.

6. In (top-down/bottom-up) processing, we construct a whole stimulus from its parts. (p. 127)

7. Name the processing model taking place when you look at this image with a caption of "woman" versus a caption of "saxophone player." (p. 127)

8. The process by which we perceive stimuli consistently across varied conditions is _____ _____. (p. 128)

9. What does the cocktail party effect tell us about our ability to monitor stimuli outside of our immediate attention? (p. 129)

4.3 ANALYZE THE SCIENTIFIC SUPPORT FOR AND AGAINST ESP.

Most people accept the existence of ESP without the need for scientific evidence, in part because they greatly underestimate how likely it is that a coincidence, like two people at a gathering sharing a birthday, occurs by chance.

10. Research suggests that the extraordinary claim of ESP (is/isn't) matched by equally extraordinary evidence. (p. 134)

SEEING: THE VISUAL SYSTEM 135–148

4.4 EXPLAIN HOW THE EYE STARTS THE VISUAL PROCESS.

The lens in the eye accommodates to focus on images both near and far by changing from "fat" to "flat." The lens optimally focuses light on the retina, which lies at the rear of the eye. The retina contains rods and cones filled with pigments. Additional cells in the retina transmit information about light to ganglion cells, and the axons of these cells combine to form the optic nerve.

11. The _____ spectrum refers to the range of wavelengths of light that humans can see. (p. 136)

12. The intensity of reflected light that reaches our eyes is called _____. (p. 136)

13. Consisting of cells that are completely transparent, the _____ changes its curvature to keep images in focus. (p. 137)

14. We can think of the _____ as a "movie screen" onto which light from the world is projected. (p. 138)

15. _____ are receptor cells that allow us to see in low light, and _____ are receptor cells that allow us to see in color. (p. 138)

16. Identify each eye component and its function. (p. 137)

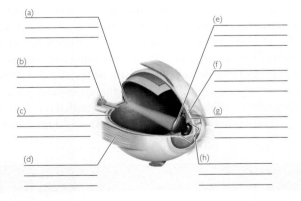

4.5 IDENTIFY THE DIFFERENT KINDS OF VISUAL PERCEPTION.

Our visual system is sensitive to shape, color, and motion. We use different parts of the visual cortex to process these different aspects of visual perception. Cells in the primary visual cortex, called V1, are sensitive to lines of a particular orientation, like a horizontal line or a vertical line. Color perception involves a mixture of trichromatic and opponent processing. Our visual system detects motion by comparing individual "still frames" of visual content.

17. Apply what you have learned about the Gestalt principles of visual perception by identifying each rule as shown. (p. 141)

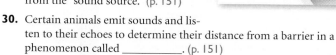

18. The idea that color vision is based on our sensitivity to three different colors is called the _____ theory. (p. 142)

19. Our ability to see spatial relations in three dimensions is called _____ _____. (p. 144)

4.6 DESCRIBE DIFFERENT VISUAL PROBLEMS.

Blindness is a worldwide problem, especially in underdeveloped countries. There are several types of color blindness; red-green color blindness is the most common type, and it affects mostly males. People with motion blindness can't seamlessly string still images into the perception of ongoing motion. The phenomenon of blindsight demonstrates that even some blind people can make decent guesses about the location of objects in their environments.

20. A person with _____ _____ can tell us the shape and color of an object, but can't recognize or name it. (p. 147)

HEARING: THE AUDITORY SYSTEM 148–151

4.7 EXPLAIN HOW THE EAR STARTS THE AUDITORY PROCESS.

Sound waves created by vibration of air molecules are funneled into the outer ear. These vibrations perturb the eardrum, causing the three small bones in the middle ear to vibrate. This process creates pressure in the cochlea, which contains the basilar membrane and organ of Corti, in which hair cells are embedded. The hair cells then bend, thereby exciting them. The message is relayed through the auditory nerve.

21. _____ refers to the frequency of the sound wave, and is measured in hertz (Hz). (p. 148)

22. The height of the sound wave corresponds to _____ and is measured in decibels (dB). (p. 149)

23. We refer to _____ to describe the complexity or quality of a sound. (p. 149)

24. The _____ lies in the inner ear and converts vibration into neural activity. (p. 149)

25. The organ of Corti and basilar membrane are especially critical to hearing because _____ _____ are embedded within them. (p. 149)

26. Identify both the component and its function in the hearing process. (p. 150)

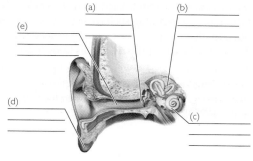

4.8 IDENTIFY THE DIFFERENT KINDS OF AUDITORY PERCEPTION.

We accomplish pitch perception in three ways. Place theory is pitch perception based on where along the basilar membrane hair cells are maximally excited. Frequency theory is based on hair cells reproducing the frequency of the pitch in their firing rates. In volley theory, groups of neurons stagger their responses to follow a pitch. We also perceive where a sound is coming from, a phenomenon called "sound localization."

27. The perception of high-pitched tones by the basilar membrane can be explained by the _____ theory. (p. 150)

Sound source

28. We use various brain centers to _____ sounds with respect to our bodies. (p. 150)

29. Map out, showing direction lines and steps, how we locate sound starting from the "sound source." (p. 151)

30. Certain animals emit sounds and listen to their echoes to determine their distance from a barrier in a phenomenon called _____. (p. 151)

SMELL AND TASTE: THE SENSUAL SENSES 152–155

4.9 IDENTIFY HOW WE SENSE AND PERCEIVE ODORS AND TASTES.

Gustation (taste) and olfaction (smell) are chemical senses because our sense receptors interact with molecules containing flavor and odor. The tongue contains taste receptors for sweet, sour, bitter, salty, umami (a "meaty" or "savory" flavor), and perhaps fat. Our ability to taste foods relies largely on smell. Olfactory receptors in our noses are sensitive to hundreds of different airborne molecules. We use our senses of taste and smell to sample our food. We react to extremely sour tastes, which may be due to food spoilage, with disgust. We also appear sensitive to pheromones, odorless molecules that can affect sexual responses.

31. Airborne chemicals that interact with receptors in the lining of our nasal passages are called _____. (p. 152)

32. We detect taste with _____ _____ that are on our tongue. (p. 152)

33. We're sensitive to _____ basic tastes, the last of which, _____, was recently discovered. (p. 152)

34. There is a (weak/strong) tendency for individual taste receptors to concentrate at certain locations on the tongue. (p. 152)

35. Our taste perception (is/isn't) dependent largely on our sense of smell. (p. 153)

36. A region of the _____ _____ is a site of convergence for smell and taste. (p. 153)

37. Label the brain components involved in the processes of smell and taste. (p. 154)

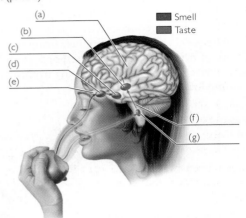

- (a)
- (b)
- (c)
- (d)
- (e)
- (f)
- (g)

■ Smell
■ Taste

38. Both tasting disgusting food and viewing facial expressions of disgust activate the _____ _____. (p. 154)

39. What chemicals do some perfume advertisers inaccurately claim are contained in their products which, when worn, allegedly trigger a physical response from others? (p. 154)

40. Researchers have showed that cancer patients who lose their sense of taste have a (better/worse) prognosis. (p. 154)

OUR BODY SENSES: TOUCH, BODY POSITION, AND BALANCE 155–159

4.10 DESCRIBE THE THREE DIFFERENT BODY SENSES.

We process information about touch to the skin, muscle activity, and acceleration. These are called "somatosensory" for body sensation, "proprioception" for muscle position sense, and "vestibular sense" for the sense of balance and equilibrium. The somatosensory system responds to light touch, deep pressure, hot and cold temperature, and tissue damage. Our muscles contain sense receptors that detect stretch and others that detect force. We calculate where our bodies are located from this information. We're typically unaware of our sense of equilibrium.

41. The body's system for touch and pain is the _____ system. (p. 155)

42. Our sense of body position is called _____. (p. 155)

43. The _____ _____, also called the sense of equilibrium, enables us to sense and maintain our balance. (p. 155)

4.11 EXPLAIN HOW PAIN PERCEPTION DIFFERS FROM TOUCH PERCEPTION.

The perception of pain differs from the perception of touch because there's a large emotional component to pain not present with touch. This is because pain information activates parts of the limbic system in addition to the somatosensory cortex. There's evidence that pain perception can be reduced by a "stoic" mind-set as well as cultural and genetic factors. Disorders of pain perception, called pain insensitivities, are associated with an increased risk of injury. As unpleasant as pain may be, it's essential to our survival.

44. We sense touch, temperature, and especially pain, with _____ _____ _____. (p. 155)

45. Our fingertips have the (least/most) nerve endings. (p. 156)

46. Explain the process by which humans detect physical pressure, temperature, and pain. (p. 156)

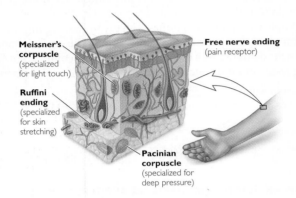

Meissner's corpuscle (specialized for light touch)

Free nerve ending (pain receptor)

Ruffini ending (specialized for skin stretching)

Pacinian corpuscle (specialized for deep pressure)

47. Touch information travels more (slowly/quickly) than pain stimuli information. (p. 156)

48. Information about body touch, temperature, and painful stimuli travels in the _____ nerves before entering the spinal cord. (p. 156)

49. Describe the "mirror box" treatment and identify its role in helping people who have lost limbs. (p. 157)

4.12 DESCRIBE THE FIELD OF PSYCHOLOGY CALLED HUMAN FACTORS.

Many everyday objects aren't designed optimally to capitalize on humans' sensory and perceptual capacities. The field of human factors starts with what psychologists have learned about sensation and perception, and then designs user-friendly devices, like computer keyboards and airplane cockpits, with this knowledge in mind.

50. Psychologists can use what we know about human psychology and sensory systems—ranging from our body position sense to vision—to build more _____, or worker-friendly, gadgets and tools of the trade. (p. 159)

- illusion (p. 124)
- sensation (p. 124)
- perception (p. 124)
- transduction (p. 125)
- sense receptor (p. 125)
- sensory adaptation (p. 125)
- psychophysics (p. 125)
- absolute threshold (p. 125)
- just noticeable difference (JND) (p. 125)
- Weber's Law (p. 125)
- signal detection theory (p. 126)
- synesthesia (p. 127)
- parallel processing (p. 127)
- bottom-up processing (p. 127)
- top-down processing (p. 127)

- perceptual set (p. 128)
- perceptual constancy (p. 128)
- selective attention (p. 129)
- inattentional blindness (p. 130)
- subliminal perception (p. 130)
- extrasensory perception (ESP) (p. 132)
- hue (p. 136)
- pupil (p. 136)
- cornea (p. 137)
- lens (p. 137)
- accommodation (p. 138)
- retina (p. 138)
- fovea (p. 138)
- acuity (p. 138)
- rods (p. 138)

- dark adaptation (p. 138)
- cones (p. 138)
- optic nerve (p. 138)
- blind spot (p. 139)
- feature detector cell (p. 140)
- trichromatic theory (p. 142)
- color blindness (p. 142)
- opponent process theory (p. 143)
- depth perception (p. 144)
- monocular depth cues (p. 144)
- binocular depth cues (p. 144)
- audition (p. 148)
- timbre (p. 149)
- cochlea (p. 149)

- organ of Corti (p. 149)
- basilar membrane (p. 149)
- place theory (p. 150)
- frequency theory (p. 150)
- olfaction (p. 152)
- gustation (p. 152)
- taste bud (p. 152)
- pheromone (p. 154)
- somatosensory (p. 155)
- gate control model (p. 156)
- phantom pain (p. 157)
- proprioception (p. 158)
- vestibular sense (p. 158)
- semicircular canals (p. 159)

APPLY YOUR SCIENTIFIC THINKING SKILLS

Use your scientific thinking skills to answer the following questions, referencing specific scientific thinking principles and common errors in reasoning whenever possible.

1. We can find scores of subliminal self-help tapes and mp3s advertised online despite the fact that studies show they are ineffective. Locate two examples of these products and examine their claims scientifically. Apart from the illusory placebo effect, what are other reasons that people who purchase these products might think they work?

2. Go online and locate psychic predictions for the *upcoming* year from at least two different sites. What common techniques do they employ (such as multiple end points)? Now try to find predictions for the *past* year. How many of them were accurate? And how might those who made the predictions try to explain why they didn't come true?

3. Research the claims that proponents of aromatherapy make about the health benefits of essential oils. What does scientific research tell us about these claims?

5 CONSCIOUSNESS
expanding the boundaries of psychological inquiry

Sleep paralysis = inability to move right after falling asleep or just after being woken up.

Consciousness = subjective experience of world and self, including ever-changing awareness of thoughts, emotions, sensations, events, and actions. *Wow, insanity!* *obviously not.*

ruling out rival hypotheses

**HAVE IMPORTANT ALTERNATIVE EXPLANATIONS
FOR THE FINDINGS BEEN EXCLUDED?**

Sleep paralysis has been reported in many
cultures, with the terrifying nighttime visitors
ranging from an "old hag" to demonlike entities,
as depicted in this painting, *The Nightmare*, by
Henry Fuseli.

sleep paralysis
state of being unable to move just after falling
asleep or right before waking up

consciousness
our subjective experience of the world, our
bodies, and our mental perspectives

Consider this fascinating story related by a subject in Susan Clancy's (2005) landmark research on people who come to believe they were kidnapped by aliens.

"I had this terrible nightmare—at least I think it was a nightmare. Something was on top of me. It wasn't human. It was pushing into me, I couldn't move, I couldn't scream, I was being suffocated. It was the worst dream I ever had. When I told my therapist about it she basically asked me if anything had happened to me as a kid . . . Well, for some reason, I started to have images of aliens pop into my head. Did you see that movie *Signs*—the one with Mel Gibson? The aliens looked more like those, not the more typical ones. I'd be walking to school and then—POP—an alien head would be in my head . . . Once I started thinking maybe I was abducted I couldn't stop. Finally I told my therapist about what was going on and she said she couldn't help me with this, but she referred me to a psychologist in Somerville, someone who worked with people who believed this. The first time, when he asked me why I was there I opened my mouth to talk but I started crying and I couldn't stop . . . He said that I shouldn't be afraid, that this was very common, that it was the first stage of coming to realize what happened to me, that in some people the memories only get partially erased and that those people can access them if they are willing to do the work, to undergo hypnosis and allow yourself to find out." (Clancy, 2005, pp. 30–31)

This person isn't alone. Nearly one-fifth of college students in one survey endorsed the belief that extraterrestrials (ETs) can actually visit us in dreams, and 10 percent claimed to have "experienced or met an extraterrestrial" (Kunzendorf et al., 2007–2008). But did they *really* encounter ETs, as Clancy's subjects claimed? Clancy and her Harvard University colleagues (Clancy et al., 2002; McNally & Clancy, 2005) say there's a slim chance at best. But they happened on a startling discovery that may explain the abduction reports.

Many of their subjects shared a history of **sleep paralysis**—a strange experience of being unable to move just after falling asleep or immediately upon awakening. This puzzling phenomenon is surprisingly common. One-third to one-half of college students have had at least one episode of sleep paralysis, which typically is no cause for concern (Fukuda et al., 1998). Sleep paralysis is caused by a disruption in the sleep cycle and is often associated with anxiety or even terror, feelings of vibrations, humming noises, and the eerie sense of menacing figures close to or on top of the immobile person. There are cultural differences in how people interpret this strange experience. In Thailand, people attribute it to a ghost, but in Newfoundland, people attribute it to an "old hag"—an elderly witch sitting on the person's chest. According to Susan Blackmore (2004), the "latest sleep paralysis myth may be alien abduction" (p. 315).

Unfortunately, the therapist that Clancy's subject consulted wasn't aware of sleep paralysis. Nor did he know that hypnosis isn't a trustworthy means of unearthing accurate memories. In fact, we'll soon learn that hypnosis can often help to create false memories. In many of the cases Clancy reported, it's not a big leap for people who suspect they were abducted to elaborate on their story during hypnosis and to imagine that aliens performed medical experiments on them. After all, that's what the media often lead people to believe happens when the aliens come calling. *This is ridiculous. Aliens? Really?*

Sleep paralysis is only one of many remarkable sleep-related experiences we'll encounter in this chapter, along with other fascinating examples of alterations in **consciousness**—our subjective experience of the world and ourselves. Consciousness encompasses our ever-changing awareness of thoughts, emotions, bodily sensations, events, and actions. Some biologists (Bray, 2009) argue that even single-celled organisms are conscious and capable of learning, knowledge, and a primitive form of awareness. Intriguing as such speculations are, we'll restrict our discussion to the nature and mysteries of human consciousness. Puzzling phenomena, such as out-of-body, near-death, and mystical experiences, once at the outermost fringes of scientific psychology, are now receiving increasing attention as leading-edge scientists strive to comprehend the intricate links between our brains and our perceptions of the world and ourselves (Cardeña, Lynn, & Krippner, 2000).

It's easy to see why many scientists describe sleep, hypnosis, and other phenomena we'll examine as radical departures from our ordinary state of consciousness. Yet our sleeping and waking experiences shade subtly into one another; for example, research shows that our waking thoughts are sometimes bizarre, fragmented, and laced with captivating images, much as sleep thoughts are (Klinger, 1990, 2000; Klinger & Cox, 1987/1988). Across a typical day, we experience many altered states in our stream of consciousness, ranging from subtle to profound (Banks, 2009; Neher, 1990). The spotlight of our awareness and level of alertness changes continually in response to external (sights, sounds) and internal (bodily processes) stimuli to meet the shifting demands of daily living. Honed by hundreds of thousands of years of natural selection, our fine-tuned mental apparatus is prepared to respond to virtually any situation or threat efficiently, seamlessly, and often unconsciously, allowing us to do many things, such as walking and talking, simultaneously (But please don't drive and text message at the same time!) (Kihlstrom, 2009; Kirsch & Lynn, 1998; Wegner, 2004).

In this chapter, we'll encounter numerous examples of how consciousness is sensitively attuned to changes in our brain chemistry, expectations and memories, and culture. We'll learn how scientists are taking advantage of sophisticated tools to measure neural events and our intensely personal experience of ourselves and the events that shape our lives (Paller, Voss, & Westerberg, 2009). We'll also examine how the unity of consciousness can break down in unusual ways, such as during sleepwalking, when we're unconscious yet move about as if awake, and déjà vu, when we feel as though we're reliving an event we've never experienced (Voss, Baym, & Paller, 2008). As in many cases in psychology (see Chapter 15), abnormalities in functioning can often shed light on normal functioning (Cooper, 2003; Harkness, 2007).

THE BIOLOGY OF SLEEP

5.1 Explain the role of the circadian rhythm and how our bodies react to a disruption in our biological clocks.

5.2 Identify the different stages of sleep and the neural activity and dreaming behaviors that occur in each.

5.3 Identify the features and causes of sleep disorders.

We spend as much as one-third or more of our lives in one specific state of consciousness. No, we don't mean zoning out during a boring lecture. We're referring to sleep. Although it's clear that sleep is of central importance to our health and daily functioning, psychologists still don't know for sure why we sleep. Some theories suggest that sleep plays a critical role in memory consolidation (see Chapter 6); others suggest that it's critical for the immune system (see Chapter 12), neural development, and neural connectivity more generally (see Chapter 3; Mignot, 2008; Siegel, 2009). Some evolutionary theorists have proposed that sleep contributes to our survival by conserving our energy, taking us out of circulation at times when we might be most vulnerable to unseen predators, and restoring our strength to fend them off (Siegel, 2005). There may be some truth to several or even all of these explanations.

■ The Circadian Rhythm: The Cycle of Everyday Life

Long before scientists began to probe the secrets of sleep in the laboratory, primitive hunters were keenly aware of daily cycles of sleep and wakefulness. **Circadian rhythm** is a fancy term ("circadian" is Latin for "about a day") for changes that occur on a roughly 24-hour basis in many of our biological processes, including hormone release, brain waves, body temperature, and drowsiness. Popularly known as the brain's **biological clock**, the meager 20,000 neurons located in the *suprachiasmatic nucleus* (SCN) in the hypothalamus (see Chapter 3) make us feel drowsy at different times of the day and night. Many of us have noticed that we feel like taking a nap at around three or four in the afternoon. Indeed, in many European and Latin American countries, a midafternoon nap (a "siesta" in Spanish) is part of the daily ritual. This sense of fatigue is triggered by our biological clocks. The urge to snooze comes over us at night as well because levels of the hormone *melatonin* (see Chapter 3), which triggers feelings of sleepiness, increase after dark. ((•⊢ **Listen**

circadian rhythm
cyclical changes that occur on a roughly 24-hour basis in many biological processes

biological clock
term for the suprachiasmatic nucleus (SCN) in the hypothalamus that's responsible for controlling our levels of alertness

((•⊢ **Listen** to the Brain Time audio file on **mypsychlab.com**

jet lag = disruption in Circadian rhythm.

When we travel east, we're especially likely to experience jet lag: losing time and the shorter days throw off our sleep and other routines more than heading in the opposite direction (Eastman et al., 2005).

If you've ever taken a long flight across several time zones, you'll be no stranger to *jet lag*, the result of a disruption of our body's circadian rhythms. Imagine traveling cross-country and "losing" three hours in the flight from California to Florida. When we wake up at eight the next morning, we probably won't feel rested because our bodies' clocks are set for five A.M., the time it would be in California. The more time zones we pass through, the longer it takes our bodies' clocks to reset.

Our biological clocks can also be disrupted when we work late shifts, which disturb sleep and increase the risk of injuries, fatal accidents, and health problems, including diabetes and heart disease (Åkerstedt et al., 2002; Kirkady, Levine, & Shephard, 2000). Scientists are in hot pursuit of drugs that target melatonin receptors in the brain to re-sync the biological clocks of travelers and shift workers (Rajaratanam et al., 2009). That's because melatonin plays a key role in regulating circadian rhythms.

How much sleep do we need? Most of us need about seven to 10 hours. Newborns are gluttons for sleep and need about 16 hours over the course of a day. At the other extreme are the lucky few—less than 1 percent of the population—who carry a mutation in a gene called DEC2 that allows them to get away with sleeping as little as six hours a night without "crashing" the next day (He et al., 2009). College students may need as many as nine hours of sleep a night, although most sleep no more than six hours (Maas, 1999), creating a powerful urge to nap the next day (Rock, 2004). One common misconception is that the elderly need less sleep than the rest of us, only six or seven hours a night. But in reality, they probably need just as much sleep, but they sleep more fitfully (Ohayon, 2002).

Ordinarily, there don't seem to be many negative consequences of losing one night's sleep other than feeling edgy, irritable, and unable to concentrate well the next day. Yet after a few nights of sleep deprivation, we feel more "out of it" and begin to accumulate a balance of "sleep debt." People deprived of multiple nights of sleep, or who cut back drastically on sleep, often experience depression, difficulties in learning new information and paying attention, and slowed reaction times (Cohen, et al., 2010; Gangswisch et al., 2010). After more than four days of severe sleep deprivation, we may even experience brief hallucinations, such as hearing voices or seeing things (Wolfe & Pruitt, 2003). Sleep deprivation is associated with a variety of adverse health outcomes: weight gain (we burn off a lot of calories just by sleeping); increased risk for high blood pressure, diabetes, and heart problems; and a less vigorous immune response to viral infections (Dement & Vaughan, 1999; Motivala & Irwin, 2007). Some researchers even believe that the massive increase in obesity in the United States over the past few decades (see Chapter 11) is due largely to Americans' chronic sleep deprivation (Hasler et al., 2004), although this claim is scientifically controversial.

■ Stages of Sleep

For much of human history, people believed there was something like a switch in our brains that turned consciousness on when we were awake and off when we snoozed. But one night in 1951, a discovery in Nathaniel Kleitman's sleep laboratory at the University of Chicago changed how we think about sleep and dreaming. Eugene Aserinsky, Kleitman's graduate student, monitored his son Armond's eye movements and brain waves while he slept. Aserinsky was astonished to observe that Armond's eyes danced periodically back and forth under his closed lids, like the eyes of the sleeping babies Aserinsky had seen on other occasions. Whenever the eye movements occurred, Armond's brain pulsed with electrical activity, as measured by an electroencephalogram (EEG; see Chapter 3), much as it did when Armond was awake (Aserinsky, 1996).

The fledgling scientist had the good sense to know that he was onto something of immense importance. The slumbering brain wasn't an inert tangle of neurons; rather, it was abuzz with activity, at least at various intervals. Aserinsky further suspected that Armond's eye movements reflected episodes of dreaming. Aserinsky and Kleitman (1953) confirmed this hunch when they awakened subjects while they were

Sleep deprivation in night-shift workers may have been responsible for the Three Mile Island nuclear reactor plant accident in Pennsylvania in 1979 (*top*) and the Exxon Valdez shipwreck (*bottom*) that caused a massive oil spill in Alaska in 1989 (Coren, 1996).

Rapid Eye Movement (REM) sleep / more vivid = dream more in that stage than non-REM stages of sleep

displaying **rapid eye movements** (REM). In almost all cases, they reported vivid dreams. In contrast, subjects were much less likely to report vivid dreams when researchers awakened them from **non-REM (NREM) sleep**, although later research showed that vivid dreams occasionally happened during NREM sleep, too.

In landmark research using all night-recording devices, Kleitman and William Dement (Dement & Kleitman, 1957) went on to discover that during sleep we repeatedly pass through five stages every night. Each cycle lasts about 90 minutes, and each stage of sleep is clearly distinguishable from awake states, as shown in **FIGURE 5.1**.

STAGE 1 SLEEP. Has someone ever nudged you to wake up, and you weren't even sure whether you were awake or asleep? Perhaps you even replied, "No, I wasn't really sleeping," but your friend insisted, "Yes, you were. You were starting to snore." If so, you were probably in stage 1 sleep. In this light stage of sleep, which lasts for five to 10 minutes, our brain activity powers down by 50 percent or more, producing *theta* waves, which occur four to seven times per second. These waves are slower than the *beta* waves of 13 or more times per second produced during active alert states, and the *alpha* waves of eight to 12 times per second when we're quiet and relaxed. As we drift off to deeper sleep, we become more relaxed, and we may experience *hypnagogic imagery*—scrambled, bizarre, and dreamlike images that flit in and out of consciousness. We may also experience sudden jerks (sometimes called myoclonic jerks) of our limbs as if being startled or falling. In this state of sleep, we're typically quite confused. Some scientists speculate that many reports of ghosts stem from hypnagogic imagery that sleepers misinterpret as human figures (Hines, 2003).

STAGE 2 SLEEP. In stage 2 sleep, our brain waves slow down even more. Sudden intense bursts of electrical activity called *sleep spindles* of about 12–14 cycles a second, and occasional sharply rising and falling waves known as *K-complexes*, first appear in the EEG (Aldrich, 1999). K-complexes appear only when we're asleep. As our brain activity decelerates, our heart rate slows, our body temperature decreases, our muscles relax even more, and our eye movements cease. We spend as much as 65 percent of our sleep in stage 2.

STAGES 3 AND 4 SLEEP. After about 10 to 30 minutes, light sleep gives way to much deeper slow-wave sleep, in which we can observe *delta waves,* which are as slow as one to two cycles a second, in the EEG. In stage 3, delta waves appear 20 to 50 percent of the time, and in stage 4, they appear more than half the time. To feel fully rested in the morning, we need to experience these deeper stages of sleep throughout the night. A common myth is that drinking alcohol is a good way to catch up on sleep. Not quite. Having several drinks before bed usually puts us to bed sooner, but it usually makes us feel more tired the next day, because alcohol suppresses delta sleep. Children are famously good sleepers because they spend as much as 40 percent of their sleep time in deep sleep, when they may appear "dead to the world" and are difficult to awaken. In contrast, adults spend only about one-quarter of their sleep "sleeping like a baby," in deep sleep.

STAGE 5: REM SLEEP. After 15 to 30 minutes, we return to stage 2 before our brains shift dramatically into high gear, with high frequency, low-amplitude waves resembling those of wakefulness. We've entered stage 5, known commonly as **REM sleep**.

Our hyped brain waves during REM sleep are accompanied by increased heart rate and blood pressure, as well as rapid and irregular breathing, a state that occupies about 20 to 25 percent of our night's sleep. After 10 to 20 minutes of REM sleep, the cycle starts up again, as we glide back to the early stages of sleep and then back into deeper sleep yet again.

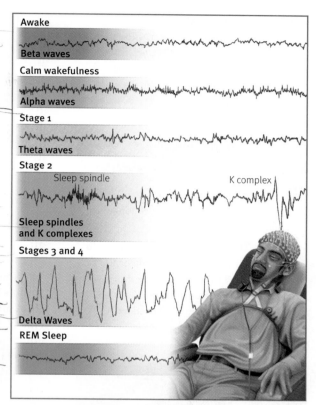

FIGURE 5.1 The Stages of Sleep. The EEG allows scientists to distinguish among the major stages of sleep, along with two levels of wakefulness. As we can see, brain activity during REM sleep is similar to that when we're awake and alert, because our brains during REM are typically engaged in vivid dreaming.

(Labels in figure: Awake; Beta waves; Calm wakefulness; Alpha waves; Stage 1; Theta waves; Stage 2; Sleep spindle; K complex; Sleep spindles and K complexes; Stages 3 and 4; Delta Waves; REM Sleep)

Electrical recording devices make it possible to study the relations among brain activity, eye movements, and physical relaxation.

rapid eye movement (REM)
darting of the eyes underneath closed eyelids during sleep

non-REM (NREM) sleep
stages 1 through 4 of the sleep cycle, during which rapid eye movements do not occur and dreaming is less frequent and vivid

REM sleep
stage of sleep during which the brain is most active and during which vivid dreaming most often occurs

FIGURE 5.2   Stages of Sleep in a Typical Night. The graph shows the typical progression through the night of stages 1–4 and REM sleep. Stages 1–4 are indicated on the y-axis, and REM stages are represented by the green curves on the graph. The REM periods occur about every 90 minutes throughout the night (Dement, 1974).

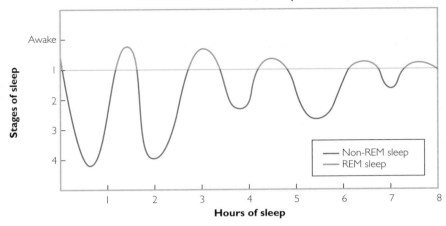

FICTOID ✕

MYTH: Dreams occur in only a few seconds, although they take much longer to recount later.

REALITY: This belief, held by Sigmund Freud and others, is wrong. In fact, our later REM periods toward the early morning typically last for half an hour or more. So if it seems like one of your dreams has lasted for 45 minutes, that's often because it has.

 Research demonstrates that REM and non-REM dreams tend to differ in content. Which dream image above is most likely to be a REM dream, and which is most likely to be a non-REM dream? (See answer upside down below.)

Answer: Photo on the top is more likely to be a non-REM dream; photo on the bottom is more likely to be a REM dream.

The amount of time spent in REM sleep increases with each cycle. By morning, we may spend as much as an hour in REM sleep compared with the 10 to 20 minutes we spend in REM after falling asleep. Each night, we circle back to REM sleep five or six times (see **FIGURE 5.2**).

We don't dream *only* during REM sleep, although we dream *more* in REM (Domhoff, 1996, 1999). Across many studies, 82 percent of REM periods are associated with dream reports compared with only 43 percent of non-REM periods (time spent in stages 1 through 4 sleep) (Nielsen, 1999). Many REM dreams are emotional, illogical, and prone to sudden shifts in "plot" (Foulkes, 1962; Hobson, Pace-Schott, & Stickgold, 2000). In contrast, non-REM dreams often are shorter (Antrobus, 1983; Foulkes & Rechtschaffen, 1964), are more thought-like and repetitive, and deal with everyday topics of current concern to us, like homework, shopping lists, or taxes (Hobson, 2002; Rechtschaffen, Verdone, & Wheaton, 1963).

Nevertheless, as the night wears on, dream reports from NREM sleep (starting with stage 2) resemble REM dream reports, leading some researchers to suggest that REM and NREM dreams aren't as distinct as once believed (Antrobus, 1983; Foulkes & Schmidt, 1983; McNamara et al., 2005). Thus, consciousness during sleep may vary with our level of brain activity and sleep stage (Siegel, 2005; Wamsley et al., 2007).

REM sleep is biologically important, probably essential. Depriving rats of REM sleep typically leads to their death within a few weeks (National Institute on Alcohol Use and Alcoholism, 1998), although rats die even sooner from total sleep deprivation (Rechtschaffen, 1998). When we humans are deprived of REM for a few nights, we experience *REM rebound*: The amount and intensity of REM sleep increases, suggesting that REM serves a critical biological function (Ocampo-Garces et al., 2000). Many of us have observed REM rebound when we haven't slept much for a few nights in a row. When we finally get a good night's sleep, we often experience much more intense dreams, even nightmares, probably reflecting a powerful bounce-back of REM sleep. Yet scientists are still debating the biological functions of REM sleep.

The function of the rapidly darting eye movements of REM sleep is unknown (Rechtschaffen, 1998; Siegel, 2005). Some researchers once believed they served to scan the images of dreams (Dement, 1974). William Dement once observed a subject during REM engaging in a striking pattern of back-and-forth horizontal eye movements. When Dement awakened him, he reported dreaming of a Ping-Pong match. Nevertheless, the evidence for this "scanning hypothesis" of REM is mixed, and the fact that subjects blind from birth engage in REM calls it into question (Gross, Byrne, & Fisher, 1965). Also occurring during REM is a phenomenon called *middle ear muscle activity* (MEMA), in which the muscles of our middle ears become active, almost as though they're assisting us to hear sounds in the dream (Pessah & Roffwarg, 1972; Slegel et al., 1991).

[Handwritten notes at top of page:]
REM sleep is Paradoxical sleep because brain is active by body is inactive.

REM behavior disorder (RBD) = 1/200 people have this (men over 50 in particular)
→ brain stem structures that are supposed to prevent movement during REM sleep don't function correctly

During REM sleep, our supercharged brains are creating dreams, but our bodies are relaxed and, for all practical purposes, paralyzed. For this reason, scientists sometimes call REM sleep *paradoxical sleep* because the brain is active at the same time the body is inactive. If REM didn't paralyze us, we'd act out our dreams, something that people with a strange—and very rare—condition called REM behavior disorder (RBD) do on occasion. In one case of RBD, for 20 years a 77-year-old minister acted out violent dreams in his sleep and occasionally injured his wife (Mahowald & Schenck, 2000). Fortunately, only about one person in 200 has symptoms of RBD, which occurs most frequently in men over the age of 50. In this condition, the brain stem structures (see Chapter 3) that ordinarily prevent us from moving during REM sleep don't function properly.

■ Lucid Dreaming

We've been talking about sleeping and waking as distinct stages, but they may shade gradually into one another (Antrobus, Antrobus, & Fischer, 1965; Voss et al., 2009). Consider a phenomenon that challenges the idea that we're either totally asleep or totally awake: lucid dreaming. If you've ever dreamed and known you were dreaming, you've experienced **lucid dreaming** (Blackmore, 1991; LaBerge, 1980, 2000; Van Eeden, 1913).

Most of us have experienced at least one lucid dream, and about one-fifth of Americans report dreaming lucidly on a monthly basis (Snyder & Gackenbach, 1988). Many lucid dreamers become aware they're dreaming when they see something so bizarre or improbable that they conclude (correctly) that they're having a dream. In one survey, 72 percent of lucid dreamers felt they could control what was happening in their dreams compared with 34 percent of non-lucid dreamers (Kunzendorf et al., 2006–2007). Still, researchers haven't resolved the question of whether lucid dreamers are asleep when they're aware of their dream content or whether some merely report that their dreams have a lucid quality after they awaken (LaBerge et al., 1981). Watch

Lucid dreaming opens up the possibility of controlling our dreams. The ability to become lucid during a nightmare usually improves the dream's outcome (Levitan & LeBerge, 1990; Spoormaker & van den Bout, 2006). Nevertheless, there's no good evidence that changing our lucid dreams can help us to overcome depression, anxiety, or other adjustment problems, despite the claims of some popular psychology books (Mindell, 1990).

■ Disorders of Sleep

Nearly all of us have trouble falling asleep or staying asleep from time to time. When sleep problems recur, interfere with our ability to function at work or school, or affect our health, they can exact a dear price. The cost of sleep disorders in terms of health and lost work productivity amounts to as much as $35 billion per year (Athius et al., 1998). We can also gauge the cost in terms of human lives, with an estimated 1,500 Americans who fall asleep at the wheel killed each year (Fenton, 2007). These grim statistics are understandable given that 30 to 50 percent of people report some sort of sleep problem (Althius et al., 1998; Blay, Andreoli, & Gastal, 2008).

INSOMNIA. The most common sleep disturbance is insomnia. **Insomnia** can take the following forms: (a) having trouble falling asleep (regularly taking more than 30 minutes to doze off), (b) waking too early in the morning, and (c) waking up during the night and having trouble returning to sleep. An estimated 9 to 15 percent of people report severe or longstanding problems with insomnia (Morin & Edinger, 2009).

People who suffer from depression, pain, or a variety of medical conditions report especially high rates of insomnia (Ford & Kamerow, 1989; Katz & McHorney, 2002; Smith & Haythornwaite, 2004). Brief bouts of insomnia are often due to stress and relationship problems, medications and illness, working late or variable shifts, jet lag, drinking caffeine,

Classic work by Michel Jouvet (1962) showed that lesioning a brain stem region called the locus coeruleus, which is responsible for keeping us paralyzed during REM, leads cats to act out their dreams. If Jouvet gave cats a ball of yarn to play with during the day, they'd often reenact this play behavior in their dreams.

ruling out rival hypotheses

HAVE IMPORTANT ALTERNATIVE EXPLANATIONS FOR THE FINDINGS BEEN EXCLUDED?

Watch Lucid Dreaming on **mypsychlab.com**

FACTOID +

Dolphins "sleep" with one of their brain's hemispheres asleep and the other awake. The eye on the side opposite the sleeping hemisphere typically remains shut, with the other eye remaining open. After a few hours, the other hemisphere and eye take over as sleep continues. This strange arrangement permits dolphins to sleep while remaining on the lookout for predators and obstacles, as well as to rise periodically to the surface of the water to breathe (Ridgway, 2002).

lucid dreaming
experience of becoming aware that one is dreaming

insomnia
difficulty falling and staying asleep

To ensure that the effects of sleeping pills don't carry over to when we're awake, it's important to monitor how we react to them and ensure that we have plenty of time to sleep before needing to be active again.

This dog is experiencing an episode of narcolepsy, which can occur after playful fighting. People and animals with narcolepsy can experience cataplexy when they become excited.

narcolepsy
disorder characterized by the rapid and often unexpected onset of sleep

sleep apnea
disorder caused by a blockage of the airway during sleep, resulting in daytime fatigue

or napping during the day. Insomnia can become recurrent if we become frustrated and anxious when we can't fall asleep right away (Spielman, Conroy, & Glovinsky, 2003). Many people don't realize that even most "good sleepers" take 15 to 20 minutes to fall asleep. To combat insomnia, James Maas (1999) recommends hiding clocks to avoid becoming preoccupied with the inability to fall asleep quickly, sleeping in a cool room, going to sleep and waking up at regular times, and avoiding caffeine, naps during the day, reading in bed, and watching television or surfing the Web right before bedtime.

Although sleeping pills can be effective in treating insomnia, researchers have discovered that brief psychotherapy is more effective than Ambien, a popular sleeping pill (Jacobs et al., 2004). Recently, it's come to light that in rare instances, people who use Ambien engage in eating, walking, and even driving while asleep, and that Lunesta, another popular sleeping medication, can cause amnesia for events that occur after taking it (Schenck, 2006). Longstanding use of many sleeping pills can create dependency and make it more difficult to sleep once people stop taking them, a phenomenon called *rebound insomnia*. So, in an ironic twist, sleeping pills can actually cause insomnia (Bellon, 2006).

NARCOLEPSY. **Narcolepsy** is a dramatic disorder in which people experience episodes of sudden sleep lasting anywhere from a few seconds to several minutes and, less frequently, as long as an hour. Consider a patient (treated by one of us) who fell asleep in all sorts of situations: at his favorite movies, in the shower, and while driving. He was a prison guard, but he couldn't stay awake on the job. He feared his boss would fire him and stifled many a yawn in his presence.

In people with narcolepsy, the overwhelming urge to sleep can strike at any moment. Surprise, elation, or other strong emotions—even those associated with laughing at a joke or engaging in sexual intercourse—can lead some people with narcolepsy to experience *cataplexy,* a complete loss of muscle tone. During cataplexy, people can fall because their muscles become limp as a rag doll. Cataplexy occurs in healthy people during REM sleep. But in narcolepsy, people experiencing cataplexy remain alert the whole time, even though they can't move. Ordinarily, sleepers don't enter REM sleep for more than an hour after they fall asleep. But when people who experience an episode of narcolepsy doze off, they plummet into REM sleep immediately, suggesting that it results from a sleep–wake cycle that's badly off-kilter. Vivid hypnagogic hallucinations often accompany the onset of narcoleptic episodes, raising the possibility that REM intrusions are one cause of brief waking hallucinations.

Genetic abnormalities boost the risk of narcolepsy, and some people develop narcolepsy after an accident that causes brain damage. The hormone *orexin* plays a key role in triggering sudden attacks of sleepiness (Mieda et al., 2004). Indeed, people with narcolepsy have abnormally few brain cells that produce orexin. When researchers administered orexin in a nasal spray to sleep-deprived rhesus monkeys, these animals' performance on cognitive tasks equaled that of well-rested monkeys (Deadwyler et al., 2007). Medications that either replace orexin or mimic its effects in the brain may one day cure narcolepsy. Meanwhile, narcolepsy sufferers can benefit from taking the medication modafinil (its brand name is Provigil), which promotes wakefulness and is quite effective in treating narcolepsy.

SLEEP APNEA. In 2008, a 53-year-old Go Airlines pilot and his copilot fell asleep during the flight, failed to respond to air traffic controllers for nearly 20 minutes, and overshot the runway by about 30 miles before they woke up (CNN, August 3, 2009). What happened? The pilot suffered from **sleep apnea**, a serious sleep disorder that afflicts between 2 and 20 percent of the general population, depending on how broadly or narrowly it's defined (Shamsuzzaman, Gersh, & Somers, 2003; Strohl & Redline, 1996). Apnea is caused by a blockage of the airway during sleep, as shown in **FIGURE 5.3**. This problem causes people with apnea to snore loudly, gasp, and sometimes stop breathing for more than 20 seconds. Struggling to breathe rouses the person many times—often several hundred times—during the night and interferes with sleep, causing fatigue the next day. Yet most people with sleep apnea have no awareness of these multiple awakenings. A lack of oxygen and the buildup of carbon dioxide can lead to many prob-

Night Terrors = harmless events that happen mostly in children, or in adults when intensely stressed.

Sleepwalking —walking while asleep but function/act like an awake person

the biology of sleep **173**

lems, including night sweats, weight gain, fatigue, hearing loss, and an irregular heartbeat (Sanders & Givelber, 2006). A 10-year study of 6,441 men and women underscored the dangerous effects of sleep apnea. The researchers found that the disorder raised the overall risk of death by 17 percent; in men 40–70 years old with severe apnea, the increase in risk shot up to 46 percent compared with healthy men of the same age (Punjabi et al., 2009).

Because apnea is associated with being overweight, doctors typically recommend weight loss as a first treatment option. When enlarged tonsils cause apnea in children, doctors can remove them surgically. But in adults, surgical procedures often don't work well. Many people benefit from wearing a face mask attached to a machine that blows air into their nasal passages, forcing the airway to remain open. Nevertheless, adjusting to this rather uncomfortable machine can be challenging (Wolfe & Pruitt, 2003).

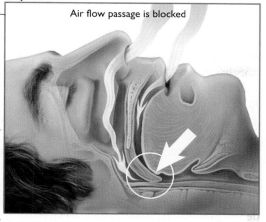

Air flow passage is blocked

FIGURE 5.3 Flow of Air and Quality of Sleep. When the flow of air is blocked, as in sleep apnea, the quality of sleep can be seriously disrupted.

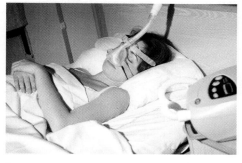

Person using a device to combat sleep apnea at home.

NIGHT TERRORS. Night terrors are often more disturbing to onlookers than to sleepers. Parents who witness a child's night terrors can hardly believe that the child has no recollection of what occurred. Screaming, perspiring, confused, and wide-eyed, the child may thrash about before falling back into a deep sleep. Such episodes usually last for only a few minutes, although they may seem like an eternity to a distraught parent.

Despite their dramatic nature, **night terrors** are typically harmless events that occur almost exclusively in children. Parents often learn not to overreact and even ignore the episodes if the child isn't in physical danger. Night terrors occasionally occur in adults, especially when they're under intense stress.

SLEEPWALKING. For many of us, the image of a "somnambulist," or sleepwalker, is a person with eyes closed, arms outstretched, and both hands at shoulder height, walking like a zombie. In actuality, a sleepwalking person often acts like any fully awake person, although a sleepwalker may be somewhat clumsier. Some 15 to 30 percent of children and 4 to 5 percent of adults sleepwalk occasionally (Mahowald & Bornemann, 2005). **Sleepwalking**—walking while fully asleep—often involves relatively little activity, but sleepwalkers have been known to drive cars, turn on computers, or even have sexual intercourse while asleep (Underwood, 2007). In fact, a few people who committed murder have used sleepwalking as a legal defense. In one controversial case, a young man who drove almost 20 miles, removed a tire iron from a car, and killed his mother-in-law and seriously injured his father-in-law with a knife, was declared innocent because he maintained (and the judges agreed) that he slept through the whole event and wasn't responsible for his behavior (McCall, Smith, & Shapiro, 1997). People deprived of sleep are more likely to exhibit sleepwalking the following night (Zadra, Pilon, & Montplaisir, 2008).

FACTOID +

Moms and dads typically worry about their sleep-deprived teenagers. But the parents of 15-year-old Louisa Ball, who lives in south England, were concerned for another reason—their daughter routinely slept for two weeks straight without interruptions, unless she received medication. Louisa suffers from a rare neurological condition called Kleine-Levin Syndrome, aptly nicknamed "Sleeping Beauty Disorder." Her parents needed to wake her every 22 hours to feed her and take her to the bathroom, after which she fell immediately asleep.

FICTOID ✕

MYTH: Night terrors occur when people act out nightmares in their sleep.

FACT: Night terrors aren't caused by nightmares. Nightmares typically occur only during REM sleep, whereas night terrors take place during deep non-REM sleep (stages 3 and 4). Night terrors occur more frequently in children than in adults because children spend more time in deep stages of sleep (Wolfe & Pruit, 2003).

? What's wrong with this picture? Does it capture how a sleepwalking person would actually appear to an onlooker? (See answer upside down at bottom of page.)

Answer: Sleepwalkers typically walk just like regular people, not like zombies.

night terrors
sudden waking episodes characterized by screaming, perspiring, and confusion followed by a return to a deep sleep

sleepwalking
walking while fully asleep

FACTOID +

We can fall asleep with our eyes open. In a 1960 study, an investigator taped the eyes of three volunteers—one of them severely sleep-deprived—wide open while flashing bright lights at them, blasting loud music into their ears, and administering periodic electric shocks to their legs. They fell sound asleep within 12 minutes (Boese, 2007).

✔ Study and Review on mypsychlab.com

Sleepwalking is most frequent in childhood; about 2 to 3 percent of children are frequent sleepwalkers, and up to 30 percent of children have sleepwalked at least once (American Psychiatric Association, 2000). Contrary to popular misconception, sleepwalkers aren't acting out their dreams, because sleepwalking almost always occurs during non-REM (especially stage 3 or 4) sleep. For most people, sleepwalking is harmless, and sleepwalkers rarely remember their actions after awakening. But for children and adults who engage in potentially dangerous activities (such as climbing out an open window) while sleepwalking, doors and windows can be wired with alarms to alert others to direct them back to bed. If someone is sleepwalking, it's perfectly safe to wake him or her up, despite what we may have seen in movies (Wolfe & Pruitt, 2003).

assess your knowledge   FACT OR FICTION?

1. The average adult needs about six hours of sleep a night. True / **False**
2. People move slowly through the first four stages of sleep but then spend the rest of the night in REM sleep. True / **False**
3. When we dream, our brains are much less active than when awake. True / **False**
4. Sleep apnea is more common in thin than in overweight people. True / **False**
5. Night terrors usually last only a few minutes and are typically harmless. **True** / False

Answers: 1. F (p. 168); 2. F (p. 169); 3. F (p. 171); 4. F (p. 173); 5. T (p. 173)

DREAMS

5.4   Describe Freud's theory of dreams.

5.5   Explain three major modern theories of dreaming.

Dreaming is a virtually universal experience. Some people insist they never dream, but research shows this phenomenon is almost always due to a failure to recall their dreams rather than a failure to experience them. When brought into a sleep laboratory, just about everyone reports vivid dreaming when awakened during a REM period (Dement, 1974; Domhoff & Schneider, 2004), although a mysterious handful of people don't (Butler & Watson, 1985; Pagel, 2003). Even blind people dream. But whether their dreams contain visual imagery depends on when they became blind. People blinded before age four don't experience visual dream imagery, whereas those blinded after age seven do so, suggesting that between ages four to six is the window within which the ability to generate visual imagery develops (Kerr, 1993; Kerr & Domhoff, 2004).

Whether we're researchers in Timbuktu or New York City, we'll find cross-culturally consistent patterns in dreaming. Virtually all of us experience dreams that contain more aggression than friendliness, more negative than positive emotions, and more misfortune than good fortune. Women's dreams generally contain more emotion than men's dreams, and their dream characters are about evenly divided between men and women. In contrast, men are more likely to dream about men by a 2:1 ratio (Hall, 1984). At least a few differences in dreams are associated with cultural factors. For example, the dreams of people in more technologically advanced societies feature fewer animals than those in small, traditional societies (Domhoff, 1996, 2001a).

Scientists still don't know for sure why we dream, but evidence from a variety of sources suggests that dreams are involved in (a) processing emotional memories (Maquet & Franck, 1997); (b) integrating new experiences with established memories to make sense of and create a virtual reality model of the world (Hobson, 2009; Stickgold, James, & Hobson, 2002); (c) learning new strategies and ways of doing things, like swinging a golf club (Walker et al., 2002); (d) simulating threatening events so we can better cope with them in everyday life (Revonsuo, 2000); and (e) reorganizing and consolidating memories (Crick & Mitchison, 1983, Diekelmann & Born, 2010). Still, the function of dreams remains a puzzle because research evidence concerning the role of learning and memory in dreams is mixed. We'll discuss four major theories of dreams, beginning with one by Sigmund Freud.

■ Freud's Dream Protection Theory

We've been trying to decipher the meaning of dreams for thousands of years. The Babylonians believed that dreams were sent by the gods, the Assyrians thought that dreams contained signs or omens, the Greeks built dream temples in which visitors awaited prophecies sent by the gods during dreams, and North American Indians believed that dreams revealed hidden wishes and desires (Van de Castle, 1994).

Sigmund Freud sided with the Native Americans. In his landmark book, *The Interpretation of Dreams* (1900), Freud described dreams as the guardians (protectors) of sleep. During sleep, the ego (see Chapter 14), which acts as a sort of mental censor, is less able than when awake to keep sexual and aggressive instincts at bay by repressing them. If not for dreams, these instincts would bubble up, disturbing sleep. The *dream-work* disguises and contains the pesky sexual and aggressive impulses by transforming them into symbols that represent *wish fulfillment*—how we wish things could be (see Chapter 14).

According to Freud, dreams don't surrender their secrets easily—they require interpretation to reverse the dream-work and reveal their true meaning. He distinguished between the details of the dream itself, which he called the *manifest content,* and its true, hidden meaning, which he called the *latent content.* For example, a dream about getting a flat tire (manifest content) might signify anxiety about the loss of status at our job (latent content).

Most scientists have rejected the dream protection and wish fulfillment theories of dreams (Domhoff, 2001a). Contrary to Freud's dream protection theory, some patients with brain injuries report that they don't dream, yet sleep soundly (Jus et al., 1973). If, as Freud claimed, "wish fulfillment is the meaning of each and every dream" (Freud, 1900, p. 106), we'd expect dream content to be mostly positive. Yet although most of us have occasional dreams of flying, winning the lottery, or being with the object of our wildest fantasies, these themes are less frequent than dreams of misfortune. Freud believed that many or most dreams are sexual in nature. But sexual themes account for as little as 10 percent of the dreams we remember (see **TABLE 5.1**) (Domhoff, 2003).

In addition, many dreams don't appear to be disguised, as Freud contended. As many as 90 percent of dream reports are straightforward descriptions of everyday activities and problems, like talking to friends (Domhoff, 2003; Dorus, Dorus, & Rechtschaffen, 1971). A further challenge to wish fulfillment theory is that people who've experienced highly traumatic events often experience repetitive nightmares (Barratt, 1996). But nightmares clearly aren't wish fulfillments, and they aren't at all uncommon in either adults or children. So, if you have an occasional nightmare, rest assured: It's perfectly normal.

■ Activation–Synthesis Theory

Starting in the 1960s and 1970s, Alan Hobson and Robert McCarley developed the **activation–synthesis theory** (Hobson & McCarley, 1977; Hobson, Pace-Schott, & Stickgold, 2000), which proposes that dreams reflect brain activation in sleep, rather than a repressed unconscious wish, as Freud claimed. Far from having deep, universal meaning, Hobson and McCarley maintained that dreams reflect the activated brain's attempt to make sense of random and internally generated neural signals during REM sleep.

Throughout the day and night, the balance of neurotransmitters in the brain shifts continually. REM is turned on by surges of the neurotransmitter acetylcholine, as the neurotransmitters serotonin and norepinephrine are shut down. Acetylcholine activates nerve cells in the pons, located at the base of the brain (see Chapter 3), while dwindling levels of serotonin and norepinephrine decrease reflective thought, reasoning, attention, and memory. The activated pons sends incomplete signals to the lateral geniculate nucleus of the

TABLE 5.1 Most Frequent Dream Themes.

1. Being chased or pursued
2. Being lost, late, or trapped
3. Falling
4. Flying
5. Losing valuable possessions
6. Sexual dreams
7. Experiencing great natural beauty
8. Being naked or dressed oddly
9. Injury or illness

(*Source:* Domhoff, 2003)

> **activation–synthesis theory**
> theory that dreams reflect inputs from brain activation originating in the pons, which the forebrain then attempts to weave into a story

falsifiability

CAN THE CLAIM BE DISPROVED?

FACTOID +

People express consistent biases in interpreting their dreams. Individuals are most likely to believe that their negative dreams are meaningful when they're about someone they dislike, and that their positive dreams are meaningful when they're about a friend (Morewedge & Norton, 2009).

Nightmares are most frequent in children, but are also common in adults.

FIGURE 5.4 Activation–Synthesis Theory. According to activation–synthesis theory, the pons transmits random signals to the thalamus, which relays information to the forebrain of the cerebral cortex. The forebrain in turn attempts to create a story from the incomplete information it receives.

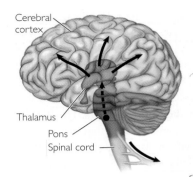

Cerebral cortex

Thalamus

Pons

Spinal cord

thalamus, a relay for sensory information to the language and visual areas of the forebrain, as shown in **FIGURE 5.4** (see Chapter 3). The forebrain does its best to cobble together the signals it receives into a meaningful story. Nevertheless, the bits of information it receives are haphazard and chaotic, so the narrative is rarely coherent or logical. The amygdala is also ramped up, adding the emotional colors of fear, anxiety, anger, sadness, and elation to the mix (see Chapters 3 and 11). According to activation-synthesis theory, the net result of these complex brain changes is what we experience as a dream.

■ Dreaming and the Forebrain

ruling out rival hypotheses

HAVE IMPORTANT ALTERNATIVE EXPLANATIONS
FOR THE FINDINGS BEEN EXCLUDED?

Dreaming happens by the forebrain

An alternative to the activation-synthesis theory emphasizes the role of the forebrain in dreaming. Mark Solms (1997; Solms & Turnbull, 2002) surveyed 332 cases of patients with brain damage from stroke, tumors, and injury. From this gold mine of data, he determined that damage to (a) the deep frontal white matter, which connects different parts of the cortex to the lower parts of the brain, and (b) the parietal lobes can lead to a complete loss of dreaming. It's likely that the damaged brain areas are pathways that allow brain centers involved in dreaming to communicate. When they're disconnected, dreaming stops.

falsifiability

CAN THE CLAIM BE DISPROVED?

Thus, damage to the forebrain can eliminate dreams entirely, even when the brain stem is working properly. This finding seems to refute the claim that the brain stem plays an exclusive role in producing dreams and underscores the role of the forebrain in dreaming. According to Solms, dreams are driven largely by the motivational and emotional control centers of the forebrain as the logical "executive" parts of the brain snooze.

■ Neurocognitive Perspectives on Dreaming

neurocognitive theory
theory that dreams are a meaningful product of our cognitive capacities, which shape what we dream about

Scientists who've advanced a **neurocognitive theory** of dreaming argue that explaining dreams only in terms of neurotransmitters and random neural impulses doesn't tell the full story. Instead, they contend, dreams are a meaningful product of our cognitive capacities, which shape what we dream about. For example, children under the age of seven or eight recall dreaming on only 20 to 30 percent of occasions when awakened from REM sleep com-

Answers are located at the end of the text.

DREAM INTERPRETATIONS   evaluating CLAIMS

We all dream, and many of us are curious about what, if anything, our dreams mean. According to many popular websites and books, our dreams are trying to tell us something through their symbols. Let's evaluate some of these claims, which are modeled after actual dream interpretation books and websites.

"Your dreams are *hidden messages* sent from your subconscious to help guide your life." Is there extraordinary evidence to support this extraordinary claim? In fact, most dream reports are straightforward descriptions of everyday activities and problems rather than hidden or disguised messages.

"*Seeing a coconut in your dreams means* that you will receive an unexpected sum of money." Scientific evidence doesn't support the claim that specific symbols in our dreams possess a deeper meaning or predict something in our lives. Many dreams have no special meaning at all, and some dreams reflect everyday preoccupations.

"Using the *ancient art of dream analysis*, we can uncover hidden meanings in your dreams." Does the fact that dream interpretations have been around a long time mean they're valid?

pared with 80 to 90 percent of adults (Foulkes, 1982, 1999). Until they reach the age of nine or 10, children's dreams tend to be simple, lacking in movement, and less emotional and bizarre than adult dreams (Domhoff, 1996). A typical five-year-old's dream may be of a pet or animal in a zoo. Apart from an occasional nightmare, children's dreams feature little aggression or negative emotion (Domhoff, 2003; Foulkes, 1999). According to the neurocognitive perspective, complex dreams are "cognitive achievements" that parallel the gradual development of visual imagination and other advanced cognitive abilities. We begin to dream like adults when our brains develop the "wiring" to do so (Domhoff, 2001a).

Content analyses of tens of thousands of dreams (Hall & Van de Castle, 1966) reveal that many are associated with everyday activities, emotional concerns, and preoccupations (Domhoff, 1996; Hall & Nordby, 1972; Smith & Hall, 1964), including playing sports, preparing for tests, feeling self-conscious about our appearance, and being single (Pano, Hilscher, & Cupchik, 2008–2009). Moreover, dream content is surprisingly stable over long time periods. In a journal containing 904 dreams that a woman kept for more than five decades, six themes (eating or thinking of food, the loss of an object, going to the toilet, being in a small or messy room, missing a bus or train, doing something with her mother) accounted for more than three-fourths of the contents of her dreams (Domhoff, 1993). Additionally, 50 to 80 percent of people report recurrent dreams, like missing a test, over many years (Cartwright & Romanek, 1978; Zadra, 1996). The bottom line? Although dreams are sometimes bizarre, they're often rather ordinary in content and seem to reflect more than random neural impulses generated by the brain stem (Domhoff, 2001b; Foulkes, 1985; Revonsuo, 2000; Strauch & Meier, 1996).

As we've seen, there are sharp disagreements among scientists about the role of the brain stem and REM sleep, and the role that development plays in dreaming. Nevertheless, scientists generally agree that (1) acetylcholine turns on REM sleep and (2) the forebrain plays an important role in dreams.

[handwritten margin notes: Neurocognitive Perspectives on Dreaming Theory → dreams become more complex as cognitive capacities increase → dreams are ordinary, consistent, and mainly of everyday concerns.]

---

assess your knowledge   FACT OR FICTION?

1. Dreams often reflect unfulfilled wishes, as Freud suggested. **True / ~~False~~**

2. Activation–synthesis theory proposes that dreams result from incomplete neural signals being generated by the pons. **~~True~~ / False**

3. REM sleep is triggered by the neurotransmitter acetylcholine. **~~True~~ / False**

4. Damage to the forebrain can eliminate dreams. **~~True~~ / False**

5. Recurrent dreams are extremely rare. **True / ~~False~~**

Answers: 1. F (p. 175); 2. T (pp. 175–176); 3. T (p. 175); 4. T (p. 176); 5. F (p. 177)

✓— Study and Review on mypsychlab.com

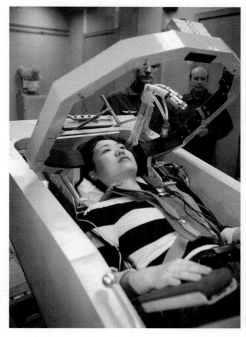

When astronauts train for missions in whirling centrifuge devices that force oxygen enriched blood out of their brains as they accelerate, some experience vivid hallucinations (Birbaumer et al., 2005).

OTHER ALTERATIONS OF CONSCIOUSNESS AND UNUSUAL EXPERIENCES

5.6 Determine how scientists explain unusual and seemingly "mystical" alterations in consciousness.

5.7 Distinguish myths from realities concerning hypnosis.

As the stages of sleep demonstrate, consciousness is far more complicated than just "conscious" versus "unconscious." Moreover, there are other variations on the theme of consciousness besides sleep and waking. Some of the more radical alterations in consciousness include hallucinations, as well as out-of-body, near-death, and déjà vu experiences.

■ Hallucinations: Experiencing What Isn't There

What do Attila the Hun; Robert Schumann, the famous music composer; and Winston Churchill have in common? The answer: They all experienced hallucinations in the form of visions or voices. *Hallucinations* are realistic perceptual experiences in the absence of

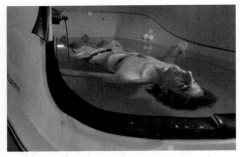

People who float in lukewarm saltwater in dark and silent sensory deprivation tanks, hallucinate to compensate for the lack of sensory stimulation (Smith, 2009).

Hallucination: realistic perceptual experience in the absence of external stimuli [handwritten annotation]

any external stimuli. Hallucinations can occur in any sensory modality and be "as real as real." Brain scans reveal that when people report visual hallucinations, their visual cortex becomes active, just as it does when they see a real object (Allen et al., 2008; Bentall, 2000). The same correspondence holds true for other sense modalities, like hearing, underscoring the link between our perceptual experiences and brain activity.

A frequent misconception is that hallucinations occur only in psychologically disturbed individuals (Aleman & Laroi, 2008). But hallucinations are far more common than many people realize. Surveys reveal that between 10 and 14 percent (Tien, 1991) to as many as 39 percent (Ohayon, 2000; Posey & Losch, 1983) of college students and people in the general population report having hallucinated during the day at least once—even when not taking drugs or experiencing psychological problems (Ohayon, 2000). Some non-Western cultures, including some in Africa, value hallucinations as gifts of wisdom from the gods and incorporate them into their religious rituals. People in these societies may even go out of their way to induce hallucinations by means of prayer, fasting, and hallucinogenic drugs (Al-Issa, 1995; Bourguignon, 1970).

Visual hallucinations can also be brought about by oxygen and sensory deprivation. As we'll learn in Chapter 15, auditory hallucinations (those involving sound) can occur when patients mistakenly attribute their thoughts, or inner speech, to an external source (Bentall, 1990, 2000; Frith, 1992). Healthy adults and college students who report having engaged in a great deal of fantasizing and imaginative activities since childhood—so-called fantasy-prone persons—report having problems distinguishing fantasy from reality, and hallucinate persons and objects on occasion (Wilson & Barber, 1981, 1983; Lynn & Rhue, 1988).

■ Out-of-Body and Near-Death Experiences

Carlos Alvarado (2000) described a 36-year-old police officer's account of an **out-of-body experience (OBE)**, an extraordinary sense of her consciousness leaving her body, when she pursued an armed suspect on her first night on patrol. "When I and three other officers stopped the vehicle and started getting (to) the suspect . . . I was afraid. I promptly went out of my body and up into the air maybe 20 feet above the scene. I remained there, extremely calm, while I watched the entire procedure—including myself—do exactly what I had been trained to do." Alvarado reported that "[s]uddenly, [she] found herself back in her body after the suspect had been subdued" (p. 183).

OBEs are surprisingly common: About 25 percent of college students and 10 percent of the general population report having experienced one or more of them (Alvarado, 2000). In many cases, individuals describe themselves as floating above their bodies, calmly observing themselves from above, implying that our sense of ourselves need not be subjectively locked into our bodies (Smith, 2009). People who are prone to OBEs frequently report other unusual experiences, including vivid fantasies, lucid dreams, hallucinations, perceptual distortions, and strange body sensations in everyday life (Blackmore, 1984, 1986). Some people also experience OBEs when they're medicated, using psychedelic drugs, experiencing migraine headaches or seizures, or either extremely relaxed or under extreme stress.

Yet are people really able to roam outside their bodies during an OBE? Laboratory studies have compared what's reported during an OBE against sights and sounds known to be present in a given location, like a hidden ledge 10 feet above a bed. Interestingly, even though many participants report they can see or hear what's occurring at a distant place, their reports are generally inaccurate or, at best, a "good guess" when they are accurate. When researchers have reported positive results, these results have virtually never been replicated (Alvarado, 2000). So there's no good evidence that people are truly floating above their bodies during an OBE, although it certainly seems that way to them (Cheyne & Girard, 2009). These findings appear to falsify the claim that people genuinely emerge from their bodies during OBEs.

What, then, are some possible explanations for these dramatic changes in consciousness? Our sense of self depends on a complex interplay of sensory information. But what happens when our senses of touch and vision are scrambled? Research suggests that

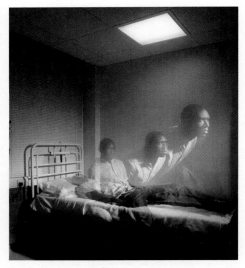

As real as an out-of-body experience seems to the person having it, research has found no evidence that consciousness exists outside the body.

out-of-body experience (OBE)
sense of our consciousness leaving our body

replicability ▶
CAN THE RESULTS BE DUPLICATED IN OTHER STUDIES?

falsifiability ▶
CAN THE CLAIM BE DISPROVED?

TABLE 5.2 Common Elements in Adult Near-Death Experiences.

- Difficulty describing the experience in words
- Hearing ourselves pronounced dead
- Feelings of peace and quiet
- Hearing unusual noises
- Meeting "spiritual beings"
- Experiencing a bright light as a "being of light"
- Panoramic "life review," that is, seeing our entire life pass before our eyes
- Experiencing a realm in which all knowledge exists
- Experiencing cities of light
- Experiencing a realm of ghosts and spirits
- Sensing a border or limit
- Coming back "into the body"

(*Source:* Moody, 1975, 1977; adapted from Greyson, 2000)

Although there are many variations of a "near-death experience," most people in our culture believe it involves moving through a tunnel and toward a white light.

the result is a disruption of our experience of our physical body with striking similarities to an OBE. H. Henrik Ehrsson (2007) provided participants with goggles that permitted them to view a video display of themselves relayed by a camera placed behind them. This set-up created the weird illusion that their bodies, viewed from the rear, actually were standing in front of them. Ehrrson touched participants with a rod in the chest while he used cameras to make it appear that the visual image was being touched at the same time. Participants reported the eerie sensation that their video double was also being touched. In short, individuals reported they could experience the touch in a location outside their physical bodies (see also Lenggenhager et al., 2007). OBEs remind us (see Chapter 4) that one of the human brain's great achievements is its ability to integrate sensory information from different pathways into a unified experience. Yet when visual sensory impressions combine with physical sensations, they can trick us into thinking our physical selves are separate from our bodies (Cheyne & Girard, 2009; Terhune, 2009).

OBEs also sometimes occur in **near-death experiences (NDEs)** reported by people who've nearly died or thought they were going to die. In fact, about one quarter of patients with NDEs experience their consciousness outside their bodies (van Lommel et al., 2001). Ever since Raymond Moody (1975) cataloged them over 30 years ago, Americans have become familiar with the classical elements of the NDE that are widely circulated in books and movies—passing through a dark tunnel, experiencing a bright light as a "being of light," the *life review* (seeing our lives pass before our eyes), and meeting spiritual beings or long-dead relatives, all before "coming back into the body" (see **TABLE 5.2**). Roughly 6 to 33 percent of people who've been close to death report NDEs (Blanke & Dieguez, 2009; Greyson, 2000; Ring, 1984; Sabom, 1982; van Lommel et al., 2001).

NDEs differ across persons and cultures, suggesting they don't provide a genuine glimpse of the afterlife, but are constructed from prevalent beliefs about the hereafter in response to the threat of death (Ehrenwald, 1974; Noyes & Kletti, 1976). People from Christian and Buddhist cultures frequently report the sensation of moving through a tunnel, but native people in North America, the Pacific Islands, and Australia rarely do (Kellehear, 1993).

It's tempting to believe that NDEs prove that when we die we'll all be ushered into the afterlife by friends or loved ones. Nevertheless, the evidence is insufficient to support this extraordinary claim. Scientists have offered alternative explanations for NDEs based on changes in the chemistry of the brain associated with cardiac arrest, anesthesia, and other physical traumas (Blackmore, 1993). For example, a feeling of complete peace that can accompany an NDE may result from the massive release of *endorphins* (see Chapter 3) in a dying brain, and buzzing, ringing, or other unusual sounds may be the rumblings of an oxygen-starved brain (Blackmore, 1993).

(© www.CartoonStock.com)

> **near-death experience (NDE)**
> out-of-body experience reported by people who've nearly died or thought they were going to die

◄ extraordinary claims

IS THE EVIDENCE AS STRONG AS THE CLAIM?

◄ ruling out rival hypotheses

HAVE IMPORTANT ALTERNATIVE EXPLANATIONS FOR THE FINDINGS BEEN EXCLUDED?

Moreover, many, if not all, of the experiences associated with NDEs occur in circumstances in which people don't face imminent death. For example, NDE-like experiences can be triggered by (a) electrical stimulation of the brain's temporal lobes (Persinger, 1994); (b) lack of oxygen to the brain in rapid acceleration during fighter pilot training (Whinnery, 1997); and (c) psychedelic (such as LSD and mescaline) and anesthetic (such as ketamine) drugs (Jansen, 1991). Until more definitive evidence is marshaled to demonstrate that NDEs reflect anything more than changes in physiology in the dying brain, there seems to be no reason to discard this more parsimonious explanation for NDEs.

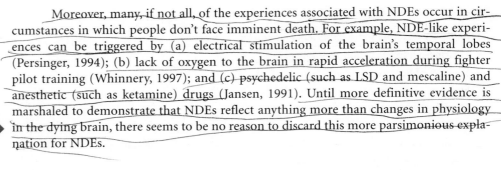

occam's razor

DOES A SIMPLER EXPLANATION FIT THE DATA JUST AS WELL?

■ Déjà Vu Experiences

Have you ever had the mind-boggling sense that you've "been there" or "done that" before? Or have you ever felt you were reliving something, scene by scene, even though you knew that the situation was new or unfamiliar? When your text's first author first visited his undergraduate alma mater, Cornell University, he had the unmistakable feeling of having seen the campus even though he'd never been there before. If you've had one or more of these eerie flashes of familiarity, you've experienced **déjà vu**, which is French for "already seen." More than two-thirds of us have experienced at least one episode of déjà vu (Adachi et al., 2008). These fleeting 10–30 second illusions are especially likely to be reported by people who remember their dreams, travel frequently, are young, and have liberal political and religious beliefs, a college education, and a high income (Brown, 2003, 2004a).

An excess of the neurotransmitter dopamine in the temporal lobes may play a role in déjà vu (Taiminen & Jääskeläinen, 2001). In addition, people who experience small seizures in the right temporal lobe, which is largely responsible for feelings of familiarity, sometimes experience déjà vu right before a seizure (Bancaud et al., 1994). Déjà vu may also arise when a present experience resembles an earlier one. The familiar feeling arises because we don't consciously recall the previous experience, which may have originated in childhood, or, in later life, when we may have been distracted and don't consciously remember what we're seeing. Perhaps we've driven by a park many times without ever noticing it, but our minds processed the information unconsciously (Strayer, Drews, & Johnston, 2003). So when we drive by the park some time later, it's "déjà vu all over again." Although some have proposed that the déjà vu experience is a memory from a past life, this explanation is unfalsifiable and therefore outside the boundaries of science (Stevenson, 1960).

(© Chris Slane)

falsifiability

CAN THE CLAIM BE DISPROVED?

■ Mystical Experiences

Mystical experiences can last for only a few moments yet often leave lasting, even lifelong, impressions. These experiences involve a common core of features that include a sense of unity or oneness with the world, transcendence of time and space, and feelings of wonder and awe. These phenomena often have strong spiritual overtones and may have contributed to the formation of many world religions. Yet they differ across religious faiths. Christians often describe mystical experiences in terms of an awe-inspiring merging with God's presence. In contrast, Buddhists, whose spiritual practices focus more on achieving personal enlightenment than worship of a deity, often describe mystical incidents in terms of bliss and selfless peace. Although shaped by learning and culture, each person's mystical experience is probably unique. As many as 35 percent of Americans say they've felt very close to a powerful, uplifting spiritual force at least once (Greeley, 1975).

Because intense mystical experiences are rare, unpredictable, difficult to put into words, and often fleeting, they're difficult to study in the laboratory (Wulff, 2000). Nevertheless, scientists have recently begun to probe their mysteries. One approach they've adopted is to study people who report a history of mystical experiences; another is to induce mystical experiences and examine their consequences.

Adopting the first approach, researchers used fMRI to scan the brains of fifteen Roman Catholic nuns after asking them to close their eyes and relive the most intense mystical occur-

FACTOID +

Some people experience a phenomenon called *jamais vu*, French for "never seen," which is essentially the opposite of déjà vu. In *jamais vu*, the person reports feeling as though a previously familiar experience suddenly seems unfamiliar. *Jamais vu* is sometimes seen in neurological disorders, such as amnesia (see Chapter 7) and epilepsy (Brown, 2004).

déjà vu
feeling of reliving an experience that's new

mystical experience
feelings of unity or oneness with the world, often with strong spiritual overtones

rence they'd ever experienced (Beauregard & Paquette, 2006). They also instructed them to relive the most intense state of union with another human they'd felt as a nun. Compared with a condition in which the nuns sat quietly with eyes closed and the condition in which the nuns relived the interpersonal experience, the "mystical experiences" condition produced distinctive patterns of brain activation. In fact, at least 12 areas of the brain associated with emotion, perception, and cognition became active when the nuns relived mystical experiences.

We can question whether the researchers actually captured mystical experiences. Reliving an experience in the laboratory may differ from more spontaneous mystical events produced by fasting, prayer, fevers, seizures in the temporal lobes, or meditation (Geschwind, 1983; Persinger, 1987). Still, brain scanning techniques clearly hold promise in studying mystical states of consciousness and in revealing links between these states and biological mechanisms.

In the second approach, neuroscientists asked 36 participants without any personal or family history of mental illness to ingest psilocybin (Griffiths et al., 2008). Psilocybin is a hallucinogenic drug that affects serotonin receptors and is the active ingredient in the "sacred mushroom," used for centuries in religious ceremonies. Three key findings emerged at the follow-up 14 months later. First, 58 percent of participants who ingested psilocybin reported a mystical experience. Second, 58 percent felt that the mystical experience was one of the most meaningful events of their lives, and 67 percent rated the experience as one of their top five most spiritually significant moments. Third, 64 percent of participants reported increases in life satisfaction. The percentages of mystical and positive experiences were much lower among participants who ingested a placebo.

But we should keep in mind that 31 percent of participants who ingested psilocybin reported extreme fears and paranoia during the session. In the placebo condition, none reported such fears. This research offers a glimpse of the promise of studying mystical experiences in the laboratory, while reminding us that caution is warranted in studying hallucinogenic drugs that can induce negative as well as positive feelings.

■ Hypnosis

Hypnosis is a set of techniques that provides people with suggestions for alterations in their perceptions, thoughts, feelings, and behaviors (Kirsch & Lynn, 1998). To increase people's suggestibility, most hypnotists use an *induction method*, which typically includes suggestions for relaxation and calmness (Kirsch, 1994).

Consider the following scenario that unfolds after Jessica experiences a relaxation-based induction ("You are feeling relaxed, more and more relaxed, as you go deeper into hypnosis"): The hypnotist drones, "Your hand is getting lighter, lighter, it is rising, rising by itself, lifting off the resting surface." Slowly, slowly, Jessica's hand lifts in herky-jerky movements, in sync with the suggestions. After hypnosis, she insists that her hand moved by itself, without her doing anything to lift it. Two more suggestions follow: one for numbness in her hand, after which she appears insensitive to her hand being pricked lightly with a needle, and another for her to hallucinate seeing a dog sitting in the corner. With little prompting, she walks over to the imaginary dog and pets him (Lynn & Rhue, 1991). At the end of the session, after Jessica opens her eyes, she still appears a bit sleepy.

Now consider a clever study in which Jason Noble and Kevin McConkey (1995) used hypnosis to suggest a change of sex. Most of the highly suggestible people who received the suggestion claimed that they were a person of the opposite sex, even after they were confronted with an image of themselves on a video monitor, and their sex transformation was challenged by an authority figure. One male subject commented, "Well, I'm not as pretty as I thought, but I have long, blond hair."

MYTHS AND MISCONCEPTIONS ABOUT HYPNOSIS: WHAT HYPNOSIS IS AND ISN'T. Do the remarkable changes in consciousness described in these examples signify a trance or sleeplike state? Might it be possible to exploit suggestibility for therapeutic purposes—say, for pain relief? These sorts of questions have stoked the curiosity of laypersons, scientists, and therapists for more than 200 years and stimulated scientific studies of hypnosis around the world (Cardeña, 2005; Nash & Barnier, 2008).

Hypnosis has fascinated scientists and clinical practitioners for more than two centuries, yet the basic methods for inducing hypnosis have changed little over the years.

hypnosis
set of techniques that provides people with suggestions for alterations in their perceptions, thoughts, feelings, and behaviors

FIGURE 5.5 Anti-Smoking Ad. Many advertisements for the effectiveness of hypnosis in treating smoking are misleading and exaggerated. Still, hypnosis can sometimes be combined with well-established treatment approaches as a cost-effective means of helping some people quit smoking.

Stop Smoking Forever with Hypnosis.

ruling out rival hypotheses

HAVE IMPORTANT ALTERNATIVE EXPLANATIONS FOR THE FINDINGS BEEN EXCLUDED?

FICTOID ✕

MYTH: Most hypnotists use a swinging watch to lull subjects into a state of relaxation.

REALITY: Few hypnotists today use a watch; any procedure that effectively induces expectancies of hypnosis can boost suggestibility in most people (Kirsch, 1991).

People who perform in stage hypnosis shows are carefully selected before the performance for high suggestibility.

Indeed, once regarded as largely pseudoscientific, hypnosis has moved into the mainstream of science and clinical practice, encouraged by the development of reliable and valid measures of hypnotic suggestibility. Typical suggestions on such scales call for changes in perceptions and sensations (such as hallucinating a person or object), movements (such as experiencing heaviness in the eyes and eye closure), and memory (experiencing amnesia for all or part of the session). Based on standardized scales, scientists have established that approximately 15 to 20 percent of people pass very few (0–3 out of 12) suggestions (low suggestibles); another 15 to 20 percent pass 9–12 of the suggestions (high suggestibles); and the remaining 60 to 70 percent pass 5–8 suggestions (medium suggestibles).

Hypnosis enjoys a wide range of clinical applications. Studies show that hypnosis enhances the effectiveness of psychodynamic and cognitive-behavioral psychotherapies (Kirsch, 1990; Kirsch, Montgomery, & Sapirstein, 1995), which we'll discuss in Chapter 16. Hypnosis is also useful for treating pain, medical conditions, and habit disorders (such as smoking addiction) (see **FIGURE 5.5**), and it boosts the effectiveness of therapies for anxiety, obesity, and other conditions (Lynn & Kirsch, 2006). Nevertheless, the extent to which the benefits associated with hypnosis in these cases are attributable to relaxation or enhanced expectancies for improvement remains unclear. Moreover, because there's no evidence that hypnosis is an effective treatment by itself, we should be skeptical of professional "hypnotherapists" (many of whom we can find in our local Yellow Pages who use nothing but hypnosis to treat serious psychological problems).

Despite the increasingly warm embrace of hypnosis by the professional community, public knowledge about hypnosis hasn't kept pace with scientific developments. We'll first examine six misconceptions about hypnosis before evaluating two prominent theories of how it works.

Myth 1: Hypnosis Produces a Trance State in Which "Amazing" Things Happen. Consider a sampling of movies that portray the hypnotic trance state as so overpowering that otherwise normal people will: (a) commit suicide (*The Garden Murders*); (b) disfigure themselves with scalding water (*The Hypnotic Eye*); (c) assist in blackmail (*On Her Majesty's Secret Service*); (d) perceive only a person's internal beauty (*Shallow Hal*); (e) experience total bliss (*Office Space*), (f) steal (*Curse of the Jade Scorpion*); and our favorite, (g) fall victim to brainwashing by alien preachers using messages in sermons (*Invasion of the Space Preachers*).

Other popular stereotypes of hypnosis derive from *stage hypnosis* shows, in which hypnotists seemingly program people to enact commands ranging from quacking like a duck to playing a wicked air guitar to the music of U2. But the wacky actions of people in movies and onstage have nothing to do with a trance state. In stage shows, the hypnotist carefully selects potential performers by observing how they respond to waking imaginative suggestions, which are highly correlated with how people respond to hypnotic suggestions (Braffman & Kirsch, 1999). Those whose outstretched hands drop or sag when asked to imagine holding a heavy dictionary are likely to be invited onstage because they're probably highly suggestible to begin with. Moreover, "hypnotized" volunteers often feel compelled to do outlandish things because they're under intense pressure to entertain the audience. Many stage hypnotists also use the *stage whispers* technique, in which they whisper instructions ("When I snap my fingers, bark like a dog") into volunteers' ears (Meeker & Barber, 1971).

Actually, hypnosis doesn't have a great impact on suggestibility, nor does it turn people into mindless robots. A person who responds to six out of 12 suggestions without being hypnotized might respond to seven or eight after hypnosis (Kirsch & Lynn, 1995). In addition, people can resist and even oppose hypnotic suggestions at will (Lynn, Rhue, & Weekes, 1990). So, Hollywood thrillers aside, hypnosis can't turn a mild-mannered person into a cold-blooded murderer.

Myth 2: Hypnotic Phenomena Are Unique. Contrary to popular belief, subjects can experience many hypnotic phenomena, such as hallucinations and pain insensitivity, when they receive suggestions alone, even without hypnosis (Barber, 1969; Sarbin & Coe, 1979; Spanos, 1986, 1991). What's more, some of the tricks we see in stage hypnosis shows, like suspending volunteers between the tops of two chairs, are easily duplicated in highly motivated participants without hypnosis.

Scientists haven't yet identified any unique physiological states or markers of hypnosis (Dixon & Laurence, 1992; Hasegawa & Jamieson, 2002; Sarbin & Slagle, 1979; Wagstaff, 1998). So there's no clear biological distinction between hypnosis and wakefulness. Moreover, people's brain activity during hypnosis depends very much on the suggestions they receive. People who receive suggestions for deep relaxation show different patterns of brain activity from those who receive suggestions to listen to an imaginary CD with the song "Jingle Bells."

This classic picture of a person suspended between two chairs illustrates the "human plank phenomenon," often demonstrated at stage hypnosis shows as "proof" of the special powers of hypnosis. In actuality, people who stiffen their bodies can do this without hypnosis; however, we don't recommend you try it. If the chairs aren't placed properly, the person can be injured.

Myth 3: Hypnosis Is a Sleeplike State. James Braid (1843), a Scottish physician, claimed that the hypnotized brain produces a condition akin to sleep. Braid labeled the phenomenon *neurohypnosis* (from the Greek word *hypno,* meaning "sleep"), and the shortened term "hypnosis" eventually stuck. Yet people who are hypnotized don't show brain waves similar to those of sleep. What's more, people are just as responsive to hypnotic suggestions administered while exercising on a stationary bicycle as they are following hypnotic suggestions for sleep and relaxation (Bányai & Hilgard, 1976; Wark, 2006).

Myth 4: Hypnotized People Are Unaware of Their Surroundings. Another popular idea is that hypnotized people are so "entranced" that they lose touch with their surroundings. In actuality, most hypnotized people are fully aware of their immediate surroundings, and can even recall the details of a telephone conversation they overheard during hypnosis (Lynn, Weekes, & Milano, 1989).

Myth 5: Hypnotized People Forget What Happened during Hypnosis. In the 1962 film *The Manchurian Candidate,* remade in 2004, a person is programmed by hypnosis to commit an assassination and has no memory of what transpired during hypnosis. In real life, *spontaneous amnesia* for what happens during hypnosis is rare and mostly limited to people who expect to be amnesic following hypnosis (Simon & Salzberg, 1985; Young & Cooper, 1972).

Myth 6: Hypnosis Enhances Memory. In 1976 in Chowchilla, California, three young men intent on committing the "perfect crime" kidnapped 26 children and their bus driver (see Chapter 7). The blundering criminals didn't expect their captives to escape after being hidden underground for six hours. After police apprehended the criminals, the bus driver was hypnotized and correctly provided numbers from the license plate of the kidnappers' car. The media capitalized on this now famous case to publicize the power of hypnosis to enhance recall. The problem is that the anecdote doesn't tell us whether hypnosis was responsible for what the driver remembered. Perhaps the driver recalled the event because people often can remember additional details when they try to recall an event a second time, regardless of whether they're hypnotized.

Moreover, the media tend not to report the scores of cases in which hypnosis fails to enhance memory, such as a Brinks armored car robbery that took place in Boston (Kihlstrom, 1987). In this case, the witness was hypnotized and confidently recalled the license plate of the car of the president of Harvard University, where the witness was employed. Apparently, he confused a car he'd seen multiple times with the car involved in the robbery.

Scientific studies generally reveal that hypnosis doesn't improve memory (Erdelyi, 1994; Mazzoni, Heap, & Scoboria, 2010). Hypnosis does increase the amount of information we recall, but much of it is inaccurate (Erdelyi, 1994; Steblay & Bothwell, 1994; Wagstaff, 2008). To make matters worse, hypnosis tends to increase eyewitnesses' confidence in inaccurate, as well as accurate, memories (Green & Lynn, 2005). Indeed, courts in most U.S. states have banned the testimony of hypnotized witnesses out of concerns that their inaccurate statements will sway a jury and lead to wrongful convictions.

Hypnotists frequently present subjects with the suggestion that one of their arms is lifting involuntarily.

FICTOID

MYTH: People can become "stuck" in hypnosis, and may remain in a permanent hypnotized state if the hypnotist leaves.

REALITY: There's no evidence that people can become stuck in a hypnotic state; this misconception assumes erroneously that hypnotized people are in a distinct trance.

◄ ruling out rival hypotheses

HAVE IMPORTANT ALTERNATIVE EXPLANATIONS FOR THE FINDINGS BEEN EXCLUDED?

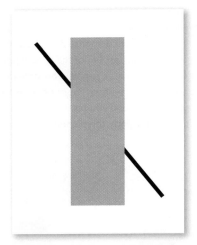

Researchers have used the Poggendorf illusion, shown above, to study the effects of hypnotic age regression. Adults tend to see the two segments of the black line as misaligned (in reality, they're perfectly aligned), whereas children don't. When adult subjects are age-regressed to childhood, they still see the two segments of the black line as misaligned, suggesting that hypnotic age regression doesn't make adults' perceptions more childlike (Ascher, Barber, & Spanos, 1972; Nash, 1987).

AGE REGRESSION AND PAST LIVES

One of the most popular myths of hypnosis is that it can help people retrieve memories of events as far back in time as birth. A televised documentary (Bikel, 1995) showed a group therapy session in which a woman was age-regressed through childhood, to the womb, and eventually to being trapped in her mother's fallopian tube. The woman provided a highly emotional demonstration of the discomfort that one would experience if one were indeed stuck in such an uncomfortable position. Although the woman may have believed in the reality of her experience, we can be quite certain that it wasn't memory based (after all, she didn't have a brain yet, because she wasn't even a fertilized egg at this point). Instead, age-regressed subjects behave the way they think children should behave. Age-regressed adults don't show the expected patterns on many indices of development. For example, when regressed to childhood, they exhibit the brain waves (EEGs; see Chapter 3) typical of adults rather than of children. No matter how compelling, age-regressed experiences aren't exact mental replicas of childhood experiences (Nash, 1987).

Some therapists believe that they can trace their patients' current problems to previous lives and practice **past life regression therapy** (Weiss, 1988). Typically, they hypnotize and age-regress patients to "go back to" the source of their present-day psychological and physical problems. For example, some practitioners of past life regression therapy claim that neck and shoulder pains may be signs of having been executed by hanging or by a guillotine in a previous life.

With rare exceptions (Stevenson, 1974), researchers believe that reports of a past life are the products of imagination and what hypnotized participants know about a given time period. When checked against known facts (such as whether the country was at war or peace, the face on the coin of the time), subjects' descriptions of the historical circumstances of their supposed past lives are rarely accurate. When they are, we can often explain this accuracy by "educated guesses" and knowledge of history (Spanos et al., 1991). One participant regressed to ancient times claimed to be Julius Caesar, emperor of Rome, in 50 B.C., even though the designations of B.C. and A.D. weren't adopted until centuries later and even though Julius Caesar died decades before the first Roman emperor came to power. Moreover, one of the best predictors of whether people will experience a past life memory while regressed is whether they accept the existence of reincarnation (Baker, 1992), bolstering the claim that past life memories are products of people's beliefs and expectancies.

past life regression therapy
therapeutic approach that hypnotizes and supposedly age-regresses patients to a previous life to identify the source of a present-day problem

sociocognitive theory
approach to explaining hypnosis based on people's attitudes, beliefs, and expectations

THEORIES OF HYPNOSIS. Researchers have attempted to explain hypnosis by a host of factors, including (a) unconscious drives and motivations (Baker, 1985; Fromm & Nash, 1997); (b) a willingness to overlook logical inconsistencies (Orne, 1959); (c) receptivity to suggestion (McConkey, 1991; Sheehan, 1991); and (d) inhibition of the brain's frontal lobes (Farvolden & Woody, 2004; Woody & Bowers, 1994). Each of these theories has contributed valuable insights into hypnotic phenomena and generated useful research (Kihlstrom, 2003; Nash & Barnier, 2008). Nevertheless, two other models, the sociocognitive theory and the dissociation theory, have received the lion's share of attention.

Sociocognitive Theory. Sociocognitive theorists (Barber, 1969; Coe & Sarbin, 1991; Lynn, Kirsch, & Hallquist, 2008; Spanos, 1986) reject the idea that hypnosis is a trance state or unique state of consciousness. Instead, they explain hypnosis in the same way they explain everyday social behaviors. According to **sociocognitive theory**, people's attitudes, beliefs, motivations, and expectations about hypnosis, as well as their ability to respond to waking imaginative suggestions, shape their responses to hypnosis.

Theories of hypnosis, including sociocognitive theory, must address why some people are highly responsive to hypnotic suggestions whereas others aren't. Peoples' expectations of whether they'll respond to hypnotic suggestions are correlated with how they respond (Kirsch & Council, 1992). Still, this correlation doesn't necessarily mean that people's expectations cause them to be susceptible to hypnosis. Studies in which participants' responses vary as a function of what they're told about hypnosis provide more convincing evidence of causality. Participants told that hypnotized people can resist suggestions find themselves able to resist, whereas those told that hypnotized people can't resist suggestions often fail to resist (Lynn et al., 1984; Spanos, Cobb, & Gorassini, 1985).

Sociocognitive theory proposes that attitudes, beliefs, and motivations influence people's suggestibility. Studies show that a training program that increases people's positive feelings and expectancies about hypnosis and their willingness to imagine along with suggestions increases their ability to respond to hypnosis (Gorassini & Spanos, 1998). About half of subjects who initially score at the lowest range of suggestibility test at the top range of suggestibility after training. These findings challenge the idea that hypnotic suggestibility is a stable trait that can't be modified (Piccione, Hilgard, & Zimbardo, 1989) and offer support for sociocognitive theory.

Dissociation Theory. Ernest Hilgard's (1977, 1986, 1994) **dissociation theory** is an influential alternative to sociocognitive theories of hypnosis (Kihlstrom, 1992, 1998; Woody & Sadler, 2008). Hilgard (1977) defined *dissociation* as a division of consciousness, in which attention, effort, and planning are carried out without awareness. He hypothesized that hypnotic suggestions result in a separation between personality functions that are normally well integrated.

Hilgard (1977) happened on a discovery that played a key role in the development of his theory. During a demonstration of hypnotically suggested deafness, a student asked whether some part of the person could hear. Hilgard then told the subject that when he touched the subject's arm he'd be able to talk to the part that could hear if such a part existed. When Hilgard placed his hand on the subject's arm, the subject described what people in the room said. However, when Hilgard removed his hand, the subject was again "deaf." Hilgard invented the metaphor of the *hidden observer* to describe the dissociated, unhypnotized "part" of the mind that he could access on cue. Much of the support for dissociation theory derives from hidden observer studies of hypnotic blindness, pain, and hallucinations. For example, in studies of hypnotic analgesia (inability to experience pain), experimenters bring forth hidden observers, which report pain even though the "hypnotized part" reports little or no pain (Hilgard, 1977).

Later researchers suggested an alternative explanation for the hidden observer phenomenon (Kirsch & Lynn, 1998; Spanos, 1986, 1991). Nicholas Spanos (1991) believed that the hidden observer arises because the hypnotist suggests it directly or indirectly. That is, subjects pick up on the fact that the instructions used to bring forth the hidden observer imply they should act as though a separate, nonhypnotized "part" of the person can communicate with the hypnotist. Spanos hypothesized that changing the instructions should change what the hidden observer reports.

That's exactly what he found. Changing the instructions led hidden observers to experience more pain or less pain, or to perceive a number normally or in reverse (Spanos & Hewitt, 1980), leading Irving Kirsch and Steven Jay Lynn (1998) to dub the phenomenon the *flexible observer*. From their perspective, the hidden observer is no different from any other suggested hypnotic response: It's shaped by what we expect and believe.

According to a revision of Hilgard's dissociation theory (Woody & Bowers, 1994), hypnosis bypasses the ordinary sense of control we exert over our behaviors. Thus, suggestions directly bring about responses with little or no sense of effort or conscious control (Jamieson & Sheehan, 2004; Sadler & Woody, 2010). This theory does a good job of describing what people experience during hypnosis, and fits nicely with sociocognitive theories that emphasize the unconscious, automatic nature of most behaviors both within and apart from the context of hypnosis (Kirsch & Lynn, 1998; see Chapter 1).

correlation vs. causation
CAN WE BE SURE THAT A CAUSES B?

Socio cognitive theory
→ people respond to hypnosis with influences from attitudes, beliefs, and motivations

Dissociation Theory
→ hypnotic suggestions result in separation between personality functions that are usually integrated

ruling out rival hypotheses
HAVE IMPORTANT ALTERNATIVE EXPLANATIONS FOR THE FINDINGS BEEN EXCLUDED?

dissociation theory
approach to explaining hypnosis based on a separation between personality functions that are normally well integrated

✔●—[Study and Review on mypsychlab.com

DRUGS AND CONSCIOUSNESS

5.8　Identify possible influences on alcohol abuse and dependence.

5.9　Distinguish different types of drugs and their effects on consciousness.

Virtually every culture has discovered that certain plant substances can alter consciousness, often dramatically. Knowledge of the mind-bending qualities of fermented fruits and grains, the juice of the poppy, boiled coffee beans and tea leaves, the burning tobacco or marijuana leaf, certain molds that grow on crops, and the granulated extract of the coca leaf has been handed down to us from ancient times. We now know that these **psychoactive drugs** contain chemicals similar to those found naturally in our brains and that their molecules alter consciousness by changing chemical processes in neurons (see Chapter 3). Some psychoactive drugs are used to treat physical and mental illness, but others are used almost exclusively for recreational purposes. The precise psychological and physical effects depend on the type of drug and dosage, as we've summarized in **TABLE 5.3**.

But as we'll see, the effects of drugs depend on far more than their chemical properties. *Mental set*—beliefs and expectancies about the effects of drugs—and the settings in which people take these drugs also account for people's responses to them. People's reactions to drugs are also rooted in their cultural heritage and genetic endowment.

■ Substance Abuse and Dependence

Drugs are substances that change the way we think, feel, or act. It's easy to forget that alcohol and nicotine are drugs, because they're typically commonplace and legal. Still, the misuse of both legal and illegal drugs is a serious societal problem. According to a national survey (Johnston et al., 2009a), 66 percent of young people (ages 29–30) reported having tried marijuana, and 48 percent report having tried other illegal drugs, like cocaine, heroin, and hallucinogens.

psychoactive drug
substance that contains chemicals similar to those found naturally in our brains that alter consciousness by changing chemical processes in neurons

TABLE 5.3 Major Drug Types and Their Effects.

DRUG TYPE	EXAMPLES	EFFECT ON BEHAVIOR
Depressants	Alcohol, barbiturates, Quaaludes, Valium	Decreased activity of the central nervous system (initial high followed by sleepiness, slower thinking, and impaired concentration)
Stimulants	Tobacco, cocaine, amphetamines, methamphetamine	Increased activity of the central nervous system (sense of alertness, well-being, energy)
Opiates	Heroin, morphine, codeine	Sense of euphoria, decreased pain
Psychedelics	Marijuana, LSD, Ecstasy	Dramatically altered perception, mood, and thoughts

ABUSE VERSUS DEPENDENCE: A FINE LINE. There's often a fine line between drug use and abuse. What starts out as experimentation with drugs to "get high" and be sociable with friends can become a pattern of intensified use, and lead to substance abuse and dependence (dependence on alcohol is commonly known as "alcoholism"). Generally speaking, people qualify for a diagnosis of *substance abuse* when they experience recurrent problems associated with the drug (APA, 2000). Problems often surface in the family, with friends, on the job, in fulfilling life responsibilities, and with the law.

Substance dependence is a more serious pattern of use, leading to clinically significant impairment, distress, or both. **TABLE 5.4** shows the complete set of symptoms required for a diagnosis of substance dependence. **Tolerance** is a key feature of dependence and occurs when people need to consume an increased amount of a drug to achieve intoxication. Alternatively, people who develop tolerance may not obtain the same reaction or "kick" from a drug after using it for some time. Tolerance is often associated with increases in the amount of drugs people consume. ◉─Watch

When people use drugs for long periods of time and then either stop or cut down on their use, they're likely to experience **withdrawal** symptoms that vary with the drug they use. Alcohol withdrawal symptoms, for example, can range from insomnia and mild anxiety to more severe symptoms such as seizures, confusion, and hallucinations (Bayard et al., 2004). People exhibit **physical dependence** on a drug when they continue to take it to avoid withdrawal symptoms. In contrast, people can develop **psychological dependence** when their continued use of a drug is motivated by intense cravings.

According to one survey (Knight et al., 2002), within a 12-month period, 6 percent of college students met the criteria for a diagnosis of alcohol dependence, and 31 percent for the diagnosis of alcohol abuse. Still, most people don't fit neatly into categories of substance abuse versus dependence and vary a great deal in the severity of their symptoms (Harford & Muthen, 2001; Sher, Grekin, & Williams, 2006).

EXPLANATIONS FOR DRUG USE AND ABUSE. People often begin using drugs when they become available, when their family or peers approve of them, and when they don't anticipate serious consequences from their use (Pihl, 1999). Illegal drug use typically starts in early adolescence, peaks in early adulthood, and declines sharply thereafter. Young adults may turn to drugs for novel experiences, as a way of rebelling against their parents, and as a means of gaining peer approval (Deater-Deckard, 2001; Fergusson, Swain-Campbell, & Horwood, 2002). Fortunately, later in life, pressures to be employed and establish a family often counteract earlier pressures and attitudes associated with drug use (Newcomb & Bentler, 1988). In the sections to come, we'll focus on the causes of alcohol abuse and alcohol dependence because they're the forms of drug misuse that scientists best understand.

◉─Watch the Alcoholism video on
mypsychlab.com

TABLE 5.4 Symptoms of Substance Dependence. A maladaptive pattern of substance use, leading to clinically significant impairment or distress, as manifested by at least three of the following (in the same 12-month period).

1. Tolerance
2. Withdrawal
3. The substance is often taken in larger amounts or over a longer period than was intended
4. Persistent desire or unsuccessful efforts to cut down or control substance use
5. A great deal of time is spent in activities necessary to obtain the substance
6. Important social, occupational, or recreational activities are given up or reduced because of substance use
7. Substance use is continued despite knowledge of having a persistent or recurrent physical or psychological problem related to the substance

(*Source:* From *Diagnostic and Statistical Manual of Mental Disorders*, 4th ed., American Psychiatric Association, 2000)

tolerance
reduction in the effect of a drug as a result of repeated use, requiring users to consume greater quantities to achieve the same effect

withdrawal
unpleasant effects of reducing or stopping consumption of a drug that users had consumed habitually

physical dependence
dependence on a drug that occurs when people continue to take it to avoid withdrawal symptoms

psychological dependence
dependence on a drug that occurs when continued use of the drug is motivated by intense cravings

Sociocultural Influences. Cultures or groups in which drinking is strictly prohibited, such as Muslims or Mormons, exhibit low rates of alcoholism (Chentsova-Dutton & Tsai, 2006). In Egypt, the annual rate of alcohol dependence is only .2 percent, that is, about one in 500 people (World Health Organization, 2004). The situation differs markedly in some so-called vinocultural or "wet" societies, such as France and Italy, which view drinking as a healthy part of daily life (*vino* refers to wine in many languages). In Poland, a "wet" country, the annual rate of alcohol dependence among adults is 11.2 percent. Some researchers attribute these differences to cultural differences in attitudes toward alcohol and its abuse. Nevertheless, these differences could also be due in part to genetic influences, and the cultural attitudes themselves may reflect these differences.

Unemployed people are at relatively high risk for alcohol abuse, and may use alcohol to cope with being out of work. Nevertheless, the converse is also likely to be true: People who abuse alcohol are more likely than other people to perform poorly at work and lose their jobs (Forcier, 1988). So in this case cause and effect may be difficult to separate.

Is There an Addictive Personality? Important as they are, sociocultural factors don't easily explain individual differences *within* cultures. We can find alcoholics in societies with strong sanctions against drinking and teetotalers in societies in which drinking is widespread. To explain these facts, popular and scientific psychologists alike have long wondered whether certain people have an "addictive personality" that predisposes them to abuse alcohol and other drugs (Shaffer, 2000). On the one hand, research suggests that common wisdom to the contrary, there's no single addictive personality profile (Rozin & Stoess, 1993). On the other hand, researchers have found that certain personality traits predispose to alcohol and drug abuse. In particular, studies have tied substance abuse to impulsivity (Baker & Yardley, 2002; Kanzler & Rosenthal, 2003; Kollins, 2003), sociability (Wennberg, 2002), and a propensity to experience negative emotions, like anxiety and hostility (Jackson & Sher, 2003). But some of these traits may partly result from, rather than cause, substance misuse. Also, as we'll soon learn, genetic influences appear to account at least in part for both antisocial behavior and alcoholism risk (Slutske et al., 1998). ◉ Watch

Learning and Expectancies. According to the *tension reduction hypothesis* (Cappell & Herman, 1972; Sayette, 1999; Sher, 1987), people consume alcohol and other drugs to relieve anxiety. Such "self-medication" reinforces drug use and increases the probability of continued use. Alcohol affects brain centers involved in reward (Koob, 2000) as well as dopamine, which plays a crucial role in reward (see Chapter 3). Nevertheless, people probably drink to relieve anxiety only when they believe alcohol is a stress reducer (Greeley & Oei, 1999), so expectancies almost certainly play a role, too. But once individuals become dependent on alcohol, the discomfort of their withdrawal symptoms can motivate drug-seeking behavior and continued use.

Genetic Influences. Alcoholism tends to run in families (Sher, Grekin, & Williams, 2005). But this doesn't tell us whether this finding is due to genes, shared environment, or both. Twin and adoption studies have resolved the issue: They show that genetic factors play a key role in the vulnerability to alcoholism (McGue, 1999). Multiple genes are probably involved (NIAAA, 2000), but what's inherited? No one knows for sure, but researchers have uncovered a genetic link between people's response to alcohol and their risk of developing alcoholism. A strong negative reaction to alcohol use decreases the risk of alcoholism, whereas a weak response increases this risk. A mutation in the aldehyde 2 (ALDH2) gene causes a distinctly unpleasant response to alcohol: facial flushing, heart palpitations (feeling one's heart beating), and nausea (Higuchi et al., 1995). This gene is present in about 40 percent of people of Asian descent, who are at low risk for alcoholism and drink less alcohol than people in most other ethnic groups (Cook & Wall, 2005).

ruling out rival hypotheses

HAVE IMPORTANT ALTERNATIVE EXPLANATIONS FOR THE FINDINGS BEEN EXCLUDED?

correlation vs. causation

CAN WE BE SURE THAT A CAUSES B?

correlation vs. causation

CAN WE BE SURE THAT A CAUSES B?

◉ Watch Addicted to Video Games on mypsychlab.com

ruling out rival hypotheses

HAVE IMPORTANT ALTERNATIVE EXPLANATIONS FOR THE FINDINGS BEEN EXCLUDED?

Marc Schuckit (1994) argued that a genetically influenced weak response to alcohol contributes to a later desire to drink heavily to achieve the pleasurable effects of intoxication. Schuckit (1988) discovered that nearly 40 percent of people with an alcoholic parent, compared with less than 10 percent of people with nonalcoholic parents, showed few signs of intoxication after drinking, even when they consumed the equivalent of about three alcoholic drinks. To determine whether reactions to alcohol predict alcohol abuse, Schuckit (1998) followed 435 20-year-olds for 10 years. Those with an initial weak response to alcohol displayed a fourfold increase in their risk for alcoholism at age 30. Recently, researchers confirmed Schuckit's claim and identified a gene on chromosome 15 that may be associated with a weak response to alcohol (Josslyn et al., 2008). In coming years, scientists may better understand how the genetic predisposition to heavy drinking and the use of other substances is activated by environmental factors, such as life stressors, peer pressure, and drug availability (Sher et al., 2005).

■ Depressants

Alcohol and sedative-hypnotics (barbiturates and benzodiazepines) are depressant drugs, so-called because they depress the effects of the central nervous system. In contrast, stimulant drugs, like nicotine and cocaine, which we'll review in the next section, rev up our central nervous systems. We'll learn that the effects of alcohol are remarkably wide-ranging, varying from stimulation at low doses to sedation at higher doses. By the way, **sedative** means "calming," and **hypnotic** means "sleep-inducing" (despite its name, it doesn't mean "hypnosis-inducing").

ALCOHOL. Humanity has long had an intimate relationship with alcohol. Some scientists speculate that a long-forgotten person from the late Stone Age, perhaps 10,000 years ago, accidentally partook of a jar of honey that had been left out too long (Vallee, 1988). He or she became the first human to drink alcohol, and the human race has never been quite the same since. Today, alcohol is the most widely used and abused drug. Almost two-thirds (62 percent) of adult men in our society report using alcohol in the past month (Centers for Disease Control, 2009), and 39 percent of 8th graders report that they tried alcohol at one time (Johnston et al., 2009b). _wow._

We must look to the effects of alcohol to understand its powerful appeal. Although many people believe that alcohol is a stimulant, physiologically it's primarily a depressant. Alcohol behaves as an emotional and physiological stimulant only at relatively low doses because it depresses areas of the brain that inhibit emotion and behavior (Pohorecky, 1977; Tucker, Vucinich, & Sobell, 1982). Small amounts of alcohol can promote feelings of relaxation, elevate mood, increase talkativeness and activity, lower inhibitions, and impair judgment. At higher doses, when the blood alcohol content (BAC)—the concentration of alcohol in the blood—reaches .05 to .10, the sedating and depressant effects of alcohol generally become more apparent. Brain centers become depressed, slowing thinking and impairing concentration, walking, and muscular coordination (Erblich et al., 2003). At higher doses, users sometimes experience a mix of stimulating and sedating effects (King et al., 2002).

The short-term effects of intoxication are directly related to the BAC. Contrary to popular myth, switching among different types of alcohol—like beer, wine, and hard liquor—is no more likely to lead to drunkenness than sticking with one type of alcohol (see **TABLE 5.5** on page 190). The feeling of intoxication depends largely on the rate of absorption of alcohol by the bloodstream, mostly through the stomach and intestines. The more food in our stomach, the less quickly alcohol is absorbed. This fact explains why we feel more of an effect of alcohol on an empty stomach. Compared with men, women have more body fat (alcohol isn't fat-soluble) and less water in which to dilute alcohol. So a woman whose weight equals that of a man, and who's consumed the same amount of alcohol, will

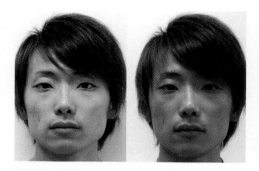

? Like some people of Asian heritage, this person shows a pronounced flushing response after having a drink, as seen in this before and after panel. **Based on the research literature, is he likely to be at increased or decreased risk for alcohol problems in later life compared with most people?** (See answer upside-down at bottom of page).

---

sedative
drug that exerts a calming effect

hypnotic
drug that exerts a sleep-inducing effect

Answer: Decreased.

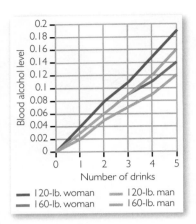

FIGURE 5.6   Influences on BAC.   A person's blood alcohol content (BAC) depends on a variety of factors beyond the number of drinks consumed. The person's weight, gender, and stomach contents all play a role. This graph shows how body weight and gender influence BAC. For both men and women, heavier people have a lower BAC, but at both 120 pounds and 160 pounds, women have a higher BAC than men.

Research shows that when driving down a highway, our hands are almost constantly performing minor adjustments to the steering wheel of which we're not consciously aware. Excessive alcohol can inhibit these adjustments, causing us to weave or swerve into other lanes without realizing it (Brookhuis, 1998).

TABLE 5.5 Five Other Alcohol Myths.   Although we've addressed some popular misconceptions about alcohol in the text, there are scores of others. How many of these have you heard?

MISCONCEPTION	TRUTH
1. Every time we drink, we destroy about 10,000 brain cells.	Scientists haven't precisely determined the effect of a single drink on brain cell loss. Heavy drinking over time is associated with brain damage and memory problems.
2. It's okay to drive a few hours after drinking.	Coordination can be affected as much as 10–12 hours after drinking, so it's not safe to drink and drive. Binge-drinking (five or more drinks at a time if male; four, if female) is associated with 80 percent of traffic accidents (Marczinski, Harrison, & Fillmore, 2008).
3. To avoid a hangover, take two or three acetaminophen tablets, a common alternative to aspirin.	Taking acetaminophen tablets can increase the toxicity of alcohol to the liver.
4. Our judgment isn't impaired until we're extremely drunk.	Impaired judgment can occur well before obvious signs of intoxication appear.
5. A "blackout" is passing out from drinking.	A "blackout" is a loss of memory for a period of time while drunk, and has nothing to do with passing out.

have a higher BAC than he will (Kinney & Leaton, 1995). **FIGURE 5.6** shows the relationship between the amounts of beverage consumed and alcohol concentration in the blood. Because absorption varies as a function of variables like stomach contents and body weight, these effects vary across persons and occasions.

In most states, a BAC of .08 is the cutoff for legal intoxication while operating a vehicle; at this point the operation of an automobile is hazardous. In the BAC range of .20 to .30, impairment increases to the point at which strong sedation occurs; at .40 to .50, unconsciousness may set in. Blood alcohol levels of .50 to .60 may prove fatal. The body metabolizes alcohol at the rate of about one-half ounce per hour (the equivalent of about an ounce of whiskey). We'll explore other health risks associated with alcohol consumption in Chapter 12.

Although drug effects are influenced by the dose of the drug, the user's expectancies also play a substantial role. The *balanced placebo design* is a four-group design (see **FIGURE 5.7**) in which researchers tell participants they either are, or aren't, receiving an active drug and, in fact, either do or don't receive it (Kirsch, 2003). This clever design allows researchers to tease apart the relative influence of expectancies (placebo effects) and the physiological effects of alcohol and other drugs.

The results of balanced placebo studies show that at low alcohol dose levels, culturally learned expectancies influence mood and complex social behaviors. Remarkably, participants who ingest a placebo drink mixed to taste just like alcohol display many of the same subjective effects of drunkenness as participants who ingest an actual alcoholic drink.

FIGURE 5.7   The Four Groups of the Balanced Placebo Design.   The balanced-placebo design includes four groups in which participants (a) are told they're receiving a drug and in fact receive a drug, (b) are told they're receiving a drug but actually receive a placebo, (c) are told they're receiving a placebo but actually receive a drug, and (d) are told they're receiving a placebo and in fact receive a placebo.

Expectancies are often more important than the physiological effects of alcohol in influencing social behaviors, such as aggression (Lang et al., 1975). Alcohol may provide some people with an excuse to engage in actions that are socially prohibited or discouraged, like flirting (Hull & Bond, 1986). In males, expectancies may override the pharmacological effects of alcohol in enhancing humor, anxiety reduction, and sexual responsivity. In contrast, nonsocial behaviors, such as reaction time and motor coordination, are more influenced by alcohol itself than by expectancies (Marlatt & Rosenow, 1980). Expectancies that drinking will produce positive outcomes predict who'll drink and how much they'll drink, and expectancies that drinking will produce negative outcomes predict who'll abstain (Goldman, Darkes, & Del Boca, 1999; Leigh & Stacy, 2004).

The *setting*, or social context in which people consume alcohol, also influences its effects. For example, subjects tested in a barlike situation with drinking companions feel more friendly and elated when they drink, and consume nearly twice as much alcohol as subjects who drink by themselves (Lindman, 1982; Sher et al., 2005).

THE SEDATIVE-HYPNOTICS. When people have problems falling asleep or are excessively anxious, they may consult a physician to obtain sedative-hypnotic drugs. Because these drugs produce depressant effects, they're dangerous at high dosages and can produce unconsciousness, coma, and even death.

Researchers usually group sedative-hypnotics into three categories: *barbiturates* (for example, Seconal, Nembutal, and Tuinal); *nonbarbiturates* (for example, Sopor and Methaqualone, better known as Quaalude); and *benzodiazepines*. Benzodiazepines, including Valium, were extremely popular in the 1960s and 1970s and are still widely used today to relieve anxiety. Barbiturates produce a state of intoxication very similar to that of alcohol. Barbiturates have the greatest abuse potential, which is troubling because the consequences of overdose are often fatal.

■ Stimulants

Nicotine, contained in tobacco, as well as cocaine and amphetamines, are **stimulants** because they rev up our central nervous system. In contrast to depressants, they increase heart rate, respiration, and blood pressure.

NICOTINE. Over the course of human history, people have consumed tobacco in various ways: smoking, chewing, dipping, licking, and even drinking (Gritz, 1980). As cigarette companies have long known but were reluctant to admit, the nicotine in tobacco is a potent and addictive drug. It reaches the brain about 10 seconds after it's inhaled, and its effects register at the spinal cord, peripheral nervous system, heart, and other bodily organs shortly thereafter. Nicotine activates receptors sensitive to the neurotransmitter acetylcholine, and smokers often report feelings of stimulation as well as relaxation and alertness.

Like many other drugs taken for nonmedical purposes, nicotine has *adjustive value*, meaning it can enhance positive emotional reactions and minimize negative emotional reactions, including the distress experienced when the nicotine level drops (Leventhal & Cleary, 1980). For many young people, positive images associated with smoking enhance its appeal. In Chapter 12, we'll examine the many negative health consequences of tobacco use. ◉ Watch

COCAINE. Cocaine is the most powerful natural stimulant. Cocaine users commonly report euphoria, enhanced mental and physical capacity, stimulation, a decrease in hunger, indifference to pain, and a sense of well-being accompanied by diminished fatigue. These effects peak quickly and usually fade within a half hour.

Cocaine grows in abundance in the mountainous region of South America, where it's obtained from the leaves of a shrub, *Erythroxylum coca*. By the late 1800s, doctors hailed cocaine as a cure-all and prescribed it for a wide range of illnesses. Around the turn of the

For years, cigarette companies published advertisements claiming that smoking is good for people's health, as in this 1946 ad boasting of Camel's popularity among physicians.

◉ Watch Smoking Damage on mypsychlab.com

stimulant
drug that increases activity in the central nervous system, including heart rate, respiration, and blood pressure

At the turn of the twentieth century, many nonprescription products, such as the then-new soft drink Coca-Cola, contained tiny amounts of cocaine.

FACTOID +

Recent research suggests that trace (tiny) amounts of cocaine are present on 90 percent of dollar bills (and other paper money) in the United States. These amounts are highest in U.S. cities with the highest prevalence of drug problems; in Washington, DC, for example, 96 percent of paper money contained at least some cocaine (Raloff, 2009).

Smoking crack, a highly concentrated form of cocaine, is more dangerous than snorting regular cocaine.

century, medicines, wines, and alcoholic tonics containing cocaine and coca extracts were popular. Until 1903, Coca-Cola contained small amounts of cocaine, and was advertised to "cure your headache and relieve fatigue for only 5 cents."

Even Sigmund Freud advocated the use of cocaine to treat morphine addiction and used cocaine to improve his mood. However, he came out against its use after dependence problems surfaced shortly after the drug became popular. Cocaine came under strict government control in the United States in 1906.

According to surveys, 5 percent of 12th graders reported having used cocaine in the past year, and 40 percent of people by the age of 50 report having used cocaine at least once (Johnston et al, 2009a,b). Cocaine is a powerful reinforcer. When conditioned to self-inject cocaine, rhesus monkeys remain intoxicated for long periods of time. They may even "dose themselves to death" when unlimited quantities of cocaine are available (Johanson, Balster, & Bonese, 1976). Heavy intake of cocaine by humans also produces an intense drive to use it (Spotts & Shontz, 1976, 1983). Cocaine increases the activity of the neurotransmitters dopamine and perhaps serotonin, which contribute to its reinforcing effects.

Cocaine users can inject it intravenously. But they more commonly inhale or "snort" it through the nose, where the nasal mucous membranes absorb it. *Crack cocaine* is a highly concentrated dose of cocaine produced by dissolving cocaine in an alkaline (basic) solution and boiling it until a whitish lump, or "rock" remains that can be smoked. Crack's popularity is attributable to the intense euphoria it generates and its relative affordability. But the "high" is short-lived and followed by unpleasant feelings, which often leads to consuming cocaine whenever available to regain the high (Gottheil & Weinstein, 1983).

AMPHETAMINES. Amphetamines are among the most commonly abused of all drugs, with 37 percent of Americans trying them at least once by age 50 (Johnston et al., 2009a). Amphetamines illustrate how different patterns of use can produce different subjective effects. The first pattern involves occasional use of small doses of oral amphetamines to postpone fatigue, elevate mood while performing an unpleasant task, cram for a test, or experience well-being. In this case, intake of amphetamines doesn't become a routine part of the users' lifestyle.

In the second pattern, users obtain amphetamines from a doctor, but ingest them on a regular basis for euphoria-producing effects rather than for their prescribed purpose. In these cases, a potent psychological dependence on the drug may occur, followed by depression if regular use is interrupted.

The third pattern is associated with street users—"speed freaks"—who inject large doses of amphetamines intravenously to achieve the "rush" of pleasure immediately following the injection. These users are likely to be restless, talkative, and excited, and to inject amphetamines repeatedly to prolong euphoria. Inability to sleep and loss of appetite are also hallmarks of the so-called speed binge. Users may become increasingly suspicious and hostile and develop paranoid delusions (believing that others are out to get them).

In recent years, *methamphetamine*, a drug closely related chemically to amphetamines, has emerged as a widely used drug of abuse. As many as one in 20 high school students report using methamphetamine (Johnston et al., 2009b). In its crystalline and highly addictive form, it's known as crystal meth or simply "meth." When they smoke it, users experience intense exhilaration, followed by euphoria that can last 12 to 16 hours. Crystal meth is more powerful than amphetamines, generally has a higher purity level, and carries a high risk of overdose and dependence. Meth can destroy tissues and blood vessels and cause acne; it can also lead to weight loss, tremors, and dental problems.

■ Narcotics

The opiate drugs heroin, morphine, and codeine are derived from the opium poppy, a plant found in abundance in Asia. Morphine is the major ingredient in opium. The action of heroin is virtually identical to that of morphine, but heroin is about three times as powerful and now accounts for 90 percent of opiate abuse. The opiates often are called **narcotics** because they relieve pain and induce sleep.

At first glance, heroin's psychological effects might appear mostly pleasurable: "Heroin is the king of drugs. . . . It leaves you floating on a calm sea where nothing seems to matter and everything is okay. . . . Suddenly the emptiness disappears. . . . The terrible growing inadequacy has vanished. And in its place is the power and comfort that's called confidence. No one can get to you when you keep nodding" (Rosenberg, 1973, pp. 25–26). This description conveys a sense of the euphoria that opiate users may experience. But these pleasurable effects are limited to the three or four hours that the usual dose lasts. If people addicted to heroin don't take another dose within four to six hours, they experience *heroin withdrawal syndrome,* with symptoms like abdominal cramps, vomiting, craving for the drug, yawning, runny nose, sweating, and chills. With continued heroin use, the drug's euphoric effects gradually diminish. The addict may continue using heroin as much to avoid withdrawal symptoms as to experience the intense high of the first few injections (Hutcheson et al., 2001; Julien, 2004).

About 1 to 2 percent of young adults have tried heroin (Johnston, O'Malley, & Bachman, 2003; Johnston et al., 2009a). The sleep-inducing properties of heroin derive largely from its depressant effects on the central nervous system: drowsiness follows injection, breathing and pulse rate slow, and pupils constrict. At higher doses, coma and death may follow.

Even infrequent users risk becoming addicted to heroin. But as we'll discover in Chapter 6, contrary to popular conception, heroin addiction isn't inevitable (Sullum, 2003). For example, people who use opiates for medical purposes don't necessarily become addicted.

Since the introduction of the powerful opiate pain reliever OxyContin in the mid-1990s, drug abusers have turned to it increasingly for "highs." Unfortunately, injecting or taking OxyContin in pill form in combination with alcohol and other depressant drugs can be lethal (Cone et al., 2004).

■ Psychedelics

Scientists describe such drugs as LSD, mescaline, PCP, and Ecstasy as **hallucinogenic** or *psychedelic* because they produce dramatic alterations in perception, mood, and thought. Because the effects of marijuana aren't as "mind-bending" as those of LSD, some researchers don't classify marijuana as a hallucinogen. In contrast, others describe it as a "mild hallucinogen." Interestingly, marijuana may also have sedative or hypnotic qualities.

MARIJUANA. Marijuana is the most frequently used illegal drug in the United States. By the age of 50, 74 percent of adults report having used it at least once (Johnston et al., 2009a). Known in popular culture as pot, grass, herb, Mary Jane, 420, and weed, marijuana comes from the leaves and flowering part of the hemp plant (*Cannabis sativa*). The subjective effects of marijuana are produced by its primary ingredient, THC (delta-9-tetrahydrocannabinol). People experience a "high" feeling within a few minutes, which peaks within a half hour. Hashish, manufactured from the buds and flowers of female plants, contains much greater concentrations of THC than marijuana and is more potent.

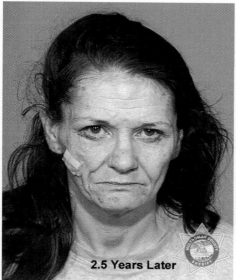

2.5 Years Later

The photo of 42-year-old Theresa Baxter on the top was taken before she became a methamphetamine addict. The photo on the bottom was taken two and a half years later, after she was arrested for fraud and identity theft to support her addiction.

narcotic
drug that relieves pain and induces sleep

hallucinogenic
causing dramatic alterations of perception, mood, and thought

The ground-up leaves of the hemp plant are the source of marijuana.

Whether marijuana is smoked or, less frequently, eaten or consumed in tea, users report short-term effects, including a sense of time slowing down, enhanced sensations of touch, increased appreciation for sounds, hunger ("the munchies"), feelings of well-being, and a tendency to giggle. Later, they may become quiet, introspective, and sleepy. At higher doses, users may experience disturbances in short-term memory, exaggerated emotions, and an altered sense of self. Some reactions are more unpleasant, including difficulty concentrating, slowed thought, depersonalization (a sense of being "out of touch" or disconnected from the self; see Chapter 15), and, more rarely, extreme anxiety, panic, and psychotic episodes (Earleywine, 2005). Driving while intoxicated with marijuana is hazardous, especially at high doses (Ramaekers et al, 2006).

The intoxicating effects of marijuana can last for two or three hours, but begin when THC courses through the bloodstream and travels to the brain, where it stimulates cannabinoid receptors. These specialized receptors are concentrated in areas of the brain that control pleasure, perception, memory, and coordinated body movements (see Chapter 3). The most prominent physiological changes are increases in heart rate, reddening of the eyes, and dryness of the mouth.

Scientists are striving to better understand the long-term physical and psychological effects of marijuana use. Although marijuana produces more damage to cells than tobacco smoke (Maertens et al., 2009), aside from an increased risk of lung and respiratory disease (Tetrault et al., 2007), scientists haven't found consistent evidence for serious physical health or fertility consequences of marijuana use. Still, chronic, heavy use of marijuana can impair attention and memory. Fortunately, normal cognitive functioning is typically restored after a month of abstinence (Pope, Gruber, & Yurgelun-Todd, 2001). Questions about cause-and-effect relationships come into play when interpreting research regarding the dangers of marijuana use. High school students who use marijuana earn lower grades and are more likely to get in trouble with the law than other students (Kleinman et al., 1988; Substance Abuse and Mental Health Services Administration, 2001). But high school students who use marijuana might do so because they have troubled home lives or psychological problems and do poorly in school *before* using marijuana (Shedler & Block, 1990). Indeed, there may be some truth to both scenarios.

Some researchers have argued that marijuana is a "gateway" drug that predisposes users to try more serious drugs, like heroin and cocaine (Kandel, Yamaguchi, & Chen, 1992). In a study of identical twin pairs (see Chapter 3) in which one twin tried marijuana in adolescence but the other didn't, the twin who tried marijuana was later at heightened risk for abusing alcohol and other drugs (Lynskey et al., 2003). Nevertheless, evaluating whether marijuana is a gateway drug isn't easy. Merely because one event precedes another doesn't mean it causes it (see Chapter 10). For example, eating baby foods in infancy doesn't cause us to eat "grown-up" foods in adulthood. Teens may tend to use marijuana before other drugs because it's less threatening, more readily available, or both. The scientific debate continues.

correlation vs. causation
CAN WE BE SURE THAT A CAUSES B?

LSD AND OTHER HALLUCINOGENS. On Friday, April 16, 1943, an odd thing happened to Swiss chemist Albert Hofmann. In 1938, Hofmann synthesized a chemical compound, d-lysergic acid diethylamide-25 (LSD), from chemicals found in a fungus that grows on rye. Five years later, when Hofmann again decided to work on the compound, he absorbed some of it unknowingly through his skin. When he went home, he felt restless, dizzy, and "perceived an uninterrupted stream of fantastic pictures, extraordinary shapes with intense, kaleidoscopic play of colors. After some two hours this condition faded away" (Hofmann,1980, p. 5).

Hofmann was the first of millions of people to experience the mind-altering effects of LSD. By the age of 40, about 20 percent of Americans have tried LSD (Johnston, O'Malley, & Bachman, 2002). The psychedelic effects of LSD may stem from its interference with the action of the neurotransmitter serotonin (see Chapter 3) at the synapse. The effects of LSD are also associated with areas of the brain rich in receptors for the neurotransmitter dopamine. As Hofmann discovered, even tiny amounts of LSD can produce dramatic shifts in our perceptions and consciousness. Pills about the size of two aspirins can provide more than 6,000 "highs." Some users report astonishingly clear thoughts and fascinating changes in sensations and perceptions, including synesthesia (the blending of senses—for example, the "smelling of noises;" see Chapter 4). Some users also report mystical experiences (Pahnke et al., 1970).

But LSD and other hallucinogens can also produce panic, paranoid delusions, confusion, depression, and bodily discomfort. Occasionally, psychotic reactions persist long after a psychedelic experience, most often in people with a history of psychological problems (Abraham & Aldridge, 1993). People who are suspicious and insecure before ingesting LSD are most anxious during an LSD session (Linton & Langs, 1964). *Flashbacks*—recurrences of a psychedelic experience—occur occasionally. Curiously, there's no known pharmacological basis for their occurrence. One explanation is that they're triggered by something in the environment or an emotional state associated with a past psychedelic experience.

Unlike LSD, Ecstasy, also known as MDMA (methylenedioxymethamphetamine), has both stimulant and hallucinogenic properties. It produces cascades of the neurotransmitter serotonin in the brain, which increases self-confidence and well-being, and produces powerful feelings of empathy for others. But its use has a serious downside: Its side effects can include high blood pressure, depression, nausea, blurred vision, liver problems, sleep disturbance, and possibly memory loss and damage to neurons that rely on serotonin (Kish, 2002; Soar, Parrott, & Fox, 2004).

Drugs, like other means of altering consciousness, remind us that the "brain" and the "mind" are merely different ways of looking at the same phenomenon (see Chapters 1 and 3). They also illustrate the fluid way we experience the world and ourselves. Although a precise grasp of consciousness eludes us, appreciating the nuances of consciousness and their neurological correlates bring us closer to understanding the biological and psychological underpinnings of our waking and sleeping lives.

✓● **Study** and **Review** on **mypsychlab.com**

All-night dance parties termed "raves," in which Ecstasy and other psychedelic drugs are widely available, became popular in the mid-1990s in the United States.

assess your knowledge — FACT OR FICTION?

1. The effects of many drugs depend on the expectations of the user. **True** / **False**

2. Alcohol is a central nervous system depressant. **True** / **False**

3. Tobacco is the most potent natural stimulant drug. **True** / **False** *Cocaine*

4. A causal link between marijuana and unemployment has been well established. **True** / **False** *Correlational*

5. Drug flashbacks are common among people who use LSD. **True** / **False** *or occasion*

Answers: 1. T (p. 186); 2. T (p. 189); 3. F (p. 191); 4. F (p. 194); 5. F (p. 195)

✔●─[Study and Review on mypsychlab.com

THE BIOLOGY OF SLEEP 167–174

5.1 EXPLAIN THE ROLE OF THE CIRCADIAN RHYTHM AND HOW OUR BODIES REACT TO A DISRUPTION IN OUR BIOLOGICAL CLOCKS.

Sleep and wakefulness vary in response to a circadian rhythm that regulates many bodily processes over a 24-hour period. The "biological clock" is located in the suprachiasmatic nucleus in the hypothalamus.

1. As a college student you may like to sleep late in the morning because your _____ _____ is set that way. (p. 167)

2. The result of a disruption of our body's circadian rhythms that occurs when you fly across the country is called _____ _____. (p. 168)

5.2 IDENTIFY THE DIFFERENT STAGES OF SLEEP AND THE NEURAL ACTIVITY AND DREAMING BEHAVIORS THAT OCCUR IN EACH.

In the 1950s, researchers identified five stages of sleep that include periods of dreaming in which subjects' eyes move rapidly back and forth (rapid eye movement, or REM, sleep). Although vivid, bizarre, and emotional dreams are most likely to occur in REM sleep, dreams occur in non-REM sleep as well. In stage 1 sleep, we feel drowsy and quickly transition to stage 2 sleep in which our brain waves slow down, heart rate slows, body temperature decreases, and muscles relax. In stages 3 and 4 ("deep") sleep, large amplitude delta waves (1 or 2 cycles/second) become more frequent. In stage 5, REM sleep, the brain is activated much as it is during waking life.

3. Label the types of brain waves displayed at each sleep stage. (p. 169)

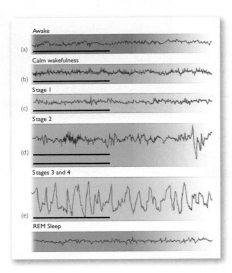

Awake
(a)

Calm wakefulness
(b)

Stage 1
(c)

Stage 2
(d)

Stages 3 and 4
(e)

REM Sleep

4. REM and non-REM dreams differ in that _____ dreams tend to be emotional and illogical and _____ dreams are shorter, more repetitive, and deal with everyday topics of current concern. (p. 170)

5. When humans are deprived of REM for a few nights, we experience _____ _____, during which the amount and intensity of REM sleep increases. (p. 170)

((•─[Listen to an audio file of your chapter mypsychlab.com

5.3 IDENTIFY THE FEATURES AND CAUSES OF SLEEP DISORDERS.

Insomnia (problems falling asleep, waking in the night, or waking early) is the most common sleep disorder and is costly to society in terms of fatigue, missed work, and accidents. Episodes of narcolepsy, which can last as long as an hour, are marked by the rapid onset of sleep. Sleep apnea is also related to daytime fatigue and is caused by a blockage of the airways during sleep. Night terrors and sleepwalking, both associated with deep sleep, are typically harmless and are not recalled by the person on awakening.

6. Researchers have discovered that brief psychotherapy is (more/less) effective than Ambien, a popular sleeping pill, in the treatment of insomnia. (p. 172)

7. People who have _____ fall asleep suddenly and at inopportune times, like while driving a car. (p. 172)

8. What factors can contribute to cataplexy in people or animals with narcolepsy? (p. 172)

9. During a _____ _____, a child can experience a dramatic episode of crying or thrashing during non-REM sleep, and won't remember it in the morning. (p. 173)

10. Sleepwalking is most frequent in (childhood/adulthood). (p. 173)

DREAMS 174–177

5.4 DESCRIBE FREUD'S THEORY OF DREAMS.

Freud theorized that dreams represent disguised wishes. However, many dreams involve unpleasant or undesirable experiences, and many involve uninteresting reviews of routine daily events. Thus, Freud's dream theory hasn't received much empirical support.

11. In the era before rigorous laboratory research, *The Interpretation of Dreams*, by _____ _____ played an influential role in how people thought about dreams. (p. 175)

12. Freud distinguished between the details of the dream itself, which he called the _____ _____, and the true, hidden meaning, which he called the _____ _____. (p. 175)

13. Nightmares, which are common in both children and adults, challenge which theory about dreams? (p. 175)

5.5 EXPLAIN THREE MAJOR MODERN THEORIES OF DREAMING.

According to activation-synthesis theory, the forebrain attempts to interpret meaningless signals from the brain stem (specifically, the pons). Another theory of dreaming suggests that reduction of activity in the prefrontal cortex results in vivid and emotional, but logically disjointed, dreams. Neurocognitive theories hold that our dreams depend in large part on our cognitive and visuospatial abilities.

14. Evidence suggests that dreams (are/are not) involved in processing emotional memories and integrating new experiences with established memories to make sense of the world. (p. 174)

15. Hobson and McCarley's activation synthesis theory links dreams to _____ _____. (p. 175)

16. REM sleep is activated by surges of the neurotransmitter _____, which activates nerve cells in the pons. (p. 175)

17. Label the brain components (a, b, c, d) that the activation-synthesis theory suggests are involved in dreaming. (p. 176)

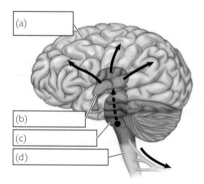

18. People who have an injury to the _____, as researched by Solms, do not dream. (p. 176)

19. Scientists who take a _____ view of dreaming contend that we must consider our cognitive capacities, which shape the content of our dreams. (p. 176)

20. Children's dreams tend to be (less/more) emotional and bizarre than adult dreams. (p. 177)

OTHER ALTERATIONS OF CONSCIOUSNESS AND UNUSUAL EXPERIENCES 177–186

5.6 DETERMINE HOW SCIENTISTS EXPLAIN UNUSUAL AND SEEMINGLY "MYSTICAL" ALTERATIONS IN CONSCIOUSNESS.

Hallucinations and mystical experiences are associated with fasting, sensory deprivation, hallucinogenic drugs, prayer, and like near-death experiences, vary considerably in content across cultures. During out of body experiences, people's consciousness doesn't actually exit their bodies, and some NDEs are experienced by people who aren't near death. Déjà vu experiences don't represent a memory from a past life, but may be triggered by small seizures in the temporal lobe or unconscious information processing.

21. _____ are realistic perceptual experiences in the absence of any external stimuli. (pp. 177–178)

22. Why do people who float in lukewarm saltwater in dark and silent sensory deprivation tanks (such as the one pictured here) hallucinate? (p. 178)

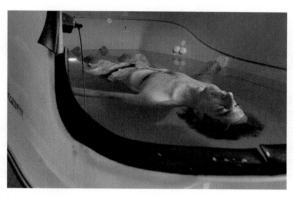

23. Although there are many variations depending on one's religion and culture, many people in our culture associate a _____ experience with approaching a white light. (p. 179)

24. One of the most common alterations in consciousness, _____ _____ is the sensation that you're reliving something even though you know the situation is new, or that you've been somewhere even though you've never been there before. (p. 180)

5.7 DISTINGUISH MYTHS FROM REALITIES CONCERNING HYPNOSIS.

Contrary to popular belief, hypnosis isn't a sleeplike state, subjects generally don't report having been in a "trance," people are aware of their surroundings and don't forget what happened during hypnosis, the type of induction has little impact, and hypnosis doesn't improve memory. In fact, hypnosis can lead to more false memories that are held with confidence, regardless of their accuracy. According to the sociocognitive model of hypnosis, the often dramatic effects associated with hypnosis may be attributable largely to preexisting expectations and beliefs about hypnosis. The dissociation model is another influential explanation for hypnosis. This model emphasizes divisions of consciousness during hypnosis.

25. To increase people's suggestibility, most hypnotists use an _____ _____, which typically includes suggestions for relaxation and calmness. (p. 181)

26. Hypnosis in clinical practice (has/has not) demonstrated positive effects in treating pain and habit disorders, such as smoking. (p. 182)

27. Would the person shown in this drawing have to be in an altered state of consciousness to achieve this position? Why or why not? (p. 183)

Answers are located at the end of the text.

28. One of the most popular myths about hypnosis is that it can make people remember a past life using a therapy called _____ _____ _____ _____ . (p. 184)

29. For _____ theorists, people's expectations about hypnosis, including the cues they receive from hypnotists, shape their responses. (p. 184)

30. Hilgard's _____ theory explains hypnosis based on a separation of the part of the personality responsible for planning from the part of the personality that controls awareness. (p. 185)

DRUGS AND CONSCIOUSNESS 186–195

5.8 IDENTIFY POSSIBLE INFLUENCES ON ALCOHOL ABUSE AND DEPENDENCE.

Substance abuse is associated with recurrent problems related to the drug. Substance dependence is associated with symptoms of tolerance and withdrawal. Cultures that prohibit drinking, such as Muslim cultures, generally exhibit low rates of alcoholism. Many people take drugs and alcohol in part to reduce tension and anxiety.

31. People qualify for a diagnosis of _____ _____ when they experience recurrent problems related to the drug. (p. 187)

32. _____ _____ is a more serious pattern of use that is associated with symptoms of tolerance and withdrawal. (p. 187)

33. Cultures in which drinking is strictly prohibited exhibit (low/high) rates of alcoholism. (p. 188)

34. According to the _____ _____ _____ people consume alcohol and other drugs to relieve anxiety. (p. 188)

5.9 DISTINGUISH DIFFERENT TYPES OF DRUGS AND THEIR EFFECTS ON CONSCIOUSNESS.

The effects of drugs are associated with the dose of the drug, as well as with users' expectancies, personality, and culture. Nicotine, a powerful stimulant, is responsible for the effects of tobacco on consciousness. Smokers often report feeling stimulated as well as tranquil, relaxed, and alert. Cocaine is the most powerful natural stimulant, with effects similar to those of amphetamines. Cocaine is highly addictive. Alcohol is a central nervous system depressant, like the sedative-hypnotic drugs such as Valium. Sedative-hypnotic drugs reduce anxiety at low doses and induce sleep at moderate

doses. Expectancies influence how people react to alcohol. Heroin and other opiates are highly addictive. Heroin withdrawal symptoms range from mild to severe. The effects of marijuana, sometimes classified as a mild hallucinogen, include mood changes, alterations in perception, and disturbances in short-term memory. LSD is a potent hallucinogen. Although flashbacks are rare, LSD can elicit a wide range of positive and negative reactions.

35. To show the balanced placebo design, insert the proper drug conditions in each of the four boxes. (p. 190)

		Received	
		Drug	No drug
Told	Drug		
	No drug		

36. Some people abuse _____ to postpone fatigue or elevate their mood while performing an unpleasant task. (p. 192)

37. In recent years, as many as one in 20 high school students report using methamphetamine, which in its crystalline form is known as _____ _____. (p. 192)

38. Opiate drugs—heroin, morphine, and codeine—are often called _____ because they relieve pain and induce sleep. (p. 193)

39. Hoffman created the mind-altering hallucinogenic drug _____ by accident while creating a compound from chemicals in a fungus. (p. 194)

40. Complete the table by adding the effects and examples for each drug type listed. (p. 186)

DRUG TYPE	EXAMPLES	EFFECT ON BEHAVIOR
Depressants	_____	_____
Stimulants	_____	_____
Opiates	_____	_____
Psychedelics	_____	_____

DO YOU KNOW THESE TERMS?

- sleep paralysis (p. 166)
- consciousness (p. 166)
- circadian rhythm (p. 167)
- biological clock (p. 167)
- rapid eye movement (REM) (p. 169)
- non-REM (NREM) sleep (p. 169)
- REM sleep (p. 169)
- lucid dreaming (p. 171)
- insomnia (p. 171)
- narcolepsy (p. 172)

- sleep apnea (p. 172)
- night terrors (p. 173)
- sleepwalking (p. 173)
- activation–synthesis theory (p. 175)
- neurocognitive theory (p. 176)
- out-of-body experience (OBE) (p. 178)
- near-death experience (NDE) (p. 179)
- déjà vu (p. 180)

- mystical experience (p. 180)
- hypnosis (p. 181)
- past life regression therapy (p. 184)
- sociocognitive theory (p. 184)
- dissociation theory (p. 185)
- psychoactive drug (p. 186)
- tolerance (p. 187)
- withdrawal (p. 187)
- physical dependence (p. 187)

- psychological dependence (p. 187)
- sedative (p. 189)
- hypnotic (p. 189)
- stimulant (p. 191)
- narcotic (p. 193)
- hallucinogenic (p. 193)

APPLY YOUR SCIENTIFIC THINKING SKILLS

Use your scientific thinking skills to answer the following questions, referencing specific scientific thinking principles and common errors in reasoning whenever possible.

1. As we've learned in this chapter, insomnia is the most common sleep disorder. Locate three treatment options for insomnia, being sure to include both behavioral and biomedical or drug treatments. Use your scientific thinking skills to determine which of these treatments would be the most effective and why.

2. Hypnosis has a wide range of clinical applications, including pain management and smoking cessation. Using the Internet or self-help books, choose two examples of hypnosis being used in a clinical setting and evaluate whether each example accurately portrays the benefits and limitations of hypnosis. Be sure to refer to this chapter's list of common misconceptions about hypnosis.

3. The debate surrounding marijuana as a "gateway" drug rests largely on the scientific thinking principle of correlation vs. causation. Research this debate further and find several media articles on both sides of the issue. What arguments does each side make to support its viewpoint? What rival hypotheses, if any, might each side have neglected to consider?

6 LEARNING

how nurture changes us

THINK ABOUT IT

HOW DO PHOBIAS AND FETISHES DEVELOP?

HOW DO TRAINERS GET ANIMALS TO DO CUTE TRICKS, LIKE DANCING OR WATER SKIING?

DOES WATCHING VIOLENCE ON TV REALLY TEACH CHILDREN TO BECOME VIOLENT?

WHY DO WE SOMETIMES AVOID A DELICIOUS FOOD FOR DECADES AFTER ONLY ONE NEGATIVE EXPERIENCE WITH IT?

CAN WE LEARN IN OUR SLEEP?

Learning the information in this textbook is altering your brain in ways that psychologists are increasingly coming to understand.

learning
change in an organism's behavior or thought as a result of experience

habituation
process of responding less strongly over time to repeated stimuli

Before reading further, try your hand at the following three items.

1. Ivan Pavlov, the discoverer of classical conditioning, was well known as a
   a. slow eater.
   b. fast walker.
   c. terrible cook.
   d. I have no idea.

2. John B. Watson, the founder of behaviorism, was tossed out of Johns Hopkins University for
   a. plagiarizing a journal article.
   b. stabbing one of his faculty colleagues.
   c. having an affair with his graduate student.
   d. I have no idea.

3. As a college student, B. F. Skinner, the founder of radical behaviorism, once spread a false rumor that which of the following individuals was coming to campus?
   a. silent movie comedian Charlie Chaplin
   b. psychoanalyst Sigmund Freud
   c. President Theodore Roosevelt
   d. I have no idea.

Now, read the following paragraph.

The three most famous figures in the psychology of learning were each colorful characters in their own way. The discoverer of classical conditioning, Ivan Pavlov, was a notoriously compulsive fellow. He ate lunch every day at precisely 12 noon, went to bed at exactly the same time every night, and departed St. Petersburg, Russia, for vacation the same day every year. Pavlov was also such a rapid walker that his wife frequently had to run frantically to keep up with him. The life of the founder of behaviorism, John B. Watson, was rocked with scandal. Despite becoming one of the world's most famous psychologists, he was unceremoniously booted out of Johns Hopkins University for having an affair with his graduate student, Rosalie Rayner. B. F. Skinner, the founder of radical behaviorism, was something of a prankster during his undergraduate years at Hamilton College in New York. He and a friend once spread a false rumor that comedian Charlie Chaplin was coming to campus. This rumor nearly provoked a riot when Chaplin didn't materialize as expected.

Now go back and try again to answer the three questions at the beginning of this chapter.

If you got more questions right the second time than the first—and odds are you did—then you've experienced something we all take for granted: learning. (The answers, by the way, are b, c, and a.) By **learning**, we mean a change in an organism's behavior or thought as a result of experience. As we learned in Chapter 3, when we learn our brains change along with our behaviors. Remarkably, your brain is physically different now than it was just a few minutes ago, because it underwent chemical changes that allowed you to learn novel facts. Learning lies at the heart of just about every domain of psychology. As we discovered in Chapter 1, virtually all behaviors are a complex stew of genetic predispositions and learning. Without learning, we'd be unable to do much; we couldn't walk, talk, or read an introductory psychology textbook chapter about learning.

Psychologists have long debated how many distinct types of learning there are. We're won't try to settle this controversy here. Instead, we'll review several types of learning that psychologists have studied in depth, starting with the most basic.

Before we do, place your brain on pause, put down your pen or highlighter, close your eyes, and attend to several things that you almost never notice: the soft buzzing of the lights in the room, the feel of your clothing against your skin, the sensation of your tongue on your teeth or lips. Unless someone draws our attention to these stimuli, we don't even realize they're there, because we've learned to ignore them. **Habituation** is the process by which we respond less strongly over time to repeated stimuli. It helps explain why loud snorers can sleep peacefully through the night while keeping their irritated roommates wide awake. Chronic snorers have become so accustomed to the sound of their own snoring that they no longer notice it.

Habituation is the simplest and probably earliest form of learning to emerge in humans. Unborn fetuses as young as 32 weeks display habituation when we apply a gentle vibrator to the mother's stomach. At first, the fetus jerks around in response to the stimulus, but after repeated vibrations it stops moving (Morokuma et al., 2004). What was first a shock to the fetus's system later became a mere annoyance that it could safely ignore.

In research that earned him the Nobel Prize in 2000, neurophysiologist Eric Kandel uncovered the biological mechanism of habituation of *Aplysia,* a five-inch-long sea slug. Prick an *Aplysia* on a certain part of its body, and it retracts its gill in a defensive maneuver. Touch *Aplysia* in the same spot repeatedly, and it begins to ignore the stimulus. This habituation, Kandel found, is accompanied by a progressive decrease in release of the neurotransmitter serotonin (see Chapter 3) at the *Aplysia*'s synapses (Siegelbaum, Camardo, & Kandel, 1982). This discovery helped psychologists unravel the neural bases of learning (see **FIGURE 6.1**).

Habituation makes good adaptive sense. We wouldn't want to attend to every tiny sensation that comes across our mental radar screens, because most pose no threat. Yet we wouldn't want to habituate to stimuli that might be dangerous. Fortunately, not all repeated stimuli lead to habituation, only those that we deem safe or worth ignoring do. We typically don't habituate to powerful stimuli, like extremely loud tones or painful electric shocks.

Psychologists have studied habituation using the skin conductance response, a measure of the electrical conductivity of the fingertips. As our fingertips moisten with sweat, they become better conductors of electricity. Scientists measure this moistening with electrodes placed on the fingertips. Because sweating generally indicates anxiety (Fowles, 1980), researchers often use the skin conductance response in studies of habituation. Most research shows that we stop sweating sooner for weak than for strong stimuli, meaning that weak stimuli stop producing anxiety fairly quickly. In the case of very strong stimuli, like painful electric shocks, we often see no habituation at all—people continue to sweat anxiously at the same high levels—even across many trials (Lykken et al., 1988). That also makes good adaptive sense, because we wouldn't want to habituate to stimuli that pose a serious threat to us.

Indeed, some cases of repeated exposure to stimuli lead to *sensitization*—that is, responding more strongly over time—rather than habituation. Sensitization is most likely when a stimulus is dangerous, irritating, or both. *Aplysia* show sensitization as well as habituation. Have you ever tried to study when the person next to you was whispering, and the whispering kept getting more annoying to the point that you couldn't concentrate? If so, you've experienced sensitization.

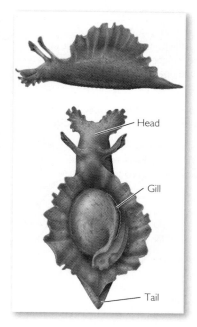

Head

Gill

Tail

FIGURE 6.1   Habituation in a Simple Animal. *Aplysia californicus* is a sea slug about five inches long that retracts its gill when pricked, but then habituates (stops retracting its gill) if pricked repeatedly.

Habituating to background noise while studying can be difficult, especially if the noise is loud.

(handwritten note: habituation and sensitization are opposites.)

CLASSICAL CONDITIONING

6.1   Describe Pavlov's model of classical conditioning and discriminate conditioned stimuli and responses from unconditioned stimuli and responses.

6.2   Explain the major principles and terminology associated with classical conditioning.

6.3   Explain how complex behaviors can result from classical conditioning and how they emerge in our daily lives.

The story of habituation could hardly be more straightforward. We experience a stimulus, respond to it, and then stop responding after repeated exposure. We've learned something significant, but we haven't learned to forge connections between two stimuli. Yet a great deal of learning depends on associating one thing with another. If we never learned to connect one stimulus, like the appearance of an apple, with another stimulus, like its taste, our world would be what William James (1890) called a "blooming, buzzing confusion"—a world of disconnected sensory experiences.

classical (Pavlovian) conditioning
form of learning in which animals come to respond to a previously neutral stimulus that
had been paired with another stimulus that
elicits an automatic response

unconditioned stimulus (UCS)
stimulus that elicits an automatic response

unconditioned response (UCR)
automatic response to a nonneutral stimulus
that does not need to be learned

conditioned response (CR)
response previously associated with a nonneutral stimulus that is elicited by a neutral
stimulus through conditioning

conditioned stimulus (CS)
initially neutral stimulus that comes to elicit a
response due to association with an unconditioned stimulus

◉ **Watch** Classic Footage of Pavlov on
mypsychlab.com

The rock band Barenaked Ladies accurately
described classical conditioning in their song,
Brian Wilson. The lyrics go:
"It's a matter of instinct, it's a matter of
conditioning, it's a matter of fact. You can call
me Pavlov's dog. Ring a bell and I'll salivate—
how'd you like that?"
Not bad for a group of nonpsychologists!

FACTOID ✚

Classical conditioning can occur even
among people who are in a vegetative state
(see Chapter 3). In a recent study,
researchers repeatedly delivered a musical
note, followed by a puff of air to the eyes—
a UCS that produces a UCR of blinking—
to 22 patients in vegetative or minimally
conscious states (Bekinschtein et al., 2009).
Eventually, the musical note became a CS,
producing eye blinking even in these largely
or entirely unconscious individuals.

Several centuries ago, a school of thinkers called the *British Associationists* believed that we acquire virtually all of our knowledge by *conditioning,* that is, by forming
associations among stimuli. Once we form these associations, like the connection between our mother's voice with her face, we need only recall one element of the pair to
retrieve the other. The British Associationists, like John Stuart Mill (1806–1873), believed that simple associations provided the mental building blocks for all of our more
complex ideas.

■ Pavlov's Discoveries

The history of science teaches us that many discoveries arise from *serendipity,* or accident.
Yet it takes a great scientist to capitalize on serendipitous observations that others regard as
meaningless flukes. As French microbiologist Louis Pasteur, who discovered the process of
pasteurizing milk, observed, "Chance favors the prepared mind." So it was with the discoveries of Russian scientist Ivan Pavlov. His landmark understanding of classical conditioning
emerged from a set of unforeseen observations that were unrelated to his main research interests.

Pavlov's primary research was digestion in dogs—in fact, his discoveries concerning digestion, not classical conditioning, earned him the Nobel Prize in 1904. Pavlov
placed dogs in a harness and inserted a *cannula,* or collection tube, into their salivary
glands to study their salivary responses to meat powder. In doing so, he observed something unexpected: He found that dogs began salivating (more informally, they started to
drool) not only to the meat powder itself, but to previously neutral stimuli that had become associated with it, such as research assistants who brought in the powder. Indeed,
the dogs even salivated to the sound of these assistants' footsteps as they approached the
laboratory. The dogs seemed to be anticipating the meat powder and responding to stimuli that signaled its arrival. ◉ **Watch**

We call this process of association **classical conditioning** (or
Pavlovian conditioning): a form of
learning in which animals come to
respond to a previously neutral
stimulus that had been paired with
another stimulus that elicits an automatic response. Yet Pavlov's initial
observations were merely anecdotal,
so like any good scientist he put his
informal observations to a more rigorous test.

Here's how Pavlov first demonstrated classical conditioning systematically (see
FIGURE 6.2).

1. He started with an initially neutral stimulus, one that didn't elicit any particular
   response. In this case, Pavlov used a metronome, a clicking pendulum that keeps
   time (in other studies, Pavlov used a tuning fork or whistle; contrary to popular
   belief, Pavlov didn't use a bell).
2. He then paired the neutral stimulus again and again with an **unconditioned
   stimulus (UCS)**, a stimulus that elicits an automatic—that is, a reflexive—response. In the case of Pavlov's dogs, the unconditioned stimulus is the meat
   powder, and the automatic, reflexive response it elicits is the **unconditioned
   response (UCR)**. For Pavlov's dogs, the unconditioned response was salivation. The key point is that the animal doesn't need to learn to respond to the
   unconditioned stimulus with the unconditioned response: Dogs naturally
   drool in response to food. The animal generates the unconditioned response
   without any training at all, because the response is a product of nature
   (genes), not nurture (experience).

3. As Pavlov repeatedly paired the neutral stimulus with the unconditioned stimulus, he observed something remarkable. If he now presented the metronome alone, it elicited a response, namely, salivation. This new response is the **conditioned response (CR)**: a response previously associated with a nonneutral stimulus that comes to be elicited by a neutral stimulus. Lo and behold, learning has occurred. The metronome had become a **conditioned stimulus (CS)**—a previously neutral stimulus that comes to elicit a conditioned response as a result of its association with an unconditioned stimulus. The dog, which previously did nothing when it heard the metronome except perhaps turn its head toward it, now salivates when it hears the metronome. The conditioned response, in contrast to the unconditioned response, is a product of nurture (experience), not nature (genes).

? Like many people, this girl found her first ride on a roller coaster terrifying. Now, all she needs to do is to see a photograph of a roller coaster for her heart to start pounding. In this scenario, what three classical conditioning terms describe (a) her first roller coaster ride, (b) a photograph of a roller coaster, and (c) her heart pounding in response to this photograph? (See answers upside down at bottom of page.)

FIGURE 6.2 Pavlov's Classical Conditioning Model. UCS (meat powder) is paired with a neutral stimulus (metronome clicking) and produces UCR (salivation). Then the metronome is presented alone, and CR (salivation) occurs.

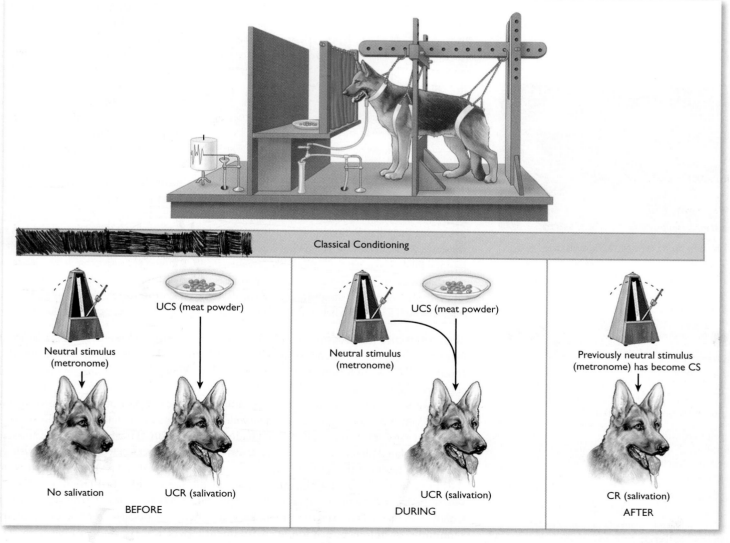

Classical Conditioning

UCS (meat powder)

Neutral stimulus (metronome)

No salivation   UCR (salivation)

BEFORE

UCS (meat powder)

Neutral stimulus (metronome)

UCR (salivation)

DURING

Previously neutral stimulus (metronome) has become CS

CR (salivation)

AFTER

Acquisition = learn the conditioned response
Extinction = eventual disappearance of conditioned response after conditioned stimulus present w/o the CR. The CR is now overshadowed by new response. Spontaneous Recovery = extinct CR reappears

In most cases, the CR is fairly similar to the UCR but it's rarely identical to it. For example, Pavlov found that dogs salivated less in response to the metronome (the CS) than to the meat powder (the UCS).

Few findings in psychology are as replicable as classical conditioning. We can apply the classical conditioning paradigm to just about any animal with an intact nervous system, and demonstrate it repeatedly without fail. If only all psychological findings were so dependable!

■ Principles of Classical Conditioning

We'll next explore the major principles underlying classical conditioning. Pavlov noted, and many others have since confirmed, that classical conditioning occurs in three phases—acquisition, extinction, and spontaneous recovery.

ACQUISITION. In **acquisition**, we gradually learn—or acquire—the CR. If we look at **FIGURE 6.3a**, we'll see that as the CS and UCS are paired over and over again, the CR increases progressively in strength. The steepness of this curve varies somewhat depending on how close together in time we present the CS and UCS. In general, the closer in time the pairing of CS and UCS, the faster learning occurs, with about a half second delay typically being the optimal pairing for learning. Longer delays usually decrease the speed and strength of the organism's response.

EXTINCTION. In a process called **extinction**, the CR decreases in magnitude and eventually disappears when the CS is repeatedly presented alone, that is, without the UCS (see **FIGURE 6.3b**). After numerous presentations of

FIGURE 6.3 Acquisition and Extinction. Acquisition is the repeated pairing of UCS and CS, increasing the CR's strength (a). In extinction, the CS is presented again and again without the UCS, resulting in the gradual disappearance of the CR (b).

A person hiking through the woods may experience fear when she approaches an area if she's previously spotted a dangerous animal there.

acquisition
learning phase during which a conditioned response is established

extinction
gradual reduction and eventual elimination of the conditioned response after the conditioned stimulus is presented repeatedly without the unconditioned stimulus

spontaneous recovery
sudden reemergence of an extinct conditioned response after a delay in exposure to the conditioned stimulus

renewal effect
sudden reemergence of a conditioned response following extinction when an animal is returned to the environment in which the conditioned response was acquired

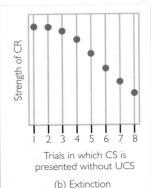

Strength of CR

1 2 3 4 5 6 7 8
Trials in which CS is paired with UCS
(a) Acquisition

Strength of CR

1 2 3 4 5 6 7 8
Trials in which CS is presented without UCS
(b) Extinction

the metronome without meat powder, Pavlov's dogs eventually stopped salivating. Most psychologists once believed that extinction was similar to forgetting: The CR fades away over repeated trials, just as many memories gradually decay (see Chapter 7). Yet the truth is more complicated and interesting than that. Extinction is an active, rather than passive, process. During extinction a new response, which in the case of Pavlov's dogs was the *absence* of salivation, gradually "writes over" or inhibits the CR, namely, salivation. The extinguished CR doesn't vanish completely; it's merely overshadowed by the new behavior. This contrasts with many forms of traditional forgetting, in which the memory itself disappears. Interestingly, Pavlov had proposed this hypothesis in his writings, although few people believed him at the time. How do we know he was right? Read on.

SPONTANEOUS RECOVERY. In a phenomenon called **spontaneous recovery**, a seemingly extinct CR reappears (often in somewhat weaker form) if we present the CS again. It's as though the CR were lurking in the background, waiting to appear following another presentation of the CS. In a classic study, Pavlov (1927) presented the CS (tone from a metronome) alone again and again and extinguished the CR (salivation) because there was no UCS (mouth-watering meat powder) following it. Two hours later, he presented the CS again and the CR returned. The animal hadn't really forgotten the CR, it just suppressed it.

A related phenomenon is the **renewal effect**, which occurs when we extinguish a response in a setting different from the one in which the animal acquired it. When we restore the animal to the original setting, the extinguished response reappears (Bouton, 1994). The renewal effect may help to explain why people with *phobias*—intense, irrational fears (see Chapter 15)—who've overcome their phobias often experience a reappearance of their symptoms when they return to the environment in which they acquired their fears (Denniston, Chang, & Miller, 2003). Even though it may sometimes lead to a return of phobias,

[handwritten margin notes at top: Stimulus Generalization - one stimulus elicit a response, so other stimuli similar to the conditioned stimulus give way to the same conditioned response / Stimulus Discrimination - stimuli that are less similar to CS elicit different responses from CR.]

the renewal effect is often adaptive. If we've been bitten by a snake in one part of a forest, it makes sense to experience fear when we find ourselves there again, even years later. That same snake or his slithery descendants may still be lying in wait in the same spot.

STIMULUS GENERALIZATION. Pavlov found that following classical conditioning, his dogs salivated not merely to the original metronome sound, but to sounds similar to it. This phenomenon is **stimulus generalization**: the process by which CSs that are similar, but not identical, to the original CS elicit a CR. Stimulus generalization occurs along a *generalization gradient*: The more similar to the original CS the new CS is, the stronger the CR will be (see **FIGURE 6.4**). Pavlov found that his dogs showed their largest amount of salivation to the original sound, with progressively less salivation to sounds that were less and less similar to it in pitch. Stimulus generalization is adaptive, because it allows us to transfer what we've learned to new things. For example, once we've learned to drive our own car, we can borrow a friend's car without needing a full tutorial on how to drive it.

STIMULUS DISCRIMINATION. The flip side of the coin to stimulus generalization is **stimulus discrimination**; it occurs when we exhibit a less pronounced CR to CSs that differ from the original CS. Stimulus discrimination helps us understand why we can enjoy scary movies. Although we may hyperventilate a bit while watching television footage of a ferocious tornado tearing through a small town, we'd respond much more strongly if the tornado were headed straight for our home. Thankfully, we've learned to discriminate between a televised stimulus and the real-world version of it, and to modify our response as a result. Like stimulus generalization, stimulus discrimination is adaptive, because it allows us to distinguish among stimuli that share some similarities but that differ in important ways. Without it, we'd be scared to pet a new dog if we were bitten by a similar-looking dog last week.

■ Higher-Order Conditioning *[handwritten: = Conditioned response in response to a conditioned stimulus / association to another CS]*

Taking conditioning a step further, organisms learn to develop conditioned associations to CSs that are associated with the original CS. If after conditioning a dog to salivate to a tone, we pair a picture of a circle with that tone, a dog eventually salivates to the circle as well as to the tone. That's **higher-order conditioning**: the process by which organisms develop classically conditioned responses to CSs that later become associated with the original CS (Gewirtz & Davis, 2000). As we might expect, second-order conditioning—in which a new CS is paired with the original CS—tends to be weaker than garden-variety classical conditioning, and third-order conditioning—in which a third CS is in turn paired with the second-order CS—is even weaker. Fourth-order conditioning and beyond are typically difficult or impossible.

Higher-order conditioning allows us to extend classical conditioning to a host of new stimuli. It helps explain why we feel thirsty after someone merely says "Coke" on a sweltering summer day. We've already come to associate the sight, sound, and smell of a Coca-Cola with quenching our thirst, and we eventually came to associate the word *Coke* with these CSs.

Higher-order conditioning also helps to explain some surprising findings concerning addictions to cigarettes, heroin, and other drugs. Many addictions are shaped in part by higher-order conditioning, with the context in which people take the drugs serving as a higher-order CS. People who don't generally smoke cigarettes may find themselves craving one at a party because they've smoked occasionally at previous parties with their friends who smoke. Behaviorists refer to these higher-order CSs as *occasion setters*, because they refer to the setting in which the CS occurs.

Although public perception has it that "breaking the grip" of heroin addiction is essentially impossible, research suggests that this is true for only some addicts (Sullum, 2003). Lee Robins and her colleagues (Robins, Helzer, & Davis, 1975) examined 451 Vietnam veterans who returned to the United States with cases of serious heroin addiction. Although many mental health experts confidently predicted an epidemic of heroin addiction following the veterans' return to America, the problem was much less serious than expected. In Robins' sample,

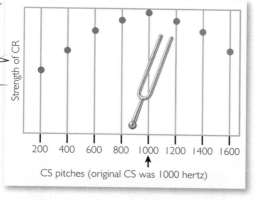

[Figure 6.4 graph: vertical axis "Strength of CR", horizontal axis "CS pitches (original CS was 1000 hertz)" with values 200, 400, 600, 800, 1000, 1200, 1400, 1600; arrow pointing to 1000]

FIGURE 6.4 Generalization Gradient. The more similar to the original CS the new CS is (for example, Pavlov using a tone pitched close to the original tone's pitch), the stronger the CR will be.

[handwritten notes near Coke image: "So jump in my step as I rush to see you." "I'll do anything... Goodbye, Apathy." "Don't you stop pushing me?"]

Higher-order conditioning helps explain the seemingly mysterious "power of suggestion." Merely hearing "Want a Coke?" on a hot summer day can make us feel thirsty.

stimulus generalization
process by which conditioned stimuli similar, but not identical, to the original conditioned stimulus elicit a conditioned response

stimulus discrimination
process by which organisms display a less pronounced conditioned response to conditioned stimuli that differ from the original conditioned stimulus

higher-order conditioning
developing a conditioned response to a conditioned stimulus by virtue of its association with another conditioned stimulus

86 percent of heroin-addicted Vietnam veterans lost their addiction shortly after returning to the United States. What happened? Because the occasion setters had changed from Vietnam to the United States, the veterans' classically conditioned responses to heroin extinguished. Of course, this fact doesn't take away from the seriousness of the addiction for the 14 percent of Robins' sample who remained addicted and often went on to abuse other drugs.

Applications of Classical Conditioning to Daily Life

Without classical conditioning, we couldn't develop physiological associations to stimuli that signal biologically important events, like things we want to eat—or that want to eat us. Many of the physiological responses we display in classical conditioning contribute to our survival. Salivation, for instance, helps us to digest food. Although skin conductance responses aren't especially important for us today, they probably were to our primate ancestors (Stern, Ray, & Davis, 1980), who found that moist fingers and toes came in handy for grasping tree limbs while fleeing from predators. Slightly wet fingertips help us adhere to things, as you'll discover if you moisten the tip of your index finger while turning to the next page of this book.

Classical conditioning isn't limited to salivating dogs in old Russian laboratories; it applies to daily life, too. We'll consider four everyday applications of classical conditioning here: advertising, the acquisition of fears and phobias, the acquisition of fetishes, and disgust reactions.

CLASSICAL CONDITIONING AND ADVERTISING. Few people grasp the principles of classical conditioning, especially higher-order conditioning, better than advertisers. By repeatedly pairing the sights and sounds of products with photographs of handsome hunks and scantily clad beauties, marketing whizzes try to establish classically conditioned connections between their brands and positive emotions. They do so for a good reason: Research shows that it works. So does another favorite trick of advertisers: repeatedly pairing pictures of products with pictures our favorite celebrities (Till, Stanley, & Priluck, 2008).

One researcher (Gorn, 1982) paired slides of either blue or beige pens (the CSs) with music that participants had rated as either enjoyable or not enjoyable (the UCSs). Then he gave participants the opportunity to select a pen upon departing the lab. Whereas 79 percent of participants who heard music they liked picked the pen that had been paired with music, only 30 percent of those who heard music they disliked picked the pen that had been paired with music.

Nevertheless, not all researchers who've paired products with pleasurable stimuli have succeeded in replicating classical conditioning effects (Smith, 2001). Two researchers (Gresham & Shimp, 1985) paired various products, like Coke, Colgate toothpaste, and Grape Nuts cereal, with television commercials that previous subjects had rated as generating pleasant, unpleasant, or neutral emotions. They found little evidence that these pairings affected participants' preferences for the ads. Nevertheless, their negative findings are open to a rival explanation: latent inhibition. **Latent inhibition** refers to the fact that when we've experienced a CS alone many times, it's difficult to classically condition it to another stimulus (Palsson et al., 2005; Vaitl & Lipp, 1997). Because the investigators relied on brands with which participants were already familiar, their negative findings may be attributable to latent inhibition. Indeed, when researchers have used novel brands, they've generally been able to show classical conditioning effects (Stuart, Shimp, & Engle, 1987).

THE ACQUISITION OF FEARS AND PHOBIAS: THE STRANGE TALE OF LITTLE ALBERT. Can classical conditioning help explain how we come to fear or avoid stimuli? John B. Watson, the founder of behaviorism (see Chapter 1), answered this question in 1920 when he and his graduate student, Rosalie Rayner, performed what must be regarded as one of the most ethically questionable studies in the history of psychology. Here's what they did.

Watson and Rayner (1920) set out in part to falsify the Freudian view (see Chapters 1 and 14) of phobias, which proposes that phobias stem from deep-seated conflicts buried in the unconscious. To do so, they recruited a nine-month-old infant who'll be forever known in the psychological literature as Little Albert. Little Albert was fond of furry little creatures, like white rats. But Watson and Rayner were about to change that. ⊕ Explore

Advertisers use higher-order classical conditioning to get customers to associate their products with an inherently enjoyable stimulus.

replicability

CAN THE RESULTS BE DUPLICATED IN OTHER STUDIES?

ruling out rival hypotheses

HAVE IMPORTANT ALTERNATIVE EXPLANATIONS FOR THE FINDINGS BEEN EXCLUDED?

latent inhibition
difficulty in establishing classical conditioning to a conditioned stimulus we've repeatedly experienced alone, that is, without the unconditioned stimulus

falsifiability

CAN THE CLAIM BE DISPROVED?

⊕ Explore the Classical Conditioning of Little Albert on **mypsychlab.com**

Watson and Rayner first allowed Little Albert to play with a rat. But only seconds afterward, Watson snuck up behind Little Albert and struck a gong with a steel hammer, creating an earsplitting noise, startling him out of his wits, and making him cry. After seven such pairings of the rat and UCS (loud sound from gong), Little Albert displayed a CR (crying) to the rat alone, demonstrating that the rat had now become a CS. The conditioned response was still present when Watson and Rayner exposed Little Albert to the rat five days later. Little Albert also displayed stimulus generalization, crying not only in response to rats, but also to a rabbit, a dog, a furry coat, and, to a lesser extent, a Santa Claus mask and John B. Watson's hair. Fortunately, Little Albert also demonstrated at least some stimulus discrimination, as he didn't display much fear toward cotton balls or the hair of Dr. Watson's research assistants.

Incidentally, no one knows for sure what became of poor Little Albert (see Factoid). His mother withdrew him from the study about a month after it began, never to be heard from again. Needless to say, because inducing a phobia-like condition in an infant raises a host of serious ethical questions, Watson and Rayner's Little Albert study would never get past a modern-day college or university Institutional Review Board (see Chapter 2).

Stimulus generalization, like that experienced by Little Albert, allows our learning to be remarkably flexible—which is often, although not always, a good thing. It allows us to develop fears of many stimuli, although certain phobias, such as those of snakes, spiders, heights, water, and blood, are considerably more widespread than others (American Psychiatric Association, 2000). Other, more exotic phobias, like fear of being tickled by feathers (*pteronophobia*), fear of clowns (*coulrophobia*), fear of flutes (*aulophobia*), and fear of bald people (*peladophobia*), are exceedingly rare.

The good news is that if classical conditioning can contribute to our acquiring phobias, it can also contribute to our overcoming them. Mary Cover Jones, a student of Watson, treated a three-year-old named Little Peter, who had a phobia of rabbits. Jones (1924) treated Peter's fear successfully by gradually introducing him to a white rabbit while giving him a piece of his favorite candy. As she moved the rabbit increasingly close to him, the sight of the rabbit eventually came to elicit a new CR: pleasure rather than fear. Modern-day psychotherapists, although rarely feeding their clients candy, use similar practices to eliminate phobias. They may pair feared stimuli with relaxation or other pleasurable stimuli (Wolpe, 1990; see Chapter 16).

FETISHES. There's also good reason to believe that **fetishism**—sexual attraction to nonliving things—often arises in part from classical conditioning (Akins, 2004). Like phobias, fetishes come in a bewildering variety of forms: They can become attached to shoes, stockings, dolls, stuffed animals, automobile engines (yes, that's right), and just about anything else (Lowenstein, 2002).

Although the origins of human fetishes are controversial, Michael Domjan and his colleagues managed to classically condition fetishes in male Japanese quails. In one study, they presented male quails with a cylindrical object made of terrycloth, followed by a female quail with which they happily mated. After 30 such pairings, about half of the male quails attempted to mate with the cylindrical object when it appeared alone (Köksal et al., 2004). Although the generalizability of these findings to humans is unclear, there's good evidence that at least some people develop fetishes by the repeated pairing of neutral objects with sexual activity (Rachman & Hodgson, 1968; Weinberg, Williams, & Calhan, 1995).

DISGUST REACTIONS. Imagine that a researcher asked you to eat a piece of fudge. No problem, right? Well, now imagine the fudge were shaped like dog feces. If you're like most subjects in the studies of Paul Rozin and his colleagues, you'd hesitate (D'Amato, 1998; Rozin, Millman, & Nemeroff, 1986).

Rozin (who's earned the nickname "Dr. Disgust") and his colleagues have found that we acquire disgust reactions with surprising ease. In most cases, these reactions are probably a product of classical conditioning. CSs—like a photograph of rotten eggs—that are associated with disgusting UCSs—like the smell and taste of rotten eggs in our

Classic study in which a nine-month-old boy was conditioned to fear white furry objects. Here, Little Albert, with John B. Watson and Rosalie Rayner, is crying in response to a Santa Claus mask.

FACTOID

One team of psychologists has recently claimed that Little Albert was actually "Douglas Merritte," the son of a nurse who was born in 1919 at Johns Hopkins University Hospital and died at age 6 due to a build-up of fluid in his brain (Beck, Levinson, & Irons, 2009). But other psychologists doubt that Little Albert has been discovered (Powell, 2010; Reese, 2010).

Michael Domjan and his colleagues used classical conditioning to instill a fetish in male quails.

fetishism
sexual attraction to nonliving things

mouths—may themselves come to elicit disgust. In many cases, disgust reactions are tied to stimuli that are biologically important to us, like animals or objects that are dirty or potentially poisonous (Connolly et al., 2008; Rozin & Fallon, 1987).

In another study, Rozin and his collaborators asked participants to drink from two glasses of water, both of which contained sugar (sucrose). In one case, the sucrose came from a bottle labeled "Sucrose"; in another, it came from a bottle labeled "Sodium Cyanide, Poison." The investigators told subjects that both bottles were completely safe. They even asked subjects to select which label went with which glass, proving the labels were meaningless. Even so, subjects were hesitant to drink from the glass that contained the sucrose labeled as poisonous (Rozin, Markwith, & Ross, 1990). Participants' responses in this study were irrational, but perhaps understandable: They were probably relying on the heuristic "better safe than sorry." Classical conditioning helps keep us safe, even if it goes too far on occasion.

psychomythology

ARE WE WHAT WE EAT?

Many of us have heard that "we are what we eat," but in the 1950s the psychologist James McConnell took this proverb quite literally. McConnell became convinced he'd discovered a means of chemically transferring learning from one animal to another. Indeed, for many years psychology textbooks informed undergraduates that scientists could chemically transfer learning across animals.

McConnell's animal of choice was the *planaria*, a flatworm that's typically no more than a few inches long. Using classical conditioning, McConnell and his colleagues exposed planaria to a light, which served as the CS, while pairing it with a one-second electric shock, which served as the UCS. When planaria receive an electric shock, they contract reflexively. After numerous pairings between light and shock, the light itself causes planaria to contract (Thompson & McConnell, 1955).

McConnell wanted to find out whether he could chemically transfer the memory of this classical conditioning experience to another planaria. His approach was brutally simple. Relying on the fact that many planaria are miniature cannibals, he chopped up the trained planaria and fed them to their fellow worms. Remarkably, McConnell (1962) reported that planaria who'd gobbled up classically conditioned planaria acquired classically conditioned reactions to the light more quickly than planaria who hadn't.

Understandably, McConnell's memory transfer studies generated enormous excitement. Imagine if McConnell were right! You could sign up for your introductory psychology class, swallow a pill containing all of the psychological knowledge you'd need to get an A, and ... voila, you're now an expert psychologist. Indeed, McConnell went directly to the general public with his findings, proclaiming in *Time, Newsweek,* and other popular magazines that scientists were on the verge of developing a "memory pill" (Rilling, 1996).

Yet it wasn't long before the wind went out of McConnell's scientific sails: Although researchers at over 50 labs tried to replicate his findings, many couldn't (Stern, 2010). What's more, researchers brought up a host of alternative explanations for his results. For one, McConnell hadn't ruled out the possibility that his findings were attributable to *pseudoconditioning*, which occurs when the CS by itself triggers the UCR. That is, he hadn't excluded the possibility that the light itself caused the planaria to contract (Collins & Pinch, 1993), perhaps leading him to the false conclusion that the cannibalistic planaria had acquired a classically conditioned reaction to the light. Eventually, after years of intense debate and mixed or negative results, the scientific community concluded that McConnell may have fooled himself into seeing something that was never there: He'd become a likely victim of confirmation bias (see Chapter 2). His planaria lab closed its doors in 1971, and was never heard from again.

Still, McConnell may yet have the last laugh. Even though his studies may have been flawed, some scientists have conjectured that memory may indeed be chemically transferrable in some cases (Smalheiser, Manev, & Costa, 2001). As is so often the case in science, the truth will eventually win out.

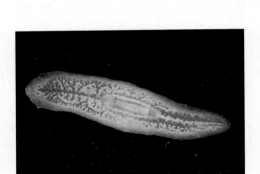

James McConnell and his colleagues paired a light with an electric shock, which caused the *planaria* worm to contract reflexively.

replicability ▶

CAN THE RESULTS BE DUPLICATED IN OTHER STUDIES?

ruling out rival hypotheses ▶

HAVE IMPORTANT ALTERNATIVE EXPLANATIONS FOR THE FINDINGS BEEN EXCLUDED?

assess your knowledge   FACT OR FICTION?

1. Habituation to meaningless stimuli is generally adaptive. **True / False**

2. In classical conditioning, the conditioned stimulus (CS) initially yields a reflexive, automatic response. **True / False**

3. Conditioning is generally most effective when the CS precedes the UCS by a short period of time. **True / False**

4. Extinction is produced by the gradual "decay" of the CR over time. **True / False**

5. Heroin addiction may sometimes be "broken" by dramatically altering the setting in which addicts inject the drug. **True / False**

Answers: 1. T (p.203); 2. F (p.205); 3. T (p.206); 4. F (p.206); 5. T (p.208)

[handwritten notes]: This has got to be a good life :)

[handwritten notes]: Operant Conditioning = learning is controlled by consequences of organism's behavior- (reward)

OPERANT CONDITIONING

6.4 Distinguish operant conditioning from classical conditioning.

6.5 Describe Thorndike's law of effect.

6.6 Describe reinforcement and its effects on behavior and distinguish negative reinforcement from punishment.

6.7 Identify the four schedules of reinforcement and the response pattern associated with each.

6.8 Describe some applications of operant conditioning.

What do the following four examples have in common?

- Using bird feed as a reward, a behavioral psychologist teaches a pigeon to distinguish paintings by Monet from paintings by Picasso. By the end of the training, the pigeon is a veritable art aficionado.

- Using fish as a treat, a trainer teaches a dolphin to jump out of the water, spin three times, splash in the water, and propel itself through a hoop.

- In his initial attempt at playing tennis, a frustrated 12-year-old hits his opponent's serve into the net the first 15 times. After two hours of practice, he returns his opponent's serve successfully more than half the time.

- A hospitalized patient with dissociative identity disorder (formerly known as multiple personality disorder), displays features of an "alter" personality whenever staff members pay attention to him. When they ignore him, his alter personality seemingly vanishes.

The answer: All are examples of operant conditioning. The first, incidentally, comes from an actual study (Watanabe, Sakamoto, & Wakita, 1995). **Operant conditioning** is learning controlled by the consequences of the organism's behavior (Staddon & Cerutti, 2003). In each of these examples, superficially different as they are, the organism's behavior is shaped by what comes after it, namely, reward. Psychologists also refer to operant conditioning as *instrumental conditioning*, because the organism's response serves an instrumental function. That is, the organism "gets something" out of the response, like food, sex, attention, or avoiding something unpleasant.

Behaviorists refer to the behaviors produced by the animal to receive a reward as *operants*, because the animal "operates" on its environment to get what it wants. Dropping a dollar into a soda machine is an operant, as is asking out an appealing classmate. In the first case, our reward is a refreshing drink and in the second, a hot date—if we're lucky. *[handwritten: haha]*

■ Distinguishing Operant Conditioning from Classical Conditioning

Operant conditioning differs from classical conditioning in three important ways, which we've highlighted in **TABLE 6.1** on page 212.

Through operant conditioning, researchers taught pigeons to distinguish paintings by Monet (*top*) from those of Picasso (*bottom*).

operant conditioning
learning controlled by the consequences of the organism's behavior

"I'm begining to salivate just thinking about applying here."

TABLE 6.1 Key Differences between Operant and Classical Conditioning.

	CLASSICAL CONDITIONING	OPERANT CONDITIONING
Target behavior is . . .	Elicited automatically	Emitted voluntarily
Reward is . . .	Provided unconditionally	Contingent on behavior
Behavior depends primarily on . . .	Autonomic nervous system	Skeletal muscles

Classical Conditioning
- → elicited reflexive and automatic responses
- → reward is given regardless of response
- → depends on autonomic nervous system.

Operant Conditioning
- → emitted voluntary responses
- → reward is given dependent on behavior
- → depends on voluntary motor behavior

1. In classical conditioning, the organism's response is *elicited*, that is, "pulled out" of the organism by the UCS, and later the CS. Remember that in classical conditioning the UCR is a reflexive and automatic response that doesn't require training. In operant conditioning, the organism's response is *emitted*, that is, generated by the organism in a seemingly voluntary fashion.

2. In classical conditioning, the animal's reward is independent of what it does. Pavlov gave his dogs meat powder regardless of whether, or how much, they salivated. In operant conditioning, the animal's reward is contingent—that is, dependent—on what it does. If the animal doesn't emit a response, it comes out empty-handed (or in the case of a dog, empty-pawed).

3. In classical conditioning, the organism's responses depend primarily on the autonomic nervous system (see Chapter 3). In operant conditioning, the organism's responses depend primarily on the skeletal muscles. That is, in contrast to classical conditioning, in which learning involves changes in heart rate, breathing, perspiration, and other bodily systems, in operant conditioning learning involves changes in voluntary motor behavior.

■ The Law of Effect

The famous **law of effect**, put forth by psychologist E. L. Thorndike, forms the basis of much of operant conditioning: *If a response, in the presence of a stimulus, is followed by a satisfying state of affairs, the bond between stimulus and response will be strengthened.* This statement means simply that if we're rewarded for a response to a stimulus, we're more like to repeat that response to the stimulus in the future. Psychologists sometimes refer to early forms of behaviorism as S-R psychology (S stands for *stimulus*, R for *response*). According to S-R theorists, most of our complex behaviors reflect the progressive accumulation of associations between stimuli and responses: the sight of a close friend and saying hello, or the smell of a delicious hamburger and reaching for it on our plate. S-R theorists maintain that almost everything we do voluntarily—driving a car, eating a sandwich, or planting a kiss on someone's lips—results from the gradual buildup of S-R bonds due to the law of effect. Thorndike (1898) discovered the law of effect in a classic study of cats and puzzle boxes. Here's what he did.

Thorndike placed a hungry cat in a box and put a tantalizing piece of fish just outside. To escape from the box, the cat needed to hit upon (literally) the right solution, which was pressing on a lever or pulling on a string inside the box (see **FIGURE 6.5**).

When Thorndike first placed the cat in the puzzle box, it typically flailed around aimlessly in a frantic effort to escape. Then, by sheer accident, the cat eventually found the correct solution, scurried out of the box, and gobbled up its delectable treat. Thorndike wanted to find out what would happen to the cat's behavior over time. Once it figured out the solution to the puzzle, would it then get it right every time?

Thorndike found that the cat's time to escape from the puzzle box decreased *gradually* over sixty trials. There was no point at which the cat abruptly realized what it

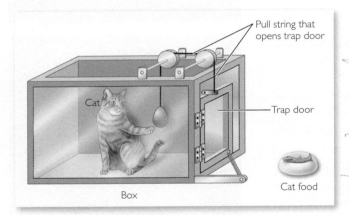

FIGURE 6.5 Thorndike's Puzzle Box.
Thorndike's classic puzzle box research seemed to suggest that cats solve problems solely through trial and error.

Law of effect: stimulus is preceded by multiple repeats the strength between stimulus and response will increase

→ S-R Psychology

law of effect
principle asserting that if a stimulus followed by a behavior results in a reward, the stimulus is more likely to give rise to the behavior in the future

needed to do to escape. According to Thorndike, his cats were learning by trial and error through the steady buildup of associations. Indeed, Thorndike and many other S-R theorists went so far as to conclude that all learning, including all human learning, occurs by trial and error. For them, S-R bonds are gradually "stamped into" the organism by reward.

These findings, Thorndike concluded, provide a crushing blow to the hypothesis that cats learn by **insight**, that is, by grasping the underlying nature of the problem. Had his cats possessed insight into the nature of the problem, the results presumably would have looked like what we see in **FIGURE 6.6**. This figure illustrates what psychologists term the *aha reaction:* "Aha—I got it!" Once the animal solves the problem, it gets it correct just about every time after that. Yet Thorndike never found an Aha! moment: The time to a correct solution decreased only gradually.

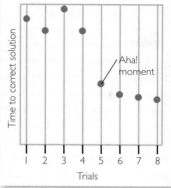

FIGURE 6.6 "Aha Reaction." Insight learning: Once an individual solves the problem, he or she gets the answer right almost every time after that.

insight
grasping the underlying nature of a problem

Skinner box
small animal chamber constructed by Skinner to allow sustained periods of conditioning to be administered and behaviors to be recorded unsupervised

reinforcement
outcome or consequence of a behavior that strengthens the probability of the behavior

positive reinforcement
presentation of a stimulus that strengthens the probability of the behavior

negative reinforcement
removal of a stimulus that strengthens the probability of the behavior

■ B. F. Skinner and Reinforcement

Thorndike's pioneering discoveries on the law of effect laid the groundwork for research on operant conditioning. B. F. Skinner then kicked it up a notch using electronic technology.

Skinner found Thorndike's experimental setup unwieldy because the researcher needed to stick around to place the unhappy cat back into the puzzle box following each trial. This limitation made it difficult to study the buildup of associations in ongoing operant behavior over hours, days, or weeks. So he developed what came to be known as a **Skinner box** (more formally, an operant chamber), which electronically records an animal's responses and prints out a *cumulative record*, or graph, of the animal's activity. A Skinner box typically contains a bar that delivers food when pressed, a food dispenser, and often a light that signals when reward is forthcoming (see **FIGURE 6.7**). With this setup, Skinner studied the operant behavior of rats, pigeons, and other animals and mapped out their responses to reward. By allowing a device to record behavior without any direct human observation, Skinner ran the risk of missing some important behaviors that the box wasn't designed to record. Nonetheless, his discoveries forever altered the landscape of psychology.

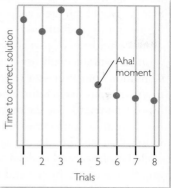

FIGURE 6.7 Rat in Skinner Box and Electronic Device for Recording the Rat's Behavior. B. F. Skinner devised a small chamber (the Skinner box) containing a bar that the rat presses to obtain food, a food dispenser, and often a light that signals when reward is forthcoming. An electronic device graphs the rat's responses in the researcher's absence.

■ Terminology of Operant Conditioning

To understand Skinner's research, you need to learn a bit of psychological jargon. Here we'll discuss three key concepts in Skinnerian psychology: reinforcement, punishment, and discriminative stimulus.

REINFORCEMENT. Up to this point, we've used the term *reward* to refer to any consequence that makes a behavior more likely to occur. But Skinner found this term imprecise, because it doesn't tell us how the organism's behavior changes in response to the reward. He preferred the term **reinforcement**, meaning any outcome that strengthens the probability of a response (Skinner, 1953, 1971).

Skinner distinguished **positive reinforcement**, when we administer a stimulus, from **negative reinforcement**, when we take away a stimulus. Positive reinforcement could be giving a child a Hershey's Kiss when he picks up his toys; negative reinforcement could be ending a child's time-out for bad behavior once she's stopped whining. In both cases, the

FICTOID

MYTH: Skinner raised his daughter in a Skinner box in infancy, causing her to develop severe mental illness later in life.

REALITY: Skinner designed what he called a baby tender (he jokingly called it an "heir conditioner") for his daughter, a modified crib that was glassed in on the top and sides and was heated and humidified. This arrangement allowed her to sleep, play with toys, and crawl around comfortably when she was in her crib wearing only her diaper. Skinner attempted unsuccessfully to market his invention to new parents. Incidentally, Skinner's daughter is alive and well—and quite psychologically normal.

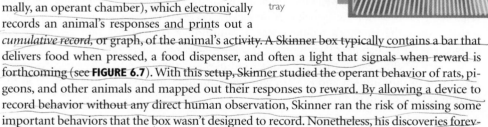

"Oh, not bad. The light comes on, I press the bar, they write me a check. How about you?"

(© The New Yorker Collection 1993 Tom Cheney from cartoonbank.com. All Rights Reserved.)

Forcing a student to see the principal is typically a form of punishment; nevertheless, it can instead serve as a negative reinforcement if it allows the student to escape from an unpleasant class.

punishment
outcome or consequence of a behavior that weakens the probability of the behavior

Table 6.2 Answers: (1) punishment; because the boy's teacher reduced his rate of noise-making.
(2) negative reinforcement; because her doctor increased the woman's rates of eating well and exercising.
(3) negative reinforcement; because the parole board increased the prisoner's rate of law-abiding behavior.
(4) punishment; because the woman decreased her roommate's rate of messy behavior.

most frequent outcome is an increase or strengthening of the response. Note, though, that Skinner would call these actions "reinforcements" *only* if they make the response more likely to occur in the future.

Hundreds of psychology students over the years have demonstrated the power of positive reinforcement using an unconventional participant: their professor. In the game Condition Your Professor (Vyse, 1997), a class of introductory psychology students agrees to provide positive reinforcement—such as smiling or nodding their heads—to their professor whenever he or she moves in a particular direction, such as to the far left side of the room. Your authors know of one famous introductory psychology teacher who spent almost all of his time lecturing from behind his podium. During one class, his students smiled profusely and nodded their heads whenever he ventured out from behind the podium. Sure enough, by the end of class the professor was spending most of his time away from the podium. You and your classmates might want to attempt a similar stunt with your introductory psychology professor: Just don't mention we suggested it.

PUNISHMENT. We shouldn't confuse negative reinforcement with **punishment**, which is any outcome that weakens the probability of a response. Punishments, like reinforcements, can be either positive or negative depending on whether they involve administering a stimulus—positive—or taking one away—negative.

Positive punishment typically involves administering a stimulus that the organism wishes to avoid, such as a physical shock or a spanking, or an unpleasant social outcome, like laughing at someone. Negative punishment involves the removal of a stimulus that the organism wishes to experience, such as a favorite toy or article of clothing.

We also shouldn't confuse punishment with the disciplinary practices often associated with it; discipline is punishment only if it decreases the probability of the behavior. Skinner, who insisted on precision in language, argued that certain actions that might superficially appear to be punishments are actually reinforcers. He defined reinforcers and punishments solely in terms of their consequences. Consider this scenario: A mother rushes into her three-year-old son's bedroom and yells "Stop that!" each time she hears him kicking the wall. Is she punishing his demanding behavior? There's no way to tell without knowing the effect on his behavior. If he kicks the wall more often following the scolding, then the mother is actually reinforcing his behavior. Nevertheless, if his kicking decreases or stops altogether after he was scolded, then the mother's scolding was a punishment. Remember that reinforcement strengthens the probability of a response, punishment weakens it (see **TABLE 6.2**).

Try labeling each of the following examples as an instance of either negative reinforcement or punishment and explain why (you can find the answers upside down in the margin at the bottom of this page):

1. A boy keeps making noise in the back of a classroom despite a teacher's repeated warnings. The teacher finally sends him to the principal's office. When he returns two hours later, he's much quieter.

TABLE 6.2 Distinguishing Reinforcement from Punishment.

	PROCEDURE	EFFECT ON BEHAVIOR	TYPICAL EXAMPLE
Positive Reinforcement	Presenting a stimulus	Increases target behavior	Giving a gold star on homework, resulting in a student studying more
Negative Reinforcement	Removing a stimulus	Increases target behavior	Static on phone subsides when you stand in a specific spot in your room, causing you to stand there more often
Positive Punishment	Presenting a stimulus	Decreases target behavior	Scolding by a pet owner, reducing a dog's habit of chewing on shoes
Negative Punishment	Removing a stimulus	Decreases target behavior	Confiscating a favorite toy, stopping a child from throwing future tantrums

2. A woman with diabetes works hard to control her blood sugar through diet and exercise. As a result, her doctor allows her to discontinue administering her unpleasant daily insulin shots, which increases her attempts to eat healthily and exercise. *negative reinforcement*

3. A parole board releases a previously aggressive criminal from prison early for being a "model citizen" within the institution over the past five years. Following his release, he continues to behave in a law-abiding manner. *negative reinforcement*

4. A woman yells at her roommate for leaving dirty clothing scattered all around her apartment. Her roommate apologizes and never makes a mess again. *negative punishment.*

Does punishment work in the long run? Popular wisdom tells us that it usually does: "Spare the rod, spoil the child." Yet Skinner (1953) and most of his followers argued against the routine use of punishment to change behavior. They believed that reinforcement alone could shape most human behaviors for the better. ((•⸱—**Listen**

According to Skinner and others (Azrin & Holz, 1966), punishment has several disadvantages:

1. Punishment tells the organism only what *not* to do, not what *to* do. A child who's punished for throwing a tantrum won't learn how to deal with frustration more constructively.

2. Punishment often creates anxiety, which can interfere with future learning.

3. Punishment may encourage subversive behavior, prompting people to become sneakier about the situations in which they can and can't display forbidden behavior. A child who's punished for grabbing his brother's toys may learn to grab his brother's toys only when his parents aren't looking.

4. Punishment from parents may provide a model for children's aggressive behavior (Straus, Sugarman, & Giles-Sims, 1997). A child whose parents slap him when he misbehaves may "get the message" that slapping is acceptable.

Numerous researchers have reported that the use of physical punishment by parents is positively correlated with aggressive behavior in children (Fang & Corso, 2007; Gershoff, 2002), although scientists disagree about how large this correlation is (Paolucci & Violato, 2004). Across many studies, Murray Straus and his colleagues (for example, Straus & McCord, 1998) found that physical punishment is associated with more behavioral problems in children. In a study of 1,575 subjects drawn from the general population, Cathy Widom and her colleagues further found that physically abused children are at heightened risk for aggressiveness in adulthood (Widom, 1989a, 1989b). Many researchers interpreted this finding as implying that early physical abuse causes aggression.

Widom (1989a) concluded that her findings reveal the operation of a "cycle of violence," whereby parental aggression begets childhood aggression. When these children become parents, many become abusers themselves. Similarly, Elizabeth Gershoff (2002) reviewed 88 studies of corporal punishment based on a whopping 39,309 participants. Although she found that corporal punishment is sometimes associated with short-term improvements in children's behavior, she also found that a history of such punishment in childhood is associated with an increased probability of becoming an abuser in adulthood.

Yet we must remember that these studies are correlational and don't demonstrate causality. Other interpretations are possible. For example, because children share half of their genes with each parent, and because aggression is partly heritable (Krueger, Hicks, & McGue, 2001), the correlation between parents' physical aggression and their children's aggression may be due to the fact that parents who are physically aggressive pass on this genetic predisposition to their children (DiLalla & Gottesman, 1991; Lynch et al., 2006). It's also conceivable that the causal arrow is reversed: Aggressive children may be difficult to control and therefore evoke physical abuse from their parents. This hypothesis doesn't in any way excuse physical abuse or imply that it's acceptable, but it may help to explain why it occurs. In addition, it's possible that mild levels of punishment are effective, but that severe forms of punishment, including abuse, aren't (Baumrind, Larzelere, & Cowan, 1992; Lynch et al., 2006).

((•⸱—**Listen** to the Punishment and Reinforcement Podcast on **mypsychlab.com**

Skinner and his followers believed that reinforcement is generally much more effective than punishment in shaping children's behavior.

◄ **correlation vs. causation**

CAN WE BE SURE THAT A CAUSES B?

"They're in the wrong place, trying to make it right." [handwritten]

In some countries, such as China and Thailand, spanking is uncommon.

discriminating stimuli → signals the presence of reinforcement [handwritten]

When parents stop giving this boy his favorite toy when he screams, he'll initially scream harder to get what he wants. Eventually he'll realize it won't work and give up the screaming behavior.

Making matters more complicated, the association between physical punishment and childhood behavior problems may depend on race and culture. Spanking and other forms of physical discipline are correlated positively with childhood behavior problems in Caucasian families, but correlated negatively in African American families (Lansford et al., 2004). Moreover, spanking tends to be more predictive of higher levels of childhood aggression and anxiety in countries in which spanking is rare, like China or Thailand, than in countries in which it's common, like Kenya or India (Lansford et al., 2005). The reasons for this difference aren't clear, although children who are spanked in countries in which spanking is more culturally accepted may feel less stigmatized than children in countries in which it's culturally condemned.

Still, that's not to say that we should never use punishment, only that we should use it sparingly. Most research suggests that punishment works best when it's delivered consistently and follows the undesired behavior promptly (Brennan & Mednick, 1994). In particular, immediate punishment sometimes tends to be effective, whereas delayed punishment is often useless (Church, 1969; McCord, 2006; Moffitt, 1983). Punishment of an undesired behavior also works best when we simultaneously reinforce a desired behavior (Azrin & Holz, 1966).

DISCRIMINATIVE STIMULUS. Another critical term in operant conditioning lingo is the **discriminative stimulus**, any stimulus that signals the presence of reinforcement. When we snap our fingers at a dog in the hope of having it come over to us, the dog may approach us for a much-appreciated petting. For the dog, our finger snapping is a discriminative stimulus: It's a signal that if it comes near us, it will receive reinforcement. According to behaviorists, we're responding to discriminative stimuli virtually all the time, even if we're not consciously aware of it. A friend's waving at us from across campus is another common discriminative stimulus: It often signals to us that our friend wants to chat with us, thereby reinforcing us for responding to her wave.

SAME SONG, SECOND VERSE. *Acquisition, extinction, spontaneous recovery, stimulus generalization,* and *stimulus discrimination* are all terms with which we've crossed paths in our discussion of classical conditioning. These terms apply just as much to operant conditioning, too. We can find their definitions in **TABLE 6.3**. Below, we'll examine how three of these concepts apply to operant conditioning.

Extinction. In operant conditioning, extinction occurs when we stop delivering reinforcers following a previously reinforced behavior. Gradually, this behavior declines in frequency and disappears. If parents give a screaming child a toy to quiet her, they may be inadvertently reinforcing her behavior, because she's learning to scream to get something. If parents buy earplugs and stop placating the child by giving toys, the screaming behavior gradually extinguishes. In such cases we often see an *extinction burst.* That is, shortly after withdrawing the reinforcer the undesired behavior initially increases in intensity, probably because the child is trying harder to get reinforced. So there's some truth to the old saying that things sometimes need to get worse before they get better.

TABLE 6.3 Definition Reminders of Key Concepts in Both Classical and Operant Conditioning.

TERM	DEFINITION
Acquisition	Learning phase during which a response is established
Extinction	Gradual reduction and eventual elimination of the response after a stimulus is presented repeatedly
Spontaneous Recovery	Sudden reemergence of an extinguished response after a delay
Stimulus Generalization	Displaying response to stimuli similar to but not identical to the original stimulus
Stimulus Discrimination	Displaying a less pronounced response to stimuli that differ from the original stimulus

discriminative stimulus
stimulus associated with the presence of reinforcement

[Handwritten notes in top margin: "No sleep today. Can't even rest when the sun's down. No time. Just not enough. And nobody's watching you now. When we children were kids we'd play out in the street. Just dipped in late when we were children. Say that I know the fear..."]

Stimulus Discrimination. As we mentioned earlier, one group of investigators used food reinforcement to train pigeons to distinguish paintings by Monet from those of Picasso (Watanabe et al., 1995). That's *stimulus discrimination*, because the pigeons learned to tell the difference between two different types of stimuli.

Stimulus Generalization. Interestingly, these investigators found that their pigeons also displayed stimulus generalization. Following operant conditioning, they distinguished paintings by impressionist artists whose styles were similar to Monet's, such as Renoir, from paintings by cubist artists similar to Picasso, such as Braque.

[Handwritten: smart pigeons]

Schedules of Reinforcement

Skinner (1938) found that animals' behaviors differ depending on the **schedule of reinforcement**, that is, the pattern of delivering reinforcement. In the simplest pattern, **continuous reinforcement**, we reinforce a behavior every time it occurs. **Partial reinforcement**, sometimes called *intermittent reinforcement*, occurs when we reinforce responses only some of the time.

Try answering this question: If we want to train a dog to perform a trick, like catching a Frisbee, should we reinforce it for (a) each successful catch or (b) only some of its successful catches? If you're like most people, you'd answer (a), which seems to match our commonsense notions regarding the effects of reinforcement. It seems logical to assume that the more consistent the reinforcement, the more consistent will be the resulting behavior.

Nevertheless, Skinner's principle of partial reinforcement shows that our commonplace intuitions about reinforcement are backward. According to the principle of partial reinforcement, behaviors we reinforce only occasionally are slower to extinguish than those we reinforce continuously, that is, every time. Although this point may seem counterintuitive, consider that an animal that expects to be rewarded every time it performs the target behavior may become reluctant to continue performing the behavior if the reinforcement becomes undependable. However, if an animal has learned that the behavior will be rewarded only occasionally, it's more likely to continue the behavior in the hope of getting reinforcement.

So if we want an animal to maintain a trick for a long time, we should actually reinforce it for correct responses only every once in a while. Skinner (1969) noted that continuous reinforcement allows animals to learn new behaviors more quickly, but that partial reinforcement leads to a greater resistance to extinction. This principle may help to explain why some people remain trapped for years in terribly dysfunctional, even abusive, relationships. Some relationship partners provide intermittent reinforcement to their significant others, treating them miserably most of the time but treating them well on rare occasions. This pattern of partial reinforcement may keep individuals "hooked" in relationships that aren't working—and aren't likely to work in the long run.

Although there are numerous schedules of reinforcement, we'll discuss the four major ones here. Remarkably, the effects of these reinforcement schedules are consistent across species as diverse as cockroaches, pigeons, rats, and humans. That's impressive replicability. The principal reinforcement schedules vary along two dimensions:

1. *The consistency of administering reinforcement.* Some reinforcement contingencies are *fixed,* whereas others are *variable.* That is, in some cases experimenters provide reinforcement on a regular (fixed) basis, whereas in others they provide reinforcement on an irregular (variable) basis.

2. *The basis of administering reinforcement.* Some reinforcement schedules operate on *ratio* schedules, whereas others operate on *interval* schedules. In ratio schedules, the experimenter reinforces the animal based on the *number of responses* it's emitted. In interval schedules, the experimenter reinforces the animal based on the *amount of time* elapsed since the last reinforcement.

---

schedule of reinforcement
pattern of reinforcing a behavior

continuous reinforcement
reinforcing a behavior every time it occurs, resulting in faster learning but faster extinction than only occasional reinforcement

partial reinforcement
only occasional reinforcement of a behavior, resulting in slower extinction than if the behavior had been reinforced continually

[?] If we want this dog to retain this basketball twirling trick in the future, should we reinforce it each time if performs the trick, or only some of the time? (See answer upside down at bottom of page.)

replicability

CAN THE RESULTS BE DUPLICATED IN OTHER STUDIES?

[Handwritten: ratio = responses, interval = time]

Answer: Only some of the time

FIGURE 6.8   Four Major Reinforcement Schedules.   The four major reinforcement schedules are (a) fixed ratio, (b) fixed interval, (c) variable ratio, and (d) variable interval.

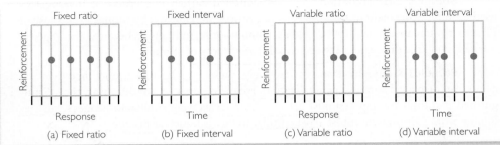

(a) Fixed ratio   (b) Fixed interval   (c) Variable ratio   (d) Variable interval

? Imagine that this football player received a salary bonus for every five touchdowns he scored. What reinforcement schedule would he be on?   (See answer upside down on bottom of page.)

fixed ratio (FR) schedule
pattern in which we provide reinforcement following a regular number of responses

fixed interval (FI) schedule
pattern in which we provide reinforcement for producing the response at least once following a specified time interval

variable ratio (VR) schedule
pattern in which we provide reinforcement after a specific number of responses on average, with the number varying randomly

variable interval (VI) schedule
pattern in which we provide reinforcement for producing the response at least once during an average time interval, with the interval varying randomly

We can combine these two dimensions to arrive at four major schedules of reinforcement (see **FIGURE 6.8**):

1. In a **fixed ratio (FR) schedule**, we provide reinforcement after a regular number of responses. For example, we could give a rat a pellet after it presses the lever in a Skinner box fifteen times.

2. In a **fixed interval (FI) schedule**, we provide reinforcement for producing the response at least once after a specified amount of time has passed. For example, a worker in a clock factory might get paid every Friday for the work she's done, as long as she's generated at least one clock during that one-week interval.

3. In a **variable ratio (VR) schedule**, we provide reinforcement after a specific number of responses on average, but the precise number of responses required during any given period varies randomly. A pigeon on a variable ratio schedule with an average ratio of 10 might receive a piece of bird feed after six pecks, then after 12 pecks, then after one peck, then after 21 pecks, with the average of these ratios being 10.

4. In a **variable interval (VI) schedule**, we provide reinforcement for producing the response after an average time interval, with the actual interval varying randomly. For example, we could give a dog a treat for performing a trick on a variable interval schedule with an average interval of eight minutes. This dog may have to perform the trick sometime during a seven-minute interval the first time, then a one-minute interval the second time, then a 20-minute interval, and then a four-minute interval, with the average of these intervals being eight minutes.

Skinner discovered that different reinforcement schedules yield distinctive patterns of responding (see **FIGURE 6.9**). Ratio schedules tend to yield higher rates of responding than do interval schedules. This finding makes intuitive sense. If a dog gets a treat every five times he rolls over, he's going to roll over more often than if he gets a treat every five minutes, regardless of whether he rolls over once or 20 times during that interval. In addition, variable schedules tend to yield more consistent rates of responding than do fixed schedules. This finding also makes intuitive sense. If we never know when our next treat is coming, it's in our best interests to keep emitting the response to ensure we've emitted it enough times to earn the reward.

Two other features of reinforcement schedules are worth noting. First, fixed interval schedules are associated with a "scalloped" pattern of responding. This *FI scallop* reflects the fact that the animal "waits" for a time after it receives reinforcement, and then increases its rate of responding just before the interval is up as it begins to anticipate reinforcement.

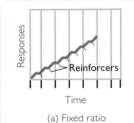 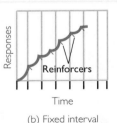 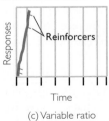 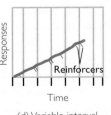

(a) Fixed ratio   (b) Fixed interval   (c) Variable ratio   (d) Variable interval

FIGURE 6.9   Typical Response Patterns for the Four Reinforcement Schedules.   Note the "scalloped" pattern in (b), the fixed interval response pattern. The subject decreases the reinforced behavior immediately after receiving a reinforcer, then increases the behavior in anticipation of reinforcement as the time for reinforcement approaches.

[handwritten margin notes: "On a Wednesday, in cafe, I watched I begin again..." "Break and burn and end" "but on a Wednesday in cafe, I watched it begin again" "Monday?!"]

Second, variable ratio (VR) schedules usually yield the highest rates of responding of all. It's for this reason that there's one place where we can be guaranteed to find a VR schedule: A casino. Roulette wheels, slot machines, and other casino devices deliver cash rewards on an irregular basis, and they do so based on the gambler's responses. Sometimes the gambler has to pull the arm of the slot machine (the "one-armed bandit") hundreds of times before receiving any money at all. At other times, the gambler pulls the arm only once and makes out like a bandit himself, perhaps walking away with thousands of dollars for a few seconds of work. The extreme unpredictability of the VR schedule is precisely what keeps gamblers hooked, because a huge reinforcement can come at any time.

VR schedules keep pigeons hooked, too. Skinner (1953) found that pigeons placed on VR schedules sometimes continue to peck on a disk for food after more than 150,000 nonreinforced responses. In some cases, they literally ground down their beaks in the process. Like desperate gamblers in a Las Vegas casino hoping for a huge payoff, they don't give up despite repeated disappointments. For Skinner, much of what we call "persistence" or "determination" in everyday life is merely a consequence of being on a reinforcement schedule that's difficult to extinguish, especially a VR schedule. ⊙→ Simulate

■ Applications of Operant Conditioning

Operant conditioning plays a role in a surprising number of everyday experiences and in some special circumstances, as well. As we've already noted, operant conditioning is central to some parenting practices. It's also relevant to a wide array of other situations ranging from animal training to weight loss plans—and even to learning to master a video game. Here we'll explore a few well-studied examples of operant conditioning in action.

ANIMAL TRAINING. If you've ever seen animals perform at a circus, zoo, or aquarium, you might wonder how on earth they learned such elaborate routines. There's an old joke that just as magicians pull rabbits out of hats, behaviorist pull habits out of rats—and other animals, too. They typically do so by means of a procedure called **shaping by successive approximations**, or *shaping* for short. Using shaping, we reinforce behaviors that aren't exactly the target behavior but that are progressively closer versions of it. Typically, we shape an organism's response by initially reinforcing most or all responses that are close to the desired behavior, and then gradually *fading* (that is, decreasing the frequency of) our reinforcement for the not-exactly-right behaviors over time.

Animal trainers often combine shaping with a technique called *chaining,* in which they link a number of interrelated behaviors to form a longer series. Each behavior in the chain becomes a cue for the next behavior in the chain, just as A becomes a cue for B, B for C, and so on when we're learning the alphabet. ⊙→ Simulate

By means of shaping and chaining, Skinner taught pigeons to play Ping-Pong, although they weren't exactly Olympic-caliber table tennis players. To do so, he first reinforced them for turning toward the paddles, then approaching the paddles, then placing the paddles in their beaks, then picking up the paddles with their beaks, and so on. Then, he chained later behaviors, like swinging the paddle and then hitting the ball, to the earlier behaviors. During World War II, Skinner also taught pigeons to guide missiles from airplanes to enemy targets by pecking at an image on a screen whenever the missile got closer to the target, although the U.S. military never adopted his creative approach to aerial warfare. In both cases, Skinner began by reinforcing initial approximations to the desired response. As we might imagine, shaping and chaining complex animal behaviors requires patience, as the process can take days or weeks. Still, the payoff can be substantial, because we can train animals to engage in numerous behaviors that lie well outside their normal repertoires. Indeed, all contemporary animal trainers rely on Skinnerian principles. *— Yay for B.F. Skinner.*

OVERCOMING PROCRASTINATION. Be honest: Did you put off reading this chapter until the last moment? If so, don't feel ashamed, because procrastination is one of the most frequent study problems that college students report. Although widespread, procrastination may not be harmless. The stress it causes may be bad for our physical and psychological health. Moreover,

⊙→ Simulate Schedules of Reinforcement on **mypsychlab.com**

Skinner's shaping principles are used today to train service animals.

⊙→ Simulate Shaping on **mypsychlab.com**

shaping by successive approximations
conditioning a target behavior by progressively reinforcing behaviors that come closer and closer to the target

correlation vs. causation

CAN WE BE SURE THAT A CAUSES B?

procrastinators tend to perform more poorly in their classes than do early birds (Tice & Baumeister, 1997). Although these findings are correlational and don't establish that procrastination causes bad grades, they certainly suggest that putting things off isn't ideal.

How can we overcome procrastination? Don't put off reading the rest of this paragraph, because we have a possible remedy for dilly-dallying. Although there are several potential solutions for procrastination, among the best is probably the one discovered by David Premack (1965). In his research on monkeys, Premack found that we can positively reinforce a less frequently performed behavior with a more frequently performed behavior (Danaher, 1974). Although not a foolproof rule (Knapp, 1976), this principle typically works surprisingly well. Research suggests this approach may help people to stop putting off things they've long avoided, like going to the dentist (Ramer, 1980).

If you find yourself putting off a reading or writing task, think of behaviors you'd typically perform if given the chance—perhaps hanging out with a few close friends, watching a favorite TV program, or treating yourself to an ice cream cone. Then, reinforce yourself with these higher frequency behaviors *only* after you've completed your homework.

SUPERSTITIOUS BEHAVIOR. How many of the following behaviors do you perform?

- Never opening an umbrella indoors
- Not walking under a ladder
- Crossing the street whenever you see a black cat
- Carrying a lucky charm or necklace
- Going out of your way not to step on cracks in the sidewalk
- Knocking on wood
- Crossing your fingers
- Avoiding the number 13 (like not stopping on the thirteenth floor of a building)

If you've engaged in several of these actions, you're at least somewhat superstitious. So are many Americans. Twelve percent of Americans are afraid of walking under a ladder, while 14 percent are afraid of crossing paths with a black cat (Vyse, 1997). So many people are afraid of the number 13 (a fear called *triskaidekaphobia*) that the floor designations in many tall buildings skip directly from 12 to 14 (Hock, 2002). This phobia isn't limited to North America; in Paris, triskaidekaphobics who are going out to dinner with 12 other people can hire a *quatorzieme,* a person paid to serve as a fourteenth guest.

How do superstitions relate to operant conditioning? In a classic study, Skinner (1948) placed eight food-deprived pigeons in a Skinner box while delivering reinforcement (bird feed) *every 15 seconds independent of their behavior.* That is, the birds received reinforcement regardless of what they did. After a few days, Skinner found that six of the eight pigeons had acquired remarkably strange behaviors. In the words of Skinner:

> One bird was conditioned to turn counterclockwise about the cage, making two or three turns between reinforcements. Another repeatedly thrust its head into one of the upper corners of the cage. A third developed a tossing response as if placing its head beneath an invisible bar and lifting it repeatedly. Two birds developed a pendulum motion of the head and body in which the head was extended forward and swung from right to left. (p. 168)

You may have observed similarly odd behaviors in pigeons that people are feeding in city parks; some may prance around or walk rapidly in circles in anticipation of reinforcement. According to Skinner, his pigeons had developed *superstitious behavior:* Actions linked to reinforcement by sheer coincidence (Morse & Skinner, 1957). There's no actual association between superstitious behavior and reinforcement, although the animal acts as though there is. The behavior that the pigeon just happened to be performing immediately prior to being reinforced was strengthened—remember that reinforcement increases the probability of a response—so the pigeon kept on doing it (this kind of accidental operant conditioning is sometimes called *superstitious conditioning*). Not all studies have been able to replicate these findings in pigeons (Staddon & Simmelhag, 1971), although it's likely that at least some animal—and human—superstitions develop in the fashion Skinner described (Bloom et al., 2007; Garcia-Montes et al., 2008).

So many people are afraid of the number 13 that many buildings don't have a thirteenth floor.

replicability

CAN THE RESULTS BE DUPLICATED IN OTHER STUDIES?

"...and not another" *goodbye - not to* *call - operant conditioning* *everything* *I don't* *almost* *do:*

Few people are more prone to superstitions than athletes. That's probably because the outcome of so many sporting events, even those requiring a great deal of skill, depends heavily on chance. As we learned in Chapter 2, baseball Hall of Famer Wade Boggs became famous for eating chicken before each game. Hall of Fame football player Jim Kelly forced himself to vomit before every game, and basketball player Chuck Person ate exactly two candy bars (always Snickers or Kit Kats) before every game (Vyse, 1997). Superstar golfer Tiger Woods always wears a red shirt when playing on Sundays. It's not just athletes; sports fans also have their share of superstitions, like the football fan who wears his "lucky" T-shirt before a big game.

Interestingly, the prevalence of superstitions in sports depends on the extent to which the outcomes are due to chance. That's exactly what Skinner would have predicted, because, as we've already discovered, partial reinforcement schedules are more likely to produce enduring behaviors than are continuous reinforcement schedules. In baseball, hitting is much less under players' control than is fielding: Even the best hitters succeed only about three out of 10 times, whereas the best fielders succeed 9.8 or even 9.9 out of 10 times. So hitting is controlled by a partial reinforcement schedule, whereas fielding is controlled by something close to a continuous reinforcement schedule. As we might expect, baseball players have far more hitting-related superstitions—like drawing a favorite symbol in the sand in the batter's box—than fielding-related superstitions (Gmelch, 1974; Vyse, 1997).

Of course, human superstitions aren't due entirely to operant conditioning. Many superstitions are spread partly by word-of-mouth (Herrnstein, 1966). If our mother tells us over and over again that black cats bring bad luck, we may become wary of them. Still, for many superstitions, operant conditioning probably plays an important role.

THERAPEUTIC USES OF OPERANT CONDITIONING. We can apply operant conditioning to clinical settings as well. One of the most successful applications of operant conditioning has been the *token economy.* Token economies are systems, often set up in psychiatric hospitals, for reinforcing appropriate behaviors and extinguishing inappropriate ones (Carr, Frazier, & Roland, 2005; Kazdin, 1982). Typically, psychologists who construct token economies begin by identifying *target behaviors,* that is, actions they hope to make more frequent. Staff members reinforce patients who exhibit these behaviors using tokens, chips, points, or other **secondary reinforcers.** Secondary reinforcers are neutral objects that become associated with **primary reinforcers**—things, like a favorite food or drink, that naturally increase the target behavior.

For instance, one of the authors of your textbook worked in a psychiatric hospital unit consisting of children with serious behavior problems, including yelling and cursing. In this unit, one target behavior was being polite to staff members. So whenever a child was especially polite to a staff member, he was rewarded with points, which he could trade in for something he wanted, like ice cream or attending a movie with staff members. Whenever a child was rude to a staff member, he was punished with a loss of points.

Research suggests that token economies are often effective in improving behavior in hospitals, group homes, and juvenile detention units (Ayllon & Milan, 2002; Paul & Lentz, 1977). Nevertheless, token economies are controversial, because the behaviors learned in institutions don't always transfer to the outside world (Carr et al., 2005; Wakefield, 2006). That's especially likely if the patients return to settings, like deviant peer groups, in which they're reinforced for socially inappropriate behaviors.

Operant conditioning has also been helpful in the treatment of individuals with autism, especially in improving their language deficits (see Chapter 2). *Applied behavior analysis* (ABA) for autism makes extensive use of shaping techniques; mental health professionals offer food and other primary reinforcers to individuals with autism as they reach progressively closer approximations to certain words and, eventually, complete sentences.

Ivar Lovaas and his colleagues have pioneered the best-known ABA program for autism (Lovaas, 1987; McEachin, Smith, & Lovaas, 1993). The results of Lovaas's work have been promising. Children with autism who undergo ABA training emerge with better language and intellectual skills than do control groups of children with autism who don't undergo such training (Green, 1996; Matson et al., 1996; Romanczyk et al., 2003).

Like many athletes, former major league pitcher Turk Wendell had a host of superstitions, including chewing exactly four pieces of black licorice while pitching and—shown here—jumping over the foul line on the way back to the dugout.

The token economy is one of the most successful applications of operant conditioning.

2° reinforcer = neutral objects associated with 1° reinforcer

1° reinforcer = object that increases target behavior

secondary reinforcer
neutral object that becomes associated with a primary reinforcer

primary reinforcer
item or outcome that naturally increases the target behavior

ruling out rival hypotheses

HAVE IMPORTANT ALTERNATIVE EXPLANATIONS FOR THE FINDINGS BEEN EXCLUDED?

Amygdala: classically conditioned fear
Brain areas with dopamine
- operant conditioned responses (i.e. reward)

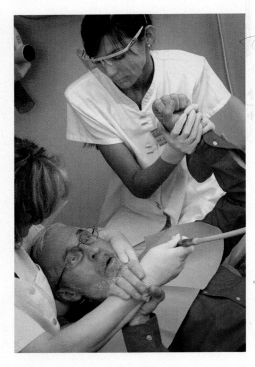

Fears of dental procedures are often reinforced by avoidance behavior over many years, such as a refusal to go to the dentist until it's absolutely necessary.

✓ **Study** and **Review** on mypsychlab.com

Nevertheless, because Lovaas didn't randomly assign children with autism to experimental and control groups, his findings are vulnerable to a rival explanation: Perhaps the children in the experimental group had higher levels of functioning to begin with. Indeed, there's evidence this was the case (Schopler, Short, & Mesibov, 1989). The current consensus is that ABA isn't a miracle cure for the language deficits of autism, but that it can be extremely helpful in many cases (Herbert, Sharp, & Gaudiano, 2002).

■ Putting Classical and Operant Conditioning Together

Up to this point, we've discussed classical and operant conditioning as though they were two entirely independent processes. Yet the truth is more complicated. The similarities between classical and operant conditioning, including the fact that we find acquisition, extinction, stimulus generalization, and so on, in both, have led some theorists to argue that these two forms of learning aren't as different as some psychologists believe (Brown & Jenkins, 1968; Staddon, 2003).

Although there are certainly important similarities between classical and operant conditioning, brain imaging studies demonstrate that these two forms of learning are associated with activations in different brain regions. Classically conditioned fear reactions are based largely in the amygdala (LeDoux, 1996; Likhtik et al., 2008; Veit et al., 2002), whereas operantly conditioned responses are based largely in brain areas rich in dopamine, which are linked to reward (Robbins & Everitt, 1998; Simmons & Neill, 2009; see Chapter 3).

These two types of conditioning often interact. We've already discovered that certain phobias arise in part by classical conditioning: A previously neutral stimulus (the CS)—say, a dog—is paired with an unpleasant stimulus (the UCS)—a dog bite—resulting in the CR of fear. So far, so good.

But this tidy scheme doesn't answer an important question: Why doesn't the CR of fear eventually extinguish? Given what we've learned about classical conditioning, we might expect the CR of fear to fade away over time with repeated exposure to the CS of dogs. Yet this often doesn't happen (Rachman, 1977). Many people with phobias remain deathly afraid of their feared stimulus for years, even decades. Indeed, only about 20 percent of untreated adults with phobias ever get over their fears (American Psychiatric Association, 2000). Why?

Enter *two-process theory* to the rescue as an explanation (Mowrer, 1947). According to two-process theory, we need both classical and operant conditioning to explain the persistence of anxiety disorders. Here's how: People acquire phobias by means of classical conditioning. Then, once they have a phobia, they start to avoid their feared stimulus whenever they see it. If they have a dog phobia, they may cross the street whenever they see someone walking toward them with a large German shepherd. When they do, they experience a reduction in anxiety, which *negatively reinforces* their fear. Recall that negative reinforcement involves the removal of a stimulus, in this case anxiety, that makes the behavior associated with it more likely. So, by avoiding dogs whenever they see them, people with a dog phobia are negatively reinforcing their fear. Ironically, they're operantly conditioning themselves to make their fears more likely to persist. They're exchanging short-term gain for long-term pain.

assess your knowledge   FACT OR FICTION?

1. In classical conditioning, responses are emitted; in operant conditioning, they're elicited. **True / False**
2. Negative reinforcement and punishment are superficially different, but they produce the same short-term effects on behavior. **True / False**
3. The correlation between spanking and children's behavioral problems appears to be positive in Caucasians but negative in African Americans. **True / False**
4. The principle of partial reinforcement states that behaviors reinforced only some of the time extinguish more rapidly than behaviors reinforced continuously. **True / False**
5. We can reinforce less frequent behaviors with more frequent behaviors. **True / False**

Answers: 1. F (p. 212); 2. F (p. 214); 3. T (p. 216); 4. F (p. 217); 5. T (p. 220)

COGNITIVE MODELS OF LEARNING

6.9 Outline the evidence that supports latent learning and observational learning.

6.10 Identify evidence of insight learning.

Thus far, we've omitted one word when discussing how we learn: *thinking*. That's not accidental, because early behaviorists didn't believe that thought played much of a causal role in learning. An advocate of what he called *radical behaviorism*, Skinner (1953) believed that observable behavior, thinking, and emotion are all governed by the same laws of learning, namely, classical and operant conditioning. For radical behaviorists, thinking and emotion *are* behaviors, they're just covert—that is, unobservable—behaviors. One frequent misconception about Skinner is that he didn't believe in thinking. On this and a host of other issues, Skinner isn't merely one of the most famous of all psychologists; he's also one of the most misunderstood (DeBell & Harless, 1992; Wyatt, 2001; see **TABLE 6.4**).

On the contrary, Skinner clearly thought—he wouldn't have objected to our use of that word here—that humans and other intelligent animals think, but that thinking is no different in principle from any other behavior. For Skinner, this view is far more parsimonious than invoking different laws of learning for thinking than for other behaviors. At times, Skinner went even further. In a talk delivered eight days before his death, Skinner (1990) likened proponents of cognitive psychology, who believe that thinking plays a central role in causing behavior (see Chapter 1), to pseudoscientists. Cognitive psychology, he argued, invokes unobservable and ultimately meaningless concepts—like "mind"—to explain behavior. Skinner claimed that doing so doesn't bring us any closer to the true causes of behavior.

Despite widespread misconception, Skinner and other radical behaviorists acknowledged that people and other intelligent animals think. Nevertheless, they viewed thinking as no different from other behaviors, except that it just happens to be unobservable.

occam's razor

DOES A SIMPLER EXPLANATION FIT THE DATA JUST AS WELL?

■ S-O-R Psychology: Throwing Thinking Back into the Mix

Few psychologists today share Skinner's harsh assessment of cognitive psychology. In fact, most psychologists now agree that the story of learning in humans is incomplete without at least some role for cognition, that is, thinking (Bolles, 1979; Kirsch et al., 2004; Pinker, 1997).

TABLE 6.4 Widespread Myths about the Psychology of B. F. Skinner.

FICTION	FACT
Skinner believed that genes played no role in human behavior	Skinner acknowledged that genes affect the ease with which people learn habits, although he believed the study of genes was of little relevance to psychology
Skinner didn't believe in thinking or emotion	Skinner believed that humans and other intelligent animals think and experience emotions, although he regarded thinking and feeling merely as covert (unobservable) behaviors
Skinner favored the use of punishment as a behavioral technique	Skinner opposed the use of punishment for shaping human behaviors, and believed that reinforcement should be used whenever possible
Skinner believed that any human behavior could be conditioned	Skinner never argued this, although his predecessor John B. Watson came close to doing so
Skinner denied the uniqueness of individuals	Skinner openly acknowledged that all individuals are unique, as they are the product of unique genetic predispositions and unique learning histories
Skinner's vision of society was devoid of morality	Skinner advocated a society in which people would be reinforced for ethical and cooperative behavior

(*Sources:* DeBell & Harless, 1992; Wyatt 2001)

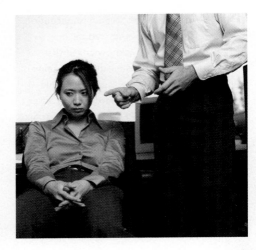

Although few of us enjoy criticism, some of us react to it well, whereas others of us don't. According to S-O-R psychologists, this difference hinges on our interpretation of what the criticism means.

latent learning
learning that's not directly observable

FIGURE 6.10 Tolman and Honzik's Maze Trials. Graph from Tolman and Honzik's classic study of latent learning in rats. Pay particular attention to the blue line. The rats in this group weren't reinforced until day 11; note the sudden drop in the number of their errors on receiving reinforcement. The rats were learning all along, even though they weren't showing it. (*Source:* Tolman & Honzik, 1930)

Over the past 30 or 40 years, psychology has moved increasingly away from a simple S-R (stimulus-response) psychology to a more complex S-O-R psychology, with *O* being the organism that interprets the stimulus before producing a response (Mischel, 1973; Woodworth, 1929). For S-O-R psychologists, the link between S and R isn't mindless or automatic. Instead, the organism's response to a stimulus depends on what this stimulus *means* to it. The S-O-R principle helps to explain a phenomenon we've probably all encountered. You've probably had the experience of giving two friends the same mild criticism (like, "It bothers me a little when you show up late") and found that they reacted quite differently: One was apologetic, the other defensive.

To explain these differing reactions, Skinner would probably have invoked your friends' differing *learning histories,* in essence how each friend had been trained to react to criticism. In contrast, S-O-R theorists, who believe that cognition is central to explaining learning, would contend that the differences in your friends' reactions stem from how they *interpreted* your criticism. Your first friend may have viewed your criticism as constructive feedback, your second friend as a personal attack.

S-O-R theorists don't deny that classical and operant conditioning occur, but they believe that these forms of learning usually depend on thinking. Take a person who's been classically conditioned by tones and shock to sweat in response to the tones. Her skin conductance response will extinguish suddenly if she's told that no more shocks are on the way (Grings, 1973). This phenomenon of *cognitive conditioning,* whereby our interpretation of the situation affects conditioning, suggests that conditioning is more than an automatic, mindless process (Brewer, 1974; Kirsch et al., 2004).

S-O-R theorists also emphasize the role of expectations in learning. For example, they point out that classical conditioning occurs only if the CS regularly predicts the occurrence of the UCS (Rescorla, 1990; Rescorla & Wagner, 1972). If we repeatedly present the CS and UCS close together in time, that alone won't do the trick when it comes to producing classical conditioning. Organisms show classically conditioned reactions only when the CS reliably forecasts the UCS, suggesting that they're building up expectations about what comes next. So according to S-O-R theorists, whenever Pavlov's dogs heard the ticking of the metronome, they thought—and the word "thought" is crucial here—"Ah, I think some meat powder is on the way."

To explain psychology's gradual transition from behaviorism to cognitivism, we need to tell the story of a pioneering psychologist and his rats.

■ Latent Learning

One of the first serious challenges to the radical behaviorist account of learning was mounted by Edward Chace Tolman (1886–1959), whose contribution to the psychology of learning can't be overestimated. Tolman suspected that reinforcement wasn't the be-all and end-all of learning. To understand why, answer this question: "Who was one of the first psychologists to challenge the radical behaviorist account of learning?" If you've been paying attention, you answered "Tolman." Yet immediately before we asked that question, you knew the answer, even though you had no opportunity to demonstrate it. According to Tolman (1932), you engaged in **latent learning**: learning that isn't directly observable (Blodgett, 1929). We learn many things without showing them. Putting it a bit differently, there's a crucial difference between *competence*—what we know—and *performance*—showing what we know (Bradbard et al., 1986).

Why is this distinction important? Because it implies that *reinforcement isn't necessary for learning.* Here's how Tolman and C. H. Honzik (1930) demonstrated this point systematically.

They randomly assigned three groups of rats to go through a maze over a three-week period (see **FIGURE 6.10**). One group always received reinforcement in the form of cheese when it got to the end of the maze. A second group never received reinforcement when it got to the end of the maze. The first group made far fewer errors; that's no great surprise. The third group of rats received no reinforcement for the first 10 days, and then started receiving reinforcement on the eleventh day.

As we can see in Figure 6.10, the rats in the third group showed a large and abrupt drop in their number of errors after receiving their very first reinforcer. In fact, within only a few days their number of errors didn't differ significantly from the number of errors among the rats who were always reinforced.

According to Tolman, this finding means that the rats in the third group had been learning all along. They just hadn't bothered to show it because they had nothing to gain. Once there was a payoff for learning, namely, a tasty morsel of cheese, they promptly became miniature maze masters.

According to Tolman (1948), the rats had developed **cognitive maps**—that is, spatial representations—of the maze. If you're like most college students, you were hopelessly confused the first day you arrived on your campus. Over time, however, you probably developed a mental sense of the layout of the campus, so that you now hardly ever become lost. That internal spatial blueprint, according to Tolman, is a cognitive map.

In a clever demonstration of cognitive maps, three investigators (McNamara, Long, & Wilke, 1956) had one set of rats run repeatedly through a maze to receive reinforcement. They put another set of rats in little moving "trolley cars," in which the rats could observe the layout of the maze but not obtain the experience of running through it. When the researchers gave the second group of rats the chance to run through the maze, they did just as well as the rats in the first group. As rodent tourists in trolley cars, they'd acquired cognitive maps of the maze.

The latent learning research of Tolman and others challenged strict behavioral models of learning, because their work suggested that learning could occur without reinforcement. To many psychologists, this research falsified the claim that reinforcement is necessary for all forms of learning. It also suggested that thinking, in the form of cognitive maps, plays a central role in at least some forms of learning.

■ Observational Learning

According to some psychologists, one important variant of latent learning is **observational learning**: learning by watching others (Bandura, 1965). In many cases, we learn by watching *models:* parents, teachers, and others who are influential to us. Many psychologists regard observational learning as a form of latent learning because it allows us to learn without reinforcement. We can merely watch someone else being reinforced for doing something and take our cues from them.

Observational learning spares us the expense of having to learn everything firsthand (Bandura, 1977). Most of us aren't experts in skydiving, but from our observations of people who've gone skydiving we learn that it's generally a wise idea to have a parachute on before jumping out of a plane. Note that we didn't need to learn this useful tidbit of advice by trial and error, or else we wouldn't be here to talk about it. Observational learning can spare us from serious, even life-threatening, mistakes. But it can also contribute to our learning of maladaptive habits.

OBSERVATIONAL LEARNING OF AGGRESSION. In classic research in the 1960s, Albert Bandura and his colleagues demonstrated that children can learn to act aggressively by watching aggressive role models (Bandura, Ross, & Ross, 1963).

These researchers asked preschool boys and girls to watch an adult (the model) interact with a large Bobo doll, a wobbly doll that bounces back to its original upright position after being hit (Bandura, Ross, & Ross, 1961). The experimenters randomly assigned some children to watch the adult model playing quietly and ignoring the Bobo doll, and others to watch the adult model punching the Bobo doll in the nose, hitting it with a mallet, sitting on it, and kicking it around the room. As though that weren't enough, the model in the latter condition shouted out insults and vivid descriptions of his actions while inflicting violence: "Sock him in the nose," "Kick him," "Pow."

Cats have cognitive maps, too. (© Hilary B. Price. King Features Syndicate)

falsifiability

CAN THE CLAIM BE DISPROVED?

Children acquire a great deal of their behavior by observational learning of adults, especially their parents.

cognitive map
mental representation of how a physical space is organized

observational learning
learning by watching others

Bandura and his coworkers then brought the children into a room with an array of appealing toys, including a miniature fire engine, a jet fighter, and a large doll set. Just as children began playing with these toys, the experimenter interrupted them, informing them that they needed to move to a different room. This interruption was intentional, as the investigators wanted to frustrate the children to make them more likely to behave aggressively. Then the experimenter brought them into a second room, which contained a Bobo doll identical to the one they'd seen. ◉ Watch

On a variety of dependent measures, Bandura and his colleagues found that previous exposure to the aggressive model triggered significantly more aggression against the Bobo doll than did exposure to the nonaggressive model. The children who'd watched the aggressive model yelled at the doll much as the model had done, and they even imitated many of his verbal insults. In a later study, Bandura and his colleagues (Bandura, Ross, & Ross, 1963) replicated these results when they displayed the aggressive models to children on film rather than in person.

MEDIA VIOLENCE AND REAL-WORLD AGGRESSION. The Bandura studies and scores of later studies of observational learning led psychologists to examine a theoretically and socially important question: Does exposure to media violence, such as in films, movies, or video games, contribute to real-world violence—or what Bushman and Anderson (2001) called violence in the "reel world"? The research literature addressing this question is as vast as it is confusing, and could easily occupy an entire book by itself. So we'll only briefly touch on some of the research highlights here.

Hundreds of investigators using correlational designs have reported that children who watch many violent television programs are more aggressive than other children (Wilson & Herrnstein, 1985). But do these findings demonstrate that media violence causes real-world violence? If you answered "No," give yourself a favored reinforcer. They could indicate merely that highly aggressive children are more likely than other children to tune in to aggressive television programs (Freedman, 1984). Alternatively, these findings could be due to a third variable, such as children's initial levels of aggressiveness. That is, highly aggressive children may be more likely than other children to both watch violent television programs *and* to act aggressively.

Investigators have tried to get around this problem by using longitudinal designs (see Chapter 10), which track individuals' behavior over time. Longitudinal studies show that children who choose to watch many violent television shows commit more aggressive acts years later than do children who choose to watch fewer violent television shows, even when researchers have equated children in their initial levels of aggression (Huesmann et al., 2003; see **FIGURE 6.11**). These studies offer somewhat more compelling evidence for a causal link between media violence and aggression than do traditional correlational studies. But even they don't demonstrate a causal association, because they're not true experiments (see Chapter 2). Participants in these studies aren't randomly assigned to conditions, but instead select which television shows to watch. As a consequence, unmeasured personality variables, like impulsivity, or social variables, like weak parental supervision, might account for these findings. Moreover, just because variable A precedes variable B doesn't mean that variable A *causes* variable B (see Chapter 10). For example, if we found that most common colds start with a scratchy throat and a runny nose, we shouldn't conclude that scratchy throats and runny noses cause colds, only that they're early signs of a cold.

Still other investigators have examined whether the link between media models and later aggression holds up under the tightly controlled conditions of the laboratory. In most of these studies, researchers have exposed subjects to either violent or nonviolent media presentations and seen whether subjects in the former groups behaved

◉ Watch Bandura's Bobo Doll Experiment on **mypsychlab.com**

replicability

CAN THE RESULTS BE DUPLICATED IN OTHER STUDIES?

correlation vs. causation

CAN WE BE SURE THAT A CAUSES B?

ruling out rival hypotheses

HAVE IMPORTANT ALTERNATIVE EXPLANATIONS FOR THE FINDINGS BEEN EXCLUDED?

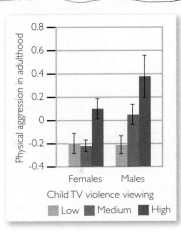

FIGURE 6.11 Longitudinal Study of Individuals Who Watched Violent TV as Children. In both females and males, there's a positive correlation between viewing violent television in childhood and violent behavior in adulthood. But this correlation doesn't demonstrate causality. Why? (*Source:* Huesmann et al., 2003)

more aggressively, such as by yelling at the experimenter or delivering electric shocks to another subject when provoked. In general, these studies strongly suggest a causal association between media violence and laboratory aggression (Wood, Wong, & Chachere, 1991; see Chapter 13). The same conclusion appears to hold for the relation between violent video games and aggression (Bushman & Anderson, 2001; Anderson, Gentile, & Buckley, 2007; see Chapter 13), although the causal link here is less well established (Ferguson, 2009).

Finally, some investigators have conducted *field studies* of the link between media violence and aggression (Anderson & Bushman, 2002). In field studies, researchers examine the relation between naturally occurring events and aggression in the real world. For example, sociologist David Phillips (1983) found that the number of homicides increased by approximately one-eighth following widely publicized boxing matches. Moreover, when a Caucasian boxer defeated an African American, the victim of the murder was more likely to be an African American, whereas the converse was true when an African American boxer defeated a Caucasian. Nevertheless, some researchers have questioned these findings because the spike in homicides was evident only on the third day after these fights, but not on other days (Baron & Reiss, 1985). Thus, these results may have been due to chance.

Another investigator (Williams, 1986) conducted a field study of a small, isolated mountain town in Canada that had no television before 1973. She called it "Notel," short for "*no television.*" Compared with school-age children in two other Canadian towns that already had television, children in Notel showed a marked increase in physical and verbal aggression two years later. Nevertheless, these findings are difficult to interpret in light of a potential confound: At around the same time that Notel received television, the Canadian government constructed a large highway that connected Notel to nearby towns. This highway might have introduced the children in Notel to negative outside influences, including crime from other cities.

So what can we make of all of the research on media violence and aggressive behaviors? We're confronted with four lines of evidence—correlational studies, longitudinal studies, laboratory studies, and field studies—each with its own strengths and weaknesses. Correlational, longitudinal, and field studies tend to be strong in *external validity,* that is, generalizability to the real world, but weak in *internal validity,* that is, the extent to which they permit cause-and-effect inferences (see Chapter 2). Laboratory studies, in contrast, tend to be weak in external validity but strong in internal validity. Yet despite their shortcomings, all four types of studies point in the same direction: at least some causal relation between media violence and aggression (Anderson et al., 2003; Carnegay, Anderson, & Bartholow, 2007). Scientific conclusions are usually the most convincing when we base them on findings from different research designs, each with a slightly different set of imperfections (Shadish, Cook, & Campbell, 2002). As a result, most psychological scientists today agree that media violence contributes to aggression in at least some circumstances (Anderson & Bushman, 2002a; Bushman & Anderson, 2001).

Nevertheless, it's equally clear that media violence is only one small piece of a multifaceted puzzle. We can't explain aggression by means of media violence alone because the substantial majority of individuals exposed to high levels of such violence don't become aggressive (Freedman, 2002; Wilson & Herrnstein, 1985). We'll examine other influences on aggression in Chapter 13. ⊙→ Simulate

> ◄ ruling out rival hypotheses
> **HAVE IMPORTANT ALTERNATIVE EXPLANATIONS FOR THE FINDINGS BEEN EXCLUDED?**

⊙→ Simulate Media Violence on mypsychlab.com

■ Mirror Neurons and Observational Learning

You find yourself alone in a new city, standing in line behind someone using an ATM. Like so many other cash machines, this one is slightly—and annoyingly—different from all the other ones you've seen. You watch as the person in front of you inserts her card, pushes a few buttons, and grabs her money from the slot at the bottom of the machine. Now it's your turn, and you know exactly what to do. You learned by watching. But how? Although the question of how our brains engage in observational learning is still shrouded in mystery, neuroscientists have recently begun to pinpoint a potential physiological basis for it.

When a monkey watches another monkey perform an action, such as reaching for an object, a group of neurons in its prefrontal cortex, near its motor cortex (see Chapter 3), becomes active (Rizzolatti et al., 1996). These cells are called **mirror neurons** because they're the

mirror neuron
cell in the prefrontal cortex that becomes activated by specific motions when an animal both performs and observes that action

Mirror neurons become active when we watch someone similar to us performing a behavior.

same cells that would have become active had the monkey performed the same movement. It's as though these neurons are "imagining" what it would be like to perform the behavior.

Mirror neurons appear to be remarkably selective. They don't become active when a monkey sees another monkey that remains stationary or sees a piece of food that another monkey grabbed. Instead, they become active only when a monkey sees another monkey engaging in an action, like grabbing. Moreover, these neurons seem tuned to extremely specific behaviors. Investigators have found one mirror neuron in monkeys that fires only when the monkey himself or a person he's observing grabs a peanut, and a different mirror neuron that fires only when the monkey himself or a person he's observing eats a peanut (Winerman, 2005).

Using PET scanning, researchers have identified a similar mirror neuron system in humans (Gallese & Goldman, 1998), but they've yet to identify individual mirror neurons, as they have in monkeys. No one knows for sure what mirror neurons do or why they're in our brains. But some neuroscientists have conjectured that such neurons play a central role in empathy (Azar, 2005; Iacoboni, 2009; Ramachandran, 2000), including feeling others' emotional states and emulating their movements (Fabbri-Destro & Rizzolatti, 2008). When we see an athlete suffer an injury during a sporting event, like a baseball player grimacing in agony after a bruising slide into home plate, we wince in pain along with him. In some sense, we may be "feeling his pain," because the mirror neurons that correspond to the neurons in his motor areas are becoming activated. Some authors have gone further to speculate that mirror neuron abnormalities play a key role in infantile autism (see Chapters 2 and 15), which is often associated with difficulties in adopting the perspectives of others (Dingfelder, 2005). But whether these neurons play a role in causing autism is unknown, as the findings are only correlational (Dinstein et al., 2008).

Even so, the discovery of mirror neurons may ultimately provide valuable insights into how we learn from others. This discovery also helps us appreciate that even when we're alone, we're often not really alone. Even when we're sitting by ourselves watching television, our brain and the brain of that baseball player sliding into home plate may be in sync, our mirror neurons and his lighting up in unison.

correlation vs. causation

CAN WE BE SURE THAT A CAUSES B?

Köhler found that Sultan, his "star" chimpanzee, discovered how to insert one bamboo stick inside another to create an extra-long stick, thereby allowing him to obtain food.

Köhler's apes also figured out how to get to a banana suspended well above their heads: Stack a bunch of boxes atop each other, and climb to the top box.

■ Insight Learning

Latent learning and observational learning were by no means the only holes poked in behaviorist theory. Another serious challenge came from a German psychologist during World War I: Wolfgang Köhler.

Around the same time that psychologists were conducting the first latent learning studies, Köhler (1925), a founder of Gestalt psychology (see Chapter 4), was posing various problems to four chimpanzees in the Canary Islands off the coast of Africa. His favorite of the four was a genius of an ape named Sultan, who was especially adept at solving puzzles. In one case Köhler placed a tempting bunch of bananas outside of the cage, well out of Sultan's reach, along with two bamboo sticks inside the cage. Neither stick was long enough to reach the bananas. After what appeared to be some heavy-duty pondering, Sultan suddenly hit on the solution: Stick one bamboo stick inside the other, creating one extra-long bamboo stick.

What was notable, according to Köhler, was that his chimpanzees appeared to experience the "aha reaction" we discussed earlier. Their solutions to his problems didn't appear to reflect trial and error, as it did with Thorndike's cats, but rather *insight,* the sudden understanding of the solution to a problem. That is, their solutions resembled what we saw back in Figure 6.6. The chimps seemed to suddenly "get" the solution to the problem, and from then on they got it right just about every time.

Still, Köhler's findings and conclusions weren't without their shortcomings. His observations were anecdotal, and he didn't measure them systematically. Because Köhler videotaped only some of his chimpanzees' problem solving, it's difficult to rule out the possibility that at least some of his chimps had engaged in trial and error before figuring out each problem (Gould & Gould, 1994). Moreover, because the chimps were often in the same cage, they might have engaged in observational learning. Still, Köhler's work suggests that at least some smart animals can learn through insight rather than trial and error. There's good evidence that humans can, too (Dawes, 1994).

assess your knowledge   FACT OR FICTION?

1. According to Skinner, animals don't think or experience emotions. **True / False**

2. Proponents of latent learning argue that reinforcement isn't necessary for learning.
   True / False

3. Research on observational learning demonstrates that children can learn aggression by
   watching aggressive role models. **True / False**

4. There's no good research evidence for insight learning. **True / False**

Answers: 1. F (p. 223); 2. T (p. 224); 3. T (p. 225); 4. F (p. 228)

BIOLOGICAL INFLUENCES ON LEARNING

6.11   Explain how biological predispositions can facilitate learning of some associations.

For many decades, most behaviorists regarded learning as entirely distinct from biology.
The animal's learning history and genetic makeup were like two ships passing in the night.
Yet we now understand that our biology influences the speed and nature of our learning in
complex and fascinating ways. Here are three powerful examples.

■ Conditioned Taste Aversions

One day in the 1970s, psychologist Martin Seligman went out to dinner with his wife. He
ordered a filet mignon steak flavored with sauce béarnaise, his favorite topping. Approximately six hours later, while at the opera, Seligman felt nauseated and became violently ill.
He and his stomach recovered, but his love of sauce béarnaise didn't. From then on, Seligman couldn't even think of, let alone taste, sauce béarnaise without feeling like vomiting
(Seligman & Hager, 1972).

   The *sauce béarnaise syndrome,* also known as *conditioned taste aversion,* refers to the
fact that classical conditioning can lead us to develop avoidance reactions to the taste of
food. Before reading on, ask yourself a question: Does Seligman's story contradict the other
examples of classical conditioning we've discussed, like that of Pavlov and his dogs?

   In fact, it does in at least three ways (Garcia & Hankins, 1977):

1. In contrast to most classically conditioned reactions, which require repeated
   pairings between CS and UCS, conditioned taste aversions typically require *only
   one trial* to develop.

2. The delay between CS and UCS in conditioned taste aversions can be as long as
   six or even eight hours (Rachlin & Logue, 1991).

3. Conditioned taste aversions tend to be remarkably specific and display little evidence of stimulus generalization. One of the earliest childhood memories of
   one of your text's authors is that of eating a delicious piece of lasagna and then
   becoming violently ill several hours later. For more than 20 years, he avoided
   lasagna at all costs while thoroughly enjoying spaghetti, manicotti, veal parmigiana, and virtually every other Italian dish despite its similarity to lasagna. He
   finally forced himself to get over his lasagna phobia, but not without a momentous struggle.

   These differences make good sense. We wouldn't want to have to experience horrific food poisoning again and again to learn a conditioned association between taste and illness. Doing so would not only be incredibly unpleasant, but we'd sometimes be dead after
the first trial. The long lag time between eating and illness violates typical classical conditioning because close timing between the CS and UCS is usually necessary for learning. But
in this case, the delayed association between CS and UCS is adaptive, because it teaches to
avoid dangerous foods we might have ingested hours earlier. ●—Explore

Handwritten margin notes:
Conditioned taste aversion
(sauce béarnaise syndrome)
- require only one trial to develop
- CS and UCS can have delays of up to 8 hours.
- specific yet little evidence of stimulus generalization

●—Explore Conditioned Taste Aversions
on mypsychlab.com

Psychological science has helped many cancer patients undergoing chemotherapy to minimize conditioned taste aversions to their favorite foods.

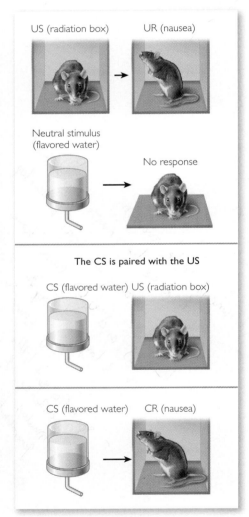

US (radiation box)   UR (nausea)

Neutral stimulus
(flavored water)

No response

The CS is paired with the US

CS (flavored water)   US (radiation box)

CS (flavored water)   CR (nausea)

FIGURE 6.12   Conditioned Taste Aversion. The work of John Garcia and his colleagues demonstrated that animals tend to develop conditioned taste aversions only to certain stimuli, namely, those that trigger nausea in the real world.

Conditioned taste aversions are a particular problem among cancer patients undergoing chemotherapy, which frequently induces nausea and vomiting. As a result, they often develop an aversion to any food that preceded chemotherapy, even though they realize it bears no logical connection to the treatment. Fortunately, health psychologists (see Chapter 12) have developed a clever way around this problem. Capitalizing on the specificity of conditioned taste aversions, they ask cancer patients to eat an unfamiliar *scapegoat food*—a novel food of which they aren't fond—prior to chemotherapy. In general, the taste aversion becomes conditioned to the scapegoat food rather than to patients' preferred foods (Andresen, Birch, & Johnson, 1990).

John Garcia and one of his colleagues helped to demonstrate biological influences on conditioned taste aversions (Garcia & Koelling, 1966). They found that rats exposed to X-rays, which make them nauseated, developed conditioned aversions to a specific taste but not to a specific visual or auditory stimulus presented after the X-rays (Garcia & Koelling, 1966). In other words, the rats more readily associated nausea with taste than with other sensory stimuli after a single exposure. Conditioned taste aversions aren't much fun, but they're often adaptive. In the real world, poisoned drinks and foods, not sights and sounds, make animals feel sick. As a consequence, animals more easily develop conditioned aversions to stimuli that tend to trigger nausea in the real world (see **FIGURE 6.12**).

This finding contradicts the assumption of *equipotentiality*—the claim that we can classically condition all CSs equally well to all UCSs—a belief held by many traditional behaviorists (Plotkin, 2004). Garcia and others had found that certain CSs, such as those associated with taste, are easily conditioned to certain UCSs, such as those associated with nausea (Rachman, 1977; Thorndike, 1911). Recall that following his night out with his wife, Martin Seligman felt nauseated at the thought of sauce béarnaise, but not at the thought of the opera or—thankfully, for his marriage—his wife.

■ Preparedness and Phobias

A second challenge to the equipotentiality assumption comes from research on phobias. If we look at the distribution of phobias in the general population, we'll find something curious: People aren't always afraid of things with which they've had the most frequent unpleasant experiences. Phobias of the dark, heights, snakes, spiders, deep water, and blood are commonplace, even though many people who fear these stimuli have never had a frightening encounter with them. In contrast, phobias of razors, knives, the edges of furniture, ovens, and electrical outlets are extremely rare, although many of us have been cut, bruised, burned, or otherwise hurt by them.

Seligman (1971) proposed that we can explain the distribution of phobias in the population by means of **preparedness**: We're evolutionarily predisposed to fear certain stimuli more than others. According to Seligman, that's because certain stimuli, like steep cliffs and poisonous animals, posed a threat to our early human ancestors (Hofmann, 2008; Ohman & Mineka, 2001). In contrast, household items and appliances didn't, because they weren't around back then. In the words of Susan Mineka (1993), prepared fears are "evolutionary memories": emotional legacies of natural selection.

Mineka and Michael Cook (1993) showed lab-reared rhesus monkeys, who had no previous exposure to snakes, a videotape of fellow monkeys reacting in horror to snakes. Within less than half an hour, the monkeys acquired a fear of snakes by observational learning (surprisingly, rhesus monkeys who've never been exposed to snakes show no fear of them). The researchers then edited the videotape to make it appear that the same monkeys were reacting in horror, but this time in response to flowers, a toy rabbit, a toy snake, or a toy crocodile. They then showed these doctored videotapes to different groups of monkeys who had no experience with flowers, rabbits, snakes, or crocodiles. The monkeys who observed these altered videotapes acquired fears of the toy snake and toy crocodile, but not

the flowers or toy rabbit. From the standpoint of preparedness, this finding is understandable. Snakes and crocodiles were dangerous to our primate ancestors, but flowers and rabbits weren't (Ohman & Mineka, 2003).

This coyote, eating from a sheep carcass that's been tainted with a mild poison, will become sick several hours later. The coyote will avoid sheep from then on. Ranchers have made use of this technique to keep coyotes from attacking their livestock.

Preparedness may render us likely to develop *illusory correlations* between fear-provoking stimuli and negative consequences (Fiedler, Freytag, & Meiser, 2009; Tomarken, Mineka, & Cook, 1989). Recall from Chapter 2 that an illusory correlation is a statistical mirage; it's the perception of a nonexistent association between two variables. One team of investigators administered intermittent electrical shocks to subjects—some of whom feared snakes and some of whom didn't—while they watched slides of snakes and damaged electrical outlets. The pairings of the slide stimuli with the shocks were random, so that the actual correlation between them was zero. Yet subjects with high levels of snake fear perceived a marked correlation between the occurrence of the snake slides, but not the electrical outlets, with the electric shocks. Subjects with low levels of snake fear didn't fall prey to this illusory correlation (Tomarken, Sutton, & Mineka, 1995).

Snake-fearful people were on the lookout for any threatening stimuli that might signal snakes, so they overestimated how often snake slides co-occurred with electric shock. Interestingly, they showed no such overestimation for electrical outlets, even though they're more closely linked in our minds than are snakes to electric shock. This finding suggests that preparedness may be at work, because snakes, but not electrical outlets, posed threats to our primate ancestors.

Still, the laboratory evidence for preparedness isn't completely consistent. When researchers have paired either prepared stimuli—like snakes or spiders—or unprepared stimuli—like flowers or mushrooms—with electric shocks, they haven't invariably replicated the finding that subjects more rapidly acquire fears to prepared than unprepared stimuli (Davey, 1995; McNally, 1987). Moreover, some authors have proposed that preparedness findings may be due to an alternative explanation that isn't evolutionary in nature: latent inhibition. As we'll recall from earlier in the chapter, latent inhibition refers to the fact that CSs that have appeared alone (that is, without a UCS) many times are especially difficult to classically condition to a stimulus. Because we routinely encounter electric sockets, stoves, knives, and the like, without experiencing any negative consequences, these stimuli may be resistant to classical conditioning. In contrast, because few of us have regular encounters with snakes, cliffs, deep water, and so on, these stimuli may be more easily classically conditioned to aversive outcomes (Bond & Siddle, 1996).

Aside from preparedness, genetic influences probably play a role in the acquisition of certain phobias. Individuals with a dog phobia don't differ from those without a dog phobia in their number of negative experiences with dogs, such as bites (DiNardo et al., 1988). Moreover, only about half of people with a dog phobia have ever had a scary encounter with a dog; the same holds for people with many other phobias. These results make it unlikely that classical conditioning alone can explain all cases of phobia. Instead, some people appear predisposed genetically to develop phobias *given* a history of certain classical conditioning experiences (Kendler et al., 1992).

When we were children we'd play out in the streets just dipped in ink.

preparedness = evolutionary predisposition to fear of certain stimuli more than others.

◄ replicability

CAN THE RESULTS BE DUPLICATED IN OTHER STUDIES?

◄ ruling out rival hypotheses

HAVE IMPORTANT ALTERNATIVE EXPLANATIONS FOR THE FINDINGS BEEN EXCLUDED?

Mineka and Cook (1993) showed that monkeys can acquire fears of snakes by means of observational learning. Nevertheless, these monkeys didn't acquire fears of nondangerous stimuli, like flowers, suggesting a role for evolutionary predispositions in the development of fears.

■ Instinctive Drift

Animal trainers Marian and Keller Breland taught pigeons, chickens, raccoons, pigs, and a host of other creatures to perform a variety of tricks—much like those we might see on David Letterman's Stupid Pet Tricks segment—for circuses and television advertisers. As students of B. F. Skinner at Harvard, they relied on traditional methods of operant conditioning to shape their animals' behavior.

---

preparedness
evolutionary predisposition to learn some pairings of feared stimuli over others owing to their survival value

Instinctive drift is the tendency to return to an evolutionarily selected behavior.

In the process of their animal training adventures, the Brelands discovered that their little charges didn't always behave as anticipated. In one case they tried to train raccoons to drop tokens into a piggy bank. Although they successfully trained the raccoons to pick up the coins using food reinforcement, they soon ran headfirst into a surprising problem. Despite repeated reinforcement for dropping the coins into the piggy bank, the raccoons began rubbing the coins together, dropping them, and rubbing them together again instead.

The raccoons had reverted to an innate behavior, namely, rinsing. They were treating the tokens like pieces of food, like the small hard shells they extract from the beds of ponds and streams (Timberlake, 2006). Breland and Breland (1961) referred to this phenomenon as **instinctive drift**: the tendency for animals to return to innate behaviors following repeated reinforcement. Researchers have observed instinctive drift in other animals, including rats (Powell & Curley, 1984). Psychologists don't fully understand the reasons for such drift. Nevertheless, instinctive drift suggests that we can't fully understand learning without taking into account innate biological influences, because these influences place limits on what kinds of behaviors we can train through reinforcement.

✔ Study and Review on mypsychlab.com

assess your knowledge   FACT OR FICTION?

1. Many conditioned taste aversions are acquired in only a single trial. **True / False**

2. Most research suggests that the assumption of equipotentiality is false. **True / False**

3. The phenomenon of preparedness helps explain why virtually all major phobias are equally common in the general population. **True / False**

4. With progressively more reinforcement, animals typically drift further and further away from their instinctive patterns of behavior. **True / False**

Answers: 1. T (p. 229); 2. T (p. 230); 3. F (p. 230); 4. F (p. 232)

LEARNING FADS: DO THEY WORK?

6.12   Evaluate popular techniques marketed to enhance learning.

If you've made it all the way to this point in the chapter (congratulations!), you know that learning new information is hard work. Perhaps because learning new things requires so much time and effort on our part, many mental health professionals have marketed a motley assortment of techniques that supposedly help us to learn more quickly, or more easily, than we currently do. Do these newfangled methods work? We'll find out by examining four popular techniques.

■ Sleep-Assisted Learning

Imagine that you could master all of the information in this book while getting a few nights of sound sleep. You could pay someone to audio-record the entire book, play the recording over the span of several weeknights, and you'd be all done. You could say goodbye to those late nights in the library or dorm room reading about psychology.

As in many areas of psychology, hope springs eternal. Many proponents of *sleep-assisted learning*—learning new material while asleep—have made some extraordinary claims regarding this technique's potential. Some companies market CDs that can purportedly help us to learn languages, stop smoking, lose weight, reduce stress, or become a better lover, all while we're comfortably catching up on our *zzzzs*.

These assertions are certainly quite remarkable. Does the scientific evidence for sleep-assisted learning stack up to its proponents' impressive claims?

instinctive drift
tendency for animals to return to innate behaviors following repeated reinforcement

extraordinary claims ➤

IS THE EVIDENCE AS STRONG AS THE CLAIM?

As is so often the case in life, things that sound too good to be true often are. Admittedly, the early findings on sleep-assisted learning were encouraging. One group of investigators exposed sailors to Morse code (a shorthand form of communication that radio operators sometimes use) while asleep. These sailors mastered Morse code three weeks faster than did other sailors (Simon & Emmons, 1955). Other studies from the former Soviet Union seemingly provided support for the claim that people could learn new material, such as tape-recorded words or sentences, while asleep (Aarons, 1976).

Nevertheless, these early positive reports neglected to rule out a crucial alternative explanation: The recordings may have awakened the subjects. The problem is that almost all of the studies showing positive effects didn't monitor subjects' electroencephalograms (EEGs; see Chapter 3) to ensure they were asleep while listening to the tapes (Druckman & Swets, 1988; Druckman & Bjork, 1994; Lilienfeld et al., 2010). Better-controlled studies that monitored subjects' EEGs to make sure they were asleep offered little evidence for sleep-assisted learning. So to the extent that sleep-learning tapes "work," it's probably because subjects hear snatches of them while drifting in and out of sleep. As for that quick fix for reducing stress, we'd recommend skipping the audio recordings and just getting a good night's rest.

> ◄ **ruling out rival hypotheses**
>
> **HAVE IMPORTANT ALTERNATIVE EXPLANATIONS FOR THE FINDINGS BEEN EXCLUDED?**

Answers are located at the end of the text.

SLEEP-ASSISTED LEARNING

evaluating **CLAIMS**

When you think of learning, what's the first thing that pops into your head—textbooks, classrooms, or late-night study sessions? For proponents of sleep-assisted learning, it might be a cozy bed. Numerous websites and books claim that you can master a foreign language, become a better public speaker, and even improve your marriage while you're sound asleep. Let's evaluate some of these claims, which are modeled after actual ads for sleep-assisted learning products.

"Join the *thousands of people* who have increased their learning."
Does the fact that thousands of people believe in a claim make it true? What logical fallacy does this ad commit (see Chapter 1)?

"Sleep learning is a more efficient way to learn because *the information flows directly to our subconscious mind.* (While your conscious mind relaxes!)"
What's the problem with this extraordinary claim?

"Risk-free, 100% money-back *guarantee.*"
We should be skeptical of guarantees, as virtually no psychological technique is foolproof.

"Designed using *proven research* conducted all over the world ..."
What questions should you ask about how this research was conducted? Can we assume that "proven" means the research has been replicated?

"Use your brain's full potential. The average mind uses only *5% of its* capacity."
Is there scientific support for the claim that we use only a small portion of our brain (see Chapter 3)?

■ Accelerated Learning

Still other companies promise consumers ultrafast techniques for learning. These methods, known as Superlearning or Suggestive Accelerative Learning and Teaching Techniques (SALTT), supposedly allow people to pick up new information at anywhere from 25 to several hundred times their normal learning speeds (Wenger, 1983). SALTT relies on a mixture of several techniques, such as generating expectations for enhanced learning (telling students they'll learn more quickly), getting students to visualize information they're learning, playing classical music during learning, and breathing in a regular rhythm while learning (Lozanov, 1978). When combined, these techniques supposedly allow learners to gain access to intuitive aspects of their minds that otherwise remain inaccessible.

Again, however, the evidence for the effectiveness of SALTT and similar methods doesn't come close to matching the extraordinary claims (Della Sala, 2006). Almost all studies show that SALTT doesn't produce enhanced learning (Dipamo & Job, 1990; Druckman & Swets, 1988). Even when researchers have reported positive results for SALTT, these findings have been open to rival explanations. That's because many of the studies conducted on SALTT compared this method with a control condition in which students did little or nothing. As a result, the few positive results reported for SALTT could be attributable to placebo effects (see Chapter 2), especially because one of the major components of SALTT is raising learners' expectations (Druckman & Swets, 1988).

extraordinary claims
IS THE EVIDENCE AS STRONG AS THE CLAIM?

ruling out rival hypotheses
HAVE IMPORTANT ALTERNATIVE EXPLANATIONS FOR THE FINDINGS BEEN EXCLUDED?

■ Discovery Learning

As we've discovered throughout this text, learning how to *rule out rival explanations* for findings is a key ingredient of scientific thinking. But science educators haven't always agreed on how to teach this crucial skill.

One increasingly popular way of imparting this knowledge is *discovery learning*: giving students experimental materials and asking them to figure out the scientific principles on their own (Klahr & Nigram, 2004). For example, a psychology professor who's teaching operant conditioning might set her students up with a friendly rat, a maze, and a plentiful supply of cheese and ask them to figure out which variables affect the rat's learning. For instance, does the rat learn the maze most quickly when we reinforce it continuously or only occasionally?

Nevertheless, as David Klahr and his colleagues have shown, the old-fashioned method of *direct instruction,* in which we simply tell students how to solve problems, is often more effective and efficient than discovery learning. In one study, they examined third- and fourth-graders' ability to isolate the variables that influence how quickly a ball rolls down a ramp, such as the ramp's steepness or length. Only 23 percent of students assigned to a discovery learning condition later solved a slightly different problem on their own, whereas 77 percent of students assigned to a direct instruction condition did (Klahr & Nigram, 2004).

That's not to say that discovery learning has no role in education, as in the long-term it may encourage students to learn how to pose scientific questions on their own (Alferink, 2007; Kuhn & Dean, 2005). But because many students may never figure out how to solve certain scientific problems independently, it's ill-advised as a stand-alone approach (Kirschner, Sweller, & Clark, 2006; Mayer, 2004).

ruling out rival hypotheses
HAVE IMPORTANT ALTERNATIVE EXPLANATIONS FOR THE FINDINGS BEEN EXCLUDED?

■ Learning Styles

Few claims about learning are as wide-spread as the belief that all individuals have their own distinctive **learning styles**—their preferred means of acquiring information. According to proponents of this view, some students are "analytical" learners who excel at breaking down problems into different components, whereas others are "holistic" learners who excel at viewing problems

as a whole. Still others are "verbal" learners who prefer to talk through problems, whereas others are "spatial" learners who prefer to visualize problems in their heads (Cassidy, 2004; Desmedt & Valcke, 2004). Some educational psychologists have claimed to boost learning dramatically by matching different methods of instruction to students' learning styles. According to them, children who are verbal learners should learn much faster and better with written material, children who are spatial learners should learn much faster and better with visual material, and so on.

Appealing as these assertions are, they haven't stood the test of careful research (Lilienfeld et al., 2009; Pashler et al., 2009). For one thing, it's difficult to assess learning style reliably (Snider, 1992; Stahl, 1999). As we'll recall from Chapter 2, *reliability* refers to consistency in measurement. In this case, researchers have found that different measures designed to assess people's learning styles often yield very different answers about their preferred mode of learning. In part, that's probably because few of us are purely analytical or holistic learners, verbal or spatial learners, and so on; most of us are a blend of multiple styles. Moreover, studies have generally revealed that tailoring different methods to people's learning styles doesn't result in enhanced learning (Kavale & Forness, 1987; Kratzig & Arbuthnott, 2006; Tarver & Dawson, 1978). Instead, most research shows that certain teaching approaches, like setting high standards for students and providing them with the motivation and skills to reach these standards, work best regardless of students' learning styles (Geake, 2008; Zhang, 2006). Like a number of other fads in popular psychology, the idea of learning styles seems to be more fiction than fact (Alferink, 2007; Pashler et al., 2009; Stahl, 1999).

The view that students with certain learning styles benefit from specific types of instructional materials is popular in educational psychology. Yet scientific research provides little evidence for this belief.

✓—Study and Review on mypsychlab.com

assess your knowledge   FACT OR FICTION?

1. Sleep-assisted learning techniques only work if subjects stay completely asleep during learning. True / **False**

2. The few positive results for accelerated learning in the SALTT program may be due to placebo effects. **True** / False

3. Discovery learning tends to be more efficient than direct instruction for solving most scientific problems. True / **False**

4. There's little evidence that matching teaching methods to people's learning styles enhances learning. **True** / False

Answers: 1. F (p.233); 2. T (p.234); 3. F (p.234); 4. T (p.235)

learning style
an individual's preferred or optimal method of acquiring new information

✓• Study and Review on mypsychlab.com   ((•• Listen to an audio file of your chapter mypsychlab.com

CLASSICAL CONDITIONING 203–211

6.1 DESCRIBE PAVLOV'S MODEL OF CLASSICAL CONDITIONING AND DISCRIMINATE CONDITIONED STIMULI AND RESPONSES FROM UNCONDITIONED STIMULI AND RESPONSES.

In classical conditioning, animals come to respond to a previously neutral stimulus that had been paired with another stimulus (the CS) that elicits a reflexive, automatic response. After repeated pairings with the UCS, which elicits an automatic, reflexive response (the UCR) from the organism, the CS comes to elicit a conditioned response (CR).

1. A change of an organism's behavior or thought as a result of experience is called _____. (p. 202)

2. The process of _____ occurs when we respond less strongly over time to repeated stimuli. (p. 202)

3. Identify the steps of the classical conditioning model used in Pavlov's dog research. (p. 205)

4. If the dog continues to salivate at the sound of the metronome when the meat powder is absent, psychologists call this process _____ _____. (p. 205)

6.2 EXPLAIN THE MAJOR PRINCIPLES AND TERMINOLOGY ASSOCIATED WITH CLASSICAL CONDITIONING.

Acquisition is the process by which we gradually learn the CR. Extinction is the process whereby following repeated presentation of the CS alone, the CR decreases in magnitude and eventually disappears. Extinction appears to involve an "overwriting" of the CR by new information rather than a forgetting of this information.

5. The learning phase during which a conditioned response is established is called _____. (p. 206)

6. After numerous presentations of the metronome without meat powder, Pavlov's dogs eventually stopped salivating; this is the process of _____. (p. 206)

7. A sudden reemergence of an extinguished conditioned response after a delay in exposure to the conditioned stimulus is called _____ _____. (p. 206)

8. Being able to enjoy a scary movie while still being scared of real world stimuli is an example of stimulus (generalization/ discrimination). (p. 207)

6.3 EXPLAIN HOW COMPLEX BEHAVIORS CAN RESULT FROM CLASSICAL CONDITIONING AND HOW THEY EMERGE IN OUR DAILY LIVES.

Higher-order conditioning occurs when organisms develop classically conditioned responses to CSs associated with the original CS.

9. Many addictions (are/are not) shaped in part by higher-order conditioning. (p. 207)

10. Describe the methods used by Watson and Rayner to condition fear in Little Albert and explain why their work couldn't be replicated today for ethical reasons. (p. 209)

OPERANT CONDITIONING 211–222

6.4 DISTINGUISH OPERANT CONDITIONING FROM CLASSICAL CONDITIONING.

Operant conditioning is learning controlled by its consequences. Operant conditioning involves many of the same processes, including acquisition and extinction, as does classical conditioning. Nevertheless, in operant conditioning, responses are emitted rather than elicited, the reinforcement is contingent on behavior, and responses mostly involve skeletal (voluntary) muscles rather than the autonomic nervous system.

11. Complete the table to show the differences between classical and operant conditioning. (p. 212)

	CLASSICAL CONDITIONING	OPERANT CONDITIONING
Target behavior is ...		
Reward is ...		
Behavior depends primarily on ...		

12. In (classical/operant) conditioning, the reward is contingent on behavior. (p. 212)

6.5 DESCRIBE THORNDIKE'S LAW OF EFFECT.

Thorndike's law of effect tells us that if a response, in the presence of a stimulus, is followed by a reward, it's likely to be repeated, resulting in the gradual "stamping in" of S-R (stimulus-response) connections.

13. Thorndike's findings provided a crushing blow to the hypothesis that cats invariably learn by _____, that is, by grasping the nature of the problem. (p. 213)

6.6 DESCRIBE REINFORCEMENT AND ITS EFFECTS ON BEHAVIOR AND DISTINGUISH NEGATIVE REINFORCEMENT FROM PUNISHMENT AS INFLUENCES ON BEHAVIOR.

Reinforcement can be either positive (presentation of an outcome) or negative (withdrawal of an outcome). Negative reinforcement increases the rate of a behavior, whereas punishment decreases it. One disadvantage of punishment is that it tells the organism only what *not* to do, not what *to* do.

14. A physics professor announces to his class that students who are earning 90 percent or higher in the class don't have to take the midterm. This is an example of (positive/negative) reinforcement. (p. 213)

15. Reinforcement _____ the probability of a response, whereas punishment _____ the probability of a response. (p. 214)

16. According to Skinner, one disadvantage of punishment is that it often creates _____, which interferes with future learning. (p. 215)

6.7 IDENTIFY THE FOUR SCHEDULES OF REINFORCEMENT AND THE RESPONSE PATTERN ASSOCIATED WITH EACH.

There are four major schedules of reinforcement: fixed ratio, fixed interval, variable ratio, and variable interval. These four schedules differ along two dimensions: consistency of administering reinforcement (fixed or variable) and the basis of administering reinforcement (ratio or interval).

17. Identify the typical response patterns for the four reinforcement schedule types. (p. 218)

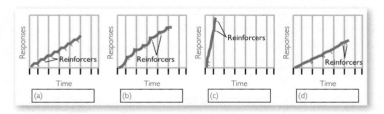

18. Casino gambling is a prime example of a _____ _____ schedule. (p. 219)

6.8 DESCRIBE SOME APPLICATIONS OF OPERANT CONDITIONING.

Operant conditioning has a number of applications to everyday life, including shaping by successive approximations and overcoming procrastination.

19. Animal trainers often combine the technique of _____, when they reinforce behaviors that aren't exactly the target behav-

ior but that are progressively closer versions of it, with _____, in which they link a number of interrelated behaviors to form a longer series. (p. 219)

20. One of the most successful applications of operant conditioning has been the _____ _____, which is a system, often set up in psychiatric hospitals, for reinforcing appropriate behaviors and extinguishing inappropriate ones. (p. 221)

COGNITIVE MODELS OF LEARNING 223–229

6.9 OUTLINE THE EVIDENCE THAT SUPPORTS LATENT LEARNING AND OBSERVATIONAL LEARNING.

S-O-R psychologists believe that the organism's interpretation of stimuli plays a central role in learning. Tolman's work on latent learning, which showed that animals can learn without reinforcement, challenged the radical behaviorists' view of learning. Research suggests that individuals can acquire aggressive behavior by observational learning. Correlational studies, longitudinal studies, laboratory studies, and field studies suggest that media violence contributes to aggression.

21. Skinner was an advocate of _____ behaviorism, in which observable behavior, thinking, and emotion are all governed by the same laws of learning. (p. 223)

22. Early behaviorists (believed/didn't believe) that thought played an important causal role in learning. (p. 223)

23. In the past few decades, psychology has increasingly moved away from a simple S-R (stimulus-response) psychology to a more complex _____ psychology, where the link between S and R isn't automatic. (p. 224)

24. When talking to employees about their performance, why might managers want to adapt their style depending on the person to whom they're talking/? (p. 224)

25. According to Tolman, the rats in his study had developed spatial representations of the maze termed _____ _____. (p. 225)

26. What type of learning is taking place in this photo, and what is the basis of the learning process shown? (p. 225)

Answers are located at the end of the text.

27. In classic research in the 1960s, _____ _____ and his colleagues demonstrated that children can learn to act aggressively by watching aggressive role models. (p. 225)

28. Longitudinal studies that correlate the amount of violent TV watched in childhood with the amount of aggressive acts committed in adulthood (have/have not) demonstrated causality. (p. 226)

29. Cells in the prefrontal cortex that become activated by specific motions when an animal performs or observes that an action are called _____ _____. (p. 227)

6.10 IDENTIFY EVIDENCE OF INSIGHT LEARNING.

Kohler's work suggested that apes can learn through insight, and later work with humans suggests the same conclusion. This research calls into question Thorndike's conclusion that all learning occurs through trial and error.

30. Kohler's work with chimpanzees suggested that at least some smart animals can learn through _____ rather than trial and error. (p. 228)

BIOLOGICAL INFLUENCES ON LEARNING 229–232

6.11 EXPLAIN HOW BIOLOGICAL PREDISPOSITIONS CAN FACILITATE LEARNING OF SOME ASSOCIATIONS.

Psychologists have increasingly recognized that our genetic endowment influences learning. Conditioned taste aversions refer to the phenomenon whereby classical conditioning can lead us to develop avoidance reactions to the taste of food. John Garcia and his colleagues showed that conditioned taste aversions violate the principle of equipotentiality, because they demonstrate that certain CSs are more easily conditioned than others to certain UCSs. Research on preparedness suggests that we are evolutionarily predisposed to learn to fear some stimuli more easily than others.

31. Conditioned taste aversions typically require (one trial/many trials) to develop. (p. 229)

32. Explain how health psychologists can help cancer patients undergoing chemotherapy to minimize conditioned taste aversions to their favorite foods. (p. 230)

33. Through his research with rats, Garcia helped to demonstrate the _____ influences on conditioned taste aversions. (p. 230)

34. The rats in Garcia's study more readily associated nausea with _____ than with any other sensory stimuli. (p. 230)

35. Conditioned taste aversions aren't much fun, but they're often _____ in the real world. An example would be an animal that develops a conditioned taste aversion to a poisoned food or drink. (p. 230)

36. Garcia and others challenged the assumption of _____, the belief of many behaviorists that we can pair all CSs equally well with all UCSs. (p. 230)

37. According to Seligman, we're evolutionarily predisposed to fear certain stimuli more than others by means of _____. (p. 230)

38. In Mineka's and Cook's study, the monkeys (acquired/didn't acquire) fears of nondangerous stimuli, such as flowers. (p. 231)

39. Mineka's and Cook's study was clearly a case of learning because the monkeys were (afraid/unafraid) of snakes prior to the experiment. (p. 230)

40. Describe the phenomenon whereby animals return to evolutionarily selected behaviors, and how that phenomenon has affected researchers' understanding of learning. (p. 232)

LEARNING FADS: DO THEY WORK? 232–235

6.12 EVALUATE POPULAR TECHNIQUES MARKETED TO ENHANCE LEARNING.

Proponents of sleep-assisted learning claim that individuals can learn new material while asleep. Nevertheless, well-controlled studies of sleep-assisted learning have yielded negative results. Early reports of successful learning during sleep appear attributable to a failure to carefully monitor subjects' EEGs to ensure that they were actually asleep. Studies of accelerated learning techniques also show few or no positive effects, and positive results appear attributable to placebo effects and other artifacts. Although popular in science education, discovery learning approaches are often less effective and efficient than direct instruction. Some educational psychologists claim to be able to boost learning by matching individuals' learning styles with different teaching methods. Nevertheless, learning styles are difficult to assess reliably; moreover, studies that have matched learning styles with teaching methods have typically yielded negative results.

41. The problem with early findings on sleep-assisted learning is that almost all of the studies showing positive effects didn't monitor subjects' _____ to ensure they were asleep while listening to the tapes. (p. 233)

42. Explain the extraordinary claims about how sleep-assisted learning works and identify shortcomings in researchers' attempts to validate those claims. (p. 233)

43. Methods of accelerated learning, such as _____ _____ _____ _____ _____ supposedly allow people to pick up new information anywhere from 25 to several hundred times their normal learning speed. (p. 234)

44. SALTT relies on such techniques as getting students to _____ information they're learning, and playing _____ music while they're learning. (p. 234)

45. Any scattered positive results for SALTT could be due in part to _____ effects because one of the components of the program is raising learners' expectations. (p. 234)

46. When you give students experimental materials and ask them to figure out a scientific principle on their own, this is known as _____ _____. (p. 234)

47. Klahr and his colleagues have shown that the old-fashioned method of _____ _____, in which we simply tell students how to solve problems, is often most efficient and effective. (p. 234)

48. Individuals' preferred or optimal method of acquiring new information are referred to as _____ _____. (p. 235)

49. Proponents of this view believe that some students are _____ learners who excel at breaking down problems into different components, while others are _____ learners who excel at viewing problems as a whole. (p. 235)

50. Provide a valid argument against teaching to students' learning styles. (p. 235)

APPLY YOUR SCIENTIFIC THINKING SKILLS

Use your scientific thinking skills to answer the following questions, referencing specific scientific thinking principles and common errors in reasoning whenever possible.

1. Skinner and his followers believed that reinforcement is more effective than punishment in shaping children's behavior. Yet there still exists a wide variety of opinion over the best way to raise and discipline children. Read several sources of parenting advice offered in the popular media, locating some examples that favor reinforcement and others that favor punishment. What arguments does each side use to support its preferred parenting style? What claims do they make about shaping children's behaviors, and are they supported by scientific evidence?

2. Researchers have used different types of studies to examine the connection between exposure to media violence and aggressive behavior. Read a few newspaper, magazine, or Internet articles on this topic (their focus can be on violent television, movies, songs, or video games), choosing at least one that argues for a connection between media violence and aggression and at least one that argues against such a connection. What arguments does each side make? How accurately did they interpret the research? Are there explanations or variables that these articles neglected to consider?

3. This chapter discussed four popular learning fads: sleep-assisted learning, accelerated learning, discovery learning, and learning styles. Identify and evaluate some other popular learning techniques (Hint: Perform a Google search for "learning techniques" or "learning methods"). Do these techniques make extraordinary claims regarding their benefits? What research support, if any, do they offer for their claims?

7 MEMORY

constructing and reconstructing our pasts

THINK ABOUT IT

DO WE REALLY REMEMBER EVERYTHING THAT'S EVER HAPPENED TO US?

DO MEMORY AIDS LIKE "ROY G. BIV" (FOR THE COLORS OF THE RAINBOW) REALLY HELP US TO REMEMBER?

WHAT ARE INFANTS' EARLIEST MEMORIES?

DO WITNESSES TO A CRIME ALWAYS REMEMBER WHAT THEY OBSERVED ACCURATELY?

CAN PEOPLE RECOVER REPRESSED MEMORIES OF TRAUMATIC EXPERIENCES?

Consider the following memorable two tales of memory, both true.

True Story 1. A woman in her forties, known only by the initials A.J., has such an astounding memory that she's left even seasoned psychological researchers shaking their heads in bewilderment. Although emotionally quite normal, A.J. is markedly abnormal in one way: She remembers just about everything she's ever experienced. When researchers give her a date, like March 17, 1989, she can tell them precisely what she was doing on that day—taking a test, eating dinner with a good friend, or traveling to a new city. Researchers have confirmed that she's almost always right. Moreover, she remembers on what day of the week that date fell. In 2003, a team of investigators asked A.J. to remember all of the dates of Easter over the past 24 years. She got all but two correct and reported accurately what she'd done each day (Parker, Cahill, & McCaugh, 2006).

A.J. "suffers" from an exceedingly rare condition called hyperthymestic syndrome: memory that's too good. Or does she really suffer? It's not entirely clear, because she regards her remarkable memory as both a curse and a blessing (Price & Davis, 2008). A.J. says that she sometimes remembers painful events that she'd prefer to forget, but also that she'd never want to give up her special memory "gift." As to the causes of hyperthymestic syndrome, scientists are baffled (Foer, 2007).

True Story 2. In 1997, Nadean Cool, a 44-year-old nurse's aide in Wisconsin, won a $2.4 million malpractice settlement against her psychotherapist. Nadean entered treatment with relatively mild emotional problems, such as depressed mood and binge eating. Yet after five years of treatment, Nadean supposedly "recovered" childhood memories of having been a member of a murderous satanic cult, of being raped, and of witnessing the murder of her eight-year-old childhood friend. Her therapist also persuaded her that she harbored more than 130 personalities, including demons, angels, children, and a duck. (Her therapist apparently even listed her treatment as group therapy on the grounds that he needed to treat numerous different personalities.)

All of these memories surfaced after Nadean participated in repeated sessions involving *guided imagery*—in which therapists ask clients to imagine past events—and *hypnotic age regression*—in which therapists use hypnosis to "return" clients to the psychological state of childhood (see Chapter 5). The therapist also subjected Nadean to an exorcism and 15-hour marathon therapy sessions. As therapy progressed, she became overwhelmed by images of terrifying memories she was convinced were genuine. Eventually, however, Nadean came to doubt the reality of these memories, and she terminated treatment.

In a very real sense, we *are* our memories. Our memories define not only our past, but our sense of identity. For A.J., life is like "a movie in her mind that never stops," as she puts it. Her recollections of her life and interactions with friends are remarkably vivid and emotionally intense. A.J.'s memory has shaped her personality in profound ways.

Moreover, when our memories change, as did Nadean Cool's, so do our identities. Following psychotherapy, Nadean came to believe she was a victim of brutal and repeated child abuse. She even came to believe she suffered from a severe condition, namely, *dissociative identity disorder*, or DID (known formerly as multiple personality disorder; see Chapter 15), which is supposedly characterized by the existence of "alter" personalities, or *alters*.

HOW MEMORY OPERATES: THE MEMORY ASSEMBLY LINE

7.1 Identify the ways that memories do and don't accurately reflect experiences.

7.2 Explain the function, span, and duration of each of the three memory systems.

7.3 Differentiate the subtypes of long-term memory.

We can define **memory** as the retention of information over time. We have memories for many different kinds of information, ranging from our sixteenth birthday party, to how to ride a bike, to the shape of a pyramid. Our memories work pretty well most of the time. Odds are high that tomorrow you'll find your way into school or work just fine and that, with a little luck, you'll even remember some of what you read in this chapter. Yet in other cases, our memories fail us, often when we least expect it. How many times have you mis-

memory
retention of information over time

placed your keys or cellphone? Or forgotten the names of people you've met over and over again? We call this seeming contradiction the *paradox of memory:* Our memories are surprisingly good in some situations and surprisingly poor in others.

■ The Paradox of Memory

To a large extent, this chapter is the story of this paradox. As we'll see, the answer to the paradox of memory hinges on a crucial fact: *The same memory mechanisms that serve us well in most circumstances can sometimes cause us problems in others.*

WHEN OUR MEMORIES SERVE US WELL. Research shows that our memories are often astonishingly accurate. Most of us can recognize our schoolmates decades later and recite the lyrics to dozens, even hundreds, of songs. Consider a study by a group of investigators (Standing, Conezio, & Haber, 1970) who showed college students 2,560 photographs of various objects or scenes for only a few seconds each. Three days later, the researchers showed these students each of the original photographs paired with one new photograph, and asked them to say which was which. Remarkably, the students picked out the original photographs correctly 93 percent of the time. In another case, a researcher contacted subjects 17 years (!) after they'd viewed over one hundred line drawings for one to three seconds in a laboratory study. They identified these drawings at better-than-chance rates when compared with a control group of participants who'd never seen the drawings (Mitchell, 2006).

The memories of a small subset of individuals with a condition known as *infantile autism* are even more astonishing. Contrary to popular misconception, most individuals with autism lack specialized memory abilities, but there are impressive exceptions. Take the case of Kim Peek, who was the inspiration for the 1998 Academy Award–winning film, *Rain Man* (Peek died in 2009). Peek's IQ was 87, noticeably below the average of approximately 100. Yet Peek memorized about 12,000 books word for word, the zip codes of every town in the United States, and the number of every highway connecting every city in the United States (Foer, 2007; Treffert & Christiansen, 2005). Kim Peek was also a *calendar calculator:* If you gave him any past or future date, like October 17, 2094, and he'd give you the correct day of the week in a matter of seconds. Not surprisingly, Kim earned the nickname of "Kim-puter" among researchers who studied his astonishing memory feats.

Yet as we learned with A.J., it's not only people with autism who possess remarkable memory capacities. Consider the case of Rajan Mahadevan (better known simply as Rajan), now a lecturer in the psychology department of the University of Tennessee. Rajan's memory feats were so spectacular that they were spoofed on an episode of the cartoon show *The Simpsons.* Rajan had somehow managed to memorize the number *pi*—the ratio of a circle's diameter to its radius—to 38,811 digits (see **FIGURE 7.1**). When he recited them, it took him three hours at a rate of more than three digits per second. In sharp contrast to Kim Peek, Rajan is entirely normal emotionally.

In the mid-1990s, one of the authors of this text had the opportunity to watch Rajan show off his pi memorization talents. And show off he did. Someone would read 10 random, sequential digits of pi, and Rajan was off and running: He effortlessly reeled off the next hundred or so digits of pi. Yet Rajan also provides a wonderful illustration of the paradox of memory. Despite finding pi to be a piece of cake, he kept forgetting the location of the men's restroom at the University of Minnesota psychology department although he'd been tested down the hall from it repeatedly (Biederman et al., 1992).

How did Rajan pull off his amazing feat? We'll find out later in the chapter.

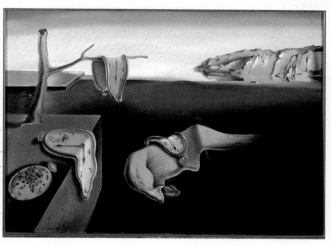

Salvador Dali's classic painting, *The Persistence of Memory,* is a powerful reminder that our memories are much more like melting wax than hardened metal. They often change over time, far more than we realize.

Kim Peek, the "real Rain Man" (who passed away in 2009), exhibited phenomenal memory despite low overall intelligence.

Pi=3.					
1415926535	8979323846	2643383279	5028841971	6939937510	(50)
5820974944	5923078164	0628620899	8628034825	3421170679	(100)
8214808651	3282306647	0938446095	5058223172	5359408128	(150)
4811174502	8410270193	8521105559	6446229489	5493038196	(200)
4428810975	6659334461	2847564823	3786783165	2712019091	(250)
4564856692	3460348610	4543266482	1339360726	0249141273	(300)
7245870066	0631558817	4881520920	9628292540	9171536436	(350)
7892590360	0113305305	4882046652	1384146951	9415116094	(400)
3305727036	5759591953	0921861173	8193261179	3105118548	(450)
0744623799	6274956735	1885752724	8912279381	8301194912	(500)
9833673362	4406566430	8602139494	6395224737	1907021798	(550)
6094370277	0539217176	2931767523	8467481846	7669405132	(600)
0005681271	4526356082	7785771342	7577896091	7363717872	(650)
1468440901	2249534301	5654958537	1050792279	6892589235	(700)
4201995611	2129021960	8640344181	5981362977	4771309960	(750)
5187072113	4999999837	2978049951	0597317328	1609631859	(800)
5024459455	3469083026	4252230825	3344685035	2619311881	(850)
7101000313	7838752886	5875332083	8142061717	7669147303	(900)
5982534904	2875546873	1159562863	8823537875	9375195778	(950)
1857780532					(1000)

FIGURE 7.1 Rajan's Demonstration Sheet of Digits of Pi.
Rajan's feats demonstrate the uppermost end of the capacity of human memory.

WHEN OUR MEMORIES FAIL US. In some exceedingly rare cases, as with A.J., memory is virtually perfect. Many others of us have extremely good memories in one or two narrow domains, like art history, baseball batting averages, or Civil War trivia. Yet as the case of Nadean Cool illustrates, memory can be surprisingly malleable and prone to error.

Most and perhaps all of us are vulnerable to false memories under the right conditions. Here's a simple demonstration that requires only a pen or pencil and a piece of paper (for maximum effect, you may want to try this demonstration along with a group of friends). Read the list of words below, taking about a second per word. Read the left column first, then the middle column, then the right. Ready? Okay, begin.

Bed	Cot	Sheets
Pillow	Dream	Rest
Tired	Snore	Yawn
Darkness	Blanket	Couch

Now, put down your textbook, and take a minute or so to jot down as many of these words as you can recall.

Did you remember *couch*? If so, give yourself a point. How about *snore*? If so, good—give yourself another point.

Okay, how about *sleep*? If you're like about a third of typical subjects, you "remembered" seeing the word *sleep*. But now take a close look at the list. The word *sleep* isn't there.

If you or your friends remembered seeing this word on the list, you experienced a **memory illusion**: a false but subjectively compelling memory (Deese, 1959; Roediger & McDermott, 1995, 1999). Like visual illusions (see Chapter 4), most memory illusions are byproducts of our brain's generally adaptive tendency to go beyond the information available to it. By doing so, our brain helps us to make sense of the world, but it sometimes leads us astray (Gilovich, 1991; Kida, 2006). In this case, you may have remembered seeing the word *sleep* because it was linked closely in meaning to the other words on the list—namely, sleeping, dreaming, and resting. As a consequence, you may have been fooled into remembering that the word *sleep* was there. By relying on the *representativeness heuristic* (Chapter 2)—like goes with like—we simplify things to make them easier to remember. In this case, though, our use of this handy heuristic comes with a modest price: a memory illusion.

■ The Reconstructive Nature of Memory

This demonstration drives home a crucial point: Our memories frequently fool us and fail us. Indeed, a central theme of this chapter is that our memories are far more reconstructive than reproductive. When we try to recall an event, we *actively reconstruct* our memories using the cues and information available to us. We don't *passively reproduce* our memories, as we would if we were downloading information from a Web page. Remembering is largely a matter of patching together our often fuzzy recollection with our best hunches about what really happened. When we recall our past experiences, we rarely, if ever, reproduce precise replicas of them (Neisser & Hyman, 1999). We should therefore be skeptical of claims that certain vivid memories or even dreams are exact "photocopies" of past events (van der Kolk et al., 1984).

In fact, it's easy to show that our memories are often reconstructive. After reading this sentence, close your eyes for a few moments and picture your most recent walk along a beach, lake, or pond. Then, after opening your eyes, ask yourself what you "saw."

Did you see yourself as if from a distance? If so, you experienced what psychologists Georgia Nigro and Ulric Neisser termed an *observer memory*, meaning a memory in which we see ourselves as an outside observer would (Nigro & Neisser, 1983). As Sigmund Freud noted well over a century ago, observer memories provide an existence proof (see Chapter 2) that at least some of our memories are reconstructive (Schacter, 1996). You couldn't possibly have *seen* yourself from a distance, because you don't see yourself when you look at your surroundings: You must have constructed that memory rather than recalled in its

memory illusion
false but subjectively compelling memory

original form. If you instead pictured the scene as you would have seen it through your own eyes, you experienced what Nigro and Neisser called a *field memory:* seeing the world through your visual field (Willander & Larrson, 2007). Interestingly, Asians are more likely than European Americans to experience observer memories (Cohen & Gunz, 2002), whereas European Americans are more likely than Asians to experience field memories. This result fits with findings that members of many Asian cultures are more likely than members of Western cultures to adopt others' perspectives (see Chapters 1 and 10). So our memories are probably shaped by not only our hunches and expectations, but by our cultural backgrounds.

The science of memory offers yet another striking example of how research contradicts popular opinion. Surveys indicate that many or most people believe our memories operate like video cameras or DVDs, replaying events precisely as we saw them. Moreover, 36 percent of us believe our brains contain perfect records of everything we've ever experienced (Alvarez & Brown, 2001). Even most psychotherapists believe that everything we learn is permanently stored in the mind (Loftus & Loftus, 1980; Yapko, 1994). Yet as we'll soon discover, research raises serious questions concerning all of these assumptions.

How can our memories be so good in some cases and so bad in others? How can we explain both the astonishing memories of people like A.J. and Rajan and the faulty memories of people like Nadean Cool? To grasp the paradox of memory, we need to figure out how some of our experiences make it into our memories, whereas so many others never do. To do so, let's embark on a guided tour of the factory assembly line inside our heads.

■ The Three Systems of Memory

Up to this point, we've been talking about memory as though it were a single thing. It isn't. Most psychologists distinguish among three major *systems* of memory: sensory memory, short-term memory, and long-term memory, as depicted in **FIGURE 7.2** (Atkinson & Shiffrin, 1968; Waugh & Norman, 1965). These systems serve different purposes and vary along at least two important dimensions: *span*—how much information each system can hold—and *duration*—over how long a period of time that system can hold information.

In reality, the distinctions among these three memory systems aren't always clear-cut. Moreover, many modern researchers suspect that there are more than three memory systems (Baddeley, 1993; Healy & McNamara, 1996). For the sake of simplicity, we'll begin by discussing the three-systems model, although we'll point out some ambiguities along the way.

We can think of these three systems much like different factory workers along an assembly line. The first system, *sensory memory,* is tied closely to the raw materials of our experiences, our perceptions of the world; it holds these perceptions for just a few seconds or less before passing *some* of them on to the second system. This second system, *short-term memory,* works actively with the information handed to it, transforming it into more meaningful material before passing *some* of it on to the third system. Short-term memory holds on to information longer than sensory memory does, but not much longer. The third and final system, *long-term memory,* permits us to retain important information for minutes, days, weeks, months, or even years. In some cases, the information in long-term memory lasts for a lifetime. The odds are high, for example, that you'll remember your first kiss and your high school graduation for many decades, perhaps until the last day of your life. As you can tell from our use of the word *some* in the previous sentences, we lose a great deal of information at each relay station in the memory assembly line. ●⎯Explore

SENSORY MEMORY. If you're anywhere near a television set, turn it on for 10 seconds or so. What did you see?

Regardless of what program you were watching, you almost certainly experienced a steady and uninterrupted stream of visual information. In reality, that continuous stream of images was an illusion, because television programs and movies consist of

When you picture yourself taking a recent walk on the beach, do you see yourself as an outside observer would (an "observer memory")? If so, such a recollection provides compelling evidence that memory can be reconstructive.

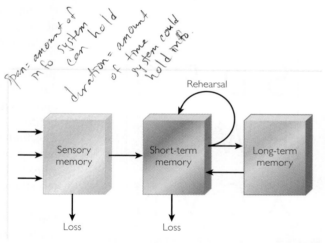

FIGURE 7.2 **The Three-Memory Model.** This model subdivides memory into sensory, short-term, and long-term memory. Information flows from left to right, but also from right to left in the case of information retrieved from long-term memory and moved into short-term memory. (*Source:* Atkinson & Shiffrin, 1968)

●⎯**Explore** the Key Processes in Stages of Memory on **mypsychlab.com**

Iconic memory: After a lightning strike, we retain a visual image of it for about one second. (*Source:* © Ralph Wetmore.)

FIGURE 7.3 Display of Twelve Letters as Used in Sperling's 1960 Study. Sperling's partial report method demonstrated that all displayed letters were held in sensory memory, but decayed rapidly before all of them could be transferred to short-term memory. (*Source:* Sperling, 1960)

sensory memory
brief storage of perceptual information before it is passed to short-term memory

iconic memory
visual sensory memory

a series of disconnected frames, each separated by an extremely brief interlude of darkness you can't perceive. Yet your brain sees these frames as blending together into a seamless whole, in part because it continues to detect each frame for an extremely brief period of time after it disappears.

That is, our brains retain each frame in our **sensory memory**, the first factory worker in the assembly line of memory. Sensory memory briefly maintains our perceptions in a "buffer" area before passing them on to the next memory system, which is short-term memory. Sensory memory is a helpful system, because it buys our brains a bit of extra time to process incoming sensations. It also allows us to "fill in the blanks" in our perceptions and see the world as an unbroken stream of events.

Psychologists believe each sense, including vision, hearing, touch, taste, and smell, has its own form of sensory memory. In the case of television or movie clips, we experience an **iconic memory**, the type of sensory memory that applies to vision. Iconic memories last for only about a second, and then they're gone forever.

Psychologist George Sperling (1960) conducted a pioneering study that demonstrated the existence of iconic memory. He quickly flashed participants a display of 12 letters, with four letters arranged in three rows, as shown in **FIGURE 7.3**. The display lasted only about one-twentieth of a second. Sperling found that most participants could remember four or five letters. Surprisingly, different participants remembered different letters. This finding suggested to Sperling that all 12 letters had an equal chance of being recalled but that no one person could recall them all. This finding was puzzling. After all, if participants had remembered the whole visual display, why could they recall only a handful of letters and no more?

To find out, Sperling had a "flash" of insight, pun intended. As he flashed the 12 letters, he used a tone (high, medium, or low) to signal participants which of the three rows (top, middle, or bottom) to report. Then he randomly instructed participants to report only one of the three rows. When he used this technique, which he termed the *method of partial report,* he found that virtually all participants now got almost all letters in that row correct. This finding confirmed Sperling's clever hunch: Participants had access to all 12 letters in their memories. Sperling concluded that our iconic memories fade so quickly that we can't access all the information before it disappears. So Sperling's participants were able to take in all of the information, but retained it in memory only long enough to read off a few letters.

Iconic memory may help to explain the remarkable, and exceedingly rare, phenomenon of *eidetic imagery,* popularly called "photographic memory." People with eidetic memory, most of them children, can supposedly hold a visual image in their minds with such clarity that they can describe it perfectly or almost perfectly (see **FIGURE 7.4**). Some psychologists believe that eidetic memory reflects an unusually long persistence of the iconic image in some fortunate people. Nevertheless, recent evidence raises questions about whether any memories are truly photographic because these memories often contain minor errors, including information that wasn't in the original visual stimulus (Minsky, 1986).

Sensory memory also applies to hearing. Now read that last sentence out loud: "Sensory memory also applies to hearing." If you pause for a few moments after saying it, you'll be able to replay the words precisely as you heard them for a few seconds, much like a soft echo reverberating from a mountaintop. That's why psychologists call this form of sensory memory **echoic memory** (Neisser, 1967). In contrast to iconic memories, echoic memories can last as long as five to 10 seconds (Cowan, Lichty, & Grove, 1990), conveniently permitting you to take notes on your psychology professor's most recent sentence even after he or she has finished saying it. Interestingly, there's also some evidence of eidetic memories for hearing, in which a few fortunate individuals report that their echoic memories persist for unusually long periods of time. Now, wouldn't that make taking lecture notes a breeze?

SHORT-TERM MEMORY. Once information makes it past our sensory buffers, it passes into our **short-term memory**, a second system for retaining information in our memories for brief periods of time. Short-term memory is the second factory worker in our memory assembly line. Short-term memory is closely related to what psychologists call *working memory*, which refers to our ability to hold on to information we're currently thinking about, attending to, or processing actively (Baddeley, 1993; Baddeley & Hitch, 1974; Unsworth & Engle, 2007). If sensory memory is what feeds raw materials into the assembly line, then short-term memory is the workspace where construction happens. After construction takes place, we either move the product into the warehouse for long-term storage or, in some cases, scrap it altogether.

FIGURE 7.4 Alice with Cheshire Cat. Memory psychologists have used variations of this drawing from Lewis Carroll's *Alice's Adventures in Wonderland* to test for eidetic imagery. To find out if you have eidetic memory, look for no longer than 30 seconds at the drawing and then cover it with a sheet of paper. Do that now before reading on. Now, can you remember how many stripes were on the cat's tail? Few adults can remember such details (Gray & Gummerman, 1975), although eidetic memory is much more prevalent among elementary school children (Haber, 1979).

If short-term memory is a short stop on the assembly line, just how brief is it? In the late 1950s, a husband-and-wife team decided to find out.

The Duration of Short-Term Memory. Lloyd and Margaret Peterson (1959) presented participants with lists of three letters each, such as MKP or ASN, and then asked them to recall these three-letter strings. In some cases, they made participants wait only three seconds before recalling the letters; in other cases, they made them wait up to 18 seconds. Each time, they told participants to count backward by threes while they were waiting.

Many psychologists were surprised by the Petersons' results, and you may be, too. They found that after about 10 or 15 seconds, most participants *did no better than chance*. So the duration of short-term memory is quite brief; it's probably no longer than about 20 seconds. Some researchers believe it's even shorter than that, perhaps even less than five seconds, because some subjects in the Peterson and Peterson study may have been able to silently rehearse the letters even when counting backward (Sebrects, Marsh, & Seamon, 1989). Incidentally, many people misuse the term *short-term memory* in everyday language. For example, they may say that their "short-term memory isn't working" because they forgot what they had for dinner yesterday. As we've seen, the duration of short-term memory is far briefer than that.

Memory Loss from Short-Term Memory: Decay versus Interference. Why did the Petersons' participants lose their short-term memories so quickly, just as we quickly lose our memories of phone numbers we've just heard? The most obvious explanation is that short-term memories **decay**, that is, fade away over time. The longer we wait, the less is left. Yet there's a competing explanation for the loss of information from short-term memory: **interference**. According to this view, our memories get in the way of each other. That is, our memories are very much like radio signals. They don't change over time, but they're harder to detect if they're jammed by other signals.

As it turns out, there's evidence for both decay and interference. Recent physiological evidence for decay comes from research suggesting that the birth of new neurons in the hippocampus (see Chapter 3) leads to the decay of memories in that brain region (Kitamura et al., 2009). As we create new memories, we our old ones gradually fade away. Nevertheless, there's even stronger evidence for the role of interference in memory loss. For example, two

echoic memory
auditory sensory memory

short-term memory
memory system that retains information for limited durations

decay
fading of information from memory over time

interference
loss of information from memory because of competition from additional incoming information

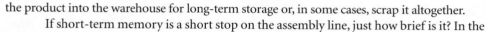

ruling out rival hypotheses

HAVE IMPORTANT ALTERNATIVE EXPLANATIONS FOR THE FINDINGS BEEN EXCLUDED?

investigators (Waugh & Norman, 1965) presented subjects with many different lists of 16 digits, such as 6 2 7 1 8 5 3 4 2 6 9 7 4 5 8 3. Right after subjects saw each list, the researchers gave them one "target" digit to focus on, and then asked subjects which digit came after this target digit. In all cases, this target digit appeared twice in the list, and subjects had to remember the digit that came after its *first* presentation in the list. In the digit list above, the target item might be "8," so we'd search for the first 8 in the list—and the correct response would be 5.

ruling out rival hypotheses

HAVE IMPORTANT ALTERNATIVE EXPLANATIONS FOR THE FINDINGS BEEN EXCLUDED?

As an ingenious means of ruling out alternative hypotheses, the experimenters manipulated two variables to figure out which of them influenced forgetting. Specifically, they manipulated both (1) where in the list the target digit appeared (early or late) and (2) how rapidly they presented digits to subjects—either quickly (one digit every second) or slowly (one digit every four seconds). They told subjects to listen carefully to each digit, but not to rehearse it mentally. Now, if decay were the principal culprit in forgetting, participants' performance should become worse when researchers read the list slowly because more time had passed between digits. In contrast, if interference were the principal culprit, participants' performance should become worse when the target digit appeared later rather than earlier in the list, regardless of speed, because memory for later digits is hampered by memory for earlier digits.

The results showed that interference is the major factor in forgetting. Participants' forgetting is due almost entirely to where in the list the target digit appears, rather than to the speed of presentation (Keppel & Underwood, 1962). Still, most researchers believe that both decay and interference play some role in short-term memory loss (Altmann & Schunn, 2002).

We're not quite done with our examination of interference yet, because it turns out that there are two different kinds of interference (Underwood, 1957). One kind, **retroactive interference**, occurs when learning something new hampers earlier learning: The new interferes with the old (think of the prefix *retro-*, because retroactive interference works in a reverse direction). If you've learned one language, say Spanish, and then later learned a somewhat similar language, perhaps Italian, you've probably found that you started making mistakes in Spanish you'd never made before. Specifically, you may have found yourself using Italian words, like *buono*, for Spanish words, like *bueno* (both *buono* and *bueno* mean "good").

In contrast, **proactive interference**, occurs when earlier learning gets in the way of new learning: The old interferes with the new. For example, knowing how to play tennis might interfere with our attempt to learn to play racquetball, which requires a much smaller racquet. Not surprisingly, both retroactive and proactive interference are more likely to occur when the old and new stimuli that we've learned are similar. Learning a new language doesn't much affect our ability to master a new spaghetti recipe.

The Capacity of Short-Term Memory: The Magic Number. We've already seen that short-term memory doesn't last very long. Twenty seconds, or even less, and—poof!—the memory is gone, unless we've made an extra-special effort to retain it. But how large is the *span* of short-term memory?

Try reading each of the following rows of numbers, one row at a time, at a rate of one number per second. Once you're done with each row, close your eyes and try writing down what you remember. Ready? Okay, begin.

$$9 - 5 - 2$$
$$2 - 9 - 7 - 3$$
$$5 - 7 - 4 - 9 - 2$$
$$6 - 2 - 7 - 3 - 8 - 4$$
$$2 - 4 - 1 - 8 - 6 - 4 - 7$$
$$3 - 9 - 5 - 7 - 4 - 1 - 8 - 9$$
$$8 - 4 - 6 - 3 - 1 - 7 - 4 - 2 - 5$$
$$5 - 2 - 9 - 3 - 4 - 6 - 1 - 8 - 5 - 7$$

You've just taken a test of "digit span." How'd you make out? Odds are that you breezed through three digits, started to find four digits a bit tricky, and maxed out at somewhere between five and nine digits. It's unlikely you got the 10-digit list completely right; if you did, you've earned the right to call yourself a memory superstar.

? This player is actively engaged in a racquetball match. If she was an experienced tennis player before attempting racquetball, the odds are high that her tennis swings would initially get in the way of her learning how to swing a racquetball racquet properly. That is, it will take her a while to "unlearn" her tennis swings. **What kind of interference is she experiencing?** (See answer upside down.)

retroactive interference
interference with retention of old information due to acquisition of new information

[handwritten: new interfering with old]

proactive interference
interference with acquisition of new information due to previous learning of information

[handwritten: old interfering with new]

Answer: Proactive interference (the old interfering with the new).

That's because the digit span of most adults is between five and nine digits, with an average of seven digits. Indeed, this finding is so consistent across people that psychologist George Miller (1956) referred to seven plus or minus two pieces of information as the **Magic Number**.

According to Miller, the Magic Number is the universal limit of short-term memory, and it applies to just about all information we encounter: Numbers, letters, people, vegetables, and cities. Because it's hard to retain much more than seven plus or minus two pieces of information in our short-term memory, it's almost surely not a coincidence that telephone numbers in North America are exactly seven digits long, not counting the area code (some European phone numbers are slightly longer, but few exceed nine, the upper limit for the Magic Number). Some psychologists have since argued that Miller's Magic Number may overestimate the capacity of short-term memory, and that the true Magic Number may be as low as four (Cowan, 2001). Regardless of who's right, it's clear that the capacity of short-term memory is extremely limited.

Chunking. If our short-term memory capacity is no more than nine digits, and perhaps much less, how do we manage to remember larger amounts of information than this for brief periods of time? Read the following sentence, then wait a few seconds and recite it back to yourself: **Harry Potter's white owl Hedwig flew off into the dark and stormy night.** Were you able to remember most or even all of it? The odds are high that you were. Yet this sentence contained thirteen words, which exceeds the Magic Number. How did you accomplish this feat?

We can expand our ability to remember things in the short term by using a technique called **chunking**: organizing material into meaningful groupings. For example, look at the following string of 15 letters for a few seconds, and then try to recall them:

K A C F J N A B I S B C F U I

How'd you do? Odds are you didn't do too well, probably right around the Magic Number, that is, only a subset of the letters listed. Okay, now try this 15-letter string instead.

C I A U S A F B I N B C J F K

Did you do any better this time? It's the same 15 letters, but you probably noticed something different about this group than the first group: They consisted of meaningful abbreviations. So you probably "chunked" these 15 letters into five meaningful groups of three letters each: CIA, USA, FBI, NBC, JFK. In this way, you reduced the number of items you needed to remember from 15 to only five. In fact, you might have even gotten this number down to less than five by combining CIA and FBI (both the initials of U.S. government intelligence agencies) into one chunk.

Chunking explains how Rajan performed his remarkable pi memorization feats. He memorized enormous numbers of area codes, dates of famous historical events, and other meaningful numbers embedded within the list of pi digits to effectively reduce more than 30,000 digits to a much smaller number.

Experts rely on chunking to help them recall complicated information. For example, chess masters recall *realistic* chess positions far better than do novices, yet do no better than novices at recalling random chess positions, suggesting that experts organize meaningful chess positions into broader patterns (Chase & Simon, 1973).

Rehearsal. Whereas chunking increases the span of short-term memory, a strategy called rehearsal extends the duration of information in short-term memory. **Rehearsal** is repeating the information mentally, or even out loud. In that way, we keep the information "alive" in our short-term memories, just as a juggler keeps a bunch of bowling pins "alive" by continuing to catch them and toss them back into the air. Of course, if he pauses for a second to scratch his nose, the bowling pins come crashing to the ground. Similarly, if we stop rehearsing and shift our attention elsewhere, we'll quickly lose material from our short-term memory.

There are two major types of rehearsal. The first, **maintenance rehearsal**, simply involves repeating the stimuli in their original form; we don't attempt to change the original stimuli in any way. We engage in maintenance rehearsal whenever we hear a phone

Magic Number
the span of short-term memory, according to George Miller: seven plus or minus two pieces of information

chunking
organizing information into meaningful groupings, allowing us to extend the span of short-term memory

rehearsal
repeating information to extend the duration of retention in short-term memory

maintenance rehearsal
repeating stimuli in their original form to retain them in short-term memory

FACTOID

One man named S.F. was able to get his digit span memory up to 79 digits using chunking. Among other tricks, S.F., who was a runner, memorized enormous numbers of world record times for track events and used them to chunk numbers into bigger units. Yet S.F. hadn't really increased his short-term memory capacity at all, only his chunking ability. His memory span for letters was only a measly six, well within the range of the Magic Number achieved by the rest of us memory slackers.

Chunking numbers = grouping numbers and such to memorize better.

Master chess players recall realistic chess positions, like the one above, better than do beginners. But they do no better than beginners at recalling unrealistic chess positions. So the experts' edge stems not from raw memory power, but from chunking.

number and keep on repeating it—either out loud or in our minds—until we're ready to dial the number. In this way, we keep the information "alive" in our short-term memory. Of course, if someone interrupts us while we're rehearsing, we'll forget the number.

The second type of rehearsal, **elaborative rehearsal**, usually takes more effort. In this type of rehearsal, we "elaborate" on the stimuli we need to remember by linking them in some meaningful way, perhaps by visualizing them or trying to understand their interrelationship (Craik & Lockhart, 1972).

To grasp the difference between maintenance and elaborative rehearsal, let's imagine that a researcher gave us a *paired-associate task*. In this task, the investigator first presents us with various pairs of words, such as dog–shoe, tree–pipe, key–monkey, and kite–president. Then, she presents us with the first word in each pair—dog, tree, and so on—and asks us to remember the second word in the pair. If we used maintenance rehearsal, we'd simply repeat the words in each pair over and over again as soon as we heard it—dog–shoe, dog–shoe, dog–shoe, and so on. In contrast, if we used elaborative rehearsal, we'd try to link the words in each pair in a meaningful way. One effective way of accomplishing this goal is to come up with a meaningful, perhaps even absurd, visual image that combines both stimuli (Ghetti et al., 2008; Paivio, 1969) (see **FIGURE 7.5**). Research shows that we're especially likely to remember the two stimuli if we picture them interacting in some fashion (Wollen, Weber, & Lowry, 1972). That's probably because doing so allows us to chunk them into a single integrated stimulus. So to remember the word pair dog–rocket, for example, we could picture a dog piloting a rocket ship or a rocket ship barking like a dog.

Elaborative rehearsal usually works better than maintenance rehearsal (Harris & Qualls, 2000). This finding demolishes a widely held misconception about memory: that rote memorization is typically the best means of retaining information. There's a take-home lesson here when it comes to our study habits. To remember complex information, it's almost always better to connect that information with things we already know than to merely keep repeating it.

FIGURE 7.5 Word Pairs. Using elaborative rehearsal helps us recall the word pair dog–shoe. (*Source:* Paivio, 1969)

Depth of Processing. This finding is consistent with a **levels-of-processing** model of memory. According to this model, the more deeply we process information, the better we tend to remember it. This model identifies three levels of processing of verbal information (Craik & Lockhart, 1972): visual, phonological (sound-related), and semantic (meaning-related). Visual processing is the most shallow, phonological somewhat less shallow, and semantic the deepest. To understand the differences among these three levels, try to remember the following sentence:

ALL PEOPLE CREATE THEIR OWN MEANING OF LIFE.

If you relied on *visual* processing, you'd hone in on how the sentence looks. For example, you might try to focus on the fact that the sentence consists entirely of capital letters. If you relied on *phonological* processing, you'd focus on how the words in the sentence sound. Most likely, you'd repeat the sentence again and again until it began to sound boringly familiar. Finally, if you relied on *semantic* processing, you'd emphasize the sentence's meaning. You might elaborate on how you've tried to create your own meaning of life and how doing so has been helpful to you. Research shows that deeper levels of processing, especially semantic processing, tend to produce more enduring long-term memories (Craik & Tulving, 1975). ⊙➤ Simulate

Still, some psychologists have criticized the levels-of-processing model as largely unfalsifiable (Baddeley, 1993). According to them, it's virtually impossible to determine how deeply we've processed a memory in the first place, so we could never independently test the claim that more deeply processed memories are better remembered. Moreover, critics claim that proponents of the levels-of-processing model are merely equating "depth" with how well subjects later remember. There may well be some truth to this criticism. Still, it's safe to say that the more meaning we can supply to a stimulus, the more likely we are to recall it in the long term.

LONG-TERM MEMORY. Now that the second factory assembly line worker—short-term memory—has finished her construction job, what does she pass on to the third and final worker? And how does what the third worker receives differ from what the second worker

⊙➤ **Simulate** Depth Processing on **mypsychlab.com**

falsifiability

CAN THE CLAIM BE DISPROVED? ➤

elaborative rehearsal
linking stimuli to each other in a meaningful way to improve retention of information in short-term memory

levels of processing
depth of transforming information, which influences how easily we remember it

started out with? **Long-term memory**, the third worker, is our relatively enduring store of information. It includes the facts, experiences, and skills we've acquired over our lifetimes.

Differences between Long-Term and Short-Term Memory. Long-term memory differs from short-term memory in several important ways. First, in contrast to short-term memory, which can typically hold at most seven to nine stimuli in hand at a single time, the capacity of long-term memory is huge. Just how huge? No one knows for sure. Some scientists estimate that a typical person's memory holds about as much information as 500 complete sets of *Encyclopaedia Britannica* (Cordón, 2005). So if someone praises you on your "encyclopedic memory," accept the compliment. They're probably right.

Second, although information in short-term memory vanishes after only about 20 seconds at most, information in long-term memory often endures for years, even decades—and sometimes permanently. Consider the work of psychologist Harry Bahrick, who has studied individuals' memory for languages they learned in school over many decades. In **FIGURE 7.6**, we can see that people's memory declines markedly about two to three years after taking a Spanish course. Yet after about two years, the decline becomes quite gradual. Indeed, it begins to level out after a while, with almost no additional loss for up to 50 years after they took the course (Bahrick & Phelps, 1987). Bahrick referred to this kind of long-term memory, which remains "frozen" over time, as **permastore**, as an analogy to the permafrost found in the Arctic or Antarctic that never melts.

Third, the types of mistakes we commit in long-term memory differ from those we make in short-term memory. Long-term memory errors tend to be *semantic*, that is, based on the meaning of the information we've received. So we might misremember a "poodle" as a "terrier." In contrast, short-term memory errors tend to be *acoustic*, that is, based on the sound of the information we've received (Conrad, 1964; Wickelgren, 1965). So, we might misremember hearing "noodle" rather than "poodle."

Primacy and Recency Effects. When we try to remember a large number of items, such as a grocery list or a schedule of events, we often forget some of them. To some extent, psychologists can predict which items we're more likely to forget and which we're more likely to remember.

To demonstrate this point, read the list of twenty words below, either to yourself or out loud. Read the left column first, then the middle column, then the right one. Then, turn away from your book and take a few minutes to try to recall as many of these words as you can in any order you'd like. Ready? Begin.

Ball	Sky	Store
Shoe	Desk	Pencil
Tree	Car	Grass
Dog	Rope	Man
Paper	Dress	Cloud
Bird	Xylophone	Hat
House	Knife	Vase

If you're like most people, you probably did a bit better with the early words, like ball, shoe, and tree, than with the words in the middle of the list. That's the **primacy effect**: the tendency to remember stimuli, like words, early in a list. Also, you may have done a bit better with the later words, like cloud, hat, and vase. That's the **recency effect**: the tendency to remember stimuli later in a list. As an aside, there's a decent chance you remembered the word *xylophone*, which seems to be something of an oddball in the list. That's because we tend to remember stimuli that are distinctive in some way (Neath & Surprenant, 2003). ●→ Simulate

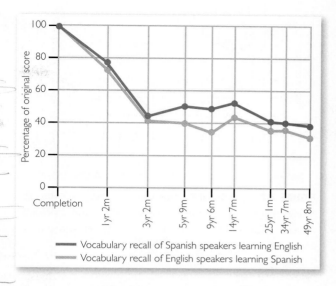

FIGURE 7.6 Long-term Memory Retention. The classic work of Harry Bahrick (1984) shows that retention of a foreign language remains remarkably constant for spans of almost 50 years after an initial drop. (*Source:* Bahrick, 1984)

●→ **Simulate** the Serial Position Effect on **mypsychlab.com**

long-term memory
relatively enduring (from minutes to years) retention of information stored regarding our facts, experiences, and skills

permastore
type of long-term memory that appears to be permanent

primacy effect
tendency to remember words at the beginning of a list especially well

recency effect
tendency to remember words at the end of a list especially well

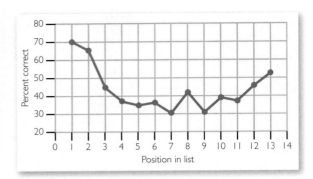

FIGURE 7.7 The Serial Position Curve. Most psychologists believe that the primacy and recency effects in this curve are the telltale signs of two different memory systems: long-term and short-term memory, respectively.

 Simulate the Serial Position Curve on **mypsychlab.com**

FACTOID ✚

There's even a serial position curve for U.S. presidents. If given the chance to name as many presidents as they can, most people list early presidents, like Washington, Jefferson, and Adams, and recent presidents, like Clinton, Bush, and Obama more than middle presidents, with good old Abe Lincoln being a striking exception (Roediger & Crowder, 1976).

? During a 2009 rock concert in Michigan, Bruce Springsteen referred repeatedly to being in Ohio (and even greeted the audience by yelling "Hello Ohio!"). "The Boss" committed an error in which subtype of long-term memory? (See answer upside down on bottom of page.)

serial position curve
graph depicting both primacy and recency effects on people's ability to recall items on a list

semantic memory
our knowledge of facts about the world

episodic memory
recollection of events in our lives

explicit memory
memories we recall intentionally and of which we have conscious awareness

implicit memory
memories we don't deliberately remember or reflect on consciously

Answer: Semantic memory.

If we averaged your results along with those of a few hundred other subjects, we'd end up with the graph depicted in **FIGURE 7.7**, called the **serial position curve**. As we can see, this curve clearly displays the primacy and recency effects.

Most researchers agree that primacy and recency effects reflect the operation of different memory systems. Because the last few words in the list were probably lingering in your short-term memory, you were probably especially likely to recall them. So the recency effect seems to reflect the workings of short-term memory.

What explains the primacy effect? This one is trickier, but there's good evidence that you were more likely to recall the earlier words in the list because you had more opportunity to rehearse them silently—and perhaps even to chunk them. As a consequence, these words were more likely to be transferred from short-term memory into long-term memory. So the primacy effect seems to reflect the operation of long-term memory. ◉▸ Simulate

Types of Long-Term Memory. As we mentioned earlier, some psychologists argue that there are actually more than three memory systems. In particular, they claim that long-term memory isn't just one system, but many.

To find out why, try your hand at the following four questions.

1. In what year did the United States become independent from Great Britain?
2. What Republican candidate for president did Barack Obama defeat in the 2008 election?
3. How old were you when you first tried to ride a bicycle?
4. Where did you celebrate your last birthday?

According to Endel Tulving (1972) and many other memory researchers, our answers to the first two questions rely on different memory systems than our answers to the last two. Our answers to the first two questions

(1776 and John McCain) depend on **semantic memory**, our knowledge of facts about the world. In contrast, our answers to the last two questions, which are unique to us, depend on **episodic memory**, our recollection of events in our lives. A.J., whom we discussed at the beginning of the chapter, experiences remarkably accurate episodic memories. There's good evidence that these two types of memory are housed in different brain regions. Semantic memory tends to activate the left frontal cortex more than the right frontal cortex, and vice versa for episodic memory (Cabeza & Nyberg, 1997). Still, semantic and episodic memory both require conscious effort and awareness. Whether we're trying to recall the definition of "chunking" from earlier in this chapter or our first kiss, we *know* we're trying to remember. Moreover, when we recall this information, we have a conscious experience of accessing it. That is, both semantic and episodic memory are examples of **explicit memory**, the process of recalling information intentionally. (Some researchers refer to the information recalled by explicit memory as *declarative memory*.)

Explicit memory differs from **implicit memory**, the process of recalling information we don't remember deliberately. Implicit memories don't require conscious effort on our part. For example, each of us can go through the steps of unlocking our front doors without consciously recalling the sequence of actions required to do so. In fact, we probably can't tell without reenacting it in our heads or actually standing in front of our doors which way the key turns in the lock and how we'd hold the key in our hands while unlocking the door.

Studies of people with brain damage provide remarkable *existence proofs* (see Chapter 2) for the distinction between implicit and explicit memory. Antonio Damasio (2000) has studied a patient named David, whose left and right temporal lobes were largely obliterated by a virus. David has virtually no explicit memory for anyone he's met; when Damasio shows him photographs of people with whom he's recently interacted, he can't recognize any of them. Yet when Damasio asks David which of these people he'd ask for help if he needed it, he points to those who've been kind to him, utterly clueless of who they are. David has no explicit memory for who's helped him, but his implicit memory remains intact.

Procedural memory is memory for how to do things, even things we do automatically without thinking about how to do them.

To make matters still more complicated, there are several subtypes of implicit memory. We'll discuss two here: procedural memory and priming. However, according to most psychologists, implicit memory also includes habituation, classical conditioning, and other forms of learning we've encountered in Chapter 6.

One subtype of implicit memory, **procedural memory**, refers to memory for motor skills and habits. Whenever we ride a bicycle or open a soda can, we're relying on procedural memory. In contrast to semantic memory, which is "know what" memory, procedural memory is "know how" memory. Our procedural and semantic memories for the same skills are sometimes surprisingly different. For those of you who are avid typists, find a computer keyboard or typewriter and type the word *the*. That's a breeze, right? Now turn away from the keyboard for a moment, and try to remember where the *t, h,* and *e* are located, but without moving your fingers. If you're like most people, you'll draw a blank. You may even find that the only way to remember their location is to use your fingers to type the imaginary letters in midair. Although your procedural memory for locating letters on a keyboard is effortless, your semantic memory for locating them is a different story.

A second subtype of implicit memory, **priming**, refers to our ability to identify a stimulus more easily or more quickly when we've previously encountered similar stimuli. Imagine that a researcher flashes the word QUEEN, interspersed with a few hundred other words, very quickly on a computer screen. An hour later, she asks you to perform a *stem completion task,* which requires you to fill in the missing letters of a word. In this case, the stem completion task is K _____. Research shows that having seen the word QUEEN, you're more likely to complete the stem with KING (as opposed to KILL or KNOW, for example) than are subjects who haven't seen QUEEN (Neely, 1976). This is true, incidentally, even for subjects who insist they can't even remember having seen the word QUEEN (Bargh, 1994). This memory is implicit because it doesn't require any deliberate effort on our part.

If you're having a hard time keeping all of these subtypes of long-term memory straight, **FIGURE 7.8** summarizes the major subtypes of explicit and implicit memory.

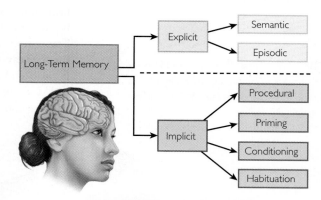

(A)   (B)

Priming: A Demonstration Is the drawing at the bottom a duck or a rabbit? This illusion, originally concocted by psychologist Joseph Jastrow around the turn of the century, affords a good illustration of priming you can try on your friends. Show some of your friends only Photograph A (covering up Photograph B), and then show other friends only Photograph B (covering up Photograph A). Then ask them what they see in the drawing below. Your friends primed with Photograph A will be more likely to "see" the related image of a duck, and your friends primed with Photograph B will be more likely to "see" the related image of a rabbit (see Chapter 4).

FIGURE 7.8 The Many Subtypes of Memory. A summary of the subtypes of explicit and implicit memory.

procedural memory
memory for how to do things, including motor skills and habits

priming
our ability to identify a stimulus more easily or more quickly after we've encountered similar stimuli

assess your knowledge   FACT OR FICTION?

1. Most of us can accurately recognize thousands of faces we've seen only a few days earlier. **True / False**

2. Memory is more reconstructive than reproductive. **True / False**

3. The major reason for forgetting information from short-term memory appears to be the decay of memories. **True / False**

4. Chunking can permit us to greatly increase the number of digits or letters we hold in our short-term memories. **True / False**

5. Information in long-term memory often lasts for years or decades. **True / False**

Answers: 1. T (p. 243); 2. T (p. 244); 3. F (p. 247); 4. T (p. 249); 5. T (p. 251)

THE THREE PROCESSES OF MEMORY

7.4 Identify methods for connecting new information to existing knowledge.

7.5 Identify the role that schemas play in the storage of memories.

7.6 Distinguish ways of measuring memory.

7.7 Describe how the relation between encoding and retrieval conditions influences remembering.

How do we get information into our long-term memories? Memory psychologists agree that there are three major *processes* of memory: *Encoding, storage,* and *retrieval.* By the way, we shouldn't confuse these three processes with the three *systems* of memory we've just discussed (sensory, short-term, and long-term). Whereas the three systems refer to the *what* of memory, the three processes we're about to discuss refer to the *how* of memory. They explain how information gets transferred into long-term memory and gets back out again when we need it (see **FIGURE 7.9**). ●─Explore

To understand these three processes of memory, picture yourself working as a librarian at your college or university library. When a new book arrives, you first give it a number to identify it; that's encoding. Then you file it away on the bookshelf; that's storage. Then, when you want to find the book a few weeks, months, or even years later, you go to the shelves and fetch it; that's retrieval. Of course, like all metaphors, this one is an oversimplification, because the memories we retrieve are rarely identical to those we initially encoded. Some of the "books" in our mental library may become yellow with age; others become marked up or even damaged beyond recognition.

FIGURE 7.9 Three Processes of Memory. The process of remembering is similar in some ways to the process of filing and fetching a library book.

Process 1 Encoding: Using a computer, a librarian enters the cataloguing information for a book into the library's database. In the process, the librarian finds out where the book needs to be shelved. The computer prints out a label (what we might think of as an encoding label) that the librarian affixes to the book's spine so that everyone will know where the book should be stored.

Process 2 Storage: The librarian puts the books in the proper section of the library, according to how they've been catalogued.

Process 3 Retrieval: When the librarian wants to access the book, he looks up the cataloguing information and then goes to the appropriate shelf with his computer printout showing the catalogue location of the book to retrieve it.

■ Encoding: The "Call Numbers" of the Mind

Encoding refers to the process of getting information into our memory banks. To remember something, we first need to make sure the information is in a format our memories can use. To a far greater extent than we realize, many of our memory failures are actually failures of encoding. To go back to our library analogy, imagine that the librarian assigns some of the books that come in for processing an identification number but later decides to toss some of them in the trash instead. These books never make it to the shelves. Once we lose the chance to encode an event, we'll never remember it. No encoding, no memory.

THE ROLE OF ATTENTION. To encode something, we must first attend to it. Have you ever had the embarrassing experience of going to a party and being introduced to several people at the same time, and then immediately realizing that you'd forgotten all of their names? Odds are high you were so nervous or distracted that you never encoded their names in the first place.

That principle helps to explain why the popular belief that our brains preserve a record of every event we've ever encountered (Alvarez & Brown, 2001) is almost surely a myth. Most events we've experienced are never encoded, and almost all events we do encode include only some of the details of the experience. Much of our everyday experience never gets into our brains in the first place. For instance, consider this example of an everyday object we've seen hundreds, even thousands, of times. Take a look at **FIGURE 7.10**, where you'll see an array of six pennies. Which of these pennies is the real one?

If you flunked this miniature test of "common cents," don't feel too bad. When two researchers conducted a similar version of this test about three decades ago, they found that fewer than half of 203 Americans identified the correct penny (Nickerson & Adams, 1979). We see pennies almost every day, yet how often do we actually pay attention to the details of them?

Encoding also helps to explain the familiar *next-in-line effect*. You've experienced this phenomenon if you've ever been in a class when the instructor called on several students in a row to answer a question or say their names. You probably found that your memory was especially poor for what the person immediately before you said (Bond, Pitre, & van Leeuwen, 1991). That's because you were so preoccupied with what you were going to say that you weren't paying much attention to what the person right before you was saying.

MNEMONICS: VALUABLE MEMORY AIDS. What do the following strange passages have in common? *PEMDAS*

1. Please Excuse My Dear Aunt Sally.
2. Thirty days hath September, April, June, and November. All the rest have 31, except for February, which has 28, and you probably think it's great. Or maybe it's when fine, on leap year, it has 29.
3. Every Good Boy Does Fine.

Each is a **mnemonic** (pronounced "nee-muh-nik"): a learning aid, strategy, or device that enhances recall. Mnemonics help us encode memories in a way that makes them easier to recall. From time to time, virtually all of us use recall boosters, like making lists or writing appointments on a calendar or portable computer (Intons-Peterson & Fournier, 1986). Nevertheless, mnemonics differ from these "external" memory aids in that they rely on internal mental strategies, namely, strategies we use during encoding that help us later retrieve useful information. Item 1 specifies the proper order of mathematical operations (parentheses, exponents, multiplication, division, addition, subtraction) by having each word start with the same letter as the mathematical operation. Item 2 is a rhyme that's a handy way of remembering the number of days in each month. Item 3 stands for the note names on the lines of the treble clef in musical notation (E, G, B, D, F).

Mnemonic devices share two major features. First, we can apply them to just about anything and everything: the names of planets, the elements of the periodic table, the bones of the hand, the order of geological time periods, and the colors of the rainbow (the last

"In one ear and out the other," so the saying goes. If you've met someone and have forgotten his or her name a minute later, you probably never encoded it in the first place.

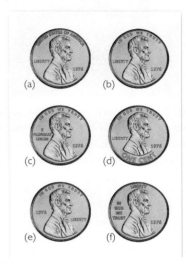

? **FIGURE 7.10** Penny Array from Nickerson and Adams (1979). Which of these pennies is the real one? Try to guess before pulling one out of your pocket. (*Source:* Nickerson & Adams, 1979)

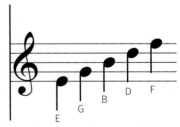

Music students use the mnemonic "Every good boy does fine" to remember the names of the lines (E, G, B, D, F) in the treble clef.

encoding
process of getting information into our memory banks

mnemonic
a learning aid, strategy, or device that enhances recall

Answer: The correct answer is (b)

FIGURE 7.11 Pegword Method. The pegword method can be a useful mnemonic for helping us recall lists of objects in order. See the text for an explanation of this fanciful illustration.

being ROY G. BIV for red, orange, yellow, green, blue, indigo, and violet). Second, most mnemonics depend on having a store of knowledge to begin with. We need to know something about mathematical operations for the mnemonic about Aunt Sally to make any sense. So in general, mnemonics are most helpful as mental shortcuts for recalling lists of information we've already learned. There are many other mnemonic approaches in addition to those we've discussed: We'll review three here.

Pegword Method. By elementary school age, most of us were well acquainted with the exploits of Jack and Jill, Little Bo Peep, and Little Jack Horner. Songs ranging from "Twinkle, Twinkle Little Star" to the hip-hop songs of the Black Eyed Peas are easy to remember because they contain rhymes.

Rhyming is a key component of the *pegword method,* often used to recall lists of words. To master this mnemonic, first associate each number in a list with a word that rhymes with each number, such as "One is a bun." The word associated with the number is a "pegword." It's essential to memorize a list like the one that follows, but the fact that the numbers and words rhyme makes it easy to do so: (1) One is a bun, (2) Two is a shoe, (3) Three is a tree, and (4) Four is a door.

Suppose you need to learn four words associated with memory concepts for your psychology class (don't you wish there were only four new terms in this chapter?) and that you need to recall them in the following order: chunking, elaboration, hippocampus, and decay. After you've memorized the pegword associated with each number (such as "one is a bun"), create an image that associates the word you want to remember with the pegword (such as *bun*). For the first word, *chunking,* you could imagine a bun (the pegword) with a chunk missing or broken up into chunks. For two—*elaboration*—you might imagine a shoe with elaborate beading, sequins, and bows. For three—*hippocampus*—imagine a tree with a hippo camping under it. For number four, *decay,* you might picture a rotting, decaying door on an old house. When you need to remember the third thing on your list, for example, you'd say to yourself that three is a tree, which would prompt recall of the hippo camping under it, and you'd know that the third word on the list is hippocampus (see **FIGURE 7.11**).

Method of Loci. The *method of loci* (pronounced low-sigh) relies on imagery of places, that is, *locations,* hence the name of the mnemonic (Bellezza, 1999). The method is straightforward: Think of a path with which you're familiar and can imagine vividly. Perhaps it's the route from your dorm to the cafeteria, or a stroll through the rooms in your apartment. Think of the path you take and the things that you encounter in a set order. For example, to get to the cafeteria, first you get in the elevator, then you walk under a huge tree before you pass by a fountain, and so on. If you need to remember five words in a particular order, think of five things you'll encounter on your way to the cafeteria; if you need to recall ten words, imagine ten locations along your route. If you were trying to remember the list of memory terms with the method of loci, you might imagine chunks of rock or glass on the floor of the elevator.

Keyword Method. If you've taken a foreign language course, you may be familiar with the *keyword method.* This strategy depends on your ability to think of an English word (the keyword) that reminds you of the word you're trying to remember. Take the Spanish word *casa,* which means "house" in English. Think of an English word, like case, that sounds like or brings to mind "casa." Now think of an image that combines "case" (or another word of your choice) and "house." Perhaps you can picture a case of soda on the roof of your house. When you think of this image, it should help you retrieve the meaning of *casa.* People who learn foreign vocabulary benefit from the keyword strategy compared with more traditional methods (Gruneberg & Sykes, 1991). The keyword method also helps elderly individuals to improve their recall of Spanish words (Gruneberg & Pascoe, 1996).

Generally speaking, mnemonics can be helpful if we're motivated to practice them on a regular basis. Many people seem to prefer external aids, such as making lists (Park, Smith, & Cavanaugh, 1990) to mnemonics, probably because they take less work and effort. Mnemonics require training, patience, and even a dash of creativity.

psychomythology

SMART PILLS

The next time you're in your local drug store, stop by the aisle containing herbal remedies. There you'll find a virtual museum of so-called smart pills designed to enhance memory: ginkgo, vitamin E, and even drugs with unpronounceable, but scientific-sounding, names like phosphatidylserine, citicoline, and piracetam. Can any of them help us remember where we mislaid our keys this morning, memorize the names of the ten people we met at last night's party, or recall how to spell "phosphatidylserine"?

Probably the best-known herbal remedy for memory is ginkgo (whose scientific name is *Ginkgo biloba*), an ancient Chinese medicine extracted from the leaves of the ginkgo tree. Although it might be tempting to assume that ginkgo is effective because it's been used for many centuries, this would be an example of the *argument from antiquity fallacy* (see Chapter 1), the error of concluding that something must be effective because it's been around for a long time. The manufacturers of ginkgo claim that it can markedly improve normal people's memory in as little as four weeks. Like many other memory boosters, ginkgo presumably works in part by increasing the level of the brain's acetylcholine, a neurotransmitter that plays a key role in memory (see Chapter 3).

Ginkgo is remarkably popular; Americans spend several hundred million dollars on it per year. Yet controlled studies comparing ginkgo with a placebo show that its effects on memory in normal individuals are minimal, even nonexistent (Gold, Cahill, & Wenk, 2002; Solomon et al., 2002). If ginkgo produces any effects on normal memory at all, they appear to be about equal to those of drinking a glass of lemonade or any sugary liquid (as you'll recall from Chapter 3, sugar is the brain's fuel). Ginkgo's effects on memory in people with Alzheimer's disease or other forms of dementia are slight (Gold et al., 2002) and perhaps even nonexistent (DeKosky et al., 2008). There's no good evidence that it can reverse severe memory loss. Moreover, like many herbal remedies, ginkgo can be harmful in certain cases; it can interfere with the effects of blood-thinning medicines and thereby cause excessive bleeding. As for the other smart pills we mentioned with fancy names, the evidence for their effects on memory is too preliminary to draw strong conclusions (McDaniel, Maier, & Einstein, 2002).

Finally, what about pills designed to boost attention and keep us awake, perhaps just long enough to study for that dreaded final exam? Not surprisingly, some of these drugs are becoming popular on college campuses. Surveys show that up to 25 percent of college students have used Ritalin, Adderall, and similar stimulants, widely prescribed for attention-deficit/hyperactivity disorder (see Chapter 15), to help them concentrate while studying or taking exams (Greely et al., 2008). One team of investigators compared students taking the SAT, some of whom believed they were ingesting Ritalin and some whom believed they were ingesting a dummy pill. The former students reported better mental functioning and attention—but their SAT scores weren't any higher. Yet *both* groups had actually received a dummy pill, suggesting that Ritalin's "impact" on test-taking may be due to a placebo effect (Gowin, 2009; see Chapter 2). Modafinil (its brand name is Provigil), commonly prescribed for narcolepsy, sleep apnea, and other sleep disorders (see Chapter 5), is also popular as an aid for maintaining wakefulness and alertness. Nevertheless, research suggests that although Modafinil may be about as effective as caffeine for enhancing attention in sleep-deprived people, at least some of its effects on fatigue may not exceed those of a placebo (Kumar, 2008). Because the Food and Drug Administration (FDA) no longer regulates diet supplements and herbal remedies, including those intended to enhance memory, it's anybody's guess whether they work, or even whether any might be harmful (Bent, 2008). As is so often the case in pop psychology, the best advice for those of us hoping to become memory whizzes overnight is *caveat emptor:* Let the buyer beware.

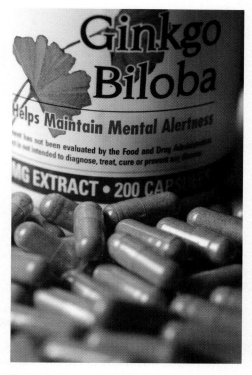

Ginkgo and other supposed memory-enhancing drugs are a multimillion-dollar industry in the United States. These pills are popular, but do they work?

■ Storage: Filing Away Our Memories

Once we've filed away a library book on the shelf, it sits there, often for years at a time, collecting dust and cobwebs. We've stored it, perhaps to be retrieved one day by a student or professor who needs it for a writing project. **Storage** refers to the process of keeping information in memory.

Yet where in the library we choose to file this book depends on our *interpretation and expectations* regarding the book's content. Let's imagine a new book entitled *The Psychology of Dating* has just arrived in the library. Should we file this book in the psychology section, along with books on personality, emotion, and social psychology, or in the relationships section, along with books on dating, attraction, and marriage? The answer depends on what we think is most important or relevant about the book's content. Similarly, how we store our experiences in memory depends on our interpretations and expectations of these events.

THE VALUE OF SCHEMAS. Consider this scenario. You and your friends go to a brand new sit-down restaurant. Although this is your first visit, you've got a pretty good idea of what's in store. That's because you possess a schema for eating at a nice restaurant. A **schema** is an organized knowledge structure or mental model that we've stored in memory. Our schema for restaurants is characterized by a set order of events, sometimes called a *script* (Schank & Abelson, 1977). You're seated at a table, given menus from which you

storage
process of keeping information in memory

schema
organized knowledge structure or mental model that we've stored in memory

---

Answers are located at the end of the text.

MEMORY BOOSTERS

evaluating CLAIMS

Many of us would love to improve our memories—to perform better in our courses or at work, remember birthdays, anniversaries, and other important dates, or just to remember where we left our keys. Scores of products on the market purport to improve our memories and overall brain functioning. Let's evaluate some of these claims, which are modeled after actual ads for memory-enhancing supplements.

"Never misplace your keys again! Use our product and *cure your absentmindedness!*"
The claim that this product is a cure is extraordinary. What kind of evidence is needed to support this claim?

"*Scientifically proven* to improve your memory."
The claim talks of "proof" yet scientific knowledge is rarely, if ever, conclusive. What information would you need to evaluate whether the studies were conducted properly?

"Our formula is a *synergistic blend of antioxidants, gotu kola, brainy aromatics, amino acids, and specific neurotransmitter nutrients* to help maintain *healthy cellular energy production by promoting healthy mitochondrial function, scavenging free radicals, and promoting blood circulation* to the brain."
We should beware of meaningless "psychobabble" that uses scientific-sounding words that are lacking in substance.

"*75% of Americans are turning to complementary and alternative medicine to* improve their memory—by taking our all-natural memory enhancers you can be one of them."
Does the claim that a large portion of Americans use complementary and alternative medicines mean this product is effective? Why or why not?

order food, wait while your food is prepared, eat the food, get the check, and pay for the food before leaving. And don't forget the tip! There's even a standard sequence in ordering, at least in U.S. culture. We order drinks first, followed by appetizers, soup or salad, entrees, and finally dessert and coffee.

Schemas serve a valuable function: They equip us with frames of reference for interpreting new situations. Without schemas, we'd find some information almost impossible to comprehend. Read the following paragraph (Bransford & Johnson, 1972, p. 719), to see if you can figure out what it's describing. But be sure not to turn the page upside down before you do.

> If the balloons popped, the sound would not be able to carry since everything would be too far away from the correct floor. A closed window would also prevent the sound from carrying since most buildings tend to be well insulated. Since the whole operation depends on a steady flow of electricity, a break in the middle of the wire would also cause problems. Of course the fellow could shout, but the human voice is not loud enough to carry that far. An additional problem is that a string could break on the instrument. Then there could be no accompaniment to the message. It is clear that the best situation would involve less distance. Then there would be fewer potential problems. With face-to-face contact, the least number of things could go wrong.

Okay, do you have any clue what this is all about? Almost certainly, you were unable to make heads or tails of it. Now turn the page upside down and look at **FIGURE 7.12**. Does it make any more sense now? Indeed, when John Bransford and Meriette Johnson (1972) showed a very similar drawing to participants before reading them this passage, participants understood the story better and remembered more of it than did those who hadn't seen this drawing. The drawing enhances memory, because it provides us with a schema for interpreting a story that's otherwise virtually impossible to understand.

SCHEMAS AND MEMORY MISTAKES. Valuable as they are, schemas can sometimes create problems for us, because they can lead us to remember things that never happened. Schemas simplify, which is good because they help to make sense of the world. But schemas sometimes *oversimplify,* which is bad because they can produce memory illusions. Schemas provide one key explanation for the paradox of memory: They enhance memory in some cases, but lead to memory errors in others.

For example, Mark Snyder and Seymour Uranowitz (1978) presented participants with a case study of the life of a woman, Betty K. After reading this case study, some participants learned that Betty was now living a heterosexual lifestyle, others that she was living a homosexual lifestyle. Snyder and Uranowitz then gave subjects a recognition test for the details in the passage. They found that participants distorted their memories of the original information, such as her relationship with her father and past dating habits, to be in line with their schema—their beliefs about her current lifestyle. For example, participants who believed Betty to be homosexual mistakenly recalled her never having dated men in high school. If we're not careful, our schemas can lead us to overgeneralize, painting all members of a category with the same broad brush (see Chapter 13).

■ Retrieval: Heading for the "Stacks"

To remember something, we need to fetch it from our long-term memory banks. This is **retrieval**, the third and final process of memory. Yet, as we mentioned earlier, this is where our metaphor of a library begins to break down, because what we retrieve from our memory often doesn't match what we put into it. Our memories are reconstructive, often transforming our recollections to fit our beliefs and expectations.

Many types of forgetting result from failures of retrieval: Our memories are still present, but we can't access them. It's pretty easy to demonstrate this point. If a friend is nearby, try the following demonstration, courtesy of psychologist Endel Tulving (even if you don't have a friend handy, you can still follow along). Read each category

Our interpretation of ambiguous events in everyday life, like an animated conversation on the street, depends in part on our schemas.

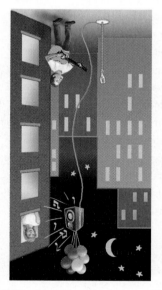

FIGURE 7.12   The Value of Schemas. After reading the passage in the text on this page, turn the page upside down, and take a look at the drawing. Now reread the passage. This drawing makes the point that, without schemas, much of what we read is incomprehensible. (*Source:* Adapted from Bransford & Johnson, 1972)

retrieval
reactivation or reconstruction of experiences from our memory stores

TABLE 7.1 Demonstration of Retrieval Cues. Find a friend and read each category, followed by the word that goes along with it. Then, ask your friend to recall only the words, in any order. For each word your friend forgot, ask whether he or she remembers something from that word's category. As you'll see, this demonstration helps to make a simple point: Many memory failures are actually failures of retrieval.

CATEGORY	WORD
A metal	Silver
A precious stone	Pearl
A relative	Niece
A bird	Canary
Type of reading material	Journal
A military title	Major
A color	Violet
A four-legged animal	Mouse
A piece of furniture	Dresser
A part of the body	Finger
A fruit	Cherry
A weapon	Cannon
A type of dwelling	Mansion
An alcoholic beverage	Brandy
A crime	Kidnapping
An occupation	Plumber
A sport	Lacrosse
An article of clothing	Sweater
A musical instrument	Saxophone
An insect	Wasp

retrieval cue
hint that makes it easier for us to recall information

recall
generating previously remembered information

recognition
selecting previously remembered information from an array of options

relearning
reacquiring knowledge that we'd previously learned but largely forgotten over time

[handwritten margin notes: "writing an essay on the..."; "the multiple choice"]

FIGURE 7.13 Ebbinghaus's Curve of Forgetting. This graph from Ebbinghaus' classic memory research shows the percent "savings," or how much faster information he relearned the second time following various delays (plotted in hours).

in **TABLE 7.1** to your friend, followed by the word that goes along with it. Tell your friend that after you're done reading all of the categories and their corresponding words, you'll ask him or her to recall just the words—in any order—not the categories.

After you read the list to your friend, ask him or her to take a few minutes to write down as many words as he or she can remember. Almost certainly, your friend missed some of them. For those missing words, prompt your friend with the category. So if your friend missed *Finger,* ask, "Do you remember the word that went with 'A part of the body'?" You'll probably find that these prompts help your friend to remember some of the forgotten words. In psychological lingo, the category names serve as **retrieval cues**: hints that make it easier for us to recall information. So your friend's long-term memory contained these missing words, but he or she needed the retrieval cues to remember them.

MEASURING MEMORY. Psychologists assess people's memory in three major ways: recall, recognition, and relearning. Think of them as the three Rs (another mnemonic device, by the way).

Recall and Recognition. What kind of exam do you find the toughest: essay or multiple choice? For sure, we've all taken multiple-choice tests that are "killers." Still, all else being equal, essay tests are usually harder than multiple-choice tests. That's because **recall**, that is, generating previously remembered information on our own, tends to be more difficult than **recognition**, selecting previously remembered information from an array of options (Bahrick, Bahrick, & Wittlinger, 1975). To demonstrate what we mean, try recalling the sixth president of the United States. Unless you're an American history buff, you may be stumped. If so, try this question instead.

The sixth president of the United States was:

(a) George Washington   (c) Barack Obama
(b) John Quincy Adams   (d) Sarah Palin

With a bit of thought, you probably figured out that (b) was the correct answer. You could safely eliminate (a) because you know George Washington was the first president, (c) because you know Barack Obama is the current president, and (d) because you know Sarah Palin hasn't been president. Moreover, you may well have recognized John Quincy Adams as an early U.S. president, even if you didn't know he was number six.

Why is recall usually harder than recognition? In part, it's because recalling an item requires two steps—generating an answer and then determining whether it seems correct—whereas recognizing an item takes only one step: determining which item from a list seems most correct (Haist, Shimamura, & Squire, 1992).

Relearning. A third way of measuring memory is **relearning**: how much more quickly we learn information when we study something we've already studied relative to when we studied it the first time. For this reason, psychologists often call this approach the method of *savings:* Now that we've studied something, we don't need to take as much time to refresh our memories of it (that is, we've "saved" time by studying it).

The concept of relearning originated with the pioneering work of German researcher Hermann Ebbinghaus (1885) well over a century ago. Ebbinghaus used hundreds of "nonsense syllables," like ZAK and BOL, to test his own recollection across differing time intervals. As we can see in **FIGURE 7.13**, he found that most of

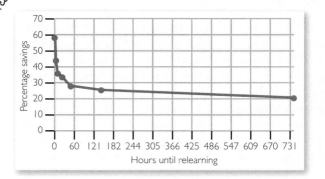

our forgetting occurs almost immediately after learning new material, with less and less forgetting after that. However, he also found that when he attempted to relearn the nonsense syllables he'd forgotten after a delay, he learned them much more quickly the second time around.

Imagine you learned to play the guitar in high school but haven't played it for several years. When you sit down to strum an old song, you're rusty at first. Although you need to go back to your notes to remind yourself the first couple of times you sit down to play, you'll probably find that it doesn't take you nearly as long to get the hang of the song the second time around. That's relearning. Relearning shows that a memory for this skill was still lurking in your brain—somewhere.

Relearning is a more sensitive measure of memory than either recall or recognition. That's because relearning allows us to assess memory using a relative amount (how much faster was material learned the second time?) rather than the simple "right" or "wrong" we obtain from recall or recognition (Nelson, 1985). It also allows us to measure memory for procedures, like driving a car or playing a piano piece, as well as for facts and figures.

When memorizing his nonsense syllables, Ebbinghaus happened on a crucial principle that applies to most forms of learning: the law of **distributed versus massed practice** (Donovan & Radosevich, 1999; Willingham, 2002). Simply put, this law tells us that we tend to remember things better in the long run when we spread our learning over long intervals than when we pack it into short intervals. This principle is probably one of the best-replicated effects in all of psychology (Cepeda et al., 2006). Even infants show it (Cornell, 1980). ◉⎯**Watch**

Herein lies another word to the wise. Cramming for an exam helps us remember the information for *that exam*, but it typically produces poor long-term retention. If you want to master the information in your psychology course—or any course, for that matter—you should spread out your review of the material over long intervals. So, when one of your teachers nags you to "start studying at least a week before the exam rather than waiting until the last minute," you have Ebbinghaus to thank—or blame.

A final studying hint is to test yourself frequently on the material you've read. Indeed, research shows that although most students believe that repeatedly studying material is more helpful than repeated testing, they're wrong. Studying helps retention in the short-run, but self-testing helps in the long-run (Karpicke & Roediger, 2008; Roediger & Karpicke, 2006). So before reading the next paragraph, you might want to pause and give yourself a little quiz on what you've just read! **TABLE 7.2** provides a handy list of studying pointers based on several memory concepts introduced in this chapter.

◉⎯**Watch** the Cramming video on **mypsychlab.com**

replicability

◀ **CAN THE RESULTS BE DUPLICATED IN OTHER STUDIES?**

TABLE 7.2 Helpful Study Hints Derived from Memory Research.

MEMORY CONCEPT	POINTER
(1) Distributed versus massed study	Spread your study time out—review your notes and textbook in increments rather than cramming.
(2) Testing effect	Test yourself frequently on the material you've read.
(3) Elaborative rehearsal	Connect new knowledge with existing knowledge rather than simply memorizing facts or names.
(4) Levels of processing	Work to process ideas deeply and meaningfully—avoid writing notes down word for word from instructors' lectures or slides. Try to capture the information in your own words.
(5) Mnemonic devices	The more reminders or cues you can connect from your knowledge base to new material, the more likely you are to recall new material when tested.

Psychological research demonstrates that testing oneself frequently on the material one has just read is a good way of enhancing long-term retention—even better than repeated studying.

distributed versus massed practice
studying information in small increments over time (distributed) versus in large increments over a brief amount of time (massed)

TABLE 7.3 TOT Phenomenon. First try to come up with the capital of each state. Then, return to the text for some hints. (Answers are located upside-down at the bottom of the page)

STATE	CAPITAL
Georgia	
Wisconsin	
California	
Louisiana	
Florida	
Colorado	
New Jersey	
Arizona	
Nebraska	
Kentucky	

FACTOID +

TOT occurs in those who use sign language as well as spoken language; psychologists call this the *tip-of-the-fingers* phenomenon. Deaf signers who are unable to retrieve the names of fairly famous people but feel that they're on the verge of remembering can depict at least some part of the famous person's name with their fingers about 80 percent of the time (Thompson, Emmorey, & Gollan, 2005).

FIGURE 7.14 Research Shows That the Word Learning of Scuba Divers Depends on Context. If the divers learned words underwater, they recalled them best when underwater again.

replicability

CAN THE RESULTS BE DUPLICATED IN OTHER STUDIES?

TIP-OF-THE-TONGUE PHENOMENON. We've all experienced retrieval failure in the form of the frustrating **tip-of-the-tongue (TOT) phenomenon**, in which we're sure we know the answer to a question, but can't come up with it (Brown, 1991; Ecke, 2009; Schwartz, 1999). It's surprisingly easy to generate this phenomenon (Baddeley, 1993). Read the names of the 10 U.S. states in **TABLE 7.3**, and try to name their capital cities. Now focus on the states for which you're *unsure* of whether you know the right answer, and keep trying. If you're still stuck, look at the list that follows, which gives you the first letter of the capital of each state: Georgia (A), Wisconsin (M), California (S), Louisiana (B), Florida (T), Colorado (D), New Jersey (T), Arizona (P), Nebraska (L), and Kentucky (F).

Did the first letters help? Research shows when we experience the TOT phenomenon, they often will. The fact that we sometimes experience TOT tells us that there's a difference between something we've forgotten because it didn't get *stored* in memory and something that's in there somewhere that we can't quite *retrieve*.

Two investigators showed that when people believe that something is on the tip of their tongues, they're frequently right (Brown & McNeill, 1966). They presented subjects with the definitions of relatively rare words (such as "to give up the throne") and asked them to come up with the word (in this case, *abdicate*). About 10 percent of the time, subjects reported a TOT experience; they were pretty sure they "knew" the word, but couldn't generate it. In these cases, the researchers asked participants to guess the first letter of the word or the number of syllables in it. Interestingly, the participants did much better than chance. So subjects *did* know something about the word; they just couldn't spit it out whole.

ENCODING SPECIFICITY: FINDING THINGS WHERE WE LEFT THEM. Why is it easier to retrieve some things from memory than others? One answer to this mystery lies in the principle of **encoding specificity** introduced by Endel Tulving (1982; Tulving & Thompson, 1973). We're more likely to remember something when the conditions present at the time we encoded it are also present at retrieval. We can see this principle at work in several psychological phenomena, two of which we'll examine here: context-dependent learning and state-dependent learning.

Context-Dependent Learning. Context-dependent learning refers to superior retrieval when the external context of the original memories matches the retrieval context. Duncan Godden and Alan Baddeley (1975) provided an example of this effect in an inge-

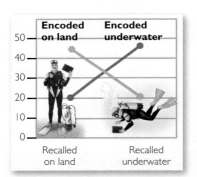

nious study of scuba divers. They presented divers with 40 unrelated words while the divers were either standing on the beach or submerged in about 15 feet of water. Godden and Baddeley then tested the divers in either the same or a different context from which they originally presented the words. The divers' memory was best when the original context matched the retrieval context, regardless of whether they were on land or underwater, as shown in **FIGURE 7.14**.

There's even evidence for context-dependent learning when undergraduates take exams. Students tend to do slightly better on their exams when tested in the same classroom in which they learned the material (Smith, 1979). You may want to gently remind your introductory psychology instructor of this fact when he or she schedules the room for your next test. Still, this effect isn't all that powerful, and not all researchers have replicated it (Saufley, Otaka, & Bavaresco, 1985). That's probably because you've acquired the information not only in the classroom but in other settings, such as the room in which you're now reading this textbook.

State-Dependent Learning. Despite its name, state-dependent learning doesn't mean that if you learned something while on vacation in Montana, you need to go back to Montana to recall it. Instead, state-dependent learning is similar to context-dependent learning, except that it refers to the internal "state" of the organism rather than the external context. That is, **state-dependent learning** refers to superior retrieval of memories when the organism is in the same physiological or psychological state as it was during encoding.

There's anecdotal evidence for this phenomenon among alcoholics, who often report that they need to get drunk to locate items—including their favorite bottles of liquor—that they'd hidden while drinking (Goodwin, 1995). Of course, we've learned that anecdotes are limited as sources of scientific evidence (see Chapter 2). However, in this case, controlled studies bear out the anecdotes: People who've learned a task while under the influence of alcohol tend to remember it better when under the influence than when sober (Goodwin et al., 1969). Still, researchers haven't always replicated these findings (Lisman, 1974), suggesting that state-dependent effects probably depend in complex ways on the participants tested and stimuli administered.

State-dependent learning sometimes extends to mood, in which case it's termed *mood-dependent learning* (Bower, 1981). Studies show that most people find it easier to recall unpleasant memories than pleasant ones when they're sad, and easier to recall pleasant memories than unpleasant ones when they're happy (Guenther, 1998; Nelson & Craighead, 1977).

Mood-dependent learning can create nasty difficulties for researchers who want to draw conclusions about people's life histories. Specifically, it can result in a *retrospective bias:* Our current psychological state can distort memories of our past (Dawes, 1988; Ross, 1989; Taylor, Russ-Eft, & Taylor, 2009). For example, most individuals with clinical depression report having been treated more harshly by their parents in childhood than do individuals without clinical depression. One explanation for this finding is that harsh parental treatment predisposes to later depression. But there's another explanation: Perhaps people's bad moods distort their memories of their childhoods.

To evaluate this possibility, researchers asked three groups of participants—(1) people who had clinical depression, (2) people who had a history of depression but weren't currently depressed, and (3) people who'd never been depressed—about how their parents treated them as children. Currently depressed participants recalled their parents as having been more rejecting and domineering toward them as children than did participants in the other two groups (Lewinsohn & Rosenbaum, 1987). So participants' moods seem to have influenced their evaluations of how their parents had treated them. In this case, we don't know whether the subjects with clinical depression were less *accurate* than the participants in the other groups, only that their memories were different (although as we'll learn in Chapter 15, mildly—but not severely—depressed people may sometimes be *more* accurate in their memories than nondepressed people).

> ◀ **replicability**
> CAN THE RESULTS BE
> DUPLICATED IN OTHER STUDIES?

> ◀ **ruling out rival hypotheses**
> HAVE IMPORTANT ALTERNATIVE EXPLANATIONS
> FOR THE FINDINGS BEEN EXCLUDED?

---

assess your knowledge   FACT OR FICTION?

✓● Study and Review on mypsychlab.com

1. We encode virtually all of our life experiences, even though we can't retrieve more than a tiny proportion of them. **True / False**

2. We need to practice mnemonics to use them successfully. **True / False**

3. Schemas only distort memories, but don't enhance them. **True / False**

4. In general, recall is more difficult than recognition. **True / False**

5. Cramming for exams, although stressful, is actually a good strategy for enhancing long-term recall of material. **True / False**

Answers: 1. F (p. 255); 2. T (p. 256); 3. F (p. 259); 4. T (p. 260); 5. F (p. 261)

THE BIOLOGY OF MEMORY

7.8 Describe the role of long-term potentiation in memory.

7.9 Distinguish different types of amnesia and the relevance of amnesia to the brain's organization of memory.

7.10 Identify the key impairments of Alzheimer's disease.

Although few of us think about it, the biology of memory plays a pivotal role in our daily lives, whether it's remembering where we left our keys or the name of that friendly person we met at last night's party. What's more, understanding how our brains store memory may help us find ways of treating devastating diseases that impair our ability to recall everyday events.

tip-of-the-tongue (TOT) phenomenon
experience of knowing that we know something but being unable to access it

encoding specificity
phenomenon of remembering something better when the conditions under which we retrieve information are similar to the conditions under which we encoded it

context-dependent learning
superior retrieval of memories when the external context of the original memories matches the retrieval context

state-dependent learning
superior retrieval of memories when the organism is in the same physiological or psychological state as it was during encoding

ruling out rival hypotheses

HAVE IMPORTANT ALTERNATIVE EXPLANATIONS FOR THE FINDINGS BEEN EXCLUDED?

long-term potentiation (LTP)
gradual strengthening of the connections among neurons from repetitive stimulation

correlation vs. causation

CAN WE BE SURE THAT A CAUSES B?

■ The Neural Basis of Memory Storage

Locating where a library book is stored is generally pretty easy. We look it up in our library's computer system, write down its number, go to the shelf, and—unless someone's recently plucked it away—find it. If we're lucky, it's right there on the shelf where it's supposed to be. Yet as we'll soon see, memory storage in the brain isn't quite this cut and dry.

THE ELUSIVE ENGRAM. Beginning in the 1920s, psychologist Karl Lashley went in search of the *engram*: the physical trace of each memory in the brain (see Chapter 6). He taught rats how to run mazes, and lesioned different parts of their brains to see if they forgot how to find their way. By doing so, Lashley hoped to discover where memory is stored in the brain. Yet after years of painstaking work, he came up empty-handed.

Still, Lashley learned two important things. First, the more brain he removed, the worse the rat performed on the maze: There's no great surprise there. Second, no matter where he removed brain tissue, the rats retained at least some memory of the maze (Lashley, 1929). Even removing up to half of the rat's cortex didn't erase the memory. These findings led Lashley to conclude that we can't simply point to a spot in the brain and say, "There's the memory of my first kiss," because that memory isn't located in a single place, like a library book sitting on a shelf. Instead, as scientists have since learned, memories of different features of experiences, like their sound, sight, and smell, are almost certainly stored in different brain regions (see Chapter 3).

Over a half century ago, Donald Hebb (1949) suggested that the engram is instead located in *assemblies* (organized groups) of neurons in the brain. According to Hebb, one neuron (A) becomes connected to another neuron (B) when it repeatedly activates that neuron. As we learned in Chapter 3, neurons, fed by a rich blend of neurotransmitters, form circuits, integrate sensory information in meaningful ways, and transform our experience of the world into lasting, perhaps even lifelong, memories.

LONG-TERM POTENTIATION—A PHYSIOLOGICAL BASIS FOR MEMORY. As we learned also in Chapter 3, **long-term potentiation (LTP)** refers to a gradual strengthening of the connections among neurons by repetitive stimulation over time (Abrari et al., 2009; Bliss, Collingridge, & Morris, 2004). Terje Lomo first observed LTP in the hippocampus of rabbits in 1966, and researchers have since identified it in the hippocampus and other brain structures of humans and other mammals. The gist of what neuroscientists have learned since the discovery of LTP is that neurons that "fire together wire together" (Malenka & Nicoll, 1999). To a large extent, Hebb was right.

Today, many researchers believe that our ability to store memories depends on strengthening the connections among neurons arranged in sprawling networks that extend to the far and deep recesses of our brains (Shors & Matzels, 1999). The question of whether LTP is directly responsible for the storage of memories, or whether it affects learning indirectly by increasing arousal and attention, remains unresolved (Shors & Matzel, 1999). Still, most scientists agree that LTP plays a key role in learning, and that the hippocampus plays a key role in forming lasting memories.

LTP and the Hippocampus. To tell what cells are responsible for LTP, many researchers use thin slices of the hippocampus (Kandel, Schwartz, & Jessell, 2000). These slices come from young animals, usually rats or mice, and are bathed in solutions containing nutrients that keep the tissue alive. In a typical LTP experiment, researchers first establish how hippocampal cells respond at baseline. This is much like determining how we respond to someone asking us a question. Researchers then apply a strong stimulus, much like having someone yell at us. After the strong stimulus, hippocampal neurons respond at an enhanced level to ordinary stimuli, much as we might respond to a neutral question with a louder voice than usual after someone yelled at us. That's LTP.

Like the hippocampus, the amygdala and parts of the association cortex (see Chapter 3) exhibit LTP-like activity. Moreover, there's an LTP-like response in the amygdala following the creation of a fear memory (Maren, 2005; Sigurdsson et al., 2007). These results establish LTP-like activity as a correlate of memory, but don't demonstrate that LTP serves as the basis of memory.

LTP and Glutamate. LTP tends to occur at synapses where the sending neuron releases the neurotransmitter glutamate into the synaptic cleft—the space between the sending and receiving neuron (see Chapter 3). As shown in **FIGURE 7.15**, glutamate interacts with receptors for NMDA and another substance (AMPA). LTP enhances the release of glutamate into the synaptic cleft, resulting in enhanced learning (Lisman & Raghavachari, 2007). Joe Tsien and his colleagues were even able to create a "smart mouse" (called the "Doogie mouse" after *Doogie Howser, M.D.* a television show based on a brilliant teenage doctor) by manipulating its genes to create extra receptors for NMDA. Compared with everyday mice, the Doogie mouse is an especially quick and effective learner (Lee & Silva, 2009; Tsien, 2000).

■ Where is Memory Stored?

Clearly, the hippocampus is critical to memory. As we saw in Chapter 4, some researchers have even identified neurons in the hippocampus that fire in response only to certain celebrities, such as actress Halle Berry (Quiroga et al., 2005). (See **FIGURE 7.16**.)

But is the hippocampus, or any single brain structure, the site of the elusive engram? We can say with some certainty that the answer is no. fMRI studies reveal that learned information isn't stored permanently in the hippocampus itself. Rather, the prefrontal cortex seems to be one of the major "banks" from which we withdraw our memories (Zeinah et al., 2003). But as Lashley discovered, damage to isolated areas of the prefrontal cortex—or other cortical regions, for that matter—doesn't wipe out long-established memories. Much as the smell of a rose diffuses throughout a room, our memories distribute themselves throughout many areas of the cortex.

AMNESIA—BIOLOGICAL BASES OF EXPLICIT AND IMPLICIT MEMORY. Earlier we learned about explicit and implicit memory. Research demonstrates that two forms of memory are governed largely by different brain systems (Squire, 1987; Voss & Paller, 2008). The best evidence comes from individuals with severe amnesia. The two most common types of amnesia are **retrograde amnesia**, in which we lose some memories of our past, and **anterograde amnesia**, in which we lose the capacity to form new memories.

Amnesia Myths. The general public holds a host of misconceptions about amnesia. Perhaps the most prevalent myth is that many people with amnesia have lost all memories of their previous life, even of who they are. In fact, such *generalized amnesia* is exceedingly rare (American Psychiatric Association [APA], 2000), although it's a favorite plot device of Hollywood moviemakers (Baxendale, 2004). Another myth, also perpetuated by Hollywood, is that memory recovery from amnesia is usually abrupt. Although sudden recoveries from amnesia make for good drama, they don't make for good science. In fact, memory recovery from amnesia tends to occur gradually, if at all (APA, 2000). A final myth is that most people with amnesia suffer primarily from retrograde amnesia (Lilienfeld et al., 2010); in fact, anterograde amnesia is a far more common and troubling problem.

Case Studies of Amnesia: H.M. and Clive Wearing. By far the best-known person with amnesia in the psychological literature was a man from Connecticut known only by the initials of H.M., who suffered from severe

The 2000 film *Memento* offers a largely accurate portrayal of an individual with virtually complete anterograde amnesia stemming from an accident. The main character in the movie tattooed numerous messages on his body in a desperate effort to remind himself of his pre-amnesia life. In reality, such messages rarely help people with anterograde amnesia, because they usually don't remember to look at them.

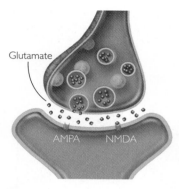

FIGURE 7.15 Neural Basis of Long-Term Potentiation. LTP enhances the release of glutamate and activates postsynaptic receptors for NMDA and AMPA.

FIGURE 7.16 Halle Berry Neuron. Scientists have discovered cells in the human hippocampus that respond preferentially to actress Halle Berry, including when she's dressed as Catwoman and even to her name (see *top row*). These cells don't respond to other celebrities or other beautiful women (see *bottom row*). The graphs below each figure show the firing rates of the neuron to the picture above it. (*Source:* Quiroga et al., 2005)

retrograde amnesia
loss of memories from our past

anterograde amnesia
inability to encode new memories from our experiences

epileptic seizures that his doctors couldn't control with medication. In March 1953, in a last-ditch attempt to eliminate these seizures, surgeons removed large chunks of H.M.'s temporal lobes, including both his left and right hippocampi, where they had reason to believe the seizures originated. (The surgeons of the time didn't anticipate the disastrous impact of this radical operation, which would probably never be performed today.) At the time, H.M. was 26 years old. Following the operation, H.M. developed virtually complete anterograde amnesia: He could recall almost no new information. Although he also experienced some retrograde amnesia for the 11 years prior to the surgery (Corkin, 1984), his memories from the first 15 years of his life remained pretty much intact.

In the decades following his surgery, H.M.'s life was, for all intents and purposes, frozen in time. H.M. himself put it eloquently: "Every day is alone by itself, whatever enjoyment I have had, whatever sorrow I have had." Among other things, he was oblivious to the fact that he had undergone surgery. Two years after the operation, in 1955, he reported the current date as March 1953. H.M. read the same magazines and completed the same jigsaw puzzles over and over again without any awareness of having seen them before. He didn't recall having met physicians whom he met just a few minutes earlier, or remember what he ate for lunch 30 minutes ago (Milner, 1972; Scoville & Milner, 1957). Even when informed repeatedly of the death of his uncle, he showed the same dramatic grief reaction to the news each time (Shimamura, 1992). H.M.'s true identity was revealed as Henry Molaison only after his death in December 2008 at the age of 82. For 55 years, he acquired virtually no new explicit memories.

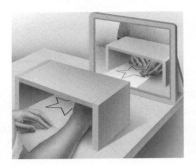

FIGURE 7.17 A Mirror Tracing Task Similar to That Administered to H.M. How well can you draw while looking in a mirror? On this task, used to assess implicit memory, subjects must trace a star while looking only at a mirror.

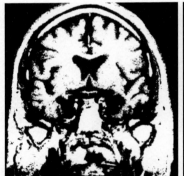

H.M.'s brain damage as imaged in 1997. The scan shows severe damage to his hippocampi and nearby regions. (*Source:* Corkin et al., 1997)

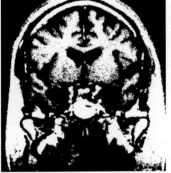

H.M.'s tragic case, like that of Damasio's patient David, illustrates a striking dissociation between explicit and implicit memory. Researchers asked H.M. to trace simple geometrical shapes from a mirror (**FIGURE 7.17**), a task that just about all people find infuriatingly difficult when they first try it. Although H.M. had no recollection of ever having performed this task before, his performance improved steadily over time (Milner, 1964, 1965). So although H.M. had no explicit memory for this task, he displayed clear-cut implicit—specifically, procedural—memory for it.

When researchers examined H.M.'s brain using imaging techniques, they found that not only his hippocampus but his surrounding cortex and neighboring amygdala (see Chapter 3) were damaged (Corkin et al., 1997). This finding and others led researchers to hypothesize that large circuits connecting different parts of the limbic system, including the hippocampus, and amygdala, are critical to memory (see **FIGURE 7.18**).

Similar evidence for a distinction between explicit and implicit memory comes from the case of Clive Wearing, a former music producer in Great Britain whose hippocampi (along with several other brain structures) were destroyed by a herpes virus in 1985 (D. Wearing, 2005). Like H.M., Clive has virtually complete anterograde amnesia. When his wife leaves the room for a few minutes and returns, he showers her with immense affection, as though he hasn't seen her in years. Yet Clive shows implicit memory in the form of priming effects. When his wife says "St. Mary's," he quickly responds "Padding-ton," entirely oblivious of why he says that. The name of the hospital to which Clive Wearing was taken after his viral infection was—you guessed it—St. Mary's Paddington (D. Wearing, 2005). The bottom line: Damage to the hippocampus impairs explicit memory, but leaves implicit memory intact.

EMOTIONAL MEMORY. We usually think of memory as our good friend, as a lifelong companion that helps us to store useful information, allowing us to cope with our environment. Yet our memories can also bring us distress, as in the case of a 53-year-old woman who reported olfactory (smell) memories tracking back to a brutal gang rape decades earlier (Vermetten & Bremner, 2003). Olfactory hallucinations of leather, alcohol, and the aftershave "Old Spice"—all of which were present at the rape scene—triggered intense fear responses that led her to retreat to a closet and engage in self-destructive behavior.

The Role of the Amygdala The amygdala is where the emotional components of these and other memories, especially those governing fear, are stored. The amygdala interacts with the hippocampus during the formation of memory, but each structure contributes slightly different information (refer again to Figure 7.18). Researchers uncovered the specific roles of the amygdala and hippocampus in a study of two patients identified by their initials, S.M. and W.S. The first suffered damage to the amygdala, the second to the hippocampus (LeBar & Phelps, 2005). The patient with amygdala damage (S.M.) remembered facts about the fear-producing experience, but not the fear. In contrast, the patient with hippocampal damage (W.S.) remembered the fear, but not the facts about the fear-producing experience. So the amygdala and hippocampus play distinctive roles in memory, with the amygdala helping us recall the emotions associated with fear-provoking events and the hippocampus helping us recall the events themselves (Marschner et al., 2008).

Erasing Painful Memories What if it were possible to erase or take the sting out of traumatic or painful memories, like witnessing someone's death or experiencing the devastating break-up of a relationship? This question raises some fascinating ethical issues: Is erasing all traces of pain in life always a good thing? Or is emotional suffering instead an essential part of being human? These questions have taken on new urgency with the discovery of a drug that appears to block the formation of traumatic memories.

As we've learned, emotional memories can persist, even if they often become distorted over time. The hormones adrenaline and norepinephrine (see Chapter 3) are released in the face of stress and stimulate protein (beta-adrenergic) receptors on nerve cells, which solidify emotional memories.

Lawrence Cahill and James McGaugh (1995) demonstrated the staying power of emotional memories in an elegant study. They created two stories regarding 12 slides they showed to participants. They told half of the participants an emotionally neutral story about a boy's visit to a hospital where his father works. They told the other half a far more disturbing story about the same slides; in the middle of the story, they informed participants that the boy was injured and operated on at a hospital to reattach his severed legs. Participants returned for a memory test 24 hours later, and Cahill and McGaugh asked them what they remembered about the slides. Participants who heard the emotionally arousing story displayed the best recall for the part of the story about the boy's trauma. In contrast, participants who heard the neutral story recalled the same amount of detail for all parts of the story.

Cahill and McGaugh (Cahill et al., 1994) repeated this experiment with an interesting twist. This time, they gave some participants a drug called *propranolol*, which blocks the effects of adrenaline on beta-adrenergic receptors (doctors also use it to treat high blood pressure). When participants' adrenaline was inhibited by propranolol, they didn't display especially good recall for the emotionally arousing part of the story. In fact, their recall was no different from that of individuals who listened to the emotionally neutral story.

Psychiatrist Roger Pitman reasoned that propranolol might blunt the memories of real-life traumas, such as automobile accidents. Pitman and his colleagues (Pitman et al., 2002) administered propranolol to people for 10 days after they experienced a traumatic event, such as a car accident and, a month later, examined their physical reactions to individually prepared tapes that replayed key aspects of the event. Forty-three percent of participants who received a placebo showed a physical response to the tape that re-created their traumatic experience. Yet none of the people who received the drug did.

Pitman's pill only dampened the effects of traumatic memories; it didn't erase them. These findings have been replicated by other investigators using different designs (Kindt, Soeter, & Vervliet, 2009). Still, this research hasn't laid to rest questions about whether such procedures are ethical, much less desirable. After all, if we could choose to forget every negative experience, would be learn and grow from our mistakes? The mere fact that we *can* do something doesn't mean we *should*, so the debate continues.

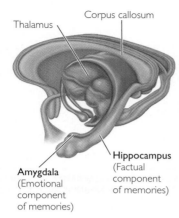

FIGURE 7.18 Emotional Memories and the Brain. Research suggests that the amygdala helps us recall the fear associated with scary experiences, and the hippocampus helps us recall the experiences themselves. (*Source:* Adapted from Kalat, 2007)

replicability

CAN THE RESULTS BE
DUPLICATED IN OTHER STUDIES?

■ The Biology of Memory Deterioration

As we humans pass the ripe old age of 65 years, we usually begin to experience memory problems and some degeneration in the brain. Yet despite what many people believe (Lilienfeld et al., 2010), senility isn't an unavoidable part of aging, and some manage to make it past 100 with only modest amounts of everyday forgetfulness. But scientists disagree as to how much memory loss is "normal" during the advanced years. Some argue that we needn't accept any memory impairment as normal. Nevertheless, a longitudinal study of subjects aged 59 to 84 years at baseline showed small but consistent reductions in the overall area of the cortex at two-year and four-year intervals (Resnick et al., 2003). We might assume that subtle cognitive decline would accompany these tissue losses, but alternative hypotheses are possible. For example, cognition may be fully preserved until a critical amount of tissue loss occurs.

Many people equate senility with one cause: Alzheimer's disease. Yet Alzheimer's disease is only the most frequent cause of senility, accounting for about 50 to 60 percent of cases of *dementia,* that is, severe memory loss (another common cause of senility is the accumulation of multiple strokes in the brain). Alzheimer's disease occurs at alarming rates as people age—one American develops Alzheimer's disease every 72 seconds (Alzheimer's Disease Facts and Fictions, 2007). The risk for Alzheimer's disease is 13 percent for those over 65 years of age, but a whopping 42 percent for those over 85 years of age. The cognitive impairments of Alzheimer's disease are both memory and language related, which corresponds to the patterns of cortical loss in this illness (see **FIGURE 7.19**). The memory loss begins with recent events, with memories of the distant past being the last to go. Alzheimer's patients forget their grandchildren's names well before forgetting their children's names. Alzheimer's disease patients also experience disorientation and are frequently at a loss as to where they are, what year it is, or who the current president is. ◉─│Watch

As we learned in Chapter 3, the Alzheimer's brain contains many senile plaques and neurofibrillary tangles. These abnormalities contribute to the loss of synapses and death of cells in the hippocampus and cerebral cortex. They may also contribute to memory loss and intellectual decline. Loss of synapses is correlated with intellectual status, with greater loss as the disease progresses (Scheff et al., 2007). But this result doesn't necessarily mean that the reduction in synapses causes the memory decline. Along with loss of synapses comes degeneration and death of acetylcholine neurons in the forebrain. Accordingly, the most common treatments for Alzheimer's disease today are drugs that boost the amount of acetylcholine in the brain by inhibiting its breakdown. There are also experimental procedures, such as gene therapies that enhance the production of neurotrophic (growth) factors, which enable acetylcholine neurons to survive and thrive (see Chapter 3). Still other promising medications block the actions of the neuorotransmmitter glutamate (Francis, 2008), which as we learned in Chapter 3 tends to be toxic to neurons in high doses. Yet no treatment to date halts or reverses the course of Alzheimer's disease. At best, these treatments only slow its progression slightly.

For this reason, researchers have evaluated people's lifestyles to see if anything can be done to reduce the risk of Alzheimer's disease. A massive study assessing over 4,000 people over 65 years of age showed that being physically active reduces the risk of cognitive impairment and Alzheimer's disease (Laurin et al., 2001). This large study dovetails with earlier findings from a small, but telling study of 678 nuns who were hard working, active, and had strong social networks. What's most remarkable about these nuns is their advanced ages—ranging from 87 to over 100 years—along with their low inci-

ruling out rival hypotheses

HAVE IMPORTANT ALTERNATIVE EXPLANATIONS FOR THE FINDINGS BEEN EXCLUDED?

FIGURE 7.19 Changes in the Brain of Patients with Alzheimer's Disease.
Changes include enlargement of the ventricles and severe loss of the cortex in areas involved in language and memory. (*Source:* Courtesy of Alzheimer's Disease Research, a program of the American Health Assistance Foundation)

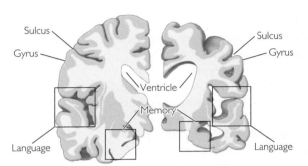

Sulcus

Gyrus

Ventricle

Memory

Language

Sulcus

Gyrus

Language

Normal   Alzheimer's

◉─│**Watch** What Happens with Alzheimer's on **mypsychlab.com**

correlation vs. causation

CAN WE BE SURE THAT A CAUSES B?

In 2001, the year of the *Time* magazine photoessay on the "Nun Study," Sister Ester was 106, the oldest nun in the order. The results of this study suggest that physical and mental activity may protect against memory loss.

dence of cognitive impairment, including Alzheimer's disease (Snowdon, 2003). Numerous other studies suggest that people who are highly educated and intellectually active are at decreased risk of Alzheimer's disease (Ngandu et al., 2007). Admittedly, these correlational findings are ambiguous in their causal direction: Perhaps people who are more mentally and physically fit have more brain capacity to begin with. Yet these findings certainly raise the possibility that the old maxim "use it or lose it" may contain more than a grain of truth (Cracchiolo, Mori, & Nazian, 2007; Wilson et al., 2007).

◀ **correlation vs. causation**

CAN WE BE SURE THAT A CAUSES B?

assess your knowledge   FACT OR FICTION?

✓● **Study** and **Review** on **mypsychlab.com**

1. Long-term potentiation appears to play a key role in learning. **True / False**

2. The hippocampus is the site of the engram. **True / False**

3. Memory recovery from amnesia is usually quite sudden. **True / False**

4. Explicit and implicit memory are controlled by the same brain structure. **True / False**

5. Alzheimer's disease is only one cause of dementia. **True / False**

Answers: 1. T (p. 264); 2. F (p. 265); 3. F (p. 265); 4. F (p. 266); 5. T (p. 268)

THE DEVELOPMENT OF MEMORY: ACQUIRING A PERSONAL HISTORY

7.11   Identify how children's memory abilities change with age.

How early can children remember, and what do they remember? The answer depends on what kind of memory we're discussing. In one sense, we can remember information even before we're born. That's because fetuses display *habituation*—a decrease in attention to familiar stimuli. As we learned in Chapter 6, fetuses as young as 32 weeks exhibit a decline in their reactions to vibratory stimulators over time. Habituation is a form of implicit memory—to interpret a stimulus as familiar, we need to recall we've experienced it before. It's a far cry from explicitly recalling the words to a song or remembering what we wore to our last birthday party, but it's still a form of remembering.

■ Memory over Time

Memory changes as we age, but there's considerable continuity over the course of development. On average, infants have worse memories than children, who have worse memories than adults, and young adults have better memories than older adults. But the same basic processes operate across the life span. For example, infants display a serial position curve just as adults do (Cornell & Bergstrom, 1983; Gulya et al., 2001). Nevertheless, the span of memory and the ability to use strategies increase dramatically across the infant, toddler, preschool, and elementary school years.

Over time, children's memories become increasingly sophisticated. Several factors explain why. First, children's memory spans increase with age (Pascual-Leone, 1989). In fact, their Magic Number doesn't become seven plus or minus two until age 12 or so. If we ask a three-year-old to remember a string of letters or numbers, she'll remember only about three on average. A five-year-old will remember about four. By age nine, children are getting close to the adult's Magic Number, remembering six items on average.

Is this increase in span a result of better use of strategies, like rehearsal? That's certainly part of the story (Flavell, Beach, & Chinsky, 1966; McGilly & Siegler, 1989), but there's a large physical maturational component, too. So in an odd turn of events, shoe size is actually more highly correlated with memory span in children than with either age or intelligence. Nevertheless, we can assure you that this correlation isn't a causal one! Because different children grow at different rates, this correlation reflects a biological maturity component to memory span, for which variables like shoe size or height are the best predictors.

◀ **correlation vs. causation**

CAN WE BE SURE THAT A CAUSES B?

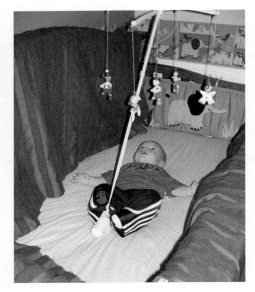

Carolyn Rovee-Collier and other researchers have used mobiles to study infants' implicit memory. Although infants can't tell you they remember the mobiles, their memories "vote with their feet."

? Some people claim to remember their own birth. What well-established psychological phenomenon renders this claim extremely implausible? (See answer upside down on bottom of page.)

meta-memory
knowledge about our own memory abilities and limitations

infantile amnesia
inability of adults to remember personal experiences that took place before an early age

Second, our conceptual understanding increases with age. This fact is important because our ability to chunk related items and store memories in meaningful ways depends on our knowledge of the world. For example, without knowing that "CIA" stands for Central Intelligence Agency, children can't chunk the letters C, I, and A into one unit.

Third, over time children develop enhanced **meta-memory** skills: knowledge about their memory abilities and limitations. These skills help children to identify when they need to use strategies to improve their memories, as well as which strategies work best (Schneider, 2008; Schneider & Bjorklund, 1998; Weinert, 1989; Zabrucky & Ratner, 1986). If we show a four-year-old 10 pictures and ask her how many she thinks she can remember, she'll probably tell you with supreme confidence that she can remember all 10. She can't. Children at this age don't appreciate their own memory limitations and overestimate their capacities as a result. Older children, who actually remember *more* than younger children, estimate they'll remember *less*. As a result, they're more accurate in their ability to gauge their recall (Flavell, Friedrichs, & Hoyt, 1970).

■ Infants' Implicit Memory: Talking with their Feet

Carolyn Rovee-Collier developed an innovative technique to study infants' implicit memory. Her research capitalizes on the fact that we can operantly condition (see Chapter 6) infants to perform specific behaviors. Rovee-Collier placed infants in a crib with a mobile positioned over their heads. She first watched their behaviors for a few minutes to assess their activity levels in a "baseline" condition. Then, she took a ribbon tied to the mobile and attached it to the infant's ankle. The next time the infant kicked her foot, she was in for a pleasant surprise: The mobile shook and jiggled in response. Infants find the motion of the mobile inherently reinforcing. Because the movement is dependent on infants' behavior, they quickly become conditioned to kick their legs to get the mobile moving.

Once she conditioned infants to kick their legs in response to the mobile, Rovee-Collier sent them home. Then, after a delay—of a day, a week, or even a month—she brought them back to the lab and placed them in the crib again. This time, the mobile wasn't attached to the infant's leg, so there was no reinforcement. The question was: Would infants show an increased kicking rate in response to seeing the mobile? If so, it would imply that they remembered the conditioning experience.

Rovee-Collier (1993) found that children as young as two months retained a memory of this experience, although they forgot it after just a few days. Nevertheless, their span of recall increased quickly. Three-month-olds could remember the conditioning for over a week, and six-month-olds for over two weeks. Infants' memories of the experience were surprisingly specific. If researchers modified even a few elements of the mobile or changed the pattern of the crib liner ever so slightly, infants didn't seem to recognize the mobile: Their kicking rate returned to baseline.

■ Infantile Amnesia

Take a brief break from reading this chapter, and try to recall your earliest memory. What was it, and how old were you? Most students say their earliest memory falls somewhere between three and five years of age. **Infantile amnesia** is the inability of adults to retrieve accurate memories before an early age (Malinoski, Lynn, & Sivec, 1998; Wetzler & Sweeney, 1986).

Few, if any, of us correctly recall events before two or three years of age, the lowest cutoff for infantile amnesia (West & Bauer, 1999; Winograd & Killinger, 1983). Memories before that age just aren't trustworthy. So if you have a distinct memory of something that happened at age one or before, it's almost certainly either a false memory or a true memory of something that happened later.

Recent research suggests that culture may shape the age and content of our first memories. European Americans report earlier first memories than do people from Taiwan. Moreover, European Americans' earliest memories more often focus on themselves, whereas Taiwanese's earliest memories more often focus on others (Wang, 2006). These findings dovetail with research we'll describe later in the text (see Chapter 10) showing that European American cultures tend to be individually oriented, whereas many Asian cultures tend to be other-oriented (Lehman, Chiu, & Schaller, 2004).

INFANTILE AMNESIA AND POP PSYCHOLOGY. Proponents of some fringe psychological treatments have largely ignored the scientific evidence concerning infantile amnesia. Many advocates of hypnotic age regression, which Nadean Cool's therapist used, claim to be able to retrieve memories from well before age two, sometimes even before birth (Nash, 1987). At least one therapist even tried to recover his female client's memory of being trapped as an egg in her mother's fallopian tube prior to fertilization (*Frontline*, 1995). Similarly, proponents of the school of Scientology, popular among many Hollywood celebrities, believe that long-buried memories of negative statements overheard by fetuses, embryos, and even zygotes can be reactivated in adulthood, especially under stress. These memories, Scientologists claim, can trigger low self-esteem and other psychological problems (Carroll, 2003; Gardner, 1958). For example, if a fetus overhears her mother say "I hate you" during a bitter argument with her husband, the grown adult may later misinterpret this statement as referring to herself rather than to her father. Fortunately, for both fetuses and adults, there's no evidence for this extraordinary claim. Fetuses can't accurately make out most sentences they hear from outside the womb (Smith et al., 2003), let alone remember them decades later.

EXPLANATIONS FOR INFANTILE AMNESIA. No one knows for sure why the first few years of our lives are lost to us forever, but psychologists have a few promising leads (Bauer, 2006). The hippocampus, which as we've learned plays a key role in long-term memory, especially episodic memory, is only partially developed in infancy (Mishkin, Malamut, & Bachevalier, 1984; Schacter & Moscovitch, 1984; Zola, 1997). So before age two or so, we may not possess the brain architecture needed to retain memories of events (see Chapter 10).

Also, as infants, we possess little or no concept of self (Fivush, 1988; Howe & Courage, 1993). Before about 18 months of age, infants can't recognize themselves in mirrors (Lewis, Brooks-Gunn, & Jaskir, 1985). Without a well-developed sense of self, some psychologists maintain, infants can't encode or store memories of their experiences in a meaningful fashion.

▶ **extraordinary claims**
IS THE EVIDENCE AS STRONG AS THE CLAIM?

Research suggests that other than humans, gorillas, orangutans, dolphins, and perhaps elephants are among the handful of species that exhibit mirror self-recognition—often regarded as one important indicator of the presence of a self-concept (Plotnik, deWaal, & Reiss, 2006). Here a baby reacts to his mirror image.

✓— **Study** and **Review** on **mypsychlab.com**

---

assess your knowledge   **FACT OR FICTION?**

1. Most young children underestimate their memory abilities. **True / False**

2. Children as young as two months have implicit memories of their experiences. **True / False**

3. Most adults can accurately recall events that took place before they were three years old. **True / False**

4. One explanation for infantile amnesia is that the hippocampus is only partially developed in infancy. **True / False**

Answers: 1. F (p. 270); 2. T (p. 270); 3. F (p. 270); 4. T (p. 271)

FALSE MEMORIES: WHEN GOOD MEMORY GOES BAD

7.12 Identify factors that influence people's susceptibility to false memories and memory errors.

7.13 Describe some of the real-world implications of false memories and memory errors.

We generally trust our memories to provide us with an accurate recounting of our past. In many cases, our memories do the job well enough. Over the past few decades, however, researchers have shown that our memories can be more fallible than any of us could have imagined. Moreover, we're often far more confident of our recollections of events than we should be.

A photo of then-president George W. Bush being told about the September 11th terrorist attacks by his chief of staff, Andrew Card. Two months later, while answering a question, Bush said that he vividly recalled watching the first plane hit the World Trade Center tower on television. Yet Bush's recollection must have been a false memory, because video footage of the first plane hitting the tower wasn't released until a number of days after the attacks (Chabris & Simons, 2010; Greenberg, 2004).

---

flashbulb memory
emotional memory that is extraordinarily vivid and detailed

source monitoring confusion
lack of clarity about the origin of a memory

---

replicability

CAN THE RESULTS BE DUPLICATED IN OTHER STUDIES?

occam's razor

DOES A SIMPLER EXPLANATION FIT THE DATA JUST AS WELL?

■ False Memories

At first blush, our everyday experience strongly suggests that we can safely rely on our memories, because many of our recollections seem to be as crisp as scenes from a movie. Do you remember where you were and what you were doing when you heard about the terrorist attacks on September 11, 2001? Most Americans say yes, and many say that, even today, they can "relive" those frightening moments with astonishing clarity. Many older Americans report equally vivid memories of the assassination of President John F. Kennedy on November 22, 1963. Powerful memories of the attempted assassination of President Ronald Reagan (Pillemer, 1984), the explosion of the space shuttle *Challenger* (McCloskey, Wible, & Cohen, 1988), and the deaths of Princess Diana (Krackow, Lynn, & Payne, 2006) and singer Michael Jackson are other examples.

FLASHBULB MEMORIES. It's no wonder that Roger Brown and James Kulik (1977) referred to these recollections as **flashbulb memories**, emotional memories that seem so vivid that people seem able to recount them in remarkable, even photographic, detail. They further argued that flashbulb memories don't decay over time like ordinary memories. So flashbulb memories suggest that our memories sometimes operate like video cameras or DVDs after all, right?

Maybe not. Ulric Neisser and Nicole Harsch (1992) decided to find out whether extremely vivid memories were accurate by studying college students' recollection of the explosion of the space shuttle *Challenger* in 1986. For many people, this was a particularly tragic and memorable event because, for the first time, a non-astronaut—a schoolteacher named Christa McAuliffe—was on board. Neisser and Harsch discovered that two and a half to three years after the *Challenger* explosion, 75 percent of college students' reports of the event didn't match their recollections from only a few days following this event. Moreover, about a third of the students' stories changed dramatically over time. Consider this recollection from one of their subjects almost immediately after the *Challenger* explosion.

Initial Recollection (January 1986): "I was in my religion class and some people walked in and started talking about the explosion. I didn't know any details except that it had exploded and the schoolteacher's students had all been watching, which I thought was so sad. Then after class I went to my room and watched the TV program talking about it and I got all the details from that."

Here's the recollection from the *same* student more than two and a half years later:

Later Recollection (September 1988): "When I first heard about the explosion I was sitting in my freshman dorm room with my roommate and we were watching TV. It came on a news flash and we were both totally shocked. I was really upset and went upstairs to talk to a friend of mine, and then I called my parents."

When Neisser and Harsch presented students with their written recollections from several years earlier, some insisted that they must have been written by someone else! The authors coined the term *phantom flashbulb memory* to capture the idea that many seeming flashbulb memories are false. This phenomenon has been replicated with a group of students asked to recall their memory of the 1995 verdict of the O. J. Simpson murder trial (Schmolk, Buffalo & Squire, 2000). After 32 months, 40 percent of the memory reports contained "major distortions" relative to their initial recollection only three days after the verdict.

This research indicates that so-called flashbulb memories change over time, just like all other memories. They remind us that much as our memories may seem to work like video cameras, they don't. We don't need to invoke an entirely new set of explanations to explain vivid recollections. The most parsimonious hypothesis is that flashbulb memories aren't a separate class of memories; they're much like other memories, just more intense.

SOURCE MONITORING: WHO SAID THAT? Think back to a conversation you had yesterday with a friend. How do you know it really happened? About 25 percent of undergraduates report experiencing a distinct memory of an event but feeling unsure of whether it actually occurred or was part of a dream (Rassin, Merckelbach, & Spaan, 2001). This is an example of a **source monitoring confusion**, a lack of clarity about the origin of a memory.

According to a *source monitoring* view of memory (Johnson, Hashtroudi, & Lindsay, 1993; Johnson & Raye, 1981), we try to identify the origins of our memories by seeking cues about how we encoded them. Source monitoring refers to our efforts to identify the origins (sources) of a memory. We rely on source monitoring to recall which information source provided the information—did you hear it on the news or from a friend? Have you ever started to tell someone a joke or story only to realize that he was the one who told it to you in the first place? That's an example of a source monitoring failure. Whenever we try to figure out whether a memory really reflects something that happened or whether we merely imagined it, we're engaging in source monitoring. For example, we typically rely on cues regarding how vivid and detailed our memories are. All things being equal, memories of our recent past that are more vivid and detailed are more likely to reflect actual events (Lynn et al., 2003a), although as we've learned even these memories are sometimes inaccurate. If our memory of a conversation with a friend on campus is vague and fuzzy, we may begin to wonder whether it really happened or it was merely a product of our overactive imagination.

In many cases, source monitoring works well, by helping us avoid confusing our memories with our fantasies. This ability comes in handy when we're trying to recall whether we actually punched our obnoxious boss in the nose or just fantasized about doing so. Yet because cues regarding the vividness and detail of memories are far from perfect, source monitoring isn't perfect, either. We can sometimes be fooled, and false memories can result.

A source monitoring perspective helps us understand why some people are especially receptive to false memories. Remember the memory illusion test with all of the sleepy words earlier in the chapter? (No, it's not a false memory.) Some studies suggest that people who are fantasy-prone are more likely to experience memory illusions on this task (Geraerts et al., 2005; Winograd, Peluso, & Glover, 1998). So are the elderly (Jacoby & Rhodes, 2006) and even people who believe they've been abducted by space aliens (Clancy et al., 2002). All of these groups of people are probably more likely to confuse their imaginations with reality.

Many other memory errors reflect confusions in source monitoring. Take the phenomenon of **cryptomnesia** (literally meaning "hidden memory"), whereby we mistakenly forget that one of "our" ideas originated with someone else. Some cases of plagiarism probably reflect cryptomnesia. When the late George Harrison, a former member of the Beatles, wrote his hit song, "My Sweet Lord," he apparently forgot that the melody of this song was virtually identical to that of the Chiffons' song, "He's So Fine," which had appeared about 10 years earlier. After the copyright owners of the Chiffons' song sued Harrison, he used cryptomnesia as a legal defense, arguing that he mistakenly believed he'd invented the melody himself. The judge awarded money to the copyright owners of the original song, although he ruled that Harrison probably didn't commit the plagiarism intentionally.

■ Implanting False Memories in the Lab

Three decades ago, psychologist Elizabeth Loftus (Loftus, 1979; Loftus, Miller, & Burns, 1978; Wells & Loftus, 1984) opened researchers' eyes to the dramatic effects of misleading suggestions on both everyday memories and eyewitness reports. She found that **suggestive memory techniques**—procedures that strongly encourage people to recall memories—often create recollections that were never present to begin with (Lynn et al., 2003a). Her pioneering work demonstrated that our memories are far more malleable than most psychologists had assumed. ◉ ⌐Watch

MISINFORMATION EFFECT. In a classic study, Loftus and John Palmer (1974) showed participants brief clips of traffic accidents and asked them to estimate the speed of the vehicles involved. They varied the wording of the question, "About how fast were the cars going

cryptomnesia
failure to recognize that our ideas originated with someone else

suggestive memory technique
procedure that encourages patients to recall memories that may or may not have taken place

In 2006, Kaavya Viswanathan, a Harvard sophomore and author of the book *How Opal Mehta Got Kissed, Got Wild, and Got a Life,* was accused of plagiarism when reporters revealed that numerous passages in her book were suspiciously similar to those in several other books. Viswanathan's defense was cryptomnesia: She claimed to have read these books and forgotten their source (she also claimed to possess a photographic memory, making it difficult for her to forget the original passages).

◉─⌐Watch Memory: Elizabeth Loftus on **mypsychlab.com**

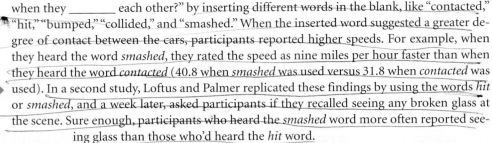

when they _____ each other?" by inserting different words in the blank, like "contacted," "hit," "bumped," "collided," and "smashed." When the inserted word suggested a greater degree of contact between the cars, participants reported higher speeds. For example, when they heard the word *smashed*, they rated the speed as nine miles per hour faster than when they heard the word *contacted* (40.8 when *smashed* was used versus 31.8 when *contacted* was used). In a second study, Loftus and Palmer replicated these findings by using the words *hit* or *smashed*, and a week later, asked participants if they recalled seeing any broken glass at the scene. Sure enough, participants who heard the *smashed* word more often reported seeing glass than those who'd heard the *hit* word.

replicability

CAN THE RESULTS BE DUPLICATED IN OTHER STUDIES?

In a later study, Loftus and her colleagues asked participants to watch a slide sequence of an accident in which a car passed through an intersection and struck a pedestrian. They asked participants questions about the event. Some of the questions contained misleading suggestions. For example, in the actual slide sequence, the sign at the intersection was a yield sign. Yet Loftus and her colleagues phrased one of the questions, "While the car was stopped at the stop sign, did a red Datsun pass by?" Afterward, participants who received the misleading questions were more likely to say that the sign was a stop sign than a yield sign. In contrast, most subjects who didn't receive the phony information recalled the yield sign accurately. This phenomenon is the **misinformation effect:** Providing people with misleading information after an event can lead to fictitious memories (Loftus, Miller, & Burns, 1978).

In the 1978 study by Loftus and her colleagues, subjects saw a car stopped at a yield sign (*top*). Yet when prompted with the information that the car had been stopped at a stop sign (*bottom*), they later "remembered" seeing the stop sign.

LOST IN THE MALL AND OTHER IMPLANTED MEMORIES. Loftus's famous "lost in the mall study" demonstrates that we can implant elaborate memories of a made-up event that never happened. Loftus and her colleagues (Loftus, Coan, & Pickrell, 1996; Loftus & Pickrell, 1995) asked the relatives of 24 participants to describe events that participants had experienced in childhood. They then presented participants with a booklet that contained the details of three events the relatives reported, along with a fourth event that the relatives verified never occurred: being lost in a shopping mall as a child. Participants wrote about each event they could recall. In follow-up interviews, a quarter of the subjects claimed to distinctly remember being lost in the mall as a child. Some even provided surprisingly detailed accounts of the event.

Many investigators followed in the path of Loftus's groundbreaking work. Using suggestive questions and statements, researchers have successfully implanted memories of a wide variety of events, ranging from accidentally spilling a bowl of punch on the parents of the bride at a wedding reception to a serious animal attack to demonic possession, in about 20 to 25 percent of college students (Bernstein et al., 2005; DeBreuil, Garry, & Loftus, 1998; Hyman, Husband, & Billings, 1995; Mazzoni, Loftus, & Kirsch, 2001; Porter, Yuille, & Lehman, 1999).

Do participants' reports in false memory studies reflect actual changes in their memories? Or could they merely reflect demand characteristics, attempts to please experimenters or give experimenters the answers participants believe they're seeking (see Chapter 2)? Probably not, because even when researchers have told subjects they implanted the memories, many continue to insist that the memories are genuine (Ceci et al., 1994). Moreover, the fact that many investigators, using different experimental designs, have replicated the finding that memories are malleable provides strong support for the claim that memory is reconstructive.

replicability

CAN THE RESULTS BE DUPLICATED IN OTHER STUDIES?

misinformation effect
creation of fictitious memories by providing misleading information about an event after it takes place

EVENT PLAUSIBILITY. As we might imagine, there are limits to how far we can go in implanting false memories. Much of what we recall hinges on our beliefs, hunches, and "best guesses" about what we've experienced (Hirt et al., 1999). Given what we know, it's easier for us to believe some things than others.

Let's say we asked you to imagine vividly and repeatedly that your instructor wore a Mexican sombrero to your last class, and interrupted her lecture to do the Mexican hat dance. We suspect you wouldn't buy the suggestion for two reasons. First, it's easier to implant a memory of something that's plausible than of something that isn't (Pezdek, Finger, & Hodge, 1997). Second, it's easier to implant a fictitious memory of an event from the distant past for which we have hazy or no recall than of an event from the recent past we remember well.

MEMORIES OF IMPOSSIBLE EVENTS. Most of the studies we've reviewed are open to at least one major criticism. Perhaps participants actually experienced the suggested event, such as being lost in a mall, but forgot about it until the suggestion reminded them of it. Studies of impossible or highly implausible memories rule out this alternative hypothesis. Indeed, researchers have devised clever *existence proofs* (see Chapter 2) demonstrating that it's possible to create elaborate memories of events that never happened. Here are two "memorable" examples.

One team of researchers (Wade et al., 2002) showed participants a fake photograph of a hot-air balloon, into which they'd pasted photographs of the participant and a relative (ah, the wonders of computers!). Family members had confirmed that the participant had never experienced a hot-air balloon ride. The investigators showed participants the fake photograph and asked them to describe "everything you can remember without leaving anything out, no matter how trivial it may seem." After two further interviews, 50 percent of subjects recalled at least some of the fictitious hot-air balloon ride, and some embellished their reports with sensory details, like seeing a road from high up in the air. In another study (Braun, Ellis, & Loftus, 2002), investigators showed participants ads for Disneyland that featured Bugs Bunny and asked them about seeing Bugs at Disneyland as a child. Sixteen percent of subjects said they remembered meeting and shaking hands with Bugs Bunny; some even remembered hearing him say, "What's up, doc?" What's so strange about that? Bugs Bunny is a Warner Brothers, not a Disney, cartoon character, so the memories must have been false.

In another study, investigators suggested to some participants that they'd become ill in childhood after eating egg salad (Geraerts et al., 2008). Later on, these participants ate significantly fewer egg salad sandwiches than participants who didn't receive this suggestion—even up to four months later. These findings demonstrate that suggestive memory procedures can affect not only our recollections, but our behaviors (Bernstein et al., 2005).

■ Generalizing from the Lab to the Real World

Studies like these we've reviewed, and dramatic cases like that of Nadean Cool, provide vivid examples of how suggestive memory recovery techniques can shape our memories and identities. Ethical limitations render it difficult, if not impossible, to determine whether we can implant memories of sexual and physical abuse inside or outside the laboratory. So we should be cautious about generalizing experimental findings to the real world, because these laboratory studies may be low in *external validity* (see Chapter 2). Still, these studies raise the possibility that memory errors bear important implications for real-world situations, like eyewitness identifications. Do they?

EYEWITNESS TESTIMONY. As of today, 255 prisoners have been acquitted of a crime and released because their DNA didn't match genetic material left by perpetrators. Consider Gene Bibbons, "Number 125," sentenced to life imprisonment for the sexual assault of a 16-year-old girl. The victim described the perpetrator as a man with long curly hair, wearing jeans, even though Bibbons had short, cropped hair at the time and was wearing shorts.

> ◄ ruling out rival hypotheses
>
> **HAVE IMPORTANT ALTERNATIVE EXPLANATIONS FOR THE FINDINGS BEEN EXCLUDED?**

Research using fake photographs shows that we can "rewrite" parts of people's life histories. In one case, subjects became convinced that they'd experienced a hot-air balloon ride as a child even when they hadn't.

In 1984, Jennifer Thompson, a 22-year-old college student, was raped. Shortly after, she confidently identified Ronald Cotton (*right*) as the man who raped her, and he was imprisoned following a trial. In 1995, a DNA test showed conclusively that Bobby Poole (*left*) was the actual rapist, and Cotton was released after spending 11 years in prison for a crime he didn't commit. Consumed by guilt, Thompson sought out Cotton following his release from prison; they've since become friends.

Still, she identified Bibbons as the assailant. Years later, investigators located a biological specimen, and genetic testing confirmed that Bibbons's DNA didn't match the DNA at the crime scene. After maintaining his innocence for 16 years, Bibbons walked out of prison a free man.

If there's a thread that ties Bibbons to the more than 250 other unjustly imprisoned individuals, it's that an eyewitness misidentified him as guilty. Three-quarters or more of prisoners acquitted by DNA testing are mistakenly identified by eyewitnesses (Scheck, Neufeld, & Dwyer, 2000), in about a third of cases by two or more eyewitnesses (Arkowitz & Lilienfeld, 2009). This fact isn't surprising when we consider that when witnesses seem sure they've identified a culprit, juries tend to believe them (Smith et al., 2001; Wells & Bradford, 1998). Yet contrary to popular (mis)conception, the correlation between witnesses' confidence and the accuracy of their testimony is often modest (Bothwell, Deffenbacher, & Brigham, 1987; Kassin, Ellsworth, & Smith, 1989; Sporer et al., 1995).

Eyewitnesses sometimes provide invaluable evidence, especially when they have ample time to observe the perpetrator under good lighting conditions, when the criminal isn't disguised, and when little time elapses between witnessing the crime and identifying the guilty party (Memon, Hope, & Bull, 2003). But eyewitness testimony is far from accurate when these optimal conditions aren't met. Moreover, eyewitness testimony is less likely to be accurate when people observe individuals of races different from their own (Kassin et al., 2001; Meissner & Brigham, 2001; Pezdek, Blandon-Gitlin, & Moore, 2003), when they talk to other witnesses (Wells, Memon, & Penrod, 2006), when they catch only a brief glimpse of the criminal (Wells, Memon, & Penrod, 2006), or when they view a crime under stressful circumstances, such as when they feel threatened (Deffenbacher et al., 2004). Sometimes eyewitnesses also mistake someone they've seen shortly before the crime for the actual criminal (Deffenbacher, Bornstein, & Penrod, 2006). Eyewitness accuracy is also often impaired by the phenomenon of *weapon focus:* When a crime involves a weapon, people understandably tend to focus on the weapon rather than the perpetrator's appearance (Steblay, 1992). Psychologists can play a critical role in educating jurors about the science of eyewitness recall, so that they can better weigh the evidence (Arkowitz & Lilienfeld, 2009).

Psychologists also can inform juries about the best way to conduct eyewitness lineups, a common fixture of television crime shows. As we learned in Chapter 1, most research suggests that identification of suspects is more accurate with *sequential lineups,* in which witnesses view one person at a time (Lindsay & Wells, 1985) than with *simultaneous lineups,* in which witnesses make the selection from a group of both suspects and decoys (Steblay et al., 2001). The major problem is that when the real criminal isn't in the lineup, witnesses are likely to mistakenly identify the person who most closely resembles the real perpetrator. Nevertheless, because this finding hasn't been universally replicated, some researchers have argued that it may be premature to substitute sequential with simultaneous line-ups in real-world settings (McQuiston-Surrett, Malpass, & Tredoux, 2006). In addition, line-ups tend to be more accurate when police tell witnesses that the true criminal either might or might not be present in the line-up, as this procedure reduces demand characteristics (see Chapter 2) on witnesses to "help" investigators by fingering a guilty person (Wells et al., 2006). A final crucial consideration is that the person who conducts the lineup should be blind to who the suspect is, because this knowledge could unintentionally bias eyewitnesses.

? Even though the teller may have a good look at the face of this bank robber, her eyewitness memory of his face is likely to be impaired by what factor? (See answer upside down at bottom of page.)

replicability ▷

CAN THE RESULTS BE DUPLICATED IN OTHER STUDIES?

Answer: Weapon focus

■ Suggestibility and Child Testimony

Probably because they sometimes confuse fantasy with reality, children are especially vulnerable to suggestions to recall events that didn't occur (Ceci & Bruck, 1993). Stephen Ceci and his colleagues (Ceci et al., 1994) asked preschool children to imagine real and fictitious events. Once a week, for a total of seven to ten interviews, they instructed children to "think real hard" about whether the events had occurred. For example, they asked the children to try to remember made-up events, like going to the hospital with a mousetrap on their fingers. Fifty-eight percent of children generated stories regarding at least one of these fictitious events. Interestingly, about a quarter of the children continued to insist their memories were real even when their parents and the experimenter assured them the events never happened. The fact that children cling to their false memories even when an authority figure tells them the memories are wrong suggests that such memories can be convincing. These findings are important for another reason: Many social workers and police officers who suspect that a child was abused question the child about this abuse repeatedly. Repeated questioning comes with a risk: Children may give investigators the answers they're seeking, even if these answers are wrong.

This research carries a key practical suggestion: Psychologists and other health care workers need to use less suggestive procedures when questioning children. Indeed, most research demonstrates that many children can provide reasonably accurate memories when they're simply asked about an event once in a non-leading fashion (for example, "Can you tell me what happened?") (Ornstein et al., 1997).

Children's memories are also affected by schemas, especially their expectations about how others will act. To demonstrate this point, two researchers (Leichtman & Ceci, 1995) provided three- to six-year-old children with information that led them to hold a negative stereotype about a man, "Sam Stone," before he visited the classroom several weeks later. They told the children various stories about Sam, a clumsy character who did things like accidentally break Barbie dolls and rip sweaters. When Sam actually visited, he didn't act clumsily at all, but the next day, the teacher showed the children a soiled teddy bear and a torn book. Afterward, the investigators interviewed some of the children on different occasions about what Sam did during the visit. They asked the children suggestive questions, such as "Did Sam Stone rip the book or did he use scissors?" Then, during the final interview, they asked children to describe Sam's visit. In response to open-ended questions, 46 percent of three- and four-year-olds and 30 percent of five- and six-year-olds reported that Sam had ripped the book, soiled the teddy bear, or both. With further prompts, 72 percent of the younger preschoolers and 44 percent of the older preschoolers responded to the suggestion. Children in a control condition, who weren't interviewed or provided with negative stereotypes, rarely made these errors.

THE FALSE MEMORY CONTROVERSY. One of the most divisive controversies in all of psychology centers on the possibility that memories of child abuse and other traumatic experiences can be shaped by suggestive techniques in psychotherapy (see Chapter 16). In fact, debates concerning false memories have become so bitter that some writers have referred to them as the "memory wars" (Crews, 1990).

On one side of the battle are memory recovery therapists, who claim that patients *repress* memories of traumatic events, such as childhood sexual abuse, and then *recover* them years, even decades, later (Brown, Scheflin, & Hammond, 1997). As we'll learn in Chapter 14, most followers of Sigmund Freud believe that repression is a form of forgetting in which people push painful memories into their unconscious. According to recovered memory therapists, these repressed memories are the root cause of current life problems and must be addressed to make progress in psychotherapy (McHugh, 2008; McNally, 2003). Some, like Nadean Cool's therapist, even claim their clients have repressed memories of murderous satanic cults, even though investigations by the FBI have consistently failed to unearth any evidence of these cults (Lanning, 1989). By the

FICTOID

MYTH: All people who've experienced a traumatic event recall it as less terrifying as time passes.

REALITY: Some people remember an experience as *more* frightening as time passes. One research team studied a group of women who'd witnessed a school shooting. They first asked the women to describe the shooting five months after it happened, and again 12 months later. Some of these women had become more emotionally distressed in the intervening year. They recalled the shooting as having been more terrifying at 17 months than they had at five months (Schwarz, Kowalski, & McNally, 1993), probably because their current mood state influenced their memories of the event.

Gary Ramona, a successful California wine executive, was accused by his daughter, Holly, of sexually abusing her in childhood. Siding with her daughter, his wife divorced him. Ramona eventually won a half-million-dollar lawsuit against Holly's psychiatrist. The jury agreed with Ramona that the psychiatrist's suggestive techniques had triggered false memories of sexual abuse in Holly.

FICTOID ✕

MYTH: People who think they might have been sexually abused, but aren't sure, can use symptom checklists in self-help books to help them find out.

REALITY: Many therapists who treat patients with suspected sexual abuse histories prescribe "survivor books"—self-help books that often contain checklists of supposed telltale symptoms of past sexual abuse, such as fears of sex, low self-esteem, insecurity about one's appearance, or excessive dependency (Lynn et al., 2003b). Yet research shows that most of these symptoms are so vague and general that they can apply to virtually everyone (Emery & Lilienfeld, 2004).

mid-1990s, approximately 25 percent of psychotherapists reported in surveys (Polosny & Follette, 1996; Poole et al., 1995) that they used two or more potentially suggestive procedures, including dream interpretation, repeated questioning, guided imagery, and hypnosis, to help patients who had no recollection of sexual abuse to recover memories of it.

Lined up on the opposing side of the false memory debate is a growing chorus of researchers who claim that there's slim evidence that people repress traumatic memories, including childhood sexual abuse. These researchers point to a mounting body of evidence that painful memories, such as memories of the Holocaust (Golier et al., 2002), are well remembered and, if anything, remembered too well (Loftus, 1993; McNally, 2003; Pope et al., 2007; see Chapter 16). According to them, there's serious reason to doubt that many memories can be repressed and then recovered years or decades later. These researchers have also voiced serious concerns about whether suggestive procedures can lead patients to conclude erroneously that family members abused them in childhood. Indeed, hundreds of individuals have been separated from their families, and in some cases even imprisoned, solely on the basis of recovered memory claims of child sexual abuse.

From a scientific and ethical standpoint, this state of affairs is deeply troubling, often tragic. Given what we now know about how fallible human memory is, recovered memories of child abuse shouldn't be trusted completely unless they're accompanied by clear-cut corroborating evidence. In the past decade, the false memory controversy has subsided somewhat, largely because a consensus has emerged that suggestive procedures can create false memories of childhood events in many, although perhaps not all, psychotherapy clients.

■ The Seven Sins of Memory

By this point in the chapter, we hope we've persuaded you that although our memories generally work well and are often accurate, they're anything but perfect. Daniel Schacter (2001) elegantly summarized the tricks that memory can play on us by describing the "seven sins of memory." Schacter's analogy to the ancient seven deadly sins (pride, anger, envy, greed, gluttony, lust, and sloth) is hardly accidental. Just as these sins can get us into big trouble, the seven sins of memory, which we've listed below, can lead to a host of memory errors.

1. **Suggestibility.** As we've learned, misleading information following events, leading questions, and explicit information and suggestions can increase the chances of our believing that fictitious events occurred.

2. **Misattribution.** Suggestions are often effective because they lead us to misattribute memories to incorrect sources, mistaking what we've imagined for a real memory. We can also misremember where we've read or heard about an event.

3. **Bias.** As we've seen, our schemas can bias our memories. For example, information that conveys stereotypes about people can influence our memories of them. If we expect people to act unethically, we may remember them as acting unethically even when they didn't.

4. **Transience.** One thing is certain: Many of our memories will fade with time. This loss affects both short- and long-term memories. As we age, it's increasingly difficult to access memories. In cases of massive brain injury or dementia, the ability to access memories can be severely impaired.

5. **Persistence.** The great author William Faulkner once wrote, "The past is never dead; it's not even past." Remember the last time someone "stole your parking space," that is, snuck in front of you even though you got there first? Or when someone insulted you in front of your friends? These events can linger in our minds for days or weeks and intrude into our thoughts, even disrupting our ability to sleep.

6. **Blocking.** Most of us have had the experience of starting to say something, and then suddenly and inexplicably losing all memory of what we intended to say. Although this experience can be embarrassing, most of us recover quickly from *blocking,* a temporary inability to access information. The TOT phenomenon is another example of blocking.

7. **Absentmindedness.** Virtually all of us suffer from occasional absentmindedness, such as forgetting an appointment when we're tired or distracted. People who get caught up in fantasies or daydream frequently are especially likely to report being absentminded (Lynn & Rhue, 1988; Wilson & Barber, 1981). Absentmindedness can stem from a failure either to encode memories because we're not paying attention or to retrieve memories we've already stored.

Absentmindedness afflicts all of us occasionally, as it did to star violinist Philippe Quint, shown here chatting with taxi driver Mohammed Khalil in 2008. A few weeks earlier, Quint had left something fairly important in Khalil's cab following a concert performance: a four-million-dollar Stradivarius violin built in 1723. Fortunately, Khalil kept the violin and returned it to Quint the next day.

The seven sins of memory needn't lead us to despair. As Schacter (2001) pointed out, if we look at the flip side of each of the seven sins, we'll find an adaptive function. So these seven sins help us resolve the paradox of memory, because most memory errors stem from basic mechanisms of memory that usually serve us well. For instance, the fact that older memories aren't as accessible as new ones is adaptive, because many new memories are relevant to current life tasks and challenges. In this way, we're likely to keep in mind memories that are distinctive, interesting, and emotionally meaningful. Even absentmindedness has its upside, because paying attention to unnecessary details can derail us from pursuing important life goals. In short, the same mechanisms that falter when memory is imperfect help to explain our ability to use memory as a bridge between the past and the present, and as a gateway to the future.

---

assess your knowledge · **FACT OR FICTION?**   ✓ **Study** and **Review** on **mypsychlab.com**

1. Flashbulb memories almost never change over time. **True/False**

2. People sometimes find it difficult to tell the difference between a true and a false memory. **True/False**

3. It's almost impossible to create false memories of complex events, like undergoing a painful medical procedure. **True/False**

4. One powerful way of creating false memories is to show people fake photographs of events that didn't happen. **True/False**

5. Repeatedly asking children if they were abused leads to more accurate answers than asking them only once. **True / False**

Answers: 1. F (p. 272); 2. T (p. 273); 3. F (p. 275); 4. T (p. 275); 5. F (p. 277)

YOUR COMPLETE REVIEW SYSTEM

✓● Study and Review on mypsychlab.com

HOW MEMORY OPERATES: THE MEMORY ASSEMBLY LINE 242–254

7.1 IDENTIFY THE WAYS THAT MEMORIES DO AND DON'T ACCURATELY REFLECT EXPERIENCES.

Memories can be surprisingly accurate over very long periods of time, but tend to be reconstructive rather than reproductive.

1. A _____ _____ is a false but subjectively compelling memory. (p. 244)

2. Our memories are far more (reproductive/reconstructive) rather than (reproductive/reconstructive). (p. 244)

7.2 EXPLAIN THE FUNCTION, SPAN, AND DURATION OF EACH OF THE THREE MEMORY SYSTEMS.

Sensory memory, short-term memory, and long-term memory are stages of information processing that vary in how much information they hold and for how long they retain it. Short-term memory has a limited span of seven plus or minus two items that can be extended by grouping things together into larger, meaningful units called chunks.

3. The three major systems of memory are measured by _____, or, how much information each system can hold, and _____, or, how long a period of time the system can hold information. (p. 245)

4. Map out the three-memory model process proposed by Atkinson and Shiffrin depicting memory flow. (p. 245)

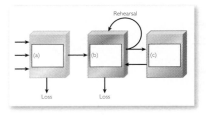

5. _____ memory is the brief storage of perceptual information before it's passed to _____ memory. (p. 246)

6. _____ _____ is a type of sensory memory that applies to vision. (p. 246)

7. To extend the span of short-term memory, we organize information into meaningful groupings using a process called _____. (p. 249)

8. The tendency to remember words at the beginning of a list better than those in the middle is known as the _____ _____. (p. 251)

7.3 DIFFERENTIATE THE SUBTYPES OF LONG-TERM MEMORY.

Explicit memory subtypes include semantic and episodic memory. Implicit memory types include procedural and priming memory.

9. _____ memory is the process of recalling information intentionally, and _____ memory is the process of recalling information we don't remember deliberately. (p. 252)

((●● Listen to an audio file of your chapter on mypsychlab.com

10. Complete the diagram to show the many subtypes of explicit and implicit memory. (p. 253)

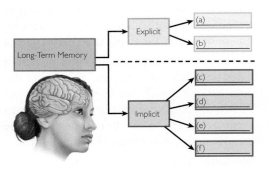

THE THREE PROCESSES OF MEMORY 254–263

7.4 IDENTIFY METHODS FOR CONNECTING NEW INFORMATION TO EXISTING KNOWLEDGE.

Mnemonics are memory aids that link new information to more familiar knowledge. There are many kinds of mnemonics; they take effort to use but can assist recall.

11. The three major processes of memory are _____, _____, and _____. (p. 254)

12. _____ is the process of organizing information in a format that our memories can use. (p. 255)

13. If we use the phrase "Every good boy does fine" to remember the names of the lines (E, G, B, D, F) in the treble clef, we're using a _____. (p. 255)

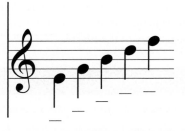

7.5 IDENTIFY THE ROLE THAT SCHEMAS PLAY IN THE STORAGE OF MEMORIES.

Schemas equip us with frames of reference for interpreting new situations. Nevertheless, they can sometimes lead to memory errors.

14. Organized knowledge structures that we've stored in memory are called _____. (p. 258)

7.6 DISTINGUISH WAYS OF MEASURING MEMORY.

Recall requires generating previously encountered information on our own, whereas recognition simply requires selecting the correct information from an array of choices. How quickly we relearn material previously learned and forgotten provides another measure of memory.

15. _____ is the reactivation or reconstruction of experiences from our memory stores. (p. 259)

16. _____ is reacquiring knowledge that we'd previously learned but largely forgotten over time. (p. 260)

17. The law of _____ _____ _____ _____ explains why cramming for a test is not the best way to remember things well in the long run. (p. 261)

18. Identify the concepts from memory researchers that can help you in studying for this and other courses. (p. 261)

MEMORY CONCEPT	POINTER
1. _____	Spread your study time out—review your notes and textbook in increments rather than cramming.
2. _____	Connect new knowledge with existing knowledge rather than simply memorizing facts or names.
3. _____	Work to process ideas deeply and meaningfully—avoid writing notes down word-for-word from instructors' lectures or slides. Try to capture the information in your own words.
4. _____	The more reminders or cues you can connect from your knowledge base to new material, the more likely you are to recall new material when tested.
5. _____	Test yourself frequently on the material you've read.

7.7 DESCRIBE HOW THE RELATION BETWEEN ENCODING AND RETRIEVAL CONDITIONS INFLUENCES REMEMBERING.

Individuals tend to remember better if they're tested under the same physical and emotional conditions as when they encoded the information.

18. _____ _____ is the phenomenon of remembering something better when the conditions under which we retrieve information are similar to the conditions under which we encoded it. (p. 262)

19. In _____ _____, our retrieval of memories is superior when the external context of the original memories matches the retrieval context. (p. 262)

THE BIOLOGY OF MEMORY 263–269

7.8 DESCRIBE THE ROLE OF LONG-TERM POTENTIATION IN MEMORY.

Most scientists believe that long-term potentiation—a gradual strengthening of the connections among neurons from repetitive stimulation—plays a key role in the formation of memories and memory storage.

21. Lashley's studies with rats demonstrated that memory (is/isn't) located in one part of the brain. (p. 264)

22. Today most scientists agree that LTP plays a key role in _____. (p. 264)

23. The _____ plays a key role in forming lasting memories. (p. 264)

7.9 DISTINGUISH DIFFERENT TYPES OF AMNESIA AND THE RELEVANCE OF AMNESIA TO THE BRAIN'S ORGANIZATION OF MEMORY.

Evidence from studies of amnesia patients demonstrates that there are distinct memory systems, because people with amnesia for declarative memory can often still form new procedural memories. Retrograde amnesia causes forgetting of past experiences, whereas anterograde amnesia prevents us from forming memories of new experiences.

24. A person with _____ amnesia has lost some memories of his/her past. (p. 265)

25. The inability to encode new memories from our experiences is called _____ amnesia. (p. 265)

26. On this task, subjects must trace a star while looking only at a mirror. What type of memory is this task designed to assess? (p. 266)

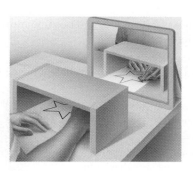

27. Damage to the hippocampus impairs _____ memory but leaves _____ memory intact. (p. 266)

28. Label and describe each component of the limbic system and its role in memory. (p. 267)

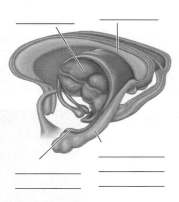

7.10 IDENTIFY THE KEY IMPAIRMENTS OF ALZHEIMER'S DISEASE

The memory loss of patients with Alzheimer's disease begins with that of recent events, with memories of events of the distant past typically being the last to go. Alzheimer's disease is marked by loss of synapses and acetylcholine neurons.

29. Senility (is/isn't) an unavoidable part of aging. (p. 268)

30. Alzheimer's disease accounts for only 50 to 60 percent of cases of _____, or severe memory loss. (p. 268)

THE DEVELOPMENT OF MEMORY: ACQUIRING A PERSONAL HISTORY 269–271

7.11 IDENTIFY HOW CHILDREN'S MEMORY ABILITIES CHANGE WITH AGE.

Infants display implicit memory for events; both infants' and children's memories are influenced by some of the same factors as adults' memory. Children's memory improves in part because of maturational changes in the brain that extend the span of memory. Over time, children become better able to use mnemonic and rehearsal strategies and become more aware of their memory limitations.

31. Over time, children develop their enhanced _____ skills that provide knowledge about their memory ability and limitations. (p. 270)

32. Rovee-Collier's experiments utilized operant conditioning to study infants' _____ _____. (p. 270)

33. How did Carolyn Rovee-Collier and others use infants' kicking behavior to study memory in infants? (p. 270)

34. Rovee-Collier found that infants' memories of the experience were surprisingly (general/specific). (p. 270)

35. _____ _____ is the inability to remember personal experiences that took place before the age of three or so. (p. 270)

36. European Americans report (earlier/later) first memories than do people from Taiwan. (p. 270)

37. There (is/isn't) evidence that we can remember things that took place at or prior to birth (p. 271)

38. The _____, which is critical for the establishment of long-term memory, is only partially developed in infancy. (p. 271)

39. Infants have little sense of _____, which makes it difficult for them to encode or store experiences in ways that are meaningful. (p. 271)

40. Which important indicator of the presence of a self-concept do humans and chimpanzees exhibit? (p. 271)

FALSE MEMORIES: WHEN GOOD MEMORY GOES BAD 271–279

7.12 IDENTIFY FACTORS THAT INFLUENCE PEOPLE'S SUSCEPTIBILITY TO FALSE MEMORIES AND MEMORY ERRORS.

Flashbulb memories for highly significant events seem more crisp and vivid than other memories but may be just as vulnerable to errors as other kinds of memory. One source of memory errors is source monitoring difficulty; we can't always remember where or from whom we learned something, or whether it was a figment of our imagination, sometimes resulting in cryptomnesia. Our memories for events are easily influenced by suggestions from others that the events happened differently than our observations suggested.

41. _____ _____ are memories that are extremely vivid and detailed, and often highly emotional. (p. 272)

42. Whenever we try to figure out whether a memory reflects something that really happened, we're engaging in _____ _____. (p. 273)

43. The failure to recognize that our ideas come from another source is called _____. (p. 273)

44. Explain Elizabeth Loftus' misinformation effect and its influence on our memory. (p. 274)

45. Explain how we could have vivid memories of events we never experienced. (p. 275)

46. Research has shown that it's (impossible/possible) to implant memories of a made-up event that never happened. (p. 275)

7.13 DESCRIBE SOME OF THE REAL-WORLD IMPLICATIONS OF FALSE MEMORIES AND MEMORY ERRORS.

The fact that we're receptive to suggestions about whether and how events took place bears important implications for eyewitness testimony. Many scientists have argued that apparent "recovered memories" of early trauma may actually be due to the tendency of suggestive therapeutic procedures to induce false recollections.

47. The correlation between eyewitnesses' confidence in their testimony and the accuracy of this testimony is (weak/strong). (p. 276)

48. Research suggests that some _____ may be unintentionally implanting memories of traumatic events by m means of suggestive procedures. (p. 278)

49. Most of us recover quickly from _____, a temporary inability to access information. (p. 279)

50. In a well-known example of _____, violinist Philippe Quint once left his four-million dollar violin in a cab. (p. 279)

DO YOU KNOW THESE TERMS?

- memory (p. 242)
- memory illusion (p. 244)
- sensory memory (p. 246)
- iconic memory (p. 246)
- echoic memory (p. 247)
- short-term memory (p. 247)
- decay (p. 247)
- interference (p. 247)
- retroactive interference (p. 248)
- proactive interference (p. 248)
- Magic Number (p. 249)
- chunking (p. 249)
- rehearsal (p. 249)
- maintenance rehearsal (p. 249)

- elaborative rehearsal (p. 250)
- levels of processing (p. 250)
- long-term memory (p. 251)
- permastore (p. 251)
- primacy effect (p. 251)
- recency effect (p. 251)
- serial position curve (p. 252)
- semantic memory (p. 252)
- episodic memory (p. 252)
- explicit memory (p. 252)
- implicit memory (p. 252)
- procedural memory (p. 253)
- priming (p. 253)
- encoding (p. 255)

- mnemonic (p. 255)
- storage (p. 258)
- schema (p. 258)
- retrieval (p. 259)
- retrieval cue (p. 260)
- recall (p. 260)
- recognition (p. 260)
- relearning (p. 260)
- distributed versus massed practice (p. 261)
- tip-of-the-tongue (TOT) phenomenon (p. 262)
- encoding specificity (p. 262)
- context-dependent learning (p. 262)

- state-dependent learning (p. 262)
- long-term potentiation (LTP) (p. 264)
- retrograde amnesia (p. 265)
- anterograde amnesia (p. 265)
- meta-memory (p. 270)
- infantile amnesia (p. 270)
- flashbulb memory (p. 272)
- source monitoring confusion (p. 272)
- cryptomnesia (p. 273)
- suggestive memory technique (p. 273)
- misinformation effect (p. 274)

APPLY YOUR SCIENTIFIC THINKING SKILLS

Use your scientific thinking skills to answer the following questions, referencing specific scientific thinking principles and common errors in reasoning whenever possible.

1. As we've learned, our memories are often not as accurate as we assume. Think back to an early memory of an event (such as a childhood vacation) that you shared with friends or family. Write down as many details of the memory as you can. Now ask those friends or family members to write down their memories of the event. In what ways do the memories differ? How can you explain the differences given what you now know about memory?

2. Search the Internet or popular magazines and find several examples of products designed to improve your memory, such as so-called "memory pills" or "smart pills." What kinds of claims do

the promoters of these products make? Are their claims scientifically plausible given what you've learned about how memory works?

3. Locate at least three magazine articles or Internet sites that discuss repressed and recovered memory. What arguments do they make to support the existence and accuracy of these memories? Are these arguments supported by scientific knowledge? Are there rival hypotheses to consider?

8 LANGUAGE, THINKING, AND REASONING

getting inside our talking heads

THINK ABOUT IT

IS THE BABBLING OF BABIES MEANINGFUL?

DO NONHUMAN ANIMALS HAVE LANGUAGE?

ARE CHILDREN WHO LEARN TWO LANGUAGES AT A DISADVANTAGE?

DOES SPEED-READING WORK?

WHICH ARE MORE ACCURATE: FIRST IMPRESSIONS OR IN-DEPTH ANALYSES?

More than we typically realize, our ability to follow a conversation depends on a host of sophisticated inferences.

TABLE 8.1 How's That Again? Ambiguous News Headlines. Language can be ambiguous and even unintentionally humorous when taken out of context. The examples in (A) are ambiguous because they use words that possess multiple meanings. The examples in (B) possess ambiguous grammar, resulting in two possible interpretations.

(A) Ambiguous Word Meaning
Drunk Gets Nine Months in Violin Case
Iraqi Head Seeks Arms
Man Struck by Lightning Faces Battery Charge
Old School Pillars Are Replaced by Alumni
Two Convicts Evade Noose, Jury Hung

(B) Grammatically Ambiguous
Eye Drops Off Shelf
British Left Waffles on Falkland Islands
Killer Sentenced to Die for Second Time in 10 Years
Ban on Soliciting Dead in Trotwood
Include Your Children When Baking Cookies

One of the most valuable lessons psychology can teach us is to appreciate mental capacities we normally take for granted. Take language and thinking. We rely on them almost every second of our waking hours, but rarely notice the complexity that goes into them.

Picture this brief conversation between two students:

MALE STUDENT: "Just scored us some free tickets to the game!"

FEMALE STUDENT: "Shut up! How?"

MALE STUDENT: "I heard this guy at the bank say he had some he couldn't use, did a little backslapping and high-fiving and . . . ta-da!"

Most native speakers of English can follow that conversation with ease. Yet all sorts of complex cognitive processes go into understanding that conversation. Let's look at some of the behind-the-scenes thinking that was probably going on as you read that passage.

1. You filled in the gaps in grammar. For example, "Just scored us some free tickets" is an incomplete phrase that needs the word "I" at the beginning to make it grammatical, but you realized that the male student was referring to himself.

2. You figured out that "the game" is either important to the students, about to take place in the near future, or both. You also figured out that the female student knew which game the male was talking about, even though you didn't know which one it was.

3. You inferred that "shut up" wasn't a literal command to be quiet, but instead an expression of surprise, even skepticism.

4. You realized that the male student engaged in a bit of friendly social interaction to persuade the man at the bank to hand over his tickets. This realization goes well beyond the literal action reported in the conversation—he reported only backslapping and high-fiving.

What enables us to draw these and other sophisticated inferences in our everyday conversations? Our ability to access knowledge, draw conclusions, make decisions, and interpret new phrases—all largely outside of our conscious awareness—play crucial roles.

We tend to think that words possess fixed meanings, like the ones we find in the dictionary. But how we interpret a word depends on its context. Many funny (and sometimes not so funny) misunderstandings can arise when contextual information is missing. **TABLE 8.1** presents examples of actual newspaper headlines in which interpreting the words literally can result in unintentionally humorous interpretations.

In this chapter, we'll examine how we communicate and comprehend meaning using words, and the challenges we face when doing so. Then, we'll explore our thinking and reasoning processes in everyday life, and learn to avoid commonplace pitfalls in logic that can lead us to draw mistaken conclusions about the world around us.

HOW DOES LANGUAGE WORK?

8.1 Describe the four levels of analysis that make up language.

8.2 Trace the development of language acquisition in children.

8.3 Determine how sign language in deaf individuals relates to spoken language acquisition in hearing individuals.

8.4 Identify the pros and cons of bilingualism.

8.5 Compare and contrast theories of language acquisition.

8.6 Distinguish human language from nonhuman animal communication.

Language is a system of communication that combines symbols, such as words or gestural signs, in rule-based ways to create meaning. One hallmark of language is that it tends to be arbitrary: Its sounds, words, and sentences bear no clear relation to their meaning. For example, there's nothing about the word *dog* that resembles a friendly, furry animal that barks, and the word *tarantula* is a lot longer than the word *pig*, even though tarantulas are (thankfully) a lot smaller than pigs. Language serves several crucial functions. The most obvious is the transmission of information. When we tell our roommate "The party starts at nine" or place an order at a coffee shop for a "skim latte," we're communicating information that enables us or someone else to accomplish a goal, like getting to the party on time or making sure our latte is nonfat.

Language serves key social and emotional functions, too. It enables us to express our thoughts about social interactions, such as conveying, "I thought you were mad at me" or "That guy was hilarious." We spend much of our conversational time establishing or maintaining our relationships with others (Dunbar, 1996).

■ The Features of Language

We take language for granted because it's a highly practiced and automatic cognitive process. By *automatic*, we mean that using and interpreting language usually require little attention, enabling us to perform other tasks like walking, cooking, or exercising without speech getting in the way (Posner & Snyder, 1975; see Chapter 1). We don't realize how complex language is until we try to learn or use a new one. In fact, our ability to use language requires the coordination of an enormous number of cognitive, social, and physical skills. Even the mere ability to produce the sounds of our language requires the delicate interplay among breath control, vocal cords, throat and mouth position, and tongue movement.

We can think about language at four levels of analysis, all of which we need to coordinate to communicate effectively. These levels are (1) **phonemes**, the sounds of our language; (2) **morphemes**, the smallest units of meaningful speech; (3) **syntax**, the grammatical rules that govern how we compose words into meaningful strings; and (4) **extralinguistic information**, elements of communication that aren't part of the content of language but are critical to interpreting its meaning, such as facial expressions and tone of voice. We can think of each level as similar to the different levels of specificity involved in preparing a meal, ranging from the individual ingredients to the menu items to the meal itself and, last but not least, to the overall dining experience.

PHONEMES: THE INGREDIENTS. Phonemes are categories of sounds our vocal apparatus produces. These categories are influenced by elements of our vocal tract, including our lips, teeth, tongue placement, vibration of the vocal cords, opening and closing of our throat, and other physical manipulations of our throat and mouth.

Experts disagree on the total number of phonemes across all of the world's languages—probably around 100 in total—but they agree that each language includes only a subset of them. English contains between 40 and 45 phonemes, depending on how we count them. Some languages have as few as about 15, others more than 60. Although there's some overlap across languages, some languages contain sounds that don't occur in other languages. This fact certainly adds to the challenge of learning a second language. **TABLE 8.2** provides examples of phoneme differences across the world's languages.

language
largely arbitrary system of communication that combines symbols (such as words or gestural signs) in rule-based ways to create meaning

phoneme
category of sounds our vocal apparatus produces

morpheme
smallest meaningful unit of speech

syntax
grammatical rules that govern how words are composed into meaningful strings

extralinguistic information
elements of communication that aren't part of the content of language but are critical to interpreting its meaning

"Sorry, but I'm going to have to issue you a summons for reckless grammar and driving without an apostrophe."

(© The New Yorker Collection 1987 Michael Maslin from cartoonbank.com. All Rights Reserved.)

TABLE 8.2 Cross-Linguistic Differences in Phoneme Distinctions. Often, speakers of one language perceive speech sounds as belonging to a single phoneme category, whereas speakers of another language break the category into two or more distinct phonemes. In cases in which English is the language that *doesn't* make a distinction, it's difficult for native English-speakers to imagine that the sounds are distinct.

PHONEME DISTINCTION	EXAMPLE	DOES HAVE DISTINCTION	DOES NOT HAVE DISTINCTION
R / L	Rid / Lid	ENGLISH	JAPANESE
S / Z	Ice / Eyes	ENGLISH	SPANISH
K / Kh	Keep / Cool	ARABIC	ENGLISH
D / T / TH	Doll / Tall / no example in English; mouth shaped as if pronouncing the letter *d* but with the tongue against back of teeth	HINDI	ENGLISH

MORPHEMES: THE MENU ITEMS. Morphemes are the smallest units of meaning in a language. They're created by stringing phonemes together. Most of our morphemes are words, such as "dog" and "happy." Morphemes convey information about **semantics**—meaning derived from words and sentences. Nevertheless, we also have strings of sounds that aren't words by themselves but modify the meaning of words when they're tacked onto them. These are morphemes, too, although they don't stand alone as words. For example, the morpheme *re-* as in *recall* or *rewrite* means "to do again," and the morpheme *-ish* as in *warmish* or *pinkish* means "to a moderate degree."

SYNTAX: PUTTING TOGETHER A MEAL. Syntax is the set of rules of a language by which we construct sentences. For instance, the string of words, "I ate pizza for dinner" forms a complete sentence that follows the syntactic rules of English. In contrast, "Pizza ate I for dinner" doesn't follow English syntax, although it follows the syntactic rules of some other languages. Syntax isn't just word order, though; it also includes *morphological markers* and sentence structure. Morphological markers are grammatical elements that modify words by adding sounds to them that change their meaning. For example, in English, we add *s* for plural, *ed* for past tense, and *ing* for ongoing action.

Although syntactic rules describe how language is organized, real-world language rarely follows them perfectly. If you were to write down word for word what your psychology professor says at the beginning of your next class, you'll find that he or she will certainly violate at least one or two syntactic rules. So syntax describes an idealized form of language, much like the formal language we read in written documents, like this textbook.

EXTRALINGUISTIC INFORMATION: THE OVERALL DINING EXPERIENCE. We often think of language as self-explanatory: We say what we mean, and mean what we say (most of the time, anyway). Yet, we take an awful lot of additional information for granted when understanding language. Extralinguistic information isn't part of language, but it plays an essential role in allowing us to interpret it. Some examples include previous statements by others in the conversation and the speaker's nonverbal cues—such as his facial expression, posture, gestures, and tone of voice. Misunderstandings can easily arise if people aren't attentive to this information or if some of it's blocked, such as during a phone conversation or in a text or e-mail (see Chapter 11).

Suppose we hear someone say, "It's just awful in here!" This sentence doesn't provide enough information to figure out what the speaker means. To understand her, we need to look at her facial expressions and gestures and take into account where she is, what she's doing, and what people were talking about just prior to this statement. If she's waving her hand in front of her face and wiping her forehead while standing in a hot kitchen, we'd probably infer that she's referring to the temperature of the room. If she's holding her nose and making a disgusted face while standing in a seafood shop, we'd probably infer she's referring to a really awful smell. And if she has a frustrated look on her face and someone had just commented on the huge number of people at the event she's attending, we might infer she's referring to how crowded the room is.

LANGUAGE DIALECTS: REGIONAL AND CULTURAL DIFFERENCES IN DINING HABITS. Although each language has its own set of phonemes, morphemes, and syntactic rules, there's variability in these elements within, as well as across, languages. **Dialects** are variations of the same language used by groups of people from specific geographic areas, social groups, or ethnic backgrounds. Dialects aren't distinct languages, because speakers of two different dialects can (mostly) understand each other (Labov, 1970). Different dialects may employ slight variations of the standard pronunciations, vocabulary, and syntax of the language. For instance, many people from Boston (and from England) are known for dropping their *r*'s ("I pahked my cah") and many Texans are known for their "twang." Similarly, you may refer to the same drink as either "soda," "pop," "tonic," or

How we interpret a sentence depends a great deal on the context. How would your interpretation of the sentence "It's just awful in here!" differ in these two contexts?

semantics
meaning derived from words and sentences

dialect
language variation used by a group of people who share geographic proximity or ethnic background

"Coke" depending on where you live. It's important to be aware that speakers of dialects that differ from the "standardized" version of the native language aren't making pronunciation or grammatical errors.

Many people assume that speakers of nondominant dialects are trying but failing to speak the majority (standard) version of the dialect (Smitherman-Donaldson & van Dijk, 1988). This assumption can lead to unwarranted and misguided prejudice (Baugh, 2000). Speakers of these dialects are using consistent syntactic rules in their speech, even though these rules differ from those used by the "mainstream" dialect (Ellis, 2006; Rickford & Rickford, 2000). For example, speakers of African American Vernacular English might say "plug it *up*" instead of "plug it *in.*" Speakers of Appalachian Dialect (spoken by many people living in the Appalachian Mountains) might say, "He had *went* to the store" instead of "He had *gone* to the store." As long as they're using these constructions systematically, they're using an equally valid, rule-based form of communication.

How Did Language Come About and Why?

Scientists have long debated the question of how language evolved and the possible advantages that such a complicated communication system affords. One clear advantage is that language allows us to communicate extremely complex thoughts. Some evolutionary theorists argue that language

Frank and Ernest

WORDS DOWN GOT WE'VE GOOD PRETTY -- SHOULD NOW INVENT WE SYNTAX!

(© 1997 Thaves. Reprinted with permission.)

evolved into a complex system as our early apelike ancestors began to engage in increasingly complex social organizations and activities like coordinated group hunting. One thing on which evolutionary theorists agree is that language must offer the human species a strong survival advantage to offset its many disadvantages. For example, language requires a lengthy learning period and hefty brainpower. In addition, possessing a vocal tract that allows us to make a wide array of sounds actually increases our chances of choking (Hauser & Fitch, 2003).

One challenge to explaining how language evolved is that phonemes, words, and syntactic rules are generally arbitrarily related to things to which they refer. That seems like an unintuitive "design feature." Many scholars argue that language is arbitrary for a good reason. Using arbitrary words allows us more flexibility to express complex ideas that may not contain sounds that obviously resemble them.

Still, there are intriguing examples of nonarbitrary language in which words *do* resemble their meaning. The most obvious is *onomatopoeia,* or words that resemble the sounds to which they refer, like "buzz," "meow," "beep," and "zoom." Another example is that across the world's languages, the word for mother nearly always starts with an *m* or *n,* whereas the word for father nearly always starts with a *b, p,* or *d.* This fact is probably more than a coincidence, particularly because these phonemes tend to be those that children acquire earliest; moreover, in the case of mother, the sound "m" is the sound that babies make when sucking on mom's nipple. Research on *sound symbolism*—the fact that certain word sounds seem to have intrinsic meanings—challenges the idea of language as completely arbitrary (Imai et al., 2008; Nygaard, Cook, & Namy, 2009; Parault & Parkinson, 2008; see **FIGURE 8.1**). For example, one research team found that native English speakers who were learning Japanese words and their English translations learned the words faster and more easily if they were taught the correct translation than if they were taught an incorrect translation (Nygaard et al., 2009). This finding suggests that the words sounded more like their *real* meanings. The fact that at least some sound symbolism appears consistent across languages raises the intriguing possibility that connections between auditory and other sensory systems in the brain (see Chapter 4) influenced how languages evolved.

FIGURE 8.1 A Classic Example of Sound Symbolism. Which object looks like a "maluma" and which looks like a "takete"? If you're like most people (children *and* adults the world over), you'll say that the "maluma" is on the left and the "takete" is on the right.

FACTOID

Related words often have similar-sounding initial consonant clusters, a phenomenon termed phonesthemes (Hutchins, 1999). For example, in English the *sn* sound is associated with a large number of nose-related activities, including sneeze, sniff, snore, snooze, snicker, snoop (what a "nosy" person does, after all), and even snot! Can you think of other sound sequences that occur in a cluster of related words?

Fetuses can learn about the melody and rhythm of their native language and learn to recognize their mother's voice before birth. They can even learn to recognize a specific story read to them before birth (DeCasper & Spence, 1988).

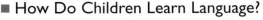

■ How Do Children Learn Language?

Language is among the few documented cases in which children are more efficient learners than adults. The language-learning process starts long before children begin talking. In fact, it begins even before they're born! By the fifth month of pregnancy, the auditory systems of unborn infants are developed enough that they can begin to make out their mothers' voices, learn to recognize some characteristics of their mothers' native language, and even recognize specific songs or stories they've heard repeatedly (DeCasper & Spence, 1988).

We know this to be true because researchers have developed a clever way to test newborn infants' ability to distinguish sounds, namely, a method that capitalizes on operant conditioning (see Chapter 6). The technique is the *high-amplitude sucking procedure* and takes advantage of one of the few behaviors over which infants have good control at birth—sucking. Two-day-old infants suck more on a pacifier when they hear their mothers' native language than when they hear a foreign language, even when total strangers speak both languages. Even at this early age, they display a clear preference for their mothers' native language. This is true of infants of both English-speaking and Spanish-speaking mothers: Infants whose mothers speak English suck harder when they hear English than Spanish, and those whose mothers speak Spanish suck harder when they hear Spanish than English (Moon, Cooper, & Fifer, 1993). The fact that researchers tested babies whose mothers speak multiple languages is an elegant experimental design feature. It allowed them to rule out the possibility that all babies prefer English over another language, regardless of which language their mothers speak.

◉—Watch Stimulating Language Development on **mypsychlab.com**

ruling out rival hypotheses

HAVE IMPORTANT ALTERNATIVE EXPLANATIONS FOR THE FINDINGS BEEN EXCLUDED?

Babies often engage in vocal exchanges such as nonsense "conversations" and turn-taking imitation sequences with others as they approach their first birthdays. Doing so helps cement the social function of language even before they can speak.

babbling
intentional vocalization that lacks specific meaning

one word stage
early period of language development when children use single-word phrases to convey an entire thought

PERCEIVING AND PRODUCING THE SOUNDS OF LANGUAGE. During the first year or so after birth, infants learn much more about the sounds of their native languages. They begin to figure out the phonemes of their languages and how to use their vocal apparatus to make specific sounds. Although children's babbling seems like nonsense—and it usually is—it plays an important role in language development by enabling babies to figure out how to move their vocal tracts to generate specific sounds. **Babbling** refers to any intentional vocalization (sounds other than crying, burping, sighing, and laughing, which are less intentional) that lacks specific meaning. Babbling evolves over the first year of life and follows a progression of stages demonstrating infants' increasing control of their vocal tracts (Kent & Miolo, 1995). By the end of their first year, infants' babbling takes on a conversational tone that sounds meaningful even though it isn't (Goldstein & Schwade, 2008). ◉—Watch

As infants are fine-tuning their vocal tracts, they're also fine-tuning their ears. As we've learned, different languages have different phoneme categories, so to be successful users of their native languages infants must learn which sets of sounds are relevant for their own language. All babies initially share the same basic phoneme categories regardless of their parents' native language. The only problem is that some languages don't use the sound categories with which infants are born. Such babies are actually born with the wrong phonemes for their language (Lasky, Suradal-Lasky, & Klein, 1975). For example, all infants are born being able to distinguish two sound categories that are relevant for Hindi but not English (Werker et al., 1981). Luckily, babies learning any language can adjust their phonemes rapidly over the course of the first year to match their native language. By 10 months, infants' phonemes are very much like those of the adult speakers of their native language (Werker & Tees, 1984).

LEARNING WORDS. Infants acquire the sounds of their language during their first year of life. But how and when do children begin to use these sounds to communicate? One key principle characterizes early word learning: *Comprehension precedes production.* Children are learning to recognize and interpret words well before— sometimes months before—they can produce them (see **FIGURE 8.2**). That's because they have only a limited ability to coordinate sounds to produce recognizable words. They may be perfectly aware that "elephant" refers to a large gray animal with a long trunk and large ears, but be unable to produce this big word.

One of the first words that children understand is their own name. Although most infants don't clearly start comprehending words until nine or 10 months, they recognize their own names by as early as six months (Tincoff & Jucszyk, 1999). They begin to recognize other commonly used and important (to them!) words like "bottle," "mama," and "doggie" by 10 to 12 months.

Children start to *produce* their first words around their first birthdays, although there's considerable variability in this milestone. They acquire their first words slowly. Between one and one and a half years of age, they gradually accumulate a vocabulary of between 20 and 100 words. As children become more experienced in learning new words, the rate at which they acquire words increases (Golinkoff et al., 2000; Smith, 2000). By the time they turn two, most children can produce several hundred words. By kindergarten, their vocabularies have ballooned to several thousand words.

Yet children typically make some mistakes in interpreting what words mean and how to use them. In particular, they often over- and underextend, applying words in a broader sense (overextension, like referring to all adult men as "Daddy") than adults do, or a narrower sense (underextension, like thinking that the word "cat" applies only to their pet cat). And nearly every child gets at least one word's meaning completely wrong at first. One of our favorite examples is of a child who cried out ecstatically, "Downtown!" every time he saw a fountain, because there was a large fountain located in his city's downtown area. Of course, most of the time children manage to get word meanings exactly right, which is a remarkable achievement.

SYNTACTIC DEVELOPMENT: PUTTING IT ALL TOGETHER. The first major milestone in children's syntactic development is combining words into phrases. Children start off speaking in the **one word stage**, during which they use just individual words to conveys entire thoughts. A child may use the word "doggie" to mean "There's a doggie!" "Where's the doggie?" or even "The doggie licked me!" Interpreting what children mean in the one-word stage can be a monumental challenge. By the time children turn two, most start to combine words into simple two-word phrases. Although these phrases are still far from complete sentences, they go a long way toward improving comprehensibility. For example, the child can now say

Very young children with limited vocabularies can't talk very well and are often shy about talking in front of strangers. **Can you think of ways that researchers could measure what words children understand without depending on their ability to tell us?** (See answer upside down at bottom of page.)

A child who uses the word "grandpa" to apply to any gray-haired man is committing what kind of mistake? (See answer upside down at right.)

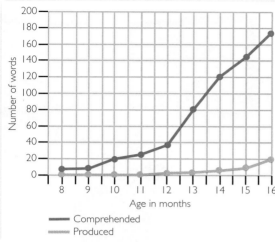

FIGURE 8.2 Word Comprehension between 8 and 16 Months of Age. In the early stages of word learning, children learn to comprehend new words before they figure out how to say them. This graph depicts the number of words that at least 50 percent of children at each month between 8 and 16 months can comprehend and say. Although not shown on this graph, the discrepancy between the number of words children know and those they can say continues to narrow as they approach 24 months. (*Source:* Adapted from Fenson et al., 1994)

FACTOID

When children acquire their first words, most also begin producing "baby signs"— meaningful gestures that stand for things like "more," "juice," or "fish." These aren't examples of sign language, because they're made up by the infant and don't have a syntax. But they seem to improve infants' communicative effectiveness. Baby signs, or symbolic gestures, as they're often called, are probably easier to produce early on because infants have better physical control of their hands than of their vocal tracts. In fact, many parents have begun teaching their children baby signs to improve their children's ability to communicate.

Answer: Overextension.

Answer: Researchers often ask infants to *show* what they know ("Which one is the ball?") or measure whether children look longer at the right object when hearing a familiar word.

FIGURE 8.3 Children Display Comprehension of Word Order Prior to Sentence Production. Children can display their grasp of syntax by pointing to a video that matches a sentence they have heard. Here, a 17-month-old child is displaying her comprehension of the sentence "The pig is tickling the dog" by pointing to the video that corresponds to the sentence.

FICTOID ✕

MYTH: Some people engage in *glossolalia*, that is, speaking in tongues or in *xenoglossia*, that is, speaking in a language they've never encountered.

REALITY: Scientific research can't resolve the question of whether glossolalia or xenoglossia is of supernatural origin. Nevertheless, careful analyses indicate that glossalalia doesn't exhibit the features of an actual language (Nickell, 1993), and that there are no documented cases of people suddenly acquiring a language they've never spoken (Malony & Lovekin, 1985).

sign language
language developed by members of a deaf community that uses visual rather than auditory communication

"more juice" to request a refill or "uh-oh juice" to notify mom that his juice just spilled. Although these phrases are still simplistic, children at this stage have already grasped something about syntactic rules. For example, they tend to use words in the correct order, even if they're leaving some of them out.

As is the case with word learning, children comprehend some basic syntactic rules before they can display them. Among other things, they understand how word order relates to meaning before they can generate complete sentences. Two researchers showed 17-month-olds two videos side-by-side, one that showed Cookie Monster tickling Big Bird and another that showed Big Bird tickling Cookie Monster. The experimenter asked the children, "Show me where Big Bird is tickling Cookie Monster." The children pointed toward the correct video, demonstrating they could determine from word order who was the "tickler" and who was the "ticklee" (Hirsch-Pasek & Golinkoff, 1996). (See **FIGURE 8.3** for a different example using a pig and a dog.)

Several months after they've begun using two-word phrases, children use more complex sentences involving three- or four-word combinations. Around the same time, they begin to produce morphological markers such as -*s* for plural and -*ed* for past tense in English. They acquire most syntactic rules by preschool age, but continue to acquire more complex rules in their early school years (Dennis, Sugar, & Whitaker, 1982).

■ Special Cases of Language Learning

Children learning language sometimes confront special challenges. These challenges may prevent, slow down, or complicate acquiring a language. We'll review two of them: Sign language learning in deaf children and bilingual language acquisition.

SIGN LANGUAGE. Sign language is a type of language developed by members of deaf communities that allows them to use visual rather than auditory communication. It involves using the hands, face, body, and "sign space"—the space immediately in front of the signer—to communicate. Just as there are many spoken languages, there are many sign languages spoken in different countries and deaf communities.

Many people hold a variety of misconceptions about sign languages (see **TABLE 8.3**). People often think of sign language as an elaborate form of gesturing, a charades-type

TABLE 8.3 Common Misconceptions about Deafness and Sign Language.

MYTH	REALITY
1. Deaf people don't need sign language because they can lip read.	Even the most skilled lip-readers can pick up only about 30 to 35 percent of what's being said because most of the work is done behind the scenes by the throat, tongue, and teeth. Our lips look virtually identical when saying "nice" and "dice"—even words like "queen" and "white" look the same to lip readers.
2. Learning to sign slows down deaf children's ability to learn to speak.	Historically, deaf education programs tried to prevent deaf children from learning to sign because they feared children would never learn to talk. It's now clear that learning a sign language actually speeds up the process of learning to talk.
3. American Sign Language is English translated word-for-word into signs.	American Sign Language (ASL) bears no resemblance to English; the syntax in particular differs completely from English syntax. Some deaf communities use what's called Signed English instead of ASL which translates English sentences word-for-word into signs from ASL.

attempt to act out silently what people would otherwise speak. This couldn't be further from the truth. Sign language is called "language" for a reason. It's a linguistic system of communication with its own phonemes, words, syntax, and extralinguistic information (Newport & Meier, 1985; Poizner, Klima, & Bellugi, 1987; Stokoe, Casterline, & Croneberg, 1976). Linguists who've analyzed the structure and organization of various sign languages (American Sign Language, French Sign Language, even Nicaraguan Sign Language) have confirmed that sign languages exhibit all of the same features as spoken languages, including a complex set of syntactic rules that determine when a string of signs is a grammatical sentence.

Further evidence that sign language works just like any other language comes from two sources. First, the same brain areas involved in processing spoken languages become active in sign languages (Petitto et al., 2000; Poizner et al., 1987). In fact, native signers' brains involve both traditional "language areas" and other brain areas that play roles in visual or spatial processing (Newman et al., 2002). Second, babies who learn sign languages pass through the same developmental stages at about the same ages as babies who learn spoken languages (Newport & Meier, 1985; Orlanksy & Bonvillian, 1984; Petitto & Marentette, 1991). They babble with their hands (Petitto & Marentette, 1991), acquire their first "words" (signs) at around the same time as hearing babies (Orlanksy & Bonvillian, 1984), and pass through the same stages of syntactic development at the same ages as hearing babies (Newport & Meier, 1985).

BILINGUALISM. Many of us have tried to learn a second language, and some of us are **bilingual**, adept at speaking and comprehending two languages. Given that so many of us have attempted to master a second language, why can so few of us call ourselves bilingual? Part of the answer lies in how we encounter a second language. We usually master a language more easily by living in a foreign country than by learning it in a classroom (Baker & MacIntyre, 2000; Genesee, 1985). Not surprisingly, our motivation to learn a new language also plays a key role (Piske, MacKay, & Flege, 2001). But the best predictor of whether we'll become fluent is the age of acquisition: All things being equal, the earlier, the better (Johnson & Newport, 1989).

In most bilingual persons, one language is dominant. It's typically the first language learned, the one they heard most often as a child, and the one they use most often. Children exposed to two languages may learn one language at home with their parents but hear a different language when they attend school. In this case, the home language is probably dominant. Or a student who speaks one language may spend a year abroad and learn a second language through immersion in this different-language community. The first language the student learned as a child would probably be dominant as well. Nevertheless, there are cases in which the child is introduced to two languages from the outset, as when her parents speak two languages or she has a full-time caretaker who speaks a different language from her parents. How do bilingual persons fluent in two languages keep them straight, and how are these languages organized in their brain? ⊙—⎡**Watch**

Children learning two languages follow the same stages in the same order for each language as do *monolingual* children—those learning a single language. There's some evidence that bilingual children experience some delay in each of their languages relative to their monolingual counterparts (Gathercole, 2002a, b). However, this delay depends on which aspects of language researchers measure. Vocabulary development is relatively unimpaired (Pearson & Fernández, 1994; Pearson, Fernández, & Oller, 1993), whereas syntax is more affected (Gathercole, 2002a, b). Moreover, despite popular claims that children are slowed down in their overall cognitive development, the delays that occur early in development are restricted only to language, and are balanced out by a variety of long-term benefits (Sorace, 2007). Not only can bilingual individuals converse with two language communities rather than one, but the process of figuring out how two languages work gives them heightened **metalinguistic** insight—awareness of how language is structured and used. As a result, they tend to perform better on language tasks in general (Bialystok, 1988; Galambos & Hakuta, 1988; Ricciardelli, 1992).

Unlike this deaf child, whose parent is a fluent signer, most deaf babies are born to hearing parents who don't begin learning sign language until after their babies are born (or sometimes even later).

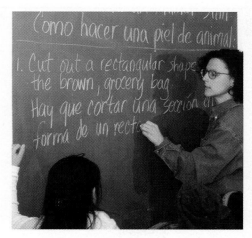

A growing number of children hear one language spoken at home and another at school. Some are instructed in two different languages at school. Although bilingualism may slow the learning of some aspects of both languages, it promotes metalinguistic insight in the long run.

⊙—⎡**Watch** Bilingual Education on **mypsychlab.com**

bilingual
proficient and fluent at speaking and comprehending two distinct languages

metalinguistic
awareness of how language is structured and used

Studies of brain activation during language processing demonstrate that bilingual persons who learned a second language early in development process the two languages using similar brain areas (Fabbro, 1999). In contrast, those who learned their second language later in development use different brain areas (Kim et al. 1997), suggesting that the brain may segregate different, later-learned languages into different regions. An alternative hypothesis is that the distinct brain areas observed for later-age exposure to second language are due to the fact that people who acquire languages later are less proficient and require more brain involvement to master their second language as a result (Abutalebi, Cappa, & Perani, 2005).

LANGUAGE DEPRIVATION. How much of language is due to nature as opposed to nurture? One way to understand how much nature versus nurture contributes to a given behavior is to perform "deprivation" experiments in which we deprive individuals of "nurture" and look to see whether the behavior occurs anyway. If it does, there's evidence that nature has endowed the individual with a tendency to exhibit that behavior. For obvious ethical reasons, we'd never intentionally deprive a child of language exposure.

Nevertheless, several tragic cases have served as "natural experiments" in this regard. Genie was a girl chained to a potty seat in a back bedroom for much of the first 13 years of her life and deprived almost entirely of social interaction or language input (Curtiss, 1977). Once rescued from this abusive situation and exposed to language, Genie displayed a rudimentary ability to communicate. But she, and others like her, failed to become fluent language users. Nevertheless, there are alternative explanations for impairment in these cases, such as the severe emotional and physical neglect these children experienced. As we learned in Chapter 2, case studies like Genie's tend to be limited in their ability to exclude rival explanations.

Susan Goldin-Meadow discovered an alternative way to study language deprivation, one that ruled out many of the rival explanations that plague cases like Genie's. She began studying deaf children of hearing parents who didn't know any sign language. Unlike Genie, these children are loved, cared for, fed, and given the opportunity to develop normally in all respects besides language. Goldin-Meadow found that many deaf children invent their own signs, even when not instructed in sign language. This phenomenon, called **homesign**, shows impressive ingenuity (and motivation to communicate) on the part of children, because they've invented these signs without guidance from adults (Goldin-Meadow et al., 2009). Still, without being exposed systematically to a language model, such as American Sign Language, homesigners never develop full-blown language. Pieces of the language puzzle are independent of experience, but to complete the whole puzzle, exposure to language is required. So as is so often the case, both nature and nurture play crucial roles.

■ Critical Periods for Language Learning

As we noted earlier, younger children are better at learning language than are older children and adults. Much of the evidence for this conclusion derives from studies of second language acquisition. This research has focused on whether there's a *critical period* for developing language. Critical periods are windows of time in development during which an organism must learn an ability if it's going to learn it at all (see Chapter 10). We can look at the age of exposure to language to discover whether such exposure must occur during a specific time window for language to be learned.

In a classic study, researchers examined the critical period for language by testing the English grammar skills of adults who'd immigrated to the United States from China and Korea at various ages. The test required participants to detect grammatical errors such as "The man climbed the ladder up carefully" and "The little boy is speak to a policeman." The investigators found that overall language proficiency was near native levels for adults first exposed to English between one and seven years of age. But skills dropped off for adults exposed to English after age seven (Johnson & Newport, 1989; see **FIGURE 8.4**).

---

ruling out rival hypotheses

HAVE IMPORTANT ALTERNATIVE EXPLANATIONS FOR THE FINDINGS BEEN EXCLUDED?

ruling out rival hypotheses

HAVE IMPORTANT ALTERNATIVE EXPLANATIONS FOR THE FINDINGS BEEN EXCLUDED?

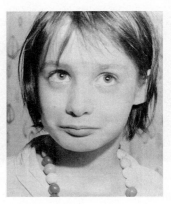

A young girl named Genie was deprived of language until adolescence. Genie's failure to learn to use language fluently is consistent with the idea that there is a critical period for language learning, although the severe abuse and emotional deprivation she experienced make it difficult to draw firm conclusions.

homesign
system of signs invented by deaf children of hearing parents who receive no language input

Notice, however, in Figure 8.4 that after the age of seven the drop-off is gradual rather than abrupt. Syntax and pronunciation are more vulnerable to effects of the age of exposure than is vocabulary (Johnson & Newport, 1989; Piske, MacKay, & Flege, 2001).

More recently, researchers have examined evidence of critical periods by studying deaf children born to hearing parents who've received *cochlear implants* at various ages. Cochlear implants are a relatively recent innovation; they're small computers that digitize sound and feed that sound activation directly to the auditory nerve (see Chapter 4), bypassing the inner ear. As a result, deaf children's brains can receive auditory input. Cochlear implants have yielded mixed results, with many recipients experiencing difficulties with learning spoken language (Svirsky et al., 2000). Cochlear implants produce more positive effects on language among younger than older children (Svirsky, Chin, & Jester, 2007). It's not clear whether these age effects are due to the brain's ability to interpret the auditory stimulation in general or to the ability to learn language specifically. Either way, children with cochlear implants provide additional evidence that age of exposure influences children's learning success.

It's clear that age of acquisition influences language learning. But there's no evidence in humans for strict critical periods, at least when it comes to language. Instead, language learning is typically marked by what psychologists call a *sensitive period*, a period during which people are more receptive to learning and can acquire new knowledge more easily. We don't fully understand why older children and adults are less capable of learning new languages than younger children. The most promising account is Elissa Newport's (1990) "less is more" hypothesis (Newport, Bavelier, & Neville, 2001). According to this hypothesis, children have more limited information-processing abilities, fewer analytic skills, and less specific knowledge about how language works than do adults. As a result, they learn language more naturalistically and gradually from the "ground up." In contrast, adults try to impose more organization and structure on their learning, ironically making learning a language more challenging.

■ Theoretical Accounts of Language Acquisition

Given children's impressive ability to learn to use such a complex system at such an early age, what explanations can we generate for children's language learning? Some explanations fall more heavily on the nature side of the nature–nurture debate, others on the nurture side. Yet even the strongest nature account acknowledges that children aren't born knowing their specific language; they learn what they hear. Similarly, the strongest nurture account acknowledges that children's brains are set up in a way that's receptive to learning and organizing language input. Here, we'll review four major theoretical accounts of language acquisition.

THE IMITATION ACCOUNT. The simplest explanation of children's language learning is that they learn through imitation. In this respect, this account is the most parsimonious of the four we'll examine. Babies hear language used in systematic ways and learn to use language as adults use it. This is certainly true in one sense, because babies learn the language they hear. Behaviorists (see Chapters 1 and 6) took this account one step further by arguing that babies don't just imitate what they hear, but imitate what they're reinforced for saying (Skinner, 1953). But a purely imitation-based explanation is unlikely tell the whole story

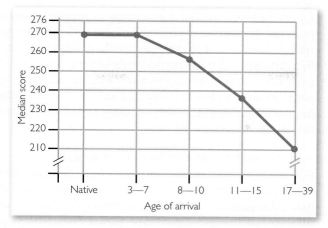

FIGURE 8.4 Proficiency in Second Language Depends on the Age of Exposure. Adults first exposed to English before age seven displayed proficiency comparable to that of native English speakers, whereas those who learned English after age seven were significantly less proficient. (*Source:* Johnson & Newport, 1989)

ruling out rival hypotheses

HAVE IMPORTANT ALTERNATIVE EXPLANATIONS FOR THE FINDINGS BEEN EXCLUDED?

Language clearly has an important learned component, because children adopted from a different country learn to speak the language of their adopted rather than biological parents.

occam's razor

DOES A SIMPLER EXPLANATION FIT THE DATA JUST AS WELL?

for one reason: Language is **generative**. *Generativity* means that language isn't just a set of predefined sentences that we can pull out and apply in appropriate contexts. Instead, it's a system that allows us to create an infinite number of sentences, producing new statements, thoughts, and ideas never previously uttered (indeed, it's unlikely that anyone has ever written the exact sentence you just read). The fact that even very young children use language in generative ways—creating sentences or combinations of words they've never heard—means they're producing things for which they were never directly reinforced, refuting a strictly behavioral view.

THE NATIVIST ACCOUNT. The strongest nature view is the **nativist** account, which says that children come into the world with some basic knowledge of how language works. Nativists propose that children are born with expectations that there will be syntactic rules that influence how sentences are constructed (Chomsky, 1972), although the precise rules for their native language need to be learned through exposure. Noam Chomsky, who essentially invented the field of contemporary linguistics, even hypothesized that humans possess a specific language "organ" in the brain that houses these rules. He called it the **language acquisition device**, and argued that it comes preprogrammed to enable children to use language. Nativists point out that children often make *overregularization* errors, applying syntactic rules when they shouldn't. For example, children may say "foots" instead of "feet" or "goed" instead of "went" even though they've (hopefully!) never heard these word forms from adults. Chomsky took this finding as evidence that children follow syntactic rules in their heads rather than imitating what they hear.

A key weakness of the nativist view is that many of its claims are difficult to falsify. Critics point out that children learn syntax gradually and that even adults use grammatically incorrect sentences. The nativist could reply that different aspects of grammar take more or less time to "set," and that ungrammatical sentences don't imply lack of knowledge of grammar. These are certainly reasonable explanations, but the theory's weakness is that it's hard to think of an outcome that nativists couldn't explain. As we've noted in earlier chapters, a theory that can explain every conceivable outcome essentially explains nothing.

THE SOCIAL PRAGMATICS ACCOUNT. The **social pragmatics** account suggests that specific aspects of the social environment structure language learning. According to this account, children use the context of a conversation to infer its topic from the actions, expressions, gestures, and other behaviors of speakers. Children can figure out word meaning in these situations as early as 24 months of age (Bloom, 2000). Still, this account has its weaknesses. Explaining child language on the basis of social understanding requires us to assume that infants understand an awful lot about how other people are thinking. In addition, we can explain most social pragmatic abilities without requiring as much insight on the part of the child (Samuelson & Smith, 1998). For example, social pragmatic theorists might say that children learn to interpret meaning from pointing by inferring the speaker's intentions. Alternatively, children might use a simpler process; they might notice that every time their caretakers point to a specific object, they utter the same word. In this way, children may infer that where someone is pointing is correlated with word meaning. This deduction doesn't require children to take into account the social context or communicative intentions of others.

THE GENERAL COGNITIVE PROCESSING ACCOUNT. Another explanation for how children learn language is the *general cognitive processing* account. It proposes that children's ability to learn language results from general skills that children apply across a variety of activities. For example, children's ability to perceive, learn, and recognize patterns may be all they need to learn language. If so, there'd be no need to propose a language acquisition device as Chomsky did.

Still, there are challenges to this account, too. One is that children are better at learning languages than adults, whereas adults are better at learning things in general. Another is that specific areas of the brain (see Chapter 3), especially the left temporal lobe

---

falsifiability

CAN THE CLAIM BE DISPROVED? →

falsifiability

CAN THE CLAIM BE DISPROVED? →

generative
allowing an infinite number of unique sentences to be created by combining words in novel ways

nativist
account of language acquisition that suggests children are born with some basic knowledge of how language works

language acquisition device
hypothetical organ in the brain in which nativists believe knowledge of syntax resides

social pragmatics
account of language acquisition that proposes children infer what words and sentences mean from context and social interactions

occam's razor

DOES A SIMPLER EXPLANATION FIT THE DATA JUST AS WELL? →

psychomythology

DO TWINS HAVE THEIR OWN LANGUAGE?

The idea of being a twin has a certain appeal and allure. It's only natural to expect there to be a special bond between two people who've been together from the moment of conception. One commonly held belief is that this special bond enables twins to invent their own secret language, one only they can understand—a phenomenon known as *cryptophasia*.

As fascinating as this notion is, the truth is less exotic, but no less interesting. Cases of apparent cryptophasia among twins turn out to be a result of phonological impairment and other types of language delay (Bishop & Bishop, 1998; Dodd & McEvoy, 1994) that are more prevalent among twins than among singletons (children born one at a time). Twin pairs who've supposedly developed a secret language are simply attempting to use their native language, but with poor articulation and significant pronunciation errors. These difficulties are serious enough to render their speech largely incomprehensible to the rest of us. This problem sometimes results in longer-term language impairment well into elementary school. Because twin pairs tend to make similar kinds of phonological errors, their speech is more understandable to each other than it is to their parents or nonrelated children (Dodd & McEvoy, 1994; Thorpe, et al., 2001).

? Popular psychology tells us that twins sometimes develop their own language. What does research indicate is really going on here? (See answer upside down at bottom of page.)

(see **FIGURE 8.5**), are more active in language processing than in other types of learning, memory, and pattern recognition activities (Gazzaniga, Ivry, & Mangun, 2002). This finding implies that at least some distinct cognitive processes occur during language as opposed to other cognitive activities.

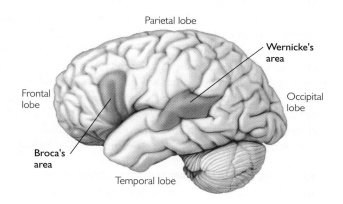

FIGURE 8.5 Language Processing Areas of the Brain. Two areas of the brain that play key roles in language processing are Broca's area, involved in speech production, and Wernicke's area, involved in speech comprehension (see Chapter 3).

EVALUATING THE THEORIES SCIENTIFICALLY. Each theoretical view offers a persuasive argument. Which is correct? As we've seen, we can rule out a purely imitation-based account because it can't explain the complexity and generativity of language. Nativism, although plausible, is difficult to falsify and not particularly parsimonious because it requires infants to be born with knowledge about all of the rules that govern the world's remarkably diverse languages. There are probably some elements of the ability to use language that are inborn, as suggested by the fact that language-deprived deaf children develop homesign, which includes some aspects of language. The remaining two perspectives are receiving by far the most attention among researchers, who are generating experiments that investigate which of them best accounts for children's language development (Namy & Waxman, 2000; Samuelson & Smith, 1998). Still other researchers have proposed interactionist accounts, which acknowledge a role for both social pragmatics and general cognitive learning (Hirsh-Pasek & Golinkoff, 2008).

ruling out rival hypotheses

HAVE IMPORTANT ALTERNATIVE EXPLANATIONS FOR THE FINDINGS BEEN EXCLUDED?

falsifiability

CAN THE CLAIM BE DISPROVED?

occam's razor

DOES A SIMPLER EXPLANATION FIT THE DATA JUST AS WELL?

■ Nonhuman Animal Communication

The communication systems of different animal species differ in type and complexity. Some species use scent marking as their primary form of communication. Others rely on visual displays, such as baring their teeth or flapping their wings. Still others, like we humans, use vocal communication. But human language is much is more complex in its

Answer: Twins aren't developing their own language but are instead displaying very similar sounding speech production disorders.

FIGURE 8.6 Communication among Honeybees. Honeybees use the waggle dance to communicate to other bees the location of a food source: in which direction it lies, how far away it is, and how plentiful it is.

structure and rules than other animals' communication systems. It's also more generative. Most species have a fixed number of ways of expressing a fixed number of messages, but no means of communicating completely new ideas.

HOW ANIMALS COMMUNICATE. If we humans want to grab others' attention, we need only say the words "sex" and "violence." Similarly, in most nonhuman animals, the two circumstances in which communication most often takes place are—you guessed it—mating and aggression. Male songbirds, such as canaries and finches, produce a specific song to attract mates and another to convey the message, "This is my territory, back off" (Kendeigh, 1941). Chimpanzees use a combination of vocalizations and visual displays, such as facial expressions and slapping the ground, to convey aggression (de Waal, 1989). When it comes to mating rituals, male chimpanzees squat with their knees spread to display their penises as an invitation to mate (admittedly, chimpanzees aren't known for their subtlety). Of course, we humans have our own ways of attracting mates, although we usually call this something more polite like "flirting" when it comes to our own species.

A fascinating example of nonhuman communication that provides information exchange beyond aggression and mating is the waggle dance of honeybees. Bees use this dance to communicate with their fellow bees about the location of a food source (see **FIGURE 8.6**). Bees that locate a food source fly back to their hive and perform an intricate series of figure-eight movements, moving the hind segment of their bodies back and forth rapidly (waggling) as they walk. The direction the bee faces indicates which direction to fly, and the duration and intensity of the waggle indicate how far and how plentiful the food supply is (Riley et al., 2005; von Frisch, 1967). The bee's waggle dance is one of the few non-human examples of communication about something beyond the here and now.

The vervet monkey provides another example. Many bird and mammal species let out a specific vocalization when a predator is nearby, but what makes vervet monkeys distinctive is their use of different alarm calls for different predators (Seyfarth & Cheney, 1997). They produce one type of call when they see a leopard, a second when they see a snake, and a third when they see a hawk or other flying predator. These alarm calls are the closest thing to words scientists have observed outside of human language, because specific sounds correspond to specific meanings. 👁—Watch

👁—Watch Birds and Language on mypsychlab.com

TEACHING HUMAN LANGUAGE TO NONHUMAN ANIMALS. Concerted efforts to teach animals human language have been largely unsuccessful. The earliest attempts to teach chimpanzees, one of our nearest living genetic relatives, fell flat. The researchers assumed incorrectly that chimpanzees possess a vocal apparatus similar to ours: Chimpanzees' vocal apparatus doesn't permit anywhere near the range and coordination of sounds we can achieve (Lieberman, Crelin, & Klatt, 1972). Later researchers tried to teach chimpanzees to use either sign language or a lexigram board, which allows them to point to printed visual symbols that stand for specific words (see **FIGURE 8.7**). 👁—Watch

👁—Watch the Sign Language video on mypsychlab.com

These attempts were more promising, but there were still crucial limits:

1. Chimpanzees, unlike human infants, require thousands of trials to learn to associate signs or lexigrams with their meanings.

2. The vast majority of chimpanzees' attempts to communicate seem to be requests for food or other pleasurable activities, like being tickled or chased.

3. Chimpanzees combine words into more complex utterances, but they never master syntactic rules.

FIGURE 8.7 A Chimpanzee Uses Lexigrams to Communicate with Caretakers. This ape has been trained to associate colored shapes with meanings such as "juice," "fruit," and "tickle."

Two animal species may do a bit better. One is the bonobo (formerly called the pygmy chimpanzee), once thought to be a type of chimpanzee but now recognized as a distinct species that's genetically even more closely related to humans. The few studies conducted on bonobos suggest a different learning pathway, which more closely resembles human learning (Savage-Rumbaugh, 1986). Bonobos (1) learn better as young animals than as adults, (2) tend to learn through observation rather than direct reinforcement, and

(3) use symbols to comment on or engage in social interactions, rather than simply for food treats. Yet bonobos, like their chimpanzee cousins, seem to get stuck when learning syntax. Even the most proficient of the bonobos trained with human language can't master syntactic rules beyond the level of about a two-and-a-half-year-old human child. One species that may be able to use spoken language much as we do is the African gray parrot. An Einstein of a parrot named Alex, who died in 2007 at the age of 31, was renowned for his ability to speak and to solve cognitive tasks. Parrots are, of course, famous, and sometimes infamous, for their ability to mimic sounds. They can reproduce (or "parrot") human speech, barking dogs, vacuum cleaners, and locomotive whistles. This mimicry doesn't equate to understanding language. But at least some African gray parrots, including Alex, appear to go beyond mere mimicry. They use language in a more humanlike manner, generating new and meaningful combinations of words and even mastering syntactic rules (Pepperberg, 2006). Yet their learning process is more similar to that of chimpanzees than bonobos and humans. It's a result of many repetitions rather than of observing and interacting with the world.

We humans are indeed unique in our ability to use language in such sophisticated ways. Of course, complexity in and of itself doesn't make us better, although it may make us "smarter" in some crucial ways. Squirrels and cockroaches do a pretty decent job of keeping themselves going with whatever communication systems they have to work with. For their purposes, they're every bit as effective in their communication as we are.

Alex (an African gray parrot) was famous for his impressive language skills.

---

assess your knowledge   FACT OR FICTION?

✓•—[**Study** and **Review** on **mypsychlab.com**

1. Nonstandard dialects of English follow syntactic rules that differ from but are just as valid as the rules in standard American English. **True / False**

2. Children's two-word utterances typically violate syntactic rules. **True / False**

3. Children who are deaf learn to sign at an older age than hearing children who are learning to talk. **True / False**

4. Bilingual individuals usually have one dominant language, which they learned earlier in development. **True / False**

5. Few nonhuman animal communication systems involve exchanges of information beyond the here and now. **True / False**

Answers: 1. T (p. 289); 2. F (p. 292); 3. F (p. 293); 4. T (p. 293); 5. T (p. 298)

DO WE THINK IN WORDS? THE RELATION BETWEEN LANGUAGE AND THOUGHT

8.7 Identify how our language may influence our thinking.

We've all had times when we realized we were conversing with ourselves; we may have even started talking out loud to ourselves. Clearly, we sometimes think in words. What about the rest of the time? Do we usually think in a nonlinguistic fashion or just not notice our internal conversation? One early hypothesis, proposed by John B. Watson, the founder of behaviorism (see Chapters 1 and 6), is that thinking is a form of internal speech. For Watson, there's no thinking without language, and all of our thoughts—our memories, decisions, ruminations, and fantasies—are merely verbal descriptions in our minds. Watson believed that thinking is simply subvocal talking, moving the vocal tract as if talking, but below hearing level.

The proposal that all thought is represented verbally implies that children don't think at all until they've mastered language, and that the language we speak shapes how we perceive and interact with the world. What does the evidence say?

■ Linguistic Determinism: We Speak, Therefore We Think

The view that we represent all thinking linguistically is called **linguistic determinism**. One of the best-known examples of how language can influence thought is the belief that Inuits (formerly called Eskimos) possess about a thousand words for snow. Linguistic determinists argue that having so many words for snow enables Inuits to perceive incredibly subtle distinctions among types of snow. It's a good story. But there are several reasons to believe it's all a myth.

1. Although Inuits make several fine distinctions among types of snow, research shows that a thousand is a substantial exaggeration of these types.

2. English speakers actually use many terms to describe different types of snow, such as "slush," "powder," or even "crud." In fact, we have just about as many terms as do the Inuits.

3. Even assuming that the Inuits have more terms for snow than we do, we can't infer that the greater number of terms *caused* the Inuit to make finer distinctions. It's just as likely that Inuits and other people who work in snowy conditions, like skiers and hikers, find it helpful to draw fine distinctions among types of snow. If so, language may reflect people's thinking about snow rather than the other way around. The correlation between the number of words and number of distinctions doesn't mean that the words produced distinctions that wouldn't otherwise have been there.

It's challenging to think of ways to test linguistic determinism. One strong test would be to compare the thought processes of people who can use language with those of people who can't to see if their thinking is similar. Of course, nearly everyone learns language, and those few who don't are typically either severely cognitively impaired or have suffered such serious abuse and neglect that they're deeply disturbed emotionally. So we need to look to other evidence to see whether normal thinking can exist without language.

Helen Keller offers a fascinating case example. She lost her hearing and her sight at 19 months due to illness, leaving her unable to communicate either vocally or gesturally. With the help of her teacher, Annie Sullivan, she discovered that signs performed against the palm of her hand were a form of communication. Keller eventually learned several languages and went on to write multiple books about her experiences. In her writings, Keller revealed herself to be a believer in linguistic determinism. She wrote that before learning language, "I did not know that I am. I lived in a world that was a no-world. . . . I did not know that I knew aught [anything] or that I lived or acted or desired. I had neither will nor intellect" (Keller, 1910, pp. 113–114). Of course, this is merely one anecdote, not systematic scientific evidence. Most of us have poor memories of our childhood mental states, thoughts, and perspectives. So there are alternative explanations for Keller's recalling a lack of thought. Moreover, there are reasons to doubt linguistic determinism. One of the earliest tests of linguistic determinism is one you won't want to try at home; it prevented someone from engaging in subvocal speech by paralyzing him temporarily. The researchers used a drug called *curare,* which paralyzes the muscles and skeleton but leaves the patient conscious. The brave—or should we say foolish?—subject was an anesthesiologist (scientists and physicians have a long history of attempting experiments on themselves before trying anything dangerous on others). After the drug had worn off, he accurately reported events he'd observed, and described thoughts and sensations he'd experienced while paralyzed (Smith et al., 1947). Clearly, thought isn't completely dependent on subvocalizing. This finding soundly falsified Watson's hypothesis that thought is merely subvocal language. Yet it didn't entirely rule out linguistic determinism. For example, we may think by simulating speech in our minds without moving our vocal tracts to produce sounds.

Later evidence was more conclusive. First, contrary to the predictions of linguistic determinism, children can perform many complex cognitive tasks long before they can talk about them. For that reason, psychologists have developed cognitive performance tests for infants and children that minimize testers' reliance on verbal instructions

correlation vs. causation
CAN WE BE SURE THAT A CAUSES B?

The Inuit live in Arctic climates in Siberia, Alaska, northern Canada, and Greenland. It's common lore that the Inuit have a thousand words to refer to different types of snow, and as a result, they make finer distinctions among types of snow than do people who speak English. In fact, this claim is a myth: Inuit languages have about the same number of words for snow as does English.

ruling out rival hypotheses
HAVE IMPORTANT ALTERNATIVE EXPLANATIONS FOR THE FINDINGS BEEN EXCLUDED?

falsifiability
CAN THE CLAIM BE DISPROVED?

linguistic determinism
view that all thought is represented verbally and that, as a result, our language defines our thinking

and verbal responses. A second compelling argument against linguistic determinism comes from neuroimaging studies of problem solving, thinking, remembering, and reading (see **FIGURE 8.8**). These studies show that although language areas often become activated when people engage in certain cognitive tasks, such as reading, they aren't activated during others, such as spatial tasks or visual imagery (Gazzaniga, Ivry, & Mangun, 2002). These studies suggest that thought can occur without language.

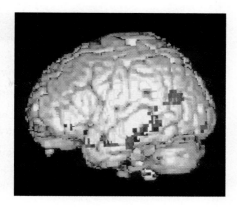

FIGURE 8.8 Brain Activation during Language Tasks. This PET scan shows the areas in the left temporal lobe that become especially active when people are trying to figure out the meanings of words.

FICTOID

MYTH: Language impairment as a result of stroke or other brain injury occurs only following left hemisphere damage.

REALITY: Although more obvious language deficits tend to occur in left-hemisphere-damaged patients, damage to the right temporal and frontal lobes can also disrupt the ability to interpret or use nonliteral speech, such as sarcasm.

■ Linguistic Relativity: Language Gives Thought a Gentle Nudge

Clearly, linguistic determinism—at least in its original form—doesn't have a lot going for it. Nevertheless, there's some promise for a less radical perspective, called **linguistic relativity**. Proponents of linguistic relativity maintain that characteristics of language shape our thought processes. This idea is also known as the *Sapir-Whorf hypothesis*, named after the two scholars who proposed it (Sapir, 1929; Whorf, 1956). There's evidence both for and against linguistic relativity. Sapir and Whorf might have argued that this mixed evidence is to be expected, because some aspects of thinking are more vulnerable to language influence than others.

Several studies suggest that language can affect thinking (Majid, 2010; McDonough, Choi, & Mandler, 2003). Two researchers examined the memories of Russians who moved to the United States and achieved fluency in Russian and English. These participants recalled events that happened in Russia more accurately when speaking Russian, and recalled events that happened in the United States more accurately when speaking English even though they recalled both events while in the United States (Marian & Neisser, 2000). Yet in other cases, researchers have been surprised to discover that language sometimes doesn't influence thought. One example is color categorization (Lenneberg, 1967). Different languages contain different numbers of basic color terms. In English, we generally use a set of 11 basic color terms: red, blue, green, yellow, white, black, purple, orange, pink, brown, and gray. Nevertheless, some languages contain fewer basic color terms. A language community may use a single word to refer to all things that are either blue or green. When it becomes important to distinguish blue from green things, speakers may say "blue/green like the sky" versus "blue/green like the leaves." In a small number of non-Westernized cultures, such as the Dani of New Guinea, there are no true color terms at all, only "dark" and "bright."

The Dani language has only words for "dark" and "bright," not individual colors, but Dani people can distinguish colors, just as we do.

The fact that there are different numbers of color terms in different languages affords a clever test case for the Sapir-Whorf hypothesis. If language influences thought, someone from the Dani, whose language contains only two color terms, should have a harder time distinguishing blue from green than those of us whose language contains separate terms for these two colors. Nevertheless, Eleanor Rosch (1973) demonstrated that the Dani perceive colors as dividing up into roughly the same color categories as do English speakers.

So does this mean that speakers of all languages end up thinking in precisely the same ways? No. The evidence suggests that language shapes some, but not all, aspects of perception, memory, and thought. Nevertheless, when researchers identify language-related differences in thought, it's not easy to disentangle the influences of language from culture. Different language communities also have different priorities, emphases, and values that shape how they think about the world. Because nearly all cross-linguistic comparisons are correlational rather than experimental, language and culture are nearly always confounded. We therefore must be careful when drawing causal conclusions about the impact of language on thinking.

linguistic relativity
view that characteristics of language shape our thought processes

◄ **correlation vs. causation**
CAN WE BE SURE THAT A CAUSES B?

✓•—Study and Review on mypsychlab.com

Control Condition	Stroop Interference Condition
Rabbit	Red
House	Blue
Blanket	Green
Dance	Yellow
Flower	Purple
Key	Orange
Seven	Black
Dance	Yellow
House	Blue
Key	Orange
Seven	Purple
Flower	Black
Rabbit	Red
Blanket	Green

FIGURE 8.9 The Stroop Effect. The Stroop task demonstrates that reading is automatic. Go down each column and say aloud the color of ink in which each word is printed. Try the control list first—you'll find that it's relatively straightforward task. Next, try the Stroop interference list. You'll probably find the task considerably more difficult.

whole word recognition
reading strategy that involves identifying common words based on their appearance without having to sound them out

phonetic decomposition
reading strategy that involves sounding out words by drawing correspondences between printed letters and sounds

FIGURE 8.10 Learning How Writing Moves. Before learning to read, children must learn which writing direction is correct for their language. English is written from left to right (a); Hebrew from right to left (b); and Japanese from top to bottom (c).

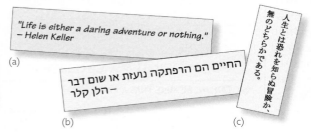

(a) "Life is either a daring adventure or nothing." – Helen Keller

(b) החיים הם הרפתקה נועזת או שום דבר – הלן קלר

(c) 人生とは恐れを知らぬ冒険か、無のどちらかである。

assess your knowledge **FACT OR FICTION?**

1. We can't determine whether the fine distinctions Inuits make among different kinds of snow are a cause or a consequence of the many terms for *snow* in their language. **True / False**

2. The curare experiment falsified linguistic determinism. **True / False**

3. According to the Sapir-Whorf hypothesis, all aspects of thinking are slightly, but not strongly, influenced by language. **True / False**

4. People who speak languages that lack terms for distinguishing colors can't tell these colors apart. **True / False**

Answers: 1. T (p. 300); 2. F (p. 300); 3. F (p. 301); 4. F (p. 301)

READING: RECOGNIZING THE WRITTEN WORD

8.8 Identify the skills required to learn to read, and understand the debate concerning reading strategies.

8.9 Analyze the relationship between reading speed and reading comprehension.

Reading, like spoken language, eventually becomes an automatic process, one that doesn't consume our attentional resources, except when we're reading something particularly challenging or engaging. Odds are high you could munch on potato chips while reading this chapter without having it affect your comprehension. In fact, reading becomes so automatic by the time we reach college-age that we can't turn it off even when we want to. Usually, this is a good thing because it means we can read street signs while driving even when the person sitting next to us is gabbing away. But the automatic nature of reading can be less than ideal when we accidentally glimpse someone's open diary or intimately personal Facebook message on a nearby computer. In these cases, we almost can't help but violate others' privacy, because we can't put the brakes on our brains to stop us from processing what we see.

A compelling demonstration of the automaticity of language—for better or for worse—is the Stroop color-naming task, named after the researcher who invented it, J. Ridley Stroop (1935). This task requires participants to suppress their attention to printed words to identify the color of the ink. The catch is that the printed words are color names that contradict the ink color (see **FIGURE 8.9**). Most people experience enormous difficulty ignoring the printed words, even though the task doesn't require them to read. The Stroop task shows that reading is automatic and hard to inhibit (MacLeod, 1991). Interestingly, children who are still getting the hang of reading don't experience interference in the Stroop task, so they do better on this task than adults (Schadler & Thissen, 1981). Because their reading is effortful, they can turn off their attention to the words and pay attention only to ink color. As children become more practiced readers, they actually begin to do worse on the Stroop.

■ Learning to Read

Before we learn to read, we must realize several things. Some seem self-evident to us, but they aren't always obvious to new learners, including young children, particularly those whose caretakers don't often read to them. To be reading ready, we must:

1. Realize that writing is meaningful. Young children looking at books and signs may not realize that the seeming gobbledy-gook printed below pictures or on street signs is something more than scribbles (Stanovich & West, 1989).

2. Understand that writing moves in a specific direction (see **FIGURE 8.10**). Those learning English must figure out that writing moves from left to right, children learning Hebrew that writing moves from right to left, and children learning Japanese that writing moves from top to bottom. We must also realize that breaks in the print separate distinct words. These aspects of writing are our basic starting points for reading (Clay, 1975).

3. Learn to recognize the letters of the alphabet. This task is harder than it seems because we must figure out what basic features distinguish an *N* from an *M,* for example, despite the fact that we see both *N*s and *M*s printed in a variety of confusingly different sizes and styles (Chall, 1983).

4. Learn that printed letters correspond to specific sounds. The relation between sounds and letters isn't anywhere near perfect, but figuring out what sounds an *F, B,* and *L* make is another crucial starting point. Experiments have shown that training children to be aware of sound–letter correspondences enhances reading (Bradley & Bryant, 1983; Gibb & Randall, 1988; Lunberg, Frost, & Persen, 1988).

Once all of these pre-reading insights are in place, we must master two skills to become *experts* at reading. The first is learning to recognize how whole printed words look on the page. Without this skill, reading isn't easy or automatic. We need to recognize common words without having to sound out each word as if it were the first time we've seen it. The average reader uses **whole word recognition** to read the vast majority of printed words (LaBerge & Samuels, 1974). Still, this obviously can't be the whole story because we need to develop strategies for reading new words. For these words, we use a second strategy, called **phonetic decomposition** or *phonics* (National Research Council, 1998). This strategy involves sounding out words by figuring out the correspondences between printed letters and sounds. For words like *livid,* this task is simple because each printed consonant (*l, v,* and *d*) corresponds to a single phoneme in English and the vowel (*i*) has the same sound in both instances. Nevertheless, not all sounds in the English language are linked to a unique letter (or even combination of letters) corresponding to them. For example, sounding out the word *pleasure* based on letter-to-phoneme correspondences won't get us far; we'll end up with something way off base, like "plee-ah-sir-eh." In these cases, we need to memorize how the word's spelling translates to the spoken word. Watch

There's been heated debate about whether whole word recognition or phonics is the best strategy for teaching reading. For a long time, educators believed that teaching children to recognize whole words was the best way to get them to become proficient readers. As a consequence, a great deal of U.S. educational policy was based on whole word learning. Although these educators were right that mature readers rely mostly on whole word recognition, they mistook the correlation between reading proficiency and the whole word recognition strategy as causal. They concluded incorrectly that whole word recognition *leads to* better reading. In fact, learning to analyze and recognize sound–letter correspondences, even though they're not perfect, is a much more effective way to get and keep children reading (Rayner et al., 2002).

■ Speed-Reading—A Hoax in Sheep's Clothing?

Arguably, one of the biggest hoaxes perpetuated on educated people is that speed-reading courses are effective. We can find training programs in speed-reading, also known as photoreading, megaspeed-reading, and alphanetics, almost everywhere. Some universities even offer sponsored courses to boost students' reading rates. Here's a hot tip: Save your money! Speed-reading "works" in the sense that it speeds up our reading rate. So what's the catch? Our comprehension suffers enormously (Graf, 1973). Reading is subject to a speed–accuracy trade-off: The faster we read, the more we miss. The average college student reads about 200–300 words per minute (Carver, 1990). Controlled studies indicate that reading faster than 400 words per minute results in comprehension rates below 50 percent (Cunningham, Stanovich, & Wilson, 1990).

FICTOID

MYTH: *Dyslexia* is defined as a tendency to transpose letters in words (like spelling the word *read* as "raed") or to perceive letters or numbers backward (like seeing a *b* as a *d*).

REALITY: Only some people with dyslexia (which means "reading difficulty") display these reversal problems; moreover, many children display these problems at a young age but don't develop dyslexia. Nor do people with dyslexia literally perceive words backward.

FACTOID +

Children who frequently hear and recite nursery rhymes tend to be earlier readers (Bryant et al., 1989), perhaps because the rhyming words (like *cat* and *hat*) increase their awareness of separate phonemes in words. Alternatively, better verbal skills may underlie both abilities.

◀ **correlation vs. causation**
CAN WE BE SURE THAT A CAUSES B?

? We can often spot posters and fliers like this one on college campuses, in coffee shops, and in our spam e-mail. Such speed-reading programs claim to increase our reading rate from 2 to 100 times over the average reading rate (which is 200 to 300 words per minute). **Why should we not trust these claims?** (See answer upside down below.)

 Watch the Literacy video on **mypsychlab.com**

Answer: Although our reading rate will increase, our comprehension suffers.

Answers are located at the end of the text.

SPEED-READING COURSES

evaluating CLAIMS

How much time do you spend reading textbooks, lecture notes, and other course materials? Probably more than you care to remember. Wouldn't it be great to cut that time in half—or even more—and spend more time hanging out with your friends? Let's evaluate some of these claims, which are modeled after actual advertisements for speed-reading courses.

"Improve your *reading speed, comprehension*, retention, and recall with our course."
Claims to improve reading speed and comprehension, but research shows that speed-reading has negative consequences on our comprehension.

"Learn how to *double or triple* your reading speed in *under 15 minutes*."
What kind of evidence would you need to support this extraordinary claim?

"This course was developed by a *team of professionals who researched* speed-reading at colleges and universities around the world."
What would you need to know about these "professionals" and how they conducted their research?

"Our course will teach you how to *skim* excessively detailed documents."
Note that this claim acknowledges that most of the success of "speed-reading" actually comes from skimming—that is, not reading some material at all.

correlation vs. causation
CAN WE BE SURE THAT A CAUSES B?

extraordinary claims
IS THE EVIDENCE AS STRONG AS THE CLAIM?

So why are speed-reading programs so popular? Because they're based on a genuine finding, namely, that reading speed is correlated with comprehension. Nevertheless, this correlation doesn't imply that if we start reading faster, we'll comprehend more. Proficient readers tend to be both faster at reading and better at comprehending than poorer readers, but reading speed doesn't cause comprehension.

Speed-reading programs promise to increase our reading rates many times over, to 1,000 or even 2,000 words per minute. There have even been extraordinary claims of people who can read between 15,000 and 30,000 words per minute. Yet the truth turns out to be far less than extraordinary. Researchers tested two such readers on their identification of specific words and comprehension within a written text (Homa, 1983). These supposed whizzes were no better than average readers at finding specific words. Moreover, both failed the comprehension test miserably, understanding less than 50 percent of what they read. Is there any hope of improving our reading speed while not diminishing our comprehension? Fortunately, several approaches are effective. An old study demonstrated that the slowest 10 percent of readers in the Harvard freshman class improved their reading speed from an average of 215 words per minute to 335 words per minute after 10 weeks of tutoring for their reading skills (Bond, 1941). Even more important, these students' comprehension improved, too. Why did speeding up their reading boost their comprehension? Because their reading rate was still below 400 words per minute, their comprehension didn't suffer. At the same time, they covered more material, so they weren't running out of time by the end of the exam.

FICTOID ✖

MYTH: Subvocalizing (silently pronouncing words in our heads) increases reading comprehension.

REALITY: Subvocalizing slows down our reading because we speak much slower than we can read. As a result, people who subvocalize tend to complete less of a text within a given time period, resulting in lower comprehension.

assess your knowledge

FACT OR FICTION?

1. The Stroop color-naming task demonstrates that reading is automatic. **True / False**

2. Phonetic decomposition is a straightforward linking of printed letters to phonemes. **True / False**

3. Whole word recognition is the most efficient reading strategy for fluent readers and the best way to teach children to read. **True / False**

4. Increasing our reading speed can increase our comprehension as long as we stay under 400 words per minute. **True / False**

Answers: 1. T (p. 302); 2. F (p. 303); 3. F (p. 303); 4. T (p. 304)

THINKING AND REASONING

8.10   Identify methods for achieving cognitive economy.

8.11   Describe what factors affect how we make decisions.

8.12   Describe some common problem-solving strategies and challenges.

8.13   Describe various models of the human mind.

Nearly all of the chapters of this text thus far, and more still to come, describe aspects of thinking. Generally speaking, we can define **thinking** as any mental activity or processing of information. It includes learning, remembering, perceiving, communicating, believing, and deciding. All are fundamental aspects of what psychologists call cognition (see Chapter 1).

As we discovered in Chapter 6, behaviorists attempted to explain mental activity in terms of stimulus and response, reinforcement and punishment. Yet psychologists have long known that our minds often go beyond the available information, making leaps of insight and drawing inferences. Our minds fill in the gaps to create information that isn't present in its environmental inputs (see Chapters 2 and 4). Behaviorism's "black box psychology" (see Chapter 1) can't easily account for these phenomena.

■ Cognitive Economy—Imposing Order on Our World

Given the complexity of the cognitive tasks we must perform, our brains have adapted by finding ways to streamline the process. That's where cognitive economy enters the picture. As we learned in Chapter 2, we're *cognitive misers*. We economize mentally in a variety of ways that reduce our mental effort, but that enable us to get things right most of the time. Yet as we've also seen, cognitive economy can occasionally get us in trouble, especially when it leads us not merely to simplify, but to oversimplify. Here we'll review two forms of cognitive economy: heuristics and top-down processing.

HEURISTICS: MENTAL SHORTCUTS.   As we discovered in Chapter 2, our minds use a variety of *heuristics*, or shortcuts, to increase our thinking efficiency (Ariely, 2008). From an evolutionary perspective, heuristics may have enhanced our survival. We've already encountered several heuristics and biases that can lead us to draw faulty conclusions about scientific evidence. For example, the availability heuristic tells us to judge the likelihood of an event on the basis of how easy it is to generate an example of it. Confirmation bias leads us to seek evidence that fits with, rather than contradicts, what we believe. Even though these shortcuts can backfire if we're not careful (see Chapter 2), we've developed them for a reason: They're often useful in everyday life (Gigerenzer, 2007; Gilovich, Griffin, & Kahneman, 2002).

We process an enormous amount of information every minute of every day. From the moment we wake up, we must take into account what time it is, notice if there are any obstacles on the floor (like a roommate's shoes) between us and the shower, plan what time we need to get to class or work, and collect everything we need to bring with us. Of course, that's all before we've even stepped out the door. If we were to attend to and draw conclusions about every aspect of our experience all the time, we'd be so overwhelmed that we'd be paralyzed psychologically.

We draw inferences that provide mental shortcuts many times a day and, most of the time, they steer us right. If a roommate's keys are lying on the dining table, we might infer that our roommate is home without actually checking. We might infer that the stressed-out looking woman walking briskly by might not be the best person to stop and ask to contribute to our charity. We typically can decide that the week-old milk in our refrigerator has gone bad based on its smell without actually tasting it (or better yet, conducting a microscopic bacterial analysis). Each of these conclusions is unwarranted under rigorous standards of evidence-based reasoning. Yet most of these guesses are probably safe.

Cognitive economy allows us to simplify what we attend to and keep the information we need for decision making to a manageable minimum. Gerd Gigerenzer (2001, 2007; Gigerenzer & Goldstein, 1996) referred to this type of cognitive economy as "fast and frugal" thinking. He argued that it serves us well most of the time. In fact, in many cases, the heuristics we use are more valid than an exhaustive (and exhausting!) analysis of all potential factors (Gladwell, 2005).

thinking
any mental activity or processing of information, including learning, remembering, perceiving, communicating, believing, and deciding

Research by Samuel Gosling and his collaborators suggests that observers can often infer people's personality traits at better than chance levels merely by inspecting their rooms. What might you guess about the level of conscientiousness of this room's occupant?

FIGURE 8.11 Top-Down Processing. Our brains engage in perceptual completion, the use of top-down processing to perceive something that isn't there. Most people see this drawing as a perfectly fine drawing of an elephant, but look closely at its legs. (*Source:* Shepard, 1990)

Another example of top-down processing comes from mondegreens—commonly misheard song lyrics. For example, in his song Purple Haze, many people think that Jimi Hendrix sings "Excuse me while I kiss this guy." In fact, Hendrix sings "Excuse me while I kiss the sky."

One study revealed that untrained observers can make surprisingly accurate judgments about people on the basis of limited information. Samuel Gosling and his colleagues asked a group of untrained observers to make personality judgments about students by viewing their dorm rooms or bedrooms for only a few minutes. They gave observers no instructions about what features of the room to focus on, and covered all photos in the rooms so that observers couldn't determine the sex, race, or age of the rooms' occupants. Yet observers accurately gauged several aspects of the occupants' personalities, such as their emotional stability, openness to new experiences, and conscientiousness (Gosling, 2008; see Chapter 14). Presumably, observers were relying on mental shortcuts to draw conclusions about occupants' personalities because they had no firsthand experience with them.

Nalini Ambady and Robert Rosenthal (1993) provided another remarkable example of how cognitive economy serves us well. They showed participants 30-second silent clips of instructors teaching and asked them to evaluate their nonverbal behaviors. Participants' ratings on the basis of only 30 seconds of exposure were correlated significantly with the teachers' end-of-course evaluations by their students; in fact, their ratings were still predictive of course evaluations even when the clips were only six seconds long! Ambady and Rosenthal referred to our ability to extract useful information from small bits of behavior as "thin slicing." John Gottman and his colleagues also showed that they could predict with more than 90 percent accuracy which couples will divorce within the next 15 years after observing just 15 minutes of a couple's videotaped interaction. It turns out that the emotion of contempt—but perhaps surprisingly, not anger—is one of the best predictors (Carrère & Gottman, 1999; see Chapter 11).

But cognitive economy is a mixed blessing, because it can also lead us to faulty conclusions (Lehrer, 2009; Myers, 2002). Although our snap judgments of people are usually more accurate than we'd expect by chance, we can occasionally be wildly wrong. This fact probably helps to explain why brief open-ended interviews of people, such as college students, job applicants, and psychiatric patients, often yield inaccurate judgments of their personalities (Garb, 1998; see Chapter 14). We should listen to our first impressions but not be imprisoned by them.

TOP-DOWN PROCESSING. Another way our minds streamline their processing is by filling in the gaps using our experience and background knowledge. As we learned in Chapter 4, psychologists call this phenomenon *top-down processing*. We can contrast top-down processing with bottom-up processing, in which our brain processes only the information it receives and constructs meaning from it slowly and surely by building up knowledge through experience. In Chapter 4, we saw how perception is distinct from sensation because our perceptual experiences rely not only on raw sensory input but on stored knowledge that our brains call up to interpret it (see **FIGURE 8.11**). In Chapter 7, we encountered chunking, another form of top-down processing. Chunking is a memory aid that relies on our ability to organize information into larger units, expanding the span and detail of our memories. The Stroop effect and automaticity of reading, which we've discussed in this chapter, are also examples of top-down knowledge, because we access the knowledge of printed words we've stored instead of analyzing the printed word forms as we read (refer back to Figure 8.9). Each of these examples highlights our brain's tendency to simplify our cognitive functioning by using preexisting knowledge to spare us from reinventing the wheel.

One common source of top-down processing that aids our thinking and reasoning is our use of concepts and schemas. **Concepts** are our knowledge and ideas about objects, actions, and characteristics that share core properties. We have concepts of what properties all motorcycles share, or of all purple things. As we learned in Chapter 7, schemas are concepts we've stored in memory about how certain actions, objects, and ideas are related to each other. Schemas help us to mentally organize *events* that share core features, say, going to a restaurant, cleaning the house, and visiting the zoo. As we acquire knowledge, we create stored schemas that enable us to draw on our knowledge when we experience something new. When encountering an animal we've never seen, we use our knowledge of its features to recognize whether it's a mammal or a reptile, harmless or dangerous.

A concept allows us to have all of our general knowledge about dogs at our disposal when dealing with Rover. We don't need to discover from scratch that Rover barks, pants when he's hot, and has a stomach. These things all come "for free" once we recognize Rover as a dog. Similarly, when we go to a new doctor's office, no one has to tell us to sit in the waiting room and that someone will call us when an examining room is ready, because our schema for doctors' visits tells us this is the standard script. Of course, our concepts and schemas don't apply to all real-world situations. Rover may be unable to bark because of a throat disorder. Yet most of the time, our concepts and schemas safely allow us to exert less cognitive effort over basic knowledge, freeing us up to engage in more complex reasoning and emotional processing.

■ Decision Making: Choices, Choices, and More Choices

Decision making is the process of selecting among a set of possible alternatives. Will I order fries or a salad with my sandwich? Should I major in philosophy or physics? Which outfit looks better? Each decision that we make seems deceptively simple on the surface: It's an either/or choice. But lots of factors enter in to most decisions. Let's take a seemingly straightforward question, such as whether to order a salad or fries. Such a choice often depends on a variety of factors, such as whether we're watching our weight, whether we like the type of fries and salad dressings available at a particular restaurant, and maybe even what everyone else at our table is eating. For many such small, daily decisions, we often weigh the various considerations quickly and implicitly, that is, below conscious awareness. But for some other decisions, such as where to go to college or whether to get married, the decisions have much larger consequences and require more careful deliberation. In these cases, the decision-making process often becomes more explicit. We mull over the options, sometimes identify and list the pros and cons of each option, and may solicit the advice and opinions of friends, family, and trusted advisors such as professors, clergy, and coaches.

Is this a good idea? It depends (Lehrer, 2009). Timothy Wilson and his colleagues gave female college students a choice among five art posters to take home. Two of the posters were by famous artists (Monet and van Gogh) and three were posters of cats. The investigators asked half the students to just "go with their guts" and pick which poster they liked, and the other half to carefully list each of the pros and cons of each poster. When the researchers re-contacted the subjects a few weeks later, the ones who went with their guts were much happier with their choices (Wilson et al., 1993). When it comes to emotional preferences, like which art we like or which people we find attractive, thinking too much may get us in trouble. Ironically, this may be especially true for complex emotionally laden decisions, like which car to buy, because our brains can easily become overwhelmed by excessive information (Dijksterhuis et al., 2006). In such cases, listing all of the pros and cons can confuse us, leading to "paralysis by analysis." Yet when it comes to evaluating scientific claims in the laboratory and real life, trusting our guts is usually a bad idea (Lilienfeld et al., 2010; Myers, 2002). As we've learned throughout this text, our intuitions can easily mislead us into accepting seductive but false claims, like those concerning bogus diet plans or ineffective self-help programs.

Marketing researchers, advertising executives, and political pollsters have long known that an additional factor influences our decision making: **framing**, that is, how we formulate the question about what we need to decide (Tversky & Kahnemann, 1986). Imagine a pollster asked you "Would you support an initiative to provide guaranteed access to health care for 95 percent of American citizens?" Most of us would probably agree that this sounds like a pretty good idea. But now imagine that the pollster reworded the question to emphasize a different aspect of the issue: "Would you support a health care initiative that failed to cover more than 15 million Americans?" Suddenly, this idea doesn't sound so good, does it? But guess what? The questions are based on exactly the same information. An initiative that covered 95 percent of Americans would leave 5 percent without access, and 5 percent of the population of the United States is 15 million people. Even though both questions

concept
our knowledge and ideas about a set of objects, actions, and or characteristics that share core properties

decision making
the process of selecting among a set of possible alternatives

framing
the way a question is formulated which can influence the decisions people make

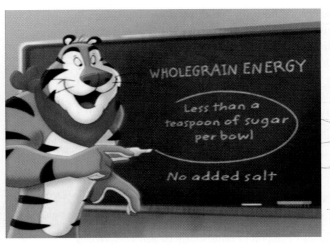

The ad on the left emphasizes a percent reduction in sugar, the ad on the right highlights the total amount. Both emphasize the low amount of sugar in the product but present the information differently. **What concept do the differences between these two ads demonstrate?** (See answer upside down at bottom of page.)

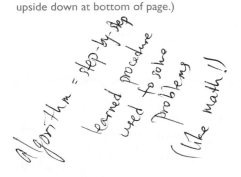

👁 **Watch** the Water Lily video on **mypsychlab.com**

problem solving
generating a cognitive strategy to accomplish a goal

algorithm
step-by-step learned procedure used to solve a problem

ask about access to health care, one emphasizes the percentage of people covered, and the other the sheer scale of who wouldn't be. That's framing.

Researchers in a newly minted field called *neuroeconomics* have become interested in how the brain works when making financial decisions (Glimcher et al., 2008). By using fMRI (see Chapter 3), to identify brain areas that become active in specific decision-making situations—such as when interacting with a person who's stingy or selfish—researchers hope to better predict and understand how emotion, reasoning, and arousal influence our decisions (Kato et al., 2009). One team of investigators imaged the brains of participants asked to make risky monetary decisions. When participants received advice from a financial expert, brain regions involved in decision making—such as certain areas of their frontal lobes (see Chapter 3)—became less active than when they received no financial advice (Engelmann et al., 2009). This finding reminds us that trusting authorities may sometimes be hazardous, as it can lead us to forego our critical thinking capacities (see Chapter 1).

■ Problem Solving: Accomplishing Our Goals

Many times a day, we're faced with problems to solve. Some are as simple as figuring out where we left our favorite pair of shoes, but others involve attempting to recover a corrupted computer file or figuring out how to get to a new restaurant in an unfamiliar part of town. **Problem solving** is generating a cognitive strategy to accomplish a goal.

APPROACHES TO SOLVING PROBLEMS. We've encountered a variety of heuristics, like availability and representativeness, that we use to draw conclusions and solve problems in a "fast and frugal" way. Although these heuristics can often be effective, we can draw on a variety of more deliberate solutions, too. In particular, we can solve many problems following step-by-step learned procedures known as **algorithms**. Algorithms come in handy for problems that depend on the same basic steps for arriving at a solution every time the solution is required, such as replacing the starter on a car, performing a tonsillectomy, or making a peanut-butter-and-jelly sandwich. Algorithms ensure that we address all steps when we solve a problem, but they're pretty inflexible. Imagine you have an algorithm for cooking a mushroom omelet that includes melting some butter, but you run out of butter. You'd be stuck. As a result, you could either give up—or instead "use your head" to engage in a more flexible solution. 👁 **Watch**

One approach is to try breaking a problem down in to subproblems that are easier to solve. If we're trying to construct a doghouse, we might break the problem into: (1) identifying the size and dimensions of the doghouse, (2) purchasing the materials, (3) constructing the floor, and so on. By breaking the problem into bite-sized chunks, we can often solve it more quickly and easily. Another effective approach involves reasoning from related examples, such as realizing that because oil is often substituted for butter in baking recipes, it might work for an omelet, too (Gentner et al., 2009). Many breakthroughs in scientific problems in the laboratory and real world have come from drawing *analogies* between two distinct topics. These analogies solve problems with similar structures. For example, George deMestral invented Velcro in 1948 after observing how burrs stuck to his dog's fur by using a series of tiny hooks that attached to individual strands of fur.

OBSTACLES TO PROBLEM SOLVING. Although we use a variety of effective strategies to solve problems, we also face a variety of hurdles—cognitive tendencies that can interfere with use of effective problem-solving strategies. We'll consider three obstacles to solving problems correctly: salience of surface similarities, mental sets, and functional fixedness.

Salience of Surface Similarities. Salience refers to how attention-grabbing something is. We tend to focus our attention on the surface-level (superficial) properties of a problem, such as the topic of an algebra word problem, and try to solve problems in the same way we solved problems that exhibited similar surface characteristics. When one algebra word problem calls for subtraction and another calls for division, the fact that they both deal with trains isn't going to help us. Ignoring the surface features of a problem and focusing on the underlying reasoning needed to solve it can be challenging.

The two problems in **TABLE 8.4** involve the same reasoning processes, so learning how to solve one problem provides us with the solution to the other. Yet in one study, only 20 percent of students who saw the fortress problem figured out the tumor problem (Gick & Holyoak, 1983). When researchers told students that the fortress problem could help them solve the tumor problem, their success shot up to 92 percent. The students hadn't noticed that the fortress solution was relevant. ⊙➤ Simulate

⊙➤ **Simulate** Intuition and Discovery in Problem Solving on **mypsychlab.com**

TABLE 8.4 Fortress and Tumor Problems. Students who read the first problem rarely used it to solve the second problem because the surface features (a general and a fortress versus radiation and a tumor) were too different. But when researchers encouraged students to use the fortress problem as a basis for solving the tumor problem, they usually generated the correct solution.

PROBLEM	DESCRIPTION
The Fortress Problem	A small country was ruled from a strong fortress by a dictator. The fortress was situated in the middle of the country, surrounded by farms and villages. Many roads led to the fortress through the countryside. A rebel general vowed to capture the fortress. The general knew that an attack by his entire army would capture the fortress. He gathered his army at the head of one of the roads, ready to launch a full-scale direct attack. However, the general then learned that the dictator had planted mines on each of the roads. The mines were set so that small bodies of men could pass over them safely, since the dictator needed to move his troops and workers to and from the fortress. However, any large force would detonate the mines. Not only would this blow up the road, but it would also destroy many neighboring villages. It therefore seemed impossible to capture the fortress. However, the general devised a simple plan. He divided his army into small groups and dispatched each group to the head of a different road. When all was ready he gave the signal and each group marched down a different road. Each group continued down its road to the fortress so that the entire army arrived together at the fortress at the same time. In this way, the general captured the fortress and overthrew the dictator.
The Tumor Problem	Suppose you are a doctor faced with a patient who has a malignant tumor in his stomach. It is impossible to operate on the patient, but unless the tumor is destroyed, the patient will die. There is a kind of ray that can be used to destroy the tumor. If the rays reach the tumor all at once at sufficiently high intensity, the tumor will be destroyed. Unfortunately, at this intensity, the healthy tissue that the rays pass through on the way to the tumor will also be destroyed. At a lower intensity the rays are harmless to healthy tissue but they will not affect the tumor either. What type of procedure might be used to destroy the tumor with the rays and at the same time avoid destroying the healthy tissue?

(*Source*: Gick & Holyoak, 1983)

[Handwritten margin notes:]

Problem-Solving Methods
→ algorithms
→ creating subproblems and then solving
→ using (making) analogies/examples

Truth

Problem-Solving Obstacles
→ salience of surface similarities
→ mental sets
→ functional fixedness.

FIGURE 8.12 Mental Set Problems. Solve these problems by figuring out how to add and remove precise amounts of water using the jars provided. The first two problems use the same formula: Add the amount in the first jug (A), subtract the amount from the second jug (B), and then subtract the amount from the third jug (C) twice (A – B – C – C = Target amount). The third problem requires a different solution. Can you figure it out? If you're stuck, you may be experiencing a "mental set."

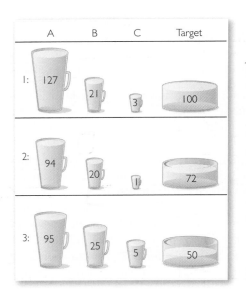

FIGURE 8.13 Functional Fixedness. A classic demonstration of functional fixedness requires participants to figure out how to mount a candle on a wall given only a candle, book of matches, and box of tacks (Duncker, 1945). To see the solution, see the upside-down figure on the next page.

Mental Sets. Once we find a workable solution that's dependable, we often get stuck in that solution mode; we have trouble generating alternatives or "thinking outside the box." Psychologists term this phenomenon a **mental set**. When attempting to pick a topic for a term paper, we may have trouble thinking of topics that the professor hasn't already covered in class. Ironically, a friend who hasn't taken the class may be able to come up with more creative ideas because our thinking has become "boxed in" by our experiences. In a classic study of mental sets, participants had to solve a series of problems that required measuring out a precise amount of water by adding and subtracting water, given only three odd measuring jars (such as filling a jug with precisely 100 quarts using only a 21-quart jar, a 127-quart jar, and a 3-quart jar; see **FIGURE 8.12**). Participants either solved eight problems that used the same formula (A – B – C – C = Target amount) before working on a problem that used a different formula, or they solved the ninth problem without working on the first eight. Only 36 percent of participants who solved the first eight problems the same way generated the correct solution on the ninth one. In contrast, participants who solved the ninth problem first generated a correct solution 95 percent of the time (Luchins, 1946). Solving the first eight problems actually made solving the ninth more difficult, because the eight problems created a mental set from which subjects had a hard time breaking free.

Functional Fixedness. **Functional fixedness** occurs when we experience difficulty conceptualizing that an object typically used for one purpose can be used for another (German & Defeyter, 2000). That is, we become "fixated" on one conventional use for an object. Have you ever needed a hammer, tape, or scissors but didn't have any of these items around? Were you able to come up with any alternative solutions? Functional fixedness can prevent us from realizing that we could use a shoe as a hammer, a mailing label as tape, or a key to cut a piece of string.

One famous demonstration asked participants to figure out a way to mount a candle on a wall given only a candle, book of matches, and box of tacks, as shown in **FIGURE 8.13** (Duncker, 1945). Can you think of how to do it? Most of us find this problem difficult because it forces us to use conventional objects in unconventional ways. Nevertheless, one study challenged the idea of functional fixedness as an explanation for this finding. The researchers showed that individuals from a rural area of Ecuador who live in a traditional nontechnological society and consequently have few expectations about the functional roles of these objects still had difficulty solving the problem (German & Barrett, 2005). So functional fixedness may occur even when we've had little or no experience with the objects in question.

■ Models of the Mind

Given everything we've learned about our fast and frugal processing, our heuristics and biases, and our abilities and limitations as problem solvers, what's the best model—or unifying explanation—for how the mind works? In the 1980s, many psychologists adopted a computer analogy to explain the mind's tendency to process information, fill in gaps, and draw inferences. Perhaps thinking is akin to running data through a computer program. From this perspective, the brain's algorithms are like preprogrammed abilities; the brain runs data through its "software program" and spits out an answer.

Although some modern psychologists still rely on the computer model, most believe that a computer analogy isn't the best for explaining how we think (Searle, 1990). In fact, some of the tasks that humans find simplest are among the most difficult for computers. Although we can perceive and recognize speech without difficulty, anyone who's attempted to use voice commands

ruling out rival hypotheses

HAVE IMPORTANT ALTERNATIVE EXPLANATIONS FOR THE FINDINGS BEEN EXCLUDED?

mental set
phenomenon of becoming stuck in a specific problem-solving strategy, inhibiting our ability to generate alternatives

functional fixedness
difficulty conceptualizing that an object typically used for one purpose can be used for another

on an automated phone menu knows that computers are notoriously poor at this task. One reason that humans beat out computers on such tasks is that we can take context into account and draw subtle inferences that computers can't. For example, we might hear someone speak a sentence that sounds a lot like "I frog," but that occurs in the context of him apologizing for not bringing you something he promised. So we might be able to guess that he meant to say "I forgot." In contrast, a computer won't be able to use top-down knowledge to resolve this ambiguity.

Another important way that human thinking differs from computers is that computers, unlike humans, don't have a chance to explore and interact with the world. From infancy, we act on the world and observe the consequences of our actions. We learn that sitting on a surface that isn't designed to hold our weight can cause us to fall, or that telling someone "You're a jerk" usually produces a different emotional reaction than telling her "I'm upset about what you said."

Recent models of the mind have attempted to reflect the physically interactive nature of our knowledge and experience by developing *embodied* accounts of thinking. According to embodiment models, our knowledge is organized and accessed in a manner that enables us to simulate our actual experiences. For example, people who hear the sentence "The man saw the eagle in the sky" and then see a picture of an eagle are faster to label the eagle if the eagle has its wings spread (consistent with how it would look in the scenario described in the sentence) than if its wings are folded close to its body (Fischer & Zwaan, 2008). Neuroimaging studies of brain activation are consistent with an embodied approach to understanding thinking (Barsalou, 2008). Specifically, these studies show that the brain's sensory areas (for example, visual, auditory, and motor cortex; see Chapter 3) become activated when people think about objects, actions, and events.

Human cognitive processing is remarkably flexible and creative, taking advantage of past experience, context, imagination, and mental shortcuts to provide rapid and efficient solutions to problems. Our fast and frugal thinking serves us remarkably well much of the time. Nevertheless, one of our major goals in this textbook is to raise awareness about how our cognitive systems can lead us astray and how we can guard against it. Such awareness can help us recognize situations in which we're vulnerable to faulty reasoning and think twice about our intuitions. When we hear on the news that vaccines cause autism or that watching violent television shows can turn entirely normal kids into violent monsters, we should stop to think about the information on which the media based these conclusions. When evaluating political candidates' extravagant promises ("If I'm elected, you'll all have another $5,000 in your pockets by the end of the year!") or deciding whether that incredible deal on laptops ("Laptops for only $200 apiece, and they're five times faster than your home computer!") is too good to be true, we should consider whether the information is sufficient to warrant the remarkable claims. When deciding whether the car we're thinking of buying is safe or the diet plan we're considering is effective, we should stop to think about what extensive consumer and scientific research says instead of concentrating on a handful of anecdotes from friends. Cognitive economy has a lot going for it, but being aware of its pitfalls will make us more informed consumers of information in our everyday lives.

extraordinary claims

IS THE EVIDENCE AS STRONG AS THE CLAIM?

assess your knowledge   FACT OR FICTION?

✔ Study and Review on mypsychlab.com

1. "Fast and frugal" processing almost always leads to false conclusions. True / **False**

2. Top-down processing involves drawing inferences from previous experience and applying them to current situations. **True** / False

3. Decision making is always an implicit process influenced subtly by how we frame the problem. True / **False**

4. Comparing problems that require similar reasoning processes but different surface characteristics can help us overcome deceptive surface similarities. **True** / False

5. Functional fixedness is a product of Western technology-dependent society. True / **False**

Answer to Figure 8.13

✓• Study and Review on mypsychlab.com

(•• Listen to an audio file of your chapter on mypsychlab.com

HOW DOES LANGUAGE WORK? 286–299

8.1 DESCRIBE THE FOUR LEVELS OF ANALYSIS THAT MAKE UP LANGUAGE.

To fully understand the complexity of language, we must analyze phonemes, morphemes, syntax, and extralinguistic information. These four levels work together to create meaning and transmit information. Morphemes are the smallest units of language that convey meaning, known as semantics. Extralinguistic information, such as tone of voice, facial expression, gestures, contextual cues, and cultural conventions, all enter into how we interpret language. Dialects are regional, social, and ethnic group variations in the ways that a language is spoken, all of which are equally valid versions of the language.

1. List the four levels of analysis we use to analyze language. (p. 287)

   1. _____

   2. _____

   3. _____

   4. _____

2. English contains between 40 and 45 categories of sounds, or _____. (p. 287)

3. _____ is the set of rules of a language by which we construct sentences. (p. 288)

4. A language variation used by a group of people who share geographic proximity or ethnic background is a _____. (p. 288)

8.2 TRACE THE DEVELOPMENT OF LANGUAGE ACQUISITION IN CHILDREN.

Infants' babbling becomes more sophisticated over the course of their first year as control over their vocal tracts increases. They also fine-tune their perception of phonemes over the course of the first year of listening to their native language. Children's word and syntax comprehension precedes their production of language. They acquire their first words around their first birthdays and typically begin combining words into rudimentary phrases by their second birthdays. Understanding of extralinguistic aspects of communication develops gradually over the preschool and elementary school years.

5. By what month of pregnancy are fetuses' auditory systems developed enough for them to detect sounds, and how much do they learn about their mothers' languages and voices in utero? (p. 290)

8.3 DETERMINE HOW SIGN LANGUAGE IN DEAF INDIVIDUALS RELATES TO SPOKEN LANGUAGE ACQUISITION IN HEARING INDIVIDUALS.

Sign languages possess the same linguistic features and complexity as spoken languages. Children learning sign language from native signing parents acquire their language at the same age and same rate as children learning spoken language.

6. The (same/different) brain areas involved in processing spoken languages become active in sign languages. (p. 293)

8.4 IDENTIFY THE PROS AND CONS OF BILINGUALISM.

Bilingual individuals typically have one dominant language. Learning two languages slows some aspects of the acquisition process, but ultimately results in stronger metalinguistic skills. Children learn a second language faster and more fluently than adults. Nevertheless, there's no specific critical period during which language learning must take place.

7. Bilingual individuals tend to perform (better/worse) on metalinguistic tasks than individuals that speak only one language. (p. 293)

8.5 COMPARE THEORIES OF LANGUAGE ACQUISITION.

Imitation accounts of language acquisition can't account for the generativity of language. Nativist accounts posit that language would be too hard to learn without some "pre-programming" of the structure of language in the brain. Nativist approaches are difficult to falsify and appear to underestimate both the amount of information that children can use to discover the structure of language from their social environment and their ability to remember patterns in the language they hear. Social pragmatics and general cognitive learning accounts appear to offer the best-supported explanations for how children acquire language.

8. Even very young children use language in _____ ways, producing sentences or combinations of words they've never heard before. (p. 296)

9. Noam Chomsky theorized that humans possess a specific language "organ" in the brain called the _____ _____ _____. (p. 296)

8.6 DISTINGUISH HUMAN LANGUAGE FROM NONHUMAN ANIMAL COMMUNICATION.

Most nonhuman animal communication systems involve aggression and mating displays, but little else, and lack the generativity of human language systems. Attempts to teach language to nonhuman animals have been only modestly successful. Chimpanzees and African gray parrots can learn the basics of linguistic communication but learn very differently from humans. Bonobos seem to learn more like humans do, but don't exceed the proficiency level of about a two-and-a-half-year-old human.

10. Unlike chimpanzees, _____ have a learning pathway that more closely resembles human learning. (p. 298)

DO WE THINK IN WORDS? THE RELATION BETWEEN LANGUAGE AND THOUGHT

299–302

8.7 IDENTIFY HOW OUR LANGUAGE MAY INFLUENCE OUR THINKING.

The notion that language completely determines our thinking (linguistic determinism) has little or no scientific support. Nevertheless, evidence supports the idea that language can influence some aspects of our thinking (linguistic relativity).

11. John B. Watson, the founder of behaviorism, believed that thinking is a form of _____ speech. (p. 299)

12. The view that all thought is represented linguistically, as evidenced by the different Inuit words for snow, is called _____ _____. (p. 300)

13. Recent neuroimaging studies suggest that thought (can/can't) occur without language. (p. 301)

14. Compared with linguistic determinism _____ _____ is a less radical perspective on how language relates to thought. (p. 301)

15. Does Helen Keller's view of thought without language correspond more closely to the idea of linguistic determinism or linguistic relativity, and why? (p. 300)

16. According to the Sapir-Whorf hypothesis, characteristics of _____ shape our thought process. (p. 301)

17. One case in which researchers found that language doesn't influence thought is _____ categorization. (p. 301)

18. The Dani language has words for _____ and _____ but does not have words for individual colors. (p. 301)

19. How does the fact that the Dani of New Guinea can perceive different color categories present a challenge to the Sapir-Whorf hypothesis? (p. 301)

20. When researchers identify language-related differences in thought, it (is/isn't) easy to disentangle the influences of language from culture. (p. 301)

READING: RECOGNIZING THE WRITTEN WORD

302–304

8.8 IDENTIFY THE SKILLS REQUIRED TO LEARN TO READ AND UNDERSTAND THE DEBATE CONCERNING READING STRATEGIES.

Before children can begin to read, they must realize that writing is meaningful. They must also learn to recognize individual letters, and figure out which printed letters tend to correspond to which sounds. We generally use two strategies when learning to read: whole word recognition and phonetic decomposition. Whole word recognition is more efficient when reading familiar words, but phonetic decomposition is critical for less familiar words. There is no perfect correspondence between printed letters and spoken sounds, which makes sounding out printed words challenging.

21. The Stroop task shows that reading is _____. (p. 302)

22. Go down each column and say aloud the color of ink in which each word is printed. Try the control list first, then try the Stroop interference list. What did you notice about the level of difficulty of each list? Why the discrepancy? (p. 302)

Control Condition	Stroop Interference Condition
Rabbit	Red
House	Blue
Blanket	**Green**
Dance	**Yellow**
Flower	Purple
Key	Orange
Seven	Black
Dance	**Yellow**
House	**Blue**
Key	Orange
Seven	Purple
Flower	Black
Rabbit	Red
Blanket	Green

23. Children must learn which _____ is right for their language. (p. 302)

24. Match up the language with the direction in which it should read. (p. 302)

"Life is either a daring adventure or nothing." – Helen Keller

English is read from _____   a. top to bottom

Hebrew is read from _____   b. left to right

Japanese is read from _____   c. right to left

Answers are located at the end of the text.

25. Children must learn that printed letters correspond to specific _____. (p. 302)

26. The average reader uses _____ _____ _____ to read the vast majority of printed words. (p. 303)

27. With a reading strategy called _____ _____, we sound out new words by drawing correspondences between printed letters and sounds. (p. 303)

28. There's been heated debate about whether awareness of sound–letter correspondences, known as _____, is the best strategy for teaching children to read. (p. 303)

8.9 ANALYZE THE RELATIONSHIP BETWEEN READING SPEED AND READING COMPREHENSION.

Speed-reading courses are ineffective. Although we can learn to increase our speed as readers, reading faster than 400 words per minute seriously impairs text comprehension.

29. Reading speeds (are/aren't) correlated with comprehension. (p. 304)

30. Controlled studies indicate that reading faster than _____ words per minute results in comprehension rates below 50 percent. (p. 304)

THINKING AND REASONING 305–311

8.10 IDENTIFY METHODS FOR ACHIEVING COGNITIVE ECONOMY.

Cognitive economy is a necessary aspect of our cognitive functioning. We would be unable to function effectively without some way of streamlining our information processing. Heuristics and top-down processing are examples of cognitive economy that we use routinely. There are downsides to cognitive economy, including the reasoning errors outlined in Chapters 1 and 2 as obstacles to scientific thinking. Heuristics and biases are often useful, but can lead us to make costly mistakes if we apply them uncritically.

31. We define _____ as any mental activity or processing of information. (p. 305)

32. _____ _____ allows us to simplify what we need to attend to and keep the information we need to make decisions to a manageable minimum. (p. 305)

33. Ambady and Rosenthal referred to our ability to extract useful information from small bits of behavior as _____ _____. (p. 306)

34. What phenomenon does this drawing of an elephant help to demonstrate? When you first looked at it, did you perceive something different from what was actually there? (p. 306)

35. A mental representation of a set of objects, actions, or events that share core features is a _____. (p. 306)

8.11 DESCRIBE WHAT FACTORS AFFECT HOW WE MAKE DECISIONS.

Many of our daily decisions are made implicitly (without conscious awareness) and based on cognitive economy. For bigger decisions, we may attempt to analyze the pros and cons on a more explicit level, and consult experts, trusted friends, and advisors. Although it makes sense to make bigger decisions more carefully, overanalyzing can sometimes overwhelm us. When evaluating scientific evidence, it is crucial not to simply follow our "gut" reactions. Framing, which refers to how decisions are presented to us, has a substantial impact on these decisions even when the underlying information relevant to these decisions is identical.

36. As these two cereal advertisements demonstrate, _____ can affect decision making. (p. 308)

8.12 DESCRIBE SOME COMMON PROBLEM-SOLVING STRATEGIES AND CHALLENGES.

Many daily problems are solved using heuristics, but others involve more deliberate strategies. Algorithms are step-by-step procedures for solving routine problems, but aren't very flexible. Other solutions involve breaking down problems into subproblems and reasoning based on analogies to other problems in seemingly unrelated areas. Three hurdles to effective problem solving are being distracted by the salience of surface similarities, being stuck in a mental set, and falling prey to functional fixedness.

37. When we generate a cognitive strategy to accomplish a specific goal, we are engaging in _____ _____. (p. 308)

38. The phenomenon of becoming entrenched in a particular problem-solving strategy that inhibits generating alternative strategies is called a _____ _____. (p. 310)

39. _____ _____ occurs when we experience difficulty conceptualizing that an object typically used for one purpose can be used for another. (p. 310)

8.13 DESCRIBE VARIOUS MODELS OF THE HUMAN MIND.

Scientists once believed that the mind worked much like a computer, running programs to compute answers to problems and execute mental commands. Nevertheless, it's is now clear that the computer is a poor analogy for the human mind. We draw inferences, instantly take context in to account, and draw on top-down knowledge in a way that computers don't. Our ability to interact physically with the world also exerts a big impact on our thinking abilities. Embodied accounts of thinking seem to better explain our thinking and reasoning abilities, and are supported by neuroimaging studies demonstrating that our brain's perceptual and motor areas are activated during thought.

40. According to _____ _____ of cognition, our knowledge is organized and accessed in a manner that enables us to simulate our actual experiences. (p. 311)

DO YOU KNOW THESE TERMS?

- language (p. 286)
- phoneme (p. 287)
- morpheme (p. 287)
- syntax (p. 287)
- extralinguistic information (p. 287)
- semantics (p. 288)
- dialect (p. 288)
- babbling (p. 290)

- one word stage (p. 291)
- sign language (p. 292)
- bilingual (p. 293)
- metalinguistic (p. 293)
- homesign (p. 294)
- generative (p. 296)
- nativist (p. 296)
- language acquisition device (p. 296)

- social pragmatics (p. 296)
- linguistic determinism (p. 300)
- linguistic relativity (p. 301)
- whole word recognition (p. 303)
- phonetic decomposition (p. 303)
- thinking (p. 305)
- concept (p. 306)
- decision making (p. 307)

- framing (p. 307)
- problem solving (p. 308)
- algorithm (p. 308)
- mental set (p. 310)
- functional fixedness (p. 310)

APPLY YOUR SCIENTIFIC THINKING SKILLS

Use your scientific thinking skills to answer the following questions, referencing specific scientific thinking principles and common errors in reasoning whenever possible.

1. Communication depends on more than just our words. It also includes our facial expressions, posture, gestures, and tone of voice. Create a list of several different ways we communicate in our personal, academic, and professional lives (for example, face-to-face conversations, text messages, e-mail, Facebook). Which aspects of communication are preserved and omitted in each of these communication forms, and what types of communication errors might arise as a result? How can we use scientific thinking and our knowledge of language and communication to prevent these errors?

2. Examine the role that framing plays in our decision making. Select a current topic of debate, like health care, foreign policy, or gun control laws, and research how each opposing side frames its arguments. How can you use your knowledge of decision making and your scientific thinking skills to make an informed decision about this issue?

3. Try to think of a recent time when you were trying to solve a problem—say a problem in your personal life, or a homework problem assigned to you in one of your classes—and simply got stuck despite repeated attempts. To which of the obstacles to effective problem solving discussed in this chapter might you have fallen prey? What helped you, or might have helped you, find your way out of this problem?

9 INTELLIGENCE AND IQ TESTING

controversy and consensus

THINK ABOUT IT

IS HUMAN INTELLIGENCE RELATED TO BRAIN SIZE?

ARE IQ SCORES STABLE OVER TIME?

DO IQ TESTS PREDICT ANYTHING USEFUL?

ARE IQ TESTS BIASED AGAINST CERTAIN MINORITY GROUPS?

ARE ALL INTELLIGENT PEOPLE CREATIVE?

Exam 3
Ch 10
Ch 9
Ch 8 (305-315)
Ch 12

This ex–bar bouncer may not look like someone with one of the highest IQs in the United States. But Chris Langan scores so highly on standard IQ tests that his measured intelligence can only be estimated.

Galton invented/studied eugenics.

If you were to see Chris Langan on the street, you'd almost surely pass right by him. Now in his late 50s, Langan's face is unfamiliar to the overwhelming majority of the general public. Yet according to some psychologists, Langan may be the smartest person in the United States (Gladwell, 2009). Like many geniuses, Langan was a *child prodigy:* an individual who displays astounding intellectual achievements at an early age (Morelock & Feldman, 1993). According to reports, he began speaking at six months old and taught himself to read by age three. When tested on a standard intelligence test, his estimated IQ—intelligence quotient—was an astonishing 195; the psychologist who examined him had to estimate it because the scores on standard IQ tests don't go up that high. Langan received a perfect score of 1600 on his SAT, a widely used college admissions test, and he dropped out of two colleges in part because he felt that he was more knowledgeable than his professors. In 2008, Langan won $250,000 on NBC's game show, "1 vs. 100." In his spare time, Langan wrote a book introducing his "Cognitive-Theoretical Model of the Universe," a comprehensive theory linking the mind to reality, which contains sentences like "No matter what else happens in this evolving universe, it must be temporally embedded in this dualistic self-inclusion operation" (no, we don't understand it, either).

What, you might ask, does Chris Langan do for a living? Is he a laboratory scientist, a university professor, or a famous computer programmer? If you guessed any of these three, you'd be wrong. For about 20 years, Chris Langan worked as a bar bouncer while holding other jobs, including construction worker and firefighter. Today, he works on a farm in Missouri with his wife. Even though Langan long yearned to earn a doctoral degree and to become a great scientist, he never got close. Why? Langan seemed to have a knack for offending others, including his college professors, without intending to. Moreover, he appeared unwilling to tolerate the minor bureaucratic frustrations of academic life. To this day, Langan's grand theory remains obscure, as he's never submitted it to a peer-reviewed journal.

How do people like Chris Langan achieve stratospheric levels of IQ? And how can we explain why Langan, in contrast to many others with extremely high IQs, failed to achieve great academic success? In this chapter, we won't find definitive answers, but we'll uncover a few tantalizing cues.

WHAT IS INTELLIGENCE? DEFINITIONAL CONFUSION

9.1 Identify different models and types of intelligence.

9.2 Describe the connection between intelligence and brain size and efficiency.

One of the problems that renders psychology so challenging—and at times exasperating—is the lack of clear-cut definitions for many of its concepts. No area of psychology illustrates this ongoing challenge better than the field of intelligence. Even today, psychologists can't agree on the precise definition of intelligence (Sternberg, 2003b; Sternberg & Detterman, 1986).

Psychologist Edwin Boring (1923) discovered an easy away around the nagging question of what intelligence is. According to Boring, intelligence is whatever intelligence tests measure. Yes, it's that simple. Some modern psychologists have embraced this definition, which lets us off the hook from having to figure out what intelligence is. Yet because this definition sidesteps the central question of what makes some people smarter than others—or whether some people are really smarter than others across the board—it doesn't really get us all that far. The definition of intelligence must go beyond Boring's definition. With that point in mind, let's examine the most influential attempts to define and understand intelligence.

■ Intelligence as Sensory Capacity: Out of Sight, Out of Mind

Sir Francis Galton (1822–1911) was a prominent scientist, inventor, and cousin of the great biologist Charles Darwin, codeveloper of the theory of evolution by natural selection. Following in the footsteps of his older cousin, Galton—himself a creative genius in many respects—was interested in the potential adaptive advantages of high intellect. Perhaps as a consequence of his own exceptional intelligence, he was fascinated by the question of what makes some people especially smart.

Galton proposed a radical hypothesis: Intelligence is the by-product of sensory capacity. He reasoned that most knowledge first comes through the senses, especially vision and hearing. Therefore, he assumed, people with superior sensory capacities, like better eyesight, should acquire more knowledge than other people.

For a six-year period beginning in 1884, Galton set up a laboratory at a museum in London, England. There, he administered a battery of 17 sensory tests to more than 9,000 visitors (Gillham, 2001). He measured just about everything under the sun relating to sensory ability: the highest and lowest pitch of sounds that individuals could detect; their reaction times to various stimuli; their ability to discriminate the weights of similar objects; and their capacity to differentiate the smells of various roses. James McKeen Cattell, who worked under and was influenced substantially by Galton, shortly thereafter imported Galton's tests to America, administering them to thousands of college students to find out what they were measuring. Like his teacher, Cattell assumed that intelligence was a matter of raw sensory ability.

Yet later research showed that different measures of sensory capacities, like the ability to distinguish similar sounds from one another or similar colors from one another, are only weakly correlated (Acton & Schroeder, 2001): That is, one exceptional sense, like heightened hearing, doesn't bear much of a relation to other exceptional senses, like heightened vision. Nor are measures of sensory ability highly correlated with assessments of overall intelligence (Li, Jordanova, & Lindenberger, 1998). These findings falsify Galton's and Cattell's claim that intelligence equals sensory ability. Whatever intelligence is, it's more than just good eyesight, hearing, smell, and taste. A moment's reflection reveals that this must be the case: According to Galton, Helen Keller, the blind and deaf woman who became a brilliant author and social critic (see Chapter 8), would almost by definition have had mental retardation. Galton's definition can't be right.

Still, as we'll learn later, Galton may have been onto something. Recent research suggests that some forms of sensory ability relate modestly to intelligence, although these two concepts clearly aren't identical.

Intelligence as Abstract Thinking

Early in the last century, the French government wanted to find a way to identify children in need of special educational assistance. In 1904, the Minister of Public Instruction in Paris tapped two individuals, Alfred Binet (pronounced "Bee-NAY") and Théodore Simon (pronounced "See-MOAN"), to develop an objective psychological test that would separate "slower" learners from other children without having to rely on the subjective judgments of teachers.

Binet and Simon experimented with many different items (an item is a question on a measure, including an intelligence or personality test) designed to distinguish students whom teachers perceived as plodding learners from other students. In 1905, they developed what most psychologists today regard as the first **intelligence test**, a diagnostic tool designed to measure overall thinking ability.

Binet and Simon's items were remarkably diverse in content. They involved naming objects, generating the meanings of words, drawing pictures from memory, completing incomplete sentences ("The man wrote a letter using his _____"), determining the similarities between two objects ("In what way are a dog and a rose alike?"), and constructing a sentence from three words ("woman," "house," and "walked"). Despite the superficial differences among these items, they had one thing in common that Binet and Simon (1905) recognized: *higher mental processes*. These processes included reasoning, understanding, and judgment (Siegler, 1992). In this respect, their items differed sharply from those of Galton, which had relied solely on sensation. Virtually all items on modern intelligence tests have followed Binet and Simon's lead.

Intelligence theorists later built on Binet and Simon's notions. Indeed, most experts agree that whatever intelligence is, it has something to do with **abstract thinking**: the capacity to understand hypothetical concepts, rather than concepts in the here-and-now

falsifiability

CAN THE CLAIM BE DISPROVED?

Galton's laboratory on display at the International Health Exhibition in London in 1884. The exhibit later moved to the South Kensington Museum where, between 1886 and 1890, thousands of visitors took a battery of 17 sensory tests.

intelligence test
diagnostic tool designed to measure overall thinking ability

abstract thinking
capacity to understand hypothetical concepts

Ken Jennings (top), who broke the record for winnings on the game show *Jeopardy!*, would be regarded as especially intelligent by most individuals in Western culture. In contrast, a village elder (bottom) who can impart wisdom would be regarded as especially intelligent by many individuals in Chinese culture.

g (general intelligence)
hypothetical factor that accounts for overall differences in intellect among people

(Gottfredson, 1997; Sternberg, 2003b). In 1921, a panel of 14 American experts generated a list of definitions of intelligence. They didn't succeed in hammering out a single definition, but they mostly agreed that intelligence consists of the abilities to:

- reason abstractly
- learn to adapt to novel environmental circumstances
- acquire knowledge
- benefit from experience

Interestingly, research on how laypeople view intelligence yields similar conclusions, at least in the United States. Most Americans view intelligence as consisting of the capacity to reason well and reason quickly ("to think on one's feet"), as well as to amass large amounts of knowledge in brief periods of time (Sternberg et al., 1981). In contrast, in some non-Western countries, laypersons view intelligence as reflecting people's wisdom and judgment more than their intellectual brilliance (Baral & Das, 2003). For example, in China people tend to view intelligent individuals as those who perform actions for the greater good of the society and are humble (Yang & Sternberg, 1997). Geniuses who toot their own horns might be showered with fame and fortune in the United States, but they might be viewed as hopeless braggarts in the eyes of many Chinese. This difference is consistent with findings that Chinese culture tends to be more focused on group harmony than American culture (Triandis, 2001; see Chapter 10).

■ Intelligence as General versus Specific Abilities

There was one other crucial way that Binet and Simon's items differed from Galton's. When researchers looked at the correlations among these items, they were in for a surprise. Even though Binet and Simon's items differed enormously in content, the correlations among them were all positive: People who got one item correct were more likely than chance to get the others correct. Admittedly, most of these correlations were fairly low, say .2 or .3 (as we learned in Chapter 2, correlations have a maximum of 1.0), but they were almost never zero or negative. Interestingly, this finding has held up with items on modern IQ tests (Alliger, 1988; Carroll, 1993). Given that some of Binet and Simon's items assessed vocabulary, others assessed spatial ability, and still others assessed verbal reasoning, this finding was puzzling.

The phenomenon of positive correlations among intelligence test items caught the attention of psychologist Charles Spearman (1927). To account for these correlations, Spearman hypothesized the existence of a single shared factor across all these aspects—*g*, or **general intelligence**—that accounted for the overall differences in intellect among people. All intelligence test items are positively correlated, he thought, because they reflect the influence of overall intelligence.

Spearman wasn't sure what produces individual differences in *g*, although he speculated that it has something to do with "mental energy" (Sternberg, 2003b). For Spearman, *g* corresponds to the strength of our mental engines. Just as some cars possess more powerful engines than others, he thought, some people have more "powerful"—more effective and efficient—brains than others. They have more *g*.

The meaning of *g* remains exceedingly controversial (Gould, 1981; Herrnstein & Murray, 1994; Jensen, 1998). All because of this little letter, some intelligence researchers are barely on speaking terms. Why? Because *g* implies that some people are just plain smarter than others. Many people find this view distasteful, because it smacks of elitism. Others, like the late Stephen Jay Gould, have argued that *g* is merely a statistical artifact. In his influential book, *The Mismeasure of Man*, Gould (1981) maintained that the idea that all people can be ranked along a single dimension of general intelligence is mistaken. Yet Gould's critics have responded that *g* is unlikely to be a statistical illusion, because scientists have consistently found that intelligence test items are positively correlated with each other regardless of their content (Gottfredson, 2009). Later in the chapter, we'll revisit the controversies swirling around *g* in the context of possible sex and race differences in intelligence.

Spearman didn't believe that *g* tells the whole story about intelligence. For every intelligence test item, Spearman (1927) also proposed the existence of a factor called *s* or **specific abilities** that are unique to each item. That is, according to Spearman, how well we perform on a given mental task depends not only on our general smarts (*g*), but also on our particular skills in narrow domains (*s*). For example, our ability to solve the spatial problem in **FIGURE 9.1** is due not only to our general problem-solving ability but to our specific talents with spatial tests, tasks examining the location of objects in physical space. Even if we're really smart—high in overall *g*—we might flunk this item because we have a specific deficiency when it comes to spatial problems. That deficiency may mean either that we're not inherently adept at spatial tasks or that we haven't had much experience with them.

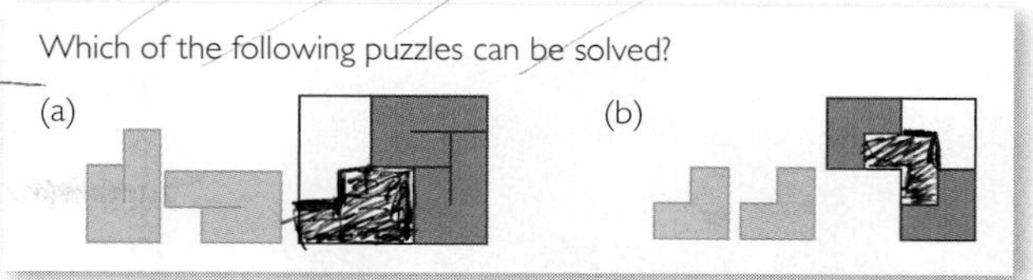

Which of the following puzzles can be solved?

(a)   (b)

FIGURE 9.1   Spatial Task. Try it! For each of the two puzzles shown, try to fit the yellow shapes into the white space to complete the red figure (*Source:* Smith, 2001).

■ Fluid and Crystallized Intelligence

Later researchers found that Spearman's *g* wasn't as uniform as he'd believed (Carroll, 1993; Vernon, 1971). In the 1930s, Louis Thurstone (1938) discovered that some intelligence test items relate more highly to each other than do other items: These items form clumps corresponding to different intellectual capacities. Later, Raymond Cattell (no relation to James McKeen Cattell) and John Horn distinguished fluid from crystallized intelligence, arguing that what we call "intelligence" is actually a mixture of two capacities.

Fluid intelligence refers to the capacity to learn new ways of solving problems. We rely on our fluid intelligence the first time we try to solve a puzzle we've never seen or the first time we try to operate a type of vehicle, like a motorcycle, we've never driven. In contrast, **crystallized intelligence** refers to the accumulated knowledge of the world we acquire over time (Cattell, 1971; Horn, 1994). We rely on our crystallized intelligence to answer questions such as "What's the capital of Italy?" or "How many justices sit on the U.S. Supreme Court?" According to Cattell and Horn, knowledge from newly learned tasks "flows" into our long-term memories, "crystallizing" into lasting knowledge (**FIGURE 9.2**). Most modern researchers don't believe that the existence of fluid and crystallized intelligence undermines the existence of *g*. They view them as "facets" or more specific aspects of *g* (Messick, 1992).

There's some evidence for the fluid–crystallized distinction. Fluid abilities are more likely to decline with age than are crystallized abilities (see Chapter 10). In fact, some researchers have found that crystallized abilities increase with age, including old age (Salthouse, 1996; Schaie, 1996). In addition, fluid abilities are more highly related to *g* than crystallized abilities (Blair, 2006; Gustafsson, 1988). This finding suggests that of the two abilities, fluid intelligence may better capture the power of the "mental engine" to which Spearman referred.

Crystallized intelligence, but not fluid intelligence, is moderately and positively associated (a correlation of about .3) with a personality trait we'll encounter in Chapter 14: *openness to experience* (Ackerman & Heggestad, 1997; DeYoung, Peterson, & Higgins, 2005; Gignac, Stough, & Lovkonitis, 2004). People high in openness to experience are imaginative, intellectually curious, and excited about exploring new ideas, places, and things (Goldberg, 1993). We don't fully understand the causal direction here. Higher crystallized intelligence could give rise to greater openness to experience, as people who know more things to begin with may find learning new things to be easier and therefore more enjoyable. Alternatively, greater openness to experience could give rise to greater crystallized intelligence, as people who are intellectually curious may expose themselves to more knowledge and learn more things.

Fluid IQ

Crystallized IQ

FIGURE 9.2   Knowledge "Flowing" into a Flask. According to Cattell and Horn's model, there are two kinds of intelligence, fluid and crystallized. Fluid intelligence "flows" into crystallized intelligence over time.

Specific skills from experience/ learning

? According to Cattell and Horn, would this bird IQ test primarily be a measure of (a) fluid or (b) crystallized intelligence? Why? (See answer upside down on bottom of page.)

I.Q. TEST FOR BIRDS

1. IT IS BEST TO MIGRATE IN
   ☐ JANUARY
   ☐ OCTOBER
   ☐ FEBRUARY
2. WHICH HAS THE MOST PROTEIN?
   ☐ GRASS
   ☐ SEEDS
   ☐ WORMS
3. YOU ARE RELATED TO A
   ☐ MOOSE
   ☐ OWL
   ☐ SNAKE

s (specific abilities)
particular ability level in a narrow domain

fluid intelligence
capacity to learn new ways of solving problems

crystallized intelligence
accumulated knowledge of the world acquired over time

◄ **correlation vs. causation**

CAN WE BE SURE THAT A CAUSES B?

Answer: Crystallized, because it assesses accumulated knowledge of the world.

(a)

(b)

(c)

According to Gardner, individuals vary in the types of intelligence at which they excel. (a) Martin Luther King Jr. was a great orator with high linguistic (and probably interpersonal) intelligence; (b) Taylor Swift is a musician with renowned musical intelligence; and (c) professional tennis player Serena Williams has impressive bodily-kinesthetic intelligence.

multiple intelligences
idea that people vary in their ability levels across different domains of intellectual skill

triarchic model
model of intelligence proposed by Robert Sternberg positing three distinct types of intelligence: analytical, practical, and creative

■ Multiple Intelligences: Different Ways of Being Smart

Up to this point, we've been talking about "intelligence" as though it were one and only one overarching intellectual ability. But in recent decades, several prominent psychologists have argued for the existence of **multiple intelligences**: entirely different domains of intellectual skill. According to them, the concept of g is wrong, or at least incomplete. For them, we need multiple intelligences to explain the story of people like Chris Langan, who are extremely successful in some intellectual domains yet unsuccessful in others. Moreover, these psychologists maintain that we can't simply say that Sally is smarter than Bill, because there are many ways of being smart (Guilford, 1967). Even Spearman's concept of s is a partial acknowledgement of the existence of multiple intelligences, because it recognizes that even people with equal levels of g can have different intellectual strengths and weaknesses. But in contrast to Spearman, most proponents of multiple intelligences insist that g is only one component of intelligence.

FRAMES OF MIND. Howard Gardner's (1983, 1999) theory of multiple intelligences has been enormously influential in educational practice and theory over the past two decades. According to Gardner, there are numerous "frames of mind," or different ways of thinking about the world. Each frame of mind is a different and fully independent intelligence in its own right.

Gardner (1983) outlined a number of criteria for determining whether a mental ability is a separate intelligence. Among other things, he maintained, researchers must demonstrate that different intelligences can be isolated from one another in studies of people with brain damage; people with damage to a specific brain region must show deficits in one intelligence, but not others. In addition, Gardner argued that different intelligences should be especially pronounced in people with exceptional talents. For example, Gardner believed that the presence of *autistic savants,* about whom we learned in Chapter 7, provides support for the existence of multiple intelligences. These individuals show remarkable abilities in one or two narrow domains, such as knowing the precise batting averages of all active baseball players, but not in most other domains. Gardner also suggested that different intelligences should make sense from an evolutionary standpoint: They should help organisms survive or make it easier for them to meet future mates.

Gardner (1999) proposed eight different intelligences ranging from linguistic and spatial to musical and interpersonal, as described in **TABLE 9.1**. He's also tentatively proposed the existence of a ninth intelligence, called *existential* intelligence: the ability to grasp deep philosophical ideas, like the meaning of life.

Gardner's model has inspired thousands of teachers to tailor their lesson plans around children's individual profiles of multiple intelligences, an effort with which Gardner has said he isn't entirely comfortable (Willingham, 2004). For example, in a class of students with high levels of bodily-kinesthetic intelligence, but low levels of logico-mathematical intelligence, a teacher might encourage students to learn arithmetic problems, like $3 + 4 = 7$, by dividing them into groups of three and four, having them stand up in front of the class, and all join hands to form a bigger group of seven.

TABLE 9.1 Howard Gardner's Multiple Intelligences.

INTELLIGENCE TYPE	CHARACTERISTICS OF HIGH SCORERS
Linguistic	Speak and write well
Logico-mathematical	Use logic and mathematical skills to solve problems, such as scientific questions
Spatial	Think and reason about objects in three-dimensional space
Musical	Perform, understand, and enjoy music
Bodily-kinesthetic	Manipulate the body in sports, dance, or other physical endeavors
Interpersonal	Understand and interact effectively with others
Intrapersonal	Understand and possess insight into self
Naturalistic	Recognize, identify, and understand animals, plants, and other living things

Yet this approach may not be a good idea. After all, if a child has a weakness in a specific skill domain, like vocabulary or mathematics, it may make more sense to try to teach "to" that domain rather than "away" from it. Otherwise, we may allow his already poor skills to decay, much like a weak muscle we choose not to exercise. In addition, as we learned in Chapter 6, research hasn't supported the claim that matching teaching styles to students' learning styles enhances learning outcomes (Stahl, 1999).

The scientific reaction to Gardner's model has been mixed. All researchers agree with Gardner that we vary in our intellectual strengths and weaknesses. Gardner also deserves credit for highlighting the point that intelligent people aren't all smart in the same way. But much of Gardner's model is vague and difficult to test. In particular, it's not clear why certain mental abilities, but not others, qualify as multiple intelligences. According to Gardner's criteria, there should probably also be "humor" and "memory" intelligences (Willingham, 2004). Or, given Gardner's emphasis on evolutionary adaptiveness, why not "romantic" intelligence, the ability to attract sexual partners? It's also not clear that all of Gardner's "intelligences" are genuinely related to intelligence. Some, such as bodily-kinesthetic intelligence, seem much closer to talents that depend heavily on nonmental abilities, like athletic skills (Scarr, 1985; Sternberg, 1988b).

Moreover, because Gardner hasn't developed formal tests to measure his intelligences, his model is virtually impossible to falsify (Klein, 1998). In particular, there's no good evidence that his multiple intelligences are truly independent, as he claims (Lubinski & Benbow, 1995). If measures of these intelligences were all positively correlated, that could suggest that they're all manifestations of g, just as Spearman argued. Even research on autistic savants doesn't clearly support Gardner's model, because autistic savants tend to score higher on measures of general intelligence than do other individuals with autism (Miller, 1999). This finding suggests that their highly specialized abilities are due at least partly to g.

THE TRIARCHIC MODEL. Like Gardner, Robert Sternberg has argued that there's more to intelligence than g. Sternberg's (1983, 1988b) **triarchic model** posits the existence of three largely distinct intelligences (see **FIGURE 9.3**). Moreover, in conjunction with the College Board, he's been developing measures of the second and third intelligence, which he believes are largely unrepresented in standard IQ tests. These three intelligences are:

1. **Analytical intelligence:** the ability to reason logically. In essence, analytical intelligence is "book smarts." It's the kind of intelligence we need to do well on traditional intelligence tests and college admissions exams, the kind of intelligence possessed by Chris Langan. According to Sternberg, this form of intelligence is closely related to g. But, for him, it's only one component of intelligence and not necessarily the most crucial. Indeed, Sternberg has long complained about a "g-ocentric" view of intelligence, one in which school-related smarts is the only kind of intelligence that psychologists value (Sternberg & Wagner, 1993).

2. **Practical intelligence:** also called "tacit intelligence"; the ability to solve real-world problems, especially those involving other people. In contrast to analytical intelligence, this form of intelligence is akin to "street smarts." It's the kind of smarts we need to "size up" people we've just met or figure out how to get ahead on the job. Practical intelligence also relates to what some researchers call *social intelligence,* or the capacity to understand others (Guilford, 1967). Sternberg and his colleagues have developed measures of practical intelligence to assess how well employees and bosses perform in business settings, how well soldiers perform in military settings, and so on (see **FIGURE 9.4**).

3. **Creative intelligence:** also called "creativity"; our ability to come up with novel and effective answers to questions. It's the kind of intelligence we need to find new and effective solutions to problems, like composing an emotionally moving poem or exquisite piece of music. Sternberg argues that practical and creative intelligences predict outcomes, like job performance, that analytical intelligence doesn't (Sternberg & Wagner, 1993; Sternberg et al., 1995).

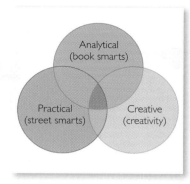

FIGURE 9.3 Sternberg's Triarchic Model of Intelligence. Sternberg's model proposes three kinds of intelligence: analytical, practical, and creative.

falsifiability

CAN THE CLAIM BE DISPROVED?

It's your second year as a manager in a company in the communications industry. You head a department of about 30 people. The evaluation of your first year on the job has been generally favorable. Performance ratings for your department are at least as good as they were before you took over, and perhaps even a little better. You have two assistants. One is quite capable. The other just seems to go through the motions and has been of little real help. You believe that although you are well-liked, there is little that would distinguish you in the eyes of your superiors from the nine other managers at the same level in your company. Your goal is quick promotion to the top of the company. The following is a list of things you are considering doing in the next 2 months. You can't do them all. Rate the importance of each activity (from 1 being the highest, 5 being the lowest) as a means of attaining your goal.

____ (a) Find a way to get rid of the "dead wood" in your company; that is, the unhelpful assistant and a few others.

____ (b) Participate in a series of panel discussions to be shown on local public television.

____ (c) Find ways to make sure your superiors are aware of your accomplishments.

____ (d) Try to better match the work that needs to be done with the strengths and weaknesses of your employees.

____ (e) Write an article on productivity for your company newsletter.

FIGURE 9.4 Sample Item from Test of Practical Intelligence (Item for Business Managers). According to Robert Sternberg, items assessing practical intelligence, like this one, predict real-world behaviors that standard IQ items don't. (*Source:* Adapted from Wagner & Sternberg, 1986)

Our intuitions tell us that these three types of intellect don't always go hand in hand. We can all think of people who are extremely book smart but who possess all of the social skills of a block of concrete. Similarly, we can think of people who have high levels of street smarts but who do poorly on school-related tests.

Yet, like virtually all anecdotes (see Chapter 1), such examples have their limitations. Indeed, many scientists have questioned the bases of Sternberg's claims. In particular, Sternberg hasn't demonstrated convincingly that practical intelligence is independent of *g* (Gottfredson, 2003; Jensen, 1993). Like crystallized intelligence, it may merely be one specialized subtype of *g*. Furthermore, Sternberg's work-related measures of practical intelligence may actually be measures of job knowledge. Not surprisingly, people who know the most about a job tend to perform it the best (Schmidt & Hunter, 1993). Moreover, the causal direction of this correlation isn't clear. Although more practical knowledge may lead to better job performance, better job performance may lead to more practical knowledge (Brody, 1992).

Thus, the concept of multiple intelligences remains controversial. Unquestionably, we all possess different intellectual strengths and weaknesses, but it's not clear that they're as independent of each other as Gardner and Sternberg assert. So there may still be a general intelligence dimension after all.

Revisiting Chris Langan, we can see how Spearman, on the one hand, and Gardner and Sternberg, on the other, would conceptualize his genius. Spearman would have viewed Langan as possessing extremely high *g*, as well as high specific abilities (*s*) in language, theoretical understanding, and other mental capacities. Gardner and Sternberg, while acknowledging that Langan has remarkable analytical abilities and book smarts, might emphasize that he appears to have difficulty understanding others and therefore may be below average in interpersonal (Gardner) or practical (Sternberg) intelligence.

■ Biological Bases of Intelligence

One popular notion about intelligence is that it's related positively to brain size. We speak of smart people as "brainy" or having "lots of marbles upstairs." But to what extent is intelligence related to the brain's size and efficiency?

INTELLIGENCE AND BRAIN STRUCTURE AND FUNCTION. For years, almost all psychology textbooks informed students that although brain size correlates with intelligence *across* species, it's uncorrelated with intelligence *within* species, including humans. But several studies demonstrate that brain volume, as measured by structural MRI scans (see Chapter 3), correlates positively—between .3 and .4—with measured intelligence (McDaniel, 2005; Willerman et al., 1991). So when we refer to the supersmart kid in class who gets 100s on all of his exams without studying as a "brain," we may not be entirely off base. Still, the correlation between brain volume and IQ is complicated, and may hold more for verbal than for spatial abilities (Witelson, Beresh, & Kiger, 2006).

Moreover, we don't know whether these findings reflect a direct causal association. Perhaps bigger brains lead to higher intelligence. Or perhaps some third variable, like better nutrition before or shortly after birth, leads to both. In addition, a correlation of less than .4 tells us that the association between brain size and intelligence is far less than perfect. For example, Albert Einstein's brain actually weighed about 1,230 grams, slightly less than the average brain. Interestingly, though, the lower part of Einstein's parietal cortex, an area that becomes active during spatial reasoning tasks, was 15 percent wider than normal (Witelson, Kigar, & Harvey, 1999). This finding may explain Einstein's remarkable capacity for visual imagery (Falk, 2009). In addition, Einstein's brain also had an unusually high density of neurons and glial cells (see Chapter 3), suggesting that his brain packed more mass than the average brain (Anderson & Harvey, 1996).

Recent studies on brain development suggest that there may be more to the story. A study using structural MRI revealed that highly intelligent (IQs in the top 10 percent) seven-year-olds have a *thinner* cerebral cortex than other children. The cortexes of these children then thicken rapidly, peaking at about age 12 (Shaw et al., 2006). We don't yet know what these findings mean, and independent investigators haven't replicated them. But they may indicate that, like fine wines, intelligent brains take longer to mature than others.

---

correlation vs. causation

CAN WE BE SURE THAT A CAUSES B?

FICTOID ✕

MYTH: Albert Einstein had dyslexia.

REALITY: Scores of popular psychology sources, including many organizations for dyslexia, claim that Albert Einstein had this learning disability, which is marked by difficulties with word recognition and reading in the absence of other intellectual deficits. Although there's some anecdotal but inconsistent evidence that Einstein was an abnormally late talker, there's no good evidence that he had dyslexia or any other learning disability (Thomas, 2004).

---

correlation vs. causation

CAN WE BE SURE THAT A CAUSES B?

---

replicability

CAN THE RESULTS BE DUPLICATED IN OTHER STUDIES?

Functional brain imaging studies and laboratory studies of information processing offer intriguing clues regarding what intelligence is and where in the brain it resides. Over the span of about a month, Richard Haier and his colleagues (Haier et al., 1992) taught a group of eight undergraduates to play the computer video game Tetris. All subjects improved over time, and those with the highest scores on a measure of intelligence improved the most. Surprisingly, subjects with higher levels of intelligence exhibited *less* brain activity in many areas than subjects with lower levels of intelligence (Haier et al., 2009). Haier's explanation? The brains of the more intelligent students were especially efficient. Much like well-conditioned athletes who barely break a sweat while running a five-mile race, they could afford to slack off a bit while learning the task (Haier, 2009). Admittedly, not all researchers have replicated Haier's findings (Fidelman, 1993), but they raise the possibility that intelligence in part reflects efficiency of mental processing.

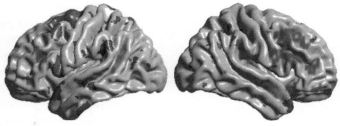

Here are functional brain images (see Chapter 3) of two people who've been playing the computer game *Tetris*. As is standard in brain images, red depicts high levels of brain activation, blue low levels of brain activation. According to research by Richard Haier and colleagues, which brain is likely to come from someone with a high IQ, and why? (See answer upside down on bottom of page.)

replicability

CAN THE RESULTS BE DUPLICATED IN OTHER STUDIES?

INTELLIGENCE AND REACTION TIME. When speaking loosely, we sometimes refer to people who don't seem as intelligent as other people as "slow." Psychologists have brought this folk belief to the laboratory by studying the relation of intelligence to *reaction time,* or the speed of responding to a stimulus (Jensen, 2006). Imagine being seated in front of the reaction time box shown in **FIGURE 9.5** (Hick, 1952), which features a semicircle of eight buttons, with lights alongside of them. On each trial, anywhere from one to eight of the lights turn on, and then one of them suddenly turns off. Your job is to hit the button next to the light that turned off, and to do so as quickly as possible. The results of numerous studies indicate that measured intelligence correlates negatively (about –.3 to –.4) with reaction time on this task (Deary, Der, & Ford, 2001; Detterman, 1987): People with higher intelligence react more quickly than other people when the light turns off (Brody, 1992). So Galton may not have been completely wrong in believing that speed of sensory processing contributes to intelligence, although these two concepts clearly aren't identical.

FIGURE 9.5 Reaction-Time Apparatus. Psychologists have used a reaction-time box to study the relation between intelligence and response to simple stimuli. Typically, the red lights turn on and then, as soon as one turns off, the participant tries as quickly as possible to press the blue button next to the unlit light.

INTELLIGENCE AND MEMORY. Intelligence also bears an intimate connection to memory capacity. Many researchers have examined the relation of tasks that assess "working memory" to intelligence. As we learned in Chapter 7, this type of memory is closely related to short-term memory. A typical working memory task might require subjects to perform a test of digit span (see Chapter 7) while trying to figure out the meaning of a proverb (such as "What does the saying 'A bird in the hand is worth two in the bush' mean?"). Scores on working memory tasks are moderately correlated (about .5) with scores on intelligence tests (Ackerman, Beier, & Boyle, 2005; Engle, 2002; Kane, Hambrick, & Conway, 2005).

THE LOCATION OF INTELLIGENCE. Where in the brain is intelligence located? This may seem like a silly question, as it's unlikely that a neurosurgeon can point to a specific region of the brain and say "Right there ... that's what makes us smart." Yet intelligence is more localized to certain areas of the cortex than others. One group of investigators administered a number of reasoning tasks that are highly "g-loaded"—substantially related to general intelligence (see **FIGURE 9.6**). These tasks all activated the prefrontal cortex (Duncan et al., 2000), a brain region

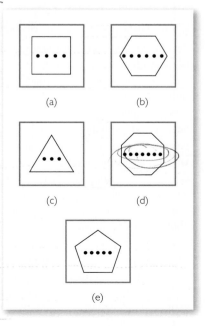

(a) (b) (c) (d) (e)

FIGURE 9.6 Sample Task (a Highly *g-*Loaded Item). This sample item is similar to items that researchers have identified as highly "*g*-loaded," meaning that it's a good predictor of general intelligence. In this item, one of the five choices differs from the others. **Can you figure out which one it is?** (The answer is printed upside down at the bottom of the page.)

Answer to Figure 9.6: d

Answer: The brain on the right; people with high IQs tend to have more efficient brains, which in turn need to work less hard.

that plays key roles in planning, impulse control, and short-term memory (see Chapter 3). Nevertheless, the prefrontal cortex doesn't tell the whole story when it comes to intelligence. For example, regions of the parietal lobe, which is intimately involved in spatial abilities (see Chapter 3), also appear to be associated with intelligence (Haier, 2009; Jung & Haier, 2007).

PULLING IT ALL TOGETHER. If there's one central theme to these diverse findings, it's that intelligence is related to efficiency or speed of information processing (Schmiedek et al., 2007; Vernon, 1987). So here, common sense may be partly correct: People who are quick thinkers tend to be especially intelligent. Still, the associations are far less than a perfect correlation of 1.0, which tells us that intelligence is more than quickness of thinking. These results also suggest that the capacity to retrieve short-term information is related to intelligence, although the causal direction of this association isn't clear.

✓—Study and Review on mypsychlab.com

assess your knowledge   FACT OR FICTION?

1. Most research suggests that intelligence is almost entirely a function of sensory ability. True / False

2. All or almost all items on modern intelligence tests tend to be positively correlated with each other. True / False

3. According to Sternberg, practical intelligence is essentially the same thing as book smarts. True / False

4. Within humans, brain size tends to be moderately positively correlated with measured intelligence. True / False

5. Intelligence is unrelated to reaction time. True / False

Answers: 1. F (p.319); 2. T (p.320); 3. F (p.323); 4. T (p.324); 5. F (p.325)

INTELLIGENCE TESTING: THE GOOD, THE BAD, AND THE UGLY

9.3 Determine how psychologists calculate IQ.

9.4 Explain the history of misuse of intelligence tests in the United States.

9.5 Describe tests of intelligence used today and evaluate the reliability and validity of IQ scores.

9.6 Distinguish the unique characteristics of mental retardation and genius.

Psychologists have long struggled with the thorny question of how to measure people's intelligence. The simplest way to do so would, of course, be to ask them "How smart are you?". Tempting as this approach might be, it's unlikely to work. Self-estimates of IQ correlate only .2 to .3 with objective measures of intelligence (Hansford & Hattie, 1982). Making matters more complicated, recent evidence suggests that people with poor cognitive skills are especially likely to overestimate their intellectual abilities, a phenomenon called the *double curse of incompetence* (Dunning, Heath, & Suls, 2004; Kruger & Dunning, 1999). This curse may explain why some people perform poorly in school and on the job, even though they're convinced they're performing well. It may also explain the embarrassing behavior of our Uncle Ernie, who keeps telling jokes that aren't funny— and keeps laughing at them (Goode, 2000). *Metacognitive skills* play a key role in the double curse of incompetence (Koriat & Bjork, 2005). Metacognition refers to knowledge of our own knowledge (see Chapter 8). People with poor metacognitive skills in a given domain may overestimate their performance, because they don't know what they don't know (Dunning et al., 2004; Sinkavich, 1995).

These findings confirm the intuitions of Binet, Simon, and other psychologists that we need systematic tests to measure intelligence. When Binet and Simon created the first intelligence test more than a century ago, however, they had no inkling that they'd alter the landscape of psychology. Yet their invention has changed how we select people for schools, jobs, and the

[Handwritten margin notes:] double curse of incompetence – people think they are performing well when they actually are not.

Metacognitive skills – overestimate own skills

military; it's changed schooling and social policies; and it's changed how we think about ourselves. The history of intelligence testing begins where Binet and Simon left off.

How We Calculate IQ

Shortly after Binet and Simon introduced their test to France, Lewis Terman of Stanford University developed a modified and translated version called the **Stanford-Binet IQ test**, first published in 1916 and still used today in its revised fifth edition. Originally developed for children but since extended to adults, the Stanford-Binet consists of a wide variety of tasks like those Binet and Simon used, such as tests of vocabulary, memory for pictures, naming of familiar objects, repeating sentences, and following commands (Janda, 1998). Terman's great achievement was to establish a set of *norms*, baseline scores in the general population from which we can compare each individual's score. Using norms, we can ask whether a given person's score on intelligence test items are above or below those of similar-aged people, and by how much. All modern intelligence tests contain norms for different age groups, such as adults between 30 and 54, 55 and 69, and so on.

Shortly before World War I, German psychologist Wilhelm Stern (1912) invented the formula for the **intelligence quotient**, which will forever be known by two letters: *IQ*. Stern's formula for computing IQ was simple: Divide *mental age* by *chronological age* and multiply the resulting number by 100. **Mental age**, a concept introduced by Binet, is the age corresponding to the average person's performance on an intelligence test. A girl who takes an IQ test and does as well as the average six-year-old has a mental age of six, regardless of her actual age. Her chronological age is simply her actual age, in years. So, if a 10-year-old child does as well on an IQ test as the average eight-year-old, his IQ according to Stern's formula would be 80 (a mental age of eight divided by a chronological age of 10, multiplied by 100). Conversely, if an eight-year-old child does as well on an IQ test as the average 10-year-old, his IQ according to Stern's formula would be 125 (a mental age of 10 divided by a chronological age of eight multiplied by 100). ◉ ⎯ Watch

Although Stern's formula does a respectable job of estimating intelligence for children and young adolescents, it soon became evident that the formula contains a critical flaw. Mental age scores increase progressively in childhood, but start to level out at around age 16 (Eysenck, 1994). Once we hit 16 or so, our performance on IQ test items doesn't increase by much. Because our mental age levels off but our chronological age increases with time, Stern's formula would result in everyone's IQ getting lower and lower as they get older.

That's why almost all modern intelligence researchers rely on a statistic called **deviation IQ** when computing IQ for adults (Wechsler, 1939). Basically, using a statistical measure of variability (see Chapter 2), the deviation IQ expresses each person's IQ relative to the norms for his or her age group. An IQ of 100, which is average, means that a person's IQ is exactly typical of people of his age group. An IQ of 80 is a standard amount below average for any age group, and an IQ of 120 is a standard amount above. In this way, the deviation IQ gets rid of the problem posed by Stern's formula, because it doesn't result in IQs decreasing after age 16.

The Eugenics Movement: Misuses and Abuses of IQ Testing

Soon after French psychologists Binet and Simon had developed their test, researchers in other countries began translating it into various languages. Among the first was American psychologist Henry Goddard, who translated it into English in 1908. In only a matter of years, IQ testing became a booming business in the United States. It was no longer merely a vehicle for targeting schoolchildren in need of special help, however, but a means of identifying adults deemed intellectually inferior.

The IQ testing movement quickly spiraled out of control. Examiners frequently administered these tests in English to new American immigrants who barely knew the language. It's hardly surprising, then, that about 40 percent of these immigrants were classified as having mental retardation. Moreover, Goddard and others adapted childhood tests for use in testing adults, without fully understanding how the IQ scores applied to adults (Kevles, 1985). As a consequence, legions of adults given his tests, including prison inmates and delinquents, scored in

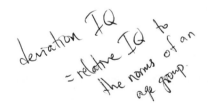

[handwritten note: IQ = intelligence quotient]

$$\left(\frac{\text{mental age}}{\text{chronological age}}\right) \times 100 = IQ$$

◉ ⎯ **Watch** the Classic Video: Assessment of Memory with the Stanford-Binet Intelligence Scale on **mypsychlab.com**

[handwritten note: deviation IQ = relative IQ to the norms of an age group]

Stanford-Binet IQ test
intelligence test based on the measure developed by Binet and Simon, adapted by Lewis Terman of Stanford University

intelligence quotient (IQ)
systematic means of quantifying differences among people in their intelligence

mental age
age corresponding to the average individual's performance on an intelligence test

deviation IQ
expression of a person's IQ relative to his or her same-aged peers

eugenics
movement in the early twentieth century to improve a population's genetic stock by encouraging those with good genes to reproduce, preventing those with bad genes from reproducing, or both

Total number of operations to January 1, 1935: 21,539

- ▇ Laws in effect January 1, 1935
- ▇ Sterilization laws in effect January 1, 1935
- ▇ States with no sterilization laws
- * Sterilization laws repealed

FIGURE 9.7   A Sterilization Map of the United States in 1935. As of 1935, most U.S. states had mandatory sterilization laws, a legacy of the eugenics movement, either on the books or pending. (*Source:* Dolan DNA Learning Center)

Addie Lee Anderson, 87, shown August 8, 2006, at her home in Fayetteville, North Carolina, was involuntarily sterilized in 1950 by the Eugenics Board of North Carolina after the birth of her last child.

the range of mental retardation. In one especially embarrassing episode, a psychologist administered Goddard's IQ test to the mayor of Chicago, as well as to his running mates and opponents. Almost all scored in the mentally retarded range, creating a public relations disaster for Goddard when the newspapers found out about it (Wood, Garb, & Nezworski, 2006).

Eventually, concern with the low IQs of many immigrants and even many Americans led to a social movement called **eugenics** (meaning "good genes"), a term coined by none other than Sir Francis Galton (Gillham, 2001). Eugenics was the effort to improve a population's "genetic stock" by encouraging people with "good genes" to reproduce (*positive eugenics*), by discouraging people with "bad genes" from reproducing (*negative eugenics*), or both. Galton had been a proponent of only positive eugenics, but many later psychologists advocated negative eugenics.

Although eugenics was by no means unique to America (Kuntz & Bachrach, 2006), it became immensely popular there in the early twentieth century, especially from 1910 to 1930. Dozens of universities, among them Harvard, Cornell, Columbia, and Brown, offered courses in eugenics to approximately 20,000 undergraduates (Selden, 1999). Most high school and college biology texts presented eugenics as a scientific enterprise.

Eugenics came to be associated with at least two disturbing practices. First, many users of early IQ tests didn't consider sufficiently the problems introduced by administering items in English to largely non-English-speaking respondents, leading them to underestimate their intelligence. Beginning in the 1920s, the U.S. Congress passed laws designed to restrict immigration from other countries supposedly marked by low intelligence, especially those in eastern and southern Europe (Gould, 1981). Second, beginning in 1907 and continuing through the next few decades, 33 U.S. states passed laws requiring the sterilization of low-IQ individuals (see **FIGURE 9.7**). Some of the surgeons who performed these sterilizations tricked their patients into believing they were undergoing emergency appendectomies (removal of their appendices) (Leslie, 2000). The assumption behind mandatory sterilization was that IQ was genetically influenced, so preventing low-IQ individuals from reproducing would halt the supposed deterioration of the population's intelligence. When all was said and done, about 66,000 North Americans, many of them African Americans and other poor minorities, underwent forced sterilizations (Reynolds, 2003). Disturbingly, the U.S. Supreme Court upheld these sterilization practices in 1927 in a case called *Buck v. Bell*. Ruling to uphold the sterilization of 18-year-old Carrie Buck, who'd come from two generations of purportedly "feeble-minded" ancestors, Justice Oliver Wendell Holmes wrote that "three generations of imbeciles are enough." Fortunately, the practice of sterilization slowed in the 1940s and had subsided almost completely by the early 1960s, although involuntary sterilization laws remained on the books in America for years. Virginia became the last state to repeal them in 1974.

We can still feel the impact of the eugenics movement today. Many people are understandably suspicious of claims regarding IQ and its genetic bases, as these claims remind them of the unethical efforts by eugenics advocates to "purge" low-IQ individuals from the gene pool. Still, we must be careful not to confuse a claim's validity with the people who advocate it (otherwise known as the error of "guilt by association"). It's true that many eugenics supporters were strong proponents of IQ testing and research on the genetic bases of IQ. But this fact doesn't, by itself, imply that we should dismiss the science of IQ testing or research on genetic bases of IQ. Although it's entirely appropriate to be dismayed by the tragic history of the eugenics movement in America, the two issues are logically separable.

■ IQ Testing Today

Today, the IQ test stands as one of psychology's best-known, yet most controversial, accomplishments. In 1989, the American Academy for the Advancement of Science listed the IQ test as one of the 20 greatest scientific achievements of the twentieth century (Henshaw, 2006). Whether or not we agree with this assessment, there's no question that IQ testing has been remarkably influential. Although psychologists have developed dozens of IQ tests, a mere handful have come to dominate the modern testing scene. We'll discuss these tests next, along with standardized tests like the SAT and measures of infant intelligence.

COMMONLY USED ADULT IQ TESTS. The IQ test administered most widely to assess intelligence in adults is the **Wechsler Adult Intelligence Scale**, or **WAIS** (Watkins et al., 1995). Ironically, David Wechsler, a psychologist who developed this test, was a Romanian immigrant to the United States who was among those classified as feebleminded by early, flawed IQ tests. Perhaps not surprisingly, Wechsler's negative experience led him to construct an IQ test based on more than verbal abilities. The most recent version of his test, the WAIS-IV (Wechsler, 2008), consists of 15 "subtests," or specific tasks, designed to assess such varied mental abilities as vocabulary, arithmetic, spatial ability, reasoning about proverbs, and general knowledge about the world. We can find sample items from several of these subtests in **FIGURE 9.8**. The WAIS-IV yields five major scores: (1) overall IQ, (2) verbal comprehension, (3) perceptual reasoning, (4) working memory, and (5) processing speed. Verbal comprehension relates primarily to crystallized intelligence, while perceptual reasoning, working memory, and processing speed relate primarily to fluid intelligence.

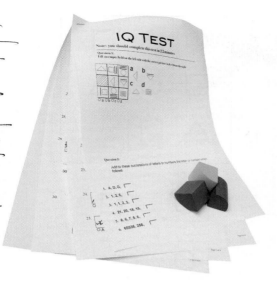

We can find dozens of informal "Test Yourself" IQ tests on the Internet, in magazines, or in self-help books. Most of these tests haven't been validated, so we shouldn't put much stock in the IQ scores they yield.

	Wechsler Adult Intelligence Scale (WAIS) Sample Items*	
Test	**Description**	**Example**
Information	Taps general range of information	On which continent is France?
Comprehension	Tests understanding of social conventions and ability to evaluate past experience	Why do people need birth certificates?
Arithmetic	Tests arithmetic reasoning through verbal problems	How many hours will it take to drive 150 miles at 50 miles per hour?
Similarities	Asks in what way certain objects or concepts are similar; measures abstract thinking	How are a calculator and a typewriter alike?
Digit span	Tests attention and rote memory by orally presenting series of digits to be repeated forward or backward	Repeat the following numbers backward: 2 4 3 5 1 8 6
Vocabulary	Tests ability to define increasingly difficult words	What does *repudiate* mean?
Digit symbol	Tests speed of learning through timed coding tasks in which numbers must be associated with marks of various shapes	Shown / Fill in
Picture completion	Tests visual alertness and visual memory through presentation of an incompletely drawn figure; the missing part must be discovered and named	Tell me what is missing:
Block design	Tests ability to perceive and analyze patterns presenting designs that must be copied with blocks	Assemble blocks to match this design:
Visual Puzzles	Tests ability to organize parts of a figure into a larger spatial array	Which three of these pieces go together to make this puzzle?
Figure Weights	Tests ability to reason logically about numbers	Which one of these goes here to balance the scale?

Wechsler Adult Intelligence Scale (WAIS)
most widely used intelligence test for adults today, consisting of 15 subtests to assess different types of mental abilities

FIGURE 9.8 Sample Items from WAIS. Eleven of 15 subtests of the WAIS-IV (the newest version), along with items similar to those on the test.

*Note: For copyright reasons, we can't present the items on the actual test. (Source: NCS Pearson, Inc.)

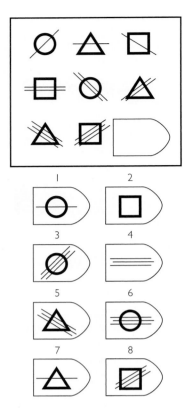

FIGURE 9.9 Item Similar to That on Raven's Progressive Matrices. An item similar to those in the *Raven's Progressive Matrices—Advanced Progressive Matrices*. The answer is positioned upside down at the bottom of the page.
(*Source:* NCS Pearson, Inc., 1998)

culture-fair IQ test
abstract reasoning measure that doesn't depend on language and is often believed to be less influenced by cultural factors than other IQ tests

COMMONLY USED CHILDHOOD IQ TESTS. Two widely used IQ tests for children are the Wechsler Intelligence Scale for Children (WISC) and the Wechsler Primary and Preschool Scale of Intelligence (WPPSI; pronounced "WHIP-see"), the former in its fourth edition and latter in this third edition. Both measures are versions of the WAIS adapted for older children and adolescents (the WISC-IV) or younger children aged two and a half to seven years old (the WPPSI-III) (Kaplan & Sacuzzo, 2008).

CULTURE-FAIR IQ TESTS. Going all the way at least to the days of David Wechsler, one major criticism of IQ tests has been their heavy reliance on language. Test takers who aren't fluent in the native language may do poorly on IQ tests largely because they don't comprehend the test instructions or the questions themselves. Moreover, cultural factors can affect people's familiarity with test materials, and in turn their performance on intellectual tasks (Neisser et al., 1996). In one study, a researcher asked schoolchildren in England and Zambia (a country in southern Africa) to reproduce a series of visual patterns using both paper and pencil—a medium with which British children tend to be familar—and wire—a medium with which Zambian children tend to be familiar. The British children did better than the Zambian children when using paper and pencil, but the Zambian children did better than the British children when using wire (Serpell, 1979).

As a consequence of these problems, psychologists have developed a variety of **culture-fair IQ tests**, which consist of abstract-reasoning items that don't depend on language (Cattell, 1949). Presumably, these tests are less influenced by cultural differences than standard IQ tests are.

Perhaps the best-known culture-fair test is Raven's Progressive Matrices, used widely in Great Britain as a measure of intelligence (Raven, Raven, & Court, 1998). As **FIGURE 9.9** shows, this test requires examinees to pick out the final geometrical pattern in a sequence (the matrices are "progressive" because they start off easy and become increasingly difficult). Raven's Progressive Matrices is an excellent measure of *g* (Neisser et al., 1996).

psychomythology

DO COLLEGE ADMISSIONS TESTS PREDICT GRADES?

Psychologists designed the SAT, ACT, Graduate Record Exam (GRE), and other admissions tests to forecast performance in undergraduate and graduate courses. Yet the correlations between these tests and college grades are often below .5 and in a few cases close to zero (Morrison & Morrison, 1995). Moreover, although SATs and GREs tend to predict first-year grades at reasonable levels, they generally do a worse job of predicting performance in later years of college (Kuncel & Hezlett, 2007).

These low correlations have prompted many critics to conclude that the SAT and GRE aren't helpful for making predictions about grades (Oldfield, 1998; Sternberg & Williams, 1997). More than one-fourth of major liberal arts colleges in the United States no longer require the SAT, and these numbers are growing (Lewin, 2006). Ralph Nader, a consumer advocate and former presidential candidate, argued that the SAT is so invalid that it should be banned (Kaplan, 1982; Nairn, 1980). In 2001, the chancellor of the University of California State system, Richard Atkinson—himself a prominent psychologist, argued that the SAT is only weakly predictive of students' actual achievement (Atkinson, 2001).

Are Nader and Atkinson right? Yes and no. They're right that the SAT and GRE are highly imperfect predictors and that they don't correlate highly with future grades. But they're wrong that this fact renders the tests largely useless. To understand why, let's look at the graph in **Figure 9.10a**. We call this graph a *scatterplot* (see Chapter 2), because it's a plot of the correlation between two variables, in this case between SAT scores and grade point average (GPA) in college. As we can see, the SAT scores (combined across all three subtests) range from 700 to 2,300, and GPA ranges from 1.5 to almost 4.0. The correlation in this scatterplot is .65, which is fairly high. Recall from Chapter 2 that high positive correlations display a pronounced upward tilt.

But let's now look at **Figure 9.10b**, which is a close-up of the dots that are 1,500 or higher on the x (horizontal) axis. As we can see, the range of SAT scores is now only between 1,500 and 2,300 combined. This range is typical of what we find at many highly competitive colleges. That's

■ College Admissions Tests: What Do They Measure?

The odds are high you've taken at least one, and perhaps many, college admissions tests in your life. In fact, to get into college you may have endured the misery of the SAT, once called the Scholastic Assessment Test and before that, the Scholastic Aptitude Test (oddly enough, the initials "SAT" no longer stand for anything), or the ACT (which formerly stood for the American College Test). The SAT now consists of three sections—Mathematics, Reading, and Writing—with scores on each ranging from 200 to 800.

Companies that provide coaching for standardized tests often promise to raise students' scores by a substantial margin. What does the research say?

COLLEGE ADMISSIONS TESTS AND IQ. College admissions tests are designed either to test overall competence in a specific domain or to predict academic success. For many years, the Educational Testing Service apparently collected data on the correlation between the SAT and IQ, but didn't release them until recently (Seligman, 2004). Until that time, we knew little or nothing about the SAT–IQ relationship. Murphy Frey and Douglas Detterman (2004) found that the SAT correlates highly (between about .7 and .8) with two standard measures of intelligence, including the Raven's Progressive Matrices. So the SAT is clearly linked to measured intelligence.

Among professional basketball players, height isn't an especially good predictor of who scores the most points, because the range of heights is dramatically restricted.

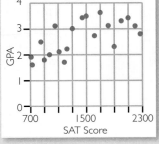

because few people with SAT scores much below 1,500 combined get into these colleges. What does the correlation look like now? As we can see, it's much lower than that in Figure 9.10a; in fact, the correlation is close to zero (it's even slightly negative). The upward tilt of this correlation has clearly disappeared.

These two scatterplots illustrate a crucial phenomenon overlooked by many critics of the SAT and GRE (for example, Sternberg & Williams, 1997): restriction of range. *Restriction of range* refers to the fact that correlations tend to go down when we limit the range of scores on one or both variables (Alexander et al., 1987). To understand restriction of range, think of the relation of height to basketball playing ability. In a group of ordinary people playing a pickup basketball game on a Saturday afternoon, height will correlate highly with who scores more points. But in a game of professional basketball players, height barely matters, because almost everyone who makes it to a professional basketball team is tall.

Restriction of range helps to explain why the SAT and GRE aren't highly predictive of scores in college and graduate school: Colleges and graduate schools rarely admit low scorers (Camara, 2009). Indeed, when two researchers examined the validity of the GRE in a graduate department that admitted applicants regardless of their GRE scores, the GRE correlated highly (between .55 and .70) with measures of graduate GPA (Huitema & Stein, 1993). So when we remove restriction of range, the GRE becomes highly predictive of later grades. Restriction of range also probably accounts for why SATs and GREs are less predictive of later grades than of first-year grades. When students get to pick the classes in which they do well, they tend to obtain higher grades, thereby limiting the range of GPAs (Sackett, Borneman, & Connelly, 2008).

To return to the question we posed at the outset—Do standardized tests predict grades?—the answer is, "When we measure the full range of scores, yes, although by no means perfectly."

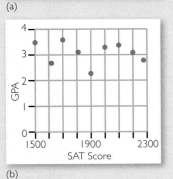

(a)

(b)

FIGURE 9.10 Scatterplot of Correlation between SAT Scores and College GPA. In the graph depicted in (a), SAT scores are clearly correlated with GPA. We can see an upward slant to the data points as we move from lower to higher scores. In the graph depicted in (b), the same data are depicted but only for the narrow range of higher SAT scores (1,500–2,300). As we can see, there is no clear correlation between SAT scores and GPA in this range.

COACHING ON COLLEGE ADMISSIONS TESTS. You've probably heard of companies, such as Princeton Review or Kaplan, that prepare students for the SAT and other college admissions tests. These companies charge sizable chunks of money and make some pretty lavish claims. For example, Princeton Review has guaranteed 100 point increases on the SAT, and Kaplan has asserted that more than a quarter of students improve by 170 points or more when taking the SAT a second time (Powers & Rock, 1999).

Do these courses really work? The answer isn't clear (DerSimonian & Laird, 1983), which is surprising given how long these programs have been around. There's definitely a positive *correlation* between whether people taking coaching courses and their SAT scores, but this correlation may be due to a third variable: Students who take coaching courses tend to be more educated and better prepared for these tests to begin with (Camara, 2009). Still, the evidence suggests that commercial coaching improves SAT scores slightly, probably by 10 to 15 points on average per section (Kulik, Bangert-Drowns, & Kulik, 1984; Powers, 1993). ◉ | **Watch**

Are the companies deliberately exaggerating? Not necessarily. It's true that some people improve by 100 points or more after taking SAT preparation courses. But the companies are probably neglecting to consider an alternative explanation for these increases: practice effects (Shadish, Cook, & Campbell, 2002). By *practice effects,* we mean that people frequently improve on tests as a result of practice alone. So the companies may be concluding mistakenly that people who take their courses are improving *because* of these courses rather than merely *after* them. When researchers have controlled for practice effects by including a control group of people who take the SAT a second time but haven't taken an SAT preparation course, the improvements resulting from these courses has been much smaller than claimed by the companies (Camara, 2009; Powers & Rock, 1999). So if you want to gain a slight edge on the SAT or similar standardized tests, by all means consider enrolling in one of these courses, or buy some practice tests of your own. But if you're looking for a 200- or 300-point increase, you'd do best to hold on to your money.

■ Reliability of IQ Scores: Is IQ Forever?

We often think of people's IQ scores in much the same way we think of their social security numbers: as sticking with them for life. Joe's a 116, Maria's a 130, and Bill's a 97. Yet IQ scores aren't fixed. They almost never remain exactly the same over time; in fact, they occasionally shift within the same person by as much as 10 points or more over a matter of months.

STABILITY OF IQ IN ADULTHOOD. IQ scores usually remain reasonably stable in adulthood. As we learned in Chapter 2, *reliability* refers to consistency of measurement. As we also learned, one important type of reliability is *test-retest reliability,* which refers to the extent to which scores on a measure remain stable over time. For adult IQ tests like the WAIS-IV, test-retest reliabilities tend to be about .95 over a several week interval (Wechsler, 1997). As you'll recall, .95 is an extremely high correlation, nearly but not quite perfect. Even across long stretches of time, IQ scores tend to be reasonably stable. In one study of 101 Scottish schoolchildren followed up over time, IQ scores obtained at age 11 correlated .73 with their IQ scores at age 77 (Deary et al., 2000).

STABILITY OF IQ IN INFANCY AND CHILDHOOD. There's a key exception to the rule regarding the high test-retest reliability of IQ tests. Prior to age two or three, IQ tests aren't stable over time. In fact, IQ measured in the first six months of life correlates just about zero with adult IQ (Brody, 1992). Nor do IQ scores obtained in the first few years of life do a good job of forecasting outcomes, unless they're extremely low, such as under 50; such scores tend to be predictive of later mental retardation. IQ tests designed for very young children assess the sensory abilities that Galton and Cattell emphasized, which bear little association with intelligence. In contrast, IQ tests designed for older children and beyond assess the abstract reasoning emphasized by Binet, Simon, and others. This reasoning, as we've seen, lies at the heart of what we call intelligence.

---

correlation vs. causation
CAN WE BE SURE THAT A CAUSES B?

◉ | **Watch** SAT Alternatives: Robert Sternberg on **mypsychlab.com**

ruling out rival hypotheses
HAVE IMPORTANT ALTERNATIVE EXPLANATIONS FOR THE FINDINGS BEEN EXCLUDED?

FACTOID +

Technically, you can receive a score of zero on the SAT if you answer every question incorrectly (you'll receive a score of 200 if you answer the questions randomly). Nevertheless, because the Educational Testing Service, which administers and scores the SAT, doesn't report scores below 200, you'll receive a score of 200 on your SAT just for signing your name.

Seated comfortably on mom's lap, a baby takes an experimental measure of infant intelligence that assesses response to novelty. The baby had previously viewed a number of identical pairs of photos of two people playing with toys, and is now viewing two different photos (containing different toys). The extent to which infants look at the novel photo modestly predicts their adult intelligence.

Some measures of infant intelligence are slightly more promising when it comes to predicting later IQ. One is speed of habituation. As we discovered in Chapter 6, habituation refers to the tendency to stop responding to repeated presentations of the same stimulus. Infants who habituate to a visual stimulus (like a red circle) more quickly—as measured by how long they stare at it—turn out to have higher IQs in later childhood and adolescence, with correlations typically in the .3 to .5 range (McCall &Carriger, 1993; Slater, 1997).

It's not entirely clear why this is so. Perhaps this correlation reflects a direct causal association between intelligence and habituation: Infants who are smart "take in" information from novel stimuli quickly, so they're ready to move on to new things. Alternatively, this correlation may reflect the influence of a third variable, like interest in new stimuli (Colombo, 1993). Perhaps infants who are more interested in new things both habituate more quickly *and* learn more things, resulting in higher intelligence later on.

A related approach presents babies with pairs of pictures, like photos of faces. For many trials, the two faces are the same. Then suddenly, a novel face appears along with the familiar face. Infants who attend more to the new face later tend to have higher IQs in childhood and adolescence than other infants (DiLalla et al., 1990; Smith, Fagan, & Ulvund, 2002). Still, this measure has its problems. In particular, its test-retest reliability is fairly low (Benasich & Bejar, 1992).

It remains to be seen whether researchers will develop even better measures of infant intelligence. Ultimately, these measures may yield clues regarding how intelligence develops and perhaps even what intelligence is.

■ Validity of IQ Scores: Predicting Life Outcomes

Whatever we think of IQ tests, there's little question that they're valid for at least some purposes. As we learned in Chapter 2, *validity* refers to the extent to which a test measures what it purports to measure. One important indicator of a test's validity is its ability to relate to outcomes measured at about the same time the test is administered, or what psychologists call "concurrent" validity (think of the word "current"). Modern IQ tests have strong concurrent validity; for example, they correlate moderately to highly with other IQ tests given during the same session (Wechsler, 1988). ◉─ Watch

Another important indicator is its capacity to forecast future outcomes, or what psychologists call "predictive" validity. IQ scores do a good job of predicting academic success; they correlate about .5 with grades in high school and college (Neisser et al., 1997). Still, because this correlation is considerably lower than 1.0, it tells us there's more to school success than IQ. Motivation, intellectual curiosity, effort, and *mental energy*—the ability to focus on difficult problems for long periods of time (Lykken, 2005) —also play crucial roles.

How typical are people like Chris Langan, who have extremely high IQs but unremarkable occupational success? Less than we might think. IQ scores predict performance across a wide variety of occupations, with the average correlation again being about .5 (Ones, Viswesveran, & Dilchert, 2005; Sackett et al., 2008). By comparison, the correlation between ratings of how well people do in job interviews and job performance is only about .15, which is ironic given that many employers place heavier weight on interviews than on IQ when selecting job applicants (Hunter & Hunter, 1984). The correlation between IQ and job performance is higher in more mentally demanding occupations, such as physician or lawyer, than in less mentally demanding occupations, like clerk or newspaper delivery person (Salgado et al., 2003). Using estimates from biographers and historians (see **TABLE 9.2**), one researcher even found that presidents' estimated IQ predicted the quality of leadership among U.S. presidents, with correlations in the .3 to .4 range (Simonton, 2006).

IQ also predicts a variety of important real-world behaviors outside the classroom and workplace. For example, IQ is associated with health-related outcomes, including sickness and car accidents (Gottfredson, 2004; Lubinski & Humphreys, 1992). At least some of the negative correlation between IQ and illness may be attributable to *health literacy,* the ability to understand health-related information, such as instructions from doctors or on drug labels. People with low health literacy may have difficulty maintaining good health behaviors, such as getting

correlation vs. causation
CAN WE BE SURE THAT A CAUSES B?

◉─⎜Watch Are Intelligence Tests Valid?:
Robert Guthrie on **mypsychlab.com**

TABLE 9.2 Estimated IQ of Selected U.S. Presidents. Based on biographical and historical information, Dean Keith Simonton (2006) derived estimates of the IQs of all U.S. presidents up to and including George W. Bush. This table presents the estimated IQ range for some presidents, meaning their true IQs probably fall somewhere between the two numbers.

PRESIDENT	ESTIMATED IQ
George Washington	125–140
Thomas Jefferson	145–160
John Quincy Adams	165–175
Millard Fillmore	121–149
Abraham Lincoln	125–150
Ulysses S. Grant	110–130
Warren Harding	108–140
Franklin Delano Roosevelt	127–151
Harry Truman	116–140
John F. Kennedy	139–160
Richard M. Nixon	119–143
Jimmy Carter	130–157
Ronald Reagan	118–142
Bill Clinton	136–159
George W. Bush	111–139

(*Source:* Simonton, 2006)

enough exercise, eating the right foods, or taking the right dosage of their medications. IQ is also associated with criminal tendencies: The IQs of delinquent adolescents are about seven points lower than those of other adolescents (Wilson & Herrnstein, 1985).

But there's a potential confound here (see Chapter 2). IQ is positively associated with social class, as poorer people tend to have lower IQs. So poverty, rather than IQ, may explain at least some of the associations we've discussed. Researchers have tried to address this rival hypothesis by determining whether the correlations hold up even when accounting for social class. In most cases, including health outcomes and crime, they do (Herrnstein & Murray, 1994; Neisser et al., 1997). Still, to some extent, the causal arrow probably runs in both directions. Poverty may contribute to low IQs, but low IQs may also contribute to poverty, because people with low IQs may lack some of the cognitive abilities that allow them to obtain and keep well-paying jobs.

Some people, like journalist Malcolm Gladwell, author of the best-selling book *Outliers* (2009), claim that the correlation between high IQ and life achievement holds only to up to moderate IQ level, after which the correlation becomes essentially nonexistent. This phenomenon, which psychologists call a *threshold effect*, implies that above a certain level of IQ, intelligence is no longer predictive of important real-world accomplishments. Yet the evidence doesn't support Gladwell's claim: The correlation between IQ and life achievements remains essentially identical even at extremely high levels of IQ (Lubinksi, 2009; Sackett et al., 2008).

ruling out rival hypotheses

HAVE IMPORTANT ALTERNATIVE EXPLANATIONS FOR THE FINDINGS BEEN EXCLUDED?

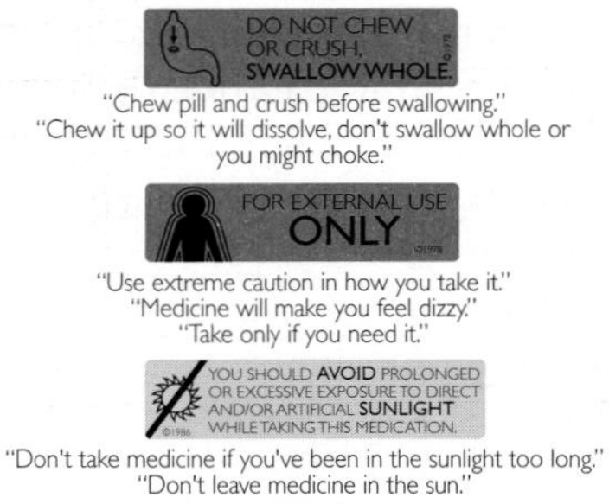

Low levels of health literacy, which are associated with IQ, can lead to dangerous misunderstandings of medication instructions. On the top are actual warning labels attached to certain medications; underneath each warning label are actual interpretations of these warnings by some subjects in a published study (Davis et al., 2006). (*Source:* Franklin, 2005)

Reading Confusion Into Drug Warnings
When researchers asked consumers to interpret prescription warning stickers, these are among the responses they gave:

DO NOT CHEW OR CRUSH, SWALLOW WHOLE
"Chew pill and crush before swallowing."
"Chew it up so it will dissolve, don't swallow whole or you might choke."

FOR EXTERNAL USE ONLY
"Use extreme caution in how you take it."
"Medicine will make you feel dizzy."
"Take only if you need it."

YOU SHOULD **AVOID** PROLONGED OR EXCESSIVE EXPOSURE TO DIRECT AND/OR ARTIFICIAL SUNLIGHT WHILE TAKING THIS MEDICATION.
"Don't take medicine if you've been in the sunlight too long."
"Don't leave medicine in the sun."

■ A Tale of Two Tails: From Mental Retardation to Genius

Within a population, IQ scores are distributed in a **bell curve**, across the range of possible IQ scores. In this distribution, discovered by the German mathematician Karl Friedrich Gauss (1777-1855), the bulk of the scores fall toward the middle, with progressively fewer scores toward the "tails" or extremes, forming the shape of a bell.

FIGURE 9.11 shows that the bell curve fits the distribution of IQ scores in the population fairly well, with one minor exception. The bulk of scores fall in the broad middle of the distribution; about 95 percent of people have IQs between 70 and 130. The curve contains a small bump on the left, indicating that there are more very low IQ scores than we'd expect from a perfect bell curve. These extreme scores are probably the result of *assortative mating* (Mackintosh, 1998): the tendency of individuals with similar genes to have children. In this case, individuals with mental retardation are especially likely to parent a child with other individuals with mental retardation, probably because they frequent the same locations (such as special schools), then develop a relationship, and have children.

Let's now look at what we know about the two tails of the IQ score distribution: mental retardation and genius.

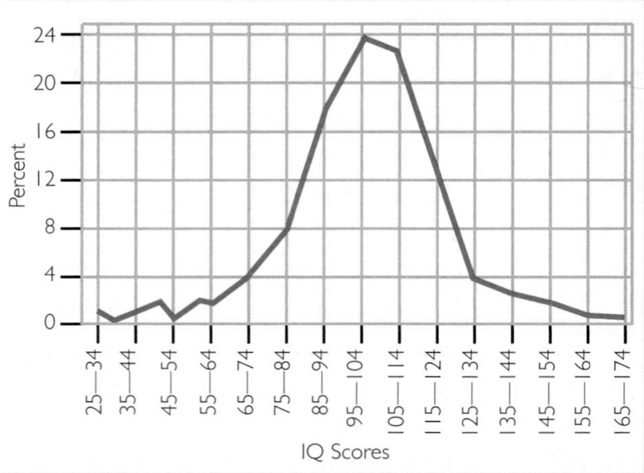

MENTAL RETARDATION. Psychologists define **mental retardation**, sometimes now termed "intellectual disability," by three criteria, all of which must be present: (1) onset prior to adulthood, (2) IQ below approximately 70, and (3) inadequate adaptive functioning, as assessed by difficulties with dressing and feeding oneself, communicating with others, and other basic life skills (Greenspan & Switzky, 2003). The adaptive functioning criterion largely explains why about two-thirds of children with mental retardation lose this diagnosis in adulthood (Grossman, 1983); as individuals acquire life-functioning skills, they no longer qualify for this diagnosis. Some experts have also recently placed heightened emphasis on *gullibility* (the susceptibility to being duped by others) as a criterion for mental retardation,

bell curve
distribution of scores in which the bulk of the scores fall toward the middle, with progressively fewer scores toward the "tails" or extremes

mental retardation
condition characterized by an onset prior to adulthood, an IQ below about 70, and an inability to engage in adequate daily functioning

FIGURE 9.11 Distribution of IQ Scores in the General Population. The bell curve roughly approximates the distribution of IQ scores in the general population.

in part for social policy reasons. A diagnosis of mental retardation qualifies individuals for additional government services. For this reason, the inability to protect oneself from being taken advantage of by others should be weighted heavily in determining whether a person has mental retardation (Greenspan, Loughlin, & Black, 2001).

About one percent of persons in the United States, most of them males, fulfill the criteria for mental retardation (American Psychiatric Association, 2000). The current system of psychiatric diagnosis classifies mental retardation into four categories: mild (once called "educable"), moderate (once called "trainable"), severe, and profound. Contrary to popular conception, most individuals with mental retardation—at least 85 percent—fall into the "mild" category. In most cases, children with mild retardation can be integrated or *mainstreamed* into regular classrooms. Still, the term "mild mental retardation" is misleading, because individuals in this category still have significant deficits in adaptive functioning.

Contrary to what we might expect, the more severe the mental retardation, the *less* likely it is to run in families (Reed & Reed, 1965). Mild forms of mental retardation are typically due to a mix of genetic and environmental influences that parents pass on to their children. In contrast, severe forms of mental retardation are more often the result of rare genetic mutations or accidents during birth, neither of which tend to be transmitted within families.

There are at least 200 different causes of mental retardation. Two of the most common genetic conditions associated with mental retardation are fragile X syndrome, which is produced by a mutation on the X chromosome (females have two copies of this chromosome, males only one), and Down syndrome, which is the result of an extra copy of chromosome 21. Most children with Down syndrome have either mild or moderate retardation. Nevertheless, a subset of individuals with Down syndrome known as *mosaics* (so called because only some of their cells contain an extra chromosome 21) have relatively normal IQs. People with Down syndrome typically exhibit a distinctive pattern of physical features, including a flat nose, upwardly slanted eyes, a protruding tongue, and a short neck. The prevalence of Down syndrome rises sharply with the birth mother's age; at age 30, it's less than one in 1,000, but by age 49, it's about one in 12 (Hook & Lindjso, 1978).

Societal attitudes toward individuals with mental retardation have improved dramatically over the past century. The Americans with Disabilities Act (ADA), passed in 1990, outlawed job and educational discrimination on the basis of mental and physical disabilities, and the Individuals with Disabilities Education Act (IDEA), passed in 1996, provided federal aid to states and local educational districts for accommodations to youth with mental and physical disabilities. Both ADA and IDEA have helped bring those with mental retardation out of institutions and into our workplaces and schools. As we increase our regular contact with these individuals, such laws may further erode the lingering stigma that some Americans feel toward these members of society.

GENIUS AND EXCEPTIONAL INTELLIGENCE. Let's now turn to the opposite tail of the bell curve. If you're fortunate enough to score in the top two percent of the IQ range, you'll qualify for membership in an organization called Mensa. A large proportion of individuals with IQs at or near this range populate certain occupations, such as doctors, lawyers, engineers, and college professors (Herrnstein & Murray, 1994) (see **FIGURE 9.12**). Yet we know relatively little about the psychological characteristics of individuals with high IQs or their academic, occupational, and social performance over time. Several research studies offer tantalizing clues.

Most individuals with Down syndrome have mild or moderate mental retardation. Nevertheless, many have been successfully mainstreamed into traditional classrooms.

FACTOID

The terms "moron," "imbecile," and "idiot," today used in everyday language as insults, once referred to differing levels of mental retardation: moron (mild), moderate to severe (imbecile), and profound (idiot) (Scheerenberger, 1983).

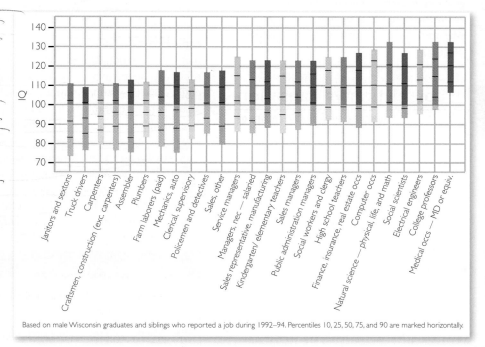

Based on male Wisconsin graduates and siblings who reported a job during 1992–94. Percentiles 10, 25, 50, 75, and 90 are marked horizontally.

FIGURE 9.12 IQ Scores among Select Professions. A study of IQ scores reveals that among a range of professions, college-level teaching, law, engineering, and medicine attract those with the highest average IQs. However, at least 25 percent of those in every profession score above 90 on IQ tests. There are intelligent people in every profession. (*Source:* Adapted from Hauser, 2002)

In the 1920s, Lewis Terman and his colleagues (Terman & Oden, 1959) initiated one of the classic studies of intellectually gifted individuals. From some 250,000 junior high school students in California, Terman selected about 1,500 who had IQs of about 135 or higher. He tracked these individuals, known affectionately as Terman's "Termites," for several decades (some are still alive today). Although Terman's study was flawed, in part because he didn't recruit a control group of individuals with average or low IQs, it refuted two common misconceptions regarding people with high IQs.

First, contradicting the common claim that almost all child prodigies "burn out" in adulthood, Terman's subjects became a highly distinguished group: 97 earned doctoral degrees, 57 earned medical degrees, and 92 earned law degrees. These numbers are all much higher than what we'd expect from the general population (Leslie, 2000). A later study of an even more select group—young adolescents who scored in the top .001 percent (that's one in 10,000) on tests of verbal or mathematical ability—generated similar results. By their early twenties, these individuals were attending graduate school at a rate more than 50 times higher than that in the general population and many had already published scientific or literary articles (Lubinski, 2009; Lubinski et al., 2006). Second, Terman's results disputed the popular notion that there's an intimate link between genius and madness. Although the absence of a control group makes it difficult to know for certain, his findings pointed to slightly lower rates of mental illness and suicide among his adult Termites compared with the general population. Later researchers have found broadly similar results (Simonton & Song, 2009), although a few have reported that exceedingly intelligent children, such as those with IQs over 180, may be at heightened risk for selected mental health problems, especially loneliness and depression (Janos & Robinson, 1985; Winner, 1999). These negative outcomes may be a consequence of the greater ridicule and isolation that these children experience. Still, there's scant evidence that high intelligence is associated with high levels of severe mental illness.

What's the recipe for creating a genius, like Chris Langan? We don't know, although as we'll soon discover, genetic factors probably play a significant role. Still, as the brilliant inventor Thomas Edison said famously, "genius is one percent inspiration, 99 percent perspiration." Here common wisdom is correct: Practice makes perfect, or at least pretty darned good. The best predictor of exceptional career success in violin, piano, ballet, chess, and sports is the sheer amount of time we spend in practice. The most talented musicians practice twice as much as the less talented ones (Ericsson, Krampe, & Tesch-Romer, 1993; Gladwell, 2009). Of course, the causal arrow here isn't clear. Greater amounts of practice could be causing greater success, or greater levels of initial talent could be causing greater amounts of practice. We won't spend 10 hours a day perfecting our guitar playing unless we're decent at it to begin with. In addition, research shows that across many domains, such as science, art, and music, individuals almost never attain remarkable intellectual accomplishments until they've dedicated themselves intensely for at least 10 years—or, to be a bit more precise, 10,000 hours—in that domain (Gladwell, 2009; Simonton, 1997). So the familiar Hollywood stereotype of the teenager or young adult who achieves astonishing intellectual brilliance with virtually no effort is exceedingly unrealistic.

? Are Hollywood movies like the 1997 movie *Good Will Hunting* accurate in their portrayal of childhood or adolescent geniuses as exerting minimal effort to make astonishing intellectual discoveries? Why or why not? (See answer upside down on bottom of page.)

correlation vs. causation

CAN WE BE SURE THAT A CAUSES B?

✓ **Study** and **Review** on **mypsychlab.com**

assess your knowledge — FACT OR FICTION?

1. Today, IQ is measured as mental age divided by chronological age, multiplied by 100. **True / False**

2. Standard IQ tests administered in infancy tend not to be highly predictive of later IQ scores. **True / False**

3. Although IQ scores predict school achievement, they're almost useless for predicting occupational success. **True / False**

4. The most prevalent form of mental retardation is mild retardation. **True / False**

5. Research suggests a close link between extremely high intelligence and many forms of severe mental illness. **True / False**

Answers: 1. F (p. 327); 2. T (p. 332); 3. F (p. 333); 4. T (p. 335); 5. F (p. 336)

GENETIC AND ENVIRONMENTAL INFLUENCES ON IQ

9.7   Explain how genetic influences can be determined from family, twin, and adoption studies.

9.8   Identify potential environmental influences on IQ.

Up to this point, we've talked at length about what intelligence is and how we measure it. But we've said little about its causes, or about the relative roles of nature and nurture in its development. Over the past few decades, psychologists have obtained a much better handle on the genetic and environmental contributors to IQ. As we'll discover, however, significant flash points of controversy remain. ⊕ Explore

Explore Factors Affecting Intelligence on **mypsychlab.com**

■ Exploring Genetic Influences on IQ

As we learned in Chapter 3, scientists can study genetic influences on psychological characteristics in three major ways: family studies, twin studies, and adoption studies. They've done so for intelligence, with surprisingly consistent results.

FAMILY STUDIES.   As we saw in Chapter 3, *family studies* allow us to examine the extent to which a trait "runs" or goes together in intact families, those in which all family members live together in the same home. Sir Francis Galton, who coined the phrase "nature and nurture" (Galton, 1876), conducted one of the first family studies of intelligence in his book *Hereditary Genius.* Galton (1869) gathered data on the extent to which persons renowned for their intellectual accomplishments had biological relatives who were also renowned for their intellectual accomplishments. He found that the proportion of relatives who'd achieved intellectual greatness declined steadily with increasing biological distance. Intellectually brilliant individuals had many first-degree relatives (parents, siblings, and children) who were also brilliant, but fewer second-degree relatives (such as cousins), and still fewer third-degree relatives (such as second cousins) who were brilliant. Later studies have confirmed that IQ runs in families: The correlation of IQ for brothers and sisters raised in the same family is about .5, whereas for cousins it's about .15 (Bouchard & McGue, 1981). Galton concluded that these findings demonstrated a genetic basis to intellectual greatness, but he overlooked a crucial limitation that applies to all family studies: *Studies of intact families don't allow us to distinguish the effects of genes from those of the environment.* As a consequence, when a trait runs in families, we don't know whether it's for genetic reasons, environmental reasons, or both (see Chapter 3).

TWIN STUDIES.   Because family studies don't permit investigators to disentangle the effects of nature from those of nurture, they've turned to more informative research designs. These include *twin studies,* which as we've seen (Chapter 3) compare correlations in a trait in two types of twins: identical (monozygotic) and fraternal (dizygotic).

The logic of the twin design is straightforward. Because identical twins share twice as many of their genes on average as fraternal twins, we can compare the correlations in IQ in these two different twin types. Given a handful of assumptions, higher identical than fraternal twin correlations strongly suggest genetic influence. In almost all cases, studies of twins reared together have offered evidence of considerably higher identical than fraternal twin correlations for IQ (Bouchard & McGue, 1981; Loehlin, Willerman, & Horn, 1988; Toga & Thompson, 2005). In typical studies of IQ, identical twin correlations have been in the .7 to .8 range, whereas fraternal twin correlations have been in the .3 to .4 range. Nevertheless, in all studies of twins raised together, identical twin correlations have been lower than 1.0.

These findings tell us two things. First, the higher identical than fraternal twin correlations tell us that IQ is influenced by genetic factors. The best estimate for the heritability of IQ lies somewhere between 40 and 70 percent (Brody, 1992; Devlin, Daniels, & Roeder, 1997). Interestingly, the heritability of IQ seems to increase from childhood to adulthood (McClearn et al., 1997), perhaps because people become less influenced by their environments, especially their parents, as they move away from home. Although the twin findings don't tell us which genes are relevant to intelligence, the past decade has witnessed progress in identifying specific genes for intelligence. These genes appear to cut across multiple domains of mental ability,

Twin studies of intelligence compare the mental performance of identical (*top*) versus fraternal (*bottom*) twins.

including attention, working memory, and perhaps even risk for Alzheimer's disease (Plomin & Kovas, 2005; Posthuma & de Gues, 2006). There is, however, one notable exception to the moderate to high heritability of IQ. Relatively recent evidence suggests that the heritability of IQ may be very low in people at or below the poverty line (Turkheimer et al., 2003). These findings raise the possibility that at high levels of environmental deprivation, the effects of environment on intelligence may largely swamp out the effects of genes.

Explore Correlations of IQ Scores of Persons of Varying Relationships on mypsychlab.com

Second, twin findings provide even more convincing evidence for environmental influences on IQ, because the identical twin correlations for IQ are less than perfect. Given that identical twins share 100 percent of their genes, they would correlate 1.0 if genetic influences alone were operative (assuming the IQ tests are reliable). The fact that they correlate less than 1.0 tells us that environmental influences also play a role, although the studies don't tell us what these influences are. Explore

ruling out rival hypotheses
HAVE IMPORTANT ALTERNATIVE EXPLANATIONS FOR THE FINDINGS BEEN EXCLUDED?

Up to this point, we've discussed only studies of twins raised together. These studies are vulnerable to a rival hypothesis: Perhaps identical twins are more similar than fraternal twins because they spend more time together. To exclude this possibility, investigators have conducted studies of identical and fraternal twins reared apart since birth or shortly after birth. Thomas Bouchard and his colleagues at the University of Minnesota conducted the landmark study of twins reared apart in the 1980s and 1990s. Remarkably, the results of this study revealed that a sample of over 40 identical twin pairs reared apart were just as similar on three measures of IQ (including the WAIS and Raven's Progressive Matrices) as identical twins reared together (Bouchard et al., 1990). Other investigators have replicated these findings (Pederson et al., 1992), although because twins reared apart are extremely rare, the sample sizes of these studies are relatively low.

replicability
CAN THE RESULTS BE DUPLICATED IN OTHER STUDIES?

ADOPTION STUDIES. Studies of intact family members are limited because they can't disentangle genetic from environmental influences. To address this shortcoming, psychologists have turned to *adoption studies* (Chapter 3), which examine the extent to which children adopted into new homes resemble their adoptive versus biological parents. Adoption studies allow us to separate environmental from genetic effects on IQ, because adoptees are raised by parents with whom they share an environment, but not genes. One potential confound in adoption studies is *selective placement:* Adoption agencies frequently place children in homes similar to those of the biological parents (DeFries & Plomin, 1978; Tully, Iacono, & McGue, 2008). This confound can lead investigators to mistakenly interpret the similarity between adoptive children and adoptive parents as an environmental effect. In adoption studies of IQ, researchers often try to control for selective placement by correcting statistically for the correlation in IQ between biological and adoptive parents.

Adoption studies have established a clear contribution of the environment in IQ. For example, adopted children who come from extremely deprived environments show an increase in IQ when adopted into homes that provide more enriched environments (Capron & Duyme, 1989). In one study of French children raised in an extremely deprived environment, children who were adopted showed an average 16-point IQ edge over children who weren't (Schiff et al., 1982).

But do adopted children's IQs resemble their biological parents' IQs? The results of adoption studies indicate that the IQs of adopted children tend to be similar to the IQs of their biological parents, offering evidence of genetic influence. As young children, adoptees tend to resemble the adoptive parents in IQ, but this resemblance dissipates once these children become older and approach adolescence (Loehlin, Horn, & Willerman, 1989; Phillips & Fulker, 1989; Plomin et al., 1997).

Many children adopted from environments of severe deprivation, such as this orphanage in Romania, show increases in IQ after immersion in a healthier and more attentive adoptive environment (see Chapter 10).

■ Exploring Environmental Influences on IQ

As we've learned, twin and adoption studies paint a consistent picture: Both genes and environment affect IQ scores. But these studies leave a mysterious question unanswered: What environmental factors influence IQ? Psychologists don't know for sure, although they've made significant inroads toward identifying promising candidates. As we'll see, environmental influences can include not only the *social* environment, such as school and parents, but also the *biological* environment, such as the availability of nutrients and exposure to toxic substances, such as lead. We'll also see that the evidence for some of these environmental influences is more convincing than for others.

DOES HOW WE THINK ABOUT INTELLIGENCE AFFECT IQ? Some recent research suggests that how we conceptualize intelligence may actually influence our intelligence. Carol Dweck (2002, 2006) showed that people who believe that intelligence is a fixed entity that doesn't change tend to take fewer academic risks, such as enrolling in challenging classes. According to Dweck, they think, "If I do really poorly in a class, it probably means I'm stupid, and I can't do anything about that." After failing on a problem, they tend to become discouraged and give up, probably because they assume they can't boost their intelligence. In contrast, people who believe that intelligence is a flexible process that can increase over time tend to take more academic risks; they think, "If I do really poorly in a class, I can still do better next time." They tend to persist after failing on a problem, probably because they believe that effort can pay off. As a consequence, they may perform better in the long run on challenging intellectual tasks. Nevertheless, because not all researchers have found that beliefs about intelligence are associated with performance on mental tests, these claims require further investigation (Glenn, 2010).

BIRTH ORDER: ARE OLDER SIBLINGS WISER? In the 1970s, Robert Zajonc (whose name, oddly enough, rhymes with "science"), created a stir by arguing that later-born children tend to be less intelligent than earlier-born children (Zajonc, 1976). According to Zajonc, IQ declines steadily with increasing numbers of children in a family. He even authored an article in the popular magazine *Psychology Today* entitled "Dumber by the Dozen" (Zajonc, 1975).

In one respect, Zajonc was right: Later-born children tend to have slightly lower IQs (on the order of a few points) than earlier-born children (Kristensen & Bjerkedal, 2007). But it's not clear that he interpreted this correlation correctly. Here's the problem. Parents with lower IQs are slightly more likely to have many children than are parents with higher IQs. As a consequence, when we look across families, birth order is associated with IQ, but only because low-IQ families have a larger number of later-born children than do high-IQ families. In contrast, when we look *within* families, the relationship between birth order and IQ becomes smaller and may even vanish (Michalski & Shackelford, 2001; Rodgers et al., 2000). So a more accurate way to state the correlation is that children who come from larger families have slightly lower IQs than do children who come from smaller families.

DOES SCHOOLING MAKE US SMARTER? Autopsy studies show that educated people have more synapses, that is, neural connections (see Chapter 3), than less-educated people (Orlovskaya et al., 1999). In addition, the number of years of schooling correlates between .5 and .6 with IQ scores (Neisser et al., 1996). Although some authors have interpreted this correlation as meaning that schooling leads to higher IQ and perhaps even more synapses—it's equally possible that the causal arrow is reversed. Indeed, there's evidence that individuals with high IQ scores enjoy taking classes more than individuals with low IQ scores (Rehberg & Rosenthal, 1978). As a consequence, they may be more likely to stay in school and go on to college and beyond. This wouldn't be terribly surprising given that individuals with high IQ scores tend to do better in their classes.

Still, several lines of evidence suggest that schooling exerts a causal influence on IQ (Ceci, 1991; Ceci & Williams, 1997; Nisbett, 2009):

1. Researchers have examined pairs of children who are almost exactly the same age, but in which one child attended an extra year of school because he was born just a few days earlier (say, August 31 as opposed to September 2). This can occur because public schools often have hard-and-fast cutoff dates for how old children must be to begin school. In such cases, children who've attended an extra year of school tend to have higher IQs, despite being nearly identical in chronological age.

2. Children's IQs tend to drop significantly during summer vacations.

3. Students who drop out of school end up with lower IQs than students who stay in school, even when they start out with the same IQ.

replicability
CAN THE RESULTS BE DUPLICATED IN OTHER STUDIES?

correlation vs. causation
CAN WE BE SURE THAT A CAUSES B?

Children's IQs tend to drop significantly during summer vacations, suggesting an environmental influence on IQ.

The federal Head Start program was launched in the 1960s to give disadvantaged preschoolers a jump-start on their education. Studies show that Head Start programs typically produce short-term increases in IQ, but that these increases fade with time.

BOOSTING IQ BY EARLY INTERVENTION. In a controversial article in the late 1960s, Arthur Jensen contended that IQ is highly heritable and therefore difficult to modify by means of environmental intervention (Jensen, 1969). In making this argument, Jensen fell prey to a logical error we debunked earlier in this book (see Chapter 3): namely, that heritability implies that a trait can't be changed. Yet he raised an important question: Can we boost IQ with early educational interventions?

Some of the best evidence comes from studies of *Head Start,* a preschool program launched in the 1960s to give disadvantaged children a "jump start" by offering them an enriched educational experience. The hope was that this program would allow them to catch up intellectually to other children. Dozens of studies of Head Start programs have yielded consistent results, and they've been largely disappointing. Although these programs produce short-term increases in IQ (Ludwig & Phillips, 2008), these increases don't typically persist after the programs end (Caruso, Taylor, & Detterman, 1982; Royce, Darlington, & Murray, 1983). Similar results emerge from studies of other early-intervention programs (Brody, 1992; Herrnstein & Murray, 1994). At the same time, these programs may not be entirely worthless. Several studies indicate that Head Start and similar early-intervention programs result in lower rates of high school dropout and of being held back a grade compared with control conditions (Campbell & Raney, 1995; Darlington, 1986; Neisser et al., 1996). They may also yield higher levels of early literacy and understanding of others' emotions (Bierman et al., 2008).

A SELF-FULFILLING PROPHECY: EXPECTANCY EFFECTS ON IQ. In the 1960s, Robert Rosenthal and Lenore Jacobson wanted to examine the effects of teacher expectancies on IQ. As we saw in Chapter 2, the *experimenter expectancy effect* refers to the tendency of researchers to unintentionally influence the outcome of studies. In this case, Rosenthal and Jacobson (1966) looked at the expectancies of teachers rather than researchers. They administered an IQ test to students in the first through sixth grades, disguising it with a fake name ("The Harvard Test of Inflected Acquisition"). Then they gave teachers the results, which indicated that 20 percent of their students would show remarkable gains in intelligence during the subsequent eight months: These students were "bloomers" who'd soon reach their full intellectual potential. But Rosenthal and Jacobson misled the teachers. They had *randomly* selected these 20 percent of students to be classified as bloomers, and these students' initial scores didn't differ from those of other students. Yet when Rosenthal and Jacobson retested all students a year later with the same IQ test, the 20 percent labeled as bloomers scored about four IQ points higher than the other students. Expectations had become reality.

replicability >

CAN THE RESULTS BE DUPLICATED IN OTHER STUDIES?

This effect has now been replicated in a number of studies, although the size of the effect isn't large (Rosenthal, 1994; Smith, 1980). We don't know how this effect occurs, although there's evidence that teachers more often smile at, make eye contact with, and nod their heads toward students they incorrectly believe are smart compared with other students (Chaiken, Sigler, & Derlega, 1974). As a consequence, they may positively reinforce (see Chapter 6) these students' learning. Nevertheless, the effects of expectancy on IQ have their limits. These effects are substantial only when teachers don't know their students well; when teachers have worked with students for at least a few weeks, the effects often disappear (Raudenbush, 1984). Once teachers form definite impressions of how smart their students are, it's hard to persuade them their impressions are off base.

POVERTY AND IQ: SOCIOECONOMIC AND NUTRITIONAL DEPRIVATION. It's difficult to put a firm number on the effects of poverty, but there's reason to believe that social and economic deprivation can adversely affect IQ. Arthur Jensen (1977) studied a group of families in an extremely poor area of rural Georgia. For African American (but not Caucasian) children, he found evidence for a *cumulative deficit,* a difference that grows over time. Older siblings consistently had lower IQs than younger siblings, with a steady decrease of about 1.5 IQ points per year. Jensen's explanation was that siblings in this impoverished region experienced progressively more intellectual deprivation as they aged, leading them to fall further behind other children (Willerman, 1979).

Along with poverty often comes inadequate diet. Studies from poor areas in Central America suggest that malnutrition in childhood, especially if prolonged, can lower IQ (Eysenck & Schoenthaler, 1997). In one investigation, researchers gave nutritional (protein) supplements to preschool children from an impoverished region of Guatemala. These children's school-related test scores were significantly higher than those of similar children who didn't receive supplements (Pollitt et al., 1993).

Poor children are also especially likely to be exposed to lead as a result of drinking lead-contaminated water, breathing lead-contaminated dust, or eating lead paint chips. Such exposure is also associated with intellectual deficits (Bellinger & Needleman, 2003; Canfield et al., 2003; Ris et al., 2004). Nevertheless, it's unclear how much of this correlation is due to the direct effects of lead itself as opposed to poverty or other factors, like malnutrition.

Scientific controversy has swirled around another potential nutritional influence: breast-feeding. On the one side are researchers who claim that infants who are breast-fed end up with higher IQs—perhaps on the order of a few points—than children who are bottle-fed (Mortensen et al., 2002; Quinn et al., 2001). Indeed, mothers' milk contains about 100 ingredients absent from milk formula, including several that speed up the myelinization of neurons (see Chapter 3). On the other side are researchers who contend that this IQ difference is due to one or more confounds: For example, mothers who breast-feed their babies tend to be somewhat higher in social class and IQ than mothers who bottle-feed their babies (Der, Batty, & Deary, 2006; Jacobson, Chiodo, & Jacobson, 1999). These confounds could account for the seeming effect of breast-feeding on IQ. The debate rages on (Caspi et al., 2007).

GETTING SMARTER ALL THE TIME: THE MYSTERIOUS FLYNN EFFECT. In the 1980s, political scientist James Flynn noticed something decidedly odd (Dickens & Flynn, 2001; Flynn, 1981, 1987). Over time, the average IQ of the population was rising at a rate of about three points per decade, a phenomenon now known as the **Flynn effect** (Herrnstein & Murray, 1994). The magnitude of the Flynn effect is mind-boggling. It

> **Flynn effect**
> finding that average IQ scores have been rising at a rate of approximately three points per decade

ruling out rival hypotheses

HAVE IMPORTANT ALTERNATIVE EXPLANATIONS FOR THE FINDINGS BEEN EXCLUDED?

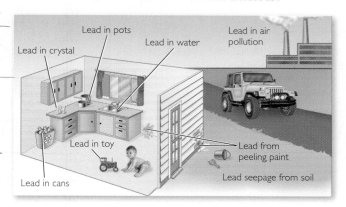

Lead exposure can arise from many sources in everyday life and may contribute to decreased IQ. Nevertheless, the causal association between lead intake and IQ remains controversial.

Answers are located at the end of the text.

IQ BOOSTERS

A wide variety of books and websites claim to increase your IQ in a matter of days—some by as much as 200 points! Let's evaluate some of these claims, which are modeled after actual ads for products designed to increase your IQ.

evaluating CLAIMS

"While the 'experts' argue about whether you can increase IQ or not, we promise real results!"
A warning sign of pseudoscience is the absence of connectivity to other research. This claim implies that the test developers can simply ignore what others have tried before—possible, but unlikely.

"Become a genius in 5 simple steps."
Does this claim seem plausible given what you know about the probable reaction range (see Chapter 3) of intelligence? What kind of evidence would you need to support it?

"Credibly synthesize process-centric quantum wave outsourcing."
Beware of psychobabble; this claim sounds sophisticated, but has little or no scientific meaning.

"Take our IQ test and expose your true creativity."
This claim implies that intelligence and creativity are similar, if not identical. What does the scientific research say (see p. 350)?

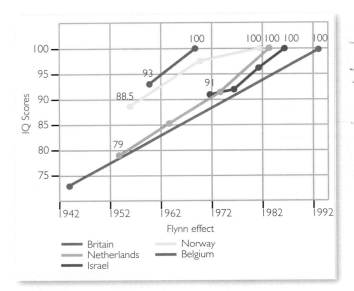

FIGURE 9.13   Flynn Effect. Research on the Flynn effect demonstrates that IQ scores have been increasing in many countries across several decades. The causes of this effect remain unclear. (*Source:* Flynn, 1999)

One American differs from his Civil War ancestor.

Typical Civil War soldier	Typical modern American
(5 feet, 6 inches, 145 pounds)	(5 feet, 11 inches, 235 pounds)

As can be seen in the sizes of these men and their uniforms, most people are considerably larger today than they were in the era of the U.S. Civil War (1861–1865). That difference reflects dramatic differences in nutrition over the past 150 years. Some psychologists propose that enhanced nutrition may account for the Flynn effect.

suggests that, on average, our IQs are a full 10 to 15 points higher than those of our grandparents (see **FIGURE 9.13**). With a few exceptions (Mingroni, 2007; Rushton, 1999), most researchers agree that this effect is a result of unidentified environmental influences on IQ, because it's unlikely that genetic changes could account for such rapid rises in IQ over brief time periods.

What could these environmental influences be? Psychologists have proposed at least four explanations:

1. **Increased test sophistication.** According to this explanation, the rise in IQ scores results not from people becoming smarter, but becoming more experienced at taking tests (Flynn, 1998). There may be some truth to the test sophistication hypothesis, but there's a fly in the ointment. The Flynn effect is most pronounced on "culture-fair" tests, such as Raven's Progressive Matrices, to which people have had the least exposure (Brouwers, de Vijver, & Van Hemert, 2009; Neisser, 1998).

2. **Increased complexity of the modern world.** With television, e-mail, the Internet, fax machines, cellphones, and the like, we're forced to process far more information far more quickly than our parents and grandparents ever did. So the modern information explosion may be putting pressure on us to become more intelligent (Greenfield, 1998; Schooler, 1998).

3. **Better nutrition.** Most evidence suggests that the Flynn effect is affecting primarily the lower, but not the upper, tail of the bell curve. One potential explanation for this finding is diet. People are better fed than ever before, and the rates of severe malnutrition in many (although not all) parts of the world are declining (Lynn, 1998; Sigman & Whaley, 1998). As we've already learned, there's good evidence that nutrition can affect IQ.

4. **Changes at home and school.** Over the past several decades in the United States, families have become smaller, allowing parents to devote more time to their children. Parents also have more access to intellectual resources than ever. In addition, children and adolescents spend more years in school than in previous generations (Bronfenbrenner et al., 1996).

We don't fully understand the causes of the Flynn effect, and there may be some truth to several of these explanations. But the mystery doesn't end here. Recent data suggest that the Flynn effect may be subsiding or even reversing, at least in Europe (Sundet, Barlaug, & Torjussen, 2004). Some investigators have suggested that children's decreasing amounts of play with other children, perhaps resulting from greater computer and video game use, may be the culprit (Schneider, 2006), but no one knows for sure. The causes of the apparent end to the Flynn effect are as puzzling as the causes of its beginning.

✓ **Study** and **Review** on **mypsychlab.com**

assess your knowledge   FACT OR FICTION?

1. Identical twins reared apart appear to be about as similar on IQ tests as identical twins reared together. True / False

2. Children adopted at birth bear almost no resemblance in IQ to their biological parents. True / False

3. There's good evidence that being removed from school can lower IQ scores. True / False

4. Head Start programs produce lasting increases in IQ scores. True / False

5. People's average performance on IQ tests have remained virtually unchanged over the past several decades. True / False

Answers: 1. T (p. 338); 2. F (p. 338); 3. T (p. 339); 4. F (p. 340); 5. F (p. 341)

GROUP DIFFERENCES IN IQ: THE SCIENCE AND THE POLITICS

9.9 Identify similarities and differences in mental ability between men and women.

9.10 Evaluate the evidence concerning racial differences in IQ.

Thus far, we've focused almost entirely on the thorny question of *individual differences* (see Chapter 1) in IQ: Why does measured intelligence differ among people within a population? If you think that what we've discussed so far is controversial, fasten your seat belts. The topic of *group differences* in IQ is perhaps the most bitterly disputed in all of psychology. Here we'll look at what the research says about two group differences in IQ: (1) differences between men and women and (2) differences among races.

As we'll discover, the issues are as emotionally charged as they are scientifically complex. They've also become deeply entangled with politics (Hunt, 1999), with people on differing sides of these debates accusing each other of biases and bad intentions. Some have even gone so far to argue that scientists should keep away altogether from studying group differences in IQ (Rose, 2009). When evaluating these issues, it's crucial that we try to be as objective as possible. That is, we must try to avoid *emotional reasoning*, or the affect heuristic (see Chapter 1), the tendency to judge the validity of an idea by our emotional reactions to it. Just because some of the ideas we'll encounter regarding intelligence may make us feel uneasy or even angry doesn't mean we should dismiss them out of hand. Difficult as it may be, we must try to evaluate these issues objectively and with an open mind to scientific evidence.

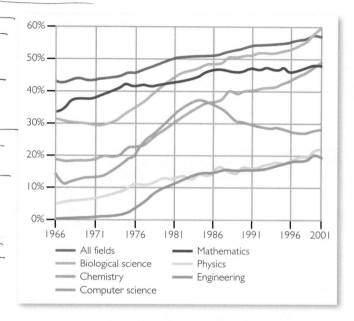

FIGURE 9.14 Bachelor's Degrees Earned by Women in Selected Fields, 1966–2001. Across a 35-year period, women have been underrepresented in most of the "hard" sciences, comprising only a minority of those graduating with a degree in these areas of study. (*Source:* Ivie & Ray, 2005)

■ Sex Differences in IQ and Mental Abilities

In January 2005, then Harvard University President Lawrence Summers created a furor. Speaking at an informal meeting of university faculty from around the country, Summers wondered aloud why there were so few women in the "hard" sciences, like physics, chemistry, and biology (see **FIGURE 9.14**). He tentatively proposed a few reasons, one involving discrimination against women and a second involving women's preference for raising families rather than for competing in grueling, cutthroat occupations. But it was Summers' third reason that really got people going. Summers conjectured that perhaps women enter the world with a genetic disadvantage in science and mathematics. Many people were appalled. One prominent woman biologist from the Massachusetts Institute of Technology stormed out of Summers' talk in protest. Within days, hundreds of Harvard faculty members were calling for his head (he resigned shortly thereafter). A firestorm of controversy regarding sex differences in mental abilities followed on the heels of Summers' provocative statements. In this section, we'll take a scientifically balanced look at the evidence.

SEX DIFFERENCES IN IQ. Do men and women differ in overall IQ? A handful of researchers have recently reported that men have slightly higher IQs than women—perhaps between three and five points (Jackson & Rushton, 2005; Lynn & Irwing, 2004)—but these claims are controversial, to put it mildly. Indeed, most researchers have found few or no average sex differences in IQ (Jensen, 1998).

Yet average differences don't tell the whole story. Numerous studies indicate that men are more *variable* in their overall IQ scores than women (Hedges & Nowell, 1995; Johnson, Carothers, & Deary, 2009). So although men don't appear to have higher average IQs than women, there are more men at both the low and the high ends of IQ bell curve (see **FIGURE 9.15**). We don't know the reason for this difference; researchers have, not surprisingly, proposed both genetic and environmental explanations.

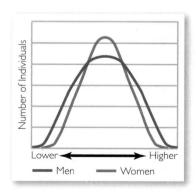

FIGURE 9.15 Distributions of Men and Women in IQ Tests. The IQ distribution of men is wider than the distribution of women. As a consequence, there are more men than women with both low and high IQ scores and more women with scores in the middle.

SEX DIFFERENCES IN SPECIFIC MENTAL ABILITIES. Even though there's little, if any, difference in overall IQ between men and women, the picture becomes more interesting—and more complicated—when we get to specific mental abilities. Men and women are quite similar when it comes to most intellectual abilities (Hyde, 2005; Maccoby & Jacklin, 1974), but a closer look reveals some consistent sex differences (Block, 1976; Halpern, 1992; Halpern et al., 2007; Pinker, 2005). ⊙ Watch

Women tend to do better than men on some verbal tasks, like spelling, writing, and pronouncing words (Feingold, 1988; Halpern et al., 2007; Kimura, 1999). This sex difference may have a hormonal component; even within women, some research suggests that verbal ability ebbs and flows along with the level of estrogen, a sex hormone that's more plentiful in women than men (see Chapter 3). In one study, women were best at quickly repeating tongue twisters (like "A box of mixed biscuits in a biscuit mixer") when their estrogen levels were at their peak (Hampson & Kimura, 1988). Nevertheless, not all investigators have found that current levels of sex hormones are associated with mental abilities within males or females (Halari et al., 2005). On average, females also do better than males in arithmetic calculation, like adding or subtracting numbers, although this difference is present only in childhood (Hyde, Fennema, & Lamon, 1990). Finally, females tend to be better than males in detecting and recognizing feelings in others, especially when they reach adulthood (Hall, 1978; McClure, 2000). For example, they're usually better than men at distinguishing among faces that display different emotions, such as fear and anger. Incidentally, despite popular stereotypes, there's no good evidence that women talk more than men. A recent study that tracked six samples of men and women in the United States and Mexico found that both sexes speak about 16,000 words per day (Mehl et al., 2007).

In contrast, men tend to do better than women on most tasks requiring spatial ability (Halpern et al., 2007). The largest difference emerges on *mental rotation* tasks, like the one shown in **FIGURE 9.16**, which require subjects to determine which of a series of rotated blocks matches a target group of rotated blocks (Voyer, Voyer, & Bryden, 1995). Interestingly, one of the largest reported psychological sex differences is in geography, an area of study that relies heavily on spatial ability. Among the five million children who've participated in the National Geography Bee, 77 percent have been boys (Zernike, 2000). Males also tend to do better than females on mathematics tasks that involve complicated reasoning, like deriving proofs in geometry (Benbow & Stanley, 1980). This difference doesn't emerge until adolescence (Hyde et al., 1990), perhaps reflecting hormonal changes that occur around puberty. At the extreme tails of the bell curve, this difference is magnified. For example, in one study of students who received scores of 700 or above on the SAT math section, males outnumbered females by 13 to 1 (Benbow & Stanley, 1983). But there are more males than females in the low tail of the test, too. ⊙ Simulate

⊙ Watch Gender Differences: Robert Sternberg on **mypsychlab.com**

replicability >

CAN THE RESULTS BE DUPLICATED IN OTHER STUDIES?

FICTOID ✕

MYTH: Women are worse, or at least more dangerous, drivers than men.

REALITY: Men's better average spatial ability may have contributed to the popular belief that men are better—especially safer—drivers than women. In fact, even when controlling for the fact that men drive more miles than women, men get into about 70 percent more car accidents than women (Meyer, 2006), perhaps because they take more risks when driving.

⊙ Simulate Mental Rotation on **mypsychlab.com**

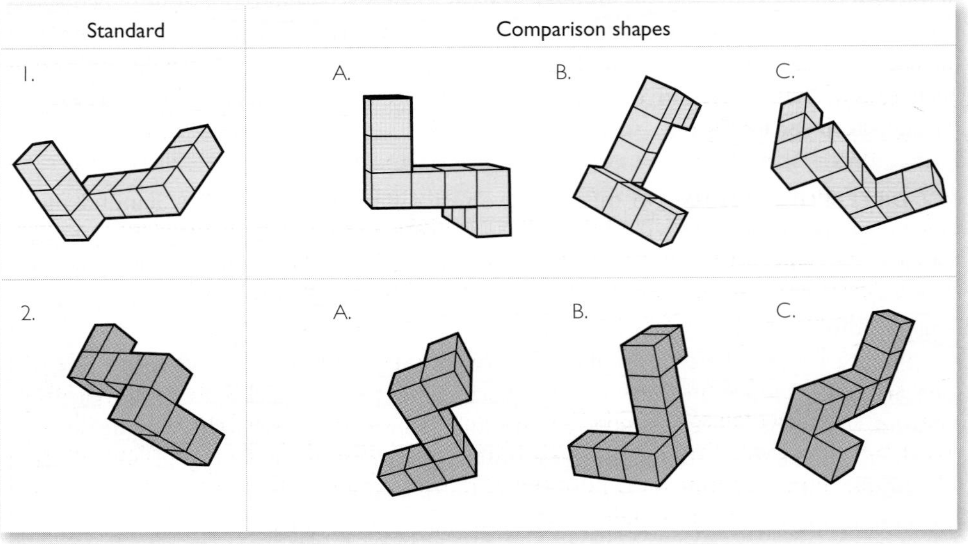

? FIGURE 9.16 Mental Rotation Task. Men tend to do better than women on tests of mental rotation, which require subjects to figure out which "comparison" shape on the right matches the "standard" shape on the left. You may want to try your hand (or your mind, to be more exact) at these two items. Turn the book upside down and see the bottom of this page for the answers. (*Source:* Metzler & Shepard, 1974)

Answers to Figure 9.16: 1. A; 2. B.

Standard	Comparison shapes		
1.	A.	B.	C.
2.	A.	B.	C.

POTENTIAL CAUSES OF SEX DIFFERENCES So what's the bottom line? On the one hand, it's possible that some sex differences in mental abilities, such as women's higher scores on certain verbal tasks and men's higher scores on spatial and complex math-solving tasks, are rooted in genes. Indeed, despite many changes in men's and women's roles over the past several decades, sex differences in spatial ability haven't decreased over time (Voyer et al., 1995). Moreover, some studies indicate that excess levels of prenatal testosterone, a hormone of which males have more than females, is associated with better spatial ability (Hampson, Rovert, & Altman, 1998; Jones, Braithwaite, & Healy, 2003), although not all researchers have replicated this finding.

On the other hand, there's ample reason to suspect that some, perhaps even most, of the sex differences in science and math ability are environmental (Levine et al., 2006). For one thing, male and female infants show few or no differences in spatial or counting ability (Spelke, 2005). Even when sex differences in these abilities emerge later in life, they may be due more to sex differences in problem-solving strategies than in inherent abilities. For example, when researchers have encouraged both men and women to solve math problems using spatial imagery (which men usually prefer) rather than verbal reasoning (which women usually prefer), the sex difference in math performance becomes noticeably smaller (Geary, 1996). Moreover, if we look back at the graph in Figure 9.14, we can see something striking. From 1966 to 2001, the percentage of women entering the "hard" sciences has been increasing steadily. This finding suggests that at least some of the underrepresentation of women in the "hard" sciences is the result of societal factors, such as discrimination and society's expectations, rather than women's weaker science skills. It also makes us wonder what this graph will look like in 10 years. Stay tuned.

■ Racial Differences in IQ

Perhaps one of the most controversial, and at times troubling, findings in the study of intelligence is that average IQ scores differ among races. The differences vary in size but have been replicated multiple times (Loehlin, Lindzey, & Spuhler, 1977; Gottfredson, 2009; Wickerts, Dolan, & van der Maas, 2010). On average, African Americans and Hispanic Americans score lower than Caucasians on standard IQ tests (Hunt & Carlson, 2007; Lynn, 2006; Neisser et al., 1996), and Asian Americans score higher than Caucasians (Lynn, 1996; Sue, 1993). Among Caucasians in the United States, the IQs of Jews are slightly higher than those of non-Jews (Lynn, 2003). The average IQ difference between Caucasians and African Americans, which some researchers have estimated to be as high as 15 points, has received the most attention. What do these differences tell us about the abilities and potential of individuals from different races, and why these differences exist?

FOR WHOM THE BELL CURVE TOLLS. Over the years, some sectors of society have attempted to use these findings in a misguided attempt to argue that some races are innately superior to others. There are several problems with this claim. First, claims of inherent racial "superiority" lie outside the boundaries of science and can't be answered by data. Scientists can determine only the origins of racial differences, namely, whether they're genetic, environmental, or both. Second, the IQ differences among races may be narrowing over recent decades (Dickens & Flynn, 2006; Hauser, 1998). Third, the variability *within* any given race tends to be considerably larger than the variability *between* races (Nisbett, 1995, 2009). This finding means that the distributions of IQ scores for different races overlap substantially (see **FIGURE 9.17**). As a result, many African Americans and Hispanic Americans have higher IQs than many Caucasians and Asian Americans. The bottom line is clear: We can't use race as a basis for inferring any given person's IQ.

In 1994, Richard Herrnstein and Charles Murray touched off a bitter dispute among scientists and politicians alike. In their explosive book, *The Bell Curve*, they argued that IQ plays a much more important role in society than most people are willing to admit. People at the upper tail of the IQ bell curve, they maintained, tend to "rise to the top" of the social ladder, because they possess high levels of cognitive skills. As a consequence, they make more money, assume more positions of leadership, and enter more powerful occupations than people at the lower tail.

replicability

CAN THE RESULTS BE DUPLICATED IN OTHER STUDIES?

Men and women tend to differ in how they solve spatial problems.

replicability

CAN THE RESULTS BE DUPLICATED IN OTHER STUDIES?

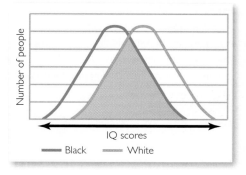

FIGURE 9.17 Diagram of African American and Caucasian Distributions for IQ. African American and Caucasian IQ distributions differ by an average of 15 IQ points—but they show substantial overlap, as indicated by the shaded area.

Had Herrnstein and Murray (1994) stopped there, their book would probably have attracted scant public attention. But they went further, conjecturing that at least some of the IQ gap between races might be genetic in origin. Herrnstein and Murray were hardly the first to make this suggestion (Jensen, 1973; Rushton & Bogaert, 1987). Nevertheless, their claims received unprecedented press coverage, reawakening a bitter debate that had arisen in the 1960s when Arthur Jensen proposed a genetic basis for racial differences in IQ. Jensen's work aroused widespread suspicions of racism, and was even interpreted by some White supremacists as supporting claims that Caucasians are genetically superior to Blacks. J. Philippe Rushton (1995) also became a controversial figure in the 1980s and 1990s when he offered an evolutionary explanation for racial differences in IQ. Although some researchers have advanced strong arguments for a genetic basis for racial differences in IQ, we'll soon discover that the preponderance of evidence supports the idea that racial differences in IQ are largely or entirely environmental in origin, perhaps reflecting the difference resources and opportunities available to individuals of different races.

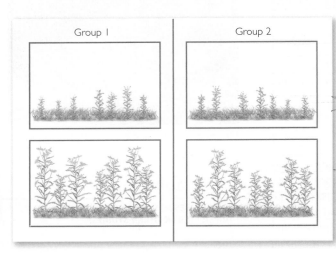

FIGURE 9.18   Drawings of Two Groups of Plants.   These two groups of plants are well matched in height to start, but one outstrips the other over time due to different environmental conditions. This demonstrates how group differences in IQ could be "real" but completely environmentally determined. (*Source:* Based on Lewontin, 1970)

RECONCILING RACIAL DIFFERENCES.   To see why racial differences in IQ don't necessarily imply genetic differences in intelligence or learning potential, let's look at the two groups of plants in the upper panel of **FIGURE 9.18** (Lewontin, 1970). As we can see, in this "thought experiment" the plants within each group differ in height. These differences in height reflect (at least in part) genetic influences on plants' tendencies to grow and flourish. Note, however, that at this point in the growth cycle, the plants in the two groups are, on average, roughly equal in height. Now let's imagine that we provide one of these groups of plants, in this case the one on the left, with plenty of water and light, but provide the other group with minimal water and light. We twiddle our thumbs and wait a few weeks, and then voila: We now find that the plants on the left are, on average, much taller than the plants on the right. Although the two groups each had equal potential to grow and flourish, environmental influences resulted in one group growing taller than the other.

So what's the take-home message? The difference in height between these groups is *entirely environmental*—it's due to watering and light—so we can't explain the difference between the two groups in genetic terms. In other words, the between-group differences aren't at all heritable. If we think of children as little "human plants" (after all, the word "kindergarten" means "child garden" in German), we can easily imagine that different races begin life with no average genetic differences in IQ. But over time, the cumulative effects of factors such as social deprivation and prejudice may produce a notable difference in IQ between racial groups, one that's entirely environmental in origin.

It's also important to point out that although one group of plants in our example grew taller than the other, one or two individual plants in the shorter group actually grew taller than some plants from the taller group. This point highlights the overlapping distributions of heights in the two groups, demonstrating that even within a relatively "deprived" group, some plants exceed the growth of some members of the more "privileged" group. This point reminds us why we can't use group differences in IQ to infer the IQ of any given person. Although this example demonstrates that racial differences in IQ *could* be entirely environmental in nature, it doesn't demonstrate that they *are*. We need to look at the scientific evidence for answers to that question.

WHAT ARE THE CAUSES OF RACIAL DIFFERENCES IN IQ?   Some researchers have pointed out that IQ is heritable and have argued from this finding that racial differences must be due at least partly to genetic influences. However, this is a faulty conclusion based on a misunderstanding of how the heritability of a trait among individuals *within* a group relates to the heritability of this trait *between* groups.

Within-group heritability is the extent to which a trait, like IQ, is heritable within groups, such as Asian Americans or women. **Between-group heritability** is the extent to which the difference in this trait between groups, such as between Asian Americans and Caucasians or between men and women, is heritable. It's critical to keep in mind that *within-group heritability doesn't necessarily imply between-group heritability.* That is, just because IQ is heritable within groups doesn't imply that the difference between these groups has anything to do with their genes. Some researchers have confused within-group and between-group heritability, assuming mistakenly that because IQ is heritable within any group such as a race or gender, racial differences in IQ must themselves be heritable (Lilienfeld & Waldman, 2000; Nisbett, 1995, 2009). To return to our plant analogy, we must remember that within each, some plants grew taller than others. These differences were caused by differences in the heartiness of the genetic strain of the individual plants within each group. Nevertheless, the differences between the two groups of plants were due entirely to environmental factors, even though within-group differences were due entirely to genes.

So what's the evidence that racial differences in IQ result from environmental and *not* genetic factors? Most of this research comes from analyses of differences between African Americans and Caucasians, and it largely points away from a genetic explanation of racial IQ gaps.

One study conducted in Germany shortly after World War II compared the IQ scores of children of African American soldiers and Caucasian German mothers with the children of Caucasian American soldiers and Caucasian German mothers. In both groups, mothers raised the children, so the societal environment was approximately the same. The IQs of these two groups of children didn't differ (Eyferth, 1961). Thus, the differing race-related genes appeared to have no bearing on children's IQ when environment was roughly equated. Other studies have examined whether African Americans with Caucasian European ancestry obtain a "boost" in IQ relative to those with few European ancestors, which would be expected if racial differences were genetic. The research shows that African Americans with more ancestors of Caucasian descent don't differ significantly in IQ from those with few or no such ancestors (Nisbett, 2009; Scarr et al., 1977; Witty & Jenkins, 1934). One group of researchers even found a slight tendency in the opposite direction: African Americans with more Caucasian European ancestry had *lower* IQs (Loehlin, Vandenberg, & Osborne, 1973). In any case, these findings provide no evidence for a genetic explanation of the IQ gap between African Americans and Caucasians.

Another study examined the effect of cross-racial adoption on IQ. This study showed that the IQs of African American children adopted by middle-class Caucasian parents were higher at age seven than those of either the average African American or Caucasian child (Scarr & Weinberg, 1976). This finding suggests that what appears to be a race-related effect may actually be more related to socioeconomic status, because a much higher percentage of African and Hispanic Americans than Caucasians and Asian Americans are living in poverty. A follow-up of these children revealed that their IQs declined over a 10-year period (Weinberg, Scarr, & Waldman, 1992), which may mean that the effects of socioeconomic status are short-lived. Or it may mean that the negative effects (such as discrimination) of being a member of an ethnic minority group in a predominantly Caucasian community gradually counteract the effects of a changed environment.

TEST BIAS. One popular explanation for race differences in IQ is that the tests are biased against certain groups and in favor of others. Test bias has a specific meaning for psychologists, which differs from the popular use of the term. In scientific terms, a test isn't biased merely because some groups perform better on it than others. Psychologists don't regard a tape measure as biased, even though men obtain higher average scores than women when we use it to measure height. When psychologists refer to **test bias**, they instead mean that a test predicts outcomes—such as grades or occupational success—

University of California at Berkeley psychologist Frank Worrell (2006) on the controversial topic of race differences in IQ: "Scientists and practitioners must begin to give greater weight to data, even when the data clash with deeply held beliefs. All of us must be willing to have respectful conversations with those who do not agree with us."

within-group heritability ~~in one group~~
extent to which the variability of a trait within a group is genetically influenced

between-group heritability ~~comparing groups~~
extent to which differences in a trait between groups is genetically influenced

test bias
tendency of a test to predict outcomes better in one group than another

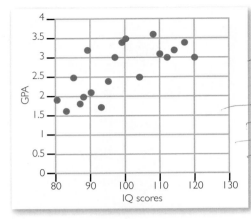

(a)

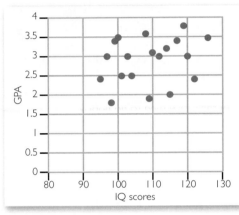

(b)

FIGURE 9.19 Two Scatterplots Representing Test Bias. These two scatterplots display a made-up example of test bias. In (a) IQ scores correlate highly with GPA for Caucasians (.7 correlation), whereas in (b) correlations between IQ scores and GPA are much lower for Asian Americans (.25). Even though Asian Americans display higher IQs on average in this example, the test is biased against them because it's a weaker predictor of GPA in that group.

stereotype threat
fear that we may confirm a negative group stereotype

better in one group than in another (Anastasi & Urbina, 1996; Reynolds, 1999; Kaplan & Saccuzzo, 2008). Putting it a bit differently, a biased test means different things in one group than in another. Let's suppose that the correlation between IQ scores and college grade point average (GPA) in Caucasians was .7, as shown in **FIGURE 9.19a**, but only .25 for Asian Americans, as shown in **FIGURE 9.19b**. This finding would imply that IQ was a better predictor of GPA in Caucasians than in Asian Americans. In this case, the IQ test would be biased *against* Asian Americans, even though the average IQ scores for that group were higher than those of Caucasians. Thus, average differences between groups *do not* necessarily indicate test bias.

So are IQ tests racially biased? The answer seems to be no (Brody, 1992; Lilienfeld et al., 2010; Neisser et al., 1996). In almost all studies, researchers have found that the correlations between IQ tests and both academic and occupational achievement are about equal across races (Brown, Reynolds, & Whitaker, 1999; Gottfredson, 2009; Hunter, Schmidt, & Hunter, 1979). This finding leads to the conclusion that IQ differences among races go hand in hand with differences in average *achievement* among races. Unfortunately, in U.S. society some races tend to do better in school and have higher-ranking and higher-paying jobs than others. According to some psychologists, the most likely explanation for why both IQ and achievement vary across races is that *society,* not IQ tests themselves, is biased, leading both to differences in IQ test performance and to differences in grades and career achievement among races. For example, African Americans and Hispanic Americans may receive lower scores on IQ tests because of prejudice, inferior schooling, and other environmental disadvantages. These disadvantages, in turn, leave many African and Hispanic Americans less prepared to compete in higher education and the job market. Nevertheless, the finding that IQ tests are also equally correlated with reaction time measures across races suggests that this explanation may not tell the whole story, because these measures are unlikely to be affected by social disadvantage (Jensen, 1980).

STEREOTYPE THREAT. One other environmental factor that may affect how individuals perform and achieve is **stereotype threat**. Stereotype threat refers to the fear that we may confirm a negative group stereotype, such as a stereotype of our group as less intelligent or less athletic than others. Stereotype threat creates a self-fulfilling prophecy, in which those who are anxious about confirming a negative stereotype actually increase their likelihood of doing so. According to Claude Steele, stereotype threat can impair individuals' performance on IQ tests and standardized tests, like the SAT. Here's his reasoning: If we're members of a group that has a reputation for doing poorly on IQ tests, the mere thought that we're taking an IQ test will arouse stereotype threat. We think, "I'm supposed to do really badly on this test." This belief, Steele (1997) contends, can itself influence behavior, leading some people who would otherwise do well to display reduced performance.

Research shows that in virtually every country ever studied, girls are better readers than boys (Halpern, 2004). **Does this finding show that tests of reading are biased against boys? Why or why not?** (See answer upside down at left.)

Steele has shown that stereotype threat can indeed depress African Americans' IQ scores, at least in the laboratory. When researchers gave African Americans items from an IQ test but told them the items were measuring something other than IQ, like "the ability to solve puzzles," they performed better than when told the items were measuring IQ (Steele & Aronson, 1995). Stereotype threat manipulations may cause African American participants to become stressed, preoccupied, or overly self-conscious, thereby impeding their performance (Logel et al., 2009; Schmader, Johns, & Forbes, 2008).

Also, giving African Americans and Caucasians an in-class writing assignment designed to boost their personal identity—by asking them to identify their most important personal value, like friends, family, or expressing themselves through art—reduced the racial gap in academic performance by 40 percent (Cohen et al., 2006). The meaning of these intriguing findings isn't clear. One possibility is that thinking about what's important to us, or focusing on ourselves as individuals rather than as members of a group, renders us less vulnerable to stereotype threat. Still, most of these findings come from the tightly controlled world of the psychological laboratory and therefore may be of limited external validity (see Chapter 2). The extent to which stereotype threat findings generalize to the real world remains an active area of investigation and debate (Danaher & Crandall, 2008; Stricker & Ward, 2004).

Some researchers (McCarty, 2001) and writers in the popular media (Chandler, 1999) have gone so far as to suggest that racial differences between African Americans and Caucasians on IQ tests are due completely to stereotype threat and self-fulfilling prophecies (Brown & Day, 2006). Nevertheless, most studies suggest that the effects of stereotype threat aren't large enough to account fully for this gap (Sackett, Hardison, & Cullen, 2004).

Our discussion leads us to the conclusion that broader societal differences in resources, opportunities, attitudes, and experiences are probably responsible for much, if not all, of the racial differences in IQ. The encouraging news, however, is that nothing in the research literature implies that racial differences in IQ are unchangeable. If environmental disadvantages can contribute to IQ differences, eradicating the disadvantages may eliminate these differences.

Research suggests that stereotype threat can lead African American students to perform worse on tests on which they believe members of their race tend to do poorly.

assess your knowledge — FACT OR FICTION?

✔ Study and Review on mypsychlab.com

1. There are few or no sex differences on spatial tasks, such as mental rotation.
   True / False

2. The IQ difference between African Americans and Caucasians is smaller than the IQ difference within each group. **True / False**   *between is smaller than variability within.*

3. Within-group heritability necessarily implies between-group heritability. **True / False**

4. Average differences between groups on a test don't necessarily indicate that the test is biased. **True / False**

5. Stereotype threat may account for part of the IQ difference between African Americans and Caucasians. **True / False**

Answers: 1. F (p.344); 2. T (p.345); 3. F (p.347); 4. T (p.347); 5. T (p.348)

THE REST OF THE STORY: OTHER DIMENSIONS OF INTELLECT

9.11 Describe how creativity and emotional intelligence relate to intelligence.

9.12 Identify reasons why intelligence doesn't protect us from errors in thinking.

IQ, IQ, and still more IQ. Pretty much everything we've discussed in this chapter presumes that IQ is a good measure of intelligence. Although there's strong evidence that IQ tests are valid indicators of what psychologists call intelligence, it's clear that there's far more than high IQ to living our lives intelligently. Many people without sky-high IQs are wise and thoughtful citizens of society, and many people with sky-high IQs behave in foolish, even disastrous ways. If you have any doubt about the latter, just look at the string of high-profile political sex scandals over the past decade, in which well-educated and highly intelligent people got caught red-handed doing remarkably dumb things. We'll conclude the chapter with a survey of other psychological variables that can make us act intelligently—and not so intelligently.

Bernard Madoff, shown here after his arrest in 2009, swindled thousands of extremely intelligent and well-educated investors out of huge amounts of money—in some cases many millions of dollars each. Research shows that high levels of intelligence offer no guarantee against gullibility and uncritical thinking.

[handwritten margin note: divergent thinking → like divergence in calc!! generating many different solutions to a problem]

Frank Lloyd Wright's architectural masterpiece, "Fallingwater," is a prime example of a remarkable creative achievement. It still stands proudly in rural Pennsylvania.

⊙ ▶ Simulate Creativity at
mypsychlab.com

[handwritten margin note: Convergent thinking → Convergence" the capacity to think of the best solution to a problem]

divergent thinking
capacity to generate many different solutions to a problem

convergent thinking
capacity to generate the single best solution to a problem

■ Creativity

By age 54, German composer Ludwig van Beethoven was almost completely deaf. Yet when he reached that age in 1824, he somehow managed to compose his monumental Ninth Symphony, even though while conducting the orchestra performing its world premiere, he couldn't hear a note of it.

"Beethoven's Ninth," as musicologists call it, was astonishing in its originality and brilliance: It was completely unlike any piece of music ever written. No one had thought of composing a symphony more than an hour long (most symphonies were less than half that long), let alone including singers and a full chorus in a musical form that had always been purely instrumental. Nor had anyone been so daring—or brash—as to switch the long-established order of the symphony's traditional four movements, with the slow movement coming third instead of second. As is often the case in response to works of music, art, and literature that break the mold, some critics condemned Beethoven's Ninth as too abrasive, too reckless, and too "different." One wrote that the piece "sounds to me like the upsetting of a bag of nails, with here and there also a dropped hammer" (Goulding, 1992). Yet today, many experts consider Beethoven's Ninth Symphony the greatest piece of music ever written.

Beethoven's music personifies creativity. But like former Supreme Court Justice Potter Stewart, who defined obscenity by saying, "I know it when I see it" (*Jacobellis v. Ohio*, 1964), psychologists have found creativity easier to identify than define. Nevertheless, most psychologists agree that creative accomplishments consist of two features: They are *novel* and *successful*. When we hear an exceptionally creative piece of music, like Beethoven's Ninth, or see an exceptionally creative painting, we nod our heads and say "Wow, that's amazing. He—or she—got it exactly right."

Psychologists often measure creativity using tests of **divergent thinking** (Guilford, 1967; Razoumnikova, 2000): the capacity to generate many different solutions to problems. For this reason, psychologists sometimes call it "outside the box" thinking. For example, in the "Uses for Objects" test, subjects must generate as many uses for an ordinary object, like a paper clip or a brick, as they can (Hudson, 1967). It's likely, though, that tests of divergent thinking don't capture everything about creativity. To be creative, we also need to be good at **convergent thinking**: the capacity to find the single best answer to a problem (Bink & Marsh, 2000). As two-time Nobel Prize–winner Linus Pauling said, to be creative we need to first come up with lots of ideas, and then toss out all the bad ones.

We shouldn't confuse intelligence with creativity: Measures of these two capacities are only weakly or moderately associated, with correlations often in the .2 or .3 range (Furnham et al., 2006; Willerman, 1979). Many intelligent people aren't especially creative, and vice versa.

Highly creative people are an interesting lot. They tend to be bold and willing to take intellectual risks (Sternberg & Lubart, 1992). They also tend to be emotionally troubled while possessed of high self-esteem. Not surprisingly, they're not always the easiest folks in the world to get along with (Barron, 1969; Cattell, 1971). ⊙ ▶ Simulate

There's evidence of a link between creativity and *bipolar disorder*, about which we'll learn more in Chapter 15. People with bipolar disorder (once called manic depression) experience episodes of greatly elevated exuberance, energy, self-esteem, and risk taking (Furnham et al., 2008). They frequently report that their thoughts race through their heads more quickly than they can speak them, and they can go for days without much sleep. During these dramatic bursts of heightened mood and activity (called manic episodes), individuals with bipolar disorder who have artistic talents may become especially productive. Nevertheless, there's not much evidence that their work increases in quality, only quantity (Weisberg, 1994).

Biographical evidence suggests that many great painters such as Vincent van Gogh, Paul Gauguin, and Jackson Pollack; great writers such as Emily Dickinson, Mark Twain, and Ernest Hemingway; and great composers such as Gustav Mahler, Peter Iylich

Tchaikovsky, and Robert Schumann, probably suffered from bipolar disorder (Jamison, 1993; McDermott, 2001). Moreover, studies show that highly creative individuals in artistic and literary professions have higher than expected levels of bipolar disorder and closely related conditions (Andreasen, 1987; Jamison, 1989 see **FIGURE 9.20**).

Because they're willing to take intellectual risks, creative people typically fall flat on their faces more often than do uncreative people. Even Beethoven composed a few notable clunkers. Probably the best predictor of the *quality* of a person's creative accomplishments is the *quantity* of that person's output (Simonton, 1999). Extremely creative artists, musicians, and scientists produce far more stuff than other people. Some of it isn't especially good, but much of it is. And every once in a while, some of it is truly great.

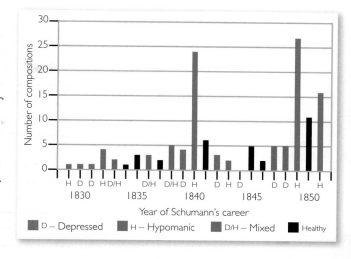

FIGURE 9.20   A Graph of Robert Schumann's Productivity. The German composer Robert Schumann almost certainly had bipolar disorder. As we can see, his productivity increased dramatically during "hypomanic" (mild manic) episodes and decreased dramatically during depressive episodes (which most people with bipolar disorder also experience; see Chapter 15). (*Source:* Weisberg, 1994)

■ Interests and Intellect

Research shows that people with different intellectual strengths tend to exhibit different personality traits and interest patterns (Ackerman & Beier, 2003). When we get to the level of specific mental abilities, we find that people with different intellectual strengths typically display different intellectual interests. People with high levels of scientific and mathematical ability tend to be especially interested in investigating the workings of nature and often describe themselves as enjoying the practical deeds of everyday life, like balancing checkbooks or fixing things around the house. People with high levels of verbal ability tend to be interested in art and music. And people who are poor at math and spatial ability tend to be especially interested in going into professions that involve helping others (Ackerman & Heggestad, 1997; Ackerman, Kanfer, & Goff, 2005). What we're good at—and not good at—tells us quite a bit about what we like to do.

■ Emotional Intelligence: Is EQ as Important as IQ?

Emotional intelligence—the ability to understand our emotions and those of others, and to apply this information to our everyday lives (Goleman, 1995; Mayer, Salovey, & Caruso, 2008; Salovey & Mayer, 1990)—is one of the most active topics in popular psychology today. According to some researchers, emotional intelligence consists of several subcomponents, such as the capacities to understand and recognize one's emotions, to appreciate others' emotions, to control one's emotions, and to adapt one's emotions to diverse situations (Bar-On, 2004). Most proponents of emotional intelligence maintain that "EQ" (one's emotional quotient) is just as, if not more, important as IQ for effective functioning in the world.

Some items on emotional intelligence tests ask subjects to report how good they are at handling their emotions under stress. Others ask subjects to identify which emotion a face is expressing (a skill on which women usually outperform men, as we've already seen). Still others ask subjects to predict what emotion a person will experience in a given situation, like meeting future in-laws for the first time or being asked an embarrassing question during a job interview (**FIGURE 9.21**). Many American companies now provide their

> **emotional intelligence**
> ability to understand our own emotions and those of others, and to apply this information to our daily lives

FIGURE 9.21   Item Similar to That on a Test of Emotional Intelligence. How would you do on a test of emotional intelligence? Try your hand at this item, modeled after those on actual emotional intelligence measures. The correct answer is upside down at the bottom of the page.

When Anne's friend Maggie was feeling depressed over a recent break-up with her boyfriend, Anne took several hours off from studying for a big test to drive to Maggie's apartment and comfort her. Two weeks later, Anne was upset over an argument with her sister, and phoned Maggie to talk about it. Maggie told Anne she was busy packing for an upcoming trip and asked if they could put off talking until the following week. Anne felt _____. (Select the best choice.)

(a) sad   (b) nervous   (c) embarrassed   (d) resentful   (e) envious

employees and bosses with formal training for boosting their emotional intelligence (Locke, 2005). Among other things, EQ training seminars teach workers to "listen" to their emotions in making decisions, find better means of coping with stressful job situations, and express empathy to coworkers.

Few would dispute the claim that these are helpful skills on the job. In addition, people with low emotional intelligence are prone to some psychological problems, like depression and substance abuse (Hertel, Schutz, & Lammers, 2009). Still, the emotional intelligence concept has its critics. In particular, it's not clear that this concept offers much beyond personality (Matthews, Zeidner, & Roberts, 2002). Most measures of emotional intelligence assess personality traits, such as extraversion, agreeableness, and openness to experience, at least as much they do intelligence (Conte, 2005). Moreover, although advocates of emotional intelligence claim that this concept predicts job performance beyond general intelligence (Mayer, Roberts, & Barsade, 2008), most research suggests otherwise (Van Rooy & Viswesvaran, 2004). Nor is there much evidence that different measures of emotional intelligence are highly correlated (2005). The most parsimonious hypothesis is that emotional intelligence isn't anything new, and that it's instead a mixture of personality traits that psychologists have studied for decades.

occam's razor

DOES A SIMPLER EXPLANATION FIT THE DATA JUST AS WELL?

■ Wisdom

Being intelligent isn't the same as being wise. Indeed, measures of intelligence are only moderately correlated with measures of wisdom (Helson & Srivastava, 2002). Robert Sternberg (2002) defined **wisdom** as the application of intelligence toward a common good. Wise people have learned to achieve a delicate balance among three often-competing interests: (1) concerns about oneself (self-interest), (2) concerns about others, and (3) concerns about the broader society. Wise persons channel their intelligence into avenues that benefit others. To accomplish this end, they come to appreciate alternative points of view, even as they may disagree with them. To a substantial extent, wisdom is marked by an awareness of our biases and cognitive fallibilities (Meacham, 1990). In these respects, we can think of wise people as good scientific thinkers in everyday life (Lilienfeld, Ammirati, & Landfield, 2009). Wisdom sometimes, but by no means always, comes with age (Erikson, 1968).

tolerant

Abraham Lincoln, although an emotionally troubled man prone to bouts of severe depression (Shenk, 2005), was a wise person who's justifiably regarded as one of America's greatest presidents. He managed to balance his own views about slavery with those of his citizens, rarely making bold political moves until he'd successfully mobilized public opinion in his favor. Lincoln also bent over backward to solicit the views of those who disagreed with him, going so far as to include former opponents in his cabinet (Goodwin, 2005). In all of these cases, Lincoln kept his eye on the ball: the long-term unity of the country.

■ Why Smart People Believe Strange Things

As Keith Stanovich (2009) observed, IQ tests do a good job of assessing how efficiently we process information, but they don't assess the ability to think scientifically. For example, measures of confirmation bias, like the Wason selection task (see Chapter 2), are barely correlated, if at all, with IQ (Stanovich & West, 2008). Indeed, high levels of intelligence afford no guarantee against beliefs for which there's scant evidence (Hyman, 2002). People with high IQs are at least as prone as other people to beliefs in conspiracy theories, such as the belief that President Kennedy's assassination was the result of a co-ordinated plot within the U.S. government (Goertzel, 1994) or that the Bush administration orchestrated the September 11 attacks (Molé, 2006). Moreover, the history of

wisdom
application of intelligence toward a common good

science is replete with examples of brilliant individuals holding strange beliefs. Two-time Nobel Prize–winning chemist Linus Pauling, whom we encountered when discussing creativity, insisted that high levels of vitamin C can cure cancer, despite overwhelming evidence to the contrary.

In many cases, smart people embrace odd beliefs because they're adept at finding plausible-sounding reasons to bolster their opinions (Shermer, 2002). IQ is correlated positively with the ability to defend our positions effectively, but correlated negatively with the ability to consider alternative positions (Perkins, 1981). High IQ may be related to the strength of the **ideological immune system**: our defenses against evidence that contradicts our views (Shermer, 2002; Snelson, 1993). We've all felt our ideological immune systems kicking into high gear when a friend challenges our political beliefs (say, about capital punishment) with evidence we'd prefer not to hear. First we first feel defensive, and then we frantically search our mental knowledge banks to find arguments that could refute our friend's irksome evidence. Our knack for defending our positions against competing viewpoints can sometimes lead to confirmation bias, blinding us to information we should take seriously.

Robert Sternberg (2002) suggested that people with high IQs are especially vulnerable to the *sense of omniscience* (knowing everything). Because intelligent people know many things, they frequently make the mistake of thinking they know just about everything. For example, the brilliant writer Sir Arthur Conan Doyle, who invented the character Sherlock Holmes, got taken in by an embarrassingly obvious photographic prank (Hines, 2003). In the 1917 "Cottingley fairies" hoax, two young British girls insisted that they'd photographed themselves along with dancing fairies. Brushing aside the criticisms of doubters, Conan Doyle wrote a book about the Cottingley fairies and defended the girls against accusations of trickery. He'd forgotten the basic principle that extraordinary claims require extraordinary evidence. The girls eventually confessed to doctoring the photographs after someone discovered they'd cut the fairies out of a book (Randi, 1982). Conan Doyle, who had a remarkably sharp mind, may have assumed that he couldn't be duped. Yet, as we've learned throughout this book, none of us is immune from errors in thinking. When intelligent people neglect the safeguards afforded by the scientific method, they'll often be fooled.

One of the photographs from the famous Cottingley fairies hoax that took in writer Arthur Conan Doyle. Even extremely intelligent people can be fooled by fake claims.

◀ extraordinary claims

IS THE EVIDENCE AS STRONG AS THE CLAIM?

---

assess your knowledge   FACT OR FICTION?

1. Intelligence and creativity are highly correlated. True / False

2. The work of highly creative people is almost always high in quality. True / False

3. Emotional intelligence and personality aren't entirely independent. True / False

4. People with high IQs are almost always better at considering alternative points of view than people with low IQs. True / False

Answers: 1. F (p. 350); 2. F (p. 351); 3. T (p. 352); 4. F (p. 353).

✓ Study and Review on mypsychlab.com

ideological immune system
our psychological defenses against evidence that contradicts our views

✓—Study and Review on mypsychlab.com

WHAT IS INTELLIGENCE? DEFINITIONAL CONFUSION 318–326

9.1 IDENTIFY DIFFERENT MODELS AND TYPES OF INTELLIGENCE.

Sir Francis Galton proposed that intelligence stems from sensory capacity. Binet and Simon, who developed the first intelligence test, argued that intelligence consists of higher mental processes, such as reasoning, understanding, and judgment. Spearman observed that tests of mental ability tend to be positively correlated. To explain this pattern, he invoked the existence of *g*, or general intelligence, but also posited the existence of *s*, or specific factors unique to particular mental tasks. Some psychologists have argued for the existence of multiple intelligences. According to them, there are different ways of being smart. Nevertheless, , it's not clear whether these proposed intelligences are independent of each other or of a more general intelligence factor.

1. According to Galton's conception of intelligence, someone who has excellent eyesight and hearing would also have (high/low) intelligence. (p. 319)

2. Binet and Simon developed what is considered to be the first _____ _____, which served as a model for many intelligence researchers who followed in their footsteps. (p. 319)

3. In trying to define intelligence, early 20th century researchers agreed that it was related to _____ _____. (p. 319)

4. The theory of _____ _____, developed by Charles Spearman, which accounted for the differences in intellect among people, could be explained by a single common factor. (p. 320)

5. According to Spearman, someone's intelligence is not only dependent on his/her general intelligence, or *g*, but also on his/her _____ or _____ _____. (p. 321)

6. When driving a vehicle you've never driven, you're relying on your capacity for _____ _____, but when you answer a question on a history test, you're relying on your capacity for _____ _____. (p. 321)

7. According to Gardner's model of multiple intelligences, there are many different types of intelligence, which he refers to as _____ _____ _____. (p. 322)

8. Identify the three kinds of intelligence in Sternberg's Triarchic Model of Intelligence. (p. 323)

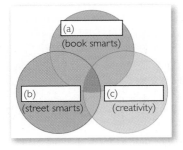

(a) (book smarts)

(b) (street smarts)   (c) (creativity)

((•—Listen to an audio file of your chapter on **mypsychlab.com**

9.2 DESCRIBE THE CONNECTION BETWEEN INTELLIGENCE AND BRAIN SIZE AND EFFICIENCY.

Brain size and intelligence are moderately positively correlated in humans. Some evidence suggests that people with high levels of intelligence possess especially efficient brains. Intelligence also seems related to faster reaction times, as well as working memory capacity, and probably stems in part from the activity of the prefrontal cortex.

9. Haier's study of college students who played the video game *Tetris* indicated that the brains of the more intelligent students were especially _____ at mental processing. (p. 325)

10. Which of these images displays a different pattern than the others? What underlying abilities might be required to enable someone to answer this *g*-loaded question correctly? (p. 325)

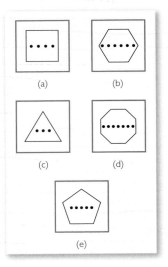

INTELLIGENCE TESTING: THE GOOD, THE BAD, AND THE UGLY 326–336

9.3 DETERMINE HOW PSYCHOLOGISTS CALCULATE IQ.

Stern defined the intelligence quotient (IQ) as mental age divided by chronological age, with the result multiplied by 100. This simple formula becomes problematic in adolescence and adulthood, because mental age tends to level out at around age 16. As a consequence, most modern intelligence tests define IQ in terms of deviation IQ.

11. Using Wilhelm Stern's IQ formula, complete the equation and calculate IQ for the example provided. Next explain the flaw in this formula when applying it to two adults with a mental age of 18, the first an 18-year-old, and the second a 35-year-old. (p. 327)

$$8 \div 10 = \underline{\qquad} \times \underline{\qquad} = \underline{\qquad}$$

(mental age)   (chronological age)   (total)   (IQ)

12. When computing IQ, modern researchers rely on a statistic called _____ _____. (p. 327)

9.4 EXPLAIN THE HISTORY OF MISUSE OF INTELLIGENCE TESTS IN THE UNITED STATES.

Eugenics was the effort to improve a population's "genetic stock" by encouraging people with "good genes" to reproduce, by discouraging people with "bad genes" from reproducing, or both. IQ tests became an important tool of the eugenics movement, because many proponents of eugenics wished to minimize the reproduction and immigration of individuals with low IQs. In part because of eugenics, many people today view IQ tests with skepticism.

13. _____ _____ is one of the extremely disturbing practices that came about as a result of the eugenics movement. (p. 328)

9.5 DESCRIBE TESTS OF INTELLIGENCE USED TODAY AND EVALUATE THE RELIABILITY AND VALIDITY OF IQ SCORES.

Psychologists have developed IQ tests for both adults, such as the WAIS-IV, and for children, such as the WISC-IV. IQ scores are reasonably stable in adulthood, although they aren't especially stable in infancy or early childhood. IQ tests predict a variety of important real-world outcomes, including job performance and physical health.

14. Psychologists have developed many different adult IQ tests, but the most commonly used is the _____ _____ _____. (p. 329)

15. Apply your knowledge of the WAIS by viewing each visual example and identifying its corresponding test and description. (p. 329)

16. The _____ of IQ tests indicates whether these tests accurately measure what they purport to measure. (p. 333)

9.6 DISTINGUISH THE UNIQUE CHARACTERISTICS OF MENTAL RETARDATION AND GENIUS.

There are four categories of mental retardation: mild, moderate, severe, and profound. At least 85 percent of individuals with mental retardation fall into the mild category. Terman's study of gifted schoolchildren helped to debunk widespread ideas that child prodigies "burn out" in adulthood and that genius often leads to insanity.

17. There are three criteria that define mental retardation: (1) onset prior to adulthood, (2) IQ below approximately _____, and (3) inadequate adaptive functioning. (p. 334)

18. About one percent of persons in the United States, most of them (females/males), fulfill the criteria for mental retardation. (p. 335)

19. _____ is an organization whose members score in the top _____ percent of the IQ range. (p. 335)

20. The results of Lewis Terman's classic studies of intellectually gifted individuals disputed the popular notion that there's an intimate link between genius and _____. (p. 336)

GENETIC AND ENVIRONMENTAL INFLUENCES ON IQ 337–342

9.7 EXPLAIN HOW GENETIC INFLUENCES CAN BE DETERMINED FROM FAMILY, TWIN, AND ADOPTION STUDIES.

Twin and adoption studies suggest that at least some of the tendency for IQ to run in families is genetically influenced, although they also offer convincing evidence of environmental effects on IQ. The heritability of IQ appears be relatively low, however, among extremely poor individuals, perhaps reflecting the adverse effects of environmental deprivation on the expression of genetic potential.

21. Galton conducted one of the first _____ _____ of intelligence to determine whether intellectual brilliance runs in families. (p. 337)

22. Twin studies tell us that IQ is influenced both by _____ and _____ factors. (pp. 337–338)

23. _____ studies are a way for researchers to separate environmental effects from genetic effects on IQ and other psychological traits. (p. 338)

24. If a child from a deprived environment is adopted into an enriched family environment, we would expect this child's IQ to (increase/decrease/stay the same). (p. 338)

9.8 IDENTIFY POTENTIAL ENVIRONMENTAL INFLUENCES ON IQ.

Schooling is related to high IQ scores. Research suggests that both poverty and nutrition are causally related to IQ, although disentangling the effects of nutrition from other factors, such as social class, is challenging.

25. Environmental influences on intelligence can be divided into two types: the _____ environment, such as school and parents, and the _____ environment, such as nutrition and exposure to toxins. (p. 339)

26. What effect, according to Ceci, does summer vacation have on a child's IQ and what does this finding suggest about the factors contributing to performance on IQ tests? (p. 339)

27. According to studies like Rosenthal and Jacobson's, if a teacher thinks a student has obtained a high IQ score, that teacher will give (more/less) attention to that student. This finding is related to the _____ _____ effect. (p. 340)

Answers are located at the end of the text.

28. Studies from poor areas in Central America suggest that _____ in childhood can lower IQ. (p. 341)

29. If your IQ is higher than your grandparent's IQ, this difference may be attributable to the _____ _____. (p. 341)

30. Identify four possible environmental influences on IQ as seen in the Flynn effect. (p. 342)

1. _____
2. _____
3. _____
4. _____

GROUP DIFFERENCES IN IQ: THE SCIENCE AND THE POLITICS 343–349

9.9 IDENTIFY SIMILARITIES AND DIFFERENCES IN MENTAL ABILITY BETWEEN MEN AND WOMEN.

Most research suggests little, if any, overall average sex difference in IQ between men and women. Nevertheless, studies indicate that men are more variable in their IQ scores than women. Women tend to do better than men on some verbal tasks, whereas men tend to do better than women on some spatial tasks.

31. Comments about women in science and mathematics made by a former president of Harvard University sparked a firestorm about _____ differences in IQ. (p. 343)

32. Men and women (are/aren't) similar when it comes to most intellectual abilities. (p. 344)

33. Men tend to do better than women on some tasks requiring _____ ability, and women tend to do better than men on some tasks requiring _____ ability. (p. 344)

34. There's little evidence for sex differences in IQ overall, but research has revealed consistent differences between the sexes in some specific skills. Indicate below which sex (M/F) scores higher on each of the skills listed. (p. 344)

_____ Spelling
_____ Arithmetic calculation *(in childhood)*
_____ Complex mathematical tasks *(in adolescence)*
_____ Safe driving
_____ Geography
_____ Sociability
_____ Reading facial expression for emotion
_____ Spatial ability

35. From 1966–2001, the number of women entering the "hard" sciences (increased/decreased) steadily. (p. 345)

9.10 EVALUATE THE EVIDENCE CONCERNING RACIAL DIFFERENCES IN IQ.

On average, African Americans score about 15 points lower than Caucasians on standard IQ tests. Asian Americans score about five points higher than Caucasians. Nevertheless, there's substantial overlap in the IQ distributions across races. Test bias does not appear to be a viable interpretation of the IQ test gap between African Americans and Caucasians because IQ scores predict the same criteria in African Americans and Caucasians. Nevertheless, several studies offer good reasons to believe that much of the IQ between African Americans and Caucasians is is environmental.

36. The authors of *The Bell Curve* revived a bitter public debate when they speculated that the IQ gap between races might be _____ in origin. (p. 346)

37. How can environmental influences explain how two sets of plants that started out at the same height can end up so different? What does this thought experiment tell us about potential environmental effects on IQ? (p. 346)

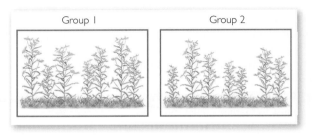

Group 1   Group 2

38. To demonstrate that there's no genetic explanation for the IQ gap between African Americans and Caucasian Americans, one needs to understand the difference between _____ heritability and _____ heritability. (p. 347)

39. When a test predicts outcomes better in one group than in another, this is known as _____ _____. (pp. 347–348)

40. If you're a member of a group that has a reputation for doing poorly on standardized tests, you may do poorly when you take one merely because of _____ _____. (p. 348)

THE REST OF THE STORY: OTHER DIMENSIONS OF INTELLECT 349–353

9.11 DESCRIBE HOW CREATIVITY AND EMOTIONAL INTELLIGENCE RELATE TO INTELLIGENCE.

Creative accomplishments consist of two features: They are novel and successful. Psychologists often measure creativity using tests of divergent thinking, which assess the capacity to generate many different solutions to a problem. Nevertheless, creativity also requires convergent thinking, the capacity to find the single best answer to a problem. Emotional intelligence refers to the ability to understand our own emotions and those of others, and to apply this information to our daily lives. Although emotional intelligence is relevant to job performance, it's not clear how much it contributes beyond either intelligence or personality traits, such as extraversion.

41. Intelligence, as measured by IQ, (is/isn't) the only dimension of intellect. (p. 349)

42. If you're good at thinking "outside the box," you'd probably score highly on a test that measures _____ thinking. (p. 350)

43. The ability to find the best single answer to a problem is called _____ _____. (p. 350)

44. Correlations between measures of intelligence and creativity tend to be (low/high). (p. 350)

45. Creative people tend to be (willing/not willing) to take intellectual risks. (p. 350)

46. What traits do highly creative people possess that other noncreative people lack? (p. 350)

47. There (is/isn't) evidence that different measures of emotional intelligence are highly correlated. (p. 352)

9.12 IDENTIFY REASONS WHY INTELLIGENCE DOESN'T PROTECT US FROM ERRORS IN THINKING.

Wisdom is the application of intelligence toward a common good. Wisdom isn't identical to intelligence and it sometimes, but not always, comes with age. Even highly intelligent people can believe strange things because standard IQ tests aren't especially good measures of scientific thinking capacity. Some people have even suggested that high intelligence may allow people to find false, but plausible-sounding, arguments to bolster their unsupported views.

48. Nobel Prize–winning chemist Linus Pauling's belief that vitamin C cures cancer, despite overwhelming evidence to the contrary, suggests that he had a strong _____ immune system. (p. 353)

49. Why was the writer Arthur Conan Doyle fooled by the famous Cottingley fairies hoax? (p. 353)

50. Sternberg suggested that people with high IQs are vulnerable to the _____ _____ _____ . (p. 353)

DO YOU KNOW THESE TERMS?

- intelligence test (p. 319)
- abstract thinking (p. 319)
- *g* (general intelligence) (p. 320)
- *s* (specific abilities) (p. 321)
- fluid intelligence (p. 321)
- crystallized intelligence (p. 321)
- multiple intelligences (p. 322)
- triarchic model (p. 323)

- Stanford-Binet IQ test (p. 327)
- intelligence quotient (IQ) (p. 327)
- mental age (p. 327)
- deviation IQ (p. 327)
- eugenics (p. 328)
- Wechsler Adult Intelligence Scale (WAIS) (p. 329)

- culture-fair IQ test (p. 330)
- bell curve (p. 334)
- mental retardation (p. 334)
- Flynn effect (p. 341)
- within-group heritability (p. 347)
- between-group heritability (p. 347)
- test bias (p. 347)

- stereotype threat (p. 348)
- divergent thinking (p. 350)
- convergent thinking (p. 350)
- emotional intelligence (p. 351)
- wisdom (p. 352)
- ideological immune system (p. 353)

APPLY YOUR SCIENTIFIC THINKING SKILLS

Use your scientific thinking skills to answer the following questions, referencing specific scientific thinking principles and common errors in reasoning whenever possible.

1. There's a widely held myth that highly stimulating early environments are critical for infant intellectual development (see Chapter 10). In reality, most normal environments provide adequate stimulation for infant development. Although research suggests a negative effect of severely deprived environments on intelligence, adding *more* stimulation to already healthy environments may not help much. Look for websites marketing "infant stimulation" products. In what way are these sites' claims consistent—or inconsistent—with scientific evidence?

2. Research three examples of companies or products that claim to improve your score on standardized tests. What methods do they recommend for improving your score? Are there other explanations for the improvements in scores they advertise? Do they make any guarantees or exaggerated claims about how much your score will improve?

3. As the chapter notes, even highly intelligent people sometimes behave in foolish ways. Locate an example of a famous person—say, a political figure, scientist, or artist—who's clearly intelligent but who engaged in spectacularly unintelligent actions. What potential scientific explanations might you offer for the causes of his or her behavior?

10 HUMAN DEVELOPMENT

how and why we change

THINK ABOUT IT

DO EMOTIONALLY TRAUMATIC EXPERIENCES IN INFANCY TYPICALLY SCAR CHILDREN FOR LIFE?

DO AMERICAN PARENTING AND SCHOOLING TECHNIQUES GIVE CHILDREN A DEVELOPMENTAL ADVANTAGE RELATIVE TO APPROACHES IN OTHER COUNTRIES?

CAN ADOLESCENTS MAKE MATURE DECISIONS?

HOW DOES BECOMING A PARENT AFFECT PEOPLE'S QUALITY OF LIFE?

IS THE AGING PROCESS ALL DOWNHILL?

The story of the Genain quadruplets raises fascinating and complex questions regarding the interplay of nature and nurture in development.

correlation vs. causation

CAN WE BE SURE THAT A CAUSES B?

Nora, Iris, Myra, and Hester Genain are sisters. They're in their early eighties now. And all of them are emotionally disturbed in some way that's hard to put a finger on. In reality, Nora, Iris, Myra, and Hester aren't their actual names. The first letter of each of their names combine to form an acronym: NIMH. That's because scientists at NIMH—the National Institute of Mental Health, outside of Washington, DC—gave them these false names to safeguard their identities. Scientists at NIMH have been studying them for several decades, measuring their early and later development, personality traits, and even brain activity using functional imaging.

Why have scientists at NIMH been so interested in Nora, Iris, Myra, and Hester? It turns out that these four women have two striking things in common. First, they are identical quadruplets and born within 17 minutes of each other. Second, Nora, Iris, Myra, and Hester all have schizophrenia.

The Genain quadruplets, as they're known in the psychological literature, offer a classic illustration of the interplay between nature and nurture over the course of development (Rosenthal, 1963). Both of their parents suffered from serious psychological problems. Given what we know about the genetics of schizophrenia—which as we'll learn in Chapter 15 is a severe disorder of thinking and emotion that usually results in a loss of contact with reality—it's likely that the Genain quadruplets inherited a predisposition toward this condition.

Yet the timing and expression of each quadruplet's disorder differed. This finding, as NIMH researchers recognized, offers powerful evidence for the role of the environment in the manifestation of schizophrenia. That's because identical quadruplets, like identical twins, possess the same DNA; in effect they're genetic clones of one another (see Chapter 3). So any behavioral differences among the Genains must be due to differences in their environments.

Although three of the sisters—Nora, Iris, and Hester—were hospitalized for their disorder, one of them—Myra—wasn't. Indeed, Myra was clearly disturbed but better adjusted than the others. Unlike the other quadruplets, she'd once married and even held a job for many years. In contrast, Hester was the most seriously ill of the sisters; she was disoriented, confused, and almost completely incapable of caring for herself. Nora, although also disturbed, was healthier than Iris, who like Hester was frequently bewildered and out of touch with reality.

What environmental variables might account for these differences? From birth, the four sisters differed in weight. The two severely afflicted sisters—Hester and Iris—weighed less than Myra and Nora (Rosenthal, 1963). Moreover, their mother clearly favored Myra and Nora over Hester and Iris. In particular, she regarded Myra as psychologically healthier and smarter than the other quadruplets. In contrast, their mother frequently punished Hester and Iris for what she perceived as inappropriate behavior (Bernheim & Lewine, 1979; Stierlin, 1972). Yet even today, the role that these environmental factors played in the development of the Genain quadruplets' schizophrenia remains a mystery.

The fascinating story of the Genain quadruplets underscores the enormous challenges that psychologists confront in disentangling nature from nurture throughout development. Was the mother's harsher treatment of Hester and Iris compared with Myra and Nora a *cause* of their more severe schizophrenia? It's certainly possible. Nevertheless, we can't conclude that with certainty, because we know only that unsupportive parental treatment in the Genain family was associated with more severe outcomes in the children. It's equally possible that their mother's harsher treatment of Hester and Iris was a *reaction* to their more severe symptoms in the first place. After all, parents may be less nurturing of their children if their children are difficult to begin with. In these cases, harsher treatment from parents may cause difficult children to become even more disturbed, resulting in even harsher treatment from parents, thereby creating a vicious cycle (Bell, 1968; Rutter, 1997). The tale of the Genain quadruplets, like those of other case studies, raises far more questions than answers—in this case, about how the same genes and similar environments can result in different patterns of psychological adjustment. As we discovered in Chapter 2, case studies are almost always better suited for raising questions than for answering them. Fortunately, as we'll soon learn, psychologists have developed methods for shedding light on the causes of development over time.

SPECIAL CONSIDERATIONS IN HUMAN DEVELOPMENT

10.1 Identify ways to think scientifically about developmental findings.

10.2 Clarify how nature and nurture can contribute to development.

Developmental psychology is the study of how behavior changes over the life span. Before we explore issues of how we develop, we need to come to grips with several challenges that often arise when investigating psychological development. Understanding these challenges, along with the scientific thinking principles we've encountered throughout this book, will provide us with the equipment we need to evaluate the causes of physical, cognitive, emotional, and social changes from childhood to old age.

■ Post Hoc Fallacy

One critical consideration to bear in mind is that things that occur first don't necessarily cause things that come later. It would be silly to conclude, for example, that because nearly 100 percent of serial killers drank milk as children, milk drinking creates mass murderers. Yet this type of reasoning becomes tempting when the earlier behavior seems logically related to the later one. For example, if we learned that children who are shy are more likely to become engineers as adults, we could easily imagine plausible arguments for how shyness might lead to interests in engineering. But we wouldn't have grounds for inferring causation from this correlation, because many factors could have influenced both behaviors. This logical error—the mistake of assuming that because A comes before B, A must cause B—is called the **post hoc fallacy** (*post hoc* is Latin for "after this").

■ Bidirectional Influences

Human development is almost always a two-way street: Developmental influences are bidirectional. Children's experiences influence their development, but their development also influences their experiences. As we saw with the Genain quadruplets, psychological traffic from parents to children runs in both directions: Parents influence their children's behavior, which in turn feeds back to influence their parents, and so on (Bell, 1968; Collins et al., 2000; O'Connor et al., 1998). Children also change their environments by acting in ways that create changes in the behaviors of their parents, siblings, friends, and teachers (Plomin, DeFries, & Loehlin, 1977). Furthermore, as children grow older, they play an increasingly active role in altering and selecting their environments.

It's crucial to keep bidirectional influences in mind, because pop psychology is chock full of *unidirectional* explanations: those that attempt to explain development in terms of a one-headed arrow. Parents fight with each other → their children react negatively. Children witness violence at school → they become more aggressive. There's probably a kernel of truth in each of these explanations. Yet they typically tell only part of the story. That's why so many arrows in psychology contain two heads (↔), not one. In the study of human development, two "heads" are almost always better—or least more accurate—than one, at least as far as arrows are concerned.

■ Keeping an Eye on Cohort Effects

Imagine we conduct a study designed to examine how people's knowledge of computers changes with age. We enter our study armed with a reasonable hypothesis: People's knowledge of computers should increase steadily from adolescence until early adulthood, after which it should level off at about age 30. After about age 30, we predict, knowledge of computers should remain about the same or increase slightly. To test our hypothesis, we sample 100,000 people in the U.S. population, with a broad age range of 18 to 80. We carefully screen out people with dementias or other forms of brain damage to ensure that we're not accidentally including people with faulty memories. However, contrary to our hypothesis, we find that people's knowledge of computers declines dramatically with age, especially between the ages of 60 and 80. What did we do wrong?

correlation vs. causation
CAN WE BE SURE THAT A CAUSES B?

> **developmental psychology**
> study of how behavior changes over the life span
>
> **post hoc fallacy**
> false assumption that because one event occurred before another event, it must have caused that event

Can you think of both an environmental and a genetic explanation for why adolescents in gangs become trouble makers? (See answer upside down at bottom of page.)

Answer: Environmental explanation—kids who hang out with troublemakers can be persuaded to engage in troubled behaviors. Genetic explanation—kids who are genetically predisposed to engage in destructive acts are driven to seek out other like-minded kids.

ruling out rival hypotheses

HAVE IMPORTANT ALTERNATIVE EXPLANATIONS FOR THE FINDINGS BEEN EXCLUDED?

Older adults may be less comfortable or skilled with technology because it wasn't around when they were growing up, limiting our ability to compare performance of older with younger adults in a cross-sectional study.

The classic "Up Series" directed by Michael Apted traces the lives of 14 British people over time, from age seven all the way up through age 49. Here, three "stars" of the documentary, Jackie, Lynn, and Sue, now in their forties, proudly display photographs of themselves at younger ages. The longitudinal designs used by psychologists work in the same way: They track the lives of the same groups of people over time.

cross-sectional design
research design that examines people of different ages at a single point in time

cohort effect
effect observed in a sample of participants that results from individuals in the sample growing up at the same time

longitudinal design
research design that examines development in the same group of people on multiple occasions over time

It turns out that we forgot to consider an alternative explanation for our findings. We started out by asking a perfectly sensible question. But in science, we also must make sure that the design we select is the right one for answering it. In this case, it wasn't. We used a **cross-sectional design**, a design in which researchers examine people of different ages at a single point in time (Achenbach, 1982; Raulin & Lilienfeld, 2008). In a cross-sectional design, we obtain a "snapshot" of each person at a single age; we assess some people when they're 24, some when they're 47, others when they're 63, and so on.

The major problem with cross-sectional designs is that they don't control for **cohort effects**: effects due to the fact that sets of people who lived during one time period, called *cohorts*, can differ in some systematic way from sets of people who lived during a different time period. For example, Baby Boomers (born in the decades after World War II, when the population boomed following the soldiers' return) grew up in a very different technological age than did the members of the Millennial Generation (those born in the 1980s and 1990s). In the study we've described, cohort effects are a serious shortcoming, because before the late 1980s, few Americans used computers. So those over 60 years old may not be as computer savvy as younger folks. This has nothing to do with the effects of aging, but everything to do with the effects of the era in which they grew up.

A longitudinal design is the only sure way around this problem. In a **longitudinal design**, psychologists track the development of the same group of subjects over time (Shadish, Cook, & Campbell, 2002). Rather than obtaining a snapshot of each person at only one point in time, we obtain the equivalent of a series of home movies, taken at different ages. This design allows us to examine true *developmental* effects: changes over time within individuals as a consequence of growing older. Without longitudinal designs, we can be tricked into concluding that event A comes before result B even when it doesn't. For example, much of the pop psychology literature warns us that divorce leads to *externalizing behaviors*—behaviors such as breaking rules, defying authority figures, and committing crimes—in children (Wallerstein, 1989). Yet a longitudinal study that tracked a sample of boys over several decades revealed otherwise: Boys whose parents divorced exhibited externalizing behaviors *years before* the divorce even occurred (Block & Block, 2006; Block, Block, & Gjerde, 1986).

Although longitudinal designs are ideal for studying change over time, they can be costly and time-consuming. For example, our study of computer literacy would take about six decades to complete. Such studies also can result in *attrition*—participants dropping out of the study before it's completed. When longitudinal designs aren't feasible, we should remember to interpret the results of cross-sectional studies with healthy skepticism, bearing in mind that cohort effects may account for any observed changes at different ages. Nevertheless, there are some research questions for which cross-sectional designs are more useful than longitudinal designs. For example, when comparing the performance of two-year-olds with two-and-a-half-year-olds on a memory test, the potential for cohort effects seems low. In fact, in such a study, a longitudinal design could be more problematic because administering the same memory task to the same children twice so close together would probably result in better performance on the second test simply because the task was familiar. We should also bear in mind that longitudinal designs aren't experimental designs (see Chapter 2), so we can't use these studies to infer cause-and-effect relationships.

■ The Influence of Early Experience

There's no doubt that early life experiences can sometimes shape later development in powerful ways. Indeed, early input from the outside world exerts a significant impact on brain development. Yet these influences on brain and behavior don't stop after the first few years, but operate throughout the life span. We shouldn't overestimate the impact of experiences in infancy on long-term development, because such experiences are influential but rarely irreversible (Bruer, 1999; Clarke & Clarke, 1976; Kagan, 1998; Paris, 2000).

In particular, we must be careful to avoid two myths concerning development. The first is the myth of *infant determinism*, the widespread assumption that extremely early experiences—especially in the first three years of life—are almost always more influential than later experiences in shaping us as adults. For example, contrary to popular psychology sources, there's no evidence that separating an infant from its mother during the first few hours after birth can produce lasting negative consequences for emotional adjustment (Klaus & Kennell, 1976). There's no question that early experience plays an important role in children's physical, cognitive, and social development. But there's no reason to believe that later experiences play any less of a role in development. In fact, later experiences can often offset the negative effects of early deprivation (Kagan, 1975). Neuroscience research shows that the brain changes in important ways in response to experience throughout childhood and well into early adulthood (Greenough, 1997), supporting the notion that later experiences in life can be as influential as those in early childhood.

The second myth is *childhood fragility*, which holds that children are delicate little creatures who are easily damaged (Paris, 2000; Sommers & Satel, 2005). Research shows most children are remarkably *resilient*, or capable of withstanding stress (see Chapter 12), and that most children emerge from potentially traumatic situations, including kidnappings, in surprisingly good shape (Bonanno, 2004; Cicchetti & Garmezy, 1993; Garmezy, Masten, & Tellegen, 1984). Remarkably, even many children who experience sexual abuse eventually emerge without severe psychological problems, although some almost surely experience long-term negative effects (Rind, Tromovitch, & Bauserman, 1998; Salter et al., 2003).

■ Clarifying the Nature–Nurture Debate

As we learned in Chapter 1, both *nature*—our genetic endowment—and *nurture*—the environments we encounter—play powerful roles in shaping development. Yet as we'll soon see, disentangling their effects is far from simple, because nature and nurture intersect in a variety of fascinating ways, which we've summarized in **TABLE 10.1**.

In the mid-1990s, Betty Hart and Todd Risley (1995) conducted a six-month longitudinal investigation that showed that parents who speak a lot to their children produce children with larger vocabularies than parents who don't. Hart and Risley's study provides evidence for a powerful environmental influence on children's vocabulary, right? Well, not so fast. In intact families, parents and children share not only an environment but also genes. To borrow a term we learned in Chapter 2, genes and environment are *confounded*. So there's an alternative explanation for Hart and Risley's findings: Perhaps they reflect the fact that parents who speak a lot to their children have higher vocabularies themselves. Vocabulary is partly influenced by genetic factors (Stromswold, 2001), so these parents may merely be passing on their genetic predisposition for better vocabularies to their children. Many studies of human development are subject to the same confound.

GENE-ENVIRONMENT INTERACTION. Nature and nurture sometimes *interact* over the course of development, meaning that the effect of one depends on the contribution of the other. For example, some genetic research shows that people who possess a gene that results

ruling out rival hypotheses

HAVE IMPORTANT ALTERNATIVE EXPLANATIONS FOR THE FINDINGS BEEN EXCLUDED?

TABLE 10.1 Intersections of Nature and Nurture. Nature and nurture are hard to disentangle—it's easy to mistake an environmental effect for a genetic effect, and vice versa. Here are some of the ways that genes and environment can intersect, making it difficult to separate out the influence of each.

NATURE–NURTURE INTERSECTIONS	DEFINITIONS
Gene-Environment Interactions	The impact of genes on behavior depends on the environment in which the behavior develops.
Nature via Nurture	Genetic predispositions can drive us to select and create particular environments, leading to the mistaken appearance of a pure effect of nature.
Gene Expression	Some genes "turn on" only in response to specific environmental events.

in low production of an enzyme called *monoamine oxidase* (MAO) are at heightened risk for developing into violent criminals (Moore, Scarpa, & Raine, 2002). In 2002, Avshalom Caspi and his colleagues conducted a longitudinal study of children who possessed this gene, some of whom committed violent crimes and some of whom didn't. They discovered that whether this genetic risk factor is associated with violent behavior depends on whether children were exposed to a specific environmental factor. Specifically, children with *both* the low MAO gene *and* a history of maltreatment (such as physical abuse) were at heightened risk for antisocial behaviors, like stealing, assault, and rape. Children with the low MAO gene alone weren't at heightened risk (Caspi et al., 2002; Kim-Cohen et al., 2006). This finding illustrates **gene-environment interaction**: In many cases, the effects of genes depend on the environment, and vice versa.

NATURE VIA NURTURE. As we learned in Chapter 1, nature and nurture are rarely independent. In particular, children with certain genetic predispositions often seek out and create their own environments, a phenomenon termed **nature via nurture** (Lykken, 1995; Ridley, 2003). In this way, nurture affords children the opportunity to express their genetic tendencies (Scarr & McCartney, 1983). For example, as they grow older, highly fearful children tend to seek out environments that protect them from their anxieties (Rose & Ditto, 1983). Because highly fearful children select safer environments, it may appear that growing up in safe environments helps to create fearfulness, when the environment is actually a consequence of children's genetic predispositions.

GENE EXPRESSION. Strange as it may sound, environmental experiences actually turn genes on and off throughout development. This phenomenon of **gene expression** is one of the most significant discoveries to hit psychology over the past several decades (Champagne & Mashoodh, 2009; Plomin & Crabbe, 2000). Every one of the 100 trillion or so (give or take a few trillion) cells in our bodies contains every one of our genes. Yet only some of these genes are active at any given time, and it sometimes takes environmental experiences to flip their switches to "on." For example, children with genes that predispose them to anxiety may never become anxious unless a highly stressful event, like the death of a parent early in development, triggers these genes to become active. Gene expression reminds us that nurture affects nature. In turn, nature affects how we react to nurture, and so on.

✓— **Study** and **Review** on mypsychlab.com

assess your knowledge — FACT OR FICTION?

1. Just because one event precedes a second event doesn't necessarily mean that it causes it. **True** / **False**

2. Research shows that most children are passive recipients of their parents' influence. **True** / **False**

3. Most children exposed to severe stressors end up with healthy patterns of psychological adjustment. **True** / **False**

4. Environmental experiences can turn genes on and off throughout the course of development. **True** / **False**

Answers: 1. T (p. 361); 2. F (p. 361); 3. T (p. 363); 4. T (p. 364)

THE DEVELOPING BODY: PHYSICAL AND MOTOR DEVELOPMENT

10.3 Track the trajectory of prenatal development and identify barriers to normal development.

10.4 Describe how infants learn to coordinate motion and achieve major motor milestones.

10.5 Describe physical maturation during childhood and adolescence.

10.6 Explain which aspects of physical ability decline during aging.

The human body begins to take shape long before birth, as does the ability to perform coordinated movements. Learning, memory, and even preferences—for certain sounds or

---

gene-environment interaction
situation in which the effects of genes depend on the environment in which they are expressed

nature via nurture
tendency of individuals with certain genetic predispositions to seek out and create environments that permit the expression of those predispositions

gene expression
activation or deactivation of genes by environmental experiences throughout development

prenatal
prior to birth

zygote
fertilized egg

blastocyst
ball of identical cells early in pregnancy that haven't yet begun to take on any specific function in a body part

embryo
second to eighth week of prenatal development, during which limbs, facial features, and major organs of the body take form

fetus
period of prenatal development from ninth week until birth after all major organs are established and physical maturation is the primary change

body positions, for example—are also well under way in unborn infants. Nevertheless, the form and structure of the body, including the brain, undergo radical changes throughout the life span, influencing the range of behaviors across development.

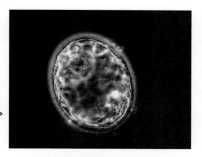

■ Conception and Prenatal Development: From Zygote to Baby

During the **prenatal** (prior to birth) period of development, the human body acquires its basic form and structure.

The most dramatic changes in prenatal development occur in the earliest stages of pregnancy. Following conception, when a sperm cell fertilizes an egg to produce a **zygote**, prenatal physical development unfolds in three stages. In the *germinal stage*, the zygote begins to divide and double, forming a **blastocyst**—a ball of identical cells that haven't yet begun to take on any specific function in a body part. The blastocyst keeps growing as cells continue to divide for the first week and a half or so after fertilization (see **FIGURE 10.1**). Around the middle of the second week, the cells begin to differentiate, taking on different roles as the organs of the body begin to develop.

Once different cells start to assume different functions, the blastocyst becomes an **embryo**. The *embryonic stage* continues from the second to the eighth week of development, during which limbs, facial features, and major organs (including the heart, lungs, and brain) begin to take shape. During this stage, many things can go awry in fetal development. Spontaneous miscarriages often occur when the embryo doesn't form properly (Roberts & Lowe, 1975), frequently without the mother even knowing she was pregnant.

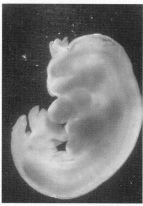

By the ninth week, the major organs are established, and the heart begins to beat. This final milestone is called the *fetal stage* because it's the point at which the embryo becomes a **fetus**. The fetus's "job" for the rest of the pregnancy is physical maturation. This phase is more about fleshing out what's already there than establishing new structures. The last third of pregnancy in particular is devoted almost entirely to "bulking up." ◉—⎡Watch

BRAIN DEVELOPMENT: 18 DAYS AND BEYOND. The human brain begins to develop a mere 18 days after fertilization. Unlike most organs, which are completely formed by birth and continue to grow only in size, our brains continue to develop into adolescence and probably even early adulthood (Caviness et al., 1996).

Between the eighteenth day of pregnancy and the end of the sixth month, neurons begin developing at an astronomical rate, a process called *proliferation*. Some estimates place the rate of neural development as high as an astonishing 250,000 brain cells per minute during peak times. The fetus ends up manufacturing many, many more neurons than it will need as an infant. In addition to producing all of these cells, the brain must organize them to perform coordinated functions. Starting in the fourth month and continuing throughout pregnancy, migration of cells begins to occur. Neurons start to sort themselves out, moving to their final positions in a specific structure of the brain, such as the hippocampus and cerebellum (see Chapter 3).

This series of photos depicts the transition from blastocyst (a mass of identical cells) (*top*) to embryo (preliminary development of skeleton, organs, and limbs) (*middle*) to fetus (recognizably human form) (*bottom*) during the first three months of pregnancy.

◉—⎡Watch Fetal Development on **mypsychlab.com**

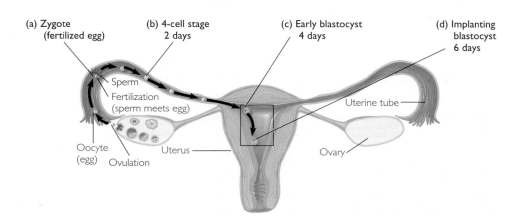

(a) Zygote (fertilized egg)
(b) 4-cell stage 2 days
(c) Early blastocyst 4 days
(d) Implanting blastocyst 6 days
Sperm
Fertilization (sperm meets egg)
Uterine tube
Oocyte (egg)
Ovulation
Uterus
Ovary

FIGURE 10.1   The Journey of a Fertilized Egg from Ovary to Uterus.   After an egg is fertilized by a sperm cell, it begins traveling through the fallopian tube to the uterus. As it travels, cells begin to divide and duplicate, becoming a blastocyst. The blastocyst implants itself in the uterus by the sixth day. (*Source:* Adapted from Marieb and Hoehn, 2007)

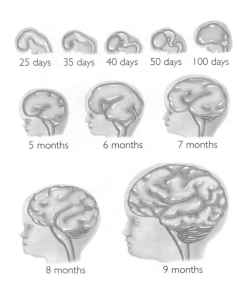

25 days 35 days 40 days 50 days 100 days

5 months 6 months 7 months

8 months 9 months

The fetal brain begins as a long tube that develops into a variety of different structures with the brain stem (which controls basic functions like breathing and digestion) developing first, followed by cortical structures later in pregnancy. (*Source:* Restak, 1984).

⦿→ **Simulate** Teratogens and their Effects on **mypsychlab.com**

Different teratogens adversely affect different systems and may vary in their effects at different stages of pregnancy. For example, high levels of alcohol exposure can result in a collection of symptoms known as *fetal alcohol syndrome*. Fetal alcohol syndrome includes learning disabilities, physical growth retardation, facial malformations, and behavioral disorders (Abel & Sokol, 1986).

teratogen
an environmental factor that can exert a negative impact on prenatal development

fetal alcohol syndrome
condition resulting from high levels of prenatal alcohol exposure, causing learning disabilities, physical growth retardation, facial malformations, and behavioral disorders

OBSTACLES TO NORMAL FETAL DEVELOPMENT. Although most babies are born healthy and fully intact, fetal development can be disrupted in three ways: (1) exposure to hazardous environmental influences, (2) biological influences resulting from genetic disorders or errors in cell duplication during cell division, and (3) premature birth.

Teratogens: Hazards to Fetal Health. Most women don't even realize they're pregnant until after the fetus's body and brain development are well under way. As a result, women often engage unknowingly in activities that are potentially harmful to the fetus. **Teratogens** are environmental factors that can exert a negative impact on prenatal development. They run the gamut from drugs and alcohol to chicken pox and X-rays. Even anxiety and depression in the mother are potential teratogens because they alter the fetus's chemical and physiological environment (Bellamy, 1998). For example, alcohol exposure can result in **fetal alcohol syndrome**, which includes a host of symptoms, such as learning disabilities, physical growth retardation, facial malformations, and behavioral disorders (Abel, 1998). Cigarette smoking during pregnancy is one of the most prevalent teratogens. Mothers who smoke cigarettes or marijuana, or use other recreational drugs during pregnancy, are particularly likely to deliver low-birth-weight babies (Pringle et al., 2005; Windham et al., 2000). Low birth weight, defined as less than five and a half pounds (compared with an average birth weight of about seven and a half pounds) for a full-term baby, poses a high risk of death, infection, and developmental disorders (Copper et al., 1993; Schothorst & van Engeland, 1996). ⦿→ Simulate

Depending on the teratogen and when the embryo or fetus is exposed to it, teratogens can influence how specific parts of the brain develop. Others exert a more general impact on brain development. Because the brain has such a long period of maturation relative to most other organs, it's particularly vulnerable to teratogens.

Genetic Disruptions of Fetal Development. Genetic disorders or random errors in cell division are a second adverse influence on prenatal development. Often, a single cell, including the egg or sperm cell prior to fertilization, or even a family of cells, is copied with some error or break in the genetic material. Like a page with a smudge that keeps being photocopied with that smudge preserved, these cells go on to replicate with the error retained, resulting in impaired development of organs or organ systems. Any number of irregularities can result, some as minor as a birthmark and others as major as mental retardation, including Down syndrome, a disorder marked by specific facial and body malformations (see Chapter 9).

Prematurity. A full-term baby is born after 40 weeks of pregnancy—actually closer to nine and a half months than nine months, as is commonly believed. Premature infants ("preemies") are those born at fewer than 36 weeks' gestation. The *viability* point, the point in pregnancy at which infants can typically survive on their own, is around 25 weeks. In rare cases, fetuses as young as 22 weeks have survived, but only with serious physical and cognitive impairments. Preemies have underdeveloped lungs and brains and are often unable to engage in basic physiological functions, such as breathing and maintaining a healthy body temperature. They often experience serious delays in cognitive and physical development. With each week of pregnancy, the odds of fetal survival increase and the odds of developmental disorders decrease (Hoekstra et al., 2004).

■ Infant Motor Development: How Babies Get Going

Starting at birth, infants begin to learn how to make use of their bodies through movement and coordinate interactions with their environment. Some aspects of motor coordination are evident even at birth, but others develop gradually throughout infancy and early childhood.

SURVIVAL INSTINCTS: INFANT REFLEXES. Infants are born with a large set of automatic motor behaviors—or *reflexes* (see Chapter 3)—that are triggered by specific types of stimulation and fulfill important survival needs (Swaiman & Ashwal, 1999). One example is the *sucking reflex,* an automatic response to oral stimulation. If we put something in a

baby's mouth (including a finger—try it sometime ...
with the parents' permission, of course!), she'll clamp
down and begin sucking. A related reflex is the
rooting reflex, which serves the same survival
need: eating. If we softly stroke a hungry infant's cheek, she'll automatically turn her head
toward our hand and begin casting about with
her mouth, eagerly seeking a nipple to suck.
These reflexes help keep infants alive because if
they needed to learn through trial and error that sucking
on an object yields nourishment, they might starve trying
to get the hang of it.

**LEARNING TO GET UP AND GO: COORDINATING
MOVEMENT.** But reflexes can only get babies only so
far; they must learn other motor behaviors through
trial and error. **Motor behaviors** are bodily motions
that occur as result of self-initiated force that moves
the bones and muscles. The major motor milestones during development include sitting up,
crawling, standing unsupported, and walking.
The age at which different children reach these
milestones varies enormously, although almost all
acquire them in the same order (see **FIGURE 10.2**).

We take for granted how easy it is to reach
for a cup of coffee sitting on a table, yet the calculations our body makes—the physical adjustments that
control our body's positioning and the direction and
speed of our movements—to accomplish that act are incredibly complex.
They're also customized to fit each situation, or we'd end up knocking our coffee to
the floor most of the time (Adolph, 1997). As total novices, babies haven't yet learned to
perform the lightning-quick calculations needed for good hand-eye coordination and
motor planning. Crawling and walking are even more complicated than reaching, because
they involve supporting the infant's weight, coordinating all four limbs, and somehow
keeping track of where she's heading.

FACTORS INFLUENCING MOTOR DEVELOPMENT. There's a wide range in the rate and
manner in which children achieve motor milestones. Some crawl and walk much earlier
than others, and a few skip the crawling stage entirely. These findings suggest that these skills
don't necessarily build on each other in a causal fashion, as the post hoc fallacy might lead us
to believe. What remains to be explained, then, is why all children acquire motor milestones
in the same order.

Physical maturation plays a key role in allowing children to becoming increasingly
steady and flexible in their movements. One explanation for this role is that motor patterns
are innately programmed and become activated at specific time points. Some motor
achievements, such as crawling and walking, also depend on the physical maturation of the
body, allowing children to acquire the necessary strength and coordination. Differences
among children in the rate at which motor development unfolds are also influenced by
their body weight. Heavier babies tend to achieve milestones more gradually than lighter
babies because they need to build up their muscles more before they can support their
weight (Thelen & Ulrich, 1982).

Cultural and parenting practices also play crucial roles in motor development
(Thelen, 1995). Considerable variability exists across cultures in the timing of developmental milestones. In Peru and China, infants are tightly swaddled in blankets that provide warmth and a sense of security, but that prevent free movement of the limbs (Li et al.,

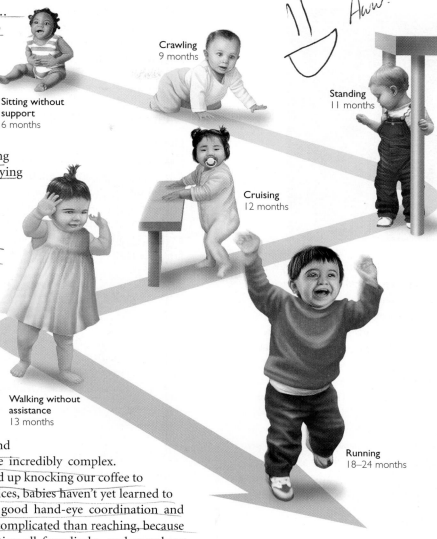

Sitting without support
6 months

Crawling
9 months

Standing
11 months

Cruising
12 months

Walking without assistance
13 months

Running
18–24 months

FIGURE 10.2 The Progression of Motor
Development. Different children typically
achieve major motor milestones in the same
order, although each milestone requires an
entirely new set of motor coordination skills.
For example, cruising, walking, and running look
similar but require very different muscle groups
and shifts in weight to accomplish movement.

motor behavior
bodily motion that occur as result of self-initiated force that moves the bones and muscles

The practices of swaddling and stretching infants can seem extreme to many Americans, but these are our cultural perspectives. Although cultural variability in these practices influences the rate of motor development, none of these early physical experiences result in long-term advantages or impairments.

FIGURE 10.3 Changes in Body Proportions over Development. This figure displays the proportional size of the head, torso, and limbs across the life span when scaled to the same overall height. The size of the head relative to the body decreases dramatically over the course of development, whereas the relative length of the legs increases dramatically.

2000). Swaddled babies tend to cry less and sleep more soundly, but prolonged swaddling over the first year of life slows down their motor development. In contrast, many African and West Indian mothers engage in a variety of stretching, massage, and strength-building exercises with their infants. This practice, which looks harmful to American eyes, speeds up infants' motor development (Hopkins & Westra, 1988).

■ Growth and Physical Development throughout Childhood

Our bodies continue to change dramatically through early childhood and adolescence. Careful inspection of an infant reveals that he has no apparent neck, a head almost half the size of his torso, and arms that don't even reach the top of his head. Over the course of childhood, different parts of the body grow at different rates and the ultimate proportions of the body are quite different than at birth. For example, the absolute size of the head continues to increase with development, but it grows at a slower pace than the torso or legs. As a result, an adolescent or young adult has a smaller head-size-to-body-size ratio than an infant (see **FIGURE 10.3**).

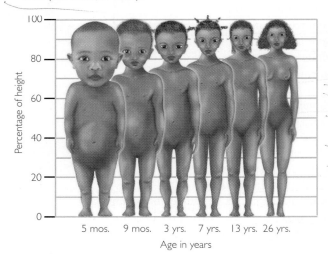

Throughout this text, we've sprinkled numerous examples of popular psychology wisdom that are false. Well, here's some common knowledge that's *true*: Growth spurts are real. Michael Hermanussen and his colleagues found "mini growth spurts" occurring every 30 to 55 days in children ages three to 16, followed by lulls during which growth is much slower (Hermanussen, 1998; Hermanussen et al., 1988). One study that measured three infants daily found that infants' growth occurs much more suddenly. They showed no growth at all for days at a time, followed by overnight increases of as much as an inch (Lampl, Veldhuis, & Johnson, 1992)! Nevertheless, other studies have failed to replicate this finding, leading some researchers to propose that growth is actually more gradual, with shifts in the *rate* of growth at various points in development (Heinrichs et al., 1995; Hermanussen & Geiger-Benoit, 1995). The evidence suggests that there are spurts, but that the periods between aren't marked by a total absence of growth.

replicability

CAN THE RESULTS BE DUPLICATED IN OTHER STUDIES?

■ Physical Maturation in Adolescence: The Power of Puberty

Our bodies don't reach full maturity until **adolescence**—the transitional period between childhood and adulthood commonly associated with the teenage years. In fact, adolescence is a time of profound physical changes. Many of these changes are hormonal. The pituitary gland stimulates physical growth and the reproductive system releases sex hormones—estrogens and androgens (see Chapters 3 and 11)—into the bloodstream, triggering growth and other physical changes. Many people think of androgens, such as testosterone, as male hormones and estrogens as female hormones. In fact, both types of hormones are present in both sexes in varying proportions. In boys, testosterone promotes increases in muscle tissue, growth of facial and body hair, and broadening of the shoulders. In girls, estrogens promote breast growth, uterus and vaginal maturation, hip broadening, and the onset of menstruation. Androgens in girls also induce physical growth and the growth of pubic hair (see **FIGURE 10.4**). Boys' muscle strength begins to exceed girls' in adolescence, and boys undergo a variety of changes in lung function and blood circulation. These changes result in greater average physical strength and en-

adolescence
the transition between childhood and adulthood commonly associated with the teenage years

puberty
the achievement of sexual maturation resulting in the potential to reproduce

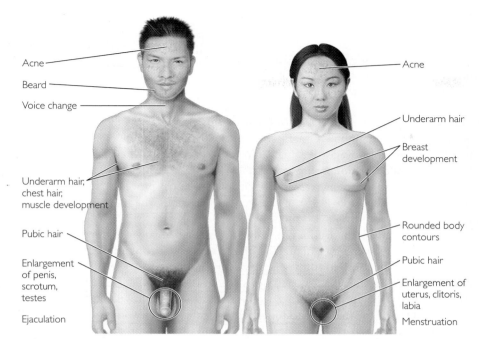

Acne

Beard

Voice change

Underarm hair; chest hair; muscle development

Pubic hair

Enlargement of penis, scrotum, testes

Ejaculation

Acne

Underarm hair

Breast development

Rounded body contours

Pubic hair

Enlargement of uterus, clitoris, labia

Menstruation

FIGURE 10.4   Physical and Sexual Maturation during the Preteen and Teenage Years. Physical and sexual maturation during the preteen and teenage years. Hormones result in rapid growth to full adult height. They also trigger changes in the reproductive system and in secondary sex characteristics, such as increased breast size, and broader hips in girls, and broader shoulders in boys.

In 2005, professional golfer Michelle Wie, who is 6 feet, 1 inch tall, became the first ever female golfer to qualify to play in a *men's* United States Golf Association tournament. Men's greater strength, on average, makes it challenging for women to compete at men's level in athletics.

FACTOID

The age of menarche has decreased over the past 100 years, moving from around 15 to around 13 years of age on average. This change is probably due primarily to better nutrition and health care (Tanner, 1998).

These seventh-grade students vary in physical height, but the girl (on the right) is the tallest of the bunch. Girls tend to mature earlier and more rapidly than boys. The girl is probably close to reaching her adult height, whereas the boys still have lots of growing to do.

durance in boys than in girls, explaining the divergence between boys' and girls' athletic ability that emerges in adolescence (Beunen & Malina, 1996; Malina & Bouchard, 1991).

A crucial component of hormonal changes in adolescence is **puberty** or *sexual maturation*—the attainment of physical potential for reproduction. Maturation includes changes in **primary sex characteristics**, which include the reproductive organs and genitals. It also includes changes in **secondary sex characteristics**, which include sex-differentiating characteristics that don't relate directly to reproduction, such as breast enlargement in girls, deepening voices in boys, and pubic hair in both genders. In girls, **menarche**—the onset of menstruation—tends not to begin until they've achieved full physical maturity. Menarche is the body's insurance plan against allowing girls to become pregnant before their bodies can carry an infant to term and give birth safely (Tanner, 1990). There's variability in when menstruation begins because girls reach full physical maturity at different ages.

Spermarche, the first ejaculation, is the comparable milestone in boys and occurs, on average, at around 13 years of age. Because boys need not be fully physically mature to bear children, spermarche isn't as closely tied to physical maturity as is menarche. In fact, boys often take a much longer time to mature fully than girls, which is why we'll often see sixth- and seventh-grade girls towering above their male counterparts. The first signs of sexual maturation in boys are enlargement of the testicles and penis, and growth of pubic hair (Graber, Petersen, & Brooks-Gunn, 1996). Later, boys begin to see signs of facial and body hair, and their voices deepen.

The timing of puberty in boys and girls is genetically influenced; identical twins tend to begin menstruating within a month of each other, whereas fraternal twins average about a year's difference in onset (Tanner, 1990). Still, a variety of environmental factors, some relating to physical health, affect when adolescents reach puberty. Adolescents from higher socioeconomic status households generally have access to better nutrition and health care, and reach puberty earlier as a result (Eveleth & Tanner, 1976). Girls from wealthier countries tend to begin menstruating earlier than those from poorer countries. Girls in Japan and the United States usually start menstruating between $12\frac{1}{2}$ and $13\frac{1}{2}$; years of age, whereas girls in the poorest regions of Africa don't usually start menstruating until between 14 and 17 years of age (Eveleth & Tanner, 1990).

primary sex characteristic
a physical feature such as the reproductive organs and genitals that distinguish the sexes

secondary sex characteristic
a sex-differentiating characteristic that doesn't relate directly to reproduction, such as breast enlargement in women and deepening voices in men

menarche
start of menstruation

spermarche
boys' first ejaculation

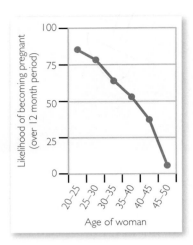

FIGURE 10.5 Fertility Peaks in the Twenties and Declines Thereafter. Women reach peak fertility between the ages of 20 and 25. The likelihood of a woman becoming pregnant drops dramatically between 30 and 50. This figure shows how the success of women in becoming pregnant during one year's time declines with age.

⊙▸ Simulate Aging and Changes in Physical Appearance on **mypsychlab.com**

■ Physical Development in Adulthood

After reaching full physical and sexual maturation during puberty, most of us reach our physical peak in the early twenties (Larsson, Grimby, & Karlsson, 1979; Lindle et al., 1997). Strength, coordination, speed of cognitive processing, and physical flexibility also attain their highest levels in early adulthood.

PHYSICAL CHANGES IN MIDDLE ADULTHOOD. Americans spend millions of dollars each year on products and gimmicks marketed to make them look younger as they attempt to stave off the inevitable ravages of aging. Unfortunately, some of the effects of age on physical appearance and functioning are inescapable facts of life. As we age, we experience a decline in muscle tone and an increase in body fat. Basic sensory processes, such as vision and hearing tend to decline, too. Even our sense of smell declines when we reach our sixties or seventies. ⊙▸ Simulate

Fertility in women declines sharply during their thirties and forties (see **FIGURE 10.5**), which has become a challenge for many women in contemporary society who opt to delay childbearing until they achieve career success. As a result, fertility treatments have been on the rise. The bad news is that the risks of serious birth defects in babies increase substantially among women who become pregnant in their thirties and forties. One of the major milestones of physical aging in women is **menopause**—the termination of menstruation, signaling the end of a woman's reproductive potential. Menopause is triggered by a reduction in estrogen, which can result in "hot flashes" marked by becoming incredibly hot, sweaty, and dry-mouthed. Many women report mood swings, sleep disruption, and temporary loss of sexual drive or pleasure.

Answers are located at the end of the text.

ANTI-AGING TREATMENTS   evaluating CLAIMS

Many of us are in search of a "fountain of youth"—a quick, easy, and affordable way to reduce or even reverse the signs of aging. A wide variety of products, such as creams and serums, purport to do exactly this, yet which of them—if any—are effective? Let's evaluate some of these claims, which are modeled after actual ads for anti-aging products.

"We are affiliated with *various medical schools* and our product is *used by thousands of physicians* nationwide."
This claim indicates that the program is affiliated with medical schools and used by physicians, creating a sense of legitimacy, but neglects to mention which medical schools they are. Moreover, this claim commits the argument from authority fallacy (see Chapter 1).

"We hold *exclusive worldwide rights* to a highly refined supplement and are making it *available to the public for a limited time* only so act now!"
Beware of ads that claim to have a scarcity of resources or promise you exclusive access to a product (see Chapter 13 for the "scarcity heuristic").

"See how natural looking and youthful our product will make you. We offer *no overnight miracles or quick-fixes*, but subtle results over time."
By explaining that the results may take time, this ad avoids exaggerated claims. It also doesn't promise any specific quantifiable results, only that your appearance will be more "natural looking" and "youthful."

"In a *randomized, double-blind human study* our product showed a significant effect on the signs of aging."
Randomization and double-blind condition assignment are crucial components of experimental research (see Chapter 2). What additional information would you need to know about this experiment to evaluate whether the product's claims are legitimate?

Interestingly, the prevalence of these effects varies across cultures. Although about 50 percent of North American women report hot flashes, less than 15 percent of Japanese women do (Lock, 1998). Perhaps because of these changes, a common misconception is that menopause is a period of heightened depression. In fact, research suggests that women in menopause are no more prone to depression than women at other phases of life (Busch, Zonderman, & Costa, 1994; Dennerstein, Lehert, & Guthrie, 2002).

Men experience nothing equivalent to menopause; they can continue to reproduce well into old age. Still, there's a gradual decline in sperm production and testosterone levels with age, and maintaining an erection and achieving ejaculation can become a challenge—as the popularity of Viagra and Cialis television ads targeted toward elderly males attests (see Chapter 11). Like older women, older men are at heightened risk for having children with developmental disorders. Despite changes in the reproductive equipment of aging adults, most senior citizens experience healthy sex drives (see Chapter 11).

CHANGES IN AGILITY AND PHYSICAL COORDINATION WITH AGE. There are individual and task-specific differences in the effects of aging on motor coordination. Complex tasks show greater effects of age than simpler ones (Luchies et al., 2002; Welford, 1977); simple motor tasks, such as tapping a finger to a beat, show relatively small declines (Ruff & Parker, 1993). Elderly adults also become less flexible in learning new motor skills, like learning to drive a new car (Guan & Wade, 2000).

Some individuals display greater age-related declines than others. Strength training and increased physical activity may minimize some of these declines and increase life span (Fiatarone et al., 1990; Frontera et al., 1988). Many of the changes we typically associate with aging are actually due to diseases that are correlated with age, like heart disease and arthritis. Although chronological age and physical health are correlated, the great variability in how people age refutes the popular notion that old age invariably produces physical decline. 👁 Watch

Research suggests that physical activity and strength training are valuable in minimizing age-related declines.

👁 **Watch** an interview with a Centenarian on **mypsychlab.com**

◀ **falsifiability**
CAN THE CLAIM BE DISPROVED?

✓ **Study** and **Review** on **mypsychlab.com**

---

assess your knowledge   **FACT OR FICTION?**

1. A fetus's brain produces only as many neurons as it will need as an infant. **True / False**

2. Fetuses exposed to teratogens, such as cigarette smoke from their mothers, tend to be low-birth-weight infants at birth. **True / False**

3. Children tend to achieve motor milestones in the same order even though the age of acquisition varies within and across cultures. **True / False**

4. *Testosterone* Androgens cause changes in boys at puberty, whereas estrogens cause changes in girls. **True / False**

5. Elderly people's hearing, sight, and other senses decline, but their ability to learn new motor skills are still intact. **True / False**
   decline

Answers: 1. F (p. 365); 2. T (p. 366); 3. T (p. 367); 4. F (p. 368); 5. F (p. 371)

THE DEVELOPING MIND: COGNITIVE DEVELOPMENT

10.7 Understand major theories of how children's thinking develops.

10.8 Explain how children acquire knowledge in important cognitive domains.

10.9 Describe how attitudes toward knowledge change during adolescence.

Cognitive development—how we acquire the ability to learn, think, communicate, and remember over time—explains the mystery of how we come to understand our worlds. Yet only relatively recently have psychologists constructed systematic theories of cognitive development across the life span.

menopause
the termination of menstruation, marking the end of a woman's reproductive potential

cognitive development
study of how children acquire the ability to learn, think, reason, communicate, and remember

Jean Piaget was the first to develop a comprehensive theory of cognitive development. His ideas rested on the assumption that children's thinking was not just an immature form of adult thinking but was fundamentally different from that of adults.

Equilibration = balance between experience of the world and thoughts about the world.

Piaget Day

assimilation
Piagetian process of absorbing new experience into current knowledge structures

accommodation
Piagetian process of altering a belief to make it more compatible with experience

sensorimotor stage
stage in Piaget's theory characterized by a focus on the here and now without the ability to represent experiences mentally

object permanence
the understanding that objects continue to exist even when out of view

preoperational stage
stage in Piaget's theory characterized by the ability to construct mental representations of experience, but not yet perform operations on them

■ Theories of Cognitive Development

Psychologists have generated a variety of theoretical perspectives to explain how our thinking develops. Cognitive developmental theories differ in three core ways:

1. Some propose *stagelike* changes in understanding (sudden spurts in knowledge followed by periods of stability), others more *continuous* (gradual, incremental) changes in understanding.

2. Some adopt a *domain-general* account of development, others a *domain-specific* account. The former propose cross-cutting changes in children's cognitive skills that affect most or all areas of cognitive function at once (domain-general), the latter propose that children's cognitive skills develop independently and at different rates across different domains, such as reasoning, language, and counting (domain-specific).

3. Cognitive developmental models differ in their views of the principal source of learning. Some models emphasize physical experience, others social interaction, and still others biological maturation.

PIAGET: HOW CHILDREN CONSTRUCT THEIR WORLDS. The pioneering Swiss psychologist Jean Piaget (1896–1980) was the first to present a comprehensive account of cognitive development. He attempted to identify the stages that children pass through on their way to adultlike thinking. Piaget's theory led to the formation of cognitive development as a distinct discipline, and for decades most research in this field focused on substantiating—or more recently, refuting—his claims.

Perhaps Piaget's greatest contribution was his insight that children aren't miniature adults. He showed that children's understanding of the world differs fundamentally from adults', but is perfectly rational given their limited experience with the world. For example, children often believe that their teachers live at school, a reasonable assumption given that's the only place they've seen their teachers. Piaget also altered our view of children's learning by demonstrating that children aren't passive observers of their worlds, but rather active learners who seek information and observe the consequences of their actions.

Piaget was a *stage theorist*. He believed that children's development is marked by radical reorganizations of thinking at specific transition points—stages—followed by periods during which their understanding of the world stabilizes. He also believed that the end point of cognitive development is achieving the ability to reason logically about hypothetical problems. As we'll soon see, each stage is characterized by a certain level of abstract reasoning capacity, with the ability to think beyond the here and now increasing at each stage. Piaget's stages are domain-general, slicing across all areas of cognitive capacity. Thus, a child capable of a certain level of abstract reasoning in mathematics can also achieve this level in a spatial problem-solving task.

Piaget proposed that cognitive change is marked by *equilibration:* maintaining a balance between our experience of the world and our thoughts about it. Children, he said, are motivated to match their thinking about the world with their observations. When the child experiences something new, she checks whether that experience fits with her *schema* (see Chapter 8), her understanding of and expectations about how the world works. If the information is inconsistent, as when a child has a schema of the world as flat but learns in school that the earth is round, something must give way. Piaget suggested that children use two processes—assimilation and accommodation—to keep their thinking about the world in tune with their experiences.

Assimilation and Accommodation. The process of absorbing new experience into current schemas is **assimilation**. If a child who believes the earth is flat (see **FIGURE 10.6a**) learns that the earth is round, she might assimilate this knowledge into her schema by picturing a flat disk, like a coin (see **FIGURE 10.6b**). This adjustment allows her to absorb this fact without changing her belief that the earth is flat. Children use assimilation to acquire new knowledge within a stage. During assimilation, the child's cognitive skills and worldviews remain unchanged, so she reinterprets new experiences to fit into what she already knows.

The assimilation process can continue for only so long. Eventually, the child can no longer reconcile what she believes with what she experiences. A child confronted with a globe will have a difficult time assimilating this information into her schema that the earth is flat. When a child can no longer assimilate experiences into her existing knowledge structures, something has to budge. She's forced to engage in accommodation.

Accommodation is the altering of a schema to make it more compatible with experience. Accommodation drives stage change by forcing children to enter a new way of looking at the world, in this case, by changing their conception from flat to round (see **FIGURE 10.6c**). This process of assimilating and accommodating in tandem ensures a state of harmony between the world and mind of the child—equilibration.

Piaget's Stages of Development. Piaget identified four stages, each marked by a specific way of looking at the world and a specific set of cognitive limitations (see **TABLE 10.2**).

1. **Sensorimotor stage:** From birth to about two years, the **sensorimotor stage** is marked by a focus on the here and now. Children's main sources of knowledge, thinking, and experience are their physical interactions with the world. They acquire all information through perceiving information from the world and observing the physical consequences of their actions. The major milestone of this stage, which forces children to accommodate and enter a new stage, is *mental representation*—the ability to think about things that are absent from immediate surroundings, such as remembering previously encountered objects. Children in this stage lack **object permanence**, the understanding that objects continue to exist even when out of view. A ball that disappears behind the television is, for all intents and purposes, gone. For them, it's "out of sight, out of mind." *Deferred imitation,* the ability to perform an action observed earlier, is also absent from the sensorimotor stage. Both object permanence and deferred imitation require children to think beyond the here and now.

2. **Preoperational stage:** Piaget proposed that from two until about seven years, children pass through the **preoperational stage**, marked by an ability to construct mental representations of experience. Children in this stage can use such symbols as language, drawings, and objects as representations of ideas. When a child holds a banana and pretends it's a phone, he's displaying symbolic behavior. He has a mental representation that differs from his physical experience. Similarly, playing house in which one child pretends to be the mommy, one the daddy, and one the baby demonstrates an ability to assume imaginary roles that differ from actual roles.

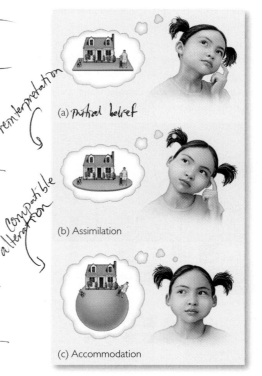

(a) initial belief

(b) Assimilation

(c) Accommodation

FIGURE 10.6 An Example of Assimilation and Accommodation in Action. A child's initial belief that the earth is flat (a) is adjusted through assimilation (b) when she learns the earth is round. Once her assimilated belief no longer fits with her experience, her belief undergoes accommodation (c).

? This child appears to have forgotten the blocks continue to exist after they've been hidden from view. What Piagetian concept does this photograph illustrate? (See answer upside down at bottom of page.)

Answer: Object permanence

TABLE 10.2 Descriptions of the Four Stages of Cognitive Development in Piaget's Theory.

STAGE	TYPICAL AGES	DESCRIPTION
Sensorimotor	Birth to 2 years	No thought beyond immediate physical experiences
Preoperational	2 to 7 years	Able to think beyond the here and now, but egocentric and unable to perform mental transformations
Concrete Operations	7 to 11 years	Able to perform mental transformations but only on concrete physical objects
Formal Operations	11 years to adulthood	Able to perform hypothetical and abstract reasoning

FIGURE 10.7 Piaget's Three Mountain Task. Piaget's three mountain task requires children to look at a display from one perspective (View 1) and infer what someone would see if viewing the mountains from a different perspective, such as View 2. Piaget argued that egocentric reasoning in the preoperational stage prevents children from succeeding at this task.

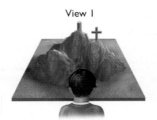
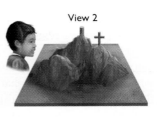

View 1 View 2

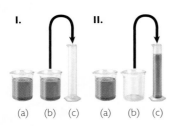

Which has more, row A or row B, or do they both have the same?

Now which has more, row A or row B, or do they both have the same?

FIGURE 10.8 Piaget's Conservation Tasks. Piaget's conservation tasks ask the child to examine two equal amounts and then watch as the researcher manipulates one of the two amounts in some way. The researcher then asks the child to compare the two quantities. The conservation of liquid task is on the top, the conservation of number task on the bottom. To succeed at the conservation task, children need to say that the amounts remain the same even though they appear unequal. (*Source:* Reprinted with permission from *Human Development*, 7e, by Diane E. Papalia et al. © 1998 The McGraw-Hill Companies, Inc.)

egocentrism
inability to see the world from others' perspectives

conservation
Piagetian task requiring children to understand that despite a transformation in the physical presentation of an amount, the amount remains the same

concrete operations stage
stage in Piaget's theory characterized by the ability to perform mental operations on physical events only

Although the preoperational stage witnesses clear advances in thinking, Piaget believed children in this stage were hampered by **egocentrism**—an inability to see the world from others' point of view (see **FIGURE 10.7**). The preoperational stage is called "preoperational" because of another limitation, the inability to perform mental operations. Although preoperational children have mental representations, they can't perform mental transformations ("operations") on them. For example, they can generate a mental image of a vase on a table if the vase isn't there. But they can't imagine what would happen to the vase if someone knocked it off the table. Piaget developed a set of **conservation** tasks like those shown in **FIGURE 10.8** to test children's ability to perform mental operations. These tasks ask children to determine whether a certain amount will be "conserved"—stay the same—following a physical transformation. Preoperational children routinely fail conservation tasks that older children find to be a breeze.

3. **Concrete operational stage:** Between seven and 11 years old, children enter the **concrete operations stage**, characterized by the ability to perform mental operations, but only for actual physical events. Children in this stage can now pass conservation tasks. They can also perform organizational tasks that require mental operations on physical objects, like sorting coins by size or setting up a battle scene with toy soldiers. But they're still poor at performing mental operations in abstract or hypothetical situations. They need physical experience as an anchor to which they can tether their mental operations.

4. **Formal operations stage:** Piaget's fourth and final stage, which he believed didn't emerge until adolescence, is the **formal operations stage**. It's then that children can perform what Piaget regarded as the most sophisticated type of thinking: hypothetical reasoning beyond the here and now, as in the pendulum task shown in **FIGURE 10.9**. This task requires children to experiment systematically with hypotheses and explain outcomes. Children at this stage can understand logical concepts, such as if–then statements ("If I'm late for school, I'll get sent to the principal's office") and either–or statements ("Mom says I can either go to the game tonight or go to the sleepover tomorrow night."). They can also begin to think about abstract questions, like the meaning of life.

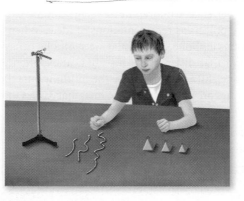

FIGURE 10.9 Pendulum Task. Piaget's pendulum task requires children to answer the question: "What makes a pendulum swing faster or slower?" Children have the opportunity to construct a pendulum using longer and shorter strings with heavier and lighter weights. Children in the formal operations stage can systematically manipulate various combinations of weights and lengths to observe how they influenced the speed of the swing.

Pros and Cons of Piaget's Theory. Piaget's theory was a significant landmark in psychology, as it helped us understand how children's thinking evolves into more adultlike thinking. Nevertheless, his theory turned out to be inaccurate in several ways. For example, much of development is more continuous than stagelike (Flavell, 1992; Klahr & MacWhinney, 1998; Siegler, 1995). Developmental change is also less general than Piaget proposed. In fact, Piaget was aware that development didn't always result in the cross-cutting changes he'd proposed. He used the term *horizontal décalage* to refer to cases in which a child is more advanced in one cognitive domain than another. As some critics have noted (Fischer, 1978), the concept of horizontal décalage renders Piaget's claim that development proceeds in domain-general stages difficult to falsify. Imagine a child performing at a preoperational level on one task and at a concrete operational level on another, a frequent occurrence. In response, a follower of Piaget could simply invoke horizontal décalage rather than acknowledge that this inconsistency calls into question the idea of domain-general stages.

Another criticism of Piaget's theory is that some phenomena he observed appeared to be at least partly a product of task demands. He often relied on children's ability to reflect and report on their reasoning processes. As a result, he probably underestimated children's underlying competence. Investigators have found it difficult to replicate the developmental progression he identified using tasks that are less dependent on language than those he used.

Piaget's methodologies may also have been culturally biased in that they elicited more sophisticated responses from children in Westernized societies with formal education than from those in non-Westernized societies. Indeed, non-Westernized children often reveal sophisticated insights when interviewed in a more culturally sensitive manner (Cole, 1990; Gellatly, 1987; Luria, 1976; Rogoff & Chavajay, 1995). Meanwhile, even in Western societies, a significant proportion of adolescents and even adults fail some formal operational tasks (Byrnes, 1988; Kuhn et al., 1995), suggesting that Piaget may have been overly optimistic about the typical course of cognitive development. Perhaps Piaget based his conclusions on a particularly educated sample that skewed his estimates of the typical developmental trajectory. Piaget's observations themselves may also have been biased because many were based on tests of his own three children.

Despite these shortcomings, Piaget justifiably remains a towering figure in the field of cognitive development (Lourenco & Machado, 1996). As a result of his legacy, psychologists today have reconceptualized cognitive development by:

1. viewing children as different in kind rather than degree from adults;

2. characterizing learning as an active rather than passive process; and

3. exploring general cognitive processes that may cut across multiple domains of knowledge, thereby accounting for cognitive development in terms of fewer—and more parsimonious—underlying processes.

VYGOTSKY: SOCIAL AND CULTURAL INFLUENCES ON LEARNING. At around the same time that Piaget was developing his theory, Russian researcher Lev Vygotsky (1896–1936) was developing a different but equally comprehensive theory of cognitive development.

Vygotsky was particularly interested in how social and cultural factors influence learning. He noted that parents and other caretakers tend to structure the learning environment for children in ways that guide them to behave as if they've learned something before they have. This process has come to be

> **formal operations stage**
> stage in Piaget's theory characterized by the ability to perform hypothetical reasoning beyond the here and now

◄ **falsifiability**

CAN THE CLAIM BE DISPROVED?

horizontal décalage = Piaget's acceptance that a child is more advanced in one cognitive domain than another.

◄ **replicability**

CAN THE RESULTS BE DUPLICATED IN OTHER STUDIES?

◄ **occam's razor**

DOES A SIMPLER EXPLANATION FIT THE DATA JUST AS WELL?

Lev Vyogotsky (pictured here with his daughter) developed a theory of cognitive development that emphasized social and cultural information as the key sources of learning. Although Vygotsky's scholarly career was shortened by an early death (he died of tuberculosis at age 37), his theory is still extremely influential.

The term *scaffolding* is used to refer to the way parents structure the learning environment for children. Here, the father is instructing the child how to fit the shape onto a peg, but allowing the child to insert the shape himself.

◉⎯**Watch** the Zone of Proximal Development: Cognitive on **mypsychlab.com**

known as **scaffolding**, a term borrowed from building construction (Wood, Bruner, & Ross, 1976). Just as builders provide external scaffolds for support while a building is under construction, parents provide a structure to aid their children. Over time, parents gradually remove structure as children become better able to complete tasks on their own, much like training wheels on a bicycle.

One of Vygotsky's most influential notions was developmental readiness for learning. He identified the **zone of proximal development** as the phase when children are receptive to learning a new skill but aren't yet successful at it. He suggested that for any given skill, children move from a phase when they can't learn it, even with assistance, to the zone of proximal development, during which they're ready to make use of scaffolding. In his view, children gradually learn to perform a task independently, but require guidance when getting started. Vygotsky also believed that different children can acquire skills and master tasks at different rates. For him, there were no domain-general stages. ◉⎯|Watch

Vygotsky's work has had a substantial impact on European, British, and American researchers and remains influential today, especially in educational settings, where guided learning and peer collaboration are popular (Jaramillo, 1996, Rogoff, 1995; Tomasello, 2008). Whereas Piaget emphasized physical interaction with the world as the primary source of learning, Vygotsky emphasized social interaction.

CONTEMPORARY THEORIES OF COGNITIVE DEVELOPMENT. Theoretical accounts today are much more diverse than when the field of cognitive development got off the ground, and few are strictly Piagetian or Vygotskian. Still, we can trace the roots of each theory to one of these two theorists.

General Cognitive Accounts. Several modern theories resemble Piaget's theories in that they emphasize general cognitive abilities and acquired rather than innate knowledge (Bloom, 2000; Elman, 2005). Contemporary theorists share Piaget's commitment to general cognitive processes and experience-based learning. Nevertheless, they differ from Piaget in regarding learning as gradual rather than stagelike.

Sociocultural Accounts. These theories emphasize the social context and the ways in which interactions with caretakers and other children guide children's understanding of the world (Rogoff, 1998; Tomasello, 2000). Some sociocultural theorists emphasize experience-based learning, others innate knowledge. But along with Vygotsky, they share a focus on the child's interaction with the social world as the primary source of development.

Modular Accounts. Like Vygotsky's theory, this class of theories emphasizes the idea of domain-specific learning, that is, separate spheres of knowledge in different domains (Carey, 1985; Waxman & Booth, 2001). For example, the knowledge base for understanding language may be independent of the ability to reason about space, with no overlapping cognitive skills between them.

■ Cognitive Landmarks of Early Development

We've already learned about some of the major cognitive accomplishments within the realms of perception (Chapter 4), memory (Chapter 7), and language (Chapter 8). But children must attain a variety of other cognitive skills to make sense of their worlds. Here, we'll review some of the highlights.

PHYSICAL REASONING: FIGURING OUT WHICH WAY IS UP. To understand their physical worlds, children must learn to reason about them. They need to learn that objects are solid, they fall when dropped, and one object can disappear behind another and reappear on the other side. Adults take all of these concepts for granted, but they aren't obvious to novice experiencers of the world.

scaffolding
Vygotskian learning mechanism in which parents provide initial assistance in children's learning but gradually remove structure as children become more competent

zone of proximal development
phase of learning during which children can benefit from instruction

psychomythology

THE MOZART EFFECT, BABY EINSTEIN, AND CREATING "SUPERBABIES"

For years, parents have yearned for a quick and easy educational method to boost their infants' intelligence. After all, in today's cutthroat world, what parents wouldn't want to place their child at a competitive advantage? To get a jump-start, of course, parents must begin early, ideally soon after birth. This seemingly far-fetched hope that parents can turn their babies into miniature geniuses turned into apparent reality in 1993 with the publication of an article in the prestigious journal *Nature*. That paper reported that college students who listened to about 10 minutes of a Mozart piano sonata showed a significant improvement on a spatial reasoning task compared with a group of students who listened to a relaxation tape (Rauscher, Shaw, & Ky, 1993). The *Mozart Effect*—the supposed enhancement in intelligence after listening to classical music (Campbell, 1997)—was born.

The 1993 finding didn't say anything about long-term enhancement of spatial ability, let alone intelligence in general. It applied only to a task administered almost immediately after listening to Mozart's music. And the findings were based entirely on college students. But this didn't stop the popular press or toy companies from taking the Mozart Effect ball and running with it. Companies soon marketed scores of Mozart Effect CDs and cassettes targeted toward babies, featuring claims that listening to the music of Mozart and other composers boosts infant intelligence. In 1998, then Georgia Governor Zell Miller added $105,000 to the state budget to allow each newborn in Georgia to receive a free Mozart CD or cassette.

Miller's decision was premature. In fact, researchers had a devil of a time replicating the Mozart Effect. Many couldn't find the effect at all, and those who did discovered that it was trivial in magnitude (two IQ points or less) and of short duration (an hour or less; Chabris, 1999; Steele, Bass, & Crook, 1999). Zell Miller (1999) urged advocates of the Mozart Effect to ignore these negative findings, imploring them not "to be misled or discouraged by some academics debunking other academics." But this is precisely how science works at its best: by trying to falsify claims made by other investigators.

Later researchers helped to explain the Mozart Effect. The results of one study suggested that the effect may be due to the greater emotional arousal produced by listening to Mozart relative to either other composers or silence (Thompson, Schellenberg, & Husain, 2001). Another researcher found that listening to Mozart was no better for improving spatial ability than listening to a passage from a scary story. These findings suggest that a more parsimonious explanation for the Mozart Effect is short-term arousal. Anything that boosts alertness is likely to increase performance on mentally demanding tasks, but it's unlikely to produce long-term effects on spatial ability or, for that matter, overall intelligence (Gray & Della Sala, 2007). Our advice: It's a wonderful idea to expose infants and children to great music. But don't expect it to turn babies into little geniuses.

The Mozart Effect is only one example of a research finding being overhyped to capitalize on parents' desires to boost their baby's intellect. In the 1980s, thousands of parents bombarded their newborn infants with foreign languages and advanced math in an effort to create "superbabies" (Clarke-Stewart, 1998). Alleged intelligence-improving products such as "Baby Einstein" toys and videos are a $100-million-a-year industry (Minow, 2005; Quart, 2006). Yet there's no evidence that these products work, either. In fact, research suggests that babies learn less from videos than from playing actively for the same time period (Anderson & Pempek, 2005; Zimmerman, Christakis, & Meltzoff, 2008).

Claims for the Mozart Effect have contributed to a huge industry of products for babies and young children, yet the scientific evidence for this effect is surprisingly weak.

◀ replicability

CAN THE RESULTS BE DUPLICATED IN OTHER STUDIES?

◀ falsifiability

CAN THE CLAIM BE DISPROVED?

◀ occam's razor

DOES A SIMPLER EXPLANATION FIT THE DATA JUST AS WELL?

FIGURE 10.10 Habituation Event. If infants understand that the box continues to exist even when it's out of sight, they should be surprised to see the platform continue to rotate in a way that seems to pass through the box. Contrary to Piaget's claims about the age of object permanence, infants as young as four months look longer at the full rotation event, suggesting that they're surprised when the platform appears to rotate through the box. (*Source:* Baillargeon, Spelke, & Wasserman, 1985)

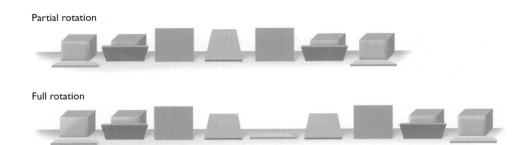

Partial rotation

Full rotation

Piaget proposed that children don't master object permanence until between eight and 12 months of age, because children younger than eight months old don't search for an object hidden under a cloth. Nevertheless, Renee Baillargeon (1987) showed that by five months and possibly younger, infants display an understanding of object permanence if given a task that doesn't require a physically coordinated search for the object (see **FIGURE 10.10**). Baillargeon based her conclusions on studies of how long infants look at displays that are either consistent or inconsistent with object permanence. Her findings suggest that Piaget underestimated when children achieve object permanence, because his tasks require not only an understanding of object permanence, but also an ability to plan and perform a physical search for the hidden toy. When Baillargeon eliminated these task demands, an earlier mastery of object permanence emerged.

Infants possess a basic understanding of some other aspects of how physical objects behave, a set of beliefs called *naive physics*. For example, they know that objects that are unsupported should fall (Spelke, 1994). This knowledge becomes more refined with experience (see **FIGURE 10.11**) (Baillargeon & Hanko-Summers, 1990; Needham & Baillargeon, 1993). In particular, as we age we become less reliant on intuitions and more reliant on evidence of how things actually work. Yet as Michael McCloskey (1983) showed, even many adults hold inaccurate ideas about naive physics, suggesting that we don't totally outgrow certain scientific misconceptions (Bloom & Weisberg, 2007) (see **FIGURE 10.12**).

CONCEPTS AND CATEGORIES: CLASSIFYING THE WORLD. One of the most basic cognitive accomplishments is learning to categorize objects by kind. Children learn to recognize dogs even though they come in all shapes, sizes, and colors. They also learn to distinguish dogs from cats, horses, and goats. Categorization is crucial because it frees us from having to explore every object to find out what it is and does (see Chapter 8). Imagine if every time a baby were given a new bottle, she had to discover through trial and error what it was. Kids, not to mention adults, wouldn't get very far without categories.

ruling out rival hypotheses

HAVE IMPORTANT ALTERNATIVE EXPLANATIONS FOR THE FINDINGS BEEN EXCLUDED?

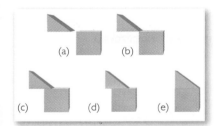

(a) (b)
(c) (d) (e)

FIGURE 10.11 Children Learn Gradually That Unsupported Objects Will Fall. As early as four and a half months, infants expect objects that are completely unsupported, as in (a), to fall and objects that are completely supported, as in (e), not to fall. An understanding of how much support must be present to prevent an object from falling develops over time. Early on, infants expect that any contact with a support surface will prevent the object from falling, as in (b), (c), and (d). With experience, infants learn to expect that only those in (d) and (e), in which the majority of the weight is on the support surface, won't fall.

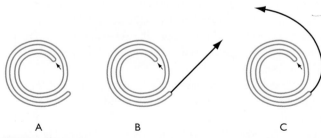

A   B   C

FIGURE 10.12 Naive Physics. Michael McCloskey (1983) posed the following problem to undergraduates:
Imagine a ball enters a tube, as shown in drawing A. **Which drawing illustrates how it will exit from the tube, B or C?** (See answer upside down on left.) If you got this one wrong, don't feel bad, because many college students do, too, committing the same error that many school-age children do. This finding suggests that even as adults we often don't fully outgrow mistaken notions of how the world works (Bloom & Weisberg, 2007).

Answer: B. Most people find C more intuitive, as this answer suggests that objects will continue in the same path of motion in which they began.

Even infants can categorize. When shown a series of bird pictures, infants eventually get bored with them and look away, but show fresh interest when shown a picture of a dinosaur. This finding implies that they've categorized birds as all of the same kind and therefore no longer new, but the dinosaur as belonging to a different category (Quinn & Eimas, 1996). Over the course of development, conceptual knowledge becomes richer, more detailed, and more flexible (Nelson, 1977). Children learn how objects are thematically related to each other, such as a dog and a bone being related because dogs eat bones (Nelson, 1977). They also learn more about aspects of categories that explain how members of categories connect, such as that fruits both taste sweet and grow on trees. This increased conceptual knowledge about categories assists them in reasoning about the world (see Chapter 8).

Children acquire concepts of events as well as objects. For example, young children rapidly learn what's likely to occur during routine events such as birthday parties, doctors' office visits, and trips to fast-food restaurants. Children depend so heavily on their expectations of events that they'll sometimes incorrectly recall a typical feature of an event that didn't occur (Fivush & Hudson, 1990; Nelson & Hudson, 1988; see Chapter 7).

SELF-CONCEPT AND THE CONCEPT OF "OTHER": WHO WE ARE, AND WHO WE AREN'T. Developing a sense of self as different from others is critical for children's development. Their ability to understand themselves as possessing unique identities unfolds gradually during the toddler and preschool years. But even by three months of age, infants possess some sense of self as distinct from others. Babies at this age who view videos of themselves side by side with another baby prefer to look at the image of the other baby (Bahrick, Moss, & Fadil, 1996; Rochat, 2001), suggesting that they recognize the other baby as different from themselves. Indeed, infants who see a live-action video of only their legs side by side with a recording of another infant's legs still prefer to watch the video of the other baby's legs, even if both sets of legs are dressed identically. This finding reveals that babies aren't just demonstrating a novelty preference for the other baby's face because they've seen their own face before in the mirror or in photographs.

Infants who view a video image of their own legs side by side with a videotape of another infant's legs will look longer at the video of the other baby. This finding suggests infants recognize the correspondence between the video images and their own bodies (Bahrick & Watson, 1985) and find their own actions less interesting to watch.

◄ **ruling out rival hypotheses**

HAVE IMPORTANT ALTERNATIVE EXPLANATIONS FOR THE FINDINGS BEEN EXCLUDED?

As early as their first birthdays, children can recognize their images in a mirror (Amsterdam, 1972; Priel & deSchonen, 1986; see Chapter 7). By two years, they can recognize pictures of themselves and refer to themselves by name (Lewis & Brooks-Gunn, 1979). These accomplishments appear to be tied to development in a specific brain region, namely, the junction of the left temporal and parietal lobes (Lewis & Carmody, 2008). Well before their first birthdays, children begin to understand that people are a distinct category. They smile more at people than at objects (Ellsworth, Muir, & Hains, 1993) and imitate people's behaviors more often than the same actions displayed by moving objects (Legerstee, 1991). Imitation implies that children can translate someone else's actions into their own and grasp a correspondence between self and other.

A further milestone is children's ability to understand that others' perspectives can differ from theirs—a capacity called **theory of mind** (Premack & Woodruff, 1978). Theory of mind refers to children's ability to reason about what other people believe. (Note that according to Chapter 1, this "theory" isn't really a theory!) The big challenge for children on this front is to realize that "other people may not know what I know." In some sense, children know this fact by the time they're one or two years old, because they ask their parents questions like "Where's Daddy?" and "What's this?" revealing that they expect parents to know things they don't. Yet it's particularly challenging for children to realize that sometimes *they* know things that others don't.

A classic test of theory of mind is the *false-belief task* (Birch & Bloom, 2007; Wimmer & Perner, 1983), which tests children's ability to understand that someone else believes something they know to be wrong. In this task, children hear a story (often accompanied by

theory of mind
ability to reason about what other people know or believe

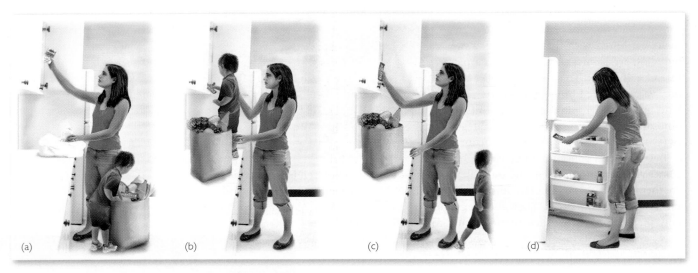

(a)　(b)　(c)　(d)

FIGURE 10.13 The False-Belief Task. In the false-belief task, the child participant knows something about which someone else is unaware. In this scenario, the child learns that Joey in the story believes the candy bar is in the cabinet. But because she's heard the whole story, the child knows the candy bar is really in the refrigerator. When asked where Joey thinks the candy is, will the child respond with her own knowledge of the true location, or will she realize that Joey is unaware of this change?

illustrations like those in **FIGURE 10.13**) about a child who stores a special treat in one place, but a third party (such as the child's mother), unbeknownst to the child, moves the treat to another place. Researchers then ask the child where the child in the story will look for the treat when he returns. Children who pass this task understand that although they themselves know where the treat is actually hidden, the child in the story holds an incorrect belief about the treat's location. Those who fail the task believe that if they know where the treat is, the child in the story must know as well.

Children typically don't succeed at this task until around age four or five. Yet how early children succeed on false-belief tasks varies depending on seemingly minor variations in the task (Wellman, Cross, & Watson, 2001). If researchers arrange the false-belief task so that it's more of a real-world situation and less of a story, most children can pass it. Also, if researchers tell children the reason for the change was to "trick" someone, they're more successful at an earlier age. Thus, children's failure on the classic false-belief task before age four may be due to aspects of the task rather than their inadequate understanding of others' knowledge. Still, it's clear that the ability to understand others' perspectives increases with age.

ruling out rival hypotheses ▷

HAVE IMPORTANT ALTERNATIVE EXPLANATIONS FOR THE FINDINGS BEEN EXCLUDED?

NUMBERS AND MATHEMATICS: WHAT COUNTS. Counting and math are relatively recent achievements in human history. Humans developed the first counting system only a few thousand years ago. Unlike many cognitive skills that children acquire, counting and mathematics don't inevitably develop. In a few nonindustrialized cultures such as the Pirahã, a tribe in Brazil, conventional counting and mathematics appear not to exist (Gordon, 2004).

Learning to count is a lot more complex than it seems. Of course, many children learn to "count to ten" at a very early age, reciting "1-2-3-4-5-6-7-8-9-10" in rapid succession and waiting for applause to follow. But children must also learn a variety of more complex aspects of number such as that (1) numbers are about amount, (2) number words refer to specific quantities (and not just "a bunch" or "a few"), and (3) numbers are ordered from smallest to largest in quantity (Gelman & Gallistel, 1978). Children must also master the idea that two elephants is the same number as two grains of rice—that the *size* of entities isn't relevant to quantity. Kelly Mix and her colleagues showed that this insight is extremely difficult for children (Mix, 1999; Mix,

Members of the Pirahã culture don't have a system for calculating precise amounts.

Huttenlocher, & Levine, 1996). Children find it easier to match two sets of the same quantity when the objects to be counted closely resemble each other than when they don't (see **FIGURE 10.14**). When similarity among the objects is high, children master this task at three years of age, but when the objects look different, they don't succeed until three and a half years. And when they have to match the quantity of a visual set with sets of sounds, they don't succeed until after age four.

Counting and other mathematical skills in preschool- and school-aged children develop at different rates across cultures. Cross-cultural differences in how parents and teachers introduce counting to children seem to account at least in part for these differences. Differences in how the linguistic counting systems are structured also play a role. For example, the English word "twelve" doesn't convey any information about what quantity it represents, whereas in Chinese, it's literally translated as "one ten, two," which appears to help children understand what quantity it represents (Gladwell, 2009; Miller et al., 1995).

■ Cognitive Changes in Adolescence

As Piaget noted, it's not until adolescence that we achieve our most abstract levels of reasoning ability. There are many reasons why cognitive development continues well into the teenage years. Part of the story here is about brain development, and part is about the kinds of problems, opportunities, and experiences we only encounter for the very first time during adolescence.

Although most brain maturation occurs prenatally and in the first few years of life, the frontal lobes don't mature fully until late adolescence or early adulthood (Casey et al., 2000; Johnson, 1998). As we discovered in Chapter 3, the frontal lobes are largely responsible for planning, decision making, and impulse control. The fact that the frontal lobes are still maturing during adolescence may explain some of the impulsive behaviors, like skateboarding down a steep incline, for which teens are notorious (Weinberger, Elvevag, & Giedd, 2005). Even on the simplest tasks, such as inhibiting the impulse to look at a flashing light, teens have a more difficult time and require more brain processing than do adults (Luna & Sweeney, 2004). In addition, during adolescence, limbic structures of the brain (see Chapter 3) involved in social rewards become more active, probably rendering teens susceptible to deviant peer group influences, such as drug use and delinquency (Steinberg, 2007).

Adolescents routinely encounter new adultlike opportunities to engage in potentially harmful activities, but their brains aren't ready to make well-reasoned decisions. For example, they're often faced with making decisions such as whether to have sex, engage in vandalism, or drive drunk. Adolescents must negotiate these choices without a "full deck" of decision-making cards. Nevertheless, there's debate over whether we can blame teen behavioral problems entirely on the "teen brain." Some researchers argue that these impulsive behaviors don't routinely appear in adolescents in non-Westernized cultures, suggesting that the causes of this phenomenon may be as much cultural as biological (Epstein, 2007; Schlegel & Barry, 1991).

According to David Elkind (1967), adolescent behavioral problems stem in part from the *personal fable*, teenagers' feelings of profound uniqueness and of living out a story that others are watching. This feeling of "specialness" can sometimes lead to a sense of invincibility. Nevertheless, recent research calls the notion of a personal fable into question (Vartanian, 2000). Increasing evidence suggests that most adolescents don't actually underestimate the risks of such behaviors as driving fast or having early sex; they're often aware they're taking chances, but don't care (Reyna & Farley, 2006). Moreover, not all adolescents who see themselves as invulnerable take foolish chances, probably because they can inhibit their impulses (Vartanian, 2000).

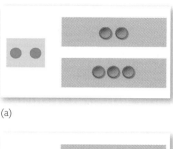

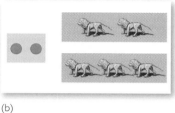

(a)

(b)

FIGURE 10.14 Children Find It Easier to Match Quantities When the Objects Resemble Each Other. In Mix's studies, children match the display on the left with one of the displays on the right. Children find this much easier in the top (a) in which the disks resemble the dots, than in the bottom (b), in which the stimuli are different. (*Source:* Mix, 1999)

FACTOID

Not all cultures count to 10 on their fingers; many have much more elaborate systems of tracking amounts on their fingers, hands, arms, heads, and other body parts. Some systems have specific body locations assigned for numbers from 1 to as high as 74!

▶ ruling out rival hypotheses

HAVE IMPORTANT ALTERNATIVE EXPLANATIONS FOR THE FINDINGS BEEN EXCLUDED?

Lee Boyd Malvo participated in the Washington, DC, sniper killings in October 2002. He was 17 years old at the time of the crimes. Some researchers argue that adolescents who commit crimes should be considered "less guilty by reason of adolescence" because their frontal lobes aren't fully mature, preventing them from making mature decisions regarding the consequences of their actions (Steinberg & Scott, 2003). Others disagree, noting that the overwhelming majority of adolescents don't commit violent crimes. What do you think?

ATTITUDES TOWARD KNOWLEDGE IN ADOLESCENTS AND YOUNG ADULTS. Another critical cognitive change that takes place during the late high school and college years is in adolescents' and young adults' perspectives toward knowledge. Students starting college are often frustrated to find few black-and-white answers to questions. One of the hardest things for them to appreciate is that the answer to questions like "Which theory is better?" is often "It depends." William Perry (1970) cataloged the transitions that students undergo during the college years as they discover that their professors have few absolute answers to offer. He noted that over the course of their college years, students pass through a variety of "positions," or perspectives, on knowledge.

Students who expect clear right or wrong answers to all questions may initially resist changing their views and instead try to reconcile their expectations with what they're learning in the classroom (recall Piaget's assimilation process). They may understand that the "it depends" perspective is the one their professors want them to embrace. So they'll often say the "right things" on exams to get good grades, but believe deep down that there's a right and a wrong answer to most questions. With time and experience, students relax their expectations for absolute answers and construe knowledge as relative.

Over time, though, students typically come to realize that they can't abandon the idea of "truth" or "reality" completely, but that they can appreciate and respect differing points of view (but recall the pitfalls discussed in Chapter 1 of dismissing evidence on the grounds that "everyone is entitled to my opinion"). Although the past three decades have witnessed minor modifications to Perry's stages, his overall model has withstood the test of time (Cano, 2005; Cano & Cardelle-Elawar, 2004).

Cognitive Function in Adulthood

There are minuses and pluses to growing older. On the downside, many aging adults complain they just can't remember things they used to. They're right: Many aspects of cognitive function *do* decline as people get older. Our ability to recall information begins to decrease after age 30. Still, there's considerable variability in how much memory declines, with most people experiencing only modest decreases with age (Shimamura et al., 1995). People's overall speed of processing also declines, which is why teenagers can regularly beat older adults at video games and other speed-sensitive tasks (Cerella, 1985; Salthouse, 2004). These age-related declines are probably a result of brain changes that occur with age, because overall brain matter decreases over the course of adulthood. Age-related declines in brain volume are particularly pronounced in certain areas (Scahill et al., 2003), including the cortex (see Chapter 3) and the hippocampus, which plays a key role in memory (see Chapter 7).

On the upside, some aspects of cognitive function are largely spared from age-related decline, and others actually improve with age:

1. Although free recall (being asked to generate items from memory; see Chapter 6) declines with age, cued recall and recognition remain intact (Schonfield & Robertson, 1966).

2. Aging adults show relatively little decline when asked to remember material that's pertinent to their everyday lives, as opposed to the random lists of words often used in memory research (Graf, 1990; Perlmutter, 1983).

3. Older adults perform better on most vocabulary and knowledge tests than do younger adults (Cattell, 1963). Crystallized intelligence (see Chapter 9), our accumulated knowledge and experience, tends to stay the same or increase with age, giving older adults a greater database of information on which to draw when solving problems (Baltes, Saudinger, & Lindenberger, 1999; Beier & Ackerman, 2001; Horn & Hofer, 1992). Here's a case in which common sense is true: Older *is* wiser!

replicability

CAN THE RESULTS BE DUPLICATED IN OTHER STUDIES?

When we consider that older adults have decades of accumulated knowledge and crystallized intelligence outstripping that of younger adults, we can see why many of the world's cultures honor and revere the elderly.

✓ Study and Review on mypsychlab.com

assess your knowledge   FACT OR FICTION?

1. Piaget argued that development was domain-general and continuous. **True / False**

2. Vygotsky's theory proposes that individual children vary in the age at which they achieve developmental readiness for particular cognitive abilities. **True / False**

3. The ability to count precise quantities is absent in some cultures. **True / False**

4. Adolescents may not always make mature decisions about engaging in risky behaviors because their frontal lobes aren't fully mature. **True / False**

5. Older adults perform worse than younger adults on tests that require memory for random lists of words, but perform better on tests of knowledge and vocabulary. **True / False**

Answers: 1. F (p. 372); 2. T (p. 376); 3. T (p. 380); 4. T (p. 381); 5. T (p. 382).

THE DEVELOPING PERSONALITY: SOCIAL AND MORAL DEVELOPMENT

10.10 Describe how and when children establish emotional bonds with their caregivers.

10.11 Explain the environmental and genetic influences on social behavior and social style in children.

10.12 Determine how morality and identity develop during adolescence and emerging adulthood.

10.13 Identify developmental changes during major life transitions in adults.

10.14 Summarize different ways of conceptualizing old age.

We humans are inherently social beings. Our work lives, school lives, romantic lives, and family lives all involve interaction with others. Because social relationships are so central to our everyday functioning, it's not surprising that our interpersonal relations change as we develop.

■ Social Development in Infancy and Childhood

Not long after birth, infants soon take a keen interest in others. Infants prefer looking at faces over just about all other visual information. As early as four days after birth, infants show a marked preference for Mommy's face compared with that of other women (Pascalis et al., 1995). Infants' interest in others is a good thing because people—particularly familiar people, like their parents—are valuable sources of information and provide the love and support they need to flourish.

As sociable as infants are, something changes dramatically over the course of only a few months. The same infant who was giggling on the floor with a perfect stranger at six months may scream in terror if approached by that same stranger only a few months later. This phenomenon is known as **stranger anxiety**. Known also as *eight months anxiety,* this behavior manifests itself in a fear of strangers beginning at about eight or nine months of age (Greenberg, Hillman, & Grice, 1973; Konner, 1990). It generally increases up until about 12 to 15 months of age, and then declines steadily. Interestingly, the onset of stranger anxiety appears to be virtually identical across all cultures (Kagan, 1976) (see **FIGURE 10.15**). Eight months anxiety makes good evolutionary sense, because it's at about this age that most infants begin to crawl around on their own. As a result, it's the age at which infants can—and usually do—find a way to get themselves into trouble. So this anxiety may be an adaptive mechanism for keeping infants away from dangers, including unknown adults.

TEMPERAMENT AND SOCIAL DEVELOPMENT: BABIES' EMOTIONAL STYLES. As anyone who's spent time with infants can attest, babies vary widely in their social interaction styles. Some are friendly, others are shy and wary, and still others ignore most people altogether. These individual differences in children's social and emotional styles reflect differences in **temperament** (Mervielde et al., 2005). By definition, temperament is *early appearing* (in contrast to some other personality characteristics) and *largely genetic* in origin.

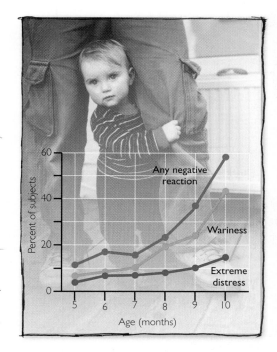

FIGURE 10.15 Stranger Anxiety. As we can see in this graph from one published study, infants' anxiety and negative reactions when confronted with a stranger first begin at around eight or nine months and continue to increase. Typically, they won't begin to decline until about 12 or 15 months. (*Source:* Waters, Matas, & Sroufe, 1975)

stranger anxiety
a fear of strangers developing at eight or nine months of age

temperament
basic emotional style that appears early in development and is largely genetic in origin

The majority of children fall into one of three temperament categories: (a) easy, (b) difficult, and (c) slow to warm up.

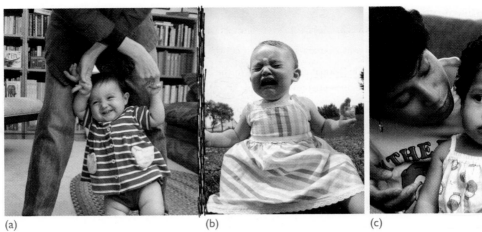

(a)   (b)   (c)

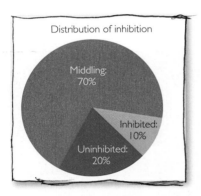

Distribution of inhibition

Middling; 70%

Inhibited: 10%

Uninhibited: 20%

FIGURE 10.16 Behaviorally Inhibited Children. About 10 percent of children are behaviorally inhibited, with the majority either uninhibited or somewhere in between. (*Source:* Kagan, Reznick, & Snidman, 1988)

Watch a Temperament video on **mypsychlab.com**

---

ruling out rival hypotheses

HAVE IMPORTANT ALTERNATIVE EXPLANATIONS FOR THE FINDINGS BEEN EXCLUDED?

Watch Attachment in Infants on **mypsychlab.com**

attachment
the strong emotional connection we share with those to whom we feel closest

In their studies of American children, Alexander Thomas and Stella Chess (1977) identified three major temperamental styles. *Easy* infants (about 40 percent of babies) are adaptable and relaxed; *difficult* infants (about 10 percent of babies) are fussy and easily frustrated; and *slow-to-warm-up* infants (about 15 percent of babies) are disturbed by new stimuli at first but gradually adjust to them. The remaining 35 percent of children don't fit neatly into any of these three categories.

Based initially on research with cats, Jerome Kagan identified another temperamental style he termed *behavioral inhibition* (Kagan et al., 2007). Like "scaredy cats," who crawl under the nearest bed at the sight of a new moving toy, behaviorally inhibited human infants become frightened at the sight of novel or unexpected stimuli, like unfamiliar faces, loud tones, or little moving robots (Kagan, Reznick, & Snidman, 1988). Their hearts pound, their bodies tense up, and their amygdalae become active (Schwartz et al., 2003). This last finding makes sense, because we'll recall from Chapter 3 that the amygdala plays a key role in processing fear. According to Kagan and his colleagues, we can find this temperamental style in about 15 percent of cats and in about 10 percent or slightly more of human children (see **FIGURE 10.16**). Infants with high levels of behavioral inhibition are also at heightened risk for shyness and anxiety disorders in childhood or adolescence (Biederman et al., 2001; Turner, Beidel, & Wolff, 1996). Still, behavioral inhibition isn't all bad. Infants with extremely *low* levels of behavioral inhibition may be at increased risk for impulsive behaviors in later childhood (Burgess et al., 2003), so a certain amount of behavioral inhibition may be healthy. **Watch**

There are also cultural differences in temperament (Freedman & DeBoer, 1979). Daniel Freedman (1978; Freedman & Freedman, 1969) compared how Chinese American and European American four-day-old infants reacted when researchers placed a cloth over their faces. Chinese American infants were considerably calmer than European American infants, many of whom struggled mightily to remove the offending cloths. These and other findings (Kagan et al., 1994) don't demonstrate that these cultural differences in temperament are genetic, as they could be a consequence of different intrauterine (within the womb) hormonal environments across cultures. Still, they demonstrate that differences in infants' basic personality styles emerge almost immediately after birth. Although temperament forms early in development and is genetically influenced, it can be shaped by environmental influences. For example, behaviorally inhibited children placed in day care settings often adapt to this more social environment by becoming less inhibited (Martin & Fox, 2006).

ATTACHMENT: ESTABLISHING BONDS. With rare exceptions, such as infantile autism (see Chapters 2 and 15), all infants forge close emotional bonds with significant adults, usually their parents. This emotional connection we share with those to whom we feel closest is called **attachment**. There may be a good evolutionary reason for the attachment bond. As psychiatrist John Bowlby (1973) noted, it ensures that infants and children don't stray too far from the powerful others who feed and protect them. To understand the origins of attachment, we need to begin with the story of an Austrian zoologist and his birds. **Watch**

Imprinting. In the 1930s, Konrad Lorenz—who went on to win a Nobel Prize for the work we're about to describe—was observing the behaviors of geese. By sheer accident, he discovered that goslings (young geese) seemed to follow around the first large, moving object they saw after hatching. Although Lorenz (1937) referred to this phenomenon as "stamping in" in German, it's come to be known in English as *imprinting*. Once a gosling has imprinted on something or someone, it becomes largely fixated on it, and is unlikely to follow or bond with anything else. Fortunately, 99 percent or more of the time, the first large, moving object that a gosling sees after emerging from the egg is none other than Mother Goose. But Lorenz showed that goslings will cheerfully imprint onto whatever large, moving object they see following birth—including Lorenz himself. Newborn goslings will even imprint onto moving objects, such as large white bouncing balls and boxes on wheels if they have nothing better to choose from (Johnson, 2002).

We humans don't imprint onto our mothers in the way that geese do: We don't bond automatically to the first moving thing we see. Still, human infants and most mammalian infants exhibit a "softer" form of imprinting, in which they forge strong bonds with those who tend to them shortly after birth.

Lorenz discovered that imprinting occurs only during a *critical period* (Almli & Finger, 1987): a specific window of time during which an event must occur (see Chapter 8). In the case of Lorenz's goslings, this critical period was about 36 hours. If the goslings didn't see their mothers until after that window closed, they never imprinted to her, or to anything else for that matter.

In reality, most critical periods don't end as abruptly as Lorenz believed (Bruer, 1999). That's especially true of intelligent mammals, like cats, dogs, and humans, whose behaviors are more flexible than those of geese. That's why most psychologists now use the term *sensitive period* to refer to developmental windows in creatures with a greater range of behaviors.

Do humans have sensitive periods for the development of healthy interpersonal relationships? This question is controversial. As we'll recall from Chapter 8, there's some evidence for a sensitive period for human language. There's also some evidence that early and prolonged separation from attachment figures can produce detrimental effects on psychological adjustment, including social bonding. Some of the best evidence comes from a longitudinal study of infants adopted from Romanian orphanages. In the 1970s and 1980s, all forms of birth control were banned in Romania, resulting in catastrophic numbers of unplanned pregnancies and babies whose parents couldn't support them. Romanian orphanages were overwhelmed by the number of infants for whom they had to provide care. As a result, these orphanages offered little social interaction or emotional care and infants were often left in their cribs all day and night. These infants had no opportunity to develop bonds with adult caretakers until much later, when thousands of them were adopted by families in the United States and England. Sir Michael Rutter and his colleagues found that although infants from these orphanages adopted before six months of age fared well later, those older than six months of age when adopted often exhibited what appeared to be negative effects of their early environment, including serious emotional problems, such as inattention, hyperactivity, and difficulties becoming attached to their adult caregivers (Kreppner, O'Connor, & Rutter, 2001; O'Connor & Rutter, 2000). Nevertheless, there may be another explanation for these findings: The children who were adopted later may have had more emotional difficulties to begin with. As a consequence, they may have been more difficult to place in adoptive families. Nevertheless, the finding that early institutionalization is associated with later emotional problems has been replicated in numerous studies using different methodologies (Ames, 1997; Kreppner et al., 2001).

Contact Comfort: The Healing Touch. Given that human infants don't imprint onto attachment figures, on what basis do they bond to their parents? For decades, psychologists assumed that the primary basis for the attachment bond is the nourishment supplied by mothers. Children bond to those who provide them with milk and food, and in most cases this happens to be Mommy. This view fit with the assumptions of behaviorism (see Chapter 6), which posited that reinforcement is the primary shaping influence on our preferences.

As Nobel Prize–winning biologist Konrad Lorenz goes for a swim, he's followed by three geese who imprinted on him almost immediately after they hatched.

"IT'S AN INTERESTING PSYCHOLOGICAL PHENOMENON. THEY THINK HE'S THEIR MOTHER. SO DOES HE."

> **ruling out rival hypotheses**
>
> **HAVE IMPORTANT ALTERNATIVE EXPLANATIONS FOR THE FINDINGS BEEN EXCLUDED?**
>
> **replicability**
>
> **CAN THE RESULTS BE DUPLICATED IN OTHER STUDIES?**

? When frightened by a novel object, Harlow's infant monkeys almost always preferred the terry cloth mother over the wire mother. **What does this finding tell us about the basis for attachment?** (See answer upside down at bottom of page.)

Harry Harlow overturned this assumption in the 1950s with his pioneering research on infant rhesus monkeys, which are close genetic relatives of humans (Blum, 2002). Harlow (1958) separated baby monkeys from their mothers only a few hours after birth. He then placed them in a cage with two "surrogate" mothers, both inanimate. One—the "wire mother"—consisted of an angular face and a cold, mangled mesh of uncomfortable metal wires. This wire mother did have one thing going for her, though: nourishment. She sported a little bottle of milk from which the baby monkey could drink. In sharp contrast, the second mother, the "terry cloth mother," had a round face and was made of foam rubber, overlaid with a comfortable layer of terry cloth, and heated with a lightbulb. Harlow found that although baby monkeys routinely went to wire mothers for milk, they spent much more of their time with terry cloth mothers. In addition, when Harlow exposed monkeys to a scary stimulus, like a toy robot playing a drum, they were much more likely to run to the terry cloth mother and cling to her for reassurance. Harlow termed this phenomenon **contact comfort**: the positive emotions afforded by touch. Contact comfort may help us to understand why we human primates find simple touch, like holding the hand of a romantic partner, so reassuring. Indeed, Tiffany Field (2003) and her colleagues showed that gentle massage helps premature babies to gain weight, sleep better, and bond more closely with their parents than attention alone.

Attachment Styles: The Strange Situation. As every professional babysitter or day care worker knows, infants attach to their parents in radically different ways. Some are cuddly and affectionate, whereas others are distant and standoffish. Some are calm, whereas others are jittery.

Although these anecdotal observations offer useful insights, it wasn't until Mary Ainsworth and her colleagues developed the *Strange Situation* that psychologists settled on a systematic way of quantifying infants' attachment styles (Ainsworth et al., 1978). The Strange Situation is a laboratory procedure for examining one-year-olds' reactions to separation from their attachment figures, usually their mothers. Here's how it works. First, researchers place the infant in an unfamiliar room with his or her mother. The room is loaded with all kinds of interesting toys, and the mother gives the infant the chance to play with them. Then a stranger enters. On two different occasions, the mother exits the room, leaving the infant alone with the stranger before reuniting with her infant. The Strange Situation takes advantage of infants' stranger anxiety, which as we've learned tends to peak at about one year. Today, most attachment researchers rely on the Strange Situation to measure infants' attachment styles (see **FIGURE 10.17**).

During the Strange Situation, trained research assistants code the infant's emotional and physical reactions to the mother's departure and return. Most researchers find that infants' behaviors fall into one of four categories: ◉→ **Simulate**

FIGURE 10.17 Physical Setup of the Strange Situation. In the Strange Situation, both the mother and a stranger are present before the mother leaves the child with the stranger. The child's response to the mother's departure, and reaction when she returns are used to determine the child's attachment style (*Source:* Ainsworth et al., 1978)

◉→ **Simulate** Attachment Classifications in the Strange Situation on **mypsychlab.com**

contact comfort
positive emotions afforded by touch

1. **Secure attachment** (about 60 percent of U.S. infants). The infant reacts to mom's departure by becoming upset, but greets her return with joy. In essence, the infant uses mom as a *secure base:* a rock-solid source of support to which to turn in times of trouble (Bowlby, 1990).

2. **Insecure-avoidant attachment** (about 15–20 percent of U.S. infants). The infant reacts to mom's departure with indifference and shows little reaction on her return.

Answer: Attachment is based on contact comfort, not nourishment.

3. **Insecure-anxious attachment** (about 15–20 percent of U.S. infants). The infant reacts to mom's departure with panic. He then shows a mixed emotional reaction on her return, simultaneously reaching for her yet squirming to get away after she picks him up (for this reason, some psychologists refer to this style as "anxious-ambivalent").

4. **Disorganized attachment** (about 5–10 percent of U.S infants). This rarest of attachment styles wasn't included in the original classification, but was added later by Mary Main and her colleagues (Main & Cassidy, 1988). Children with this pattern react to mom's departure and return with an inconsistent and confused set of responses. They may appear dazed when reunited with her.

Note that we wrote "U.S. infants" in parentheses following each classification. That's because there are cultural differences in attachment style. For example, more infants in Japan than in the United States fall into the insecure-anxious category, whereas more infants in the United States than in Japan fall into the insecure-avoidant category (Rothbaum et al., 2000). These differences may stem in part from the fact that Japanese babies experience fewer separations from Mom in everyday life than do American babies. As a consequence, Japanese babies may find the Strange Situation even "stranger"—and more stressful—than do American babies (van Ijzendoorn & Sagi, 1999).

The attachment styles derived from the Strange Situation predict children's later behavior. Infants with a secure attachment style tend to grow up to be more well adjusted, helpful, and empathic than infants with other attachment styles (LaFreniere & Sroufe, 1985; Sroufe, 1983). In contrast, infants with an anxious attachment style are more likely to be disliked and mistreated by their peers later in childhood than infants with other attachment styles.

Infants form attachment bonds with both mothers and fathers, and with siblings, grandparents, and other caregivers. Developing an attachment to one adult figure in the infant's life doesn't necessarily undermine the ability to form others. Infants placed in day care may establish secure attachment relationships with their caretakers, although secure attachments are more likely with parents. Moreover, the quality of attachment to day care workers depends on the quality and type of day care (Anhert et al., 2006). In two-parent households, infants typically display a strong early preference for the primary caregiver (usually the mother) that disappears by around 18 months.

Despite its popularity, the Strange Situation has its shortcomings. Researchers must be careful to avoid **mono-operation bias** (Shadish, Cook, & Campbell, 2002): the mistake of relying on only a single measure to draw conclusions. The Strange Situation is, after all, merely one indicator of attachment. To *equate* it with attachment, as some psychologists have done, is a serious error. Indeed, some researchers have begun to develop alternative measures of attachment, such as interviews in adulthood designed to assess bonding to one's parents (Hesse, 1999).

The Strange Situation also isn't especially *reliable*. As we learned in Chapter 2, reliability refers to the consistency of a measuring instrument. If the Strange Situation were a highly reliable measure of attachment, babies who are securely attached at age one, for example, should tend to remain that way for a short time afterward. Yet many infants switch their attachment classifications over brief time periods (Lamb et al., 1984; Paris, 2000). In general, attachment styles remain consistent only when parents' living circumstances stay the same. If parents undergo a change in job status, their children's attachment style often changes along with it (Bruer, 1999; Thompson, 1998). Moreover, almost 40 percent of children display a different attachment style with their mother than with their father (van Ijzendorn & De Wolff, 1997), suggesting that many children can't simply be pigeonholed into a single attachment classification.

Most attachment theorists begin with a central assumption: Infants' attachment styles attributable largely to their parents' responsiveness to them. For example, infants whose parents respond to their signals of distress by comforting them are supposedly more

mono-operation bias
drawing conclusions on the basis of only a single measure

likely to develop a secure attachment style than other infants (Ainsworth et al., 1978). For most attachment theorists, the cause → effect arrow runs from parent to child. In contrast, some psychologists have argued that the causal arrow is reversed, and that children's temperament influences their attachment styles. That is, infants with certain temperaments may elicit certain attachment behaviors from their parents (Paris, 2000; Rutter, 1995). For example, irritable infants may provoke frustration in their parents, which in turn makes these infants still more irritable, and so on. This bidirectional influence may result in an insecure attachment style. So temperament may be a third variable (see Chapter 2) predisposing to both certain parenting practices and certain attachment styles.

PARENTING: WHAT'S RIGHT AND WHAT'S WRONG? Over the past century, self-proclaimed parenting experts have bombarded nervous mothers and fathers with contradictory advice about how to raise their children (Hulbert, 2003; Rankin, 2005). In the 1950s and 1960s, pediatrician Dr. Benjamin Spock became a major proponent of a *child-centered* or "soft" approach to parenting, in which parents should be highly responsive to their children's needs (Hulbert, 2003). Other experts have instead called for a *parent-centered* or "hard" approach to parenting, in which parents don't indulge or reinforce children's calls for attention. Making matters more confusing, some parenting advice seems to be at odds with psychological research. For example, child psychologist Dr. James Dobson advocates spanking children as a disciplinary technique (Dobson, 1992), even though there's not much evidence that physical punishment is effective for promoting long-term behavioral change (see Chapter 6). What does research say about which parenting styles are most effective for promoting healthy development?

Parenting Styles and Later Adjustment. Diana Baumrind's (1971, 1991) work may offer partial answers to this perennial question. Based on her observations of Caucasian middle-class families, Baumrind identified the following three major parenting styles:

- **Permissive.** Permissive parents tend to be lenient with their children, allowing them considerable freedom inside and outside the household. They use discipline sparingly, if at all, and often shower their children with affection.

- **Authoritarian.** Authoritarian parents tend to be strict with their children, giving their children little opportunity for free play or exploration, and punishing them when they don't respond appropriately to their demands. They show little affection toward their children.

- **Authoritative.** Authoritative parents combine the best features of both permissive and authoritarian worlds. They're supportive of their children but set clear and firm limits with them.

Some authors refer to these three styles as "too soft," "too hard," and "just right," respectively. Since Baumrind developed her initial threefold classification, some authors (Maccoby & Martin, 1983) identified a fourth style of parenting:

- **Uninvolved.** Neglectful parents tend to ignore their children, paying little attention to either their positive or negative behaviors.

Baumrind (1991) and other investigators (Weiss & Schwarz, 1996) found that children with *authoritative* parents exhibit the best social and emotional adjustment and the lowest levels of behavior problems, at least among Caucasian middle-class American families. Children with uninvolved parents tend to fare the worst, and children with either permissive or authoritarian parents fall in between.

Superficially, these findings seem to suggest that parents should raise their children authoritatively. Yet Baumrind's findings are only correlational and don't permit us to draw cause-and-effect inferences. In fact, the correlations that Baumrind reported could be at least partly genetic in origin. For example, permissive parents may tend to be impulsive and pass on genes predisposing to impulsivity to their children. Research shows that fussiness of children in infancy forecasts whether parents will engage in physical punishment, such as spanking, raising the possibility that child temperament may partly influence parenting style (Berlin et al., 2009).

correlation vs. causation
CAN WE BE SURE THAT A CAUSES B?

A host of newsstand magazines provide parents with advice about different parenting behaviors and styles. Psychological science can help them evaluate the validity of this advice.

correlation vs. causation
CAN WE BE SURE THAT A CAUSES B?

There's another limitation to Baumrind's conclusions: Her findings may not hold up well outside of middle-class, Caucasian American families. For example, the relationships between parenting style and children's adjustment aren't as strong in *collectivist* cultures, like China, as in *individualistic* cultures, like the United States. Collectivist cultures place a high premium on group harmony, whereas individualist cultures place a high premium on achievement and independence (Triandis & Suh, 2002;). Some data suggest that authoritarian parenting is associated with better outcomes in collectivist than in individualist societies (Sorkhabi, 2005; Steinberg, 2001). Other research suggests that a hybrid parenting approach, one that includes harsh (often physical) punishments alongside a warm emotional bond, is prevalent in African American families (Deater-Deckard & Dodge, 1997). As a result, harsh punishments tend to be associated with better outcomes for African American children than for American children of European descent.

So what's the bottom line on parenting styles? The bulk of the research suggests that specific parenting styles may not matter as much as experts had once thought. By and large, if parents provide their children with what Heinz Hartmann (1939) termed the **average expectable environment**—an environment that provides children with basic needs for affection and appropriate discipline—most of their children will probably turn out just fine. Or, as Donald Winnicott (1958) argued, parenting need only be *good enough*, not necessarily excellent (Paris, 2000). So contrary to what they may hear from parenting gurus on *Oprah*, parents needn't lose sleep about everything they do or every word they say.

Yet if parenting falls well below the range of the average expectable environment—if it's especially poor—children's social development can suffer. There's good reason to believe that many children raised by extremely abusive (so-called toxic) parents often experience ill effects later on (Downey & Coyne, 1990; Lykken, 2000). In addition, parenting quality matters when children enter the world with a strong genetic predisposition toward psychological disturbance or aggressiveness. For example, when children are genetically prone to high levels of impulsivity and violent behavior, parents probably need to exert especially firm and consistent discipline (Collins et al., 2000; Lykken, 1995). As we noted earlier, the effects of genes sometimes interact with those of the environment (Caspi et al., 2002; Kagan, 1994; Suomi, 1997).

Peers versus Parents. In 1995, a controversy erupted when Judith Rich Harris published a paper in one of psychology's premier journals, *Psychological Review*, claiming that peers play an even more important role than parents in children's social development. According to Harris's (1995, 1998) controversial *group socialization theory* of development, most environmental transmission is "horizontal"—from children to other children—rather than "vertical"—from parents to children. Harris's model implies that parents may play much less of a role in children's development than previously believed. Nevertheless, twins who share many of the same peers are only slightly more similar in personality than are twins who share only a few of the same peers (Loehlin, 1997), raising questions about Harris's claims. Furthermore, the causal direction of this association isn't clear: Do similar peers lead twins to develop similar personalities, or do twins with similar personalities seek out similar peers? It remains to be seen whether Harris's bold claims regarding the power of peers in shaping development will stand the test of time.

The Role of the Father. Fathers differ from mothers in several ways in their interactions with children. First, fathers tend to be less attentive and affectionate than mothers toward their babies. Second, they spend less time with their babies than mothers, even in households in which both mothers and fathers are at home (Golombok, 2000). Third, when fathers interact with their children, they spend more of their time than do mothers in physical play (Parke, 1996). Fourth, both boys and girls tend to choose their fathers over their mothers as playmates (Clarke-Stewart, 1980). Despite these differences between mothers and fathers, fathers exert an important impact on

In collectivist cultures, where obedience to authority is highly valued, authoritarian parenting may be associated with better outcomes than authoritative parenting.

Fathers tend to be less affectionate with their children than mothers, but both girls and boys tend to prefer their father over their mother as a playmate.

correlation vs. causation

CAN WE BE SURE THAT A CAUSES B?

average expectable environment
environment that provides children with basic needs for affection and discipline

children's psychological well-being and adjustment. Children benefit from warm, close relationships with their father regardless of how much time they spend with him (Lamb & Tamis-LeMonda, 2003).

"Nontraditional" Families: Science and Politics. Most child development research has been conducted on children in "traditional" families—living in a household with two parents of opposite sexes. But many children grow up in single parent households, or are the offspring of a same-sex couple. Politicians and the media have had much to say about the demise of the American family and the need to protect traditional family values. What does research have to say about the effects of "nontraditional" parenting configurations?

The impact of single-parenthood on children is unclear. On the one hand, there's evidence that children from single-parent families have more behavior problems, such as aggression and impulsivity, than do children from two-parent families (Golombok, 2000). Moreover, their risk for crime is about seven times higher than for children in two-parent families (Lykken, 1993, 2000). Some researchers argue that the higher proportion of single-parent families today is a key reason for the higher rates of violent crime in the United States today compared with the 1960s (Wilson & Herrnstein, 1985; Lykken, 1995).

On the other hand, data comparing single-parent with two-parent families are only correlational, so we can't draw causal inferences from them. Single mothers differ from married mothers in many ways; they tend to be poorer, less well educated, and marked by higher levels of life stress (Aber & Rappaport, 1994). They also move around much more often than married moms, making it difficult for their children to form stable social bonds with peers (Harris, 1998). Any or all of these factors—or factors researchers haven't considered—could account for the differences between these two groups of women in their children's adjustment.

Moreover, children raised by single mothers whose husbands died—rather than by divorced or separated mothers—generally exhibit no higher rates of emotional or behavioral problems than do children from two-parent households (Felner et al., 1981; McLeod, 1991). This finding suggests that the apparent effects of single-mother parenting could be attributable to characteristics of the *father* or to maternal distress associated with having no second parent in the home.

So we can safely conclude that many single mothers do a fine job of raising their children, and that being raised by a single mom doesn't necessarily doom children to later behavior problems. In addition, children raised by single fathers don't appear to differ in their behaviors from children raised by single mothers (Golombok, 2000; Hetherington & Stanley-Hagan, 1995). Although some single parents have children with more behavioral problems than do other mothers, the causes of this difference are unknown.

The evidence regarding the impact of same-sex parents on children's development is clearer. Children raised by same-sex couples don't differ from those raised by opposite-sex couples in social adjustment outcomes, academic performance, or sexual orientation (Gottman, 1990; Wainright et al., 2004). Despite the distinctive roles that mothers and fathers often play in children's lives, same-sex couples generally divide up their labor and parenting similarly to opposite-sex couples. In fact, in opposite-sex couples in which the father is the primary caregiver and the mother is the primary breadwinner, we see a different division of labor, in which the mother takes on the role of the "fun" parent. The bottom line is that having one primary parental attachment figure and one secondary attachment figure who plays a different role appears to impact infants' development similarly, regardless of the gender composition of the parents.

correlation vs. causation

CAN WE BE SURE THAT A CAUSES B?

ruling out rival hypotheses

HAVE IMPORTANT ALTERNATIVE EXPLANATIONS FOR THE FINDINGS BEEN EXCLUDED?

Although the popular stereotype of a family includes a husband, wife, and several children, a surprisingly small number of families fit this mold. Single-parent families, same-sex parents, blended families following a second marriage, and childless couples are far more common than most people think.

Effects of Divorce on Children. Much of the popular psychology literature informs us that divorce often exacts a serious emotional toll on children. On September 25, 2000, *Time* magazine featured a cover story entitled "What Divorce Does to Kids," accompanied by the ominous warning that "the long-term damage is worse than you thought." This story was sparked by a 25-year study of 60 families by Judith Wallerstein (1989), who reported that the negative effects of divorce were enduring: Many years later, the children of divorced parents had difficulties with establishing career goals and stable romantic relationships. Yet Wallerstein didn't include a control group of families in which one or both parents had been separated from their children for reasons other than divorce, such as accidental death. As a result, we can't tell whether her findings reflect the effects of divorce itself rather than the general effects of stressful disruption in the family.

Better-designed studies show that the substantial majority of children survive their parents' divorce without long-term emotional damage (Cherlin et al., 1991; Hetherington, Cox, & Cox, 1985). In addition, the apparent effects of divorce depend on the severity of conflict between parents before the divorce. When parents experience only mild conflict before the divorce, the seeming effects of divorce are actually *more* severe than when parents experience intense conflict before the divorce (Amato & Booth, 1997; Rutter, 1972). In the latter case, divorce typically produces no ill effects on children, probably because they find the divorce to be a welcome relief from their parents' incessant arguing. ◉ Watch

Still, divorce can surely produce negative effects on *some* children. One group of investigators compared the children of identical twins, only one of whom had been divorced. The design provides an elegant control for genetic effects, because these twins are genetically identical. The researchers found that children of identical twins who'd divorced had higher levels of depression and substance abuse, as well as poorer school performance, than the children of identical twins who hadn't divorced (D'Onofrio et al., 2006). These findings suggest that divorce can exert negative effects on some children, although they don't rule out the possibility that parental conflict prior to and during the divorce, rather than divorce itself, accounts for the differences (Hetherington & Stanley-Hagan, 2002).

SELF-CONTROL: LEARNING TO INHIBIT IMPULSES. A crucial ingredient of social development, and one that parents begin wishing for long before it emerges, is **self-control**: the ability to inhibit our impulses (Eigsti et al., 2006). We may be tempted to snag that unclaimed coffee at the Starbucks counter or tell our unbearably arrogant boss what we really think of him, but we usually—and thankfully—restrain our desires to do so. Other times, we must put our desires on the back burner until we fulfill our obligations.

As we all know, children are notoriously bad at delaying gratification, but some are better at it than others. As Walter Mischel and his colleagues have discovered, our capacity to delay gratification is a good predictor of later social adjustment. To study delay of gratification, they leave a child all alone in a room with a small reward, like one cookie, and a little bell. Next, they tell the child that if she can wait 15 minutes, she can get an even bigger reward, like two cookies. If she can't wait that long, she can ring the bell to summon the experimenter. The children have several options: wait patiently, ring the bell and sacrifice the big reward, or throw caution to the wind and stuff the cookie in their mouths.

Children's ability to wait for the bigger reward at the age of four years forecasts superior ability to cope with frustration in adolescence, probably because handling difficult situations hinges on an ability to inhibit negative reactions to distress. It even predicts teenagers' SAT scores (Mischel, Shoda, & Peake, 1988; Mischel, Shoda, & Rodriguez, 1989). Of course, these findings don't prove that self-control causes these later outcomes. But they suggest that the capacity to delay gratification in childhood is an early indicator of the capacity to restrain impulses, which in turn is rooted in frontal lobe functioning (Eigsti et al., 2006; Mischel & Ayduk, 2004).

THE DEVELOPMENT OF GENDER IDENTITY. Gender concepts are crucial to children's understanding of themselves as social beings. Before addressing how we develop a sense of ourselves as boys or girls, men or women, we need to sort through a bit of confusing

◀ **ruling out rival hypotheses**

HAVE IMPORTANT ALTERNATIVE EXPLANATIONS FOR THE FINDINGS BEEN EXCLUDED?

◉ **Watch** Pam: a Divorced Mother of a Nine-Year-Old, Part 1 on **mypsychlab.com**

◀ **ruling out rival hypotheses**

HAVE IMPORTANT ALTERNATIVE EXPLANATIONS FOR THE FINDINGS BEEN EXCLUDED?

Children in Mischel's delay-of-gratification task must inhibit their desire to eat a cookie if they want to receive a bigger reward—eating both cookies—later.

◀ **correlation vs. causation**

CAN WE BE SURE THAT A CAUSES B?

self-control
ability to inhibit an impulse to act

terminology. Most psychologists distinguish sex from gender, with *sex* referring to individuals' biological status as male or female and *gender* referring to the psychological characteristics—behaviors, thoughts, and emotions—that tend to be associated with being male or female. But we're not done yet. **Gender identity** refers to people's sense of being male or female. Some people with *gender identity disorder,* sometimes called *transsexualism* in adulthood, report feeling "trapped" in the body of the opposite sex. They may be biologically male, yet feel like a woman, or vice versa. In contrast, **gender role** refers to the behaviors that tend to accompany being male or female. Gender identity and gender role don't always go together. An adolescent may see herself as female, yet engage in "stereotypically" masculine behaviors, like playing football and playing the role of class clown.

Researchers have observed that when monkeys are given a choice of toys to play with, female monkeys *(left)* tend to prefer dolls, whereas male monkeys *(right)* tend to prefer trucks.

Biological Influences on Gender. A popular misconception is that gender differences don't emerge until socializing influences, like parenting practices, have had the opportunity to act on children. Yet some gender differences are evident in early infancy, rendering this explanation unlikely.

As early as one year of age or less, boys and girls prefer to play with different types of toys, even if they've been exposed only to gender-neutral toys or have had equal access to toys associated with both genders. Boys generally like balls, guns, and fire trucks; girls like dolls, stuffed animals, and cookware (Caldera, Huston, & O'Brien, 1989; Smith & Daglish, 1977). Infants as young as three months prefer to look at gender-consistent toys (Alexander et al., 2009). Remarkably, investigators have observed these preferences in nonhuman primates, including vervet monkeys. When placed in cages with toys, boy monkeys tend to choose trucks and balls, whereas girl monkeys tend to choose dolls and pots (Alexander & Hines, 2002). This finding suggests that toy preferences may reflect differences in biological predispositions, such as aggressiveness and nurturance, shared by many primates. Indeed, in humans, monkeys, and even mice, adult females exposed to excess levels of testosterone (see Chapter 3) during birth tend to engage in more rough-and-tumble play than other females (Berenbaum & Hines, 1992; Edwards, 1970; Young, Goy, & Phoenix, 1964).

As early as age three, boys prefer to hang out with other boys, and girls with other girls (LaFreniere, Strayer, & Gauthier, 1984; Whiting & Edwards, 1988). This phenomenon of *sex segregation* suggests that children understand the differences between genders and are aware that they fit better with one gender than the other. Sex segregation emerges in rhesus monkeys between six and 12 months of age (Rupp, 2003), raising the possibility that this phenomenon has biological roots.

Research suggests that parents tend to be more accepting of "tomboyish" behaviors among girls than "sissyish" behavior among boys.

Social Influences on Gender. As we've discovered throughout this chapter, nature rarely if ever operates in a vacuum. Nature is almost always amplified by nurture, such as the reinforcing influences of parents and teachers. Research shows that parents tend to encourage children to engage in gender-stereotyped behaviors, such as achievement and independence among boys and dependence and nurturance among girls. Fathers are more likely than mothers to enforce these stereotypes (Lytton & Romney, 1991).

Social expectations for how members of each gender should behave also matter. In one study, two researchers (Condry & Condry, 1976) showed adults videos of an infant reacting to several emotionally arousing stimuli, like a jack-in-the-box toy popping open suddenly. They told some adults that the infant was a boy ("David") and other adults that the infant was a girl ("Dana"). The investigators randomly assigned the adults to these two conditions, making the study a true experiment (see Chapter 2). They found that observers' beliefs about the infant's gender colored their interpretations of the infant's behavior. Adults who thought the infant was named David rated "his" startled reaction to the jack-in-the-box as reflecting anger, whereas adults who thought the infant was named Dana rated "her" startled reaction to the jack-in-the-box as reflecting fear.

Teachers also tend to respond to boys and girls in accord with prevailing gender stereotypes. They give boys more attention when they exhibit aggression and girls more attention when they exhibit dependent or "needy" behaviors (Serbin & O'Leary, 1975). Even when boys and girls are equally assertive and equally verbal, teachers tend to lavish assertive boys and verbal girls with greater amounts of attention (Fagot et al., 1985). In modern-day America, gender-role socialization tends to be stricter for boys than for girls. Parents toler-

gender identity
individuals' sense of being male or female

gender role
a set of behaviors that tend to be associated with being male or female

identity
our sense of who we are, and our life goals and priorities

psychosocial crisis
dilemma concerning an individual's relations to other people

ate and may even encourage cross-sex "tomboy" behavior in girls, like playing with both trucks and dolls, more than in boys, who tend to be stereotyped as "sissies" if they play with dolls (Langlois & Downs, 1980; Wood et al., 2002).

■ Social and Emotional Development in Adolescence

Common wisdom regards adolescence as one of the most traumatic times in development, and it's certainly a time of dramatic changes in body, brain, and social activities. Yet the teenage years can also be a wonderful time of discovery, of opportunity to participate in adultlike activities, and of deep friendships. We might characterize adolescence in the words of Charles Dickens: "It was the best of times, it was the worst of times." There's plenty of conflict with parents (Laursen, Coy, & Collins, 1998), risk-taking (Arnett, 1995), and anxiety (Larson & Richards, 1994) relative to younger children and adults. Yet most evidence suggests that the idea of adolescence as an inevitable roller-coaster ride is a myth (Arnett, 1999; Epstein, 2007): Only about 20 percent of adolescents experience marked turmoil (Offer & Schonert-Reichl, 1992). The remainder ride out the teenage years surprisingly smoothly.

BUILDING AN IDENTITY. We've all asked ourselves "Who am I?" at some point. Indeed, one of the central challenges of adolescence is to get a firm handle on our **identity**, our sense of who we are, as well as our life goals and priorities. Erik Erikson (1902–1994) developed the most comprehensive theory of how identity develops.

Erikson's Model of Identity: The Identity Crisis.
As an adolescent, Erikson wrestled with more than his share of identity issues. Although of Danish descent and unmistakably Scandinavian in his appearance (he was tall, with blue eyes and blonde hair), Erikson was raised Jewish. Largely as a consequence, he felt like an outsider at his synagogue, where he was teased for being Scandinavian, and his school, where he was teased for being Jewish (Hunt, 1993; Kushner, 1993). It's probably not merely coincidental that Erikson (1963, 1970) coined the term *identity crisis* to describe the confusion that most adolescents experience regarding their sense of self.

Erikson's theoretical work went well beyond the topic of adolescence. In contrast to Sigmund Freud, who as we'll learn in Chapter 14 believed that personality development stopped largely in late childhood, Erikson believed that personality growth continues throughout the life span. Erikson formulated an eight-stage model of human development from "womb to tomb," as psychologists like to say. In each of his "Eight Stages," we confront a different **psychosocial crisis**: a dilemma concerning our relations to other people, be they parents, teachers, friends, or society at large. For example, Erikson believed that infants face a dilemma about whether the world is a safe place in which they can depend on caregivers to treat them well. Later, children face a dilemma about whether to feel confident in their abilities. As we negotiate each stage, we acquire a more fleshed-out sense of who we are.

As we can see in **FIGURE 10.18**, the fifth stage, "Identity versus Role Confusion," is the period during which adolescents grapple with perhaps the most fundamental question of all: who they are. In most cases, they emerge from this crisis relatively unscathed. But if

According to Erikson, adolescence is a time of exploring who we are. Trying on different identities by acting and dressing in particular ways is part of this process.

1. Infancy
Trust versus mistrust
Developing general security, optimism, and trust in others

2. Toddlerhood
Autonomy versus shame and doubt
Developing a sense of independence and confident self-reliance, taking setbacks in stride

3. Early childhood
Initiative versus guilt
Developing initiative in exploring and manipulating the environment

4. Middle childhood
Industry versus inferiority
Enjoyment and mastery of the developmental tasks of childhood, in and out of school

5. Adolescence
Identity versus role confusion
Achievement of a stable and satisfying sense of role and direction

6. Young adulthood
Intimacy versus isolation
Development of the ability to maintain intimate personal relationships

7. Adulthood
Generativity versus stagnation
Satisfaction of personal and familial needs supplemented by development of interest in the welfare of others and the world in general

8. Aging
Ego integrity versus despair
Recognizing and adjusting to aging and the prospect of death with a sense of satisfaction about the future

FIGURE 10.18 Erikson's Eight Stages of Human Development. (*Source:* Good and Brophy, 1995)

Explore Erikson's Last Four Stages of Psychosocial Development on **mypsychlab.com**

correlation vs. causation
CAN WE BE SURE THAT A CAUSES B?

they don't, they may be at risk for later psychological conditions marked by confusion regarding identity (such as borderline personality disorder, which we'll encounter in Chapter 15). For Erikson, the successful resolution of each stage holds crucial implications later on down the line. If we don't solve the challenges posed by earlier stages, we'll experience difficulty solving the challenges posed by later stages. **Explore**

Although Erikson's theorizing has been influential, the research basis for many of his claims is slim. There's not much evidence that there are exactly eight stages or that we pass through them in the same order. There's some evidence that individuals who don't successfully negotiate the early stages of development, like identity versus role confusion, experience more difficulty with later stages than do other individuals (Vaillant & Milosky, 1980). Although consistent with Erikson's model, these findings are only correlational. As a consequence, they don't demonstrate that problems with early stages *produce* problems in later stages, as the post hoc fallacy reminds us.

Emerging Adulthood. Until recently, developmental researchers regarded individuals under 18 as adolescents and those over 18 as adults. Most psychological research is based on adults between 18 and 22, especially those in college (Henrich et al., 2010). But scientists have increasingly recognized that many changes in identity and emotional development distinct from later adult experiences occur in early adulthood. Researchers now define the period of life between 18 and 25 as **emerging adulthood**, during which many aspects of emotional development, identity, and personality become solidified (Arnett, 2004).

Many emerging adults struggle to figure out their identities and life goals, "trying on different hats" in an effort to see which one fits best. Psychologists call this process *role experimentation*. We may juggle "nerdy," "cool," and "jock" friends at varying times, scope out different potential majors, and even explore alternative religious and philosophical beliefs. Our identities undergo a variety of important changes over the course of emerging adulthood as we acquire the opportunity to fine-tune the fit between who we are and who we want to be.

MORAL DEVELOPMENT: KNOWING RIGHT FROM WRONG.

Children begin to develop ideas of right and wrong as toddlers and preschoolers. But *moral dilemmas*—situations in which there are no clear right or wrong answers—arise much more frequently in the teen and young adult years. Should I lie to my parents about where I've been so they don't worry about me? Should I avoid my nice but nerdy friend so that my popular friends will like me better? The approach we adopt to these and other moral problems changes over the course of development.

Children's Moral Development. There's good reason to believe that we can trace the roots of our moral understanding to *fear*. In infancy and childhood, we associate right with reward and wrong with punishment, so we learn not to do bad things to avoid punishment. Over time, our fears become internalized. We come to fear not merely the recriminations of our parents and teachers, but the recriminations of our own moral sensibilities (Lykken, 1995). As Freud (1932) observed, we become afraid of ourselves (Freud called guilt "moral anxiety"). Indeed, one of the best predictors of the strength of children's sense of morality is their level of fear years earlier (Frick & Marsee, 2006; Kochanska et al., 2002).

Piaget believed that children's moral development, like other aspects of their development, is constrained by their level of cognitive development (Loevinger, 1987). For example, he argued that children in the concrete operational stage tend to evaluate people in terms of *objective responsibility*—how much harm they've done. As they approach formal operations, though, they tend to evaluate people in terms of *subjective responsibility*—their intentions to produce harm (Piaget, 1932).

If we ask a six- or seven-year-old who's more to blame, (a) a child who accidentally knocks over 20 kitchen plates in his parents' cabinet or (b) a child who purposefully knocks over 10 kitchen plates because he was hopping mad at his parents, she's more likely to say (a), because it produced more damage. In contrast, a 12- or 13-year-old is more likely to say (b), because it was intentional. With age, children become better able to understand that there's more to personal responsibility than the sheer amount of damage one has wrought. Whether they mean to inflict damage also counts.

emerging adulthood
period of life between the ages of 18 and 25 during which many aspects of emotional development, identity, and personality become solidified

Kohlberg and Morality: Finding the Moral High Ground. Lawrence Kohlberg extended Piaget's thinking to identify how morality unfolds across the life span. He studied how morality changes with development by exploring how participants wrestle with moral dilemmas. Because Kohlberg's moral dilemmas don't have clear right or wrong answers, he didn't score the answers based on what participants judged to be morally right or wrong; he scored only the *reasoning processes* they used to decide what was right or wrong. For Kohlberg, what matters are the underlying principles that people invoke to solve moral problems.

We'll explain this point using one famous moral problem developed by Kohlberg. Consider Heinz's dilemma and think about how you'd handle it.

Heinz and the Drug

In Europe, a woman was near death from a special kind of cancer. There was one drug that the doctors thought might save her. It was a form of radium that a druggist in the same town had recently discovered. The drug was expensive to make, but the druggist was charging 10 times what the drug cost him to make. He paid $400 for the radium and charged $4,000 for a small dose of the drug. The sick woman's husband, Heinz, went to everyone he knew to borrow the money and tried every legal means, but he could only get together about $2,000, which is half of what it cost. He told the druggist that his wife was dying, and asked him to sell it cheaper or let him pay later. But the druggist said, "No, I discovered the drug and I'm going to make money from it." So, having tried every legal means, Heinz gets desperate and considers breaking into the man's store to steal the drug.

Question: Should Heinz steal the drug? Why or why not?

After testing many children, adolescents, and adults on this and other dilemmas, Kohlberg (1976, 1981) concluded that morality develops in three major stages. We can see these stages, along with sample answers to the Heinz dilemma that go along with them, in **TABLE 10.3**. The first level, *preconventional morality,* is marked by a focus on punishment and reward. What's right is what we're rewarded for; what's wrong is what we're punished for. The second level, *conventional morality,* is marked by a focus on societal values. What's right is what society approves of; what's wrong is what society disapproves of. The third level, *postconventional morality,* is marked by a focus on internal moral principles that transcend society. What's right is what accords with fundamental human rights and values; what's wrong is what contradicts these rights and values. Kohlberg believed the sequence of these levels was invariant, although he acknowledged that different people pass through them at different rates. In fact, Kohlberg's research indicated that most adults never get past conventional morality to achieve postconventional morality. ⊙—Watch

Another moral dilemma, in this case adapted slightly from one of Kohlberg's: Imagine you've just learned that one of your next-door neighbors, whom you've known for many years as an extremely kind and caring person, is wanted for an attempted murder she committed as a young woman three decades ago (this scenario describes Sara Jane Olson, ex-member of a violent revolutionary organization, shown here with her daughter). Would you turn her in to the police? Why or why not?

TABLE 10.3 Kohlberg's Scheme of Moral Development and Sample Explanations. Kohlberg scored the reasoning processes underlying the answer to the Heinz dilemma, not the answers themselves.

LEVEL	HEINZ SHOULD STEAL THE DRUG BECAUSE ...	HEINZ SHOULD *NOT* STEAL THE DRUG BECAUSE ...
Preconventional Morality	He can get away with it	He might get caught
Conventional Morality	Others will look down on him if he lets his wife die	It's against the law
Postconventional Morality	The protection of human life is a higher moral principle that can overrule laws against stealing	Doing so violates a basic social contract needed to preserve civilization: Thou shalt not steal

⊙—Watch Moral Development: Postconventional on **mypsychlab.com**

Criticisms of Kohlberg's Work. Kohlberg's work has been enormously influential; his research has shed light on the development of morality and informed educational efforts to enhance people's moral reasoning (Kohlberg & Turiel, 1971; Loevinger, 1987). Still, Kohlberg's findings have met with more than their share of criticism; we'll examine five criticisms here.

1. **Cultural Bias.** By and large, studies have confirmed Kohlberg's claim that people pass through his levels in the same order, regardless of their country or culture of origin (Snarey, 1982). But some critics have accused Kohlberg of cultural bias, because people from different cultures tend to achieve different scores on his moral development scheme. For example, people from individualistic societies often score somewhat higher than do those in collectivist societies (Shweder, Mahapatra, & Miller, 1990). Still, as we learned in Chapter 9, group differences don't always indicate bias, so the meaning of this finding is unclear.

"Like thunder and lightning ... together we make the perfect storm."

Carol Gilligan suggested that women's more caring orientation may affect their responses to moral dilemmas. Yet, women appear to score just as highly as men on Kohlberg's moral development scheme.

falsifiability

CAN THE CLAIM BE DISPROVED?

ruling out rival hypotheses

HAVE IMPORTANT ALTERNATIVE EXPLANATIONS FOR THE FINDINGS BEEN EXCLUDED?

correlation vs. causation

CAN WE BE SURE THAT A CAUSES B?

2. **Sex Bias.** Kohlberg's student Carol Gilligan (1982) broke from her mentor to argue that his system was biased against women. For Gilligan, Kohlberg's scheme unfairly favors males, who are more likely than women to adopt a "justice" orientation based on abstract principles of fairness, whereas women are more likely than men to adopt a "caring" orientation based on concrete principles of nurturance. Yet despite gender differences in strategies toward moral problems, there's little evidence that men score higher than women on Kohlberg's scheme (Moon, 1986; Sunar, 2002).

3. **Low Correlation with Moral Behavior.** Scores on Kohlberg's scheme are only modestly related to real-world moral behavior (Krebs & Denton, 2005). For example, the correlation between Kohlberg's levels and moral behavior, such as honest and altruistic actions, tends to be only about .3 (Blasi, 1980). Kohlberg argued that his moral development system *shouldn't* correlate highly with real-world actions, because it measures people's thinking about moral problems, not their moral behaviors. People may perform the same behaviors for very different reasons: A person may steal a coat from a store because he wants to add it to his fashion collection or because he wants to keep his freezing children warm in the winter. Still, this kind of reasoning raises problems for the falsifiability of Kohlberg's system. If the scores in this system correlate with behavior, they provide evidence for it; if they don't correlate with behavior, they don't necessarily provide evidence against it.

4. **Confound with Verbal Intelligence.** Responding effectively to Kohlberg's moral dilemmas requires some basic smarts. But that fact should make us a bit uneasy, because Kohlberg's scheme may be measuring people's ability to understand and talk about problems in general rather than moral problems in particular (Blasi, 1980). There's only one way to rule out this possibility: measure verbal intelligence in the same study as we measure moral development, and see whether it washes out the findings. Some studies have found that intelligence may explain Kohlberg's findings (Sanders, Lubinski, & Benbow, 1995), but others have found strong relations between scores on Kohlberg's scheme and moral behavior even after taking intelligence into account (Gibbs, 2006). The issue remains unresolved.

5. **Causal Direction.** Kohlberg's model assumes that our moral reasoning precedes our emotional reactions to moral issues. Yet in some cases, our emotional reactions to morally laden stimuli, like photographs of assaults on innocent people, occur almost instantaneously (Luo et al., 2006). Moreover, we can know something is wrong without being able to explain why; for example, many people "know" intuitively that incest is immoral but can't offer a reason (Haidt, 2007). These findings suggest that moral reasoning may sometimes come after, rather than before, our emotional reactions.

■ Life Transitions in Adulthood

As we "emerge" into full-blown adults, many aspects of our lives begin to stabilize, but others begin to change even more dramatically. These changes tend to be associated with major transitions in lifestyle or societal status, such as shifting from student to wage earner, entering a serious relationship, or becoming a parent. Many of these transitions are wonderful experiences, but they can be stressful. We often think of adults as following a predictable life trajectory: attending college in the late teens and early twenties, getting that first job after graduation, falling in love with someone of the opposite sex, getting married, having children, watching them grow up, and growing old gracefully while rocking on the front porch. In reality, we vastly overestimate how many of us adhere to this tidy stereotype of the road of life (Coontz, 1992). Many college students are in their late twenties, thirties, or forties, attending school while maintaining a job, and have families who are financially dependent on them. Many family units consist of single parents, same-sex parents, unmarried parents, second families following a divorce, and childless couples. Census reports (U.S. Census Bureau, 2005) indicate that fewer than 25 percent of adults live in conventional nuclear families (mom, dad, and children).

CAREERS. One of the biggest sources of anxiety for young adults graduating from college—particularly those who haven't served in the workforce—is what they're going to do for a living. Many recent graduates cast around a bit for a career path that matches their qualifications and interests. For some, this strategy can be beneficial, because they end up discovering unexpected careers that are good fits for their skills and passions. Although it was once the norm for people to work for one company or in one career for their entire lives, this is no longer the case. A longitudinal study conducted by the Bureau of Labor Statistics (2006) revealed that the average American worker changed jobs 10.5 times between the ages of 18 and 40. Although changes were more frequent in the teens and early twenties, people between 36 and 40 changed jobs at least once on average.

Finding a job that is satisfying—that is, stimulating, draws on the employee's skills, and creates a supportive work environment—can be a challenge. But job satisfaction (or lack thereof) can have a big impact on our emotional well-being (Faragher, et al., 2005). Overall levels of job satisfaction change over the course of adulthood. Emerging adults who are starting their first professional positions often report high levels of job satisfaction, but rates of satisfaction decline during middle adulthood, perhaps in part because the novelty has worn off. Nevertheless, job satisfaction increases again prior to retirement age, creating what psychologists call a U-shaped curve, in which satisfaction is high early and late in the game but hits a dip in the middle (Clark et al., 1996).

LOVE AND COMMITMENT. One of the most momentous adult transitions is finding a life mate. Romantic relationships, although often exciting and fulfilling, typically call for a major shift in lifestyle. Even something as simple as integrating our music collections with our partners' can be a stressful experience. Nevertheless, there may be benefits to sharing life with a significant other. Physical and emotional intimacy are associated with greater physical health and lower stress (Coombs, 1991). Overall, those in serious long-term relationships—both homosexual and heterosexual—report higher overall levels of happiness than those who are single (Gove, Hughes, & Style, 1983; Wayment & Peplau, 1995). Nevertheless, this finding is only correlational and could reflect a tendency for happier people to enter into stable relationships (see Chapter 11).

Although the average age of marriage in the United States is increasing, from 20 for women and 22 for men in 1960 to about 25 for women and 27 for men today, more than 50 percent of adults in the United States are married, and about 5 percent are cohabitating but unmarried. About 11 percent of unmarried couples are same-sex partnerships, almost evenly divided between male and female relationships (U.S. Census Bureau, 2000). The vast majority of people become part of a long-term committed relationship at some point during adulthood.

PARENTHOOD. Becoming a parent is probably the biggest transition that adults can undergo. Having a child involves a fundamental shift in lifestyle because, suddenly, adults are completely responsible for the well-being of someone other than themselves. Although this experience is incredibly rewarding for most parents, it's also anxiety provoking. Becoming a parent requires a huge change in schedule, a reduction in sleep, and challenges associated with balancing competing demands of work and family. New parents are often unprepared for these changes, imagining that they'll just stick to their routine and bring baby along with them wherever they go—which almost never works the way they envision it. Research indicates that new parents who have the easiest time adjusting to parenthood are those whose expectations about the amount of change involved are the most realistic (Belsky & Kelly, 1994). ⊙ **Watch**

Most parents make the adjustment, although each year—and sometimes each month—can bring new challenges as children develop. Although most adults adjust to parenthood, longitudinal studies of couples' marital satisfaction reveal that satisfaction drops

Although we usually think of college students as being in their late teens or early twenties and financially dependent on their parents, many "nontraditional" students enroll in college while working full-time and supporting families.

◄ **correlation vs. causation**
CAN WE BE SURE THAT A CAUSES B?

Having a baby is a significant and wonderful life event, but becoming a new parent is also a significant source of stress.

⊙ **Watch** Jess: Expecting First Child, Part 1 on **mypsychlab.com**

for both parents during the year following the birth of a child and remains low throughout the first several years of their child's life (Cowan & Cowan, 1995; Shapiro, Gottman, & Carrere, 2000). Couples matched on initial level of marital satisfaction but who don't have a child display no such decline (Schulz, Cowan, & Cowan, 2006). The good news is that parents' overall level of satisfaction with *life* doesn't decline after the birth of a child. The decline in marital satisfaction seems to be specifically a marriage-related phenomenon, perhaps stemming from parents paying less attention to each other or conflicts over approaches to child rearing. Marital satisfaction typically rebounds once children reach school age.

MIDLIFE TRANSITIONS. Major adjustments also take place as adults reach middle age and begin to see the first signs of gray hairs and wrinkles. As adults begin to feel their age, they confront new challenges, such as having their children leave home or caring for aging parents whose health is declining. The "sandwich generation" refers to adults (typically in their thirties and forties) who are caring for *both* growing children and aging parents, a particularly difficult situation given multiple competing demands.

One popular misconception about middle age is that most men, and some women, undergo a **midlife crisis**, marked by emotional distress about the aging process and an attempt to regain their youth. The stereotype is of a man in his forties or fifties impulsively buying a motorcycle or leaving his similarly-aged wife for a 25-year-old woman. Although psychologists once viewed this period of transition as a normal part of adult development (Gould, 1978), researchers have failed to replicate findings of an increase in emotional distress during middle age (Eisler & Ragsdale, 1992; Rosenberg, Rosenberg, & Farrell, 1999). The midlife crisis is more myth than reality.

The parallel female version of the midlife crisis in popular psychology is the **empty-nest syndrome**, a supposed period of depression in mothers following the "flight" of their children from the home as they reach adulthood. The idea of the empty-nest syndrome, like the midlife crisis, is overstated. Most research suggests that there are cohort effects on the incidence of empty-nest syndrome. Women whose children left the "nest" during or just after World War II seem to have been less affected by the change in role than those whose children moved out of the home in the 1960s and 1970s. This cohort effect appears to relate to the extent to which women were likely to have joined the workforce or were primarily homemakers, because a large percentage of women were employed outside the home during and just after World War II to aid in war efforts, followed by a decline in outside employment during the 1960s and 1970s (Borland, 1982).

Women who define themselves less exclusively in their roles as parents, even those who aren't employed outside the home, are less vulnerable to empty-nest syndrome than those who have more traditional attitudes toward women's roles in society (Harkins, 1978). Some researchers have even speculated that empty-nest syndrome is specific to Caucasian women who don't work outside the home. The social norms, lifestyles, and extended family demands common among African American and Mexican American women, and of women of lower socioeconomic status who more commonly work outside the home, may buffer them against the feeling of being at loose ends once their children fly the nest (Borland, 1982; Woehrer, 1982). Fortunately, and contrary to popular belief, most empty nesters experience an *increase* in life satisfaction following their newfound flexibility and freedom (Black & Hill, 1984). Nonetheless, the shift in role, not to mention the sudden increase in free time, takes some adjustment (Walsh, 1999).

SOCIAL TRANSITIONS IN LATER YEARS. In the early 21st century, people are living longer than ever. The life expectancy of the average American man is 75.3; for the American woman it's 80.4 (Centers for Disease Control and Prevention, 2009). Contrast those numbers with those only a century ago, when the average life span was 48 for men and 51 for women (National Center for Health Statistics, 2005). A greater percentage of the population is elderly than ever before, now that the "baby boomers" are coming of age. Moreover, the elderly now have more options for living out their later years. Many opt not to retire until well after 70. Some retire and take on part-time work or become volunteers for chari-

---

replicability

CAN THE RESULTS BE DUPLICATED IN OTHER STUDIES?

For women who have worked throughout the years spent raising their children, the "empty-nest" transition tends to be easier than for stay-at-home mothers.

midlife crisis
supposed phase of adulthood characterized by emotional distress about the aging process and an attempt to regain youth

empty-nest syndrome
alleged period of depression in mothers following the departure of their grown children from the home

ties. Many enter retirement communities and assisted living facilities that allow them to maintain active social lives even when they can no longer drive, shop, or cook. Contrary to popular belief, depression is actually less common among the elderly than it is among younger people (Lilienfeld et al., 2010). Across the population, happiness tends to increase through the sixties and perhaps even seventies (Nass, Brave, & Takayama, 2006). Nevertheless, about 15 percent of the elderly experience significant problems with depression. Perhaps not surprisingly, those with declining health and sleep disturbances are especially vulnerable to depression (Cole & Dendukuri, 2003).

How can we predict how aging will affect us? Chronological age doesn't necessarily forecast the behavioral or biological changes that accompany aging (Birren & Renner, 1977). Other ways of measuring age may do a better job of capturing the impact of changes in later life. Let's consider four indices other than chronological age (Birren & Renner, 1977): ◉ Watch

Every day, 98-year-old Mitchell Namy (the great-uncle of one of your book's authors) sends e-mails, Web surfs, and trades stocks online. He drives himself to his weekly bridge games. Although his hearing and his knees have declined, his "functional age" is well below his chronological age.

◉ **Watch** a 92-Year-Old Volunteer on **mypsychlab.com**

1. **Biological age:** the estimate of a person's age in terms of biological functioning. How efficiently are the person's organ systems, such as heart and lungs, functioning? When a 65-year-old brags, "My doctor says I have the body of a 40-year-old," this is what his doctor is talking about.

2. **Psychological age:** a person's mental attitudes and agility, and the capacity to deal with the stresses of an ever-changing environment. Some people display little change in memory, ability to learn, and personality from adolescence to old age, whereas others deteriorate substantially.

3. **Functional age:** a person's ability to function in given roles in society. Functional age may provide a better basis for judging readiness to retire, replacing the arbitrary criterion of chronological age (for example, that people should retire at 65 or 70).

4. **Social age:** whether people behave in accord with the social behaviors appropriate for their age. When people judge a woman as "dressing too young for her age" or roll their eyes at an 80-year-old man cruising around downtown in a sports car looking for young women, they're invoking expectations about social age.

Growing old isn't entirely a "state of mind," as the saying goes, because a host of physical and social factors influence how comfortably we age. But there no's question that remaining physically and mentally active can promote a younger body and mind, no matter how many candles appear on our birthday cake.

assess your knowledge   FACT OR FICTION?

✓ **Study** and **Review** on **mypsychlab.com**

1. Studies of contact comfort suggest that nourishment isn't the principal basis for attachment in primates. True / False

2. Studies suggest that within the broad range of the average expectable environment, parenting style may not be a crucial determinant of children's development. True / False

3. Gender differences don't emerge until parenting practices have the opportunity to influence children's behavior. True / False

4. When evaluating Kohlberg's moral dilemmas, the answers people give are more important than the reasoning processes they used to arrive at these answers. True / False

5. Marriage and becoming a parent both exert an overall positive impact on adults' stress levels. True / False

Answers: 1. T (p. 386); 2. T (p. 389); 3. F (p. 392); 4. F (p. 395); 5. F (p. 397)

SPECIAL CONSIDERATIONS IN HUMAN DEVELOPMENT 361–364

10.1 IDENTIFY WAYS TO THINK SCIENTIFICALLY ABOUT DEVELOPMENTAL FINDINGS.

In evaluating how and why children change, we must resist the temptation to assume that events that happened prior necessarily cause events that happen later, and keep in mind that cause and effect is often a two-way street.

1. The study of how behavior changes over time is called _____ _____ . (p. 361)

2. The _____ _____ fallacy is the assumption that because one event happened before another event, the two events are causally related. (p. 361)

3. In a _____ design, researchers obtain a "snapshot" of people of different ages at a single point in time. (p. 362)

4. _____ _____ can be observed when different samples of participants show different effects because they grew up during different time periods. (p. 362)

5. How was the classic "Up Series" documentary set up similar to longitudinal designs in psychology? Can you identify at least one positive and one negative aspect of utilizing longitudinal designs? (p. 362)

6. Research shows that most children (are/aren't) remarkably resilient and capable of withstanding stress. (p. 363)

10.2 CLARIFY HOW NATURE AND NURTURE CAN CONTRIBUTE TO DEVELOPMENT.

Genes and environment intersect in complex ways, so we can't always conclude that one or the other is driving behavior. For example, as children develop, how their genes are expressed often depends on their experiences.

7. Both _____, our genetic endowment, and _____, the environments we encounter, play powerful roles in shaping our development. (p. 363)

8. Many studies of human development are subject to a _____, meaning it is difficult to identify the relative effects of genes and environment. (p. 363)

9. Caspi and colleagues' longitudinal study of children with low levels of MAO illustrates the phenomenon of _____ _____ , in which the effect of genes depends on environment, and vice versa. (p. 364)

10. Apply what you've learned about the nature–nurture debate by matching each nature-nurture intersection with the appropriate description. (pp. 363–364)

____ Gene Expression	1. The impact of genes on behavior depends on the environment in which the behavior develops.
____ Gene-Environment Interactions	2. Genetic predispositions can drive us to select and create particular environments, leading to the mistaken appearance of a pure effect of nature.
____ Nature via Nurture	3. Some genes "turn on" only in response to specific environmental events.

THE DEVELOPING BODY: PHYSICAL & MOTOR DEVELOPMENT 364–371

10.3 TRACK THE TRAJECTORY OF PRENATAL DEVELOPMENT AND IDENTIFY BARRIERS TO NORMAL DEVELOPMENT.

Many important aspects of fetal development occur early in pregnancy. The brain begins to develop 18 days after conception and continues to mature into adolescence. Teratogens such as drugs, alcohol, and even maternal stress can damage or slow fetal development. Although premature infants often experience developmental delays, low-birthweight babies tend to have the least positive outcomes.

11. Early in pregnancy, a ball of identical cells that hasn't yet taken on any specific function is called the _____. (p. 365)

12. The embryo becomes a _____ once the major organs are established and the heart has begun to beat. (p. 365)

13. Environmental factors that can have a negative effect on prenatal development are called _____. (p. 366)

14. The _____ point at which infants can typically survive on their own is 25 weeks, but a full-term baby is born at _____ weeks. (p. 366)

10.4 DESCRIBE HOW INFANTS LEARN TO COORDINATE MOTION AND ACHIEVE MAJOR MOTOR MILESTONES.

Children tend to achieve motor milestones such as crawling and walking in roughly the same order, although the ages when they accomplish these milestones vary. Infants are born with reflexes that help them get started, but experience plays a critical role in building up children's muscles and motor coordination.

15. Children rely on _____ _____ as they learn how to coordinate their movements in order to reach or crawl. (p. 367)

16. Plot the progression of development in the figure by listing the age and major motor milestone depicted by each child. (p. 367)

(a) _____

(b) _____

(c) _____

(d) _____

(e) _____

(f) _____

17. How do child-rearing practices in other cultures (such as swaddling in Peru), compared with those in the United States, affect children's short- and long-term motor development? (p. 368)

10.5 DESCRIBE PHYSICAL MATURATION DURING CHILDHOOD AND ADOLESCENCE.

During childhood, different parts of the body grow at different rates, with the head-to-body-size ratio becoming smaller than in infancy. Adolescence is marked by sexual maturation and significant physical changes.

18. Sexual maturation includes changes in _____ _____ _____ , such as the reproductive organs and genitals, and _____ _____ _____, such as breast enlargement in girls and deepening voices in boys. (p. 369)

10.6 EXPLAIN WHICH ASPECTS OF PHYSICAL ABILITY DECLINE DURING AGING.

There are large individual differences in age-related changes in agility and physical coordination. One of the major milestones of physical aging in women is menopause.

19. Some aspects of physical decline may be related to decreasing _____ capacities. (p. 370)

20. Research suggests that women in menopause are (more/no more) prone to depression than women at other phases of life. (p. 371)

THE DEVELOPING MIND: COGNITIVE DEVELOPMENT 371–383

10.7 UNDERSTAND MAJOR THEORIES OF HOW CHILDREN'S THINKING DEVELOPS.

Piaget believed that development unfolds in four stages that influence all aspects of cognitive development. Vygotsky believed that different children develop skills in different domains at different rates, and that social structuring on the part of the parent facili-

tates children's learning and development. Researchers continue to debate whether learning happens in more general or domain-specific ways, whether learning is gradual or stage-like, and how much innate cognitive knowledge children possess.

21. According to Piaget, when children can no longer use _____ to absorb a new experience into their current knowledge structures, they will engage in _____ by altering an existing belief to make it more compatible with the new experience. (p. 373)

22. Using the descriptions provided, complete the table to show Piaget's four stages of cognitive development. (p. 373)

STAGE	TYPICAL AGES	DESCRIPTION
_____	_____	No thought beyond immediate physical experiences
_____	_____	Able to think beyond the here and now, but egocentric and unable to perform mental transformations
_____	_____	Able to perform mental transformations but only on concrete physical objects
_____	_____	Able to perform hypothetical and abstract reasoning

23. What ability does Piaget's three mountains task (below) measure? In what stage can children pass this task? (p. 374)

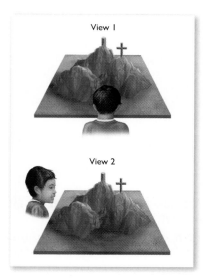

View 1

View 2

24. Modern research suggests that cognitive development is (less/more) continuous and (less/more) general than Piaget theorized. (p. 375)

25. Whereas Piaget emphasized children's exploration of the physical world, Vygotsky believed that _____ and _____ factors were children's primary source of learning. (p. 375)

26. Vygotsky identified the zone of _____ _____ as the phase when a child is receptive to learning a new skill and can make use of _____, the structure provided by parents to aid the child's learning. (p. 376)

Answers are located at the end of the text.

10.8 EXPLAIN HOW CHILDREN ACQUIRE KNOWLEDGE IN IMPORTANT COGNITIVE DOMAINS.

Physical reasoning in infants involves both basic, apparently innate, knowledge, and refinement of knowledge based on experience. Conceptual development requires children to acquire knowledge of how things look, how they are used, and in what contexts they appear. Self-recognition becomes increasingly sophisticated as children move from understanding they are physically distinct entities to understanding that others have minds distinct from their own. Numerical development requires a complex understanding of counting rules and the nature of precise quantities. This ability develops slowly and is easily disrupted. The ability to count doesn't appear in all cultures.

27. Work by Renee Baillargeon shows that infants (do/don't) have a basic understanding of the physics of an object's behavior. (p. 378)

28. A classic test of _____ _____ _____ is the false-belief task, which examines children's ability to reason about what other people know or believe. (p. 379)

10.9 DESCRIBE HOW ATTITUDES TOWARD KNOWLEDGE CHANGE DURING ADOLESCENCE.

Adolescents are confronted with more adult-like opportunities and decisions that their brain's relatively immature frontal lobes aren't always prepared to handle.

29. According to David Elkind, adolescent behavioral problems stem in part from what he termed the _____ _____, teenagers' feelings of profound uniqueness and of living out a story that others are watching. (p. 381)

30. William Perry noted that students pass through a variety of _____, or perspectives, on knowledge during their college years as they discover that their professors have few absolute answers to offer. (p. 382)

THE DEVELOPING PERSONALITY: SOCIAL AND MORAL DEVELOPMENT 383–399

10.10 DESCRIBE HOW AND WHEN CHILDREN ESTABLISH EMOTIONAL BONDS WITH THEIR CAREGIVERS.

Although infants may recognize and react positively to their caregivers, they don't develop a specific attachment bond until around eight months of age. The type of attachment that infants form with their caregivers varies depending on parental style and the infant's temperament.

31. Usually starting at eight or nine months, babies can develop _____ _____, which may be an adaptive mechanism for keeping infants away from danger. (p. 383)

32. Lorenz showed that newborn goslings bonded to the first moving thing they saw, a phenomenon called _____. (p. 385)

33. Define Harlow's notion of contact comfort and describe the role each "mother" played in helping meet the monkey's needs. (p. 386)

34. Complete the table by describing the four attachment styles identified in Ainsworth's Strange Situation research. (pp. 386–387)

ATTACHMENT STYLE	DESCRIPTION/CHILD'S REACTION
1. Secure attachment	
2. Insecure-avoidant attachment	
3. Insecure-anxious attachment	
4. Disorganized attachment	

10.11 EXPLAIN THE ENVIRONMENTAL AND GENETIC INFLUENCES ON SOCIAL BEHAVIOR AND SOCIAL STYLE IN CHILDREN.

Parenting style (permissive, authoritative, authoritarian, or uninvolved), family structure, and peers may all influence children's behaviors and emotional adjustment, although their precise causal role is controversial. Aspects of children, such as temperament and self-control, also affect their long-term social development.

35. Research suggests that specific parenting styles may not matter so much as whether the parent can provide the _____ _____ environment. (p. 389)

10.12 DETERMINE HOW MORALITY AND IDENTITY DEVELOP DURING ADOLESCENCE AND EMERGING ADULTHOOD.

Children's initial concepts of morality are based largely on fear of punishment, but over time become more sophisticated and based on intentions rather than consequences. Getting a handle on identity is one of the challenges of adolescence.

36. Erikson coined the term _____ _____ to describe the confusion that most adolescents experience regarding their sense of self. (p. 393)

37. According to Erikson's theory of human development, we travel through _____ stages and we face a different _____ crisis at each stage. (p. 393)

38. Kohlberg studied the development of _____ by scoring the _____ _____ people used as they wrestled with a moral dilemma. (p. 395)

10.13 IDENTIFY DEVELOPMENTAL CHANGES DURING MAJOR LIFE TRANSITIONS IN ADULTS.

Major life transitions, including career changes, finding a romantic partner, and having children, can be stressful for adults. Nevertheless, contrary to the claims of popular psychology, midlife crises are relatively rare.

39. One of the biggest transitions an adult can go through is becoming a _____. (p. 397)

10.14 SUMMARIZE DIFFERENT WAYS OF CONCEPTUALIZING OLD AGE.
Chronological age isn't a perfect predictor of physical, social, or cognitive ability in the elderly. Some aspects of cognitive and physical functions begin to decline as early as age 30. However, other cognitive abilities increase with age; how much we slow down depends on a host of factors, including our activity levels.

40. A 65-year-old person who is in excellent health and top physical condition may have a _____ _____ of 45 years old. (p. 399)

DO YOU KNOW THESE TERMS?

- developmental psychology (p. 361)
- post hoc fallacy (p. 361)
- cross-sectional design (p. 362)
- cohort effect (p. 362)
- longitudinal design (p. 362)
- gene-environment interaction (p. 364)
- nature via nurture (p. 364)
- gene expression (p. 364)
- prenatal (p. 365)
- zygote (p. 365)
- blastocyst (p. 365)
- embryo (p. 365)
- fetus (p. 365)

- teratogen (p. 366)
- fetal alcohol syndrome (p. 366)
- motor behavior (p. 367)
- adolescence (p. 368)
- puberty (p. 369)
- primary sex characteristic (p. 369)
- secondary sex characteristic (p. 369)
- menarche (p. 369)
- spermarche (p. 369)
- menopause (p. 370)
- cognitive development (p. 371)
- assimilation (p. 372)
- accommodation (p. 373)

- sensorimotor stage (p. 373)
- object permanence (p. 373)
- preoperational stage (p. 373)
- egocentrism (p. 374)
- conservation (p. 374)
- concrete operations stage (p. 374)
- formal operations stage (p. 374)
- scaffolding (p. 376)
- zone of proximal development (p. 376)
- theory of mind (p. 379)
- stranger anxiety (p. 383)
- temperament (p. 383)
- attachment (p. 384)

- contact comfort (p. 386)
- mono-operation bias (p. 387)
- average expectable environment (p. 389)
- self control (p. 391)
- gender identity (p. 392)
- gender role (p. 392)
- identity (p. 393)
- psychosocial crisis (p. 393)
- emerging adulthood (p. 394)
- midlife crisis (p. 398)
- empty-nest syndrome (p. 398)

APPLY YOUR SCIENTIFIC THINKING SKILLS

Use your scientific thinking skills to answer the following questions, referencing specific scientific thinking principles and common errors in reasoning whenever possible.

1. Parents now have an amazing amount of parenting advice at their disposal in books, on websites, and through parent listservs and chat rooms. Research three sources of parenting information and create a list of the key topics they address (such as getting one's infant to sleep or eat better, or disciplining one's child). What assumptions do they make about the role of nature versus nurture in parenting and how do these assumptions correspond to scientific research? Are there rival hypotheses about children's behaviors that these sources neglected to consider?

2. As we've learned, the frontal lobes don't fully mature until late adolescence or early adulthood, a biological reality that may affect teenage decision making. There is active debate regarding how many teenage behavioral problems stem from the "teen brain." Find three examples of media articles related to this issue, such as debates over changing the age at which teens can enlist in the military, drink alcohol legally, obtain a driving license, or even stay out during an age-related "curfew." What arguments does each side use to support its case? What scientific or logical errors, if any, does each side make?

3. Based on the research that we've discussed regarding the changes that come with age, what features would you include if someone asked you to design a senior center to help healthy aging adults maintain their physical, cognitive, and social well-being? What evidence would you cite to support each of your decisions?

11 | EMOTION AND MOTIVATION

what moves us

THINK ABOUT IT

ARE EMOTION AND REASON OPPOSITES OF EACH OTHER?

IS THE POLYGRAPH TEST REALLY A "LIE DETECTOR"?

ARE PEOPLE WHO HAVE GOOD THINGS HAPPEN TO THEM HAPPIER THAN OTHER PEOPLE?

DOES SEXUAL DESIRE DISAPPEAR IN OLD AGE?

DO OPPOSITES ATTRACT IN ROMANTIC RELATIONSHIPS?

T O X I C
E M O T I O N S
A T   W O R K

And What You Can Do About Them

P E T E R   J.   F R O S T

Pop psychology books often tell us that many emotions, especially in the extreme, are "toxic." Are they right?

Meet Elliott. He's a Caucasian male, 30 years of age. At first blush, Elliott looks and acts pretty much like everyone else. He's well dressed and socially appropriate, and his scores on tests of intelligence, memory, and language are boringly normal. Yet Elliott is different—very different—from the average person in two ways.

First, Elliott has recently recovered from brain surgery. Diagnosed with a frontal lobe tumor that had ballooned to the size of a small orange, Elliott underwent a radical operation to remove not only the tumor but also a sizable chunk of surrounding brain tissue. In many respects, Elliott is a contemporary version of Vermont railroad worker Phineas Gage, who, as we'll recall from Chapter 3, lost much of his frontal cortex in a catastrophic accident in 1848 (Damasio, 1994; Eslinger & Damasio, 1985).

Second, like Gage, Elliott's behavior differs strikingly from what it was before he lost a goodly portion of his brain. Before the operation, Elliott was a successful businessman with a happy and balanced home life. Yet Elliott is now different in one crucial way: He seems entirely devoid of emotion. As Antonio Damasio (1994), who studied Elliott in depth, remarked: "I never saw a tinge of emotion in my many hours of conversation with him: no sadness, no impatience, no frustration …" (p. 45). When Damasio's colleague Daniel Tranel showed Elliott a series of upsetting photographs, including pictures of gruesome injuries, buildings crumbling during earthquakes, and houses in flames, Elliott displayed virtually no emotional response, as measured by either his subjective report or his physiological reactions. Nor does Elliott express much joy when describing the wonderful moments of his life. As Damasio (1994) put it:

> Try to imagine not feeling pleasure when you contemplate a painting you love or hear a favorite piece of music. Try to imagine yourself forever robbed of that possibility and yet aware of the intellectual contents of the visual or musical stimulus, and also aware that it once did give you pleasure. We might summarize Elliott's predicament as *to know but not to feel.* (p. 45)

What's more, Elliott's life, like that of Phineas Gage, is in utter shambles. Elliott has made foolish decisions in his personal life, investing all of his savings in a risky business venture and going bankrupt. He married a woman who was a poor match for him, resulting in an abrupt divorce. His on-the-job performance is no better.

Elliott's case imparts a valuable lesson: Emotion and reason aren't necessarily opposites. To the contrary, emotion is often the servant of reason (Levine, 1998). Without feelings, we have scant basis for rational decisions. Recent research suggests that college students made a bit angry (by having been asked to write about past infuriating experiences) are actually better than non-angry students at distinguishing strong from weak scientific arguments in research studies (Moons & Mackie, 2007). Elliott married the wrong woman in part because he'd lost access to his "gut feelings" concerning his attraction to members of the opposite sex. He based his choice of a romantic partner largely on reason alone, which is typically a recipe for disaster (Gigerenzer, 2007). Even though Mr. Spock of *Star Trek* fame is the epitome of pure reason, research suggests that a real-life version of Mr. Spock would actually be far more irrational than rational. His absence of emotional reactions would ultimately do him in as he attempted to generate solutions to everyday problems.

Popular wisdom teaches us that many emotions, especially negative ones, are bad for us. A litany of pop psychology books encourages us not to feel angry, guilty, ashamed, or sad. Such emotions, the books inform us, are unhealthy, even "toxic." Pop psychologists are right to remind us that excessive anger, guilt, and the like can be self-destructive. "Everything in moderation," as our grandmother reminded us. But they're wrong to suggest we'd be better off without these feelings, because many emotions—even negative ones—are crucial to our survival.

THEORIES OF EMOTION: WHAT CAUSES OUR FEELINGS?

11.1 Describe the major theories of emotion.

11.2 Identify unconscious influences on emotion.

Elliott and Mr. Spock aside, virtually all of us experience **emotions**—mental states or feelings associated with our evaluation of our experiences. Although psychologists don't agree fully on what causes our emotions, we'll soon discover that they've made significant strides toward unraveling this and many other enduring mysteries.

emotion
mental state or feeling associated with our evaluation of our experiences

■ Discrete Emotions Theory: Emotions as Evolved Expressions

According to **discrete emotions theory**, humans experience a small number of distinct emotions, even if they combine in complex ways (Griffiths, 1997; Izard, 1994; Tomkins, 1962). Advocates of this theory propose that emotions have distinct biological roots and serve evolutionary functions. Each emotion, they suggest, is associated with a distinct "motor program": a set of genetically influenced physiological responses that are essentially the same in all of us (Ekman & Friesen, 1971). They further argue that because the brain's cortex, which plays a key role in thinking, evolved later than the limbic system, which plays a key role in emotion, our emotional reactions to situations precede our thoughts about them (Zajonc, 1984, 2000).

SUPPORT FOR AN EVOLUTIONARY BASIS OF EMOTIONS. The fact that some emotional expressions emerge even without direct reinforcement suggests that they may be by-products of innate motor programs (Freedman, 1964; Panksepp, 2007). Newborn infants smile spontaneously during REM sleep, the sleep stage during which most vivid dreaming occurs (see Chapter 5). At about six weeks, babies start to smile whenever they see a favorite face, and at about three months, they may smile when they're learning to do something new, even when no one's around (Plutchik, 2003). Irenäus Eibl-Eibesfeldt (1973) showed that even three-month-old babies who are blind from birth smile in response to playing and tickling, and frown and cry when left alone.

Consider the emotion of *disgust*, which derives from the Latin term for "bad taste" (see Chapter 4). Imagine we asked you to swallow a piece of food that you find repulsive, like a dried-up cockroach (apologies to those of you reading this chapter over lunch or dinner). The odds are high you'd wrinkle your nose, contract your mouth, stick out your tongue, turn your head slightly to one side, and close your eyes at least partly (Phillips et al., 1997). Discrete emotions theorists would say that this coordinated set of reactions is evolutionarily adaptive. When you wrinkle your nose and contract your mouth, you're reducing the chances you'll ingest this substance; by sticking out your tongue, you're increasing the chances you'll expel it; by turning your head, you're doing your best to avoid it; and by closing your eyes, you're limiting the damage it can do to your visual system. Other emotions similarly prepare us for biologically important actions (Frijda, 1986). When we're afraid, our eyes open wide, allowing us to better spot potential dangers, like predators, lurking in our environment. When we're angry, our teeth and fists often become clenched, readying us to bite and fight.

Charles Darwin (1872) was among the first to point out the similarities between the emotional expressions of humans and many nonhuman animals. He noted that the angry snarl of dogs, marked by the baring of their fangs, is reminiscent of the dismissive sneer of humans. Eugene Morton (1977, 1982) showed deep-seated similarities in communication across most animal species, especially mammals and birds, further suggesting that the emotions of humans and nonhuman animals share the same evolutionary heritage. For example, across the animal kingdom high-pitched sounds are associated with friendly interactions, and low-pitched sounds with hostile interactions. Jaak Panksepp (2005) discovered that rats emit a high-pitched chirp, perhaps similar to human laughter, when tickled. The high-pitched panting of dogs during play also seems similar in many ways to human laughter.

Of course, the mere fact that two things are superficially similar doesn't prove that they share evolutionary roots. Birds and bats both have wings, but their wings evolved independently of each other. In the case of emotions, however, we know that all mammals share an evolutionary ancestor. The fact that many mammals display similar emotional reactions during similar social behaviors, such as tickling and play, lends itself to a parsimonious hypothesis: Perhaps these reactions share the same evolutionary origins.

CULTURE AND EMOTION. Another way of evaluating claims that discrete emotions are products of evolution is to examine the *universality* of emotional expressions. If we humans evolved to express emotions a certain way, we'd expect expressions to communicate the same meaning across cultures.

Recognition of Emotions across Cultures. One telling piece of evidence for discrete emotions theory derives from research showing that people recognize and generate the same emotional expressions across cultures (Izard, 1971). Nevertheless, this re-

People have recognized the facial reaction of disgust for centuries. This is a photograph from Charles Darwin's book on the expression of emotions, published in 1872.

David Matsumoto and Bob Willingham, themselves former national judo competitors, examined the facial expressions of judo competition winners and losers at the 2004 Athens Olympics. They found that competitors in 35 countries across six continents displayed extremely similar smiles and other facial reactions after winning a match or receiving a medal (Matsumoto & Willingham, 2006).

occam's razor
DOES A SIMPLER EXPLANATION FIT THE DATA JUST AS WELL?

discrete emotions theory
theory that humans experience a small number of distinct emotions that are rooted in our biology

ruling out rival hypotheses

HAVE IMPORTANT ALTERNATIVE EXPLANATIONS FOR THE FINDINGS BEEN EXCLUDED?

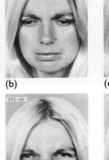
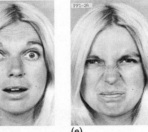
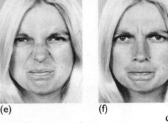

(a) (b) (c)

(d) (e) (f)

? Six of the seven primary emotions identified by Paul Ekman and his colleagues. **Can you match each face to the corresponding emotions of anger, disgust, fear, happiness, sadness, and surprise?** (See answer upside down at bottom of page.)

⊙▸ Simulate Recognizing Facial Expressions of Emotions on **mypsychlab.com**

Some psychologists believe that pride is also a discrete emotion. Pride tends to be associated with a smile, along with the head pushed back, the chest pushed forward, and one's hands on the hips or in the air (Tracy & Robins, 2007)—as shown here.

primary emotions
small number (perhaps seven) of emotions believed by some theorists to be cross-culturally universal

display rules
cross-cultural guidelines for how and when to express emotions

Answers: (a) happiness; (b) sadness; (c) fear; (d) surprise; (e) disgust; (f) anger.

search is vulnerable to a rival explanation: Because these people have all been exposed to Western culture, the similarities may be due to shared experiences rather than a shared evolutionary heritage.

To rule out this explanation, in the late 1960s American psychologist Paul Ekman traveled to the wilds of southeastern New Guinea to study a group of people who'd been essentially isolated from Western culture and still used Stone Age tools. With the aid of a translator, Ekman read them a brief story (for example, "His mother has died, and he feels very sad"), along with a display of photographs of Americans depicting various emotions, like happiness, sadness, and anger. Then, Ekman asked them to select the photograph that matched the story. He later went further, asking U.S. college students to guess which emotions the New Guineans were displaying (Ekman & Friesen, 1971).

Ekman (1999) and his colleagues (Ekman & Friesen, 1986) concluded that a small number of **primary emotions**—perhaps seven—are cross-culturally universal. Specifically, they found that the facial expressions associated with these emotions are recognized across most, if not all, cultures. Discrete emotions theorists call these emotions "primary" because they're presumably the biologically based emotions from which other emotions arise:

- Happiness
- Sadness
- Surprise
- Anger
- Disgust
- Fear
- Contempt

Recent research suggests that pride may also be a cross-culturally universal emotion, although the evidence for this claim is preliminary (Tracy & Robins, 2007).

Ekman and his colleagues found that certain primary emotions are easier to detect than others. Happiness tends to be the most easily recognized emotion (Elfenbein & Ambady, 2002); their New Guinea subjects correctly recognized happiness in Americans more than 90 percent of the time (Ekman, 1994). In contrast, negative emotions are more

difficult to recognize; many subjects confuse disgust with anger, anger with fear, and fear with surprise (Elfenbein & Ambady, 2002; Tomkins & McCarter, 1964). Although people across widely different cultures don't always agree on which facial expressions go with which emotions (Feldman Barrett & Bliss-Moreau, 2009; Russell, 1994), they agree often enough to provide support for discrete emotions theory. ⊙▸ Simulate

Primary emotions don't tell the whole story of our feelings. Just as talented painters create a magnificently complex palette of secondary paint colors, like various shades of green and purple, from a few primary paint colors, like blue and yellow (see Chapter 4), our brains "create" an enormous array of *secondary emotions* from a small number of primary emotions. The secondary emotion of "alarm" seems to be a mixture of fear and surprise, and the secondary emotion of "hatred" seems to be a mixture of anger and disgust (Plutchik, 2000).

Some of these complex emotion blends possess names in other languages, but lack an equivalent in English. Take *schadenfreude*, a German term referring to the glee we experience at witnessing the misfortune of others, especially those we see as arrogant (Ortony, Clore, & Collins, 1988). It seems to be a hybrid of several emotions, like happiness, anger, and pride. We experience *schadenfreude* when we feel secretly happy when a classmate who brags about getting A-pluses on his exams unexpectedly gets an F.

Cultural Differences in Emotional Expression: Display Rules. The finding that certain emotions exist across most or all cultures doesn't mean that cultures are identical in their emotional expressions. In part, that's because cultures differ in **display rules**, societal guidelines for how and when to express emotions (Ekman & Friesen, 1975; Matsumoto et al., 2005). In Western culture, parents teach most boys not to cry, whereas they typically teach girls that crying is acceptable (Plutchik, 2003). Americans can be taken aback when a visitor from South America, the Middle East, or some European countries, like Russia, greets them by planting a kiss on their cheek.

In a study of display rules, Wallace Friesen (1972) videotaped Japanese and American college students without their knowledge. He asked both groups of students to watch two film clips, one of a neutral travel scene (the control condition) and one of an incredibly gory film depicting a ritual genital mutilation (the experimental condition). When these students were alone, their facial reactions to the films were similar: Both groups showed little emotional reaction to the neutral film but clear signs of fear, disgust, and distress to the gory film. Yet when an older experimenter entered the room, the role of culture became apparent. Although American students' reactions to the films didn't change, Japanese students typically smiled during the gory film, concealing their negative emotional reactions. In Japanese culture, deference to authority figures is the norm, so the students acted as though they were happy to see the films. In many cases, culture doesn't influence emotion itself; it influences its overt expression (Fok et al., 2008).

ACCOMPANIMENTS OF EMOTIONAL EXPRESSIONS. According to discrete emotions theorists, each primary emotion is associated with a distinctive constellation of facial expressions. In anger, our lips consistently narrow and our eyebrows move downward. In contempt, we frequently lift and tighten our lips on one side of our face, generating a smirk (Matsumoto & Ekman, 2004), or roll our eyes upward, in effect communicating "I'm above (superior to) you" (see **FIGURE 11.1**). Interestingly, John Gottman and his colleagues have found that contempt, and the facial expressions that go along with it, are among the best predictors of divorce in married couples (Gottman & Levenson, 1999).

Emotions and Physiology. We can differentiate at least some primary emotions by their patterns of physiological responding (Ax, 1953; Rainville et al., 2006). The mere act of making a face associated with a specific emotion alters our bodily reactions in characteristic ways (Ekman, Levenson, & Friesen, 1983). Our heart rates tend to increase more when we make angry and fearful than happy or surprised facial expressions (Cacioppo et al., 1997), probably because the first two emotions are more closely linked to the emergency reactions we experience when threatened (see Chapters 3 and 12). Our heart kicks into high gear when we're in danger, mobilizing us for action (Frijda, 1986). Yet even fear and anger differ physiologically. When we're afraid, our digestive systems tend to slow down. In contrast, when we're angry, our digestive systems tend to speed up, which explains why our "stomachs churn" when we're furious (Carlson & Hatfield, 1992).

Brain imaging data also provide at least some evidence for discrete emotions. Fear, disgust, and anger tend to show different patterns of brain activation (Murphy, Nimmo-Smith, & Lawrence, 2003). Fear is relatively specific to the amygdala (see Chapter 3), disgust to the *insula*, a region within the limbic system, and anger to a region of the frontal cortex behind our eyes.

Yet in other cases we can't distinguish different emotions by means of their physiology (Cacioppo, Tassinary, & Bernstson, 2000; Feldman Barrett et al., 2007). Surprisingly, happiness and sadness aren't terribly different in their patterns of brain activation (Murphy et al., 2003). Moreover, there's almost certainly no single "fear processor," "disgust processor," and so on, in the brain, because multiple brain regions participate in all emotions (Schienle et al., 2002).

Pair 1

Pair 2

FIGURE 11.1 **Which Mask Conveys a Threat?** In hunter–gatherer societies, people often construct masks to convey threat, especially anger. These two pairs of shapes are based on wooden masks worn in these societies. In both cases, the shape on the left communicates more threat. Even American college students can distinguish the threatening from nonthreatening mask at higher than chance levels. (*Source:* Aronoff, Barclay, & Stevenson, 1988)

In April 2007, American actor Richard Gere scandalized much of India by kissing Indian actress Shilpa Shetty's cheek on stage at an AIDS awareness rally. This action even resulted in a warrant being placed for Gere's arrest in India; it was later dropped. Gere was apparently unaware of display rules in India that strictly forbid kissing in public.

FACTOID

The word "supercilious," which refers to feeling contemptuously superior to others, literally means "above the eyebrow." Facial expressions associated with contempt often communicate a sense that others are "beneath" us.

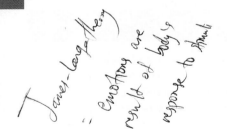

Psychologist Paul Ekman, shown here, is demonstrating two smiles: a Duchenne (genuine) smile and a non-Duchenne smile. Which is the Duchenne smile? (See answer upside down at bottom of page.)

cognitive theories of emotion
theories proposing that emotions are products of thinking

James-Lange theory of emotion
theory proposing that emotions result from our interpretations of our bodily reactions to stimuli

correlation vs. causation

CAN WE BE SURE THAT A CAUSES B?

replicability

CAN THE RESULTS BE DUPLICATED IN OTHER STUDIES?

Answer: Photo on top. One simple clue is more movement of the eyes in a Duchenne smile.

Real versus Fake Emotions. We can use certain components of facial expressions to help us distinguish real from fake emotions. In genuine happiness, we see an upward turning of the corners of the mouth, along with a drooping of the eyelids and a crinkling of the corners of the eyes (Ekman, Davidson, & Friesen, 1990). Emotion theorists distinguish this genuine expression, called the *Duchenne smile* after the neurologist who discovered it, from the fake or *Pan Am smile*, which is marked by a movement of the mouth but not the eyes. The term *Pan Am smile* derives from an old television commercial featuring the now defunct airline Pan Am, in which all of the flight attendants flashed obviously fake smiles. If you page through your family albums, you'll probably find an abundance of Pan Am smiles, especially in posed photographs. Interestingly, among subjects asked to produce facial expressions, only Duchenne smiles are associated with increased activity of the front region of the left hemisphere, which appears specialized for positive emotions (Ekman et al., 1990).

■ Cognitive Theories of Emotion: Think First, Feel Later

As we've seen, discrete emotions theorists emphasize the biological underpinnings of emotion. For them, emotions are largely innate motor programs triggered by certain stimuli, and our emotional reactions to these stimuli precede our interpretation of them. Advocates of **cognitive theories of emotion** disagree. For them, emotions are products of thinking rather than the other way around. What we feel in response to a situation is determined by how we interpret it (Scherer, 1988). As we'll learn in Chapter 12, the way we appraise situations influences whether we find them stressful (Lazarus & Folkman, 1984). If we see an upcoming job interview as a potential catastrophe, we'll be hopelessly stressed out; if we see it as a healthy challenge, we'll be appropriately geared up for it. Moreover, for cognitive theorists, there are no discrete emotions, because the boundaries across emotions are fuzzy and there are as many different emotions as there are kinds of thoughts (Feldman Barrett & Russell, 1999; Ortony & Turner, 1990).

JAMES-LANGE THEORY OF EMOTION. Perhaps the oldest cognitive theory of emotion owes its origins to the great American psychologist William James (1890), whom we met in Chapter 1. Because Danish researcher Carl Lange (1885) advanced a similar version of this theory around the same time, psychologists refer to it as the **James-Lange theory of emotion**. According to the James-Lange theory, emotions result from our interpretations of our bodily reactions to stimuli.

To take James's example, let's imagine that while hiking through the forest, we come upon a bear. What happens next? Common wisdom tells us that we first become scared and then run away. Yet as James recognized, the link between our fear and running away is only a correlation; this link doesn't demonstrate that our fear *causes* us to run away. Indeed, James and Lange argued that the causal arrow is reversed: *We're afraid because we run away.* That is, we observe our physiological and behavioral reactions to a stimulus, in this case our hearts pounding, our palms sweating, and our feet running, and then conclude that we must have been scared (see **FIGURE 11.2**).

In support of this theory, a researcher examined five groups of patients with injuries in different regions of their spinal cord (Hohmann, 1966). Patients with injuries high in their spinal cord had lost almost all of their bodily sensation, and those with lower injuries had lost only part of their bodily sensation. Just as James and Lange would have predicted, patients with higher spinal cord damage reported less emotion—fear and anger—than those with lower spinal cord damage. Presumably, patients with lower injuries could feel more of their bodies, which allowed them a greater range of emotional reactions. Still, some researchers have criticized these findings because of a possible experimenter expectancy effect (see Chapter 2): the researcher knew which spinal cord patients were which when he assessed their emotions, which could have biased the results (Prinz, 2004). Moreover, some investigators haven't replicated these findings: One research team found no differences in the happiness of patients with or without spinal cord injuries (Chwalisz, Diener, & Gallagher, 1988).

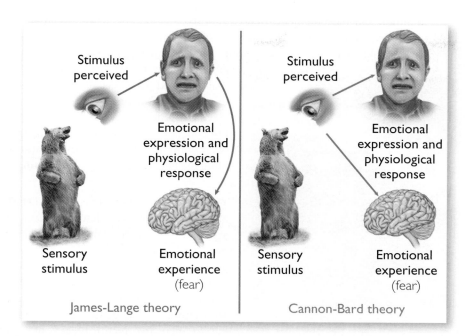

FIGURE 11.2 What Triggers Emotions? The James-Lange and Cannon-Bard theories differ in their views of how emotions are generated. (*Source:* Adapted from Cardoso)

Somatic marker theory — autonomic responses assist in decision-making and figuring how to act next.

Cannon-Bard theory = emotion-provoking event leads to emotion which and bodily reactions happen at the same time.

Few scientists today are strict believers in the James-Lange theory, but it continues to influence modern-day thinking about emotion. Antonio Damasio's (1994) **somatic marker theory** (*somatic* means "physical") proposes that we unconsciously and instantaneously use our "gut reactions"—especially our autonomic responses, like our heart rate and sweating (see Chapter 3)—to gauge how we should act. According to Damasio, if we feel our hearts pounding during a first date, we use that information as a "marker" or signal to help us decide what to do next, like ask that person out for a second date. Elliott, whom we met in this chapter's opening, may have made irrational decisions because he'd lost much of his frontal cortex, the input station for information from the brain's sensory regions. In turn, he may have lost access to somatic markers of emotion (Damasio, 1994). Still, there's evidence that people can make decisions solely on the basis of external knowledge and without any bodily feedback (Maia & McClelland, 2004). One team of investigators examined patients who suffered from a rare condition called *pure autonomic failure* (PAF), which is marked by a deterioration of autonomic nervous system neurons beginning in middle age (Heims et al., 2004). These patients don't experience increases in autonomic activity, such as heart rate or sweating, in response to emotional stimuli. Yet these patients had no difficulty on a gambling task that required them to make decisions about monetary risks. These findings don't completely falsify somatic marker theory, as it's possible that somatic markers are helpful to us when making decisions. But they suggest that somatic markers aren't *necessary* for wise choices, even if they sometimes give us a bit of extra guidance.

falsifiability

CAN THE CLAIM BE DISPROVED?

CANNON-BARD THEORY OF EMOTION. Walter Cannon (1929) and Philip Bard (1942) pointed out several flaws with James's and Lange's reasoning. They noted that most physiological changes occur too slowly—often taking at least a few seconds—to trigger emotional reactions, which happen almost instantaneously. Cannon and Bard also argued that we aren't aware of many of our bodily reactions, like the contractions of our stomach or liver. As a consequence, we can't use them to infer our emotions.

Cannon and Bard proposed a different model for the correlation between emotions and bodily reactions. According to the **Cannon-Bard theory**, an emotion-provoking event leads simultaneously to both an emotion and bodily reactions. To return to James's example, Cannon and Bard would say that when we see a bear while hiking in the forest, the sight of that bear triggers both fear and running at the same time (again refer to Figure 11.2).

somatic marker theory
theory proposing that we use our "gut reactions" to help us determine how we should act

Cannon-Bard theory
theory proposing that an emotion-provoking event leads simultaneously to an emotion and to bodily reactions

Cannon and Bard further proposed that the *thalamus*, which is a relay station for the senses (see Chapter 3), triggers both an emotion and bodily reactions. Cannon and Bard were probably wrong about that, because later researchers showed that numerous regions of the limbic system, including the hypothalamus and the amygdala, also play key roles in emotion (Carlson & Hatfield, 1992; Lewis, Haviland-Jones, & Feldman Barrett, 2008; Plutchik & Kellerman, 1986). Still, their model of emotion has encouraged investigators to explore the bases of emotion in the brain.

According to Schachter and Singer's two-factor theory of emotion, we first experience arousal after an emotion-provoking event, like a car accident, and then seek to interpret the cause of that arousal. The resulting label we attach to our arousal is the emotion.

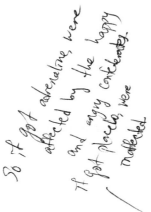

TWO-FACTOR THEORY OF EMOTION. Stanley Schachter and Jerome Singer (1962) argued that both the James-Lange and Cannon-Bard models were too simple. They agreed with James and Lange that our cognitive interpretations of our bodily reactions play a crucial role in emotions, but disagreed with James and Lange that these bodily reactions are sufficient for emotion. According to their **two-factor theory** of emotion (Schachter & Singer, 1962), two psychological events are required to produce an emotion:

1. After encountering an emotion-provoking event, we experience an undifferentiated state of arousal, that is, alertness. By "undifferentiated," Schachter and Singer meant that this arousal is the same across all emotions.

2. We seek to explain the source of this autonomic arousal. Once we attribute the arousal to an occurrence, either one within us or in the external environment, we experience an emotion. Once we figure out what's making us aroused, we "label" that arousal with an emotion. This labeling process, Schachter and Singer proposed, typically occurs so rapidly that we're not aware of it. According to this view, emotions are the explanations we attach to our arousal.

To illustrate, imagine we're hiking in the forest yet again (you'd think we'd have learned by now that we might find a bear there!). Then, sure enough, we come upon a bear. According to Schachter and Singer, we first become physiologically aroused; evolution assures that we do so that we're ready to fight—probably not an especially smart idea in this case—or flee (see Chapter 12). Then, we try to figure out the source of that arousal. One need not have a Ph.D. in psychology to infer that our arousal probably has something to do with the bear. So we label this arousal as fear, and that's the emotion we experience.

It's a good story, but do our emotions really work this way? In a classic study, Schachter and Singer (1962) decided to find out. As a "cover story," they informed subjects that they were testing the effectiveness of a new vitamin supplement—"Suproxin"—on vision. In reality, they were testing the effects of *adrenaline*, a chemical that produces physiological arousal (see Chapter 3). Schachter and Singer randomly assigned some subjects to receive an injection of Suproxin (again, actually adrenaline) and others an injection of placebo. While the adrenaline was entering their systems, Schachter and Singer randomly assigned subjects to two additional conditions: one in which a confederate (an undercover research assistant) acted in a happy fashion while completing questionnaires, and second in which a confederate acted in an angry fashion while completing questionnaires. The confederate was blind to whether subjects had received adrenaline or placebo. Finally, Schachter and Singer asked participants to describe how strongly they were experiencing different emotions.

Schachter and Singer's results dovetailed with two-factor theory. The emotions of subjects who'd received the placebo weren't influenced by the behavior of the confederate, but the emotions of the subjects who received adrenaline were. Subjects exposed to the

two-factor theory
theory proposing that emotions are produced by an undifferentiated state of arousal along with an attribution (explanation) of that arousal

happy confederate reported feeling happier, and those exposed to the angry confederate reported feeling angrier—but in both cases *only* if they'd received adrenaline. Emotion, Schachter and Singer concluded, requires *both* physiological arousal *and* an attribution of that arousal to an emotion-inducing event.

The award for the most creative test of the two-factor theory probably goes to two researchers (Dutton & Aron, 1974), who asked an attractive female confederate to approach male undergraduates on the University of British Columbia campus. She asked them for help with a survey and gave them her phone number in case they had any questions. Half of the time, she approached them on a sturdy bridge that didn't move, and half of the time she approached them on a swaying bridge suspended 200 feet above a river. Although only 30 percent of males in the first condition called her, 60 percent of males in the second condition did. The wobbly bridge in the second condition presumably increased male students' arousal, leading them to feel more intense romantic emotions. In a related study of "love at first fright," investigators approached participants immediately either before or after a roller-coaster ride, and showed them a photograph of an attractive member of the opposite sex. Participants who'd just gotten off the roller coaster rated the person in the photograph as more attractive—and indicated more of an interest in dating him or her—than did those who were just about to get on the roller coaster (Meston & Frohlich, 2003).

Still, the support for two-factor theory has been mixed. Not all researchers have replicated Schachter and Singer's (1962) results (Marshall & Zimbardo, 1979; Maslach, 1979). Moreover, research suggests that although arousal often intensifies emotions, emotions can occur in the absence of arousal (Reisenzein, 1983). Contrary to what Schachter and Singer claimed, arousal isn't necessary for all emotional experiences.

PUTTING IT ALL TOGETHER. So which of these theories should we believe? As is so often the case in psychology, there's probably a kernel of truth in several explanations. Discrete emotions theory is probably correct that our emotional reactions are shaped in part by natural selection and that these reactions serve crucial adaptive functions. Nevertheless, discrete emotions theory doesn't exclude the possibility that our thinking influences our emotions in significant ways, as cognitive theorists propose. Indeed, the James-Lange and somatic marker theories are probably correct in assuming that our inferences concerning our bodily reactions can influence our emotional states. Finally, two-factor theory may be right that physiological arousal plays a key role in the intensity of our emotional experiences, although it's unlikely that all emotions require such arousal.

■ Unconscious Influences on Emotion

In recent decades, researchers have become especially interested in *unconscious influences on emotion*: variables outside our awareness that can affect our feelings. One piece of evidence for unconscious influences on emotion comes from research on *automatic behaviors*.

AUTOMATIC GENERATION OF EMOTION. As we learned in Chapter 1, research suggests that a good deal of our behavior is produced automatically, that is, with no voluntary influence on our part (Bargh & Ferguson, 2000; see Chapter 14). Yet we often perceive such behavior as intentional (Kirsch & Lynn, 1999; Wegner, 2002). The same may hold for our emotional reactions; many may be generated automatically, much like the knee-jerk reflex that our doctor elicits when she taps on our knees with a hammer.

Two investigators presented some subjects visually with a set of words describing positive stimuli (like *friends* and *music*) and other subjects with words describing negative stimuli (like *cancer* and *cockroach*). These stimuli appeared so quickly that they were *subliminal*, that is, below the threshold for awareness (see Chapter 4). Even though subjects couldn't identify what they saw at better than chance levels, those exposed to positive stimuli reported being in a better mood than those exposed to negative stimuli

This swaying suspension bridge on the University of British Columbia campus allowed psychologists to test Schachter and Singer's two-factor theory of emotion.

replicability

◄ **CAN THE RESULTS BE DUPLICATED IN OTHER STUDIES?**

arousal intensifies emotions but not all emotions require arousal.

like in our lab.

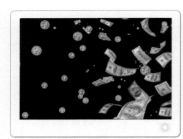

Stimuli can influence our emotional behavior even when we don't recognize them as the culprits. In one study, subjects subtly reminded of money by watching a computer screensaver of floating currency (*above*) later put more physical distance between themselves and a stranger than did subjects who watched a screensaver of floating fish (*below*), presumably because thinking of money makes people more self-centered (Vohs, Meade, & Goode, 2006).

replicability

CAN THE RESULTS BE DUPLICATED IN OTHER STUDIES?

Polygon pairs

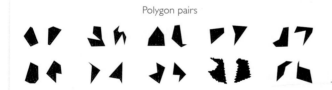

FIGURE 11.3 Which Polygon Do You Prefer? Pairs of polygons used in the mere exposure research of Robert Zajonc and his colleagues. Subjects exposed repeatedly to only one polygon within the pair prefer that polygon, even if they don't recall having seen it. (*Source:* Epley, 2006)

mere exposure effect
phenomenon in which repeated exposure to a stimulus makes us more likely to feel favorably toward it

(Bargh & Chartrand, 1999). Other research shows that subliminal exposure to faces displaying a specific emotion, like fear, happiness, or disgust, changes participants' moods in the direction of that emotion (Ruys & Stapel, 2008) and even produces changes in facial muscles corresponding to that emotion (Dimberg, Thunberg, & Elmehed, 2000).

MERE EXPOSURE EFFECT.

Psychology: From Inquiry to Understanding
Psychology: From Inquiry to Understanding
Psychology: From Inquiry to Understanding
Psychology: From Inquiry to Understanding

After reading the four lines above, how do you feel about our textbook? Do you like it better or worse than you did before? (We hope you answered "better.")

Popular wisdom would say no. It tells us that "familiarity breeds contempt": The more often we've seen or heard something, the more we come to dislike it. There's surely a grain of truth to this notion, as most of us have had the experience of hearing a jingle on the radio that grates on our nerves increasingly with each passing repetition. Yet research by Robert Zajonc and others on the **mere exposure effect** suggests that the opposite is more common: that is, familiarity breeds *comfort* (Zajonc, 1968). The mere exposure effect refers to the fact that repeated exposure to a stimulus makes us more likely to feel favorably toward it (Bornstein, 1989; Kunst-Wilson & Zajonc, 1980).

Of course, the finding that we like things we've seen many times before isn't itself terribly surprising. This correlation could be due to the fact that we repeatedly seek out things we like. If we love ice cream, we're likely to spend more time seeking ice cream than are people who hate ice cream, assuming such human beings actually exist. Better evidence for the mere exposure effect derives from experiments using meaningless material, for which individuals are unlikely to have any prior feelings. Experiments show that repeated exposure to various stimuli, such as nonsense syllables (like "zab" and "gar"), Chinese letters (to non-Chinese subjects), and polygons of various shapes, results in greater liking toward these stimuli compared with little or no exposure (see **FIGURE 11.3**). These effects have been replicated by multiple investigators using quite different stimuli, attesting to their generality. The mere exposure effect even extends to faces. We tend to prefer an image of ourselves as we appear in the mirror to an image of ourselves as we appear in a photograph (Mita, Dermer, & Knight, 1977), probably because we see ourselves in the mirror just about every day. Our friends, in contrast, generally prefer the photographic image. Of course, advertisers are well aware of the mere exposure effect and capitalize on it mercilessly (Baker, 1999; Fang, Singh, & Ahluwalia, 2007). Repetitions of a commercial tend to increase our liking for the product, especially if we're positively inclined toward it to begin with.

There's evidence that the mere exposure effect can operate unconsciously, because it emerges even when experimenters present meaningless stimuli subliminally (Bornstein, 1992; Zajonc, 2001). Even when people aren't aware of having seen a stimulus, like a specific polygon, they report liking it better than stimuli, like slightly different polygons, they've never seen. Mere exposure effects may be even larger for subliminally than for *supraliminally* (consciously) presented stimuli (Bornstein, 1989). Still, there's controversy about just how enduring the mere exposure effect is. It seems to influence short-term preferences, but not long-term emotions (Lazarus, 1984).

No one knows why mere exposure effects occur. They may reflect *habituation*, a primitive form of learning we encountered in Chapter 6. The more frequently we encounter a stimulus without anything bad happening, the more comfortable we feel in its presence. Alternatively, we may prefer things we find easier to process (Harmon-Jones & Allen, 2001; Mandler, Nakamura, & Van Zandt, 1987). The more often we experience something, the less effort it typically takes to comprehend it. Recall from Chapter 2 that we're *cognitive misers:* We prefer less mental work to more. So all else being equal, you'll like this paragraph better after having read it a few times than after you read it the first time. That's a not-so-subtle hint to read it again!

FACIAL FEEDBACK HYPOTHESIS. If no one is near you, and you're not afraid of looking foolish, make a big smile and hold it for a while, maybe for 15 seconds. How do you feel (other than silly)? Next, make a big frown, and again hold it for a while. How do you feel now?

According to the **facial feedback hypothesis**, you're likely to feel emotions that correspond to your facial features—first happy, and then, sad or angry (Adelmann & Zajonc, 1989; Goldman & de Vignemont, 2009; Niedenthal, 2007). This hypothesis originated with none other than Charles Darwin (1872), although Robert Zajonc revived it in the 1980s. Zajonc went beyond Darwin by proposing that changes in the blood vessels of the face "feed back" temperature information to the brain, altering our emotions in predictable ways. Like James and Lange, Zajonc argued that our emotions typically arise from our behavioral and physiological reactions. But unlike James and Lange, Zajonc viewed this process as purely biochemical and noncognitive, that is, as involving no thinking. Moreover, according to Zajonc, it operates outside of our awareness (Zajonc, Murphy, & Inglehart, 1989).

There's scientific support for the facial feedback hypothesis. In one study, researchers asked subjects to rate how funny they found various cartoons (Strack, Martin, & Stepper, 1988). They randomly assigned some subjects to watch cartoons while holding a pen with their teeth, others to watch cartoons while holding a pen with their lips. If you try this one at home, you'll discover that when you hold a pen with your teeth, you tend to smile; when you hold a pen with your lips, you tend to frown. Sure enough, subjects who held a pen with their teeth rated the cartoons as funnier than did other subjects.

Still, it's not clear that these effects work by means of facial feedback to the brain, as Zajonc claimed. An alternative hypothesis for these effects is classical conditioning (see Chapter 6). Over the course of our lives, we've experienced countless conditioning "trials" in which we smile while feeling happy and frown while feeling unhappy. Eventually, smiles become conditioned stimuli for happiness, frowns for unhappiness.

✔ **Study** and **Review** on **mypsychlab.com**

Most people prefer their mirror image to their image as taken by a photographer. In this case, this subject is more likely to prefer the photograph on the left, presumably because he is more accustomed to this view of himself.

> **facial feedback hypothesis**
> theory that blood vessels in the face feed back temperature information in the brain, altering our experience of emotions

 ◀ ruling out rival hypotheses

HAVE IMPORTANT ALTERNATIVE EXPLANATIONS FOR THE FINDINGS BEEN EXCLUDED?

---

assess your knowledge   FACT OR FICTION?

1. Psychological research demonstrates that emotion and reason are direct opposites of each other. **True / False**

   emotion → reason (leads to)

2. Some emotions, like happiness, appear to be recognized by a substantial majority of people in all cultures. **True / False**

3. According to the James-Lange theory, emotions follow from our bodily reactions. **True / False**

4. Two-factor theory proposes that arousal is necessary for emotion. **True / False**

5. The mere exposure effect refers to the finding that repeated presentations of a stimulus lead to less liking of that stimulus. **True / False**

   show

Answers: 1. F (p. 406); 2. T (p. 408); 3. T (p. 410); 4. T (p. 412); 5. F (p. 414)

FACTOID ✚

The results of a small study suggest that the chemical *Botox*, used to treat wrinkles by paralyzing the skin around them, may be helpful in treating depression (Finzi & Wasserman, 2006). Although this finding requires replication, it's consistent with the facial feedback hypothesis, because *Botox* may decrease the sad facial expressions of depressed people, in turn dampening their sad emotions.

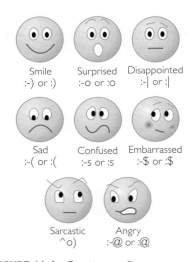

FIGURE 11.4 Emoticons. Because e-mail messages are devoid of nonverbal cues, people have developed a variety of "emoticons" to convey various emotions that might not be obvious over e-mail and instant messaging. (*Source:* Microsoft Corporation)

nonverbal leakage
unconscious spillover of emotions into nonverbal behavior

NONVERBAL EXPRESSION OF EMOTION: THE EYES, BODIES, AND CULTURES HAVE IT

11.3 Explain the importance of nonverbal expression of emotion.

11.4 Identify major lie detection methods and their pitfalls.

Much of our emotional expression is nonverbal. Not only do our facial expressions change frequently when we experience a strong emotion, so do our gestures and postures. As baseball Hall of Famer Yogi Berra (known for his funny words of wisdom) said, "You can observe a lot just by watching." What's more, our nonverbal behaviors are often more valid indicators of our emotions than our words, largely because we're better at disguising our verbal language than our gestures and tone of voice (DePaulo, 1992). **Nonverbal leakage**—an unconscious spillover of emotions into nonverbal behavior—is often a powerful cue that we're trying to hide an emotion. So when we ever so subtly roll our eyes while agreeing to our boss's unreasonable request to house-sit her dogs over the weekend ("Sure, I'd be happy to do it"), we can be confident that the "eyes have it."

■ The Importance of Nonverbal Cues

We often take for granted how important nonverbal behavior is to our everyday communication—until, that is, when we don't have access to it (see Chapter 8). Without nonverbal cues to our emotions, embarrassing miscommunications can arise. Many of us have experienced this effect when a person to whom we send an innocuous or humorous text message or e-mail misinterprets it as hostile. Without being able to hear our vocal inflections or see our facial emotions, recipients may misinterpret what we meant to say. This problem is compounded by the fact that we overestimate how easily others can figure out the intended meanings of our e-mail messages (Kruger et al., 2005). More broadly, psychologists refer to this problem as the *curse of knowledge:* When we know something, in this case what we intend to say, we often make the mistake of assuming others know it, too (Birch & Bloom, 2003) (see **FIGURE 11.4**).

■ Body Language and Gestures

Our postures can convey a lot about our emotional states (see **FIGURE 11.5**). Slumped posture can convey sadness and upright posture can convey happiness or excitement, although an upright posture involving a lot of body tension may also convey anger (Duclos et al, 1989). This nonverbal leakage is largely unconscious. When interpreting the emotional states of others, we typically take both facial and body information into account. Research on embodied cognition (see Chapter 7) even shows that our postures affect our readiness to engage in certain behaviors. When participants are insulted, they're more likely to display brain responses typical of anger (activation of the left frontal lobes) when sitting straight up than when reclining (Harmon-Jones & Peterson, 2009). That's probably because we're more prepared to strike others when upright than when lying down.

Gestures come in a seemingly endless variety of forms (Ekman, 2001). When talking, we often use *illustrators* (Ekman, 2001), gestures that highlight or accentuate speech, such as when we forcefully move our hands forward to make an important point. When stressed out, we may engage in *manipulators*, gestures in which one body part strokes, presses, bites, or otherwise

FIGURE 11.5 Emotional Expression through Posture. Even in these stick figure drawings with no facial features, we can easily interpret their emotional states from their "body language" (Duclos et al., 1989).

[Handwritten margin notes:] Illustrators = gestures that accentuate speech. manipulators = gestures in which one part of body interacts with another. emblems = gestures that convey conventional meanings.

touches another body part. For example, while cramming for an exam, we may twirl our hair or bite our fingernails.

We're all familiar with *emblems* (Ekman, 2001), gestures that convey conventional meanings recognized by members of a culture, such as the hand wave and nodding of the head. Some of these gestures are consistent across cultures, such as crossing one's fingers when hoping for good luck (Plutchik, 2003). Yet others differ across cultures, which should serve as a word of warning to unwary foreign travelers (Archer, 1997). The "thumbs up" is a sign of approval among Westerners, but an insult in much of the Muslim world. Some surprised American soldiers quickly discovered this awkward fact upon greeting Iraqi civilians following the U.S. invasion in 2003. The familiar American "hello" wave means "go away" in some European countries, and the American "OK sign" is a vulgar insult in Turkey. Nodding "yes" means "no" in parts of Yugoslavia and Iran, which can cause embarrassing problems if your host asks if you enjoyed the meal he just served (Axtell, 1997).

As useful as body language can be in communicating information about emotional states, we must be careful in drawing conclusions about its meaning for any given person (Ekman, 2001). Some pop psychologists specialize in "translating" body language into emotions, as if there were a universal dictionary of body language. Yet these psychologists overlook the fact that within a given culture, people differ greatly in the body language they use to express certain emotions. For instance, in November 2008 body language expert Tonya Reiman interpreted the fact that then President-Elect Barack Obama put his hand on the shoulder of outgoing president George W. Bush during a White House meeting as evidence that Obama was trying to assume a power role. But Reiman may not have considered alternative explanations for this behavior; perhaps Obama likes to touch others as a means of showing liking or appreciation.

■ Personal Space

Have you ever walked into a virtually empty movie theater and taken a seat, only to find that someone sits right next to you? Or have you ever approached someone to whom you were attracted, only to find them taking a step away from you? These are among the phenomena addressed by **proxemics**—the study of personal space.

Anthropologist Edward Hall (1966) observed that personal distance is correlated positively with emotional distance. The further we stand from a person, the less emotionally close we usually feel to him or her, and vice versa. But there are exceptions. When we're trying to intimidate people, we typically get closer to them. For example, lawyers tend to stand closer to witnesses they're challenging (Brodsky et al., 1999).

According to Hall, there are four levels of personal space. Nevertheless, like most distinctions in psychology, the separations between these levels aren't clear-cut:

1. **Public distance** (12 feet or more): typically used for public speaking, such as lecturing;
2. **Social distance** (4–12 feet): typically used for conversations among strangers and casual acquaintances;
3. **Personal distance** (1.5–4 feet): typically used for conversations among close friends or romantic partners;
4. **Intimate distance** (0–1.5 feet): typically used for kissing, hugging, whispering "sweet nothings," and affectionate touching.

When these implicit rules are violated, we usually feel uncomfortable, as when a stranger gets "in our face" to ask us for a favor.

Hall (1976) argued that cultures differ in personal space. In many Latin and Middle Eastern countries, personal space is relatively close, whereas in many Scandinavian and Asian countries, personal space is more distant. Nevertheless, data suggest that although these cultural differences are genuine, they aren't as large as Hall believed (Jones, 1979). There are also sex differences in personal space, with women preferring closer space than

(Sydney Harris, www.CartoonStock.com. Used by permission.)

◄ **ruling out rival hypotheses**

HAVE IMPORTANT ALTERNATIVE EXPLANATIONS FOR THE FINDINGS BEEN EXCLUDED?

Research points to cultural differences in personal space. For example, people from Middle Eastern countries often talk slightly closer to others than do people from European countries.

proxemics
study of personal space

men (Vrught & Kerkstra, 1984). Personal space also increases from childhood to early adulthood (Hayduk, 1983), perhaps because the young haven't yet developed clear interpersonal boundaries.

■ Lying and Lie Detection

We all lie. Diary studies suggest that college students tell an average of about two lies per day (DePaulo et al., 1996). Lying is so commonplace that the English language contains 112 different words for lying (Henig, 2006). Psychologists have long been interested in finding a dependable means of detecting lying. But how successful have they been?

HUMANS AS LIE DETECTORS. We spend a sizable amount of our everyday lives trying to figure out if others are "being straight" with us or putting us on. To do so, we frequently rely on people's nonverbal behaviors. When researchers ask people to lie about something, like whether they enjoyed watching a gruesome film, their illustrators tend to decrease, whereas their manipulators and emblems tend to increase (Ekman, 2001). Yet none of these gestures are foolproof indicators of dishonesty, so we shouldn't place too much stock in any one of them. Indeed, despite what most police officers believe, nonverbal cues tend to be less valid indicators of lying than verbal cues (Vrij, 2008). The best way of finding out whether someone is lying is to listen to what they're saying rather than how they're saying it; for example, dishonest statements tend to contain fewer details and fewer qualifiers (such as "I'm not sure about this, but I think that ...") than do truthful statements (DePaulo, Lindsay, Malone, et al., 2003).

Although many of us are confident of our ability to detect lies, research suggests given a 50-50 chance of being right, most of us achieve only about 55 percent accuracy and few exceed 70 percent (Ekman, 2001; Zuckerman, DePaulo, & Rosenthal, 1981). Moreover, occupational groups we might expect to be especially accurate detectors of lies, like people who administer so-called lie detector (polygraph) tests, customs officials, and psychiatrists, usually do no better than the rest of us—meaning not much better than chance (Ekman & O'Sullivan, 1991; Kraut & Poe, 1980; DePaulo & Pfeifer, 1986). Researchers have found only a few groups, including secret service agents, clinical psychologists who study deception, and perhaps some judges and law enforcement officials, to be especially adept at lie detection (Ekman & O'Sullivan, 1991; Ekman, O'Sullivan, & Frank, 1999). These correlational findings may indicate that years of experience in spotting lies make people better at it: Practice makes perfect. Or perhaps the causal arrow is reversed: People who are interpersonally perceptive may pursue professions that allow them to exercise this talent (see **FIGURE 11.6**).

Another sobering finding is that there's typically little or no correlation between people's confidence in their ability to detect lies and their accuracy (Ekman, 2001). So when a juror proclaims with utmost confidence, "I could tell that the witness was lying; I'm positive about it," we should take it with a grain of salt. As in research on eyewitness memory (see Chapter 7), we shouldn't confuse confidence with correctness.

The television show "Lie to Me" features Dr. Cal Lightman, a psychologist who can supposedly use nonverbal cues to detect lying with exceptional accuracy. Why does scientific evidence raise doubts about Lightman's character? (See answer upside down on bottom of page.)

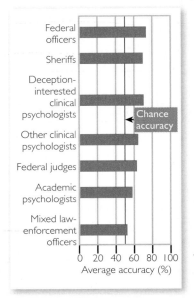

FIGURE 11.6 Who Can Catch a Liar? Data from Paul Ekman and his colleagues on the accuracy levels of different occupational groups in detecting deception; the chance rate of accuracy in these studies is 50 percent. Several groups do only somewhat better than chance, with law enforcement officers (including police) actually doing slightly worse than chance. (*Source:* Ekman, O'Sullivan, & Frank, 1999)

correlation vs. causation

CAN WE BE SURE THAT A CAUSES B? ›

Answer: Research shows that even professionals with substantial expertise in detecting lies have high error rates.

THE POLYGRAPH TEST. The polygraph or "lie detector" test has long been one of the icons of popular psychology. It makes frequent cameo appearances in television courtroom dramas and daytime talk shows. Even popular psychologist Dr. Phil has promoted the polygraph test on his television show as a means of finding out which partner in a relationship is lying (Levenson, 2005).

The Modern Polygraph Test.

The polygraph test was born in 1915 and remains popular today. The largest organization of polygraph examiners in the United States claims the test is 98 percent accurate (Koerner, 2002). Does research support this extraordinary claim?

The polygraph test, like most lie-detection techniques, rests on the assumption of the **Pinocchio response**: a perfect physiological or behavioral indicator of lying (Lykken, 1998; Ruscio, 2005). Like Pinocchio's nose, people's bodily reactions supposedly give them away whenever they lie.

The modern polygraph test measures several physiological signals that often reflect anxiety, most typically blood pressure, respiration, and skin conductance, a measure of palm sweating. The assumption is that dishonest suspects experience anxiety—and heightened autonomic activity—when confronted with questions that expose their falsehoods.

The most widely administered version of the polygraph test, the Controlled Question Test (CQT), measures suspects' physiological responses following three major types of yes–no questions (Lykken, 1998).

1. **Relevant questions,** or "Did you do it" questions, those bearing on the crime in question ("Did you rob the bank on the afternoon of August 16?");

2. **Irrelevant questions,** those not bearing on the crime in question or on suspects' lies ("Is your name Sam Jones?");

3. **Control questions,** those reflecting probable lies. They typically inquire about trivial flaws—misdeeds about which most people will lie, especially under intense pressure ("Have you ever been tempted to steal anything from a store?"). Suspects' physiological activity following these questions supposedly provides a "baseline" for gauging their bodily responses during known lies.

If the suspect's autonomic activity following the relevant questions is higher than that following irrelevant and control questions, polygraph examiners label the CQT results "deceptive." Otherwise, they label them "truthful" (or inconclusive if the responses to irrelevant and control questions are about equal).

Evaluating the Polygraph Test: What's the Truth?

Although the polygraph test usually does better than chance for detecting lies (Kircher, Horowitz, & Raskin, 1988), it yields a high rate of *false positives*, that is, innocent individuals whom the test labels incorrectly as guilty (Iacono & Patrick, 2006; National Research Council, 2003). Putting it less technically, *the polygraph test is biased against the innocent.* Studies comparing the test results of known criminals with those of known noncriminals show that the test misclassifies a large proportion of innocent individuals (perhaps 40 percent or more) as guilty (Patrick & Iacono, 1991). As a consequence, the results of polygraph tests aren't admissible in most U.S. courts (Saxe & Ben-Shakhar, 1999).

The problem is that the polygraph test confuses arousal with evidence of guilt. The polygraph test is misnamed: It's an "arousal detector," not a lie detector (Iacono, 2009; Saxe, 1991). Many people display arousal following relevant questions for reasons other than the anxiety associated with lying, such as the fear of being convicted for a crime they didn't commit. Polygraph enthusiasts' claims to the contrary, there *is* no Pinocchio response, at least none that psychologists have discovered.

The polygraph test assumes the existence of a Pinocchio response, a physiological reaction uniquely associated with lying. But does such a response exist?

> **Pinocchio response**
> supposedly perfect physiological or behavioral indicator of lying

extraordinary claims

IS THE EVIDENCE AS STRONG AS THE CLAIM?

FACTOID ✚

The principal developer of the polygraph test, William Marston (1893–1947), also created the comic-book character Wonder Woman, who proudly sported a "lasso of truth." When Wonder Woman wrapped the lasso around the waist of a potential criminal, she compelled him to tell the truth ("Yes, I did rob the bank ... I admit it"). For Marston (1938), the polygraph test was the equivalent of Wonder Woman's lasso: It was an infallible detector of lies.

The modern polygraph test relies on the assumption of a Pinocchio response, a perfect indicator of lying—much like that of Pinocchio's nose, which became longer whenever he fibbed. Yet psychological research calls the existence of the Pinocchio response into serious question. Some people exhibit physiological arousal when they don't lie, and some people don't exhibit physiological arousal when they do lie.

These problems plague most other popular lie-detection methods. Some agencies use *voice stress analysis* to detect lies on the basis of findings that people's voices increase in pitch when they lie. Yet because most people's voices also go up in pitch when they're stressed out (Long & Krall, 1990), voice stress analyzers barely do better than chance at detecting lies (Gamer et al., 2006; Sackett & Decker, 1979).

The polygraph test may also yield a nontrivial number of *false negatives*, that is, guilty individuals whom the test incorrectly labels innocent. Many properly trained subjects can "beat" the test by using *countermeasures*—methods designed to alter their responses to control questions. To pass the polygraph test, as we've seen, we must exhibit a more pronounced physiological response to control questions than to relevant questions. Given less than 30 minutes of preparation, half or more of subjects can accomplish this goal by biting their tongues, curling their toes, or performing difficult mental arithmetic problems (such as counting backward from 1,000 by 17s) during control questions (Honts, Raskin, & Kircher, 1994; Iacono, 2001). Some psychologists have also suggested that people with psychopathic personality, who have low levels of guilt and fear (see Chapter 15), may be especially adept at beating the polygraph test because of their low levels of arousal in response to incriminating questions (Lykken, 1978), although research bearing on this conjecture is mixed (Patrick & Iacono, 1989; Waid & Orne, 1982).

If the polygraph is so flawed, why are polygraph examiners persuaded of its validity? The answer probably lies in the fact that the polygraph is often effective for eliciting confessions, especially when people fail the test (Lykken, 1998; Ruscio, 2005). As a result, polygraph examiners may come to believe the test works, because many people who fail the test later "admit" they were lying. Yet there's good evidence that many criminal confessions are false (Kassin & Gudjonsson, 2004). Moreover, polygraph examiners frequently conclude that suspects who failed the test and who didn't confess to crimes must actually be guilty. But without hard-and-fast criminal evidence against these suspects, this assertion is unfalsifiable.

falsifiability
CAN THE CLAIM BE DISPROVED?

OTHER METHODS OF LIE DETECTION. The serious limitations of the polygraph test have led researchers to seek out alternatives to this technique.

Here we'll examine three other widely used lie detection methods.

Guilty Knowledge Test. To get around the polygraph test's shortcomings, David Lykken developed the **guilty knowledge test (GKT)**, which relies on the premise that criminals harbor concealed knowledge about the crime that innocent people don't (Lykken, 1959, 1960). In contrast to the polygraph, the GKT doesn't hinge on the assumption of a Pinocchio response, because it measures only suspects' recognition of concealed knowledge, not lying.

If we were to administer the GKT to a suspect, we'd concoct a series of multiple-choice questions in which only one choice contains the object at the crime scene, such as a red handkerchief, and we'd measure his physiological responses—like his skin conductance—following each choice. If, across many items, the suspect consistently shows pronounced physiological responses to only the objects at the crime scene, we can be reasonably certain that he was present at the crime—and probably committed it.

In contrast to the polygraph, the GKT has a low false-positive rate, that is, it misidentifies few innocent people as guilty. In this respect, it may be a useful investigative device for law enforcement officials. Nevertheless, the GKT has a fairly high false-negative rate, because many criminals may have either not noticed or since forgotten key aspects of the crime scene (Ben-Shakhar & Elaad, 2003; Iacono & Patrick, 2006).

Tests Using Brain Scanning Techniques. Several researchers have attempted to improve on the traditional GKT by measuring suspects' brain waves following each item (Bashore & Rapp, 1993; Farwell & Donchin, 1991), a technique called *brain fingerprinting*. Brain waves may be a more sensitive measure of the recognition of concealed knowledge than skin conductance or other indices used in the traditional GKT (Farwell & Smith, 2001). Nevertheless, the scientific support for brain fingerprinting is preliminary. One problem is that most of the evidence for this technique comes from laboratory studies in which participants are forced to rehearse details of a simulated crime (like the color of a

guilty knowledge test (GKT)
alternative to the polygraph test that relies on the premise that criminals harbor concealed knowledge about the crime that innocent people don't

psychomythology

IS "TRUTH SERUM" REALLY A TRUTH SERUM?

Scores of Hollywood movies portray truth serum as the chemical version of Wonder Woman's magical lasso (see Factoid, p. 419). In the 1994 movie *True Lies*, terrorists capture a CIA agent and inject him with "truth serum," forcing him to disclose deep dark secrets of his past. In the 2004 comedy *Meet the Fockers*, a father injects his daughter's fiancé with truth serum to test whether he is worthy of marrying her. After a person receives truth serum, the embarrassing truth supposedly emerges, whether or not he wants it to.

Truth serum is a term for a broad class of drugs called *barbiturates*, such as Sodium Pentothal. These drugs typically relax people and, in high doses, make them fall asleep. During the 1930s and 1940s, truth serum was a popular tool in psychotherapy for unearthing supposedly unconscious material (Dysken et al., 1979; Mann, 1969; Winter, 2005). For several decades, the police and military occasionally administered truth serum to suspects in the hopes of dredging up concealed information. In 1963, the U.S. Supreme Court ruled that criminal confessions induced under truth serum were scientifically questionable and unconstitutional, effectively putting a halt to its use for most purposes. Still, fascination with truth serum never died. Following the terrorist attacks of September 11, 2001, some U.S. government organizations displayed a renewed interest in truth serum, largely for the purpose of interrogating suspected terrorists (Brown, 2006). In 2008, Indian police reportedly administered truth serum to the lone surviving gunman in the horrific Mumbai terrorist attacks (Borrell, 2008).

Yet scientific evidence demonstrates that truth serum is anything but infallible. Studies show that people can lie under the influence of truth serum, falsifying the claim that this chemical invariably produces truthful statements (Piper, 1993). Even more problematic is evidence suggesting that truth serum, like many suggestive memory-recovery techniques (see Chapter 7), doesn't enhance memory: It merely lowers the threshold for reporting all memories, both true and false (Lynn et al., 2003a; Piper, 1993). As a consequence, memories retrieved under the influence of truth serum aren't any more trustworthy—and may be less trustworthy—than other memories (Borrell, 2008). Indeed, because the physiological effects of barbiturates are similar to those of alcohol, the effects of truth serum are comparable to those of getting rip-roaring drunk. Our inhibitions are lowered, but what we say can't always be trusted.

◄ **falsifiability**

CAN THE CLAIM BE DISPROVED?

---

stolen purse or the type of jacket worn by a victim). In the real world, many criminals may forget these details, leading to lower accuracy rates (Rosenfeld, 2005).

Other companies, like the California-based "No Lie MRI," claim to be able to use fMRI methods (see Chapter 3) to distinguish truths from falsehoods (Stix, 2008). Yet these techniques aren't ready for widespread public consumption, because different studies often find activations in different brain regions during lying (Greely & Illes, 2007). Moreover, the brain activations associated with lying may be similar or identical to those associated with merely *thinking* about lying (Greene & Paxton, 2009). If so, fMRI methods may suffer from the same false-positive problem as the traditional polygraph.

Integrity Tests. Rather than use complex equipment designed to measure people's physiological responses, some employers administer paper-and-pencil **integrity tests**, questionnaires that presumably assess workers' tendency to steal or cheat. About 6,000 American companies, including McDonald's, administer them to several million people each year (Cullen & Sackett, 2004). Integrity test questions fall into several categories, including potential employees':

1. **History of stealing** ("Have you ever stolen anything from your place of work?");

2. **Attitudes toward stealing** ("Do you think that workers who steal property from a store should always be fired?");

3. **Perceptions of others' honesty** ("Do you believe that most people steal from their companies every now and then?").

integrity test
questionnaire that presumably assesses workers' tendency to steal or cheat

"Yes" responses to questions 1 and 3, and a "no" response to question 2 will put you well on your way to a "dishonest" score on integrity tests.

Integrity tests predict employee theft, absenteeism, and other workplace misbehavior at better-than-chance levels (Berry, Sackett, & Wiemann, 2007; Ones, Viswesvaran, & Schmidt, 1993; Sackett & Wanek, 1996). Yet these tests yield numerous false positives (Lilienfeld, Alliger, & Mitchell, 1995; Office of Technology Assessment, 1990). Ironically, some of these false positives may be people who are especially forgiving of others, such as those who believe in giving a second chance to desperate employees who steal a tiny amount of money to feed their families. These people might well answer "No" to question 2. So integrity tests, like the polygraph, may be biased against the innocent.

that's still wrong.

✓ Study and Review on mypsychlab.com

---

assess your knowledge   **FACT OR FICTION?**

1. Almost all emblems are cross-culturally universal. **True / False**

2. Personal distance from others is usually correlated positively with emotional distance. **True / False**

3. People who've had a great deal of experience with liars are almost always better at detecting them than are other people. **True / False**

4. The polygraph test has a very low false-positive rate. **True / False**

5. The effects of "truth serum" are quite similar to those of ingesting several alcoholic drinks. **True / False**

Answers: 1. F (p. 417); 2. T (p. 417); 3. F (p. 418); 4. F (p. 419); 5. T (p. 421)

HAPPINESS AND SELF-ESTEEM: SCIENCE CONFRONTS POP PSYCHOLOGY

11.5   Describe the emerging discipline of positive psychology.

11.6   Identify common myths and realities about happiness and self-esteem.

The ruler of the tiny country of Bhutan, nestled in the Himalayan mountain range, recently had an unconventional idea (see **FIGURE 11.7**). Rather than focusing on increasing his nation's gross national product (GNP, a measure of economic success), the king decided to try to improve his nation's gross national happiness (GNH; Nettle, 2005). He hopes to boost Bhutan's GNH, as it's called, by preserving the beauty of its natural environment, promoting positive cultural values, and giving citizens more of a voice in government decisions. Until recently, almost all psychologists would have probably viewed the king as a naive idealist. Not anymore. *Did he manage to raise the GNH?*

■ Positive Psychology: Psychology's Future or Psychology's Fad?

Much of contemporary psychology has focused on minimizing severe distress and on returning disturbed people to adequate levels of functioning. But it's done little to encourage adequately functioning people to achieve their full emotional potential—to become "better than well" (Keyes & Haidt, 2003). Some authors have also argued that popular psychology has underestimated people's resilience in the face of stressful life events (Bonanno et al., 2002; Garmezy, Masten, & Tellegen, 1984; see Chapter 12). Since about the turn of the 21st century, the emerging discipline of **positive psychology** has sought to change that state of neglect by emphasizing human strengths, such as resilience, coping, life satisfaction, love, and happiness (Myers & Diener, 1996; Seligman & Csikszentmihalyi, 2000). This field also focuses on helping people to find ways of enhancing positive emotions, like happiness and fulfillment, as well as on building psychologically healthy communities (Sheldon & King,

FIGURE 11.7   Bhutan, Home of Gross National Happiness. In the Himalayan country of Bhutan, the king has made increasing his country's Gross National Happiness a major domestic policy goal.

positive psychology
discipline that has sought to emphasize human strengths

2001). Christopher Peterson and Martin Seligman (2004) outlined numerous "character strengths and virtues" they view as essential to positive psychology. Several of them, such as curiosity, love, and gratitude, are positively associated with long-term life satisfaction (Park, Peterson, & Seligman, 2004). Across the country, positive psychologists have begun to teach students to incorporate these strengths and virtues into their daily lives (Max, 2007).

Yet some psychologists have condemned positive psychology as a "fad" (Lazarus, 2003) whose claims have outstripped the scientific evidence (Held, 2004; Max, 2007). They argue that positive psychology's "look on the bright side of life" approach may have its downside. As Julie Norem (2001) observed, **defensive pessimism** serves a valuable function for many anxious people. Defensive pessimism is the strategy of anticipating failure and then compensating for this expectation by mentally overpreparing for negative outcomes. For example, defensive pessimists tend to respond "True" to items like "I spend lots of time imagining what could go wrong" and "I often start out expecting the worst, even though I will probably do okay." This strategy helps certain people to improve their performance, probably because it encourages them to work harder (Norem & Cantor, 1986). Robbing defensive pessimists of their pessimism—say, by cheering them up—makes them perform worse (Norem & Chang, 2002).

Moreover, optimists' rose-colored glasses and tendency to gloss over their mistakes may sometimes prevent them from seeing reality clearly. For example, optimists tend to recall feedback about their social skills as better than it was (Norem, 2001), which could prevent them from learning from their interpersonal errors, like inadvertently offending others. In addition, optimists sometimes display greater physiological responses to stressors, like bad health news, than do pessimists, perhaps because they don't spend enough time preparing for the worst (Segerstrom, 2005).

None of this takes away from the value of positive psychology for many people. But the problem of *individual differences* (see Chapter 1) reminds us to be wary of "one size fits all" solutions to life's multifaceted problems. Positive thinking is a key ingredient in many people's recipe for happiness, but it may not be for everyone.

■ What Happiness Is Good For

For most of the 20th century, psychologists largely dismissed happiness as a "fluffy" topic better suited to self-help books and motivational seminars than rigorous research. Yet over the past few decades, a growing body of research has suggested that happiness—generally defined as people's subjective sense of how satisfied they are with life—may produce enduring psychological and physical benefits (see **FIGURE 11.8**).

Consider the results of a study that has tracked a group of 180 nuns in Wisconsin for six decades (see Chapter 7). These nuns had kept daily diaries starting in the 1930s, when they were in their early twenties. Nuns whose sentences featured many positive words—such as those dealing with love, joy, and hope—outlived other nuns by an average of almost 10 years (Danner, Snowdon, & Friesen, 2001). Of course, correlation doesn't imply causation, and the nuns who used more happy words may have differed in subtle ways from other nuns, such as in their exercise or health practices. Still, the findings are tantalizing.

Like all primary emotions, happiness may serve evolutionarily adaptive functions. According to Barbara Fredrickson's (2001, 2003) **broaden and build theory**, happiness predisposes us to think more openly, allowing us to see the "big picture" we might have otherwise overlooked. As one test of this theory, doctors who received a small bag of candy made more accurate diagnoses of liver disease than other doctors, apparently because being in a good mood allowed them to consider alternative diagnostic possibilities (Isen, Rosenzweig, & Young, 1991). So broader thinking may permit us to find novel solutions to problems. When we're happy, we see more of the world and seek out more opportunities, like romantic partners we wouldn't have previously considered. (Lyubomirsky, King, & Diener, 2005).

Happiness leads to acceptance

FICTOID

MYTH: Positive affirmations, like "I'm a good person" or "I really like myself," are a good way of enhancing self-esteem.

REALITY: Research suggests that such affirmations don't do much to enhance the self-esteem of people already high in self-esteem and may actually diminish the self-esteem of people low in self-esteem, perhaps they remind these people of their shortcomings (Wood, Perunovic, & Lee, 2009)

be a realist (be straight forward with yourself) know your flaws.

Measure Your Happiness: Take the *Satisfaction with Life Scale*

Below are five statements that you may agree or disagree with. Using the 1 to 7 scale below, indicate your agreement with each item by placing the appropriate number on the line preceding that item. Please be open and honest in your responding.

1	Strongly disagree	4	Neither agree nor disagree	5	Slightly agree
2	Disagree			6	Agree
3	Slightly disagree			7	Strongly agree

___6___ In most ways my life is close to my ideal.

___6___ The conditions of my life are excellent.   *33 ✓*

___7___ I am satisfied with my life.

___7___ So far I have gotten the important things I want in life.

___7___ If I could live my life over, I would change almost nothing.

Scoring:
- 31–35 Extremely satisfied • 26–30 Satisfied
- 21–25 Slightly satisfied • 20 Neutral • 15–19 Slightly dissatisfied
- 10–14 Dissatisfied • 5–9 Extremely dissatisfied

FIGURE 11.8 Satisfaction with Life Scale (SWLS). Do you wonder how happy you are? Take this quick test developed by psychologist Ed Diener and his colleagues to help you find out. (*Source:* Diener et al., 1985)

correlation vs. causation

CAN WE BE SURE THAT A CAUSES B?

defensive pessimism
strategy of anticipating failure and compensating for this expectation by mentally overpreparing for negative outcomes

broaden and build theory
theory proposing that happiness predisposes us to think more openly

FIGURE 11.9 Happily Living Longer. Happiness is associated with living longer. Does this finding reflect a direct causal effect? Could we ever know? (*Source:* Duenwald, 2002)

FACTOID

Although money itself won't buy happiness, more money *relative to other people* we know just might. Research shows that although our absolute amount of wealth isn't much related to our happiness, our position (ranking) of our wealth compared with those around us is (Boyce, Brown, & Moore, 2010).

? According to psychological research, what's wrong—or at least misleading—about this photo? (See answer upside down on bottom of page.)

Contrary to popular conception, older adults are happier, on average, than younger people.

Answer: Research suggests that money and material gifts don't buy us happiness, at least once we're financially comfortable.

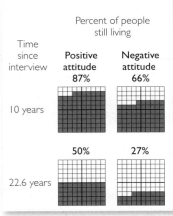

A study of 660 people over 50 in Ohio found that those with positive attitudes about aging lived, on average, 7.5 years longer.

Percent of people still living

Time since interview	Positive attitude 87%	Negative attitude 66%
10 years		
	50%	27%
22.6 years		

All else being equal, life is easier for those of us who are optimists (see Chapter 12). Optimists tend to be happier in everyday life than pessimists (Seligman & Pawelski, 2003) and find it easier than pessimists to cope with life's rocky road (Watson & Clark, 1984). For example, when given threatening medical information (such as their risk for developing cancer), optimists tend to pay more attention to it and remember it better than pessimists (Aspinwall & Brunhart, 2000). This finding may partly explain why optimists tend to live longer than pessimists (Maruta et al., 2000); they may be less likely to ignore risks to their health (see **FIGURE 11.9**). Optimism is even a plus in the bruising world of politics. One of the best predictors of who'll win a presidential election is which candidate's speeches contain the more hopeful language (Zullow et al., 1988). When we close the door on the voting booth, we tend to pull the lever for the candidate who promises us a better tomorrow.

■ What Makes Us Happy: Myths and Realities

Given that Americans spend about $750 million a year on self-help books designed to make them happy and another $1 billion a year on motivational speakers, we might assume that we have all of the advice about happiness we need. Yet as psychologist Daniel Gilbert observed, "People have a lot of bad theories about happiness" (Martin, 2006). So to understand happiness, we first need to burst some pop psychology bubbles.

Misconception 1: *The prime determinant of happiness is what happens to us.* This is arguably the single most widespread myth in all of popular psychology. Ed Diener and Martin Seligman screened more than 200 college students for their levels of happiness, and compared the upper 10 percent with the middle and lowest 10 percent. The happiest students didn't experience any more positive life events than the other groups (Diener & Seligman, 2002). In another study, Daniel Kahneman and his colleagues tracked the moods and activities of over 909 women by asking them to record their experiences. They found that life circumstances, such as their income and features of their job—like whether their jobs included good benefits—were essentially uncorrelated with women's current levels of happiness. In contrast, women's sleep quality and tendencies toward depression were good predictors of happiness (Kahneman, Krueger, Schkade, Schwarz, & Stone, 2004).

Misconception 2: *Money makes us happy.* From what psychological research tells us, money can't buy long-term happiness (Kesebir & Diener, 2008; Wilson, 2002). Admittedly, when we're running short of it, money is a bit related to happiness. Below about $50,000, there's a modest association between how wealthy we are and how happy we are. But above about $50,000, additional money doesn't make us much happier (Helliwell & Putnam, 2004) (see **FIGURE 11.10**). Still, most unhappy people are mistakenly convinced they'd be happier if they could only have more money. They may forget that higher salaries often require longer hours, which in turns means less free time—and in turn, often less happiness (Kahneman et al. 2006).

Misconception 3: *Happiness declines in old age.* We're all familiar with the widespread stereotype of the sad old man or woman, sitting all alone in a sparsely decorated room with no one to talk to. Yet happiness tends to increase with age, at least through the late sixties and perhaps seventies (Mroczek & Kolarz, 1998). Indeed, surveys suggest that the happiest group of people is men aged 65 and older (Martin,

2006). Only when people become quite old, typically in their eighties, does happiness decrease noticeably. Interestingly, happiness drops dramatically in the last year of life (Mroczek & Spiro, 2005). Although this correlation may reflect a causal effect of unhappiness on health, it may also reflect a causal effect of declining health on unhappiness.

The increase in happiness with old age appears to be due to the **positivity effect**: the tendency for individuals to remember more positive than negative information with age (Carstensen & Lockenhoff, 2003; Charles, Mather, & Carstensen, 2003). This effect, in turn, is accompanied by diminished activity of the amygdala (Mather et al., 2004), which plays a key role in the processing of negative emotions (see Chapter 3).

Misconception 4: *People on the West Coast are the happiest.* Beautiful beaches, sunshine, warm weather, great celebrity watching ... who could ask for a better recipe for happiness? Maybe some Southern Californians. Even though non-Californians believe that Southern Californians are especially happy, Southern Californians are no happier than anyone else, including people in the chilly upper Midwest (Schkade & Kahneman, 1998). Non-Californians are probably falling prey to the *availability heuristic* (see Chapter 2). When we think of the West Coast, we think of surfers, glamorous actresses, and millionaires sipping martinis on the beach. We forget about the high cost of living, high crime rates, traffic congestion, and all of the other things that come with living in popular areas.

We've talked about four things that don't make us happy, but we haven't said much about what *does* make us happy. Fortunately, research offers some helpful clues (Martin, 2006; Myers, 1993b; Myers & Diener, 1996):

- **Marriage.** Married people tend to be happier than unmarried people (Mastekaasa, 1994), a well-replicated finding that holds across 42 countries studied by researchers (Diener et al., 2000). Moreover, among people who are married, happiness is a good predictor of marital satisfaction (Myers, 2000).

- **Friendships.** People with many friends tend to be happier than people with few friends (Diener & Seligman, 2002).

- **College.** People who graduate from college tend to be happier than people who don't (Martin, 2006).

- **Religion.** People who are deeply religious tend to be happier than people who aren't (Myers, 1993b). This finding might reflect the fact that religious individuals often feel connected to a larger community, as well as to a higher power.

- **Political affiliation.** Republicans tend to be happier than Democrats, both of whom tend to be happier than Independents (Pew Research Center, 2006), although the reasons for these differences are unclear.

- **Exercise.** People who exercise regularly tend to be happier and less depressed than people who don't (Babyak et al., 2000; Stathopoulou et al., 2006), perhaps because exercise itself seems to be an antidepressant (Salmon, 2001).

- **Gratitude.** Merely asking participants on a daily basis to list reasons why they should be grateful about their lives, like having good friends, intimate romantic partners, and a fulfilling job, can enhance short-term happiness (Emmons & McCullough, 2003; Sheldon & Lyubomirsky, 2006), probably because doing so reminds them of what they have.

- **Giving.** Experimental research in which experimenters give participants cash shows that spending money on others produces greater happiness than does spending it on ourselves (Dunn, Akmin, & Norton, 2008). This finding dovetails with research showing that we find performing empathic behaviors toward others pleasurable (de Waal, 2009; see Chapter 13).

correlation vs. causation
CAN WE BE SURE THAT A CAUSES B?

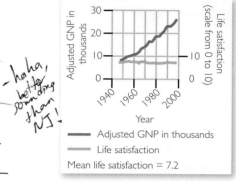

FIGURE 11.10 Does Wealth Bring Happiness? Over a 60-year span, the U.S. gross national product (a measure of economic prosperity) has increased dramatically. Yet Americans' average level of life satisfaction has stayed remarkably constant over the same time period. (*Source:* Diener & Seligman, 2004.)

replicability
CAN THE RESULTS BE DUPLICATED IN OTHER STUDIES?

FACTOID

The world champions of happiness appear to be the Danes. For unknown reasons, people in Denmark report the highest level of satisfaction in the world, with Swiss a close second. Americans come in at 23rd (White, 2006).

positivity effect
tendency for people to remember more positive than negative information with age

The state of "flow," in which we're totally absorbed in an activity and don't notice time passing, is associated with high levels of satisfaction and subjective well-being. We can experience flow in many work situations and enjoyable pastimes.

correlation vs. causation

CAN WE BE SURE THAT A CAUSES B?

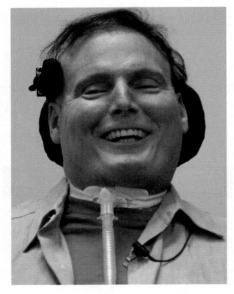

Research shows that following accidents, people with paraplegia typically regain much of their preaccident levels of happiness. The upbeat attitude of actor Christopher Reeve, who died in 2004, nine years after being paralyzed in a horse-riding accident, was both a surprise and an inspiration to many Americans.

affective forecasting
ability to predict our own and others' happiness

durability bias
belief that both our good and bad moods will last longer than they do

• **Flow.** Mihaly Csikszentmihalyi (pronounced "cheeks sent me high") has found that individuals in the midst of *flow*, a mental state in which we're completely immersed in what we're doing, tend to be especially happy (Csikszentmihalyi, 1990, 1997). Some of us experience flow while writing, others while reading, others while performing manual labor, and still others while playing sports, performing music, or creating works of art. During moments of flow, we're so intensely engaged in a rewarding activity that we screen out unpleasant distractions. We also feel a powerful sense of control over our actions.

Still, we should bear two cautions in mind when interpreting these findings. First, the associations between these variables and happiness are typically modest in magnitude, and there are many exceptions to the trends. For example, although there's a slight tendency for married people to be happier than unmarried people, there are plenty of unhappy married people and happy unmarried people (Lucas et al., 2003).

Second, many of these findings derive from correlational research, so the direction of the causal arrow is often unclear. For example, although religious people tend to be happier than nonreligious people, happier people may find it easier than unhappy people to embrace a meaningful religious faith. Moreover, although frequent flow experiences probably contribute to long-term happiness, happy people may be especially prone to flow experiences.

If research tells us anything about how to find happiness, it's that consciously going out of our way to seek it out rarely works. As the concept of flow implies, happiness often emerges from the sheer act of enjoying what we do best, whether it's our work, hobbies, or romantic partners. Happiness lies in the pursuit of the prize, not the prize itself.

True.

■ Forecasting Happiness

We're remarkably poor at **affective forecasting**: predicting our own and others' happiness (Gilbert et al., 1998; Wilson, 2002). We engage in affective forecasting whenever we make a life decision, like picking a college, entering into a long-term relationship, or buying a car. We tell ourselves that each of our choices will boost our happiness, but we're typically no more accurate than a meteorologist who tries to forecast next week's weather by poking his head out the window.

Our affective forecasts aren't merely wrong; they're consistently wrong in one direction. Specifically, *we overestimate the long-term impact of events on our moods* (Gilbert, 2006; Sevdalis & Harvey, 2007). That is, we display a **durability bias**: We believe that both our good and bad moods will last longer than they do (Frederick & Loewenstein, 1999; Gilbert et al., 1998; Wilson, 2002). Consider the following counterintuitive findings:

• Every month, tens of thousands of Americans wait on hour-long lines in the hopes of winning multi-million-dollar lotteries—and guaranteeing a life of never-ending bliss. Sure enough, lottery winners' happiness shoots up sky-high immediately after hitting the big jackpot. Yet by two months, their happiness is back to normal—and not much higher than anyone else's (Brickman, Coates, & Janoff-Bulman, 1978).

• Most people with paraplegia—people paralyzed from the waist down—have returned largely (although not entirely) to their baseline levels of happiness only a few months after their accidents (Brickman et al., 1978). People with other major physical disabilities similarly cope surprisingly well; for example, people who are blind are on average just as happy as people who can see (Feinman, 1978).

• Before taking an HIV test, people understandably predict that they'd be profoundly distressed were they to turn up HIV-positive. Yet only five weeks after discovering they're HIV-positive, people are considerably happier than they expected to be. Moreover, people who discovered they were HIV-negative are considerably less happy than they expected to be (Sieff, Dawes, & Loewenstein, 1999).

What's going on here? We underestimate how rapidly we adjust to our baseline levels of happiness or unhappiness. We forget that we're stuck on what Philip Brickman and Donald Campbell (1971) termed the **hedonic treadmill**: the tendency for our moods to adapt to external circumstances (*hedonic* means "associated with pleasure"). Just as our running speeds adjust quickly to match the speed of a treadmill—or else we'll fall flat on our faces—our levels of happiness adjust quickly to our ongoing life situations. When something good happens to us, we feel better in the short term. Yet we soon adapt to our positive life circumstances, bringing us back to emotional square one (Helson, 1948).

The hedonic treadmill hypothesis proposes that we begin life with a genetically influenced happiness "set point" from which we bounce up and down in response to short-term life events (Lykken, 2000; Lykken & Tellegen, 1996). With few exceptions, we return to that set point after a few days or weeks. We differ from each other in our happiness set points. Studies reveal that most of us are relatively happy most of the time, but others of us are chronically unhappy (Diener, Lucas, & Scollon, 2006) (see **FIGURE 11.11**). Our happiness set points are quite stable, but they can occasionally shift over time, especially following momentous life events. Getting divorced, widowed, or laid off from work often seem to result in lasting increases in unhappiness that don't dissipate completely (Diener et al., 2006).

There's a life lesson lurking in all of this. Here popular wisdom is correct: The grass *is* greener on the other side. It seems greener, that is, until we've been on the other side for a while and realize that the grass is still greener on yet another lawn.

Self-Esteem: Important or Overhyped?

Many pop psychology sources tie virtually all psychological difficulties to one, and only one, core problem: low self-esteem (Branden, 1994; Reasoner, 2000). If you log on to Amazon.com, you'll find over 150,000 books, tapes, and other products devoted to boosting **self-esteem**, typically defined as people's evaluation of their worth. You can even find a self-esteem cereal bowl emblazoned with positive affirmations, like "I'm talented!" and "I'm good-looking!" One American company has even established "Celebration Voice Mailboxes" to offer continual praise to its employees (Zaslow, 2007).

THE GREAT MYTHS OF SELF-ESTEEM. Certainly, all things being equal, high self-esteem isn't a bad thing: Self-esteem is positively correlated with happiness, and negatively correlated with loneliness (Furnham & Cheng, 2000; Hudson, Elek, & Campbell-Grossman, 2000). Yet despite what the popular psychology industry tells us, there's no evidence that low self-esteem is the root of all unhappiness. This assertion is a prime example of a *single-variable explanation*, which as we noted in Chapter 1 reduces complex problems, like depression or aggression, to one cause. Although low self-esteem may play some causal role in these problems, it's unlikely to be the sole culprit. Indeed, the correlations between self-esteem and these difficulties tend to be only modest in size.

What's more, the evidence linking self-esteem to life success is feeble (Dawes, 1994; Sommers & Satel, 2005). People with high self-esteem aren't much more likely than people with low self-esteem to have good social skills or to do well in school. They're also just about as likely to abuse alcohol and other drugs (Baumeister et al., 2003).

When it comes to aggression, the story becomes more interesting. Most of the popular psychology literature links aggression to low self-esteem. There may be some truth to this view (Donnellen et al., 2005). Yet most evidence suggests that a subset of *high* self-esteem people is especially prone to aggression, especially when confronted with "ego threats": challenges to their self-worth.

In one study, Brad Bushman and Roy Baumeister asked participants to write essays concerning their attitudes toward abortion, and told them that another participant would be evaluating their essay. In fact, Bushman and Baumeister had randomly assigned participants to receive either positive evaluations ("No suggestions, great essay!") or negative evaluations ("This is one of the worst essays I have read!"). Then, participants played a game in

FIGURE 11.11   How Happy Are Americans?
Research shows that most Americans are pretty happy, with about a third describing themselves as "very happy." (*Source:* Pew Research Center Report, 2006)

Happiness is largely a matter of comparison, as this photograph from the 2008 Beijing Summer Olympics demonstrates. Research shows that third place finishers, such as American swimmer Ryan Lochte (*right*), tend to be happier—and in this case just about as happy as first place finisher Michael Phelps (*middle*)—than second place finishers, like Hungarian Laszlo Cseh (*left*). The second place finishers are probably especially disappointed because they compare their outcome with what "might have been" (Medvec, Madey, & Gilovich, 1995).

hedonic treadmill
tendency for our moods to adapt to external circumstances

self-esteem
evaluation of our worth

As the name of this bookstore attests, the notion that self-esteem is important to mental health is central to popular psychology.

positive illusions
tendencies to perceive ourselves more favorably than others do

correlation vs. causation

CAN WE BE SURE THAT A CAUSES B?

On April 20, 1999, Eric Harris and Dylan Klebold murdered 12 students and a teacher at Columbine High School in Colorado. Although much of the popular press attributed the murders to low self-esteem, Harris and Klebold's diaries (released after their suicides) indicated that they perceived themselves as superior to their classmates.

FACTOID +

Yes, folks, it's true: Hollywood celebrities *are* self-centered. Dr. Drew Pinsky (better known as "Dr. Drew") and S. Mark Young found that celebrities scored 17 percent higher on a self-report measure of narcissism than did members of the general population. Reality-show contestants scored the highest (Young & Pinsky, 2006).

which they could retaliate against their essay evaluator with a loud blast of noise. High self-esteem subjects who also had high levels of *narcissism*—extreme self-centeredness—responded to negative evaluations by bombarding their opponents with louder noises, but low self-esteem subjects didn't (Bushman & Baumeister, 1998). In addition, in prisons, narcissistic inmates are especially likely to respond with verbal aggression when given orders by guards (Cale & Lilienfeld, 2006).

THE REALITIES OF SELF-ESTEEM. Still, research suggests that self-esteem affords several apparent benefits along with somewhat greater happiness and social connectedness (Baumeister et al., 2003). High self-esteem is associated with greater initiative and persistence—that is, a willingness to attempt new challenges and to stick with them even when the going gets rough—and with resilience in the face of stress. Nevertheless, these findings are correlational and may not be causal.

Self-esteem is also related to **positive illusions**: tendencies to perceive ourselves more favorably than others do. Most high self-esteem individuals see themselves as more intelligent, attractive, and likable than do low self-esteem individuals. Yet they don't score any higher than low-self-esteem individuals on objective measures of these characteristics (Baumeister et al., 2003).

The association between positive illusions and psychological adjustment is controversial. Some researchers believe that unrealistically favorable views of ourselves are healthy (Taylor & Brown, 1988, 1994), because they imbue us with self-confidence. Others disagree (Colvin & Block, 1994), contending that positive illusions make it hard for us to see reality clearly. Indeed, people who view themselves much more positively than their peers tend to be self-centered (John & Robins, 1994). Similarly, children who are aggressive and bully their peers usually overestimate their popularity (Barry, Frick, & Killian, 2003; Emler, 2001).

There may be some truth to both positions. A slight positive bias may be adaptive, as it may lend us the self-assurance we need to take healthy risks, like asking people out for dates or applying for jobs. Yet when our positive biases become too extreme, they may lead to psychological difficulties, including extreme self-centeredness, because these biases may prevent us from benefiting from constructive feedback (Kistner et al., 2006).

✓ **Study** and **Review** on **mypsychlab.com**

assess your knowledge   FACT OR FICTION?

1. Pessimism is an adaptive strategy for some people. **True** / **False**

2. Good moods often allow us to consider novel alternatives to problems. **True** / **False**

3. Money is highly correlated with happiness, especially at high levels of income. **True** / **False**   *nope, not at high levels*

4. Happiness tends to decline sharply after age 50. **True** / **False**   *after 80*

5. A few months after hitting it big in a lottery, lottery winners aren't much happier than anyone else. **True** / **False**

6. High self-esteem is essential for good mental health. **True** / **False**

Answers: 1. T (p. 423); 2. T (p. 423); 3. F (p. 424); 4. F (p. 424); 5. T (p. 426); 6. F (p. 427)

MOTIVATION: OUR WANTS AND NEEDS

11.7 Explain basic principles and theories of motivation.

11.8 Describe the determinants of hunger, weight gain, and obesity.

11.9 Identify the symptoms of bulimia and anorexia.

11.10 Describe the human sexual response cycle and factors that influence sexual activity.

11.11 Identify common misconceptions about and potential influences on sexual orientation.

Up to this point, we've discussed how and why we experience emotions. Yet to explain why we do things, we also need to understand the psychological forces that pull and push us in various, and sometimes opposing, directions. **Motivation** refers to the drives—especially wants and needs—that propel us in specific directions. When we're motivated to do something, like read an interesting book, talk to a friend, or avoid studying for an exam, we're driven to *move* toward or away from that act—both psychologically and physically. Most of us wish we could be more motivated to perform the tasks of life that we ought to do but manage to put off, like pay our bills or begin work on that long-overdue term paper.

So it's no surprise that the world of popular psychology is bursting at the seams with "motivational speakers" who line their pockets with cash from people hoping to receive inspiration in love or work. Although such speakers may get our adrenaline flowing and make us feel good in the short term, there's no evidence that they deliver long-term benefits (Wilson, 2003).

■ Motivation: A Beginner's Guide

One doesn't need to be a psychologist to realize that two of the most overpowering motivators in life are food and sex. We'll soon learn about the whys and the hows of these two great "facts of life." Before we do, we first need to learn about a few basic principles of motivation. Does our little teaser motivate you to read on? We hope so. *Haha.*

DRIVE REDUCTION THEORY. One of the most influential motivational concepts in psychology is **drive reduction theory**, formulated by Clark Hull (1943), Donald Hebb (1949), and others. According to this theory, certain *drives*, like hunger, thirst, and sexual frustration, motivate us to minimize aversive states (Dollard & Miller, 1950). Note that all of these drives are unpleasant, but that satisfaction of them results in pleasure.

From the standpoint of evolutionary theory, drives are geared to ensure our survival and reproduction. Yet some drives are more powerful than others. Thirst is more potent than hunger, and for good reason. Natural selection has probably ensured that our drive to quench our thirst is stronger than our drive to satisfy our hunger because most of us can survive only a few days without water but over a month without food. Most drive reduction theories propose that we're motivated to maintain a given level of psychological **homeostasis**, that is, equilibrium. To understand homeostasis, think of how a thermostat works to control the temperature in your house or apartment. It's set to a given temperature, say 68 degrees Fahrenheit, and when the room temperature deviates up or down from that set point, the thermostat "tells" your cooling or heating system to restore the equilibrium. Similarly, when we're hungry, we're motivated to satisfy that drive by eating, but ideally not too much. If we eat too much, our brain signals to us that we've overdone things and doesn't allow us to become hungry again for a while.

Drives and Arousal: Not Getting ahead of the Curve. One factor that affects the strength of our drives is arousal. According to the **Yerkes-Dodson law** (Yerkes & Dodson, 1908; see Chapter 14), formulated about a century ago, there's an inverted U-shaped relation between arousal, on the one hand, and mood and performance, on the other (although its developers actually referred to the strength of stimuli rather than the strength of arousal; Winton, 1987). As we can see in **FIGURE 11.12**, for each of us there's an optimal point of arousal, usually near the middle of the curve. If we're below that optimal point, we

Motivational speakers, like Anthony Robbins, are adept at persuading their audiences that they can accomplish just about anything with enough drive and effort. Nevertheless, there's no solid research evidence that such speakers produce long-term changes in people's behavior.

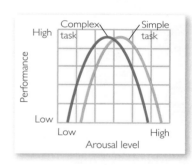

FIGURE 11.12 Yerkes-Dodson Law. This law describes an inverted U-shaped relation between arousal on the one hand, and performance or affect, on the other. We tend to do our best—and are most content—when we experience intermediate levels of arousal.

motivation
psychological drives that propel us in a specific direction

drive reduction theory
theory proposing that certain drives, like hunger, thirst, and sexual frustration motivate us to act in ways that minimize aversive states

homeostasis
equilibrium

Yerkes-Dodson law
inverted U-shaped relation between arousal on the one hand, and mood and performance on the other

Sports psychology research indicates that athletes who are too calm often don't perform at maximum capacity. So getting athletes "pumped up" —but not too pumped up—is a key goal for coaches and trainers.

typically experience low motivation and don't perform well. If we're above that optimal point, we typically feel too anxious or stimulated and likewise don't perform well. Only when we're moderately aroused do we experience the ideal balance of motivation and control to accomplish our goals. Moreover, even within each of us, our arousal level often shifts depending on the time of day, substances we've ingested (like caffeine), and complexity of the tasks we're confronting (Revelle et al., 1980).

The Yerkes-Dodson law is popular among sports psychologists. Think of a swimmer who's underaroused before a major meet. She's unlikely to perform as well as she could, because she's not sufficiently motivated to do her best. So her sports psychologist may try to nudge her into the "psyched up" range of the Yerkes-Dodson curve, where she's feeling just aroused enough to want to do well, but not so aroused she can't concentrate (Anderson, Revelle, & Lynch, 1989).

According to the Yerkes-Dodson law, when we're underaroused we frequently experience "stimulus hunger," that is, a drive for stimulation. We can satisfy this desire in any number of ways: fidgeting, fantasizing, listening to music, socializing with friends, or doing wheelies on a motorcycle. As Daniel Berlyne (1960) noted, underarousal can heighten our sense of curiosity, motivating us to explore stimuli that are complex or novel, like a challenging book or a piece of abstract art. In classic studies of *sensory deprivation* (see Chapter 5) in the 1950s and 1960s, volunteers who entered isolation tanks for several hours often managed to create their own mental stimulation in this state of extreme underarousal (Jones, 1969; Zuckerman & Hopkins, 1966). Many experienced rich sensory images, and a few began to see or hear things that weren't there. Their brains yanked them out of the low end of the Yerkes-Dodson curve.

When Our Drives Clash: Approach and Avoidance. It's way past midnight. We're incredibly hungry, but too exhausted to get up off the couch to pop a dessert into the microwave. So we sit there frozen pathetically in place, spending several minutes deciding whether to remain on the couch or exert the monumental effort needed to walk the 10 feet over to the kitchen. We're experiencing the often psychologically painful effects of conflicting drives.

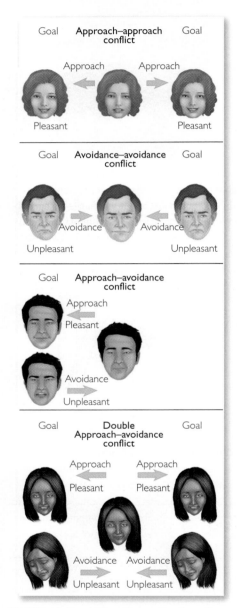

FIGURE 11.13 When Drives Conflict. Four types of conflict can arise when approach and avoidance drives clash. (*Source:* Pettijohn, 1998)

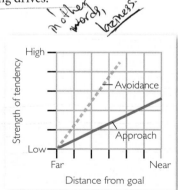

in other words, laziness.

FIGURE 11.14 Approach and Avoidance over Time. As we get closer to a goal, the avoidance gradient becomes steeper than the approach gradient. Projects that seem desirable a few weeks in the future become more undesirable as the deadline approaches. (*Source:* Dr. Ronald Mayer, www.sfsu.edu)

Certain drives generate tendencies toward *approach,* that is, a predisposition toward certain stimuli, like food or objects of our sexual desire. In contrast, others generate tendencies toward *avoidance,* that is, a disposition away from certain stimuli, like rude people or frightening animals (Gray, 1982). As Kurt Lewin (1935) observed, approach and avoidance drives often conflict, as when we want to introduce ourselves to an attractive person across the room but are terrified of rejection. In other cases, two approach drives can conflict, as can two avoidance drives (see **FIGURE 11.13**). As a general rule, the avoidance gradient is steeper than the approach gradient (Bogartz, 1965) (see **FIGURE 11.14**). In less technical terms, this means that as we get closer to our goals, our tendencies to avoid increase more rapidly than our tendencies to approach. This phenomenon helps explain why we often agree to do things months in advance, only to regret them later. When we volunteer enthusiastically in June to organize our club's holiday party in December, the idea sounds like a lot of fun. But as the date of the party draws near, our sense of enjoyment is swamped by our sense of dread regarding all of the drudge work that lies ahead.

INCENTIVE THEORIES. Valuable as drive reduction theories have been to psychology, they don't explain why we often engage in behaviors even when our drives are satisfied. For example, drive reduction theories would predict that once Maya Angelou, Pablo Picasso, or Wolfgang Amadeus Mozart completed a masterpiece, their desire to generate another one would decrease, because they would have quenched their creative thirsts. Yet the opposite often happens; creative success seems to breed an even greater desire to create.

As a consequence, psychologists have come to recognize that drive reduction theories of motivation need to be supplemented by **incentive theories**, which propose that we're often motivated by positive goals, like the pleasure of creating a great painting or the glory of finishing first in a track meet. Many of these theories, in turn, distinguish *intrinsic motivation,* in which people are motivated by internal goals, from *extrinsic motivation,* in which people are motivated by external goals. If we're intrinsically motivated to do well in a psychology class, we're driven primarily by our desire to master the material; if we're extrinsically motivated to do well in this class, we're driven primarily by our desire to get a good grade.

As we learned in Chapter 6, behaviorists define reinforcement as any outcome that makes the behavior that preceded it more likely. Yet there's evidence that certain rewards that we might expect to be reinforcers may *undermine* intrinsic motivation, rendering us less likely to perform behaviors we once enjoyed (Deci, 1971; Deci, Koestner, & Ryan, 1999). Mark Lepper and his colleagues (Lepper, Greene, & Nisbett, 1973) identified preschool children who were especially interested in drawing and randomly assigned them to three conditions: (1) one in which children agreed to draw pictures to receive an award (a fancy certificate with a gold seal and red ribbon); (2) one in which children drew pictures without knowing they'd receive an award, which they later all received; or (3) one in which no children received an award. Two weeks later, the experimenters again gave children the chance to draw pictures and observed them behind a one-way mirror. Interestingly, children in the first condition—who engaged in the activity to achieve a reward—showed significantly less interest in drawing than did children in the other two conditions. Many psychologists and some popular writers have interpreted these findings as implying that when we see ourselves performing a behavior to obtain an external goal, we conclude that we weren't all that interested in that behavior in the first place (Kohn, 1993). "I was only doing it to get the reward," we tell ourselves, "so I guess I wasn't really interested in it for its own sake." As a result, our intrinsic motivation for that behavior decreases.

Not all psychologists accept this interpretation (Carton, 1996; Eisenberger & Cameron, 1996). For one thing, some researchers haven't replicated the undermining effect (Cameron & Pierce, 1994). Still others have offered rival explanations for these findings. One is a *contrast effect:* Once we receive reinforcement for performing a behavior, we anticipate that reinforcement again. If the reinforcement is suddenly withdrawn, we're less likely to perform the behavior. So we're not that different from a rat that's reinforced with a chunk of cheese for completing a maze. When the rat gets to the end of the maze and unexpectedly finds no cheese (the origin of the expression, "Rats!" perhaps?), he's less likely to run the maze quickly the next time (Crespi, 1942; Shoemaker & Fagen, 1984).

OUR NEEDS: PHYSICAL AND PSYCHOLOGICAL URGES. As anyone who's hungry or thirsty knows, some human needs take precedence over others. Starting with psychiatrist Henry Murray (1938), theorists have distinguished *primary needs*—biological necessities, like hunger and thirst, from *secondary needs*—psychological desires. Murray identified more than 20 secondary needs, including the *need for achievement*, about which we'll learn in Chapter 14 (McClelland et al., 1958).

According to Abraham Maslow's **hierarchy of needs** (1954, 1971), we must satisfy our primary needs, such as physiological needs and needs for safety and security,

 Children who are motivated to draw by the fun of it rather than by an outside reward have what kind of motivation?
(See answer upside down on bottom of page.)

replicability
CAN THE RESULTS BE DUPLICATED IN OTHER STUDIES?
ruling out rival hypotheses
HAVE IMPORTANT ALTERNATIVE EXPLANATIONS FOR THE FINDINGS BEEN EXCLUDED?

incentive theories
theories proposing that we're often motivated by positive goals

hierarchy of needs
model, developed by Abraham Maslow, proposing that we must satisfy physiological needs and needs for safety and security before progressing to more complex needs

Answer: Intrinsic

FIGURE 11.15 Maslow's Hierarchy of Needs. According to Abraham Maslow, our needs are arranged in a hierarchy or pyramid, with the most "basic" needs at the bottom. If our basic needs aren't satisfied, Maslow claimed, we can't progress up the hierarchy. Does research support this assertion?

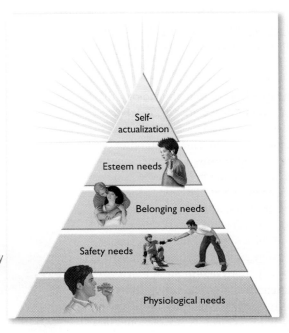

Self-actualization

Esteem needs

Belonging needs

Safety needs

Physiological needs

⊕ Explore Maslow's Hierarchy of Needs on **mypsychlab.com**

before we can progress to more complex secondary needs. These more complex needs include desires for belongingness and love, self-esteem, and finally self-actualization, the drive to realize our full psychological potential (see Chapter 14). As we progress up Maslow's hierarchy, we move away from needs produced by drives, and toward needs produced by incentives. Maslow's hierarchy reminds us of an often overlooked point: When people are starving or malnourished, they often aren't concerned about abstract principles of psychological growth, such as achieving self-knowledge or obtaining democratic freedoms. First things must come first (see **FIGURE 11.15**). ⊕ Explore

Although Maslow's hierarchy is a helpful starting point, we shouldn't take it literally. Some needs are more crucial than others, but there's evidence that people who haven't achieved lower levels of his hierarchy can sometimes attain higher levels (Rowan, 1998; Soper, Milford, & Rosenthal, 1995). The numerous cases of starving artists, who continue to paint masterworks despite being hungry and poor, appear to falsify Maslow's claim of an invariant hierarchy of needs (Zautra, 2003).

falsifiability

CAN THE CLAIM BE DISPROVED?

■ Hunger, Eating, and Eating Disorders

If we're lucky, we don't experience the pangs of hunger very often or for very long, and can refuel with a Big Mac, a veggie sandwich, or whatever satisfies our cravings. But for billions of less privileged people, hunger is a fact of everyday life. As unpleasant as feelings of hunger can be, our very survival depends on it. We experience hunger and thirst to motivate us to acquire food and drink, which provide us with nutrients and energy needed to be active and alert, and maintain a properly functioning immune system (Mattes et al., 2005).

HUNGER AND EATING: REGULATORY PROCESSES. If food is available, we eat when we're hungry. And when we feel full (satiated), we stop eating. Simple, right? Not when we consider that inside our bodies, a complex series of events governing hunger and eating unfolds. One early idea, suggested by Walter Cannon and Alfred Washburn (1912), is that stomach contractions, which occur when our stomach is empty, cause hunger. To test this hypothesis, Washburn, Cannon's graduate student, swallowed a balloon (we don't recommend trying this at home) that was inflated inside his stomach by means of a tube. The intrepid student's reports of hunger were associated with muscle contractions, measured by pressure on the balloon. Nevertheless, as we've learned, we can't infer causation from a correlational finding. Scientists have since observed that people still report hunger pangs when their stomachs are surgically removed, and when surgeons cut the nerve to the stomach responsible for stomach contractions (Bray, 1985). These findings falsify the stomach contraction hypothesis.

correlation vs. causation

CAN WE BE SURE THAT A CAUSES B?

falsifiability

CAN THE CLAIM BE DISPROVED?

Children often point to their stomachs when they're hungry, but the brain is far more influential than the stomach as a command and control center for food cravings. Scientists began to get an inkling of this truth more than 50 years ago, when they learned that two areas of the hypothalamus play different roles in eating. Consider two rats in the same cage that couldn't look more different. Rat 1 is very large, some might say humongous. Rat 2 is scrawny to the point of requiring force-feeding to survive. Scientists supersized the first rat by electrically stimulating the lateral (side) parts of its hypothalamus (Delgado & Anand, 1952). The second rat became slimmer than a supermodel rodent when researchers destroyed its lateral hypothalamus by making a small lesion in it (Anand & Brobeck, 1951; Teitelbaum & Epstein, 1962). Based on these findings, scientists concluded that the lateral hypothalamus plays a key role in initiating eating (see photo at right).

Something remarkable happens when researchers stimulate the *ventromedial* or lower middle part of rats' hypothalamus: The furry creatures eat very little or stop eating entirely (Olds, 1959). When researchers lesion the same part of the brain, the rats become so hefty they look like they're about to burst (Hetherington & Ranson, 1940; King, 2006). The ventromedial hypothalamus seems to let rats know when to stop eating.

Many psychology books have labeled the lateral hypothalamus a "feeding center" and the ventromedial hypothalamus a "satiety center," but this distinction is too simple. Other regions of the hypothalamus, including the arcuate nucleus and paraventricular nucleus, also respond to hunger and satiety signals (Coppari et al., 2005; Scott, McDade, & Luckman, 2007). In reality, a complex sequence of events mediated by different brain areas and body regions choreographs eating (Grill & Kaplan, 2002). A distended or full stomach activates neurons in the hypothalamus, and in response we resist our impulses to reach for that second cookie (Jordan, 1969; Smith, 1996; Stunkard, 1975). A hormone produced in the stomach called *ghrelin* communicates with the hypothalamus to increase hunger, whereas another hormone, called cholecystokinin (CCK), counteracts the effects of ghrelin and decreases hunger (Badman & Flier, 2005).

Glucose (blood sugar) provides our cells with high-octane energy to score a touchdown or flee from a hungry lion. Our bodies produce glucose from proteins, fats, and carbohydrates in the foods we eat. The hypothalamus is in tune with changing levels of glucose, signaled by receptors for glucose in the liver and hypothalamus (Schwartz et al., 2000; Woods et al., 1998). According to **glucostatic theory** (Campfield et al., 1996; van Litalie, 1990), when our blood glucose levels drop, typically after we haven't eaten for some time, hunger creates a drive to eat to restore the proper level of glucose. In this way, we achieve homeostasis, the balance of energy we take in and expend. People gain weight when there's an imbalance, such that more energy is taken into the body than expended by way of exercise or the body's ability to "burn" excess calories through metabolic processes.

When our glucose levels drop substantially, we generally feel hungry (Levin, Dunn-Meynell, & Routh, 1999). But levels of blood glucose can be quite variable and don't always mirror the amount or types of food we eat. In fact, our self-reported hunger and desire for a meal are better predictors of our energy intake in our meals over a three-day period than are our glucose levels (Pittas et al., 2005). Far more than glucose is involved in regulating eating.

WEIGHT GAIN AND OBESITY: BIOLOGICAL AND PSYCHOLOGICAL INFLUENCES. When we go "people watching" in the mall, we can't help but notice that adults and children come in more shapes and sizes than varieties of Campbell's soup. If that mall or supermarket is in the United States, we'll also observe that about two-thirds of the passersby are overweight or obese. In our evolutionary history, stocking up on tasty and energy-loaded fatty foods was probably necessary for survival, and may partly explain our preference for such foods. In today's food-rich society of all-you-can-eat buffets and oversized portions, however, people typically consume far more calories than they need to ensure their survival (Capaldi, 1996; Konner, 2003). We'll explore obesity in Chapter 12, but here we'll examine the physiology and psychology of eating and overeating.

Chemical Messengers and Eating. When we eat a candy bar, some of the glucose from the treat may get converted into fat, which stores energy for the long term. The more stored energy in fat cells, the more they produce a hormone called **leptin**. Leptin signals the hypothalamus and brain stem to reduce appetite and increase the amount of energy used (Grill et al., 2002). Researchers discovered a clue to the causes of obesity when they found that mice that lacked the gene for leptin become obese at an early age (Hamann & Matthaei, 1996). Interestingly, people who are obese seem resistant to the effects of leptin.

Individuals who are obese also find food difficult to resist because they think about food a lot, and find the tasty qualities of food especially rewarding. The mere sight, taste, smell, and thought of plentiful food in our environment can trigger the release of

Haha, people watching

glucostatic theory
theory that when our blood glucose levels drop, hunger creates a drive to eat to restore the proper level of glucose

leptin
hormone that signals the hypothalamus and brain stem to reduce appetite and increase the amount of energy used

neurotransmitters, including serotonin, that activate the brain's pleasure circuits (Ciarella et al., 1991; Lowe & Levine, 2005). People who are obese also may overeat to provide comfort or distraction to counter negative emotions (Hoppa & Hallstrom, 1981; Stice et al., 2005).

The Set Point. Another reason why the battle of the bulge isn't easy to win is that each of us may have a genetically programmed **set point**, a value—much like that on our car's fuel gauges—that establishes a range of body fat and muscle mass we tend to maintain (Mrosovsky & Powley, 1977). When we eat too little and drop below our set point, regulatory mechanisms kick in to increase our appetite or decrease our metabolism (Knecht, Elllger, & Levine, 2007). In this way, our bodies defend against weight loss. According to Richard Nisbett, people who are obese try to keep their weight below their set point. Consequently, they're hungry much of the time, which increases the appeal of tasty, high-calorie foods and makes dieting difficult (Nisbett, 1972). When we eat too much, the opposite occurs. Without our ever realizing it, our bodies tune down our appetite and increase our metabolism.

According to the set point hypothesis, an obese person has a biological predisposition toward greater weight than does a thin person. No one knows for sure what "sets" the set point, but individuals who are obese may be born with more fat cells, with lower metabolic rates at which their bodies burn calories, or with less sensitivity to leptin than thin people. Some people seem to bulk up like Sumo wrestlers no matter how little they eat, whereas others remain thin as a reed no matter how much they eat.

Still, some findings raise suspicions about the set point hypothesis. David Levitsky and his colleagues (Levitsky et al., 2005) determined how many calories study subjects consumed during a 14-day baseline period, and then overfed the subjects so that they consumed 35 percent more calories than they did at baseline. During a third period, in which subjects could eat whatever they wanted, they didn't restrict their food intake enough to return to baseline levels, as predicted by set point theory. What's clear is that we're not fated to remain at a fixed weight; there's a range of weights we can "settle into." Most of us can control and modify our weight, within limits, by staying active and eating a healthy diet.

The Role of Genes in Obesity. Genes probably exert a substantial influence on our weight. In about 6 percent of cases of severe obesity, a mutation in a major *melanocortin-4 receptor gene* is responsible (Todorovic & Haskell-Lueuvano, 2005). People born with this mutation never seem to feel full, regardless of whether they've eaten a strawberry or half a strawberry pie. In effect, their brains don't let them know when to stop eating. Scientists have identified other genes, including the leptin gene, but a combination of many genes associated with appetite, amount of fat stored in the body, and metabolism probably work together to increase the likelihood of obesity.

Twin studies point to a genetic predisposition toward obesity. Researchers have found correlations for fat mass in the range of .7–.9 for identical twins, and a range of .35–.45 for fraternal twins (Lee, 2009; Stunkard, Foch, & Hrubec, 1986). Because twins are raised in the same family and often share the same general diet and lifestyle, it's especially important for researchers to study identical twins raised in different families. When they've done so, they've found correlations of .4–.7 for body mass (Maes, Neale, & Eaves, 1997). Adoption studies lend further support for the role of genes. People's body mass is correlated with their biological, but not adoptive, parents' body mass (Allison et al., 1996).

Sensitivity to Cues and Expectations. But genes don't completely determine our weight. External cues, such as the time of day, observing others sample multiple portions of tempting desserts, and expectations also play prominent roles in food consumption. The supersizing of portions—called *portion distortion*—has probably contributed to the supersizing of Americans (Geier, Rozin, & Doris, 2006; Wansink, 2009). In the United States, from 1977 to 1996, portion sizes of food served on dinner plates in restaurants ballooned by 25 percent (Young & Nestle, 2002). When people are served M&Ms with a large spoon,

People differ in their genetic tendency toward obesity, so differences in food consumption and weight may be apparent at an early age. A mutation in the melanocortin-4 receptor gene may play a role in some early cases of obesity.

ruling out rival hypotheses

HAVE IMPORTANT ALTERNATIVE EXPLANATIONS FOR THE FINDINGS BEEN EXCLUDED?

set point
value that establishes a range of body and muscle mass we tend to maintain

they eat substantially more of them than when they're served in a small spoon (Geier et al., 2006). Brian Wansick and his colleagues (Wansink, Painter, & North, 2005) fooled participants by have them unknowingly drink soup from "bottomless bowls"—bowls that remained full by means of a flowing tube containing soup connected to the bottom of the bowl. They consumed a whopping 73 percent more soup than participants who consumed soup from regular bowls. Because we think in terms of "units" of things as the optimal amount—a heuristic called *unit bias* (Geier et al., 2006)—controlling portions of food consumed is a good way to control our weight. A nifty trick to keep in mind is to eat food on a smaller plate: Doing so will make portions appear bigger and limit the amount we eat.

Brian Wansink, shown here, has shown that people tend to eat more popcorn when it's served in a large rather than a small bucket—an example of what psychologists call "unit bias." So beware of those "You can get an extra-large portion for only 75 cents more" pitches from movie vendors.

Stanley Schachter proposed the **internal–external theory**, which holds that relative to other people, people with obesity are motivated to eat more by external cues like portion size, as well as the taste, smell, and appearance of food, than by internal cues like a growling stomach or feelings of fullness (Canetti, Bachar, & Berry 2002; Schachter, 1968). According to this theory, individuals are at risk for obesity when they continue to eat even after being full, and base their food choices on the appealing qualities of food, time of day, or social circumstances. In the laboratory, people who are obese are more likely than other people to gorge themselves after researchers manipulate clocks in the room to fool participants into thinking it's dinnertime (Schachter & Gross, 1968). Nevertheless, another possibility, which research favors, is that the oversensitivity to external cues is a consequence rather than a cause of eating patterns (Nisbett, 1972).

> **internal–external theory**
> theory holding that obese people are motivated to eat more by external cues than internal cues

◄ **ruling out rival hypotheses**

HAVE IMPORTANT ALTERNATIVE EXPLANATIONS FOR THE FINDINGS BEEN EXCLUDED?

Answers are located at the end of the text.

DIETS AND WEIGHT-LOSS PLANS

evaluating CLAIMS

We Americans are always looking for a new, quicker way to lose weight and achieve our ideal body size and shape. The creators of diets and weight-loss plans are only too happy to oblige. Some claim we can lose weight by avoiding carbohydrates, others by drinking protein shakes, and still others by consuming only one type of soup or grapefruit. How many of these diet tips have you heard? Let's evaluate some of these claims, which are modeled after actual ads for diets and weight-loss plans.

"We help you lose weight by changing your everyday habits. Learn how to eat *smaller portions*, choose more *nutritious foods*, and make *exercise* a part of your daily routine."
This ad doesn't make any promises about how much weight you'll lose and correctly notes that reducing calories (through smaller portions of nutritious foods) and exercise are necessary components of a sensible diet.

"I have a whole new lease on life— I lost *98 pounds in only four months!*"
The anecdotal claim that someone lost almost 100 pounds in four months is extraordinary— that would be an average of over six pounds lost each and every week. Note that the ad doesn't mention potential adverse health effects of such dramatic weight loss. In addition, no reason is given for the weight loss, so we can't assume the diet is the cause. What rival explanations can you think of for such a drastic weight loss?

"Our *revolutionary research* shows that you can lose weight without dieting or exercise. Click here to learn more."
Beware of claims based on "revolutionary" new studies. The principle of connectivity reminds us that science builds with previous research. Moreover, to be trusted, results should be replicated in independent studies.

bulimia nervosa
eating disorder associated with a pattern of bingeing and purging in an effort to lose or maintain weight

anorexia nervosa
eating disorder associated with excessive weight loss and the irrational perception that one is overweight

👁 Watch Eating Disorders on **mypsychlab.com**

EATING DISORDERS: BULIMIA AND ANOREXIA. People who try to lose a lot of weight over a short period of time are especially prone to binge eating (Lowe, Gleaves, & Murphy-Eberenz, 1998). The eating disorder of **bulimia nervosa** (better known simply as *bulimia*) is associated with a pattern of *bingeing*—eating large amounts of highly caloric foods in brief periods of time—followed by *purging*—vomiting or other means of drastic weight loss, like frantic exercise or extreme dieting. During a binge, some people gorge themselves with food equaling more than 10,000 calories in a two-hour period and average about 3,500 calories per binge. That amounts to about six Big Macs (Walsh, 1993; Walsh et al., 1992). 👁 Watch

Bulimia literally means "ox hunger." Bingeing can be frightening because it's often accompanied by the feeling that it's impossible to stop eating. After a binge, most people with bulimia feel guilt and anxiety over the loss of control and the prospect of gaining weight. Frequently, their answer to this problem is to purge, which typically takes the form of self-induced vomiting, but sometimes involves abusing laxatives or diet pills or excessive exercise (Williamson et al., 2002).

Bingeing and purging set up a vicious cycle. Purging is reinforcing because it relieves anxious feelings after overeating and sidesteps weight gain. But it sets the stage for bouts of overeating. For example, vomiting allows people with bulimia to "undo" the binge and rationalize later bouts of overeating ("I can always get rid of the ice cream"). After bingeing, they may resolve to go on a strict diet. Yet severe dieting leads to hunger and increases preoccupation with food and the temptation to binge (Stice et al., 1999; Stice et al., 2005). When eating spirals out of control, concerns about dieting and the likelihood of another binge escalate, thereby completing the self-destructive circle (Fairburn, Cooper, & Sharfan, 2003; Lynn & Kirsch, 2006). This binge-purge cycle can be physically hazardous, resulting in heart problems (which can be fatal), tears to the esophagus, and wearing away of tooth enamel (Mehler, 2003).

Bulimia is the most common eating disorder, afflicting 1 to 3 percent of the population (Craighead, 2002; Keski-Rahkonen et al., 2008). About 95 percent of people with this diagnosis are women. An additional 8 percent to 16 percent of young women, including many in college, fall short of a diagnosis of bulimia, but show signs of disordered eating, such as repeated bingeing. Many women with bulimia are perfectionists with low self-esteem, and have an especially strong need for approval (Friedman & Wishman, 1998; Joiner et al., 1997).

People with bulimia report high levels of body dissatisfaction and often see themselves as obese when they're of normal weight (Johnson & Wardle, 2005). Twin studies suggest that bulimia is influenced by genetic factors (Bulik, Sullivan, & Kendler, 1998). Nevertheless, bulimia is probably also triggered in part by sociocultural expectations concerning the ideal body image. In modern society, the media equate beauty with a slender female figure. Movies, sitcoms, and magazines feature extremely underweight females, typically 15 percent below women's average weight (Johnson, Tobin, & Steinberg, 1989). So it's no wonder that women who frequently view television programs featuring extremely thin women experience higher levels of body image dissatisfaction than other women (Himes & Thompson, 2007; Thompson et al., 2004; Tiggeman & Pickering, 1996) (see **FIGURE 11.16**). Nevertheless, women who are already concerned about their body image may tend to watch television programs featuring idealized images of women, so the causal arrow could run in the opposite direction. Still, there's compelling circumstantial evidence for at least some causal effect of the media on eating disorders. Following the introduction of American and British television onto the remote Pacific island of Fiji, the symptoms of eating disorders in teenage girls increased fivefold within only fours years (Becker et al., 2002).

Anorexia nervosa, or anorexia, is less common than bulimia, with rates ranging from 0.5 percent to 1 percent of the population (Craighead, 2002). But like bulimia, anorexia usually begins in adolescence, is much more common in girls than boys, and is

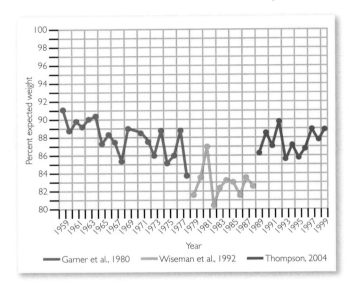

FIGURE 11.16 Data from Three Studies on the Weights of *Playboy* Centerfolds from 1959 to 1999. *Playboy* centerfold models have consistently been markedly below average in weight, reaching a low point in the mid- to late 1980s and rebounding somewhat in the 1990s. These centerfold models' images may provide women with unrealistic ideals of thinness. (The y-axis shows the percentage of expected weight, with 100 percent being average.) (*Source:* Sypeck et al., 2006)

correlation vs. causation

CAN WE BE SURE THAT A CAUSES B?

sometimes fueled by sociocultural pressures to be thin. Whereas individuals with bulimia tend to be in the normal weight range, those with anorexia become emaciated in their relentless pursuit of thinness (Golden & Sacker, 1984). Along with a "fear of fatness," individuals with anorexia—like those with bulimia—have a distorted perception of their body size. Even those with bones showing through their skin may describe themselves as fat.

Psychologists diagnose anorexia when individuals display a refusal to maintain body weight at or above a minimally normal weight for age and height (specifically, their body weight is less than 85 percent of that expected). Individuals with anorexia often lose between 25 percent and 50 percent of their body weight.

Concerns about body shape can become so all-consuming that individuals with anorexia stubbornly deny the seriousness of their condition and resist pressure from family and friends to gain weight. Starvation can actually produce symptoms of anorexia. In the "starvation study," 36 healthy young men volunteered to restrict their food intake severely for half a year as an alternative to serving in the military (Keys et al., 1950). On average, they lost about 25 percent of their weight. Their preoccupation with food increased dramatically, and some spent a great deal of time planning how, when, and where to eat their daily food portion. Some ate very slowly, whereas others hoarded food or gulped it down as if it were their final meal. Some men broke the eating rules and binged, followed by intense guilt or self-induced vomiting. It's clear that once people severely reduce their food intake, starvation itself can lead to many of the symptoms of anorexia and bulimia (Fairburn et al., 2003; Garner, 1997).

With continued low weight, a loss of menstrual periods, hair loss, heart problems, life-threatening electrolyte imbalances, and fragile bones may result (Gottdiener et al., 1978; Katzman, 2005). A patient treated by your text's second author broke her femur (the long bone in the thigh) during an ordinary game of tennis. Some researchers put the mortality rate for anorexia at 5 percent to 10 percent, making it one of the most life-threatening of all psychological conditions (Birmingham et al., 2005; Sullivan, 1995).

Anorexia is present not only in Western countries but also in regions that have had little exposure to Western media, including some Middle Eastern nations and parts of India (Keel & Klump, 2003; Lynn et al., 2007). Although anorexia appears to be more culturally and historically universal than bulimia, societal *explanations* for its causes have differed across time and place. For example, historical descriptions suggest that some young Catholic nuns in medieval times who starved themselves probably had anorexia. Yet they explained their fasting behaviors as efforts to purify their souls for God (Keel & Klump, 2003; Smith, Spillane, & Annus, 2006).

■ Sexual Motivation

Sexual desire—called *libido*—is a wish or craving for sexual activity and sexual pleasure (Regan & Berscheid, 1999). Sexual desire is deeply rooted in our genes and biology, but as we'll see, it's also influenced by social and cultural factors.

SEXUAL DESIRE AND ITS CAUSES. The sex hormone testosterone can sometimes enhance sexual interest in the short-term (see Chapter 3), but other biological influences are also at play. A team of researchers (Houle et al., 2006) suggested that the neurotransmitter serotonin is the key to explaining an intriguing link between migraine headaches and increased libido. Based on findings that low sexual desire is associated with high levels of serotonin, and that migraine headaches are associated with low levels of serotonin, they hypothesized that people with migraines would report high levels of sexual desire. The investigators compared participants with migraine headaches with participants matched for age and gender who suffered from tension headaches, which are unrelated to serotonin levels. Sufferers of migraine headaches reported 20 percent higher levels of sexual desire than did sufferers of tension headaches.

Researchers have discovered that variations in a gene that produces DRD4, a protein related to dopamine transmission, are correlated with students' reports of sexual desire and arousal (Zion et al., 2006). The scientists estimated that approximately 20 percent of

Anorexia isn't limited to women, although it's comparatively rare among men. It's associated with body image distortion, which contributes to a fear of being fat despite being severely underweight.

FICTOID

MYTH: People with anorexia (which means "without hunger" in Greek) aren't hungry.

REALITY: People with anorexia nervosa experience hunger, sometimes quite intensely, but rigidly deny themselves food. They feel anxious and guilty when they give in to the urge to eat, and may exercise excessively or abuse laxatives on such occasions to avoid weight gain.

FICTOID

MYTH: The average man thinks about sex every seven seconds.

REALITY: Although this claim and others very much like it (you may have heard "every eight seconds," or "every 15 seconds") are widespread, there's no research evidence for them. Some survey data indicate that 54 percent of men say they think about sex at least once a day or more (http://kinseyinstitute.org/resources/FAQ.html), but offer no support for the "every seven seconds" claim (http://www.snopes.com/science/stats/thinksex.asp).

excitement phase

phase in human sexual response in which people experience sexual pleasure and notice physiological changes associated with it

plateau phase

phase in human sexual response in which sexual tension builds

orgasm (climax) phase

phase in human sexual response marked by involuntary rhythmic contractions in the muscles of genitals in both men and women

resolution phase

phase in human sexual response following orgasm, in which people report relaxation and a sense of well-being

the population possesses the mutation for increased sexual desire, whereas another 70 percent possesses a variant of the gene that depresses sexual desire. These findings dovetail with research showing that dopamine plays a key role in reward (see Chapter 3).

Many people believe that men have a stronger desire for sex than women. This stereotype may hold more than a kernel of truth (Baumeister, Catanese, & Vohs, 2001). Compared with women, men desire sex more frequently and experience more sexual arousal (Hiller, 2005; Klusman, 2002;), have a greater number and variety of sexual fantasies (Laumann et al., 1994; Leitenberg & Henning, 1995), masturbate more frequently (Oliver & Hyde, 1993), want to have more sexual partners (Buss & Schmidt, 1993), and desire sex earlier in a relationship (Sprecher, Barbee, & Schwartz, 1995). Interestingly, women tend to experience greater variability than men in their sex drive (Lippa, 2009), and women with high sex drives tend to be attracted to both men and women (Chivers & Bailey, 2005). In contrast, men with high sex drives tend to be attracted to only one sex or the other, depending on their sexual orientation (Lippa, 2006). In contrast to men, women's appetite for sex—but not their need for romantic tenderness—appears to decline after they form a secure relationship. From an evolutionary perspective, relatively high sex drive at the beginning of a relationship cements the pair bond, and when sex drive falters, it may pique men's sexual interest. Meanwhile, men's sexual interest remains stable, perhaps to equal that of potential sexual competitors. Of course, none of these findings about sex necessarily apply to any individual man or woman, and there's tremendous variability in sexual interest among men and women—indeed, at least as much variability as there is between men and women.

Socialization may help explain why men and women appear to differ in sexual desire. Women are socialized to be less assertive and aggressive in many spheres of life, including the expression of their sexual desires. So perhaps women and men actually experience comparable sexual drives, but women don't express or admit their desires as much (Fisher, 2009). Although the evidence tilts toward the conclusion that men have an inherently stronger sex drive than women, the evidence isn't definitive.

THE PHYSIOLOGY OF THE HUMAN SEXUAL RESPONSE. In 1954, the husband and wife team of William Masters and Virginia Johnson launched their pioneering investigations of sexual desire and the human sexual response. Their observations included sexual behaviors under virtually every imaginable condition, and some virtually unimaginable. Masters and Johnson's laboratory wasn't exactly a prescription for romantic intimacy: In addition to a bed, it contained monitoring equipment to measure physiological changes, cameras, and a probe that contained a camera to record changes in the vagina during intercourse. Yet most people who volunteered for their studies accommodated to the laboratory with surprising ease.

Masters and Johnson (1966) reported that the basic sexual arousal cycle was the same for men and women. Based on their research and other observations (Kaplan, 1977), scientists define the *sexual response cycle* in terms of four phases: (1) excitement, (2) plateau, (3) orgasm, and (4) resolution (see **FIGURE 11.17**).

The **excitement phase** is initiated by whatever prompts sexual interest. People often experience little sexual desire when they're tired, distracted, stressed out, in pain, or ill. Lack of attraction to a partner, depression, anxiety, and resentment can also inhibit sexual desire. In the excitement phase, people experience sexual pleasure and start to notice physiological changes, such as penile erection in men and vaginal swelling and lubrication in women. During the **plateau phase**, sexual tension builds, and if it continues, ultimately leads to orgasm. In the **orgasm (climax) phase**, sexual pleasure and physical changes peak, there are involuntary rhythmic contractions in the muscles of the genitals in men and women, and men ejaculate. Brain scans reveal that when individuals achieve orgasm, the areas that control fear in the amygdala become less active than when people aren't sexually aroused (Georgiadis et al., 2006). This finding may explain why in the **resolution phase**, after orgasm, people report relaxation

ruling out rival hypotheses

HAVE IMPORTANT ALTERNATIVE EXPLANATIONS FOR THE FINDINGS BEEN EXCLUDED?

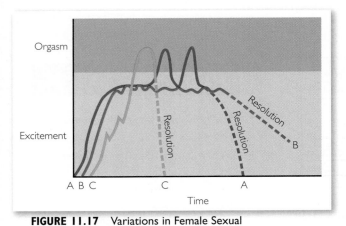

FIGURE 11.17 Variations in Female Sexual Response Cycle. This figure depicts the sexual arousal cycle for four different women, each represented by a different color. Three of the four women experienced at least one orgasm. The woman whose response is traced by the red line experienced excitement but no orgasm. (*Source:* Rathus, Nevid, & Fichner-Rathus, 2008)

and a sense of well-being as the body returns to its unstimulated state (Belliveau & Richter, 1970; Resnick & Ithman, 2009).

Masters and Johnson's groundbreaking efforts didn't capture a crucial fact: People's sexuality is deeply embedded in their relationships and feelings for one another. People experience more frequent and consistent orgasms when they love their partner and feel loved in return (Birnbaum, Glaubman, & Mikulincer. 2001) and feel satisfied in their relationship (Young et al., 2000). But we can question the causal direction between relationship quality and the frequency and consistency of orgasms. Frequent orgasms may not merely reflect healthy relationships but contribute to them. ⊕—Explore

correlation vs. causation
CAN WE BE SURE THAT A CAUSES B?

⊕—**Explore** the Sexual Response Cycle on
mypsychlab.com

FREQUENCY OF SEXUAL ACTIVITIES AND AGING. Early in their marriage, couples have sex on average about twice a week (Laumann et al., 1994). As people age, the frequency of their sexual activities decreases but their sexual satisfaction doesn't. Perhaps people expect their sexual activity to decrease as they age, so they're not disappointed by this change.

Contrary to the myth that sexual activities virtually cease for senior citizens, many people are sexually active well into their seventies and eighties, especially when they're healthy, are in happy marriages, and perceive that their partners desire a sexual relationship (Call, Sprecher, & Schwartz, 1995). Three-fourths of married men and 56 percent of married women are sexually active over age 60, and 30 percent of women 80 to 102 (!) years old and 63 percent of men in that age range are sexually active (Meston, 1997). Women experience complex and sometimes striking changes in hormones during menopause, although there's another explanation for the difference between older men's and women's sexual activities. By the age of 80, women have less opportunity to find male partners; for every 100 women, there are only 39 men (Meston, 1997).

ruling out rival hypotheses
**HAVE IMPORTANT ALTERNATIVE EXPLANATIONS
FOR THE FINDINGS BEEN EXCLUDED?**

There are at least three problems with much of the research on sex and aging. First, many surveys haven't disentangled age from the length of time people are in relationships (Burgess, 2004). The frequency of sexual activity tends to decrease the longer people are in a relationship. Second, scientists haven't examined the effects of poor health on sexual activity in the elderly. Third, many studies on seniors aren't based on random samples, so it's not clear how representative they are of the elderly (Hayes & Dennerstein, 2005).

SEXUALITY AND CULTURE. People's expression of sexual desires is shaped by social norms and culture. Clellan Ford and Frank Beach's (1951) fascinating observations reveal how cultural norms influence people's ideas of what's sexually appropriate or inappropriate. When members of the Tsonga tribe in Africa first saw Europeans kissing, they laughed and remarked, "Look at them—they eat each other's saliva and dirt" (Ford & Beach, 1951). Admittedly, they have a point. Members of the Apinaly society in Brazil don't kiss, but women of the tribe may bite off their lovers' eyebrows and noisily spit them to one side. Women of the island Turk are even less kind, at least by Western standards: They customarily poke a finger into the man's ear when they're sexually excited.

David Buss (1989) found that residents of non-Western societies, including India, Iran, and China, place a much greater value on chastity in a potential partner than do individuals in Western European countries, including Sweden, Holland, and France. Americans are divided on whether they approve (59 percent) or disapprove (41 percent) of premarital sex (Widmer, Treas, & Newcomb, 1998). This latter percentage stands at odds with the prevalence of premarital sex in the United States, with men reporting rates of 85 percent and women rates of 80 percent (Laumann et al., 1994).

SEXUAL ORIENTATION: SCIENCE AND POLITICS. Same-sex romantic relationships develop in virtually all cultures and have done so since the dawn of recorded history. Biologists have documented homosexual behaviors in some 450 species (Bagemihl, 1999). People differ in their sexual orientation or interest in same (homosexual), opposite (heterosexual), or both (bisexual) sex sexual partners. We should keep in mind that sexual orientation isn't the same as sexual activity. For example, people may restrict their sexual partners to opposite sex individuals, yet be sexually attracted to same-sex individuals. Alfred Kinsey, in his famous

"Kinsey Report" of the 1940s and 1950s, cautioned against categorizing people as heterosexual or homosexual, but "as individuals who have had certain amounts of homosexual experience and certain amounts of heterosexual experience" (quoted by Haeberle, 1978, p. 230). Indeed, if we were to categorize as homosexual all persons with one homosexual experience, a sizable number of people would fall into this category (McConaghy, 2005).

People also differ in how they think and feel about their homosexuality. Many people who engage in occasional homosexual activities don't view themselves as gay (Bell & Weinberg, 1978).

Prevalence of Different Sexual Orientations. Research suggests that about 2.8 percent of males and 1.4 percent of females 18 or older identify themselves as gay, lesbian, or bisexual (Laumann et al., 1994; National Opinion Research Center, 2003). Nevertheless, even the best estimates may not represent the general population, because researchers often conduct surveys in prisons, college dorms, military barracks, or under the sponsorship of gay organizations, all of which may result in sampling bias.

Since Kinsey's groundbreaking research, scientists have acquired a better understanding of homosexuality and challenged common misconceptions about gay men, lesbians, and bisexuals. Contrary to the stereotype that one person in a gay relationship adopts a masculine role, whereas the other adopts a feminine role, less than a fourth of gay men and women fit neatly into these categories (Jay & Young, 1979; Lever, 1995). A good deal of media coverage also implies that gay individuals recruit others to become gay, or are especially likely to sexually abuse children and adolescents. Yet scientific evidence supports neither view (Freund, Watson, & Rienzo, 1989; Jenny, Roesler, & Poyer, 1994). Another myth is that gay individuals are unfit to be parents. In fact, homosexual and heterosexual adults don't differ in their approach to parenting (Bos, van Balen, & van den Boom, 2007; Patterson, 1992) and are equally likely to provide supportive environments for their children (Gartrell & Bos, 2010; Patterson & Chan, 1996; Weston, 1991; see Chapter 10).

Can Sexual Orientation Be Changed? Masters and Johnson (1979; Schwartz & Masters, 1984), among others, examined whether it's possible to change the sexual orientation of gay men and women who wish to become heterosexual. Their work was methodologically problematic, in part because most participants were bisexual rather than homosexual. Later, Robert Spitzer (2003) evaluated 200 cases of people who underwent sexual reorientation therapy and reported many instances in which people changed from a predominantly homosexual to heterosexual orientation for a five-year period or longer. Nevertheless, only 11 percent of the men and 37 percent of the women reported a complete change in orientation. Moreover, it's not clear whether these apparently successful individuals were exclusively homosexual before therapy, and whether their sexual orientation changed much beyond their self-reports. Spitzer's sample was far from a random sample of gay individuals: Most were college graduates, 76 percent of the men and 47 percent of the women were married, and less than half were openly gay at some point prior to the study. Still, Spitzer's research suggests that some degree of sexual reorientation might be possible in certain motivated individuals.

Critics of sexual reorientation therapies contend that such treatments promote the misconception that homosexuality is a disease that requires a cure (Davison, 1976; Haldeman, 1994). Prior to 1973, homosexuality was included in the American Psychiatric Association's formal list of mental disorders, the Diagnostic and Statistical Manual (Bayer & Spitzer, 1985; see Chapter 15), but scientific and social attitudes have changed markedly over the past three and a half decades. Although gay men and women report relatively high rates of anxiety and depression (Biernbaum & Ruscio, 2004; Ferguson, Horwood, & Beautrais, 1999), this fact doesn't indicate that homosexuality itself is a disease, let alone that it requires treatment. Moreover, the higher rates of psychological problems in gay populations holds true only in Caucasians, not Blacks or Latinos (Meyer, Dietrich, & Schwartz, 2007). In many or most cases, gay individuals' psychological problems may reflect their reaction to social oppression and intolerance of their lifestyles rather than preexisting mental disturbance. Accordingly, gay individuals who participate in reorientation therapy and don't achieve the changes they seek may become even more dissatisfied.

Research indicates that gay people are as likely as heterosexual people to provide supportive environments for children.

ruling out rival hypotheses

HAVE IMPORTANT ALTERNATIVE EXPLANATIONS FOR THE FINDINGS BEEN EXCLUDED?

The American Psychological Association (2009) recently affirmed that same-sex sexual and romantic attractions are normal variations of human sexuality, and concluded that there's insufficient evidence to support the use of psychological interventions to change sexual orientation. There's growing consensus that evidence-based treatments that value cultural diversity are well-positioned to help many currently distressed people accept and live with their homosexuality, rather than change their sexual orientation (Bartoli & Gillem, 2008; Glassgold et al., 2009).

GENETIC AND ENVIRONMENTAL INFLUENCES ON SEXUAL ORIENTATION. Bearing in mind the caveat that heritability doesn't imply that a characteristic can't be changed (see Chapter 3), most scientists are skeptical about the ability of gay individuals to change their sexual orientation because there are indications of inborn differences between homosexual and heterosexual individuals. Because many gay men and women report they've felt different from others for as long as they can remember, it's plausible that biological differences are sometimes present even before birth.

Sexual Orientation: Clues from Twin Studies. Indeed, twin studies offer support for a role of genetic influences on male homosexuality. Michael Bailey and Richard Pillard (1991) found a concordance rate of 52 percent in identical twins, in contrast with a concordance rate of 22 percent in fraternal twins (*concordance* refers to the proportion of co-twins who exhibit a characteristic, in this case, homosexuality, when the other twin also exhibits this characteristic). In a later study conducted in Australia with 1,538 male twin pairs, Bailey and his associates (Bailey, Dunne, & Martin, 2000) used a strict standard for defining sexual orientation and found a concordance rate of 20 percent for homosexuality in identical twins and 0 percent in fraternal twins. In still another study, they found concordance rates for lesbians of 48 percent in identical twins and 16 percent in fraternal twins (Bailey et al., 1993). The finding that a substantial percentage of identical twins aren't concordant tells us that environmental influences play a key role in homosexuality, although it doesn't tell us what these influences are.

Exotic Becomes Erotic. Nestled within Bailey's studies are clues related to the causes of sexual orientation. Gay men reported that they were often feminine boys and lesbians that they were often masculine girls, suggesting a potential genetic influence on childhood gender nonconformity.

Daryl Bem (1996) and others (Bailey & Zucker, 1995; Green, 1987; Zuger, 1988) proposed that childhood gender nonconformity plays a pivotal role in homosexuality. Boys who lack aggressiveness and avoid rough-and-tumble play may prefer the company of girls, and thus be gender-nonconforming. According to Bem's theory, called *exotic becomes erotic,* nonconforming children feel different and estranged from their peers, and perceive their same-sex peers as unfamiliar and exotic (Bem, 2000). Children's sense of being different from their same-sex peers, and possibly being the subject of teasing or ridicule, arouses their autonomic nervous systems (see Chapter 3). Later in life, this arousal is transformed into attraction for same-sex peers. It's unlikely that Bem's theory accounts for all or even most gay individuals' sexual preferences, because only about half of gay men and lesbian women report having been feminine and masculine, respectively, in childhood (Bell et al., 1981). Still, one strength of Bem's theory is its acknowledgement of the interplay of genetic and environmental influences, including play activities and peers' reactions.

Sex Hormones, Prenatal Influences, and Sexual Orientation. To trace the biological roots of homosexuality, researchers have turned to a different environment—the womb. When the fetus develops, sex hormones called androgens (see Chapter 3) influence whether the brain sets the child on a path toward more masculine than feminine characteristics, or vice versa. According to one theory, girls exposed to excessive testosterone in the womb develop masculinized brains, and boys exposed to too little testosterone develop feminized brains (Ellis & Ames, 1987). These hormonal influences affect temperament and set the stage for childhood gender nonconformity and a homosexual orientation in later life (Bem, 1996).

Canadian singers and songwriter twins, Tegan and Sarah Quin, who are openly gay, don't want their music to be defined by their sexual orientation.

FACTOID   +

Can people guess sexual orientation by looking at pictures of faces? Researchers have found that college students who viewed equal numbers of homosexual and heterosexual women on Internet dating sites guessed right about 64 percent of the time (Rule, Amaday, & Hallett, 2009). A study with male faces confirmed this finding (Rule & Amaday, 2008). It's unclear whether people perform above chance because of subtle social cues, biologically influenced differences in facial appearance, or differences in posed facial expressions.

correlation vs. causation

CAN WE BE SURE THAT A CAUSES B?

replicability

CAN THE RESULTS BE DUPLICATED IN OTHER STUDIES?

correlation vs. causation

CAN WE BE SURE THAT A CAUSES B?

Having older brothers increases the odds of male homosexuality by 33 percent for each older brother, amounting to an increase in the rate of homosexuality from about 3 to 5 percent (Blanchard & Bogaert, 1996). One explanation is that male fetuses produce substances, called antigens, that trigger the mother's immune system to develop anti-male antibodies that affect the sexual differentiation of the fetus's brain, with the effect intensifying with the birth of each succeeding male child. Researchers recently qualified the original finding by showing that older brothers increase the odds of homosexuality in right-handed but not left-handed males (Blanchard, 2008). Perhaps left-handed fetuses may not be sensitive to the anti-male antibodies, or the mothers of left-handed fetuses may not produce these antibodies.

Several unusual lines of research—related to fingers and hands—also provide support for prenatal influences on sexual orientation. On average, gay individuals have more fingerprint ridges on their left hand than do heterosexual individuals (Hall & Kimura, 1994). And on average, lesbian women have a more masculine (lower) ratio of the length of the index finger to the ring finger (Williams et al., 2000). Male homosexuals are nearly one and a half times more likely than heterosexual men to be left-handed, whereas lesbians are almost twice as likely as heterosexual women to be left-handed (Lalumière, Blanchard, & Zucker, 2000). Fingerprints, finger length, and handedness are all determined largely before birth. So there's some justification for pointing the finger (pun intended) at prenatal influences, even though we can't yet specify which influences, such as exposure to sex hormones, are most important.

Sexual Orientation: Brain Differences. In 1981, Simon LeVay created a stir among scientists and laypersons alike by reporting that a small cluster of neurons in the hypothalamus, no larger than a millimeter, was less than half the size in gay compared with heterosexual men. The study is open to several criticisms: LeVay examined gay men's brains at autopsy, and the men died from AIDS-related complications. Still, it's unlikely that the differences LeVay uncovered are due entirely to AIDS, because a number of the heterosexual men also died of AIDS-related complications. The changes LeVay observed in the hypothalamus might also have been the result, rather than the cause, of homosexuality and differences in lifestyles between gay and heterosexual men. Yet another limitation was that LeVay's sample of gay men with AIDS wasn't representative of all gay men, so replicating his results will be especially important.

Some of the concerns about LeVay's research are tempered by a brain imaging study (Savic, Berglund, & Lindstrom, 2005) in which investigators exposed gay men and heterosexual men and women to substances believed to be *pheromones* (see Chapter 4). When heterosexual men smelled chemicals produced in women's urine, their hypothalamuses became active. When heterosexual women smelled a substance derived from testosterone produced in men's sweat, the same thing happened. The most intriguing finding was that gay men's brains responded like women's when they smelled the substance derived from male sweat. These results are consistent with LeVay's finding that the hypothalamus is related to sexual orientation.

Researchers have looked beyond the hypothalamus to find biological indicators of sexual orientation, and discovered that the brain's corpus callosum (see Chapter 3) is larger in homosexual than heterosexual men (Witelson et al., 2008). The scientists suggested that this finding implies that homosexuality is influenced by genetic factors, because the size of the corpus callosum is inherited. Nevertheless, we should again bear in mind that both brain size and brain activity could be a consequence, rather than a cause, of sexual orientation.

Scientists have yet to discover a dependable biological marker of sexual orientation. The great majority of left-handed individuals aren't gay, many gay men have more older sisters than older brothers, many non-lesbians have masculine (lower) index finger to ring finger ratios, and the size of the hypothalamus is comparable in most gay and non-gay individuals. In all likelihood, social and cultural influences that remain to be understood, in conjunction with genetic factors, play important roles in shaping people's sexual orientation.

✓●─[Study and Review on **mypsychlab.com**

assess your knowledge   FACT OR FICTION?

1. According to the Yerkes-Dodson law, we generally do best when we're at our highest levels of arousal. **True / False**

2. Obese individuals seem resistant to the effects of leptin. **True / False**

3. Starvation can lead to at least some symptoms of anorexia nervosa. **True / False**

4. Few people are sexually active into their seventies and eighties. **True / False**

5. Scientists have yet to discover a dependable biological marker of sexual orientation. **True / False**

Answers: 1. F (pp. 429–430); 2. T (p. 433); 3. T (p. 437); 4. F (p. 439); 5. T (p. 442)

ATTRACTION, LOVE, AND HATE: THE GREATEST MYSTERIES OF THEM ALL

11.12 Identify principles and factors that guide attraction and relationship formation.

11.13 Describe the major types of love and the elements of love and hate.

In 1975, psychologists Ellen Berscheid and Elaine Hatfield received a dubious distinction (Benson, 2006). They became the first individuals to receive the Golden Fleece Award, an "honor" (actually, a dishonor) bestowed on them by then Wisconsin Senator William Proxmire. Proxmire had cooked up this award as a way of drawing public attention to projects that he regarded as colossal wastes of taxpayer money. Berscheid and Hatfield, it so happens, had won this award for their government-funded research on the psychological determinants of attraction and love (look for their names in the section you're about to read). Proxmire found the very idea of studying these topics scientifically to be absurd:

> "I'm strongly against this," he said, "not only because no one—not even the National Science Foundation—can argue that falling in love is a science; not only because I am sure that even if they spend 84 million or 84 billion they wouldn't get an answer that anyone would believe. I'm also against it because I don't *want* to know the answer!" (Hatfield & Walster, 1978, viii)

Of course, Proxmire was entitled not to know the answer. Yet more than three decades of research have since shown that Proxmire was woefully wrong in one crucial respect: Psychologists *can* study love scientifically. None of this takes away from the profound mysteries of falling in love, but it suggests that love may not be quite as unfathomable as we—or the thousands of poets who've written about it across the centuries—might believe.

■ Social Influences on Interpersonal Attraction

How can two people meet and become lovers in a world teeming with nearly seven billion people? Of course, attraction is only the initial stage in a relationship, but we need to feel a twinkle of chemistry with someone before deciding whether we're compatible enough with him or her in our core values and attitudes before proceeding any further (Murstein, 1977). We might ascribe finding our true love to the fickle finger of destiny, but scientists suggest that friendship, dating, and mate choices aren't random. Three major principles guide attraction and relationship formation: proximity, similarity, and reciprocity (Berscheid & Reis, 1998; Luo & Klohnen, 2005; Sprecher, 1998). ◉─[Watch

The origins of love are remarkably old, even ancient. In 2007, archaeologists unearthed these skeletons of a male and female couple in Italy (ironically, only 25 miles from Verona, the site of Shakespeare's legendary *Romeo and Juliet*), frozen in an embrace over 5,000 years ago.

◉─[Watch the video Interpersonal Attraction on **mypsychlab.com**

Psychological research shows that physical proximity, such as being seated next to each other in a classroom, can set the stage for later attraction.

proximity
physical nearness, a predictor of attraction

similarity
extent to which we have things in common with others, a predictor of attraction

PROXIMITY: WHEN NEAR BECOMES DEAR. A simple truth of human relationships is that our closest friends often live, study, work, or play closest to us. Many years after high school, the second author of your textbook married the woman who sat in front of him in numerous classes. Because their last names started with the letter L, the fact that the seats were arranged alphabetically ensured they'd have an opportunity to become acquainted. After their 30-year high school reunion brought them together again, they fell in love and married.

This example illustrates how physical nearness—or **proximity**—affords the opportunity for relationship formation. Like reunited schoolmates, people in classrooms with alphabetically assigned seats tend to have friends with last names that start with the same letter or a letter close in the alphabet (Segal, 1974). We're most likely to be attracted to and befriend people nearby, whom we see on a regular basis (Nahemow & Lawton, 1975). Leon Festinger, Stanley Schachter, and Kurt Back (1950) asked individuals living in apartments for married students at the Massachusetts Institute of Technology to name three of their closest friends. Of these friends, 65 percent lived in the same building, and 41 percent lived next door.

The effects of mere exposure we encountered earlier in the chapter may explain why seeing someone on a frequent basis, whether in the supermarket or workout room, heightens attraction. In a study conducted in a college classroom, four women with similar appearances posed as students and attended zero, five, ten, or fifteen sessions (Moreland & Beach, 1992). At the end of the semester, the experimenters showed participants slides of the women and asked them to rate attendees' attractiveness. Although the posers didn't interact with any of the students, participants judged women who attended more classes as more attractive.

© Mike Baldwin / Cornered

Andy Oxidant meets Free Radical.

? This cartoon portrays a couple whose "chemistry" stems from their being opposite to each other in important respects. **According to the research literature, in what way is this couple atypical?** (See answer upside down on bottom of page.)

Answer: Studies show that opposites don't attract in romantic relationships.

SIMILARITY: LIKE ATTRACTS LIKE. Would you rather be stranded on a desert island with someone very much like yourself or very different? Perhaps if you like Mozart and your island mate prefers hip-hop, you'd have a lot to talk or at least debate about. Yet with little in common, you might find it difficult to establish a personal connection. This point brings us to our next principle: **similarity**, the extent to which we have things in common with others.

Scientists have found that there's much more truth to the adage "Birds of a feather flock together" than the equally well-worn proverb "Opposites attract." Whether it's art, music, food preferences, educational level, physical attractiveness, or values, we're attracted to people who are similar to us (Byrne, 1971; Montoya, Horton, & Kirchner, 2008; Swann & Pelham, 2002). We're also more likely to befriend, date, and marry compatible people (Curran & Lippold, 1975; Knox, Zusman, & Nieves, 1997). There's even evidence that pet owners tend to select dogs who resemble them (Roy & Christenfeld, 2004), although not all researchers are convinced by these findings (Levine, 2005).

Online dating services have caught on to the fact that similarity breeds content (Hill, Rubin & Peplau, 1976). One popular service, eHarmony.com, tries to match prospective partners on the basis of personality similarity, although there's no good evidence that they're especially successful at doing so (Epstein, 2007). Similarity pays off in the long run, too. Married couples who share similar traits are more likely to stay together than dissimilar couples (Meyer & Pepper, 1977).

Similarity greases the wheels of social interaction for a few reasons. First, when people's interests and attitudes overlap, the foundation is paved for mutual understanding. Second, we assume we'll be readily accepted and liked by others who see eye-to-eye with us. Third, people who share our likes and dislikes provide validation for our views and help us feel good about ourselves. There may be even considerable truth to the saying "The enemy of my enemy is my friend" (Heider, 1958). Research demonstrates that a glue that binds friendships, especially in the early stages, is sharing negative impressions about others (Bosson et al., 2006). Negative gossip may permit us to elevate ourselves at the expense of others, thereby enhancing our self-esteem. 👁 Watch

👁 Watch Dating and Finding a Mate: Ralf, 33 on **mypsychlab.com**

RECIPROCITY: ALL GIVE AND NO TAKE DOES NOT A GOOD RELATIONSHIP MAKE. For a relationship to move to deeper levels, the third principle of attraction—**reciprocity**, or the rule of give and take—is often crucial. Across cultures, there's a norm of reciprocity (Gouldner, 1960) that begins to kick into motion as early as 11 years of age (Rotenberg & Mann, 1986). That is, we tend to feel obligated to give what we get and maintain equity in a relationship (Walster, Berscheid, & Walster, 1973). Liking begets liking, and revealing personal information begets disclosure. When we believe people like us, we're inclined to feel attracted to them (Brehm et al., 2002; Carlson & Rose, 2007). When we believe that our partner finds us attractive or likable, we generally act more likable in response to this ego-boosting information (Curtis & Miller, 1986). Talking about meaningful things is a vital element of most friendships. In particular, disclosure about intimate topics often brings about intimacy. When one person talks about superficial topics or discusses intimate topics in a superficial way, low levels of disclosure often result (Lynn, 1978). Although a complete lack of reciprocity can put a relationship into the deep freeze, absolute reciprocity isn't required to make a relationship hum, especially when one partner responds to our disclosures with sympathy and concern (Berg & Archer, 1980).

PHYSICAL ATTRACTION: LIKE IT OR NOT, WE JUDGE BOOKS BY THEIR COVERS. As we saw in Chapter 6, some important scientific discoveries arise from *serendipity*, that is, sheer luck. So it was with a study that Elaine Hatfield and her colleagues conducted over 40 years ago (Hatfield et al., 1966). They administered a battery of personality, attitude, and interest measures to 725 incoming college men and women during freshman "Welcome Week." Hatfield and her coworkers paired these students randomly for a leisurely date and dance lasting two and a half hours, giving them the chance to get acquainted. Which variables, the researchers wondered, would predict whether the partners were interested in a second date? Much to their surprise, the only variable that significantly predicted attraction was one the researchers had included only as an afterthought (Gangestad & Scheyd, 2005): people's level of physical attractiveness as rated by their partners (Hatfield et al., 1966).

As we learned in Chapter 2, physically attractive people tend to be more popular than physically unattractive people (Dion, Berscheid, & Walster, 1972; Fehr, 2008). Yet what makes us find others attractive? Is it all merely a matter of "chemistry," an inexplicable process that lies beyond the grasp of science, as Senator Proxmire believed? Or is there a science to "love at first sight," or at least attraction at first sight? ▶ Simulate

▶ Simulate Perceptions of Attractiveness on **mypsychlab.com**

SEX DIFFERENCES IN WHAT WE FIND ATTRACTIVE: NATURE OR NURTURE? Although physical attractiveness is important to both sexes when it comes to choosing our romantic partners, it's especially important to men (Buunk et al., 2002; Feingold, 1992). David Buss (1989) conducted a comprehensive survey of mate preferences among heterosexuals in 37 cultures across six continents, with countries as diverse as Canada, Spain, Finland, Greece, Bulgaria, Venezuela, Iran, Japan, and South Africa. Although he found that the importance people attach to physical attractiveness varies across cultures, men consistently place more weight on looks in women than women do in men. Men also prefer women who are somewhat younger than they are. Conversely, Buss found that women tend to place more emphasis than do men on having a partner with a high level of financial resources. In contrast to men, women prefer partners who are somewhat older than they are. Still, men and women value many of the same things. Both sexes put a premium on having a partner who's intelligent, dependable, and kind (Buss, 1994).

reciprocity
rule of give and take, a predictor of attraction

Evolutionary Models of Attraction. Putting aside these commonalities, how can we make sense of sex differences in mate preferences? Evolutionary theorists point out that because most men produce enormous numbers of sperm—an average of about 300 million per ejaculation—they typically pursue a mating strategy that maximizes the chances that at least one of these sperm will find a receptive egg at the end of its long journey (Symons, 1979). As a consequence, evolutionary psychologists contend, men are on the lookout for cues of potential health and fertility, such as physical attractiveness and youth. Women, in contrast, typically produce only one egg per month, so they must be choosy. In a study of speed dating—a technique invented by Los Angeles Rabbi Yaacov Deyo in 1998 to help Jewish singles get acquainted—men and women interacted with potential dates for three minutes (Kurzban & Weeden, 2005). Men chose to have further contact with half of the women they met, whereas women were decidedly pickier, selecting one in three men to meet again. Women tend to pursue a mating strategy that maximizes the chances that the man with whom they mate will provide well for their offspring. Hence women's preference for men who are well off monetarily, and a bit more experienced in the ways of life (Buunk et al., 2002).

Social Role Theory. Still, some researchers have offered alternatives to evolutionary models of attraction. According to Alice Eagly and Wendy Wood's (1999) *social role theory*, biological variables play a role in men's and women's preferences, but not in the way that evolutionary psychologists contend. Instead, biological factors constrain the roles that men and women adopt (Eagly, Wood & Johannesen-Schmidt, 2004). Because men tend to be bigger and stronger than women, they've more often ended up playing the roles of hunter, food provider, and warrior. Moreover, because men don't bear children, they have considerable opportunities to pursue high-status positions. In contrast, because women bear children, they've more often ended up playing the role of child care provider and have been more limited in pursuing high-status positions.

Some of these differences in traditional roles may help to explain men's and women's differing mate preferences. For example, because women have typically held fewer high-status positions than men, they may have preferred men who are dependable financial providers (Eagly et al., 2004). Consistent with social role theory, men and women have become more similar in their mate preferences over the past half century (Buss et al., 2001), perhaps reflecting the increasing social opportunities for women across that time period. So although nature may channel men and women into somewhat different roles and therefore different mate preferences, nurture may shape these roles and preferences in significant ways.

IS BEAUTY IN THE EYE OF THE BEHOLDER? Popular wisdom tells us that "beauty is in the eye of the beholder." To some extent that saying is true. Yet it's also an oversimplification. People tend to agree at considerably higher than chance levels about who is, and isn't, physically attractive (Burns & Farina, 1992). This is the case not only within a race but across races; Caucasian and African American men tend to agree on which women are attractive, as do Caucasian and Asian American men (Cunningham et al., 1995). Even across vastly different cultures, men and women tend to agree on whom they find physically attractive (Langlois et al., 2000).

Furthermore, men and women prefer certain body shapes in members of the opposite sex. Men tend to be especially attracted to women with a waist-to-hip ratio of about .7, that is, with a waist about 70 percent as large as their hips (Singh, 1993), although this ratio is often less important than other variables, like body weight (Furnham, Petrides, & Constantinides, 2005; Tassinary & Hansen, 1998). In contrast, women generally prefer men with a higher waist-to-hip ratio (Singh, 1995). According to evolutionary psychologist Donald Symons (1979), these findings imply that "beauty lies in the adaptations of the beholder." Women's waist-to-hip ratio tends to decline as they become older, so this ratio is a cue—although a highly imperfect one—to fertility.

ruling out rival hypotheses

HAVE IMPORTANT ALTERNATIVE EXPLANATIONS FOR THE FINDINGS BEEN EXCLUDED?

Although standards of beauty differ somewhat within and across cultures, research suggests that both most African American men and most Caucasian men agree on which African American women (such as Halle Berry, *left*) and Caucasian women (such as Jennifer Aniston, *right*) are physically attractive.

FACTOID +

Across the world, most people display a *cute response*: a positive emotional reaction to faces that display certain characteristics, especially (a) large eyes; (b) a small, round nose; (c) big round ears; and (d) a large head relative to the body (Lorenz, 1971). These are the same facial features we find in infants, so natural selection may have predisposed us to find these features irresistibly adorable (Angier, 2006).

Still, there are differences in physical preferences within and across cultures (Swami & Furnham, 2008). For example, men from African American and Caribbean cultures often find women with a large body size more physically attractive than do men of European cultures (Rosenblum & Lewis, 1999). Furthermore, preferences toward thinness have frequently shifted over historical time, as even a casual inspection of paintings of nude women over the past few centuries reveals.

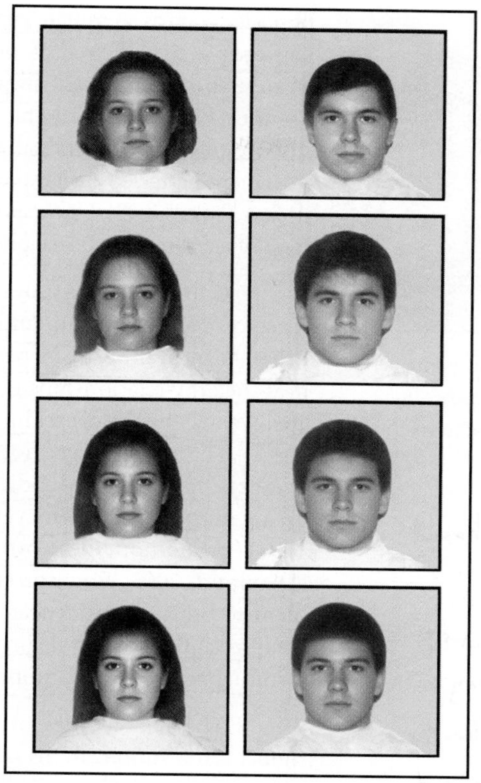

WHEN BEING "JUST AVERAGE" IS JUST FINE. Which person are we more likely to find attractive: (a) someone who's exotic, unusual, or distinctive in some way or (b) someone who's just plain average? If you're like most people, you'd assume (a). Indeed, we sometimes insult people's appearance by calling women "plain Janes," and men "average Joes."

Yet as Judith Langlois and Lori Roggman (1990) showed, being average has its pluses. By using a computer to digitize the faces of students and then combine them progressively, they found that people generally prefer faces that are the most average. In their study, people preferred average faces a whopping 96 percent of the time (see **FIGURE 11.18**; to try your hand at averaging faces, see a demonstration at www.faceresearch.org/tech/demos/average). Although some psychologists found these results difficult to believe, many investigators have replicated them for European, Japanese, and Chinese faces (Gangestad & Scheyd, 2005; Rhodes, Halberstadt, & Brajkovich, 2001). Average faces are also more symmetrical than non-average faces, so our preferences for average faces might be due to their greater symmetry. Yet studies show that even when faces are symmetrical, people still prefer faces that are more average (Valentine, Darling, & Donnelly, 2004).

Evolutionary psychologists have speculated that "averageness" in a face tends to reflect an absence of genetic mutations, serious diseases, and other abnormalities. As a consequence, we could be drawn to people with such faces, as they're often better "genetic catches." Maybe. But there's a fly in the ointment. Studies show that people prefer not merely average faces, but average animals, like birds and fish, and even average objects, like cars and watches (Halberstadt & Rhodes, 2003). So our preference for average faces may be due to an alternative mechanism, namely, a more general preference for anything that's average. Perhaps we find average stimuli to be more familiar and easier to process mentally, because they reflect stimuli we've seen before many times (Gangestad & Scheyd, 2005).

FIGURE 11.18   Which Face Is Most Attractive? The two columns depict faces that have been averaged with other faces (from *top* to *bottom*) 4, 8, 16, and 32 times. Most people find the faces on the bottom, which are the most "average," to be the most attractive (Langlois & Roggman, 1990). Remarkably, Sir Francis Galton (1878), whom we met in Chapter 9, anticipated these findings well over a century ago. (*Source:* Langlois & Roggman, 1990)

replicability

CAN THE RESULTS BE DUPLICATED IN OTHER STUDIES?

ruling out rival hypotheses

HAVE IMPORTANT ALTERNATIVE EXPLANATIONS FOR THE FINDINGS BEEN EXCLUDED?

Average faces are preferred to non-average faces.

ruling out rival hypotheses

HAVE IMPORTANT ALTERNATIVE EXPLANATIONS FOR THE FINDINGS BEEN EXCLUDED?

■ Love: Science Confronts the Mysterious

Elizabeth Barrett Browning wrote famously: "How do I love thee? Let me count the ways." According to some psychologists, we may not need to count all that high. We'll explain.

LOVE: A MANY-SPLENDORED THING? Psychologists are no different from the rest of us. They've tried to understand the myriad varieties of love, with some concluding that there's only one type of love, and others that love comes in many shapes and sizes. According to Elaine Hatfield and Richard Rapson (1996), there are two major types of love: passionate and companionate. Robert Sternberg, as we'll soon see, puts the number at seven.

Passionate Love: Love as a Hollywood Romance. Passionate love is marked by a powerful, even overwhelming, longing for one's partner. It's a strange mix of delirious happiness when we're around the object of our desire and utter misery when we're not. It's the stuff of which Hollywood movies are made. As Romeo and Juliet knew all too well, passionate love is fueled when

and Bollywood (lol).

passionate love
love marked by powerful, even overwhelming, longing for one's partner

Companionate love is often the primary form of love among the elderly. It can be a powerful emotional bond between couples across the life span.

Uncertainty fuels attachment and desire.

→ emotional attachment ~~caused~~ influenced by oxytocin.

→ sexual desire is influenced by testosterone and estrogen

obstacles, such as seemingly insurmountable physical distance or the strenuous objection of parents, are placed in the way of romance (Driscoll, Davis, & Lipetz, 1972). Such hurdles may heighten arousal, thereby intensifying passion, as Schachter and Singer's two-factor theory would predict (Kenrick, Neuberg, & Cialdini, 2005). In a study that followed participants for one month after a speed dating event, individuals who experienced anxiety about a potential partner's romantic involvement expressed greater preference for a serious relationship than for a one-night stand (Eastwick & Finkel, 2008). Uncertainty about how relationships will unfold, combined with hope that romantic feelings will be reciprocated, fuel attachment and desire (Tennov, 1979).

Companionate Love: Love as Friendship. **Companionate love** is marked by a sense of deep friendship and fondness for one's partner. Romantic relationships tend to progress over time from passionate to companionate love (Wojciszke, 2002), although most healthy relationships retain at least a spark of passion. In older couples, companionate love may be the overriding emotion in the relationship.

There's growing evidence that companionate and passionate love are psychologically independent. Studies indicate that people can "fall in love" with partners in the sense of caring deeply about them, yet experience little or no sexual desire toward them (Diamond, 2004). In addition, these two forms of love may be associated with differing brain systems (Diamond, 2003; Gonzaga et al., 2006). Animal research suggests that emotional attachment to others is influenced largely by such hormones as oxytocin, which as we noted in Chapter 3 plays a key role in pair bonding and interpersonal trust. In contrast, sexual desire is influenced by sex hormones, such as testosterone and estrogen.

The Three Sides of Love. Robert Sternberg believes that the "two types of love" model is too simple. In his *triangular theory of love*, Sternberg (1986, 1988a) proposed three major elements of love: (1) intimacy ("I feel really close to this person"); (2) passion ("I'm crazy about this person"); and (3) commitment ("I really want to stay with this person"). These elements combine to form seven varieties of love (see **FIGURE 11.19**). Sternberg's

FIGURE 11.19 **What Is Love?** According to Sternberg's triangular theory of love, intimacy, passion, and commitment combine to form seven varieties of love, with "consummate love" being the ultimate form of love marked by high levels of all three components.

Companionate
Intimacy = closeness (liking)
Passion = craziness, insanity (infatuation)
Commitment = loyalty. (empty love)
→ Romantic love
→ Fatuous love
All 3 = Consummate love.

companionate love
love marked by a sense of deep friendship and fondness for one's partner

model is more of a description of love types than an explanation of why people fall in love, but it's a helpful road map toward understanding one of life's great mysteries. ◉ Watch

HATE: A NEGLECTED TOPIC.

Until recently, psychologists didn't want to have much to do with the topic of hate. Most introductory psychology textbooks don't even list the word *hate* in their indices. Yet with the horrific events of September 11, 2001, and the burgeoning problem of terrorism around the globe, it's clear that psychologists can no longer turn a blind eye to the question of why some people despise others, at times to the point of wanting to destroy them (Sternberg, 2004). Of course, hate can assume a variety of less violent but still pernicious forms in everyday life, including extreme forms of racism, sexism, anti-Semitism, homophobia, and occasionally even excessive political partisanship (see Chapter 13).

Using his triangular theory of love as a starting point, Robert Sternberg (2003) developed a theory of hate, with hatred consisting of three elements:

1. negation of intimacy ("I would never want to get close to these people");
2. passion ("I absolutely and positively despise these people"); and
3. commitment ("I'm determined to stop or harm these people").

As in his theory of love, differing forms of hate arise from combinations of these three elements, with "burning hate"—the most severe—reflecting high scores on all three. For Sternberg, the key to fueling hate is propaganda. Groups and governments that "teach" hatred of other groups are experts at portraying these groups as evil and worthy of disdain (Keen, 1986; Sternberg, 2003a).

As Paul Bloom (2004) noted, the emotion of disgust probably evolved as a means of helping us to avoid dangerous substances, like rotting meats, or repulsive animals, like cockroaches (see Chapters 4 and 6). Yet he observed that we can extend the emotion of disgust to entire groups of people we dislike. In this way, we perceive them as "subhuman" and worthy of extermination, like insects and other pests (Hodson & Costello, 2007; Sternberg, 2003a). Not surprisingly, people who detest other groups frequently refer to them with terms that reinforce perceptions of disgust, like *vermin, pigs,* or *scum.* Doing so probably makes it easier for us to hate them.

The good news is that if we can learn hate, we can probably unlearn it. Teaching individuals to overcome their confirmation bias (see Chapter 2) toward perceiving only the negative attributes of individuals or groups they dislike may be an essential first step (Harrington, 2004). Recognizing that "there's good and bad in everyone," as the saying goes, may help us combat our deep-seated animosity toward our enemies—and more broadly, members of other races, cultures, and groups whose views differ from our own.

◉ Watch Triangular Theory of Love: Robert Sternberg on **mypsychlab.com**

---

assess your knowledge   FACT OR FICTION?

1. When it comes to romantic chemistry, opposites attract. **True / False**
2. In general, people find average faces the most physically attractive. **True / False**
3. Companionate and passionate love appear to be psychologically and physiologically independent. **True / False**
4. Passion and commitment play a key role in love, but are irrelevant to hate. **True / False**

Answers: 1. F (p. 444); 2. T (p. 447); 3. T (p. 448); 4. F (p. 449)

✓ Study and Review on **mypsychlab.com**

THEORIES OF EMOTION: WHAT CAUSES OUR FEELINGS? 406–415

11.1 DESCRIBE THE MAJOR THEORIES OF EMOTION.

According to discrete emotions theory, people experience a small number (perhaps seven) of distinct biologically influenced emotions. According to cognitive theories, including the James-Lange theory, emotions result from our interpretation of stimuli or our bodily reactions to them. According to the Cannon-Bard theory, emotion-provoking events lead to both emotions and bodily reactions. Schachter and Singer's two-factor theory proposes that emotions are the explanations we attach to our general state of arousal following an emotion-provoking event.

1. According to _____ _____ theory, humans experience a small number of distinct emotions that combine in complex ways. (p. 407)

2. One of the first researchers to study how emotional expressions of humans and nonhumans are similar, _____ _____ observed that the angry snarl of dogs bears a resemblance to the dismissive sneer of humans. (p. 407)

3. What kind of smile, marked by the turning upward of the corners of the mouth and changes in the eyelids and corners of the eye, is Paul Ekman displaying in this photo? (p. 410)

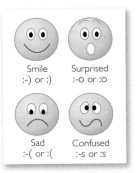

4. According to _____ theories of emotion, emotions are products of thinking. (p. 410)

5. According to the _____ theory of emotion, emotions result from our interpretations of our bodily reactions to stimuli. (p. 410)

6. According to Damasio's somatic marker theory, we (do/don't) use our "gut reactions" to help us determine how we should act. (p. 411)

7. According to the Cannon-Bard theory, an emotion-provoking event leads _____ to both an emotion and to bodily reactions. (p. 411)

8. Describe how we experience emotions during an event like a car accident, according to Schachter and Singer's two-factor theory of emotion. (p. 412)

11.2 IDENTIFY UNCONSCIOUS INFLUENCES ON EMOTION.

Many emotional experiences are generated automatically and operate unconsciously, as illustrated by research on the mere exposure effect and the facial feedback hypothesis.

9. According to the mere exposure effect, repeated exposure to a stimulus makes us (more/less) likely to feel favorably toward it. (p. 414)

10. According to the facial feedback hypothesis, we're more likely to feel emotions that correspond to our _____ _____. (p. 415)

NONVERBAL EXPRESSION OF EMOTION: THE EYES, BODIES, & CULTURES HAVE IT 416–422

11.3 EXPLAIN THE IMPORTANCE OF NONVERBAL EXPRESSION OF EMOTION.

Much of emotional expression is nonverbal; gestures highlight speech (illustrators), involve touches of our bodies (manipulators), or convey specific meanings (emblems). Nonverbal expressions are often more valid indicators of emotions than are words.

11. The unconscious spillover of emotions into nonverbal behavior is known as _____ _____. (p. 416)

12. How do emoticons help to ensure that an e-mail or text message is interpreted in the manner it was intended? (p. 416)

Smile
:-) or :)

Surprised
:-o or :o

Sad
:-(or :(

Confused
:-s or :s

13. When talking, we often use _____, gestures that highlight or accentuate speech. (p. 416)

14. When stressed or nervous, you may engage in _____, such as biting your fingernails or twirling your hair. (p. 416)

15. Gestures that convey specific meanings, such as a hand wave or the OK sign, are called _____. (p. 417)

11.4 IDENTIFY MAJOR LIE DETECTION METHODS AND THEIR PITFALLS.

The polygraph test measures physiological responses to questions designed to expose falsehoods. The Controlled Question Test (CQT) contains questions relevant and irrelevant to the crime, and control questions that reflect presumed lies. Greater physiological reactivity in response to relevant questions supposedly suggests deception. Nevertheless, the CQT detects general arousal rather than guilt and results in numerous false positives—innocent individuals mistakenly identified as guilty. False negatives (guilty individuals mistakenly identified as innocent) can result when individuals employ countermeasures (such as biting the tongue or curling the toes). The Guilty Knowledge Test (GKT) instead relies on the premise that criminals harbor concealed knowledge about the crime that innocent people don't. The GKT has a low false-positive rate, but a fairly high false-negative rate.

16. Typically, the correlation between people's confidence in their ability to detect lies and their accuracy in doing so is (low/high). (p. 418)

17. The most widely administered version of the polygraph test, the

_____ _____

_____, measures subjects' physiological responses following three major types of yes-no questions. (p. 419)

18. Research shows that the primary problem with the polygraph test is its high rate of (false positives/false negatives). (p. 419)

19. How does the polygraph rely on the assumption of the Pinocchio response? (p. 419)

20. Some employers administer paper-and-pencil _____ tests in an attempt to assess workers' tendency to steal or cheat. (p. 421)

HAPPINESS AND SELF-ESTEEM: SCIENCE CONFRONTS POP PSYCHOLOGY 422–428

11.5 DESCRIBE THE EMERGING DISCIPLINE OF POSITIVE PSYCHOLOGY.

Positive psychology emphasizes strengths, love, and happiness. Happiness is often adaptive; it allows us to build on strengths and opportunities (broaden and build theory).

21. Explain how the King of Bhutan plans to increase the Gross National Happiness of his country and why this initiative may be beneficial to all. (p. 422)

22. Peterson and Seligman identified numerous

_____ _____

and _____ as essential to positive psychology. (p. 423)

23. According to Fredrickson's _____ _____ _____ theory, happiness predisposes us to think more openly. (p. 423)

11.6 IDENTIFY COMMON MYTHS AND REALITIES ABOUT HAPPINESS AND SELF-ESTEEM.

Myths: The prime determinant of happiness is what happens to us; money makes us happy; happiness declines in old age; and people on the West Coast are the happiest. Realities: Happiness is associated with marriage, college education, and religious beliefs; voting Republican; exercise; gratitude; and immersion in what we're doing ("flow"). We tend to overestimate the long-term impact of events on our happiness. Myth: Low self-esteem is the root of all unhappiness. Reality: Self-esteem is only modestly associated with mental health but is associated with greater initiative, persistence, and positive illusions—the tendency to perceive ourselves more favorably than others do.

24. _____ _____ is a strategy of anticipating failures and compensating for this expectation by mentally overpreparing for negative outcomes. (p. 423)

25. According to psychological research, money (can/can't) buy long-term happiness. (p. 424)

26. The increase in happiness with old age appears to be due to the _____ effect. (p. 425)

27. The ability to predict our own and others' happiness is called _____ _____. (p. 426)

28. When we believe that both our good and bad moods will last longer than they do, we're suffering from a _____ _____ . (p. 427)

29. Why do second-place finishers tend to be less happy than third-place finishers? (p. 427)

30. Most individuals with high self-esteem have

_____

_____, in that they see themselves as more intelligent, attractive, and likeable than other individuals. (p. 428)

MOTIVATION: OUR WANTS AND NEEDS 429–443

11.7 EXPLAIN BASIC PRINCIPLES AND THEORIES OF MOTIVATION.

Motivation refers to the drives—especially our wants and needs—that propel us in specific directions. Drive reduction theory states that drives (such as hunger and thirst) pull us to act in certain ways. The Yerkes-Dodson law posits an inverted U-shaped relation between arousal and mood/performance. Approach and avoidance often drive conflict. According to incentive theories, positive goals are motivators. These motivators include primary (biological) and secondary (psychological desires/achievement, self-actualization) needs.

Answers are located at the end of the text.

31. Is there any research evidence that motivational speakers, like Anthony Robbins, produce long-term changes in people's behavior? (p. 429)

32. Most drive reduction theories propose that we're motivated to maintain a given level of psychological _____. (p. 429)

33. The _____ law describes an inverted U-shaped relation between arousal on the one hand, and performance and mood, on the other. (p. 429)

34. _____ theories propose that we're often motivated by positive goals. (p. 431)

35. Using Maslow's Hierarchy of Needs, insert the appropriate need at each level of the pyramid in the path to achieving self-actualization. (p. 432)

11.8 DESCRIBE THE DETERMINANTS OF HUNGER, WEIGHT GAIN, AND OBESITY.

The lateral hypothalamus has been called a "feeding center" and the ventromedial hypothalamus a "satiety center," although these descriptions oversimplify scientific reality. Hunger is also associated with hormones (ghrelin), low glucose levels, neurotransmitters (leptin, serotonin), a genetically programmed set point for body fat and muscle mass, specific genes (melanocortin-4 receptor gene, leptin gene), and sensitivity to food cues and expectations.

36. According to _____ theory, when our blood glucose levels drop, hunger creates a drive to eat to restore the proper level of glucose. (p. 433)

37. Each of us may have a genetically programmed _____ _____ that establishes a range of body and muscle mass we tend to maintain. (p. 434)

11.9 IDENTIFY THE SYMPTOMS OF BULIMIA AND ANOREXIA.

Bulimia nervosa is marked by recurrent binge eating, followed by attempts to minimize weight gain. Anorexia nervosa is characterized by a refusal to eat, resulting in body weight less than 85 percent of that expected for age and height.

38. _____ is the most common eating disorder, and 95 percent of the people with this diagnosis are women. (p. 436)

11.10 DESCRIBE THE HUMAN SEXUAL RESPONSE CYCLE AND FACTORS THAT INFLUENCE SEXUAL ACTIVITY.

Masters and Johnson described four stages of the sexual response cycle: excitement, plateau, orgasm, and resolution. Frequency of sexual activity decreases with age, but sexual satisfaction doesn't. Expression of sexual desire is shaped by social norms and culture.

39. Masters and Johnson reported in their pioneering investigation that the basic sexual arousal cycle is (the same/different) for men and women. (p. 438)

11.11 IDENTIFY COMMON MISCONCEPTIONS ABOUT AND POTENTIAL INFLUENCES ON SEXUAL ORIENTATION.

Common myths include the notions that gay individuals: (a) typically adopt a masculine or feminine role; (b) are especially likely to sexually abuse children and adolescents; and (c) are usually inadequate parents. Potential influences on sexual orientation are an inherited tendency toward childhood gender nonconformity; sex hormones; prenatal influences; and brain differences.

40. According to one theory of influences on sexual orientation, girls exposed to excessive testosterone in the womb develop _____ brains, and boys exposed to too little testosterone develop _____ brains. (p. 441)

ATTRACTION, LOVE, AND HATE: THE GREATEST MYSTERIES OF THEM ALL 443–449

11.12 IDENTIFY PRINCIPLES AND FACTORS THAT GUIDE ATTRACTION AND RELATIONSHIP FORMATION.

Factors guiding attraction and relationship formation are proximity (physical closeness), similarity (like attracts like), reciprocity (give what we get), physical attractiveness (more important to men than to women), evolutionary influences, social roles, and preference for "average" faces.

41. Physical nearness, or _____, affords the opportunity for relationship formation. (p. 444)

42. We're often attracted to people with whom we have high levels of _____, or things in common. (p. 444)

43. For a relationship to move to deeper levels, the rule of give and take, or _____ is often crucial. (p. 445)

44. According to Buss, across cultures, (men/women) attach more importance to physical attractiveness? (p. 445)

45. Across vastly different cultures, men and women tend to (agree/disagree) on whom they find physically attractive. (p. 446)

46. Average faces are rated as (less/more) attractive than distinctive or exotic faces? (p. 447)

11.13 DESCRIBE THE MAJOR TYPES OF LOVE AND THE ELEMENTS OF LOVE AND HATE.

The major love types are passionate and companionate. According to Sternberg's model of love, the major love elements are intimacy, passion, and commitment. The major hate elements are negation of intimacy, passion, and commitment.

47. _____ love can be a mix of delirious happiness when we're near the object of our desire, and misery when separated from it. (p. 447)

48. A relationship marked by a sense of deep friendship and fondness for our partner is called _____. (p. 448)

49. Using Sternberg's triangular theory of love, complete this figure by identifying the three major elements of love (forming the points of the triangle) illustrated here. According to Sternberg, which is the ultimate form of love (box d)? (p. 448)

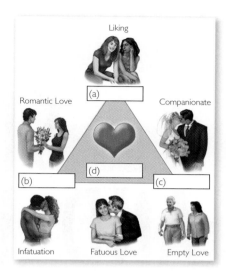

50. Teaching individuals to overcome their _____ _____ toward perceiving only negative attributions of groups they dislike may be an essential first step in unlearning hate. (p. 449)

DO YOU KNOW THESE TERMS?

- emotion (p. 406)
- discrete emotions theory (p. 407)
- primary emotions (p. 408)
- display rules (p. 408)
- cognitive theories of emotion (p. 410)
- James-Lange theory of emotion (p. 410)
- somatic marker theory (p. 411)
- Cannon-Bard theory (p. 411)
- two-factor theory (p. 412)
- mere exposure effect (p. 414)
- facial feedback hypothesis (p. 415)

- nonverbal leakage (p. 416)
- proxemics (p. 417)
- Pinocchio response (p. 419)
- guilty knowledge test (GKT) (p. 420)
- integrity test (p. 421)
- positive psychology (p. 422)
- defensive pessimism (p. 423)
- broaden and build theory (p. 423)
- positivity effect (p. 425)
- affective forecasting (p. 426)
- durability bias (p. 426)
- hedonic treadmill (p. 427)

- self-esteem (p. 427)
- positive illusions (p. 428)
- motivation (p. 429)
- drive reduction theory (p. 429)
- homeostasis (p. 429)
- Yerkes-Dodson law (p. 429)
- incentive theories (p. 431)
- hierarchy of needs (p. 431)
- glucostatic theory (p. 433)
- leptin (p. 433)
- set point (p. 434)
- internal–external theory (p. 435)
- bulimia nervosa (p. 436)

- anorexia nervosa (p. 436)
- excitement phase (p. 438)
- plateau phase (p. 438)
- orgasm (climax) phase (p. 438)
- resolution phase (p. 438)
- proximity (p. 444)
- similarity (p. 444)
- reciprocity (p. 445)
- passionate love (p. 447)
- companionate love (p. 448)

APPLY YOUR SCIENTIFIC THINKING SKILLS

Use your scientific thinking skills to answer the following questions, referencing specific scientific thinking principles and common errors in reasoning whenever possible.

1. Research three books or training programs designed to enhance self-esteem. How do they connect self-esteem to happiness and success in life? Do they confuse correlation with causation? Have they considered rival hypotheses for how people become happy or successful in life? If so, which ones?

2. The popular media is filled with examples of body language experts claiming to identify which celebrity couples are truly in love and which are headed for a break-up. Find a few examples of Internet sites devoted to interpreting body language. Are their claims about their ability to interpret nonverbal communication

extraordinary? Are there more parsimonious explanations for these claims?

3. Select a current debate surrounding sexual orientation, such as the "Don't ask, don't tell" policy in the military or the issue of civil unions and gay marriage, and examine at least two scientific arguments on both sides of the issue. What assumptions does each side make regarding the role of genetic and environmental influences in sexual orientation? Has either side misrepresented the scientific research or neglected to consider alternative interpretations? Explain.

12 STRESS, COPING, AND HEALTH

the mind–body interconnection

THINK ABOUT IT

DO MOST PEOPLE WHO ENCOUNTER HIGHLY AVERSIVE EVENTS DEVELOP POSTTRAUMATIC STRESS DISORDER?

ARE SOME PEOPLE MORE PRONE TO HEART ATTACKS THAN OTHERS?

ARE CRASH DIETS THAT PROMISE QUICK AND ENDURING WEIGHT LOSS EFFECTIVE?

ARE ACUPUNCTURE AND OTHER ALTERNATIVE MEDICAL TREATMENTS MORE EFFECTIVE THAN TRADITIONAL MEDICAL PROCEDURES?

CAN PLACEBOS AFFECT BRAIN ACTIVITY?

Firefighters and police officers who merely witness traumatic events often experience high levels of stress.

Tuesday, September 11, 2001, is a day that few Americans will forget. Across the country, people were glued to their television sets watching in horror as two loaded passenger planes flew into the Twin Towers of the World Trade Center (WTC) in New York City. In the worst terrorist attack in American history, more than 2,700 people were killed at the WTC alone. Hundreds more were killed when terrorists crashed two other planes into the Pentagon and a field in rural Pennsylvania, where passengers had attempted to regain control of the plane.

In the aftermath of this tragedy, inspiring stories emerged of courageous first responders—firefighters, paramedics, police, and emergency service workers—who risked their lives to save others. Nearly 400 people who participated in rescue operations died on 9/11. Many others survived to tell their stories. The following accounts by first responders at the WTC (McNally, 2001) are a sample of reactions to some of the most stressful circumstances imaginable—and some unimaginable.

- Juana Lomi, a paramedic, raced to the WTC and survived the collapse of the towers. "It was an overwhelming feeling of fear, horror—and not being able to do more. There were hundreds of people that needed to be treated. I was at risk of losing my life, but I had to stay and help other people."

- Louie Cacchioli, a firefighter, saved the lives of many people. "I stepped outside after bringing about 40 or 50 people down a stairway. I looked around. It was crazy. Somebody yelled, 'Look out! The tower's coming down!' I started running. I tossed my air mask away to make myself lighter. Next thing I know, there's a big black ball of smoke. I threw myself on my knees, and I'm crying. I said to myself, 'Oh, my God, I'm going to die.' I was crawling. Then—the biggest miracle thing in the world. My hands came onto an air mask. It still had air. Another 15 seconds, I wouldn't have made it."

- Mike Hanson, a member of the Emergency Services Unit of the New York Police Department, used a torch to cut through steel to rescue people. "Emotionally, it's taken a toll. Just like I work in small sectors of massive destruction, I have to take it in little pieces mentally. That's the only way I can manage it."

These stories raise fascinating questions that are crucial to the study of stress, coping, and health. What happens after we experience a traumatic event? How do people like Louie Cacchioli fare following a close brush with death? Do the effects reverberate long afterward, producing lasting psychological or physical illnesses? Or can many people manage to cope, even thrive, in the aftermath of harrowing circumstances?

In this chapter, we'll explore the myriad ways in which people cope with stressful circumstances, ranging from the annoyance of a computer crash to the terror of surviving a plane crash. We'll also examine the complex interplay between stress and physical health. Ronald Kessler and his colleagues (Kessler et al., 1995) studied nearly 6,000 men and women in the general population and found that most (60–90 percent) had experienced at least one potentially traumatic event, such as a sexual or physical assault or car accident. So it's actually the unusual person who doesn't experience severe stress in his or her lifetime (de Vries & Olff, 2009; Ozer et al., 2003). Groups at especially high risk for stressful events include young and unmarried people, African Americans, and people of low socioeconomic status (Kessler et al., 1994; Miranda & Green, 1999; Turner, Wheaton, & Lloyd, 1995). Women are more likely than men to experience sexual assault and child abuse, but less likely to experience nonsexual assaults, accidents, disasters, fires, or wartime combat (Tolin & Foa, 2006). Many people assume that individuals who live in rural areas or nonindustrialized countries experience minimal stress compared with residents of urban and more developed areas. Yet scientists have discovered no support for this popular belief: Stress-producing events are widespread among all sectors of society (Bigbee, 1990).

Fortunately, exposure to events like Hurricane Katrina, frontline combat in Afghanistan, or the 2010 earthquake in Haiti doesn't guarantee that people will be traumatized for life. Herein lies another case in which scientific research contradicts popular psychology. Many self-help books inform us that most people require psychological help in the face of stressful circumstances (Sommers & Satel, 2005). Some companies dispense squadrons of grief counselors to help people cope with the upshot of stressful events; these companies often assume that without psychological help, most witnesses to trauma are doomed to serious psychological problems. In

2007, grief counselors arrived at the scene to help traumatized college students deal with the horrific shootings at Virginia Tech, and in 1998 they even traveled to the Boston Public Library to help librarians deal with their feelings of loss following the destruction of books in a flood.

Yet we'll discover in this chapter that even in the face of horrific circumstances, like shootings and natural disasters, most of us are surprisingly resilient (Bonanno, 2004). Even most victims of child sexual abuse turn out to be psychologically healthy adults, although there are certainly exceptions (Rind, Tromovitch, & Bauserman, 1998). Because practicing psychologists tend to see only those people who react emotionally to stress—after all, the healthy people don't come for help—they probably overestimate most people's fragility and underestimate their resilience, an error sometimes called the *clinician's illusion* (Cohen & Cohen, 1984).

Before we discuss why some people thrive and others nosedive when confronted with stressful life events, we'll consider the fundamental question of what stress is. We'll then explore competing views of stress, the mind–body link responsible for stress-related disorders, how we cope with stressful situations, and the rapidly growing fields of health psychology and alternative medicine.

WHAT IS STRESS?

12.1   Explain how stress is defined and approached in different ways.

12.2   Identify different approaches to measuring stress.

Before we proceed further, it's important to distinguish two terms—stress and trauma—that are commonly confused. **Stress**—a type of response—consists of the tension, discomfort, or physical symptoms that arise when a situation, called a *stressor*—a type of stimulus—strains our ability to cope effectively. A *traumatic* event is a stressor that's so severe that it can produce long-term psychological or health consequences.

The field's thinking about stress has evolved over the years (Cooper & Dewe, 2004). Before the 1940s, scientists rarely used the term *stress* outside of the engineering profession (Hayward, 1960), where it referred to stresses on materials and building structures. A building was said to withstand stress if it didn't collapse under intense pressure. It wasn't until 1944 that the term *stress* found its way into the psychological literature (Jones & Bright, 2001). This engineering analogy highlights the notion that "if the body were like a machine and machines are subject to wear and tear then so too would be the body" (Doublet, 2000, p. 48). But just as two buildings can withstand differing amounts of stress before weakening and collapsing, people differ widely in their personal resources, the significance they attach to stressful events, and their ability to grapple with them.

■ Stress in the Eye of the Beholder: Three Approaches

Researchers have approached the study of stress in three different, yet interrelated and complementary ways (Kessler, Price, & Wortman, 1985). Each approach has yielded valuable insights, and, when considered together, illuminate the big and small events that generate distress and the ways we perceive and respond to stressful situations.

STRESSORS AS STIMULI. The *stressors as stimuli* approach focuses on identifying different types of stressful events, ranging from job loss to combat. This approach has pinpointed categories of events that most of us find dangerous and unpredictable, as well as the people who are most susceptible to stress following different events (Collins et al., 2003; Costa & McCrae, 1990). For example, college freshmen show a greater response to such negative life events as the breakup of a relationship than do older men or women (Jackson & Finney, 2002). Pregnancy is often a joyous yet stressful event, fraught with uncertainties, including concerns about the child's health. Women who are highly anxious or experience negative life events during pregnancy are more likely to deliver their babies early—3–5 weeks before normal gestation of 40–42 weeks—compared with women who experience more typical worries (Dunkel-Schetter, 2009). When people retire, the combination of low income and physical disability can make matters worse, suggesting that stressful situations can produce cumulative effects (Smith et al., 2005; Ubel, 2005).

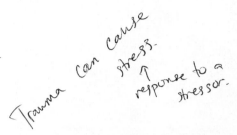

Some researchers call the psychological and physical response to a stressor "strain," much as a material can be said to be strained when under stress.

The stress of unemployment includes not only the frustration and despair of looking for a new job, but the economic hardship of living on a sharply reduced income.

stress
the tension, discomfort, or physical symptoms that arise when a situation, called a stressor—a type of stimulus—strains our ability to cope effectively

Hurricane Katrina devastated much of New Orleans in 2005, forcing many displaced residents to relocate as far away as Michigan and California.

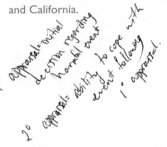

 [Explore] the Effect of Cognitive Appraisal on Responses to Stressors on **mypsychlab.com**

Emotion-focused coping may encourage people who've divorced to begin dating again.

primary appraisal
initial decision regarding whether an event is harmful

secondary appraisal
perceptions regarding our ability to cope with an event that follows primary appraisal

problem-focused coping
coping strategy by which we problem solve and tackle life's challenges head-on

emotion-focused coping
coping strategy that features a positive outlook on feelings or situations accompanied by behaviors that reduce painful emotions

corticosteroid
stress hormone that activates the body and prepares us to respond to stressful circumstances

Victims of natural disasters sometimes suffer from collective trauma that damages the bonds among them. In 2005, Hurricane Katrina separated family members for long periods of time and spawned chaos in the streets of New Orleans. But disasters can also unify communities and bring out the best in us, as our examples of first responders underscores. Christopher Peterson and Martin Seligman (2003) conducted a survey of character strengths (see Chapter 11) of 4,817 Americans before the 9/11 terrorist attacks, and within two months afterward. After the attacks, kindness, teamwork, leadership, gratitude, hope, love, and spirituality increased. One team of researchers performed a linguistic analysis on the diaries of 1,084 users of an online journaling service two months before and two months after the 9/11 attacks. Forty-five percent of the entries after the attack dealt with a larger social group, such as the community and nation, in contrast with none of the entries before the attack (Cohen, Mehl, & Pennebaker, 2004). These findings suggest that stressful circumstances that touch the lives of an entire community can increase social awareness and cement interpersonal bonds.

STRESS AS A TRANSACTION. Stress is a subjective experience. Some people are devastated by the breakup of a meaningful relationship, whereas others are optimistic about the opportunity to start afresh. People's varied reactions to the same event suggest that we can view stress as a transaction between people and their environments (Coyne & Holroyd, 1982; Lazarus, 1999; Lazarus & Folkman, 1984). Researchers who study *stress as a transaction* examine how people interpret and cope with stressful events. Richard Lazarus and his coworkers contended that a critical factor influencing whether we experience an event as stressful is our appraisal, that is, evaluation, of the event. When we encounter a potentially threatening event, we initially engage in **primary appraisal**. That is, we first decide whether the event is harmful before making a **secondary appraisal** about how well we can cope with it (Lazarus & Folkman, 1984). [Explore]

When we believe we can't cope, we're more likely to experience a full-blown stress reaction than when we believe we can (Lazarus, 1999). When we're optimistic and think we can achieve our goals, we're especially likely to engage in **problem-focused coping**, a coping strategy in which we tackle life's challenges head-on (Carver & Scheier, 1999; Lazarus & Folkman, 1984). When we earn a disappointing grade on a test, we may analyze why we fell short and devise a workable plan to improve our performance on the next exam. When situations arise that we can't avoid or control, we're more likely to adopt **emotion-focused coping**, a coping strategy in which we try to place a positive spin on our feelings or predicaments and engage in behaviors to reduce painful emotions (Carver, Scheier, & Weintraub, 1989; Lazarus & Folkman, 1984). After the breakup of a relationship, we may remind ourselves that we were unhappy months before it occurred and reenter the dating arena.

STRESS AS A RESPONSE. Stress researchers also study *stress as a response*—they assess people's psychological and physical reactions to stressful circumstances. Typically, scientists expose subjects to stress-producing stimuli in the laboratory; in other cases, they study people who've encountered real-life stressors. Then they measure a host of outcome variables: stress-related feelings such as depression, hopelessness, and hostility, and physiological responses such as increases in heart rate and the release of stress hormones called **corticosteroids**. These hormones activate the body and prepare us for stressful circumstances (see Chapter 3).

No Two Stresses Are Created Equal: Measuring Stress

Measuring stress is a tricky business, largely because what's exceedingly stressful for one person, like an argument with a boss, may be a mere annoyance for another. Two scales—the Social Readjustment Rating Scale and the Hassles Scale—endeavor to gauge the nature and impact of differing stressful events.

MAJOR LIFE EVENTS. Adopting the view that stressors are stimuli, David Holmes and his colleagues developed the Social Readjustment Rating Scale (SRRS) questionnaire based on 43 life events ranked in terms of their stressfulness as rated by participants (Holmes & Rahe, 1967; Miller & Rahe, 1997). The first of many efforts to measure life events systematically, the SRRS scale is scored by adding the numbers to the right of each item experienced over the preceding year. Before reading further, try your hand at the SRRS in **FIGURE 12.1.**

1. Death of a spouse	100	12. Pregnancy	40	26. Spouse begins or stops work	26
2. Divorce	73			27. Begin or end school	26
3. Marital separation	65	13. Sex difficulties	39	28. Change in living conditions	25
4. Jail term	63	14. Gain of a new family member	39	29. Revision of personal habits	24
5. Death of a close family member	63	15. Business readjustments	39	30. Trouble with boss	23
6. Personal injury or illness	53	16. Change in financial state	38	31. Change in work hours or conditions	20
7. Marriage	50	17. Death of a close friend	37	32. Change in residence	20
8. Fired at work	47	18. Change to different line of work	36	33. Change in school	20
9. Marital reconciliation	45	19. Change in number of arguments with spouse	35	34. Change in recreation	19
10. Retirement	45	20. Mortgage over $50,000	31	35. Change in religious activities	19
11. Change in health of family member	44	21. Foreclosure of mortgage	30	36. Change in social activities	18
		22. Change in responsibilities at work	29	37. Loan less than $50,000	17
		23. Son or daughter leaving home	29	38. Change in sleeping habits	16
		24. Trouble with in-laws	29	39. Change in number of family get-togethers	15
		25. Outstanding personal achievements	28	40. Change in eating habits	15
				41. Vacation	13
				42. Holidays	12
				43. Minor violation of laws	11

FIGURE 12.1 Forty-Three Stressful Life Events from the Social Readjustment Rating Scale. Scoring: Each event should be considered if it's taken place in the past 12 months. Add values to the right of each item to obtain the total score. Your susceptibility to illness and mental health problems: Low < 149; Mild = 150–199; Moderate = 200–299; Major ≥ 300. Bear in mind that very high scores indicate only a susceptibility to certain emotional problems, not the presence of these problems themselves. (*Source:* Holmes & Rahe, 1967)

Getting stuck in traffic is one of many "hassles" we encounter in our daily lives. Research suggests that such hassles can be quite stressful over the long haul.

The fact that many events on the SRRS involve life transitions suggests that the scale may be measuring how we adapt to changing circumstances, many of which tax our ability to cope effectively. Studies using the SRRS and related measures indicate that the number of stressful events people report over the previous year or so is associated with a variety of physical disorders (Dohrenwend & Dohrenwend, 1974; Holmes & Masuda, 1974) and psychological disorders, like depression (Coyne, 1992; Holahan & Moos, 1991; Schmidt et al., 2004). Nevertheless, the sheer number of stressful life events is far from a perfect predictor of who'll become physically or psychologically ill (Coyne & Racioppo, 2000). That's because this approach to measuring stressors doesn't consider other crucial factors, including people's interpretation of events, coping behaviors and resources, and difficulty with recalling events accurately (Coyne & Racioppo, 2000; Lazarus, 1999). In addition, it neglects to take into account some of the more "chronic" ongoing stressors that many individuals experience. Even subtle forms of discrimination or differential treatment based on race, gender, sexual orientation, or religion, for example, can be a significant source of stress even though they rarely are prompted by or lead to a single stressful event we can check off on a list. This approach also neglects the fact that some stressful life events, like divorce or troubles with bosses, can be *consequences* rather than *causes* of people's psychological problems (Depue & Monroe, 1986).

correlation vs. causation
CAN WE BE SURE THAT A CAUSES B?

HASSLES: DON'T SWEAT THE SMALL STUFF. We've all had days when just about everything goes wrong and everybody seems to get on our nerves: Our daily lives are often loaded with **hassles**, minor nuisances that strain our ability to cope. But can lots of hassles add up to be as taxing as the monumental events that shake the foundations of our world?

Researchers developed the Hassles Scale to measure how stressful events, ranging from small annoyances to major daily pressures, impact our adjustment (DeLongis, Folkman, & Lazarus, 1988; Kanner et al., 1981). Both major life events and hassles are associated with poor general health. Nevertheless, the frequency and perceived severity of hassles are actually better predictors of physical health, depression, and anxiety than are major life events (Fernandez & Sheffield, 1996; Kanner et al., 1981).

ruling out rival hypotheses
HAVE IMPORTANT ALTERNATIVE EXPLANATIONS FOR THE FINDINGS BEEN EXCLUDED?

Still, it's possible that major stressful events are the real culprits because they set us off when we already feel hassled, or create hassles with which we then need to cope. To test this alternative hypothesis, researchers have used statistical procedures to show that even when the influence of major life events is subtracted from the mix, hassles still predict psychological adjustment (Forshaw, 2002; Kanner et al., 1981).

ruling out rival hypotheses
HAVE IMPORTANT ALTERNATIVE EXPLANATIONS FOR THE FINDINGS BEEN EXCLUDED?

Yet questions about the measurement of hassles remain. Some items on the Hassles scale, such as difficulties with relaxing and insomnia, may reflect symptoms of psychological disorders, such as depression or anxiety, rather than hassles (Monroe, 1983). Nevertheless, when the scale developers (DeLongis et al., 1988) revised the scale by removing all words related to symptoms, they found that hassles were still associated with health outcomes.

We've learned that measuring stress is no easy feat. In response to this challenge, researchers have devised interview-based methods, which provide a more in-depth picture of life stress than self-report measures. Interviewers can identify the positive and negative events people experience as stressful, distinguish ongoing from "one-shot" stressors, and consider how events interact to produce physical and psychological problems (Dohrenwend, 2006; Monroe, 2008). Still, in assessing stress, researchers must balance the rich information yield from interviews with the ease of administration and efficiency of questionnaires.

hassle
minor annoyance or nuisance that strains our ability to cope

✓—Study and Review on **mypsychlab.com**

assess your knowledge   **FACT OR FICTION?**

1. Most people at one time or another will experience an extremely stressful event. **True** / **False**

2. The effects of stressors can be cumulative. **True** / **False**

3. Natural disasters may sometimes result in stronger community bonds. **True** / **False**

4. According to the stress as a transaction viewpoint, almost all people respond to stressful events in the same way. **True** / **False**

5. Major life events have a greater effect on adjustment than do everyday hassles. **True** / **False**   *Can be similar effect depending on severity and frequency of hassles.*

Answers: 1. T (p. 456); 2. T (p. 457); 3. T (p. 458); 4. F (p. 458); 5. F (p. 460)

emotional brain = amygdala, hypothalamus, and hippocampus. produces fear.

HOW WE ADAPT TO STRESS: CHANGE AND CHALLENGE

12.3   Describe Selye's general adaptation syndrome.

12.4   Describe the diversity of stress responses.

As any of us who's had to confront a harrowing event, like a car accident or high-pressure interview for a big job, knows, adapting to stress isn't easy. Yet natural selection has endowed us with a set of responses for coping with anxiety-provoking circumstances.

■ The Mechanics of Stress: Selye's General Adaptation Syndrome

In 1956, Canadian physician Hans Selye ignited the field of modern-day stress research by publishing *The Stress of Life*, a landmark book that unveiled his decades of study on the effects of prolonged stress on the body. Selye's genius was to recognize a connection between the stress response of animals, including stomach ulcers and increases in the size of the adrenal gland, which produces stress hormones, and that of physically ill patients, who showed a consistent pattern of stress-related responses. Dovetailing with the engineering analogy we've already discussed, Selye believed that too much stress leads to breakdowns. He argued that we're equipped with a sensitive physiology that responds to stressful circumstances by kicking us into high gear. He called the pattern of responding to stress the **general adaptation syndrome (GAS)**. According to Selye, all prolonged stressors take us through three stages of adaptation: *alarm, resistance,* and *exhaustion* (see **FIGURE 12.2**). To illustrate key aspects of the GAS and the extent to which our appraisals determine our reactions to stress, let's consider the experience of a hypothetical person, named Mark, who's terrified of flying.

THE ALARM REACTION. Selye's first stage, the *alarm reaction*, involves excitation of the autonomic nervous system, the discharge of the stress hormone adrenaline, and physical symptoms of anxiety. Joseph LeDoux (1996) and others have identified the seat of anxiety within the limbic system—dubbed the *emotional brain*—that includes the amygdala, hypothalamus, and hippocampus (see Chapter 3). Once in flight, Mark feels the plane moving through pockets of turbulence and his cold, clammy hands clutch the shaking seat. His mouth is dry. His heart pounds. His breathing is rapid and shallow. He feels lightheaded and dizzy. Images of plane crashes he's seen on television pop uncontrollably into his mind. Mark's swift emotional reaction to the turbulence is tripped largely by his amygdala, where vital emotional memories are stored (see Chapters 7 and 11) and create gut feelings of a possible crash.

The hypothalamus sits atop a mind-body link known as the *hypothalamus-pituitary-adrenal* (HPA) axis, shown in **FIGURE 12.3**. When the

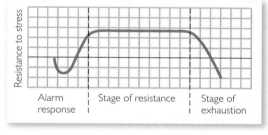

FIGURE 12.2   Selye's General Adaptation Syndrome.   According to Selye's general adaptation syndrome, our level of resistance to stress drops during the alarm phase, increases during the resistance phase, and drops again during the exhaustion phase. (*Source:* Selye, 1956)

general adaptation syndrome (GAS)
stress-response pattern proposed by Hans Selye that consists of three stages: alarm, resistance, and exhaustion

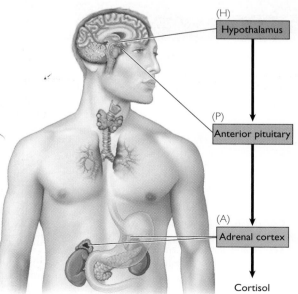

FIGURE 12.3   The Hypothalamus-Pituitary-Adrenal (HPA) Axis.

hypothalamus (H) receives signals of fear, the sympathetic nervous system activates the adrenal gland (A), which secretes the stress hormones epinephrine (adrenaline) and norepinephrine (noradrenalin). In a matter of moments, Mark's blood pressure rises, his pupils dilate, and his heart pumps blood to vital organs, readying Mark for the **fight-or-flight response** (see Chapter 3). This response, first described by Walter Cannon in 1915, is a set of physiological and psychological reactions that mobilize us to either confront or leave a threatening situation. Cannon noted that when animals, including humans, face a threat, they have two options: *fight* (actively attack the threat or cope in the immediate situation) or *flee* (escape). Of course, Mark can't flee, so his fear escalates. The hypothalamus and pituitary gland (P) orchestrate the adrenal gland's release of another stress hormone, cortisol, which floods Mark with energy, while his hippocampus retrieves terrifying images from news stories of planes going down in flames.

RESISTANCE. After the initial rush of stress hormones, Mark enters Selye's second stage of the GAS: *resistance.* He adapts to the stressor and finds ways to cope with it. The instant Mark's hippocampus detected danger from the first apparent jolt of rough air, it opened up a gateway to portions of his cerebral cortex, which neuroscientist Joseph LeDoux (1996) called the "thinking brain." At one point, Mark experiences a sudden impulse to bolt from his seat, but his basal ganglia, linked to the frontal cortex of his thinking brain, wisely leads him to think better of it. Mark slowly but surely gets a handle on his fears. He reminds himself that flying is statistically much safer than driving and that he's flown through choppy air in the past without being injured. He looks around and notices that most of the passengers look calm. He reminds himself to breathe slowly, and with each breath his relaxation replaces tension.

EXHAUSTION. Mark calms down, and is able to get through his flight without panicking. But what happens when a stressor, such as wartime combat lasting months, is more prolonged and uncontrollable? Here's when the third stage of Selye's GAS—*exhaustion*—sets in. If our personal resources are limited and we lack good coping measures, our resistance may ultimately break down, causing our levels of activation to bottom out. The results can range from damage to an organ system, to depression and anxiety, to a breakdown in the immune system (which we'll discuss later in the chapter).

■ The Diversity of Stress Responses

Not all of us react to stressors with a fight-or-flight response. Our reactions vary from one stressor to another, and these reactions are shaped by gender.

FIGHT OR FLIGHT OR TEND AND BEFRIEND? Shelley Taylor and her colleagues coined the catchy phrase **tend and befriend** to describe a common pattern of reacting to stress among women (Taylor et al., 2000), although some men display it, too. Taylor observed that in times of stress, women generally rely on their social contacts and nurturing abilities—they *tend* to those around them and to themselves—more than men do. When stressed out, women typically *befriend*, or turn to others for support.

That's not to say that women lack a self-preservation instinct, or that they don't experience a fight-or-flight pattern when endangered. They certainly don't shirk from defending themselves and their children or from attempting to escape when physically threatened. Nevertheless, compared with men, women generally have more to lose—especially when they're pregnant, nursing, or caring for children—if they're injured or killed when fighting or fleeing. Therefore, over the course of evolutionary history, they've developed a tend-and-befriend response to threat which, along with the fight-or-flight response, boosts the odds of their and their offspring's survival. Oxytocin (see Chapter 3), the "love and bonding hormone," further counters stress and promotes the tend-and-befriend response (Kosfeld et al., 2005; Taylor et al., 2000). Researchers discovered that women with high levels of oxytocin during pregnancy and in the first month after the birth of their children are more likely to touch them affectionately, sing special songs to them, and bathe and feed them in special ways (Feldman et al., 2007).

In stressful times, women often rely on friendships for support and comfort, a pattern that psychologist Shelley Taylor called "tend and befriend."

fight-or-flight response
physical and psychological reaction that mobilizes people and animals to either defend themselves (fight) or escape (flee) a threatening situation

tend and befriend
reaction that mobilizes people to nurture (tend) or seek social support (befriend) under stress

LONG-LASTING STRESS REACTIONS. Bad things happen to all of us. For most of us, life goes on. But others of us experience long-lasting psychological repercussions, including posttraumatic stress disorder (Comijs et al., 2008; Meichenbaum, 1994; Yehuda et al., 1993).

When Stress Is Too Much: Posttraumatic Stress Disorder. On April 16, 2007, 23-year-old Cho Seung-Hui, a student at Virginia Tech, went on a shooting rampage, killing 31 classmates and professors before taking his own life. When Marjorie Lindholm, 24, heard the news of the massacre, she immediately relived the terror she experienced as a student at Columbine High School on April 20, 1999. On that day, two students, Eric Harris and Dylan Klebold, shot 12 of her classmates and a teacher before turning the guns on themselves. In a television interview she said, "I started crying, then shaking. I remembered everything I saw at Columbine. I got physically ill. There is no way I'm going to forget that day" (Stepp, 2007).

The horrific 2007 shooting spree at Virginia Tech left some survivors with symptoms of posttraumatic stress disorder.

psychomythology

ARE ALMOST ALL PEOPLE TRAUMATIZED BY HIGHLY AVERSIVE EVENTS?

A widespread view in popular psychology is that most people exposed to trauma develop PTSD or other serious psychological disorders. Immediately following the 9/11 attacks, for example, many mental health professionals predicted an epidemic of PTSD across the United States (Sommers & Satel, 2005). Were they right? ◉ ─|Watch

George Bonanno and his colleagues conducted a study that underscores the remarkable resilience of survivors of extremely aversive events (Bonanno et al., 2006). Using a random-digit dialing procedure, the researchers sampled 2,752 adults in the New York City area about six months after the 9/11 attacks. They conducted their assessments using a computer-assisted telephone interview system. People were judged to be resilient if they reported zero or one PTSD symptoms during the first six months after the attack. Bonanno's results offered surprising evidence for psychological adjustment; 65.1 percent of the sample was resilient. A quarter of the people who were in the World Trade Center at the time of the attack developed probable PTSD, although more than half of the people in this category were resilient. Other research indicates that although most Americans were profoundly upset for several days following the 9/11 attacks, nearly all quickly regained their equilibrium and returned to their previous level of functioning (McNally, 2003). So when it comes to responses to trauma, resilience is the rule rather than the exception.

People who cope well in the aftermath of a serious stressor tend to display relatively high levels of functioning before the event (Bonanno et al., 2005). Yet resilience isn't limited to a few particularly well-adjusted, brave, or tough-minded people, nor to a single type or class of events. Instead, it's the most common response to traumatic events. Most people who take care of a partner dying of AIDS, suffer the death of a spouse, or survive a physical or sexual assault report few long-term psychological symptoms (Bonanno, 2004).

Resilience is the rule rather than the exception even among children, who are commonly regarded as fragile and vulnerable to stress (Sommers & Satel, 2005). William Copeland and his associates interviewed 1,420 children aged 9, 11, and 13, and reinterviewed them every year through 16 years of age. More than two-thirds of the children had been exposed to at least one potentially traumatic event such as abuse, a serious accident, or the violent death of a loved one. Nevertheless, only a tiny fraction of the children (less than 0.5 percent) met criteria for PTSD, and few children showed signs of any traumatic reaction at all (Copeland et al., 2007).

TABLE 12.1 presents the rates of PTSD and acute stress disorder (a disorder similar to, although briefer in duration than, PTSD) associated with a number of disturbing events. Although most of us will experience a potentially traumatic stressor at some time in our lives, the lifetime prevalence of PTSD is only 5 percent in men and 10 percent in women (Keane, Marshall, & Taft, 2006; Kessler et al., 1995).

Combat ranks with sexual assault as one of two events producing the highest risk for PTSD.

◉ ─|Watch PTSD 911 on **mypsychlab.com**

TABLE 12.1 Percentages of People Who Develop Posttraumatic Conditions as a Function of the Event.

PERCENTAGE OF PEOPLE WHO DEVELOP PTSD	
Natural disaster	4%–5%
Bombing	34%
Plane crash into hotel	29%
Mass shooting	28%

PERCENTAGE OF PEOPLE WHO DEVELOP ACUTE STRESS DISORDER	
Typhoon	7%
Industrial accident	6%
Mass shooting	33%
Violent assault	19%
Vehicle accident	14%
Assault, severe burns	13%

(*Source:* Bryant, 2000, National Center for PTSD)

Marjorie displays some of the hallmark symptoms of *posttraumatic stress disorder* (PTSD), a condition that sometimes follows extremely stressful life events. Its telltale symptoms include vivid memories, feelings, and images of traumatic experiences, known commonly as *flashbacks*. Other symptoms of PTSD, which we'll consider in greater depth in Chapter 15, include efforts to avoid reminders of the trauma, feeling detached or estranged from others, and symptoms of increased arousal, such as difficulty sleeping and startling easily. The severity, duration, and nearness to the stressor all affect people's likelihood of developing PTSD (American Psychiatric Association, 2000; Ozer et al., 2003).

✓• Study and Review on mypsychlab.com

THE BRAIN—BODY REACTION TO STRESS

12.5   Describe how the immune system is affected by stress.

12.6   Identify how physical disorders such as ulcers are related to stress.

12.7   Describe the role of personality, everyday experiences, and socioeconomic factors in coronary heart disease.

In 1962, two Japanese physicians conducted a study demonstrating the intimate connection between brain and body. Their study, which researchers today might find difficult to carry out for ethical reasons, showed how hypnotic and direct suggestions from a respected authority figure could produce dramatic skin reactions. The researchers selected 13 boys who contracted a red, itchy skin reaction when touched with the leaves of a tree with effects similar to poison ivy. Five boys received a hypnotic induction with suggestions for relaxation and drowsiness, and another eight boys received no prior hypnotic induction—just suggestions administered while they were awake and alert.

All boys sat with their eyes closed and weren't aware of what types of leaves were touching them. A respected physician told all the boys he was touching them with the leaves of the poison ivy–type tree, when in fact he was touching them with leaves from a harmless tree. In the second phase, the researchers reversed the conditions: They rubbed the boys' arms with the poison–ivy type leaves, but told them the leaves were harmless.

The reactions were remarkable. In the first phase, all hypnotic subjects and all suggestion-alone subjects showed significant skin disturbance as a result of believing they were touched by the poison ivy–type leaves. As is so often the case in psychology, beliefs can create reality, in this case a *nocebo effect* (see Chapter 2). In the second phase, four of five hypnotic subjects and seven of eight suggestion-alone subjects didn't show any skin reactions to the leaves, even though all had developed skin reactions to the leaves prior to the study (Ikemi & Nakagawa, 1962).

This study demonstrates how psychological factors, in this case the stressful idea of contracting an itchy rash, can influence physical processes. Indeed, much of what we call a "psychological" response to events manifests itself in physiological reactions. In this chapter and others, we'll see that stress can spill over into multiple domains of life, creating

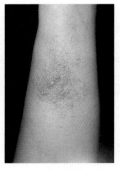

Suggestion alone can produce an uncomfortable rash much like that produced by poison ivy in people who are highly sensitive to leaves of a tree with effects similar to poison ivy.

physical difficulties that disrupt our sleep (see Chapter 5) and sexual functioning (see Chapter 11). But can stress seep into our cells and weaken our body's defenses against infections? A number of fascinating studies tell us that the answer is yes.

■ The Immune System

Ordinarily (and thankfully!), we never have to think about the billions of viruses, fungi, protozoa, and bacteria that share our environment or inhabit our body. That's because our **immune system** neutralizes or destroys them. The immune system is our body's defense against invading bacteria, viruses, and other potentially illness-producing organisms and substances. Our first shield from these foreign invaders, called *antigens*, is the skin, which blocks the entry of many disease-producing organisms, called *pathogens*. When we cough or sneeze, our lungs expel harmful bacteria and viruses. Saliva, urine, tears, perspiration, and stomach acid also rid our body of pathogens.

Some viruses or bacteria penetrate these defenses, but our immune system is wily and has other means of safeguarding us. *Phagocytes* and *lymphocytes* are two types of specialized white blood cells manufactured in the marrow of the bones. First at the scene of an infection, phagocytes engulf an invader. Longer-lived *macrophages* wander through the body as scavengers, destroying remaining antigens and dead tissue. Two types of lymphocytes, *T cells* and *B cells*, are also stalwart soldiers in the night-and-day battle to keep us healthy. Substances called cytokines signal natural killer T cells, as they're called, to move through the body and attach to proteins on the surface of virus- and cancer-infected cells, popping them like balloons. B cells produce proteins called *antibodies*, which stick to the surface of invaders, slow their progress, and attract other proteins that destroy the foreign organisms.

Under ordinary circumstances, the immune system is remarkably effective. But it's not a perfect barrier against infection. For example, many early-stage forms of breast and other cancers vanish or get smaller without treatment (Esserman, Shieh, & Thompson, 2009), yet some cancer cells can suppress an effective immune response, multiply, and wreak havoc in the body. Serious disorders of the immune system, such as **acquired immune deficiency syndrome (AIDS)**, are life threatening. AIDS is an incurable yet often treatable condition in which the human immunodeficiency virus (HIV) attacks and damages the immune system. When the immune system is overactive, it can launch an attack on various organs of the body, causing *autoimmune diseases* like arthritis, in which the immune system causes swelling and pain at the joints, and multiple sclerosis, in which the immune system attacks the protective myelin sheath surrounding neurons (see Chapter 3).

■ Psychoneuroimmunology: Our Bodies, Our Environments, and Our Health

The study of the relationship between the immune system and central nervous system—the seat of our emotions and reactions to the environment (see Chapter 3)—goes by a mouthful of a name: **psychoneuroimmunology** (Cohen & Herbert, 1996). When evaluating psychoneuroimmunology, we must be careful not to fall prey to exaggerated claims. For example, physical diseases aren't the result of negative thinking, nor can positive thinking reverse serious illnesses like cancer (Hines, 2003; Lilienfeld et al., 2010)—despite assertions by immensely popular alternative medical practitioners like Andrew Weil (2000) and Deepak Chopra (1989). Nor, despite early and widely publicized claims (Fawzy et al., 1993; Spiegel et al., 1989), does psychotherapy appear to prolong the survival of women with breast cancer (Coyne, Stefanek, & Palmer, 2007). Nevertheless, researchers using rigorous designs have discovered fascinating links between our life circumstances and our ability to fend off illnesses.

People from all walks of life can contract the HIV virus and develop AIDS.

immune system
our body's defense system against invading bacteria, viruses, and other potentially illness-producing organisms and substances

acquired immune deficiency syndrome (AIDS)
a life-threatening, incurable, yet treatable condition in which the human immunodeficiency virus (HIV) attacks and damages the immune system

psychoneuroimmunology
study of the relationship between the immune system and central nervous system

◄ **extraordinary claims**

IS THE EVIDENCE AS STRONG AS THE CLAIM?

Dr. Andrew Weil (*far left*) and Dr. Deepak Chopra have popularized the idea that the "mind" can cure serious illnesses. Yet most of their optimistic claims aren't supported by scientific evidence.

FICTOID ✖

MYTH: Sudden stress or trauma can turn one's hair white.

REALITY: There's no evidence that intense stress can make one's hair turn white overnight or even over a short period of time. Nor is there any known physical mechanism by which this process could occur (Radford, 2007).

ruling out rival hypotheses ▷

HAVE IMPORTANT ALTERNATIVE EXPLANATIONS FOR THE FINDINGS BEEN EXCLUDED?

Caretakers of people with Alzheimer's disease experience high levels of stress, are at heightened risk of developing depression, and even show decreases in their blood's ability to clot (associated with having a stroke) in response to stressful life events (von Känel et al., 2003). For reasons that are unknown, the negative pyschological effects of such caretaking seem to be lower among African Americans than Caucasians (Janevic & Connell, 2001).

STRESS AND COLDS. Many people believe they're more likely to get a cold when they're really stressed out—and they're right. Sheldon Cohen and his associates placed cold viruses into volunteers' nasal passages (Cohen, Tyrell, & Smith, 1991). Other volunteers, in a placebo condition, didn't receive the virus, but received nasal drops with a saline solution. Stressful life events in the year preceding the study predicted the number of colds people developed when exposed to the virus. Exposure to the virus was also important. People in the placebo condition didn't develop as many colds, even when they experienced stressful events in the year before the study. The researchers (Cohen et al., 1998) later discovered that significant stressors, such as unemployment and interpersonal difficulties lasting at least a month, were the best predictors of who developed a cold, perhaps because long-term stressors are especially likely to promote an inflammatory response known to increase the risk of colds and other diseases (Doyle & Cohen, 2009). But a network of friends and relatives and close ties to the community afforded protection against colds (Cohen et al., 1997; Cohen et al., 2003).

It's possible that stress affects health-related behaviors but has no direct impact on the immune system. For instance, our susceptibility to a cold may increase because when we're under stress we tend to sleep poorly, eat non-nutritious foods, and smoke and drink alcohol excessively, all of which depress the immune system. In a recent study, Cohen and his colleagues (Cohen et al., 2009) found that people who slept an average of seven hours a night before they were exposed to a cold virus were almost three times more likely to catch a cold than were people who slept for eight hours or more. Still, the investigators found that even when they controlled for sleep quality and other health-related behaviors, the relation between stress and colds remained.

STRESS AND IMMUNE FUNCTION: BEYOND THE COMMON COLD. Janice Kiecolt-Glaser and her associates are pioneers in the study of the connection between stressors and the immune system. Caring for a family member with Alzheimer's disease, a severe form of dementia (see Chapters 3 and 7), can be exceedingly stressful and cause long-term disruption of the immune system. Kiecolt-Glaser demonstrated that a small wound (standardized for size) took 24 percent longer to heal in Alzheimer's caregivers compared with a group of people who weren't taking care of a relative with Alzheimer's (Kiecolt-Glaser et al., 1995). All of the following stressors can lead to disruptions in the immune system (Kiecolt-Glaser et al., 2002):

- taking an important test
- death of a spouse
- unemployment
- marital conflict
- living near a damaged nuclear reactor
- natural disasters

The good news is that positive emotions and social support, which we'll consider later in the chapter, can fortify our immune systems (Esterling, Kiecolt-Glaser, & Glaser, 1996; Kennedy, Kiecolt-Glaser, & Glaser, 1990).

■ Stress-Related Illnesses: A Biopsychosocial View

Not long ago a common myth of popular psychology was that beliefs and mental states were the root causes of many physical ailments. Certain illnesses or disorders were once called *psychosomatic,* because psychologists believed that deep-seated conflicts and emotional reactions were the culprits. For example, Franz Alexander (1950) argued that stomach ulcers are linked to infantile cravings to be fed and feelings of dependency. In adulthood, these conflicts become reawakened and activate the gastrointestinal system (stomach and intestines), which has been associated with feeding.

The result, according to Alexander, is a **peptic ulcer**—an inflamed area in the gastrointestinal tract that can cause pain, nausea, and loss of appetite. Even today, many or most people believe that ulcers are produced by stress (Lilienfeld et al., 2010).

Yet we now know that ulcers aren't caused by dependency or stress, nor by eating spicy foods like salsas and hot chicken wings. Rather, Helicobacter pylori (*H. pylori*)—an unusual bacterium that thrives in stomach acid—is actually the cause of as many as 90 percent of stomach ulcers. Still, stress may play some role in contributing to ulcers—perhaps by reducing the efficiency of the immune system and increasing vulnerability to the bacterium. Higher rates of ulcers are associated with earthquakes, being a prisoner of war, economic crises, and other anxiety-provoking events (Levenstein et al., 1999).

Psychologists use the term **psychophysiological** to describe authentic illnesses like ulcers in which emotions and stress contribute to, maintain, or aggravate physical conditions. Scientists widely acknowledge that emotions and stress are associated with physical disorders, including coronary heart disease and AIDS. Most psychologists have adopted a **biopsychosocial perspective**, which proposes that most medical conditions are neither all physical nor all psychological. Numerous physical illnesses depend on the complex interplay of genes, lifestyle, immunity, social support, everyday stressors, and self-perceptions (Engel, 1977; Fava & Sonino, 2008; Turk, 1996).

CORONARY HEART DISEASE. Scientists have learned that psychological factors, including stress and personality traits, are key risk factors for **coronary heart disease (CHD)**. CHD is the complete or partial blockage of the arteries that provide oxygen to the heart, and is the number one cause of death and disability in the United States (Kung et al., 2008). It accounts for an astonishing one in every two and a half deaths, and almost a million deaths every year (Gatchel & Oordt, 2003). CHD develops when deposits of *cholesterol*—a waxy, fatty substance that travels in the bloodstream—collect in the walls of arteries, narrowing and blocking the coronary arteries, creating a condition called *atherosclerosis*. Atherosclerosis is associated with an inflammatory response in the artery walls, and if the condition worsens, it can lead to chest pain and the deterioration and death of heart tissue, otherwise known as a heart attack (see **FIGURE 12.4**).

The Role of Stress in CHD. A host of factors are associated with CHD. Researchers examined 18,863 men in 1967–70 and followed them for 38 years (Clarke et al., 2009). From age 50 onward, the men with a history of smoking, high cholesterol, and high blood pressure lived an average of 10 years less, and died at twice the rate from heart attacks, as men with none of these risk factors. A family history of CHD, diabetes, and low levels of vitamin D—the "sunshine vitamin"—can also boost the risk of heart disease (Wang et al., 2008).

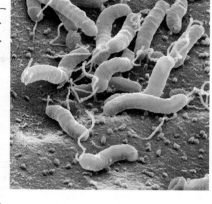

Contrary to popular belief, stress isn't the major cause of ulcers. Instead, the bacterium *Helicobacter pylori* is the prime culprit.

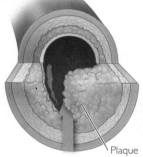

FIGURE 12.4 Atherosclerosis. Cholesterol deposits in the large arteries form plaque, restricting the flow of blood. This condition, called *atherosclerosis*, can result in stroke, heart attack, and serious chest pain.

Normal artery

Blood flow

Artery narrowed by atherosclerosis

Plaque

The pioneering Framingham Study, which began in 1948, is one of most influential investigations of health in America. This longitudinal study has provided a treasure trove of data on risk factors for CHD, and continues to examine the health of over 5,000 men and women in Framingham, Massachusetts.

peptic ulcer
inflamed area in the gastrointestinal tract that can cause pain, nausea, and loss of appetite

psychophysiological
illnesses such as asthma and ulcers in which emotions and stress contribute to, maintain, or aggravate the physical condition

biopsychosocial perspective
the view that an illness or medical condition is the product of the interplay of biological, psychological, and social factors

coronary heart disease (CHD)
damage to the heart from the complete or partial blockage of the arteries that provide oxygen to the heart

correlation vs. causation
CAN WE BE SURE THAT A CAUSES B?

Stress deserves a prominent place on the list of CHD risk factors. Stressful life events predict recurrences of heart attacks, high blood pressure, and enlargement of the heart (Repetti, Taylor, & Seeman, 2002; Schnall et al., 1990; Troxel et al., 2003). Although only correlational, these data suggest that stressors may sometimes produce negative physiological effects. Moreover, high levels of stress hormones triggered by extreme stress can lead to disruptions in normal heart rhythm and even sudden death, as well as to atherosclerosis in people who are highly reactive to everyday stressors (Carney, Freedland, & Veith, 2005; Sarafino, 2006). People with CHD also show signs of a hyped-up autonomic nervous system, with elevated heart rates and exaggerated responses to physical stressors (Carney et al., 2005). Even though stress may exert a direct effect on CHD, stress is also associated with behavioral risk factors for CHD, including poor diet and inadequate exercise (Chandola et al., 2008). So at least some of the effects of stress on CHD may actually be due to the overlap between stress and these risk factors.

ruling out rival hypotheses
HAVE IMPORTANT ALTERNATIVE EXPLANATIONS FOR THE FINDINGS BEEN EXCLUDED?

The ABCs of Personality in CHD. In addition to stress, researchers have suggested that longstanding behavior patterns contribute to risk for CHD. When we picture someone at risk for a heart attack, certain personality characteristics come to mind: competitive, hard driving, ambitious, and impatient. The media have widely popularized the so-called **Type A personality** (as opposed to the calmer and mellower *Type B personality*) who fits this description.

Two cardiologists, Meyer Friedman and Ray Rosenman (1959), coined this term to describe a curious behavior pattern they observed among CHD patients. They noticed that the chairs in their hospital waiting room were rapidly becoming worn out around the edges. Many of their CHD patients were literally sitting and bouncing on the edges of their seats because of restlessness. But long before Friedman and Rosenman dubbed some of their patients Type A, in 1892, Canadian physician William Osler described the heart attack–prone person as "a keen and ambitious man, the indicator of whose engines are set a full speed ahead" (Chesney & Rosenman, 1980, p. 188). Later, Friedman and Rosenman (1974) identified additional characteristics that clustered under the Type A description: perfectionistic, prone to hostility, stubborn, opinionated, cynical, and controlling.

? Why can chronic anger be bad for our health? (See answer upside down at bottom of page.)

Rosenman and Friedman launched a study (Rosenman et al., 1975; Rosenman et al., 1964) of 3,500 males to determine whether Type A personality traits predict CHD risk over an eight-and-a-half-year period. Even when they took other risk factors, like smoking and diet, into account, Type A traits were still associated with later heart disease risk. Although early studies revealed high rates of CHD among extreme Type A individuals, later studies yielded many negative results (Gatchel & Oordt, 2003). Scientists began to question whether the fact that a constellation of traits is associated with increased risk means that each trait is equally important. Is a person who hustles to meet deadlines equally at risk for a heart attack as one who's cynical and hostile? Scientists soon turned to the question of which Type A traits are most associated with heightened risk.

replicability
CAN THE RESULTS BE DUPLICATED IN OTHER STUDIES?

Type A personality
personality type that describes people who are competitive, driven, hostile, and ambitious

ruling out rival hypotheses
HAVE IMPORTANT ALTERNATIVE EXPLANATIONS FOR THE FINDINGS BEEN EXCLUDED?

Anger and Hostility. Of all Type A traits, hostility is the most predictive of heart disease (Matthews et al., 2004; Myrtek, 2001; Nabi et al., 2008; Smith & Gallo, 2001). In one study, researchers gave medical students a test of hostility and tracked them down 25 years later. Those with high hostility scores were more likely to have suffered and died from CHD than those with low scores (Barefoot, Dahlstrom, & Williams, 1983). Hostility is associated with well-documented risk factors for CHD, such as alcohol consumption, smoking, and weight gain (Bunde & Suls, 2006), so an alternative hypothesis is that its effects on CHD are indirect. Nevertheless, in a study of older white men, hostility surpassed these traditional risk factors in predicting CHD (Niaura et al., 2002). Luckily, there's a silver lining to this gray cloud: Tamping down hostility and practicing forgiveness of others helps to reduce CHD risk (McCullough et al., 2009). When researchers taught CHD patients techniques to curtail their hostility, they found a 37 percent decrease in deaths from heart attacks compared with other patients (Dusseldorp et al., 1999; Friedman et al., 1987).

CHD, EVERYDAY EXPERIENCES, AND SOCIOECONOMIC FACTORS. Hostility and other negative emotions don't always arise from enduring personality traits. Negative emotions can stem from the many pressures and demands we confront in our fast-paced, competitive society. Let's consider three sources of support for the claim that everyday experiences set the stage for many physical problems, including heart disease. First, people who experience even one significant drop in their income over a five-year period face a 30 percent increase in their risk of dying from any cause. Two such drops in income jack up the risk to a whopping 70 percent (Duncan, 1996). Second, African American women who report discrimination, unfair treatment, and high stress levels have more narrowing and blockage of their arteries than other African American women (Troxel et al., 2003). Third, CHD is associated with substantial job stress and dissatisfaction (Quick et al., 1997). Although job stress is correlated with CHD, it may not cause it in all circumstances. Interesting possibilities that have yet to be fully explored are that the causal arrow is reversed: Perhaps CHD causes job stress in some people. Another hypothesis is that a third variable, such as personality makeup, attitudes toward others, or early experiences with trauma, contribute to both job stress and CHD.

◀ **correlation vs. causation**
CAN WE BE SURE THAT A CAUSES B?

Still, these findings, along with the others we've examined, point to another possibility that's been well supported by research: The poor share the burden of most health problems disproportionately. Researchers have established a strong correlation between poverty and poor health (Antonovsky, 1967; Repetti, Taylor, & Seeman, 2002), but we still need to ask, "What's responsible for this association?"

◀ **ruling out rival hypotheses**
HAVE IMPORTANT ALTERNATIVE EXPLANATIONS FOR THE FINDINGS BEEN EXCLUDED?

Linda Gallo and Karen Matthews (2003) addressed this question. They noted that life can prove immensely challenging for people who have little education, struggle in a bad job with a nasty supervisor, and barely make enough money to make ends meet. People from low SES backgrounds who regularly encounter these circumstances experience a powerful drain on their personal and interpersonal resources. This state of affairs decreases their ability to cope with stressors and with depression, hopelessness, and hostility, which increase the risk of poor health and CHD. To make matters worse, negative thoughts and feelings can promote unhealthy habits like smoking, drinking, and lack of exercise, which further increase the risk of physical problems (Gallo & Matthews, 2003).

ILLNESS CAN CREATE STRESS. We've seen that stress can contribute to physical disorders, such as CHD. But of course, physical disorders can also create stress. Not surprisingly, being diagnosed with a potentially fatal illness that has an uncertain outcome, like cancer or AIDS, can be unimaginably stressful and pose innumerable challenges. Conversely, when the treatment for severe illnesses is successful, the transition from poor to dramatically improved health can introduce new and difficult decisions, like whether to return to work or to begin or end relationships (Catz & Kelly, 2001).

---

assess your knowledge   **FACT OR FICTION?**   ✓—[**Study** and **Review** on **mypsychlab.com**

1. Overactivity of the immune system sometimes leads to disease. **True / False**

2. One major cause of ulcers is eating hot, spicy foods late at night. **True / False**

3. Most psychologists adopt a biopsychosocial perspective, which proposes that most medical conditions are neither all physical nor all psychological. **True / False**

4. The number one cause of death and disability in the United States is coronary heart disease. **True / False**

5. Social and economic factors are largely or entirely unrelated to risk for physical diseases. **True / False**

Answers: 1. T (p. 465); 2. F (p. 467); 3. T (p. 467); 4. T (p. 467); 5. F (p. 469)

social support
relationships with people and groups that can provide us with emotional comfort and personal and financial resources

COPING WITH STRESS

12.8 Describe the role of social support and different types of control in coping with stress.

12.9 Explain how our attitudes, beliefs, and personality may influence our responses to stress.

Clearly, some of us adapt better in the face of challenge and change than others. Why is this so, and what can we do to reduce stress, manage our lives, and stay healthy? We'll next take stock of how we can use social support and coping strategies to deal with stressful circumstances.

■ Social Support

Imagine that you survived the 9/11 World Trade Center attack. What would be helpful? When we ask our students this question, many say the support of family, friends, neighbors, teachers, coworkers, and clergy would be invaluable. **Social support** encompasses interpersonal relations with people, groups, and the larger community. Social support can provide us with emotional comfort, financial assistance, and information to make decisions, solve problems, and contend with stressful situations (Schaefer, Coyne, & Lazarus, 1981; Stroebe, 2000; Wills & Fegan, 2001). Lisa Berkman and Leonard Syme (1979) conducted a landmark study of the hypothesis that social support buffers us against the adverse effects of stress on health. They analyzed data from nearly 5,000 men and women in Alameda County, California, over a nine-year period. They honed in on four kinds of social ties: marriage, contact with friends, church membership, and formal and informal group associations. They then created a social network index reflecting the number of social connections and social supports available to each person.  **Watch**

Support and comfort from others can buffer the effects of highly aversive situations.

Watch Socializing and Stress on **mypsychlab.com**

ruling out rival hypotheses

> **HAVE IMPORTANT ALTERNATIVE EXPLANATIONS FOR THE FINDINGS BEEN EXCLUDED?**

Berkman and Syme found a strong relationship between the number of social connections, across every age group, and the probability of dying during the nine-year period. But do these findings mean that isolation increases our chances of dying? A rival hypothesis is that poor health results in few social bonds, rather than the other way around. To rule out this possibility, the researchers surveyed participants when they started the study. People with high and low levels of support reported a comparable illness history, suggesting that poor initial health can't explain why people with the least social support are later more likely to die. Nevertheless, people aren't necessarily accurate when they judge their health.

To address this concern, James House, Cynthia Robbins, and Helen Metzner (1982) ensured that their 2,700 participants received a medical examination *before* their study got under way. This exam provided a more objective assessment of health status. The researchers replicated Berkman and Syme's (1979) findings: Even when they took initial health status into account, people with less social support had higher mortality rates.

replicability

> **CAN THE RESULTS BE DUPLICATED IN OTHER STUDIES?**

Fortunately, the positive influence of social support isn't limited to health outcomes. Supportive and caring relationships can help us cope with short-term crises and life transitions. A happy marriage, for example, is protective against depression, even when people encounter major stressors (Alloway & Bebbington, 1987; Gotlib & Hammen, 1992). But the breakup of close relationships through separation, divorce, discrimination, or bereavement ranks among the most stressful events we can experience (Gardner, Gabriel, & Deikman, 2000).

(Copyright 2003 by Randy Glasbergen. www.glasbergen.com)

STRESS MANAGEMENT TECHNIQUES

1. _____
2. _____
3. _____
4. _____

—GLASBERGEN

"Howl at an ambulance or fire siren every chance you get. Run around the room in circles with a sock in your mouth. Eat a messy meal without using your hands or utensils. Ask a friend to scratch your belly..."

■ Gaining Control

As mentioned earlier, we can also relieve stress by acquiring control of situations. Next, we'll discuss five types of control we can use, either alone or in conjunction, in different situations (Bonanno, 2004; Cohen et al., 1986; Higgins & Endler, 1995; Lazarus & Folkman, 1984; Sarafino, 2006).

BEHAVIORAL CONTROL. Behavioral control is the ability to step up and do something to reduce the impact of a stressful situation or prevent its recurrence. As we'll recall, this type of active coping is called *problem-focused* and is generally more effective in relieving stress than *avoidance-oriented coping*—avoiding action to solve our problems or giving up hope (Lazarus & Folkman, 1984; Roth & Cohen, 1986). Research in the United States and Iceland shows that the more high school and college students use problem-focused coping techniques, the less likely they are to develop drinking problems (Rafnsson, Jonsson, & Windle, 2006).

[handwritten: Behavioral Control = do something to reduce impact of stressful problem. (problem-focused)]

[handwritten: Cognitive Control = think (non-negatively) emotions that result from stressful events]

COGNITIVE CONTROL. Cognitive control is the ability to *cognitively restructure or think differently about* negative emotions that arise in response to stress-provoking events (Higgins & Endler, 1995; Lazarus & Folkman, 1984; Skinner et al., 2003). This type of control includes *emotion-focused coping,* which we introduced earlier, a strategy that comes in handy when adjusting to uncertain situations or aversive events we can't control or change. In a novel study, Thomas Strentz and Stephen Auerbach (1988) exposed airline pilots and flight attendants to a simulated hijacking attempt and four days of captivity. During captivity, subjects who received instructions before the abduction to use emotion-focused coping strategies reported less distress than did those who received instructions to use problem-focused coping.

DECISIONAL CONTROL. Decisional control is the ability to choose among alternative courses of action (Sarafino, 2006). We can consult with trusted friends about which classes to take and which professors to avoid, and make decisions about which surgeon to consult to perform a high-stakes operation. *[handwritten: Decisional Control = Ability to choose]*

INFORMATIONAL CONTROL. Informational control is the ability to acquire information about a stressful event. Knowing what types of questions are on the SAT or GRE can help us prepare for them, as can knowing something about the person we're "fixed up with" on an upcoming date. We engage in **proactive coping** when we anticipate stressful situations and take steps to prevent or minimize difficulties before they arise (Greenglass, 2002; Karasek & Theorell, 1990; Schwarzer & Taubert, 2002). People who engage in proactive coping tend to perceive stressful circumstances as opportunities for growth (Greenglass, 2002).

[handwritten: Informational Control = getting info about stressful event]

GRE preparation classes can be one useful source of informational control.

EMOTIONAL CONTROL. Emotional control is the ability to suppress and express emotions. Writing in a diary, for example, can facilitate emotional control and has a host of long-lasting benefits (Pennebaker, 1997). In a now classic study, James Pennebaker and his colleagues (Pennebaker, Kiecolt-Glaser, & Glaser, 1988) asked one group of college students to write about their deepest thoughts and feelings about past traumas for four consecutive days, for 20 minutes a day. They asked another group of students to write about superficial topics. Six weeks after the study, students who "opened up" about their traumatic experiences made fewer visits to the health center and showed signs of improved immune functioning compared with the students who wrote about trivial topics. Replications in laboratories around the world have confirmed that writing about traumatic events can influence a variety of academic, social, and cognitive variables, and improve the health and well-being of people ranging from arthritis sufferers to maximum security prisoners (Campbell & Pennebaker, 2003; Pennebaker & Graybeal, 2001; Smyth et al., 1999); although scientific debate regarding the size of these effects continues (Frisina, Borod, & Lepore, 2004).

The work of James Pennebaker suggests that writing about our stressors can ward off physical illness, although this effect is only modest.

[handwritten: Emotional Control = suppress and express emotions.]

Still, there may be times when it's best to conceal our emotions, such as cloaking our fears when we're giving a speech and suppressing our anger, at least for the moment, when trying to resolve a problem with a coworker (Bonanno et al., 2004; Gross & Muñoz, 1995). As the old saying goes, "There's a time and a place for everything."

replicability

◄ **CAN THE RESULTS BE DUPLICATED IN OTHER STUDIES?**

proactive coping
anticipation of problems and stressful situations that promotes effective coping

? According to research on the expression of anger, how will this girl feel after punching this pillow repeatedly? (See answer upside down at bottom of page.)

Crisis debriefing sessions, in which people discuss their reactions to a traumatic event in a group, may actually increase PTSD risk.

IS CATHARSIS A GOOD THING? Contrary to the popular notion that expressing what we feel is always beneficial, disclosing painful feelings, called *catharsis*, is a double-edged sword. When it involves problem solving and constructive efforts to make troubling situations "right," it can be beneficial. But when catharsis reinforces a sense of helplessness, as when we voice our rage about something we can't or won't change, catharsis can actually be harmful (Littrell, 1998). This finding is worrisome, because a slew of popular psychotherapies rely on catharsis, encouraging clients to "get it out of your system," "get things off your chest," or "let it all hang out." Some of these therapies instruct clients to yell, punch pillows, or throw balls against walls when they become upset (Bushman, Baumeister, & Phillips, 2001; Lewis & Bucher, 1992; Lohr et al., 2007). Yet research shows that these activities rarely reduce our long-term stress, although they may make us feel slightly better for a few moments. In other cases, they actually seem to heighten our anger or anxiety in the long run (Tavris, 1989), perhaps because emotional upset often generates a vicious cycle: We can become distressed about the fact that we're distressed.

DOES CRISIS DEBRIEFING HELP? Some therapists—especially those employed by fire, police, or other emergency services—administer a popular treatment called *crisis debriefing*, which is designed to ward off PTSD among people exposed to trauma. Several thousand crisis debriefers descended on lower Manhattan in the wake of the 9/11 attacks in a well-meaning effort to help traumatized witnesses of the attacks. Crisis debriefing is a single-session procedure, typically conducted in groups, that usually lasts three to four hours. Most often, therapists conduct this procedure within one or two days of a traumatic event, such as a terrible accident. It proceeds according to standardized steps, including strongly encouraging group members to discuss and "process" their negative emotions, listing the posttraumatic symptoms that group members are likely to experience, and discouraging group members from discontinuing participation once the session has started.

Recent studies indicate that crisis debriefing isn't effective for trauma reactions. What's worse, several studies suggest that it may actually increase the risk of PTSD among people exposed to trauma, perhaps because it gets in the way of people's natural coping strategies (Lilienfeld, 2007; Litz et al., 2002; McNally, Bryant, & Ehlers, 2003).

Nor is there much evidence that merely talking about our problems when we're upset is helpful. A systematic review of 61 studies (Meads & Nouwen, 2005) revealed no overall benefits for emotional disclosure (compared with nondisclosure) on a variety of measures of physical and psychological health. None of this implies that we should never discuss our feelings with others when we're upset. But it does mean that doing so is most likely to be beneficial when it allows us to think about and work through our problems in a more constructive light.

■ Flexible Coping

The ability to adjust coping strategies as the situation demands is critical to contending with many stressful situations (Bonanno & Kaltman, 2001; Cheng, 2003; Westphal & Bonanno, 2004). George Bonanno and his colleagues studied students who'd just started college in New York City when terrorists destroyed the World Trade Center in 2001 (Bonanno et al., 2004). They predicted that students who had difficulties with managing their emotions would find the transition to college life particularly difficult. Participants completed a checklist of psychological symptoms at the start of the study and two years later. Those who were better at flexibly controlling their emotions by suppressing or expressing them on demand on a laboratory task reported less distress at the two-year follow-up.

Expending a great deal of effort to suppress and avoid emotions can distract us from problem solving and lead to an unintended consequence: The emotions may return in full or greater force. In fact, the attempt to suppress negative emotions and thoughts associated with aversive events tends to backfire and increase the very negative experiences we're struggling so hard to avoid (Beck et al., 2006; Richards, Bulter, & Gross, 2003; Wegner, 2005). Accepting circumstances and feelings we can't change, and finding positive ways of thinking about our problems, can be a potent means of contending with stressful situations (Skinner et al., 2003).

■ Individual Differences: Attitudes, Beliefs, and Personality

Some people survive almost unimaginably horrific circumstances with few or no visible psychological scars, whereas others view the world through the dark lens of pessimism and crumble when the little things in life don't go their way. Our attitudes, personality, and socialization shape our reactions—for better and worse—to potential stressors.

HARDINESS: CHALLENGE, COMMITMENT, AND CONTROL. More than three decades ago, Salvatore Maddi and his colleagues (Kobasa, Hiller, & Maddi, 1979) initiated a study of the qualities of stress-resistant people. They found that resilient people possess a set of attitudes they called **hardiness**. Hardy people view change as a challenge rather than a threat, are committed to their life and work, and believe they can control events (Maddi, 2004).

Suzanne Kobasa and Maddi asked 670 managers at a public utility to report their stressful experiences on a checklist. Then they selected executives who scored high on both stress and illness, and another group who scored equally high on stress but reported below-average levels of illness. Managers who showed high stress but low levels of illness were more oriented to challenge and higher in their sense of control over events, and felt a deep sense of involvement in their work and social lives.

When we're physically ill, we don't usually feel especially hardy. So we can appreciate the fact that another explanation for Kobasa and Maddi's findings is that illness creates negative attitudes, rather than the other way around. To address the question of causal direction, Maddi and Kobasa (1984) conducted a longitudinal study (see Chapter 10) of changes in health and attitudes over time. At the end of two years, people whose attitudes toward life reflected high levels of control, commitment, and challenge remained healthier than those whose attitudes didn't. Hardiness also can boost stress resistance among nurses in hospice settings, immigrants adjusting to life in the United States, and military personnel who survive life-threatening stressors (Atri, Sharma, & Cottrell, 2006; Bartone, 1999; Maddi, 2002). Still, because hardiness is closely associated with low levels of anxiety-proneness, it's not entirely clear whether hardiness itself—as opposed to a general tendency to react calmly to life stressors—is the major predictor of successful coping (Coifman et al., 2007; Sinclair & Tetrick, 2000; Smeets et al., 2010).

OPTIMISM. We know them when we meet them. Optimistic people have a rosy outlook and don't dwell on the dark side of life. Even on a cloudy day, we can bask in their sunshine. As we learned in Chapter 11, there are some distinct advantages to being optimistic. Optimistic people are more productive, focused, persistent, and better at handling frustration than pessimists (Peterson, 2000; Seligman, 1990). Optimism is also associated with a lower mortality rate (Stern, Dhanda, & Hazunda, 2001), a more vigorous immune response (Segerstrom et al., 1998), lower distress in infertile women trying to have a child (Abbey, Halman, & Andrews, 1992), better surgical outcomes (Scheier et al., 1989), and fewer physical complaints (Scheier & Carver, 1992).

SPIRITUALITY AND RELIGIOUS INVOLVEMENT. Spirituality is the search for the sacred, which may or may not extend to belief in God. Spiritual and religious beliefs play vital roles in many of our lives. According to a Harris Poll (Taylor, 2009), 82 percent of Americans believe in God. Compared with nonreligious people, people who describe themselves as religious (who say they believe in God) have lower mortality rates, improved immune system functioning, lower blood pressure, and a greater ability to recover from illnesses (Koenig, McCullough, & Larson, 2001; Levin, 2001; Matthews, Larson, & Barry, 1993). One explanation for these findings is that religious involvements activate a healing energy that scientists

Research suggests that instructing someone *not* to think of something, like a white bear, often results in increases in the very thought the person is trying to suppress (Wegner et al., 1987).

> **hardiness**
> set of attitudes marked by a sense of control over events, commitment to life and work, and courage and motivation to confront stressful events

correlation vs. causation
CAN WE BE SURE THAT A CAUSES B?

> **spirituality**
> search for the sacred, which may or may not extend to belief in God

ruling out rival hypotheses
HAVE IMPORTANT ALTERNATIVE EXPLANATIONS FOR THE FINDINGS BEEN EXCLUDED?

Optimists—who proverbially see the glass as "half full," rather than "half empty"—are more likely than pessimists to view change as a challenge.

falsifiability

CAN THE CLAIM BE DISPROVED?

can't measure (Ellison & Levin, 1998). As we'll see in our discussion of energy medicines, however, explanations that depend on an undetectable force or energy can't be falsified and therefore lie outside the boundaries of science.

The correlation between religiosity and physical health isn't easy to interpret. Some authors have measured religiosity by counting how often people attend church or other religious services and found that such attendance is associated with better physical health. But this correlation is potentially attributable to a confound: People who are sick are less likely to attend religious services than healthy people, so the causal arrow may be reversed (Sloan et al., 1999).

correlation vs. causation

CAN WE BE SURE THAT A CAUSES B?

Research on the links between spirituality and religious involvement, on the one hand, and health, on the other, is limited (Powell, Shahabi, & Thoresen, 2003). But until more definitive evidence is available, let's consider several potential reasons why spirituality and religious involvements may be a boon to many people. ◉ Watch

◉ Watch Religion and Longevity on mypsychlab.com

1. Many religions foster self-control and prohibit risky health behaviors, including alcohol, drugs, and unsafe sexual practices (McCullough, & Willoughby, 2009).

2. Religious engagement, such as attendance at services, often boosts social support and increases marital satisfaction (Orathinkal & Vansteenwegen, 2006).

3. A sense of meaning and purpose, control over life, positive emotions, and positive appraisals of stressful situations associated with prayer and religious activities may enhance coping (Potts, 2004).

RUMINATION: RECYCLING THE MENTAL GARBAGE. So far we've considered adaptive ways of coping with taxing circumstances without becoming unhinged. But some ways of reacting to stressful situations are clearly counterproductive. Susan Nolen-Hoeksema

Answers are located at the end of the text.

STRESS REDUCTION AND RELAXATION TECHNIQUES

evaluating CLAIMS

We all have stress in our lives, whether it comes from our coursework, jobs, families, or all three. The Internet offers a wide array of techniques for reducing stress, but it's often difficult to identify which techniques are supported by sound science. Let's evaluate some of these claims, which are modeled after actual stress-reduction websites.

"Here are some helpful tips for reducing stress. Remember, there is *no 'one size fits all' solution* and all of these methods require that you *change the way you approach and deal with potential stressors* in your life."
This site avoids exaggerated claims by acknowledging that there's no miracle cure for stress. The methods of stress reduction and relief differ for every person and require us to make changes in our lives.

"Our *all-natural pills* allow you to *wipe away all the stress in your life—instantly and naturally.*"
What's wrong with this advertiser's claim that the pills offer an "all-natural" approach to stress-reduction? Does the promise to eliminate all forms of stress in your life seem plausible? Why or why not?

"*Top experts agree that Trans-Cortex space-dimensional music CDs can relax up to 90% of overstressed listeners!*"
How much weight should we give to statements that appeal to the authority of unnamed "top experts" who endorse a product with a fancy-sounding, made-up name? What might be the problem with statistics that claim a success rate of "up to 90%"?

(1987) suggested that recycling negative events in our minds can lead us to become depressed. More specifically, some of us spend a great deal of time *ruminating*—focusing on how bad we feel and endlessly analyzing the causes and consequences of our problems.

 Nolen-Hoeksema (2000, 2003) contended that women have much higher rates and more frequent bouts of depression than men (see Chapter 15) because they tend to ruminate more than men. In contrast, when stressed out, men are more likely to focus on pleasurable or distracting activities such as work, watching football games, or drinking copious amounts of alcohol (which we don't recommend). They also adopt a more direct approach to solving their problems than do women (Nolen-Hoeksema, 2002). Early socialization may in part pave the way for these differing reactions (Nolen-Hoeksema & Girgus, 1994). Although parents encourage girls to analyze and talk about their problems, they often actively discourage boys from expressing their feelings and instead encourage them to take action or tough it out. Still, men and women alike can benefit from cutting down on rumination and confronting their problems head-on.

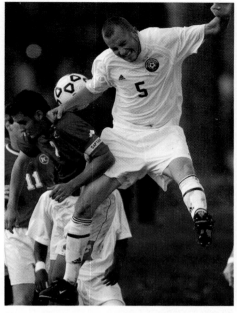

Men may be more likely than women to play sports, which often decreases the tendency to ruminate when stressed out.

✔ **Study** and **Review** on **mypsychlab.com**

assess your knowledge — FACT OR FICTION?

1. Researchers have found a strong connection between social support and people's chance of dying over a nine-year period. **True** / **False**
2. One general coping strategy tends to work for all situations. **True** / **False**
3. Optimistic people are especially skilled at tolerating frustration. **True** / **False**
4. Participation in religious activities can increase social support. **True** / **False**
5. Rumination is usually an adaptive strategy for dealing with anxiety and depression. **True** / **False**

Answers: 1. T (p. 470); 2. F (p. 472); 3. T (p. 473); 4. T (p. 474); 5. F (p. 475).

PROMOTING GOOD HEALTH—AND LESS STRESS!

12.10 Identify four behaviors that contribute to a healthy lifestyle.

12.11 Identify reasons why it is difficult to change our lifestyles.

12.12 Describe different alternative and complementary medical approaches and compare their effectiveness with placebos.

If we could all reduce or eliminate stress in our lives, the public health consequences would be enormous. Stress is a risk factor for many behaviors, such as smoking and alcohol abuse, which are themselves risk factors for many illnesses. What can we do to decrease stress-related diseases and modify our health-destructive habits? **Health psychology**, also called *behavioral medicine*, is a rapidly growing field that has contributed to our understanding of the influences of stress and other psychological factors on physical disorders.

 Health psychologists integrate behavioral sciences with the practice of medicine (Gatchel & Baum, 1983). They also combine educational and psychological interventions to promote and maintain health, and prevent and treat illness (France et al., 2008; Leventhal et al. 2006; Matarazzo, 1980). Health psychologists work in hospitals, rehabilitation centers, medical schools, industry, government agencies, and academic and research settings. Interventions developed within health psychology include teaching patients stress management skills and pain reduction techniques, and helping people to mobilize social support, comply with medical regimens, and pursue healthy lifestyles.

"I'm learning how to relax, doctor — but I want to relax *better* and *faster*! I want to be on the cutting edge of relaxation!"

(Randy Glasbergen, www.glasbergen.com. Used by permission.)

health psychology
field of psychology, also called behavioral medicine, that integrates the behavioral sciences with the practice of medicine

Health psychologists use a variety of educational and behavioral interventions to promote and maintain health, and assist people in coping with serious illnesses.

■ Toward a Healthy Lifestyle

Health psychologists help patients break the grip of unhealthy habits. Smoking, excessive drinking, and overeating can be triggered by stress, and can be maintained when these activities reduce stress (Polivy, Schueneman, & Carlson, 1976; Young, Oei, & Knight, 1990). Among women who are sexual assault survivors, drinking to reduce distress places them at risk for alcoholism (Ullman et al., 2005). Smokers are four times more likely to suffer from clinical depression as nonsmokers and may smoke in part to relieve distress (Breslau, Kilby, & Andreski, 1993). According to a survey of more than 2,000 adults (American Psychological Association, 2006), one in four Americans uses food to relieve stress and cope with problems. Unfortunately, when we engage in unhealthy behaviors that reduce stress in the short run, we place ourselves at risk for health and stress-related problems in the long run. We'll next examine four behaviors that can counteract these negative cycles and promote health.

HEALTHY BEHAVIOR #1: STOP SMOKING. Smoking ranks as the leading cause of preventable disease and death in the United States (Centers for Disease Control and Prevention, 2005). In America, about 24 percent of men and 18 percent of women smoke cigarettes (Centers for Disease Control and Prevention, 2007b). These statistics are alarming given that one in four regular smokers dies of a smoking-related disease (Woloshin, Schwartz, & Welch, 2002). A 30- to 40-year-old male cigarette smoker with a two-pack-a-day habit loses about eight years of his life on average (Green, 2000). Smoking doubles our chances of dying from either CHD or stroke (McBride, 1992) and is responsible for one-third of all cancer deaths (Haxby, 1995). Smoking is also the primary cause of lung disease among men and women (U.S. Department of Health and Human Services, 1990; Woloshin et al., 2002).

Although as many as 80 percent of smokers want to stop smoking, only about 5 percent of the approximately 40 percent of U.S. smokers who try to stop each year on their own succeed (American Psychiatric Association, 2000; Schoenborn et al., 2004). Mark Twain captured the challenges that smokers face in his famous quote: "Giving up smoking is the easiest thing in the world. I know because I've done it thousands of times."

Health psychologists make smoking treatment and prevention a high priority. Stop-smoking approaches typically educate people about the health consequences of smoking and teach smokers to manage stress. They also help smokers to pinpoint and avoid high-risk situations associated with past smoking, such as parties and bars (Marlatt & Gordon, 1985; Miller & Rollnick, 2002). These strategies are effective with 25 to 35 percent of long-term smokers and are also helpful for people who eat or drink excessively.

Each time people try to stop smoking, their chances of their succeeding improve (Lynn & Kirsch, 2006). People who stop smoking live longer than those who don't, and women who stop smoking during the first few months of pregnancy reduce their risk of problem pregnancies (such as low-birth-weight babies) to that of women who've never smoked. After 10 to 15 years of nonsmoking, an ex-smoker's risk of premature death approaches that of someone who's never smoked (National Cancer Institute, 2000). So, if you're a smoker, don't quit your attempts to quit!

HEALTHY BEHAVIOR #2: CURB ALCOHOL CONSUMPTION. According to a recent survey, more than 60 percent of adults reported having drunk alcohol in the past year (National Center for Health Statistics, 2003). Repeated bouts of heavy drinking, especially *heavy episodic drinking* (formerly called binge drinking)—defined as drinking five or more drinks on one occasion for men and four or more drinks on one occasion for women—is associated with increases in many different types of cancer, serious and sometimes fatal liver problems, pregnancy complications, and brain shrinkage and other neurological problems (Bagnardi et al., 2001).

Several controversial studies (French & Zavala, 2007; Mukamal et al., 2003, 2005) suggest that light to moderate drinking—defined as two drinks per day for men and one drink per day for women—lessen the risk of heart disease and stroke. Nevertheless, a rival explanation for these findings is that people who drink only moderate amounts of alcohol, such as wine, may have higher incomes and healthier lifestyles compared with people who either abstain from drinking or drink more than two drinks at a sitting (Lieber, 2003; Saarni et al., 2008).

Evidence is clear that heavy drinking can produce long-term physical problems.

ruling out rival hypotheses

HAVE IMPORTANT ALTERNATIVE EXPLANATIONS FOR THE FINDINGS BEEN EXCLUDED?

Another hypothesis is that people who abstain are in poorer health to begin with than are light or moderate drinkers. Nevertheless, systematic reviews of studies comparing drinkers with nondrinkers who abstained because they chose to do so (not because of poor health, disability, or weakness) found no health differences between drinkers and teetotalers (Fillmore et al., 2006).

At this time, we can't be sure that any amount of alcohol is safe, much less good for our health. One thing's reasonably certain, however: Drinking heavily is associated with a heightened risk of cardiovascular disease (Bagnardi et al., 2001). Fortunately, many of the negative effects of alcohol, including changes in the brain, can be reversed or minimized when we abstain from drinking (Tyas, 2001).

HEALTHY BEHAVIOR #3: ACHIEVE A HEALTHY WEIGHT. The statistics tell the grim story. As of 2006, two-thirds of adult Americans were overweight, and about a third of these Americans are obese, as indicated by a statistic known as the *body mass index (BMI)* (see **FIGURE 12.5**) (Ogden et al., 2007). The number of obese children and adolescents has tripled over the past decade or so, signaling an ominous trend (Ogden et al., 2006). According to some researchers, our society faces an "obesity epidemic" of enormous proportions, due in large measure to decreases in our physical activity (Heini & Weinsier, 1997; Wing & Polley, 2001).

The Effects of Weight on Health. People who are obese are at heightened risk of heart disease, stroke, high blood pressure, arthritis, some types of cancer, respiratory problems, and diabetes (Klein et al., 2004; Kurth et al., 2003). Exercise is one of the best means of shedding that annoying fat around the belly and of losing weight over the long haul (Pronk & Wing, 1994). The more inactive we are and the more time we spend watching television, the more likely we are to be obese (Ching et al., 1996; Gortmaker et al., 1993). Of course, these findings are only correlational; it's also possible that people who are obese are weaker and less energetic, and become couch potatoes as a result. Indeed, there's considerable controversy over how much of the negative association between obesity and physical health is due to obesity itself as opposed to the behaviors that often go along with it, such as inactivity and poor nutrition (Campos, 2004; Johnson, 2005).

If an obese person, say a 300-pound man, sheds even 10 percent of his weight, his health will improve (Wing & Polley, 2001). Losing weight reduces blood pressure, cholesterol, and the risk of diabetes (Kanders & Blackburn, 1992), and often has the added benefit of reducing anxiety and improving mood (Wadden & Stunkard, 1993).

Overweight individuals suffer from a variety of social and emotional problems, too. Many obese children are subject to teasing (Thompson et al., 2005). When they become adolescents and adults, they often experience discrimination in the social arena and workplace (Crandall, 1994; Schwartz, et al., 2006). In one study of 9,125 adults, obese people were 25 percent more likely to suffer from depression or an anxiety disorder compared with people of normal weight (Simon et al., 2006). It's not clear whether depression triggers obesity, or whether obesity sets the stage for depression. Yet the positive association between obesity and depression counters the popular stereotype of the obese person as cheerful or "jolly" (Roberts et al., 2002). Our negative attitudes toward obesity run so deep that 46 percent of people say they'd rather give up at least a year of their lives than be obese, and 30 percent would rather be divorced than obese (Schwartz et al., 2006).

Clearly, overweight people suffer in many respects. Researchers followed a group of people age 16 to 24 for seven years (Gortmaker et al., 1993). At the end of the study, individuals who were overweight were less wealthy, didn't progress as far in school, and were

Calculate BMI by dividing weight in pounds (lbs) by height in inches (in) squared and multiplying by a conversion factor of 703.

Example: Weight = 155 lbs, height = 5'9" (69)
Calculation: $[155 \div (69)^2] \times 703 = 22.89$

BMI	Weight Status
Below 18.5	Underweight
18.5 to 24.9	Normal
25.0 to 29.9	Overweight
30.0 and above	Obese

Height	Weight Range	BMI	Weight Status
	124 lbs or less	Below 18.5	Underweight
5'9"	125 lbs to 168 lbs	18.5 to 24.9	Normal
	169 lbs to 202 lbs	25.0 to 29.9	Overweight
	203 lbs or more	30 or higher	Obese

FIGURE 12.5 Body Mass Index (BMI) and Weight Status. (*Source:* Centers for Disease Control and Prevention, 2007a, Division of Nutrition and Physical Activity National Center for Chronic Disease Prevention and Health Promotion)

◄ **correlation vs. causation**
CAN WE BE SURE THAT A CAUSES B?

Being overweight or obese increases the risk of various physical health problems, and is also associated with depression and other adjustment difficulties.

◄ **correlation vs. causation**
CAN WE BE SURE THAT A CAUSES B?

TABLE 12.2 Reasons for Obesity in America Aside from Diet and Lack of Exercise.

(1) Lack of adequate sleep, which directly causes weight gain.

(2) Endocrine disruptors in foods that modify fats in the body.

(3) Comfortable temperatures as a result of heating/air conditioning that decrease calories burned from sweating and shivering.

(4) Use of medicines that contribute to weight gain.

(5) Increases in certain segments of the population, including Hispanics and middle-aged people, who have higher rates of obesity.

(6) Increase in mothers who give birth at older ages, which is associated with heavier children.

(7) Genetic influences during pregnancy.

(8) Moderately overweight people may have an evolutionary advantage over very thin people and be more likely to survive: Darwinian natural selection.

(9) People tend to marry people with a similar body type, a phenomenon called *assortative mating*. When heavy people reproduce, they're likely to give birth to relatively heavy children.

ruling out rival hypotheses

HAVE IMPORTANT ALTERNATIVE EXPLANATIONS FOR THE FINDINGS BEEN EXCLUDED?

replicability

CAN THE RESULTS BE DUPLICATED IN OTHER STUDIES?

less likely to be married. These changes occurred independently of intelligence and financial status at the start of the study, bolstering the claim that prejudice and discrimination account for the plight of overweight people (see **TABLE 12.2**).

Tips for Achieving a Healthy Weight. Given the many social and medical reasons for losing weight, it's no wonder that people have tried all manner of products and diets touted as effective for weight loss. The fad treatments include appetite-suppressing eyeglasses, magic weight-loss earrings, electrical muscle stimulators, and "magnet diet pills" to flush fat out of the body—all of which are entirely devoid of scientific support (Corbett, 2006). Many fad diets offer conflicting and confusing recommendations based on little more than someone's pet theory, rather than careful research that's been replicated. Some of our favorite fad diets include the "cabbage soup" diet, in which you feast on little more than—guess what?—cabbage soup (sounds yummy, doesn't it?), the popcorn diet (ideal for compulsive movie-goers), and the grapefruit diet (Danbrot, 2004; Herskowitz, 1987; Thompson & Ahrens, 2004). Some people on these diets may experience dramatic short-term weight loss, but this loss is almost always followed by a gradual return of the initial weight (Brownell & Rodin, 1994), resulting in the well-known "yo-yo effect" that often accompanies dieting. *Crash diets*—those in which people severely restrict calories (often down to 1,000 calories per day for several weeks)—aren't likely to result in long-term weight loss and are unhealthy (Shade et al., 2004).

Recently, researchers found that overweight people on the popular Atkins high-fat, low-carbohydrate diet lost more weight than their counterparts on other diets, including a low-fat, high-carbohydrate diet with plenty of fruits, vegetables, and pasta (Gardner et al., 2007). Nevertheless, people who follow a low-fat diet for one year report more positive moods and a greater sense of well-being compared with people who follow a low-carbohydrate diet (Brinkworth et al., 2009). Importantly, after six months, people on most or all diets begin to regain their weight and stray from their diet plans. The bottom line? It's a challenge to lose weight, on a long-term basis, on any diet (Mann et al., 2007). Yet about 20 percent of people can lose at least 10 percent of their body weight and keep it off for at least a year (Wing & Hill, 2001).

One variable affecting our dieting success is our genes. Perhaps as much as half of the differences in people's tendency to become overweight is genetically influenced

The huge number of diet books published each year can be bewildering to people who are trying to lose weight. How many of these books are based on adequate science?

(Bouchard, 1995; Wing & Polley, 2001). Researchers have pinpointed genes associated with obesity, which appear related to appetite and energy use (Bouchard et al., 2004; Campfield, Smith, & Burn, 1996). These discoveries suggest that it might one day be possible to develop drugs that switch genes on and off to control weight. But while we're waiting, there's much we can do to achieve a stable, healthy weight, regardless of our genetic heritage.

Here's some basic yet scientifically supported advice to follow for controlling our weight and eating a healthy diet:

1. Exercise regularly.
2. Monitor total calories and body weight (Wing & Hill, 2001).
3. Eat foods with "good fats," such as olive oil and fish oil to protect against heart disease, lower your salt and caffeine intake to reduce blood pressure, and eat high fiber foods to lower the risk of CHD and diabetes (Cook, 2008; Covas, Konstantinidou, & Fito, 2009; Vuksan et al., 2009).
4. Get lots of help from your social network to support your efforts to lose weight (Wing & Jeffrey, 1999).
5. Control portion size. By all means, don't make a habit of "supersizing" your cheeseburgers and fries (see Chapter 11).

HEALTHY BEHAVIOR #4: EXERCISE. Help for some psychological ailments may be as close as our running shoes. Jogging, swimming, bicycling and other regular **aerobic exercises**, which promote the use of oxygen in the body, can lower blood pressure and risk for CHD, improve lung function, relieve the symptoms of arthritis, decrease diabetes risk, and cut the risk of breast and colon cancer (Barbour, Houle, & Dubbert, 2003; Wei et al., 1999). Running, weight lifting, and yoga for eight weeks or longer can also improve cardiovascular recovery from stress (Chafin, Christenfeld & Gerin, 2008), and relieve depression (Mutrie, 1988; Palmer, 1995; Stathopoulou et al., 2006) and anxiety (Landers, 1998; Phillips, Kiernan, & King, 2001).

Contrary to the popular "no pain, no gain" belief that exercise must be vigorous and sustained to do any good, 30 minutes of activity on most days of the week, including gardening and cleaning our rooms, can lead to improved fitness and health (Blair et al., 1992; Pate et al., 1995). In a study in Finland (Paffenbarger et al., 1986), middle-aged men who didn't get much physical activity on the job but who burned off 2,000 calories (the equivalent of about four Big Macs) a week in their spare time lived two and a half years longer on average than men who were less active in their leisure hours. Of course, people who are less active may be less physically fit to begin with, so the causal arrow may run in both directions. Although even moderate exercise—at about the level of a brisk walk—can reap health benefits, including improved cognitive functioning in older adults and perhaps even the growth of neurons (Erickson & Kramer, 2009), more sustained and vigorous exercise is needed to reach our fitness potential.

Aerobic exercise, including rowing, swimming, and biking, is an excellent way to lose weight, stay fit, and maintain or even improve cardiovascular health.

aerobic exercise
exercise that promotes the use of oxygen in the body

correlation vs. causation

CAN WE BE SURE THAT A CAUSES B?

BUT CHANGING LIFESTYLES IS EASIER SAID THAN DONE. Why do we have difficulty changing our lifestyles, even when we know that bad habits can endanger our health? As many as 30 to 70 percent of patients don't take their physician's medical advice (National Heart, Lung, and Blood Institute, 1998), and as many as 80 percent don't follow their physician's recommendations to exercise, stop smoking, change their diet, or take prescribed medications (Berlant & Pruitt, 2003). The extent of some medical noncompliance is truly staggering. Paula Vincent (1971) found that 58 percent of patients with glaucoma, a serious eye disease, didn't take their prescribed eye drops, even though they knew that their failure to do so could make them go blind!

Personal Inertia. One reason for noncompliance is that it's difficult to overcome personal inertia—to try something new. Many self-destructive habits relieve stress and don't create an imminent health threat, so it's easy for us to "let things be." Eating a heaping portion of ice cream doesn't seem terribly dangerous when we view heart disease as a distant and uncertain catastrophe. John Norcross and his colleagues found that only 19 percent of those who made a New Year's resolution to change a problem behavior, including changing their diet or exercising more, maintained the change when followed up two years later (Norcross, Ratzin, & Payne, 1988; Norcross & Vangerelli, 1989).

Misestimating Risk. Another reason we maintain the status quo is that we underestimate certain risks to our health and overestimate others. To illustrate this point, try answering the following three questions before reading on:

In the United States, which causes more deaths?

1. All types of accidents combined, or strokes?

2. All motor vehicle (car, truck, bus, and motorcycle) accidents combined, or digestive cancer?

3. Diabetes, or homicide?

The answers are (1) strokes (by about twofold), (2) digestive cancer (by about threefold), and (3) diabetes (by about fourfold). If you got one or more of these questions wrong (and most people do), the odds are you relied on the *availability heuristic* (see Chapter 2)—the mental shortcut by which we judge the likelihood of an event by the ease with which it comes to mind (Hertwig, Pachur, & Kurzenhauser, 2005; Tversky & Kahneman, 1974). Because the news media provide far more coverage of dramatic accidents and homicides than strokes, digestive cancer, or diabetes, we overestimate the probability of accidents and homicides and underestimate the probability of many diseases. And because the media feature so many emotional and memorable stories of famous women who've developed breast cancer, we're likely to think of breast cancer as a more frequent and deadly illness than heart disease (Ruscio, 2000). Heart disease is less newsworthy precisely because it's more commonplace, and perhaps less terrifying, than cancer with its troubling treatment-related side effects, including very obvious hair loss.

In general, we underestimate the frequency of the most common causes of death, and overestimate the frequency of the least common causes of death (Lichtenstein et al., 1978). These errors in judgment can be costly: If women believe heart disease isn't a threat, they may not change their lifestyle.

Many of us are well aware of health risks, but don't take them to "heart," pun intended. Smokers greatly overestimate their chances of living to the age of 75 (Schoenbaum, 1997). Others of us rationalize our lifestyle choices by telling ourselves, "Something's going to kill me anyway, so I might as well enjoy my life and do whatever I want."

Feeling Powerless. Still others of us feel powerless to change, perhaps because our habits are so deeply ingrained. Consider a person who's smoked a pack of cigarettes a day for the last 15 years. She's inhaled cigarette smoke over a million times. It's no wonder she feels helpless to change her habit.

If we told you that four fully loaded jumbo jets were crashing every day in the United States, you'd be outraged. Yet the equivalent of that number—about 1,200 people—die each day in America from smoking-related causes (Centers for Disease Control and Prevention, 2005). How likely is it we'll actually die in a plane crash? Not likely at all, even if we spend years racking up our frequent-flier miles. We'd need to fly in commercial airliners for about 10,000 years straight—that is, around the clock without any breaks—before the odds of our dying in a plane crash exceed 50 percent. But because plane crashes make big news, we overestimate their frequency.

FICTOID ✕

MYTH: Being a postal worker is among the most dangerous of all occupations.

REALITY: Despite sensational media reports of shootings in mailroom offices (the origin of the phrase "going postal"), deaths among postal workers from violence are extremely rare. For example, the lifetime odds of a postal worker being killed on the job are one in 370,000, compared with the lifetime odds of one in 15,000 for a farmer and one in 7,300 for a construction worker (Ropeik & Gray, 2002). But because postal shootings tend to garner considerable publicity, we overestimate their frequency.

PREVENTION PROGRAMS. Because modifying such deeply entrenched behaviors can be so difficult, we're best off not developing them in the first place. Prevention efforts should begin by adolescence, if not earlier, because the earlier in life we develop unhealthy habits, the more likely they'll create problems, like alcohol abuse, for us later in life (Hingson, Heeren, & Winter, 2006). Health psychologists have developed prevention programs that contain the following elements:

- educating young people about the risks and negative consequences of obesity, smoking, and excessive drinking;
- educating young people about positive health behaviors, such as good nutrition and the importance of exercise;
- teaching young people to recognize and resist peer pressure to engage in unhealthy behaviors;
- exposing young people to positive role models who don't drink or smoke;
- teaching effective coping skills for daily living and dealing with stressful life events.

But not all prevention efforts are successful. The Drug Abuse Resistance Education, or DARE, program is used in schools nationwide to teach students how to avoid getting into drugs, gangs, and violent activities (Ringwalt & Greene, 1993). The program uses police officers and targets fifth and sixth graders. It emphasizes the negative aspects of excessive drinking and substance abuse, and the positive aspects of self-esteem and healthy life choices. The program is popular with school administrators and parents; there's a good chance you've seen DARE bumper stickers on cars in your neighborhood. Nevertheless, researchers have repeatedly found that the program doesn't produce positive long-term effects on substance abuse or boost self-esteem (Lynam et al., 1999). A few researchers have even found that it may occasionally backfire to produce increases in substance abuse (Lilienfeld, 2007; Werch & Owen, 2002). Programs that focus on coping skills and managing stress generally show better treatment and prevention outcomes (MacKillop et al., 2003). These findings remind us that we need to evaluate programs carefully before they're widely promoted based on their intuitive appeal alone.

Despite its popularity, the DARE program isn't effective for preventing substance abuse or enhancing self-esteem.

■ Complementary and Alternative Medicine

What do the following three practices have in common?

1. Drinking a solution of snake venom that's diluted to the point that it's not harmful.
2. Placing thin needles in the external ear to relieve nausea following an operation.
3. Manipulating the spine to treat pain and prevent disease.

The answer: Each is an alternative or nonstandard treatment that falls outside the mainstream of modern medicine. **Alternative medicine** refers to health care practices and products used *in place of* conventional medicine, that is, medicine for which there's solid evidence of safety and effectiveness. **Complementary medicine**, in contrast, refers to products and practices that are used *together with* conventional medicine (National Center for Complementary and Alternative Medicine, 2002). Together, both forms of medicine are known as CAM (complementary and alternative medicine). What unites them is that they've not yet been shown to be safe and effective using scientific standards (Bausell, 2007; Singh & Ernst, 2008).

THE SCOPE OF ALTERNATIVE HEALTH CARE. Each year, Americans fork out about $34 billion to CAM practitioners and to purchase CAM products (Nahin et al., 2009). In the National Health Interview Survey, 38 percent of adults and 12 percent of children reported using some form of CAM (not including prayer) over the preceding year (Barnes, Bloom, & Nahin, 2008). We can examine various CAM therapies in **TABLE 12.3** (on page 482).

alternative medicine
health care practices and products used in place of conventional medicine

complementary medicine
health care practices and products used together with conventional medicine

TABLE 12.3 Use of CAM Therapies among American Adults

TYPE OF THERAPY	PERCENTAGE OF USERS DURING THE PREVIOUS YEAR
Natural Products	17.7%
Deep Breathing	12.7%
Meditation	9.4%
Chiropractic and Related Methods	8.6%
Massage	8.3%
Yoga	6.1%
Diet-Based Therapies	3.6%
Progressive Relaxation	2.9%
Guided Imagery	2.2%
Homeopathy	1.8%
Acupuncture	1.4%
Biofeedback	0.2%

Statistics taken from 2007 National Health Interview Survey (Barnes et al., 2008)

FICTOID

MYTH: Magnets, such as those embedded in shoe insoles, can reduce pain.

REALITY: Most controlled studies show that magnets are useless in alleviating pain, including foot pain, when compared with fake (placebo) magnets (Winemiller et al., 2003).

BIOLOGICALLY BASED THERAPIES: VITAMINS, HERBS, AND FOOD SUPPLEMENTS. Americans shell out more than $22 billion each year for herbal treatments of uncertain effectiveness (Gupta, 2007; Walach & Kirsch, 2003). Yet many herbal and natural preparations that some once viewed as promising have generally been found to be no more effective than a placebo (Bausell, 2007; see Chapter 2). Negative findings have challenged still-popular beliefs that:

- the herb St. John's Wort can alleviate the symptoms of moderate to severe depression (Davidson et al., 2002);
- shark cartilage can cure some cancers (Loprinzi et al., 2005);
- the widely used supplements glucosamine and chondroitin, found naturally in the body but extracted from animal tissue, relieve mild arthritis pain (Reichenbach et al., 2007);
- acai berries can improve sexual performance, increase energy, and aid digestion and weight loss (Bender, 2008; Cassileth, Heitzer, & Wesa, 2009); and
- an extract from the leaves of the ginkgo biloba tree slows cognitive decline in aging adults, prevents Alzheimer's disease, and reduces heart attacks or strokes (DeKosky et al., 2008; Kuller et al., 2010; see Chapter 7).

Many vitamins and dietary supplements haven't fared well, either. Dietary supplementation with calcium doesn't prevent much bone loss in women (Jackson et al., 2006); vitamin C doesn't markedly decrease the severity or duration of colds (Douglas et al., 2004); and high doses of vitamin E may actually increase the risk of death from many causes (Miller et al., 2005). Vitamin deficiencies can cause serious health problems, but there isn't much benefit in taking "mega doses" of vitamins or minerals far in excess of recommended amounts. Even two-time Nobel Prize–winner Linus Pauling was convinced that taking huge doses of vitamin C—up to 10 grams, well over 100 times the recommended daily allowance—could ward off cancer and other diseases. Yet research suggests that these and similar practices may be bad for our health (Bjelakovic et al., 2007; Lawson et al., 2007).

The U.S. Food and Drug Administration (FDA) carefully regulates most medicines. But because of controversial congressional legislation passed in 1999, it no longer monitors the safety, purity, or effectiveness of herbs, vitamins, or dietary supplements. So if we go to our local drugstore and purchase a bottle of St. John's Wort or ginkgo (see Chapter 7), we're gambling with our safety. Some impure herbal preparations contain dangerous amounts of lead and even the poison arsenic (Ernst, 2002). Still other supplements, such as kava (extracted from a shrub, and used for anxiety and insomnia), prompted the FDA to issue a warning about liver damage (Saper et al., 2004). Some natural products can also interfere with the actions of conventional medicines. For example, St. John's Wort can block the effectiveness of drugs used to combat AIDS and blood clots (Gupta, 2007). Just because something is natural doesn't mean that it's necessarily safe or healthy for us (as we note in Chapter 13, Table 13.3, this false belief is called the *natural commonplace*). Finally, because the FDA doesn't monitor these products, there's no guarantee that they even contain what they claim to contain.

MANIPULATIVE AND BODY-BASED METHODS: THE EXAMPLE OF CHIROPRACTIC MEDICINE.

Chief among body-based methods is *chiropractic manipulation*, which is, not surprisingly, practiced by chiropractors. Chiropractors are health professionals who manipulate the spine to treat a wide range of pain-related conditions and injuries and often provide nutritional and lifestyle counseling. Nearly 20 percent of Americans report having visited a chiropractor (Barnes et al., 2004). Unlike medical doctors, chiropractors can't perform surgeries or prescribe medications. Historically, the practice of chiropractic medicine was based on the idea that irregularities in the alignment of the spine, known as *subluxations,* prevent the nervous and immune systems from functioning properly. The subluxation theory has no scientific support, and even some chiropractors don't subscribe to it. Moreover, although chiropractic procedures may sometimes be helpful, they're no better than standard

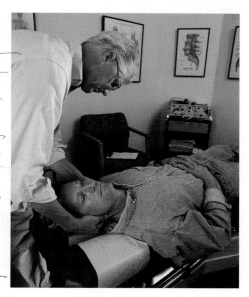

Chiropractors typically manipulate the spine and muscles to treat a variety of health problems. But there's little evidence that their approaches are more effective than those derived from traditional medicine.

approaches, including exercise, general practitioner care, pain relievers, and physical therapy (Assendelft et al., 2003; Astin & Ernst, 2002). More important, there's no evidence that these procedures can cure cancers or other diseases not associated with back problems. Still, some people may benefit from the attention, support, and advice they receive from chiropractors, which may relieve stress and create a strong placebo effect.

MIND-BODY MEDICINE: BIOFEEDBACK AND MEDITATION.

Biofeedback is feedback by a device that provides almost an immediate output of a biological function, such as heart rate or skin temperature (Miller, 1978). Over time, some patients can learn to use this feedback to modify physiological responses associated with stress or illness. Nevertheless, health psychologists have raised questions about whether biofeedback yields beneficial effects beyond the relaxation associated with sitting quietly. In fact, relaxation training and biofeedback are about equally effective in reducing stress and treating anxiety, headaches, insomnia, and the side effects associated with cancer chemotherapy (Gatchel, 2001).

Meditation refers to a variety of practices that train attention and awareness (Shapiro & Walsh, 2003). Meditative practices are embedded in many world religions and integrated into the lives of people of all races and creeds. In Western countries, people typ-

biofeedback
feedback by a device that provides almost an immediate output of a biological function, such as heart rate or skin temperature

meditation
a variety of practices that train attention and awareness

Biofeedback of forehead muscle tension can provide substantial control of this tension, thereby offering relief from muscle contraction headaches. But biofeedback may often be no more effective than relaxation.

In 2007, meditation was practiced by nearly 10 percent of people in the United States, reflecting increased perceptions of the possible benefits of meditation by the general public and the scientific community (National Institutes of Health, 2008).

FICTOID ✖

MYTH: "Alpha consciousness" is associated with a state of heightened relaxation.

REALITY: Although meditation and other states of relaxation are associated with increases in alpha waves (Cahn & Polich, 2006), it's not true that high levels of alpha waves increase relaxation. Correlation, as we've learned, isn't always causation. Indeed, there's no good evidence that increasing alpha waves using commercially available EEG devices boosts relaxation. What's more, children with attention-deficit/hyperactivity disorder (see Chapter 15), who tend to be anything but relaxed, generate especially large numbers of alpha waves (Beyerstein, 1999).

◉→ Simulate Stress and Heath on **mypsychlab.com**

ically practice meditation to achieve stress reduction, whereas in non-Western countries people typically practice meditation to achieve insight and spiritual growth. Contrary to stereotypes, there's no one "right" way to meditate.

In *concentrative meditation,* the goal is to focus attention on a single thing, such as the flame of a candle, a *mantra* (an internal sound), or one's breath. In fact, slow and deep rhythmic breathing to relieve stress is an increasingly popular CAM technique, which can be used in the practice of meditation and in the face of stressful circumstances to promote relaxation (Barnes et al., 2008). In *awareness meditation,* attention flows freely and examines whatever comes to mind.

For centuries, meditation fell well outside the scientific mainstream. Yet in the 1960s, scientists began to take a serious look at its possible benefits. Since then, they've identified a wide range of positive effects. These effects include heightened creativity, empathy, alertness, and self-esteem (Haimerl & Valentine, 2001; So & Orme-Johnson, 2001), along with decreases in anxiety, interpersonal problems (Tloczynski & Tantriella, 1998), and recurrences of depression (Segal, Williams, & Teasdale, 2001). Clinicians have added meditative techniques to a variety of psychotherapies and used them with some success in treating pain and numerous medical conditions (Baer, 2003; Kabat-Zinn, 2003). Meditation can also enhance blood flow in the brain (Newberg et al., 2001) and immune function (Davidson et al, 2003). ◉→ Simulate

Many people seem to benefit from meditation, although it's not clear why: Its positive effects may derive from a greater acceptance of our troubling thoughts and feelings (Kabat-Zinn, 2003). They may also derive not from meditation itself, but from sitting quietly, resting, and relaxing with eyes closed (Farthing, 1992; Holmes, 1987). People's positive attitudes and expectancies about meditation may also account for why it's beneficial. Few studies have followed meditators for long periods of time, so we don't know whether positive effects persist, generalize to different situations, or apply to large numbers of meditators. When researchers find differences between experienced meditators and nonmeditators, they need to be careful about how they interpret the results. Meditation might create specific changes in brain wave activity, but people who show certain brain wave patterns may be especially attracted to meditation in the first place (Lutz et al., 2004). Therefore, the direction of the causal arrow is difficult to determine.

correlation vs. causation ▶

CAN WE BE SURE THAT A CAUSES B?

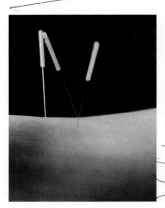

Acupuncture needles are thin and can be inserted virtually any place on the skin.

acupuncture
ancient Chinese practice of inserting thin needles into more than 2,000 points in the body to alter energy forces believed to run through the body

ENERGY MEDICINE: THE EXAMPLE OF ACUPUNCTURE. *Energy medicines* are increasingly popular (refer back to Table 12.3) and are based on the idea that disruptions in our body's energy field can be mapped and treated. Chinese physicians first developed and practiced **acupuncture** at least 2,000 years ago. In acupuncture, practitioners insert thin needles into specific points in the body. More than 4 percent of Americans (Barnes et al., 2004) have consulted acupuncturists. These practitioners place the needles on specific spots called *meridians,* which they believe channel a subtle energy or life force called "*qi*" (pronounced "chee"). Acupuncturists claim to relieve blockages of qi by applying needles or electrical, laser, or heat stimulation, to one or more of 2,000 points on the body.

Acupuncture can help to relieve nausea following surgical operations and treat pain-related conditions (Berman & Straus, 2004). Still, there's no reason to believe that any of its positive effects are due to energy changes (Posner & Sampson, 1999). The acupuncture points were mapped long before the rise of modern science. Even today, scientists haven't been able to measure, much less identify, the energy associated with specific illnesses. We'll recall that if a concept can't be measured and isn't falsifiable—in this case, it's impossible to disprove that "qi" is the effective mechanism—then it's not scientific.

PLACEBOS AND CAM. R. Barker Bausell (2007), a former advocate of CAM, reviewed research on acupuncture and other CAM treatments and concluded that they've mostly failed to demonstrate that they're more effective than placebos or "sham" (fake) treatment. For example, patients with low back pain (Brinkhaus et al., 2006) and migraine headaches (Diener, Kronfeld, & Boewing, 2006) benefit from sham acupuncture treatment in which researchers place needles at locations that don't match the acupuncture points or in which needles don't actually penetrate the skin. Indeed, most research suggests that sham acupuncture relieves symptoms as much as standard acupuncture (Hall, 2008; Hines, 2003). The placebo effect is a simpler explanation that better accounts for the data than the hypothesis that an undetectable energy field is responsible for acupuncture's effects.

Indeed, placebo effects are often impressive in their own right, and exert a measurable impact on brain chemistry and activity (see Chapter 2; Kirsch, 2010). Placebos and acupuncture both stimulate the release of endorphins (see Chapter 3), although many activities, including eating hot chili, laughter, vigorous running, and hitting one's finger with a hammer do, too (Cabyoglu, Ergene, & Tan, 2006; Hall, 2008; Pert, 1997). Pain, often the target of CAM treatments, is notoriously responsive to placebos. Tor Wager and his colleagues told patients that a cream would reduce the pain of heat or electric shock (Wager et al., 2004). After the scientists applied the placebo cream to patients' skin, patients reported less pain, and brain imaging (fMRI) detected less activity in brain areas that register pain.

Now consider another impressive demonstration of "placebo power" in Parkinson's disease, a serious and irreversible illness. It produces slow movements, rigid muscles, and tremors associated with decreased levels of the neurotransmitter dopamine (see Chapter 3). Parkinson's disease generally afflicts people over 60 years of age, but can occasionally strike people in their twenties and thirties, as in the case of actor Michael J. Fox.

In a remarkable study (McRae et al., 2004), scientists transplanted dopamine neurons from a fetus into the brains of patients with Parkinson's disease. They hoped this procedure would stimulate dopamine production and improve patients' quality of life. The patients learned before the surgery that they might receive a sham (fake) treatment in which holes would be drilled in their skull, but the cells would not be transplanted. (It's worth noting that the question of whether such operations are ethical is controversial [Miller, 2003].) Half the patients received the real surgery, half the sham surgery. A year later, the researchers asked all patients to guess whether they'd received the real or sham procedure. Patients who erroneously *thought* they underwent the real surgery had a better quality of life—for example, better physical functioning and social support—than those who received the real surgery but thought they received the sham surgery.

◄ **falsifiability**

CAN THE CLAIM BE DISPROVED?

FACTOID +

According to some historical accounts, acupuncture was discovered on ancient Chinese battlefields, when soldiers pierced by arrows and sharp stones reported relief from their other ailments (Gori & Firenzuoli, 2007).

◄ **occam's razor**

DOES A SIMPLER EXPLANATION FIT THE DATA JUST AS WELL?

◄ **ruling out rival hypotheses**

HAVE IMPORTANT ALTERNATIVE EXPLANATIONS FOR THE FINDINGS BEEN EXCLUDED?

? Reiki is a Japanese energy therapy and spiritual healing practice in which practitioners first suggest that patients relax and then place their hands on or above them to rebalance and focus reiki energy (qi) on different body parts. Researchers have not found evidence that reiki is helpful in treating medical or stress-related conditions (Lee, Pittler, Ernst, 2008). **What explanation, other than energy transfer, could account for reports of stress reduction or symptom improvement following reiki treatment?** (See answer upside down at bottom of page.)

Answer: Alternative explanations include: the placebo effect, relaxation, and naturally occurring changes in the course of an illness.

Doctors may be able to harness the power of placebos—by increasing patients' hope and positive expectancies to alleviate some physical symptoms and enhance the effects of available treatments. Researchers, in turn, need to carefully control for placebo effects in evaluating any new medical treatment, be it CAM or conventional, to rule out the possibility that they account for the treatment's effectiveness (Bausell, 2007).

ruling out rival hypotheses

HAVE IMPORTANT ALTERNATIVE EXPLANATIONS FOR THE FINDINGS BEEN EXCLUDED?

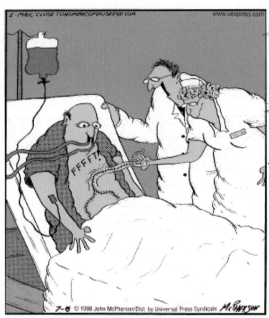

"Now that you're fully recovered, Mr. Dawkins, we can tell you the truth. The 12-hour operation, the intravenous meals, the three weeks of bed rest ... all were part of an elaborate placebo effect."

WHOLE MEDICAL SYSTEMS: THE EXAMPLE OF HOMEOPATHY. Entire medical systems have developed apart from conventional medicine for thousands of years in China and India. A more recent example of such a system is **homeopathic medicine**, practiced in the United States since the early 1800s. Nearly 4 percent of Americans report having used homeopathic remedies (Barnes et al., 2004). These remedies are based on the premise that consuming an extremely diluted dose of a substance known to produce an illness in a healthy person will alleviate that illness. To understand how homeopathy supposedly works, we should recall the joke about the patient who forgot to take his homeopathic remedy and died of an underdose. The principle behind homeopathy is that "like cures like." This is a good example of the *representativeness heuristic* (see Chapter 2), a mental shortcut with which we judge the similarity between two things by gauging the extent to which they resemble each other ("like goes with like").

When we rely too heavily on the representativeness heuristic, we can make errors in judgment. In this case, we might assume that the treatment for a disorder must resemble its cause—so if a disorder is caused by too much of chemical A, we should treat it by presenting the patient with as little of chemical A as possible. Nevertheless, homeopaths often dilute remedies to the point that not even a single molecule of the original substance remains. Homeopaths' belief that the "memory" of the substance is enough to stimulate the body's defenses is an extraordinary claim that makes utterly no sense from a scientific perspective. Medicine that contains no medicine isn't medicine.

extraordinary claims

IS THE EVIDENCE AS STRONG AS THE CLAIM?

Not surprisingly, homeopathic remedies haven't been shown to be effective for any medical condition (Giles, 2007). Yet they remain popular, as do many other CAM treatments that have little or no scientific support.

Why is this so? Here are five probable reasons for the apparent effectiveness of homeopathy and other unsupported CAM treatments (Bausell, 2007; Beyerstein, 1997):

1. They produce a placebo effect by instilling hope.

2. People may assume that natural products like herbs and megavitamins improve their health because they perceive no adverse effects to counter this belief.

3. The symptoms of many physical disorders come and go, so consumers may attribute symptom relief to the treatment, rather than to changes in the natural course of the illness.

4. When CAM treatments accompany conventional treatments, people may attribute their improvement to the CAM treatment, rather than to the less dramatic or interesting conventional treatment.

5. The problem may be misdiagnosed in the first place, so the condition isn't as severe as initially believed.

homeopathic medicine
remedies that feature a small dose of an illness-inducing substance to activate the body's own natural defenses

Hamlet.

CAM TREATMENTS: TO USE OR NOT TO USE, THAT IS THE QUESTION. Choosing scientifically unsupported alternative treatments over well-established traditional ones can be hazardous to our health. The popular media often serves up misinformation about CAM with potentially far-reaching public health consequences. For example, in numerous talk show appearances and a best-selling book, former sitcom actress Suzanne Somers (2009) has rejected the use of standard—and often highly effective—chemotherapy for breast and prostate cancer, and touted alternative treatments and vitamin supplements that research has shown to be worthless or even dangerous.

Should we uncritically accept medical opinion and advice we encounter in the media or elsewhere? By now, you should be able to guess our answer: No! Conversely, should we conclude that all CAM treatments are worthless? Not at all. As we learned in Chapter 1, it's essential that we keep an open mind and not dismiss new treatments out of hand. Many drugs derive from plant and natural products, and many effective medicines surely remain to be discovered. Every year, drug companies screen thousands of natural products for disease-fighting properties, and a few prove worthy of further testing. For example, *taxol*, derived from the Pacific yew tree, has been shown to be effective as an anticancer drug. Although St. John's Wort isn't especially effective for severe depression, it appears to be somewhat helpful for mild depression (Kasper et al., 2007; Wallach & Kirsch, 2003). These and other herbal medicines may eventually become part of mainstream treatment if they turn out to be safe and effective.

The same is true of psychological practices. Meditation, once regarded as an alternative approach, now appears to be an effective means of reducing stress and has increasingly blended into the spectrum of conventional approaches.

Barry Beyerstein (1997) recommended that we ask the following two questions before trying an alternative approach:

1. Does it lack a scientific rationale, or contradict well-accepted scientific laws or principles?

2. Do carefully done studies show that the product or treatment is less effective than conventional approaches?

If the answer to both questions is "yes," we should be especially skeptical. When in doubt, it's wise to consult a physician about a CAM treatment. Doing so will give us confidence that the treatment we select, regardless of whether it's conventional, is genuinely a "good alternative."

? Some celebrities have expressed strong opinions against conventional medical practices. For example, Bill Maher has voiced strong opposition to the swine flu vaccine despite the medical establishment's call for preventive vaccination. **What might be a public health consequence of Maher's opinion about vaccination?** (See answer upside down at bottom of page.)

Since the late 1700s, physicians have known that digitalis, a drug that comes from the purple foxglove plant, can control heart rate and treat heart disease. Some, but by no means all, natural plants are effective medicines.

<table>
<tr><td>

assess your knowledge
</td><td>

FACT OR FICTION?
</td></tr>
</table>

1. Most smokers who want to stop smoking each year succeed on their own without professional help. **True / False**

2. Obese people tend to be "jollier" than non-obese people. **True / False**

3. Women tend to overestimate their risk of dying from breast cancer as opposed to heart disease. **True / False**

4. The fact that a health product is "natural" means it's likely to be safe. **True / False**

5. The effects of acupuncture appear to be due to the redistribution of energy in the body. **True / False**

Answers: 1. F (p. 476); 2. F (p. 477); 3. T (p. 480); 4. F (p. 483); 5. F (p. 485).

✓ **Study** and **Review** on **mypsychlab.com**

WHAT IS STRESS? 457–461

12.1 EXPLAIN HOW STRESS IS DEFINED AND APPROACHED IN DIFFERENT WAYS.

Stress is a part of daily life. Most people experience one or more extremely stressful events in their lifetimes. People experience stress when they feel physically threatened, unsafe, or unable to meet the perceived demands of life. Stress can be viewed as a stimulus, a response, or a transaction with the environment. Reactions to stressful events and their consequences are important in studying the response aspects of stress, whereas identifying specific categories of stressful events (unemployment, natural disasters) is the focus of stressors as stimuli view of stress. The stress as a transaction view holds that the experience of stress depends on both primary appraisal (the decision regarding whether the event is harmful) and secondary appraisal (perceptions of our ability to cope with the event) of the potentially stressful event.

1. The tension, discomfort, or physical symptoms that arise when a situation strains our ability to cope is called _____. (p. 457)

2. Survivors of Hurricane Katrina might be of particular interest to researchers who study stress from which viewpoint? (p. 458)

3. People's varied reactions to the same event suggest that we can view stress as a _____ between people and their environments. (p. 458)

4. When we encounter a potentially threatening event, we initially engage in _____ _____ to decide whether the event is harmful. (p. 458)

5. We make a _____ _____ to determine how well we can cope with a harmful event. (p. 458)

6. _____ _____ is a coping strategy people use to tackle life's challenges head-on. (p. 458)

7. When we try to put a positive spin on our feelings or predicaments and engage in behaviors to reduce painful emotions, we are engaging in _____ _____. (p. 458)

12.2 IDENTIFY DIFFERENT APPROACHES TO MEASURING STRESS.

Psychologists often assess life events that require major adaptations and adjustments, such as illness and unemployment. They also assess hassles—annoying, frustrating daily events, which may be more related to adverse psychological and health outcomes than major stressors. Interview-based methods provide a more in-depth picture of life stress than questionnaires.

8. The _____ _____ _____ Scale is based on 43 life events ranked in terms of how stressful participants rated them. (p. 458)

9. How can daily hassles such as traffic, a difficult relationship with a boss, or getting the wrong order at a drive-through restaurant affect our health? (p. 460)

10. The frequency and perceived severity of hassles are (better/worse) predictors of physical health than are major life events. (p. 460)

HOW WE ADAPT TO STRESS: CHANGE AND CHALLENGE 461–464

12.3 DESCRIBE SELYE'S GENERAL ADAPTATION SYNDROME (GAS).

The GAS consists of three stages: (1) Alarm: the autonomic nervous system is activated; (2) resistance: adaptation and coping occurs; and (3) exhaustion: when resources and coping abilities are depleted, which can damage organs and contribute to depression and posttraumatic stress disorder (PTSD).

11. Identify the brain and body components activated in the alarm reaction proposed by Selye's GAS, depicted here. (p. 461)

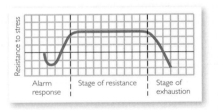

12. The _____ response is a set of physiological or psychological reactions that mobilize us to either confront or escape a threatening situation. (p. 462)

13. During the _____ stage of the GAS we adapt to the stressor and try to find a way to cope with it. (p. 462)

14. During the _____ stage of the GAS, resources and coping abilities are limited, and stress can damage organs and engender depression and posttraumatic stress disorder. (p. 462)

12.4 DESCRIBE THE DIVERSITY OF STRESS RESPONSES.

Our stress reactions vary from one stressor to another, and may be shaped by gender. The tend-and-befriend response is more common in women than in men. In times of stress, women often rely more on their social contacts, nurture others, and befriend or turn to others for support. About 5 percent (men) to 10 percent (women) of people experience PTSD in the face of a potentially traumatic stressor. Yet as many as two-thirds of people are resilient in the face of powerful stressors.

15. What are the similarities and differences between Shelley Taylor's tend-and-befriend response and the fight-or-flight response? (p. 462)

16. The hormone _____ further counters stress and promotes the tend-and-be-friend response. (p. 462)

17. In a survey of NYC area residents after 9/11, researchers found that (25 percent/65 percent) of the sample were resilient. (p. 463)

18. People who cope well in the aftermath of a stressor tend to display relatively (high/low) levels of functioning before the event. (p. 463)

19. The severity, duration, and nearness to the stressor affect people's likelihood of developing _____ _____ _____. (p. 464)

20. The telltale symptoms of PTSD include vivid memories, feelings, and images of traumatic experiences, known commonly as _____. (p. 464)

THE BRAIN—BODY REACTION TO STRESS

464–469

12.5 DESCRIBE HOW THE IMMUNE SYSTEM IS AFFECTED BY STRESS.

The immune system is the body's defensive barrier against disease. Phagocytes and lymphocytes neutralize antigens, such as viruses and bacteria, and produce proteins called antibodies that fight infection. Diseases of the immune system include AIDS and autoimmune diseases in which the immune system is overactive. Stress can decrease resistance to illness, delay healing, and impair the immune system.

21. AIDS is a life-threatening, incurable, yet treatable condition in which the _____ _____ _____ attacks and damages the immune system. (p. 465)

22. An example of an autoimmune disease in which the immune system is over-active is (arthritis/alcoholism). (p. 465)

23. Psychoneuroimmunology is the study of the relationship between the immune system and the _____ _____ system. (p. 465)

24. Research has shown that stress (can/can't) decrease resistance to the cold virus. (p. 466)

12.6 IDENTIFY HOW PHYSICAL DISORDERS SUCH AS ULCERS ARE RELATED TO STRESS.

Psychologists use the term psychophysiological to describe illnesses like ulcers in which emotions and stress contribute to, maintain, or aggravate physical conditions. Ulcers, which appear to be caused by the H. pylori bacterium and exacerbated by stress, can

be understood in terms of a biopsychosocial perspective, which considers both physical and psychological factors.

25. Ulcers (are/are not) caused by hot, spicy foods. (p. 467)

26. A biopsychosocial perspective proposes that most medical conditions are neither all physical nor all _____. (p. 467)

12.7 DESCRIBE THE ROLE OF PERSONALITY, EVERYDAY EXPERIENCES, AND SOCIOECONOMIC FACTORS IN CORONARY HEART DISEASE.

For many years, the Type A personality was thought to promote risk of CHD, but more recent work points to chronic hostility as a more central risk factor. Socioeconomic factors and everyday life experience can set the stage for many physical problems, including coronary heart disease.

27. Scientists have learned that psychological factors, including stress and personality traits are key risk factors for _____ _____ _____. (p. 467)

28. What are the characteristics of a Type A personality and what health risks are associated with such a personality? (p. 468)

29. Although job stress is correlated with CHD, it may not _____ it in all circumstances. (p. 469)

30. Researchers have established a (weak/strong) correlation between poverty and poor health. (p. 469)

COPING WITH STRESS 470–475

12.8 DESCRIBE THE ROLE OF SOCIAL SUPPORT AND DIFFERENT TYPES OF CONTROL IN COPING WITH STRESS.

Social support and the following types of stress control are important: (1) behavioral control (taking action to reduce stress), (2) cognitive control (reappraising stressful events that can't be avoided), (3) decisional control (choosing among alternatives), (4) informational control (acquiring information about a stressor), and (5) emotional control (suppressing and expressing emotions at will). Flexible coping (adjusting coping strategies to specific situations) is also helpful.

31. _____ _____ encompasses our relationships with people and groups that provide emotional and financial assistance as we contend with important decisions or stressful situations. (p. 470)

32. What are the benefits of a strong social network when an individual is undergoing stressful or challenging life events? (p. 470)

33. The ability to step up and take action to reduce the impact of a stressful situation is an example of _____ _____. (p. 471)

34. _____ _____ is the ability to think differently about negative emotions that arise in response to stress-provoking events. (p. 471)

35. We engage in _____ _____ when we anticipate stressful situations and take steps to prevent or minimize difficulties before they arise. (p. 471)

36. What is crisis debriefing and how effective is it for people who have experienced a traumatic event? (p. 472)

12.9 EXPLAIN HOW OUR ATTITUDES, BELIEFS, AND PERSONALITIES MAY INFLUENCE OUR RESPONSES TO STRESS.

Hardy people view change as challenge, have a deep sense of commitment to their life and work, and believe they can control events. Optimism and spirituality boost stress resistance, whereas rumination is not an adaptive way of coping with stressful circumstances.

37. _____ is a set of attitudes, marked by a sense of control over events, commitment to life and work, and motivation and courage to confront stressful events. (p. 473)

38. Optimistic people are (better/worse) at handling frustration than pessimists. (p. 473)

39. _____ is the search for the sacred, which may or may not extend to belief in God. (p. 473)

40. Spending a good deal of time ruminating is a (productive/counter-productive) way of reacting to a stressful situation. (pp. 474–475)

PROMOTING GOOD HEALTH—AND LESS STRESS! 475–487

12.10 IDENTIFY FOUR BEHAVIORS THAT CONTRIBUTE TO A HEALTHY LIFESTYLE.

Behaviors that can promote health include not smoking, curbing alcohol consumption, maintaining a healthy weight, and exercising.

41. The field of psychology that integrates the behavioral sciences with the practice of medicine is called _____ _____. (p. 475)

42. Health psychologists make the treatment and prevention of _____ a high priority, because it's the leading cause of preventable disease and deaths in the United States. (p. 476)

43. Research has shown that heavy _____ is associated with significant increases in many different types of cancer, serious and sometimes fatal liver problems, and brain shrinkage and other neurological problems. (p. 476)

44. Follow the formula below to calculate your BMI and determine your weight status from the categories listed. (p. 477)

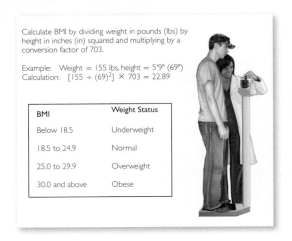

Calculate BMI by dividing weight in pounds (lbs) by height in inches (in) squared and multiplying by a conversion factor of 703.

Example: Weight = 155 lbs, height = 5'9" (69")
Calculation: $[155 \div (69)^2] \times 703 = 22.89$

BMI	Weight Status
Below 18.5	Underweight
18.5 to 24.9	Normal
25.0 to 29.9	Overweight
30.0 and above	Obese

45. Genes (play/do not play) a role in people's tendency to become overweight. (pp. 477–478)

12.11 IDENTIFY REASONS WHY IT IS DIFFICULT TO CHANGE OUR LIFESTYLES.

Reasons why it's difficult to change our lifestyles include personal inertia, misestimating risk, and feelings of powerlessness.

46. Because of the _____ heuristic, we tend to underestimate certain risks to our health and overestimate others. (p. 480)

12.12 DESCRIBE DIFFERENT ALTERNATIVE AND COMPLEMENTARY MEDICAL APPROACHES AND COMPARE THEIR EFFECTIVENESS WITH PLACEBOS.

Alternative medicine approaches include biologically based therapies (vitamins, herbs, food supplements), manipulative and body-based methods (chiropractic medicine), mind-body medicine (biofeedback and meditation), energy medicine (acupuncture), and whole medical systems (homeopathy). Many alternative approaches are no more effective than placebos. Alternative medical products and procedures can become part of conventional medicine when demonstrated to be safe and effective.

47. _____ _____ refers to health care practices and products that are used in place of conventional medicine. (p. 481)

48. Herbs, vitamins, and dietary supplements (are/are not) regulated by the FDA for safety, purity, and effectiveness. (p. 482)

49. List some of the positive effects of meditation and possible explanations for each. (p. 484)

50. _____ _____ is based on the premise that consuming an extremely diluted dose of an illness-inducing substance will activate the body's own natural defenses against it. (p. 486)

DO YOU KNOW THESE TERMS?

- stress (p. 457)
- primary appraisal (p. 458)
- secondary appraisal (p. 458)
- problem-focused coping (p. 458)
- emotion-focused coping (p. 458)
- corticosteroid (p. 458)
- hassle (p. 460)
- general adaptation syndrome (GAS) (p. 461)

- fight-or-flight response (p. 462)
- tend and befriend (p. 462)
- immune system (p. 465)
- acquired immune deficiency syndrome (AIDS) (p. 465)
- psychoneuroimmunology (p. 465)
- peptic ulcer (p. 467)
- psychophysiological (p. 467)

- biopsychosocial perspective (p. 467)
- coronary heart disease (CHD) (p. 467)
- Type A personality (p. 468)
- social support (p. 470)
- proactive coping (p. 471)
- hardiness (p. 473)
- spirituality (p. 473)

- health psychology (p. 475)
- aerobic exercise (p. 479)
- alternative medicine (p. 481)
- complementary medicine (p. 481)
- biofeedback (p. 483)
- meditation (p. 483)
- acupuncture (p. 484)
- homeopathic medicine (p. 486)

APPLY YOUR SCIENTIFIC THINKING SKILLS

Use your scientific thinking skills to answer the following questions, referencing specific scientific thinking principles and common errors in reasoning whenever possible.

1. There are a wide variety of support groups that people can attend, both in person and online. Research at least two of them and describe the types of social support that each offers. What scientifically supported methods do they use to help individuals gain control over their problems?

2. An estimated 24 percent of American men and 18 percent of women smoke cigarettes, despite scientific research that shows the negative impact that smoking has on our health. Compare the approaches used by three different anti-smoking programs (such as those using behavior modification, hypnosis, or drugs in a patch or gum). Are their methods and claims about success rates supported by research?

3. Many websites advertise products or methods designed to enhance people's ability to cope with stress. First, identify three such ads and evaluate the scientific support for each of the techniques or approaches recommended. Second, create a brief ad for a product or approach that's well supported by scientific evidence.

13 SOCIAL PSYCHOLOGY

how others affect us

THINK ABOUT IT

WHAT CAUSES MASS HYSTERIA OVER RUMORS ABOUT THINGS LIKE MARTIAN LANDINGS?

HOW DO CULTS PERSUADE PEOPLE TO BECOME FANATICS?

WERE THE NAZIS PARTICULARLY EVIL, OR WOULD WE HAVE DONE THE SAME THING IN THEIR BOOTS?

HOW CAN A WOMAN BE RAPED IN PLAIN VIEW OF MANY PEOPLE WITHOUT ANYONE COMING TO HER AID?

WHAT'S THE BEST WAY TO PERSUADE OTHERS TO DO SOMETHING FOR US?

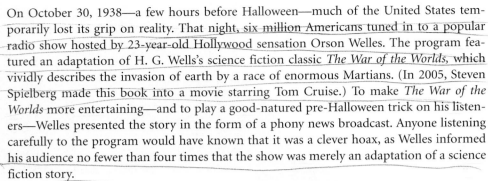

On October 30, 1938—a few hours before Halloween—much of the United States temporarily lost its grip on reality. That night, six million Americans tuned in to a popular radio show hosted by 23-year-old Hollywood sensation Orson Welles. The program featured an adaptation of H. G. Wells's science fiction classic *The War of the Worlds,* which vividly describes the invasion of earth by a race of enormous Martians. (In 2005, Steven Spielberg made this book into a movie starring Tom Cruise.) To make *The War of the Worlds* more entertaining—and to play a good-natured pre-Halloween trick on his listeners—Welles presented the story in the form of a phony news broadcast. Anyone listening carefully to the program would have known that it was a clever hoax, as Welles informed his audience no fewer than four times that the show was merely an adaptation of a science fiction story.

As the broadcast unfolded over the next hour, a newscaster periodically interrupted live orchestral music with increasingly alarming news bulletins that first reported a series of explosions on the surface of Mars and later the landing of a mysterious metal capsule on a farm in Grover's Mill, New Jersey, some 50 miles from New York City. Against the backdrop of screaming witnesses, a terrified reporter described a large alien with tentacles emerging from a hatch in the capsule. By the program's end, the newscaster informed listeners that an army of giant Martians was launching a full-scale invasion of New York City.

The War of the Worlds triggered a mass panic (Bartholomew, 1998). Hundreds of frightened listeners fled into the streets, while others hid in their basements. Still others called the police or loaded their guns. Some even wrapped their heads in towels in preparation for a Martian chemical attack (Cantril, 1947). Although most listeners didn't panic, at least tens of thousands did (Bainbridge, 1987). Surprisingly, many listeners apparently never bothered to consider alternative explanations for the program or to seek out evidence that could have falsified claims of a massive alien invasion. Had they tuned their radios to a different station, they would have heard no coverage of this presumably momentous event in human history. That surely would have tipped them off that Welles's program was a huge practical joke. Instead, many listeners fell prey to confirmation bias (see Chapter 1), focusing on only one hypothesis—that the news bulletins were real—at the expense of all others.

In addition to alarming listeners, the show caused many to misinterpret familiar stimuli as unfamiliar. For example, some residents of Grover's Mill panicked at the sight of a tall water tower that they'd surely passed hundreds of times. In their intense fright, they mistook it for a space ship and shot it to smithereens. Our shared beliefs about reality can affect our interpretation of it.

Welles had pulled off the most successful Halloween prank of all time. How did he do it? One thing's for certain: Welles had never taken an introductory psychology course, so he didn't rely on formal scientific research. Yet he understood the power of social influence, although even he was caught off guard by just how potent it was.

social psychology
study of how people influence others' behavior, beliefs, and attitudes

for good and bad.

ruling out rival hypotheses

HAVE IMPORTANT ALTERNATIVE EXPLANATIONS FOR THE FINDINGS BEEN EXCLUDED?

falsifiability

CAN THE CLAIM BE DISPROVED?

Orson Welles created mass panic in 1938 when he persuaded tens of thousands of Americans of the existence of a widespread Martian invasion. Although residents of Grover's Mill, New Jersey, had surely passed by this water tower (*right*) many times, their panic led them to mistake it for an alien rocket ship (see poster from *The War of the Worlds, left*). Social factors can shape how we interpret reality.

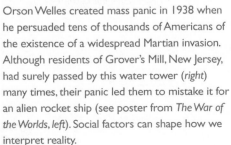

WHAT IS SOCIAL PSYCHOLOGY?

13.1 Identify the ways in which social situations influence the behavior of individuals.

13.2 Explain how the fundamental attribution error can cause us to misjudge others' behaviors.

Social psychology helps us to understand not only why *The War of the Worlds* hoax succeeded, but why many forms of social influence are so powerful. **Social psychology** is the study of how people influence others' behavior, beliefs, and attitudes—for both good and bad (Lewin, 1951). Social psychology helps us understand not only why we sometimes act helpfully and even heroically in the presence of others, but also why we occasionally show our worst sides, caving in to group pressure or standing by idly while others suffer. It also sheds light on why we're prone to accept blindly irrational, even pseudoscientific, beliefs.

There's a catch here, however. Research shows that we tend to believe that only others, but not ourselves, are vulnerable to social influence (Pronin, 2008; see Chapter 1). So we may initially resist some social psychological findings because they seem to apply to everyone else but us. In reality, they're relevant to us, too.

In this chapter, we'll begin by examining the social animals we call human beings (Aronson, 1998) and discuss how and why we often underestimate the impact of social influence on others' behavior. We'll move on to examine two especially potent social influences, conformity and obedience, and then address the question of why we help people at some times and harm them at others. Then, we'll discuss our attitudes and how social pressure shapes them. We'll end by exploring the troubling question of how prejudice toward others arises and, more optimistically, how we can combat it.

■ Humans as a Social Species

Social psychology is important for one reason: We humans are a highly social species. Most evidence suggests that as early hominids in Africa hundreds of thousands of years ago, we evolved in relatively small and tight social bands (Barchas, 1986). Even as modern-day humans, most of us naturally gravitate to small groups. In forming cliques, or groups that include some people—in-group members—we by extension exclude others—out-group members.

GRAVITATING TO EACH OTHER—TO A POINT. Anthropologist Robin Dunbar (1993) has become famous for a number: 150. This number is the approximate size of most human social groups, from the hunter–gatherers of days of yore to today's scientists working in a specialized research area (Gladwell, 2005). Research suggests that 150 is also close to the average number of people that each of us knows reasonably well. Interestingly, the number of "friends" in the average person's Facebook profile is about 130, not far from Dunbar's number (Marlow, 2009). Dunbar argued that the size of our cortex (see Chapter 3) relative to the rest of our brain places limits on how many people with whom we can closely associate. For animals with smaller cortices relative to the rest of their brains, such as chimpanzees and dolphins, the number of relations may be smaller (Dunbar, 1993; Marino, 2005). Whether or not 150 is the universal "magic number," Dunbar is probably right that our highly social brains are predisposed to forming intimate interpersonal networks that are large—but only so large.

THE NEED TO BELONG: WHY WE FORM GROUPS. When we're deprived of social contact for a considerable length of time, we usually become lonely. According to Roy Baumeister and Mark Leary's (1995) *need-to-belong theory*, we humans have a biologically based need for interpersonal connections. We seek out social bonds when we can and suffer negative psychological and physical consequences when we can't. Stanley Schacter (1959) discovered the power of this social need in a small pilot study. He asked five male volunteers to live alone in separate rooms for an extended time period. All five were miserable. One bailed out after only 20 minutes, and three lasted only two days. The lone holdout, who reported feeling extremely anxious, made it to eight days. Research on inmates placed in solitary confinement suggests that they experience more psychological symptoms, especially mood and anxiety problems, than other inmates (Andersen et al., 2000), although because the former inmates may be more emotionally maladjusted to begin with, this finding is difficult to interpret.

More systematic research shows that the threat of social isolation can lead us to behave in self-destructive ways and even impair our mental functioning. In a series of experiments, Jean Twenge and her colleagues asked undergraduates to complete a personality measure and gave them bogus feedback based on their test results: They told participants either that "You're the type who will end up alone later in life" or "You're likely to be accident prone later in life." Students who received feedback that they'd be isolated toward the end of their lives were significantly more likely than other students to engage in unhealthy behaviors, like eating a fattening snack or procrastinating on an assignment (Twenge, Catanese, & Baumeister, 2002). The same negative feedback is so upsetting that it even impairs students' performance on IQ tests (Baumeister, Twenge, & Nuss, 2002).

◄ ruling out rival hypotheses

HAVE IMPORTANT ALTERNATIVE EXPLANATIONS FOR THE FINDINGS BEEN EXCLUDED?

Brain imaging research goes a step further, shedding light on the commonplace observation that being cut off from social contact "hurts," literally and figuratively. Kip Williams and his coworkers placed participants in an fMRI scanner while they played a computerized ball tossing game with other "participants," who didn't actually exist. In a "virtual" version of the popular television show *Survivor*, the researchers rigged the game so that all participants were eventually excluded. Upon experiencing the sting of social rejection, participants displayed pronounced activation in a brain region called the cingulate cortex, which becomes active during physical pain. So that "ouch" we feel after being thrown out of a group may bear more than a coincidental similarity to the pain we feel after stubbing our toe (Eisenberger, Lieberman, & Williams, 2003). Recent research using the ball tossing game even suggests that the pain-killer Tylenol—compared with a placebo—blunts the activity of the cingulate cortex in response to social rejection (DeWall et al., 2010).

HOW WE CAME TO BE THIS WAY: EVOLUTION AND SOCIAL BEHAVIOR. Because we'll soon be examining many unhealthy forms of social influence, such as how unquestioning acceptance of authority figures can lead us to do foolish things, we might be tempted to conclude that almost all social influence is negative. That would be a serious mistake. Virtually all of the social influence processes we'll discuss are adaptive under most circumstances and help to regulate cultural practices. From the perspective of an evolutionary approach to social behavior, many social influence processes have been naturally selected, because they've generally served us well over the course of evolution (Buss & Kenrick, 1998). Even if we're skeptical of the view that evolution helps to explain much of social behavior, we can still accept a core premise: Social influence processes serve us well most of the time, but they can occasionally backfire on us if we're not careful.

An evolutionary perspective on social behavior leads us to one crucial conclusion: *Conformity, obedience, and many other forms of social influence become maladaptive only when they're blind or unquestioning.* From this standpoint, irrational group behavior—like the disastrous obedience of thousands of German citizens during the Nazi regime of the 1930s and 1940s and the massive genocide in Rwanda in the 1990s—are by-products of adaptive processes that have gone terribly wrong. There's nothing wrong with looking to a persuasive leader for guidance, as long as we don't stop asking questions. Once we accept social influence without evaluating it critically, though, we place ourselves at the mercy of powerful others.

SOCIAL COMPARISON: WHERE DO I STAND? One reason others affect us is that they often serve as a mirror of sorts, providing us with helpful information about ourselves (Cooley, 1902; Schrauger & Schoeneman, 1979). According to Leon Festinger's (1954) **social comparison theory**, we evaluate our abilities and beliefs by comparing them with those of others. Doing so helps us to understand ourselves and our social worlds better. If you want to find out if you're a good psychology student, it's only natural to compare your exam performance with that of your classmates (Kruglanski & Mayseless, 2000). Doing so gives you a better sense of how you stack up relative to them, and can spur you on to make needed improvements in your study habits.

Social comparison comes in two different "flavors." In *upward social comparison*, we compare ourselves with people who seem superior to us in some way, as when a new member of the women's college basketball compares herself with the team's top two superstars. In *downward social comparison*, we compare ourselves with others who seem inferior to us in some way, as when the same basketball player compares herself with her clumsy friends who keep bouncing basketballs off of their feet.

Despite their differences, both upward and downward social comparison sometimes boost our self-concepts (Buunk, et al., 1990; Suls, Martin, & Wheeler, 2002). When we engage in upward social comparison, especially with people who aren't too different from us, we may feel better because we conclude that "If he can achieve that, I bet I can achieve it too." When we engage in downward social comparison, we often end up feeling

Orderly evacuation of a building in an emergency highlights how conformity and obedience can be constructive.

[handwritten margin notes] Upward social comparison = compare self to people who are superior to us in some way. downward social comparison = compare self to people who are inferior to us in some way.

social comparison theory
theory that we seek to evaluate our abilities and beliefs by comparing them with those of others

mass hysteria
outbreak of irrational behavior that is spread by social contagion

Collective delusions *Many people simultaneously become convinced of bizarre things, which are actually false*

Don't you wait for me? ··· And you wait for me.

superior to our peers who are less competent than us in an important domain of life. Downward social comparison probably accounts in part for the popularity of televised reality shows, which often feature the daily lives of people who are spectacularly unsuccessful in their romantic relationships or friendships. Interestingly, even when social comparison makes us look inferior relative to someone else, we may buffer our self-concepts by persuading ourselves that it's only because the other person is exceptionally talented (Alicke et al., 1997). In one study, some participants learned—falsely—that another person had outperformed them on a test of intelligence. Relative to observers, these participants markedly overestimated that persons' intelligence. By concluding that "the person who outperformed me is a genius" (p. 781), participants salvaged their self-esteem: "It's not that I'm dumb, it's that he's incredibly smart."

SOCIAL CONTAGION. Just as we often turn to others to better understand ourselves, we often look to them when a situation is ambiguous to figure out what to believe—and how to act. That's only natural, and it's often a pretty good idea. When we experience severe turbulence on an airplane flight, we often look to the faces of other passengers as cues for how to react. If they appear calm, we'll generally relax; if they appear nervous or panicked, we'll probably start looking around for the nearest emergency exit. But what if others are thinking and behaving irrationally? Then, we may do the same, because social behavior is often contagious. *The War of the Worlds* might seem like an isolated case of human irrationality, but that's far from the truth. It's merely one example of *mass hysteria*.

Mass Hysteria: Irrationality at a Group Level. **Mass hysteria** is a contagious outbreak of irrational behavior that spreads much like a flu epidemic. Because we're most likely to engage in social comparison when a situation is ambiguous, many of us are prone to mass hysteria under the right circumstances. In some cases, episodes of mass hysteria lead to *collective delusions*, in which many people simultaneously come to be convinced of bizarre things that are false. Consider how the frequency of unidentified flying objects (UFOs) sightings shot up at times when societal consciousness of space travel was heightened (see **FIGURE 13.1**).

This trend started on June 24, 1947, when pilot Kenneth Arnold spotted nine mysterious shiny objects while flying over the ocean near Mount Rainier in Washington State. Interestingly, Arnold told reporters that these objects were shaped like *sausages*. Nevertheless, he also made the offhand observation that they'd "skipped over the water like saucers."

probably dolphins or something

Within days, the phrase "flying saucers" appeared in over 150 newspapers across the United States (Bartholomew & Goode, 2000). Even more interestingly, within only a few years thousands of people were claiming to see saucer-shaped objects in the sky. Had the newspapers been more accurate in their coverage of Arnold's words, we might today be hearing unidentified flying object (UFO) reports of flying sausages rather than flying saucers. But once the media introduced the term "flying saucers," the now familiar circular shape of UFOs took hold in the American consciousness and never let go.

Another collective delusion occurred in the spring of 1954, when the city of Seattle, Washington, experienced an epidemic of "windshield pitting." Thousands of residents noticed tiny indentations, or pits, in their car windshields that they suspected were the result of a secret nuclear test performed by the federal government. Their concerns spun so out of control that Seattle's mayor eventually sought emergency help from President Eisenhower (Bartholomew & Goode, 2000). Although the residents of Seattle hadn't realized it, the windshield pits had been there all along, as they are on most cars. The windshield-pitting epidemic offers another illustration of how shared societal beliefs can influence our interpretations of reality, making the familiar seem unfamiliar. When confronted with two explanations for the pitting—a secret nuclear explosion or the impact of dirt particles hitting the windshield—Seattle residents would have been better off picking the simpler one.

FICTOID ✕

MYTH: There's no adequate scientific explanation for most UFO reports.

REALITY: Ninety-eight percent of UFO reports can be accounted for by misinterpretations of ordinary phenomena, including lenticular cloud formations (which resemble saucers), the planet Venus, meteors, airplanes, satellites, weather balloons, and even swarms of insects. Perceptual factors play a role, too. To correct for movements of our eye muscles, our brain constantly alters the perceived position of the external world. Against an entirely dark background, our brain is fooled into perceiving the world as moving. In extreme darkness, we mistakenly perceive stars in the sky as moving, and may misinterpret them as extraterrestrial vehicles (Carroll, 2003; Hines, 2003).

wow.

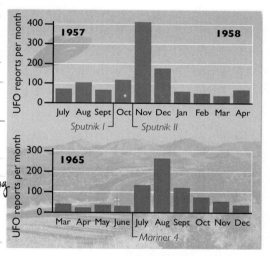

FIGURE 13.1 Graph of UFO Sightings. In the 1950s and 1960s, the number of UFO sightings shot up dramatically following the launches of *Sputnik I* and *II* (the Russian satellites that were the first objects launched into space) and following the U.S. launch of the space probe *Mariner 4*. Although these data don't permit definite cause-and-effect conclusions, they're consistent with the possibility that UFO sightings are of social origin. (*Source:* Hartmann, 1992)

occam's razor

DOES A SIMPLER EXPLANATION FIT THE DATA JUST AS WELL?

Urban Legends. Another demonstration of the power of social contagion comes from *urban legends:* false stories repeated so many times that people believe them to be true (Brunvand, 1999). As Gordon Allport and Leo Postman (1947) noted over six decades ago, rumors tend to grow less accurate with repeated retellings, often becoming oversimplified to make for a good story. With the increasing popularity of the Internet, YouTube, and social media, urban legends and other erroneous rumors can now spread "virally," becoming virtual overnight sensations in the absence of any objective evidence (Fernback, 2003; Sunstein, 2009). How many of the urban legends in **FIGURE 13.2** have you heard? ● Explore

All of the false stories in Figure 13.2 are too bizarre to be true, yet people consistently believe them. Urban legends are convincing in part because they're surprising, yet plausible (Gilovich, 1991). Urban legends also make good stories because they tug on our emotions, especially negative ones (Heath & Heath, 2007; Rosnow, 1980). Research shows that the most popular urban legends contain a heavy dose of material relevant to the emotion of disgust, probably because they arouse our perverse sense of curiosity. As a result, they often spread like wildfire. It's perhaps not coincidental that many feature rats and other animals that we don't exactly find appealing (Heath, Bell, & Sternberg, 2001).

A woman heated her poodle in a microwave oven in a well-meaning attempt to dry it off following a rainstorm. It exploded.

While still alive, Walt Disney arranged to have his body frozen after his death so that it could be unfrozen at a future date when advanced technology will permit him to live again.

Outside her home, a woman found a stray Chihuahua. She cared for the pet for several weeks and eventually brought it to a veterinarian, who informed her that her cute little "dog" was actually a giant rat.

Many gang members drive around late at night without their car lights on and then shoot people who flash their lights at them.

A woman on a transatlantic flight was trapped in the bathroom for over 2 hours after flushing the toilet created a vacuum, binding her to the seat.

● Explore Urban Legends on mypsychlab.com

FIGURE 13.2 Urban Legend? Some popular urban legends: All are widely known, yet all are false. Incidentally, if you ever want to find out whether a remarkable rumor from the Internet or media is true, check the high-quality website www.snopes.com, which continually tracks the accuracy of urban legends.

social facilitation
enhancement of performance brought about by the presence of others

The presence of others enhances our performance on simple or familiar tasks. These cyclists will probably ride faster together than either would alone.

SOCIAL FACILITATION: FROM BICYCLISTS TO COCKROACHES. Because we're social creatures, being surrounded by others can make us perform better. Indeed, the mere presence of others can enhance our performance in certain situations, a phenomenon that Robert Zajonc called **social facilitation**. In the world's first social psychological study, Norman Triplett (1897) found that bicycle racers obtained faster speeds (32.6 miles per hour on average) when racing along with other bicyclists than when racing against only the clock (24 miles per hour on average). Zajonc (1965) reported that social facilitation applies to birds, fish, and even insects. In what's surely one of the most creative studies in the history of psychology, Zajonc and two colleagues randomly assigned cockroaches to two conditions: one in which they ran a maze alone and in another in which they ran a maze while being observed by an audience of fellow cockroaches from a "spectator box." Compared with the lone cockroaches, cockroaches in the second condition ran the maze significantly faster and committed fewer errors (Zajonc, Heingartner, & Herman, 1969).

Yet the impact of others on our behavior isn't always positive (Bond & Titus, 1983). Social facilitation occurs only on tasks we find easy, whereas *social disruption*—a worsening of performance in the presence of others—occurs on tasks we find difficult. You've probably discovered this principle if you've ever "choked" in the company of others while singing a difficult song or telling a joke with a complicated punch line. One team of five researchers watched people playing pool (Michaels et al., 1982). The experienced pool players did better in the presence of others, but the inexperienced pool players did worse. So the effects of social influence can be either positive or negative depending on the situation. We're especially likely to "choke" on a difficult task when we're distracted—such as by the knowledge that others are watching us—which can limit the working memory (see Chapter 7) we can devote to solving this problem (Beilock, 2008; Beilock & Carr, 2005).

■ The Fundamental Attribution Error: The Great Lesson of Social Psychology

When we try to figure out why people, ourselves included, did something, we're forming **attributions**, or assigning causes to behavior. We make attributions every day. Some attributions are internal (inside the person), such as when we conclude that Joe Smith robbed a bank because he's impulsive. Other attributions are external (outside the person), such as when we conclude that Bill Jones robbed a bank because his family was broke (Kelley, 1973). We can explain a great deal of our everyday behavior by situational factors, like peer pressure, that are external to us.

When we read about the frenzied behavior of some Americans during *The War of the Worlds,* we shake our heads in amazement and pat ourselves on the back with the confident reassurance that we'd never have acted this way. Yet if the field of social psychology imparts one lesson that we should take with us for the rest of our lives (Myers, 1993a), it's the **fundamental attribution error**. Coined by Lee Ross (1977), this term refers to the tendency to overestimate the impact of *dispositional influences* on others' behavior. By dispositional influences, we mean enduring characteristics, such as personality traits, attitudes, and intelligence. Because of this error, we attribute too much of people's behavior to who they are.

Because of the fundamental attribution error, we also tend to underestimate the impact of situational influences on others' behavior, so we also attribute too little of their behavior to what's going on around them. We may assume incorrectly that a boss in a failing company who fired several of his loyal employees to save money must be callous, when in fact he was under enormous pressure to rescue his company—and spare the jobs of hundreds of other loyal employees. Similarly, we may assume that we'd never have panicked during *The War of the Worlds* hoax, even though we might well have.

No one knows for sure why we commit the fundamental attribution error, but one likely culprit is the fact that we're rarely aware of all of the situational factors impinging on others' behavior at a given moment (Gilbert & Malone, 1995; Pronin, 2008). When we witness a senator caving into political influence on a vote, we may think to ourselves, "What a coward!," because we may not recognize—or appreciate—the social pressure he was feeling.

Interestingly, we're less likely to commit the fundamental attribution error if we've been in the same situation ourselves (Balcetis & Dunning, 2008) or been encouraged to feel empathic toward those we're observing (Regan & Totten, 1975), perhaps because taking a walk in others' shoes helps us grasp what they have to contend with. This explanation dovetails with a curious finding. We tend to commit the fundamental attribution error only when explaining *others'* behavior; when explaining the causes of our *own* behavior, we typically invoke situational influences, probably because we're well aware of all of the situational factors affecting us (Jones & Nisbett, 1972). For example, if we ask you why your best friend in college chose to attend this school, you'll most likely mention dispositional factors; "She's a really motivated person and likes to work hard." In contrast, if we ask *you* why you chose to attend this school, you'll most likely mention situational factors: "When I visited the college, I really liked the campus and was impressed by what I heard about the professors." Still, this difference isn't large in size, and tends to hold only when we're describing people we know well (Malle, 2006).

EVIDENCE FOR THE FUNDAMENTAL ATTRIBUTION ERROR. Edward E. Jones and Victor Harris (1967) conducted the first study to demonstrate the fundamental attribution error. They asked undergraduates to serve as "debaters" in a discussion of U.S. attitudes toward Cuba and its controversial leader, Fidel Castro. In full view of the other debaters, they randomly assigned students to read aloud debate speeches that adopted either a pro-Castro or an anti-Castro position. ◆—[Explore]

After hearing these speeches, the researchers asked the other debaters to evaluate each debater's *true* attitudes toward Castro. That is, putting aside the speech he or she read, what do you think each debater *really* believes about Castro? Students fell prey to the fundamental attribution error; they inferred that what debaters said reflected their true

(a)

(b)

(c)

(d)

The 1960s television show "Candid Camera," which placed ordinary people in absurd situations, illustrates the *fundamental attribution error* (Maas & Toivanen, 1978). Viewers laugh at people's often silly reactions, underestimating how likely most of us are to fall victim to situational influences—in this case, group pressure. In one classic episode (shown here), an unsuspecting person enters an elevator filled with Candid Camera staff (a and b). Suddenly and for no reason, all of the staff turn to the right (c). Sure enough, the bewildered person turns to the right also (d).

◆—[Explore] the Fundamental Attribution Error on **mypsychlab.com**

attribution
process of assigning causes to behavior

fundamental attribution error
tendency to overestimate the impact of dispositional influences on other people's behavior

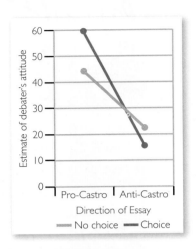

FIGURE 13.3 Participants' Performance in Jones & Harris (1967) Castro Study. Participants inferred that debaters' pro-Castro positions reflected their actual attitudes even though debaters couldn't choose which position to adopt—an example of the fundamental attribution error. (*Source:* Jones & Harris, 1967)

✓━ **Study** and **Review** on **mypsychlab.com**

conformity
tendency of people to alter their behavior as a result of group pressure

position regarding Castro *even though they knew that the assignment to conditions was entirely random* (see **FIGURE 13.3**). They forgot to take the situation—namely, the random assignment of participants to the experimental condition—into account when evaluating debaters' attitudes (Ross, Amabile, & Steinmetz, 1977).

THE FUNDAMENTAL ATTRIBUTION ERROR: CULTURAL INFLUENCES. Interestingly, the fundamental attribution error is associated with cultural factors. Although almost everyone is prone to this error, Japanese and Chinese people seem to be less so (Nisbett, 2003). That may be because they're more likely than those in Western cultures to view behaviors within a context (see Chapter 1). As a result, they may be more prone to seeing others' behavior as a complex stew of both dispositional and situational influences.

For example, after reading newspaper descriptions of mass murderers, Chinese participants are considerably less likely to invoke dispositional explanations for their behavior ("He must be an evil person") and more likely to invoke situational explanations ("He must have been under terrible stress in his life"). In contrast, U.S. participants show the opposite pattern (Morris & Peng, 1994). This cultural difference even extends to inanimate objects. When shown a circle moving in various directions, Chinese students are more likely to say that the circle's movement is due to situational or external factors ("Something is pushing on the circle") than to dispositional or internal factors ("The circle wants to move to the right"). We again find the opposite pattern among U.S. students (Nisbett, 2003).

assess your knowledge — FACT OR FICTION?

1. From the standpoint of an evolutionary approach to social behavior, conformity and obedience are inherently maladaptive. **True / False**

2. Social comparison <u>almost always</u> involves comparing ourselves with people who are worse off than we are. **True / False**

3. The presence of other people always enhances our performance. **True / False**

4. The fundamental attribution error reminds us that we tend to attribute others' behavior primarily to their personality traits and attitudes. **True / False**

Answers: 1. F (p. 496); 2. F (p. 496); 3. F (p. 498); 4. T (p. 499)

SOCIAL INFLUENCE: CONFORMITY AND OBEDIENCE

13.3 Determine the factors that influence when we conform to others.

13.4 Recognize the dangers of group decision making and identify ways to avoid mistakes common in group decisions.

13.5 Identify the factors that maximize or minimize obedience to authority.

Think of an organization or group to which you've belonged, like a club, school committee, fraternity, or sorority. Have you ever just gone along with one of the group's ideas even though you knew that it was bad, perhaps even unethical? If you have, don't feel ashamed, because you're in good company. **Conformity** refers to the tendency of people to alter their behavior as a result of group pressure (Kiesler & Kiesler, 1969; Pronin, Burger, & Molouki, 2007; Sherif, 1936). We all conform to social pressure from time to time. Yet as we'll soon see, we occasionally take this tendency too far.

■ Conformity: The Asch Studies

Solomon Asch conducted the classic study of conformity in the 1950s. Asch's (1955) research design was as straightforward as it was elegant. In some social psychological studies, such as Asch's, participants are lured in by a cover story that conceals the study's true goal.

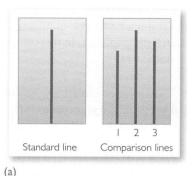

Standard line   Comparison lines

(a)

(b)

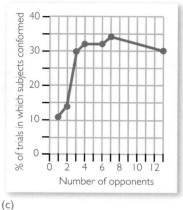

(c)

Often, other "participants" in the study are actually *confederates*, or undercover agents of the researcher. But the actual participants are unaware of that deception.

In this chapter, we'll ask you to imagine yourself as a participant in several classic social psychological studies. Let's begin with Asch's.

The Setup: Asch invites participants to a "study of perceptual judgments" that asks eight participants—including you—to compare a standard line with three comparison lines: 1, 2, and 3. Unbeknownst to you, the other "participants" are actually confederates. A researcher explains that your job is to say out loud which of three comparison lines matches the standard line. The researcher starts with a person across the table, so you're always the fifth to be called.

The Study: On the first trial (figure not shown) the correct answer is clearly "1." You listen intently as the first few participants call out their answers. Participant 1: "1." Participant 2: "1." Participant 3: "1." Participant 4: "1." As Participant 5, you simply follow, and say "1." The three participants following you give the same answer: 1. "This study's going to be a breeze," you say to yourself.

The second trial displays a similar problem, just as easy to answer, in which the correct answer is clearly "2" (see **FIGURE 13.4a**). Again, you listen while the participants call out their answers. Participant 1: "3." Participant 2: "3." Participant 3: "3." Participant 4: "3."

You can hardly believe your eyes (see **FIGURE 13.4b**). It seems obvious that "2" is the correct answer, but everyone is calling "3." What on earth is going on? Are your eyes deceiving you? What are you going to do?

The Results: If you're like 75 percent of participants in the original Asch study, you'd conform to the incorrect norm on at least one of 12 trials. Across all 12 trials in the Asch study, participants conformed to the wrong answer 37 percent of the time. Some conformed even when the comparison line differed from the standard line by more than six inches! Understandably, participants reported being confused and even distressed because they experienced a sharp conflict between their perceptions and what they believed to be others' perceptions.

SOCIAL INFLUENCES ON CONFORMITY. Asch (1955) and later researchers went on to pinpoint some of the social factors that influence how likely we are to conform. They concluded that conformity was influenced by the following independent variables: ◉ Watch

- **Unanimity:** If all confederates gave the wrong answer, the participant was more likely to conform. Nevertheless, if one confederate gave the correct response, the level of conformity plummeted by three-fourths.

- **Difference in the wrong answer:** Knowing that someone else in the group differed from the majority—*even if that person held a different view from the participant*—made the participant less likely to conform.

- **Size:** The size of the majority made a difference, but only up to about five or six confederates. People were no more likely to conform in a group of 10 than in a group of five (see **FIGURE 13.4c**).

FIGURE 13.4 Asch's Conformity Study. (a) Which of the "comparison lines" is the same length as the "standard line"? If several other participants said it was line #3, would you go along with them? (b) Here we see the lone actual participant (middle), barely believing his eyes, straining to look at the stimulus cards after the confederates gave the wrong answer. This participant was one of only 25 percent of Asch's participants who stuck to his guns and gave the correct answer in all 12 trials. After the study, he insisted, "I have to call them as I see them." (c) In Asch's studies, conformity increased as the size of the majority increased—but only up to about five or six confederates. (*Source:* Asch, 1955)

◉ Watch Conformity and Influence in Groups on **mypsychlab.com**

ruling out rival hypotheses

HAVE IMPORTANT ALTERNATIVE EXPLANATIONS
FOR THE FINDINGS BEEN EXCLUDED?

replicability

CAN THE RESULTS BE
DUPLICATED IN OTHER STUDIES?

Asch also tried to rule out alternative hypotheses for his findings. To determine whether group norms affected participants' *perceptions* of the lines, he replicated his original study but asked participants to write, rather than call out, their responses. In this condition, their answers were right more than 99 percent of the time.

IMAGING STUDIES: PROBING FURTHER INFLUENCES. Nevertheless, relatively recent brain imaging technology raises the possibility that social pressure can sometimes influence perception. Gregory Berns and his colleagues (Berns et al., 2005) placed participants in an fMRI scanner (see Chapter 3) and showed them two figures. They asked participants to determine whether the figures were the same or different. To do so, they had to mentally rotate one or both of them. The researchers led participants to believe that four other people were making the same judgments along with them; in fact, these judgments were preprogrammed into a computer.

On some trials, the other "participants" gave unanimously correct answers; on others, they gave unanimously incorrect answers. Like Asch, Berns and his collaborators found high levels of conformity: Participants went along with others' wrong answers 41 percent of the time. Their conforming behavior was associated with activity in the amygdala, which triggers anxiety in response to danger cues (see Chapter 3). This finding suggests that conformity may come with a price tag of negative emotions, particularly anxiety. Berns and his colleagues also found that conformity was associated with activity in the parietal and occipital lobes, the areas of the brain responsible for visual perception. This finding suggests that social pressure might sometimes affect how we perceive reality, although activity in these brain areas may have instead reflected participants' tendency to doubt and then recheck their initial perceptions.

ruling out rival hypotheses

HAVE IMPORTANT ALTERNATIVE EXPLANATIONS
FOR THE FINDINGS BEEN EXCLUDED?

INDIVIDUAL, CULTURAL, AND GENDER DIFFERENCES IN CONFORMITY. People's responses to social pressure are also associated with individual and cultural differences. People with low self-esteem are especially prone to conformity (Hardy, 1957). Asians are also more likely to conform than Americans (Bond & Smith, 1996), probably because most Asian cultures are more collectivist than American culture (Oyserman, Coon, & Kemmelmeier, 2002; see Chapter 10). This greater collectivism probably leads many Asians to be more concerned about peer opinion than Americans. In addition, people in individualistic cultures, like the United States, generally prefer to stand out from the crowd, whereas those in collectivist cultures prefer to blend in. In one study, researchers presented American and Asian participants with a bunch of orange and green pens that had a majority of one color and a minority of the other. Americans tended to pick the minority-colored pens, whereas Asians tended to pick the majority-colored pens (Kim & Markus, 1999).

Many early studies suggested that women are more likely to conform than men (Eagly & Carli, 1981). Nevertheless, this sex difference may have been due to an alternative explanation: The experimenters were all male. When later studies were conducted by female experimenters, the sex difference in conformity largely vanished (Feldman-Summers et al., 1980; Javornisky, 1979).

ruling out rival hypotheses

HAVE IMPORTANT ALTERNATIVE EXPLANATIONS
FOR THE FINDINGS BEEN EXCLUDED?

■ Deindividuation: Losing Our Typical Identities

One process that can make us more vulnerable to conformity is **deindividuation**: The tendency of people to engage in atypical behavior when stripped of their usual identities (Festinger, Pepitone, & Newcomb, 1952). Several factors contribute to deindividuation, but the most prominent are a feeling of anonymity and a lack of individual responsibility (Dipboye, 1977; Postmes & Spears, 1998). When we're deindividuated, we become more vulnerable to social influences, including the impact of social roles. The advent of e-mail, text messaging, and other largely impersonal forms of communication may contribute to deindividuation, in turn leading to a heightened risk of "flaming"—sending insulting messages to others (Kato, Kato, & Akahori, 2007). The face painting of warriors and the masks donned by the Ku Klux Klan may also fuel deindividuation by fostering anonymity (Wat-

deindividuation
tendency of people to engage in uncharacteristic behavior when they are stripped of their usual identities

son, 1973). The results of one study showed that children asked to wear masks were more likely than other children to help themselves to forbidden Halloween candy (Miller & Rowold, 1979).

Every day, we play multiple social roles: student or teacher, son or daughter, roommate, athlete, and club member, to name but a few. What happens when we temporarily lose our typical social identities and are forced to adopt different identities?

STANFORD PRISON STUDY: CHAOS IN PALO ALTO. Philip Zimbardo and his colleagues first approached this question over three decades ago (Haney, Banks, & Zimbardo, 1973). Zimbardo knew about the dehumanizing conditions in many prisons and wondered whether they stemmed from peoples' personalities, or from the roles they're required to adopt. The roles of prisoner and guard, which are inherently antagonistic, may carry such powerful expectations that they generate self-fulfilling prophecies. What would happen if ordinary people played the roles of prisoner and guard? Would they begin to assume the identities assigned to them?

Setup: Zimbardo and his colleagues advertised for volunteers for a two-week "psychological study of prison life" (see **FIGURE 13.5**). Using a coin toss, he randomly assigned 24 male undergraduates, prescreened for normal adjustment using personality tests, to be either prisoners or guards.

The Study: Zimbardo transformed the basement of the Stanford psychology department in Palo Alto, California, into a simulated prison, complete with jail cells. To add to the realism, actual Palo Alto police officers arrested the would-be prisoners at their homes and transported them to the simulated prison. The prisoners and guards were forced to dress in clothes befitting their assigned roles. Zimbardo, who acted as the prison "superintendent," instructed guards to refer to prisoners only by numbers, not by names.

The Results: The first day passed without incident, but something soon went horribly wrong. Guards began to treat prisoners cruelly and subject them to harsh punishments. Guards forced prisoners to perform humiliating lineups, do push-ups, sing, strip naked, and clean filthy toilets with their bare hands. In some cases, they even placed bags over prisoners' heads.

By day two, the prisoners mounted a rebellion, which the guards quickly quashed. Things went steadily downhill from there. The guards became increasingly sadistic, using fire extinguishers on the prisoners and forcing them to simulate sodomy. Soon, many prisoners began to display signs of emotional disturbance, including depression, hopelessness, and anger. Zimbardo released two prisoners from the study because they appeared to be on the verge of a psychological breakdown. One prisoner went on a hunger strike in protest.

At day six, Zimbardo—after some prodding from one of his former graduate students, Christina Maslach—ended the study eight days early. Although the prisoners were relieved at the news, some guards were disappointed (Haney et al., 1973). Perhaps Zimbardo was right; once prisoners and guards had been assigned roles that deemphasized their individuality, they adopted their designated roles more easily than anyone might have imagined.

Nevertheless, Zimbardo's study wasn't carefully controlled: In many respects, it was more of a demonstration than an experiment. In particular, his prisoners and guards may have experienced demand characteristics (see Chapter 2) to behave in accord with their assigned roles. Among other things, they may have assumed that the investigators wanted them to play the parts of prisoners and guards and obliged. Moreover, at least one attempt to replicate the Stanford prison study was unsuccessful, suggesting that the effects of deindividuation may not be inevitable (Reicher & Haslam, 2006).

THE REAL WORLD: CHAOS IN ABU GHRAIB. The Stanford prison study wasn't an isolated event (Zimbardo, 2007). In 2004, the world witnessed disturbingly similar images in the now-infamous Iraqi prison of Abu Ghraib. There, we saw guards—this

 Research on deindividuation suggests that irresponsible behavior would probably be more likely to occur in which of these two settings, and why? (See answer upside down on bottom of page.)

FACTOID +

In a recent study, participants were more likely to cheat in a dim room than in a fully lit room. Oddly enough, they even were more likely to behave selfishly—helping themselves to more than their fair share of money—when asked to wear sunglasses, even though they were no less anonymous than when not wearing sunglasses (Zhong, Bohns, & Gino, 2010). Apparently, even the mere illusion of anonymity can foster deindividuation.

> Male college students needed for psychological study of prison life. $15 per day for 1-2 weeks beginning Aug. 14. For further information & application come to Room 218, Jordan Hall, Stanford U.

FIGURE 13.5 Newspaper Ad for Zimbardo's Prison Study. A facsimile of the newspaper advertisement for Zimbardo's Stanford Prison Study, 1972. (*Source:* Zimbardo, 1972)

◀ replicability

CAN THE RESULTS BE DUPLICATED IN OTHER STUDIES?

Answer: Situation on right, because (1) people aren't wearing name tags and aren't easily identifiable and (2) the room is dark and may foster greater anonymity.

To some observers, some of the behaviors documented at Abu Ghraib prison in Iraq (photos at right) are eerily similar to those of Zimbardo's prison study (photos at left). Were the same processes of deindividuation at work?

time, actual U.S. soldiers—placing bags over Iraqi prisoners' heads, leading them around with dog leashes, pointing mockingly at their exposed genitals, and arranging them in human pyramids for their amusement. These similarities weren't lost on Zimbardo (2004b, 2007), who maintained that the Abu Ghraib fiasco was a product of situational forces. According to Zimbardo, the dehumanization of prisoners and prison guards made it likely they'd lose themselves in the social roles to which superiors assigned them.

That said, the overwhelming majority of U.S. prison guards during the Iraqi War didn't engage in abuse, so the reasons for such abuse don't lie entirely in the situation. As research using Asch's studies reminds us, individual differences in personality play a key role in conformity. Indeed, several guards who perpetrated the Abu Ghraib abuses had a long history of irresponsible behavior (Saletan, 2004).

Furthermore, deindividuation doesn't necessarily make us behave badly; it makes us more likely to conform to whatever norms are present in the situation (Postmes & Spears, 1998). A loss of identity actually makes people more likely to engage in prosocial, or helping, behavior when others are helping out (Johnson & Downing, 1979). For good or bad and often both, deindividuation makes us behave more like a member of the group and less like an individual.

CROWDS: MOB PSYCHOLOGY IN ACTION. Deindividuation helps explain why crowd behavior is so unpredictable: The actions of people in crowds depend largely on whether others are acting prosocially or antisocially (against others). A myth that's endured for centuries is that crowds are always more aggressive than individuals. In the late 19th century, sociologist Gustav Le Bon (1995) argued that crowds are a recipe for irrational and even destructive behavior. According to Le Bon, people in crowds are more anonymous and therefore more likely to act on their impulses than individuals.

In some cases, crowds do become aggressive. In November 2008, a Long Island, New York, Wal-Mart employee was trampled to death by a stampeding crowd of over 200 people after the store doors opened for post-Thanksgiving shopping. Four other people, including a pregnant woman, were injured. Some shoppers, eager to get good deals on discounted products, ran over emergency workers assisting the victims. Yet in other cases, crowds are less aggressive than individuals (de Waal, 1989; de Waal, Aurelli, & Judge, 2000), perhaps because deindividuation can make people either more or less aggressive, depending on prevailing social norms. Moreover, people in crowds typically limit their social interactions to minimize conflict (Baum, 1987). For example, people on crowded buses and elevators generally avoid staring at one another, instead preferring to stare at the road or the floor. This behavior is probably adaptive, because people are less likely to say or do something that could offend others.

groupthink
emphasis on group unanimity at the expense of critical thinking

Although crowds *sometimes* engage in irrational, even violent, behavior, research suggests that crowds aren't necessarily more aggressive than individuals. The January 2009 inauguration of President Barack Obama, shown here, was marked by no arrests despite an estimated crowd size of 1.8 million people.

■ Groupthink

Closely related to conformity is a phenomenon that Irving Janis (1972) termed **groupthink**: an emphasis on group unanimity at the expense of critical thinking. Groups sometimes become so intent on ensuring that everyone agrees with everyone else that they lose their capacity to evaluate issues objectively. To be sure, groups sometimes make good decisions, especially when group members are free to contribute opinions that aren't influenced—and potentially contaminated—by peer pressure (Surowiecki, 2004). On television shows like "Who Wants to Be a Millionaire," for example, contestants poll audience members, who then submit independent responses. In most cases, the audience's favorite answer is right. Yet groups often make poor decisions, especially when members' judgments aren't independent of each other. Research shows that when groups combine information from members, they typically rely on "common knowledge"—information that group members share—rather than unique knowledge, resulting in no net gain in new information (Stasser & Titus, 2003). As we learned in Chapter 1, widely held knowledge is often incorrect knowledge.

GROUPTHINK IN THE REAL WORLD. Janis arrived at the concept of groupthink after studying the reasoning processes behind the failed 1961 invasion of the Bay of Pigs in Cuba. Following lengthy discussions with cabinet members, President John F. Kennedy recruited 1,400 Cuban immigrants to invade Cuba and overthrow its dictator, Fidel Castro. But Castro found out about the invasion in advance and nearly all the invaders were captured or killed. It was an enormous humiliation for the United States, and Kennedy apologized for it on national television.

The members of Kennedy's cabinet weren't dumb; to the contrary, they were an uncommonly brilliant group of politicians and diplomats. Yet their actions were astonishingly foolish. After the failed invasion, Kennedy asked, "How could I have been so stupid?" (Dallek, 2003). Janis had a simple answer: Kennedy and his cabinet fell prey to groupthink.

The Bay of Pigs invasion wasn't the last time that groupthink led intelligent people to make catastrophic decisions. In 1986, the space shuttle *Challenger* exploded, killing the seven astronauts aboard a mere 73 seconds after takeoff. Following group discussions, project managers of the *Challenger* agreed to launch it after a series of bitterly cold days in January, despite warnings from NASA engineers that the shuttle might explode because rubber rings on the rocket booster could fail in freezing temperatures (Esser & Lindoerfer, 1989).

TABLE 13.1 depicts some of the "symptoms" identified by Janis (1972) that render groups vulnerable to groupthink. Nevertheless, some psychologists have pointed out that Janis's descriptions of groupthink derived from anecdotal observations, which we've learned are often flawed as sources of evidence (see Chapter 2). Moreover, groupthink

"All those in favor say 'Aye.'"   "Aye."   "Aye."   "Aye."   "Aye."   "Aye."

? What symptom of groupthink does this cartoon illustrate? (See answer upside down at bottom of page.) (© *The New Yorker Collection 1979 Henry Martin from cartoonbank.com*. All Rights Reserved.)

TABLE 13.1 Symptoms of Groupthink.

SYMPTOM	EXAMPLE
An illusion of the group's invulnerability	"We can't possibly fail!"
An illusion of the group's unanimity	"Obviously, we all agree."
An unquestioned belief in the group's moral correctness	"We know we're on the right side."
Conformity pressure—pressure on group members to go along with everyone else	"Don't rock the boat!"
Stereotyping of the out-group—a caricaturing of the enemy	"They're all morons."
Self-censorship—the tendency of group members to keep their mouths shut even when they have doubts	"I suspect the group leader's idea is stupid, but I'd better not say anything."
Mindguards—self-appointed individuals whose job it is to stifle disagreement	"Oh, you think you know better than the rest of us?"

Answer: Self-censorship

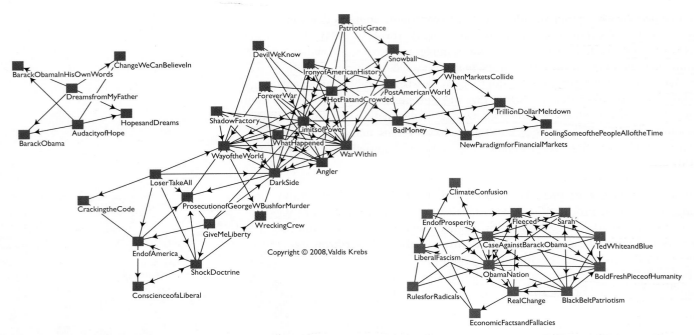

Copyright © 2008, Valdis Krebs

Research on book-buying habits shows that people who purchase liberal books—depicted in blue—tend to buy other liberal books; people who purchase conservative books—depicted in red—tend to buy other conservative books (Krebs, 2008). The closer the books are to each other in the diagram, the more likely they've both been purchased by the same person. Such selective exposure of information may foster polarization of political views in the electorate.

group polarization
tendency of group discussion to strengthen the dominant positions held by individual group members

doesn't always lead to bad decisions, just overconfident ones (Tyson, 1987). Seeking group consensus isn't always a bad idea, but doing so before all of the evidence is available is (Longley & Pruitt, 1980).

TREATMENTS FOR GROUPTHINK. As a psychological condition, groupthink is often treatable. Janis (1972) noted that the best way to avoid groupthink is to encourage active dissent within an organization. He recommended that all groups appoint a "devil's advocate"—a person whose role is to voice doubts about the wisdom of the group's decisions. In addition, he suggested having independent experts on hand to evaluate whether the group's decisions make sense. Finally, holding a follow-up meeting to evaluate whether the decision reached in the first meeting still seems reasonable can serve as a helpful check against errors in reasoning.

GROUP POLARIZATION: GOING TO EXTREMES. Related to groupthink is **group polarization**, which occurs when group discussion strengthens the dominant position held by individual group members (Isenberg, 1986; Myers & Lamm, 1976). In one study, a group of students who were slightly unprejudiced became less prejudiced after discussing racial issues, whereas a group that was slightly prejudiced became *more* prejudiced after discussing racial issues (Myers & Bishop, 1970). Contrary to what our intuitions tell us, talking things over with others isn't always a good idea. Group polarization can be helpful if it leads to efficient decisions when there's no time to waste. Yet in other cases, it can be destructive, as when juries rush to unanimous decisions before they've considered all the evidence (Myers & Kaplan, 1976).

There's evidence that the American electorate is becoming increasingly polarized, with left-leaning citizens becoming more liberal, and right-leaning citizens becoming more conservative (Abramowitz & Saunders, 2008). At least some of this polarization may be due to the increasing accessibility of Internet blogs, radio talk shows, and cable television, which provide political partisans on both sides with a steady diet of information that supports their views—and fuels their confirmation bias (Jamieson & Cappella, 2007; Lilienfeld, Ammirati, & Landfield, 2009). Moreover, research on book-buying habits shows that liberals read almost exclusively liberal books and conservatives read almost exclusively conservative books (Eakin, 2004). Few people on either end of the political spectrum expose themselves to information that challenges their views, probably generating further polarization.

CULTS AND BRAINWASHING. In extreme forms, groupthink can lead to **cults**: groups that exhibit intense and unquestioning devotion to a single cause. Although most cults aren't dangerous (Bridgstock, 2009), they can occasionally have disastrous consequences. Consider Heaven's Gate, a southern California–based group founded in 1975 by Marshall Applewhite, a former psychiatric patient. Cult members believed that Applewhite was a reincarnated version of Jesus Christ. Applewhite, they were convinced, would take them to a starship in their afterlives. In 1997, a major comet approached Earth, and several false reports circulated in the media that a spaceship was tailing it. The Heaven's Gate members believed this was their calling. Virtually all of the cult members—39 of them—committed suicide by drinking a poisoned cocktail.

Because cults are secretive and difficult to study, we know relatively little about them. But evidence suggests that cults promote groupthink in four major ways (Lalich, 2004): having a persuasive leader who fosters loyalty; disconnecting group members from the outside world; discouraging questioning of the group's assumptions; and establishing training practices that gradually indoctrinate members (Galanter, 1980).

Cults: Common Misconceptions. Misconceptions about cults abound. One is that cult members are usually emotionally disturbed. Studies show that most cult members are psychologically normal (Aronoff, Lynn, & Malinowski, 2000; Lalich, 2004), although many cult *leaders* probably suffer from serious mental illness. This erroneous belief probably stems from the fundamental attribution error. In trying to explain why people join cults, we overestimate the role of personality traits and underestimate the role of social influences.

Many people hold the same beliefs about suicide bombers, like the September 11 terrorists or those who detonated bus and subway bombs in London in 2005. Research on suicide bombers suggests that most aren't mentally disordered (Gordon, 2002; Sageman, 2004), although many appear to be marked by rigidity of thinking, reluctance to question authority, and a tendency to blame others (Lester, Yang, & Lindsay, 2004).

A second misconception is that all cult members are *brainwashed,* or transformed by group leaders into unthinking zombies. Although some psychologists have argued that many cults use brainwashing techniques (Singer, 1979), there's considerable scientific controversy about the existence of brainwashing. For one thing, there's not much evidence that brainwashing permanently alters victims' beliefs (Melton, 1999). Moreover, there's reason to doubt whether brainwashing is a unique means of changing people's behavior. Instead, the persuasive techniques of brainwashing probably aren't all that different from those used by effective political leaders and salespeople (Zimbardo, 1997). We'll have more to say about these techniques later in the chapter.

Resisting Cult Influence: Inoculation. How can we best resist the indoctrination that leads to cults? Here, the psychological research is clear, although counterintuitive: first expose people to information consistent with cult beliefs, and then debunk it. In his work on the **inoculation effect**, William McGuire (1964) demonstrated that the best way of immunizing people against an undesirable belief is to first gently introduce them to reasons why this belief seems to be correct, which gives them the chance to generate their own counterarguments against these reasons. In this way, they'll be more resistant to arguments for this belief—and more open to arguments against it—in the future (Compton & Pfau, 2005). This approach works much like a vaccine, which inoculates people against a virus by presenting them with a small dose of it, thereby activating the body's defenses (McGuire, 1964; McGuire & Papageorgis, 1961). For example, if we want to persuade someone that sleep-assisted learning doesn't work (see Chapter 6), we might first point out that the brain remains active during sleep, so it's possible that such learning could take place. This inoculation makes people more receptive to learning that there's no evidence that we can learn outside information while sleep.

Cult membership involves following the cult's practices without question. Reverend Sun Yung Moon of the Unification Church has united thousands of total strangers in mass wedding ceremonies. The couples are determined by pairing photos of prospective brides and grooms. They meet for the first time during the week leading up to the wedding day, often on the day of the ceremony itself.

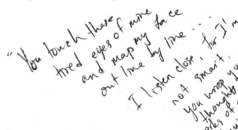

FICTOID ✕

MYTH: Poverty and poor education are key causes of terrorism, including suicide bombings.

REALITY: Most suicide bombers in the Middle East, including the September 11 hijackers and many Al Qaida members, are relatively well off and well educated (Sageman, 2004).

cult
group of individuals who exhibit intense and unquestioning devotion to a single cause

inoculation effect
approach to convincing people to change their minds about something by first introducing reasons why the perspective might be correct and then debunking them

Two sides of the coin of obedience: Lt. William Calley (*left*) was charged with murder by the Army for ordering his platoon to massacre unarmed civilians in the My Lai massacre in 1968. Calley was the only one in the platoon to be charged with a crime. Hugh Thompson (*right*), along with his fellow crew members, landed their helicopter between their fellow Army platoon and the civilians in the My Lai massacre in an effort to save the lives of the unarmed villagers. Thompson and crew were awarded the Soldier's Medal for bravery.

■ Obedience: The Psychology of Following Orders

In the case of conformity, we go along to get along. The transmission is "horizontal"—the group influence originates from our peers. In the case of **obedience**, we take our marching orders from people who are above us in the hierarchy of authority, such as a teacher, parent, or boss. Here the transmission is "vertical"—the group influence springs not from our peers, but from our leaders (Loevinger, 1987). Many groups, such as cults, acquire their influence from a potent combination of both conformity and obedience.

OBEDIENCE: A DOUBLE-EDGED SWORD. Obedience is a necessary, even essential, ingredient in our daily lives. Without it, society couldn't run smoothly. You're reading this book in part because your professor told you to, and you'll obey the traffic lights and stop signs on your next trip to school or work (we hope!) because you know you're expected to. Yet like conformity, obedience can produce troubling consequences when people stop asking questions about *why* they're behaving as others want them to. As British writer C. P. Snow wrote, "When you look at the dark and gloomy history of man, you will find that more hideous crimes have been committed in the name of obedience than have ever been committed in the name of rebellion." Let's look at one infamous example.

During the Vietnam War, U.S. Lieutenant William Calley commanded a platoon of a division named Charlie Company that had encountered heavy arms fire for weeks. Understandably, the members of Charlie Company were on edge during the morning of March 16, 1968 as they entered the village of My Lai (pronounced "Me Lie"), expecting to find a hideout for North Vietnamese soldiers. Although the platoon located no enemy soldiers in My Lai, Calley ordered soldiers to open fire on villagers, none of whom had initiated combat. They bludgeoned several old men to death with the butts of their rifles and shot praying children and women in the head. When all was said and done, the American platoon had brutally slaughtered about 500 innocent Vietnamese ranging in age from one to 82 years.

Calley insisted that he was merely taking orders from his superiors and bore no direct responsibility for the massacre: "I was ordered to go in there and destroy the enemy. That was my job that day. That was the mission I was given. I did not sit down and think in terms of men, women, and children. They were all classified the same" (Calley, 1971). In turn, the soldiers in Calley's platoon claimed they were merely taking orders from Calley. Calley was convicted in 1971 of murder and sentenced to life in military prison, but President Richard Nixon commuted his sentence.

In sharp contrast to Calley's behavior, Officer Hugh Thompson Jr. attempted to halt the massacre by landing his U.S. Army helicopter between Calley's troops and the innocent villagers. Risking their lives, Thompson and his two crewmen ordered the troops to stop shooting and evacuated the village, saving scores of innocent lives.

The My Lai massacre may seem inexplicable to us. Yet it's only one instance of the perils of unthinking obedience. How can we make sense of this behavior?

STANLEY MILGRAM: SOURCES OF DESTRUCTIVE OBEDIENCE. Stanley Milgram was a graduate student of Solomon Asch's who wanted to understand the principles underlying irrational group behavior. The child of Jewish parents who grew up during World War II, Milgram became preoccupied with the profoundly troubling question of how the Holocaust could have occurred. The prevailing wisdom in the late 1940s and 1950s was that the Holocaust was primarily the product of twisted minds that had perpetuated dastardly deeds. Yet Milgram suspected that the truth was far subtler. He agreed that the actions of the Germans during the Holocaust were grossly unethical, of course, but he came to believe that the underlying psychological processes that give rise to destructive obedience are surprisingly commonplace. Milgram was fond of the writings of German author Hannah Arendt, who regarded the Holocaust as an example of "the banality of evil." Ac-

obedience
adherence to instructions from those of higher authority

cording to Arendt, most of the world's wickedness originates not from a handful of cold-blooded villains, but from large numbers of perfectly normal citizens who follow orders blindly.

The Milgram Paradigm. In the early 1960s, Milgram began to tinker with a laboratory paradigm (a model experiment) that could provide a window into the causes of obedience (Blass, 2004). Although influenced by Asch's work, Milgram was more interested in obedience than in conformity, because he believed that unquestioning acceptance of authority figures is the crucial ingredient in explaining unjustified violence against innocent individuals. Milgram also believed that Asch's paradigm wasn't sufficiently engrossing to simulate the real-life power of dangerous social influence. After a few years of pilot testing, Milgram finally hit on the paradigm he wanted, not knowing that it would become one of the most influential in the history of psychology (Cialdini & Goldstein, 2004; Slater, 2004).

The Setup: You spot an advertisement in a local New Haven, Connecticut, newspaper, asking for volunteers for a study of memory. The ad notes that participants will be paid $4.50, which in the 1960s was a hefty chunk of change. You arrive at the laboratory at Yale University, where a tall and imposing man in a white lab coat, Mr. Williams, greets you. You also meet another friendly, middle-aged participant, Mr. Wallace, who unbeknownst to you is actually a confederate. The cover story is that you and Mr. Wallace will be participating in a study of the effects of "punishment on learning," with one of you being the teacher and the other the learner. You draw lots to see who'll play which role, and get the piece of paper that says "teacher" (in fact, the lots are rigged). From here on in, Mr. Williams refers to you as the "teacher" and to Mr. Wallace as the "learner."

As the teacher, Mr. Williams explains, you'll present Mr. Wallace with what psychologists call a *paired-associate task*. In this task, you'll read a long list of word pairs, like strong–arm and black–curtain. Then you'll present the learner with the first word in each pair (such as "strong") and ask him to select the second word ("arm") from a list of four words. Now here's the surprise: To evaluate the effects of punishment on learning, you'll be delivering a series of painful electric shocks to the learner. With each wrong answer, you'll move up one step on a shock generator. The shocks range from 15 volts up to 450 volts and are accompanied by labels ranging from "Slight Shock" and "Moderate Shock," to "Danger: Severe Shock" and finally, and most ominously, "XXX."

The Study: You watch as Mr. Williams brings the learner into a room and straps his arm to a shock plate. The learner, Mr. Williams explains, will push a button corresponding to his answer to the first word in each pair. His answer will light up in an adjoining room where you sit. For a correct answer, you'll do nothing. But for an incorrect answer, you'll give the learner an electric shock, with the intensity increasing with each mistake. At this point, the learner mentions to Mr. Williams that he has "a slight heart condition" and asks anxiously how powerful the shocks will be. Mr. Williams responds curtly that although the shocks will be painful, they "will cause no permanent tissue damage."

You're led into the adjoining room and seated in front of the shock generator. Following Milgram's plan, the learner makes a few correct responses, but soon begins to make errors. If, at any time, you turn to Mr. Williams to ask if you should continue, he responds with a set of prearranged prompts that urge you to go on ("Please go on," "The experiment requires that you continue," "You have no other choice; you *must* go on"). Milgram standardized the verbal statements of the learner, which also unbeknownst to you, have been prerecorded on audiotape (Milgram, 1974). At 75 volts, the learner grunts "Ugh!" and by 330 volts, he frantically yells "Let me out of here!" repeatedly and complains of chest pain. From 345 volts onward, there's nothing—only silence. The learner stops responding to your items, and Mr. Williams instructs you to treat these nonresponses as incorrect answers and to keep administering increasingly intense shocks.

Four panels from Milgram's obedience study:

The shock generator.

The "learner" Mr. Wallace, being strapped to the shock plate by Mr. Williams and an assistant.

Mr. Williams delivering instructions to the "teacher," the actual participant.

The "teacher" breaking off the study after refusing to comply with Mr. Williams' orders.

FIGURE 13.6 Milgram's Obedience Study: The Shocking Findings. This graph displays the percentage of participants in Milgram's obedience study who complied with the experimenter's commands at different shock levels. As we can see, about two thirds of participants obeyed until the bitter end.

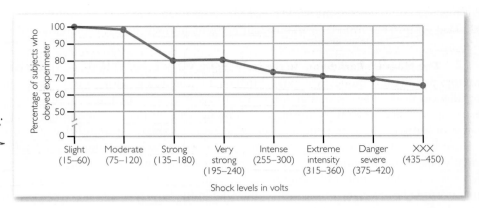

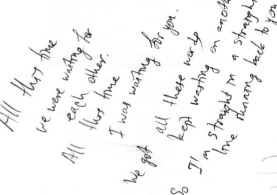

The Results: When Milgram first designed this study, he asked 40 psychiatrists at Yale University to forecast the outcome. Their predictions? Most participants, they predicted, would break off at 150 volts and only .1 percent (that's 1 in 1,000), representing a "pathological fringe" (Milgram, 1974), would go all the way to 450 volts. Before reading on, you may want to ask yourself what you would have done had you been a participant in Milgram's study. Would you have delivered any shocks? If so, how far would you have gone?

In fact, in the original Milgram study, *all* participants administered at least some shocks. Most went up to at least 150 volts, and a remarkable 62 percent displayed complete compliance, going all the way up 450 volts (see **FIGURE 13.6**). This means that the Yale psychiatrists were off by a factor of several hundred.

These results were, well, shocking. Milgram himself was startled by them (Blass, 2004). Before Milgram's study, most psychologists assumed that the overwhelming majority of normal people would disobey what were obviously cruel and outrageous orders. But like the Yale psychiatrists, they committed the fundamental attribution error: They underestimated the impact of the situation on participants' behaviors.

There were other surprises. Many participants showed uncontrollable tics and fits of nervous laughter. Yet few appeared to be sadistic. Even those who complied until the bitter end seemed reluctant to deliver shocks, asking or begging the experimenter to allow them to stop. Yet most participants still followed Mr. Williams's orders despite these pleas, often assuming no responsibility for their actions. One person's responses were illustrative; after the study was over he claimed, "I stopped, but he [the experimenter] made me go on" (Milgram, 1974).

The Milgram Paradigm: Themes and Variations. Like his mentor Solomon Asch, Milgram conducted a variety of follow-up studies to pinpoint the situational factors that affected obedience and to rule out alternative explanations for his findings. These studies provide an elegant demonstration of social psychological research at its best. In addition, they afford a powerful test of the replicability of Milgram's paradigm and its generalizability across situations.

We've summarized the major variations Milgram conducted on his original paradigm in **TABLE 13.2**. As we can see, the level of participants' obedience varied substantially depending on a number of independent variables, including the amount of feedback and proximity from the learner to the teacher, and the physical proximity and prestige of the experimenter. Although this table displays numerous variations, two key themes emerge. First, the greater the "psychological distance" between teacher (the actual participant) and experimenter, the *less* the obedience. As the experimenter became more psychologically distant, as when he gave instructions by telephone, compliance plummeted. Second, the greater the psychological distance between teacher and learner, the *more* the obedience. Most striking was the level of compliance when Milgram increased the psychological distance between teacher and learner by having the teacher di-

ruling out rival hypotheses

HAVE IMPORTANT ALTERNATIVE EXPLANATIONS FOR THE FINDINGS BEEN EXCLUDED?

replicability

CAN THE RESULTS BE DUPLICATED IN OTHER STUDIES?

TABLE 13.2 The Milgram Paradigm: Themes and Variations.

VARIATION/CONDITION	DESCRIPTION	PERCENTAGE WHO COMPLIED TO 450 VOLTS
Remote feedback condition (initial study)	No verbal feedback from the learner; teacher hears only the learner pounding the wall in protest after being shocked	65%
Voice feedback condition	Teacher hears the learner's screams of pain and complaints	62%
Proximity condition	Learner is in the same room as the teacher, so that teacher not only hears but observes the learner's agony	40%
Touch proximity condition	Teacher is required to hold the learner's hand on a shock plate; whenever the learner's hand flies off the shock plate, the teacher must jam it back down to ensure electrical contact	30%
Telephone condition	Experimenter gives instructions by telephone from a separate room (*Note:* some participants "cheated" by giving less intense shocks than what the experimenter directed)	30%
Second experimenter condition	A second experimenter is present and begins disagreeing with the first experimenter about whether to carry on with the session	0%
Less prestigious setting for study	Study is conducted (voice feedback condition is replicated) in a rundown office building in nearby Bridgeport, Connecticut, removing all affiliation with Yale University	48%
Ask teacher to direct a different participant to administer shock	Teacher is asked to give orders to another "participant" (actually a confederate), who then delivers the shocks. In this condition, teachers can reassure themselves, "I'm not actually giving any shocks; I'm just telling him to do it"	93%

rect someone else to administer the shocks. Here the level of complete compliance shot up to 93 percent. Like Lieutenant Calley, whose defense during the My Lai massacre was that he was "just taking orders," participants in this condition probably felt relieved of personal responsibility. Many Nazis, like Adolph Eichmann, offered similar excuses for their orders to kill thousands of Jews: They were just following instructions from their superiors (Aronson, 1998). When people do immoral things, they often look to pass the buck on to somebody else.

In the "touch proximity" condition (see Table 13.2), participants were instructed to hold the "learner's" hand on a shock plate. Here the level of obedience plummeted. This condition illustrates the point that decreasing the psychological distance between teacher and learner leads to decreased obedience.

The Milgram Paradigm: Individual, Gender, and Cultural Differences. When evaluating Milgram's findings, it's only natural to focus on the sizable proportion of participants who followed orders. Yet many of his participants didn't go along with the experimenter's commands despite intense pressure to do so. Recall that at My Lai, some American soldiers disobeyed Calley's orders by ordering his soldiers to stop firing. Moreover, during the Holocaust thousands of European families risked their lives to offer safe haven to Jewish civilians in clear defiance of Nazi laws (Wilson, 1993). So despite powerful situational pressures, some people disobey authority figures who give unethical orders. Who are they?

Surprisingly, Milgram (1974) found that obedient and disobedient participants were similar on most personality variables. For example, he found no evidence that obedient participants were more sadistic than disobedient participants, suggesting that participants didn't follow orders because they enjoyed doing so (Aronson, 1998).

FACTOID

In a disturbing study, a research team told 32 undergraduates to deliver electric shocks to a small male dog (Larsen et al., 1974). Only two refused, and the average voltage level delivered was slightly over 100 volts. Males administered significantly more intense shocks than did females. You'll be relieved to know, however, that the dog didn't actually receive shocks, although participants believed he did.

Rosa Parks (1913–2005) became a role model for "civil disobedience" during the 1950s and 1960s when she refused to give up her seat on a bus to a White man as was required by law. Morality, for her, overrode law.

Nevertheless, researchers have identified a few predictors of obedience in Milgram's paradigm. Lawrence Kohlberg found that the level of moral development using his interview-based scheme (see Chapter 10) was negatively correlated with compliance; more morally advanced participants were more willing to defy the experimenter (Kohlberg, 1965; Milgram, 1974). Especially moral people may sometimes be more willing to violate rules than less moral people, especially if they view them as unreasonable. Another researcher found that people with high levels of a personality trait called *authoritarianism* are more likely to comply with the experimenters' demands (Elms, 1972). People with high levels of authoritarianism see the world as a big hierarchy of power. For them, authority figures are to be respected, not questioned (Adorno et al., 1950; Dillehay, 1978). It makes sense that authoritarian individuals would display high levels of obedience in Milgram's paradigm, as they presumably viewed Mr. Williams as an authority figure whose orders they shouldn't question.

Milgram found no consistent sex differences in obedience; this finding has held up in later studies using his paradigm (Blass, 1999). Milgram's findings have also been replicated in many countries. The overall rates of obedience among Americans don't differ significantly from those of non-Americans (Blass, 2004), including people in Italy (Ancona & Pareyson, 1968), South Africa (Edwards et al., 1969), Spain (Miranda et al., 1981), Germany (Mantell, 1971), Australia (Kilham & Mann, 1974), and Jordan (Shanab & Yahya, 1977). ◉ Watch

Milgram's Studies: Lessons. Psychologists have learned a great deal from Milgram's work. They've learned that the power of authority figures is greater than almost anyone had imagined, and that obedience doesn't typically result from sadism. Milgram's research also reminds us of the power of the fundamental attribution error. Most people, even psychiatrists, underestimate situational influences on behavior (Bierbrauer, 1973; Sabini & Silver, 1983).

Psychologists continue to debate whether Milgram's study offers an adequate model of what happened during the Holocaust and My Lai. Milgram's critics correctly note that, in contrast to Milgram's participants, some concentration camp guards actively enjoyed torturing innocent people (Cialdini & Goldstein, 2004). These critics further argue that destructive obedience on a grand scale probably requires not only an authority figure bearing an official stamp of approval, but also a core group of genuinely wicked people. They may well be right. These controversies aside, there's no doubt that Stanley Milgram has forever changed how we think about ourselves and others. He's made us more keenly aware of the fact that good people can do bad things and that rational people can behave irrationally (Aronson, 1998). By warning us of these perils, Milgram may have steered us on the path toward guarding against them.

replicability

CAN THE RESULTS BE DUPLICATED IN OTHER STUDIES?

◉ **Watch** the Milgram Obedience Study Today on **mypsychlab.com**

✓ **Study** and **Review** on **mypsychlab.com**

---

assess your knowledge   FACT OR FICTION?

1. Asch's studies demonstrated that several allies are required to counteract the effects of conformity on an individual. **True / False**

2. Deindividuation can make people more likely to engage in prosocial, as well as antisocial, behavior. **True / False**

3. Groups almost always make less extreme decisions than do individuals. **True / False**

4. Obedience is by itself maladaptive and unhealthy. **True / False**

Answers: 1. F (p. 501); 2. T (p. 504); 3. F (p. 505); 4. F (p. 508)

HELPING AND HARMING OTHERS: PROSOCIAL BEHAVIOR AND AGGRESSION

13.6   Explain which aspects of a situation increase or decrease the likelihood of bystander intervention.

13.7   Describe the social and individual difference variables that contribute to human aggression.

For centuries, philosophers have debated the question of whether human nature is good or bad. Yet scientific truth rarely falls neatly into one of two extremes. Indeed, mounting evidence suggests that human nature is a blend of both socially constructive and destructive tendencies.

Primate researcher Frans de Waal (1982, 1996) argues that our two closest animal relatives, the bonobo (pygmy chimpanzee; see Chapter 8) and the chimpanzee, display the seeds of both prosocial and antisocial behavior. Because we share more than 98 percent of our DNA with both species, they offer a slightly fuzzy evolutionary window onto our own nature. Although these species overlap in their social behaviors, the bonobo is more of a model for *prosocial behavior*—behavior intended to help others—and the chimpanzee is more of a model for antisocial behavior, including aggressive acts. Bonobos are veritable experts at reconciling after arguments, often making peace by making love—literally. They also engage in helping behaviors that we ordinarily associate with humans. De Waal described a remarkable event at the San Diego Zoo, where bonobo caretakers

> were filling up the water moat. The juveniles of the [bonobo] group were playing in the empty moat, and the caretakers had not noticed. When they went to the kitchen to turn on the water, all of a sudden in front of the window they saw Kakowet, the old male of the group, and he was waving and screaming at them to draw their attention. [The caretakers] looked at the moat and saw the juveniles and then got them out of there, before the moat filled up. (p. 4)

Chimpanzees engage in prosocial behavior, too, like making up after fights. Yet they're far more prone to aggression than are bonobos. In the 1970s, Jane Goodall (1990) stunned the scientific world by reporting that chimpanzees occasionally wage all-out wars against other chimpanzee groups, replete with brutal murders, infanticide, and cannibalism.

To which species are we more similar, the peace-loving bonobo or the belligerent chimpanzee? In reality, we're a bit of both. De Waal (2006) is fond of calling the human species "the bipolar ape," because our social behavior is a blend of that of our closest ape relatives.

In this next section, we'll examine the roots of prosocial and antisocial actions, with a particular emphasis on situational factors that contribute to both behaviors. We'll begin by examining why we fail to help in some situations, but why we help in others. We'll then explore why we occasionally act aggressively toward members of our species. As we've seen, Milgram's obedience research sheds light on the social influences that can lead us to harm others. But we'll soon discover that obedience to authority is only part of the story.

■ Safety in Numbers or Danger in Numbers? Bystander Nonintervention

You've probably heard the saying, "There's safety in numbers." Popular wisdom teaches us that when we find ourselves in danger, it's best to be in the company of others. Is that true? Let's look at two real-life examples.

TWO TRAGIC STORIES OF BYSTANDER NONINTERVENTION.

- On March 13, 1964, at three A.M., 28-year-old Catherine (Kitty) Genovese was returning to her apartment in New York City, having just gotten off work. Suddenly, a man appeared and began stabbing her. He came and left no fewer than three times over a 35-minute time span. Kitty repeatedly screamed and pleaded for help as the lights from nearby apartments flipped on. Although the precise facts remain in dispute and some early reports appear to have been exaggerated (Manning, Levine, & Collins, 2007), most of the evidence suggests that at least half a dozen—and perhaps many more—of her 30 or so neighbors heard the events but failed to come to her aid. Most didn't even bother to call the police. By the end of the gruesome attack, Kitty Genovese was dead (see **FIGURE 13.7**).

This remarkable photo by primate researcher Frans de Waal shows a male chimpanzee (*left*) extending a hand of appeasement to another chimpanzee after a fight. Many psychologists have argued that our tendency toward prosocial behavior has deep roots in our primate heritage.

FIGURE 13.7   The Murder of Kitty Genovese. Place in Kew Gardens, New York, where Kitty Genovese was murdered on March 13, 1964, at 3:20 A.M. She drove into the parking lot at the Kew Gardens train station and parked her car at spot 1. Noticing a man in the lot, she became nervous and headed toward a police telephone box. The man caught her and attacked her with a knife at spot 2. She managed to get away, but he attacked her again at spot 3 and again at spot 4.

One familiar example of pluralistic ignorance is the "silent classroom scenario," which often occurs after a professor has delivered a lecture that has left everyone in the class thoroughly confused. Following the lecture, the professor asks "Are there are any questions?" and no one responds. Each student in the class looks nervously at the other students, all of whom are sitting quietly, and assumes mistakenly that he or she is the only one who didn't understand the lecture (Wardell, 1999). *True.*

? What social psychological principles help explain why these people don't stop to help the man lying on the ground? (See answer upside down on bottom of page.)

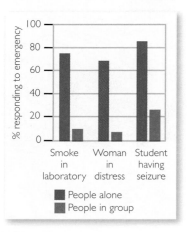

FIGURE 13.8 Bystander Intervention. Across three classic experiments on bystander intervention, the percentage of people helping when in groups was markedly lower than the percentage of people helping when alone.

Answer: Pluralistic ignorance (people walking by may assume the man is drunk or asleep rather than injured) and diffusion of responsibility (the presence of numerous people present makes each person feel less responsible for the consequences of not helping).

- On October 23, 2009, as many as 20 bystanders stood and watched while a 16-year-old girl was brutally gang-raped for over two hours outside a school dance in Richmond, California. According to reports, no one called the police, even though many of the onlookers had cellphones. *Sick People. Hmm.*

CAUSES OF BYSTANDER NONINTERVENTION: WHY WE DON'T HELP. Like most anecdotes, these real-world stories are useful for illustrating concepts, but they don't allow for scientific generalizations. For years, many psychologists assumed that the nonresponsiveness of bystanders was due simply to a lack of caring; some even referred to the phenomenon as "bystander apathy." But psychologists John Darley and Bibb Latané suspected that the *bystander effect* was less a consequence of apathy than of "psychological paralysis." According to Darley and Latané (1968a), bystanders in emergencies typically want to intervene, but often find themselves frozen, seemingly helpless to help. Darley and Latané also suspected that popular psychology was wrong—that there's actually danger rather than safety in numbers. Bucking conventional wisdom, they hypothesized that the presence of others makes people *less*, not more, likely to help in emergencies. Why?

Pluralistic Ignorance: It Must Just Be Me. Darley and Latané maintained that two major factors explain bystander nonintervention. The first is **pluralistic ignorance**: the error of assuming that no one in the group perceives things as we do. To intervene in an emergency, we first need to recognize that the situation is really an emergency. Imagine that on your way to class tomorrow you see a student in dirty clothing slumped across a bench. As you stroll by, thoughts whiz through your mind: Is he asleep? Is he drunk? Could he be seriously ill, even dead? Could my psychology professor be conducting a study to examine my responses to emergencies? Here's where pluralistic ignorance comes into play. We look around, notice that nobody is responding, and assume—perhaps mistakenly—that the situation isn't an emergency. We assume we're the only one who thinks the situation might be an emergency. Reassured that the coast is clear and that there's nothing to worry about, we continue on our merry way to class.

So pluralistic ignorance is relevant when we're trying to figure out whether an ambiguous situation is really an emergency. But it doesn't fully explain the behavior of bystanders in the Kitty Genovese or Richmond, California, gang rape tragedies, because those situations were clearly emergencies. Even once we've recognized that the situation is an emergency, the presence of others still tends to inhibit helping.

Diffusion of Responsibility: Passing the Buck. A second step is required for us to intervene in an emergency. We need to feel a burden of responsibility for the consequences of *not* intervening. Here's the rub: The more people present at an emergency, *the less each person feels responsible for the negative consequences of not helping*. Darley and Latané called this phenomenon **diffusion of responsibility**: The presence of others makes each person feel less responsible for the outcome. If you don't assist someone in a crowded park who's having a heart attack and that person dies, you can always say to yourself, "Well, that's a terrible tragedy, but it wasn't really *my* fault. After all, plenty of other people could have helped, too." The participants in Milgram's study who complied with the experimenter's commands when instructing someone else to deliver shocks probably experienced diffusion of responsibility: They could reassure themselves "Well, I wasn't the only one who did it."

So we can experience pluralistic ignorance, which prevents us from interpreting a situation as an emergency, *and* we can experience diffusion of responsibility, which discourages us from offering assistance in an emergency. From this perspective, it's perhaps surprising that any of us helps in emergencies, because the obstacles to intervening are considerable.

Studies of Bystander Nonintervention. To get at the psychological roots of the bystander effect, Darley, Latané, and their colleagues tested the effect of bystanders on participants' willingness to (1) report that smoke was filling a room (Darley & Latané, 1968b); (2) react to what sounded like a woman falling off a ladder and injuring herself (Latané & Rodin, 1969); and (3) respond to what sounded like another student experiencing an epileptic seizure (Darley & Latané, 1968a). In all of these studies, participants were significantly more likely to seek or offer help when they were alone than in a group (see **FIGURE 13.8**).

Researchers have replicated these findings many times using slightly different designs. In an analysis of almost 50 studies of bystander intervention involving close to 6,000 participants, Bibb Latané and Steve Nida (1981) found that people were more likely to help when alone than in groups about 90 percent of the time. That's an impressive degree of replicability. Even *thinking* about being in a large group makes us less likely to help in an emergency (Garcia et al. 2002). ◆─[Explore

replicability

CAN THE RESULTS BE DUPLICATED IN OTHER STUDIES?

◆─[**Explore** Bystander Intervention on **mypsychlab.com**

■ Social Loafing: With a Little Too Much Help from My Friends

Have you ever been a member of a group that got virtually nothing accomplished? (All four authors of your textbook regularly attend meetings of university faculty, so we're particular experts on this topic.) If so, you may have been a victim of **social loafing**, a phenomenon in which people slack off in groups (Latané, Williams, & Harkins, 1979; North, Linley, & Hargreaves, 2000). As a consequence of social loafing, the whole is less than the sum of its parts.

Some psychologists believe that social loafing is a variant of bystander nonintervention. That's because social loafing appears to be due in part to diffusion of responsibility: People working in groups typically feel less responsible for the outcome of a project than they do when working alone. As a result, they don't invest as much effort.

[handwritten: haha HS Group projects. Typical.]

psychomythology

IS BRAINSTORMING IN GROUPS A GOOD WAY TO GENERATE IDEAS?

Imagine that you've been hired by an advertising firm to cook up a new marketing campaign for Mrs. Yummy's Chicken Noodle Soup. The soup hasn't been selling well of late and your job is to come up with an advertising jingle that will instill in every American an uncontrollable urge to reach for the nearest cup of chicken noodle soup.

Although you initially plan to come up with slogans on your own, your boss walks into your cubicle and informs you that you'll be participating in a "group brainstorming" meeting later that afternoon in the executive suite. There, you and 12 other firm members will let your imaginations run wild, saying whatever comes to mind in the hopes of hitting on a winning chicken noodle soup advertising formula. Indeed, companies across the world regularly use group brainstorming as a means of generating novel ideas. They assume that several heads that generate a flurry of ideas are better than one. In a book entitled *Applied Imagination*, which influenced many companies to adopt brainstorming, Alex Osborn (1957) argued that "the average person can think up twice as many ideas when working with a group than when working alone" (p. 229).

Although the idea behind group brainstorming is intuitively appealing, it turns out to be wrong. Numerous studies demonstrate that group brainstorming is actually less effective than individual brainstorming (Brown & Paulus, 2002; Diehl & Stroebe, 1987). When brainstorming, groups tend to come up with fewer ideas, and often fewer good ones, than individuals (Paulus, 2004; Putman & Paulus, 2009). Group brainstorming generally also results in less creative ideas than those generated by individual brainstorming. Making matters worse, groups often overestimate how successful they are at producing new ideas, which may help to explain brainstorming's popularity (Paulus, Larey, & Ortega, 1995).

There are at least two reasons why group brainstorming is less effective than individual brainstorming. One is that group members may be anxious about being evaluated by others, leading them to hold back potentially good ideas. The second is social loafing. When brainstorming in groups, people frequently engage in what's called "free riding": They sit back and let others do the hard work (Diehl & Stroebe, 1987). Whatever the reason, research suggests that when it comes to brainstorming, one brain may be better than two—or many more—at least when the brains can communicate with each other.

pluralistic ignorance
error of assuming that no one in a group perceives things as we do

diffusion of responsibility
reduction in feelings of personal responsibility in the presence of others

social loafing
phenomenon whereby individuals become less productive in groups

Studies of social loafing demonstrate that in large groups, individuals often work (or in this case, pull) less hard than they do when alone.

Psychological research suggests that we sometimes engage in genuine altruism—helping largely out of empathy.

Psychologists have demonstrated social loafing in numerous experiments. In one, a researcher placed blindfolds and headphones on six participants and asked them to clap or yell as loudly as possible. When participants thought they were making noises as part of a group, they were less loud than when they thought they were making noises alone (Williams, Harkins, & Latané, 1981). Cheerleaders also cheer less loudly when they believe they're part of a group than when they believe they're alone (Hardy & Latané, 1986). Investigators have also identified social loafing effects in studies of rope-pulling (the "tug-of-war" game), navigating mazes, identifying radar signals, and evaluating job candidates (Karau & Williams, 1995). Like many other social psychological phenomena, social loafing may be influenced by cultural factors. People in individualistic countries, like the United States, are more prone to social loafing than people in collectivist countries, like China, probably because people in the latter countries feel more responsible for the outcomes of group successes or failures (Earley, 1989).

One of the best antidotes to social loafing is to ensure that each person in the group is identifiable, for example, by guaranteeing that managers and bosses can evaluate each individual's performance. By doing so, we can help "diffuse" the diffusion of responsibility that often arises in groups.

■ Prosocial Behavior and Altruism

Even though there's usually danger rather than safety in numbers when it comes to others helping us, many of us do help in emergencies even when others are around (Fischer et al., 2006). In the Kitty Genovese tragedy, at least one person apparently did call police (Manning et al., 2007). Indeed, there's good evidence that many of us engage in **altruism**, that is, helping others for unselfish reasons (Batson, 1987; Dovidio et al., 2006; Penner et al., 2005).

ALTRUISM: HELPING SELFLESSLY. Over the years, some scientists have argued that we help others entirely for egoistic (self-centered) reasons, like relieving our own distress, experiencing the joy of others we've helped (Hoffman, 1981), or anticipating that people we've helped will be more likely to reciprocate by helping us later (Gintis et al., 2003). From this perspective, we help others only to benefit ourselves, either by improving our moods or boosting the odds that someone will assist us in the future when we're in a jam. Yet in a series of experiments, Daniel Batson and his colleagues showed that we sometimes engage in genuine altruism. That is, in some cases we help others in discomfort primarily because we feel empathic toward them (Batson et al., 1991; Batson & Shaw, 1991; Fischer et al., 2006). In some studies, they exposed participants to a female victim (actually a confederate) who was receiving painful electric shocks and gave them the option of either (a) taking her place and receiving shocks themselves or (b) turning away and not watching her receive shocks. When participants were made to feel empathic toward the victim (for example, by learning that their values and interests were similar to hers), they generally offered to take her place and receive shocks rather than turn away (Batson et al., 1981). In some cases we seem to help not only to relieve our distress but to relieve the distress of others.

Along with empathy, a number of psychological variables increase the odds of helping. Let's look at some of the most crucial ones.

HELPING: SITUATIONAL INFLUENCES. People are more likely to help in some situations than in others. They're more likely to help others when they can't easily escape the situation—for example, by running away, driving away, or as in the case of the Kitty Genovese murder, turning off their lights and drifting back to sleep. They're also more likely to help someone who collapses on a crowded subway than on the sidewalk. Characteristics of the victim also matter. In one study, bystanders helped a person with a cane 95 percent of the time, but helped an obviously drunk person only 50 percent of the time (Piliavin, Rodin, & Piliavin, 1969). Being in a good mood also makes us more likely to help (Isen, Clark, & Schwartz, 1976). So does exposure to role models who help others (Bryan & Test, 1967; Rushton & Campbell, 1977).

altruism
helping others for unselfish reasons

One striking study examined seminary students who were on their way across campus to deliver a sermon on the Biblical story of the Good Samaritan, which describes the moral importance of assisting injured people (Darley & Batson, 1973). The investigators led some students to believe that they needed to rush over to give the lecture, others to believe they had some extra time. While walking across campus, the students came across a man (actually a confederate) slumped over in a doorway who twice coughed and moaned loudly. The seminary students were significantly less likely to offer assistance to the man if they were in a hurry (only 10 percent) than if they had time to spare (63 percent). Some of the students simply stepped over him on their way to the lecture. So much for the Good Samaritan!

If there's a silver lining to the gray cloud of bystander nonintervention, it's that exposure to research on bystander effects may increase the chances of intervening in emergencies. This is an example of what Kenneth Gergen (1973) called an **enlightenment effect**: Learning about psychological research can change real-world behavior for the better (Katzev & Brownstein, 1989). A group of investigators (Beaman et al., 1978) presented the research literature on bystander intervention effects to one psychology class—containing much of the same information you've just read—but didn't present this literature to a very similar psychology class. Two weeks later, the students, accompanied by a confederate, came upon a person slumped over on a park bench. Compared with 25 percent of students who hadn't received the lecture on bystander intervention, 43 percent of students who'd received the lecture intervened to help. This study worked, probably because it imparted new knowledge about bystander intervention and perhaps also because it made people more aware of the importance of helping. So the very act of reading this chapter may have made you more likely to become a responsive bystander.

HELPING: INDIVIDUAL AND GENDER DIFFERENCES. Individual differences in personality also influence the likelihood of helping. Participants who are less concerned about social approval and less traditional are more likely to go against the grain and intervene in emergencies even when others are present (Latané & Darley, 1970). Extraverted people are also more prone to help others than introverted people (Krueger, Hicks, & McGue, 2001). In addition, people with lifesaving skills, such as trained medical workers, are more likely to offer assistance to others in emergencies than are other people, even when they're off duty (Huston et al., 1981). Some people may not help on certain occasions simply because they don't know what to do.

Some researchers have reported a slight tendency for men to help more than women (Eagly & Crowley, 1986). This difference isn't especially consistent across studies (Becker & Eagly, 2004), and it seems to be accounted for by an alternative explanation, namely the tendency of men to help more than women only in situations involving physical or social risk. Moreover, men are especially likely to help women rather than other men, especially if the women are physically attractive (Eagly & Crowley, 1986).

◄ ruling out rival hypotheses

HAVE IMPORTANT ALTERNATIVE EXPLANATIONS FOR THE FINDINGS BEEN EXCLUDED?

■ Aggression: Why We Hurt Others

Like our primate cousins, the chimpanzees, we occasionally engage in violence toward others. And like them, we're a war-waging species; as we write this chapter, there are at least 15 full-scale wars raging across the globe. Psychologists define **aggression** as behavior intended to harm others, either verbally or physically. To account for aggressive behavior on both large and small scales, we need to examine the role of both situational and dispositional factors.

AGGRESSION: SITUATIONAL INFLUENCES. Using both laboratory and naturalistic designs (see Chapter 2), psychologists have pinpointed a host of situational influences—some short-term, others long-term, on human aggression. Here are some of the best-replicated findings.

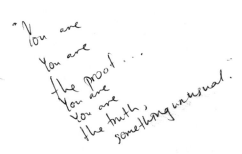

enlightenment effect
learning about psychological research can change real-world behavior for the better

aggression
behavior intended to harm others, either verbally or physically

◄ replicability

CAN THE RESULTS BE DUPLICATED IN OTHER STUDIES?

Both interpersonal provocation and frustration from being stuck in traffic probably contribute to "road rage."

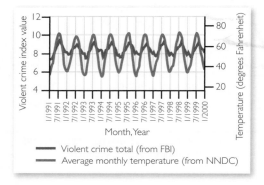

FIGURE 13.9   Monthly Violent Crime versus Average Temperature, 1991–1999. Research demonstrates that violent crime rates coincide with outdoor temperatures. How might we determine whether this correlation indicates a causal effect? (*Source:* Nienberg)

ruling out rival hypotheses

HAVE IMPORTANT ALTERNATIVE EXPLANATIONS FOR THE FINDINGS BEEN EXCLUDED?

- **Interpersonal Provocation:** Not surprisingly, we're especially likely to strike out aggressively against those who have provoked us, say, by insulting, threatening, or hitting us (Geen, 2001).

- **Frustration:** We're especially likely to behave aggressively when frustrated, that is, thwarted from reaching a goal (Anderson & Bushman, 2002b; Berkowitz, 1989). In one study, a research assistant asked participants to perform a difficult paper-folding (origami) task at an unreasonably rapid rate, and either apologized for moving participants along too quickly or told them to pick up the pace ("I would like to hurry and get this over with"). Frustrated participants—those in the second condition—were later more likely to give the assistant a low job-related evaluation (Dill & Anderson, 1995).

- **Media Influences:** As we learned in Chapter 6, an impressive body of laboratory and naturalistic evidence points to the conclusion that watching media violence increases the odds of violence through observational learning (Anderson et al., 2003; Bandura, 1973). A number of laboratory experiments suggests that playing violent video games also boosts the odds of violence in both Western and Asian cultures (Anderson et al., 2010; Gentile & Anderson, 2006), although some have questioned how well these findings generalize to the real world (Ferguson, 2009; Ferguson & Kilburn, 2010; Freedman, 2002).

- **Aggressive Cues:** External cues associated with violence, such as guns and knives, can serve as discriminative stimuli (see Chapter 6) for aggression, making us more likely to act violently in response to provocation (Carlson, Marcus-Newhall, & Miller, 1990). Leonard Berkowitz and Anthony LePage (1967) found that the mere presence of a gun—as opposed to a badminton racket—on a table triggered more aggression in participants who'd been provoked by mild electric shocks for supposed poor performance on a task.

- **Arousal:** When our autonomic nervous systems (see Chapters 3 and 12) are hyped up, we may mistakenly attribute this arousal to anger, leading us to act aggressively (Zillman, 1988). Dolf Zillmann and his colleagues found that participants who pedaled an exercise bicycle delivered more intense electric shocks to someone who'd annoyed them than did participants who sat still (Zillmann, Katcher, & Milavsky, 1972).

- **Alcohol and Other Drugs:** Certain substances can disinhibit our brain's prefrontal cortex (see Chapter 3), lowering our inhibitions toward behaving violently (Begue & Subra, 2008; Kelly et al., 1988). After being provoked with electric shocks by an "opponent" (who was actually fictitious) during a competitive game, participants chose more intense electric shocks after consuming alcohol or benzodiazepines, such as Valium (see Chapter 16), than after consuming a placebo (Taylor, 1993). But alcohol is likely to trigger aggression only when the target of our aggression occupies the focus of our attention, as when someone is threatening us directly (Giancola & Corman, 2007).

- **Temperature:** Rates of violent crime in different regions of the United States mirror the average temperatures in these regions (Anderson, Bushman, & Groom, 1997). Because warm temperatures increase irritability, they may make people more likely to lose their tempers when provoked or frustrated (Anderson & Bushman, 2002b). Nevertheless, because extremely warm temperatures are more common in the southern United States, in which violent crime rates are especially high (see the Cultural Differences section on page 519), investigators have had to rule out the rival hypothesis that this "heat effect" is due to geographical region. They've generally succeeded in doing so by demonstrating that even within the same geographical region, warmer temperatures are associated with higher rates of violence (Anderson & Anderson, 1996; see **FIGURE 13.9**). Even getting people to think about words associated with heat (like sunburn)—compared with words associated with cold or neutral words—makes them more likely to act aggressively (DeWall & Bushman, 2009).

AGGRESSION: INDIVIDUAL, GENDER, AND CULTURAL DIFFERENCES. On a typical day in the United States, there are between 40 and 45 murders; that's one about every half hour. There are also about 230 reported rapes, or one about every five or six minutes (Federal Bureau of Investigation, 2005). These statistics paint a grim picture. Yet the substantial majority of people are generally law-abiding, and only a tiny percentage ever engage in serious physical aggression toward others. Across a wide swath of societies that scientists have studied, only a small percentage of people—perhaps 5 or 6 percent—account for a half or more of all crimes, including violent crimes (Wilson & Herrnstein, 1985). Why?

Personality Traits. When confronted with the same situation, like an insult, people differ in their tendencies to behave aggressively. Certain personality traits can combine to create a dangerous cocktail of aggression-proneness. People with high levels of negative emotions (such as irritability and mistrust), impulsivity, and a lack of closeness to others are especially prone to violence (Krueger et al., 1994).

Sex Differences. One of the best replicated sex differences in humans, and across the animal kingdom for that matter, is the higher level of physical aggressiveness among males than females (Eagly & Steffen, 1986; Maccoby & Jacklin, 1980; Storch et al., 2004). In conjunction with biological sex, age plays a role: The rates of crime, including violent crime, would drop by two-thirds if all males between the ages of 12 and 28 were magically placed into a state of temporary hibernation (Lykken, 1995).

The reasons for the sex difference in aggression are controversial, although some researchers have traced it to higher levels of the hormone testosterone in males (Dabbs, 2001). Nevertheless, the correlation between testosterone and aggression is controversial, because aggression may cause higher testosterone rather than the other way around (Sapolsky, 1998). One of the precious few exceptions to the sex difference in aggression is the spotted hyena (or "laughing hyena"), in which females are more aggressive than males. This exception may prove the rule, because the female spotted hyena has unusually high levels of a hormone closely related to testosterone (Glickman et al., 1987). Social factors almost surely play a role, too, at least in humans: Parents and teachers pay more attention to boys when they engage in aggression and to girls when they engage in dependent behaviors, like clinginess (Eagly, Wood, & Diekman, 2000; Serbin & O'Leary, 1975).

Yet the well-replicated male predominance in aggression may apply only to direct aggression, like physical violence and bullying, not indirect aggression—which is typically marked by "stabbing others in the back." Nicki Crick (1995) discovered that girls tend to be higher than boys in **relational aggression**, a form of indirect aggression marked by spreading rumors, gossiping, social exclusion, and nonverbal putdowns (like giving other girls "the silent treatment") for the purposes of interpersonal manipulation. Crick's findings dovetail with results suggesting that females are just as likely, if not more, than males to express anger in subtle ways (Archer, 2004; Eagly & Steffen, 1986; Frieze et al., 1978). In contrast, boys have much higher rates of bullying than girls (Olweus, 1993).

Cultural Differences. Culture also shapes aggression. Physical aggression and violent crime are less prevalent among Asian individuals, such as Japanese and Chinese, than among Americans or Europeans (Wilson & Herrnstein, 1985; Zhang & Snowdon, 1999). Richard Nisbett, Dov Cohen, and colleagues have also found that people from the southern regions of the United States are more likely than those from other regions of the country to adhere to a *culture of honor*, a social norm of defending one's reputation in the face of perceived insults (Nisbett & Cohen, 1996; Vandello, Cohen, & Ransom, 2008). The culture of honor may help to explain why the rates of violence are higher in the South than in other parts of the United States. Interestingly, these rates are higher only for violence that arises in the context of disputes, not in robberies, burglaries, or other crimes (Cohen & Nisbett, 1994). The culture of honor even shows itself in the relatively safe confines of the laboratory. In three experiments, a male confederate bumped into a male college student in a narrow hallway, muttering a profanity about him before storming

relational aggression
form of indirect aggression, prevalent in girls, involving spreading rumors, gossiping, and nonverbal putdowns for the purpose of social manipulation

replicability
CAN THE RESULTS BE DUPLICATED IN OTHER STUDIES?

correlation vs. causation
CAN WE BE SURE THAT A CAUSES B?

replicability
CAN THE RESULTS BE DUPLICATED IN OTHER STUDIES?

Research suggests although males tend to be more physically aggressive than females, girls are more likely than boys to engage in relational aggression, which includes gossiping and making fun of others behind their backs.

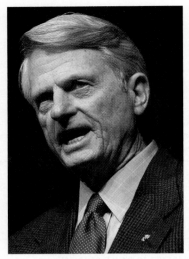

In a heated television interview in 2004 with host Chris Matthews, former Georgia governor Zell Miller stunned viewers by saying that he wished he could challenge Matthews to a duel. Yet social psychologists familiar with the "culture of honor" could not have been surprised, as Southern gentlemen of days past frequently settled challenges to their reputation in this manner.

People's expressed voting preferences to pollsters don't always predict their actual voting behavior.

attitude
belief that includes an emotional component

away. Students from southern states were more likely than students from other states to react with a boost in testosterone and to display aggressive behavior against another confederate (Cohen et al., 1996).

✔•⦿ **Study** and **Review** on **mypsychlab.com**

assess your knowledge   **FACT OR FICTION?**

1. Research suggests that the old saying that "there's safety in numbers" is wrong.
   True / False

2. The primary reason for bystander nonintervention is the apathy of onlookers.
   True / False

3. Most people tend to work especially hard in groups. True / False

4. People who have lifesaving skills are more likely to help than those without.
   True / False

5. Drinking can calm us down, lowering our risk for aggression. True / False

6. The "culture of honor" may contribute to lower levels of violent crime in the U.S. South.
   True / False

Answers: 1. T (p. 514); 2. F (p. 514); 3. F (p. 515); 4. T (p. 517); 5. F (p. 518); (6) F (p. 519)

ATTITUDES AND PERSUASION: CHANGING MINDS

13.8 Describe how attitudes relate to behavior.

13.9 Evaluate theoretical accounts of how and when we alter our attitudes.

13.10 Identify common and effective persuasion techniques and how they're exploited by pseudoscientists.

First, answer the following question: Do you think the death penalty is an effective deterrent against murder? Second, answer this question: How do you feel about the death penalty?

Having gone through this exercise, you can now grasp the difference between beliefs and attitudes. The first question assessed your *beliefs* about the death penalty, the second question assessed your *attitudes* toward the death penalty. A belief is a conclusion regarding factual evidence, whereas an **attitude** is a belief that includes an emotional component. Attitudes reflect how we feel about an issue or person. For that reason, they're an important part of our social worlds.

■ Attitudes and Behavior

A prevalent misconception is that attitudes are good predictors of behavior. For example, most people believe that how we feel about a political candidate predicts with a high level of certainty whether we'll vote toward or against that candidate. It doesn't (Wicker, 1969). In part, this finding explains why even carefully conducted political polls are rarely foolproof.

WHEN ATTITUDES DON'T PREDICT BEHAVIOR. In a study conducted over 70 years ago, Robert LaPiere surveyed 128 American hotel and restaurant owners to find out whether they'd be willing to serve guests who were Chinese, who at the time were widely discriminated against. Over 90 percent of LaPiere's participants said no. Yet when LaPiere had previously toured the country with a Chinese couple, 127 of 128 owners of the same establishments had already served them (LaPiere, 1934). To be sure, LaPiere's study was imperfect; for example, there's no way to know if the people who filled out the survey were the same people who'd served them (Dockery & Bedeian, 1989). Still, his conclusion has stood the test of time. Indeed, a review of 88 studies revealed that the average correlation between attitudes and behavior is about .38 (Kraus, 1995), which is only a moderate association. So although attitudes forecast behavior at better-than-chance levels, they're far from powerful predictors. This finding probably reflects the fact that our behaviors are the outcome of many factors, only one of which is our attitudes. For example, LaPiere's prejudiced participants may not have been especially fond of the idea of serving Chinese guests. Yet when they met these guests in person, they may have found them more likable than they expected. Or when push came to shove, they may have been reluctant to pass up the chance for good business.

WHEN ATTITUDES DO PREDICT BEHAVIOR. Occasionally, though, our attitudes predict our behaviors reasonably well. Attitudes that are highly *accessible*—which come to mind easily—tend to be strongly predictive of our behavior (Fazio, 1995). Imagine that we asked you two questions: (1) How do you feel about the idea of buying a new brand of yogurt that's been scientifically demonstrated to decrease our levels of low-density cholesterol? and (2) How do you feel about the idea of buying chocolate ice cream? If you're like most people, you'll find the second question easier to answer than the first question, because you've thought more about it. If so, your attitude toward chocolate ice cream is more likely to predict your purchasing behavior than your attitude toward the new-fangled yogurt. Perhaps not surprisingly, attitudes also tend to predict behavior when they're firmly held and stable over time (Conner et al., 2000; Kraus, 1995).

Attitudes predict behavior when:
→ firmly held and stable over time
→ low self-monitors

Attitudes also predict behavior well for a group of people called low *self-monitors* (Kraus, 1995). **Self-monitoring** is a trait that assesses the extent to which people's behaviors reflect their true feelings and attitudes (Gangestad & Snyder, 2000; Snyder, 1974). Low self-monitors tend to be straight shooters, whereas high self-monitors tend to be social chameleons. We can more often trust low self-monitors' actions to mirror their attitudes.

correlation vs. causation
CAN WE BE SURE THAT A CAUSES B?

Still, the fact that attitudes are correlated with behaviors doesn't mean they cause them. Other explanations are possible; for example, our behaviors may sometimes cause our attitudes. Imagine that we start out with a negative attitude toward homeless persons. If a friend persuades us to volunteer to help the homeless for three hours a week and we end up enjoying this type of work, our attitudes toward homeless people may improve.

Origins of Attitudes

Our attitudes stem from a variety of sources, including our prior experience and personalities. Here, we'll review some of the key influences on our attitudes.

recognition heuristic = more likely to believe something we've heard many times

RECOGNITION. Our experiences shape our attitudes. The *recognition heuristic* makes us more likely to believe something we've heard many times (Arkes, 1993). Like most heuristics (mental shortcuts or rules of thumb; see Chapter 2), the recognition heuristic generally serves us well, because things we hear many times from many different people often *are* true. Moreover, this heuristic can help us make snap judgments that are surprisingly accurate. To test this possibility, two researchers asked a group of students in Chicago and in Munich, Germany, the following question: *Which city has a larger population: San Diego, California, or San Antonio, Texas?* Unexpectedly, only 62 percent of American students got the correct answer (San Diego), whereas 100 percent of German students did (Goldstein & Gigerenzer, 1999). The German students didn't get it right more often than the Americans because they had more knowledge of U.S. cities; they got it right because they had *less* knowledge of U.S. cities. Most German students had never heard of San Antonio, so they relied on the recognition heuristic ("The city I've heard of probably has more people in it"). In contrast, the American students had heard of both cities and then tried to guess which had a larger population. For the German students, at least, the recognition heuristic worked.

But when a story is persuasive or interesting, the recognition heuristic can get us into trouble. It can lead us to fall for stories that are too good to be true, like some urban legends, or buy products that seem familiar just because we've heard their names over and over again. All good advertisers make use of this heuristic by cooking up catchy, easily repeated jingles. If we recall the *bandwagon fallacy* from Chapter 1, we'll remember that we shouldn't believe—or buy—something merely because most people do. Moreover, hearing

self-monitoring
personality trait that assesses the extent to which people's behavior reflects their true feelings and attitudes

one person express an opinion 10 times ("Grandma Sally's Spaghetti Tastes Delicious!") can lead us to conclude falsely that this view is as widely held as hearing 10 people express it only once (Weaver et al., 2007).

ATTITUDES AND PERSONALITY. Our attitudes are associated in important ways with our personality traits. Although we may persuade ourselves that our political attitudes derive from completely objective analyses of social issues, these attitudes are often affected by our personalities.

In an article that stirred up more than its share of controversy, one team of researchers (Jost, Glaser, Kruglanski, & Sulloway, 2003) reported that across many studies, political conservatives tend to be more fearful, more sensitive to threat, and less tolerant of uncertainty than political liberals. They suggested that these personality traits are the "psychological glue" that binds together conservatives' political attitudes toward the death penalty, abortion, gun control, school prayer, national defense, and a host of seemingly unrelated issues. Other research shows that conservatives show a higher skin conductance response—a measure of arousal (see Chapter 6)—than do liberals following threatening stimuli, like sudden loud noises or pictures of large spiders or badly wounded people (Oxley et al., 2008). Nevertheless, some researchers have questioned whether findings comparing conservatives and liberals are due to an alternative hypothesis: They might reflect political extremism in general rather than right-wing conservatism specifically (Greenberg & Jonas, 2003). According to them, left-wing extremists are just as likely to be fearful, dogmatic, and the like, as right-wing extremists are. Because there are few studies of left-wing extremists, we don't know who's right.

Our personalities even relate to, and perhaps influence, our attitudes toward religion. The specific religion we adopt is largely a function of our religious exposure while growing up and is mostly independent of our personalities. Nevertheless, our *religiosity*—the depth of our religious convictions—is linked to certain personality traits. Adolescents with high levels of conscientiousness (see Chapter 14) are especially likely to become deeply religious adults (McCullough, Tsang, & Brion, 2003).

ruling out rival hypotheses

HAVE IMPORTANT ALTERNATIVE EXPLANATIONS FOR THE FINDINGS BEEN EXCLUDED?

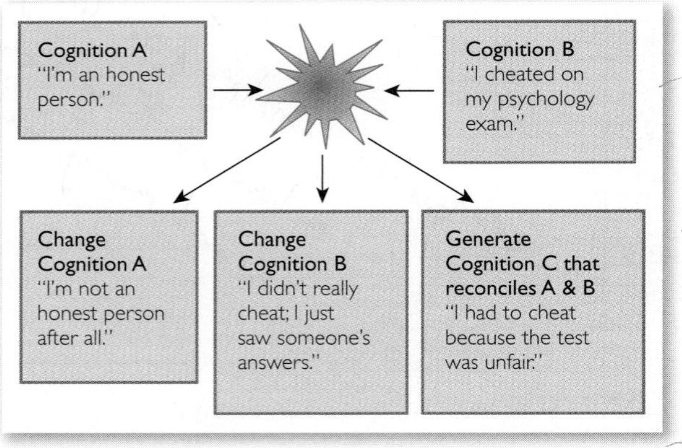

FIGURE 13.10 Cognitive Dissonance Theory. According to cognitive dissonance theory, we can reduce the conflict between two cognitions (beliefs) in multiple ways—by changing the first cognition, changing the second cognition, or introducing a third cognition that resolves the conflict.

cognitive dissonance
unpleasant mental experience of tension resulting from two conflicting thoughts or beliefs

■ Attitude Change: Wait, Wait, I Just Changed My Mind

Many of us are surprised to discover that our attitudes on many topics, like the death penalty and abortion, change over the years. We tend to perceive ourselves as more consistent over time in our attitudes than we really are (Bem & McConnell, 1970; Goethals & Reckman, 1973; Ross, 1989), perhaps in part because we don't like to think of ourselves as weak-willed flip-floppers. Yet this point raises a question that psychologists have long struggled to answer: Why and how do our attitudes change?

COGNITIVE DISSONANCE THEORY. In the 1950s, Leon Festinger developed *cognitive dissonance theory,* an influential model of attitude change. According to this theory, we alter our attitudes because we experience an unpleasant state of tension—**cognitive dissonance**—between two or more conflicting thoughts (cognitions). Because we dislike this state of tension, we're motivated to reduce or eliminate it. If we hold an attitude or belief (cognition A) that's inconsistent with another attitude or belief (cognition B), we can reduce the anxiety resulting from this inconsistency in three major ways: change cognition A, change cognition B, or introduce a new cognition, C, that resolves the inconsistency between A and B (see **FIGURE 13.10**).

Let's move from As, Bs, and Cs to a real-world example. Imagine you believe that your new friend, Sandy, is a nice person. You learn from another friend, Chris, that Sandy recently stole a wallet from a fellow classmate. According to Festinger, this news should produce cognitive dissonance, because it creates a conflict between cognition A (Sandy is a nice person) and cognition B (Sandy stole money from someone and therefore isn't such a nice person after all). To resolve this nagging sense of tension, you can change cognition A and decide that Sandy actually isn't such a nice person. Or you can change cognition B, perhaps by deciding that the news that Sandy stole money must be a false rumor spread by her enemies. Or you can instead introduce a new thought, cognition C, that resolves the discrepancy between cognitions A and B. For example, you could persuade yourself that Sandy is still a nice person but that she took her classmate's wallet be-

cause she was starving and in desperate need of a short-term infusion of cash ("I'm sure she'll return the wallet and all of the money in a day or two once she's grabbed something to eat," you reassure yourself).

Festinger, along with J. Merrill Carlsmith, conducted the first systematic test of cognitive dissonance theory in the late 1950s (Festinger & Carlsmith, 1959).

The Setup: You sign up for a two-hour study of "Measures of Performance." At the lab, an experimenter provides you with instructions for some manual tasks—all mind-numbingly boring, like inserting 12 spools into a tray, emptying the tray, refilling the tray, and so on, for half an hour. Now here's the twist: The experimenter explains that a research assistant normally informs the next participant waiting in the hallway about the study and, to help recruit this participant, he says how interesting and enjoyable the study was. Unfortunately, the research assistant couldn't make it into the lab today. So, the experimenter wonders, would you be kind enough to substitute for him?

The Study: Festinger and Carlsmith randomly assigned some participants to receive $1 to perform this favor and others to receive $20. Afterward, they asked participants how much they enjoyed performing the tasks. From the perspective of learning theory, especially operant conditioning (see Chapter 6), we might expect participants paid $20 to say they enjoyed the task more. Yet cognitive dissonance theory makes the counterintuitive prediction that participants paid $1 should say they enjoyed the task more. Why? Because all participants should experience cognitive dissonance: They performed an incredibly boring task but told the next participant it was fun. Yet participants given $20 had a good *external justification* for telling this little fib, namely, that the experimenter bribed them to do it. In contrast, participants given $1 have almost no external justification. As a result, the only easy way to resolve their cognitive dissonance is to persuade themselves that they must have enjoyed the task after all. They deceive themselves.

The Results: The results supported this surprising prediction. Participants given less money reported enjoying the task more, presumably because they needed to justify their lies to themselves. Their behaviors had changed their attitudes. Since Festinger and Carlsmith's study, hundreds of experiments have yielded results consistent with cognitive dissonance theory (Cooper, 2007; Harmon-Jones & Mills, 1999). ⊕ Explore

ALTERNATIVES TO COGNITIVE DISSONANCE THEORY. Cognitive dissonance theory is alive and well, although researchers continue to debate whether alternative processes account for attitude change. Some scholars contend that it's not dissonance itself that's responsible for shifting our attitudes, but rather threats to our self-concepts (Aronson, 1992; Wood, 2000). In Festinger and Carlsmith's (1959) study, perhaps what motivated participants in the $1 condition to change their attitudes was a discrepancy between who they believed they were (a decent person) and what they did (lie to another participant). From this perspective, only certain conflicts between attitudes produce cognitive dissonance, namely, those that challenge our views of who we are.

There are at least two other explanations for cognitive dissonance effects. The first, **self-perception theory,** proposes that we acquire our attitudes by observing our behaviors (Bem, 1967). According to this model, Festinger and Carlsmith's participants in the $1

 How would cognitive dissonance theory explain why some fraternities ask their members to perform bizarre and embarrassing hazing rituals before joining? If you're curious, one classic study investigated this issue (Aronson & Mills, 1959). (See answer upside down on bottom of page.)

FACTOID ✚

In one of the most creative demonstrations of cognitive dissonance theory, four researchers asked participants to taste fried grasshoppers (Zimbardo et al., 1965). They randomly assigned some participants to receive this bizarre request from a friendly person, and others to receive it from an unfriendly person. Consistent with cognitive dissonance theory, the latter participants reported liking the fried grasshoppers more than the former participants did. Participants who tasted the grasshoppers at the behest of the friendly person had a good external justification ("I did it to help out a nice person"), but the other participants didn't. So the latter participants resolved their dissonance by changing their attitudes— hmmm, those little critters were delicious.

⊕ Explore Cognitive Dissonance on **mypsychlab.com**

◄ **replicability**
CAN THE RESULTS BE DUPLICATED IN OTHER STUDIES?

◄ **ruling out rival hypotheses**
HAVE IMPORTANT ALTERNATIVE EXPLANATIONS FOR THE FINDINGS BEEN EXCLUDED?

self-perception theory
theory that we acquire our attitudes by observing our behaviors

Answer: People who willingly undergo a severe initiation to a group feel a need to justify this action, and thereby convince themselves that the group must be worthwhile.

Dual Process Models of persuasion:
(1) Central = careful, thoughtful information is key
(2) Peripheral = surface features

condition looked at their behavior and said to themselves, "I told the other participant that I liked the task, and I got paid only one lousy buck to do so. So I guess I must have really liked the task." The second, **impression management theory** (Goffman, 1959), proposes that we don't really change our attitudes in cognitive dissonance studies; we only tell the experimenters we have. We do so because we don't want to appear inconsistent (Tedeschi, Schlenker, & Bonoma, 1971). According to this model, Festinger and Carlsmith's participants in the $1 condition didn't want to look like hypocrites. So they told the experimenter they enjoyed the task even though they didn't. As is often the case in psychology, there may be some truth to each explanation. Some participants may exhibit attitude change because of cognitive dissonance, others because of self-perception, and still others because of impression management (Bem & Funder, 1978).

■ Persuasion: Humans as Salespeople

Whether or not we realize it, we encounter attempts at persuasion every day. If you're like the average student entering college, you've already watched 360,000 commercials; that number will reach a staggering two million by the time you turn 65. Each time you walk into a store or supermarket, you see hundreds of products that marketers have crafted carefully to make you more likely to purchase them.

ROUTES TO PERSUASION. According to *dual process models* of persuasion, there are two alternative pathways to persuading others (Petty & Cacioppo, 1986; Petty & Wegener, 1999). One, the *central* route, leads us to evaluate the merits of persuasive arguments carefully and thoughtfully. Here, we focus on the *informational content* of the arguments: Do they hold up under close scrutiny? We're especially likely to take this route when we're motivated to evaluate information carefully and able do so, as when we're deciding between two colleges we like very much, and have plenty of time and relevant information on our hands. The attitudes we acquire via this route tend to be strongly held and relatively enduring.

The other, the *peripheral* route, leads us to respond to persuasive arguments on the basis of snap judgments. Here, we focus on *surface aspects* of the arguments: For example, how appealing or interesting are they? We're especially likely to take this route when we're not motivated to weigh information carefully and don't have the ability to do so, as when we're distracted while watching a commercial. Although the attitudes we acquire via this route tend to be weaker and relatively unstable, they can affect our short-term choices in powerful ways. The danger of persuasive messages that travel through the peripheral route is that we can be easily fooled by superficial factors, such as how physically attractive, famous, or likable the communicator is or how many times we've heard the message (Hemsley & Doob, 1978; Hovland, Janis, & Kelly, 1953; Kenrick, Neuberg, & Cialdini, 2005).

PERSUASION TECHNIQUES. Drawing on the research literature concerning attitudes and attitude change, psychologists have identified a host of effective techniques for persuading others. Many of these methods operate by means of the peripheral persuasion route, largely bypassing our scientific thinking capacities. Interestingly, successful businesspeople have used many of these techniques for decades (Cialdini, 2001). Let's look at three of them.

Start small, then go big.

- **Foot-in-the-door technique:** Following on the heels of cognitive dissonance theory (Freedman & Fraser, 1966; Gorassini & Olson, 1995), the **foot-in-the-door technique** suggests that we start with a small request before making a bigger one. If we want to get our classmate to volunteer five hours a week for the "Helping a Starving Psychologist" charity organization, we can first ask her to volunteer one hour a week. Once we've gotten her to agree to that request, we have our "foot in the door," because from the perspective of cognitive dissonance theory she'll feel a need to justify her initial commitment. As a consequence, she'll probably end up with a positive attitude toward the organization, boosting the odds that she'll volunteer even more of her time.

impression management theory
theory that we don't really change our attitudes, but report that we have so that our behaviors appear consistent with our attitudes

foot-in-the-door technique
persuasive technique involving making a small request before making a bigger one

door-in-the-face technique
persuasive technique involving making an unreasonably large request before making the small request we're hoping to have granted

low-ball technique
persuasive technique in which the seller of a product starts by quoting a low sales price, and then mentions all of the "add-on" costs once the customer has agreed to purchase the product

- **Door-in-the-face technique:** Alternatively, we can start with a large request, like asking for a $100 donation to our charity, before asking for a small one, like a $10 donation (Cialdini et al., 1975; O'Keefe & Hale, 2001). One reason this **door-in-the-face technique** works may be that the initial large request often induces guilt in recipients (O'Keefe & Figge, 1997). But if the initial request is so outrageous that it appears insincere or unreasonable, this method can backfire (Cialdini & Goldstein, 2004). Research suggests that the foot-in-the-door and door-in-the-face techniques work about equally well (Pascual & Guequen, 2005).

- **Low-ball technique:** In the **low-ball technique**, the seller of a product starts by quoting a price well below the actual sales price (Burger & Petty, 1981; Cialdini, 2001). Once the buyer agrees to purchase the product, the seller mentions all of the desirable or needed "add-ons" that come along with the product. By the time the deal is done, the buyer may end up paying twice as much as he'd initially agreed to pay. We can even use this technique to obtain favors from friends. In one study, a confederate asked strangers to look after his dog while he visited a friend in the hospital. In some cases, he first got the stranger to agree to the request, and only then told him he'd be gone for half an hour; in other cases, he told the stranger up front he'd be gone for half an hour. The first tactic worked better (Gueguen, Pascual, & Dagot, 2002). 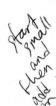 Watch

This car salesperson begins the deal by quoting the base price, and then once the customer has agreed to purchase the car, he mentions all of the added features that cost more. **What persuasion technique is he using?** (See answer upside down at bottom of page.)

When asking for a raise, one approach is to request a much larger raise than one expects in the hopes that boss will offer a raise close to what one wants. **What do psychologists call this technique?** (See answer upside down on bottom of page.)

Watch a Car Salesman Example: Robert Cialdini on **mypsychlab.com**

CHARACTERISTICS OF THE MESSENGER. Research demonstrates that we're more likely to swallow a persuasive message if famous or attractive people deliver it—whether or not they'd logically know something about the product they're hawking.

Fortunately, we can safeguard consumers against this error by teaching them to distinguish legitimate from illegitimate authorities (Cialdini & Sagarin, 2005). We're also more likely to believe messages when the source possesses high credibility, such as presumed expertise (Heesacker, Petty, & Cacioppo, 1983; Pornpitakpan, 2004). That's almost surely why so many drug commercials feature physicians dressed in white lab coats, and why so many product advertisements assure that us "Four out of five doctors recommend . . ."

In addition, messages are especially persuasive if the messenger seems similar to us. In one study, researchers asked students to read a description of the bizarre and not especially likable Russian mystic, Grigory Rasputin. Some students were randomly assigned a description of Rasputin that featured his birth date (December 16), whereas others were randomly assigned a description of Rasputin that featured the student's birth date. Students who believed they shared a birth date with Rasputin thought more positively of him than students who didn't (Finch & Cialdini, 1989).

Researchers have now reported this *implicit egotism* effect—the finding that we're more positively disposed toward people, places, or things that resemble us—across many domains (Pelham, Carvallo, & Jones, 2005). This effect appears to influence not only our attitudes, but our life choices. In matters of love and friendship, we're more likely than chance would predict to select people whose names contain the first letters of our first or last names. All things being equal, Johns tend to be fond of Jessicas, Roberts of Ronalds, and so on. Nevertheless, most people are unaware of this *name-letter effect* (Nuttin, 1985). People even seem to gravitate to places

Endorsements from attractive celebrities, like Hilary Duff, can lead us to prefer some products over others for irrational reasons.

that are similar to their names. One group of researchers found a higher than expected number of Louises living in Louisiana, Virginias in Virginia, Georgias in Georgia, and Florences in Florida (Pelham, Mirenberg, & Jones, 2002; see **FIGURE 13.11**). Moreover, the investigators ruled out an alternative explanation for this finding, namely, the possibility that parents tended to name their children after the state in which they were born, by determining that adults tend to move into states with names similar to their own.

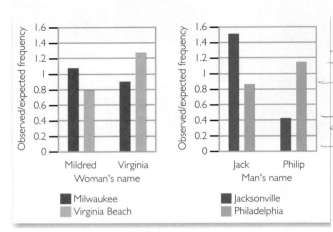

FIGURE 13.11 Graph Illustrating Implicit Egotism Effect. Research shows a statistical tendency for us to choose to live in cities and other geographical regions with names similar to ours. (*Source:* Pelham, Mirenberg, & Jones, 2002)

Answers are located at the end of the text.

THE MARKETING OF PSEUDOSCIENCE. Many proponents of pseudoscience make good use of persuasion tactics, although they may sometimes do so with the best of intentions. The appeal of these tactics helps to explain why so many intelligent people fall prey to pseudoscientific claims. To resist these tactics, we must first be able to recognize them. Anthony Pratkanis (1995) identified a variety of persuasion tactics to watch out for when evaluating unsubstantiated claims. **TABLE 13.3** lists seven of them; we should bear in mind that people can use these tactics to persuade us of a wide variety of claims of both the pseudoscientific and everyday variety.

As we can see, several of these tactics make use of heuristics—mental shortcuts (see Chapter 2) that are appealing and seductive, but occasionally misleading. Many also take the peripheral route to persuasion, rendering it less likely we'll evaluate these claims scientifically. For example, by using vivid testimonials, advertisers exploit the availability heuristic (see Chapter 2). As a result, one dramatic case report of a person's psychological improvement following an herbal remedy can be more compelling than 20 carefully controlled studies showing that this remedy is worthless. Or by manufacturing source credibility, advertisers can fool consumers into believing that a source is more trustworthy than it is. For example, a commercial for a weight loss plan might present a person who received a certificate at a weekend workshop ("Robert Smith, Officially Certified Dietary Trainer") as a scientific expert.

WORK-FROM-HOME JOBS

evaluating CLAIMS

The internet is chock-full of advertisements for jobs that offer us the chance to earn huge sums of money from the comfort of your own home. Many of these ads use social psychological persuasion techniques to persuade us that we can achieve instant wealth, typically with little more than a phone or Internet connection. Let's evaluate some of these claims, which are modeled after actual ads for home business opportunities.

"Download our guide to starting your own business now *before they run out*."
Just because there are limited copies of this guide doesn't mean it must be valuable—perhaps the manufacturer printed only a small quantity of the guides in the first place. What marketing tactic does this claim employ (see Table 13.3 for a hint.)?

"Want to use the power of the Internet to become rich? Now you can with this report *developed by a well-known sales executive*. "
What would you want to know about the background and success of this sales executive? Should the fact that an expert created this report make you more likely to trust it? What logical fallacy does this claim commit (see Chapter 1)?

"I started out with almost no savings and now *make $5,000-$6,000 every month* working from home."
Beware of claims that rely heavily on anecdotal evidence. It would be hard to verify that this person makes $70,000 per year working from home. This person's sales results may also be unrepresentative of most people, who could earn far less (or even lose money) working from home.

TABLE 13.3 Pseudoscience Marketing Techniques.

PSEUDOSCIENCE TACTIC	CONCEPT	EXAMPLE	PROBLEM
Creation of a "phantom" goal	Capitalize on desire to accomplish unrealistic objectives	"Master the complete works of Shakespeare while sleeping!"	Extreme claims are usually impossible to achieve
Vivid testimonials	Learning about someone else's personal experience	"Sandra Sadness was severely depressed for 5 years until she underwent rebirthing therapy!"	A single person's perspective is virtually worthless as scientific evidence but can be extremely persuasive (see Chapter 2)
Manufacturing source credibility	We're more likely to believe sources that we judge to be trustworthy or legitimate	"Dr. Jonathan Nobel from Princeton endorses this subliminal tape to build self-esteem."	Advertisers may present source in a deceptive fashion
Scarcity heuristic	Something that's rare must be especially valuable	"Call before midnight to get your copy of Dr. Genius's Improvement Program; it's going to sell out fast!"	Scarcity may be false or a result of low production because of low anticipated demand
Consensus heuristic	If most people believe that something works, it must work	"Thousands of psychologists use the Rorschach Inkblot Test, so it must be valid."	Common "knowledge" is often wrong (see Chapter 1)
The natural commonplace	A widely held belief that things that are natural are good	"Mrs. Candy Cure's new over-the-counter antianxiety medication is made from all-natural ingredients!"	*Natural* doesn't mean healthy—just look at poisonous mushrooms
The goddess-within commonplace	A widely held belief that we all possess a hidden mystical side that traditional Western science neglects or denies	"The Magical Mind ESP Enhancement program allows you to get in touch with your unrecognized psychic potential!"	Carefully controlled tests fail to support supernatural ability or potential (see Chapter 4)

assess your knowledge   FACT OR FICTION?

✓ **Study** and **Review** on mypsychlab.com

1. People's attitudes often don't predict their behaviors especially well. ~~True~~ False
   correlate sometimes – not too strongly

2. We're less likely to believe something we've heard many times. True ~~False~~
   more

3. The best way to change people's minds on an issue is to pay them a large sum of money for doing so. True ~~False~~

4. Using the door-in-the-face technique, we begin with a small request before making a larger one. True ~~False~~
   large request right away

Answers: 1. T (p. 520); 2. F (p. 521); 3. F (p. 523); 4. F (p. 525).

PREJUDICE AND DISCRIMINATION

13.11 Distinguish prejudice and stereotypes as beliefs from discrimination as a behavior.

13.12 Identify some of the causes of prejudice and describe methods for combating it.

The term **prejudice** means to prejudge something negatively—to arrive at an unfavorable conclusion before we've evaluated all of the evidence. If we're prejudiced toward a specific class of persons, whether they be women, African Americans, Norwegians, or hair stylists, it means we've jumped to a premature and negative conclusion about them.

■ Stereotypes

To understand prejudice, we need to begin with stereotypes. A **stereotype** is a belief—positive or negative—about a group's characteristics that we apply to most members of that group. Like many mental shortcuts, stereotypes typically stem from adaptive psychological

prejudice
drawing negative conclusions about a person, group of people, or situation prior to evaluating the evidence

stereotype
a belief, positive or negative, about the characteristics of members of a group that is applied generally to most members of the group

Demonizing an outgroup (such as all immigrants) is a frequent manifestation of in-group bias.

FIGURE 13.12   The Danger of Stereotypes. Gordon Allport and Leo Postman (1956) used a drawing similar to this one to show how negative stereotypes can distort the transmission of information across people. They asked one White participant to look at the drawing—which clearly depicts a White man wielding a razor at an African American man—and then relay the scene to a string of five or six other White participants in a "game of telephone." As the story was passed from participant to participant, it became progressively warped—with over half of the retellings of the story describing the African American man as holding the razor.

FIGURE 13.13   Scene from Correll et al. Study on Stereotypes Quick—Is this man armed or unarmed? In the study by Correll et al. (2002), participants asked to make a split-second decision were more likely to incorrectly judge an African-American man than a White man as holding a gun—and to shoot at him. The man in the computerized scene above, by the way, is holding a cell phone.

processes. As we learned in Chapter 2, we humans are *cognitive misers*—we strive to save mental energy by simplifying reality. By lumping enormous numbers of people who share a single characteristic, like skin color, nationality, or religion, into a single category, stereotypes help us make sense of our often confusing social worlds (Macrae & Bodenhausen, 2000). In this regard, they're like other schemas (see Chapter 7) in that they help us to process information.

Yet stereotypes can be the seeds from which prejudice grows. They can mislead us when we paint them with too broad a brush, as when we assume that *all* members of a group share a given characteristic. They can also mislead us when we cling to them too rigidly and are unwilling to modify them in light of disconfirming evidence. In such cases, stereotypes fuel confirmation bias (see Chapter 2) about people who differ from us. Stereotypes, like other schemas (see Chapter 7), can also lead to us to spread erroneous negative information about members of other groups, as the classic study described in **FIGURE 13.12** demonstrates.

Stereotypes can even affect our split-second interpretations of ambiguous stimuli. One line of research demonstrating this point was inspired by a real-life tragedy. In 1999,

Western African immigrant Amadou Diallo was shot 41 times by four New York City police officers who believed mistakenly that he was reaching for a gun. In fact, he was reaching for his wallet, presumably in a desperate attempt to display his identification to the officers. As displayed in **FIGURE 13.13**, Joshua Correll and his colleagues brought the Diallo incident into the laboratory by showing participants a video of a man—in some cases White, in some cases African-American—reaching for a cell-phone, a wallet, or a handgun. Participants had less than a second to decide whether to "shoot" the man in a simulated computer game. Participants were more likely to shoot unarmed African-American than unarmed White men; this finding held true even for African-American participants (Correll et al., 2002).

Many stereotypes contain a kernel of truth, and still others are largely accurate. For instance, laypersons' estimates of the magnitude of sex differences on various psychological traits, such as aggression, helpfulness, talkativeness, and conformity, correspond closely to the actual magnitude of these differences found by researchers (Swim, 1994).

Nevertheless, some stereotypes are massive overgeneralizations. These stereotypes reflect the presence of *illusory correlation* (see Chapter 2), because they indicate the perception of an erroneous association between a minority group and a given characteristic (Hamilton & Rose, 1980). For example, although most people believe that there's a powerful correlation between mental illness and violence, studies indicate that the risk of violence is markedly elevated only among a small subset of mentally ill individuals, particularly those with paranoid beliefs or substance misuse (Douglas, Guy, & Hart, 2009; Monahan, 1984; see Chapter 15). Similarly, surveys demonstrate that most Americans believe that lesbian women are at especially high risk for HIV infection, even though lesbian women actually have lower rates of HIV infection than heterosexuals of both sexes and homosexual men (Aronson, 1992).

Stereotypes can also result in what Thomas Pettigrew (1979) called the **ultimate attribution error**: The mistake of attributing the negative behavior of entire groups—like women, Christians, or African Americans—to their dispositions ("All people of race X are unsuccessful because they're lazy"). When we commit this error, we also tend to attribute any positive behaviors of disliked groups to luck ("Unlike other members of race Y, she was successful because she was fortunate to be raised by extremely supportive parents") or to rare exceptions that prove the rule ("He's not greedy like all of the other members of race Z"). Like the fundamental attribution error, after which it's named, the ultimate attribution error leads us to underestimate the impact of situational factors on people's behavior. For example, Caucasian students are more likely to interpret a shove as intentionally aggressive, as opposed to accidental, when it originates from an African American than from another Caucasian (Duncan, 1976).

Once we've learned them, stereotypes come to us naturally. Research suggests that overcoming stereotypes takes hard mental work. The key difference between prejudiced and nonprejudiced people isn't that the former have stereotypes of minority groups and the latter don't, because both groups harbor such stereotypes. Instead, it's that prejudiced people don't try hard to resist their stereotypes, but nonprejudiced people do (Devine, 1989; Devine et al., 1991). Neuroimaging research shows that presenting White participants with extremely quick (30 milliseconds, or about one-thirtieth of a second) images of African Americans triggers activation in the amygdala, a region linked to the perception of threat (Cunningham et al., 2004; see Chapter 3). Yet presenting Whites with these images for a longer duration (525 milliseconds, or about half a second) results in lower amygdala activation, as well as higher levels of activation in the frontal lobes, which inhibit the amygdala (Ochsner et al., 2002). This provocative finding suggests that many Whites experience an automatic negative reaction to Black faces, which they suppress moments later.

■ The Nature of Prejudice

It's safe to say that we all hold at least some prejudices against certain groups of people (Aronson, 2000). Some have argued that a tendency toward prejudice is deeply rooted in the human species. From the standpoint of natural selection, organisms benefit from forging close alliances with insiders and mistrusting outsiders (Cottrell & Neuberg, 2005). This is part of a broader evolutionary principle called **adaptive conservatism** (Henderson, 1985; Mineka, 1992): better safe than sorry. Indeed, members of one race are more likely to show pronounced skin conductance responses (see Chapter 6) to fear-relevant stimuli—a snake and a spider—than to fear-irrelevant stimuli—a bird and a butterfly—that have been paired repeatedly with faces of a different race (Olsson et al., 2005). We quite easily, and perhaps quite naturally, associate people from other races with scary things.

Still, notice that we wrote "tendency" in the previous paragraph. Even if there's an evolutionary predisposition toward fearing or mistrusting outsiders, that doesn't mean that prejudice is inevitable. Two major biases are associated with our tendency to forge alliances with people like ourselves. ◉ Watch

The first is **in-group bias**, the tendency to favor individuals inside our group relative to members outside our group (Van Bavel, Packer, & Cunningham, 2008). If you've ever watched a sporting event, you've observed in-group bias. There, you'll witness thousands of red-faced fans (the term "fan," incidentally, is short for "fanatic") cheering their home team wildly and booing the visiting team with equal gusto, even though most of these fans have no financial stake in the game's outcome—and have never met a single player on either team. Yet the home team is their "tribe," and they'll happily spend several hours out of their day to cheer them on against their mortal enemy.

In-group bias may be reinforced by our tendency to "turn off" our compassion toward out-group members. In one study, researchers using functional magnetic resonance imaging (fMRI) imaged the brains of liberal college students while they pondered the description of someone similar to themselves—a liberal person—and then someone dissimilar from themselves—a Christian conservative. The medial prefrontal cortex, which tends to become active when we feel empathy toward others, became more active when participants thought about the liberal. But it became less active when they thought about the Christian conservative (Mitchell, Macrae, & Banaji, , 2006).

The second bias is **out-group homogeneity**, the tendency to view all people outside of our group as highly similar (Park & Rothbart, 1982). Out-group homogeneity makes it easy for us to dismiss members of other groups, such as different races, in one fell swoop, because we can simply tell ourselves that they all share at least one undesirable characteristic—like greediness or laziness ("All people of Race X look and act the same way"). In this way, we don't need to bother getting to know them.

◉ **Watch** the Prejudice video on **mypsychlab.com**

ultimate attribution error
assumption that behaviors among individual members of a group are due to their internal dispositions

adaptive conservatism
evolutionary principle that creates a predisposition toward distrusting anything or anyone unfamiliar or different

in-group bias
tendency to favor individuals within our group over those from outside our group

out-group homogeneity
tendency to view all individuals outside our group as highly similar

Thanks largely to psychological research, most U.S. orchestras now use blind auditions as a safeguard against sex bias and discrimination.

■ Discrimination

Just as stereotypes can lead to prejudice, prejudice in turn can lead to discrimination, a term with which it's often confused. **Discrimination** is the act of treating members of out-groups differently from members of in-groups. *Whereas prejudice refers to negative attitudes toward others, discrimination refers to negative behaviors toward others.* We can be prejudiced against people without discriminating against them.

CONSEQUENCES OF DISCRIMINATION. Discrimination has significant real-world consequences. For example, far fewer women than men are members of major American orchestras. To find out why, one research team examined how music judges evaluated female musicians during auditions. In some cases, judges could see the musicians; in others, the musicians played behind a screen. When judges were blind to musicians' sex, women were 50 percent more likely to pass auditions (Goldin & Rouse, 2000). For this reason, most major American orchestras today use blind auditions (Gladwell, 2005).

In another study, investigators (Word, Zanna, & Cooper, 1974) observed Caucasian undergraduates as they interviewed both Caucasian and African American applicants (who were actually confederates) for a job. When interviewing African American applicants, interviewers sat farther away from the interviewee, made more speech errors, and ended the interview sooner.

These findings, which focused on interviewer behavior, didn't demonstrate whether the different treatment affected the applicants' behavior. So the researchers trained Caucasian interviewers to treat Caucasian job applicants in the same way they'd treated African American applicants. Independent evaluators blind to the behavior of the interviewers coded the behavior of applicants from videotaped interviews. The results were striking. The evaluators rated job applicants who received the "African American treatment" as significantly more nervous and less qualified for the job than job applicants who received the "Caucasian treatment." This study shows how subtle discriminatory behaviors can adversely affect the quality of interpersonal interactions. Discrimination can be subtle, yet powerful.

CREATING DISCRIMINATION: DON'T TRY THIS AT HOME. It's remarkably easy to cook up discrimination. The recipe? Just create two groups that differ on any characteristic, no matter how trivial. To demonstrate this point, Henry Tajfel (1982) developed the *minimal intergroup paradigm,* a laboratory method for creating groups based on arbitrary differences. In one study, Tajfel and colleagues flashed groups of dots on a screen and asked participants to estimate how many dots they saw. In reality, the researchers ignored participants' answers, randomly classifying some as "dot overestimators" and others as "dot underestimators." They then gave participants the opportunity to distribute money and resources to other participants. People within each group allotted more goodies to people inside than outside their dot estimator group (Tajfel et al., 1971).

Iowa schoolteacher Jane Elliott created similarly random discrimination in her third-grade classroom in 1969. The day after civil rights leader Reverend Martin Luther King, Jr. was assassinated, she divided her class into favored and disfavored groups based solely on their eye color (Monteith & Winters, 2002). Informing her pupils that brown-eyed children are superior because of excess melanin in their eyes, Elliott deprived blue-eyed children of basic rights, such as second helpings at lunch or drinking from the water fountain. She also insulted blue-eyed children, calling them lazy, dumb, and dishonest. According to Elliott, the results were dramatic; most brown-eyed children quickly become arrogant and condescending, and most blue-eyed children became submissive and insecure.

Teachers across the United States used the now-famous blue eyes–brown eyes demonstration in the late 1960s and 1970s to teach students about the dangers of discrimination (the first author of your textbook was a participant in one of these demonstrations as an elementary school student in New York City). One follow-up study investigating the effects of this demonstration suggests that Caucasian students who experience it report less prejudice toward minorities than do Caucasian students in a control group (Stewart et al., 2003). Nevertheless, because students who underwent this demonstration may have felt demand characteristics to report less prejudice, additional studies are needed to rule out this alternative explanation.

Jane Elliott's classic blue eyes–brown eyes demonstration highlighted the negative interpersonal effects of discrimination.

discrimination
negative behavior toward members of out-groups

ruling out rival hypotheses >

HAVE IMPORTANT ALTERNATIVE EXPLANATIONS FOR THE FINDINGS BEEN EXCLUDED?

■ Roots of Prejudice: A Tangled Web

The roots of prejudice are complex and multifaceted. Nevertheless, psychologists have honed in on several crucial factors that may contribute to prejudice. We'll now examine a few of the prime culprits.

SCAPEGOAT HYPOTHESIS. According to the **scapegoat hypothesis**, prejudice arises from a need to blame other groups for our misfortunes. It can also stem from competition over scarce resources (Jackson, 1993). Between 1882 and 1930, for instance, the number of lynchings of African Americans in the U.S. South rose when the price of cotton went up (Tolnay & Beck, 1995). This finding suggests that some Caucasians may have blamed African Americans for the bad prices, although we don't know this for certain. For example, it's possible that higher cotton prices were associated with greater violence toward all members of society, not just African Americans. Nevertheless, there's more direct research support for the scapegoat hypothesis. In an experiment disguised as a study of learning, Caucasian students administered more intense electric shocks to an African American student than to a Caucasian student, but only when the African American student was unfriendly (Rogers & Prentice-Dunn, 1981). This finding is consistent with the possibility that frustration can trigger aggression, which people then displace onto minority groups.

JUST-WORLD HYPOTHESIS. Melvin Lerner's (1980) **just-world hypothesis** implies that many of us have a deep-seated need to perceive the world as fair—to believe that all things happen for a reason. Ironically, this need for a sense of fair play, especially if powerful, may foster prejudice. That's because it can lead us to place blame on groups that are already in a one-down position. Many people with a strong belief in a just world are likely to believe that victims of serious illnesses, including cancer and AIDS, are responsible for their plights (Hafer & Begue, 2005). Sociologists and psychologists have referred to this phenomenon as "blaming the victim" (Ryan, 1976).

CONFORMITY. Some prejudiced attitudes and behaviors probably stem from conformity to social norms. A study conducted in South Africa half a century ago revealed that Caucasians with a high need for conformity were especially likely to be prejudiced against Blacks (Pettigrew, 1958). Such conformity may stem from a need for social approval. In a study of college fraternities and sororities, researchers found that established members of Greek organizations were about equally likely to express negative views of out-groups (other fraternities and sororities) regardless of whether their opinions were public or private. In contrast, new pledges were more likely to express negative views of out-groups when their opinions were public (Noel, Wann, & Branscombe, 1995). Presumably, the pledges wanted to be liked by in-group members and went out of their way to voice their dislike of the "outsiders."

INDIVIDUAL DIFFERENCES IN PREJUDICE. Some people exhibit high levels of prejudice against a wide variety of out-groups. For example, people with authoritarian personality traits (which we discussed earlier), are prone to high levels of prejudice against many groups, including Native Americans and homosexuals (Altemeyer, 2004; Whitley & Lee, 2000), as are people with a strong need to "pigeonhole" people into distinct categories (Schaller et al., 1995). In addition, people with high levels of *extrinsic religiosity*, who view religion as a means to an end, such as obtaining friends or social support, tend to have high levels of prejudice (Batson & Ventis, 1982). In contrast, people with high levels of *intrinsic religiosity*—for whom religion is a deeply ingrained part of their belief system—tend to have equal or lower levels of prejudice than nonreligious people (Gorsuch, 1988; Pontón & Gorsuch, 1988).

■ Prejudice "Behind the Scenes"

Surveys demonstrate that interracial prejudice has declined substantially in the United States over the past four to five decades (Schuman et al., 1997). Nevertheless, some scholars contend that much prejudice, particularly that of Caucasians toward African Americans, has merely "gone underground"—that is, become subtler (Dovidio et al., 1997; Fiske, 2002; Hackney, 2005; Sue et al., 2007). One approach to studying subtle prejudice is to measure

ruling out rival hypotheses

HAVE IMPORTANT ALTERNATIVE EXPLANATIONS FOR THE FINDINGS BEEN EXCLUDED?

FACTOID

The term *scapegoat* originates from Biblical times, when rabbis engaged in an unusual practice for eliminating sin on the Jewish holy day of Yom Kippur. They brought forth two goats, one of which they sacrificed to God. The other goat lucked out. The rabbis grabbed the lucky goat's head while recounting all of the sins of the people, symbolically transferring these sins onto it. They then released the escaping goat—the *scapegoat*—into the woods, where it carried away the burden of society's moral errors.

FACTOID

People with high levels of prejudice toward multiple ethnic groups may display prejudice toward entirely fictitious groups of people (Bishop, Tuchfarber, & Oldendick, 1986). In a classic study, a researcher found that people who were prejudiced against Jews and African Americans also expressed dislike of the Pireneans, Danireans, and Wallonians—all of which are nonexistent ethnic groups (Hartley, 1946).

scapegoat hypothesis
claim that prejudice arises from a need to blame other groups for our misfortunes

just-world hypothesis
claim that our attributions and behaviors are shaped by a deep-seated assumption that the world is fair and all things happen for a reason

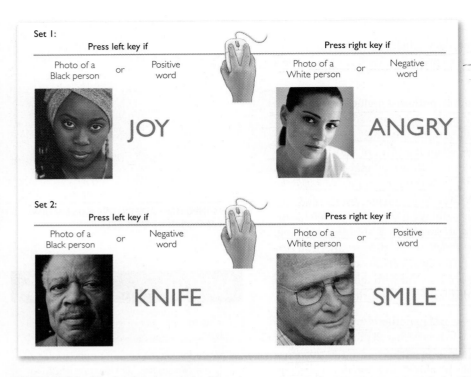

FIGURE 13.14 The Implicit Association Test. The Implicit Association Test (IAT) is the most widely researched measure of implicit or unconscious prejudice. This is a rendered example: Many people (across races) associate negative words more readily with African American than Causasian faces. But does the test really measure unconscious prejudice, or does it measure something else?

falsifiability

CAN THE CLAIM BE DISPROVED?

explicit prejudice
unfounded negative belief of which we're aware regarding the characteristics of an out-group

implicit prejudice
unfounded negative belief of which we're unaware regarding the characteristics of an out-group

implicit (unconscious) prejudice (Fazio & Olson, 2003; Vanman et al., 2004). In contrast to **explicit prejudices**, of which we're aware, **implicit prejudices** are those of which we're unaware. For example, one research team asked Whites to cooperate with Blacks on a task. Although White participants claimed to like their Black partners, sensitive measures of their facial activity implied otherwise: Their forehead muscles involved in frowning became active (Vanman et al., 1997).

Another implicit prejudice technique that's received an enormous amount of attention in recent years is the Implicit Association Test (IAT) developed by Anthony Greenwald and Mahzarin Banaji. As shown in **FIGURE 13.14**, researchers might ask a participant to press a key on the computer keyboard with his left hand if he sees either a photograph of an African American or a positive word (like *joy*) and to press a different key with his right hand if he sees a photograph of a Caucasian or a negative word (like *bad*). After performing this task for a number of trials, researchers ask participants to again press the left and right keys, but this time for the reverse pairing (that is, to press the left key for a photograph of either an African American or a negative word, and the right key for a photograph of either a Caucasian or a positive word) (Greenwald, McGhee, & Schwartz, 1998). The results of numerous studies demonstrate that most Caucasian participants respond more quickly to pairings in which African American faces are paired with negative words and Caucasian faces are paired with positive words (Banaji, 2001). Investigators have recently expanded the IAT to test a variety of forms of prejudice, including racism, sexism, homophobia, religious discrimination, and ageism (prejudice against older individuals). Many authors argue that the results of the IAT reflect unconscious prejudice (Gladwell, 2005; Greenwald & Nosek, 2001). If you want to try out the IAT, check out the website https://implicit.harvard.edu/implicit/demo.

Nevertheless, things may not be quite that simple (De Houwer et al., 2009). For one thing, the IAT often doesn't correlate significantly with explicit measures of prejudice, such as questionnaire measures of racist attitudes (Arkes & Tetlock, 2004). Proponents of the IAT argue that this absence of a correlation actually supports the IAT's validity, because the IAT supposedly measures unconscious rather than conscious racial attitudes. Yet this reasoning raises questions regarding the falsifiability of the IAT because IAT proponents could presumably interpret either a positive or a zero correlation as evidence for the IAT's validity. Moreover, it's unclear whether the IAT measures prejudice as much as *awareness* of stereotypes. Unprejudiced persons may correctly perceive that much of mainstream American society links Muslims, for example, with many negative characteristics and Christians with many positive characteristics, yet they may personally reject these associations as biased (Arkes & Tetlock, 2004; Redding, 2004).

Another problem is at least some of positive findings linking the IAT to real-world racism may stem from only a handful of participants with extreme scores; as a result, the IAT may not measure implicit prejudice for the substantial majority of people (Blanton et al., 2009). So scholars continue to debate whether the IAT and similar measures genuinely measure prejudice (Blanton & Jaccard, 2008; De Houwer et al., 2009; Gawronski, LeBel, & Peters, 2007).

■ Combating Prejudice: Some Remedies

Having traversed some pretty depressing ground—blind conformity, destructive obedience, bystander nonintervention, social loafing, and now prejudice—we're pleased to close our chapter with a piece of good news: We can overcome prejudice, at least to some extent. But how?

ROBBERS CAVE STUDY. We can find some clues in a study that Muzafer Sherif and his colleagues conducted in Robbers Cave, Oklahoma (so named because robbers once used these caves to hide from law enforcement authorities). Sherif split 22 well-adjusted fifth grade students into two groups, the Eagles and the Rattlers, and sent them packing to summer camp. After giving the boys within each group the chance to form strong bonds, Sherif introduced the groups to each other and engaged them in a four-day sports and games tournament. When he did, pandemonium ensued. The Eagles and Rattlers displayed intense animosity toward one another, eventually manifesting in name-calling, food throwing, and fistfights.

Sherif next wanted to find out whether he could "cure" the prejudice he'd helped to create. His treatment was simple: Engage the groups in activities that required them to cooperate to achieve an overarching goal. For example, he rigged a series of mishaps, such as a breakdown of a truck carrying food supplies, that forced the Eagles and Rattlers to work together. Sure enough, such cooperation toward a shared goal produced a dramatic decrease in hostility between the groups (Sherif et al., 1961). The Robbers Cave study imparts a valuable lesson: One means of reducing prejudice is to encourage people to work toward a shared higher purpose. By doing so, they can feel that they're no longer members of completely separate groups, but part of a larger and more inclusive group: "We're all in this together" (Fiske, 2000).

JIGSAW CLASSROOMS. Elliott Aronson (Aronson et al., 1978) incorporated the lessons of the Robbers Cave study into his educational work on **jigsaw classrooms**, in which teachers assign children separate tasks that all need to be fitted together to complete a project. A teacher might give each student in a class a different piece of history to investigate regarding the U.S. Civil War. One might present on Virginia's role, another on New York's, another on Georgia's, and so on. The students then cooperate to assemble the pieces into an integrated lesson. Numerous studies reveal that jigsaw classrooms result in significant decreases in racial prejudice (Aronson, 2004; Slavin & Cooper, 1999).

The Robbers Cave study and Aronson's work on jigsaw classrooms underscore a lesson confirmed by many other social psychology studies: *Increased contact between racial groups is rarely sufficient to reduce prejudice.* Indeed, during the early Civil Rights era in the United States, many attempts to reduce prejudice by means of desegregation backfired, resulting in increases in racial tension (Stephan, 1978). The advocates of these well-intended efforts assumed mistakenly that contact by itself could heal the deep wounds of prejudice. We now know that interventions are most likely to reduce prejudice only if they satisfy several conditions (see **TABLE 13.4**). These conditions lead to an optimistic conclusion: Prejudice is neither inevitable nor irreversible. ((•— **Listen**

Beginning with the classic Robber's Cave study, research shows that campers from diverse groups who work together toward shared goals will end up with lower levels of prejudice.

In jigsaw classrooms, children cooperate on a multipart project, with each child assuming a small but essential role.

TABLE 13.4 Ideal Conditions for Reducing Prejudice.

- The groups should cooperate toward shared goals
- The contact between groups should be enjoyable
- The groups should be of roughly equal status
- Group members should disconfirm the other group's negative stereotypes
- Group members should have the potential to become friends

(*Source:* Kenrick et al., 2005; Pettigrew, 1998)

((•— **Listen** to the Jigsaw Technique audio file on **mypsychlab.com**

✓•— **Study** and **Review** on **mypsychlab.com**

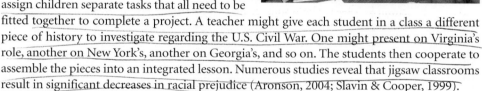

assess your knowledge   FACT OR FICTION?

1. Prejudice refers to negative behavior against out-group members. **True / False**

2. By definition, all stereotypes are inaccurate. **True / False**

3. Research demonstrates that nonprejudiced people lack stereotypes of other groups. **True / False**

4. Cooperation toward shared goals is a key ingredient in reducing prejudice. **True / False**

5. Research suggests that increased contact between groups is sufficient to reduce prejudice. **True / False**

Answers: 1. F (p. 527); 2. F (p. 528); 3. F (p. 529); 4. T (p. 533); 5. F (p. 533)

jigsaw classroom
educational approach designed to minimize prejudice by requiring all children to make independent contributions to a shared project

WHAT IS SOCIAL PSYCHOLOGY? 494–500

13.1 IDENTIFY THE WAYS IN WHICH SOCIAL SITUATIONS INFLUENCE THE BEHAVIORS OF INDIVIDUALS.

The need-to-belong theory proposes that humans have a biological need for interpersonal connections. According to social comparison theory, we're motivated to evaluate our beliefs, attitudes, and reactions by comparing them with the beliefs, attitudes, and reactions of others. Mass hysteria and urban legends reflect outbreaks of irrational behavior spread largely by social contagion. Social facilitation refers to the presence of others enhancing our performance in certain situations.

1. Social psychologists study how people influence others' _____, _____, and _____, for both good and bad. (p. 494)

2. The idea that we have a biologically based need for interpersonal connections is known as the _____ theory. (p. 495)

3. According to Festinger's _____ _____ theory, we evaluate our abilities and beliefs largely by judging how we rank relative to others. (p. 496)

4. The flying saucer craze is arguably one of the most widespread cases of what phenomenon? (p. 497)

5. What factors contribute to the rise and spread of urban legends? (p. 498)

While still alive, Walt Disney arranged to have his body frozen after his death so that it could be unfrozen at a future date when advanced technology will permit him to live again.

6. A worsened performance in the presence of others is explained by _____ _____. (p. 498)

7. Researchers have found that our performance in front of others is influenced by our level of _____ in that performance area. (p. 498)

13.2 EXPLAIN HOW THE FUNDAMENTAL ATTRIBUTION ERROR CAN CAUSE US TO MISJUDGE OTHERS' BEHAVIORS.

Attributions refer to our efforts to explain behavior; some attributions are internal, others external. The great lesson of social psychology is the fundamental attribution error—the tendency to overestimate the impact of dispositions on others' behavior. As a result of this error, we also tend to underestimate the impact of situations on others' behavior.

8. We tend to form _____ in our desire to assign causes to other people's behavior. (p. 499)

9. The tendency to overestimate the impact of _____ _____ on others' behavior is called the fundamental attribution error. (p. 499)

10. The fundamental attribution error (does/doesn't) apply to people's attributions about themselves. (p. 499)

SOCIAL INFLUENCE: CONFORMITY AND OBEDIENCE 500–512

13.3 DETERMINE THE FACTORS THAT INFLUENCE WHEN WE CONFORM TO OTHERS.

Conformity refers to the tendency of people to change their behavior as a result of group pressure. Asch's conformity studies underscore the power of social pressure, although there are individual and cultural differences in conformity. Deindividuation refers to the tendency of people to engage in atypical behavior when stripped of their usual identities. The Stanford prison study is a powerful demonstration of the effects of deindividuation on behavior.

11. Changing your personal style, habits, or behavior to fit into a social or peer group is an example of _____. (p. 500)

12. Under what circumstances discussed in the text would you identify line 3 as equal in length to the standard line? (p. 501)

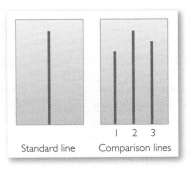

Standard line   Comparison lines
1 2 3

13. According to research by Berns and his colleagues, conformity is associated with activity in the _____ and _____ lobes of the brain. (p. 502)

14. People with (high/low) self-esteem are especially prone to conformity. (p. 502)

15. Researchers like Phil Zimbardo found that two prominent factors that contribute to deindividuation are a feeling of _____ and a lack of _____ _____. (p. 502)

16. The Stanford prison study results have been compared with the prison guard atrocities at _____ _____ in Iraq. (p. 503)

13.4 RECOGNIZE THE DANGERS OF GROUP DECISION MAKING AND IDENTIFY WAYS TO AVOID MISTAKES COMMON IN GROUP DECISIONS.

Groupthink is a preoccupation with group unanimity that impairs critical thinking. It can be "treated" by interventions that encourage dissent within the group. Group polarization refers to the tendency of group discussion to strengthen the dominant positions of individual group members. Cults are groups of individuals who exhibit extreme groupthink, marked by intense and unquestioning devotion to a single individual.

17. NASA's decision to launch the 1986 *Challenger* shuttle despite warnings of potential problems from engineers may have resulted from _____. (p. 505)

18. The best way to resist the indoctrination that leads to cults is through the _____ _____, which involves first introducing reasons why the perspective might be correct, then debunking them. (p. 507)

13.5 IDENTIFY THE FACTORS THAT MAXIMIZE OR MINIMIZE OBEDIENCE TO AUTHORITY.

Milgram's classic work on authority demonstrates the power of destructive obedience to authority and helps to clarify the situational factors that both foster and impede obedience.

19. Milgram's study testing the effects of "punishment on learning" was, in reality, designed to measure _____. (p. 509)

20. What factors in the Milgram study increased the likelihood that subjects would refuse to comply with orders to shock the "learner"? (pp. 510–511)

HELPING AND HARMING OTHERS: PROSOCIAL BEHAVIOR AND AGGRESSION 513–520

13.6 EXPLAIN WHICH ASPECTS OF A SITUATION INCREASE OR DECREASE THE LIKELIHOOD OF BYSTANDER INTERVENTION.

Although common wisdom suggests that there's "safety in numbers," research suggests otherwise. Bystander nonintervention results from two major factors: pluralistic ignorance and diffusion of responsibility. The first affects whether we recognize ambiguous situations as emergencies, and the second affects how we respond once we've identified situations as emergencies. People are more likely to help when they're unable to escape from a situation, have adequate time to intervene, are in a good mood, and have been exposed to research on bystander intervention.

21. What phenomenon did primate researcher Frans de Waal capture in this photo of two chimpanzees? (p. 513)

22. The presence of others tends to make people (less/more) likely to help someone in need. (p. 514)

23. What steps could you take to improve your chances of obtaining help if you were badly hurt or seriously ill in a public place? (p. 514)

24. As diffusion of responsibility occurs, each individual feels (more/less) accountable for helping someone in need. (p. 514)

25. The phenomenon in which people exert less effort on a task when in a group than when alone is known as _____ _____ . (p. 515)

26. Prior exposure to psychological research (can/can't) change an individual's real-world behavior for the better. (p. 517)

27. Extraverted people are (more/less) prone to help others than introverted people. (p. 517)

13.7 DESCRIBE THE SOCIAL AND INDIVIDUAL DIFFERENCE VARIABLES THAT CONTRIBUTE TO HUMAN AGGRESSION.

A variety of situational variables, including provocation, frustration, aggressive cues, media influences, arousal, and temperature, increase the likelihood of aggression. Men tend to be more physically aggressive than women, although girls are more relationally aggressive than boys. The southern "culture of honor" may help to explain why murder rates are higher in the southern United States than in other regions of the country.

28. Aggressive behavior, both at the individual and group levels, is influenced by _____ and _____ factors. (p. 517)

29. Because warm temperatures increase _____, they may make people more likely to lose their tempers when provoked or frustrated. (p. 518)

30. _____ aggression is a form of indirect aggression that involves spreading rumors, gossiping, and nonverbal putdowns for the purpose of social manipulation. (p. 519)

ATTITUDES AND PERSUASION: CHANGING MINDS 520–527

13.8 DESCRIBE HOW ATTITUDES RELATE TO BEHAVIOR.

Attitudes aren't typically good predictors of behavior, although attitudes predict behavior relatively well when they're highly accessible, firmly held, and stable over time.

31. The major distinction between a belief and an attitude is that an attitude involves a(n) _____ component. (p. 520)

32. LaPiere's research suggested that people's stated attitudes (did/didn't) accurately predict their situational behavior. (p. 520)

33. The behavior of someone who is a (low/high) self-monitor is likely to reflect his/her true feelings and attitudes. (p. 521)

34. The _____ _____, which makes us more likely to believe something we've heard many times, generally reflects accurate information. (p. 521)

13.9 EVALUATE THEORETICAL ACCOUNTS OF HOW AND WHEN WE ALTER OUR ATTITUDES.

According to cognitive dissonance theory, a discrepancy between two beliefs leads to an unpleasant state of tension that we're motivated to reduce. In some cases, we reduce this state by altering our attitudes. Two alternative views are self-perception theory, which proposes that we infer our attitudes from observing our behaviors, and impression management theory, which proposes that we don't really change our attitudes but report that we have so that we appear consistent.

Answers are located at the end of the text.

35. Using your knowledge of cognitive dissonance, complete the bottom set of boxes with statements geared toward resolving the stated conflict. (p. 522)

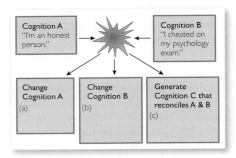

36. In Festinger and Carlsmith's test of cognitive dissonance theory, participants given less money reported enjoying the task (more/less). (p. 523)

13.10 IDENTIFY COMMON AND EFFECTIVE PERSUASION TECHNIQUES AND HOW THEY'RE EXPLOITED BY PSEUDOSCIENTISTS.

According to dual process models of persuasion, there are two routes to persuasion: a central route that involves careful evaluation of arguments and a peripheral route that relies on superficial cues. Effective persuasion techniques include the foot-in-the-door technique, the door-in-the-face technique, and the low-ball technique. Many techniques designed to market pseudoscientific products largely make use of the peripheral route to persuasion.

37. Match up the technique to the definition. (pp. 524–525)

_____	Foot-in-the-door technique	1. Making an unreasonably large request with the goal of getting someone to agree to a lesser request
_____	Door-in-the-face technique	2. "Adding on" costs hidden until an agreement to buy the item at lower cost is reached
_____	Low-ball technique	3. Making a small request of someone followed by a bigger request

38. Once a friend has agreed to help you select paint colors for your dorm room, asking her to help you actually paint the room is an example of the _____ technique. (p. 524)

39. Messages are especially persuasive if the messenger seems (similar/different) to us. (p. 524)

40. By manufacturing _____ _____, advertisers can fool consumers into believing that a source is more trustworthy than it is. (p. 525)

PREJUDICE AND DISCRIMINATION 527–533

13.11 DISTINGUISH PREJUDICE AND STEREOTYPES AS BELIEFS FROM DISCRIMINATION AS A BEHAVIOR.

Prejudice is coming to a negative conclusion before we've evaluated all the evidence. Prejudice is accompanied by several other biases, including in-group bias and out-group homogeneity. Stereotypes are beliefs about a group's characteristics that we apply to most members of that group. They can be either positive or negative. Discrimination is the act of treating out-group members differently from in-group members.

41. Concluding that all Americans are loud, materialistic, and arrogant without ever having spent time with any of them is an example of _____. (p. 527)

42. A belief that all cheerleaders are ditzy, flirty, and interested only in dating is a(n) _____. (p. 527)

43. Our tendency to view all people outside of our group as highly similar is known as (in-group bias/out-group homogeneity). (p. 529)

44. Believing—without first-hand knowledge—that teens with nose piercings who frequent the local mall are all troublemakers is a form of _____, and refusing to serve them in your mall restaurant is a form of _____. (p. 530)

45. How did one school teacher use her pupils' eye color to demonstrate how discrimination arises ? (p. 530)

13.12 IDENTIFY SOME OF THE CAUSES OF PREJUDICE AND DESCRIBE METHODS FOR COMBATING IT.

There's evidence for various explanations of prejudice, including scapegoating, belief in a just world, and conformity. One of the most effective means of combating prejudice is to make members of different groups work together toward achieving shared overarching goals.

46. According to the _____ _____, prejudice arises from a need to blame other groups for our misfortunes. (p. 531)

47. The idea that our behaviors and attributions are based on the assumption that all things happen for a reason supports the _____ hypothesis. (p. 531)

48. The _____ _____ _____ is a technique to measure implicit prejudice. (p. 532)

49. How do Aronson's jigsaw classrooms work to reduce prejudice? (p. 533)

50. One condition for reducing prejudice is to (encourage/discourage) group members from becoming friends. (p. 533)

DO YOU KNOW THESE TERMS?

- social psychology (p. 494)
- social comparison theory (p. 496)
- mass hysteria (p. 497)
- social facilitation (p. 498)
- attribution (p. 499)
- fundamental attribution error (p. 499)
- conformity (p. 500)
- deindividuation (p. 502)
- groupthink (p. 504)
- group polarization (p. 506)

- cult (p. 507)
- inoculation effect (p. 507)
- obedience (p. 508)
- pluralistic ignorance (p. 514)
- diffusion of responsibility (p. 514)
- social loafing (p. 515)
- altruism (p. 516)
- enlightenment effect (p. 517)
- aggression (p. 517)
- relational aggression (p. 519)
- attitude (p. 520)

- self-monitoring (p. 521)
- cognitive dissonance (p. 522)
- self-perception theory (p. 523)
- impression management theory (p. 524)
- foot-in-the-door technique (p. 524)
- door-in-the-face technique (p. 525)
- low-ball technique (p. 525)
- prejudice (p. 527)
- stereotype (p. 527)
- ultimate attribution error (p. 528)

- adaptive conservatism (p. 529)
- in-group bias (p. 529)
- out-group homogeneity (p. 529)
- discrimination (p. 530)
- scapegoat hypothesis (p. 531)
- just-world hypothesis (p. 531)
- explicit prejudice (p. 532)
- implicit prejudice (p. 532)
- jigsaw classroom (p. 533)

APPLY YOUR SCIENTIFIC THINKING SKILLS

Use your scientific thinking skills to answer the following questions, referencing specific scientific thinking principles and common errors in reasoning whenever possible.

1. Although we like to think of ourselves as individuals, we all belong to groups that require some form of conformity. List a few of the groups to which you belong (such as religious institutions, college clubs, or fraternities or sororities) and describe the advantages and disadvantages of being a part of each group. How does each group promote conformity?

2. Sadly, we can read or hear about acts of violence in the news every day. Select an aggressive act (like a high-profile murder or bombing) that has been in the headlines recently, and read at least two articles about it. What situational influences does each article list as possible causes of the act? Have the articles considered rival hypotheses for the aggressive actions, such as individual, gender, or cultural differences?

3. Visit three or four websites that promote a political candidate or party. What persuasive techniques do they use to attempt to gain your support (including your donation, volunteering, or vote)? How effective are these techniques in each case?

14 PERSONALITY

who we are

THINK ABOUT IT

DOES A SIMILAR UPBRINGING LEAD TO
SIMILARITIES IN CHILDREN'S PERSONALITIES?

CAN WE REDUCE THE ENORMOUS VARIATION IN
PEOPLE'S PERSONALITIES TO A MERE HANDFUL
OF UNDERLYING FACTORS?

HOW CONSISTENT IS OUR BEHAVIOR ACROSS
SITUATIONS?

CAN WE USE RESPONSES TO INKBLOTS TO
INFER PEOPLE'S PERSONALITY TRAITS?

IS CRIMINAL PROFILING SCIENTIFIC?

Oskar Stohr and Jack Yufe, identical twins
reared apart, obtained extremely similar scores
on personality tests. But the outward
expressions of their personality traits were
remarkably different. Why?

Radio and talk show personalities, like Dr. Laura
Schlessinger ("Dr. Laura"), often provide single-
cause explanations for complex, multiply-
determined psychological problems.

Born in 1933, Jack and Oskar are alike in two crucial ways. The first is obvious when you meet them: They're identical twins, genetic clones of each other. In contrast to most identical twins, though, they didn't grow up together. Instead, along with several dozen twin pairs studied by Thomas Bouchard and his colleagues at the University of Minnesota during the 1980s and 1990s, Jack and Oskar were separated almost immediately after birth and reunited decades later (Begley & Kasindorf, 1979). There's another similarity: Despite not having known each other for 40 years (they met once only briefly in 1954), Jack and Oskar have nearly identical personalities. Their scores on the Minnesota Multiphasic Personality Inventory, a personality questionnaire about which we'll learn later in the chapter, are about as similar as that of the same person taking the test twice.

That's about where the similarities end. Jack was raised by a Jewish family in the Caribbean until age 17, when he moved to Israel and joined a kibbutz. Oskar was raised by his maternal grandmother in a region of the former Czechoslovakia that was under Hitler's control during World War II. Although Jack's and Oskar's personalities are similar, their political attitudes are as different as night and day. Jack was a devoutly religious Jew who enjoyed war movies that portrayed Germans in a bad light. While in Israel, he worked to help build the Jewish state. In stark contrast, Oskar was an ardent Nazi and anti-Semite who became a dedicated member of the Hitler Youth movement as World War II drew to a close. So although Jack and Oskar had similar personalities—intense, loyal, and politically engaged—they manifested these personalities in dramatically different ways.

The case of Jack and Oskar is just that—a case. As we learned in Chapter 2, case studies have their limitations. For one thing, it's hard to know how far we can generalize the Jack and Oskar story to other twins, let alone to all other people. Yet like some case studies, Jack and Oskar's story raises a host of fascinating questions that psychologists can examine using rigorous research designs. Why were Jack and Oskar so similar in personality despite having had no contact with each other for decades? How can two people with such similar personalities end up with such dissimilar political attitudes? How did environmental influences shape the expression of their personalities?

The answers to these questions, we'll soon learn, aren't simple. Although most of us believe we can explain why people act as they do, we're wrong at least as often as we're right (Nisbett & Wilson, 1977).

Few are more confident in their abilities to explain behavior than radio and television "advice experts," many of whom liberally sprinkle their shows with off-the-cuff psychological accounts for people's behavior (Heaton & Wilson, 1995; Williams & Ceci, 1998). Consider the following statements typical of those offered by talk show psychologists: "He murdered all of those people because he had an unhappy childhood." "She overeats because she has low self-esteem." Intuitively appealing as these explanations are, we must beware of *single-cause explanations* of human behavior (see Chapter 1). When trying to uncover the root causes of people's actions, we must keep in mind that personality is multiply determined. Indeed, personality is the unimaginably complicated outcome of hundreds of causal factors: genetic, prenatal, parenting, peer influences, life stressors, and plain old luck, both good and bad.

PERSONALITY: WHAT IS IT AND HOW CAN WE STUDY IT?

14.1 Describe how twin and adoption studies shed light on genetic and environmental influences on personality.

In Chapter 13, we learned how the social context can influence our behavior in profound ways. There, we met up with the *fundamental attribution error,* the tendency to attribute too much of others' behavior to their dispositions, including their personalities, and not enough to the situations they confront.

Even bearing this error in mind, most psychologists agree that there *is* such a thing as **personality**—people's typical ways of thinking, feeling, and behaving. We aren't exclusively a product of the social factors impinging on us at any given moment, although we're certainly influenced by them. Most also agree with the American psychologist Gordon Allport's (1966) definition of personality as consisting of relatively enduring predispositions that influence our behavior across many situations (Funder, 1991; John, Robins, & Pervin, 2008; Tellegen, 1991). These predispositions, also called **traits**—like introversion, aggressiveness, and conscientiousness—account in part for consistencies in our behavior, across both time and situations. ((•—[Listen]

There are two major approaches to studying personality. A **nomothetic approach** strives to understand personality by identifying general laws that govern the behavior of all individuals. Most modern personality research, including most of the research we'll examine in this chapter, is nomothetic because it attempts to derive principles that explain the thinking, emotions, and behaviors of all people. This approach typically allows for generalization across individuals, but limited insight into the unique patterning of attributes within one person.

In contrast, an **idiographic approach** (think of "idiosyncratic") strives to understand personality by identifying the unique configuration of characteristics and life history experiences within a person. Most case studies are idiographic. Gordon Allport (1965) presented a classic example of the idiographic approach in his book *Letters from Jenny,* which features an analysis of 301 letters written by one woman over 12 years. In these letters, Allport uncovered themes that characterized Jenny's attitudes toward her son, Ross. When Jenny wrote about Ross in positive terms, themes of her early life often emerged; when she wrote about him in negative terms, themes of her unappreciated sacrifices for him often emerged. The idiographic approach reveals the richly detailed tapestry of one person's life, but allows for limited generalizability to other people. Moreover, it generates hypotheses that are often difficult to falsify, because these hypotheses are frequently post hoc ("after the fact") explanations about events that have already occurred.

How do personality traits originate? We'll first approach this question from the vantage point of behavior-genetic studies of personality and move on to various theories of personality, including Freudian, behavioral, and humanistic models, that offer competing answers to this question. As we'll discover, all of these theories strive to explain *both commonalities and differences* among people in their personalities. For example, they try to account for not only how we develop a conscience, but why some of us have a stronger conscience than others.

Behavior-genetic methods, with which we first crossed paths in Chapter 3, help psychologists to disentangle three broad influences on personality:

- *genetic* factors;

- *shared environmental* factors—experiences that make individuals within the same family more alike. If parents try to make both of their children more outgoing by reinforcing them with attention and succeed in doing so, their parenting in this case is a shared environmental factor; and

- *nonshared environmental* factors—experiences that make individuals within the same family less alike. If a parent treats one child more affectionately than another, and as a consequence this child ends up with higher self-esteem than the other child, the parenting in this case is a nonshared environmental factor. For much of the 20th century, most psychologists put their money on shared environmental influences as causal factors, as they believed that the most important environmental influences are transmitted from parents to children (Harris, 1994; Rowe, 1991).

■ Investigating the Causes of Personality: Overview of Twin and Adoption Studies

To distinguish among these three influences, behavior geneticists have applied twin studies and adoption studies (see Chapter 3) to personality. Because identical (monozygotic) twins are more similar genetically than fraternal (dizygotic) twins, a higher correlation of a trait among identical than fraternal twins—assuming that the environmental influences on

((•—[Listen] to the Personality podcast on **mypsychlab.com**

falsifiability
CAN THE CLAIM BE DISPROVED?

personality
people's typical ways of thinking, feeling, and behaving

trait
relatively enduring predisposition that influences our behavior across many situations

nomothetic approach
approach to personality that focuses on identifying general laws that govern the behavior of all individuals

idiographic approach
approach to personality that focuses on identifying the unique configuration of characteristics and life history experiences within a person

TABLE 14.1 Comparison of Correlations of Twins Reared Together and Apart for Selected Personality Traits.

	TWINS REARED TOGETHER		TWINS REARED APART	
	IDENTICAL TWIN CORRELATION	FRATERNAL TWIN CORRELATION	IDENTICAL TWIN CORRELATION	FRATERNAL TWIN CORRELATION
Anxiety proneness	.52	.24	.61	.27
Aggression	.43	.14	.46	.06
Alienation	.55	.38	.55	.38
Impulse control	.41	.06	.50	.03
Emotional well-being	.58	.23	.48	.18
Traditionalism	.50	.47	.53	.39
Achievement orientation	.36	.07	.36	.07

(*Source:* Tellegen et al., 1988)

both sets of twins are comparable—suggests a genetic influence. In contrast, identical twin correlations that are equal to or less than fraternal twin correlations suggest the absence of a genetic component, and instead point to nonshared environmental influences—those that make people within a family (including twins) different.

REARED-TOGETHER TWINS: GENES OR ENVIRONMENT? From the findings of one landmark twin study of personality, we can see that numerous personality traits—including anxiety proneness, impulse control, and traditionalism—are influenced substantially by genetic factors (see the left side of **TABLE 14.1**). This study examined identical twin pairs raised together and fraternal twins who were either both male or both female (Tellegen et al., 1988). A number of researchers have replicated these findings in twin samples from intact families (Loehlin, 1992; Plomin, 2004).

> **replicability**
> **CAN THE RESULTS BE DUPLICATED IN OTHER STUDIES?**

The results in Table 14.1 impart another lesson. What do the identical twin correlations have in common? The answer is so self-evident that we can easily overlook it: All are substantially less than 1.0. This finding demonstrates that nonshared environment plays an important role in personality (Krueger, 2000; Plomin & Daniels, 1987; Turkheimer, 2000). If heritability were 1.0 (that is, 100 percent), the identical twin correlations would also be 1.0. Because they're considerably less than 1.0, nonshared environmental influences must play a key role in personality. Regrettably, these twin findings don't tell us what these nonshared environmental influences are.

> **falsifiability**
> **CAN THE CLAIM BE DISPROVED?**

REARED-APART TWINS: SHINING A SPOTLIGHT ON GENES. Table 14.1 might tempt us to conclude that the similarities between identical twins are primarily a result of their similar upbringing rather than their shared genes. But this explanation is refuted by studies of identical and fraternal twins raised apart.

In an extraordinary investigation, researchers at the University of Minnesota spent more than two decades accumulating the largest ever sample of identical and fraternal twins reared apart—about 130 in total (Bouchard et al., 1990). Many had been separated almost immediately after birth, raised in different states and sometimes even different countries, and reunited for the first time decades later in the Minneapolis–St. Paul airport. Jack and Oskar, whom we met at the outset of this chapter, were among those in the "Minnesota Twins" study, as it came to be known. ◉ Watch

> ◉ **Watch** Twins Separated at Birth, Reunited on **mypsychlab.com**

Before psychologists conducted these studies, some prominent social scientists predicted confidently that identical twins reared apart would barely resemble each other in personality (Mischel, 1981). Were they right? The right side of Table 14.1 displays some of the principal findings from the Minnesota Twins study. Two findings in the right side of this table stand out. First, identical twins reared apart tend to be strikingly similar in their personality traits. They're also far more similar than fraternal twins reared apart (Tellegen et al., 1988). A more convincing case for the role of genetic influences on personality would be hard to come by.

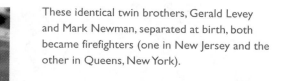

These identical twin brothers, Gerald Levey and Mark Newman, separated at birth, both became firefighters (one in New Jersey and the other in Queens, New York).

Second, when comparing the results in the left and right sides of Table 14.1, it's evident that identical twins reared apart are about as similar as identical twins reared together. This remarkable finding suggests that shared environment plays little or no role in the causes of adult personality. Behavior-genetic researchers have replicated this result in other twin samples (Loehlin, 1992; Pederson et al., 1988; Vernon et al., 2008).

This finding is sufficiently surprising that it bears repeating: *Shared environment plays little or no role in adult personality.* In many respects, this may be the most stunning finding in recent personality psychology, although it's yet to exert a substantial impact on popular psychology (Harris, 2006; Pinker, 2002; Rowe, 1994). Shared environment plays some role in childhood personality, but this role generally dissipates as we grow older. By the time we reach adulthood, the impact of shared environment on our personalities is weak at best (Plomin & McClearn, 1993; Torgesen et al., 2008). This finding suggests that if parents try to make all of their children outgoing, for example, by exposing them to friendly children and encouraging them to attend parties, they're likely to fail in the long run.

ADOPTION STUDIES: FURTHER SEPARATING GENES AND ENVIRONMENT. *Adoption studies* (see Chapter 3) permit investigators to separate the effects of genes and environment by examining children who were separated at an early age from their biological families. The finding that an adopted child's personality is similar to that of his or her biological parents points to genetic influence; in contrast, the finding that an adopted child's personality is similar to that of his or her adoptive parents points to shared environmental influence.

In one adoption study conducted in Texas, investigators examined several personality traits as measured by a widely used measure, the California Psychological Inventory, which we'll encounter later in the chapter. In **TABLE 14.2**, we'll focus on one such trait: *sociability*, or the extent to which people enjoy being with others.

As we can see in Table 14.2, the correlations between biological parents and their adopted-away children in their sociability levels are slightly higher than the correlations between adoptive parents and their adopted children *even though the biological parents had essentially no environmental contact with their children after birth* (Loehlin & Horn, 2010). Most other researchers have obtained similar findings for other personality traits (Loehlin, 1992; Scarr et al., 1981). These results run counter to the intuitively plausible hypothesis that shared environment is influential in personality: Being raised together doesn't lead to much similarity in personality between parents and offspring.

■ Birth Order: Does It Matter?

As we've seen, nonshared environmental influences play a key role in personality. Yet the question of what psychological variables make up these influences remains a mystery (Turkheimer & Waldron, 2000). One long-time candidate for a nonshared environmental factor has been birth order. Many popular books, such as *The New Birth Order Book* (Leman, 1998), claim that firstborns tend toward achievement, middle-borns toward diplomacy, and later-borns toward risk taking. Yet virtually all of these claims are exaggerated, because most researchers have failed to uncover strong or consistent associations between birth order and personality (Ernst & Angst, 1983; Jefferson, Herbst, & McCrae, 1998).

FACTOID

One pair of male identical twins separated at birth in the Minnesota Twins study (both named "Jim" by their adoptive parents) both constructed similar-looking tree houses in their backyards, named their dogs "Toy," and were married twice, both to women named Linda and Betty. Another pair of separated adult identical twins in that study—in this case, female—both attempted to conquer their fear of the ocean by entering the water backward up to their ankles and then turning around (Segal, 1999). Yet because these are anecdotes and could reflect chance coincidences (Wyatt et al., 1984), we need to turn to systematic analyses of reared apart twins.

Crazy coincidences

TABLE 14.2 Correlations among Various Relatives in an Adoption Study of Sociability.

CORRELATION	
Mother and biological child	.15
Mother and adopted child	.01
Father and biological child	.20
Father and adopted child	.08

(*Source:* Loehlin & Horn, 2010)

Molecular Genetic Studies
→ genes code for proteins
that influence the
functioning of neurotransmitters
→ functioning of neurotransmitters
is associated with certain
personality traits

Nevertheless, popular claims regarding the importance of birth order received a boost from the work of science historian Frank Sulloway (1996). He examined the association between birth order and attitudes toward revolutionary scientific theories, such as Copernicus' theory of the sun-centered universe and Darwin's theory of natural selection. Sulloway asked panels of historians to evaluate how 4,000 scientists reacted to these and other scientific controversies when their developers proposed them between the years 1543 and 1967. He found that later-borns were 3.1 times more likely than firstborns to favor revolutionary ideas; for extremely radical ideas, this ratio increased to 4.7. In contrast, firstborns usually supported the status quo. Sulloway's findings raise the possibility that birth order is an important nonshared environmental influence, but it's not clear how much we can generalize his findings to nonscientific disciplines. Moreover, some scientists have raised questions about Sulloway's methods. For example, when rating whether scientists were revolutionaries, his panel of scientists may not have been blind to their birth order (Harris, 1998). In addition, some scientists haven't replicated Sulloway's finding that later-borns are more rebellious than firstborns (Freese, Powell, & Steelman, 1999).

replicability

> **CAN THE RESULTS BE DUPLICATED IN OTHER STUDIES?**

■ Behavior-Genetic Studies: A Note of Caution

Researchers using twin and adoption studies have found that genes influence a variety of behaviors often associated with personality traits. These behaviors include divorce (McGue & Lykken, 1992), religiosity (Waller et al., 1990), and even the tendency to watch television (Plomin et al., 1990). Perhaps surprisingly, many social attitudes, including those concerning the death penalty and nudist colonies, are moderately heritable (Martin et al., 1986). For each of these characteristics, identical twin correlations are considerably higher than fraternal twin correlations.

Twin studies demonstrate that religiosity has a substantial genetic component. But does that finding mean there are specific genes for religiosity?

Do these findings mean, as the popular press often implies, that there are specific genes for divorce, religiosity, death penalty attitudes, and the like? Don't bet on it. Genes code for proteins, not specific behaviors or attitudes, and therefore affect most psychological characteristics in a highly indirect fashion (N. Block, 1995). As we learned from Jack and Oskar, genes probably exert an indirect influence on certain personality traits—like a tendency to experience deep emotions—but the environment influences how these traits play out in our lives, such as becoming either an observant Jew or a passionate anti-Semite. The pathways from genes to behavior are long and circuitous. So when we hear media reports of a "gay gene," "alcoholism gene," or "divorce gene," we should be skeptical. Although there are probably genetic influences on homosexuality (see Chapter 11) and even divorce, it's exceedingly unlikely that a single gene codes directly for these or other multifaceted behaviors (Kendler, 2005; Nigg & Goldsmith, 1994).

Although twin and adoption studies provide remarkably useful information concerning the heritability of personality traits, they tell us little about *which* genes are related to personality. In an attempt to answer this question, researchers have turned to **molecular genetic studies**, which may allow them to pinpoint which genes are associated with specific personality traits (Canli, 2008; Plomin et al., 1997). These studies rest on two premises:

↳ serotonin activity.
more impulsive and aggressive

1. Genes code for proteins that in turn often influence the functioning of neurotransmitters, like dopamine and serotonin (see Chapter 3).

2. The functioning of many neurotransmitters is associated with certain personality traits (Cloninger, 1987; Gardini, Cloninger, & Venneri, 2009). For example, people with low levels of serotonin activity tend to be more impulsive and aggressive than other persons (Carver & Miller, 2006; Dolan, Anderson, & Deakin, 2001).

molecular genetic study
investigation that allows researchers to pinpoint genes associated with specific personality traits

Although the methodology of molecular genetic studies is complicated, most of them work by examining the linkage between specific genes and known genetic markers on each chromosome. At this point, however, there have been relatively few consistently replicated associations between specific genes and personality traits.

replicability

> **CAN THE RESULTS BE DUPLICATED IN OTHER STUDIES?**

dopamine = reward seeking neurotransmitter.

One notable exception is the connection between *novelty seeking*—a trait that refers to the tendency to search out and enjoy new experiences—and genetic markers of the dopamine system, which is intimately involved in reward seeking (see Chapter 3). Several researchers have reported significant associations between measures of novelty seeking and various genes influencing the activity of the neurotransmitter dopamine (Epstein et al., 1996; Munafo et al., 2008; see Chapter 3). In addition, some investigators have reported a linkage between symptoms of attention-deficit/hyperactivity disorder, a childhood disorder associated with novelty seeking (see Chapter 15), and genes influencing the dopamine system (Waldman & Gizer, 2006). Nevertheless, findings linking dopamine-related genes to novelty seeking haven't always been consistently replicated (Pogue-Geile et al., 1998; Waldman & Gizer, 2006) and tend to be weak in magnitude, so we should view them with a bit of caution. It's likely that we'll see more progress linking specific genes, such as those of the serotonin system (Lesch et al., 1996) to specific personality traits in the coming decade.

◄ replicability

CAN THE RESULTS BE DUPLICATED IN OTHER STUDIES?

assess your knowledge   FACT OR FICTION?

1. Identical twins reared together tend to be about as similar in their personality traits as identical twins reared apart. (True) / False

2. Environmental factors shared among members of the same family play an important role in the causes of most personality traits in adulthood. True / (False)

3. Birth order is weakly related to most personality traits. (True) / False

4. We shouldn't trust the findings from molecular genetic studies of personality until independent investigators have replicated them. (True) / False

Answers: 1. T (p. 543); 2. F (p. 543); 3. T (p. 543); 4. T (p. 544)

✓ Study and Review on mypsychlab.com

PSYCHOANALYTIC THEORY: THE CONTROVERSIAL LEGACY OF SIGMUND FREUD AND HIS FOLLOWERS

14.2 Describe the core assumptions of psychoanalytic theory.

14.3 Describe key criticisms of psychoanalytic theory and the central features of neo-Freudian theories.

Long before researchers stepped in to conduct controlled studies of the causes of personality, psychologists, psychiatrists, and many other thinkers had generated theoretical models that sought to explain the development and workings of personality. These models address three key questions:

1. How do our personalities develop?

2. What are the core driving forces in our personalities or, more informally, what makes us tick?

3. What accounts for individual differences in personality?

We'll examine and evaluate four influential models of personality, starting with the grand-daddy of them all: Sigmund Freud's psychoanalytic theory.

To most nonpsychologists, psychoanalytic theory—indeed, much of personality theory itself—is virtually synonymous with the writings of a Viennese physician named Sigmund Freud (1856–1939), who is undeniably one of the most influential figures in all of psychology. Yet ironically, Freud's training wasn't in psychology or psychiatry—specialties that scarcely existed in his day—but in neurology. Largely as a consequence of his neurological background, Freud initially believed that mental disorders were physiologically caused. Yet his views changed dramatically in 1885, when he spent a year in Paris studying under neurologist Jean Charcot. Charcot had been treating patients, most of them women, who had a condition then known as "grande hysteria." They exhibited an assortment of spectacular physical symptoms.

Sigmund Freud, the founder of simultaneously the most worsh criticized figure in personality

TABLE 14.3 Examples of "Freudian Slips" from notes by Freud.

"A member of the House of Commons referred to another as the honorable member for Central Hell instead of Central Hull."

"A soldier said to a friend that 'I wish there were a thousand men mortified on that hill' instead of 'fortified on that hill.'"

"A lady, attempting to compliment another, says that 'I am sure that you must have thrown this delightful hat together' instead of 'sewn it together,' thereby betraying her thought that the hat was poorly made."

"A lady states that few gentlemen know how to value the 'ineffectual' qualities in a woman, as opposed to 'intellectual.'"

(*Source:* Freud, 1901)

paralyses of the arms and legs, fainting spells, and seizures. Careful investigation failed to turn up any physical causes of these symptoms, some of which made little or no physiological sense. For example, some of Charcot's patients exhibited *glove anesthesia*, a loss of sensation in the hand alone, with no accompanying loss of sensation in the arm. Glove anesthesia defies standard neurological principles because the sensory pathways extending to the hand run through the arm. If the hand lacks sensation, the arm should, too.

This and related observations led Freud to conclude that many mental disorders were produced by psychological rather than physiological factors. He developed a theoretical model to explain these disorders, traditionally called *psychoanalytic theory*, and an accompanying treatment called *psychoanalysis* (see Chapter 16).

■ Freud's Psychoanalytic Theory of Personality

Psychoanalytic theory rests on three core assumptions (Brenner, 1973; Loevinger, 1987). These assumptions, especially the second and third, set this theory apart from most other personality theories.

- *Psychic Determinism.* Freudians believe in **psychic determinism**: the assumption that all psychological events have a cause. Psychic determinism is a specific case of determinism as a general concept (see Chapter 1), which states that all events are caused. We aren't free to choose our actions, Freudians claim, because we're at the mercy of powerful inner forces that lie outside of our awareness (Custer & Aarts, 2010). Dreams, neurotic symptoms, and "Freudian slips" of the tongue are all reflections of deep psychological conflict bubbling up to the surface (see **TABLE 14.3**). Moreover, for Freudians, many key influences on adult personality stem from early childhood experiences, especially parenting.

- *Symbolic Meaning.* For Freudians, no action, no matter how seemingly trivial, is meaningless. All are attributable to preceding mental causes, even if we can't always figure out what they are. If while teaching a class, your male professor manages to crack a long piece of chalk in two, some might be inclined to disregard this action as uninteresting. Freudians, in contrast, would be likely to argue that this piece of chalk is *symbolic* of something else, most likely something sexual in nature. Yet even strict Freudians agree that not all behaviors are symbolic. In response to a questioner who asked Freud why he enjoyed smoking cigars, Freud supposedly responded that "a cigar is sometimes just a cigar" (some scholars, however, argue that this quotation is an urban legend; see Chapter 13).

- *Unconscious Motivation.* Freudians argue for the central importance of *unconscious motivation.* According to Freud (1933), we rarely understand why we do what we do, although we quite readily cook up explanations for our actions after the fact. Some authors have likened the Freudian view of the mind (Freud, 1923) to an iceberg, with the unconscious—the part of personality of which we're entirely unaware—being the vast and largely uncharted area of the psyche submerged entirely underwater (see **FIGURE 14.1**). The conscious component of the mind, the part of personality of which we're aware, is merely the "tip of the iceberg," barely visible above the water's surface. For Freud, the unconscious is of immensely greater importance in the causes of our personality than the conscious.

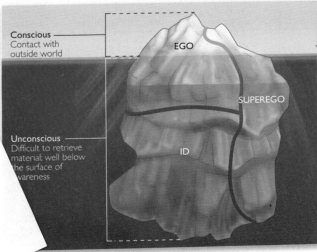

Conscious
Contact with outside world

EGO

SUPEREGO

ID

Unconscious
Difficult to retrieve material; well below the surface of awareness

■ The Id, Ego, and Superego: The Structure of Personality

Freud (1933, 1935) hypothesized that the human psyche consists of three *agencies* or components: id, ego, and superego. For Freud, the interplay among these three agencies gives rise to our personalities, and differences in the strength of these agencies account largely for individual differences in personality.

THE ID: BASIC INSTINCTS. The **id**, according to Freud, is the reservoir of our most primitive impulses, a seething cauldron of desires that provides the driving force much of our behavior. The id is entirely unconscious; it's the part of the iceberg submerged underwater. It contains a variety of drives, particularly the sexual drive or *libido* (see Chapter 11) and aggressive drive. Although critics have sometimes accused Freud of saying that "everything is sex," this allegation is only partly true. Freud believed the libido to be of crucial importance in personality, but he maintained that other impulses, particularly aggression, also play significant shaping roles. According to Freud, the id operates by means of the **pleasure principle**. The pleasure principle strives for immediate gratification: The word *no* isn't in the id's vocabulary.

THE EGO: THE BOSS. The **ego** is the boss of the personality, its principal decision maker. The ego's primary tasks are interacting with the real world and finding ways to resolve the competing demands of the other two psychic agencies. We shouldn't confuse the Freudian ego with the ego, or inflated sense of self-worth ("Wow, that athlete has a big ego"), that's crept into everyday language.

The ego, unlike the id, is governed by the **reality principle**. The reality principle strives to delay gratification until it can find an appropriate outlet. If you find today's introductory psychology lecture to be inordinately frustrating, your id may want to satisfy your aggressive impulses by screaming out loud in class (we don't recommend doing this, by the way). This is the pleasure principle rearing its ugly head. But the ego's reality principle requires that you delay this gratification until you can find a socially appropriate outlet for your aggression, such as throwing darts at a dartboard—ideally one featuring your professor's face as the bull's-eye—when you get home from class.

THE SUPEREGO: MORAL STANDARDS. The **superego** is our sense of morality. The term literally means "above ego," and Freud conceptualized this agency much like a judgmental parent looking down upon the ego. The superego contains the sense of right and wrong we've internalized from our interactions with society, particularly our parents. According to Freudians, people with overly developed superegos are guilt-prone, whereas particularly guilt-free people are at risk for developing psychopathic personality (see Chapters 11 and 15). ◉—⌐Explore

HOW THE PSYCHIC AGENCIES INTERACT. Much of the time, id, ego, and superego interact harmoniously, much like a chamber music trio playing in perfect synchrony. Yet the agendas of these agencies sometimes collide (see **FIGURE 14.2**). Indeed, Freud (1935) hypothesized that psychological distress results from conflict among these three agencies. If you're attracted to your best friend's partner, your id is at odds with your ego and (hopefully!) your superego. You might fantasize about a romantic fling with this person (id), but feel frightened about what would happen to you (ego) and stricken with pangs of guilt about hurting your friend's feelings (superego) if you were foolish enough to act on your impulses.

For an intimate view of the three psychic agencies in action, we have only to look to the third of our lives we spend asleep. Dreams, Freud (1900) suggested, are the "royal road to the unconscious mind" (see Chapter 5) because they not only reveal the inner workings of our id in action, but illustrate how ego and superego cooperate to keep the id's wishes in check. According to Freud, all dreams are *wish fulfillments*, that is, expressions of the id's impulses. Yet they don't always seem that way on the surface, said Freud, because these wishes are disguised. When the superego perceives the id's desires to be

[handwritten note:] "I want you to burn my bridges down." Yeah, set me on fire

psychic determinism
the assumption that all psychological events have a cause

id
reservoir of our most primitive impulses, including sex and aggression

pleasure principle ⌐ (NO)
tendency of the id to strive for immediate gratification

ego
psyche's executive and principal decision maker

reality principle
tendency of the ego to postpone gratification until it can find an appropriate outlet

superego
our sense of morality

[handwritten notes:]
Id = primitive impulses
ego = decision maker
Superego = morality.

◉—⌐Explore the Id, Ego, and Superego on mypsychlab.com

FIGURE 14.2   Id, Ego, and Superego. Many works of art portray an individual trying to make a difficult moral decision, with a devil on one shoulder—urging immoral behavior—and an angel—urging moral behavior—on the other. Freudians would say that such artwork captures the distinction among ego (the person trying to make the decision), id (demon), and superego (angel).

Most dream dictionaries available in bookstores imply that there are universal meanings for dream symbols. Even most psychoanalysts reject this claim.

threatening, it "commands" the ego to plaster over these wishes with symbols. We sometimes draw these symbols from our distant past, but in other cases we draw them from what Freud called the "day residue," the accumulation of events we experienced on the day of the dream. So rather than having an explicit dream about a romantic encounter with a classmate, a male might dream of driving a car through a tunnel, a favorite Freudian symbolic representation of sex.

But beware: Popular psychology books notwithstanding, most Freudians don't regard dream symbols as universal. If we peruse the section of our local bookstores devoted to dreams, we'll find several dictionaries of dream symbols. One such dictionary (Schoenewolf, 1997) offers the following rules for interpreting dream symbols: a duck, icicle, spear, umbrella, or tie symbolizes the penis; a pocket, tunnel, jug, or gate symbolizes the vagina; and a kangaroo symbolizes sexual vitality (please don't ask us to explain this one). These and other dream dictionaries (Ackroyd, 1993) vastly oversimplify Freudian theory, because Freudians believe that different symbols can mean different things to different dreamers.

ANXIETY AND THE DEFENSE MECHANISMS A principal function of the ego, according to Freud, is to contend with threats from the outside world. When danger arises, the ego experiences anxiety, signaling it to undertake corrective actions. Sometimes these actions are straightforward, like jumping out of the way of an oncoming car. In other cases, though, we can't do much to correct the situation, so we must change our *perception* of it.

In these cases, the ego engages in **defense mechanisms**: unconscious maneuvers intended to minimize anxiety. The concept of defense mechanisms has crept into our everyday language ("Stop being so defensive"). Contrary to popular belief, Freud held that defense mechanisms are essential for psychological health. Indeed, the person lacking any defense mechanisms would be at the mercy of uncontrollable anxiety. Nonetheless, an excessive reliance on one or two defense mechanisms, Freud insisted, is pathological. Freud and his daughter, Anna, who became a prominent psychoanalyst in her own right, outlined the principal defense mechanisms (A. Freud, 1937). We'll present a brief tour of them here (see **TABLE 14.4**). ⊕─ Explore

Explore Defense Mechanisms on **mypsychlab.com**

- **Repression**, the most critical defense mechanism in psychoanalytic theory, is the *motivated forgetting* of emotionally threatening memories or impulses. Unlike the types of forgetting we discussed in Chapter 7, repression is presumably triggered by anxiety: We forget because we want to forget. According to Freud, we repress unhappy memories of early childhood to avoid the pain they produce. This repression leads us to experience *infantile amnesia* (see Chapter 7), the inability to remember anything prior to about age three (Fivush & Hudson, 1990). Early childhood, Freud contended, is too anxiety provoking for us to remember fully. We now know this explanation is unlikely, because investigators have identified infantile amnesia in other animals, including mice and rats (Berk, Vigorito, & Miller, 1979; Richardson, Riccio, & Axiotis, 1986). A committed Freudian could presumably argue that mice and other rodents also repress traumatic memories of early childhood (perhaps memories of seeing too many cats?), but Occam's razor renders this explanation implausible.

- In contrast to repression, which is the motivated forgetting of distressing internal experiences, **denial** is the motivated forgetting of distressing *external* experiences. We most often observe denial in people with psychotic disorders, such as schizophrenia (see Chapter 15), although individuals undergoing extreme stress occasionally engage in denial, too. It's not uncommon, for example, for the relatives of individuals who have recently died in a tragic accident to insist that their loved ones must somehow, somewhere, be alive.

- **Regression** is the act of returning psychologically to a younger age, typically early childhood, when life was simpler and safer. Older children who've long since stopped sucking their thumbs sometimes suddenly resume thumb sucking under stress.

defense mechanisms
unconscious maneuvers intended to minimize anxiety

repression
motivated forgetting of emotionally threatening memories or impulses

occam's razor ▸

DOES A SIMPLER EXPLANATION FIT THE DATA JUST AS WELL?

denial
motivated forgetting of distressing external experiences

regression
the act of returning psychologically to a younger, and typically simpler and safer, age

TABLE 14.4 Major Freudian Defense Mechanisms and an Example of Each.

DEFENSE MECHANISM	DEFINITION	EXAMPLE
Repression	Motivated forgetting of emotionally threatening memories or impulses	A person who witnesses a traumatic combat scene finds himself unable to remember it.
Denial	Motivated forgetting of distressing experiences	A mother who loses a child in a car accident insists her child is alive.
Regression	Returning psychologically to a younger and safer time	A college student starts sucking his thumb during a difficult exam.
Reaction-formation	Transforming an anxiety-producing experience into its opposite	A married woman who's sexually attracted to a coworker experiences hatred and revulsion toward him.
Projection	Unconscious attribution of our negative qualities onto others	A married man with powerful unconscious sexual impulses toward females complains that other women are always "after him."
Displacement	Directing an impulse from a socially unacceptable target onto a more acceptable one	A golfer angrily throws his club into the woods after he misses an easy putt.
Rationalization	Providing reasonable-sounding explanations for unreasonable behaviors or failures	A political candidate who loses an election convinces herself that she didn't really want the position after all.
Intellectualization	Avoiding the emotions associated with anxiety-provoking experiences by focusing on abstract and impersonal thoughts	A woman whose husband cheats on her reassures herself that "according to evolutionary psychologists, men are naturally sexually promiscuous, so there's nothing to worry about."
Identification with the aggressor	Adopting the psychological characteristics of people we find threatening	A college basketball player who initially fears his tyrannical coach comes to admire him and adopts his dictatorial qualities.
Sublimation	Transforming a socially unacceptable impulse into an admired and socially valued goal	A boy who enjoys beating up on other children grows up to become a successful professional boxer.

- **Reaction-formation** is the transformation of an anxiety-provoking emotion into its opposite. The observable emotion we see actually reflects the opposite emotion the person feels unconsciously. Freud contended that we can infer the presence of reaction-formation by the intensity with which the person expresses the emotion, as this emotion displays an exaggerated or "phony" quality.

  In a remarkable study, Henry Adams and his colleagues found that males with high levels of *homophobia*—a dislike (not technically a fear, as the word implies) of homosexuals—showed significantly *greater* increases in penile circumference than males with low levels of homophobia in response to sexually explicit videotapes of homosexual stimuli, such as men engaging in sex with other men (Adams, Wright, & Lohr, 1996). This finding is tantalizingly consistent with the Freudian concept of reaction-formation; some homophobics may harbor unconscious homosexual impulses that they find unacceptable and transform them into a conscious dislike of homosexuals. Still, there's an alternative explanation: Anxiety can increase sexual arousal and perhaps trigger penile erections (Barlow, Sakheim, & Beck, 1983). So future investigators will need to rule out this rival hypothesis.

- **Projection** is the unconscious attribution of our negative characteristics to others. According to psychoanalysts, people with paranoia are projecting their unconscious hostility onto others. Deep down they want to harm others, but because they can't accept these impulses they perceive others as wanting to harm them.

reaction-formation
transformation of an anxiety-provoking emotion into its opposite

projection
unconscious attribution of our negative characteristics to others

◄ ruling out rival hypotheses

HAVE IMPORTANT ALTERNATIVE EXPLANATIONS FOR THE FINDINGS BEEN EXCLUDED?

In this photograph from a 2008 game, frustrated player Prince Fielder throws his bat to the ground after popping out. Freudians would say that Fielder is engaging in which defense mechanism? (See answer upside down at bottom of page.)

FIGURE 14.3 "Sour Grapes." According to psychoanalysts, rationalization often involves a psychological minimization of previously desired outcomes. This etching from Aesop's fables illustrates one example of rationalization, namely, the famous "sour grapes" phenomenon: The fox, who can't reach the previously desired grapes, tells himself, "These grapes are much too green and sour. Even if I could reach them, I would not eat them."

Answer: Displacement

- Closely related to projection is **displacement**, in which we direct an impulse from a socially unacceptable target onto a safer and more socially acceptable target. After a frustrating day at work, we may pound our fist against the punching bag at the gym rather than into the faces of our annoying coworkers.

- **Rationalization** provides a reasonable-sounding explanation for our unreasonable behaviors or for failures. Some people who receive *posthypnotic suggestions* (see Chapter 5) to perform bizarre actions engage in rationalizations to explain these actions. A subject given a posthypnotic suggestion to bark like a dog after emerging from hypnosis may do so. When the hypnotist asks him why he barked, he may rationalize his behavior: "Hmmm ... I was just thinking about how much I missed my dog, so I felt like barking" (see **FIGURE 14.3**). A related defense mechanism, *intellectualization*, allows us to avoid anxiety by thinking about abstract and interpersonal thoughts (refer back to Table 14.4).

- **Identification with the aggressor** is the process of adopting the characteristics of individuals we find threatening: "If you can't beat 'em, join 'em." Anna Freud (1937) observed identification with the aggressor in concentration camp survivors, some of whom seemed to assume their guards' personality characteristics. Identification with the aggressor may underlie some cases of *Stockholm syndrome*—named after a 1973 hostage crisis in Stockholm, Sweden, in which some hostages developed emotional attachments toward their captors (Kuleshnyk, 1984). Nevertheless, journalists and pop psychologists have often used this term loosely to refer to any friendships that hostages forge with their captors (McKenzie, 2004), which may have little or nothing to do with identification with the aggressor.

- **Sublimation** transforms a socially unacceptable impulse into an admired goal. George Vaillant's (1977) book, *Adaptation to Life,* which is a 40-year longitudinal study of Harvard University graduates, features several striking examples of sublimation. Among them is the story of a man who set fires in childhood and went on to become chief of his local fire department.

■ Stages of Psychosexual Development

No aspect of Freud's theory is more controversial than his model of psychosexual development. Nor has any aspect of his theory been more widely criticized as pseudoscientific (Cioffi, 1998). According to Freud, personality development proceeds through a series of stages. He termed these stages *psychosexual* because each focuses on an **erogenous zone**, or sexually arousing zone of the body. Although we're accustomed to thinking of our genitals as our primary sexual organs, Freud believed that other bodily areas are sources of sexual gratification in early development. Contrary to prevailing wisdom at the time, Freud insisted that sexuality begins in infancy. He maintained that the extent to which we resolve each stage successfully bears crucial implications for later personality development (see **TABLE 14.5**). He believed that individuals can become *fixated*, or "stuck," in an early stage of development. Fixations can occur because children were either deprived of sexual gratification

TABLE 14.5 Freud's Stages of Psychosexual Development.

STAGE	APPROXIMATE AGE	PRIMARY SOURCE OF SEXUAL PLEASURE
Oral	Birth to 12–18 months	Sucking and drinking
Anal	18 months to 3 years	Alleviating tension by expelling feces
Phallic*	3 years to 6 years	Genitals (penis or clitoris)
Latency	6 years to 12 years	Dormant sexual stage
Genital	12 years and beyond	Renewed sexual impulses; emergence of mature romantic relationships

*Includes Oedipus and Electra complexes.

they were supposed to receive during that stage, or excessively gratified during that stage; in either case, they experience difficulty moving ahead to the next stage. Let's examine the five psychosexual stages as Freud conceptualized them, bearing in mind that many modern critics don't share his views.

THE ORAL STAGE. The first stage of psychosexual development, the **oral stage**, which generally lasts from birth to 12–18 months, focuses on the mouth. During this stage, infants obtain sexual pleasure primarily by sucking and drinking. Freud believed that adults who are orally fixated tend to react to stress by becoming intensely dependent on others for reassurance—a form of regression, according to Freud—just as infants depend on their mother's breast as a source of satisfaction. They're also prone to unhealthy "oral" behaviors, like overeating, drinking excessively, or smoking.

THE ANAL STAGE. At the **anal stage**, which lasts from about 18 months to three years, children first come face-to-face with psychological conflict. During this stage, children want to alleviate tension and experience pleasure by moving their bowels, but soon discover that they can't do so whenever nature calls. Instead, they must learn to inhibit their urges and wait to move their bowels in a socially appropriate place—ideally, the toilet. If children's toilet training is either too harsh or too lenient, they'll become fixated and prone to regressing to this stage during anxiety-provoking circumstances. Freudians believe that anally fixated individuals—*anal personalities*—tend toward excessive neatness, stinginess, and stubbornness in adulthood.

THE PHALLIC STAGE. The **phallic stage**, which lasts from approximately three to six years, is of paramount importance to Freudians in explaining personality. During this stage, the penis (for boys) and clitoris (for girls) become the primary erogenous zones for pleasure. Simultaneously, children develop a powerful attraction for the opposite-sex parent, as well as a desire to eliminate the same-sex parent as a rival. Here's where things get complicated, so fasten your seat belts.

In boys, the phallic stage is termed the **Oedipus complex** after the tragic Greek character who unknowingly killed his father and married his mother. The boy, who wants Mommy all for himself, wants to kill or at least rid himself of Daddy. The boy comes to believe that his father perceives him as a rival for his mother's affection and fears that his father will castrate him as a result. Ultimately, these castration anxieties and the impossibility of ever attaining mother as a love object lead the boy to abandon this love. He then identifies with the aggressor, in this case his father, and adopts his characteristics: Like father, like son. The Oedipus complex is thereby resolved. Nevertheless, if children don't resolve this complex, claimed Freud, the stage is set for psychological problems later in life.

In girls, in contrast, the phallic stage is often termed the **Electra complex** after the Greek character who avenged her father's murder by killing her mother. Girls, like boys, desire the affections of the opposite-sex parent and fantasize about doing away with the same-sex parent. In girls, however, the phallic stage takes the form of *penis envy,* in which the girl desires to possess a penis, just like Daddy has. For reasons that Freud never clearly explained, girls believe themselves inferior to boys because of their "missing" organ. According to Freud, this sense of inferiority persists beyond childhood for years or even decades. Penis envy is probably Freud's most ridiculed concept, and with good reason, largely because there's no research support for it.

THE LATENCY STAGE. The fourth psychosexual stage, the **latency stage**, is a period of calm following the stormy phallic stage. In latency, which lasts from about six to 12 years, sexual impulses are submerged into the unconscious. Consistent with this belief, most boys and girls during this stage find members of the opposite sex to be "yucky" and utterly unappealing.

THE GENITAL STAGE. During the fifth and final psychosexual stage, the **genital stage**—which generally begins at around age 12—sexual impulses reawaken. If development up to this point has proceeded without major glitches, this stage witnesses the emergence of mature romantic relationships. In contrast, if serious problems weren't resolved at earlier stages, difficulties with establishing intimate love attachments are likely.

displacement
directing an impulse from a socially unacceptable target onto a safer and more socially acceptable target

rationalization
providing a reasonable-sounding explanation for unreasonable behaviors or for failures

identification with the aggressor
process of adopting the characteristics of individuals we find threatening

sublimation
transforming a socially unacceptable impulse into an admired goal

erogenous zone
sexually arousing zone of the body

oral stage
psychosexual stage that focuses on the mouth

anal stage
psychosexual stage that focuses on toilet training

phallic stage
psychosexual stage that focuses on the genitals

Oedipus complex
conflict during phallic stage in which boys supposedly love their mothers romantically and want to eliminate their fathers as rivals

Electra complex
conflict during phallic stage in which girls supposedly love their fathers romantically and want to eliminate their mothers as rivals

latency stage
psychosexual stage in which sexual impulses are submerged into the unconscious

genital stage
psychosexual stage in which sexual impulses awaken and typically begin to mature into romantic attraction toward others

In the classic Greek tragedy by Sophocles, Oedipus blinds himself soon after discovering that he'd unknowingly murdered his father and married his mother. Freud was so influenced by this play that he referred to the supposed love of all boys for their mothers as the Oedipus complex.

■ Psychoanalytic Theory Evaluated Scientifically

Freudian theory has been enormously influential in the thinking of psychologists and laypersons about personality, and for that reason alone his ideas merit careful examination (Kramer, 2007). Even Freud's most vocal detractors acknowledge that he was an ingenious thinker. But ingenuity shouldn't be confused with scientific support. Indeed, an outpouring of articles and books over the past few decades has raised troubling questions concerning the scientific status of psychoanalytic theory. Here we'll examine five major criticisms.

falsifiability

CAN THE CLAIM BE DISPROVED?

UNFALSIFIABILITY. Critics have noted that many hypotheses derived from Freudian theory are difficult or impossible to refute. To take just one example, the concept of reaction-formation offers a convenient escape hatch that allows many psychoanalytic hypotheses to evade falsification. If we were to find evidence that most five-year-old boys report being sexually repulsed by their mothers, would this observation refute the existence of the Oedipus complex? Superficially, the answer would seem to be yes, but Freudians could respond that these boys are engaging in reaction-formation and are attracted to their mothers at an unconscious level.

Indeed, Freud often used *ad hoc maneuvers* (see Chapter 1) to protect his pet hypotheses from refutation. One of Freud's patients intensely disliked her mother-in-law and took pains to ensure that she wouldn't spend a summer vacation with her. Yet while in therapy with Freud she dreamt of spending a summer vacation with her mother-in-law. This dream seemingly falsifies Freud's theory that all dreams are wish fulfillments. Yet Freud argued that her dream *supported* his theory because her underlying wish was to prove Freud incorrect (Dolnick, 1998)! Although we might marvel at Freud's ingenuity, this "heads I win, tails you lose" reasoning renders psychoanalytic theory difficult to falsify.

FAILED PREDICTIONS. Although much of Freudian theory is difficult to falsify, those portions of the theory that can be falsified often have been (Grunbaum, 1984). For example, Freud claimed that children exposed to overly harsh toilet training would grow up to be rigid and perfectionistic. Yet most investigators have found no association between toilet training practices and adult personality (Fisher & Greenberg, 1996). Similarly, there's little scientific support for many Freudian defense mechanisms, including repression. In particular, laboratory research shows that people are no more likely to forget negative life experiences than equally arousing, but positive, life experiences (Holmes, 1974, 1990).

QUESTIONABLE CONCEPTION OF THE UNCONSCIOUS. There's increasing reason to doubt the existence of the unconscious as Freud conceived of it. It's true that we're often unaware of why we do things. Richard Nisbett and Timothy Wilson (1977) reviewed a broad range of studies demonstrating that we often convince ourselves that we behave for reasons that are plausible, but incorrect. For example, in the context of a memory study investigators randomly exposed some participants, but not others, to the word pair "ocean–moon" embedded in a list of word pairs. When later asked to name their favorite detergent, the former participants were significantly more likely than the latter to name "Tide." Yet when asked the reasons for their choice, none came up with the correct explanation, namely, that the word "moon" triggered an association to "tide." Instead, participants came up with presumably false but plausible explanations (such as "I recently saw a Tide commercial on television").

Recent evidence suggests that subliminally presented stimuli (see Chapters 4 and 11), that is, stimuli presented below the threshold for awareness, can affect our behavior. Other evidence derives from priming paradigms, in which researchers observe the effects of subtle stimuli on people's behavior (see Chapter 7). In one study, researchers primed some participants, but not others, with words relevant to old age (like "Florida" and "wrinkle") in the context of a language task. Remarkably, after the study was over, primed participants walked down the hallway more slowly than did unprimed participants (Bargh & Chartrand, 1999)!

[handwritten margin note: He seems like quite the difficult guy. He cannot be wrong, now can he?]

[handwritten margin note: Subliminally presented stimuli are presented below the threshold for awareness.]

These findings may seem to support Freudian theory because they suggest that factors of which we're unaware influence our behavior (Westen, 1998). Yet they don't provide evidence for *the* unconscious: a massive reservoir of impulses and memories submerged beneath awareness (Wilson, 2002). Freud viewed the unconscious as a "place" where sexual and aggressive energies, along with repressed memories, are housed. Nevertheless, research doesn't support the existence of this place, let alone tell us where it's located (Kihlstrom, 1987).

RELIANCE ON UNREPRESENTATIVE SAMPLES. Many authors have charged that Freud based his theories on atypical samples and generalized them to the rest of humanity. Most of Freud's patients were upper-class, neurotic Viennese women, a far cry from the average Nigerian man or Malaysian woman. Freud's theories may therefore possess limited *external validity*, that is, generalizability (see Chapter 2), for people from other cultural backgrounds. Moreover, although Freud's methods of inquiry were idiographic, his theory was nomothetic: He studied a relatively small number of individuals in depth, but applied his theories to virtually all of humanity.

FLAWED ASSUMPTION OF SHARED ENVIRONMENTAL INFLUENCE. Many Freudian hypotheses presume that shared environment plays a key role in molding personality. For example, Freudians claim that the child emerging from the phallic stage assumes the personality characteristics of the same-sex parent. Nevertheless, as behavior-genetic studies have shown, shared environment plays scant role in adult personality, contradicting a key proposition of Freudian theory.

In summary, Freudian theory has had a profound influence on modern conceptions of the mind, but much of it is problematic from a scientific standpoint. The one insight of Freud that's best stood the test of time is that we're often unaware of why we do what we do. But this insight wasn't original to Freud (Crews, 1998), and as we'll learn later in the chapter, it's consistent with other models of personality, including behaviorism.

■ Freud's Followers: The Neo-Freudians

Largely in reaction to criticisms of Freudian theory, a number of theorists—many of them Freud's own students—broke from their mentor to forge their own models of personality. Because these thinkers modified Freud's views in significant ways, they're typically referred to as neo-Freudians.

NEO-FREUDIAN THEORIES: CORE FEATURES. Most neo-Freudian theories share with Freudian theory an emphasis on (a) unconscious influences and (b) the importance of early experience in shaping personality. Nevertheless, **neo-Freudian theories** differ from Freudian theory in two key ways:

1. Neo-Freudian theories place less emphasis than Freudian theory on sexuality as a driving force in personality, and more emphasis on social drives, such as the need for approval; and

2. Most neo-Freudian theories are more optimistic than Freudian theory concerning the prospects for personality growth throughout the life span. Freud was notoriously pessimistic about the possibility of personality change after childhood; he once wrote that the goal of psychoanalysis was to turn neurotic misery into ordinary, everyday unhappiness (Breuer & Freud, 1895).

ALFRED ADLER: THE STRIVING FOR SUPERIORITY. The first major follower of Freud to defect from the fold was Viennese psychiatrist Alfred Adler (1870–1937). According to Adler (1931), the principal motive in human personality is not sex or aggression, but the *striving for superiority*. Our overriding goal in life, said Adler, is to be better than others. We aim to accomplish this goal by crafting our distinctive **style of life**, or longstanding pattern of achieving superiority over our peers. People may try to satisfy their superiority strivings by becoming famous entertainers, great athletes, or outstanding parents.

One of Freud's best-known patients, known as "Anna O.," was Bertha Pappenheim, who later became the founder of social work in Germany (she was even honored with her own postage stamp). Because many of Freud's patients, like Pappenheim, were relatively wealthy Viennese women, critics have questioned the generalizability of his conclusions to other cultures.

neo-Freudian theories
theories derived from Freud's model, but that placed less emphasis on sexuality as a driving force in personality and were more optimistic regarding the prospects for long-term personality growth

style of life
according to Adler, each person's distinctive way of achieving superiority

Alfred Adler probably would have argued that German dictator Adolph Hitler's desire to dominate others was due to a striving for superiority and an effort to compensate for deep-seated inferiority feelings.

Adler (1922) maintained that neurotic difficulties stem from early childhood; children who are pampered or neglected by their parents are later at risk for an **inferiority complex**, a popular term inspired by Adler. People with an inferiority complex are prone to low self-esteem and tend to overcompensate for this feeling. As a result, they often attempt to demonstrate their superiority to others at all costs, even if it means dominating them. For Adler, most forms of mental illness are unhealthy attempts to overcompensate for the inferiority complex.

Adler's hypotheses, like Freud's, are difficult to falsify (Popper, 1965). Critics once asked Adler to explain how someone's decision to become a homeless person with alcoholism supported his theory that people always try to attain superiority over others. He responded that such a person has selected a lifestyle that affords a convenient excuse for being unable to achieve greatness. In effect, he can tell himself, "If only I didn't drink, I would have become successful." As we can see, with a little creativity, we can cook up an Adlerian explanation after the fact for almost any behavior.

falsifiability

CAN THE CLAIM BE DISPROVED?

Jung believed that the collective unconscious is our shared storehouse of ancestral memories. He even claimed that episodes of synchronicity, which involve the simultaneous occurrence of thoughts and events, reflect the actions of the collective unconscious. Is this claim falsifiable? (© ScienceCartoonPlus.com)

CARL JUNG: THE COLLECTIVE UNCONSCIOUS. Another pupil of Freud who parted ways with his mentor was Swiss psychiatrist Carl Gustav Jung (1875–1961). Although Freud originally anointed Jung to be the standard-bearer of the next generation of psychoanalysts, Jung became disenchanted with Freud's overemphasis on sexuality. Jung's views have become enormously influential in popular psychology, and Jung is something of a cult figure in New Age circles. Jung's theory is extraordinarily complicated—indeed, it may be the only major theory of personality more complex than Freud's—so we'll touch on only a few of the highlights here. ◉ **Watch**

Jung (1936) argued that in addition to Freud's version of the unconscious—which Jung termed the *personal unconscious*—there's also a **collective unconscious.** For Jung, the collective unconscious comprises the memories that ancestors have passed down to us across the generations. It's our shared storehouse of ancestral memories, and accounts for cultural similarities in myths and legends. We recognize our mothers immediately after birth, Jung argued, because the memories of thousands of generations of individuals who've seen their mothers after birth have been passed down to us genetically.

Jung further believed that the collective unconscious contains numerous **archetypes**, or cross-culturally universal symbols, which explain the similarities across people in their emotional reactions to many features of the world. Archetypes include the mother, the goddess, the hero, and the mandala (circle), which Jung believed symbolized a desire for wholeness or unity (Campbell, 1988; Jung, 1950). Jung (1958) even speculated that the modern epidemic of flying saucer reports stems from an unconscious desire to achieve a sense of unity with the universe, because flying saucers are shaped like mandalas.

Provocative as it is, Jung's theory suffers from some of the same shortcomings as those of Freud and Adler. It's difficult to falsify, as it generates few clear-cut predictions

FACTOID +

Some psychotherapists use *Jungian sandplay therapy* (Steinhardt, 1998) to uncover children's deep-seated conflicts. These practitioners try to infer the existence of archetypes on the basis of shapes that children draw in sand, and use them as a springboard for therapy. Nevertheless, there's no evidence that Jungian sandplay therapy is effective (Lilienfeld, 1999b), even though it's probably a lot of fun for children, not to mention therapists.

◉ **Watch** Carl Jung: Unconscious on **mypsychlab.com**

A mandala symbol similar to one drawn by one of Jung's patients. This drawing reminds us that therapists can influence their clients. As a consequence, therapists must be careful not to mistake their clients' drawings or statements as evidence for their preferred theories.

inferiority complex
feelings of low self-esteem that can lead to overcompensation for such feelings

collective unconscious
according to Jung, our shared storehouse of memories that ancestors have passed down to us across generations

archetype
cross-culturally universal symbols

(Gallo, 1994; Monte, 1995). For example, it's hard to imagine what evidence could falsify Jung's claim that flying saucer sightings stem from an underlying wish for wholeness with the universe. In addition, although Jung hypothesized that archetypes are transmitted to us from our ancestral past, he may not have sufficiently considered a rival explanation. Perhaps archetypes are cross-culturally universal because they represent crucial elements of the environment—mothers, wise elders, the sun, and moon (the sun and moon are, after all, shaped like mandalas)—that people across all cultures experience. Shared experiences rather than shared genes may account for commonalities in archetypes across the world.

KAREN HORNEY: FEMINIST PSYCHOLOGY. German physician Karen Horney (1885–1952) was the first major feminist personality theorist. Although not departing drastically from Freud's core assumptions, Horney (1939) took aim at those aspects of his theory that she saw as gender biased. She viewed Freud's concept of penis envy as especially misguided. Horney maintained that women's sense of inferiority stems not from their anatomy but their excessive dependency on men, which society has ingrained in them from an early age. She similarly objected to the Oedipus complex on the grounds that it's neither inevitable nor universal. This complex, she maintained, is a *symptom* rather than a *cause* of psychological problems, because it arises only when the opposite-sex parent is overly protective and the same-sex parent overly critical.

FREUD'S FOLLOWERS EVALUATED SCIENTIFICALLY. Many neo-Freudian theorists tempered some of the excesses of Freudian theory. They pointed out that anatomy isn't always destiny when it comes to the psychological differences between the sexes, and argued that social influences must be reckoned with in the development of personality. Nevertheless, as we've seen, falsifiability remains a serious concern for neo-Freudian theories, especially those of Adler and Jung. As a consequence, their scientific standing remains about as controversial as that of Freudian theory.

Karen Horney, the first major feminist psychological theorist, believed that Freud greatly underemphasized social factors as causes of inferiority feelings in many women.

◄ **falsifiability**
CAN THE CLAIM BE DISPROVED?

◄ **ruling out rival hypotheses**
HAVE IMPORTANT ALTERNATIVE EXPLANATIONS FOR THE FINDINGS BEEN EXCLUDED?

◄ **falsifiability**
CAN THE CLAIM BE DISPROVED?

✓ Study and Review on **mypsychlab.com**

---

assess your knowledge   **FACT OR FICTION?**

1. Freud believed that sex is the only important drive in personality. **True / False**
2. Freudians would say that most persons with very high opinions of themselves have overdeveloped egos. **True / False**
3. According to Freudians, a given dream symbol such as a snake doesn't have the same underlying meaning for every dreamer. **True / False**
4. According to Freud, a person who is orally fixed would be likely to drink excessively. **True / False**
5. One criticism of Freudian theory is that many of its predictions are difficult to falsify. **True / False**
6. Most neo-Freudian theorists, like Adler, placed less emphasis than did Freud on social influences on personality development. **True / False**

Answers: 1. F (p. 547); 2. F (p. 547); 3. T (p. 547); 4. T (p. 548); 5. T (p. 551); 6. F (p. 553)

BEHAVIORAL AND SOCIAL LEARNING THEORIES OF PERSONALITY

14.4 Identify the core assumptions of behavioral and social learning theories of personality.

14.5 Describe key criticisms of behavioral and social learning approaches.

We've already encountered behavioral models, including radical behaviorism, in Chapter 6. So why are we again crossing paths with behaviorism? After all, behaviorism is a theory of learning rather than a theory of personality, isn't it?

Actually, behaviorism is both. Radical behaviorists, like B. F. Skinner (see Chapter 6), believe that differences in our personalities stem largely from differences in our learning histories. Unlike Freudians, radical behaviorists reject the notion that the first few years of

(handwritten margin note: Why personalities differ? → genetic factors → contingencies (reinforcers and punishers) in environment)

life are especially critical in personality development. Childhood certainly matters, but learning continues to mold our personalities throughout the life span.

For radical behaviorists, our personalities are bundles of habits acquired by classical and operant conditioning. In contrast to other personality theorists, radical behaviorists don't believe that personality plays a role in *causing* behavior. For them, personality *consists of* behaviors. These behaviors are both overt (observable) and covert (unobservable), such as thoughts and feelings. A radical behaviorist wouldn't have much trouble accepting the idea that some people are extraverted, or that extraverted people tend to have many friends and attend many parties. But a radical behaviorist would strongly dispute the conclusion that certain people have many friends and attend many parties *because* they're extraverted.

Behavioral Views of the Causes of Personality

Radical behaviorists view personality as under the control of two major influences: (a) genetic factors and (b) *contingencies* in the environment, that is, reinforcers and punishers (see Chapter 6). Together, these influences explain why our personalities differ.

BEHAVIORAL VIEWS OF DETERMINISM. Like psychoanalysts, radical behaviorists are determinists: They believe all of our actions are products of preexisting causal influences. This is one of the precious few issues on which Freud and Skinner would likely have agreed if we could magically bring them back to life for a debate, one that most modern psychologists would probably pay a sizable chunk of their life savings to witness. For radical behaviorists, free will is an illusion (see Chapter 1). We may believe we're free to either continue reading this sentence or to instead stop to grab a long-awaited bowl of ice cream, but we're fooling ourselves. We're convinced that we're free to select our behaviors only because we're usually oblivious to the situational factors that trigger them.

Although this person may perceive her decision to either eat or not eat a piece of candy as under her control, radical behaviorists would regard her perception as an illusion.

BEHAVIORAL VIEWS OF UNCONSCIOUS PROCESSING. The belief in unconscious processing is another rare point of consensus between Freudians and Skinnerians (Overskeid, 2007), although their views of this processing differ sharply. For Skinner, we're unconscious of many things because we're often unaware of immediate situational influences on our behavior (Skinner, 1974). We may have had the experience of suddenly humming a song to ourselves and wondering why we were doing so, until we realized that this song had been playing softly on a distant radio. According to Skinner, we were initially unconscious of the reasons for our behavior because we were unaware of the external cause of this behavior, in this case, the song in the background.

Such unconscious processing is a far cry from the Freudian unconscious, which is a vast storehouse of inaccessible thoughts, memories, and impulses. For radical behaviorists, there's no such storehouse because the unconscious variables that play a role in causing behavior lie *outside*, not inside, of us.

Social Learning Theories of Personality: The Causal Role of Thinking Resurrected

social learning theorists
theorists who emphasize thinking as a cause of personality

(handwritten margin note: believe classical and operant conditioning are cognitively mediated)

Although influenced by radical behaviorists, **social learning theorists** (also sometimes called social cognitive theorists) believed that Skinner had gone too far in his wholesale rejection of the influence of thoughts on behavior. Spurred on by Edward Chase Tolman and others who believed that learning depends on our plans and goals (see Chapter 6), these theorists emphasized thinking as a cause of personality. How we interpret our environments affects how we react to them; if we perceive others as threatening, we'll typically be hostile and suspicious in return. According to social learning theorists, classical and operant conditioning are cognitively mediated. As we acquire information in classical and operant conditioning, we're actively thinking about and interpreting what it means. ⊕ Explore

⊕ Explore Behavioral versus Social Learning Theories of Personality on **mypsychlab.com**

SOCIAL LEARNING VIEWS OF DETERMINISM. Most social learning theorists hold a more complex view of determinism than do radical behaviorists. As we learned in Chapter 1, Albert Bandura (1986) made a compelling case for **reciprocal determinism**, a form of causation whereby personality and cognitive factors, behavior, and environmental variables mutually influence one another. Our high levels of extraversion may motivate us to introduce ourselves to our introductory psychology classmates and thereby make new friends. In turn, our newfound friends may reinforce our extraversion, encouraging us to attend parties we'd otherwise skip. Attending these parties may result in our acquiring additional friends who further reinforce our extraversion, and so on.

OBSERVATIONAL LEARNING AND PERSONALITY. Social learning theorists proposed that much of learning occurs by watching others. As we learned in Chapter 6, *observational learning* appears to be a key form of learning neglected by traditional behaviorists (Bandura, 1965). Observational learning expands greatly the range of stimuli from which we can benefit. It also means that our parents and teachers can play significant roles in shaping our personalities, because we acquire both good and bad habits by watching and, later, emulating them. For example, through observational learning, we can learn to behave altruistically by seeing our parents donate money to charities.

SENSE OF PERCEIVED CONTROL. Social learning theorists emphasized individuals' sense of control over life events. Julian Rotter (1966) introduced the concept of **locus of control** to describe the extent to which we believe that reinforcers and punishers lie inside or outside of our control. People with an internal locus of control ("internals") believe that life events are due largely to their own efforts and personal characteristics. In contrast, people with an external locus of control ("externals") believe that life events are largely a product of chance and fate, or what Hamlet termed the "slings and arrows of outrageous fortune" (see **TABLE 14.6**).

Rotter hypothesized that internals are less prone than externals to emotional upset following life stressors, because they're more likely to believe they can remedy problems on their own. Indeed, almost all forms of psychological distress, including depression and anxiety, are associated with an external locus of control (Benassi, Sweeney, & Dufour, 1988; Carton & Nowicki, 1996). It's not clear, though, whether these correlational findings reflect a causal relationship between external locus of control and mental disorders, as Rotter believed. Perhaps once people develop depression or anxiety, they begin to feel their lives are spiraling out of control. Or perhaps people who doubt their abilities are prone to both an external locus of control, on the one hand, and depression and anxiety, on the other.

When people in difficult circumstances obtain a measure of control over their lives, their adjustment improves. Ellen Langer and Judith Rodin (1976) gave residents on one floor of a nursing home control over several aspects of their environment. Residents on that floor had more freedom in arranging their rooms, lodging complaints, and attending films, whereas residents on a different floor had minimal control over these matters. Langer and Rodin found that residents afforded greater control showed better emotional adjustment

In observational learning, parents, teachers, and other adults play significant roles in shaping children's personalities: Children learn good and bad habits by watching and later emulating adults. This child may learn early that charitable giving is a worthy endeavor.

correlation vs. causation

CAN WE BE SURE THAT A CAUSES B?

[handwritten margin notes] locus of control → internal = life events are due to their own efforts and personal characteristics → external = life events are a product of chance and fate.

reciprocal determinism
tendency for people to mutually influence each other's behavior

locus of control
extent to which people believe that reinforcers and punishers lie inside or outside of their control

TABLE 14.6 Sample Items from a Measure of Locus of Control.

	TRUE OR FALSE
(1) Many people live miserable lives because of their parents.	True/False
(2) If you set realistic goals, you can succeed no matter what.	True/False
(3) One can climb the professional ladder just by being around at the right time.	True/False
(4) If I study hard enough, I can pass any exam.	True/False

For items 1 and 3, a "True" response is scored in the direction of an external locus of control, and a "False" response is scored in the direction of an internal locus of control. Items 2 and 4 are scored in the opposite fashion.
(*Source*: Reprinted with permission of Psychtests.com)

than other residents. Remarkably, one year later, fewer residents in the former condition had died. Although these results seem to suggest that a heightened sense of control enhances psychological and physical health, they're a bit difficult to interpret. Perhaps residents given greater control actually took advantage of it by sprucing up their rooms or voicing concerns to staff. So it may not be perceived control as much as *actual* control that matters.

ruling out rival hypotheses

HAVE IMPORTANT ALTERNATIVE EXPLANATIONS FOR THE FINDINGS BEEN EXCLUDED?

■ Behavioral and Social Learning Theories Evaluated Scientifically

B. F. Skinner and his fellow radical behaviorists agreed with Freud that our behavior is determined, but maintained that the primary causes of our behavior—contingencies—lie outside rather than inside of us. Even critics of radical behaviorism acknowledge that Skinner and his followers placed the field of psychology on firmer scientific footing. Many of them charged, however, that radical behaviorists went too far in their exclusion of any causal role for thinking. Indeed, the claim that our thoughts play no causal role in our behavior strikes most modern thinkers as implausible from an evolutionary perspective. Natural selection has endowed us with an enormous cerebral cortex (see Chapter 3), which is specialized for problem solving, planning, reasoning, and other high-level cognitive processes. It seems difficult to comprehend why our huge cortexes would have evolved if our thoughts were merely by-products of contingencies.

Social learning theorists rekindled psychologists' interests in thinking and argued that observational learning is a crucial form of learning in addition to classical and operant conditioning. Nevertheless, social learning theory isn't immune to criticism. In particular, the claim that observational learning exerts a powerful influence over our personalities implies an important causal role of shared environment. After all, if we learn largely by modeling the behaviors of our parents and other relatives, we should become like them. Yet, as we've learned, behavior-genetic studies have shown that the effects of shared environment on adult personality are weak or nonexistent.

Although social learning theorists believe that learning processes depend on cognition (thinking; see Chapter 8), scientists have observed these processes in animals with tiny cerebral cortexes and even with no cortexes at all. For example, they've documented classical conditioning in honeybees (Alcock, 1999) and starfish (McClintock & Lawrence, 1983). There's even evidence that classical conditioning occurs in such microscopic organisms as protozoa (Bergstrom, 1968) and hydra (Tanaka, 1966), although not all researchers have replicated these findings (Applewhite et al., 1972). There have also been reports of observational learning in the octopus (Fiorito & Scotto, 1993), although these findings are scientifically controversial.

The fact that learning occurs in relatively simple animals implies any one of three things. First, perhaps social learning theorists are wrong that basic forms of learning depend on cognition. Second, perhaps the thinking processes involved in these forms of learning are primitive in certain cases, although we might justifiably question whether a starfish, let alone a protozoan, is capable of genuine "thought." Third, the learning processes of simple animals may rely on different mechanisms from those of humans. At this point, the scientific evidence doesn't permit a clear answer.

How much of the daughter's personality and mannerisms are due to social learning from her mother? The scientific verdict is still out.

replicability

CAN THE RESULTS BE DUPLICATED IN OTHER STUDIES?

✓ Study and Review on mypsychlab.com

assess your knowledge   FACT OR FICTION?

1. For radical behaviorists, our personalities are bundles of habits influenced by learning. **True** / **False**

2. Radical behaviorists argue that we're sometimes "unconscious" of the true causes of our behavior. **True** / **False**

3. Social learning theorists believe that observational learning is a key form of learning in addition to classical and operant conditioning. **True** / **False**

4. According to social learning theorists, individuals with an internal locus of control are more prone to depression than individuals with an external locus of control. **True** / **False**

Answers: 1. T (p. 556); 2. T (p. 556); 3. T (p. 557); 4. F (p. 557).

HUMANISTIC MODELS OF PERSONALITY: THE THIRD FORCE

14.6 Explain the concept of self-actualization and its role in humanistic models.

14.7 Describe key criticisms of humanistic approaches.

Psychoanalytic theory, along with behavioral and social learning models, dominated personality psychology throughout the first half of the 20th century. In the 1950s and 1960s, however, *humanistic models* emerged as a "third force" in personality psychology. Humanistic psychologists rejected the determinism of psychoanalysts and behaviorists and embraced the notion of free will. We're perfectly free, they maintained, to choose either socially constructive or destructive paths in life.

Most humanistic psychologists propose that the core motive in personality is **self-actualization**: the drive to develop our innate potential to the fullest possible extent (see Chapter 11). Freudians would say that self-actualization would be disastrous for society because our innate drives, housed in the id, are selfish and potentially harmful if not controlled. For Freudians, a society of self-actualized people would result in sheer pandemonium, with citizens expressing their sexual and aggressive urges with reckless abandon. Humanistic theorists, in contrast, view human nature as inherently constructive, so they see self-actualization as a worthy goal.

■ Rogers and Maslow: Self-Actualization Realized and Unrealized

The best-known humanistic theorist was Carl Rogers (1902–1987), who, as we'll learn in Chapter 16, used his personality theory as a point of departure for an influential form of psychotherapy. Ever the optimist, Rogers believed that we could all achieve our full potential for emotional fulfillment if only society allowed it.

ROGERS'S MODEL OF PERSONALITY. According to Rogers (1947), our personalities consist of three major components: organism, self, and conditions of worth.

1. The *organism* is our innate—and substantially genetically influenced—blueprint. In this regard, it's like the Freudian id, except that Rogers viewed the organism as inherently positive and helpful toward others. Rogers wasn't terribly specific, however, about the makeup of the organism.

2. The *self* is our self-concept, the set of beliefs about who we are.

3. **Conditions of worth** are the expectations we place on ourselves for appropriate and inappropriate behavior. Like the Freudian superego, they emanate from our parents and society, and eventually we internalize them. Conditions of worth arise—typically in childhood—when others make their acceptance of us conditional (that is, dependent) only on certain behaviors, but not others. As a result, we accept ourselves only if we act in certain ways. A child who enjoys writing poetry may develop conditions of worth if taunted by peers. "When I'm teased for writing poetry, I'm not worthwhile. When I stop, I'm not teased so I become worthwhile." For Rogers, individual differences in personality stem largely from differences in the conditions of worth that others impose on us. Although in his idealistic moments Rogers envisioned a world in which conditions of worth no longer existed, he reluctantly acknowledged that in modern society even the best adjusted among us inevitably harbor certain conditions of worth. Conditions of worth result in **incongruence** between self and organism. Incongruence means that our personalities are inconsistent with our innate dispositions: We're no longer our genuine selves, because we're acting in ways that are inconsistent with our underlying potentialities.

MASLOW: THE CHARACTERISTICS OF SELF-ACTUALIZED PEOPLE. Whereas Rogers focused largely on pathological individuals whose tendencies toward self-actualization were thwarted, Abraham Maslow (1908–1970) focused on individuals who were

Carl Rogers, pioneer of humanistic psychology, held an optimistic view of human nature, although some critics have accused him of being naive in minimizing the dark side of human nature.

self-actualization
drive to develop our innate potential to the fullest possible extent

conditions of worth
according to Rogers, expectations we place on ourselves for appropriate and inappropriate behavior

incongruence
inconsistency between our personalities and innate dispositions

Mahatma Gandhi is one of the historical figures whom Abraham Maslow considered to be self-actualized.

? The motto of this army recruitment poster ("Be all that you can be") captures the essence of what humanistic psychology concept? (See answer upside down on bottom of page.)

---

peak experience
transcendent moment of intense excitement and tranquility marked by a profound sense of connection to the world

---

falsifiability ›

CAN THE CLAIM BE DISPROVED?

self-actualized, especially historical figures. Among those whom Maslow considered self-actualized were Thomas Jefferson, Abraham Lincoln, Martin Luther King Jr., Helen Keller, and Mahatma Gandhi.

According to Maslow (1971), self-actualized people tend to be creative, spontaneous, and accepting of themselves and others. They're self-confident but not self-centered. They focus on real-world and intellectual problems and have a few deep friendships rather than many superficial ones. Contrary to what we might expect, self-actualized individuals typically crave privacy and can come off as aloof or even difficult to deal with, because they've outgrown the need to be popular. As a consequence, they're not afraid to "rock the boat" when necessary or express unpopular opinions. They're also prone to **peak experiences**—transcendent moments of intense excitement and tranquility marked by a profound sense of connection to the world.

■ Humanistic Models Evaluated Scientifically

Humanistic models of personality boldly proclaimed the importance of free will and personal choice, and appealed to a generation of young people disenchanted with the determinism of psychoanalysis and behaviorism. Yet investigators in *comparative psychology*, the branch of psychology that compares behavior across species, have challenged Rogers's claim that human nature is entirely positive. Their research suggests that the capacity for aggression is inherent in our close primate cousins, the chimpanzees (Goodall & van Lawick, 1971; see Chapter 13). There's also evidence from twin studies that aggression is probably part of humans' genetic heritage (Krueger, Hicks, & McGue, 2001). Therefore, actualization of our full genetic potential is unlikely to bring about the state of eternal bliss that Rogers imagined. At the same time, research suggests that the capacity for altruism is intrinsic to both chimpanzees and humans (de Waal, 1990, 2009; Wilson, 1993). Human nature, it seems, is a complex mix of selfish and selfless motives.

Rogers's research demonstrated that the discrepancy between people's descriptions of their actual versus ideal selves is greater for emotionally disturbed than for emotionally healthy individuals. This difference decreases over the course of psychotherapy (Rogers & Dymond, 1954). Rogers interpreted this finding as reflecting a lessening of conditions of worth. Yet these results are hard to interpret, because the people who showed decreases in incongruence following therapy weren't the same people who improved (Loevinger, 1987).

Maslow's research on the characteristics of self-actualized individuals paved the way for today's "positive psychology" movement (see Chapter 11). Indeed, although he rarely receives credit for it, Maslow (1954) was the first person to use this term. Yet his work is problematic on methodological grounds. In beginning with the assumption that self-actualized individuals tend to be creative and spontaneous, Maslow may have limited his search to historical figures who displayed these traits. As such, he may have fallen prey to confirmation bias (see Chapter 2): Because he wasn't blind to his hypothesis concerning the personality features of self-actualized individuals, he had no easy way of guarding against this bias.

Humanistic models are also difficult to falsify. If a study of the general population showed that many people were self-actualized, humanistic psychologists could interpret this finding as evidence that self-actualization is a key influence on personality. But if this study showed that virtually no one was self-actualized, humanistic psychologists could explain away this finding by saying that most individuals' drives toward self-actualization had been stifled. Although the claim that self-actualization is the central motive in personality may not be testable scientifically, the principle that we should develop our potential to the fullest may have considerable value as a philosophy of life.

✓• [**Study** and **Review** on mypsychlab.com]

assess your knowledge — FACT OR FICTION?

1. According to Rogers, human nature is inherently positive. **True** / **False**

2. Rogers believed that only severely disturbed individuals acquire conditions of worth.
   True / **False**

3. Maslow argued that almost all self-actualized individuals are sociable and easy to get along with. **True** / **False**

4. Many claims of humanistic models are difficult to falsify. **True** / **False**

Answers: 1. T (p. 559); 2. F (p. 560); 3. F (p. 560); 4. T (p. 560)

TRAIT MODELS OF PERSONALITY: CONSISTENCIES IN OUR BEHAVIOR

14.8 Describe trait models of personality, including the Big Five.

14.9 Identify key criticisms of trait models.

In contrast to most personality theorists we've reviewed, proponents of trait models are interested primarily in describing and understanding the *structure* of personality. Much like early chemists who strove to identify the elements of the periodic table, trait theorists aim to pinpoint the major traits of personality, which as we've learned are relatively enduring dispositions that affect our behaviors across situations.

■ Identifying Traits: Factor Analysis

Invoking personality traits as causes of behavior has its challenges. To start with, we must avoid the *circular reasoning fallacy* (see Chapter 1). We might conclude that a child who kicks others on the playground is aggressive. But in asking how we know that this child is aggressive, we might respond "because he kicks other children on the playground." Note that this answer merely restates the same evidence we used to infer that the child was aggressive in the first place. To avoid this logical trap, we need to demonstrate that personality traits predict behaviors in novel situations or correlate with biological or laboratory measures.

From there, we need to narrow down the pool of possible traits. As Gordon Allport observed, there are over 17,000 terms in the English language referring to personality traits: shy, stubborn, impulsive, greedy, cheerful, and so on (Allport & Odbert, 1936). To reduce this enormous diversity of traits to a much smaller of underlying traits, trait theorists use a statistical technique called **factor analysis**. This method analyzes the correlations among responses on personality measures to identify the underlying "factors" that give rise to these correlations.

TABLE 14.7 presents the correlations among six different variables—sociability, popularity, liveliness, risk-taking, sensation seeking, and impulsivity—in a hypothetical

Claiming that a child is "aggressive" merely because he engages in aggressive behavior gives us no new information and is an example of circular reasoning. To be meaningful, personality traits must do more than merely describe behaviors we've already observed.

factor analysis
statistical technique that analyzes the correlations among responses on personality inventories and other measures

TABLE 14.7 An "Eyeball" Factor Analysis of Six Variables. Follow along as we describe this correlation matrix of six personality measures (the 1.00s on the diagonal represent the correlation of each variable with itself, which is a perfect correlation).

	MEASURES					
	VARIABLE 1 SOCIABILITY	**VARIABLE 2 POPULARITY**	**VARIABLE 3 LIVELINESS**	**VARIABLE 4 RISK-TAKING**	**VARIABLE 5 SENSATION SEEKING**	**VARIABLE 6 IMPULSIVITY**
Variable 1	1.00	.78	.82	.12	.07	−.03
Variable 2		1.00	.70	.08	.02	.11
Variable 3			1.00	.05	.11	.18
Variable 4				1.00	.69	.85
Variable 5					1.00	.72
Variable 6						1.00

FACTOID ✚

Individuals' handshakes can tell us something about their Big Five personality traits. Research demonstrates that people with firm handshakes tend to be somewhat higher in extraversion and openness to experience, and lower in neuroticism, than people with limp handshakes (Chaplin, 2000).

❓ Research shows that the Big Five trait of openness to experience predicts art preferences (Feist & Brady, 2004). Which painting above would a person high in openness to experience be most likely to prefer, and why? (See answer upside down on bottom of page.)

Big Five
five traits that have surfaced repeatedly in factor analyses of personality measures

lexical approach
approach proposing that the most crucial features of personality are embedded in our language

Answer: Painting on the top. Openness to experience is correlated with preference for abstract art, probably because this trait is related to unconventionality and tolerance for ambiguity.

correlation matrix: A table of correlations. As we look over this correlation matrix, we'll notice that only some of the cells contain numbers; that's because correlation matrixes present each correlation only once. (That's why, for example, the matrix displays the correlation between variables 1 and 4 only once.) We can see that variables 1 through 3 are highly correlated, as are variables 4 through 6. But these two sets of variables aren't correlated much with one another, so the correlation matrix suggests the presence of two factors. We might call the factor comprising variables 1 through 3 (in blue) "extraversion," and we might call the factor comprising variables 4 through 6 (in green) "fearlessness." The formal technique of factor analysis uses much more rigorous statistical criteria to accomplish the same goal as the "eyeball method" we just walked you through.

■ The Big Five Model of Personality: The Geography of the Psyche

Although there's no complete consensus among trait theorists regarding the most scientifically supported model of personality structure, one model has amassed an impressive body of research evidence. This model, the **Big Five**, consists of five traits that have surfaced repeatedly in factor analyses of personality measures.

The Big Five were uncovered using a **lexical approach** to personality, which proposes that the most crucial features of human personality are embedded in our language (Goldberg, 1993). The logic here is simple. If a personality trait is important in our daily lives, it's likely that we talk a lot about it. The Big Five emerged from factor analyses of trait terms in dictionaries and works of literature. According to Paul Costa, Robert McCrae, and their collaborators (Costa & McCrae, 1992; Widiger, 2001), these five dimensions are:

- *Openness to Experience,* sometimes just called "Openness"—open people tend to be intellectually curious and unconventional;
- *Conscientiousness*—conscientious people tend to be careful and responsible;
- *Extraversion*—extraverted people tend to be social and lively;
- *Agreeableness*—agreeable people tend to be sociable and easy to get along with; and
- *Neuroticism*—neurotic people tend to be tense and moody.

We can use either of two waterlogged acronyms—OCEAN or CANOE—as a handy mnemonic for remembering the Big Five. According to Big Five advocates, we can use these factors to describe all people, including those with psychological disorders. Each of us occupies some location on all five of these dimensions. A severely depressed person, for example, may be low in Extraversion, high in Neuroticism, and about average on the other three dimensions.

The Big Five appear in people's ratings of personality even when researchers ask participants to describe people they've only seen, not met (Passini & Norman, 1966). This finding suggests that we harbor *implicit personality theories,* that is, intuitive ideas concerning personality traits and their associations with behavior. The popular dating website eHarmony.com uses the Big Five to match prospective partners, although the research evidence for its success is minimal (see Chapter 11). The work of Samuel Gosling and others suggests that the Big Five, plus a sixth trait of dominance, also emerge in studies of chimpanzee personality (Gosling, 2001, 2008; King & Figueredo, 1997), although it's difficult to exclude the possibility that raters in these studies are *anthropomorphizing*—that is, unintentionally imposing their implicit personality theories on chimpanzees.

THE BIG FIVE AND BEHAVIOR. The Big Five predict many important real-world behaviors. High Conscientiousness, low Neuroticism, and perhaps high Agreeableness are associated with successful job performance (Barrick & Mount, 1991; Tett, Jackson, & Rothstein, 1991) and grades in school (Conard, 2006; Heaven, Ciarrochi, & Vialle, 2007). In some but not all studies, Extraversion has been positively correlated with successful performance among salespersons (Furnham & Fudge, 2008). Three researchers (Rubenzer, Fashingbauer, & Ones, 2000) asked presidential biographers to rate the U.S. presidents from George

Washington through George W. Bush. Scores on Openness to Experience were correlated positively with independently assessed ratings of presidents' historical greatness. Interestingly, Agreeableness was (slightly) *negatively* correlated with historical greatness, suggesting that the best presidents often aren't always the easiest to get along with. In addition, conscientiousness is positively associated with physical health and even life span (Martin & Friedman, 2000), probably because conscientious people are more likely than others to engage in healthy behaviors, like exercising regularly and avoiding smoking (Bogg & Roberts, 2004).

CULTURAL INFLUENCES ON THE BIG FIVE In seeking to address enduring questions concerning the cross-cultural relevance of personality, researchers have discovered that the Big Five are identifiable in China, Japan, Italy, Hungary, and Turkey (De Raad et al., 1998; McCrae & Costa, 1997; Triandis & Suh, 2002). Nevertheless, there may be limits to the Big Five's cross-cultural universality. Openness to experience doesn't emerge clearly in all cultures (De Raad et al., 2002) and some investigators have found dimensions in addition to the Big Five. For example, personality studies in China have revealed an additional "Chinese tradition" factor that encompasses aspects of personality distinctive to Chinese culture, including an emphasis on group harmony and saving face to avoid embarrassment (Cheung & Leung, 1998). Moreover, studies in Germany, Finland, and several other countries suggest the presence of a factor comprising honesty and humility in addition to the Big Five (Lee & Ashton, 2004).

Are you a dog person or a cat person? Recent research suggests that scores on the Big Five can help predict the answer: Dog people tend to have somewhat higher scores than cat people on extraversion, agreeableness, and conscientiousness, whereas cat people tend to have somewhat higher scores than dog people on neuroticism and openness to experience (Gosling & Sandy, 2010).

Individualism-Collectivism and Personality. Cross-cultural researchers have devoted considerable attention to a key dimension relevant to personality we first encountered in Chapter 10: *individualism-collectivism.* People from largely individualistic cultures, like the United States, tend to focus on themselves and their personal goals, whereas those from largely collectivist cultures, primarily in Asia, tend to focus on their relations with others (Triandis, 1989). People from individualistic cultures usually report higher self-esteem than those from collectivist cultures (Heine et al., 1999). In addition, personality traits may be less predictive of behavior in collectivist than individualistic cultures, probably because people's behavior in collectivist cultures is more influenced by social norms (Church & Katigbak, 2002).

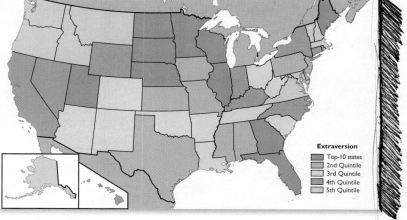

Still, we shouldn't oversimplify the distinction between individualistic and collectivist cultures. Only about 60 percent of people in individualist cultures possess individualist personalities, and only about 60 percent of people in collectivist cultures possess collectivist personalities (Triandis & Suh, 2002). Furthermore, Asian countries differ markedly in their levels of collectivism, reminding us of the perils of stereotyping and overgeneralization (see Chapter 13). For example, although Chinese are generally more collectivist than Americans, Japanese and Koreans aren't (Oyserman, Coon, & Kemmelmeier, 2002).

Research by Peter Rentfrow, Samuel Gosling, and Jeff Potter (2008) shows that the Big Five traits differ across geographical regions. Here, for example, is a map of the levels of extraversion across the 50 U.S. states. This research raises intriguing questions: For example, does living in relatively isolated states, like Idaho or Alaska, make one introverted, or are introverted people drawn to living in isolated states?

ALTERNATIVES TO THE BIG FIVE. The Big Five is a useful system for organizing individual differences in personality. Nevertheless, there's reason to question the lexical approach, as people may not be consciously aware of all important features of personality (J. Block, 1995). As a consequence, our language may not adequately reflect these features. In addition, there's no Big Five factor corresponding to morality (Loevinger, 1993), despite the centrality of this variable to many theories of personality, including those of Freud and his followers. Still other psychologists, like Hans Eysenck (1991), Auke Tellegen (1982), and

C. Robert Cloninger (1987) maintain that three dimensions rather than five offer the most accurate model of personality structure. According to them, the Big Five dimensions of Agreeableness, Conscientiousness, and (low) Openness to Experience combine to form one larger dimension of impulse control or fearfulness along with the dimensions of Extraversion and Neuroticism. The "Big Three" model of personality structure is a worthy alternative to the Big Five (Harkness et al., 2008).

■ Basic Tendencies versus Characteristic Adaptations

Personality traits don't tell the whole story of why we differ from each other. The story of Jack and Oskar underscores the distinction between *basic tendencies* and *characteristic adaptations* (Harkness & Lilienfeld, 1997; McCrae & Costa, 1995). Basic tendencies are underlying personality traits, whereas characteristic adaptations are their behavioral manifestations. The key point is that people can express their personality traits in dramatically different ways. In Jack and Oskar's case, the same basic tendencies—intense loyalty and devotion to social causes—were expressed in markedly different characteristic adaptations: Jack's Judaism and profound dislike of Germans and Oskar's Nazism and profound dislike of Jews.

Sensation seeking (Zuckerman, 1979), or the tendency to seek out new and exciting stimuli, offers another example of this distinction. High sensation seekers enjoy parachute jumping, sampling spicy foods, and living life in the fast lane. In contrast, low sensation seekers dislike risk, adventure, and novelty; when they go out to eat, they always go to the same restaurant and they always order chicken parmigiana, for example. Interestingly, the average sensation-seeking scores of firefighters and prisoners are essentially identical, but significantly higher than those of average college students (Zuckerman, 1994). Apparently, people can express tendencies toward risk taking and danger seeking in either socially constructive (firefighting) or destructive (crime) outlets. Why some sensation seekers end up in firehouses and others in prisons remains mysterious.

■ Can Personality Traits Change?

Longitudinal studies (see Chapter 10) demonstrate that prior to age 30, personality traits sometimes change over time. Openness, extraversion, and neuroticism tend to decline a bit from the late teens to early thirties, whereas conscientiousness and agreeableness tend to increase a bit (Costa & McCrae, 1992; Srivastava et al., 2003). Yet studies also show that the levels of most traits don't change much after age 30 and change even less after about age 50 (McCrae & Costa, 1994; Roberts & DelVecchio, 2000). We don't know whether psychotherapy can change personality, although many psychologists today are even less optimistic about this prospect than they were in Freud's day.

In the best seller *Listening to Prozac*, Peter Kramer (1993) sparked interest in the possibility that medication can change personality traits. He coined the term *cosmetic psychopharmacology* to describe the use of medications to produce long-term alterations in personality. According to Kramer, there's anecdotal evidence that certain mood-altering medications, like Prozac, Paxil, and Zoloft (see Chapter 16), produce calmness and decreased shyness, even among people without mental illness (Concar, 1994). He argued that these drugs may allow us to become "better than well." Although the evidence is preliminary, the results of one study demonstrate that well-adjusted people who ingest Paxil experience less hostility and more interest in socializing than those who ingested a placebo (Knutson et al., 1988). In a more recent study, Paxil—compared with a placebo—increased levels of extraversion and decreased levels of neuroticism among people with clinical depression (Tang et al., 2009).

Kramer's arguments raise intriguing scientific, practical, and ethical questions. On the scientific side, might our personalities, which we think of as being an intrinsic part of ourselves, be more malleable than we supposed? On the practical and ethical sides, could cosmetic psychopharmacology have any important disadvantages? As we learned in Chapter 11, evolutionary psychologists argue that many emotions serve essential adaptive

Personality research reveals that prisoners and firefighters tend to receive equally high scores on measures of sensation seeking, suggesting that they may have channeled their basic tendencies into dramatically different characteristic adaptations.

functions. Anxiety, for example, may be a crucial warning signal of potential danger. If we reduced most people's anxiety levels, could we inadvertently produce a civilization of passive citizens blissfully unconcerned about impending disaster? Although this alarmist scenario seems unlikely in anything other than a science fiction thriller, it's clear that cosmetic psychopharmacology poses significant challenges that have yet to be resolved.

■ Trait Models Evaluated Scientifically

Trait theory was highly influential through the early and mid-twentieth century. Then in a bombshell 1968 book, *Personality and Assessment,* Walter Mischel called the very notion of personality traits into question, embroiling the field of trait psychology in heated controversy for over a decade.

WALTER MISCHEL'S ARGUMENT: BEHAVIORAL INCONSISTENCY. As we noted earlier, psychologists had long assumed that traits influence behavior across many situations. But in his review of the literature, Mischel found low correlations among different behaviors presumed to reflect the same trait. For example, he cited a study by Hugh Hartschorne and Mark May (1928) that had examined the correlations among behavioral indicators of honesty among children. Hartschorne and May concocted situations that allowed children to behave either honestly or dishonestly, giving them the opportunity to steal a dime, change answers on an exam, and lie. Surprisingly, the correlations among children's behavior across these situations were low, with none exceeding .30. So children who steal, for example, aren't much more likely than other children to cheat. Numerous researchers have reported similar findings in adults for such traits as dependency, friendliness, and conscientiousness (Bem & Allen, 1974; Diener & Larson, 1984; Mischel, 1968). People, it seems, aren't nearly as consistent across situations as most of us believe.

Mischel concluded that measures of personality aren't especially helpful for what they were designed to do—forecast behavior. Some psychologists later tried to explain our persistent belief in the predictive power of personality traits in terms of our cognitive biases, especially the fundamental attribution error (see Chapter 13). For them, we "see" people's personalities all around us because we mistake situational influences on their behavior, such as peer pressure, for personality influences (Bem & Allen, 1974; Ross & Nisbett, 1991). ⊕ Explore

Explore Mischel's Theory of Personality on **mypsychlab.com**

PERSONALITY TRAITS REBORN: PSYCHOLOGISTS RESPOND TO MISCHEL. Were Mischel's criticisms valid? Yes and no. As Seymour Epstein (1979) noted, Mischel was correct that personality traits aren't highly predictive of isolated behaviors, such as lying or cheating in a single situation. Nevertheless, in several studies Epstein showed that personality traits are often highly predictive of *aggregated* behaviors, that is, composites of behavior averaged across many situations. If we use a measure of extraversion to predict whether our friend will attend a party next Saturday night, we'll probably do only slightly better than chance. In contrast, if we use this measure to predict our friend's behavior across an average of many situations—attendance at parties, friendliness in small seminars, and willingness to engage in conversations with strangers—we'll probably do rather well. Contrary to Mischel's initial conclusions, personality traits can be useful for predicting overall behavioral trends—such as whether someone will be a responsible employee or a difficult marital partner (Kenrick & Funder, 1988; Rushton, Brainerd, & Presley, 1983; Tellegen, 1991).

In contrast to other personality theories we've reviewed, trait models are primarily efforts to *describe* individual differences in personality rather than to *explain* their causes. This emphasis on description is both a strength and a weakness. On the one hand, these models have advanced our understanding of personality structure and helped psychologists to predict performance in jobs, even the job of leader of the world's largest superpower. On the other hand, some trait models don't provide much insight into the causes of personality. Although the Big Five, for example, do a decent job of capturing personality differences among people, they don't shed much light on the origins of these differences.

Some researchers, like Hans Eysenck, have tried to remedy this shortcoming. For example, according to Eysenck (1973), the personality dimension of extraversion–introversion is produced by differences in the threshold of arousal of the reticular activating system (RAS). As we learned in Chapter 3, the RAS controls alertness and is responsible for keeping us awake. If your RAS is still functioning at this late point in the chapter, you might be wondering how RAS activity is related to extraversion and introversion. Although the following hypothesis is paradoxical, Eysenck argued that extraverts have an *underactive* RAS: They're habitually underaroused and bored. So they seek out stimulation, including other people, to jack up their arousal (recall the Yerkes-Dodson law from Chapter 11). In contrast, introverts tend to have an overactive RAS: They're habitually overaroused, and try to minimize or shut out stimulation, again including other people. Interestingly, extraverts, unlike introverts, prefer loud to soft music (Geen, 1984; Kageyama, 1999). Although the evidence for Eysenck's hypothesis isn't entirely consistent (Gray, 1981; Matthews & Gilliland, 1999), his theorizing demonstrates that trait theories can generate fruitful hypotheses concerning the relations between personality traits and biological variables.

✔•—Study and Review on mypsychlab.com

assess your knowledge   FACT OR FICTION?

1. One limitation of the Big Five model is that researchers have identified these traits only in American culture. **True / False**

2. Research demonstrates that after late childhood, the levels of most personality traits virtually never change over the life span. **True / False**

3. Personality traits typically predict behavior in a single situation with high levels of accuracy. **True / False**

4. According to Eysenck, extraverts tend to be less aroused than introverts. **True / False**

Answers: 1. F (p. 563); 2. F (p. 564); 3. F (p. 565); 4. T (p. 566)

PERSONALITY ASSESSMENT: MEASURING AND MISMEASURING THE PSYCHE

14.10 Describe structured personality tests, such as the MMPI-2, and their methods of construction.

14.11 Describe projective tests, particularly the Rorschach, and their strengths and weaknesses.

14.12 Identify common pitfalls in personality assessment.

Personality wouldn't be helpful to psychologists if they had no way of measuring it. That's where personality assessment enters into the picture: It offers us the promise of detecting individual differences in personality in a scientifically rigorous fashion. But developing accurate tools to measure personality is easier said than done.

■ Famous—and Infamous—Errors in Personality Assessment

Indeed, personality psychology has long been plagued by a parade of dubious assessment methods. Phrenology, which we encountered in Chapter 3, purported to detect people's personality traits by measuring the patterns of bumps on their heads. Related to phrenology was *physiognomy,* popular in the 18th and 19th centuries, which claimed to detect people's personality traits from their facial characteristics (Collins, 1999). The term "lowbrow," which today refers to someone who's uncultured, derives from the old belief that most nonintellectual people have protruding foreheads and a low brow line. This claim, like virtually all other claims of physiognomy, has been falsified. Still, physiognomy may contain a tiny kernel of truth. Research suggests that women do better than chance at figuring out which men are most interested in children merely by looking at still photographs of their faces (Roney et al., 2006), although it's not clear to which features of men's faces observers

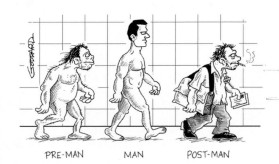

PRE-MAN   MAN   POST-MAN

Traditional beliefs persist that those with protruding foreheads and low brow lines are less intelligent or cultured than other people. (© Clive Goddard/www.CartoonStock.com)

falsifiability ▶
CAN THE CLAIM BE DISPROVED?

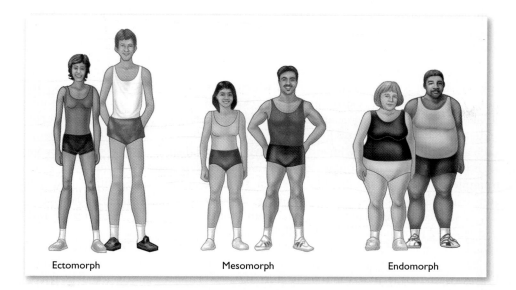

Ectomorph   Mesomorph   Endomorph

FIGURE 14.4 Sheldon's Body Types. According to William Sheldon, three major body types are associated with different personality traits. Yet research hasn't borne out most of Sheldon's claims. Because Sheldon wasn't blind to body type when rating people's personality traits, his findings may have been due largely to confirmation bias.

based these judgments. In another study, observers accurately gauged men's tendencies toward physical aggressiveness by glancing briefly at their faces (Carre, McCormick, & Mondloch, 2009). Interestingly, these estimates were highly correlated with the ratio of the width to the length of men's faces (with faces that are wider than longer reflecting more aggressiveness) perhaps because this ratio reflects the influence of hormones secreted during puberty than also affect aggressiveness.

In the vein of physiognomy, psychologist William Sheldon believed he could draw inferences about people's personalities from their body types (see **FIGURE 14.4**). Highly muscular people (mesomorphs), he thought, tend to be assertive and bold, whereas lean and skinny people (ectomorphs) tend to be introverted and intellectual (Sheldon, 1971). Yet Sheldon failed to consider an alternative explanation: He wasn't blind to people's body types when he judged their personality traits and may have fallen prey to confirmation bias. Perhaps not surprisingly, well-controlled studies later found the correlations between Sheldon's body types and personality traits to be weak or nonexistent (Deabler, Hartl, & Willis, 1974; Lester, Kaminsky, & McGovern, 1994).

With these errors of the past in mind, how can we distinguish scientific from unscientific or even pseudoscientific personality assessment methods? Two key criteria for evaluating all tests, including personality tests, are reliability and validity (see Chapter 2). *Reliability*, we'll recall, refers to consistency of measurement and *validity* to the extent to which a test measures what it purports to measure. We'll keep these dual criteria in mind as we survey the two major types of personality tests: structured and projective.

Tests must be reliable and valid

■ Structured Personality Tests

The best-known personality instruments are **structured personality tests**. These are typically paper-and-pencil tests consisting of questions that respondents answer in one of a few fixed ways. By fixed ways, we mean choosing between true and false answers, or by selecting options on a scale with, for example, 1 being "always true," 2 being "somewhat true," and so on, until 5, which is "always false" (these numerical scales are called *Likert* formats). Structured personality tests have several advantages: They're typically easy to administer and score, and they allow researchers to collect data from many participants simultaneously.

MMPI AND MMPI-2: DETECTING ABNORMAL PERSONALITY. The **Minnesota Multiphasic Personality Inventory** or **MMPI** (Hathaway & McKinley, 1940) is the most extensively researched of all structured personality tests. Psychologists across the world use the MMPI to detect symptoms of mental disorders. Developed in the early 1940s by psychologist Starke

◀ ruling out rival hypotheses

HAVE IMPORTANT ALTERNATIVE EXPLANATIONS FOR THE FINDINGS BEEN EXCLUDED?

FICTOID

MYTH: Informal (unstructured) interviews, which lack standard questions and scoring criteria, are the best means of assessing personality traits among prospective college students and job employees.

REALITY: Informal interviews are a problematic method of assessing personality, largely because different interviewers frequently disagree on their impressions of interviewees (McDaniel et al., 1994; Weisner & Cronshaw, 1988).

structured personality test
paper-and-pencil test consisting of questions that respondents answer in one of a few fixed ways

Minnesota Multiphasic Personality Inventory (MMPI)
widely used structured personality test designed to assess symptoms of mental disorders

Hathaway and neurologist J. Charnley McKinley of the University of Minnesota, the MMPI was revised in the 1980s by James Butcher and his colleagues (Butcher et al., 1989). This revised test, the MMPI-2, consists of 567 true-false items.

MMPI and MMPI-2: Construction and Content. The MMPI-2, like its predecessor, consists of ten *basic* scales, eight of which assess mental disorders, such as paranoia, depression, and schizophrenia (see Chapter 15). Hathaway and McKinley developed these scales by means of an **empirical (or data-based) method of test construction.** Using this approach, researchers begin with two or more criterion groups, such as a group of people with a specific psychological disorder and a group of people with no psychological disorder, and examine which items best distinguish them. For example, the items on the MMPI depression scale are those that best differentiate persons with clinical depression from people with no diagnosed mental disorder.

One consequence of the empirical method of test construction is that many MMPI and MMPI-2 items possess low **face validity.** Face validity refers to the extent to which respondents can tell what the items are measuring. In a face valid test, we can take the items on "face value": They assess what they seem to assess. Face validity is actually a misnomer, because it isn't really a form of validity at all. Because Hathaway and McKinley were concerned only with *whether*, not *why*, the MMPI items differentiated among criterion groups, they ended up with some items that bear little obvious connection with the disorder they supposedly assess. To take an example of an item with low face validity from another structured personality test, can you guess which personality trait the following item assesses: "I think newborn babies look very much like little monkeys"? The answer is nurturance, that is, a tendency to care for others—with a "True" answer reflecting low nurturance and a "False" answer reflecting high nurturance—although few test-takers can figure that out (Jackson, 1971, p. 238).

Researchers don't agree on whether low face validity is an overall advantage or disadvantage. Some believe that items with low face validity assess key aspects of personality that are subtle or lie outside of respondents' awareness (Meehl, 1945). Moreover, such items have the advantage of being difficult for respondents to fake. In contrast, other researchers believe that these items don't add to the MMPI's diagnostic capacity (Jackson, 1971; Weed, Ben-Porath, & Butcher, 1990).

The MMPI-2 contains three major *validity* scales. These scales detect various *response sets*, which are tendencies to distort responses to items (see Chapter 2). Response sets, which can diminish the validity of psychological tests, include *impression management*—making ourselves look better than we really are—and *malingering*—making ourselves appear psychologically disturbed. The MMPI *L* (Lie) Scale consists of items assessing the denial of trivial faults (such as "I occasionally become angry"). If you deny a large number of such faults, it's likely that you're either (a) engaging in impression management or (b) a promising candidate for sainthood. Given that (a) is more likely than (b), psychologists typically use scores on the *L* scale to detect a dishonest approach to test-taking. The *F* (Frequency) Scale consists of items that people in the general population rarely endorse (such as "I have a cough most of the time"). High scores on *F* can indicate malingering, although they can also reflect serious psychological disturbance or carelessness in responding to items. The *K* (Correction) Scale consists of items that are similar to, although subtler than, those on the *L* scale; this scale measures defensive or guarded responding.

As we can see in **FIGURE 14.5**, psychologists plot the ten basic scales and three validity scales of the MMPI-2 in profile form, which displays the pattern of each person's scale scores. Although many clinicians enjoy interpreting MMPI-2 profiles, research demonstrates that simple statistical formulas that can be programmed into a computer yield interpretations that are equally, if not more, valid than those of experienced clinicians (Garb, 1998; Goldberg, 1969). Nevertheless, these findings, which hold not only for the MMPI-2 but for most or even all personality tests, haven't exerted an appreciable impact on clinical practice (Dawes, Faust, & Meehl, 1989; Vrieze & Grove, 2009).

empirical method of test construction
approach to building tests in which researchers begin with two or more criterion groups, and examine which items best distinguish them

face validity
extent to which respondents can tell what the items are measuring

What's in a signature?

They are what they write? Maybe, according to handwriting experts who have examined the scrawls of the presidential candidates in search of meaningful clues:

Sen. John McCain
His writing reflects his "maverick" political status as well as a sense of pride; he is intense yet private.

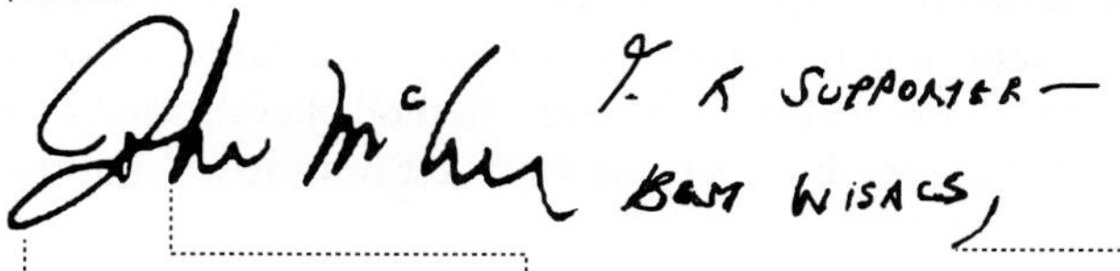

■ First-name letters change direction, indicating he will go his own way

■ The tall H shows pride, ambition; overlap of upward/downward strokes suggests a need for privacy

■ Slashing comma reveals a possible temper

Sen. Hillary Rodham Clinton
Her signature indicates that she is controlled, smart and forceful, and doesn't suffer fools.

■ Two Ls in Hillary are simple sticks rather than loops, projecting efficiency

■ Style is upright, but has no emotional pull

■ The I's are dotted and Ts crossed, showing discipline

Sen. Barack Obama
A flexible, limber, smooth style indicates he deals with different people and situations well.

■ Overall style implies emotion and a conversational capacity

■ The B cutting through the O signifies more weight given to personal achievements than to family legacy

FIGURE 14.8 Handwriting Sample. Graphologists often rely substantially on the representativeness heuristic. These graphologists analyzed the handwriting of the major candidates in the 2008 presidential election, and concluded, for example, that John McCain's "slashing comma" reveals a possible temper problem and that Barack Obama's "smooth" writing style reflects an ability to handle situations well.

FACTOID

One of the most unconventional, yet still popular, projective tests is the Luscher Color Test, which is premised on the notion that respondents' color preferences reveal their personality traits (Luscher & Scott, 1969). For example, people who like blue supposedly harbor needs for tranquility, whereas people who like green supposedly harbor needs to impress others. Research suggests that this test is essentially worthless for assessing personality (Holmes et al., 1984).

■ Common Pitfalls in Personality Assessment

Imagine that as part of a research requirement for your introductory psychology class you've just completed a structured personality test, like the MMPI-2. You look on with anxious anticipation as the research assistant inputs your data into a computer, which spits out the following personality description:

> Some of your hopes and dreams are pretty unrealistic. You have a great deal of unused potential that you have not yet turned to your advantage. Although you sometimes enjoy being around others, you value your privacy. You prize your independence and dislike being hemmed in by rules and restrictions. You are an independent thinker and do not accept others' opinions without strong evidence. You sometimes have serious doubts about whether you have made the right decision or done the right thing. Despite these doubts, you are a strong person whom others can count on in times of trouble.

After reading this description, you turn to the research assistant with a mixture of amazement and awe, and exclaim, "This description fits me perfectly. You've hit the nail on the head!"

But there's a catch. This description, the research assistant informs you, wasn't based on your test results at all. Instead, this description is identical to one that all 100 previous participants have received. You've been the victim of a devilish hoax. This example illustrates what Paul Meehl (1956) termed the *P. T. Barnum effect,* after the circus entrepreneur who said "I try to give a little something to everyone."

THE P.T. BARNUM EFFECT: THE PERILS OF PERSONAL VALIDATION. The **P. T. Barnum effect** is the tendency of people to accept high base rate descriptions—descriptions that apply to almost everyone—as accurate. It demonstrates that *personal validation*—the use of subjective judgments of accuracy (Forer, 1949)—is a flawed method of evaluating a test's validity. We may be convinced that the results of a personality test fit us to a T, but that doesn't mean the test is valid.

The P. T. Barnum effect probably accounts largely for the popularity of astrological horoscopes, palmistry, and crystal ball, tea leaf, and tarot card readings (see Chapter 4). Despite the widespread use of all of these methods, there's no evidence for their validity (Hines, 2003; Park, 1982). People are especially likely to accept P. T. Barnum descriptions they believe are tailored specifically to them (Snyder, Shenkel, & Lowery, 1977). This finding probably helps to explain why horoscopes—which specify the precise year, month, day, and occasionally even time of the person's birth—are often so convincing.

The popularity of tarot card reading, crystal ball reading, palmistry, and many similar techniques probably stems largely from the P.T. Barnum effect.

In an illustration of the P. T. Barnum effect, Susan Blackmore (1983) found that clients couldn't pick out their own tarot card readings from nine other readings at better-than-chance levels. Yet when tarot card readers gave their readings to clients on a face-to-face basis, clients found them extremely accurate. Because each reading contained general statements that apply to everyone, clients who heard only one reading found it believable.

The same principle applies to astrology. People can't pick out their horoscope from others at better-than-chance levels (Dean, 1987). Nevertheless, when people read their horoscope in the newspaper, they're often certain it applies to them. One probable reason for this curious discrepancy is that people tend to read only the horoscope for their own sign, but not others. If they didn't fall prey to confirmation bias and forced themselves to read all 12 horoscopes, they'd probably realize that most or even all of these horoscopes fit them equally well. Although astrology makes extraordinary claims, namely, that it can divine people's personality traits with nearly perfect accuracy, the evidence for these claims is virtually nonexistent.

extraordinary claims

IS THE EVIDENCE AS STRONG AS THE CLAIM?

The P. T. Barnum effect can also fool psychologists into believing that certain traits describe specific groups of people even when they don't. Many pop psychologists claim that adult children of alcoholics (ACOAs) display a distinctive constellation of personality traits. ACOAs are supposedly perfectionistic, concerned about others' approval, overly protective of others, and prone to hiding their feelings. But when three researchers (Logue, Sher, & Frensch, 1992) administered a questionnaire consisting of presumed ACOA characteristics (such as "You sometimes project a front, hiding your own true feelings") to both ACOAs and non-ACOAs, they found no significant differences between these groups. Both

P.T. Barnum effect
tendency of people to accept high base rate descriptions as accurate

groups found the supposed ACOA statements to fit them well and just about as well as a set of P. T. Barnum statements. Because these traits are so widespread in the general population, the commonly accepted personality profile of the ACOA is probably attributable to the P. T. Barnum effect.

PERSONALITY ASSESSMENT EVALUATED SCIENTIFICALLY. Personality assessment has contributed to psychologists' ability to detect personality traits, both normal and abnormal, and has helped them to predict significant real-world behaviors. Moreover, psychologists have succeeded in developing numerous personality measures, especially structured personality tests, with adequate reliability and validity. Research also indicates that a few projective techniques can achieve satisfactory reliability and validity. For instance, scores on certain *sentence completion tests,* which ask respondents to complete a sentence stem (for example, "My father was ..."), are associated with delinquency, moral development, and other important characteristics (Cohn & Westenberg, 2004; Loevinger, 1987).

FACTOID

The word *disaster,* which means "bad star" in Latin, originates from astrology. Many ancient people believed that catastrophic events often resulted from unfortunate configurations of stars in the night sky.

psychomythology

HOW ACCURATE IS CRIMINAL PROFILING?

Another practice whose popularity may derive in part from the P.T. Barnum effect is *criminal profiling,* a technique depicted in the 1991 movie *The Silence of the Lambs* and such television shows as *Criminal Minds* and *Law and Order.* Criminal profilers at the FBI and other law enforcement agencies claim to draw detailed inferences about perpetrators' personality traits and motives from the pattern of crimes committed.

It's true that we can often guess certain characteristics of criminals at better-than-chance levels. If we're investigating a homicide, we'll do better than flipping a coin by guessing that the murderer was a male (most murders are committed by men) between the ages of 15 and 25 (most murders are committed by adolescents and young adults) who suffers from psychological problems (most murderers suffer from psychological problems). But criminal profilers purport to go considerably beyond such widely available statistics. They typically claim to possess unique expertise and to be able to harness their years of accumulated experience to outperform statistical formulas.

Nevertheless, their assessments sometimes echo P.T. Barnum. In the fall of 2002, when the Washington, DC, area was paralyzed by random sniper shootings at gas stations and in parking lots, one former FBI profiler predicted that the sniper would turn out to be someone who is "self-centered" and "angry" at others (Kleinfield & Goode, 2002)—both obvious guesses that most laypersons could make.

Indeed, research demonstrates that police officers can't distinguish genuine criminal profiles from bogus criminal profiles consisting of vague and general personality characteristics (such as "he has deep-seated problems with hostility"). This finding suggests the parsimonious hypothesis that profilers often base their conclusions about criminals on little more than P.T. Barnum statements (Alison, Smith, & Morgan, 2003; Gladwell, 2007). Moreover, although some researchers have found that profilers sometimes perform better than untrained individuals in identifying criminal suspects, others have found that professional profilers are no more accurate in gauging the personality features of murderers than are college students with no training in criminology (Homant & Kennedy, 1998; Snook et al., 2008). In one study, chemistry majors actually produced more accurate profiles of a murderer than did experienced homicide detectives and police officers (Kocsis, Hayes, & Irwin, 2002). Perhaps most important, there's no persuasive evidence that criminal profilers do better than statistical formulas that take into account the psychological traits of known murderers.

Criminal profiling may therefore be more of an urban legend than a scientifically demonstrated ability. Yet tradition dies hard, and the FBI and other crime organizations remain in the full-time business of training criminal profilers.

Hit shows such as *CSI: New York* have stimulated Americans' interest in criminal profiling. Nevertheless, research suggests that criminal profiling is more art than science.

◄ occam's razor

DOES A SIMPLER EXPLANATION FIT THE DATA JUST AS WELL?

Given the scientific progress that psychologists have made in assessing personality, however, why do many continue to use measures with weak scientific support (Lilienfeld et al., 2001)? In particular, why do some clinicians still rely on scores derived from the Myers-Briggs and several projective tests, like the Rorschach, TAT, and human figure drawings, that are of questionable reliability and validity?

The answer is that they're prone to the same errors in thinking as the rest of us (Lilienfeld, Wood, & Garb, 2007). One such error is *illusory correlation*, the perception of nonexistent statistical associations between variables (see Chapter 2). An illusory correlation is a mirage that leads us to see something, namely, a relationship between two variables, that isn't there.

Loren and Jean Chapman (1967) showed college students a series of concocted human figure drawings containing certain physical features (such as large eyes and large genitals) along with a description of the personality traits of the person of who supposedly produced each drawing (such as paranoid and overly concerned about sexuality). They

Answers are located at the end of the text.

ONLINE PERSONALITY TESTS

evaluating **CLAIMS**

The Internet offers a wide array of personality tests, including ones that claim to identify your personality based on your facial features, color preferences, or responses to word-association tests. Some even claim to "diagnose" your personality based on your preferences for movies, fictional characters, or animals. Let's evaluate some of these claims, which are modeled after actual personality tests found online.

"This color test has been *used for decades* and *given to thousands of people* worldwide."
Does the fact that a test has been used by many people for many years tell us anything about its validity? What two logical fallacies does this claim commit (see Chapter 1)?

"Over 70% of *people who take this test rate it* as very accurate."
What's the danger of asking people who take the test determine its accuracy? What other methods should we use when evaluating personality assessment methods?

"Results: You are *confident, self-reliant, prudent, and have strong instincts* in life."
This test's results include descriptors typical of the P. T. Barnum effect. Who doesn't like to think of themselves as "confident," "self-reliant," "prudent," or having "strong instincts"?

"The self-scoring inventories on this site allow you to approximate your MBTI Type preferences, but *have not commonly accepted psychometric standards for reliability and validity*. Therefore, they should not be used as a substitute for taking an MBTI®."
This site includes an appropriate disclaimer that reminds those taking the tests of the importance of reliability and validity.

then asked participants to estimate the extent to which these physical features and personality traits co-occurred in the drawings. Unbeknownst to participants, there was *no* correlation between the drawing features and personality traits, because the researchers had paired these two sets of variables randomly.

Yet students consistently saw certain drawing features as associated with certain personality traits. Interestingly, these were the same drawing features that experienced clinicians tend to believe are related to these traits—and which research has shown to be invalid (Kahill, 1984). For example, students reported incorrectly that people who produced drawings with large eyes tended to be paranoid and that people who produced drawings with large genitals tended to be overly concerned with sexuality.

Like graphologists, the students in the Chapmans' study probably relied on the representativeness heuristic: Like goes with like. As a result, they were fooled, because things that seem similar on the surface don't always go together in real life. These students probably also relied on availability heuristic (see Chapter 2) recalling the cases in which drawing signs correspond to personality traits and forgetting the cases in which they don't. Clinicians, being mere mortals like the rest of us, can easily fall victim to these heuristics too, which may explain why some of them are convinced that certain personality tests are much more valid than the scientific evidence indicates.

These commonplace errors in thinking remind us of a theme we've underscored throughout this book: Personal experience, although useful in generating hypotheses, can be misleading when it comes to testing them. Only scientific methods, which are essential safeguards against human error, allow us to determine whether we should trust our personal experience or disregard it in favor of evidence to the contrary.

FICTOID

MYTH: A practitioner's number of years of experience with using a personality test, like the MMPI-2 or Rorschach, is positively correlated with the accuracy of his or her clinical judgments using that test.

REALITY: For most personality measures, including the MMPI-2 and Rorschach, there's essentially no correlation between experience with using a test and clinical accuracy (Garb, 1998). Once a person has been thoroughly trained in how to administer and interpret a personality measure, additional years of experience typically makes little or no difference. The results of one study showed that a psychologist who'd authored two books on a widely used human figure drawing test did worse than hospital secretaries when using this test to diagnose children's psychological problems (Levenberg, 1975).

---

assess your knowledge   FACT OR FICTION?

✓—Study and Review on **mypsychlab.com**

1. Items with low face validity tend to be especially easy for respondents to fake. **True** / **False**

2. Simple formulas that can be programmed into computers yield MMPI-2 interpretations equal or superior to those of experienced clinicians. **True** / **False**

3. Adding the Rorschach Inkblot Test to other measures in a test battery sometimes produces decreases in validity. **True** / **False**

4. The more detailed and specific an astrological horoscope is about someone's personality traits, the more likely that person will perceive it as accurate. **True** / **False**

5. Research suggests that although students sometimes fall victim to illusory correlation, experienced clinicians don't. **True** / **False**

Answers: 1. F (p. 568); 2. T (p. 568); 3. T (p. 571); 4. F (p. 574); 5. F (p. 576)

✓●─ **Study** and **Review** on **mypsychlab.com**

PERSONALITY: WHAT IS IT AND HOW CAN WE STUDY IT? 540–545

14.1 DESCRIBE HOW TWIN AND ADOPTION STUDIES SHED LIGHT ON GENETIC AND ENVIRONMENTAL INFLUENCES ON PERSONALITY.

Twin and adoption studies suggest that many personality traits are heritable and point to a key role for nonshared environment, but not shared environment for adult personality.

1. Name the major influences (factors) on personality discussed by behavior geneticists. (p. 541)

    1. _____
    2. _____
    3. _____

2. _____ _____ influences make individuals within the same family less alike. (p. 541)

3. To distinguish the effects of genes from the effects of environment, behavior geneticists have conducted _____ studies and _____ studies of personality. (p. 541)

4. If the heritability of personality were 1.0 (that is, 100 percent), then correlations of personality traits in identical twins would be _____. (p. 542)

5. The Minnesota Twins study found that identical twins reared apart tend to be strikingly (similar/dissimilar) in their personality traits. (p. 543)

6. According to the Minnesota Twins study, _____ environment plays little to no role in adult personality. (p. 543)

7. Adoption studies permit investigators to separate the effects of _____ and _____ by comparing adopted children's similarities to their adoptive versus biological parents. (p. 543)

8. In one adoption study of sociability conducted in Texas, the correlations between biological parents and their adopted-away children were slightly (lower/higher) than the correlations between adoptive parents and their adopted children. (p. 543)

9. How would you challenge the notion that a specific gene exists for divorce, religiosity, or political attitudes? (p. 544)

10. In an attempt to identify which genes are associated with specific personality traits, some researchers have turned to _____ _____ studies, but the findings of these studies have often not been replicated. (p. 544)

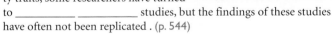

PSYCHOANALYTIC THEORY: THE CONTROVERSIAL LEGACY OF SIGMUND FREUD AND HIS FOLLOWERS 545–555

14.2 DESCRIBE THE CORE ASSUMPTIONS OF PSYCHOANALYTIC THEORY.

Freud's psychoanalytic theory rests on three core assumptions: psychic determinism, symbolic meaning, and unconscious moti-

((●─ **Listen** an audio file of your chapter on **mypsychlab.com**

vation. According to Freud, personality results from the interactions among id, ego, and superego. The ego copes with threat by deploying defense mechanisms. Freud's five psychosexual stages are oral, anal, phallic, latency, and genital.

11. Freudians believe in _____ _____, the assumption that all psychological events have a cause. (p. 546)

12. The _____, according to Freud, is the reservoir of our most primitive impulses (like sex and aggression), whereas the _____ is the psyche's executive and principal decision maker. (p. 547)

13. Freud hypothesized that _____ _____ results from conflicts among the id, ego, and superego. (p. 547)

14. Freud believed that the ego maintains psychological health by engaging in _____ _____, unconscious maneuvers intended to minimize anxiety. (p. 548)

15. Complete the table by indicating the approximate age ranges for each of Freud's psychosexual stages of development. (p. 550)

STAGE	APPROXIMATE AGE
Oral	_____
Anal	_____
Phallic *	_____
Latency	_____
Genital	_____

*Includes Oedipus & Electra Complexes

16. The conflict during Freud's phallic stage in which boys supposedly love their mothers romantically and want to eliminate their fathers as rivals is termed the _____ _____. (p. 551)

14.3 DESCRIBE KEY CRITICISMS OF PSYCHOANALYTIC THEORY AND THE CENTRAL FEATURES OF NEO-FREUDIAN THEORIES.

Psychoanalytic theory has been criticized for unfalsifiability, failed predictions, questionable conception of the unconscious, lack of evidence, and a flawed assumption of shared environmental influence. Neo-Freudians shared with Freud an emphasis on unconscious influences and the importance of early experience, but placed less emphasis on sexuality as a driving force in personality.

17. Recent research has shown that many aspects of Freud's psychoanalytic theory (are/aren't) supported when scientific standards, such as falsifiability, are applied. (p. 552)

18. There's increasing reason to doubt the existence of the _____ as Freud conceived of it, namely as a "place" where sexual and aggressive energies, along with repressed memories, are housed. (p. 552)

19. According to Alfred Adler, the principal motive in human personality is not sex or aggression, but the _____ _____ _____. (p. 553)

20. Describe Jung's theory of archetypes and the collective unconscious, and identify a possible shortcoming in this theory. (pp. 554–555)

BEHAVIORAL AND SOCIAL LEARNING THEORIES OF PERSONALITY 555–558

14.4 IDENTIFY THE CORE ASSUMPTIONS OF BEHAVIORAL AND SOCIAL LEARNING THEORIES OF PERSONALITY.

Radical behaviorists view personality as under the control of two major influences: genetic factors and contingencies in the environment. Radical behaviorists, like psychoanalysts, are determinists and believe in unconscious processing, but deny the existence of "the" unconscious. In contrast to radical behaviorists, social learning theorists accord a central role to thinking in the causes of personality, and argue that observational learning and a sense of personal control play key roles in personality.

21. Radical behaviorists like Skinner believe that our personalities stem largely from differences in our learning _____. (p. 555)

22. Radical behaviorists believe that personality (causes/consists of) behaviors. (p. 556)

23. One of the few things on which Freud and Skinner would have agreed is the concept of _____, the belief that all our actions are products of preexisting causal influences. (p. 556)

24. Unlike Skinner, social learning theorists emphasize _____ as a cause of personality. (p. 556)

25. Albert Bandura made a compelling case for _____ _____, a form of causation whereby personality and cognitive factors, behavior, and environmental variables mutually influence one another. (p. 557)

26. Summarize the role of observational learning in shaping children's personalities. (p. 557)

27. Rotter introduced the concept of _____ _____ _____ to describe the extent to which individuals believe that reinforcers and punishers lie inside or outside of their control. (p. 557)

28. Identify whether each response from a measure of locus of control indicate an internal or an external locus of control. (p. 557)

SAMPLE ITEM	SAMPLE RESPONSE (TRUE/FALSE)	INTERNAL OR EXTERNAL LOCUS OF CONTROL
(1) Many people live miserable lives because of their parents.	True	
(2) If you set realistic goals, you can succeed no matter what.	True	
(3) One can climb the professional ladder just by being around at the right time.	False	
(4) If I study hard enough, I can pass any exam.	False	

29. Someone with an internal locus of control is (more/less) prone than someone with an external locus of control to emotional upset following life stressors. (p. 557)

14.5 DESCRIBE KEY CRITICISMS OF BEHAVIORAL AND SOCIAL LEARNING APPROACHES.

Critics have accused radical behaviorists of going too far in their exclusion of thinking in the causes of personality. The social learning theory claim that observational learning plays a crucial role in personality runs counter to findings that shared environmental influence on adult personality is minimal.

30. Social learning theorists' claim that observational learning plays a powerful role in adult personality is subject to criticism because it implies that _____ _____ plays a causal role. (p. 558)

HUMANISTIC MODELS OF PERSONALITY: THE THIRD FORCE 559–561

14.6 EXPLAIN THE CONCEPT OF SELF-ACTUALIZATION AND ITS ROLE IN HUMANISTIC MODELS.

Most humanistic psychologists argue that the core motive in personality is self-actualization. According to Carl Rogers, unhealthy behavior results from the imposition of conditions of worth, which block drives toward self-actualization. According to Abraham Maslow, self-actualized individuals are creative, spontaneous, accepting, and prone to peak experiences.

31. Humanistic psychologists rejected the determinism of psychoanalysts and behaviorists and embraced the notion of _____ _____. (p. 559)

32. Freudians would say that self-actualization would be (disastrous/helpful) for society. (p. 559)

33. Carl Rogers, pioneer of humanistic psychology, held an (optimistic/pessimistic) view of human nature. (p. 559)

34. Complete the table by listing and describing the three major components of personality, according to Rogers's model. (p. 559)

MAJOR COMPONENT OF PERSONALITY	DESCRIPTION
1. _____	_____
2. _____	_____
3. _____	_____

35. _____ occurs when our personalities are inconsistent with our innate dispositions. (p. 559)

36. Maslow studied self-actualized people and found they were prone to _____ _____, transcendent moments of intense excitement. (p. 560)

37. Followers of Maslow would probably argue that Mahatma Gandhi is a good example of a self-actualized person. Name three to five traits of self-actualized people. (p. 560)

Answers are located at the end of the text.

14.7 DESCRIBE KEY CRITICISMS OF HUMANISTIC APPROACHES.

Critics have attacked humanistic models for being naive about human nature and for advancing theories that are difficult to falsify.

38. Investigators in _____ _____, the branch of psychology that compares behavior across species, have challenged Rogers's claim that human nature is entirely positive. (p. 560)

39. Critics argue that actualization of our full genetic potential is (likely/unlikely) to bring about the state of bliss that Rogers imagined. (p. 560)

40. Maslow may have fallen prey to _____ _____ because he limited his study to individuals who displayed the traits he hypothesized were associated with self-actualized people. (p. 560)

TRAIT MODELS OF PERSONALITY: CONSISTENCIES IN OUR BEHAVIOR 561–566

14.8 DESCRIBE TRAIT MODELS OF PERSONALITY INCLUDING THE BIG FIVE.

Trait theories use factor analysis to identify groups of personality features that tend to correlate with each other. These groupings often correspond to broader traits such as extraversion and agreeableness. One influential model of personality is the Big Five, which predicts many important aspects of real-world behavior, including job performance. Nevertheless, the Big Five may be limited as a model of personality structure because people may not have conscious access to all important features of personality.

41. Trait theorists are interested primarily in describing and understanding the _____ of personality. (p. 561)

42. Claiming that a child is "aggressive" merely because he engages in aggressive behavior gives us no new information and is an example of circular reasoning. What must personality traits do to be meaningful? (p. 561)

43. A statistical technique called _____ _____ analyzes the correlations among responses on personality inventories. (p. 561)

44. A group of traits that have surfaced repeatedly in factor analyses of personality measures is known as the _____ _____. (p. 562)

45. Using the acronym OCEAN as a mnemonic device, the traits in this group are: _____ _____, _____, _____, _____, and _____. (p. 562)

46. Match the appropriate personality trait and description using the Big Five measure. (p. 562)

___ Extraversion	a. tendency to be careful and responsible
___ Neuroticism	b. tendency to be intellectually curious and unconventional
___ Conscientiousness	c. tendency to be friendly and easy to get along with
___ Agreeableness	d. tendency to be sociable and lively
___ Openness to Experience	e. tendency to be tense and moody

47. In studying cultural influences on personality, researchers have found that _____ _____ _____, doesn't emerge clearly in all cultures. (p. 563)

14.9 IDENTIFY KEY CRITICISMS OF TRAIT MODELS.

In the late 1960s, Walter Mischel pointed out that personality traits rarely predict isolated behaviors with high levels of accuracy; later research vindicated his claim, but demonstrated that personality traits are often helpful for predicting long-term behavioral trends. Some models of personality structure, including the Big Five, are more descriptive than explanatory.

48. Mischel's review suggested that people's behaviors (are/aren't) very consistent across different situations. (p. 565)

49. Personality traits can be useful predictors of real-world behaviors, but only when they're _____ across different situations. (p. 565)

50. Although the Big Five do a decent job of capturing personality differences among people, they don't shed much light on the _____ of these differences. (p. 565)

PERSONALITY ASSESSMENT: MEASURING AND MISMEASURING THE PSYCHE 566–577

14.10 DESCRIBE STRUCTURED PERSONALITY TESTS, SUCH AS THE MMPI-2, AND THEIR METHODS OF CONSTRUCTION.

Structured personality tests consist of questions that people can answer in only one of a few fixed ways. Some, like the MMPI-2 and CPI, are developed empirically, others, like the NEO-PI-R, are developed rationally/theoretically.

51. The _____ _____ _____ _____ is widely used to assess mental disorders and consists of ten basic scales. (p. 567)

52. Hathaway and McKinley developed these scales using an _____ method of test construction. (p. 568)

53. Many MMPI and MMPI-2 items possess low _____ _____, which refers to the extent to which respondents can tell what the items are measuring. (p. 568)

54. Extensive research (supports/doesn't support) the reliability of most MMPI-2 scales, as well as their validity for differentiating among mental disorders. (p. 569)

55. The _____ method of test construction requires test developers to begin with a clear-cut conceptualization of a trait and then write items to assess that conceptualization. (p. 569)

14.11 DESCRIBE PROJECTIVE TESTS, PARTICULARLY THE RORSCHACH, AND THEIR STRENGTHS AND WEAKNESSES.

Projective tests consist of ambiguous stimuli that the examinee must interpret. Many of these tests lack adequate levels of reliability, validity, and incremental validity.

56. The _____ hypothesis assumes that in the process of interpreting ambiguous stimuli, examinees inevitably project aspects of their personality onto the stimulus. (p. 570)

57. In what situations might investigators or social workers use these dolls? What are the pitfalls of this technique? (p. 570)

58. The widely used _____ _____ test consists of 10 symmetrical inkblots, and remains scientifically controversial. (p. 570)

59. From which projective test of personality does this item derive? (p. 571)

14.12 IDENTIFY COMMON PITFALLS IN PERSONALITY ASSESSMENT.

Two common pitfalls in personality assessment are the P. T. Barnum effect and illusory correlation, which highlight the need for scientific methods as safeguards against human error.

60. The tendency of people to endorse high base rate descriptions—descriptions that apply to almost everyone—is called the _____ _____ _____. (p. 574)

DO YOU KNOW THESE TERMS?

- personality (p. 541)
- trait (p. 541)
- nomothetic approach (p. 541)
- idiographic approach (p. 541)
- molecular genetic study (p. 544)
- psychic determinism (p. 546)
- id (p. 547)
- pleasure principle (p. 547)
- ego (p. 547)
- reality principle (p. 547)
- superego (p. 547)
- defense mechanism (p. 548)
- repression (p. 548)
- denial (p. 548)
- regression (p. 548)
- reaction-formation (p. 549)

- projection (p. 549)
- displacement (p. 550)
- rationalization (p. 550)
- identification with the aggressor (p. 550)
- sublimation (p. 550)
- erogenous zone (p. 550)
- oral stage (p. 551)
- anal stage (p. 551)
- phallic stage (p. 551)
- Oedipus complex (p. 551)
- Electra complex (p. 551)
- latency stage (p. 551)
- genital stage (p. 551)
- neo-Freudian theories (p. 553)
- style of life (p. 553)

- inferiority complex (p. 554)
- collective unconscious (p. 554)
- archetype (p. 554)
- social learning theorists (p. 556)
- reciprocal determinism (p. 557)
- locus of control (p. 557)
- self-actualization (p. 559)
- conditions of worth (p. 559)
- incongruence (p. 559)
- peak experience (p. 560)
- factor analysis (p. 561)
- Big Five (p. 562)
- lexical approach (p. 562)
- structured personality test (p. 567)

- Minnesota Multiphasic Personality Inventory (MMPI) (p. 567)
- empirical method of test construction (p. 568)
- face validity (p. 568)
- rational/theoretical method of test construction (p. 569)
- projective test (p. 570)
- projective hypothesis (p. 570)
- Rorschach Inkblot Test (p. 570)
- incremental validity (p. 571)
- Thematic Apperception Test (TAT) (p. 571)
- graphology (p. 572)
- P. T. Barnum effect (p. 574)

APPLY YOUR SCIENTIFIC THINKING SKILLS

Use your scientific thinking skills to answer the following questions, referencing specific scientific thinking principles and common errors in reasoning whenever possible.

1. Consult two or three books or websites designed to help parents identify and understand their child's personality. What emphasis do they place on genetic factors, shared environmental factors, and nonshared environmental factors in shaping personality? To what extent are their claims consistent with evidence from behavior-genetic studies? Have they considered alternative explanations and avoided confusing correlation with causation? Explain.

2. As we've learned in this chapter, Freud's writings have exerted an enormous impact on popular culture, although many modern psychologists have questioned their scientific basis. Find two or three recent articles in the popular press that refer to Freudian theory in explaining the causes or treatment of a psychological

disorder. To what extent is the press coverage consistent with contemporary scientific evidence regarding Freudian theory?

3. Studies show that people can't pick out their horoscope from others at better-than-chance levels (Dean, 1987), yet are often certain their horoscope applies to them. Look up the astrology section in at least three different newspapers or websites and read the horoscopes for all 12 astrological signs. What commonalities do you see across the horoscopes (both across signs and across the sources that you consulted)? How accurately do the horoscopes for your sign describe your personality? Now think of other people who share your birthday or astrological sign—does the horoscope apply equally well to their personalities?

15 PSYCHOLOGICAL DISORDERS

when adaptation breaks down

THINK ABOUT IT

ARE PSYCHIATRIC DIAGNOSES MEANINGFUL, OR ARE THEY JUST LABELS FOR UNDESIRABLE BEHAVIORS?

IS THE INSANITY DEFENSE SUCCESSFUL MOST OF THE TIME?

DOES EVERYONE WHO ATTEMPTS SUICIDE WISH TO DIE?

IS SCHIZOPHRENIA THE SAME AS SPLIT PERSONALITY?

ARE ALL PEOPLE WITH PSYCHOPATHIC PERSONALITY VIOLENT?

Below are descriptions of five actual patients (with names changed to safeguard their identity) drawn from the clinical experiences of two of your textbook's authors. Read each description, and ask yourself what these people have in common.

Ida, 43 years old, was strolling around a shopping mall by herself. Suddenly and out of the blue, she experienced a burst of incredibly intense anxiety that left her feeling terrified, faint, and nauseated. She thought she was having a heart attack and took a taxi to the nearest emergency room. The doctors found nothing wrong with her heart and told her the problem was "all in her head." Ida has since refused to leave her house or go anywhere without her husband. She's scared to drive or take buses. Ida's diagnosis: *panic disorder (with agoraphobia)*.

Bill, 45 years old, hasn't shaved or showered in over 10 years. His beard is several feet long. Bill doesn't want to shave or shower because he's terrified that tiny "metal slivers" from the water will find their way into his skin. As much as possible, Bill avoids talking on the telephone or walking through doorways because he's petrified of acquiring germs. Whenever he experiences a thought he feels he shouldn't be having—such as a desire to kiss a married woman—he counts backward from 100 by sevens. Bill recognizes these behaviors as irrational, but hasn't been able to change them despite two decades of treatment. Bill's diagnosis: *obsessive-compulsive disorder.*

A few days after having a baby at age 30, Ann became incredibly giddy. She felt on top of the world, barely needed any sleep, and for the first time began sleeping with men she'd just met. Ann also became convinced she'd turned into a clown—literally. She was even persuaded that she had a bright red round nose, even though her nose was entirely normal. Ann's diagnosis: *bipolar disorder.*

Terrell, 28 years old, has just been released from the intensive care unit of a city hospital. He had shot himself in the stomach after becoming convinced that fish were swimming there. He suspects these fish are part of a government conspiracy to make him physically ill. Terrell's diagnosis: *schizophrenia.*

Johnny is 13 years old. He's charming, articulate, and fun loving. Yet he's furious that his parents have helped commit him to the inpatient unit of a psychiatric hospital, and he blames them for his problems. Johnny is well aware that his actions, like cursing at teachers, holding live cats under water until they drown, and attempting to blow up his junior high school with stolen dynamite, aren't exactly popular among adults. Yet he sees nothing especially wrong with these behaviors and admits he's never felt guilty about anything. Johnny's diagnosis: *conduct disorder (with probable psychopathic personality)*.

CONCEPTIONS OF MENTAL ILLNESS: YESTERDAY AND TODAY

15.1 Identify criteria for defining mental disorders.

15.2 Describe conceptions of diagnoses across history and cultures.

15.3 Identify common misconceptions about psychiatric diagnoses, and the strengths and limitations of the current diagnostic system.

These brief sketches don't do justice to the extraordinarily rich and complex lives of these five people, but they give us some sense of the broad scope of *psychopathology,* or mental illness. In almost all mental disorders, we witness a failure of adaptation to the environment. In one way or another, people with mental disorders aren't adjusting well to the demands of daily life. Many psychopathology researchers adopt a *failure analysis approach* to mental disorders (Harkness, 2007). Just as engineers use accidents, such as plane crashes, to help them understand how mechanical systems work properly, psychopathology researchers examine breakdowns in adaptation to help them understand healthy functioning.

But what do Ida, Bill, Ann, Terrell, and Johnny have in common? Putting it differently, what distinguishes psychological abnormality from normality?

What Is Mental Illness? A Deceptively Complex Question

The answer to this question isn't as simple as we might assume, because the concept of *mental disorder* doesn't lend itself to a clear-cut dictionary definition. Instead, psychologists and psychiatrists have proposed a host of criteria for what mental disorder is. We'll review five of them here. Each criterion captures something important about mental disorder, but each has its shortcomings (Gorenstein, 1984; Wakefield, 1992). ◉—Watch

◉—Watch the Current Diagnostic Models: Sue Mineka on **mypsychlab.com**

STATISTICAL RARITY. Many mental disorders, like schizophrenia—Terrell's condition—are uncommon in the population. Yet we can't rely on statistical rarity to define mental disorder, because not all infrequent conditions—such as extraordinary creativity—are pathological, and many mental illnesses—such as mild depression—are quite common (Kendell, 1975).

SUBJECTIVE DISTRESS. Most mental disorders, including mood and anxiety disorders, produce emotional pain for individuals afflicted with them. But not all psychological disorders generate distress. For example, during the manic phases of bipolar disorder, which Ann experienced, people frequently feel better than normal and perceive nothing wrong with their behaviors. Similarly, many adolescents with conduct disorder, like Johnny, experience less distress than the typical adolescent.

IMPAIRMENT. Most mental disorders interfere with people's ability to function in everyday life. These disorders can destroy marriages, friendships, and jobs. Yet the presence of impairment by itself can't define mental illness, because some conditions, like laziness, can produce impairment but aren't mental disorders.

SOCIETAL DISAPPROVAL. Nearly 50 years ago, psychiatrist Thomas Szasz (1960) argued famously that "mental illness is a myth" and that "mental disorders" are nothing more than conditions that society dislikes. He even proposed that psychologists and psychiatrists use diagnoses as weapons of control: By attaching negative labels to people whose behaviors they find objectionable, they're putting these people "in their place." Szasz was both right and wrong. He was right that our negative attitudes toward those with serious mental illnesses are often deep-seated and widespread. Szasz was also right that societal attitudes shape our views of abnormality.

Psychiatric diagnoses have often mirrored the views of the times. For centuries, some psychiatrists invoked the diagnosis of *masturbational insanity* to describe individuals whose compulsive masturbation supposedly drove them mad (Hare, 1962). Homosexuality was classified as a mental illness until members of the American Psychiatric Association voted to remove it from their list of disorders in 1973 (Bayer, 1981; see Chapter 11). As society became more accepting of homosexuality, mental health professionals came to reject the view that such behavior is indicative of psychological disorder. ◉—Watch

But Szasz was wrong that society regards all disapproved conditions as mental disorders (Wakefield, 1992). To take just one example, racism is justifiably deplored by society, but isn't considered a mental disorder by either lay persons or mental health professionals (Yamey & Shaw, 2002). Neither is messiness or rudeness even though they're both considered undesirable by society.

BIOLOGICAL DYSFUNCTION. Many mental disorders probably result from breakdowns or failures of physiological systems. For example, we'll learn that schizophrenia is often marked by an underactivity in the brain's frontal lobes. In contrast, some mental disorders, like specific *phobias* (intense and irrational fears; see Chapter 6), appear to be acquired largely through learning experiences and often require only a weak genetic predisposition to trigger them.

In fact, it's unlikely that any one criterion distinguishes mental disorders from normality, which explains why mental disorder is difficult or impossible to define. As a consequence, some authors have argued for a *family resemblance view* of mental disorder

In the mid-1800s, some psychiatrists applied the diagnosis of *drapetomania* to describe the "disorder" of slaves who attempted repeatedly to escape from their masters. In a journal article, a physician even prescribed whipping and toe amputation as "treatments" for this condition (Cartwright, 1851). Psychiatric diagnoses are often shaped by the views—and biases—of the historical period.

◉—Watch Drapetomania: Robert Guthrie on **mypsychlab.com**

Brothers and sisters share a family resemblance; they look like each other but don't have any one feature in common. The broad category of "mental disorders" may be similar. Different mental disorders aren't alike in the same exact way, but they share a number of features.

The infamous "dunking test" for witches, popular during the witch scares of the 16th and 17th centuries. According to the dunking test, if a woman drowned, it meant she wasn't a witch. In contrast, if she floated to the top of the water, it meant she was a witch and needed to be executed. Either way, she died.

demonic model
view of mental illness in which odd behavior, hearing voices, or talking to oneself was attributed to evil spirits infesting the body

medical model
view of mental illness as due to a physical disorder requiring medical treatment

asylum
institution for people with mental illnesses created in the 15th century

(Kirmayer & Young, 1999; Lilienfeld & Marino, 1995; Rosenhan & Seligman, 1989). According to this perspective, mental disorders don't all have one thing in common. Just as brothers and sisters within a family look similar but don't all possess exactly the same eyes, ears, or noses, mental disorders share a loose set of features. These features include those we've described—statistical rarity, subjective distress, impairment, societal disapproval, and biological dysfunction—as well as others, such as a need for treatment, irrationality, and loss of control over one's behavior (Bergner, 1997). So Ida, Bill, Ann, Terrell, and Johnny aren't alike in precisely the same way. Yet they overlap enough in their features that we recognize each of them as having a mental disorder.

■ Historical Conceptions of Mental Illness: From Demons to Asylums

Throughout history, people have recognized certain behaviors as abnormal. Yet their explanations and treatments for these behaviors have shifted in tune with prevailing cultural conceptions. The history of society's evolving views of mental illness tells the fascinating story of a bumpy road from nonscience to science.

THE DEMONIC MODEL. During the Middle Ages, many people in Europe and later in America viewed mental illnesses through the lens of a **demonic model**. They attributed hearing voices, talking to oneself, and other odd behaviors to the actions of evil spirits infesting the body (Hunter & Macalpine, 1963). They also viewed at least some, but not all (Schoeneman, 1984), witches as having a mental illness. In 1486, two German priests released a detailed manual, the *Malleus Malleficarum* ("The Witches' Hammer"), to assist in identifying witches, whom many religious figures believed were possessed by the devil. For decades, this text was second only to the Bible as the world's best-selling book. According to the *Malleus Malleficarum*, one could detect witches by means of such foolproof indicators as the *Devil's Mark,* a spot on the skin that's insensitive to pain. The *Malleus Malleficarum* played a key role in the witch hunts of the 16th and 17th centuries, which resulted in the executions of tens of thousands of innocent individuals.

The often bizarre "treatments" of the day, including exorcisms, flowed directly from the demonic model. Yet the legacy of the demonic model lives on today in the thousands of exorcisms still performed in Italy, Mexico, and other countries (Harrington, 2005).

THE MEDICAL MODEL. As the Middle Ages faded and the Renaissance took hold, views of those with mental illness became more enlightened. Over time, more people came to perceive mental illness primarily as a physical disorder requiring medical treatment—a view that some scholars refer to as the **medical model** (Blaney, 1975). Beginning in the 15th century and especially in later centuries, European governments began to house these individuals in **asylums**—institutions for those with mental illness (Gottesman, 1991). Although the term *asylum* means a place of safety, it's acquired a considerably more negative connotation because many institutions were massively overcrowded and understaffed. Indeed, the term *bedlam,* meaning "utter chaos," derives from a shortened version of "Bethlehem," the name of an insane asylum in London established in the Middle Ages (Scull, MacKenzie, & Hervey, 1996).

Moreover, the medical treatments of that era were scarcely more scientific than those of the demonic era, and several were equally barbaric. One gruesome treatment was "bloodletting," which was premised on the mistaken notion that excessive blood causes mental illness. In some cases, physicians drained patients of nearly four pounds of blood, about 40 percent of the body's total. In still other cases, staff workers tried to frighten patients "out of their diseases" by tossing them into a pit of snakes, hence the term *snake pit* as a synonym for an insane asylum (Szasz, 2006).

Not surprisingly, most patients of this era deteriorated, and in the case of bloodletting, some died. Even those who improved in the short term may have merely been responding to the *placebo effect*—improvement resulting from the expectation of improvement (see Chapter 2). Yet few physicians of the day considered the placebo effect as a rival explanation for these treatments' seeming effectiveness. Although most of these treatments seem preposterous to us today, it's crucial to recognize that psychological and medical treatments are products of the times. Society's beliefs about the causes of mental illness shape its interventions.

Fortunately, reform was on the way. Thanks to the heroic efforts of Phillippe Pinel (1748–1826) in France and Dorothea Dix (1802–1887) in America, an approach called **moral treatment** gained a foothold in Europe and America. Advocates of moral treatment insisted that those with mental illness be treated with dignity, kindness, and respect. Prior to moral treatment, patients in asylums were often bound in chains; following moral treat-

◀ **ruling out rival hypotheses**

HAVE IMPORTANT ALTERNATIVE EXPLANATIONS FOR THE FINDINGS BEEN EXCLUDED?

Dorothea Dix, a Massachusetts schoolteacher whose lobbying efforts resulted in the establishment of more humane psychiatric facilities in the 1800s.

ment, they were free to roam the halls of hospitals, get fresh air, and interact freely with staff and other patients. Still, effective treatments for mental illnesses were virtually nonexistent, so many people continued to suffer for years with no hope of relief.

THE MODERN ERA OF PSYCHIATRIC TREATMENT. It wasn't until the early 1950s that a dramatic change in society's treatment of individuals with mental illness arrived on the scene. It was then that psychiatrists introduced a medication imported from France called *chlorpromazine* (its brand name is Thorazine) into mental hospitals (see Chapter 16). Chlorpromazine wasn't a miracle cure, but it offered a modestly effective treatment for some symptoms of schizophrenia and other disorders marked by a loss of contact with reality. Many patients with these conditions became able to function independently, and some returned to their families. Others held jobs for the first time in years, even decades.

By the 1960s and 1970s, the advent of chlorpromazine and similar medications (see Chapter 16) became the primary impetus for a governmental policy called **deinstitutionalization**. Deinstitutionalization featured two major components: releasing hospitalized psychiatric patients into the community and closing mental hospitals (Torrey, 1997). Following deinstitutionalization, the number of hospitalized psychiatric patients plummeted through the beginning of the 21st century (see **FIGURE 15.1**). But deinstitutionalization was a decidedly mixed blessing. Some patients returned to a semblance of a regular life, but tens of thousands of others spilled into cities and rural areas without adequate follow-up care. Many went off their medications and wandered the streets aimlessly. Some of the homeless people we can see today on the streets of major American cities are a tragic legacy of deinstitutionalization (Leeper, 1988). Today, psychologists, social workers, and other mental health professionals are working to improve the quality and availability of community care for severely affected psychiatric patients. Among the consequences of these efforts are *community mental health centers* and *halfway houses,* which are free or low-cost care facilities in which people can obtain treatment.

Thankfully, our understanding of mental illness and its treatment today is considerably more sophisticated than it was centuries ago. Still, precious few of today's treatments are genuine cures.

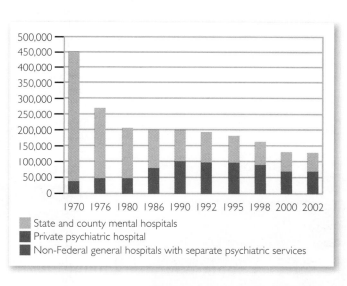

FIGURE 15.1 Decline in Psychiatric Inpatients. Over the past several decades, the number of hospitalized psychiatric patients has gradually declined. (*Source:* http://www.ahrq.gov/about/annualconf09/vandivort_mark_owens/slide4.jpg)

moral treatment
approach to mental illness calling for dignity, kindness, and respect for those with mental illness

deinstitutionalization
1960s and 1970s governmental policy that focused on releasing hospitalized psychiatric patients into the community and closing mental hospitals

■ Psychiatric Diagnoses Across Cultures

Psychiatric diagnoses are shaped not only by history, but also by culture (Chentsova-Dutton & Tsai, 2006; Watters, 2010). Psychologists have increasingly recognized that certain conditions are *culture-bound*—specific to one or more societies—although most of these conditions remain poorly researched (see **TABLE 15.1**) (Kleinman, 1988; Simons & Hughes, 1986).

CULTURE-BOUND SYNDROMES. For example, some parts of Malaysia and several other Asian countries, including China and India, have witnessed periodic outbreaks of a strange condition known as *koro.* The victims of *koro,* most of whom are male, typically believe that their penis and testicles are disappearing and receding into their abdomen (female victims of *koro* sometimes believe that their breasts are disappearing). *Koro* is spread largely by social contagion. Once one man begins to experience its symptoms, others often follow suit, triggering widespread panics (see Chapter 13). In one region of India in 1982, the *koro* epidemic spun so out of control that the local government took to the streets with loudspeakers to reassure terrified civilians that their genitals weren't vanishing. Government officials even measured male residents' penises with rulers in an attempt to prove their fears unfounded (Bartholomew, 1994).

Another disorder specific to Malaysia, the Philippines, and some African countries is *amok.* This condition is marked by episodes of intense sadness and brooding followed by uncontrolled behavior and unprovoked attacks on people or animals (American Psychiatric Association, 2000). This condition gave rise to the popular phrase "running amok," meaning "going wild."

Other culture-bound syndromes seem to be variants of conditions in Western culture. In Japan, for example, social anxiety is typically expressed as a fear of offending others (called *taijin kyofushu*), such as by saying something offensive or giving off a terrible body odor (Kleinknecht et al. 1994). But in the United States, social anxiety is more commonly generated by fear of public embarrassment, such as what we might experience when giving a speech. Culture may influence how people express interpersonal anxiety. Because Japanese culture is more collectivistic (see Chapters 10 and 14) than Western culture, Japanese tend to be more concerned about their impact on others than are Westerners.

In contrast, Western culture is more individualistic, so people tend to worry more about what may happen to them as individuals. European-Canadian patients report more psychological symptoms than their Chinese counterparts, perhaps suggesting a tendency to

"*Mal de ojo,*" or the "evil eye," is a culture-bound syndrome common in many Mediterranean and Latin countries. Believed by its victims to be brought on by the glance of a malicious person, *mal de ojo* is marked by insomnia, nervousness, crying for no reason, and vomiting. Here, customers in Egypt select pendants for warding off the evil eye.

TABLE 15.1 A Sampling of Common Culture-Bound Syndromes Not Discussed in the Text.

SYNDROME	REGION/POPULATION AFFECTED	DESCRIPTION
Arctic Hysteria	Alaska Natives (Inuit)	Abrupt episode accompanied by extreme excitement and frequently followed by convulsive seizures and coma.
Ataque de Nervios	Latin America	Symptoms include uncontrollable shouting, attacks of crying, trembling, heat in the chest rising to the head, and verbal or physical aggression.
Brain Fog	West Africa	Symptoms include difficulties in concentrating, remembering, and thinking.
Latah	Malaysia and Southeast Asia	Found mostly among women; marked by an extreme startle reaction, followed by a loss of control, cursing, and mimicking of others' actions and speech.
Mal de Ojo (Evil Eye)	Spain and Latin America	A common term to describe the cause of disease, misfortune, and social disruption.
Windigo	Native Americans Central and N.E. Canada	Morbid state of anxiety with fears of becoming a cannibal.

(*Source:* Data, DSM-IV APA, 2000; Hall, 2001)

"psychologize" symptoms of distress. Because Chinese patients frequently focus their thoughts "externally," as opposed to "internally" on their emotional states, they may be more likely to notice somatic symptoms like aches and pains when distressed (Ryder et al., 2008). The focus on the self in individualistic societies may also contribute to certain culture-bound disorders in Western countries. Some eating disorders are largely specific to the United States and Europe, where the media bombard viewers with images of thin models, probably making already self-conscious women even more self-conscious (see Chapter 11) (Keel & Klump, 2003; McCarthy, 1990).

CULTURAL UNIVERSALITY. Despite the cultural differences we've noted, we shouldn't exaggerate the cultural relativity of mental disorders. Many mental disorders, especially those that are severe, appear to exist in most and perhaps all cultures. Jane Murphy (1976) conducted a classic study of two isolated societies—a group of Yorubas in Nigeria and a group of Inuit Eskimos near the Bering Strait—that had experienced essentially no contact with Western culture. These cultures possessed terms for disorders that are strikingly similar to schizophrenia, alcoholism, and *psychopathic personality,* a condition marked by dishonesty, manipulativeness, and an absence of guilt and empathy (see Chapters 11 and 14). For example, in Inuit *kunlangeta* describes a person who lies, cheats, steals, is unfaithful to women, and doesn't obey elders—a description that fits almost perfectly the Western concept of psychopathic personality. When Murphy asked one of the Inuit how they dealt with such individuals, he replied that "somebody would have pushed him off the ice when no one was looking." Apparently, Inuit aren't much fonder of psychopaths than we are.

Special Considerations in Psychiatric Classification and Diagnosis

Because there are so many ways in which psychological adaptation can go awry, we'd be hopelessly lost without some system of diagnostic classification. Psychiatric diagnoses serve at least two crucial functions. *First,* they help us pinpoint the psychological problem a person is experiencing. Once we've identified this problem, it's often easier to select a treatment. *Second,* psychiatric diagnoses make it easier for mental health professionals to communicate. When a psychologist diagnoses a patient with schizophrenia, she can be reasonably certain that other psychologists know his or her principal symptoms. Diagnoses operate as forms of mental shorthand, simplifying complex descriptions of problematic behaviors into convenient summary phrases.

Still, there are a host of misconceptions regarding psychiatric diagnosis. Before turning to our present system of psychiatric classification, we'll examine four prevalent misconceptions.

Misconception 1: *Psychiatric diagnosis is nothing more than pigeonholing, that is, sorting people into different "boxes."* According to this criticism, when we diagnose people with a mental disorder, we deprive them of their uniqueness: We imply that all people within the same diagnostic category are alike in all important respects. To the contrary, a diagnosis implies only that all people with that diagnosis are alike in at least *one* important respect (Lilienfeld & Landfield, 2008). Psychologists recognize that even within a diagnostic category, like schizophrenia or bipolar disorder, people differ dramatically in their other psychological difficulties, race and cultural background, personality traits, interests, and cognitive skills. People are far more than their disorders.

Misconception 2: *Psychiatric diagnoses are unreliable.* As we learned in Chapter 2, *reliability* refers to consistency of measurement. In the case of psychiatric diagnoses, the form of reliability that matters most is *interrater reliability:* the extent to which different raters (such as different psychologists) agree on patients' diagnoses. The widespread perception that psychiatric diagnosis is unreliable is probably fueled by high-profile media coverage of "dueling expert witnesses" in criminal trials, in which one expert witness diagnoses a defendant as experiencing schizophrenia and another diagnoses him as free of this disorder.

FACTOID

Another potential culture-bound syndrome is the unusual condition of body integrity identity disorder (also known as *apotemnophilia;* in Greek, *apotemno/*"cut off" + philia/"love of"), in which people experience persistent desires to undergo operations to amputate their limbs or body parts. Although responsible physicians won't perform such operations, many patients with body integrity identity disorder have found doctors willing to amputate their limbs (First, 2004). This disorder has thus far been reported only in the United States and Europe (Littlewood, 2004).

Trials involving "dueling expert witnesses" may contribute to the erroneous public perception that psychologists can't agree on the diagnoses of individuals with suspected mental disorders.

Actor David Duchovny and golfer Tiger Woods are among the many celebrities who've reportedly sought treatment for "sexual addiction," which is not an official psychiatric diagnosis. Is sexual addiction a genuine condition, or is it merely a descriptive label for problematic behavior? Many psychologists argue the latter.

In fact, for major mental disorders, like schizophrenia, mood disorders, anxiety disorders, and alcoholism, interrater reliabilities are typically about as high—correlations between raters of 0.8 or above out of a maximum of 1.0—as for most medical disorders (Matarazzo, 1983). Still, the picture isn't entirely rosy. For many personality disorders, a class of disorders we'll discuss later, interrater reliabilities tend to be lower (Zimmerman, 1994).

Misconception 3: *Psychiatric diagnoses are invalid.* From the standpoint of Thomas Szasz (1960) and other critics, psychiatric diagnoses are largely useless because they don't provide us with much, if any, new information. They're merely descriptive labels for behaviors we don't like.

When it comes to some pop psychology labels, Szasz probably has a point. Consider the explosion of diagnostic labels that are devoid of scientific support such as codependency, sexual addiction, internet addiction, road rage disorder, and compulsive shopping disorder (Cocarro et al., 2006; Granello & Beamish, 1998; Koran et al., 2006; McCann, Shindler, & Hammond, 2003). Although frequently used in talk shows, television programs, movies, and self-help books, these labels aren't recognized as formal psychiatric diagnoses.

Yet there's now considerable evidence that many psychiatric diagnoses *do* tell us something new about the person. In a classic paper, psychiatrists Eli Robins and Samuel Guze (1970) outlined several criteria for determining whether a psychiatric diagnosis is valid. According to Robins and Guze, a valid diagnosis:

1. distinguishes that diagnosis from other, similar diagnoses;
2. predicts diagnosed individuals' performance on laboratory tests, including personality measures, neurotransmitter levels, and brain imaging findings (Andreasen, 1995);
3. predicts diagnosed individuals' family history of psychiatric disorders;
4. predicts diagnosed individuals' *natural history*—that is, what tends to happen to them over time.

In addition, some authors have argued that a valid diagnosis ideally:

5. predicts diagnosed individuals' response to treatment (Waldman, Lilienfeld, & Lahey, 1996).

There's good evidence that unlike most pop psychology labels, many mental disorders fulfill Robins and Guze's criteria for validity. **TABLE 15.2** illustrates these criteria using the example of *attention-deficit/hyperactivity disorder (ADHD)*, a disorder we'll encounter later in the chapter that's characterized by inattention, impulsivity, and overactivity.

TABLE 15.2 Criteria for Validity: The Case of ADHD. Although controversial in many respects, the diagnosis of attention-deficit/hyperactivity disorder (ADHD) largely satisfies the Robins and Guze criteria for validity.

ROBINS & GUZE CRITERIA	FINDINGS CONCERNING THE ADHD DIAGNOSIS
1. Distinguishes a particular diagnosis from other similar diagnoses	The child's symptoms can't be accounted for by other diagnoses, such as substance abuse and anxiety disorders
2. Predicts performance on laboratory tests (personality measures, neurotransmitter levels, brain imaging findings)	The child is likely to perform poorly on laboratory measures of concentration
3. Predicts family history of psychiatric disorders	The child has a higher probability than the average child of having biological relatives with ADHD
4. Predicts what happens to the individual over time	The child is likely to show continued difficulties with inattention in adulthood, but improvements in impulsivity and overactivity in adulthood
5. Predicts response to treatment	The child has a good chance of responding positively to stimulant medications, like Ritalin (see Chapter 16)

Misconception 4: *Psychiatric diagnoses stigmatize people.* According to **labeling theorists**, psychiatric diagnoses exert powerful negative effects on people's perceptions and behaviors (Scheff, 1984; Slater, 2004). Labeling theorists argue that once a mental health professional diagnoses us, others perceive us differently. Suddenly, we're "weird," "strange," even "crazy." This diagnosis leads others to treat us differently, in turn often leading us to behave in weird, strange, or crazy ways. The diagnosis thereby becomes a self-fulfilling prophecy.

In a sensational study, David Rosenhan (1973) asked eight individuals with no symptoms of mental illness (himself included) to pose as fake patients in 12 psychiatric hospitals. These "pseudopatients" (fake patients) presented themselves to admitting psychiatrists with a single complaint: They were hearing a voice saying "empty, hollow, and thud." In all 12 cases, the psychiatrists admitted these pseudopatients to the hospital, almost always with diagnoses of schizophrenia (one received a diagnosis of manic depression, or what would today be called bipolar disorder). Remarkably, they remained there for an average of three weeks despite displaying no further symptoms of mental illness. The diagnosis of schizophrenia, Rosenhan concluded, became a self-fulfilling prophecy, leading doctors and nursing staff to view these individuals as disturbed. For example, the nursing staff interpreted one pseudopatient's note taking as "abnormal writing behavior."

It's true that there's still stigma attached to some psychiatric diagnoses. If someone tells us that a person has schizophrenia, for instance, we may be wary of him at first or misinterpret his behaviors as consistent with this diagnosis. Yet the negative effects of labels last only so long. Even in Rosenhan's study, all pseudopatients were released from hospitals with diagnoses of either schizophrenia or manic depression "in remission" ("in remission" means without any symptoms) (Spitzer, 1975). These discharge diagnoses tell us that psychiatrists eventually recognized that these individuals were behaving normally. Overall, there's not much evidence that psychiatric diagnoses themselves generate long-term negative effects (Ruscio, 2003).

■ Psychiatric Diagnosis Today: The DSM-IV

The official system for classifying individuals with mental disorders is the ***Diagnostic and Statistical Manual of Mental Disorders*** (DSM), which originated in 1952 and is now in its fourth edition, called DSM-IV (APA, 2000). The next edition, DSM-V, is due out in 2013. There are 17 different classes of disorders in the DSM-IV (see **TABLE 15.3**), several of which we'll be discussing in the pages to come.

labeling theorists
scholars who argues that psychiatric diagnoses exert powerful negative effects on people's perceptions and behaviors

***Diagnostic and Statistical Manual of Mental Disorders* (DSM)**
diagnostic system containing the American Psychiatric Association (APA) criteria for mental disorders

TABLE 15.3 The 17 Major Classes of Disorders in DSM-IV.

1. Disorders Usually First Diagnosed in Infancy, Childhood, or Adolescence—mental retardation, attention deficit and disruptive behavior disorders, tic disorders
2. Delirium, Dementia, and Amnestic, and Other Cognitive Disorders—Dementia due to Alzheimer's disease and Parkinson's Disease
3. Mental Disorders due to a General Medical Condition
4. Substance-Related Disorders
5. Schizophrenia and Other Psychotic Disorders
6. Mood Disorders
7. Anxiety Disorders
8. Somatoform Disorders
9. Factitious Disorders
10. Dissociative Disorders
11. Sexual and Gender Identity Disorders
12. Eating Disorders
13. Sleep Disorders
14. Impulse-Control Disorders Not Elsewhere Classified
15. Adjustment Disorders
16. Personality Disorders
17. Other Conditions That May Be a Focus of Clinical Attention—problems related to abuse or neglect, personality traits that affect coping style, or medical conditions

(*Source:* From *Diagnostic and Statistical Manual of Mental Disorders*, 4th ed., American Psychiatric Association, 2000)

DIAGNOSTIC CRITERIA AND DECISION RULES. Psychiatric classification has come a long way since the days of the *Malleus Malleficarum*. DSM-IV provides psychologists and psychiatrists with a list of diagnostic criteria for each condition, and a set of decision rules for deciding how many of these criteria need to be met. In **TABLE 15.4**, we'll find the DSM-IV criteria for the diagnosis of *major depression*, a condition we'll encounter later in the chapter. As we can see in Criterion A, to diagnose a person with major depression, DSM-IV requires this person to exhibit at least five of nine symptoms over a two-week period, with the requirement that at least one of the first two symptoms (depressed mood and diminished interest or pleasure) be present.

"THINKING ORGANIC." DSM-IV warns diagnosticians about physical—or "organic," that is, medically induced—conditions that can simulate certain psychological disorders (Morrison, 1997). As we can see in Criterion D in Table 15.4, DSM-IV notes that certain substance use or medical disorders can mimic the clinical picture of depression. For example, it informs readers that *hypothyroidism,* a disorder marked by underactivity of the thyroid gland (in our lower necks), can produce depressive symptoms. If a patient's depression appears due to hypothyroidism, the psychologist shouldn't diagnose major depression. It's essential to "think organic," or to first rule out medical causes of a disorder, when diagnosing psychological conditions.

THE DSM-IV: OTHER FEATURES. DSM-IV is more than a tool for diagnosing mental disorders; it's a valuable source of information concerning the characteristics, such as the **prevalence**, of many mental disorders. Prevalence refers to the percentage of people in the population with a disorder. In the case of major depression, the lifetime prevalence is at least 10 percent among women and at least 5 percent among men (some estimates are even higher). That means that for a woman, the odds are at least one in 10 she'll experience an episode of major depression at some point in her life; for a man, the odds are at least one in 20 (APA, 2000). ⊕ ⌐Explore

DSM-IV also recognizes that there's more to people than their disorders. Accordingly, it asks psychologists and psychiatrists to assess patients along multiple **axes**, or dimensions of functioning. DSM-IV contains axes not only for major mental disorders (Axis I), but also for personality disorders and mental retardation (Axis II), associated

⊕ ⌐**Explore** the Axes of the DSM on **mypsychlab.com**

TABLE 15.4 The DSM-IV Criteria for Major Depressive Disorder.

A. Five (or more) of the following (must include one of the symptoms [1] or [2])
  1. depressed mood most of the day
  2. markedly diminished interest or pleasure in all, or almost all, activities
  3. significant weight loss when not dieting or weight gain (more or less than 5% per month)
  4. insomnia or hypersomnia (excessive sleep) nearly every day
  5. psychomotor agitation or retardation (slowing) nearly every day
  6. fatigue or loss of energy nearly every day
  7. feelings of worthlessness or excessive or inappropriate guilt nearly every day
  8. diminished ability to think or concentrate, or indecisiveness, nearly every day
  9. recurrent thoughts of death (not just fear of dying), recurrent suicidal ideation

B. Symptoms do not meet criteria for a mixed episode (simultaneous depression and mania)

C. Symptoms cause clinically significant distress or impairment in social, occupational, or other important areas of functioning.

D. Symptoms are not due to the physiological effects of a substance or a medical condition

E. Symptoms are not better accounted for by bereavement (loss of a loved one); that is, after a loss, symptoms persist for longer than two months or are characterized by marked functional impairment, morbid preoccupation with worthlessness, suicidal ideation, psychotic symptoms, or psychomotor retardation

(*Source:* From *Diagnostic and Statistical Manual of Mental Disorders,* 4th ed., American Psychiatric Association, 2000)

prevalence
percentage of people within a population who have a specific mental disorder

axis
dimension of functioning

medical conditions (Axis III), life stressors (Axis IV), and overall level of daily functioning (Axis V). In this respect, DSM-IV adopts a *biopsychosocial approach* (see Chapter 12), which acknowledges the interplay of biological (like hormonal abnormalities), psychological (like irrational thoughts), and social (interpersonal interactions) influences.

Finally, DSM-IV acknowledges that we live in a diverse world filled with people from different ethnic, socioeconomic, and cultural backgrounds. Some of them embrace unconventional beliefs, sexual identities, and behaviors that are "abnormal" from the vantage point of our contemporary society. DSM-IV provides information about how differing cultural backgrounds can affect the content and expression of symptoms. This information is vital to ensuring that diagnosticians don't "incorrectly judge as psychopathology those normal variations in behavior, belief, or experience that are particular to the individual's culture" (p. xxiv).

THE DSM-IV: CRITICISMS. There's little dispute that DSM-IV is a helpful system for slicing up the enormous pie of psychopathology into more meaningful and manageable pieces. Yet DSM-IV has received more than its share of criticism, and sometimes for good reason (Widiger & Clark, 2000).

There are well over 350 diagnoses in DSM-IV, not all of which meet the Robins and Guze criteria for validity. To take only one example, the DSM-IV diagnosis of "Mathematics Disorder" describes little more than difficulties with performing arithmetic or math reasoning problems. It seems to be more of a label for learning problems than a diagnosis that tells us something new about the person. In addition, although the diagnostic criteria and decision rules for many DSM-IV disorders are based primarily on scientific findings, others are based largely on subjective committee decisions. Another problem with DSM-IV is the high level of **comorbidity** among many of its diagnoses (Angold, 1999; Cramer et al., 2010; Lilienfeld, Waldman, & Israel, 1994), meaning that individuals with one diagnosis frequently have one or more additional diagnoses. For example, it's extremely common for people with a major depression diagnosis to meet criteria for one or more anxiety disorders. This extensive comorbidity raises the troubling question of whether DSM-IV is diagnosing genuinely independent conditions as opposed to slightly different variations of one underlying condition.

Another problem with DSM-IV is its reliance on a **categorical model** of psychopathology (Trull & Durett, 2005). In a categorical model, a mental disorder—such as major depression—is either present or absent, with no in between. Categories differ from each other in kind, not degree. Pregnancy fits a categorical model, because a woman is either pregnant or she's not. Yet scientific evidence suggests that some disorders in DSM-IV better fit a **dimensional model**, meaning they differ from normal functioning in degree, not kind (Krueger & Piasecki, 2002). Height fits a dimensional model, because although people differ in height, these differences aren't all or none. The same may be true of many forms of depression and anxiety, which most research suggests lie on a continuum with normality (Kollman et al., 2006; Slade & Andrews, 2005). These findings square with our everyday experience, because we all feel at least a bit depressed and anxious from time to time.

Some authors have proposed that the Big Five, a system of personality dimensions we encountered in Chapter 14, may better capture the true "state of nature" than many of the categories in DSM-IV (Widiger & Clark, 2000). For example, depression is typically characterized by high levels of neuroticism and introversion. Indeed, DSM-V is likely to include a system of personality dimensions similar to the Big Five (Krueger et al., 2007). Yet many psychologists have resisted a dimensional model, perhaps because they, like the rest of us, are *cognitive misers* (see Chapter 2); they strive to simplify the world. Most of us find it easier to think of the world in terms of simple black or white categories than complex shades of gray (Lilienfeld & Waldman, 2004; Macrae & Bondenhausen, 2000).

Like virtually all documents crafted by human beings, DSM-IV is vulnerable to political influences (Kirk & Kutchins, 1992). For example, some researchers have lobbied successfully for the inclusion of their "favorite" disorder or area of specialty. But like all scientific

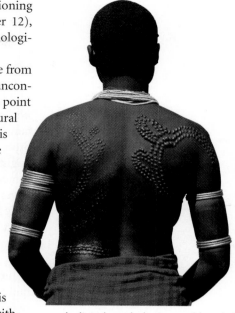

A clinical psychologist would probably perceive cutting oneself as pathological, but the DSM-IV reminds clinicians that in some cultures, such practices are used to produce tribal scars and should be regarded as normal.

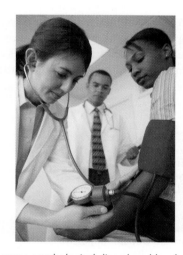

Like some psychological disorders, blood pressure better fits a dimensional than a categorical model, as there's no sharp dividing line between normal and high blood pressure.

comorbidity
co-occurrence of two or more diagnoses within the same person

categorical model
model in which a mental disorder differs from normal functioning in kind rather than degree

dimensional model
model in which a mental disorder differs from normal functioning in degree rather than kind

endeavors, the system of psychiatric classification tends to be self-correcting. Just as homosexuality was stricken from the DSM in the 1970s, science will continue to weed out invalid disorders, ensuring that future editions of the DSM will be based on better evidence.

NORMALITY AND ABNORMALITY: A SPECTRUM OF SEVERITY. As you read case histories or descriptions in this chapter, you may wonder, "Is my behavior abnormal?" or "Maybe my problems are more serious than I thought." At times like this, it's useful to be aware of *medical students' syndrome* (Howes & Salkovskis, 1998). As medical students first become familiar with the symptoms of specific diseases, they often begin to focus on their bodily processes. Soon they find it hard to stop wondering whether a slight twinge in their chest might be an early warning of heart trouble or a mild headache the first sign of a brain tumor. Similarly, as we learn about psychological disorders, it's only natural to "see ourselves" in some patterns of behavior, largely because in meeting the complex demands of daily life we all experience disturbing impulses, thoughts, and fears from time to time. So don't become alarmed as you learn about these conditions, as many are probably extremes of psychological difficulties we all experience on occasion.

But at some point in your life, you may experience a psychological problem that's so disturbing and persistent that you'll want to talk with someone about it. If so, you'll probably find it worthwhile to consult with a family member, friend, physician, dormitory counselor, clergy person, or mental health professional, such as a social worker, psychologist, or psychiatrist. In Chapter 16, we'll present some tips for what to look for and avoid in a psychotherapist.

Answers are located at the end of the text.

ONLINE TESTS FOR MENTAL DISORDERS — evaluating CLAIMS

We're all familiar with medical websites that allow us to type in our symptoms ("itchy throat, headache, no fever") and receive a free, instant diagnosis of our physical ailments. But did you know that similar sites exist for the diagnosis of mental illnesses, including attention-deficit/hyperactivity disorder? Let's evaluate some claims and statements, which are modeled after information on actual sites devoted to the self-diagnosis of adult ADHD.

"This 20 question self-test is *the most valid and reliable* screening measure for adult ADHD available on the Internet!"
Be suspicious of claims like "most valid and reliable" put forward with no supportive evidence. Because information on the Internet is vast and constantly subject to change, it's difficult to evaluate this extraordinary claim. Moreover, most online diagnostic tests have never been evaluated in peer reviewed studies.

"*High scores on the self-test may result from* depression, anxiety, and bipolar disorder, so *it's important* to *rule out these conditions* before a diagnosis of ADHD can be made with confidence."
The site states accurately that ADHD symptoms often overlap with those of other disorders, and that it may be challenging to distinguish the symptoms of ADHD, anxiety, depression, and bipolar disorder.

"Keep in mind that this is a screening test. Remember, it's *only the first step in arriving at an accurate diagnosis* of ADHD."
This statement rightly cautions against arriving at an ADHD diagnosis based on information contained in a brief questionnaire: It's often necessary to consider historical information and current behaviors and performance in different settings (such as school, workplace, and home), as well as tests of attention and input from different professionals (such as physicians, teachers, and family members).

MENTAL ILLNESS AND THE LAW: A CONTROVERSIAL INTERFACE. Psychological problems not only affect our mental functioning; they can place us at risk for legal problems. There are few topics about which the general public is certain it knows more, yet actually knows less, than the interface between mental illness and the law.

Mental Illness and Violence. One of the most pervasive myths in psychology is that people with mental illness are at greatly heightened risk for violence (Link et al., 1999). In fact, the overwhelming majority of people with schizophrenia and other psychotic disorders aren't physically aggressive toward others (Friedman, 2006; Steadman et al., 1998; Teplin, 1985). One might have hoped that the seemingly endless parade of "real crime" shows on television would have helped to combat this misconception, but it's probably done the opposite. Although only a few percent of people with mental disorders commit aggressive acts, about 75 percent of televised characters with mental illness are violent (Wahl, 1997).

Still, like many misconceptions, this one contains a kernel of truth. Although most people with mental illness aren't at increased risk for violence, a subset—especially those who are convinced they are being persecuted (by the government, for example), and those with substance abuse—are (Douglas, Guy, & Hart, 2009; Monahan, 1992; Steadman et al., 1998).

psychomythology

THE INSANITY DEFENSE: FREE WILL VERSUS DETERMINISM

In courts of law, mental illnesses and the law occasionally collide head-on, often with unpredictable consequences. The best-known example of this clash is the **insanity defense**, which is premised on the idea that we shouldn't hold people legally responsible for their crimes if they weren't of "sound mind" when they committed them. The insanity defense comes in many forms, which differ across state and federal courts. Forty-six U.S. states use some version of this defense, with four—Utah, Montana, Idaho, and Kansas—opting out of it.

Most contemporary forms of this defense are based loosely on the *M'Naghten rule,* formulated during an 1843 British trial. This rule requires that to be declared insane, persons must either have (1) not known what they were doing at the time of the crime or (2) not known that what they were doing was wrong (Melton et al., 1997). A defendant (accused person) who was so disoriented during an epileptic seizure that he didn't realize he was attacking a police officer might fulfill the first prong of M'Naghten; a defendant who believed he was actually murdering Adolf Hitler when he shot his next-door neighbor might fulfill the second. Several other versions of the insanity defense strive to determine whether defendants were incapable of controlling their impulses at the moment of the crime. Because this judgment is exceedingly difficult (how can we know whether a man who murdered his wife in the heat of overwhelming anger *could* have controlled his temper had he really tried?), some courts ignore it.

The insanity defense is controversial, to put it mildly. To its proponents, this defense is necessary for defendants whose mental state is so deranged that it impairs their freedom to decide whether to commit a crime (Sadoff, 1992; Stone, 1982). To its critics, this defense is nothing more than a legal cop-out that excuses criminals of responsibility (Lykken, 1982; Szasz, 1991). These divergent perspectives reflect a more deep-seated disagreement about free will versus determinism (see Chapter 1). The legal system assumes that our actions are freely chosen, whereas scientific psychology assumes that our actions are completely determined by prior variables, including our genetic makeup and learning history. So lawyers and judges tend to view the insanity defense as a needed exception for the small minority of defendants who lack free will. In contrast, many psychologists view this defense as illogical, because they see all crimes, including those committed by people with severe mental disorders, as equally "determined."

Following an initial conviction and later appeal, Andrea Yates was acquitted on the basis of an insanity verdict in a 2006 trial. Diagnosed with postpartum depression (depression following childbirth), Yates drowned her five young children in the bathtub, apparently convinced that she'd received commands to do so from Satan. The intense publicity surrounding the Yates' trials and several others involving the insanity verdict has probably contributed to public misperceptions regarding this verdict's prevalence.

insanity defense
legal defense proposing that people shouldn't be held legally responsible for their actions if they weren't of "sound mind" when committing them

There are numerous misconceptions regarding the insanity verdict (see **TABLE 15.5**). For example, although most people believe that a sizable proportion, perhaps 15–20 percent, of criminals are acquitted (found innocent) on the basis of the insanity verdict, the actual percentage is less than 1 percent (Silver, Cirincione, & Steadman, 1994). This erroneous belief probably stems from the *availability heuristic* (see Chapter 2): Because we hear a great deal about a few widely publicized cases of defendants acquitted on the grounds of insanity, we overestimate this verdict's prevalence (Butler, 2006).

TABLE 15.5 Popular Misconceptions Regarding the Insanity Defense.

MYTH	REALITY
Insanity is a psychological or psychiatric term.	Insanity is a purely legal term that refers only to whether the person was responsible for the crime, not to the nature of his or her psychiatric disorder.
The determination of insanity rests on a careful evaluation of the person's current mental state.	The determination of insanity rests on a determination of the person's mental state at the time of the crime.
The insanity defense requires a judgment of the defendant's incompetence to stand trial.	Competence to stand trial bears on defendant's ability to assist in his/her own defense.
A large proportion of criminals escape criminal responsibility by using the insanity defense.	The insanity defense is raised in only about 1% of criminal trials and is successful only about one-fourth of the time.
Most people acquitted on the basis of an insanity defense quickly go free.	The average insanity acquittee spends close to three years in a psychiatric hospital, often longer than the length of a criminal sentence for the same crime.
Insanity defenses are complicated and frequently fool juries as a result.	Most successful insanity verdicts are delivered by judges, not juries.
Most people who use the insanity defense are faking mental illness.	The rate of faking mental illness among insanity defendants appears to be low.

(*Sources:* Butler, 2006; Grisso, 2003; McCutcheon & McCutcheon, 1994; Pasewark & Pantle, 1979; Phillips, Wolf, & Coons, 1998; Silver et al., 1994)

Involuntary Commitment. We're all familiar with *criminal commitment,* which is just a fancy term for putting someone in jail or prison. Yet society possesses another mechanism for committing individuals against their will. Known as **involuntary commitment** or *civil commitment,* it's a procedure for protecting us from certain people with mental disorders, and protecting them from themselves. Most U.S. states specify that individuals with mental illness can be committed against their will only if they (1) pose a clear and present threat to themselves or others or (2) are so psychologically impaired that they can't care for themselves (Appelbaum, 1997; Werth, 2001). Although psychiatrists (but not psychologists) can recommend involuntary commitment to a hospital, only a judge can formally approve it following a hearing. Nevertheless, in most states, two psychiatrists or other physicians can place an emergency "hold" on patients to hospitalize them involuntarily for a brief period of time, typically three days. When that period expires, the patient is legally entitled to a judicial hearing.

Involuntary commitment raises difficult ethical questions. Advocates of this procedure contend that the government has the right to assume the role of "parent" over individuals with mental illness who are dangerous and don't possess sufficient insight to appreciate the impact of their actions (Chodoff, 1976; Satel, 1999). In contrast, critics argue that by involuntarily institutionalizing people who haven't committed crimes, the government is depriving them of their civil liberties (Schaler, 2004; Szasz, 1978). Critics of involuntary

involuntary commitment
procedure of placing some people with mental illnesses in a psychiatric hospital or other facility based on their potential danger to themselves or others, or their inability to care for themselves

commitment also point to research demonstrating that mental health professionals typical-ly do a poor job of forecasting violence (Monahan, 1992), often predicting that patients will commit violence when they won't. Research suggests that African American psychiatric pa-tients are especially likely to be misclassified as potentially violent (Garb, 1998). Still, mental health professionals can predict violence at better than chance levels, especially when pa-tients have very recently engaged in, or are immediately threatening, violence (Kramer, Wol-bransky, & Heilbrun, 2007; Lidz, Mulvey, & Gardner, 1993; Monahan et al., 2000).

somatoform disorder
condition marked by physical symptoms that suggest an underlying medical illness, but that are actually psychological in origin

✓—[**Study** and **Review** on mypsychlab.com

assess your knowledge — FACT OR FICTION?

1. According to a family resemblance view, no one criterion distinguishes mental disorder from normality. **True** / **False**

2. Once the medical model began to take hold in the Renaissance, treatments for mental disorders came to be based on strong scientific evidence. **True** / **False**

3. Almost all deinstitutionalized patients returned successfully to their families and communities. **True** / **False**

4. Some mental disorders appear to be present in most, if not all, cultures. **True** / **False**

5. Virtually all psychiatric diagnoses are unreliable. **True** / **False**

6. Most individuals with severe mental illness are not prone to violence. **True** / **False**

Answers: 1. T (p. 586); 2. F (p. 586); 3. F (p. 587); 4. T (p. 589); 5. F (p. 590); 6. T (p. 595)

Many anxiety disorders, including phobias, frequently have an initial onset in childhood.

ANXIETY DISORDERS: THE MANY FACES OF WORRY AND FEAR

15.4 Describe the many ways people experience anxiety.

We'll begin our tour of psychological disorders with problems stemming from anxiety. For-tunately, most everyday anxieties generally don't last long or feel especially uncomfortable. Anxiety in small doses can even be adaptive. It can permit a lightning-quick response to danger, steer us away from harmful behaviors, and inspire us to solve festering problems. Yet sometimes anxiety spirals out of control, becoming excessive and inappropriate. It may even feel life-threatening (Mendelowicz & Stein, 2000).

Anxiety disorders are among the most prevalent of all mental disorders; 29 percent of us will meet the diagnostic criteria for one or more such disorders at some point in our lives (Kessler et al., 2005). The average age of onset for anxiety disorders (11 years) is earlier than for most other disorders, including substance use disor-ders (20 years) and mood disorders (30 years; Kessler et al., 2005). **TABLE 15.6** displays the lifetime prevalence of anxiety disorders, along with many other disorders we'll consider in this chapter.

Yet anxiety isn't limited to anxiety disorders. Anxiety can seep into numerous aspects of our functioning, including our perceived physical health. In a mysterious class of condi-tions called **somatoform disorders**, people experience physi-cal symptoms that suggest an underlying medical illness, but that are actually of psychological origin (see Table 15.6). The condition known in Freud's day as "grande hysteria," which we encountered in Chapter 14 (most of these cases today would be diagnosed as a condition called conversion disor-der), is one example. High levels of physical anxiety are perva-sive in many somatoform disorders. For example, people

The term *hypochondriasis* literally means "under the chondria," or rib cage, the site of many of the physical symptoms that hypochondriacs report (Vilenski.org).

TABLE 15.6 Lifetime Prevalence of DSM-IV Disorders (in percent).

Disorder	%
Panic disorder	4.7
Specific phobia	12.5
Social phobia	12.1
Generalized anxiety disorder	5.7
Obsessive-compulsive disorder	1.6
Posttraumatic stress disorder	6.8
Major depressive disorder	16.6
Dysthymic disorder	2.5
Bipolar I-II disorder	3.9
Attention-deficit/hyperactivity disorder	8.1
Alcohol abuse	13.2
Alcohol dependence (Alcoholism)	5.4
Drug abuse	7.9
Drug dependence	3.0
Any disorder	46.4
Two or more disorders	27.7
Three or more disorders	17.3

(*Source:* Kessler, et al., 2005)

with **hypochondriasis** are preoccupied with the idea that they're suffering from a serious physical disease (Asmundson & Taylor, 2005). Much like radar operators who stay on their toes for signs of incoming enemy planes, they seem continually to be on the alert for a new symptom. Despite repeated medical reassurance and physical examinations, those with hypochondriasis insist that their mild aches, pains, and twinges are signs of serious diseases, like cancer, AIDS, or heart disease (APA, 2000).

■ Generalized Anxiety Disorder: Perpetual Worry

We all get caught up with worry from time to time. Yet for the 3 percent of us who have **generalized anxiety disorder (GAD)**, worry is a way of life. People with GAD spend an average of 60 percent of each day worrying, compared with 18 percent for the rest of the general population (Craske et al., 1989). Many describe themselves as "worry warts." They tend to think anxious thoughts, feel irritable and on edge, have trouble sleeping, and experience considerable bodily tension and fatigue (Barlow, Chorpita, & Turovsky, 1996; Wittchen, 2002). Often they worry too much about the small things in life, like an upcoming meeting at work or social event. One-third of those with GAD develop it following a major stressful event—like a wedding, illness, physical abuse, or death of a relative—or as the result of lifestyle changes, such as completing school and embarking on a career (Mellinger & Lynn, 2003; Hazlett-Stevens, Pruitt, & Collins, 2008). People with GAD are more likely to be female than male—as is the case with most anxiety disorders—as well as middle-aged, widowed or divorced, poor, and prone to "self medication" with alcohol and drugs to relieve symptoms (Grant et al., 2005; Noyes, 2001). Asians, Hispanics, and African Americans are at relatively low risk for GAD (Grant et al., 2005).

GAD may be the core anxiety disorder out of which all others develop (Barlow, 2002). Indeed, people with GAD often experience other anxiety disorders, including phobias and panic disorder, which we'll consider next. ((•─│Listen

■ Panic Disorder: Terror That Comes Out of the Blue

The Greek god Pan was a mischievous spirit who popped out of the bushes to scare the living daylights out of travelers. Pan lent his name to **panic attacks**, which occur when nervous feelings gather momentum and escalate into intense bouts of fear, even terror. Panic attacks can occur only rarely, or on a daily basis, for weeks, months, or even years at a time. People are diagnosed with **panic disorder** when they experience panic attacks that are repeated and unexpected, and when they either experience persistent concerns about panicking or change their behavior (for example, change jobs) as a result of the attacks (APA, 2000).

Panic attacks peak in less than 10 minutes and can include sweating, dizziness, light-headedness, a racing or pounding heart, shortness of breath, feelings of unreality, and fears of going crazy or dying. Because many patients experiencing their initial panic attacks believe they're having heart attacks, many first go to emergency rooms, only to be sent home and—like Ida, whom we met at the outset of the chapter—told "it's all in your head." Some panic attacks are associated with specific situations, such as riding in elevators or shopping in supermarkets, but others come entirely out of the blue, that is, without warning, often generating fears of the situations in which they occur.

Panic can occur in every anxiety disorder, as well as in mood and eating disorders. Even high-functioning people can experience panic attacks in anticipation of stressful events (Cox & Taylor, 1998): About 20–25 percent of college students report at least one panic attack in a one-year period, with about half that number reporting unexpected attacks (Lilienfeld, 1997). Panic disorder often develops in early adulthood (Kessler et al., 2005), and is associated with a history of fears of separation from a parent during childhood (Lewinsohn et al., 2008).

■ Phobias: Irrational Fears

A **phobia** is an intense fear of an object or situation that's greatly out of proportion to its actual threat. Many of us have mild fears—of things like spiders and snakes—that aren't severe enough to be phobias. For a fear to be diagnosed as a phobia, it must restrict our lives, create considerable distress, or both.

hypochondriasis
an individual's continual preoccupation with the notion that he has a serious physical disease

generalized anxiety disorder (GAD)
continual feelings of worry, anxiety, physical tension, and irritability across many areas of life functioning

panic attack
brief, intense episode of extreme fear characterized by sweating, dizziness, light-headedness, racing heartbeat, and feelings of impending death or going crazy

panic disorder
repeated and unexpected panic attacks, along with either persistent concerns about future attacks or a change in personal behavior in an attempt to avoid them

phobia
intense fear of an object or situation that's greatly out of proportion to its actual threat

((•─│**Listen** to a Generalized Anxiety
Podcast at **mypsychlab.com**

First Person Account:
PANIC DISORDER

For me, a panic attack is almost a violent experience. I feel disconnected from reality. I feel like I'm losing control in a very extreme way. My heart pounds really hard, I feel like I can't get my breath, and there's an overwhelming feeling that things are crashing in on me.
(Dickey, 1994)

Symptoms of a panic attack include a pounding or racing heart, shortness of breath, and faintness or dizziness. This can lead people to believe they are having a heart attack.

Phobias are the most common of all anxiety disorders. One in nine of us has a phobia of an animal, blood or injury, or a situation like a thunderstorm. Social fears are just as common (Kessler et al., 1994). Agoraphobia, which we'll examine next, is the most debilitating of the phobias, and occurs in about one in 20 of us (Keller & Craske, 2008; Kessler et al., 2006).

AGORAPHOBIA. Some 2,700 years ago in the city-states of ancient Greece, agoraphobia acquired its name as a condition in which certain fearful citizens couldn't pass through the central city's open-air markets (*agoras*). A common misconception is that agoraphobia is a fear of crowds or public places. But **agoraphobia** actually refers to a fear of being in a place or situation in which escape is difficult or embarrassing, or in which help is unavailable in the event of a panic attack (APA, 2000).

Agoraphobia typically emerges in the midteens and is usually a direct outgrowth of panic disorder. In fact, most people with panic disorder develop agoraphobia (Cox & Taylor, 1999) and become apprehensive in a host of settings, such as malls, crowded movie theaters, tunnels, bridges, or wide-open spaces. The manifestation of agoraphobia seems to differ across cultures. For example, some Eskimos in Greenland suffer from a condition called "kayak angst," marked by a pronounced fear of going out to sea by oneself in a kayak (Barlow, 2000; Gusow, 1963).

In some cases, agoraphobia reaches extreme proportions. Two clinicians saw a 62-year-old woman with agoraphobia who hadn't left her house—even once—for 25 years (Jensvold & Turner, 1988). Having experienced severe panic attacks and terrified by the prospect of still more, she spent almost all of her waking hours locked away in her bedroom, with curtains drawn. The therapists attempted to treat her agoraphobia by encouraging her to take short trips out of her house, but she repeatedly refused to walk even a few steps past her front door.

SPECIFIC AND SOCIAL PHOBIA. Phobias of objects, places, or situations—called **specific phobias**—commonly arise in response to animals, insects, thunderstorms, water, elevators, and darkness. Many of these fears, especially of animals, are widespread in childhood but disappear with age (APA, 2000).

Surveys show that most people rank public speaking as a greater fear than dying (Wallechinsky, Wallace, & Wallace, 1977). Given that statistic, imagine how people with **social phobia**, also called social anxiety disorder, must feel. They experience a marked fear of public appearances in which embarrassment or humiliation seems likely, such as speaking or performing in public, or more rarely, swimming, swallowing, or signing their checks in public (Mellinger & Lynn, 2003). Their anxiety goes well beyond the stage fright that most of us feel occasionally (Heimberg & Juster, 1995).

■ Posttraumatic Stress Disorder: The Enduring Effects of Experiencing Horror

When people experience or witness a traumatic event, such as front-line combat, an earthquake, or sexual assault, they may develop **posttraumatic stress disorder** (PTSD; see Chapter 12). To qualify for a diagnosis of PTSD, the event must be physically dangerous or life-threatening, either to oneself or someone else (APA, 2000).

We learned in Chapter 12 that flashbacks are among the hallmarks of PTSD. The terror of war can return decades after the original trauma and be reactivated by everyday stressful experiences (Foa & Kozak, 1986). In recounting his war experiences, Vietnam veteran Tim O'Brien (1990) commented: "The hardest part, by far, is to make the bad pictures go away. In war time, the world is one big long horror movie, image after image, and if it's anything like Vietnam, I'm in for a lifetime of wee-hour creeps" (p. 56).

Posttraumatic stress disorder involves a constellation of symptoms that can be quite debilitating. Combat veterans are at high risk for developing this disorder.

Some of the most common fears involve insects and animals, such as spiders and snakes.

First Person Account:
SOCIAL PHOBIA

"*When I would walk into a room full of people, I'd turn red and it would feel like everybody's eyes were on me. I was embarrassed to stand off in a corner by myself, but I couldn't think of anything to say to anybody. It was humiliating. I felt so clumsy, I couldn't wait to get out.*"

(Dickey, 1994)

agoraphobia
fear of being in a place or situation from which escape is difficult or embarrassing, or in which help is unavailable in the event of a panic attack

specific phobia
intense fear of objects, places, or situations that is greatly out of proportion to their actual threat

social phobia
marked fear of public appearances in which embarrassment or humiliation seems likely

posttraumatic stress disorder (PTSD)
marked emotional disturbance after experiencing or witnessing a severely stressful event

Other symptoms include efforts to avoid thoughts, feelings, places, and conversations associated with the trauma; recurrent dreams of the trauma; and increased arousal, such as sleep difficulties and startling easily (APA, 2000). Reminders of the incident can trigger full-blown panic attacks, as in the case of a Vietnam veteran who hid under his bed whenever he heard a city helicopter in the distance—over 20 years after the war ended (Baum, Cohen, & Hall, 1993; Foa & Rothbaum, 1998; Jones & Barlow, 1990). PTSD isn't easy to diagnose. Some of its symptoms, such as anxiety and difficulty sleeping, may have been present *before* the stressful event. Moreover, some people *malinger* (fake) PTSD to obtain government benefits, so diagnosticians must rule out this possibility (Rosen, 2006).

■ Obsessive–Compulsive Disorder: Trapped in One's Thoughts

Just about all of us have had a thought or even a silly song jingle that we just couldn't get out of our heads. Patients with **obsessive-compulsive disorder** (**OCD**) know all too well what this experience is like, except that their symptoms are much more severe. Like Bill, whom we'll recall from the opening of the chapter, they typically suffer from **obsessions**: persistent ideas, thoughts, or impulses that are unwanted and inappropriate and cause marked distress. Unlike typical worries, obsessions aren't extreme responses to everyday stressors. They usually center on "unacceptable" thoughts about such topics as contamination, sex, aggression, or religion (Franklin & Foa, 2008). For example, individuals with OCD may be consumed with fears of being dirty or thoughts of killing others. Unlike ordinary worriers, or people who experience compulsions that aren't especially disturbing to them—such as checking repeatedly to see whether a door is locked—people with OCD typically are disturbed by their thoughts and usually see them as irrational or nonsensical (Fullana et al., 2009). They often label themselves "crazy" or dangerous. Despite their best efforts, people with OCD can't find a way to make these thoughts stop.

Most OCD patients also experience symptoms linked closely to obsessions, namely, **compulsions**: repetitive behaviors or mental acts that they undertake to reduce or prevent distress, or relieve shame and guilt (Abramowitz, Taylr, & McKay, 2009). In most cases, patients feel driven to perform the action that accompanies an obsession, prevent some dreaded event, or "make things right." A patient treated by one of your text's authors awoke early each morning to wash the hood of his car until it was spotless, and felt compelled to repeat this ritual as soon as he arrived home at the end of the workday. Common OCD rituals include:

- repeatedly checking door locks, windows, electronic controls, and ovens
- performing tasks in set ways, like putting on one's shoes in a fixed pattern
- repeatedly arranging and rearranging objects
- washing and cleaning repeatedly and unnecessarily
- counting the number of dots on a wall or touching or tapping objects
- hoarding newspapers, books, letters, soda cans, or other objects

Many people without OCD occasionally engage in one or more of these activities (Mataix-Cols, Rosario-Campos, & Leckman, 2005). Nevertheless, by definition, individuals diagnosed with OCD spend at least an hour a day immersed in obsessions, compulsions, or both; one patient spent 15–18 hours per day washing his hands, showering, getting dressed, and cleaning money. Still, many individuals with OCD lead remarkably successful lives. Howard Hughes, the billionaire industrialist, struggled for years with severe, untreated symptoms of

---

HAVE IMPORTANT ALTERNATIVE EXPLANATIONS FOR THE FINDINGS BEEN EXCLUDED?

First Person Account:
OBSESSIVE-COMPULSIVE DISORDER

"*I couldn't do anything without rituals. They transcended every aspect of my life. Counting was big for me. When I set my alarm at night, I had to set it to a number that wouldn't add up to a 'bad' number. I would wash my hair three times as opposed to once because three was a good-luck number and one wasn't. It took me longer to read because I'd count the lines in a paragraph. If I was writing a term paper, I couldn't have a certain number of words on a line if it added up to a bad number. I was always worried that if I didn't do something, my parents were going to die.***"**

(Dickey, 1994)

Some dogs suffer from a condition called canine lick acral dermatitis, in which they lick themselves compulsively, resulting in severe skin damage (Derr, 2010). Some scientists believe that this condition may be an animal variant of obsessive-compulsive disorder; interestingly, this condition sometimes responds to the same medications used to treat human obsessive-compulsive disorder (see Chapter 16).

obsessive-compulsive disorder (OCD)
condition marked by repeated and lengthy (at least one hour per day) immersion in obsessions, compulsions, or both

obsession
persistent idea, thought, or impulse that is unwanted and inappropriate, causing marked distress

compulsion
repetitive behavior or mental act performed to reduce or prevent stress

OCD. As his disorder progressed, he became so obsessed with possible contamination by germs that he refused to leave the expensive hotel rooms in which he lived. He refused to shake hands with anyone and instructed his servants to engage in elaborate rituals concerning food and utensils. For example, he insisted that they wrap the handle of a spoon in tissue paper and seal it with tape. Yet Hughes rarely bathed or brushed his teeth, and cut his hair and fingernails only once a year (Bartlett & Steele, 2004; Brownstein & Solyom, 1986). More recently, celebrities like Cameron Diaz, Billy Bob Thornton, and David Beckham have spoken publicly about their struggles with the disorder.

Howard Hughes, the billionaire industrialist, suffered from debilitating obsessive-compulsive disorder later in his life.

■ Explanations for Anxiety Disorders: The Roots of Pathological Worry and Fear

How do anxiety disorders arise? Differing theories propose explanations focusing on the environment, catastrophic thinking, and biological influences.

LEARNING MODELS OF ANXIETY: ANXIOUS RESPONSES AS ACQUIRED HABITS. According to learning theories, fears are—you guessed it—learned. John B. Watson and Rosalie Rayner's (1920) famous demonstration of classical conditioning of the fear of a small furry animal (remember poor little Albert from Chapter 6?) powerfully conveys how people learn fears.

Operant conditioning, which relies on reinforcements and punishments (see Chapter 6), offers another account of how fears are maintained. If a socially awkward girl repeatedly experiences rejection when she asks boys to go to movies, she may become shy around them. If this pattern of rejection continues, she could develop a full-blown social phobia. Paradoxically, her avoidance of boys provides negative reinforcement, because it allows her to escape the unpleasant consequences of social interaction. This sense of relief perpetuates her avoidance, and ultimately her anxiety.

Learning theorists (Rachman, 1977) believe that fears can arise in two additional ways. First, we can acquire fears by observing others engage in fearful behaviors (Mineka & Cook, 1993). A father's fear of dogs might instill the same in his child. Second, fears can stem from information or misinformation from others. If a mother tells her children that riding in elevators is dangerous, they may end up taking the stairs.

CATASTROPHIZING AND ANXIETY SENSITIVITY. People with social phobias predict that many social encounters will be interpersonal disasters, and some people with fears of lightning are so fearful that they seek the shelter of a basement when mild thunderstorms are detected on radar 50 miles away (Voncken, Bogels, & deVriees, 2003). As these examples illustrate, *catastrophizing* is a core feature of anxious thinking (Beck, 1976; Ellis, 1962; Ellis & Dryden, 1997). People catastrophize when they predict terrible events—such as contracting a life-threatening illness from turning a doorknob—despite their low probability (A. T. Beck, 1964; J. Beck, 1995).

People with anxiety disorders tend to interpret ambiguous situations in a negative light (Matthews & MacLeod, 2005; see **TABLE 15.7**). Many people with anxiety disorders harbor high levels of **anxiety sensitivity**, a fear of anxiety-related sensations (Reiss & McNally, 1985; Stein, Jang, & Livesley, 1999). Think of the times you felt a bit dizzy when you stood up quickly or your heart raced after climbing a flight of stairs. You probably dismissed these physical symptoms as harmless. Yet people with high anxiety sensitivity tend

Have you ever been unable to get a song or a snatch of a tune out of your head? Psychologists have a term for this phenomenon; it's called an "earworm." A recent study revealed that 98 percent of students have experienced earworms, with the jingle "It's a small world after all" being one of the most frequent (Kellaris, 2003).

TABLE 15.7 Anxiety and Interpretation of Ambiguity.

Anxiety leads us to interpret ambiguous stimuli negatively. Researchers have asked anxious and nonanxious subjects to listen to *homophones*— words that sound the same but have two different meanings and spellings—and to write down the word they heard. In these studies, they've used homophone pairs in which one meaning (and spelling) is threatening and the other is nonthreatening. Compared with nonanxious subjects, anxious subjects are more likely to write down the version of the homophone that's threatening, such as "bury" as opposed to "berry" (Blanchette & Richards, 2003; Mathews, Richard, & Eysenck, 1989).

SELECTED HOMOPHONES	
THREATENING MEANING/ SPELLING	**NONTHREATENING MEANING/ SPELLING**
Bury	Berry
Die	Dye
Patients	Patience
Bruise	Brews
Flu	Flew
Sword	Soared
Bore	Boar

anxiety sensitivity
fear of anxiety-related sensations

to misinterpret them as dangerous—perhaps as early signs of a heart attack or stroke—and react with intense worry (Clark, 1986; Lilienfeld, 1997; McNally & Eke, 1996). As a result, their barely noticeable physical sensations or minor anxiety can spiral into full-blown panic attacks (Schmidt, Zvolensky, & Maner, 2006).

ANXIETY: BIOLOGICAL INFLUENCES. Twin studies show that many anxiety disorders, including panic disorder, phobias, and OCD, are genetically influenced (Andrews et al., 1990; Roy et al., 1995; Van Grootheest et al., 2007). In particular, genes influence people's levels of neuroticism—a tendency to be high strung and irritable (see Chapter 14)—which can set the stage for excessive worry (Anderson, Taylor, & McLean, 1996; Zinbarg & Barlow, 1996). On a genetic basis, people who experience GAD are virtually indistinguishable from those who experience major depression, which is also associated with elevated neuroticism (Kendler & Karkowski-Shuman, 1997). This finding suggests a shared genetic pathway for these disorders.

Family studies show that people with OCD are twice as likely as people without OCD to inherit a specific overactive gene related to the transport of the neurotransmitter serotonin (Goldman et al., 2006). The obsessive-compulsive response in the brain involves a malfunction of the caudate nucleus, a portion of the brain that initiates and controls body movement (Hansen et.al., 2002; Pigott, Myers, & Williams, 1996). A glitch in the caudate nucleus also seems to create problems in setting aside doubts and misgivings. Much like a car that's stuck in gear, people with OCD experience problems with shifting thoughts and behaviors (Schwartz & Bayette, 1996). Brain scans also reveal increased activity in portions of the frontal lobes where information is filtered, prioritized, and organized. Under these circumstances, people can't seem to get troubling thoughts out of their minds or inhibit repeated rituals.

Some children with OCD and related anxiety disorders also meet criteria for *Tourette's Disorder*, a condition marked by motor tics, like twitching and facial grimacing, and vocal tics, like grunting or throat clearing (although Tourette's Disorder sometimes occurs without OCD). This finding has led some researchers to suggest that OCD and Tourette's Disorder share biological roots (Mell, Davis, & Owens, 2005). A number of children develop OCD or Tourette's Disorder after experiencing strep throat or scarlet fever infections caused by streptococcal (strep) bacteria. Scientists are seeking to determine whether strep triggers an immune system response that affects the brain and brings about OCD symptoms, or whether the relationship between strep and OCD symptoms is coincidental (Gause et al., 2009; Kurlan & Kaplan, 2004). Another possibility is that children with strep feel irritable and uncomfortable, which worsens OCD symptoms.

Campers participate in a team building exercise during a summer camp for children with Tourette's Disorder, a syndrome marked by motor and vocal tics.

FICTOID ✕

MYTH: Most individuals with Tourette's Disorder engage in frequent cursing, a symptom known as coprolalia.

REALITY: Seventy percent or more of patients with Tourette's Disorder do not curse (Goldenberg, Brown, & Weiner, 2004).

ruling out rival hypotheses

HAVE IMPORTANT ALTERNATIVE EXPLANATIONS FOR THE FINDINGS BEEN EXCLUDED?

✓ Study and Review on mypsychlab.com

assess your knowledge · FACT OR FICTION?

1. According to some theorists, GAD is the core anxiety disorder out of which others develop. **True** / **False**

2. Panic attacks typically peak in 10 minutes or less. **True** / **False**

3. Because PTSD is characterized by dramatic symptoms, it's typically an easy disorder to diagnose. **True** / **False**

4. Catastrophizing is a core feature of anxious thinking. **True** / **False**

5. Genes exert little influence on obsessive-compulsive disorder. **True** / **False**

Answers: 1. T (p. 598); 2. T (p. 598); 3. F (p. 600); 4. T (p. 601); 5. F (p. 602).

MOOD DISORDERS AND SUICIDE

15.5   Identify the characteristics of different mood disorders.

15.6   Describe how life events can interact with characteristics of the individual to produce depression symptoms.

15.7   Identify common myths and misconceptions about suicide.

Imagine we're therapists interviewing someone who's come to us for help. As the client begins to talk about his life, it becomes clear that even the simplest activities, like dressing or driving to work, have become enormous acts of will. He reports difficulty sleeping and unaccountably wakes up before dawn each day. He refuses to answer the telephone. He lies listlessly for hours staring at the television set. His mood is downcast, and occasionally tears well up in his eyes. He's recently lost a fair amount of weight. His world is gray, a void. Toward the end of the interview, he tells us he's begun to contemplate suicide.

We've just interviewed a person with a *mood disorder,* so called because his difficulties center on his bleak mood, which colors all aspects of his existence. When we check his symptoms against those in Table 15.4 (refer to p. 592), we can see that he meets the criteria for a **major depressive episode**. We'll soon encounter another mood disorder, *bipolar disorder,* in which people's mood is often the mirror image of depression. **TABLE 15.8** outlines the range of mood disorders in DSM-IV.

TABLE 15.8 Mood Disorders and Conditions.

DISORDER	SYMPTOMS
Major Depressive Disorder	Chronic or recurrent state in which a person experiences a lingering depressed mood or diminished interest in pleasurable activities, along with symptoms that include weight loss and sleep difficulties
Manic Episode	Markedly inflated self-esteem or grandiosity, greatly decreased need for sleep, much more talkative than usual, racing thoughts, distractibility, increased activity level or agitation, and excessive involvement in pleasurable activities that can cause problems (like unprotected sex, excessive spending, reckless driving)
Bipolar Disorder I	Presence of one or more manic episodes
Dysthymic Disorder	Low-level depression of at least two years' duration; feelings of inadequacy, sadness, low energy, poor appetite, decreased pleasure and productivity, and hopelessness
Hypomanic Episode	A less intense and disruptive version of a manic episode; feelings of elation, grouchiness or irritability, distractability, and talkativeness
Bipolar Disorder II	Patients must experience at least one episode of major depression and one hypomanic episode.
Cyclothymic Disorder	Moods alternate between numerous periods of hypomanic symptoms and numerous periods of depressive symptoms. To remember cyclothymia, think of "cycles" of up and down moods. Cyclothymia increases the risk of developing bipolar disorder.
Postpartum Depression	A depressive episode that occurs within a month after childbirth. As many as 15% of women develop postpartum depression. A much more serious condition, postpartum psychosis, occurs in about one or two per 1,000 childbirths, with psychotic symptoms, including command hallucinations to kill the infant or delusions that the infant is possessed by an evil spirit (Beck & Gable, 2001).
Seasonal Affective Disorder	Depressive episodes that display a seasonal pattern, most commonly beginning in fall or winter and improving in spring. There must be two consecutive years in which the episode appears on a seasonal basis. Symptoms often include weight gain, lack of energy, carbohydrate craving, and excessive sleep.

(*Source:* Data from DSM-IV, APA, 2000)

Manic Episode

Postpartum Depression

major depressive episode
state in which a person experiences a lingering depressed mood or diminished interest in pleasurable activities, along with symptoms that include weight loss and sleep difficulties

In most cultures, women are generally at greater risk for developing depression than men. Nevertheless, the reasons for this difference aren't fully understood.

Watch Helen: Major Depression on **mypsychlab.com**

ruling out rival hypotheses

HAVE IMPORTANT ALTERNATIVE EXPLANATIONS FOR THE FINDINGS BEEN EXCLUDED?

FACTOID +

Following birth, perhaps as many as 2 to 3 percent of new mothers experience a condition called postpartum obsessive-compulsive disorder. In some cases, the infant becomes the focus of the mother's bizarre thoughts and compulsive behaviors. These symptoms can include repeatedly checking the child to ensure her safety, hiding knives for fear of stabbing the child, and excessive cleaning. Some mothers become so fearful of what they might do to their children that they're reluctant to take care of them (Arnold, 1999). Fortunately, such women almost never harm their children, and effective treatments are available.

■ Major Depressive Disorder: Common, But Not the Common Cold

Over the course of a lifetime, more than 20 percent of us will experience a mood disorder. Major depression alone darkens the lives of more than 16 percent of Americans (Kessler et al., 2005). Due to its frequency, some have dubbed depression the "common cold" of psychological disorders (Seligman, 1975). Yet we'll soon see that this description doesn't begin to capture the profound depths of suffering that people with this condition experience. Depressive disorders can begin at any age, but are most likely to strike people in their thirties. Contrary to popular misconception, they're less common in elderly adults than in younger people (Klerman, 1986).

As we mentioned earlier, women are about twice as likely to experience depression as men. In Chapter 12, we learned that this gender difference may be associated with women's tendency to ruminate more than men (Nolen-Hoeksema, 2002, 2003). Yet it may also be associated with differences between men and women in economic power, sex hormones, social support, and history of physical or sexual abuse (Howland & Thase, 1998). The sex difference in depression is widespread but not universal. In some cultures, such as certain Mediterranean populations, Orthodox Jews, and the Amish, this sex difference is largely absent (Piccinelli & Wilkinson, 2000). But researchers don't know why. One possibility is that the differences in the rates of depression across genders in Western cultures reflect an underdiagnosis of depression in men. In the United States, women are more willing to admit to depression and seek psychological services than men, who are socialized to "act tough" (Kilmartin, 2006). ●—**Watch**

Over the past century, the rate of diagnosed major depression has gradually creeped up, and psychologists have diagnosed depression at earlier ages with succeeding generations (Compton et al., 2006; Klerman et al., 1985). Nevertheless, the earlier onset of depression, which today peaks at 15–24 years of age, may be more illusory than real. Older people may have difficulty remembering past depressive episodes, leading scientists to underestimate the prevalence of depression among the elderly (Giuffra & Risch, 1994).

The symptoms of depression may develop gradually over days or weeks; in other cases, they may surface rather suddenly. Depression, like the common cold, is recurrent. The average person with major depression experiences five or six episodes over the course of a lifetime. Most episodes last from six months to a year. But in as many as a fifth of cases, depression is *chronic,* that is, present for decades with no relief (Ingram, Scott, & Seigel, 1998). Generally, the earlier depression strikes the first time, the more likely it will persist or recur (Coryell et al., 2009). In sharp contrast to the common cold, depression can produce severe impairment. In extreme cases, people may fail to feed or clothe themselves or take care of basic health needs, like brushing their teeth or showering.

■ Explanations for Major Depressive Disorder: A Tangled Web

The multifaceted phenomenon of depression illustrates the biopsychosocial approach (see Chapter 12), underscoring how multiple factors can combine to produce psychological symptoms. Let's reconsider the depressed man we imagined interviewing at the beginning of this section. From his severely depressed father and perpetually anxious mother, he may have inherited a tendency to respond to stressful situations with negative emotions (neuroticism). He felt that a competitive colleague tried continually to undermine his authority as a television producer. In response, he felt insecure, and began to second-guess his every decision. Each day he wasted hours ruminating about losing his job. The quality of his work nose-dived. He withdrew socially and began to refuse invitations to go golfing with his buddies. His friends tried to cheer him up, but the black cloud that hung over his head wouldn't budge. Feeling rebuffed, his friends stopped inviting him to do anything. His once-bright social world became a black void, and he moped around doing virtually nothing. He felt helpless. Eventually, his dark thoughts turned to suicide.

This example highlights a key point. To fully understand depression, we must appreciate the complex interplay of inborn tendencies, stressful events, interpersonal relationships, the loss of reinforcers in everyday life, negative thoughts, and feelings of helplessness (Akiskal & McKinney, 1973; Ilardi & Feldman, 2001).

DEPRESSION AND LIFE EVENTS. Sigmund Freud (1917) suggested that early loss can render us vulnerable to depression later in life. He may have been on to something, because the loss of beloved people or even the threat of loss can trigger depression in adulthood. Stressful life events that represent loss or threat of separation are especially tied to depression (Brugha, 1995; Mazure, 1998; Paykel, 2003). But the loss created by a blow to our sense of self-worth can sting every bit as much as the loss of a close relationship (Finlay-Jones & Brown, 1981). A crucial determinant of whether we'll become depressed is whether we've lost or are about to lose something we value dearly, like someone we love, financial support, or self-esteem (Beck, 1983; Blatt, 1974; Prince et al., 1997; Zuroff, Mongrain, & Santor, 2004). Although the lack or loss of social support better predicts depression in women than men, the flip side is that nurturing relationships are more likely to protect women against depression compared with men (Kendler, Myers, & Prescott, 2005).

As we learned in Chapter 12, pessimism and other symptoms of depression can set the stage for negative life circumstances, like getting fired from a job or losing a close relationship (Hammen, 1991; Harkness & Luther, 2001). The causal arrow of this association thus points in both directions. Negative life events set us up to bring us down, but depression can create problems in living.

correlation vs. causation

CAN WE BE SURE THAT A CAUSES B?

INTERPERSONAL MODEL: DEPRESSION AS A SOCIAL DISORDER. James Coyne hypothesized that depression creates interpersonal problems (1976; Joiner & Coyne, 1999; Rudolf et al., 2006). When people become depressed, he argued, they seek excessive reassurance, which in turn leads others to dislike and reject them. Coyne (1976) asked undergraduates to talk on the telephone for 20 minutes with patients with depression, patients without depression, or nonpatient women drawn from the community. He didn't inform students they'd be interacting with patients with depression. Yet following the interaction, students who spoke with these patients became more depressed, anxious, and hostile than those who interacted with individuals without depression. Moreover, subjects were more rejecting of patients with depression and expressed much less interest in interacting with them in the future. For Coyne, depression is a vicious cycle. People with depression often elicit hostility and rejection from others, which in turn maintains or worsens their depression.

Many, but not all, studies have replicated Coyne's findings that people with depression seek excessive reassurance and tend to stir up negative feelings in others (Burns et al., 2006; Joiner & Coyne, 1999; Starr & Davilla, 2008). Constant worrying, mistrust, fears of rejection and abandonment, and socially inappropriate behaviors can also be a social turn-off to many people (Wei et al., 2005; Zborowski & Garske, 1993).

replicability

CAN THE RESULTS BE DUPLICATED IN OTHER STUDIES?

BEHAVIORAL MODEL: DEPRESSION AS A LOSS OF REINFORCEMENT. Peter Lewinsohn's (1974) *behavioral model* proposes that depression results from a low rate of response-contingent positive reinforcement. Put in simpler terms, when people with depression try different things and receive no payoff for them, they eventually give up. They stop participating in many pleasant activities, affording them little opportunity to obtain reinforcement from others. In time, their personal and social worlds shrink, as depression seeps into virtually every nook and cranny of their lives. Lewinsohn later observed that some people with depression lack social skills (Segrin, 2000; Youngren & Lewinsohn, 1980), making it harder for them to obtain reinforcement from people they value. To make matters worse, if others respond to individuals with depression with sympathy and concern, they may reinforce and maintain their withdrawal. This view implies a straightforward recipe for breaking the grip of depression: pushing ourselves to engage in pleasant activities. Sometimes merely getting out of bed can be the first step toward conquering depression (Dimidjian et al., 2006).

According to James Coyne's interpersonal model of depression, depression can trigger rejection from others, in turn contributing to further depression.

Most people have an illusion of control; for example, they mistakenly believe that they're more likely to win a gamble if they toss the dice than if someone else does. Interestingly, people who have mild or moderate depression tend not to fall prey to this thinking error (Golin, Terrell, & Johnson, 1977), suggesting they may actually be more realistic than people without depression under certain circumstances.

COGNITIVE MODEL: DEPRESSION AS A DISORDER OF THINKING. In contrast, Aaron Beck's influential **cognitive model of depression** holds that depression is caused by negative beliefs and expectations (Beck, 1967, 1987). Beck focused on the *cognitive triad*, three components of depressed thinking: negative views of oneself, the world, and the future. These habitual thought patterns, called *negative schemas*, presumably originate in early experiences of loss, failure, and rejection. Activated by stressful events in later life, these schemas reinforce people with depression's negative experiences (Scher, Ingram, & Segal, 2005).

A depressed person's view of the world is bleak because they put a decidedly negative mental spin on their experiences. They also suffer from *cognitive distortions*, which are skewed ways of thinking. One example is selective abstraction, in which people come to a negative conclusion based on only an isolated aspect of a situation. A man might consistently single out a trivial error he committed in a softball game and blame himself completely for the loss. It's as though people with depression are wearing glasses that filter out all of life's positive experiences and bring all of life's negative experiences into sharper focus.

There's considerable support for Beck's idea that people with depression hold negative views of themselves, the future, and the world (Haaga, Dyck, & Ernst, 1991; Ingram, 2003). But the evidence for the role of cognitive distortions in nonhospitalized, or not seriously depressed, individuals isn't as strong (Haack et al., 1996). In fact, some research suggests that compared with people without depression, individuals with mild depression actually have a *more* accurate view of circumstances, a phenomenon called *depressive realism*. In contrast, people who aren't depressed experience *illusory control* over their environments. This surprising conclusion comes from research in which people without depression were more likely than people with depression to believe they controlled a lightbulb when it came on, even though experimenters rigged when it turned on and off (Alloy & Abramson, 1979, 1988). Thus, people with depression were more realistic in their estimates of personal control, because they had no control over the bulb. Researchers (Msetfi et al., 2005) replicated this finding, but suggested that depressed individuals experience difficulties attending to and processing information about the light. So rather than being more realistic, people with depression may be less attentive to "reality," a finding consistent with cognitive models.

Not tuning into reality may exact serious costs. Janet Kistner and her colleagues (Kistner et al., 2006) studied nine- and 10-year-old children's perceptions of how their classmates felt about them. The researchers discovered that children with accurate perceptions of their level of social acceptance were less likely to develop depression than those with inaccurate perceptions. Beck's theory implies that negative schemas shape emotional tone rather than the other way around. Nevertheless, Kistner's research suggests that depression itself can create a negative bias. As time went on, children who were depressed at the outset of the study became more negatively biased about how much others liked and perceived them. These findings point to a cycle in which inaccurate perceptions lead to depression, and depression leads to inaccurate perceptions.

LEARNED HELPLESSNESS: DEPRESSION AS A CONSEQUENCE OF UNCONTROLLABLE EVENTS. Martin Seligman (1975; Seligman & Maier, 1967) accidentally stumbled across an unusual finding related to depression in his work with dogs. He was testing dogs in a shuttle box, depicted in **FIGURE 15.2**; one side of the box was electrified and the other side, separated by a barrier, wasn't. Ordinarily, dogs avoid painful shocks by jumping over

replicability

CAN THE RESULTS BE DUPLICATED IN OTHER STUDIES?

correlation vs. causation

CAN WE BE SURE THAT A CAUSES B?

FIGURE 15.2 The Shuttle Box. Using an apparatus like this, Martin Seligman found that dogs who were first prevented from escaping the shock gave up trying to escape electric shocks even when they were free to do so. He called this phenomenon "learned helplessness."

Light dims, warning of impending shock

Grid floor—shocks can be administered

Dog will be safe from shock on this side

Bars on this side will be electrified

cognitive model of depression
theory that depression is caused by negative beliefs and expectations

the barrier to the nonelectrified side of the box. Yet Seligman found something surprising. Dogs first restrained in a hammock and exposed to shocks they couldn't escape later often made no attempt to escape shocks in the shuttle box, even when they could easily get away from them. Some of the dogs just sat there, whimpering and crying, passively accepting the shocks as though they were inescapable. They'd learned to become helpless.

Bruce Overmier and Seligman (1967) described **learned helplessness** as the tendency to feel helpless in the face of events we can't control and argued that it offers an animal model of depression. Seligman noted striking parallels between the effects of learned helplessness and depressive symptoms: passivity, appetite and weight loss, and difficulty learning that one can change circumstances for the better. But we must be cautious in drawing conclusions from animal studies because many psychological conditions, including depression, may differ in animals and humans (Raulin & Lilienfeld, 2008).

Provocative as it is, Seligman's model can't account for all aspects of depression. It doesn't explain why people with depression make internal attributions (explanations) for failure. In fact, the tendency to assume personal responsibility for failure contradicts the notion that people with depression regard negative events as beyond their control. The original model also doesn't acknowledge that the mere expectation of uncontrollability isn't sufficient to induce depression. After all, people don't become sad when they receive large amounts of money in a lottery, even though they have no control over this event (Abramson, Seligman, & Teasdale, 1978).

When data don't fit a model, good scientists revise it. Seligman and his colleagues (Abramson et al., 1978) altered the learned helplessness model to account for the attributions people make to explain their worlds. They argued that persons prone to depression attribute failure to *internal* as opposed to external factors, and success to *external* as opposed to internal factors. A person with depression might blame a poor test grade on a lack of ability, an internal factor, and a good score on the ease of the exam, an external factor. The researchers also observed that depression-prone persons make attributions that are *global* and *stable:* They tend to see their failures as general and fixed aspects of their personalities. Still, internal, global, and stable attributions may be more a consequence than a cause of depression (Harvey & Weary, 1984). The depression brought on by undesirable life events may skew our thinking, leading us to make negative attributions (Beidel & Turner, 1986; Gibb & Alloy, 2006; Ilardi & Craighead, 1994).

correlation vs. causation
CAN WE BE SURE THAT A CAUSES B?

Whether we develop depression depends not only on our attributions of outcomes, but also on the difference between how we feel—our actual affect—and how we want to feel—our ideal affect (Tsai, 2007). Jeanne Tsai and her colleagues found that cultural factors influence people's ideal affect (Tsai, Knutson, & Fung, 2006). Compared with Hong Kong Chinese, European Americans and Asian Americans value excitement, whereas compared with European Americans, Hong Kong Chinese and Asian Americans value calm. Yet across all three cultural groups, the size of the gap between ideal and actual affect predicts depression.

DEPRESSION: THE ROLE OF BIOLOGY. Twin studies indicate that genes exert a moderate effect on the risk of major depression (Kendler et al., 1993). Some researchers have suggested that specific variations in the serotonin transporter gene (which affects the rate of reuptake of serotonin; see Chapter 3) play a role in depression, especially in conjunction with life experiences. Scientists first reported that people who inherit two copies of this stress-sensitive gene are two and a half times more likely to develop depression following four stressful events than people with another version of the gene that isn't sensitive to stress (Caspi et al., 2003). The stress-sensitive gene appears to affect people's ability to dampen negative emotions in the face of stress (Kendler, Gardner, & Prescott, 2003). Nevertheless, researchers who recently reviewed all the available evidence concluded that there was no basis for a link between the gene and stressful life events, on the one hand, and depression, on the other (Risch et al., 2009). In response, other scientists challenged how these authors analyzed previous findings (Rutter, 2009). To resolve questions regarding the role of gene-life events interactions in depression, researchers will need to conduct

learned helplessness
tendency to feel helpless in the face of events we can't control

replicability

CAN THE RESULTS BE DUPLICATED IN OTHER STUDIES?

well-designed studies to determine whether the initially promising findings are replicable. Hopefully, these studies will clarify whether any genetic irregularities that surface are specific to depression; they may be associated with anxiety, too (Hariri et al., 2002).

Depression also appears linked to low levels of the neurotransmitter norepinephrine (Leonard, 1997; Robinson, 2007) and diminished neurogenesis (growth of new neurons), which brings about reduced hippocampal volume (see Chapter 3) (Pittinger & Duman, 2008; Videbech & Ravnkilde, 2004). Many patients with depression have problems in the brain's reward and stress-response systems (Depue & Iacono, 1989; Forbes, Shaw, & Dahl, 2007), and decreased levels of dopamine, the neurotransmitter most closely tied to reward (Martinot et al., 2001). This finding may help to explain why depression is often associated with an inability to experience pleasure.

■ Bipolar Disorder: When Mood Goes to Extremes

Ann, the giddy patient with bipolar disorder whom we met at the beginning of the chapter, experienced many classic symptoms of a **manic episode**. These episodes are typically marked by dramatically elevated mood (feeling "on top of the world"), decreased need for sleep, greatly heightened energy, inflated self-esteem, increased talkativeness, and irresponsible behavior. People in a manic episode often display "pressured speech," as though they can't get their words out quickly enough, and are difficult to interrupt (Goodwin & Jamison, 1990). Their ideas often race through their heads quickly, which may account for the heightened rate of creative accomplishments in some individuals with bipolar disorder (see Chapter 9). These and other symptoms, which we can find in Table 15.8 (refer to page 603), typically begin with a rapid increase over only a few days. People usually experience their first manic episode after their early twenties (Kessler et al., 2005).

Bipolar disorder, formerly called manic-depressive disorder, is diagnosed when there's a history of at least one manic episode (APA, 2000). In contrast to major depression, bipolar disorder is equally common in men and women. In the great majority of cases—upward of 90 percent (Alda, 1997)—people who've had one manic episode experience at least one more. Some have episodes separated by many years and then have a series of episodes, one rapidly following the other. More than half the time, a major depressive episode precedes or follows a manic episode. Manic episodes often produce serious problems in social and occupational functioning, such as substance abuse and unrestrained sexual behavior. Because their judgment is so impaired, people in the midst of manic episodes may go on wild spending sprees, or drive while intoxicated. One of your book's authors treated a manic patient who passed himself off to a financial company as his own father, gained access to his father's savings for retirement, and gambled away his entire family fortune. Another frittered away most of his life's savings by purchasing more than 100 bowling balls, none of which he needed. The negative effects of a manic episode, including loss of employment, family conflicts, and divorce, can persist for many years (Coryell et al., 1993).

Bipolar disorder is among the most genetically influenced of all mental disorders (Miklowitz & Johnson, 2006). Twin studies suggest that its heritability may be as high as 85 percent (Alda, 1997; McGuffin et al., 2003). Scientists believe that genes that increase the sensitivity of the dopamine receptors (Willner, 1995) and decrease the sensitivity of serotonin receptors may boost the risk of bipolar disorder (Ogden et al., 2004).

Brain imaging studies suggest that people with bipolar disorder experience increased activity in structures related to emotion, including the amygdala (Chang et al., 2004; Yergelun-Todd et al., 2000), and decreased activity in structures associated with planning, such as the prefrontal cortex (Kruger et al., 2003). Still, the cause–effect relationship between physiological findings and mood disorders isn't clear. For example, the high levels of norepinephrine and differences in brain activity observed in people with bipolar disorder may be an effect rather than a cause of the disorder (Thase, Jindal, & Howland, 2002).

Bipolar disorder is influenced by more than biological factors. Stressful life events are associated with an increased risk of manic episodes, more frequent relapse, and a longer recovery from manic episodes (Johnson & Miller, 1997). Interestingly, some manic

People in the midst of manic episodes frequently go on uncontrolled spending sprees and may "max out" multiple credit cards in the process.

First Person Account:
BIPOLAR DISORDER

"When I start going into a high, I no longer feel like an ordinary [homemaker]. Instead I feel organized and accomplished and I begin to feel I am my most creative self. I can write poetry easily ... melodies without effort ... paint ... I feel a sense of euphoria or elation.... I don't seem to need much sleep ... I've just bought six new dresses ... I feel sexy and men stare at me. Maybe I'll have an affair, or perhaps several.... However, when I go beyond this state, I become manic.... I begin to see things in my mind that aren't real.... One night I created an entire movie.... I also experienced complete terror ... when I knew that an assassination scene was about to take place.... I went into a manic psychosis at that point. My screams awakened my husband.... I was admitted to the hospital the next day."

(Cheve, 1976)

correlation vs. causation

CAN WE BE SURE THAT A CAUSES B?

episodes appear to be triggered by *positive* life events associated with striving for and achieving goals, such as job promotions or winning poetry contests (Johnson et al., 2000; Johnson et al., 2008). Once again, we can see that psychological disorders arise from the intersection of biological, psychological, and sociocultural forces. 👁—Watch

👁—**Watch** Nathan: Bipolar Disorder on **mypsychlab.com**

■ Suicide: Facts and Fictions

Major depression and bipolar disorder are associated with a higher risk of suicide than most other disorders (Miklowitz & Johnson, 2006; Wolfsdorf et al., 2003). Estimates suggest that the suicide rate of people with bipolar disorder is about 15 times higher than that of the general population (Harris & Barraclough, 1997). Some anxiety disorders, like panic disorder and social phobia, and substance abuse are also associated with heightened suicide risk (Spirito & Esposito-Smythers, 2006). In 2001, scientists ranked suicide as the 11th leading cause of death in the United States (NIMH, 2004), and the third leading cause of death for children, adolescents, and young adults (Kochanek et al., 2004). ((•—Listen

((•—**Listen** to the Suicide audio file on **mypsychlab.com**

Typically, more than 30,000 people commit suicide in the United States each year, a number that surely underestimates the problem because relatives report many suicides as accidents. For each completed suicide, there are an estimated eight to 25 attempts. Contrary to what many believe, most people are more of a threat to themselves than others. For every two people who are victims of homicide, three take their own lives (NIMH, 2004). In **TABLE 15.9**, we present a number of other common myths and misconceptions about suicide. It's essential to try to predict suicide attempts because most people are acutely suicidal for only a short window of time (Schneidman, Faberow, & Litman, 1970; Simon, 2006), and intervention during that time can be critical. Unfortunately, the prediction of suicide poses serious practical problems. First, we can't easily conduct longitudinal studies (see Chapter 10) to determine which people will attempt suicide. It would be unethical to allow people believed to be at high suicide risk to go through with attempts to allow us to pinpoint predictors of suicide. Second, it's difficult to study the psychological states associated with suicide because the period of high risk for a suicide attempt is often brief. Third, the low prevalence of suicide makes predicting it difficult (Finn & Kamphuis, 1995; Meehl & Rosen, 1955). Most estimates put the rate of completed suicide at 12 or 13 out of 100,000 people in the general population. So if only about one-hundredth of 1 percent of the population completes a suicide, our best guess—with about 99.9 percent accuracy—is that no one

FICTOID ✕

MYTH: Suicide rates increase around the Christmas holidays, largely because people without close family members feel especially lonely.

REALITY: There's little support for this view; in fact, several studies suggest a slight *decrease* in suicide attempts and completions around Christmas (Ajdacic-Gross et al., 2003; Phillips & Wills, 1987).

TABLE 15.9 Common Myths and Misconceptions about Suicide.

MYTH	REALITY
Talking to persons with depression about suicide often makes them more likely to commit the act.	Talking to persons with depression about suicide makes them more likely to obtain help.
Suicide is almost always completed with no warning.	Many or most individuals who commit suicide communicate their intent to others, which gives us an opportunity to seek help for a suicidal person.
As a severe depression lifts, people's suicide risk decreases.	As a severe depression lifts, the risk of suicide may actually increase, in part because individuals possess more energy to attempt the act.
Most people who threaten suicide are seeking attention.	Although attention seeking motivates some suicidal behaviors, most suicidal acts stem from severe depression and hopelessness.
People who talk a lot about suicide almost never commit it.	Talking about suicide is associated with a considerably greater risk of suicide.

manic episode
experience marked by dramatically elevated mood, decreased need for sleep, increased energy, inflated self-esteem, increased talkativeness, and irresponsible behavior

bipolar disorder
condition marked by a history of at least one manic episode

will commit suicide. Nevertheless, the social costs of failing to predict a suicide are so great that efforts to accurately predict suicide attempts continue (see **FIGURE 15.3**).

Fortunately, research has taught us a great deal about risk factors for suicide. The single best predictor of suicide is a previous attempt, because 30 to 40 percent of all people who kill themselves have made at least one prior attempt (Maris, 1992; Pelkonen & Marttunen, 2003). About three times as many men as women commit suicide, but nearly three times as many women try it (NIMH, 2004). Interestingly, hopelessness may be an even better predictor of suicide than depressed mood (Beck et al., 1990; Goldston et al., 2001), because people are most likely to try to kill themselves when they see no escape from their pain. Intense agitation is also a powerful predictor of suicide risk (Fawcett, 1997). A list of risk factors for suicide appears in **TABLE 15.10**.

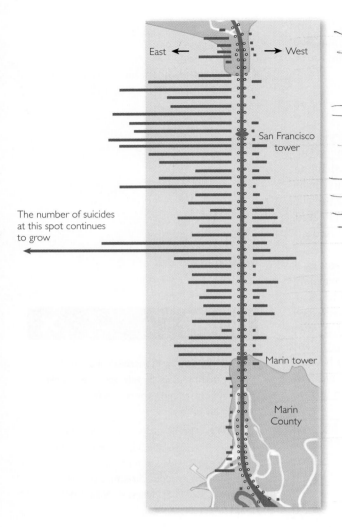

East ← → West

San Francisco tower

The number of suicides at this spot continues to grow

Marin tower

Marin County

TABLE 15.10 Major Suicide Risk Factors.

1. Depression
2. Hopelessness
3. Substance abuse
4. Schizophrenia
5. Homosexuality, probably because of social stigma
6. Unemployment
7. Chronic, painful, or disfiguring physical illness
8. Recent loss of a loved one; being divorced, separated, or widowed
9. Family history of suicide
10. Personality disorders, such as borderline personality disorder (see later discussion)
11. Anxiety disorders, such as panic disorder and social phobia
12. Old age, especially in men
13. Recent discharge from a hospital

FIGURE 15.3   Suicides by Location. The famed Golden Gate Bridge in San Francisco has been the site of well over 1,200 suicides. One inch on each of the blue lines equates to about 20 suicides. (*Source:* SFGate.com)

✓ **Study** and **Review** on **mypsychlab.com**

PERSONALITY AND DISSOCIATIVE DISORDERS: THE DISRUPTED AND DIVIDED SELF

15.8   Identify the characteristics of borderline and psychopathic personality disorders.

15.9   Explain the controversies surrounding dissociative disorders, especially dissociative identity disorder.

Most of us are accustomed to thinking of ourselves as one coherent unified identity. But some individuals—especially those with personality and dissociative disorders—experience a serious disruption in their thoughts or behaviors that prevents them from experiencing a healthy, consistent identity. Distinguishing normal variations in personality and sense of self from personality and identity disorders isn't easy because we all have our personal quirks.

■ Personality Disorders

Of all psychiatric conditions, personality disorders are historically the least reliably diagnosed (Fowler, O'Donohue & Lilienfeld, 2007; Perry, 1984; Zimmerman, 1994). DSM-IV states that we should diagnose a **personality disorder** only when personality traits first appear by adolescence; are inflexible, stable, and expressed in a wide variety of situations; and lead to distress or impairment (APA, 2000). But more than most patterns of behavior we've described, whether we perceive someone with a personality disorder as abnormal depends on the context in which their behavior occurs (Price & Bouffard, 1974). The suspiciousness of a person with a paranoid personality disorder may be a liability in a cooperative work group, but an asset in a private investigator.

In **TABLE 15.11**, we list the major personality disorders in DSM-IV. In contrast to the other conditions we've discussed, which are coded on Axis I of DSM-IV, personality disorders are coded on Axis II. This distinction supposedly reflects the fact that whereas Axis I refers to major mental disorders, like major depression and panic disorder, Axis II refers to longstanding personality traits that may color the expression of these disorders (Widiger & Frances, 1985). Although personality disorders are separable, they often exhibit substantial

At least in mild doses, features of some personality disorders may be adaptive in certain occupations. For example, the traits of obsessive-compulsive personality disorder, which include attention to detail and perfectionism, may come in handy for accountants.

TABLE 15.11 The DSM-IV Classification of Major Personality Disorders.

ODD, ECCENTRIC CLUSTER	
Paranoid personality disorder	Distrust, suspiciousness, oversensitivity
Schizotypal personality disorder	Intense discomfort in social situations; odd thinking, perception, communication, behaviors
Schizoid personality disorder	Detachment from social relationships, bland or limited expression of emotion
DRAMATIC, EMOTIONAL, ERRATIC CLUSTER	
Histrionic personality disorder	Attention seeking, overemotional, dramatic, shallow, seductive, suggestible
Narcissistic personality disorder	Grandiose sense of self-importance or uniqueness, need for constant attention and admiration, lacks empathy, preoccupation with fantasies of unlimited success or power
Antisocial personality disorder	Antisocial behavior, violates or disregards rights of others, lying, stealing, irresponsibility, lack of remorse
Borderline personality disorder	Instability in various areas of life, tense and unstable relationships, recurrent suicide attempts, efforts to avoid being abandoned, unstable self-image/identity disturbance
ANXIOUS, FEARFUL CLUSTER	
Avoidant personality disorder	Unwilling to enter into relationships unless guarantee of uncritical acceptance; social withdrawal; fear of social criticism or rejection; reluctant to take risks or try new things that may bring about embarrassment
Dependent personality disorder	Difficulty making everyday decisions; excessive reliance on and need for reassurance, support, nurturance from others; feels helpless when alone
Obsessive-compulsive personality disorder	Preoccupied with order, organization, rules, small details; perfectionistic; rigid and stubborn; overinvolved in work; inflexible

(*Source:* From *Diagnostic and Statistical Manual of Mental Disorders*, 4th ed., American Psychiatric Association, 2000)

personality disorder
condition in which personality traits, appearing first in adolescence, are inflexible, stable, expressed in a wide variety of situations, and lead to distress or impairment

The homicidal and unstable character in the movie *Fatal Attraction* would probably qualify for a diagnosis of borderline personality disorder, although most people with this diagnosis aren't violent.

borderline personality disorder
condition marked by extreme instability in mood, identity, and impulse control

psychopathic personality
condition marked by superficial charm, dishonesty, manipulativeness, self-centeredness, and risk taking

antisocial personality disorder (ASPD)
condition marked by a lengthy history of irresponsible and/or illegal actions

comorbidity with each other and with many Axis I disorders, such as major depression and generalized anxiety disorder (Lenzenweger et al., 2007), leading some to question whether the distinction between Axis I and Axis II disorders is scientifically justifiable (Harkness & Lilienfeld, 1997).

Based mostly on superficial similarities among personality disorders, DSM-IV groups these conditions into three clusters—odd or eccentric; dramatic, erratic, or emotional; and anxious or fearful. We'll consider in detail two major and extensively researched personality disorders—borderline personality disorder and psychopathic personality.

BORDERLINE PERSONALITY DISORDER: STABLE INSTABILITY. About two percent of adults, most of them women (Swartz et al., 1990), develop **borderline personality disorder**, a condition marked by instability in mood, identity, and impulse control. Individuals with borderline personality disorder tend to be extremely impulsive and unpredictable, although many are married and hold down good jobs. Their relationships frequently alternate from extremes of worshipping partners one day to hating them the next. Some have aptly described this disorder as a pattern of "stable instability" (Grinker & Werble, 1977). The name *borderline personality* stems from the now outmoded belief that this condition lies on the border between psychotic and "neurotic"—relatively normal, yet mildly disabled—functioning (Stern, 1938).

Borderline Personality: A Volatile Blend of Traits. Persons with borderline personality's impulsivity and rapidly fluctuating emotions often have a self-destructive quality: Many engage in drug abuse, sexual promiscuity, overeating, and even self-mutilation, like cutting themselves when upset. They may threaten suicide to manipulate others, reflecting the chaotic nature of their relationships. Because many experience intense feelings of abandonment when alone, they may jump frantically from one unhealthy relationship to another.

Explanations of Borderline Personality Disorder. Psychoanalyst Otto Kernberg (1967, 1973) traced the roots of borderline personality to childhood problems with developing a sense of self and bonding emotionally to others. According to Kernberg, individuals with borderline personality disorder can't integrate differing perceptions of people, themselves included. This defect supposedly arises from an inborn tendency to experience intense anger and frustration from living with a cold, unempathetic mother. Kernberg argued that borderline individuals experience the world and themselves as unstable because they tend to "split" people and experiences into either all good or all bad. Although influential, Kernberg's model of borderline personality remains inadequately researched.

According to Marsha Linehan's (1993) sociobiological model, individuals with borderline personality disorder inherit a tendency to overreact to stress and experience lifelong difficulties with regulating their emotions (Crowell, Beauchaine, & Linehan, 2009). Indeed, twin studies suggest that borderline personality traits are substantially heritable (Torgerson et al., 2000). Difficulties in controlling emotions may be responsible for the rejection many individuals with borderline personality disorder encounter, as well as their concerns about being validated, loved, and accepted. Edward Selby and Thomas Joiner's emotional cascade model holds that intense rumination about negative events or emotional experiences may result in uncontrolled "emotional cascades," which prompt self-injurious actions, like cutting. Although these impulsive and desperate actions succeed in providing brief distraction from rumination, they often fuel further bouts of rumination, creating a vicious cycle of problems with regulating emotions (Selby et al., 2009; Selby & Joiner, 2009).

PSYCHOPATHIC PERSONALITY: DON'T JUDGE A BOOK BY ITS COVER. We don't intend to alarm you. Yet the odds are high that in your life you've met—perhaps even dated—at least one person whom psychologists describe as a **psychopathic personality**, which used to be known informally as a *psychopath* or *sociopath*. Psychopathic personality overlaps with the DSM-IV diagnosis of **antisocial personality disorder (ASPD)**, although it's not identical to it. In contrast to ASPD, which is marked by a lengthy history of illegal and irresponsible actions, psychopathic personality is marked by a distinctive set of personality traits (Lilienfeld, 1994). Because most psychological research has concentrated on psychopathic personality rather than ASPD (Hare, 2003)—a strange irony as only the latter diagnosis is in DSM-IV—we'll focus on psychopathy here.

Psychopathic Personality: A Dangerous Mixture of Traits. Those with psychopathic personality—most of them male—are guiltless, dishonest, manipulative, callous, and self-centered (Cleckley, 1941/1988; Lykken, 1995). Because of these distinctly unpleasant personality traits, one might assume we'd all go out of our way to avoid individuals with this disorder—and we'd probably be better off if we did. However, many of us seek out people with psychopathic personality as friends and even romantic partners because they tend to be charming, personable, and engaging (Hare, 1993). This was certainly the case with Johnny, whom we'll recall from the beginning of the chapter. Like Johnny, many people with this condition have a history of *conduct disorder,* marked by lying, cheating, and stealing in childhood and adolescence.

If the traits we've described fit someone you know to a T, there's no need to panic. Despite popular conception, most people with psychopathic personality aren't physically aggressive. Nevertheless, they are at heightened risk for crime compared with the average person, and a handful—probably a few percent—are habitually violent. Mass murderer Ted Bundy almost certainly met the criteria for psychopathic personality disorder, as do about 25 percent of prison inmates (Hare, 2003). Also, despite scores of movie portrayals of crazed serial killers, people with this disorder typically aren't psychotic. To the contrary, most are entirely rational. They know full well that their irresponsible actions are morally wrong; they just don't care.

There's reason to suspect that people with this condition populate not only much of the criminal justice system, but also positions of leadership in corporations and politics (Babiak & Hare, 2006). Many psychopathic traits, such as interpersonal skills, superficial likability, ruthlessness, and risk taking, may give people with this disorder a leg up for getting ahead of the rest of the pack. Still, there's surprisingly little research on "successful psychopaths"—people with high levels of psychopathic traits who function well in society (Hall & Benning, 2006; Widom, 1977).

Causes of Psychopathic Personality. Despite over five decades of research, the causes of psychopathic personality remain mysterious. Classic research shows that individuals with this disorder don't show much classical conditioning to unpleasant unconditioned stimuli, like electric shocks (Lykken, 1957). Similarly, when asked to sit patiently in a chair for an impending electric shock or loud blast of noise, their levels of skin conductance—an indicator of arousal—increase only about one-fifth as much as those without psychopathic personality (Hare, 1978; Lorber, 2004). These abnormalities probably stem from a deficit in fear, which may give rise to many of the other features of the disorder (Fowles & Dindo, 2009; Lykken, 1995; Patrick, 2006). Perhaps as a consequence of this dearth of fear, people with psychopathic personality aren't motivated to learn from punishment and tend to repeat the same mistakes in life (Newman & Kosson, 1986).

An alternative explanation is that individuals with this disorder are underaroused. As we learned in Chapter 11, the *Yerkes-Dodson law* describes a well-established psychological principle: an inverted U-shaped relationship between arousal, on the one hand, and mood and performance, on the other. As this law reminds us, people who are habitually underaroused experience *stimulus hunger:* They're bored and seek out excitement. The underarousal hypothesis may help to explain why those with psychopathic personality tend to be risk takers (Zuckerman, 1989), as well as why they frequently get in trouble with the law and abuse all manner of substances (Taylor & Lang, 2006). Nevertheless, the causal arrow between underarousal and psychopathy may run in the opposite direction: If people with psychopathic traits are fearless, they may experience little arousal in response to stimuli (Lykken, 1995).

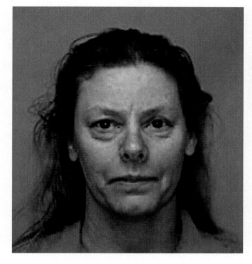

In rare cases, violent individuals with psychopathic personality are women (Arrigo & Griffin, 2004). Aileen Wuornos (pictured above), a serial killer called the Damsel of Death, was executed for the murders of six men she lured to their death by posing as a stranded driver. Charlize Theron won an Academy Award for her portrayal of Wuornos in the movie *Monster.*

FICTOID

MYTH: All people with psychopathic personality disorder are untreatable and can't be rehabilitated.

REALITY: Although the view that individuals with psychopathic personality are "hopeless cases" is widely accepted, recent evidence suggests that at least some people with this disorder may improve as a consequence of psychotherapy (Salekin, 2002; Skeem, Monahan, & Mulvey, 2002).

◀ ruling out rival hypotheses

HAVE IMPORTANT ALTERNATIVE EXPLANATIONS FOR THE FINDINGS BEEN EXCLUDED?

◀ correlation vs. causation

CAN WE BE SURE THAT A CAUSES B?

■ Dissociative Disorders

When speaking about ourselves, we use the words *me* and *I* without giving it a second thought. That's not the case in most **dissociative disorders**, which involve disruptions in consciousness, memory, identity, or perception (APA, 2000). The idea that one person can have more than one identity—let alone more than a hundred, as in the case of Nadean Cool whom we met in Chapter 7, is an extraordinary claim. So it's no wonder that dissociative identity disorder (DID) is one of the most controversial of all diagnoses. Before we consider the debate that swirls around this condition, we'll consider several other dissociative disorders.

extraordinary claims

IS THE EVIDENCE AS STRONG AS THE CLAIM?

dissociative disorder
condition involving disruptions in consciousness, memory, identity, or perception

depersonalization disorder
condition marked by multiple episodes of depersonalization

dissociative amnesia
inability to recall important personal information—most often related to a stressful experience—that can't be explained by ordinary forgetfulness

dissociative fugue
sudden, unexpected travel away from home or the workplace, accompanied by amnesia for significant life events

DEPERSONALIZATION DISORDER. If you've ever felt detached from yourself, as though you're living in a movie or dream or observing your body from the perspective of an outsider, you've experienced *depersonalization*. More than half of adults have experienced one brief episode of depersonalization, and such experiences are especially common among adolescents and college students (APA, 2000; Simeon et al., 1997). Only if experiences of depersonalization are frequent do people qualify for a diagnosis of **depersonalization disorder**. *Derealization*, the sense that the external world is strange or unreal, often accompanies both depersonalization and panic attacks.

DISSOCIATIVE AMNESIA. In **dissociative amnesia**, people can't recall important personal information—most often following a stressful experience—that isn't due to ordinary forgetting. Their memory loss is extensive, and can include suicide attempts or violent outbursts (Sar et al, 2007). More commonly, psychologists diagnose dissociative amnesia when adults report gaps in their memories for child abuse.

This diagnosis has proven controversial for several reasons. First, memory gaps regarding nontraumatic events are common in healthy individuals and aren't necessarily stress-related or indicative of dissociation (Belli et al., 1998). Second, most people may not be especially motivated to recall child abuse or other upsetting events. As Richard McNally (2003) pointed out, not thinking about something isn't the same as being *unable* to remember it, which is amnesia. Third, careful studies have turned up no convincing cases of amnesia that can't be explained by other factors, like disease, brain injury, normal forgetting, or an unwillingness to think about disturbing events (Kihlstrom, 2005; Pope et al., 2007).

ruling out rival hypotheses

HAVE IMPORTANT ALTERNATIVE EXPLANATIONS FOR THE FINDINGS BEEN EXCLUDED?

Jeffrey Ingram, age 40, experienced a dissociative fugue in which he claimed for over a month that he couldn't remember anything about his life. He was reunited with his fiancée in 2006 only after he appeared on television shows asking the public to identify him.

DISSOCIATIVE FUGUE. At times, we've all felt like running away from our troubles. In **dissociative fugue**, people not only forget significant events in their lives, but flee their stressful circumstances (*fugue* is Latin for "flight"). In some cases, they move to another city or another country, assuming a new identity. Fugues can last for hours or, in unusual cases, years. Dissociative fugue is rare, occurring in about two of every 1,000 people (APA, 2000), with more prolonged fugue states even rarer (Karlin & Orne, 1996).

In 2006, a 57-year-old husband, father, and Boy Scout leader from New York was found living under a new name in a homeless shelter in Chicago after he left his garage near his office and disappeared. When a tip to *America's Most Wanted* uncovered his true identity six months later, his family contacted him, but he claimed to have no memory of who they were (Brody, 2007).

In this and other fugue cases, it's essential to find out whether the fugue resulted from a head injury, stroke, or other neurological cause. Moreover, some people merely claim amnesia to avoid responsibilities or stressful circumstances, relocate to a different area, and get a fresh start in life. Even when fugues occur shortly after a traumatic event, it's difficult to know whether the trauma caused the amnesia. Scientists don't fully understand the role trauma, psychological factors, and neurological conditions play in fugue states (Kihlstrom, 2005).

correlation vs. causation

CAN WE BE SURE THAT A CAUSES B?

dissociative identity disorder (DID)
condition characterized by the presence of two or more distinct identities or personality states that recurrently take control of the person's behavior

DISSOCIATIVE IDENTITY DISORDER: MULTIPLE PERSONALITIES, MULTIPLE CONTROVERSIES. According to DSM-IV, **dissociative identity disorder (DID)** is characterized by the presence of two or more distinct identities or personality states, which are more temporary patterns of behavior. The identities or personality states recurrently assume control over the person's behavior. These alternate identities or "alters," as they're called, are often very different from the primary or "host" personality and may be of different names, ages, genders, and even races. In some cases, these features are the opposite of those exhibited by the host personality. For example, if the host personality is shy and retiring, one or more alters may be outgoing or flamboyant. Psychologists have reported the number of alters to range from one (the so-called split personality) to hundreds or even thousands, with one reported case of 4,500 personalities (Acocella, 1999). In general, women are more likely to receive a DID diagnosis and report more alters than men (APA, 2000).

Researchers have identified intriguing differences among alters in their respiration rates (Bahnson & Smith, 1975), brain wave activity (EEG; Ludwig et al., 1972), eyeglass prescriptions (Miller, 1989), handedness (Savitz et al., 2004), skin conductance responses (Brende, 1984), voice patterns, and handwriting (Lilienfeld & Lynn, 2003). Fascinating as these findings are, they don't provide conclusive evidence for the existence of alters. These differences could stem from changes in mood or thoughts over time or to bodily changes, such as muscle tension, that people can produce on a voluntary basis (Allen & Movius, 2000; Merkelbach, Devilly, & Rassin, 2002). Moreover, scientists have falsified claims that alters are truly distinct. When psychologists have used objective measures of memory, they've typically found that information presented to one alter is available to the other, providing no evidence for amnesia across alters (Allen & Moravius, 2000; Huntjens et al., 2006).

The primary controversy surrounding DID revolves around one question: Is DID a response to early trauma, or is it a consequence of social and cultural factors (Merskey, 1992)? According to the *posttraumatic model* (Gleaves, May, & Cardeña, 2001; Ross, 1997), DID arises from a history of severe abuse—physical, sexual, or both—during childhood. This abuse leads individuals to "compartmentalize" their identity into distinct alters as a means of coping with intense emotional pain. In this way, the person can feel as though the abuse happened to someone else. ⊕ **Explore**

Advocates of the posttraumatic model claim that 90 percent or more of individuals with DID were severely abused in childhood (Gleaves, 1996). Nevertheless, many studies that reported this association didn't check the accuracy of abuse claims against objective information, such as court records of abuse (Coons, Bowman, & Milstein, 1988). Moreover, researchers haven't shown that early abuse is specific to DID, as it's present in many other disorders (Pope & Hudson, 1992). These considerations don't exclude a role for early trauma in DID, but they suggest that researchers must conduct further controlled studies before drawing strong conclusions (Gleaves, 1996; Gleaves et al., 2001).

According to advocates of the competing *sociocognitive model* (see Chapter 5), the claim that some people have hundreds of personalities is extraordinary, but the evidence for it is unconvincing (Giesbrecht et al., 2008; Lilienfeld et al., 1999; McHugh, 1993; Merskey, 1992; Spanos, 1994, 1996). According to this model, people's expectancies and beliefs—shaped by certain psychotherapeutic procedures and cultural influences, rather than early traumas—account for the origin and maintenance of DID. Advocates of this model claim that some therapists—like those of Nadean Cool (see Chapter 7), use procedures, like hypnosis and repeated prompting of alters, that suggest to patients that their puzzling symptoms are the products of indwelling identities

"I HAVE 25 PATIENTS IN MY COUNSELING GROUP—MRS. SHERMAN, MR. MARTIN, AND MR. MARTIN'S 23 OTHER PERSONALITIES."

(*Source:* Dan Rosandich, www.CartoonStock.com)

▶ **ruling out rival hypotheses**

HAVE IMPORTANT ALTERNATIVE EXPLANATIONS FOR THE FINDINGS BEEN EXCLUDED?

▶ **falsifiability**

CAN THE CLAIM BE DISPROVED?

⊕ **Explore** Dissociative Identity Disorder on **mypsychlab.com**

like Sibyl? yeah, Sybil →

▶ **extraordinary claims**

IS THE EVIDENCE AS STRONG AS THE CLAIM?

▶ **ruling out rival hypotheses**

HAVE IMPORTANT ALTERNATIVE EXPLANATIONS FOR THE FINDINGS BEEN EXCLUDED?

Sheri Storm was diagnosed with dissociative identity disorder, but later became convinced that a therapist had inadvertently implanted her alter personalities using suggestive techniques. This painting—completed by Storm during therapy—depicts the seemingly endless parade of her alters emerging in treatment.

(Lilienfeld & Lynn, 2003; Lilienfeld et al., 1999). The following observations and findings support this hypothesis:

- Many or most DID patients show few or no clear-cut signs of this condition, such as alters, prior to psychotherapy (Kluft, 1984).
- Mainstream treatment techniques for DID reinforce the idea that the person possesses multiple identities. These techniques include using hypnosis to "bring forth" hidden alters, communicating with alters and giving them different names, and encouraging patients to recover repressed memories supposedly housed in dissociated selves (Spanos, 1994, 1996).
- The number of alters per DID individual tends to increase substantially when therapists use these techniques (Piper, 1997).

As of 1970, there were 79 documented cases of DID in the world literature. As of 1986, the number of DID cases had mushroomed to approximately 6,000 (Lilienfeld et al., 1999), and some estimates in the early 21st century are in the hundreds of thousands. The sociocognitive model holds that the popular media have played a pivotal role in the DID epidemic (Elzinga et al., 1998). Indeed, much of the dramatic increase in DID's prevalence followed closely on the release of the best-selling book *Sybil* (Schreiber, 1973) in the mid-1970s, later made into an Emmy Award–winning television movie starring Sally Field. The book and later film told the heartbreaking story of a young woman with 16 personalities who reported a history of sadistic child abuse. Interestingly, subsequently released audiotapes of Sybil's therapy sessions suggested that she had no alters or memories of child abuse prior to treatment, and that her therapist urged her to behave differently on different occasions (Rieber, 1999).

Over the past two decades, media coverage of DID has skyrocketed (Showalter, 1997; Spanos, 1996; Wilson, 2003), with some celebrities, like comedian Roseanne Barr and football star Hershel Walker, claiming to suffer from the disorder. Although DID is virtually nonexistent in Japan and India, it is now diagnosed with considerable frequency in some countries, such as Holland, in which it has recently received more publicity (Lilienfeld et al., 1999). In summary, there's considerable support for the sociocognitive model and the claim that therapists, along with the media, are creating alters rather than discovering them. The dissociative disorders provide a powerful, although troubling, example of how social and cultural forces can shape psychological disorders.

✓— **Study** and **Review** on **mypsychlab.com**

assess your knowledge　　　　　　　　　FACT OR FICTION?

1. Personality disorders are almost always reliably diagnosed. **True** / **False**
2. Borderline personality is among the most unstable of the personality disorders. **True** / **False**
3. Most people with psychopathic personality disorder are not habitually violent. **True** / **False**
4. Child abuse clearly causes DID. **True** / **False**
5. The media have played little role in the recent increase in DID diagnoses. **True** / **False**

Answers: 1. F (p. 611); 2. T (p. 612); 3. T (p. 613); 4. F (p. 615); 5. F (p. 616)

THE ENIGMA OF SCHIZOPHRENIA

15.10 Recognize the characteristic symptoms of schizophrenia.

15.11 Explain how psychosocial, neural, biochemical, and genetic influences create the vulnerability to schizophrenia.

schizophrenia
severe disorder of thought and emotion associated with a loss of contact with reality

Psychiatrist Daniel Weinberger has called **schizophrenia** the "cancer" of mental illness: It's perhaps the most severe of all disorders, and the most mysterious (Levy-Reiner, 1996). As we'll discover, it's a devastating disorder of thought and emotion associated with a loss of contact with reality. ⊙→ **Simulate**

⊙→ **Simulate** a Schizophrenia Overview on **mypsychlab.com**

■ Symptoms of Schizophrenia: The Shattered Mind

Even today, many people confuse schizophrenia with DID (Wahl, 1997). Swiss psychiatrist Eugen Bleuler gave us the modern term *schizophrenia* in 1911. The term literally means "split mind," which no doubt contributed to the popular myth that the symptoms of schizophrenia stem from a split personality. You may have even heard people refer to a "schizophrenic attitude" when explaining that they're "of two minds" regarding an issue. Don't be misled. As Bleuler recognized, the difficulties of individuals with schizophrenia arise from disturbances in attention, thinking, language, emotion, and relationships with others. In contrast to DID, which is supposedly characterized by multiple intact personalities, schizophrenia is characterized by one personality that's shattered.

Schizophrenia causes most of its sufferers' levels of functioning to plunge. More than half suffer from serious disabilities, such as an inability to hold a job and maintain close relationships (Harvey, Reichenberg, & Bowie, 2006). Indeed, a large proportion of homeless people would receive diagnoses of schizophrenia (Cornblatt, Green, & Walker, 1999). Individuals who experience schizophrenia comprise less than 1 percent of the population, with most estimates ranging from .4 to .7 percent (Saha et al., 2005). Yet they make up half of the approximately 100,000 patients in state and county mental institutions in the United States (Grob, 1997). But there's some good news. Today, more than ever, people with schizophrenia can function in society, even though they may need to return periodically to hospitals for treatment (Harding, Zubin, & Strauss, 1992; Lamb & Bachrach, 2001; Mueser & McGurk, 2004).

Researchers have struggled with the problem of describing schizophrenia since the 18th century, when Emil Kraepelin first outlined the features of patients with *dementia praecox,* meaning psychological deterioration in youth. But Kraepelin didn't get it quite right. Even though the typical onset of schizophrenia is in the mid-twenties for men and the late twenties for women, schizophrenia can also strike after age 45 (APA, 2000). Moreover, as many as one-half to two-thirds of people with schizophrenia improve significantly, although not completely, and a small percentage recover completely after a single episode (Harrow et al., 2005; Robinson et al., 2004).

DELUSIONS: FIXED FALSE BELIEFS. Among the hallmark symptoms of schizophrenia are **delusions**—strongly held fixed beliefs that have no basis in reality. Delusions are called **psychotic symptoms** because they represent a serious distortion of reality. Terrell, whom we met at the beginning of the chapter, experienced delusions that led to a suicide attempt.

Michael Medved
Culture Clash

WORLDNETDAILY EXCLUSIVE COMMENTARY

Liberals show schizophrenic approach to religion

Posted: December 23, 2002

A quick glance at the American left reveals a movement in the midst of a nervous breakdown, displaying behavior that goes beyond inconsistency into the realm of bipolar moods and multiple personality disorders.

Nowhere do these violently conflicting impulses manifest themselves more clearly than in the contradictory attitude toward religion.

? What's wrong with the headline of this opinion column (selected by the website, not the author), which refers to the conflicting attitudes of some liberals toward religion? (See answer upside down on bottom of page.)

First Person Account:
SCHIZOPHRENIA

"*The reflection in the store window—it's me, isn't it? I know it is, but it's hard to tell. Glassy shadows, polished pastels, a jigsaw puzzle of my body, face, and clothes, with pieces disappearing whenever I move.... Schizophrenia is painful, and it is craziness when I hear voices, when I believe people are following me, wanting to snatch my very soul. I am frightened, too, when every whisper, every laugh is about me; when newspapers suddenly contain cures, four-letter words shouting at me; when sparkles of light are demon eyes.*"

(McGrath, 1984)

British artist Louis Wain (1860–1939), famous for his paintings of cats, developed a severe psychiatric disorder—perhaps schizophrenia—relatively late in life. Some of his paintings, like the two shown here, seem to capture the profound psychological confusion and fragmentation typical of schizophrenia (although despite widespread claims, there's no good evidence that his paintings became more disturbed as he became increasingly ill).

delusion
strongly held, fixed belief that has no basis in reality

psychotic symptom
psychological problem reflecting serious distortions in reality

FACTOID

One of the more unusual delusions is *folie a deux* (French for the "folly of two"), known technically as "shared psychotic disorder" in DSM-IV. In *folie a deux,* one person in a close relationship, often a marriage, induces the same delusion in his or her partner. For example, both partners may end up convinced that the government is poisoning their food (Silveira & Seeman, 1995). Rare cases of *folie a deux* in identical twins, *folie a trois* (involving three people) and *folie a famille* (involving an entire family) have also been reported.

Delusions commonly involve themes of persecution. One of your book's authors treated a man who believed that coworkers tapped his phone and conspired to get him fired. Another was convinced that a helicopter in the distance beamed the Beatles song "All You Need Is Love" into his head to make him feel jealous and inadequate. The authors of your book have also treated patients who reported delusions of grandeur (greatness), including one who believed that she'd discovered the cure for cancer even though she had no medical training. Other delusions center on the body and may include a firm belief that one is infested with brain parasites or even that one is dead (so-called Cotard's syndrome). Still others involve elaborate themes of sexuality or romance. John Hinckley, the man who nearly assassinated then President Ronald Reagan in 1981, was convinced that murdering the president would gain him the affection of actress Jodie Foster.

HALLUCINATIONS: FALSE PERCEPTIONS. Among the other serious symptoms of schizophrenia are **hallucinations:** sensory perceptions that occur in the absence of an external stimulus. They can be auditory (involving hearing), olfactory (involving smell), gustatory (involving taste), tactile (involving the sense of feeling), or visual. Most hallucinations in schizophrenia are auditory, usually consisting of voices. In some patients, hallucinated voices express disapproval or carry on a running commentary about the person's thoughts or actions. *Command hallucinations,* which tell patients what to do ("Go over to that man and tell him to shut up!"), may be associated with a heightened risk of violence toward others (McNiel, Eisner, & Binder, 2000). Incidentally, extremely vivid or detailed visual hallucinations—especially in the absence of auditory hallucinations—are usually signs of an organic (medical) disorder or substance abuse rather than schizophrenia (Shea, 1998).

? In the 2001 film, "A Beautiful Mind," actor Russell Crowe (*left*) portrays Nobel Prize–winning mathematician John Nash, who was diagnosed with schizophrenia. In this scene, Nash is shown talking to a friend whom he sees—but does not exist. **What's scientifically unrealistic about this scene?** (See answer upside down on bottom of page.)

Do your thoughts sound like voices in your head? Many people experience their thoughts as inner speech, which is entirely normal. Some researchers suggest that auditory hallucinations occur when people with schizophrenia believe mistakenly that their inner speech arises from a source outside themselves (Bentall, 2000; Frith, 1992; Thomas, 1997). Brain scans reveal that when people experience auditory hallucinations, brain areas associated with speech perception and production become activated (McGuire, Shah, & Murray, 1993).

DISORGANIZED SPEECH. Consider a 39-year-old patient with schizophrenia's reply to the question of whether he felt that people imitated him. "Yes ... I don't quite gather. I know one right and one left use both hands but I can't follow the system that's working. The idea is meant in a kind way, but it's not the way I understand life. It seems to be people taking sides. If certain people agree with me they speak, and if not, they don't. Everybody seems to be the doctor and Mr. H. [his own name] in turn" (Mayer-Gross, Slater, & Roth, 1969, p. 177).

We can see that his language skips from topic to topic in a disjointed way. Most researchers believe that this peculiar language results from thought disorder (Meehl, 1962; Stirk et al., 2008). The usual associations that we forge between two words, such as mother–child, are considerably weakened or highly unusual for individuals with schizophrenia (for example, mother–rug) (Kuperberg et al., 2006). In severe forms, the resulting speech is so jumbled that it's almost impossible to understand, leading psychologists to describe it as *word salad.* Language problems, like thought disorder, point to fundamental impairments in schizophrenia in the ability to shift and maintain attention, which influence virtually every aspect of affected individuals' daily lives (Cornblatt & Keilp, 1994; Fuller et al., 2006).

hallucination
sensory perception that occurs in the absence of an external stimulus

Answer: Extremely vivid or detailed visual hallucinations are very rare in schizophrenia.

TABLE 15.12 Main Subtypes of Schizophrenia.

Paranoid Type	Characterized primarily by prominent delusions or auditory hallucinations. Most commonly, the delusions are persecutory or grandiose, but often the two types of delusions are combined, and organized around a consistent theme. Apart from specific delusions, the person's ability to think, reason, and express feelings may not be impaired. Accordingly, paranoid schizophrenics function at a higher level than individuals with other types of schizophrenia.
Disorganized Type	Characterized by disorganized speech and behavior, as well as flat or inappropriate affect, such as unpredictable giggling. Delusions and hallucinations, if present, are not well organized into a single theme and often are short-lived.
Catatonic Type	Characterized by one or more catatonic symptoms. Catatonic patients can harm themselves or others when they are in a stupor and are immobile or when they are extremely excited and agitated. Malnutrition, exhaustion, and self-inflicted injuries are possible.

(*Source:* Data, *DSM-IV*, APA, 2000)

GROSSLY DISORGANIZED BEHAVIOR AND CATATONIA. When people develop schizophrenia, self-care, personal hygiene, and motivation often deteriorate. They may avoid conversation; laugh, cry, or swear inappropriately; or wear a warm coat on a sweltering summer day.

Catatonic symptoms involve motor (movement) problems, such as extreme resistance to complying with even simple suggestions, holding the body in bizarre or rigid postures, or curling up in a fetal position. Catatonic individuals' withdrawal can be so severe that they refuse to speak and move, or they may pace aimlessly. They may also repeat a phrase in conversation in a parrotlike manner, a symptom called *echolalia.* At the opposite extreme, they may occasionally engage in bouts of frenzied, purposeless motor activity (see **TABLE 15.12**).

■ Explanations for Schizophrenia: The Roots of a Shattered Mind

Today, virtually all scientists believe that psychosocial factors play some role in schizophrenia. Nevertheless, they also agree that these factors probably trigger the disorder only in people with a genetic vulnerability.

THE FAMILY AND EXPRESSED EMOTION. Early theories of schizophrenia mistakenly laid the blame for the condition on mothers, with so-called *schizophrenogenic* (schizophrenia-producing) mothers being the prime culprits. Based on informal observations of families of children with schizophrenia, some authors described such mothers as overprotective, smothering, rejecting, and controlling (Arieti, 1959; Lidz, 1973). Other theorists pointed the finger of blame at the interactions among all family members (Dolnick, 1998).

But as important as clinical experience can be in generating hypotheses, it doesn't provide an adequate arena for testing them (see Chapter 2). Indeed, these early studies were severely flawed, largely because they lacked control groups of people without schizophrenia. A now widely accepted rival hypothesis is that family members' responses aren't the cause of schizophrenia, but instead are typically a response to the stressful experience of living with a severely disturbed person.

It's widely acknowledged that parents and family members don't "cause" schizophrenia (Gottesman, 1991; Walker et al., 2004). Still, families may influence whether patients with the disorder relapse. After leaving hospitals, patients experience more than twice the likelihood of relapse (50 to 60 percent) when their relatives display high *expressed emotion* (EE)—that is, criticism, hostility, and overinvolvement (Brown et al., 1962; Butzlaff & Hooley, 1998). Criticism is especially predictive of relapse (Halweg et al., 1989; McCarty et

Catatonic individuals, like the one shown here, may permit their limbs to be moved to any position, and maintain this posture for lengthy periods of time, a condition called *waxy flexibility.*

ruling out rival hypotheses
HAVE IMPORTANT ALTERNATIVE EXPLANATIONS FOR THE FINDINGS BEEN EXCLUDED?

catatonic symptom
motor problem, including extreme resistance to complying with simple suggestions, holding the body in bizarre or rigid postures, or curling up in a fetal position

al., 2004), and may result in part from relatives' frustrations in living with a person with schizophrenia who displays disruptive behaviors. Indeed, EE may reflect family members' reactions to their loved one's schizophrenia as much as contribute to their loved one's relapse (King, 2000).

The apparent effects of EE vary across ethnic groups. Critical comments from family members may undermine recovering patients' confidence and sense of independence, which are valued in Caucasian American culture (Chentsova-Dutton & Tsai, 2007). In contrast, in Mexican American culture, independence isn't as highly valued, so criticism doesn't predict relapse. Nevertheless, a lack of family warmth, which is prized in Mexican American families, does predict relapse (Lopez et al., 2004). Moreover, in African American families, high levels of EE predict *better* outcomes among individuals with schizophrenia, perhaps because family members perceive EE as an expression of openness, honesty, and caring (Rosenfarb, Bellack, & Aziz, 2006). Although EE often predicts relapse, well-controlled studies don't support the hypothesis that child rearing directly *causes* schizophrenia, any more than does extreme poverty, childhood trauma, or parental conflict, all of which are correlated with schizophrenia (Cornblatt, Green, & Walker, 1999; Schofield & Balian, 1959).

SCHIZOPHRENIA: BRAIN, BIOCHEMICAL, AND GENETIC FINDINGS. Research using a variety of technologies has uncovered intriguing biological clues to the causes of schizophrenia. We'll focus on three such clues: brain abnormalities, neurotransmitter differences, and genetic findings.

Brain Abnormalities. Research indicates that one or more of four fluid-filled structures called *ventricles* (see Chapter 3), which cushion and nourish the brain, are typically enlarged in individuals with schizophrenia. This finding is important for two reasons. First, these brain areas frequently expand when others shrink (Barta et al., 1990; Raz & Raz, 1990), suggesting that schizophrenia is a disorder of brain deterioration. Second, deterioration in these areas is associated with thought disorder (Vita et al., 1995).

Other brain abnormalities in schizophrenia include increases in the size of the *sulci,* or spaces between the ridges of the brain (Cannon, Mednick, & Parnas, 1989), and decreases in (a) the size of the temporal lobes (Boos et al., 2007; Job et al., 2005), (b) activation of the amygdala and hippocampus (Hempel et al., 2003), and (c) in the symmetry of the brain's hemispheres (Luchins, Weinberger, & Wyatt, 1982; Zivotofsky et al., 2007). Functional brain imaging studies show that the frontal lobes of people with schizophrenia are less active than those of nonpatients when engaged in demanding mental tasks (Andreasen et al., 1992; Knyazeva et al., 2008), a phenomenon called *hypofrontality.* Still, it's not clear whether these findings are causes or consequences of the disorder. For example, hypofrontality could be due to the tendency of patients with schizophrenia to concentrate less on tasks compared with other individuals. Researchers also need to rule out alternative explanations for brain underactivity that could arise from patients' diet, drinking and smoking habits, and medication use (Hanson & Gottesman, 2005).

Some studies have suggested that marijuana use in adolescence can bring about schizophrenia and other psychotic disorders in genetically vulnerable individuals (Compton et al., 2009; Degenhardt et al., 2009; Degenhardt & Hall, 2006). Nevertheless, it's difficult to pin down a causal relationship between marijuana use and schizophrenia for three reasons: (1) people who use marijuana are likely to use a variety of other drugs, which they may be reluctant to report on surveys; (2) individuals with schizophrenia may be more likely to use marijuana, so the causal arrow may be reversed, and (3) the rates of schizophrenia remained stable between 1970–2005 in the United Kingdom, although marijuana use increased over this period (Frisher et al., 2009). Still, people with a personal or family history of psychotic disorders, including schizophrenia, would be particularly ill advised to use marijuana.

Neurotransmitter Differences. The biochemistry of the brain is one of the keys to unlocking the mystery of schizophrenia. One early explanation was the *dopamine hypothesis* (Carlsson, 1995; Keith et al., 1976; Nicol & Gottesman, 1983). The evidence for the role of dopamine in schizophrenia is mostly indirect. First, most antischizophrenic drugs block dopamine receptor sites. To put it crudely, they "slow down" nerve impulses by partially

---

correlation vs. causation

CAN WE BE SURE THAT A CAUSES B?

correlation vs. causation

CAN WE BE SURE THAT A CAUSES B?

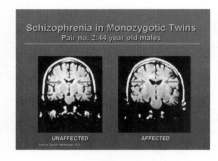

In one identical twin with schizophrenia, the fluid-filled ventricles of the brain (*see red arrows*) are enlarged relative to his or her co-twin without schizophrenia. Such enlargement probably reflects a deterioration in brain tissue surrounding the ventricles, which expand to fill the missing space.

correlation vs. causation

CAN WE BE SURE THAT A CAUSES B?

ruling out rival hypotheses

HAVE IMPORTANT ALTERNATIVE EXPLANATIONS FOR THE FINDINGS BEEN EXCLUDED?

correlation vs. causation

CAN WE BE SURE THAT A CAUSES B?

blocking the action of dopamine (see Chapters 3 and 16). Second, amphetamine, a stimulant (see Chapter 5) that blocks the reuptake of dopamine, tends to worsen the symptoms of schizophrenia (Lieberman & Koreen, 1993; Snyder, 1975).

Nevertheless, the hypothesis that a simple excess of dopamine creates the symptoms of schizophrenia doesn't seem to fit the data. A better-supported rival hypothesis is that abnormalities in dopamine *receptors* produce these symptoms. Receptor sites in the brain appear to be highly specific for dopamine transmission. These sites respond uniquely to drugs designed to reduce psychotic symptoms and are associated with difficulties in attention, memory, and motivation (Busatto, 1995; Keefe & Henry, 1994; Reis et al., 2004).

These findings provide evidence for a direct tie between dopamine pathways and symptoms of schizophrenia, such as paranoia. As we've seen, some symptoms of schizophrenia represent excesses of normal functions and include hallucinations, delusions, and disorganized speech and behavior. We can contrast these *positive symptoms* with *negative symptoms,* which reflect decreases or losses of normal functions. These symptoms include social withdrawal and diminished motivations, decreased expression of emotions, and brief and limited speech (Andreasen et al., 1995). People with schizophrenia are less impaired when their symptoms are predominantly positive rather than negative (Harvey, Reichenberg, & Bowie, 2006). There's evidence that positive symptoms result from dopamine excesses in some brain regions, and negative symptoms from dopamine deficits in other brain regions (Davis et al., 1991). However, the causes of negative symptoms are difficult to pinpoint, because they may arise from prolonged institutionalization and medication side effects (see Chapter 16). Dopamine is probably only one of several neurotransmitters that play a role in schizophrenia; other likely candidates are norepinephrine, glutamate, and serotonin (Cornblatt, Green, & Walker, 1999; Grace, 1991).

Genetic Influences. Still unresolved is the question of which biological deficits are present prior to schizophrenia and which appear after the disorder begins (Seidman et al., 2003). The seeds of schizophrenia are often sown well before birth and lie partly in individuals' genetic endowment. As we can see in **FIGURE 15.4**, being the offspring of someone diagnosed with schizophrenia greatly increases one's odds of developing the disorder. If we have a sibling with schizophrenia, we have about a one in 10 chance of developing the disorder; these odds are about 10 times higher than those of the average person. As genetic similarity increases, so does the risk of schizophrenia. **Watch**

Still, it's possible the environment accounts for these findings because siblings not only share genes, but also grow up in the same family. To eliminate this ambiguity, researchers have conducted twin studies, which provide convincing support for a genetic influence on schizophrenia. If we have an identical twin with schizophrenia, our risk rises to about 50 percent. An identical twin of a person with schizophrenia is about three times as likely as a fraternal twin of a person with schizophrenia to develop the disorder, and about 50 times as likely as an average person (Gottesman & Shields, 1972; Kendler & Diehl, 1993; Meehl, 1962). Adoption data also point to a genetic influence. Even when children who have a biological parent with schizophrenia are adopted by parents with no hint of the disorder, their risk of schizophrenia is greater than that of a person with no biological relative with schizophrenia (Gottesman, 1991). Interestingly, scientists have identified structural brain abnormalities, like ventricular enlargement and decreases in brain volume, in the healthy close relatives of patients with schizophrenia, further suggesting that genetic influences produce a vulnerability to schizophrenia (Staal et al., 2000).

ruling out rival hypotheses
HAVE IMPORTANT ALTERNATIVE EXPLANATIONS FOR THE FINDINGS BEEN EXCLUDED?

"Hey you: you gotta breathe; you gotta we'll be okay" ♥

correlation vs. causation
CAN WE BE SURE THAT A CAUSES B?

Watch Genetic Schizophrenia on mypsychlab.com

ruling out rival hypotheses
HAVE IMPORTANT ALTERNATIVE EXPLANATIONS FOR THE FINDINGS BEEN EXCLUDED?

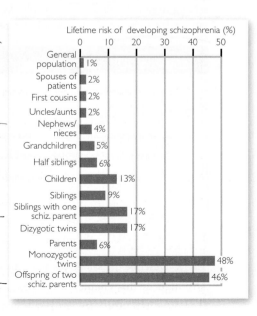

Lifetime risk of developing schizophrenia (%)

General population	1%
Spouses of patients	2%
First cousins	2%
Uncles/aunts	2%
Nephews/ nieces	4%
Grandchildren	5%
Half siblings	6%
Children	13%
Siblings	9%
Siblings with one schiz. parent	17%
Dizygotic twins	17%
Parents	6%
Monozygotic twins	48%
Offspring of two schiz. parents	46%

FIGURE 15.4 Schizophrenia Risk and the Family. The lifetime risk of developing schizophrenia is largely a function of how closely an individual is genetically related to a person with schizophrenia. (*Source:* Feldman, 1991)

Many people with schizotypal personality disorder are prone to "magical thinking"—the belief that their thoughts can influence actions through supernatural or otherwise mysterious processes. For example, they may believe that stepping on a crack in the sidewalk will create misfortune.

FACTOID ✚

Data show that more people with schizophrenia are born in the winter and spring than at other times of the year (Davies et al., 2003; Torrey et al., 1997). The reason for this strange finding doesn't appear to lie in astrology: Certain viral infections that affect pregnant women and that may trigger schizophrenia in vulnerable fetuses are most common in winter months.

VULNERABILITY TO SCHIZOPHRENIA: DIATHESIS-STRESS MODELS. Diathesis-stress models incorporate much of what we know about schizophrenia. Such models propose that schizophrenia, along with many other mental disorders, is a joint product of a genetic vulnerability, called a *diathesis,* and stressors that trigger this vulnerability (Meehl, 1962; Walker & DiForio, 1997; Zubin & Spring, 1977).

Paul Meehl (1990) suggested that approximately 10 percent of the population has a genetic predisposition to schizophrenia. What are people with this predisposition like? During adolescence and adulthood, they may strike us as "odd ducks." They may seem socially uncomfortable, and their speech, thought processes, and perceptions may impress us as unusual. They're likely to endorse items on psychological tests such as "Occasionally, I have felt as though my body did not exist" (Chapman, Chapman, & Raulin, 1978). Such individuals display symptoms of psychosis-proneness or *schizotypal personality disorder* (refer to Table 15.11 on page 611). Most people with schizotypal personality disorder don't develop full-blown schizophrenia, perhaps because they have a weaker genetic vulnerability or because they've experienced fewer stressors.

Well before people experience symptoms of schizophrenia, we can identify "early warning signs" or markers of vulnerability to this condition. People with schizotypal personality disorder display some of these markers, which include social withdrawal, thought and movement abnormalities (Mittal et al., 2007; Walker, Baum, & DiForio, 1998), learning and memory deficits (Volgmaier et al., 2000), elevated neuroticism (Lonnqvist et al., 2009), temporal lobe abnormalities (Siever & Davis, 2004), impaired attention (Keefe et al., 1997), and eye movement disturbances when tracking moving objects (Iacono, 1985; Lenzenweger, McLachlan, & Rubin, 2007). Their difficulties begin early in life. Elaine Walker and Richard Lewine (1990) found that people who viewed home movies of siblings interacting could identify which children later developed schizophrenia at better-than-chance levels. Even at an early age, vulnerable children's lack of emotions and decreased eye contact and social responsiveness tipped off observers. This design is valuable because it gets around the retrospective bias (see Chapter 7) introduced by asking adults to report on their childhood experiences.

But most people with a vulnerability to schizophrenia don't develop it. Whether someone ends up with the disorder depends, in part, on the impact of events that interfere with normal development. Children of women who had the flu during their second trimester of pregnancy (Brown et al., 2004; Mednick et al., 1988), suffered starvation early in pregnancy (Susser & Lyn, 1992), or experienced complications while giving birth (Weinberger, 1987) are at a somewhat heightened risk of schizophrenia. Viral infections in the uterus may also play a key role in triggering certain cases of schizophrenia (Walker & DiForio, 1997). But the great majority of people exposed to infection or trauma before birth never show signs of schizophrenia. So these events probably create problems only for people who are genetically vulnerable to begin with (Cornblatt, Green, & Walker, 1999; Verdoux, 2004).

✔●—**Study** and **Review** on **mypsychlab.com**

| assess your knowledge | FACT OR FICTION? |

1. Delusions are rare in schizophrenia. **True / False**
2. Most hallucinations in schizophrenia are visual. **True / False**
3. Schizophrenogenic mothers often cause schizophrenia. **True / False**
4. The evidence for the dopamine hypothesis is mostly indirect. **True / False**
5. There's little support for the genetic transmission of schizophrenia. **True / False**

Answers: 1. F (p. 617); 2. F (p. 618); 3. F (p. 619); 4. T (p. 620); 5. F (p. 621)

diathesis-stress model
perspective proposing that mental disorders are a joint product of a genetic vulnerability, called a diathesis, and stressors that trigger this vulnerability

CHILDHOOD DISORDERS: RECENT CONTROVERSIES

15.12 Describe the symptoms and debate surrounding disorders diagnosed in childhood.

Although in this chapter we've focused primarily on disorders of adulthood, we'll now close with a few words about childhood disorders, especially those that have been front and center in the public eye. Each of the disorders we'll consider—autistic disorder, attention-deficit/hyperactivity disorder, and early onset bipolar disorder—have garnered their share of controversy in the popular media and the scientific community.

■ Autistic Disorders

One in 100. That's the proportion of individuals with **autistic disorder** (better known as autism) in the population that you may have seen on television commercials or read about in magazines. Although this proportion may not seem all that high, it's remarkably high compared with the figure of one in 2,000 to 2,500, which researchers had until recently accepted for many years (Wing & Potter, 2002). Across a mere 10-year period—from 1993 to 2003—statistics from the United States Department of Education revealed a 657 percent increase in the rates of autism (technically called infantile autism) across the country (see **FIGURE 15.5**). In Wisconsin, the increase was a staggering 15,117 percent (Rust, 2006). These dramatic upsurges in the prevalence of autism have led many researchers and educators, and even some politicians, to speak of an autism "epidemic" (Kippes & Garrison, 2006). But is the epidemic real? ◉ **Watch**

As we learned in Chapter 2, individuals with autism are marked by severe deficits in language, social bonding, and imagination, usually accompanied by mental retardation (APA, 2000). The causes of autism remain mysterious, although twin studies suggest that genetic influences play a prominent role (Rutter, 2000). Still, genetic influences alone can't easily account for an astronomical rise in a disorder's prevalence over the span of a decade. It's therefore not surprising that researchers have looked to environmental variables to explain this bewildering increase. In particular, some investigators have pointed their fingers squarely at one potential culprit: vaccines (Rimland, 2004). Much of the hype surrounding the vaccine–autism link was fueled by a study of only 12 children in the late 1990s (Wakefield et al., 1998) demonstrating an apparent linkage between autistic symptoms and the MMR vaccine, the vaccine for mumps, measles, and rubella, also known as German measles (the journal *Lancet*, which published the study, officially retracted it in 2010, saying that Wakefield never received ethical clearance for the investigation and that the article contained false claims about subject recruitment). The symptoms of autism usually become most apparent shortly after the age of two, not long after infants have received MMR and other vaccinations for a host of diseases. Indeed, tens of thousands of parents insist that their children developed autism following the MMR vaccine, or following vaccines containing a preservative known as *thimerosol*, which is present in many mercury-bearing vaccines. Nevertheless, studies in the United States, Europe, and Japan failed to replicate the association between the MMR vaccine and autism, strongly suggesting that the seeming correlation between vaccinations and autism was a mirage (Offit, 2008). The results of several large American, European, and Japanese studies show that even as the rate of MMR

Many parents remain convinced that vaccines trigger autism, despite scientific evidence to the contrary.

◉ **Watch** Autistic Children on **mypsychlab.com**

replicability

CAN THE RESULTS BE DUPLICATED IN OTHER STUDIES?

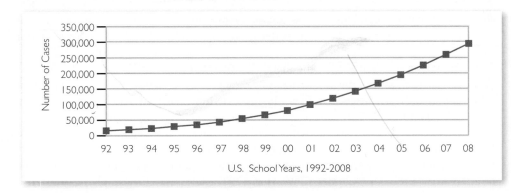

FIGURE 15.5 **The Autism Epidemic in America from 1992 to 2008.** The fact that autism diagnoses have been skyrocketing isn't controversial—but the reasons for the increase are.

autistic disorder
disorder (also known as autism) marked by severe deficits in language, social bonding, and imagination, usually accompanied by mental retardation

vaccinations remained constant or declined, the rate of autism diagnoses continued to soar (Herbert, Sharp, & Gaudiano, 2002; Honda, Shimizu, & Rutter, 2005). Moreover, even after the Danish government stopped administering thimerosol-containing vaccines, the prevalence of autism still skyrocketed (Madsen et al., 2002).

Many parents of children with autism probably fell prey to *illusory correlation* (see Chapter 2); they'd "seen" a statistical association that didn't exist. Their error was entirely understandable. Given that their children had received vaccines and developed autistic symptoms at around the same time, it was only natural to perceive an association between the two events.

Making matters more complex, recent research calls into question the very existence of the autism epidemic (Grinker, 2007; Wilson, 2005). Most previous investigators had neglected to take into account an alternative explanation—changes in diagnostic practices over time, which have expanded the autism diagnosis to include more mildly affected children, including some with a condition called *Asperger's disorder* (which appears to be a mild form of autism). Evidence suggests that more liberal diagnostic criteria rather than vaccines can account for most, if not all, of the reported autism epidemic (Gernsbacher, Dawson, & Goldsmith, 2005; Lilienfeld & Arkowitz, 2007). In addition, the Americans with Disabilities Act and Individuals with Disabilities Education Act, both passed in the 1990s, indirectly encouraged school districts to classify more children as having autism and other developmental disabilities, as these children could now receive more extensive educational accommodations.

Of course, at least a small part of the epidemic might be genuine, and some still unidentified environmental cause could account for the increase. But in evaluating the evidence, we should ask ourselves a critical question. Which is more parsimonious as an explanation of a 657 percent increase within one decade, a vaccine that's yet to be shown to produce any increase in the symptoms of autism, or a simple change in diagnostic practices?

ruling out rival hypotheses

HAVE IMPORTANT ALTERNATIVE EXPLANATIONS FOR THE FINDINGS BEEN EXCLUDED?

occam's razor

DOES A SIMPLER EXPLANATION FIT THE DATA JUST AS WELL?

■ Attention-Deficit/Hyperactivity Disorder and Early-Onset Bipolar Disorder

Even the best-adjusted children often appear overactive, energetic, and restless. But children with **attention-deficit/hyperactivity disorder (ADHD)** often behave like caricatures of the exuberant child. You probably know or have known someone with ADHD: 3 to 7 percent of school-age children satisfy the diagnostic criteria for the disorder (Barkley, 2006; Bird, 2002). The male to female ratio of ADHD ranges from 3.4 to 1 across studies, and between 30 and 80 percent of children with ADHD continue to display ADHD symptoms into adolescence and adulthood (Barkley, 2006; Monastra, 2006). The ADHD diagnosis subsumes two subtypes, one with hyperactivity, and one without hyperactivity, in which inattention is predominant (APA, 2000).

SYMPTOMS OF ADHD. The first signs of ADHD may be evident as early as infancy. Parents often report that children with ADHD are fussy, cry incessantly, and frequently move and shift their position in the crib (Wolke, Rizzo, & Woods, 2002). By three years of age, they're constantly walking or climbing, restless, and prone to emotional outbursts. But it's not until elementary school that their behavior patterns are likely to be labeled "hyperactive" and a treatment referral made. Teachers complain that such children won't remain in their seats, follow directions, or pay attention, and that they display temper tantrums with little provocation. Such children often struggle with learning disabilities, difficulties with processing verbal information, and poor balance and coordination (Jerome, 2000; Mangeot et al., 2001). By middle childhood, academic problems and disruptive behavior are frequently evident.

A high level of physical activity often diminishes as children with ADHD mature and approach adolescence. Nevertheless, by adolescence, impulsiveness, restlessness, inattention, problems with peers, delinquency, and academic difficulties comprise a patchwork of adjustment problems (Barkley, 2006; Hoza, 2007; Kelly, 2009). Alcohol and substance abuse are frequent (Molina & Pelham, 2003), and many adolescents with ADHD appear in juvenile courts as a result of running away from home, school truancy, and theft (Foley,

---

FICTOID ✖

MYTH: Children with ADHD can't concentrate.

REALITY: Sit with a child with ADHD playing her favorite computer game, and you'll probably be impressed with her intense concentration. If you were to interrupt her play, don't be surprised if she gets frustrated, edgy, and angry. This curious phenomenon occurs because children with ADHD can indeed concentrate, and even "hyperfocus," when something captures their attention; however, they experience difficulty shifting their attention to focus on tasks that *aren't* attention-grabbing, like homework or chores (Barkley, 1997).

---

attention-deficit/hyperactivity disorder (ADHD)
childhood condition marked by excessive inattention, impulsivity, and activity

Carlton, & Howell, 1996). Adults with ADHD are at increased risk for accidents and injuries (Woodward, Fergusson, & Horwood, 2000), divorce (Wymbs et al., 2008), unemployment, and contacts with the legal system (Hinshaw, 2002).

ADHD appears to be genetically influenced in many cases, with estimates of its heritability as high as .80 (Swanson & Castellanos, 2002). What may be inherited are abnormalities in genes that influence (a) serotonin, dopamine, and norepinephrine; (b) a smaller brain volume; and (c) decreased activation in the frontal areas of the brain (Monastra, 2008).

As we'll see in Chapter 16, people with ADHD can be treated successfully with stimulant medications. Nevertheless, these medications occasionally have serious side effects, making accurate diagnosis a serious public health issue. Yet an accurate diagnosis of ADHD can be dicey. A host of conditions that can cause problems in attention and behavioral control, including traumatic brain injuries, diabetes, thyroid problems, vitamin deficiencies, anxiety, and depression, must first be ruled out (Monastra, 2008). Additionally, there's sometimes a fine line between highly energetic children and those with mild ADHD. As a consequence, some scholars have expressed concerns that ADHD is overdiagnosed in some settings (Lefever, Arcona, & Antonuccio, 2004), although others point to evidence that some children with ADHD are actually overlooked by many diagnosticians (Sciutto & Eisenberg, 2007).

Many children have problems concentrating. There can be a fine line between children who have trouble paying attention in class and children diagnosed with ADHD.

THE CONTROVERSY OVER EARLY-ONSET BIPOLAR DISORDER. Perhaps the most controversial diagnostic challenge is distinguishing children with ADHD from children with bipolar disorder (Meyer & Carlson, 2008). The diagnosis of early-onset bipolar disorder was once rare, but ballooned from only .42 percent of cases of outpatient mental health visits in the early 1990s to 6.67 percent of such visits in 2003 (Moreno et al., 2007), raising concerns about its overdiagnosis. Children are particularly likely to receive a diagnosis of early-onset bipolar disorder when they show rapid mood changes, reckless behavior, irritability, and aggression (McClellan, Kowatch, & Findling, 2007). Popular books like *The Bipolar Child* (Papolos & Papolos, 2007), which list these and other symptoms, catch the eye of many parents with troubled children and raise concerns about bipolar disorder. Yet a moment's reflection suggests that many children fit this description, and surely many children with ADHD can be so characterized. Because 60 to 90 percent of children with bipolar disorder share an ADHD diagnosis, a hypothesis to consider is that many children diagnosed with bipolar disorder are merely those with severe symptoms of ADHD, such as extreme temper outbursts and mood swings (Geller et al., 2002; Kim & Miklowitz, 2002).

◀ ruling out rival hypotheses

HAVE IMPORTANT ALTERNATIVE EXPLANATIONS FOR THE FINDINGS BEEN EXCLUDED?

Research that tracks children diagnosed with bipolar disorder to determine whether they display classic symptoms of the disorder, such as manic episodes, in adulthood, may help to resolve the question of whether the symptoms observed in childhood are truly early expressions of bipolar disorder. Meanwhile, a thorough evaluation involving parents, teachers, and mental health professionals is essential to an accurate diagnosis of early-onset bipolar disorder, as well as ADHD.

---

assess your knowledge   FACT OR FICTION?

✓● Study and Review on mypsychlab.com

1. The rates of diagnosed autism have sharply declined in recent years. **True** / **False**

2. Most cases of autism are ~~caused~~ *correlated* by vaccines. **True** / **False**

3. More boys than girls are diagnosed with ADHD. **True** / **False**

4. Parents first notice their children's attention problems in elementary *3 yr rs* school. **True** / **False**

5. Children with bipolar disorder are likely to also be diagnosed with ADHD. **True** / **False**

Answers: 1. F (p. 623); 2. F (p. 624); 3. T (p. 624); 4. F (p. 624); 5. T (p. 625).

YOUR COMPLETE REVIEW SYSTEM

✓● Study and Review on mypsychlab.com

CONCEPTIONS OF MENTAL ILLNESS: YESTERDAY AND TODAY 584–597

15.1 IDENTIFY CRITERIA FOR DEFINING MENTAL DISORDERS.

The concept of mental disorder is difficult to define. Nevertheless, criteria for mental disorders include statistical rarity, subjective distress, impairment, societal disapproval, and biological dysfunction. Some scholars argue that mental illness is best captured by a family resemblance view.

1. Describe the family resemblance view of mental disorder. (p. 586)

15.2 DESCRIBE CONCEPTIONS OF DIAGNOSES ACROSS HISTORY AND CULTURES.

The demonic model of mental illness was followed by the medical model of the Renaissance. In the early 1950s, medications to treat schizophrenia led to deinstitutionalization. Some psychological conditions are culture-specific. Still, many mental disorders, such as schizophrenia, can be found in most or all cultures.

2. During the Middle Ages, _____ was often used to treat mental illness. (p. 586)

3. Institutions for the mentally ill created in the 15th century were known as _____. (p. 586)

4. In America in the 19th century, Dorothea Dix advocated for _____ _____, an approach calling for dignity, kindness, and respect for those with mental illness. (p. 587)

5. In the early 1950s, medications that treated schizophrenia, like chlorpromazine, led to a government policy called _____. (p. 587)

6. Some eating disorders are examples of a _____ disorder specific to Western cultures. (p. 589)

15.3 IDENTIFY COMMON MISCONCEPTIONS ABOUT PSYCHIATRIC DIAGNOSES, AND THE STRENGTHS AND LIMITATIONS OF THE CURRENT DIAGNOSTIC SYSTEM.

Misconceptions include the ideas that a diagnosis is nothing more than pigeonholing, and that diagnoses are unreliable, invalid, and stigmatizing. The Diagnostic and Statistical Manual of Mental Disorders (DSM-IV) is a valuable tool that contains separate axes for psychiatric diagnoses, medical conditions, life stressors, and overall life functioning. Its limitations include high levels of comorbidity and an assumption of a categorical model in the absence of compelling evidence.

7. What misconception regarding psychiatric diagnosis is fueled by high-profile media coverage of "dueling expert witnesses" in criminal trials? (p. 589)

(((•● Listen to an audio file of your chapter on mypsychlab.com

8. The DSM-IV asks psychologists and psychiatrists to assess patients along multiple _____, or dimensions of functioning. (p. 592)

9. The diagnostic criteria used to classify individuals with mental disorders in DSM-IV (are/are not) based completely on scientific evidence. (p. 593)

10. One of the problems with the DSM-IV is the high level of _____ among many of its diagnoses. (p. 593)

ANXIETY DISORDERS: THE MANY FACES OF WORRY AND FEAR 597–602

15.4 DESCRIBE THE MANY WAYS PEOPLE EXPERIENCE ANXIETY.

Panic attacks involve intense yet brief rushes of fear that are greatly out of proportion to the actual threat. People with generalized anxiety disorder spend much of their day worrying. In phobias, fears are intense and highly focused. In posttraumatic stress disorder, extremely stressful events produce enduring anxiety. Obsessive-compulsive disorder is marked by intensely disturbing thoughts, senseless or irrational rituals, or both. Learning theory proposes that fears can be learned via classical and operant conditioning and observation. Anxious people tend to catastrophize or exaggerate the likelihood of negative events. Many anxiety disorders are genetically influenced.

11. People with _____ _____ _____ spend an average of 60 percent of each day worrying. (p. 598)

12. People suffer from _____ _____ when they experience panic attacks that are repeated and unexpected and when they change their behavior in an attempt to avoid panic attacks. (p. 598)

13. A _____ is an intense fear of an object or a situation that's greatly out of proportion to its actual threat. (p. 598)

14. What are the symptoms of PTSD? Who is at high risk for developing this disorder? (p. 599)

15. Persistent ideas, thoughts, or impulses that are unwanted and inappropriate and cause distress are called _____. (p. 600)

16. Repetitive behaviors or mental acts initiated to reduce or prevent stress are called _____. (p. 600)

17. What anxiety disorder did the billionaire industrialist Howard Hughes suffer from? Can you name some other well-known people who suffer from this disorder? (p. 601)

18. People _____ when they predict terrible events, despite the low probability of their actual occurrence. (p. 601)

19. Anxious people tend to interpret ambiguous situations in a (negative/positive) light. (p. 601)

20. Many people with anxiety disorders harbor high levels of _____ _____, a fear of anxiety-related sensations. (p. 601)

MOOD DISORDERS AND SUICIDE 603–610

15.5 IDENTIFY THE CHARACTERISTICS OF DIFFERENT MOOD DISORDERS.

The sad mood of major depression is the mirror image of the expansive mood associated with a manic episode, seen in bipolar disorder. Depression can be recurrent or, more rarely, chronic. Manic episodes are often preceded or followed by bouts of depression. The diagnosis of the type of mood disorder depends in part on the intensity of the depressive or manic experience.

21. The state in which a person experiences a lingering depressed mood or diminished interest in pleasurable activities is called a(n) _____ _____ _____. (p. 603)

22. Over the course of a lifetime, more than _____ percent of us will experience a mood disorder. (p. 604)

23. Bipolar disorder is (equally common/more common) in women compared with men. (p. 608)

24. Twin studies suggest that the _____ of bipolar disorder may be as high as 85 percent. (p. 608)

15.6 DESCRIBE HOW LIFE EVENTS CAN INTERACT WITH CHARACTERISTICS OF THE INDIVIDUAL TO PRODUCE DEPRESSION SYMPTOMS.

Stressful life events are linked to depression. Depressed people may face social rejection, which can amplify depression. According to Lewinsohn's behavioral model, depression results from a low rate of response-contingent positive reinforcement. Aaron Beck's cognitive model holds that negative schemas play an important role in depression, whereas Martin Seligman's model emphasizes learned helplessness. Genes exert a moderate effect on the risk of developing depression.

25. Describe James Coyne's interpersonal model of depression. (p. 605)

26. Lewinsohn's behavioral model assumes that depression results from a (low/high) rate of response-contingent positive reinforcement. (p. 605)

27. Aaron Beck's cognitive model focused on three components of depressed thinking: negative views of _____, the _____, and the _____. (p. 606)

28. Identify and describe the theory Martin Seligman proposed based on his shuttle box research. (p. 606)

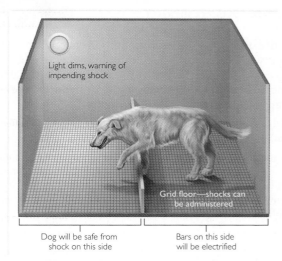

Light dims, warning of impending shock

Grid floor—shocks can be administered

Dog will be safe from shock on this side

Bars on this side will be electrified

15.7 IDENTIFY COMMON MYTHS AND MISCONCEPTIONS ABOUT SUICIDE.

Myths about suicide include the misconception that talking to depressed people about suicide makes them more likely to commit the act, suicide is almost always completed with no warning, suicide risk decreases as severe depression lifts, most people who threaten suicide are seeking attention, and people who talk a lot about suicide almost never commit it.

29. _____ _____ and _____ _____ are associated with a higher risk of suicide than most other disorders. (p. 609)

30. Many or most individuals who commit suicide (communicate/do not communicate) their intent to others. (p. 609)

PERSONALITY AND DISSOCIATIVE DISORDERS: THE DISRUPTED AND DIVIDED SELF 610–616

15.8 IDENTIFY THE CHARACTERISTICS OF BORDERLINE AND PSYCHOPATHIC PERSONALITY DISORDERS.

Borderline personality disorder is marked by instability in mood, identity, and impulse control. People with psychopathic personality are guiltless, dishonest, callous, and self-centered.

31. Of all psychiatric conditions, personality disorders are historically (least/most) reliably diagnosed. (p. 611)

32. Persons with borderline personality disorder's impulsivity and rapidly fluctuating emotions often have a _____ quality. (p. 612)

33. A diagnosis of _____ personality disorder is characterized by a lengthy history of illegal and irresponsible actions. (p. 613)

34. Most people with psychopathic personalities (are/are not) physically aggressive. (p. 613)

Answers are located at the end of the text.

35. From a psychological perspective, what's rare about the case of serial killer Aileen Wuornos? (p. 613)

15.9 EXPLAIN THE CONTROVERSIES SURROUNDING DISSOCIATIVE DISORDERS, ESPECIALLY DISSOCIATIVE IDENTITY DISORDER.

Dissociative disorders involve disruptions in consciousness, memory, identity, or perception. The role of severe child abuse in DID is controversial. The sociocognitive model holds that social influences, including the media and suggestive procedures in psychotherapy, shape symptoms of DID.

36. In DID, the alternate identities are often very (similar to/different from) the primary personality. (p. 615)

37. The intriguing differences that researchers have identified among alters in their respiration rates, brain wave activity, eyeglass prescription, handedness, skin conductance responses, voice patterns, and handwriting (do/don't) provide conclusive evidence for the existence of different alters. (p. 615)

38. According to the _____ model, DID arises from a history of severe abuse during childhood. (p. 615)

39. According to the sociocognitive model, how might a therapist contribute to the origin and maintenance of DID, as the artist of this painting claimed? (pp. 615–616)

40. Some psychologists hold that the _____ _____ have played a pivotal role in the DID epidemic. (p. 616)

THE ENIGMA OF SCHIZOPHRENIA 616–622

15.10 RECOGNIZE THE CHARACTERISTIC SYMPTOMS OF SCHIZOPHRENIA.

The symptoms of schizophrenia include delusions, hallucinations, disorganized speech, and grossly disorganized behavior or catatonia.

41. Despite the origin of the term "schizophrenia," it shouldn't be confused with _____ _____ _____ . (p. 617)

42. Strongly held, fixed beliefs that have no basis in reality are called _____. (p. 617)

43. _____ symptoms represent serious reality distortions. (p. 617)

44. Most _____ in schizophrenia are auditory, usually consisting of voices. (p. 618)

45. People with schizophrenia can exhibit _____ _____, in which their language becomes severely jumbled and skips from topic to topic in a disjointed way. (p. 618)

46. _____ symptoms involve motor problems, extreme resistance to complying with simple suggestions, holding the body in rigid postures, and refusing to speak or move. (p. 619)

15.11 EXPLAIN HOW PSYCHOSOCIAL, NEURAL, BIOCHEMICAL, AND GENETIC INFLUENCES CREATE THE VULNERABILITY TO SCHIZOPHRENIA

Scientists have discovered brain abnormalities in patients with schizophrenia. Individuals with schizophrenia are prone to relapse when their relatives display high expressed emotion (criticism, hostility, and over-involvement).

47. It is widely acknowledged today that parents and family members (cause/don't cause) schizophrenia. (p. 619)

48. Research indicates that one or more of four fluid-filled structures called ventricles, which cushion and nourish the brain, are typically (enlarged/diminished) in individuals with schizophrenia. (p. 620)

49. As illustrated in this figure, the lifetime risk of developing schizophrenia is largely a function of what? (p. 621)

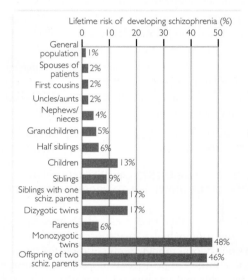

50. A _____ model proposes that schizophrenia, along with many other mental disorders, is a product of genetic vulnerability, and stressors that trigger this vulnerability. (p. 622)

CHILDHOOD DISORDERS: RECENT CONTROVERSIES 622–625

15.12 DESCRIBE THE SYMPTOMS AND DEBATE SURROUNDING DISORDERS DIAGNOSED IN CHILDHOOD.

Individuals with autistic disorder are marked by severe deficits in language, social bonding, and imagination, usually accompanied by mental retardation. Children with ADHD experience problems with inattention, impulsivity, and hyperactivity, and often struggle with learning disabilities, difficulties processing verbal information, and poor balance and coordination. Some scholars have expressed concerns that ADHD is overdiagnosed in some settings, although others point to evidence that some children with ADHD are actually overlooked by many diagnosticians. One of the most controversial diagnostic challenges is distinguishing children with ADHD from children with bipolar disorder.

51. Genetic influences alone (can/can't) easily account for an astronomical rise in autism's prevalence over the span of a decade. (p. 623)

52. Research studies have (failed/succeeded) in replicating the association between the MMR vaccine and autism. (pp. 623–624)

53. Many parents of children with autism probably fall prey to _____ _____; they "see" a statistical association that didn't exist. (p. 624)

54. What really accounts for most of the reported autism epidemic, despite many parents' conviction that vaccines trigger the disorder? (p. 624)

55. The diagnosis of ADHD subsumes two subtypes, one with _____, and one without in which _____ is predominant. (p. 624)

56. The first signs of hyperactivity may be evident in _____. (p. 624)

57. Although a high level of physical activity often diminishes as children with ADHD mature and approach adolescence, adjustment problems such as _____ and _____ _____ are frequent. (p. 624)

58. ADHD is associated with (increased/decreased) activation in the frontal areas of the brain. (p. 625)

59. List at least three conditions that must be first ruled out before an accurate diagnosis of ADHD can be made. (p. 625)

1. _____

2. _____

3. _____

60. Because _____ to _____ percent of children with bipolar disorder share an ADHD diagnosis, a hypothesis to consider is that many children diagnosed with bipolar disorder are merely those with more severe symptoms of ADHD. (p. 625)

DO YOU KNOW THESE TERMS?

- demonic model (p. 586)
- medical model (p. 586)
- asylum (p. 586)
- moral treatment (p. 587)
- deinstitutionalization (p. 587)
- labeling theorists (p. 591)
- *Diagnostic and Statistical Manual of Mental Disorders* (DSM) (p. 591)
- prevalence (p. 592)
- axis (p. 592)
- comorbidity (p. 593)
- categorical model (p. 593)
- dimensional model (p. 593)
- insanity defense (p. 595)
- involuntary commitment (p. 596)

- somatoform disorder (p. 597)
- hypochondriasis (p. 598)
- generalized anxiety disorder (GAD) (p. 598)
- panic attack (p. 598)
- panic disorder (p. 598)
- phobia (p. 598)
- agoraphobia (p. 599)
- specific phobia (p. 599)
- social phobia (p. 599)
- posttraumatic stress disorder (PTSD) (p. 599)
- obsessive-compulsive disorder (OCD) (p. 600)
- obsession (p. 600)

- compulsion (p. 600)
- anxiety sensitivity (p. 601)
- major depressive episode (p. 603)
- cognitive model of depression (p. 606)
- learned helplessness (p. 607)
- manic episode (p. 608)
- bipolar disorder (p. 608)
- personality disorder (p. 611)
- borderline personality disorder (p. 612)
- psychopathic personality (p. 612)
- antisocial personality disorder (ASPD) (p. 612)
- dissociative disorder (p. 614)

- depersonalization disorder (p. 614)
- dissociative amnesia (p. 614)
- dissociative fugue (p. 614)
- dissociative identity disorder (DID) (p. 614)
- schizophrenia (p. 616)
- delusion (p. 617)
- psychotic symptom (p. 617)
- hallucination (p. 618)
- catatonic symptom (p. 619)
- diathesis-stress model (p. 622)
- autistic disorder (p. 623)
- attention-deficit/hyperactivity disorder (ADHD) (p. 624)

APPLY YOUR SCIENTIFIC THINKING SKILLS

Use your scientific thinking skills to answer the following questions, referencing specific scientific thinking principles and common errors in reasoning whenever possible.

1. The popular media uses many diagnostic labels, such as codependency or sexual or Internet addiction, that have minimal scientific support. Go online or to your local bookstore and locate at least three examples of these labels. How is each disorder or addiction diagnosed? Do the disorders fulfill the criteria for validity outlined by Robins and Guze (refer to Table 15.2)? Why or why not?

2. As the text notes, the insanity defense is the subject of many popular misconceptions. Locate two popular articles that discuss

the use of this defense in a recent legal case. To what extent was the coverage of the insanity defense factually accurate? Did it fall prey to any of the myths described in the chapter? Explain.

3. Locate two to three articles or websites that argue for a connection between childhood vaccinations and the increase in autism rates. What evidence do they provide to support a link between vaccines and autism? Have the sources considered alternative explanations for the increase in autism rates?

16 PSYCHOLOGICAL AND BIOLOGICAL TREATMENTS

helping people change

THINK ABOUT IT

ARE MORE EXPERIENCED THERAPISTS BETTER THAN INEXPERIENCED THERAPISTS?

DO ALL PSYCHOTHERAPIES REQUIRE PEOPLE TO ACHIEVE INSIGHT TO IMPROVE?

IS ALCOHOLICS ANONYMOUS BETTER THAN OTHER TYPES OF TREATMENT FOR ALCOHOLISM?

ARE SOME PSYCHOTHERAPIES HARMFUL?

DOES ELECTROSHOCK TREATMENT PRODUCE LONG-TERM BRAIN DAMAGE?

Popular portrayals of psychotherapy have a long history in the media. (*top:* © Cathy Gaines *bottom:* © CartoonBank.com)

psychotherapy
a psychological intervention designed to help people resolve emotional, behavioral, and interpersonal problems and improve the quality of their lives

Before reading on, picture a typical psychotherapy session. What's the person in therapy—often called the "client" —doing? The therapist? What does the room look like? Perhaps your first thought is of the proverbial client on a couch, with the therapist sitting behind her, pen and pad in hand, intent on unearthing long-forgotten memories, analyzing dreams, and encouraging the client to vent painful feelings.

If this scenario comes to mind, it's no wonder. From the early days of psychotherapy (often simply called "therapy"), these images have been etched into our cultural consciousness. But we'll discover that this picture doesn't begin to tell the story of the vast array of psychotherapeutic approaches that encompass individual therapy, treatments conducted in groups and with families, and even art, dance, and music therapy. Nor does the scenario capture the powerful biological treatments that have changed the lives of people with psychological disorders by targeting the brain's functioning. In this chapter, we'll examine a broad spectrum of therapies, both psychological and biological, that are designed to alleviate emotional suffering.

Like many concepts in psychology, *psychotherapy* isn't easy to define. Over a half century ago, one pioneer in psychotherapy wrote, half-jokingly, "Psychotherapy is an undefined technique applied to unspecified problems with unpredictable outcomes. For this technique, we recommend rigorous training" (Raimy, 1950, p. 63). Some might contend that things haven't changed much since then. Still, for our purposes, we can define **psychotherapy** as a psychological intervention designed to help people resolve emotional, behavioral, and interpersonal problems and improve the quality of their lives (Engler & Goleman, 1992, p. 15). Although the popular media often speak of therapy as though it were one thing, there are well over 500 "brands" of psychotherapy (Eisner, 2000), about three times as many as there were in the 1970s. As we'll learn, research demonstrates that many of these therapies are effective, but many others haven't been tested. In the pages to come, we'll offer critical thinking tools for distinguishing both psychological and biomedical therapies that are scientifically supported from those are ineffective or scientifically unsupported but promising.

PSYCHOTHERAPY: CLIENTS AND PRACTITIONERS

16.1 Describe who seeks treatment, who benefits from psychotherapy, and who practices psychotherapy.

16.2 Distinguish between professionals and paraprofessionals and describe what it takes to be an effective therapist.

We'll begin by considering several questions: Who seeks and benefits from psychotherapy? How is psychotherapy practiced? What makes a psychotherapist effective?

■ Who Seeks and Benefits from Treatment?

A 2006 *Newsweek* poll found that about 20 percent of Americans have received psychological treatment at some point, and that about 4 percent are currently in psychotherapy. People grapple with specific problems in psychotherapy, but they also contend frequently with feelings of helplessness, social isolation, and a sense of failure (Garfield, 1978; Lambert, 2003). Still others turn to therapy to expand their self-awareness, learn better ways of relating to others, and consider lifestyle changes.

GENDER, ETHNIC, AND CULTURAL DIFFERENCES IN ENTERING TREATMENT. Some people are more likely to enter psychological treatment than others. Women are more likely to seek treatment than men (Addis & Mahalik, 2003; DuBrin & Zastowny, 1988), although both sexes benefit equally from psychotherapy (Petry, Tennen, & Affleck, 2000). Members of many racial and ethnic minority groups, particularly Asian Americans and Hispanic Americans, are less likely to seek mental health services than Caucasian Americans (Sue & Lam, 2002), perhaps because of the lingering stigma surrounding psychotherapy in these groups. Socioeconomic factors also predict who seeks therapy. Therapy can be very costly for those without health insurance or whose health plans don't include mental health coverage (Wang et al., 2008). Nevertheless, when individuals hailing from diverse cultural and ethnic backgrounds obtain psychotherapy, they're likely to benefit from it (Navarro, 1993; Prochaska & Norcross, 2007).

Culturally sensitive psychotherapists tune their interventions to clients' cultural values and the difficulties they encounter in adapting to a dominant culture that may differ vastly from their own (Sue & Sue, 2003; Whaley & Davis, 2007). Although ethnic minorities prefer therapists with a similar ethnic background (Coleman, Wampold, & Casali, 1995), there's no consistent evidence that client-therapist ethnic (Shin et al., 2005) or gender (Bowman et al., 2001) matches enhance therapy outcome. Still, when clients are relative newcomers to a culture and not well acquainted with its traditions, therapist–client ethnic match may play a greater role in therapy's effectiveness (Sue, 1998). The good news is that people can be helped by therapists who differ from them in significant ways, including ethnicity and gender (Cardemil, 2010; Whaley & Davis, 2007).

REAPING BENEFITS FROM TREATMENT. The effectiveness of therapy depends on a host of individual differences. Clients who are better adjusted to begin with, realize they may be contributing to their problems, and are motivated to work on those problems are most likely to improve (Prochaska & DiClemente, 1982; Prochaska & Norcross, 2002). Clients who experience some anxiety do better in psychotherapy—probably because their distress fuels their motivation to make life changes (Frank, 1974; Miller et al., 1995)—as do clients with temporary or situational problems, such as relationship upheavals (Gasperini et al., 1993; Steinmetz, Lewinsohn, & Antonuccio, 1983).

■ Who Practices Psychotherapy?

As we learned in Chapter 1, licensed professionals, especially clinical psychologists, psychiatrists, mental health counselors, and clinical social workers, are the mainstays of the mental health profession (see **TABLE 16.1**). But unlicensed religious, vocational, and rehabilitation counselors, as well as art therapists also provide psychological services. ◆ Explore

The ideal client? A 1964 study (Schofield, 1964) found that many therapists preferred to treat people who were relatively young, attractive, verbal, intelligent, and successful (YAVIS clients). Nevertheless, therapists have recently become more aware of the importance of assisting a broad clientele of all ages and cultural backgrounds.

◆ **Explore** Psychotherapy Practitioners and their Activities on **mypsychlab.com**

TABLE 16.1 Occupations, Degrees, Roles, and Work Settings of Mental Health Professionals. Not all therapists are the same: Mental health consumers are often unaware of the substantial differences in education, training, and roles of different psychotherapists. This table provides some guidance.

OCCUPATION	DEGREE/LICENSE	SETTINGS/ROLE
Clinical Psychologist	PhD/PsyD, MA	Private practice, hospitals, schools, community agencies, medical settings, academic, other
Psychiatrist	MD or DO	Physicians, private practice, hospitals, medical centers, schools, academic, other
Counseling Psychologist	PhD, EdD, MA, MS, MC	University clinics, mental health centers; treat people with less severe psychological problems
School Psychologist	PhD, PsyD, EdD, EdS, MA, MS, MEd	In-school interventions, assessment, prevention programs, work with teachers, students, parents
Clinical Social Worker	Training varies widely; BSW, MSW, DSW, LCSW	Private practice following supervised experience, psychiatric facilities, hospitals/community agencies, schools, case managers; help with social and health problems
Mental Health Counselor	MSW, MS, MC	Private practice, community agencies, hospitals, other; career counseling, marriage issues, substance abuse
Psychiatric Nurse	Training varies widely; associate's degree, BSN, MSN, DNP, PhD	Hospitals, community health centers, primary care facilities, outpatient mental health clinics; manage medications, with advanced degrees can diagnose, treat mental patients
Pastoral Counselor	Training varies; from bachelor's degree to more advanced degrees	Counseling, support in spiritual context, wellness programs; group, family, and couples therapy

Degree Key: BSN, bachelor of science in nursing; BSW, bachelor of social work; DNP, doctorate nurse practitioner; DO, doctor of osteopathy; DSW, doctor of social work; EdD, doctor of education; EdS, specialist in education; LCSW, licensed clinical social worker; MA, master of arts; MC, master of counseling; MD, doctor of medicine; MEd, master of education; MS, master of science; MSN, master of science in nursing; MSW, master of social work; PhD, doctor of philosophy; PsyD, doctor of psychology.

? In the HBO television series, *In Treatment*, Laura (played by Melissa George), develops sexual feelings for her therapist, Paul (played by Gabriel Byrne). Paul doesn't have a sexual relationship with her, because he experiences a panic attack. A sexual relationship with a client is highly unethical. **Which of the following behaviors is also unethical?** A) Revealing a client's plan to commit suicide to a family member to prevent the suicide. B) Revealing a client's plan to assault another person to prevent the assault. C) Informing a client's elderly father that she harbors hateful feelings toward him. (See answer upside down at bottom of page.)

paraprofessional
person with no professional training who provides mental health services

PROFESSIONALS VERSUS PARAPROFESSIONALS. Contrary to the myth that all psychotherapists have advanced degrees in mental health, volunteers and **paraprofessionals**, helpers who have no formal professional training, often provide psychological services in such settings as crisis intervention centers and other social service agencies. In most states, the term *therapist* isn't legally protected, so virtually anyone can hang up a shingle and offer treatment. Many paraprofessionals obtain agency-specific training and attend workshops that enhance their educational backgrounds. They may also be trained to recognize situations that require consultation with professionals with greater expertise. Paraprofessionals help to compensate for the sizable gap between the high demand for and meager supply of licensed practitioners (den Boer et al., 2005).

Again contrary to popular belief, therapists don't need to be professionally trained or have many years of experience to be effective (Berman & Norton, 1985; Blatt et al., 1996; Christensen & Jacobson, 1994). Indeed, most studies reveal few or no differences in effectiveness between more and less experienced therapists (Dawes, 1994; McFall, 2006). Why is this so? As Jerome Frank (1961) noted, regardless of level of professional training, people who fulfill the role of therapist may provide clients with hope, empathy, advice, support, and opportunities for new learning experiences (Frank & Frank, 1991; Lambert & Ogles, 2004).

Even if there are few or no differences in therapy outcome as a function of professional training, there are clear advantages to consulting with a professional. Professional helpers (1) understand how to operate effectively within the mental health system; (2) appreciate complex ethical, professional, and personal issues; and (3) can select treatments of demonstrated effectiveness (Garske & Anderson, 2003). Moreover, trained and experienced therapists may be more confident, less defensive, and better able to appreciate clients' world-view than less experienced therapists (Teyber & McClure, 2000).

WHAT DOES IT TAKE TO BE AN EFFECTIVE PSYCHOTHERAPIST? Given that training and years of experience aren't critical determinants of what makes a good therapist, what is? Effective therapists (Garske & Anderson, 2003) are likely to be warm and direct (Westerman, Foote, & Winston, 1995), establish a positive working relationship with clients (Kazdin, Marciano, & Whitley, 2005; Luborsky et al., 1997), and tend not to contradict clients (Friedlander, 1984). Effective therapists also select important topics to focus on in sessions (Goldfried, Raue, & Castonguay, 1998), and match their treatments to the needs and characteristics of clients (Beutler & Harwood, 2002). Differences among therapists in their abilities and characteristics may be so great that they overshadow differences in the effectiveness of the treatments they provide (Ahn & Wampold, 2001; Luborsky et al., 1986). So when it comes to the success of psychotherapy, the choice of *therapist* is every bit as important as the choice of *therapy* (Blow, Sprenkle, & Davis, 2007).

What makes a good therapist from the client's point of view? The composite view of the "good" therapist is that of an expert who's warm, respectful, caring, and engaged (Littauer, Sexton, & Wyan, 2005; Strupp, Fox, & Lessler, 1969). This description fits exactly the sort of therapist we advise you or your loved ones to seek. In **TABLE 16.2**, we present some tips for both selecting good therapists and avoiding bad ones.

TABLE 16.2 What Should I Look for in a Therapist, and What Type of Therapist Should I Avoid? Tens of thousands of people call themselves therapists, and it's often hard to know what kind of therapist to seek out or avoid. This checklist may help you, your friends, or your loved ones to select a good therapist—and to steer clear of a bad one.

If your answer is yes to most of the following statements, the therapist should be in a good position to help you:

1. I can talk freely and openly with my therapist.
2. My therapist listens carefully to what I say and understands my feelings.
3. My therapist is warm, direct, and provides useful feedback.
4. My therapist explains up front what he or she will be doing and why, and is willing to answer questions about his or her qualifications and training, my diagnosis, and our treatment plan.
5. My therapist encourages me to confront challenges and solve problems.
6. My therapist uses scientifically based approaches and discusses the pros and cons of other approaches.
7. My therapist monitors how I'm doing regularly and is willing to change course when treatment isn't going well.

If your answer is yes to one or more of the following statements, the therapist may *not* be in a good position to help you, and even may be harmful:

1. My therapist gets defensive and angry when challenged.
2. My therapist has a "one size fits all" approach to all problems.
3. My therapist spends considerable time each session making "small talk," telling me exactly what to do, and sharing personal anecdotes.
4. My therapist isn't clear about what is expected of me in the treatment plan, and our discussions lack any focus and direction.
5. My therapist doesn't seem willing to discuss the scientific support for what he or she is doing.
6. There are no clear professional boundaries in my relationship with my therapist; for example, my therapist talks a lot about his or her personal life or asks me for personal favors.

assess your knowledge   FACT OR FICTION?

✓•—Study and Review on **mypsychlab.com**

1. Asian Americans are more likely to seek psychotherapy than Caucasian Americans. **True / False**
2. Clients who are poorly adjusted to begin with are most likely to improve with therapy. **True / False**
3. All people who practice therapy have advanced degrees in mental health. **True / False**
   workshops are also good
4. Professional training is necessary to produce good therapy outcomes. **True / False**
5. The choice of a therapist is as important as the choice of therapy. **True / False**

Answers: 1. F (p.632); 2. F (p.633); 3. F (p.634); 4. F (p.634); 5. T (p.634)

INSIGHT THERAPIES: ACQUIRING UNDERSTANDING

16.3 Describe the core beliefs and criticisms of psychodynamic therapies.

16.4 Describe and evaluate the effectiveness of humanistic therapies.

16.5 List the advantages of group methods and describe the research evidence concerning the effectiveness of Alcoholics Anonymous.

16.6 Identify different approaches to treating the dysfunctional family system.

In much of the chapter that lies ahead, we'll examine some of the more prominent therapeutic approaches and evaluate their scientific status. We'll begin with *psychodynamic therapies*, treatments inspired by classical psychoanalysis and influenced by Freud's techniques. Nevertheless, compared with psychoanalysis, which tends to be expensive, lengthy (often lasting years or even decades), and often involves meeting most days of the week, psychodynamic therapy is typically less costly, briefer—weeks or months or open-ended—and involves meeting only once or twice a week (Shedler, 2010). After we examine Freud's techniques, we'll consider a group of therapists called *neo-Freudians* (see Chapter 14), who adopted Freud's psychodynamic perspective but modified his approach in distinctive ways. Psychodynamic therapies, and the humanistic therapies we'll also discuss, are often called **insight therapies**, as their goal is to cultivate insight, that is, expanded awareness.

FICTOID

MYTH: Psychotherapy didn't exist prior to Freud.

REALITY: Therapies based on self-improvement principles were popular in the United States decades before Freud was born (Cautin, 2010).

insight therapies
psychotherapies, including psychodynamic, humanistic, and group approaches, with the goal of expanding awareness or insight

The Freudian concept of free association is a bit like a magician pulling kerchiefs out of a hat, with one thought leading to the next, in turn leading to the next, and so on.

It's always the same dream. I'm in therapy, analyzing my recurring dream.

■ Psychoanalytic and Psychodynamic Therapies: Freud's Legacy

Psychodynamic therapists share the following three approaches and beliefs, which form the core of their approach (Blagys & Hilsenroth, 2000; Shedler, 2010; see Chapter 14):

1. They believe the causes of abnormal behaviors, including unconscious conflicts, wishes, and impulses, stem from traumatic or other adverse childhood experiences.

2. They strive to analyze: (a) distressing thoughts and feelings clients avoid, (b) wishes and fantasies, (c) recurring themes and life patterns, (d) significant past events, and (e) the therapeutic relationship.

3. They believe that when clients achieve insight into previously unconscious material, the causes and the significance of symptoms will become evident, often causing symptoms to disappear.

PSYCHOANALYSIS: KEY INGREDIENTS. Freud's psychoanalysis was one of the first forms of psychotherapy. According to Freud, the goal of psychoanalysis is to decrease guilt and frustration and *make the unconscious conscious* by bringing to awareness previously repressed impulses, conflicts, and memories (Bornstein, 2001; Mellinger & Lynn, 2003). Psychoanalytic therapists, sometimes called "analysts," attempt to fill this tall order using six primary approaches.

(1) Free Association. As clients lie on a couch in a comfortable position, therapists instruct them to say whatever thoughts come to mind, no matter how meaningless or nonsensical they might seem. This process is called **free association**, because clients are permitted to express themselves without censorship.

(2) Interpretation. From the client's string of free associations, analysts form hypotheses regarding the origin of the client's difficulties and share them with him or her as the therapeutic relationship evolves. Therapists also formulate *interpretations*—explanations—of the unconscious bases of a client's dreams, emotions, and behaviors. They point out the supposedly disguised expression of a repressed idea, impulse, or wish, as in the following interpretation of a client's repeated "accidents" resulting in injury: "Having these accidents perhaps served an unconscious purpose; they assured you of getting the attention you felt you could not get otherwise." As in comedy, timing is everything. If the therapist offers the interpretation before the client is ready to accept it, psychoanalysts maintain, anxiety may derail the flow of new associations.

(3) Dream Analysis. According to Freud, dreams express unconscious themes that influence the client's conscious life. The therapist's task is to interpret the relation of the dream to the client's waking life and the dream's symbolic significance. In Chapter 5, we discussed the distinction between a dream's manifest (observable) and latent (hidden) content. Thus, the therapist might interpret the appearance of an ogre in a dream—the manifest content—as representing a hated and feared parent—the latent content.

(4) Resistance. As treatment progresses and people become aware of previously unconscious and often feared aspects of themselves, they often experience **resistance**: they try to avoid further confrontation. Clients express resistance in many ways, including skipping therapy sessions or drawing a blank when the therapist asks a question about painful moments in their past, but all forms of resistance stall their progress. To minimize resistance, psychoanalysts attempt to make clients aware they're unconsciously blocking therapeutic efforts and make clear *how* and *what* they're resisting (Anderson & Stewart, 1983; Reich, 1949).

(5) Transference. As analysis continues, clients begin to experience **transference**: They project intense, unrealistic feelings and expectations from their past onto the therapist. The ambiguous figure of the analyst supposedly becomes the focus of emotions once directed at significant persons from the client's childhood. In one example, a client brought a gun into treatment and pointed it at the therapist. The therapist replied: "This is what I meant about your murderous feelings toward your father (Laughs). Do you see it now?" (Monroe, 1955). Freud believed that transference provides a vehicle for clients to understand their irrational expectations and demands of others, including the therapist.

Research suggests that we indeed often react to people in our present lives in ways similar to people in our past (Berk & Andersen, 2000; Luborsky, et al., 1985). These findings may suggest that Freud was right about the transference; alternatively, they may mean that our stable personality traits (see Chapter 14) lead us to react to people in similar ways over time. These lingering questions aside, therapists' interpretations of the transference may be helpful for some clients (Ogrodniczuk & Piper, 1999).

(6) Working Through. In the final stage of psychoanalysis, therapists help clients *work through,* or process, their problems. The insight gained in treatment is a helpful starting point, but it's not sufficient. As a consequence, therapists must repeatedly address conflicts and resistance to achieving healthy behavior patterns and help clients confront old and ineffective coping responses as they reemerge in everyday life (Menninger, 1958; Wachtel, 1997).

DEVELOPMENTS IN PSYCHOANALYSIS: THE NEO-FREUDIAN TRADITION. Freud's ideas spawned new therapeutic approaches in the psychodynamic tradition (Ellis, Abrams, & Abrams, 2008). In contrast to Freudian therapists, neo-Freudian therapists are more concerned with conscious aspects of the client's functioning. For example, according to neo-Freudian Carl Jung (see Chapter 14), the goal of psychotherapy is *individuation*—the integration of opposing aspects of the personality into a harmonious "whole," namely, the self. To help clients achieve individuation, Jung considered their future goals as well as past experiences. Neo-Freudians also emphasize the impact of cultural and interpersonal influences on behavior across the life span (Adler, 1938; Mitchell & Black, 1995). Beyond Freud's emphasis on sexuality and aggression, neo-Freudians acknowledge the impact of other needs, including love, dependence, power, and status. They're also more optimistic than was Freud regarding people's prospects for achieving healthy functioning (see Chapter 14).

The emphasis on interpersonal relationships is the hallmark of Harry Stack Sullivan's *interpersonal psychotherapy.* According to Sullivan (1954), psychotherapy is a collaborative undertaking between client and therapist. Sullivan contended that the analyst's proper role is that of *participant observer.* Through her ongoing observations, the analyst discovers and communicates to clients their unrealistic attitudes and behaviors in everyday life.

Sullivan's work influenced the contemporary approach of **interpersonal therapy (IPT).** Originally a treatment for depression (Klerman et al., 1984; Santor & Kusumakar, 2001), IPT is a short-term (12 to 16 sessions) intervention designed to strengthen people's social skills and assist them in coping with interpersonal problems, conflicts (such as disputes with family members), and life transitions (such as childbirth and retirement). In addition to effectively treating depression (Klerman et al., 1984; Hinrichsen, 2008), IPT has demonstrated success in treating substance abuse and eating disorders (Klerman & Weissman, 1993; Weissman, Markowitz, & Klerman, 2000).

? ** This client began crying after his therapist gently suggested that he take more risks in life. "That's exactly what my father used to tell me as a child," he says, and "now I feel criticized by you the same way I felt criticized by my father." **According to psychoanalysts, the client is experiencing what phenomenon? (See answer upside down on bottom of page.)

ruling out rival hypotheses

HAVE IMPORTANT ALTERNATIVE EXPLANATIONS FOR THE FINDINGS BEEN EXCLUDED?

free association
technique in which clients express themselves without censorship of any sort

resistance
attempts to avoid confrontation and anxiety associated with uncovering previously repressed thoughts, emotions, and impulses

transference
projecting intense, unrealistic feelings and expectations from the past onto the therapist

interpersonal therapy (IPT)
treatment that strengthens social skills and targets interpersonal problems, conflicts, and life transitions

Interpersonal therapy aims to resolve interpersonal problems and conflicts and to teach people social skills.

Answer: Transference

falsifiability ➤
CAN THE CLAIM BE DISPROVED?

ruling out rival hypotheses ➤
HAVE IMPORTANT ALTERNATIVE EXPLANATIONS
FOR THE FINDINGS BEEN EXCLUDED?

ruling out rival hypotheses ➤
HAVE IMPORTANT ALTERNATIVE EXPLANATIONS
FOR THE FINDINGS BEEN EXCLUDED?

Is Insight Necessary? As we've seen, psychodynamic therapies rely heavily on insight. Many Hollywood films, like *Good Will Hunting* (1997) and *Analyze This* (1999), reinforce the impression that insight—especially into the childhood origins of problems—is always the crucial ingredient in therapeutic change. Yet extensive research demonstrates that understanding our emotional history, however deep and gratifying, isn't required to relieve psychological distress (Weisz et al., 1995). To improve, clients typically need to practice new and more adaptive behaviors in everyday life—that is, to engage in *working through* (Wachtel, 1977).

Some psychodynamic concepts, including therapeutic interpretations, are difficult to falsify (see Chapter 14). How can we demonstrate that a person's dream of his father scowling at him, for example, points to repressed memories of child abuse, as a therapist might infer? A client might respond, "Aha, that's it!" but this reaction could reflect transference or an attempt to please the therapist. If the client improves, the therapist might conclude that the interpretation is accurate, but the timing could be coincidental rather than causal (Grunbaum, 1984).

The failure to rule out rival hypotheses may lead both therapist and client to attribute progress mistakenly to insight and interpretation when other influences, like placebo effects (see Chapter 2), are responsible (Meyer, 1981). Research supports this caution. In one long-term study of psychoanalytic treatment (Bachrach et al., 1991), half of 42 clients improved but failed to show insight into their "core conflicts." Yet the support the therapist provided was more related to improvement than was insight.

Are Traumatic Memories Repressed? Although many psychodynamic therapists believe that current difficulties often stem from the repression of traumatic events, such as childhood abuse (Frederickson, 1992; Levis, 1995), research doesn't bear out this claim (Lynn et al., 2004; McHugh, 2008). Try this thought experiment. Which event would you be more likely to forget: An instance when your peers ridiculed you and beat you up in third grade for being the class know-it-all, or a time when the teacher praised you in class for your participation? Odds are you thought you'd be better able to recall the unsettling event, and you'd be right. As we learned in Chapter 7, disturbing events are actually *more* memorable and *less* subject to forgetting than everyday occurrences (Loftus, 1993; Lynn et al., 2004; Porter & Peace, 2007). After reviewing the research evidence, Richard McNally (2003) concluded that the scientific support for repressed memories is weak, and that many memories, especially those that stretch to the distant past, are often subject to distortion (see Chapter 7). Nevertheless, the issue remains controversial (Anderson & Green, 2001; Erdelyi, 2006).

Psychodynamic Therapies Evaluated Scientifically. Valuable as they've been, many psychodynamic therapies are questionable from a scientific standpoint. Freud and Jung based their therapeutic observations largely on small samples of wealthy, intelligent, and successful people, rendering their external validity (see Chapter 2) unclear. Their clinical sessions weren't observed by others or conducted on a systematic basis that permitted replication by others, as would be the case with rigorously controlled research.

replicability ➤
CAN THE RESULTS BE
DUPLICATED IN OTHER STUDIES?

The concerns we've raised aside, research indicates that brief versions of psychodynamic therapy are better than no treatment (Leichsenring, Rabung, & Leibing, 2004; Shedler, 2010), although they may be somewhat less effective than cognitive-behavioral therapies, which don't emphasize insight (Grawe, Donati, & Bernauer, 1998; Shapiro & Shapiro, 1982). Moreover, psychodynamic therapy isn't especially effective for psychotic disorders, like schizophrenia, even though some practitioners continue to use it for this purpose (Karon, 1994).

■ Humanistic Therapies: Achieving Our Potential

Under the umbrella of **humanistic therapies**, we can find a variety of approaches rooted in the humanistic perspective on personality (see Chapter 14). Therapies within this orientation share an emphasis on insight, self-actualization, and the belief that human nature is basically positive (Maslow, 1954; Rogers, 1961; Shlien & Levant, 1984). Humanistic therapists reject the interpretive techniques of psychoanalysis. Instead, they strive to understand clients' inner

humanistic therapies
therapies that emphasize the development
of human potential and the belief that human
nature is basically positive

worlds through empathy and focus on clients' thoughts and feelings in the present moment.

Humanistic therapists share a desire to help people overcome the sense of alienation so prevalent in our culture; to develop their sensory and emotional awareness; and express their creativity and help them become loving, responsible, and authentic. Humanistic therapists stress the importance of assuming responsibility for decisions, not attributing our problems to the past, and living fully and finding meaning in the present.

According to Rogers, if a father gives his child love only when he receives a good grade, but not when he receives a poor grade, is the father expressing conditional regard or unconditional regard? (See answer upside down at bottom of page.)

PERSON-CENTERED THERAPY: ATTAINING ACCEPTANCE.

No therapist better exemplifies the practice of humanistic therapy than Carl Rogers (see Chapter 14). His therapy is *nondirective* because therapists don't define or diagnose clients' problems or try to get at the root cause of their difficulties. His approach, once called client-centered therapy, is called **person-centered therapy** because therapists don't tell clients how to solve their problems, and clients can use the therapy hour however they choose (Rogers, 1942). To ensure a positive outcome, the therapist must satisfy three conditions: ◉—**Watch**

1. The therapist must be an authentic, genuine person who reveals his or her own reactions to what the client is communicating.

    Client: I think I'm beyond help.

    Therapist: Huh? Feel as though you're beyond help. I know. You feel just completely hopeless about yourself. I can understand that. I don't feel hopeless, but I realize you do (Meador & Rogers, 1979, p. 157).

2. The therapist must express *unconditional positive regard,* that is, a nonjudgmental acceptance of all feelings the client expresses. Rogers was convinced that unconditional positive regard elicits a more positive self-concept. He maintained that it allows clients to reclaim aspects of their "true selves" that they disowned earlier in life due to others placing conditions of worth (see Chapter 14) on them.

3. The therapist must relate to clients with empathic understanding. In Rogers' words: "To sense the patient's world as if it were our own, but without ever losing the 'as if' quality. This is empathy" (Rogers, 1957, p. 98).

One way to communicate empathy is by way of *reflection,* that is, mirroring back the client's feelings—a technique for which Rogers was famous. Here's an example.

Client: I was small and I envied people who were large. I was—well, I took beatings by boys and I couldn't strike back. ...

Therapist: You've had plenty of experience in being the underdog. (Rogers, 1942, pp. 145–146)

With increased awareness and heightened self-acceptance, people hopefully come to think more realistically, become more tolerant of others, and engage in more adaptive behaviors (Rogers, 1961). Some researchers have developed computer programs that attempt to simulate Rogers' person-centered therapy, especially Rogers' method of reflection (see **TABLE 16.3**).

Person-centered interviewing techniques, including warmth and empathy, reflective listening, unconditional acceptance, and avoiding confrontation, lie at the heart of *motivational interviewing* (Miller & Rollnick, 2002). This one- to two-session procedure recognizes that many clients are ambivalent about changing longstanding behaviors and is geared toward clarifying and bringing forth their reasons for changing—and not

TABLE 16.3 Simulated Conversation between Client and Computer Therapist, Eliza. Some researchers have developed computer programs that attempt to simulate Rogers' person-centered therapy, especially Rogers' method of reflection. Here, we can read excerpts from a conversation between a client and the computer therapist, Eliza, developed by computer scientist Joseph Weizenbaum. Would Eliza make a good therapist?

[handwritten: No, it is screening]

Client: Men are all alike.
Eliza: IN WHAT WAY?
Client: They're always bugging us about something or other.
Eliza: CAN YOU THINK OF A SPECIFIC EXAMPLE?
Client: Well, my boyfriend made me come here.
Eliza: YOUR BOYFRIEND MADE YOU COME HERE?
Client: He says I'm depressed much of the time.
Eliza: I AM SORRY TO HEAR YOU ARE DEPRESSED.
Client: It's true. I am unhappy.
Eliza: DO YOU THINK COMING HERE WILL HELP YOU NOT TO BE UNHAPPY?
Client: I need some help, that much seems certain.
Eliza: WHAT WOULD IT MEAN TO YOU IF YOU GOT SOME HELP?
Client: Perhaps I could learn to get along with my mother.
Eliza: TELL ME MORE ABOUT YOUR FAMILY.
Client: My mother takes care of me.
Eliza: WHO ELSE IN YOUR FAMILY TAKES CARE OF YOU?
Client: My father.
Eliza: YOUR FATHER?
Client: You are like my father in some ways.
Eliza: WHAT RESEMBLANCE DO YOU SEE?

(*Source:* http://i5.nyu.edu/~mm64/x52.9265/january1966.html; Weizenbaum)

◉—**Watch** Carl Rogers: Role of a Therapist on **mypsychlab.com**

person-centered therapy
therapy centering on the client's goals and ways of solving problems

changing—their lives. Motivational interviewing, initially shown to be helpful in treating alcohol-related problems (Project MATCH Research Group, 1997), has been successful in modifying a variety of health-related behaviors, including exercise and diet (Burke, Arkowitz, & Dunn, 2002; Burke, Arkowitz, & Menchola, 2003).

GESTALT THERAPY: BECOMING WHOLE. Fritz Perls, the flamboyant founder of **Gestalt therapy**, was trained as a psychodynamic therapist, but imported some concepts from Gestalt psychology, a theory of perception we encountered in Chapter 4, into a new brand of therapy. The word *gestalt* (configuration) means an organized whole. Gestalt therapists believe that people with psychological difficulties are "incomplete gestalts" because they've excluded from their awareness experiences and aspects of their personalities that trigger anxiety. As a consequence, Gestalt therapists aim to integrate differing and sometimes opposing aspects of clients' personalities into a unified sense of self.

For Gestalt therapists, the key to personal growth is accepting responsibility for one's feelings and maintaining contact with the here and now. Gestalt therapy was the first of many therapies that recognize the importance of awareness, acceptance, and expression of feelings. In the *two-chair technique,* Gestalt therapists ask clients to move from chair to chair, creating a dialogue with two conflicting aspects of their personalities (see **FIGURE 16.1**). The "good boy" versus the "spoiled brat" may serve as the focal point for such an interchange. Gestalt therapists believe this procedure allows a synthesis of the opposing sides to emerge. For example, the good boy, always eager to please others, may learn from a conversation with the spoiled brat that it's acceptable in certain instances to be assertive, even demanding. Thus, the "good brat" may be more effective and authentic than either personality aspect alone.

HUMANISTIC THERAPIES EVALUATED SCIENTIFICALLY. The core concepts of humanistic therapies, such as meaning and self-actualization, are difficult to measure and falsify. For example, at exactly what point can we say a person is self-aware and authentic?

To his credit, however, Rogers specified three conditions for effective psychotherapy that could be falsified. Research has shown that he was largely on the mark when it comes to the therapeutic relationship. Establishing a strong alliance is helpful to the ultimate success of therapy (Horvath & Bedi, 2002; Wampold, 2001). In fact, the therapeutic relationship is typically a stronger predictor of success in therapy than the use of specific techniques (Bohart et al., 2002). But Rogers was wrong in one key respect: The three core conditions he specified aren't "necessary and sufficient" for improvement (Bohart, 2003; Norcross & Beutler, 1997). Although he overstated their impact, empathy (Bohart, Elliott, & Greenberg, 2002) and positive regard (Farber & Lane, 2002) are modestly related to therapy outcome (Orlinsky & Howard, 1986). Some studies have revealed a positive relation between genuineness and therapeutic outcome, but others haven't (Klein et al., 2002; Orlinsky, Grawe, & Parks, 1994). As we'll learn later, some people can derive considerable benefits from self-help programs that don't even involve therapists (Gould & Clum, 1993), so the therapeutic relationship isn't necessary for improvement. Moreover, research suggests that the causal direction of the relation between the therapeutic alliance and improvement may often be the reverse of what Rogers proposed: Clients may first improve and then develop a stronger emotional bond with the therapist as a result (DeRubeis & Feeley, 1990; Kazdin, 2007).

Person-centered therapy is more effective than no treatment (Greenberg, Elliot, & Lietaer, 1994). But findings concerning the effectiveness of person-centered therapy are inconsistent, with some suggesting it may not help much more than a placebo treatment, such as merely chatting for the same amount of time with a nonprofessional (Smith, Glass, & Miller, 1980). In contrast, other studies suggest that person-centered therapies often result in substantial improvement and may be comparable in effectiveness to the cognitive-behavioral therapies we'll encounter later (Elliott, 2002; Greenberg & Watson, 1998).

FIGURE 16.1 The Two-Chair Technique. Gestalt therapy's two-chair technique aims to integrate opposing aspects of the client's personality, such as the "good boy" and the "spoiled brat."

falsifiability

CAN THE CLAIM BE DISPROVED?

correlation vs. causation

CAN WE BE SURE THAT A CAUSES B?

Gestalt therapy
therapy that aims to integrate different and sometimes opposing aspects of personality into a unified sense of self

■ Group Therapies: The More, the Merrier

Since the early 1920s, when Viennese psychiatrist Jacob Moreno introduced the term **group therapy**, helping professionals have appreciated the value of treating more than one person at a time. The popularity of group approaches has paralleled the increased demand for psychological services in the general population. Group therapies, which typically range in size from three to as many as 20 clients, are efficient, time-saving, and less costly than individual treatments, and span all major schools of psychotherapy (Levine, 1979). In a safe group environment, participants can provide and receive support, exchange information and feedback, model effective behaviors and practice new skills, and recognize that they're not alone in struggling with adjustment problems (Yalom, 1985).

Today, psychologists conduct group sessions in a variety of settings, including homes, hospitals, inpatient and residential settings, community agencies, and professional offices. They reach people who are divorced, experiencing marital problems, struggling with gender identity, and are experiencing problems with alcoholism and eating disorders, among many others (Dies, 2003; Lynn & Frauman, 1985). The most recent trend is for self-help groups to form over the Internet, especially for people with problems that may be embarrassing to share in face-to-face encounters (Davison, Pennebaker, & Dickerson, 2000; Golkaramnay et al., 2007). Research suggests that group procedures are effective for a wide range of problems and about as helpful as individual treatments (McEvoy, 2007; Fuhriman & Burlingame, 1994). ((•─│Listen

ALCOHOLICS ANONYMOUS. *Self-help groups* are composed of peers who share a similar problem; often they don't include a professional mental illness specialist. Over the past several decades, these groups, of which **Alcoholics Anonymous** (AA) is the best known, have become remarkably popular. AA was founded in 1935 and is now the largest organization for treating people with alcoholism, with more than 1.7 million members worldwide (Humphreys, 2000). At AA meetings, people share their struggles with alcohol, and new members are "sponsored" or mentored by more senior members, who've often achieved years of sobriety.

The program is organized around the famous "Twelve Steps" toward sobriety and is based on the assumptions that alcohol is a physical disease and "once an alcoholic, always an alcoholic," which require that members never drink another drop after entering treatment. Several of the Twelve Steps ask members to place their trust in a "higher power" and to acknowledge their powerlessness over alcohol. AA also offers a powerful social support network (Vaillant & Milofsky, 1982). Groups based on the Twelve-Step model have been established for drug users (Narcotics Anonymous), gamblers, overeaters, spouses and children of alcoholics, "shopaholics" (compulsive shoppers), sexual addicts, and scores of others experiencing problems with impulse control. Nevertheless, there's virtually no research on the effectiveness of these other Twelve-Step approaches.

Although AA appears to be helpful for some people, many claims regarding its success aren't supported by data. People who attend AA meetings or receive treatment based on the Twelve Steps fare about as well as, but no better than, people who receive other treatments, including cognitive–behavioral therapy (Brandsma, Maultsby, & Welsh, 1980; Ferri, Amoto, & Davoli, 2006; Project MATCH Research Group, 1997). Moreover, AA members who end up in studies are usually the most active participants and have received prior professional help, resulting in an overestimate of how well AA works. Also, as many as 68 percent of participants drop out within three months of joining AA (Emrick, 1987), and those who remain in treatment are probably those who've improved (MacKillop et al., 2003).

CONTROLLED DRINKING AND RELAPSE PREVENTION. Contrary to the AA philosophy, the behavioral view assumes that excessive drinking is a learned behavior that therapists can modify and control without total abstinence (Marlatt, 1983). There's bitter controversy about whether *controlled drinking,* that is, drinking in moderation, is even an appropriate treatment goal. Nevertheless, there's considerable evidence that treatment programs that

Group therapy procedures are efficient, time-saving, and less costly than many individual treatment methods.

((•─│**Listen** to the audio file e-therapy on **mypsychlab.com**

WE ARE THE FACES OF RECOVERY
Recovery is *everywhere.*   Made possible as a public service by

Alcoholics Anonymous has been in existence since the 1930s, and provides self-help to people of all ages and backgrounds.

---

group therapy
therapy that treats more than one person at a time

Alcoholics Anonymous
Twelve-Step, self-help program that provides social support for achieving sobriety

encourage people with alcoholism to set limits, drink moderately, and reinforce their progress can be effective for many clients (MacKillop, et al., 2003; Miller & Hester, 1980; Sobell & Sobell, 1973, 1976). Programs that teach people skills to cope with stressful life circumstances and tolerate negative emotions (Monti, Gulliver, & Myers, 1994) are at least as effective as Twelve-Step programs (Project MATCH Research Group, 1997).

Bucking the popular belief, sometimes repeated in the AA community, of "one drink, one drunk," *relapse prevention* (RP) treatment assumes that many people with alcoholism will at some point experience a lapse, or slip, and resume drinking (Larimer, Palmer, & Marlatt, 1999; Marlatt & Gordon, 1985). RP teaches people to not feel ashamed, guilty, or discouraged when they lapse. Negative feelings about a slip can lead to continued drinking, called the *abstinence violation effect* (Marlatt & Gordon, 1985; Polivy & Herman, 2002). Once someone slips up, he figures, "Well, I guess I'm back to drinking again," and goes back to drinking at high levels. RP therapists teach people to rebound after a lapse and avoid situations in which they're tempted to drink. Thus, they learn that a *lapse* doesn't mean a *relapse*. Research suggests that relapse prevention programs are often effective (Irvin et al., 1999). Still, total abstinence may be the best goal for people with severe dependence on alcohol or for whom controlled drinking has failed (Rosenberg, 1993).

■ Family Therapies: Treating the Dysfunctional Family System

Family therapists see most psychological problems as rooted in a dysfunctional family system. For them, treatment must focus on the family context out of which conflicts presumably arise. In *family therapy*, the "patient"—the focus of treatment—isn't one person, but rather the family unit itself. Family therapists therefore focus on interactions among family members. 👁 Watch

STRATEGIC FAMILY THERAPY. **Strategic family interventions** are designed to remove barriers to effective communication. According to strategic therapists, including Virginia Satir (1964), Jay Haley (1976), and Paul Watzlawick (Watzlawick, Weakland, & Fisch, 1974), families often scapegoat one family member as the *identified patient* with the problem. For these therapists, the real source of difficulties lies in the dysfunctional ways in which family members communicate, solve problems, and relate to one another (see **FIGURE 16.2**).

Strategic therapists first identify the family's unhealthy communication patterns and its unsuccessful approaches to problem solving. Then, they invite family members to carry out planned tasks known as *directives*. Directives shift how family members solve problems and interact. They often involve *paradoxical requests*, which many of us associate with the concept of "reverse psychology." Some researchers (Beutler, Clarkin, & Bongar, 2000) have found that therapists often achieve success when they command their "resistant" or uncooperative clients to intentionally produce the thought, feeling, or behavior that troubled them.

Consider a therapist who "reframed" (cast in a positive light) a couple's arguments by interpreting them as a sign of their emotional closeness. The therapist gave the couple the paradoxical directive to *increase* their arguing to learn more about their love for one another. To show the therapist they were "not in love," they stopped arguing, which was, of course, the therapist's goal in the first place. Once their arguments ceased, their relationship improved (Watzlawick, Beavin, & Jackson, 1967).

STRUCTURAL FAMILY THERAPY. In **structural family therapy** (Minuchin, 1974), the therapist actively immerses herself in the everyday activities of the family to make changes in how they arrange and organize interactions. Salvatore Minuchin and his colleagues successfully treated a 14-year-old girl named Laura who obtained her father's attention by refusing to eat. Eventually, Laura could express in words the message that her refusal to eat conveyed indirectly, and she no longer refused to eat to attain affection (Aponte & Hoffman, 1973). Research indicates that family therapy is more effective than no treatment (Hazelrigg, Cooper, & Borduin, 1987; Vetere, 2001) and at least as effective as individual therapy (Foster & Gurman, 1985; Shadish, 1995).

FIGURE 16.2 Where's the Problem?
According to the strategic family therapy approach, families often single out one family member as "the problem" when the problem is actually rooted in the interactional patterns of all family members.

👁 Watch a Family Therapist on **mypsychlab.com**

In structural family therapy, the therapist immerses herself in the family's everyday activities. Having observed what goes on in the family, the therapist can then advocate for changes in how the family arranges and organizes its interactions.

strategic family intervention
family therapy approach designed to remove barriers to effective communication

structural family therapy
treatment in which therapists deeply involve themselves in family activities to change how family members arrange and organize interactions

✓•─[**Study** and **Review** on **mypsychlab.com**]

assess your knowledge | FACT OR FICTION?

1. An important criticism of psychoanalytic therapy is that many of its key concepts aren't falsifiable. **True** / **False**

2. Reflection is a central component of person-centered therapy. **True** / **False**

3. Group psychotherapies are generally as effective as individual psychotherapies. **True** / **False**

4. Alcoholics Anonymous is no more effective than many other alcohol abuse treatments. **True** / **False**

5. Family therapies focus on the one person in the family with the most problems. **True** / **False**

Answers: 1. T (p. 638); 2. T (p. 639); 3. T (p. 641); 4. T (p. 641); 5. F (p. 642)

A behavior therapist treating a bad habit, like nail biting, would try to determine the situations in which nail-biting occurs, as well as the consequences of nail-biting for the person—such as distraction from anxiety.

BEHAVIORAL APPROACHES: CHANGING MALADAPTIVE ACTIONS

16.7   Describe the characteristics of behavior therapy and identify different behavioral approaches.

16.8   Describe the features of cognitive-behavioral therapies (CBT).

In sharp contrast to psychotherapists who hold that insight is the key to improvement, **behavior therapists** are so named because they focus on the specific behaviors that lead the client to seek therapy and the current variables that maintain problematic thoughts, feelings, and behaviors (Antony & Roemer, 2003). Behavior therapists assume that behavior change results from the operation of basic principles of learning, especially classical conditioning, operant conditioning, and observational learning (see Chapter 6). For example, the client's problematic behaviors, such as crossing the street whenever he sees a dog in the case of someone with a dog phobia, are maintained by reinforcement (see Chapter 6). Avoiding the dog helps the person to obtain negative reinforcement—in this case, escaping anxiety—although the person is often unaware of this function.

Behavior therapists use a wide variety of *behavioral assessment* techniques to pinpoint environmental causes of the person's problem, establish specific and measurable treatment goals, and devise therapeutic procedures. The emphasis is on current, rather than past, behaviors and on specific behaviors, rather than broad traits. Behavior therapists may use direct observations of behaviors, verbal descriptions of the nature and dimensions of the problem, scores on paper-and-pencil tests, standardized interviews (First et al., 1996), and physiological measures (Yartz & Hawk, 2001) to plan treatment and monitor its progress. A complete assessment considers clients' gender, race, socioeconomic class, culture, sexual orientation, and ethnic factors (Ivey, Ivey, & Simek-Morgan, 1993), as well as information about their interpersonal relationships and drug use (Lazarus, 2003). Evaluation of treatment effectiveness is integrated seamlessly into all phases of therapy, and therapists encourage clients to apply their newly acquired coping skills to everyday life. Let's now examine the nuts and bolts of several behavioral approaches.

■ Systematic Desensitization and Exposure Therapies: Learning Principles in Action

Systematic desensitization is an excellent example of how behavior therapists apply learning principles to treatment. Psychiatrist Joseph Wolpe developed systematic desensitization (SD) in 1958 to help clients manage phobias. SD gradually exposes clients to anxiety-producing situations through the use of imagined scenes. This technique was the earliest **exposure therapy**, a class of procedures that confronts clients with what they fear with the goal of reducing this fear.

behavior therapist
therapist who focuses on specific problem behaviors, and current variables that maintain problematic thoughts, feelings, and behaviors

systematic desensitization
clients are taught to relax as they are gradually exposed to what they fear in a stepwise manner

exposure therapy
therapy that confronts clients with what they fear with the goal of reducing the fear

In vivo desensitization: Clients gradually approach and handle any fears, as these clients are doing as they overcome their fear of flying.

ruling out rival hypotheses ⟩

HAVE IMPORTANT ALTERNATIVE EXPLANATIONS FOR THE FINDINGS BEEN EXCLUDED?

HOW DESENSITIZATION WORKS: ONE STEP AT A TIME. SD is based on the principle of *reciprocal inhibition*, which says that clients can't experience two conflicting responses simultaneously. We can't be anxious and relaxed at the same time because relaxation inhibits anxiety. Wolpe described his technique as a form of classical conditioning (see Chapter 6) and called it *counterconditioning*. By pairing an incompatible relaxation response with anxiety, we condition a more adaptive response to anxiety-arousing stimuli.

A therapist begins SD by teaching the client how to relax. She might imagine pleasant scenes, focus on breathing and maintaining a slow breathing rate, and alternately tense and relax her muscles (Bernstein, Borkovec, & Hazlett-Stevens, 2000; Jacobson, 1938). Next, the therapist helps the client to construct an *anxiety hierarchy*—a "ladder" of situations that climbs from least to most anxiety provoking. We can find a hierarchy used to treat a person with height phobia in **TABLE 16.4**. The therapy proceeds in a stepwise manner. The therapist asks the client to relax and imagine the first scene, and moves to the next, more anxiety-producing scene only after the client reports feeling relaxed while imagining the first scene.

Consider the following example of how a client moves stepwise up the anxiety hierarchy, from the least to most anxiety-producing scene.

> **Therapist:** "Soon I shall ask you to imagine a scene. After you hear a description of the situation, please imagine it as vividly as you can, through your own eyes, as if you were actually there. Try to include all the details in the scene. While you're visualizing the situation, you may continue feeling as relaxed as you are now … After 5, 10, or 15 seconds, I'll ask you to stop imagining the scene … and to just relax. But if you begin to feel even the slightest increase in anxiety or tension, please signal this to me by raising your left forefinger … I'll step in and ask you to stop imagining the situation and then will help you get relaxed once more" (Goldfried & Davison, 1976, pp. 124–125).

If the client reports anxiety at any point, the therapist interrupts the process and helps her relax again. Then, the therapist reintroduces the scene that preceded the one that caused anxiety. This process continues until the client can confront the most frightening scenes without anxiety.

Desensitization can also occur *in vivo*, that is, in "real life." In vivo SD involves gradual exposure to what the client actually fears, rather than imagining the anxiety-provoking situation. SD is effective for a wide range of phobias, insomnia, speech disorders, asthma attacks, nightmares, and some cases of problem drinking (Spiegler & Guevremont, 2003).

The Effectiveness of Systematic Desensitization. Behavior therapists strive to discover not only what works, but why. Researchers can evaluate many therapeutic procedures by isolating the effects of each component and comparing these effects with that of the full treatment package (Wilson & O' Leary, 1980). This approach is called **dismantling**, because it enables researchers to examine the effectiveness of isolated components of a broader treatment. Dismantling helps rule out rival hypotheses about the effective mechanisms of SD and other treatments.

dismantling
research procedure for examining the effectiveness of isolated components of a larger treatment

TABLE 16.4 A Systematic Desensitization Hierarchy of a Person with a Fear of Heights.

1. You are beginning to climb the ladder leaning against the side of your house. You plan to work on the roof.
2. You are driving with the family on a California coastal highway with a dropoff to the right.
3. You are in a commercial airliner at the time of takeoff.
4. You are in an airliner at an altitude of 30,000 feet experiencing considerable turbulence.
5. You are on a California seaside cliff, approximately two feet (judged to be a safe distance) from the edge and looking down.
6. You are climbing the water tower to assist in painting, about 10 feet from the ground.
7. You are on the catwalk around the water tank, painting the tank.

(*Source:* Rimm & Masters, 1979)

Dismantling studies show that no single component of desensitization (relaxation, imagery, an anxiety hierarchy) is essential: We can eliminate each without affecting treatment outcome. Therefore, the door is open to diverse interpretations for the treatment's success (Kazdin & Wilcoxon, 1976; Lohr, DeMaio, & McGlynn, 2003). One possibility is that the credibility of the treatment creates a strong placebo effect (see Chapter 2; Mineka & Thomas, 1999). Interestingly, desensitization may fare no better than a placebo procedure designed to arouse an equivalent degree of positive expectations (Lick, 1975). Alternatively, when therapists expose clients to what they fear, clients may realize their fears are irrational, or their fear response may extinguish (see Chapter 6) following repeated uneventful contact with the feared stimulus (Casey, Oei, & Newcombe, 2004; Rachman, 1994; Zinbarg, 1993).

FLOODING AND VIRTUAL REALITY EXPOSURE. Flooding therapies provide a vivid contrast to SD. Flooding therapists jump right to the top of the anxiety hierarchy and expose clients to images of the stimuli they fear the most for prolonged periods, often for an hour or even several hours. Flooding therapies are based on the idea that fears are maintained by avoidance. For example, because individuals with a height phobia continually avoid high places, they never learn that the disastrous consequences they envision won't occur. Ironically, their avoidance only perpetuates their fears by means of negative reinforcement (see Chapter 6). The flooding therapist provokes anxiety repeatedly in the absence of actual negative consequences, so that extinction of the fear can proceed.

Like SD, flooding can be conducted in vivo. To paraphrase the Nike slogan ("Just do it"): "If you're afraid to do it, do it!" (Chambless & Goldstein, 1980). During the first session, a therapist who practices in vivo flooding might accompany a person with a height phobia to the top of a skyscraper and look down for an hour, or however long it takes for anxiety to dissipate. Remarkably, many people with specific phobias—including those who were in psychodynamic therapy for decades with no relief—have been essentially cured of their fears after only a single session (Antony & Barlow, 2002; Williams, Turner, & Peer, 1985). Therapists have successfully used flooding with numerous anxiety disorders, including obsessive-compulsive disorder, social phobia, posttraumatic stress disorder, and agoraphobia.

A crucial component of flooding is **response prevention** (more recently called "ritual prevention" in the case of obsessive-compulsive disorder, or OCD), in which therapists prevent clients from performing their typical avoidance behaviors (Spiegler, 1983). A therapist may treat a person with a hand-washing compulsion by exposing her to dirt and preventing her from washing her hands (Franklin & Foa, 2002). Research demonstrates that this treatment is effective for OCD and closely related conditions (Chambless & Ollendick, 2001). Some therapists have applied exposure plus response prevention to clients with bulimia (see Chapter 11) by having them eat large amounts of food, but preventing them from purging, exercising, or otherwise trying to lose weight. Research on the effectiveness of this approach for bulimia is mixed (Carter et al., 2003).

Virtual reality exposure therapy is the new kid on the block of exposure therapies. With high-tech equipment, which provides a "virtually lifelike" experience of fear-provoking situations, therapists can treat many anxiety-related conditions, including height phobia (Emmelkamp et al., 2001), storm phobia (Botella et al., 2006), flying phobia (Emmelkamp et al., 2002), and posttraumatic stress disorder (Rothbaum et al., 2001). Virtual reality exposure not only rivals the effectiveness of traditional in vivo exposure, but also provides repeated exposure to situations that often aren't feasible in real life, like flying in airplanes.

EXPOSURE: FRINGE AND FAD TECHNIQUES. Traditionally, behavior therapists have been careful not to exaggerate claims of the effectiveness of exposure therapies and promote them to the public as cure-alls. We can contrast this cautious approach with that of recent proponents of fringe therapeutic techniques, some of who've made extraordinary claims that don't stack up well against the evidence.

ruling out rival hypotheses

HAVE IMPORTANT ALTERNATIVE EXPLANATIONS FOR THE FINDINGS BEEN EXCLUDED?

"But I'm barely breathing... I don't break even"

Flooding therapies = immediately exposes clients to fearing stimuli b/c of avoidance.

Exposure therapies provide clients with cutting-edge virtual reality technology to confront their fears of spiders and other potentially frightening stimuli. Does this virtual reality scene cause you extreme anxiety?

Flooding component ↓

response prevention
technique in which therapists prevent clients from performing their typical avoidance behaviors

extraordinary claims

IS THE EVIDENCE AS STRONG AS THE CLAIM?

Thought Field Therapists claim that touching of body parts in a set order can play a role in treating longstanding phobias resistant to treatment by other means.

Roger Callahan, who developed *Thought Field Therapy* (TFT), claimed that his procedure can cure phobias in as little as five minutes (Callahan, 1995, 2001) and cure not only human fears, but also fears of horses and dogs. In TFT, the client thinks of a distressing problem while the therapist taps specific points on her body in a predetermined order. Meanwhile, the client hums parts of "The Star Spangled Banner," rolls her eyes, or counts (how TFT therapists accomplish these feats with animals is unknown). These decidedly strange procedures supposedly remove invisible "energy blocks" associated with a specific fear. There's no research evidence for the assertion that the technique cures anxiety by manipulating energy fields, which have never been shown to exist, or for the implausible claim of virtually instantaneous cures for the vast majority of phobia sufferers (Lohr et al., 2003). Because the "energy blocks" of TFT aren't measurable, the theoretical claims of TFT are unfalsifiable.

falsifiability
CAN THE CLAIM BE DISPROVED?

Some other exposure-based therapies feature numerous "bells and whistles" that provide them with the superficial veneer of science. Take *eye movement desensitization and reprocessing* (EMDR), which has been marketed widely as a "breakthrough" treatment for anxiety disorders (Shapiro, 1995; Shapiro & Forrest, 1997). As of 2010, more than 80,000 therapists have been trained in EMDR. EMDR proponents claim that clients' lateral eye movements, made while they imagine a past traumatic event, enhance their processing of painful memories. Yet systematic reviews of research demonstrate that the eye movements of EMDR play no role in this treatment's effectiveness. Moreover, EMDR is no more effective than standard exposure treatments (Davidson & Parker, 2001; Lohr, Tolin, & Lilienfeld, 1998; Rubin, 2003). Accordingly, a parsimonious hypothesis is that the active ingredient of EMDR isn't the eye movements for which it's named, but rather the exposure the technique provides.

In EMDR, the client focuses on the therapist's fingers as they move back and forth. Nevertheless, studies indicate that such eye movements play no useful role in EMDR's effectiveness.

occam's razor
DOES A SIMPLER EXPLANATION FIT THE DATA JUST AS WELL?

■ Modeling in Therapy: Learning by Watching

Clients can learn many things by observing therapists model positive behaviors. Modeling is one form of *observational or vicarious learning* (see Chapters 6 and 14). Albert Bandura (1971, 1977) has long advocated **participant modeling**, a technique in which the therapist models a calm encounter with the client's feared object or situation, and then guides the client through the steps of the encounter until she can cope unassisted.

ASSERTION TRAINING. Modeling is an important component of assertion and social skills training programs designed to help clients with social anxiety. The primary goals of assertion training are to facilitate the expression of thoughts and feelings in a forthright and socially appropriate manner and to ensure that clients aren't taken advantage of, ignored, or denied their legitimate rights (Alberti & Emmons, 2001). In assertion training, therapists teach clients to avoid extreme reactions to others' unreasonable demands, such as submissiveness, on the one hand, and aggressiveness, on the other. Assertiveness, the middle ground between these extremes, is the goal.

BEHAVIORAL REHEARSAL. Therapies commonly use behavioral rehearsal in assertion training and other participant modeling techniques. In behavioral rehearsal, the client engages in role-playing with a therapist to learn and practice new skills. The therapist plays the role of a relevant person such as a spouse, parent, or boss. The client reacts to the character enacted by the therapist, and in turn the therapist offers coaching and feedback. To give the client an opportunity to model assertive behav-

participant modeling
technique in which the therapist first models a problematic situation and then guides the client through steps to cope with it unassisted

iors, therapist and client reverse roles, with the therapist playing the client's role. By doing so, the therapist models not only what the client might say, but how the client might say it.

To transfer what clients learn to everyday life, therapists encourage them to practice their newfound skills outside of therapy sessions. Modeling and social skills training can make valuable contributions to treating (although not curing) schizophrenia, autism, depression, attention-deficit/hyperactivity disorder (ADHD), and social anxiety (Antony & Roemer, 2003; Scattone, 2007; Monastra, 2008).

■ Operant Procedures: Consequences Count

As you may recall from Chapter 6, psychologists have used operant conditioning procedures to good effect among children with autism. Another example of an operant procedure is the **token economy** (again see Chapter 6), widely used in treatment programs in institutional and residential settings, as well as the home. In token economies, certain behaviors, like helping others, are consistently rewarded with tokens that clients can later exchange for more tangible rewards, whereas other behaviors, like screaming at hospital staff, are ignored or punished. In this way, such programs shape, maintain, or alter behaviors by the consistent application of operant conditioning principles (Kazdin, 1978). Critics of token economies argue that the benefits don't necessarily generalize to other settings, and they're difficult and impractical to administer (Corrigan, 1995). Nevertheless, token economies have shown some success in the classroom (Boniecki & Moore, 2003), in treating children with ADHD at home and at school (Mueser & Liberman, 1995), and in treating clients with schizophrenia who require long-term hospitalization (Dixon et al., 2010; Paul & Lentz, 1977).

Aversion therapies use punishment to decrease the frequency of undesirable behaviors. Aversion therapies are aptly named. While a person engages in a problem behavior, therapists introduce stimuli that most people experience as painful, unpleasant, or even revolting. For example, therapists have used medications, such as disulfiram—better known as Antabuse—to make people vomit after drinking alcohol (Brewer, 1992), electric shocks to treat psychologically triggered recurrent sneezing (Kushner, 1968), and verbal descriptions of feeling nauseated while people imagine smoking cigarettes (Cautela, 1971).

Research provides at best mixed support for the effectiveness of aversive procedures (Spiegler & Guevremont, 2003). For example, people with alcoholism often simply stop taking Antabuse rather than stop drinking (MacKillop et al., 2003). In general, therapists attempt minimally unpleasant techniques before moving on to more aversive measures. The decision to implement aversion therapies should be made only after carefully weighing their costs and benefits relative to alternative approaches.

■ Cognitive-Behavioral Therapies: Learning to Think Differently

Advocates of **cognitive-behavioral therapies** hold that beliefs play the central role in our feelings and behaviors. These therapies share three core assumptions: (1) cognitions are identifiable and measureable, (2) cognitions are the key players in both healthy and unhealthy psychological functioning, and (3) irrational beliefs or catastrophic thinking, such as "I'm worthless, and will never succeed at anything," can be replaced by more rational and adaptive cognitions. ◉ ▭Watch

THE ABCS OF RATIONAL EMOTIVE BEHAVIOR THERAPY. Beginning in the mid-1950s, pioneering therapist Albert Ellis (Ellis, 1958, 1962) advocated *rational emotive therapy* (RET), later renamed *rational emotive behavior therapy* (REBT). In many respects, REBT is a prime example of a cognitive-behavioral approach. It's cognitive in its emphasis on changing how we think (that's the "cognitive" part), but also focuses on changing how we act (that's the "behavioral" part).

◉ ▭**Watch** Cognitive Behavioral Therapy on **mypsychlab.com**

token economy
method in which desirable behaviors are rewarded with tokens that clients can exchange for tangible rewards

aversion therapy
treatment that uses punishment to decrease the frequency of undesirable behaviors

cognitive-behavioral therapies
treatments that attempt to replace maladaptive or irrational cognitions with more adaptive, rational cognitions

FIGURE 16.3 The ABCs of Rational Emotive Behavior Therapy. How someone feels about an event is determined by his or her beliefs about the event.

A Activating event	**B** Beliefs	**C** Consequences
Exam	Oh no! I thought I did well, but I really bombed.	I'm feeling really depressed, now I'll never succeed in college..
	Phew, I did better than I thought. This stuff doesn't come easily to me.	I feel great! Now I know I can do better in my other classes.

LOVE ME, LOVE ME, ONLY ME!

Love me, love me, only me
Or I'll die without you!
Make your love a guarantee,
So I can never doubt you!
Love me, love me totally
Really, really try dear.
But if you demand love, too,
I'll hate you till I die, dear!
Love me, love me all the time,
Thoroughly and wholly!
Life turns into slushy slime
Less you love me solely!
Love me with great tenderness,
With no ifs or buts dear.
If you love me somewhat less,
I'll really hate your guts, dear!

Albert Ellis wrote a number of humorous song lyrics to demonstrate REBT principles (Ellis even recorded them commercially, although it's unlikely that he'd make it to the finals of *American Idol*). This song, set to the tune of Yankee Doodle, pokes fun at the widespread but irrational belief that all romantic relationships should be characterized by promises of complete, unconditional, and never-ending love. (Adapted from "Love Me, Love Me, Only Me!" by Albert Ellis. Reprinted with permission of Albert Ellis Institute)

falsifiability

CAN THE CLAIM BE DISPROVED?

Ellis argued that we respond to an unpleasant activating (internal or external) event (A) with a range of emotional and behavioral consequences (C). As we all know, people often respond very differently to the same objective event; some students respond to an 75 on an exam by celebrating, whereas others respond by berating themselves for not getting a 90 or even a 100. For Ellis, the differences in how we respond to the same event stem largely from differences in (B)—our belief systems (see **FIGURE 16.3**). The ABCs Ellis identified lie at the heart of most, if not all, cognitive-behavior therapies.

Some beliefs are rational: They're flexible, logical, and promote self-acceptance. In contrast, others are irrational: They're associated with unrealistic demands about the self ("I must be perfect"), others ("I must become worried about other people's problems"), and life conditions ("I must be worried about things I can't control."). Ellis also maintained that psychologically unhealthy people frequently "awfulize," that is, engage in catastrophic thinking about their problems ("If I don't get this job, it would be the worst thing that ever happened to me"). We can find examples of 12 irrational beliefs outlined by Ellis in **TABLE 16.5**. According to Ellis, our vulnerability to psychological disturbance is a product of the frequency and strength of our irrational beliefs (David, Lynn, & Ellis, 2010).

To his ABC scheme, Ellis added a (D) and (E) component to describe how therapists treat clients. REBT therapists encourage clients to actively dispute (D) their irrational beliefs and adopt more effective (E) and rational beliefs to increase adaptive responses. To modify clients' irrational beliefs, the therapist forcefully encourages them to rethink their assumptions and personal philosophy. REBT therapists often assign "homework" designed to falsify clients' maladaptive beliefs. For example, they may give shy clients an assignment to talk to an attractive man or woman to falsify their belief that "If I'm rejected by someone I like, it will be absolutely terrible."

OTHER COGNITIVE-BEHAVIORAL APPROACHES. Cognitive-behavioral therapists differ in the extent to which they incorporate behavioral methods. Aaron Beck's enormously popular *cognitive therapy*, which many credit as playing an instrumental role in creating the field of cognitive-behavioral therapy (Smith, 2009), emphasizes identifying and modifying

TABLE 16.5 Irrational Beliefs:"The Dirty Dozen."   Albert Ellis identified 12 irrational ideas ("The Dirty Dozen") that are widespread in our culture. You may find it interesting to see which of these beliefs you've entertained at some point in your life. Because these ideas are so much a part of many people's thinking, don't be surprised if you hold a number of them.

1. You must have sincere love and approval almost all the time from all the people you find significant.
2. You must prove yourself thoroughly competent, adequate, and achieving; or you must at least have real competence or talent at something important.
3. People who harm you or commit misdeeds rate as generally bad, wicked, or villainous individuals, and you should severely blame, damn, and punish them for their sins.
4. Life proves awful, terrible, horrible, or catastrophic when things do not go the way you would like them to go.
5. Emotional misery comes from external pressures and you have little ability to control your feelings or rid yourself of depression and hostility.
6. If something seems dangerous or fearsome, you must become terribly occupied with and upset about it.
7. You will find it easier to avoid facing many of life's difficulties and self-responsibilities than to undertake some rewarding forms of self-discipline.
8. Your past remains all-important and, because something once strongly influenced your life, it has to keep determining your feelings and behavior today.
9. People and things should turn out better than they do; and you have to view it as awful and horrible if you do not quickly find good solutions to life's hassles.
10. You can achieve happiness by inaction or by passively and uncommitedly "enjoying yourself."
11. You must have a high degree of order or certainty to feel comfortable.
12. You give yourself a global rating as a human, and your general worth and self-acceptance depends on the goodness of your performance and the degree that people approve of you.

(*Source:* Ellis, 1977)

PERSONAL 110(

About 9 months ago I began to notice a man wearing sunglasses who was watching me from a parking lot across the street. I thought he was suspicious and eventually concluded that he and his colleagues were following me everywhere I went. Even when I went on vacation to California 3000 miles away, I noticed that the same man and his colleagues were not far behind. After several weeks of careful investigation, I decided to leave home and travel to Europe in an attempt to escape him. Even while in Paris, I felt his eyes on me and was quite sure that I even saw him on television one night. I fear he has already contacted my employer and possibly some of my friends, because they all seem more distant from me lately. I want you all to know that everything he says about me is a lie.

---

distorted thoughts and long-held negative core beliefs ("I'm unlovable") (Beck et al., 1979; J. Beck, 1995). Nevertheless, cognitive therapy places somewhat greater weight on behavioral procedures than does Ellis's REBT (Stricker & Gold, 2003). Researchers have found Beck's approach helpful for people with depression and perhaps even bipolar disorder and schizophrenia (A. T. Beck, 2005; Hollon, Thase, & Markowitz, 2002).

In Donald Meichenbaum's (1985) *stress inoculation training*, therapists teach clients to prepare for and cope with future stressful life events. In this approach, therapists "inoculate" clients against an upcoming stressor by getting them to anticipate it and develop cognitive skills to minimize its harm, much as we receive a vaccine (inoculation) containing a small amount of a virus to ward off illness. Therapists modify clients' *self-statements*, that is, their ongoing mental dialogue (Meichenbaum, 1985). Clients fearful of giving a speech may learn to say things to themselves like, "Even though it's scary, the outcome probably won't be as bad as I fear." Therapists have applied stress inoculation successfully to children and adults facing medical and surgical procedures, public speaking, and exams (Meichenbaum, 1996), as well as to clients with anger problems (Cahill et al., 2003; Novaco, 1995).

Two pioneers of cognitive-behavioral therapy, Aaron Beck (*left;* 1921–) and Albert Ellis (1913–2007).

? Each of the three statements below—provided by therapists in response to the person who placed the personal ad—is typical of a different psychotherapy. **Match each statement with the therapy (A. client-centered, B. Freudian, C. REBT) it best represents:** (See answer upside down on bottom of page.)

1. You're being irrational and jumping to conclusions. Even if someone were following you, why conclude that he's contacted your friends just because they're more distant?
2. You've told me that during childhood, your father constantly judged you; and when he stared at you, it brought about tremendous guilt. Perhaps this man you can't escape symbolizes your father?
3. Starting nine months ago, you became suspicious of a man you're now pretty sure will damage relationships you prize. How terrible it must feel to think he's telling lies about you!

Answers: 1-C, 2-B, 3-A

FACTOID

There's at least some evidence that therapists' theoretical orientation is correlated with their personality traits. Several, although not all, studies suggest that compared with other therapists, psychoanalytic therapists tend to be especially insecure and serious, behavior therapists tend to be especially assertive and self-confident, and cognitive-behavioral therapists tend to be especially rational (Keinan, Almagor, & Ben-Porath, 1989; Walton, 1978).

TABLE 16.6 Primary Theoretical Orientations of Practicing Clinical Psychologists in the United States. As we can see, the largest proportion of clinical psychologists calls themselves eclectic/integrative.

ORIENTATION	% CLINICAL PSYCHOLOGISTS
Eclectic/Integrative	29
Cognitive	28
Psychodynamic	12
Behavioral	10
Other	7
Interpersonal	4
Psychoanalytic	3
Family Systems	3
Existential-Humanistic	2
Person-Centered	1

(*Sources:* Prochaska & Norcross, 2007; derived from Bechtold et al., 2001; Norcross, Karpiak, & Santoro, 2005; Norcross, Strausser, & Missar, 1988)

ruling out rival hypotheses

HAVE IMPORTANT ALTERNATIVE EXPLANATIONS FOR THE FINDINGS BEEN EXCLUDED?

[handwritten notes: 3rd wave Therapies: ACT = acceptance and commitment therapy. DBT = dialectical behavior therapy.]

ACCEPTANCE: THE THIRD WAVE OF COGNITIVE-BEHAVIORAL THERAPY. The past few decades have witnessed a surge of interest in so-called *third wave therapies* that represent a shift from both the first (behavioral) and second (cognitive) waves of the cognitive-behavioral tradition (Hayes, 2004). Instead of trying to change maladaptive behaviors and negative thoughts, third wave therapies embrace a different goal: to assist clients with accepting all aspects of their experience—thoughts, feelings, memories, and physical sensations—they've avoided or suppressed. Consistent with this goal, research suggests that avoiding and suppressing disturbing experiences, rather than accepting or confronting them, often backfires, creating even greater emotional turmoil (Amir et al., 2001; Teasdale, Segal, & Williams, 2003). Steven Hayes and colleagues' (Hayes, Follette, & Linehan, 2004; Hayes, Strosahl, & Wilson, 1999) acceptance and commitment therapy (ACT) stands at the vanguard of such approaches. ACT practitioners teach clients that negative thoughts such as "I'm worthless" are merely thoughts, not "facts," while encouraging them to accept and tolerate the full range of their feelings, and act in keeping with their goals and values.

Marsha Linehan's (Linehan 1993) dialectical behavior therapy (DBT), used frequently in the treatment of clients with borderline personality disorder (see Chapter 15) at risk for suicide, addresses the *dialectic*—the apparent contradiction between opposing tendencies—of changing problematic behavior and accepting it. Linehan encourages clients to accept their intense emotions while actively attempting to cope with these emotions by making changes in their lives.

It remains to be seen whether these new techniques are more effective than standard behavioral and cognitive-behavioral therapies, and critics have raised concerns that they've been overhyped in the absence of convincing scientific evidence (Hofmann & Asmundson, 2008; Ost, 2008). Nevertheless, these methods, and their potential unique contributions, are worthy of further investigation.

Many third wave therapies fall in line with the current trend in psychotherapy for therapists to create individually tailored, *eclectic* approaches—treatments that integrate techniques and theories from more than one existing approach (Lazarus, 2006; Stricker & Gold, 2003; Wachtel, 1997). For example, ACT and DBT therapists adopt behavioral techniques and meditation practices from a Buddhist tradition (see Chapter 5), and borrow from humanistic psychology's emphasis on awareness and emotional expression. As we can see in **TABLE 16.6**, the largest percentage of practicing clinical psychologists describes their theoretical orientation as eclectic/integrative (Norcross, 2005; Prochaska & Norcross, 2007).

Only recently have psychologists come to learn which specific therapeutic components contribute to treatment success. For example, *behavioral activation*—getting clients, such as those who are depressed, to participate in reinforcing activities—is a key component of many third wave and cognitive-behavioral approaches, and is emerging as a key element of successful psychotherapy (Dimidjian et al., 2006; Hopko, Robertson, & Lejuez, 2006). Still, the more ingredients are tossed into the therapeutic mix, the more challenging it becomes to dismantle integrative approaches and evaluate rival hypotheses regarding which ingredients matter.

CBT AND THIRD WAVE APPROACHES EVALUATED SCIENTIFICALLY. Research allows us to draw the following conclusions about the effectiveness of behavioral and cognitive-behavioral therapies:

1. They're more effective than no treatment or placebo treatment (Bowers & Clum, 1988; Smith, Glass, & Miller, 1980)

2. They're at least as effective (Sloane et al., 1975; Smith & Glass, 1977), and in some cases more effective, than psychodynamic and person-centered therapies (Grawe, Donati, & Bernauer, 1998).

3. They're at least as effective as drug therapies for depression (Elkin, 1994).

4. In general, CBT and behavioral treatments are about equally effective for most problems (Feske & Chambless, 1995; Jacobson et al., 1996).

Haha.

5. Third wave approaches have scored successes in treating a variety of disorders, including depression and alcoholism (Marlatt, 2002; Segal, Williams, & Teasdale, 2002), and CBT and ACT achieve comparable outcomes in treating depression and anxiety (Forman et al., 2007).

✓● **Study** and **Review** on **mypsychlab.com**

assess your knowledge — FACT OR FICTION?

1. Behavior therapies place a great deal of importance on insight. **True / False** *behavior/actions*
2. One commonly used assertion training technique is behavioral rehearsal. **True / False**
3. Token economy programs are based on operant conditioning principles. **True / False**
4. According to Albert Ellis, feelings create irrational beliefs. **True / False**
5. Acceptance and commitment therapy borrows techniques from a Buddhist tradition. **True / False**

Answers: 1. F (p.643); 2. T (p.646); 3. T (p.647); 4. F (p.648); 5. T (p.650)

IS PSYCHOTHERAPY EFFECTIVE?

16.9 Evaluate the claim that all psychotherapies are equally effective.

16.10 Explain how ineffective therapies can sometimes appear to be effective.

In Lewis Carroll's book *Alice in Wonderland,* the Dodo bird proclaimed after a race that "All have won, and all must have prizes." Seventy years ago, Saul Rosenzweig (1936) delivered the same verdict regarding the effectiveness of different psychotherapies. That is, all appear to be helpful, but are roughly equivalent in their outcomes: "All have won, and all must have prizes" (see **FIGURE 16.4**).

■ The Dodo Bird Verdict: Alive or Extinct?

Are all therapies equivalent in their effects?

Before the mid-1970s, there was considerable controversy regarding whether psychotherapy was effective at all. Some investigators concluded that it was virtually worthless (Eysenck, 1952), whereas others concluded the opposite.

Beginning in the late 1970s, a scientific consensus emerged that psychotherapy works in alleviating human suffering (Landman & Dawes, 1982; Smith & Glass, 1977)—a consensus that holds to this day. This conclusion derived from studies using a technique called *meta-analysis*. A **meta-analysis**, meaning "analysis of analysis," is a statistical method that helps researchers to interpret large bodies of psychological literature. By pooling the results of many studies as though they were one big study, meta-analysis allows researchers to seek patterns across large numbers of studies and draw general conclusions that hold up across independent laboratories (Hunt, 1997; Rosenthal & DiMatteo, 2001).

Today, some researchers using meta-analysis have claimed to support the Dodo bird verdict. Their results suggest that a wide range of psychotherapies are about equal in their effects (Garske & Anderson, 2003; Grissom, 1996; Wampold et al., 1997, 2002). Studies with experienced therapists who've practiced behavioral, psychodynamic, and person-centered approaches have found that all are more successful in helping clients compared with no treatment, but no different from each other in their effects (DiLoretto, 1971; Sloane et al.,1975).

Other researchers aren't convinced. They contend that the Dodo bird verdict, like the real Dodo bird, is extinct. Although most forms of psychotherapy work well, and many are about equal in their effects, there are notable exceptions (Beutler, 2002; Hunsley & DiGuilio, 2002). For example, behavioral and cognitive-behavioral treatments are clearly more effective than other treatments for children and adolescents with behavior problems

In Lewis Carroll's book *Alice in Wonderland,* the Dodo bird declared, following a race, that "All have won, and all must have prizes." Psychotherapy researchers use the term *dodo bird verdict* to refer to the conclusion that all therapies are equivalent in their effects. Not all investigators accept this verdict.

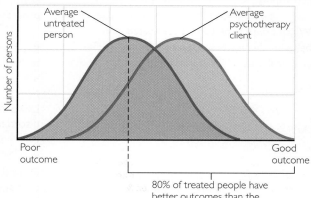

FIGURE 16.4 The Effectiveness of Psychotherapy. This graph shows two normal distributions (see Chapter 2) derived from nearly 500 studies of psychotherapy outcomes. The distribution on the left shows people who haven't received psychotherapy, and the distribution on the right shows people who've received psychotherapy. As we can see, across a variety of treatments and samples, 80 percent of people who receive therapy do better than people who don't. (*Source:* Smith, Glass, & Miller, 1980)

meta-analysis
statistical method that helps researchers to interpret large bodies of psychological literature

Helped reach a consensus to conclude that psychotherapy works in alleviating human suffering.

Scared Straight programs expose adolescents to prisoners and prison life in an effort to "scare them" away from criminal careers. Despite their popularity, research suggests that such programs are not merely ineffective, but harmful in some cases. Which principle of learning associated with behavior therapy best explains this finding? (See answer upside down at bottom of page.)

(Garske & Anderson, 2003; Weisz et al., 1995). Moreover, behavioral and cognitive-behavioral therapies consistently outperform most other therapies for anxiety disorders, including phobias, panic disorder, and obsessive-compulsive disorder (Addis et al., 2004; Chambless & Ollendick, 2001).

Also calling into question the Dodo bird verdict are findings that some psychotherapies can make people worse (Barlow, 2010; Dimidjian & Hollon, 2010; Lilienfeld, 2007). Although we might assume that doing something is always better than doing nothing for psychological distress, research suggests otherwise. A nontrivial proportion of clients, perhaps 5 to 10 percent, become worse following psychotherapy, and some may become worse *because of* psychotherapy (Castonguay et al., 2010; Rhule, 2005; Strupp, Hadley, & Gomez-Schwartz, 1978). For example, several researchers have found that crisis debriefing (see Chapter 12) can sometimes increase the risk of posttraumatic stress symptoms in people exposed to trauma. The same appears to be true of Scared Straight interventions, which try to "scare away" at-risk adolescents from a life a life of crime by introducing them to actual prisoners (Petrosino, Turpin-Petrosino, & Buehler, 2003). We can see a number of other potentially harmful therapies in **TABLE 16.7**.

TABLE 16.7 List of Potentially Harmful Therapies. Research suggests that some psychotherapies are potentially harmful for certain individuals.

THERAPY	INTERVENTION	POTENTIAL HARM
Facilitated communication	A facilitator holds the hands of children with autism or other developmental disabilities as they type messages on a keyboard (Chapter 2).	False accusations of child abuse against family members
Scared Straight programs	At-risk adolescents are exposed to the harsh realities of prison life to frighten them away from a life of future crime.	Worsening of conduct problems
Recovered-memory techniques	Therapists use methods to recover memories, including prompting of memories, leading questions, hypnosis, and guided imagery.	Production of false memories of trauma
Dissociative identity disorder (DID)–oriented psychotherapy	Therapists use techniques that imply to clients that they harbor "alter" personalities. Therapists attempt to summon and interact with alters.	Production of alters, creation of serious identity problems
Critical incident stress (crisis) debriefing	Shortly after a traumatic event, therapists urge group members to "process" their negative emotions, describe posttraumatic stress disorder symptoms that members are likely to experience, and discourage members from discontinuing participation.	Heightened risk for posttraumatic stress symptoms
DARE (Drug Abuse and Resistance Education) programs	Police officers teach schoolchildren about the risks of drug use and social skills to resist peer pressure to try drugs (Chapter 12).	Increased intake of alcohol and other substances (such as cigarettes)
Coercive restraint therapies	Therapists physically restrain children who have difficulty forming attachments to their parents. These therapies include rebirthing (see Chapter 1) and holding therapy, in which the therapist holds children down until they stop resisting or begin to show eye contact.	Physical injuries, suffocation, death

(*Source:* Lilienfeld, 2007)

The bottom line? Many therapies are effective, and many do about equally well. Yet there are clear-cut exceptions to the Dodo bird verdict. Moreover, because at least some therapies are harmful, we shouldn't assume that we'll always be safe picking a random therapist out of the telephone book.

■ How Different Groups of People Respond to Psychotherapy

A void exists in our knowledge of how certain segments of the population respond to psychotherapy (Brown, 2006; Olkin & Taliaferro, 2005; U.S. Surgeon General, 2001). Research suggests that socioeconomic status (SES), gender, race, ethnicity, and age typically have little or no bearing on the outcome of therapy (Beutler, Machado, & Neufeldt, 1994; Cruz et al., 2007; Petry, Tennen, & Affleck, 2000; Rabinowitz & Renert, 1997; Schmidt & Hancey, 1979). Still, we must be tentative in our conclusions because researchers haven't studied these variables in depth. Many controlled studies of psychotherapy don't report participants' race, ethnicity, disability status, or sexual orientation, nor do they analyze whether the effectiveness of psychotherapy depends on these variables (Cardemil, 2010; Sue & Zane, 2006). So we can't be completely confident that therapies effective for Caucasians are equally effective for other populations.

■ Common Factors

One probable reason why many therapies are comparable in effectiveness is that certain *common factors*—those that cut across many or most therapies—are responsible for improvement across diverse treatments. As Jerome Frank (1961) noted in his classic book, *Persuasion and Healing*, these common factors include empathic listening, instilling hope, establishing a strong emotional bond with clients, providing a clear theoretical rationale for treatment, and implementing techniques that offer new ways of thinking, feeling, and behaving (Lambert & Ogles, 2004; Miller, Duncan, & Hubbel, 2005; Wampold, 2001). Frank observed that these common factors are also shared by many forms of faith healing, religious conversion, and interpersonal persuasion over the centuries, and that they extend across most, if not all, cultures. Although we might be tempted to dismiss these factors as "placebos," this would miss the crucial point that they're essential in instilling in clients the motivation to change. Indeed, studies show that common factors typically account for a hefty chunk of improvement in therapy (Cuijpers et al., 2008; Sparks, Duncan, & Miller, 2008).

In contrast, *specific factors* are those that characterize only certain therapies: They include exposure, challenging irrational beliefs, and social skills training. In some cases, specific factors may be key ingredients in psychotherapeutic change; in other cases, they may not enhance treatment effectiveness beyond common factors (Stevens, Hynan, & Allen, 2000). Psychologists are divided about the extent to which common versus specific factors influence the outcome of psychotherapy (Craighead, Sheets, & Bjornsson, 2005; DeRubeis, Brotman, & Gibbons, 2005; Kazdin, 2005), although most agree that both matter.

■ Empirically Supported Treatments

Psychologists are also split on the extent to which they should base their treatments on subjective experience and intuition as opposed to carefully controlled research. The *scientist-practitioner gap* (Fox, 1993; Tavris, 2003) refers to the sharp cleft between psychologists who view psychotherapy as more an art than a science and those who believe that clinical practice should primarily reflect well-replicated scientific findings (Dawes, 1994; Lilienfeld, Lynn, & Lohr, 2003; Baker, McFall, & Shoham, 2009). Clearly, subjective judgment plays a crucial role in therapy, but such judgment should be informed by scientific evidence. But what kind of evidence should therapists consider? Over the past 15 years or so, researchers have responded to this question by putting forth lists of **empirically supported treatments (ESTs)**, now sometimes called "research supported treatments"—interventions for specific disorders backed by high-quality scientific evidence derived from controlled studies (Chambless et al., 1996; Lebow, 2010).

Good psychotherapists keep up with the current state of the research literature, staying informed about which therapies do and don't have strong scientific support.

replicability

CAN THE RESULTS BE DUPLICATED IN OTHER STUDIES?

empirically supported treatment (EST)
intervention for specific disorders supported by high-quality scientific evidence

FICTOID ✕

MYTH: Most psychotherapists use empirically supported treatments.

REALITY: Survey data suggest that only a minority of therapists use empirically supported treatments (Baker et al., 2009; Freiheit et al., 2004). For example, a survey of practitioners who treat clients with eating disorders (especially anorexia and bulimia) indicated that most don't regularly administer either cognitive-behavioral or interpersonal therapies, the primary interventions found to be helpful for these conditions (Pederson et al., 2000).

Behavior therapy and cognitive-behavioral therapy have emerged as ESTs for depression, anxiety disorders, obesity, marital problems, sexual dysfunction, and alcohol problems. Interpersonal therapy has considerable support for depression and bulimia, as do acceptance-based approaches for borderline personality disorder. Still, we shouldn't conclude that a treatment that's not on the EST list isn't effective. The fact that a treatment isn't on the list may mean only that investigators haven't yet conducted research to demonstrate its effectiveness (Arkowitz & Lilienfeld, 2006).

The movement to develop lists of ESTs is controversial. Critics of this movement contend that the research literature isn't sufficiently well developed to conclude that certain treatments are clearly superior to others for certain disorders, so why not base one's treatment on subjective feelings and intuition about "what works?" (Levant, 2004; Westen, Novotny, & Thompson-Brenner, 2004). In response, proponents of this movement argue that the best scientific evidence available should inform clinical practice (Baker et al., 2009). Because current data suggest that at least some treatments are superior to others for some disorders, such as exposure therapy for anxiety disorders, they contend, practitioners have an ethical obligation to rely on ESTs unless there's a compelling reason not to (Chambless & Ollendick, 2001; Crits-Christoph, Wilson, & Hollon, 2005; Hunsley & DiGuilio, 2002). The authors of your text find the latter argument more compelling, because the burden of proof for selecting and administering a treatment should always fall on therapists. Therefore, if there's reasonable evidence that certain treatments are better than others for certain disorders, therapists should be guided by this evidence. In **TABLE 16.8**, we list and describe several research-supported treatments.

TABLE 16.8 Empirically Supported Therapies. Selected therapies deemed "empirically supported" by the American Psychological Association Division 12 committee.

THERAPY AND PROBLEM	DESCRIPTION OF THERAPY
Behavior therapy for depression	• Monitor and increase positive daily activities • Improve communication skills • Increase assertive behaviors • Increase positive reinforcement for nondepressed behaviors • Decrease life stresses
Cognitive-behavioral therapy for depression	• Teach clients to identify, reevaluate, and change negative thinking associated with depressed feelings • Conduct between-session experiments to test thoughts for accuracy • Monitor and increase daily activities
Interpersonal therapy for depression	• Help clients identify and resolve interpersonal difficulties associated with depression
Cognitive-behavioral therapy for bulimia	• Teach clients ways to prevent binge eating and create alternative behaviors • Develop a plan for a regular pattern of eating • Support skills to deal with high-risk situations for binge eating and purging • Modify attitudes toward eating and one's physical appearance
Cognitive-behavioral therapy for panic disorder	• Produce panic attacks during sessions to help clients perceive them as less "dangerous" (to reassure them that they will not, for example, "go crazy" or die) • Introduce breathing retraining (slow deep breaths) to prevent hyperventilation • Control exposure to situations that trigger panic attacks

(*Source:* Arkowitz & Lilienfeld, 2006)

■ Why Can Ineffective Therapies Appear to Be Helpful? How We Can Be Fooled

Some therapists have successfully marketed a wide variety of interventions that lack research support (Lilienfeld, Lynn, & Lohr, 2003; Norcross, Garofalo, & Koocher, 2006; Singer & Nievod, 2003). They include treatments as seemingly bizarre as dolphin therapy, laughter therapy, treatment for the trauma of abduction by aliens (Appelle, Lynn, & Newman, 2000), and even treatment for resolving problems due to traumas in a past life (Mills & Lynn, 2000). ⊙ Simulate

Many of these treatments rest on questionable premises. For example, advocates of "primal scream therapy" (sometimes called primal therapy) believe that the only way to achieve relief from psychological pain is to release pent up rage in one's nervous system, including rage stemming from the trauma of birth. Therapists who practice neurolinguistic programming (NLP) claim to treat psychological problems by matching their nonverbal behaviors, like their tone of voice, eye movements, and facial gestures, to those of their clients. In this way, therapists presumably develop a direct communication pathway permitting them to influence clients more easily. Yet there's virtually no research support for primal scream therapy or NLP (Singer & Lalich, 1996; Witkowski, in press).

How might clients and therapists alike come to believe that treatments that are ineffective are helpful? The following five reasons can help us understand why bogus therapies can gain a dedicated public following (Arkowitz & Lilienfeld, 2006; Beyerstein, 1997).

1. **Spontaneous remission.** The client's recovery may have nothing at all to do with the treatment. All of us have our "ups and downs." Similarly, many psychological problems are self-limiting or cyclical and improve without intervention. A breakup with our latest "crush" may depress us for a while, but most of us will improve even without professional help. This phenomenon is known as *spontaneous remission*, and occasionally occurs even in serious medical conditions, including cancer (Silverman, 1987).

    Spontaneous remission is surprisingly common in psychotherapy. In the first formal review of psychotherapy outcomes, Hans Eysenck (1952) reported the findings of two uncontrolled studies of neurotic (mildly disturbed) clients who received no formal therapy. The rate of spontaneous remission in these studies was a staggering 72 percent! Admittedly, the studies Eysenck selected may have had unusually high rates of spontaneous remission because the individuals he claimed were "untreated" received reassurance and suggestion. Still, there's no question that many people with psychological problems, like depression, often improve without treatment. Only if people who are treated improve at a rate that exceeds that of untreated people, or those on a wait list, can we rule out the effects of spontaneous remission.

2. **The placebo effect.** The pesky placebo effect (see Chapters 2 and 12) can lead to significant symptom relief. By instilling hope and the conviction that we can rise to life's challenges, virtually any credible treatment can be helpful in alleviating our demoralization.

⊙ **Simulate** Ineffective Therapies on mypsychlab.com

Some therapists claim that contact with dolphins can treat a variety of psychological problems, including autism. However, research does not support the idea that dolphin therapy is effective for any problem or disorder (Marino & Lilienfeld, 1998; 2007).

Positive life events that occur outside of therapy sessions, like major job promotions, can help to explain spontaneous remissions of some psychological problems, such as depression. As neo-Freudian theorist Karen Horney observed, "Life itself still remains a very effective therapist" (Horney, 1945, p. 240; see Chapter 14).

FACTOID +

One of the strangest psychotherapies of all time is surely "direct analysis," developed by psychiatrist John Rosen as a treatment for schizophrenia. Called direct analysis because Rosen claimed to speak directly to clients' unconscious minds, this method required therapists to yell at clients, call them crazy, and threaten to slice them into pieces. In some cases, Rosen even enlisted psychiatric aides to dress up as FBI agents to question clients about their fantasies. Although once highly influential—Rosen received the 1971 American Academy of Psychotherapy "Man of the Year" award—direct analysis is no longer accepted in the therapeutic community (Dolnick, 1998). The science of psychotherapy, like other domains of science, is self-correcting.

 ruling out rival hypotheses

HAVE IMPORTANT ALTERNATIVE EXPLANATIONS FOR THE FINDINGS BEEN EXCLUDED?

3. **Self-serving biases.** Even when they don't improve, clients who are strongly invested in psychotherapy and have shelled out a lot of money in the pursuit of well-being can persuade themselves they've been helped. Because it would be too troubling to admit to oneself (or others) that it's all been a waste of time, energy, and effort, there's often a strong psychological pull to find value in a treatment (Axsom & Cooper, 1985). Clients may also overestimate their apparent successes while ignoring, downplaying, or explaining away their failures as a means of maintaining their self-esteem (Beyerstein & Hadaway, 1991).

4. **Regression to the mean.** It's a statistical fact of life that extreme scores tend to become less extreme on retesting, a phenomenon known as *regression to the mean*. If you receive a zero on your first psychology exam, there's a silver lining to this gray cloud: You'll almost surely do better on your second exam! Conversely, if you receive a 100 on your first exam, odds are also high you won't do as well the second time around. Scores on measures of psychopathology are no different. If a client comes into treatment extremely depressed, the chances are high she'll be less depressed in a few weeks. Regression to the mean can fool therapists and clients into believing that a useless treatment is effective. It's an especially tricky problem in evaluating whether psychotherapy is effective, because most clients enter psychotherapy when their symptoms are most extreme.

5. **Retrospective rewriting of the past.** In some cases, we may believe we've improved even when we haven't because we misremember our initial (pretreatment) level of adjustment as worse than it was. We *expect* to change after treatment, and may adjust our memories to fit this expectation. In one study, investigators randomly assigned college students to either take a study skills

---

Answers are located at the end of the text.

PSYCHOTHERAPIES

evaluating **CLAIMS**

There are over 500 different therapies on the market, yet only a small percentage of them are empirically supported. How can you identify which therapies might be helpful, which aren't, and which might even be harmful? Let's evaluate some of these claims, which are modeled after actual advertisements for therapies found online.

"Our *breakthrough energy therapy* is *far superior* to any short-term therapy available for anxiety."
What types of control groups would be especially important to include in research evaluating this claim?

"Our *debriefing process* allows those involved in the incident to process the event and *vent their fears and anger* associated with it."
What does scientific research tell us about crisis debriefing (see Chapter 12 and 16)? Is the "venting" of fears and anger always a good thing?

"Cognitive-behavioral therapy *may not be effective in all cases,* but studies have shown that CBT *is equally as effective in the treatment of depression as anti-depressant medication.*"
This claim avoids exaggerating the benefits of cognitive-behavioral therapy (CBT) by noting that it may not be effective in all cases. The ad notes correctly that CBT is about as effective as antidepressant medication for clinical depression.

course or serve in a wait-list control group. On objective measures of grades, the course proved worthless. Yet students who took the course—but not students in the control group—thought they'd improved. Why? They mistakenly recalled their initial study skills as worse than they actually were (Conway & Ross, 1984; Ross, 1990). The same phenomenon may sometimes occur in psychotherapy.

psychomythology

ARE SELF-HELP BOOKS ALWAYS HELPFUL?

Each year Americans can choose from about 3,500 newly published self-help books that promise everything from achieving everlasting bliss and expanded consciousness to freedom from virtually every human failing and foible imaginable. Self-help books are only one piece of the massive quilt of the self-improvement industry that extends to Internet sites, magazines, radio and television shows, CDs, DVDs, lectures, workshops, and advice columns. It's no mystery why self-help books are so popular that Americans spend $650 million a year on them, and at least 80 percent of therapists recommend them to their clients (Arkowitz & Lilienfeld, 2007).

Researchers have studied the effects of reading self-help books, known in psychology lingo as "bibliotherapy." The relatively small number of studies conducted on self-help books suggests that bibliotherapy and psychotherapy often lead to comparable improvements in depression, anxiety, and other problems (Gould & Clum, 1993).

Still, we should bear three points in mind. First, we can't generalize the limited findings to all of the books on the shelves of our local bookstore, because the overwhelming majority of self-help books are untested (Rosen, Glasgow, & Moore, 2003). Second, people who volunteer for research on self-help books may be more motivated to read the entire book and benefit from it than the curious person who purchases the book under more casual circumstances. Third, many self-help books address relatively minor problems, like everyday worries and public speaking. When researchers (Menchola, Arkowitz, & Burke, 2007) have examined more serious problems, like major depression and panic disorder, psychotherapy has fared better than bibliotherapy, although both do better than no treatment.

Some people don't respond at all to self-help books (Febbraro et al., 1999), and many self-help books promise far more than they can deliver. Readers who fall short of how the promotional materials on the cover assure them they'll respond may feel like failures and be less likely to seek professional help or make changes on their own. Bearing this possibility in mind, Hal Arkowitz and Scott Lilienfeld (2007) offered the following recommendations about selecting self-help books.

The "secret" to the 2007 best seller *The Secret* by Rhonda Byrne (*left*) is the so-called *law of attraction*—good thoughts attract good things and bad thoughts attract bad things. Yet there's no evidence that merely wishing for something good to happen without taking concrete steps to accomplish it is effective. We should be skeptical of self-help books that promise simple answers to complex problems.

- Use books that have research support and are based on valid psychological principles of change (Gambrill, 1992). Make sure the author refers to published research that supports the claims made. Books that have shown positive effects in studies include *Feeling Good* by David Burns, *Mind over Mood* by Dennis Greenberger and Christine Padesky, and *Coping with Panic* by George Clum.
- Evaluate the author's credentials. Does he or she have the professional training and expertise to write on the topic at hand?
- Be wary of books that make far-fetched promises, such as curing a phobia in five minutes. The 2007 blockbuster best seller *The Secret* (Byrne, 2007), popularized by Oprah Winfrey, informs readers that positive thinking alone can cure cancer, help one become a millionaire, or achieve just about any goal one wants. Yet there's not a shred of research evidence that this kind of wishful thinking is helpful (Smythe, 2007). 👁—Watch
- Beware of books that rely on a "one size fits all" approach. A book that tells us to always express anger to our relationship partner fails to take into account the complexity and specifics of the relationship.
- Serious problems like clinical depression, obsessive-compulsive disorder, or schizophrenia warrant professional help rather than self-help alone.

👁—Watch the Secret on **mypsychlab.com**

✓●—[Study and Review on mypsychlab.com

BIOMEDICAL TREATMENTS: MEDICATIONS, ELECTRICAL STIMULATION, AND SURGERY

16.11 Recognize different types of drugs and cautions associated with drug treatment.

16.12 Outline key considerations in drug treatment.

16.13 Identify misconceptions about biomedical treatments.

Biomedical treatments—including medications, electrical stimulation techniques, and brain surgery—directly alter the brain's chemistry or physiology. Just as the number of psychotherapy approaches has more than tripled since the 1970s, antidepressant prescriptions have tripled from 1988 to 1994 and from 1990 to 2000 (Smith, 2005). Today, close to 10 percent of Americans take antidepressants (Barber, 2008). Many people are surprised to learn that about 10 percent of inpatients with major depression still receive electroconvulsive therapy (ECT)—informally called "shock therapy"—which delivers small electric shocks to people's brains to lift their mood (Olfson et al., 1998; Pagnin et al., 2008). By the 1950s, as many as 50,000 patients received psychosurgery, in which the frontal lobes or other brain regions were damaged or removed in an effort to control serious psychological disorders (Tooth & Newton, 1961; Valenstein, 1973). Today, surgeons rarely perform such operations, reflecting the controversies surrounding psychosurgery, and the fact that less risky and more effective treatments are available. As we consider the pros and cons of various biomedical treatments, we'll see that each approach has attracted ardent critics and defenders.

■ Psychopharmacotherapy: Targeting Brain Chemistry

We'll begin our tour of biomedical treatments with **psychopharmacotherapy**—the use of medications to treat psychological problems. For virtually every psychological disorder treated with psychotherapy, there's an available medication. In 1954, the widespread marketing of the drug Thorazine (chlorpromazine) ushered in the "pharmacological revolution" in the treatment of serious psychological disorders (see Chapter 15). For the first time, professionals could prescribe powerful medications to ease the symptoms of schizophrenia and related conditions. By 1970, it was unusual for any patient with schizophrenia not to be treated with Thorazine or other "major tranquilizers," as they came to be known.

Pharmaceutical companies soon sensed the promise of medicines to treat a broad spectrum of patients, and their efforts paid off handsomely. Researchers discovered that the emotional storms that torment people with bipolar disorder could be tamed with Lithium, Tegretol, and a new generation of mood stabilizer drugs. Medications are now available for people with more common conditions, ranging from anxiety about public speaking to the harsh realities of stressful circumstances. As of 2004, 10 percent of adult women and 4 percent of adult men were taking antidepressants (Smith, 2005). We can attribute the staggering number of prescriptions for depression largely to the phenomenal popularity of the selective serotonin reuptake inhibitor (SSRI) antidepressants, including Prozac, Zoloft, and Paxil, which boost levels of the neurotransmitter serotonin.

In **TABLE 16.9**, we present commonly used drugs and their presumed mechanisms of action to treat anxiety disorders (anxiolytics or *antianxiety drugs*), depression (*antidepressants*), bipolar disorders (*mood stabilizers*), psychotic conditions (neuroleptics/ *an-*

psychopharmacotherapy
use of medications to treat psychological problems

tipsychotics or major tranquilizers), and attention problems (*psychostimulants*, which stimulate the nervous system yet paradoxically treat symptoms of attention-deficit/hyperactivity disorder). As we can see from this table, many of these medications ease the symptoms of multiple psychological conditions. ⊕ Explore

⊕ **Explore** Drugs Commonly Used to Treat Psychiatric Disorders on **mypsychlab.com**

TABLE 16.9 Commonly Used Medications for Psychological Disorders, Mechanisms of Action, and Other Uses.

	MEDICATION	EXAMPLES	ACTION	OTHER USES
Antianxiety Medications	Benzodiazepines	Diazepam (Valium), alprazolam (Xanax), clonazepam (Klonopin), lorazepam (Ativan)	Increase efficiency of GABA binding to receptor sites	Use with antipsychotic medications, treat medication side effects, alcohol detox
	Buspirone (Buspar)		Stabilizes serotonin levels	Depressive and anxiety states; sometimes used with antipsychotics; aggression in people with brain injuries and dementia
	Beta blockers	Atenolol (Tenormin), propranolol (Inderal)	Compete with norepinephrine at receptor sites that control heart and muscle function; reduce rapid heartbeat, muscle tension	Control blood pressure, regulate heart beat
Antidepressants	Monoamine oxidase (MAO) inhibitors	Isocarboxazid (Marplan), phenelzine (Nardil), tranylcypromine (Parnate)	Inhibit action of enzymes that metabolize norepinephrine and serotonin; inhibit dopamine	Panic and other anxiety disorders
	Cyclic antidepressants	Amitriptyline (Elavil), imipramine (Tofranil), desipramine (Norpramine), nortriptyline (Pamelor)	Inhibit reuptake of norepinephrine and serotonin	Panic and other anxiety disorders, pain relief
	SSRIs (selective serotonin reuptake inhibitors)	Fluoxetine (Prozac), citalopram (Celexa), sertraline (Zoloft)	Selectively inhibit reuptake of serotonin	Eating disorders (especially bulimia), obsessive-compulsive disorder, social phobia
Mood Stabilizers	Mineral salts	Lithium carbonate (Lithium)	Decrease noradrenaline, increase serotonin	
	Anticonvulsant medications	Carbamazepine (Tegretol), lamotrigine (Lamictal), divalproex sodium (Depakote)	Increase levels of neurotransmitter GABA, inhibit norepinephrine reuptake (Tegretol)	Bipolar disorder
Antipsychotics	Conventional antipsychotics	Chlorpromazine (Thorazine), haloperidol (Haldol)	Block postsynaptic dopamine receptors	Tourette syndrome (Haldol), bipolar disorder with the exception of Clozaril
	Serotonin-dopamine antagonists (atypical antipsychotics)	Clozapine (Clozaril), risperidone (Risperdal), olanzapine (Zyprexa), ziprasidone (Geodon), quetiapine (Seroquel)	Block activity of both serotonin and/or dopamine; also affect norepinephrine, acetylcholine	
Psychostimulants and Other Medications for Attentional Problems	Methylphenidate (Ritalin, Concerta), amphetamine (Adderall), dexmethylphenidate (Focalin)		Release norepinephrine, dopamine, serotonin in frontal regions of the brain, where attention and behavior are regulated	
	Atomoxetine (Strattera)		Selectively inhibit reuptake of norepinephrine	

Medication

Most modern medications for depression, like fluoxetine (whose brand name is Prozac), appear to work by increasing the amount of serotonin in the brain. Yet this medication for depression, tianeptine (whose brand name is Stablon), appears to work by *decreasing* the amount of serotonin. The fact that medications can treat depression by either raising or lowering serotonin levels suggests that popular "chemical imbalance" theories of depression are oversimplified.

Nevertheless, we should bear in mind that we don't know for sure how most of these medications work. Although drug company advertisements, including those we've seen on television, often claim that medications—especially antidepressants—correct a "chemical imbalance" in the brain, this notion is almost surely oversimplified (Kirsch, 2010). For one thing, most medications probably work on multiple neurotransmitter systems. Moreover, there's no scientific evidence for an "optimal" level of serotonin or other neurotransmitters in the brain (Lacasse & Leo, 2005). Finally, many medications, including antidepressants, may exert their effects largely by affecting the sensitivity of neuron receptors (see Chapter 3) rather than the levels of neurotransmitters.

Today, psychologists often refer patients to psychiatrists and other professionals who can prescribe medications and consult with prescribers to plan treatment. Until recently, only psychiatrists and a few other mental health professionals, like psychiatric nurse practitioners, could prescribe medications. But beginning in 1999, psychologists in the U.S. territory of Guam were granted legal permission to prescribe medications followed by two U.S. states (New Mexico in 2002 and Louisiana in 2004). Before being allowed to prescribe, these psychologists must first complete a curriculum of coursework on physiology, anatomy, and psychopharmacology (the study of medications that affect psychological functioning). Nevertheless, the growing movement to allow psychologists to prescribe medications has been controversial, in part because many critics charge that psychologists don't possess sufficient knowledge of the anatomy and physiology of the human body to adequately evaluate the intended effects and side effects of medications (Robiner et al., 2003; Stuart & Heiby, 2007).

CAUTIONS TO CONSIDER: DOSAGE AND SIDE EFFECTS. Psychopharmacotherapy isn't a cure-all. Virtually all medications have side effects that practitioners must weigh against their potential benefits. Most adverse reactions, including nausea, drowsiness, weakness, fatigue, and impaired sexual performance, are reversible when medications are discontinued or when their dosage is lowered. Nevertheless, this isn't the case with *tardive dyskinesia* (TD), a serious side effect of some older antipsychotic medications, those used to treat schizophrenia and other psychoses. The symptoms of TD include grotesque involuntary movements of the facial muscles and mouth and twitching of the neck, arms, and legs. Most often, the disorder begins after several years of high-dosage treatment (*tardive*, like *tardy*, means late-appearing), but it occasionally begins after only a few months of therapy at low dosages (Simpson & Kline, 1976). Newer antipsychotic medicines such as Risperdal, which treat the negative, as well as positive, symptoms of schizophrenia (see Chapter 15), generally produce fewer serious adverse effects. But they too occasionally produce serious side effects, including sudden cardiac deaths, and the verdict is out regarding whether they're more effective than earlier and less costly medications (Correll & Schenk, 2008; Lieberman et al., 2005; Schneeweiss & Avorn, 2009).

One Dose Doesn't "Fit All": Differences in Responses to Medication. People don't all respond equally to the same dose of medication. Weight, age, and even racial differences often affect drug response. African Americans tend to require lower doses of certain antianxiety and antidepressant drugs and have a faster response than do Caucasians, and Asians metabolize (break down) these medications more slowly than do Caucasians (Baker & Bell, 1999; Campinha-Bacote, 2002; Strickland et al., 1997). Because some people become physically and psychologically dependent on medications, such as the widely prescribed antianxiety medications Valium and Xanax (known as benzodiazepines), physicians must proceed with caution and determine the lowest dose possible to achieve positive results and minimize unpleasant side effects (Wigal et al., 2006). Discontinuation of certain drugs, such as those for anxiety and depression, should be performed gradually to minimize withdrawal reactions, including anxiety and agitation (Lejoyeux & Ades, 1997).

Medications on Trial: Harmful and Overprescribed? Some psychologists have raised serious questions about the effectiveness of the SSRIs, especially among children and adolescents (Healy, 2004; Kendall, Pilling, & Whittington, 2005). There also are widely publicized indications that SSRIs increase the risk of suicidal thoughts in people younger than 18 years of age, although there's no clear evidence that they increase the risk of *completed* suicide (Goldstein & Ruscio, 2010). For this reason, the U.S. Food and Drug Administration (FDA) now requires drug manufacturers to include warnings of possible suicide risk on the labels of SSRIs. Following these "black box" warnings (so called because they're enclosed in a box with black borders on the medication label), antidepressant prescriptions dropped by nearly 20 percent (Nemeroff et al., 2007). ((•▬ **Listen**

Scientists don't understand why antidepressants increase suicidal thoughts in some children and adolescents. These drugs sometimes produce agitation, so they may make already depressed people even more distressed and possibly suicidal (Brambilla et al., 2005). Yet the risk of suicide attempts and completions among people prescribed SSRIs remains very low. Physicians frequently prescribe SSRIs to treat anxiety disorders, including panic disorder and OCD. Fortunately, anxious patients without depression aren't at especially high risk for suicide (Mellinger & Lynn, 2003).

Another area of public concern is overprescription. Parents, teachers, and helping professionals have expressed particular alarm that psychostimulants for attention-deficit/hyperactivity disorder (ADHD; see Chapter 15), such as Ritalin (methylphenidate), are overprescribed and may substitute for teaching effective coping strategies for focusing attention (LeFever, Arcona, & Antonuccio, 2003; Safer, 2000). Since the early 1990s, the number of prescriptions for ADHD has increased fourfold. Although little is known about the long-term safety of Ritalin with children under six, the number of prescriptions for children ages two (!) to four nearly tripled between 1991 and 1995 alone (Bentley & Walsh, 2006). Critics of psychostimulants have pointed to their potential for abuse. Moreover, their adverse effects include insomnia, irritability, heart-related complications, and stunted growth.

Children should be diagnosed with ADHD and placed on stimulants only after they've been evaluated with input from parents and teachers (see Chapter 15). Yet 70 to 80 percent of children with ADHD can be treated effectively with stimulants (Steele et al., 2006), which can sometimes be combined to good advantage with behavior therapy (Jensen et al., 2005).

A final area of concern is *polypharmacy:* prescribing many medications—sometimes five or more—at the same time. This practice can be hazardous if not carefully monitored, because certain medications may interfere with the effects of others or interact with them in dangerous ways. Polypharmacy is a particular problem among the elderly, who tend to be especially susceptible to drug side effects (Fulton & Allen, 2005).

EVALUATING PSYCHOPHARMACOTHERAPY. To medicate or not medicate, that is the question. In many instances, psychotherapy, with no added medications, can successfully treat people with many disorders. CBT is at least as effective as antidepressants, even for severe depression, and perhaps more effective than antidepressants in preventing relapse (DeRubeis, Brotman, & Gibbons, 2005; Hollon, Thase, & Markowitz, 2002). Psychotherapy alone is also effective for a variety of anxiety disorders, dysthymia, bulimia, and insomnia (Otto, Smits, & Reese, 2005; Thase, 2000).

((•▬ **Listen** to Antidepressant Warning Labels audio file on **mypsychlab.com**

Parenting a child with attention-deficit/hyperactivity disorder (ADHD) can be challenging and often requires support from teachers and medical professionals.

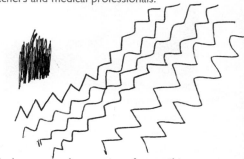

Polypharmacy—the practice of prescribing multiple medications at the same time—can increase the risk of infrequent yet serious side effects produced by interactions among drugs. The tragic death of actor Heath Ledger in 2008 highlights the possibility of overdose by taking multiple medications that aren't carefully monitored by medical professionals.

FICTOID

MYTH: One way of treating patients with ADHD effectively is by reducing the amount of sugar in their diets.

REALITY: There's no convincing evidence that reducing the amount of sugar in the diets of children with ADHD—or instituting other dietary changes (like eliminating artificial food coloring or flavors)—improves their symptoms (Waschbusch & Hill, 2003).

Scientists are finding that when patients benefit from psychotherapy, this change is reflected in the workings of their brains. In some cases, psychotherapy and medication produce similar brain changes, suggesting that different routes to improvement share similar mechanisms (Kumari, 2006) and reminding us that "mind" and "brain" describe the same phenomena at different levels of explanation (see Chapters 1 and 3).

For instance, scientists observed that patients with OCD who received behavior therapy showed brain changes similar to those who received an SSRI (Prozac) (Baxter et al., 1992). Interestingly, researchers detected decreased metabolic activity in the caudate nucleus, a brain region overactive in OCD. Shortly thereafter, they confirmed these findings with patients with OCD who received CBT (Schwartz et al., 1996). Researchers have reported similar results in studies of participants with social phobias receiving either CBT or treatment with an antianxiety medication (Citalopram). Regardless of whether participants received CBT or medication, they showed reduced activity in limbic system structures that house the brain's reaction to threat (Furmark et al., 2002).

This research cautions us against a widespread logical error, namely, inferring a disorder's optimal treatment from its cause (Ross & Pam, 1995). Many people believe mistakenly that a condition that's largely biological in its causes, like schizophrenia, should be treated with medication and that a condition that's largely environmental in its causes, like a specific phobia (see Chapter 15), should be treated with psychotherapy. Yet the research we've reviewed shows that this logic is erroneous, because psychological treatments affect our biology, just as biomedical treatments affect our psychology.

Critics of pharmacotherapy claim that medications are of little value in helping patients learn social skills, modify self-defeating behaviors, or cope with conflict. For example, when patients with anxiety disorders discontinue their medications, half or more may relapse (Marks et. al., 1993). Over the long haul, psychotherapy may be much less expensive than medications, so it often makes sense to try psychotherapy first (Arkowitz & Lilienfeld, 2007).

Still, there are often clear advantages of combining medication with psychotherapy (Thase, 2000). If people's symptoms interfere greatly with their functioning, or if psychotherapy alone hasn't worked for a two-month period, adding medication is frequently justified. Generally, research suggests that combining medication with psychotherapy is warranted for schizophrenia, bipolar disorder, longterm major depression, and major depression with psychotic symptoms (Otto, Smits, & Reese, 2005; Thase, 2000).

It's a logical error to infer a disorder's cause from its treatment, or vice versa. Headaches can be treated with aspirin, but that doesn't imply that headaches are due to a deficiency of aspirin in the body.

■ Electrical Stimulation: Conceptions and Misconceptions

Consider the following account of **electroconvulsive therapy** (ECT), which we introduced at the outset of our discussion of biomedical treatments:

> Strapped to a stretcher, you are wheeled into the ECT room. The electroshock machine is in clear view. The nurse places the electrodes on you. An injection (to promote anesthesia or lack of conscious awareness) is given.... You awaken in your hospital bed. You are confused to find it so difficult to recover memories. Finally you stop struggling in the realization that you have no memory for what has transpired. You were scheduled to have ECT, but something must have happened. Perhaps it was postponed. But the nurse keeps asking, 'How are you feeling?' You think to yourself: 'It must have been given;' but you can't remember (Taylor, 1975, p. 33).

ELECTROCONVULSIVE THERAPY: FACT AND FICTION. What happened here? As in other cases of modern ECT, medical personnel first injected a muscle relaxant and anesthetic and then administered brief electrical pulses to the patient's brain to relieve severe depression that hadn't responded to other treatments. This patient, like others receiving ECT, experienced a full-blown seizure lasting about a minute, much like that experienced by patients with epilepsy. Physicians typically recommend ECT for individ-

electroconvulsive therapy (ECT)
patients receive brief electrical pulses to the brain that produce a seizure to treat serious psychological problems

uals with serious depression, bipolar disorder, schizophrenia, and severe catatonia (see Chapter 15), and only then as a last resort when all other treatments have failed. A typical course of ECT is six to 10 treatments, given three times a week.

Misconceptions about ECT abound, including the erroneous beliefs that ECT is painful or dangerous and that it invariably produces long-term memory loss, personality changes, and even brain damage (Dowman, Patel, & Rajput, 2005; Malcom, 1989; Santa Maria, Baumeister, & Gouvier, 1999). Media characterizations of ECT, such as in the Academy Award–winning 1975 film *One Flew Over the Cuckoo's Nest,* promote the mistaken idea that ECT is little more than a brutal means of punishment or behavioral control, with no redeeming value. Not surprisingly, most Americans hold negative attitudes about ECT (Walter & McDonald, 2004).

Nevertheless, the picture looks quite different when researchers interview individuals who've undergone ECT. In one study of 24 patients, 91 percent reported being happy to have received ECT (Goodman et al., 1999). In another study, 98 percent of patients said they'd seek ECT again if their depression returned, and 62 percent said that the treatment was less frightening than a visit to the dentist (Pettinati et al., 1994). More important, researchers report improvement rates as high as 80 to 90 percent following ECT for severe depression (APA, 2001).

Although harsh public perceptions about ECT may be unwarranted, we should note a few cautions. About 50 percent of people with an initially positive response relapse within six months or so (Bourgon & Kellner, 2000), so ECT isn't a cure-all. In addition, people who experience ECT may be motivated to convince themselves that the treatment helped. Although many patients report feeling better after ECT, they don't always show parallel changes on objective measures of depression and mental functioning (Scovern & Kilmann, 1980). ECT may be helpful because it increases the levels of serotonin in the brain (Rasmussen, Sampson, & Rummans, 2002) and stimulates growth of brain cells in the hippocampus (Bolwig, 2009). A rival hypothesis is that ECT induces strong expectations of improvement and serves as an "electrical placebo." But studies showing that ECT works better than "sham" (fake) ECT render this explanation less likely (Carney et al., 2003).

In prescribing ECT, the physician's challenge is to determine whether the therapeutic gains outweigh the potential adverse effects. As the case we read suggests, ECT can create short-term confusion and cloud memory. In most cases, memory loss is restricted to events that occur right before the treatment and generally subsides within a few weeks (Sackeim, 1986). However, in the first long-term study of patients in the community who received ECT, memory and attention problems persisted in some patients for six months after treatment (Sackeim et al., 2007). Placing electrodes on the right side of the brain (unilateral ECT) rather than on both sides (bilateral ECT) reduced, but didn't entirely eliminate, these impairments. When psychiatrists use ECT, it's crucial that patients and their family members understand the procedure, as well as its potential benefits and risks.

VAGUS NERVE AND TRANSCRANIAL STIMULATION. In a recent development, surgeons can implant a small electrical device under the skin near the breastbone to stimulate the *vagus nerve* to treat severe depression. The vagus nerve projects to many brain areas, and electrical pulses to this nerve may stimulate serotonin and increase brain blood

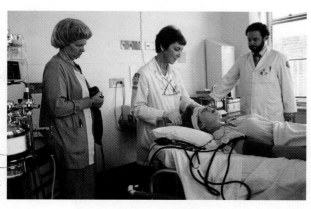

A team of professionals administer electroconvulsive therapy.

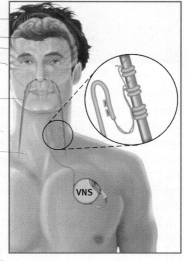

A small vagus nerve stimulator can be implanted under the breastbone in cases of serious treatment-resistant depression.

◀ **ruling out rival hypotheses**

HAVE IMPORTANT ALTERNATIVE EXPLANATIONS FOR THE FINDINGS BEEN EXCLUDED?

FICTOID

MYTH: Patients who receive ECT display violent convulsions, sometimes leading to serious injuries.

REALITY: Although this was true decades ago and is still the case in some developing countries (Giles, 2002), the muscle relaxant and anesthesia now administered along with ECT prevent violent convulsions. In Western countries today, ECT is no more physically dangerous than anesthesia itself.

ruling out rival hypotheses

HAVE IMPORTANT ALTERNATIVE EXPLANATIONS FOR THE FINDINGS BEEN EXCLUDED?

flow (George et al., 2000). The FDA has approved this procedure, as well as repeated transcranial magnetic stimulation (see Chapter 3), for depression that hasn't responded to other treatments. Well-controlled, large-scale studies on these procedures are mostly lacking. Studies comparing these methods with devices that don't provide any stimulation suggest that improvement may be due to placebo effects (Herwig et al., 2007; Rush et al., 2005). Researchers have recently experimented with deep brain stimulation of regions of the frontal cortex and other brain structures with treatment-resistant depressed patients, but it's too early to draw firm conclusions about this procedure's value (Mayberg et al., 2005). Each of these experimental methods carries the risk of side effects, ranging from headaches, coughs, and apathy to hallucinations and seizures, suggesting that their risks and benefits must be weighed carefully.

■ Psychosurgery: An Absolute Last Resort

Psychosurgery, or brain surgery to treat psychological disorders, is the most radical and controversial of all biomedical treatments (see Chapter 2). As is often the case with new treatments, psychosurgery was hailed as a promising innovation not long after it was introduced. As we learned in Chapter 2, most of the early psychosurgical operations were prefrontal lobotomies. Psychosurgery remained popular until the mid-1950s, when the tide of enthusiasm receded in the face of reports of scores of "dehumanized zombies" and the availability of medicines as alternatives to surgery (Mashour, Walker, & Matura, 2005; Valenstein, 1973). To most critics, the benefits of psychosurgery rarely, if ever, outweighed the costs of impairing memory, diminishing emotion and creativity, and the risks of brain surgery (Neville, 1978).

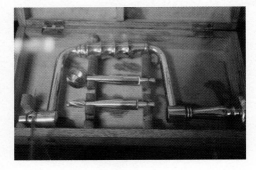

Surgeons used tools like these to perform early lobotomies before sophisticated surgical techniques were developed.

Psychosurgery has a long history, as this photo of a 2,000-plus-year-old skull from Peru shows. As we can see, this skull contains a huge hole produced by a procedure called "trephining." Scientists believe that trephining may have been performed in an effort to heal mental disorders or to relieve brain diseases, like epilepsy or tumors (Alt et al., 1997).

Critics also noted that the motives for conducting psychosurgery weren't always benign (Valenstein, 1973). In the past, surgeons sometimes performed lobotomies on vio-

lent sexual criminals, homosexual child abusers, and aggressive prison inmates (Mashour et al., 2005). Punitive and therapeutic motives were sometimes difficult to separate. Social goals, such as the control of behavior, were occasionally confused with therapeutic goals.

In the 1960s, surgeons ushered new forms of psychosurgery to the forefront. The procedures involved creating small lesions in the amygdala or in other parts of the limbic system, such as the cingulate cortex, which plays a key role in controlling emotions (see Chapter 3). Surgeons replaced primitive procedures with ultrasound, electricity, freezing of tissues, and implants of radioactive materials. Automated surgical devices added precision to delicate brain surgery. With the advent of modern psychosurgical techniques, negative physical side effects became less frequent.

Today, surgeons sometimes perform psychosurgery as an absolute last resort for patients with a handful of conditions, such as severe OCD, major depression, and bipolar disorder. In a study using strict criteria for improvement, 25 to 30 percent of 33 patients with OCD who'd failed to respond to all other treatments benefited substantially from psychosurgery (Janice et al., 1991). Still, there are few well-controlled long-term studies of psychosurgery and an absence of data about which patients respond best. Even when psychosurgery appears successful, we can generate alternative explanations, including placebo effects and self-serving biases, to account for apparent treatment gains (Dawes, 1994).

psychosurgery
brain surgery to treat psychological problems

ruling out rival hypotheses

HAVE IMPORTANT ALTERNATIVE EXPLANATIONS FOR THE FINDINGS BEEN EXCLUDED?

Recognizing the need to protect patient interests, institutional review boards (IRBs; see Chapter 2) in hospitals where surgeons perform psychosurgery must approve each operation. IRBs help ensure that (a) there's a clear rationale for the operation, (b) the patient has received an appropriate preoperative and postoperative evaluation, (c) the patient has consented to the operation, and (d) the surgeon is competent to conduct the procedure (Mashour et al., 2005). Scientific research may one day lead to more effective forms of psychosurgery, but the scientific and ethical debates surrounding such surgery are likely to endure.

---

assess your knowledge   FACT OR FICTION?

✓●—[**Study** and **Review** on **mypsychlab.com**

1. The first major drug for psychological conditions was developed to treat bipolar disorder. **True** / **False**   *Schizophrenia*

2. One serious side effect of antipsychotic medications is tardive dyskinesia. **True** / **False**

3. People of different races and cultures respond similarly to the same dose of medication. **True** / **False**

4. Most people experience long-lasting brain damage after a course of ECT. **True** / **False**

5. Most early psychosurgery operations were prefrontal lobotomies. **True** / **False**

Answers: 1. F (p. 658); 2. T (p. 660); 3. F (p. 660); 4. F (p. 663); 5. T (p. 664)

✓ ━ **Study** and **Review** on **mypsychlab.com**

PSYCHOTHERAPY: CLIENTS AND PRACTITIONERS 632–635

16.1 **DESCRIBE WHO SEEKS TREATMENT, WHO BENEFITS FROM PSYCHOTHERAPY, AND WHO PRACTICES PSYCHOTHERAPY.**

Therapists treat people of all ages and social, cultural, and ethnic backgrounds. Individuals with anxiety, and those with minor and temporary problems, are most likely to benefit from therapy. Socioeconomic status, gender, age, and ethnicity don't predict treatment outcome.

1. _____ can be defined as a psychological intervention designed to help people resolve emotional, behavioral, and interpersonal problems and improve the quality of their lives. (p. 632)

2. In general, (women/men) are more likely to seek psychotherapy. (p. 632)

3. Hispanic Americans are (less/more) likely than non–Hispanic Americans to seek mental health services. (p. 632)

4. People (can/can't) be helped by therapists who differ from them in significant ways. (p. 633)

5. Individuals who experience some anxiety or minor, temporary problems are (not likely/likely) to benefit from therapy. (p. 633)

6. What was the ideal client like, according to a 1964 study of people in therapy? Has that view changed today? (p. 633)

16.2 **DISTINGUISH BETWEEN PROFESSIONALS AND PARAPROFESSIONALS AND DESCRIBE WHAT IT TAKES TO BE AN EFFECTIVE THERAPIST.**

Unlicensed paraprofessionals with no formal training, as well as licensed professionals, can be equally effective as trained therapists. Warmth, selecting important topics to discuss, not contradicting clients, and the ability to establish a positive relationship are more important determinants of a therapist's effectiveness than formal training or being licensed.

7. A person with no professional training who provides mental health services is called a _____. (p. 634)

8. In most states, the term *therapist* (is/isn't) legally protected. (p. 634)

9. How ethical was the client–therapist relationship in the television drama, *In Treatment*? (p. 634)

10. A therapist who talks a lot about his/her personal life is likely to be (effective/ineffective). (p. 635)

((•━ **Listen** to an audio file of your chapter **mypsychlab.com**

INSIGHT THERAPIES: ACQUIRING UNDERSTANDING 635–643

16.3 **DESCRIBE THE CORE BELIEFS AND CRITICISMS OF PSYCHODYNAMIC THERAPIES.**

The core beliefs of psychodynamic therapies are the importance of the unconscious, childhood experiences, expressing emotions and reexperiencing past events, and acquiring insight. Evidence for psychodynamic therapies is based largely on small and highly select patients samples, anecdotal studies, and the questionable curative value of insight, although controlled studies suggest that these therapies may be helpful in some cases.

11. In the technique of _____ _____, clients are allowed to express themselves without censorship of any sort. (p. 636)

12. Neo-Freudians placed (more/less) emphasis on the unconscious than did Freudians. (p. 637)

13. Acccording to Jung, _____ is the integration of opposing aspects of the patient's personality into a harmonious "whole," namely, the self. (p. 637)

14. Critics of psychodynamic therapies assert that understanding our emotional history (is/isn't) required to relieve psychological distress. (p. 638)

16.4 **DESCRIBE AND EVALUATE THE EFFECTIVENESS OF HUMANISTIC THERAPIES.**

Humanistic therapies hold that self-actualization is a universal human drive, and adopt an experience-based approach in which clients work to fulfill their potential. Research suggests that genuineness, unconditional positive regard, and empathic understanding are related to improvement.

15. In Rogers' _____ therapy, the therapist uses reflection to communicate empathy to the client. (p. 639)

16. Explain the two-chair technique as used by Gestalt therapists. (p. 640)

16.5 **LIST THE ADVANTAGES OF GROUP METHODS AND DESCRIBE THE RESEARCH EVIDENCE CONCERNING THE EFFECTIVENESS OF ALCOHOLICS ANONYMOUS.**

Group methods span all schools of psychotherapy and are efficient, time-saving, and less costly than individual methods. Participants learn from others' experiences, benefit from feedback and modeling others, and discover that problems and suffering are widespread. AA is helpful for some clients, but appears to be no more effective than other treatments, including CBT. Research suggests that controlled drinking approaches can be effective with some people with alcoholism.

17. It is (rare/common) for self-help groups to form on the Internet. (p. 641)

18. The relapse prevention approach teaches people to not feel ashamed or discouraged when they lapse, in an effort to avoid the _____ _____ effect. (p. 642)

16.6 IDENTIFY DIFFERENT APPROACHES TO TREATING THE DYSFUNCTIONAL FAMILY SYSTEM.

Family therapies treat problems in the family system. Strategic family therapists remove barriers to effective communication, whereas structural family therapists plan changes in the way family interactions are structured.

19. _____ _____ _____ are designed to remove barriers to effective communication. (p. 642)

20. In _____ family therapy, the therapist is actively involved in the everyday activities of the family to change the structure of their interactions. (p. 642)

BEHAVIORAL APPROACHES: CHANGING MALADAPTIVE ACTIONS 643–651

16.7 DESCRIBE THE CHARACTERISTICS OF BEHAVIOR THERAPY AND IDENTIFY DIFFERENT BEHAVIORAL APPROACHES.

Behavior therapy is grounded in the scientific method and based on learning principles. Exposure therapies confront people with their fears. Exposure can be gradual and stepwise or start with the most frightening scenes imaginable. Modeling techniques, based on observational learning principles, include behavioral rehearsal and role-playing to foster assertiveness. Token economies and aversion therapies are based on operant conditioning principles.

21. A class of procedures that confronts patients with what they fear with the goal of reducing this fear is called _____ _____. (p. 643)

22. During _____ _____, clients are taught to relax as they are gradually exposed to what they fear in a stepwise manner. (p. 644)

23. What is in vivo exposure therapy and how can it help people with a fear of flying? (p. 644)

24. Patients are exposed right away to images of stimuli that they fear the most for prolonged periods during _____. (p. 645)

25. A crucial component of flooding is _____ _____, in which the therapist blocks clients from performing their typical avoidance behaviors. (p. 645)

26. What is EMDR therapy, and what role do eye movements play in treatment outcome? (p. 646)

27. During _____ _____, the therapist first models a problematic situation and then guides the client through steps to cope with it. (p. 646)

28. In _____ _____ programs, desirable behaviors are rewarded through the consistent application of operant conditioning principles. (p. 647)

16.8 DESCRIBE THE FEATURES OF COGNITIVE-BEHAVIORAL THERAPIES (CBT).

Cognitive-behavioral therapists modify irrational and negative beliefs and distorted thoughts that contribute to unhealthy feelings and behaviors. Ellis's rational emotive behavior therapy, Beck's cognitive therapy, and Meichenbaum's stress inoculation training are influential variations of CBT.

29. Ellis's rational emotive-behavior therapy (REBT) emphasizes that our _____ systems play a key role in how we function psychologically. (p. 648)

30. In Meichenbaum's (1985) _____ _____ _____, therapists teach clients to prepare for and cope with future stressful life events. (p. 649)

IS PSYCHOTHERAPY EFFECTIVE? 651–658

16.9 EVALUATE THE CLAIM THAT ALL PSYCHOTHERAPIES ARE EQUALLY EFFECTIVE.

Many therapies are effective. Nevertheless, some therapies, including behavioral and cognitive-behavioral treatments, are more effective than other treatments for specific problems, such as anxiety disorders. Still other treatments, like crisis debriefing, appear to be harmful in some cases.

31. The Dodo bird verdict suggests that all types of psychotherapies are equally _____. (p. 651)

32. Among researchers there is (strong consensus/no consensus) that the Dodo bird verdict is correct. (p. 651)

33. Research shows that behavioral and cognitive behavioral therapies are (more/less) effective than other treatments for children and adolescents with behavioral problems. (p. 651)

34. Most studies show that (20 percent/80 percent) of people who receive psychotherapy do better than the average person who does not. (p. 651)

35. What does the research suggest about the effectiveness of Scared Straight programs? (p. 652)

Answers are located at the end of the text.

36. _____ _____ _____ are treatments for specific disorders that are supported by high-quality scientific evidence. (p. 653)

16.10 EXPLAIN HOW INEFFECTIVE THERAPIES CAN SOMETIMES APPEAR TO BE EFFECTIVE.

Ineffective therapies can appear to be helpful because of spontaneous remission, the placebo effect, self-serving biases, regression to the mean, and retrospective rewriting of the past.

37. What kind of effect can positive life events, like major job promotions, have on psychological problems? (p. 655)

38. Even when they don't improve, clients who have invested time, money, and emotional effort in psychotherapy may convince themselves they've been helped, a psychological phenomenon known as the _____ _____. (p. 656)

39. According to the regression to the mean phenomenon, if a client comes into treatment extremely depressed, the chances are (high/low) that she'll be less depressed in a few weeks. (p. 656)

40. Americans spend $650 million a year on _____ _____ that promise self-improvement. (p. 657)

BIOMEDICAL TREATMENTS: MEDICATIONS, ELECTRICAL STIMULATION, AND SURGERY

658–665

16.11 RECOGNIZE DIFFERENT TYPES OF DRUGS AND CAUTIONS ASSOCIATED WITH DRUG TREATMENT.

Medications are available to treat psychotic conditions (neuroleptics/antispsychotics or major tranquilizers), bipolar disorder (mood stabilizers), depression (antidepressants), anxiety (anxiolytics), and attentional problems (psychostimulants).

41. The use of medications to treat psychological problems is called _____. (p. 658)

42. The first major drug for a psychological disorder, Thorazine, was used to treat _____. (p. 658)

43. Prozac and Zoloft are among the best-known _____ _____ _____ inhibitors. (p. 658)

44. There (is/is not) scientific evidence for an "optimal level" of serotonin or other neurotransmitters in the brain. (p. 660)

16.12 OUTLINE KEY CONSIDERATIONS IN DRUG TREATMENT.

People who prescribe drugs must be aware of side effects, not overprescribe medications, and carefully monitor the effects of multiple medications (polypharmacy).

45. People of different races and cultures (do/do not) respond equally to the same dose of medication. (p. 660)

46. The safety and effectiveness of SSRIs when prescribed to _____ and _____ have been called into question because of increased risk of suicidal thoughts. (p. 661)

47. The drug Ritalin, used to treat ADHD, is an example of a medication that many feel has been _____ and may substitute for effective coping strategies for focusing attention. (p. 661)

16.13 IDENTIFY MISCONCEPTIONS ABOUT BIOMEDICAL TREATMENTS.

Contrary to popular belief, electroconvulsive therapy (ECT) is not painful or dangerous, and doesn't invariably produce memory loss, personality changes, or brain damage. Psychosurgery may be useful as a treatment of absolute last resort.

48. During _____ _____, patients receive brief electrical pulses to the brain that produce a seizure to treat serious psychological problems. (p. 662)

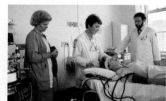

49. How does electrical stimulation to the vagus nerve work? Has research shown it to be an effective treatment? (pp. 663–664)

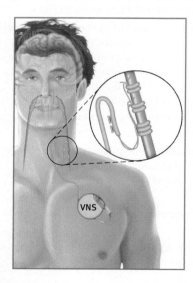

50. Define psychosurgery and explain its potential side effects. (p. 664)

- psychotherapy (p. 632)
- paraprofessional (p. 634)
- insight therapies (p. 635)
- free association (p. 636)
- resistance (p. 636)
- transference (p. 636)
- interpersonal therapies (p. 637)
- humanistic therapies (p. 638)

- person-centered therapy (p. 639)
- Gestalt therapy (p. 640)
- group therapy (p. 641)
- Alcoholics Anonymous (p. 641)
- strategic family intervention (p. 642)
- structural family therapy (p. 642)
- behavior therapist (p. 643)

- systematic desensitization (p. 643)
- exposure therapy (p. 643)
- dismantling (p. 644)
- response prevention (p. 645)
- participant modeling (p. 646)
- token economy (p. 647)
- aversion therapy (p. 647)

- cognitive–behavioral therapies (p. 647)
- meta-analysis (p. 651)
- empirically supported treatment (EST) (p. 653)
- psychopharmacotherapy (p. 658)
- electroconvulsive therapy (ECT) (p. 662)
- psychosurgery (p. 664)

APPLY YOUR SCIENTIFIC THINKING SKILLS

Use your scientific thinking skills to answer the following questions, referencing specific scientific thinking principles and common errors in reasoning whenever possible.

1. There's been a lot of media coverage recently on the overprescription of drugs, particularly to younger children with ADHD. Read articles on both sides of this issue and summarize their arguments. What scientific evidence does each side offer? Has each interpreted the research correctly?

2. Browse through some of the self-help books at your local bookstore or online and select three or four of them (ideally, select books on a wide variety of issues). What scientific research does each book use to support its claims? Do any of the books make extraordinary claims or rely on a "one size fits all" approach to psychological problems? What professional training or expertise, if any, do the authors have?

3. Research one of the potentially harmful therapies in Table 16.7. To what do the proponents of this therapy attribute their success? Have they considered alternate hypotheses? Do they discuss any of the potentially negative effects of the therapy on their websites or in articles?

absolute refractory period time during which another action potential is impossible; limits maximal firing rate

absolute threshold lowest level of a stimulus needed for the nervous system to detect a change 50 percent of the time

abstract thinking capacity to understand hypothetical concepts

accommodation (Chapter 4) changing the shape of the lens to focus on objects near or far

accommodation (Chapter 10) Piagetian process of altering a belief to make it more compatible with experience

acquired immune deficiency syndrome (AIDS) a life-threatening, incurable, yet treatable condition in which the human immunodeficiency virus (HIV) attacks and damages the immune system

acquisition learning phase during which a conditioned response is established

action potential electrical impulse that travels down the axon triggering the release of neurotransmitters

activation–synthesis theory theory that dreams reflect inputs from brain activation originating in the pons, which the forebrain then attempts to weave into a story

acuity sharpness of vision

acupuncture ancient Chinese practice of inserting thin needles into more than 2,000 points in the body to alter energy forces believed to run through the body

ad hoc immunizing hypothesis escape hatch or loophole that defenders of a theory use to protect their theory from falsification

adaptive conservatism evolutionary principle that creates a predisposition toward distrusting anything or anyone unfamiliar or different

adolescence the transition between childhood and adulthood commonly associated with the teenage years

adoption study analysis of how traits vary in individuals raised apart from their biological relatives

adrenal gland tissue located on top of the kidneys that releases adrenaline and cortisol during states of emotional arousal

aerobic exercise exercise that promotes the use of oxygen in the body

affective forecasting ability to predict our own and others' happiness

aggression behavior intended to harm others, either verbally or physically

agoraphobia fear of being in a place or situation from which escape is difficult or embarrassing, or in which help is unavailable in the event of a panic attack

Alcoholics Anonymous Twelve-Step, self-help program that provides social support for achieving sobriety

algorithm step-by-step learned procedure used to solve a problem

alternative medicine health care practices and products used in place of conventional medicine

altruism helping others for unselfish reasons

amygdala part of limbic system that plays key roles in fear, excitement, and arousal

anal stage psychosexual stage that focuses on toilet training

anorexia nervosa eating disorder associated with excessive weight loss and the irrational perception that one is overweight

anterograde amnesia inability to encode new memories from our experiences

antisocial personality disorder (ASPD) condition marked by a lengthy history of irresponsible and/or illegal actions

anxiety sensitivity fear of anxiety-related sensations

apophenia tendency to perceive meaningful connections among unrelated phenomena

applied research research examining how we can use basic research to solve real-world problems

archetype cross-culturally universal symbols

assimilation Piagetian process of absorbing new experience into current knowledge structures

association cortex regions of the cerebral cortex that integrate simpler functions to perform more complex functions

asylum institution for people with mental illnesses created in the 15th century

attachment the strong emotional connection we share with those to whom we feel closest

attention-deficit/hyperactivity disorder (ADHD) childhood condition marked by excessive inattention, impulsivity, and activity

attitude belief that includes an emotional component

attribution process of assigning causes to behavior

audition our sense of hearing

autistic disorder disorder (also known as autism) marked by severe deficits in language, social bonding, and imagination, usually accompanied by mental retardation

autonomic nervous system part of the nervous system controlling the involuntary actions of our internal organs and glands, which (along with the limbic system) participates in emotion regulation

availability heuristic heuristic that involves estimating the likelihood of an occurrence based on the ease with which it comes to our minds

average expectable environment environment that provides children with basic needs for affection and discipline

aversion therapy treatment that uses punishment to decrease the frequency of undesirable behaviors

axis dimension of functioning

axon portion of neuron that sends signals

babbling intentional vocalization that lacks specific meaning

basal ganglia structures in the forebrain that help to control movement

base rate how common a characteristic or behavior is in the general population

basic research research examining how the mind works

basilar membrane membrane supporting the organ of Corti and hair cells in the cochlea

behavior therapists therapist who focuses on specific problem behaviors, and current variables that maintain problematic thoughts, feelings, and behaviors

behaviorism school of psychology that focuses on uncovering the general laws of learning by looking at observable behavior

belief perseverance tendency to stick to our initial beliefs even when evidence contradicts them

bell curve distribution of scores in which the bulk of the scores fall toward the middle, with progressively fewer scores toward the "tails" or extremes

between-group heritability extent to which differences in a trait between groups is genetically influenced

Big Five five traits that have surfaced repeatedly in factor analyses of personality measures

bilingual proficient and fluent at speaking and comprehending two distinct languages

binocular depth cues stimuli that enable us to judge depth using both eyes

biofeedback feedback by a device that provides almost an immediate output of a biological function, such as heart rate or skin temperature

biological clock term for the suprachiasmatic nucleus (SCN) in the hypothalamus that's responsible for controlling our levels of alertness

bipolar disorder condition marked by a history of at least one manic episode

biopsychosocial perspective the view that an illness or medical condition is the product of the interplay of biological, psychological, and social factors

blastocyst ball of identical cells early in pregnancy that haven't yet begun to take on any specific function in a body part

blind unaware of whether one is in the experimental or control group

blind spot part of the visual field we can't see because of an absence of rods and cones

borderline personality disorder condition marked by extreme instability in mood, identity, and impulse control

bottom-up processing processing in which a whole is constructed from parts

brain stem part of the brain between the spinal cord and cerebral cortex that contains the midbrain, pons, and medulla

broaden and build theory theory proposing that happiness predisposes us to think more openly

Broca's area language area in the prefrontal cortex that helps to control speech production

bulimia nervosa eating disorder associated with a pattern of bingeing and purging in an effort to lose or maintain weight

Cannon-Bard theory theory proposing that an emotion-provoking event leads simultaneously to an emotion and to bodily reactions

case study research design that examines one person or a small number of people in depth, often over an extended time period

catatonic symptom motor problem, including extreme resistance to complying with simple suggestions, holding the body in bizarre or rigid postures, or curling up in a fetal position

categorical model model in which a mental disorder differs from normal functioning in kind rather than degree

central nervous system (CNS) part of nervous system containing brain and spinal cord that controls the mind and behavior

central tendency measure of the "central" scores in a data set, or where the group tends to cluster

cerebellum brain structure responsible for our sense of balance

cerebral cortex outermost part of forebrain, responsible for analyzing sensory processing and higher brain functions

cerebral hemispheres two halves of the cerebral cortex, each of which serve distinct yet highly integrated functions

cerebral ventricles pockets in the brain that contain cerebrospinal fluid (CSF), which provide the brain with nutrients and cushion against injury

chromosome slender thread inside a cell's nucleus that carries genes

chunking organizing information into meaningful groupings, allowing us to extend the span of short-term memory

circadian rhythm cyclical changes that occur on a roughly 24-hour basis in many biological processes

classical (Pavlovian) conditioning form of learning in which animals come to respond to a previously neutral stimulus that had been paired with another stimulus that elicits an automatic response

cochlea bony, spiral-shaped sense organ used for hearing

cognitive biases systematic errors in thinking

cognitive development study of how children acquire the ability to learn, think, reason, communicate, and remember

cognitive dissonance unpleasant mental experience of tension resulting from two conflicting thoughts or beliefs

cognitive map mental representation of how a physical space is organized

cognitive model of depression theory that depression is caused by negative beliefs and expectations

cognitive neuroscience relatively new field of psychology that examines the relation between brain functioning and thinking

cognitive psychology school of psychology that proposes that thinking is central to understanding behavior

cognitive theories of emotion theories proposing that emotions are products of thinking

cognitive-behavioral therapies treatments that attempt to replace maladaptive or irrational cognitions with more adaptive, rational cognitions

cohort effect effect observed in a sample of participants that results from individuals in the sample growing up at the same time

collective unconscious according to Jung, our shared storehouse of memories that ancestors have passed down to us across generations

color blindness inability to see some or all colors

comorbidity co-occurrence of two or more diagnoses within the same person

companionate love love marked by a sense of deep friendship and fondness for one's partner

complementary medicine health care practices and products used together with conventional medicine

compulsion repetitive behavior or mental act performed to reduce or prevent stress

computed tomography (CT) a scanning technique using multiple X-rays to construct three-dimensional images

concept our knowledge and ideas about a set of objects, actions, and or characteristics that share core properties

concrete operations stage stage in Piaget's theory characterized by the ability to perform mental operations on physical events only

conditioned response (CR) response previously associated with a nonneutral stimulus that is elicited by a neutral stimulus through conditioning

conditioned stimulus (CS) initially neutral stimulus that comes to elicit a response due to association with an unconditioned stimulus

conditions of worth according to Rogers, expectations we place on ourselves for appropriate and inappropriate behavior

cones receptor cells in the retina allowing us to see in color

confirmation bias tendency to seek out evidence that supports our hypotheses and deny, dismiss, or distort evidence that contradicts them

conformity tendency of people to alter their behavior as a result of group pressure

consciousness our subjective experience of the world, our bodies, and our mental perspectives

conservation Piagetian task requiring children to understand that despite a transformation in the physical presentation of an amount, the amount remains the same

contact comfort positive emotions afforded by touch

context-dependent learning superior retrieval of memories when the external context of the original memories matches the retrieval context

continuous reinforcement reinforcing a behavior every time it occurs, resulting in faster learning but faster extinction than only occasional reinforcement

control group in an experiment, the group of participants that doesn't receive the manipulation

convergent thinking capacity to generate the single best solution to a problem

cornea part of the eye containing transparent cells that focus light on the retina

coronary heart disease (CHD) damage to the heart from the complete or partial blockage of the arteries that provide oxygen to the heart

corpus callosum large band of fibers connecting the two cerebral hemispheres

correlation–causation fallacy error of assuming that because one thing is associated with another, it must cause the other

correlational design research design that examines the extent to which two variables are associated

corticosteroid stress hormone that activates the body and prepares us to respond to stressful circumstances

critical thinking set of skills for evaluating all claims in an open-minded and careful fashion

cross-sectional design research design that examines people of different ages at a single point in time

cryptomnesia failure to recognize that our ideas originated with someone else

crystallized intelligence accumulated knowledge of the world acquired over time

cult group of individuals who exhibit intense and unquestioning devotion to a single cause

culture-fair IQ test abstract reasoning measure that doesn't depend on language and is often believed to be less influenced by cultural factors than other IQ tests

déjà vu feeling of reliving an experience that's new

dark adaptation time in dark before rods regain maximum light sensitivity

decay fading of information from memory over time

decision making the process of selecting among a set of possible alternatives

defense mechanisms unconscious maneuvers intended to minimize anxiety

defensive pessimism strategy of anticipating failure and compensating for this expectation by mentally overpreparing for negative outcomes

deindividuation tendency of people to engage in uncharacteristic behavior when they are stripped of their usual identities

deinstitutionalization 1960s and 1970s governmental policy that focused on releasing hospitalized psychiatric patients into the community and closing mental hospitals

delusion strongly held, fixed belief that has no basis in reality

demand characteristics cues that participants pick up from a study that allow them to generate guesses regarding the researcher's hypotheses

demonic model view of mental illness in which odd behavior, hearing voices, or talking to oneself was attributed to evil spirits infesting the body

dendrite portion of neuron that receives signals

denial motivated forgetting of distressing external experiences

dependent variable variable that an experimenter measures to see whether the manipulation has an effect

depersonalization disorder condition marked by multiple episodes of depersonalization

depth perception ability to judge distance and three-dimensional relations

descriptive statistics numerical characterizations that describe data

developmental psychology study of how behavior changes over the life span

deviation IQ expression of a person's IQ relative to his or her same-aged peers

Diagnostic and Statistical Manual of Mental Disorders **(DSM)** diagnostic system containing the American Psychiatric Association (APA) criteria for mental disorders

dialect language variation used by a group of people who share geographic proximity or ethnic background

diathesis-stress model perspective proposing that mental disorders are a joint product of a genetic vulnerability, called a diathesis, and stressors that trigger this vulnerability

diffusion of responsibility reduction in feelings of personal responsibility in the presence of others

dimensional model model in which a mental disorder differs from normal functioning in degree rather than kind

discrete emotions theory theory that humans experience a small number of distinct emotions that are rooted in our biology

discrimination negative behavior toward members of out-groups

discriminative stimulus stimulus associated with the presence of reinforcement

dismantling research procedure for examining the effectiveness of isolated components of a larger treatment

displacement directing an impulse from a socially unacceptable target onto a safer and more socially acceptable target

display rules cross-cultural guidelines for how and when to express emotions

dissociation theory approach to explaining hypnosis based on a separation between personality functions that are normally well integrated

dissociative amnesia inability to recall important personal information—most often related to a stressful experience—that can't be explained by ordinary forgetfulness

dissociative disorder condition involving disruptions in consciousness, memory, identity, or perception

dissociative fugue sudden, unexpected travel away from home or the workplace, accompanied by amnesia for significant life events

dissociative identity disorder (DID) condition characterized by the presence of two or more distinct identities or personality states that recurrently take control of the person's behavior

distributed versus massed practice studying information in small increments over time (distributed) versus in large increments over a brief amount of time (massed)

divergent thinking capacity to generate many different solutions to a problem

dominant gene gene that masks other genes' effects

door-in-the-face technique persuasive technique involving making an unreasonably large request before making the small request we're hoping to have granted

double-blind when neither researchers nor participants are aware of who's in the experimental or control group

drive reduction theory theory proposing that certain drives, like hunger, thirst, and sexual frustration motivate us to act in ways that minimize aversive states

durability bias belief that both our good and bad moods will last longer than they do

echoic memory auditory sensory memory

ego psyche's executive and principal decision maker

egocentrism inability to see the world from others' perspectives

elaborative rehearsal linking stimuli to each other in a meaningful way to improve retention of information in short-term memory

Electra complex conflict during phallic stage in which girls supposedly love their fathers romantically and want to eliminate their mothers as rivals

electroconvulsive therapy (ECT) patients receive brief electrical pulses to the brain that produce a seizure to treat serious psychological problems

electroencephalograph (EEG)   recording of brain's electrical activity at the surface of the skull

embryo   second to eighth week of prenatal development, during which limbs, facial features, and major organs of the body take form

emerging adulthood   period of life between the ages of 18 and 25 during which many aspects of emotional development, identity, and personality become solidified

emotion   mental state or feeling associated with our evaluation of our experiences

emotional intelligence   ability to understand our own emotions and those of others, and to apply this information to our daily lives

emotion-focused coping   coping strategy that features a positive outlook on feelings or situations accompanied by behaviors that reduce painful emotions

empirical method of test construction   approach to building tests in which researchers begin with two or more criterion groups, and examine which items best distinguish them

empirically supported treatment (EST)   intervention for specific disorders supported by high-quality scientific evidence

empty-nest syndrome   alleged period of depression in mothers following the departure of their grown children from the home

encoding   process of getting information into our memory banks

encoding specificity   phenomenon of remembering something better when the conditions under which we retrieve information are similar to the conditions under which we encoded it

endocrine system   system of glands and hormones that controls secretion of blood-borne chemical messengers

endorphin   chemical in the brain that plays a specialized role in pain reduction

enlightenment effect   learning about psychological research can change real-world behavior for the better

episodic memory   recollection of events in our lives

erogenous zone   sexually arousing zone of the body

eugenics   movement in the early twentieth century to improve a population's genetic stock by encouraging those with good genes to reproduce, preventing those with bad genes from reproducing, or both

evolutionary psychology   discipline that applies Darwin's theory of natural selection to human and animal behavior

excitement phase   phase in human sexual response in which people experience sexual pleasure and notice physiological changes associated with it

existence proof   demonstration that a given psychological phenomenon can occur

experiment   research design characterized by random assignment of participants to conditions and manipulation of an independent variable

experimental group   in an experiment, the group of participants that receives the manipulation

experimenter expectancy effect   phenomenon in which researchers' hypotheses lead them to unintentionally bias the outcome of a study

explicit memory   memories we recall intentionally and of which we have conscious awareness

explicit prejudice   unfounded negative belief of which we're aware regarding the characteristics of an out-group

exposure therapy   therapy that confronts clients with what they fear with the goal of reducing the fear

external validity   extent to which we can generalize findings to real-world settings

extinction   gradual reduction and eventual elimination of the conditioned response after the conditioned stimulus is presented repeatedly without the unconditioned stimulus

extralinguistic information   elements of communication that aren't part of the content of language but are critical to interpreting its meaning

extrasensory perception (ESP)   perception of events outside the known channels of sensation

face validity   extent to which respondents can tell what the items are measuring

facial feedback hypothesis   theory that blood vessels in the face feed back temperature information in the brain, altering our experience of emotions

factor analysis   statistical technique that analyzes the correlations among responses on personality inventories and other measures

falsifiable   capable of being disproved

family study   analysis of how characteristics run in intact families

feature detector cell   cell that detects lines and edges

fetal alcohol syndrome   condition resulting from high levels of prenatal alcohol exposure, causing learning disabilities, physical growth retardation, facial malformations, and behavioral disorders

fetishism   sexual attraction to nonliving things

fetus   period of prenatal development from ninth week until birth after all major organs are established and physical maturation is the primary change

fight-or-flight response   physical and psychological reaction that mobilizes people and animals to either defend themselves (fight) or escape (flee) a threatening situation

fitness   organisms' capacity to pass on their genes

fixed interval (FI) schedule   pattern in which we provide reinforcement for producing the response at least once following a specified time interval

fixed ratio (FR) schedule   pattern in which we provide reinforcement following a regular number of responses

flashbulb memory   emotional memory that is extraordinarily vivid and detailed

fluid intelligence   capacity to learn new ways of solving problems

Flynn effect   finding that average IQ scores have been rising at a rate of approximately three points per decade

foot-in-the-door technique   persuasive technique involving making a small request before making a bigger one

forebrain (cerebrum)   forward part of the brain that allows advanced intellectual abilities

formal operations stage   stage in Piaget's theory characterized by the ability to perform hypothetical reasoning beyond the here and now

fovea   central portion of the retina

framing   the way a question is formulated which can influence the decisions people make

free association   technique in which clients express themselves without censorship of any sort

frequency theory   rate at which neurons fire the action potential reproduces the pitch

frontal lobe   forward part of cerebral cortex responsible for motor function, language, memory, and planning

functional fixedness   difficulty conceptualizing that an object typically used for one purpose can be used for another

functional MRI (fMRI)   technique that uses magnetic fields to visualize brain activity using the BOLD response

functionalism   school of psychology that aimed to understand the adaptive purposes of psychological characteristics

fundamental attribution error   tendency to overestimate the impact of dispositional influences on other people's behavior

g (general intelligence)   hypothetical factor that accounts for overall differences in intellect among people

gate control model   idea that pain is blocked or gated from consciousness by neural mechanisms in the spinal cord

gender identity   individuals' sense of being male or female

gender role   a set of behaviors that tend to be associated with being male or female

gene   genetic material, composed of deoxyribonucleic acid (DNA)

gene expression   activation or deactivation of genes by environmental experiences throughout development

gene-environment interaction   situation in which the effects of genes depend on the environment in which they are expressed

general adaptation syndrome (GAS)   stress-response pattern proposed by Hans Selye that consists of three stages: alarm, resistance, and exhaustion

generalized anxiety disorder (GAD)   continual feelings of worry, anxiety, physical tension, and irritability across many areas of life functioning

generative   allowing an infinite number of unique sentences to be created by combining words in novel ways

genital stage   psychosexual stage in which sexual impulses awaken and typically begin to mature into romantic attraction toward others

genotype   our genetic makeup

Gestalt therapy   therapy that aims to integrate different and sometimes opposing aspects of personality into a unified sense of self

glial cell   cell in nervous system that plays a role in the formation of myelin and the blood–brain barrier, responds to injury, removes debris, and enhances learning and memory

glucostatic theory   theory that when our blood glucose levels drop, hunger creates a drive to eat to restore the proper level of glucose

graphology   psychological interpretation of handwriting

group polarization   tendency of group discussion to strengthen the dominant positions held by individual group members

group therapy   therapy that treats more than one person at a time

groupthink   emphasis on group unanimity at the expense of critical thinking

guilty knowledge test (GKT)   alternative to the polygraph test that relies on the premise that criminals harbor concealed knowledge about the crime that innocent people don't

gustation   our sense of taste

habituation   process of responding less strongly over time to repeated stimuli

hallucination   sensory perception that occurs in the absence of an external stimulus

hallucinogenic   causing dramatic alterations of perception, mood, and thought

hardiness   set of attitudes marked by a sense of control over events, commitment to life and work, and courage and motivation to confront stressful events

hassle   minor annoyance or nuisance that strains our ability to cope

health psychology   field of psychology, also called behavioral medicine, that integrates the behavioral sciences with the practice of medicine

hedonic treadmill   tendency for our moods to adapt to external circumstances

heritability   percentage of the variability in a trait across individuals that is due to genes

heuristic   mental shortcut that helps us to streamline our thinking and make sense of our world

hierarchy of needs   model, developed by Abraham Maslow, proposing that we must satisfy physiological needs and needs for safety and security before progressing to more complex needs

higher-order conditioning   developing a conditioned response to a conditioned stimulus by virtue of its association with another conditioned stimulus

hindbrain   region below the midbrain that contains the cerebellum, pons, and medulla

hindsight bias   tendency to overestimate how well we could have successfully forecasted known outcomes

hippocampus   part of the brain that plays a role in spatial memory

homeopathic medicine   remedies that feature a small dose of an illness-inducing substance to activate the body's own natural defenses

homeostasis   equilibrium

homesign   system of signs invented by deaf children of hearing parents who receive no language input

hormone   chemical released into the bloodstream that influences particular organs and glands

hue   color of light

humanistic therapies   therapies that emphasize the development of human potential and the belief that human nature is basically positive

hypnosis   set of techniques that provides people with suggestions for alterations in their perceptions, thoughts, feelings, and behaviors

hypnotic   drug that exerts a sleep-inducing effect

hypochondriasis   an individual's continual preoccupation with the notion that he has a serious physical disease

hypothalamus   part of the brain responsible for maintaining a constant internal state

hypothesis   testable prediction derived from a scientific theory

iconic memory   visual sensory memory

id   reservoir of our most primitive impulses, including sex and aggression

identification with the aggressor   process of adopting the characteristics of individuals we find threatening

identity   our sense of who we are, and our life goals and priorities

ideological immune system   our psychological defenses against evidence that contradicts our views

idiographic approach   approach to personality that focuses on identifying the unique configuration of characteristics and life history experiences within a person

illusion   perception in which the way we perceive a stimulus doesn't match its physical reality

illusory correlation   perception of a statistical association between two variables where none exists

immune system   our body's defense system against invading bacteria, viruses, and other potentially illness-producing organisms and substances

implicit memory   memories we don't deliberately remember or reflect on consciously

implicit prejudice   unfounded negative belief of which we're unaware regarding the characteristics of an out-group

impression management theory   theory that we don't really change our attitudes, but report that we have so that our behaviors appear consistent with our attitudes

inattentional blindness   failure to detect stimuli that are in plain sight when our attention is focused elsewhere

incentive theories   theories proposing that we're often motivated by positive goals

incongruence   inconsistency between our personalities and innate dispositions

incremental validity   extent to which a test contributes information beyond other, more easily collected, measures

independent variable   variable that an experimenter manipulates

individual differences   variations among people in their thinking, emotion, personality, and behavior

infantile amnesia   inability of adults to remember personal experiences that took place before an early age

inferential statistics   mathematical methods that allow us to determine whether we can generalize findings from our sample to the full population

inferiority complex   feelings of low self-esteem that can lead to overcompensation for such feelings

informed consent   informing research participants of what is involved in a study before asking them to participate

in-group bias   tendency to favor individuals within our group over those from outside our group

inoculation effect   approach to convincing people to change their minds about something by first introducing reasons why the perspective might be correct and then debunking them

insanity defense   legal defense proposing that people shouldn't be held legally responsible for their actions if they weren't of "sound mind" when committing them

insight   grasping the underlying nature of a problem

insight therapies   psychotherapies, including psychodynamic, humanistic, and group approaches, with the goal of expanding awareness or insight

insomnia   difficulty falling and staying asleep

instinctive drift   tendency for animals to return to innate behaviors following repeated reinforcement

integrity test   questionnaire that presumably assesses workers' tendency to steal or cheat

intelligence quotient (IQ)   systematic means of quantifying differences among people in their intelligence

intelligence test   diagnostic tool designed to measure overall thinking ability

interference   loss of information from memory because of competition from additional incoming information

internal validity   extent to which we can draw cause-and-effect inferences from a study

internal–external theory   theory holding that obese people are motivated to eat more by external cues than internal cues

interneuron   neuron that sends messages to other neurons nearby

interpersonal therapy (IPT)   treatment that strengthens social skills and targets interpersonal problems, conflicts, and life transitions

introspection   method by which trained observers carefully reflect and report on their mental experiences

involuntary commitment   procedure of placing some people with mental illnesses in a psychiatric hospital or other facility based on their potential danger to themselves or others, or their inability to care for themselves

James-Lange theory of emotion   theory proposing that emotions result from our interpretations of our bodily reactions to stimuli

jigsaw classroom   educational approach designed to minimize prejudice by requiring all children to make independent contributions to a shared project

just noticeable difference (JND)   the smallest change in the intensity of a stimulus that we can detect

just-world hypothesis   claim that our attributions and behaviors are shaped by a deep-seated assumption that the world is fair and all things happen for a reason

labeling theorists   scholars who argue that psychiatric diagnoses exert powerful negative effects on people's perceptions and behaviors

language   largely arbitrary system of communication that combines symbols (such as words or gestural signs) in rule-based ways to create meaning

language acquisition device   hypothetical organ in the brain in which nativists believe knowledge of syntax resides

latency stage   psychosexual stage in which sexual impulses are submerged into the unconscious

latent inhibition   difficulty in establishing classical conditioning to a conditioned stimulus we've repeatedly experienced alone, that is, without the unconditioned stimulus

latent learning   learning that's not directly observable

lateralization   cognitive function that relies more on one side of the brain than the other

law of effect   principle asserting that if a stimulus followed by a behavior results in a reward, the stimulus is more likely to give rise to the behavior in the future

learned helplessness   tendency to feel helpless in the face of events we can't control

learning   change in an organism's behavior or thought as a result of experience

learning style   an individual's preferred or optimal method of acquiring new information

lens   part of the eye that changes curvature to keep images in focus

leptin   hormone that signals the hypothalamus and brain stem to reduce appetite and increase the amount of energy used

levels of analysis   rungs on a ladder of analysis, with lower levels tied most closely to biological influences and higher levels tied most closely to social influences

levels of processing   depth of transforming information, which influences how easily we remember it

lexical approach   approach proposing that the most crucial features of personality are embedded in our language

limbic system   emotional center of brain that also plays roles in smell, motivation, and memory

linguistic determinism   view that all thought is represented verbally and that, as a result, our language defines our thinking

linguistic relativity   view that characteristics of language shape our thought processes

locus of control   extent to which people believe that reinforcers and punishers lie inside or outside of their control

longitudinal design   research design that examines development in the same group of people on multiple occasions over time

long-term memory   relatively enduring (from minutes to years) retention of information stored regarding our facts, experiences, and skills

long-term potentiation (LTP)   gradual strengthening of the connections among neurons from repetitive stimulation

low-ball technique   persuasive technique in which the seller of a product starts by quoting a low sales price, and then mentions all of the "add-on" costs once the customer has agreed to purchase the product

lucid dreaming   experience of becoming aware that one is dreaming

Magic Number   the span of short-term memory, according to George Miller: seven plus or minus two pieces of information

magnetic resonance imaging (MRI)   technique that uses magnetic fields to indirectly visualize brain structure

magnetoencephalography (MEG)   technique that measures brain activity by detecting tiny magnetic fields generated by the brain

maintenance rehearsal   repeating stimuli in their original form to retain them in short-term memory

major depressive episode   state in which a person experiences a lingering depressed mood or diminished interest in pleasurable activities, along with symptoms that include weight loss and sleep difficulties

manic episode   experience marked by dramatically elevated mood, decreased need for sleep, increased energy, inflated self-esteem, increased talkativeness, and irresponsible behavior

mass hysteria   outbreak of irrational behavior that is spread by social contagion

mean   average; a measure of central tendency

median   middle score in a data set; a measure of central tendency

medical model   view of mental illness as due to a physical disorder requiring medical treatment

meditation   a variety of practices that train attention and awareness

medulla   part of brain stem involved in basic functions, such as heartbeat and breathing

memory   retention of information over time

memory illusion   false but subjectively compelling memory

menarche   start of menstruation

menopause   the termination of menstruation, marking the end of a woman's reproductive potential

mental age   age corresponding to the average individual's performance on an intelligence test

mental retardation   condition characterized by an onset prior to adulthood, an IQ below about 70, and an inability to engage in adequate daily functioning

mental set   phenomenon of becoming stuck in a specific problem-solving strategy, inhibiting our ability to generate alternatives

mere exposure effect   phenomenon in which repeated exposure to a stimulus makes us more likely to feel favorably toward it

meta-analysis   statistical method that helps researchers to interpret large bodies of psychological literature

metalinguistic   awareness of how language is structured and used

meta-memory   knowledge about our own memory abilities and limitations

metaphysical claims   assertions about the world that are not testable

midbrain   part of the brain stem that contributes to movement, tracking of visual stimuli, and reflexes triggered by sound

midlife crisis   supposed phase of adulthood characterized by emotional distress about the aging process and an attempt to regain youth

Minnesota Multiphasic Personality Inventory (MMPI)   widely used structured personality test designed to assess symptoms of mental disorders

mirror neuron   cell in the prefrontal cortex that becomes activated by specific motions when an animal both performs and observes that action

misinformation effect   creation of fictitious memories by providing misleading information about an event after it takes place

mnemonic   a learning aid, strategy, or device that enhances recall

mode   most frequent score in a data set; a measure of central tendency

molecular genetic study   investigation that allows researchers to pinpoint genes associated with specific personality traits

monocular depth cues   stimuli that enable us to judge depth using only one eye

mono-operation bias   drawing conclusions on the basis of only a single measure

moral treatment   approach to mental illness calling for dignity, kindness, and respect for the mentally ill

morpheme   smallest meaningful unit of speech

motivation   psychological drives that propel us in a specific direction

motor behavior   bodily motion that occurs as result of self-initiated force that moves the bones and muscles

motor cortex   part of frontal lobe responsible for body movement

multiple intelligences   idea that people vary in their ability levels across different domains of intellectual skill

multiply determined   caused by many factors

myelin sheath   glial cells wrapped around axons that act as insulators of the neuron's signal

mystical experience   feelings of unity or oneness with the world, often with strong spiritual overtones

naive realism   belief that we see the world precisely as it is

narcolepsy   disorder characterized by the rapid and often unexpected onset of sleep

narcotic   drug that relieves pain and induces sleep

nativist   account of language acquisition that suggests children are born with some basic knowledge of how language works

natural selection   principle that organisms that possess adaptations survive and reproduce at a higher rate than other organisms

naturalistic observation   watching behavior in real-world settings without trying to manipulate the situation

nature via nurture   tendency of individuals with certain genetic predispositions to seek out and create environments that permit the expression of those predispositions

near-death experience (NDE)   out-of-body experience reported by people who've nearly died or thought they were going to die

negative reinforcement   removal of a stimulus that strengthens the probability of the behavior

neo-Freudian theories   theories derived from Freud's model, but that placed less emphasis on sexuality as a driving force in personality and were more optimistic regarding the prospects for long-term personality growth

neurocognitive theory   theory that dreams are a meaningful product of our cognitive capacities, which shape what we dream about

neurogenesis   creation of new neurons in the adult brain

neuron   nerve cell specialized for communication

neurotransmitter   chemical messenger specialized for communication from neuron to neuron

night terrors   sudden waking episodes characterized by screaming, perspiring, and confusion followed by a return to a deep sleep

nomothetic approach   approach to personality that focuses on identifying general laws that govern the behavior of all individuals

non-REM (NREM) sleep   stages 1 through 4 of the sleep cycle, during which rapid eye movements do not occur and dreaming is less frequent and vivid

nonverbal leakage   unconscious spillover of emotions into nonverbal behavior

obedience   adherence to instructions from those of higher authority

object permanence   the understanding that objects continue to exist even when out of view

observational learning   learning by watching others

obsession   persistent idea, thought, or impulse that is unwanted and inappropriate, causing marked distress

obsessive-compulsive disorder (OCD)   condition marked by repeated and lengthy (at least one hour per day) immersion in obsessions, compulsions, or both

occipital lobe   back part of cerebral cortex specialized for vision

Oedipus complex   conflict during phallic stage in which boys supposedly love their mothers romantically and want to eliminate their fathers as rivals

olfaction   our sense of smell

one word stage   early period of language development when children use single-word phrases to convey an entire thought

operant conditioning   learning controlled by the consequences of the organism's behavior

operational definition   a working definition of what a researcher is measuring

opponent process theory   theory that we perceive colors in terms of three pairs of opponent colors: either red or green, blue or yellow, or black or white

optic nerve   nerve that travels from the retina to the brain

oral stage   psychosexual stage that focuses on the mouth

organ of Corti   tissue containing the hair cells necessary for hearing

orgasm (climax) phase   phase in human sexual response marked by involuntary rhythmic contractions in the muscles of genitals in both men and women

out-group homogeneity   tendency to view all individuals outside our group as highly similar

out-of-body experience (OBE)   sense of our consciousness leaving our body

overconfidence   tendency to overestimate our ability to make correct predictions

P. T. Barnum effect   tendency of people to accept high base rate descriptions as accurate

panic attack   brief, intense episode of extreme fear characterized by sweating, dizziness, light-headedness, racing heartbeat, and feelings of impending death or going crazy

panic disorder   repeated and unexpected panic attacks, along with either persistent concerns about future attacks or a change in personal behavior in an attempt to avoid them

parallel processing   the ability to attend to many sense modalities simultaneously

paraprofessional   person with no professional training who provides mental health services

parasympathetic nervous system   division of autonomic nervous system that controls rest and digestion

pareidolia   tendency to perceive meaningful images in meaningless visual stimuli

parietal lobe   upper middle part of the cerebral cortex lying behind the frontal lobe that is specialized for touch and perception

partial reinforcement   only occasional reinforcement of a behavior, resulting in slower extinction than if the behavior had been reinforced continually

participant modeling   technique in which the therapist first models a problematic situation and then guides the client through steps to cope with it unassisted

passionate love   love marked by powerful, even overwhelming, longing for one's partner

past life regression therapy   therapeutic approach that hypnotizes and supposedly age-regresses patients to a previous life to identify the source of a present-day problem

peak experience   transcendent moment of intense excitement and tranquility marked by a profound sense of connection to the world

peptic ulcer   inflamed area in the gastrointestinal tract that can cause pain, nausea, and loss of appetite

perception   the brain's interpretation of raw sensory inputs

perceptual constancy   the process by which we perceive stimuli consistently across varied conditions

perceptual set   set formed when expectations influence perceptions

peripheral nervous system (PNS)   nerves in the body that extend outside the central nervous system (CNS)

permastore   type of long-term memory that appears to be permanent

personality   people's typical ways of thinking, feeling, and behaving

personality disorder   condition in which personality traits, appearing first in adolescence, are inflexible, stable, expressed in a wide variety of situations, and lead to distress or impairment

person-centered therapy   therapy centering on the client's goals and ways of solving problems

phallic stage   psychosexual stage that focuses on the genitals

phantom pain   pain or discomfort felt in an amputated limb

phenotype   our observable traits

pheromone   odorless chemical that serves as a social signal to members of one's species

phobia   intense fear of an object or situation that's greatly out of proportion to its actual threat

phoneme   category of sounds our vocal apparatus produces

phonetic decomposition   reading strategy that involves sounding out words by drawing correspondences between printed letters and sounds

physical dependence   dependence on a drug that occurs when people continue to take it to avoid withdrawal symptoms

Pinocchio response   supposedly perfect physiological or behavioral indicator of lying

pituitary gland   master gland that, under the control of the hypothalamus, directs the other glands of the body

place theory   specific place along the basilar membrane matches a tone with a specific pitch

placebo effect   improvement resulting from the mere expectation of improvement

plasticity   ability of the nervous system to change

plateau phase   phase in human sexual response in which sexual tension builds

pleasure principle   tendency of the id to strive for immediate gratification

pluralistic ignorance   error of assuming that no one in a group perceives things as we do

pons   part of the brain stem that connects the cortex with the cerebellum

positive illusions   tendencies to perceive ourselves more favorably than others do

positive psychology   discipline that has sought to emphasize human strengths

positive reinforcement   presentation of a stimulus that strengthens the probability of the behavior

positivity effect   tendency for people to remember more positive than negative information with age

positron emission tomography (PET)   imaging technique that measures consumption of glucose-like molecules, yielding a picture of neural activity in different regions of the brain

post hoc fallacy   false assumption that because one event occurred before another event, it must have caused that event

posttraumatic stress disorder (PTSD)   marked emotional disturbance after experiencing or witnessing a severely stressful event

prefrontal cortex   part of frontal lobe responsible for thinking, planning, and language

prefrontal lobotomy   surgical procedure that severs fibers connecting the frontal lobes of the brain from the underlying thalamus

prejudice   drawing negative conclusions about a person, group of people, or situation prior to evaluating the evidence

prenatal   prior to birth

preoperational stage   stage in Piaget's theory characterized by the ability to construct mental representations of experience, but not yet perform operations on them

preparedness   evolutionary predisposition to learn some pairings of feared stimuli over others owing to their survival value

prevalence   percentage of people within a population who have a specific mental disorder

primacy effect   tendency to remember words at the beginning of a list especially well

primary appraisal   initial decision regarding whether an event is harmful

primary emotions   small number (perhaps seven) of emotions believed by some theorists to be cross-culturally universal

primary reinforcer   item or outcome that naturally increases the target behavior

primary sensory cortex   regions of the cerebral cortex that initially process information from the senses

primary sex characteristic   a physical feature such as the reproductive organs and genitals that distinguish the sexes

priming   our ability to identify a stimulus more easily or more quickly after we've encountered similar stimuli

proactive coping   anticipation of problems and stressful situations that promotes effective coping

proactive interference   interference with acquisition of new information due to previous learning of information

problem solving   generating a cognitive strategy to accomplish a goal

problem-focused coping   coping strategy by which we problem solve and tackle life's challenges head-on

procedural memory   memory for how to do things, including motor skills and habits

projection   unconscious attribution of our negative characteristics to others

projective hypothesis   hypothesis that in the process of interpreting ambiguous stimuli, examinees project aspects of their personality onto the stimulus

projective test   test consisting of ambiguous stimuli that examinees must interpret or make sense of

proprioception   our sense of body position

proxemics   study of personal space

proximity   physical nearness, a predictor of attraction

pseudoscience   set of claims that seems scientific but isn't

psychic determinism   the assumption that all psychological events have a cause

psychoactive drug   substance that contains chemicals similar to those found naturally in our brains that alter consciousness by changing chemical processes in neurons

psychoanalysis   school of psychology, founded by Sigmund Freud, that focuses on internal psychological processes of which we're unaware

psychological dependence   dependence on a drug that occurs when continued use of the drug is motivated by intense cravings

psychology   the scientific study of the mind, brain, and behavior

psychoneuroimmunology   study of the relationship between the immune system and central nervous system

psychopathic personality   condition marked by superficial charm, dishonesty, manipulativeness, self-centeredness, and risk taking

psychopharmacotherapy   use of medications to treat psychological problems

psychophysics   the study of how we perceive sensory stimuli based on their physical characteristics

psychophysiological   illnesses such as asthma and ulcers in which emotions and stress contribute to, maintain, or aggravate the physical condition

psychosocial crisis   dilemma concerning an individual's relations to other people

psychosurgery   brain surgery to treat psychological problems

psychotherapy   a psychological intervention designed to help people resolve emotional, behavioral, and interpersonal problems and improve the quality of their lives

psychotic symptom   psychological problem reflecting serious distortions in reality

puberty   the achievement of sexual maturation resulting in the potential to reproduce

punishment   outcome or consequence of a behavior that weakens the probability of the behavior

pupil   circular hole through which light enters the eye

random assignment   randomly sorting participants into two groups

random selection   procedure that ensures every person in a population has an equal chance of being chosen to participate

range   difference between the highest and lowest scores; a measure of dispersion

rapid eye movement (REM)   darting of the eyes underneath closed eyelids during sleep

rational/theoretical method of test construction   approach to building tests that requires test developers to begin with a clear-cut conceptualization of a trait and then write items to assess that conceptualization

rationalization   providing a reasonable-sounding explanation for unreasonable behaviors or for failures

reaction-formation   transformation of an anxiety-provoking emotion into its opposite

reality principle   tendency of the ego to postpone gratification until it can find an appropriate outlet

recall   generating previously remembered information

recency effect   tendency to remember words at the end of a list especially well

receptor site   location that uniquely recognizes a neurotransmitter

recessive gene   gene that is expressed only in the absence of a dominant gene

reciprocal determinism   tendency for people to mutually influence each other's behavior

reciprocity   rule of give and take, a predictor of attraction

recognition   selecting previously remembered information from an array of options

reflex   an automatic motor response to a sensory stimulus

regression   the act of returning psychologically to a younger, and typically simpler and safer, age

rehearsal   repeating information to extend the duration of retention in short-term memory

reinforcement   outcome or consequence of a behavior that strengthens the probability of the behavior

relational aggression   form of indirect aggression, prevalent in girls, involving spreading rumors, gossiping, and nonverbal putdowns for the purpose of social manipulation

relearning   reacquiring knowledge that we'd previously learned but largely forgotten over time

reliability   consistency of measurement

REM sleep   stage of sleep during which the brain is most active and during which vivid dreaming most often occurs

renewal effect   sudden reemergence of a conditioned response following extinction when an animal is returned to the environment in which the conditioned response was acquired

replicability   when a study's findings are able to be duplicated, ideally by independent investigators

representativeness heuristic   heuristic that involves judging the probability of an event by its superficial similarity to a prototype

repression   motivated forgetting of emotionally threatening memories or impulses

resistance   attempts to avoid confrontation and anxiety associated with uncovering previously repressed thoughts, emotions, and impulses

resolution phase   phase in human sexual response following orgasm, in which people report relaxation and a sense of well-being

response prevention   technique in which therapists prevent clients from performing their typical avoidance behaviors

response set   tendency of research participants to distort their responses to questionnaire items

resting potential   electrical charge difference (–60 millivolts) across the neuronal membrane, when the neuron is not being stimulated or inhibited

reticular activating system (RAS)   brain area that plays a key role in arousal

retina   membrane at the back of the eye responsible for converting light into neural activity

retrieval   reactivation or reconstruction of experiences from our memory stores

retrieval cue   hint that makes it easier for us to recall information

retroactive interference   interference with retention of old information due to acquisition of new information

retrograde amnesia   loss of memories from our past

reuptake   means of recycling neurotransmitters

rods   receptor cells in the retina allowing us to see in low levels of light

Rorschach Inkblot Test   projective test consisting of ten symmetrical inkblots

_s_ (specific abilities)   particular ability level in a narrow domain

scaffolding   Vygotskian learning mechanism in which parents provide initial assistance in children's learning but gradually remove structure as children become more competent

scapegoat hypothesis   claim that prejudice arises from a need to blame other groups for our misfortunes

scatterplot   grouping of points on a two-dimensional graph in which each dot represents a single person's data

schedule of reinforcement   pattern of reinforcing a behavior

schema   organized knowledge structure or mental model that we've stored in memory

schizophrenia   severe disorder of thought and emotion associated with a loss of contact with reality

scientific skepticism   approach of evaluating all claims with an open mind but insisting on persuasive evidence before accepting them

scientific theory   explanation for a large number of findings in the natural world

secondary appraisal   perceptions regarding our ability to cope with an event that follows primary appraisal

secondary reinforcer   neutral object that becomes associated with a primary reinforcer

secondary sex characteristic   a sex-differentiating characteristic that doesn't relate directly to reproduction, such as breast enlargement in women and deepening voices in men

sedative   drug that exerts a calming effect

selective attention   process of selecting one sensory channel and ignoring or minimizing others

self-actualization   drive to develop our innate potential to the fullest possible extent

self-control   ability to inhibit an impulse to act

self-esteem   evaluation of our worth

self-monitoring   personality trait that assesses the extent to which people's behavior reflects their true feelings and attitudes

self-perception theory   theory that we acquire our attitudes by observing our behaviors

semantic memory   our knowledge of facts about the world

semantics   meaning derived from words and sentences

semicircular canals   three fluid-filled canals in the inner ear responsible for our sense of balance

sensation   detection of physical energy by sense organs, which then send information to the brain

sense receptor   specialized cell responsible for converting external stimuli into neural activity for a specific sensory system

sensorimotor stage   stage in Piaget's theory characterized by a focus on the here and now without the ability to represent experiences mentally

sensory adaptation   activation is greatest when a stimulus is first detected

sensory memory   brief storage of perceptual information before it is passed to short-term memory

serial position curve   graph depicting both primacy and recency effects on people's ability to recall items on a list

set point   value that establishes a range of body and muscle mass we tend to maintain

shaping by successive approximations   conditioning a target behavior by progressively reinforcing behaviors that come closer and closer to the target

short-term memory   memory system that retains information for limited durations

sign language   language developed by members of a deaf community that uses visual rather than auditory communication

signal detection theory   theory regarding how stimuli are detected under different conditions

similarity   extent to which we have things in common with others, a predictor of attraction

Skinner box   small animal chamber constructed by Skinner to allow sustained periods of conditioning to be administered and behaviors to be recorded unsupervised

sleep apnea   disorder caused by a blockage of the airway during sleep, resulting in daytime fatigue

sleep paralysis   state of being unable to move just after falling asleep or right before waking up

sleepwalking   walking while fully asleep

social comparison theory   theory that we seek to evaluate our abilities and beliefs by comparing them with those of others

social facilitation   enhancement of performance brought about by the presence of others

social learning theorists   theorists who emphasize thinking as a cause of personality

social loafing   phenomenon whereby individuals become less productive in groups

social phobia   marked fear of public appearances in which embarrassment or humiliation seems likely

social pragmatics   account of language acquisition that proposes children infer what words and sentences mean from context and social interactions

social psychology   study of how people influence others' behavior, beliefs, and attitudes

social support   relationships with people and groups that can provide us with emotional comfort and personal and financial resources

sociocognitive theory   approach to explaining hypnosis based on people's attitudes, beliefs, and expectations

somatic marker theory   theory proposing that we use our "gut reactions" to help us determine how we should act

somatic nervous system part of the nervous system that conveys information between the CNS and the body, controlling and coordinating voluntary movement

somatoform disorder condition marked by physical symptoms that suggest an underlying medical illness, but that are actually psychological in origin

somatosensory our sense of touch, temperature, and pain

source monitoring confusion lack of clarity about the origin of a memory

specific phobia intense fear of objects, places, or situations that is greatly out of proportion to their actual threat

spermarche boys' first ejaculation

spinal cord thick bundle of nerves that conveys signals between the brain and the body

spirituality search for the sacred, which may or may not extend to belief in God

split-brain surgery procedure that involves severing the corpus callosum to reduce the spread of epileptic seizures

spontaneous recovery sudden reemergence of an extinct conditioned response after a delay in exposure to the conditioned stimulus

standard deviation measure of dispersion that takes into account how far each data point is from the mean

Stanford-Binet IQ test intelligence test based on the measure developed by Binet and Simon, adapted by Lewis Terman of Stanford University

state-dependent learning superior retrieval of memories when the organism is in the same physiological or psychological state as it was during encoding

statistics application of mathematics to describing and analyzing data

stem cell a cell, often originating in embryos, having the capacity to differentiate into a more specialized cell

stereotype threat fear that we may confirm a negative group stereotype

stereotype a belief, positive or negative, about the characteristics of members of a group that is applied generally to most members of the group

stimulant drug that increases activity in the central nervous system, including heart rate, respiration, and blood pressure

stimulus discrimination process by which organisms display a less pronounced conditioned response to conditioned stimuli that differ from the original conditioned stimulus

stimulus generalization process by which conditioned stimuli similar, but not identical, to the original conditioned stimulus elicit a conditioned response

storage process of keeping information in memory

stranger anxiety a fear of strangers developing at eight or nine months of age

strategic family intervention family therapy approach designed to remove barriers to effective communication

stress the tension, discomfort, or physical symptoms that arise when a situation, called a stressor—a type of stimulus—strains our ability to cope effectively

structural family therapy treatment in which therapists deeply involve themselves in family activities to change how family members arrange and organize interactions

structuralism school of psychology that aimed to identify the basic elements of psychological experience

structured personality test paper-and-pencil test consisting of questions that respondents answer in one of a few fixed ways

style of life according to Adler, each person's distinctive way of achieving superiority

sublimation transforming a socially unacceptable impulse into an admired goal

subliminal perception perception below the limen or threshold of conscious awareness

suggestive memory technique procedure that encourages patients to recall memories that may or may not have taken place

superego our sense of morality

sympathetic nervous system division of the autonomic nervous system engaged during a crisis or after actions requiring fight or flight

synapse space between two connecting neurons through which messages are transmitted chemically

synaptic cleft a gap into which neurotransmitters are released from the axon terminal

synaptic vesicle spherical sac containing neurotransmitters

synesthesia a condition in which people experience cross-modal sensations

syntax grammatical rules that govern how words are composed into meaningful strings

systematic desensitization clients are taught to relax as they are gradually exposed to what they fear in a stepwise manner

taste bud sense receptor in the tongue that responds to sweet, salty, sour, bitter, umami, and perhaps fat

temperament basic emotional style that appears early in development and is largely genetic in origin

temporal lobe lower part of cerebral cortex that plays roles in hearing, understanding language, and memory

tend and befriend reaction that mobilizes people to nurture (tend) or seek social support (befriend) under stress

teratogen an environmental factor that can exert a negative impact on prenatal development

terror management theory theory proposing that our awareness of our death leaves us with an underlying sense of terror with which we cope by adopting reassuring cultural worldviews

test bias tendency of a test to predict outcomes better in one group than another

thalamus gateway from the sense organs to the primary sensory cortex

Thematic Apperception Test (TAT) projective test requiring examinees to tell a story in response to ambiguous pictures

theory of mind ability to reason about what other people know or believe

thinking any mental activity or processing of information, including learning, remembering, perceiving, communicating, believing, and deciding

threshold membrane potential necessary to trigger an action potential

timbre complexity or quality of sound that makes musical instruments, human voices, or other sources sound unique

tip-of-the-tongue (TOT) phenomenon experience of knowing that we know something but being unable to access it

token economy method in which desirable behaviors are rewarded with tokens that clients can exchange for tangible rewards

tolerance reduction in the effect of a drug as a result of repeated use, requiring users to consume greater quantities to achieve the same effect

top-down processing conceptually driven processing influenced by beliefs and expectancies

trait relatively enduring predisposition that influences our behavior across many situations

transcranial magnetic stimulation (TMS) technique that applies strong and quickly changing magnetic fields to the surface of the skull that can either enhance or interrupt brain function

transduction the process of converting an external energy or substance into electrical activity within neurons

transference projecting intense, unrealistic feelings and expectations from the past onto the therapist

triarchic model   model of intelligence proposed by Robert Sternberg positing three distinct types of intelligence: analytical, practical, and creative

trichromatic theory   idea that color vision is based on our sensitivity to three primary colors

twin study   analysis of how traits differ in identical versus fraternal twins

two-factor theory   theory proposing that emotions are produced by an undifferentiated state of arousal along with an attribution (explanation) of that arousal

Type A personality   personality type that describes people who are competitive, driven, hostile, and ambitious

ultimate attribution error   assumption that behaviors among individual members of a group are due to their internal dispositions

unconditioned response (UCR)   automatic response to a nonneutral stimulus that does not need to be learned

unconditioned stimulus (UCS)   stimulus that elicits an automatic response

validity   extent to which a measure assesses what it purports to measure

variability   measure of how loosely or tightly bunched scores are

variable   anything that can vary

variable interval (VI) schedule   pattern in which we provide reinforcement for producing the response at least once during an average time interval, with the interval varying randomly

variable ratio (VR) schedule   pattern in which we provide reinforcement after a specific number of responses on average, with the number varying randomly

vestibular sense   our sense of equilibrium or balance

Weber's Law   there is a constant proportional relationship between the JND and original stimulus intensity

Wechsler Adult Intelligence Scale (WAIS)   most widely used intelligence test for adults today, consisting of 15 subtests to assess different types of mental abilities

Wernicke's area   part of the temporal lobe involved in understanding speech

whole word recognition   reading strategy that involves identifying common words based on their appearance without having to sound them out

wisdom   application of intelligence toward a common good

withdrawal   unpleasant effects of reducing or stopping consumption of a drug that users had consumed habitually

within-group heritability   extent to which the variability of a trait within a group is genetically influenced

Yerkes-Dodson law   inverted U-shaped relation between arousal on the one hand, and mood and performance on the other

zone of proximal development   phase of learning during which children can benefit from instruction

zygote   fertilized egg

1: PSYCHOLOGY AND SCIENTIFIC THINKING

WHAT IS PSYCHOLOGY? SCIENCE VERSUS INTUITION?

1. believing is seeing
2. These tables are identical in size—one can be directly superimposed on top of the other. Even though our perceptions are often accurate, we can't always trust them to provide us with an error-free picture of the world.
3. isn't
4. approach
5. scientific theory
6. theories; hypotheses
7. 1: H; 2:T; 3:T; 4: H; 5: H
8. confirmation bias
9. belief perseverance
10. testable

PSYCHOLOGICAL PSEUDOSCIENCE: IMPOSTERS OF SCIENCE

11. misinformation
12. 95
13. psychotherapy
14. widespread
15. 1b; 2c; 3e; 4g; 5d; 6a; 7f
16. adaptive
17. unrelated
18. chance
19. pareidolia
20. terror management

SCIENTIFIC THINKING: DISTINGUISHING FACT FROM FICTION

21. scientific skepticism
22. critical (or scientific) thinking
23. can
24. explanations
25. correlation–causation fallacy
26. falsifiable
27. replicability
28. parsimony
29. There are two explanations for crop circles—one supernatural and the other natural. According to Occam's Razor, we should generally select the simplest explanation.
30. 1f; 2c; 3a; 4e; 5d; 6b

PSYCHOLOGY'S PAST AND PRESENT: WHAT A LONG, STRANGE TRIP IT'S BEEN

31. introspection
32. black box
33. interpretation
34. don't need
35. Developmental psychologists spend most of their time in the lab, collecting and analyzing data on children's behavior.
36. Evolutionary psychology
37. illusion
38. Basic; applied
39. Human faces better capture readers' attention on the left rather than on the right side of pages. Written text, in contrast, better captures readers' attention on the right side.
40. SAT; ACT

2: RESEARCH METHODS

THE BEAUTY AND NECESSITY OF GOOD RESEARCH DESIGN

1. By relying on a mental shortcut or a heuristic based on the knowledge that California is on the West Coast, most people forget or don't know that a large chunk of California is east of Nevada.
2. heuristics
3. representativeness
4. base rate
5. availability
6. Cognitive biases
7. hindsight bias; overconfidence
8. hindsight bias
9. overconfidence
10. Hitler's rise to power

THE SCIENTIFIC METHOD: TOOLBOX OF SKILLS

11. external validity; internal validity
12. The pollsters got it wrong largely because they based their results on telephone surveys. Back in 1948, considerably more Republicans (who tended to be richer) owned telephones than Democrats, resulting in a biased sampling and a skewed pre-election prediction.
13. reliability; validity
14. self-report measures; response sets
15. the same
16. can; can't
17. experiment
18. control
19. placebo; blind
20. The nocebo effect is harm resulting from the mere expectation of harm. People who believe in voodoo may experience pain when one of their enemies inserts a pin into a doll symbolizing them.

ETHICAL ISSUES IN RESEARCH DESIGN

21. syphilis; antibiotics
22. All research with human subjects requires approval from an IRB before it can be conducted. IRBs evaluate the ethics of the study and require a procedure called informed consent: Researchers must tell subjects what they're getting into before asking them to participate.
23. informed consent
24. deception
25. Debriefing
26. American Psychological Association
27. invasive
28. 7-8
29. scientific gains
30. Arguments for: Some animal research has led to direct benefits to humans as well as immensely useful knowledge in its own right; many psychological treatments were derived from animal research that could not have been developed using human participants. Arguments against: The deaths of approximately 20 million lab animals a year aren't worth the benefits; many critics argue that the knowledge gleaned from animal research is of such doubtful external validity to humans as to be virtually useless.

STATISTICS: THE CURRENCY OF PSYCHOLOGICAL RESEARCH

31. descriptive; central tendency
32. Mode: 2; Mean: 3; Median: 1
33. mean
34. variability
35. range
36. standard deviation
37. a) negative skew; b) positive skew
38. conclusions
39. greater
40. truncated line graph

EVALUATING PSYCHOLOGICAL RESEARCH

41. peer reviewer
42. independent variable
43. control
44. placebo
45. experimenter expectancy
46. blind
47. are not
48. source
49. sharpening; leveling
50. pseudosymmetry

3: BIOLOGICAL PSYCHOLOGY

NERVE CELLS: COMMUNICATION PORTALS

1. cell body
2. dendrites
3. axons; send
4. synapse
5. myelin sheath
6. resting potential
7. a) axon is long extension in middle of diagram; b) arrow should go left to right; c) neurotransmitter release is represented by dots on right side of diagram
8. reuptake
9. endorphins
10. neurons

THE BRAIN-BEHAVIOR NETWORK

11. central nervous system
12. peripheral nervous
13. a) cortex; b) basal ganglia; c) limbic system; d) cerebellum; e) brain stem; f) spinal cord
14. cerebral cortex
15. a) generates signals responsible for voluntary movements; b) receives data about sensations in skin, muscles, and joints; c) analyzes visual data to form images; d) receives information from the optic nerve, transmitted through the visual thalamus; e) interprets spoken and written language; f) analyzes data about sound, so that we can recognize words or melodies; g) detects discrete qualities of sound, such as pitch and volume; h) vital for the formation of speech; i) influences various aspects of behavior, personality, planning, and reasoning
16. basal ganglia
17. reticular activating
18. somatic nervous
19. sympathetic
20. respiration; perspiration

THE ENDOCRINE SYSTEM

21. endocrine system
22. pituitary gland
23. a) hypothalamus; b) pineal gland; c) pituitary; d) thyroid; e) adrenal

glands; f) pancreas; g) testes; h) ovaries
24. oxytocin
25. adrenal glands
26. The nerves of the sympathetic nervous system signal the adrenal glands to release adrenaline, which prepares us for counterattack (fight) or escape (flight).
27. cortisol
28. testosterone; estrogen
29. do
30. accept

MAPPING THE MIND: THE BRAIN IN ACTION
31. phrenology
32. electroencephalograph (EEG)
33. wouldn't
34. the change in blood oxygen level
35. aren't
36. lateralization
37. split-brain
38. The subject's right hemisphere recognizes the snow scene, leading her to point with her left hand

(controlled by the right, hemisphere) to the shovel, but her left hemisphere recognizes the claw, leading her to indicate verbally that the chicken is the matching object.
39. right; left
40. aren't

NATURE AND NURTURE: DID YOUR GENES—OR PARENTS—MAKE YOU DO IT?
41. 46; just 1 pair

42. chromosomes
43. Genes
44. phenotype; genotype
45. dominant
46. natural selection
47. behavioral genetics
48. groups of people
49. No, because environmental manipulation is still possible and could result in substantial changes. In fact, heritability can actually change over time.
50. adoption studies

4: SENSATION AND PERCEPTION

TWO SIDES OF THE COIN: SENSATION AND PERCEPTION
1. transduction
2. sense receptor
3. absolute threshold
4. just noticeable difference
5. synesthesia
6. bottom-up
7. top-down processing: the top-down influence that we're thinking of a jazz musician biases our bottom-up processing of the shapes in this figure and increases the chances we'll perceive a saxophone player
8. perceptual constancy
9. The *cocktail party effect* refers to our ability to pick out an important message, like our name, in a conversation that doesn't involve us. This finding tells us that the filter inside our brain, which selects what will and won't receive our attention, is more complex than just an "on" or "off" switch.
10. isn't

SEEING: THE VISUAL SYSTEM
11. visible
12. brightness
13. lens
14. retina
15. Rods; cones

16. a) fovea: part of the retina where light rays are most sharply focused; b) optic nerve: transmits impulses from the retina to the rest of the brain; c) retina: innermost layer of the eye, where incoming light is converted into nerve impulses; d) eye muscle: one of six surrounding muscles that rotate the eye in all directions; e) lens: transparent disk that focuses light rays for near or distant vision; f) cornea: curved, transparent dome that bends incoming light; g) iris: colored area containing muscles that control the pupil; h) pupil: opening in the center of the iris that lets in light
17. a) proximity; b) closure
18. trichromatic
19. depth perception
20. visual agnosia

HEARING: THE AUDITORY SYSTEM
21. Pitch
22. loudness
23. timbre
24. cochlea
25. hair cells
26. a) eardrum: membrane that vibrates in response to sound waves; b) semicircular canal: one of three fluid-filled structures that play a role in balance; c) cochlea: converts vibration into neural activity; d) pinna:

flexible outer flap of the ear, which channels sound waves into the ear canal; e) ear canal: conducts sound waves to the eardrum
27. place
28. localize
29. See figure on p. 151; When someone standing to our left speaks to us, the sound reaches our left ear slightly earlier than it reaches our right. Also the intensity detected by the left ear is greater than the intensity detected by the right ear, because the right ear lies in a sound shadow produced by the head and shoulders. The amount of discrepancy in timing and intensity enables us to determine where the sound originated.
30. echolocation

SMELL AND TASTE: THE SENSUAL SENSES
31. odors
32. taste buds
33. five; umami
34. weak
35. is
36. orbitofrontal cortex
37. a) somatosensory cortex; b) thalamus; c) olfactory cortex; d) olfactory bulb; e) orbitofrontal cortex; f) pons; g) medulla oblongata

38. gustatory cortex
39. Pheromones
40. worse

OUR BODY SENSES: TOUCH, BODY POSITION, AND BALANCE
41. somatosensory
42. proprioception
43. vestibular sense
44. free nerve endings
45. most
46. The skin contains many different types of receptors and free nerve endings specialized for detecting mechanical pressure, stretching, and pain.
47. quickly
48. somatic
49. The mirror box consists of a two-chamber box with a mirror in the center. When the subject looks at her right hand in the box, it creates the illusion that the mirror image of her right hand is her left hand. This box can sometimes alleviate the discomfort of phantom limb pain by positioning the intact limb as the phantom limb appears to be positioned, and then moving it to a more comfortable position.
50. ergonomic

5: CONSCIOUSNESS

THE BIOLOGY OF SLEEP
1. biological clock
2. jet lag
3. a) Beta waves; b) Alpha waves; c) Theta waves; d) Sleep spindles & K complexes; e) Delta waves
4. REM, non-REM
5. REM rebound
6. more
7. narcolepsy
8. Surprise, elation, or other strong emotions can lead people or animals with narcolepsy to

experience cataplexy, a complete loss of muscle tone.
9. night terror
10. childhood

DREAMS
11. Sigmund Freud
12. manifest content, latent content
13. Freud's wish fulfillment theory
14. are
15. brain activity
16. acetylcholine
17. a) cerebral cortex; b) thalamus; c) pons; d) spinal cord

18. forebrain
19. neurocognitive
20. less

OTHER ALTERATIONS OF CONSCIOUSNESS AND UNUSUAL EXPERIENCES
21. Hallucinations
22. To compensate for the lack of sensory stimulation
23. near-death
24. déjà vu
25. induction method
26. has

27. No, people who stiffen their bodies can do this without hypnosis
28. past life regression therapy
29. sociocognitive
30. dissociation

DRUGS AND CONSCIOUSNESS
31. substance abuse
32. Substance dependence
33. low
34. tension reduction hypothesis
35.

Drug effect + Placebo effect	Placebo effect
Drug effect	Baseline

36. amphetamines

37. crystal meth

38. narcotics

39. LSD

40.

DRUG TYPE	EXAMPLES	EFFECT ON BEHAVIOR
Depressants	alcohol, barbiturates, Quaaludes, Valium	decreased activity of the central nervous system (initial high followed by sleepiness, slower thinking, and impaired concentration)
Stimulants	tobacco, cocaine, amphetamines, methamphetamine	increased activity of the central nervous system (sense of alertness, well-being, energy)
Opiates	heroin, morphine, codeine	sense of euphoria, decreased pain
Psychedelics	Marijuana, LSD, Ecstasy	dramatically altered perception, mood, and thoughts

6: LEARNING

CLASSICAL CONDITIONING

1. learning

2. habituation

3. a) neutral stimulus (metronome); b) no salivation; c) UCS (meat powder); d) UCR (salivation); e) neutral stimulus; f) UCS; g) UCR (salivation); h) previously neutral stimulus is now CS; i) CR (salivation)

4. classical conditioning

5. acquisition

6. extinction

7. spontaneous recovery

8. discrimination

9. are

10. Little Albert initially liked small furry animals. Watson and Rayner first allowed Little Albert to play with a white rat. But only seconds afterward, Watson sneaked up behind Little Albert and struck a gong with a steel hammer, creating an earsplitting noise and startling him out of his wits. After seven such pairings of CS (rat) and UCS (loud sound from gong), Little Albert displayed a CR (fear) to the rat alone. Because inducing a prolonged fear response in an infant raises a host of serious ethical questions, the study would never get past a modern IRB.

OPERANT CONDITIONING

11.

	CLASSICAL CONDITIONING	OPERANT CONDITIONING
Target behavior is …	Elicited automatically	Emitted voluntarily
Reward is …	Provided unconditionally	Contingent on behavior
Behavior depends primarily on …	Autonomic nervous system	Skeletal muscles

12. operant

13. insight

14. negative

15. strengthens; weakens

16. anxiety

17. a) fixed ratio; b) fixed interval; c) variable ratio; d) variable interval

18. variable ratio

19. shaping; chaining

20. token economy

COGNITIVE MODELS OF LEARNING

21. radical

22. didn't believe

23. S-O-R

24. S-O-R theorists believe that cognition is central to explaining learning and contend that people respond differently because they interpret the criticism in different ways. So managers need to take into account individual reactions when offering performance evaluations.

25. cognitive maps

26. Observational learning takes place by watching others. Children acquire a great deal of their behavior by observing and imitating the behaviors of adults, especially their parents.

27. Albert Bandura

28. have not

29. mirror neurons

30. insight

BIOLOGICAL INFLUENCES ON LEARNING

31. one trial

32. By using a scapegoat food, they can minimize conditioned taste aversions to their favorite foods.

33. biological

34. taste

35. adaptive

36. equipotentiality

37. preparedness

38. didn't acquire

39. unafraid

40. Instinctive drift is the tendency for animals to return to innate behaviors following repeated reinforcement to perform a different behavior. Psychologists don't fully understand the reasons for such drift, but it does suggest that we can't fully understand learning without taking into account innate biological influences, as these influences often place limits on what kind of behaviors we can train.

LEARNING FADS: DO THEY WORK?

41. electroencephalograms (EEGs)

42. Proponents of sleep-assisted learning claim we can learn languages, or learn how to stop smoking, lose weight, or reduce stress while asleep. The problem with almost all of the studies showing positive effects of sleep-assisted learning is they didn't monitor subjects' EEGs to ensure they were actually asleep while listening to the tapes.

43. Suggestive Accelerative Learning and Teaching Techniques

44. visualize; classical

45. placebo

46. discovery learning

47. direct instruction

48. learning style

49. analytical; holistic

50. Scientific research provides little evidence that tailoring teaching to individual learning styles enhances learning. In addition, it's difficult to assess students' learning styles reliably.

7: MEMORY

HOW MEMORY OPERATES: THE MEMORY ASSEMBLY LINE

1. memory illusion

2. reconstructive; reproductive

3. span; duration

4. a) sensory memory; b) short-term memory; c) long-term memory

5. Sensory; short-term

6. Iconic memory

7. chunking

8. primacy effect

9. Explicit; implicit

10. a) semantic; b) episodic; c) procedural; d) priming; e) conditioning; f) habituation

THE THREE PROCESSES OF MEMORY

11. encoding; storage; retrieval

12. Encoding

13. mnemonic

14. schemas

15. Retrieval

16. Relearning

17. distributed versus massed practice

18. 1) distributed versus massed study; 2) elaborative rehearsal; 3) levels of processing; 4) mnemonic devices; 5) testing effect

19. Encoding specificity

20. context-dependent learning

THE BIOLOGY OF MEMORY

21. isn't
22. learning
23. hippocampus
24. retrograde
25. anterograde
26. implicit memory
27. explicit; implicit
28. top left: thalamus; top right: corpus callosum; bottom left: amygdala/ helps us recall the emotions associated with fear-provoking events; bottom right: hippocampus/ helps us recall the events themselves
29. isn't
30. dementia

THE DEVELOPMENT OF MEMORY: ACQUIRING A PERSONAL HISTORY

31. metamemory
32. implicit memory
33. Rovee-Collier and others used mobiles to study infants' implicit memory. She conditioned infants to kick in a circular setting to see a mobile move. Although infants can't tell you they remember the mobile when they later see it again, their kicking behavior gives us insight into whether they recall the mobile and for how long.
34. specific
35. Infantile amnesia
36. earlier
37. isn't
38. hippocampus
39. self
40. mirror self-recognition

FALSE MEMORIES: WHEN GOOD MEMORY GOES BAD

41. Flashbulb memories
42. source monitoring
43. cryptomnesia
44. The misinformation effect is the creation of fictitious memories by providing misleading information about an event after it takes place.
45. By using powerful suggestions and fake photographs, researchers have demonstrated that it's possible to create elaborate memories of events that never happened.
46. possible
47. weak
48. therapists
49. blocking
50. absentmindedness

8: LANGUAGE, THINKING, AND REASONING

HOW DOES LANGUAGE WORK?

1. 1) phonemes; 2) morphemes; 3) syntax; 4) extralinguistic information
2. phonemes
3. Syntax
4. dialect
5. Babies begin to hear inside the womb by the fifth month of pregnancy. They can learn to recognize their mother's voices and some characteristics of their mother's native language, and can even recognize specific songs or stories they've heard over and over again.
6. same
7. better
8. generative
9. language acquisition device
10. bonobos

DO WE THINK IN WORDS? THE RELATION BETWEEN LANGUAGE AND THOUGHT

11. internal
12. linguistic determinism
13. can
14. linguistic relativity
15. Helen Keller's writings suggest she did not recall experiencing much in the way of mental life before learning to communicate—a view that corresponds with the notion of linguistic determinism.
16. language
17. color
18. dark; bright
19. If language influences thought, someone from the Dani, whose language only contains two color terms, should have a harder time distinguishing blue from green than those of us whose language contains separate terms for these two colors. But Rosch (1973) demonstrated that the Dani perceive colors as dividing up into roughly the same color categories as do English speakers.
20. isn't

READING: RECOGNIZING THE WRITTEN WORD

21. automatic
22. The control list is relatively easy but the Stroop interference list is considerably more difficult. The Stroop task requires participants to suppress their attention to printed words to identify the color of the ink. This is easier when the printed words don't "compete" than when the printed words are also color names. The level of difficulty of the Stroop interference list shows that reading is automatic and not easy to inhibit.
23. direction
24. b; c; a
25. sounds
26. whole word recognition
27. phonetic decomposition
28. phonics
29. are
30. 400

THINKING AND REASONING

31. thinking
32. Cognitive economy
33. thin slicing
34. Our brains engage in perceptual completion, the use of top-down processing to perceive something that isn't there, or perceive something the way we expect it to appear. Most people see this drawing as a perfectly fine drawing of an elephant, even though there are actually too many legs for the number of feet.
35. concept
36. framing
37. problem solving
38. mental set
39. Functional fixedness
40. embodiment models

9: INTELLIGENCE AND IQ TESTING

WHAT IS INTELLIGENCE? DEFINITIONAL CONFUSION

1. high
2. intelligence test
3. abstract thinking
4. general intelligence
5. s; specific abilities
6. fluid intelligence; crystallized intelligence
7. frames of mind
8. a) analytical; b) practical; c) creative
9. efficient
10. d. General abilities such as reasoning, short-term memory, and pattern recognition could explain people's ability to answer this question correctly.

INTELLIGENCE TESTING: THE GOOD, THE BAD, AND THE UGLY

11. In the example provided, .8 x 100 = 80. If we apply this formula to an 18-year-old with a mental age of 18, we'd have the following: 18 (mental age)/18 (chronological age) = 1 x 100 = 100 (IQ). If we apply it to a 35-year-old who also has a mental age of 18, we'd have: 18 (mental age)/35 (chronological age) = .51 x 100 = 51 (IQ). Because our mental age levels off but our chronological age increases with time, Stern's formula would result in everyone's IQ getting lower and lower as they got older.
12. deviation IQ
13. Mandatory sterilization
14. Wechsler Adult Intelligence Scale (WAIS)
15. a) Digit symbol: tests speed of learning through timed coding tasks in which numbers must be associated with marks of various shapes; b) Picture completion: tests visual alertness and visual memory through presentation of an incompletely drawn figure; the missing part must be discovered and named; c) Block design: tests ability to perceive and analyze patterns by presenting designs that must be copied with blocks.
16. validity
17. 70
18. males
19. Mensa; two
20. madness

GENETIC AND ENVIRONMENTAL INFLUENCES ON IQ

21. family studies
22. genetic; environmental
23. Adoption
24. increase
25. social; biological
26. Children's IQ tends to drop significantly during summer vacations, suggesting an environmental influence on IQ.
27. more; experimenter expectancy
28. malnutrition
29. Flynn Effect
30. 1) increased test sophistication; 2) increased complexity of the modern world; 3) better nutrition; 4) changes at home and school

GROUP DIFFERENCES IN IQ: THE SCIENCE AND THE POLITICS

31. sex
32. are
33. spatial; verbal
34. F: spelling; M: arithmetic calculation; M: complex mathematical tasks; M: safe driving, M: geography, F: sociability; F: reading facial expression in emotion; M: spatial ability

35. increased
36. genetic
37. The two groups of plants started at the same height but were exposed to different environmental conditions. This demonstrates how group differences in IQ could be "real" but completely environmentally influenced.

38. within-group; between-group
39. test bias
40. stereotype threat

THE REST OF THE STORY: OTHER DIMENSIONS OF INTELLECT
41. isn't
42. divergent
43. convergent thinking

44. low
45. willing
46. Creative people tend to be bold and willing to take intellectual risks. They also tend to be emotionally troubled while possessed of high self-esteem.
47. isn't
48. ideological

49. Because people with high IQs are especially vulnerable to the sense of omniscience—because intelligent people know many things, they frequently make the mistake of thinking they know everything.
50. sense of omniscience

10: HUMAN DEVELOPMENT

SPECIAL CONSIDERATIONS IN HUMAN DEVELOPMENT
1. developmental psychology
2. post hoc
3. cross-sectional
4. Cohort effects
5. Like a longitudinal design, the series traces the lives of the same group of British people over time, from age 7 all the way up through age 49. Longitudinal design allows us to examine true developmental effects: changes over time as a consequence of growing older. However, this type of design is time consuming and is not experimental, so it can't be used to infer cause-and-effect relationships.
6. are
7. nature; nurture
8. confound
9. gene-environment interaction
10. 3 (Gene Expression); 1 (Gene-Environment Interaction); 2 (Nature via Nurture)

THE DEVELOPING BODY: PHYSICAL AND MOTOR DEVELOPMENT
11. blastocyst

12. fetus
13. teratogens
14. viability; 40
15. motor behaviors
16. a) sitting without support (6 months); b) crawling (9 months); c) standing (11 months); d) cruising (12 months); e) walking without assistance (13 months); f) running (18–24 months)
17. Although cultural variability in practices such as swaddling or stretching influences the rate of motor development, none of these early physical experiences results in long-term advantages or impairments.
18. primary sex characteristics; secondary sex characteristics
19. sensory
20. no more

THE DEVELOPING MIND: COGNITIVE DEVELOPMENT
21. assimilation; accommodation
22. From top to bottom: sensorimotor (birth to two years); preoperational (two to seven years); concrete operations (seven to 11 years); formal operations (11 years to adulthood)

23. The task measures egocentrism—the inability to see the world from others' perspectives. Children in the concrete operational stage can pass this task.
24. more; less
25. social; cultural
26. proximal development; scaffolding
27. do
28. theory of mind
29. personal fable
30. positions

THE DEVELOPING PERSONALITY: SOCIAL AND MORAL DEVELOPMENT
31. stranger anxiety
32. imprinting
33. Contact comfort refers to positive emotions afforded by touch. When frightened by a novel object, Harlow's infant monkeys almost always preferred the terry cloth mother over the wire mother even though the wire mother was the monkeys' source of food. Contact comfort prevails over nourishment.
34. 1) The infant becomes upset upon mom's departure but greets her return with joy; 2) The infant

reacts with indifference to mom's departure and shows little reaction upon her return; 3) The infant reacts to mom's departure with panic and shows a mixed emotional reaction on her return; 4) The infant reacts to mom's departure and return with an inconsistent and confused set of responses. The infant may appear dazed when reunited with her.
35. average expectable
36. identity crisis
37. eight; psychosocial
38. morality; reasoning processes
39. parent
40. biological age

11: EMOTION AND MOTIVATION

THEORIES OF EMOTION: WHAT CAUSES OUR FEELINGS?
1. discrete emotions
2. Charles Darwin
3. The Duchenne smile
4. cognitive
5. James-Lange
6. do
7. simultaneously
8. We first experience arousal after an emotion-provoking event and then look to the situation to determine the cause of that arousal. The emotional label we attach to our arousal based on our interpretation of the situation is the emotion we experience.
9. more
10. facial features

NONVERBAL EXPRESSION OF EMOTION: THE EYES, BODIES, AND CULTURES HAVE IT
11. nonverbal leakage
12. Because e-mail messages are devoid of nonverbal cues, people have

developed a variety of emoticons to convey various emotions that might not be obvious over e-mail or instant messaging.
13. illustrators
14. manipulators
15. emblems
16. low
17. Controlled Question Test (CQT)
18. false positives
19. The Pinocchio response is a perfect physiological or behavioral indicator of lying. Like Pinocchio's nose, people's bodily reactions supposedly give them away whenever they lie.
20. integrity

HAPPINESS AND SELF-ESTEEM: SCIENCE CONFRONTS POP PSYCHOLOGY
21. The King plans to boost GNH in Bhutan by preserving the beauty of its natural environment, promoting cultural values, and giving citizens more of a voice in government decisions. This is beneficial because

happiness often breeds both health and success in our work, family, and love lives.
22. character strengths; virtues
23. broaden and build
24. Defensive pessimism
25. can't
26. positivity
27. affective forecasting
28. durability bias
29. Probably because silver medal winners compare their outcome with what "might have been."
30. positive illusions

MOTIVATION: OUR WANTS AND NEEDS
31. No
32. homeostasis
33. Yerkes-Dodson
34. Incentive
35. a) physiological needs; b) safety needs; c) belonging needs; d) esteem needs
36. glucostatic
37. set point

38. bulimia
39. the same
40. masculinized; feminized

ATTRACTION, LOVE, AND HATE: THE GREATEST MYSTERIES OF THEM ALL
41. proximity
42. similarity
43. reciprocity
44. men
45. agree
46. more
47. Passionate
48. companionate love
49. a) Intimacy; b) Passion; c) Commitment; d) Consummate love
50. confirmation bias

12: STRESS, COPING, AND HEALTH

WHAT IS STRESS?

1. stress
2. stressors as stimuli approach
3. transaction
4. primary appraisal
5. secondary appraisal
6. Problem-focused coping
7. emotion-focused coping
8. Social Readjustment Rating
9. Daily hassles and minor annoyances can add up and strain our ability to cope.
10. better

HOW WE ADAPT TO STRESS: CHANGE AND CHALLENGE

11. The alarm reaction involves the excitation of the autonomic nervous system, the discharge of the stress hormone adrenaline, and physical symptoms of anxiety.
12. fight-or-flight
13. resistance
14. exhaustion
15. Both responses refer to ways of coping with stressors. During the fight-or-flight responses, a person is physically and psychologically mobilized to either fight the enemy or flee from the situation. In contrast, during times of stress women often rely on their social supports and nurturing abilities (the tend-and-befriend response) to help them cope with stressful situations.
16. oxytocin
17. 65 percent
18. high
19. posttraumatic stress disorder (PTSD)
20. flashbacks

THE BRAIN–BODY REACTION TO STRESS

21. human immunodeficiency virus
22. arthritis
23. central nervous
24. can
25. are not
26. psychological
27. coronary heart disease
28. Type A personality type describes people who are competitive, driven, hostile, ambitious, and impatient. Research indicates that the anger component of the Type A personality can be deadly, increasing our risk for coronary heart disease.
29. cause
30. strong

COPING WITH STRESS

31. Social support
32. Social support can provide us with emotional comfort, financial assistance, and information to make decisions, solve problems, and contend with stressful situations.
33. behavioral control
34. Cognitive control
35. proactive coping
36. Crisis debriefing sessions, in which a facilitator structures a group discussion of people's reactions to a shared traumatic event, may actually increase PTSD risk.
37. Hardiness
38. better
39. Spirituality
40. counterproductive

PROMOTING GOOD HEALTH—AND LESS STRESS!

41. health psychology
42. smoking
43. drinking
44. Answers will vary based on weight/height
45. play
46. availability
47. Alternative medicine
48. are not
49. Positive effects include increases in creativity, empathy, alertness, and self-esteem, as well as decreases in anxiety, interpersonal problems, and recurrence of depression. It can also enhance blood flow in the brain and immune function. Its positive effects may derive from a greater acceptance of our troubling thoughts and feelings. The effects may not be due to meditation itself, but from sitting quietly, resting, and relaxing with eyes closed. Positive attitudes, beliefs, and expectancies about meditation may also account for why it's beneficial.
50. Homeopathic medicine

13: SOCIAL PSYCHOLOGY

WHAT IS SOCIAL PSYCHOLOGY?

1. behavior; beliefs; attitudes
2. need-to-belong
3. social comparison
4. collective delusion
5. Urban legends are convincing in part because they fit our preconceptions. They make good stories because they tug on our emotions, especially negative ones (such as disgust).
6. social disruption
7. experience
8. attributions
9. dispositional influences
10. doesn't

SOCIAL INFLUENCE: CONFORMITY AND OBEDIENCE

11. conformity
12. If others responding before you all consistently supplied this same (obviously incorrect) answer, you'd be extremely likely to provide the same wrong answer yourself.
13. parietal; occipital
14. low
15. anonymity; individual responsibility
16. Abu Ghraib
17. groupthink
18. inoculation effect
19. obedience
20. The greater the psychological distance between the teacher and experimenter, the less the obedience. For instance, obedience plummeted when the experimenter gave instructions by telephone. Obedience also varied depending on the psychological distance between the teacher and learner. For example, if the teacher was in the same room with the learner, obedience decreased, but if the teacher was instructed to have a third person administer the shock, obedience increased.

HELPING AND HARMING OTHERS: PROSOCIAL BEHAVIOR AND AGGRESSION

21. prosocial behavior
22. less
23. Address a specific person ("Man in the blue shirt, please help me!") to decrease the chances of bystander nonintervention.
24. less
25. social loafing
26. can
27. more
28. situational; dispositional
29. irritability
30. Relational

ATTITUDES AND PERSUASION: CHANGING MINDS

31. emotional
32. didn't
33. low
34. recognition heuristic
35. a) "I'm not an honest person after all"; b) "I didn't really cheat; I just saw someone's answers"; c) "I had to cheat because the test was unfair"
36. more
37. 3) foot-in-the-door; 1) door-in-the-face; 2) low-ball;
38. foot-in-the-door
39. similar
40. source credibility

PREJUDICE AND DISCRIMINATION

41. prejudice
42. stereotype
43. out-group homogeneity
44. prejudice; discrimination
45. Jane Elliott divided her class into favored and disfavored groups based solely on their eye color, informing her students that children with brown eyes are superior because of excess melanin in their eyes. The results were dramatic: The brown-eyed children quickly become arrogant and condescending, and the blue-eyed children became submissive and insecure.
46. scapegoat hypothesis
47. just-world
48. Implicit Association Test (IAT)
49. In jigsaw classrooms, children cooperate on a multipart project, with each child assuming a small but essential role.
50. encourage

14: PERSONALITY

PERSONALITY: WHAT IS IT AND HOW CAN WE STUDY IT?

1. 1) genetic factors; 2) shared environmental factors; 3) nonshared environmental factors
2. Nonshared environmental
3. twin; adoption
4. 1.0
5. similar
6. shared
7. genes; environment
8. higher
9. Genes code for proteins, not specific behaviors or attitudes. It's far more likely that genes influence behaviors and attitudes in a highly indirect fashion.
10. molecular genetic

PSYCHOANALYTIC THEORY: THE CONTROVERSIAL LEGACY OF SIGMUND FREUD AND HIS FOLLOWERS

11. psychic determinism
12. id; ego
13. psychological distress
14. defense mechanisms
15. Oral: birth to 12–18 months; Anal: 18 months to 3 years; Phallic: 3–6 years; Latency: 6–12 years; Genital: 12 years and beyond
16. Oedipus complex
17. aren't
18. unconscious
19. striving for superiority

20. Jung argued that in addition to Freud's version of the unconscious, there's also a collective unconscious that comprises all of the memories that ancestors have passed down to us across the generations. Jung believed the collective unconscious contains numerous archetypes, or cross-culturally universal emotional symbols, which explain the similarities across people in their emotional reactions to many features of the world. Jung's theory is difficult to falsify and does not rule out rival hypotheses.

BEHAVIORAL AND SOCIAL LEARNING THEORIES OF PERSONALITY

21. histories
22. consists of
23. determinism
24. thinking
25. reciprocal determinism
26. In observational learning, parents, teachers and others play significant roles in shaping children's personalities: Children learn good and bad habits by watching and later emulating adults. This child may learn early that charitable giving is a worthy endeavor.
27. locus of control
28. 1) external; 2) internal; 3) external; 4) internal
29. less
30. shared environment

HUMANISTIC MODELS OF PERSONALITY: THE THIRD FORCE

31. free will
32. disastrous
33. optimistic
34. 1) organism/our innate blueprint; 2) self/our self-concept, the set of beliefs about who we are; 3) conditions of worth/expectations we place on ourselves for appropriate and inappropriate behavior
35. Incongruence
36. peak experiences
37. Self-actualized people tend to be creative, spontaneous, and accepting of themselves and others. They're self-confident (but not self-centered) and focus on real-world and intellectual problems and have a few deep friendships rather than many superficial ones. They typically crave privacy and can come off as introverted or aloof.
38. comparative psychology
39. unlikely
40. confirmation bias

TRAIT MODELS OF PERSONALITY: CONSISTENCIES IN OUR BEHAVIOR

41. structure
42. Personality traits must do more than merely describe behaviors we've already observed—they must predict behaviors in novel situations or correlate with biological or laboratory measures.

43. factor analysis
44. Big Five
45. openness to experience, conscientiousness, extraversion, agreeableness, neuroticism
46. d: Extraversion; e: Neuroticism; a: Conscientiousness: c: Agreeableness; b: Openness to Experience
47. openness to experience
48. aren't
49. aggregated
50. origins

PERSONALITY ASSESSMENT: MEASURING AND MISMEASURING THE PSYCHE

51. Minnesota Multiphasic Personality Inventory
52. empirical
53. face validity
54. supports
55. rational/theoretical
56. projective
57. Investigators and social workers allow children to play freely with anatomically detailed dolls to try to infer whether the children have been sexually abused based. This projective test has led to numerous false accusations, because many nonabused children engage in sexualized doll play.
58. Rorschach Inkblot
59. Thematic Apperception Test (TAT)
60. P.T. Barnum effect

15: PSYCHOLOGICAL DISORDERS

CONCEPTIONS OF MENTAL ILLNESS: YESTERDAY AND TODAY

1. Brothers and sisters share a family resemblance; they look like each other but don't have any one feature in common. The broad category of "mental disorders" may be similar. Different mental disorders aren't alike in the same exact way, but they share a number of features.
2. exorcism
3. asylums
4. moral treatment
5. deinstitutionalization
6. culture-bound
7. Trials involving dueling expert witnesses may contribute to the erroneous public perception that psychologists can't agree on the diagnoses of individuals with suspected mental disorders.
8. axes
9. are not
10. comorbidity

ANXIETY DISORDERS: THE MANY FACES OF WORRY AND FEAR

11. generalized anxiety disorder
12. panic disorder
13. phobia

14. PTSD is marked by emotional disturbance after experiencing or witnessing a severely stressful event. Symptoms include flashbacks to the event; efforts to avoid thoughts, feelings, places and conversations associated with the trauma; recurrent dreams of the trauma; and increased arousal, such as sleep difficulties and startling easily. Combat veterans and those who have experienced a natural disaster or sexual assault are at high risk.
15. obsessions
16. compulsions
17. OCD; also Cameron Diaz, Billy Bob Thornton, and David Beckham
18. catastrophize
19. negative
20. anxiety sensitivity

MOOD DISORDERS AND SUICIDE

21. major depressive episode
22. 20
23. equally common
24. heritability
25. According to this model, depression can trigger rejection from others, in turn contributing to further depression.

26. low
27. oneself; world; future
28. Using the shuttle box, Seligman found that dogs that were first prevented from escaping the shock gave up trying to escape electric shocks even when they were free to do so. He called this phenomenon "learned helplessness" and hypothesized that this might be one way that depression develops in humans.
29. Major depression; bipolar disorder
30. communicate

PERSONALITY AND DISSOCIATIVE DISORDERS: THE DISRUPTED AND DIVIDED SELF

31. least
32. self-destructive
33. antisocial
34. are not
35. She's a woman—individuals with psychopathic personality disorder are usually men.
36. different from
37. don't
38. posttraumatic
39. Mainstream treatment techniques for DID reinforce the idea that the

person possesses multiple identities. These techniques include using hypnosis to "bring forth" hidden alters, communicating with alters and giving them different names, and encouraging patients to recover repressed memories supposedly housed in dissociated selves.
40. popular media

THE ENIGMA OF SCHIZOPHRENIA

41. dissociative identity disorder
42. delusions
43. Psychotic
44. hallucinations
45. word salad
46. Catatonic
47. don't cause
48. enlarged
49. It is a function of how closely an individual is genetically related to a person with schizophrenia.
50. diathesis-stress

CHILDHOOD DISORDERS: RECENT CONTROVERSIES

51. can't
52. failed
53. illusory correlation
54. Evidence suggests that more liberal

diagnostic criteria rather than vaccines can account for most, if not all, of the reported autism epidemic. In addition, the Americans with Disabilities Act and Individuals with Disabilities Education Act, both passed in the 1990s, indirectly encouraged school districts to classify more children as having autism and other developmental disabilities, as these children could now receive more extensive educational accommodations

55. hyperactivity; inattention
56. infancy
57. alcohol, substance abuse
58. decreased
59. Possible answers: traumatic brain injuries, diabetes, thyroid problems, vitamin deficiencies, anxiety, and depression
60. 60, 90

16: PSYCHOLOGICAL AND BIOLOGICAL TREATMENTS

PSYCHOTHERAPY: CLIENTS AND PRACTITIONERS

1. Psychotherapy
2. women
3. less
4. can
5. likely
6. A 1964 study found that many therapists preferred to treat people who were relatively young, attractive, verbal, intelligent, and successful. Therapists have recently become more aware of the importance of assisting a broad clientele of all ages and cultural backgrounds.
7. paraprofessional
8. isn't
9. In this show, the character Laura develops sexual feelings for her therapist, Paul. Paul almost follows through with a sexual relationship with her, but doesn't do so because he experiences a panic attack. Clearly, had he done so, such behavior would have been unethical.
10. ineffective

INSIGHT THERAPIES: ACQUIRING UNDERSTANDING

11. free association
12. less
13. individuation
14. isn't
15. person-centered
16. Gestalt therapy's two-chair technique aims to integrate opposing aspects of the client's personality, such as the "good boy" and the "spoiled brat."
17. common
18. abstinence violation
19. Strategic family interventions
20. structural

BEHAVIORAL APPROACHES: CHANGING MALADAPTIVE ACTIONS

21. exposure therapy
22. systematic desensitization
23. Clients gradually approach and handle any fears, as these clients are doing as they overcome their fear of flying. In vivo desensitization involves real-life, gradual exposure to what the patient actually fears, rather than imagining the anxiety-provoking situation.
24. flooding
25. response prevention
26. In EMDR, the patient focuses on the therapist's fingers as they move back and forth, while reliving a traumatic memory. Studies indicate that such eye movements play no useful role in EMDR's effectiveness.
27. participant modeling
28. token economy
29. belief
30. stress inoculation training

IS PSYCHOTHERAPY EFFECTIVE?

31. effective
32. no consensus
33. more
34. 80 percent
35. Scared Straight programs expose adolescents to prisoners and prison life in an effort to scare them away from criminal careers. Despite their popularity, research suggests that such programs are not merely ineffective, but can actually increase the rate of problem behaviors in teens.
36. Empirically supported therapies
37. Positive life events can help to explain spontaneous remission, the phenomenon of a psychological problem improving without any intervention.
38. self-serving bias
39. high
40. self-help books

BIOMEDICAL TREATMENTS: MEDICATIONS, ELECTRICAL STIMULATION, AND SURGERY

41. psychopharmacotherapy
42. schizophrenia
43. selective serotonin reuptake
44. is not
45. do not
46. children; adolescents
47. overprescribed
48. electroconvulsive therapy
49. A small electrical device is implanted under the skin near the breastbone to stimulate the vagus nerve (which projects into many brain areas) and is believed to stimulate serotonin release. It is used to treat severe depression. Well-controlled, large-scale studies are mostly lacking.
50. Psychosurgery is brain surgery used to treat psychological problems. Psychosurgery once involved destruction of significant portions of the brain, resulting in impaired memory, diminished emotion and creativity, and personality change. Psychosurgery today is much more sophisticated and associated with significantly milder side effects. Nonetheless, the stigma surrounding psychosurgery remains.

1: EVALUATING CLAIMS Health Benefits of Fruits and Vegetables

"Studies show that eating walnuts *may reduce your risk and delay the on-set of Alzheimer's."*

The use of the qualifying word "may" renders the claim difficult or impossible to falsify. What would we need to know about how these studies to validate the claim?

ANSWER: We'd need to know that Alzheimer's disease was measured objectively, and that people who ate walnuts were compared systematically with people who didn't eat walnuts.

"Eating peaches gives you energy and makes you feel light and fresh throughout the year."

This claim is vague and difficult to falsify. How would you define or measure "light and fresh"?

"Avoid drugs or surgery and find a completely natural cure to your disease."

The phrase "completely natural" implies that the cure is safer than drugs or surgery. Can you think of any natural substances (including fruits and vegetables) that are dangerous or even fatal?

ANSWER: Poisonous mushrooms, arsenic, poison ivy, and a host of other natural substances are all dangerous to one's health.

"These natural cures come from ancient cultures and have been handed down for thousands of years."

Does the fact that something has been around for a long time mean it's trustworthy? What logical fallacy does this ad commit?

ANSWER: No. This ad commits the argument from antiquity fallacy (see Chapter 1)—assuming that a belief must be valid because it's been around for a long time.

2: EVALUATING CLAIMS Hair-Loss Remedies

"Call us now to learn more about the *advantages and highlights* of our product."

Beware of ads that only focus on the advantages of their products. What questions would you have about potential disadvantages or side effects?

ANSWER: What are the most common side effects, and how frequent are they? How dangerous are these side effects? Might the product work only for certain people with hair loss?

"Thousands of others have seen results—read their *testimonials.*"

Can we rely on testimonial or anecdotal evidence alone? Why or why not?

ANSWER: Testimonials alone are often misleading; in this case, they may be inaccurate, unrepresentative, or both. Moreover, there may be alternative explanations for these results: Perhaps the hair regrowth was due to other influences, including the use of other hair loss treatments.

"Use our supplements and grow back your hair *without the use of chemicals* or surgery."

Why is the claim that this supplement doesn't contain chemicals implausible?

ANSWER: By definition, all supplements contain chemicals!

"Our hair-loss cure is *doctor approved* and recommended."

Does the fact that doctors approve this cure make it more legitimate in your eyes? What questions would you ask about the number and type of doctors who approve of this product?

ANSWER: Beware of the appeal to authority fallacy (see Chapter 1)—just because a doctor or other authority figure endorses a product doesn't make the product's claims valid. The ad doesn't indicate how many doctors endorse the product, so we have no way of knowing if the number is small or large. We also don't know the doctors' background or training, so it's unclear if they're qualified to recommend the product.

3: EVALUATING CLAIMS Diagnosing Your Brain Orientation

"Left-brained people are more likely to focus on details and logic and to follow rules and schedules. They do well in math and science. *Right-brained people* are more likely to be deep thinkers or dreamers, and to act more spontaneously. They excel in the social sciences and the arts."

The ad implies incorrectly that some people are left-brained and others right-brained, when in fact the left and right hemispheres differ only in emphasis.

This *quick test* can help you determine your dominant side in just a few seconds.

This extraordinary claim isn't supported by extraordinary evidence. Furthermore, what would we need to know about this test to determine if it's valid?

ANSWER: Does the test correlate with other measures of left versus right brain preference, such as brain activity assessed in brain imaging studies?

"Use these exercises to improve the information flow between your left and right brain and improve your performance on spelling tests and listening comprehension."

There's no research to support the claim that these exercises will improve your academic performance.

4: EVALUATING CLAIMS Subliminal Persuasion CDs

"Over one million people have discovered the power of our CDs."

Does the sheer number of people who purchase a product provide evidence of its effectiveness? Is there necessarily a correlation between how many people use a product and its effectiveness?

ANSWER: No and no. This ad commits the bandwagon fallacy (Chapter 1). The number of people who use a product is a highly undependable measure of its effectiveness.

"Our CDs will improve all aspects of your life. You will conquer your fears, increase your IQ, lose weight, and attract a mate."

Extraordinary claims about subliminal persuasion require extraordinary evidence, and the ad provides no such evidence. To date, scientists have failed to document the ability of subliminal persuasion to produce profound personal changes.

"Your CDs are the best I've ever tried—they changed my life!"—Andrew from Atlanta, GA

Why are claims based only on testimonials and anecdotal evidence not trustworthy?

ANSWER: We have no idea whether Andrew's testimonial is genuine. Moreover, even if it is, we have no idea whether many other people might have experienced different results than Andrew. We also don't know if there are rival explanations for Andrew's reported positive results; perhaps Andrew was receiving psychotherapy at the same time or perhaps the CDs contained helpful advice that wasn't presented subliminally.

5: EVALUATING CLAIMS Dream Interpretations

"Your dreams are hidden messages sent from your subconscious to help guide your life."

Is there extraordinary evidence to support this extraordinary claim? In fact, most dream reports are straightforward descriptions of everyday activities and problems rather than hidden or disguised messages.

"Seeing a coconut in your dreams means that you will receive an unexpected sum of money."

Scientific evidence doesn't support the claim that specific symbols in our dreams possess a deeper meaning or predict something in our lives. Many dreams have no special meaning at all, and some dreams reflect everyday preoccupations.

"Using the ancient art of dream analysis, we can uncover hidden meanings in your dreams."

Does the fact that dream interpretations have been around a long time mean they're valid?

ANSWER: No. The error of assuming something is valid because it's been around a long time is the argument from antiquity fallacy (see Chapter 1).

6: EVALUATING CLAIMS Sleep-Assisted Learning

"Join the thousands of people who have increased their learning."

Does the fact that thousands of people believe in a claim make it true? What logical fallacy does this ad commit (see Chapter 1)?

ANSWER: No. This ad commits the bandwagon fallacy.

"Designed using proven research conducted all over the world . . ."

What questions should you ask about how this research was conducted? Can we assume that "proven" means the research has been replicated?

ANSWER: Is this claim based on genuine experimental research, with random assignment to conditions? What was the nature of the control group? Were participants and experimenters blind to the condition to which participants were assigned? Also, be suspicious of claims that products are "proven," as genuine "proof" is extremely rare in psychology. There's no guarantee that the research has been replicated by independent investigators.

"Use your brain's full potential. The average mind uses only 5% of our brain capacity."

Is there scientific support for the claim that we use only a small portion of our brain (see Chapter 3)?

ANSWER: No; to the contrary, there's overwhelming evidence that we use most or all of our brain most of the time.

"Sleep learning is a more efficient way to learn because *the information flows directly to our subconscious mind (while your conscious mind relaxes!)*"
What's the problem with this extraordinary claim?
ANSWER: As presently stated, this claim is difficult or impossible to falsify. It's hard to know what evidence could refute the assertion that information is flowing to people's subconscious.

"Risk-free, 100% money-back *guarantee.*"
We should be skeptical of guarantees, as virtually no psychological technique is foolproof.

7: EVALUATING CLAIMS Memory Boosters

"**Never misplace your keys again!** Use our product and *cure your absent-mindedness!*"
The claim that this product is a cure is extraordinary. What kind of evidence is needed to support this claim?
ANSWER: For the ad to demonstrate a true "cure," researchers would need to show that absentminded people would never or virtually never commit a mental error again after using the product. Needless to say, this is a tall order. They would also need to conduct an experimental study with random assignment to experimental and control conditions.

"*Scientifically proven to improve your memory.*"
The claim talks of "proof," yet scientific knowledge is rarely, if ever, conclusive. What information would you need to evaluate whether the studies were conducted properly?
ANSWER: One would need to show that the studies were true experiments that were properly conducted, with random assignment to conditions and a double-blind design.

"**Our formula is a *synergistic blend of antioxidants, gotu kola, brainy aromatics, amino acids, and specific neurotransmitter nutrients* to help maintain healthy cellular energy production by promoting healthy mitochondrial function, scavenging free radicals, and promoting blood circulation to the brain.**"
We should beware of meaningless "psychobabble" that uses scientific-sounding words that are lacking in substance.

"**75% of Americans are turning to complementary and alternative medicine to improve their memory—by taking our all-natural memory enhancers you can be one of them.**"
Does the claim that a large portion of Americans use complementary and alternative medicines mean this product is effective? Why or why not?
ANSWER: This claim commits the bandwagon fallacy (see Chapter 1). The mere fact that many people use these products doesn't imply they work. At best, it might imply that many people *assume* they work.

8: EVALUATING CLAIMS Speed-Reading Courses

"**Improve your *reading speed, comprehension,* retention and recall with our course.**"
Claims to improve reading speed and comprehension, but research shows that speed reading has negative consequences on our comprehension.

"**Learn how to *double or triple* your reading speed in *under 15 minutes.*"
What kind of evidence would you need to support this extraordinary claim?
ANSWER: First, is there experimental evidence to support this claim? Ideally, we would want to see a direct comparison of learners' reading speeds before and after 15 minutes of exposure to the technique. Second, we would want to measure not only reading *speed* but also reading *comprehension* after learning the technique. If reading comprehension decreases, the technique accomplishes very little by increasing speed.

"**This course was developed by a *team of professionals who researched speed reading at colleges and universities around the world.***"
What would you need to know about these "professionals" and how they conducted their research?
ANSWER: Are they trained scientists who understand how to conduct an experiment, or are they merely paid employees of the company? Was the research published in a peer reviewed journal?

"**Our course will teach you how to *skim excessively detailed documents.***"
Note that this claim acknowledges that most of the success of "speed reading" actually comes from skimming—that is, not reading some material at all.

9: EVALUATING CLAIMS IQ Boosters

"*While the 'experts' argue about whether you can increase IQ or not, we promise real results!*"
A warning sign of pseudoscience is the absence of connectivity to other research. This claim implies that the test developers can simply ignore what others have tried before—possible, but unlikely.

"*Become a genius in 5 simple steps.*"
Does this claim seem plausible given what you know about the probably reaction range (see Chapter 3) of intelligence? What kind of evidence would you need to support it?
ANSWER: Virtually all genetically influenced psychological traits have a reaction range, meaning there are probably limits to how much they can be changed given environmental input. It's exceedingly unlikely that any program can turn anyone into a genius, let alone a program that contains only five quick steps.

"**Credibly synthesize *process-centric quantum wave outsourcing.***"
Beware of psychobabble; this claim sounds sophisticated, but has little or no scientific meaning.

"**Take our IQ test and *expose your true creativity.***"
This claim implies that intelligence and creativity are similar, if not identical. What does the scientific research say (see p. 350)?
ANSWER: The ad confuses intelligence with creativity; research shows that intelligence and creativity are only moderately associated.

10: EVALUATING CLAIMS Anti-Aging Treatments

"**We are affiliated with *various medical schools* and our product is *used by thousands of physicians* nationwide.**"
This claim indicates that the program is affiliated with medical schools and used by physicians, creating a sense of legitimacy, but neglects to mention which medical schools they are. Moreover, this claim commits the argument from authority fallacy (see Chapter 1).

"**See how natural looking and youthful our product will make you. We offer *no overnight miracles or quick-fixes,* but subtle results over time.**"
By explaining that the results may take time, this ad avoids exaggerated claims. It also doesn't promise any specific quantifiable results, only that your appearance will be more "natural looking" and "youthful."

"**We hold *exclusive worldwide rights* to a highly refined supplement and are making it *available to the public for a limited time* only so act now!**"
Beware of ads that claim to have a scarcity of resources or to promise you exclusive access to a product (see Chapter 13 for the "scarcity heuristic").

"**In a *randomized, double-blind human study* our product showed a significant effect on the signs of aging.**"
Randomization and double-blind condition assignment are crucial components of experimental research (see Chapter 2). What additional information would you need to know about this experiment to evaluate whether the product's claims are legitimate?
ANSWER: Who conducted the study? Were they independent or "in-house" experts, scientists or non-scientists? What was the comparison or control condition?

11: EVALUATING CLAIMS Diets and Weight-Loss Plans

"**We help you lose weight by changing your everyday habits. Learn how to eat *smaller portions,* choose more *nutritious foods,* and make *exercise* a part of your daily routine.**"
This ad doesn't make any promises about how much weight you'll lose and correctly notes that reducing calories (through smaller portion of nutritious foods) and exercise are necessary components of a sensible diet.

"**I have a whole new lease on life—I lost *98 pounds in only four months!*"
The anecdotal claim that someone lost almost 100 pounds in four months is extraordinary—that would be an average of over six pounds lost each week. Note that the ad doesn't mention potential adverse health effects of such dramatic weight loss. In addition, no reason is given for the weight loss, so we can't assume the diet is the cause. What rival explanations can you think of for such a drastic weight loss?
ANSWER: Perhaps the person exercised frantically during that time, tried other diets, or both. Also, various medical conditions as well as psychological problems (such as severe depression) can lead to substantial weight loss.

"**Our *revolutionary research* shows that you can lose weight without dieting or exercise. Click here to learn more.**"
Beware of claims based on "revolutionary" new studies. The principle of connectivity reminds us that science builds with previous research. Moreover, to be trusted, results should be replicated in independent studies.

12: EVALUATING CLAIMS Stress Reduction and Relaxation Techniques

"**Here are some helpful tips for reducing stress. Remember, there is *no 'one size fits all' solution* and all of these methods require you to *change the way you approach and deal with potential stressors* in your life.**"

This site avoids exaggerated claims by acknowledging that there's no miracle cure for stress. The methods of stress reduction and relief differ for every person and require us to make changes in our lives.

"Our *all-natural pills* allow you to *wipe away all the stress in your life—instantly* and naturally."

What's wrong with this advertiser's claim that the pills offer an "all-natural" approach to stress-reduction? Does the promise to eliminate all forms of stress in your life seem plausible? Why or why not?

ANSWER: The claim relies on the mistaken idea that just because something is natural means it's safe or healthy (see discussion of the "natural commonplace" in Chapter 13). Stress is a natural part of life, so the promise to eliminate all forms of stress is implausible—and perhaps ill-advised.

"*Top experts agree that* Trans-Cortex space-dimensional music CDs can *relax up to 90% of overstressed listeners!*"

How much weight should we give to statements that appeal to the authority of unnamed "top experts" who endorse a product with a fancy-sounding, made-up name? What might be the problem with statistics that claim a success rate of "up to 90%"?

ANSWER: Appeals to authority by unnamed "top experts" should carry little weight, as should scientific-sounding names that have no bearing on a product's effectiveness. Vague statistics can be misleading. "Overstressed" can mean just about anything, and it's unclear whether the claim is based on anecdotes or carefully conducted research.

13: EVALUATING CLAIMS Work-from-Home Jobs

"Download our guide to starting your own business now *before they run out.*"

Just because there are limited copies of this guide doesn't mean it must be valuable—perhaps the manufacturer printed only a small quantity of the guides in the first place. What marketing tactic does this claim employ (see Table 13.3 for a hint)?

ANSWER: The scarcity heuristic—if a product is scarce, people often assume it must be valuable.

"Want to use the power of the Internet to become rich? Now you can with this report *developed by a well-known sales executive.*"

Should the fact that an expert created this report make you much more likely to trust it? What logical fallacy does this claim commit (see Chapter 1)?

ANSWER: Not necessarily. This claim commits the genetic fallacy—the fact that the report was crafted by a well-known sales executive might provide a reason to take a closer look at it, but it wouldn't guarantee its effectiveness.

"I started out with almost no savings and now *make $5,000–$6,000 every month* working from home."

Beware of claims that rely heavily on anecdotal evidence. It would be hard to verify that this person makes $70,000 per year working from home. This person's sales results may also be unrepresentative of most people, who could earn far less—or even lose money—working from home.

14: EVALUATING CLAIMS Online Personality Tests

"This color test has been *used for decades* and *given to thousands of people* worldwide."

Does the fact that a test has been used by many people for many years tell us anything about its validity? What two logical fallacies does this claim commit (see Chapter 1)?

ANSWER: No. This claim commits the bandwagon and argument from antiquity fallacies.

"Over 70% of *people who take this test rate it* as very accurate."

What's the danger of asking people who take the test determine its accuracy? What other methods should we use when evaluating personality assessment methods?

ANSWER: The ad erroneously implies that "personal validation"—determining a test's validity by asking people who've taken it to judge its validity—is accurate. In fact, people who've taken the test may be fooled by the P.T. Barnum effect. We instead need to find out whether the test is reliable and valid using well controlled studies. For example, in the case of validity, does the test predict ratings of people's personality by others who know them well? Does it predict their real-world behavior?

"Results: You are *confident, self-reliant, prudent, and have strong instincts* in life."

This test's results include descriptors typical of the P.T. Barnum effect. Who doesn't like to think of themselves as "confident," "self-reliant," "prudent," or having "strong instincts"?

"The self-scoring inventories on this site allow you to approximate your MBTI Type preferences, but *have not met commonly accepted psychometric standards for reliability and validity.* Therefore, they should not to be used as a substitute for taking an MBTI ®."

This site includes an appropriate disclaimer that reminds test-takers of the importance of reliability and validity.

15: EVALUATING CLAIMS Online Tests for Mental Disorders

"This 20 question self-test is *the most valid and reliable* screening measure for adult ADHD available on the Internet!"

Be suspicious of claims like "most valid and reliable" put forward with no supportive evidence. Because information on the Internet is vast and constantly subject to change, it's difficult to evaluate this extraordinary claim. Moreover, most online diagnostic tests have never been evaluated in peer reviewed studies.

"*High scores on the self-test may result from* depression, anxiety, and bipolar disorder, so *it's important to rule out these conditions* before a diagnosis of ADHD can be made with confidence."

The site accurately states that ADHD symptoms often overlap with those of other disorders, and that it may be challenging to distinguish the symptoms of ADHD, anxiety, depression, and bipolar disorder.

"Keep in mind that this is a screening test. Remember, it's *only the first step in arriving at an accurate diagnosis* of ADHD."

This statement rightly cautions against arriving at an ADHD diagnosis based on information contained in a brief questionnaire: It's often necessary to consider historical information and current behaviors and performance in different settings (such as school, workplace, and home), as well as tests of attention and input from different professionals (such as physicians, teachers, and family members).

16: EVALUATING CLAIMS Psychotherapies

Our breakthrough energy therapy is far superior to any short-term therapy available for anxiety.

What types of control groups would be especially important to include in research evaluating this claim?

ANSWER: (1) Participants who undergo alternative well-established empirically supported treatments, (2) groups that control for placebo effects, and (3) wait-list groups that control for spontaneous remission.

"Our *debriefing process* allows those involved in the incident to process the event and *vent their fears and anger* associated with it."

What does scientific research tell us about crisis debriefing (see Chapters 12 and 16)? Is the "venting" of fears and anger always a good thing?

ANSWER: Crisis debriefing can sometimes be harmful and may increase the risk of posttraumatic symptoms in people exposed to trauma. Venting fears can interfere with the use of natural coping strategies to recover from traumatic experiences.

"Cognitive-behavioral therapy *may not be effective in all cases,* but studies have shown that CBT *is equally as effective in the treatment of depression as anti-depressant medication.*"

This claim avoids exaggerating the benefits of cognitive-behavioral therapy (CBT) by noting that it may not be effective in all cases. The ad notes correctly that CBT is about as effective as antidepressant medication for clinical depression.

Aamodt, S., & Wang, S. (2008). *Welcome to your brain: Why you lose your car keys but never forget how to drive and other puzzles of everyday life.* London: Bloomsbury.

Aarons, L. (1976). Sleep-assisted instruction. *Psychological Bulletin, 83,* 1–40.

Abbey, A., Halman, L., & Andrews, F. (1992). Psychosocial, treatment and demographic predictors of the stress associated with infertility. *Fertility and Sterility, 57,* 122–127.

Abbot, N. C., Harkness, E. F., Stevinson, C., Marshall, F. P., Conn, D. A., & Ernst, E. (2001). Spiritual healing as a therapy for chronic pain: A randomized, clinical trial. *Pain, 91,* 79–89.

Abel, E.L. (1998). *Fetal alcohol abuse syndrome.* New York, NY: Plenum Press.

Abel, E. L., & Sokol, R. J. (1986). Fetal alcohol syndrome is now leading cause of mental retardation. *Lancet, 2,* 1222.

Aber, M., & Rappaport, J. (1994). The violence of prediction: The uneasy relationship between social science and social policy. *Applied and Preventive Psychology, 3,* 43–54.

Abraham, H. D., & Aldridge, A. M. (1993). Adverse consequences of lysergic acid diethylamide. *Addiction, 88,* 1327–1334.

Abramowitz, A. I., & Saunders, K. L. (2008). Is polarization a myth? *Journal of Politics, 70,* 542-555.

Abramowitz, J. S., Taylor, S., & McKay, D. (2009). Obsessive-compulsive disorder. *Lancet, 374,* 491–499.

Abramson, L. Y., Seligman, M. E. P., & Teasdale, J. D. (1978). Learned helplessness in humans: Critique and reformulation. *Journal of Abnormal Psychology, 87,* 49–74.

Abrari, K., Rashidy-Pour, A., Semnanian, S., & Fathollahi, Y. (2009). Post-training administration of corticosterone enhances consolidation of contextual fear memory and hippocampal long-term potentiation in rats. *Neurobiology of Learning and Memory, 91,* 260–265.

Abutalebi, J., Cappa, S. F., & Perani, D. (2005). What can functional neuroimaging tell us about the bilingual brain? In Kroll, J. F., & de Groot, A. M. B. (Eds.), *Handbook of bilingualism: Psycholinguistic approaches* (pp. 497–515). New York, NY: Oxford University Press.

Achenbach, T. M. (1982). Research methods in developmental psychopathology. In P. C. Kendall & J. Butcher (eds.), *Handbook of research methods in clinical psychology* (pp. 127–181). New York: Wiley.

Ackerman, P. L., & Beier, M. E. (2003). Intelligence, personality, and interests in the career choice process. *Journal of Career Assessment, 11,* 205–218.

Ackerman, P. L., Beier, M. E., & Boyle, M. O. (2005). Working memory and intelligence: The same or different constructs? *Psychological Bulletin, 131,* 30–60.

Ackerman, P. L., & Heggestad, E. D. (1997). Intelligence, personality, and interests: Evidence for overlapping traits. *Psychological Bulletin, 121,* 219–245.

Ackerman, P. L., Kanfer, R., & Goff, M. (1995). Cognitive and non-cognitive determinants of complex skill acquisition. *Journal of Experimental Psychology: Applied, 1,* 270–304.

Ackerman, S. J., Hilsenroth, M. J., Clemence, A. J., Weatherill, R., & Fowler J. C. (2001). Convergent validity of Rorschach and TAT scales of object relations. *Journal of Personality Assessment, 77,* 295–306.

Ackroyd, E. (1993). *A dictionary of dream symbols.* London: Blanford.

Acocella, J. (1999). *Creating hysteria: Women and multiple personality disorder.* San Francisco: Jossey-Bass Publishers.

Acton, G. S., & Schroeder, D. H. (2001). Sensory discrimination as related to general intelligence. *Intelligence, 29,* 263–271.

Adachi, N., Akanu, N., Adachi, T., Takekawa, Y., Adachi, Y., Ito, M., & Ikeda, H. (2008). Déjà vu experiences are rarely associated with pathological dissociation. *Journal of Nervous and Mental Disease, 196,* 417–419.

Adams, H. E., Wright, L. E., & Lohr, B. A. (1996). Is homophobia associated with homosexual arousal? *Journal of Abnormal Psychology, 105,* 440–445.

Addis, M. E., Hatgis, C., Krasnow, A. D., Jacob, K., Bourne, L., & Mansfield, A. (2004). Effectiveness of cognitive-behavioral treatment for panic disorder versus treatment as usual in a managed care setting. *Journal of Consulting and Clinical Psychology, 72,* 625–635.

Addis, M. E., & Mahalik, J. R. (2003). Men, masculinity, and the contexts of help seeking. *American Psychologist, 58,* 5–14.

Adelmann, P. K., & Zajonc, R. B. (1989). Facial efference and the experience of emotion. *Annual Review of Psychology, 40,* 249–280.

Adler, A. (1922). *Practice and theory of individual psychology.* London: Routledge and K. Paul.

Adler, A. (1931). *What life should mean to you.* Boston: Little Brown.

Adler, A. (1938). *Social interest: A challenge of mankind.* London: Faber & Faber.

Adolph, K. E. (1997). Learning in the development of infant locomotion. *Monographs of the Society for Research in Child Development, 63,* Serial No. 251.

Adolphs, R., Tranel, D., Damasio, H., & Damasio, A. (1994). Impaired recognition of emotion in facial expressions following bilateral damage to the human amygdala. *Nature, 372,* 669–672.

Adorno, T. W., Frenkel-Brunswik, E., Levinson, D., & Sanford, R. N. (1950). *The authoritarian personality.* New York: Harper & Row.

Ahn, H., & Wampold, B. E. (2001). Where oh where are the specific ingredients? A meta-analysis of component studies in counseling and psychotherapy. *Journal of Counseling Psychology, 48,* 251–257.

Ahnert, L., Pinquart, M., & Lamb, M. E. (2006). Security of children's relationships with nonparental care providers: A meta-analysis. *Child Development, 77,* 664–679.

Aimone, J. B., Wiles, J., & Gage, F. H. (2006). Potential role for adult neurogenesis in the encoding of time in new memories. *Nature Neuroscience, 9,* 723–727.

Ainsworth, M. D. S., Blehar, M. C., Waters, E., & Wall, S. (1978). *Patterns of attachment: A psychological study of the Strange Situation.* Hillsdale, NJ: Erlbaum.

Ajdacic-Gross, V., Wang, J., Bopp, M., Eich, D., Rossler, W., & Gutzwiller, F. (2003). Are seasonalities in suicide dependent on suicide methods? A reappraisal. *Social Science and Medicine, 57,* 1173–1181.

Åkerstedt T, Fredlund, P., Gillberg, M., Jansson, B. (2002). A prospective study of fatal occupational accidents – relationship to sleeping difficulties and occupational factors. *Journal of Sleep Research, 11,* 69–71.

Akins, C. K. (2004). The role of Pavlovian conditioning in sexual behavior: A comparative analysis of human and nonhuman animals. *International Journal of Comparative Psychology, 17,* 241–262.

Akiskal, H. S., & McKinney, W. T. (1973). Depressive disorders: Toward a unified hypothesis. *Science, 182,* 20–29.

Alberti, R. E., & Emmons, M. L. (2001). *Your perfect right: Assertiveness and equality in your life and relationships* (8th ed.). New York: Impact Publishers.

Alcock, J. E. (1990). *Science and supernature: A critical appraisal of parapsychology.* Buffalo, NY: Prometheus Books.

Alcock, J. E. (1995). The belief engine. *Skeptical Inquirer, 19*(3), 14–18.

Alcock, J. (1999) The nesting behaviour of Dawson's burrowing bee Amegilla dawsoni (Hymenoptera: Anthophorini) and the production of offspring of different sizes. *Journal of Insect Behavior, 12,* 363–384.

Alda, M. (1997). Bipolar disorder: From families to genes. *Canadian Journal of Psychiatry, 42,* 378–387.

Aldrich, M. S. (1999). *Sleep medicine.* New York: Oxford University Press.

Aleman, A., & Laroi, F. (2008). *Hallucinations: The science of idiosyncratic perception.* Washington, DC: American Psychological Association.

Alexander, F. (1950). *Psychosomatic medicine: Its principles and applications.* New York: W. W. Norton.

Alexander, G. M., & Hines, M. (2002). Sex differences in response to children's toys in non-human primates (*cercopithecus aethiops sabaeus*). *Evolution and Human Behavior, 23,* 467–479.

Alexander, G. M., Wilcox, T., & Woods, R. (2009). Sex differences in infants' visual interest in toys. *Archives of Sexual Behavior, 38,* 427–433.

Alexander, R. A., Carson, K. P., Alliger, G. M., & Carr, L. (1987). Correcting doubly truncated correlations: An improved approximation for correcting the bivariate normal correlation when truncation has occurred on both variables. *Educational and Psychological Measurement, 47,* 309–315.

Alferink, L. A. (2007). Educational practices, superstitious behavior, and mythed opportunities. *Scientific Review of Mental Health Practice, 5*(2), 21–30.

Alicke, M. D., LoSchiavo, F. M., Zerbst, J. I., & Zhang, S. (1997). The person who outperforms me is a genius: Esteem maintenance in upward social comparison. *Journal of Personality and Social Psychology, 73*, 781–789.

Alison, L. J., Smith, M. D., & Morgan, K. (2003). Interpreting the accuracy of offender profiles. *Psychology, Crime & Law, 9*, 185–195.

Al-Issa, I. (1995). The illusion of reality or the reality of illusion: Hallucinations and culture. *British Journal of Psychiatry, 166*, 368–373.

Allen, J. J. B., & Movius, H. L. (2000). The objective assessment of amnesia in dissociative identity disorder using event-related potentials. *International Journal of Psychophysiology, 38*, 21–41.

Allen, P., Laroi, F., McGuire, P. K., & Aleman, A. (2008). The hallucinating brain: A review of structural and functional neuroimaging studies of hallucinations. *Neuroscience & Biobehavioral Reviews, 32*, 175–191.

Alliger, G. M. (1988). Do zero correlations really exist among measures of different intellectual abilities? *Educational & Psychological Measurement, 48*, 275–280.

Allison, D. B., Kaprio, J., Korkeila, M., Koskenvuo, M., Neale, M. C., & Hayakawa, K. (1996). The heritability of body mass index among an international sample of monozygotic twins reared apart. *International Journal of Obesity and Related Disorders, 20*, 501–506.

Alloway, R., & Bebbington, P. (1987). The buffer theory of social support: A review of the literature. *Psychological Medicine, 17*, 91–108.

Alloy, L. B., & Abramson, L. Y. (1979). Judgment of contingency in depressed and nondepressed students: Sadder but wiser? *Journal of Experimental Psychology: General, 108*, 441–485.

Alloy, L. B., & Abramson, L. Y. (1988). Depressive realism: Four theoretical perspectives. In L. B. Alloy (ed.), *Cognitive process in depression* (pp. 223–265). New York: Guilford.

Allport, G. W. (1965). *Letters from Jenny.* New York: Harcourt, Brace, & World.

Allport, G. W. (1966). Traits revisited. *American Psychologist, 21*, 1–10.

Allport, G. W., & Odbert, H. S. (1936). Trait names, a psycholexical study. *Psychological Monographs, 47* (1, Whole No. 211).

Allport, G. W., & Postman, L. J. (1956). The basic psychology of rumor. *Journal of Abnormal and Social Psychology, 53*, 27–33.

Almli, C. R., & Finger, S. (1987). Neural insult and critical period concepts. In M. H. Bornstein (Ed.), *Sensitive periods in development: Interdisciplinary perspectives* (pp. 123–143). Hillsdale, NJ: Lawrence Erlbaum.

Alt, K. W., Jeunesse, C., Buitrago-Téllez, C. H., Wächter, R., Boes, E., & Pichler, S. L. (1997). Evidence for Stone Age cranial surgery. *Nature, 387*, 360.

Altemeyer, B. (2004). Highly dominating, highly authoritarian personalities. *Journal of Social Psychology, 14*, 421–427.

Althius, M. D., Fredman, L., Langenberg, P. W., & Magaziner, J. (1998). The relationship between insomnia and mortality among community-dwelling older women. *Journal of the American Geriatric Society, 46*, 1270–1273.

Altmann, E. M., & Schunn, C. D. (2002). Integrating decay and interference: A new look at an old interaction. In the *Proceedings of the 24th Annual Conference of the Cognitive Science Society*. Mahwah, NJ: Erlbaum.

Alvarado, C. S. (2000). Out of body experiences. In E. Cardeña, S. J. Lynn, & S. Krippner (eEds.), *The variety of anomalous experiences* (pp. 183–218). Washington, DC: American Psychological Association.

Alvarez, C. A., & Brown, S. W. (2001). *What people believe about memory despite the research evidence*. Paper presented at the Annual Convention of the American Psychological Association, San Francisco, CA.

Alvarez, L. W. (1965). A pseudo experience in parapsychology. *Science, 148*(3677), 1541.

Alzheimer's Disease Facts and Fictions (2007). Alzheimer's disease information: Retrieved from http://www.psychtreatment.com/alzheimer.htm on December 4, 2007.

Amato, P. R., & Booth, A. (1997). *A generation at risk: Growing up in an era of family upheaval*. Cambridge, MA: Harvard University Press.

Ambady, N., & Rosenthal, R. (1993). Half a minute: Predicting teacher evaluations from thin slices of nonverbal behavior and physical attractiveness. *Journal of Personality and Social Psychology, 64*, 431–441.

American Psychiatric Association. (2000). *Diagnostic and statistical manual of mental disorders: DSM-IV-TR* (4th ed.). Washington, DC: Author.

American Psychological Association (2002). Ethical principles of psychologists and code of conduct. *American Psychologist, 57*, 1060–1073.

American Psychological Association. (2003). Fire trucks are supposed to be red, right? Not if you want to reduce accidents. Retrieved September 10, 2008, from www.psychologymatters.org/solomon.html.

American Psychological Association. (2006). Americans engage in unhealthy behaviors to manage stress. *APA Practice Media Room.* Retrieved from http://apahelpcenter.mediaroom.com/index.php?s=press_releases&item=23.

American Psychological Association. (2007). The changing gender composition of psychology. Retrieved March 20, 2010, from http://www.apa.org/monitor/jun07/changing.aspx.

American Psychological Association (2009). *Resolution on appropriate affirmative responses to sexual orientation distress and change efforts.* APA Online. http://www.apa.org/pi/lgbc/publications/resolution. Retrieved December 12, 2009.

Ames, A. Jr., (1946) Binocular vision as affected by relations between uniocular stimulus-patterns in commonplace environments. *American Journal of Psychology, 59*, 333–357.

Ames, E. (1997). *The development of Romanian orphanage children adopted to Canada. Final report to National Welfare Grants Program: Human Resources Development, Canada*. Barnaby, British Columbia, Canada: Simon Fraser University.

Amir, N., Coles, M. E., Brigidi, B., & Foa, E. B. (2001). The effect of practice on recall of emotional information in individuals with generalized social phobia. *Journal of Abnormal Psychology, 110*, 76–78.

Amsterdam, B. (1972). Mirror self-image reactions before the age of two. *Developmental Psychobiology, 5*, 297–305.

Anand, B. K., & Brobeck, J. R. (1951). Hypothalamic control of food intake in rats and cats. *Yale Journal of Biological Medicine, 24*, 123.

Anastasi, A., & Urbina, S. (1996). *Psychological testing.* New York: Prentice Hall.

Ancona, L., & Pareyson, R. (1968). Contributo allo studio della aggressione: La dinamica della obbedienza distruttiva [Contribution to the study of aggression: The dynamics of destructive obedience]. *Archivio di Psicologia, Neurologia, e Psichiatria, 29*, 340–372.

Andersen, H. S., Sestoft, D., Lillebaek, T., Gabrielsen, G., Hemmingsen, R., & Kramp, P. (2000). A longitudinal study of prisoners on remand: psychiatric prevalence, incidence and psychopathology in solitary vs. non-solitary confinement. *Acta Psychiatrica Scandinavica, 102*, 19–25.

Anderson, A. K., Christoff, K., Stappen, I., Panitz, D., Ghahremani, D. G., Glover, G., et al. (2003). Dissociated neural representations of intensity and valence in human olfaction. *Nature Neuroscience, 6*, 196–202.

Anderson B., & Harvey T. (1996). Alterations in cortical thickness and neuronal density in the frontal cortex of Albert Einstein. *Neuroscience Letters, 210*, 161–164.

Anderson, C. A., & Anderson, K. B. (1996). Violent crime rate studies in philosophical context: A destructive testing approach to heat and southern culture of violence effects. *Journal of Personality and Social Psychology, 70*, 740–756.

Anderson, C. A., Berkowitz, L., Donnerstein, E., Huesmann, L. R., Johnson, J. D., Linz, D., et al. (2003). The influence of media violence on youth. *Psychological Science in the Public Interest, 4*, 81–110.

Anderson, C. A., & Bushman, B. J. (2002a). The effects of media violence on society. *Science, 295*, 2377–2378.

Anderson, C. A., & Bushman, B. J. (2002b). Human aggression. *Annual Review of Psychology, 53*, 27–51.

Anderson, C. A., & Bushman, B. J. (2002c). Media violence and the American public revisited. *American Psychologist, 57*, 448–450.

Anderson, C. A., Bushman, B. J., & Groom, R. W. (1997). Hot years and serious and deadly assault: Empirical tests of the heat hypothesis. *Journal of Personality and Social Psychology, 73*, 1213–1223.

Anderson, C. A., Gentile, D. A., & Buckley, K. E. (2007). Violent video game effects on children and adolescents: Theory, research, and public policy. Oxford, U.K.: Oxford University Press.

Anderson, C. A., Lindsay, J. J., & Bushman, B. J. (1999). Research in the psychological laboratory: Truth or triviality? *Current Directions in Psychological Science, 8*, 3–9.

Anderson, C. A., Shibuya, A., Ihiri, N., Swing, E. L., Bushman, B. J., Sakamoto, A., Rothstein, H. R., & Saleem, M. (2010). Violent video game effects on aggression, empathy, and prosocial behavior in Eastern and Western countries. *Psychological Bulletin, 136*, 151–173.

Anderson, C. M., & Stewart, S. (1983). *Mastering resistance.* New York: Guilford Press.

Anderson, D. R., & Pempek, T. A. (2005). Television and very young children. *American Behavioral Scientist, 48,* 505–522.

Anderson, K. J., Revelle, W., & Lynch, M. J. (1989). Caffeine, impulsivity, and memory scanning: A comparison of two explanations for the Yerkes-Dodson effect. *Motivation and Emotion, 13,* 1–20.

Anderson, K. W., Taylor, S., & McLean, P. (1996). Panic disorder associated with blood-injury-reactivity: The necessity of establishing functional relationships among maladaptive behaviors. *Behavior Therapy, 27,* 463–472.

Anderson, M. C., & Green, C. (2001). Suppressing unwanted memories by executive control. *Nature, 410,* 366–369.

Andreasen, N. C. (1987). Creativity and mental illness: Prevalence rates in writers and their first-degree relatives. *American Journal of Psychiatry, 144,* 1288–1292.

Andreasen, N. C. (1995). The validation of psychiatric-diagnosis: New models and approaches. *American Journal of Psychiatry, 152,* 161–162.

Andreasen. N. C., O'Leary, D. S., Flaum, M., Nopoulos, P., Watkins, G. L., Boles Ponto, L. L., & Hichwa, R. D, (1997). Hypofrontality in schizophrenia: Distributed dysfunctional circuits in neuroleptic-naive patients. *Lancet, 349,* 1730–1734.

Andreasen, N. C., Rezai, K., Alliger, R., Swayze, V. W. II, Flaum, M., Kirchner, P., et al. (1992). Hypofrontality in neuroleptic-naive patients and in patients with chronic schizophrenia: Assessment with xenon 133 single-photon emission computed tomography and the Tower of London. *Archives of General Psychiatry, 49,* 943–958.

Andresen, G. V., Birch, L. L., & Johnson, P. A. (1990). The scapegoat effect on food aversions after chemotherapy. *Cancer, 66,* 1649–1653.

Andrews, G., Stewart, G., Morris-Yates, A., Holt, P., & Henderson, S. (1990). Evidence for a general neurotic syndrome. *The British Journal of Psychiatry, 157,* 6–12.

Angier, N. (2006, January 3). The cute factor. *New York Times.* Retrieved from http://www.nytimes.com/2006/01/03/science/03cute.html?ex=1293944400&en=9942fdaf51f1211c&ei=5090&partner=rssuserland&emc=rss.

Angier, N. (2009, June 22). When an ear witness decides the case. *New York Times.* http://www.nytimes.com/2009/06/23/science/23angi.html.

Angold, A. (1999). Comorbidity. *Journal of Child Psychology and Psychiatry, 40,* 57–87.

Antonovsky, A. (1967). Social class, life expectancy and overall mortality. *Milbank Memorial Fund Quarterly,* 45, 31–73.

Antony, M. A., & Barlow, D. H. (2002). Specific phobia. In D. H. Barlow (ed.), *Anxiety and its disorders: The nature and treatment of anxiety and panic* (2nd ed., pp. 380–417). New York: Guilford Press.

Antony, M. A., & Roemer, L. (2003). Behavior therapy. In A. S. Gurman & S. B. Messer (eds.), *Essential psychotherapies: Theory and practice* (2nd ed., pp. 182–223). New York: Guilford Press.

Antrobus, J. S. (1983). REM and NREM sleep reports: Comparison of word frequencies by cognitive classes. *Psychophysiology, 20,* 562–568.

Antrobus, J. S., Antrobus, J. S., & Fisher, C. (1965). Discrimination of dreaming and nondreaming sleep. *Archives of General Psychiatry, 12,* 395–401.

Aponte, H., & Hoffman, L. (1973). The open door: A structural approach to a family with an anorectic child. *Family Process, 12,* 1–44.

Appelbaum, P. S. (1997). Almost a revolution: An international perspective on the law of involuntary commitment. *Journal of the American Academy of Psychiatry and Law, 25,* 135–147.

Appelle, S., Lynn, S. J., & Newman, L. (2000). The alien abduction experience: Theoretical and empirical issues. In E. Cardeña, S. J. Lynn, & S. Krippner (eds.), *The varieties of anomalous experience: Examining the scientific evidence* (pp. 253–283). Washington, DC: American Psychological Association.

Applewhite, P. B., Gardner, F., Foley, D., & Clendenin, M. (1971). Failure to condition tetrahymena. *Scandinavian Journal of Psychology, 12,* 65–67.

Archer, D. (1997). *A world of differences: Understanding cross-cultural communication* [video]. Berkeley, CA: University of California, Extension Center for Media and Independent Learning.

Archer, J. (2004). Sex differences in aggression in real-world settings: A meta-analytic review. *Review of General Psychology, 8*(4), 291–322.

Ariely, D. (2008). *Predictably irrational: The hidden forces that shape our decisions.* New York: HarperCollins.

Arieti, S. (1959). Manic-depressive psychosis. In S. Arieti (ed.), *American handbook of psychiatry* (pp. 439-444). New York: Basic Books.

Arkes, H. R. (1993). Some practical judgment and decision-making research. In N. J. Castellan (ed.), *Individual and Group Decision Making: Current Issues* (pp. 3-19). Hillsdale, NJ: Lawrence Erlbaum Assoc Inc.

Arkes, H. R., & Tetlock, P. E. (2004). Attributions of implicit prejudice or "Would Jesse Jackson 'fail' the Implicit Association Test?" *Psychological Inquiry, 15,* 257–278.

Arkowitz, H., & Lilienfeld, S. O. (2006). Psychotherapy on trial. *Scientific American Mind, 3,* 42–49.

Arkowitz, H., & Lilienfeld, S. O. (2007). A pill to fix your ills? *Scientific American Mind, 18,* 80–81.

Arkowitz, H., & Lilienfeld, S. O. (2009, January). Why science tells us not to rely on eyewitness accounts. *Scientific American Mind.* http://www.scientificamerican.com/article.cfm?id=do-the-eyes-have-it.

Arnett, J. J. (1995). The young and the reckless: Adolescent reckless behavior. *Current Directions in Psychological Science, 4,* 67–71.

Arnett, J. J. (1999). Adolescent storm and stress, reconsidered. *American Psychologist, 4,* 317–326.

Arnett, J. J. (2004). *Emerging adulthood: The winding road frm the late teens through the twenties.* Oxford: Oxford University Press.

Arnold L. M. (1999). A case series of women with postpartum-onset obsessive-compulsive disorder. Primary Care Companion. *Journal of Clinical Psychiatry, 1,* 103–108.

Aronoff, J., Barclay, A. M., & Stevenson, L. A. (1988) The recognition of threatening facial stimuli. *Journal of Personality and Social Psychology, 54,* 647–655.

Aronoff, J., Lynn, S. J., & Malinowski, P. (2000). Are cultic environments psychologically harmful? *Clinical Psychology Review, 20,* 91–111.

Aronson, E. (1992). *The social animal* (6th ed.). New York: W. H. Freeman.

Aronson, E. (1998). *The social animal* (8th ed.). New York: Worth.

Aronson, E. (2000) The jigsaw strategy: Reducing prejudice in the classroom. *Psychology Review 7,* 2–5.

Aronson, E. (2004). Reducing hostility and building compassion: Lessons from the jigsaw classroom. In A. G. Miller (ed.), *The social psychology of good and evil* (pp. 469–488). New York: Guilford Press.

Aronson, E., Blaney, N., Stephan, C., Sikes, J., & Snapp, M. (1978). *The jigsaw classroom.* Beverly Hills, CA: Sage.

Aronson, E., & Mills, J. (1959). The effect of severity of initiation on liking for a group. *Journal of Abnormal and Social Psychology, 59,* 177–181.

Arrigo, B., & Griffin, A. (2004). Serial murder and the case of Aileen Wuornos: Attachment theory, psychopathy, and predatory aggression. *Behavioral Sciences and the Law, 22,* 375–393.

Asch, S. E. (1955). Opinions and social pressure. *Scientific American, 193,* 31–35.

Ascher, L. M., Barber, T. X., & Spanos, N. P. (1972). Two attempts to replicate the Parrish-Lundy-Leibowitz experiment on hypnotic age regression. *American Journal of Clinical Hypnosis, 14,* 178–185.

Aserinsky, E. (1996). Memories of famous neuropsychologists: The discovery of REM sleep. *Journal of the History of the Neurosciences, 5,* 213–227.

Aserinsky, E., & Kleitman, N. (1953). Regularly occurring periods of ocular motility and concomitant phenomena during sleep. *Science, 118,* 361–375.

Ashton, S. G., & Goldberg, L. W. (1973). In response to Jackson's challenge: The comparative validity of personality scales constructed by the external (empirical) strategy and scales developed intuitively by experts, novices, and laymen. *Journal of Research in Personality, 7,* 1–20.

Asmundson, J. G., & Taylor, S. (2005). *It's not all in your head: How worrying about your health can make you sick—And what you can do about it.* New York: Guilford.

Aspinwall, L., & Brunhart, S. (2000). What I don't know won't hurt me. In J. Gillham (ed.), *The science of optimism and hope: Research essays in honor of Martin E. P. Seligman* (pp. 163–200). Philadelphia: Templeton Foundation Press.

Assendelft, W. J. J., Morton, S. C., Yu, E. I., Suttorp, M. J., & Shekelle, P. G. (2003). Spinal manipulative therapy for low back pain: A meta-analysis of effectiveness relative to other therapies. *Annals of Internal Medicine, 138,* 871–881.

Astin, J. A., & Ernst, E. (2002). The effectiveness of spinal manipulation for the treatment of headache disorders: A systematic review of randomized clinical trials. *Cephalalgia, 22,* 617–623.

Atkinson, R. C. (2001, February 18). *Standardized tests and access to American universities.* The 2001 Robert H. Atwell Distinguished Lecture delivered at the 83rd Annual Meeting of the American Council on Education, Washington, DC. http://www.ucop.edu/news/sat/speech.html.

Atkinson, R. C., & Shiffrin, R. M. (1968). Human memory: A proposed system and its control processes. In K. W. Spence and J. T. Spence (eds.), *The psychology of learning and motivation: Advances in research and theory* (Vol. 2, pp. 89–195). New York: Academic Press.

Atri, A., Sharma, M., & Cottrell, R. (2006). Role of social support, hardiness, and acculturation as predictors of mental health among international students of Asian Indian origin. *International Quarterly of Community Health Education, 27*, 59–73.

Audebert, O., Deiss, V., & Rousset, S. (2006). Hedonism as a predictor of attitudes of young French women towards meat. *Appetite, 46*, 239–247.

Ax, A. F. (1953). The physiological differentiation between fear and anger in humans. *Psychosomatic Medicine, 55*, 433–442.

Axsom, D., & Cooper, J. (1985). Cognitive dissonance and psychotherapy: The role of effort justification in inducing weight loss. *Journal of Experimental Social Psychology, 21*, 149–160.

Axtell, R. E. (1997). *Do's and taboos of body language around the world.* New York: Wiley.

Ayllon, T., & Milan, M. (2002). Token economy: Guidelines for operation. In M. Hersen & W. Sledge, Encyclopedia of psychotherapy (pp. 829–833). New York: Academic Press.

Azar, B. (1999, July/August). Destructive lab attack sends a wake-up call. *APA Monitor.* Retrieved October 22, 2007, from www.apa.org/monitor/julaug99/sc1.html.

Azar, B. (2005, October). How mimicry begat culture. *American Psychological Association Monitor, 36*(9). Retrieved from http://www.apa.org/monitor/oct05/mirror.html on March 27, 2010.

Azevedo, F. A., Carvalho, L. R. B., Grinberg, L. T., Farfel, J. M., Ferretti, R. E. L., Leite, R. E. P., et al. (2009). Equal numbers of neuronal and nonneuronal cells make the human brain an isometrically scaled-up primate brain. *Journal of Comparative Neurology, 513*, 532–541.

Azrin, N. H., & Holz, W. C. (1966). Punishment. In W. K. Honig (ed.), *Operant behavior: Areas of research and application* (pp. 380–447). New York: Appleton-Century-Crofts.

Babiak, P., & Hare, R. D. (2006). *Snakes in suits: When psychopaths go to work.* New York: Regan Books.

Babyak, M. A., Blumenthal, J. A., Herman, S., Khatri, P., Doraiswamy, P. M., Moore, K. A., et al. (2000). Exercise treatment for major depression: Maintenance of therapeutic benefit at 10 months. *Psychosomatic Medicine, 62*, 633–638.

Bachrach, H., Galatzer-Levy, R., Skolnikoff, A., & Waldron, S. (1991). On the efficacy of psychoanalysis. *Journal of the American Psychoanalytic Association, 39*, 871–916.

Baddeley, A. D. (1993). *Your memory: A user's guide* (2nd ed.). London: Lifecycle Publications.

Baddeley, A. D., & Hitch, G. J. (1974). Working memory. In G. A. Bower (ed.), *Recent advances in learning and motivation, Vol. 8* (pp. 47–90). New York: Academic Press.

Badman, M. K., & Flier, J. S. (2005). The gut and energy balance: Visceral allies in the obesity wars. *Science, 307*, 1909–1914.

Baer, R. A. (2003). Mindfulness training as a clinical intervention: A conceptual and an empirical review. *Clinical Psychology: Science and Practice, 10*, 125–143.

Bagemihl, B. (1999). *Biological exuberance, animal homosexuality and natural diversity.* London: Profile Books.

Bagnardi, V., Blangiardo, M., LaVecchia, C. L., & Corrado, G. (2001). *Alcohol consumption and the risk of cancer: A meta-analysis.* Bethesda, MD: National Institute on Alcohol Abuse and Alcoholism.

Bahnson, C. B., Smith, K. (1975). Autonomic changes in a multiple personality. *Psychosomatic Medicine, 37*, 85–86.

Bahrick, H. P. (1984). Semantic memory content in permastore: Fifty years of memory for Spanish learning in school. *Journal of Experimental Psychology: General, 113*, 1–29.

Bahrick, H. P., Bahrick, P. O., & Wittlinger, R. P. (1975). Fifty years of memory for names and faces: A cross-sectional approach. *Journal of Experimental Psychology: General, 104*, 54–75.

Bahrick, H. P., & Phelps, E. (1987). Retention of Spanish vocabulary over 8 years. *Journal of Experimental Psychology: Learning, Memory, & Cognition, 13*, 344–349.

Bahrick, L. E., Moss, L., & Fadil, C. (1996). The development of self recognition in infancy. *Ecological Psychology, 8*, 189–208.

Bahrick, L. E., & Watson, J. S. (1985). Detection of intermodal proprioceptive visual contingency as a potential basis of self-perception in infancy. *Developmental Psychology, 21*, 963–973.

Bailey, J. M., Dunne, M. P., & Martin, N. G. (2000). Genetic and environmental influences on sexual orientation and its correlates in an Australian twin sample. *Journal of Personality and Social Psychology, 78*, 524–536.

Bailey, J. M., & Pillard, R. C. (1991). A genetic study of male sexual orientation. *Archives of General Psychiatry, 48*, 1089–1096.

Bailey, J. M., Pillard, R. C., Neale, M. C., & Agyei, Y. (1993). Heritable factors influence sexual orientation in women. *Archives of General Psychiatry, 50*, 217–223.

Bailey, J. M., & Zucker, K. J. (1995). Childhood sex-typed behavior and sexual orientation: A conceptual analysis and quantitative review. *Developmental Psychology, 31*, 43–55.

Baillargeon, R. (1987). Object permanence in 6 and 8-month-old infants. *Developmental Psychology, 23*, 655–664.

Baillargeon, R., & Hanko-Summers, S. (1990). Is the top object adequately supported by the bottom object? Young infants' understanding of support relations. *Cognitive Development, 5*, 29–53.

Baillargeon, R., Spelke, E., & Wasserman, S. (1985). Object permanence in five-month-old infants. *Cognition, 20*, 191–208.

Bainbridge, W. S. (1987). Collective behavior and social movements. In R. Stark (ed.), *Sociology* (pp. 544–576). Belmont, CA: Wadsworth.

Baker, E. (1985). Psychoanalysis and psychoanalytic psychotherapy. In S. J. Lynn & J. P. Garske (eds.), *Contemporary psychotherapies: Models and methods* (pp. 19–26). Columbus, OH: Charles E. Merrill.

Baker, F. M., & Bell, C. C. (1999). Issues in the psychiatric treatment of African Americans. *Psychiatry Services, 50*, 362–368.

Baker, J. R., & Yardley, J. K. (2002). Moderating effect of gender on the relationship between sensation-seeking impulsivity and substance use in adolescents. *Journal of Child and Adolescence Substance Abuse, 12*, 27–43.

Baker, R. A. (1992). *Hidden memories: Voices and visions from within.* Buffalo, NY: Prometheus Books.

Baker, S. C., & MacIntyre, P. D. (2000). The role of gender and immersion in communication and second language orientations. *Language Learning, 50*, 311–341.

Baker, T. B., McFall, R. M. & Shoham, V. (2009). Current status and future prospects of clinical psychology toward a scientifically principled approach to mental and behavioral health care. *Perspectives on Psychological Science, 9*, 67–103.

Baker, W. E. (1999). When can affective conditioning and mere exposure directly influence brand choice? *Journal of Advertising, 28*, 31–47.

Balcetis, E., & Dunning, D. A. (2008). A mile in moccasins: How situational experience diminishes dispositionism in social inference. *Personality and Social Psychology Bulletin, 34*, 102–144.

Baldwin, M. W., Carrell, S. E., & Lopez, D. F. (1990). Priming relationship schemas: My advisor and the Pope are watching me from the back of my mind. *Journal of Experimental Social Psychology, 26*, 435–454.

Ball, J. D., Archer, R. P., & Imhoff, E. A. (1994). Time requirements of psychological testing: A survey of practitioners. *Journal of Personality Assessment, 63*, 239–249.

Baltes, P. B., Staudinger, U. M., & Lindenberger, U. (1999). Lifespan psychology: Theory and application to intellectual functioning. *Annual Review of Psychology, 50*, 471–507.

Banaji, M. R. (2001). Implicit attitudes can be measured. In H. D. Roediger III, J. S. Naime, I. Neath, & A. Surprenant (eds.), *The nature of remembering: Essays in honor of Robert G. Crowder* (pp. 117–150). Washington, DC: American Psychological Association.

Bancaud, J., Brunet-Bourgin, F., Chauvel, P., & Halgren, E. (1994). Anatomical origin of déjà vu and vivid "memories" in human temporal lobe epilepsy. *Brain, 117*, 71–90.

Bancroft, J. (2005). The endocrinology of sexual arousal. *Journal of Endocrinology, 186*, 411–427.

Bandura, A. (1965). Vicarious processes: A case of no-trial learning. In L. Berkowitz (ed.), *Advances in experimental social psychology* (Vol. 2, pp. 3–55). New York: Academic Press.

Bandura, A. (1971). *Psychological modeling.* Chicago: Aldine/Atherton.

Bandura, A. (1973). *Aggression: A social learning analysis.* Oxford, England: Prentice-Hall.

Bandura, A. (1977). Self-efficacy: Toward a unifying theory of behavioral change. *Psychological Review, 84*, 191–215.

Bandura, A. (1986). *Social foundations of thought and action: A social-cognitive theory.* Englewood, Cliffs, NJ: Prentice Hall.

Bandura, A., Ross, D., & Ross, S. A. (1961). Transmission of aggression through imitation of aggressive models. *Journal of Abnormal and Social Psychology, 63*, 575–582.

Bandura, A., Ross, D., & Ross, S. A. (1963). Imitation of film mediated aggressive models. *Journal of Abnormal and Social Psychology, 66*, 3–11.

Banks, W. (ed.) (2009). *Encyclopedia of consciousness.* New York: Academic Press.

Bányai, É. I., & Hilgard, E. R. (1976). A comparison of active-alert hypnotic induction with traditional relaxation induction. *Journal of Abnormal Psychology, 85*, 218–224.

Bar-Eli, M., Avugos, S., & Raab, M. (2006). Twenty years of "hot hand" research: Review and critique. *Psychology of Sport and Exercise, 7*, 525–553.

Bar-On, R. (2004). The Bar-On Emotional Quotient Inventory (EQ-i): Rationale, description, and psychometric properties. In G. Geher (ed.), *Measuring emotional intelligence: Common ground and controversy* (pp. 115-145). Hauppauge, NY: Nova Science.

Baral, B. D., & Das, J. P. (2003). Intelligence: What is indigenous to India and what is shared? In R. J. Sternberg (ed.), *International handbook of intelligence* (pp. 270–301). Cambridge, England: Cambridge University Press.

Barber, C. (2008). The medicated Americans: Antidepressant prescriptions on the rise. *Scientific American Mind, 19*, 41–51.

Barber, T. X. (1969). *Hypnosis: A scientific approach.* New York: Van Nostrand Reinhold.

Barbour, K. A., Houle, T. T., & Dubbert, P. M. (2003). Physical inactivity as a risk factor for chronic disease. In L. M. Cohen, D. E. McCargie, & F. L. Collins (eds.), *The health psychology handbook* (pp. 146–168). Thousand Oaks, CA: Sage.

Barchas, P. (1986). A sociophysiological orientation to small groups. In E. Lawler (ed.), *Advances in group processes* (Vol. 3, pp. 209–246). Greenwich, CT: JAI Press.

Bard, P. (1942). Neural mechanisms in emotional and sexual behavior. *Psychosomatic Medicine, 4*, 171–172.

Barefoot, J. C., Dahlstrom, W. G., & Williams, R. B. (1983). Hostility, CHD incidence, and total mortality. A 25-year follow-up study of 255 physicians. *Psychosomatic Medicine, 45,* 559–563.

Bargh, J. A. (1994). The four horsemen of automaticity: Awareness, efficiency, intention, and control in social cognition. In R. S. Wyer Jr. & T. K. Srull (eds.), *Handbook of social cognition* (2nd ed., pp. 1–40). Hillsdale, NJ: Erlbaum.

Bargh, J. A., & Chartrand, T. L. (1999). The unbearable automaticity of being. *American Psychologist, 54*, 462–479.

Bargh, J. A., & Ferguson, M. L. (2000). Beyond behaviorism: On the automaticity of higher mental processes. *Psychological Bulletin, 126*, 925–945.

Bargh, J. A., & Pietromonaco, P. (1982). Automatic information processing and social perception: The influence of trait information presented outside of conscious awareness on impression formation. *Journal of Personality and Social Psychology, 43*, 437–449.

Barkley, R. A. (1997). *ADHD and the nature of self-control.* New York: Guilford Press.

Barkley, R. A. (2006). *Attention-deficit-hyperactivity disorder: A handbook for diagnosis and treatment.* New York: Guilford Press.

Barkow, J. H., Cosmides, L., & Tooby, J. (1992). *The adapted mind: Evolutionary psychology and the generation of culture.* New York: Oxford University Press.

Barlow, D. H. (2000). Unraveling the mysteries of anxiety and its disorders from the perspective of emotion theory. *American Psychologist, 55*, 1247–1263.

Barlow, D. H. (2002). *Anxiety and its disorders: The nature and treatment of anxiety and panic.* New York: Guilford.

Barlow, D. H. (2010). Negative effects from psychological treatment: A perspective. *American Psychologist, 65,* 13–20.

Barlow, D. H., Chorpita, B. F., & Turovsky, J. (1996). Fear, panic, anxiety, and disorders of emotion. In D. A. Hope (ed.), *Perspectives on anxiety, panic, and fear* (The 43rd Annual Nebraska Symposium on Motivation) (pp. 251–328). Lincoln: University of Nebraska Press.

Barlow, D. M., Sakheim, D. K. and Beck, J. G. (1983). Anxiety increases sexual arousal. *Journal of Abnormal Psychology, 92,* 49–54.

Barnes, P. M., Bloom, B., & Nahin, R. (2008). CDC National Health Statistics Report #12. *Complementary and alternative medicine use among adults and children: United States, 2007.* Available at nccam.nih.gov/news/camstats.htm.

Barnes, P. M., Powell-Griner, E., McFann, K., & Nahin, R. L. (2004). *Complementary and alternative medicine use among adults: United States, 2002.* CDC Advance Data Report #343.

Barnett, R. C., & Rivers, C. (2004, October 13). The persistence of gender myths in math. *Education Week, 24*(7), 39.

Baron, J. N., & Reiss, P. C. (1985) Same time, next year - Aggregate analyses of the mass-media and violent behavior. *American Sociological Review, 50*, 347-363.

Baron-Cohen, S., Harrison, J., Goldstein, L. H., & Wyke, M. (1993). Coloured speech-perception: Is synaesthesia what happens when modularity breaks down? *Perception, 22*, 419–426.

Barratt, D. (1996). *Trauma and dreams.* Cambridge, MA: Harvard University Press.

Barrick, M. R., & Mount, M. K. (1991). The Big Five personality dimensions and job performance: A meta-analysis. *Personnel Psychology, 44*, 1–26.

Barron, F. (1969). *Creative person and creative process.* New York: Holt, Rinehart and Winston.

Barry, C. T., Frick, P. J., & Killian, A. L. (2003). The relation of narcissism and self-esteem to conduct problems in children. *Journal of Clinical Child and Adolescent Psychology, 32,* 139–152.

Barsalou, L. W. (2008). Cognitive and neural contributions to understanding the conceptual system. *Current Directions in Psychological Science, 17,* 91–95.

Barta, P. E., Pearlson, G. D., Powers, R. E., Richards, S. S., & Tune, L. E. (1990). Auditory hallucinations and smaller superior temporal gyral volume in schizophrenia. *American Journal of Psychiatry, 147*, 1457–1462.

Bartels, A., & Zeki, S. (2006). The temporal order of binding visual attributes. *Vision Research, 46*, 2280–2286.

Bartlett, D., & Steele, J. L. (2004*). Howard Hughes: His life and madness.* London: Andre Deutsch.

Bartholomew, R. E. (1994). The social psychology of "epidemic" koro. *International Journal of Social Psychiatry, 40*, 46–60.

Bartholomew, R. E. (1998). The Martian panic sixty years later: What have we learned? *Skeptical Inquirer, 22*(6), 40–43.

Bartholomew, R. E., & Goode, E. (2000). Mass delusions and hysterias: Highlights from the past millennium. *Skeptical Inquirer, 24*, 20–28.

Bartoshuk, L. M. (2004). Psychophysics: A journey from the laboratory to the clinic. *Appetite, 43,* 15–18.

Bartley, J. (2009). Could glial activation be a factor in migraine? *Medical Hypotheses, 72*, 255–257.

Bartoli, E., & Gillem, A. R. (2008). Continuing to depolarize the debate on sexual orientation and religious identity and the therapeutic process. *Professional Psychology: Research and Practice, 39*, 202–209.

Bartone, P. T. (1999). Hardiness protects against war-related stress in army reserve forces. *Consulting Psychology Journal, 51*, 72–82.

Bartz, W. R. (2002, September/October). Teaching skepticism via the CRITIC acronym and the *Skeptical Inquirer. Skeptical Inquirer, 17*, 42–44.

Bashore, T. T., & Rapp, P. E. (1993). Are there alternatives to traditional polygraph procedures? *Psychological Bulletin, 113*, 2–22.

Basil, J. A., Kamil, A. C., Balda, R., & Fite, K. V. (1996). Differences in hippocampal volume among food storing corvids. *Brain Behavior and Evolution, 47,* 156–154.

Batson, C. D. (1987). Prosocial motivation: Is it ever truly altruistic? In L. Berkowitz (ed.), *Advances in experimental social psychology* (Vol. 20, pp. 65–122). New York: Academic Press.

Batson, C. D., Batson, J., Singlsby, J., Harrell, K., Peekna, H., & Todd, R. (1991). Empathic joy and the empathy-altruism hypothesis. *Journal of Personality and Social Psychology, 61*, 413–426.

Batson, C. D., Duncan, B. D., Ackerman, P., Buckley, T., & Birch, K. (1981). Is empathic emotion a source of altruistic motivation? *Journal of Personality and Social Psychology, 40*, 290–302.

Batson, C. D., & Shaw, L. (1991). Evidence for altruism: Toward a pluralism of prosocial motives. *Psychological Inquiry, 2*, 107–122.

Batson, C. D., & Ventis, W. L. (1982). *The religious experience: A social psychological perspective.* New York: Oxford University Press.

Bauer, H. (1992). *Scientific literacy and the myth of the scientific method.* Urbana, IL: University of Illinois Press.

Bauer, P. J. (2006). Constructing a past in infancy: A neuro-developmental account. *Trends in Cognitive Sciences, 10,* 175–181.

Baugh, J. (2000). *Beyond Ebonics: Linguistic pride and racial prejudice.* New York: Oxford University Press.

Baum, A., Cohen, L., & Hall, M. (1993). Control and intrusive memories as possible determinants of chronic stress. *Psychosomatic Medicine, 55,* 274–286.

Baum, H. S. (1987). *The invisible bureaucracy.* Oxford, England: Oxford University Press.

Baumeister R. F. (2008). Free will in scientific psychology. *Perspectives on Psychological Science, 3,* 14–19.

Baumeister, R. F., Catanese, K. R., & Vohs, K. D. (2001). Is there a gender difference in strength of sex drive? Theoretical views, conceptual distinctions, and a review of relevant evidence. *Personality and Social Psychology Review, 5,* 242–273.

Baumeister, R. F., Campbell, J. D., Krueger, J. I., & Vohs, K. D. (2003). Does high self-esteem cause better performance, interpersonal success, happiness, or healthier lifestyles? *Psychological Science in the Public Interest, 4,* 1–44.

Baumeister, R. F., & Leary, M. R. (1995). The need to belong: Desire for interpersonal attachments as a fundamental human motivation. *Psychological Bulletin, 117,* 497–529.

Baumeister, R. F., Twenge, J. M., & Nuss, C. (2002). Effects of social exclusion on cognitive processes: Anticipated aloneness reduces intelligent thought. *Journal of Personality and Social Psychology, 83,* 817–827.

Baumrind, D. (1964). Some thoughts on ethics of research: After reading Milgram's "Behavioral study of obedience." *American Psychologist, 19,* 421–423.

Baumrind, D. (1971). Current patterns of parental authority. *Developmental Psychology Monographs, 4* (Pts. 1 & 2).

Baumrind, D. (1991). The influence of parenting style on adolescent competence and substance use. *Journal of Early Adolescence, 11,* 56–95.

Baumrind, D., Larzelere, R. E., & Cowan, P. A. (2002) Ordinary physical punishment: Is it harmful? Comment on Gershoff (2002). *Psychological Bulletin, 128,* 580–589.

Bausell, R. B. (2007). *The truth about complementary and alternative medicine.* Oxford: Oxford University Press.

Baxendale, S. (2004). Memories aren't made of this: Amnesia at the movies. *British Medical Journal, 18,* 1480–1483.

Baxter, L. R., Schwartz, J. M., Bergman, K. S., Szuba, M. P., Guze, B. H., Mazziotta, J. C. et al. (1992). Caudate glucose metabolic rate changes with both drug and behavior therapy for obsessive-compulsive disorder. *Archives of General Psychiatry, 49,* 681–689.

Bayer, R. (1981). *Homosexuality and American psychiatry: The politics of diagnosis.* Princeton, NJ: Princeton University Press.

Bayer, R., & Spitzer, R. L. (1985). Neurosis, psychodynamics, and DSM-III: A history of the controversy. *Archives of General Psychiatry, 42,* 187–196.

Bayard, M, Mcintyre, J., Hill, K. R., & Woodside, J. (2004). Alcohol withdrawal syndrome. *American Family Physician, 69,* 1442–1450.

Beaman, A., Barnes, P., Klentz, B., & McQuirk, B. (1978). Increasing helping rates through information dissemination: Teaching pays. *Personality and Social Psychology Bulletin, 4,* 406–411.

Beaman, C. P., Bridges, A. M., & Scott, S. K. (2007). From dichotic listening to the irrelevant sound effect: A behavioural and neuroimaging analysis of the processing of unattended speech. *Cortex, 43,* 124–134.

Beatty, J. (1982). Task-evoked pupillary responses, processing load, and the structure of processing resources. *Psychological Bulletin, 91,* 276–292.

Beauregard, M., & Paquette, V. (2006). Neural correlates of a mystical experience in Carmelite nuns. *Neuroscience Letters, 405,* 186–190.

Bechtoldt, H., Norcross, J. C., Wyckoff, L. A., Pokrywa, M. L., & Campbell, L. F. (2001). Theoretical orientations and employment settings of clinical and counseling psychologists: A comparative study. *The Clinical Psychologist, 54,* 3–6.

Beck, A. T., (1964). Thinking and depression: 2. Theory and therapy. *Archives of General Psychiatry, 10,* 561–571.

Beck, A. T. (1976). *Depression: Clinical, experimental, and theoretical aspects.* New York: Harper & Row.

Beck, A. T. (1976). *Cognitive therapy and the emotional disorders.* New York: International Universities Press.

Beck, A. T. (1983). Treatment of depression. *New York Times Book Review, 88*(10), 35.

Beck, A. T. (1987) Cognitive models of depression. *Journal of Cognitive Psychotherapy, 1,* 5–37.

Beck, A. T. (2005). The current state of cognitive therapy: A 40-year retrospective. *Archives of General Psychiatry, 62,* 953–959.

Beck, A. T., Brown, G., Berchick, R. J., Stewart, B. L., & Steer, R. A. (1990). Relationship between hopelessness and ultimate suicide: A replication with psychiatric outpatients. *American Journal of Psychiatry, 147,* 190–195.

Beck, A. T., Rush, A. J., Shaw, B. F., & Emery, G. (1979). *Cognitive therapy of depression.* New York: Guilford Press.

Beck, C. T., & Gable, R. K. (2001). Comparative analysis of the performance of the Postpartum Depression Screening Scale with two other depression instruments. *Nursing Research, 50,* 242–250.

Beck, H. P., Levinson, S., & Irons, G. (2009). A journey to John B. Watson's infant laboratory. American Psychologist, 64, 605–614.

Beck, J. G., Gudmundsdottir, B. Palyo, S. A., Miller, L. M., & Grant, D. M. (2006). Rebound effects following deliberate thought suppression: Does PTSD make a difference? *Behavior Therapy, 37,* 170–180.

Beck, J. S. (1995). *Cognitive therapy: Basics and beyond.* New York: Guilford Press.

Becker, A. E., Burwell, R. A., Gilman, S. E., Herzog, D. B., & Hamburg, P. (2002). Eating behaviors and attitudes following prolonged television exposure among ethnic Fijian adolescent girls. *British Journal of Psychiatry, 180,* 509–514.

Becker, S. W., & Eagly, A. H. (2004). The heroism of women and men. *American Psychologist, 59,* 163–178.

Begley, S., & Kasindorf, M. (1979, December 3). Twins: Nazi and Jew. *Newsweek,* 139.

Bègue, L., & Subra, B. (2008). Alcohol and aggression: Perspectives on controlled and uncontrolled social information processing. *Social and Personality Psychology Compass, 2,* 511–538.

Beidel, D. C., & Turner, S. M. (1986). A critique of the theoretical bases of cognitive–behavioral theories and therapy. *Clinical Psychology Review, 6,* 177–197.

Beier, M. E., & Ackerman, P. L. (2001). Current events knowledge in adults: An investigation of age, intelligence and non-ability determinants. *Psychology and Aging, 16,* 615–628.

Beilock, S. L. (2008). Math performance in stressful situations. *Current Directions in Psychological Science, 17,* 339–343.

Beilock, S. L., & Carr, T. H. (2005). When high-powered people fail: Working memory and "choking under pressure" in math. *Psychological Science, 16,* 101–105.

Békésy, G. (1949). On the resonance curve and the decay period at different points along the cochlear partition. *Journal of the Acoustical Society of America, 21,* 245–254.

Bekinschtein, T. A., Shalom, D.E., Forcato, C., Herrera, M., Coleman, M. R., Manes, F. F., et al., (2009). Classical conditioning in the vegetative and minimally conscious state. *Nature Neuroscience, 12,* 1343–1349.

Bell, A., P., & Weinberg, M. S. (1978). *Homosexualities: A study of diversity among men and women.* New York: Simon & Schuster.

Bell, A. P., Weinberg, M. S., & Hammersmith, S. K. (1981). *Sexual preference: Its development in men and women.* Bloomington, IN: Indiana University Press.

Bell, R. (1968). A reinterpretation of the direction of effects in studies of socialization. *Psychological Review, 75,* 81–95.

Bellamy, C. (1998). *The state of the world's children 1998.* New York: Oxford University Press.

Bellezza, F. S. (1999). Mnemonic devices. In A. E. Kazdin (ed.), *Encyclopedia of psychology.* Washington, DC: American Psychological Association.

Belli, R. F., Winkielman, P., Read, J. D., Schwarz, N., & Lynn, S. J. (1998). Recalling more childhood events leads to judgments of poorer memory: Implications for the recovered/false memory debate. *Psychonomic Bulletin & Review, 5,* 318–323.

Bellinger, D. C., & Needleman, H. L. (2003). Intellectual impairment and blood lead levels. *New England Journal of Medicine, 349,* 500–502.

Belliveau, F., & Richter, L. (1970). *Understanding human sexual inadequacy.* New York: Bantam Books.

Bellon, A. (2006). Searching for new options for treating insomnia: Are melatonin and ramelteon beneficial? *Journal of Psychiatric Practice, 12,* 229–243.

Belsky, J. (1988). The "effects" of infant day care reconsidered. *Early Childhood Research Quarterly, 3,* 235–272.

Belsky, J., & Kelly, J. (1994). *The transition to parenthood.* New York: Delacourte.

Bem, D. J. (1967). Self-perception: An alternative interpretation of cognitive dissonance phenomena. *Psychological Review, 74,* 183–200.

Bem, D. J. (1996). Exotic becomes erotic: A developmental theory of sexual orientation. *Psychological Review, 103,* 320–335.

Bem, D. J. (2000). Exotic becomes erotic: Interpreting the biological correlates of sexual orientation. *Archives of Sexual Behavior, 29,* 531–548.

Bem, D. J., & Allen, A. (1974). On predicting some of the people some of the time: The search for cross-situational consistencies in behavior. *Psychological Review, 81,* 506–520.

Bem, D. J., & Funder, D. C. (1978). Predicting more of the people more of the time: Assessing the personality of situations. *Psychological Review, 85,* 485–500.

Bem, D. J., & Honorton, C. (1994). Does psi exist? Replicable evidence for an anomalous process of information transfer. *Psychological Bulletin, 115,* 4–18.

Bem, D. J., & McConnell, H. K. (1970). Testing the self-perception explanation of dissonance phenomena: On the salience of premanipulation attitudes. *Journal of Personality and Social Psychology, 14,* 23–31.

Ben-Shakhar, G., & Elaad, E. (2003). The validity of psychophysiological detection of information with the Guilty Knowledge Test: A meta-analytic review. *Journal of Applied Psychology, 88,* 131–151.

Ben-Shakhar, G., Bar-Hillel, M., Bilu, Y., Ben-Abba, E., & Flug, A. (1986). Can graphology predict occupational success? Two empirical studies and some methodological ruminations. *Journal of Applied Psychology, 71,* 645–653.

Benasich, A. A., & Bejar, I. I. (1992). The Fagan Test of Infant Intelligence: A critical review. *Journal of Applied Developmental Psychology, 13,* 153–171.

Benassi, V. A., Sweeney, P. D., & Dufour, C. L. (1988). Is there a relation between locus of control orientation and depression? *Journal of Abnormal Psychology, 8,* 357–367.

Benbow, C. P., & Stanley, J. C. (1980). Sex differences in mathematical ability: Fact or artifact? *Science, 210,* 1262–1264.

Bender, D. A. (2008). What we don't know that we need to know. *Healthwatch. Newsletter, 71,* 4-5.

Benedetti, F., Lanotte, M., Lopiano, L., & Colloca, L. (2007). When words are painful: Unraveling the mechanisms of the nocebo effect. *Neuroscience, 147,* 260–271.

Benjamin, L. T., & Baker, D. B. (2004). From séance to science: A history of the profession of psychology in America. Belmont, CA: Wadsworth.

Bennett, C. M., Baird, A. A., Miller, M. B., & Wolford, G. L. (2009, June). *Neural correlates of interspecies perspective taking in the post-mortem Atlantic Salmon: An argument for multiple comparisons correction.* Poster presented at the 15th Annual Meeting of the Organization for Human Brain Mapping, San Francisco, CA.

Bennett, M. R. (1998). Monoaminergic synapses and schizophrenia: 45 years of neuroleptics. *Journal of Psychopharmacology, 12,* 289–304.

Benson, E. (2006, June). All that's gold doesn't glitter: How the Golden Fleece tarnished psychological science. *APS Observer.* Retrieved from www.psychologicalscience.org/observer/getArticle.cfm?id=1998.

Bent, S. (2008). Herbal medicine in the United States: review of efficacy, safety, and regulation: Grand rounds at University of California, San Francisco Medical Center. *Journal of General Internal Medicine, 23,* 854–859.

Bentall, R. P. (1990). The illusion of reality: A review and integration of psychological research on hallucinations. *Psychological Bulletin, 107,* 82–95.

Bentall, R. P. (2000). Hallucinatory experiences. In E. Cardeña, S. J. Lynn, & S. Krippner (eds.), *Varieties of anomalous experience: Examining the scientific evidence* (pp. 85–120). Washington, DC: American Psychological Association.

Bentley, K. J., & Walsh, J. (2006). *The social worker and psychotropic medication: Toward effective collaboration with mental health clients, families, and providers* (3rd ed.). Belmont, CA: Thompson.

Berenbaum, S. A., & Hines, M. (1992). Early androgens are related to childhood sex-typed toy preference. *Psychological Science, 3,* 203–206.

Berg, J. H., & Archer, R. L. (1980). Disclosure or concern: A second look at liking for the norm breaker. *Journal of Personality, 48,* 245–257.

Berger, H. (1929). Ueber das Elektroenkephalogramm des Menschen. *Archiv für Psychiatrie und Nervenkrankheiten, 87,* 527–570.

Bergner, R. M. (1997). What is psychopathology? And so what? *Clinical Psychology: Science and Practice, 4,* 235–248.

Bergstrom, S. R. (1968). Acquisition of an avoidance reaction to the light in the protozoa tetrahymena. *Scandinavian Journal of Psychology, 9,* 220–224.

Berk, A. M., Vigorito, M., & Miller, R. R. (1979). Retroactive stimulus interference with conditioned emotional response retention in infant and adult rats: Implications for infantile amnesia. *Journal of Experimental Psychology: Animal Behavior Processes, 3,* 284–299.

Berk, M. S., & Andersen, S. M. (2000). The impact of past relationships on interpersonal behavior: Behavioral confirmation in the social-cognitive process of transference. *Journal of Personality and Social Psychology, 79,* 546–562.

Berkman, L. F., & Syme, S. L. (1979). Social networks, host resistance, and mortality: A nine year follow-up study of Alameda County residents. *American Journal of Epidemiology, 109,* 186–204.

Berkowitz, L. (1989). Frustration-aggression hypothesis: Examination and reformulation. *Psychological Bulletin, 106,* 59–73.

Berkowitz, L., & LePage, A. (1967). Weapons as aggression-eliciting stimuli. *Journal of Personality and Social Psychology, 7,* 202–207.

Berlant, N. E., & Pruitt, S. D. (2003). Adherence to medical recommendations. In L. M. Cohen, D. E. McChargue, & F. L. Collins (eds.), *The health psychology handbook* (pp. 208–224). Thousand Oaks, CA: Sage Publications.

Berlin, L. J., Ispa, J. M., Fine, M. A., Malone, P. S., Brooks-Gunn, J., Brady-Smith, C., et al. (2009). Correlates and consequences of spanking and verbal punishment for low-income White, African American, and Mexican American toddlers. *Child Development, 80,* 1403–1420.

Berlyne, D. E. (1960). *Conflict, arousal, and curiosity.* New York: McGraw-Hill.

Berman, J. D., & Straus, S. E. (2004). Implementing a research agenda for complementary and alternative medicine. *Annual Review of Medicine, 55,* 239–254.

Berman, J. S., & Norton, N. C. (1985). Does professional training make a therapist more effective? *Psychological Bulletin, 98,* 401–406.

Bernhardt, P. C., Dabbs, J. M., Fielden, J. A., & Lutter, C. D. (1998). Testosterone changes during vicarious experiences of winning and losing among fans at sporting events. *Physiology and Behavior, 65,* 59–62.

Bernheim, K. F., & Lewine, R. R. (1979). *Schizophrenia: symptoms, treatment, causes.* New York: Norton.

Berns, G. S., Chappelow, J., Zink, C. F., Pagnoni, G., Martin-Skurski, M. E., & Richards, J. (2005). Neurobiological correlates of social conformity and independence during mental rotation. *Biological Psychiatry, 58,* 245–253.

Bernstein, D. A., Borkovec, T. D., & Hazlett-Stevens, H. (2000). *New directions in progressive relaxation training: A guidebook for helping professionals.* Westport, CT: Praeger.

Bernstein, D. M., Laney, C., Morris, E. K., & Loftus, E. F. (2005). False memories about food can lead to food avoidance. *Social Cognition, 23,* 11–34.

Berry, C. M., Sackett, P. R., and Wiemann, S. A. (2007). A review of recent developments in integrity test research. *Personnel Psychology, 60,* 270–301.

Berscheid, E., & Reis, H. T. (1998). Attraction and close relationships. In D. Gilbert, S. Fiske, & G. Lindzey (eds.), *The handbook of social psychology* (Vol. 2, 4th ed., pp. 193–281). New York: McGraw-Hill.

Beunen, G., & Malina, R. M. (1996). *The child and adolescent athlete.* Oxford, England: Blackwell.

Beutler, L. E. (2002). The dodo bird is extinct. *Clinical Psychology: Science and Practice, 9,* 30–34.

Beutler, L. E., Clarkin, J. F., & Bongar, B. (2000). *Guidelines for the systematic treatment of the depressed person.* Oxford, England: Oxford University Press.

Beutler, L. E., & Harwood, T. M. (2002). What is and can be attributed to the therapeutic relationship. *Journal of Contemporary Psychotherapy, 32,* 25–33.

Beutler, L. E., Machado, P. P., & Neufeldt, S. A. (1994). Therapist variables. In A. E. Bergin & S. L. Garfield (eds.), *Handbook of psychotherapy and behavior change* (4th ed., pp. 259–260). New York: John Wiley & Sons.

Beyerstein, B. (1996). Graphology. In G. Stein (ed.), *The encyclopedia of the paranormal* (pp. 309–324). Buffalo, NY: Prometheus Books.

Beyerstein, B. L. (1997, September/October). Why bogus therapies seem to work. *Skeptical Inquirer, 21,* 29–34.

Beyerstein, B. L. (1999). Whence cometh the myth that we only use ten percent of our brains? In S. Della Sala (ed.), *Mind myths: Exploring everyday mysteries of the mind and brain* (pp. 1–24). Chichester, England: John Wiley and Sons.

Beyerstein, B. L., & Beyerstein, D. F. (1992). *The write stuff: Evaluations of graphology—The study of handwriting analysis.* Buffalo, NY: Prometheus.

Beyerstein, B., & Hadaway, P. (1991). On avoiding folly. *Journal of Drug Issues, 20,* 689–700.

Bialystok, E. (1988). Levels of bilingualism and levels of linguistic awareness. *Developmental Psychology, 24,* 560–567.

Biasi, E., Silvotti, L., & Tirindelli, R. (2001). Pheromone detection in rodents. *Neuroreport, 12,* A81–A84.

Biederman, I., Cooper, E. E., Fox, P. W., & Mahadevan, R. S. (1992). Unexceptional spatial memory in an exceptional memorist. *Journal of Experimental Psychology: Learning, Memory, and Cognition, 18,* 654–657.

Biederman, J., Hirshfeld-Becker, D. R., Rosenbaum, J. F., Herot, C., Friedman, D., Snidman, N., et al. (2001). Further evidence of association between behavioral inhibition and social anxiety in children. *American Journal of Psychiatry, 158,* 1673–1679.

Bierbrauer, G. (1973). *Effect of set, perspective, and temporal factors in attribution.* Unpublished doctoral dissertation, Stanford University, Palo Alto, CA.

Bierman, K. L., Domitrovich, C. E., Nix, R., Gest, S. D., Welsh, J. A., Greenberg, M. T., et al. (2008). Promoting academic and social-emotional school readiness: The Head Start REDI program. *Child Development, 79,* 1802–1807.

Biernbaum, M. A., & Ruscio, M. (2004). Differences between matched heterosexual and non-heterosexual college students on measures of defense mechanisms and psychopathological symptoms. *Journal of Homosexuality, 48,* 125–141.

Bigbee, J. (1990). Stressful life events and illness occurrence in rural versus urban women. *Journal of Community Health Nursing, 7,* 105–113.

Bikel, O. (Producer). (1995, April 11). *Frontline* [Television broadcast: "Divided Memories"]. New York: Public Broadcasting Service.

Biklen, D. (1990). Communication unbound: Autism and praxis. *Harvard Educational Review, 60,* 291–314.

Binet, A., & Simon, T. A. (1905). Méthode nouvelle pour le diagnostic du niveau intellectuel des anormaux. *L'Année Psychologique, 11,* 191–244.

Bink, M. L., & Marsh, R. L. (2000). Cognitive regularities in creative activity. *Review of General Psychology, 4,* 59–78.

Birbaumer, N., Gruzelier, J., Jamieson, G. A., Kotchoubey, B., Kubler, A., Lehmann, D., et al. (2005). Psychobiology of altered states of consciousness. *Psychological Bulletin, 131,* 98–127.

Birch, S. A. J., & Bloom, P. (2003). Children are cursed: An asymmetric bias in mental state attribution. *Psychological Science, 14,* 283–286.

Birch, S. A. J., & Bloom, P. (2007). The curse of knowledge in reasoning about false beliefs. *Psychological Science, 18,* 382–386.

Bird, H. R. (2002), The diagnostic classification, epidemiology, and cross-cultural validity of ADHD. In P. S. Jensen & J. R. Cooper (eds.) *Attention Deficit Hyperactivity Disorder: State of the science, best practices* (pp. 212–216). Kingston, NJ: Civil Research Institute.

Birmingham, C. L., Su, J., Hlynsky, J. A., Goldner, E. M., & Gao, M. (2005). The mortality rate from anorexia nervosa. *International Journal of Eating Disorders, 38,* 143–146.

Birnbaum, G., Glaubman, H., & Mikulincer, M. (2001). Women's experience of heterosexual intercourse—Scale construction, factor structure, and relations to orgasmic disorder. *Journal of Sex Research, 38,* 191–204.

Birren, J. E., & Renner, V. J. (1977). Research on the psychology of aging: Principles and experimentation. In J. E. Birren & K. W. Schaie (eds.), *Handbook of the psychology of aging* (pp. 3–38). New York: Van Nostrand Reinhold.

Bishop, D. V. M., & Bishop, S. J. (1998). "Twin language": A risk factor for language impairment? *Journal of Speech, Language & Hearing Research, 41,* 150–160.

Bishop, G. F., Oldendick, R. W., & Tuchfarber, A. J. (1986). Opinions on fictitious issues: The pressure to answer survey questions. *Public Opinion Quarterly, 50,* 240–250.

Bjelakovic, G., Nikolova, D., Gluud, L. L., Simonetti, R. G., & Gluud, C. (2007). Mortality in randomized trials of antioxidant supplements for primary and secondary prevention: Systematic review and meta-analysis. *Journal of the American Medical Association, 297,* 842–847.

Black, S. M., & Hill, C. E. (1984). The psychological well-being of women in their middle years. *Psychology of Women Quarterly, 8,* 282–292.

Blackmore, S (1984). Accounting for out-of-body experiences. *Bulletin of the British Psychological Society, 37,* A53.

Blackmore, S. (1986). Out-of-body experiences in schizophrenia: A questionnaire surevey. *Journal of Nervous and Mental Disease, 174,* 615–619.

Blackmore, S. (1991). Lucid dreaming: Awake in your sleep? *Skeptical Inquirer, 15,* 362–370.

Blackmore, S. (1993). *Dying to live: Near-death experiences.* Buffalo, NY: Prometheus.

Blackmore, S. (2004). *Consciousness: An introduction.* New York: Oxford University Press.

Blagys, M. D. & Hilsenroth, M. J. (2000). Distinctive features of short-term psychodynamic-interpersonal psychotherapy: A review of the comparative psychotherapy process literature. *Clinical Psychology-Science and Practice, 7,* 167–188.

Blair, C. (2006). How similar are fluid cognition and general intelligence? A developmental neuroscience perspective on fluid cognition as an aspect of human cognitive ability. *Behavioral and Brain Sciences, 29,* 109–160.

Blair, S. N., Kohl, H. W., Gordon, N. F., & Paffenberger, R. S. (1992). How much physical activity is good for health? *Annual Review of Public Health, 13,* 99–126.

Blanchard, R. (2008). Review and theory of handedness, birth order, and homosexuality in men. *Laterality: Asymmetries of Body, Brain, and Cognition, 13,* 51–70.

Blanchard, R., & Bogaert, A. F. (1996). Homosexuality in men and number of older brothers. *American Journal of Psychiatry, 153,* 27–31.

Blanchette, I., & Richards, A. (2003). Anxiety and the interpretation of ambiguous stimuli: Beyond the emotion-congruent effect. *Journal of Experimental Psychology: General, 13,* 294–309.

Blaney, P. H. (1975). Implications of the medical model and its alternatives. *American. Journal of Psychiatry. 132,* 911–914.

Blanke, O., & Dieguez, S. (2009). Leaving body and life behind: Out-of-body and near death experience. In S. Laureys (ed.), The neurology of consciousness (pp. 303–325). Amsterdam: Elsevier.

Blanton, H., Klick, J., Mitchell, G., Jaccard, J., Mellers, B., & Tetlock, P. E. (2009). Strong claims and weak evidence: Reassessing the predictive validity of the IAT. *Journal of Applied Psychology, 94*(3), 567–582.

Blanton, H., & Jaccard, J. (2008). Representing versus generalizing: Two approaches to external validity and their implications for the study of prejudice. *Psychological Inquiry, 19,* 99–105.

Blasi, A. (1980). Bridging moral cognition and moral action: A critical review of the literature. *Psychological Bulletin, 88,* 593–637.

Blass, T. (1999). The Milgram paradigm after 35 years. *Journal of Applied Social Psychology, 29,* 955–978.

Blass, T. (2004). *The man who shocked the world: The life and legacy of Stanley Milgram.* New York: Perseus.

Blatt, S. J. (1974). Levels of object representation in anaclitic and introjective depression. *Psychoanalytic Studies of the Child, 29,* 107–157.

Blatt, S. J., Sanislow, C. A., Zuroff, D. C., & Pilkonis, P. A. (1996). Characteristics of effective therapists: Further analyses of data from the NIMH. *TDCRP, Journal of Consulting and Clinical Psychology, 64,* 1276–1284.

Blay, S. L., Andreoli, S. B., & Gastal, F. L. (2008). Prevalence of self-reported sleep disturbance among older adults and the association of sleep with service demand and medical conditions. *International Psychogeriatrics, 20,* 582–595.

Bliss, T., Collingridge, G., & Morris, R. (2004). Long-term potentiation: Enhancing neuroscience for 30 years. Oxford, England: Oxford University Press.

Block, J. (1976). Issues, problems and pitfalls in assessing sex differences: A critical review of "The Psychology of Sex Differences." *Merrill Palmer Quarterly, 22,* 283–340.

Block, J. (1995). A contrarian view of the five-factor approach to personality description. *Psychological Bulletin, 117,* 187–215.

Block, J. (2006). In whom should Americans trust? Jeff Block's personal idea fountain. Retrieved June 10, 2008, from http://jeffblock.wordpress.com/category/military/.

Block, J., & Block, J. H. (2006). Venturing a 30-year longitudinal study. *American Psychologist, 61,* 315–327.

Block, J. H., Block, J., & Gjerde, P. F. (1986). The personality of children prior to divorce: A prospective study. *Child Development, 57,* 827–840.

Block, N. (1995). How heritability misleads about race. *Cognition, 56,* 99–128.

Blodgett, H. C. (1929). The effect of the introduction of reward upon the maze performance of rats. *University of California Publications in Psychology, 4,* 113–134.

Blood, A. J., & Zatorre, R. J. (2001). Intensely pleasurable responses to music correlate with activity in brain regions implicated in reward and emotion. *Proceedings of the National Academy of Sciences, U. S. A., 98,* 11818–11823.

Bloom, C., Venard, J., Harden, M., & Seetharaman, S. (2007). Non-contingent positive and negative reinforcement schedules of superstitious behaviors. *Behavioural Processes, 75,* 8–13.

Bloom, P. (2000). *How children learn the meanings of words.* Boston, MA: MIT Press.

Bloom, P. (2004). *Descartes' baby: How the science of child development explains what makes us human.* New York: Basic Books.

Bloom, P. & Weisberg, D. S. (2007, May 18). Childhood origins of adult resistance to science. *Science, 316,* 996–997.

Blow, A. J., Sprenkle, D. H., & Davis, S. D. (2007). Is who delivers the treatment more important than the treatment itself? The role of the therapist in common factors. *Journal of Marital and Family Therapy, 33,* 298–317.

Blum, D. (2002). *Love at Goon Park: Harry Harlow and the science of affection.* Cambridge, MA: Perseus Publishing.

Blum, D. (2006). *Ghost hunters: William James and the search for scientific proof of life after death.* New York: Penguin Press.

Boese, A. (2007, November 3). The whacko files. *New Scientist, 196,* 49–55.

Bogartz, R. S. (1965). The criterion method: Some analyses and remarks. *Psychological Bulletin, 64,* 1–14.

Bogg, T. & Roberts, B. W. (2004). Conscientiousness and health behaviors: A meta-analysis. *Psychological Bulletin, 130,* 887–919.

Bohart, A. C. (2003). Person-centered psychotherapy and related experiential approaches. In A. S. Gurman & S. B. Messer (eds.), *Essential psychotherapies: Theory and practice* (2nd ed., pp. 107–148). New York: Guilford Press.

Bohart, A., Elliott, R., Greenberg, L. S., & Watson, J. C. (2002). Empathy redux. In J. Norcross & M. Lambert (eds.), *Psychotherapy relationships that work* (pp. 89–109). Oxford, England: Oxford University Press.

Bolles, R. C. (1962). The difference between statistical hypotheses and scientific hypotheses. *Psychological Reports, 11,* 639–645.

Bolles, R. C. (1979). *Learning theory.* New York: Holt, Rinehart and Winston.

Bolwig, T. (2009). Electroconvulsive therapy: The role of hippocampal neurogenesis. *European Psychiatry, 24,* Supplement 1, S 75.

Bonanno, G. A. (2004). Loss, trauma, and human resilience: Have we underestimated the human capacity to thrive after extremely aversive events? *American Psychologist, 59,* 20–28.

Bonanno, G. A., Field, N. P., Kovacevic, A., & Kaltman, S. (2002). Self-enhancement as a buffer against extreme adversity: Civil war in Bosnia and traumatic loss in the United States. *Personality and Social Psychology Bulletin, 28,* 184–196.

Bonanno, G. A., Galea, S., Bucciarelli, A., & Vlahov, D. (2006). Psychological resilience after disaster: New York City in the aftermath of the September 11th terrorist attack. *Psychological Science, 17,* 181–186.

Bonanno, G. A., & Kaltman, S. (2001). The varieties of grief experience. *Clinical Psychology Review, 21,* 705–734.

Bonanno, G. A., Moskowitz, J. T., Papa, A., & Folkman, S. (2005). Resilience to loss in bereaved spouses, bereaved parents, and bereaved gay men. *Journal of Personality and Social Psychology, 88,* 827–843.

Bonanno, G. A., Papa, A., Lalande, K., Westphal, M., & Coifman, K. (2004). The importance of being flexible: The ability to enhance and suppress emotional expression predicts long-term adjustment. *Psychological Science, 157,* 482–487.

Bond, C. F. (2006). A world of lies. *Journal of Cross-Cultural Psychology, 30,* 60–74.

Bond, C. F., Pitre, U., & Van Leeuwen, M. D. (1991). Encoding operations and the next-in-line effect. *Personality and Social Psychology Bulletin, 17,* 435–441.

Bond, E. A. (1941). The Yale-Harvard freshman speed reading experiment. *School & Society, 54,* 107–111.

Bond, N. W., Siddle, D. A. T. (1996). The preparedness account of social phobia: some data and alternative explanations. In R. M. Rapee (ed.), *Current Controversies in the Anxiety Disorders* (pp. 291-316). Guilford Press, London.

Bond, R., & Smith, R. P. (1996). Culture and conformity: A meta-analysis of studies using Asch's line judgment task. *Psychological Bulletin, 119,* 111–137.

Bond, R., & Titus, L. J. (1983). Social facilitation: A meta-analysis of 241 studies. *Psychological Bulletin, 94,* 265–292.

Bonham, V. L. (2001). Race, ethnicity, and pain treatment: Striving to understand the causes and solutions to the disparities in pain treatment. *Journal of Law & Medical Ethics, 29,* 52–68.

Boniecki, K. A., & Moore, S. (2003). Breaking the silence: Using a token economy to reinforce classroom participation. *Teaching of Psychology, 30,* 224–227.

Boos, H. B. M., Aleman, A., Pol, H. H., Cahn, W., & Kahn, R. (2007). Brain volumes in relatives of patients with schizophrenia: A meta-analysis. *Schizophrenia Bulletin, 33,* 329.

Boring, E. G. (1923). Intelligence as the tests test it. *New Republic, 35,* 35–37.

Boring, E. G. (1930). A new ambiguous figure. *American Journal of Psychology, 42,* 444.

Borland, D. C. (1982). A cohort analysis approach to the empty nest syndrome among three ethnic groups of women: A theoretical position. *Journal of Marriage and the Family, 44,* 117–129.

Bornstein, R. F. (1989). Exposure and affect: Overview and meta-analysis of research, 1968–1987. *Psychological Bulletin, 106,* 265–289.

Bornstein, R. F. (2001). The impending death of psychoanalysis. *Psychoanalytic Psychology, 18,* 3–20.

Borrell, B. (2008). What is truth serum? *Scientific American.* http://www.scientificamerican.com/article.cfm?id=what-is-truth-serum.

Bos, H. M. W., van Balen, F., & van den Boom, D. C. (2007). Child adjustment and parenting in planned lesbian-parent families. *American Journal of Orthopsychiatry, 77,* 38–48.

Bosson, J. K., Johnson, A. B., Niederhoffer, K., & Swann, W. B., Jr. (2006). Interpersonal chemistry through negativity: Bonding by sharing negative attitudes about others. *Personal Relationships, 13,* 135–150.

Botella, C., Banos, R. M., Guerrero, B., Garcia-Palacio, A., Quero, S., & Alcaniz, M. (2006). Using a flexible virtual environment for treating a storm phobia. *PsychNology, 4,* 129–144.

Bothwell, R. K., Deffenbacher, K. A., & Brigham, J. C. (1987). Correlation of eyewitness accuracy and confidence: Optimality hypothesis revisited. *Journal of Applied Psychology, 72,* 691–695.

Bouchard, C. (1995). Genetics and the metabolic syndrome. *International Journal of Obesity, 19,* 552–559.

Bouchard, T. J., Jr. (2004). Genetic influence on human psychological traits. *Current Directions in Psychological Science, 4,* 148–151.

Bouchard, T. J., Lykken, D. T., McGue, M., Segal, N. L., & Tellegen, A. (1990, October 12). Sources of human psychological differences: The Minnesota study of twins reared apart. *Science, 250,* 223–228.

Bouchard, T. J., & McGue, M. (1981). Familial studies of intelligence: A review. *Science, 212,* 1055–1059.

Bourgon, L. N., & Kellner, C. H. (2000). Relapse of depression after ECT: A review. *Journal of ECT, 16,* 19-31.

Bourguignon, E. (1970). Hallucinations and trance: An anthropologist's perspective. In W. Keup (ed.), *Origins and mechanisms of hallucination* (pp. 183–190). New York: Plenum Press.

Bouton, M. E. (1994). Context, ambiguity, and classical conditioning. *Current Directions in Psychological Science, 3,* 1–5.

Bower, G. H. (1981). Mood and memory. *American Psychologist, 36,* 129–148.

Bowers, T., & Clum, G. A. (1988). Specific and nonspecific treatment effects in controlled psychotherapy research. *Psychological Bulletin, 103,* 315–323.

Bowlby, J. (1973). *Attachment and loss. Vol. 2: Separation: Anxiety & anger.* London: Hogarth.

Bowlby, J. (1990). The study and reduction of group tensions in the family. In E. Trist, H. Murray, & B. Trist (eds.), *The social engagement of social science: A Tavistock anthology, Vol. I: The socio-psychological perspective* (pp. 291–298). Philadelphia: University of Pennsylvania Press.

Bowman, D., Scogin, F., Floyd, M., & McKendree-Smith, N. (2001). Psychotherapy length of stay and outcome: A meta-analysis of the effect of therapist sex. *Psychotherapy, 38,* 142–150.

Boyce, C. J., Brown, G. D. A., & Moore, S. C. (in press). Money and happiness: Rank of income, not income, affects life satisfaction. *Psychological Science.*

Boyer, P. (2003). Religious thought and behavior as by-products of brain function. *Trends in Cognitive Sciences, 7,* 119–124.

Boyke, J., Driemeyer, J., Gaser, C., Büchel, C., & May, A. (2008). Training-induced brain structure changes in the elderly. *Journal of Neuroscience, 28,* 7031-7035.

Bradbard, M. R., Martin, C. L., Endsley, R. C., & Halverson, C. F. (1986). Influence of sex stereotypes on children's exploration and memory: A competence versus performance distinction. *Developmental Psychology, 22,* 481–486.

Bradbury, E. J., & McMahon, S. B. (2006). Spinal cord repair strategies: Why do they work? *Nature Reviews Neuroscience, 7,* 644–653.

Bradbury, J. (2005). Molecular insights into human brain evolution. *PLoS Biology 3,* 50.

Bradley, L., & Bryant, P. E. (1983). Categorizing sounds and learning to read: A causal connection. *Nature, 301,* 419–421.

Braffman, W., & Kirsch, I. (1999). Imaginative suggestibility and hypnotizability: An empirical analysis. *Journal of Personality and Social Psychology, 77,* 578–587.

Braid, J. (1843). *Neurypnology or the rationale of nervous sleep considered in relation with animal magnetism illustrated by numerous cases of its successful application in the relief and cure of disease.* London: John Churchill.

Brambilla, P., Cipriani, A., Hotopf, M., & Barbui, C. (2005). Side-effect profile of fluoxetine in comparison with other SSRIs, tricyclic, and newer antidepressants: A meta-analysis of clinical trial data. *Pharmacopsychiatry, 38,* 69–77.

Branden, N. (1994). *Six pillars of self-esteem.* New York: Bantam Books.

Bransford, J. D., & Johnson, M. K. (1972). Contextual prerequisites for understanding: Some investigations of comprehension and recall. *Journal of Verbal Learning and Verbal Behavior, 11,* 717–726.

Brandsma, J. M., Maultsby, M. C., & Welsh, R. J. (1980). Alcoholics Anonymous: An empirical outcome study. *Addictive Behaviors, 5,* 359–370.

Braun, K. A., Ellis, R., & Loftus, E. F. (2002). Make my memory. *Psychology and Marketing, 19,* 1–23.

Bray, D. (2009). *Wetware: A computer in every living cell.* New Haven, CT: Yale University Press.

Bray G. A. (1985). Complications of obesity. *Journal of the American Medical Association, 240,* 1607–1634.

Brehm, S. S., Miller, R. S., Perlman, D., & Campbell, S. M. (2002). *Intimate relationships* (3rd ed.). New York: McGraw-Hill.

Breland, K., & Breland, M. (1961). The misbehavior of organisms. *American Psychologist, 16*(11), 681–684.

Brende, J. O. (1984). The psychophysiologic manifestations of dissociation: Electrodermal responses in a multiple personality patient. *Psychiatry Clinics of North America, 7,* 41–50.

Brennan, P. A., & Mednick, S. A. (1994). Learning theory approach to the deterrence of criminal recidivism. *Journal of Abnormal Psychology, 103,* 430–440.

Brenner, C. (1973). *An elementary textbook of psychoanalysis.* New York: International Universities Press.

Breslau, N., Kilbey, K. M., & Andreski, P. (1993). Nicotine dependence and major depression. *Archives of General Psychiatry, 50,* 31–35.

Breuer, J., & Freud, S. (1895). *Studies on hysteria.* In J. Strachey et al. (trans. and ed.), *The standard edition of the complete psychological works of Sigmund Freud (1953–74)* (Vol. 2). London: Hogarth.

Brewer, C. (1992). Controlled trials of Antabuse in alcoholism: The importance of supervision and adequate dosage. *Acta Psychiatrica Scandinavica, 86,* 51–58.

Brewer, W. F. (1974). There is no convincing evidence for operant or classical conditioning in adult humans. In W. B. Weimer & D. S. Palemo (eds.), *Cognition and the symbolic processes* (pp. 1–42). Hillsdale, NJ: Erlbaum.

Brickman, P., & Campbell, D. T. (1971). Hedonic relativism and planning the good society. In M. H. Appley (ed.), *Adaptation level theory: A symposium* (pp. 287–305). New York: Academic Press.

Brickman, P., Coates, D., & Janoff-Bulman, R. (1978). Lottery winners and accident victims: Is happiness relative? *Journal of Personality and Social Psychology, 36,* 917–927.

Bridgestock, M. (2009). *Beyond belief: Skepticism, science and the paranormal.* Cambridge: Cambridge University Press.

Brinkhaus, B., Witt, C. M., Jena, S., Linde, K., Streng, A., Wagenpfeil, S., et al. (2006). Acupuncture in patients with chronic low back pain: A randomized controlled trial. *Archives of Internal Medicine, 166,* 450–457.

Brinkworth, G. D., Buckley, J. D., Noakes, M., Clifton, P. M., Wilson, C. J. (2009). Long-term effects of a very low carbohydrate diet and a low-fat diet on mood and cognitive function. *Archives of Internal Medicine, 169,* 1873–1880.

Broadbent, D. E. (1957). A mechanical model for human attention and immediate memory. *Psychological Review, 54,* 205–215.

Broca, P. P. (1861). Loss of speech, chronic softening and partial destruction of the anterior left lobe of the brain. *Bulletin de la Société Anthropologique, 2,* 235–238.

Brodsky, S. L., Hooper, N., Tipper, D., and Yates, B. (1999). Attorney invasion of witness space. *Law and Psychology Review, 23,* 49–69.

Brody, J. (2007, April 17). When a brain forgets where memory is. *New York Times.* Retrieved August 2, 2007, from www.nytimes.com/2007/04/17/health/psychology/17brody.html.

Brody, N. (1992). *Intelligence* (2nd ed.). San Diego, CA: Academic Press.

Bronfenbrenner, U., McClelland, P., Wethington, E., Moen, P., & Ceci, S. J. (1996). *The state of Americans: This generation and the next.* New York: Free Press.

Brookhuis, K. A. (1998). How to measure driving ability under the influence of alcohol and drugs, and why. *Human Psychopharmacology, 13,* 64–69.

Brouwers, S. A., Van de Vijver, F. J. R., & Van Hemert, D. A. (2009). Variation in Raven's Progressive Matrices scores across time and place. *Learning and Individual Differences, 19,* 330–338.

Brown, A. S. (1991). A review of the tip of the tongue phenomenon. *Psychological Bulletin, 109,* 204–223.

Brown, A. S. (2003). A review of the déjà vu experience. *Psychological Bulletin, 129,* 394–413.

Brown, A. S. (2004a). *The déjà vu experience.* New York: Psychology Press.

Brown, A. S. (2004b). The déjà vu illusion. *Current Directions in Psychological Science, 13,* 256–259.

Brown, A. S., Begg, M. D., Gravenstein, S., Schaefer, C. A., Wyatt, W. J., Bresnahan, M., et al. (2004). Serologic evidence for prenatal influenza in the etiology of schizophrenia. *Archives of General Psychiatry, 61,* 774–780.

Brown, D. (2006, November 20). Some believe "truth serums" will come back. *Washington Post,* A08.

Brown, D., Scheflin, A. W., & Hammond, C. (1997). *Trauma, memory, treatment, and the law.* New York: W. W. Norton.

Brown, G. W., Monck, E. M., Carstairs, G. M., & Wing, J. K. (1962). Influence of family life on the course of schizophrenic illness. *British Journal of Preventive and Social Medicine, 16,* 55–68.

Brown, P. K., & Wald, G. (1964). Visual pigments in single rods and cones of the human retina. *Science, 144,* 45–52.

Brown, P. L. & Jenkins, H. M. (1968). Auto-shaping of pigeons key-peck. *Journal of the Experimental Analysis of Behavior, 11,* 1–18.

Brown, R., & Kulik, J. (1977). Flashbulb memories. *Cognition, 5,* 73–99.

Brown, R. P., & Day, E. A. (2006). The difference isn't Black and White: Stereotype threat and the race difference on Raven's Progressive Matrices. *Journal of Applied Psychology, 91,* 979–985.

Brown, R. T., Reynolds, C. R., & Whitaker, J. S. (1999). Bias in mental testing since Bias in Mental Testing. *School Psychology Quarterly, 14,* 208–238.

Brown, R. W., & McNeill, D. (1966). The "tip-of-the-tongue" phenomenon. *Journal of Verbal Learning and Verbal Behavior, 5,* 325–337.

Brown, V. R., & Paulus, P. B. (2002). Making group brainstorming more effective: Recommendations from an associative memory perspective. *Current Directions in Psychological Science, 11,* 208–212.

Brownell, K. D., & Rodin, J. (1994). The dieting maelstrom: Is it possible and advisable to lose weight? *American Psychologist, 49,* 781–791.

Brownstein, M., & Solyom, L. (1986). The dilemma of Howard Hughes: Paradoxical behavior in compulsive disorders. *Canadian Journal of Psychiatry, 31,* 238–240.

Bruer, J. T. (1999). *The myth of the first three years: A new understanding of brain development and lifelong learning.* New York: Free Press.

Brugha, T. S. (ed.). (1995). *Social support and psychiatric disorder research findings and guidelines for clinical practice.* Cambridge, England: Cambridge University Press.

Brunvand, J. H. (1999). *Too good to be true: The colossal book of urban legends.* New York: W. W. Norton.

Bryan, J. H., & Test, M. A. (1967). Models and helping: Naturalistic studies in aiding behavior. *Journal of Personality and Social Psychology, 6*, 400–407.

Bryant, P. E., Bradley, L., MacLean, M., & Crossland, J. (1989). Nursery rhymes, phonological skills, and reading. *Journal of Child Language, 16*, 407–428.

Bryant, R. A. (2000). Cognitive behavioral therapy of violence-related post-traumatic stress disorder. *Aggression and Violent Behavior, 5*, 79–97.

Buck, L., & Axel, R. (1991). A novel multigene family may encode odorant receptors: A molecular basis for odor recognition. *Cell, 65*, 175–183.

Buckalew, L. W., & Ross, S. (1981). Relationship of perceptual characteristics to efficacy of placebos. *Psychological Reports, 49*, 955–961.

Buckle, S., Dawson, K., & Singer, P. (1989). The syngamy debate: when precisely does a human life begin? *Law, Medicine, and Health Care, 17*, 174–181.

Bulik, C. M., Sullivan, P. F., & Kendler, K. S. (1998). Heritability of binge-eating and broadly defined bulimia nervosa. *Biological Psychiatry, 44*, 1210–1218.

Bunde, J., & Suls, J. (2006). A quantitative analysis of the relationship between the Cook-Medley Hostility Scale and traditional coronary artery disease risk factors. *Health Psychology, 25*, 493–500.

Bunge, M. (1998). *Philosophy of science: From problem to theory* (Vol. 1). Piscataway, NJ: Transaction Publishers.

Bureau of Labor Statistics. (2006). *Number of jobs held, labor market activity, and earnings growth among the youngest baby boomers: Results from a longitudinal survey*. Retrieved from www.bls.gov/news.release/nlsoy.nr0.htm.

Burger, J. M., & Petty, R. E. (1981). The low-ball compliance technique: Task or person commitment? *Journal of Personality and Social Psychology, 40*, 492–500.

Burgess, E. O. (2004). Sexuality in midlife and later life couples. In J. H. Harvey, A. Wenzel, & S. Sprecher (eds.), *The handbook of sexuality in close relationships* (pp. 437–454). Mahwah, NJ: Lawrence Erlbaum Associates.

Burgess, K. B., Marshall, P., Rubin K. H., & Fox, N. A. (2003). Infant attachment and temperament as predictors of subsequent behavior problems and psychophysiological functioning. *Journal of Child Psychology and Psychiatry and Allied Disciplines, 44*, 1–13.

Burke, B. L., Arkowitz, H., & Dunn, C. (2002). The efficacy of motivational interviewing. In W. R. Miller & S. Rollnick (eds.), *Motivational interviewing: Preparing people for change* (2nd ed., pp. 217–250). New York: Guilford Press.

Burke, B. L., Arkowitz, H., & Menchola, M. (2003). The efficacy of motivational interviewing: A meta-analysis of controlled clinical trials. *Journal of Consulting and Clinical Psychology, 71*, 843–861.

Burns, A. B., Brown, J. S., Plant, A., Sachs-Ericsson, N., & Joiner, T. E. (2006). On the specific depressotypic nature of excessive reassurance-seeking. *Personality and Individual Differences, 40*, 135–145.

Burns, G. L., & Farina, A. (1992). The role of physical attractiveness in adjustment. *Genetic, Social, and General Psychology Monographs, 118*, 157–194.

Busatto, G. F., Pilowsky, L. S., Costa, D. C., Ell, P. J., Lingford-Hughes, A., & Kerwin, R. W. (1995). In vivo imaging of GABAA receptors using sequential whole-volume iodine-123 iomazenil single-photon emission tomography. *European Journal of Nuclear Medicine, 22*, 1–26.

Busch, C. M., Zonderman, A. B., & Costa, P. T. (1994). Menopausal transition and psychological distress in a nationally representative sample: Is menopause associated with psychological distress? *Journal of Aging and Health, 6*, 209–228.

Bushman, B. J., & Anderson, C. A. (2001). Media violence and the American public: Scientific facts versus media misinformation. *American Psychologist, 56*, 477–489.

Bushman, B. J., & Baumeister, R. F. (1998). Threatened egotism, narcissism, self-esteem, and direct and displaced aggression: Does self-love or self-hate lead to violence? *Journal of Personality and Social Psychology, 75*, 219–229.

Bushman, B. J., Baumeister, R. F., & Phillips, C. M. (2001). Do people aggress to improve their mood? Catharsis beliefs, affect regulation opportunity, and aggressive responding. *Journal of Personality and Social Psychology, 81*, 17–32.

Bushnell, M. C., Duncan, G. H., Hofbauer, R. K., Ha, B., Chen, J. I., & Carrier, B. (1999). Pain perception: Is there a role for primary somatosensory cortex? *Proceedings of the National Academy of Sciences, U.S.A., 96*, 7705–7709.

Buss, D. M. (1989). Sex differences in human mate preferences: Evolutionary hypotheses tested in 37 cultures. *Behavioral and Brain Sciences, 12*, 1–14.

Buss, D. M. (1994). *The evolution of desire: Strategies of human mating*. New York: Basic Books.

Buss, D. M. (1995). Evolutionary psychology: A new paradigm for psychological science. *Psychological Inquiry, 6*, 1–30.

Buss, D. M., & Kenrick, D. T. (1998). Evolutionary social psychology. In D. T. Gilbert, S. T. Fiske, & G. Lindzey (eds.), *The handbook of social psychology* (4th ed., Vol. 1, pp. 982–1026). Boston: McGraw Hill.

Buss, D. M., & Schmitt, D. P. (1993). Sexual strategies theory: An evolutionary perspective on human mating. *Psychological Review, 100*, 204–232.

Buss, D. M., Shackelford, T. K., Kirkpatrick, L. A., & Larsen, R. J. (2001). A half-century of mate preferences: The cultural evolution of values. *Journal of Marriage and Families, 63*, 492–503.

Butcher, J. N., Dahlstrom, W. G., Graham, J. R., Tellegen, A., & Kaemmer, B. (1989). *MMPI-2: Manual for administration and scoring*. Minneapolis: University of Minnesota Press.

Butler, B. (2006). NGRI revisited: Venirepersons' attitudes toward the insanity defense. *Journal of Applied Social Psychology, 36*, 1833–1847.

Butler, S., & Watson, R. (1985). Individual differences in memory for dreams: The role of cognitive skills. *Perceptual and Motor Skills, 53*, 841–864.

Butzlaff, R. L., & Hooley, J. M. (1998). Expressed emotion and psychiatric relapse: A meta-analysis. *Archives of General Psychiatry, 55*, 547–552.

Buunk, B. P, Collins, R. L., Taylor, S. E., VanYperen, N. C. & Dakof, G. A. (1990). The affective consequences of social comparison: Either direction has its ups and downs. Journal of Personality-and Social Psychology, 59, 1238–1249.

Buunk, B. P., Dijkstra, P., Fetchenhauer, D., & Kenrick, D. (2002). Age and gender differences in mate selection criteria for various involvement levels. *Personal Relationships, 9*, 271–278.

Byrne, D. (1971). *The attraction paradigm*. New York: Academic Press.

Byrne, R. (2007). *The secret*. New York: Atria Books.

Byrnes, J. P. (1988). Formal operations: A systematic reformulation. *Developmental Review, 8*, 66–87.

Cabeza, R., & Nyberg, L. (1997). Imaging cognition: An empirical review of PET studies with normal subjects. *Journal of Cognitive Neuroscience, 9*, 1–26.

Cabyoglu, M. T., Ergene, N., Tan, U. (2006). The mechanism of acupuncture and clinical applications. *International Journal of Neuroscience, 116*, 115–125.

Cacioppo, J. T. (2004). Common sense, intuition, and theory in personality and social psychology. *Personality and Social Psychology Review, 8*, 114–122.

Cacioppo, J. T., Berntson, G. G., Klein, D. J., & Poehlmann, K. M. (1997). The psychophysiology of emotion across the lifespan. *Annual Review of Gerontology and Geriatrics, 17*, 27–74.

Cacioppo, J. T., Berntson, G. G., Sheridan, J. F., & McClintock, M. K. (2000). Multilevel integrative analyses of human behavior: Social neuroscience and the complementing nature of social and biological approaches. *Psychological Bulletin, 126*, 829–843.

Cacioppo, J. T., Berntson, G. G., Lorig, T. S., Norris, C. J., Rickett, E., & Nusbaum, H. (2003). Just because you're imaging the brain doesn't mean you can stop using your head: A primer and set of first principles. *Journal of Personality and Social Psychology, 85*, 650–661.

Cacioppo, J. T., Tassinary, L. G., & Berntson, G. G. (2000). *Handbook of psychophysiology*. Cambridge, England: Cambridge University Press.

Cahill, L., & McGaugh, J. L. (1995). A novel demonstration of enhanced memory associated with emotional arousal. *Consciousness and Cognition, 4*, 410–421.

Cahill, L., Prins, B., Weber, M., & McGaugh, J. L. (1994). Beta-adrenergic activation and memory for emotional events. *Nature, 371*, 702–704.

Cahill, S. P., Rauch, S. A. M., Hembree, E. A., & Foa, E. B. (2003). Effectiveness of cognitive behavioral treatments for PTSD on anger. *Journal of Cognitive Psychotherapy, 17*(2), 113–131.

Cahn, B. R., & Polich, J. (2006). Meditation states and traits: EEG, ERP, and neuroimaging studies. *Psychological Bulletin, 132*, 180–211.

Calder, A. J., Keane, J., Manes, F., Antoun, N., & Young, A. W. (2000). Impaired recognition and experience of disgust following brain injury. *Nature Neuroscience, 3*, 1077–1078.

Caldera, Y. M., Huston, A. C., & O'Brien, M. (1989). Social interactions and play patterns of parents and toddlers with feminine, masculine and neutral toys. *Child Development, 60*, 70–76.

Cale, E. M., & Lilienfeld, S. O. (2006). Psychopath factors and risk for aggressive behavior: A test of the "threatened egotism" hypothesis. *Law and Human Behavior, 30*, 51–74.

Call, V., Sprecher, S., & Schwartz, P. (1995). The incidence and frequency of marital sex in a national sample. *Journal of Marriage and the Family, 57*, 639–652.

Callahan, R. J. (1995, August). *A thought field therapy (TFT) algorithm for trauma: A reproducible experiment in psychotherapy.* Paper presented at the 105th Annual Convention of the American Psychological Association, Chicago, IL.

Callahan, R. J. (2001). The impact of thought field therapy on heart rate variability (HRV). *Journal of Clinical Psychology, 57,* 1153–1170.

Calley, W. (1971). From William Calley: Court Martial. Retrieved October 29, 2007, from http://law.jrank.org/pages/3208/William-Calley-Court-Martial-1970.html.

Calvin, W. H. (2004). *A brief history of the mind: From apes to intellect and beyond.* New York: Oxford University Press.

Camara, W. J. (2009). College admission testing: Myths and realities in an age of admissions hype. In R. Phelps (ed.), *Correcting fallacies about educational and psychological testing* (pp. 147–180). Washington, DC: American Psychological Association.

Cameron, J., & Pierce, W. D. (1994). Reinforcement, reward, and intrinsic motivation: A meta-analysis. *Review of Educational Research, 64,* 363–423.

Campbell, D. (1997). *The Mozart effect: Tapping the power of music to heal the body, strengthen the mind, and unlock the creative spirit.* New York: Avon Books.

Campbell, J. (1988). *The power of myth.* New York: Doubleday.

Campbell, F. A., & Ramey, C. T. (1995). Cognitive and school outcomes for high-risk African-American students at middle adolescence: Positive effects of early intervention. *American Educational Research Journal, 32,* 743–772.

Campbell, R. S., & Pennebaker, J. (2003). The secret life of pronouns: Flexibility in writing style and physical health. *Psychological Science, 14,* 60–65.

Campfield, L. A., Smith, F. J., & Burn, P. (1996). The OB protein (leptin) pathway—A link between adipose tissue mass and central neural networks. *Hormone and Metabolic Research, 28,* 619–632.

Campfield, L. A., Smith, F. J., Rosenbaum, M., & Hirsch, J. (1996). Human eating: Evidence for a physiological basis using a modified paradigm. *Neuroscience Biobehavioral Review, 20,* 133–137.

Campinha-Bacote, J. (2002). *Resources in transcultural care and mental health* (13th ed.). Cincinnati, OH: Transcultural Care Associated.

Campos, P. (2004). The obesity myth: *Why America's obsession with weight is hazardous to your health.* New York: Gotham Books.

Canetti, L., Bachar, E., & Berry, E. M. (2002). Food and emotion. *Behavioural Processes, 60,* 157–164.

Canfield, R. L., Henderson, C. R., Jr., Cory-Slechta, D. A., Cox, C., Jusko, T. A., & Lanphear, B. P. (2003). Intellectual impairment in children with blood lead concentrations below 10 microg per deciliter. *New England Journal of Medicine, 348,* 1517–1526.

Canli, T. (2008, March/April). The character code. *Scientific American Mind, 19,* 52–57.

Cannon, T. D., Mednick, S. A., & Parnas, J. (1989). Genetic and perinatal determinants of structural brain deficits in schizophrenia. *Archives of General Psychiatry, 46,* 883–889.

Cannon, W. B. (1929). *Bodily changes in pain, hunger, fear and rage.* New York: D. Appleton.

Cannon, W. B., & Washburn, A. L. (1912). An explanation of hunger. *American Journal of Physiology, 29,* 441–454.

Cano, F. (2005). Epistemological beliefs and approaches to learning: Their change through secondary school and their influence on academic performance. *British Journal of Educational Psychology, 75,* 203–221.

Cano, F., & Cardelle-Elawar, M. (2004). An integrated analysis of secondary school students' conceptions and beliefs about learning. *European Journal of Psychology of Education, 19,* 167–187.

Cantril, H. (1947). *The invasion from Mars.* Princeton, NJ: Princeton University Press.

Capaldi, E. D. (1996). Conditioned food preferences. In E. D. Capaldi (ed.), *Why we eat what we eat: The psychology of eating* (pp. 53–80). Washington, DC: American Psychological Association.

Cappell, H., & Herman, C. (1972). Alcohol and tension reduction: A review. *Quarterly Journal of Studies in Alcohol, 33,* 33–64.

Cappella, J. N., & Jamieson, K. H. (1997). *Spiral of cynicism: The press and the public good.* Oxford, UK: Oxford University Press.

Capron, C., & Duyme, M. (1989). Assessment of effects of socioeconomic status on IQ in a full cross-fostering study. *Nature, 340,* 552–553.

Cardemil, E. V. (in press). Cultural adaptations to empirically supported treatments: A research agenda. *Scientific Review of Mental Health Practice.*

Cardeña, E., Lynn, J. S., & Krippner, S. (eds.) (2000). *Varieties of anomalous experience.* Washington, DC: American Psychological Association.

Carey, S. (1985). *Conceptual change in childhood.* Cambridge, MA: Bradford Books, MIT Press.

Carlson, J. G., & Hatfield, E. (1992). *Psychology of emotion.* New York: Harcourt, Brace, Jovanovich.

Carlson, M., Marcus-Newhall, A., & Miller, N. (1990). The effects of situational aggression cues: A quantitative review. *Journal of Personality and Social Psychology, 58,* 622–633.

Carlson, N. R., Heth, C. D., Miller, H. L., Donahoe, J. W., Buskist, W., & Martin, G. N. (2007). *Psychology: The Science of Behavior* (6th ed.). Boston: Allyn & Bacon.

Carlson, W., & Rose, A. J. (2007). The role of reciprocity in romantic relationships in middle childhood and early adolescence. *Merrill-Palmer Quarterly, 53,* 262–290.

Carlsson, A. (1995). Towards a new understanding of dopamine receptors. Symposium: Dopamine receptor subtypes in neurological and psychiatric diseases. *Clinical Neuropharmacology, 18*(Suppl.), 65–135.

Carnagey, N. L., Anderson, C. A., & Bartholow, B. D. (2007). Media violence and social neuroscience: New questions and new opportunities. *Current Directions in Psychological Science, 16,* 178–182.

Carney, R. M., Freedland, K. E., & Veith, R. C. (2005). Depression, the autonomic nervous system, and coronary heart disease. *Psychosomatic Medicine, 67,* 29–33.

Carney, S., Cowen, P., Geddes, J., Goodwin, G., Rogers, R., Dearness, K., et al. (2003). Efficacy and safety of electroconvulsive therapy in depressive disorders: A systematic review and meta-analysis. *Lancet, 361,* 799–808.

Carr, J. E., Fraizer, T. J., & Roland, J. P. (2005). Token economy. In A. M. Gross & R. S. Drabman (eds.) *Encyclopedia of behavior modification and cognitive behavior therapy—Volume 2: Child clinical applications* (pp. 1075–1079). Thousand Oaks, CA: Sage.

Carre, J. M., McCormick, C. M., & Mondloch, C. J. (2009). Facial structure is a reliable cue of aggressive behavior. *Psychological Science, 20,* 1194–1198.

Carrère, S., & Gottman, J. (1999). Predicting divorce among newlyweds from the first three minutes of a marital conflict discussion. *Family Process, 30,* 293–301.

Carroll, J. B. (1993). *Human cognitive abilities: A survey of factor analytic studies.* Cambridge, England: Cambridge University Press.

Carroll, R. T. (2003). *The skeptic's dictionary: A collection of strange beliefs, amusing deceptions, and dangerous delusions.* New York: Wiley.

Carstensen, L. L., & Lockenhoff, C. E. (2003). Aging, emotion, and evolution. *Annals of the New York Academy of Science, 1000,* 152–179.

Carter, F. A., McIntosh, V. V. W., Joyce, P. R., Sullivan, P. F., & Bulik, C. M. (2003). Role of exposure with response prevention in cognitive-behavioral therapy for bulimia nervosa: Three-year follow-up results. *International Journal of Eating Disorders, 33,* 127–135.

Carton, J. S. (1996). The differential effects of tangible rewards and praise on intrinsic motivation: A comparison of cognitive evaluation theory and operant theory. *The Behavior Analyst, 19,* 237–255.

Carton, J. S., & Nowicki, S., Jr. (1996). Origins of generalized control expectancies: Reported child stress and observed maternal control and warmth. *Journal of Social Psychology, 136,* 753–760.

Cartwright, J. (2000). *Evolution and human behaviour.* London: Macmillan.

Cartwright, R., & Romanek, I. (1978). Repetitive dreams of normal subjects. *Sleep Research, 7,* 7–15.

Cartwright, S. A. (1851, May). Report on the diseases and physical peculiarities of the Negro race. *The New Orleans Medical and Surgical Journal,* 691–715.

Caruso, D. R., Taylor, J., & Detterman, D. K. (1982). Intelligence research and intelligent policy. In D. K. Detterman & R. J. Sternberg (eds.), *How and how much can intelligence be increased?* (pp. 45–65). Norwood, NJ: Ablex.

Carver, C. S., & Miller, C. J. (2006). Relations of serotonin function to personality: Current views and a key methodological issue. *Psychiatry Research, 144,* 1–15.

Carver, C. S., & Scheier, M. F. (1999). Themes and issues in the self-regulation of behavior. In R. S. Wyer, Jr. (ed.), *Advances in social cognition* (Vol. 12). Mahwah, NJ: Erlbaum.

Carver, C. S., Scheier, M. F., & Weintraub, J. K. (1989). Assessing coping strategies: A theoretically based approach. *Journal of Personality and Social Psychology, 56*, 267–283.

Carver, R. P. (1990). *Reading rate: A review of research and theory.* San Diego, CA: Academic Press.

Caryl, P. G., Bean, J. E., Smallwood, E. B., Barron, J. C., Tully, L., & Allerhand, M. (2009). Women's preference for male pupil-size: Effects of conception risk, sociosexuality and relationship status. *Personality and Individual Differences. 46*, 50–508.

Casey, B., Giedd, J. N., & Thomas, K. M. (2000). Structural and functional brain development and its relation to cognitive development. *Biological Psychology, 54*, 241–257.

Casey, L. M., Oei, T. P. S., & Newcombe, P. A. (2004). An integrated cognitive model of panic disorder: The role of positive and negative cognitions. *Clinical Psychology Review, 24*, 529–555.

Caspi, A., McClay, J., Moffitt, T., Mill, J., Martin, J., Craig, I. W., et al. (2002). Role of genotype in the cycle of violence in maltreated children. *Science, 297*, 851–854.

Caspi, A., Sugden, K., Moffitt, T. E., Taylor, A., Craig, I., Harrington, H. L., et al. (2003). Influence of life stress on depression: Moderation by a polymorphism in the 5-HTT gene. *Science, 301*, 386–389.

Caspi, A., Williams, B., Kim-Cohen J., Craig, I. W., Milne, B. J., Poulton, R., et al. (2007). Moderation of breastfeeding effects on the IQ by genetic variation in fatty acid metabolism. *Proceedings of the National Academy of Sciences, 10*, 1073.

Cassidy, K. L. (2004). The adult learner rediscovered: Psychiatry residents' push for cognitive–behavioral therapy training and a learner-driven model of educational change. *Academic Psychiatry, 28*, 215–220.

Cassileth, B. R., Heitzer, M., & Wesa, K. (2009). The public health impact of herbs and nutritional supplements. *Pharmaceutical Biology, 47*, 761–767.

Castonguay, L. G., Boswell, J. F., Constantino, M. J., Goldfried, M. R., & Hill, C. E. (2010). Training implications of harmful effects of psychological treatments. *American Psychologist, 65*, 34–49.

Catania, K. C. (2006). Olfaction: Underwater "sniffing" by semi-aquatic mammals. *Nature, 444*, 1024–1025.

Catz, S. L., & Kelly, J. A. (2001). Living with HIV disease. In A. Baum, T. A. Revenson, & J. E. Singer (eds.), *Handbook of health psychology* (pp. 841–849). Mahwah, NJ: Lawrence Erlbaum.

Cattell, R. B. (1949). *Culture Free Intelligence Test, Scale 1, Handbook.* Champaign, IL: Institute of Personality and Ability.

Cattell, R. B. (1963). Theory of fluid and crystallized intelligence: A critical experiment. *Journal of Educational Psychology, 54*, 1–22.

Cattell, R. B. (1971). *Abilities: Their structure, growth, and action.* Boston: Houghton-Mifflin.

Cautela, J. R. (1971). Covert conditioning. In A. Jacobs & L. B. Sachs (eds.), *The psychology of private events: Perspectives on covert response systems.* New York: Academic Press.

Cautin, R. L. (2010). Shyness: How normal behavior became a sickness. *Journal of the History of the Behavioral Sciences, 46*, 109–111.

Caviness, V. S. Jr., Kennedy, D. N., Bates, J. F., & Makris, N. (1996). The developing human brain: A morphometric profile. In R. W. Thatcher, G. R. Lyon, J. Rumsey, & N. Krasnegor (eds.), *Developmental neuroimaging: Mapping the development of brain and behavior* (pp. 3–14). San Diego, CA: Academic Press.

Ceci, S. J. (1991). How much does schooling influence general intelligence and its cognitive components? A reassessment of the evidence. *Developmental Psychology, 27*, 703–722.

Ceci, S. J., & Bruck, M. (1993). Suggestibility of the child witness: A historical review and synthesis. *Psychological Bulletin, 113*, 403–439.

Ceci, S. J., Crotteau-Huffman, M., Smith, E., & Loftus, E. W. (1994). Repeatedly thinking about non-events. *Consciousness & Cognition, 3*, 388–407.

Ceci, S. J., & Williams, W. M. (1997). Schooling, intelligence, and income. *American Psychologist, 52*, 1051–1058.

Centers for Disease Control and Prevention (2005). *Cigarette smoking among adults: United States, 2003.* MMWR Highlights, Vol. 54, No. 20. United States Department of Health and Human Services. Atlanta, GA: Author.

Centers for Disease Control and Prevention (2007a). About BMI for adults. Retrieved January 31, 2008 from http://www.edc.gov/nccdphp/dnpa/bmi/adult_BMI/about_adult_BMI.htm.

Centers for Disease Control and Prevention (2007b). Cigarette smoking among adults: United States, 2006. *MMWR Highlights, 56*, 1157–1161.

Centers for Disease Control and Prevention (2008). *Behavioral Risk Factor Surveillance System prevalence data.* Atlanta, GA: Centers for Disease Control and Prevention. Available at www.cdc.gov/brfss. Retrieved March 28, 2008.

Centers for Disease Control and Prevention (2009). *NCHS Data Brief: Death in the United States, 2007.* Retrieved April 17, 2010 from http://www.cdc.gov/NCHS/data/databriefs/db26.htm.

Centers for Disease Control and Prevention (2009). Summary Health Statistics for U.S. Adults: National Health Interview Survey, 2008. Retrieved March 26, 2010 from http://www.cdc.gov/NCHS/fastats/alcohol.htm.

Cepeda, N. J., Pashler, H., Vul, E., Wixted, J. T., & Rohrer, D. (2006). Distributed practice in verbal recall tasks: A review and quantitative synthesis. *Psychological Bulletin, 132*, 354–380.

Cerella, J. (1985). Information processing rates in the elderly. *Psychological Bulletin, 98*, 67–83.

Chabris, C., & Simons, D. (2010). *The invisible gorilla and other ways our intuitions deceive us.* New York: Crown Publishers.

Chabris, C. F. (1999). Prelude or requiem for the "Mozart effect"? *Nature, 400*, 826–827.

Chafin, S., Christenfeld, N., & Gerin, W. (2008). Improving cardiovascular recovery from stress with brief post-stress exercise. *Health Psychology, 27*, 64–72.

Chaiken, A. L., Sigler, F., & Derlega, V. J. (1974). Nonverbal mediators of supervisor expectancy effects. *Journal of Personality and Social Psychology, 30*, 144–149.

Chall, J. S. (1983). *Stages of reading development.* New York: McGraw-Hill.

Chambless, D. L., & Goldstein, A. (1980). The treatment of agoraphobia. In A. Goldstein & E. B. Foz (eds.), *Handbook of behavioral interventions* (pp. 322-415). New York: John Wiley & Sons.

Chambless, D. L., & Ollendick, T. H. (2001). Empirically supported psychological interventions: Controversies and evidence. *Annual Review of Psychology, 52*, 685–716.

Chambless, D. L., Sanderson, W. C., Shoham, V., Bennett Johnson, S., Pope, K. S., Crits-Christoph, P., et al. (1996). An update on empirically validated therapies. *The Clinical Psychologist, 49*, 5–18.

Champagne, F. A., & Mashoodh, R. (2009). Genes in context: Gene-environment interplay and the origins of individual differences in behavior. *Current Directions in Psychological Science, 18*, 127–131.

Chandler, M. (Writer & Director). (1999, October 4). "Secrets of the SAT." In M. Sullivan (Executive Producer), *Frontline.* Boston: WGBH.

Chandola, T., Britton, A., Brunner, E., Hemingway, H., Malik, M., Kumari, M., et al. (2008). Work stress and coronary heart disease: What are the mechanisms? *European Heart Journal, 29* , 640–648.

Chandrashekar, J., Hoon, M. A., Ryba, N. J., & Zuker, C. S. (2006). The receptors and cells for mammalian taste. *Nature, 444*, 288–294.

Chang, K., Adleman, N. E., Dienes, K., Simeonova, D. I., Menon, V., & Reiss, A. (2004) Anomalous prefrontal-subcortical activation in familial pediatric bipolar disorder - A functional magnetic resonance imaging investigation. *Archives of General Psychiatry, 61*, 781–792.

Chaplin, W. F., Phillips, J. B., Brown, J. D., Clanton, N. R., & Stein, J. L. (2000). Handshaking, gender, personality, and first impressions. *Journal of Personality and Social Psychology, 79*, 110–117.

Chapman, L. J., & Chapman, J. P. (1967). Genesis of popular but erroneous diagnostic observations. *Journal of Abnormal Psychology, 72*, 193–204.

Chapman, L. J., & Chapman, J. P. (1969). Illusory correlation as an obstacle to the use of valid psychodiagnostic signs. *Journal of Abnormal Psychology, 74*, 271–280.

Chapman, L. J., Chapman J. P., & Raulin M. L. (1978). Body-image aberration in schizophrenia. *Journal of Abnormal Psychology, 87*, 399–407.

Charles, S. T., Mather, M., & Carstensen, L. L. (2003). Aging and emotional memory: The forgettable nature of negative images for older adults. *Journal of Experimental Psychology: General, 132*, 310–324.

Chase, W. G., & Simon, H. A. (1973). The mind's eye in chess. In W. G. Chase (ed.), *Visual information processing* (pp. 215–281). New York: Academic Press.

Chayer, C., & Freedman, M. (2001). Frontal lobe functions. *Current Neurology & Neuroscience Reports, 1*, 547–552.

Cheesman, J., & Merikle, P. M. (1986). Distinguishing conscious from unconscious perceptual processes. *Canadian Journal of Psychology, 40,* 343–367.

Cheng, C. (2003). Cognitive and motivational processes underlying coping flexibility: A dual-process model. *Journal of Personality and Social Psychology, 84,* 425–438.

Chentsova-Dutton, Y. E., & Tsai, J. L. (2007). Cultural factors influence the expression of psychopathology. In S. O. Lilienfeld & W. O'Donohue (eds.), *The great ideas of clinical science: 17 principles that every mental health professional should understand* (pp. 375–396). New York: Brunner-Taylor.

Cherlin, A. J., Furstenberg, F. F., Chase-Lansdale, P. L., Kiernan, K. E., Robins, P.K., Morrison, D. R., et al. (1991) Longitudinal studies of effects of divorce on children in Great Britain and the United States. *Science, 252,* 1386–1389.

Chesney, M. A., & Rosenman, M. D. (1980). Type A behavior in the work setting. In C. L. Cooper & R. Payne (eds.), *Current concerns in occupational stress* (pp. 187–212). Chichester, England: Wiley.

Cheung, F. M., & Leung, K. (1998). Indigenous personality measures: Chinese examples. *Journal of Cross-Cultural Psychology, 29,* 233–248.

Cheyne, J. A., & Girard, T. A. (2009). The body unbound: Vestibular-motor hallucinations and out of body experiences. *Cortex, 45,* 201–215.

Ching, P. I., Willett, W. C., Rimm, E. B., Colditz, G. A., Gortmaker, S. L., & Stampfer, M. J. (1996). Activity level and risk of overweight in male health professionals. *American Journal of Public Health, 86,* 25–30.

Chivers, M. L., & Bailey, J. M. (2005). A sex difference in features that elicit genital response. *Biological Psychology, 70,* 115–120.

Chodoff, P. (1976). The case for involuntary hospitalization of the mentally ill. *American Journal of Psychiatry, 133,* 396–501.

Chomsky, N. (1972). *Language and mind.* New York: Harcourt Brace Jovanovich.

Chopra, D. (1989). *Quantum healing: Exploring the frontiers of mind/body medicine.* New York: Bantam.

Christakis, N. A., & Fowler, J. H. (2007). The spread of obesity in a large social network over 32 years. *New England Journal of Medicine, 357,* 370–379.

Christensen, A., & Jacobson, N. S. (1994). Who (or what) can do psychotherapy: The status and challenge of nonprofessional therapies. *Psychological Science, 5,* 8–14.

Chua, H. F., Boland, J. E., & Nisbett, R. E. (2005). Cultural variation in eye movements during scene perception. *Proceedings of the National Academy of Sciences, 102,* 12629–12633.

Church, A. T., & Katigbak, M. S. (2002). The five-factor model in the Philippines: Investigating trait structure and levels across cultures. In R. R. McCrae & J. Allik (eds.), *The five-factor model across cultures* (pp. 129–154). New York: Kluwer Academic/Plenum Publishers.

Church, R. M. (1969). Response suppression. In B. Campbell & R. Church (eds.), *Punishment and aversive behavior* (pp. 111–156). New York: Appleton-Century-Crofts.

Chwalisz, K., Diener, E., & Gallagher, D. (1988). Autonomic arousal feedback and emotional experience: Evidence from the spinal cord injured. *Journal of Personality and Social Psychology, 54,* 820–828.

Cialdini, R. B. (2001). *Influence: Science and practice* (4th ed.). Boston: Allyn & Bacon.

Cialdini, R. B., & Goldstein, N. J. (2004). Social influence: Compliance and conformity. *Annual Review of Psychology, 55,* 591–621.

Cialdini, R. B., & Sagarin, B. J. (2005). Interpersonal influence. In T. Brock & M. Green (eds.), *Persuasion: Psychological insights and perspectives* (pp. 143–169). Newbury Park, CA: Sage Press.

Cialdini, R. B., Vincent, J. E., Lewis, S. K., Catalan, J., Wheeler, D., & Darby, B. L. (1975). Reciprocal concessions procedure for inducing compliance: The door-in-the-face technique. *Journal of Personality and Social Psychology, 31,* 206–215.

Ciarella, G., Ciarella, M., Graziani, P., & Mirante, M. (1991). Changes in food consumption of obese patients induced by dietary treatment combined with dexfenfluramine. *International Journal of Obesity, 15,* 69.

Cicchetti, D., & Garmezy, N. (1993). Prospects and promises in the study of resilience. *Development and Psychopathology, 5,* 497–502.

Cioffi, F. (1998). *Freud and the question of pseudoscience.* Chicago: Open Court.

Clancy, S. A. (2005). *Abducted: How people come to believe they were kidnapped by aliens.* Cambridge, MA: Harvard University Press.

Clancy, S. A., McNally, R. J., Schachter, D. L., Lenzenweger, M. F., & Pitman, R. K. (2002). Memory distortion in people reporting abduction by aliens. *Journal of Abnormal Psychology, 111,* 455–461.

Clark, A., Oswald, A., & Warr, P. (1996). Is job satisfaction U-shaped in age? *Journal of Occupational and Organizational Psychology, 69,* 57–81.

Clark, D. M. (1986). A cognitive approach to panic. *Behaviour Research and Therapy, 24,* 156–163.

Clark, K. B. & Clark, M. P. (1950) Emotional factors in racial identification and preference in Negro children. *Journal of Negro Education, 19,* 506–513.

Clark, M. (1997). *Reason to believe.* New York: Avon Books.

Clarke, R., Emberson, J., Fletcher, A., Breeze, E., Marmot, M., & Shipley, M. J. (2009). Life expectancy in relation to cardiovascular risk factors: 38 year follow-up of 19,000 men in the Whitehall study. *British Medical Journal, 339,* b 3513.

Clark, R. D. (2005). An examination of the "hot hand" in professional golfers. *Perceptual and Motor Skills, 101,* 365–372.

Clarke, A. M., & Clarke, A. D. B. (1976). *Early experience: Myth and evidence.* London: Open Books.

Clarke-Stewart, K. A. (1980). The father's contribution to children's cognitive and social development in early childhood. In F. A. Pedersen (ed.), *The father-infant relationship: Observational studies in the family setting* (pp. 111–146). New York: Praeger.

Clay, M. M. (1975). *What did I write?* Auckland, New Zealand: Heinemann.

Clay, R. A. (2002). Advertising as science. *American Psychological Association Monitor, 33,* 38.

Cleckley, H. (1941/1988). *The mask of sanity.* St. Louis, MO: Mosby.

Cloninger, C. R. (1987) A systematic method for clinical description and classification of personality variants. A proposal. *Archives of General Psychiatry, 44,* 573–588.

CNN (August 3, 2009). *Apnea, early starts blamed in Hawaii pilot's nap.* http://www.cnn.com/2009/US/08/03/sleepy.pilots.apnea/.

Coccaro, E. F., & Danehy, M. (2006). Intermittent explosive disorder. In E. Hollander & D. J. Stein (Eds.), Clinical manual of impulse-control disorders (pp. 19-37). Washington, DC: American Psychiatric Publishing.

Coe, W. C., & Sarbin, T. R. (1991). Role theory: Hypnosis from a dramaturgical and narrational perspective. In S. J. Lynn & J. W. Rhue (eds.), *Theories of hypnosis: Current models and perspectives* (pp. 303–323). New York: Guilford Press.

Cohen, D. & Gunz, A. (2002). As seen by the other . . . : Perspectives on the self in the memories and emotional perceptions of Easterners and Westerners. *Psychological Science, 13,* 55–59.

Cohen, D., & Nisbett, R. E. (1994). Self-protection and the culture of honor: Explaining Southern violence. *Personality and Social Psychology Bulletin, 20,* 551–567.

Cohen, D. A., Wang, W., Wyatt, J. K., Kronauer, R. E., Dijk, D. J., Czeisler, et al. (2010). Uncovering residual effects of chronic sleep loss on human performance. *Science Translational Medicine, 2,* 14ra3.

Cohen, G. L., Garcia, J., Apfel, N., & Master, A. (2006). Reducing the racial achievement gap: A social-psychological intervention. *Science, 313,* 1307–1310.

Cohen, M. A., Mehl, M. R., & Pennebaker, J. W. (2004). Linguistic markers of psychological change surrounding September 11, 2001. *Psychological Science, 15,* 687–693.

Cohen, P., & Cohen, J. (1984). The clinician's illusion. *Archives of General Psychiatry, 41,* 1178–1182.

Cohen, S., Doyle, W. J., Alper, C. M., Janicki-Deverts, D., & Turner, R. B. (2009). Sleep habits and susceptibility to the common cold. *Archives of Internal Medicine, 169,* 62–67.

Cohen, S., Doyle, W. J., Skoner, D. P., Rabin, B. S., & Gwaltney, J. M. (1997). Social ties and susceptibility to the common cold. *Journal of the American Medical Association, 277,* 1940–1944.

Cohen, S., Doyle, W. J., Turner, R. B., Alper, C. M., & Skoner, D. P. (2003). Emotional style and susceptibility to the common cold. *Psychosomatic Medicine, 65,* 652–657.

Cohen, S., Evans, G. W., Stokols, D., & Krantz, D. S. (1986). *Behavior, health, and environmental stress.* New York: Plenum.

Cohen, S., Frank, E., Doyle, B. J., Skoner, D. P., Rabin, B. S. & Gwaltney, J. M. (1998). Types of stressors that increase susceptibility to the common cold. *Health Psychology, 17,* 214–223.

Cohen, S., & Herbert, T. B. (1996). Health psychology: Psychological factors and physical disease from the perspective of human psychoneuroimmunology. *Annual Review of Psychology, 47,* 113–142.

Cohen, S., Tyrell, D. A. J., & Smith, A. P. (1991). Psychological stress and susceptibility to the common cold. *New England Journal of Medicine, 325,* 606–612.

Cohn, L. D., & Westenberg P. M. (2004). Intelligence and maturity: Meta-analytic evidence for the incremental and discriminant validity of Loevinger's measure of ego development. *Journal of Personality and Social Psychology, 86,* 760–772.

Coifman, K. G., Bonanno, G. A., Ray, R. D., & Gross, J. J. (2007). Does repressive coping promote resilience? Affective-autonomic response discrepancy during bereavement. *Journal of Personality and Social Psychology, 92,* 745–758.

Cole, M. (1990). Cultural psychology: A once and future discipline? In J. J. Berman (ed.), *Nebraska Symposium on Motivation, 1989: Cross-cultural perspectives* (pp. 279–335). Lincoln, NE: University of Nebraska Press.

Cole, M. G., & Dendukuri, N. (2003). Risk factors for depresson among elderly community subjects: A systematic review and meta-analysis. *American Journal of Psychiatry, 160,* 1147–1156.

Coleman, H. L. K., Wampold, B. E., & Casali, S. L. (1995). Ethnic minorities' ratings of ethnically similar and European American counselors: A meta-analysis. *Journal of Counseling Psychology, 42,* 55–64.

College Board. (1976–1977). *Student descriptive questionnaire.* Princeton, NJ: Educational Testing Service.

Collins, A. F. (1999). The enduring appeal of physiognomy: Physical appearance as a sign of temperament, character, and intelligence. *History of Psychology, 2,* 251–276.

Collins, A. W., Maccoby, E. E., Steinberg, L., Hetherington, M. E., & Bornstein, M. H. (2000). Contemporary research on parenting. *American Psychologist, 55,* 218–232.

Collins, F. L., Sorocco, K. H., Haala, K. R., Miller, B. I., & Lovallo, W. R. (2003). Stress and health. In L. M. Cohen, D. E. McChargue, & F. L. Collins (eds.), *The health psychology handbook: Practical issues for the behavioral medicine specialist* (pp. 169–186). London: Sage Publications.

Collins, H., & Pinch, T. (1993) *The Golem: What you should know about science.* Cambridge, UK: Cambridge University Press.

Colombo, J. (1993). *Infant cognition: Predicting later intellectual functioning.* Newbury Park, CA: Sage.

Colvin, C. R., & Block, J. (1994). Do positive illusions foster mental health? An examination of the Taylor and Brown formulation. *Psychological Bulletin, 116,* 3–20.

Comijs, H., Beekman, A., Smits, F., Bremmer, M., Tilburg, T., & Deeg, D. (2008). Childhood adversity, recent life events, and depression in later life. *Journal of Affective Disorders, 103,* 243–246.

Compton, A. M., Conway, K. P., Stinson, F. S., & Grant, B. F. (2006). Changes in the prevalence of major depression and comorbid substance use disorders in the United States between 1991–1992 and 2001–2002. *American Journal of Psychiatry, 163,* 2141–2147.

Compton, J. A., & Pfau, M. (2005). Inoculation theory of resistance to influence at maturity: Recent progress in theory development and application and suggestions for future research. *Communication Yearbook, 29,* 97–145.

Compton, M.T., & Broussard, B. (2009). *The first episode of psychosis: A guide for patients and their families.* New York: Oxford University Press.

Compton, M. T., Kelley, M. E., Ramsay, C. E., Pringle, M., Goulding, S. M., Esterberg, M. L., et al. (2009). Association of pre-onset cannabis, alcohol, and tobacco use with age at onset of prodrome and age at onset of psychosis in first-episode patients. *American Journal of Psychiatry, 166,* 1251–1257.

Concar, D. (1994). Design your own personality. *New Scientist, 141,* 22–26.

Condry, J. C., & Condry, S. (1976). Sex differences: A study in the eye of the beholder. *Child Development, 47,* 812–819.

Cone, E. J., Fant, R. V., Rohay, J. M., Caplan, Y, Ballina, M., Reder, R. F., et al.. Oxycodone involvement in drug abuse deaths. II. Evidence for toxic multiple drug-drug interactions. *Journal of Analytical Toxicology, 28,* 217–225.

Conrad, R. (1964). Acoustic confusion and immediate memory. *British Journal of Psychology, 55,* 75–84.

Conner, M., Sheeran, P., Norman, P., & Armitage, C. J. (2000). Temporal stability as a moderator of relationships in the Theory of Planned Behaviour. *British Journal of Social Psychology, 39,* 469–493.

Connolly, K. M., Lohr, J. M., & Olatunji, B. O. (2008). Information processing in contamination fear: A covariation bias examination of fear and disgust. *Journal of Anxiety Disorders, 23,* 60–68.

Consumer Reports. (2006, November 1). *Flip up or flip out.* Retrieved May 26, 2008, from www.accessmylibrary.com/coms2/summary_0286-29406170_ITM.

Conte, J. M. (2005). A review and critique of emotional intelligence measures. *Journal of Organizational Behavior, 26,* 433–440.

Conway, M., & Ross, M. (1984). Getting what you want by revising what you had. *Journal of Personality and Social Psychology, 47,* 783–748.

Cook, N. R. (2008). Salt intake, blood pressure, and clinical outcomes. *Current Opinion in Nephrology and Hypertension, 17,* 310–314.

Cook, T. D. (1985). Post-positivist critical multiplism. In R. L. Shotland & M. M. Mark (eds.), *Social science and social policy* (pp. 21–62). Beverly Hills, CA: Sage.

Cook, T. A. R., & Wall, T. L. (2005). Ethnicity and the subjective effects of alcohol. In M. Earleywine (ed.), *Mind-altering drugs: The science of subjective experience* (pp. 154–182). Washington, DC: American Psychological Association.

Cooley, C. H. (2002). *Human Nature and the Social Order.* New York: Scribner's.

Coombs, R. H. (1991). Marital status and personal well-being: A literature review. *Family Relations: Journal of Applied Family and Child Studies, 40,* 17–102.

Coon, D. J. (1992). Testing the limits of sense and science: American experimental psychologists combat spiritualism: 1880–1920. *American Psychologist, 47,* 143–151.

Coons, P. M., Bowman, E. S., & Milstein, V. (1988). Multiple personality disorder: A clinical investigation of 50 cases. *Journal of Nervous and Mental Disease, 176,* 519–527.

Coontz, S. (1992). *The way we never were: American families and the nostalgia trap.* New York: Basic Books.

Cooper, C. L., & Dewe, P. (2004). *Stress: A brief history.* Malden, MA: Blackwell Publishing.

Cooper, J. (2007). *Cognitive dissonance: Fifty years of a classic theory.* New York: Sage.

Cooper, R. P. (2003). Mechanisms for the generation and regulation of sequential behavior. *Philosophical Psychology, 16,* 389–416.

Coover, J. E. & Angell, F. (1907). General practice effect of special exercise. *American Journal of Psychology, 18,* 328–340.

Copeland, W. E., Keeler, G., Angold, A., & Costello, E. J. (2007). Traumatic events and posttraumatic stress in childhood. *Archives of General Psychiatry, 64,* 577–584.

Coppari, R., Ichinose, M., Lee, C. E., Pullen, A. E., Kenny, C. D., McGovern, et al. (2005). The hypothalamic arcuate nucleus: A key site for mediating leptin's effects on glucose homeostasis and locomotor activity. *Cell Metabolism, 1,* 63–72.

Copper, R. L., Goldenberg, R. L., Creasy, R. K., DuBard, M. B., Davis, R. O., Entman, S. S., et al. (1993). A multicenter study of preterm, birth weight, and gestational age-specific neonatal mortality. *American Journal of Obstetrics and Gynecology, 168,* 78–84.

Corballis, M. C. (1999). Are we in our right minds? In S. Della Sala (ed.), *Mind myths* (pp. 26–42). Chichester, England: John Wiley & Sons.

Corbett, T. (2006). The facts about weight loss products and programs. Federal Trade Commission, Food and Drug Administration. www.attorneygeneral.gov/uploadedFiles/Consumers/weight_loss. Retrieved June 30, 2006.

Cordón, L. A. (2005). *Popular psychology: An encyclopedia.* Westport, CT: Greenwood.

Coren, S. (1996). *Sleep thieves.* New York: Free Press.

Corkin, S. (1984). Lasting consequences of bilateral medial temporal lobectomy: Clinical course and experimental findings. In S. M. Kosslyn & R. A. Anderson (eds.), *Frontiers in cognitive neuroscience* (pp. 516–526). London: The MIT Press.

Corkin, S., Amaral, D. G., Gonzalez, R. G., Johnson, K. A., & Hyman, B. T. (1997). H.M.'s medial temporal lobe lesion: Findings from magnetic resonance imaging. *Journal of Neuroscience, 17,* 3964–3979.

Cornblatt, B. A., & Keilp, J. G. (1994). Impaired attention, genetics, and the pathophysiology of schizophrenia. *Schizophrenia Bulletin, 20,* 31–46.

Cornblatt, B. A., Green, M. F., & Walker, E. F. (1999). Schizophrenia: Etiology and neurocognition. In T. Millon, P. H. Blaney, & R. D. Davis (eds.), *Oxford textbook of psychopathology* (pp. 227–310). New York: Oxford University Press.

Cornell, E. H. (1980). Distributed study facilitates infants' delayed recognition memory. *Memory and Cognition, 8,* 539–542.

Cornell, E. H., & Bergstrom, L. I. (1983). Serial-position effects in infants' recognition memory. *Memory and Cognition, 11,* 494–499.

Correll, J., Park, B., Judd, C. M., & Wittenbrink, B. (2002). The police officer's dilemma: Using ethnicity to disambiguate potentially threatening individuals. *Journal of Personality and Social Psychology, 83,* 1314–1329.

Correll, C. U., & Schenk, E. M. (2008). Tardive dyskinesia and new antipsychotics. *Current Opinion in Psychiatry, 21,* 151–156.

Corrigan, P. W. (1995). Use of a token-economy with seriously mentally-ill patients: Criticisms and misconceptions. *Psychiatric Services, 46,* 1258–1263.

Corsini, R. J. (1999). *Dictionary of psychology.* Philadelphia: Brunner/Mazel.

Coryell, W., Scheftner, W., Keller, M., Endicott, J., Maser, J., & Klerman, G. L. (1993). The enduring psychosocial consequences of mania and depression. *American Journal of Psychiatry, 150,* 720–727.

Coryell, W., Solomon, S., Leon, A., Fiedorowicz, J. G., Schettler, P., Judd, L, et al. (2009). Does major depressive disorder change with age? *Psychological Medicine, 39,* 1689–1695.

Costa, P. T. Jr., & McCrae, R. R. (1990). Personality disorders and the five-factor model of personality. *Journal of Personality Disorders, 4,* 362–371.

Costa, P. T., & McCrae, R. R. (1992). 4 ways 5 factors are basic. *Personality and Individual Differences, 13,* 653–665.

Costa, P. T., Jr., & McCrae, R. R. (1992). *NEO PI-R professional manual.* Odessa, FL: Psychological Assessment Resources, Inc.

Costa, P. T., & McCrae, R. R. (1998). Trait theories of personality. In D. F. Barone, M. Hersen, & V. B. Van Hasselt (eds.), *Advanced Personality* (pp. 103–121). New York: Plenum.

Cotter, D. R., Pariante, C. M., & Eerall, I. P. (2001). Glial cell abnormalities in major psychiatric disorders: The evidence and implications. *Brain Research Bulletin, 55,* 585–595.

Cottrell, C. A., & Neuberg, S. L. (2005). Different emotional reactions to different groups: A sociofunctional threat-based approach to "prejudice." *Journal of Personality and Social Psychology, 88,* 770–789.

Covas, M. I., Konstantinidou, V., & Fito, M. (2009). Olive oil and cardiovascular health. *Journal of Cardiovascular Pharmacology, 54,* 477–482.

Cowan, C. P., & Cowan, P. A. (1995). Interventions to ease the transition to parenthood: Why they are needed and what they can do. *Family Relations, 44,* 412–423.

Cowan, N. (2001). The magical number 4 in short-term memory: A reconsideration of mental storage capacity. *Behavioral and Brain Sciences, 24,* 87–185.

Cowan, N., Lichty, W., & Grove, T. R. (1990). Properties of memory for unattended spoken syllables. *Journal of Experimental Psychology: Learning, Memory, & Cognition, 16,* 258–269.

Cox, B. J., & Taylor, S. (1998). Anxiety disorders: Panic and phobias. In T. Millon, P. H. Blaney, & R. D. Davis (eds.), *Oxford textbook of psychopathology* (pp. 81–113). New York: Oxford University Press.

Coyne, J. C. (1976). Depression and the response of others. *Journal of Abnormal Psychology, 85,* 186–193.

Coyne, J. C. (1992). Cognition in depression: A paradigm in crisis. *Psychological Inquiry, 3,* 232–235.

Coyne, J. C., & Holroyd, K. (1982). Stress, coping, and illness: A transactional perspective. In T. Millon, C. Green, & R. Meachem (eds.), *Handbook of clinical health psychology* (pp. 103–127). New York: Plenum Press.

Coyne, J. C., & Racioppo, M. W. (2000). Never the twain shall meet? Closing the gap between coping research and clinical intervention research. *American Psychologist, 55,* 655–664.

Coyne, J. C., Stefanek, M., & Palmer, S. C. (2007). Psychotherapy and survival in cancer: The conflict between hope and evidence. *Psychological Bulletin, 133,* 367–394.

Cracchiolo, J. J., Mori, T., Nazian, S., Tan, J., Potter, H. G., Adrendash, G. W., et al. (2007). Enhanced cognitive activity-over and above social or physical activity-is required to protect Alzheimer's mice against cognitive impairment, reduce Ab deposition, and increase synaptic immunostaining. *Neurobiology of Learning & Memory, 88,* 277–294.

Craighead, E., Sheets, E. S., & Bjornsson, A. S. (2005). Specificity and non-specificity in psychotherapy. *Clinical Psychology: Science and Practice, 12,* 189–193.

Craighead, L. W. (2002). Obesity and eating disorders. In M. M. Antony & D. H. Barlow (eds.), *A guide to treatments that work* (2nd ed., pp. 245–262). New York: Oxford.

Craik, F. I. M., & Lockhart, R. (1972). Levels of processing: A framework for memory research. *Journal of Verbal Learning & Verbal Behavior, 11,* 671–684.

Craik, F. I. M., & Tulving, E. (1975). Depth of processing and the retention of words in episodic memory. *Journal of Experimental Psychology: General, 104,* 268–294.

Cramer, V., Torgersen, S., & Kringlen, E. (2010). Mood disorders and quality of life: A community study. *Nordic Journal of Psychiatry, 64,* 58–62.

Crandall, C. S. (1994). Prejudice against fat people: Ideology and self-interest. *Journal of Personality and Social Psychology, 66,* 882–894.

Craske, M. G., Rapee, R. M., Jackel, L., & Barlow, D. H. (1989). Qualitative dimensions of worry in DSM-III-R generalized anxiety disorder subjects and nonanxious controls. *Behaviour Research and Therapy, 27,* 397–402.

Crespi, L. P. (1942). Quantitative variation of incentive and performance in the white rat. *American Journal of Psychology, 55,* 467–517.

Cressen, R. (1975). Artistic quality of drawings and judges' evaluations of the DAP. *Journal of Personality Assessment, 39,* 132–137.

Crews, F. (1990). *The memory wars: Freud's legacy in dispute.* New York: New York Times Review of Books.

Crews, F. C. (ed.) (1998). *Unauthorized Freud: Doubters confront a legend.* New York: Viking Press.

Crews, F. (2005). Response to Holland. *Scientific Review of Alternative Medicine, 10,* 24–28.

Crick, F., & Mitchison, G. (1983). The function of dream sleep. *Nature, 304,* 111–114.

Crick, N. (1995). Relational aggression: The role of intent attributions, feelings of distress, and provocation type. *Development and Psychopathology, 7,* 313–322.

Crits-Christoph, P., Wilson, G. T., & Hollon, S. D. (2005). Empirically supported psychotherapies: Comment on Westen, Novotny, and Thompson-Brenner (2004). *Psychological Bulletin, 131,* 412–417.

Cross, P. (1977). Not can but will college teaching be improved? *New Directions for Higher Education, 17,* 1–15.

Crowell, S. E., Beauchaine, T. P., & Linehan, M. M. (2009). A biosocial developmental model of borderline personality disorder: Elaborating and extending Linehan's theory. *Psychological Bulletin, 135,* 495–510.

Cruz, M., Scott, J., Houck, P., Reynolds, C. F., Frank, E., & Shear, M. K. (2007). Clinical presentation and treatment outcome of African Americans with complicated grief. *Psychiatric Services, 58,* 700–702.

Csikszentmihalyi, M. (1990). *Flow, the psychology of optimal experience.* New York: Harper & Row.

Csikszentmihalyi, M. (1997). *Finding flow: The psychology of engagement with everyday life.* New York: Basic Books.

Cuijpers, P., Vanstraten, A., Warmerdam, L., & Smits, N. (2008). Characteristics of effective psychological treatments of depression: A metaregression analysis. *Psychothreapy Research, 18,* 225–236.

Culham, J. C., & Valyear, K. F. (2006). Human parietal cortex in action. *Current Opinion in Neurobiology, 16,* 205–212.

Cullen, M. J., & Sackett, P. R. (2004). Integrity testing in the workplace. In J. C. Thomas & M. Hersen (eds.), Comprehensive handbook of psychological assessment, Volume 4: Industrial and organizational psychology (pp. 149–165). Hoboken, NJ: John Wiley & Sons.

Cunningham, A. E., Stanovich, K. E., & Wilson, M. R. (1990). Cognitive variation in adult college students differing in reading ability. In T. H. Carr & B. A. Levy (eds.), *Reading and its development: Component skills approaches* (pp. 129–159). San Diego, CA: Academic Press.

Cunningham, M. R., Roberts, A. R., Wu, H., Barbee, A. P., & Bruen, P. B. (1995). Their ideas of beauty are, on the whole, the same as ours: Consistency and variability in the cross-cultural perception of female physical attractiveness. *Journal of Personality and Social Psychology, 68,* 261–279.

Cunningham, P. F. (1993, October). *Can the use of animals in neuropsychological and psychopharmacological experiments continue to be justified?* Paper presented at the New England Psychological Association 33rd Annual Meeting, Goffstown, NH.

Cunningham, W. A., Nezlek, J. B., & Banaji, M. R. (2004). Implicit and explicit ethnocentrism: Revisiting the ideologies of prejudice. *Personality and Social Psychology, 30,* 1332–1346.

Curran, J. P., & Lippold, S. (1975). The effects of physical attraction and attitude similarity on attraction in dating dyads. *Journal of Personality, 43,* 528–539.

Curtis, R. C., & Miller, K. (1986). Believing another likes or dislikes you: Behavior making the beliefs come true. *Journal of Personality and Social Psychology, 51,* 284–290.

Curtiss, S. (1977). Genie: Psycholinguistic study of a modern-day "wild child." London: Academic Press.

Custer, R., & Aarts, H. (2010). The unconscious will: How the pursuit of goals operates outside of conscious awareness. Science, 329, 47–50.

Cutler, B. L., & Wells, G. L. (2009). Expert testimony regarding eyewitness identification. In J. L. Skeem, K. S. Douglas, & S. O. Lilienfeld (eds.), Psychological science in the courtroom: Consensus and controversy (pp. 100–123). New York: Guilford.

Cytowic, R. E. (1993). The man who tasted shapes: A bizarre medical mystery offers revolutionary insights into emotions, reasoning, and consciousness. New York: G. P. Putnam's Sons.

Cytowic, R. E., & Eagleman, D. M. (2009). Wednesday is indigo blue. Cambridge and London: MIT Press.

D'Amato, E. (1998, January/February). Mystery of disgust. Psychology Today. Retrieved from http://www.psychologytoday.com/articles/200909/mystery-disgust on March 27, 2010.

D'Onofrio, B. M., Turkheimer, E. N, Emery, R., Slutske, W., Heath, A., Madden, P. A. F., et al. (2006). A genetically informed study of the processes underlying the association between parental marital instability and offspring adjustment. Developmental Psychology, 42, 486–499.

Dabbs, J. B. (2001). Heroes, rogues, and lovers: Testosterone and behavior. New York: McGraw Hill.

Dabbs, J. M., Jr., & Dabbs, M. G. (2000) Heroes, rogues, and lovers: Testosterone and behavior. New York: McGraw-Hill.

Dallek, R. (2003). An unfinished life: John F. Kennedy, 1917–1963. Boston: Little, Brown and Company.

Damasio, A. (1994). Descartes' error. New York: G. P. Putnam's Sons.

Damasio, A. (2000). The feeling of what happens: Body, emotion and the making of consciousness. Cambridge, MA: MIT Press.

Damasio, H., Grabowski, T., Frank, R., Galaburda, A. M., & Damasio, A. R. (1994). The return of Phineas Gage: Clues about the brain from the skull of a famous patient. Science, 264, 1102–1105.

Danaher, B. C. (1974). Theoretical foundations and clinical applications of the Premack principle: Review and critique. Behavior Therapy, 5, 307–324.

Danaher, K. & Crandall, C. S. (2008). Stereotype threat in applied settings re-examined. Journal of Applied Social Psychology, 38, 1639–1655.

Danbrot, M. (2004). The new cabbage soup diet. New York: St. Martin's Press.

Danner, D. D., Snowdon, D. A., & Friesen, W. V. (2001). Positive emotions in early life and longevity: Findings from the nun study. Journal of Personality and Social Psychology, 80, 804–813.

Darley, J. M., & Batson, D. (1973). From Jerusalem to Jericho: A study of situational and dispositional variables in helping behavior. Journal of Personality and Social Psychology, 27, 100–108.

Darley, J. M., & Latané, B. (1968a). Bystander intervention in emergencies: Diffusion of responsibility. Journal of Personality and Social Psychology, 8, 377–383.

Darley, J. M., & Latané, B. (1968b). When will people help in a crisis? Psychology Today, 2, 54–57, 70–71.

Darlington, R. B. (1986). Long-term effects of preschool programs. In U. Neisser (ed.), The school achievement of minority children. Hillsdale, NJ: Erlbaum.

Darwin, C. (1859). On the origin of species. London: John Murray.

Darwin, C. R. (1872). The expression of the emotions in man and animals. London: John Murray.

Davey, G. C. L. (1995). Rumination and the enhancement of fear: Some laboratory findings. Behavioural and Cognitive Psychotherapy, 23, 203–215.

David, D., Lynn, S. J., & Ellis, A. (2010). Rational and irrational beliefs. New York: Oxford University Press.

Davidson, J. R., Gadde, K. M., Fairbank, J. A., Krishnan, R. R., Califf, R. M., Binanay, C., et al. (2002). Hypericum Depression Trial Study Group. Effect of Hypericum perforatum (St. John's wort) in major depressive disorder: A randomized, controlled trial. Journal of the American Medical Association, 287, 1807–1814.

Davidson, P. R., & Parker, K. C. (2001). Eye movement desensitization and reprocessing (EMDR): A meta-analysis. Journal of Consulting and Clinical Psychology, 69, 305–316.

Davidson, R. J., Kabat-Zinn, J., Schumacher, J., Rosenkranz, M., Muller, D., Santorelli, S. F., et al. (2003). Alternations in brain and immune function produced by mindfulness meditation. Psychosomatic Medicine, 65, 564–570.

Davies, G., Welham, J., Chant, D., Torrey, E. F., & McGrath, J. (2003). A systematic review and meta-analysis of northern hemisphere season of birth in schizophrenia. Schizophrenia Research, 29, 587–593.

Davis, D. M. (2006, February). Intrigue at the immune synapse. Scientific American Mind. http://www.scientificamerican.com/article.cfm?id=intrigue-at-the-immune-sy.

Davis, H. (2009). Caveman logic: The persistence of primitive thinking in a modern world. Amherst, New York: Prometheus.

Davis, K. L., Kahn, R. S., Ko, G., & Davidson, M. (1991). Dopamine in schizophrenia: Review and reconceptualization. American Journal of Psychiatry, 148, 1474–1486.

Davis, M., & Shi, C. (2000). The amygdala. Current Biology, 10, R131.

Davis, S. R., Davison, S. L., Donath, S., & Bell, R. J. (2005). Circulating androgen levels and self-reported sexual function in women. Journal of the American Medical Association, 294, 91–96.

Davis, T. C., Wolf, M. S., Bass, P. F., Middlebrooks, M., Kennen, E., Baker, D. W., et al. (2006). Low literacy impairs comprehension of prescription drug warning labels. Journal of General Internal Medicine, 21, 847–851.

Davison, G. C. (1976). Homosexuality: The ethical challenge. Journal of Consulting and Clinical Psychology, 44, 157–162.

Davison, G. C., & Lazarus, A. A. (2007). Clinical case studies are important in the science and practice of psychotherapy. In S. O. Lilienfeld & W. T. O'Donohue (eds.), The great ideas of clinical science: 17 principles that every mental health professional should understand (pp. 149–162). New York: Routledge.

Davison, K. P., Pennebaker, J. W., & Dickerson, S. S. (2000). Who talks? The social psychology of illness support groups. American Psychologist, 55, 205–217.

Dawes, R. M. (1988). Rational choice in an uncertain world. Orlando, FL: Harcourt-Brace Jovanovich.

Dawes, R. M. (1994). House of cards: Psychology and psychotherapy built on myth. New York: Free Press.

Dawes, R. M. (1998, June). "Listening to Prozac but hearing placebo": Commentary on Kirsch and Sapirstein. Prevention & Treatment, 1(2).

Dawes, R. M. (2006). Experience and validity of clinical judgement: The illusory correlation. Behavioral Sciences and the Law, 7, 457–467.

Dawes, R. M., Faust, D., & Meehl, P. E. (1989). Clinical versus actuarial judgment. Science, 243, 1668–1674.

De Houwer, J., Teige-Mocigemba, S., Spruyt, A., & Moors, A. (2007). Implicit measures: A normative analysis and review. Psychological Bulletin, 135, 347–368.

De Raad, B., & Perugini, M. (2002). Big Five assessment. Ashland, OH: Hogrefe & Huber.

De Raad, B., Perugini, M., Hrebickova, M., & Szarota, P. (1998). The lingua franca of personality: Taxonomies and structure. Journal of Cross Cultural Psychology, 29, 212–232.

de Vries, G. J., & Olff, M. (2009). The lifetime prevalence of traumatic events and posttraumatic stress disorder in the Netherlands. Journal of Traumatic Stress, 22, 259–267.

de Waal, F. B. M. (1982). Chimpanzee politics: Power and sex among apes. Baltimore: Johns Hopkins University Press.

de Waal, F. B. M. (1989). The myth of a simple relation between space and aggression in captive primates. Zoo Biology, 8, 141–148.

de Waal, F. B. M. (1990). Peacemaking among primates. Cambridge, MA: Harvard University Press.

de Waal, F. B. M. (1996). Good natured: The origins of right and wrong in humans and other animals. Cambridge, MA: Harvard University Press.

de Waal, F. B. M. (2002). Evolutionary psychology: The wheat and the chaff. Current Directions in Psychological Science, 11, 187–191.

de Waal, F. B. M. (2006). Primates and philosophers: How morality evolved (S. Macedo & J. Ober, eds.). Princeton, NJ: Princeton University Press.

de Waal, F. B. M. (2009). The age of empathy: Nature's lessons for a kinder society. New York: Random House.

de Waal, F. B. M., Aureli, F., & Judge, P. G. (2000, May). Coping with crowding. Scientific American, 282, 76–81.

Deabler, H. L., Hartl, E. M., & Willis, C. A. (1973). Physique and personality: Somatotype and the 16PF. Perceptual and Motor Skills, 36, 927–933.

Deadwyler, S. A., Porrino, L., Siegel, J. M., & Mampson, R. (2007). Systemic and nasal delivery of orexin-A (Hypocretin-I) reduces the effects of sleep deprivation on cognitive performance in nonhuman primates. *Journal of Neuroscience, 27,* 14239–14247.

Dean, C. (2005, August 23). Scientists speak up on mix-up of God and science. *New York Times.* http://personal.bgsu.edu/~edwards/NYTimesCSL.pdf.

Dean, G. (1987). Does astrology need to be true? Part 2: The answer is no. *Skeptical Inquirer, 11,* 257–273.

Deary, I. J., Der, G., & Ford, G. (2001). Reaction time and intelligence differences: A population based cohort study. *Intelligence, 29,* 1–11.

Deary, I. J., Whalley, L. J., Lemmon, H., Crawford, J. R., & Starr, J. M. (2000). The stability of individual differences in mental ability from childhood to old age: Follow-up of the 1932 Scottish Mental Survey. *Intelligence, 28,* 49–55.

Deater-Deckard, K. (2001). Annotation: Recent research examining the role of peer relationships in the development of psychopathology. *Journal of Child Psychology and Psychiatry, 42,* 565–579.

Deater-Deckard, K., & Dodge, K. A. (1997). Externalizing behavior problems and discipline revisited: Nonlinear effects and variation by culture, context, and gender. *Psychological Inquiry, 8,* 161–175.

DeBell, C. S., & Harless, D. K. (1992) B. F. Skinner: Myth and misperception. *Teaching of Psychology, 19*(2), 68–73.

DeBreuil, S. C., Garry, M., & Loftus, E. F. (1998). Tales from the crib: Age regression and the creation of unlikely memories. In S. J. Lynn & K. M. McConkey (eds.) *Truth in memory.* (pp. 137–160). New York: Guilford Press.

DeCasper, A. J., & Spence, M. J. (1988). Prenatal maternal speech influences newborns' perception of speech sounds. In S. Chess, A. Thomas, & M. Hertzig (eds.), *Annual progress in child psychiatry and child development, 1987* (pp. 5–25). Philadelphia: Brunner/Mazel.

Deci, E. L. (1971). Effects of externally mediated rewards on intrinsic motivation. *Journal of Personality and Social Psychology, 18,* 105–115.

Deci, E. L., Koestner, R., & Ryan, R. M. (1999). A meta-analytic review of experiments examining the effects of extrinsic rewards on intrinsic motivation. *Psychological Bulletin, 125,* 627–668.

Deese, J. (1959). On the prediction of occurrence of particular verbal intrusions in immediate recall. *Journal of Experimental Psychology, 58,* 17–22.

Deffenbacher, K. A., Bornstein, B. H., & Penrod, S. D. (2006). Mugshot exposure effects: retroactive interference, mugshot commitment, source confusion, and unconscious transference. *Law and Human Behavior, 30,* 287–307.

Deffenbacher, K. A., Bornstein, B. H., Penrod, S. D., & McGorty, E. K. (2004). A meta-analytic review of the effects of high stress on eyewitness memory. *Law and Human Behavior, 28,* 687–706.

DeFries, J. C., & Plomin, R. (1978). Behavioral genetics. *Annual Review of Psychology, 29,* 473–515.

Degenhardt, L., & Hall, W. (2006). Is cannabis a contributory cause of psychosis? *Canadian Journal of Psychiatry, 51,* 556–565.

Degenhardt, L., Hall, W. D., Lynskey, M., McGrath, J. M., McLaren, J., Calabria, B., et al. (2009). Should burden of disease estimates include cannabis use as a risk factor for psychosis? *PLOS Medicine, 6*(9): e1000133.doi:10.1371/journal.pmed.1000133.

DeKosky, S. T., Williamson, J. D., Fitzpatrick, A. L. et al. (2008). Ginkgo biloba for prevention of dementia - A randomized controlled trial. *Journal of the American Medical Association, 300,* 2253–2262.

Delgado, J. M. R., & Anand, B. K. (1952). Increase of food intake induced by electrical stimulation of the lateral hypothalamus. *American Journal of Physiology, 172,* 162–168.

Della Sala, S. (2007). *Tall tales about the mind and brain: Separating fact from fiction.* Oxford, UK: Oxford University Press.

DeLongis, A., Folkman, S., & Lazarus, R. (1988). The impact of daily stress on health and mood psychological and social resources as mediators. *Journal of Personality and Social Psychology, 54,* 486–495.

Dement, W. C. (1974). *Some must watch while some must sleep.* San Francisco: W. H. Freeman.

Dement, W. C., & Kleitman, N. (1957). The relation of eye movements during sleep to dream activity: An objective method for the study of dreaming. *Journal of Experimental Psychology, 53,* 339–346.

Dement, W. C., & Vaughan, C. (1999*). The promise of sleep: A pioneer in sleep medicine explores the vital connection between health, happiness, and a good night's sleep*. New York: Dell Trade Paperbacks.

den Boer, P. C. A. M., Wiersma, D., Russo, S. & van den Bosch, R. J. (2005). Paraprofessionals for anxiety and depressive disorders: A meta-analysis. *The Cochrane Database of Systematic Reviews,* Issue 2. Art No: CD004688.

Dennerstein, L., Lehert, P., & Guthrie, J. (2002). The effects of the menopausal transition and biopsychosocial factors on well-being. *Archives of Women's Mental Health, 5,* 15–22.

Dennett, D. C. (1995). *Darwin's dangerous idea: Evolution and the meanings of life.* New York: Simon and Schuster.

Dennis, M., Sugar, J., & Whitaker, H. A. (1982). The acquisition of tag questions. *Child Development, 53,* 1254–1257.

Denniston, J. C., Chang, R., & Miller, R. R. (2003). Massive extinction prevents the renewal effect. *Learning and Motivation, 34,* 68–86.

DeNoon, D. (2005): *Experts: Chelation therapy not worth the risk.* Medscape Psychiatry and Mental Health. Retrieved November 11, 2007, from http://www.medscape.com/viewarticle/511713.

DePaulo, B. (1992). Nonverbal behavior and self-presentation. *Psychological Bulletin, 111,* 203–243.

DePaulo, B. M., Kashy, D. A., Kirkendol, S. E., Wyer, M. M., & Epstein, J. A. (1996). Lying in everyday life. *Journal of Personality and Social Psychology, 70,* 979–995.

DePaulo, B. M., Lindsay, J. J., Malone, B. E., Muhlenbruck, L., Charlton, K., & Cooper, H. (2003). Cues to deception. *Psychological Bulletin, 129,* 74–118.

DePaulo, B. M., & Pfeifer, R. L. (1986). On-the-job experience and skill at detecting deception. *Journal of Applied Social Psychology, 16,* 249–267.

Depue, R. A., & Iacono, W. G. (1989). Neurobehavioral aspects of affective disorders. *Annual Review of Psychology, 40,* 457–492.

Depue, R. A., & Monroe, S. M. (1986). Conceptualization and measurement of human disorder in life stress research—The problem of chronic disturbance. *Psychological Bulletin, 99,* 36–51.

Der, G., Batty, G. D., & Deary, I. J. (2006). Effect of breast feeding on intelligence in children: Prospective study, sibling pairs analysis, and meta-analysis. *British Medical Journal, 333,* 945–950.

Derr, M. (2010, January 18). Study finds a shared gene in dogs with compulsive behavior. *The New York Times.* Retrieved from http://www.nytimes.com/2010/01/19/science/19dogs.html on May 7, 2009.

DerSimonian, R., & Laird, N. M. (1983). Evaluating the effect of coaching on SAT scores: A meta-analysis. *Harvard Educational Review, 53,* 1–15.

DeRubeis, R. J., Brotman, M. A., & Gibbons, C. J. (2005). A conceptual and methodological analysis of the nonspecifics argument. *Clinical Psychology: Science & Practice, 12,* 174–183.

DeRubeis, R. J., & Feeley, M. (1990). Determinants of change in cognitive therapy for depression. *Cognitive Therapy and Research, 14,* 469–482.

Desmedt, E., & Valcke, M. (2004). Mapping the learning styles "jungle": An overview of the literature based on citation analysis. *Educational Psychology, 24,* 445–464.

Despres, O., Candas, V., & Dufour, A. (2005). Auditory compensation in myopic humans: Involvement of binaural, monaural, or echo cues? *Brain Research, 1041,* 56–65.

Detterman, D. K. (1987). What does reaction time tell us about intelligence? In P. Vernon (ed.), *Speed of information-processing and intelligence.* Norwood, NJ: Ablex.

Devilbiss, D. M., & Berridge, C. W. (2006). Low-dose methylphenidate actions on tonic and phasic locus coeruleus discharge. *Journal of Pharmacology & Experimental Therapeutics, 319,* 1327–1335.

Devine, P. G. (1989). Stereotypes and prejudice: Their automatic and controlled components. *Journal of Personality and Social Psychology, 56,* 5–18.

Devine, P. G., Monteith, M. J., Zuwerink, J. R., & Elliot, A. J. (1991). Prejudice with and without compunction. *Journal of Personality and Social Psychology, 60,* 817–830.

Devlin, B., Daniels, M., Roeder, K. (1997). The heritability of IQ. *Nature, 388,* 468–471.

DeWall, C. N., & Bushman, B. J. (2009). Hot under the collar in a lukewarm environment: Words associated with hot temperature increase aggressive thoughts and hostile perceptions. *Journal of Experimental Social Psychology, 45,* 1045–1047.

DeWall C. N., MacDonald, G., Webster, G. D., Masten, C.L., Baumeister, R. F., et al. (2010). Acetaminophen reduces social pain: Behavioral and neural evidence. *Psychological Science, 21,* 1–7

DeYoung, C. G., Peterson, J. B., & Higgins, D. M. (2005). Sources of openness/intellect: Cognitive and neuropsychological correlates of the fifth factor of personality. *Journal of Personality, 73*, 825–858.

Diamond, L. M. (2003). What does sexual orientation orient? A biobehavioral model distinguishing romantic love and sexual desire. *Psychological Review, 110*, 173–192.

Diamond, L. M. (2004). Emerging perspectives on distinctions between romantic love and sexual desire. *Current Directions in Psychological Science, 13*, 116–119.

Dickens, W. T., & Flynn, J. R. (2001). Heritability estimates versus large environmental effects: The IQ paradox resolved. *Psychological Review, 108*, 346–369.

Dickens, W. T., & Flynn, J. R. (2006). Black Americans reduce the racial IQ gap: Evidence from standardization samples. *Psychological Science, 17*, 1101–1107.

Dickey, M. (1994). *Anxiety disorders.* National Institute of Mental Health. Washington, DC: U.S. Government Printing Office.

Diehl, M., & Stroebe, W. (1987). Productivity loss in brainstorming groups: Toward the solution of a riddle. *Journal of Personality and Social Psychology, 53*, 497–509.

Diekelmann, S., & Born, J. (2010). The memory function of sleep. *Nature Reviews Neuroscience, 11*, 114–126.

Diener, E., Emmons, R. A., Larsen, R. J., & Griffin, S. (1985). The satisfaction with life scale. *Journal of Personality Assessment, 49*, 71–75.

Diener, E., Gohm, C. L., Suh, E., & Oishi, S. (2000). Similarity of the relations between marital status and subjective well-being across cultures. *Journal of Cross-Cultural Psychology, 31*, 419–436.

Diener, E. & Larsen, R. J. (1984). Temporal stability and cross-situational consistency of affective, cognitive, and behavioral responses. *Journal of Personality and Social Psychology, 47*, 871–883.

Diener, E., Lucas, R., & Scollon, C. N. (2006). Beyond the hedonic treadmill: Revising the adaptation theory of well-being. *American Psychologist, 61*, 305–314.

Diener, E., & Seligman, M. E. P. (2002). Very happy people. *Psychological Science, 13*, 81–84.

Diener, E., & Seligman, M. E. P. (2004). Beyond money: Toward an economy of well-being. *Psychological Science in the Public Interest, 5*, 1–31.

Diener, H. C., Kronfeld, K., & Boewing, G. (2006). Efficacy of acupuncture for the prophylaxis of migraine: A multi-center randomized controlled trial. *The Lancet Neurology,* Online, March 2.

Dienes, Z. (2008). *Understanding psychology as a science: An introduction to scientific and statistical inference.* New York: Palgrave Macmillan.

Dies, R. R. (2003). Group psychotherapies. In A. S. Gurman & S. B. Messer (eds.), *Essential psychotherapies*: Theory and practice (2nd ed., pp. 515–550). New York: Guilford Press.

Dijksterhuis, A., Aarts, H., & Smith, P. K. (2005). The power of the subliminal: On subliminal persuasion and other potential applications. In R. R. Hassin, J. S. Uleman, & J. A. Bargh (eds.), *The new unconscious* (pp. 77–106). New York: Oxford University Press.

Dijksterhuis, A., Bos, M. W., Nordgren, L. F., & van Baaren, R. B., (2006). On making the right choice: The deliberation-without-attention effect. *Science, 311*, 1005–1007.

DiLalla, L. F., & Gottesman, I. I. (1991). Biological and genetic contributors to violence—Widom's untold tale. *Psychological Bulletin, 109*, 125–129.

DiLalla, L. F., Thompson, L. A., Plomin, R., Phillips, K., Fagan, J. F., Haith, M. M., et al. (1990). Infant predictors of preschool and adult IQ: A study of infant twins and their parents. *Developmental Psychology, 26*, 759–769.

Dill, J. C., & Anderson, C. A. (1995). Effects of frustration justification on hostile aggression. *Aggressive Behavior, 21*, 359–369.

Dillehay, R. C. (1978). Authoritarianism. In H. London & J. E. Exner (eds.), *Dimensions of personality* (pp. 85–127). New York: John Wiley & Sons.

DiLoretto, A. O. (1971). *Comparative psychotherapy: An experimental analysis.* Chicago: Aldine-Atherton.

Dimberg, U., Thunberg, M., & Elmehed, K. (2000). Unconscious facial reactions to emotional facial expressions. *Psychological Science, 11*, 86–89.

Dimidjian, S., & Hollon, S. D. (2010). How would we know if psychotherapy were harmful? *American Psychologist, 65*, 21–33.

Dimidjian, S., Hollon, S. D., Dobson, K. S., Schmaling, K. B., Kohlenberg, R.J., Addis, M. E., et al. (2006). Randomized trial of behavioral activation, cognitive therapy and antidepressant medication in the acute treatment of adults with mild depression. *Journal of Consulting and Clinical Psychology, 74*(4) 658–670.

DiNardo, P. A., Guzy, L. T., & Bak, R. M. (1988). Anxiety response patterns and etiological factors in dog-fearful and non-fearful subjects. *Behaviour Research and Therapy, 26*, 245–251.

Dingfelder, S. F. (2005, October). Autism's smoking gun? *American Psychological Association Monitor, 36*(9). Retrieved from http://www.apa.org/monitor/oct05/autism.html on March 27, 2010.

Dinstein, I., Thomas, C., & Behrmann, M. (2008) A mirror up to nature. *Current Biology, 18*, R13–R18.

Dion, K., Berscheid, E., & Walster, E. (1972). What is beautiful is good. *Journal of Personality and Social Psychology, 24*, 285–290.

Dipamo, B., Job RFS. (1991). A methodological review of studies of SALT (suggestive accelerative learning and teaching) techniques. *Australian Journal of Educational Technology, 7*, 127–143.

Dipboye, R. L. (1977). Alternative approaches to deindividuation. *Psychological Bulletin, 85*, 1057–1075.

Dixon, L. B., Dickerson, F., Bellack, A. S., Bennett, M., Dickinson, D., Goldberg, R. W. et al. (2010). The 2009 Schizophrenia PORT psychosocial treatment recommendations and summary statements. *Schizophrenia Bulletin, 36*, 48–70.

Dixon, M., & Laurence, J. (1992). Two hundred years of hypnosis research: Questions resolved? Questions unanswered! In E. Fromm and M. Nash (eds.), *Contemporary hypnosis research* (pp. 34–66). New York: Guilford.

Dobson, J. (1992). *The strong-willed child.* Carol Stream, IL: Tyndale.

Dockery, T. M., & Bedeian, A. G. (1989). Attitudes versus actions: LaPiere (1934) classic study revisited. *Social Behavior and Personality, 17*, 9–16.

Dodd, B., & McEvoy, S. (1994). Twin language or phonological disorder? *Journal of Child Language, 21*, 273–289.

Dohrenwend, B. P. (2006). Inventorying stressful life events as risk factors for psychopathology: toward resolution of the problem of intracategory variability. *Psychological Bulletin, 132*, 477–495.

Dohrenwend, B. S., & Dohrenwend, B. P. (eds.) (1974). *Stressful life events: Their nature and effects* (pp. 245–258). New York: Wiley.

Dolan, M., Anderson, I. M., & Deakin, J. F. (2001). Relationship between 5-HT function and impulsivity and aggression in male offenders with personality disorders. *British Journal of Psychiatry, 178*, 352–359.

Dollard, J., & Miller, N. (1950). *Personality and psychotherapy: An analysis in terms of learning, thinking and culture.* New York: McGraw-Hill.

Dolnick, E. (1998). *Madness on the couch: Blaming the victim in the heyday of psychoanalysis.* New York: Simon & Schuster.

Domhoff, G. W. (1993). The repetition of dreams and dream elements: A possible clue to a function of dreams. In A. Moffitt, M. Kramer, & R. Hoffman (eds.), *The functions of dream*s (pp. 293–320). Albany, NY: SUNY Press.

Domhoff, G. W. (1996). *Finding meaning in dreams: A quantitative approach.* New York: Plenum.

Domhoff, G. W. (1999). *The scientific study of dreams: Neural networks, cognitive development, and content analysis.* Washington, DC: American Psychological Association.

Domhoff, G. W. (2001a). A new neurocognitive theory of dreams. *Dreaming, 11*, 13–33.

Domhoff, G. W. (2003). Dreaming—An introduction to the science of sleep. *Science, 299*, 1987–1988.

Domhoff, G. W., & Schneider, A. (2004). Much ado about very little: The small effect size when home and laboratory dreams are compared. *Dreaming, 19*, 139–151.

Domjan, M., & Purdy, J. E. (1995). Animal research in psychology. *American Psychologist, 50*, 496–503.

Donnellen, M. B., Trzesniewski, K. H., Robins, R. W., Moffitt, T. E., & Caspi, A. (2005). Exploring the link between self-esteem and externalizing behaviors: Low self-esteem is related to antisocial behavior, conduct disorder, and delinquency. *Psychological Science, 16*, 328–335.

Donovan, J. J., & Radosevich, D. R. (1999). A meta-analytic review of the distribution of practice effect: Now you see it, now you don't. *Journal of Applied Psychology, 84*, 795–805.

Dorus, E., Dorus, W., & Rechtschaffen, A. (1971). The incidence of novelty in dreams. *Archives of General Psychiatry, 25*, 364–368.

Dosajh, N. L. (1996). Projective techniques with particular reference to inkblot tests. *Journal of Projective Psychology and Mental Health, 3*, 59–68.

Doty, R. L., Deems, D., & Stellar, S. (1988). Olfactory dysfunction in Parkinson's disease: A general deficit unrelated to neurologic signs, disease stage, or disease duration. *Neurology, 38,* 1237–1244.

Doublet, S. (2000). *The stress myth.* Freemans Reach, New South Wales, Australia: Ipsilon Publishing.

Douglas, K. S., Guy, L. S., & Hart, S. D. (2009). Psychosis as a risk factor for violence to others: A meta-analysis. *Psychological Bulletin, 135,* 679–706.

Douglas, R. M., Hemilä, H., D'Souza, R., Chalker, E. B., & Treacy, B. (2004). Vitamin C for preventing and treating the common cold. *Cochrane Database System Review, 4,* CD000980.

Dovidio, J., Kawakami, K., Johnson, C., Johnson, B., & Howard, A. (1997). On the nature of prejudice: Automatic and controlled processes. *Journal of Experimental Social Psychology, 33,* 510–540.

Dovidio, J., Piliavin, J., Schroeder, D., & Penner, L. (2006). *The social psychology of prosocial behavior.* Mahwah, NJ: Erlbaum.

Dowman, J., Patel, A., & Rajput, K. (2005). Electroconvulsive therapy: Attitudes and misconceptions. *The Journal of ECT, 21,* 84–87.

Downey, G., & Coyne, J. C. (1990). Children of depressed parents: An integrative review. *Psychological Bulletin, 108,* 50–76.

Doyle, W. J., & Cohen, S. C. (2009). *Etiology of the common cold: Modulating factors.* Basel, Switzerland: Birkhäuser Basel.

Driscoll, R., Davis, K. E., & Lipetz, M. E. (1972). Parental interference and romantic love: The Romeo and Juliet effect. *Journal of Personality and Social Structure, 24,* 1–10.

Drory, A. (1986). Graphology and job performance: A validation study. In B. Nevo (ed.), *Scientific aspects of graphology* (pp. 165–173). Springfield, IL: Charles C. Thomas.

Druckman, D., & Bjork, R. A. (eds.). (1994). *Learning, remembering, believing: Enhancing human performance.* Washington, DC: National Academy Press.

Druckman, D., & Swets, J. A. (eds.). (1988). *Enhancing human performance: Issues, theories, and techniques.* Washington, DC: National Academy Press.

DuBrin, J. R., & Zastowny, T. R. (1988). Predicting early attrition from psychotherapy: An analysis of a large private practice cohort. *Psychotherapy, 25,* 393–498.

Duclos, S.., Laird, J., Schneider, E., Sexter, M., Stern, L. & van Lighten, O. (1989). Emotion-specific effects of facial expressions and postures on emotional experience. *Journal of Personality and Social Psychology, 57,* 100–108.

Duenwald, M. (2002, May 7). Religion and health: New research revives an old debate. *New York Times,* D5.

Duggal S., & Sroufe L. A. (1998). Recovered memory of childhood sexual trauma: A documented case from a longitudinal study. *Journal of Traumatic Stress, 11,* 301–321.

Dunbar, R. (1993). Coevolution of neocortical size, group size, and language in humans. *Behavioral and Brain Sciences, 16,* 681–735.

Dunbar, R. (1996). *Grooming, gossip, and the evolution of language.* London: Faber & Faber.

Dunbar, R. (2003). Psychology: Evolution of the social brain. *Science, 302,* 1160–1161.

Duncan, B. (1976). Differential social perception and attribution of intergroup violence. *Journal of Personality and Social Psychology, 34,* 590–598.

Duncan, G. (1996). Income dynamics and health. *International Journal of Health Services, 26,* 419–444.

Duncan, J., Seitz, R. J., Kolodny, J., Bor, D., Herzog, H., Ahmed, A., et al. (2000). A neural basis for general intelligence. *Science, 289,* 457–460.

Duncker, K. (1945). *On problem-solving.* Psychological Monographs (No. 270).

Dunkel-Schetter, C. (2009). Stress processes in pregnancy and preterm birth. *Current Directions in Psychological Science, 18,* 205–209.

Dunn, E. W., Aknin, L., & Norton, M. I. (2008). Spending money on others promotes happiness. *Science, 319,* 1687–1688.

Dunning, D., Heath, C., & Suls, J. (2004). Flawed self-assessment: Implications for health, education, and the workplace. *Psychological Science in the Public Interest, 5,* 69–106.

Dusseldorp, E., van Elderen, T., Maes, S., Meulman, J., & Kraaij, V. (1999). A meta-analysis of psychoeducational programs for coronary heart disease patients. *Health Psychology, 18,* 506–519.

Dutton, D. G., & Aron, A. (1974). Some evidence for heightened sexual attraction under conditions of high anxiety. *Journal of Personality and Social Psychology, 30,* 510–517.

Dweck, C. S. (2002). Beliefs that make smart people dumb. In R. Sternberg (ed.), *Why smart people can be so stupid* (pp. 24–41). New Haven. CT: Yale University Press.

Dweck, C. S. (2006). *Mindset: The new psychology of success.* New York: Random House.

Dysken, M. W., Kooser, J. A., Haraszti, J. S., & Davis, J. M. (1979). Clinical usefulness of sodium amobarbitol interviewing. *Archives of General Psychiatry, 36,* 789–794.

Eagly, A. H., Ashmore, R. D., Makhijani, M. G., & Longo, L. C. (1991). What is beautiful is good, but . . . : A meta-analytic review of research on the physical attractiveness stereotype. *Psychological Bulletin, 110,* 109–128.

Eagly, A. H., & Carli, L. L. (1981). Sex of researchers and sex-typed communications as determinants of sex differences in influenceability: A meta-analysis of social influence studies. *Psychological Bulletin, 90,* 1–20.

Eagly, A. H., & Crowley, M. (1986). Gender differences in helping behavior: A meta-analytic review of the social psychological literature. *Psychological Bulletin, 100,* 283–308.

Eagly, A. H., & Steffen, V. J. (1986). Gender and aggressive behavior: A meta-analytic review of the social psychological literature. *Psychological Bulletin, 100,* 309–330.

Eagly, A. H., & Wood, W. (1999). The origins of sex differences in human behavior: Evolved dispositions versus social roles. *American Psychologist, 54,* 408–423.

Eagly, A. H., Wood, W., & Diekman, A. B. (2000). Social role theory of sex differences and similarities: A current appraisal. In T. Eckes & H. M. Trauntner (eds.), *The developmental social psychology of gender* (pp. 123-174). Longon: Erlbaum.

Eagly, A. H., Wood, W., & Johannesen-Schmidt, M. C. (2004). Social role theory of sex differences and similarities: Implications for the partner preferences of women and men. In A. H. Eagly, A. Beall, & R. S. Sternberg (eds.), *The psychology of gender* (2nd ed., pp. 269–295). New York: Guilford Press.

Eakin, P. J. (2004). What are we reading when we read autobiography? *Narrative, 12,* 121–132.

Earley, P. C. (1989). Social loafing and collectivism: A comparison of the United States and the People's Republic of China. *Administrative Science Quarterly, 34,* 565–581.

Earleywine, M. (2005). *Mind-altering drugs: The science of subjective experience.* Oxford: Oxford University Press.

Eastman, C., Gazda, C. J., Burgess, H. J., Crowley, S., & Fogg, L. F. (2005). Circadian rhythms before eastward flight: A strategy to reduce jet lag. *Sleep, 28,* 33–44.

Eastwick, P. W, & Finkel, E. J. (2008). The attachment system in fledgling relationships: An activating role for attachment anxiety. *Journal of Personality and Social Psychology, 95,* 628–647.

Ebbinghaus, H. (1885). Memory: A contribution to experimental psychology. New York: Teachers College, Columbia University.

Eccleston, C., & Crombez, G. (1999). Pain demands attention: A cognitive-affective model of the interruptive function of pain. *Psychological Bulletin, 125,* 356–366.

Ecke, P. (2009). The tip-of-the-tongue phenomenon as a window on (bilingual) lexical retrieval. In A. Pavlenko (ed.), *The bilingual mental lexicon: Interdisciplinary approaches* (pp. 185–208). Bristol, UK: Multilingual Matters.

Edens, J. F., Buffington, J. K., Tomicic, T. L., & Riley, B. D. (2001), Effects of positive impression management on the Psychopathic Personality Inventory. *Law and Human Behavior, 25,* 235–256.

Edwards, D. A. (1970). Post-neonatal androgenization and adult aggressive behavior in female mice. *Physiology and Behavior, 5,* 465–467.

Edwards, D. M., Franks, P., Friedgood, D., Lobban, G., & Mackay, H. C. G. (1969). *An experiment on obedience.* Unpublished student report, University of the Witwatersrand, Johannesburg, South Africa.

Egan, L. C., Santos, L. R., & Bloom, P. (2007). The origins of cognitive dissonance: Evidence from children and monkeys. *Psychological Science, 18,* 978–983.

Ehrenwald, J. (1974). Out-of-the-body experiences and the denial of death. *Journal of Nervous and Mental Disease, 159,* 227–233.

Ehrsson, H. H. (2007). The experimental induction of out-of-body experiences. *Science, 317,* 1048.

Ehrsson, H. H., Spence, C., & Passingham, R. E. (2004). That's my hand! Activity in premotor cortex reflects feeling of ownership of a limb. *Science, 305,* 875–877.

Eibl-Eibesfeldt, I. (1973). The expressive behaviour of the deaf-and-blind-born. In M. von Cranach & I. Vine (eds.), *Social communication and movement* (pp. 163–194). London: Academic Press.

Eich, E., & Hyman, R. (1991). Subliminal self help. In D. Druckman & R. A. Bjork (eds.), *In the mind's eye: Enhancing human performance* (pp. 107–119). Washington, DC: National Academy Press.

Eigsti, I. M., Zayas, V., Mischel, W., Shoda, Y., Ayduk, O., Dadlani, M. B., et al. (2006). Predicting cognitive control from preschool to late adolescence and young adulthood. *Psychological Science, 17,* 478–484.

Eippert, F., Finsterbusch, J., Binger, U., & Buchel, C. (2009). Direct evidence for spinal cord involvement in placebo analgesia. *Science, 326,* 404.

Eisenberger, N. I., Lieberman, M. D., & Williams, K. D. (2003). Does rejection hurt? An fMRI study of social exclusion. *Science, 302,* 290–292.

Eisenberger, R., & Cameron, J. (1996). Detrimental effects of reward: Reality or myth? *American Psychologist, 51,* 1153–1166.

Eisler, R. M., & Ragsdale, K. (1992). Masculine gender role and midlife transition in men. In V. B. Van Hasselt & M. Hersen (eds.), *Handbook of social development: A lifespan perspective* (pp. 455–471). New York: Plenum Press.

Eisner, D. A. (2000). *The death of psychotherapy: From Freud to alien abductions.* Westport, CT: Praeger.

Ekman, P. (1994). Strong evidence for universals in facial expressions: A reply to Russell's mistaken critique. *Psychological Bulletin, 115,* 268–287.

Ekman, P. (1999). Facial expressions. In T. Dalgleish & M. J. Power (eds.), *Handbook of cognition and emotion* (pp. 301–320). New York: John Wiley & Sons.

Ekman, P. (2001). *Telling lies: Clues to deceit in the marketplace, politics, and marriage.* New York: Norton.

Ekman, P., Davidson, R. J., & Friesen, W. V. (1990). Duchenne's smile: Emotional expression and brain physiology II. *Journal of Personality and Social Psychology, 58,* 342–353.

Ekman, P., & Friesen, W. V. (1971). Constants across cultures in the face and emotion. *Journal of Personality and Social Psychology, 17,* 124–129.

Ekman, P., & Friesen, W. V. (1975). *Unmasking the face: A guide to recognizing emotions from facial clues.* Englewood Cliffs, NJ: Prentice-Hall.

Ekman, P., & Friesen, W. V. (1986). A new pancultural facial expression of emotion. *Motivation and Emotion, 10,* 159–168.

Ekman, P., Levenson, R. W., & Friesen, W. V. (1983). Autonomic nervous system activity distinguishes between emotions. *Science, 221,* 1208–1210.

Ekman, P., & O'Sullivan, M. (1991). Who can catch a liar? *American Psychologist, 46,* 913–920.

Ekman, P., O'Sullivan, M., & Frank, M. G. (1999). A few can catch a liar. *Psychological Science, 10,* 263–266.

Elfenbein, H. A., & Ambady, N. (2002). On the universality and cultural specificity of emotion recognition: A meta-analysis. *Psychological Bulletin, 128,* 203–235.

Elkin, I. (1994). The NIMH Treatment of Depression Collaborative Research Program: Where we began and where we are now. In A. E. Bergin & S. L. Garfield (eds.), *Handbook of psychotherapy and behavior change* (4th ed., pp. 114–135). New York: Wiley.

Elkind, D. (1967). Egocentrism in adolescence. *Child Development, 38,* 1025–1034.

Ellenberger, H. F. (1970). *The discovery of the unconscious: The history and evolution of dynamic psychiatry.* New York: Basic Books.

Elliott, R. (2002). The effectiveness of humanistic therapies: A meta-analysis. In D. J. Cain & J. Seeman (eds.), *Humanistic psychotherapies: Handbook of research and practice* (pp. 57–81). Washington, DC: American Psychological Association.

Ellis, A. (1958). *Sex without guilt.* New York: Lyle Stuart.

Ellis, A. (1962). *Reason and emotion in psychotherapy.* New York: Lyle Stuart.

Ellis, A. (1977). The basic clinical theory of rational-emotive therapy. In A. Ellis & R. Grieger (eds.), *Handbook of rational-emotive therapy* (pp. 3–34). New York: Springer.

Ellis, A., Abrams, M., & Abrams, L. D. (2008). *Personality theories: Critical perspectives.* New York: Sage.

Ellis, A., & Dryden, W. (1997). *The practice of rational-emotive behavior therapy.* New York: Springer Publishing.

Ellis, L., & Ames, M. A. (1987). Neurohormonal functioning and sexual orientation: A theory of homosexuality-heterosexuality. *Psychological Bulletin, 101,* 233–258.

Ellis, M. (2006). Appalachian English and Ozark English. In R. Abramson & J. Haskell (eds.), *The Encyclopedia of Appalachia* (pp. 1008–1011). Knoxville, TN: University of Tennessee Press.

Ellison, C. G., & Levin, S. L. (1998). The religion-health connection: Evidence, theory, and future directions. *Health Education and Behavior, 25,* 700–720.

Ellsworth, C. P., Muir, D. W., & Hains, S. M. (1993). Social competence and person-object differentiation: An analysis of the still-face effect. *Developmental Psychology, 29,* 63–73.

Elman, J. L. (2005). Connectionist models of cognitive development: Where next? *Trends in Cognitive Science, 9,* 111–117.

Elzinga, B. M., van Dyck, R., & Spinhoven, P. (1998). Three controversies about dissociative identity disorder. *Clinical Psychology and Psychotherapy, 5,* 13–23.

Emery, C., & Lilienfeld, S. O. (2004). The validity of child sexual abuse survivor checklists in the popular psychology literature: A Barnum effect? *Professional Psychology: Science and Practice, 35,* 268–274.

Emery, G. (2005). Psychic predictions 2005. *Skeptical Inquirer, 29*(2), 7–8.

Emler, N. (2001). *Self-esteem: The costs and causes of low self-worth.* York, North Yorkshire, England: Joseph Rowntree Foundation.

Emmelkamp, P. M. G., Bruynzeel, M., Drost, L., & van der Mast, C. A. P. G. (2001). Virtual reality treatment in acrophobia: A comparison with exposure in vivo. *CyberPsychology & Behavior, 4,* 335–339.

Emmelkamp, P. M. G., Krijn, M., Hulsbosch, A. M., de Vries, S., Schuemie, M. J. & Van der Mast, C. A. P. G. (2002). Virtual reality treatment versus exposure in vivo: A comparative evaluation in acrophobia. *Behaviour Research and Therapy, 40,* 509–516.

Emmons, R. A., & McCullough, M. E. (2003). Counting blessings versus burdens: An experimental investigation of gratitude and subjective well-being in daily life. *Journal of Personality and Social Psychology, 84,* 377–389.

Emrick, C. D. (1987). Alcoholics Anonymous: Affiliation processes and effectiveness as treatment. *Alcoholism: Clinical and Experimental Research, 11,* 416–423.

Engel, A. K., & Singer, W. (2001). Temporal binding and the neural correlates of sensory awareness. *Trends in Cognitive Science, 5,* 6–25.

Engel, G. L. (1977). The need for a new medical model: A challenge for biomedicine. *Science, 196,* 129–136.

Engelmann, J. B., Capra, M. S., Noussair, C. & Berns, G. S. (2009). Expert financial advice neurobiologically "offloads" financial decision-making under risk. *PLoS one 4(3): e4957.doi:10.1371/journal.pone.0004957.*

Engle, R. W. (2002). Working memory capacity as executive attention. *Current Directions in Psychological Science, 11,* 19–23.

Engler, J., & Goleman, D. (1992). *A consumer's guide to psychotherapy.* New York: Simon & Schuster.

Epstein, R. (2007). Giving psychology away: A personal journey. *Perspectives on Psychological Science, 1,* 389–400.

Epstein, R. P., Novick, O., Umansky, R., Priel, B., Osher, Y., Blaine, D., et al. (1996). Dopamine D4 receptor (D4DR) exon III polymorphism associated with the human personality trait of novelty seeking. *Nature Genetics, 12,* 78–80.

Epstein, S. (1979). The stability of behavior: I. On predicting more of the people more of the time. *Journal of Personality and Social Psychology, 37,* 1097–1126.

Erblich, J., Earlywine, M., Erblich, B., & Bovjerg, D. H. (2003). Biphasic stimulant and sedative effects of ethanol: Are children of alcoholics really different? *Addictive Behaviors, 28,* 1129–1139.

Erdelyi, M. (1994). Hypnotic hypermnesia: The empty set of hypermnesia. *International Journal of Clinical and Experimental Hypnosis, 42,* 379–390.

Erdelyi, M. H. (2006). The unified theory of repression. *Behavioral and Brain Sciences, 29,* 499–551.

Erickson, K. I., & Kramer, A. F. (2009). Aerobic exercise effects on cognitive and neural plasticity in older adults. *British Journal of Sports Medicine, 43,* 22–24.

Ericsson, K. A., Krampe, R. Th., & Tesch-Römer, C. (1993). The role of deliberate practice in the acquisition of expert performance. *Psychological Review, 100,* 363–406.

Erikson, E. H. (1963). *Childhood and society* (2nd ed.). New York: W. W. Norton.

Erikson, E. H. (1968). *Identity: Youth and crisis*. London: Faber & Faber.

Erikson, E. H. (1970). Reflections on the dissent of contemporary youth. *International Journal of Psychoanalysis, 51*, 11–22.

Ernst, C., & Angst, J. (1983). *Birth order*. Berlin, Germany: Springer-Verlag.

Ernst, E. (2002). Heavy metals in traditional Indian remedies. *European Journal of Clinical Pharmacology, 57*, 891–896.

Esch, T., & Stefano, G. B. (2005). The neurobiology of love. *Neuro Endocrinology Letters, 26*, 175–192.

Eslinger, P. J., & Damasio, A. R. (1985). Severe disturbance of higher cognition after bilateral frontal lobe ablation. Patient EVR. *Neurology, 35*, 1731–1741.

Esser, J. K., & Lindoerfer, J. L. (1989), Groupthink and the Space Shuttle Challenger accident: toward a quantitative case analysis. *Journal of Behavioral Decision Making, 2*, 167–177.

Esserman, L., Shieh, Y., & Thompson, I. (2009). Rethinking screening for breast cancer and prostate cancer. *Journal of the American Medical Association, 302*(15), 1685–1692.

Esterling, B. A., Kiecolt-Glaser, J. K., & Glaser, R. (1996). Psychosocial modulation of cytokine-induced natural killer cell activity in older adults. *Psychosomatic Medicine, 58*, 264–272.

Esterson, A. (1993). *Seductive mirage: An exploration of the work of Sigmund Freud*. Chicago: Open court.

Evans, C. J. (2004). Secrets of the opium poppy revealed. *Neuropharmacology, 47*(Suppl. 1), 293–299.

Evans, R. B. (1972). Titchener and his lost system. *Journal of the History of the Behavioral Sciences, 8*, 168–180.

Eveleth, P. B., & Tanner, J. M. (1976). *Worldwide variation in human growth*. Cambridge, England: Cambridge University Press.

Eveleth, P. B., & Tanner, J. M. (1990). *Worldwide variation in human growth* (2nd ed.). Cambridge, England: Cambridge University Press.

Eyferth, K. (1961). Leistungen verschiedener Gruppen von Besatzungskindern in Hamburg-Wechsler Intelligenztest fur Kinder (HAWIK) [Performance of different groups of occupation children on the Hamburg-Wechsler Intelligence Test for Children]. *Archhiv fur die gesamte Psychologie, 113*, 222–241.

Eysenck, H. J. (1952). The effects of psychotherapy: An evaluation. *Journal of Consulting Psychology, 16*, 319–324.

Eysenck, H. J. (1973). *Eysenck on extraversion*. New York: Wiley.

Eysenck, H. J. (1991). Dimensions of personality: 16, 5, or 3?—Criteria for a taxonomic paradigm. *Personality and Individual Differences, 12*, 773–790.

Eysenck, H. J. (1994). *Test your IQ*. Toronto, Ontario, Canada: Penguin Books.

Eysenck, H. J., & Schoenthaler, S. J. (1997). Raising IQ level by vitamin and mineral supplementation. In R. Sternberg & E. Grigorenko (eds.), *Intelligence, heredity, and environment* (pp. 363–392). Cambridge, England: Cambridge University Press.

Fabbri-Destro, M. & Rizzolatti, G. (2008). Mirror neurons and mirror systems in monkeys and humans. *Physiology, 23*, 171–179.

Fabbro, F. (1999). *The neurolinguistics of bilingualism. An introduction*. Hove, England: Psychology Press.

Fagg, G. E., & Foster, A. C. (1983). Amino acid neurotransmitters and their pathways in the mammalian central nervous system. *Neuroscience, 9*, 701–719.

Fagot, B., Hagan, R., Leinbach, M., & Kronsberg, S. (1985). Differential reactions to assertive and communicative acts of toddler girls and boys. *Child Development, 56*, 1499–1505.

Fairburn, C. G., Cooper, Z., & Shafran, R. (2003). Cognitive behaviour therapy for eating disorders: A "transdiagnostic" theory and treatment. *Behaviour Research and Therapy, 41*, 509–528.

Falk, D. (2009). New information about Einstein's brain. Frontiers in Evolutionary Neuroscience. http://frontiersin.org/evolutionaryneuroscience/paper/10.3389/neuro.18/003.2009/html/.

Fang, X., & Corso, P. S. (2007). Child maltreatment, youth violence, and intimate partner violence: Developmental relationships. *American Journal of Preventive Medicine, 33*, 281–290.

Fang, X., Singh, S., & AhluWalia, R. (2007). An examination of different explanations for the mere exposure effect. *Journal of Consumer Research, 34*, 97–103.

Faragher, E. B., Cass, M., & Cooper C. L. (2005). The relationship between job satisfaction and health: A meta-analysis. *Occupational and Environmental Medicine, 62*, 105–112

Farber, B. A., & Lane, J. S. (2002). Effective elements of the therapy relationship: Positive regard and support. In J. Norcross (ed.), *Psychotherapy relationships that work: Therapists' relational contributions to effective psychotherapy* (pp. 175–194). New York: Oxford.

Farthing, G. W. (1992). *The psychology of consciousness*. Englewood Cliffs, NJ: Prentice Hall.

Farvolden, P., & Woody, E. Z. (2004). Hypnosis, memory and frontal executive functioning. *International Journal of Clinical and Experimental Hypnosis, 52*, 3–26.

Farwell, L. A., & Donchin, E. (1991). The truth will out: Interrogative polygraphy ("lie detection") with event-related brain potentials. *Psychophysiology, 28*, 531–547.

Farwell, L. A., & Smith, S. S. (2001). Using brain MERMER testing to detect knowledge despite efforts to conceal. *Journal of Forensic Science, 46*, 135–143.

Fava, G., & Sonino, N. (2008). The biopsychosocial model thirty years later. *Psychotherapy and Psychosomatics, 77*, 1–2.

Fawcett, J. (1997). The detection and consequences of anxiety in clinical depression. *Journal of Clinical Psychiatry, 58*, 35–40.

Fawzy, F. I., Fawzy, N. W., Hyun, C. S., Elashoff, R., Guthrie, D., Fahey, J. L., et al. (1993). Malignant melanoma. Effects of an early structured psychiatric intervention, coping, and affective state on recurrence and survival 6 years later. *Archives of General Psychiatry, 50*, 681–689.

Fazio, R. H. (1995). Attitudes as object-evaluation associations: Determinants, consequences, and correlates of attitude accessibility. In R. E. Petty & J. A. Krosnick (eds.), *Attitude strength: Antecedents and consequences* (pp. 247–283). Mahwah, NJ: Erlbaum.

Fazio, R. H., & Olson, M. A. (2003). Implicit measures in social cognition: Their meaning and use. *Annual Review of Psychology, 54*, 297–327.

Febbraro, G. A. R., Clum, G. A., Roodman, A. A., & Wright, J. H. (1999). The limits of bibliotherapy: A study of the differential effectiveness of self-administered interventions in individuals with panic attacks. *Behavior Therapy, 30*, 209–222.

Federal Bureau of Investigation. (2005). *Crime in the United States*. Washington, DC: Author.

Fehr, B. (2008). Friendship formation. In S. Sprecher, A. Wenzel, & J. Harvey (eds.), *Handbook of relationship formation* (pp. 29–55). New York: Psychology Press.

Feingold, A. (1988). Cognitive gender differences are disappearing. *American Psychologist, 43*, 95–103.

Feingold, A. (1992). Good-looking people are not what we think. *Psychological Bulletin, 111*, 304–341.

Feinman, S. (1978). The blind as "ordinary people." *Journal of Visual Impairment and Blindness, 72*, 231–238.

Feist, G. J., & Brady, T. R. (2004). Openness to experience, non-conformity, and the preference for abstract art. *Empirical Studies of the Arts, 22*, 77–89.

Feldman, E. (1991). Identifying the genes for diabetes and schizophrenia. *British Medical Journal, 303*(6794), 124.

Feldman Barrett, L. & Bliss-Moreau, E. (2009). She's emotional. He's having a bad day: Attributional explanations for emotion stereotypes. *9*, 649-658.

Feldman Barrett, L., Lindquist, K., Bliss-Moreau, E., Duncan, S., Gendron, M., Mize, J., et al. (2007). Of mice and men: Natural kinds of emotion in the mammalian brain? *Perspectives on Psychological Science, 2*, 297–312.

Feldman Barrett, L. & Russell, J. A. (1999). Structure of current affect. *Current Directions in Psychological Science, 8*, 10–14.

Feldman, R., Weller, A., Zagoory-Sharon, O., & Levine, A. (2007). Evidence for a neuroendocrinological foundation of human affiliation: Plasma oxytocin levels across pregnancy and the postpartum period predict mother-infant bonding. *Psychological Science, 18*, 965–970.

Feldman-Summers, S., Montano, D. E., Kasprzyk, D., & Wagner, B. (1980). Influence attempts when competing views are gender-related: Sex as credibility. *Psychology of Women Quarterly, 5*, 311–320.

Felner, R. D., Ginter, M. A., Boike, M. F., & Cowen, E. L. (1981). Parental death or divorce in childhood: Problems, interventions, and outcomes in a school based mental health project. *Journal of Primary Prevention, 1*, 240–246.

Fenson, L., Dale, P. S., Reznick, J. S., Bates, E., Thal, D. J., & Pethick, S. J. (1994). Variability in early communicative development. *Monographs of the Society for Research in Child Development, 59* (5, Serial No. 173).

Fenton, R. (2007, November 2). Drowsy driving is big killer in U.S. *ABC News*. Retrieved November 8, 2007, from http://abcnews.go.com/Health/wireStory?id=3811426.

Ferguson, C. J. (2009) Violent video games; Dogma, fear, and pseudoscience. *Skeptical Inquirer, 33(5)*, 38–54.

Ferguson, C. J., & Kilburn, J. (2010). Much ado about nothing: The misestimation and overinterpretation of violent video game effects in Eastern and Western nations: Comment on Anderson et al. (2010). *Psychological Bulletin, 136*, 174–178.

Ferguson, D. M., Horwood, L. J., & Beautrais, A. L. (1999). Is sexual orientation related to mental health problems and suicidality in young people? *Archives of General Psychiatry, 56*, 876–880.

Fergusson, D. M., Swain-Campbell, N. R., & Horwood, L. (2002). Deviant peer affiliations, crime, and substance use: A fixed effects regression analysis. *Journal of Abnormal Child Psychology, 30*, 419–430.

Fernandez, E., & Sheffield, J. (1996). Relative contributions of life events versus daily hassles to the frequency and intensity of headaches. *Headache, 36*, 595–602.

Fernback, J. (2003). Legends on the net: An examination of computer-mediated communication as a locus of oral culture. *New Media & Society, 5*, 29-45.

Ferri, M., Amoto, L., & Davoli, M. (2006). Alcoholics Anonymous and other 12-step programmes for alcohol dependence. The Cochrance Review. Art. No: CDOO5032.DOI: 10.1002/14651858. CD005032.pub2.

Ferris, C. F. (1996). The rage of innocents. *The Sciences, 36*, 22–26.

Feske, U., & Chambless, D. L. (1995*)*. Cognitive behavioral versus exposure only treatment for social phobia: A meta-analysis. *Behavior Therapy, 26*, 695–720.

Festinger, L. (1954). A theory of social comparison processes. *Human Relations, 7*, 117–140.

Festinger, L., & Carlsmith, J. M. (1959). Cognitive consequences of forced compliance. *Journal of Abnormal and Social Psychology, 58*, 202–210.

Festinger, L., Pepitone, A., & Newcomb, T. (1952). Some consequences of deindividuation in a group. *Journal of Abnormal and Social Psychology, 47*, 382–389.

Festinger, L., Schachter, S., & Back, K. (1950). *Social pressures in informal groups*. New York: Harper.

Fiatarone, M. A., Marks, E. C., Ryan, N. D., Meredith, C. N., Lipsitz, L. A., & Evans, W. J. (1990). High-intensity strength training in nonagenarians. *Journal of the American Medical Association, 263*, 3029–3034.

Fidelman, U. (1993). Intelligence and the brain's consumption of energy: What is intelligence? *Personality and Individual Differences, 14*, 283–286.

Fiedler, K., Freytag, P., & Meiser, T. (2009). Pseudocontingencies: An integrative account of an intriguing cognitive illusion. *Psychological Review, 116*, 187–206.

Field, T. (2003). Stimulation of preterm infants. *Pediatrics in Review, 24*, 4–10.

Fields, R. D. (2007, February/March). Sex and the secret nerve. *Scientific American Mind*, 21–27.

Fields, R.D. (2009). *The other brain: From dementia to schizophrenia, how discoveries about the brain are revolutionizing medicine and science*. New York: Simon & Schuster.

Figueredo, A. J. (1993). Critical multiplism, meta-analysis, and generalization: An integrative commentary. *New Directions for Program Evaluation, 60*, 3–12.

Fillmore, K. M., Kerr, W. C., Stockwell, T., Chikritzhs, T., & Bostrom, A. (2006). Moderate alcohol use and reduced mortality risk: Systematic error in prospective studies. *Addiction Research and Theory, 14*, 101–132.

Finch, J. F., & Cialdini, R. B. (1989). Another indirect tactic of (self-)image management: Boosting. *Personality and Social Psychology Bulletin, 15*, 222–232.

Finger, S. (2000). *Minds behind the brain: A history of the pioneers and their discoveries*. New York: Oxford University Press.

Finlay-Jones, R. A., & Brown, G. W. (1981). Types of stressful life event and the onset of anxiety and depressive disorder. *Psychological Medicine, 11*, 803–815.

Finn, S. E., & Kamphuis, J. H. (1995). What a clinician needs to know about base rates. In J. N. Butcher (ed.), *Clinical personality assessment: Practical approaches* (pp. 224–235). New York: Oxford University Press.

Finzi, E., & Wasserman, E. (2006). Treatment of depression with botulinum toxin A: A case series. *Dermatologic Surgery, 32*, 645–650.

Fiorito, G., & Scotto, P. (1993). Observational learning in *Octopus vulgaris*. *Science, 256*, 545–546.

First, M. B. (2004) Desire for amputation of a limb: paraphilia, psychosis, or a new type of identity disorder. *Psychological Medicine, 35*, 919–928.

First, M. B., Spitzer, R. L., Gibbon, M., & Williams, J. B. W. (1996). *Structured clinical interview for DSM-IV Axis I disorders—Patient Edition (SCID-I/P, Version 2.0)*. New York: Biometrics Research Department, New York State Psychiatric Institute.

Fischer, K. W. (1978). The question of decalage between object permanence and person permanence. *Developmental Psychology, 14*, 1–10.

Fischer, P., Greitemeyer, T., Pollozek, F., & Frey, D. (2006). The unresponsive bystander: Are bystanders more responsive in dangerous emergencies? *European Journal of Social Psychology, 36*, 267–278.

Fischer, M.H. & Zwaan, R.A. (2008). Embodied language: A review of the role of the motor system in language comprehension. *Quarterly Journal of Experimental Psychology, 61*, 825–850.

Fischoff, B. (1975). Hindsight does not equal foresight: The effect of outcome knowledge on judgment under uncertainty. *Journal of Experimental Psychology: Human Perception and Performance, 1*, 288–299.

Fisher, J. P., Hassan, D. T., & O'Connor, N., (1995). Minerva. *BMJ: British Medical Journal, 310*, 70.

Fisher, S., & Greenberg, R. (1996). *Freud scientifically appraised*. New York: Wiley.

Fisher, T. D. (2009). The impact of socially conveyed norms on the reporting of sexual behavior and attitudes by men and women. *Journal of Experimental Social Psychology, 45*, 567–572.

Fiske, S. T. (2002). What we know about bias and intergroup conflict, problem of the century. *Current Directions in Psychological Science, 11*, 123–128.

Fiske, S. T. (2000). Stereotying, prejudice, and discrimination at the seam between the centuries: Evolution, culture, mind, and brain. *European Journal of Social Psychology, 30*, 299–322.

Fiske, S. T., & Taylor, S. E. (1991). *Social cognition* (2nd ed.). New York: McGraw Hill.

Fivush, R. (1988). The functions of event memory: Some comments on Nelson and Barsalou. In U. Neisser & E. Winograd (eds.), *Remembering reconsidered: Ecological and traditional approaches to the study of memory* (pp. 277–282). New York: Cambridge University Press.

Fivush, R., & Hudson, J. A. (eds.). (1990). *Knowing and remembering in young children*. New York: Cambridge University Press.

Flavell, J. H. (1992). Cognitive development: Past, present and future. *Developmental Psychology, 28*, 998–1005.

Flavell, J. H., Beach, D. H., & Chinsky, J. M. (1966). Spontaneous verbal rehearsal in a memory test as a function of age. *Child Development, 37*, 283–299.

Flavell, J., Friedrichs, A., & Hoyt, J. (1970). Developmental changes in memorization processes. *Cognitive Psychology, 1*, 324–340.

Flynn, J. R. (1981). The mean IQ of Americans: Massive gains 1932 to 1978. *Psychological Bulletin, 95*, 29–51.

Flynn, J. R. (1987). Massive IQ gains in 14 nations: What IQ tests really measure. *Psychological Bulletin, 101*, 171–191.

Flynn, J. R. (1998). IQ gains over time: Toward finding the causes. In U. Neisser (ed.), *The rising curve* (pp. 25–66). Washington, DC: American Psychological Association.

Flynn, J. R. (1999). Searching for justice: The discovery of IQ gains over time. *American Psychologist, 54*, 5–20.

Foa, E. B., & Kozak, M. J. (1986). Emotional processing of fear: Exposure to corrective information. *Psychological Bulletin, 99*, 20–35.

Foa, E. B., & Rothbaum, B. O. (1998). *Treating the trauma of rape: Cognitive behavioral therapy for PTSD*. New York: Guilford Press.

Foer, J. (2007). Remember this. *National Geographic, 212*, 32–57.

Fok, H. K., Hui, C. M., Bond, M. H., Matsumoto, D., & Yoo, S. H. (2008). Integrating personality, context, relationship, and emotion type into a model of display rules. *Journal of Research in Personality, 42*, 133–150.

Foley, H. A., Carlton, C. O., & Howell, R. J. (1996). The relationship of attention deficit hyperactivity disorder and conduct disorder to juvenile delinquency: Legal implications. *Bulletin of the American Academy of Psychiatry and the Law, 24*, 333–345.

Fontana, L., Eagon, J. C., Trujilio, M. E., Scherer, P. E., & Klein, S. (2007). Visceral fat adipokine secretion is associated with systemic inflammation in obese humans. *Diabetes, 56*, 1010–1013.

Forbes, E. E., Shaw, D. S., & Dahl, R. E. (2007). Alterations in reward-related decision making in boys with recent and future depression. *Biological Psychiatry, 61,* 633–639.

Forcier, M. W. (1988). Unemployment and alcohol abuse: A review. *Journal of Occupational Medicine, 30,* 246–251.

Ford, C. S., & Beach, F. (1951). *Patterns of sexual behavior.* New York: Harper and Row.

Ford, D. E., & Kamerow, D. B. (1989). Epidemiologic study of sleep disturbances and psychiatric disorders: An opportunity for prevention. *Journal of the American Medical Association, 263,* 1479–1484.

Forer, B. R. (1949). The fallacy of personal validation. *Journal of Abnormal and Social Psychology, 44,* 118–123.

Forman, E. M., Herbert, J. D., Moltra, E., Yeomans, P.D., & Geller, P. A. (2007). A randomized controlled effectiveness trial of acceptance and commitment therapy and cognitive therapy for anxiety and depression. *Behavior Modification, 31,* 772–799.

Forshaw, M. (2002). *Essential health psychology.* New York: Oxford University Press.

Foster, S., & Gurman, A. (1985). Family therapies. In S. Lynn & J. P. Garske (eds.), *Contemporary psychotherapies: Models and methods* (pp. 377–418). Columbus, OH: Charles E. Merrill.

Foulkes, D. (1962). Dream reports from different stages of sleep. *Journal of Abnormal and Social Psychology, 65,* 14–25.

Foulkes, D. (1982). *Children's dreams.* New York: Wiley.

Foulkes, D. (1985). *Dreaming: A cognitive-psychological analysis.* New York: Erlbaum.

Foulkes, D. (1999). *Children's dreaming and the development of consciousness.* Cambridge, MA: Harvard University Press.

Foulkes, D., & Rechtschaffen, A. (1964). Presleep determinants of dream content: Effects of two films. *Perceptual and Motor Skills, 19,* 983–1005.

Foulkes, D. & Schmidt, M. (1983) Temporal sequence and unit composition in dream reports from different stages of sleep. *Sleep, 6,* 265–280.

Fournier, J. C., DeRubeis, R. J., Hollon, S. D., Dimidjian, S., Amsterdam, J. D., Shelton, R. C., & Fawcett, J. (2010). Antidepressant drug effects and depression severity. *Journal of the American Medical Association, 303,* 47–53.

Fowler, K. A., Lilienfeld, S. O., & Patrick, C. P. (2009). Detecting psychopathy from thin slices of behavior. *Psychological Assessment, 21,* 68–78.

Fowler, K. A., O'Donohue, W. T., & Lilienfeld, S. O. (2007). Personality disorders in perspective. In W. T. O'Donohue, K. A. Fowler, & S. O. Lilienfeld (eds.), *Personality disorders: Toward the DSM-V* (pp. 1–19). Los Angeles, CA: Sage.

Fowles, D. C. (1980). The three arousal model: Implications of Gray's two-factor learning theory for heart rate, electrodermal activity, and psychopathy. *Psychophysiology, 17,* 87–104.

Fowles, D. C., & Dindo, L. (2009). Temperament and psychopathy: A dual-pathway model. *Current Directions in Psychological Science, 18,* 179–183.

Fox, M. J. (2002). *Lucky man: A memoir.* New York: Hyperion.

France, C. R., Masters, K. S., Belar, C.D., Kerns, R.D., Klonoff, E. A., Larkin, K., et al. (2008). Application of the competency model to clinical health psychology. *Professional Psychology: Research and Practice, 39,* 573–580.

Francis P.T. (2008). Glutamatergic approaches to the treatment of cognitive and behavioural symptoms of Alzheimer's disease. *Neurodegenerative Diseases, 5,* 241–243.

Frank, J. D. (1961). *Persuasion and healing: A comparative study of psychotherapy* (2nd ed.). Baltimore: Johns Hopkins University Press.

Frank, J. D. (1974). Common features of psychotherapies and their patients. *Psychotherapy and Psychosomatics, 24,* 368–371.

Frank, J. D., & Frank, J. B. (1991). *Persuasion and healing: A comparative study of psychotherapy* (3rd ed.). Baltimore: Johns Hopkins University Press.

Frank, L. K. (1948). *Projective methods.* Springfield, IL: Charles C Thomas.

Franklin, M. (2005, September 27). In heeding health warnings, memory can be tricky. *New York Times.* Retrieved November 12, 2007, from www.nytimes.com/2005/09/27/health/27cons.html?_r=1&oref=slogin.

Franklin, M. E., & Foa, E. B. (2002). Cognitive behavioral treatment of obsessive-compulsive disorder. In P. Nathan & J. Gorman (eds.), *A guide to treatments that work* (2nd ed., pp. 367–386). Oxford, UK: Oxford University Press.

Franklin, M. E., & Foa, E. B. (2008). Obsessive compulsive disorder. In D. Barlow (ed.), *Clinical handbook of psychological disorders: A step-by-step treatment manual* (pp. 164–215). New York: Guilford Press.

Franz, V. H., Bulthoff, H. H., & Fahle, M. (2003). Grasp effects of the Ebbinghaus illusion: Obstacle avoidance isn't the explanation. *Experimental Brain Research, 149,* 470–477.

Frederick, S., & Loewenstein, G. (1999). Hedonic adaptation. In D. Kahneman, E. Diener, & N. Schwarz (eds.), *Well-being: The foundations of hedonic psychology* (pp. 302–329). New York: Russell Sage Foundation.

Frederickson, R. (1992). *Repressed memories.* New York: Fireside/Parkside.

Fredrickson, B. L. (2001). The role of positive emotions in positive psychology: The broaden-and-build theory of positive emotions. *American Psychologist, 56,* 218–226.

Fredrickson, B. L. (2003). The value of positive emotions. *American Scientist, 91,* 330–335.

Freedman, D. G. (1964). Smiling in blind infants and the issue of innate versus acquired. *Journal of Child Psychology and Psychiatry, 5,* 171–184.

Freedman, D. G. (1978). Ethnic differences in babies. *Human Nature, 2,* 36–43.

Freedman, D. G., & DeBoer, M. (1979). Biological and cultural differences in early child development: A review. *Annual Review of Anthropology, 8,* 579–600.

Freedman, D. G., & Freedman, N. C. (1969). Behavioral differences between Chinese-American and European-American newborns. *Nature, 224,* 122.

Freedman, J. L. (1984). Effect of television violence on aggressiveness. *Psychological Bulletin, 96,* 227–246.

Freedman, J. L. (2002). *Media violence and its effects on aggression: Assessing the scientific evidence.* Toronto, Ontario, Canada: University of Toronto Press.

Freedman, J. L., & Fraser, S. C. (1966). Compliance without pressure: The foot-in-the-door technique. *Journal of Personality and Social Psychology, 4,* 195–203.

Freese, J., Powell, B., & Steelman, L. C. (1999). Rebel without a cause or effect: Birth order and social attitudes. *American Sociological Review, 64,* 207–231.

Freiheit, S. R., Vye, D., Swan, R., & Cady, M. (2004). Cognitive-behavioral therapy for anxiety: Is dissemination working? *The Behavior Therapist, 27,* 25–32.

Freire, R., & Cheng, H. W. (2004). Experience-dependent changes in the hippocampus of domestic chicks: A model for spatial memory. *European Journal of Neuroscience, 20,* 1065–1068.

French, C. C. (1992). Population stereotypes and belief in the paranormal: Is there a relationship? *Australian Psychologist, 27,* 57–58.

French, M. T., & Zavala, S. K. (2007). The health benefits of moderate drinking revisited: Alcohol use and self-reported health status. *American Journal of Health Promotion, 21,* 484–491.

Freud, A. (1937). *The ego and the mechanisms of defense.* London: Hogarth.

Freud, S. (1900). *The interpretation of dreams* (J. Crick, Trans.). London: Oxford University Press.

Freud, S. (1901). *The psychopathology of everyday life* (Vol. VI). London: Hogarth.

Freud, S. (1917/1953). "Mourning and Melancholia" in *The Standard Edition of the Complete Psychological Works of Sigmund Freud* (Vol. 14, pp. 239–258). (James Strachey, trans. and ed.). London: Hogarth Press.

Freud, S. (1923). *The ego and the id. Standard Edition, 19,* 3–66.

Freud, S. (1932). *New introductory lectures in psychoanalysis.* New York: W. W. Norton.

Freud, S. (1933). *New introductory lectures on psychoanalysis.* New York: Carleton House.

Freud, S. (1935). *A general introduction to psychoanalysis.* New York: Washington Square Press.

Freund, K., Watson, R., & Rienzo, D. (1989). Heterosexuality, homosexuality, and erotic age preference. *The Journal of Sex Research, 26,* 107–117.

Frey, M. C., & Detterman, D. K. (2004). Scholastic assessment or g? The relationship between the SAT and general cognitive ability. *Psychological Science, 15,* 373–398.

Frick, P. J., & Marsee, M. A. (2006). Psychopathy and developmental pathways to antisocial behavior in youth. In C. J. Patrick (ed.), *Handbook of psychopathy* (pp. 353–374). New York: Guilford Press.

Friedlander, M. L. (1984). Psychotherapy talk as social control. *Psychotherapy, 21,* 335–341.

Friedman, M., & Rosenman, R. H. (1959). Association of a specific overt behavior pattern with increases in blood cholesterol, blood clotting time, incidence of arcus senilis and clinical coronary artery disease. *Journal of the American Medical Association, 169,* 1286–1296.

Friedman, M., & Rosenman, R. H. (1974). *Type A behavior and your heart.* New York: Alfred A. Knopf.

Friedman, M., Powell, L. H., Thoreson, C. E., Ulmer, D., Price, V., Gill, J. J., et al. (1987). Effect of discontinuance of Type A behavioral counseling on Type A behavior and cardiac recurrence rate of post myocardial infarction patients. *American Heart Journal, 114,* 483–490.

Friedman, M. A., & Wishman, M. A. (1998). Sociotropy, autonomy, and bulimic symptomatology. *International Journal of Eating Disorders, 23,* 439–442.

Friedman, R. A. (2006). Mental illness and violence: How strong is the link? *New England Journal of Medicine, 355,* 2064–2066.

Friedman, R. S., & Arndt, J. (2005). Reexploring the connection between terror management theory and dissonance theory. *Personality and Social Psychology Bulletin, 31,* 1217–1225.

Friesen, W. V. (1972). *Cultural differences in facial expressions in a social situation: An experimental test of the concept of display rules.* Unpublished doctoral dissertation, University of California, San Francisco.

Frieze, I. H., Peterson, J. E., Johnson, P. B., Ruble, D. N., & Zellman, G. (1978). *Women and sex roles: A social psychological perspective.* New York: W. W. Norton.

Frijda, N. H. (1986). *The emotions.* Cambridge, England: Cambridge University.

Frisher M., Crome, I., Martino, O., & Croft, P. (2009). Assessing the impact of cannabis use on trends in diagnosed schizophrenia in the United Kingdom from 1996 to 2005. *Schizophrenia Research, 113,* 123–128.

Frisina, P. G., Borod, J. C., & Lepore, S. J. (2004). A meta-analysis of the effects of written disclosure on the health outcomes of clinical populations. *Journal of Nervous and Mental Disease, 192,* 629–634.

Frith, C. D. (1992). *The cognitive neuropsychology of schizophrenia.* Hillsdale, NJ: Erlbaum.

Fromm, E., & Nash, M. R. (1997). *Hypnosis and psychoanalysis. Mental Health Library Series, No. 5.* Guilford, CT: International Universities Press.

Frontera, W. R., Meredith, C. N., O'Reilly, K. P., Knuttgen, H. H., & Evans, W. J. (1988). Strength conditioning in older men: Skeletal muscle hypertrophy and improved function. *Journal of Applied Physiology, 64,* 1038–1044.

Fu, K. M., Johnston, T. A., Shah, A. S., Arnold, L., Smiley, J., Hackett, T. A., et al. (2003). Auditory cortical neurons respond to somatosensory stimulation. *Journal of Neuroscience, 23,* 7510–7515.

Fuhriman, A., & Burlingame, G. M. (1994). Group psychotherapy: Research and practice. In A. Fuhriman & G. M. Burlingame (eds.), *Handbook of group psychotherapy: An empirical and clinical synthesis* (pp. 3–40). New York: John Wiley & Sons.

Fukuda, H., & Takahashi, J. (2005). Embryonic stem cells as a cell source for treating Parkinson's disease. *Expert Opinion on Biological Therapy, 5,* 1273–1280.

Fukuda, K., Ogilvie, R., Chilcott, L., Venditteli, A., & Takeuchi, T. (1998). High prevalence of sleep paralysis in Canadian and Japanese college students. *Dreaming, 8,* 59–66.

Fullana, M. A., Mataix-Cols, D., Caspi, A., Harrington, H., Grisham, J. R., Moffitt, T. E., et al. (2009). Obsessions and compulsions in the community: Prevalence, interference, help seeking, developmental stability, and co-occurring psychiatric conditions. *The American Journal of Psychiatry, 166,* 329–336.

Fuller, R. L., Luck, S. J., Braun, E. L., Robinson, B. M., McMahon, R. P., & Gold, J. M. (2006). Impaired control of visual attention in schizophrenia. *Journal of Abnormal Psychology, 115,* 266–275.

Fulton, M. M., & Allen, E. R. (2005). Polypharmacy in the elderly: A literature review. *Journal of the American Academy of Nurse Practitioners, 17,* 123–132.

Funder, D. C. (1991). Global traits: A neo-Allportian approach to personality. *Psychological Science, 2,* 31–39.

Furmark, T., Tillfors, M., Marteinsdottir, I., Fischer, H., Pissiota, A., Langstrom, B., et al. (2002). Common changes in cerebral blood flow in patients with social phobia treated with citalopram or cognitive-behavioral therapy. *Archives of General Psychiatry, 59,* 425–433.

Furnham, A., Batey, M., Anand, K., & Manfield, J. (2008). Personality, hypomania, intelligence and creativity. *Personality and Individual Differences, 44,* 1060–1069.

Furnham, A., & Cheng, H. (2000). Perceived parental behavior, self-esteem and happiness. *Social Psychiatry and Psychiatric Epidemiology, 35,* 463–470.

Furnham, A., & Fudge, C. (2008). The Five Factor model of personality and sales performance. *Journal of Individual Differences, 29,* 11–16.

Furnham, A., Petrides, K. V., & Constantinides, A. (2005). The effects of body mass index and waist-to-hip ratio on ratings of female attractiveness, fecundity, and health. *Personality and Individual Differences, 38,* 1823–1834.

Furnham, A., Zhang, J., & Chamorro-Premuzic, T. (2006) The relationship between psychometric and self-estimated intelligence, creativity, personality and academic achievement. *Imagination, Cognition and Personality, 25,* 119–145.

Fuster, J. M. (2000). Executive frontal functions. *Experimental Brain Research, 133,* 66–70.

Gage, F. H. (2002). Neurogenesis in the adult brain. *Journal of Neuroscience, 22,* 612–613.

Galambos, S. J., & Hakuta, K. (1988). Subject-specific and task-specific characteristics of metalinguistic awareness in bilingual children. *Applied Psycholinguistics, 9,* 141–162.

Galanter, M. (1980). Psychological induction into the large group: Findings from a modern religious sect. *American Journal of Psychiatry, 137,* 1574–1579.

Gallese, V., & Goldman, A. (1998) Mirror neurons and the simulation theory of mind-reading. *Trends in Cognitive Sciences, 2,* 493–501.

Gallo, E. (1994). Synchronicity and the archetypes: The imprecision of C. G. Jung's language and concepts. *Skeptical Inquirer, 18,* 376–403.

Gallo, L. C., & Matthews, K. A. (2003). Understanding the association between socioeconomic status and physical health: Do negative emotions play a role? *Psychological Bulletin, 129,* 10–51.

Gallup, G. G., Jr. (1979). Self-awareness in primates. *American Scientist, 67,* 417–421.

Gallup, G. G., Jr., & Suarez, S. D. (1985). Alternatives to the use of animals in psychological research. *American Psychologist, 40,* 1104–1111.

Galton, F. (1876). The history of twin, as a criterion of the relative powers of nature and nurture. *Journal of the Anthropological Institute of Great Britain and Ireland, 5,* 391–406.

Galton, F. (1869). *Hereditary genius: An inquiry into its laws and consequences.* London: Macmillan.

Galton, F. (1878). Composite portraits made by combining those of many different persons into a single resultant figure. *Journal of the Anthropological Institute of Great Britain and Ireland, 8,* 132.

Galton, F. (1880). Statistics of mental imagery. *Mind, 5,* 301–318.

Gambrill, E. D. (1992). Self-help books: Pseudoscience in the guise of science? *Skeptical Inquirer 16*(4), 389–399.

Gamer, M., Rill, H. G., Vossel, G., & Gödert, H. W. (2006). Psychophysiological and vocal measures in the detection of guilty knowledge. *International Journal of Psychophysiology, 60,* 76–87.

Gangestad, S., & Scheyd, G. J. (2005). The evolution of human physical attractiveness. *Annual Review of Anthropology, 34,* 523–548.

Gangestad, S. W., & Snyder, M. (2000). Self-monitoring: Appraisal and reappraisal. *Psychological Bulletin, 126,* 530–555.

Gangswisch, J. E., Babiss, L. A., Malaspina, D., Turner, J. B., Zammit, G. K., & Posner, K. (2010). Earlier parental set bedtimes as a protective factor against depression and suicidal ideation, *Sleep, 33,* 97–106.

Garb, H. N. (1984). The incremental validity of information used in personality assessment. *Clinical Psychology Review, 4,* 641–655.

Garb, H. N. (1998). *Studying the clinician: Judgment, research, and psychological assessment.* Washington, DC: American Psychological Association.

Garb, H. N., Wood, J. M., Lilienfeld, S. O., & Nezworski, T. (2005). Roots of the Rorschach controversy. *Clinical Psychology Review, 25,* 97–118.

Garcia, J., & Hankins, W. G. (1977). On the origin of food aversion paradigms. In L. M. Barker, M. R. Best, & M. Domjan (eds.), *Learning mechanisms in food selection* (pp. 3–22). Houston, TX: Baylor University Press.

Garcia, J., & Koelling, R. A. (1966). The relation of cue to consequence in avoidance learning. *Psychonomic Science, 4,* 123–124.

Garcia, S. M., Weaver, K., Moskowitz, G. B., & Darley, J. M. (2002). Crowded minds: The implicit bystander effect. *Journal of Personality and Social Psychology, 83,* 843–853.

García-Montes, J. M., Álvarez, M. P., Sass, L. A., & Cangas, A. J. (2008). The role of superstition in psychopathology. *Philosophy, Psychiatry, & Psychology, 15,* 227–237.

Gardini, S., Cloninger, C. R., & Venneri, A. (2009). Individual differences in personality traits reflect structural variance in specific brain regions. *Brain Research Bulletin, 79,* 265–270.

Gardner, C. D., Kiazand, A., Alhassan, S., Kim, S., Stafford, R. S., Balise, R., et al. (2007). Comparison of the Atkins, Zone, Ornish, and LEARN diets for change in weight and related risk factors among overweight premenopausal women. *Journal of the American Medical Association, 297,* 969–977.

Gardner, H. (1983). *Frames of mind: The theory of multiple intelligences.* New York: Basic Books.

Gardner, H. (1999). *Intelligence reframed: Multiple intelligences for the 21st century.* New York: Basic Books.

Gardner, M. (1958). *Fads and fallacies in the name of science.* New York: Dover.

Gardner, W. L., Gabriel, S., & Diekman, A. B. (2000). Interpersonal processes. In J. T. Cacioppo, L. G. Tassinary, & G. G. Berntson (eds.), *Handbook of psychophysiology* (2nd ed., pp. 643–664). New York: Cambridge University Press.

Garfield, S. L. (1978). Research on client variables. In S. Garfield & A. Bergin (eds.), *Handbook of psychotherapy and behavior change* (pp. 191–232). New York: John Wiley & Sons.

Garmezy, N., Masten, A. S., & Tellegen, A. (1984). The study of stress and competence in children: A building block for developmental psychopathology. *Child Development, 55,* 97–111.

Garner, D. M. (1997). Psychoeducational principles in the treatment of eating disorders. In D. M. Garner & P. E. Garfinkel (eds.), *Handbook for treatment of eating disorders* (pp. 145–177). New York: Guilford Press.

Garske, J. P., & Anderson, T. (2003). Toward a science of psychotherapy research: Present status and evaluation. In S. O. Lilienfeld, S. J. Lynn, & J. M. Lohr (eds.), *Science and pseudoscience in clinical psychology* (pp. 145–175). New York: Guilford Press.

Gartrel, N., & Bos, H. (2010). U.S. National Longitudinal Lesbian Family Study: Psychological adjustment of 17-year-old adolescents. *Pediatrics, 126,* 1–9.

Gasperini, M., Scherillo, P., Manfredonia, M. G., Franchini, L., & Smeraldi, E. (1993). A study of relapse in subjects with mood disorder on lithium treatment. *European Neuropsychopharmacology, 3,* 103–110.

Gatchel, R. J. (2001). Biofeedback and self-regulation of physiological activity: A major adjunctive treatment modality in health psychology. In A. Baum, T. A. Revenson, & J. E. Singer (eds.), *Handbook of health psychology* (pp. 95–103). Mahwah, NJ: Lawrence Erlbaum.

Gatchel, R. J., & Baum, A. (1983). *An introduction to health psychology.* Reading, MA: Addison-Wesley.

Gatchel, R. J., & Oordt, M. S. (2003). *Clinical psychology and primary health care.* Washington, DC: American Psychological Association.

Gathercole, V. C. M. (2002a). Command of the mass/count distinction in bilingual and monolingual children: An English morphosyntactic distinction. In D. K. Oller & R. E. Eilers (eds.), *Language and literacy in bilingual children* (pp. 175–206). Clevedon, England: Multilingual Matters.

Gathercole, V. C. M. (2002b). Grammatical gender in bilingual and monolingual children: A Spanish morphosyntactic distinction. In D. K. Oller & R. E. Eilers (eds.), *Language and literacy in bilingual children* (pp. 207–219), Clevedon, England: Multilingual Matters.

Gause, C., Morris, C., Vernekar, S., Pardo-Villamizar, C., Grados, M. A., & Singer, H. S. (2009). Antineuronal antibodies in OCD: Comparisons in children with OCD-only, OCD+chronic tics and OCD+PANDAS. *Journal of Neuroimmunology, 214,* 118–124.

Gawronski, B., LeBel, E. P., & Peters, K. R. (2007). What do implicit measures tell us? Scrutinizing the validity of three common assumptions. *Perspectives on Psychological Science, 2,* 181–193.

Gazzaniga, M. S. (2000). Cerebral specialization and interhemispheric communication: Does the corpus callosum enable the human condition? *Brain, 123,* 1293–1326.

Gazzaniga, M. S., Ivry, R., Mangun, G.R. (1988). *Fundamentals of cognitive neuroscience.* New York: W.W. Norton.

Gazzaniga, M. S., Ivry, R., & Mangun, G. R. (2002). *Fundamentals of cognitive neuroscience* (2nd ed.). New York: W. W. Norton.

Geake, J. (2008). Neuromythologies in education. *Educational Research, 80,* 123–133.

Geary, D. C. (1996). Sexual selection and sex differences in mathematical abilities. *Behavioral and Brain Sciences, 19,* 229–284.

Geen, R. G., (1984). Preferred stimulation levels in introverts and extroverts: Effects on arousal and performance. *Journal of Personality and Social Psychology, 46,* 1303–1312.

Geen, R. G. (2001). *Human aggression* (2nd ed.). New York: Taylor & Francis.

Geier, A. B., Rozin, P., & Doros, G. (2006). Unit bias: A new heuristic that helps explain the effect of portion size on food intake. *Psychological Science, 17,* 521–525.

Geiser, S. & Studley, R. (2002). UC and the SAT: Predictive validity and differential impact of the SAT I and SAT II at the University of California. *Educational Assessment, 8,* 1–26.

Gellatly, A. R. (1987). Acquisition of a concept of logical necessity. *Human Development, 30,* 32–47.

Geller, B., Zimmerman, B., Williams, M., Bolhofner, K., Craney, J. L. Frazer, J., et al. (2002). DSM-IV mania symptoms in a prepubertal and early adolescent bipolar disorder phenotype compared to attention deficit hyperactive and normal controls. *Journal of the American Academy of Child and Adolescent Psychopharmacology, 12,* 11–25.

Gelman, R., & Gallistel, C. (1978). *The child's understanding of number.* Cambridge, MA: Harvard University Press.

Genesee, F. (1985). Second language learning through immersion: A review of U.S. programs. *Review of Educational Research, 55,* 541–561.

Gentile, D. A., & Anderson, C. A. (2003). Violent video games: The newest media violence hazard. In D. A. Gentile (ed.), *Media violence and children* (pp. 131–152). Westport, CT: Praeger Publishing.

Gentner, D., Loewenstein, J., Thompson, L., & Forbus, K. D. (2009). Reviving inert knowledge: Analogical abstraction supports relational retrieval of past events. *Cognitive Science, 33,* 1343–1382.

George, M. S., Sackeim, H., Rush, A. J., Marangell, L. B., Nahas, Z., Husain, M. M., et al. (2000). Vagus nerve stimulation: A new tool for treatment-resistant depression. *Biological Psychiatry, 47,* 287–295.

Georgiadis, J. R., Kortekaas, R., Kuipers, R., Nieuwenburg, A., Pruim, J., Reinders, A. A., et al. (2006). Regional cerebral blood flow changes associated with clitorally induced orgasm in healthy women. *European Journal of Neuroscience, 24,* 3305–3316.

Geraerts, E., Bernstein, D. M., Merckelbach, H., Londers, C., Raymaekers, L., & Loftus, E. F. (2008). Lasting beliefs and their behavioral consequences. *Psychological Science, 19,* 749–753.

Geraerts, E., Smeets, E., Jelicic, M., van Heerden, J., & Merckelbach, H. (2005). Fantasy proneness, but not self-reported trauma is related to DRM performance of women reporting recovered memories of childhood sexual abuse. *Consciousness and Cognition, 14,* 602–612.

Gerard, S., & Aybala, S. (2007). GABAergic contributions to the pathophysiology of depression and the mechanism of antidepressant action. *CNS & Neurological Disorders-Drug Targets, 6,* 127–140.

Gerard, S., Smith, B. H., & Simpson, J. A. (2003). A randomized controlled trial of spiritual healing in restricted neck movement. *Journal of Alternative and Complementary Medicine, 9,* 467–477.

Gergen, K. J. (1973). Social psychology as history. *Journal of Personality and Social Psychology, 26,* 309–320.

German, T. P., & Barrett, H. C. (2005). Functional fixedness in a technologically sparse culture. *Psychological Science, 16,* 1–5.

German, T. P., & Defeyter, M. A. (2000). Immunity to functional fixedness in young children. *Psychonomic Bulletin & Review, 7,* 707–712.

Gernsbacher, M. A., Dawson, M., & Goldsmith, H. H. (2005). Three reasons not to believe in an autism epidemic. *Current Directions in Psychological Science, 14,* 55–58.

Gershoff, E. T. (2002). Corporal punishment by parents and associated child behaviors and experiences: A meta-analytic and theoretical review. *Psychological Bulletin, 128,* 539–579.

Geschwind, N. (1983). Interictal behavior changes in epilepsy. *Epilepsia, 24*(Suppl. 1), S23–S30.

Gewirtz, J. C., & Davis, M. (2000). Using Pavlovian "higher-order" conditioning paradigms to investigate the neural substrates of emotional learning and memory. *Learning and Memory, 7,* 257–266.

Ghetti, S., Lyons, K.E., Lazzarin, F., & Cornoldi, C. (2008). The development of metamemory monitoring during retrieval: The case of memory strength and memory absence. *Journal of Experimental Child Psychology, 99,* 157–181.

Giancola, P. R., & Corman, M. D. (2007). Alcohol and aggression: A test of the attention-allocation model. *Psychological Science, 18,* 649–655.

Gibb, B. E., & Alloy, L. B. (2006). A prospective test of the hopelessness theory of depression in children. *Journal of Clinical Child and Adolescent Psychology, 35,* 264–274.

Gibb, C., & Randall, P. E. (1988). Metalinguistic abilities and learning to read. *Educational Research, 30,* 135–141.

Gibbs, J. C. (2006). Should Kohlberg's cognitive developmental approach to morality be replaced with a more pragmatic approach? Comment on Krebs and Denton (2005). *Psychological Review, 113,* 666–671.

Gibbs, M. E., & Bowser, D. N. (2009). Astrocytes and interneurons in memory processing in the chick hippocampus: Roles for G-coupled protein receptors, GABA(B) and mGluRi. *Neurochemical Research, 34.*

Gibson, E. J. (1991). *An odyssey in learning and perception.* Cambridge, MA: MIT Press.

Gibson, E. J., & Walk, R. D. (1960). The "visual cliff." *Scientific American, 202,* 64–71.

Gick, M. L., & Holyoak, K. J. (1983). Schema induction and analogical transfer. *Cognitive Psychology, 14,* 1–38.

Giesbrecht, T., Lynn, S. J., Lilienfeld, S. O., & Merckelbach, H. (2008). Cognitive processes in dissociation: An analysis of core theoretical assumptions. *Psychological Bulletin, 134,* 617–647.

Gigerenzer, G. (2001). The adaptive toolbox. In G. Gigerenzer & R. Selten (eds.), *Bounded rationality: The adaptive toolbox* (pp. 37–50). Cambridge, MA: MIT Press.

Gigerenzer, G. (2007). *Gut feelings: The intelligence of the unconscious.* New York: Viking Press.

Gigerenzer, G., & Goldstein, D. G. (1996). Reasoning the fast and frugal way: Models of bounded rationality. *Psychological Review, 103,* 650–669.

Gignac, G. E., Stough, C., & Loukomitis, S. (2004). Openness, intelligence, and self-report intelligence, *Intelligence, 32,* 133–143.

Gilbert, D. T. (2006). *Stumbling on happiness.* New York: Knopf.

Gilber, D. T., & Malone, P. S. (1995). The correspondence bias. *Psychological Bulletin, 117,* 21–38.

Gilbert, D. T., Pinel, E. C., Wilson, T. D., Blumberg, S. J., & Wheatley, T. (1998). Immune neglect: A source of durability bias in affective forecasting. *Journal of Personality and Social Psychology, 75,* 617–638.

Gilbertson, T. A., Fontenot D. T., Liu, L., Zhang, H., & Monroe, W. T. (1997). Fatty acid modulation of K+ channels in taste receptor cells: Gustatory cues for dietary fat. *American Journal of Physiology, 272*(4 Pt. 1), C1203–C1210.

Giles, J. (2002). Electroconvulsive therapy and the fear of deviance. *Journal for the Theory of Social Behaviour, 32,* 61–87.

Giles, J. (2007). Degrees in homeopathy slated as unscientific. *Nature, 446,* 352–352.

Gillham, N. W. (2001). *A life of Sir Francis Galton: From African exploration to the birth of eugenics.* New York: Oxford University Press.

Gilligan, C. (1982). *In a different voice: Psychological theory and women's development.* Cambridge, MA: Harvard University Press.

Gilovich, T. (1991). *How we know what isn't so: The fallibility of human reason in everyday life.* New York: Free Press.

Gilovich, T., Griffin, D., & Kahneman, D. (eds.). (2002). *Heuristics and biases: The psychology of intuitive judgment.* New York: Cambridge University Press.

Gilovich, T., Vallone, R., & Tversky, A. (1985). The hot hand in basketball – On the misperception of random sequences. *Cognitive Psychology, 17,* 295–314.

Gintis, H., Bowles, S., Boyd, R., & Fehr, E. (2003). Explaining altruistic behavior in humans. *Evolution and Human Behavior, 24,* 153–172.

Giuffra, L. A., & Risch, N. (1994). Diminished recall and the cohort effect of major depression: A simulation study. *Psychological Medicine, 24,* 375–383.

Gizewski, E. R., Gasser, T., de Greiff, A., Boehm, A., & Forsting, M. (2003). Cross-modal plasticity for sensory and motor activation patterns in blind subjects. *Neuroimage, 19,* 968–975.

Gladwell, M. (2005). *Blink: The power of thinking without thinking.* Boston: Little, Brown, & Company.

Gladwell, M. (2007, November 12). Dangerous minds: Criminal profiling made easy. *New Yorker.* Retrieved November 9, 2007, from www.newyorker.com/reporting/2007/11/12/071112fa_fact_gladwell.

Gladwell, M. (2009). *Outliers: The story of success.* Boston: Little, Brown, and Company.

Glaser, J., & Kihlstrom, J. F. (2005). Compensatory automaticity: Unconscious volition is not an oxymoron. In R. Hassin, J. S. Uleman, & J. A. Bargh (eds.), *The new unconscious* (pp. 171–195). Oxford: Oxford University Press.

Glasser, S. P., & Frishman, W. (2008). The placebo and nocebo effect. In S. P. Glasser (ed.), *Essentials of clinical research* (pp. 111–128). Netherlands: Springer.

Glassgold, J. M., Beckstead, L., Drescher, J., Greene, B., Miller, R. L., & Worthington, R. L. (2009). *Report of the American Psychological Association Task Force on the appropriate therapeutic responses to sexual orientation.* Washington, DC: American Psychological Association.

Gleaves, D. H. (1996). The sociocognitive model of dissociative identity disorder: A reexamination of the evidence. *Psychological Bulletin, 120,* 42–59.

Gleaves, D. H., May, M. C., & Cardeña, E. (2001). An examination of the diagnostic validity of dissociative identity disorder. *Clinical Psychology Review, 21,* 577–608.

Glenn, D. (2010, May 9). Carol Dweck's attitude: It's not about how smart you are. *Chronicle of Higher Education.* http://chronicle.com/article/Carol-Dwecks-Attitude/65405/

Glickman, S. E., Frank, L. G., Davidson, J. M., Smith, E. R., & Siiteri, P. K. (1987). Androstenedione may organize or activate sex-reversed traits in female spotted hyenas. *Proceedings of the National Academy of Sciences, 84,* 3444–3447.

Glimcher, P. W., Camerer, C. F., Fehr, E., & Poldrack, R. A. (2008). *Neuroeconomics: Decision-making and the brain.* San Diego, CA: Academic Press.

Glynn, I. (1999). *An anatomy of thought: The origin and machinery of the mind.* New York: Oxford University Press.

Gobel, S. M., & Rushworth, M. F. (2004). Cognitive neuroscience: Acting on numbers. *Current Biology, 14,* R517–R519.

Godden, D. R., & Baddeley, A. D. (1975). Context dependency in two natural environments: On land and underwater. *British Journal of Psychology, 91,* 99–104.

Goertzel, T. (1994). Belief in conspiracy theories. *Political Psychology, 15,* 733–744.

Goethals, G. R., & Reckman, R. F. (1973). The perception of consistency in attitudes. *Journal of Experimental Social Psychology, 9,* 491–501.

Goff, D. C., & Coyle, J. T. (2001). The emerging role of glutamate in the pathophysiology and treatment of schizophrenia. *American Journal of Psychiatry, 158,* 1367–1377.

Goffman, E. (1959). *The presentation of self in everyday life.* London: Penguin.

Gold, J. M., Murray, R. F., Bennett, P. J., & Sekuler, A. B. (2000). Deriving behavioural receptive fields for visually completed contours. *Current Biology, 10,* 663–666.

Gold, P. E., Cahill, L., & Wenk, G. L. (2002). Gingko biloba: A cognitive enhancer? *Psychological Science in the Public Interest, 3,* 2–11.

Goldberg, L. (1986). Some informal explorations and ruminations about graphology. In B. Nevo (ed.), *Scientific aspects of graphology* (pp. 281–293). Springfield, IL: Charles C. Thomas.

Goldberg, L. R. (1969). The search for configural relationships in personality assessment: The diagnosis of psychosis vs. neurosis from the MMPI. *Multivariate Behavioral Research, 4,* 523–536.

Goldberg, L. R. (1993). The structure of phenotypic personality traits. *American Psychologist, 48,* 26–34.

Golden, N., & Sacker, I. M. (1984). An overview of the etiology, diagnosis, and management of anorexia nervosa. *Clinical Pediatrics, 23,* 209–214.

Goldenberg, J. N., Brown, S. B., & Weiner, W. J. (1994). Coprolalia in younger patients with Gilles de la Tourette syndrome. *Movement Disorders, 9,* 622–625.

Goldfried, M. R., & Davison, G. C. (1976). *Clinical behavior therapy.* New York: Holt, Rinehart, & Winston.

Goldfried, M. R., Raue, P. J., & Castonguay, L. G. (1998). The therapeutic focus in significant sessions of master therapists: A comparison of cognitive-behavioral and psychodynamic-interpersonal interventions. *Journal of Consulting and Clinical Psychology, 66,* 803–810.

Goldin, C., & Rouse, C. (2000). Orchestrating impartiality. *American Economic Review, 90,* 715–741.

Goldin-Meadow, S., Ozyurek, A., Sancar, B., & Mylander, C. (2009). Making language around the globe: A crosslinguistic study of homesign in the United States, China, and Turkey. In J. Guo, E. Lieven, N. Budwig, S. Ervin-Tripp, K. Nakamura, & S. Ozcaliskan, (eds.) *Crosslinguistic approaches to the psychology of language: Research in the tradition of Dan Isaac Slobin* (pp. 27–39). New York, NY: Psychology Press.

Golding, J., Steer, C., Emmett, P., Bartoshuk, L. M., Horwood, J., & Smith, G. D. (2009). Associations between the ability to detect a bitter taste, dietary behavior, and growth: A preliminary report. *Annals of the New York Academy of Sciences, 1170,* 553–557.

Goldman, M. S., Darkes, J., & Del Boca, F. K. (1999). Expectancy mediation of biopsychosocial risk for alcohol use and alcoholism. In I. Kirsch (ed.), *How expectancies shape experience* (pp. 232–262). Washington, DC: American Psychological Association.

Goldman, A. I. & de Vignemont, F. (2009). Is social cognition embodied? *Trends in Cognitive Sciences, 13,* 154–159.

Goldman, D., Hu, X., Kennedy, J., & Murphy, D. (2006). Linkage of gain-of-function serotonin transporter alleles to obsessive compulsive disorder. *Biological Psychiatry, 59,* 99S–100S.

Goldreich, D., & Kanics, I. M. (2003). Tactile acuity is enhanced in blindness. *Journal of Neuroscience, 23,* 3439–3445.

Goldstein, D. G., & Gigerenzer, G. (1999). The recognition heuristic: How ignorance makes us smart. In G. Gigerenzer, P. M. Todd, & the ABC Research Group (eds.), *Simple heuristics that make us smart* (pp. 37–58). London: Oxford University Press.

Goldstein, L., & Ruscio, J. (2009). Thinking outside the Black Box: The relative risk of suicide with antidepressant use. *Scientific Review of Mental Health Practice, 7,* 3-16.

Goldstein, M. H., & Schwade, J. A. (2008). Social feedback to infants' babbling facilitates rapid phonological learning. *Psychological Science, 19,* 515–523.

Goldston, D. B., Daniel, S. S., Reboussin, B., Reboussin, D., Frazier, P. H., & Harris, A. (2001). Cognitive risk factors and suicide attempts among formerly hospitalized adolescents: A prospective naturalistic study. *Journal of the American Academy of Child and Adolescent Psychiatry, 40,* 155–162.

Goleman, D. (1995). *Emotional Intelligence.* New York: Bantam Books.

Golier, J. A., Yehuda, R., Lupien, S. J., & Harvey. P. D., Grossman, R., & Elkin, A. (2002). Memory performance in Holocaust survivors with posttraumatic stress disorder. *American Journal of Psychiatry, 159,* 1682–1688.

Golin, S., Terrell, T., & Johnson, B. (1977). Depression and the illusion of control. *Journal of Abnormal Psychology, 86,* 440–442.

Golinkoff, R. M., Hirsh-Pasek, K., Bloom, L., Smith, L. B., Woodward, A. L., Akhtar, N., et al. (2000). *Becoming a word learner: A debate on lexical acquisition.* New York, NY: Oxford University Press.

Golkaramnay, V., Bauer, S., Haug, S., Wolf, M., Kordy, H. (2007). The exploration of the effectiveness of group therapy through an Internet chat as aftercare: A controlled naturalistic study. *Psychotherapy and Psychosomatics, 76,* 219–225.

Golombok, S. (2000). *Parenting: What really counts?* London: Routledge.

Gonzaga, G. C., Turner, R. A., Keltner, D., Campos, B., & Altemus, M. (2006). Romantic love and sexual desire in close relationships. *Emotion, 6,* 163–179.

Good, T. L., & Brophy, J. (1995). *Contemporary educational psychology.* Boston: Longman.

Goodall, J. (1990). *Through a window.* Boston: Houghton Mifflin.

Goodall, J., & van Lawick, H. (1971). *In the shadow of man.* Boston: Houghton-Mifflin.

Goode, E. (2000, January 18). Among the inept, researchers discover, ignorance is bliss. New York Times. http://www.nytimes.com/2000/01/18/health/among-the-inept-researchers-discover-ignorance-is-bliss.html?pagewanted=all.

Goodman, J. A., Krahn, L. E., Smith, G. G., Rummans, T. A., & Pileggi, T. S. (1999). Patient satisfaction with electroconvulsive therapy. *Mayo Clinic Proceedings, 74,* 967–971.

Goodwin, D. K. (2005). *Team of rivals: The political genius of Abraham Lincoln.* New York: Simon & Schuster.

Goodwin, D. W. (1995). Alcohol amnesia. *Addiction, 90,* 315–317.

Goodwin, D. W., Powell, B., Brenner, D., Hoine, H., & Sterne, J. (1969). Alcohol and recall: State dependent effects in man. *Science, 163,* 1358–1360.

Goodwin, F. K., & Jamison K. R. (1990), *Manic-depressive illness.* New York: Oxford University Press.

Gorassini, D., & Olson, J. (1995). Does self-perception change explain the foot-in-the-door effect? *Journal of Personality and Social Psychology, 69,* 91–105.

Gorassini, D. R., & Spanos, N. P. (1998). The Carleton Skill Training Program. In I. Kirsch, A. Capafons, E. Cardeña, & S. Amigo (eds.), *Clinical hypnosis and self-regulation: Cognitive-behavioral perspectives* (pp. 141–177). Washington, DC: American Psychological Association.

Gordon, H. (2002). The suicide bomber: Is it a psychiatric phenomenon? *Psychiatric Bulletin, 26,* 285–287.

Gordon, P. (2004). Numerical cognition without words: Evidence from Amazonia. *Science, 306,* 496–499.

Gorenstein, E. E. (1984). Debating mental illness: Implications for science, medicine, and social policy. *American Psychologist, 39,* 50–56.

Gori, L., & Firenzuoli, F. (2007). Ear acupuncture in European traditional medicine. *Evidence-Based Complementary and Alternative Medicine, 4,* 13–16.

Gorn, G. J. (1982). The effects of music in advertising on choice behavior: A classical conditioning approach. *Journal of Marketing, 46,* 94–101.

Gorsuch, R. L. (1988). Psychology of religion. *Annual Review of Psychology, 39,* 201–221.

Gortmaker, S. L., Must, A., Perrin, J. M., Sobol, A. M., & Dietz, W. H. (1993). Social and economic consequences of overweight in adolescence and young adulthood. *New England Journal of Medicine, 329,* 1009–1012.

Gosling, S. D. (2001). From mice to men: What can we learn about personality from animal research? *Psychological Bulletin, 127,* 45–86.

Gosling, S. D. (2008). Personality in non-human animals. *Social and Personality Psychology Compass, 2,* 985–1002.

Gosling, S. D. (2008). *Snoop: What your stuff says about you.* New York: Basic Books.

Gosling, S. D., Rentfrow, P. J., & Swann, W. B. (2003). A very brief measure of the Big-Five personality domains. *Journal of Research in Personality, 36,* 504–528.

Gosling, S. D., Sandy, C. J., & Potter, J. (in press). Personalities of self-identified "dog people" and "cat people." *Anthrozoos.*

Gotlib, I. H., & Hammen, C. (1992). *Psychological aspects of depression: Toward a cognitive-interpersonal integration.* New York: Wiley.

Gottdiener, J. S., Gross, H. A., Henry, W. L., Borer, J. S., & Ebert, M. H. (1978). Effects of self-induced starvation on cardiac size and function in anorexia nervosa. *Circulation, 58,* 425–433.

Gottfredson, L. S. (1997). Why g matters: The complexity of everyday life. *Intelligence, 24,* 79–132.

Gottfredson, L. S. (2003). On Sternberg's "Reply to Gottfredson." *Intelligence, 31,* 415–424.

Gottfredson, L. S. (2004). Intelligence: Is it the epidemiologists' elusive "fundamental cause" of social class inequalities in health? *Journal of Personality and Social Psychology, 86,* 174–199.

Gottfredson, L. S. (2009). Logical fallacies used to dismiss the evidence on intelligence testing. In R. Phelps (ed.), *Correcting fallacies about educational and psychological testing* (pp. 11–65). Washington, DC: American Psychological Association.

Gottesman, I. I. (1991). *Schizophrenia genesis: The origins of madness.* New York: W. H. Freeman.

Gottesman, I. I., & Shields, J. (1972). *Schizophrenia and genetics: A twin study vantage point.* New York: Academic Press.

Gottesmann, C. (2002). GABA mechanisms and sleep. *Neuroscience, 111,* 231–239.

Gottheil, E., & Weinstein, S. O. (1983). Cocaine: An emerging problem. In S. Akhtar (ed.), *New psychiatric syndromes; DSM III and beyond.* New York: Jason Aronson.

Gottlieb, G. (2003). On making behavioral genetics truly developmental. *Human Development, 46,* 337–355.

Gottman, J. S. (1990). Children of gay and pesbian parents. In F. W. Bozett, & M. B. Sussman, (eds.), *Homosexuality and Family Relations* (pp. 177–196). London, England: The Hawthorne Press.

Gottman, J. M., & Levenson, R. W. (1999). What predicts change in marital interaction over time? A study of alternative models. *Family Processes, 38,* 143–158.

Gough, H. G. (1957). *California Psychological Inventory manual.* Palo Alto, CA: Consulting Psychologists Press.

Gould, E., & Gross, C. G. (2002). Neurogenesis in adult mammals: Some progress and problems. *Journal of Neuroscience, 22,* 619–623.

Gould, J. L., & Gould, C. G. (1994) *The animal mind*. New York: Scientific American Library/Scientific American Books.

Gould, R. (1978). *Transformations: Growth and change in adult life*. New York: Simon and Schuster.

Gould, R. A., & Clum, G. A. (1993). A meta-analysis of self-help treatment approaches. *Clinical Psychology Review, 13*, 169–186.

Gould, S. J. (1981). *The mismeasure of man*. New York: W. W. Norton.

Gould, S. J. (1997). Nonoverlapping magisteria. *Natural History, 106*, 16–22.

Goulding, P. (1992). *Classical music: The 50 greatest composers and their 1000 greatest works*. New York: Ballantine.

Gouldner, A. W. (1960). The norm of reciprocity: A preliminary statement. *American Sociological Review, 25*, 161–178.

Gove, W. R., Hughes, M., & Style, C. B. (1983). Does marriage have positive effects on the psychological well-being of the individual? *Journal of Health and Social Behavior, 24*, 122–131.

Gowin, J. (2009, September 29). How "smart drugs" enhance us. *Psychology Today*. http://www.psychologytoday.com/blog/you-illuminated/200909/how-smart-drugs-enhance-us.

Graber, J. A., Petersen, A. C., & Brooks-Gunn, J. (1996). Pubertal processes: Methods, measures, and models. In J. A. Graber, J. Brooks-Gunn, & A. C. Petersen (eds.), *Transitions through adolescence: Interpersonal domains and context* (pp. 23–53). Hillsdale, NJ: Erlbaum.

Grace, A. A. (1991). The cortical regulation of dopamine system responsivity - A hypothesis regarding its role in the etiology of schizophrenia. *Schizophrenia Research, 4*, 345.

Graf, P. (1990). Life-span changes in implicit and explicit memory. *Bulletin of the Psychonomic Society, 28*, 353–358.

Graf, R. G. (1973). Speed reading: Remember the tortoise. *Psychology Today, 7*, 112–113.

Graham, J. R. (2006). *MMPI-2: Assessing personality and psychopathology* (3rd ed.). New York: Oxford University Press.

Granello, D. H., & Beamish, P. M. (1998). Reconceptualizing codependency in women: A sense of connectedness, not pathology. *Journal of Mental Health Counseling, 20*, 344–358.

Grant, B. F., Hasin, D. S., Stinson, F. S., Dawson D. A., Ruan, W. J., Goldstein, R. B., et al., (2005). Prevalence, correlates, co-morbidity, and comparative disability of DSM-IV generalized anxiety disorder in the USA: Results from the National Epidemiologic Survey on alcohol and related conditions. *Psychological Medicine, 35,* 1747–1759.

Grawe, K., Donati, R., & Bernauer, F. (1998). *Psychotherapy in transition*. Seattle, WA: Hogrefe & Huber.

Gray, C. R., & Gummerman, K. (1975). The enigmatic eidetic image: A critical examination of methods, data, and theories. *Psychological Bulletin, 82*, 383–407.

Gray, G., & Della Sala, S. (2007). The Mozart effect: It's time to face the music! In S. Della Sala (ed.), *Tall tales about the mind and brain: Separating fact from fiction* (pp. 148–157). Oxford, UK: Oxford University Press.

Gray, J. (1981). A critique of Eysenck's theory of personality. In H. J. Eysenck (ed.), *A model for personality* (pp. 246–276). New York: Springer.

Gray, J. (1992). *Men are from mars, women are from venus*. New York: HarperCollins.

Gray, J. A. (1982). *The neuropsychology of anxiety: An enquiry into the functions of the septo-hippocampal system*. Oxford, UK: Oxford University Press.

Graybiel, A. M., Aosaki, T., Flaherty, A. W., & Kimura, M. (1994). The basal ganglia and adaptive motor control. *Science, 265*, 1826–1831.

Greeley, A. M. (1975*). The sociology of the paranormal: A reconnaissance* (Sage Research Papers in the Social Sciences, Vol. 3, Series No. 90-023). Beverly Hills, CA: Sage.

Greeley, A. M. (1987). Mysticism goes mainstream. *American Health, 6*, 47–49.

Greely H., Sahakian, B., Harris, J., Kessler, R. C., Gazzaniga, M., Campbell, P., et al. (2008). Towards responsible use of cognitive-enhancing drugs by the healthy. *Nature, 456*, 702–705.

Greely H. T., & Illes, J. (2007). Neuroscience-based lie detection: The urgent need for regulation. *American Journal of Law & Medicine, 33*, 377–431.

Greeley, J., & Oei, T. (1999). Alcohol and tension reduction: 1987–1997. In K. E Leonard & H. T. Blane (eds.), *Psychological theories of drinking and alcoholism* (2nd ed., pp.14–53). New York: Guilford.

Green, C. D. (1992). Is unified positivism the answer to psychology's disunity? *American Psychologist, 48,* 1057–1058.

Green, D. M., & Swets, J. A. (1966). *Signal detection theory and psychophysics*. New York: Wiley.

Green, G. (1996). Early behavioral intervention for autism: What does research tell us? In C. Maurice, G. Green, & S. Luce (Eds.), *Behavioral intervention for young children with autism: A manual for parents and professionals* (pp. 29–44). Austin, TX: PRO-E.

Green, J. P. (2000). Treating women who smoke: The benefits of using hypnosis. In L. Hornyak & J. P. Green (eds.), *Healing from within: The use of hypnosis in women's health care* (pp. 91–118). Washington, DC: American Psychological Association.

Green, J. P., & Lynn, S. J. (2005). Hypnosis vs. relaxation: Accuracy and confidence in dating international news events. *Applied Cognitive Psychology, 19*, 679–691.

Green, R. (1987). *The "sissy boy syndrome" and the development of homosexuality*. New Haven, CT: Yale University Press.

Greenberg, D. J., Hillman, D., & Grice, D. (1973). Infant and stranger variables related to stranger anxiety in the first year of life. *Development Psychology, 9*, 207–212.

Greenberg, D. L. (2004). President Bush's False 'Flashbulb' Memory of 9/11/01. Applied Cognitive Psychology, 18, 363–370.

Greenberg, J., & Jonas, E. (2003). Psychological motives and political orientation: The left, the right, and the rigid: Comment on Jost et al. (2003). *Psychological Bulletin, 129*, 376–382.

Greenberg, L. S., Elliot, R., & Lietaer, G. (1994). Research on humanistic and experiential psychotherapies. In A. E. Bergin & L. S. Garfield (eds.), *Handbook of psychotherapy and behavior change* (4th ed., pp. 509–539). New York: Wiley.

Greenberg, L. S., & Watson, J. C. (1998). Experiential therapy of depression: Differential effects of client-centered relationship conditions and process experiential interventions. *Psychotherapy Research, 8*, 210–224.

Greene, J. D., & Paxton, J. M. (2009). Patterns of neural activity associated with honest and dishonest moral decisions. *Proceedings of the National Academy of Sciences USA, 106*, 12506–12511.

Greene, R. L. (2000). *The MMPI-2: An interpretive manual* (2nd ed.). Boston: Allyn & Bacon.

Greenfield, P. (1998). The cultural evolution of IQ. In U. Neisser (ed.), *The rising curve: Long-term gains in IQ and related measures* (pp. 81–122). Washington, DC: American Psychological Association.

Greenglass, E. (2002). Proactive coping. In E. Frydenberg (ed.), *Beyond coping: Meeting goals, vision, and challenges* (pp. 37–62). London: Oxford University Press.

Greenough, W. T. (1997). We can't just focus on the first three years. *American Psychological Association Monitor on Psychology, 28*, 19.

Greenspan, S., & Switzky, H. N. (eds.). (2003). *What is mental retardation? Ideas for the new century*. Washington, DC: American Association on Mental Retardation.

Greenspan, S., Loughlin, G., & Black, R. S. (2001). Credulity and gullibility in people with developmental disabilities: A framework for future research. In L. M. Glidden (ed.), *International review of research in mental retardation, Vol. 24* (pp. 101–135). New York: Academic Press.

Greenwald, A. G., & Gillmore, G. M. (1997). Grading leniency is a removable contaminant of student ratings. *American Psychologist, 52*, 1209–1217.

Greenwald, A. G., Leippe, M. R., Pratkanis, A. R., & Baumgardner, M. H. (1986). Under what conditions does theory obstruct research progress? *Psychological Review, 93*, 216–229.

Greenwald, A. G., McGhee, D. E., & Schwartz, J. L. K. (1998). Measuring individual differences in implicit cognition: The implicit association test. *Journal of Personality and Social Psychology, 74*, 1464–1480.

Greenwald, A. G., & Nosek, B. A. (2001). Health of the Implicit Association Test at age 3. *Zeitschrift für Experimentelle Psychologie, 48*, 85–93.

Greenwald, A. G., Spangenberg, E. R., Pratkanis, A. R., & Eskenazi, J. (1991). Double-blind tests of subliminal self-help audio tapes. *Psychological Science, 2*, 119–122.

Gregory, R. J., Canning, S. S., Lee, T. W., & Wise, J. (2004). Cognitive bibliotherapy for depression: A meta-analysis. *Professional Psychology: Research and Practice, 35*, 275–280.

Gresham, L. G., & Shimp, T. A. (1985). Attitude toward the advertisement and brand attitudes: A classical conditioning perspective. *Journal of Advertising, 14*, 10–17, 49.

Greyson, B. (2000). Near-death experiences. In E. Cardeña, S. J. Lynn, & S. Krippner (eds.), *Varieties of anomalous experiences* (pp. 315–352). Washington, DC: American Psychological Association.

Griffiths, P. E. (1997). *What emotions really are: The problem of psychological categories.* Chicago: Chicago University Press.

Griffiths, R. R., Richards, W. A., Johnson, M. W., McCann, U. D., & Jesse, R. (2008). Mystical-type experiences occasioned by psilocybin mediate the attribution of personal meaning and spiritual significance 14 months later. *Journal of Psychopharmacology, 22,* 621–632.

Grill, H. J., & Kaplan, J. M. (2002). The neuroanatomical axis for control of energy balance. *Frontiers in Neuroendocrinology, 21,* 2–40.

Grill, H. J., Schwartz, M. W., Kaplan, J. M., Foxhall, J. S., Breininger, J., & Baskin, D. G. (2002). Evidence that the caudal brainstem is a target for the inhibitory effect of leptin on food intake. *Endocrinology, 143,* 239–246.

Grings, W. W. (1973). Cognitive factors in electrodermal conditioning. *Psychological Bulletin, 79,* 200–210.

Grinker, R. R., & Werble, B. (1977). *The borderline patient.* New York: Aronson.

Grinker, R. R. (2007). *Unstrange Minds: Remapping the world of autism.* New York, NY, US: Basic Books.

Grisso, T. (2003). *Evaluating competencies: Forensic assessments and instruments* (2nd ed). New York: Kluwer.

Grissom, R. J. (1996). The magical number, 7±2 meta-analysis of the probability of superior outcome in comparisons involving therapy, placebo, and control. *Journal of Consulting and Clinical Psychology, 64,* 973–982.

Gritz, E. R. (1980). Smoking behavior and tobacco abuse. In N. K. Mello (ed.), *Advances in substance abuse, Vol. 1* (pp. 91–158). Greenwich, CT: JAI Press.

Grob, G. N. (1997). Deinstitutionalization: The illusion of policy. *Journal of Policy History, 9,* 48–73.

Gross, J., Byrne, J., & Fisher, C. (1965). Eye movements during emergent Stage 1 EEG in subjects with lifelong blindness. *Journal of Nervous and Mental Disease, 141,* 365–370.

Gross, J. J., & Muñoz, R. F. (1995). Emotional regulation and mental health. *Clinical Psychology: Science & Practice, 2,* 151–164.

Grossman, H. J. (ed.). (1983). *Classification in mental retardation* (Rev. ed.). Washington, DC: American Association on Mental Deficiency.

Grove, W. M., & Tellegen, A. (1991). Problems in the classification of personality disorders. *Journal of Personality Disorders, 5,* 31–41.

Grunbaum, A. (1984). *The foundations of psychoanalysis: A philosophical critique.* Berkeley: University of California Press.

Gruneberg, M. M., and Pascoe, K. (1996). The effectiveness of the keyword method for receptive and productive foreign vocabulary learning in the elderly. *Contemporary Educational Psychology, 21,* 102–109.

Gruneberg, M. M., and Sykes, R. N. (1991). Individual differences and attitudes to the keyword method of foreign language learning. *Language Learning Journal, 4,* 60–62.

Gu, Q. (2002). Neuromodulatory transmitter systems in the cortex and their role in cortical plasticity. *Neuroscience, 111,* 815–835.

Guan, J. H., & Wade, M. G. (2000). The effect of aging on adaptive eye–hand coordination. *Journals of Gerontology Series B—Psychological Sciences and Social Sciences, 55,* P151–P162.

Guéguen, N., Pascual A., & Dagot L. (2002). The low-ball technique: An application in a field setting, *Psychological Reports, 91,* 81–84.

Guenther, R. K. (1998). *Human cognition.* Upper Saddle River, NJ: Prentice Hall.

Guilford, J. P. (1954). *Psychometric methods* (2nd ed.). New York: McGraw-Hill.

Guilford, J. P. (1967). *The nature of human intelligence.* New York: McGraw-Hill.

Gulya, M., Galluccio, L., Wilk, A., & Rovee-Collier, C. (2001). Infants' long-term memory for a serial list: Recognition and reactivation. *Developmental Psychobiology, 38,* 174–185.

Gupta, S. (2007, May 24). Herbal remedies' potential dangers. Time Inc. Retrieved from www.time.com/time/magazine/article/0,9171,1625175,00.html.

Gusow, W. (1963). A preliminary report of kayak-angst among the Eskimo of West Greenland: A study in sensory deprivation. *International Journal of Social Psychiatry, 9,* 18–26.

Gustafsson, J. E. (1988). Hierarchical models of individual differences in cognitive abilities. In R. J. Sternberg (ed.), *Advances in the psychology of human intelligence, Vol. 4* (pp. 35–71). Hillsdale, NJ: Erlbaum.

Haack, L. J., Metalsky, G. I., Dykman, B. M., & Abramson, L. Y. (1996). Use of current situational information and causal inference: Do dysphoric indi-viduals make "unwarranted" causal inferences? *Cognitive Therapy and Research, 20,* 309–331.

Haaga, D. A., Dyck, M. J., & Ernst, D. (1991). Empirical status of cognitive theory of depression. *Psychological Bulletin, 110,* 215–236.

Haber, R. N. (1979). Twenty years of haunting eidetic imagery: Where's the ghost? *Behavioral and Brain Sciences, 2,* 583–629.

Hackney, A. (2005). Teaching students about stereotypes, prejudice, and discrimination: An interview with Susan Fiske. *Teaching of Psychology, 32,* 196–199.

Haeberle, E. J. (1978). *The sex atlas.* New York: Seabury Press.

Haeffel, G. (2010). When self-help is no help: Traditional cognitive skills training does not prevent depressive symptoms in people who ruminate. *Behaviour Research and Therapy, 48,* 152–157.

Hafer, C. L., & Begue, L. (2005). Experimental research on just-world theory: Problems, developments, and future challenges. *Psychological Bulletin, 131,* 128–167.

Hagen, M. (2001). Damaged goods? What, if anything, does science tell us about the long-term effects of childhood sexual abuse? *Skeptical Inquirer, 24*(1), 54–59.

Haidt, J. (2007) The new synthesis in moral psychology. *Science, 316,* 998–1002.

Haier, R. J. (2009, November/December). What does a smart brain look like? *Scientific American Mind,* 26–33.

Haier, R. J., Siegel, B. V., MacLachlan, A., Soderling, E., Lottenberg, S., & Buchsbaum, M. S. (1992). Regional glucose metabolic changes after learning a complex visuospatial/motor task: A positron emission tomographic study. *Brain Research, 570,* 134–143.

Haimerl, C. J., & Valentine, E. (2001). The effect of contemplative practice on interpersonal, and transpersonal dimensions of the self-concept. *Journal of Transpersonal Psychology, 33,* 37–52.

Haist, F., Shimamura, A. P., & Squire, L. R. (1992). On the relationship between recall and recognition memory. *Journal of Experimental Psychology: Learning, Memory, and Cognition, 18,* 691–702.

Halari, R., Hines, M., Kumari, V., et al. (2005) Sex differences and individual differences in cognitive performance and their relationship to endogenous gonadal hormones and gonadotropins. *Behavioral Neuroscience, 119,* 104–117.

Halberstadt, J., & Rhodes, G. (2003). It's not just the average face that's attractive: The attractiveness of averageness of computer-manipulated birds, fish, and automobiles. *Psychonomic Bulletin and Review, 10,* 149–156.

Haldeman, D. (1994). The practice and ethics of sexual orientation conversion therapy. *Journal of Consulting and Clinical Psychology, 62,* 221–227.

Haley, J. (1976). *Problem-solving therapy.* San Francisco: Jossey-Bass.

Hall, C. S., & Nordby, V. J. (1972). *The individual and his dreams.* Winnipeg, Manitoba, Canada: New American Library.

Hall, C. S., & Van de Castle, R. (1966). *Content analysis of dreams.* New York: Appleton-Century-Crofts.

Hall, C. S. (1984). A ubiquitous sex difference in dreams, revisited. *Journal of Personality and Social Psychology, 46,* 1109–1117.

Hall, E. T. (1966). *The hidden dimension.* New York: Anchor Books.

Hall, E. T. (1976). *Beyond culture.* New York: Doubleday.

Hall, H. (2008). Puncturing the acupuncture myth. *Skeptic, 14,* 5.

Hall, J. A. (1978). Gender effects in decoding nonverbal cues. *Psychological Bulletin, 85,* 845–857.

Hall, J. A. Y., & Kimura, D. (1994). Dermatoglyphic asymmetry and sexual orientation in men. *Behavioral Neuroscience, 108,* 1203–1206.

Hall, J. R., & Benning, S. D. (2006). The "successful" psychopath: Adaptive and subclinical manifestations of psychopathy in the general population. In C. J. Patrick (ed.), *Handbook of psychopathy* (pp. 459–478). New York: Guilford Press.

Hall, L. E. (2005). *Dictionary of Multicultural Psychology: Issues, Terms, and Concepts.* Thousand Oaks, CA: Sage.

Halpern, D. F. (1992). *Sex differences in cognitive abilities* (2nd ed.). Hillsdale, NJ: Erlbaum.

Halpern, D. F. (2004). A cognitive-process taxonomy for sex differences in cognitive abilities. *Current Directions in Psychological Science, 13,* 135–139.

Halpern, D. F., Benbow, C. P., Geary, D. C., Gur, R. C., Hyde, J. S., & Gernsbacher, M. A. (2007). The science of sex differences in science and mathematics. *Psychological Science in the Public Interest, 8,* 1–51.

Halweg, K., Goldstein, M. J., Neuchterlein, K. H., Magana, A. B., Mintz, J., Doane, J. A., et al. (1989). Expressed emotion and patient-relative interaction in families of recent onset schizophrenics. *Journal of Consulting and Clinical Psychology, 57,* 11–18.

Hamann, A., & Matthaei, S. (1996). Regulation of energy balance by leptin. *Experimental Clinical Endocrinology Diabetes, 104,* 293–300.

Hamilton, D. L., & Rose, T. L. (1980). Illusory correlation and the maintenance of stereotypic beliefs. *Journal of Personality and Social Psychology, 39,* 832–845.

Hamilton, R. H., & Pascual-Leone, A. (1998). Cortical plasticity associated with Braille learning. *Trends in Cognitive Neuroscience, 2,* 168–174.

Hamm, A. O., Weike, A. I., Schupp, H. T., Treig, T., Dressel, A., & Kessler, C. (2003). Affective blindsight: intact fear conditioning to a visual cue in a cortically blind patient, *Brain, 126,* 267–275.

Hammen, C. (1991). Generation of stress in the course of unipolar depression. *Journal of Abnormal Psychology, 100,* 555–561.

Hampson, E., & Kimura, D. (1988) Reciprocal effects of hormonal fluctuations on human motor and perceptual-spatial skills. *Behavioral Neuroscience, 102,* 456–459.

Hampson, E., Rovet, J. F., & Altmann, D. (1998). Spatial reasoning in children with congenital adrenal hyperplasia due to 21-hydroxylase deficiency. *Developmental Neuropsychology, 14,* 299–320.

Haney, C., Banks, W. C., & Zimbardo, P. G. (1973). Interpersonal dynamics in a simulated prison. *International Journal of Criminology & Penology, 1,* 69–97.

Hansen, E. S., Hasselbalch, S., Law, J., & Bolwig, T. G. (2002). The caudate nucleus in obsessive-compulsive disorder. Reduced metabolism following treatment with paroxetine: A PET study. *International Journal of Neuropsychopharmacology, 5,* 1–10.

Hansford, B., & Hattie, J. (1982). The relationship between self and achievement performance measures. *Review of Educational Research, 52,* 123–142.

Hanson, D. R., & Gottesman, I. I. (2005). Theories of schizophrenia: A genetic-inflammatory-vascular synthesis. *Biomed Central Medical Genetics, 6,* Published online February 11, 2005. Doi: 10.1186/1471-2350-6-7.

Haraldsson, E., & Houtkooper, J. (1991). Psychic experience in the multinational human-values study – who reports them. *Personality and Individual Differences, 13,* 1085–1096.

Harding, C. M., Zubin, J., & Strauss, J. S. (1992). Chronicity in schizophrenia: Revisited. *British Journal of Psychiatry Supplement, 18,* 27–37.

Hardy, C., & Latane, B. (1986). Social loafing on a cheering task. *Social Science, 71,* 165–172.

Hardy, K. R. (1957). Determinants of conformity and attitude change. *Journal of Abnormal and Social Psychology, 4,* 289–294.

Hare, E. H. (1962). Masturbatory insanity: The history of an idea. *Journal of Mental Science, 108,* 2–25.

Hare, R. D. (1978). Electrodermal and cardiovascular correlates of psychopathy. In R. D. Hare & D. Schalling (eds.), *Psychopathic behavior: Approaches to research* (pp. 107–144). Chichester, England: John Wiley & Sons.

Hare, R. D. (1993). *Without conscience: The disturbing world of the psychopaths among us.* New York: Simon & Schuster.

Hare, R. D. (2003). *The Hare Psychopathy Checklist—Revised.* Toronto, Ontario, Canada: Multi-Health Systems.

Harford, T., & Muthen, B. O. (2001). The dimensionality of alcohol abuse and dependence: A multivariate analysis of DSM-IV symptoms in the National Longitudinal Survey of Youth. *Journal of Studies in Alcohol, 62,* 150–157.

Hariri, A. R., Mattay, V. S., Tessitore, A., Kolachana, B., Fera, F., Goldman, D., et al. (2002). Serotonin transporter genetic variation and the response of the human amygdala. *Science, 297,* 400–403.

Harkins, E. B. (1978). Effects of empty nest transition on self-report of psychological and physical well-being. *Journal of Marriage and the Family, 40,* 549–556.

Harkness, A. R. (2007). Personality traits are essential for a complete clinical science. In S. O. Lilienfeld and W. O'Donohue (eds.), *The great ideas of clinical science: 17 concepts that every mental health professional should understand* (pp. 263–290). New York: Routledge.

Harkness, A. R., & Lilienfeld, S. O. (1997). Individual differences science for treatment planning: Personality traits. *Psychological Assessment, 9,* 349–360.

Harkness, K. L., & Luther, J. (2001). Clinical risk factors for the generation of life events in major depression. *Journal of Abnormal Psychology, 110,* 564–572.

Harlow, H. F. (1958). The nature of love. *American Psychologist, 13,* 673–685.

Harlow, J. M. (1848). Passage of an iron rod through the head. *Boston Medical and Surgical Journal, 39,* 389–393. (Republished in *Journal of Neuropsychiatry and Clinical Neuroscience, 1991, 11,* 281–283.)

Harmon-Jones, E., & Allen, J. J. B. (2001). The role of affect in the mere exposure effect: Evidence from psychophysiological and individual differences approaches. *Personality and Social Psychology Bulletin, 27,* 889–898.

Harmon-Jones, E., & Mills, J. (eds.). (1999). *Cognitive dissonance: Progress on a pivotal theory in social psychology.* Washington, DC: American Psychological Association.

Harmon-Jones, E., & Peterson, C. K. (2009). Supine body position reduces neural response to anger evocation. *Psychological Science, 20,* 1209–1210.

Harrington, E. R. (2004). The social psychology of hatred. *Journal of Hate Studies, 3,* 49–82.

Harrington, P. (2005, December). Exorcisms rise in Mexico, keeping Father Mendoza, healers busy. *Bloomberg News.* Retrieved June 2, 2008, from www.banderasnews.com/0512/nr-mexorcisms.htm.

Harris, E. C., & Barraclough, B. (1997). Suicide as an outcome for mental disorders—A meta-analysis. *British Journal of Psychiatry, 170,* 205–228.

Harris, J. L., & Qualls, C. D. (2000). The association of elaborative or maintenance rehearsal with age, reading comprehension, and verbal working memory performance. *Aphasiology, 14,* 515–526.

Harris, J. R. (1995). Where is the child's environment? A group socialization theory of development. *Psychological Review, 102,* 458–489.

Harris, J. R. (1998). *The nurture assumption: Why children turn out the way they do.* New York: Free Press.

Harris, J. R. (2002). *The nurture assumption: Why children turn out the way they do (2nd ed).* New York: Free Press.

Harris, J. R. (2006). *No two alike: Human nature and human individuality.* New York: W. W. Norton.

Harris, M. (1976). History and significance of the emic/etic distinction. *Annual Review of Anthropology, 5,* 329–350.

Harris, P. L. (1994). The child's understanding of emotion: Developmental-change and the family environment. *Journal of Child Psychology and Psychiatry and Allied Disciplines, 35,* 3–28.

Harrow, M., Grossman, L. S., Jobe, T. H., & Herbener, E. S. (2005) Do patients with schizophrenia ever show periods of recovery? A 15-year multi-follow-up study. *Schizophrenia Bulletin, 31,* 723–734.

Hart, B., & Risley, T. R. (1995). *Meaningful differences in the everyday experience of young American children.* Baltimore: Paul H. Brookes.

Hartley, E. (1946). *Problems in prejudice.* New York: King's Crown Press.

Hartmann, H. (1939). *Ego psychology and the problem of adaptation.* New York: International Universities Press.

Hartmann, W. K. (1992). *Astronomy: The cosmic journey.* Belmont, CA: Wadsworth.

Hartshorne, H., & May, M. A. (1928). *Studies in the nature of character: Vol. 1. Studies in deceit.* New York: Macmillan.

Harvey, J. H., & Weary, G. (1984). Current issues in attribution theory and research. *Annual Review of Psychology, 35,* 427–460.

Harvey, P. D., Reichenberg, A., & Bowie, C. R. (2006). Cognition and aging in psychopathology: Focus on schizophrenia and depression. In S. Nolen-Hoeksema, T. D. Cannon, & T. Widiger (eds.), *Annual Review of Clinical Psychology* (Vol. 2 pp. 389–409). Palo Alto, CA: Annual Reviews.

Hasegawa, H., & Jamieson, G. A. (2002). Conceptual issues in hypnosis research: Explanations, definitions and the state/non-state debate. *Contemporary Hypnosis, 19,* 103–117.

Hasler, G., Buysse, D. J., Klaghofer, R., Gamma, A., Ajdacic, V., Eich, D., et al. (2004). The association between short sleep duration and obesity in young adults: A 13-year prospective study. *Sleep, 27,* 661–666.

Hassin, R. R., Uleman, J. S., & Bargh, J. A. (2005). *The new unconscious.* New York: Oxford University Press.

Hastorf, A. H., & Cantril, A. H. (1954). They saw a game – A case study. *Journal of Abnormal and Social Psychology, 49,* 129–134.

Hatfield, E., Aronson, V., Abrahams, D., & Rottman, L. (1966). The importance of physical attractiveness in dating behavior. *Journal of Personality and Social Psychology, 4,* 508–516.

Hatfield, E., & Rapson, R. (1996). *Love and sex: Cross-cultural perspectives.* Boston: Allyn & Bacon.

Hatfield, E., & Walster, G. W. (1978). *A new look at love.* Reading, MA: Addison-Wesley.

Hathaway, S. R., & McKinley, J. C. (1940). A multiphasic personality schedule (Minnesota): I. Construction of the schedule. *Journal of Psychology, 14,* 73–84.

Hauser, M. D. (2002). Nature vs. nurture redux. *Science, 298,* 1554–1555.

Hauser, M. D., & Fitch, W. T. (2003). What are the uniquely human components of the language faculty? In M. H. Christiansen & S. Kirby (eds.), *Language evolution. Studies in the evolution of language* (pp. 158–181). London: Oxford University Press.

Hauser, R. M. (1998). Trends in black-white test score differences: I. Uses and misuses of NAEP/SAT data. In U. Neisser (ed.), *The rising curve: Long-term gains in IQ and related measures* (pp. 219–249). Washington, DC: American Psychological Association.

Hawkley, L. C., & Cacioppo, J. T. (2007). Aging and loneliness: Downhill quickly? *Current Directions in Psychological Science, 16,* 187–191.

Haxby, D. G. (1995). Treatment of nicotine dependence. *American Journal of Health-System Pharmacy, 52,* 265–281.

Hayduk, L. (1983). Personal space: Where we now stand. *Psychological Bulletin, 94,* 293–335.

Hayes, R., & Dennerstein, L. (2005). The impact of aging on sexual function and sexual dysfunction in women: A review of population-based studies. *Journal of Sex Research, 2,* 317–330.

Hayes, S. C. (2004). Acceptance and Commitment Therapy, relational frame theory, and the third wave of behavioral and cognitive therapies. *Behavior Therapy, 35*(4), 639–665.

Hayes, S. C., Follette, V. M., & Linehan, M. M. (eds.) (2004). *Mindfulness and acceptance: Expanding the cognitive-behavioral tradition.* New York: Guilford.

Hayes, S. C., Strosahl, K., & Wilson, K. G. (1999). *Acceptance and commitment therapy.* New York: Guilford Press.

Hayward, L. R. C. (1960). The subjective meaning of stress. *British Journal of Psychology, 33,* 185–194.

Hazelrigg, M. D., Cooper, H. M., & Borduin, C. M. (1987). Evaluating the effectiveness of family therapies: An integrative review and analysis. *Psychological Bulletin, 101,* 428–442.

Hazlett-Stevens, H., Pruitt, L. D., & Collins, A. (2008). Phenomenology of generalized anxiety disorder. In M. M. Anthony & M. B. Stein (eds.), *Oxford handbook of anxiety and related disorders* (pp. 47–64). New York: Oxford University Press.

He, Y., Jones, C. R., Fujiki, N., Xu, Y., Guo, B., Holder, J. L., et al. (2009). The transcriptional repressor DEC2 regulates sleep length in mammals. *Science, 325,* 866–870.

Healy, A. F., & McNamara, D. S. (1996). Verbal learning and memory: Does the modal model still work? *Annual Review of Psychology, 47,* 143–172.

Healy, D. (2004). SSRI and suicide? Reply. *Psychotherapy and Psychosomatics, 73,* 262.

Heath, C., & Heath, D. (2007). *Made to stick: Why some ideas survive and others die.* New York: Random House.

Heath, C. B., Bell, C., & Sternberg, E. (2001). Emotional selection in memes: The case of urban legends. *Journal of Personality and Social Psychology, 81,* 1028–1041.

Heath, T. P., Melichar, J. K., Nutt, D. J., & Donaldson, L. F. (2006). Human taste thresholds are modulated by serotonin and noradrenaline. *Journal of Neuroscience, 26,* 12664–12671.

Heaton, J. A., & Wilson, N. L. (1995). *Tuning in trouble: Talk TV's destructive impact on mental health.* San Francisco: Jossey-Bass.

Heaven, P. C. L., Ciarrochi, J., & Vialle, W. (2007). Conscientiousness and Eysenckian Psychoticism as predictors of school grades: A one-year longitudinal study. *Personality and Individual Differences, 42,* 535–546.

Hebb, D. O. (1949). *The organization of behavior.* New York: John Wiley.

Hedges, L. V., & Nowell, A. (1995). Sex differences in mental test scores, variability, and numbers of high-scoring individuals. *Science, 269,* 41–45.

Heesacker, M, Petty, R. E., & Cacioppo, J. T. (1983). Field-dependence and attitude-change: Source credibility can alter persuasion by affecting message-relevant thinking. *Journal of Personality, 51,* 653–666.

Heider, F. (1958). *The psychology of interpersonal relations.* New York: Wiley.

Heimberg, R. G., & Juster, H. R. (1995). Cognitive-behavioral treatments: Literature review. In R. G. Heimberg, M. R. Liebowitz, D. A. Hope, & F. R. Schneier (eds.), *Social phobia: Diagnosis, assessment, and treatment.* New York: Guilford Press.

Heims, H. C., Critchley, H. D., Dolan, R., Mathias, C. J., & Cipolotti, L. (2004). Social and motivational functioning is not critically dependent on feedback of autonomic responses: Neuropsychological evidence from patients with pure autonomic failure. *Neuropsychologia, 42,* 1979–1988.

Heine, S. J., Lehman, D. R., Markus, H. R., & Kitayama, S. (1999). Is there a universal need for positive self-regard? *Psychological Review, 106,* 766–794.

Heini, A. F., & Weinsier, R. L. (1997). Divergent trends in obesity and fat intake patterns: The American paradox. *American Journal of Medicine, 102,* 259–264.

Heinrichs, C., Munson, P., Counts, D., Cutler, G., Jr., & Baron, J. (1995). Patterns of human growth. *Science, 268,* 442–447.

Held, B. (2004). The negative side of positive psychology. *Journal of Humanistic Psychology, 44,* 9–46.

Helliwell, J. F., & Putnam, R. D. (2004). The social context of well-being. *Philosophical Transactions of the Royal Society (London) Series B, 359,* 1435–1446.

Helmes, E., & Reddon, J. R. (1993). A perspective on developments in assessing psychopathology: A critical review of the MMPI and MMPI-2. *Psychological Bulletin, 113,* 453–471.

Helmholtz, H. (1850). Ueber die Fortpflanzungsgeschwindigkeit der Nervenreizung. *Annalen der Physik, 155,* 329–330.

Helson, H. (1948). Adaptation-level as a basis for a quantitative theory of frames of reference. *Psychological Review, 55,* 297–313.

Helson, R., & Srivastava, S. (2002). Creativity and wisdom: Similarities, differences, and how they develop. *Personality and Social Psychology Bulletin, 28,* 1430–1440.

Hempel, A., Hempel, E., Schönknecht, P., Stippich, C., & Schröder, J. (2003). Impairment in basal limbic function in schizophrenia during affect recognition. *Psychiatry Research, 122,* 115–124.

Hemsley, G. D., & Doob, A. N. (1978). The effect of looking behavior on perceptions of a communicator's credibility. *Journal of Applied Social Psychology, 8,* 136–144.

Henderson, J. M., & Hollingworth, A. (1999). The role of fixation position in detecting scene changes across saccades. *Psychological Science, 10,* 438–443.

Henderson, R. W. (1985). Fearful memories: The motivational significance of forgetting. In F. R. Brush & J. B. Overmier (eds.), *Affect, conditioning, and cognition: Essays on the determinants of behavior* (pp. 43–53). Hillsdale, NJ: Erlbaum.

Henig, R. M. (2006, February 5). Looking for the lie. *New York Times Magazine,* 46–53, 76, 83.

Henrich, J., Heine, S., & Norenzayan, A. (2010). The weirdest people in the world? Behavioral and Brain Sciences, 33(2-3), 61–83.

Henriques, G. (2004). Psychology defined. *Journal of Clinical Psychology, 60,* 1207–1221.

Henshaw, J. M. (2006). *Does measurement measure up? How numbers reveal and conceal the truth.* Baltimore: Johns Hopkins University Press.

Herbert, M. R. (2005). Large brains in autism: The challenge of pervasive abnormality. *Neuroscientist, 11,* 417–440.

Herbert, J. D., Sharp, I. R., & Gaudiano, B. A. (2002). Separating fact from fiction in the etiology and treatment of autism: A scientific review of the evidence. *Scientific Review of Mental Health Practice, 1,* 25–45.

Hergenhahn, B. R. (2000). *An introduction to the history of psychology* (4th ed.). Pacific Grove, CA: Wadsworth.

Hermanussen, M. (1998). The analysis of short-term growth. *Hormone Research, 49,* 53–64.

Hermanussen, M., & Geiger-Benoit, K. (1995). No evidence for saltation in human growth. *Annals of Human Biology, 22,* 341–345.

Hermanussen, M., Geiger-Benoit, K., Burmeister, J., & Sippell, W. G. (1988). Knemometry in childhood: Accuracy and standardization of a new technique of lower leg length measurement. *Annals of Human Biology, 15,* 1–16.

Herrmann, C. S., & Friederici, A. D. (2001). Object processing in the infant brain. *Science, 292,* 163.

Herrmann, N. (1996). *The whole brain business book.* New York: McGraw-Hill.

Herrnstein, R. J. (1966). Superstition: A corollary of the principles of operant conditioning. In W. K. Honig (ed.), *Operant behavior: Areas of research and application* (pp. 33–51). New York: Appleton-Century-Crofts.

Herrnstein, R. J., & Murray, C. (1994). *The bell curve: Intelligence and class structure in American life.* New York: Free Press.

Herskowitz, J. (1987). *The popcorn diet plus*. New Delhi, India: Pharos Books.

Hertel, J., Schutz, A., & Lammers, C. H. (2009). Emotional intelligence and mental disorder. *Journal of Clinical Psychology, 65*, 942–954.

Hertwig, R., Pacur, T., & Kurzenhauser, S. (2005). Judgments of risk frequencies: Tests of possible cognitive mechanisms. *Journal of Experimental Psychology: Learning, Memory, and Cognition, 31*, 621–642.

Herwig, U., Fallgatter, A. J., Hoppner, J., Eschweiler, G. W., Kron, M., Hajak, G., et al. (2007). Antidepressant effects of augmentative transcranial magnetic stimulation. A randomized multicenter trial. *British Journal of Psychiatry, 191*, 441–448.

Hess, E. H. (1965). Attitude and pupil size. *Scientific American, 212*(4), 46–54.

Hess, R. A. (2003). Estrogen in the adult male reproductive tract: A review. *Reproductive and Biological Endocrinology, 9*, 1–52.

Hesse, E. (1999). The adult attachment interview: Historical and current perspectives. In J. Cassidy & P. Shaver (eds.), *Handbook of attachment: Theory, research, and clinical applications* (pp. 395–433). New York: Guilford Press.

Hetherington, A. W., & Ranson, S. W. (1940). Hypothalamic lesions and adiposity in the rat. *Anatomical Record, 78*, 149–158.

Hetherington, E. M., Cox, M., & Cox, R. (1985). Long-term effects of divorce and remarriage on the adjustment of children. *Journal of the American Academy of Child Psychiatry, 24*, 518–530.

Hetherington, E. M. & Stanley-Hagan, M. (2002). Parenting in divorced and remarried families. In M. Bornstein (ed.), *Handbook of parenting: Being and becoming a parent, Vol. 3*, 287–316. Mahwah, NJ: Lawrence Erlbaum Associates.

Hick, W. E. (1952). On the rate of gain of information. *Quarterly Journal of Experimental Psychology, 4*, 11–26.

Higgins, J. E., & Endler, N. (1995). Coping, life stress, and psychological and somatic distress. *European Journal of Personality, 9*, 253–270.

Highstein, S. M., Fay, R. R., & Popper A. N. (2004). *The vestibular system*. Berlin, Germany: Springer-Verlag.

Hilgard, E. R. (1977). *Divided consciousness: Multiple controls in human thought and action*. New York: Wiley.

Hilgard, E. R. (1986). *Divided consciousness: Multiple controls in human thought and action* (expanded ed.). New York: Wiley.

Hilgard, E. R. (1994). Neodissociation theory. In S. J. Lynn & J. W. Rhue (eds.), *Dissociation: Clinical, theoretical and research perspectives* (pp. 32–51). New York: Guilford Press.

Higuchi, S., Matsushita, S., Murayama, M., Takagai, S., & Hayashida, M. (1995). Alcohol and aldehyde dehydrogenase polymorphisms and the risk for alcoholism. *American Journal of Psychiatry, 152*, 1219–1221.

Hill, C., Rubin, Z., & Peplau, L. A. (1976). Breakups before marriage: The end of 103 affairs. *Journal of Social Issues, 32*, 147–168.

Hill, E. L., & Frith, U. (2003). Understanding autism: Insights from mind and brain. In U. Frith & E. Hill (eds.), *Autism: Mind and brain* (pp. 1–19). New York: Oxford University Press.

Hill, W. E. (1915). "My Wife and My Mother-in-Law." *Puck*, 11.

Hiller, J. (2005). Gender differences in sexual motivation. *Journal of Men's Health and Gender, 2*, 339–345.

Himes, S. M., & Thompson, J. K. (2007). Fat stigmatization in television shows and movies: A content analysis. *Obesity, 15*, 712–718.

Hines, T. (1987). Left brain/right brain mythology and implications for management and training. *The Academy of Management Review, 12*, 600–606.

Hines, T. (2003). *Pseudoscience and the paranormal: A critical examination of the evidence* (2nd ed.). Buffalo, NY: Prometheus.

Hingson, R., Heeren, T., & Winter, M. R. (2006). Drinking onset and alcohol dependence: Age at onset, duration, and severity. *Archives of Pediatrics and Adolescent Medicine, 160*, 739–746.

Hinrichsen, G. A. (2008). Interpersonal psychotherapy for late life depression: Current status and new applications. *Journal of Rational-Emotive & Cognitive-Behavior Therapy, 26*, 263–275.

Hinshaw, S. P. (2002). Is ADHD an impairing condition in childhood and adolescence? In P. S. Jensen & J. R. Cooper (Eds.), *Attention deficit hyperactivity disorder: State of the science—best practices* (pp. 515–521). Kingston, NJ: Civic Research Institute.

Hirsch, A. R., (2003). Handbook of Olfaction and Gustation. *Journal of the American Medical Association, 290*, 3257–3258.

Hirsh-Pasek, K., & Golinkoff, R. (1996). *The origins of grammar*. Cambridge, MA: MIT Press.

Hirsh-Pasek, K. & Golinkoff, R. M. (2008) Language acquisition in childhood. In W. Donsbach (ed.), *The Blackwell international encyclopedia of communication, Vol. VI* (pp. 2636–2638). Oxford, UK and Malden, MA: Wiley-Blackwell.

Hirt, E. R., Lynn, S. J., Payne, D. G., Krackow, E., & McCrea, S. M. (1999) Expectancies and memory: Inferring the past from what must have been. In I. Kirsch (ed) *How expectancies shape experience* (pp. 93–124). Washington, DC: American Psychological Association.

Hite, S. (1987). *The Hite report on women and love: A cultural revolution in progress*. New York: Alfred A. Knopf.

Hoagland, R. C. (1987). *The monuments of mars: A city on the edge of forever*. Berkeley, CA: North Atlantic

Hobson, J. A. (2002). *Dreaming: An introduction to the science of sleep*. New York: Oxford University Press.

Hobson, J. A. (2009). REM sleep and dreaming: Towards a theory of protoconsciousness. *Nature Reviews Neuroscience, 10*, 803–813.

Hobson, J. A., & McCarley, R. M. (1977). The brain as a dream state generator: An activation-synthesis hypothesis. *American Journal of Psychiatry, 134*, 1335–1348.

Hobson, J. A., Pace-Schott, E., & Stickgold, R. (2000). Dreaming and the brain: Towards a cognitive neuroscience of conscious states. *Behavioral and Brain Sciences, 23*, 793–842.

Hock, R. R. (2002). *Forty studies that changed psychology: Explorations into the history of psychological research* (4th ed.). Upper Saddle River, NJ: Prentice Hall.

Hodson, G., & Costello, K. (2007). Interpersonal disgust, ideological orientations, and dehumanization as predictors of intergroup attitudes. *Psychological Science, 18*, 691–698.

Hoekstra, R. E., Ferrara, T. B., Couser, R. J., Payne, N. R., & Connett, J. E. (2004). Survival and long-term neurodevelopmental outcome of extremely premature infants born at 23–26 weeks' gestation age at a tertiary center. *Pediatrics, 113*, e1–e6.

Hofer, T., Przyrembel, H., & Verleger, S. (2004). New evidence for the theory of the stork. *Paediatric and Perinatal Epidemiology, 18*, 88–92.

Hoffman, H., & Patterson, D. (2005). Virtual reality pain distraction. APS Bulletin, 15. http://www.ampainsoc.org/pub/bulletin/spr05/inno1.htm. Retrieved November 7, 2009.

Hoffman, M. B., & Morse, S. J. (2006, July 30). The insanity defense goes back on trial. Retrieved October 22, 2007, from www.nytimes.com/2006/07/30/opinion/30hoffman.html?_r=1&oref=slogin.

Hoffman, M. L. (1981). Is altruism part of human nature? *Journal of Personality and Social Psychology, 40*, 121–137.

Hoffrage, U. (2004). Overconfidence. In R. F. Pohl (ed.), *Cognitive illusions: Fallacies and biases in thinking, judgment, and memory* (pp. 235–254). Hove, England: Psychology Press.

Hofmann, A. (1980). *LCD: My problem child*. New York: McGraw-Hill.

Hofmann, S. G. (2008). Cognitive processes in fear acquisition and extinction in animals and humans: Implications for exposure therapy of anxiety disorders. *Clinical Psychology Review, 28*, 199–210.

Hofmann, S. G., & Asmundson, G. J. G. (2008). Acceptance and mindfulness-based therapy: New wave or old hat? *Clinical Psychology Review, 28*, 1–16.

Hohmann, G. W. (1966). Some effects of spinal cord lesions on experienced emotional feelings. *Psychophysiology, 3*, 143–156.

Holahan, C., & Moos, R. H. (1991). Life stressors, personal and social resources and depression: A four-year structural model. *Journal of Abnormal Psychology, 100*, 31–38.

Holahan, M. R., Rekart, J. L., Sandoval, J., & Routtenberg, A. (2006). Spatial learning induces presynaptic structural remodeling in the hippocampal mossy fiber system of two rat strains. *Hippocampus, 16*, 560–570.

Holden, J. E., Jeong, Y., & Forrest, J. M. (2005). The endogenous opioid system and clinical pain management. *AACN Clinical Issues, 16*, 291–301.

Hollon, S. D., Thase, M. E., & Markowitz, J. C. (2002). Treatment and prevention of depression. *Psychological Science in the Public Interest, 3*, 2002.

Holloway, R. L. (1983). Cerebral brain endocast pattern of *Australopithecus afarensis* hominid. *Nature, 303*, 420–422.

Holmes, C., Wurtz, P., Waln, R., Dungan, D., & Joseph, C. (1984). Relationship between the Luscher Color Test and the MMPI. *Journal of Clinical Psychology, 40*, 126–128.

Holmes, D. S. (1974). Investigation of repression: Differential recall of material experimentally or naturally associated with ego threat. *Psychological Bulletin, 81,* 632–653.

Holmes, D. S. (1987). The influence of meditation versus rest on physiological arousal. In M. West (ed.), *The psychology of meditation* (pp. 81–103). Oxford, England: Clarendon Press.

Holmes, D. S. (1990). The evidence for repression: An examination of sixty years of research. In J. L. Singer (ed.), *Repression and dissociation* (pp. 85–102). Chicago: University of Chicago Press.

Holmes, E. A., James, E. E., Coode-Bate, T., & Deeprose, C. (2009). Can playing the computer game "Tetris" reduce the build-up of flashbacks for trauma? A proposal from Cognitive Science. *PloS ONE, 4:*e4153.

Holmes, T. H., & Masuda, M. (1974). Life change and illness susceptibility. In B. S. Dohrenwend & P. P. Dohrenwend (eds.), *Stressful life events: Their nature and effects* (pp. 45–72). New York: Wiley.

Holmes, T. H., & Rahe, R. H. (1967). The Social Readjustment Scale. *Journal of Psychosomatic Research, 11,* 213–218.

Homa, D. (1983). An assessment of two extraordinary speed-readers. *Bulletin of the Psychonomic Society, 21,* 123–126.

Homant, R. J., & Kennedy, D. B. (1998). Psychological aspects of crime scene profiling. *Criminal Justice and Behavior, 25,* 319–343.

Honda, H., Shimizu, Y., & Rutter, M. (2005). No effect of MMR withdrawal on the incidence of autism: A total population study. *Journal of Child Psychology and Psychiatry, 46,* 572–579.

Honts, C. R., Raskin, D. C., & Kircher, J. C. (1994). Mental and physical countermeasures reduce the accuracy of polygraph tests. *Journal of Applied Psychology, 79,* 252–259.

Hook, E. B., & Lindsjo, A. (1978). Down syndrome in live births by single year maternal age interval in a Swedish study: Comparison with results from a New York State study. *American Journal of Human Genetics, 30,* 19–27.

Hopkins, B., & Westra, T. (1988). Maternal handling and motor development: An intracultural study. *Genetic, Social, and General Psychology Monographs, 114,* 377–408.

Hopko, D. R., Robertson, S. M. C. & Lejuez, C. W. (2006). Behavioral activation for anxiety disorders. *The Behavior Analyst Today, 7,* 212–224.

Hoppa, H., & Hallstrom, T. (1981). Weight gain in adulthood in relation to socioeconomic factors, mental illness, and personality traits: A prospective study of middle-aged men. *Journal of Psychosomatic Research, 25,* 83–89.

Horgan, J. (1999). *The undiscovered mind: How the human brain defies replication, medication, and explanation.* New York: Free Press.

Horgan, J. (2005, June). Can a single brain cell think? *Discover Magazine.* http://cbcl.mit.edu/news/files/kreiman-hogan-5-05.htm

Horn, J. L. (1994). The theory of fluid and crystallized intelligence. In R. J. Sternberg (ed.), *The encyclopedia of intelligence* (pp. 443–451). New York: Macmillan.

Horn, J. L., & Hofer, S. M. (1992). Major abilities and development in the adult period. In R. J. Sternberg & C. A. Berg (eds.), *Intellectual development* (pp. 44–99). New York: Cambridge University Press.

Horney, K. (1939). *New ways in psychoanalysis.* New York: Norton.

Horney, K. (1945). *Our inner conflicts: A constructive theory of neurosis.* New York: Summit Books.

Horvath, A. O., & Bedi, R. P. (2002). The alliance. In J. C. Norcross (ed.), *Psychotherapy relationships that work: Therapist contributions and responsiveness to patients* (pp. 37–69). New York: Oxford University Press.

Houle, T. T., Dhingra, L. K., Remble, T. A., Rokicki, L. A., & Penzien, D. B. (2006). Not tonight, I have a headache? *Headache: The Journal of Head and Face Pain, 46,* 983–990.

Hounsfield, G. N. (1973). Computerized transverse axial scanning (tomography). 1. Description of system. *British Journal of Radiology, 46,* 1016–1022.

House, J. S., Robbins, C., & Metzner, H. L. (1982). The association of social relationships and activities with mortality: Prospective evidence from the Tecumseh Community Health Study. *American Journal of Epidemiology, 116,* 123–140.

Hovland, C. I., Janis, I. L., & Kelley, H. H. (1953). *Communication and persuasion: Psychological studies of opinion change.* New Haven, CT: Yale University Press.

Howard, K. I., Kopta, S. M., Krause, M. S., Orlinsky, D. E. (1986). The dose-effect relationship in psychotherapy. *American Psychologist, 41,* 159–164.

Howe, M., & Courage, M. (1993). On resolving the enigma of infantile amnesia. *Psychological Bulletin, 113,* 305–326.

Howes, O. D., & Salkovskis, P. M. (1998). Health anxiety in medical students. *Lancet, 351,* 1332.

Howland, R. H., & Thase, M. E. (1998). Cyclothymic disorder. In T. A. Widiger (ed.), *DSM-IV Sourcebook* (pp. 37–51). Washington, DC: American Psychiatric Association.

Hoza, B. (2007). Peer functioning in children with ADHD. *Journal of Pediatric Psychology, 32,* 665–663.

Hróbjartsson, A., & Götzsche, P. C. (2001). Is the placebo powerless? An analysis of clinical trials comparing placebo with no treatment. *New England Journal of Medicine, 344,* 1594–1602.

Hubel, D. H, & Wiesel, T. N. (1962). Receptive fields, binocular interaction and functional architecture in the cat's visual cortex. *Journal of Physiology, 160,* 106–154.

Hubel, D. H., & Wiesel, T. N. (1963). Shape and arrangement of columns in cat's striate cortex. *Journal of Physiology, 165,* 559–568.

Huck, S. W. (2008). *Statistical misconceptions.* New York: Routledge.

Huck, S. W., & Sandler, H. M. (1979). *Rival hypotheses: Alternative interpretation of data based conclusions.* New York: Harper and Row.

Hudson, D. B., Elek, S., & Campbell-Grossman, C. (2000). Depression, self-esteem, loneliness, and social support among adolescent mothers participating in the new parents project. *Adolescence, 35,* 445–453.

Hudson, L. (1967). *Contrary imaginations: A psychological study of the English schoolboy.* Harmondsworth, England: Penguin.

Huesmann, L. R., Moise-Titus, J., Podolski, C., & Eron, L. D. (2003). Longitudinal relations between children's exposure to TV violence and their aggressive and violent behavior in young adulthood: 1977–1992. *Developmental Psychology, 39,* 201–221.

Huff, D. (1954). *How to lie with statistics.* New York: W. W. Norton.

Huitema, B. E., & Stein, C. R. (1993). Validity of the GRE without restriction of range. *Psychological Reports, 72,* 123–127.

Hulbert, A. (2003). *Raising America: Experts, parents, and a century of advice about children.* New York: Knopf.

Hull, C. L. (1943). *Principles of behavior.* New York: Appleton-Century-Crofts.

Hull, J. G., & Bond, C. F. (1986). Social and behavioral consequences of alcohol consumption and expectancy: A meta-analysis. *Psychological Bulletin, 99,* 347–360.

Humphreys, K. (2000). Community narratives and personal stories in Alcoholics Anonymous. *Journal of Community Psychology, 28,* 495–506.

Hunsley, J., & Bailey, J. M. (1999). The clinical utility of the Rorschach: Unfulfilled promises and an uncertain future. *Psychological Assessment, 11,* 266–277.

Hunsley, J., & DiGuilio, G. (2002). Dodo bird, phoenix, or urban legend? *Scientific Review of Mental Health Practice, 1,* 11–22.

Hunsley, J., Lee, C. M., & Wood, J. (2003). Controversial and questionable assessment techniques. In S. O. Lilienfeld, J. M. Lohr, & S. J. Lynn (eds.), *Science and pseudoscience in contemporary clinical psychology* (pp. 39–76). New York: Guilford.

Hunt, E. (1999). Intelligence and human resources: Past, present, and future. In P. L. Ackerman, P. C. Kyllonen, & R. D. Roberts (eds.), *Learning and individual differences: Process, trait, and content determinants* (pp. 3–30). Washington, DC: American Psychological Association.

Hunt, E., & Carlson, J. (2007). Considerations relating to the study of group differences in intelligence. *Perspectives on Psychological Science, 2,* 194–213.

Hunt, M. (1993). *The story of psychology.* New York: Doubleday.

Hunt, M. (1997). *How science takes stock: The story of meta-analysis.* New York: Russell Sage Foundation.

Hunt, M. (1999). *The new know-nothings: The political foes of the scientific study of human nature.* New Brunswick, NJ: Transaction Publishers.

Hunter, J. E., & Hunter, R. F. (1984). Validity and utility of alternative predictors of job performance. *Psychological Bulletin, 96,* 72–98.

Hunter, J. E., Schmidt, F. L., & Hunter, R. (1979). Differential validity of employment tests by race: A comprehensive review and analysis. *Psychological Bulletin, 85,* 721–735.

Hunter, R. A., & Macalpine, I. (1963). *Three hundred years of psychiatry: 1535–1860.* London: Oxford University Press.

Huston, T. L., Ruggiero, M., Conner, R., & Geis, G. (1981). Bystander intervention into crime: A study based on naturally-occurring episodes. *Social Psychology Quarterly, 44,* 14–23.

Hutcheson, D. M., Everitt, B. J., Robbins, T. W., & Dickinson, A. (2001). The role of withdrawal in heroin addiction: Enhances reward or promotes avoidance? *Nature Neuroscience, 4,* 943–947.

Hutchins, S. S. (1999). *The psychosocial reality, variability, and the compositionality of English phonesthemes.* Unpublished doctoral dissertation, Emory University, Atlanta, GA.

Hyde, J. S. (2005). The gender similarities hypothesis. *American Psychologist, 60,* 581–592.

Hyde, J. S., Fennema, E., & Lamon, S. J. (1990). Gender differences in mathematics performance: A meta-analysis. *Psychological Bulletin, 107,* 139–155.

Hyman, I. E., Husband, T. H., & Billings, F. J. (1995). False memories of childhood experiences. *Applied Cognitive Psychology 9,* 181–197.

Hyman, R. (1977). Cold reading: How to convince strangers that you know all about them. *The Zetetic, 1*(2), 18–37.

Hyman, R. (1996). The evidence for psychic functioning: Claims vs. reality. *Skeptical Inquirer, 20,* 24–26.

Hyman, R. (1989). *The elusive quarry: A scientific appraisal of psychical research.* Buffalo, NY: Prometheus Books.

Hyman, R. (2002). When and why are smart people stupid? In R. Sternberg (ed.), *Why smart people can be so stupid* (pp. 1–23). New Haven, CT: Yale University Press.

Hyman, R. (2003, January/February). How not to test mediums: Critiquing the afterlife experiments. *Skeptical Inquirer, 27*(1), 20–30.

Iacoboni, M., (2009). Imitation, empathy, and mirror neurons. *Annual Review of Psychology, 60,* 653–670.

Iacono, W. G. (1985). Psychophysiologic markers of psychopathology: A review. *Canadian Psychology, 26,* 96–112.

Iacono, W. G. (2001). Forensic "lie detection": Procedures without scientific basis. *Journal of Forensic Psychology Practice, 1,* 75–86.

Iacono, W. G. (2009). Psychophysiological detection of deception and guilty knowledge. In J. L. Skeem, K. S. Douglas, & S. O. Lilienfeld (eds.), *Psychological science in the courtroom: Consensus and controversy* (pp. 224–241). New York: Guilford Press.

Iacono, W. G., & Patrick, C. J. (2006). Polygraph ("lie detector") testing: Current status and emerging trends. In I. B. Weiner & A. Hess (eds.), *Handbook of forensic psychology* (3rd ed., pp. 552–588). New York: Wiley.

Ikemi, Y., & Nakagawa, S. (1962). A psychosomatic study of contagious dermatitis. *Kyushu Journal of Medical Science, 13,* 335–350.

Ilardi, S. S., & Craighead, W. E. (1994). The role of nonspecific factors in cognitive therapy for depression. *Clinical Psychology: Science and Practice, 9,* 138–156.

Ilardi, S. S., & Feldman, D. (2001). The cognitive neuroscience paradigm: A unifying meta-theoretical framework for the science and practice of clinical psychology. *Journal of Clinical Psychology, 57,* 1067–1088.

Ilardi, S. S., Rand, K., & Karwoski, L. (2007). The cognitive neuroscience perspective allows us to understand abnormal behavior at multiple levels of complexity. In S. O. Lilienfeld & W. O. O'Donohue (eds.), *The great ideas of clinical science: 17 principles that all mental health professionals should understand* (pp. 291–309). New York: Routledge.

Imai, M., Kita, S., Nagumo, M., & Okada, H. (2008). Sound symbolism facilitates early verb learning. *Cognition, 109,* 54–65.

Ingram, R. (2003). Origins of cognitive vulnerability to depression. *Cognitive Therapy and Research, 27,* 77–88.

Ingram, R. E., Scott, W., & Siegle, G. (1999). Depression: Social and cognitive aspects. In T. Millon, P. H. Blaney, & R. D. Davis (eds.), *Oxford textbook of psychopathology* (pp. 203–226). New York: Oxford Press.

Intons-Peterson, M. J., & Fournier, J. (1986). External and internal memory aids: When and how often do we use them? *Journal of Experimental Psychology: General, 115,* 267–280.

Ioannidis, J. P. A. (2005). Contradicted and initially stronger effects in highly cited clinical research. *Journal of the American Medical Association, 294,* 218–228.

Irvin, J. E., Bowers, C. A., Dunn, M. E., & Wang, M. C. (1999). Efficacy of relapse prevention: A meta-analytic review. *Journal of Consulting and Clinical Psychology, 67,* 563–570.

Isen, A. M., Clark, M., & Schwartz, M. F. (1976). Duration of the effect of good mood on helping: Footprints in the sand of time. *Journal of Personality & Social Psychology, 34,* 385–393.

Isen, A. M., Rosenzweig, A. S., & Young, M. J. (1991). The influence of positive affect on clinical problem solving. *Medical Decision Making, 11,* 221–227.

Isenberg, D. J. (1986). Group polarization: A critical review and meta-analysis. *Journal of Personality and Social Psychology, 50,* 1141–1151.

Ivey, A. E., Ivey, M. B., & Simek-Morgan, L. (1993). *Counseling and psychotherapy: A multi-cultural perspective* (3rd ed.). Boston: Allyn & Bacon.

Ivie, R., & Ray, K. N. (2005). *Women in physics and astronomy, 2005.* College Park, MD: American Institute of Physics.

Izard, C. E. (1971). *The face of emotion.* New York: Appleton-Century-Crofts.

Izard, C. E. (1994). Innate and universal facial expressions: Evidence from developmental and cross-country research. *Psychological Bulletin, 115,* 288–299.

Jackson, D. N. (1971). The dynamics of structured personality tests: 1971. *Psychological Review, 78,* 229–248.

Jackson, D. N., & Rushton, J. P. (2006). Males have greater g: Sex differences in general mental ability from 100,000 17- to 18-year-olds on the Scholastic Assessment Test. *Intelligence, 34,* 479–486.

Jackson, J. W. (1993) Realistic group conflict theory: A review and evaluation of the theoretical and empirical literature. *Psychological Record, 43,* 395–414.

Jackson, K. M., & Sher, K. J. (2003). Alcohol use disorders and psychological distress: A prospective state-trait analysis. *Journal of Abnormal Psychology, 112,* 599–613.

Jackson, P. B., & Finney, M. (2002). Negative life events and psychological distress among young adults. *Social Psychology Quarterly, 65,* 186–201.

Jackson, R. D., LaCroix, A. Z., Gass, M., Wallace, R. B., Robbins, J., Lewis, C.E., et al. (2006). Calcium plus vitamin D supplementation and risk of fractures. *New England Journal of Medicine, 354,* 669–683.

Jacobs, G. D., Pace-Schott, E. F., Stickgold, R., & Otto, M. W. (2004). Cognitive behavior therapy and pharmacotherapy for insomnia: A randomized controlled trial and direct comparison. *Archives of Internal Medicine, 164,* 1888–1896.

Jacobson, E. (1938). *Progressive relaxation.* Chicago: University of Chicago Press.

Jacobson, J., Mulick, J., & Schwartz, A. (1995). A history of facilitated communication. *American Psychologist, 50,* 750–765.

Jacobson, L. H., Kelly, P. H., Bettler, B., Kaupmann, K., & Cryan, J. F. (2007). Specific roles of GABA B(1) receptor isoforms in cognition. *Behavioural Brain Research, 181,* 158–162.

Jacobson, N. S., Dobson, K. S., Truax, P. A., Addis, M. E., Koerner, K., Gollan, J. K., et al. (1996). A component analysis of cognitive-behavioral treatment for depression. *Journal of Consulting and Clinical Psychology, 64,* 295–304.

Jacobson, S. W., Chiodo, L. M., & Jacobson, J. L. (1999). Breastfeeding effects on intelligence quotient in 4- and 11-year-old children. *Pediatrics, 103,* e71.

Jacoby, L. L., & Rhodes, M. G. (2006). False remembering the aged. *Current Directions in Psychological Science, 15,* 49–53.

Jaffe, E. (2004). What was I thinking? Kahneman explains how intuition leads us astray. *Association for Psychological Science Observer, 17,* 5.

James, W. (1890). *The principles of psychology.* Cambridge, MA: Harvard University Press.

Jameson, K. A., Highnote, S., & Wasserman, L. (2001). Richer color experience in observers with multiple photopigment opsin genes. *Psychonomic Bulletin and Review, 8,* 244–261.

Jamieson, G. A., & Sheehan, P. W. (2004). An empirical test of Woody and Bowers's dissociated-control theory of hypnosis. *International Journal of Clinical and Experimental Hypnosis, 52,* 232–249.

Jamison, K. R. (1989). Mood disorders and patterns of creativity in British writers and artists. *Psychiatry, 52,* 125–134.

Jamison, K. R. (1993). *Touched with fire: Manic-depressive illness and the artistic temperament.* New York: Free Press.

Janda, L. H. (1998). *Psychological testing, theory, and applications.* Boston: Allyn & Bacon.

Janevic, M. R., & Connell, C. M. (2001). Racial, ethnic, and cultural differences in the dementia caregiving experience. *The Gerontologist, 41,* 334–347.

Janis, I. L. (1972). *Victims of groupthink.* Boston: Houghton Mifflin.

Janos, P. M., & Robinson, N. M. (1985). Psychosocial development in intellectually gifted children. In F. D. Horowitz & M. O'Brien (eds.), *The gifted and talented: Developmental perspectives* (pp. 149–195). Washington, DC: American Psychological Association.

Jansen, K. L. R. (1991). Transcendental explanations and the near-death experience. *Lancet, 337,* 207–243.

Jaramillo, J. A., (1996). Vygotsky's sociocultural theory and contributions to the development of constructivist curricula. *Education, 117,* 133–140.

Javornisky, G. (1979). Task content and sex differences in conformity. *Journal of Psychology, 108*, 213–220.

Jay, K., & Young, A. (1979). *Out of the closets: Voices of gay liberation*. New York: BJ Publishing Group.

Jefferson, T., Herbst, J. H., & McCrae, R. R. (1998). Associations between birth order and personality traits: Evidence from self-reports and observer ratings. *Journal of Research in Personality, 32*, 498–509.

Jenike, M. A., Baer, L., Ballantine, T., Martuza, R. L., Tynes, S., Giriunas, I., et al. (1991). Cingulotomy for refractory obsessive compulsive disorder. A long term follow-up of 33 patients. *Archives of General Psychiatry, 48*, 548–555.

Jenny, C., Roesler, T. A., & Poyer, K. L. (1994). Are children at risk for sexual abuse by homosexuals? *Pediatrics, 94*, 41–44.

Jensen, A. R. (1969). How much can we boost I.Q. and scholastic achievement? *Harvard Educational Review, 33*, 1–123.

Jensen, A. R. (1973). *Educability and group differences*. London: Methuen.

Jensen, A. R. (1977). Cumulative deficit of blacks in the rural south. *Developmental Psychology, 13*, 184–191.

Jensen, A. R. (1980). *Bias in mental testing*. New York: Free Press.

Jensen, A. R. (1993). Test validity: g versus "tacit knowledge." *Current Directions in Psychological Science, 2*, 9–10.

Jensen, A. R. (1998). *The g factor: The science of mental ability*. Westport, CT: Praeger.

Jensen, A. R. (2006). *Clocking the mind: Mental chronometry and individual differences*. Oxford, England: Elsevier.

Jensen, P. S., Garcia, J. A., Glied, S., Crow, M., Foster, M., Schlander, M., et al. (2005). Cost-effectiveness of ADHD treatments: Findings from the multimodal treatment study of children with ADHD. *American Journal of Psychiatry, 162*, 1628–1636.

Jensvold, M. F., & Turner, S. M. (1988). The woman who hadn't been out of her house in 25 years. In J. A. Talbott & A. Z. A. Manevitz (eds.), *Psychiatric house calls* (pp. 161–167). Washington, DC: American Psychiatric Association Press.

Jerison, H. J. (1983). The evolution of the mammalian brain as an information processing system. In J. F. Eisenberg & D. G. Kleiman (eds.), Advances in the study of mammalian behavior. *American Society of Mammalogists Special Publication, 7*, 632–661.

Jerome, L. (2000). Central auditory processing disorder and ADHD. *Journal of the American Academy of Child & Adolescent Psychiatry, 39*, 399–400.

Job, D., Whalley, H. C., Johnstone, E. C., & Lawrie, S. M. (2005). Grey matter changes over time in high risk subjects developing schizophrenia. *NeuroImage, 25*, 1023–1030.

Johanson, C. E. Balster, R. L., & Bonese, K. (1976). Self-administration of psychomotor stimulant drugs: The effects of unlimited access. *Pharmacology, Biochemistry, and Behavior, 4*, 45–51.

John, O. P., & Robins, R. W. (1994). Accuracy and bias in self-perception: Individual differences in self-enhancement and the role of narcissism. *Journal of Personality and Social Psychology, 66*, 206–219.

John, O. P., Robins, R. W., & Pervin, L. A. (2008). *Handbook of personality: Theory and research* (3rd Edition). New York: Guilford.

Johnson, C. L., Tobin, D. L., & Steinberg, S. L. (1989). Etiological, developmental and treatment considerations for bulimia. Special issue: The bulimic college student: Evaluation, treatment and prevention. *Journal of College Student Psychotherapy, 3*, 57–73.

Johnson, F., & Wardle, J. (2005). Dietary restraint, body dissatisfaction, and psychological distress: A prospective analysis. *Journal of Abnormal Psychology, 114*, 119–125.

Johnson, J. S., & Newport, E. L. (1989). Critical period effects in second language learning: The influence of maturational state on the acquisition of English as a second language. *Cognitive Psychology, 21*, 60–99.

Johnson, M. H. (1992). Imprinting and the development of face recognition: From chick to man. *Current Directions in Psychological Science, 1*, 52–55.

Johnson, M. H. (1998). The neural basis of cognitive development. In W. Damon (ed.), *Handbook of child psychology: Vol. 2: Cognition, perception, and language* (pp. 1–49). Hoboken, NJ: Wiley.

Johnson, M. K., Hashtroudi, S., & Lindsay, D. S. (1993). Source monitoring. *Psychological Bulletin, 114*, 3–28.

Johnson, M. K., & Raye, C. L. (1981). Reality monitoring. *Psychological Review, 88*, 67–85.

Johnson, P. (2005). Obesity: Epidemic or myth? *Skeptical Inquirer, 29*, 25–29.

Johnson, R. D., & Downing, L. L. (1979). Deindividuation and valence of cues: Effects on prosocial and anti-social behavior. *Journal of Personality and Social Psychology, 37*, 1532–1538.

Johnson, S. L., Cueller, A. K., Ruggero, C., Winett-Perlman, C., Goodnick, P., & White, R. (2008). Life events as predictors of mania and depression in bipolar 1 disorder. *Journal of Abnormal Psychology, 117*, 268–277.

Johnson, S. L., & Miller, I. (1997). Negative life events and time to recovery from episodes of bipolar disorder. *Journal of Abnormal Psychology, 106*, 449–457.

Johnson, S. L., Sandrow, D., Meyer, B., Winters, R., Miller, I., Solomon D., et al. (2000). Increases in manic symptoms after life events involving goal attainment. *Journal of Abnormal Psychology, 109*, 721–727.

Johnson, W., Carothers, A., & Deary, I. J. (2009). A role for the X chromosome in sex differences in variability in general intelligence? *Perspectives on Psychological Science, 4*, 598–611.

Johnston, L. D., O'Malley, P. M., & Bachman, J. G. (2002). *Monitoring the future national results on adolescent drug use: Overview of key findings, 2001*. Bethesda, MD: National Institute on Drug Abuse (DHHS/PHS).

Johnston, L. D., O'Malley, P. M., & Bachman, J. G. (2003). *Monitoring the future national results on adolescent drug use: Overview of key findings, 2002*. Bethesda, MD: National institute on Drug Abuse (DHHS/PHS).

Johnston, L. D., O'Malley, P. M., Bachman, J. G., & Schulenberg, J. E. (2008). *Monitoring the future national survey results on drug use, 1975–2007. Volume II: College students and adults ages 19–45*. (NIH Publication No. 08-6418B). Bethesda, MD: National Institute on Drug Abuse.

Johnston, L. D., O'Malley, P. M., Bachman, J. G., & Schulenberg, J. E. (2009). *Monitoring the future national survey results on drug use, 1975–2007. Volume I: Secondary school students* (NIH Publication No. 08-6418A). Bethesda, MD: National Institute on Drug Abuse.

Joiner, T. E., & Coyne, J. C. (1999). *The interactional nature of depression: Advances in interpersonal approaches*. Washington, DC: American Psychological Association.

Joiner, T. E., Heatherton, T. F., Rudd, M. D., & Schmidt, N. B. (1997). Perfectionism, perceived weight status, and bulimic symptoms: Two studies testing a diathesis–stress model. *Journal of Abnormal Psychology, 106*, 145–153.

Jones, A. (1969). Stimulus-seeking behavior. In J. Zubek (ed.), *Sensory deprivation: Fifteen years of research* (pp. 167–206). New York: Appleton-Century-Crofts.

Jones, B. E. (2003). Arousal systems. *Frontiers in Bioscience, 8*, 438–451.

Jones, C. M., Braithwaite, V. A., & Healy, S. D. (2003). The evolution of sex differences in spatial ability. *Behavioral Neuroscience, 117*, 403–411.

Jones, E. E., & Harris, V. A. (1967). The attribution of attitudes. *Journal of Experimental Social Psychology, 3*, 1–24.

Jones, E. E., & Nisbett, R. E. (1972). The actor and the observer: Divergent perceptions of the causes of the behavior. In E. E. Jones, D. E. Kanouse, H. H. Kelley, R. E. Nisbett, S. Valins, & B. Weiner (eds.), *Attribution: Perceiving the causes of behavior* (pp. 79–94). Morristown, NJ: General Learning Press.

Jones, F., & Bright, J. (2001). *Stress: Myth, theory, and research*. Harlow, England: Prentice Hall.

Jones, J., & Callan, D. (2003). Brain activity during audiovisual speech perception: An fMRI study of the McGurk effect. *NeuroReport, 14*, 1129–1133.

Jones, J. C., & Barlow, D. H. (1990). The etiology of posttraumatic stress disorder. *Clinical Psychology Review, 10*, 299–328.

Jones, J. H. (1993). *Bad blood: The Tuskegee syphilis experiment* (2nd ed.). New York: Free Press.

Jones, L. L., Oudega, M., Bunge, M. B., & Tuszynski, M. H. (2001). Neurotrophic factors, cellular bridges and gene therapy for spinal cord injury. *Journal of Physiology, 15*, 83–89.

Jones, M. C. (1924). The elimination of children's fears. *Journal of Experimental Psychology, 7*, 382–390.

Jones, S. E. (1979). Integrating etic and emic approaches in the study of intercultural communication. In M. Asante, E. Newmark, & C. Blake (eds.), Handbook of intercultural communication. Beverly Hills, CA: Sage.

Jordan, H. A. (1969). Voluntary intragastric feeding: Oral and gastric contributions to food intake and hunger in man. *Journal of Comparative and Physiological Psychology, 68*, 498–506.

Joseph, R. (1988). Dual mental functioning in a split-brain patient. *Journal of Clinical Psychology, 44*, 770–779.

Joslyn, G., Brusch, G., Robertson, M., Smith, T. L., Kalmijn, J., Schuckit, M., & White, R. L. (2008). Chromosome 15q25.1 genetic markers associated with level of response to alcohol in humans. *Proceedings of the National Academy of Sciences*, DOI: 10.1073/pnas.0810970105.

Jost, J. T., Glaser, J., Kruglanski, A. W., & Sulloway, F., (2003). Political conservatism as motivated social cognition. *Psychological Bulletin, 129*, 339–375.

Jouvet, M. (1962). Recherches sur les structures nerveuses et les mechanismes responsables des differentes phases du sommeil physiologique. *Archives italiannes de Biologie, 100*, 125–206.

Julien, R. M. (2004). *A primer of drug action* (10th ed.). San Francisco: W. H. Freeman.

Jung, C. G. (1936). *Archetypes and the collective unconscious*. Princeton, NJ: Princeton University Press.

Jung, C. G. (1950). On mandalas. In *The collected works of C. G. Jung* (Vol. 9ii). Princeton, NJ: Princeton University Press.

Jung, C. G. (1958). Flying saucers: A modern myth of things seen in the skies. In *The collected works of C. G. Jung* (Vol. 14). Princeton, NJ: Princeton University Press.

Jung, R., & Haier, R. J. (2007). The parieto-frontal integration theory (P-FIT) of intelligence: Converging neuroimaging evidence. *Behavioral and Brain Sciences, 30*, 135–187.

Jus, A., Jus, K., Gautier, J., Villenueve, A., Pires, P., Lachance, R., et al. (1973). Dream reports after reserpine in chronic lobotomized schizophrenic patients. *Vie médicale au Canada français, 2*, 843–848.

Kabat-Zinn, J. (2003). Mindfulness-based interventions in context: Past, present, and future. *Clinical Psychology: Science & Practice, 10*, 144–156.

Kagan, J. (1975). Resilience in cognitive development. *Ethos, 3*, 231–247.

Kagan, J. (1976). Emergent themes in human development. *American Scientist, 64*, 186–196.

Kagan, J. (1994). *Three seductive ideas*. Cambridge, MA: Harvard University Press.

Kagan, J. (1998). Biology and the child. In W. Damon & N. Eisenberg (eds.), *Handbook of child psychology, Vol. 3: Social, emotional, and personality development* (5th ed., pp. 177–235). Hoboken, NJ: John Wiley.

Kagan, J., Reznick, J. S., & Snidman, N. (1988). Biological bases of childhood shyness. *Science, 240*, 167–171.

Kagan, J., Snidman, N., Arcus, D., & Reznick, J. S. (1994). *Galen's prophecy: Temperament in human nature*. New York: Basic Books.

Kagan, J., Snidman, N., Kahn, V., & Towsley, S. (2007). The preservation of two infant temperaments into adolescence. *SRCD Monographs, 72*(2).

Kageyama, T. (1999). Loudness in listening to music with portable headphone stereos. *Perceptual and Motor Skills, 88*, 423.

Kahill, S. (1984). Human figure drawing in adults: An update of the empirical evidence, 1967–1982. *Canadian Psychology, 25*, 395–410.

Kahneman, D., & Klein, G. (2009). Conditions for intuitive expertise: A failure to disagree. *American Psychologist, 64*, 515–526.

Kahneman, D., Krueger, A., Schkade, D., Schwarz, N., & Stone, A. (2006). Would you be happier if you were richer? A focusing illusion. *Science, 312*, 1908–1910.

Kahneman, D., Slovic, P., & Tversky, A. (eds.). (1982). *Judgment under uncertainty: Heuristics and biases*. New York: Cambridge University Press.

Kahneman, D., Krueger, A. B., Schkade, D. A. Schwarz, N., & Stone, A. A. (2004). A survey method for characterizing daily life experience: The day reconstruction method. *Science, 306*, 1776–1780.

Kalat, J. W. (2007). *Biological psychology* (9th ed.). Belmont, CA: Thomson Wadsworth.

Kamrin, M. A. (1988). *Toxicology: A primer on toxicology principles and applications*. Boca Raton, FL: Lewis Publishers.

Kandel, D., Yamaguchi, K., & Chen, K. (1992). Stages of progression in drug involvement from adolescence to adulthood: Further evidence for the gateway theory. *Journal of Studies of Alcohol, 53*, 447–457.

Kandel, E. R., Schwartz, J. H., & Jessell, T. M. (1991). Principles of Neural Science. Norwalk, CT: Appleton and Lange.

Kanders, B. S., & Blackburn, G. L. (1992). Reducing primary risk factors by therapeutic weight loss. In T. A. Wadden & T. B. Van Itallie (eds.), *Treatment of the seriously obese patient* (pp. 213–230). New York: Guilford Press.

Kane, M. J., Hambrick, D. Z., & Conway, A. R. A. (2005). Working memory capacity and fluid intelligence are strongly related constructs: Comment on Ackerman, Beier, and Boyle (2004). *Psychological Bulletin, 131*, 66–71.

Kanner, A. D., Coyne, J. C., Schaefer, C., & Lazarus, R. S. (1981). Comparison of two modes of stress measurement: Daily hassles and uplifts versus major life events. *Journal of Behavioral Medicine, 4*, 1–39.

Kanzler, H. R., & Rosenthal, R. N. (2003). Dual diagnosis: Alcoholism and co-morbid psychiatric disorders. *American Journal of Addiction, 12*(Suppl. 1), 21–40.

Kaplan, H. S. (1977). Hypoactive sexual desire. *Journal of Sex and Marital Therapy, 3*, 3–9.

Kaplan, R. M. (1982). Nader's raid on the testing industry: Is it in the best interests of the consumer? *American Psychologist, 37*, 15–23.

Kaplan, R. M. & Saccuzzo, D. P. (2005). *Psychological testing: Principles, applications, and issues.* (6th edition). Belmont, CA: Wadsworth/Thomson.

Kaplan, R. M. & Saccuzzo, D. P. (2008). *Psychological testing: Principles, applications, and issues.* (7th edition). Belmont, CA: Wadsworth/Thomson.

Kaptchuk, T. J. (2002). The placebo effect in alternative medicine: Can the performance of a healing ritual have clinical significance? *Annals of Internal Medicine, 136*, 817–825.

Karasek, R., & Theorell, T. (1990). *Health work: Stress, productivity and the reconstruction of life*. New York: Basic Books.

Karatekin, C. (2004). Development of attentional allocation in the dual task paradigm. *International Journal of Psychophysiology, 52*, 7–21.

Karau, S. J., & Williams, K. D. (1995). Social loafing—Research findings, implications, and future directions. *Current Directions in Psychological Science, 4*, 134–140.

Karlen, S. J., & Krubitzer, L. (2006). The evolution of the neocortex in mammals: Intrinsic and extrinsic contributions to the cortical phenotype. *Novartis Found Symposium 270*, 159–169.

Karlin, R. A., & Orne, M. T. (1996). Commentary on *Borawick v. Shay*: Hypnosis, social influence, incestuous child abuse, and satanic ritual abuse: The iatrogenic creation of horrific memories for the remote past. *Cultic Studies Journal, 13*, 42–94.

Karlsson, R. M., Tanaka, K., & Hellig, M., & Holmes, A. (2008). Loss of glial glutamate and aspartate transporter (Excitatory amino acid transporter 1) causes locomotor hyperactivity and exaggerated responses to psychotomimetics: Rescue by haloperidol and metabotropic glutamate 2/3 agonist. *Biological Psychiatry, 64*, 810–814.

Karon, B. P. (1994). *Effective psychoanalytic therapy of schizophrenia and other severe disorders* (APA Videotape Series). Washington, DC: American Psychological Association.

Karon, B. P. (2000). A clinical interpretation of the Thematic Apperception Test, Rorschach, and other clinical data: A reexamination of statistical versus clinical prediction. *Professional Psychology: Research and Practice, 31*, 230–233.

Karpicke, J. D., & Roediger, H. L. (2008). The critical importance of retrieval for learning. *Science, 319*, 966–968.

Kasper, S., Gastpar, M., Muller, W. E., Volz, H. P., Dienel, A., Kieser, M., et al. (2007). Efficacy of St. John's wort extract WS 5570 in acute treatment of mild depression. *European Archives of Psychiatry and Clinical Neuroscience, 258*, 59–63.

Kassin, S. (2004). *Psychology* (4th ed.). Upper Saddle River, NJ: Prentice Hall.

Kassin, S. M., & Gudjonsson, G. H. (2004). The psychology of confession: A review of the literature and issues. *Psychological Science in the Public Interest, 5*, 33–67.

Kassin, S. M., Ellsworth, P. C., & Smith, V. L. (1989). The "general acceptance" of psychological research on eyewitness testimony: A survey of the experts. *American Psychologist, 44*, 1089–1098.

Kassin, S. M., Tubb, V. A., Hosch, H. M., & Memon, A. (2001). On the "general acceptance" of eyewitness testimony research. *American Psychologist, 56*, 405–416.

Kato, J., Ide, H., Kabashima, I., Kadota, H., Takano, K., & Kansaku, K. (2009). Neural correlates of attitude change following positive and negative advertisements. *Frontiers in Behavioral Neuroscience, 3*, ArtID 6.

Kato, Y., Kato, S., & Akahori, K. (2007). Effects of emotional cues transmitted in e-mail communication on the emotions experienced by senders and receivers. *Computers in Human Behavior, 23*, 1894–1905.

Katz, D. A., & McHorney, C. A. (2002). The relationship between insomnia and health-related quality of life in patients with chronic illness. *Journal of Family Practice, 51*, 229–235.

Katz, J. (1988). *Seductions of crime: Moral and sensual attractions in doing evil*. New York: Basic Books.

Katzev, R., & Brownstein, R. (1989). The influence of enlightenment on compliance. *Journal of Social Psychology, 129,* 335–347.

Katzman, D. K. (2005). Medical complications in adolescents with anorexia nervosa: A review of the literature. *International Journal of Eating Disorders, 37*(Suppl.), S52–S59.

Kavale, K. A., & Forness, S. R. (1987). Substance over style—Assessing the efficacy of modality testing and teaching. *Exceptional Children, 54,* 228–239.

Kayser, C., Petkov, C. I., Augath, M., & Logothetis, N. K. (2007). Functional imaging reveals visual modulation of specific fields in auditory cortex. *Journal of Neuroscience, 27,* 1824–1835.

Kazdin, A. E. (1978). The application of operant techniques in treatment, rehabilitation, and education. In S. L. Garfield & A. E. Bergin (eds.), *Handbook of psychotherapy and behavior change* (2nd ed.). New York: John Wiley & Sons.

Kazdin, A. E. (1982). The token economy: A decade later. *Journal of Applied Behavior Analysis, 15,* 431–445.

Kazdin, A. E. (2005). Treatment outcomes, common factors, and continued neglect of mechanisms of change. *Clinical Psychology: Science and Practice, 12,* 184–188.

Kazdin, A. E., & Hersen, M. (1980). The current status of behavior therapy. *Behavior Modification, 4,* 283–302.

Kazdin, A. E. (2007). Mediators and mechanisms of change in psychotherapy research. *Annual Review of Clinical Psychology, 3,* 1–27.

Kazdin, A. E., Marciano, P. L., & Whitley, M. K. (2005). The therapeutic alliance in cognitive-behavioral treatment of children referred for oppositional, aggressive, and antisocial behavior. *Journal of Consulting and Clinical Psychology, 73,* 725–730.

Kazdin, A. E., & Wilcoxon, L. A. (1976). Systematic desensitization and non-specific treatment effects: A methodological evaluation. *Psychological Bulletin, 83,* 729–758.

Keane, T., Marshall, A. D., & Taft, C. T. (2006). Posttraumatic stress disorder: Etiology, epidemiology, and treatment outcome. *Annual Review of Clinical Psychology, 2,* 161–197.

Keefe, R. & Henry, P. S. (1994). Understanding schizophrenia: A guide to the new research on causes and treatment. New York: Free Press.

Keefe, R. S., Silverman, J. M., Mohs, R. C., Siever, L. J., Harvery, P. D., Friedman, L., et al. (1997). Eye tracking, attention, and schizotypal symptoms in nonpsychotic relatives of patients with schizophrenia. *Archives of General Psychiatry, 54,* 169–176.

Keel, P. K., & Klump, K. L. (2003). Are eating disorders culture-bound syndromes? Implications for conceptualizing their etiology. *Psychological Bulletin, 129,* 747–769.

Keen, S. (1986). *Faces of the enemy: Reflections of the hostile imagination.* San Francisco: Harper & Row.

Keil, F. C., Lockhart, K. L., & Schlegel, E. (2010). A bump on a bump?: Emerging intuitions concerning the relative difficulty of the sciences. *Journal of Experimental Psychology: General, 139,* 1–15.

Keinan, G., Almagor, M. & Ben-Porath, Y. S. (1989). A reevaluation of the relationships between psychotherapeutic orientation and perceived personality characteristics. *Psychotherapy, 26,* 218–226.

Keith, S. J., Gunderson, J. G., Reifman, A., Buchsbaum, S., & Mosher, L. R. (1976). Special report: Schizophrenia, 1976. *Schizophrenia Bulletin, 2,* 510–565.

Kellaris, J. J. (2003). *Dissecting earworms: Further evidence on the song-stuck-in-your-head phenomenon.* Paper presented at the the Society for Consumer Psychology Winter 2003 Conference, New Orleans, LA.

Kellehear, A. (1993). Culture, biology, and the near-death experience: A reappraisal. *Journal of Nervous and Mental Disease, 181,* 148–156.

Keller, H. (1910). Before the soul dawn. *The world I live in* (pp. 113–114). New York: Century.

Keller, M. L., & Craske, M. G. (2008). Panic disorder and agoraphobia. In J. Hunsley & E. J. Mash (eds.), *A guide to assessments that work* (pp. 229–253). New York: Oxford University Press.

Kelly, E. (2009). *Encyclopedia of attention deficit hyperactivity disorder.* New York: Greenwood.

Kelley, H. H. (1973). Processes of causal attribution. *American Psychologist, 28,* 107–128.

Kelly, T. H., Cherek, D. R., Steinberg, J. L., & Robinson, D. (1988). Effects of provocation and alcohol on human aggressive behavior. *Drug and Alcohol Dependence, 21,* 105–112.

Kendall, T., Pilling, S., & Whittington, C. J. (2005). Are the SSRIs and atypical antidepressants safe and effective for children and adolescents? *Current Opinion in Psychiatry, 18,* 21–25.

Kendeigh, S. C. (1941). Territorial and mating behavior of the house wren. *Illinois Biographical Monographs, 18*(3) (Serial No. 120).

Kendell, R. E. (1975). The concept of disease and its implications for psychiatry. *British Journal of Psychiatry, 127,* 305–315.

Kendler, K. S. (2005). Toward a philosophical structure for psychiatry. *American Journal of Psychiatry, 162,* 433–440.

Kendler, K. S., & Diehl, S. R. (1993). The genetics of schizophrenia: A current, genetic-epidemiologic perspective. *Schizophrenia Bulletin, 19,* 261–285.

Kendler, K. S., Gardner, C. O., & Prescott, C. A. (2003). Personality and the experience of environmental adversity. *Psychological Medicine, 33,* 1193–1202.

Kendler, K. S., & Karkowski-Shuman, L. (1997). Stressful life events and genetic liability to major depression: Genetic control of exposure to the environment? *Psychological Medicine, 27,* 539–547.

Kendler, K. S., Myers, J., & Prescott, C. A. (2005). Sex differences in the relationship between social support and risk for major depression: A longitudinal study of opposite-sex twin pairs. *American Journal of Psychiatry, 162,* 250–256.

Kendler, K. S., Neale, M. C., Kessler, R. C., Heath, A. C., & Eaves, L. J. (1992) The genetic epidemiology of phobias in women: The interrelationship of agoraphobia, social phobia, situational phobia, and simple phobia. *Archives of General Psychiatry, 49,* 273–281.

Kendler, K. S., Neale, M. C., Kessler, R. C., Heath, A. C., & Eaves, L. J. (1993). A test of the equal-environment assumption in twin studies of psychiatric illness. *Behavior Genetics, 23,* 21–27.

Kenneally, C. (2006). The deepest cut—Radical neurosurgery and the brain's adaptability. *New Yorker, 82*(20), 36–42.

Kennedy, S., Kiecolt-Glaser, J. K., & Glaser, R. (1990). Social support, stress, and the immune system. In B. R. Sarason, I. G. Sarason, & G. R. Pierce (eds.), *Social support: An interactional view* (pp. 253–266). New York: Wiley.

Kenrick, D. T., & Funder, D. C. (1988). Profiting from controversy: Lessons from the person-situation debate. *American Psychologist, 43,* 23–34.

Kenrick, D. T., Neuberg, S. L., & Cialdini, R. B. (2005). *Social psychology: Unraveling the mystery* (3rd ed.). Boston: Allyn & Bacon.

Kent, R. D., & Miolo, G. (1995). Phonetic abilities in the first year of life. In P. Flether & B. MacWhinney (eds.), *The handbook of child language* (pp. 303–334). San Diego, CA: Academic Press.

Keppel, G., & Underwood, B. J. (1962). Proactive inhibition in short-term retention of single items. *Journal of Verbal Learning and Verbal Behavior, 1,* 153–161.

Kernberg, O. F. (1967). Borderline personality organization. *Journal of the American Psychoanalytic Association, 15,* 641–685.

Kernberg, O. F. (1975). *Borderline conditions and pathological narcissism.* New York: Jason Aronson.

Kerr, N. H. (1993) Mental imagery, dreams, and perception. In C. Cavallero, & D. Foulkes, (eds.). *Dreaming as cognition* (pp. 18–37). Hertfordshire, England: Harvester Wheatsheaf.

Kerr, N. H. & Domhoff, G. W. (2004). Do the blind literally "see" in their dreams? A critique of a recent claim that they do. *Dreaming, 14,* 230–233.

Kesebir, P., & Diener, E. D. (2008). In pursuit of happiness: Empirical answers to philosophical questions. *Perspectives on Psychological Science, 3,* 117–125.

Keski-Rahkonen, A., Hoek, H. W., Linna, M. S., Raevuori, A., Sihvola, E., Bulik, C. M., et al. (2008). Incidence and outcomes of bulimia nervosa: A nationwide population-based study. *Psychological Medicine, 8,* 1–9.

Kessler, R. C., Berglund, P., Demler, O., Jin, R., & Walters, E. E. (2005). Lifetime prevalence and age-of-onset distributions of DSM-IV disorders in the National Comorbidity Survey Replication. *Archives of General Psychiatry, 62,* 593–602.

Kessler, R. C., Chiu, W. T., Jin, R., Ruscio, A. M., Shear, K., & Walters, E. E. (2006). The epidemiology of panic attacks, panic disorder, and agoraphobia in the National Comorbidity Survey Replication. *Archives of General Psychiatry, 63,* 415–424.

Kessler, R. C., McGonagale, K. A., Zhao, S., Nelson, C. B., Hughes, M., Eshleman, S., et al. (1994). Lifetime and 12-month prevalence of DSM-III-R psychiatric disorders in the United States: Results from the National Comorbidity Survey. *Archives of General Psychiatry, 51,* 8–19.

Kessler, R. C., Price, R. H., & Wortman, C. B. (1985). Social factors in psychopathology: Stress, social support and coping processes. *Annual Review of Psychology, 36,* 351–372.

Kessler, R. C., Sonnega, A., Bromet, E., Hughes, M., & Nelson, C. B. (1995). Post-traumatic stress disorder in the National Comorbidity Survey. *Archives of General Psychiatry, 52,* 1048–1060.

Kessler, R. C., Soukup, J., Davis, R. B., Foster, D. F., Wilkey, S. A., van Rompay, M. I., et al. (2001). The use of complementary and alternative therapies to treat anxiety and depression in the United States. *American Journal of Psychiatry, 158,* 289–294.

Kevles, D. J. (1985). *In the name of eugenics: Genetics and the uses of human heredity.* New York: Knopf.

Keyes, C. L. M., & Haidt, J. (eds.). (2003). *Flourishing: Positive psychology and the life well lived.* Washington, DC: American Psychological Association.

Keys, A., Brozek, J., Henschel, A., Mickelsen, O., & Taylor, H. L. (1950). *The biology of human starvation* (2 vols.). Minneapolis, MN: University of Minnesota Press.

Kida, T. (2006). *Don't believe everything you think: The 6 basic mistakes we make in thinking.* Amherst, NY: Prometheus Books.

Kiecolt-Glaser, J. K., Marucha, P. T., Malarkey, W. B., Mercado, A. M., & Glaser, R. (1995). Slowing of wound healing by psychological stress. *Lancet, 346,* 1194–1196.

Kiecolt-Glaser, J. K., McGuire, L., Robles, T. F., & Glaser, R. (2002). Psychoneuroimmunology: Psychological influences on immune function and health. *Journal of Consulting and Clinical Psychology, 70,* 537–547.

Kiesler, C. A., & Kiesler, S. B. (1969). *Conformity.* Menlo Park, CA: Addison-Wesley.

Kihlstrom, J. F. (1987). The cognitive unconscious. *Science, 237,* 1445–1452.

Kihlstrom, J. F. (1992). Hypnosis: A sesquicentennial essay. *International Journal of Clinical and Experimental Hypnosis, 40,* 301–314.

Kihlstrom, J. F. (1998). Dissociations and dissociation theory in hypnosis: Comment on Kirsch & Lynn (1998). *Psychological Bulletin, 123,* 186–191.

Kihlstrom, J. F. (2003). The fox, the hedgehog, and hypnosis. *International Journal of Clinical & Experimental Hypnosis, 51,* 166–189.

Kihlstrom, J. F. (2005). Dissociative disorders. In S. Nolen-Hoeksema, T. D. Cannon, & T. Widiger (eds.), *Annual Review of Clinical Psychology, 1,* 227–254.

Kihlstrom, J. W. (2009). Unconscious cognition. In W. Banks (ed.), *Encyclopedia of consciousness.* New York: Academic Press.

Kilgore, W., & Yurgelun-Todd, D. (2005). Social anxiety predicts amygdala activation in adolescents viewing fearful faces. *Neuroreport, 16,* 1671–1675.

Kilham, W., & Mann, L. (1974). Level of destructive obedience as a function of transmitter and executant roles in the Milgram obedience paradigm. *Journal of Personality and Social Psychology, 29,* 696–702.

Kilmartin, C. (2006). Depression in men: Communication, diagnosis and therapy. *The Journal of Men's Health & Gender, 2,* 95–99.

Kim, E. Y., & Miklowitz, D. J. (2004). Expressed emotion as a predictor of outcome among bipolar patients undergoing family therapy. *Journal of Affective Disorders, 82,* 343–352.

Kim, H., & Markus, H. R. (1999). Deviance or uniqueness, harmony or conformity? A cultural analysis. *Journal of Personality and Social Psychology, 77,* 785–800.

Kim, J. H. S., Relkin, N. R., Lee, K. M., & Hirsch, J. (1997). Distinct cortical areas associated with native and second languages. *Nature, 388,* 171–174.

Kim-Cohen, J., Caspi, A., Taylor, A., Williams, B., Newcombe, R., Craig, I., et al. (2006). MAOA, maltreatment, and gene-environment interaction predicting children's mental health: New evidence and a meta-analysis. *Molecular Psychiatry, 11,* 903–913.

Kimura, D. (1999). *Sex and cognition.* Cambridge, MA: MIT Press.

Kindt, M., Soeter, M., & Vervliet, B. (2009). Beyond extinction: Erasing human fear responses and preventing the return of fear. *Nature Neuroscience, 12,* 256–258.

King, A. C., Houle, T., de Wit, H., Holdstock, L., & Schuster, A. (2002). Biphasic alcohol response differs in heavy versus light drinkers. *Alcoholism: Clinical and Experimental Research, 26,* 827–835.

King, B. (2006). The rise, fall, and resurrection of the ventromedial hypothalamus in the regulation of feeding behavior and body weight. *Physiology & Behavior, 87,* 221–224.

King, J. (2000) Treatment of schizophrenia - What in fact is schizophrenia? *British Medical Journal, 320,* 800.

King, J. E., & Figueredo, A. J. (1997). The five-factor model plus dominance in chimpanzee personality. *Journal of Research in Personality, 31,* 257–271.

Kinney, J., & Leaton, G. (1995). *Loosening the grip: A handbook of alcohol information* (5th ed.). St. Louis, MO: Mosby.

Kippes, C., & Garrison, C. B. (2006). Are we in the midst of an autism epidemic? A review of prevalence data. *Missouri Medicine, 103,* 65–68.

Kircher, J. C., Horowitz, S. W., & Raskin, D. C. (1988). Meta-analysis of mock crime studies of the control question polygraph technique. *Law and Human Behavior, 12,* 79–90.

Kirk, S. A., & Kutchins, H. (1992). *The selling of DSM: The rhetoric of science in psychiatry.* Hawthorne, NY: Aldine de Gruyter.

Kirkcaldy, B. D., Levine, R., Shephard, R. J. (2000). The impact of working hours on physical and psychological health of German managers. *European Review of Applied Psychology, 50,* 443–449.

Kirmayer, L. J., & Young, A. (1999). Culture and context in the evolutionary concept of mental disorder. *Journal of Abnormal Psychology, 108,* 446–452.

Kirsch, I. (1990). *Changing expectations: A key to effective psychotherapy.* Pacific Grove, CA: Brooks/Cole.

Kirsch, I. (1991). The social learning theory of hypnosis. In S. J. Lynn & J. Rhue (eds.), *Theories of hypnosis: Current models and perspectives* (pp. 439–466). New York: Guilford Press.

Kirsch, I. (1994). Clinical hypnosis as a nondeceptive placebo: Empirically derived techniques. *American Journal of Clinical Hypnosis, 37,* 95–106.

Kirsch, I. (1999). *How expectancies shape experience.* Washington, DC: American Psychological Association.

Kirsch, I. (2003). Hidden administration as ethical alternatives to the balanced placebo design. *Prevention & Treatment, 6,* Article 5. Available from http://journals.apa.org/prevention/volume6/pre0060005c.html.

Kirsch, I. (2010). *The emperor's new drugs.* New York: Basic Books.

Kirsch, I., & Council, J. R. (1992). Situational and personality correlates of suggestibility. In E. Fromm & M. Nash (eds.), *Contemporary hypnosis research* (pp. 267–292). New York: Guilford.

Kirsch, I., Deacon, B. J., Huedoo-Medina, T.B., Scoboria, A. Moore, T. J., & Johnson, B. T. (2008). Meta-analysis of data submitted to the food and drug administration. PloS Medicine (5) (2); e45.doi: 10.1371/journal.pmed.0050045.

Kirsch, I., & Lynn, S. J. (1995). The altered state of hypnosis: Changes in the theoretical landscape. *American Psychologist, 50,* 846–858.

Kirsch, I., & Lynn, S. J. (1998). Dissociation theories of hypnosis. *Psychological Bulletin, 123,* 100–115.

Kirsch, I., & Lynn, S. J. (1999). Automaticity in clinical psychology. *American Psychologist, 54,* 504–515.

Kirsch, I., Lynn, S. J., Vigorito, M., & Miller, R. R. (2004). The role of cognition in classical and operant conditioning. *Journal of Clinical Psychology, 60,* 369–392.

Kirsch, I., Montgomery, G., & Sapirstein, G. (1995). Hypnosis as an adjunct to cognitive behavioral psychotherapy: A meta-analysis. *Journal of Consulting and Clinical Psychology, 63,* 214–220.

Kirsch, I., & Sapirstein, G. (1998). Listening to Prozac but hearing placebo: A meta-analysis of antidepressant medication. *Prevention & Treatment, 1,* art. 0002a. Retrieved February 15, 2003, from journals.apa.org/prevention/volume1/pre0010002a.html.

Kirschner, P. A., Sweller, J., & Clark, R. E. (2006). Why minimal guidance during instruction does not work: An analysis of the failure of constructivist, discovery, problem-based, experiential, and inquiry-based teaching. *Educational Psychologist, 41,* 75–86.

Kish, S. J. (2002). How strong is the evidence that brain serotonin neurons are damaged in human users of ecstasy? *Pharmacology, Biochemistry, and Behavior, 71,* 845–855.

Kistner, J. A., David-Ferdon, C. F., Repper, K. K., & Joiner, T. E., Jr. (2006). Bias and accuracy of children's perceptions of peer acceptance: Prospective associations with depressive symptoms. *Journal of Abnormal Child Psychology, 34,* 349–361.

Kitamura T., et al. (2009). Adult neurogenesis modulates the hippocampus-dependent period of associative fear memory. *Cell, 139,* 814–827.

Kitcher, P. (1985). *Vaulting ambition: Sociobiology and the quest for human nature.* Cambridge, MA: MIT Press.

Kitcher, P. (2009, October 25). The fact of evolution. *New York Times Book Review,* 6.

Klahr, D., & MacWhinney, B. (1998). Information processing. In W. Damon (ed.), *Handbook of child psychology: Vol. 2: Cognition, perception, and language* (pp. 631–678). Hoboken, NJ: Wiley.

Klahr, D., & Nigam, M. (2004). The equivalence of learning paths in early science instruction: Effects of direct instruction and discovery learning. *Psychological Science, 15*, 661–667.

Klaus, M. H., & Kennell, J. H. (1976). *Maternal–infant bonding.* St. Louis, MO: Mosby.

Klein, D. F. (1998). Listening to meta-analysis but hearing bias. *Prevention & Treatment, 1*, art. 0006c. Retrieved May 12, 2006, from journals.apa.org/prevention/volume1/pre0010006c.html.

Klein, M. H., Kolden, G. G., Michels, J., & Chisholm-Stockard, S. (2002). Effective elements of the therapy relationship: Congruence/genuineness. In J. C. Norcross (ed.), *Psychotherapy relationships that work: Therapists' relational contributions to effective psychotherapy* (pp. 195–215). London: Oxford University Press.

Klein, S., Burke, L. E., Bray, G. A., Blair, S., Allison, D. B., Pi-Sunyer, X., et al. (2004). AHA scientific statement: Clinical implications of obesity with specific focus on cardiovascular disease. *Circulation, 1110*, 2952–2967.

Kleinfield, N. R., & Goode, E. (2002, October 28th). Retracing a trail: The sniper suspects. New York Times. http://www.nytimes.com/2002/10/28/us/retracing-trail-sniper-suspects-serial-killing-s-squarest-pegs-not-solo-white.html?page-wanted=1.

Kleinknecht, R. A., Dinnel, D. L., Tanouye-Wilson, S., & Lonner, W. J. (1994). Cultural variation in social anxiety and phobia: A study of Taijin Kyofusho. *The Behavior Therapist, 17*, 175–178.

Kleinman, A. (1988). *Rethinking psychiatry: From cultural category to personal experience.* New York: Free Press.

Klerman, G. L. (1986). The National Institute of Mental Health - Epidemiologic Catchment Area (NIMH-ECA) Program - Background, preliminary findings and implications. *Social Psychiatry, 21*, 159–166.

Klerman, G. L., Lavori, P.W., Rice, J. Reich, T., Endicot, J., Andreasen, N., et al. (1985). Birth-cohort trends in rates of major depressive disorder among relatives of patients with affective disorder. *Archives of General Psychiatry, 42*, 689–693.

Klerman, G. L., & Weissman, M. M. (Eds.). (1993). *New applications of interpersonal psychotherapy.* Washington, DC: American Psychiatric Press.

Klerman, G. L., Weissman, M. M., Rounsaville, B. J., & Chevron, E. S. (1984). *Interpersonal psychotherapy of depression.* New York: Basic Books.

Klimoski, R. (1992). Graphology in personnel selection. In B. L. Beyerstein & D. F. Beyerstein (Eds.), *The write stuff: Evaluations of graphology—The study of handwriting analysis* (pp. 232–268). Buffalo, NY: Prometheus Books.

Klinger, E. (1999) Thought flow: Properties and mechanisms underlying shifts in content. In Singer, J. A., & Salovey, P. (Eds) *At play in the fields of consciousness: Essays in honor of Jerome L. Singer* (pp. 29–50). Mahwah, NJ: Lawrence Erlbaum Associates Publishers.

Klinger (2000). Daydreams. In A.E. Kazdin (Ed.), *Encyclopedia of psychology.* New York: Oxford University Press/American Psychological Association.

Klinger, E., & Cox, W. M. (1987-1988) Dimensions of thought flow in everyday life. *Imagination, Cognition and Personality*, 7, 105–128.

Kluft, R. P. (1984). Multiple personality in childhood. *Psychiatric Clinics of North America, 7*, 121–134.

Kluger, A. N., & Tikochinsky, J. (2001). The error of accepting the "theoretical" null hypothesis: The rise, fall and resurrection of common sense hypotheses in psychology. *Psychological Bulletin, 127*, 408–423.

Klusmann, D. (2002). Sexual motivation and the duration of partnership. *Archives of Sexual Behavior, 31*, 275–287.

Knapp, T. J. (1976). Premack principle in human experimental and applied settings. *Behaviour Research and Therapy, 14*, 133–147.

Knecht, S., Ellger, T., & Levine, J. A. (2007). Obesity in neurobiology. *Progress in Neurobiology, 84*, 85–103.

Knight, J. R., Wechsler, H., Kuo, M., Seibring, M., Weitzman, E. R., & Schuckit, M. (2002). Alcohol abuse and dependence among U.S. college students. *Journal of Studies on Alcohol, 63*, 263–270.

Knox, D., Zusman, M., & Nieves, W. (1997). College students' homogamous preferences for a date and mate. *College Student Journal, 31*, 445–448.

Knox, J. J., Coppieters, M. W., & Hodges, P. W. (2006). Do you know where your arm is if you think your head has moved? *Experimental Brain Research, 173*, 94–101.

Knutson, B., Wolkowitz, O. M., Cole, S. W., Chan, T., Moore, E. A., Johnson, R. C., et al. (1988). Selective alteration of personality and social behavior by serotonergic intervention. *American Journal of Psychiatry, 155*, 373–379.

Knyazeva, M. G., Jalili, M. Meuli, R. Hasler, M. DeFeo, Ol, & Do, K. Q. (2008) Alpha rhythm and hypofrontality in schizophrenia. *Acta Psychiatrica Scandinavica, 118*, 188–199.

Kobasa, S. C., Hilker, R. R., & Maddi, S. R. (1979). Who stays healthy under stress? *Journal of Occupational Medicine, 21*, 595–598.

Koch, C. (1993). Computational approaches to cognition: The bottom-up view. *Current Opinion in Neurobiology, 3*, 203–208.

Kochanek, K. D., Murphy, S. L., Anderson, R. N., & Scott, C. (2004). Deaths: Final data for 2002. *National Vital Statistics Report, 53*, 1–116.

Kochanska, G., Gross, J. N., Lin, M.-H., & Nichols, K. E. (2002). Guilt in young children: Development, determinants, and relations with a broader system of standards. *Child Development, 73*, 461–482.

Kocsis, R. N., Hayes, A. F., & Irwin, H. J. (2002). Investigative experience and accuracy in psychological profiling of a violent crime. *Journal of Interpersonal Violence, 17*, 811–823.

Koenig, H. G., McCullough, M. E., & Larson, D. B. (2001). *Handbook of religion and health.* New York: Oxford University Press.

Koerner, B. I. (2002, November 1). Lie detector roulette. *Mother Jones.* Retrieved from http://www.newamerica.net/publications/articles/2002/lie_detector_roulette.

Kohlberg, L. (1965, March 26). *Relationships between the development of moral judgment and moral conduct.* Paper presented at the Annual Meeting of the Society for Research in Child Development, Minneapolis, MN.

Kohlberg, L. (1976). Moral stages and moralization: The cognitive-developmental approach. In T. Lickona (Ed.), *Moral development and behavior: Theory, research and social issues* (pp. 31–53). New York: Holt, Rinehart and Winston.

Kohlberg, L. (1981). *The philosophy of moral development: Moral stages and the idea of justice.* San Francisco: Harper & Row.

Kohlberg, L., & Turiel, E. (1971). Moral development and moral education. In G. Lesser (Ed.), *Psychology and educational practice.* Chicago: Scott Foresman.

Köhler, W. (1925) An aspect of Gestalt psychology. *Pediatric Seminars, 32*, 691–723.

Köhler, W. (1929) *Gestalt psychology.* New York: Liveright.

Kohn, A. (1993). *Punished by rewards: The trouble with gold stars, incentive plans, As, praise and other bribes.* Boston: Houghton Mifflin.

Koivisto, M., & Revonsuo, A. (2007). How meaning shapes seeing. *Psychological Science, 18*, 845–849.

Köksal, F., Domjan, M., Kurt, A., Sertel, O., Orüng, S., Bowers, R., & Kumru, G. (2004). An animal model of fetishism. *Behaviour Research and Therapy, 42*, 1421–1434.

Kollins, S. H. (2003). Delay discounting is associated with substance use in college students. *Addictive Behaviors, 28*, 1167–1173.

Kollman, D. M., Brown, T. A., Liverant, G. I., & Hofmann, S. G. (2006). A taxometric investigation of the latent structure of social anxiety disorder in outpatients with anxiety and mood disorders. *Depression and Anxiety, 23*, 190–199.

Konner, M. (1990). *Why the reckless survive—And other secrets of human nature.* New York: Viking.

Konner, M. (2003). *The tangled wing: Biological constraints on the human spirit.* New York: Henry Holt.

Koob, A. (2009). *The root of thought: Unlocking glia—the brain cell that will help us sharpen our wits, heal injury, and treat brain disease.* New York: FT Press.

Koob, G. F. (2000) Animal models of craving for ethanol. *Addiction, 95*, S73–S81.

Koran, L. M., Faber, R. J., Aboujaoude, E., Large, M. D., & Serpe, R. T. (2006). Estimated prevalence of compulsive buying behavior in the United States. *American Journal of Psychiatry, 163*, 1806–1812.

Koriat, A., & Bjork, R. A. (2005). Illusions of competence in monitoring one's knowledge during study. *Journal of Experimental Psychology: Learning, Memory, and Cognition, 31*, 187–194.

Kosfeld, M., Heinrichs, M., Zaks, P., Fischbacher, U., & Fehr, E. (2005). Oxytocin increases trust in humans. *Nature, 435*, 673–676.

Kounios, J., Frymiare, J. L., Bowden, E. M., Fleck, J. I., Subramaniam, K., Parrish, T. B., et al. (2006). The prepared mind: Neural activity prior to problem presentation predicts subsequent solution by sudden insight. *Psychological Science, 17*, 882–890.

Kozorovitskiy, Y., & Gould, E. (2003). Adult neurogenesis: A mechanism for brain repair? *Journal of Clinical & Experimental Neuropsychology, 25,* 721–732.

Krackow, E., Lynn, S. J., & Payne, D. (2005–2006). Death of Princess Diana: The effects of memory enhancement procedures on flashbulb memories. *Imagination, Cognition, and Personality, 25,* 197–220.

Kramer, P. (1993). *Listening to Prozac.* New York: Penguin Books.

Kramer, P. (2007). *Freud: Inventor of the modern mind.* New York: HarperCollins.

Kramer, G. M., Wolbransky, M., Heilbrun, K. (2007) Plea bargaining recommendations by criminal defense attorneys: Evidence strength, potential sentence, and defendant preference. *Behavioral Sciences & the Law, 25,* 573–585.

Kratzig, G. P., & Arbuthnott, K. D. (2006). Perceptual learning style and learning proficiency: A test of the hypothesis. *Journal of Educational Psychology, 98,* 238–246.

Kraus, S. J. (1995). Attitudes and the prediction of behaviour: A meta-analysis of the empirical literature. *Personality and Social Psychology Bulletin, 21,* 58–75.

Kraut, R. E., & Poe, D. (1980). Behavioral roots of person perception: The deception judgments of customs inspectors and laymen. *Journal of Personality and Social Psychology, 39,* 784–798.

Krebs, D. L., & Denton, K. (2005). Toward a more pragmatic approach to morality: A critical evaluation of Kohlberg's model. *Psychological Review, 112,* 629–649.

Krebs, V. (2008). *Political Polarization During the 2008 US Presidential Campaign.* Retrieved May 2, 2010, from http://www.orgnet.com/divided.html.

Kristensen, P., & Bjerkedal, T. (2007). Explaining the relation between birth order and intelligence. *Science, 316,* 1717.

Kreppner, J. M., O'Connor, T. G., & Rutter, M. (2001). Can inattention/overactivity be an institutional deprivation syndrome? *Journal of Abnormal Child Psychology, 29,* 513–528.

Krubitzer, L., & Kaas, J. (2005). The evolution of the neocortex in mammals: How is phenotypic diversity generated? *Current Opinion in Neurobiology, 15,* 444–453.

Krueger, J. I., & Funder, D. C. (2004). Towards a balanced social psychology: Causes, consequences and cures for the problem-seeking approach to social behavior and cognition. *Behavioral and Brain Sciences 27,* 313–327.

Krueger, R., & Piasecki, T., M. (2002). Toward a dimensional and psychometrically-informed approach to conceptualizing psychopathology. *Behaviour Research and Therapy, 40,* 485–499.

Krueger, R. F. (2000). Phenotypic, genetic, and nonshared environmental parallels in the structure of personality: A view from the Multidimensional Personality Questionnaire. *Journal of Personality and Social Psychology, 79,* 1057–1067.

Krueger, R. F., Hicks, B. M., & McGue, M. (2001). Altruism and antisocial behavior: Independent tendencies, unique personality correlates, distinct etiologies. *Psychological Science, 12,* 397–402.

Krueger, R. F., Schmutte, P. S., Caspi, A., Moffitt, T. E., Campbell, K., & Silva P. A. (1994). Personality traits are linked to crime among men and women: Evidence from a birth cohort. *Journal of Abnormal Psychology, 103,* 328–338.

Krueger, R. F., Skodol, A. E., Livesley, W. J., Shrout, P. E., & Huang, Y. (2007). Synthesizing dimensional and categorical approaches to personality disorders: Refining the research agenda for DSM-V Axis II. *International Journal of Methods in Psychiatric Research, 16*(S1), S65–S73.

Kruger, J., & Dunning, D. (1999). Unskilled and unaware of it: How difficulties in recognizing one's own incompetence lead to inflated self-assessments. *Journal of Personality and Social Psychology, 77,* 1121–1134.

Kruger, J., Epley, N., Parker, J., & Ng, Z. (2005). Egocentrism over email: Can we communicate as well as we think? *Journal of Personality and Social Psychology, 89,* 925–936.

Kruger, J., Savitsky, K., & Gilovich, T. (1999). Superstition and the regression effect. *Skeptical Inquirer, 23,* 24–29.

Kruger, S., Seminowicz, D., Goldapple, K., Kennedy, S. H., & Mayberg, H. S. (2003). State and trait influences on mood regulation in bipolar disorder: Blood flow differences with an acute mood challenge. *Biological Psychiatry, 54,* 1274–1283.

Kruglanski, A. W., & Mayseless, O. (1990). Classic and current social comparison research: Expanding the perspective. *Psychological Bulletin, 108,* 195–208.

Kuhn, D. (2007). Jumping to conclusions. *Scientific American Mind, 18*(1), 44–51.

Kuhn, D., & Dean, D. (2005). Is developing scientific thinking all about learning to control variables? *Psychological Science, 16,* 866–870.

Kuhn, D., Garcia-Mila, M., Zohar, A., & Andersen, C. (1995). Strategies of knowledge acquisition. *Monographs of the Society for Research in Child Development, 60,* Serial No. 4.

Kuleshnyk, I. (1984). The Stockholm syndrome: Toward an understanding. *Social Action & the Law, 10,* 37–42.

Kulik, J. A., Bangert-Drowns, R. L., & Kulik, C.-L. C. (1984). Effectiveness of coaching for aptitude tests. *Psychological Bulletin, 95,* 179–188.

Kuller, L. H., Ives, D. G., Fitzpatrick, A. L., Carlson, M. C., Mercado, C., Lopez, O. L., et al. (2010). Does gingo biloba reduce the risk of cardiovascular events? *Circulation: Cardiovascular Quality and Outcomes, 3,* 41–71.

Kumar, R. (2008) Approved and investigational uses of modafinil : An evidence-based review. *Drugs. 68,* 1803–1839.

Kumari, V. (2006). Do psychotherapies produce neurobiological effects? *Acta Neuropsychiatrica, 18,* 61–70.

Kuncel, N. R., & Hezlett, S. A. (2007). Standardized tests predict graduate students' success. *Science, 315,* 1080–1081.

Kunda, Z. (1999). *Social cognition: Making sense of people.* Cambridge, MA: The MIT Press.

Kung, H. C., Hoyert, D. L., Xu, J., & Murphy, S. L. (2008). Deaths: Final data for 2005. *National Vital Statistics Reports, 56,* 1–120.

Kunst-Wilson, W. R., & Zajonc, R. B. (1980). Affective discrimination of stimuli that cannot be recognized. *Science, 207,* 557–558.

Kuntz, D.., & Bachrach, S. (2006). *Deadly medicine: Creating the master race.* Washington, D.C: United States Holocaust Memorial Museum.

Kunzendorf, R. G., Treantafel, N., Taing, B., Flete, A., Savoie, S., Agersea, S., et al. (2006-2007). The sense of self in lucid dreams: "Self as subject" vs. "self as agent" vs. "self as object." *Imagination, Cognition, and Personality, 26,* 303–323.

Kunzendorf, R. G., Watson, G., Monroe, L., Tassone, S., Papoutsakis, E., McArdle, E., et al. (2007-2008). The archaic belief in dream visitations as it relates to "seeing ghosts," meeting the lord," as well as "encountering extraterrestrials." *Imagination, Cognition, and Personality, 27,* 71–85.

Kuperberg, G. R., Sitnikova, T., Goff, D., & Holcomb, P. J. (2006). Making sense of sentences in schizophrenia: Electrophysiological evidence for abnormal interactions between semantic and syntactic processing. *Journal of Abnormal Psychology, 115,* 251–265.

Kurlan, R., & Kaplan, E. L. (2004). The pediatric autoimmune neuropsychiatric disorders associated with streptococcal infection (PANDAS) etiology for tics and obsessive-compulsive symptoms: hypothesis or entity. Practical considerations for the clinician. *Pediatrics, 112,* 884–886.

Kurth, T., Gaziano, J. M., Berger, K., Kase, C. S., Rexrode, K. M., Cook, N. R., et al. (2003). Body mass index and the risk of stroke in men. *Archives of Internal Medicine, 163,* 2557–2662.

Kurtus, R. (2000). I walked on fire and lived to tell about it. Retrieved May 24, 2007, from www.school-for-champions.com/excellence/firewalk.htm.

Kurzban, R., & Weeden, J. (2005). HurryDate: Mate preferences in action. *Evolution and Human Behavior, 26,* 227–244.

Kushner, M. (1968). The operant control of intractable sneezing. In C. D. Spielberger, R. Fox, & B. Masterson (Eds.), *Contributions to general psychology*: Selected readings for introductory psychology. New York: Roland Press.

Kushner, H. I. (1993). Taking Erikson's identity seriously: Psychoanalyzing the psychohistorian. *Psychohistory Review, 22,* 7–34.

LaBerge, D., & Samuels, S. J. (1974). Towards a theory of automatic information processing in reading. *Cognitive Psychology, 6,* 293–323.

LaBerge, S. (1980). *Lucid dreaming: An exploratory study of consciousness during sleep.* Unpublished doctoral dissertation, Stanford University, Stanford, CA.

LaBerge, S. (2000). Lucid dreaming: Evidence and methodology. *Behavioral and Brain Sciences, 23,* 962–963.

LaBerge, S., Nagel, L., Dement, W., & Zarcone, V. (1981). Lucid dreaming verified by volitional communication during REM sleep. *Perceptual and Motor Skills, 52,* 727–732.

Labov, W. (1970). The logic of non-standard English. In F. Williams (ed.), *Language and Poverty,* 153–189. Chicago: Markham.

Lacasse, J. R., & Leo, J. (2005). Serotonin and depression: A disconnect between the advertisements and the scientific literature. *PLOS Medicine, 2,* 101–106.

LaFreniere, P. J., & Sroufe, L. A. (1985). Profiles of peer competence in the pre-school: Interrelations among measures, influence of social ecology, and relation to attachment history. *Developmental Psychology, 21,* 56–69.

LaFreniere, P. L., Strayer, F. F., & Gauthier, R. (1984). The emergence of same-sex affiliative preference among preschool peers: A developmental/etho-logical perspective. *Child Development, 55,* 1958–1965.

Lalich, J. (2004). *Bounded choice: True believers and charismatic cults.* Berkeley: University of California Press.

Lalumière, M. L., Blanchard, R., & Zucker, K. L. (2000). Sexual orientation and handedness in men and women: A meta-analysis. *Psychological Bulletin, 126,* 575–592.

Lamb, H. R., & Bachrach, L. L. (2001). Some perspectives on deinstitutionaliza-tion. *Psychiatric Services, 52,* 1039–1045.

Lamb, M. & Tamis-LeMonda, C. (2003). The role of the father. In Lamb, M. (ed.), *The Role of the father in child development, 4th Edition* (pp. 1–31). Hoboken, NJ: John Wiley & Sons, Inc.

Lamb, M. E., Thompson, R. A., Gardner, W. P., Charnov, E. L., & Estes, D. (1984). Security of infantile attachment as assessed in the "strange situa-tion": Its study and biological interpretation. *Behavioral and Brain Sciences, 7,* 127–171.

Lamb, T. D. & Pugh, E. N., Jr (2004). Dark adaptation and the retinoid cycle of vision. *Progress in Retinal and Eye Research, 23,* 307–380.

Lambert, K. G. (2003). The life and career of Paul MacLean: A journey toward social and neurobiological harmony. *Physiology & Behavior, 79,* 373–381.

Lambert, M. J. (2003). *Bergin and Garfield's handbook of psychotherapy and behavior change.* New York: John Wiley.

Lambert, M. J., & Ogles, B. M. (2004). The efficacy and effectiveness of psy-chotherapy. In M. J. Lambert (ed.), *Bergin and Garfield's handbook of psy-chotherapy and behavior change* (5th ed., pp. 139–193). New York: Wiley.

Lampl, M., Veldhuis, J. D., & Johnson, M. L. (1992). Saltation and stasis—A model of human growth. *Science, 258,* 801–803.

Landers, D. M. (1998). Exercise and mental health. *Exercise Science, 7,* 131–146.

Landman, J. T., & Dawes, R. M. (1982). Psychotherapy outcome: Smith and Glass conclusions stand up under scrutiny. *American Psychologist, 37,* 504–516.

Lang, A. R., Goeckner, D. J., Adesso, V. J., & Marlatt, G. A. (1975). Effects of alcohol on aggression in male social drinkers. *Journal of Abnormal Psychology, 84,* 509–518.

Lange, C. G. (1885). *Om sindsbevaegelser: et psyko-fysiologisk studie.* Kjbenhavn: Jacob Lunds. Reprinted in C. G. Lange and W. James (eds.), *The emotions.* I. A. Haupt (trans.). Baltimore: Williams & Wilkins.

Langer, E. J., & Rodin, J. (1976). The effects of choice and enhanced personal responsibility for the aged: A field experiment in an institutional setting. *Journal of Personality and Social Psychology, 34,* 191–198.

Langlois, J. H., & Downs, A. C. (1980). Mothers, fathers, and peers as socializa-tion agents of sex-typed play behaviors in young children. *Child Development, 51,* 1237–1247.

Langlois, J. H., Kalakanis, L., Rubenstein, A. J., Larson, A., Hallam, M., & Smoot, M. (2000). Maxims or myths of beauty? A meta-analytic and theo-retical review. *Psychological Bulletin, 126,* 390–423.

Langlois, J. H., & Roggman, L. A. (1990). Attractive faces are only average. *Psychological Science, 1,* 115–121.

Lanning, K. V. (1989). *Child sex rings: A behavioral analysis.* Washington, DC: National Center for Missing and Exploited Children.

Lansford, J. E., Chang, L., Dodge, K. A., Malone, P. S., Oburu, P., Palmerus, K., et al. (2005). Physical discipline and children's adjustment: Cultural nor-mativeness as a moderator. *Child Development, 76,* 1234–1246.

Lansford, J. E., Deater-Deckard, K., Dodge, K. A., Bates, J. E., & Pettit, G. S. (2004). Ethnic differences in the link between physical discipline and later adolescent externalizing behaviors. *Journal of Child Psychology and Psychiatry, 45,* 801–812.

LaPiere, R. T. (1934). Attitudes vs. action. *Social Forces, 13,* 230–237.

Larimer, M. E., Palmer, R. S., & Marlatt, G. A. (1999). Relapse prevention: An overview of Marlatt's cognitive-behavioural model. *Alcohol Research and Health, 23,* 151–160.

Larsen, K. S., Ashlock, J., Carroll, C., Foote, S., Keller, J., Seese, G., et al. (1974). Laboratory aggression where the victim is a small dog. *Social Behavior and Personality, 2,* 174–176.

Larson, R., & Richards, M. (1994). *Divergent realities: The emotional lives of mothers, fathers, and adolescents.* New York: Basic Books.

Larsson, L. G., Grimby, G., & Karlsson, J. (1979). Muscle strength and speed of movement in relation to age and muscle morphology. *Journal of Applied Physiology, 46,* 451–456.

Lashley, K. S. (1929). *Brain mechanisms and intelligence.* Chicago: University of Chicago Press.

Lasky, R. E., Suradal-Lasky, A., & Klein, R. E. (1975). VOT discrimination by four to six and a half month old infants from Spanish environments. *Journal of Experimental Child Psychology, 20,* 215–225.

Latané, B., & Darley, J. M. (1970). *The unresponsive bystander: Why doesn't he help?* New York: Appleton-Century-Crofts.

Latané, B., & Nida, S. (1981). Ten years of research on group size and helping. *Psychological Bulletin, 89,* 308–324.

Latané, B., & Rodin, J. (1969). A lady in distress: Inhibiting effects of friends and strangers on bystander intervention. *Journal of Experimental Social Psychology, 5,* 189–302.

Latané, B., Williams, K., & Harkins, S. (1979). Many hands make light the work: The causes and consequences of social loafing. *Journal of Personality and Social Psychology, 37,* 822–832.

Laumann, E. O., Gagnon, J. H., Michael, R. T., & Michaels, S. (1994). *The social organization of sexuality: Sexual practices in the United States.* Chicago: University of Chicago Press.

Laurin, D., Verreault, R., Lindsay, J., MacPherson, K., & Rockwood, K. (2001). Physical activity and risk of cognitive impairment and dementia in elderly persons. *Archives of Neurology, 58,* 498–504.

Laursen, B., Coy, K. C., & Collins, W. (1998). Reconsidering changes in parent-child conflict across adolescence: A meta-analysis. *Child Development, 69,* 817–832.

Lauterbur, P. (1973). Image formation by induced local interaction; examples employing magnetic resonance. *Nature, 242,* 192.

Lawson, K. A., Wright, M. E., Subar, A., Mouw, T., Schatzkin, A., & Leitzmann, M. F. (2007). Multivitamin use and risk of prostate cancer in the National Institutes of Health–AARP Diet and Health Study. *Journal of the National Cancer Institute, 99,* 754–764.

Lazarus, A. A. (2006). *Brief but comprehensive psychotherapy: The multimodal way.* New York: Springer Publishing.

Lazarus, R. S. (1999). *Stress and emotion: A new synthesis.* New York: Springer Publishing.

Lazarus, R. S. (2003). Does the positive psychology movement have legs? *Psychological Inquiry, 14,* 93–109.

Lazarus, R. S. (1984). On the primacy of cognition. *American Psychologist, 39,* 124–129.

Lazarus, R. S., & Folkman, S. (1984). *Stress, appraisal, and coping.* New York: Springer.

Le Bon, G. (1895). *Psychology of the crowd.* New York: Viking Press.

Leavy, J. (1992). Spooky presidential coincidences contest. *Skeptical Inquirer, 16,* 316–320.

LeBar K.S. & Phelps E.A. (1998) Arousal mediated memory consolidation: Role of the medial temporal lobe in humans. *Psychological Science, 9,* 490–493.

Lebow, J. L. (2010). The effective treatment of personality disorders: Easily within our grasp. *Professional Psychology: Research and Practice, 41,* 73–74.

LeDoux, J. (1996). *The emotional brain: The mysterious underpinnings of emo-tional life.* New York: Simon & Schuster.

LeDoux, J. E. (2000). Emotion circuits in the brain. *Annual Review of Neuroscience, 23,* 155–184.

Lee, K., & Ashton, M. C. (2004). Psychometric properties of the HEXACO per-sonality inventory. *Multivariate Behavioral Research, 39,* 329–358.

Lee, M. S., Pittler, M. H., & Ernst, E. (2008). Effects of reiki in clinical practice: A systematic review of randomised clinical trials. *The International Journal of Clinical Practice, 62,* 947–954.

Lee, Y. S. (2009). The role of genes in the obesity epidemic. *Annals of the Academy of Medicine Singapore, 38,* 45–47.

Lee, Y. S., & Silva, A. J. (2009). The molecular and cellular biology of enhanced cognition. *Nature Reviews Neuroscience, 10,* 126–140.

Leek, F. F. (1969). The problem of brain removal during embalming by the ancient Egyptians. *Journal of Egyptian Archeology, SS,* 112–116.

Leeper, P. (1988). Having a place to live is vital to good health. *News Report, 38,* 5–8.

LeFever, G. B., Arcona, A. P., & Antonuccio, D. O. (2003). ADHD among American schoolchildren: Evidence of overdiagnosis and overuse of med-ication. *Scientific Review of Mental Health Practice, 2,* 49–60.

Legerstee, M. (1991). The role of person and object in eliciting early imitation. *Journal of Experimental Child Psychology, 51,* 423–433.

Leggio, M. G., Mandolesi, L., Federico, F., Spirito, F., Ricci, B., Gelfo, F., et al. (2005). Environmental enrichment promotes improved spatial abilities and enhanced dendritic growth in the rat. *Behavioral Brain Research, 163,* 78–90.

Lehman, D. R., Chiu, C. Y., & Schaller, M. (2004). Psychology and culture. *Annual Review of Psychology, 55,* 689–714.

Lehrer, J. (2009). *How we decide.* Boston: Houghton-Mifflin.

Leichsenring, F., Rabung, S., & Leibing, E. (2004). The efficacy of short-term psychodynamic psychotherapy in specific psychiatric disorders. *Archives of General Psychiatry, 61,* 1208–1216.

Leichtman, M., & Ceci, S. (1995). The effects of stereotypes and suggestions on preschoolers' reports. *Developmental Psychology, 31,* 568–578.

Leigh, B. C., & Stacy, A. (2004). Alcohol expectancies and drinking in different age groups. *Addiction, 99,* 215–227.

Leitenberg, H., & Henning, K. (1995). Sexual fantasy. *Psychological Bulletin, 117,* 469–496.

Lejoyeux, M., & Ades, J. (1997). Antidepressant discontinuation: A review of the literature. *Journal of Clinical Psychiatry, 58*(Suppl. 7), 11–15.

Leman, K. (1998). *The new birth order book: Why you are the way you are.* Grand Rapids, MI: Baker Book House.

Lenggenhager, B., Tadi, T., Metzinger, T., & Blanke, O. (2007). Video ergo sum: Manipulating bodily self-consciousness. *Science, 317,* 1096–1099.

Lenneberg, E. (1967). *Biological foundations of language.* New York: Wiley.

Lenzenweger, M. F., McLachlan, G., & Rubin, D. B. (2007). Resolving the latent structure of schizophrenia endophenotypes using expectation-maximization–based finite mixture modeling. *Journal of Abnormal Psychology, 116,* 16–29.

Leonard, B. E. (1997). The role of noradrenaline in depression: A review. *Journal of Psychopharmacology, 11,* S39–S47.

Lepper, M. R., Greene, D., & Nisbett, R. E. (1973). Undermining children's intrinsic interest with extrinsic rewards: A test of the "overjustification" hypothesis. *Journal of Personality and Social Psychology, 28,* 129–137.

Lerner, M. J. (1980). *The belief in a just world: A fundamental delusion.* New York: Plenum Press.

Lesch, K. P., Bengal, D., Heils, A., Sabol, S., Greenberg, B. D., Petri, S. et al. (1996). Association of anxiety related traits with a polymorphism in the serotonin transporter gene regulatory region. *Science, 274,* 1527–1531.

Leslie, M. (2000). The vexing legacy of Lewis Terman. Retrieved from www. stanfordalumni.org/news/magazine/2000/julaug/articles/terman.html.

Lester, D., Kaminsky, S., & McGovern, M. (1993). Sheldon's theory of personality in young children. *Perceptual and Motor Skills, 77,* 1330.

Lester, D., Yang, B., & Lindsay, M. (2004). Suicide bombers: Are psychological profiles possible? *Studies in Conflict & Terrorism, 27,* 283–295.

Lett, J. (1990, Winter). A field guide to critical thinking. *Skeptical Inquirer, 14,* 153–160.

Levant, R. F. (2004). The empirically validated treatments movement: A practitioner/educator perspective. *Clinical Psychology: Science and Practice, 11,* 219–224.

Levenberg, S. B. (1975). Professional training, psychodiagnostic skill, and kinetic family drawings. *Journal of Personality Assessment, 39,* 389–393.

Levenson, R. (2005, April). Desperately seeking Phil. *APS Observer.* Retrieved from http://www.psychologicalscience.org/observer/getArticle.cfm?id=1749.

Levenstein, S., Ackerman, S., Kiecolt-Glaser, J. K., & Dubois, A. (1999). Stress and peptic ulcer disease. *Journal of the American Medical Association, 281,* 10–11.

Leventhal, H., & Cleary, P. D. (1980) The smoking problem: A review of the research and theory in behavioral risk modification. *Psychological Bulletin, 88,* 370–405.

Leventhal, H., Weinman, J., Leventhal, E. A., & Phillips, L. A. (2006). Health psychology: The search for pathways between behavior and health. *Annual Review of Psychology, 59,* 477–505.

Lever, J. (1995, August 22). The 1995 Advocate survey of sexuality and relationship: The women. *Advocate,* 212–230.

Levin, B. E., Dunn-Meynell, A. A., & Routh, V. H. (1999). Regulatory, integrative, and comparative physiology. *American Journal of Physiology, 276,* 1223–1231.

Levin, D. T., & Simons, D. J. (1997). Failure to detect changes to attended objects in motion pictures. *Psychonomic Bulletin and Review, 4,* 501–506.

Levin, J. (2001). *God, faith, and health: Exploring the spirituality-healing connection.* New York: John Wiley & Sons.

Levine, B. (1979). *Group psychotherapy: Practice and development.* Englewood Cliffs, NJ: Prentice-Hall.

Levine, D. S. (1998). *Explorations in common sense and common nonsense.* http://www.uta.edu/psychology/faculty/levine/EBOOK/index.htm.

Levine, D. W. (2005). Do dogs resemble their owners? A reanalysis of Roy and Christenfeld. *Psychological science, 16,* 83–84.

Levis, D. J. (1995). Decoding traumatic memory: Implosive theory of psychopathology. In W. O. Donohue & L. Kranser (eds.), *Theories in behavior therapy* (pp. 173–207). Washington, DC: American Psychological Association.

Levitan, L., & LaBerge, S. (1990). Beyond nightmares: Lucid resourcefulness vs. helpless depression. *NightLight, 2,* 1–6.

Levitsky, D.A., Obarzanek, E., Mrdjenovic, G., & Strupp, B. J. (2005). Imprecise control of energy intake: Absence of a reduction in food intake following overfeeding in young adults. *Physiology and Behavior, 84,* 669–675.

Levy-Reiner, S. (1996). The decade of the brain: Library and NIMH hold symposia on mental illness. *Library of Congress Information Bulletin, 55,* 326–327.

Lewin, K. (1935). *A dynamic theory of personality.* New York: McGraw-Hill.

Lewin, K. (1951). *Field theory in social science: Selected theoretical papers.* D. Cartwright (ed.), New York: Harper & Row.

Lewin, T. (2006, August 31). Students' path to small colleges can bypass SAT. *New York Times.* Retrieved October 27, 2007, from http://www.nytimes.com/2006/08/31/education/31sat.html?_r=1&n=Top/Reference/Times%20Topics/People/L/Lewin,%20Tamar&oref=slogin.

Lewinsohn, P. M. (1974). A behavioral approach to depression. In R. J. Friedman & M. M. Katz (eds.), *Psychology of depression: Contemporary theory and research* (pp. 157–158). Oxford, England: John Wiley & Sons.

Lewinsohn, P. M., Holm-Denoma, J. M., Small, J. W., Seeley, J. R., & Joiner, T. E. (2008). Separation in childhood as a risk factor for future mental illness. *Journal of the American Academy for Child and Adolescent Psychiatry, 47*(5), 548–555.

Lewinsohn, P. M., & Rosenbaum, M. (1987). Recall of parental behavior by acute depressives, remitted depressives, and nondepressives. *Journal of Personality and Social Psychology, 52,* 611–620.

Lewis, M., & Brooks-Gunn, J. (1979). *Social cognition and the acquisition of self.* New York: Plenum.

Lewis, M., Brooks-Gunn, J., & Jaskir, J. J. (1985). Individual differences in visual self-recognition as a function of mother-infant attachment relationship. *Developmental Psychobiology, 21,* 1181–1187.

Lewis, M., & Carmody, D. P. (2008). Self-representation and brain development. *Developmental Psychology, 44,* 1329–1334.

Lewis, M., Haviland-Jones, J. M., & Barrett, L. F. (2008). *Handbook of Emotions.* New York: Guilford.

Lewis, W. A., & Bucher, A. M. (1992). Anger, catharsis, the reformulated frustration-aggression hypothesis, and health consequences. *Psychotherapy, 29,* 385–392.

Lewontin, R. C. (1970). Further remarks on race and the genetics of intelligence. *Bulletin of the Atomic Scientists, 26,* 23–25.

Lezak, M. D., Howieson, D. B., & Loring, D. W. (2004). *Neuropsychological assessment* (4th ed.). New York: Oxford University Press.

Li, S. C., Jordanova, M., & Lindenberger, U. (1998). From good senses to good sense: A link between tactile information processing and intelligence. *Intelligence, 26,* 99–122.

Li, Y., Liu, J., Liu, F., Guo, G., Anme, T., & Ushijima, H. (2000). Maternal child-rearing behaviors and correlates in rural minority areas of Yunnan, China. *Journal of Developmental & Behavioral Pediatrics, 21,* 114–122.

Libet, B. (1985). Unconscious cerebral initiative and the role of conscious will in voluntary action. *Behavioral and Brain Sciences, 8,* 529–566.

Lichtenstein, S., Slovic, P., Fischhoff, B., Layman, M., & Combs, B. (1978). Judged frequency of lethal events. *Journal of Experimental Psychology: Human Learning and Memory, 4,* 551–578.

Lick, J. (1975). Expectancy, false galvanic skin response feedback, and systematic desensitization in the modification of phobic behavior. *Journal of Consulting and Clinical Psychology, 43,* 557–557.

Lidz, C. W., Mulvey, E. P., & Gardner, W. (1993). The accuracy of predictions of violence to others. *Journal of the American Medical Association, 269,* 1007–1111.

Lidz, T. (1973). *The origin and treatment of schizophrenic disorders.* New York: Basic Books.

Lie, D. C., Song, H., Colamarino, S. A., Ming, G. L., & Gage, F. H. (2004). Neurogenesis in the adult brain: New strategies for central nervous system diseases. *Annual Review of Pharmacology & Toxicology, 44,* 399–421.

Lieber, C. M. (2003). Alcohol and health: A drink a day won't keep the doctor away. *Cleveland Clinic Journal of Medicine, 70,* 945–953.

Lieberman, J., Stroup, T. S., McEvoy, J. P., Swartz, M. S., Rosenheck, R. A., Perkins, D. O., et al. (2005). Effectiveness of antipsychotic drugs in patients with chronic schizophrenia. *New England Journal of Medicine, 353,* 1209–1203.

Lieberman, J. A., & Koreen, A. R. (1993). Neurochemistry and neuroendocrinology of schizophrenia: A selective review. *Schizophrenia Bulletin, 2,* 371–428.

Lieberman, P., Crelin, E. S., & Klatt, D. H. (1972). Phonetic ability and related anatomy of the newborn and adult human, Neanderthal man, and the chimpanzee. *American Anthropologist, 74,* 287–307.

Liem, E. B., Lin, C. M., Suleman, M. I., Doufas, A. G., Gregg, R. G., Veauthier, J. M., et al. (2004). Anesthetic requirement is increased in redheads. *Anesthesiology, 101,* 279–283.

Likhtik, D. Popa, J. & Apergis-Schoute, G.A. (2008). Amygdala intercalated neurons are required for expression of fear extinction. *Nature, 45,* 642–645.

Lilienfeld, S. O. (1994). Conceptual problems in the assessment of psychopathy. *Clinical Psychology Review, 14,* 17–38.

Lilienfeld, S. O. (1995). *Seeing both sides: Classic controversies in abnormal psychology.* Pacific Grove, CA: Brooks/Cole.

Lilienfeld, S. O. (1997). The relation of anxiety sensitivity to higher and lower order personality dimensions: Implications for the etiology of panic attacks. *Journal of Abnormal Psychology, 106,* 539–544.

Lilienfeld, S. O. (1999a, March/April). ABC's *20/20* features segment on "goggle therapy" for depression and anxiety. *Skeptical Inquirer, 23,* 8–9.

Lilienfeld, S. O. (1999b). Projective measures of personality and psychopathology: How well do they work? *Skeptical Inquirer, 23,* 32–39.

Lilienfeld, S. O. (1999c, November/December). New analyses raise doubts about replicability of ESP findings. *Skeptical Inquirer, 24,* 9–10.

Lilienfeld, S. O. (2004). Defining psychology: Is it worth the trouble? *Journal of Clinical Psychology, 60,* 1249–1253.

Lilienfeld, S. O. (2007). Psychological treatments that can cause harm. *Perspectives on Psychological Science, 2,* 53–70.

Lilienfeld, S. O., Alliger, G. M., & Mitchell, K. E. (1995). Why integrity testing remains controversial. *American Psychologist, 50,* 457–458.

Lilienfeld, S. O., Ammirati, R., & Landfield, K. (2009). Giving debiasing away: Can psychological research on correcting cognitive errors improve human welfare? *Perspectives on Psychological Science, 4,* 390–398.

Lilienfeld, S. O., & Arkowitz, H. (2007). Autism: An epidemic? *Scientific American Mind, 18*(2), 82–83.

Lilienfeld, S. O., & Fowler, K. A. (2006). The self-report assessment of psychopathy: Problems, pitfalls, and promises. In C. J. Patrick (ed.), *Handbook of psychopathy* (pp. 107–132). New York: Guilford.

Lilienfeld, S. O., & Landfield, K. (2008). Issues in diagnosis: Categorical vs. dimensional. In W. E. Craighead, D. J. Miklowitz, & L.W. Craighead (eds.), *Psychopathology: History, diagnosis, and empirical foundations* (pp. 1–33). Hoboken, NJ: Wiley.

Lilienfeld, S. O., Lohr, J. M., & Olatunji, B. O. (2008). Overcoming naive realism: Encouraging students to think critically about psychotherapy. In D.S. Dunn (ed.), *Teaching critical thinking in psychology: A handbook of best practices* (pp. 267–271). Malden, MA: Blackwell Publishing.

Lilienfeld, S. O., & Lynn, S. J. (2003). Dissociative identity disorder: Multiple personalities, multiple controversies. In S. O. Lilienfeld, S. J. Lynn, & J. M. Lohr (eds.), *Science and pseudoscience in clinical psychology* (pp. 109–143). New York: Guilford Press.

Lilienfeld, S. O., Lynn, S. J., Kirsch, I., Chaves, J. F., Sarbin, T. R., Ganaway, G. K., et al. (1999). Dissociative identity disorder and the sociocognitive model: Recalling the lessons of the past. *Psychological Bulletin, 125,* 507–523.

Lilienfeld, S. O., Lynn, S. J., & Lohr, J. M. (2003). *Science and pseudoscience in clinical psychology.* New York: Guilford Press.

Lilienfeld, S. O., Lynn, S. J., Ruscio, J., & Beyerstein, B. L. (2010). *50 great myths of popular psychology: Shattering widespread misconceptions about human behavior.* Malden, MA: Wiley-Blackwell.

Lilienfeld, S. O., & Marino, L. (1995). Mental disorder as a Roschian concept: A critique of Wakefield's "harmful dysfunction" analysis. *Journal of Abnormal Psychology, 104,* 411–420.

Lilienfeld, S. O., & Waldman, I. D. (2000, November 13). Race and IQ: What the science says. *Emory Report,* 3.

Lilienfeld, S. O., & Waldman, I. D. (2004). Comorbidity and Chairman Mao. *World Psychiatry, 3,* 26–27.

Lilienfeld, S. O., Waldman, I. D., & Israel, A. C. (1994). A critical examination of the use of the term "comorbidity" in psychopathology research. *Clinical Psychology: Science and Practice, 1,* 71–83.

Lilienfeld, S. O., Wood, J. M., & Garb, H. N. (2001). The scientific status of projective techniques. *Psychological Science in the Public Interest, 1,* 27–66.

Lilienfeld, S. O., Wood, J. M., & Garb, H. N. (2007). Why questionable psychological tests remain popular. *Scientific Review of Alternative Medicine and Aberrant Medical Practices, 10,* 6–15.

Limb, C. J. (2006). Structural and functional neural correlates of music perception. *Anatomical Record, Part A, Discoveries in Molecular, Cellular, and Evolutionary Biology, 288,* 435–446.

Lindeman, M. (1998). Motivation, cognition and pseudoscience. *Scandinavian Journal of Psychology, 39,* 257–265.

Lindle, R. S., Metter, E. J., Lynch, N. A., Fleg, J. L., Fozard, J. L., Tobin, J., et al. (1997). Age and gender comparisons of muscle strength in 654 women and men aged 20–93 yr. *Journal of Applied Physiology, 83,* 1581–1587.

Lindman, R. (1982). Social and solitary drinking: Effects on consumption and mood in male social drinkers. *Physiology and Behavior, 28,* 1093–1095.

Lindsay, R. C. L., & Wells, G. L. (1985). Improving eyewitness identifications from lineups: Simultaneous versus sequential lineup presentation. *Journal of Applied Psychology, 70,* 556–564.

Linehan, M. M. (1993). *Cognitive behavioral treatment of borderline personality disorder.* New York: Guilford Press.

Link, B. G., Phelan, J. C., Bresnahan, M., Stueve, A., & Pescosolido, B. A. (1999). Public conceptions of mental illness: Labels, causes, dangerousness and social distance. *American Journal of Public Health, 89,* 1328–1333.

Linton, H. B., & Langs, R. J. (1964). Subjective reactions to lysergic acid diethylamide (LSD-25) measured by a questionnaire. *Archives of General Psychiatry, 10,* 469–485.

Lippa, R. A. (2006). Is high sex drive associated with increased sexual attraction to both sexes? It depends on whether you are male or female. *Psychological Science, 17,* 46–52.

Lippa, R. A. (2009). Sex differences in sex drive, sociosexuality, and height across 53 nations: Testing evolutionary and social structural theories. *Archives of Sexual Behavior, 38,* 631–651.

Lisman, J., & Raghavachari, S. (2006). A unified model of the presynaptic and postsynaptic changes during LTP at CA1 synapses. *Science STKE, 10,* 11.

Lisman, S. A. (1974). Alcohol "black-out": State dependent learning? *Archives of General Psychiatry, 30,* 46–53.

Littauer, H., Sexton, H., & Wynn, R. (2005). Qualities clients wish for in their therapists. *Scandanavian Journal of Caring Science, 19,* 28–31.

Littlewood, R. (2004). Unusual psychiatric syndromes: An introduction. *Psychiatry, 3,* 1–3.

Littrell, J. (1998). Is the experience of painful emotion therapeutic? *Clinical Psychology Review, 18,* 71–102.

Litz, B. T., Gray, M. J., Bryant, R., & Adler, A. B. (2002). Early intervention for trauma: Current status and future directions. *Clinical Psychology: Science and Practice, 9,* 112–134.

Lock, M. (1998). Menopause: Lessons from anthropology. *Psychosomatic Medicine, 60,* 410–419.

Locke, E. A. (2005). Why emotional intelligence is an invalid concept. *Journal of Organizational Behavior, 26,* 425–431.

Loehlin, J. C. (1992). *Genes and environment in personality development.* Newbury Park, CA: Sage.

Loehlin, J. C. (1997). A test of J. R. Harris's theory of peer influences on personality. *Journal of Personality and Social Psychology, 72,* 1197–1201.

Loehlin, J. C., & Horn, J. M. (2010). *Personality and intelligence in adoptive families.* New York: Sage.

Loehlin, J. C., Horn, J. M., & Willerman, L. (1989) Modeling IQ change - evidence from the Texas adoption project. *Child Development, 60,* 993–1004.

Loehlin, J. C., Lindzey, G., & Spuhler, J. N. (1977). *Race differences in intelligence*. San Francisco: W. H. Freeman.

Loehlin, J. C., Vandenberg, S. G., & Osborne, R. T. (1973). Blood group genes and Negro–White ability differences. *Behavior Genetics, 3*, 263–270.

Loehlin, J. C., Willerman, L., & Horn, J. M. (1988). Human behavior genetics. *Annual Review of Psychology, 39*, 101–133.

Loevinger, J. (1987). *Paradigms of personality*. New York: W. H. Freeman.

Loevinger, J. (1993). Conformity and conscientiousness: One factor or two stages? In D. C. Funder, R. D. Parke, C. Tomlinson-Keasey, & K. Widaman (eds.), *Studying lives through time: Personality and development* (pp. 189–205). Washington, DC: American Psychological Association.

Loftus, E. F. (1979). *Eyewitness testimony*. Cambridge, MA: Harvard University Press.

Loftus, E. F. (1993). The reality of repressed memories. *American Psychologist, 48*, 518–537.

Loftus, E. F., Coan, J. A., & Pickrell, J. E. (1996). Manufacturing false memories using bits of reality. In L. M. Reder (ed.), *Implicit memory and metacognition* (pp. 195–220). Mahwah, NJ: Lawrence Erlbaum Associates.

Loftus, E. F., & Guyer, M. (2002). Who abused Jane Doe? The hazards of the single case history: Part I and Part II. *Skeptical Inquirer, 26*, 24–32.

Loftus, E. F., & Loftus, G. R. (1980). On the permanence of stored information in the human brain. *American Psychologist, 35*, 409–420.

Loftus, E. F., Miller, D. G., & Burns, H. J. (1978). Semantic integration of verbal information into a visual memory. *Human Learning and Memory, 4*, 19–31.

Loftus E. F., & Palmer, J. C. (1974). Reconstruction of automobile destruction: An example of the interaction between language and memory. *Journal of Learning and Verbal Behavior, 13*, 585–589.

Loftus, E. F., & Pickrell, J. E. (1995). The formation of false memories. *Psychiatric Annals, 25*, 720–725.

Logel, C., Iserman, E. C., Davies, P. G., Quinn, D. M., & Spencer, S. J. (2009). The perils of double consciousness: The role of thought suppression in stereotype threat. *Journal of Experimental Social Psychology, 45*, 299–312.

Logue, M. B., Sher, K. J., & Frensch, P. A. (1992). Purported characteristics of adult children of alcoholics: A possible "Barnum effect." *Professional Psychology: Research and Practice, 23*, 226–232.

Lohr, J. M., DeMaio, C., & McGlynn, F. D. (2003). Specific and nonspecific treatment factors in the experimental analysis of behavioral treatment efficacy. *Behavior Modification, 27*, 322–368.

Lohr, J. M., Hooke, W., Gist, R., & Tolin, D. F. (2003). Novel and controversial treatments for trauma-related disorders. In S. O. Lilienfeld, S. J. Lynn, & J. M. Lohr (eds.), *Science and pseudoscience in clinical psychology* (pp. 243–272). New York: Guilford Press.

Lohr, J. M., Olatunji, B. O., Baumeister, R. F., & Bushman, B. J. (2007). The pseudopsychology of anger venting and empirically supported alternatives that do no harm. *Scientific Review of Mental Health Practice 5*, 54–65.

Lohr, J. M., Tolin, D. F., & Lilienfeld, S. O. (1998). Efficacy of eye movement desensitization and reprocessing. *Behavior Therapy, 29*, 123–156.

Long, G.T. & Krall, V.L. (1990). The measurement of stress by voice analysis. *Journal of Social Behavior and Personality, 5*, 723–731.

Longley, J., & Pruitt, D. G. (1980). Groupthink: A critique of Janis's theory. In L. Wheeler (ed.), *Review of personality and social psychology* (Vol. I, pp. 74–93). Beverly Hills, CA: Sage.

Longo, M. R., Betti, V., Aglioti, S.M., & Haggard, P. (2009). Visually induced analgesia: Seeing the body reduces pain. *The Journal of Neuroscience, 29*, 12125–12130.

Lonnqvist, J. E., Verkasalo, M., Haukka, J., Nyman, K., Tihonen, J., Laaksonen, I., et al. (2009). Premorbid personality factors in schizophrenia and bipolar disorder: Results from a large cohort study of male conscripts. *Journal of Abnormal Psychology, 118*, 418–423.

Lopez, D. J. (2002). Snaring the Fowler: Mark Twain debunks phrenology. *Skeptical Inquirer, 26* (1), 33–36.

Lopez, S. R., Nelson Hipke, K., Polo, A. J., Jenkins, J. H., Karno, M., Vaughn, C., et al. (2004). Ethnicity, expressed emotion, attributions, and course of schizophrenia: Family warmth matters. *Journal of Abnormal Psychology, 113*, 428–439.

Loprinzi, C. L., Levitt, R., Barton, E. L., Sloan, J. A., Atherton, P. J., Smith, D. J., et al. (2005). Evaluation of shark cartilage in patients with advanced cancer: A North Central Center Cancer Treatment Group trial. *Cancer, 104*, 176–182.

Lorber, M. F. (2004). Autonomic psychophysiology of aggression, psychopathy, and conduct problems: A meta-analysis. *Psychological Bulletin, 130*, 531–552.

Lorenz, K. (1937). The nature of instinct. In C. H. Schiller (ed.), *Instinctive behavior: The development of a modern concept* (pp. 129–175). New York: International Universities Press.

Lorenz, K. (1971). *Studies in animal and human behavior* (Vol. 2). Cambridge, MA: Harvard University Press.

Lourenco, O., & Machado, A. (1996). In defense of Piaget's theory: A reply to 10 common criticisms. *Psychological Review, 103*, 143–164.

Lovaas, O. I. (1987) Behavioral treatment and normal educational and intellectual functioning in young autistic children. *Journal of Consulting and Clinical Psychology, 55*, 3–9.

Lowe, M. R., Gleaves, D. H., & Murphy-Eberenz, K. P. (1998). On the relation of dieting and bingeing in bulimia nervosa. *Journal of Abnormal Psychology, 107*, 263–271.

Lowe, M. R., & Levine, A. S. (2005). Eating motives and the controversy over dieting: Eating less than needed versus less than wanted. *Obesity Research, 13*, 797–806.

Lowenstein, L.F.(2002). Fetishes and their associated behavior. *Sexuality and Disability, 20*, 135–147.

Lozanov, G. (1978) *Suggestology and outlines of suggestopedy* (M. Hall-Pozharlieva & K. Pashmakova, trans.). Oxford, England: Gordon & Breach.

Lubinski, D. (2000). Scientific and social significance of assessing individual differences: Sinking shafts at a few critical points. In S. T. Fiske (ed.), *Annual Review of Psychology, 51*, 404–444.

Lubinski, D. (2009). Exceptional cognitive ability: The phenotype. *Behavior Genetics, 39*, 350–358.

Lubinski, D., & Benbow, C. P. (1995). An opportunity for empiricism: Review of Howard Gardner's *Multiple intelligences: The theory in practice. Contemporary Psychology, 40*, 935–938.

Lubinski, D., Benbow, C. P., Webb, R. M., & Bleske-Rechek, A. (2006). Tracking exceptional human capital over two decades. *Psychological Science, 17*, 194–199.

Lubinski, D., & Humphreys, L. G. (1992). Some bodily and medical correlates of mathematical giftedness and commensurate levels of socioeconomic status. *Intelligence, 16*, 99–115.

Luborsky, L., Crits-Christoph, P., McLellan, T., Woody, G., Piper, W., Imber, S., et al. (1986). Do therapists vary much in their success? Findings from four outcome studies. *American Journal of Orthopsychiatry, 56*, 501–512.

Luborsky, L., Mellon, J., van Ravenswaay, P., Childress, A. R., Colen, K., Hole, A., et al. (1985). A verification of Freud's grandest clinical hypothesis: The transference. *Clinical Psychology Review, 5*, 231–246.

Lucas, R. E., Clark, A. E., Georgellis, Y., & Diener, E. (2003). Reexamining adaptation and the set point model of happiness: Reactions to changes in marital status. *Journal of Personality and Social Psychology, 84*, 527–539.

Luchies, C. W., Schiffman, J., Richards, L. G., Thompson, M. R., Bazuin, D., & DeYoung, A. J. (2002). Effects of age, step direction, and reaction condition on the ability to step quickly. *Journals of Gerontology: Series A: Biological Sciences and Medical Sciences, 57A*, M246–M249.

Luchins, A. S. (1946). Classroom experiments on mental set. *American Journal of Psychology, 59*, 295–298.

Luchins, D. J., Weinberger, D. R., & Wyatt, R. J. (1982). Schizophrenia and cerebral asymmetry detected by computed tomography. *American Journal of Psychiatry, 139*, 753–757.

Ludwig, A. M., Brandsma, J. M., Wilbur, C. B., Bendfeldt, F., & Jameson, D. H. (1972). The objective study of a multiple personality: Or, are four heads better than one? *Archives of General Psychiatry, 26*, 298–310.

Ludwig, J., & Phillips, D. A. (2008). Long-term effects of Head Start on low-income children. *Annals of the New York Academy of Sciences, 1136*, 257–268.

Luna, B., & Sweeney, J. A. (2004). The emergence of collaborative brain function: fMRI studies of the development of response inhibition. In R. E. Dahl & L. P. Spear (eds.), *Adolescent brain development: Vulnerabilities and opportunities* (pp. 296–309). New York: New York Academy of Sciences.

Lunberg, I., Frost, J., & Petersen, O. (1988). Effects of an extensive program for stimulating phonological awareness in preschool children. *Reading Research Quarterly, 23*, 263–284.

Luo, Q., Nakic, M., Wheatley, T., Richell, R., Martin, A., & Blair, R. J. R. (2006). The neural basis of implicit moral attitude—An IAT study using event-related fMRI. *NeuroImage, 30,* 1449–1457.

Luo, S., & Klohnen, E. C. (2005). Assortative mating and marital quality in newlyweds: A couple-centered approach. *Journal of Personality and Social Psychology, 88,* 304–325.

Luria, A. (1976). *Cognitive development: Its cultural and social foundations.* (M. Lopez-Morillas & L. Solotaroff, Trans.). Cambridge, MA: Harvard University Press.

Luscher, M., & Scott, I. (1969) *The Luscher Color Test.* New York: Random House.

Lutz, A., Greischar, L. L., Rawlings, N. B., Ricard, M., & Davidson, R. J. (2004). Long-term meditators self-induce high-amplitude gamma synchrony during mental practice. *Proceedings of the National Academy of Sciences U.S.A., 101,* 16369–16373.

Lykken, D. T. (1957). A study of anxiety in the sociopathic personality. *Journal of Abnormal and Social Psychology, 55,* 6–10.

Lykken, D. T. (1959). The GSR in the detection of guilt. *Journal of Applied Psychology, 43,* 385–388.

Lykken, D. T. (1960). The validity of the guilty knowledge technique: The effects of faking. *Journal of Applied Psychology, 44,* 258–262.

Lykken, D. T. (1978). The psychopath and the lie detector. *Psychophysiology, 15,* 137–142.

Lykken, D. T. (1982). If a man be mad. *The Sciences, 22,* 11–13.

Lykken, D. T. (1993). Predicting violence in the violent society. *Applied and Preventive Psychology, 2,* 13–20.

Lykken, D. T. (1995). *The antisocial personalities.* Mahwah, NJ: Lawrence Erlbaum.

Lykken, D. T. (1998). *A tremor in the blood: Uses and abuses of the lie detector* (2nd ed.). Reading, MA: Perseus.

Lykken, D. T. (2000). The causes and costs of crime and a controversial cure. *Journal of Personality, 68,* 559–605.

Lykken, D. T. (2005). Mental energy. *Intelligence, 33,* 331–335.

Lykken, D. T., Iacono, W. G., Harioan, K., McGue, M., & Bouchard, T. J. (1988). Habituation of the skin-conductance response to strong stimuli - A twin study, *Psychophysiology, 25,* 4–15.

Lykken, D. T., & Tellegen, A. (1996). Happiness is a stochastic phenomenon. *Psychological Science, 7,* 186–189.

Lynam, D. R., Milich, R., Zimmerman, R., Novak, S. P., Logan, T. K., Martin, C., et al. (1999). Project DARE: No effects at 10-year follow-up. *Journal of Consulting and Clinical Psychology, 67,* 590–593.

Lynch, S. K., Turkheimer, E., D'Onofrio, B., Mendle, J., Emery, R. E., Slutske, W. S., et al. (2006). A genetically informed study of the association between harsh punishment and offspring behavior problems. *Family Psychology, 20,* 190–198.

Lynn, R. (1996) *Dysgenics: Genetic deterioration in modern populations.* Westport, CT: Praeger.

Lynn, R. (1998). In support of the nutrition theory. In U. Neisser (ed.), *The rising curve: Long-term gains in IQ and related measures* (pp. 207–218). Washington, DC: American Psychological Association.

Lynn, R. (2003). The intelligence of American Jews. *Personality and Individual Differences, 36,* 201–206.

Lynn, R. (2006). *Race differences in intelligence: An evolutionary analysis.* Augusta, GA: Washington Summit Books.

Lynn, R., & Irwing, P. (2004). Sex differences on the Progressive Matrices: A meta-analysis. *Intelligence, 32,* 481–498.

Lynn, S. J. (1978). Three theories of self-disclosure exchange. *Journal of Experimental Social Psychology, 14,* 466–479.

Lynn, S. J., & Frauman, D. (1985). Group psychotherapy. In S. J. Lynn, & J. P. Garske (eds.), *Contemporary psychotherapies: Models and methods* (pp. 419–458). Columbus, OH: Charles E. Merrill.

Lynn, S. J., & Kirsch, I. (2006). *Essentials of clinical hypnosis: An evidence-based approach.* Washington, DC: American Psychological Association.

Lynn, S. J., Kirsch, I., & Hallquist, M. (2008). Social cognitive theories of hypnosis. In M. R. Nash & A. M. Barnier (eds.), *Oxford handbook of hypnosis* (pp. 111–140). New York: Oxford Press.

Lynn, S. J., Knox, J. A., Fassler, O., Lilienfeld, S. O., & Loftus, E. F. (2004). Memory, trauma, and dissociation. In G. M. Rosen (ed.), *Posttraumatic stress disorder: Issues and controversies* (pp. 163–186). New York: Wiley.

Lynn, S. J., Lock, T., Loftus, E. F., Krackow, E., & Lilienfeld, S. O. (2003a). The remembrance of things past: Problematic memory recovery techniques in psychotherapy. In S. O. Lilienfeld, S. J. Lynn, & J. Lohr (eds.), *Science and pseudoscience in clinical psychology* (pp. 205–239). New York: Guilford Press.

Lynn, S. J., Matthews, A., Williams, J. C., Hallquist, M. N., & Lilienfeld, S. O. (2007). Some forms of psychopathology are partly socially constructed. In S. O. Lilienfeld & W. T. O'Donohue (eds.), *The great ideas of clinical science: 17 principles that every mental health professional should know* (pp. 347–374). New York: Routledge.

Lynn, S. J., Nash, M. R., Rhue, J. W., Frauman, D. C., & Sweeney, C. A. (1984). Nonvolition, expectancies, and hypnotic rapport. *Journal of Abnormal Psychology, 93,* 295–303.

Lynn, S. J., Pintar, J., Sandberg, D., Fite, R. F., Ecklund, K., & Stafford, J. (2003b). Towards a social narrative model of revictimization. In L. Koenig, A. O'Leary, L. Doll, & W. Pequenat (eds.), *From child sexual assault to adult sexual risk: Trauma, revictimization, and intervention* (pp. 281–313). Washington, DC: American Psychological Association.

Lynn, S. J., & Rhue, J. W. (1988). Fantasy proneness: Hypnosis, developmental antecedents, and psychopathology. *American Psychologist, 43,* 35–44.

Lynn, S. J., & Rhue, J. W. (1991). An integrative model of hypnosis. In S. J. Lynn & J. W. Rhue (eds.), *Theories of hypnosis: Current models and perspectives* (pp. 397–438). New York: Guilford Press.

Lynn, S. J., & Rhue, J. W. (1996). The fantasy-prone person: Hypnosis, imagination, and creativity. *Journal of Personality and Social Psychology, 51,* 404–408.

Lynn, S. J., Rhue, J. W., & Weekes, J. R. (1990). Hypnotic involuntariness: A social-cognitive analysis. *Psychological Review, 97,* 169–184.

Lynn, S. J., Weekes, J. R., & Milano, M. (1989). Reality versus suggestion: Pseudomemory in hypnotizable and simulating subjects. *Journal of Abnormal Psychology, 98,* 75–79.

Lynskey, M. T., Heath, A. C., Bucholz, K. K., Slutske, W. S., Madden, P. A. F., Nelson, E. C., et al. (2003). Escalation of drug use in early-onset cannabis users vs. co-twin controls. *Journal of the American Medical Association, 289,* 427–433.

Lytton, H., & Romney, D. M. (1991). Parents' differential socialization of boys and girls: A meta-analysis. *Psychological Bulletin, 109,* 267–296.

Lyubomirsky, S., King, L. A., & Diener, E. (2005). The benefits of frequent positive affect: Does happiness lead to success? *Psychological Bulletin, 131,* 803–855.

Lyvers, M., Barling, N., & Harding-Clark, J. (2006). Effect of belief in "psychic healing" on self-reported pain in chronic pain sufferers. *Journal of Psychosomatic Research, 60,* 59–61.

Maas, J. B. (1999). *Power sleep: The revolutionary program that prepares your mind for peak performance.* New York: Collins.

Maas, J., & Toivanen, K. (1978). *Candid Camera* and the behavioral sciences. *Teaching of Psychology, 5,* 226–228.

Maccoby, E. E., & Jacklin, C. N. (1974). *Psychology of sex differences.* Stanford, CA: Stanford University Press.

Maccoby, E. E., & Jacklin, C. N. (1980). Sex differences in aggression: A rejoinder. *Child Development, 51,* 964–980.

Maccoby, E. E., & Martin, J. A. (1983). Socialization in the context of the family: Parent–child interaction. In P. H. Mussen (ed.) & E. M. Hetherington (vol. ed.), *Handbook of child psychology: Vol. 4. Socialization, personality, and social development* (4th ed., pp. 1–101). New York: Wiley.

Machover, K. (1949). *Personality projection in the drawing of the human figure.* Springfield, IL: Charles C. Thomas.

MacKillop, J., Lisman, S. A., Weinstein, A., & Rosenbaum, D. (2003). Controversial treatments for alcoholism. In S. O. Lilienfeld, S. J. Lynn, & J. W. Lohr (eds.), *Science and pseudoscience in clinical psychology* (pp. 273–306). New York: Guilford.

Mackintosh, M. J. (1998). *IQ and human intelligence.* Oxford, UK: Oxford University Press.

Macknik, S. L., King, M., Randi, J., Robbins, A., Teller, Thompson, J., et al. (2008). Attention and awareness in stage magic: Turning tricks into research. *Nature Reviews/Neuroscience, 9,* 871–881.

MacLean, P. D. (1990). *The triune brain in evolution: Role in paleocerebral functions.* New York: Plenum Press.

MacLeod, C. M., (1991). Half a century of research on the Stroop effect: An integrative review. *Psychological Bulletin, 109,* 163–203.

Macmillan, M. (2000). Restoring Phineas Gage: A 150th retrospective. *Journal of the History of Neuroscience, 9*, 46–66.

Macrae, C. N., & Bodenhausen, G. V. (2000). Social cognition: Thinking categorically about others. *Annual Review of Psychology, 51*, 93–120.

Maddi, S. R. (2002). The story of hardiness: Twenty years of theorizing, research, and practice. *Consulting Psychology Journal, 54*, 173–185.

Maddi, S. R. (2004). On hardiness and other pathways to resilience. *American Psychologist, 60*, 261–262.

Maddi, S. R., & Kobasa, S. C. (1984). *The hardy executive: Health under stress.* Homewood, IL: Dow Jones-Irwin.

Madsen, K. M., Hviid, A., Vestergaard, M., Schendel, D., Wohlfart, J., Thorsen, P., et al. (2002). A population-based study of measles, mumps and rubella vaccination and autism. *New England Journal of Medicine, 347*, 1477–1482.

Maertens, R. M., White, P. A., Rickert, W, Levasseur, G., Douglas, G. R., Bellier, P. V., et al. (2009). The genotoxicity of mainstream and sidestream marijuana and tobacco smoke condensates. *Chemical Research in Toxicology, 22*, 1406–1414.

Maes, H. M., Neale, M. C., & Eaves, L. J. (1997). Genetic and environmental factors in relative body weight and human adiposity. *Behavior Genetics, 27*, 325–351.

Maguire, E. A., Gadian, D. G., Johnsrude, I. S., Good, C. D., Ashburner, J., Frackowiak, R. S., et al. (2000). Navigation-related structural change in the hippocampi of taxi drivers. *Proceedings of the National Academy of Sciences U.S.A., 97*, 4398–4403.

Mahoney, M. J., & DeMonbreun, B. G. (1977). Confirmatory bias in scientists and non-scientists. *Cognitive Therapy and Research, 1*, 176–180.

Mahowald, M. W., & Bornemann, M. A. C. (2005). NREM sleep-arousal parasomnias. In M. H. Kryger, T. Roth, & W. C. Dement (eds.), *Principles and practice of sleep medicine* (4th ed., pp. 889–896). Philadelphia: Elsevier Saunders.

Mahowald, M., & Schenck, C. (2000). *Principles and practice of sleep medicine.* New York: W. B. Saunders.

Maia, T. V., & McClelland, J. L. (2004). A re-examination of the evidence for the somatic marker hypothesis: What participants know in the Iowa gambling task. *Proceedings of the National Academy of Sciences, 101*, 16075–16080.

Maier, I. C., & Schwab, M. E. (2006). Sprouting, regeneration and circuit formation in the injured spinal cord: Factors and activity. *Philosophical Transactions of the Royal Society London B Biological Sciences, 361*, 1611–1634.

Main, M., & Cassidy, J. (1988). Categories of response to reunion with the parent at age 6: Predictable from infant attachment classifications and stable over a 1-month period. *Developmental Psychology, 24*, 415–426.

Majid, A. (2010). How words categorize the body: The mapping of perceptual parts to natural language. In B. C. Malt, & P. Wolff (eds.), *Words and the world: How words capture human experience.* New York: Oxford University Press.

Malcom, K. (1989). Patients' perceptions and knowledge of electroconvulsive therapy. *Psychiatric Bulletin, 13*, 161–165.

Malenka, R. C., & Nicoll, R. A. (1999). Long-term potentiation—A decade of progress? *Science, 285*, 1870–1874.

Malina, R. M., & Bouchard, C. (1991). *Growth, maturation, and physical activity.* Champaign, IL: Human Kinetics.

Malinoski, P., Lynn, S. J., & Sivec, H. (1998). The assessment, validity, and determinants of early memory reports: A critical review. In S. J. Lynn & K. McConkey (eds.), *Truth in memory* (pp. 109–136). New York: Guilford.

Malle, B. F. (2006). The actor-observer asymmetry in attribution: A (surprising) meta-analysis. *Psychological Bulletin, 132*, 895–919.

Malony, H. N., & Lovekin, A. A. (1985). *Glossolalia: Behavioral science perspectives on speaking in tongues.* New York: Oxford University Press.

Mandiyan, V. S., Coats. J. K., & Shah, N. M. (2005). Deficits in sexual and aggressive behaviors in Cnga2 mutant mice. *Nature Neuroscience, 8*, 1660–1662.

Mandler, G., Nakamura, Y., & Shebo-Van Zandt, B. J. (1987). Nonspecific effects of exposure on stimuli that cannot be recognized. *Journal of Experimental Psychology: Learning, Memory, & Cognition, 13*, 646–648.

Mangeot, S. D., Miller, L. J., McIntosh, D. N., McGrath-Clarke, J., Simon, J., Hagerman, R. J., et al. (2001). Sensory modulation dysfunction in children with attention-deficit-hyperactivity disorder. *Developmental Medicine & Child Neurology, 43*, 399–406.

Mann, E., & Mody, I. (2008). The multifaceted role of inhibition in epilepsy: seizure-genesis through excessive GABAergic inhibition in autosomal dominant nocturnal frontal lobe epilepsy. *Current Opinion in Neurology, 21*, 155–160.

Mann, J. (1969). The use of sodium amobarbital in psychiatry. *Ohio State Medical Journal, 65*, 700–702.

Mann, L. B. (2005, February 22). Oscar nominee: Fact or fiction? *Washington Post,* HE01.

Mann, T., Tomiyama, A. J., Westling, E., Lew, A., Samuels, B., & Chatman, J. (2007). Medicare's search for effective obesity treatments: Diets are not the answer. *American Psychologist, 62*, 220–233.

Manning, R., Levine, M. & Collins, A. (2007). The Kitty Genovese murder and the social psychology of helping: The parable of the 38 witnesses. *American Psychologist, 62*, 555–562.

Mantell, D. M. (1971). The potential for violence in Germany. *Journal of Social Issues, 27*, 101–112.

Mantella, R. C., Butters, M. A., Amico, J. A., Mazumdar, S., Rollman, B. L., et al. (2008). Salivary cortisol is associated with diagnosis and severity of late-life generalized anxiety disorder. *Psychoneuroendocrinology. 33*, 773–781.

Maquet, P., & Franck, G. (1997). REM Sleep and the amygdala. *Molecular Psychiatry, 2*, 195–196.

Marczinski, C. A., Harrison, E. L., & Fillmore, M. T. (2008). The effects of alcohol on simulated drinking and perceived driving impairment in binge drinkers. *Alcohol: Clinical and Experimental Research, 32*, 1329–1337.

Maren, S. (2005). Synaptic mechanisms of associative memory in the amygdala. *Neuron, 15*, 783–786.

Marian, V., & Neisser, U. (2000). Language-dependent recall of autobiographical memories. *Journal of Experimental Psychology: General, 129*, 361–368.

Marieb, E. N., & Hoehn, K. (2007). *Human anatomy and physiology* (7th ed.) San Francisco: Pearson.

Marino, L. (2005). Big brains matter in novel environments. *Proceedings of the National Academy of Sciences USA, 102*, 5306–5307.

Marino, L. (2009, March 20). A new kind of scientist activism. *Chronicle of Higher Education,* http://chronicle.com/article/Another-Kind-of-Scientist/24559.

Marino, L., & Lilienfeld, S. O. (1998). Dolphin-assisted therapy: Flawed data, flawed conclusions. *Anthrozoos, 11*, 194–200.

Marino, L., & Lilienfeld, S. O. (2007). Dolphin-assisted therapy: More flawed data and more flawed conclusions. *Anthrozoos, 20*, 239–249.

Marino, L., McShea, D. W., & Uhen, M. D. (2004). Origin and evolution of large brains in toothed whales. *Anatomical Record Part A: Discoveries in Molecular, Cellular, & Evolutionary Biology, 281*, 1247–1255.

Maris, R. W. (1992). The relationship of nonfatal suicide attempts to completed suicides. In R. W. Maris, A. L. Berman, J. T. Maltsberger, & R. I. Yufit (eds.), *Assessment and prediction of suicide* (pp. 362–380). New York: Guilford Press.

Marks, R. P., Swinson, M., Basoglu, K., & Kuch, H. (1993). Alprazolam and exposure alone and combined in panic disorder with agoraphobia. *British Journal of Psychiatry, 162*, 788–799.

Marlatt, G. A. (1983). The controlled-drinking controversy: A commentary. *American Psychologist, 10*, 1097–1110.

Marlatt, G. A. (2002). Buddhist philosophy and the treatment of addictive behavior. *Cognitive and Behavioral Practice, 9*, 44–47.

Marlatt, G. A., & Gordon, J. R. (eds.). (1985). *Relapse prevention: Maintenance strategies in the treatment of addictive behaviors.* New York: Guilford Press.

Marlatt, G. A., & Rosenhow, D. J. (1980). Cognitive processes in alcohol use: Expectancy and balanced placebo design. In N. K. Mello (ed.), *Advances in substance abuse: Behavioral and biological research* (pp. 159–199). Greenwich, CT: JAI Press.

Marlow, C. (2009) The size of social networks. *The Economist print edition,* Feb 26th. http://www.economist.com/science/displaystory.cfm?story_id=13176775. Retrieved 2 May, 2010.

Marschner, A., Kalisch, R., Vervliet, B., Vansteenwegen, D., & Büchel, C. (2008) Dissociable roles for the hippocampus and the amygdala in human cued vs. context fear conditioning. *Journal of Neuroscience, 28*, 9030–9036.

Marsh, A. A., Finger, E. C., Mitchell, D. G., Reid, M. E., Sims, C., Kosson, D. S., et al. (2008). Reduced amygdala response to fearful expressions in children and adolescents with callous-unemotional traits and disruptive behavior disorders. *American Journal of Psychiatry, 165*, 712–720.

Marshall, G. D., & Zimbardo, P. G. (1979). Affective consequences of inadequately explained arousal. *Journal of Personality and Social Psychology, 37*, 970–988.

Marston, W. M. (1938). *The lie detector test.* New York: Richard R. Smith.

Martin, D. (2006, November 20). *The truth about happiness may surprise you.* Retrieved from www.cnn.com/2006/HEALTH/conditions/11/10/happiness.overview/index.html.

Martin, J. N. & Fox, N. A. (2006) Temperament. In McCartney, K., & Phillips, D. (eds.), *Blackwell handbook of early childhood development*, (pp. 126–146). Malden, MA: Blackwell Publishing.

Martin, L. R., & Friedman, H. S. (2000). Comparing personality scales across time: An illustrative study of validity and consistency in life-span archival data. *Journal of Personality, 68*, 85–110.

Martin, N. G., Eaves, L. J., Heath, A. C., Jardine, R., Feingold, L. M., & Eysenck, H. J. (1986). Transmission of social attitudes. *Proceedings of the National Academy of Sciences, 83*, 4364–4368.

Martino, S. C., Collins, R. L., Elliott, M. C., Strachman, A., Kanouse, D. E., & Berry, S. H. (2006). Exposure to degrading versus nondegrading music lyrics and sexual behavior among youth. *Pediatrics, 118*, 430–441.

Martinot, M. L., Bragulat, V., Artiges, E., Dolle, F., Hinnen, F., Jouvent, R., et al. (2001). Decreased presynaptic dopamine function in the left caudate of depressed patients with affective flattening and psychomotor retardation. *American Journal of Psychiatry, 158*, 314–316.

Maruta, T., Colligan, R. C., Malinchoc, M., & Offord, K. P. (2000). Optimists vs pessimists: Survival rate among medical patients over a 30-year period. *Mayo Clinic Proceedings, 75*, 140–143.

Mashour, G. A., Walker, E. E. & Martuza, R. L. (2005). Psychosurgery: Past, present, and future. Brain Research Reviews, 48, 409–419.

Maslach, C. (1979). Negative and emotional biasing of unexplained arousal. *Journal of Personality and Social Psychology, 37*, 953–969.

Maslow, A. H. (1954). *Motivation and personality.* New York: Harper and Row.

Maslow, A. H. (1971). *The farther reaches of human nature.* New York: Viking Press.

Mastekaasa, A. (1994). The subjective well-being of the previously married: The importance of unmarried cohabitation and time since widowhood or divorce. *Social Forces, 73*, 665–692.

Masters, W. H., & Johnson, V. E. (1966). *Human sexual response.* Boston: Little, Brown.

Mataix-Cols, D., Rosario-Campos, M.C., & Lackman, J. F. (2005). A multidimensional model of obsessive-compulsive disorder. *American Journal of Psychiatry, 162*, 228–238.

Matarazzo, J. D. (1980). Behavioral health and behavioral medicine: Frontiers for a new health psychology. *American Psychologist, 35*, 807–817.

Matarazzo, J. D. (1983). The reliability of psychiatric and psychological diagnosis. *Clinical Psychology Review, 3*, 103–145.

Mather, M., Canli, T., English, T., Whitfield, S., Wais, P., Ochsner, K., et al. (2004). Amygdala responses to emotionally valenced stimuli in older and younger adults. *Psychological Science, 15*, 259–263.

Mathews, A., Richards, A., & Eysenck, M. W. (1989). Interpretation of homophones related to threat in anxiety states. *Journal of Abnormal Psychology, 98*, 31–34.

Mathews, V., Wang, Y., Kalnin, A. J., Mosier, K. M., Dunn, D. W., & Kronenberger, W. G. (2006). *Short-term effects of violent video game playing: An fMRI study.* Annual Meeting of the Radiological Society of North America, Chicago, IL.

Matson, J. L., Benavidez, D. A., Compton, L. S., Paclawskyj, T., & Baglio, C. (1996) Behavioral treatment of autistic persons: A review of research from 1980 to the present. *Research in Developmental Disabilities, 17*, 433–465.

Matsumoto, D., & Ekman, P. (2004). The relationship between expressions, labels, and descriptions of contempt. *Journal of Personality and Social Psychology, 87*, 529–540.

Matsumoto, D., & Willingham, B. (2006). The thrill of victory and the agony of defeat: Spontaneous expressions of medal winners of the 2004 Athens Olympic Games. *Journal of Personality and Social Psychology, 91*, 568–581.

Matsumoto, D., Yoo, S. H., Hirayama, S., & Petrova, G. (2005). Development and validation of a measure of display rule knowledge: The Display Rule Assessment Inventory. *Emotion, 5*, 23–40.

Mattes, R. D., Hollis, J., Hayes, D., & Stunkard, A. J. (2005). Appetite measurement and manipulation misgivings. *Journal of the American Dietetic Association, 105*, 87–97.

Matthews, A., & MacLeod, C. (2005). Cognitive vulnerability to emotional disorders. In S. Nolen-Hoeksema, T. D. Cannon, & T. Widiger (eds.), *Annual Review of Clinical Psychology* (Vol. 1, pp. 167–196). Palo Alto, CA: Annual Reviews.

Matthews, D. A., Larson, D. B., & Barry, C. P. (1993). *The faith factor: An annotated bibliography of clinical research on spiritual subjects* (Vol. 1). Rockville, MD: National Institute for Mental Healthcare Research.

Matthews, G., & Gilliland, K. (1999). The personality theories of H. J. Eyesenck and J. A. Gray: A comparative review. *Personality and Individual Differences, 26*, 583–626.

Matthews, G., Zeidner, M., & Roberts, R. (2002). *Emotional intelligence: Science and myth.* London: MIT Press.

Matthews, K. A., Gump, B. B., Harris, K. F., Haney, T. L., & Barefoot, J. C. (2004). Hostile behaviors predict cardiovascular mortality among men enrolled in the Multiple Risk Factor Intervention Trial. *Circulation, 109*, 66–70.

Max, D. T. (2007, January 7). Happiness 101. *New York Times.* Retrieved from www.nytimes.com/2007/01/07/magazine/07happiness.t.html?ex=1183608000&en=946a9bb65d8be3b7&ei=5070.

Mayberg, H. S., Lozano, A. M., Voon, V., McNeely, H. E., Seminowicz, D., Hamani, C., et al. (2005). Deep brain stimulation for treatment-resistant depression. *Neuron, 45*, 651–660.

Mayer, J., Roberts, R., & Barsade, S. G. (2008). Human abilities: Emotional intelligence. *Annual Review of Psychology, 59*, 507–536.

Mayer, J. D., Salovey, P., & Caruso, D. R. (2008). Emotional intelligence: New ability or eclectic traits? *American Psychologist, 63*, 503–517.

Mayer, R. (2004). Should there be a three-strikes rule against pure discovery learning? The case for guided methods of instruction. *American Psychologist, 59*, 14–19.

Mayer-Gross, W., Slater, E., & Roth, M. (1969). *Clinical psychiatry* (3rd ed.). Baltimore: Williams & Wilkins. Revised and reprinted 1977, Balliere, Tindall, London.

Mayberg, H. S., Silva, J. A., Brannan, S. K., Tekell, J. L., Mahurin, R. K., McGinnis, S., et al. (2002). The functional neuroanatomy of the placebo effect. *American Journal of Psychiatry, 159*, 728–737.

Mazure, C. M. (1998). Life stressors as risk factors in depression. *Clinical Psychology: Science and Practice, 5*, 291–313.

Mazzoni, G., Heap, M., & Scoboria, A. (2010). Hypnosis and memory: Theory, laboratory research, and application. In S. J. Lynn, J. W. Rhue, & I. Kirsch (eds.), *Handbook of clinical hypnosis*. Washington, DC: American Psychological Association.

Mazzoni, G. A. L., Loftus, E. F., & Kirsch, I. (2001). Changing beliefs about implausible autobiographical events: A little plausibility goes a long way. *Journal of Experimental Psychology: Applied, 7*, 31–39.

McBride, P. E. (1992). The health consequences of smoking: Cardiovascular diseases. *Medical Clinics of North America, 76*, 333–353.

McCabe, D. P., & Castel, A. D. (2008). Seeing is believing: The effect of brain images on judgements of scientific reasoning. *Cognition, 107*, 343–352.

McCall Smith, A., & Shapiro, C. M. (1997). Sleep disorders and the criminal law. In C. Shapiro & A. McCall Smith (eds.), *Forensic aspects of sleep* (pp. 29–64). Chichester, England: John Wiley & Sons.

McCall, R. B., & Carriger, M. S. (1993). A meta-analysis of infant habituation and recognition memory performance as predictors of later IQ. *Child Development, 64*, 57–79.

McCann, J. T., Shindler, K. L., & Hammond, T. R. (2003). The science and pseudoscience of expert testimony. In S. O. Lilienfeld, S. J. Lynn, & J. M. Lohr (eds.), *Science and pseudoscience in clinical psychology* (pp. 77–108). New York: Guilford.

McCarthy, M. (1990). The thin ideal, depression and eating disorders in women. *Behaviour Research and Therapy, 28*, 205–215.

McCarty, C. A., Lau, A. S., Valeri, S. M., & Weisz, J. R. (2004). Parent-child interactions proxy for behavior. *Journal of Abnormal Child Psychology, 32*, 83–93.

McCarty, R. (2001, April). Negative stereotypes: A personal view. *Monitor on Psychology, 32*(4), 31.

McCaul, K. D., & Malott, J. M. (1984). Distraction and coping with pain. *Psychological Bulletin, 95*, 516–533.

McCauley, R. N., & Henrich, J. (2006). Susceptibility to the Müller-Lyer Illusion, theory neutral observation, and the diachronic cognitive penetrability of the visual input system. *Philosophical Psychology, 19*, 79–101.

McClearn, G. E., Johansson, B., Berg, S., Pedersen, N. L., Ahern, F., Petrill, S.A. et al. (1997). Substantial genetic influence on cognitive abilities in twins 80+ years old. *Science, 276,* 1560–1563.

McClellan, J., Kowatch, R. A., & Findling, R. L. (2007). Practice parameters for the assessment and treatment of children and adolescents with bipolar disorder. *Journal of the American Academy of Child and Adolescent Psychiatry, 46,* 107–125.

McClelland, D. C., Atkinson, J. W., Clark, R. A., & Lowell, E. L. (1953). *The achievement motive.* New York: Appleton-Century-Crofts.

McClelland, D. C., Atkinson, J. W., Clark, R. A., & Lowell, E. L. (1958). A scoring manual for the achievement motive. In J. W. Atkinson (ed.), *Motives in fantasy, action, and society* (pp. 179–204). Princeton, NJ: Van Nostrand.

McClelland, J. L., & Plaut, D. C. (1993). Computational approaches to cognition: Top-down approaches. *Current Opinion in Neurobiology, 3,* 209–216.

McClintock, J. B., & Lawrence, J. M. (1982). Photoresponse and associative learning in Luidia clathrata (Say) (Echinodermata: Asteroidea). *Marine Behavior and Physiology, 9,* 13–21.

McCloskey, M. (1983). Intuitive physics. *Scientific American, 248* (4), 122–130.

McCloskey, M., Berman, M., Noblett, K., & Coccaro, E. F. (2005). Intermittent explosive disorder-integrated research diagnostic criteria: Convergent and discriminant validity. *Journal of Psychiatric Research, 40,* 231–242.

McCloskey, M., Wible, C. G., & Cohen, N. J. (1988). Is there a special flashbulb-memory mechanism? *Journal of Experimental Psychology: General, 117,* 171–181.

McClure, E. B. (2000). A meta-analytic review of sex differences in facial expression processing and their development in infants, children, and adolescents. *Psychological Bulletin, 126,* 424–453.

McConaghy, N. (2005). Time to abandon the gay/heterosexual dichotomy? [Letter to the Editor]. *Archives of Sexual Behavior, 34,* 1–2.

McConkie, G. W., & Currie, C. B. (1996). Visual stability across saccades while viewing complex pictures. *Journal of Experimental Psychology: Human Perception & Performance, 22,* 563–581.

McConkey, K. M. (1991). The construction and resolution of experience and behavior in hypnosis. In S. J. Lynn & J. W. Rhue (eds.), *Theories of hypnosis: Current models and perspectives* (pp. 542–563). New York: Guilford Press.

McConnell, J. V. (1962). Memory transfer through cannibalism in planarians. *Journal of Neuropsychiatry, 3* (Suppl. 1), 542–548.

McCord, J. (2006). Punishments and alternate routes to crime prevention. In A. K. Hess & I. B. Weiner, (eds.), *The handbook of forensic psychology* (3rd ed., pp. 701–721). Hoboken, NJ: John Wiley & Sons.

McCrae, R. R., & Costa, P. T. (1994). The stability of personality: Observation and evaluations. *Current Directions in Psychological Science, 3,* 173–175.

McCrae, R. R., & Costa, P. T. (1995). Trait explanations in personality psychology. *European Journal of Personality, 9,* 231–252.

McCrae, R. R, & Costa, P. T. (1997). Personality trait structure as a human universal. *American Psychologist, 52,* 509–516.

McCullough, M. E., Root, L. M., Tabka, B., & Witvliet, C. V. O. (2009). Forgiveness. In S. J. Lopez (ed.), *Handbook of positive psychology* (2nd ed., pp. 427–435). New York: Oxford.

McCullough, M. E., & Willoughby, B. L. B. (2009). Religion, self-regulation, and self-control: Associations, explanations, and implications. *Psychological Bulletin, 135,* 69–93.

McCullough, M. E., Tsang, J., & Brion, S. (2003). Personality traits in adolescence as predictors of religiousness in early adulthood: Findings from the Terman longitudinal study. *Personality and Social Psychology Bulletin, 29,* 980–991.

McCutcheon, L. (1996, May/June). What's that I smell? The claims of aromatherapy. *Skeptical Inquirer.* 35–37.

McCutcheon, L. E., & McCutcheon, L. E. (1994). Not guilty by reason of insanity: Getting it right or perpetuating the myths? *Psychological Reports, 74,* 764–766.

McDaniel, M. A. (2005) Big-brained people are smarter: A meta-analysis of the relationship between in vivo brain volume and intelligence. *Intelligence, 33,* 337–346.

McDaniel, M. A., Maier, S. F., & Einstein, G. O. (2002). "Brain-specific" nutrients: A memory cure? *Psychological Science in the Public Interest, 3,* 12–38.

McDaniel, M. A., Whetzel, D. L., Schmidt, F. L., & Maurer, S. D. (1994). The validity of employment interviews: A comprehensive review and meta-analysis. *Journal of Applied Psychology, 79,* 599–616.

McDermott J. F. (2001). Emily Dickinson revisited: A study of periodicity in her work. *American Journal of Psychiatry, 158,* 686–690.

McDonald, A., & Walter, G. (2004). The portrayal of ECT in American movies. *Journal of ECT, 20,* 230–236.

McDonough, L., Choi, S., & Mandler, J. M. (2003). Understanding spatial relations: Flexible infants, lexical adults. *Cognitive Psychology, 46,* 229–259.

McEachin, J. J., Smith, T., & Lovaas, O. I. (1993) Long-term outcome for children with autism who received early intensive behavioral treatment. *American Journal on Mental Retardation, 97,* 359–372.

McEvoy, P.M. (2007). Effectiveness of cognitive behavioural group therapy for social phobia in a community clinic: A benchmarking study. *Behaviour Research and Therapy, 45,* 3030–3040.

McFall, R. M. (2006). Making psychology incorruptible. *Applied & Preventative Psychology, 5,* 9–15.

McFall, R. M. (2006). Doctoral training in clinical psychology. *Annual Review of Clinical Psychology, 2,* 21–49.

McGilly, K., & Siegler, R. S. (1989). How children choose among serial recall strategies. *Child Development, 60,* 172–182.

McGrath, M. E. (1984). 1st-person account—Where did I go? *Schizophrenia Bulletin, 10,* 638–640.

McGue, M. (1999). The behavioral genetics of alcoholism. *Current Directions in Psychological Science, 8,* 109–115.

McGue, M., & Lykken, D. T. (1992). Genetic influence on risk of divorce. *Psychological Science, 3,* 368–373.

McGuffin, P., Rijsdijk, F., Andrew, M., Sham, P., Katz, R., & Cardino, A. (2003). The heritability of bipolar affective disorder and the genetic relationship to unipolar depression. *Archives of General Psychiatry, 60,* 497–502.

McGuire, P. K., Shah, G. M. S., & Murray, R. M. (1993). Increased blood flow in Broca's area during auditory hallucinations. *Lancet, 342,* 703–706.

McGuire, W. J. (1964). Inducing resistance to persuasion: Some contemporary approaches. In L. Berkowitz (ed.), *Advances in experimental social psychology* (Vol. 1, pp. 191–229). San Diego, CA: Academic Press.

McGuire, W. J., & Papageorgis, D. (1961). The relative efficacy of various types of prior belief-defense in producing immunity against persuasion. *Journal of Abnormal and Social Psychology, 62,* 327–337.

McGurk, H., & MacDonald, J. (1976). Hearing lips and seeing voices. *Nature, 264,* 746–748.

McHugh, P. R. (1993). Multiple personality disorder. *Harvard Mental Health Newsletter, 10*(3), 4–6.

McHugh P. R. (2008). *Try to remember: Psychiatry's clash over meaning, memory, and mind.* New York: Dana Press.

McKenzie, I. K. (2004). The Stockholm syndrome revisited: Hostages, relationships, prediction, control, and psychological science. *Journal of Police Crisis Negotiations, 4,* 5–21.

McKinney, M., & Jacksonville, M. C. (2005). Brain cholinergic vulnerability: Relevance to behavior and disease. *Biochemical Pharmacology, 70,* 1115–1124.

McLeod, J. D. (1991). Childhood parental loss and adult depression. *Journal of Health and Social Behavior, 32,* 205–220.

McNally, R. J. (1987). Preparedness and phobias—A review. *Psychological Bulletin, 101,* 283–303.

McNally, R. J. (2003). *Remembering trauma.* Cambridge, MA: Belknap Press.

McNally, R. J., Bryant, R. A., & Ehlers, A. (2003). Does early psychological intervention promote recovery from posttraumatic stress? *Psychological Science in the Public Interest, 4,* 45–79.

McNally, R. J., & Clancy, S. A. (2005). Sleep paralysis, sexual abuse, and space alien abduction. *Transcultural Psychiatry, 42,* 113–122.

McNally, R. J., & Lukach, B. M. (1991). Behavioral treatment of zoophilic exhibitionism. *Journal of Behavioral Research and Experimental Psychiatry, 22,* 281–284.

McNally, R. M., & Eke, M. (1996). Anxiety sensitivity, suffocation fear, and breath-holding duration as predictors of response to carbon dioxide challenge. *Journal of Abnormal Psychology, 105,* 146–149.

McNamara, H. J., Long, J. B., & Wike, E. L. (1956). Learning without response under two conditions of external cues. *Journal of Comparative and Physiological Psychology, 49,* 477–480.

McNamara, P., McLaren, D., Smith, D., Brown, A, & Stickgold, R. (2005) A "Jekyll and Hyde" within - Aggressive versus friendly interactions in REM and non-REM dreams. *Psychological Science, 16,* 130–136.

McNiel, D. E., Eisner, J. P., & Binder, R. L. (2000). The relationship between command hallucinations and violence. *Psychiatric Services, 51*, 1288–1292.

McQuiston-Surrett, D., Malpass, R. S., & Tredoux, C. G. (2006). Sequential vs. simultaneous lineups: A review of methods, data, and theory. *Psychology, Public Policy and Law, 12*, 137–169.

McRae, C., Cherin, E., Yamazaki, G., Diem, G., Vo, A. H., Russell, D., et al. (2004). Effects of perceived treatment on quality of life and medical outcomes in a double-blind placebo surgery trial. *Archives of General Psychiatry, 61*, 412–420.

Meacham, J. (1990). The loss of wisdom. In R. J. Sternberg (ed.), *Wisdom: Its nature, origins, and development* (pp. 181–211). New York: Cambridge University Press.

Meador, B. D. , & Rogers, C. R. (1979). Person centered therapy. In J. R. Corsini (ed.), *Current psychotherapies*. Itasca, IL: F. E. Peacock Publishers.

Meads, C., & Nouwen, A. (2005). Does emotional disclosure have any effects? A systematic review of the literature with meta-analyses. *International Journal of Technology Assessment in Health Care, 21*, 153–164.

Mednick, S. A., Machon, R. A., Huttunen, M. O., & Bonett, D. (1988). Adult schizophrenia following prenatal exposure to an influenza epidemic. *Archives of General Psychiatry, 45*, 189–192.

Medvec, V. H., Madey, S., & Gilovich, T. (1995). When less is more: Counterfactual thinking and satisfaction among Olympic medal winners. *Journal of Personality and Social Psychology, 69*, 603–610.

Meehl, P. E. (1945). The dynamics of "structured" personality tests. *Journal of Clinical Psychology, 1*, 296–303.

Meehl, P. E. (1956). Wanted: A good cookbook. *American Psychologist, 11*, 263–272.

Meehl, P. E. (1962). Schizotaxia, schizotypy, and schizophrenia. *American Psychologist, 17*, 827–838.

Meehl, P. E. (1967). Theory-testing in psychology and physics: A methodological paradox. *Philosophy of Science, 34*, 103–115.

Meehl, P. E. (1972). Reactions, reflections, projections. In J. N. Butcher (ed.), *Objective personality assessment: Changing perspectives* (pp. 131–189). New York: Academic Press.

Meehl, P. E. (1990). Toward an integrated theory of schizotaxia, schizotypy, and schizophrenia. *Journal of Personality Disorders, 4*, 1–99.

Meehl, P. E. (1995). Psychoanalysis is not yet a science: Comment on Shevrin. *Journal of the American Psychoanalytic Association, 43*, 1015–1023.

Meehl, P. E., & Rosen, A. (1955). Antecedent probability and the efficiency of psychometric signs, patterns, or cutting scores. *Psychological Bulletin, 52*, 194–216.

Meeker, W., & Barber, T. (1971). Toward an explanation of stage hypnosis. *Journal of Abnormal Psychology, 77*, 61–70.

Megargee, E. I. (1972). *The California Psychological Inventory handbook*. San Francisco: Jossey-Bass.

Mehl, M. R., Vazire, S., Ramírez-Esparza, N., Slatcher, R. B., & Pennebaker, J. W. (2007). Are women really more talkative than men? *Science, 317*, 82.

Mehler, P. S. (2003). Bulimia nervosa. *New England Journal of Medicine, 349*, 875–881.

Meichenbaum, D. (1985). Cognitive-behavioral therapies. In S. J. Lynn, & J. P. Garske (eds.), *Contemporary psychotherapies: Models and methods* (pp. 261–286). Columbus, OH: Charles E. Merrill.

Meichenbaum, D. (1994). *A clinical handbook/practical therapist manual for assessing and treating adults with post-traumatic stress disorder* (PTSD). Clearwater, FL: Institute Press.

Meichenbaum, D. (1996). Stress inoculation training for coping with stressors. *The Clinical Psychologist, 49*, 4–10.

Meissner, C. A., & Brigham, J. C. (2001). Thirty years of investigating the own-race bias in memory for faces: A meta-analytic review. *Psychology, Public Policy, and Law, 7*, 3–35.

Mell, L. K., Davis, R. L., & Owens, D. (2005). Association between streptococcal infection and obsessive-compulsive disorder, Tourette's syndrome, and tic disorder. *Pediatrics, 116*, 56–60.

Mellinger, D. M., & Lynn, S. J. (2003). *The monster in the cave: How to face your fear and anxiety and live your life*. New York: Berkeley.

Melton, G. B., Petrilla, J., Poythress, N. G., & Slobogin, L. A. (1997). *Psychological evaluations for the courts: A handbook for mental health professionals and lawyers* (2nd ed.). New York: Guilford Press.

Melton, G. J. (1999). *Brainwashing and the cults: The rise and fall of a theory*. Retrieved October 29, 2007, from www.cesnur.org/testi/melton.htm.

Melzack, R. (1975). The McGill Pain Questionnaire: Major properties and scoring methods. *Pain, 1*, 277–299.

Melzack, R. R., & Wall, P. (1965). Pain mechanisms: A new theory. *Science, 50*, 971–979.

Melzack, R. R., & Wall, P. (1970). Psychophysiology of pain. *International Anesthesiology Clinic, 8*, 3–34.

Memon, A., Hope, L., & Bull, R. (2003). Exposure duration: Effects on eyewitness accuracy and confidence. *British Journal of Psychology, 94*, 339–354.

Menchola, B. L., Arkowitz, H., & Burke, B. L. (2007). Efficacy of self-administered treatments for depression and anxiety: A meta-analysis. *Professional Psychology: Research and Practice, 38*, 421–429.

Mendelowicz, M. V., & Stein, M. B. (2000). Quality of life in individuals with anxiety disorders. *American Journal of Psychiatry, 157*, 669–682.

Menini, A., Picco, C., & Firestein, S. (1995). Quantal-like current fluctuations induced by odorants in olfactory receptor cells. *Nature, 373*, 435–437.

Menninger, K. (1958). *Theory of psychoanalytic technique*. New York: Basic Books.

Mercer, J. (2002). Attachment therapy: A treatment without empirical support. *The Scientific Review of Mental Health Practice, 1*, 9–16.

Mercer, J., Sarner, L., & Rosa, L. (2003). *Attachment therapy on trial: The torture and death of Candace Newmaker*. Westport, CT: Praeger.

Merckelbach, H., Devilly, G., & Rassin, E. (2002). Alters in dissociative identity disorder: Metaphors or genuine entities? *Clinical Psychology Review, 22*, 481–497.

Merikle, P. M. (1988). Subliminal auditory tapes: An evaluation. *Psychology and Marketing, 46*, 355–372.

Merskey, H. (1992). The manufacture of personalities: The production of multiple personality disorder. *British Journal of Psychiatry, 160*, 327–340.

Mervielde, I., De Clercq, B., De Fruyt, F., & Van Leeuwen, K. (2005). Temperament, personality, and developmental psychopathology as childhood antecedents of personality disorders. *Journal of Personality Disorders, 19*, 171–201.

Messick, S. (1992). Multiple intelligence or multilevel intelligence? Selective emphasis on distinctive properties of hierarchy: On Gardner's *Frames of Mind* and Sternberg's *Beyond IQ* in the context of theory and research on the structure of human abilities. *Psychological Inquiry, 3*, 365–384.

Meston, C. M. (1997). Aging and sexuality. *Western Journal of Medicine, 167*, 285–290.

Meston, C. M., & Frohlich, P. F. (2003). Love at first fright: Partner salience moderates roller coaster–induced excitation transfer. *Archives of Sexual Behavior, 32*, 537–544.

Metea, M. R., & Newman, E. A. (2006). Glial cells dilate and constrict blood vessels: A mechanism of neurovascular coupling. *The Journal of Neuroscience, 26*, 2862–2870.

Metzler, J., & Shepard, R. N. (1974). Transformational studies of the internal representation of three-dimensional objects. In R. Solso (ed.), *Theories in cognitive psychology: The Loyola Symposium* (pp. 147–201). Potomac, MD: Erlbaum.

Meyer, A. (ed.). (1981). The Hamburg Short Psychotherapy Comparison Experiment. *Psychotherapy and Psychosomatics, 35*, 81–207.

Meyer, I. H., Dietrich, J. D., & Schwartz, S. (2008). Lifetime prevalence of mental disorders and suicide attempts in diverse lesbian, gay, and bisexual populations. *American Journal of Public Health, 98*, 1004–1006.

Meyer, J. P., & Pepper, S. (1977). Need compatibility and marital adjustment in young married couples. *Journal of Personality and Social Psychology, 35*, 331–342.

Meyer, M. (2006). Commentary on "Innate sex differences supported by untypical traffic fatalities." *Chance, 19*, 18–19.

Meyer, S. E., & Carlson, G. A. (2008). Early-onset bipolar disorder. *Focus: the Journal of Lifelong Learning in Psychiatry, 6*, 271–283.

Michaels, J. W., Blommel, J. W., Brocato, R. M., Linkous, R. A., & Rowe, J. S. (1982). Social facilitation and inhibition in a natural setting. *Replications in Social Psychology, 2*, 21–24.

Michalski, R. L., & Shackelford, T. K. (2001). Methodology, birth order, intelligence, and personality. *American Psychologist, 56*, 520–521.

Mieda, M., Willie, J. T., Hara, J., Sinton, C. M., Sakurai, T., & Yanagisawa, M. (2004). Orexin peptides prevent cataplexy and improve wakefulness in an orexin neuron-ablated model of narcolepsy in mice. *Proceedings of the National Academy of Sciences, 10*, 4649–4654.

Mighty Optical Illusions. (2008). *Who says we don't have Barack Obama illusion.* Retrieved from http://www.moillusions.com/2008/12/who-says-we-dont-have-barack-obama.html, March 20, 2010.

Mignot, E. (2008). Why we sleep: The temporal organization of recovery. *PLoS Biology* 6(April): e106. doi:10.1371/journal.pbio.0060106 www.plosbiology.org.

Miklowitz, D. J., & Johnson, S. L. (2006). The psychopathology and treatment of bipolar disorder. *Annual Review of Clinical Psychology, 2,* 199–235.

Milgram, S. (1963). Behavioral study of obedience. *Journal of Abnormal and Social Psychology, 67,* 371–378.

Milgram, S. (1964). Issues in the study of obedience: A reply to Baumrind. *American Psychologist, 19,* 848–852.

Milgram, S. (1974). *Obedience to authority: An experimental view.* New York: Harper & Row.

Miller, E. R., Pastor-Barriuso, R., Dalal, D., Riemersma, R. A., Appel, L. A., & Guallar, E. (2005). Meta-analysis: High-dosage vitamin E supplementation may increase all-cause mortality. *Annals of Internal Medicine, 142,* 37–46.

Miller, F. G. (2004). Sham surgery: An ethical analysis. *Science and Engineering Ethics, 10,* 157.

Miller, F. G., & Rowold, K. L. (1979). Halloween masks and deindividuation. *Psychological Reports, 44,* 422.

Miller, G. A. (1956). The magical number seven, plus or minus two: Some limits on our capacity for processing information. *Psychological Review, 63,* 81–97.

Miller, K. F., Smith, C. M., Zhu, J., & Zhang, H. (1995). Preschool origins of cross-national differences in mathematical competence: The role of number-naming systems. *Psychological Science, 6,* 56–60.

Miller, L. K. (1999). The savant syndrome: Intellectual impairment and exceptional skill, *Psychological Bulletin, 125,* 31–46.

Miller, M. A., & Rahe, R. H. (1997). Life changes scaling for the 1990s. *Journal of Psychosomatic Research, 43,* 279–292.

Miller, N. E. (1978). Biofeedback and visceral learning. *Annual Review of Psychology* (Vol. 29). Palo Alto, CA: Annual Reviews.

Miller, R. H. (2006). The promise of stem cells for neural repair. *Brain Research, 1091,* 258–264.

Miller, S. D. (1989). Optical differences in cases of multiple personality disorder. *Journal of Nervous and Mental Disease, 177,* 480–486.

Miller, S. D., Duncan, B. L., & Hubble, M. A. (2005). Outcome-informed clinical work. In J. C. Norcross & M. R. Goldfried (eds.), *Handbook of psychotherapy integration* (2nd ed., pp. 84–102). New York: Oxford.

Miller, W. R., Brown, J. M., Simpson, T. L., Handmaker, N. S., Bien, T. H., Luckie, L. R., et al. (1995). What works? A methodological analysis of the alcohol treatment outcome literature. In R. K. Hester (ed.), *Handbook of alcoholism treatment approaches: Effective alternatives* (2nd ed., pp. 12–44). Boston: Allyn & Bacon.

Miller, W. R., & Hester, R. K. (1980). Treating the problem drinker: Modern approaches. In W. R. Miller (ed.), *The addictive behaviors: Treatment of alcoholism, drug abuse, smoking, and obesity* (pp. 11–141). Oxford, England: Pergamon Press.

Miller, W. R., & Rollnick, S. (2002). *Motivational interviewing: Preparing people for change.* New York: Guilford Press.

Miller, Z. (1999, August 31). Music fertilizes the mind. *Atlanta Journal Constitution,* A17.

Mills, A., & Lynn, S. J. (2000). Past-life experiences. In E. Cardeña, S. J. Lynn, & S. Krippner (eds.), *The varieties of anomalous experience.* New York: Guilford.

Milner, B. (1964) Some effects of frontal lobectomy in man. In J. M. Warren & K. Akert (eds.), *The frontal granular cortex and behavior* (pp. 313–334). New York: McGraw-Hill.

Milner, B. (1965) Visually guided maze learning in man: Effects of bilateral hippocampal, bilateral frontal and unilateral cerebral lesions. *Neuropsychologia, 3,* 317–338.

Milner, B. (1972). Disorders of learning and memory after temporal lobe lesions in man. *Clinical Neurosurgery, 19,* 421–446.

Milton, J., & Wiseman, R. (1999). Does psi exist? Lack of replication of an anomalous process of information transfer. *Psychological Bulletin, 125,* 387–391.

Mindell, A. (1990). *Working on yourself alone: Inner dreambody work.* New York: Arkana.

Mineka, S. (1992). Evolutionary memories, emotional processing, and the emotional disorders. In D. Medin (ed.), *The psychology of learning and motivation* (Vol. 28, pp. 161–206). San Diego, CA: Academic.

Mineka, S., & Cook, M. (1993). Mechanisms involved in the observational conditioning of fear. *Journal of Experimental Psychology: General, 122,* 23–38.

Mineka, S., & Thomas, C. (1999). Mechanisms of change in exposure therapy for anxiety disorders. In T. Dalgleish & M. J. Power (eds.), *Handbook of cognition and emotion* (pp. 747–764). Chichester, England: Wiley.

Mingroni, M. A. (2007). Resolving the IQ paradox: Heterosis as a cause of the Flynn effect and other trends. *Psychological Review, 114,* 806–829.

Minow, N. (2005, December 14). Are "educational" baby videos a scam? Research lacking to support claims. *Chicago Tribune.* Retrieved from http://blogfromthepond.blogspot.com/2005/12/are-educational-baby-videos-scam.html.

Minsky, M. (1986). *The society of mind.* New York: Simon and Schuster.

Mintz, I. (1977). A note on the addictive personality: Addiction to placebos. *American Journal of Psychiatry, 134,* 3–27.

Minuchin, S. (1974). *Families and family therapy.* Cambridge, MA: Harvard University Press.

Miranda, F. S. B., Caballero, R. B., Gomez, M. N. G., & Zamorano, M. A. M. (1981). Obediencia a la authoridad [Obedience to authority]. *Psiquis, 2,* 212–221.

Miranda, J., & Green, B. L. (1999). The need for mental health services research focusing on poor young women. *Journal of Mental Health Policy and Economics, 2,* 73–89.

Mischel, W. (1968). *Personality and assessment.* New York: Wiley.

Mischel, W. (1973). Toward a cognitive social learning reconceptualization of personality. *Psychological Review, 80,* 252–283.

Mischel, W. (1981). *Introduction to personality* (3rd ed.). New York: Holt, Rinehart and Winston.

Mischel, W., & Ayduk, O. (2004). Willpower in a cognitive-affective processing system: The dynamics of delay of gratification. In R. F. Baumeister & K. D. Vohs (eds.), *Handbook of self-regulation: Research, theory, and applications* (pp. 99–129). New York: Guilford.

Mischel, W., Shoda, Y., & Peake, P. K. (1988). The nature of adolescent competencies predicted by preschool delay of gratification. *Journal of Personality and Social Psychology, 54,* 687–696.

Mischel, W., Shoda, Y., & Rodriguez, M. L. (1989). Delay of gratification in children. *Science, 244,* 933–938.

Mishkin, M., Malamut, B., & Bachevalier, J. (1984). Memories and habits: Two neural systems. In G. Lynch, J. McGaugh, & N. Weinberger (eds.), *Neurobiology of Learning and Memory* (pp. 65–77). New York: Guilford.

Mita, T. H., Dermer, M., & Knight, J. (1977). Reversed facial images and the mere-exposure hypothesis. *Journal of Personality & Social Psychology, 13,* 89–111.

Mitchell, D. B. (2006). Nonconscious priming after 17 years—Invulnerable implicit memory? *Psychological Science, 17,* 925–929.

Mitchell, J. P., Macrae, C. N., & Banaji, M. R. (2006). Dissociable medial prefrontal contributions to judgments of similar and dissimilar others. *Neuron, 50,* 655–663.

Mitchell, S. A., & Black, M. J. (1995). *Freud and beyond: A history of modern psychoanalytic thought.* New York: Basic Books.

Mittal, V. A., Tesser, K. D., Trotman, H. D., Esterberg, M., Dhruv, S. H., Simenova, D. I., et al. (2007). Movement abnormalities and the progression of prodromal symptomatology in adolescents at risk for psychotic disorders. *Journal of Abnormal Psychology, 116,* 260–267.

Mix, K. S. (1999). Similarity and numerical equivalence appearances count. *Cognitive Development, 14,* 269–297.

Mix, K. S., Huttenlocher, J., & Levine, S. C. (1996). Do preschool children recognize auditory-visual numerical correspondences? *Child Development, 67,* 1592–1608.

Mlodinow, L. (2008). *The drunkard's walk: How randomness rules our lives.* New York: Vintage Books.

Mobbs, D., Greicius, M.D., Abdel-Azim, E., Menon, V., & Reiss, A. L. (2003) Humor modulates the mesolimbic reward centers. *Neuron, 40,* 1041–1048.

Moffitt, T. E. (1983). The learning theory model of punishment: Implications for delinquency deterrence. *Criminal Justice and Behavior, 10,* 131–158.

Molé, P. (2006). Skepticism in the classroom: A high school science teacher in the trenches. *Skeptic, 12*(3), 62–70.

Molina, B., & Pelham, W. (2003). Childhood predictors of adolescent substance use in a longitudinal study of children with ADHD. *Journal of Abnormal Psychology, 112,* 497–507.

Monahan, J. (1984). The prediction of violent behavior: Toward a second generation of theory and policy. *American Psychologist, 141,* 10–15.

Monahan, J. (1992). Mental disorder and violent behavior: Perceptions and evidence. *American Psychologist, 47,* 511–521.

Monahan, J., Steadman, H. J., Appelbaum, P. S., Robbins, P. C., Mulvey, E. P., Silver, E., et al. (2000). Developing a clinically useful actuarial tool for assessing violence risk. *British Journal of Psychiatry, 176,* 312–319.

Monastra, V. J. (2008). *Unlocking the potential of patients with ADHD.* Washington, DC: American Psychological Association.

Monroe, R. (1955). *Schools of psychoanalytic thought.* New York: Dryden.

Monroe, S. M. (1983). Major and minor events as predictors of psychological distress: Further issues and findings. *Journal of Behavioral Medicine, 6,* 189–205.

Monroe, S. M. (2008). Modern approaches to conceptualizing and measuring human life stress. In S. Nolen-Hoeksema, T. D. Cannon, & T. Widiger (eds.), *Annual Review of Clinical Psychology* (pp. 37–52). Palo Alto, CA: Annual Reviews.

Monte, C. F. (1995). *Beneath the mask: An introduction to theories of personality.* Fort Worth, TX: Harcourt Brace.

Monteith, M., & Winters, J. (2002). Why we hate. *Psychology Today, 35*(3), 44–52.

Monti, P. M., Gulliver, S. B., & Myers, M. G. (1994). Social skills training for alcoholics: Assessment and treatment. *Alcohol and Alcoholism, 29,* 627–637.

Montoya, R. M., Horton, R. S., & Kirchner, J. (2008). Is actual similarity necessary for attraction? A meta-analysis of actual and perceived similarity. *Journal of Social and Personal Relationships, 25,* 889–992.

Moody, R. A. (1975). *Life after life.* Covington, GA: Mockingbird Books.

Moody, R. A. (1977). *Reflections on life after life.* St. Simon's Island, GA: Mockingbird Books.

Mook, D. (1983). In defense of external invalidity. *American Psychologist, 38,* 379–387.

Moon, C., Cooper, R. P., & Fifer, W. P. (1993). Two-day-olds prefer their native language. *Infant Behavior & Development, 16,* 495–500.

Moon, Y. (1986). A review of cross-cultural studies on moral judgment development using the Defining Issues Test. *Behavior Science Research, 20,* 147–177.

Moons, W. G., & Mackie, D. M. (2007). Thinking straight while seeing red: The influence of anger on information processing. *Personality and Social Psychology Bulletin, 33,* 706–720.

Moore, B., & Fine, B. (eds.). (1995). *Psychoanalysis: The major concepts.* New Haven, CT: Yale University Press.

Moore, D. W. (2005, June 16). Three in four Americans believe in the paranormal. *Gallup Poll News Service.* Retrieved February 20, 2007, from www.gallup.com/poll/content/default.aspx?ci=16915.

Moore, R. J. (2008) (ed.). *Biobehavioral approaches to pain.* Netherlands: Springer.

Moore, T. E. (1992). Subliminal perception: Facts and fallacies. *Skeptical Inquirer, 16,* 273–281.

Moore, T. E. (1996). Scientific consensus and expert testimony: Lessons from the Judas Priest trial. *Skeptical Inquirer, 20,* 32–38.

Moore, T. M., Scarpa, A., & Raine, A. (2002). A meta-analysis of serotonin metabolite 5-HIAA and antisocial behavior. *Aggressive Behavior, 28,* 299–316.

Moreland, R. L., & Beach, R. (1992). Exposure effects in the classroom: The development of affinity among students. *Journal of Experimental Social Psychology, 28,* 255–276.

Morelock, M., & Feldman, D. H. (1993). Prodigies and savants: What they have to tell us about giftedness and human cognition. In K. Heller, F. Monks, & H. Passow (eds.), *International handbook for research on giftedness and talent* (pp. 161–181). Oxford, England: Pergamon Press.

Moreno, C., Laje, G., Blanco, C., Jiang, H., Schmidt, A. B., & Olfson, M. (2007). National trends in the outpatient diagnosis and treatment of bipolar disorder in youth. *Archives of General Psychiatry, 64,* 1032–1039.

Morewedge, C. K., & Norton, M. I. (2009). When dreaming is believing: The (motivated) interpretation of dreams. *Journal of Personality and Social Psychology, 96,* 249–264.

Morgan, C. D., & Murray, H. A. (1935). A method for investigating fantasies. *Archives of Neurology and Psychiatry, 34,* 289–304.

Morier, D., & Podlipentseva, J. (1997, April). Mortality salience effects on paranormal beliefs and essay ratings. Paper presented at the 77th Annual Meeting of the Western Psychological Association, Seattle, WA.

Morin, C. M., & Edinger, J. D. (2009). Sleep/wake disorders. In P. H. Blaney & T. Millon (eds.), *Oxford textbook of psychopathology* (pp. 506–526). New York: Oxford University Press.

Morokuma, S., Fukushima, K., Kawai, N., Tomonaga, M., Satoh, S., & Nakano, H. (2004). Fetal habituation correlates with functional brain development. *Behavioural Brain Research, 153,* 459–463.

Morris, M. W., & Peng, K. (1994). Culture and cause: American and Chinese attributions for social and physical events. *Journal of Personality and Social Psychology, 67,* 949–971.

Morrison, J. (1997). *When psychological problems mask medical disorders: A guide for psychotherapists.* New York: Guilford.

Morrison, T., & Morrison, M. (1995). A meta-analytic assessment of the predictive validity of the quantitative and verbal components of the Graduate Record Examination with grade point average representing the criterion of graduate success. *Educational & Psychological Measurement, 55,* 309–316.

Morse G. (1999). The nocebo effect: Scattered findings suggest that negative thinking can harm patients' health. *Hippocrates, 10.* Retrieved February 5, 2007, from http://www.hippocrates.com/archive/november1999/11departments/11integrative.html.

Morse, W. H., & Skinner, B. F. (1957). A second type of superstition in the pigeon. *American Journal of Psychology, 70,* 308–311.

Mortensen, E. L., Michaelson, K. F., Sanders, S. A., & Reinisch, J. M. (2002). The association between duration of breastfeeding and adult intelligence. *Journal of the American Medical Association, 287,* 2365–2371.

Morton, E. W. (1977). On the occurrence and significance of motivation-structural roles in some bird and mammal sounds. *American Naturalist, 111,* 855–869.

Morton, E. W. (1982). Grading, discreteness, redundancy, and motivation-structural rules. In D. E. Kroodmsa & E. H. Miller (eds.), *Acoustic communication in birds* (pp. 182–212). New York: Academic Press.

Moscovitch, M., Rosenbaum, R. S., Gilboa, A., Addis, D. R., Westmacott, R., Grady, C., et al. (2005). Functional neuroanatomy of remote episodic, semantic and spatial memory: A unified account based on multiple trace theory. *Journal of Anatomy, 207,* 35–66.

Motivala, S., & Irwin, M. R. (2007). Sleep and immunity: Cytokine pathways linking sleep and health outcomes. *Psychological Science, 16,* 21–25.

Motta, R. W., Little, S. G., & Tobin, M. I. (1993). The use and abuse of human figure drawings. *School Psychology Quarterly, 8,* 162–169.

Moulton, S. T., & Kosslyn, S. M. (2008). Using neuroimaging to resolve the psi debate. *Journal of Cognitive Neuroscience, 20,* 182–192.

Mowrer, O. H. (1947). On the dual nature of learning—A re-interpretation of "conditioning" and "problem-solving." *Harvard Educational Review, 17,* 102–148.

Mroczek, D. K., & Kolarz, C. M. (1998). The effect of age on positive and negative affect: A developmental perspective on happiness. *Journal of Personality and Social Psychology, 75,* 1333–1349.

Mroczek, D. K., & Spiro, A. (2005). Change in life satisfaction during adulthood: Findings from the Veteran Affairs normative aging study. *Journal of Personality and Social Psychology, 88,* 189–192.

Mrosovsky, N., & Powley, T. L. (1977). Set points for body weight and fat. *Behavioral Biology, 20,* 205–223.

Msetfi, R. M., Murphy, R. A., Simpson, J., & Kornbrot, D. E. (2005). Depressive realism and outcome density bias in contingency judgments: The effect of the context and inter-trial interval. *Journal of Experimental Psychology: General, 134,* 10–22.

Mueser, K. T., & Liberman, R. P. (1995). Behavior therapy in practice. In B. Bongar & L. E. Beutler (eds.), *Comprehensive textbook of psychotherapy: Theory and practice* (pp. 84–110). New York: Oxford University Press.

Mueser, K. T., & McGurk, S. R. (2004). Schizophrenia. *Lancet, 363,* 2063–2072.

Mukamal, K. J., Chung, H., Jenny, N. S., Kuller, L. H., Longstreth, W. T., Jr., Mittleman, M. A., et al. (2005). Alcohol use and risk of ischemic stroke among older adults: The cardiovascular health study. *Stroke, 36,* 1830–1834.

Mukamal, K. J., Cinigrave, K. M., Mittleman, M. A., Camargo, C. A., Stampfer, M. J., Willett, W. C., et al. (2003). Roles of drinking pattern and type of alcohol consumed in coronary heart disease in men. *New England Journal of Medicine, 348,* 109–118.

Muller, F. J., Snyder, E. Y., & Loring, J. F. (2006). Gene therapy: can neural stem cells deliver? *Nature Reviews Neuroscience, 7,* 75–84.

Munafo, M. R., Yalcin, B., Willis-Owen, S. A., & Flint, J. (2008). Association of the dopamine D4 receptor (DRD4) gene and approach-related personality traits: Meta-analysis and new data. *Biological Psychiatry, 63,* 197–206.

Murphy, C. (1999). Loss of olfactory function in dementing disease. *Physiology & Behavior, 66,* 177–182.

Murphy, F. C., Nimmo-Smith, I., & Lawrence, A. D. (2003). Functional neuroanatomy of emotion: A meta-analysis. *Cognitive, Affective, & Behavioral Neuroscience, 3,* 207–233.

Murphy, J. B. (1976). Psychiatric labeling in cross-cultural perspective: Similar kinds of disturbed behavior appear to be labeled abnormal in diverse cultures. *Science, 191,* 1019–1028.

Murray, H. A. (1938). *Explorations in personality.* New York: Oxford University Press.

Murray, H. A. (1971). *Thematic apperception test: Manual.* Cambridge, MA: Harvard University Press. (Original work published 1943).

Murstein, B. I. (1977). The stimulus-value-role (SVR) theory of dyadic relationship. In S. Duck (ed.), *Theory and practice in interpersonal attraction* (pp. 105–127). New York: Academic Press.

Muscarella, F., & Cunningham, M. R. (1996). The evolutionary significance and social perception of male pattern baldness and facial hair. *Ethology and Sociobiology, 17,* 99–117.

Musella, D. P. (2005, September/October). Gallup poll shows that Americans' belief in the paranormal persists. *Skeptical Inquirer, 29,* 5.

Mutrie, N. (1988). Exercise as a treatment for moderate depression in the UK health service. *Sport, Health, Psychology and Exercise Symposium Proceedings* (pp. 96–105). London: The Sports Council and Health Education Authority.

Myers, D. G. (1993a). *Social psychology.* New York: McGraw Hill.

Myers, D. G. (1993b). *The pursuit of happiness.* London: Aquarian.

Myers D. G. (2000). The funds, friends, and faith of happy people. *American Psychologist, 55,* 56–67.

Myers, D. G. (2002). *Intuition: Its powers and perils.* New Haven, CT: Yale University Press.

Myers, D. G., & Bishop, G. D. (1970). Discussion effects on racial attitudes. *Science, 169,* 778–789.

Myers, D. G., & Diener, E. (1996). The pursuit of happiness. *Scientific American,* 70–72.

Myers, D. G., & Kaplan, M. F. (1976). Group-induced polarization in simulated juries. *Personality and Social Psychology Bulletin, 2,* 63–66.

Myers, D. G., & Lamm, H. (1976). The group polarization phenomenon. *Psychological Bulletin, 83,* 602–627.

Myrtek, M. (2001). Meta-analyses of prospective studies on coronary heart disease, type A personality, and hostility. *International Journal of Cardiology, 79,* 245–251.

Nabi, H., Kivimaki, M., Zins, M., Elovainio, M., Consoli, S. M., Cordier, S., et al. (2008). Does personality predict mortality? Results from the GAZEL French prospective cohort study. *International Journal of Epidemiology, 37,* 386–396.

Nachev, P., & Husain, M. (2006). Disorders of visual attention and the posterior parietal cortex. *Cortex, 42,* 766–773.

Nahemow, L., & Lawton, M. P. (1975). Similarity and propinquity in friendship formation. *Journal of Personality and Social Psychology, 32,* 205–213.

Nahin, R. L., Barnes, P. M., Stussman, B. J., & Bloom, B. (2009). Costs of complementary and alternative medicine (CAM) and frequency of visits to CAM practitioners: United States, 2007. *National health statistics reports*; no. 18. Hyattsville, MD: National Center for Health Statistics.

Nairn, A. (1980). *The reign of ETS: The corporation that makes up minds.* Washington, DC: Ralph Nader.

Naito, E. (2004). Sensing limb movements in the motor cortex: How humans sense limb movement. *Neuroscientist, 10,* 73–82.

Namy, L. L., & Waxman, S. R. (2000). Naming and exclaiming: Infants' sensitivity to naming contexts. *Journal of Cognition and Development, 1,* 405–428.

Nash, M. R. (1987). What, if anything, is regressed about hypnotic age regression? A review of the empirical literature. *Psychological Bulletin, 102,* 42–52.

Nash, M. R., & Barnier, A. (eds.). (2008). *The Oxford handbook of hypnosis.* New York: Oxford Press.

Nass, C., Brave, S., & Takayama, L. (2006). Socializing consistency: From technical homogeneity to human epitome. In P. Zhang & D. Galletta (eds.), *Human-computer interactions in management information systems: Foundations* (pp. 373–391). Armonk, NY: M.E. Sharpe.

National Cancer Institute. (2000, December 12). *Fact sheet: Questions and answers about smoking cessation.* Retrieved November 2005 from http://www.cancer.gov/cancertopics/factsheet/tobacco/cessation.

National Center for Complementary and Alternative Medicine. (2002). *What is complementary and alternative medicine?* (publication no. D156). Gaithersburg, MD: NCCAM.

National Center for Health Statistics. (2005). *Life expectancy at birth, 65 and 85 years of age, United States, selected years 1900–2004.* Retrieved from http://209.217.72.34/aging/TableViewer/tableView.aspx?ReportId=438.

National Heart, Lung, and Blood Institute. (1998). *Behavioral research in cardiovascular, lung, and blood health and disease.* Washington, DC: U.S. Department of Health and Human Services.

National Institute of Mental Health. (2004). *Suicide facts and statistics, U.S., 2001.* U.S. Department of Health and Human Services. Posted April 9, 2004, at www.nimh.nih.gov/tools/helpusing.cfm.

National Institute on Alcohol Abuse and Alcoholism. (1998, July). *Alcohol and sleep,* no. 41. http://pubs.niaaa.nih.gov/publications/aa41.htm.

National Institute on Alcohol Abuse and Alcoholism. (2000, July). *Alcohol alert. From genes to geography: The cutting edge of alcohol research.* No 48. http://pubs.niaaa.nih.gov/publications/aa48.htm.

National Opinion Research Center (2003). *General social surveys, 1972–2002: Cumulative codebook.* Chicago: Author.

National Research Council. (1998). Preventing reading difficulties in young children. In C. E. Snow, M. S. Burns, & P. Griffin (eds.), Washington, DC: National Academies Press.

National Research Council. (2003). *The polygraph and lie detection.* Committee to review the scientific evidence on the polygraph. Washington, DC: National Academic Press.

National Science Foundation. (2003). Table C-2: Employed U.S. scientists and engineers, by level and field of highest degree attained, sex, and employment sector: 1999. Retrieved, 14 September 14, 2008, from http://www.nsf.gov/statistics/us-workforce/1999/dst1999.htm.

Navarro, A. M. (1993). Effectiveness of psychotherapy with Latinos in the United States: A revised meta-analysis. *Interamerican Journal of Psychology, 27,* 131–146.

Neath, I., & Surprenant, A. M. (2003). *Human memory* (2nd ed.). Pacific Grove, CA: Wadsworth.

Needham, A., & Baillargeon, R. (1993). Intuitions about support in 4.5-month-old infants. *Cognition, 47,* 121–148.

Neely, J. (1976) Semantic priming and retrieval from lexical memory: Evidence for facilitory and inhibitory processes. *Memory and Cognition, 4,* 648–654.

Neher, A. (1990). *The psychology of transcendence.* New York: Dover.

Neisser, U. (1967). *Cognitive psychology.* New York: Appleton-Century-Crofts.

Neisser, U. (1998). *The rising curve: Long-term gains in IQ and related measures.* Washington, DC: American Psychological Association.

Neisser, U., Boodoo, G., Bouchard, T. J., Jr., Boykin, A. W., Brody, N., Ceci, S. J., et al. (1996). Intelligence: Knowns and unknowns. *American Psychologist, 51,* 77–101.

Neisser, U., & Harsch, N. (1992). Phantom flashbulbs: False recollections of hearing the news about *Challenger.* In E. Winograd & U. Neisser (eds.), *Affect and accuracy in recall: Studies of flashbulb memories* (pp. 9–31). Cambridge, England: Cambridge University.

Neisser, U., & Hyman, I. (eds.). (1999). *Memory observed: Remembering in natural contexts.* New York: Worth Publishers.

Nelson, K. (1977). The syntagmatic-paradigmatic shift revisited: A review of research and theory. *Psychological Bulletin, 84,* 93–116.

Nelson, K., & Hudson, J. (1988). Scripts and memory function relationships in development. In F. E. Weinert, & M. Perlmutter (eds.) *Memory development: Universal changes and individual differences* (pp. 147–168). Hillsdale, NJ: Lawrence Erlbaum Associates.

Nelson, R. E., & Craighead, W. E. (1977), Selective recall of positive and negative feedback, self-control behaviors, and depression. *Journal of Abnormal Psychology, 86,* 379–388.

Nelson, T. O. (1985). Ebbinghaus's contribution to the measurement of retention: Savings during relearning. *Journal of Experimental Psychology: Human Learning and Memory, 11,* 472–479.

Nemeroff, C. B., Kalali, A., Keller, M. B., Charney, D. S., Lenderts, S. E., Cascade, E. F., et al. (2007). Impact of publicity concerning pediatric suicidality data on physician practice patterns in the United States. *Archives of General Psychiatry, 64,* 397.

Nesse, R., & Ellsworth, P. (2009). Evolution, emotions, and emotional disorders. *American Psychologist, 64,* 129–139.

Nettle, D. (2005). *Happiness: The science behind your smile.* Oxford, England: Oxford University Press.

Neville, R. (1978). Psychosurgery. In W. Reich (ed.), *Encyclopedia of bioethics,* Vol. 3 (pp. 1387–1391). New York: Macmillan-Free Press.

Newberg, A., Alavi, A., Baime, M., Pourdehnad, M., Santanna, J., & d'Aquili, E. (2001). The measurement of regional cerebral blood flow during the complex cognitive task of meditation: A preliminary psychiatry research study. *Neuroimaging, 106,* 113–122.

Newcomb, M. D., & Bentler, P. M. (1988). Impact of adolescent drug use and social support on problems of young adults: A longitudinal analysis. *Journal of Abnormal Psychology, 97,* 64–75.

Newman, A. J., Bavelier, D., Corina, D., Jezzard, P., & Neville, H. J. (2002). A critical period for right hemisphere recruitment in American Sign Language processing. *Nature Neuroscience, 5,* 76–80.

Newman, J. P., & Kosson, D. S. (1986). Passive avoidance learning in psychopathic and nonpsychopathic offenders. *Journal of Abnormal Psychology, 95,* 252–256.

Newport, E. L. (1990). Maturational constraints on language learning. *Cognitive Science, 14,* 11–28.

Newport, E. L., Bavelier, D., & Neville, H. J. (2001). Critical thinking about critical periods: Perspectives on a critical period for language acquisition. In E. Dupoux (ed.), *Language, brain and cognitive development: Essays in honor of Jacques Mehler.* Cambridge, MA: MIT Press.

Newport, E. L., & Meier, R. (1985). The acquisition of American Sign Language. In D. Slobin (ed.), *The cross-linguistic study of language acquisition,* Vol. 1 (pp. 881–938). Hillsdale, NJ: Erlbaum.

Ngandu, T., von Strauss, E., Helkala, E. L., Winblad, B., Nissinen, A., Tuomilehto, J., et al. (2007). Education and dementia: What lies behind the association? *Neurology, 69,* 1442–1450.

Niaura, R., Todaro, J. F., Stroud, L., Spiro, A., Ward, K. D., & Weiss, S. (2002). Hostility, the metabolic syndrome, and incident coronary heart disease. *Health Psychology, 21,* 588–593.

Nickel, J. (2000, May/June). Aura photography: A candid shot. *Skeptical Inquirer, 24,* 15–17.

Nickell, J. (1993). *Looking for a miracle: Weeping icons, relics, stigmata, visions and healing cures.* New York: Prometheus Books.

Nickerson, R. S. (1998). Confirmation bias: A ubiquitous phenomenon in many guises. *Review of General Psychology, 2,* 175–220.

Nickerson, R. S., & Adams, J. J. (1979). Long-term memory for a common object. *Cognitive Psychology, 11,* 287–307.

Nicol, S. E., & Gottesman, I. I. (1983). Clues to the genetics and neurobiology of schizophrenia. *American Scientist, 71,* 398–404.

Niedenthal, P. M. (2007). Embodying emotion. *Science, 316,* 1002–1005.

Nielsen, T. A. (1999). Mentation during sleep: The NREM/REM distinction. In R. Lydic & H. A. Baghdoyan (eds.), *Handbook of behavioral state control: Cellular and molecular mechanisms* (pp. 102–120). Boca Raton, FL: CRC Press.

Nigg, J. T., & Goldsmith, H. H. (1994). Genetics of personality disorders: Perspectives from personality and psychopathology research. *Psychological Bulletin, 115,* 346–380.

Nigro, G., & Neisser, N. (1983). Point of view in personal memories. *Cognitive Psychology, 15,* 467–482.

Nisbett, R. E. (1972). Hunger, obesity, and the ventromedial hypothalamus. *Psychological Review, 79,* 433–453.

Nisbett, R. E. (1995). Race, IQ and scientism. In S. Fraser (ed.), *The bell curve wars* (pp. 36–57). New York: HarperCollins.

Nisbett, R. E. (2003). *The geography of thought: How Asians and Westerners think differently . . . and why.* New York: Free Press.

Nisbett, R. E. (2009). *Intelligence and how to get it: Why schools and cultures count.* New York: W.W. Norton and Company.

Nisbett, R. E., & Cohen, D. (1996). *Culture of honor: The psychology of violence in the South.* Boulder, CO: Westview.

Nisbett, R. E., Peng, K. P., Choi, I., & Norenzayan, A. (2001). Culture and systems of thought: Holistic versus analytic cognition. *Psychological Review, 108,* 291–310.

Nisbett, R. E., & Ross, L. D. (1980). *Human Inference: Strategies and shortcomings of social judgment.* Englewood Cliffs, NJ: Prentice-Hall.

Nisbett, R. E., & Wilson, T. D. (1977). Telling more than we can know: Verbal reports on mental processes. *Psychological Review, 84,* 231–259.

Noble, J., & McConkey, K. M. (1995). Hypnotic sex change: Creating and challenging a delusion in the laboratory. *Journal of Abnormal Psychology, 104,* 69–74.

Noel, J. G., Wann, D. L., & Branscombe, N. R. (1995). Peripheral ingroup membership status and public negativity toward outgroups. *Journal of Personality and Social Psychology, 68,* 127–137.

Noelle-Neumann, E. (1970). Wanted: Rules for wording structured questionnaires. *Public Opinion Quarterly, 34,* 191–201.

Nolen-Hoeksema, S. (1987). Sex differences in unipolar depression: Evidence and theory. *Psychological Bulletin, 101,* 259–282.

Nolen-Hoeksema, S. (2000). The role of rumination in depressive disorders and mixed anxiety/depressive symptoms. *Journal of Abnormal Psychology, 109,* 504–511.

Nolen-Hoeksema, S. (2002). Gender differences in depression. In I. H. Gotlib & C. L. Hammen (eds.), *Handbook of depression* (pp. 492–509). New York: Guilford.

Nolen-Hoeksema, S. (2003). *Women who think too much: How to break free of overthinking and reclaim your life.* New York: Holt.

Nolen-Hoeksema, S., & Girgus, J. S. (1994). The emergence of gender differences in depression during adolescence. *Psychological Bulletin, 115,* 424–443.

Nondahl, D. M., Cruickshanks, K. J., Dalton, D. S., Klein, B., Klein, R., Schuber, C. R., et al. (2007). The impact of tinnitus on quality of life in older adults. *Journal of the American Academy of Audiology, 18,* 257–266.

Norcross, J. C. (2005). A primer on psychotherapy integration. In J. C. Norcross & M. R. Goldfried (eds.), *Handbook of psychotherapy integration* (2nd ed., pp. 3–23). New York: Oxford University Press.

Norcross, J. C., & Beutler, L. (1997). Determining the relationship of choice in brief therapy. In J. N. Butcher (ed.), *Personality assessment in managed health care* (pp. 42–60). New York: Oxford University Press.

Norcross, J. C., Garofalo, A., & Koocher, G. (2006). Discredited psychological treatments and tests: A Delphi poll. *Professional Psychology: Research and Practice, 137,* 515–522.

Norcross, J. C., Hedges, M., & Castle, P. H. (2002, Spring). Psychologists conducting psychotherapy in 2001: A study of the Division 29 membership. *Psychotherapy, 39,* 97–102.

Norcross, J. C., Karpiak, C. P., & Santoro, S. O. (2005). Clinical psychologists across the years: The Division of Clinical Psychology from 1960 to 2003. *Journal of Clinical Psychology, 61,* 1467–1483.

Norcross, J. C., Ratzin, A. C., & Payne, D. (1989). Ringing in the new year: The change processes and reported outcomes of resolutions. *Addictive Behaviors, 14,* 205–212.

Norcross, J. C., Strausser, D. J., & Missar, C. D. (1988). The process and outcomes of psychotherapists' personal treatment experiences. *Psychotherapy, 25,* 36–43.

Norcross, J. C., & Vangarelli, D. J. (1989). The resolution solution: Longitudinal examination of New Year's change attempts. *Journal of Substance Abuse, 1,* 127–134.

Norem, J. K. (2001). *The positive power of negative thinking.* New York: Basic Books.

Norem, J. K., & Cantor, N. (1986). Defensive pessimism: "Harnessing" anxiety as motivation. *Journal of Personality and Social Psychology, 52,* 1208–1217.

Norem, J. K., & Chang, E. C. (2002). The positive psychology of negative thinking. *Journal of Clinical Psychology, 37,* 1204–1238.

Norenzayan, A., & Hansen, I. G. (2006). Belief in supernatural agents in the face of death. *Personality and Social Psychology Bulletin, 32,* 174–187.

Norman, D. (1998). *The design of everyday things.* London: MIT Press.

North, A. C., Linley, P. A., & Hargreaves, D. J. (2000). Social loafing in a co-operative classroom task. *Educational Psychology, 20,* 389–392.

Novaco, R. W. (1994). Clinical problems of anger and its assessment and regulation through a stress coping skills approach. In W. O'Donohue & L.

Krasner (eds.), *Handbook of skills training* (pp. 320–338). New York: Pergamon Press.

Noyes, R., & Kletti, R. (1976). Depersonalization in the face of life-threatening danger: An interpretation. *Omega, 7,* 103–114.

Noyes, R., Jr. (2001). Comorbidity in generalized anxiety disorder. *Psychiatric Clinics of North America 24,* 41–55.

Nuttin, J. M. (1985). Narcissism beyond Gestalt and awareness: The name letter effect. *European Journal of Social Psychology, 15,* 353–361.

Nygaard, L. C., Cook, A. E., & Namy, L. L. (2009). Sound to meaning correspondences facilitate word learning. *Cognition, 112,* 181–186.

O'Brien, T. (1990). *The things they carried.* New York: Broadway.

O'Connor, T. G., Deater-Deckard, K., Fulker, D., Rutter, M., & Plomin, R. (1998). Genotype-environment correlations in late childhood and early adolescence: Antisocial behavioral problems and coercive parenting. *Developmental Psychology, 34,* 970–981.

O'Connor, T. G., & Rutter, M. (2000). Attachment disorder behavior following early severe deprivation: Extension and longitudinal follow-up. *Journal of the American Academy of Child and Adolescent Psychiatry, 39,* 703–712.

O'Donohue, W. T., Lilienfeld, S. O., & Fowler, K. A. (2007). Science is an essential safeguard against human error. In S. O. Lilienfeld & W. T. O'Donohue (eds.), *The great ideas of clinical science: 17 principles that every mental health professional should understand* (pp. 3–27). New York: Routledge.

O'Keefe, D. J., & Figge, M. (1997). A guilt-based explanation of the door-in-the-face influence strategy. *Human Communication Research, 24,* 64–81.

O'Keefe, D. J., & Hale, S. L. (2001). An odds-ratio-based meta-analysis of research on the door-in-the-face influence strategy. *Communication Reports, 14,* 31–38.

Ocampo-Garces, A., Molina, E., Rodriguez, A., & Vivaldi, E. A. (2000). Homeostasis of REM sleep after total and selective sleep deprivation in the rat. *Journal of Neurophysiology, 84,* 2699–2702.

Ochsner, K. N., Bunge, S. A., Gross, J. J., & Gabieli, J. D. E. (2002). Rethinking feelings: An fMRI study of the cognitive regulation of emotion. *Journal of Cognitive Neuroscience, 14,* 1215–1229.

Offer, D., & Schoenert-Reichl, K. A. (1992). Debunking the myths of adolescence: Findings from recent research. *Journal of the American Academy of Child and Adolescent Psychiatry, 31,* 1003–1014.

Office of Technology Assessment. (1990). *The use of integrity tests for pre-employment screening.* Washington, DC: U.S. Congress Office of Technology Assessment.

Offit, P. A. (2008). Vaccines and autism revisited: The Hanna Poling case. *New England Journal of Medicine, 358,* 2089–2091.

Ogawa, S., Lee, T. M., Kay, A. R., & Tank, D. W. (1990). Brain magnetic resonance imaging with contrast dependent on blood oxygenation. *Proceedings of the National Academy of Sciences, U.S.A., 87,* 9868–9872.

Ogden, C., Carroll, M., Curtin, L., McDowell, M., Tabak, C., & Flegal, K. (2006). Prevalence of overweight and obesity in the Unites States, 1999–2004. *Journal of the American Medical Association, 295,* 1549–1555.

Ogden, C. A., Rich, M. E., Schork, N. J., Paulus, M. P., Geyer, M. A., Lohr, J. B., et al. (2004). Candidate genes, pathways and mechanisms for bipolar (manic–depressive) and related disorders: An expanded convergent functional genomics approach. *Molecular Psychiatry, 9,* 1007–1029.

Ogden, C. L., Carroll, M. D., McDowell, M. A., & Flegal, K. M. (2007). Obesity among adults in the United States—no change since 2003–2004. *NCHS data brief no. 1* Hyattesville, MD: National Center for Health Statistics.

Ogrodniczuk, J. S., & Piper, W. E. (1999). Use of transference interpretations in dynamically oriented individual psychotherapy for patients with personality disorders. *Journal of Personality Disorders, 13,* 297–311.

Ohayon, M. M. (2000). Prevalence of hallucinations and their pathological associations in the general population. *Psychiatry Research, 97,* 153–164.

Ohayon, M. M. (2002). Epidemiology of insomnia: What we know and what we still need to learn. *Sleep Medicine Reviews, 6,* 97–111.

Ohlemiller, K. K., & Frisina, R. D. (2008). Age-related hearing loss and its cellular and molecular bases. In J. Schacht, A. N. Popper, & R. R. Fay (eds.), *Springer handbook of auditory research: Auditory trauma, protection, and repair* (pp.145–162). Netherlands: Springer.

Ohman, A., & Mineka, S. (2001). Fears, phobias, and preparedness: Toward an evolved module of fear and fear learning. *Psychological Review, 108,* 483–522.

Ohman, A., & Mineka, S. (2003). The malicious serpent: Snakes as a prototypical stimulus for an evolved module of fear. *Current Directions in Psychological Science, 12,* 5–9.

Oldfield, K. (1998). The GRE as fringe science. *Skeptic, 6*(1), 68–72.

Olds, J. (1959). Studies of neuropharmacologicals by electrical and chemical manipulation of the brain in animals with chronically implanted electrodes. In P. B. Bradley, P. Deniker, and C. Radouco-Thomas (eds.), *Neuro-Psychopharmacology,* (pp. 20–32). Amsterdam: Elsevier.

Olfson, M., Marcus, S., Sackheim, H. A., Thompson, J., & Pincus, H. A. (1998). Use of ECT for the inpatient treatment of recurrent major depression. *American Journal of Psychiatry, 155,* 22–29.

Oliver, M. B., & Hyde, J. S. (1993). Gender differences in sexuality: A meta-analysis. *Psychological Bulletin, 114,* 29–51.

Olkin, R., & Taliaferro, G. (2005). Evidence-based practices have ignored people with disabilities. In J. C. Norcross, L. E. Beutler, & R. F. Levant (eds.), *Evidence-based practices in mental health* (pp. 353–358). Washington, DC: American Psychological Association.

Olsson, A., Ebert, J. P., Banaji, M. R., & Phelps, E. A. (2005). The role of social groups in the persistence of learned fear. *Science, 309,* 785–787.

Oltmanns, T. F., & Turkheimer, E. (2009). Person perception and personality pathology. *Current Directions in Psychological Science. 18,* 32–36.

Olweus, D. (1993). *Bullying at school: What we know and what we can do.* Oxford, UK: Blackwell.

Ondeck, D. M. (2003). Impact of culture on pain. *Home Health Care Management Practice, 15,* 255–257.

Ones, D. S., Viswesvaran, C., & Dilchert, S. (2005). Personality at work: Raising awareness and correcting misconceptions. *Human Performance, 18,* 389–404.

Ones, D. S., Viswesvaran, C., & Schmidt, F. L. (1993). Comprehensive meta-analysis of integrity test validities. *Journal of Applied Psychology, 78,* 679–703.

Oppenheim, R. W. (1991). Cell death during development of the nervous system. *Annual Review of Neuroscience, 14,* 453–501.

Orathinkal, J., & Vansteenwegen, A. (2006). Religiosity and marital satisfaction. *Contemporary Family Therapy, 28,* 497–504.

Orlanksy, M. D., & Bonvillian, J. D. (1984). The role of iconicity in early sign language acquisition. *Journal of Speech and Hearing Disorders, 49,* 287–292.

Orlinsky, D. E., Grawe, K., & Parks, B. K. (1994). Process and outcome in psychotherapy—Noch einmal. In A. E. Bergin & S. L. Garfield (eds.), *Handbook of psychotherapy and behavior change* (4th ed., pp. 270–376). New York: Wiley.

Orlinksy, D. E., & Howard, K. I. (1986). Process and outcome in psychotherapy. In S. L. Garfield & A. E. Bergin (eds.), *Handbook of psychotherapy and behavior change* (3rd ed., pp. 311–384). New York: Wiley.

Orlovskaya, D. D., Uranova, N. A., Zimina, I. S., Kolomeets, N. S., Vikherva, O. V., Rachmanova, V. I., et al. (1999). Effect of professional status on the number of synapses per neuron in the prefrontal cortex of normal human and schizophrenic brain. *Society for Neuroscience Abstracts, 329,* 430.

Orne, M. T. (1959). The nature of hypnosis: Artifact and essence. *Journal of Abnormal Psychology, 58,* 277–299.

Orne, M. T. (1962). On the social psychology of the psychological experiment: With particular reference to demand characteristics and their implications. *American Psychologist, 17,* 776–783.

Ornstein, P. A., Baker-Ward, L., Gordon, B. N., & Merritt, K. A. (1997). Children's memory for medical experiences: Implications for testimony. *Applied Cognitive Psychology, 11,* S87–S104.

Ortony, A., Clore, G. L., & Collins, A. (1988). *The cognitive structure of emotions.* New York: Cambridge University Press.

Ortony, A., & Turner, T. J. (1990). What's basic about basic emotions? *Psychological Review, 97,* 315–331.

Osborn, A. F. (1957). Applied imagination: Principles and procedures of creative problem solving (Rev ed.). New York: Charles Scribner's Sons.

Ost, L. G. (2008). Efficacy of the third wave of behavioral therapies: A systematic review and meta-analysis. *Behaviour Research and Therapy, 46,* 296–321.

Ott, R. (1995). The natural wrongs about animal rights and animal liberation. *Journal of the American Veterinary Medical Association, 207,* 1023–1030.

Otto, M. W., Smits, J. A. J., & Reese, H. E. (2005). Combined psychotherapy and pharmacotherapy for mood and anxiety disorders in adults: Review and analysis. *Clinical Psychology: Science & Practice, 12*, 72–86.

Overmier, J. B., & Seligman, M. E. P. (1967). Effects of inescapable shock upon subsequent escape and avoidance responding. *Journal of Comparative and Physiological Psychology, 63*, 28–33.

Overskeid, G. (2007). Looking for Skinner and finding Freud. *American Psychologist, 65*, 590–595.

Oxley, D. R., Smith, K. B., Alford, J. R., Hibbing, M. V., Miller, J. L., Scalora, M., et al. (2008). Political attitudes vary with physiological traits. *Science, 321*, 1667–1670.

Oyserman, D., Coon, H. M., & Kemmelmeier, M. (2002). Rethinking individualism and collectivism: Evaluation of theoretical assumptions and meta-analyses. *Psychological Bulletin, 128*, 3–72.

Ozer, E. J., Best, S. R., Lipsey, T. L., & Weiss, D. S. (2003). Predictors of post-traumatic stress disorder symptoms in adults: A meta-analysis. *Psychological Bulletin, 129*, 52–73.

Paffenbarger, R. S., Hyde, R. T., Wing, A. L., & Hsieh, C. C. (1986). Physical activity, all-cause mortality, and longevity of college alumni. *New England Journal of Medicine, 314*, 605–613.

Pagel, J. F. (2003). Non-dreamers. *Sleep Medicine, 4*, 235–241.

Pagnin, D., de Queiroz, V., Pini, S., & Cassano, G. B. (2008, Winter). Efficacy of ECT in depression: A meta-analytic review. *Focus, 6*, 155–162.

Pahnke, W. N., Kurland, A. A., Unger, S., Savage, C., & Grof, S. (1970). Experimental use of psychedelic (LSD) psychotherapy. *Journal of the American Medical Association, 212*, 1856.

Paivio, A. (1969). Mental imagery in associative learning and memory. *Psychological Review, 76*, 341–363.

Paller, K. A., Voss, J. L., & Westerberg, C. E. (2009). Investigating the awareness of remembering. *Perspectives on Psychological Science, 4*, 185–199.

Palmer, L. K. (1995). Effects of a walking program on attributional style, depression, and self-esteem in women. *Perceptual and Motor Skills, 81*, 891–898.

Palmisano, S., Allison, R. S., & Howard, I. P. (2006). Illusory scene distortion occurs during perceived self-rotation in roll. *Vision Research, 46*, 4048–4058.

Palsson, E., Klamer, D., Wass C., Archer, T., Engel, J. A., & Svensen, L. (2005). The effects of phencyclidine on latent inhibition in taste aversion conditioning: differential effects of preexposure and conditioning. *Behavioural Brain Research, 157*, 139–146.

Panskepp, J. (2004). *Affective neuroscience*. New York: Oxford University Press.

Panksepp, J. (2005). Beyond a joke: From animal laughter to human joy? *Science, 208*, 62–63.

Panksepp, J. (2007). Neurologizing the psychology of affects: How appraisal-based constructivism and basic emotion theory can coexist. *Perspectives in Psychological Science, 2*, 281–296.

Panksepp, J., & Panksepp, J. B. (2000). The seven sins of evolutionary psychology. *Evolution and Cognition, 6*, 108–131.

Pano, E. G., Hilscher, M. C., & Cupchik, G. C. (2008-2009). Responding to self-consciousness: An examination of everyday and dream episodes. *Imagination, Cognition, and Personality, 28*, 173–198.

Paolucci, E. O., & Violato, C. (2004). A meta-analysis of the published research on the affective, cognitive and behavioral effects of corporal punishment. *Journal of Psychology, 138*, 197–221.

Papolos, D., & Papolos, J. (2007). *The bipolar child: The definitive and reassuring guide to childhood's most misunderstood disorder, 3rd edition*. New York: Broadway.

Parault, S. J., & Parkinson, M. M. (2008). Sound symbolic word learning in the middle grades. *Contemporary Educational Psychology, 33*, 647–671.

Paris, J. (2000). *Myths of childhood*. New York: Brunner/Mazel.

Park, B., & Rothbart, M. (1982). Perception of out-group homogeneity and levels of social categorization: Memory for the subordinate attributes of in-group and out-group members. *Journal of Personality and Social Psychology, 42*, 1051–1068.

Park, D. C., Smith, A. D., & Cavanaugh, J. C. (1990). Metamemories of memory researchers. *Memory and Cognition, 18*, 321–327.

Park, M. A. (1982). Palmistry: Science or hand jive? *Skeptical Inquirer, 5*, 198–208.

Park, N., Peterson, C., & Seligman, M. E. P. (2004). Strengths of character and well-being. *Journal of Social and Clinical Psychology, 23*, 603–619.

Park, R. (2002). *Voodoo science: The road from foolishness to fraud*. New York: Oxford University Press.

Park, R.L. (2003, January 21). The seven warning signs of bogus science. *Chronicle Review*. http://chronicle.com/article/The-Seven-Warning-Signs-of/13674.

Parke, R. (1996). *Fatherhood*. Cambridge, MA: Harvard University Press.

Parker, E. S., Cahill, L., & McGaugh, J. L. (2006). A case of unusual autobiographical remembering. *Neurocase, 12*, 35–49.

Pascalis, O., de Schonen, S., Morton, J., Deruelle, C., & Fabre-Grenet, M. (1995). Mother's face recognition by neonates: A replication and an extension. *Infant Behavior and Development, 18*, 79–85.

Pascual, A., & Guéguen, N. (2005). Foot-in-the-door and door-in-the-face: A comparative meta-analytic study. *Psychological Reports, 96*, 122–128.

Pascual-Leone, J. (1989). An organismic process model of Witkin's field dependence-independence. In T. Globerson and T. Zelniker (eds.), *Cognitive style and cognitive development* (pp. 36–70). Norwood, NJ: Ablex.

Pasewark, R. A., & Pantle, M. L. (1979). Insanity plea: Legislator's view. *American Journal of Psychiatry, 136*, 222–223.

Pashler, H., McDaniel, M., Rohrer, D., & Bjork, R. (2009). Learning styles: Concepts and evidence. *Psychological Science in the Public Interest, 9*, 105–119.

Passini, F. T., & Norman, W. T. (1966). A universal conception of personality structure? *Journal of Personality and Social Psychology, 4*, 44–49.

Pate, R. R., Pratt, M., Blair, S. N., Haskell, W. L., Macera, C. A., Bouchard, C., et al. (1995). Physical activity and public health: A recommendation from the Centers for Disease Control and the American College of Sports Medicine. *Journal of the American Medical Association, 273*, 402–407.

Patel, G. A., & Sathian, K. (2000). Visual search: Bottom-up or top-down? *Frontiers in Bioscience, 5*, D169–D193.

Patrick, C. J. (ed.). (2006). *Handbook of psychopathy*. New York: Guilford Press.

Patrick, C. J., & Iacono, W. G. (1989). Psychopathy, threat, and polygraph test accuracy. *Journal of Applied Psychology, 74*, 347–355.

Patrick, C. J., & Iacono, W. G. (1991). Validity of the control question polygraph test: The problem of sampling bias. *Journal of Applied Psychology, 76*, 229–238.

Patterson, C. J. (1992). Children of lesbian and gay parents. *Child Development, 63*, 1025–1042.

Patterson, C. J., & Chan, R. W. (1996). Gay fathers and their children. In R. P. Cabaj and T. S. Stein (eds.), *Textbook of homosexuality and mental health* (pp. 371–393). Washington, DC: American Psychiatric Press.

Paul, A. M. (2004). *The cult of personality: How personality tests are leading us to miseducate our children, mismanage our companies, and misunderstand ourselves*. New York: Free Press.

Paul, G., & Lentz, R. J. (1977). *Psychosocial treatment of chronic mental patients: Milieu versus social-learning programs*. Cambridge, MA: Harvard University Press.

Paulesu, E., Harrison, J., Baroncohen, S., Watson, J. D. G., Goldstein, L., Heather, J., Frackowiak, R. S. J., & Frith C. D. (1995). The physiology of colored hearing – A PET activation study of color-word synesthesia. *Brain, 118*, 661–676.

Paulhus, D. L. (1991). Measurement and control of response bias. In J. P. Robinson & P. R. Shaver (eds.), *Measures of personality and social psychological attitudes* (pp. 17–59). San Diego, CA: Academic Press.

Paulus, P. B., Larey, T. S., & Ortega, A. H. (1995). Performance and perceptions of brainstormers in an organizational setting. *Basic and Applied Social Psychology, 17*, 249–265.

Paulus, T. M. (2004). Collaboration or cooperation? Small group interactions in a synchronous educational environment. In T. S. Roberts (ed.), *Computer-supported collaborative learning in higher education* (pp. 100–124). Hershey, PA: Idea Group.

Pavlov, I. P. (1927). *Conditioned reflexes*. Oxford, England: Oxford University Press.

Paykel, E. S. (2003). Life events and affective disorders. *Acta Psychiatrica Scandinavia Supplement, 108*, 61–66.

Pearce, J. M. (2004). Sir Charles Scott Sherrington (1857–1952) and the synapse. *Journal of Neurology, Neurosurgery, and Psychiatry, 74*, 544.

Pearson, B. Z., & Fernàndez, S. C. (1994). Patterns of interaction in the lexical growth in two languages of bilingual infants and toddlers. *Language Learning, 44*, 617–653.

Pearson, B. Z., Fernàndez, S. C., & Oller, D. K. (1993). Lexical development in bilingual infants and toddlers: Comparison to monolingual norms. *Language Learning, 43*, 93–120.

Pearson, H. (2006). Mouse data hint at human pheromones. *Nature, 442*, 495.

Pederson, N. L., Plomin, R., Nesselroade, J. R., & McClearn, G. E. (1992). A quantitative genetic analysis of cognitive abilities during the second half of the life span. *Psychological Science, 3,* 346–352.

Pederson Mussell, M., Crosby, R. D., Crow, S. J., Knopke, A. J., Peterson, C. B., Wonderlich, S. A., et al. (2000). Utilization of empirically supported psychotherapy treatments for individuals with eating disorders: A survey of psychologists. *International Journal of Eating Disorders, 27*, 230–237.

Pelham, B. W., Carvallo, M., & Jones, J. T. (2005). Implicit egotism. *Current Directions in Psychological Science, 14*, 106–110.

Pelham, B. W., Mirenberg, M. C., & Jones, J. T. (2002). Why Susie sells seashells by the seashore: Implicit egotism and major life decisions. *Journal of Personality and Social Psychology, 82*, 469–487.

Pelkonnen, M., & Marttunen, M. (2003). Child and adolescent suicide: Epidemiology, risk factors, and approaches to prevention. *Psychiatric Drugs, 5*, 243–265.

Penfield, W. (1958). *The excitable cortex in conscious man*. Liverpool, England: Liverpool University Press.

Pennebaker, J. W. (1997). Writing about emotional experiences as a therapeutic process. *Psychological Science, 8*, 162–166.

Pennebaker, J. W., & Graybeal, A. (2001). Patterns of natural language use: Disclosure, personality, and social integration. *Current Directions, 10*, 90–93.

Pennebaker, J. W., Kiecolt-Glaser, J., & Glaser, R. (1988). Disclosure of traumas and immune function: Health implications for psychotherapy. *Journal of Consulting and Clinical Psychology, 56*, 239–245.

Penner, L. A., Dovidio, J. F., Schroeder, D. A., & Piliavin, J. A. (2005). Prosocial behavior: Multilevel perspectives. *Annual Review of Psychology, 56*, 365–392.

Pepperberg, I. M. (2006). Cognitive and communicative abilities of grey parrots. *Applied Animal Behaviour Science, 100*, 77–86.

Perkins, D. N. (1981). *The mind's best work*. Cambridge, MA: Harvard University Press.

Perlmutter, M. (1983). Learning and memory through adulthood. In M. W. Riley, B. B. Hess, & K. Bond (eds.), *Aging in society: Selected reviews of recent research*. Hillsdale, NJ: Erlbaum.

Perry, J. C. (1984). *The borderline personality disorder scale: reliability and validity*. Department of Psychiatry, Harvard Medical School at the Cambridge Hospital, Cambridge, MA. Unpublished manuscript.

Perry, W. G., Jr. (1970). *Forms of intellectual and ethical development in the college years*. Oxford, England: Holt, Rinehart & Winston.

Persinger, M. A. (1987). *Neuropsychological bases of God beliefs*. New York: Praeger.

Persinger, M. A. (1994). Near-death experiences: Determining the neuroanatomical pathways by experiential patterns and simulation in experimental settings. In L. Besette (ed.), *Healing: Beyond suffering or death* (pp. 277–286). Chabanel, Quebec, Canada: MNH.

Pert, C. (1997). *Molecules of emotion*. New York: Simon & Schuster.

Pert, C. B., Pasternak, G., & Snyder, S. H. (1973). Opiate agonists and antagonists discriminated by receptor binding in brain. *Science, 182,* 1359–1361.

Pessah, M. A., & Roffwarg, H. P. (1972). Spontaneous middle ear muscle activity in man: A rapid eye movement sleep phenomenon. *Science, 178,* 773–776.

Peterson, C. (2000). The future of optimism. *American Psychologist, 55*, 44–55.

Peterson, C., & Seligman, M. E. P. (2004). *Character strengths and virtues: A handbook and classification*. New York: Oxford University Press.

Peterson, L. R., & Peterson, M. J. (1959). Short-term retention of individual verbal items. *Journal of Experimental Psychology, 58,* 193–198.

Petitto, L. A., & Marentette, P. F. (1991). Babbling in the manual mode: Evidence for the ontogeny of language. *Science, 251,* 1493–1496.

Petitto, L. A., Zatorre, R. J., Gauna, K., Nikelski, E. J., Dostie, D., & Evans, A. C. (2000). Speech-like cerebral activity in profoundly deaf people processing sign language: Implications for the neural basis of human language. *Proceedings of the National Academy of Sciences, 97,* 13961–13966.

Petrosino. A., Turpin-Petrosino, C., & Buehler, J. (2003, November). "'Scared Straight' and other juvenile awareness programs for preventing juvenile delinquency. Campbell Review Update I." In *The Campbell Collaboration Reviews of Intervention and Policy Evaluations (C2-RIPE)*. Philadelphia, Pennsylvania: Campbell Collaboration. http://web.archive.org/web/20070927013116/http://www.campbellcollaboration.org/doc-pdf/ssrupdt.pdf.

Petry, N. M., Tennen, H., & Affleck, G. (2000). Stalking the elusive client variable in psychotherapy research. In C. R. Snyder & R. Ingram (eds.), *Handbook of psychological change: Psychotherapy processes and practices for the 21st century* (pp. 88–108). New York: John Wiley & Sons.

Pettigrew, T. F. (1958). Personality and sociocultural factors in intergroup attitudes: A cross-national comparison. *Journal of Conflict Resolution, 2*, 29–42.

Pettigrew, T. F. (1979). The ultimate attribution error: Extending Allport's cognitive analysis of prejudice. *Personality and Social Psychology Bulletin, 5*, 461–476.

Pettijohn, T. F (ed.). (1998) *Sources: Notable selections in social psychology* (2nd ed.). Guilford, CT: Dushkin/McGraw-Hill.

Pettinati, H. M., Tamburello, T. A., Ruetsch, C. R., & Kaplan, F. N. (1994). Patient attitudes toward electroconvulsive therapy. *Psychopharmacological Bulletin, 30*, 471–475.

Petty, R. E., & Cacioppo, J. T. (1986). *Communication and persuasion: Central and peripheral routes to attitude change*. New York: Springer Verlag.

Petty, R. E., & Wegener, D. T. (1999). The elaboration likelihood model: Current status and controversies. Dual-process theories in social psychology. In S. Chaiken & Y. Trope (eds.), *Dual-process theories in social psychology.* (pp. 37–72). New York: Guilford.

Pew Research Center. (2006, February 13). Are we happy yet? Retrieved from http://pewresearch.org/pubs/301/are-we-happy-yet.

Pezdek, K., Blandon-Gitlin, I., & Moore, C. (2003). Children's face recognition memory: More evidence for the cross-race effect. *Journal of Applied Psychology, 88*, 760–763.

Pezdek, K., Finger, K., & Hodge, D. (1997). Planting false childhood memories: The role of event plausibility. *Psychological Science, 8,* 437–441.

Pihl, R. O. (1999). Substance abuse: Etiological considerations. In T. Millon, P. Blaney, & R. D. Davis (eds.), *Oxford handbook of psychopathology* (pp. 249–276). New York: Oxford University Press.

Phillips, D. P. (1983) The impact of mass media violence in U.S. homicides. *American Sociological Review, 48*, 560–568.

Phillips, K., & Fulker, D. W. (1989). Quantitative genetic analysis of longitudinal trends in adoption designs with application to IQ in the Colorado Adoption Project. *Behavior Genetics, 19*, 621–658.

Phillips, D. P., & Wills, J. S. (1987). A drop in suicides around major national holidays. *Suicide and Life Threatening Behavior, 17*, 1–12.

Phillips, M. L., Young, A. W., Senior, C., Brammer, M., Andrew, A. J., Calder, J., et al. (1997). A specific neural substrate for perceiving facial expressions of disgust. *Nature, 389*, 495–498.

Phillips, M. R., Wolf, A. S., & Coons, D. J. (1988). Psychiatry and the criminal justice system: Testing the myths. *American Journal of Psychiatry, 145,* 605–610.

Phillips, W. T., Kiernan, M., & King, A. C. (2001). The effects of physical activity on physical and psychological health. In A. Baum, T. A. Revenson, & J. E. Singer (eds.), *Handbook of health psychology* (pp. 627–660). Mahwah, NJ: Lawrence Erlbaum.

Piaget, J. (1932). *The moral judgment of the child*. London: Kegan Paul.

Piatelli-Palmarini, M. (1994). *Inevitable illusions: How mistakes of reason rule our minds*. New York: John Wiley & Sons.

Piccinelli, M., & Wilkinson, G. (2000). Gender differences in depression—Critical review. *British Journal of Psychiatry, 177*, 486–492.

Piccione, C., Hilgard, E. R., & Zimbardo, P. G. (1989). On the degree of stability of measured hypnotizability over a 25-year period. *Journal of Personality and Social Psychology, 56*, 289–295.

Pigott, T. A., Myers, K. R., & Williams, D. A. (1996). Obsessive-compulsive disorder: A neuropsychiatric perspective. In R. M. Rapee (ed.), *Current controversies in the anxiety disorders* (pp. 134–160). New York: Guilford.

Piliavin, I. M., Rodin, J., & Piliavin, J. A. (1969). Good samaritanism: An underground phenomenon? *Journal of Personality and Social Psychology, 13,* 289–299.

Pillemer, D. B. (1984). Flashbulb memories of the assassination attempt on President Reagan. *Cognition, 16*, 63–80.

Pinker, S. (1997). *How the mind works*. New York: Norton.

Pinker, S. (2002). *The blank slate: The modern denial of human nature*. New York: Penguin.

Pinker, S. (2005, February 14). The science of difference: Sex ed. *The New Republic, 232,* 15–17.

Pinsk, M. A., DeSimone, K., Moore, T., Gross, C. G., & Kastner, S. (2005). Representations of faces and body parts in macaque temporal cortex: A functional MRI study. *Proceedings of the National Academy of Sciences, U.S.A., 102,* 6996–7001.

Piper, A. (1993). "Truth serum" and "recovered memories" of sexual abuse: A review of the evidence. *Journal of Psychiatry & Law, 21,* 447–471.

Piper, A. (1997). *Hoax and reality: The bizarre world of multiple personality disorder.* Northvale, NJ: Jason Aronson.

Piske, T., MacKay, I. R. A., & Flege, J. E. (2001). Factors affecting degree of foreign accent in an L2: A review. *Journal of Phonetics, 29,* 191–215.

Pitman, R. K., Sanders, K. M., Zusman, R. M., Healy, A. R., Cheema, F., Lasko, N. B., et al. (2002). Pilot study of secondary prevention of posttraumatic stress disorder with propranolol. *Biological Psychiatry, 51,* 189–192.

Pittas, A. G., Hariharan, R., Stark, P. C., Hajduk, C. L., Greenberg, A. S., & Roberts, S. B. (2005). Interstitial glucose level is a significant predictor of energy intake in free-living women with healthy body weight. *Journal of Nutrition, 135,* 1070–1074.

Pittinger, C, & Duman, R. S. (2008). Stress, depression, and neuroplasticity: A convergence of mechanisms. *Neuropsychopharmacology Reviews, 33,* 88–109.

Plait, P. C. (2002). *Bad astronomy: Misconceptions and misuses revealed from astrology to the moon landing "hoax."* New York: John Wiley & Sons.

Platt, J. R. (1964). Strong inference. *Science, 146,* 347–353.

Platt, S. A., & Sanislow, C. A. (1988). Norm-of-reaction: Definition and misinterpretation of animal research. *Journal of Comparative Psychology, 102,* 254–261.

Plomin, R. (2004). Genetics and developmental psychology. *Merrill-Palmer Quarterly Journal of Developmental Psychology, 50,* 341–352.

Plomin, R., Corley, R., DeFries, J. C., & Fulker, D. W. (1990). Individual differences in television viewing in early childhood: Nature as well as nurture. *Psychological Science, 1,* 371–377.

Plomin, R., & Crabbe, J. C. (2000). DNA. *Psychological Bulletin, 126,* 806–828.

Plomin, R., & Daniels, D. (1987). Why are children in the same family so different from one another? *Behavioral and Brain Sciences, 10,* 1–16.

Plomin, R., DeFries, J. C., & Loehlin, J. C. (1977). Genotype-environment interaction and correlation in the analysis of human behavior. *Psychological Bulletin, 84,* 309–322.

Plomin, R., DeFries, J. C., McClearn, G. E., & Rutter, M. (1997). *Behavioral genetics* (3rd ed.). New York: W. H. Freeman.

Plomin, R., & Kovas, Y. (2005). Generalist genes and learning disabilities. *Psychological Bulletin, 131,* 592–617.

Plomin, R., & McClearn, G. E. (1993). *Nature, nurture, and psychology.* Washington, DC: American Psychological Association.

Plotkin, H. (2004). *Evolutionary thought in psychology: A brief history.* Oxford, England: Blackwell.

Plotnik, J. M., de Waal, F. B. M., & Reiss, D. (2006). Self-recognition in an Asian elephant. Proceedings of the National Academy of Sciences, 103, 17053–17057.

Plutchik, R. (2000). *Emotions in the practice of psychotherapy: Clinical implications of affect theories.* Washington, DC: American Psychological Association.

Plutchik, R. (2003). *Emotions and life: Perspectives from psychology, biology, and evolution.* Washington, DC: American Psychological Association.

Plutchik, R., & Kellerman, H. (eds.). (1986). *Emotion: Theory, research, and experience: Biological foundations of emotion.* New York: Academic Press.

Podczerwinski, E. S., Wickens, C. D., & Alexander, A. L. (2002) *Technical Report ARL-01-8/NASA-01-04.* Moffett Field, CA: NASA Ames Research Center

Pogue-Geile, M., Ferrell, R., Deka, R., Debski, T., & Manuck, S. (1998). Human novelty-seeking personality traits and dopamine D4 receptor polymorphisms: a twin and genetic association study. *American Journal of Medical Genetics, 81,* 44–48.

Pohorecky, L. (1977). Biphasic action of ethanol. *Biobehavioral Review, 1,* 231–240.

Poizner, H., Klima, E. S., & Bellugi, U. (1987). *What the hands reveal about the brain.* Cambridge, MA: MIT Press.

Polivy, J., & Herman, C. P. (2002). If you first don't succeed. False hopes of self-change. *American Psychologist, 57,* 677–689.

Polivy, J., Schueneman, A. L., & Carlson, K. (1976). Alcohol and tension reduction: Cognitive and physiological effects. *Journal of Abnormal Psychology, 85,* 595–600.

Pollard, K. S., Salama, S. R., King, B., Kern, A. D., Dreszer, T., Katzman, S., et al. (2006, October 13). Forces shaping the fastest evolving regions in the human genome. *PLoS Genetics, 2*(10), 168.

Pollitt, E., Gorman, K. S., Engle, P. L., Martorell, R., & Rivera, J. (1993). Early supplementary feeding and cognition: Effects over two decades. *Monographs of the Society for Research in Child Development, 58* (7, Serial No. 235).

Polusny, M. A., & Follette, V. M. (1996). Remembering childhood sexual abuse: A national survey of psychologists' clinical practices, beliefs, and personal experiences. *Professional Psychology: Research and Practice, 27,* 41–52.

Pontón, M. O., & Gorsuch, R. L. (1988). Prejudice and religion revisited: A cross-cultural investigation with a Venezuelan sample. *Journal for the Scientific Study of Religion, 27,* 260–271.

Poole, D. A., Lindsay, D. S., Memon, A., & Bull, R. (1995). Psychotherapists' opinions, practices, and experiences with recovery of memories of incestuous abuse. *Journal of Consulting and Clinical Psychology, 68,* 426–437.

Pope, H. G., Gruber, A. J., & Yergelun-Todd, D. (2001). Residual neuropsychologic effects of cannabis. *Current Psychiatry Report, 3,* 507–512.

Pope, H. G., Jr., & Hudson, J. I. (1992). Is childhood sexual abuse a risk factor for bulimia nervosa? *American Journal of Psychiatry, 149,* 455–463.

Pope, H. G., Jr., Poliakoff, M. B., Parker, M. P., Boynes, M., & Hudson, J. I. (2007). Is dissociative amnesia a culture-bound syndrome? Findings from a survey of historical literature. *Psychological Medicine, 37,* 225–233.

Popper, K. R. (1965). *The logic of scientific discovery.* New York: Harper.

Pornpitakpan, C. (2004). The persuasiveness of source credibility: A critical review of five decades' evidence. *Journal of Applied Social Psychology, 34,* 243–281.

Porter, S., & Peace, K. A. (2007). The scars of memory: A prospective longitudinal investigation of the consistency of traumatic and positive emotional memories in adulthood. *Psychological Science, 18,* 435–441.

Porter, S., Yuille, J. C., & Lehman, D. R. (1999). The nature of real, implanted, and fabricated memories for emotional childhood events: Implications for the recovered memory debate. *Law and Human Behavior, 23,* 517–538.

Posey, T. B., & Losch, M. E. (1983). Auditory hallucinations of hearing voices in 375 normal subjects. *Imagination, Cognition and Personality, 3,* 99–113.

Posner, G. P., & Sampson, W. (1999, Fall/Winter). Chinese acupuncture for heart surgery anesthesia. *The Scientific Review of Alternative Medicine, 3,* 15–19.

Posner, M. I., & Snyder, C. R. R. (1975). Facilitation and inhibition in the processing of signals. In P. M. A. Rabbitt & S. Dornic (eds.), *Attention and performance* (pp. 669–682). New York: Academic Press.

Posthuma, D., & de Geus, E. J. C. (2006). Progress in the molecular-genetic study of intelligence. *Current Directions in Psychological Science, 15,* 151–155.

Postmes, T., & Spears, R. (1998). Deindividuation and antinormative behavior: A meta-analysis. *Psychological Bulletin, 123,* 238–259.

Potts, R. G. (2004). Spirituality, religion, and the experience of illness. In P. Camic & S. Knight (eds.), *Clinical handbook of health psychology: A practical guide to effective interventions* (pp. 297–314). Cambridge, MA: Hogrefe & Huber.

Powell, R. A. (2010). Little Albert still missing. American Psychologist, 65, 299–300.

Powell, L. H., Shahabi, L., & Thoresen, C. E. (2003). Religion and spirituality: Linkages to physical health. *American Psychologist, 58,* 36–52.

Powell, R. W., & Curley, M. (1984). Analysis of instinctive drift. 2. The development and control of species-specific responses in appetitive conditioning. *Psychological Record, 34,* 363–379.

Powers, D. E. (1993). Coaching for the SAT: A summary of the summaries and an update. *Educational Measurement: Issues and Practice, 12,* 24–39.

Powers, D. E., & Rock, D. A. (1999). Effects of coaching on SAT I: Reasoning test scores. *Journal of Educational Measurement, 36,* 93–118.

Pratkanis, A. R. (1992). The cargo-cult science of subliminal persuasion. *Skeptical Inquirer, 16,* 260–272.

Pratkanis, A. R. (1995, July/August). How to sell a pseudoscience. *Skeptical Inquirer, 19,* 19–25.

Premack, D. (1965). Reinforcement theory. In D. Levine (ed.), *Nebraska Symposium on Motivation* (pp. 123–180). Lincoln, NE: University of Nebraska Press.

Premack, D., & Woodruff, G. (1978). Does the chimpanzee have a theory of mind? *Behavioral and Brain Sciences, 1,* 515–526.

Presley, S. (1997). *Why people believe in ESP for the wrong reasons.* Retrieved October 15, 2006, from http://www.rit.org/essays/think/esp.html.

Price, J., & Davis, B. (2008). *The woman who can't forget: The extraordinary story of living with the most remarkable memory known to science.* New York: Free Press.

Price, R. H., & Bouffard, D. L. (1974). Behavioral appropriateness and situational constraint as dimensions of social behavior. *Journal of Personality and Social Psychology, 30,* 579–586.

Priel, B., & de Schonen, S. (1986). Self-recognition: A study of a population without mirrors. *Journal of Experimental Child Psychology, 41,* 237–250.

Prince, M. J., Harwood, R. H., Blizard, R. A., Thomas, A., & Mann, A. H. (1997). Social support deficits, loneliness and life events as risk factors for depression in old age. The Gospel Oak Project VI. *Psychological Medicine, 27,* 323–332.

Pringle, P. J., Geary, M. P. P., Rodeck, C. H., Kingdom, J. C. P., Kayamba-Kay's, S., & Hindmarsh, P. C. (2005). The influence of cigarette smoking on antenatal growth, birth size, and the insulin-like growth factor axis. *Journal of Clinical Endocrinology & Metabolism, 90,* 2556–2562.

Prinz, J. J. (2004). *Gut reactions: A perceptual theory of emotion.* New York: Oxford University Press.

Prochaska, J. O., & DiClemente, C. C. (1982). Transtheoretical therapy: Toward a more integrative model of change. *Psychotherapy: Theory, Research, and Practice, 20,* 161–173.

Prochaska, J. O., & Norcross, J. C. (2002). Stages of change. In J. C. Norcross (ed.), *Psychotherapy relationships that work.* New York: Oxford University Press.

Prochaska, J. O., & Norcross, J. C. (2007). *Systems of psychotherapy: A transtheoretical approach* (6th ed.). Pacific Grove, CA: Brooks/Cole.

Proctor, R. W., & Capaldi, E. J. (2006). *Why science matters: Understanding the methods of psychological research.* Malden, MA: Blackwell.

Project MATCH Research Group. (1997). Matching alcoholism treatments to client heterogeneity: Project MATCH posttreatment drinking outcomes. *Journal of Studies on Alcohol, 58,* 7–29.

Pronin, E. (2008). How we see ourselves and how we see others. *Science, 320,* 1177–1180.

Pronin, E., Berger, J., & Molouki, S. (2007). Alone in a crowd of sheep: Asymmetric perceptions of conformity and their roots in an introspective illusion. *Journal of Personality and Social Psychology, 92,* 585–595.

Pronin, E., Gilovich, T., & Ross, L. (2004). Objectivity in the eye of the beholder: Divergent perceptions of bias in self versus others. *Psychological Review, 3,* 781–799.

Pronk, N. P., & Wing, R. R. (1994). Physical activity and long-term maintenance of weight loss. *Obesity Research, 2,* 587–599.

Proske, U. (2006). Kinesthesia: The role of muscle receptors. *Muscle Nerve, 34,* 545–558.

Provine, R. R. (1996). Laughter. *American Scientist, 84,* 38–45.

Provine, R. R. (2000). *Laughter: A scientific investigation.* New York: Viking.

Punjabi, N. M., Caffo, B. S., Goodwin, J. L., Gottlieb, D. J., Newman, A. B., O'Connor, G. T., et al. (2009) Sleep-disordered breathing and mortality: A prospective cohort study. *PLoS Med, 6*(8): e1000132. doi:10.1371/journal.pmed.1000132.

Purves, D., Lotto, R. B., & Nundy, S. (2002). Why we see what we do. *American Scientist, 90,* 236.

Putman, V. L., & Paulus, P. B. (2009). Brainstorming, brainstorming rules, and decision making. *Journal of Creative Behavior, 42,* 23–29.

Pyszczynski, T., Greenberg, J., & Solomon, S. (2003). *In the wake of 9/11: The psychology of terror.* Washington, D.C.: American Psychological Association.

Quart, E. (2006, July/August). Extreme parenting. *Salon.com.* Retrieved from http://www.theatlantic.com/doc/prem/200607/parenting.

Quick, D. C. (1999, March/April). Joint pain and weather. *Skeptical Inquirer, 23,* 49–51.

Quick, J. C., Quick, J. D., Nelson, D. L., & Hurrell, J. J. (1997). *Preventive stress management in organizations.* Washington, DC: American Psychological Association.

Quinn, P. C., & Eimas, P. D. (1996). Perceptual cues that permit categorical differentiation of animal species by infants. *Journal of Experimental Child Psychology, 63,* 189–211.

Quinn, P. J., O'Callaghan, M. J., Williams, G. M., Najman, J. M., Andersen, M. J., & Bor, W. (2001). The effect of breastfeeding on child development at 5 years: A cohort study. *Journal of Paediatrics and Child Health, 37,* 465–469.

Quiroga, R. Q., Reddy, L., Kreiman, G., Koch, C., & Fried, I. (2005). Invariant visual representation by single neurons in the human brain. *Nature, 435,* 1102–1107.

Rabinowitz, J., & Renert, N. (1997). Clinicians' predictions of length of psychotherapy. *Psychiatric Services, 48,* 97–99.

Rachid, F., & Bertschy, G. (2006). Safety and efficacy of repetitive transcranial magnetic stimulation in the treatment of depression: A critical appraisal of the last 10 years. *Neurophysiologie Clinique, 36,* 157–183.

Racine, E., Bar-Ilan, O., & Illes, J. (2006). Brain Imaging: a decade of coverage in the print media. *Science Communication, 28,* 122–142.

Rachlin, H., & Logue, A. W. (1991). Learning. In M. Hersen, A. E. Kazdin, & A. S. Bellack (eds.), *The clinical psychology handbook* (2nd ed., pp. 170–184). Elmsford, NY, US: Pergamon Press.

Rachman, S. (1977). The conditioning theory of fear-acquisition: A critical examination. *Behaviour Research and Therapy, 15,* 375–387.

Rachman, S. (1994). Psychological treatment of panic: Mechanisms. In B. E. Wolfe & J. D. Maser (eds.), *Treatment of panic disorder: A consensus development conference* (pp. 133–148). Washington, DC: American Psychiatric Press.

Rachman, S., & Hodgson, R. J. (1968). Experimentally induced "sexual fetishism": Replication and development. *Psychological Record, 18,* 25–27.

Rader, C. M., & Tellegen, A. (1987). An investigation of synesthesia. *Journal of Personality and Social Psychology, 52,* 981–987.

Radford, B. (2007). Might fright cause white? *Skeptical Inquirer, 31,* 26.

Rafnsson, F. D., Jonsson, F. H., & Windle, M. (2006). Coping strategies, stressful life events, problem behaviors, and depressed affect. *Anxiety, Stress, & Coping, 19,* 241–257.

Raimy, V. C. (ed.). (1950). *Training in clinical psychology (Boulder Conference).* New York: Prentice-Hall.

Rainville, P., Bechara, A., Naqvi, N., & Damasio, A. R. (2006). Basic emotions are associated with distinct patterns of cardiorespiratory activity. *International Journal of Psychophysiology, 61,* 5–18.

Rajaratnam, S. M., Polymeropoulos, M. H., Fisher, D. M., Roth, T., Scott, C., Birznieks, G., & Klerman, E. B. (2009). Melatonin agonist tasimelteon (VEC-162) for transient insomnia after sleep-time shift: two randomised controlled multicentre trials. *Lancet, 373,* 482–491.

Raloff, J. (2009, September 12). Drugged money. *Science News, 176* (6), 9.

Ramachandran, V. S. (2000). Mirror neurons and imitation learning as the driving force behind "the great leap forward" in human evolution. Edge. Retrieved from http://www.edge.org/3rd_culture/ramachandran/ramachandran_p1.html on March 27, 2010.

Ramachandran, V. S., & Altschuler, E. L. (2009). The use of visual feedback, in particular mirror visual feedback, in restoring brain function. *Brain, 132,* 1693–1710.

Ramachandran, V. S., & Hubbard, E. M. (2001). Synaesthesia: A window into perception, thought and language. *Journal of Consciousness Studies, 8,* 33–34.

Ramachandran, V. S., & Rogers-Ramachandran, D. C. (1996). Synaesthesia in phantom limbs induced with mirrors. *Proceedings of the Royal Society of London, 263,* 377–386.

Ramaekers, J. G., Kauert, G., van Ruitenbeek, P., Theunissen, E. L., Schneider, E., & Moeller, M. R. (2006). High-potency marijuana impairs executive function and inhibitory motor control. *Neuropsychopharmacology, 31,* 2296–2303.

Ramer, D. G. (1980) The Premack Principle, self-monitoring, and the maintenance of preventive dental health behaviour. *Dissertation Abstracts International, 40*(11-B), 5415–5416.

Randi, J. (1982). *Flim-flam!* Amherst, NY: Prometheus Books.

Randoph-Seng, B., & Nielsen, M. E. (2007). Honesty: On effect of primed religious representations. *The International Journal for the Psychology of Religion, 17,* 303–315.

Randolph-Seng, B., & Mather, R. D. (2009). Does subliminal persuasion work? It depends on your motivation and awareness. *Skeptical Inquirer, 33,* 49–53.

Rankin, J. L. (2005). *Parenting experts: Their advice, the research, and getting it right.* Westport, CT: Praeger.

Rasmussen, K., Sampson, S. M., & Rummans, T. A. (2002). Electroconvulsive therapy and newer modalities for the treatment of medication-refractory mental illness. *Mayo Clinic Proceedings, 77,* 552–556.

Rassin, E., Merckelbach, H., & Spaan, V. (2001). When dreams become a royal road to confusion: Realistic dreams, dissociation, and fantasy proneness. *Journal of Nervous and Mental Disease, 189,* 478–481.

Rathus, S. A., Nevid, J. S., & Fichner-Rathus, L. (2000). *Human sexuality in a world of diversity.* Boston: Allyn & Bacon.

Raudenbush, S. W. (1984). Magnitude of teacher expectancy effects on pupil IQ as a function of the credibility of expectancy induction: A synthesis of findings from 18 experiments. *Journal of Educational Psychology, 76,* 85–97.

Raulin, M. L. (2003). *Abnormal psychology.* Boston: Allyn & Bacon.

Raulin, M. L., & Lilienfeld, S. O. (2008). Research paradigms in the study of psychopathology. In P. H. Blaney & T. Milton (eds.), *Oxford textbook of psychopathology.* (2nd ed., pp. 86–115). New York: Oxford University Press.

Rauscher, F. H., Shaw, G. L., & Ky, K. N. (1993). Music and spatial task performance. *Nature, 365,* 611.

Raven, J., Raven, J. C., & Court, J. H. (1998). *Manual for Raven's Advanced Progressive Matrices.* Oxford, England: Oxford Psychologists Press.

Rayner, K., Foorman, B. R., Perfetti, C. A., Pesetsky, D., & Seidenberg, M. S. (2002). How should reading be taught? *Scientific American, 286,* 84.

Raz, S., & Raz, N. (1990). Structural brain abnormalities in the major psychoses: A quantitative review of the evidence from computerized imaging. *Psychological Bulletin, 108,* 93–108.

Razoumnikova, O. (2000). Functional organization of different brain areas during convergent and divergent thinking: An EEG investigation. *Cognitive Brain Research, 10,* 11–18.

Reasoner, R. (2000). *Self-esteem and youth: What research has to say about it.* Port Ludlow, WA: International Council for Self-Esteem.

Rechtschaffen, A. (1998). Current perspectives on the function of sleep. *Perspectives in Biology and Medicine, 41,* 359–390.

Rechtschaffen, A., Verdone, P., & Wheaton, J. (1963). Reports of mental activity during sleep. *Canadian Psychiatry, 8,* 409–414.

Redding, R. E. (1998). How common-sense psychology can inform law and psycholegal research. *University of Chicago Law School Roundtable, 5,* 107–142.

Redding, R. E. (2004). Bias or prejudice? The politics of research on racial prejudice. *Psychological Inquiry, 15,* 289–293.

Reed, E. W., & Reed, S. C. (1965). *Mental retardation: A family study.* Philadelphia: W. B. Saunders.

Reese, H. W. (2010). Regarding Little Albert. American Psychologist, 65, 300–301.

Regan, P. C., & Berscheid, E. (1999). *Lust: What we know about human sexual desire.* Thousand Oaks, CA: Sage.

Regan, D. T., & Totten, J. (1975). Empathy and attribution: Turning observers into actors. *Journal of Personality and Social Psychology, 32,* 850–856.

Rehberg, R. A., & Rosenthal, E. R. (1978). *Class and merit in the American high school.* New York: Longman.

Reich, W. (1949). *Character analysis.* New York: Orgone Institute Press.

Reichenbach, S., Sterchi, R., Scherer, M., Trelle, S., Bürgi, E., Bürgi, U., et al. (2007). Meta-analysis: Chondroitin for osteoarthritis of the knee or hip. *Annals of Internal Medicine, 146,* 580–590.

Reicher, S. D., & Haslam, S. A. (2006). Rethinking the social psychology of tyranny: The BBC Prison Study. *British Journal of Social Psychology, 45,* 1–40.

Reid, B. (2002, April 30). The nocebo effect: Placebo's evil twin. *Washington Post,* HE01.

Reyna, V. F., & Farley, F. (2006). Risk and rationality in adolescent decision making: Implications for theory, practice, and policy. *Psychological Science in the Public Interest, 7,* 1–44.

Reis, F. L., Masson, S., deOliveira, A. R., & Brandao, M. L. (2004). Dopaminergic mechanisms in the conditioned and unconditioned fear as assessed by the two-way avoidance and light switch-off tests. *Pharmacology, Biochemistry and Behavior, 79,* 359–365.

Riesenhuber, M., & Poggio, T. (1999). Hierarchical models of object recognition in cortex. *Nature Neuroscience, 2,* 1019–1025.

Reisenzein, R. (1983). The Schachter theory of emotion: Two decades later. *Psychological Bulletin, 94,* 239–264.

Reiss, D., & Marino, L. (2001). Mirror self-recognition in the bottlenose dolphin: A case of cognitive convergence. *Proceedings of the National Academy of Sciences, 98,* 5937–5942.

Reiss, S., & McNally, R. J. (1985). The expectancy model of fear. In S. Reiss & R. R. Bootzin (eds.), *Theoretical issues in behavior therapy* (pp. 107–121). New York: Academic Press.

Rensink, R. A., O'Regan, J. K., & Clark, J. (1997). To see or not to see: The need for attention to perceive changes in scenes. *Psychological Science, 8,* 368–373.

Rentfrow, P. J., Gosling, S. D., & Potter, J. (2008). A theory of the emergence, persistence, and expression of geographic variation in psychological characteristics. *Perspectives on Psychological Science, 3*(5), 339–369.

Repetti, R., Taylor, S., & Seeman, T. (2002). Risky families: Family social environments and the mental and physical health of offspring. *Psychological Bulletin 128,* 330–366.

Rescorla, R. A. (1990). The role of information about the response-outcome relation in instrumental discrimination learning. *Journal of Experimental Psychology: Animal Behavior Processes, 16,* 262–270.

Rescorla, R. A., & Wagner, A. R. (1972). A theory of Pavlovian conditioning: Variations in effectiveness of reinforcement and non-reinforcement. In A. H. Black & W. F. Prokasy (eds.), *Classical conditioning II: Current research and theory,* (64–98). Appleton Century Crofts.

Resnick, A. G., & Ithman, M. H. (2009). The human sexual response cycle: Psychotropic side effects and treatment strategies. *Psychiatric Annals, 38,* 267–280.

Resnick, S. M., Pham, D. L., Kraut, M. A., Zonderman, A. B., & Davatzikos, C. (2003). Longitudinal magnetic resonance imaging studies of older adults: A shrinking brain. *Journal of Neuroscience, 23,* 3295–3301.

Restak, R. (1984). *The brain.* New York: Bantam Books.

Revelle, W., Humphreys, M. S., Simon, L., & Gilliland, K. (1980). The interactive effect of personality, time of day, and caffeine: A test of the arousal model. *Journal of Experimental Psychology: General, 109,* 1–31.

Revonsuo, A. (2000). The reinterpretation of dreams: An evolutionary hypothesis of the function of dreaming. *Behavioral and Brain Sciences, 23,* 877–901.

Reynolds, C. R. (1999). Cultural bias in testing of intelligence and personality. In C. Belar (ed.), Sociocultural and individual differences, Vol. 10 of M. Hersen & A. Bellack (eds.), *Comprehensive clinical psychology* (pp. 53–92). Oxford, UK: Elsevier Science.

Reynolds, D. (2003, April 25). Panel recommends counseling for sterilization survivors. *Inclusion Daily Express.* Retrieved from www.inclusiondaily. com/news/institutions/nc/eugenics.htm#042503.

Rhodes, G., Halberstadt, J., & Brajkovich, G. (2001). Generalization of mere exposure effects to averaged composite faces. *Social Cognition, 19,* 57–70.

Rhule, D. M. (2005). Take care to do no harm: Harmful interventions for youth problem behavior. *Professional Psychology: Research and Practice, 36,* 618–625.

Ricciardelli, L. A. (1992). Bilingualism and cognitive development in relation to threshold theory. *Journal of Psycholinguistic Research, 21,* 301–316.

Richards, J. M., Butler, E. A., & Gross, J. J. (2003). Emotion regulation in romantic relationships: The cognitive consequences of concealing feelings. *Journal of Social and Personal Relationships, 20,* 599–620.

Richardson, R., Riccio, C., & Axiotis, R. (1986). Alleviation of infantile amnesia in rats by internal and external contextual cues. *Developmental Psychobiology, 19,* 453–462.

Rickford, J. R., & Rickford, R. J. (2000). *Spoken soul: The story of Black English.* New York: Wiley.

Ridgway, S. H. (2002). Asymmetry and symmetry in brain waves from dolphin left and right hemispheres: Some observations after anesthesia, during quiescent hanging behavior, and during visual obstruction. *Brain, Behavior, and Evolution, 60,* 265–274.

Ridley, M. (2003). *Nature via nurture: Genes, experience, and what makes us human.* New York: HarperCollins.

Rieber, R. W. (1999). Hypnosis, false memory, and multiple personality: A trinity of affinity. *History of Psychiatry, 10,* 3–11.

Riley, J. R., Greggers, U., Smith, A. D., Reynolds, D. R., & Menzel, R. (2005) The flight paths of honeybees recruited by the waggle dance. *Nature, 435,* 205–207.

Rilling, J. K., King-Casas, B., & Sanfey, A. G. (2008). The neurobiology of social decision-making. *Current Opinion in Neurobiology, 18,* 159–165.

Rilling, M. (1996). The mystery of the vanished citations: James McConnell's forgotten 1960s quest for planarian learning, a biochemical engram, and celebrity. *American Psychologist, 51,* 1039.

Rimland, B. (2004). Association between thimerosol-containing vaccine and autism. *Journal of the American Medical Association, 291*, 180.

Rimm, D., & Masters, J. C. (1979). *Behavior therapy: Techniques and empirical findings* (2nd ed.). New York: Academic Press.

Rind, B., Tromovitch, P., & Bauserman, R. (1998). A meta-analytic examination of assumed properties of child sexual abuse using college samples. *Psychological Bulletin, 124*, 22–53.

Ring, K. (1984). *Healing toward omega: In search of the meaning of the near-death experience.* New York: Morrow.

Ringwalt, C. L., & Greene, J. M. (1993, March). *Results of school districts' drug prevention coordinators survey.* Paper presented at the Alcohol, Tobacco, and Other Drugs Conference on Evaluating School-Linked Prevention Strategies, San Diego, CA.

Ris, M. D., Dietrich, K. N., Succop, P. A., Berger, O. G., & Bornschein, R. L. (2004). Early exposure to lead and neuropsychological outcome in adolescence. *Journal of the International Neuropsychological Society, 10*, 261–270.

Risch, N., Herrell, R., Lehner, T., Liang, K. Y., Eaves, L., Hoh, J., et al.et al. (2009). The interaction between the serotonin transporter gene (5-HTTLPR), stressful life events, and risk of depression: A meta-analysis. *Journal of the American Medical Association, 301*, 2462–2471.

Risen, J., & Gilovich, T. (2007). Informal logical fallacies. In R. J. Sternberg, H. L. Roediger, & D. F. Halpern (eds.), *Critical thinking in psychology* (pp. 110–130). New York: Cambridge University Press.

Rizzolatti, G., Fadiga, L., Gallese, V., & Fogassi, L. (1996) Premotor cortex and the recognition of motor actions. *Cognitive Brain Rresearch, 3*, 131–141.

Robbins, T. W., & Everitt, B. J. (1999). Interaction of the dopaminergic system with mechanisms of associative learning and cognition: Implications for drug abuse. *Psychological Science, 10*, 199–202.

Roberts, B. W., & DelVecchio, W. F. (2000). The rank-order consistency of personality traits from childhood to old age: Review of longitudinal studies. *Psychological Bulletin, 126*, 3–25.

Roberts, C. J., & Lowe, C. R. (1975). Where have all the conceptions gone? *Lancet, i,* 498–501.

Roberts, W. M., Howard, J., & Hudspeth, A. J. (1988). Hair cells: Transduction, tuning, and transmission in the inner ear. *Annual Review of Cell Biology, 4,* 63–92.

Roberts, R. E., Strawbridge, W. J., Deleger, S., & Kaplan, G. A. (2002). Are the fat more jolly? *Annals of Behavioral Medicine, 24,* 169–180.

Robiner, W. N., Bearman, D. L., Berman, M., Grove, W. M., Colon, E., Armstrong, J., et al. (2003). Prescriptive authority for psychologists: Despite deficits in education and knowledge? *Journal of Clinical Psychology in Medical Settings, 10,* 211–221.

Robins, E., & Guze, S. B. (1970). Establishment of diagnostic validity in psychiatric illness: Its application to schizophrenia. *American Journal of Psychiatry, 126,* 983–987.

Robins, L. N., Helzer, J. E., & Davis, D. H. (1975). Narcotic use in Southeast Asia and afterward: An interview study of 898 Vietnam returnees. *Archives of General Psychiatry, 32,* 955–961.

Robinson, D. G., Woerner, M. G., McMeniman, M., Mendelowitz, A., & Bilder, R. M. (2004). Systematic and functional recovery from a first episode of schizophrenia or schizoaffective disorder. *American Journal of Psychiatry, 161,* 473–479.

Robinson, D. S. (2007). The role of dopamine and norepinephrine in depression. *Primary Psychiatry, 14,* 21–23.

Rochat, P. (2001). *The infant's world.* Cambridge, MA: Harvard University Press.

Rock, A. (2004). *The mind at night: The new science of how and why we dream.* New York: Basic Books.

Rock, I. & Kaufman, L. (1962). The moon illusion, part 2. *Science, 136,* 1023–1031.

Rodgers, J., Cleveland, H., van der Oord, E., & Rowe, D. (2000). Resolving the debate over birth order, family size, and intelligence. *American Psychologist, 55,* 599–612.

Roediger, H. L., & Crowder, R. G. (1976). A serial position effect in recall of United States presidents. *Bulletin of the Psychonomic Society, 8,* 275–278.

Roediger, H. L., & McDermott, K. B. (1995). Creating false memories: Remembering words not presented in lists. *Journal of Experimental Psychology: Learning, Memory, and Cognition, 21,* 803–814.

Roediger, H. L., & McDermott, K. B. (1999). False alarms and false memories. *Psychological Review, 106,* 406–410.

Roediger, H. L., & Karpicke, J. D. (2006). Test-enhanced learning: Taking memory tests improves long-term retention. *Psychological Science, 17,* 249–255.

Rogers, C. R. (1942). *Counseling and psychotherapy.* New York: Houghton Mifflin.

Rogers, C. R. (1947). Some observations on the organization of personality. *American Psychologist, 2,* 358–368.

Rogers, C. R. (1957). The necessary and sufficient conditions of therapeutic personality change. *Journal of Consulting Psychology, 21,* 95–103.

Rogers, C. R. (1961). *On becoming a person.* Boston: Houghton Mifflin.

Rogers, C. R., & Dymond, R. (1954). *Psychotherapy and personality change.* Chicago: University of Chicago Press.

Rogers, M., & Smith, K. H. (1993). Public perceptions of subliminal advertising. *Journal of Advertising Research, 33,* 10–18.

Rogers, R. (ed.). (1997). *Clinical assessment of malingering and deception* (2nd ed.). New York: Guilford Press.

Rogers, R. W., & Prentice-Dunn, S. (1981). Deindividuation and anger-mediated interracial aggression: Unmasking regressive racism. *Journal of Personality and Social Psychology, 41,* 63–73.

Rogoff, B. (1995). Observing sociocultural activities on three planes: Participatory appropriation, guided participation, and apprenticeship. In J. V. Wertsch, P. Pablo del Río, & A. Álvarez, (eds.), *Sociocultural studies of mind* (pp. 139–163). Cambridge, UK: Cambridge University Press.

Rogoff, B. (1998). Cognition as a collaborative process. In D. Kuhn & R. S. Seigler (eds.), *Handbook of child psychology, Vol. 2: Cognition, perception, & language* (5th ed., pp. 679–744). New York: Wiley.

Rogoff, B., & Chavajay, P. (1995). What's become of research on the cultural basis of cognitive development? *American Psychologist, 50,* 859–877.

Rolls, E. T. (2004). The functions of the orbitofrontal cortex. *Brain & Cognition, 55,* 11–29.

Romanczyk, R. G., Arnstein, L., Soorya, L. V., & Gillis, J. (2003). The myriad of controversial treatments for autism: A critical evaluation of efficacy. In S. O. Lilienfeld, S. J. Lynn, & J. M. Lohr (eds.), *Science and pseudoscience in clinical psychology* (pp. 363–395). New York: Guilford.

Roney, J. R., Hanson, K. N., Durante, K. M., & Maestripieri, D. (2006). Reading men's faces: Women's mate attractiveness judgments track men's testosterone and interest in infants. *Proceedings of the Royal Society of London B, 273,* 2169–2175.

Ropeik, D., & Gray, G. (2003). *Risk: A practical guide for deciding what's really safe and what's really dangerous in the world around you.* Boston: Houghton Mifflin.

Rosch, E. (1973). Natural categories. *Cognitive Psychology, 4,* 328–350.

Rose, R. J., & Ditto, W. B. (1983). A developmental-genetic analysis of common fears from early adolescence to early adulthood. *Child Development, 54,* 361–368.

Rose, S. (2009). Darwin 200: Should scientists study race and IQ? NO: Science and society do not benefit *Nature, 457,* 786–788.

Rosen, G. M. (1993). Self-help or hype? Comments on psychology's failure to advance self-care. *Professional Psychology: Research and Practice, 24,* 340–345.

Rosen, G. M. (2006). DSM's cautionary guideline to rule out malingering can protect the PTSD data base. *Journal of Anxiety Disorders, 20,* 530–535.

Rosen, G. M., Glasgow, R. E., & Moore, T. E. (2003). Self-help therapy: The science and business of giving psychology away. In S. O. Lilienfeld, S. J. Lynn, & J. M. Lohr (eds.), *Science and pseudoscience in clinical psychology* (pp. 399–424). New York: Guilford.

Rosenberg, H. (1993). Prediction of controlled drinking by alcoholics and problem drinkers. *Psychological Bulletin, 113,* 129–139.

Rosenberg, P. (1973). The effects of mood altering drugs: Pleasures and pitfalls. In R. E. Hardy & J. G. Cull (eds.), *Drug dependence and rehabilitation approaches.* Springfield, IL: Charles C. Thomas.

Rosenberg, S. D., Rosenberg, H. J., & Farrell, M. P. (1999). The midlife crisis revisited. *Journal of Personality and Social Psychology, 77,* 415–427.

Rosenblum, D., & Lewis, M. (1999). The relations among body image, physical attractiveness, and body mass in adolescence. *Child Development, 70,* 50–64.

Rosenfarb, I. S., Bellack, A. S., & Aziz, N. (2006). Family interactions and the course of schizophrenia in African-American and white patients. *Journal of Abnormal Psychology, 115,* 112–120.

Rosenfeld, J. P. (2005). "Brain fingerprinting": A critical analysis. *Scientific Review of Mental Health Practice, 4,* 20–37.

Rosenhan, D. L. (1973). On being sane in insane places. *Science, 179*, 250–258.

Rosenhan, D. L., & Seligman, M. E. P. (1989). *Abnormal psychology.* New York: W. W. Norton.

Rosenhow, D. J., Howland, J., Arndt, J. T., Almeida, A. B., Greece, J., Minsky, S., et al. (2010). Intoxication with bourbon versus vodka: Effects on hangover, sleep, and next-day neurocognitive performance in young adults. *Alcoholism: Clinical and Experimental Research, 34*, 509–518.

Rosenman, R. H., Brand, R. J., Jenkins, C. D., Friedman, M., Straus, R., & Wurm, M. (1975). Coronary heart disease in the Western Collaborative Group Study: Final follow-up experience of 8 1/2 years. *Journal of the American Medical Association, 233*, 872–877.

Rosenman, R. H., Friedman, M., Straus, R., Wurm, M., Kositchek, R., Hahn, W., et al. (1964). A predictive study of coronary heart disease: The Western Collaborative Group Study. *Journal of the American Medical Association, 189*, 15–22.

Rosenthal, D. (1963). *The Genain quadruplets.* New York: Basic Books.

Rosenthal, R. (1994) Interpersonal expectancy effects: A 30-year perspective. *Current Directions in Psychological Science, 3*, 176–179.

Rosenthal, R., & DiMatteo, M. R. (2001). Meta-analysis: Recent developments in quantitative methods for literature reviews. *Annual Review of Psychology, 52*, 59–82.

Rosenthal, R., & Fode, K. L. (1963). Psychology of the scientist: V. Three experiments in experimenter bias. *Psychological Reports, 12*, 491–511.

Rosenthal, R., & Jacobson, L. (1966). Teachers' expectancies: Determinants of pupils' IQ gains. *Psychological Reports, 1*, 115–118.

Rosenzweig, S. (1936). Some implicit common factors in diverse methods in psychotherapy. *American Journal of Orthopsychiatry, 6*, 412–415.

Roskies, A.L. (2007). Are neuroimages like photographs of the brain? *Philosophy of Science, 74*, 860–872.

Rosnow, R. L. (1980). Psychology of rumor reconsidered. *Psychological Bulletin, 87*, 578–591.

Rosnow, R. L. (2002). The nature and role of demand characteristics in scientific inquiry. *Prevention and Treatment, 5*(1). Retrieved March 10, 2005, from http://content.apa.org/journals/pre/5/1/37.

Ross, C. A. (1997). *Dissociative identity disorder: Diagnosis, clinical features, and treatment of multiple personality.* New York: John Wiley & Sons.

Ross, C. A., & Pam, A. (1994). *Pseudoscience in biological psychiatry: Blaming the body.* New York: Wiley.

Ross, H., & Plug, C. (2002). *The mystery of the moon illusion.* Oxford, England: Oxford University Press.

Ross, L., Amabile, T. M., & Steinmetz, J. L. (1977). Social roles, social control and biases in social perception. *Journal of Personality and Social Psychology, 35*, 485–494.

Ross, L., & Nisbett, L. E. (1991). *The person and the situation: Essential contributions of social psychology.* New York: McGraw Hill.

Ross, L., & Ward, A. (1996). Naive realism: Implications for social conflict and misunderstanding. In T. Brown, E. Reed, & E. Turiel (eds.), *Values and knowledge* (pp. 103–135). Hillsdale, NJ: Lawrence Erlbaum Associates.

Ross, M. (1989). Relation of implicit theories to the construction of personal histories. *Psychological Review, 96*, 341–357.

Rotenberg, K. J., & Mann, L. (1986). The development of the norm of the reciprocity of self-disclosure and its function in children's attraction to peers. *Child Development, 57*, 1349–1357.

Roth, S., & Cohen, L. J. (1986). Approach, avoidance, and coping with stress. *American Psychologist, 41*, 813–819.

Rothbaum, B. O., Hodges, L., Ready, D., Graap, K., & Alarcon, R. D. (2001). Virtual reality exposure therapy for Vietnam veterans with posttraumatic stress disorder. *Journal of Clinical Psychiatry, 62*, 617–622.

Rothbaum, R., Weisz, J., Pott, M., Miyake, K., & Morelli, G. (2000). Attachment and culture: Security in Japan and the U.S. *American Psychologist, 55*, 1093–1104.

Rothschild, R., & Quitkin, F. M. (1992). Review of the use of pattern analysis to differentiate true drug and placebo responses. *Psychotherapy and Psychosomatics, 58*, 170–177.

Rotter, J. B. (1966). Generalized expectancies for internal versus external control of reinforcement. *Psychological Monographs* (1, Whole No. 609).

Rotton, J., & Kelly, I. W. (1985). Much ado about the full moon: A meta-analysis of lunar-lunacy research. *Psychological Bulletin, 97*, 286–306.

Rovee-Collier, C. (1993). The capacity for long-term memory in infancy. *Current Directions in Psychological Science, 2*, 130–135.

Rowe, D. C. (1994). *The limits of family influence: Genes, experience, and behavior.* New York: Guilford Press.

Rowland, I. (2001). *The full facts on cold reading* (2nd ed.). London, England: Author.

Roy, M., McNeale, M. C., Pedersen, N. L., Mathe, A. A., & Kendler, K. S. (1995). A twin study of generalized anxiety disorder and major depression. *Psychological Medicine, 25*, 1037–1049.

Roy, M. M., & Christenfeld, N. J. S. (2004). Do dogs resemble their owners? *Psychological Science, 15*, 361–363.

Roy-Byrne, P. P. (2005). The GABA-benzodiazepine receptor complex: Structure, function, and role in anxiety. *Journal of Clinical Psychiatry, 66* (Suppl. 2), 14–20.

Royce, J., Darlington, R., & Murray, H. (1983). Pooled analyses: Findings across studies. In The Consortium for Longitudinal Studies (ed.), *As the twig is bent: Lasting effects of preschool programs* (pp. 411–459). Hillsdale, NJ: Erlbaum.

Rozin, P. (2006). The integration of biological, social, cultural, and psychological influences on food choice. In R. Shepherd & M. Raats (eds.), *The psychology of food choice* (pp. 19–40). Oxfordshire, UK: CABI

Rozin, P., & Fallon, A. (1987). A perspective on disgust. *Psychological Review, 94*, 23–41.

Rozin, P., Markwith, M., & Ross, B. (1990). The sympathetic magical law of similarity, nominal realism and neglect of negatives in response to negative labels. *Psychological Science, 1*, 383–384.

Rozin, P., Millman, L., & Nemeroff, C. (1986). Operation of the laws of sympathetic magic in disgust and other domains. *Journal of Personality and Social Psychology, 50*, 703–712.

Rozin, P., & Stoess, C. (1993). Is there a general tendency to become addicted? *Addictive Behaviors, 18*, 81–87.

Ruben, J., Schwiemann, J., Deuchert, M., Meyer, R., Krause, T., Curio, G., et al. (2001). Somatotopic organization of human secondary somatosensory cortex. *Cerebral Cortex, 11*, 463–473.

Rubenzer, S. J., Faschingbauer, T. R., & Ones, D. S. (2000, August). *Assessing the U.S. presidents using the Revised NEO Personality Inventory.* Paper presented at the Annual Convention of the American Psychological Association, Washington, DC.

Rubin, A. (2003). Unanswered questions about the empirical support for EMDR in the treatment of PTSD: A review of research. *Traumatology, 9*(1), 4–30.

Rubin, M. L., & Walls, G. L. (1969). *Fundamentals of visual science* (p. 546). Springfield, IL: Thomas.

Rudolf, K. (2009). The interpersonal context of adolescent depression. In S. Nolen Hoeksema & L. M. Hilt (eds.), Handbook of depression in adolescents (pp. 378–412). New York: Routledge.

Ruff, R. M., & Parker, S. B. (1993). Gender- and age-specific changes in motor speed and eye-hand coordination in adults: Normative values for the Finger Tapping and Grooved Pegboard tests. *Perceptual and Motor Skills, 76*, 1219–1230.

Rule, N. O., & Ambady, N. (2008). Brief exposures: Male sexual orientation is accurately perceived at 50 ms. *Journal of Experimental Social Psychology, 44*, 1100–1105.

Rule, N. O., Ambady, N., & Hallett, K. (2009). Female sexual orientation is perceived accurately, rapidly, and automatically from the face and its features. *Journal of Experimental Social Psychology, 45*, 1245–1251.

Rumelhart, D. E., & McClelland, J. L. (1987). *Parallel distributed processing* (Vol. 1). Cambridge, MA: MIT Press.

Rupp, H. (2003). *Sex segregation in rhesus monkeys* (Macaca mulatta). Unpublished Master's thesis, Emory University, Atlanta, Georgia.

Ruscio, J. (2000). Risky business: Vividness, availability, and the media paradox. *Skeptical Inquirer, 24*, 22–26.

Ruscio, J. (2003). Diagnoses and the behaviors they denote: A critical evaluation of the labeling theory of mental illness. *Scientific Review of Mental Health Practice, 3*, 5–22.

Ruscio, J. (2005). Exploring controversies in the art and science of polygraph testing. *Skeptical Inquirer, 29*, 34–39.

Rush, A. J., Marangell, L. B., Sackeim, H. A., George, M. S., Brannan, S. K., Davis, S. M., et al. (2005). Vagus nerve stimulation for treatment-resistant depression: A randomized, controlled acute phase trial. *Biological Psychiatry, 58*, 347–354.

Rushton, J. P. (1995). *Race, evolution, and behavior: An evolutionary perspective.* New Brunswick, NJ: Transaction Publishers.

Rushton, J. P. (1999). Secular gains in IQ note related to the g factor and inbreeding depression—Unlike Black-White differences: A reply to Flynn. *Personality and Individual Differences, 26,* 381–389.

Rushton, J. P., & Bogaert, A. F. (1987). Race differences in sexual behavior: Testing an evolutionary hypothesis. *Journal of Research in Personality, 21,* 529–551.

Rushton, J. P., Brainerd, C. J., & Presley, M. (1983). Behavioral development and construct validity: The principle of aggregation. *Psychological Bulletin, 94,* 18–38.

Rushton, J. P., & Campbell, A. C. (1977). Modelling, vicarious reinforcement, and extraversion on blood donating in adults: Immediate and long term effects. *European Journal of Social Psychology, 7,* 297–306.

Russell, J. A. (1994). Is there universal recognition of emotion from facial expression? A review of cross-cultural studies. *Psychological Bulletin, 115,* 102–141.

Rust, S. (2006, April 3). Autism epidemic doubted. *Milwaukee Sentinel.* Retrieved April 16, 2006, from www.jsonline.com/story/index.aspx?id=412874.

Rutter, M. (1972). *Maternal deprivation reassessed.* Oxford, England: Penguin.

Rutter, M. (1995). Maternal deprivation. In M. H. Bornstein (ed.), *Handbook of parenting, Vol. 4: Applied and practical parenting* (pp. 3–31). Hillsdale, NJ: Erlbaum.

Rutter, M. (2000). Genetic studies of autism: From the 1970s into the millennium. *Journal of Abnormal Child Psychology, 28,* 3–14.

Rutter, M. (2009). Gene-environment interactions: Biologically valid pathway or artifact. *Archives of General Psychiatry, 66,* 1287–1289.

Rutter, M. L. (1997). Nature-nurture integration: The example of anti-social behavior. *American Psychologist 52,* 390–398.

Ruys, K. I., & Stapel, D. A. (2008). Emotion elicitor or emotion messenger? Subliminal priming reveals two faces of facial expressions. *Psychological Science, 19,* 593–600.

Ryan, R. (1976). *Blaming the victim.* New York: Vintage Books.

Ryan, R. M. (1985). Thematic Apperception Test. In D. J. Keyser & R. C. Swetland (eds.), *Test critiques* (Vol. 2, pp. 799–814). Kansas City, MO: Test Corporation of America.

Ryder, A. G., Yang, J., Zhu, X., Yao, S., Yi, J., Heine, S., et al. (2008). The cultural shaping of depression: Somatic symptoms in China, psychological symptoms in North America. *Journal of Abnormal Psychology, 117,* 300–313.

Saarni, S. I., Parmanne, P., & Halila, R. (2008). Alcohol consumption, abstaining, health utility, and quality of life: A general population survey in Finland. *Alcohol and Alcoholism, 43,* 376–386.

Saba, G., Schurhoff, F., & Leboyer, M. (2006). Therapeutic and neurophysiologic aspects of transcranial magnetic stimulation in schizophrenia. *Neurophysiologie Clinique, 36,* 185–194.

Sabini, J., & Silver, M. (1983). Dispositional vs. situational interpretations of Milgram obedience experiments: The fundamental attributional error. *Journal for the Theory of Social Behavior, 13,* 147–154.

Sabom, M. (1982). *Recollections of death: A medical investigation.* New York: Harper & Row.

Sackeim, H. A. (1986). The efficacy of electroconvulsive therapy. *Annals of the New York Academy of Sciences, 462,* 70–75.

Sackeim, H. A., Prudic, J., Fuller, R., Keilp, J., Lavori, P. W., & Olfson, M. (2007). The cognitive effects of electroconvulsive therapy in community settings. *Neuropsychopharmacology, 32,* 244–254.

Sackett, P. R., Borneman, M., and Connelly, B. S. (2008). High stakes testing in education and employment: Evaluating common criticisms regarding validity and fairness. *American Psychologist, 63,* 215–227.

Sackett, P. R., & Decker, P. J. (1979). Detection of deception in the employment context: A review and critical analysis. *Personnel Psychology, 32,* 487–506.

Sackett, P. R., Hardison, C. M., & Cullen, M. J. (2004). On interpreting stereotype threat as accounting for Black-White differences on cognitive tests. *American Psychologist, 59,* 7–13.

Sackett, P. R., & Wanek, J. E. E. (1996). New developments in the use of measures of honesty, integrity, conscientiousness, dependability, trustworthiness, and reliability for personnel selection. *Personnel Psychology, 49,* 787–829.

Sacks, O. (1985). *The man who mistook his wife for a hat: And other clinical tales.* New York: Touchstone.

Sadato, N. (2005). How the blind "see" Braille: Lessons from functional magnetic resonance imaging. *Neuroscientist, 11,* 577–582.

Sadler, P., & Woody, E. Z. (2010). Dissociation in hypnosis: Theoretical frameworks and psychotherapeutic implications. In S. J. Lynn, J. W. Rhue, & I. Kirsch (eds.), *Handbook of clinical hypnosis* (2nd ed.) (pp. 151–178). Washington, DC: American Psychological Association.

Sadoff, R. L. (1992) In defense of the insanity defense. *Psychiatric Annals, 22,* 556–560.

Safer, D. J. (2000). Are stimulants overprescribed for youths with ADHD? *Annals of Clinical Psychiatry, 12,* 55–62.

Sagan, C. (1995). *The demon-haunted world: Science as a candle in the dark.* New York: Random House.

Sageman, M. (2004). *Understanding terror networks.* Philadelphia: University of Pennsylvania Press.

Saha, S., Chant, D., Welham, J., & McGrath, J. (2005). A systematic review of the prevalence of schizophrenia. *PLoS Medicine, 2,* e141doi:10.1371/journal.pmed.0020141.

Salekin, R. T. (2002). Psychopathy and therapeutic pessimism: Clinical lore or clinical reality? *Clinical Psychology Review, 22,* 79–112.

Salerno, S. (2005). *SHAM: How the self-help movement made America helpless.* New York: Crown Books.

Saletan, W. (2004, May 12). The Stanford Prison Experiment doesn't explain Abu Ghraib. *Slate.* Retrieved December 2, 2004, from http://slate.msn.com/id/2100419/.

Salgado, J. F., Anderson, N., Mocsoso, S., Bertua, C., deFruyt, F., & Rolland, J. P. (2003). A meta-analytic study of general mental ability validity for different occupations in the European community. *Journal of Applied Psychology, 88,* 1068–1081.

Salmon, P. (2001). Effects of physical exercise on anxiety, depression, and sensitivity to stress: A unifying theory. *Clinical Psychology Review, 21,* 33–61.

Salovey, P., & Mayer, J. D. (1990). Emotional intelligence. *Imagination, Cognition, and Personality, 9,* 185–211.

Salter, D., McMillan, D., Richards, M., Talbot, T., Hodges, J., Bentovim, A., et al. (2003) Development of sexually abusive behaviour in sexually victimised males: a longitudinal study. *Lancet, 361,* 471–476.

Salthouse, T. A. (1996). The processing-speed theory of adult age differences in cognition. *Psychological Review, 103,* 403–428.

Salthouse, T. A. (2004). Localizing age-related individual differences in a hierarchical structure. *Intelligence, 32,* 541–561.

Salzinger, K. (2002). Science directions: Gugelhupf. *APA Monitor on Psychology.* Retrieved May 14, 2008, from http://www.apa.org/monitor/jun02/sd.html.

Samuelson, L. K., & Smith, L. B. (1998). Memory and attention make smart word learning: An alternative account of Akhtar, Carpenter, and Tomasello. *Child Development, 69,* 94–104.

Sanchez-Andres, J. V., Olds, J. L., & Alkon, D. L. (1993). Gated informational transfer within the mammalian hippocampus: A new hypothesis. *Behavioral Brain Research, 54,* 111–106.

Sanders, C. E., Lubinski, D., & Benbow, C. P. (1995). Does the Defining Issues Test measure psychological phenomena distinct from verbal ability? An examination of Lykken's query. *Journal of Personality and Social Psychology, 69,* 498–504.

Sanders, M. H., & Givelber, R. J. (2006). Overview of obstructive sleep apnea in adults. In T. L. Lee Chiong (ed.), Sleep: *A comprehensive handbook* (pp. 231–247). Hoboken, NJ: John Wiley & Sons.

Santa Maria, M. P., Baumeister, A. A., & Gouvier, W. D. (1999). Public knowledge and misconceptions about electroconvulsive therapy: A demographically stratified investigation. *International Journal of Rehabilitation and Health, 4,* 111–116.

Santor, D. A., & Kusumakar, V. (2001). Open trial of interpersonal therapy in adolescents with moderate to severe major depression: Effectiveness of novice IPT therapists. *Journal of the American Academy of Child and Adolescent Psychiatry, 40,* 236–240.

Saper, R. B., Kales, S. N., Paquin, J., Burns, M. J., Eisenberg, D. M., Davis, R. B., et al. (2004). Heavy metal content of Ayurvedic herbal medicine products. *Journal of the American Medical Association, 292,* 2868–2873.

Sapir, E. (1929). The status of linguistics as a science. *Language, 5,* 209.

Sapolsky, R. M. (1998). Molecular neurobiology: The stress of Gulf War syndrome. *Nature, 393,* 308–309.

Sapolsky, R. M. (2007). *The trouble with testosterone: And other essays on the biology of the human predicament.* New York: Scribner.

Sappington, A. A. (1990). Recent psychological approaches to the free will versus determinism controversy. *Psychological Bulletin, 108*, 19–29.

Sar, V., Koyuncu, A., Ozturk, E, Yargic, L., Kundakci, T., Yazici, A., et al. (2007). Dissociative disorders in the psychiatric emergency ward. *General Hospital Psychiatry, 29*, 45–50.

Sarafino, E. P. (2006). *Health psychology: Biopsychosocial interactions* (5th ed.). Hoboken, NJ: John Wiley & Sons.

Sarbin, T. R., & Coe, W. C. (1979). Hypnosis and psychopathology: Replacing old myths with fresh metaphors. *Journal of Abnormal Psychology, 88*, 506–526.

Sarbin, T. R., & Slagle, R. W. (1979). Hypnosis and psychophysiological outcomes. In E. Fromm & R. E. Shor (eds.), *Developments in research and new perspectives* (pp. 273–303). New York: Aldine.

Satel, S. L. (1999). *Drug treatment: The case for coercion.* Washington, DC: American Enterprise Institute Press.

Satir, V. (1964). *Conjoint family therapy.* New York: Science and Behavior Books.

Saufley, W. H., Otaka, S. R., & Bavaresco, J. L. (1985). Context effects: Classroom tests and context independence. *Memory & Cognition, 13*, 522–528.

Savage-Rumbaugh, E. S. (1986). *Ape language: From conditioned response to symbol.* New York: Columbia University Press.

Savic, I., Berglund, H., & Lindstrom, P. (2005). Brain response to putative pheromones in homosexual men. *Proceedings of the National Academy of Sciences, U.S.A., 17*, 7356–7361.

Savitz, J., Solms, M., Pietersen, E., Ramesar, R., & Flor-Henry, P. (2004). Dissociative identity disorder associated with mania and change in handedness. *Cognitive and Behavioral Neurology, 17*, 233–237.

Saxe, L. (1991). Lying: Thoughts of an applied social psychologist. *American Psychologist, 46*, 409–415.

Saxe, L., & Ben-Shakhar, G. (1999). Admissibility of polygraph tests: The application of scientific standards post-Daubert. *Psychology, Public Policy and Law, 5*, 203–223.

Sayette, M. A. (1999). Does drinking reduce stress? *Alcohol Research and Health, 23*, 250–255.

Scahill, R. I., Frost, C., Jenkins, R., Whitwell, J. L., Rosser, M. N., & Fox, N. C. (2003). A longitudinal study of brain volume changes in normal aging using serial registered magnetic resonance imaging. *Archives of Neurology, 60*, 989–994.

Scarr, S. (1985). An author's frame of mind (Review of *Frames of mind: The theory of multiple intelligences*). *New Ideas in Psychology, 3*, 95–100.

Scarr, S., & McCartney, K. (1983). How people make their own environments: A theory of genotype-environment effects. *Child Development, 54*, 424–435.

Scarr, S., Pakstis, A. J., Katz, S. H., & Barker, W. B. (1977). Absence of a relationship between degree of White ancestry and intellectual skills within a Black population. *Human Genetics, 39*, 69–86.

Scarr, S., Webber, P. L., Weinberg, R. A., & Wittig, M. A. (1981). Personality resemblance among adolescents and their parents in biologically related and adoptive families. *Journal of Personality and Social Psychology, 40*, 885–898.

Scarr, S., & Weinberg, R. A. (1976). IQ test performance of black children adopted by white families. *American Psychologist, 31*, 726–739.

Scattone, D. (2007). Social skills interventions for children with autism. *Psychology in the Schools, 44*, 717–726.

Schachter, S. (1968). Obesity and eating. *Science, 161*, 751–761.

Schachter, S., & Gross, L. (1968). Manipulated time and eating behavior. *Journal of Personality and Social Psychology, 10*, 98–106.

Schachter, S., & Singer, J. E. (1962). Cognitive, social and physiological determinants of emotional state. *Psychological Review, 69*, 379–399.

Schacter, D. L. (1996). *Searching for memory: The brain, the mind, and the past.* New York: Basic Books.

Schacter, D. L. (2001). *The seven sins of memory.* Boston: Houghton-Mifflin.

Schacter, D. L., & Moscovitch, M. (1984). Infants, amnesics, and dissociable memory systems. In M. Moscovitch (ed.), *Infant memory* (pp. 173–216). New York: Plenum.

Schacter, S. (1959). *The psychology of affiliation: Experimental studies of the sources of gregariousness.* Stanford, CA: Stanford University Press.

Schadler, M., & Thissen, D. M. (1981). The development of automatic word recognition and reading skill. *Memory & Cognition, 9*, 132–141.

Schaefer, C., Coyne, J. C., & Lazarus R. S. (1981). The health-related functions of social support. *Journal of Behavioral Medicine, 4*, 381–406.

Schaie, K. W. (1996). *Intellectual development in adulthood: The Seattle longitudinal study.* New York: Cambridge University Press.

Schaler, J. (2004). *Addiction is a choice.* La Salle, IL: Open Court Books.

Schaller, M., Boyd, C., Yohannes, J., & O'Brien. (1995). The prejudiced personality revisited: Personal need for structure and formation of erroneous group stereotypes. *Journal of Personality and Social Psychology, 68*, 544–555.

Schank, R. C., & Abelson, R. (1977). *Scripts, plans, goals, and understanding.* Hillsdale, NJ: Erlbaum.

Schatzberg, A. F. (1998). Noradrenergic versus serotonergic antidepressants: Predictors of treatment response. *Journal of Clinical Psychiatry, 59* (Suppl. 14), 15–18.

Scheck, B., Neufeld, P., & Dwyer, J. (2000). *Actual innocence.* New York: Random House.

Scheerenberger, R. C. (1983). *A history of mental retardation.* Baltimore: P. H. Brooks Publishing.

Scheff, S. W., Price, D. A., Schmitt, F. A., DeKosky, S. T., & Mufson, E. J. (2007). Synaptic alterations in CA1 in mild Alzheimer disease and mild cognitive impairment. *Neurology, 68*, 1501–1508.

Scheff, T. J. (1984). *Being mentally ill: A sociological theory.* New York: Aldine.

Scheier, M. F., & Carver, C. S. (1992). Effects of optimism on psychological and physical well-being: Theoretical overview and empirical update. *Cognitive Therapy and Research, 16*, 201–228.

Scheier, M. F., Matthews, K. A., Owens, J. F., Magovern, G. J., Lefebvre, R. C., Abbott, R. A., et al. (1989). Dispositional optimism and recovery from coronary artery bypass surgery: The beneficial effects on physical and psychological well-being. *Journal of Personality and Social Psychology, 57*, 1024–1040.

Schenck, C. H. (2006). Paradox lost: Midnight in the battleground of sleep and dreams. Violent moving nightmares page. Retrieved January 3, 2006, from: http://www.parasomnias-rbd.com/.

Scher, C. D., Ingram, R. E., & Segal, Z. V. (2005). Cognitive reactivity and vulnerability: Empirical evaluation of construct activation and cognitive diatheses in unipolar depression. *Clinical Psychology Review, 25*, 487–510.

Scherer, K. R. (1988). Criteria for emotion-antecedent appraisal: A review. In V. Hamilton, G. H. Bower, & N. H. Frijda (eds.), *Cognitive perspectives on emotion and motivation* (pp. 89–126). Dordrecht: Nijhoff.

Schienle, A., Stark, R., Walter, B., Blecker, C., Ott, U., Kirsch, P., et al. (2002). The insula is not specifically involved in disgust processing: An fMRI study. *Neuroreport, 13*, 2023–2026.

Schiff, M., Duyme, M., Dumaret, A., & Tomkiewicz, S. (1982). How much can we boost scholastic achievement and IQ scores? A direct answer from a French adoption study. *Cognition, 12*, 165–196.

Schiffman, S. S., & Graham, B. G. (2000). Taste and smell perception affect appetite and immunity in the elderly. *European Journal of Clinical Nutrition, 54*(Suppl. 3), S54–S63.

Sciutto, M. J., & Eisenberg, M. (2007). Evaluating the evidence for and against the overdiagnosis of ADHD. *Journal of Attention Disorders, 11*, 106–113.

Schkade, D. A., & Kahneman, D. (1998). Does living in California make people happy? A focusing illusion in judgments of life satisfaction. *Psychological Science, 9*, 340–346.

Schlegel, A., & Barry, H., III. (1991). *Adolescence: An anthropological inquiry.* New York: Free Press.

Schmader, T., Johns, M., & Forbes, C. (2008). An integrated process model of stereotype threat on performance. *Psychological Review, 115*, 336–356.

Schmahmann, J. D. (2004). Disorders of the cerebellum: Ataxia, dysmetria of thought, and the cerebellar cognitive affective syndrome. *Journal of Neuropsychiatry & Clinical Neurosciences, 16*, 367–378.

Schmidt, F. L. (1992). What do data really mean? Research findings, meta-analysis, and cumulative knowledge in psychology. *American Psychologist, 47*, 1173–1181.

Schmidt, F. L., & Hunter, J. E. (1993). Tacit knowledge, practical intelligence, general mental ability and job knowledge. *Current Directions in Psychological Science, 2*, 8–9.

Schmidt, J. P., & Hancey, R. (1979). Social class and psychiatric treatment: Application of a decision-making model to use patterns in a cost-free clinic. *Journal of Consulting and Clinical Psychology, 47*, 771–772.

Schmidt, N. B., Zvolensky, M. J., & Maner, J. (2006). Anxiety sensitivity: Prospective prediction of panic attacks and Axis I pathology. *Journal of Psychiatric Research, 40,* 691–699.

Schmidt, P. J., Murphy, J. H., Haq, N., Rubinow, D. R., & Danaceau, M. A. (2004). Stressful life events, personal losses, and perimenopause-related depression. *Archives of Women's Mental Health, 7,* 19–26.

Schmidt, S. (2009). Shall we really do it again? The powerful concept of replication is neglected in the social sciences. *Review of General Psychology, 13,* 90–100.

Schmiedek F., Oberauer K., Wilhelm O., Süss H. M., Wittmann W. W. (2007). Individual differences in components of reaction time distributions and their relations to working memory and intelligence. *Journal of Experimental Psychology: General, 136,* 414–429.

Schmolk, H., Buffalo, E. A., & Squire, L. R. (2000). Memory distortions develop over time. Recollections of the O. J. Simpson trial verdict after 15 and 32 months. *Psychological Science, 11,* 39–45.

Schnall, P. L., Pieper, C., Schwartz, J. E., Karasek, R. A., Schlussel, Y., Devereux, R. B., et al. (1990). The relationship between "job strain," workplace diastolic blood pressure, and left ventricular mass index: Results of a case-control study. *Journal of the American Medical Association, 263,* 1929–1935.

Schneeweiss, S., & Avorn, J. (2009). Antipsychotic agents and sudden cardiac death—How should we manage the risk. *New England Journal of Medicine, 360,* 294–296.

Schneider, D. (2006). Smart as we can get? *American Scientist, 94,* 311–312.

Schneider, W. (2008). The development of metacognitive knowledge in children and adolescents: Major trends and implications for education. *Mind, Brain, and Education, 2,* 114–121.

Schneider, W., & Bjorklund, D. F. (1998). Memory. In W. Damon, R. S. Siegler, & D. Kuhn (eds.), *Handbook of child psychology, Vol. 2.* (pp. 467–521). New York: Wiley.

Schneidman, E. S., Farberow, N. L., & Litman, R. E. (1970). *The psychology of suicide.* New York: Science House.

Schoenbaum, M. (1997). Do smokers understand the mortality effects of smoking? Evidence from the health and retirement survey. *American Journal of Public Health, 87,* 755–759.

Schoenborn, C. A., Adams, P. F., Barnes, P. M., Vickerie, J. L., & Schiller, J. S. (2004). Health behaviors of adults: United States, 1999–2001. National Center for Health Statistics. *Vital Health Statistics, 10,* 219.

Schoeneman, T. J. (1984). The mentally ill witch in textbooks of abnormal psychology: Current status and implications of a fallacy. *Professional Psychology; Science and Practice, 15,* 299–314.

Schoenewolf, G. (1997). *The dictionary of dream interpretation, including a glossary of dream symbols.* Northvale, NJ: Jason Aronson.

Schofield, W. (1964). *Psychotherapy: The purchase of friendship.* Englewood Cliffs, NJ: Prentice-Hall.

Schonfield, D., & Robertson, B. A. (1966). Memory storage and aging. *Canadian Journal of Psychology, 20,* 228–236.

Schooler, C. (1998). Environmental complexity and the Flynn effect. In U. Neisser (ed.), *The rising curve: Long-term gains in IQ and related measures* (pp. 67–79). Washington, DC: American Psychological Association.

Schofield, W., & Balian, L. (1959). A comparative study of the personal histories of schizophrenics and non-psychiatric patients. *Journal of Abnormal and Social Psychology, 59,* 216–225.

Schooler, J. W. (1997). Reflections on a memory discovery. *Child Maltreatment, 2,* 126–133.

Schopler, E., Short, A., & Mesibov, G. (1989) Relation of behavioral treatment to "normal functioning": Comment on Lovaas. *Journal of Consulting and Clinical Psychology, 57,* 162–164.

Schothorst, P. F., & van Engeland, H. (1996). Long term behavioral sequelae of prematurity. *Journal of the American Academy of Child and Adolescent Psychiatry, 35,* 175–183.

Schreiber, F. R. (1973). *Sybil.* New York: Warner.

Schretlen, D. J. (1997). Dissimulation on the Rorschach and other projective measures. In R. Rogers (ed.), *Clinical assessment of malingering and deception* (2nd ed., pp. 208–222). New York: Guilford.

Schroeter, M. L., Abdul-Khaliq, H., Krebs, M., Dieferibacher, A., & Blasig, I. E. (2009). Neuron-specific enolase is unaltered whereas S100B is elevated in serum of patients with schizophrenia - Original research and meta-analysis. *Psychiatry Research, 167,* 66–72.

Schuckit, M. A. (1988). Reactions to alcohol in sons of alcoholics and controls. Alcoholism: *Clinical and Experimental Research, 12,* 465–470.

Schuckit, M. A. (1994). A clinical model of genetic influences in alcohol dependence. *Journal of Studies of Alcohol, 55,* 5–17.

Schulz, M. S., Cowan, C. P., & Cowan, P. A. (2006). Promoting healthy beginnings: A randomized controlled trial of preventive intervention to preserve marital quality during the transition to parenthood. *Journal of Consulting and Clinical Psychology, 74,* 20–31.

Schuman, H., Steeh, C., Bobo, L., & Krysan, M. (1997). *Racial attitudes in America: Trends and interpretations* (Rev. ed.). Cambridge, MA: Harvard University Press.

Schwartz, B. L. (1999). Sparkling at the end of the tongue: The etiology of the tip-of-the-tongue phenomenology. *Psychonomic Bulletin & Review, 6,* 379–393.

Schwartz, C. E., Wright, C. I., Shin, L. M., Kagan, J., & Rauch, S. L. (2003). Inhibited and uninhibited infants "grown up": Adult amygdalar response to novelty. *Science, 300,* 1952–1953.

Schwartz, J. M., & Bayette, B. (1996). *Brain lock: Free yourself from obsessive-compulsive behavior: A four-step self-treatment method to change your brain chemistry.* New York: HarperCollins.

Schwartz, J. M., Stoessel, P. M., Baxter, L. R., Martin, K. M., & Phelps, M. E. (1996). Systematic changes in cerebral glucose metabolic rate after successful behavior modification treatment of obsessive-compulsive disorder. *Archives of General Psychiatry, 53,* 109–113.

Schwartz, M. B., Vartanian, L. R., Nosek, B. A., & Brownell, K. D. (2006). The influence of one's own body weight on implicit and explicit anti-fat bias. *Obesity, 14,* 440–447.

Schwartz, M. F., & Masters, W. H. (1984). The Masters and Johnson treatment program for dissatisfied homosexual men. *American Journal of Psychiatry, 141,* 173–181.

Schwartz, N. W., Woods, S. C., Porte, D., Seeley, R. J., & Baskin, D. G. (2000). Central nervous system control of food intake. *Nature, 404,* 661–671.

Schwarz, E. D., Kowalski, J. M., & McNally, R. J. (1993). Malignant memories: Posttraumatic changes in memory in adults after a school shooting. *Journal of Traumatic Stress, 4,* 545–553.

Schwarz, N. (1999). Self-reports: How the questions shape the answers. *American Psychologist, 54,* 93–105.

Schwarzer, R., & Taubert, S. (2002). Tenacious goal pursuits and striving toward personal growth: Proactive coping. In E. Fydenberg (ed.), *Beyond coping: Meeting goals, visions and challenges* (pp. 19–35). London: Oxford University Press.

Schweder, R., Mahapatra, M., & Miller, J. (1990). Culture and moral development. In J. Kagan & S. Lamb (eds.), *The emergence of morality in young children* (pp. 1–83). Chicago: University of Chicago Press.

Schweder, R. A., Mahapatra, M., & Miller, J. G. (1990). Culture and moral development. In J. W. Stigler, R. A. Shweder, & G. S. Herdt (Eds.), *Cultural psychology: Essays on comparative human development* (pp. 130–204). New York: Cambridge University Press.

Scott, V., McDade, D. M., & Luckman, S. M. (2007). Rapid changes in the sensitivity of the arcuate nucleus neurons to central ghrelin in relation to feeding status. *Physiology and Behavior, 90,* 180–185.

Scovern, A. W., & Kilmann, P. R. (1980). Status of electroconvulsive therapy: Review of the outcome literature. *Psychological Bulletin, 87,* 260–295.

Scoville, W. B., & Milner, B. (1957). Loss of recent memory after bilateral hippocampal lesions. *Journal of Neurology, Neurosurgery, and Psychiatry, 20,* 11–21.

Scull, A., Mackenzie, C., & Hervey, N. (1996). *Masters of Bedlam: The transformation of the mad-doctoring trade.* Princeton, NJ: Princeton University Press.

Searle, J. (1990). Is the brain's mind a computer program? *Scientific American, 262* (1), 26–31.

Sears, D. O. (1986). College sophomores in the laboratory: Influences of a narrow data base on social-psychology's view of human nature. *Journal of Personality and Social Psychology, 51,* 515–530.

Sebrechts, M. M., Marsh, R. L., & Seamon, J. G. (1989). Secondary memory and very rapid forgetting. *Memory & Cognition, 17,* 693–700.

Sechrest, L. (1963). Incremental validity: A recommendation. *Educational and Psychological Measurement, 12,* 153–158.

Segal, M. W. (1974). Alphabet and attraction: An unobtrusive measure of the effect of propinquity in a field setting. *Journal of Personality and Social Psychology, 30,* 654–657.

Segal, N. (1999). *Twins and what they tell us about human behavior.* New York: Dutton.

Segal, Z. V., Williams, S., & Teasdale, J. (2002). *Mindfulness-based cognitive therapy for depression: A new approach to preventing relapse.* New York: Guilford.

Segall, M. H., Campbell, D. T., & Herskovits, M. J. (1966). *The influence of culture on visual perception.* Indianapolis, IN: Bobbs-Merrill.

Segerstrom, S. C. (2005). Optimism and immunity: Do positive thoughts always lead to positive effects? *Brain, Behavior, and Immunity, 19,* 195–200.

Segerstrom, S. C., Taylor, S. E., Kemeny, M. E., & Fahey, J. L. (1998). Optimism is associated with mood, coping, and immune change in response to stress. *Journal of Personality and Social Psychology, 74,* 1646–1655.

Segrin, C. (2000). Social skill deficits associated with depression. *Clinical Psychology Review, 20,* 379–403.

Seidman, L. J., Pantelis, C., Keshavan, M., Faraone, S., Goldstein, J., Horton, N. J., et al. (2003). A review and new report of medial temporal lobe dysfunction as a vulnerability indicator for schizophrenia: A magnetic resonance imaging morphometric family study of the parahippocampal gyrus. *Schizophrenia Bulletin, 29,* 803–830.

Seitz, A. R., & Watanabe, T. (2003). Psychophysics: Is subliminal learning really passive? *Nature, 422,* 36.

Selby, E. A, Anestis, M. D., Bender, T. W., & Joiner, T. E., Jr. (2009). An exploration of the emotional cascade model in borderline personality disorder. *Journal of Abnormal Psychology, 118* (2), 375–387.

Selby, E. A., & Joiner, T. E., Jr. (in press). Cascades of emotion: The emergence of borderline personality disorder from emotional and behavioral dysregulation. *Review of General Psychology.*

Selden, S. (1999). *Inheriting shame: The story of eugenics and racism in America.* New York: Teachers College Press.

Seligman, D. (1994). *A question of intelligence.* New York: Citadel Press.

Seligman, M. E. P. (1971). Phobias and preparedness. *Behavior Therapy, 2,* 307–320.

Seligman, M. E. P. (1975). *Helplessness: On depression, development, and death.* San Francisco: Freeman.

Seligman, M. E. P. (1990). *Learned optimism.* New York: Knopf.

Seligman, M. E. P., & Csikszentmihalyi, M. (2000). Positive psychology: An introduction. *American Psychologist, 55,* 5–14.

Seligman, M. E. P., & Hager, J. L. (1972). Sauce-bearnaise syndrome. *Psychology Today, 6*(3), 59.

Seligman, M. E. P., & Maier, S. F. (1967). Failure to escape traumatic shock. *Journal of Experimental Psychology, 74,* 1–9.

Seligman, M. E. P., & Pawelski, J. O. (2003). Positive psychology: FAQs. *Psychological Inquiry, 14,* 159–163.

Selye, H. (1956). *The stress of life.* New York: McGraw Hill.

Serbin, L. A., & O'Leary, K. D. (1975). How nursery schools teach girls to shut up. *Psychology Today, 9*(7), 56–58.

Serpell, R. (1979). How specific are perceptual skills? *British Journal of Psychology, 70,* 365–380.

Sevdalis, N., & Harvey, N. (2007) Biased forecasting of postdecisional affect. *Psychological Science 18,* 678–681.

Seyfarth, R. M., & Cheney, D. L. (1997). Behavioral mechanisms underlying vocal communication in nonhuman primates. *Animal Learning & Behavior, 25,* 249–267.

Shade, E. D., Ulrich, C. M., Wener, M. H., Wood, B., Yasui, Y., Lacroix, K., et al. (2004). Frequent intentional weight loss is associated with lower natural killer cell cytotoxicity in postmenopausal women: Possible long-term immune effects. *Journal of the American Dietetic Association, 104,* 903–912.

Shadish, W. R. (1995). The logic of generalization: Five principles common to experiments and ethnographies. *American Journal of Community Psychology, 23,* 419–428.

Shadish, W. R., Cook, T. D., & Campbell, D. T. (2002). *Experimental and quasi-experimental designs for generalized causal inference.* Boston, MA: Houghton Mifflin.

Shaffer, H. J. (2000). Addictive personality. In A. E. Kazdin (ed.), *Encyclopedia of psychology* (Vol. 1, pp. 35–36). Washington, DC: American Psychological Association and Oxford University Press.

Shamsuzzaman, A. S., Gersh, B. J., & Somers, V. K. (2003). Obstructive sleep apnea: Implications for cardiac and vascular disease. *Journal of the American Medical Association, 290,* 1906–1914.

Shanab, M. E., & Yahya, K. A. (1977). A behavioral study of obedience in children. *Journal of Personality and Social Psychology, 35,* 530–536.

Shapiro, A. F., Gottman, J. M., & Carrere, S. (2000). The baby and the marriage: Identifying factors that buffer against decline in marital satisfaction after the first baby arrives. *Journal of Family Psychology, 14,* 59–70.

Shapiro, D. A., & Shapiro, D. (1982). Meta-analysis of comparative therapy outcome studies: A replication and refinement. *Psychological Bulletin, 92,* 581–604.

Shapiro, F. (1989). Eye movement desensitization: A new treatment for post-traumatic stress disorder. *Journal of Behavior Therapy and Experimental Psychiatry, 20,* 211–217.

Shapiro, F. (1995). *Eye movement desensitization and reprocessing: Basic principles, protocols, and procedures.* New York: Guilford Press.

Shapiro, F., & Forrest, M. S. (1997). *EMDR: The breakthrough therapy for overcoming anxiety, stress, and trauma.* New York: Basic Books.

Shapiro, S. L., & Walsh, R. (2003). An analysis of recent meditation research and suggestions for future directions. *The Humanistic Psychologist, 31,* 86–113.

Shaw, P., Greenstein, D., Lerch, J., Clasen, L., Lenroot, R., Gogtay, N., et al. (2006). Intellectual ability and cortical development in children and adolescents. *Nature, 440,* 676–679.

Shea, S. C. (1998). *Psychiatric interviewing: The art of understanding* (2nd ed). Philadelphia: W. B. Saunders.

Shedler, J. (2010). The efficacy of psychodynamic psychotherapy. *American Psychologist, 65,* 98–109.

Shedler, J., & Block, J. (1990). Adolescent drug use and psychological health: A longitudinal inquiry. *American Psychologist, 45,* 612–630.

Sheehan, P. W. (1991). Hypnosis, context, and commitment. In S. J. Lynn & J. W. Rhue (eds.), *Theories of hypnosis: Current models and perspectives* (pp. 520–541). New York: Guilford Press.

Sheldon, K. M., & King, L. (2001). Why positive psychology is necessary. *American Psychologist, 56,* 216–217.

Sheldon, K. M., & Lyubomirsky, S. (2006). How to increase and sustain positive emotion: The effects of expressing gratitude and visualizing best possible selves. *The Journal of Positive Psychology, 1,* 73–82.

Sheldon, W. (1971). The New York study of physical constitution and psychotic pattern. *Journal of the History of the Behavioral Sciences, 7,* 115–126.

Shenk, J. W. (2005). *Lincoln's melancholy: How depression challenged a president and fueled his greatness.* Boston: Houghton Mifflin.

Shepard, R. N. (1990). *Mind sights: Original visual illusions, ambiguities, and other anomalies.* New York: W. H. Freeman.

Shepperd, J. A., & Koch, E. J. (2005). Pitfalls in teaching judgment heuristics. *Teaching of Psychology, 32,* 43–46.

Sher, K. J. (1987). Stress response dampening. In H. T. Blane & K. E. Leonard (eds.) *Psychological theories of drinking and alcoholism,* (pp. 227–271). New York: Guilford

Sher, K. J., Grekin, E. R., & Williams, N. A. (2005). The development of alcohol use disorders. In S. Nolen-Hoeksema, T. D. Cannon, & T. Widiger (eds.), *Annual Review of Clinical Psychology, 1,* 493–524.

Sher, K. J., Wood, M. D., Richardson, A. E., & Jackson, K. M. (2005). Subjective effects of alcohol 1: Effects of the drink and drinking context. In M. Earleywine (ed.), *Mind-altering drugs: The science of subjective experience* (pp. 86–134). Washington, DC: American Psychological Association.

Sherif, M. (1936). *The psychology of social norms.* New York: Harper.

Sherif, M., Harvey, O. J., White, B. J., Hood, W. R., & Sherif, C. W. (1961). *The Robbers Cave experiment: Intergroup conflict and cooperation.* Middletown, CT: Wesleyan University Press.

Sherman, R. A., Sherman, C. J., & Parker, L. (1984). Chronic phantom and stump pain among American veterans: Results of a survey. *Pain, 18,* 83–95.

Shermer, M. (2002). *Why people believe weird things: Pseudoscience, superstition, and other confusions of our time* (2nd ed.). New York: W. H. Freeman.

Shermer, M. (2008, October). Five ways brains scans mislead. *Scientific American.* http://www.scientificamerican.com/article.cfm?id=five-ways-brain-scans-mislead-us.

Sherrington, C. S. (1906). *The integrative action of the nervous system.* New York: Charles Scribner's Sons.

Shimamura, A. P. (1992). Organic amnesia. In L. Squire (ed.), *Encyclopedia of learning and memory* (pp. 30–35). New York: Macmillan.

Shimamura, A. P., Berry, J. M., Mangels, J. A., Rusting, C. L., & Jurica, P. J. (1995). Memory and cognitive abilities in university professors: Evidence for successful aging. *Psychological Science, 6,* 271–277.

Shin, S. M., Chow, C., Camacho-Gonsalves, T., Levy, R. J., Allen, E., & Leff, S. H. (2005). A meta-analytic review of racial-ethnic matching for African American and Caucasian American clients and clinicians. *Journal of Counseling Psychology, 52,* 45–56.

Shlien, J., & Levant, R. (1984). Introduction. In R. Levant & J. Shlien (eds.), *Client-centered therapy and the person-centered approach: New directions in theory, research and practice* (pp. 1–16). New York: Praeger.

Shoemaker, G. E., & Fagen, J. W. (1984). Stimulus preference and its effect on visual habituation and dishabituation in four-month-old infants. *Genetic Psychology Monographs, 109,* 3–18.

Shomstein, S., & Yantis, S. (2006). Parietal cortex mediates voluntary control of spatial and nonspatial auditory attention. *Journal of Neuroscience, 26,* 435–439.

Shors, T. J., & Matzel, L. D. (1999). Long-term potentiation: What's learning got to do with it? *Behavioral and Brain Sciences, 20,* 597–655.

Showalter, E. (1997). *Hystories: Hysterical epidemics and modern culture.* New York: Columbia University Press.

Shrauger, J. S., & Schoeneman, T. J. (1979). Symbolic interactionist view of self-concept: Through the looking glass darkly. *Psychological Bulletin, 86,* 549–573.

Sieff, E. M., Dawes, R. M., & Loewenstein, G. (1999). Anticipated versus actual reaction to HIV test results. *American Journal of Psychology, 112,* 297–311.

Siegel, J. (2005). Clues to the function of mammalian sleep. *Nature, 437,* 1264–1271.

Siegel, J. M. (2009). Sleep viewed as a state of adaptive inactivity. *Nature Reviews Neuroscience, 10,* 747–753.

Siegelbaum, S. A., Camardo, J. S., & Kandel, E. R. (1982, September 30). Serotonin and cyclic AMP close single K+ channels in Aplysia sensory neurons. *Nature, 299,* 413–417.

Siegler, R. S. (1992). The other Alfred Binet. *Developmental Psychology, 28,* 179–190.

Siegler, R. S. (1995). Children's thinking: How does change occur? In F. E. Weinert & W. Schneider (eds.), *Memory performance and competencies: Issues in growth and development* (pp. 405–430). Hillsdale, NJ: Erlbaum.

Siever, L. J., & Davis, K. L. (2004). The pathophysiology of schizophrenia disorders: Perspectives from the spectrum. *American Journal of Psychiatry, 161,* 398–413.

Sigman, M., & Whaley, S. E. (1998). The role of nutrition in the development of intelligence. In U. Neisser (ed.), *The rising curve: Long-term gains in IQ and related measures* (pp. 155–182). Washington, DC: American Psychological Association.

Sigurdsson, T., Doyere, V., Cain, C. K., & LeDoux, J. E. (2007). Long-term potentiation in the amygdala: A cellular mechanism of fear learning and memory. *Neuropharmacology, 52,* 215–227.

Silveira, J. M., & Seeman, M. V. (1995). Shared psychotic disorder: A critical review of the literature. *Canadian Journal of Psychiatry, 40,* 389–395.

Silventoinen, K., Sammalisto, S., Perola, M., Boomsma, D. I., Cornes, B. K., Davis, C., et al. (2003). Heritability of adult body height: A comparative study of twin cohorts in eight countries. *Twin Research, 6,* 399–408.

Silver, E., Cirincione, C., & Steadman, H. J. (1994). Demythologizing inaccurate perceptions of the insanity defense. *Law and Human Behavior, 18,* 63–70.

Silverman, S. (1987, July). Medical "miracles": Still mysterious despite claims of believers. *Newsletter of the Sacramento Skeptics Society,* Sacramento, CA, pp. 2–7.

Simeon, D., Gross, S., Guralnik, O., Stein, D. J., Schmeidler, J., & Hollander, E. (1997). Feeling unreal: 30 Cases of DSM-III-R depersonalization. *American Journal of Psychiatry, 154,* 1107–1113.

Simmons, D. A., & Neill. D. B. (2009) Functional interaction between the basolateral amygdala and the ventral striatum underlies incentive motivation for food reward. *Neuroscience, 159,* 1264–1273.

Simon, C. W., & Emmons, W. H. (1955). Learning during sleep? *Psychological Bulletin, 52,* 328–342.

Simon, G., von Kopff, M., Saunders, K., Miglioretti, D. L., Crane, K., Van Belle, K., et al. (2006). Association between obesity and psychiatric disorders in the U.S. population. *Archives of General Psychiatry, 63,* 824–830.

Simon, M. J., & Salzberg, H. C. (1985). The effect of manipulated expectancies on posthypnotic amnesia. *International Journal of Clinical and Experimental Hypnosis, 33,* 40–51.

Simon, R. I. (2006). Imminent suicide: The illusion of short-term prediction. *Suicide and Life-Threatening Behavior, 36,* 296–301.

Simon-Moffat, A. (2002). New fossils and a glimpse of evolution. *Science, 25,* 613–615.

Simons, D. J., & Chabris, C. F. (1999). Gorillas in our midst: Sustained inattentional blindness for dynamic events. *Perception, 28,* 1059–1074.

Simons, R. C., & Hughes, C. C. (1986). *The culture-bound syndromes: Folk illnesses of psychiatric and anthropological interest.* Boston: D. Reidel.

Simonton, D. K. (1997). Creative productivity: A predictive and explanatory model of career trajectories and landmarks. *Psychological Review, 104,* 66–89.

Simonton, D. K. (1999). *Origins of genius.* New York: Cambridge Press.

Simonton, D. K. (2006). Presidential IQ, openness, intellectual brilliance and leadership: Estimates and correlations for 42 U.S. chief executives. *Political Psychology, 27,* 511–526.

Simonton, D. K., & Song, A. V. (2009). Eminence, IQ, physical and mental health, and achievement domain: Cox's 282 geniuses revisited. *Psychological Science, 20,* 429–434.

Simpson, G. M., & Kline, N. S. (1976). Tardive dyskinesias: Manifestations, etiology, and treatment. In M. D. Yahr (ed.), *The basal ganglia* (pp. 167–183). New York: Raven Press.

Sinclair, R. R., & Tetrick, L. E. (2000). Implications of item wording for hardiness structure, relation with neuroticism, and stress buffering. *Journal of Research in Personality, 34,* 1–25.

Singer, M. (1979, January). Coming out of the cults. *Psychology Today,* 72–82.

Singer, M. T., & Lalich, J. (1996). *Crazy therapies.* Baltimore: Jossey-Bass.

Singer, M. T., & Nievod, A. (2003). New age therapies. In S. O. Lilienfeld, S. J. Lynn, & J. M. Lohr (eds.), *Science and pseudoscience in clinical psychology* (pp. 176–204). New York: Guilford.

Singh, D. (1993). Adaptive significance of female physical attractiveness: Role of waist-to-hip ratio. *Journal of Personality and Social Psychology, 65,* 293–307.

Singh, D. (1995). Female judgment of male attractiveness and desirability for relationships: Role of waist-to-hip ratio and financial status. *Journal of Personality and Social Psychology, 69,* 1089–1101.

Singh, S., & Ernst, E. (2008). *Trick or treatment: Alternative medicine on trial.* New York: Bantam.

Sinkavich, F. J. (1995). Performance and metamemory: Do students know what they don't know? *Instructional Psychology, 22,* 77–87.

Skeem, J. L., Monahan, J., & Mulvey, E. P. (2002). Psychopathy, treatment involvement, and subsequent violence among civil psychiatric patients. *Law and Human Behavior, 26,* 577–603.

Skinner, B. F. (1938). *The behavior of organisms: An experimental analysis.* New York: Appleton-Century-Crofts.

Skinner, B. F. (1948). Superstition in the pigeon. *Journal of Experimental Psychology, 38,* 168–172.

Skinner, B. F. (1953). *Science and human behavior.* New York: Macmillan.

Skinner, B. F. (1969). *Contingencies of reinforcement.* East Norwalk, CT: Appleton-Century-Crofts.

Skinner, B. F. (1971). *Beyond freedom and dignity.* New York: Knopf.

Skinner, B. F. (1974). *About behaviorism.* New York: Vintage Books.

Skinner, B. F. (1990). Can psychology be a science of mind? *American Psychologist, 4,* 1206–1210.

Skinner, E., Edge, K., Altman, J., & Sherwood, H. (2003). Searching for the structure of coping: A review and critique of category systems for classifying ways of coping. *Psychological Bulletin, 129,* 216–219.

Slade, T., & Andrews, G. (2005). Latent structure of depression in a community sample: A taxometric analysis. *Psychological Medicine, 35,* 489–497.

Slater, A. (1997). Can measures of infant habituation predict later intellectual ability? *Archives of Diseases of the Child, 77,* 474–476.

Slater, L. (2004). *Opening Skinner's box: Great psychological experiments of the 20th century.* New York: W. W. Norton.

Slavin, R. E., & Cooper, R. (1999). Improving intergroup relations: Lessons learned from cooperative learning programs. *Journal of Social Issues, 55,* 647–663.

Slegel, D. E., Benson, K. L., Zarcone, V. P., & Schubert, E. D. (1991). Middle-ear muscle activity and its association with motor activity in the extremities and head in sleep. *Lancet, 337,* 597–599.

Sloan, R. P., Bagiella, E., & Powell, T. (1999). Religion, spirituality, and medicine. *Lancet, 353,* 644–647.

Sloane, R. B., Staples, F., Cristol, A., Yorkston, N., & Whipple, K. (1975). *Psychotherapy versus behavior therapy*. Cambridge, MA: Harvard University Press.

Slovic, P., & Peters, E. (2006). Risk perception and affect. *Current Directions in Psychological Science, 15,* 322–325.

Slutske, W. S., Heath, A. C., Dinwiddie, S. H., Madden, P. A., & Bucholz, K. K. (1998). Common genetic risk factors for conduct disorder and alcohol dependence. *Journal of Abnormal Psychology, 107,* 363–374.

Smalheiser, N. R., Manev, H., & Costa, E. (2001) RNAi and memory: Was McConnell on the right track after all? *Trends in Neuroscience, 24,* 216–218.

Smeets, T., Giesbrecht, T., Raymaekers, L., Shaw, J., & Merckelbach, H. (2010). Autobiographical integration of trauma memories and repressive coping predict post-traumatic stress symptoms in undergraduate students. *Clinical Psychology and Psychotherapy, 17,* 211–218.

Smith, D., & Dumont, F. (1995). A cautionary study: Unwarranted interpretations of the Draw-A-Person Test. *Professional Psychology: Research and Practice, 26,* 298–303.

Smith, D. B. (2009, August). The doctor is in. *American Scholar.* http://www.theamericanscholar.org/the-doctor-is-in/.

Smith, D. M., Schwarz, N., Roberts, T. R., & Ubel, P. A. (2006). Why are you calling me? How study introductions change response patterns. *Quality of Life Research, 15,* 621–630.

Smith, D. M., Langa, K. M., Kabeto, M. U., & Ubel, P. A. (2005). Health, wealth, and happiness: Financial resources buffer subjective well-being after the onset of a disability. *Psychological Science, 16,* 663–666.

Smith, G. P. (1996). The direct and indirect controls of meal size. *Neuroscience Biobehavioral Review, 20,* 40–46.

Smith, G. T., Spillane, N. S., & Annus, A. M. (2006). Implications of an emerging integration of universal and culturally-specific psychologies. *Perspectives on Psychological Science, 1,* 211–233.

Smith, J. (2009). Pseudoscience and extraordinary claims of the paranormal. New York: Wiley.

Smith, J. D., & Dumont, F. (2002). Confidence in psychodiagnosis: What makes us so sure? *Clinical Psychology and Psychotherapy, 9,* 292–298.

Smith, L., Fagan, J. F., & Ulvund, S. E. (2002). The relation of recognition memory in infancy and parental socioeconomic status to later intellectual competence. *Intelligence, 30,* 247–259.

Smith, L. B. (2000). Learning how to learn words: An associative crane. In *Becoming a Word Learner.* New York: Oxford University Press.

Smith, M., & Hall, C. S. (1964). An investigation of regression in a long dream series. *Journal of Gerontology, 19,* 66–71.

Smith, M. L. (1980). Teacher expectations. *Evaluation in Education, 4,* 53–55.

Smith, M. L., & Glass, G. V. (1977). Meta-analysis of psychotherapy outcome studies. *American Psychologist, 32,* 752–760.

Smith, M. L., Glass, G. V., & Miller, T. I. (1980). *The benefits of psychotherapy.* Baltimore: Johns Hopkins University Press.

Smith, M. T., & Haythornthwaite, J. A. (2004). How do sleep disturbance and chronic pain inter-relate? Insights from the longitudinal and cognitive-behavioral clinical trials literature. *Sleep Medicine Review, 8,* 119–132.

Smith, P. K., & Daglish, L. (1977). Sex differences in parent and infant behavior in the home. *Child Development, 48,* 1250–1254.

Smith, R. A. (2001). *Challenging your preconceptions: Thinking critically about psychology.* Pacific Grove, CA: Wadsworth.

Smith, S. L., Gerhardt, K. J., Griffiths, S. K., Huang, X., & Abrams, R. M. (2003). Intelligibility of sentences recorded from the uterus of a pregnant ewe and from the fetal inner ear. *Audiology & Neuro-otology, 8,* 347–353.

Smith, S. M. (1979). Remembering in and out of context. *Journal of Experimental Psychology: Human Learning and Memory, 5,* 460–471.

Smith, S. M., Brown, H. O., Toman, J. E., & Goodman, L. S. (1947). The lack of cerebral effects of d-tubercurarine. *Anesthesiology, 8,* 1–14.

Smith, S. M., Lindsay, R. C. L., Pryke, S., & Dysart, J. E. (2001). Postdictors of eyewitness errors: Can false identifications be diagnosed in the cross race situation? *Psychology, Public Policy, and Law, 7,* 153–169.

Smith, S. S. (2005). NCHS Dataline. *Public Health Reports, 120,* 353–354.

Smith, T. (2008). Empirically supported and unsupported treatments for autism spectrum disorders. *Scientific Review of Mental Health Practice, 6,* 3–20.

Smith, T. W., & Gallo, L. C. (2001). Personality traits as risk factors for physical illness. In A. Baum, T. A. Revenson, & J. Singer (eds.), *Handbook of health psychology* (pp. 139–173). Mahwah, NJ: Erlbaum.

Smitherman-Donaldson, G., & van Dijk, T. (1988). *Discourse and discrimination.* Detroit: Wayne State University Press.

Smyth, J. M., Stonr, A. A., Hurewitz, A., & Kaell, A. (1999). Effects of writing about stressful experiences on symptom reduction in patients with asthma or rheumatoid arthritis: A randomized trial. *Journal of the American Medical Association, 281,* 1304–1309.

Smythe, I. H. (2007). The secret behind "The Secret": What is attracting millions to the "Law of Attraction"? *Skeptic, 13*(2), 8–11.

Snarey, J. (1982). *The social and moral development of kibbutz founders and Sabras: A cross-sectional and longitudinal cross-cultural study.* Thesis presented to the faculty of the Graduate School of Education, Harvard University, Cambridge, MA.

Snelson, J. S. (1993). The ideological immune system: Resistance to new ideas in science. *Skeptic, 1*(4), 44–55.

Snider, V. E. (1992). Learning styles and learning to read: A critique. *RASE: Remedial & Special Education, 13,* 6–18.

Snook, B., Cullen, R. M., Bennell, C., Taylor, P. J., & Gendreau, P. (2008). The criminal profiling illusion: What's behind the smoke and mirrors? *Criminal Justice and Behavior, 35,* 1257–1276.

Snowdon, D. A. (2003). Healthy aging and dementia: Findings from the nun study. *Annals of Internal Medicine, 139,* 450–454.

Snyder, C. R., Shenkel, R. J., & Lowery, C. R. (1977). Acceptance of personality interpretations: The "Barnum effect" and beyond. *Journal of Consulting and Clinical Psychology, 45,* 104–114.

Snyder, M. (1974). Self monitoring of expressive behavior. *Journal of Personality and Social Psychology, 30,* 526–537.

Snyder, M. & Uranowitz, S. W. (1978), Reconstructing the past: Some cognitive consequences of person perception. *Journal of Personality and Social Psychology, 36,* 941–950.

Snyder, S. H. (1975). *Madness and the brain.* New York: McGraw-Hill.

Snyder, T. J., & Gackenbach, J. (1988). Individual differences associated with lucid dreaming. In J. Gackenbach & S. Laberge (eds.), *Conscious mind, sleeping brain: Perspectives on lucid dreaming* (pp. 221–260). New York: Plenum.

So, K., & Orme-Johnson, D. (2001). Three randomized experiments on the longitudinal effects of the transcendental meditation technique on cognition. *Intelligence, 29,* 419–440.

Soar, K., Parrott, A. C., & Fox, H. C. (2004). Persistent neuropsychological problems after 7 years of abstinence from recreational ecstasy (MDMA): A case study. *Psychological Reports, 95,* 192–196.

Sobell, M. B., & Sobell, L. C. (1973). Alcoholics treated by individualized behavior therapy: One year treatment outcome. *Behaviour Research and Therapy, 11,* 599–618.

Sobell, M. B., & Sobell, L. C. (1976). Second year treatment outcome of alcoholics treated by individualized behavior therapy: Results. *Behaviour Research and Therapy, 14,* 195–215.

Solms, M. (1997). *The neuropsychology of dreams: A clinico-anatomical study.* Mahwah, NJ: Lawrence Erlbaum Associates.

Solms, M., & Turnbull, O. (2002). *The brain and the inner world.* New York: Other Press.

Solomon, P. R., Adams, F., Silver, A., Zimmer, J., & DeVeaux, R. (2002). Ginkgo for memory enhancement: A randomized controlled trial. *Journal of the American Medical Association, 288,* 835–840.

Solomon, R. (2002). *That takes ovaries! Bold females and their brazen acts.* New York: Three Rivers Press.

Solomon, S. S., & King, J. G. (1995). Influence of color on fire vehicle accidents. *Journal of Safety Research, 26,* 41–48.

Solomon, S., Greenberg, J., & Pyszczynski, T. (2000). Pride and prejudice: Fear of death and social behavior. *Current Directions in Psychological Science, 6,* 200–204.

Somers, S. (2009). *Knockout: Interviews with doctors who are curing cancer: And how to prevent getting it in the first place.* New York: Crown.

Sommers, C. H., & Satel, S. (2005). *One nation under therapy: How the helping culture is eroding self-reliance.* New York: St. Martin's Press.

Soper, B., Milford, G., & Rosenthal, G. (1995). Belief when evidence does not support theory. *Psychology & Marketing, 12,* 415–422.

Sorace, A. (2007). The more, the merrier: Facts and beliefs about the bilingual mind. In S. Della Sala (ed.), *Tall tales about the mind and the brain: Separating fact from fiction* (pp. 193–203). Oxford, England: Oxford University Press.

Sorkhabi, N. (2005). Applicability of Baumrind's parent typology to collective cultures: Analysis of cultural explanations of parent socialization effects. *International Journal of Behavioral Development, 29,* 552–563.

Spangler, W. D. (1992). Validity of questionnaire and TAT measures of need for achievement: Two meta-analyses. *Psychological Bulletin, 112,* 140–154.

Spanos, N. P. (1986). Hypnotic behavior: A social-psychological interpretation of amnesia, analgesia, and "trance logic." *The Behavioral and Brain Sciences, 9,* 499–502.

Spanos, N. P. (1991). A sociocognitive approach to hypnosis. In S. J. Lynn & J. W. Rhue (eds.), *Theories of hypnosis: Current models and perspectives* (pp. 324–361). New York: Guilford Press.

Spanos, N. P. (1994). Multiple identity enactments and multiple personality disorder: A sociocognitive perspective. *Psychological Bulletin, 116,* 143–165.

Spanos, N. P. (1996). *Multiple identities and false memories: A sociocognitive perspective.* Washington, DC: American Psychological Association.

Spanos, N. P., Cobb, P. C., & Gorassini, D. (1985). Failing to resist hypnotic test suggestions: A strategy for self-presenting as deeply hypnotized. *Psychiatry, 48,* 282–292.

Spanos, N. P., & Hewitt, E. C. (1980). The hidden observer in hypnotic analgesia: Discovery or experimental creation? *Journal of Personality and Social Psychology, 39,* 1201–1214.

Spanos, N. P., Menary, E., Gabora, M. J., DuBreuil, S. C., & Dewhirst, B. (1991). Secondary identity enactments during hypnotic past-life regression: A sociocognitive perspective. *Journal of Personality and Social Psychology, 61,* 308–320.

Sparks, J. A., Duncan, B. L., & Miller, S. D. (2008). Common factors in psychotherapy. In J. L. Lebow (ed.), *Twenty-first century psychotherapies: Contemporary approaches to theory and practice* (pp. 453–497). Hoboken, NJ: Wiley.

Spearman, C. (1927). *The abilities of man.* New York: Macmillan.

Spehr, M., Gisselmann, G., Poplawski, A., Riffel, J. A., Wetzel, C. H., Zimmer, R. K., et al. (2003). Identification of a testicular odorant receptor mediating human sperm chemotaxis. *Science, 299,* 2054–2058.

Spelke, E. S. (1994). Initial knowledge: Six suggestions. *Cognition, 50,* 431–445.

Spelke, E. S. (2005). Sex differences in intrinsic aptitude for mathematics and science: A critical review. *American Psychologist, 60,* 950–958.

Sperling, G. (1960). The information available in brief visual presentations. *Psychological Monographs: General and Applied, 74* (11, Whole No. 498), 1–29.

Sperry, R. W. (1974). Lateral specialization in the surgically separated hemispheres. In F. Schmitt & F. Worden (eds.), *Neurosciences third study program* (pp. 5–19). Cambridge, MA: MIT Press.

Spiegel, D., Bloom, J. R., Kramer, H. C., & Gottheil, E. (1989). Effect of psychosocial treatment on survival of patients with metastatic breast cancer. *Lancet, 2,* 888–891.

Spiegler, M. (1983). *Contemporary behavior therapy.* Palo Alto, CA: Mayfield.

Spiegler, M. D., & Guevremont, D. C. (2003). *Contemporary behavior therapy* (4th ed). Belmont, CA: Wadsworth/Thompson Learning.

Spielman, A., Conroy, D., & Glovinsky, P. B. (2003). Evaluation of insomnia. In M. L. Perlis, & K. L. Lichstein (eds.), *Treating sleep disorders: Principles and practice of behavioral sleep medicine* (pp. 190–213). Hoboken, NJ: John Wiley & Sons.

Spirito, A., & Esposito-Smythers, C. (2006). Attempted and completed suicide in adolescence. *Annual Review of Clinical Psychology, 2,* 237–266.

Spitzer, R. (2003). Can some gay men and lesbians change their sexual orientation? 200 participants reporting a change from homosexual to heterosexual orientation. *Archives of Sexual Behavior, 32,* 403–417.

Spitzer, R. L. (1975). On pseudoscience, science, logic in remission, and psychiatric diagnosis: A critique of Rosenhan's "On being sane in insane places." *Journal of Abnormal Psychology, 84,* 442–452.

Spoormacher, V., & Van den Bout, J. (2006). Lucid dreaming treatment for nightmares: A pilot study. *Psychotherapy and Psychosomatics, 75,* 389–394.

Spotts, J. V., & Shontz, F. C. (1976). *The lifestyles of nine American cocaine users: Trips to the land of cockaigne* [Alcohol, Drug Abuse, and Mental Health Administration, NIDA Issue No. 16]. Washington, DC: Department of Health, Education, and Welfare, PHS; U. S. Government Printing Office.

Spotts, J. F., & Shontz, F. C. (1983). Drug-induced ego states. 1. *The International Journal of the Addictions, 18,* 119–151.

Sprecher, S. (1998). Insider's perspectives on reasons for attraction to a close other. *Social Psychology Quarterly, 61,* 287–300.

Sprecher, S., Barbee, A., & Schwartz, P. (1995). "Was it good for you, too?": Gender differences in first sexual experiences. *Journal of Sex Research, 32,* 3–15.

Squire, L. R. (1987). *Memory and brain.* New York: Oxford University Press.

Srivastava, S., John, O. P., Gosling, S. D., & Potter, J. (2003). Development of personality in early and middle adulthood: Set like plaster or persistent change? *Journal of Personality and Social Psychology, 84,* 1041–1053.

Sroufe, L. A. (1983). Infant-caregiver attachment and patterns of adaptations in preschool: The roots of maladaptations and competence. In M. Perlmutter (ed.), *Minnesota Symposium on Child Psychology* (Vol. 16, pp. 41–81). Hillsdale, NJ: Erlbaum.

Staal, W. G.Pol, H.E. H., Schnack, H. G., Mechteld, L. C., Hoogendoorn, M. S. Jellema, K., et al. (2000). Structural abnormalities in patients with schizophrenia and their healthy siblings. *American Journal of Psychiatry, 157,* 416–421.

Staaddon, J. E. R. (2003) Humanism and Skinner's Radical Behaviorism. In K. A. Lattal & P. N. Chase (Ed.), *Behavior theory and philosophy,* (pp. 129–146). New York, NY: Kluwer Academic/Plenum Publishers.

Staddon, J. E. R. & Cerutti, D. T. (2003) Operant behavior. *Annual Review of Psychology, 54,* 115–144.

Staddon, J. E. R., & Simmelhag, V. L. (1971). Superstition experiment—A reexamination of its implications for principles of adaptive behavior. *Psychological Review, 78,* 3.

Stahl, S. (1999). Different strokes for different folks? A critique of learning styles. *American Educator, 23,* 27–31.

Standing, L., Conezio, J., & Haber, R. N. (1970). Perception and memory for pictures: Single-trial learning of 2500 visual stimuli. *Psychonomic Science 19,* 73–74.

Stanovich, K. E. (2009). *Decision making and rationality in the modern world.* New York: Oxford University Press.

Stanovich, K. E. (2009). *What intelligence tests miss: The psychology of rational thought.* New Haven, CT: Yale University Press.

Stanovich, K. E., & West, R. F. (2000). Advancing the rationality debate. *Behavioral and Brain Sciences, 23,* 701–726.

Stanovich, K. E, & West. R. F. (2008). On the failure of intelligence to predict myside bias and one-sided bias. *Thinking & Reasoning, 14,* 129–167.

Starr, L. R., & Davila, J. (2008). Excessive reassurance seeking, depression, and interpersonal rejection: A meta-analytic review. *Journal of Abnormal Psychology, 117,* 762–765.

Stasser, G., & Titus, W. (2003). Hidden profiles: A brief history. *Psychological Inquiry, 14,* 304–313.

Stathopoulou, G., Powers, M. B., Berry, A. C., Smits, J. A. J., & Otto, M. W. (2006). Exercise interventions for mental health: A quantitative and qualitative review. *Clinical Psychology: Science and Practice, 13,* 179–193.

Steadman, H. J., Mulvey, E. P., Monahan, J., Robbins, P. C., Appelbaum, P., Grisso, T., et al. (1998). Violence by people discharged from acute psychiatric inpatient facilities and by others in the same neighborhoods. *Archives of General Psychiatry, 55,* 1–9.

Steblay, N. M. (1992). A meta-analytic review of the weapon focus effect. *Law and Human Behavior, 16,* 413–424.

Steblay, N. M., & Bothwell, R. K. (1994). Evidence for hypnotically refreshed testimony: The view from the laboratory. *Law and Human Behavior, 18,* 635–651.

Steblay, N. M., Dysart, J., Fulero, S., & Lindsay, R. C. L. (2001). Eyewitness accuracy rates in sequential and simultaneous lineup presentations: A meta-analytic comparison. *Law and Human Behavior, 25,* 459–474.

Steblay, N. M., Dysart, J. E., Fulero, S., & Lindsay, R. C. L. (2003). Eyewitness accuracy rates in police showup and lineup presentations: A meta-analytic comparison. *Law and Human Behavior, 27,* 523–540.

Steele, C. M. (1997). A threat in the air: How stereotypes shape intellectual identity and performance. *American Psychologist, 52,* 613–629.

Steele, C. M., & Aronson, J. (1995). Stereotype threat and the intellectual test-performance of African-Americans. *Journal of Personality and Social Psychology, 69,* 797–811.

Steele, K. M., Bass, K. E., & Crook, M. D. (1999). The mystery of the Mozart effect: Failure to replicate. *Psychological Science, 10,* 366–369.

Steele, M., Weiss, M., Swanson, J., Wang, J., Prinzo, R., & Binder, C. (2006). A randomized, controlled effectiveness trial of OROS-methylphenidate compared to usual care with immediate release methylphenidate in ADHD. *Canadian Journal of Clinical Pharmacology, 14,* 50–62.

Stein, M. B., Jang, K. L., & Livesley, W. J. (1999). Heritability of anxiety sensitivity: A twin study. *American Journal of Psychiatry, 156,* 246–251.

Steinberg, L. (2001). We know some things: Adolescent-parent relationships in retrospect and prospect. *Journal of Research in Adolescence, 11,* 1–20.

Steinberg, L. (2007). Risk-taking in adolescence: New perspectives from brain and behavioral science. *Current Directions in Psychological Science, 16,* 55–59.

Steinberg, L. (2008). A social neuroscience perspective on adolescent decision-making. *Developmental Review, 28,* 78–106.

Steinberg, L., & Scott, E. S. (2003). Less guilty by reason of adolescence—Developmental immaturity, diminished responsibility, and the juvenile death penalty. *American Psychologist, 58,* 1009–1018.

Steinhardt. L. (1998). Sand, water, and universal form in sandplay and art therapy. *Art Therapy, 15,* 252–260.

Steinmetz, J. L., Lewinsohn, P. M., & Antonuccio, D. O. (1983). Prediction of individual outcome in a group intervention for depression. *Journal of Consulting and Clinical Psychology, 51,* 331–337.

Stephan, W. G. (1978). School desegregation: An evaluation of predictions made in *Brown v. Board of Education. Psychological Bulletin, 85,* 217–238.

Stepp, L. S. (2007, April 24). For Virginia Tech survivors, memories will be powerful. Washingtonpost.com. Retrieved June 18, 2007, from www.washingtonpost.com/wp-dyn/content/2007/article/04/20/AR2007042001790_pf.html.

Stern, A. (1938). Psychoanalytic investigation of and therapy in the borderline group of neuroses. *Psychoanalytical Quarterly, 7,* 467–489.

Stern, J. M., Ray, W. J., & Davis, C. M. (1980). *Psychophysiological recording.* New York: Oxford University Press.

Stern, S. L., Dhanda, R., & Hazuda, H. P. (2001). Hopelessness predicts mortality in older Mexican and European Americans. *Psychosomatic Medicine, 63,* 344–351.

Stern, W. (1912). *The psychological methods of intelligence testing* (G. Whipple, Trans.). Baltimore: Warwick and York.

Sternberg, R. J. (1983). Components of human intelligence. *Cognition, 15,* 1–48.

Sternberg, R. J. (1986). A triangular theory of love. *Psychological Review, 93,* 119–135.

Sternberg, R. J. (1988a). Triangulating love. In R. J. Sternberg & M. L. Barnes (eds.), *The psychology of love* (pp. 119–138). London: Yale University Press.

Sternberg, R. J. (1988b). *The triarchic mind: A new theory of human intelligence.* New York: Penguin Books.

Sternberg, R. J. (2002). Smart people are not stupid, but they sure can be foolish: The imbalance theory of foolishness. In R. J. Sternberg (ed.), *Why smart people can be so stupid.* New Haven, CT: Yale University Press.

Sternberg, R. J. (2003a). A duplex theory of hate: Development and application to terrorism, massacres, and genocide. *Review of General Psychology, 7,* 299–328.

Sternberg, R. J. (2003b). Intelligence. In I. B. Weiner & D. K. Freedheim (eds.), *Comprehensive handbook of psychology, Vol. 1* (pp. 135–156). New York: Wiley.

Sternberg, R. J. (2004). *Psychology* (4th ed.). Belmont, CA: Wadsworth.

Sternberg, R. J., Conway, B. E., Ketron, J. L., & Bernstein, M. (1981). People's conceptions of intelligence. *Journal of Personality and Social Psychology, 41,* 37–55.

Sternberg, R. J., & Detterman, D. K. (Eds.). (1986). *What is intelligence? Contemporary viewpoints on its nature and definition.* Norwood, NJ: Ablex.

Sternberg, R. J., & Lubart, T. I. (1992). Buy low and sell high: An investment approach to creativity. *Current Directions in Psychological Science, 1,* 1–5.

Sternberg, R. J., & Wagner, R. K. (1993). *Thinking styles inventory.* Unpublished instrument.

Sternberg, R. J., Wagner, R. K., Williams, W. M., & Horvath, J. A. (1995). Testing common sense. *American Psychologist, 50,* 912–927.

Sternberg, R. J., & Williams, W. M. (1997). Does the Graduate Record Examination predict meaningful success in the graduate training of psychologists? A case study. *American Psychologist, 52,* 630–641.

Stevens, S. E., Hynan, M. T., & Allen, M. (2000). A meta-analysis of common factor and specific treatment effects across the outcome domains of the phase model of psychotherapy. *Clinical Psychology: Science and Practice, 7,* 273–290.

Stevenson, I. (1960). The evidence for survival from claimed memories of former incarnations. Part I: Review of the data. *Journal of the American Society for Psychical Research, 54,* 51–71.

Stevenson, I. (1974). *Twenty cases suggestive of reincarnation* (2nd rev. ed.), Charlottesville, VA: University Press of Virginia.

Stewart, T. L., LaDuke, J. R., Bracht, C., Sweet, B. A. M., & Gamarel, K. E. (2003). Do the "eyes" have it? A program evaluation of Jane Elliott's "Blue-Eyes/Brown-Eyes" diversity training exercise. *Journal of Applied Social Psychology, 33,* 1898–1921.

Stice, E., Cameron, R., Killen, J. D., Hayward, C., & Taylor, C. B. (1999). Naturalistic weight reduction efforts prospectively predict growth in relative weight and onset of obesity among female adolescents. *Journal of Consulting and Clinical Psychology, 67,* 967–974.

Stice, E., Presnell, K., Shaw, H., & Rhode, P. (2005). Psychological and behavioral risk factors for obesity onset in adolescent girls: A prospective study. *Journal of Consulting and Clinical Psychology, 73,* 195–202.

Stickgold, R., James, L., & Hobson, J. A. (2002). Visual discrimination learning requires sleep after training. *Nature Neuroscience, 3,* 1235–1236.

Stierlin, H. (1972). *Conflict and reconciliation: A study in human relations and schizophrenia* (2nd ed.). New York: Science House.

Stix, G. (2008). Can fMRI really tell if you're lying? *Scientific American.* http://www.scientificamerican.com/article.cfm?id=new-lie-detector.

Stoerig, P., & Cowey, A. (1997). Blindsight in man and monkey. *Brain, 120,* 535–559.

Stokoe, W. C., Casterline, D. C., & Croneberg, C. G. (1976). *A dictionary of American Sign Language on linguistic principles.* Silver Spring, MD: Linstok.

Stone, A. A. (1982). The insanity defense on trial. *Hospital and Community Psychiatry, 33,* 636–640.

Storch, E., Bagner, D., Geffken, G., & Baumeister, A. (2004). Association between overt and relational aggression and psychosocial adjustment in undergraduate college students. *Violence and Victims, 19,* 689–700.

Strack, F., Martin, L., & Stepper, S. (1988). Inhibiting and facilitating conditions of the human smile: A nonobtrusive test of the facial feedback hypothesis. *Journal of Personality and Social Psychology, 54,* 768–777.

Strauch, I., & Meier, B. (1996). *In search of dreams: Results of experimental dream research.* Albany: SUNY Press.

Straus, M. A., & McCord, J. (1998). Do physically punished children become violent adults? In S. Nolen-Hoeksema (ed.), *Clashing views on abnormal psychology: A taking sides custom reader* (pp. 130–155). Guilford, CT: Dushkin/McGraw-Hill.

Straus, M. A., Sugarman, D. B., & Giles-Sims, J. (1997). Spanking by parents and subsequent antisocial behavior of children. *Archives of Pediatrics and Adolescent Medicine, 151,* 761–767.

Strayer, D. L., Drews, F. A., & Johnston, W. A. (2003). Cell phone-induced failures of visual attention during simulated driving. *Journal of Experimental Psychology: Applied, 9,* 23–32.

Strentz, T., & Auerbach, S. M. (1988). Adjustment to the stress of simulated captivity: Effects of emotion-focused versus problem-focused preparation on hostages differing in locus of control. *Journal of Personality and Social Psychology, 55,* 652–660.

Stricker, G., & Gold, J. (2003). Integrative approaches to psychotherapy. In A. S. Gurman & S. B. Messer (eds.), *Essential psychotherapies: Theory and practic* (2nd ed., pp. 317–349). New York: Guilford.

Stricker, L. J., & Ward, W. C. (2004) Stereotype threat, inquiring about test takers' ethnicity and gender, and standardized test performance. *Journal of Applied Social Psychology, 34,* 665–693.

Strickland, T. L., Stein, R., Lin, K. M., Risby, E., & Fong, R. (1997). The pharmacologic treatment of anxiety and depression in African Americans: Considerations for the general practitioner. *Archives of Family Medicine, 6,* 371–375.

Strik, W., Dierks, T., Hubl, D., & Horn, H. (2008). Hallucinations, thought disorders, and the language domain in schizophrenia. *Clinical EEG Neuroscience, 39,* 91–94.

Stroebe, W. (2000). *Social psychology and health* (2nd ed.). Buckingham, England: Open University Press.

Strohl, K. P., & Redline, S. (1996). Recognition of obstructive sleep apnea. *American Journal of Respiratory and Critical Care Medicine, 154,* 279–289.

Stromswold, K. (2001). The heritability of language: A review and metaanalysis of twin, adoption, and linkage studies. *Language, 77,* 647–723.

Stroop, J. R. (1935). Studies of interference in serial verbal reactions. *Journal of Experimental Psychology, 18,* 643–662.

Strupp, H. H., Fox, R. E., & Lessler, K. (1969). *Patients view their therapy*. Baltimore: Johns Hopkins University Press.

Strupp, H. H., Hadley, S. W., & Gomez-Schwartz, B. (1978). *Psychotherapy for better or worse: An analysis of the problem of negative effects*. New York: Jason Aronson.

Stuart, E. W., Shimp, T. A., & Engle, R. W. (1987). Classical conditioning of consumer attitudes: Four experiments in an advertising context. *Journal of Consumer Research, 14*, 334–349.

Stuart, R. B., & Heiby, E. M. (2007). To prescribe or not prescribe: Eleven exploratory questions. *The Scientific Review of Mental Health Practice, 5*, 4–32.

Stunkard, A. (1975). Satiety is a conditioned reflex. *Journal of Psychosomatic Medicine, 37*, 383–387.

Stunkard, A. J., Foch, T. T., & Hrubec, Z. (1986). A twin study of human obesity. *Journal of the American Medical Association, 256*, 51–54.

Substance Abuse and Mental Health Services Administration (2001). *2001 National household survey on drug abuse*. Retrieved March 26, 2010 from http://www.oas.samhsa.gov/nhsda/2k1nhsda/vol1/toc.htm.

Substance Abuse and Mental Health Services Administration. (2009). Results from the 2008 National Survey on Drug Use and Health: National Findings (Office of Applied Studies, NSDUH Series H-36, HHS Publication No. SMA 09-4434). Rockville, MD.

Sue, D. W., Capodilupo, C. M., Torino, G. C., Bucceri, J. M., Holder, A. M. B., Nadal, K. L., et al. (2007). Racial microaggressions in everyday life: Implications for clinical practice. *American Psychologist, 62*, 271–286.

Sue, D. W., & Sue, D. (2003). *Counseling the culturally diverse: Theory and practice* (4th ed.). New York: Wiley.

Sue, S. (1993, November). *Measurement, testing, and ethnic bias: Can solutions be found?* Keynote Address at the Ninth Buros-Nebraska Symposium on Measurement and Testing, Lincoln, NE.

Sue, S. (1998). In search of cultural competence in psychotherapy and counseling. *American Psychologist, 53*, 440–448.

Sue, S., & Lam, A. G. (2002). Cultural and demographic diversity. In J. C. Norcross (ed.), *Psychotherapy relationships that work* (pp. 401–421). New York: Oxford University Press.

Sue, S., & Zane, N. (2006). Ethnic minority populations have been neglected by evidence-based practices. In J. C. Norcross, L. E. Beutler, & R. F. Levant (eds.), *Evidence-based practices in mental health* (pp. 329–337). Washington, DC: American Psychological Association.

Sullivan, H. S. (1954). *The psychiatric interview*. New York: W. W. Norton.

Sullivan, P. F. (1995). Mortality of anorexia nervosa. *American Journal of Psychiatry, 152*, 1073–1074.

Sulloway, F. J. (1996). *Born to rebel: Birth order, family dynamics and creative lives*. New York: Pantheon Books.

Sullum, J. (2003). *Saying yes: In defense of drug use*. New York: Teacher/Putnam.

Suls, J., Martin, R., & Wheeler, L. (2002). Social comparison: Why, with whom and with what effect? *Current Directions in Psychological Science, 11*, 159–163.

Sultan, S., Andronikof, A., Reveillere, C., & Lemmel, G. (2006). A Rorschach stability study in a nonpatient adult sample. *Journal of Personality Assessment, 87*, 330–348.

Sunar, D. (2002). The psychology of morality. In W. J. Lonner, D. L. Dinnel, S. Hayes, & D. N. Sattler (eds.), *Online readings in psychology and culture* (Unit 2, Chap. 11) (http://www.wwu.edu/~culture), Center for Cross-Cultural Research, Western Washington University, Bellingham, WA.

Sundet, J. M., Barlaug, D. G., & Torjussen, T. M. (2004). The end of the Flynn effect? A study of secular trends in mean intelligence test scores of Norwegian conscripts during half a century. *Intelligence, 32*, 349–362.

Sunstein, C. R. (2009). On rumors: How falsehoods spread, why we believe them, and what can be done. New York: Farrar, Straus and Giroux.

Suomi, S. J. (1997). Early determinants of behaviour: Evidence from primate studies. *British Medical Bulletin, 53*, 170–184.

Surowiecki, J. (2004). Mass intelligence. *Forbes, 173*(11), 48.

Susser, E. S., & Lin, S. P. (1992). Schizophrenia after prenatal exposure to the Dutch Hunger Winter of 1944–1945. *Archives of General Psychiatry, 49*, 983–988.

Suter, M. R., Wen, Y. R., Decosterd, I., & Ji, R. R. (2007). Do glial cells control pain? *Neuron Glia Biology, 3*, 255–268.

Sutherland, S. (1992). *Irrationality: Why we don't think straight!* New Brunswick, NJ: Rutgers University Press.

Svirsky, M. A., Chin, S. B., & Jester, A. (2007). The effects of age at implantation on speech intelligibility in pediatric cochlear implant users: Clinical outcomes and sensitive periods. *Audiological Medicine, 5*, 293–306.

Svirsky, M. A., Chin, S. B., Miyamoto, R. T., Sloan, R. B., & Caldwell, M. D. (2000). Speech intelligibility of profoundly deaf pediatric hearing aid users. *The Volta Review, 102*, 175–198.

Swaiman, K. F., & Ashwal, S. (1999). *Pediatric neurology: Principles and practice* (3rd ed.). St. Louis, MO: Mosby.

Swami, V., & Furnham, A. (2008). *The body beautiful: Evolutionary and sociocultural perspectives*. UK: Palgrave Macmillan.

Swann, W. B., Jr., & Pelham, B. W. (2002). Who wants out when the going gets good? Psychological investment and preference for self-verifying college roommates. *Journal of Self and Identity, 1*, 219–233.

Swanson, J. M., & Castellanos, F. X. (2002). Biological bases of ADHD—Neuroanatomy, genetics, and pathophysiology. In P. S. Jensen & J. R. Cooper (eds.), *Attention deficit hyperactivity disorder: State of the science—best practices*. Kingston, NJ: Civic Research Institute.

Swartz, M., Blazer, D., George, L., & Winfield, I. (1990). Estimating the prevalence of borderline personality disorder in the community. *Journal of Personality Disorders, 4*, 257–272.

Swenson, C. (1968). Empirical evaluations of human figure drawings: 1957–1966. *Psychological Bulletin, 70*, 20–44.

Swim, J. K. (1994). Perceived versus meta-analytic effect sizes: An assessment of the accuracy of gender stereotypes. *Journal of Personality and Social Psychology, 66*, 21–36.

Symons, D. (1979). *The evolution of human sexuality*. New York: Oxford University Press.

Sypeck, M. F., Gray, J. J., Etu, S. F., Ahrens, A. H., Mosimann, J. E., & Wiseman, C. V. (2006) Cultural representations of thinness in women, redux: Playboy magazine's depiction of beauty from 1979 to 1999. *Body Image, 3*, 229–235.

Szasz, T. S. (1960). The myth of mental illness. *American Psychologist, 15*, 113–118.

Szasz, T. S. (1978). Should psychiatric patients ever be hospitalized involuntarily? Under any circumstances—No. In J. P. Brady & H. K. H. Brodie (eds.), *Controversy in psychiatry* (pp. 965–977). Philadelphia: W. B. Saunders.

Szasz, T. S. (1989). *Pain and pleasure: A study of bodily feelings*. Syracuse, NY: Syracuse University Press.

Szasz, T. S. (1991). *Insanity*. Chichester, England: Wiley.

Szasz, T. S. (2006). *Mental illness as a brain disease: A brief history lesson*. Cybercenter for Liberty and Responsibility. Retrieved December 22, 2006, from www.szasz.com/freeman13.html.

Taiminen, T., & Jääskeläinen, S. K. (2001). Intense and recurrent déjà vu experiences related to amantadine and phenylpropanolamine in a healthy male. *Journal of Clinical Neuroscience, 8*, 460–462.

Tajfel, H. (1982). *Social identity and intergroup relations*. Cambridge, England: Cambridge University Press.

Tajfelt, H., Billig, M., Bundy, R., & Flament, C. L. (1971). Social categorization and intergroup behavior. *European Journal of Social Psychology, 1*, 149–177.

Talbott, S. (2002). *The cortisol connection diet: The breakthrough program to control stress and lose weight*. Alameda, CA: Hunter House.

Taleb, N. N. (2004). *Fooled by randomness: The hidden role of chances in the markets and life*. New York: Texere Publishing.

Tang, T., DeRubeis, R., Hollon, S., et al. (2009). Personality change during depression treatment: A placebo-controlled trial. *Archives of General Psychiatry, 66*, 1322–1330.

Tang, Y., Nyengaard, J. R., De Groot, D. M., & Gundersen, H. J. (2001). Total regional and global number of synapses in the human brain neocortex. *Synapse, 41*, 258–273.

Tanner, J. M. (1990). *Fetus into man: Physical growth from conception to maturity* (Rev. ed.). Cambridge, MA: Harvard University Press.

Tanner, J. M. (1998). Sequence, tempo, and individual variation in growth and development of boys and girls aged twelve to sixteen. In R. E. Muuss & H. D. Porton (eds.), *Adolescent behavior and society: A book of readings* (5th ed., pp. 34–46). New York: McGraw-Hill.

Tanner, L. (2006, August 6). Sexual lyrics prompt teens to have sex. *Associated Press*. Retrieved August 6, 2006, from www.sfgate.com/cgibin/article.cgi?f=/n/a/2006/08/06/national/a215010D94.DTL.

Tarver, S. G., & Dawson, M. M. (1978). Modality preference and teaching of reading: Review. *Journal of Learning Disabilities, 11*(1), 5–17.

Tassinary, L. G., & Hansen, K. A. (1998). A critical test of the waist-to-hip ratio hypothesis of female physical attractiveness. *Psychological Science, 9,* 150–155.

Tavris, C. (1989). *Anger: The misunderstood emotion.* New York: Touchstone.

Tavris, C. (2003, September 28). Mind games: Warfare between therapists and scientists. *Chronicle Review, 45*(29), B7.

Tavris, C., & Aronson, E. (2007). *Mistakes were made (but not by me): How we justify foolish beliefs, bad decisions, and hurtful acts.* New York: Harcourt.

Taylor, H. (2009). *The religious and other beliefs of Americans 2009.* The Harris Poll #140, December 15, 2009. Rochester, NY: Harris Interactive Inc.

Taylor, J., & Lang, A. R. (2006). Psychopathy and substance use disorders. In C. J. Patrick (ed.), *Handbook of psychopathy* (pp. 495–511). New York: Guilford Press.

Taylor, P., Russ-Eft, D., & Taylor, H. (2009). Gilding the outcome by tarnishing the past: Inflationary biases in retrospective pretests. *American Journal of Evaluation, 30,* 31–43.

Taylor, R. (1975, May/June). Electroconvulsive treatment (ECT): The control of therapeutic power. *Exchange,* 32–37.

Taylor, S. E., & Brown, J. D. (1988). Illusion and well-being—A social psychological perspective on mental health. *Psychological Bulletin, 103,* 193–210.

Taylor, S. E., & Brown, J. D. (1994). Positive illusions and well-being revisited: Separating fact from fiction. *Psychological Bulletin, 116,* 21–27.

Taylor, S. E., Klein, L. C., Lewis, B. P., Gruenewald, T. L., Gurung, R. A. R., & Updegraff, J. A. (2000). Biobehavioral responses to stress in females: Tend-and-befriend, not fight-or-flight. *Psychological Review, 107,* 411–429.

Taylor, S. P. (1993). Experimental investigation of alcohol-induced aggression in humans. *Alcohol Health and Research World, 17,* 108–112.

Taylor-Clarke, M., Kennett, S., & Haggard, P. (2002). Vision modulates somatosensory cortical processing. *Current Biology, 12,* 233–236.

Teasdale, J. D., Segal, Z. V., & Williams, J. M. G. (2003). Mindfulness training and problem formulation. *Clinical Psychology: Science and Practice, 10,* 157–160.

Tedeschi, J. T., Schlenker, B. R., & Bonoma, T. V. (1971). Cognitive dissonance: Private ratiocination or public spectacle? *American Psychologist, 26,* 680–695.

Teitelbaum, P., & Epstein, A. N. (1962). The lateral hypothalamic syndrome: Recovery of feeding and drinking after lateral hypothalamic lesions. *Psychological Review, 69,* 74–90.

Tellegen, A. (1982). *Brief manual for the Multidimensional Personality Questionnaire.* Unpublished manuscript, University of Minnesota. (Original work created 1978.)

Tellegen, A., Lykken, D. T., Bouchard, T. J., Wilcox, K. J., Rich, S., & Segal, N. L. (1988). Personality similarity in twins reared apart and together. *Journal of Personality and Social Psychology, 54,* 1031–1039.

Tellegen, A. (1991). Personality traits: Issues of definition, evidence, and assessment. In D. Cicchetti & W. M. Grove (eds.), *Thinking clearly about psychology: Essays in honor of Paul Everett Meehl* (pp. 10–35). Minneapolis: University of Minnesota Press.

Tellegen, A., Lykken, D. T., Bouchard, T. J., Wilcox, K. J., Segal, N. L., & Rich, S. (1988). Personality similarity in twins reared apart and together. *Journal of Personality and Social Psychology, 54,* 1031–1039.

Tennov, D. (1979). *Love and limerence: The experience of being in love.* New York: Stein & Day.

Teplin, L. A. (1985) The criminality of the mentally ill: A dangerous misconception. *American Journal of Psychiatry, 142,* 593–599.

Teplin, L. A., McClelland, G. M., Abram, K. M., & Weiner, D. (2005). Crime victimization in adults with severe mental illness: Comparison with the national crime victimization survey. *Archives of General Psychiatry, 62,* 911–921.

Terhune, D. B. (2009). The incidence and determinants of visual phenomenology during out-of-body experiences. *Cortex, 45,* 236–242.

Terman, L. M., & Oden, M. H. (1959). *Genetic studies of genius: Vol. 5. The gifted group at mid-life.* Stanford, CA: Stanford University Press.

Tetlock, P. E. (2005). *Expert political judgment: How good is it? How can we know?* Princeton, NJ: Princeton University Press.

Tetrault, J. M., Crothers, K., Moore, B. A., Mehra, R., Concato, J., & Fiellin, D. A. (2007). Effects of marijuana smoking on pulmonary function and respira-

tory complications: A systematic review. *Archives of Internal Medicine, 167,* 221–228.

Tett, R. P., Jackson, D. N., & Rothstein, M. (1991). Personality measures as predictors of job performance: A meta-analytic review. *Personnel Psychology, 44,* 703–742.

Teyber, E., & McClure, E. T. (2000). Therapist variables. In C. R. Snyder & R. E. Ingram (eds.), *Handbook of psychological change* (pp. 62–87). New York: Wiley & Sons.

Thase, M. E. (2000). Psychopharmacology in conjunction with psychotherapy. In C. R. Snyder & R. E. Ingram (eds.), *Handbook of psychological change* (pp. 474–498). New York: Wiley & Sons.

Thase, M. E., Jindal, R., & Howland, R. H. (2002). Biological aspects of depression. In I. H. Gotlib & C. L. Hammen (eds.), *Handbook of depression* (pp. 192–218). New York: Guilford Press.

Thelen, E. (1995). Time-scale dynamics and the development of an embodied cognition. In R. F. Port & T. van Gelder (eds.), *Mind as motion: Explorations in the dynamics of cognition* (pp. 69–100). Cambridge, MA: MIT Press.

Thelen, E., & Ulrich, B. D. (1991). Hidden skills: A dynamic systems analysis of treadmill stepping during the first year. *Monographs of the Society for Research in Child Development, 56,* Serial No. 223.

Thomas, A., & Chess, S. (1977). *Temperament and development.* New York: Brunner/Mazel.

Thomas, G. V. & Jolley, R. P. (1998). Drawing conclusions: A re-examination of empirical and conceptual bases for psychological evaluation of children from their drawings. *British Journal of Clinical Psychology, 37,* 127–139.

Thomas, M. (2004). Was Einstein learning disabled? Anatomy of a myth. *Skeptic, 10*(4), 40–47.

Thomas, P. (1997). *The dialectics of schizophrenia.* Bristol, England: Free Association Books.

Thompson, D. L., & Ahrens, M. J. (2004). *The grapefruit solution: Lower your cholesterol, lose weight, and achieve optimal health with nature's wonderful fruit.* [Brochure]. Linx Corporation.

Thompson, J. K., Herbozo, S. M., Himes, S. M., & Yamamiya, Y. (2005) Weight-related teasing in adults. In K. D. Brownell, L., Rudd, R. M. Puhl, & M. B. Schwartz (eds.), *Weight bias: Nature, consequences and remedies* (pp. 137–149). New York: Guilford Press.

Thompson, J. K., Heinberg, L. J., Altabe, M. N., & Tantleff-Dunn, S. (2004). *Exacting beauty: Theory, assessment, and treatment of body image disturbance.* Washington, DC: American Psychological Association.

Thompson, R., & McConnell, J. (1955). Classical conditioning in the planarian, *Dugesia dorotocephala. Journal of Comparative and Physiological Psychology, 48,* 65–68.

Thompson, R., Emmorey, K., & Gollan, T. (2005). Tip-of-the-fingers experiences by ASL signers: Insights into the organization of a sign-based lexicon. *Psychological Science, 16,* 856–860.

Thompson, R. A. (1998). Early sociopersonality development. In W. Damon (series ed.) & N. Eisenberg (vol. ed.), *Handbook of child psychology: Vol. 3. Social, emotional, and personality development* (5th ed., pp. 25–104). New York: Wiley.

Thompson, W. F., Schellenberg, E. G., & Husain, G. (2001). Arousal, mood, and the Mozart effect. *Psychological Science, 12,* 248–251.

Thorndike, E. L. (1898). *Animal intelligence: An experimental study of the associative processes in animals.* New York: Macmillan.

Thorndike, E. L. (1911). *Animal intelligence: Experimental studies.* New York: Macmillan.

Thorpe, K., Greenwood, R., Eivers, A., & Rutter, M. (2001). Prevalence and developmental course of "secret language." *International Journal of Language & Communication Disorders, 36,* 43–62.

Thurstone, L. L. (1938). *Primary mental abilities.* Chicago: University of Chicago Press.

Tice, D. M., & Baumeister, R. F. (1997). Longitudinal study of procrastination, performance, stress, and health: The costs and benefits of dawdling. *Psychological Science, 8,* 454–458.

Tien, A. Y. (1991). Distributions of hallucinations in the population. *Social Psychiatry and Psychiatric Epidemiology, 26,* 287–292.

Tiggemann, M., & Pickering, A. S. (1996). Role of television in adolescent women's body dissatisfaction and drive for thinness. *International Journal of Eating Disorders, 20,* 199–203.

Till, B. D., Stanley, S. M., & Priluck, R. (2008). Classical conditioning and celebrity endorsers: An examination of belongingness and resistance to extinction. *Psychology & Marketing, 25,* 179–196.

Timberlake, W. (2006). Evolution-based learning mechanisms can contribute to both adaptive and problematic behavior. In S. O. Lilienfeld & W. T. O'Donohue (eds.), *The great ideas of clinical science: 17 principles that every mental health professional should understand* (pp. 187–218). New York: Routledge.

Tincoff, R., & Jusczyk, P. W. (1999). Some beginnings of word comprehension in 6-month-olds. *Psychological Science, 10,* 172–175.

Tloczynski, J., & Tantriella, M. (1998). A comparison of the effects of Zen breath meditation or relaxation on college adjustment. *Psychologia: An International Journal of Psychology in the Orient, 41,* 32–43.

Todorovic, A., & Haskell-Luevano, C. (2005). A review of melanocortin receptor small molecule ligands. *Peptides, 26,* 2026–2036.

Toga, A. W., & Thompson, P. M. (2005). Genetics of brain structure and intelligence. *Annual Review of Neuroscience, 28,* 1–23.

Tolin, D. F., & Foa, E. B. (2006). Sex differences in trauma and posttraumatic stress disorder: A quantitative review of 25 years of research. *Psychological Bulletin, 132,* 959–992.

Tolman, E. C. (1932). *Purposive behavior in animals and men.* Oxford, England: Appleton-Century.

Tolman, E. C. (1948). Cognitive maps in rats and men. *Psychological Review, 55,* 189–208.

Tolman, E. C., & Honzik, C. H. (1930). Introduction and removal of reward, and maze performance in rats. *University of California Publications in Psychology, 4,* 257–275.

Tolnay, S. E., & Beck, E. M. (1995). *A festival of violence: An analysis of Southern lynchings, 1882–1930.* Urbana-Champaign: University of Illinois Press.

Tomarken, A. J., Mineka, S., & Cook, M. (1989) Fear-relevant selective associations and covariation bias. *Journal of Abnormal Psychology, 98,* 381–394.

Tomarken, A. J., Sutton, S. K., & Mineka, S. (1995) Fear-relevant illusory correlations: What types of associations promote judgmental bias? *Journal of Abnormal Psychology, 104,* 312–326.

Tomasello, M. (2000). *The Cultural Origins of Human Cognition.* Cambridge, MA: Harvard University Press.

Tomasello, M. (2008). *Origins of Human Communication.* Cambridge, MA: MIT Press.

Tombs, S., & Silverman, I. (2004). Pupillometry—A sexual selection approach. *Evolution and Human Behavior, 25,* 221–228.

Tomkins, S. S. (1962). *Affect, imagery, consciousness: Vol. 1: The positive affects.* New York: Springer.

Tomkins, S. S., & McCarter, R. (1964). What and where are the primary affects? Some evidence for a theory. *Perceptual and Motor Skills, 18,* 119–158.

Tomlinson, N., Hicks, R. A., & Pellegrini R. J. (1978). Attributions of female college students to variations in pupil size. *Bulletin of the Psychonomic Society, 12,* 477–478.

Tooby, J., & Cosmides, L. (1989). Evolutionary psychology and the generation of culture: I. Theoretical considerations. *Ethology & Sociobiology, 10,* 29–49.

Tooth, G. C., & Newton, M. P. (1961). *Leukotomy in England and Wales 1942–1954.* London, England: Her Majesty's Stationary Office.

Torgersen, S., Czajkowski, N., Jacobson, K., Reichborn-Kjennerud, T., Roysamb, E., Neale, M. C., et al. (2008). Dimensional representations of DSM-IV cluster B personality disorders in a population-based sample of Norwegian twins: A multivariate study. *Psychological Medicine, 38,* 1–9.

Torgersen, S., Lygren, S., Oien, P. A., Skre, I., Onstad, S., Edvardsen, J., et al. (2000). A twin study of personality disorders. *Comprehensive Psychiatry, 41,* 416–425.

Torrey, E. F. (1997). *Out of the shadows: Confronting America's mental illness crisis.* New York: John Wiley.

Torrey, E. G., Miller, J., Rawlings, R., & Yolken, R. H. (1997). Seasonality of births in schizophrenia and bipolar disorder: A review of the literature. *Schizophrenia Research, 28,* 1–38.

Tracy, J. L., & Robins, R. W. (2007). Emerging insights into the nature and function of pride. *Current Directions in Psychological Science, 16,* 147–150.

Treffert, D. A., & Christensen, D. D. (2005, December). Inside the mind of a savant. *Scientific American, 293,* 108–113.

Triandis, H. C. (1989). The self and social behavior in differing cultural contexts. *Psychological Review, 96,* 506–520.

Triandis, H.C. (2001). Individiaulism-collectivism and personality. *Journal of Personality, 69,* 907–924.

Triandis, H. C., & Suh, E. M. (2002). Cultural influences on personality. *Annual Review of Psychology, 53,* 133–160.

Triplett, N. (1897). The dynamogenic factors in pacemaking and competition. *American Journal of Psychology, 9,* 507–533.

Troxel, W. M., Matthews, K. A., Bromberger, J. T., & Sutton-Tyrell, K. (2003). Chronic stress burden, discrimination, and subclinical carotid artery disease in African American and Caucasian women. *Health Psychology, 22,* 300–309.

Trull, T. J., & Durett, C. A. (2005). Categorical and dimensional models of personality disorder. *Annual Review of Clinical Psychology, 1,* 355–380.

Trull, T. J., Useda, J. D., Costa, P. T., & McCrae, R. R. (1995). Comparison of the MMPI-2 Personality Psychopathology Five (PSY-5), the NEO-PI, and the NEOPI-R. *Psychological Assessment, 7,* 508–516.

Truzzi, M. (1978). On the extraordinary: An attempt at clarification. *Zetetic Scholar, 1,* 11–22.

Tryon, W. W. (2008). Whatever happened to symptom substitution? *Clinical Psychology Review, 28,* 963–968.

Tsai, J. L. (2007). Ideal affect: Cultural causes and behavioral consequences. *Perspectives on Psychological Science, 3,* 242–259.

Tsai, J. L., Knutson, B., & Fung, H. H. (2006). Cultural variation in affect valuation. *Journal of Personality and Social Psychology, 90,* 288–307.

Tsien, J. Z. (2000). Linking Hebb's coincidence-detection to memory formation. *Current Opinions in Neurobiology, 10,* 266–273.

Tucker, J. A., Vucinich, R., & Sobell, M. (1982). Alcohol's effects on human emotions. *International Journal of the Addictions, 17,* 155–180.

Tully, E. C., Iacono, W. G., & McGue, M. (2008). An adoption study of parental depression as an environmental liability for adolescent depression and childhood disruptive disorders. *American Journal of Psychiatry, 165,* 1148–1154.

Tulving, E. (1972). Episodic and semantic memory. In E. Tulving & W. Donaldson (eds.), *Organization of memory* (pp. 378–402). New York: Academic Press.

Tulving, E. (1982). Synergistic ecphory in recall and recognition. *Canadian Journal of Psychology, 36,* 130–147.

Tulving, E., & Thomson, D. M. (1973). Encoding specificity and retrieval processes in episodic memory. *Psychological Review, 80,* 352–373.

Turk, D. C. (1996). Psychological aspects of pain and disability. *Journal of Musculoskeletal Pain, 4,* 145–154.

Turkheimer, E. (1998). Heritability and biological explanation. *Psychological Review, 105,* 782–791.

Turkheimer, E. (2000). Three laws of behavior genetics and what they mean. *Current Directions in Psychological Science, 9,* 160–163.

Turkheimer, E., Haley, A., D'Onofrio, B., Waldron, M., & Gottesman, I. (2003). Socioeconomic status modifies heritability of IQ in young children. *Psychological Science, 14,* 623–628.

Turkheimer, E., & Waldron, M. (2000). Nonshared environment: A theoretical, methodological, and quantitative review. *Psychological Bulletin, 126,* 78–108.

Turner, R. J., Wheaton, B., & Lloyd, D. A. (1995). The epidemiology of stress. *American Sociological Review, 60,* 104–125.

Turner, S. M., Beidel, D. C., & Wolff, P. L. (1996). Is behavioral inhibition related to the anxiety disorders? *Clinical Psychology Review, 16,* 57–172.

Tversky, A., & Kahneman, D. (1974). Judgment under uncertainty: Heuristics and biases. *Science, 185,* 1124–1131.

Tversky, A., & Kahneman, D. (1986). Rational choice and the framing of decisions. *Journal of Business, 59,* S251-0S278.

Twenge, J. M., Catanese, K. R., & Baumeister, R. F. (2002). Social exclusion causes self-defeating behavior. *Journal of Personality and Social Psychology, 83,* 606–615.

Tyas, S. L. (2001). Alcohol use and the risk of developing Alzheimer's disease. *Alcohol Research and Health, 25,* 299–306.

Tyson, G. A. (1987). *Introduction to psychology.* Johannesburg, South Africa: Westro Educational Books.

U.S. Census Bureau (2000). *Married-couple and unmarried-partner households: 2000.* Retrieved from http://www.census.gov/prod/2003pubs/censr-5.pdf.

U.S. Census Bureau (2005). *America's families and living arrangements: 2005.* Retrieved from http://www.census.gov/population/www/socdemo/hh-fam/cps2005.html.

U.S. Department of Health, Education, and Welfare. (1990). *Smoking and health: A report of the surgeon general* (DHEW Publication No. PHS79-50066). Washington, DC: Author.

U.S. Surgeon General. (2001). *Mental health: Culture, race, and ethnicity—A supplement to mental health: A report of the Surgeon General.* Rockville, MD: U.S. Department of Health and Human Services.

Ullman, M., Krippner, S., & Vaughan, A. (1973). *Dream telepathy.* New York: Macmillan.

Ullman, S. E., Filipas, H. H., Townsend, S. M., & Starzynski, L. L. (2005). Trauma exposure, posttraumatic stress disorder and problem drinking in sexual assault survivors. *Journal of Studies of Alcohol, 66,* 610–619.

Ulrich, R. E. (1991). Animal rights, animal wrongs and the question of balance. *Psychological Science, 2,* 197–201.

Underwood, A. (2007, June 12). It's called "sexsomnia." *Newsweek,* 53.

Underwood, B. J. (1957) Interference and forgetting. *Psychological Review, 64,* 49–60.

Unsworth, N., & Engle, R. W. (2007). On the division of short-term and working memory: An examination of simple and complex spans and their relation to higher-order abilities. *Psychological Bulletin, 133,* 1038-1066.

Uttal, W. R. (2001). *The new phrenology: The limits of localizing cognitive processes in the brain.* Cambridge, MA: Bradford Books/MIT Press.

Uttal, W. R. (2003). *Psychomythics: Sources of artifacts and misconceptions in scientific psychology.* Mahwah, NJ: Lawrence Erlbaum.

Vaillant, G. E. (1977). *Adaptation to life.* Boston: Little, Brown and Company.

Vaillant, G. E., & Milofsky, E. S. (1982). Natural history of male alcoholism IV: Paths to recovery. *Archives of General Psychiatry, 39,* 127–133.

Vaitl, D., & Lipp, O. V. (1997). Latent inhibition and autonomic responses: A psychophysiological approach. *Behavioural Brain Research, 88,* 85–93.

Valenstein, E. S. (1973). *Brain control.* New York: John Wiley & Sons.

Valenstein, E. S. (1986). *Great and desperate cures: The rise and decline of psychosurgery and other radical treatments for mental illness.* New York: Basic Books.

Valentine, T., Darling, S., & Donnelly, M. (2004). Why are average faces attractive? The effect of view and averageness on the attractiveness of female faces. *Psychonomic Bulletin & Review, 11,* 482–487.

Vallee, B. L. (1988, June). Alcohol in the Western world: A history. *Scientific American, 278,* 80–85.

Van Bavel, J. J., Packer, D. J., & Cunningham, W. A. (2008). The neural subtrates of in-group bias: A function magnetic resonance imaging investigation. *Psychological Science, 19,* 1131–1139.

Van de Castle, R. (1994). *Our dreaming mind.* New York: Ballantine Books.

van der Kolk, B., Britz, R., Burr, W., Sherry, S., & Hartmann, E. (1984). Nightmares and trauma: A comparison of nightmares after combat with lifelong nightmares in veterans. *American Journal of Psychiatry, 141,* 187–190.

Van Eeden, F. (1913). A study of dreams. *Proceedings of the Society for Psychical Research, 26,* 431–461.

Van Grootheest, D. S., Cath, D. C., Beekman, A. T., & Boomsma, D. I. (2007). *Psychological Medicine, 37,* 1635–1644.

Van Hecke, M. L. (2007). *Blind spots: Why smart people do dumb things.* Amherst, NY: Prometheus Books.

Van Ijzendoorn, M. H., & De Wolff, M. S. (1997). In search of the absent father: Meta-analyses on infant–father attachment. *Child Development, 68,* 604–609.

Van Ijzendoorn, M. H., & Sagi, A. (1999). Cross-cultural patterns of attachment: Universal and cultural dimensions. In J. Cassidy & P. R. Shaver (eds.), *Handbook of attachment: Theory, research, and clinical applications* (pp. 713–734). New York: Guilford.

Van Litalie, T. B. (1990). The glucostatic theory 1953–1988: Roots and branches. *International Journal of Obesity, 14,* 1–10.

Van Lommel, P., van Wees, R., Meyers, V., & Elfferich, I. (2001). Near-death experiences in survivors of cardiac arrest: A prospective study in the Netherlands. *Lancet, 358,* 2039–2045.

Van Rooy, D. L., & Viswesvaran, C. (2004). Emotional intelligence: A meta-analytic investigation of predictive validity and nomological net. *Journal of Vocational Behavior, 65,* 71–95.

Vandello, J. A., Cohen, D., & Random, S. (2008). US southern and northern differences in perceptions of norms about aggression: Mechanisms for the perpetuation of a culture of honor. *Journal of Cross-Cultural Psychology, 39,* 162–177.

Vane, J. R. (1981). The Thematic Apperception Test: A review. *Clinical Psychology Review, 1,* 319–336.

Vanman, E. J., Paul, B. Y., Ito, T. A., & Miller, N. (1997). The modern face of prejudice and structural features that moderate the effect of cooperation on affect. *Journal of Personality and Social Psychology, 73,* 941–959.

Vanman, E. J., Saltz, J. L., Nathan, L. R., & Warren, J. A. (2004). Racial discrimination by low-prejudiced whites: Facial movements as implicit measures of attitudes related to behavior. *Psychological Science, 15,* 711–714.

Vartanian, L. R. (2000). Revisiting the imaginary audience and personal fable constructs of adolescent egocentrism: A conceptual review. *Adolescence, 35,* 639–661.

Veit, R., Flor, H., Erb, M., Hermann, C., Lotze, M., Grodd, W., et al. (2002). Brain circuits involved in emotional learning in antisocial behavior and social phobia in humans. *Neuroscience Letters, 328*(3), 233–236.

Verdoux, H. (2004). Perinatal risk factors for schizophrenia: How specific are they? *Current Psychiatry Reports, 6,* 162–167.

Vermetten, E., & Bremner, J. D. (2003). Olfaction as a traumatic reminder in posttraumatic stress disorder: Case reports and review. *Journal of Clinical Psychiatry, 64,* 202–207.

Vernon, P. A. (1987). *Speed of information processing and intelligence.* Norwood, NJ: Ablex.

Vernon, P. A., Villani, V. C., Vickers, L. C., & Harris, J. A. (2008). A behavioral genetic investigation of the Dark Triad and the Big 5. *Personality and Individual Differences, 44,* 445–452.

Vernon, P. E. (1971). *The structure of human abilities.* London: Methuen.

Vetere, A. (2001). Structural family therapy. *Child Psychology and Psychiatry Review, 6,* 133–139.

Victor, M., & Ropper, A. H. (2005). *Adams & Victor's principles of neurology* (8th ed.). New York: McGraw Hill.

Videbech, P., & Ravnkilde, B. (2004): Hippocampal volume and depression. A meta-analysis of MRI studies. *American Journal of Psychiatry, 161,* 1957–1966.

Vincent, P. (1971). Factors influencing patient noncompliance: A theoretical approach. *Nursing Research, 20,* 509–516.

Vita, A., Dieci, G., Giobbio, A., Caputo, L., Ghrinighelli, M., & Comazzi, M., et al. (1995). Language and thought disorder in schizophrenia: Brain morphological correlates. *Schizophrenia Research, 15,* 243–251.

Vitello, P. (2006, June 12). A ringtone meant to fall on deaf ears. *New York Times.* Retrieved from www.nytimes.com/2006/06/12/technology/12ring.html?_r=1&emc=eta1&oref=slogi

Voevodsky, J. (1974). Evaluation of a deceleration warning light for reducing rear-end automobile collisions. *Journal of Applied Psychology, 59,* 270–273.

Vohs, K. D., Mead, N. L., & Goode, M. R. (2006). The psychological consequences of money. *Science, 314,* 1154–1156.

Vohs, K. D., & Schooler, J. W. (2008). The value of believing in free will: Encouraging a belief in determinism increases cheating. *Psychological Science, 19,* 49–54.

Volgmaier, M. M., Seidman, L. J., Niznikiewicz, M. A., Dickey, C. C., Shenton, M. E., & McCarley, R. W. (2000). Verbal and nonverbal neuropsychological test performance in subjects with schizotypal personality disorder. *American Journal of Psychiatry, 157,* 787–797.

Volkow, N. D., Wang, G. J., Fowler, J. S., & Ding, Y. (2005). Imaging the effects of methylphenidate on brain dopamine: New model on its therapeutic actions for attention-deficit/hyperactivity disorder. *Biological Psychiatry, 57,* 1410–1415.

Von Frisch, K. (1967). *The dance language and orientation of bees.* London: Oxford University Press.

Voncken, M. J., Bogels, S. M., & deVries, K. (2003). Interpretation and judgmental biases in social phobias. *Behavior Research and Therapy, 41,* 1481–1488.

Voss, J. L., Baym, C. L., & Paller, K. A. (2008). Accurate forced-choice recognition without awareness of memory retrieval. *Learning and Memory, 15,* 454–459.

Voss, J. L., and Paller, K. A. (2008). Brain substrates of implicit and explicit memory: the importance of concurrently acquired neural signals of both memory types. *Neuropsychologia, 46,* 3021–3029.

Voss, U., Holzmann, R., Tuin, I., & Hobson, J. A. (2009). Lucid dreaming: A state of consciousness with features of both waking and non-lucid dreaming. *Sleep, 32,* 1191–2000.

Voyer, D., Voyer, S., & Bryden, M. P. (1995). Magnitude of sex differences in spatial abilities: A meta-analysis and consideration of critical variables. *Psychological Bulletin, 117,* 250–270.

Vrba, J., & Robinson, S. E. (2001). Signal processing in magnetoencephalography. *Methods, 25,* 249–271.

Vrieze, S., & Grove, W. G. (2009). Survey on the use of clinical and mechanical prediction methods in clinical psychology. *Professional Psychology: Research and Practice, 40,* 525–531.

Vrij, A. (2008). Nonverbal dominance versus verbal accuracy: A plea to change police practice. *Criminal Justice and Behavior, 35,* 1323–1335.

Vrught, A., & Kerkstra, A. (1984). Sex differences in nonverbal communication. *Semiotica, 50, 141.*

Vuksan, V., Rogovik, A. L., Jovanovski, E., & Jenkins, A. L. (2009). Fiber facts: Benefits and recommendations for individuals with type 2 diabetes. *Current Diabetes Reports, 9,* 405–411.

Vul, E., Harris, C., Winkielman, P., & Pashler, H. (2009). Puzzlingly high correlations in fMRI studies of emotion, personality, and social cognition. *Perspectives on Psychological Science, 4,* 274–290.

Vyse, S. A. (1997). *Believing in magic: The psychology of superstition.* New York: Oxford University Press.

Vyse, S. A. (2000). *Believing in magic: The psychology of superstition.* New York: Oxford University Press.

Wachtel, P. L. (1973). Psychodynamics, behavior therapy, and the implacable experimenter: An inquiry into the consistency of personality. *Journal of Abnormal Psychology, 82,* 324–334.

Wachtel, P. L. (1977). *Psychoanalysis and behavior therapy: Toward an integration.* New York: Basic Books.

Wachtel, P. L. (1997). *Psychoanalysis, behavior therapy, and the relational world.* Washington, DC: American Psychological Association.

Wadden, T. A., & Stunkard, A. J. (1993). Psychosocial consequence of obesity and dieting: Research and clinical findings. In A. J. Stunkard & T. A. Wadden (eds.), *Obesity: Theory and therapy* (pp. 163–177). New York: Raven.

Wade, K. A., Garry, M., Read, J. D., & Lindsay, D. S. (2002). A picture is worth a thousand lies: Using false photographs to create false childhood memories. *Psychonomic Bulletin & Review, 9,* 597–603.

Wager, T. D., Rilling, J. K., Smith, E. E., Sokolik, A., Casey, K. L., Davidson, R. J., et al. (2004). Placebo-induced changes in fMRI in anticipation and experience of pain. *Science, 303,* 1162–1167.

Wagner, R. K., & Sternberg, R. J. (1986). Tacit knowledge and intelligence in the everyday world. In R. J. Sternberg & R. K. Wagner (eds.), *Practical intelligence: Nature and origins of competence in the everyday world* (pp. 51–83). Cambridge, England: Cambridge University Press.

Wagner, M. W., & Monnet, M. (1979). Attitudes of college professors toward extra-sensory perception. *Zetetic Scholar, 5,* 7–16.

Wagstaff, G. (1998). The semantics and physiology of hypnosis as an altered state: Towards a definition of hypnosis. *Contemporary Hypnosis, 15,* 149–165.

Wagstaff, G. (2008). Hypnosis and the law. *Criminal Justice and Behavior, 35,* 1277–1294.

Wahl, O. (1997). *Consumer experience with stigma: Results of a national survey.* Alexandria, VA: NAMI.

Waid, W. M., & Orne, M. T. (1982). The physiological detection of deception. *American Scientist, 70,* 402–409.

Wainright, J. L., Russell, S. T., & Patterson, C. J. (2004). Psychosocial adjustment, school outcomes, and romantic relationships of Adolescents with Same-Sex Parents. *Child Development, 75,* 1886–1898.

Wakefield, A. J., Murch, S., Anthony, A., Linnell, J., Casson, D. M., Casson, M., et al. (1998). Ileal lymphoid nodular hyperplasia, non-specific colitis, and regressive developmental disorder in children. *Lancet, 351,* 637–641.

Wakefield, J. C. (1992). The concept of mental disorder: On the boundary between biological facts and social values. *American Psychologist, 47,* 373–388.

Wakefield, J. C. (2006). Is behaviorism becoming a pseudo-science? Power versus scientific rationality in the eclipse of token economies by biological psychiatry in the treatment of schizophrenia. *Behavior and Social Issues, 15,* 202–221.

Walach, H., & Kirsch, I. (2003). Herbal treatments and antidepressant medication: Similar data, divergent conclusions. In S. O. Lilienfeld, S. J. Lynn, & J.

M. Lohr (eds.), *Science and pseudoscience in clinical psychology* (pp. 306–330). New York: Guilford.

Waldman, I. D. (2005). Statistical approaches to complex phenotypes: Evaluating neuropsychological endophenotypes for attention-deficit/hyperactivity disorder. *Biological Psychiatry, 57,* 1347–1356.

Waldman, I. D., & Gizer, I. R. (2006). The genetics of attention deficit hyperactivity disorder. *Clinical Psychology Review, 26,* 396–432.

Waldman, I. D., Lilienfeld, S. O., & Lahey, B. B. (1995). Toward construct validity in the childhood disruptive behavior disorders: Classification and diagnosis in DSM-IV and beyond. In T. H. Ollendick & R. J. Prinz (eds.), *Advances in clinical child psychology* (Vol. 17, pp. 323–363). New York: Plenum Press.

Walker, E. F., Baum, K., & Diforio, D. (1998). Developmental changes in the behavioral expression of vulnerability for schizophrenia. In M. Lenzenweger & B. Dworkin (eds.), *Experimental psychopathology and pathogenesis of schizophrenia* (pp. 469–492). Washington, DC: American Psychological Association.

Walker, E. F., & DiForio, D. (1997). Schizophrenia: A neural-diathesis stress model. *Psychological Review, 104,* 1–19.

Walker, E. F., Kestler, L., Bollini, A., & Hochman, K. (2004). Schizophrenia: Etiology and course. *Annual Review of Psychology, 55,* 401–430.

Walker, E. F., & Lewine, R. J. (1990). Prediction of adult-onset schizophrenia from childhood home movies of the patients. *American Journal of Psychiatry, 147,* 1052–1056.

Walker, M. P., Brakefield, A., Morgan, J., Hobson, J. A., & Stickgold, R. (2002). Practice, with sleep, makes perfect. *Neuron, 35,* 205–211.

Wall, P. (2000). *Pain.* New York: Columbia University Press.

Wallach, H., & Kirsch, I. (2003). Herbal treatments and antidepressant medication: Similar data, divergent conclusions. In S. O. Lilienfeld, S. J. Lynn, & J. M. Lohr (eds.), *Science and pseudoscience in clinical psychology* (pp. 306–332). New York: Guilford.

Wallechinsky, D., Wallace, D., & Wallace, H. (1977). *The book of lists.* New York: Bantam Books.

Waller, N. G., Kojetin, B. A., Bouchard, T. J., Lykken, D. T., & Tellegen, A. (1990). Genetic and environmental influences on religious interests, attitudes, and values: A study of twins reared apart and together. *Psychological Science, 1,* 1–5.

Wallerstein, J. S. (1989, January 22). Children after divorce: Wounds that don't heal. *New York Times Magazine, 19, 42.*

Walonick, D. S. (1994). *Do researchers influence survey results with their question wording choices?* Retrieved May 5, 2006, from www.statpac.com/research-papers/researcher-bias.doc.

Walsh, B. T. (1993). Binge eating in bulimia nervosa. In C. G. Fairburn & G. T. Wilson (eds.), *Binge eating: Nature, assessment, and treatment* (pp. 37–49). New York: Guilford.

Walsh, B. T., Hadigan, C. M., Kissileff, H. R., & LaChaussee, J. L. (1992). Bulimia nervosa: A syndrome of feast and famine. In G. H. Anderson & S. H. Kennedy (eds.), *The biology of feast and famine.* New York: Academic Press.

Walsh, F. (1999). Families in later life: Challenges and opportunities. In B. Carter & M. McGoldrick (eds.), *The expanded family life cycle: Individual, family and social perspectives* (3rd ed., pp. 307–326). Boston: Allyn & Bacon.

Walster, E., Berscheid, E., & Walster, G. W. (1973). New directions in equity theory and research. *Journal of Personality and Social Psychology, 25,* 151–176.

Walters, G. D., & Greene, R. L. (1988). Differentiating between schizophrenia and manic inpatients by means of the MMPI. *Journal of Personality Assessment, 52,* 91–95.

Walton, D. E. (1978). An exploratory study: Personality factors and theoretical orientations of therapists. *Psychotherapy: Theory, Research, and Practice, 15,* 390–395.

Wampold, B. E. (2001). *The great psychotherapy debate: Models, methods, and findings.* Mahwah, NJ: Lawrence Erlbaum.

Wampold, B. E., Minami, T., Baskin, T. W., & Tierney, S. C. (2002). A meta-(re)analysis of the effects of cognitive therapy versus "other therapies" for depression. *Journal of Affective Disorders, 68,* 159–165.

Wampold, B. E., Monding, W., Moody, M., Stich, I., Benson, K., & Ahn, H. (1997). A meta-analysis of outcome studies comparing bona fide psychotherapies: Empirically "all must have prizes." *Psychological Bulletin, 122,* 203–215.

Wamsley, E. J., Hirota, Y., Tucker, M. A., Smith, M. R., Antrobus, J. S. (2007). Circadian and ultradian influences on dreaming: A dual rhythm model. *Brain Research Bulletin, 71,* 347–354.

Wang, D. D., & Kriegstein, A. R. (2009). Defining the role of GABA in cortical development. *The Journal of Physiology, 187,* 1873–1879.

Wang P. S., Gruber, M. J., Powers, R. E., Schoenbaum, M., Speier, A., Wells, K. B., et al. (2008). Disruption of existing mental health treatments and failure to initiate new treatment after hurricane Katrina. *American Journal of Psychiatry, 165,* 34–41.

Wang, Q. (2006). Culture and the development of self-knowledge. *Current Directions in Psychological Science, 15,* 182–187.

Wang, T. J., Pencina, M. J., Booth, S. L., Jacques, P. F., Ingelsson, E., Lanier, K., et al. (2008). *Vitamin D deficiency and risk of cardiovascular disease. Circulation, 117,* 503–511.

Wansink, B. (2009). *Mindless eating: Why we eat more than we think.* New York: Bantam Books.

Wansink, B., Painter, J. E., & North, J. (2005). Bottomless bowls: Why visual cues of portion size may influence intake. *Obesity Research, 13,* 93–100.

Wardell, D. (1999). Children in difficulty: A guide to understanding and helping. *Contemporary Psychology, 44,* 514–515.

Wark, D. M. (2006). Alert hypnosis: A review and case report. *American Jounral of Clinical Hypnosis, 48,* 291–300.

Waschbusch, D. A., & Hill, G. P. (2003). Empirically supported, promising, and unsupported treatments for children with attention-deficit/hyperactivity disorder. In S. O. Lilienfeld, S. J. Lynn, & J. M. Lohr (eds.), *Science and pseudoscience in clinical psychology* (pp. 333–362). New York: Guilford.

Wason, P. C. (1966). Reasoning. In B. M. Foss (ed.), *New horizons in psychology* (pp. 135–151). Harmondsworth, England: Penguin.

Watanabe, S., Sakamoto, J., & Wakita, M. (1995). Pigeons' discrimination of paintings by Monet and Picasso. *Journal of the Experimental Analysis of Behavior, 63,* 65–174.

Waters, E., Matas, L., & Sroufe, L. A. (1975). Infants' reactions to an approaching stranger: Description, validation, and functional significance of wariness. *Child Development 46,* 348–356.

Watkins, C. E., Campbell, V. L., Nieberding, R., & Hallmark, R. (1995). Contemporary practice of psychological assessment by clinical psychologists. *Professional Psychology: Science and Practice, 26,* 54–60.

Watkins, L. R., & Maier, S. F. (2002). Beyond neurons: Evidence that immune and glial cells contribute to pathological pain states. *Physiological Reviews, 82,* 981–1011.

Watson, D., & Clark, L. A. (1984). Negative affectivity: The disposition to experience negative emotional states. *Psychological Bulletin, 96,* 465–490.

Watson, J. B. (1913). Psychology as the behaviorist views it. *Psychological Review, 20,* 158–177.

Watson, J. B., & Rayner, R. (1920). Conditioned emotional reactions. *Journal of Experimental Psychology, 3,* 1–14.

Watson, R. I. (1973). Investigation into deindividuation using a cross-cultural survey technique. *Journal of Personality and Social Psychology, 25,* 342–345.

Watters, E. (2010). Crazy like us: The globalization of the American psyche. New York: Free Press.

Watzlawick, P., Beavin, J., & Jackson, D. D. (1967). *Pragmatics of human communication: A study of interactional patterns, pathologies, and paradoxes.* New York: W. W. Norton.

Watzlawick, P., Weakland, J. H., & Fisch, R. (1974). *Change: Principles of problem formation and problem resolution.* New York: Norton.

Waugh, N. C., & Norman, D. A. (1965). Primary memory. *Psychological Review, 72,* 89–104.

Waxman, S. R., & Booth, A. E. (2001). On the insufficiency of domain-general accounts of word-learning: A reply to Bloom and Markson. *Cognition, 78,* 277–279.

Wayment, H. A., & Peplau, L. A. (1995). Social support and well-being among lesbian and heterosexual women: A structural modeling approach. *Personality and Social Psychology Bulletin, 21,* 1189–1199.

Wearing, D. (2005). *Forever today.* New York: Doubleday.

Weaver, K., Garcia, S. M., Schwarz, N., & Miller, D. T. (2007). Inferring the popularity of an opinion from its familiarity: A repetitive voice can sound like a chorus. *Journal of Personality and Social Psychology, 92,* 821–833.

Weaver, I. C., Cervoni, N., Champagne, F. A., D'Alessio, A. C., Sharma, S., Seckl, J. R., et al. (2004). Epigenetic programming by maternal behavior. *Nature Neuroscience, 8,* 847–854.

Wechsler, D. (1939). *The measurement of adult intelligence.* Baltimore: Williams & Wilkins.

Wechsler, D. (1988). *Wechsler Intelligence Scale for Children- Revised (WISC R).* New York: The Psychological Corporation.

Wechsler, D. (1997). *The Wechsler Adult Intelligence Scale—Third edition (WAIS-III).* San Antonio, TX: Harcourt Assessment.

Wechsler, D. (2008). *Wechsler Adult Intelligence Scale, Fourth edition (WAIS-IV).* Boston: Pearson.

Weed, N. C., Ben-Porath, Y. S., & Butcher, J. N. (1990). Failure of Weiner and Harmon MMPI subtle scales as personality descriptors and as validity indicators. *Psychological Assessment, 2,* 281–285.

Wegner, D. M. (2002). *The illusion of conscious will.* Cambridge, MA: MIT Press.

Wegner, D. M. (2004). Précis of the illusion of conscious will. *Behavioral and Brain Sciences, 27,* 649–692.

Wegner, D. M. (2005). The illusion of conscious will. *Behavioral and Brain Sciences, 27,* 649–692.

Wegner, D. M., Fuller, V. A., & Sparrow, B. (2003). Clever Hands: Uncontrolled intelligence in facilitated communication. *Journal of Personality and Social Psychology, 85,* 5–19.

Wegner, D. M., Schneider, D. J., Carter, S. R., & White, T. L. (1987). Paradoxical effects of thought supression. *Journal of Personality and Social Psychology, 53,* 5–13.

Wei, M., Kampert, J. B., Barlow, C. E., Nichaman, M. Z., Gibbons, L. W., Paffenbarger, R. S., et al. (1999). Relationship between low cardiorespiratory fitness and mortality in normal weight, overweight, and obese men. *Journal of the American Medical Association, 282,* 1547–1553.

Wei, M., Mallinckrodt, B., Larson, L. M., Zakalik, R. A. (2005). Adult attachment, depressive symptoms, and validation from self versus others. *Journal of Counseling Psychology, 52,* 368–377.

Weil, A. (2000). *Spontaneous healing: How to discover and embrace your body's natural ability to maintain and heal itself.* New York: Ballantine Books.

Weinberg, M. S., Williams, C. J., & Calhan, C. (1995). If the shoe fits . . . Exploring male-homosexual foot fetishism. *Journal of Sex Research, 31,* 17–27.

Weinberg, R. A., Scarr, S., & Waldman, I. D. (1992). The Minnesota Transracial Adoption Study: A follow-up of IQ test performance at adolescence. *Intelligence, 16,* 117–135.

Weinberger, D. R. (1987). Implications of normal brain development for the pathogenesis of schizophrenia. *Archives of General Psychiatry, 44,* 660–669.

Weinberger, D. R., Elvevag, B., & Giedd, J. N., (2005). *The adolescent brain: A work in progress, The National Campaign to Prevent Teen Pregnancy.* Retrieved from www.teenpregnancy.org/resources/reading/pdf/BRAIN.pdf.

Weinberger, N. M. (2006). Music and the brain. *Scientific American, 291*(5), 88–95.

Weiner, I. B. (1997). Current status of the Rorschach Inkblot Method. *Journal of Personality Assessment, 68,* 5–19.

Weinert, F. (1989). The impact of schooling on cognitive development: One hypothetical assumption, some empirical results, and many theoretical implications. *EARLI News, 8,* 3–7.

Weisberg, D. S., Keil, F. C., Goodstein, J., Rawson, E., & Gray, J. R. (2008). The seductive allure of neuroscience explanations. *Journal of Cognitive Neuroscience, 20,* 470–477.

Weisberg, L. A., Garcia, C., & Strub, R. L. (1996). Diseases of the peripheral nerves and motor neurons. In L. Weisberg, C. García, R. Strub, & E. Bouldin (eds.), *Essentials of clinical neurology* (pp. 458–494). St. Louis: Mosby.

Weisberg, R. W. (1994). Genius and madness? A quasi-experimental test of the hypothesis that manic-depression increases creativity. *Psychological Science, 5,* 361–367.

Weiskrantz, L. (1986). *Blindsight: A case study and its implications.* Oxford, England: Oxford University Press.

Weisner, W., & Cronshaw, S. (1988). A meta-analytic investigation of interview format and degree of structure on the validity of the employment interview. *Journal of Occupational* Psychology, 61, 275–290.

Weiss, B. L. (1988). *Many lives, many masters.* New York: Simon & Schuster.

Weiss, L. H., & Schwarz, J. C. (1996). The relationship between parenting types and older adolescents' personality, academic achievement, adjustment, and substance use. *Child Development, 67,* 2101–2114.

Weissman, M. M., Markowitz, J. C., & Klerman, G. L. (2000). *Comprehensive guide to interpersonal psychotherapy*. New York: Basic Books.

Weisz, J. R., Weiss, B., Han, S. S., Granger, D. A., & Morton, T. (1995). Effects of psychotherapy with children and adolescents revisited: A meta-analysis of treatment outcome studies. *Psychological Bulletin, 117*, 450–468.

Welford, A. (1977). Mental workload as a function of demand, capacity, strategy and skill: Synthesis report. *Travail Humain, 40*, 283–304.

Wellman, H. M., Cross, D., & Watson, J. (2001). Meta-analysis of theory-of-mind development: The truth about false belief. *Child Development, 72*, 655–684.

Wells, G. L., & Bradford, A. L. (1998). "Good, you identified the suspect": Feedback to eyewitnesses distorts their reports of the witnessing experience. *Journal of Applied Psychology, 83*, 360–376.

Wells, G. L., & Loftus, E. F. (eds.). (1984). *Eyewitness testimony: Psychological perspectives.* New York: Cambridge University Press.

Wells, G. L., Memon, A., & Penrod, S. D. (2006). Eyewitness evidence: Improving its probative value. *Psychological Science in the Public Interest, 7*, 45–75.

Wenger, W. (1983). Toward a taxonomy of methods for improving teaching and learning. *Journal of the Society for Accelerative Learning and Teaching, 8*, 75–90.

Wennberg, P. (2002). The development of alcohol habits in a Swedish male birth cohort. In S. P. Shohov (ed.), *Advances in psychology research, vol. 15* (pp. 121–155). Hauppauge, NY: Nova Science Publishers.

Werch, C. E., & Owen, D. (2002). Iatrogenic effects of alcohol and drug prevention programs. *Journal of Studies on Alcohol, 63*, 581–590.

Werker, J. F., Gilbert, J. H. V., Humphrey, K., & Tees, R. C. (1981). Developmental aspects of cross-language speech perception. *Child Development, 52*, 349–355.

Werker, J. F., & Tees, R. C. (1984). Cross-language speech perception: Evidence for perceptual reorganization during the first year of life. *Infant Behavior and Development, 7*, 49–63.

Werth, J. L. (2001). U.S. involuntary mental health commitment statutes: Requirements for persons perceived to be a potential harm to self. *Suicide and Life-Threatening Behavior, 31*, 348–357.

West, T. A., & Bauer, P. J. (1999). Assumptions of infantile amnesia: Are there differences between early and later memories? *Memory, 7*, 257–278.

Westen, D. (1991). Clinical assessment of object relations using the TAT. *Journal of Personality Assessment, 56*, 56–74.

Westen, D. (1998). The scientific legacy of Sigmund Freud: Toward a psychodynamically informed psychological science. *Psychological Bulletin, 124*, 333–371.

Westen, D., Feit, A., & Zittel, C. (1999). Methodological issues in research using projective methods. In P. C. Kendall & J. N. Butcher (eds.), *Handbook of research methods in clinical psychology* (2nd ed., pp. 224–240). New York: Wiley.

Westen, D., Kilts, C., Blagov, P., Harenski, K., & Hamann, S. (2006). The neural basis of motivated reasoning: An fMRI study of emotional constraints on political judgment during the U.S. presidential election of 2004. *Journal of Cognitive Neuroscience, 18*, 1947–1958.

Westen, D., Novotny, C. M., & Thompson-Brenner, H. (2004). The empirical status of empirically supported psychotherapies: Assumptions, findings, and reporting in controlled clinical trials. *Psychological Bulletin, 130*, 631–663.

Westerman, M. A., Foote, J. P., & Winston, A. (1995). Change in coordination across phases of psychotherapy and outcome: Two mechanisms for the role played by patients' contribution to the alliance. *Journal of Consulting and Clinical Psychology, 63*, 672–675.

Weston, K. (1991). *Families we choose: Lesbians, gays, kinship.* New York: Columbia University Press.

Westphal, M., & Bonanno, G. A. (2004). Emotional self-regulation. In M. Beauregard (ed.), *Consciousness, emotional self-regulation, and the brain* (pp. 1–34). Philadelphia: Benjamins.

Wetzler, S. E., & Sweeney, J. A. (1986). Childhood amnesia: An empirical demonstration. In D. C. Rubin (ed.), *Autobiographical memory* (pp. 191–201). New York: Cambridge University Press.

Whaley, A. L., & Davis, K. E. (2007). Cultural competence and evidence-based practice in mental health services: A complementary perspective. *American Psychologist, 62*, 563–574.

Whinnery, J. E. (1997). Psychophysiologic correlates of unconsciousness and near-death experiences. *Journal of Near-Death Studies, 15*, 231–258.

White, A. (2006). *A global projection of subjective well-being: The first published map of world happiness.* Retrieved October 30, 2007, from http://news.bbc.co.uk/2/shared/bsp/hi/pdfs/28_07_06_happiness_map.pdf.

Whiting, B. B., & Edwards, C. P. (1988). *Children of different worlds: The formation of social behavior.* Cambridge, MA: Harvard University Press.

Whitley, B. E., & Lee, S. E. (2000). The relationship of authoritarianism and related constructs to attitudes towards homosexuality. *Journal of Applied Social Psychology, 30*, 144–170.

Whitson, J. A., & Galinsky, A. D. (2008). Lacking control increases illusory pattern perception. *Science, 322*, 115–117.

Whorf, B. L. (1956). *Language, thought, and reality: Selected writings of Benjamin Lee Whorf* (J. B. Carroll, ed.). Cambridge, MA: MIT Press.

Wicherts, J. M., Dolan, C. V., & van der Maas, H. L. J. (2010). A systematic literature review of the average IQ of sub-Saharan Africans. *Intelligence, 38*, 1–20.

Wickelgren, W. A. (1965). Acoustic similarity and retroactive interference in short-term memory. *Journal of Verbal Learning and Verbal Behavior, 4*, 53–61.

Wicker, A. W. (1969). Attitudes versus actions: The relationship of verbal and overt behavioral responses to attitude objects. *Journal of Social Issues, 25*, 41–78.

Wicker, B., Keysers, C., Plailly, J., Royet, J. P., Gallese, V., & Rizzolatti, G. (2003). Both of us disgusted in my insula: The common neural basis of seeing and feeling disgust. *Neuron, 40*, 655–664.

Widiger, T. A. (2001). The best and the worst of us? *Clinical Psychology: Science and Practice, 8*, 374–377.

Widiger, T. A., & Clark, L. A. (2000). Toward DSM-V and the classification of psychopathology. *Psychological Bulletin, 126*, 946–963.

Widiger, T. A., & Frances, A. J. (1985). The DSM-III personality disorders: Perspectives from psychology. *Archives of General Psychiatry, 42*, 615–623.

Widmer, E. D., Treas, J., & Newcomb, R. (1998). Attitudes toward nonmarital sex in 24 countries. *Journal of Sex Research, 35*, 349–357.

Widom, C. S. (1977). A methodology for studying noninstitutionalized psychopaths. *Journal of Consulting and Clinical Psychology, 45*, 674–683.

Widom, C. S. (1989a). The cycle of violence. *Science, 244*, 160–166.

Widom, C. S. (1989b) Child abuse, neglect, and adult behavior: Research design and findings on criminality, violence, and child abuse. *American Journal of Orthopsychiatry, 59*, 355–367.

Wigal, T., Greenhill, L., Chuang, S., McGough, J., Vitiello, B., Skrobala, A., et al. (2006). Safety and tolerability of methylphenidate in preschool children with ADHD. *Journal of the American Academy of Adolescent Psychiatry, 45*, 1294.

Wilgus, J., & Wilgus, B. (2009). Face to face with Phineas Gage. *Journal of the History of the Neurosciences, 18*, 340–345.

Willander, J., & Larsson, M. (2007). Olfaction and emotion: The case of authobiographical memory. *Memory and Cognition, 35*, 1659–1663.

Willems, P. J. (2000). Genetic causes of hearing loss. *New England Journal of Medicine, 342*, 1101–1109.

Willerman, L. (1979). *The psychology of individual and group differences.* San Francisco: Freedman.

Willerman, R., Schultz, J. N., Rutledge, J. N., & Bigler, D. D. (1991). In vivo brain size and intelligence, *Intelligence, 15*, 223–228.

Williams, K., Harkins, S. G., & Latané, B. (1981). Identifiability as a deterrent to social loafing: Two cheering experiments. *Journal of Personality and Social Psychology, 40*, 303–311.

Williams, S. L., Turner, S. M., & Peer, D. F. (1985). Guided mastery and performance desensitization treatments for severe acrophobia. *Journal of Consulting and Clinical Psychology, 53*, 234–247.

Williams, T. J., Pepitone, M. E., Christensen, S. E., Cooke, B. M., Huberman, A. D., Breedlove, N. J., et al. (2000). Finger length patterns and human sexual orientation. *Nature, 404*, 455–456.

Williams, T. M. (ed.). (1986). *The impact of television: A naturalistic study in three communities.* Orlando, FL: Academic Press.

Williams, W. M., & Ceci, S. J. (1997, September/October). "How'm I doing?" *Change, 29*(5), 13–23.

Williams, W. M., & Ceci, S. J. (1998). *Escaping the advice trap.* Kansas City, MO: Andrews McMeel.

Williamson, D. A., Womble, L. G., Smeets, M. A. M., Netemeyer, R. G., Thaw, J. M., Kutlesic, V., et al. (2002). Latent structure of eating disorder symptoms: A factor analytic and taxometric investigation. *American Journal of Psychiatry, 159,* 412–418.

Willingham, D. T. (2002). *Allocating student study time: "Massed" versus "distributed" practice.* Retrieved May 22, 2006, from www.aft.org/american_educator/summer2002/askcognitivescientist.html.

Willingham, D. T. (2004). Reframing the mind: Howard Gardner became a hero among educators simply by redefining talents as "intelligences." *Education Next, 4,* 18–24.

Willingham, D. T. (2007, Summer). Why is critical thinking so hard to teach? *American Educator, 31*(2), 8–19.

Willner, P. (1995). Animal models of depression—Validity and applications. *Depression and Mania, 49,* 19–41.

Wills, T. A., & Fegan, M. F. (2001). Social networks and social support. In A. S. Baum, T. A. Revenson, J. E. Singer (eds.), *Handbook of Health Psychology* (pp. 209–234). Mahwah, NJ: Erlbaum.

Wilson, C. (2005). What is autism? *New Scientist, 187,* 39.

Wilson, G. T., & O'Leary, K. D. (1980). *Principles of behavior therapy.* Englewood Cliffs, NJ: Prentice-Hall.

Wilson, J. Q. (1993). *The moral sense.* New York: Free Press.

Wilson, J. Q., & Herrnstein, R. J. (1985). *Crime and human nature: The definitive study of the causes of crime.* New York: Simon & Schuster.

Wilson, N. (2003). Commercializing mental health issues: Entertainment, advertising, and psychological advice. In S. O. Lilienfeld, S. J. Lynn, & J. M. Lohr (eds.), *Science and pseudoscience in clinical psychology* (pp. 425–459). New York: Guilford.

Wilson, R. S., Scherr, P. A., Schneider, J. A., Tang, Y. & Bennett, D. A. (2007). Relation of cognitive activity to risk of developing Alzheimer disease. *Neurology, 69,* 1911–1920.

Wilson, R. S., Schneider, J. A., Arnold, S. E., Tang, Y., Boyle, P.A., & Bennett, D. A. (2007). Olfactory identification and incidence of mild cognitive impairment in older age. *Archives of General Psychiatry, 64,* 802–808.

Wilson, S. C., & Barber, T. X. (1981). Vivid fantasy and hallucinatory abilities in the life histories of excellent hypnotic subjects ("somnambules"): Preliminary report with female subjects. In E. Klinger (ed.), *Imagery: Concepts, results, and applications* (pp. 133–149). New York: Plenum Press.

Wilson, T., Lisle, D., Schooler, J., Hodges, S. D., Klaaren, K. J., & LaFleur, S. J. (1993). Introspecting about reasons can reduce post-choice satisfaction. *Personality and Social Psychology Bulletin, 69,* 331–339.

Wilson, T. D. (2002). *Strangers to ourselves: Discovering the adaptive unconscious.* Cambridge, MA: Harvard University Press.

Wimmer, H., & Perner, J. (1983). Beliefs about beliefs: Representation and constraining function of wrong beliefs in young children's understanding of deception. *Cognition, 13,* 103–128.

Windham, G. C., Hopkins, B., Fenster, L., & Swan, S. H. (2000). Prenatal active or passive tobacco smoke exposure and the risk of preterm delivery or low birth weight. *Epidemiology, 11,* 427–433.

Winemiller, M. H., Billow, R. G., Laskwoski, E. R., & Harmsen, W. S. (2003). Effect of magnetic vs. sham-magnetic insoles on plantar heel pain. *Journal of the American Medical Association, 290,* 1474–1478.

Winer, G. A., Cottrell, J. E., Gregg, V., Fournier, J. S., & Bica, L. A. (2002). Fundamentally misunderstanding visual perception. Adults' belief in visual emissions. *American Psychologist, 57,* 417–424.

Winerman, L. (2005, October). The mind's mirror. *American Psychological Association Monitor, 36*(9). Retrieved from http://www.apa.org/monitor/oct05/mirror.html on March 27, 2010.

Wing, L., & Potter, D. (2002). The epidemiology of autistic spectrum disorders: Is the prevalence rising? *Mental Retardation and Developmental Disabilities Research Reviews, 8,* 151–161.

Wing, R. R., & Hill, J. O. (2001). Successful weight loss maintenance. *Annual Review of Nutrition, 21,* 323–341.

Wing, R. R., & Jeffrey, R. W. (1999). Benefit of recruiting participants with friends and increasing social support for weight loss and maintenance. *Journal of Consulting and Clinical Psychology, 67,* 132–138.

Wing, R. R., & Polley, B. A. (2001). Obesity. In A. Baum, T. A. Revenson, & J. E. Singer (eds.), *Handbook of health psychology* (pp. 263–279). Mahwah, NJ: Erlbaum.

Winkelman, J.W., Buxton, O.M., Jensen, J.E., Benson, K.L., O'Connor, S.P., Wang, W., et al. (2008). Reduced brain GABA in primary insomnia: preliminary data from 4T proton magnetic resonance spectroscopy (1HMRS). *Sleep, 31,* 1499–1506.

Winner, E. (1999). Uncommon talents: Gifted children, prodigies, and savants. *Scientific American Presents: Exploring Intelligence, 9,* 32–37.

Winnicott, D. (1958). *Collected papers—Through pediatrics to psychoanalysis.* New York: Basic Books.

Winograd, E., & Killinger, W. A., Jr. (1983). Relating age at encoding in early childhood to adult recall: Development of flashbulb memories. *Journal of Experimental Psychology: General, 112,* 413–422.

Winograd, E., Peluso, J. P., & Glover, T. A. (1998). Individual differences in susceptibility to memory illusions. *Applied Cognitive Psychology, 12,* S5–S27.

Winter, A. (2005). The making of "truth serum." *Bulletin of the History of Medicine, 79,* 500–533.

Winton, W. M. (1987). Do introductory textbooks present the Yerkes-Dodson law correctly? *American Psychologist, 42,* 202–203.

Witelson, S. F., Beresh, H., & Kiger, D. L. (2006). Intelligence and brain size in 100 postmortem brains, sex, lateralization and age factors. *Brain, 129,* 386–398.

Witelson, S. F., Kigar, D. L., & Harvey, T. (1999). The exceptional brain of Albert Einstein. *Lancet, 353,* 2149–2153.

Witelson, S. F., Kigar, D. L., Scamvougeras, A., Kideckel, D. M., Buck, B., Stanchev, P. L., et al. (2008). Corpus callosum anatomy in right-handed homosexual and heterosexual men. *Archives of Sexual Behavior, 37,* 857–863.

Witkowski, T. (in press). Thirty-five years of research on neuro-linguistic programming. NLP research data base. State of the art or pseudoscientific decoration. Scientific Review of Mental Health Practice.

Witt, M., & Wozniak, W. (2006). Structure and function of the vomeronasal organ. *Advances in Otorhinolaryngology, 63,* 70–83.

Wittchen, H. U. (2002). Generalized anxiety disorder: Prevalence, burden, and cost to society. *Depression and Anxiety, 16,* 162–171.

Witty, P. A., & Jenkins, M. D. (1934). The educational achievements of a group of gifted Negro children. *Journal of Educational Psychology, 25,* 585–597.

Woehrer, C. E. (1982). The influence of ethnic families on intergenerational relationships and later life transitions. In F. M. Berardo (ed.), *The Annals of the American Academy of Political and Social Science* (pp. 65–78). Beverly Hills, CA: Sage.

Wojciszke, B. (2002). From the first sight to the last breath: A six-stage model of love. *Polish Psychological Bulletin, 33,* 15–25.

Wolfe, V. A., & Pruitt, S. D. (2003). Insomnia and sleep disorders. In L. M. Cohen, D. E. McChargue, & F. L. Collins (eds.), *The health psychology handbook* (pp. 425–440). Thousand Oaks, CA: Sage.

Wolfsdorf, B. A., Freeman, J., D'Eramo, K., Overholser, J., & Spirito, A. (2003). Mood states: Depression, anger, and anxiety. In A. Spirito & J. Overholser (eds.), *Evaluating and treating adolescent suicide attempters: From research to practice* (pp. 53–88). New York: Academic Press.

Wolke, D., Rizzo, P., & Woods, S. (2002). Persistent infant crying and hyperactivity problems in middle childhood. *Pediatrics, 109,* 1054–1060.

Wollen, K. A., Weber, A., & Lowry, D. H. (1972). Bizarreness versus interaction of mental images as determinants of learning. *Cognitive Psychology, 3,* 518–523.

Woloshin, S., Schwartz, L. M., & Welch, H. G. (2002). Risk charts: Putting cancer in context. *Journal of the National Cancer Institute, 94,* 799–804.

Wolpe, J. (1990). *The practice of behavior therapy* (4th ed.). Elmsford, NY: Pergamon Press.

Wood, D., Bruner, J. A., & Ross, G. (1976). Role of tutoring in problem-solving. *Journal of Child Psychology and Psychiatry and Allied Disciplines, 17,* 89–100.

Wood, E., Desmarais, S., & Gugula, S. (2002). The impact of parenting experience on gender stereotyped toy play of children. *Sex Roles, 47,* 39–49.

Wood, J. M., Garb, H. N., & Nezworski, M. T. (2006, August). *Psychometrics: Better measurement makes better clinicians.* Paper presented at the annual conference of the American Psychological Association. New Orleans, LA.

Wood, J. M., & Lilienfeld, S. O. (1999). The Rorschach Inkblot Test: A case of overstatement? *Assessment, 6,* 341–351.

Wood, J. M., Lilienfeld, S. O., Garb, H. N., & Nezworski, M. T. (2000). The Rorschach test in clinical diagnosis: A critical review, with a backward look at Garfield (1947). *Journal of Clinical Psychology, 56,* 395–430.

Wood, J. M., Lilienfeld, S. O., Garb, H. N., & Nezworski, M. T. (2010). The validity of the Rorschach Inkblot Test for discriminating psychopaths from non-psychopaths in forensic populations: A meta-analysis. *Psychological Assessment, 22,* 336–349.

Wood, J. M., Nezworski, M. T., & Stejskal, W. J. (1996). The comprehensive system for the Rorschach: A critical examination. *Psychological Science, 7,* 3–10.

Wood, J. V., Perunovic, W. E., & Lee, J. W. (2009). Positive self-statements: Power for some, peril for others. *Psychological Science, 20,* 860–866.

Wood, W., Jones, M., & Benjamin, L. T. (1986). Surveying psychological public image. *American Psychologist, 41,* 947–953.

Wood, W., Wong, F. Y., & Chachere, J. G. (1991). Effects of media violence on viewers' aggression in unconstrained social interaction. *Psychological Bulletin, 109,* 371–383.

Woods, S. C., Seeley, R. J., Porte, D., & Schwartz, N. W. (1998). Signals that regulate food intake and energy homeostasis. *Science, 280,* 1378–1383.

Woodward, L. J., Fergusson, D. M., & Horwood, L. J. (2000). Driving outcomes of young people with attentional difficulties in adolescence. *Journal of the American Academy of Child and Adolescent Psychiatry, 39,* 627–634.

Woodworth, R. S. (1929). *Psychology* (Rev. ed.). Oxford, England: Holt.

Woody, E. Z., & Bowers, K. S. (1994). A frontal assault on dissociated control. In S. J. Lynn & J. W. Rhue (eds.), *Dissociation: Clinical and theoretical perspectives* (pp. 52–79). New York: Guilford.

Woody, E. Z., & Sadler, P (2008). Dissociation theories of hypnosis. In M. R. Nash & A. J. Barnier (eds.), *The Oxford handbook of hypnosis* (pp. 81–110). New York: Oxford University Press.

Woolf, N. J. (1991). Cholinergic systems in mammalian brain and spinal cord. *Progress in Neurobiology, 37,* 475–524.

Woolf, N. J. (2006). Microtubules in the cerebral cortex: Role in memory and consciousness. In J. A. Tuszynski (ed.), *The emerging physics of consciousness* (pp. 49–94). Berlin, Germany: Springer-Verlag.

Word, C. O., Zanna, M. P., & Cooper, J. (1974). Nonverbal mediation of self-fulfilling prophecies in interracial interaction. *Journal of Experimental Social Psychology, 10,* 109–120.

World Health Organization (WHO). *The world health report 2003: shaping the future.* Geneva, Switzerland: WHO, 2003. Available from URL: http:/www.who.int/whr/en/.

World Health Organization (WHO) (2004). *Global status report on alcohol 2004.* Geneva, Switzerland: WHO, Department of Mental Health and Substance Abuse.

Worrell, F. C. (2006, Fall). Minority perspectives in psychology: The disconnect between science and practice. *The General Psychologist, 41,* 13–14.

Wulff, D. M. (2000). Mystical experiences. In E. Cardeña, S. J. Lynn, & S. Krippner (eds.), *Varieties of anomalous experience: Examining the scientific evidence.* (pp. 397–440). Washington, DC: American Psychological Association.

Wyatt, W., Posey, A., Welker, W., & Seamonds, C. (1984). Natural levels of similarities between identical twins and between unrelated people. *Skeptical Inquirer, 9,* 62–66.

Wyatt, W. J. (2001) Some myths about behaviorism that are undone by B. F. Skinner's "The Design of Cultures." *Behavior and Social Issues, 11,* 28–30.

Wymbs, B. T., Pelham, W. E., Jr., Moline, B. S. B., Gnagy, E. M., Wilson, T. K., & Greenhouse, J. B. (2008). Rate and predictors of divorce among parents of youths with ADHD. *Journal of Consulting and Clinical Psychology, 76,* 735–744.

Wysocki, C. J., & Preti, G. (2004). Facts, fallacies, fears, and frustrations with human pheromones. *Anatomical Record: Discoveries in Molecular, Cellular, & Evolutionary Biology, 281,* 1201–1211.

Yafeh, M., & Heath, C. (2003, September/October). Nostradamus' clever clairvoyance: The power of ambiguous specificity. *Skeptical Inquirer, 27,* 36–40.

Yalom, I. (1985). *The theory and practice of group psychotherapy.* New York: Basic Books.

Yamaguchi, S., & Ninomiya, K. (2000). Umami and food palatability. *Journal of Nutrition, 130*(4S Suppl.), 921S–926S.

Yamey, G., & Shaw, P. (2002). Is extreme racism a mental illness? No. *Western Journal of Medicine, 176,* 5.

Yang, S., & Sternberg, R. J. (1997). Taiwanese Chinese people's conceptions of intelligence. *Intelligence, 25,* 21–36.

Yapko, M. D. (1994). *Suggestions of abuse: True and false memories of childhood sexual trauma.* New York: Simon and Schuster.

Yartz, A. R., & Hawk, L. W., Jr. (2001). Psychophysiological assessment of anxiety: Tales from the heart. In M. M. Antony, S. M. Orsillo, & L. Roemer

(eds.), *Practitioner's guide to empirically-based measures of anxiety* (pp. 25–30). New York: Kluwer Academic/Plenum.

Yehuda, R., Resnick, H., Kahana, B., & Giller, E. L. (1993). Long-lasting hormonal alterations to extreme stress in humans: Normative or maladaptive? *Psychosomatic Medicine, 55,* 287–297.

Yerkes, R. M., & Dodson, J. D. (1908). The relation of strength of stimulus to rapidity of habit-formation. *Journal of Comparative Neurology and Psychology, 18,* 459–482.

Young, J., & Cooper, L. M. (1972). Hypnotic recall amnesia as a function of manipulated expectancy. *Proceedings of the 80th Annual Convention of the American Psychological Association, 7,* 857–858.

Young, L., & Nestle, M. (2002). The contribution of expanding portion sizes to the US obesity epidemic. *American Journal of Public Health, 92,* 246–249.

Young, L. J., & Wang, Z. X., (2004) The neurobiology of pair bonding. *Nature Neuroscience, 7,* 1048–1054.

Young, M., Denny, G., Young, T., & Luquis, R. (2000). Sexual satisfaction among married women. *American Journal of Health Studies, 16,* 73–84.

Young, R. M., Oei, T. P. S., & Knight, R. G. (1990). The tension reduction hypothesis revisited: An alcohol expectancy perspective. *British Journal of Addiction, 85,* 31–40.

Young, S. M., & Pinsky, D. (2006). Narcissism and celebrity. *Journal of Research in Personality, 40,* 463–471.

Young, T. (1802). On the theory of light and colours. *Philosophical Transactions of the Royal Society of London, 92,* 12–48.

Young, W. C., Goy, R. W., & Phoenix C. H. (1964). Hormones and sexual behavior. *Science, 143,* 212–218.

Youngren, M. A., & Lewinsohn, P. M. (1980). The functional relationship between depressed and problematic interpersonal behavior. *Journal of Abnormal Psychology, 89,* 333–341.

Yurgelun-Todd, D. A., Gruber, S. A., Kanayama, G., Killgore, W. D. S., Baird, A. A., & Young, A. D. (2000). fMRI during affect discrimination in bipolar affective disorder. *Bipolar Disorders, 2*(3), 237–248.

Zabrucky, K., & Ratner, H. H. (1986). Children's comprehension monitoring and recall of inconsistent stories. *Child Development, 57,* 1401–1418.

Zadra, A. (1996). Recurrent dreams: Their relation to life events. In D. Barrett (ed.), *Trauma and dreams* (pp. 231–247). Cambridge, MA: Harvard University Press.

Zadra, A., Pilon, M., & Montplaisir, J. (2009). Polysomnographic diagnosis of sleepwalking: Effects of sleep deprivation. *Annals of Neurology, 63,* 513–519.

Zaidel, D. W. (1994). A view of the world from a split brain perspective. In E. M. R. Critchley (ed.), *The neurological boundaries of reality* (pp. 161–174). London: Farrand Press.

Zajonc, R. B. (1965). Social facilitation. *Science, 149,* 169–274.

Zajonc, R. B. (1968). Attitudinal effects of mere exposure. *Journal of Personality and Social Psychology Monographs, 9,* 1–27.

Zajonc, R. B. (1975). Birth order and intelligence: Dumber by the dozen. *Psychology Today, 8*(8), 37–43.

Zajonc, R. B. (1976). Family configuration and intelligence: Variations in scholastic aptitude scores parallel trends in family size and the spacing of children. *Science, 192,* 227–236.

Zajonc, R. B. (1984). On the primacy of affect. *American Psychologist, 39,* 117–123.

Zajonc, R. B. (2000). Feeling and thinking: Closing the debate over the independence of affect. In J. P. Forgas (ed.), *Feeling and thinking: The role of affect in social cognition* (pp. 31–58). New York: Cambridge University Press.

Zajonc, R. B. (2001). Mere exposure: A gateway to the subliminal. *Current Directions in Psychological Science, 10,* 225–228.

Zajonc, R. B., Heingartner, A., & Herman, E. M. (1969). Social enhancement and impairment of performance in the cockroach. *Journal of Personality and Social Psychology, 13,* 83–92.

Zajonc, R. B., Murphy, S. T., & Inglehart, M. (1989). Feeling and facial efference: Implications for the vascular theory of emotion. *Psychological Review, 96,* 395–416.

Zaslow, J. (2007). The most praised generation goes to work. *Wall Street Journal.* http://online.wsj.com/article/SB117702894815776259-search.html.

Zautra, A. J. (2003). *Emotions, stress, and health.* New York: Oxford University Press.

Zborowski, M. J., & Garske, J. P. (1993). Interpersonal deviance and consequent social impact in hypothetically schizophrenia-prone men. *Journal of Abnormal Psychology, 102*, 482–489.

Zeinah, M. M., Engel, S. A., Thompson, P. M., & Bookheimer, S. Y. (2003). Dynamics of the hippocampus during encoding and retrieval of face-name pairs. *Science, 299*, 577–580.

Zernike, K. (2000, May 31). Girls a distant 2nd in geography gap among U.S. pupils. *New York Times.* http://www.nytimes.com/2000/05/31/nyregion/girls-a-distant-2nd-in-geography-gap-among-us-pupils.html?pagewanted=1.

Zhang, A. Y., & Snowden, L. R. (1999). Ethnic characteristics of mental disorders in five U.S. communities. *Cultural Diversity and Ethnic Minority Psychology, 5*, 134–136.

Zhang, L. (2006). Does student-teacher thinking style match/mismatch matter in students' achievement? *Educational Psychology, 26*, 395–409.

Zhong, C., Bohns, V. K., & Gino, F. (2010). A good lamp is the best police: Darkness increases self-interested behavior and dishonesty. *Psychological Science, 21*, 311–314.

Zillmann, D. (1988). Cognition-excitation interdependencies in aggressive behavior. *Aggressive Behavior, 14*, 51–64.

Zillmann, D., Katcher, A. H., & Milavsky, B. (1972). Excitation transfer from physical exercise to subsequent aggressive behavior. *Journal of Experimental Social Psychology, 8*, 247–259.

Zimbardo, P. G. (1972). Pathology of imprisonment. *Society, 9*(6), 4–8.

Zimbardo, P. G. (1997, May). What messages are behind today's cults? *American Psychological Association Monitor, 28*(5), 14.

Zimbardo, P. G. (2004a). Does psychology make a significant difference in our lives? *American Psychologist, 59*, 339–351.

Zimbardo, P. G. (2004b, May 9). Power turns good soldiers into "bad apples." *Boston Globe.* Retrieved May 15, 2005, from www.boston.com/news/globe/editorial_opinion/oped/articles/2004/05/09/power_turns_good_soldiers_into_bad_apples/.

Zimbardo, P. G. (2007). *The Lucifer effect: How good people turn evil.* New York: Random House.

Zimbardo, P. G., Weisenberg, M., Firestone, I., & Levy, M. (1965). Communicator effectiveness in producing public conformity and private attitude change. *Journal of Personality, 33*, 233–255.

Zimmerman, F. J., Christakis, D. A., & Meltzoff, A. N. (2007) Associations between media viewing and language development in children under age 2 years. *The Journal of Pediatrics, 151*, 364–368.

Zimmerman, M. (1994). Diagnosing personality disorders: A review of issues and research methods. *Archives of General Psychiatry, 51*, 225–245.

Zinbarg, R. (1993). Information processing and classical conditioning: Implications for exposure therapy and the integration of cognitive therapy and behavior therapy. *Journal of Behavior Therapy and Experimental Psychiatry, 24*, 129–139.

Zinbarg, R. E., & Barlow, D. H. (1996). The structure of anxiety and the anxiety disorders: A hierarchical model. *Journal of Abnormal Psychology, 105*, 81–193.

Zion, I. B., Tessler, R., Cohen, L., Lerer, E., Raz, Y., Bachner-Melman, R., et al. (2006). Polymorphisms in the dopamine D4 receptor gene (DRD4) contribute to individual differences in human sexual behavior: Desire, arousal and sexual function. *Journal for Molecular Psychiatry, 11*, 782–786.

Zivotofsky, A. Z., Edelman, S., Green, T., Fostick, L., & Strous, R. D. (2007). Hemisphere asymmetry in schizophrenia as revealed through line bisection, line trisection, and letter cancellation. *Brain Research, 1142*, 70–79.

Zola, S. (1997). The neurobiology of recovered memory, *Journal of Neuropsychiatry and Clinical Neurosciences, 9*, 449–459.

Zubin, J., & Spring, B. (1977). Vulnerability: A new view of schizophrenia. *Journal of Abnormal Psychology, 86*, 103–126.

Zuckerman, M. (1979). *Sensation seeking: Beyond the optimal level of arousal.* Hillsdale, NJ: Erlbaum.

Zuckerman, M. (1989). Personality in the third dimension: A psychobiological approach. *Personality and Individual Differences, 10*, 391–418.

Zuckerman, M. (1994). *Behavioral expressions and biosocial bases of sensation seeking.* New York: Cambridge University Press.

Zuckerman, M., DePaulo, B. M., & Rosenthal, R. (1981). Verbal and non-verbal communication of deception. In L. Berkowitz (ed.), *Advances in experimental and social psychology* (Vol. 14, pp. 1–59). New York: Academic Press.

Zuckerman, M., & Hopkins, J. (1966). Hallucinations or dreams: A study of arousal levels and reported visual sensations during sensory deprivation. *Perceptual and Motor Skills, 22*, 447–459.

Zuger, B. (1988). Is early effeminate behavior in boys early homosexuality. *Comprehensive Psychiatry, 29*, 509–519.

Zullow, H. M., Oettingen, G., Peterson, C., & Seligman, M. E. P. (1988). Pessimistic explanatory style in the historical record. *American Psychologist, 43*, 673–682.

Zuroff, D. C., Mongrain, M., & Santor, D. A. (2004). Investing in the personality vulnerability research program: Current dividends and future growth: Rejoinder to Coyne, Thompson, and Whiffen. *Psychological Bulletin, 130*, 518–522.

Note: Boldface terms and page numbers are key terms; page numbers followed by f indicate figures; those followed by t indicate tables.

TEXT AND ART

CHAPTER 1 **Figure 1.1, p. 3:** Ilardi, S. S., Rand, K., & Karwoski, L. (2007). The cognitive neuroscience perspective allows us to understand abnormal behavior at multiple levels of complexity. In S. O. Lilienfeld & W. O. O'Donohue (Eds.), *The great ideas of clinical science: 17 principles that all mental health professionals should understand* (pp. 291–309). New York: Routledge. **Figure 1.2, p. 5: Fig 1.1, p. 26** from *Mind sights: Original visual illusions, ambiguities, and other anomalies* by Roger Shepard. Copyright © 1990 by Roger Shepard. Used by permission of Henry Holt and Company. **Figure 1.4, p. 10:** Gould, S. J. (1997). Nonoverlapping magisteria. *Natural History, 106,* 16–22. **Table 1.4, p. 12:** Reprinted with the permission of The Free Press, a division of Simon & Schuster, Inc. from *How We Know What Isn't So: The Fallibility of Human Reason in Everyday Life* by Thomas Gilovich. Copyright © 1991 by Thomas Gilovich. All rights reserved. **Figure 1.6, p. 17:** Jennifer A. Whitson and Adam D. Galinsky, Lacking Control Increases Illusory Pattern Perception. *Science 3 October 2008: Vol. 322. no. 5898,* pp. 115–117 http://www.sciencemag.org/ **Figure 1.9, p. 32:** Monitor on Psychology, June 2007, Vol 38, No. 6. © 2007 American Psychological Association. Reprinted by permission.

CHAPTER 2 **Figure 2.5, p. 60:** Used with permission from Jon Mueller.

CHAPTER 3 **Figure 3.1, p. 85:** Neuron. Modified from Dorling Kindersley. **Table 3–1, p. 89:** Carlson et al, *Psychology: The Science of Behavior*, Table "Neurotransmitters", © 2007 Pearson Education, Inc. Reproduced by permission of Pearson Education, Inc. **Figure 3.3, p. 88:** Adapted from Sternberg, R. J. (2004). *Psychology* (4th ed.). Belmont, CA: Wadsworth. **Table 3.3, p. 111:** Gazzaniga, M. S. (2000). Cerebral specialization and interhemispheric communication: Does the corpus callosum enable the human condition? *Brain, 123,* 1293–1326. **Figure 3.4, p. 88:** Adapted from Sternberg, R. J. (2004). *Psychology* (4th ed.). Belmont, CA: Wadsworth. **Figure 3.6, p. 92:** Leggio, M. G., Mandolesi, L., Federico, F., Spirito, F., Ricci, B., Gelfo, F., et al. (2005). Environmental enrichment promotes improved spatial abilities and enhanced dendritic growth in the rat. *Behavioral Brain Research, 163,* 78–90. **Figure 3.8, p. 94:** Nervous system. Modified from Dorling Kindersley. **Figure 3.9, p. 95:** Human brain. Modified from Dorling Kindersley. **Figure 3.12, p. 96:** Adapted from fig. 12.9 p. 438 from *Human Anatomy & Physiology*, 7th ed. by Elaine N. Marieb and Katja Hoehn. Copyright © 2007 by Pearson Education, Inc. Reprinted by permission. **Figure 3.14 left, p. 99:** Limbic system left brain. Modified from Dorling Kindersley. **Figure 3.14 right, p. 99:** From KALAT. *Biological Psychology, International Edition* (with CD-ROM), 9E. © 2007 Wadsworth, a part of Cengage Learning, Inc. Reproduced by permission. www.cengage.com/permissions.

CHAPTER 4 **Figure 4.1, p. 124:** Glynn, I. (1999). *An anatomy of thought: The origin and machinery of the mind*. New York: Oxford University Press. Per 1st edition perm file—OUP referred us to Curtis Brown, who did not reply. 7-25-10—Per Ian Glynn's agent, Michele Topham, Felicity Bryan Associates, "The majority of the figures in Ian Glynn's book are not his copyright, so do check the Acknowledgements section at the beginning of the book to see who is the copyright holder." **Figure 4.2, p. 125:** Courtesy of The Capozzi Winery. **Figure 4.3, p. 127:** Ramachandran, V. S., & Hubbard, E. M. (2001). Synaesthesia: A window into perception, thought and language. *Journal of Consciousness Studies, 8,* 33–34. **Figure 4.8, p. 128:** The checker-shadow illusion © 1995 Edward H. Adelson. Reprinted by permission. **Figure 4.9, p. 129:** Purves, D., Lotto, R. B., & Nundy, S. (2002). Why we see what we do. *American Scientist, 90,* 236. **Figure 4.11, p. 129:** *Scientific American, December 2008,* pp. 75 and 79. Reprinted with permission. Copyright © 2008 Scientific American, a division of Nature America, Inc. All rights reserved. **Figure 4.15, p. 137:** Key parts of the eye. Adapted from Dorling Kindersley. **Figure 4.16, p. 138:** Near and farsighted eyes. Adapted from St. Luke's Cataract & Laser Institute. **Figure 4.19, p. 140:** Herrmann, C. S., & Friederici, A. D. (2001). Object processing in the infant brain. *Science, 292,* 163. **Figure 4.22, p. 142:** Moving spiral illusion. coolopticalillusions.com. **Figure 4.29, p. 150:** Human ear. Adapted from Dorling Kindersley.

CHAPTER 5 **Figure excerpt, p. 168:** Clancy, S. A. (2005). Abducted: How people come to believe they were kidnapped by aliens. Cambridge, MA: Harvard University Press. **Figure excerpt, p. 178:** Alvarado, C. S. (2000). Out of body experiences. In E. Cardena, S. J. Lynn, & S. Krippner (Eds.), The variety of anomalous experiences (pp. 183–218). Washington, DC: American Psychological Association. **Table 5.1, p. 175:** Domhoff, G. W. (2003). Dreaming—An introduction to the science of sleep. Science, 299(5615), 1987–1988. (Note—per 1st ed. perm file—created by author, no credit line needed.) **Figure 5.2, p. 170:** Dement, W. C. (1974). Some must watch while some must sleep. San Francisco: W. H. Freeman. (Note from 1st ed. perm file—redrawn so it does not resemble the original photo.) **Table 5.2, p. 179:** Moody 1975, 1977; adapted from Greyson, B. (2000). Near-death experiences. In E. Cardena, S. J. Lynn, & S. Krippner (Eds.), Varieties of anomalous experiences (pp. 315–352). Washington, DC: American Psychological Association. **Table 5.4, p. 187:** From Diagnostic and Statistical Manual of Mental Disorders, 4th ed., American Psychiatric Association, 2000.

CHAPTER 6 **Table 6.4, p. 223:** DeBell, C. S., & Harless, D. K. (1992) B. F. Skinner: Myth and misperception. *Teaching of Psychology, 19(2),* 68–73—and—Wyatt, W. J. (2001) Some myths about behaviorism that are undone by B. F. Skinner's "The Design of Cultures". *Behavior and Social Issues, 11,* 28–30. **Table 6.4, p. 223:** Wyatt, W. J. (2001) Some myths about behaviorism that are undone by B. F. Skinner's "The Design of Cultures". *Behavior and Social Issues, 11,* 28–30. **Figure 6.10, p. 224:** Tolman, E. C. (1932). *Purposive behavior in animals and men*. Oxford, England: Appleton-Century. **Figure 6.11, p. 226:** Huesmann, L. R., Moise-Titus, J., Podolski, C., & Eron, L. D. (2003). Longitudinal relations between children's exposure to TV violence and their aggressive and violent behavior in young adulthood: 1977–1992. Developmental Psychology, 39(2), 201–221.

CHAPTER 7 **Figure 7.2, p. 245:** Atkinson, R. C., & Shiffrin, R. M. (1968). Human memory: A proposed system and its control processes. In K. W. Spence and J. T. Spence (Eds.), The psychol-*ogy of learning and motivation: Advances in research and theory* (Vol. 2, pp. 89–195). New York: Academic Press. **Figure 7.3, p. 246:** Sperling, G. (1960). The information available in brief visual presentations. *Psychological Monographs: General and Applied, 74(11, Whole No. 498),* 1–29. **Figure 7.5, p. 250:** Paivio, A. (1969). Mental imagery in associative learning and memory. *Psychological Review, 76, issue 3, May 1969,* p. 241–263. With permission from Elsevier. **Figure 7.6, p. 251:** Bahrick, H. p. (1984). Semantic memory content in permastore: Fifty years of memory for Spanish learning in school. *Journal of Experimental Psychology: General, 113,* 1–29. **Figure 7.10, p. 255:** Nickerson, R. S., & Adams, J. J. (1979). Long-term memory for a common object. *Cognitive Psychology, 11,* 287–307. With permission from Elsevier. **Figure 7.12, p. 259:** Bransford, J. D., & Johnson, M. K. (1972). Contextual prerequisites for understanding: Some investigations of comprehension and recall. *Journal of Verbal Learning and Verbal Behavior, 11,* 717–726. **Figure 7.16, p. 265:** Quiroga, R. Q., Reddy, L., Kreiman, G., Koch, C., & Fried, I. (2005). Invariant visual representation by single neurons in the human brain. *Nature, 435,* 1102–1107. **Figure 7.18, p. 267:** From Kalat. *Biological Psychology, International Edition* (with CD-ROM), 9E. © 2007 Wadsworth, a part of Cengage Learning, Inc. Reproduced by permission. www.cengage.com/permissions **Figure 7.19, p. 268:** Courtesy of Alzheimer's Disease Research, a program of the American Health Assistance Foundation.

CHAPTER 8 **Figure 8.3, p. 292:** From Fenson, L., Dale, P. S., Reznick, J. S., Bates, E., Tha l, D. J., & Pethick, S. J. (1994). Developmental Trends and Variability in the Acquisition of Communicative Skills. *Monographs of the Society for Research in Child Development, 59 (5, Serial No. 173),* pp. 32–60 **Table 8.4, p. 295:** From Cognitive Psychology, 15, M.L. Glick & K.J. Holyoak, K. J. Schema induction and analogical transfer. *Cognitive Psychology, 15:1,* 1–38. Copyright © 1983, with permission from Elsevier. **Figure 8.5, p. 297:** Johnson, J.S. and Newport, E.L. 1989: Critical period effects in second language learning: the influence of maturational state on the acquisition of English as a second language. *Cognitive Psychology 21,* 60–99. **Figure 8.10, p. 302:** MacLeod, C. M., (1991). Half a century of research on the Stroop effect: An integrative review. *Psychological Bulletin, 109,* 163–203. (Note from 1st ed. perm file—Artist rendered based on author original.) **Figure 8.12, p. 310:** Shepard, R. N. (1990). *Mind sights: Original visual illusions, ambiguities, and other anomalies.* New York: W. H. Freeman.

CHAPTER 9 **Figure 9.1, p. 321: Figure 9.2, p. 357:** Smith G.G. (2001). "Interaction evokes reflection: Learning Efficiency in Spatial Visualization," selected as one of the 25 best ED-MEDIA 2001 papers by the editors of The Interactive Multimedia Electronic Journal of Computer-Enhanced Learning and published in a multimedia version in IMEJ. http://imej.edu/articles/2001/2/05/index.asp. Reprinted with permission. **Table 9.1, p. 322:** Gardner, H. (1999). *Intelligence reframed: Multiple intelligences for the 21st century.* New York: Basic Books. **Table 9.2, p. 333:** Estimated IQ of Selected US Presidents. D.K. Simonton (2006). Presidential IQ openness, intellectual brilliance and leadership: Estimates and correlations for 42 U.S. Chief Executives. *Political Psychology, 27,* 511–526. **Figure 9.3, p. 323:** Note per 1st ed. perm file—origin unknown **Figure 9.4, p. 323:** Adapted from Wagner, R. K., & Sternberg, R. J. (1986). Tacit knowledge and intelligence in the everyday world. In R. J. Sternberg & R. K. Wagner (Eds.), *Practical intelligence: Nature and origins of competence in the everyday world* (pp. 51–83). Cambridge, England: Cambridge University Press. Reprinted with permission of Cambridge University Press. **Figure 9.7, p. 328:** Reprinted with permission of the Pickler Memorial Library and the Dolan DNA Leaning Center. **Figure 9.8, p. 329:** Sample Items similar to those in the Wechsler Adult Intelligence Scale-Third Edition (WAIS-III). Copyright © 1997 by NCS Pearson, Inc. Reproduced with permission. All rights reserved. "Wechsler Adult Intelligence Scale" and "WAIS" are trademarks, in the US and/or other countries, of Pearson Education, Inc. or its affiliates(s). **Figure 9.9, p. 330:** Simulated Item similar to those in the Raven's Progressive Matrices—Advanced Progressive Matrices. Copyright 1998 by NCS Pearson, Inc. Reproduced with permission. All rights reserved. "Raven's Progressive Matrices and Vocabulary Scales" is a trademark, in the US and/or other countries, of Pearson Education, Inc. or its affiliates(s). **Figure 9.12, p. 335:** Hauser, M. D. (2002). Nature vs. nurture redux. *Science, November 2002, 298,* p. 1554–1555. **Figure 9.13, p. 342:** Flynn, J. R. (1999). Searching for justice: The discovery of IQ gains over time. *American Psychologist, 54,* 5–20, Figure I. **Figure 9.14, p. 343:** Ivie, R., & Ray, K. N. (2005). *Women in physics and astronomy, 2005.* College Park, MD: American Institute of Physics. Used with permission from the American Institute of Physics. **Figure 9.16, p. 344:** Metzler, J., & Shepard, R. N. (1974). Transformational studies of the internal representation of three-dimensional objects. In R. Solso (Ed.), *Theories in cognitive psychology: The Loyola Symposium* (pp. 147–202).Wiley & Sons. **Figure 9.18, p. 346:** Two groups of plants, based on Lewontin, R.C. (1970). Further remarks on race and the genetics of intelligence. *Bulletin of the Atomic Scientists, 26,* 23–25. (Note: redrawn).

CHAPTER 10 **Figure 10.1, p. 365:** Adapted from fig. 28.4, p. 118 from *Human Anatomy & Physiology*, 7th ed. by Elaine N. Marieb and Katja Hoehn. Copyright © 2007 by Pearson Education, Inc. Reprinted by permission. **Table 10.3, p. 395:** Kohlberg, L. (1976). Moral stages and moralization: The cognitive-developmental approach. In T. Lickona (Ed.), *Moral development and behavior: Theory, research and social issues* (pp. 31–53). New York: Holt, Rinehart and Winston. AND Kohlberg, L. (1981). *The philosophy of moral development: Moral stages and the idea of justice*. San Francisco: Harper & Row. (Note—created by authors per 1st ed. perm file). **Table 10.3, p. 395:** Kohlberg, L. (1976). Moral stages and moralization: The cognitive-developmental approach. In T. Lickona (Ed.), *Moral development and behavior: Theory, research and social issues* (pp. 31–53). New York: Holt, Rinehart and Winston. And Kohlberg, L. (1981). *The philosophy of moral development: Moral stages and the idea of justice*. San Francisco: Harper & Row. (Note—created by authors per 1st edition perm file). **Figure 10.7, p. 374:** Piaget's 3 Mountain Task Perspective from Santrock, *Child Development*, 9e, 1998. McGraw-Hill Companies, Inc. (redrawn, no permission needed) **Figure 10.8, p. 374:** Reprinted with permission from *Human Development*, 7e, by Diane E. Papalia et al. © 1998 The McGraw-Hill Companies, Inc. **Figure 10.10, p. 378:** Baillargeon, R., Spelke, E., & Wasserman, S. (1985). Object permanence in five-month-old infants. *Cognition, 20,* 3, pp. 191–208. With permission from Elsevier. **Figure 10.12, p. 378:** http://psycnet.apa.org/journals/dev/22/1/images/ dev_22_1_67_fig1a.gif. Reprinted by permission from the American Psychological Association. **Figure 10.14, p. 381:** Reprinted from Mix, K. S. (1999). Similarity and numerical equivalence: appearances count.

Cognitive Development, 14, 2, p. 269–297. With permission from Elsevier. **Figure 10.15, p. 383:** From Waters, E., Matas, L., & Sroufe, L. A. (1975). Infants' reactions to an approaching stranger: Description, validation, and functional significance of wariness. *Child Development 46(2)*, 348–356. Reprinted with permission from Blackwell Publishing. **Figure 10.16, p. 384:** Kagan, J., Reznick, J. S., & Snidman, N. (1988). Biological bases of childhood shyness. *Science, 240*, 167–171. (Per 1st edition perm file—"per Scott, not a direct lift...no credit line needed.") **Figure 10.17, p. 386:** Ainsworth, M. D. S., Blehar, M. C., Waters, E., & Wall, S. (1978). *Patterns of attachment: A psychological study of the Strange Situation.* Hillsdale, NJ: Erlbaum. **Figure 10.18, p. 393:** Good, T. L., & Brophy, J. (1995). *Contemporary Educational Psychology* 5/e published by Allyn & Bacon, Boston, MA.

CHAPTER 11 **Figure excerpt, p. 406:** Text excerpt - Antonio Demasio excerpt of 100 words, p. 45. **Figure 11.1, p. 409:** From Aronoff, J., Barclay, A. M., & Stevenson, L. A. (1988) The recognition of threatening facial stimuli. *Journal of Personality and Social Psychology, 1988, April 54 (4)*, 647–655. (FAIR USE—APA) **Figure 11.2, p. 411:** Adapted from Dr. Silvia Helena Cardosa, http://www.cerebromente.org.br./m05/mente/tub6.gif **Figure 11.3, p. 414:** Pairs of polygons used in the mere exposure research of Robert Zajonc from Laboratory Manual—Cognitive Science in Context Laboratory—Spring 2006. (Nick Epley: Cornell Univerisity), http:///www.csic.cornell.edu/201/subliminal/ **Figure 11.4, p. 416:** © 2010 Microsoft Corp. Used by permission. **Figure 11.8, p. 423:** Diener, E., Emmons, R. A., Larsen, R. J., & Griffin, S. (1985). The satisfaction with life scale. *Journal of Personality Assessment, 49*, 71–75. (No permission needed per website, material considered public domain—per 1e perm file). **Figure 11.9, p. 424:** Levy, B.R., Slade, M.D., Kunkel, S.R., and Kasl, S.V. Longevity Increased by Positive Self-Perceptions of Aging. *Journal of Personality and Social Psychology 83:* 261–270, 2002. Reprinted by permission of the author. **Figure 11.10, p. 425:** Diener, E., & Seligman, M. E. P. (2004). Beyond money: Toward an economy of well-being. *Psychological Science in the Public Interest, 5:1, July 2004*, 1–31. Reprinted by Permission of SAGE Publications. **Figure 11.11, p. 427:** How happy are Americans? From Pew Research Center Report, "Are We Happy Yet?" February 13, 2006. Reprinted by permission. **Figure 11.13, p. 430:** Adapted from the web component of Psychology: A ConnecText, 4/e, by Terry F. Pettijohn (Dushkin, 1998). Copyright © 1998 by The McGraw-Hill Companies. Reproduced by permission of McGraw-Hill Contemporary Learning Series. **Figure 11.14, p. 430:** Approach and avoidance. Dr. Ronald Mayer, San Francisco State University. **Figure 11.16, p. 436:** Sypeck, M. F., Gray, J. J., Etu, S. F., Ahrens, A. H., Mosimann, J. E., & Wiseman, C. V. (2006) Cultural representations of thinness in women, redux: Playboy magazine's depiction of beauty from 1979 to 1999. *Body Image, 3*, 229–235. With permission from Elsevier. **Figure 11.17, p. 438:** Half of fig. 5.2 p. 149, "Levels of Sexual Arousal During the Phases of the Sexual Response Cycle," female graph only. Rathus et al, *Human Sexuality in a World of Diversity*, Figure "Female Sexual Response Cycle" p. 149, © 2008 Pearson Education, Inc. Reproduced by permission of Pearson Education, Inc. **Figure 11.18, p. 447:** Langlois, J. H., & Roggman, L. A. (1990). Attractive faces are only average. *Psychological Science, 1(2)*, 115–121. **Figure 11.19, p. 448:** Sternberg, R. J. (2004). *Psychology* (4th ed.). Belmont, CA: Wadsworth.

CHAPTER 12 **Figure excerpt, p. 456:** 3 brief quotes as submitted by Juana Lomi, Louie Cacchioli and Mike Hanson as appear in Faces of Ground Zero by Joe McNally, p. 29, 93, 103. Time/Life Books, Little Brown & Co., 2002. (Fair use per Little Brown). **Figure 12.1, p. 459:** Holmes, T. H., & Rahe, R. H. (1967). The Social Readjustment Scale. *Journal of Psychosomatic Research, vol. 11, issue 2, August 1967*, p. 214. With permission from Elsevier. **Table 12.1, p. 463:** *Percentage of People Who Develop Post-Traumatic Conditions at a Function of the Event* by Bryant (2000), also sourced to http://ncptsd.va.gov/ncmain/ncdocs/fact_shts/fs_asd.html?opm=1&rr=rr105&srt=d&echorr=true (Per 1st edition perm file—author created) **Figure 12.2, p. 461:** Selye, H. (1956). *The stress of life.* New York: McGraw Hill. **Table 12.3, p. 482:** Barnes, P. M., Bloom, B., & Nahin, R. (2008). *CDC National Health Statistics Report #12. Complementary and alternative medicine use among adults and children: United States, 2007.* Available at nccam.nih.gov/news/camstats.htm.

CHAPTER 13 **Figure 13.1, p. 497:** Jones, E. E., & Harris, V. A. (1967). The attribution of attitudes. Journal of Experimental Social Psychology, 3: 1, 1–24. With permission from Elsevier. **Figure 13.2, p. 498:** Hartmann, W. K. (1992). *Astronomy: The cosmic journey.* Belmont, CA: Wadsworth. **Figure 13.4, p. 501:** Asch, S. E. (1955). Opinions and social pressure. *Scientific American, 193*, 31–35. **Table 13.4, p. 533:** Kenrick, D. T., Neuberg, S. L., & Cialdini, R. B. (2005). *Social psychology: Unraveling the mystery* (3rd ed.). Boston: Allyn & Bacon. AND Pettijohn, T. F [Ed]. (1998) Sources: *Notable selections in social psychology* (2nd ed.). Guilford, CT: Dushkin/Mcgraw-Hill. **Table 13.4, p. 533:** Kenrick, D. T., Neuberg, S. L., & Cialdini, R. B. (2005). Social psychology: Unraveling the mystery (3rd ed.). Boston: Allyn & Bacon. AND Pettijohn, T. F [Ed]. (1998) Sources: *Notable selections in social psychology* (2nd ed.). Guilford, CT: Dushkin/Mcgraw-Hill. **Figure 13.5, p. 503:** Zimbardo, P. G. (1972). Pathology of imprisonment. *Society, 9(6)*, 4–8. **Figure 13.11, p. 526:** Pelham, B. W., Mirenberg, M. C., & Jones, J. T. (2002). Why Susie sells seashells by the seashore: Implicit egotism and major life decisions. Journal of *Personality and Social Psychology, 82*, 469–487. © 2002 by the American Psychological Association. Reproduced with permission. **Figure 13.15, p. 500:** Source: www.omnivoracious.com/images/2008/10/09/election_krbs_0808polemics_2.png. © 2009, Amazon.com, Inc.

CHAPTER 14 **Table 14.1, p. 542:** Tellegen, A., Lykken, D. T., Bouchard, T. J., Wilcox, K. J., Rich, S., & Segal, N. L. (1988). Personality similarity in twins reared apart and together. *Journal of Personality and Social Psychology, 54*, 1031–1039. © 1988 by the American Psychological Association. Reproduced with permission. **Table 14.2, p. 543:** Loehlin, J. C., & Horn, J. M. (2010). *Personality and intelligence in adoptive families.* New York: Sage. **Table 14.6, p. 557:** Sample items from a measure of locus control. © 2003 psychtests.com. Locus of Control & Attribution Style test—revised. **Figure 14.5, p. 569:** Part of an MMPI. Adapted from the MMPI®-2 (Minnesota Multiphasic Personality Inventory®-2) Manual for Administration, Scoring, and Interpretation, Revised Edition. Copyright © 2001 by the Regents of the University of Minnesota. Used by permission of the University of Minnesota Press. All rights reserved. "MMPI-2" and "Minnesota Multiphasic Personality Inventory-2" are trademarks owned by the Regents of the University of Minnesota. **Figure 14.7, p. 571:** Reprinted by permission of the publishers from Henry A. Murray, Thematic Apperception Test, Card 12F. Cambridge, Mass: Harvard University Press. Copyright © 1943 by the President and Fellows of Harvard College. Copyright © 1971 by Henry A. Murray.

CHAPTER 15 **Table 15.1, p. 588:** Adaptation of table "Common Culture-Bound Syndromes" from "Introduction to Culture-Bound Syndromes" by Ronald C. Simons, *Psychiatric Times, November 2001, vol. XVIII, issue 11*, as submitted. (original found online at http://i.cmpnet.com/CME/pt/content/p011163.gif) **Table 15.2, p. 590:** Reprinted with permission from the *Diagnostic and Statistical Manual of Mental Disorders, Fourth Edition, Text Revision* (Copyright 2000). American Psychiatric Publishing. **Figure 15.4, p. 621:** Feldman, E. (1991). Identifying the genes for diabetes and schizophrenia. *British Medical Journal, 303 (6794)*, 124. **Table 15.4, p. 592:** Reprinted with permission from the Diagnostic and Statistical Manual of Mental Disorders, Fourth Edition, Text Revision (Copyright 2000). American Psychiatric Publishing. **Table 15.6, p. 597:** Kessler, R. C., Berglund, P., Demler, O., Jin, R., & Walters, E. E. (2005). Lifetime prevalence and age-of-onset distributions of DSM-IV disorders in the National Comorbidity Survey Replication. *Archives of General Psychiatry, vol. 62, June 2005*, p. 596. Copyright © 2005 American Medical Association. Reprinted by permission. **Table 15.11, p. 611:** Reprinted with permission from the *Diagnostic and Statistical Manual of Mental Disorders, Fourth Edition, Text Revision* (Copyright 2000). American Psychiatric Publishing. **Figure excerpt, p. 617:** McGrath, M. E. (1984). 1st-person account—Where did I go? *Schizophrenia Bulletin, 10(4)*, 638–640. © 1984 Oxford University Press. Reprinted by permission. **Figure excerpt, p. 618:** Mayer-Gross, W., Slater, E., & Roth, M. (1969). *Clinical psychiatry* (3rd ed.). Baltimore: Williams & Wilkins. Revised and reprinted 1977, Balliere, Tindall, London. **Table 15.12, p. 619:** Reprinted with permission from the *Diagnostic and Statistical Manual of Mental Disorders, Fourth Edition, Text Revision* (Copyright 2000). American Psychiatric Publishing. **Figure 15.29, p. 617:** Michael Medved. Liberals show schizophrenic approach to religion (headline revised per author 6-21-10)—"What's wrong with the headline of this opinion column (selected by the website, not the author) which refers to the conflicting attitudes of some liberals toward religion?") World Daily Exclusive Commentary posted December 23, 2002 WorldNetDaily.com. Reprinted by permission of the author.

CHAPTER 16 **Table 16.3, p. 639:** "Simulated conversation between client and computer, Eliza" by Joseph Weizenbaum as appeared in Communications of the ACM, Vol. 9, No. 1, January 1966:36. Used by permission of Joseph Weizenbaum. **Table 16.4, p. 644:** Rimm, D., & Masters, J. C. (1979). *Behavior therapy: Techniques and empirical findings* (2nd ed.), p. 48. New York: Academic Press. (Note per 1e perm file - unable to locate Burish and Hollon (co-authors of 3e) do not control rights, no info on Masters & Rimm. Masters left Vanderbuilt in the 1980s.) **Figure 16.4, p. 651:** Lyrics. Adapted from "Love Me, Love Me, Only Me!" by Albert Ellis. Reprinted with permission of Albert Ellis Institute. **Figure 16.4, p.651:** (to come) **Figure excerpt, p. 634:** Goldfried, M. R., & Davison, G. C. (1976). *Clinical behavior therapy.* New York: Holt, Rinehart, & Winston. **Table 16.5, p. 649:** From "The basic clinical theory of rational-emotive therapy," in A. Ellis and R. Grieger (eds.), *Handbook of Rational-Emotive Therapy.* Reprinted with permission of Albert Ellis Institute. **Table 16.7, p. 652:** Lilienfeld, S. O. (2007). Psychological treatments that can cause harm. *Perspectives on Psychological Science, 2*, 53–70. **Table 16.8, p. 654:** From "Psychotherapy on trial," by Hal Arkowitz and Scott O. Lilienfeld. *Scientific American, April/May 2006.* Copyright © 2006 by Scientific American, Inc. All rights reserved. Used by permission.

PHOTO CREDITS

WALLPAPERS: Shutterstock

COVER: Masterfile Royalty Free Division/iStockphoto.com.

CHAPTER 1 **p. 1 (CO-01a)**: © Lourens Smak/Alamy; **p. 1 (CO-01b)**: Image Source/Getty Images; **p. 3 (botton left)**: DEEPAK BUDDHIRAJA/INDIA PICTURE/CORBIS; **p. 3 (bottom center)**: Frederic Lucano/Frederic Lucano/Getty Images, Inc.; **p. 3 (bottom right)**: Mike Powell/Mike Powell/Getty Images, Inc.; **p. 4 (top center)**: Picture Partners/Alamy Images; **p. 4 (top left)**: Henry Westheim Photography/Alamy Images; **p. 4 (top bottom)**: Courtesy of Hannah Faye Chua; **p. 5**: Stuart Ramson/AP Wide World Photos; **p. 6**: www.moillusions.com; **p. 8**: Reproduced by permission, The John Rylands University Library of Manchester, and provided through the courtesy of Roger J. Wood, Faculty of Life Sciences, University of Manchester; **p. 9 (botton left)**: Press Association via AP Images; **p. 9 (bottom right)**: Bill Guggenheim/Bantam Books; **p. 9 (top)**: Courtesy of the Seattle Post-Intelligencer, original publication 10/2/02; **p. 14**: Leonard G. Horowitz, D.M.D., M.A., M.P.H. From:The CIA's Role in the Anthrax Mailings; **p. 15 (top left)**: © CORBIS All Rights Reserved; **p. 15 (top center)**: © CORBIS All Rights Reserved; **p. 15 (top right)**: Bill Steber/Bill Steber/Nashville Tennesean/AP Photo; **p. 15 (right center)**: Roger Ressmeyer/© Roger Ressmeyer/NASA/CORBIS All Rights Reserved; **p. 15 (bottom right)**: Topham/The Image Works; **p. 17**: Robert McGouey/Alamy Images; **p. 19**: AP Photo/The Olympian, Steve Bloom; **p. 20 (top)**: HO/AP Photos; **p. 20 (bottom)**: John Bazemore/AP Photos; **p. 21 (center)**: © ScienceCartoonsPlus.com; **p. 21 (top right)**: Ron Chapple Stock/© Ron Chapple/CORBIS All Rights Reserved; **p. 23**: © ScienceCartoonsPlus.com; **p. 24 (top)**: Danny Feld/Danny Feld/© NBC/Everett Collection; **p. 24 (bottom)**: Design Pics Inc./Alamy Images Royalty Free; **p. 25**: Chris Madden; **p. 25 (top)**: Mary Evans Picture Library/The Image Works; **p. 26 (top)**: Topham/The Image Works; **p. 26 (bottom)**: Viktor1/Shutterstock; **p. 27**: Archives of the History of American Psychology - The University of Akron; **p. 29 (first from top)**: Archives of the History of American Psychology - The University of Akron; **p. 29 (second from top)**: Courtesy of the Library of Congress; **p. 29 (third from top)**: Omikron/Photo Researchers, Inc.; **p. 29 (fourth from top)**: BETTMANN/CORBIS; **p. 29 (fifth from top)**: Courtesy of the Library of Congress; **p. 30**: SPL/Photo Researchers, Inc.; **p. 31 (bottom)**: JOHN STILLWELL/PA Photos/Landov/JOHN STILLWELL/PA Photos/Landov; **p. 31 (bottom)**: OJO Images/OJO Images/SuperStock; **p. 31 (top)**: Archives of the History of American Psychology - The University of Akron; **p. 32 (top)**: Freud Museum; **p. 32 (bottom 1)**: Dr. Elizabeth Loftus; **p. 32 (bottom 2)**: Leslie J. Yonce; **p. 32 (bottom 3)**: Joe Cavaretta/AP Photos; **p. 32 (bottom 4)**: Rose Hartman/Getty Images/Time Life Pictures; **p. 34**: Cartoonbank.com; **p. 36 (top)**: Dennis MacDonald/PhotoEdit Inc.; **p. 36 (bottom)**: Dennis MacDonald/PhotoEdit Inc.; **p. 37 (top)**: Fat Chance Productions/© Fat Chance Productions/CORBIS All Rights Reserved; **p. 37 (center)**: Columbia University Archives - Columbia Library.

CHAPTER 2 **p. 43 (CO-02b)**: Masterfile; **p. 44**: Alan Carey/The Image Works; **p. 45 (bottom)**: G.L. Booker/G.L. Booker/Kansas City Star/Newscom; **p. 47 (top)**: Jonas Ekstromer/Jonas Ekstromer/Pool/Ap Images; **p. 48 (top)**: Dennis MacDonald/Alamy Images Royalty Free; **p. 48 (bottom)**: Clayton Sharrard/PhotoEdit Inc.; **p. 49**: Art Resource/Art Resource; **p. 50**: Penelope Breese/Penelope